On Cooking

Techniques from Expert Chefs

Sarah R. Labensky
Alan M. Hause

Photographs by Richard Embery

Drawings by Stacey Winters Quattrone

Prentice Hall, Englewood Cliffs, New Jersey 07632

Library of Congress Cataloging-in-Publication Data

Labensky, Sarah R.
   On Cooking: techniques from expert chefs / Sarah R.
   Labensky, Alan M. Hause.
      p. cm.
   Includes bibliographical references and index.
   ISBN 0-13-195449-0
   1. Cookery.   I. Hause, Alan M.   II.   Title.
TX651.L33 1995   94-15232
641.5—dc20   CIP

Editorial/production supervision: Barbara Marttine
Interior design and electronic page layout: Laura C. Ierardi
Technical/production support: Julie Boddorf
Electronic art specialist: Rolando Corujo
Copyeditor: Nancy Velthaus
Proofreaders: Julie Boddorf/Kathryn Kasturas
Production coordinator: Ed O'Dougherty
Managing editors: Mary Carnis/Patrick Walsh
Creative director: Paula Maylahn
Cover design: Ruta Kysilewskyj
Cover photograph: Richard Embery
Acquisitions editor: Robin Baliszewski
Editorial assistant: Rose Mary Florio
Marketing manager: Ramona Sherman
Directors of production and manufacturing: Bruce Johnson/David W. Riccardi

Photo Credits:

Portrait of Fannie Farmer—courtesy of The Schlesinger Library, Radcliffe College
Portrait of Auguste Escoffier—courtesy of Musse de l'Art Culinaire, Villeneuve-Loubet (Village) France
Portraits of Alexis Soyer and Antonin Careme—courtesy of Barbara Wheaton
Drawing of the Reform Club's Kitchen—courtesy of the Reform Club, London, England

©1995 by Prentice-Hall, Inc.
A Division of Simon & Schuster
Englewood Cliffs, New Jersey 07632

Printed in the United States of America
10 9 8 7 6 5 4 3 2 1

ISBN 0-13-195449-0

Prentice-Hall International (UK) Limited, *London*
Prentice-Hall of Australia Pty. Limited, *Sydney*
Prentice-Hall Canada Inc., *Toronto*
Prentice-Hall Hispanoamericana, S.A., *Mexico*
Prentice-Hall of India Private Limited, *New Delhi*
Prentice-Hall of Japan, Inc., *Tokyo*
Simon & Schuster Asia Pte. Ltd., *Singapore*
Editora Prentice-Hall do Brasil, Ltda., *Rio de Janeiro*

PART 3
COOKING 173

CONTENTS

PART 4
BAKING   737

$\mathcal{P}$REFACE

Cooking well means more than just following recipes. That's why this book is so much more than just a collection of recipes. It is a comprehensive, authoritative guide to the culinary arts, designed to help new cooks master the essentials and experienced hands expand their repertoire.

Whether it's boning a chicken, grilling fish or finishing pastry, you'll find precise comprehensive explanations for a variety of culinary procedures. Over 1250 four-color photographs are included to assist you in choosing the right equipment, selecting the best ingredients and preparing beautiful plated presentations.

To complement the discussion of procedures and techniques, the book offers more than 550 proven recipes. These recipes, ranging from classical to contemporary preparations, are designed to bring out the full, natural flavor of fresh foods. Special features include a selection of healthful recipes and a chapter on the savory delights of Chinese, Indian, Japanese, Middle Eastern and Mexican cuisines. Favorite recipes from 30 renowned experts complete with photographs of their signature dishes are highlighted.

In addition, the book is seasoned with frequent dashes of cooking lore: sidebars on the origins of familiar traditions, the history of famous dishes, and the lives of legendaty chefs. several renowned food writers have contributed brief essays on subjects of personal interest, from a simple method of tempering chocolate to an explanation of making fresh mozzarella cheese.

Whether your looking to expand your culinary skills, refresh your memory, or create the *piéce de resistance* for a party , you'll find the answers in this exceptional volume.

ACKNOWLEDGMENTS

This book would not have been possible without the assistance and support of many people. We are particularly indebted to Steve Labenksy for his countless hours with a sharp pencil, his comments and criticism and his constant support, as well as to our photographer, Richard Embery, for his professionalism and commitment to quality. Special thanks go to Kristy Riding, Tim Moore and the entire kitchen staff of Continental Catering for their support, without which this project would not have been possible. Thanks also to Leland Atkinson, Nancy Calomiris, Gaye Ingram, Lisa Kelly, Richard Martinez, Charlotte Morrissey, Ernst Reck, Chantal van de Brug and Stacey Winters Quattrone for their help. We are also grateful to the many chefs, restaurateurs, writers and culinary professionals who provided recipes and essays for this book.

The authors wish to thank the following companies for their generous donations of equipment and supplies: J.A. Henckels Zwillingswerk, Inc., All-

===== ◆◆◆ =====
A NOTE ON RECIPES

Recipes are important and useful as a means of standardizing food preparation and recording information. We include recipes that are primarily designed to reinforce and explain techniques and procedures presented in the text.

All ingredients are listed in both U.S. and metric measurements. The metric equivalents are rounded off to even, easily measured amounts. So, you should consider these ingredient lists as separate recipes or formulas; do not measure some ingredients according to the metric amounts and other ingredients according to the U.S. amount or the proportions will not be accurate and the intended result will not be achieved.

Throughout this book, unless otherwise noted, *mirepoix* refers to a preparation of 2 parts onion, 1 part celery and 1 part carrot by weight; *pepper* refers to ground black pepper, preferably freshly ground; *butter* refers to whole, unsalted butter, and *TT* means to taste.

Detailed procedures for standard techniques are presented in the text and generally are not repeated in each recipe. (For example, "deglaze the pan" or "monte au beurre.") No matter how detailed the written recipe, however, we must assume that you have certain knowledge, skills and judgement.

Variations appear at the end of selected recipes. These give you the opportunity to see how one set of techniques or procedures can be used to prepare different dishes with only minor modifications.

While some skills and an understanding of theory can be acquired through reading and study, no book can substitute for repeated, hands-on preparation and observation.

Clad Metalcrafters, Inc. and Parrish's Cake Decorating Supplies, Inc. We also wish to thank Shamrock Foods Company, East Coast Seafood of Phoenix Inc., KitchenAid Home Appliances, Taylor Environmental Instruments, Hobart Corporation, Williams-Sonoma, architect Michael Apostolos, and Randy Dougherty of ISF International.

Finally, we wish to thank everyone involved in this project at Prentice Hall and Paramount Publishing, including Barbara Marttine, Production Editor; Ramona Sherman, Marketing Manager; Laura Ierardi, Designer; Paula Maylahn, Creative Director; and Ruta Kysilewskjy, Advertising Art Director. As for our editor, Robin Baliszewski, this book could not have been completed without her patience, her persistence and her uncommonly good sense of humor.

The authors would also like to acknowledge the following reviewers for their comments and assistance—Richard W. Alford, University of Akron; Earl Arrowood, Bucks County Community College; Mike Artlip, Culinary School of Kendall College; Leland Atkinson; James Belch, Pennsylvania Institute of Culinary Arts; Lane Berrent, Pennsylvania Institute of Culinary Arts; Thom Boehm, Pennsylvania Institute of Culinary Arts; James Bressi, New England Culinary Institute; John D. Britto, San Joaquin Delta College; Walter Bronowitz CEE, Edmonds Community College; Mark Clink, Pennsylvania Institute of Culinary Arts; George Conte, New York Restaurant School; Noel Cullen, CMC, Boston Universtiy; Jeanne Curtis, Newbury College; William Day, Johnson & Wales University; Jim Douglas CEC: CCE, Everett Community College; Rolf Epprecht, Swiss Hospitality Institute; John Fitzpatrick; Maureen Garfolo, Pennsylvania Institute of Culinary Arts; George Geary; Jeff Graves, University of Houston/Conrad N. Hilton Hotel School; Bill Greathouse, Ivy Technical College; Kimberly Harris; Brenda Harsh, Pennsylvania Institute of Culinary Arts; Elizabeth S. Leite, Scottsdale Culinary Institute; Robert Lombardi, Spokane Community College; Deborah Lynch, Middlesex County College; Sylvia Marple M.S.,R.D. , University of New Hampshire; Don McNicol, Madison Area Technical College; James Muth, Grand Rapids Community College; John Noe, Joliet Junior College; Philip H. Nudle CEC, Middlesex County College; Michael Piccinino, Shasta College; Marcia Rango; Ernst Reck; Clifford Steiner, New York Restaurant School; Christine Stamm, Johnson & Wales University; Cicely Stetson; Peter G. Tobin, Spokane Community College; and Susan Ward, Academy of Culinary Arts/Atlantic Community College.

PROFESSIONALISM

Chefs must be able to do more than properly prepare and present foods. They must understand traditions and factors influencing change. They are responsible for making sure that the food served is wholesome and safe to eat and that they and those around them work in a safe and efficient manner. Further, chefs must make sure that the foods they serve are nutritious or at least should offer his or her customers sufficient selection so they can construct a nutritious meal. And, finally, chefs are responsible for producing food in a cost-effective manner as well as accurately calculating, tracking and controlling the cost of food and labor in the kitchen.

Part I opens with a chapter on professionalism. It traces the history of chefs and restaurants, discusses the modern food service operation and factors influencing its development and explains what attributes a student chef must have to become a professional chef. The following chapters address food safety and sanitation, nutrition, menu planning and food costing.

CHAPTER 1

PROFESSIONALISM

> *"Cookery is become an art, a noble science; cooks are gentlemen."*
> —Robert Burton, British author, 1621

*S*ubstitute *"professionals"* for *"gentlemen"* and Burton's words are as true today as they were almost four hundred years ago. Like the fine arts, great cookery requires taste and creativity, an appreciation of beauty and a mastery of technique. Like the sciences, successful cookery demands a certain level of knowledge and an understanding of basic principles. And, like the "gentlemen" of Burton's days, today's professional chefs must exercise sound judgment and be committed to achieving excellence in their endeavors.

This books helps implement Burton's philosophy. It describes foods and cooking equipment, explains culinary principles and cooking techniques and provides recipes utilizing these principles and techniques. This book cannot, however, provide taste, creativity, commitment and judgment. For these we rely upon you.

◆◆◆

After studying this chapter you will be able to:

+ discuss the development of the modern food service industry
+ name key historical figures responsible for developing food service professionalism
+ explain the organization of a classical kitchen brigade
+ appreciate the role of the professional chef in modern food service operations
+ understand the attributes a student chef needs to become a professional chef

Cooking—*(1) the transfer of energy from a heat source to a food; this energy alters the food's molecular structure, changing its texture, flavor, aroma and appearance; (2) the preparation of food for consumption.*

Cookery—*the art, practice or work of cooking.*

Professional cooking—*a system of cooking based upon a knowledge of and appreciation for ingredients and procedures.*

CHEFS AND RESTAURANTS

Cooks have produced food in quantity for as long as people have eaten together. For millennia, chefs have catered to the often elaborate dining needs of the wealthy and powerful, whether they be Asian, Native American, European or African. And for centuries, vendors in China, Europe and elsewhere have sold foods they prepared themselves or bought from others to the public.

But the history of the professional chef is of relatively recent origin. Its cast is mostly French and it is intertwined with the history of restaurants. For only with the development of restaurants during the late 18th and early 19th centuries were chefs expected to produce, efficiently and economically, different dishes at different times for different diners.

The 18th Century—Boulanger's Restaurant

The word "restaurant" is derived from the French word *restaurer* (to restore). Since the 16th century, the word "restorative" had been used to describe rich and highly flavored soups or stews capable of restoring lost strength. Restoratives, like all other cooked foods offered and purchased outside the home, were made by guild members. Each guild had a monopoly on preparing certain food items. For example, during the reign of Henri IV of France (1553–1610), there were separate guilds for *rotisseurs* (who cooked *la grosse viande*, the main cuts of meat), *patissiers* (who cooked poultry, pies and tarts), *tamisiers* (who baked breads), *vinaigriers* (who made sauces and some stews, including some restoratives), *traiteurs* (who made ragouts), and *porte-chapes* (caterers who organized feasts and celebrations).

The French claim that the first modern restaurant opened one day in 1765 when a Parisian tavernkeeper, a Monsieur Boulanger, hung a sign advertising the sale of his special restorative, a dish of sheep feet in white sauce. His establishment closed shortly thereafter as the result of lawsuit brought by a guild whose members claimed that Boulanger was infringing on their exclusive right to sell prepared dishes. Boulanger triumphed in court and later reopened.

Boulanger's establishment differed from the inns and taverns that had existed throughout Europe for centuries. These inns and taverns served foods prepared (usually off-premises) by the appropriate guild. The food—of which there was little choice—was offered by the keeper as incidental to the establishment's primary function: providing sleeping accommodations or drink. Customers were served family-style and ate at communal tables. Boulanger's contribution to the food service industry was to serve a variety of foods prepared on premises to customers whose primary interest was dining.

Several other restaurants opened in Paris during the succeeding decades, including the Grande Taverne de Londres in 1782. Its owner, Antoine Beauvilliers (1754–1817), was the former steward to the Comte de Provence, later King Louis XVIII of France. He advanced the development of the modern restaurant by offering his wealthy patrons a menu listing available dishes during fixed hours. Beauvilliers' impeccably trained wait staff served patrons at small, individual tables in an elegant setting.

The French Revolution (1789–1799) had a significant effect on the budding restaurant industry. Along with the aristocracy, guilds and their monopolies were generally abolished. The revolution also allowed the public access to the skills and creativity of the well-trained, sophisticated chefs who had worked in the aristocracy's private kitchens. Although many of the aristocracy's chefs either left the country or lost their jobs (and, some, their heads), a few opened restaurants catering to the growing urbanized middle class.

The Early 19th Century— *Carême and* Grande Cuisine

As the 19th century progressed, more restaurants opened, serving a greater selection of items and catering to a wider clientele. By mid-century, there were several large, grand restaurants in Paris serving elaborate meals, decidedly reminiscent of the *grande cuisine* (also known as *haute cuisine*) of the aristocracy. **Grande cuisine**, which arguably reached its peak of perfection in the hands of Antonin Carême, was characterized by meals consisting of dozens of courses of elaborately and intricately prepared, presented, garnished and sauced foods. Other restaurateurs blended the techniques and styles of *grande cuisine* with the simpler foods and tastes of the middle class (*cuisine bourgeoisie*) to create a new cuisine simpler than *grande cuisine* but more than mere home cooking.

Grande cuisine—*the rich, intricate and elaborate cuisine of the 18th- and 19th-century French aristocracy and upper classes. It is based upon the rational identification, development and adoption of strict culinary principles. By emphasizing the how and why of cooking,* grande cuisine *was the first to distinguish itself from regional cuisines, which tend to emphasize the tradition of cooking.*

The Late 19th Century— *Escoffier and* Cuisine Classique

Following the lead set by the French in both culinary style and the restaurant business, restaurants opened in the United States and throughout Europe during the 19th century. Charles Ranhofer (1836–1899) was the first internationally renowned chef of an American restaurant, Delmonico's in New York City. In 1893 Ranhofer published his "franco-american" encyclopedia of cooking, *The Epicurean*, containing more than 3500 recipes.

Classic cuisine—*a late 19th- and early 20th-century refinement and simplification of French* grande cuisine. *Classic (or classical) cuisine relies upon the thorough exploration of culinary principles and techniques, and emphasizes the refined preparation and presentation of superb ingredients.*

♦♦♦

MARIE-ANTOINE (ANTONIN) CARÊME (1783–1833)

Carême, known as the "cook of kings and the king of cooks," was an acknowledged master of French *grande cuisine*. Abandoned on the streets of Paris as a child, he worked his way from cook's helper in a working-class restaurant to become one of the most prestigious chefs of his (or, arguably, any other) time. During his career he was chef to the famous French diplomat and gourmand Prince de Talleyrand, the Prince Regent of England (who became King George IV), Tsar Alexander I of Russia and Baron de Rothschild, among others.

His stated goal was to achieve "lightness," "grace," "order" and "perspicuity" in the preparation and presentation of food. As a *patissier*, he designed and prepared elaborate and elegant pastry and confectionery creations, many of which were based on architectural designs. (He wrote that "the fine arts are five in number, namely: painting, sculpture, poetry, music, architecture—the main branch of which is confectionery.") As a showman, he garnished his dishes with ornamental hatelets (skewers) threaded with colorful ingredients such as crayfish and intricately carved vegetables, and presented his creations on elaborate socles (bases). As a *saucier*, he standardized the use of roux as a thickening agent, perfected recipes and devised a system for sauce classification. As a *garde-manger*, Carême popularized cold cuisine, emphasizing molds and aspic dishes. As a culinary professional, he designed kitchen tools, equipment and uniforms.

As an author, he wrote and illustrated important texts on the culinary arts, including *Le Maitre d'hotel francais* (1822), describing the hundreds of dish-

Courtesy of Barbara Wheaton

es he personally created and cooked in the capitals of Europe; *Le Patissier royal parisian* (1825), containing fanciful designs for *les pieces montées*, the great decorative centerpieces that were the crowning glory of grand dinners; and his five-volume masterpiece on the state of his profession, *L'Art de la cuisine au XIXe siecle* (1833), the last two volumes of which were completed after his death by his associate Plumerey. Carême's writings almost single-handedly refined and summarized five hundred years of culinary evolution. But his treatises were not mere cookbooks. Rather, he analyzed cooking, old and new, emphasizing procedure and order and covering every aspect of the art known as *grande cuisine*.

Carême died before the age of 50, burnt out, according to Laurent Tailhade, "by the flame of his genius and the coal of the spits." But this may have been the glory he sought, for he once wrote:

> *Imagine yourself in a large kitchen at the moment of a great dinner. … [S]ee twenty chefs coming, going, moving with speed in this cauldron of heat, look at the great mass of charcoal, a cubic meter for the cooking of entrees, and another mass on the ovens for the cooking of soups, sauces, ragouts, for frying and the water baths. Add to that a heap of burning wood in front of which four spits are turning, one which bears a sirloin weighing 45–50 pounds, the other fowl or game. In this furnace everyone moves with speed; not a sound is heard, only the chef has a right to speak, and at the sound of his voice, everyone obeys. Finally, the last straw; for about half an hour, all windows are closed so that the air does not cool the dishes as they are being served. This is the way we spend the best years of our lives. We must obey even when physical strength fails, but it is the burning charcoal that kills us. … [C]harcoal kills us but what does it matter? The shorter the life, the greater the glory.*

One of the finest restaurants outside of France was the dining room at London's Savoy Hotel, opened in 1898 under the directions of Cesar Ritz (1850–1918) and Auguste Escoffier. Escoffier is generally credited with refining the *grande cuisine* of Carême to create *cuisine classique* or **classic cuisine**. By doing so, he brought French cuisine into the 20th century.

❖❖❖

AUGUSTE ESCOFFIER
(1846–1935)

Escoffier's brilliant culinary career began at the age of 13 in his uncle's restaurant and continued until his death at the age of 89. Called the "Emperor of the world's kitchens," he is perhaps best known for defining French cuisine and dining during *La Belle Epoque* (the "Gay Nineties").

Unlike Carême, Escoffier never worked in an aristocratic household. Rather, he exhibited his culinary skills in the dining rooms of the finest hotels in Europe, including the Place Vendôme in Paris and the Savoy and Carlton Hotels in London.

Escoffier did much to enhance the *grande cuisine* that arguably reached its perfection under Carême. Crediting Carême with providing the foundation for great—that is, French—cooking, Escoffier simplified the profusion of flavors, dishes and garnishes typifying Carême's work. He also streamlined some of Carême's overly elaborate and fussy procedures and classifications. For example, he reduced Carême's elaborate system of classify-

ing sauces into the five families of sauces still recognized today. Escoffier sought simplicity and aimed for the perfect balance of a few superb ingredients. Some consider his refinement of *grande cuisine* to have been so radical as to credit him with the development of a new cuisine referred to as *cuisine classique* (classic or classical cuisine).

His many writings include *Le Livre des menus* (1912), in which, discussing the principles of a well-planned meal, he analogizes a great dinner to a symphony with contrasting movements that should be appropriate to the occasion, the guests, and the season, and *Ma cuisine* (1934), surveying *cuisine bourgeoisie*. But his most important contribution is a culinary treatise intended for the professional chef entitled *Le Guide culinaire* (1903). Still in use today, it is an astounding collection of more than five thousand classic cuisine recipes and garnishes. In it, Escoffier emphasizes technique and the thorough understanding of basic cookery principles and ingredients he considers to be the building blocks professional chefs should use to create great dishes.

Escoffier was honored as a Chevalier of the French Legion of Honour in 1920 for his work in enhancing the reputation of French cuisine.

The 20th Century—Point and Nouvelle Cuisine

This century has witnessed a trend toward lighter, more naturally flavored and more simply prepared foods. Fernand Point was a master practitioner of this movement. But this master's goal of simplicity and refinement was carried to even greater heights by a generation of chefs Point trained: principally, Paul Bocuse, Jean and Pierre Troisgros, Alain Chapel, Francois Bise and Louis

❖❖❖

FERNAND POINT
(1897–1955)

A massive man with a monumental personality, Point refined and modernized the classic cuisine of Escoffier. By doing so, he laid the foundations for *nouvelle cuisine*.

Point received his early training in some of the finest hotel-restaurant kitchens in Paris. In 1922 he and his family moved to Vienne, a city in southwest France near Lyon, and opened a restaurant. Two years later his father left the restaurant to Fernand, who renamed it *La*

Pyramide. During the succeeding years it became one of the culinary wonders of the world.

Point disdained dominating sauces and distracting accompaniments and garnishes. He believed that each dish should have a single dominant ingredient, flavor or theme; garnishes must be simple and match "like a tie to a suit." Procedure was of great importance. He devoted equal efforts to frying an egg and creat-

ing the marjolaine (a light almond and hazelnut spongecake filled with chocolate and praline buttercreams). His goal was to use the finest of raw ingredients to produce perfect food that looked elegant and simple. But simplicity was not easy to achieve. As he once said, " a bearnaise sauce is simply an egg yolk, a shallot, a little tarragon vinegar, and butter, but it takes years of practice for the result to be perfect."

Nouvelle cuisine—*literally, "new cooking," a mid-20th-century movement away from many classic cuisine principles and toward a lighter cuisine based on natural flavors and simpler preparations.*

Outhier. They, along with Michel Guérard and Roger Vergé, were the pioneers of **nouvelle cuisine** in the early 1970s.

Their culinary philosophy was principled on the rejection of overly rich, needlessly complicated dishes. These chefs emphasized healthful eating. The ingredients must be absolutely fresh and of the highest possible quality; the cooking methods should be simple and direct whenever possible. The accompaniments and garnishes must be light and must contribute to an overall harmony; the completed plates must be elegantly designed and decorated. Following these guidelines, some traditional cooking methods have been applied to untraditional ingredients, and ingredients have been combined in new and previously unorthodox fashions. For chefs with taste, skill, knowledge and judgment, this works.

INFLUENCES ON MODERN FOOD SERVICE OPERATIONS

From Monsieur Boulanger's humble establishment, a great industry has grown. Today there are more than 700,000 public dining facilities in the United States alone. The dramatic growth and diversification of the food service industry is due in part to the Industrial Revolution and the social and economic changes it wrought, including the introduction of new technologies, foods, concerns and consumers.

New Technologies

Technology has always had a profound effect on cooking. For example, the development of clay and, later, metal vessels that could contain liquids and withstand as well as conduct heat offered prehistoric cooks the opportunity to stew, make soups and porridge, pickle and brine foods and control fermentation. But it was not until the rapid technological advances fostered by the Industrial Revolution that anything approaching the modern kitchen was possible.

One of the most important advancements was the introduction of the cast iron stove. Prior to the 19th century, most cooking was done on spits or grills or in cauldrons or pots set on or in a wood- or coal-burning hearth. Hearthside cooking did not lend itself well to the simultaneous preparation of many items nor to items requiring constant and delicate attention. With the introduction of cast iron stoves during the 1800s (first wood- and coal-burning, then by mid-century, gas and, by the early 20th century, electric), cooks could more comfortably and safely approach the heat source and control its temperatures. They were also able to efficiently prepare and hold a multitude of smaller amounts of items requiring different cooking methods or ingredients for later use or service, a necessity at a restaurant simultaneously catering to different diners' demands.

Also of great importance were developments in food preservation and storage techniques. For thousands of years, food had been preserved by sun-drying, salting, smoking, pickling, sugar-curing or fermenting. Although useful, these procedures destroy or distort the appearance and flavor of most foods. By the early 19th century, preserving techniques that had minimal effect on appearance and flavor began to emerge. For example, by 1800 the Frenchman François Appert successfully "canned" foods by subjecting foods stored in sterilized glass jars to very high heat. An early mechanical refrigerator was developed by the mid-1800s; soon reliable iceboxes, refrigerators and, later, freezers were available. During the 20th century, freeze-drying, vacuum-packing and irradiation have become common preservation techniques.

While advancements were being made in preservation and storage techniques, developments in transportation technology were also underway. During the 19th century, steam-powered ships and railroads were able to bring foods quickly to market from distant suppliers. Indeed, by the 1870s, Chicago meatpackers were routinely supplying Europe with beef from the western plains. During the 20th century, temperature-controlled cargo ships, trains, trucks and airplanes all have been used as part of an integrated worldwide food transportation network.

Combined with dependable food preservation and storage techniques, improved transportation networks have freed chefs from seasonal and geographic limitations in their choice of foods and have expanded consumers' culinary horizons.

Engineering advancements also have facilitated or even eliminated much routine kitchen work. Since the start of the Industrial Revolution, chefs have come to rely increasingly on mechanical and motorized food processors, mixers and cutters as well as a wealth of sophisticated kitchen equipment such as high carbon stainless steel knife blades and convection steamers.

New Foods

Modern food preservation, storage, and transportation techniques have made both fresh and exotic foods regularly available to chefs and consumers. Many of these foods are themselves more wholesome as the result of progress in agriculture and animal husbandry.

Advancements in agriculture such as the switch from organic to chemical fertilizers and the introduction of pesticides and drought- or pest-resistant strains have resulted in increased yields of healthy crops. Traditional hybridization techniques and, more recently, genetic engineering have produced new or improved grains and, for better or for worse, fruits and vegetables that have a longer shelf life and are more amenable to mass-production handling, storage and transportation methods.

Likewise, advancements in animal husbandry and aquaculture have led to a more reliable supply of leaner, healthier meat, poultry and fish. Moreover, foods found traditionally only in the wild (for example game, wild rice and many mushrooms) are now being raised commercially and are routinely available.

Food preservation and processing techniques have also led to the development of prepackaged, prepared convenience foods, some of which are actually quite good. After careful thought and testing, today's chef can rely on some of these products. Doing so allows greater flexibility and more time to devote to other preparations.

New Concerns

Consumer concerns about nutrition and diet, particularly during the last decade or so, have fueled changes in the food service industry. Obviously, what we eat affects our health. Adequate amounts of certain nutrients promote good health by preventing deficiencies; good nutrition also helps prevent chronic diseases and increases longevity. Chefs should provide their customers with nutritious foods.

The public has long been concerned about food safety. Federal, state and local governments have helped promote food safety by inspecting and grading meats and poultry, regulating label contents for packaged foods and setting sanitation standards. All these standards, especially sanitation standards, affect the way foods are prepared, stored and served.

Concerns about nutrition and food safety have also resulted in renewed interest in organically grown fruits and vegetables and free-range-raised animals.

◆◆◆

CULINARY FRENCH

Perhaps one of the most enduring legacies of French chefs and culinarians is the common usage of many French words in today's professional kitchens. Some, like *canapé* and *bain marie*, are simply the name of a food item or piece of equipment of French origin. Others, such as *sauté*, are French verbs with no equally terse and descriptive English counterpart. Still others, for example, *julienne*, are not only used as nouns (julienne of carrot), but also as verbs (to julienne a carrot) and adjectives (julienned carrot). Often we forget the origins of these words and spell them without the original accent marks.

Here we list just a few of the more commonly encountered culinary French terms. As you study this book, note how many other words are of French origin.

Bain marie (bane mah-ree)—a hot-water bath for gently cooking foods or keeping cooked foods hot; the container holding the food in the hot water bath is also referred to as a bain marie.

Brunoise (broo-nwahz)—cube-shaped cuts (1/8 inch by 1/8 inch by 1/8 inch) of vegetables or other foods.

Canapé (kahn-ah-pay)—an hors d'oeuvre (another French term, meaning appetizer) usually composed of a small piece of bread or toast topped with a savory spread and garnish.

Chef (chehf)—literally, "leader" or "chief," the person in charge of a kitchen or department.

Demi-glace (de-me glass)—literally, "half-glaze," a mixture of brown stock and brown sauce reduced by half.

Ganache (gah-nasch)—a rich pastry or candy filling made with chocolate, heavy cream, and other flavorings.

Julienne (ju-lee-en)—noun: stick-shaped cuts (1/8 inch by 1/8 inch by 1 to 2 inches) of vegetables or other foods; verb: to cut food into the stick-shaped piece; adj.: stick-shaped.

Mayonnaise (may-o-nayz)—a basic cold emulsion sauce made of egg yolks and oil and seasoned with vinegar, mustard, and seasonings.

Mirepoix (meer-pwa)—a mixture of onions, carrots, and celery, used to flavor stocks, stews, and other dishes.

Mise en place (meez on plahs)—literally, "everything in place," the preparation and assembly of all ingredients and equipment needed before a dish can be cooked.

Purée (pur-ray)—noun: food that is processed by mashing, straining or fine chopping to achieve a smooth pulp; verb: to process food to achieve a smooth pulp.

Rondeau (ron-doe)—a shallow, wide, straight-sided pot with two loop handles.

Roux (roo)—a thickener for sauces made by cooking together equal parts of fat and flour.

Sachet (sa-shay)—or Sachet d'épices (sa-shay day pees), literally "bag of spices," aromatic ingredients such as bay leaf, thyme, cloves, peppercorns and parsley stems, tied in a cheesecloth bag and used to flavor stocks and other dishes.

Sauté (saw-tay)—to cook in an open pan in a small amount of fat at high temperature.

Sous-chef (sue chehf)—literally "under chef," the chef who is second in command of a kitchen.

Vinaigrette (vih-nay-greht)—a temporary emulsion of oil and vinegar seasoned with herbs, salt and pepper.

New Consumers

Demographic and social changes have contributed to the diversification of the food service industry by creating or identifying new consumer groups with their own desires or needs. By tailoring their menu, prices and décor accordingly, food service operations cater to consumers defined by age (baby boomers and seniors, in particular), type of household (singles, couples and families), income, education and geography.

During this century, especially in the decades following World War II, there has also been a rapid increase in the number and type of institutions providing food services. These include hospitals, schools, retirement centers, hotels and resorts (which may, in turn, have fine dining, coffee shop, banquet and room service facilities), factories and office complexes. Each of these institutions presents the professional chef with unique challenges, whether they be culinary, dietary or budgetary.

Through travel or exposure to the many books and magazines about food, consumers are becoming better educated and more sophisticated. Educated consumers provide a market for new foods and cuisines as well as an appreciation for a job well done.

Although some consumers may frequent a particular restaurant because its chef or owner is a celebrity or the restaurant is riding high on a crest of fad or fashion, most consumers choose a restaurant—whether it be a fast-food burger place or an elegant French restaurant—because it provides quality food at a cost they are willing to pay. To remain successful, then, the restaurant must carefully balance its commitment to quality with marketplace realities.

THE FOOD SERVICE OPERATION

To function efficiently, a food service operation must be well organized and staffed with appropriate personnel. This staff is sometimes called a **brigade**. Although a chef will be most familiar with the back of the house or kitchen brigade, he or she should also understand how the dining room or front of the house operates. Staffing any food service facility ultimately depends on the type and complexity of the menu. (Types and styles of menus are discussed in Chapter 4, Menu Planning and Food Costing.)

Brigade—*a system of staffing a kitchen so that each worker is assigned a set of specific tasks; these tasks are often related by cooking method, equipment or the type of foods being produced.*

Escoffier is credited with developing the kitchen brigade system used in large restaurant kitchens. From the chaos and redundancy found in the private kitchens of the aristocracy, he created a distinct hierarchy of responsibilities and functions for commercial food service operations.

The Classic Kitchen Brigade

At the top is the *chef du cuisine* or *chef*, who is responsible for all kitchen operations, developing menu items and setting the kitchen's tone and tempo.

His or her principal assistant is the *sous-chef* (the under chef or second chef), who is responsible for scheduling personnel and replacing the chef and station chefs as necessary. The *sous-chef* also often functions as the *aboyeur* (expediter or announcer), who accepts the orders from the dining room, relays them to the various station chefs and then reviews the dishes before service.

The *chefs de partie* (station chefs) produce the menu items and are under the direct supervision of the chef or *sous-chef*. Previously, whenever a cook needed an item, he or his assistants produced it; thus several cooks could be making the same sauce or basic preparation. Under Escoffier's system, each station chef is assigned a specific task based upon either cooking method and equipment or the category of items to be produced. They include:

◆ The *saucier* (sauté station chef), who holds one of the most demanding jobs in the kitchen, is responsible for all sautéed items and most sauces.

◆ The *poissonier* (fish station chef) is responsible for fish and shellfish items and their sauces. This position is occasionally combined with the sauce station.

◆ The *grillardin* (grill station chef) is responsible for all grilled items.

◆ The *friturier* (fry station chef) is responsible for all fried items.

◆ The *rotisseur* (roast station chef) is responsible for all roasted items and jus or other related sauces. The grill and fry stations are sometimes subsumed into the roast station.

◆ The *potager* (soup station chef) is responsible for soups and stocks.

◆ The *legumier* (vegetable station chef) is responsible for all vegetable and starch items.

◆ The *potager* and *legumier* functions are often combined into a single vegetable station whose chef is known as the *entremetier*. *Entremets* were the courses served after the roast and were usually composed of vegetables, fruits, fritters or sweet items (the sorbet served before the main course in some contemporary restaurants is a vestigial *entremet*).

◆ The *garde-manger* (pantry chef) is responsible for cold food preparations, including salads and salad dressings, cold appetizers, charcuterie items, pâtés, terrines and similar dishes. The *garde-manger* supervises:

> The *boucher* (butcher), who is responsible for butchering meats and poultry (fish and shellfish are usually fabricated by the fish station chef).

> Also under the *garde-manger*'s supervision are the chefs responsible for hors d'oeuvre and breakfast items.

◆ The *tournant*, also known as the roundsman or swing cook, works where needed.

◆ The *patissier* (pastry chef) is responsible for all baked items, including breads, pastries and desserts. Unlike the several station chefs, the *patissier* is not necessarily under the *sous-chef*'s direct supervision. The *patissier* supervises the following:

> The *boulanger* (bread baker), who makes the breads, rolls and baked dough containers used for other menu items (for example, *bouchées* and *feuilletés*).

> The *confiseur*, who makes candies and petits fours.

> The *glacier*, who makes all chilled and frozen desserts.

> The *decorateur*, who makes showpieces and special cakes.

◆ Depending upon the size and needs of any station or area, there are one or more *demi-chefs* (assistants) and *commis* (apprentices) who work with the station chef or pastry chef to learn the area.

The Modern Kitchen Brigade

Today most food service operations utilize a simplified version of Escoffier's kitchen brigade.

The **executive chef** coordinates kitchen activities and directs the kitchen staff's training and work efforts. Taking into consideration factors such as food costs, food availability and popularity as well as labor costs, kitchen skills and equipment, the executive chef plans menus and creates recipes. He or she sets and enforces nutrition, safety and sanitation standards and participates in (or at least observes) the preparation and presentation of menu items to ensure that quality standards are rigorously and consistently maintained. He or she is also responsible for purchasing food items and, often, equipment. In some food service operations, the executive chef may assist in designing the menu, dining room and kitchen. He or she also educates the dining room staff so they can correctly answer questions about the menu. He or she may also work with food purveyors to learn about new food items and products, as well as with equipment vendors, food stylists, restaurant consultants, public relations specialists, sanitation engineers, nutritionists and dietitians.

The executive chef is assisted by a **sous-chef** or **executive sous-chef**, who participates in, supervises and coordinates the preparation of menu items. His or her primary responsibility is to make sure that the food is pre-

---

✦✦✦
THE DINING ROOM

Like the back-of-the-house (i.e., kitchen) staff, the front-of-the-house (i.e., dining room) staff is also organized into a brigade. The dining room brigade is led by the **dining room manager** (French *maître d'hotel* or *maître d'*), who generally trains all service personnel, oversees wine selections and works with the chef to develop the menu. He or she organizes the seating chart and may also seat the guests. Working subordinate to him are:

The **wine steward** (French *chef de vin* or *sommelier*), who is responsible for the wine service, including purchasing wines, assisting guests in selecting wines and then serving the wine.

The **headwaiter** (French *chef de salle*), who is responsible for service throughout the dining room or a section of it. In smaller operations, his or her role may be assumed by the *maître d'* or a captain.

The **captains** (French *chefs d'étage*), who are responsible for explaining the menu to guests and taking their orders. They are also responsible for any tableside preparations.

The **front waiters** (French *chefs de rang*), who are responsible for assuring that the tables are set properly for each course, foods are delivered properly to the proper tables and the needs of the guests are met.

The **backwaiters** (French *demi-chefs de rang* or *commis de rang*, also known as dining room attendants or buspersons), who are responsible for clearing plates, refilling water glasses and other general tasks appropriate for new dining room workers.

Whether a restaurant uses this entire array of staff depends upon the nature and size of the restaurant and the type of service provided. With **American service** there is one waiter (also called a server) who takes the order and brings the food to the table. The table is then cleaned by a dining room attendant. With **French service** there are two waiters: a captain and a waiter. The captain takes the order, does the tableside cooking and brings the drinks, appetizers, entrees and desserts to the table. The waiter serves bread and water, clears each course, crumbs the table and serves the coffee. With **Russian service**, the entree, vegetables and potatoes are served from a platter onto a plate by the waiter. With **buffet service**, usually found in specialty restaurants and some institutional settings such as schools and correctional facilities, diners generally serve themselves or are served by workers assigned to specific areas of the buffet. Restaurants offering buffet service generally charge by the meal; if they charge by the dish they are known as cafeterias.

pared, portioned, garnished and presented according to the executive chef's standards. The sous-chef may be the cook principally responsible for producing menu items and supervising the kitchen.

Large hotels and conference centers with multiple dining facilities may have one or more **area chefs**, each responsible for a specific facility or function. There could be, for instance, a restaurant chef and a banquet chef. Area chefs usually report to the executive chef. Each area chef in turn has a brigade working under him or her.

Like Escoffier's station chefs, **cooks** (or section cooks) are responsible for preparing menu items according to recipe specifications. Making the most of time, talent, space and equipment, the chef assigns responsibilities to each of the line cooks. Depending upon the size and type of operation, the sauté, broiler, fry, soup and vegetable stations may be combined into one position, as may be the pantry, cold foods and salad stations.

The **pastry chef** is responsible for developing recipes for and preparing desserts, pastries, frozen desserts and breads. He or she is usually responsible for purchasing the food items used in the bake shop.

And, as in Escoffier's days, **assistants** and **apprentices** are assigned where needed in today's kitchens.

New styles of dining have created new positions since Escoffier's days. The most notable is the **short-order cook**, who is responsible for quickly preparing foods to order in smaller operations. He or she will work the broiler, deep fryer and griddle as well as make sandwiches and even some sautéed items.

Another is the **institutional cook**, who generally works with large quantities of prepackaged or prepared foods for a captive market such as a school, hospital or prison.

THE PROFESSIONAL CHEF

Although there is no one recipe for producing a good professional chef, we believe that with knowledge, skill, taste, judgment, dedication and pride a student chef will mature into a professional chef.

Knowledge

Chefs must be able to identify, purchase, utilize and prepare a wide variety of foods. They should be able to train and supervise a safe, skilled and efficient staff. To do all this successfully, chefs must possess a body of knowledge and understand and apply certain scientific and business principles. Schooling helps. A culinary program—whether at the secondary or post-secondary level—should, at a minimum, provide the student chef with a basic knowledge of foods, food styles and the methods used to prepare foods. Student chefs should also have an understanding of sanitation, nutrition and business procedures such as food costing.

This book is designed to help you learn these basics. Many chapters have extensive sections identifying foods and equipment. Throughout this book we emphasize culinary principles, not recipes. Whenever possible, whether it be preparing puff pastry or grilling a steak, we focus on the general procedure, highlighting fundamental principles and skills; we discuss both the how and why of cooking. Only then are specific applications and sample recipes given. We also want you to have a sense of the rich tradition of cookery, so informative sidebars on food history, chef biographies and other topics are scattered throughout the book.

In this way, we follow the trail blazed by Escoffier, who wrote in the introduction to *Le Guide culinaire* that his book is not intended to be a compendium of recipes slavishly followed, but rather his treatise should be a tool that leaves his colleagues "free to develop their own methods and follow their own inspiration; ... the art of cooking ... will evolve as a society evolves, ... only basic rules remain unalterable."

As with any profession, an education does not stop at graduation. The acquisition of knowledge continues after the student chef joins the ranks of the employed. He or she should take additional classes on unique or ethnic cuisines, nutrition, business management or specialized skills. He or she should regularly review some of the many periodicals and books devoted to cooking; he or she should travel and try new dishes to broaden his or her culinary horizons. He or she should also become involved in professional organizations in order to meet his peers and exchange ideas.

Skill

Schooling alone does not make a student a chef. Nothing but practical, hands-on experience will provide even the most academically gifted student with the skills needed to produce, consistently and efficiently, quality foods or to organize, train, motivate and supervise a staff.

Many food service operations recognize that new workers, even those who have graduated from culinary programs, need time and experience to develop and hone their skills. Therefore, many graduates start at entry-level positions. They should not be discouraged; advancement will come and the training pays off in the long run. Today culinary styles and fashions change frequently. What does not go out of fashion are well-trained, skilled and knowledgeable chefs. They can adapt.

Taste

No matter how knowledgeable or skilled the chef, he or she must be able to produce food that tastes great or the consumer will not return. He or she can only do so if he is confident about his own sense of taste.

Our total perception of taste is a complex combination of smell, taste, sight, sound and texture. All senses are involved in the enjoyment of eating; all must be considered in creating or preparing a dish. The chef should develop a taste memory by sampling foods, both familiar and unfamiliar. He or she should think about what he or she tastes, making notes and experimenting with flavor combinations and cooking methods. But he or she should not be inventive simply for the sake of invention. Rather, he or she must consider how the flavors, appearances, textures and aromas of various foods will interact to create a total taste experience.

Gastronomy—*the art and science of eating well.*

Gourmet—*a connoisseur of fine food and drink.*

Gourmand—*a connoisseur of fine food and drink, often to excess.*

Gourmet foods—*foods of the highest quality, perfectly prepared and beautifully presented.*

Judgment

Selecting menu items, determining how much of what item to order, deciding whether and how to combine ingredients and approving finished items for service are all matters of judgment. Although knowledge and skill play a role in developing judgment, sound judgment comes only with experience.

Dedication

Becoming a chef is hard work; so is being one. The work is often physically taxing, the hours are usually long and the pace is frequently hectic. Despite these pressures, the chef is expected to efficiently produce consistently fine foods that are properly prepared, seasoned, garnished and presented. To do so, the chef must be dedicated to the job.

The dedicated chef should never falter. The food service industry is competitive and dependent upon the continuing good will of an often fickle public. One bad dish or one off night can result in a disgruntled diner and lost business. The chef should always be mindful of the food prepared and the customer served.

The chef must also be dedicated to his or her staff. Virtually all food service operations rely on teamwork to get the job done well. Good teamwork requires dedication to a shared goal as well as a positive attitude.

Pride

Not only is it important that the job be well done, but the professional chef should have a sense of pride in doing it well. Pride should also extend to personal appearance and behavior in and around the kitchen. The professional chef should be well-groomed and in uniform when working.

The professional chef's uniform consists of comfortable shoes, trousers (either solid white, solid black, black-and-white checked or black-and-white striped), a white double-breasted jacket, an apron and a neckerchief usually knotted or tied cravat style. The uniform has certain utilitarian aspects: Checked trousers disguise stains; the double-breasted white jacket can be rebuttoned to hide dirt, and the double layer of fabric protects from scalds and burns; the neckerchief absorbs facial perspiration; and the apron protects the uniform and insulates the body. This uniform should be worn with pride. Shoes should be polished; trousers and jacket should be pressed.

The crowning element of your uniform is your toque. The toque is the tall white hat worn by chefs almost everywhere. Although the toque traces its origin to the monasteries of the 6th century, the style worn today was introduced at the end of the 19th century. Most chefs now wear a standard six- or nine-inch-high toque, but historically a cook's rank in the kitchen dictated the type of hat worn. Beginners wore flat-topped calottes; cooks with more advanced skills wore low toques and the master chefs wore high toques called *dodin-bouffants*. Culinary lore holds that the toque's pleats—101 in all—represent the 101 ways its wearer can successfully prepare eggs.

*C*ONCLUSION

The art and science of cookery form a noble profession with a rich history and long traditions. With knowledge, skill, taste, judgment, dedication and pride, the student chef can become part of this profession. In this book we provide you with the basic knowledge and describe the techniques at which you must become skilled. Dedicate yourself to learning this information and mastering your skills. Once you have done so, take pride in your accomplishments. Good luck.

QUESTIONS FOR DISCUSSION

1. Describe the kitchen brigade system. What is its significance in today's professional kitchens?
2. What are the roles of a chef, sous-chef and line cook in a modern kitchen?
3. Describe the differences in a meal prepared by Carême and one prepared by Point.
4. List and explain three technological advances affecting food preparation.
5. Discuss the societal changes that have contributed to diversification in the modern food service industry.

CHAPTER 2 FOOD SAFETY AND SANITATION

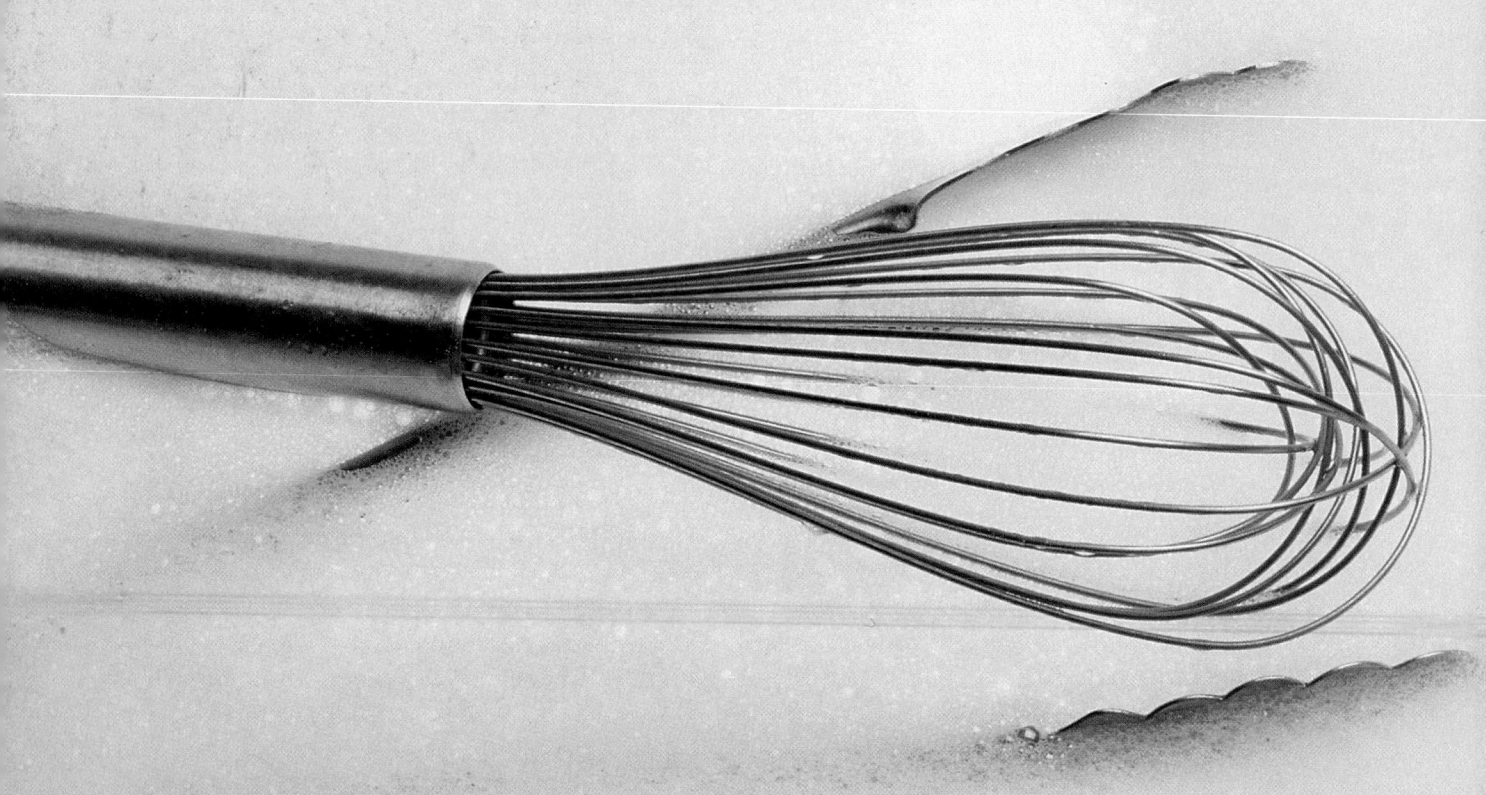

After studying this chapter, you will be able to:

♦ identify the causes of food-borne illnesses
♦ handle foods in a safe manner
♦ take appropriate actions to create and maintain a safe and sanitary working environment

*T*he United States Public Health Service identifies more than forty diseases that can be transmitted though food. Many can cause serious illness; some are even deadly. Providing consumers with safe food is the food handler's most important responsibility. Food handlers include anyone coming in contact with food or food preparation equipment. Unfortunately, food handlers are also the primary cause of food-related illnesses.

By understanding how food-borne illnesses are caused and what can be done to prevent them, you will be better able to protect your customers. This chapter is not meant to be a complete discussion of sanitation in food service operations. It should, however, alert you to practices that can result in food-borne illnesses.

Federal, state, county and municipal health, building and other codes are designed in part to ensure that food is handled in a safe and proper manner. Always consult your local health department for information and guidance. And always be conscious of what you can do to create and maintain a safe product and safe environment for your customers, your fellow employees and yourself.

Biological hazard—*a danger to the safety of food caused by disease-causing microorganisms such as bacteria, molds, yeasts, viruses or fungi.*

Chemical hazard—*a danger to the safety of food caused by chemical substances, especially cleaning agents, pesticides and toxic metals.*

Physical hazard—*a danger to the safety of food caused by particles such as glass chips, metal shavings, bits of wood or other foreign matter.*

Sanitation refers to the creation and maintenance of conditions that will prevent food contamination or food-borne illness. **Contamination** refers to the presence, generally unintentional, of harmful organisms or substances. Contaminants can be (1) biological, (2) chemical or (3) physical. When consumed in sufficient quantities, food-borne contaminants can cause illness or injury, long-lasting disease or even death.

Contamination occurs in two ways: direct contamination and cross-contamination. **Direct contamination** is the contamination of raw foods, or the plants or animals from which they come, in their natural setting or habitat. Chemical and biological contaminants such as bacteria and fungi are present in the air, soil and water. So, foods can be easily contaminated by general exposure to the environment: Grains can become contaminated by soil fumigants in the field and shellfish can become contaminated by ingesting toxic marine algae.

Chemicals and microorganisms generally cannot move on their own, however. They need to be transported, an event known as **cross-contamination**. The major cause of cross-contamination is people. Food handlers can transfer biological, chemical and physical contaminants to food while processing, preparing, cooking or serving it. It is therefore necessary to view sanitation as the correction of problems caused by direct contamination and the prevention of cross-contamination during processing and service.

DIRECT CONTAMINATION

Biological Contaminants

Biologically based food-borne illnesses can be caused by several **microorganisms**, primarily bacteria, parasites, viruses and fungi. By understanding how these organisms live and reproduce, you can better understand how to protect food from them.

Microorganism—*single-celled organisms as well as tiny plants and animals that can only be seen through a microscope.*

Bacteria

Bacteria, which are single-celled microorganisms, are the leading cause of food-borne illnesses. See Figure 2.1. Most bacteria reproduce by binary fission: Their genetic material is first duplicated and the nucleus then splits, each new nucleus taking some of the cellular material with it. See Figure 2.2. Under favorable conditions each bacterium can divide every 15–30 minutes. Within 12 hours, one bacterium can become a colony of 72 billion bacteria, more than enough to cause serious illness.

Some rod-shaped bacteria are capable of forming spores. Spores are thick-walled structures used as protection against a hostile environment. The bacteria essentially hibernate within their spores where they can survive extreme conditions that would otherwise destroy them. When conditions become favorable, the bacteria return to a viable state. This is important in food sanitation because bacterial spores may not be destroyed by heating or sanitizing techniques.

Some bacteria are beneficial, such as those that aid in digesting food or decomposing garbage. Other bacteria spoil food, but without rendering it unfit for human consumption. These bacteria, called **putrefactives**, are not a sanitation concern. (Indeed, in some cultures, they are not even a culinary concern. Cultures differ on what constitutes "bad" meat, for example, and game is sometimes hung for a time to allow bacteria to grow.)

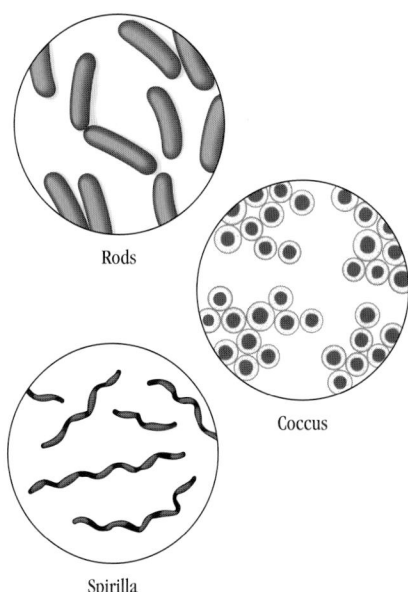

Rods

Coccus

Spirilla

FIGURE 2.1 *Bacteria can be classified by shape: Rods are short, tubular structures; coccus are discs, some of which form clusters; and spirilla are corkscrews.*

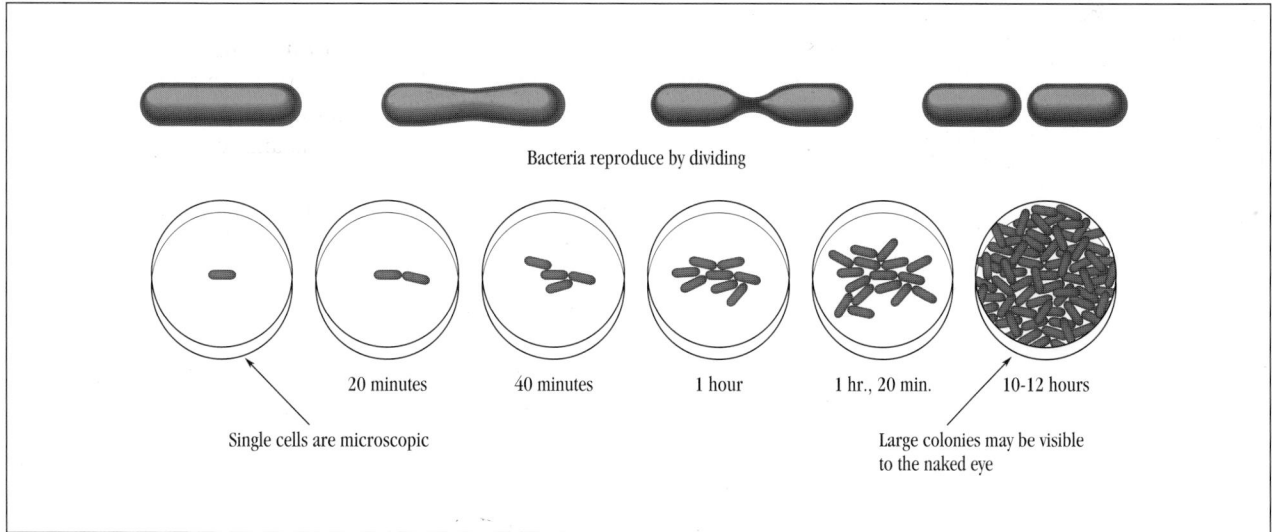

Bacteria reproduce by dividing

20 minutes   40 minutes   1 hour   1 hr., 20 min.   10-12 hours

Single cells are microscopic

Large colonies may be visible to the naked eye

FIGURE 2.2 *One bacterium divides into two; the two bacteria each divide, creating four; the four become 16 and so on. It takes only a very short time for one bacterium to produce millions more.*

Pathogen—*a living microorganism that can cause disease.*

The bacteria that are dangerous when consumed by humans are called **pathogenic**. These are the bacteria that must be destroyed or controlled in a food service operation.

Intoxications and Infections

Depending upon the particular microorganism, pathogenic bacteria can cause illnesses in humans in one of three ways: by intoxication, infection or toxin-mediated infection.

Botulism is a well-known example of an **intoxication**. Certain bacteria produce **toxins**, a byproduct of their life processes. You cannot smell, see or taste toxins. Ingesting these toxin-producing bacteria by themselves does not cause illness. But when their toxins are ingested, the toxins can literally poison the consumer. Proper food-handling techniques are critical in preventing an intoxication, because even if a food item is cooked to a sufficiently high temperature to kill all bacteria present, the toxins they leave behind are usually not destroyed.

The second type of bacterial illness is an **infection**. Salmonella is an especially well-known example. An infection occurs when live pathogenic bacteria are ingested. The bacteria then live in the consumer's intestinal tract. It is the living bacteria, not their waste products, that cause an illness. An infectant must be alive when eaten for it to do any harm. Fortunately, these bacteria can be destroyed by cooking foods to sufficiently high temperatures, usually 165°F (74°C) or higher.

The third type of bacterial illness has characteristics of both an intoxication and an infection, and is referred to as a **toxin-mediated infection**. Examples are Clostridium perfringens and Escherichia coli 0157:H7. When these living organisms are ingested they establish colonies in human or animal intestinal tracts where they then produce toxins. These bacteria are particularly dangerous for young children, the elderly or infirm.

Preventing Bacterial Intoxications and Infections

All bacteria, like other living things, need certain conditions in order to complete their life cycles. Like humans, they need food, a comfortable temperature, moisture, the proper pH, the proper atmosphere and time. The best way to prevent bacterial intoxications and infections is to attack the factors bacteria need to survive and multiply.

Food Bacteria need food for energy and growth. The foods on which bacteria thrive are referred to as **potentially hazardous foods**. Potentially hazardous foods include those high in protein such as meat, poultry, fish and shellfish. Dairy products, eggs, grains and some vegetables are also sufficiently high in protein to support bacterial growth. These foods and items containing these foods (for example, custard, hollandaise sauce and quiche) must be handled with great care.

Temperature Temperature is the most important factor in pathogenic bacteria's environment because it is the factor most easily controlled by food service workers. Most microorganisms are destroyed at high temperatures. Freezing slows, but does not stop, growth nor does it destroy bacteria.

Most of the bacteria that cause food-borne illnesses multiply rapidly at temperatures between 60°F and 120°F (16°C–49°C). Therefore, the broad range of temperatures between 40°F and 140°F (4–60°C) is referred to as the **temperature danger zone**. See Figure 2.3. By keeping foods out of the temperature danger zone you decrease the bacteria's ability to thrive and reproduce. (Regulations in some localities state that the "danger zone" begins at 45°F [7°C]. Here we use the broader range recommended by the United States Department of Agriculture—40°F–140°F—as this provides a slightly greater margin of safety.)

To control the growth of any bacteria that may be present, it is important to maintain the internal temperature of food at 140°F (60°C) or above or 40°F (4°C) or below. Simply stated: *Keep hot foods hot, keep cold foods cold.*

This is known as the **time-and-temperature principle**. Potentially hazardous foods should be heated or cooled quickly so that they are within the temperature danger zone as briefly as possible.

The high internal temperatures reached during cooking (165°F–212°F/74°C–100°C) kill most of the bacteria that can cause food-borne illnesses. When reheating foods it is important that the internal temperature reaches 165°F (74°C) or above to kill any bacteria that may have grown during storage. Once properly heated, hot foods must be held at temperatures of 140°F (60°C) or above. Foods that are to be displayed or served hot must be heated rapidly to reduce the time within the temperature danger zone. When heating or reheating foods:

◆ Heat small quantities at a time.
◆ Stir frequently.
◆ Heat foods as close to service time as possible.
◆ Use preheated ingredients whenever possible to prepare hot foods.
◆ Never use a steam table for heating or reheating foods. Bring the food to an appropriate internal temperature (at least 165°F/74°C) before placing it in the steam table for holding.

Foods that are to be displayed, stored, or served cold must be cooled rapidly. When cooling foods:

◆ Refrigerate semisolid foods at 40°F (4°C) or below in containers that are less than 2 inches deep. (Increased surface area decreases cooling time.)
◆ Avoid crowding the refrigerator; allow air to circulate around foods.
◆ Vent hot foods in an ice water bath as illustrated in Chapter 10, Stocks and Sauces.
◆ Use prechilled ingredients, for example mayonnaise, to prepare cold foods.
◆ Store cooked foods above raw foods to prevent cross-contamination.

Keep frozen foods frozen. Freezing at 0°F (–18°C) or below essentially stops bacterial growth but will not kill the bacteria. But do not place hot foods in a standard freezer. They will not cool more rapidly and the release of heat can raise the temperature of other foods in the freezer. Only a special blast freezer can be used for chilling hot items. If a special blast freezer is not available, cool hot foods as mentioned above before freezing them. When frozen foods are thawed, bacteria that are present will begin to grow. So:

◆ Never thaw foods at room temperature.
◆ Thaw foods gradually under refrigeration. Place them in a container to prevent cross-contamination from dripping or leaking liquids.
◆ Thaw foods under running water at a temperature of 70°F (21°C) or cooler.
◆ Thaw foods in a microwave *only* if the food will be prepared and served immediately.

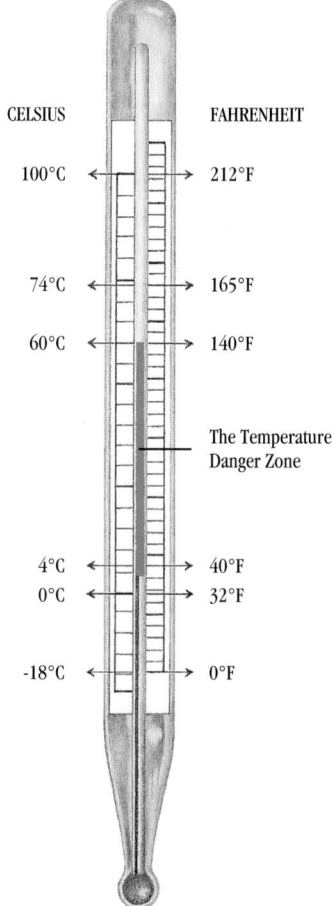

FIGURE 2.3

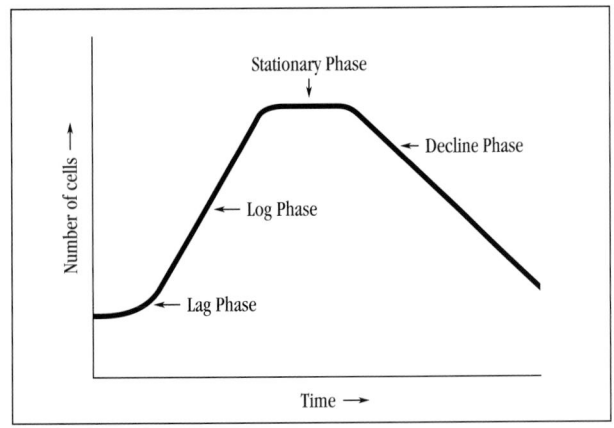

FIGURE 2.4   *Bacterial Growth Curve*

Time   When bacteria are moved from one place to another they require a period of time to adjust to new conditions. This resting period is known as the **lag phase**, when very little growth occurs. This phase may last from one to four hours. It is followed by the **log phase**, a period of accelerated growth, which lasts until the bacteria begin to crowd others within their colony, creating competition for food, space and moisture. This begins the **decline** or **negative growth phase**, during which bacteria die at an accelerated rate. See Figure 2.4.

Because of the lag phase, foods can be in the temperature danger zone for *very short periods* during preparation without an unacceptable increase in bacterial growth. Exposure to the temperature danger zone is cumulative, however, and should not exceed four hours total. The less time food is in the temperature danger zone, the less opportunity bacteria have to multiply.

Moisture   Bacteria need a certain amount of moisture, which is expressed as water activity or A_W. Water itself has an A_W of 1.0. Any food with an A_W of .85 or greater is considered potentially hazardous. See Table 2.1. Bacteria cannot flourish where the A_W is too low, usually below .85. This explains why dry foods such as flour, sugar or crackers are rarely subject to bacterial infestations. A low A_W only halts bacterial growth, however; it does not kill the microorganisms. When a dried food such as beans or rice is rehydrated, any bacteria present can flourish and the food may become potentially hazardous.

pH—*a measurement of the acid or alkaline content of a solution. Expressed on a scale of 0 to 14.0, 7.0 is considered neutral or balanced acid/alkaline; the lower the pH value, the more acidic the substance. The higher the pH value, the more alkaline the substance.*

Acid/Alkaline Balance   Bacteria are affected by the **pH** of their environment. See Table 2.2. Although they can survive in a wider range, they prefer a neutral environment with a pH of 6.6 to 7.5. Growth is usually halted if the pH is 4.6 or less. So, acidic foods such as lemon juice, tomatoes and vinegar create an unfavorable environment for bacteria. The simple addition of an acidic ingredient (such as lemon juice or vinegar) should not, however, be relied upon to destroy bacteria or preserve foods. The amount of acidity appropriate from the standpoint of taste is not sufficient to ensure destruction of bacteria. The pH level of foods also varies depending on temperature, water content, the interaction with other ingredients and a host of additional factors.

Atmosphere   Bacteria need an appropriate atmosphere. Some bacteria, known as **aerobic**, thrive on oxygen, while others, known as **anaerobic**, cannot survive in the presence of oxygen. Others, known as **facultative**, can adapt and will survive with or without oxygen. Unfortunately, most pathogenic bacteria are facultative. See Table 2.3.

Canning, which creates an anaerobic atmosphere, destroys bacteria that need oxygen. But it also creates a favorable atmosphere for anaerobic and facultative bacteria. A complete vacuum need not be formed for anaerobic bacteria to thrive, however. A tight foil covering, a complete layer of fat, even a well-fitting lid can create an atmosphere sufficiently devoid of oxygen to permit growth of anaerobic bacteria.

TABLE 2.1	WATER ACTIVITY OF COMMON FOODS
0.0	
.1	
.2	
.3	
.4	
.5	dried pasta
.6	
.7	flour, dry milk
.75	jam, jelly, crisp cooked bacon
.8	
.85	MINIMUM FOR BACTERIAL GROWTH
.9	raw bacon
.95	soft cheese
.98	poultry and meat
1.0	distilled water

TABLE 2.2   pH OF COMMON FOODS

	0	
	1.0	
A	2.0	limes, lemons
C	3.0	commercial mayonnaise
I	4.0	orange juice
D	4.6	bananas
	5.0	most vegetables (5.0 to 7.0)
	6.4	chicken and fresh meats
NEUTRAL	7.0	distilled water, fish
	8.0	crackers, hominy
A	8.5	baking soda in water
L	9.0	
K	10.0	
A	11.0	
L	12.0	household ammonia
I	13.0	
	14.0	

TABLE 2.3   CHARACTERISTICS OF BACTERIAL ILLNESSES

Common Name	Organism	Form	Common Source	Prevention
Staph	Staphylococcus aureus	Toxin	Starchy foods, cold meats, bakery items, custards, milk products, humans with infected wounds or sores	Wash hands and utensils before use; exclude unhealthy food handlers; avoid having foods at room temperature
Perfringens or CP	Clostridium perfringens	Cells and toxin	Reheated meats, sauces, stews, casseroles	Keep cooked foods at an internal temperature of 140°F (60°C) or higher; reheat leftovers to internal temperature of 165°F (74°C) or higher
Botulism	Clostridium botulinum	Toxin, cells, spores	Cooked foods held for an extended time at warm temperatures with limited oxygen, rice, potatoes, smoked fish, canned vegetables	Keep internal temperature of cooked foods above 140°F (60°C) or below 40°F (4°C); reheat leftovers thoroughly; discard swollen cans
Salmonella	Salmonella	Cells	Poultry, eggs, milk, meats, fecal contamination	Thoroughly cook all meat, poultry, fish and eggs; avoid cross-contamination with raw foods; maintain good personal hygiene
Strep	Streptococcus	Cells	Infected food workers	Do not allow employees to work if ill; protect foods from customers' coughs and sneezes
E. coli or 0157	Escherichia coli 0157:7 (enteropathogenic strains)	Cells and toxins	Any food, especially raw milk, raw vegetables, raw or rare beef, Humans	Thoroughly cook or reheat items
Listeriosis	Listeria monocytogenes	Cells	Milk products, Humans	Avoid raw milk and cheese made from unpasteurized milk

Parasites

Parasites are tiny multicelled organisms that depend on nutrients from a living host to complete their life cycle. Meat animals, fish, shellfish and humans can all play host to parasites. Several types of very small parasitic worms can enter an animal through contaminated feed, then settle in the host's intestinal tract or muscles, where they grow and reproduce. The ones most commonly found in foods are *trichinella spiralis* and *anisakis*.

Trichinosis is caused by eating undercooked game or pork infected with trichina larvae. Although trichinosis has been virtually eradicated by grain-feeding hogs and testing them before slaughter, some cases still occur each year. Traditionally it was thought that pork must be cooked to internal temperatures of 170°F (77°C) or higher to eradicate the larvae. This generally resulted in a dry, tough product. Scientists have now determined that trichina larvae are killed if held at 137°F (58°C) for 10 seconds. The United States Food and Drug Administration currently recommends cooking pork products to an internal temperature of 150°F (66°C). (All commercially packaged cured or smoked pork products must be heated to an internal temperature of 155°F [68°C] during processing.) The National Livestock and Meat Board continues to recommend cooking all pork products to 170°F (77°C), however.

Anisakiasis is another illness caused by parasitic roundworms. Anisakis worms reside in the organs of fish, especially bottom feeders or those taken from contaminated waters. Raw or undercooked fish are most often implicated in anisakiasis. Fish should be thoroughly cleaned immediately after being caught so that the parasites do not have an opportunity to spread. Thorough cooking to a minimum internal temperature of 140°F (60°C) is the only way to destroy the larvae, as they can survive even highly acidic marinades.

Viruses

Other biologically based food-borne illnesses such as hepatitis A and Norwalk virus are caused by viruses. Viruses are the smallest known form of life. They invade the living cells of a host, take over those cells' genetic material, and cause the cells to produce more viruses.

Viruses do not require a host to survive, however. They can survive—but not multiply—while lying on any food or food contact surface. Unlike bacteria, viruses can be present on any food, not just a potentially hazardous food. The food and food contact surface simply become a method of transportation between hosts.

Unlike bacteria, viruses are not affected by the water activity, pH or oxygen content of their environment. Some, however, can be destroyed by temperatures higher than 176°F (80°C). Basically, the only way to prevent food-borne viral illnesses is to prevent contamination in the first place.

Hepatitis A often enters the food supply through shellfish harvested from polluted waters. The virus is carried by humans, some of whom may never know they are infected, and is transmitted by poor personal hygiene and cross-contamination. The actual source of contamination may be hard to establish, though, because it sometimes takes months for symptoms to appear.

The Norwalk virus is spread almost entirely by poor personal hygiene among infected food handlers. The virus is found in human feces, contaminated water or vegetables fertilized by manure. The virus can be destroyed by high cooking temperatures but not by sanitizing solutions or freezing. In fact, Norwalk virus has even been found in ice cubes.

Foods most likely to transmit viral diseases are those that are not heated after handling. These include salads, sandwiches, milk, baked products, uncooked fish and shellfish and sliced meats. The best techniques for avoiding viral food-borne illnesses is to observe good personal hygiene habits, avoid cross-contamination, and use only foods obtained from reputable sources.

Fungi

Fungi are a large group of plants ranging from single-celled organisms to giant mushrooms. Fungi are everywhere: in the soil, air and water. Poisonous mushrooms, a type of fungus, can cause illness or death if consumed. The most common fungi, however, are molds and yeasts; they are the fungi of concern here.

Molds

Molds are algae-like fungi that form long filaments or strands. These filaments often extend into the air, appearing as cottony or velvety masses on food. Large colonies of mold are easily visible to the naked eye. Although many food molds are not dangerous, and some are even very beneficial, rare types known as mycotoxicoses do form toxins that have been linked to food-borne illnesses. For the most part, however, molds only affect food appearance and flavor. They cause discoloration, odors and off-flavors.

Unlike bacteria, molds can grow on almost any food at almost any temperature, moist or dry, acidic or alkaline. Mold cells can be destroyed by heating to 140°F (60°C) for 10 minutes. Their toxins are heat resistant, however, and are not destroyed by normal cooking methods. Therefore, foods that develop mold should be discarded and any container or storage area cleaned and sanitized.

Yeast

Yeast requires water and carbohydrates (sugar or starch) for survival. As the organism consumes carbohydrates it expels alcohol and carbon dioxide gas through a process known as **fermentation**. Fermentation is of great benefit in making bread and alcoholic beverages.

Although naturally occurring yeasts have not been proven to be harmful to humans, they can cause foods to spoil, developing off-flavors, odors and discoloration. Yeast is killed at temperatures of 136°F (58°C) or above.

Chemical Contaminants

The contamination of foods with a wide variety of chemicals is a very real and serious danger, one about which the public has shown a strong interest. Chemical contamination is usually inadvertent and invisible, making it extremely difficult to detect. The only way to avoid such hazards is for everyone working in a food service operation to follow proper procedures when handling foods or chemicals.

Chemical hazards include contamination with (1) the residual chemicals used in growing the food supply, (2) food service chemicals, and (3) toxic metals.

Residual Chemicals

Chemicals such as antibiotics, fertilizers, insecticides, and herbicides have brought about great progress in controlling plant, animal and human diseases, permitting greater food yields and stimulating animal growth. The benefits derived from these chemicals, however, must be contrasted with the adverse effects on humans when they are used indiscriminately or improperly.

The danger of these chemicals lies in the possible contamination of human foods, which occurs when chemical residues remain after the intended goal is achieved. Fruits and vegetables must be washed and peeled properly to reduce the risk of consuming residual chemicals.

Food Service Chemicals

A more common contamination problem involves the common chemicals found in most every food service operation. Cleaners, polishes, pesticides and abrasives are often poisonous to humans. Illness and even death can result from foods contaminated by such common items as bug spray, drain cleaner, oven cleaner or silver polish. These chemicals pose a hazard if used or stored near food supplies. Even improperly washing or rinsing dishes and utensils leaves a soap residue, which is then transmitted via food to anyone using the item.

To avoid food service chemical contamination, make sure all cleaning chemicals are clearly labeled and stored well away from food preparation and storage areas. Always use these products as directed by the manufacturer; never reuse a chemical container or package.

Toxic Metals

Another type of chemical contamination occurs when metals such as lead, mercury, copper, zinc and antimony are dispersed in food or water. For example:

♦ Metals can accumulate in fish and shellfish living in polluted waters or in plants grown in soil contaminated by the metals.
♦ Using an acid such as tomatoes or wine in a zinc (galvanized) or unlined copper container causes metal ions to be released into the food.
♦ Antimony is used in bonding enamelware; it can be released into food when the enamel is chipped or cracked, so the use of enamelware is prohibited in food service facilities.
♦ Lead enters the water supply from lead pipes and solder and is found in the glaze on some imported ceramic items.

Consuming any of these metals can cause poisoning.

To prevent metal contamination, use only approved food service equipment and utensils and re-tin copper cookware as needed. Never serve fish or shellfish that was illegally harvested or obtained from uninspected sources.

Physical Contaminants

Physical contaminants include foreign objects that find their way into foods by mistake. Examples include metal shavings created by a worn can opener, pieces of glass from a broken container, hair and dirt. Physical contaminants may be caused by intentional tampering, but they are most likely the result of poor safety and sanitation practices or a lack of training.

CROSS-CONTAMINATION

Generally, microorganisms and other contaminants cannot move by themselves. Rather, they are carried to foods and food contact surfaces by humans, rodents or insects. This transfer is referred to as cross-contamination.

Cross-contamination is the process by which one item, such as your fingers or a cutting board, becomes contaminated and then contaminates another food or tool. For example, a chef's knife and cutting board are used in butchering a potentially hazardous food such as a chicken. In this case, the chicken had been directly contaminated with salmonella at the hatchery. If the knife and board are not cleaned *and sanitized* properly, anything that touches them can also become contaminated. So, even though cooking the chicken to an appropriate internal temperature may destroy the salmonella in the chicken, the uncooked salad greens cut on the same cutting board or with the same knife can contain live bacteria.

Cross-contamination can occur with bacteria or other microorganisms, chemicals, dirt and debris. Side towels are an especially common source of cross-contamination. If a cook uses a side towel to wipe a spill off the floor, then uses that same towel to dry his hands after visiting the restroom, he has recontaminated his hands with whatever bacteria or dirt was on the floor. Cross-contamination also occurs when raw foods come in contact with cooked foods. Never store cooked food below raw food in a refrigerator, and never return cooked food to the container that held the raw food. Cross-contamination can also occur easily from smoking, drinking or eating, unless hands are properly washed after each of these activities.

Reducing Cross-Contamination

Cross-contamination can be reduced or even prevented by (1) personal cleanliness, (2) dish and equipment cleanliness and (3) pest management.

Personal Cleanliness

To produce clean, sanitary food, all food handlers must maintain high standards of personal cleanliness and hygiene. This begins with good grooming.

Humans provide the ideal environment for the growth of microorganisms. Everyone harbors bacteria in the nose and mouth. These bacteria are easily spread by sneezing or coughing, by not disposing of tissues properly and by not washing hands frequently and properly. Touching your body, then touching food or utensils, transfers bacteria. Human waste carries many dangerous microorganisms, so it is especially important to wash your hands thoroughly after visiting the restroom. An employee who is ill should not be allowed in the kitchen.

Current research shows that the human immunodeficiency virus (HIV), the causative agent of AIDS, is not spread by food. According to the United States Centers for Disease Control and Prevention, food service workers infected with HIV should not be restricted from work unless there is another infection or illness.

Here are several things you can do to decrease the risk of an illness being spread by poor personal hygiene:

◆ Wash your hands frequently and thoroughly.

◆ Keep your fingernails short, clean and neat. Do not bite your nails or wear nail polish.

◆ Keep any cut or wound antiseptically bandaged. An injured hand should also be covered with a disposable glove.

◆ Bathe daily, or more often if required.

◆ Keep your hair clean and restrained.

◆ Wear work clothes that are clean and neat. Avoid wearing jewelry or watches.

◆ Do not eat, drink, smoke or chew gum in food preparation areas.

Dish and Equipment Cleanliness

Clean—*to remove visible dirt and soil.*

Sanitize—*to reduce pathogenic organisms to safe levels.*

Sterilize—*to destroy all living microorganisms.*

The primary requirement for any food service facility is cleanability. But there is an important difference between clean and sanitary. **Clean** means that the item has no visible soil on it. **Sanitary** means that harmful substances are reduced to safe levels. Thus, something may be clean without being sanitary; the visible dirt can be removed, but disease-causing microorganisms can remain.

The cleaning of dishes, pots, pans and utensils in a food service operation involves both removing soil and sanitizing. Soil can be removed manually or by machine. Sanitizing can be accomplished with heat or chemical disinfectants.

Procedures for manually washing, rinsing and sanitizing dishes and equipment generally follow the three-compartment sink set-up shown in Figure 2.5. These procedures are:

1. Scrape and spray the item to remove soil.
2. Wash the item in the first sink compartment using an approved detergent. A brush or cloth may be used to remove any remaining soil.
3. Rinse the item in the second sink compartment using clear, hot water.
4. Sanitize the item in the third sink compartment by either:
   a. immersing it in 170°F (77°C) water for at least 30 seconds, or
   b. immersing it in an approved chemical sanitizing solution according to the manufacturer's directions.
5. Empty, clean and refill each sink compartment as necessary and check the water temperature regularly.

Food service items, dishes, silverware and utensils should always be allowed to air-dry, as towel-drying may recontaminate them.

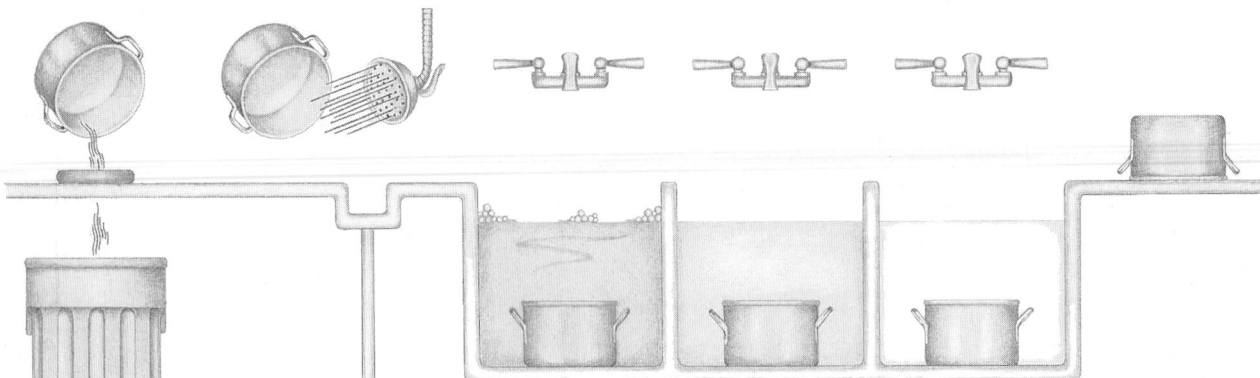

FIGURE 2.5 ***The Three-Compartment Sink*** *Procedure – scrape, spray, wash, rinse, sanitize and air-dry each item.*

Machine-washing dishes or utensils follows a similar procedure. The dish-washer should first scrape and prerinse items as needed, then load the items into dishwasher racks so that the spray of water will reach all surfaces. The machine cleans the items with a detergent, then sanitizes them with either a hot-water rinse (at least 180°F/82°C) or chemical disinfectant. When the machine cycle is complete, items should be inspected for residual soil, allowed to air-dry, and stored in a clean area.

Work tables and stationary equipment must also be cleaned and sanitized properly. Equipment and surfaces, including floors, walls and work tables, should be easily exposed for inspection and cleaning and should be con-structed so that soil can be removed effectively and efficiently with normal cleaning procedures. A thorough cleaning schedule should be implemented and closely monitored to prevent problems from developing.

The following points are important to the safety and cleanliness of any food service facility:

◆ Equipment should be disassembled for cleaning; any immersible pieces should be cleaned and sanitized like other items.

◆ All work tables or other food contact surfaces should be cleaned with deter-gent, then sanitized with a clean cloth dipped in a sanitizing solution. An acceptable sanitizing solution is made by combining one gallon (4 liters) of lukewarm water with one tablespoon (15 milliliters) of chlorine bleach. This solution must be replaced every two hours. Other chemical sanitizers should be prepared and used according to health department and manufac-turer's directions.

◆ Surfaces, especially work surfaces with which food may come in contact, should be smooth and free of cracks, crevices or seams in which soil and microorganisms can hide.

◆ Floors should be nonabsorbent and should not become slippery when wet.

◆ Walls and ceilings should be smooth and light-colored so that soil is easier to see.

◆ Light should be ample and well located throughout food preparation and storage areas. All light bulbs should be covered with a sleeve or globe to protect surroundings from shattered glass.

The design of a kitchen can also affect the sanitary habits of employees. Food preparation equipment should be arranged in such a way as to decrease the chances of cross-contamination. The work flow should eliminate crisscross-ing and backtracking. Employees should be able to reach storage, refrigeration and cleanup areas easily. Dish- and pot-washing areas and garbage facilities should be kept as far from food preparation and storage areas as possible. Cleaning supplies and other chemicals should be stored away from foods.

In most communities, the design of a food service facility is controlled in part by public health regulations. The local health and building codes should be consulted when planning any construction or remodeling, or when pur-chasing and installing new equipment.

Pest Management

Food can be contaminated by insects (e.g., roaches and flies) and rodents (e.g., mice and rats). These pests carry many harmful bacteria on their bodies, thus contaminating any surface with which they come in contact. An insect or rodent infestation is usually considered a serious health risk and should be dealt with immediately and thoroughly. Pests must be controlled by (1) building them out of the facility; (2) creating an environment in which they cannot find food, water or shelter; and (3) relying on professional extermination.

The best defense against pests is to prevent infestations in the first place by building them out. Any crack—no matter how small—in door frames, walls or window sills should be repaired immediately and all drains, pipes and vents should be well sealed. Inspect all deliveries thoroughly and reject any packages or containers found to contain evidence of pests.

Flies are the perfect method of transportation for bacteria because they feed and breed on human waste and garbage. Use screens or "fly fans" (also known as air curtains) to keep them out in the first place. Control of garbage is also essential because moist, warm, decaying organic material attracts flies and provides favorable conditions for eggs to hatch and larvae to grow.

Pest management also requires creating an inhospitable environment for pests. Store all food and supplies at least six inches off the floor and six inches away from walls. Rotate stock often to disrupt nesting places and breeding habits. Provide good ventilation in storerooms. Do not allow water to stand in drains, sinks or buckets, as cockroaches are attracted to moisture. Clean up spills and crumbs immediately and completely to reduce the food supply.

Despite your best efforts to build pests out and maintain proper housekeeping standards, it is still important to watch for the presence of pests. For example, cockroaches leave a strong, oily odor and feces that look like large grains of pepper. Cockroaches prefer to search for food and water in the dark, so seeing any cockroach on the move in the daylight is an indication of a large infestation.

Rodents (mice and rats) tend to hide during the day, so an infestation may be rather serious before any creature is actually seen. Rodent droppings, which are shiny black to brownish gray, may be evident, however. Rodent nests made from scraps of paper, hair or other soft materials may be spotted.

Should an infestation occur, consult a licensed pest control operator immediately. With early detection and proper treatment, infestations can be eliminated. Be very careful in attempting to use pesticides or insecticides yourself. These chemicals are toxic to humans as well as to pests. Great care must be used to prevent contaminating food or exposing workers or customers to the chemicals.

HACCP Systems

Now that you understand what contaminants are and how they can be destroyed or controlled, it is necessary to put this information into practice during day-to-day operations. Although local health departments inspect all food service facilities on a regular basis, continual self-inspection and control are essential for maintaining sanitary conditions.

Hazard Analysis Critical Control Points (HACCP) is proving to be an effective and efficient method for managing and maintaining sanitary conditions in all types of food service operations. Developed in 1971 for NASA to ensure food safety for astronauts, HACCP—and a similar system adopted by the National Restaurant Association known as Sanitary Assessment of the Food Environment/S.A.F.E.—is a rigorous system of self-inspection. It focuses on the *flow of food* through the food service facility, from the decision to include an item on the menu through service to the consumer.

TABLE 2.4   HACCP ANALYSIS—THE FLOW OF FOOD

Control Point	Hazard	Critical Action
Menu and recipes	Potentially hazardous foods; human hands involved in food preparation.	Plan physical work flow; train employees
Receiving	Contaminated or spoiled goods	Inspect and reject delivery if necessary
Storage	Cross-contamination to and from other foods; bacterial growth; spoilage	Maintain proper temperatures; rotate stock; discard if necessary
Preparation	Cross-contamination; bacterial growth	Wash hands and utensils; avoid temperature danger zone
Cooking	Bacterial survival; physical or chemical contamination	Cook to proper temperatures
Holding and service	Contamination; bacterial growth	Use clean equipment; maintain proper temperatures
Cooling leftovers	Bacterial survival and growth	Cool rapidly, cover and refrigerate
Reheating	Bacterial survival and growth	Heat rapidly to 165° F (74°C); maintain temperatures; do not mix old and new products

A HACCP critical control point is any step during the processing of a food when a mistake can result in the transmission, growth or survival of pathogenic bacteria. At each of these steps there is some hazard of contamination. The HACCP process begins by identifying the steps and evaluating the type and severity of hazard that can occur. It then identifies what actions can be taken to reduce or prevent each risk of hazard. See Table 2.4. The activities that present the highest risk of hazard should be monitored most closely. For example, a cook's failure to wash his hands before handling cooked food presents a greater risk of hazard than does a dirty floor. In other words, hazards must be prioritized and correction of critical concerns should take priority.

Whatever system is followed, however, all personnel must be constantly aware of and responsive to problems and potential problems associated with the safety of the food they are serving.

THE SAFE WORKER

Kitchens are filled with objects that can cut, burn, break, crush or sprain the human body. The best way to prevent work-related injuries is through proper training, adherence to good work habits and careful supervision.

The federal government enacted legislation designed to reduce hazards in the work area, thereby reducing accidents. The Occupational Safety and

Health Act (OSHA) covers a broad range of safety matters. Employers who fail to follow its rules can be severely fined. Unfortunately, human error is the leading cause of accidents, and no amount of legislation can protect someone who doesn't work in a safe manner.

Safe behavior on the job reflects pride, professionalism and consideration for fellow workers. The following list should alert you to conditions and activities aimed at preventing accidents and injuries:

+ Clean up spills as soon as they occur.
+ Learn to operate equipment properly; always use guards and safety devices.
+ Wear clothing that fits properly; avoid wearing jewelry, which may get caught in equipment.
+ Use knives and other equipment for their intended purpose only.
+ Walk, do not run.
+ Keep exits, aisles and stairs clear and unobstructed.
+ Always assume a pot or pan is hot; handle with dry towels.
+ Position pot and pan handles out of the aisles so they do not get bumped.
+ Get help or use a cart when lifting or moving heavy objects.
+ Avoid back injury by lifting with your leg muscles; stoop, don't bend, when lifting.
+ Use a well-placed ladder or stool for climbing; do not use a chair, box, drawer or shelf.
+ Keep breakable items away from food storage or production areas.
+ Warn people when you must walk behind them, especially when carrying a hot pan.

Some accidents will inevitably occur, and it is important to act appropriately in the event of an injury or emergency. This may mean calling for help or providing first aid. Every food service operation should be equipped with a complete first-aid kit. Municipal regulations may specify the exact contents of the kit. Be sure that the kit is conveniently located and well stocked at all times.

The American Red Cross and local public health departments offer training in first aid, cardiopulmonary resuscitation (CPR), and the Heimlich Maneuver used for choking victims. All employees should be trained in basic emergency procedures. A list of emergency telephone numbers should be posted by each telephone.

*C*ONCLUSION

All food service workers are responsible for supplying food that is safe to eat. Microorganisms that cause food-borne illnesses are found in all types of food; they can be destroyed or their growth can be severely limited by proper food handling procedures. By learning about food contaminants, how they are spread and how they can be prevented or controlled, you can help ensure customer safety. You are also responsible for your own physical safety as well as that of your customers and fellow workers. Maintaining sanitary and safe facilities and high standards of personal hygiene is a necessary part of this responsibility.

Questions for Discussion

1. Foods can be contaminated in several ways. Explain the differences between biological, chemical and physical contamination. Give an example of each.

2. Under what conditions will bacteria thrive? Explain what you can do to alter these conditions.

3. What is the temperature danger zone? What is its significance in food preparation?

4. Explain how improper or inadequate pest management can lead to food-borne illnesses.

5. Define HACCP. How is this system used in a typical food service facility?

CHAPTER 3
NUTRITION

After studying this chapter you will be able to:

◆ identify categories of nutrients and explain their importance in a balanced diet
◆ explain the evolution of the USDA food pyramid and its significance in planning nutritious menus
◆ understand product nutrition labels
◆ explain the effect storage and preparation techniques have on various foods' nutritional values
◆ provide diners with nutritious foods

*Ｓ*ince the days of prehistoric hunters and gatherers, people have understood that some animals and plants are good to eat and others are not. For thousands of years, cultures worldwide have attributed medicinal or beneficial effects to certain foods, particularly plants, and have recognized that foods that would otherwise be fine to eat may be unhealthy if improperly prepared or stored.

But it was not until the past few decades that people have become increasingly concerned about understanding how all foods affect their health and what foods can and should be consumed in order to promote good health. These concerns comprise the study of nutrition.

This chapter cannot provide an in-depth study of the nutritional sciences. Rather, it sets forth basic information about nutrients, food additives, and ingredient substitutes and alternatives. It also provides guidelines for reading package labels and preparing nutritious meals. Detailed nutritional information about many specific foods is found throughout the book. Also found throughout the book are recipes for dishes particularly low in calories, fat or sodium; each recipe is accompanied by a chart of nutritional values. These recipes are marked with a 👒.

Nutrition is the science that studies nutrients, the chemical substances found in food. Nutrients nourish the body by promoting growth, facilitating body functions and providing energy.

There are six categories of nutrients: carbohydrates, fats, proteins, vitamins, minerals and water. **Essential nutrients** are those that must be provided by food because the body does not produce them in sufficient quantities.

Essential nutrients—*nutrients that must be provided by food because the body does not produce them in sufficient quantities.*

The six nutrients are classified as either macronutrients or micronutrients. Macronutrients—the ones needed in large quantities—include carbohydrates, fats, proteins and water. Micronutrients—the ones the body requires only in small amounts—are vitamins and minerals.

Our bodies depend upon the various nutrients for different purposes and require different amounts of each depending on our age, sex and health. In addition, some nutrients depend on one another for proper functioning. For example, calcium and vitamin D work together in the body: Vitamin D promotes the absorption of the calcium that the body utilizes for proper bone growth. Because foods differ with regard to their nutritional content, it is important to eat a variety of foods in order to achieve a proper nutritional balance.

MACRONUTRIENTS

Calorie—*the unit of energy measured by the amount of heat required to raise 1000 grams of water one degree Celsius; it is also written as* kilocalorie *or* kcal.

Three of the macronutrients (carbohydrates, fats and proteins) provide calories or energy. A **calorie** (abbreviated *kcal*) is a unit of energy measured by the amount of heat required to rise 1000 grams of water one degree Celsius. It is the way we describe the amount of energy in food. The number of calories in food is measured by a device called a calorimeter, which burns the food and analyzes the residue.

One gram of pure fat supplies 9 kcal; one gram of pure carbohydrate supplies 4 kcal, as does one gram of pure protein. Most foods are a combination of carbohydrates, proteins and fats; their kcal content may not be easily determined unless we know how much of each macronutrient the food contains.

Carbohydrates

Carbohydrates are formed from hydrogen, oxygen and carbon; they are classified as simple or complex. **Simple carbohydrates** are single chains of naturally occurring **sugars**. These include simple sugars, called monosaccharides (mono = single; saccharide = sugar unit), and double sugars, called disaccharides (di = double). **Complex carbohydrates** are long chains of polysaccharides (poly = many). Polysaccharides consist of thousands of glucose units linked together and arranged as a **starch** or **fiber**.

The body digests (or breaks down) these sugars and starches into glucose. Glucose, also known as blood sugar, is a very important source of energy for the body.

Fiber is not digested for energy. Indeed, little is absorbed for any purpose. Undigestible fiber is known as **dietary fiber**. It generally comes from the seeds and cell walls of fruits, vegetables and cereal grains. Because the body cannot digest dietary fiber, this fiber passes through the digestive system almost completely unchanged. This helps keep the digestive tract running smoothly. Fiber increases fecal bulk, which encourages proper elimination of waste products from the large intestines and helps avoid some forms of gastrointestinal distress.

Simple carbohydrates are found in the naturally occurring sugars in fruit, vegetables and milk as well as sweeteners such as honey, corn syrup and table sugar. Complex carbohydrates are found in vegetables, fruits and cereal grains such as wheat, barley and oats.

Vegetables and fruits vary with regard to the relative amounts of sugar, starch and dietary fiber they contain. Root vegetables such as beets or potatoes have a high starch content but low fiber content. Leafy and stalk vegetables—lettuce and celery, for example—have relatively small quantities of starch, but they do contain a great deal of fiber. Fruits also vary in carbohydrate values. Most are high in sugars. Some fruits, such as dates and figs, are high in starch but low in fiber. Fruits with a high water content, such as strawberries, are low in starch but high in fiber.

Fats

Fats, like carbohydrates, are composed of carbon, hydrogen and oxygen. The differences between carbohydrates and fats are the number and arrangement of the carbon, hydrogen and oxygen atoms. Fats are found in both animal and plant foods, although fruits contain very little fat.

Depending upon their molecular structure, the fats in foods can be classified as saturated, monounsaturated or polyunsaturated. Most foods contain a combination of the three, although one kind may predominate. If saturated fat is the most abundant kind (as in the fat surrounding muscle meats), we describe the food as being saturated even though it contains a mixture of all three fats.

Saturated fats are found mainly in animal products such as milk, eggs and meats as well as in tropical oils such as coconut and palm. Monounsaturated fats come primarily from plants and plant products such as avocados and olive oil. Polyunsaturated fats come from plants (soy, corn and safflower oils, for example) and fish.

Saturated fats such a butter, lard and other animal fats are usually solid at room temperature. Monounsaturated and polyunsaturated fats are usually liquid at room temperature. Liquid vegetable oils like rapeseed (canola) and olive are high in monounsaturated fat. Cottonseed, sunflower, corn and safflower oils are high in polyunsaturated fat. All oils, however, are a combination of the three kinds of fat.

Polyunsaturated fats can become saturated through a process known as hydrogenation in which pressurized hydrogen gas is used to solidify the fat. Stick margarine, for example, is made by hydrogenating vegetable oil.

The body has more difficulty breaking down saturated fats than it does monounsaturated and polyunsaturated fats. Research suggests that high-fat diets, especially diets high in saturated fat, may be linked to heart disease, obesity and certain forms of cancer. Saturated fats are also linked to high levels of blood cholesterol, which are associated with arteriosclerosis (hardening of the arteries). Although the liver can produce all the cholesterol the body needs, additional cholesterol is often provided in the diet. Dietary cholesterol is found only in foods of animal origin. Meats, poultry, fish, shellfish, eggs and dairy products are all sources of dietary cholesterol. Fruits, vegetables and grains are cholesterol free.

Fats in moderate amounts are necessary for proper body functioning. Some transport the fat-soluble vitamins A, D, E and K throughout the body. Without fat, the body could not absorb these vitamins. Fats are also an important energy source. Fats contain 9 calories per gram, more than twice as many as carbohydrates or proteins, which each contain 4 calories per gram. Therefore, fats are an efficient way for the body to store energy.

Proteins

Proteins differ from carbohydrates and fats in that they contain nitrogen as well as carbon, hydrogen and oxygen. Protein chains are composed of various combinations of the approximately two dozen different amino acids, nine of which are essential nutrients. The specific combination of amino acids gives each protein its unique characteristics and properties. Animal proteins such as milk, dairy products, eggs, meat, poultry and fish all supply significant amounts of the essential amino acids.

Proteins are necessary for manufacturing, maintaining and repairing body tissues. They are essential for the periodic replacement of the outer layer of skin as well as for blood clotting and scar tissue formation. Hair and nails, which provide a protective cover for the body, are composed of insoluble proteins.

Another important function of protein is regulating body processes. Proteins regulate the balance of water, acids and bases and move nutrients in and out of cells. Proteins contribute to the immune system by producing antibodies, which are necessary for combating diseases. Proteins also form the enzymes that act as catalysts for body functions and the hormones that help direct body processes.

Water

The human body is approximately 60% water. Water is necessary for transporting nutrients and waste throughout the body. It cushions the cells, lubricates the joints, maintains stable body temperatures and assists waste elimination. It also promotes functioning of the nervous system and muscles.

The main sources of water are beverages such as water itself and juice. Some foods such as tomatoes, oranges, watermelon and iceberg lettuce are particularly high in water, but all foods contain it. Water is also formed by the body when other nutrients are metabolized. The average adult should consume at least 8 to 10 glasses (64 fluid ounces or 2 liters) of water a day to ensure adequate intake.

MICRONUTRIENTS

Vitamins and minerals are micronutrients. They have no calories and are consumed in small quantities. Vitamins and minerals are essential nutrients because they must be provided through the diet; the body cannot manufacture them in quantities adequate to ensure good health.

Vitamins

Vitamins are vital dietary substances needed to regulate the **metabolism** and for normal growth and body functions. They are distinct from carbohydrates, proteins and fats and are not manufactured in the body; they must be supplied by food.

Metabolism—*all of the chemical reactions and physical processes that continually occur in living cells and organisms.*

There are 13 essential vitamins. Table 3.1 lists the most important vitamins, sets forth their principal functions in the human body and identifies foods containing high concentrations of these nutrients.

Vitamins are divided into two categories: fat soluble and water soluble. The fat-soluble vitamins are A, D, E and K. Excess supplies of these vitamins are stored in fatty tissue and the liver. Water-soluble vitamins are vitamin C and the B complexes, including thiamin (B1), riboflavin (B2), niacin (B3), cobalamin (B12), pyridoxine (B6), pantothenic acid, biotin and folacin. Water-soluble vitamins are not stored to the extent that fat-soluble vitamins are, and any excess is generally excreted in the urine. Because of these differences, deficiencies in water-soluble vitamins usually develop more rapidly.

Virtually all foods contain some vitamins. Many factors contribute to a particular food's vitamin concentration: an animal's feed; the manner by which the produce is harvested, stored or processed; even the type of soil, sunlight, rainfall and temperature have significant effects on vitamin content. For example, tomatoes have a higher concentration of vitamin C when picked ripe from the vine rather than picked green. Also, different varieties of fruits and vegetables have different vitamin contents. A Wegener apple, for example, has 19 mg of vitamin C while a Red Delicious has only 6 mg.

You can control vitamin concentration and retention through careful food preparation:

1. Try to prepare vegetables as close to service time as possible; vegetables cut long before service lose more vitamins than those cut immediately before cooking.

2. Whether a vegetable is boiled, steamed or microwaved also determines the amount of vitamins it retains. Because B complex and C vitamins are water soluble, they are easily leached (washed out) or destroyed by food processing and preparation techniques such as boiling. Steaming helps retain nutrients (when steaming, keep the water level below the vegetables). But microwave cooking is best because it cooks vegetables with minimal water.

3. Roasting and grilling meats, poultry, fish and shellfish preserve more vitamins than stewing and braising. The temperatures to which foods are cooked may affect vitamin retention as well.

4. Storage affects vitamin concentrations. For example, long exposure to air and incandescent light may destroy vitamin C. Using airtight containers prevents some of this loss.

Table 3.1 identifies some of the preparation and storage techniques that help retain the maximum amount of various vitamins.

TABLE 3.1 VITAMINS: THEIR FUNCTIONS, SOURCES AND TECHNIQUES FOR RETAINING MAXIMUM NUTRIENT CONTENT

Vitamin	Functions in the Human Body	Sources	Techniques for Nutrient Retention
Vitamin A	Keeps skin healthy; protects eyes; protects mouth and nose linings; helps resist infections	Deep yellow vegetables, leafy green vegetables, egg yolks, liver, whole milk, deep yellow fruits	Serve fruits and vegetables raw; store vegetables covered and refrigerated; steam vegetables; roast or broil meats
Vitamin E	Anti-oxidant; protects membranes and cell walls	Vegetable oils, whole grains, dark leafy vegetables, legumes, peanuts	Use whole-grain flours; store foods in airtight containers; avoid exposing the food to light
Vitamin C (Ascorbic acid)	Repairs connective tissues; helps resist infections; promotes healing	Citrus fruits, raw green vegetables, strawberries, cantaloupes, tomatoes, broccoli	Serve fruits and vegetables raw; steam or microwave vegetables
Vitamin B6	Promotes enzyme functions	Meats, whole grains, dark green vegetables, potatoes, liver	Serve vegetables raw; cook foods in a minimum amount of water and for shortest possible time; roast or broil meats and fish
Vitamin B12	Helps produce red blood cells; assists metabolism; helps prevent anemia	Animal foods only, particularly milk, eggs, poultry and fish	Roast or broil meats, poultry and fish
Vitamin D	Helps absorb calcium; regulates calcium and phosphorus in bones	Milk, butter, fish oils, cream, egg yolks (exposure to sunlight produces vitamin D)	Store milk in opaque containers away from light
Vitamin K	Assists proper blood coagulation	Liver, dark green leafy vegetables (bacteria in intestinal track also produce vitamin K)	Steam or microwave vegetables; do not overcook meats
Folic Acid	Helps metabolize amino acids; promotes cell formation; prevents anemia	Dark green leafy vegetables, meats, fish, poultry, eggs, whole-grain cereals	Serve vegetables raw; steam or microwave vegetables; store vegetables covered and refrigerated
Thiamin (Vitamin B1)	Promotes normal digestion; necessary for the nervous system; helps enzymes metabolize food	Meats, poultry, dry beans and peas, peanut butter, enriched and whole-grain pastas, breads, etc.	Use enriched or whole-grain pasta or rice; do not wash whole grains before cooking or rinse afterwards; steam or microwave vegetables; roast meats at moderate temperatures; cook meats only until done
Riboflavin (Vitamin B2)	Helps usage of oxygen; promotes good vision and smooth skin; helps enzyme functions	Milk, cheese, fish, poultry, enriched and whole-grain breads, dark green leafy vegetables	Store foods in opaque containers; roast or broil meats or poultry
Niacin	Promotes normal digestion; necessary for the nervous system; helps enzymes metabolize food	Meats, poultry, fish, dark green leafy vegetables, whole grain or enriched breads and cereals	Steam or microwave vegetables; roast or broil beef, veal, lamb and poultry (pork retains about the same amount of niacin regardless of cooking method)

Minerals

Minerals cannot be manufactured by the body. They are obtained by eating plants that have drawn minerals from the ground or the flesh of animals that have eaten such plants.

Minerals are considered micronutrients because only small quantities are needed. Minerals are a critical component in hard and soft tissues (e.g., the calcium, magnesium and phosphorus present in bones and teeth). Minerals also regulate certain necessary body functions. For example, nerve impulses are transmitted through an exchange of sodium and potassium ions in the nerve cells.

Minerals are divided into two categories: trace minerals and macrominerals. Trace minerals such as iron are needed in only very small amounts. Macrominerals such as calcium are needed in relatively larger quantities. Table 3.2 lists several of the most important minerals, sets forth their principal functions and identifies foods containing high concentrations of these nutrients.

As with vitamins, food processing and preparation can reduce a food's mineral content. Soaking or cooking in large amounts of water can leach out a food's content of water-soluble minerals. Processing or refining grains, such as the wheat used to make white bread, also removes minerals. Table 3.2 identifies preparation and storage techniques for retaining maximum mineral content.

TABLE 3.2   MINERALS: THEIR FUNCTIONS, SOURCES AND TECHNIQUES FOR RETAINING MAXIMUM NUTRIENT CONTENT

Mineral	Functions in the Human Body	Sources	Techniques for Nutrient Retention
Calcium (a macromineral)	Helps build bones and teeth; helps blood clot; promotes muscle and nerve functions	Dairy products	Cook foods in minimum amount of water and for shortest possible time
Iron (a trace mineral)	Combines with protein to form hemoglobin (the red substance in blood that carries oxygen); prevents anemia	Meats, poultry, fish, dark green leafy vegetables	Cook foods in minimum amount of water and for shortest possible time
Magnesium (a trace mineral)	Promotes electrical activity of nerve cells	Green leafy vegetables, whole grains, legumes, fish and shellfish	Cook foods in minimum amount of water and for shortest possible time
Zinc (a trace mineral)	Enhances healing; a component of many enzymes; helps cells use oxygen	Organ and muscle meats, whole grain breads and cereals, oysters, peanuts, legumes	Cook foods in minimum amount of water and for shortest possible time
Phosphorus (a macromineral)	Helps build bones and teeth; helps enzymes metabolize food	Milk, meats, fish, egg yolk, legumes, nuts	Roast or broil lamb, veal, pork and poultry (beef retains the same amount of phosphorus regardless of cooking method); cook foods in minimum amount of water and for shortest possible time
Potassium (a macromineral)	Maintains electrolyte and fluid balance; promotes normal body functions	Meats, poultry, fish, bananas, dried fruits, citrus fruits, broccoli, carrots, celery, potatoes, cantaloupes	Cook foods in minimum amount of water and for shortest possible time

◆◆◆

THE FEDERAL GOVERNMENT GUARDS OUR LARDER

The federal government plays an important role in the way various foodstuffs are grown, raised, slaughtered, processed, marketed, stored and transported. The principal actors are the Food and Drug Administration of the United States Department of Health and Human Services (FDA) and the United States Department of Agriculture (USDA).

The FDA's activities are directed toward protecting the nation's health against impure and unsafe foods, as well as drugs, cosmetics, medical devices and other things. It develops and administers programs addressing food safety. For example, the FDA must approve any new food additive before a manufacturer markets it to food producers and processors. To gain FDA approval, the manufacturer must prove to the FDA's satisfaction that the additive (1) is effective for the intended purpose, (2) can be detected and measured in the final product and (3) is safe. The FDA holds public hearings during which experts and consumers provide evidence and opinions before it decides to grant or deny approval. If it grants approval, the FDA issues regulations identifying the amount of the additive that can be used and the foods to which it can be added. The FDA also sets standards for labeling foods, including nutrition labels. Labeling regulations not only address the type of information that must be conveyed, but also the way it is presented.

The USDA's principal responsibility is to make sure that individual food items are safe, wholesome and accurately labeled. It attempts to meet these responsibilities through inspection and grading procedures. The USDA also provides consumer services. It conducts and publishes research on nutrition and assists those producing our food to do so efficiently and effectively.

Other federal agencies that have a role in the nation's health and food supply include the United States Centers for Disease Control and Prevention (CDC), which track illnesses, including those caused by food-borne pathogens; the National Institutes of Health (NIH), which do basic biological and nutritional research; and the Department of the Interior, which sets environmental and land-use standards.

INGREDIENT SUBSTITUTES AND ALTERNATIVES

More and more people are becoming aware that too much of certain foods can be detrimental to their health. Many are trying to cut down on foods high in salt, fat, added sugar and cholesterol. To a degree, people can accomplish their goals—and chefs can assist them—by turning to ingredient substitutes and alternatives where possible.

Here we use the term **ingredient substitute** to mean the replacement of one ingredient with another of presumably similar—although not necessarily identical—taste, texture, appearance and other characteristics. The substitute will be more nutritious, however. So, if someone is on a low-sodium diet, for example, he can avoid the sodium found in salt (sodium chloride) by substituting potassium chloride. Or, if he is avoiding fats, he can use nonfat sour cream in place of regular sour cream when baking quick breads. The differences in taste, texture, appearance and baking quality should be minimal.

We use the term **ingredient alternative** to mean the replacement of one ingredient with another of different taste, texture, appearance or other characteristic, but one which will not compromise—although it may change—the taste of the dish. As with the ingredient substitute, the ingredient alternative will be more nutritious. Lemon juice and herbs, for instance, can be used as flavoring alternatives to salt; a salsa of fresh vegetables can replace a cream-based sauce. The dishes will not taste the same, but they will still taste good.

Salt Substitutes and Alternatives

Minerals are essential to good health, but overdosing can be dangerous. A major concern in the American diet is excessive sodium (salt). The average American consumes 3000 to 7000 mg of sodium per day. Yet the necessary daily requirement according to the RDA (the Recommended Dietary

Allowance, discussed below) is 1100 to 3300 mg per day. Research has linked excessive amounts of sodium to hypertension (high blood pressure), heart and kidney diseases and strokes.

Chefs can contribute to a more healthful diet by decreasing the use of salt and other high-sodium products like soy sauce. Salt substitutes, which contain potassium chloride instead of sodium chloride, are available. "Lite" salt has a portion of the sodium content replaced by potassium but still contains some real salt for a truer flavor.

In addition, pepper, lemon, herbs, spices, fruits and vinegars can be used as salt alternatives.

Artificial Sweeteners

Saccharin, the oldest artificial sugar substitute, has been used for nearly a century. A petroleum derivative, it has no calories and tastes 300 times sweeter than sugar. Along with its sweetness, though, come health risks. Studies have shown that saccharin causes tumors in rats.

Aspartame (also known as Nutrasweet®) was developed as a substitute for saccharin. Approved by the FDA in 1981, aspartame is composed of aspartic acid and phenylalanine, both of which are naturally occurring amino acids. Unlike saccharin, aspartame does not have an aftertaste, but it is only 180 times sweeter than sugar. It is now widely used in soft drinks, frozen yogurt, candy and similar products. Aspartame breaks down when heated, however, so it cannot be used in baked products. According to the FDA, aspartame is a safe substitute for sugar, although it is a risk for those people with the rare disease phenylketonuria (PKU), who cannot metabolize the phenylalanine in aspartame.

Another sugar substitute is Acesulfame K (also known as Sunnette®), which the FDA approved in 1988. The body cannot metabolize Acesulfame K, so it passes through the digestive system unchanged. Like aspartame, it has no aftertaste. Acesulfame K is used in chewing gum, dry beverage mixes, instant coffee and tea, gelatins and nondairy creamers.

Fat Substitutes

Several types of fat substitutes are available; they are either synthetic or derived from naturally-occurring food substances. Two of the more recent products are Olestra® and Simplesse®.

Olestra® is made of sucrose and vegetable oil. The two are bonded together and the final product consists of molecules too large to be digested. Because it cannot be digested, Olestra® does not add any calories. Following FDA approval, Olestra® will be useful in cooking oils or shortening as well as in salted snacks.

Simplesse® is a popular fat substitute used in frozen desserts such as ice creams and yogurt. Simplesse®, made from egg whites or milk proteins, has a rich, creamy texture similar to fat.

Other Ingredient Substitutes and Alternatives

There are many other ingredient substitutes, some of which are identified in Table 3.3. Often ingredient substitutes and alternatives will have a dramatic impact on the nutritional values of a completed dish. For example, in Figures 3.1 A and B we list the ingredients for a traditional sausage and cheese omelet and

TABLE 3.3   INGREDIENT SUBSTITUTES

Instead of	Use
Bacon	Canadian bacon
Butter	Powdered butter granules plus liquid (either skim milk or water)
Chocolate	Cocoa (vegetable oil may be added as needed)
Cream cheese	Reduced fat or nonfat cream cheese
Emulsified salad dressing	Start with a base of reduced-fat or nonfat yogurt, sour cream or mayonnaise, then thin with skim milk
Light cream	Equal portions of 1% milk and skim evaporated milk
Mayonnaise	Reduced-fat mayonnaise (can be mixed with reduced-fat or nonfat sour cream)
Sour cream	Reduced-fat or nonfat sour cream; drained reduced fat or nonfat plain yogurt
Whipped cream	Whipped chilled evaporated skim milk

one made with ingredient substitutes. Similarly, in Figures 3.2 A and B we list the ingredients for a sheet pan of traditional fudge brownies and one made with ingredient substitutes. We also list the nutritional values for each of the four recipes. Note the differences, especially in the values for fat and cholesterol.

TRADITIONAL SAUSAGE AND CHEESE OMELET

Yield: 1 serving

Eggs, whole	3	3
Milk	3 Tbsp.	45 ml
Breakfast sausage, cooked	2 oz.	60 g
Cheddar cheese, grated	1 oz.	30 g
Salt	1/8 tsp.	1 ml
White pepper	1/8 tsp.	1 ml
Butter*	1 Tbsp.	15 ml

*The butter is used as the fat for cooking the omelet.

Nutritional values:

Calories	686	Protein	35 g
Calories from fat	76%	Vitamin A	1745 IU
Total fat	58 g	Vitamin C	0 mg
Saturated fat	26 g	Sodium	1342 mg
Cholesterol	740 mg		

FIGURE 3.1 A

OMELET WITH INGREDIENT SUBSTITUTES

Yield: 1 serving

Egg Beaters	6 oz.	180 ml
Turkey sausage, cooked and drained	2 oz.	60 g
Reduced-fat cheddar cheese, grated	1 oz.	30 g
Salt substitute	1/8 tsp.	1 ml
White pepper	1/8 tsp.	1 ml
Pan-release spray*		

*The omelet is cooked using pan-release spray instead of butter.

Nutritional values:

Calories	284	Protein	38 g
Calories from fat	41%	Vitamin A	170 IU
Total fat	13 g	Vitamin C	0 mg
Saturated fat	5 g	Sodium	780 mg
Cholesterol	61 mg		

FIGURE 3.1 B

TRADITIONAL FUDGE BROWNIES

Yield: one sheet pan

Unsweetened chocolate	2 lbs.	1 kg
Butter	2 lbs.	1 kg
Eggs	20	20
Sugar	5 lbs. 12 oz.	2.9 kg
Vanilla extract	2 oz.	60 ml
All-purpose flour	1 lb. 10 oz.	750 g
Pecan pieces	1 lb.	500 g

Nutritional values per two-inch square:

Calories	315	Protein	4 g
Calories from fat	49%	Vitamin A	367 IU
Total fat	17 g	Vitamin C	0 mg
Saturated fat	8 g	Sodium	92 mg
Cholesterol	65 mg		

The complete recipe is produced as Recipe 30.29.

FIGURE 3.2 A

BROWNIES MADE WITH INGREDIENT SUBSTITUTES

Yield: one sheet pan

Unsweetened chocolate	4 oz.	120 g
Cake flour	1 lb.	450 g
Cocoa powder	9 oz.	270 g
Salt substitute	2 tsp.	10 ml
Egg whites	12	12
Whole eggs	8	8
Granulated sugar	2 lbs. 2 oz.	1 kg
Corn syrup	2 lbs.	900 g
Unsweetened applesauce	1 1/2 pts.	670 ml
Canola oil	7 oz.	210 g
Vanilla extract	2 Tbsp.	30 ml

Nutritional values per two-inch square:

Calories	133	Protein	2 g
Calories from fat	24%	Vitamin A	30 IU
Total fat	3 g	Vitamin C	0 mg
Saturated fat	1 g	Sodium	38 mg
Cholesterol	18 mg		

The complete recipe is produced as Recipe 30.31.

FIGURE 3.2 B

Ingredient substitutes and, especially, ingredient alternatives will change the nutritional values of a dish; they may also change its taste, texture or appearance. Sometimes these changes will be acceptable; sometimes they will not. Because some ingredient substitutes and alternatives result in unsatisfactory flavors, textures or appearance, many recipes may not be suitable for substitution or alteration. Use your judgment.

ADDITIVES

Additives are substances added to many foods to prevent spoilage or improve appearance, texture, taste or nutritional value. Some food additives are incidental; some are intentional. Incidental food additives are those inadvertently or unintentionally added to foods during processing, such as pesticide residues on fruits and vegetables. Intentional food additives are those added to foods on purpose. These include the chemicals that ensure longer shelf life in baked goods and the food colorings used to make items more visually appealing.

Additives may be synthetic, synthetic materials copied from nature, or naturally occurring substances. For example, sugar substitutes used to sweeten beverages are synthetic substances, while the vitamin C and beta carotene used to preserve foods are substances copied from nature. Lecithin, an emulsifier, comes from natural sources. Although a chef will rarely use any of these additives directly, they will undoubtedly appear in many of the packaged or prepared products you may use.

PACKAGE LABELING

FDA Labeling Requirements

In an effort to provide chefs and consumers with greater information about the nutritional values of foods they purchase, the FDA sets standards for package labels. The FDA labeling requirements address (1) product identification, (2) product claims and (3) nutritional information.

Not all foods must be labeled according to FDA regulations, however. Common exceptions are (1) foods produced by small businesses, (2) foods produced and sold on site, including vending machine food, (3) foods shipped in bulk, (4) foods such as coffee, tea and some spices that have little or no nutritional value, (5) foods sold in packages with less than 12 square inches available for labeling, (6) foods sold for immediate consumption, (7) fresh fruits and vegetables and (8) raw poultry, meat and fish (USDA controls labeling practices for these items). The manufacturers, processors, distributors or retailers of these foods can voluntarily abide by the FDA labeling regulations if they wish.

Reading the Label

Product Identification

The FDA requires that products be clearly labeled with (1) the common name of the product, (2) the name and address of the manufacturer, packer or distributor, (3) the ingredients in descending order of predominance by weight and (4) the net contents by weight, measure or count. See Figure 3.3.

◆◆◆

BACK TO BASICS

Great strides in agriculture have been made during the past two centuries. Pesticides, fungicides and herbicides now eliminate or control pests that once would have devoured, ruined or choked crops. Chemical fertilizers increase yields of many of the world's staples. But not everyone has greeted these developments with open arms.

During the past few decades, scientific and medical investigators have documented, or at least suggested, health risks associated with certain synthetic pesticides, fertilizers and other products. These findings have led to a renewed interest in a back-to-the-basics approach to farming: organic farming. Specialty farms, orchards and even wineries now offer organically grown products (or, in the case of wineries, wines made from organically grown grapes). These products come with few, if any, intentional additives and should be free of any incidental additives. Proponents argue that these products are better for you and better for the health of the farm workers.

There are no federal guidelines identifying what can be called "organic." Approximately half of the states, however, have laws addressing the production of organically grown foods. These laws vary widely, but generally, most states require that products marketed as "organically grown" must have been grown in soil certified free of synthetic pesticides, fungicides, herbicides or fertilizers. Depending on the state, the land can be certified free of these products one to three years after their use has ceased.

FIGURE 3.3   *Label Illustrating Product Identification and Product Claim Requirements*
Illustration Source: Food and Drug Administration 1993

Product Claims

The FDA requires that words such as "low fat" and "fat free" be used according to specific standards. The FDA has approved the following usages:

✦ *Free*—The food must contain no or only "physiologically inconsequential" amounts of fat, saturated fat, cholesterol, sodium, sugars or calories.

✦ *Low, Little, Few* and *Low Source of*—The food can be eaten frequently without exceeding dietary guidelines for fat, saturated fat, cholesterol, sodium or calories.

Specific usages include:

Low fat—The food has 3 grams or less of fat per serving.

Low saturated fat—The food has 1 gram or less of saturated fat per serving; not more than 15% of a serving's calories are from saturated fat.

Low sodium—The food has 140 mg or less of salt per serving.

Very low sodium—The food has 35 mg or less of salt per serving.

Low cholesterol—The food has 20 mg or less of cholesterol per serving.

Low calorie—The food has 40 calories or fewer per serving.

Reduced, less and *fewer*—The nutritionally-altered product must contain at least 25% fewer calories than the regular or reference (i.e., FDA standard) food product.

Light or *Lite*—The nutritionally altered product must contain at least one third or 50% less fat than the reference product. *Light in sodium* means that the nutritionally-altered product contains 50% or less sodium than the regular or reference product. *Light* may still be used to describe color, as in "light brown sugar."

- *High*—The food must contain 20% or more of the daily value for a desirable nutrient per serving.
- *More*—The food must contain at least 10% or more of the daily value for protein, vitamins, minerals, dietary fiber or potassium than the reference product.
- *Good Source*—The food contains 10 to 19% of the daily value per serving for the specific nutrient such as calcium or dietary fiber.
- *Lean*—The meat, poultry, game, fish or shellfish item contains less than 10 grams of fat, less than 4 grams of saturated fat and less than 95 mg cholesterol per serving and per 100 grams.
- *Extra Lean*—The meat, poultry, game, fish or shellfish item contains less than 5 grams of fat, less than 2 grams of saturated fat and less than 95 mg cholesterol per serving and per 100 grams.

TABLE 3.4   DIET–DISEASE LINKS AND APPROVED HEALTH CLAIMS FOR LABELS

Food or Nutrient	Disease	Typical Foods	FDA-Approved Claim
Calcium	Osteoporosis	Low-fat and skim milks, yogurt, tofu, calcium-fortified citrus drinks, some calcium supplements	"Regular exercise and a healthy diet with enough calcium helps teen and young adult white and Asian women maintain good bone health and may reduce their high risk of osteoporosis later in life."
Sodium	Hypertension	Unsalted tuna, salmon, fruits and vegetables, low-fat milk and yogurt, cottage cheese, sherbet, cereal, flour and pasta (not egg pasta)	"Diets low in sodium may reduce the risk of high blood pressure, a disease associated with many factors."
Dietary fiber	Cancer	Fruits, vegetables, reduced-fat milk products, cereals, flours, sherbet	"Development of cancer depends on many factors. A diet low in total fat may reduce the risk of some cancers."
Dietary saturated fat and cholesterol	Coronary heart disease	Fruits, vegetables, skim and low-fat milks, cereals, whole-grain products, pasta (not egg pasta)	"While many factors affect heart disease, diets low in saturated fat and cholesterol may reduce the risk of this disease."
Fruits, vegetables and grain products that contain fiber	Cancer	Whole-grain breads and cereals, fruits and vegetables	"Low-fat diets rich in fiber-containing grain products, fruits, and vegetables may reduce the risk of some types of cancer, a disease associated with many factors."
Fruits, vegetables and grain products that contain fiber	Coronary heart disease	Fruits, vegetables and whole-grain breads and cereals	"Diets low in saturated fat and cholesterol and rich in fruits, vegetables, and grain products that contain some types of dietary fiber, particularly soluble fiber, may reduce the risk of heart disease, a disease associated with many factors."
Fruits and vegetables	Cancer	Fruits and vegetables	"Low-fat diets rich in fruits and vegetables (foods that are low in fat and may contain dietary fiber, vitamin A, or vitamin C) may reduce the risk of some types of cancer, a disease associated with many factors. Broccoli is high in vitamins A and C, and it is a good source of dietary fiber."

The FDA recognizes that there is a linkage between some foods or nutrients and certain diseases. It allows manufacturers and retailers (or their advertising agencies) to make certain specific claims regarding their products and these **diet–disease links**. See Table 3.4. For example, because the frozen mixed vegetables in Figure 3.3 are "low fat" and "cholesterol free," the manufacturer can make a specific claim about its product and the risk of heart disease.

Nutritional Information

The FDA requires that labels identify specific nutritional information including: (1) serving size, (2) total number of calories per serving, (3) number of calories from fat per serving, and (4) the percent of daily values for certain nutrients per serving. The labels must also include reference information such as the recommended daily values for certain nutrients and the number of calories per gram of fat, protein and carbohydrate. Products with limited label space do not have to include the reference information. Figure 3.4 reproduces a sample FDA nutritional label for the frozen mixed vegetables package illustrated in Figure 3.3.

Serving Size: The FDA has defined standard serving sizes for approximately 150 food categories, making it easier for consumers to compare different brands. The serving sizes reflect the amounts people actually eat.

Percent Daily Value: This section shows how the food fits into the daily diet. Most people are concerned about getting too much fat, saturated fat, cholesterol and sodium in their daily diet. This section identifies the grams per serving for each of these nutrients and the percent of the daily recommended amount of that nutrient each serving provides. The percentage is based on a 2000-calorie daily diet. For example, a person on a 2000-calorie daily diet (the FDA standard) should consume no more than 65 grams of fat. The 3 grams of total fat per serving of this frozen-mixed-vegetables product is 5% of the person's recommended daily intake of fat.

Calories per Gram: This is placed on all labels to remind consumers that carbohydrates and protein have 4 calories per gram and fat has 9 calories per gram.

Calories from Fat: Current dietary recommendations provide that no more than 30% of a person's daily caloric intake come from fat. To help consumers meet these dietary guidelines, the number of calories per serving from fat is identified.

The Recommended Daily Intake or RDI: These values represent the percentage of the daily recommended intake of important vitamins and minerals per serving. They were selected from the Recommended Dietary Allowances (RDA), which is discussed below. But unlike the RDA, the RDI sets the recommended amount of each vitamin and mineral for a so-called standard adult; it does not account for sex, age, health or other attributes. The RDI was formerly known as the U.S. RDA but was changed because of confusion with the RDA.

Daily Values: This outlines the basics of a good diet and is used to show how the food fits into such a daily diet. Some of the recommended intakes are maximums. For example, someone on a 2000-calorie-per-day diet should consume 65 grams or less of fat; someone on a 2500-calorie-per-day diet should consume 80 grams or less of fat. Other intakes are minimums; for example, 300 grams or more of carbohydrates for someone on a 2000-calorie daily diet. This section remains the same on all labels and is intended as a guide for the consumer when reading the Percent Daily Value information.

Nutrition Facts

Serving Size ½ cup (114g)
Servings Per Container 4

Amount Per Serving

Calories 90   Calories from Fat 30

                        % Daily Value*

Total Fat 3g	**5%**
Saturated Fat 0g	**0%**
Cholesterol 0mg	**0%**
Sodium 300mg	**13%**
Total Carbohydrate 13g	**4%**
Dietary Fiber 3g	**12%**
Sugars 3g	
Protein 3g	

Vitamin A	80%	Vitamin C	60%
Calcium	4%	Iron	4%

* Percent Daily Values are based on a 2,000 calorie diet. Your daily values may be higher or lower depending on your calorie needs:

		Calories	2,000	2,500
Total Fat	Less than		65g	80g
Sat Fat	Less than		20g	25g
Cholesterol	Less than		300mg	300mg
Sodium	Less than		2,400mg	2,400mg
Total Carbohydrate			300g	375g
Fiber			25g	30g

Calories per gram:
Fat 9 • Carbohydrate 4 • Protein 4

FIGURE 3.4 *Label Illustrating Nutritional Information Requirements*
Illustration Source: Food and Drug Administration 1993

THE RECOMMENDED DIETARY ALLOWANCE

The Recommended Dietary Allowance (RDA) is the standard for the daily intake of various nutrients. The RDA, first published in 1943 by the Food and Nutrition Board of the National Research Council, is revised about every five years. The Food and Nutrition Board also publishes the Nutritive Value of Foods which identifies serving sizes and nutrient information for a wide variety of foods.

The nutrients listed on the RDA table are protein; vitamins A, D, E, C, K; selenium; thiamin; riboflavin; niacin; B6; folacin; and B12 as well as the minerals calcium, phosphorus, magnesium, iron, zinc and iodine. The RDA table identifies nutrient allowances for both sexes and 15 age categories, including pregnant and lactating women. The tables are intended as guidelines for the intake of essential nutrients based upon the known needs of most healthy people.

The RDA assists chefs and dietitians, especially in schools, hospitals and other institutions, in developing nutritious meal plans.

THE FOOD PYRAMID

For many years, nutritionists and others have attempted to define a healthy, balanced diet. Most of these models divide foods into general categories and recommend that a certain number of servings or calories be consumed from each category for a balanced diet.

Before 1956 the USDA recognized seven food groups: (1) meats, eggs, dried peas and beans, (2) milk, cheese and ice cream, (3) potatoes and other vegetables and fruits, (4) green leafy and yellow vegetables, (5) citrus fruits, tomatoes and raw cabbage, (6) breads and flours and (7) butter and fortified margarine.

In 1956 the USDA reduced the seven groups to four: (1) milk and cheese, (2) meats and fish, (3) fruits and vegetables and (4) grains. An optional fifth category was sweets and fats. From these Four Basic Food Groups, the USDA recommended the average adult eat a total of 12 servings daily. Two or more servings should come from each of the meat and milk groups, and four or more servings from each of the other two groups.

In 1992 the USDA abandoned the Four Basic Food Groups and adopted the Food Pyramid. The Food Pyramid prioritizes and proportions the food choices among the food groups and gives a visual presentation of proper daily nutrition. See Figure 3.5.

As the pyramid narrows, the recommended number of daily servings decreases.

The base of the pyramid contains the bread, cereal, rice and pasta group; recommended daily intake is 6 to 11 servings. A serving consists of 1 slice of bread; 1/2 cup of cooked rice, pasta or cereal; or 1 ounce of ready-to-eat cereal.

The second tier from the bottom is divided into two unequal sections: vegetables and fruits. You should eat 3 to 5 servings from the vegetable group every day. A serving of vegetables consists of 1/2 cup of chopped raw or cooked vegetables or 1 cup of leafy raw vegetables. You should also eat 2 to 4 servings per day of fruit. A serving consists of 1 piece of fruit or melon, 3/4 cup of juice, 1/2 cup of canned fruit or 1/4 cup of dried fruit.

The third tier from the bottom is divided in half: the milk, yogurt and cheese group, and the meat, poultry, fish, shellfish, dry beans, eggs and nuts

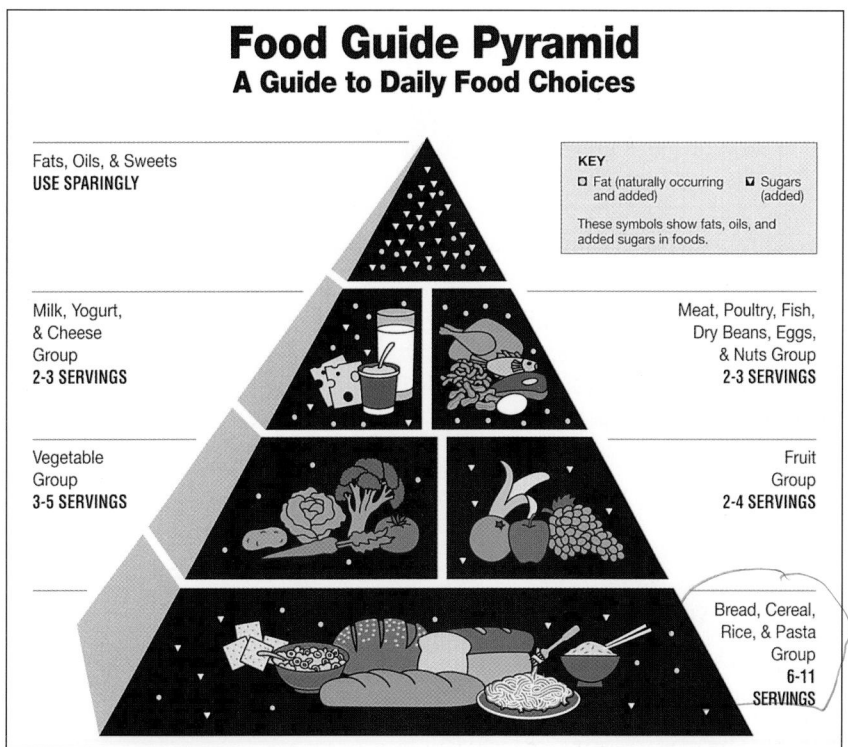

FIGURE 3.5   *The Food Pyramid*

group. You should have 2 to 3 servings from each group daily. A serving from the milk group consists of 1 cup of milk or yogurt, or 1-1/2 to 2 ounces of cheese. A serving from the meat group consists of 2-1/2 to 3 ounces of cooked lean meat, poultry, fish or shellfish; a 1/2 cup of cooked beans, 1 egg or 2 tablespoons of peanut butter counts as 1 ounce of meat.

Capping the pyramid is the fat, oil and sweets group; intake from this group should be limited. Small circles symbolizing fat and small triangles symbolizing sugar are scattered throughout the pyramid to show that some foods in these groups can add fats and sugar to the diet.

The Food Pyramid emphasizes that some foods are nutritionally better than others. It cautions against eating fats, while urging us to eat plenty of fruits, vegetables, grains, pasta and breads. These foods contain important nutrients such as vitamins, minerals, complex carbohydrates and dietary fiber.

NUTRITION AND THE CHEF

The Food Pyramid was designed to guide food consumption for a more healthful life. It presents a plan for a balanced diet. Chefs can use it to plan balanced menus as well. As the Food Pyramid suggests, chefs do not need to use only meat as the center of the plate presentation. It demands that a variety of breads, pasta and grains be included on the menu along with an interesting selection of vegetable dishes. And it cautions against the use of too much fat and sugar.

While not every food service operation can (or should) be devoted to "health food," to the extent appropriate you should offer healthful dining alternatives. Your ability to do so depends, of course, upon your facility. Chefs at hospitals, prisons and schools have much greater control over the foods their clientele consumes. Therefore, they have a far greater opportunity and responsibility to provide selections for a well-balanced diet. Chefs at most restaurants, however, do not have such captive audiences. But that does not mean that you can shirk your responsibilities.

You assist customers when you:

1. Use proper purchasing and storage techniques in order to preserve nutrients;
2. Offer a variety of foods from each tier of the Food Pyramid so that customers have a choice;
3. Offer entrees that emphasize plant instead of animal foods;
4. Offer dishes that are considerate of special dietary needs such as low fat or low salt;

◆◆◆

THE CUSTOMERS WHO COUNT

I have spent nineteen years of my professional life in the "fine dining" or "gourmet" field. As of the date of this publication, I will have completed my twentieth year in transition to what I now call a "Minimax" lifestyle.

Minimax is not the opposite of fine "gourmet dining." As a culinary philosophy it has its place about midway. *Minimax* is a constructed word that can be understood internationally. *Mini* refers to *minimum*, in this case to risks encountered by unwise or excessive consumption of food. *Max*, on the other hand, refers to *maximum* possible enhancement of food, using natural aromas, colors and textures rather than the classic western dependence on salts, fats and sugars.

Your future customers will be involved in a struggle when they read your menu. With their subjective right brains, they will be remembering former meals with enormous relish. With their objective left brains, they will apply what they know about fat, calories and sodium. Without some help they will either be confused, perplexed, rebellious or guilty.

Somehow then, you, who will make up the educated center of the restaurant business of the future, will have to address the needs of those who want to make changes and still celebrate a night out at a comforting restaurant.

My suggestion is that you devise recipes that avoid fat as a primary source of calories for *at least* two appetizers, two entrees and one dessert. I would simply describe these on the menu for what they contain and not call them "low-fat" or "diet" or, for that matter, by any special name (even Minimax!). I would then present a small, very attractive, folded menu card with a phrase such as "For Our Customers Who Count" on the outside, and then simply list the nutritional benefits from the low-fat specials in an attractive, easy-to-read manner.

If your management chooses to establish such a menu, it will be extremely important that you weigh each dish correctly and have it analyzed by an approved nutrition system such as NDS (from the University of Minnesota's Nutrition Coordinating Center, 2221 University Avenue SE, Suite 310, Minneapolis, MN 55414-3076; phone (612) 627-4862), or Heart Smart International (6617 N. Scottsdale Road, Scottsdale, AZ 85250; phone (800) 762-7819.)

The reason for accuracy is that some, if not most, of the "customers who count" do so for very critical reasons. To give someone an oversized portion of meat with a great sauce that far exceeds, say, 30% calories from fat is actually highly irresponsible and may even attract possible litigation in the future.

When you reduce fat in a classical dish, there will be a reduction in flavor, since "fat carries flavor." By drawing attention away from the taste change and enhancing the sense of smell (aroma), sight (color and presentation) and touch (texture), you can actually improve the finished dish.

I have found that the fusion idea has helped make this a reality. Fusion is simply merging seasonings from one culture with those from another. In this way it helps to see Northern European specialties that use abundant dairy products as "velvet memories," and North African and Asian seasonings as "future bright notes."

It is then possible to consider a modification to, say, sauce hollandaise by lowering the fat and adding a good Asian fish sauce to which shreds of mint and flecks of red pepper are added to spike interest with aroma, color and texture.

Whatever you choose to do, let met give you this last word of encouragement. Study hard, read the classics and see the future through them. If you've ever skipped smooth stones on flat water you'll know that the first bounce really matters. If your attitude to very rich classics is negative and condemning, then what you try to achieve will certainly fail to go the distance.

Therefore, don't condemn anyone's work. Aim to please today's customer with all the skills that our exciting profession has developed for thousands of years.

You have my very best wishes for a most successful career. Now go skip your stone . . . for your customers' sakes!

GRAHAM KERR, *author, chef and host of*
THE GALLOPING GOURMET
and GRAHAM KERR'S KITCHEN,
seen on PBS-TV and
The Discovery Channel

5. Use cooking procedures that preserve rather than destroy nutrients;

6. Use cooking procedures that minimize the use of added fat (e.g., stocks, sauces and soups can be cooled and the congealed fats removed; foods can be browned in the oven instead of being sautéed in hot fat);

7. Use equipment that minimizes the use of added fat (e.g., nonstick pans);

8. Train the wait staff to respond properly to nutritional questions diners may have about menu items, and

9. Use ingredient alternatives or substitutes where appropriate. If a dish does not lend itself to ingredient alternatives or substitutes, consider creating a new dish that replaces less nutritious traditional foods or preparations with more nutritious ones. For example, instead of serving a sauce made with butter, flour and cream, you can reduce an appropriately seasoned wine, stock or juice and then thicken it with fruit or vegetable purées or cornstarch.

Throughout this book are recipes marked with the symbol illustrated in Figure 3.6. This symbol indicates that the recipe is for a healthful dish. These dishes are generally low in calories, fat, saturated fat and/or sodium; if appropriate, they are also a good source of vitamins, protein, fiber or calcium. A table of nutritional values accompanies each recipe. These dishes are not necessarily dietetic. Rather, they should be consumed as part of a well-rounded, nutritious diet to meet the goals reflected in the Food Pyramid.

FIGURE 3.6 *The Symbol for a Healthful Recipe*

CONCLUSION

A basic understanding of and appreciation for nutrition are important for both the consumer and those who prepare the foods consumed.

What you serve is important. Carbohydrates, proteins, fats, water, vitamins and minerals, in varying amounts, are all necessary for good health. The Food Pyramid can guide selections to create and maintain a healthful diet.

How you prepare foods is also important. You should provide your customers with nutritious dishes. Remember that some cooking and storage techniques preserve nutrients; others do not. In addition, by substituting or modifying ingredients and preparation methods, many dishes can be made more nutritious.

QUESTIONS FOR DISCUSSION

1. Identify the six categories of nutrients and list two sources for each.

2. What are the differences between saturated fats and unsaturated fats? Identify two sources for each.

3. List four things you can do to reduce the loss of micronutrients when storing or preparing foods.

4. Describe the Food Pyramid. Explain how a chef can use it to plan well-balanced meals and how a consumer can use it to establish a healthful diet.

5. Create two menus for a traditional holiday dinner; one should be nutritionally well balanced and the other not. Explain your choices.

CHAPTER 4
MENU PLANNING
AND
FOOD COSTING

*T*oday's professional chef must master more than the basics of béchamel, butchering and bread baking. You must be equally skilled in the business of food services. This means knowing what products cost and how much an operation should charge for its menu items.

Although computers are almost as common in kitchens as whisks, no machine can ever replace a chef's hands-on ability to apply food cost controls. Accurate measurements, portion control and proper food handling directly affect the food service operation's bottom line. In addition, modern chefs must, at the very least, be able to conduct yield tests, calculate recipe costs and use food cost percentages.

This chapter first introduces you to various types and styles of menus. It then explains a standardized recipe format and presents the basics of food cost controls as well as information on measurements and techniques for changing or converting recipe yields. It then describes methods for determining unit and recipe costs, including calculations for raw yield tests. It concludes with a discussion of the methods for pricing menus and controlling food costs. This chapter does not attempt to cover menu design, accounting principles or computer applications. It will, however, provide a foundation of practical techniques to be used by anyone with common sense and a calculator.

THE MENU

Whether it lists Afghan dishes, hamburgers, just desserts or classic cuisine, and whether the prices range from inexpensive to exorbitant, the menu is the soul of every food service operation. Its purposes are to identify for the consumer the foods and beverages the operation offers, to create consumer enthusiasm and to increase sales. When combined with good food and good service, a good menu helps ensure success.

Most menus offer consumers sufficient selections to build an entire meal. A typical American main meal consists of three courses. The first course may be a hot or cold appetizer, soup or salad. The second course is the **entree** or main dish, usually meat, poultry, fish or shellfish accompanied by a vegetable and starch. The third course is dessert, either a sweet preparation or fruit and cheese. For a more formal meal, there may be a progression of first courses, including a hot or cold appetizer and soup, as well as a fish course served before the main dish (which, in this case, would not be fish). For a meal served in the European tradition, the salad would be presented as a palate cleanser after the main dish and before dessert.

Entree—*the main dish of an American meal, usually meat, poultry, fish or shellfish accompanied by a vegetable and starch; in France it is the first course, served before the fish and meat courses.*

Types of Menus

Menus are classified according to the regularity with which the foods are offered:

1. **Static menu**—All patrons are offered the same foods every day. Once a static menu is developed and established, it rarely changes. Static menus are typically found in fast-food operations, ethnic restaurants, steakhouses and the like.

   Static menus can also be used in institutional settings. For example, a static menu at an elementary school could offer students, along with a vegetable and dessert, the same luncheon choices every school day: a cheeseburger, fish sticks, chicken tacos, pizza wedges or a sandwich.

2. **Cycle menu**—A cycle menu is developed for a set time period; at the end of that period it repeats itself (i.e., on a seven-day cycle, the same menu is used every Monday). Some cycle menus are written on a seasonal basis, with a new menu for each season to take advantage of product availability. Cycle means are used commonly in schools, hospitals and other institutions. Although cycle menus may be repetitious, the repetition is not necessarily noticeable to diners because of the length of the cycles.

3. **Market menu**—A market menu is based upon product availability during a specific time period; it is written to use foods when they are in peak season or readily available. Market menus are becoming increasingly popular with chefs (and consumers) as they challenge the chef's ingenuity in using fresh, seasonal products. Market menus are short-lived, however, because of limited product availability and perishability. In fact, they often change daily.

4. **Hybrid menu**—A hybrid menu combines a static menu with a cycle menu or a market menu of specials.

Food service operations may have separate menus for breakfast, lunch or dinner. If all three meals are available all day and are listed on the same menu, the menu is often called a California menu; California menus are typically found in 24-hour restaurants. Depending on the food service operation's objectives, separate specialty menus for drinks, hors d'oeuvres, desserts, brunch or afternoon tea, for example, are used.

Regardless of whether the menu is static, cycle, market or hybrid, it can offer consumers the opportunity to purchase their selections à la carte, semi à la carte, table d'hôte or some combination of the three.

1. **À la carte**—Every food and beverage item is priced and ordered separately.

2. **Semi à la carte**—With this popular menu style, some food items (particularly appetizers and desserts) are priced and ordered separately, while the entree is accompanied by and priced to include other items, such as a salad, starch or vegetable.

3. **Table d'hôte** or **prix fixe**—This menu offers a complete meal at a set price. (The term *table d'hôte* is French for "host's table" and is derived from the innkeeper's practice of seating all guests at a large communal table and serving them all the same meal.) A table d'hôte meal can range from very elegant to a diner's blue-plate special.

Many menus combine à la carte, semi à la carte and table d'hôte choices. For example, appetizers, salads and desserts may be available à la carte; entrees may be offered semi à la carte (they come with a salad, starch and vegetable), while the daily special is a complete (table d'hôte or prix fixe) meal.

Menu Language

The menu is the principal way in which the food service operation, including the chef, communicates with the consumer. A well-designed menu often reflects the input of design, marketing, art and other consultants as well as the chef and management. The type of folds, cover, artwork, layout, typefaces, colors and paper are all important considerations. But the most important consideration is the language.

The menu should list the foods offered. It may include descriptions such as the preparation method, essential ingredients and service method as well as the quality, cut and quantity of product. For example, the menu can list "Porterhouse Steak" or "Mesquite Grilled 16-oz. Angus Beef Porterhouse Steak."

Federal as well as some state and local laws require that certain menu language be accurate. Areas of particular concern include statements about quantity, quality, grade and freshness as well as dietary and nutritional claims. Accurate references to an item's source are also important. If brand names are used, those brands must be served. If the restaurant claims to be serving "Fresh Dover Sole," it must be just that, not frozen sole from New England. (On the other hand, like French or Russian dressing, "English mint sauce" is a generic name for a style of food, so using that geographical adjective is appropriate even if the mint sauce is made in Arizona.) A reference to "our own fresh-baked" desserts means that the restaurant regularly bakes the desserts on premises, serves them soon after baking and does not substitute commercially prepared or frozen goods.

STANDARDIZED RECIPES

Recipe—*a set of written instructions for producing a specific food or beverage; also known as a* formula.

Standardized Recipe—*a recipe producing a known quality and quantity of food for a specific operation.*

Menu writing and **recipe** development are mutually dependent activities. Once the menu is created, standardized recipes should be prepared for each item. A **standardized recipe** is one that will produce a known quality and quantity of food for a specific operation. It specifies (1) the type and amount of each ingredient, (2) the preparation and cooking procedures, and (3) the yield and portion size.

Standardized recipes are not found in books or provided by manufacturers; they are recipes customized to your operation—cooking time, temperature and utensils should be based on the equipment actually available. Yield should be adjusted to an amount appropriate for your operation. A recipe must be tested repeatedly and adjusted to fit your facility and your needs before it can be considered standardized.

Standardized recipes are a tool for the chef and management. The written forms assist with training cooks, educating service staff and controlling financial matters. They also help ensure that the customer will receive a consistent quality and quantity of product. Accurate recipe costing and menu pricing depends on having and using standardized recipes.

Although formats differ, a standardized recipe form such as that reproduced in Figure 4.1 will usually include:

◆ Name of product
◆ Yield
◆ Portion size
◆ Presentation and garnish
◆ Ingredient quality and quantity
◆ Preparation procedures
◆ Cooking time and temperature
◆ Holding procedures

STANDARD RECIPE CARD FOR ITEM:									DATE REVISED	

QUANTITY PRODUCED   RECIPE FILE NO.

PORTION SIZE   RESTAURANT

NO. OF PORTIONS PRODUCED   SALES PRICE

INGREDIENTS	QTY/ WEIGHT	PURCH UNIT	DATE:		DATE:		DATE:		PREPARATION PROCEDURE
			UNIT COST	TOTAL	UNIT COST	TOTAL	UNIT COST	TOTAL	
TOTAL COST									
COST PER PORTION									
COST % PER PORTION									

FIGURE 4.1   *Standardized Recipe Form*

The form may also include information on costing and a photograph of the finished dish. Each form should be complete, consistent and simple to read and follow. The forms should be stored in a readily accessible place. Index cards, notebook binders or a computerized database may be used, depending on the size and complexity of the operation.

MEASUREMENTS AND CONVERSIONS

Measurement Formats

Accurate measurements are among the most important aspects of food production. Ingredients and portions must be measured correctly to ensure consistent product quality. In other words, the chef must be able to prepare a recipe the same way each time, and portion sizes must be at the same from one order to the next.

In a kitchen, measurements may be made in three ways: weight, volume and count.

Weight refers to the mass or heaviness of a substance. It is expressed in terms such as grams, ounces, pounds and tons. Weight may be used to measure liquid or dry ingredients (for example, 2 pounds of eggs for a bread recipe) and portions (for example, 4 ounces of sliced turkey for a sandwich). As weight is generally the most accurate form of measurement, portion scales or balance scales are commonly used in kitchens.

Volume refers to the space occupied by a substance. This is mathematically expressed as *height × width × length*. It is expressed in terms such as cups, quarts, gallons, teaspoons, fluid ounces, bushels and liters. Volume is most commonly used to measure liquids. It may also be used for dry ingredients when the amount is too small to be weighed accurately (for example, 1/4 teaspoon of salt). Although measuring by volume is somewhat less accurate than measuring by weight, volume measurements are generally quicker to do.

Frequently, mistakes are made in food preparation by chefs who assume wrongly that weight and volume are equal. Do not be fooled! One cup does not always equal 8 ounces. While it is true that one standard cup contains 8 *fluid* ounces, it is not true that the contents of that standard cup will *weigh* 8 ounces. For example, the weight of 1 cup of diced apples will vary depending on the size of the apple pieces. Errors are commonly made in the bakeshop by cooks who assume that 8 ounces of flour is the same as one cup of flour. In fact, one cup of flour weighs only about 4-1/2 ounces.

It is not unusual to see both weight and volume measurements used in a single recipe. When a recipe ingredient is expressed in weight, weigh it. When it is expressed as a volume, measure it. Like most rules, however, this one has exceptions. The weight and volume of water, butter, eggs and milk are, in each case, the same. For these ingredients you may use whichever measurement is most convenient.

Count refers to the number of individual items. Count is used in recipes (for example, 4 eggs) and in portion control (for example, 2 fish fillets or 1 ear of corn). Count is also commonly used in purchasing to indicate the size of the individual items. For example, a "96 count" case of lemons means that a 40-pound case contains 96 individual lemons; a "115 count" case means that the same 40-pound case contains 115 individual lemons. So, each lemon in the 96-count case is larger than those in the 115-count case. Shrimp is another item commonly sold by count. One pound of shrimp may contain from eight to several hundred shrimp, depending on the size of the individual pieces. When placing an order, the chef must specify the desired count. For example, when ordering one pound of 21–25-count shrimp the chef expects to receive not less than 21 nor more than 25 pieces.

Measurement Systems

The measurement formats of weight, volume and count are used in the imperial, U.S. and metric measurement systems. Because each of these systems is used in modern food service operations, you should be able to prepare recipes written in any of the three.

The **imperial system** is used in Great Britain, Canada and a few other countries. It uses pounds and ounces for weight, and pints and fluid ounces for volume.

The **U.S. system**, with which you are probably familiar, is the most difficult system to understand. It uses pounds for weight and cups for volume.

The **metric system** is the most commonly used system in the world. Developed in France during the late 18th century, it was intended to fill the need for a mathematically rational and uniform system of measurement. The

❖❖❖

FANNIE MERRITT FARMER
(1857–1915)

Fannie Farmer is more than the name on a cookbook. She was an early, vigorous and influential proponent of scientific cooking, nutrition and academic training for culinary professionals.

At the age of 30, Farmer enrolled in the Boston Cooking School. The school's curriculum was not designed to graduate chefs, but rather to produce cooking teachers. After graduating from the two-year course, Farmer stayed on, first as assistant principal and then as principal.

During her years there (and, indeed, for the rest of her career) she was obsessed with accurate measurements. She waged a campaign to eliminate measurements such as a "wine glass" of liquid, a "handful" of flour, a chunk of butter the "size of an egg" or a "heaping spoonful" of salt. For, as she once wrote, "correct measurements are absolutely necessary to insure the best results." Farmer also sought to replace the European system of measuring ingredients by weight with, for her, a more scientific measurement system based on volume and level measures (e.g., a level tablespoon). To a great degree, she succeeded.

Her writings reflect her concern for accurate measurements. Her first book, *The Boston Cooking School Cookbook* (1896), includes clearly written recipes with precise measurements. Later editions add recipe yields, oven temperatures and baking times.

After leaving the Boston Cooking School, she opened "Miss Farmer's School of Cookery." The curriculum listed 60 lessons divided into six courses. The first course covered the basics: laying a fire and using a gas stove; making breads, eggs, soups, potatoes and coffee. The second and third courses emphasized more advanced cooking. Pastry, desserts and salads were taught during the fourth course; presentation and service were taught during the fifth course. Quite progressively for the time, her sixth course taught cooking for nurses and emphasized nutrition and the dietary needs of the sick and elderly. (This may have reflected Farmer's personal interests, for she was partially disabled and in poor health from time to time.)

Farmer wrote other cookbooks, including *Food and Cookery for the Sick and Convalescent* (1904) and *A New Book of Cookery* (first published in 1912 and republished in several revised versions). Her writings never address the joys of cooking and eating; rather, they reflect a scientific approach to cooking and rely on clearly written, accurately measured recipes for good, solid food.

metric system is a decimal system in which the gram, liter and meter are the basic units of weight, volume and length, respectively. Larger or smaller units of weight, volume and length are formed by adding a prefix to the words *gram*, *liter* or *meter*. Some of the more commonly used prefixes in food service operations are deca- (10), kilo- (1000), deci- (1/10) and milli- (1/1000). Thus, a kilogram is 1000 grams; a decameter is 10 meters; a milliliter is 1/1000 of a liter. Because the metric system is based on multiples of 10, it is extremely easy to increase or decrease recipe amounts.

The most important thing for a chef to know about the metric system is that *you do not need to convert between the metric system and the U.S. system*

TABLE 4.1 COMMON ABBREVIATIONS AND CONVERSIONS

teaspoon	=	tsp.
tablespoon	=	Tbsp.
cup	=	c.
pint	=	pt.
quart	=	qt.
gram	=	g
milliliter	=	ml
liter	=	lt
ounce	=	oz.
fluid ounce	=	fl. oz.
pound	=	lb.
kilogram	=	kg
Dash	=	1/8 teaspoon
3 teaspoons	=	1 tablespoon
2 tablespoons	=	1 fl. oz.
4 tablespoons	=	1/4 cup (2 fl. oz.)
5-1/3 tablespoons	=	1/3 cup (2-2/3 fl. oz.)
16 tablespoons	=	1 cup (8 fl. oz.)
2 cups	=	1 pint (16 fl. oz.)
2 pints	=	1 quart (32 fl. oz.)
4 quarts	=	1 gallon (128 fl. oz.)
2 gallons	=	1 peck
4 pecks	=	1 bushel
1 gram	=	0.035 ounce (1/30 oz.)
1 ounce	=	28.35 grams
454 grams	=	1 pound
2.2 pounds	=	1 kilogram (1000 grams)
1 teaspoon	=	5 milliliters
1 tablespoon	=	15 milliliters
1 cup	=	.24 liters
1 gallon	=	3.80 liters

in recipe preparation. If a recipe is written in metric units, use metric measuring equipment; if it is written in U.S. units, use U.S. measuring equipment. Luckily, most modern measuring equipment is calibrated in both U.S. and metric increments. The need to convert amounts will arise only if the proper equipment is unavailable.

Converting Grams and Ounces

As you can see from Table 4.1, 1 ounce equals 28.35 grams. So, *to convert ounces to grams, multiply the number of ounces by 28* (rounded for convenience).

$$8 \text{ ounces} \times 28 = 224 \text{ grams}$$

And *to convert grams to ounces, divide the number of grams by 28.*

$$224 \div 28 = 8 \text{ ounces.}$$

To help you develop a framework for judging conversions, remember that:

◆ a kilogram is about 2.2 pounds
◆ a gram is about 1/30 ounce
◆ a pound is about 450 grams
◆ a liter is slightly more than a quart
◆ a centimeter is slightly less than 1/2 inch
◆ 0° Celcius is the freezing point of water (32° F)
◆ 100° Celcius is the boiling point of water (212° F)

These approximations are not a substitute for accurate conversions, however. Appendix II contains additional information on equivalents and metric conversions. There is no substitute for knowing this information. In fact, it should become second nature to you.

RECIPE CONVERSIONS

Yield—*the total amount of a product made from a specific recipe.*

Whether six servings or 60, every recipe is designed to produce or **yield** a specific amount of product. A recipe's yield may be expressed in *volume, weight* or *servings* (for example, 1 quart of sauce; 8 pounds of bread dough; 8 half-cup servings). If the expected yield does not meet your needs, you must convert (i.e., increase or decrease) the ingredient amounts. Recipe conversion is sometimes complicated by *portion size conversions.* For example, it may be necessary to convert a recipe that initially produces 24 8-ounce servings of soup into a recipe that produces 62 6-ounce servings.

Conversion Factor (C.F.)—*the number used to increase or decrease ingredient quantities and recipe yields.*

It is just as easy to change yields by uneven amounts as it is to double or halve recipes. The mathematical principle is the same: *Each ingredient is multiplied by a* **conversion factor**. Do not take shortcuts by estimating recipe amounts or conversion factors. Inaccurate conversions lead to inedible foods, embarrassing shortages or wasteful excesses. Take the time to learn and apply proper conversion techniques.

Converting Total Yield

When portion size is unimportant or remains the same, recipe yield is converted by a simple two-step process:

STEP 1: Divide the desired (new) yield by the recipe (old) yield to obtain the conversion factor.

new yield ÷ old yield = conversion factor

STEP 2: Multiply each ingredient quantity by the conversion factor to obtain the new quantity.

old quantity × conversion factor = new quantity

Example 4.1

You need to convert a recipe for cauliflower soup. The present recipe yields 1-1/2 gallons. You only need to make 3/4 gallon.

First, determine the conversion factor:

.75 gallon ÷ 1.5 gallons = .50

The same conversion factor can be obtained after first converting the recipe amounts to fluid ounces:

96 fluid ounces ÷ 192 fluid ounces = .50

Second, the conversion factor (C.F.) is applied to each ingredient in the soup recipe:

CAULIFLOWER SOUP

	old quantity	×	C.F.	=	new quantity
Cauliflower, chopped	5 lb.	×	.5	=	2-1/2 lb.
Celery stalks	4	×	.5	=	2
Onion	1	×	.5	=	1/2
Chicken stock	2 qt.	×	.5	=	1 qt.
Heavy cream	3 pt.	×	.5	=	1-1/2 pt.

Converting Portion Size

A few additional steps are necessary to convert recipes when portion sizes must also be changed.

STEP 1: Determine the total yield of the existing recipe by multiplying the number of portions by the portion size.

original portions × original portion size = total (old) yield

STEP 2: Determine the total yield desired by multiplying the new number of portions by the new portion size.

desired portions × desired portion size = total (new) yield

STEP 3: Obtain the conversion factor as described above.

total (new) yield) ÷ total (old) yield = conversion factor

STEP 4: Multiply each ingredient quantity by the conversion factor.

old quantity × conversion factor = new quantity

Example 4.2

Returning to the cauliflower soup: The original recipe produced 1-1/2 gallons or 48 4-ounce servings. Now you need 72 6-ounce servings.

STEP 1: Total original yield is $48 \times 4 = 192$ ounces

STEP 2: Total desired yield is $72 \times 6 = 432$ ounces

STEP 3: Conversion factor is calculated by dividing total new yield by total old yield:

$$432 \div 192 = 2.25$$

STEP 4: Old ingredient quantities are multiplied by conversion factor to determine new quantities:

CAULIFLOWER SOUP

	old quantity	×	C.F.	=	new quantity
Cauliflower, chopped	5 lb.	×	2.25	=	11.25 lb.
Celery stalks	4	×	2.25	=	9
Onion	1	×	2.25	=	2.25
Chicken stock	2 qt.	×	2.25	=	4.5 qt.
Heavy cream	3 pt.	×	2.25	=	6.75 pt.

Additional Conversion Problems

When making very large recipe changes—for example, from 5 to 50 portions or 600 to 36 portions—you may encounter additional problems. The mathematical conversions described above do not take into account changes in equipment, evaporation rates, unforeseen recipe errors or cooking times. Chefs learn to use their judgment, knowledge of cooking principles and skills to compensate for these factors.

Equipment

When you change the size of a recipe, you must often change the equipment used as well. Problems arise, however, when the production techniques previously used no longer work with the new quantity of ingredients. For example, if you normally make a muffin recipe in small quantities by hand and you increase the recipe size, it may be necessary to prepare the batter in a mixer. But if mixing time remains the same, the batter may become overmixed, resulting in poor-quality muffins. Trying to prepare a small amount of product in equipment that is too large for the task can also affect its quality.

Evaporation

Equipment changes can also affect product quality because of changes in evaporation rates. Increasing a soup recipe may require substituting a tilt skillet for a saucepan. But because a tilt skillet provides more surface area for evaporation than does a saucepan, reduction time must be decreased to prevent overthickening the soup. The increased evaporation caused by an increased surface area may also alter the strength of the seasonings.

Recipe Errors

A recipe may contain errors in ingredients or techniques that are not obvious when it is prepared in small quantities. When increased, however, small mistakes often become big (and obvious) ones, and the final product suffers.

The only solution is to test recipes carefully and rely on your knowledge of cooking principles to compensate for unexpected problems.

Time

Do not multiply time specifications given in a recipe by the conversion factor used with the recipe's ingredients. All things being equal, *cooking time* will not change when recipe size changes. For example, a muffin requires the same amount of baking time whether you prepare one dozen or 14 dozen. Cooking time will be affected, however, by changes in evaporation rate or heat conduction caused by equipment changes. *Mixing time* may change when recipe size is changed. Different equipment may perform mixing tasks more or less efficiently than previously used equipment. Again, rely on experience and good judgment.

CALCULATING UNIT COSTS AND RECIPE COSTS

Unit Costs

Food service operations purchase most foods from suppliers in bulk or wholesale packages. For example, canned goods are purchased by the case; produce by the flat, case or lug; and flour and sugar by 25- or 50-pound bags. Even fish and meats are often purchased in large cuts, not individual serving-sized portions. The purchased amount is rarely used for a single recipe, however. It must be broken down into smaller units such as pounds, cups, quarts or ounces.

In order to allocate the proper ingredient costs to the recipe being prepared, it is necessary to convert **as-purchased costs or prices** to **unit costs or prices**. To find the unit cost (i.e., the cost of a particular unit, say a single egg) in a package containing multiple units (e.g., a 30-dozen case), divide the as-purchased cost (A.P. cost) of the package by the number of units in the package.

As-Purchased (A.P.)—*the condition or cost of an item as it is purchased or received from the supplier.*

Unit Cost—*the price paid to acquire one of the specified units.*

$$\text{A.P. cost} \div \text{number of units} = \text{cost per unit}$$

Example 4.3

A case of #10 cans contains six individual cans. If a case of tomato paste costs $23.50, then each can costs $3.92.

$$\$23.50 \div 6 = \$3.92$$

If your recipe uses less than the total can, you must continue dividing the cost of the can until you arrive at the appropriate unit amount. Continuing with the tomato paste example, if you need only 1 cup of tomato paste, divide the can price ($3.92) by the total number of cups contained in the can to arrive at the cost per cup (unit). The list of canned good sizes in Appendix II shows that a #10 can contains approximately 13 cups. Using the formula, each cup costs $0.30.

$$\$3.92 \div 13 = .30$$

The cost of one cup can be reduced even further if necessary. If the recipe uses only 2 tablespoons of tomato paste, divide the cost per cup by the number of tablespoons in a cup. As you can see, the final cost for 2 tablespoons of this tomato paste is $0.037.

$$.30 \div 16 = .018 \times 2 = \$0.037$$

RECIPE COSTING FORM

Menu Item _____ Date _____

| Ingredient | Quantity | COST | | | TOTAL COST |
		As Purchased	Yield %	Edible Portion	

TOTAL COST OF RECIPE $ _____

Total Yield _____   Size of Portion _____
                                          Cost per Portion _____

Food Cost Percentage _____   Selling Price _____

FIGURE 4.2   *Recipe Costing Form*

Recipe Costs

With a typical recipe, you calculate the **total recipe cost** with the following two-step procedure:

STEP 1: Determine the cost for the given quantity of each recipe ingredient with the unit costing procedures described above.

STEP 2: Add all of the ingredient costs together to obtain the total recipe cost.

The total recipe cost can then be broken down into the **cost per portion**, which is the most useful figure for food cost controls. To arrive at cost per portion, divide the total recipe cost by the total number of servings or portions produced by that recipe.

total recipe cost ÷ number of portions = cost per portion

The Recipe Costing Form shown in Figure 4.2 is useful for organizing recipe costing information. It provides space for listing each ingredient, the quantity of each ingredient needed, the cost of each unit and the total cost for the ingredient. Total yield, portion size and cost per portion are listed at the bottom of the form. Note that there is no space for recipe procedures, as these are irrelevant in recipe costing.

YIELD TESTS

Computing the cost of recipe ingredients is a simple matter if the foods are used the way they are received and there is no waste or trim. This is rarely

Total Recipe Cost—*the total cost of ingredients for a particular recipe; it does not reflect overhead, labor, fixed expenses or profit.*

Cost per portion—*the amount of the total recipe cost divided by the number of portions produced from that recipe; the cost of one serving.*

the case, however. The amount of a food item **as purchased (A.P.)** and the amount of the **edible portion (E.P.)** of that same item may vary considerably, particularly with meats and fresh produce. In this context, **yield** is the usable or edible quantity remaining after processing the as-purchased quantity of the food item. That is, yield refers to the amount of usable lettuce after the case of iceberg is cleaned, or the amount of meat that is served after trimming. The **yield factor or percentage** is the ratio of the usable quantity to the purchased quantity. It is always less than 100% and may be calculated in dollars or weight/volume amounts.

Because purchase specifications and fabrication techniques vary from operation to operation, there are no precise, standard yield amounts. Each kitchen must determine its own yield factors. Yield tests must be conducted on A.P. items as they are received from purveyors. To be effective, several tests must be conducted and the results averaged to arrive at a specific operation's yield factor for that item.

The method of calculating yield varies depending on whether the item's trim is all waste (for example, vegetable peelings) or whether the trim creates usable or salable byproducts (for example, meat and poultry).

Raw Yield Tests Without Byproducts

The simplest yield test procedure is for items that have no usable or salable byproducts. These items include most produce as well as some fish and shellfish. Unless these items are ready to serve *as received* from the purveyor, trimming is required and all trim is waste. For example, one pound of apples may yield only 13 ounces of flesh after peeling and coring. If the recipe requires one pound of peeled, cored apples, the chef must start with slightly more than one pound of A.P. apples. In order to determine accurate costs for such items, the trim loss must be taken into account. Even seedless grapes do not have a 100% yield factor. The weight of stems and bad grapes must be calculated and deducted from the A.P. weight to determine the correct price per pound of servable fruit.

There are three steps for calculating yield when all trim is waste:

STEP 1: Calculate the total weight of the trim produced from the specified A.P. quantity. This is known as **trim loss**.

STEP 2: Subtract the trim loss from the A.P. weight to arrive at the total yield weight.

STEP 3: Divide the yield weight by the A.P. weight to determine the yield factor.

Example 4.4

Two pounds of fresh garlic generate 4-1/2 ounces of trim loss. Therefore, the yield weight is 27-1/2 ounces and the yield factor is 86%:

$$(2 \times 16 \text{ ounces}) = 32 \text{ ounces} - 4.5 \text{ ounces} = 27.5 \text{ ounces}$$

$$27.5 \div 32 = .859 = 86\%$$

Remember, subtract trim loss from A.P. weight, then divide yield weight by A.P. weight to arrive at the yield percentage. Note that the yield factor will always be some number less than 1, and the yield percentage will always be less than 100%.

Edible Portion (E.P.)—*the amount of a food item available for consumption after trimming or fabrication.*

Yield—*the total amount of a food item created or remaining after trimming or fabrication.*

Yield Factor or Percentage—*the ratio of the edible portion to the amount purchased.*

Trim Loss—*the amount of the product removed when preparing it for consumption.*

TABLE 4.2 COMMON PRODUCE YIELD FACTORS

Produce	Yield Factor (%)	Produce	Yield Factor (%)	Produce	Yield Factor (%)
Apples	75	Grapefruit	45	Pears	75
Apricots	94	Grapes	90	Pea pods	90
Artichokes	48	Kiwi	80	Peppers	82
Avocados	75	Leeks	50	Pineapple	50
Bananas	70	Lemons	45	Plums	75
Berries	95	Lettuce	75	Potatoes	80
Broccoli	70	Limes	45	Radishes	90
Cabbage	79	Melons	55	Rhubarb	85
Carrots	78	Mushrooms	90	Scallions	65
Cauliflower	55	Nectarines	86	Spinach	60
Celery	75	Okra	82	Squash, summer	90
Cherries	82	Onions	90	Squash, winter	70
Corn, cob	28	Oranges	60	Tomatoes	90
Cucumbers	95	Papayas	65	Turnips	75
Eggplant	85	Parsley	85	Watercress	90
Garlic	88	Peaches	75	Watermelon	45

Because each operation has its own standards for cleaning and trimming raw products, yield factors should be personalized. Lists of common yield factors are available, however, as an indication of industry norms. Some of these are included in Table 4.2.

Applying Yield Factors

Now that you understand what yield factors are and how to calculate them, we look at how they are used in costing recipes. First, yield factors are used for accurate recipe costing.

Example 4.5

Carrots cost $6.50 per 25-pound bag and have a yield factor of 78%. In other words, 22% of that 25-pound bag is waste. The price should be recalculated to account for that waste; that is, the A.P. (as purchased) unit cost must be converted to an E.P. (edible portion) unit cost. This is done by dividing A.P. cost by the yield percentage.

$$\text{A.P. Cost (\$)} \div \text{Yield Percentage} = \text{E.P. Cost (\$)}$$

$$.26/\text{pound } (6.50 \div 25) \div .78 = .33/\text{pound}$$

Thus, the carrots have an E.P. unit cost of $0.33 per pound (as compared with an A.P. price of $0.26 per pound). Note that E.P. cost is always greater than A.P. cost. When costing a recipe, you should use the $0.33-per-pound price as the accurate ingredient cost.

Second, yield factors are necessary for accurate purchasing. Most recipes list ingredients in E.P. quantities. Therefore, the chef must consider waste or trim amounts when ordering these items. If only the amounts listed in the recipe are ordered and then the item requires trimming, the number of portions (or recipe yield) will be less than the desired amount.

Example 4.6

A recipe requires 20 pounds of shredded cabbage. The yield factor for cabbage is 79%. Therefore, 20 pounds is 79% of the A.P. quantity. Divide the amount needed by the yield factor to determine the minimum A.P. quantity.

$$\text{E.P. Quantity} \div \text{Yield Percentage} = \text{A.P. Quantity}$$

$$20 \text{ pounds} \div .79 = 25.3 \text{ pounds}$$

It will take 25-1/3 pounds of cabbage to provide the 20 pounds of shredded cabbage. (This figure will be increased to an even amount for purchasing because yield factors are, at best, only an estimate.) Note that the A.P. figure must always be greater than the E.P. figure in this formula.

FOOD COST

Perhaps no other cost is emphasized as much by food service managers as **food cost**. Food cost refers to the cost of all foods used in the fabrication of menu items. This figure is also known as the **cost of goods sold** or **raw food cost** ("raw" is a bit misleading as food cost includes precooked and packaged foods as well as uncooked foods).

> **Food Cost**—*the cost of the materials that go directly into the production of the menu item.*

Food costs are calculated in two ways: (1) as a total cost of all foods used during a given time period, and (2) as a cost of one particular portion or menu item. Total cost is used as a general guideline for budgeting and menu planning. The portion or item cost is used to calculate menu prices; it helps the chef stay within cost limitations.

Cost of Goods Sold

The "goods" sold by a food service operation are, of course, the foods used in producing menu items. Before you can calculate cost of goods sold you must take a physical inventory of all foodstuffs on hand. **Inventory** should be taken periodically: at the end of each week, month, quarter or other accounting period. Taking inventory requires listing and counting all foods in the kitchen, storerooms and refrigerators. The quantities are then *extended*, that is, multiplied by the unit cost. The extended prices are then added to calculate the total inventory value.

> **Inventory**—*the listing and counting of all foods in the kitchen, storerooms and refrigerators.*

Whether prepared foods or open containers are included in the inventory depends on the operation. Often small quantities of prepared foods or open containers are not inventoried on the theory that a certain amount of such items is always on hand, the value of which is minimal but fairly consistent from one accounting period to the next.

To properly calculate the cost of goods sold you must conduct an inventory at the beginning and end of the desired period and maintain records of all purchases during the period. The time period covered by this calculation could be any duration: week, month, quarter or year. After the total value of the inventory for both the beginning and the end of the period has been established, cost of goods sold is calculated as follows:

	Value of food inventory at beginning of period
PLUS	Food purchased during period
MINUS	Inventory at end of period
	Cost of food sold

Example 4.7

The total value of food in inventory on December 1 is $7600. The restaurant purchases $2300 worth of food during December and the inventory on January 1 is worth $5600. The cost of goods sold during the month of December is $4300 (in other words, the food produced during the month of December cost $4300):

$$(7600 + 2300) - 5600 = 4300$$

Once management knows the cost of goods sold, it can compare this figure with the dollar value of sales for the same period. This comparison gives management a good idea of how the business did for that period.

Food Cost Percentages

The **food cost percentage** is the ratio of costs to sales. It shows what each dollar of sales costs. For example, a 35% food cost means that $0.35 of each dollar received went to pay for the foods the operation used. Food cost percentage is determined by dividing food cost by sales.

$$\text{food cost} \div \text{sales} = \text{food cost percentage}$$

Example 4.8

Refer back to Example 4.8 and assume that sales for December totaled $10,750. The food cost percentage for the month would be 40%:

$$4,300 \div 10,750 = .40 = 40\%$$

By itself a single food cost percentage is meaningless. To be useful, it should be compared with the food cost percentages for other months of the same year or the same month in previous years. It is also helpful to know the food cost percentages for other similarly situated food service operations.

Food cost percentages can also be calculated on individual menu items. If the food items in a sliced turkey sandwich cost $2.80 and the sandwich sells for $5.25, the food cost percentage is 53% (2.80 divided by 5.25). Many operations would find this unacceptably high. To reduce the percentage and increase gross profits, the operation must either increase the selling price or decrease the ingredient costs.

Changing menu price, raw food cost or portion size will change the food cost percentage. If the food cost percentage is too high, the gross profit will be insufficient to cover operating expenses. If the percentage is too low, customers may feel they are not getting their money's worth and take their business elsewhere. Setting an appropriate percentage requires sound judgment, knowledge of the competition and accurate cost information. Periodic evaluations are necessary to ensure that the desired objective is actually maintained.

ESTABLISHING MENU PRICES

After determining the cost of food items, you can calculate menu prices. A few of the many methods for setting menu prices are explained below. Some techniques are highly structured and closely related to food costs; others are unstructured and unrelated to actual food costs. As a practical matter, no one method is right for every operation and a combination of methods may provide the best pricing information.

Cost-Based Pricing

Food Cost Percentage Pricing

For this technique, you must first determine the food cost percentage desired for the particular facility. After calculating each item's raw food cost you determine the selling price with the following formula:

$$\text{cost per portion} \div \text{food cost percentage} = \text{selling price}$$

Example 4.9

If the raw food cost for one sandwich is $1.70 and the desired food cost percentage is 23%, the selling price must be at least $7.39:

$$1.70 \div .23 = 7.391$$

In this situation, 23% of the sales price for each item will go to cover the raw food cost for that item. The higher the food cost percentage, the lower the portion of the sales price available for labor, fixed expenses, overhead or profit. Determining the appropriate food cost percentage for the facility is critical to the successful use of this method.

Factor Pricing

A variation on food cost percentage pricing is factor pricing. First, you take the desired food cost percentage and divide it into 100 to arrive at a cost factor. The cost of each item is then multiplied by the cost factor to arrive at the menu price. Using the previous example, the factor is 4.35 (100 ÷ 23 = 4.35), and the menu price for a $1.70 item is $7.39 (1.70 × 4.35 = 7.39).

Both food cost percentage and factor pricings are fast and easy to use. But these methods are sometimes unreliable because they assume that other costs associated with preparing food stay the same for each menu item. These systems wrongly assume that the costs for labor, energy and overhead are the same for a rack of lamb entree and a seafood salad. These methods may be fine-tuned somewhat by adjusting the desired food cost percentage according to the type of food or menu category. Appetizers may be assigned a lower food cost percentage than, say, desserts or side dishes.

Prime Cost Pricing

The food service industry uses a figure known as **prime cost** to refer to the total of raw food cost plus direct labor. Direct labor is the labor actually required for an item's preparation. If, for example, food cost is $2.10 and direct labor is $1.50, then prime cost is $3.60. As with the food cost percentage example above, the prime cost percentage can be divided into the prime cost amount to determine menu price.

Prime Cost—*the combination of food costs and direct labor.*

Example 4.10

The raw food cost for a rack of lamb is $7.50; it takes a cook a total of 9 minutes to clean and trim it for service. If that cook is paid $8.50 per hour, the direct labor cost is $1.27. (8.50 per hour = .14 per minute; .14 × 9 = $1.27).

The prime cost of the rack of lamb is $8.77 (7.50 + 1.27). A selling price is then determined by dividing prime cost by the desired prime cost percentage. If management decided that the desired prime cost percentage is 48 percent, then the rack of lamb should be priced at $18.27. (8.77 ÷ .48 = 18.27)

Perceived Value Pricing

This is a rather backwards way of setting prices based on what a customer will perceive as an appropriate price. First determine what the market price is for the same or similar item. Then calculate what you can serve for that price. Assume, for example,

1. the market price for a complete fried chicken dinner is $9.95,
2. the desired profit is 7% of sales,
3. overhead expenses are 27% of sales and
4. labor is approximately 23% of sales.

Subtract the total of these items (57%) from the $9.95 selling price and you find that your total food cost for the fried chicken dinner must not be more than $4.28. This technique requires a thorough knowledge of the market and good historical information on labor and overhead costs. With the necessary information, you can determine how much to spend on raw product for each menu item and still make the desired profit.

Noncost-Based Pricing

Noncost-based pricing techniques rely on nonmonetary factors to set menu prices. Traditional prices in the area for the same or similar items may affect an operation's ability to set prices. This is particularly true for special or loss-leader items such as 79-cent jumbo sodas or 99-cent breakfast specials.

While the competition's prices are an important consideration, you should not simply copy them. Your competition's costs are not your costs no matter how similar the final food items appear. If you must charge higher prices than your competition, seek out some way to differentiate your product or service.

Virtually all food service operations are seeking to charge the highest price possible without a loss of sales. The customer's perception of value is therefore critical. The menu can be used as a tool for educating customers. Descriptive language or an explanation of unique or special dishes can be included. Customers who understand the value of service, atmosphere, out-of-season foods and specialty products will tolerate higher prices for those items.

Psychological Impact of Pricing

Regardless of how you arrive at a menu price, you may wish to round the figure up or down for psychological impact. It is human nature to perceive some prices as higher or lower than they actually are. For example, using a 9 or 5 as the last digit in a price creates the impression of a discount; prices ending in a 9 or 5 appeal to price-conscious customers. Prices ending in a 0 are perceived as more expensive and higher quality and so are often used on fine-dining menus.

The number of digits in a price is also important: $9.95 seems much less expensive than $10.25. Likewise, the first numeral in a price affects perception. When changing menu prices, an increase from $5.95 to $6.45 is seen as greater than an increase from $6.25 to $6.75, although both are 50-cent increases.

Patrons do not like to see a large spread in menu prices. It may make them think something is wrong with one of the items or may cause confusion. For example, a lobster dinner for $14.50 may be a reasonable price, but it may be inappropriate on a menu where all other items are less than $6.00. In general, the highest price should not be more than double the lowest price within the same food category. If the least expensive appetizer is $4.00, then the most expensive appetizer should not exceed $8.00.

Establishing menu prices is one of the most difficult yet important things a chef or manager can do to affect the facility's success. No one method is best for all operations, so careful study of several approaches is recommended.

CONTROLLING FOOD COSTS

Many things affect food costs in any given operation; most can be controlled by the chef or manager. These controls do not require mathematical calculations or formulas, just basic management skills and a good dose of common sense. The following factors all have an impact on the operation's bottom line:

+ menu
+ purchasing/ordering
+ receiving
+ storing
+ issuing
+ kitchen procedures
    establishing standard portions
    waste
+ sales and service

Chefs tend to focus their control efforts in the area of kitchen preparation. While this may seem logical, it is not adequate. A good chef will be involved in all aspects of the operation to help prevent problems from arising or to correct those that may occur.

Menu
A profitable menu is based upon many variables including customer desires, physical space and equipment, ingredient availability, cost of goods sold, employee skills and competition. All management personnel, including the chef, should be consulted when planning the menu. Menu changes, while possibly desirable, must be executed with as much care as the original design.

Purchasing/Ordering
Purchasing techniques have a direct impact on cost controls. On the one hand, **parstock** must be adequate for efficient operations; on the other hand, too much inventory wastes space and resources and may spoil. Before any items are ordered, purchasing specifications should be established and communicated to potential purveyors. Specifications should precisely describe the item, including grade, quality, packaging and unit size. Each operation should design its own form to best meet its specific needs. A sample specification form is shown in Figure 4.3. This information can be used to obtain price quotes from several purveyors. Update these quotes periodically to ensure that you are getting the best value for your money.

Parstock (Par)—*the amount of stock necessary to cover operating needs between deliveries.*

Receiving
Whether goods are received by a full-time clerk, as they are in a large hotel, or by the chef or kitchen manager, certain standards should be

```
Menu Item:

Product:                                    Date:

Grade/Quality:

Weight/Size:                                NAMP/IMPS #:

Packaging:

Delivery conditions:

Comments:
```

FIGURE 4.3   *Specification Form*

observed. The person signing for merchandise should first confirm that the items were actually ordered. Second, determine whether the items listed on the invoice are the ones being delivered and that the price and quantity listed are accurate. Third, the items, especially meats and produce, should be checked for quality, freshness and weight. Established purchase specifications should be readily available.

Storing

Proper storage of foodstuffs is crucial in order to prevent spoilage, pilferage and waste. Stock must be rotated so that the older items are used first. Such a system for rotating stock is referred to as FIFO: First In, First Out. Storage areas should be well ventilated and lit to prevent infestation and mold.

Issuing

It may be necessary, particularly in larger operations, to limit storeroom access to specific personnel. Maintaining ongoing inventory records or par-stock sheets helps the ordering process. Controlling issuances eliminates waste caused by multiple opened containers and ensures proper stock rotation.

Kitchen Procedures: Establishing Standard Portions

Standardizing portions is essential to controlling food costs. Unless portion quantity is uniform, it will be impossible to compute portion costs accurately. Portion discrepancies can also confuse or mislead customers.

Actual portion sizes depend on the food service operation itself, the menu, the prices and the customers' desires. Some items are generally purchased preportioned for convenience (for example, steaks are sold in uniform cuts, baking potatoes are available in uniform sizes, butter comes in preportioned pats and bread comes sliced for service). Other items must be portioned by the establishment prior to service. Special equipment makes consistent portioning easy. There are machines to slice meats, cutting guides for cakes and pies and portion scales for weighing quantities. Standardized portion scoops and ladles are indispensable for serving vegetables, soups, stews, salads and similar foods. Many of these items are discussed and illustrated in Chapter 5, Tools and Equipment.

Once acceptable portion sizes are established, employees must be properly trained to present them. If each employee of a sandwich shop prepared sandwiches the way he or she would like to eat them, customers would probably never receive the same sandwich twice. Customers may become confused and decide not to risk a repeat visit. Obviously, carelessness in portioning can also drastically affect food cost.

Kitchen Procedures: Waste

The chef must also control waste from overproduction or failure to use leftovers. With an adequate sales history, the chef can accurately estimate the quantity of food to prepare for each week, day or meal. If the menu is designed properly, the chef can also use leftovers and trim from product fabrication. The less waste generated in food preparation, the lower the overall food cost will be.

Sales and Service

An improperly trained sales staff can undo even the most rigorous of food cost controls. Front-of-the-house personnel are, after all, ultimately responsible for the sales portion of the food cost equation. Proper training is once again critical. Prices charged must be accurate and complete. Poor service can lead to the need to serve for free ("comp") an excessive amount of food. Dropped or spilled foods do not generate revenues.

CONCLUSION

No food service operation can become successful on the chef's cooking ability alone. A well-designed, enticing and accurately priced menu is also necessary. By following a standardized recipe you should be able to repeatedly produce a known quality and quantity of food for your specific food service operation. Based upon the regularity with which you offer these foods, your menu can be classified as static, cycle, market or hybrid. You can offer your menu items either à la carte, semi à la carte or table d'hôte.

You must be able to understand and apply proper techniques for converting recipes, food costing, menu pricing and loss control. Although computers are useful and are becoming more common in kitchens, no machine can substitute for a chef's watchful eye and hands-on controls.

QUESTIONS FOR DISCUSSION

1. Describe the four types of menus. Can each type of menu offer foods à la carte, semi à la carte and/or table d'hôte? Explain your answer.

2. Discuss three factors in food preparation that affect successful recipe size changes.

3. Why is it important to calculate the portion cost of a recipe in professional food service operations? Why is the full recipe cost inadequate?

4. List several factors that might cause one operation's yield factor for lettuce to be higher than another operation's. Explain why standardized yield factor lists are unreliable.

5. How is food cost percentage calculated? How can this figure be used (or misused) to evaluate the success of an operation?

6. Discuss three psychological factors used in setting menu prices.

PART TWO
PREPARATION

Mise en place *is the essence of preparation. Although it means "everything in its place," the term connotes more than merely having all ingredients and tools on hand and being ready to begin preparing a dish. Rather, it suggests that the chef can identify, appreciate and understand how the necessary tools and equipment work, how the foods are cut and what the basic flavoring ingredients and staples are.*

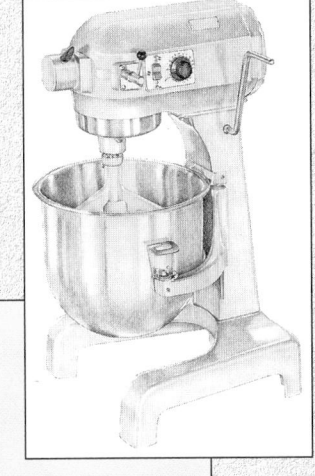

To assist you in preparing to cook, Part II presents information about the tools and equipment routinely found in professional kitchens, then discusses how a professional kitchen is organized. There is a chapter on knife skills as well as chapters on kitchen staples (herbs and spices, condiments, oils, vinegars, nuts, coffee and tea) and eggs and dairy products (including milk, cream, cultured milk products and cheese).

Understanding this information is critical before successful cooking can begin.

CHAPTER 5

TOOLS AND EQUIPMENT

After studying this chapter you will be able to:

✦ recognize a variety of professional kitchen tools and equipment
✦ select and care for knives properly
✦ understand how a professional kitchen is organized

*H*aving the proper tools and equipment for a particular task may mean the difference between a job well done and one done carelessly, incorrectly or even dangerously. This chapter introduces some of the tools and equipment typically used in a professional kitchen. Items are divided into categories according to their function: hand tools, knives, measuring and portioning devices, cookware, strainers and sieves, processing equipment, storage containers, heavy equipment and safety equipment.

A wide variety of specialized tools and equipment is available to today's chef. Breading machines, croissant shapers and doughnut glazers are designed to speed production by reducing handwork. Other devices—for instance, a duck press or a couscousière—are used only for unique tasks in preparing a few menu items. Much of this specialized equipment is quite expensive and found only in food manufacturing operations or specialized kitchens; a discussion of it is beyond the scope of this chapter. Brief descriptions of some of these specialized devices are, however, found in the Glossary. Baking pans and tools are discussed in Chapter 26, Principles of the Bakeshop.

This chapter is illustrated with generic drawings because manufacturers' designs differ. We end this chapter with a discussion of how a professional kitchen should be designed and organized.

Before using any equipment, study the operator's manual or have someone experienced with the particular item instruct you on proper procedures for its use and cleaning. And remember, always think safety.

STANDARDS FOR TOOLS AND EQUIPMENT

NSF International (NSF), previously known as the National Sanitation Foundation, promulgates consensus standards for the design, construction and installation of kitchen tools, cookware and equipment. Many states and municipalities require that food service operations use only NSF-certified equipment. Although NSF certification is voluntary, most manufacturers submit their designs to NSF for certification to show that they are suitable for use in professional food service operations. Certified equipment bears the NSF mark shown in Figure 5.1.

NSF standards reflect the following requirements:

1. Equipment must be easily cleaned.
2. All food contact surfaces must be nontoxic (under intended end use conditions), nonabsorbent, corrosion resistant and nonreactive.

FIGURE 5.1   *The NSF Mark*

3. All food contact surfaces must be smooth, that is, free of pits, cracks, crevices, ledges, rivet heads and bolts.

4. Internal corners and edges must be rounded and smooth; external corners and angles must be smooth and sealed.

5. Coating materials must be nontoxic and easily cleaned; coatings must resist chipping and cracking.

6. Waste and waste liquids must be easily removed.

SELECTING TOOLS AND EQUIPMENT

In general, only commercial food service tools and equipment should be used in a professional kitchen. Household tools and appliances not NSF certified may not withstand the rigors of a professional kitchen. Look for tools that are well constructed. For example, joints should be welded, not bonded with solder; handles should be comfortable, with rounded borders; plastic and rubber parts should be seamless.

Before purchasing or leasing any particular piece of equipment you should evaluate several factors:

1. Is this equipment necessary for producing menu items?

2. Will this equipment perform the job required in the space available?

3. Is this equipment the most economical for the operation's specific needs?

4. Is this equipment easy to clean, maintain and repair?

HAND TOOLS

Hand tools are designed to aid in cutting, shaping, moving or combining foods. They have few, if any, moving parts. Knives, discussed separately below, are the most important hand tools. Others are metal or rubber spatulas, spoons, whisks, tongs and specialized cutters. In addition to the items shown in Figure 5.2, many hand tools designed for specific tasks, such as pressing tortillas or pitting cherries, are available. Sturdiness, durability and safety are the watchwords when selecting hand tools. Choose tools that can withstand the heavy use of a professional kitchen and those that are easily cleaned.

KNIVES

Knives are the most important items in your tool kit. With a sharp knife, the skilled chef can accomplish a number of tasks more quickly and efficiently than any machine. Good-quality knives are expensive but will last for many years with proper care. Select easily sharpened, well-constructed knives that are comfortable and balanced in your hand. Knife construction and commonly used knives are discussed here; knife safety and care as well as cutting techniques are discussed in Chapter 6, Knife Skills.

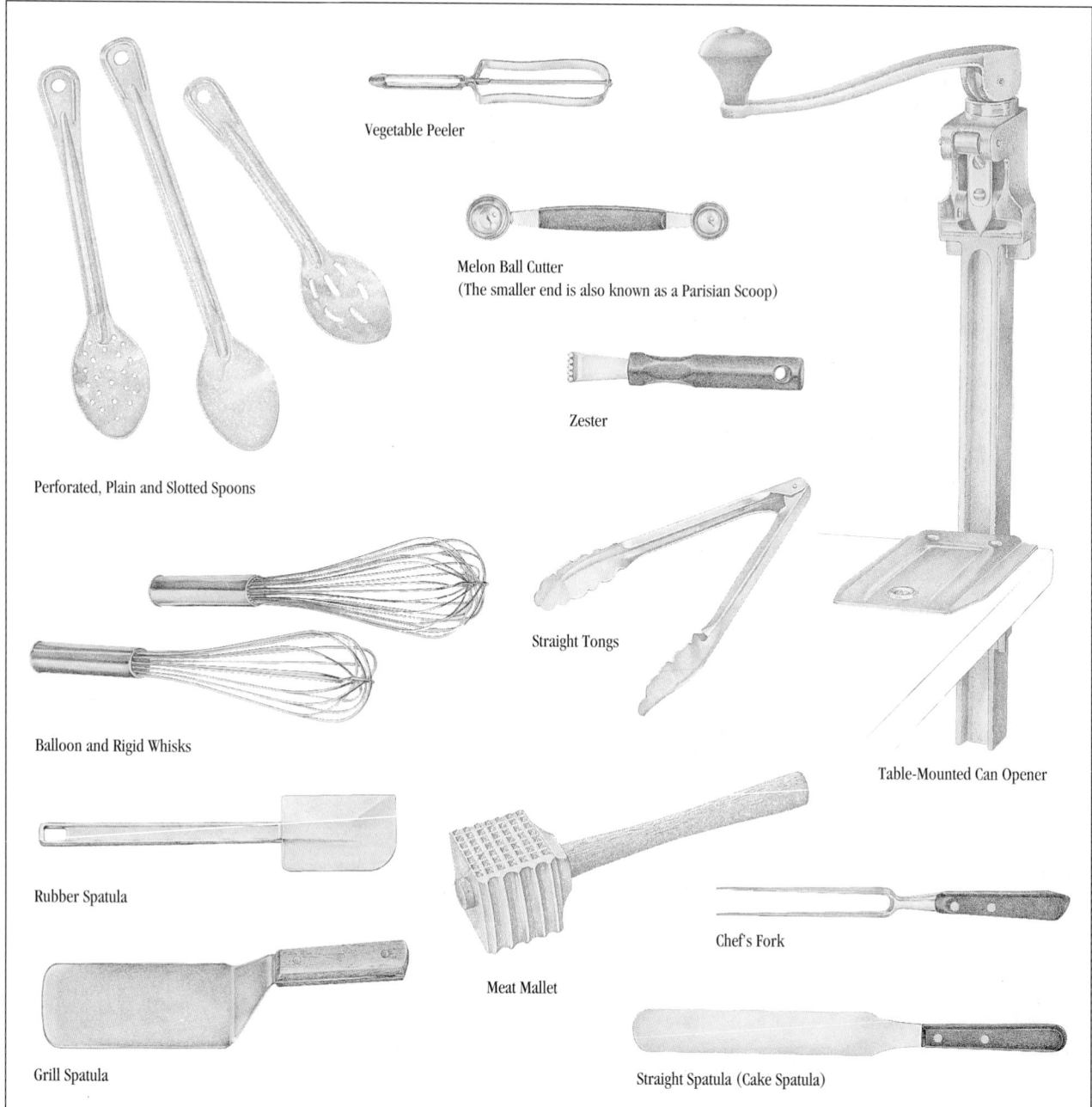

Vegetable Peeler

Melon Ball Cutter
(The smaller end is also known as a Parisian Scoop)

Zester

Perforated, Plain and Slotted Spoons

Balloon and Rigid Whisks

Straight Tongs

Table-Mounted Can Opener

Rubber Spatula

Meat Mallet

Chef's Fork

Grill Spatula

Straight Spatula (Cake Spatula)

FIGURE 5.2

Knife Construction

A good knife begins with a single piece of metal, stamped, cut or—best of all—forged and tempered into a blade of the desired shape. The metals generally used for knife blades are:

1. **Carbon steel**—An alloy of carbon and iron, it is traditionally used for blades because it is soft enough to be sharpened easily. It corrodes and discolors easily, however, especially when used with acidic foods.

2. **Stainless steel**—It will not rust, corrode or discolor and is extremely durable. But a stainless steel blade is much more difficult to sharpen than a

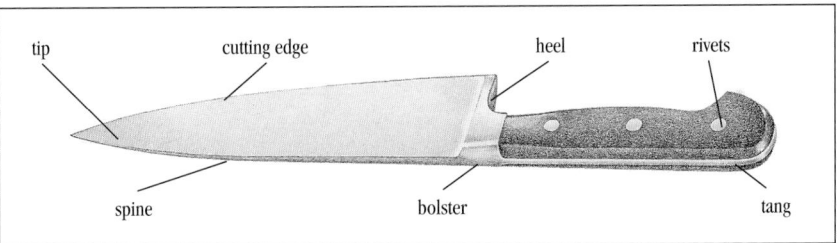

FIGURE 5.3

carbon steel one, although once an edge is established it lasts longer than the edge on a carbon steel blade.

3. **High carbon stainless steel**—An alloy combining the best features of carbon steel and stainless steel, it neither corrodes nor discolors and can be sharpened almost as easily as carbon steel. It is now the most frequently used metal for blades.

A portion of the blade, known as the tang, fits inside the handle. The best knives are constructed with a full tang running the length of the handle; they also have a bolster where the blade meets the handle (the bolster is part of the blade, not a separate collar). Less expensive knives may have a 3/4-length tang or a thin "rattail" tang. Neither provide as much support, durability or balance as a full tang.

Knife handles are often made of hard woods infused with plastic and riveted to the tang. Molded polypropylene handles are permanently bonded to a tang without seams or rivets. Any handle should be shaped for comfort and ground smooth to eliminate crevices where bacteria can grow.

Knife Shapes and Sharpening Equipment

You will collect many knives during your career, many with specialized functions not described here. This list includes only the most basic knives and sharpening equipment:

French or Chef's Knife

An all-purpose knife used for chopping, slicing and mincing. Its rigid 8- to 14-inch-long blade is wide at the heel and tapers to a point at the tip.

Utility Knife

An all-purpose knife used for cutting fruits and vegetables and carving poultry. Its rigid 6- to 8-inch-long blade is shaped like a chef's knife but narrower.

Boning Knife

A smaller knife with a thin blade used to separate meat from bone. The blade is usually 5 to 7 inches long and may be flexible or rigid.

Paring Knife

A short knife used for detail work or cutting fruits and vegetables. The rigid blade is from 2 to 4 inches long. A tournée or **bird's beak knife** is similar to a paring knife but with a curved blade; it is used for cutting curved surfaces or tournéeing vegetables.

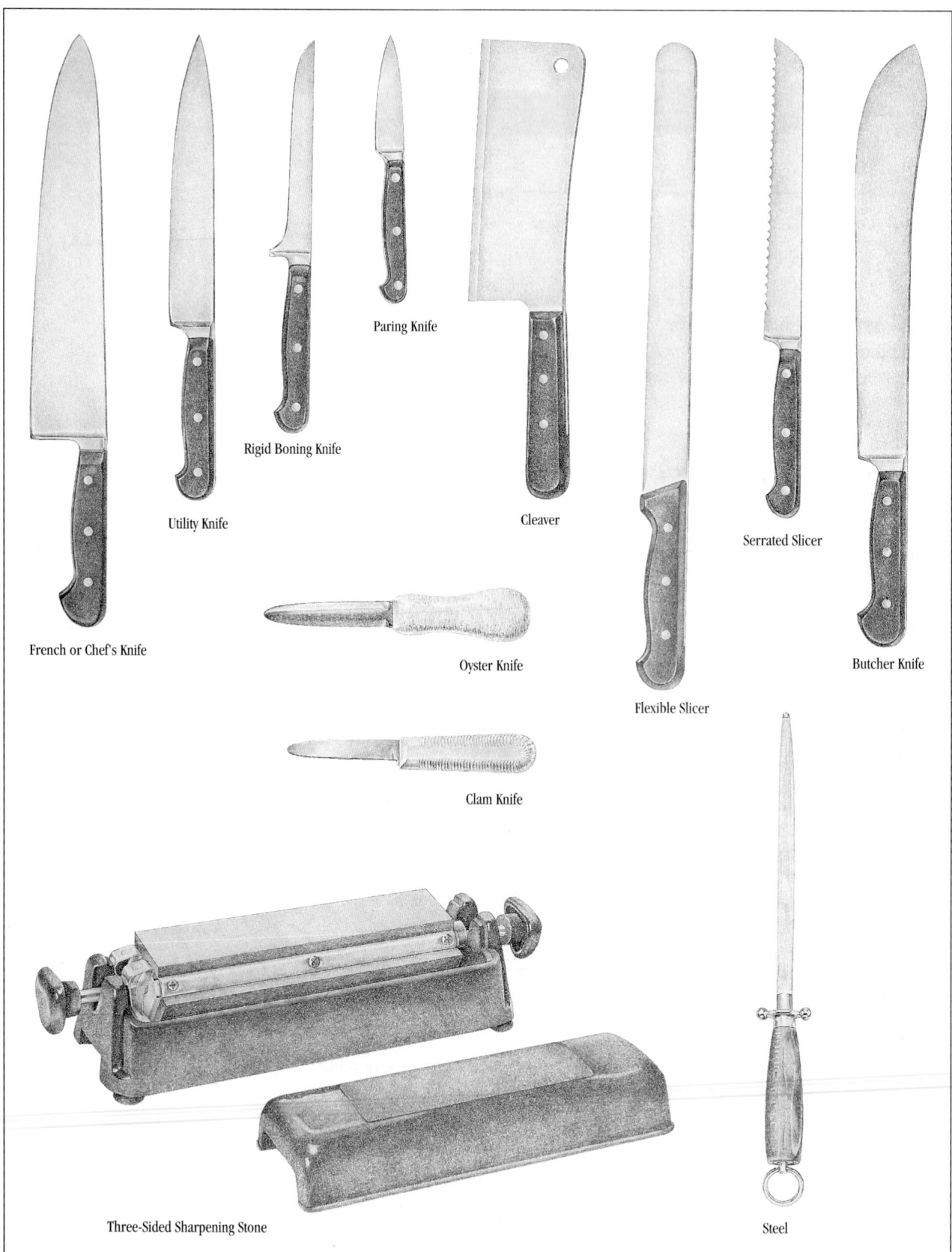

French or Chef's Knife

Utility Knife

Rigid Boning Knife

Paring Knife

Cleaver

Oyster Knife

Clam Knife

Flexible Slicer

Serrated Slicer

Butcher Knife

Three-Sided Sharpening Stone

Steel

FIGURE 5.4

Cleaver

The large, heavy rectangular blade is used for chopping or cutting through bones.

Slicer

A knife with a long, thin blade used primarily for slicing cooked meat. The tip may be round or pointed and the blade may be flexible or rigid. A similar knife with a serrated edge is used for slicing bread or pastry items.

Butcher Knife

Sometimes known as a **scimitar** because the rigid blade curves up in a 25-degree angle at the tip, it is used for fabricating raw meat and is available with 6- to 14-inch blades.

Oyster and Clam Knives

The short, rigid blades of these knives are used to open oyster and clam shells. The tips are blunt; only the clam knife has a sharp edge.

Sharpening Stone

Also known as a **whetstone**, it is used to put an edge on a dull blade.

Steel

It is used to hone or straighten a blade immediately after and between sharpenings.

MEASURING AND PORTIONING DEVICES

Recipe ingredients must be measured precisely, especially in the bakeshop, and foods should be measured when served to control portion size and cost. The devices used to measure and portion foods are, for the most part, hand tools designed to make food preparation and service easier and more precise. The accuracy they afford prevents the cost of mistakes made when accurate measurements are ignored.

Measurements may be based upon weight (e.g., grams, ounces, pounds) or volume (e.g., teaspoons, cups, gallons). Therefore it is necessary to have available several measuring devices, including liquid and dry measuring cups and a variety of scales. Thermometers and timers are also measuring devices and are discussed here. When purchasing measuring devices look for quality construction and accurate markings.

Scales

Scales are necessary to determine the weight of an ingredient or a portion of food (for example, the sliced meat for a sandwich). Portion scales use a spring mechanism, round dial and single flat tray. They are available calibrated in grams, ounces or pounds. Electronic scales also use a spring mechanism but provide digital readouts. They are often required by law where foods are priced for sale by weight. Balance scales (also known as baker's scales) use a two-tray and free-weights counterbalance system. A balance scale allows more weight to be measured at one time because it is not limited by spring capacity. Any scale must be properly used and maintained to provide an accurate reading.

TABLE 5.1   PORTION SCOOP CAPACITIES

Scoop Number	Volume		Approximate Weight*	
	U.S.	Metric	U.S.	Metric
6	2/3 c.	160 ml	5 oz.	160 g
8	1/2 c.	120 ml	4 oz.	120 g
10	3 fl. oz.	90 ml	3 to 3-1/2 oz.	85–100 g
12	1/3 c.	80 ml	2-1/2 to 3 oz.	75–85 g
16	1/4 c.	60 ml	2 oz.	60 g
20	1-1/2 fl. oz.	45 ml	1-3/4 oz.	50 g
24	1-1/3 fl. oz.	40 ml	1-1/3 oz.	40 g
30	1 fl. oz.	30 ml	1 oz.	30 g
40	0.8 fl. oz.	24 ml	0.8 oz.	23 g
60	1/2 fl. oz.	15 ml	1/2 oz.	15 g

*Weights are approximate because they vary by food.

Volume Measures

Ingredients may be measured by volume using measuring spoons and measuring cups. Measuring spoons sold as a set usually include 1/4-, 1/2-, 1-teaspoon and 1-tablespoon units (or the metric equivalent). Liquid measuring cups are available in capacities from 1 cup to 1 gallon. They have a lip or pour spout above the top line of measurement to prevent spills. Measuring cups for dry ingredients are usually sold in sets of 1/4-, 1/3-, 1/2-, and 1-cup units. They do not have pour spouts, so the top of the cup is level with the top measurement specified. Glass measuring cups are not recommended because they can break. Avoid using bent or dented measuring cups as the damage may distort the measurement capacity.

Ladles

Long-handled ladles are useful for portioning liquids such as stocks, sauces and soups. The capacity, in ounces, is stamped on the handle.

Portion Scoops

Portion scoops (also known as dishers) resemble ice cream scoops. They come in a range of standardized sizes and have a lever-operated blade for releasing their contents. Scoops are useful for portioning salads, vegetables, muffin batters or other soft foods. A number, stamped on either the handle or the release mechanism, indicates the number of level scoopfuls per quart. The higher the scoop number, the smaller the scoop's capacity.

Thermometers

Various types of thermometers are used in the kitchen.

Stem-type thermometers, including instant-read models, measure the temperature of a food. The thermometer is inserted into foods to obtain temperature readings between 0°F (–18°C) and 220°F (104°C). Temperatures are shown on either a dial noted by an arrow or a digital readout. An instant-read thermometer is a small stem-type model, designed to be carried in a pocket and used to provide quick temperature readings. An instant-read thermometer should not be left in foods that are cooking because doing so damages the thermometer.

Candy and fat thermometers measure temperatures up to 400°F (204°C) using mercury in a column of glass. A back clip attaches to the pan, keeping the chef's hands free. Be careful not to subject glass thermometers to quick temperature changes or the glass may shatter.

Because proper temperatures must be maintained for holding and storing foods, oven and refrigerator thermometers are also useful. Select thermometers with easy-to-read dials or column divisions.

Timers

Portable kitchen timers are useful for any busy chef. Small digital timers can be carried in a pocket; some even time three functions at once. Select a timer with a loud alarm signal and long timing capability.

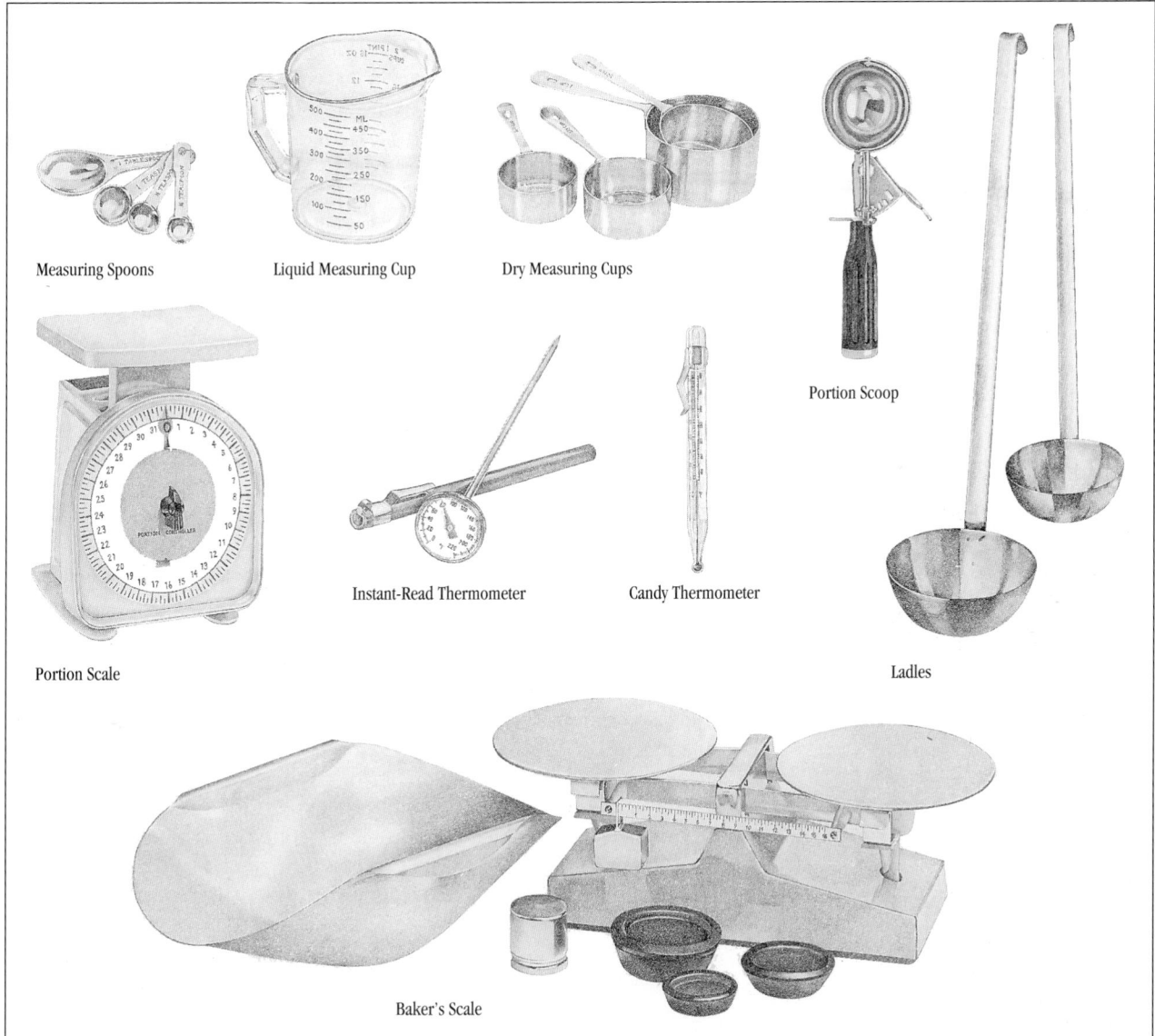

Measuring Spoons

Liquid Measuring Cup

Dry Measuring Cups

Portion Scoop

Portion Scale

Instant-Read Thermometer

Candy Thermometer

Ladles

Baker's Scale

FIGURE 5.5

COOKWARE

Cookware includes the sauté pans and stockpots used on the stove top as well as the roasting pans, hotel pans and specialty molds used inside the oven. Cookware should be selected for its size, shape, ability to conduct heat evenly and overall quality of construction.

Metals and Heat Conduction

Cookware that fails to distribute heat evenly may cause hot spots that burn foods. Because different metals conduct heat at different rates, and thicker layers of metal conduct heat more evenly than thinner ones, the most important considerations when choosing cookware are the type and thickness (known as the *gauge*) of the material used. No one cookware or material suits every process or need, however; always select the most appropriate material for the task at hand.

Copper

Copper is an excellent conductor: It heats rapidly and evenly and cools quickly. Indeed, unlined copper pots are unsurpassed for cooking sugar and fruit mixtures. But copper cookware is extremely expensive. It also requires a great deal of care and is often quite heavy. Moreover, because copper may react with some foods, copper cookware usually has a tin lining, which is soft and easily scratched. Because of these problems, copper is now often sandwiched between layers of stainless steel or aluminum in the bottom of pots and pans.

Aluminum

Aluminum is the metal used most commonly in commercial utensils. It is lightweight and, after copper, conducts heat best. Aluminum is a soft metal, though, so it should be treated with care to avoid dents. Do not use aluminum containers for storage or for cooking acidic foods because the metal reacts chemically with many foods. Light-colored foods, such as soups or sauces, may be discolored when cooked in aluminum, especially if stirred with a metal whisk or spoon.

Anodized aluminum has a hard, dark, corrosion-resistant surface that helps prevent sticking and discoloration.

Stainless Steel

Although stainless steel conducts and retains heat poorly, it is a hard, durable metal particularly useful for holding foods and for low-temperature cooking where hot spots and scorching are not problems. Stainless steel pots and pans are available with aluminum or copper bonded to the bottom or with an aluminum-layered core. Although expensive, such cookware combines the rapid, uniform heat conductivity of copper and aluminum with the strength, durability and nonreactivity of stainless steel. Stainless steel is also ideal for storage containers because it does not react with foods.

Cast Iron

Cast-iron cookware distributes heat evenly and holds high temperatures well. It is often used in griddles and large skillets. Although relatively inexpensive, cast iron is extremely heavy and brittle. It must be kept properly conditioned and dry to prevent rust and pitting.

Glass

Glass retains heat well but conducts it poorly. It does not react with foods. Tempered glass is suitable for microwave cooking provided it does not have any metal band or decoration. Commercial operations rarely use glass cookware because of the danger of breakage.

Ceramics

Ceramics, including earthenware, porcelain and stoneware, are used primarily for baking dishes, casseroles and baking stones because they conduct heat uniformly and retain temperatures well. Ceramics are nonreactive, inexpensive and generally suitable for use in a microwave oven (provided there is no metal in the glaze). Ceramics are easily chipped or cracked, however, and should not be used over a direct flame. Also, quick temperature changes may cause the cookware to crack or shatter.

Plastic

Plastic containers are frequently used in commercial kitchens for food storage or service, but they cannot be used for heating or cooking except in a microwave oven. Plastic microwave cookware is made of phenolic resin. It is easy to clean, relatively inexpensive and rigidly shaped, but its glasslike structure is brittle and it can crack or shatter.

Enamelware

Pans lined with enamel should not be used for cooking; in many areas, their use in commercial kitchens is prohibited by law. The enamel can chip or crack easily, providing good places for bacteria to grow. Also, the chemicals used to bond the enamel to the cookware can cause food poisoning if ingested.

◆◆◆

ROMAN POTS, SOUTHERN STILLS AND CRAFT FAIRS

Lead is poisonous. Ingesting it can cause severe gastrointestinal pains, anemia and central nervous system disorders including intelligence and memory deficits and behavioral changes.

The unwitting and dangerous consumption of lead is not limited to children eating peeling paint chips. Some historians suggest that the use of lead cookware and lead-lined storage vessels and water pipes may have caused pervasive lead poisoning among the elite of the Roman Empire and thus contributed to the Empire's decline. There is also ample evidence that from ancient times until just a few hundred years ago, wine was heated in lead vessels to sweeten it. This had a disastrous effect on the drinker and, for several centuries in countries throughout Europe, on the wine purveyor as well. The former could be poisoned and the latter could be punished by death for selling adulterated wine. More recently it was found that much of the moonshine whiskey produced in the American South contained lead in potentially toxic ranges. The source was determined to be the lead solder used in homemade stills, some of which even included old lead-containing car radiators as condensers.

Although commercially available cookware will not contain lead, be careful of imported pottery and those lovely hand-thrown pots found at craft fairs—there could be lead in the glaze.

Nonstick Coatings

Without affecting a metal's ability to conduct heat, a polymer (plastic) known as polytetrafluoroethylene (PTFE) and marketed under the trade-names Teflon® and Silverstone®, may be applied to many types of cookware. It provides a slippery, nonreactive finish that prevents food from sticking and allows the use of less fat in cooking. Cookware with nonstick coatings requires a great deal of care, however, as the coatings can scratch, chip and blister. Do not use metal spoons or spatulas in cookware with nonstick coatings.

Common Cookware

Pots

Pots are large round vessels with straight sides and two loop handles. Available in a range of sizes based on volume, they are used on the stove top for making stocks, soups or boiling or simmering foods, particularly where rapid evaporation is not desired. Flat or fitted lids are available.

Pans

Pans are round vessels with one long handle and straight or sloped sides. They are usually smaller and shallower than pots. Pans are available in a range of diameters and are used for general stove top cooking, especially sautéing, frying or reducing liquids rapidly.

Woks

Originally used to prepare Asian foods, woks are now found in many professional kitchens. Their round bottoms and curved sides diffuse heat and make it easy to toss or stir contents. Their large domed lids retain heat for steaming vegetables. Woks are useful for quickly sautéing strips of meat, simmering a whole fish or deep-frying appetizers. Stove top woks range in diameter from 12 to 30 inches; larger built-in gas or electric models are also available.

Hotel Pans

Hotel pans (also known as steam table pans) are rectangular stainless steel pans designed to hold food for service in steam tables. Hotel pans are also used for baking, roasting or poaching inside an oven. Perforated pans useful for draining, steaming or icing down foods are also available. The standard full-size pan is 12 by 20 inches, with pans one-half, one-third, one-sixth and other fractions of this size available. Hotel pan depth is standardized at 2 inches (referred to as a "200 pan"), 4, 6 and 8 inches.

Molds

Pâté molds are available in several shapes and sizes, and are usually made from tinned steel. Those with hinged sides, whether smooth or patterned, are more properly referred to as *pâté en croûte* molds. The hinged sides make it easier to remove the baked pâté. Terrine molds are traditionally lidded earthenware or enameled cast-iron containers used for baking ground meat mixtures. They may be round, oval or rectangular. Timbale molds are small (about 4 ounces) metal or ceramic containers used for molding aspic or baking individual portions of mousse, custard or vegetables. Their slightly flared sides allow the contents to release cleanly when inverted.

Stockpot with Spigot

Sauce Pot

Sautoir (Straight Sides)

Saucepan

Cast-Iron Skillet (Griswold)

Sauteuse (Sloped Sides)

Rondeau/Brazier

Wok

Hotel Pans

Pâté en Croûte Mold

Timbales

FIGURE 5.6

STRAINERS AND SIEVES

Strainers and sieves are used primarily to aerate and remove impurities from dry ingredients and drain or purée cooked foods. Strainers, colanders, drum sieves, china caps and chinois are nonmechanical devices with a stainless steel mesh or screen through which food passes. The size of the mesh or

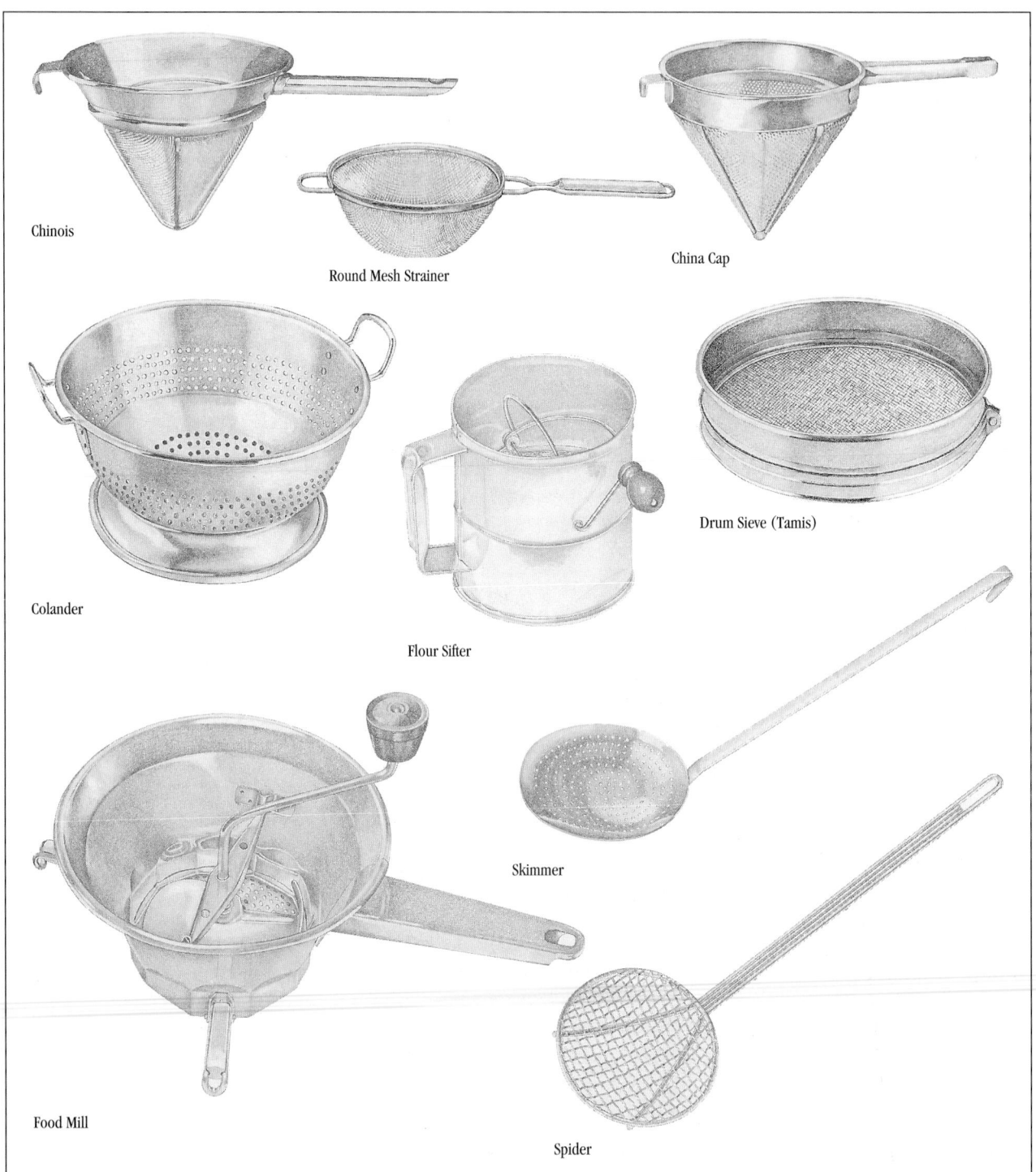

Chinois

Round Mesh Strainer

China Cap

Colander

Flour Sifter

Drum Sieve (Tamis)

Skimmer

Food Mill

Spider

FIGURE 5.7

screen varies from extremely fine to several millimeters wide; select the fineness best suited for the task at hand.

Chinois and China Cap

Both the chinois and china cap are cone-shaped metal strainers. The conical shape allows liquids to filter through small openings. A chinois is made from a very fine mesh, while a china cap has a perforated metal body. Both are used for straining stocks and sauces, with the chinois being particularly useful for consommé. A china cap can also be used with a pestle to purée soft foods.

Skimmer and Spider

Both the skimmer and spider are long-handled tools used to remove foods or impurities from liquids. The flat, perforated disk of a skimmer is used for skimming stocks or removing foods from soups or stocks. The spider has a finer mesh disk, which makes it better for retrieving items from hot fat. Wooden-handled spiders are available but are less sturdy and harder to clean than all-metal designs.

Cheesecloth

Cheesecloth is a loosely woven cotton gauze used for straining stocks and sauces and wrapping poultry or fish for poaching. Cheesecloth is also indispensable for making sachets. Always rinse cheesecloth thoroughly before use; this removes lint and prevents the cheesecloth from absorbing other liquids.

Food Mill

A food mill purées and strains food at the same time. Food is placed in the hopper and a hand-crank mechanism turns a blade in the hopper against a perforated disk, forcing the food through the disk. Most models have interchangeable disks with various-sized holes. Choose a mill that can be taken apart easily for cleaning.

Flour Sifter

A sifter is used for aerating, blending and removing impurities from dry ingredients such as flour, cocoa and leavening agents. The 8-cup hand-crank sifter shown in Figure 5.7 uses four curved rods to brush the contents through a curved mesh screen. The sifter should have a medium-fine screen and a comfortable handle.

PROCESSING EQUIPMENT

Processing equipment includes both electrical and nonelectrical devices used to chop, purée, slice, grind or mix foods. Before using any such equipment, be sure to review its operating procedures and ask for assistance if necessary. Always turn the equipment off and disconnect the power before disassembling, cleaning or moving the appliance. Any problems or malfunctions should be reported to your supervisor immediately. *Never place your hand into any machinery when the power is on. Processing equipment is powerful and can cause serious injury.*

Slicer

An electric slicer is used to cut meat, bread, cheese or raw vegetables into uniform slices. It has a circular blade that rotates at high speed. Food is placed in a carrier, then passed (manually or by an electric motor) against the blade.

Slice thickness is determined by the distance between the blade and the carrier. Because of the speed with which the blade rotates, foods can be cut into extremely thin slices very quickly. An electric slicer is convenient for preparing moderate to large quantities of food, but the time required to disassemble and clean the equipment makes it impractical when slicing only a few items.

Mandoline

A mandoline is a manually operated slicer made of stainless steel with adjustable slicing blades. It is also used to make julienne and waffle-cut slices. Its narrow, rectangular body sits on the work counter at a 45-degree angle. Foods are passed against a blade to obtain uniform slices. It is useful for slicing small quantities of fruits or vegetables when using a large electric slicer would be unwarranted. To avoid injury, always use a hand guard or steel glove when using a mandoline.

Food Chopper or Buffalo Chopper

This chopper is used to process moderate to large quantities of food to a uniform size, such as chopping onions or grinding bread for crumbs. The food is placed in a large bowl rotating beneath a hood where curved blades chop it. The size of the cut depends on how long the food is left in the machine. Buffalo choppers are available in floor or tabletop models. The motor can usually be fitted with a variety of other tools such as a meat grinder or a slicer/shredder, making it even more useful.

Food Processor

A food processor has a motor housing with a removable bowl and S-shaped blade. It is used, for example, to purée cooked foods, chop nuts, prepare compound butters and emulsify sauces. Special disks can be added that slice, shred or julienne foods. Bowl capacity and motor power vary; select a model large enough for your most common tasks.

Blender

Though similar in principle to a food processor, a blender has a tall, narrow food container and a four-pronged blade. Its design is better for processing liquids or liquefying foods quickly. A blender is used to prepare smooth drinks, purée soups and sauces, blend batters and chop ice. A **vertical cutter/mixer** (VCM) operates like a very large, powerful blender. A VCM is usually floor-mounted and has a capacity of 15 to 80 quarts.

Mixer

A vertical mixer is indispensable in the bakeshop and most kitchens. The U-shaped arms hold a metal mixing bowl in place; the selected mixing attachment fits onto the rotating head. The three common mixing attachments are the whip (used for whipping eggs or cream), the paddle (used for general mixing) and the dough hook (used for kneading bread). Most mixers have several operating speeds. Bench models range in capacity from 4.5 to 20 quarts, while floor mixers can as hold as much as 140 quarts. Some mixers can be fitted with shredder/slicers, meat grinders, juicers or power strainers, making the equipment more versatile.

Juicer

Two types of juicers are available: reamers and extractors. Reamers, also known as citrus juicers, remove juice from citrus fruits. They can be manual or electric. Manual models use a lever arm to squeeze the fruit with increased

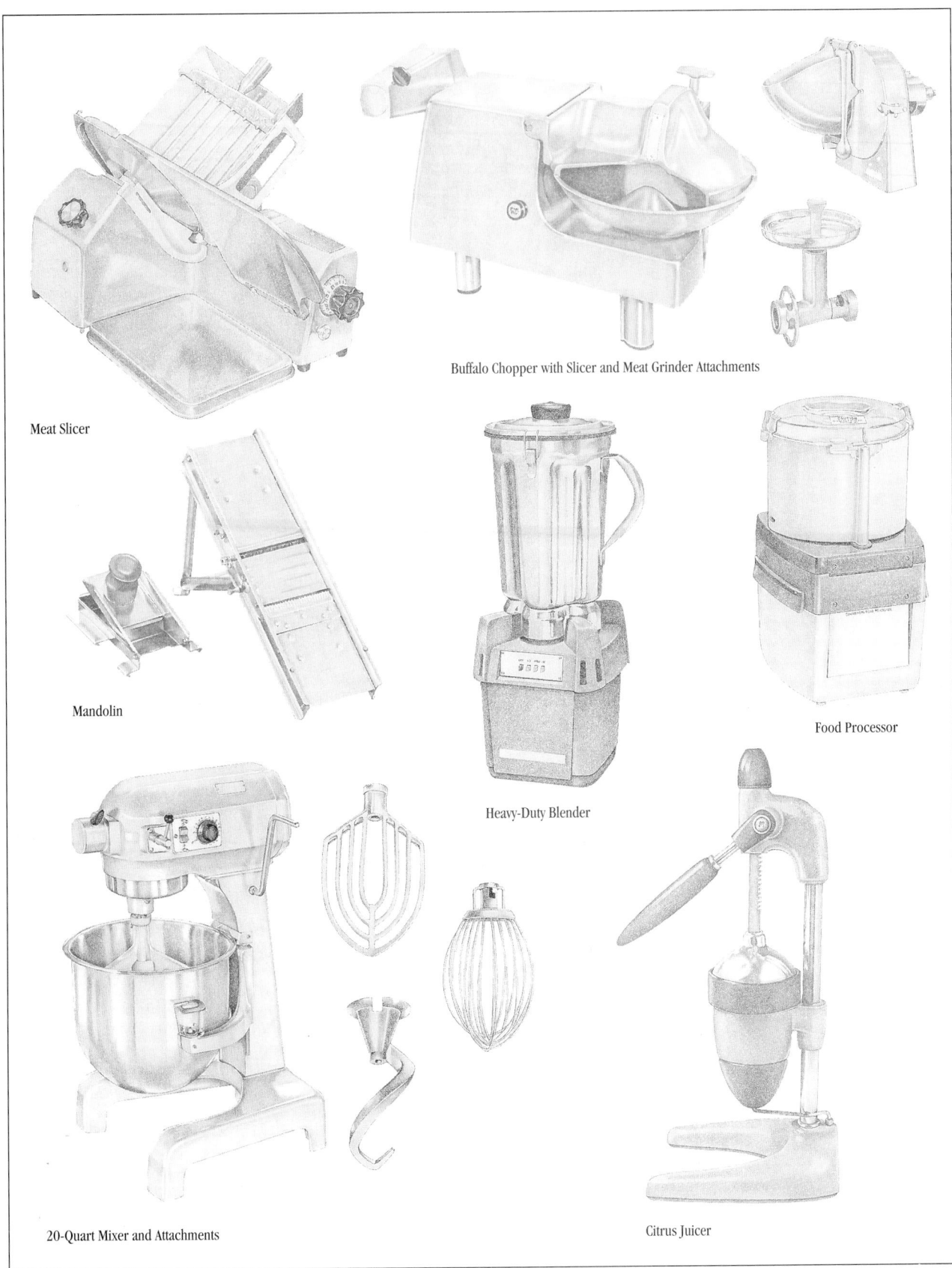

Meat Slicer

Buffalo Chopper with Slicer and Meat Grinder Attachments

Mandolin

Heavy-Duty Blender

Food Processor

20-Quart Mixer and Attachments

Citrus Juicer

FIGURE 5.8

pressure. They are most often used to prepare small to moderate amounts of juice for cooking or beverages. Juice extractors are electrical devices that create juice by liquefying raw fruits, vegetables and herbs. They use centrifugal force to filter out fiber and pulp.

STORAGE CONTAINERS

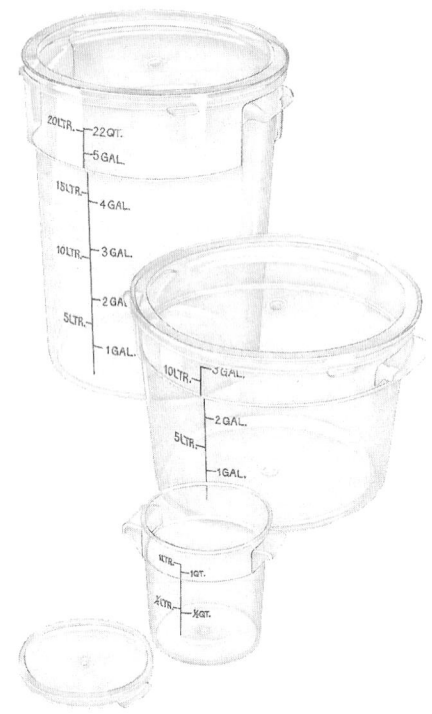

Proper storage containers are necessary for keeping leftovers and opened packages of food safe for consumption. Proper storage can also reduce the costs incurred by waste or spoilage.

While stainless steel pans such as hotel pans are suitable and useful for some items, the expense of stainless steel and the lack of air-tight lids makes these pans impractical for general storage purposes. Aluminum containers are not recommended because the metal can react with even mildly acidic items. Glass containers are generally not allowed in commercial kitchens because of the hazards of broken glass. The most useful storage containers are those made of high-density plastic (such as polyethylene and polypropylene).

Storage containers must have well-fitting lids and should be available in a variety of sizes, including some that are small enough to hold even minimal quantities of food without allowing too much exposure to oxygen. Round and square plastic containers are widely available. Flat, snap-on lids allow containers to be stacked for more efficient storage. Containers may be clear or opaque white, which helps protect light-sensitive foods. Larger containers may be fitted with handles and spigots, making them especially suited for storing stock. Some storage containers are marked with graduated measurements, so content quantity can be determined at a glance. See Figure 5.9.

Large quantities of dry ingredients, such as flour, sugar and rice, can be stored in rolling bins. The bins should be seamless with rounded corners for easy cleaning. They should have well-fitting but easy-to-open lids and should move easily on well-balanced casters.

FIGURE 5.9

HEAVY EQUIPMENT

Heavy equipment includes the gas-, electric- or steam-operated appliances used for cooking, reheating or holding foods. Heavy equipment also includes dishwashers and refrigeration units. Heavy equipment should be installed in a fixed location determined by the kitchen's traffic flow and space limitations.

Heavy equipment may be purchased or leased new or used. Used equipment is most often purchased in an effort to save money. While the initial cost is generally less for used equipment, the buyer should also consider the lack of a manufacturer's warranty or dealership guarantee and how the equipment was maintained by the prior owner. Functional used equipment is satisfactory for back-of-the-house areas, but it is usually better to purchase new equipment if it will be visible to the customer. Leasing equipment may be appropriate for some operations. The cost of leasing is less than purchasing and, if something goes wrong with the equipment, the operator is generally not responsible for repairs or service charges.

Stove Tops

Stove tops or ranges are often the most important cooking equipment in the kitchen. They have one or more burners powered by gas or electricity. The burners may be open or covered with a cast-iron or steel plate. Open burners

FIGURE 5.10   *Gas burner and flat top range with dual ovens and an overhead broiler (salamander).*

supply quick, direct heat that is easy to regulate. A steel plate, known as a **flat top**, supplies even but less intense heat. Although it takes longer to heat than a burner, the flat top supports heavier weights and makes a larger area available for cooking. Many stoves include both flat tops and open burner arrangements.

Griddles are similar to flat tops except they are made of a thinner metal plate. Foods are usually cooked directly on the griddle's surface, not in pots or pans which can nick or scratch the surface. (A griddle is illustrated in Figure 5.11.) The surface should be properly cleaned and conditioned after each use. Griddles are popular for short-order and fast-food-type operations.

Ovens

An oven is an enclosed space where food is cooked by being surrounded with hot, dry air. Conventional ovens are often located beneath the stove top. They have a heating element located at the unit's bottom or floor, and pans are placed on wire racks inside the oven's cavity. See Figure 5.10. Conventional ovens may also be separate, free-standing units or decks stacked one on top of the other. In stack ovens, pans are placed directly on the deck or floor and not on wire racks.

Convection ovens use internal fans to circulate the hot air. This tends to cook foods more quickly and evenly. Convection ovens are almost always free-standing units, powered either by gas or electricity. Because convection ovens

Griddle

Steam Kettle

Deep Fryer

Stack Oven

Overhead Broiler

Tilting Skillet

Gas Grill

Convection Steamer

FIGURE 5.11

cook foods more quickly, temperatures may need to be reduced by 25 to 50 degrees F (10 to 20°C) from those recommended for conventional ovens.

Microwave Ovens

Microwave ovens are electrically powered ovens used to cook or reheat foods. They are available in a range of sizes and power settings. Microwave ovens will not brown foods unless fitted with special browning elements. Microwave cooking is discussed in more detail in Chapter 9, Principles of Cooking.

Broilers and Grills

Broilers and grills are generally used to prepare meats, fish and poultry. For a grill, the heat source is beneath the rack on which the food is placed. For a broiler, the heat source is above the food. Most broilers are gas powered; grills may be gas or electric or may burn wood or charcoal. A **salamander** is a small overhead broiler primarily used to finish or top-brown foods. See Figure 5.10. A **rotisserie** is similar to a broiler except that the food is placed on a revolving spit in front of the heat source. The unit may be open or enclosed like an oven; it is most often used for cooking poultry or meats.

Tilting Skillets

Tilting skillets are large, free-standing, flat-bottomed pans about 6 inches deep with an internal heating element below the pan's bottom. They are usually made of stainless steel with a cover, and have a hand-crank mechanism that turns or tilts the pan to pour out the contents. Tilting skillets can be used as stockpots, braziers, fry pans, griddles or steam tables, making them one of the most versatile of modern commercial appliances.

Steam Kettles

Steam kettles (also known as steam-jacketed kettles) are similar to stockpots except they are heated from the bottom and sides by steam circulating between layers of stainless steel. The steam may be generated internally or from an outside source. Because steam heats the kettle's sides, foods cook more quickly and evenly than they would in a pot sitting on the stove top. Steam kettles are most often used for making sauces, soups, custards or stock. Steam kettles are available in a range of sizes, from a 2-gallon tabletop model to a 100-gallon floor model. Some models have a tilting mechanism that allows the contents to be poured out; others have a spigot near the bottom through which liquids can be drained.

Steamers

Pressure and convection steamers are used to cook foods rapidly and evenly, using direct contact with steam. Pressure steamers heat water above the boiling point in sealed compartments; the high temperature and sealed compartment increase the internal pressure in a range of 4 to 15 pounds per square inch. The increased pressure and temperature cook the foods rapidly. Convection steamers generate steam in an internal boiler, then release it over the foods in a cooking chamber. Both types of steamer are ideal for cooking vegetables with a minimal loss of flavor or nutrients.

Deep Fryers

Deep fryers are only used to fry foods in hot fat. The fryers may be either gas or electric and should have thermostatic controls to maintain the fat at a preset temperature. Frying procedures are discussed in Chapter 21, Deep Frying.

Refrigerators

Proper refrigeration space is an essential component of any kitchen. Many foods must be stored at low temperatures to maintain quality and safety. Most commercial refrigeration is of two types: walk-in units and reach-in or upright units.

A walk-in is a large, room-sized box capable of holding hundreds of pounds of food on adjustable shelves. A separate freezer walk-in may be positioned nearby or even inside a refrigerated walk-in.

Reach-ins may be individual units or parts of a bank of units, each with shelves approximately the size of a full sheet pan. Reach-in refrigerators and freezers are usually located throughout the kitchen to provide quick access to foods. Small units may also be placed beneath the work counters. Freezers and refrigerators are available in a wide range of sizes and door designs to suit any operation.

Other forms of commercial refrigeration include chilled drawers located beneath a work area that are just large enough to accommodate a hotel pan, and display cases used to show foods to the customer.

Dishwashers

Mechanical dishwashers are available to wash, rinse and sanitize dishware, glassware, cookware and utensils. Small models clean one rack of items at a time, while larger models can handle several racks simultaneously on a conveyor belt system. Sanitation may be accomplished with either extremely hot water (180°F/82°C) or with chemicals automatically dispensed during the final rinse cycle. Any dishwashing area should be carefully organized for efficient use of equipment and employees and to prevent recontamination of clean items.

SAFETY EQUIPMENT

There are certain items that are critical to the well-being of a food service operation although they are not used in food preparation. These are safety devices, many of which are required by state or local law. Failing to include safety equipment in a kitchen or failing to maintain it properly endangers workers and customers.

Fire Extinguishers

Fire extinguishers are canisters of foam, dry chemicals (such as sodium bicarbonate or potassium bicarbonate) or pressurized water used to extinguish small fires. They must be placed within sight of and easily reached from the work areas in which fires are more likely to occur. Different classes of extinguishers use different chemicals to fight different types of fire. The appropriate class must be used for the specific fire. See Table 5.2. Fire extinguishers must be recharged and checked from time to time. Be sure they have not been discharged, tampered with or otherwise damaged.

TABLE 5.2   FIRE EXTINGUISHERS

Class	Symbol	Use
Class A	▲	Fires involving wood, paper, cloth or plastic
Class B	■	Fires involving oil, grease or flammable chemicals
Class C	●	Fires involving electrical equipment or wiring

Combination extinguishers—AB, BC and ABC—are also available.

Ventilation Systems

Ventilation systems (also called ventilation hoods) are commonly installed over cooking equipment to remove vapors, heat and smoke. Some systems include fire extinguishing agents or sprinklers. A properly operating hood makes the kitchen more comfortable for the staff and reduces the danger of fire. The system should be designed, installed and inspected by professionals, then cleaned and maintained regularly.

First-Aid Kits

First-aid supplies should be stored in a clearly marked box, conspicuously located near food preparation areas. State and local laws may specify the kit's exact contents. Generally, they should include a first-aid manual, bandages, gauze dressings, adhesive tape, antiseptics, scissors, cold packs and other supplies. The kit should be checked regularly and items replaced as needed. In addition, cards with emergency telephone numbers should be placed inside the first-aid kit and near a telephone.

THE PROFESSIONAL KITCHEN

The kitchen is the heart of the food service operation. There, food and other items are received, stored, prepared and plated for service; dining room staff places orders, retrieves foods ready for service and returns dirty service items; dishes and other wares are cleaned and stored; and the chef conducts business. But commercial space is expensive, and most food service operators recognize that the greater number of customers served, the greater the revenues. Often this translates into a large dining area and small kitchen and storage facilities. Therefore, when designing a kitchen, it is important to use the space wisely so that each of its functions can be accomplished efficiently.

Regardless of the kitchen's size, its design begins with a consideration of the tasks to be performed. Analyzing the menu identifies these tasks. A restaurant featuring steaks and chops, for example, will need areas to fabricate and grill meats. If it relies on commercially prepared desserts and breads, it will not need a bakeshop but will still need space to hold and plate baked goods.

Once all food preparation tasks are identified, a work area for each particular task is designated. These work areas are called **work stations**. At a steak restaurant, an important work station is the broiler. If the restaurant serves fried foods, it will also need a fry station. The size and design of each work station is determined by the volume of food the operation intends to produce.

Usually work stations using the same or similar equipment for related tasks are grouped together into **work sections**. See Table 5.3. (Note that work stations correspond to the kitchen brigade system discussed in Chapter 1, Professionalism.) For example, in a typical full-service restaurant, there will be a single hot-foods

TABLE 5.3	WORK SECTIONS AND THEIR STATIONS
Sections	Stations
Hot-foods section	Broiler station Fry station Griddle station Sauté/sauce station Holding
Garde-manger section	Salad greens cleaning Salad preparation Cold foods preparation Sandwich station Showpiece preparation
Bakery section	Mixing station Dough holding and proofing Dough rolling and forming Baking and cooling Dessert preparation* Frozen dessert preparation* Plating desserts*
Banquet section	Steam cooking Dry heat cooking (roasting, broiling) Holding and plating
Short-order section	Griddle station Fry station Broiler station
Beverage section	Hot beverage station Cold beverage station Alcoholic beverage station

*These stations are sometimes found in the *garde-manger* section.

◆◆◆
ALEXIS SOYER
(1809–1858)

Alexis Soyer
Photo courtesy of Barbara Wheaton.

The father of the contemporary celebrity chef was Alexis Soyer, a Frenchman whose tragically short working life was spent mostly in London. He was a flamboyant, talented and egocentric showman. He was also a renowned chef, restaurateur, social activist, author, purveyor of prepared foods and inventor.

In 1831 Soyer left his thriving catering business and restaurant in Paris for London. (A scandal was rumored to be behind his sudden departure.) There he quickly established a reputation as a talented chef in the latest French fashion. By 1838 he was employed at a gentlemen's club called the Reform. Able to assist in planning the club's new kitchen facility, Soyer installed the most modern equipment: gas ovens with temperature controls, a steam-driven mechanical spit and a storage locker cooled by running water. From this modern kitchen he produced his signature dish: lamb chops Reform.

The Reform was founded by members of the Liberal Party, a political party interested in social reform. Their chef soon joined the party

"The Kitchen Department of the Reform Club" (1841). "To show them at one glance," wrote the *Spectator*, "the partition walls are cut away, and a bird's eye view is given of the several kitchens, larders, sculleries, and batterie de cuisine; the different functionaries are at their posts, and the accomplished chef, Monsieur Soyer, is in the act of pointing out to a favoured visitor the various contrivances suggested by his ingenuity and experience."

◆◆◆

ranks. He developed recipes for inexpensive, nutritious soups for the working class and in 1847 went to Ireland and opened soup kitchens to feed those who were starving as a result of the Potato Famine.

His most important writings reflect his interests in good food for the masses. The intended audience for *The Modern Housewife* (1849) was the middle class; the growing urban working class was the intended audience for his second book, *A Schilling Cookery for the People* (1855).

In 1851 Soyer opened his own lavishly decorated and expensively equipped restaurant called the Gastronomic Symposium of All Nations. It closed shortly thereafter, in part because of Soyer's debts, in part because he lost his operating license as a result of the rowdiness in the restaurant's American-style bar, at which customers were publicly served cocktails for the first time in London.

In addition to cooking and writing, Soyer created and marketed several prepared food items: Soyer's Sauce, Soyer's Nectar and Soyer's

Relish. He was also fascinated with kitchen gadgets and invented several, including a sink stopper, jelly mold, egg cooker and coffeepot. The most notable, however, was a portable "Magic Stove" weighing less than 4 pounds, similar to a modern chafing dish. Soyer's final triumph was in the Crimean War (1854–1857). He developed army rations, reorganized field and hospital kitchens and introduced one of his last inventions, the campaign stove. Portable, efficient and requiring little fuel, it was used by the British army for the next 90 years.

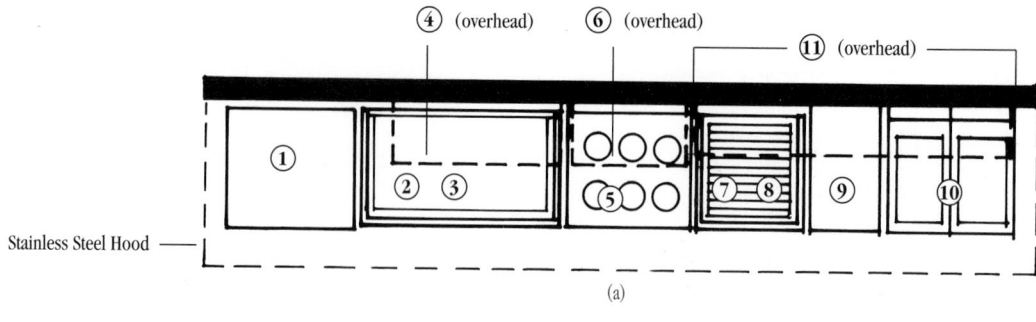

1 Convection Oven
2 Under Counter Freezer Unit
3 Griddle Top
4 Cheese Melter
5 6 Burner Top/Oven Below
6 Salamander
7 Under Counter Refrigerator
8 Broiler Top
9 Stainless Steel Work Table with Open Shelves
10 Fry Stations
11 Stainless Steel Overshelves

12 Steam Table with Open Shelves Below
13 Stainless Steel Dual Shelf with Top Heat Rod
14 Under Counter Freezer with Work Surface
15 Conveyor Toaster
16 Bain Marie with Under Counter Refrigerator
17 Microwave Table with Shelf
18 Microwave
19 Reach-in Refrigerator Unit

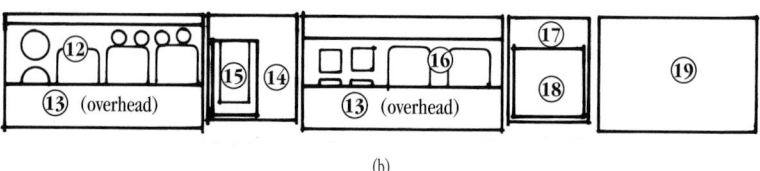

(b)

FIGURE 5.12 *Typical Hot-Foods Section Floor Plan*

section. It can consist of broiler, fry, griddle, sauté and sauce stations. Both advance preparation and last-minute cooking may be performed in the hot-foods section. The principal cooking equipment (a range, broiler, deep fryer, oven, griddle, etc.) will be arranged in a line under a ventilation hood. A typical plan for this hot-foods section is shown in Figure 5.12. Although each work station within the hot-foods section may be staffed by a different line cook, the proximity of the stations allows one line cook to cover more than one station if the kitchen is short-handed or when business is slow.

Merely considering the plan of the work station or section is not enough, however. When designing the work area, you must also consider the elevation. That is, a kitchen designer not only examines what equipment should be placed next to the other (for example, the range next to the deep fryer), but also what equipment and storage facilities can be placed beneath or on top of the other. For example, in a bakeshop, rolling storage carts for flour and sugar or an under-the-counter refrigerator for eggs and dairy products may be located beneath the work surface, while mixing bowls and dry ingredients are stored on shelves above. Figure 5.13 illustrates the elevation for the hot-foods section whose plan is shown in Figure 5.12. Ideally, each station should be designed so that the cook takes no more than three steps in any direction to perform all of his assigned station tasks.

In addition to the work sections where the menu items are produced, a typical restaurant kitchen includes areas dedicated to:

1. *Receiving and storing foods and other items.* There should be separate freezer, refrigerator and dry-goods storage facilities. Each should have

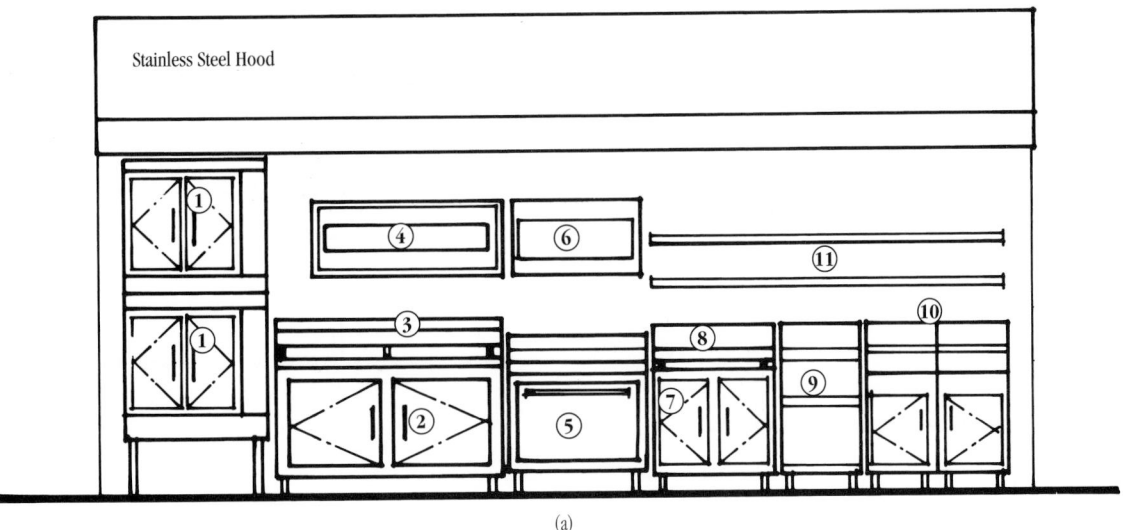

(a)

1   Convection Oven
2   Under Counter Freezer Unit
3   Griddle Top
4   Cheese Melter
5   6 Burner Top/Oven Below
6   Salamander
7   Under Counter Refrigerator
8   Broiler Top
9   Stainless Steel Work Table with Open Shelves
10 Fry Stations
11 Stainless Steel Overshelves

12 Steam Table with Open Shelves Below
13 Stainless Steel Dual Shelf with Top Heat Rod
14 Under Counter Freezer with Work Surface
15 Conveyor Toaster
16 Bain Marie with Under Counter Refrigerator
17 Microwave Table with Shelf
18 Microwave
19 Reach-in Refrigerator Unit

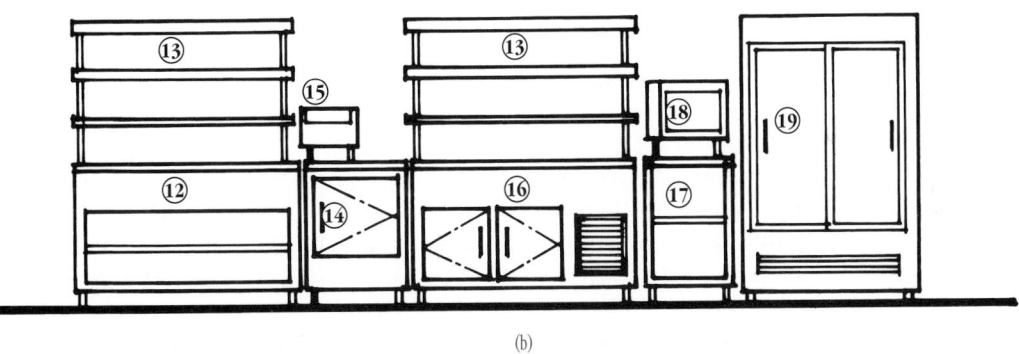

(b)

FIGURE 5.13   *Typical Hot-Foods Section Elevation*

proper temperature, humidity and light controls in order to properly and safely maintain the stored items. Depending upon the operation's size and the work stations' specific needs, there can be either a central storage area or each station or section can maintain its own storage facilities. Typically, however, there is a combination of central and section storage. For example, up to 100 pounds of flour and sugar can be stored in rolling bins under a work table in the bakeshop, while several hundreds of pounds more remain in a central dry goods area. Similarly, one box of salt can be stored near the hot line for immediate use, while the remainder of the case is stored in a central dry goods area. Additional storage space will be needed for cleaning and paper supplies, dishes and other service ware. *Never store cleaning supplies and other chemicals with foods.*

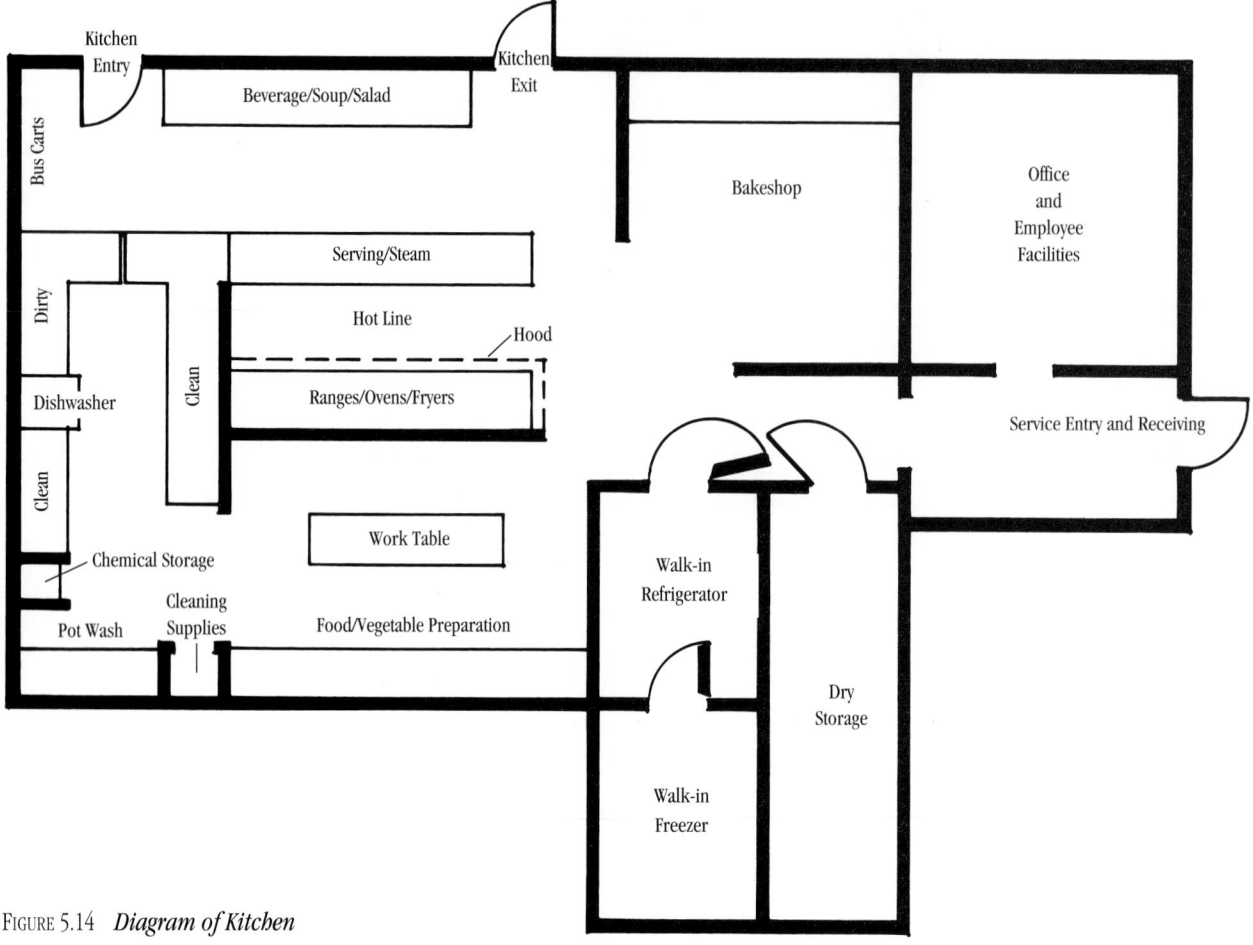

FIGURE 5.14   *Diagram of Kitchen*

2. *Washing dishes and other equipment.* These dish- and equipment-washing facilities should have their own sinks. Food-preparation and hand-washing sinks should be separate.

3. *Employee use.* Restrooms, locker facilities and an office are also found in most food service facilities.

The guiding principle behind a good kitchen design is to maximize the flow of goods and staff from one area to the next and within each area itself. Maximizing flow creates an efficient work environment and helps reduce preparation and service time.

Figure 5.14 shows the several sections of a professional kitchen. It includes an area for front-of-the-house staff to circulate, drop off orders, retrieve finished dishes and return dirty dishes. The design accounts for the flow of foods from receiving, to storage, to food preparation areas, to holding and service areas and then to the dining room as well as the flow of dirty dishes from the dining room back into the kitchen. The work sections are arranged to take advantage of shared equipment. For instance, by placing the bakeshop next to the hot-foods section, they can share ovens. The *garde-manger* and dessert sections, both of which rely on refrigerated foods, are conveniently located near the walk-in refrigerator and freezer area. The beverage station is located near the dining room entrance so that food servers do not have to walk through food preparation areas to fill beverage orders. The office is next to receiving so that the chef can easily check and receive orders. The central storage areas are easily accessible to the receiving area as well as to the food production areas, while the cleaning-supply storage is near the dishwashing area. In general, the design eliminates the need for staff from one work station or section to cross through another station or section.

Governmental building, health, fire and safety codes will dictate, to a degree, certain aspects of a professional kitchen's design. But to make the most of these spaces, the well-designed kitchen should reflect a sound understanding of the tasks to be performed and the equipment necessary to perform them.

CONCLUSION

There are hundreds of tools and pieces of equipment that can help you prepare, cook, store and present food. Every year, manufacturers offer new or improved items. Throughout your career you will use many of them. Select those that are well constructed, durable and best suited for the task at hand. Then use them in a safe and efficient manner.

The way in which equipment is arranged and stored in a kitchen is also important. Good kitchen design emphasizes the efficient flow of goods and staff from one work section to another as well as within each work section or station.

QUESTIONS FOR DISCUSSION

1. What is NSF International? What is its significance with regard to commercial kitchen equipment?
2. List the parts of a chef's knife and describe the knife's construction.
3. List six materials used to make commercial cookware and describe the advantages and disadvantages of each.
4. Describe six pieces of equipment that can be used to slice or chop foods.
5. List three classes of fire extinguishers. For each one, describe its designating symbol and identify the type or types of fire it should be used to extinguish.
6. Explain the relationship between work sections and work stations and the kitchen brigade system discussed in Chapter 1, Professionalism.

CHAPTER 6 KNIFE SKILLS

Dicing an Onion

Onions are easily peeled and diced to any size desired using the procedure shown here.

1. Using a paring knife, remove the stem end. Trim the root end but leave it nearly intact (this helps prevent the onion from falling apart while dicing). Peel away the outer skin; be careful not to remove and waste too much onion.

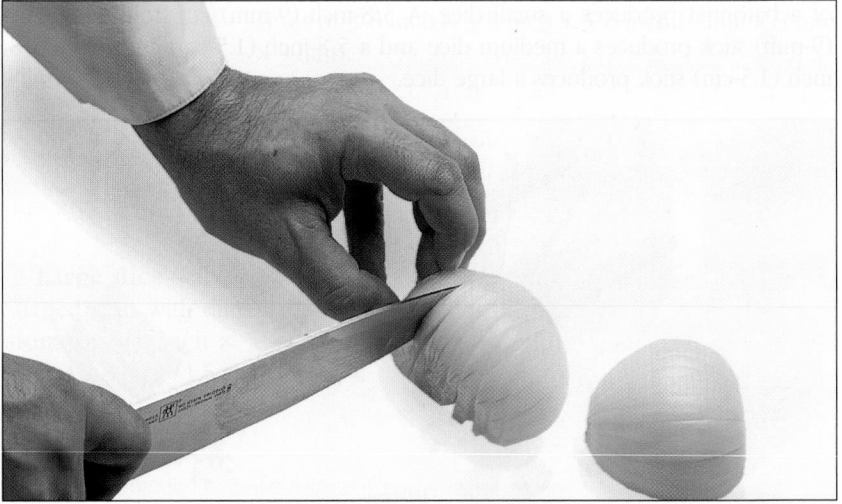

2. Cut the onion in half through the stem and root. Place the cut side down on the cutting board.

3. Cut parallel slices of the desired thickness vertically through the onion from the root toward the stem end without cutting completely through the root end.

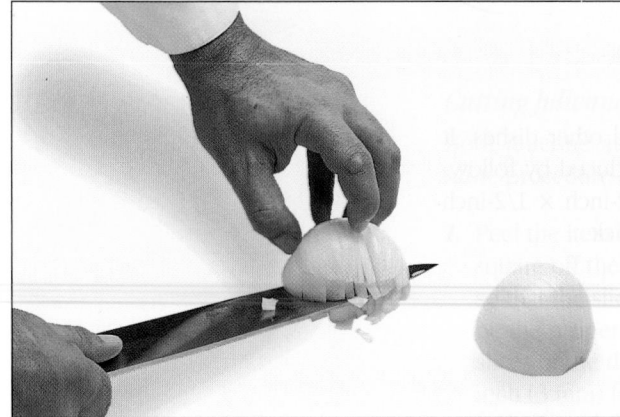

4. Make a single horizontal cut on a small onion or two horizontal cuts on a large onion through the width of the onion, again without cutting through the root end.

5. Turn the onion and cut slices perpendicular to the other slices to produce diced onion.

Mincing

To mince is to cut an item into very small pieces. The terms "finely chopped" and "minced" are often used interchangeably and are most often used when referring to garlic, shallots, herbs and other foods that do not have to be uniform in shape.

Mincing Shallots

The procedure for mincing shallots is shown here.

1. Peel and dice the shallots, following the procedure for peeling and dicing an onion.

2. With a flat hand, hold the knife's tip on the cutting board. Using a rocking motion, mince the shallots with the heel of the knife.

Tourner

Tourner ("to turn" in French) is a cutting technique that results in a football-shaped finished product with seven equal sides and blunt ends. The size of the finished product may vary, the most common being 2 inches (5 cm) long.

This is a more complicated procedure than other cuts and takes considerable practice to produce good results.

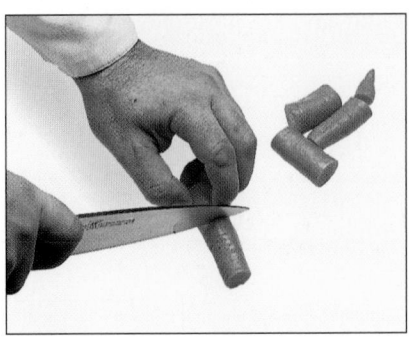

1. Cut the item being "turned" into pieces 2 inches (5 cm) × 3/4 to 1 inch (2–2.5 cm). Each piece should have flat ends. (Potatoes, turnips and beets may be cut into as many as six or eight pieces; carrots can simply be cut into 2-inch lengths.) Peeling is optional because in most cases the item's entire surface area is trimmed away.

2. Holding the item between the thumb and forefinger, use a tourné knife or a paring knife to cut seven curved sides on the item, creating a flat-ended, foot-ball-shaped product.

Oblique or Roll Cut

Oblique or roll-cut items are small pieces with two angle-cut sides. It is a relatively simple cut most often used on carrots or parsnips.

Place the peeled item on a cutting board. Holding the knife at a 45-degree angle, make the first cut. Roll the item a half turn, keeping the knife at the same angle, and make another cut. The result is a wedge-shaped piece with two angled sides.

CONCLUSION

Although many slicing and dicing machines are available, none can ever completely replace a skilled chef with a sharp knife. As a student chef, becoming efficient with your knives should be a high priority. Possessing good knife skills allows you to produce more attractive products in a safe and efficient manner. You will use the classic cuts and techniques outlined in this chapter throughout your career. You should memorize the procedures and practice them often. And remember, a dull or carelessly handled knife is dangerous.

QUESTIONS FOR DISCUSSION

1. Explain the step-by-step procedures for sharpening a knife using a three-sided whetstone.
2. What is the purpose of steel?
3. Why is it necessary to cut vegetables into uniform shapes and sizes?
4. Describe the following cutting procedures: slicing, chopping and dicing.
5. Identify the dimensions of the following cuts: julienne, batonnet, brunoise, small dice, medium dice, large dice and paysanne.
6. Describe the procedure for making tournéed vegetables.

CHAPTER 7

KITCHEN STAPLES

Although the flavors and aromas of fresh herbs are generally preferred, dried herbs are widely used because they are readily available and convenient. Purchase only the amount of dried herbs that can be used within a short time. If stored in a closed container in a cool, dry place, dried herbs should last for two to three months.

Use less dried herbs than you would fresh herbs. The loss of moisture strengthens and concentrates the flavor in dried herbs. In general, you should use only one half to one third as much dried herb as fresh in any given recipe. For example, if a recipe calls for one *tablespoon* of fresh basil, you should substitute only one *teaspoon* of dried basil. You can usually add more later if necessary.

Spices are often available whole or ground. Once ground, they lose their flavors rapidly, however. Whole spices should keep their flavors for many months if stored in air-tight containers in a cool, dry place away from direct light. Stale spices lose their spicy aroma and develop a bitter or musty aftertaste. Discard them.

Because ground spices release their flavors quickly, they should be added to cooked dishes near the end of the cooking period. In uncooked dishes that call for ground spices (for example, salad dressings), the mixture should be allowed to stand for several hours to develop good flavor.

While some combinations are timeless—rosemary with lamb, dill with salmon, nutmeg with spinach, caraway with rye bread—less common pairings can be equally delicious and far more exciting. A chef must be willing and able to experiment with new flavors. But first you must be familiar with the distinctive flavor and aroma of the herb or spice. Then you can experiment, always bearing in mind the following guidelines:

- Flavorings should not hide the taste or aroma of the primary ingredient;
- Flavorings should be combined in balance, so as not to overwhelm the palate; and
- Flavorings should not be used to disguise poor quality or poorly prepared products.

Even when following a well-tested recipe, the quantity of flavorings may need to be adjusted because of changes in brands or the condition of the ingredients. A chef should strive to develop his or palate to recognize and correct subtle variances as necessary.

Bouquet Garni and Sachet

The *bouquet garni* and the *sachet* are used to introduce flavorings, seasonings and aromatics into stocks, sauces, soups and stews.

A bouquet garni, shown in Figure 7.1, is a selection of herbs (usually fresh) and vegetables tied into a bundle with twine. The twine makes it easy to remove the bouquet when sufficient flavor has been extracted. A standard bouquet garni consists of parsley stems, celery, thyme, leeks and carrots.

A sachet (also known as a *sachet d'épices*), shown in Figure 7.2, is made by tying seasonings together in cheesecloth. A standard sachet consists of peppercorns, bay leaves, parsley stems, thyme, cloves and, optionally, garlic. The exact quantity of these ingredients is determined by the amount of liquid the sachet is meant to flavor.

Bouquets garni and sachets are used to add flavors in such a way that the ingredients can be easily removed from a dish when the flavors have been extracted. A similar technique, although less commonly used, is an **onion**

FIGURE 7.1 *Bouquet garni*

FIGURE 7.2 *Sachet*

piquet. To prepare an onion piquet, peel the onion and trim off the root end. Attach one or two dried bay leaves to the onion using whole cloves as pins. The onion piquet is then simmered in milk or stock to extract flavors.

SALT

Salt (Fr. *sel*) is the most basic seasoning and its use is universal. It preserves foods, heightens their flavors and provides the distinctive taste of saltiness. The presence of salt can be tasted easily but not smelled. Temperature affects saltiness. The cooler a food, the saltier it tastes, so it is best to undersalt hot foods that will be chilled prior to service (chilled soups, for example).

Culinary or **table salt** is sodium chloride (NaCl), one of the minerals essential to human life. Salt contains no calories, proteins, fats or carbohydrates. It is available from several sources, each with its own flavor and degree of saltiness.

Rock salt, mined from underground deposits, is available in both edible and nonedible forms. It is used for home freezing.

Common kitchen or table salt is produced by pumping water through underground salt deposits, then bringing the brine to the surface to evaporate, leaving behind crystals. Chemicals are usually added to prevent table salt from absorbing moisture and thus keep it free-flowing. Iodized salt is commonly used in the United States. The iodine has no effect on the salt's flavor or use; it is simply added to provide an easily available source of iodine, an important nutrient, to a large number of people.

Sea salt is obtained, not surprisingly, by evaporating sea water and purifying the crystals left behind. Many chefs consider its flavor stronger or purer than mined salt.

Kosher salt has large, irregular crystals and is used in the "koshering" or curing of meats. It is purified rock salt that contains no iodine or additives. It can be substituted for common kitchen salt.

Because it is nonorganic, salt keeps indefinitely. It will, however, absorb moisture from the atmosphere, which prevents it from flowing properly. Salt is

◆◆◆

ABOUT FLAVORS

Flavor is to food what hue is to color. It is what timbre is to music. Flavor is adjective; food is noun. Each ingredient has its own particular character, which is altered by every other ingredient it encounters. A secret ingredient is one that mysteriously improves the flavor of a dish without calling attention to itself. It is either undetectable or extremely subtle, but its presence is crucial because the dish would not be nearly as good without it.

Primary flavors are those that are obvious, such as the flavors of chicken and tarragon in a chicken tarragon, shrimp and garlic in a shrimp scampi, or beef and red wine in a beef *à la Bourguignon*. Secret ingredients belong to the realm of secondary flavors. However obvious it is that you need tarragon to prepare a chicken tarragon, you would not achieve the most interesting result using *only* tarragon. Tarragon, in this case, needs secondary ingredients—a hint of celery seed and anise—to make it taste more like quintessential tarragon and at the same time more than tarragon. In

this way, primary flavors often depend on secret ingredients to make them more interesting and complex. Using only one herb or spice to achieve a certain taste usually results in a lackluster dish—each mouthful tastes the same. Whether they function in a primary or secondary way, flavors combine in only three different ways: They marry, oppose, or juxtapose.

When flavors marry, they combine to form one taste. Some secondary flavors marry with primary ones to create a new flavor greater than the sum of its parts, and often two flavors can do the job better than one. It may sound like an eccentric combination, but vanilla marries with the flavor of lobster, making it taste more like the essence of lobster than lobster does on its own. And when ginger and molasses marry, they create a flavor superior to either alone.

Opposite flavors can highlight or cancel each other; they can cut or balance each other. Sweet/sour, sweet/salty, sweet/hot, salty/sour, and salty/tart are all opposites. Salt and sugar

are so opposed, in fact, that when used in equal amounts they cancel each other entirely. Sweet relish helps to cancel the salty flavor of hot dogs. Chinese sauces usually contain some sugar to help balance the saltiness of soy sauce.

Because flavors are sensed on different parts of the tongue and palate, and because they are tasted at different times, we can juxtapose them, using flavors side by side or in layers. The layering of flavors makes the food we taste more interesting because each mouthful is different.

Knowing how to combine many flavors and aromas to achieve a simple and pure result (and knowing when not to combine flavors) will make you a better, more confident cook. Good cooks over the centuries have known these things intuitively—but they've had neither the huge variety of ingredients nor the knowledge of world cuisines that we have today.

from SECRET INGREDIENTS
by CHEF MICHAEL ROBERTS

---

a powerful preservative; its presence stops or greatly slows down the growth of many undesirable organisms. Salt is used to preserve meats, vegetables and fish. It is also used to develop desirable flavors in bacon, ham, cheeses and fish products as well as pickled vegetables.

NUTS

A **nut** (Fr. *noix*) is the edible single-seed kernel of a fruit surrounded by a hard shell. A hazelnut is an example of a true nut. The term is used more generally, however, to refer to any seed or fruit with an edible kernel in a hard shell. Walnuts and peanuts are examples of non-nut "nuts" (peanuts are legumes that grow underground; walnuts have two kernels). Nuts are a good source of protein and B vitamins but are high in fat. Their high fat content makes them especially susceptible to rancidity and odor absorption. Nuts should be stored in nonmetal, air-tight containers in a cool, dark place. Most nuts may be kept frozen for up to one year.

Nuts are used in foods to provide texture and flavor. They are often roasted in a low (275°F/135°C) oven before use to heighten their flavor. Allowing roasted nuts to cool to room temperature before grinding prevents them from releasing too much oil.

Almonds (Fr. *almande*) are the seeds of a plumlike fruit. Native to western India, the almond was first cultivated by the ancient Greeks. It is now a major commercial crop in California. Almonds are available whole,

Almonds

sliced, slivered or ground. Blanched almonds have had their brown, textured skins removed; natural almonds retain their skins. Unless the brown color of natural almond skin is undesirable, the two types can be used interchangeably in recipes. Almonds are frequently used in pastries and candies and are the main ingredient in marzipan.

Cashews, native to the Amazon, are now cultivated in India and east Africa. The cashew nut is actually the seed of a plant related to poison ivy. Because of toxins in the shell, cashews are always sold shelled. They are expensive and have a strong flavor. Cashews are used in some Asian cuisines and make a wonderful addition to cookies and candies.

Cashews

Chestnuts (Fr. *marrons*) are true nuts that must be cooked before using. Available steamed, dried, boiled or roasted, they are often sold as a canned purée, with or without added sugar. Candied or glazed chestnuts are also available. Most chestnuts are grown in Europe, primarily Italy, but new varieties are beginning to flourish in North America. Their distinctive flavor is found in many sweet dishes and pastries. Because of their high starch content, chestnuts are also used in soups and sauces and may be served as a side dish.

Chestnuts

Coconuts (Fr. *noix de coco*) are the seeds from one of the largest of all fruits. They grow on the tropical coconut palm tree. The nut is a dark brown oval, covered with coarse fibers. The shell is thick and hard; inside is a layer of white, moist flesh. The interior also contains a clear liquid known as coconut water. (This is not the same as coconut milk or coconut cream, both of which are prepared from the flesh.) Coconut has a mild aroma, a sweet, nutty flavor and a crunchy, chewy texture. Fresh coconuts are readily available but require some effort to use. Coconut flesh is available shredded or flaked, with or without added sugar. Coconut is most often used in pastries and candies and is also an important ingredient in Indian and Caribbean cuisines. A good fresh coconut should feel heavy; you should be able to hear the coconut water sloshing around inside. Avoid cracked, moist or moldy coconuts.

Coconuts

Hazelnuts (Fr. *noisette*) are true nuts that grow wild in the Northeast and Upper Midwest states. The cultivated form, known as a **filbert**, is native to temperate regions throughout the Northern Hemisphere. A bit larger than the hazelnut, it has a weaker flavor than its wild cousin. Both nuts look like smooth brown marbles. Filberts are more abundant, so are generally less expensive. Hazelnuts are often ground for use in cakes or pastries. Their distinctive flavor goes well with chocolate and coffee.

Hazelnuts

To remove the hazelnut's bitter skin, roast whole nuts in a 275°F (135°C) oven for 12 to 15 minutes. They should give off a good aroma and just begin to darken. While still hot, rub the nuts in a dry towel or against a mesh sifter to remove the skin.

Macadamias, although commercially significant in Hawaii, are actually native to Australia. This small round nut is creamy white with a sweet, rich taste and high fat content. Its shell is extremely hard and must be removed by machine, so the macadamia is always sold out of the shell. Its flavor blends well with fruits, coconut and white and dark chocolate.

Macadamias

Peanuts

Pecans

Pine Nuts

Peanuts (Fr. *arachide*), also known as groundnuts, are actually legumes that grow underground. The peanut is native to South America; it made its way into North America via Africa and the slave trade. Peanuts are a good source of protein and fat and became an important source of food and oil during World War II. They may be eaten raw or roasted and are available shelled or unshelled, with or without their thin red skins. Peanuts are used in Asian cuisines and are ubiquitous ground with a bit of oil into peanut butter.

Pecans (Fr. *noix de pacane*), native to the Mississippi River Valley, are perhaps the most popular nuts in America. Their flavor is rich and mapley and appears most often in breads, sweets and pastries. They are available whole in the shell or in various standard sizes and grades of pieces.

Pine nuts (Fr. *pignon*), also known as pinon nuts and pignole, are the seeds of several species of pine tree. The small, creamy white, teardrop-shaped nuts are commonly used in dishes from Spain, Italy and the American Southwest. They are rarely chopped or ground due to their small size, and will only need roasting if being used in a dish that will not receive further cooking. Pine nuts are used in breads, pastries and salads and are essential to classic pesto sauce.

Pistachios (Fr. *pistaches*) are native to central Asia, where they have been cultivated for over 3000 years. California now produces most of the pistachios marketed in this country. Pistachios are unique for the green color of their meat. When ripe, the shell opens naturally at one end, aptly referred to as "smiling," which makes shelling the nuts quite easy. Red pistachios are dyed, not natural. Pistachios are sold whole, shelled or unshelled, and are used in pastries and meat dishes, particularly pâtés.

Pistachios

TABLE 7.2   NUTRITIONAL VALUES OF COMMON NUTS

Per 1 Ounce (28 g) Serving	Calories	Protein (g)	Carbohydrates (g)	Total Fat (g)	Saturated Fat (g)	Sodium (mg)
Almonds, whole kernels	167	5.7	5.8	14.8	1.4	3
Cashews, dry roasted	163	4.4	9.3	13.2	2.6	4
Chestnuts, roasted and peeled	70	0.9	15.0	0.6	0.1	1
Filberts, blanched	191	3.6	4.5	19.1	1.4	1
Macadamias	199	2.4	3.9	20.9	3.1	1
Peanuts, raw	159	7.2	4.5	13.8	1.9	5
Pecans	190	2.2	5.2	19.2	1.5	trace
Walnuts, English	182	4.1	5.2	17.6	1.6	3

The Corinne T. Netzer Encyclopedia of Food Values 1992

Walnuts (Fr. *noix*), relatives of the pecan, are native to Asia, Europe and North America. The black walnut, native to Appalachia, has a dark brown meat and strong flavor. The English walnut, now grown primarily in California, has a milder flavor, is easier to shell and is less expensive. Walnuts are more popular than pecans outside the United States. They are used in baked goods and are pressed for oil.

English walnuts

OILS

Oils (Fr. *huile*) are a type of fat that remains liquid at room temperature. Cooking oils are refined from various seeds, plants and vegetables. (Other fats, such as butter and margarine, are discussed in Chapter 8, Eggs and Dairy Products; animal and solid fats are discussed in Chapter 26, Principles of the Bakeshop.)

When purchasing oils you should consider their use, **smoke point**, flavor and cost. Fats, including oils and **shortenings**, are manufactured for specific purposes such as deep-frying, cake-baking, salad dressings and sautéing. Most food service operations purchase different ones for each of these needs.

Fats break down at different temperatures. The temperature at which a given fat begins to break down and smoke is known as its smoke point. Choose fats with higher smoke points for high temperature cooking such as deep-frying and sautéing. If a fat with a low smoke point is used for high temperature cooking, it may break down, burn and impart undesirable flavors.

The flavor and cost of each oil must also be considered. For example, both corn oil and walnut oil may be used in a salad dressing. Their selection may depend on balancing cost (corn oil is less expensive) against flavor (walnut oil has a stronger, more distinctive flavor).

When fats spoil they are said to go **rancid**. Rancidity is a chemical change caused by exposure to air, light or heat. It results in objectionable flavors and odors. Different fats turn rancid at different rates, but all fats benefit from refrigerated storage away from moisture, light and air. (Some oils are packaged in colored glass containers because certain tints of green and yellow block the damaging light rays that can cause an oil to go rancid.) Oils may become thick and cloudy under refrigeration. This is not a cause for concern. The oils will return to their clear, liquid states at room temperature. Stored fats should also be covered to prevent the absorption of odors.

Vegetable Oils are extracted from a variety of plants, including corn, cottonseed, peanuts and soybeans, by pressure or chemical solvents. The oil is then refined and cleaned to remove unwanted colors, odors or flavors. Vegetable oils are virtually odorless and have a neutral flavor. Because they contain no animal products they are cholesterol-free. If a commercial product contains only one type of oil it is labeled "pure" (as in "pure corn oil"). Products labeled "vegetable oil" are blended from several sources. Products labeled "salad oil" are highly refined blends of vegetable oil.

Canola oil is processed from rapeseeds. Its popularity is growing rapidly because it contains no cholesterol and has a high percentage of monounsaturated fat. Canola oil is useful for frying and general cooking because it has no flavor and a high smoke point.

Smoke point—*the temperature at which a fat begins to break down and smoke.*

Shortening—*a fat, usually made from vegetable oils, that is solid at room temperature.*

Canola oil

Nut oils are extracted from a variety of nuts and are almost always packaged as a "pure" product, never blended. A nut oil should have the strong flavor and aroma of the nut from which it was processed. Popular examples are walnut and hazelnut oils. These oils are used to give flavor to salad dressings, marinades and other dishes. But heat diminishes their flavor, so nut oils are not recommended for frying or baking. Nut oils tend to go rancid quickly and therefore are usually packaged in small containers.

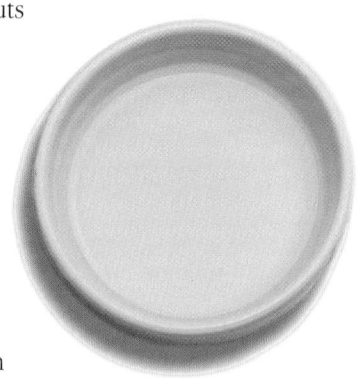

Hazelnut oil

Olive oil is the only oil that is extracted from a fruit

Extra virgin olive oil

rather than a seed, nut or grain. Olive oil is produced primarily in Spain, Italy, France, Greece and North Africa; California produces a relatively minor amount of olive oil. Like wine, olive oils vary in color and taste according to the variety of tree, the ripeness of the olives, the type of soil, the climate and the producer's preferences. Colors range from dark green to almost clear, depending on the ripeness of the olives at the time of pressing and the amount of subsequent refining. Color is not a good indication of flavor, however. Flavor is ultimately a matter of personal preference. A stronger-flavored oil may be desired for some foods, while a milder oil is better for others. Good olive oil should be thicker than refined vegetable oils, but not so thick that it has a fatty texture.

The label designations—extra virgin, virgin and pure—refer to the acidity of the oil (a low acid content is preferable) and the extent of processing used to extract the oil. The first cold-pressing of the olives results in virgin oil. (The designation "virgin" is used only when the oil is 100% unadulterated olive oil, unheated and without any chemical processing.) Virgin oil may still vary in quality depending on its acidity level. Extra virgin oil is virgin oil with an acidity level of not more than 1%; virgin oil may have an acidity level of up to 3%. Pure olive oil is processed from the pulp left after the first pressing using heat and chemicals. Pure oil is lighter in flavor and less expensive than virgin oil.

Flavored oils, also known as **infused oils**, are an interesting and increasingly popular condiment. These oils may be used as a cooking medium or flavoring accent in marinades, dressings, sauces or other dishes. Flavors include basil and other herbs, garlic, citrus and spice. Flavored oils are generally prepared with olive oil for additional flavor or canola oil, both considered more healthful than other fats.

Top-quality commercially flavored oils are prepared by extracting aromatic oils from the flavoring ingredients and then emulsifying them with a high-grade oil; any impurities are then removed by placing the oil in a centrifuge. Using the aromatic oils of the flavoring ingredients yields a more intense flavor than merely steeping the same ingredients in the oil. Flavored oils should be stored as you would any other high-quality oil.

❖❖❖
THE OLIVE

Olives are the fruit of a tree native to the Mediterranean area. Green olives are those harvested unripened; black olives are fully ripened. The raw fruit is inedibly bitter and must be washed, soaked and pickled before eating. Green olives should have a smooth, tight skin. Ripe olives will be glossy but softer, with a slightly wrinkled skin. Many varieties and flavors are available, from the tiny black Niçoise to the large purplish Kalamata. Olives are packaged in a range of sizes, from medium (the smallest) to jumbo (the largest). (Colossal and super colossal olives are actually smaller than jumbos.) Pitted olives are also available. The cavity may be filled with strips of pimento, jalapeño pepper, almonds or other foods for flavor and appearance.

Olives are used as a finger food for snacks or hors d'oeuvres, or added to salads or pasta. They may even be cooked in breads, soups, sauces, stews or casseroles. A paste made of minced ripe olives, known as tapenade, is used as a dip or condiment.

TABLE 7.3   THE SMOKE POINT AND NUTRITIONAL VALUES OF COMMON FATS

Per 1 Ounce (28 g) Serving	Smoke Point	Calories	Total Fat (g)	Saturated Fat (g)
Olive oil	437°F/225°C	251	28.4	3.8
Peanut oil	425°F/218°C	251	28.4	4.8
Lard*	370°F/188°C	230	25.6	10.0
Canola oil	425°F/218°C	251	28.4	2.0
Walnut oil	325–400°F/ 163–204°C	240	28.0	4.0
Butter, clarified*	400°F/204°C	248	28.2	17.6
Whole butter, unsalted*	260°F/127°C	200	22.8	14.2

The Corinne T. Netzer Encyclopedia of Food Values 1992

*discussed in Chapter 26

VINEGARS

Vinegar (Fr. *vinaigre*) is a thin, sour liquid used for thousands of years as a preservative, cooking ingredient, condiment and cleaning solution. Vinegar is obtained through the fermentation of wine or other alcoholic liquid. Bacteria attacks the alcohol in the solution, turning it into acetic acid. No alcohol will remain when the transformation is complete. The quality of vinegar depends upon the quality of the wine or other liquid on which it is based. Vinegar flavors are as varied as the liquids from which they are made.

Vinegars should be clear and clean looking, never cloudy or muddy. Commercial vinegars are pasteurized, so an unopened bottle should last indefinitely in a cool, dark place. Once opened, vinegars should last about three months if tightly capped. Any sediment that develops can be strained out; if mold develops, discard the vinegar.

Wine vinegars are as old as wine itself. They may be made from white or red wine, sherry or even champagne, and should bear the color and flavor hallmarks of the wine used. Wine vinegars are preferred in French and Mediterranean cuisines.

Malt vinegar is produced from malted barley. Its slightly sweet, mild flavor is used as a condiment, especially with fried foods.

Distilled vinegar, made from grain alcohol, is completely clear with a stronger vinegary flavor and higher acid content than other vinegars. It is preferred for pickling and preserving.

Cider vinegar is produced from unpasteurized apple juice or cider. It is pale brown in color with a mild acidity and fruity aroma. Cider vinegar is particularly popular in the United States.

Rice vinegar is a clear, slightly sweet product brewed from rice wine. Its flavor is clean and elegant, making it useful in a variety of dishes.

Flavored vinegars are simply traditional vinegars in which herbs, spices, fruits or other foods are steeped to infuse their flavors. They are easily produced from commercial wine or distilled vinegars, using any herb, spice or fruit desired. The use of flavored vinegars is extremely popular but definitely not new. Clove, raspberry and fennel vinegars were sold on the streets of Paris during the 13th century. Making fruit-flavored vinegars was also one of the responsibilities of American housewives during the 18th and 19th centuries.

Balsamic vinegar, Raspberry vinegar and Cider vinegar

Balsamic vinegar (It. *aceto Balsamico*) is newly popular in the United States, though it has been produced in Italy for over 800 years. To produce balsamic vinegar, red wine vinegar is aged in a succession of wooden barrels made from a variety of woods—oak, cherry, locust, ash, mulberry and juniper—for at least four, but sometimes up to 50 years. The resulting liquid is dark reddish-brown and sweet. Balsamic has a high acid level, but the sweetness covers the tart flavor, making it very mellow. True balsamic is extremely expensive because of the long aging process and the small quantities available. Most of the commercial products imported from Italy are now made by a quick carmelization and flavoring process. Balsamic is excellent as a condiment or seasoning and has a remarkable affinity for tomatoes and strawberries.

CONDIMENTS

Strictly speaking, a condiment is any food added to a dish for flavor, including herbs, spices and vinegars. Today, however, *condiments* more often refer to cooked or prepared flavorings, such as prepared mustards, relishes, bottled sauces and pickles. Several frequently used condiments are discussed here. These staples may be used to alter or enhance the flavor of a dish during cooking or added to a completed dish at the table by the consumer.

Prepared mustard is a mixture of crushed mustard seeds, vinegar or wine and salt or spices. It can be flavored in many ways—with herbs, onions, peppers and even citrus zest. It can be a smooth paste or coarse and chunky, depending on how finely the seeds are ground and whether the skins are strained out. Prepared mustard gets its tangy taste from an essential oil that forms only when the seeds are crushed and mixed with water. Prepared mustard can be used as a condiment, particularly with meat and charcuterie items, or as a flavoring ingredient in sauces, stews and marinades.

Dijon mustard takes its name from a town and the surrounding region in France that produces about half of the world's mustard. French mustard labeled "Dijon" must, by law, be produced only in that region. Dijon and Dijon-style mustards are smooth with a rich, complex flavor.

English and Chinese mustards are made from mustard flour and cool water. They are extremely hot and powerful. American or "ballpark" mustard is mild and vinegary with a bright yellow color.

Mustard never really spoils, its flavor just fades away. Because of its high acid content, mustard does not turn rancid, but it will oxidize and develop a dark surface crust. Once opened, mustard should be kept well covered and refrigerated.

Soy sauce is a thin, dark brown liquid fermented from cooked soy beans, wheat and salt. Available in several flavors and strengths, it is ubiquitous in most Asian cuisines. Light soy sauce is thin, with a light brown color and a very salty flavor. Dark soy sauce is thicker and dark brown, with a sweet, less salty flavor. Necessary for preparing many Asian dishes, soy sauce is also used in marinades and sauces and as an all-purpose condiment. Other soy-based condiments include tamari, teriyaki sauce and fermented bean paste (miso).

Ketchup (also known as catsup or catchup) originally referred to any salty extract from fish, fruits or vegetables. Prepared tomato ketchup is really a sauce, created in America and used worldwide as a flavoring ingredient or condiment. It is bright red and thick, with a tangy, sweet-sour flavor. Ketchup can be stored either in the refrigerator or at room temperature; it should keep well for up to four months after opening. Ketchup does not turn rancid or develop mold but it will darken and lose flavor as it ages.

Yellow mustard

Dijon mustard

Whole-grain mustard

Brown mustard

Even the most sophisticated food service operation occasionally uses prepared condiments or flavorings. The products described here are widely used and available from grocery stores or wholesale purveyors. Some are brand-name items that have become almost synonymous with the product itself; others are available from several manufacturers.

Barbecue sauce—Like ketchup, commercial barbecue sauce is a mixture of tomatoes, vinegar and spices; it tends to be hotter and sweeter than ketchup, however. Commercial barbecue sauce is used primarily for marinating or basting meat, poultry or fish. A tremendous variety of barbecue sauces is available, with various flavors, textures and aromas. Sample several before selecting the most appropriate for your specific needs.

Fish sauce—Fish sauce is a thin, dark brown liquid made from anchovy extract and salt. It is the quintessential Thai seasoning, but is used throughout Southeast Asia. It is extremely salty with a powerful aroma. There is no substitute; only a small amount is necessary for most dishes.

Hoisin—Hoisin sauce is a dark, thick, salty-sweet sauce made from fermented soy beans, vinegar, garlic and caramel. It is used in Chinese dishes or served as a dipping sauce.

Old Bay® seasoning—Old Bay® is a dry spice blend containing celery salt, dry mustard, paprika and other flavorings. It is widely used in shellfish preparations, especially boiled shrimp and crab.

Oyster sauce—Oyster sauce is a thick, dark sauce made from oyster extract. It has a salty-sweet flavor and rich aroma. Oyster sauce is often used with stir-fried meats and poultry.

Pickapeppa® sauce—Pickapeppa® sauce is a dark, thick, sweet-hot blend of tomatoes, onions, sugar, vinegar, mango, raisins, tamarinds and spices. Produced in Jamaica, West Indies, it is used as a condiment for meat, game or fish and as a seasoning in sauces, soups and dressings.

Tabasco® sauce—Tabasco® sauce is a thin, bright red liquid blended from vinegar, chiles and salt. Its fiery flavor is widely used in sauces, soups and prepared dishes; it is a popular condiment for Mexican, southern and southwestern cuisines. Tabasco® sauce has been produced in Louisiana since 1868. Other "Louisiana-style" hot sauces (those containing only peppers, vinegar and salt) may be substituted.

Worcestershire sauce—Worcestershire sauce is a thin, dark brown liquid made from malt vinegar, tamarind, molasses and spices. It is used as a condiment for beef and as a seasoning in sauces, soups, stews and prepared dishes. Its flavor should be rich and full, but not salty.

COFFEES AND TEAS

Coffee and tea are the staples of most beverage menus. Despite their relatively low price a good cup of coffee or tea can be extremely important to a customer's impression of your food service operation. A cup of coffee is often either the very first or the very last item consumed by a customer. Tea, whether iced or hot, is often consumed throughout the meal. Consequently, it is important that you learn to prepare and serve these beverages properly.

Coffee

Coffee (Fr. *café*) begins as the fruit of a small tree growing in tropical and subtropical regions throughout the world. The fruit, referred to as a cherry, is bright red with translucent flesh surrounding two flat-sided seeds. These seeds are the coffee beans. When ripe, the cherries are harvested by hand, then cleaned, fermented and hulled, leaving the green coffee beans. The beans are then roasted, blended, ground and brewed. Note that any coffee bean can be roasted to any degree of darkness, ground to any degree of fineness and brewed by any number of methods.

Only two species of coffee bean are routinely used: *arabica* and *robusta*. Arabica beans are the most important commercially and the ones from which the finest coffees are produced. Robusta beans do not produce as flavorful a drink as arabica. Nevertheless, robusta beans are becoming increasingly significant commercially, due in part to the fact that robusta trees are heartier and more fertile than arabica trees.

The conditions in which the beans are grown have almost as much effect on the final product as subsequent roasting, grinding and brewing. Because coffee takes much of its flavor and character from the soil, sunlight and air, the beans' origin is critical to the product's final quality. Each valley and mountain produces coffee distinct from all others, so geographic names are used to identify the beans regardless of whether they are from arabica or robusta trees. Thus, purveyors may offer beans known as Columbian, Chanchamayo (from Peru), Kilimanjaro (from Tanzania), Blue Mountain (from Jamaica), Java, Sumatra or Kona (from Hawaii), to name a few.

While many so-called gourmet coffees are made from a single type of bean, nearly all coffee sold in the United States is a blend of various qualities and types of bean.

Roasting Coffee

Roasting releases and enhances the flavors in coffee. It also darkens the beans and brings natural oils to the surface. Traditionally, almost everyone roasted their own coffee beans because all coffee beans were sold green. Today, however, roasting is left to experts who possess the necessary equipment.

It is important to recognize and understand some of the standard descriptions used for various types of roasting. No single international organization controls the naming of roasted coffee, however, so a coffee roaster may refer to products by any name. The following descriptions are based on the most common terminology.

Green coffee beans

City-roast beans

French-roast beans

- ✦ **City Roast:** Also called American or brown roast, city roast is the most widely used coffee style in this country. City roast produces a beverage that may lack brilliance or be a bit flat, yet it is the roast most Americans assume they prefer because it is the roast most often used in grocery store blends.
- ✦ **Brazilian:** Somewhat darker than a city roast, Brazilian roast should begin to show a hint of dark-roast flavor. The beans should show a trace of oil. In this context, the word Brazilian has no relationship to coffee grown in Brazil.
- ✦ **Viennese:** Also called medium-dark roast, Viennese roast generally falls somewhere between a standard city roast and French roast.
- ✦ **French Roast:** French roast, also called New Orleans or dark roast, approaches espresso in flavor without sacrificing smoothness. The beans should be the color of semi-sweet chocolate, with apparent oiliness on the surface.
- ✦ **Espresso Roast:** Espresso roast, also called Italian roast, is the darkest of all. The beans are roasted until they are virtually burnt. The beans should be black with a shiny, oily surface.

Grinding Coffee

Unlike roasting, which is best left to the experts, the grinding of coffee beans is best left to the consumer or food service operation. Whole coffee beans stay fresh longer than ground coffee. Ground coffee kept in an airtight container away from heat and light will stay fresh for three or four days. Whole beans will stay fresh for a few weeks and may be kept frozen for several months, as long as they are dry and protected from other flavors. Frozen coffee beans do not need to be thawed before grinding and brewing. Do not refrigerate coffee.

The fineness of the grind depends entirely on the type of coffee maker being used. The grind determines the length of time it takes to achieve the optimum (19%) extraction from the beans. The proper grind is simply whatever grind allows this to happen in the time it takes a specific coffee maker to complete its brewing cycle. Follow the directions for your coffee maker or ask your specialty coffee purveyor for guidance.

Brewing Coffee

Coffee is brewed by one of two methods: decoction or infusion. **Decoction** means boiling a substance until its flavor is removed. Boiling is the oldest method of making coffee, but is no longer used except in preparing extremely strong Turkish coffee. **Infusion** refers to the extraction of flavors at temperatures below boiling. Infusion techniques include steeping (mixing hot water with ground coffee), filtering (slowly pouring hot water over ground coffee held in a disposable cloth or paper filter) and dripping (pouring hot water over ground coffee and allowing the liquid to run through a strainer). Percolating is undesirable as the continuous boiling ruins the coffee's flavor.

The secrets to brewing a good cup of coffee are knowing the exact proportion of coffee to water as well as the length of time to maintain contact between the two. The best results are nearly always achieved by using two level tablespoons of ground coffee per 3/4 measuring cup (6 ounces) of water. (A standard cup of coffee is three quarters the size of a standard measuring cup; one pound of coffee yields approximately 80 level tablespoons or enough for 40 "cups" of coffee.) An Approved Coffee Measure (ACM) was developed by the Coffee Brewing Institute to measure two level tablespoons accurately. ACM scoops are readily available and are often included with retail coffee packages.

Premeasured packages of ground coffee are generally used with commercial brewing equipment. These packages are available in a range of sizes for making single pots or large urns of coffee.

If stronger coffee is desired, use more coffee per cup of water, not a longer brewing time. For weaker coffee, prepare regular-strength coffee and dilute it with hot water. Never reuse coffee grounds.

Coffeepots and carafes should be cleaned well with hot water between each use; coffee makers should be disassembled and cleaned according to the manufacturer's directions. Unless properly cleaned, oils from coffee form an invisible film on the inside of the maker and pots, imparting a rancid or stale flavor to each subsequent batch.

Finally, coffee should be served as soon as it is brewed. Oxidation takes a toll on the aroma and taste, which soon become flat and eventually bitter. Coffee may be held for a short time on the coffeemaker's hot plate at temperatures of 185° to 190°F (85° to 88°C). A better holding method, however, is to immediately pour freshly brewed coffee into a thermal carafe. Never attempt to reheat cold coffee, as drastic temperature shifts destroy flavor.

Tasting Coffee

Coffee can be judged on four characteristics: aroma, acidity, body and flavor.

As a general rule, coffee will taste the way it smells. Some coffees, particularly Colombian, are more fragrant than others, however.

Acidity, also called wininess, refers to the tartness of the coffee. Acidity is a desirable characteristic that indicates snap, life or thinness. Kenyan and Guatemalan are examples of particularly acidic coffees.

Body refers to the feeling of heaviness or thickness that coffee provides on the palate. Sumatran is generally the heaviest, with Mexican and Venezuelan being the lightest.

◆◆◆
DON'T WRECK THE ENDING

Lots of time and thought are spent on selecting the wines to accompany the various savory courses of a meal, but too often at the sweet course the dessert wine finds itself up against its worst enemy: chocolate. A good sauterne, or a good quality dessert wine of almost any kind, works best with a fruit tart or with noncitrus sorbets accompanied by "dry cookie-like things," to use Richard Olney's phrase. Chocolate, whether in the form of pastry or confection, belongs with coffee, whose aromatic bitterness is a perfect foil for it.

RICHARD H. GRAFF
Chairman, CHALONE WINE GROUP

Flavor, of course, is the most ambiguous as well as the most important characteristic. Terms such as mellow, harsh, grassy or earthy are used to describe the rather subjective characteristic of flavor.

Serving Coffee

Coffee may be served unadorned, unsweetened and black (without milk or cream). The customer then adds the desired amount of sugar and milk. Other coffee beverages are made with specific additions and provide value-added menu alternatives. The most common ways of serving coffee are described here.

- **Espresso:** Espresso (Sp. *café expreso*) refers to a unique brewing method in which hot water is forced through finely ground and packed coffee under high pressure. Properly made, it will be strong, rich and smooth, not bitter or acidic. Espresso is usually made with beans that have been roasted very dark, but any type of bean may be used. A single serving of espresso uses about 1/4 ounce (7 grams) of coffee to 1-1/2 ounces (45 milliliters) of water. Americans tend to prefer a larger portion, known as *espresso lungo*, made with 2 to 3 ounces (60–90 grams) of water.
- **Espresso machiatto:** Espresso "marked" with a tiny portion of steamed milk.
- **Cappuccino:** One third espresso, one third steamed milk and one third foamed milk; the total serving is still rather small, about 4 to 6 ounces (120–180 grams).
- **Caffe latte:** One third espresso, two thirds steamed milk without foam; usually served in a tall glass.
- **Café au lait:** the French version of the Italian *caffe latte*, café au lait (or *café creme*) is made with strong coffee instead of espresso and hot, not steamed, milk. It is traditionally served in a handleless bowl.
- **Flavored coffees:** Dried, ground chicory root has long been added to coffee, particularly by the French who enjoy its bitter flavor. Toasted barley, dried figs and spices have also been used by various cultures for years. Coffees flavored with vanilla, chocolate, liquors, spices and nuts have recently become popular in the United States. These flavors are added to roasted coffee beans by tumbling the beans with special flavoring oils. The results are strongly aromatic flavors such as vanilla hazelnut, chocolate raspberry or maple walnut.

Decaffeinated Coffee

Caffeine is an alkaloid found in coffee beans (as well as in tea leaves and cocoa beans). It is a stimulant that can improve alertness or reduce fatigue. In excess, however, caffeine can cause some people to suffer palpitations or insomnia. Regular filtered coffee contains from 85 to 100 milligrams of caffeine per cup. Robusta beans contain more caffeine than the better-quality arabica beans. Decaffeinated coffee (with 97% or more of the caffeine removed) is designed to meet consumer desires for a caffeine-free product.

Other Uses

In addition to its use as a beverage, coffee is frequently an ingredient in mixed drinks such as Irish coffee (with whiskey and cream) or café brulot (with orange, cloves and brandy). Coffee is also used in stews, sauces and pan gravy. It may be added to breads, such as rye and pumpernickel, cakes, custards, ice creams, dessert sauces and frostings. The flavor of coffee has a strong affinity for chocolate, nuts and rum.

✦✦✦

A Cup of Coffee History

Some anthropologists suggest that coffee was initially consumed by central African warriors in the form of a paste made from mashed coffee beans and animal fat rolled into balls. Eaten before battle, the animal fat and bean protein provided nourishment; the caffeine provided a stimulant.

A hot coffee drink may first have been consumed sometime during the 9th century A.D. in Persia. Made by a decoction of ripe beans, the drink was probably very thick and acrid. Nevertheless, by the year 1000, the elite of the Arab world were regularly drinking a decoction of dried coffee beans. The beans were harvested in Abyssinia (Ethiopia) and brought to market by Egyptian merchants. Within a century or so, *kahwa* became immensely popular with members of all strata of Arab society. Coffeehouses opened throughout the Levant, catering to customers who sipped the thick, brown brew while discussing affairs of heart and state.

Although European travelers to the Ottoman Empire had tasted coffee, and a few Arab or Turkish merchants living in Marseilles offered their guests a chance to sample the rare drink, coffee did not become popular in Europe until the 17th century. Its popularity is due in great part to Suleiman Aga, the Grand Panjandrum of the Ottoman Empire. In 1669 he arrived at the court of King Louis XIV of France as ambassador, bringing with him many exotic treasures, including *caffe*. Offered at his opulent parties, *caffe* soon became the drink of choice for the French aristocracy.

Coffee became popular in Vienna as a fortune of war. By 1683 the Turks were at the gates of Vienna. A decisive battle was fought and the Turks fled, leaving behind stores of gold, equipment, supplies and a barely known provision— green coffee beans. One of the victorious leaders, Franz George Kolschitzky, recognized the treasure, took it as his own and soon opened the first coffeehouse in Vienna, The Blue Bottle.

Despite its growing popularity, coffee was exorbitantly expensive, in part, the result of the Sultan's monopoly on coffee beans. His agents, principally in Marseilles, controlled the sale of beans. But the monopoly was not to survive. By the end of the 17th century, the Dutch had stolen coffee plants from Arabia and began cultivating them in Java. By the early 18th century, the French had transported seedlings to the West Indies; from there coffee plantations spread throughout the New World.

Tea

Tea (Fr. *thé*) is the name given to the leaves of *Camellia sinensis*, a tree or shrub that grows at high altitudes in damp tropical regions. Although tea comes from only one species of plant, there are three general types of tea— black, green. and oolong. The differences among the three are the result of the manner in which the leaves are treated after picking.

Black tea is amber-brown and strongly flavored. Its color and flavor result from fermenting the leaves. Black tea leaves are named or graded by leaf size. Because larger leaves brew more slowly than smaller ones, teas are sorted by leaf size for efficient brewing. *Souchong* denotes large leaves, *pekoe* denotes medium-sized leaves and *orange pekoe* denotes the smallest whole leaves. (Note that *orange pekoe* does not refer to any type of orange flavor.) Broken tea, graded as either broken orange pekoe or broken pekoe, is smaller, resulting in a darker, stronger brew. Broken tea is most often used in tea bags. These grades apply to both Chinese and Indian black teas.

Green tea is yellowish-green in color with a bitter flavor. Leaves used for green tea are not fermented. Chinese green tea leaves are also graded according to leaf size and age. The finest green tea is Gunpowder, followed by Imperial and Hyson.

Fruit tea

Gunpowder

Darjeeling

Oolong tea is partially fermented to combine the characteristics of black and green teas. Oolong is popular in China and Japan, often flavored with jasmine flowers. Oolong tea leaves are also graded by size and age.

As with coffee, tea takes much of its flavor from the geographic conditions in which it is grown. Teas are named for their place of origin, for example, Darjeeling, Ceylon (now Sri Lanka) or Assam. Many popular and commercially available teas are actually blends of leaves from various sources. Blended and unblended teas may also be flavored with oils, dried fruit, spices, flowers or herbs.

Brewing Tea

Tea may be brewed by the cup or the pot. In either case, it is important to use the following procedure.

1. Always begin with clean equipment and freshly drawn cold water. Water that has been sitting in a kettle or hot water tank contains less air and will taste flat or stale.

2. Warm the teapot by rinsing it out with hot water. This begins to relax the tea leaves and ensures that the water will stay hot when it comes in contact with the tea.

3. Place one teaspoon (5 millimeters) of loose tea or one tea bag per 3/4 cup (6 oz./180 grams) of water capacity in the warmed teapot.

4. As soon as the water comes to a boil, pour the appropriate amount over the tea. Do not allow the water to continue boiling as this removes the oxygen, leaving a flat taste. The water should be at a full boil when it comes in contact with the tea so that the tea leaves will uncurl and release their flavor.

5. Replace the lid of the teapot and allow the tea to infuse for 3 to 5 minutes. Time the brew. Color is not a reliable indication of brewing time: Tea leaves release color before flavor and different types of tea will be different colors when properly brewed.

6. Remove the tea bags or loose tea from the water when brewing is complete. This can be accomplished easily if the teapot is fitted with a removable leaf basket or if a tea bag or a perforated tea ball is used. Otherwise, decant the tea through a strainer into a second warmed teapot.

7. Serve immediately, accompanied with sugar, lemon, milk (not cream) and honey as desired. Dilute the tea with hot water if necessary.

8. Do not reuse tea leaves. One pound of tea yields 200 cups, making it the most inexpensive beverage after tap water.

For iced tea, prepare regular brewed tea using 50% more tea. Then pour into a pitcher or glass filled with ice. The stronger brew will hold its flavor better as the ice melts.

Serving Tea

Black and oolong tea may be served hot or cold, but green tea is best served hot. Black tea is served with milk or lemon and sugar; green and oolong tea are most often served plain. Adding milk to hot tea is a British preference (not normally followed in Europe or Asia) which reduces the astringency of the tea. Iced tea, an American invention, may be served plain or sweetened, and is often garnished with lemon, orange or fresh mint.

Tisanes—*herbal infusions that do not contain any "real" tea; examples include chamomile, ginseng and lemon balm. Tisanes are prepared in the same way as tea infusions.*

❖❖❖
A CUP OF TEA HISTORY

Some believe that the Chinese Emperor Shen Nung discovered tea drinking in 2737 B.C. Legend holds that the Emperor was boiling his drinking water beneath a tree when some leaves fell into the pot. Enchanted with the drink, he began to cultivate the plant. Whether myth or truth, it is known that a hot drink made from powdered dried tea leaves whipped into hot water was regularly consumed in China sometime after the 4th century. Later, decoctions of tea leaves (as well as rice, spices and nuts) became popular. But it was not until the Ming dynasty (A.D. 1368–1644) that infusions of tea leaves became commonplace.

By the 9th century, tea drinking had spread to Japan. In both Chinese and Japanese cultures, tea drinking developed into a ritual. For the Chinese, a cup of tea became the mirror of the soul. For the Japanese, it was the drink of immortality.

Tea was first transported from China to Europe by Dutch merchants during the early 1600s. By mid-century, it was introduced into England. In 1669 the East India Company was granted a charter by Queen Elizabeth I to import tea, a monopoly it held until 1833. To ensure a steady supply, the English surreptitiously procured plants from China and started plantations throughout the Indian subcontinent, as did the Dutch.

Tea drinking became fashionable in England, at least in court circles, through Charles II (raised in exile at The Hague in Holland, he reigned from 1660 until 1685) and his Portuguese wife, Catherine of Braganza. Queen Anne of England (reigned 1702–1714) introduced several concepts that eventually became part of the English tea custom. For example, she substituted tea for ale at breakfast and began using large silver pots instead of tiny china pots.

The social custom of afternoon tea began in the late 1700s, thanks to Anna, Duchess of Bedford. Historians attribute to her the late afternoon ritual of snacking on sandwiches and pastries accompanied by tea. She began the practice in order to quell her hunger pangs between breakfast and dinner (which was typically served at 9:30 or 10:00 P.M.).

Eventually two distinct types of teatime evolved. Low tea was aristocratic in origin and consisted of a snack of pastries and sandwiches, with tea, served in the late afternoon as a prelude to the evening meal. High tea was bourgeois in origin, consisting of leftovers from the typically large middle-class lunch, such as cold meats, bread and cheeses. High tea became a substitute for the evening meal.

CONCLUSION

Kitchen staples include fresh and dried herbs, spices, salt, nuts, oils, vinegars, condiments, coffees and teas. You must be able to recognize, purchase, store and use many of these staples.

The only way to determine which brand or type of staple is best for your particular needs is to taste, smell, sample and use a variety of those available. Cost, convenience and storage factors must also be considered. By maintaining a supply of seasonings, flavorings, condiments and other staples you will be able to create new dishes or enhance standard ones at a moment's notice.

QUESTIONS FOR DISCUSSION

1. What is a staple? Does every kitchen keep the same staples on hand? Explain your answer.
2. What are the differences between an herb and a spice? Give an example of a plant that is used as both an herb and a spice.
3. If a recipe calls for a fresh herb and you only have the herb dried, what do you do? Explain your answer.
4. What is the difference between a sachet and a bouquet garni? Identify the ingredients in a standard sachet and a standard bouquet garni.
5. How are condiments used by chefs and by customers?
6. Discuss the importance of using proper preparation and service techniques for coffee and tea. How can these beverages be used to improve or enhance your food service operation?

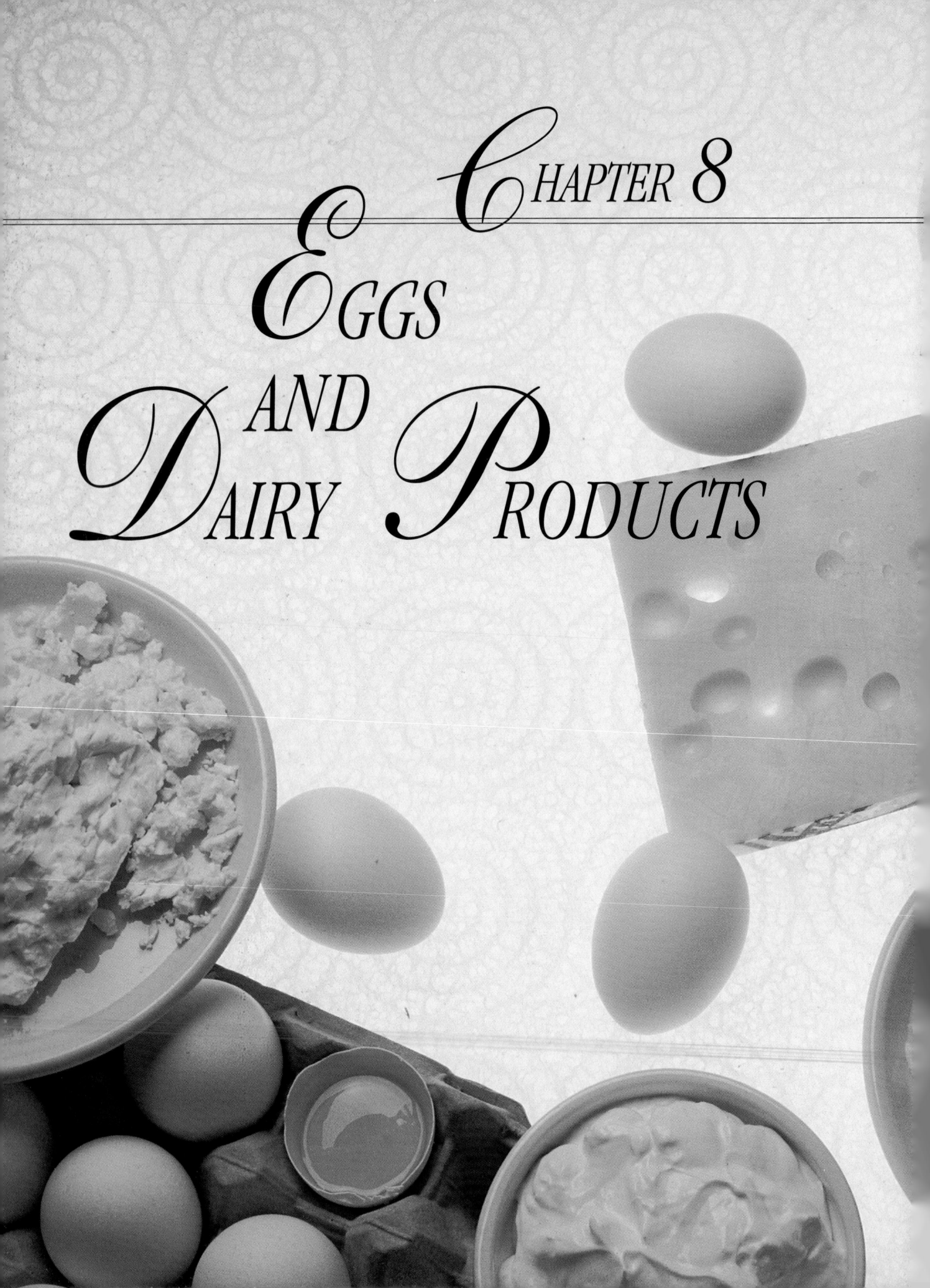

CHAPTER 8

EGGS AND DAIRY PRODUCTS

*E*ggs and milk are unique in that they, along with seeds, are the only foods that are truly designed to support life: Eggs support chick embryos; milk supports calves. Thus they are among the most nutritious of foods. Eggs as well as milk and milk-based products (known collectively as dairy products) are also extremely versatile. They are used throughout the kitchen, either served alone or as ingredients in everything from soups and sauces to breads and pastries. High quality and freshness are critical for their proper use. Learn to select the finest products, whether they are eggs, whole milk, butter or brie, and handle them with care.

EGGS

Nature designed eggs as the food source for developing chicks. Eggs, particularly chicken eggs, are also an excellent food for humans because of their high protein content, low cost and ready availability. Quail eggs are also used in food service operations. Duck and goose eggs are too fatty to be useful, however

Eggs can be cooked in a variety of ways, some of which are described in Chapter 32, Breakfast and Brunch. Eggs are also incorporated into other dishes to provide texture, structure, flavor, moisture and nutrition.

Composition

The primary parts of an egg are the shell, yolk and albumen. See Figure 8.1.

The **shell**, composed of calcium carbonate, is the outermost covering of the egg. It prevents microbes from entering and moisture from escaping, and protects the egg during handling and transport. Shell color is determined by the breed of the hen; for chickens it can range from bright white to brown. Shell color has no effect on quality, flavor or nutrition.

The **yolk** is the yellow portion of the egg. It constitutes just over one third of the egg and contains three fourths of the calories, most of the minerals and

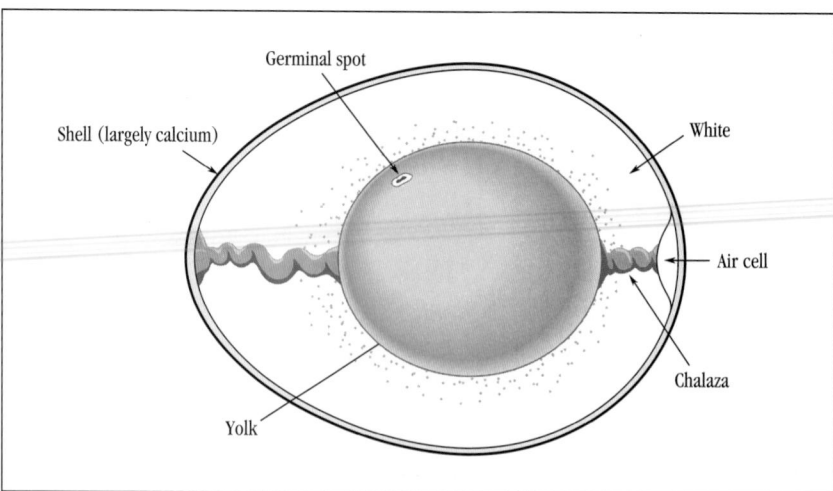

FIGURE 8.1 *An Egg*

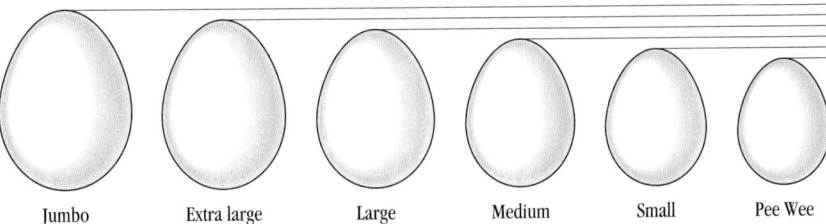

| Jumbo | Extra large | Large | Medium | Small | Pee Wee |

FIGURE 8.2 *Egg Sizes*

vitamins and all of the fat. The yolk also contains lecithin, the compound responsible for emulsification in products such as hollandaise sauce and mayonnaise. Egg yolk solidifies (coagulates) at temperatures between 149°F and 158°F (65°–70°C). Although the color of a yolk may vary depending on the hen's feed, color does not affect quality or nutritional content.

The **albumen** is the clear portion of the egg and is often referred to as the **egg white**. It constitutes about two thirds of the egg and contains more than half of the protein and riboflavin. Egg white coagulates, becoming firm and opaque, at temperatures between 144°F and 149°F (62–65°C).

An often misunderstood portion of the egg is the **chalazae cords**. These thick, twisted strands of egg white anchor the yolk in place. They are neither imperfections nor embryos. The more prominent the chalazae, the fresher the egg. Chalazae do not interfere with cooking or with whipping egg whites.

Eggs are sold in jumbo, extra large, large, medium, small and peewee sizes, as determined by weight per dozen. See Figure 8.2. Food service operations generally use large eggs.

Grading

Eggs are graded by the USDA or a state agency following USDA guidelines. The grade AA, A or B is given an egg based upon interior and exterior quality, not size. The qualities for each grade are described in Table 8.1. Grade has no effect on nutritional values.

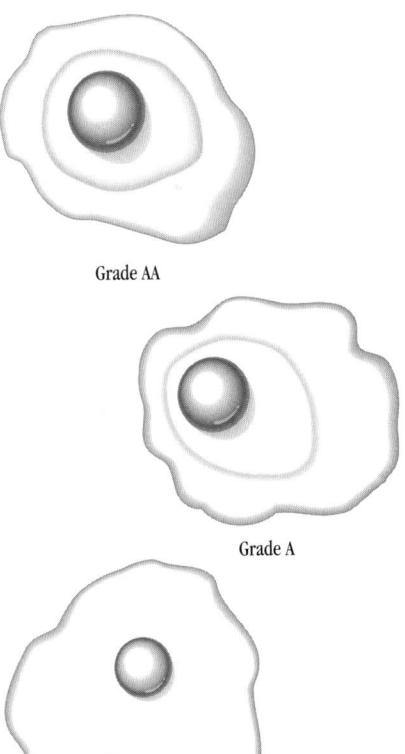

Grade AA

Grade A

Grade B

TABLE 8.1 EGG GRADES

	Grade AA	Grade A	Grade B
Spread*	Remains compact	Spreads slightly	Spreads over wide area
Albumen	Clear, thick and firm; prominent chalazae	Clear and reasonably firm; prominent chalazae	Clear; weak or watery
Yolk	Firm; centered; stands round and high; free from defects	Firm; stands fairly high; practically free from defects	Enlarged and flattened; may show slight defects
Shell	Clean; of normal shape; unbroken		Slight stains permissible; abnormal shape; unbroken
Use	Any use, especially frying, poaching and cooking in shell		Baking, scrambling, used in bulk egg products

*Spread refers to the appearance of the egg when first broken onto a flat surface.

Storage

Egg quality is quickly diminished by improper handling. Eggs should be stored at temperatures below 40°C (4°C) and at a relative humidity of 70–80%. Eggs will age more during one day at room temperature than they will during one week under proper refrigeration. As eggs age, the white becomes thinner and the yolk becomes flatter. While this will change the appearance of poached or fried eggs, age has little effect on nutrition or behavior during cooking procedures. Older eggs, however, should be used for hard-cooking, as the shells are easier to remove than on fresh eggs.

Cartons of fresh, uncooked eggs will keep for at least four to five weeks beyond the pack date if properly refrigerated. Hard-cooked eggs left in their shells and refrigerated should be used within one week.

Store eggs away from strongly flavored foods to reduce odor absorption. Rotate egg stock to maintain freshness. Do not use dirty, cracked or broken eggs as they may contain bacteria or other contaminants. Frozen eggs should be thawed in the refrigerator and used only in dishes that will be thoroughly cooked, such as baked products.

Sanitation

Eggs are a potentially hazardous food. Rich in protein, they are an excellent breeding ground for bacteria. Salmonella is of particular concern with eggs and egg products because this bacteria is commonly found in a chicken's intestinal tract. Although shells are cleaned at packing houses, some bacteria may remain. Therefore, to prevent contamination, it is best to avoid mixing a shell with the liquid egg.

Pasteurization—*the process of heating a liquid to a prescribed temperature for a specific period of time in order to destroy pathogenic bacteria.*

Inadequately cooking or improperly storing eggs may lead to food-borne illnesses. USDA guidelines indicate that **pasteurization** is achieved when the whole egg stays at a temperature of 140°F (60°C) for 3.5 minutes. Hold egg dishes below 40°F (4°C) or above 145°F (63°C). Never leave an egg dish at room temperature for more than one hour, including preparation and service time. Never reuse a container after it has held raw eggs without thoroughly cleaning and sanitizing it.

Whipped Egg Whites

Egg whites are often whipped into a foam that is then incorporated into cakes, custards, souffles, pancakes or other products. The air beaten into the egg foam gives products lightness and assists with leavening.

PROCEDURE FOR WHIPPING EGG WHITES

1. Use fresh egg whites that are completely free of egg yolk or other impurities. Warm the egg whites to room temperature before whipping; this causes a better foam to form.
2. Use a clean bowl and whisk. Even a tiny amount of fat can prevent the egg whites from foaming properly.
3. Whip the whites until very foamy, then add salt or cream of tartar as directed.
4. Continue whipping until soft peaks form, then gradually add granulated sugar as directed.
5. Whip until stiff peaks form. Properly whipped egg whites should be moist and shiny; over-whipping will make the egg whites appear dry and spongy or curdled.
6. Use the whipped egg whites immediately. If liquid begins to separate from the whipped egg whites discard them; they cannot be rewhipped successfully.

Egg whites whipped to soft peaks.

Egg whites whipped to stiff peaks.

Spongy, over-whipped egg whites.

Egg Products

Food service operations often want the convenience of buying eggs out of the shell in the exact form needed: whole eggs, yolks only or whites only. These processed items are called *egg products* and are subject to strict pasteurization standards and USDA inspections. Egg products can be frozen, refrigerated or dried. Precooked, preportioned and blended egg products are also available.

Egg Substitutes

Concerns about the cholesterol content of eggs have increased the popularity of egg substitutes. There are two general types of substitute. The first is a complete substitute made from soy or milk proteins. It should not be used in recipes where eggs are required for thickening. The second substitute contains real albumen, but the egg yolk has been replaced with vegetable or milk products. Egg substitutes have a different flavor than real eggs, but may be useful for persons on a restricted diet.

Nutrition

Eggs contain vitamins A, D, E, K and the B-complex vitamins. They are rich in minerals but also in cholesterol. The nutritional values of eggs as well as an egg substitute are listed in Table 8.2.

TABLE 8.2   NUTRITIONAL VALUES OF EGGS

	Calories	Protein (g)	Carbohydrates (g)	Total fat (g)	Saturated fat (g)	Cholesterol (mg)
Whole large egg, one approximately 1.75 ounces (53 g)	75	6.3	0.6	5	1.6	213
Yolk from one large egg	59	2.8	0.3	5	1.6	213
White from one large egg	16	3.5	0.3	0	0	0
Egg substitute (*Egg Beaters*), 1/4 cup (equivalent to one large egg)	25	5	1	0	0	0

The Corinne T. Netzer Encyclopedia of Food Values, 1992

DAIRY PRODUCTS

Dairy products include cow's milk and foods produced from cow's milk such as butter, yogurt, sour cream and cheese. The milk of other mammals, namely goats, sheep and buffaloes, is also made into cheeses that are used in commercial food service operations.

Milk

Milk is not only a popular beverage, it is also used in the preparation of many dishes. It provides texture, flavor, color and nutritional value for cooked or baked items. Indeed, milk is one of the most nutritious foods available, providing proteins, vitamins and minerals (particularly calcium). But milk is also highly perishable and an excellent bacterial breeding ground. Care must be exercised in the handling and storage of milk and other dairy products.

Whole milk—that is, milk as it comes from the cow—is composed primarily of water (about 88%). It contains approximately 3.25% milkfat and 8.25% other milk solids (proteins, milk sugar [lactose] and minerals).

Whole milk is graded A, B or C based upon standards recommended by the United States Public Health Service. Grades are assigned based on bacterial count, with Grade A products having the lowest count. Grades B and C, while still safe and wholesome, are rarely available for retail or commercial use. Fresh whole milk is not available raw, but must be processed as described below.

Processing Techniques

Pasteurization

By law, all Grade A milk must be pasteurized prior to retail sale. Pasteurization is the process of heating milk to a sufficiently high temperature for a sufficient length of time to destroy pathogenic bacteria. This typically requires holding milk at a temperature of 161°F (72°C) for 15 seconds. Pasteurization also destroys enzymes that cause spoilage thus increasing shelf life. Milk's nutritional value is not significantly affected by pasteurization.

Ultra-Pasteurization

Ultra-pasteurization is a process in which milk is heated to a very high temperature (275°F/135°C) for a very short time (2 to 4 seconds) in order to destroy virtually all bacteria. Ultra-pasteurization is most often used with whipping cream and individual creamers. Although the process may reduce cream's whipping properties, it extends its shelf life dramatically.

Ultra High Temperature Processing

UHT processing is a form of ultra-pasteurization in which milk is held at a temperature of 280° to 300°F (138°–150°C) for 2 to 6 seconds. It is then packed in sterile containers under sterile conditions and aseptically sealed to prevent bacteria from entering the container. UHT milk can be stored without refrigeration for at least three months if unopened. Although UHT milk can be stored unrefrigerated, it should be chilled before serving and stored like fresh milk once opened. UHT processing may give milk a slightly cooked taste but it has no significant effect on milk's nutritional value. Long available in Europe, it has been approved recently for sale in the United States.

Homogenization

Homogenization is a process in which the fat globules in whole milk are reduced in size and permanently dispersed throughout the liquid. This prevents the fat from clumping together and rising to the surface as a layer of cream. Although homogenization is not required, milk sold commercially is generally homogenized because it ensures a uniform consistency, a whiter color and a richer taste.

Certification

Certification is a method of controlling the quality of milk by controlling the condition of the animals from which milk is obtained. Certification is not a true processing technique; rather it requires frequent veterinary examinations of the cows and health department inspections of the dairy farm, the equipment and the employees who handle milk. Pasteurization has replaced the need for certification, but milk from certified herds is still available in a few areas.

Milkfat Removal

Whole milk can also be processed in a centrifuge to remove all or a portion of the milkfat, resulting in **lowfat milk** and **skim milk**.

Lowfat milk is whole milk from which sufficient milkfat has been removed to produce a liquid with .5% to 2.0% milkfat. (All lowfat milks must still contain approximately 8.25% milk solids.) Vitamin A is added to lowfat milk to replace that removed along with the milkfat. It will be labeled with either the fat content or the nonfat percentage. For example, milk containing 1% milkfat may be labeled "99% fat free" or "1% lowfat."

Skim milk, also referred to as **nonfat milk**, has had as much milkfat removed as possible. The fat content must be less than .5%. Skim milk must also contain at least 8.25% milk solids and be fortified with vitamin A.

Storage

Fluid milk should be kept refrigerated at or below 40°F (4°C). Its shelf life is reduced by half for every five-degree rise in temperature above 40°F (4°C). Keep milk containers closed to prevent absorption of odors and flavors. Freezing is not recommended.

Concentrated Milks

Concentrated or condensed milk products are produced by using a vacuum to remove all or part of the water from whole milk. The resulting products have a high concentration of milkfat and milk solids and an extended shelf life.

Evaporated milk is produced by removing approximately 60% of the water from whole, homogenized milk. Evaporated milk must contain at least 7.25% milkfat and 25.5% milk solids. The concentrated liquid is canned and heat-sterilized. This results in a cooked flavor and darker color. Evaporated skim milk, with a milkfat content of .5%, is also available. A can of evaporated milk requires no refrigeration until opened, although the can should be stored in a cool place. Evaporated milk can be reconstituted with an equal amount of water and used like whole milk for cooking or drinking.

Sweetened condensed milk is similar to evaporated milk in that 60% of the water has been removed. But unlike evaporated milk, sweetened condensed milk contains large amounts of sugar (40 to 45%). Sweetened condensed milk is also canned; the canning process darkens the color and adds a caramel flavor. Sweetened condensed milk cannot be substituted for whole milk or evaporated milk because of its sugar content. Its distinctive flavor is most often found in desserts and confections.

Dry milk powder is made by removing virtually all of the moisture from pasteurized milk. The moisture content must be less than 5% by weight. Dry whole milk contains between 26% and 40% milkfat. Nonfat milk powder is made from skim milk and must contain less than 1.5% milkfat by weight. Both types of dry milk are usually fortified with vitamins A and D.

The lack of moisture prevents the growth of microorganisms and allows dry whole and nonfat milk powders to be stored for extended periods without refrigeration. However, because of its high milkfat content, dried whole milk can turn rancid if not stored in a cool place. Either type of dry milk can be reconstituted with water and used like fresh milk. Milk powder may also be added to foods directly, with additional liquid included in the recipe. This procedure is typical in bread making and does not alter the function of the milk or the flavor in the finished product.

Cream

Cream is a rich, liquid milk product containing at least 18% fat. It must be pasteurized or ultra-pasteurized and may be homogenized. Cream has a slight yellow or ivory color and is more viscous than milk. It is used throughout the kitchen to give flavor and body to sauces, soups and desserts. Whipping cream, containing not less than 30% milkfat, can be whipped into a stiff foam and used in pastries and desserts. Cream is marketed in several forms with different fat contents, as described below.

Half-and-half is a mixture of whole milk and cream containing between 10% and 18% milkfat. It is often served with cereal or coffee, but does not contain enough fat to whip into a foam.

Light cream, coffee cream and **table cream** are all products with more than 18% but less than 30% milkfat. These products are often used in baked goods or soups as well as with coffee, fruit and cereal.

Light whipping cream or, simply, **whipping cream** contains between 30% and 36% milkfat. It is generally used for thickening and enriching sauces and making ice cream. It can be whipped into a foam and used as a dessert topping or folded into custards or mousses to add flavor and lightness.

Heavy whipping cream or, simply, **heavy cream** contains not less than 36% milkfat. It whips easily and holds its whipped texture longer than other creams. It must be pasteurized, but is rarely homogenized. Heavy cream is used throughout the kitchen in the same ways as light whipping cream.

Storage

Ultra-pasteurized cream will keep for six to eight weeks if refrigerated. Unwhipped cream should not be frozen. Whipped, sweetened cream can be frozen, tightly covered, for up to three months, then slowly thawed in the refrigerator. Keep cream away from strong odors and bright lights, as they can adversely affect its flavor.

Cultured Dairy Products

Cultured dairy products such as yogurt, buttermilk and sour cream are produced by adding specific bacterial cultures to fluid dairy products. The bacteria convert the milk sugar lactose into lactic acid, giving these products their body and tangy, unique flavors. The acid content also retards the growth of undesirable microorganisms; thus cultured products have been used for centuries to preserve milk.

Buttermilk originally referred to the liquid remaining after cream was churned into butter. Today buttermilk is produced by adding a culture

(*Streptococcus lactis*) to fresh, pasteurized skim or lowfat milk. This results in a tart milk with a thick texture. Buttermilk is most often used as a beverage or in baked goods.

Sour cream is produced by adding the same culture to pasteurized, homogenized light cream. The resulting product is a white, tangy gel used as a condiment or to give baked goods a distinctive flavor. Sour cream must have a milkfat content of not less than 18%.

Crème fraîche is a cultured cream popular in French cuisine. Although thinner and richer than sour cream, it has a similar tart, tangy flavor. It is used extensively in soups and sauces, especially with poultry, rabbit and lamb dishes. It is easily prepared from the following recipe.

◆◆◆

RECIPE 8.1
CRÈME FRAÎCHE

Yield: 1 pint (500 ml)

Heavy cream	16 oz.	500 g
Buttermilk, with active cultures	1 oz.	30 g

1. Heat the cream (preferably not ultra-pasteurized) to about 100°F (43°C).

2. Remove the cream from the heat and stir in the buttermilk.

3. Allow the mixture to stand in a warm place, loosely covered, until it thickens, approximately 12 to 36 hours.

4. Chill thoroughly before using. Crème fraîche will keep for up to 10 days in the refrigerator.

Yogurt is a thick, tart, custardlike product made from milk (either whole, lowfat or nonfat) cultured with *Lactobacillus bulgaricus* and *Streptococcus thermophilus*. Though touted as a health or diet food, yogurt contains the same amount of milkfat as the milk from which it is made. Yogurt may also contain a variety of sweeteners, flavorings and fruits. Yogurt is generally eaten as is, but may be used in baked products, salad dressings and frozen desserts. It is used in many Middle Eastern cuisines.

Storage

Cultured products should be kept refrigerated at 40°F (4°C) or below. Under proper conditions sour cream will last up to four weeks, yogurt up to three weeks and buttermilk up to two weeks. Freezing is not recommended for these products, but dishes prepared with cultured products generally can be frozen.

Butter

Butter is a fatty substance produced by agitating or churning cream. Its flavor is unequalled in sauces, breads and pastries. Butter contains at least 80% milkfat, not more than 16% water and 2–4% milk solids. It may or may not contain added salt. Butter is firm when chilled and soft at room temperature. It melts into a liquid at approximately 98°F (38°C) and reaches the smoke point at 260°F (127°C).

Government grading is not mandatory, but most processors submit their butters for testing. The USDA label on the package assures the buyer that the butter meets federal standards for the grade indicated:

♦ USDA Grade AA—butter of superior quality, with a fresh, sweet flavor and aroma, a smooth, creamy texture and good spreadability.
♦ USDA Grade A—butter of very good quality, with a pleasing flavor and fairly smooth texture.
♦ USDA Grade B—butter of standard quality, made from sour cream; has an acceptable flavor but lacks the taste, texture and body of Grades AA and A. Grade B is most often used in the manufacturing of foods.

Salted butter is butter with up to 2.5% salt added. This not only changes the butter's flavor, it also extends its keeping qualities. When using salted butter in cooking or baking, the salt content must be considered in the total recipe.

Whipped butter is made by incorporating air into the butter. This increases its volume and spreadability, but also increases the speed with which the butter will become rancid. Because of the change in density, whipped butter should not be substituted in recipes calling for regular butter.

Storage

Butter should be well wrapped and stored at temperatures between 32° and 35°F (0°–2°C). Unsalted butter is best kept frozen until needed. If well wrapped, frozen butter will keep for up to nine months at a temperature of 0°F (–18°C).

Clarified Butter

Unsalted whole butter is approximately 80% fat, 15% water and 5% milk solids. Although whole butter can be used for cooking or sauce making, sometimes a more stable and consistent product will be achieved by using butter that has had the water and milk solids removed by a process called clarification.

Skimming milk solids from the surface of melted butter.

PROCEDURE FOR CLARIFYING BUTTER

1. Slowly warm the butter in a saucepan over low heat without boiling or agitation. As the butter melts, the milk solids rise to the top as a foam and the water sinks to the bottom.
2. When the butter is completely melted, skim the milk solids from the top.
3. When all the milk solids have been removed, ladle the butterfat into a clean saucepan, being careful to leave the water in the bottom of the pan.
4. The clarified butter is now ready to use. One pound (454 grams) of whole butter will yield approximately 12 ounces (340 grams) of clarified butter (a yield of 75%).

Clarified butter will keep for extended periods in either the freezer or refrigerator.

Ladling the butterfat into a clean pan.

Margarine

Margarine is not a dairy product but is included in this section because it is so frequently substituted for butter in cooking, baking and table service. Margarine is manufactured from animal or vegetable fats or a combination of such fats. Flavorings, colorings, emulsifiers, preservatives and vitamins are

---

MARGARINE:
FROM LABORATORY BENCH TO DINNER TABLE

Margarine was invented by a French chemist in 1869 after Napoleon III offered a prize for the development of a synthetic edible fat. Originally produced from animal fat and milk, margarine is now made almost exclusively from vegetable fats.

In *On Food and Cooking, The Science and Lore of the Kitchen*, Harold McGee recounts the history of margarine. He explains that margarine caught on quickly in Europe and America, with large-scale production underway by 1880. But the American dairy industry and the U.S. government put up fierce resistance. First, margarine was defined as a harmful drug and its sale restricted. Then it was heavily taxed; stores had to be licensed to sell it and, like alcohol and tobacco, it was bootlegged. The U.S. government refused to purchase it for use by the armed forces. And, in an attempt to hold it to its true colors, some states did not allow margarine to be dyed yellow (animal fats and vegetable oils are much paler than butter); the dye was sold separately and mixed in by the consumer. World War II, which brought butter rationing, probably did the most to establish margarine's respectability. But it was not until 1967 that yellow margarine could be sold in Wisconsin.

Today Americans consume nearly three times as much margarine as butter. Both price and the concern about heart disease are responsible for this differential.

---

added, and the mixture is firmed or solidified by exposure to hydrogen gas at very high temperatures, a process known as hydrogenation. Generally, the firmer the margarine the greater the degree of hydrogenation and the longer its shelf life. Like butter, margarine is approximately 80% fat and 16% water. But even the finest margarine cannot match the flavor of butter.

Margarine packaged in tubs is softer and more spreadable than solid products and generally contains more water and air. Indeed, diet margarine is approximately 50% water. Because of their decreased density, these soft products should not be substituted for regular butter or margarine in cooking or baking.

Specially formulated and blended margarine is available for commercial use in making puff pastry, croissant doughs, frostings and the like.

Nutrition

Dairy products are naturally high in vitamins, minerals and protein. Often liquid products such as milk are fortified with additional vitamins and minerals. Their fat content varies depending upon the amount of milkfat left after processing. Specific nutritional values for selected dairy products are found in Table 8.3.

TABLE 8.3   NUTRITIONAL VALUES OF DAIRY PRODUCTS

Per 8-ounce (225 g) Serving	Calories	Protein (g)	Carbohydrates (g)	Total Fat (g)	Saturated fat (g)	Cholesterol (mg)	Sodium (mg)
Whole milk (3.3% milk fat)	150	8	11	8.2	5.1	33	120
Nonfat milk	85	8.4	12	0.4	0.3	4	126
Buttermilk	100	8.1	12	2.2	1.3	9	257
Heavy whipping cream	821	5	6.6	88	55	326	89
Half and half	315	7.2	10.4	27.8	17.3	89	98
Sour cream	493	7.3	9.8	48.2	30	102	123

The Corinne T. Netzer Encyclopedia of Food Values, 1992

Natural Cheeses

Cheese (Fr. *fromage*; It. *fromaggio*) is one of the oldest and most widely used foods known to man. It is served alone or as a principal ingredient in or an accompaniment to countless dishes. Cheese is commonly used in commercial kitchens, appearing in everything from breakfast to snacks to desserts.

Literally hundreds of natural cheeses are produced worldwide. Although their shapes, ages and flavors vary according to local preferences and traditions, all natural cheeses are produced in the same basic fashion as has been used for centuries. Each starts with a mammal's milk; cows, goats and sheep are the most commonly used. The milk proteins (known as *casein*) are coagulated with the addition of an enzyme, usually rennet, which is found in calves' stomachs. As the milk coagulates, it separates into solid curds and liquid whey. After draining off the whey, either the curds are made into fresh cheese, such as ricotta or cottage cheese, or the curds are further processed by cutting, kneading and cooking. The resulting substance, known as "green cheese," is packed into molds to drain. Salt or special bacteria may be added to the molded cheeses, which are then allowed to age or ripen under controlled conditions to develop the desired texture, color and flavor.

Cheeses are a product of their environment, which is why most fine cheeses cannot be reproduced outside their native locale. The breed and feed of the milk animal, the wild spores and molds in the air and even the wind currents in a storage area can affect the manner in which a cheese develops. (Roquefort, for example, develops its distinctive flavor from aging in particular caves filled with crosscurrents of cool, moist air.)

Some cheeses develop a natural rind or surface because of the application of bacteria (bloomy rind) or by repeated washing with brine (washed rind). Most natural rinds may be eaten if desired. Other cheeses are coated with an inedible wax rind to prevent moisture loss. Fresh cheeses have no rind whatsoever.

Moisture and fat contents are good indicators of a cheese's texture and shelf life. The higher the moisture content, the softer the product and the more perishable it will be. Low-moisture cheeses may be used for grating and will keep for several weeks if properly stored. (Reduced water activity levels prohibit bacterial growth.) Fat content ranges from low fat (less than 20% fat) to double cream (at least 60% fat) and triple cream (at least 72% fat). Cheeses with a high fat content will be creamier and have a richer taste and texture than low-fat products.

Most cheeses contain high percentages of fat and protein. Cheese is also rich in calcium, phosphorus and vitamin A. As animal products, natural cheeses contain cholesterol. Today, many low-fat, even nonfat, processed cheeses are available. Sodium has also been reduced or eliminated from some modern products. See Table 8.4.

Cheese Varieties

Cheeses can be classified by country of origin, ripening method, fat content or texture. Here we classify fine cheeses by texture and have adopted five categories: fresh or unripened, soft, semi-soft, firm and hard. A separate section on goat's–milk cheeses is also included.

Fresh or Unripened Cheeses

Fresh cheeses are uncooked and unripened. Referred to as *fromage blanc* or *fromage frais* in French, they are generally mild and creamy with a tart tanginess. They should not taste acidic or bitter. Fresh cheeses have a moisture content of 40% to 80% and are highly perishable.

♦♦♦
MAKING MOZZARELLA

In Italy, mozzarella is made every day; it is meant to be consumed just as often. Before there was refrigeration the balls of mozzarella were stored in well water to keep them cool, which is where the tradition originated of storing fresh mozzarella in liquid.

Once the milk is coagulated and the curds are cut, the mass is slowly stirred to enhance the whey's expulsion. A few hours later, when the curds are mature, they are removed from the whey, chopped or shredded and then mixed with hot water.

To test the exact amount of maturity, a handful of curds is dipped into a bucket of hot water for 10 seconds. When the curds are removed, they should be kneaded briefly and then, holding the mass with two hands, it should be pulled and stretched out to determine its maturity. When it is exactly ready to be strung it can be stretched as thin and opaque as tissue paper. At this point, small amounts of curd are dumped into a small vat and stirred with hot water using a paddle. This is known as "stringing" the cheese because as the curds are mixed with the water they begin to melt somewhat and become stringy. The more the cheese is stirred the longer the strings are stretched. Eventually all the strings come together to make a large mass of satiny-smooth cheese. In Italian the word *filare* means "to string"; therefore, all cheeses that are strung are members of the *pasta filata* family.

When stringing is complete the cheese is ready to be shaped and hand-formed into balls. The balls are tossed immediately into vats of cool water so they will maintain the desired shapes. When cool, the balls are immersed in brine solution and then wrapped in parchment paper.

PAULA LAMBERT, *owner*
MOZZARELLA COMPANY, Dallas, Texas

TABLE 8.4   NUTRITIONAL VALUES OF COMMON CHEESES

Per 1-ounce (28 g) Serving	Calories	Protein (g)	Carbohydrates (g)	Total Fat (g)	Saturated fat (g)	Cholesterol (mg)	Sodium (mg)
Blue	100	6.1	0.7	8.2	5.3	21	396
Cheddar	114	7.1	0.4	9.4	6	30	176
Cottage, low fat	25	3.9	1	0.5	0.3	2	115
Feta	75	4	1.2	6	4.2	25	316
Goat's milk	132	2.7	12.1	8.4	5.4	n/a	170
Mozzarella, part skim	72	6.9	0.8	4.5	2.9	16	132
Swiss	110	8	1	8	5	25	20
Processed cheese (*Velveeta*)	100	6	3	7	4	20	410

The Corinne T. Netzer Encyclopedia of Food Values, 1992

Cream cheese is soft cow's milk cheese from the United States containing approximately 35% fat. It is available in various-sized solid white blocks or whipped and flavored. It is used throughout the kitchen in baking, dips, dressings and confections and is popular as a spread for bagels or toast.

Feta is a semi-soft Greek or Italian product made from sheep's and/or goat's milk. It is a white, flaky cheese that is pickled (but not ripened) and stored in brine water, giving it a shelf life of four to six weeks. Its flavor becomes sharper and saltier with age. Feta is good for snacks and salads and melts easily for sauces and fillings.

Feta

Mozzarella is a firm Italian cheese traditionally made with water buffalo's milk (today cow's milk is more common) and containing 40% to 45% fat. Mozzarella becomes elastic when melted and is well known as "pizza cheese." Fresh mozzarella is excellent in salads or topped simply with olive oil and herbs. It is a very mild white cheese best eaten within hours of production. Commercial mozzarella is rather bland and rubbery and is best reserved for cooking, for which it may be purchased already shredded.

Mozzarella

Ricotta is a soft Italian cheese, similar to American cottage cheese, made from the whey left when other cow's-milk cheeses are produced. It contains only 4% to 10% fat. It is white or ivory in color and fluffy, with a small grain and sweet flavor. Ricotta is an important ingredient in many pasta dishes and desserts.

Soft Cheeses

Soft cheeses are characterized by their thin skins and creamy centers. They are among the most delicious and popular of cheeses. They ripen quickly and are at their peak for only a few days, sometimes less. Moisture content ranges from 50% to 75%.

Bel paese is a 20th-century Italian creation made from cow's milk and containing approximately 50% fat. It is mild and creamy with a fruity flavor. The inside is yellowish and the outside is brown or gray. Bel paese is excellent for snacking and melts easily.

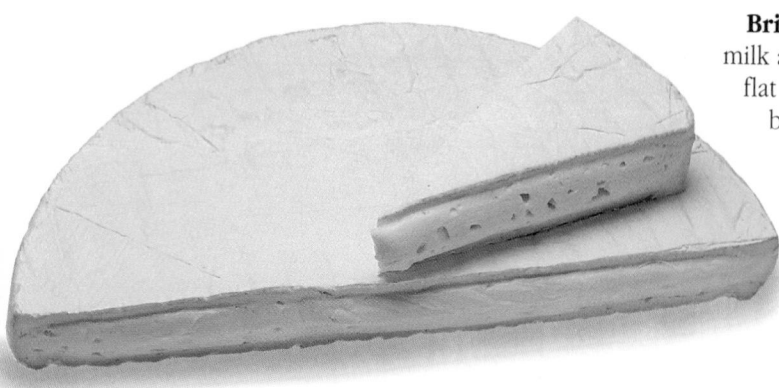

Brie

Brie is a rind-ripened French cheese made with cow's milk and containing about 60% fat. Brie is made in round, flat disks weighing 2 or 4 pounds; it is coated with a bloomy white rind. At the peak of ripeness it is creamy and rich, with a texture that oozes. Selecting a properly ripened brie is a matter of judgment and experience. Select a cheese that is bulging a bit inside its rind; there should be just the beginning of brown coloring on the rind. If underripe, brie will be bland with a hard, chalky core. Once the cheese is cut it will not ripen any further. If overripe, brie will have a brownish rind that may be gummy or sagging and will smell strongly of ammonia. The rind is edible, but trim it off if preferred. The classic after-dinner cheese, brie, is also used in soups, sauces and hors d'oeuvres.

Boursin is a triple-cream cow's-milk cheese from France containing approximately 75% fat. Boursin is usually flavored with peppers, herbs or garlic. It is rindless, with a smooth, creamy texture, and is packed in small, foil-wrapped cylinders. Boursin is a good breakfast cheese and a welcome addition to any cheese board. It is also a popular filling for baked chicken.

Camembert is a rind-ripened cheese from France containing approximately 45% fat. Bavaria also produces a Camembert, though of a somewhat lesser quality. Camembert is creamy, like brie, but milder. It is shaped in small round or oval disks and is coated with a white bloomy rind. Selecting a properly ripened Camembert is similar to selecting a brie, but Camembert will become overripe and ammoniated even more quickly than brie. Camembert is an excellent dessert or after-dinner cheese and goes particularly well with fruit.

Semisoft Cheeses

Semisoft cheeses include many mild, buttery cheeses with smooth, sliceable textures. Some semisoft cheeses are also known as monastery or Trappist cheeses because their development is traced to monasteries, some recipes having originated during the Middle Ages. The moisture content of semisoft cheeses ranges from 40% to 50%.

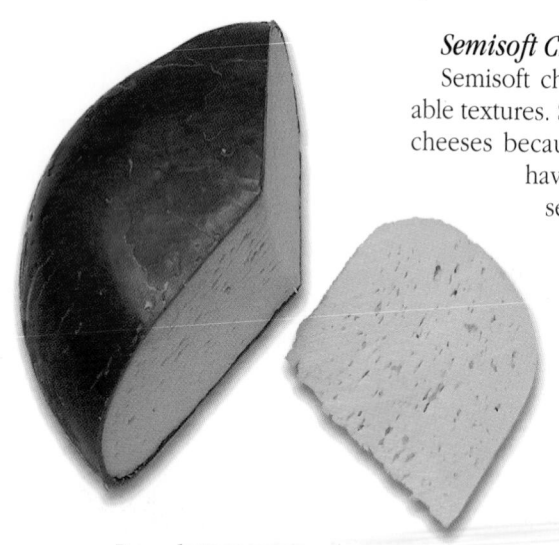

Doux de Montagne

Doux de Montagne is a cow's milk cheese from France containing approximately 45% fat. Produced in the foothills of the Pyrenees, it is also referred to as **pain de Pyrenees**. Doux de Montagne is pale yellow with irregular holes and a mellow, sweet, nutty flavor. It is sometimes studded with green peppercorns, which provide a tangy flavor contrast. It is usually shaped in large spheres and coated with brown wax. Doux de Montagne is good before dinner and for snacking.

Fontina is a cow's-milk cheese from Italy's Piedmont region containing approximately 45% fat. The original, known as **fontina Val D'Aosta**, has a dark gold, crusty rind; the pale gold, dense interior has a few small holes. It is nutty and rich. The original must have a purple trademark stamped on the rind. Imitation fontinas (known as **fontal** or **fontinella**) are produced in Denmark, France, Sweden, the United States and other regions of Italy. They tend to be softer, with less depth of flavor, and may have a rubbery texture. Real fontina is a good after-dinner cheese; the imitations are often added to sauces, soups or sandwiches.

Gorgonzola is a blue-veined cow's-milk cheese from Italy containing 48% fat. Gorgonzola has a white or ivory interior with bluish-green veins. It is creamier than Stilton or Roquefort, with a somewhat more pungent, spicy, earthy flavor. White gorgonzola has no veins but a similar flavor, while aged gorgonzola is drier and crumbly with a very strong, sharp flavor. The milder gorgonzolas are excellent with fresh peaches or pears or crumbled in a salad. Gorgonzola is also used in sauces and in the *torta con basilico*, a cakelike cheese loaf composed of layers of cheese, fresh basil and pine nuts.

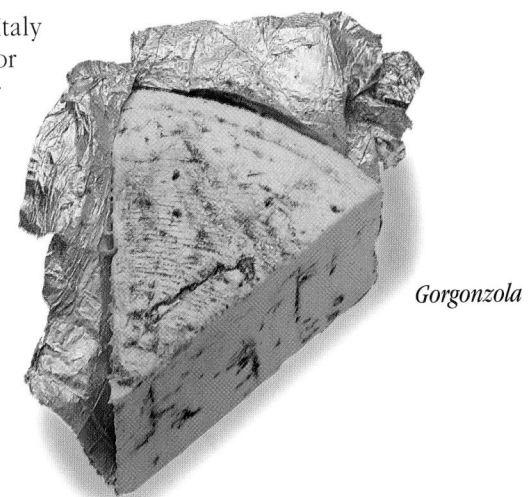

Gorgonzola

Gouda is a Dutch cheese containing approximately 48% fat. Gouda is sold in various-sized wheels covered with red or yellow wax. The cheese is yellow with a few small holes and a mild, buttery flavor. Gouda may be sold soon after production or it may be aged for several months, resulting in a firmer, more flavorful cheese. Gouda is widely popular for snacking and in **fondue.**

Havarti is a cow's-milk monastery-style cheese from Denmark containing 45% to 60% fat. Havarti is also known as **Danish Tilsit** or by the brand name **Dofino**. Pale yellow with many small, irregular holes, it is sold in small rounds, rectangular blocks or loaves. Havarti has a mild flavor and creamy texture. It is often flavored with dill, caraway seeds or peppers. Havarti is very popular for snacking and on sandwiches.

Fondue—*a Swiss specialty made with melted cheese, wine and flavorings; eaten by dipping pieces of bread into the hot mixture with long forks.*

Havarti

Port du Salut is a monastery cow's-milk product from France containing approximately 50% fat. Port du Salut (also known as Port Salut) is smooth, rich and savory. It is shaped in thick wheels with a dense, pale yellow interior and an edible, bright orange rind. The Danish version is known as **Esrom**. One of the best and most authentic Port du Saluts has the initials S.A.F.R. stamped on the rind. Lesser-quality brands may be bland and rubbery. It is popular for breakfast and snacking, especially with fruit.

Roquefort is a blue-veined sheep's-milk cheese from France containing approximately 45% fat. One of the oldest cheeses, Roquefort is intensely pungent with a rich, salty flavor and strong aroma. It is a white paste with veins of blue mold and a thin natural rind shaped into thick, foil-wrapped cylinders. Roquefort is always aged for at least three months in the limestone caves of Mount Combalou. Since 1926 no producer outside this region can legally use the name Roquefort or even "Roquefort-style." Roquefort is an excellent choice for serving before or after dinner and is, of course, essential for Roquefort dressing.

Stilton is a blue-veined cow's-milk cheese from Great Britain containing 45% fat. Stilton is one of the oldest and grandest cheeses in the world. It has a white or pale yellow interior with evenly spaced blue veins. Stilton's distinctive flavor is pungent, rich and tangy, combining the best of blues and cheddars. It is aged in cool ripening rooms for four to six months to develop the blue veining; it is then sold in tall cylinders with a crusty, edible rind. Stilton should be wrapped in a cloth dampened with salt water and stored at cool temperatures, but not refrigerated. It is best served alone, with plain crackers, dried fruit or vintage port.

Stilton

Firm Cheeses

Firm cheeses are not hard or brittle. Some are close-textured and flaky, like cheddar; others are dense, holey cheeses like Swiss Emmenthaler. Most firm cheeses are actually imitators of these two classics. Their moisture content ranges from 30% to 40%.

Cheddars are produced in both North America and Great Britain. **American Cheddar** is a cow's-milk cheese made primarily in New York, Wisconsin, Vermont and Oregon, containing from 45% to 50% fat. The best cheddars are made from raw milk and aged for several months. (Raw milk may be used in the United States provided the cheese is then aged at least 60 days.) They have a dense, crumbly texture. Cheddars may be white or colored orange with vegetable dyes, depending on local preference. Flavors range from mild to very sharp, depending on the age of the cheese. **Colby** and **longhorn** are two well-known mild, soft-textured Wisconsin cheddars. Cheddars are sold in a variety of shapes and sizes, often coated with wax. Good-quality cheddars are welcome additions to any cheese board, while those of lesser quality are better reserved for cooking and sandwiches. **English Cheddar** is a variety of cow's-milk cheese produced in Great Britain containing approximately 45% fat. Perhaps the most imitated cheese in the world, true English cheddar is rarely seen in the United States because of import restrictions. It is a moist yet sliceable cheese, aged at least six months.

American Cheddar— Wisconsin Sharp, Vermont Cabot, Canadian Black Diamond

Emmenthaler (Swiss) is a cow's-milk cheese from Switzerland containing approximately 45% fat. Emmenthaler is the original Swiss cheese; it accounts for over half of Switzerland's cheese production. It is mellow, rich and nutty with a natural rind and a light yellow interior full of large holes. It is ripened in three stages with the aid of fermenting bacteria. The holes or "eyes" are caused by gases expanding inside the cheese during fermentation. Authentic Emmenthaler is sold in 200-pound wheels with the word "Switzerland" stamped on the rind like the spokes of a wheel. Emmenthaler, one of the basic fondue cheeses, is also popular for sandwiches, snacks and after dinner with fruit and nuts.

Emmenthaler (Swiss)

Gruyère is a cow's-milk cheese made near Fribourg in the Swiss Alps and containing approximately 45% to 50% fat. Gruyère is often imitated, as the name is not legally protected. True gruyère is moist and highly flavorful, with a sweet nuttiness similar to Emmenthaler. Gruyère is aged for up to 12 months and then sold in huge wheels. It should have small, well-spaced holes and a brown, wrinkled rind. Gruyère melts easily and is often used with meats and in sauces, but is also appropriate before or after dinner.

Gruyère

Jarlsberg is a Swiss-type cow's-milk cheese from Norway containing approximately 45% fat. Jarlsberg closely resembles Swiss Emmenthaler in both taste and appearance. It is mild with a delicate, sweet taste and large holes. Jarlsberg has a pale yellow interior; it is coated with yellow wax and sold in huge wheels. It has a long shelf life and is popular for sandwiches, snacks and in cooking.

Monterey Jack is a cheddarlike cow's-milk cheese from California containing 50% fat. It is very mild and rich, with a pale ivory interior. It is sold in wheels or loaves coated with dark wax. "Jack" is often flavored with peppers or herbs and is good for snacking, sandwiches and in Mexican dishes. Dry-aged Jack develops a tough, wrinkled brown rind and a rich, firm yellow interior. It has a nutty, sharp flavor and is dry enough for grating.

Provolone is a cow's-milk cheese from southern Italy containing approximately 45% fat. Provolone *dolce*, aged only two months, is mild, with a smooth texture. Provolone *piccante*, aged up to six months, is stronger and somewhat flaky or stringy. Smoked provolone is also popular, especially for snacking. Provolone is shaped in various ways, from huge salamis to plump spheres to tiny piglets shaped by hand. It is excellent in sandwiches and for cooking, and is often used for melting and in pizza and pasta dishes.

Hard Cheeses

Hard cheeses are not simply cheeses that have been allowed to dry out. Rather, they are carefully aged for extended periods of time and have a moisture content of about 30%. Hard cheeses are most often used for grating; the best flavor will come from cheeses grated as needed. Even the finest hard cheeses begin to lose their flavor within hours of grating. The most famous and popular of the hard cheeses are those from Italy, where they are known as *grana*. Hard cheeses can also be served as a table cheese or with a salad.

Asiago is a cow's-milk cheese from Italy containing approximately 30% fat. After only one year of aging, Asiago is sharp and nutty with a cheddarlike texture. If aged for two years or more, Asiago becomes dry, brittle and suitable for grating. Either version should be an even white to pale yellow in color with no dark spots, cracks or strong aromas. It is sold in small wheels and keeps for long periods if well wrapped. Asiago melts easily and is often used in cooking.

Asiago

Parmigiano-Reggiano (Parmesan) is a cow's-milk cheese made exclusively in the region near Parma, Italy, containing from 32% to 35% fat. Parmigiano-Reggiano is one of the world's oldest and most widely copied cheeses. Used primarily for grating and cooking, it is rich, spicy and sharp with a golden interior and a hard oily rind. It should not be overly salty or bitter. Reggiano, as it is known, is produced only from mid-April to mid-November. It is shaped into huge wheels of about 80 pounds (36 kilos) each, with the name stenciled repeatedly around the rind. Imitation Parmesan is produced in the United States, Argentina and elsewhere, but none can match the distinctive flavor of freshly grated Reggiano.

Pecorino Romano is a sheep's-milk cheese from central and southern Italy containing approximately 35% fat. Romano is very brittle and sharper than other grating cheeses, with a "sheepy" tang. Its light, grainy interior is whiter than Parmesan or Asiago. It is packed in large cylinders with a yellow rind. Romano is often substituted for, or combined with, Parmesan in cooking but it is also good eaten with olives, sausages and red wine.

Parmigiano-Reggiano (Parmesan)

Goat's-Milk Cheeses

Because of their increasing popularity, cheeses made from goat's milk deserve a few words of their own. Although goats give less milk than cows, their milk is higher in fat and protein and richer and more concentrated in flavor. Cheeses made with goat's milk have a sharp, tangy flavor. They may range in texture from very soft and fresh to very hard, depending on age.

Chevre (French for "goat") refers to small, soft, creamy cheeses produced in a variety of shapes: cones, disks, pyramids or logs. Chevres are often coated with ash, herbs or seasonings. They are excellent for cooking and complement a wide variety of flavors. Unfortunately, they have a short shelf life, perhaps only two weeks. Cheese labeled *pur chevre* must be made with 100% goat's milk, while others may be a mixture of cow's and goat's milk.

The finest goat's-milk cheeses usually come from France. Preferred brands include Bucheron, exported from France in 5-pound (2-kilo) logs; Chevrotin, one of the mildest; and Montrachet, a tangy soft cheese from the Burgundy wine region. Spurred on by the increased popularity of chevre, a few American producers have developed excellent cheeses in a wide variety of shapes and styles.

Goat's Milk Cheeses

Processed Cheeses

Pasteurized processed cheese is made from a combination of aged and green cheeses that are mixed with emulsifiers and flavorings, pasteurized and poured into molds to solidify. Manufacturers can thus produce cheeses with consistent textures and flavors. Processed cheeses are commonly used in food service operations because they are less expensive than natural cheeses. And, because they will not age or ripen, their shelf life is greatly extended. Nutritionally, processed cheeses generally contain less protein, calcium and vitamin A and more sodium than natural cheeses.

Processed cheese food contains less natural cheese (but at least 51% by weight) and more moisture than regular processed cheese. Often vegetable oils and milk solids are added, making cheese food soft and spreadable.

♦♦♦

AMERICAN CHEESE PRODUCTION

The first cheese factory in the United States was built in 1851 in Oneida County, New York. Herkimer County, which adjoins Oneida County, soon became the center of the American cheese industry and remained so for the next 50 years. During this time, the largest cheese market in the world was at Little Falls, New York, where farm-produced cheeses and cheeses from over 200 factories were sold. At the turn of the century, as New York's population increased, there was a corresponding increase in demand for fluid milk. Because dairymen could receive more money for fluid milk than for cheese, cheese production declined.

While New York still produces some outstanding cheddars, the bulk of the American cheese industry gradually moved westward, eventually settling in Wisconsin's rich farmlands. The United States is now the world's largest manufacturer of cheeses, producing nearly twice as much as its nearest competitor, France.

Imitation cheese is usually manufactured with dairy byproducts and soy products mixed with emulsifiers, colorings and flavoring agents and enzymes. Although considerably less expensive than natural cheese, imitation cheese tends to be dense and rubbery, with little flavor other than that of salt.

Serving Cheeses

Cheeses may be served at any time of day. In Northern Europe they are common for breakfast; in Great Britain they are a staple at lunch. Cheeses are widely used for sandwiches, snacks and cooking in America, and they are often served following the entree or instead of dessert at formal dinners.

The flavor and texture of natural cheeses are best at room temperature. So, except for fresh cheeses, all cheeses should be removed from the refrigerator 30 minutes to an hour before service to allow them to come to room temperature. Fresh cheeses, such as cottage and cream, should be eaten chilled.

Any selection of fine cheeses should include a variety of flavors and textures: from mild to sharp, from soft to creamy to firm. Use a variety of shapes and colors for visual appeal. Do not precut the cheeses as this only causes them to become dry. Provide an adequate supply of serving knives so that stronger-flavored cheeses will not combine with and overpower milder ones. Fine cheeses are best appreciated with plain bread and crackers, as salted or seasoned crackers can mask the cheese's flavor. Noncitrus fruits are also a nice accompaniment.

Storage

Most cheeses are best kept refrigerated, well wrapped to keep odors out and moisture in. Firm and hard cheeses can be kept for several weeks; fresh cheeses will spoil in 7 to 10 days because of their high moisture content. Some cheeses that have become hard or dry may still be grated for cooking or baking. Freezing is possible but not recommended because it changes the cheese's texture, making it mealy or tough.

Cheeseboard Set for Service

◆◆◆

WINE AND CHEESE:
CLASSIC COMBINATIONS

Some cheeses are delicious with beers or ales. Others are best with strong coffee or apple cider, and nothing accompanies a cheddar cheese sandwich as well as ice-cold milk. For most cheeses, however, the ultimate partner is wine. Wine and cheese bring out the best in each other. The proteins and fats in cheeses take the edge off harsh or acidic wines, while the tannins and acids in wines bring out the creamy richness of cheeses.

Because of their natural affinity, certain pairings are universal favorites: Stilton with port, Camembert with Bordeaux, Roquefort with Sauternes and English cheddar with Burgundy. Although taste preferences are an individual matter, cheese–wine marriages follow two schools of thought: Either pair likes or pair opposites.

Pairing like with like is simple: Cheeses are often best served with wines produced in the same region. For example, a white burgundy would be an excellent choice for cheeses from Burgundy such as Montrachet; and goat cheeses from the Rhone Valley go well with wines of that region. Hearty Italian wines such as Chianti, Barolo and Valpolicella are delicious with Italian cheese—gorgonzola, provolone, taleggio. And a dry, aged Monterey Jack is perhaps the perfect mate for California zinfandel.

Opposites do attract, however. Sweet wines such as Sauternes and Gewürztraminer go well with sharp, tangy blues, especially Roquefort. And light, sparkling wines such as Champagne or Spanish Cava are a nice compliment to rich, creamy cheeses like brie and Camembert.

CONCLUSION

Eggs and dairy products are versatile foods used throughout the kitchen. They may be served as is or incorporated into many dishes, including soups, sauces, entrees, breads and desserts. Fine natural cheeses are useful in prepared dishes but are most important for buffets, as the cheese course during a meal or whenever cheese is the primary ingredient or dominant flavor. Eggs and dairy products spoil easily and must be handled and stored properly.

QUESTIONS FOR DISCUSSION

1. Explain the criteria used in grading eggs. Why might you prefer to use eggs with lower grades?
2. What are the differences between egg products and egg substitutes?
3. What is milkfat and how is it used in classifying milk-based products?
4. If a recipe calls for whole milk and you only have dried milk, what do you do? Explain your answer?
5. What is clarified butter and when is it used? Describe the procedure for clarifying butter.
6. The texture and shelf life of cheese depend on what two factors?
7. Cheeses are categorized as fresh, soft, semisoft, firm and hard. Give two examples of each and explain how they are generally used.

PART THREE
COOKING

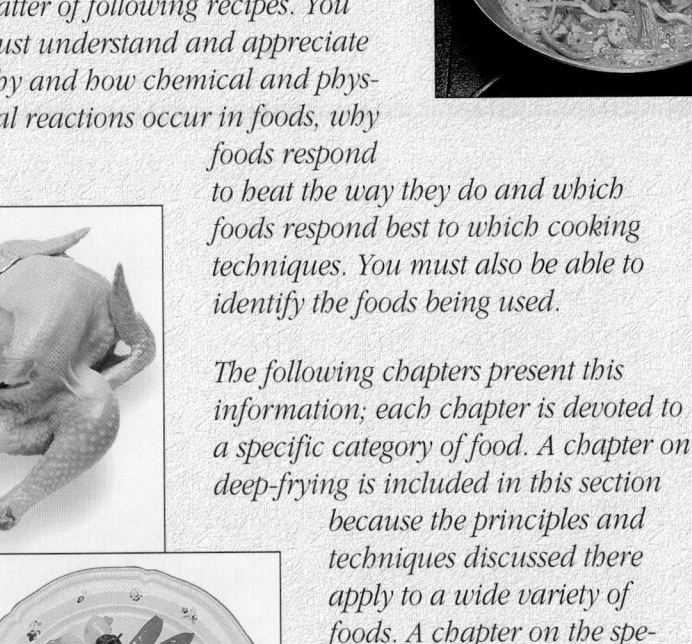

Learning to cook is not simply a matter of following recipes. You must understand and appreciate why and how chemical and physical reactions occur in foods, why foods respond to heat the way they do and which foods respond best to which cooking techniques. You must also be able to identify the foods being used.

The following chapters present this information; each chapter is devoted to a specific category of food. A chapter on deep-frying is included in this section because the principles and techniques discussed there apply to a wide variety of foods. A chapter on the specialized subject of charcuterie is also included, as its study forms part of any well-rounded culinary education.

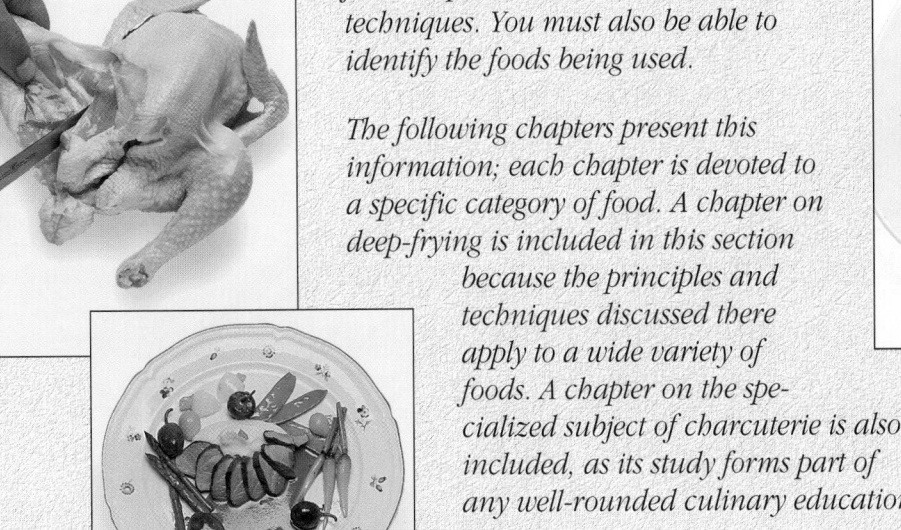

CHAPTER 9
PRINCIPLES OF COOKING

CHAPTER 10
STOCKS AND SAUCES

After studying this chapter you will be able to:

+ prepare a variety of stocks
+ recognize and classify sauces
+ use thickening agents properly
+ prepare a variety of classic and modern sauces

A **stock** *is a flavored liquid; a good stock is the key to a great soup, sauce or braised dish. The French appropriately call a stock* fond *("base"), as stocks are the basis for many classic and modern dishes.*

A **sauce** *is a thickened liquid used to flavor and enhance other foods. A good sauce adds flavor, moisture, richness and visual appeal. A sauce should complement food; it should never disguise it. A sauce can be hot or cold, sweet or savory, smooth or chunky.*

Although the thought of preparing stocks and sauces may be intimidating, the procedures are really quite simple. Carefully follow the basic procedures outlined in this chapter, use high-quality ingredients and, with practice and experience, you will soon be producing fine stocks and sauces.

This chapter addresses hot sauces as well as coulis, salsas and relishes. Cold sauces, generally based on mayonnaise, are discussed in Chapter 24, Salads and Salad Dressings; dessert sauces are discussed in Chapter 31, Custards, Creams, Frozen Desserts and Dessert Sauces.

STOCKS

There are several types of stocks. While they are all made from a combination of bones, vegetables, seasonings and liquids, each type uses specific procedures to give it distinctive characteristics.

A **white stock** is made by simmering chicken, veal or beef bones in water with vegetables and seasonings. The stock remains relatively colorless during the cooking process.

A **brown stock** is made from chicken, veal, beef or game bones and vegetables, all of which are caramelized before being simmered in water with seasonings. The stock has a rich, dark color.

Both a **fish stock** and a **fumet** are made by slowly cooking fish bones or crustacean shells and vegetables without coloring them, then adding water and seasonings and simmering for a short period of time. For a fumet, wine and lemon juice are also added. The resulting stock or fumet is a strongly flavored, relatively colorless liquid.

A **court bouillon** is made by simmering vegetables and seasonings in water and an acidic liquid such as vinegar or wine. It is used to poach fish or vegetables.

Ingredients

The basic ingredients of any stock are bones, a vegetable mixture known as a **mirepoix**, seasonings and water.

Bones

Bones are the most important ingredient for producing a good stock. Bones add flavor, richness and color. Traditionally, the kitchen or butcher shop saved the day's bones to make stock. But because many meats and poultry items are now purchased previously cut or portioned, food service operations often purchase bones specifically for stock making.

Different bones release their flavor at different rates. Even though the bones are cut into 3- to 4-inch (8 to 10 cm) pieces, a stock made entirely of beef and/or veal bones requires 6 to 8 hours of cooking time, while a stock made entirely from chicken bones requires only 5 to 6 hours.

Beef and Veal Bones

The best bones for beef and veal stock are from younger animals. They contain a higher percentage of **cartilage** and other **connective tissue** than do bones from more mature animals. Connective tissue has a high **collagen** content. Through the cooking process, the collagen is converted into **gelatin** and water. The gelatin adds richness and body to the finished stock.

The best beef and veal bones are back, neck and shank bones as they have a high collagen content. Beef and veal bones should be cut with a meat saw into small pieces, approximately 3 to 4 inches (8 to 10 cm) long, so that they can release as much flavor as possible while the stock cooks.

Chicken Bones

The best bones for chicken stock are from the neck and back. If a whole chicken carcass is used, it can be cut up for easier handling.

Fish Bones

The best bones for fish stock are from lean fish such as sole, flounder, whiting or turbot. Bones from fatty fish (e.g., salmon, tuna and swordfish) do not produce good stock because of their high fat content and distinctive flavors. The entire fish carcass can be used, but it should be cut up with a cleaver or heavy knife for easy handling and even extraction of flavors. After cutting, the pieces should be rinsed in cold water to remove blood, loose scales and other impurities.

Other Bones

Lamb, turkey, game and ham bones can also be used for white or brown stocks. While mixing bones is generally acceptable, be careful of blending strongly flavored bones, such as those from lamb or game, with beef, veal or chicken bones. The former's strong flavors may not be appropriate or desirable in the finished product.

Mirepoix

A mirepoix is a mixture of onions, carrots and celery added to a stock to enhance its flavor and aroma. Although chefs differ on the ratio of vegetables, generally a mixture of 50% onions, 25% carrots and 25% celery, by weight, is used. (Unless otherwise noted, any reference to mirepoix in this book refers to this ratio.) For a brown stock, onion skins may be used to add color. It is not necessary to peel the carrots or celery because flavor, not aesthetics, is important.

The size in which the mirepoix is chopped is determined by the stock's cooking time: The shorter the cooking time, the smaller the vegetables must be chopped to ensure that all possible flavor is extracted. For white or brown stocks made from beef or veal bones, the vegetables should be coarsely chopped into large, 1 to 2-inch (2-1/2 to 5-cm) pieces. For chicken and fish stocks, the vegetables should be more finely chopped into 1/2-inch (1-1/4-cm) pieces.

A white mirepoix is made by replacing the carrots in a standard mirepoix with parsnips and adding mushrooms and leeks. Some chefs prefer to use a

Connective tissue—*tissue found throughout an animal's body that binds together and supports other tissues such as muscles.*

Cartilage—*or gristle, a tough, elastic, whitish connective tissue that helps give structure to an animal's body.*

Collagen—*a protein found in nearly all connective tissue; it dissolves when cooked with moisture.*

Gelatin—*a tasteless, odorless and brittle mixture of proteins extracted from boiling bones, connective tissue and other animal parts; when dissolved in a hot liquid and then cooled, it forms a jellylike substance used as a thickener and stabilizer.*

FIGURE 10.1 *Mirepoix Ingredients*

white mirepoix when making a white stock, as it produces a lighter product. Sometimes parsnips, mushrooms and leeks are added to a standard mirepoix for additional flavors.

Seasonings

Principal stock seasonings are peppercorns, bay leaves, thyme, parsley stems, and optionally, garlic. These seasonings generally can be left whole. A stock is cooked long enough for all their flavors to be extracted so there is no reason to chop or grind them. Seasonings generally are added to the stock at the start of cooking. Some chefs do not add seasonings to beef or veal stock until mid-way through the cooking process, however, because of the extended cooking times. Seasonings can be added as a sachet d'épices or a bouquet garni.

Salt, an otherwise important seasoning, is not added to stock. Because a stock has a variety of uses, it is impossible for the chef to know how much salt to add when preparing it. If, for example, the stock was seasoned to taste with salt, the chef could not reduce it later; salt is not lost through reduction and the concentrated product would taste too salty. Similarly, seasoning the stock to taste with salt could prevent the chef from adding other ingredients that are high in salt when finishing a recipe. Unlike many seasonings whose flavors must be incorporated into a product through lengthy cooking periods, salt can be added at any time during the cooking process with the same effect.

Principles of Stock Making

The following principles apply to all stocks. You should follow them in order to achieve the highest-quality stock possible.

A. Start the Stock in Cold Water

The ingredients should always be covered with cold water. When bones are covered with cold water, blood and other impurities dissolve. As the water heats, the impurities coagulate and rise to the surface, where they can be removed easily by skimming. If the bones were covered with hot water, the impurities would coagulate more quickly and remain dispersed in the stock without rising to the top, making the stock cloudy.

If the water level falls below the bones during cooking, add water to cover them. No flavor can be extracted from bones not under water, and bones exposed to the air will darken and discolor a white stock.

B. Simmer the Stock Gently

The stock should be brought to a boil and then reduced to a simmer, a temperature of approximately 185°F (85°C). While simmering, the ingredients release their flavors into the liquid. If kept at a simmer, the liquid will remain clear as it reduces and a stock develops.

Never boil a stock for any length of time. Rapid boiling of a stock, even for a few minutes, causes impurities and fats to blend with the liquid, making it cloudy.

C. Skim the Stock Frequently

A stock should be skimmed often to remove the fat and impurities that rise to the surface during cooking. If they are not removed they may make the stock cloudy.

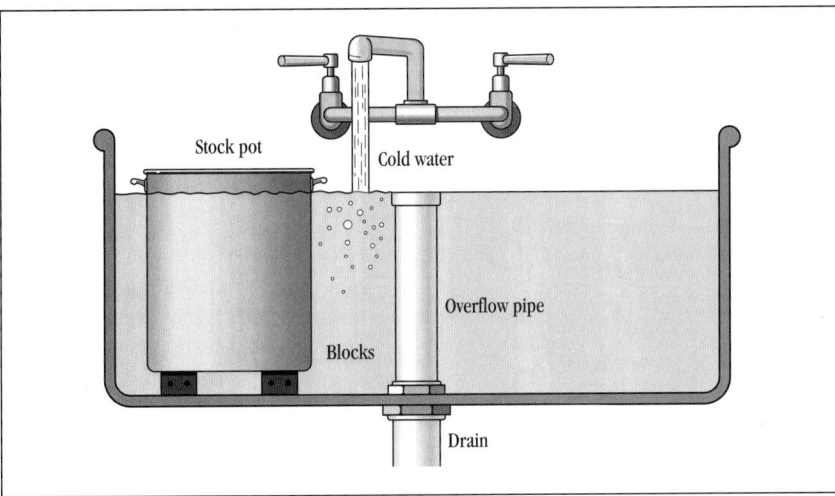

FIGURE 10.2 *Venting a Stockpot*

D. Strain the Stock Carefully

Once a stock finishes cooking, the liquid must be separated from the bones, vegetables and other solid ingredients. In order to keep the liquid clear, it is important not to disturb the solid ingredients when removing the liquid. This is easily accomplished if the stock is cooked in a steam kettle or stockpot with a spigot at the bottom.

If the stock is cooked in a standard stockpot, to strain it:

1. Skim as much fat and as many impurities from the surface as possible before removing the stockpot from the heat.
2. After removing the pot from the heat, carefully ladle the stock from the pot without stirring it.
3. Strain the stock through a china cap lined with several layers of cheesecloth.

E. Cool the Stock Quickly

Most stocks are prepared in large quantities, cooled and held for later use. Great care must be taken when cooling a stock to prevent food-borne illnesses or souring. A stock can be cooled quickly and safely with the following procedure:

1. Keep the stock in a metal container. A plastic container insulates the stock and delays cooling.
2. Vent the stockpot in an empty sink by placing it on blocks or a rack. This allows water to circulate on all sides and below the pot when the sink is filled with water. See Figure 10.2 above.
3. Install an overflow pipe in the drain and fill the sink with cold water or a combination of cold water and ice. Make sure that the weight of the stockpot is adequate to keep it from tipping over.
4. Let cold water run into the sink and drain out the overflow pipe. Stir the stock frequently to facilitate even, quick cooling.

F. Store the Stock Properly

Once the stock is cooled, transfer it to a sanitized covered container (either plastic or metal) and store it in the refrigerator. As the stock chills, fat rises to

Start the stock in cold water.
Simmer the stock gently.
Skim the stock frequently.
Strain the stock carefully.
Cool the stock quickly.
Store the stock properly.
Degrease the stock.

FIGURE 10.3 *Principles of Stock Making*

its surface and solidifies. If left intact, this layer of fat helps preserve the stock. Stocks can be stored for up to one week under refrigeration or frozen for several months.

G. Degrease the Stock

Degreasing a stock is simple: When a stock is refrigerated, fat rises to its surface, hardens and is easily lifted or scraped away before the stock is reheated.

Degrease—*to remove fat from the surface of a liquid such as a stock or sauce by skimming, scraping or lifting congealed fat.*

FIGURE 10.4 *Lifting Fat from the Surface of a Cold Stock.*

White Stock

A white or neutral stock may be made from beef, veal or chicken bones. The finished stock should have a good flavor, good clarity, high gelatin content and little or no color. Veal bones are most often used, but any combination of beef, veal or chicken bones may be used.

Blanching Bones

Chefs disagree on whether the bones for a white stock should be blanched to remove impurities. Some chefs argue that blanching keeps the stock as clear and colorless as possible; others argue that blanching removes flavor.

PROCEDURE FOR BLANCHING BONES

If you choose to blanch the bones:

1. Wash the cut-up bones; place them in a stockpot and cover them with cold water.
2. Bring the water to a boil over high heat.
3. As soon as the water boils, skim the rising impurities. Drain the water from the bones and discard it.
4. Refill the pot with cold water and proceed with the stock recipe.

◆◆◆

RECIPE 10.1

WHITE STOCK

Yield: 2 gal. (8 lt)

Bones: veal, chicken or beef	15 lb.	7 kg
Cold water	3 gal.	11 lt
Mirepoix	2 lb.	1 kg
Sachet:		
Bay leaves	2	2
Dried thyme	1/2 tsp.	2 ml
Peppercorns, crushed	1/2 tsp.	2 ml
Parsley stems	8	8

1. Cut the washed bones into pieces approximately 3–4 inches (8–10 cm) long.
2. Place the bones in a stockpot and cover them with cold water. If blanching, bring the water to a boil, skimming off the scum that rises to the surface. Drain off the water and the impurities. Then add the 3 gallons (11 liters) of cold water and bring to a boil. Reduce to a simmer.
3. If not blanching the bones, bring the cold water to a boil. Reduce to a simmer and skim the scum that forms.

4. Add the mirepoix and sachet to the simmering stock.
5. Continue simmering and skimming the stock for 6–8 hours. (If only chicken bones are used, simmer for 5–6 hours.)
6. Strain, cool and refrigerate.

Brown Stock

A brown stock is made from chicken, veal, beef or game bones. The finished stock should have a good flavor, rich dark brown color, good body and high gelatin content.

The primary differences between a brown stock and a white stock are that for a brown stock, the bones and mirepoix are caramelized before being simmered and a tomato product is added. These extra steps provide the finished stock with a rich dark color and a more intense flavor.

Caramelizing

Caramelization is the process of browning the sugars found on the surface of most foods. This gives the stock its characteristic flavor and color.

PROCEDURE FOR CARAMELIZING BONES

For caramelizing, do not wash or blanch the bones as this retards browning. To caramelize:

1. Place the cut-up bones in a roasting pan one layer deep. It is better to roast several pans of bones than to overfill one pan.
2. Roast the bones for approximately one hour in a hot oven (375°F/190°C). Stirring occasionally, brown the bones thoroughly but do not allow them to burn.
3. Transfer the roasted bones from the pan to the stockpot.

Deglazing the Pan

After the bones are caramelized, the excess fat should be removed and reserved for future use. The caramelized and coagulated proteins remaining in the roasting pan are very flavorful. To utilize them, you **deglaze** the pan.

Deglaze—*to swirl or stir a liquid (usually wine or stock) in a sauté pan or other pan to dissolve cooked food particles remaining on the bottom; the resulting mixture often becomes the base for a sauce.*

PROCEDURE FOR DEGLAZING THE PAN

1. Place the pan on the stove top over medium heat and add enough water to cover the bottom of the pan approximately 1/2 inch (12 mm) deep.
2. Stir and scrape the pan bottom to dissolve and remove all of the caramelized materials while the water heats.
3. Pour the deglazing liquid (also known as the deglazing liquor) over the bones in the stockpot.

PROCEDURE FOR CARAMELIZING MIREPOIX

1. Add a little of the reserved fat from the roasted bones to the roasting pan after it has been deglazed. (Or use a sautoir large enough to contain all of the mirepoix comfortably.)

Remouillage—*(French for "rewetting") a stock produced by reusing the bones left from making another stock. After draining the original stock from the stockpot, add fresh mirepoix, a new sachet and enough water to cover the bones and mirepoix and a second stock can be made. A remouillage is treated like the original stock; allow it to simmer for 4–5 hours before straining. A remouillage will not be as clear or as flavorful as the original stock, however. It is often used to make glazes or in place of water when making stocks.*

2. Sauté the mirepoix, browning all of the vegetables well and evenly without burning them.

3. Add the caramelized mirepoix to the stockpot.

Most any tomato product can be used in a brown stock: fresh tomatoes, canned whole tomatoes, crushed tomatoes, tomato purée or paste. If using a concentrated tomato product such as paste or purée, use approximately half the amount by weight of fresh or canned tomatoes. The tomato product should be added to the stockpot when the mirepoix is added.

◆ ◆ ◆

RECIPE 10.2
BROWN STOCK

Yield: 2 gal. (8 lt)

Bones: veal or beef,		
cut in 3–4 in. (8–10 cm) pieces	15 lb.	7 kg
Cold water	3 gal.	11 lt
Mirepoix	2 lb.	1 kg
Tomato paste	8 oz.	250 g
Sachet:		
Bay leaves	2	2
Dried thyme	1/2 tsp.	2 ml
Peppercorns, crushed	1/2 tsp.	2 ml
Garlic cloves, crushed	3	3
Parsley stems	12	12

1. Place the bones in a roasting pan, one layer deep, and brown in a 375°F (190°C) oven. Turn the bones occasionally to brown them evenly.

2. Remove the bones and place them in a stockpot. Pour off the fat from the roasting pan and reserve it.

3. Deglaze the roasting pan with part of the cold water.

4. Add the deglazing liquor and the rest of the cold water to the bones, covering them completely. Bring to a boil and reduce to a simmer.

5. Add a portion of the reserved fat to the roasting pan and sauté the mirepoix until evenly browned. Then add it to the simmering stock.

Caramelizing the bones.

Deglazing the pan with water.

Caramelizing the mirepoix.

Adding the proper amount of water.

6. Add the tomato paste and sachet to the stock and continue to simmer for 6–8 hours, skimming as necessary.

7. Strain, cool and refrigerate.

Fish Stock and Fish Fumet

A fish stock and fish fumet are similar and can be used interchangeably in most recipes. Both are clear with a pronounced fish flavor and very light body. A fumet, however, is more strongly flavored and aromatic.

The fish bones and crustacean shells used to make a fish stock or fumet should be washed but never blanched because blanching removes too much flavor. Because of the size and structure of fish bones and crustacean shells, stocks and fumets made from them require much less cooking time than even a chicken stock; 30 to 45 minutes is usually sufficient to extract full flavor. Mirepoix or other vegetables should be cut small so that all of their flavors can be extracted during the short cooking time.

The procedure for making a fish stock is very similar to that for making a white stock.

◆◆◆

RECIPE 10.3

FISH STOCK

Yield: 1 gal. (4 lt)

Fish bones or crustacean shells	10 lb.	4.5 kg
Water	5 qts.	5 lt
Mirepoix, small dice	1 lb.	450 g
Mushroom trimmings	8 oz.	250 g
Sachet:		
Bay leaves	2	2
Dried thyme	1/2 tsp.	2 ml
Peppercorns, crushed	1/4 tsp.	1 ml
Parsley stems	8	8

1. Combine all ingredients in a stockpot.

2. Bring to a simmer and skim impurities as necessary.

3. Simmer for 30 to 45 minutes.

4. Strain, cool and refrigerate.

A fish stock is sometimes used to make fish fumet; if so, the resulting product is very strongly flavored. A fish fumet is also flavored with white wine and lemon juice. When making a fumet, **sweat** the bones and vegetables before adding the cooking liquid and seasonings.

♦♦♦

RECIPE 10.4
Fish Fumet

Yield: 2 gal. (8 lt)

Whole butter	2 oz.	60 g
Onion, small dice	1 lb.	500 g
Parsley stems	12	12
Fish bones	10 lb.	5 kg
Dry white wine	1-1/2 pt.	750 ml
Lemon juice	2 oz.	60 g
Cold water or fish stock	7 qt.	7 lt
Mushroom trimmings	2 oz.	60 g
Fresh thyme	1 sprig	1 sprig
Lemon slices	10	10

1. Melt the butter in a stockpot.
2. Add the onion, parsley stems and fish bones. Cover the pot and sweat the bones on low heat.
3. Sprinkle the bones with the white wine and lemon juice.
4. Add the cold water or fish stock, mushroom trimmings, thyme and lemon slices. Bring to a boil, reduce to a simmer and cook approximately 30 minutes, skimming frequently.
5. Strain, cool and refrigerate.

1. Sweating the onions, parsley stems and fish bones.

2. Adding cold water and seasonings.

Vegetable Stock

A good vegetable stock should be clear and light-colored. Because no animal products are used, it has no gelatin content. A vegetable stock can be used instead of a meat-based stock in most recipes. This substitution is useful when preparing vegetarian dishes or as a lighter, more healthful alternative when preparing sauces and soups. Although almost any combination of vegetables can be used for stock making, more variety is not always better. Sometimes a vegetable stock made with one or two vegetables that complement the finished dish particularly well will produce better results than a stock made with many vegetables.

═══════════ ◆◆◆ ═══════════

RECIPE 10.5

VEGETABLE STOCK

Yield: 1 gal. (4 lt)

Vegetable oil	2 oz.	60 g
Mirepoix, small dice	2 lb.	900 g
Leek, whites and greens, chopped	8 oz.	250 g
Garlic cloves, chopped	4	4
Fennel, small dice	4 oz.	120 g
Turnip, diced	2 oz.	60 g
Tomato, diced	2 oz.	60 g
White wine	8 oz.	250 g
Water	1 gal.	4 lt
Sachet:		
Bay leaf	1	1
Dried thyme	1/2 tsp.	2 ml
Peppercorns, crushed	1/4 tsp.	1 ml
Parsley stems	8	8

1. Heat the oil. Add the vegetables and sweat for 10 minutes.
2. Add the white wine, water and sachet.
3. Bring the mixture to a boil, reduce to a simmer and cook for 45 minutes.
4. Strain, cool and refrigerate.

Nutritional values per 4-ounce (120 gram) serving:

Calories	38	Protein	0 g	
Calories from fat	44%	Vitamin A	2044 IU	
Total fat	2 g	Vitamin C	4 mg	
Saturated fat	0 g	Sodium	15 mg	
Cholesterol	0 g			

═══════════ ◆◆◆ ═══════════

COMMERCIAL BASES

Commercially produced flavor (or convenience) bases are widely used in food service operations. They are powdered or dehydrated flavorings added to water to create stocks or, when used in smaller amounts, to enhance the flavor of sauces and soups. Although inferior to well-made stocks, flavor bases do reduce the labor involved in the production of stocks, sauces and soups. Used properly, they also ensure a consistent product. Because bases do not contain gelatin, stocks and sauces made from them do not benefit from reduction.

Bases vary greatly in quality and price. Sodium (salt) is the main ingredient in most bases. Better bases are made primarily of meat, poultry or fish extracts. To judge the quality of a flavor base, prepare it according to package directions and compare the flavor to that of a well-made stock. The flavor base can be improved by adding a mirepoix, standard sachet and a few appropriate bones to the mixture, then simmering for one or two hours. It can then be strained, stored and used like a regular stock.

Although convenience bases are widely used in the industry, it is important to remember that even the best base is a poor substitute for a well-made stock.

Court Bouillon

A court bouillon, while not actually a stock, is prepared in much the same manner as stocks so it is included here. A court bouillon (French for "short broth") is a flavored liquid, usually water and wine or vinegar, in which vegetables and seasonings have been simmered to impart their flavors and aromas.

Court bouillon is most commonly used to poach foods such as fish and shellfish. Recipes vary depending upon the foods to be poached. Although a court bouillon can be made in advance and refrigerated for later use, its simplicity lends itself to fresh preparation whenever needed.

◆◆◆

RECIPE 10.6
COURT BOUILLON

Yield: 1 gal. (4 lt)

Water	1 gal.	4 lt
Vinegar	6 oz.	180 g
Lemon juice	2 oz.	60 g
Salt	2 oz.	60 g
Mirepoix	1 lb. 8 oz.	650 g
Peppercorns, crushed	1 tsp.	5 ml
Bay leaves	4	4
Dried thyme	pinch	pinch
Parsley stems	1 bunch	1 bunch

1. Combine all ingredients and bring to a boil.

2. Reduce to a simmer and cook for 45 minutes.

3. Strain and use immediately or cool and refrigerate.

NOTE: This recipe can be used for poaching almost any fish, but it is particularly well suited to salmon, trout or shellfish. When poaching freshwater fish, replace the water and vinegar with equal parts white wine and water.

Glaze

A glaze is the dramatic reduction and concentration of a stock. One gallon (4 liters) of stock produces only 1–2 cups (2-1/2 to 5 deciliters) of glaze. *Glace de viande* is made from brown stock, reduced until it becomes dark and syrupy. *Glace de volaille* is made from chicken stock and *glace de poisson* from fish stock.

TABLE 10.1   TROUBLESHOOTING CHART FOR STOCKS

Problem	Reason	Solution
Cloudy	Impurities	Start stock in cold water
	Stock boiled during cooking	Strain through layers of cheesecloth
Lack of flavor	Not cooked long enough	Increase cooking time
	Inadequate seasoning	Add more flavoring ingredients
	Improper ratio of bones to water	Add more bones
Lack of color	Improperly caramelized bones and mirepoix	Caramelize bones and mirepoix until darker
	Not cooked long enough	Cook longer
Lack of body	Wrong bones used	Use bones with a higher content of connective tissue
	Insufficient reduction	Cook longer
	Improper ratio of bones to water	Add more bones
Too salty	Commercial base used	Change base or make own stock; do not salt stock
	Salt added during cooking	

Glazes are added to soups or sauces to increase and intensify flavors. They are also used as a source of intense flavoring for several of the small sauces discussed below.

PROCEDURE FOR REDUCING A STOCK TO A GLAZE

1. Simmer the stock over very low heat. Be careful not to let it burn and skim it often.
2. As it reduces and the volume decreases, transfer the liquid into progressively smaller saucepans. Strain the liquid each time it is transferred into a smaller saucepan.
3. Strain it a final time, cool and refrigerate. A properly made glaze will keep for several months under refrigeration.

SAUCES

With a few exceptions, a sauce is a liquid plus thickening agent plus seasonings. Any chef can produce fine sauces by learning to:

1. Make good stocks;
2. Use thickening agents properly to achieve the desired texture, flavor and appearance; and
3. Use seasonings properly to achieve the desired flavors.

Classic hot sauces are divided into two groups: **mother** or **leading sauces** (Fr. *sauce mère*) and **small** or **compound sauces**. The five classic mother sauces are béchamel, velouté, espagnole (brown), tomato and hollandaise. Except for hollandaise, leading sauces are rarely served as is; more often they are used to create the many small sauces.

Not all sauces fall into the traditional classifications, however. Some sauces use purées of fruits or vegetables as their base; they are known as **coulis**. Others, such as **beurre blanc** (French for "white butter") and **beurre rouge** ("red butter"), are based on an acidic reduction in which whole butter is incorporated. **Flavored butters**, **salsas**, **relishes** and **pan gravy** are also used as sauces in modern food service operations.

Thickening Agents

Although there are exceptions, most sauces are thickened by the gelatinization of starches. As discussed in Chapter 9, Principles of Cooking, gelatinization is the process by which starch granules absorb moisture when placed in a liquid and heated. As the moisture is absorbed, the product thickens. Starches generally used to thicken sauces are flour, cornstarch and arrowroot. Gelatinization may sound easy, but it takes practice to produce a good sauce that

+ is lump-free,
+ has a good clean flavor that is not pasty or floury,
+ has a consistency that will coat the back of a spoon (the French call this *nappé*), and
+ will not separate or break when the sauce is held or reduced.

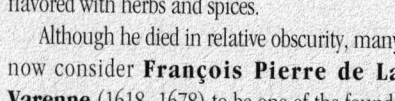

A SAUCY HISTORY

The word "sauce" is derived from the Latin word *salus*, meaning "salted." This derivation is appropriate. For millennia, salt has been the basic condiment for enhancing and/or disguising the flavor of many foods. Over the centuries, sauces have also been used for these purposes.

Cooks of ancient Rome flavored many dishes with *garum*, a golden-colored sauce made from fermented fish entrails combined with brine, condiments, water and wine or vinegar. They also used a sauce referred to as a "single" made from oil, wine and brine. When boiled with herbs and saffron it became a "double" sauce. To this the Byzantines later added pepper, cloves, cinnamon, cardamom and coriander or spikenard (a fragrant ointment made from grains).

During the Middle Ages chefs (and their employers) were fond of either very spicy or sweet-and-sour sauces. A typical sauce for roasted meat consisted of powdered cinnamon, mustard, red wine and a sweetener such as honey. It was thickened, if at all, with bits of stale or grilled bread. Other sauces were based on verjuice, an acidic stock prepared from the juice of unripe gapes. To it were added other fruit juices, honey, flower petals and herbs or spices. Indeed, most medieval sauces were heavily spiced. Perhaps this was done to showcase the host's wealth, perhaps to hide the taste of salt-cured or less-than-fresh meats.

Guillaume Tirel (c. 1312–1395), who called himself **Taillevent**, was the master chef for Charles V of France. Around 1375 Taillevent wrote *Le Viandier*, the oldest-known French cookbook. The cooking style he describes relies heavily on pounding, puréeing and spicing most foods so that the finished dish bears little resemblance in shape, texture or taste to the original ingredients. Included in his methods

for what can only be described as ways of masking poor-quality ingredients are 17 sauces. Among them is a recipe for a *cameline* sauce. It is made from grilled bread soaked in wine; the wine-soaked bread is then drained, squeeze-dried and ground with cinnamon, ginger, pepper, cloves and nutmeg; this mixture is then diluted with vinegar. There is also a recipe for a sauce called *taillemaslée*, made of fried onions, verjuice, vinegar and mustard. (Appropriately, on his grave marker Taillevent is dressed as a sergeant-at-arms whose shield is decorated with three cooking pots.)

Recipes for some sauces of the Renaissance, such as *poivrade* or *Robert*, are recognizable today. Most sauces enjoyed in Renaissance-era Italy and France consisted of some combination of concentrated cooking juices, wines, herbs and spices (especially pepper), sometimes thickened with bread. Sweet, fruit-based sauces were also popular. Most importantly for the development of modern cuisine, however, was the growing use of sauces based on broths

thickened with cream, butter and egg yolks and flavored with herbs and spices.

Although he died in relative obscurity, many now consider **François Pierre de La Varenne** (1618–1678) to be one of the founding fathers of French cuisine. His treatises, especially *Le Cuisinier français* (1651), detail the early development, methods and manners of French cuisine. His analysis and recipes mark a departure from medieval cookery and a French cuisine heavily influenced by Italian traditions. His writings were uniquely modern in that he included recipes for new foods (especially fruits and vegetables native to the Americas or the Far East) and for indigenous foods (such as saltwater fish) that were gradually becoming more popular. La Varenne is credited with introducing roux as a thickening agent for sauces, especially velouté sauces. He emphasized the importance of properly prepared *fonds* and the reduction of cooking juices to concentrate flavors. He also popularized the use of bouquets garni to flavor stocks and sauces.

Sometime during the early 18th century, the chef to the French Duc de Levis-Mirepoix pioneered the use of onions, celery and carrots to enhance the flavor and aroma of stocks. The mixture, named for the chef's employer, soon became the standard way of enriching stocks. An enriched stock greatly improves the quality of the sauces derived from it.

During the early 19th century, **Antonin Carême** developed the modern system for classifying hundreds of sauces. It is unknown how many sauces Carême actually invented himself, but he wrote treatises containing the theories and recipes for many of the sauces still used today. Carême's extravagant lists of sauces were reduced and simplified by chefs later in the 19th century, most notably by **Auguste Escoffier**.

Roux

Roux is the principal means used to thicken sauces. It is a combination of equal parts, by weight, of flour and fat, cooked together to form a paste. Cooking the flour in fat coats the starch granules with the fat and prevents them from lumping together or forming lumps when introduced into a liquid.

In large production kitchens, large amounts of roux are prepared and held for use as needed. Smaller operations may make roux as required for each recipe.

There are three types of roux:

1. **White roux**—It is cooked only briefly and should be removed from the heat as soon as it develops a frothy, bubbly appearance. It is used in white sauces, such as béchamel, or in dishes where little or no color is desired.

2. **Blond roux**—Cooked slightly longer than white roux, blond roux should begin to take on a little color as the flour caramelizes. It is used in ivory-colored sauces, such as velouté, or where a richer flavor is desired.

3. **Brown roux**—It is cooked until it develops a darker color and a nutty aroma and flavor. Brown roux is used in brown sauces and dishes where a dark color is desired. It is important to remember that cooking a starch before adding a liquid breaks down the starch granules and prevents gelatinization from occurring. Therefore, because brown roux is cooked longer than white roux, more brown roux is required to thicken a given quantity of liquid.

FIGURE 10.5 *White, Blond and Brown Roux*

PROCEDURE FOR MAKING ROUX

Whether it will be white, blond or brown, the procedure for making roux is the same:

1. Using a heavy saucepan to prevent scorching, heat the clarified butter or other fat.

2. Add all of the flour and stir to form a paste. Although all-purpose flour can be used, it is better to use cake or pastry flour because they contain a higher percentage of starch. Do not use high gluten flour because of its greatly reduced starch content. (Flours are discussed in Chapter 26, Principles of the Bakeshop.)

3. Cook the paste over medium heat until the desired color is achieved. Stir the roux often to avoid burning. Burnt roux will not thicken a liquid; it will simply add dark specks and an undesirable flavor.

Cooking the roux.

The temperature and amount of roux being prepared determine the exact length of cooking time. Generally, however, a white roux needs to cook for only a few minutes, long enough to minimize the raw flour taste. Blond roux is cooked longer, until the paste begins to change to a slightly darker color. Brown roux requires a much longer cooking time to develop its characteristic color and aroma. A good roux will be stiff, not runny or pourable.

(a)

Cold stock

Hot roux

TABLE 10.2			PROPORTIONS OF ROUX TO LIQUID					
Flour	+	Butter	=	Roux	+	Liquid	=	Sauce
6 oz./190 g	+	6 oz./190 g	=	12 oz./375 g	+	1 gal./4 lt	=	light
8 oz./250 g	+	8 oz./250g	=	1 lb./500 g	+	1 gal./4 lt	=	medium
12 oz./375 g	+	12 oz./375 g	=	24 oz./750 g	+	1 gal./4 lt	=	heavy

VARIABLES: The starch content of a flour determines its thickening power. Cake flour, being lowest in protein and highest in starch, has more thickening power than bread flour, which is high in protein and low in starch. In addition, a dark roux has less thickening power than a lighter one, so more will be needed to thicken an equal amount of liquid.

(b)

Hot stock

Cold roux

When thickening stock with roux, either:
a) add cold stock to hot roux
b) add cold roux to hot stock

INCORPORATING ROUX INTO A LIQUID

There are two ways to incorporate roux into a liquid without causing lumps:

1. Cold stock can be added to the hot roux while stirring vigorously with a whisk.
2. Room-temperature roux can be added to a hot stock while stirring vigorously with a whisk.

When the roux and the liquid are completely incorporated and the sauce begins to boil, it is necessary to cook the sauce for a period of time to remove any raw flour taste that may remain. Most chefs feel a minimum of 20 minutes is necessary.

GUIDELINES FOR USING ROUX

1. Avoid using aluminum pots. The scraping action of the whisk will turn light sauces gray and will impart a metallic flavor.
2. Use sufficiently heavy pots to prevent sauces from scorching or burning during extended cooking times.
3. Avoid extreme temperatures. Roux should be no colder than room temperature so that the fat is not fully solidified. Extremely hot roux is dangerous and can spatter when combined with a liquid. Stocks should not be ice cold when combined with roux; the roux will become very cold and the solidified pieces may be very difficult to work out with a whisk.
4. Avoid overthickening. Roux does not begin to thicken a sauce until the sauce is almost at the boiling point; the thickening action continues for several minutes while the sauce simmers. If a sauce is to cook for a long time, it will also be thickened by reduction.

Cornstarch

Cornstarch, a very fine white powder, is a pure starch derived from corn. It is used widely as a thickening agent for hot and cold sauces and is especially popular in Asian cuisines for thickening sauces and soups. Liquids thickened with cornstarch have a glossy sheen that may or may not be desirable.

One unit of cornstarch thickens about twice as much liquid as an equal unit of flour. Sauces thickened with cornstarch are less stable than those thickened with roux because cornstarch can break down and lose its thickening power after prolonged heating. Products thickened with cornstarch should not be reheated.

Incorporating Cornstarch

Cornstarch must be mixed with a cool liquid before it is introduced into a hot one. The cool liquid separates the grains of starch and allows them to begin absorbing liquid without lumping. A solution of starch and cool liquid is called a **slurry**.

The starch slurry may be added to either a hot or cold liquid. If added to a hot liquid, it must be stirred continuously during incorporation. As opposed to a roux, the gelatinization of cornstarch begins almost immediately. Sauces thickened with cornstarch must be cooked gently until the raw starch flavor disappears, usually about five minutes.

Arrowroot

Arrowroot, derived from the roots of several tropical plants, is similar in texture, appearance and thickening power to cornstarch and is used in exactly the same manner. Although it is much more expensive, arrowroot does not break down as quickly as cornstarch and it produces a slightly clearer finished product.

Beurre Manié

Beurre manié is a combination of equal amounts, by weight, of flour and soft whole butter. The flour and butter are kneaded together until smooth. The mixture is then formed into pea-sized balls and whisked into a simmering sauce. Beurre manié is used for quick thickening at the end of the cooking process. The butter also adds shine and flavor to the sauce as it melts.

Liaison

Unlike the thickeners described above, a liaison does not thicken a sauce through gelatinization. A liaison is a mixture of egg yolks and heavy cream, which adds richness and smoothness with minimal thickening. Special care must be taken to prevent the yolks from coagulating when they are added to a hot liquid because this could curdle the sauce .

1. Adding hot liquid to the egg yolks and cream mixture.

PROCEDURE FOR USING A LIAISON

1. Whisk together one part egg yolk and three parts whipping cream. Combining the yolk with cream raises the temperature at which the yolk's proteins coagulate, making it easier to incorporate them into a sauce without lumping or curdling.
2. **Temper** the egg yolk mixture by slowly adding a small amount of the hot liquid while stirring continuously.
3. When enough of the hot liquid has been added to the egg yolk mixture to warm it thoroughly, begin adding the warmed egg yolk mixture to the remaining hot liquid. Be sure to stir the mixture carefully to prevent the yolk from overcooking or lumping. Plain egg yolks coagulate at temperatures between 149 and 158°F (65–70°C). Mixing them with cream raises the temperatures at which they coagulate to approximately 180–185°F (82–85°C). Temperatures over 185°F (85°C) will cause the yolks to curdle. Great care must be taken to hold the sauce above 140°F (60°C) for food safety and sanitation reasons, yet below 185°F (85°C) to prevent curdling.

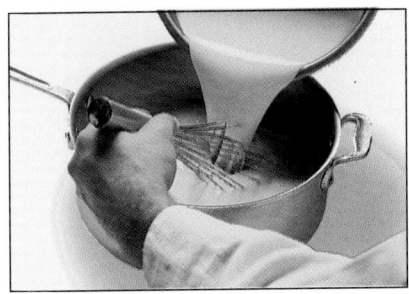

2. Adding the tempered egg yolks and cream mixture to the hot liquid.

Tempering—*gradually raising the temperature of a cold liquid by slowly stirring in a hot liquid.*

Finishing Techniques

Reduction

As sauces cook, moisture is released in the form of steam. As steam escapes, the remaining ingredients concentrate, thickening the sauce and strengthening the flavors. This process, known as **reduction**, is commonly used to thicken sauces because no starches or other flavor-altering ingredients are needed. Sauces are often finished by allowing them to reduce until the desired consistency is reached.

Straining

Smoothness is important to the success of most sauces. They can be strained through either a china cap lined with several layers of cheesecloth or a fine mesh chinois. As discussed below, often vegetables, herbs, spices and other seasonings are added to a sauce for flavor. Straining removes these ingredients as well as any lumps of roux or thickener remaining in the sauce after the desired flavor and consistency have been reached.

Monter au Beurre

Monter au beurre is the process of swirling or whisking whole butter into a sauce to give it shine, flavor and richness. Compound or flavored butters, discussed below, can be used in place of whole butter to add specific flavors. Monter au beurre is widely used to enrich and finish small sauces.

Sauce Families

Leading or mother sauces are the foundation for the entire classic repertoire of hot sauces. The five leading sauces—béchamel, velouté, espagnole (also known as brown), tomato and hollandiase—can be seasoned and garnished to create a wide variety of small or compound sauces. The five leading sauces are distinguished principally by the liquids and thickeners used to create them.

Small or **compound sauces** are grouped together into families based on their leading or mother sauce. Some small sauces have a variety of uses; others are traditional accompaniments for specific foods. A small sauce may be named for its ingredients, place of origin or creator. Although there are numerous classic small sauces, we have included only a few of the more popular ones following each of the leading sauce recipes.

TABLE 10.3	SAUCE FAMILIES	
Liquid	Thickener	Mother Sauce
Milk	Roux	Béchamel
White stock	Roux	Velouté
veal stock		Veal Velouté
chicken stock		Chicken Velouté
fish stock		Fish Velouté
Brown stock	Roux	Espagnole (Brown Sauce)
Tomato	Roux optional	Tomato sauce
Butter	Egg yolks	Hollandaise

The Béchamel Family

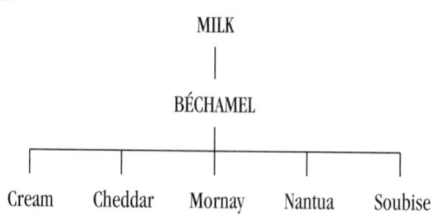

Named for its creator, Louis de Béchameil (1630–1703), steward to Louis XIV of

France, béchamel sauce is the easiest mother sauce to prepare. Traditionally it is made by adding heavy cream to a thick veal velouté. Although some chefs still believe a béchamel should contain veal stock, today the sauce is almost always made by thickening scalded milk with a white roux and adding seasonings. Often used for vegetable, egg and gratin dishes, béchamel has fallen into relative disfavor recently because of its rich, heavy nature. It is nevertheless important to understand its production and its place in traditional sauce making.

A properly made béchamel is rich, creamy and absolutely smooth with no hint of graininess. The flavors of the onion and clove used to season it should be apparent but not overwhelm the sauce's clean, milky taste. The sauce should be the color of heavy cream and have a deep luster. It should be thick enough to coat foods lightly but should not taste like the roux used to thicken it.

◆◆◆

RECIPE 10.7
BÉCHAMEL

Yield: 1 gal. (4 lt)

Onion piquet	1	1
Milk	1 gal.	4 lt
Flour	8 oz.	250 g
Clarified butter	8 oz.	250 g
Salt and white pepper	TT	TT
Nutmeg	TT	TT

1. Add the onion piquet to the milk in a heavy saucepan and simmer for 20 minutes.

2. In a separate pot, make a white roux with the flour and butter.

3. Remove the onion piquet from the milk. Gradually add the hot milk to the roux while stirring constantly with a whisk to prevent lumps. Bring to a boil.

4. Reduce the sauce to a simmer, add the seasonings and continue cooking for 30 minutes.

5. Strain the sauce through a china cap lined with cheesecloth. Melted butter can be carefully ladled over the surface of the sauce to prevent a skin from forming. Hold for service or cool in a water bath.

Small Béchamel Sauces

With a good béchamel, producing the small sauces in its family is quite simple. The quantities indicated below are for 1 quart (1 liter) of béchamel. The final step for each recipe is to season to taste with salt and pepper.

Cream Sauce   Add to béchamel 8–12 ounces (250–360 grams) scalded cream and a few drops of lemon juice.

Cheddar   Add to béchamel 8 ounces (250 grams) grated cheddar cheese, a dash of Worcestershire sauce and 1 tablespoon (15 milliliters) dry mustard.

Mornay   Add to béchamel 4 ounces (120 grams) grated Gruyère cheese and 1 ounce (30 grams) grated parmesan cheese. Thin as desired with scalded cream. Remove the sauce from the heat and swirl in 2 ounces (60 grams) whole butter.

Nantua   Add to béchamel 4 ounces (120 grams) heavy cream and 6 ounces (180 grams) crayfish butter (page 218). Add paprika to achieve the desired color. Garnish the finished sauce with diced crayfish meat.

Soubise (modern)   Sweat 1 pound (500 grams) diced onion in 1 ounce (30 grams) butter without browning. Add béchamel and simmer until the onions are fully cooked. Strain through a fine chinois.

The Velouté Family

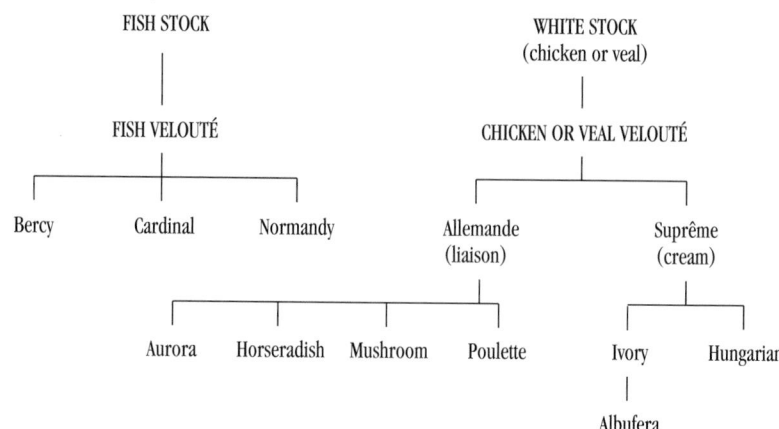

Velouté sauces are made by thickening a white stock or fish stock with roux. The white stock can be made from veal or chicken bones. A fish velouté sauce, made from fish stock, is used to create a few small sauces. A velouté sauce made from veal or chicken stock is usually used to make one of two intermediary sauces—allemande and suprême—from which many small sauces are derived. Allemande sauce is made by adding lemon juice and a liaison to either the veal or chicken velouté. (The stock used depends upon the dish with which the sauce will be served.) Suprême sauce is made by adding cream to a chicken velouté.

A properly made velouté should be rich, smooth and lump-free. If made from chicken or fish stock, it should taste of chicken or fish. A velouté made from veal stock should have a more neutral flavor. The sauce should be ivory-colored, with a deep luster. It should be thick enough to cling to foods without tasting like the roux used to thicken it.

═══════════════ ◆◆◆ ═══════════════

RECIPE 10.8
VELOUTÉ

Yield: 1 gal. (4 lt)

Clarified butter	8 oz.	250 g
Flour	8 oz.	250 g
Chicken, veal or fish stock	5 qt.	5 lt
Salt and white pepper	TT	TT

1. Melt the butter in a heavy saucepan. Add the flour and cook to make a blond roux.

2. Gradually add the stock to the roux, stirring constantly with a whisk to prevent lumps. Bring to a boil and reduce to a simmer. (Seasonings are optional; their use depends upon the seasonings in the stock and the sauce's intended use.)

3. Simmer and reduce to 1 gallon (4 liters), approximately 30 minutes.

4. Strain through a china cap lined with cheesecloth.

5. Melted butter may be carefully ladled over the surface of the sauce to prevent a skin from forming. Hold for service or cool in a water bath.

TABLE 10.4   VELOUTÉ SAUCES

Fish stock	+	Roux	=	Velouté			
Chicken stock	+	Roux	=	Velouté	+	Cream	= Suprême
Chicken stock	+	Roux	=	Velouté	+	Liaison and lemon	= Allemande
Veal stock	+	Roux	=	Velouté	+	Liaison and lemon	= Allemande

Small Fish Velouté Sauces

A few small sauces can be made from fish velouté. The quantities given are for 1 quart (1 liter) fish velouté sauce. The final step for each recipe is to season to taste with salt and pepper.

Bercy   Sauté 2 ounces (60 grams) finely diced shallots in butter. Then add 8 ounces (250 grams) dry white wine and 8 ounces (250 grams) fish stock. Reduce this mixture by one third and add the fish velouté. Finish with butter and garnish with chopped parsley.

Cardinal   Add 8 ounces (250 grams) fish stock to 1 quart (1 liter) fish velouté. Reduce this mixture by half and add 1 pint (500 milliliters) heavy cream and a dash of cayenne pepper. Bring to a boil and swirl in 1-1/2 ounces (45 grams) lobster butter (page 218). Garnish with chopped lobster coral at service time.

Normandy   Add 4 ounces (120 grams) mushroom trimmings and 4 ounces (120 milliliters) fish stock to 1 quart (1 liter) fish velouté. Reduce by one third and finish with an egg yolk and cream liaison. Strain through a fine chinois.

RECIPE 10.9

ALLEMANDE SAUCE

Yield: 1 gal. (4 lt)

Veal or chicken velouté sauce	1 gal.	4 lt
Egg yolks	8	8
Heavy cream	24 oz.	675 g
Lemon juice	1 oz.	30 g
Salt and white pepper	TT	TT

1. Bring the velouté to a simmer.

2. In a stainless steel bowl, whip the egg yolks with the cream to create a liaison. Ladle approximately one third of the hot velouté sauce into this mixture, while whisking, to temper the yolk and cream mixture.

3. When one third of the velouté has been incorporated into the now-warmed yolk and cream mixture, gradually add the liaison to the remaining velouté sauce while whisking continuously.

4. Reheat the sauce. Do not let it boil.

5. Add the lemon juice, salt and white pepper to taste.

6. Strain through a china cap lined with cheesecloth.

Small Allemande Sauces

Several small sauces are easily produced from an allemande sauce made with either a chicken or veal velouté. The quantities given are for 1 quart (1 liter) allemande. The final step for each recipe is to season to taste with salt and pepper.

Aurora Add to allemande 2 ounces (60 grams) tomato paste and finish with 1 ounce (30 grams) butter.

Horseradish Add to allemande 4 ounces (120 grams) heavy cream and 1 teaspoon (5 milliliters) dry mustard. Just before service add 2 ounces (60 grams) freshly grated horseradish. The horseradish should not be cooked with the sauce.

Mushroom Sauté 4 ounces (120 grams) sliced mushrooms in 1/2 ounce (15 grams) butter; add 2 teaspoons (10 milliliters) lemon juice. Then add the allemande to the mushrooms. Do not strain.

Poulette Sauté 8 ounces (250 grams) sliced mushrooms and 1/2 ounce (15 grams) diced shallots in 1 ounce (30 grams) butter. Add to the allemande; then add 2 ounces (60 grams) cream. Finish with lemon juice and 1 tablespoon (15 milliliters) chopped parsley.

◆◆◆

RECIPE 10.10

SUPRÊME SAUCE

Yield: 1 gal. (4 lt)

Chicken velouté sauce	1 gal.	4 lt
Mushroom trimmings	8 oz.	225 g
Heavy cream	1 qt.	1 lt
Salt and white pepper	TT	TT

1. Simmer the velouté sauce with the mushroom trimmings until reduced by one fourth.
2. Gradually whisk in the heavy cream and return to a simmer.
3. Adjust the seasonings.
4. Strain through a china cap lined with cheesecloth.

Small Suprême Sauces

The following small sauces are easily made from suprême sauce. The quantities given are for 1 quart (1 liter) suprême sauce. The final step for each recipe is to season to taste with salt and pepper.

Albufera Add to suprême 3 ounces (90 grams) glace de volaille and 2 ounces (60 grams) red pepper butter (page 219).

Hungarian Sweat 2 ounces (60 grams) diced onion in 1 tablespoon (15 milliliters) butter. Add 1 tablespoon (15 milliliters) paprika. Stir in the suprême sauce. Cook for 2–3 minutes, strain and finish with butter.

Ivory Add to suprême 3 ounces (90 grams) glace de volaille.

The Espagnole (Brown Sauce) Family

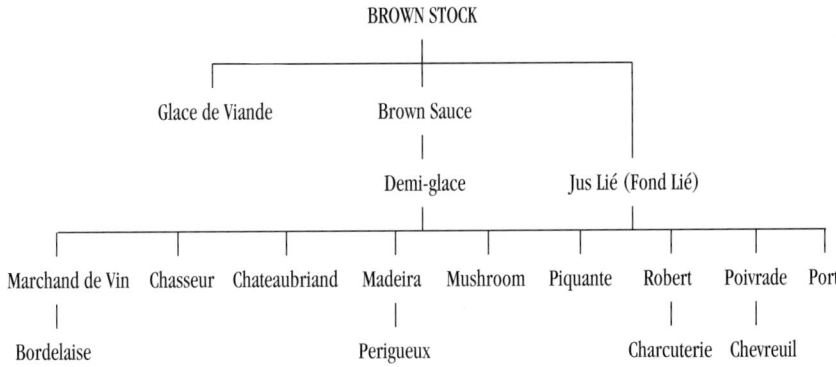

The mother sauce of the espagnole or brown sauce family is full-bodied and rich. It is made from brown stock to which brown roux, mirepoix and tomato purée are added. Most often this sauce is used to produce demi-glace. Brown stock is also used to make jus lié. Demi-glace and jus lié are usually used to create the small sauces of the espagnole family.

◆◆◆

RECIPE 10.11

ESPAGNOLE
(BROWN SAUCE)

Yield: 1 gal. (4 lt)

Mirepoix, medium dice	2 lb.	1 kg
Clarified butter	8 oz.	250 g
Flour	8 oz.	250 g
Brown stock	5 qt.	5 lt
Tomato purée	8 oz.	250 g
Sachet:		
Bay leaf	1	1
Dried thyme	1/2 tsp.	2 ml
Peppercorns, crushed	1/4 tsp.	1 ml
Parsley stems	8	8
Salt and pepper	TT	TT

1. Sauté the mirepoix in butter until well caramelized.
2. Add the flour and cook to make a brown roux.
3. Add the brown stock and tomato purée. Stir to break up any lumps of roux. Bring to a boil; reduce to a simmer.
4. Add the sachet.
5. Simmer for approximately 1-1/2 hours, allowing the sauce to reduce. Skim the surface as needed to remove impurities.
6. Strain the sauce through a china cap lined with several layers of cheesecloth. Adjust seasonings and cool in a water bath or hold for service.

Demi-Glace

Brown stock is used to make the espagnole or brown sauce described above. Espagnole sauce can then be made into demi-glace, which in turn is used to make the small sauces of the espagnole family. Demi-glace is half brown sauce, half brown stock, reduced by half. It is usually finished with a small amount of madeira or sherry wine. Because demi-glace creates a richer, more flavorful base, it produces finer small sauces than those made directly from a brown sauce.

A properly made demi-glace is rich, smooth and lump-free. Its prominent roasted flavor comes from the bones used for the brown stock. There should be no taste of roux. The caramelized bones and mirepoix as well as the tomato product contribute to its glossy dark brown, almost chocolate, color. It should be thick enough to cling to food without being pasty or heavy.

◆◆◆

RECIPE 10.12
DEMI-GLACE

Yield: 1 qt. (1 lt)

Brown stock	1 qt.	1 lt
Brown sauce	1 qt.	1 lt

1. Combine the stock and sauce in a saucepan over medium heat.
2. Simmer until the mixture is reduced by half (i.e., a yield of 1 quart or 1 liter).
3. Strain and cool in a water bath.

Jus Lié

Jus lié, also known as fond lié, is used like a demi-glace, especially to produce small sauces. Jus lié is lighter and easier to make than a demi-glace, however. It is made in one of two ways:

1. A rich brown stock is thickened with cornstarch or arrowroot and seasoned, or
2. A rich brown stock is simmered and reduced so that it thickens naturally due to concentrated amounts of gelatin and other proteins.

The starch-thickened method is a quick alternative to the long-simmering demi-glace. But because it is simply a brown stock thickened with cornstarch or arrowroot, it will only be as good as the stock with which it was begun. Sauces made from reduced stock usually have a better flavor but can be expensive to produce because of high food costs and lengthy reduction time.

A properly made jus lié is very rich and smooth. It shares many flavor characteristics with demi-glace. Its color should be dark brown and glossy from the concentrated gelatin content. Its consistency is somewhat lighter than demi-glace, but it should still cling lightly to foods.

Small Brown Sauces

Demi-glace and jus lié are used to produce many small sauces. The quantities given are for 1 quart (1 liter) demi-glace or jus lié. The final step for each recipe is to season to taste with salt and pepper.

Bordelaise Combine 1 pint (250 milliliters) dry red wine, 2 ounces (60 grams) chopped shallots, 1 bay leaf, 1 sprig thyme and a pinch of black pepper in a saucepan. Reduce by three fourths, then add demi-glace and simmer for 15 minutes. Strain through a fine chinois. Finish with 2 ounces (60 grams) whole butter and garnish with sliced, poached beef marrow.

Chasseur (Hunter's Sauce)   Sauté 4 ounces (120 grams) sliced mushrooms and 1 tablespoon (15 milliliters) diced shallots in butter. Add 8 ounces (250 grams) white wine and reduce by three fourths. Then add demi-glace and 6 ounces (170 grams) diced tomatoes; simmer for 5 minutes. Do not strain. Garnish with chopped parsley.

Chateaubriand   Combine 1 pint (500 milliliters) dry white wine and 2 ounces (60 grams) diced shallots. Reduce the mixture by two thirds. Add demi-glace and reduce by half. Season to taste with lemon juice and cayenne pepper. Do not strain. Swirl in 4 ounces (120 grams) butter to finish and garnish with chopped fresh tarragon.

Chevreuil   Prepare a poivrade sauce but add 6 ounces (170 grams) bacon or game trimmings to the mirepoix. Finish with 4 ounces (120 grams) red wine and a dash of cayenne pepper.

Madeira or Port   Bring demi-glace to a boil, reduce slightly. Then add 4 ounces (120 milliliters) madeira wine or ruby red port.

Marchand de Vin   Reduce 8 ounces (250 milliliters) dry red wine and 2 ounces (60 grams) diced shallots by two thirds. Then add demi-glace, simmer and strain.

Mushroom   Blanch 8 ounces (250 grams) mushroom caps in 8 ounces (250 milliliters) boiling water seasoned with salt and lemon juice. Drain the mushrooms, saving the liquid. Reduce this liquid to 2 tablespoons (30 milliliters) and add it to the demi-glace. Just before service stir in 2 ounces (60 grams) butter and the mushroom caps.

Périgueux   Add finely diced truffles to madeira sauce. *Périgourdine* sauce is the same, except that the truffles are cut into relatively thick slices.

Piquant   Combine 1 ounce (30 grams) shallots, 4 ounces (120 grams) white wine and 4 ounces (120 grams) white wine vinegar. Reduce the mixture by two thirds. Then add demi-glace and simmer for 10 minutes. Add 2 ounces (60 grams) diced cornichons, 1 tablespoon (15 milliliters) fresh tarragon, 1 tablespoon (15 milliliters) fresh parsley and 1 tablespoon (15 milliliters) fresh chervil. Do not strain.

Poivrade   Sweat 12 ounces (340 grams) mirepoix in 2 tablespoons (30 milliliters) oil. Add 1 bay leaf, a sprig of thyme and 4 parsley stems. Then add 1 pint (500 milliliters) vinegar and 4 ounces (120 milliliters) white wine. Reduce by half, add demi-glace and simmer for 40 minutes. Then add 20 crushed peppercorns and simmer for 5 more minutes. Strain through a fine chinois and finish with up to 2 ounces (60 grams) butter.

Robert   Sauté 8 ounces (250 grams) chopped onion in 1 ounce (30 grams) butter. Add 8 ounces (250 milliliters) dry white wine and reduce by two thirds. Add demi-glace and simmer for 10 minutes. Strain and then add 2 teaspoons (10 milliliters) prepared Dijon mustard and 1 tablespoon (15 milliliters) sugar. If the finished Robert sauce is garnished with sliced sour pickles, preferably cornichons, it is known as *Charcuterie*.

◆◆◆
POIVRADE POUR GIBIER

Poivrade is also the name given a flavorful sauce traditionally made with game stock and seasoned with peppercorns. It is used for the wonderful *Sauce Grand Veneur*, one of the most complex small sauces in the classic repertoire. For *Grand Veneur*, game stock is flavored with demi-glace and finished with cream and currant jelly. The sweetness balances the strong flavor of the game meats.

The Tomato Sauce Family

Classic tomato sauce is made from tomatoes, vegetables, seasonings and white stock and thickened with a blond or brown roux. In today's kitchens, however, most tomato sauces are not thickened with roux. Rather, they are tomatoes, herbs, spices, vegetables and other flavoring ingredients simmered together and puréed.

A properly made tomato sauce is thick, rich and full-flavored. Its texture should be grainier than most other classic sauces, but it should still be smooth. The vegetables and other seasonings should add flavor, but none should be pronounced. Tomato sauce should not be bitter, acidic or overly sweet. It should be deep red and thick enough to cling to foods.

◆◆◆

RECIPE 10.13

TOMATO SAUCE

Yield: 1 gal. (4 lt)

Salt pork, small dice	4 oz.	120 g
Mirepoix	1 lb. 8 oz.	750 g
Tomato, fresh or canned	3 qt.	3 lt
Tomato purée	2 qt.	2 lt
Sachet:		
Dried thyme	1 tsp.	5 ml
Bay leaves	3	3
Garlic cloves	3	3
Parsley stems	10	10
Peppercorns, crushed	1/2 tsp.	3 ml
Salt	1-1/2 oz.	45 g
Sugar	3/4 oz.	20 g
White stock	3 qt.	3 lt
Pork bones	2 lb.	1 kg

1. Render the salt pork over medium heat.

2. Add the mirepoix and sauté, but do not brown.

3. Add the tomatoes and tomato purée, sachet, salt and sugar.

4. Add the white stock and bones.

5. Simmer slowly for 1/2–2 hours or until the desired consistency has been reached.

6. Remove the bones and sachet and pass the sauce through a food mill. Cool in a water bath and refrigerate.

Small Tomato Sauces

The following small sauces are made by adding the listed ingredients to 1 quart (1 liter) tomato sauce. The final step for each recipe is to season to taste with salt and pepper.

Creole Sauté 6 ounces (170 grams) finely diced onion, 4 ounces (120 grams) thinly sliced celery and 1 teaspoon (5 milliliters) garlic in 1 ounce (30 milliliters) oil. Add tomato sauce, a bay leaf and a pinch of thyme; simmer for 15 minutes. Then add 4 ounces (120 grams) finely diced green pepper and a dash of hot pepper sauce; simmer for 15 minutes longer. Remove bay leaf.

Milanaise Sauté 5 ounces (140 grams) sliced mushrooms in 1/2 ounce (15 grams) butter. Add tomato sauce and then stir in 5 ounces (140 grams) cooked ham (julienne cut) and 5 ounces (140 grams) cooked tongue (julienne cut). Bring to a simmer.

Spanish Prepare creole sauce as directed, adding 4 ounces (120 grams) sliced mushrooms to the sautéed onions. Garnish with sliced black or green olives.

The Hollandaise Family

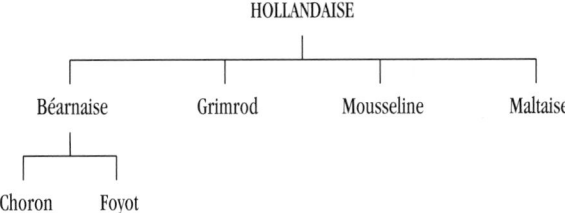

Hollandaise and the small sauces derived from it are **emulsified** sauces. Egg yolks, which contain large amounts of lecithin, a natural emulsifier, are used to emulsify warm butter and a small amount of water, lemon juice or vinegar. By vigorously whipping the egg yolks with the liquid, while slowly adding the warm butter, the lecithin coats the individual oil droplets and holds them in suspension in the liquid.

A properly made hollandaise is smooth, buttery, pale lemon-yellow-colored and very rich. It is lump-free and should not exhibit any signs of separation. The buttery flavor should dominate but not mask the flavors of the egg, lemon and vinegar. The sauce should be frothy and light, not heavy like a mayonnaise.

Emulsification—*the process by which generally unmixable liquids such as oil and water are forced into a uniform distribution.*

Temperatures and Sanitation Concerns

Temperatures play an important role in the proper production of a hollandaise sauce. As the egg yolks and liquid are whisked together, they are cooked over a bain marie until they thicken to the consistency of slightly whipped cream. Do not overheat this mixture, because even slightly cooked eggs lose their ability to emulsify. The clarified butter used to make the sauce should be warm but not so hot as to further cook the egg yolks. Although hollandaise sauce can be made from whole butter, a more stable and consistent product will be achieved by using butter that has had the water and milk solids removed through clarification. (Clarification is described in Chapter 8, Eggs and Dairy Products.)

Emulsified butter sauces are unique in that they must be held at the specific temperatures most conducive to bacterial growth: 40–140°F (4–60°C). If the sauce is heated above 150°F (65°C), the eggs will cook and the sauce will break and become grainy. If the sauce temperature falls below 45°F (7°C), the butter will solidify, making the sauce unusable. In order to minimize the risk of food-borne illnesses while maintaining the integrity of the sauce:

1. Always use clean, sanitized utensils.
2. Schedule sauce production as close to the time of service as possible. Never hold hollandaise-based sauces more than 1-1/2 hours.
3. Make small batches of sauce.
4. Never mix an old sauce with a new one.

With practice, classic hollandaise can be produced quickly and efficiently. Nevertheless, a recipe for blender hollandaise is included for those operations with a need for this technique.

◆◆◆

RECIPE 10.14

HOLLANDAISE

Yield: 1-1/2 qt. (1.5 lt)

White peppercorns, crushed	1/2 tsp.	2 ml
White wine vinegar	6 oz.	180 g
Water	4 oz.	120 g
Egg yolks	10	10
Lemon juice	2-1/2 oz.	75 g
Clarified butter, warm	1 qt.	1 lt
Salt and white pepper	TT	TT
Cayenne pepper	TT	TT

1. Combine the peppercorns, vinegar and water in a small saucepan and reduce by one half.
2. Place the egg yolks in a stainless steel bowl. Strain the vinegar and pepper reduction through a chinois, into the yolks.
3. Place the bowl over a double boiler, whipping the mixture continuously with a wire whip. As the yolks cook, the mixture will thicken. When the mixture is thick enough to leave a trail across the surface when the whip is drawn away, remove the bowl from the double boiler. Do not overcook the egg yolks.
4. Whip in 1 ounce (30 grams) lemon juice to stop the yolks from cooking.
5. Begin to add the warm clarified butter to the egg yolk mixture a drop at a time, while constantly whipping the mixture to form an emulsion. Once the emulsion is started, the butter may be added more quickly. Continue until all the butter is incorporated.
6. Whip in the remaining lemon juice. Adjust the seasonings with salt, white pepper and cayenne pepper.
7. Strain the sauce through cheesecloth if necessary and hold for service in a warm (not simmering) bain marie.

1. Combining the egg yolks with the vinegar and pepper reduction in a stainless steel bowl.

2. Whipping the mixture over a double boiler until it is thick enough to leave a trail when the whip is removed.

3. Using a kitchen towel and saucepot to firmly hold the bowl containing the yolks, add the butter slowly while whipping continuously.

4. Hollandaise at the proper consistency.

◆◆◆

RECIPE 10.15
HOLLANDAISE, BLENDER METHOD

Yield: 1 qt. (1 lt)

Egg yolks	9	9
Water, warm	3 oz.	90 g
Lemon juice	1 oz.	30 g
Cayenne pepper	TT	TT
Salt	1 tsp.	5 ml
White pepper	1/4 tsp.	1 ml
Tabasco sauce	TT	TT
Whole butter	24 oz.	750 ml

1. Place the egg yolks, water, lemon juice, cayenne pepper, salt, white pepper and Tabasco sauce in the bowl of the blender. Cover and blend on high speed for approximately 5 seconds.

2. Heat the butter to approximately 175°F (80°C). This allows the butter to cook the yolks as it is added to them.

3. Turn the blender on and immediately begin to add the butter in a steady stream. Incorporate all of the butter in 20–30 seconds. Adjust the seasonings.

4. If any lumps are present, strain the sauce through cheesecloth. Transfer the sauce to a stainless steel container and adjust the seasonings. Hold for service in a bain marie, remembering the sanitation precautions discussed above.

Procedure for Rescuing a Broken Hollandaise

Occasionally a hollandaise will break or separate and appear thin, grainy or even lumpy. A sauce breaks when the emulsion has not formed or the emulsified butter, eggs and liquid have separated. There are several reasons why this may happen: The temperature of the eggs or butter may have been too high or too low; the butter may have been added too quickly; the egg yolks may have been overcooked; too much butter may have been added or the sauce may not have been whipped vigorously enough.

Broken hollandaise can often be rescued and re-emulsified. To do so, you must first determine the cause of the problem.

Feel the bowl in which the sauce was prepared to determine if it is too hot or too cold. If the bowl is too hot, allow the sauce to cool. If it is too cold, reheat the sauce over a double boiler before attempting to rescue it.

For 1 quart (1 liter) of broken sauce, place 1 tablespoon (15 milliliters) of water in a clean stainless steel bowl and slowly beat in the broken sauce. If the problem seems to be that the eggs were overcooked or too much butter was added, add a yolk to the water before incorporating the broken sauce.

Small Hollandaise Sauces

The following small sauces are easily made by adding the listed ingredients to 1 quart (1 liter) of hollandaise. The final step for each recipe is to season to taste with salt and pepper. Béarnaise is presented here as a small sauce, although some chefs consider it a leading sauce.

Béarnaise   Combine 2 ounces (60 grams) chopped shallots, 5 tablespoons (75 milliliters) chopped fresh tarragon, 3 tablespoons (45 milliliters) chopped fresh chervil and 1 teaspoon (5 milliliters) crushed peppercorns with 8 ounces (250 milliliters) white wine vinegar. Reduce to 2 ounces (60 milliliters). Add this reduction to the egg yolks and proceed with the hollandaise recipe. Strain the finished sauce and season to taste with salt and cayenne pepper. Garnish with additional chopped fresh tarragon.

Choron   Combine 2 ounces (60 grams) tomato paste and 2 ounces (60 grams) heavy cream; add the mixture to a béarnaise.

Foyot   Add to béarnaise 3 ounces (90 grams) melted glace de viande.

Grimrod   Infuse a hollandaise sauce with saffron.

Maltaise   Add to hollandaise 2 ounces (60 grams) orange juice and 2 teaspoons (10 milliliters) finely grated orange zest. Blood oranges are traditionally used for this sauce.

Mousseline (Chantilly sauce)   Whip 8 ounces (250 grams) heavy cream until stiff. Fold it into the hollandaise just before service.

Beurre Blanc and Beurre Rouge

Beurre blanc and beurre rouge are emulsified butter sauces made without egg yolks. The small amounts of lecithin and other emulsifiers naturally found in butter are used to form an oil-in-water emulsion. Although similar to hollandaise in concept, they are not considered either classic leading or compound sauces. Beurre blancs are thinner and lighter than hollandaise and béarnaise. They should be smooth and slightly thicker than heavy cream.

Beurre blanc and beurre rouge are made from three main ingredients: shallots, white (Fr. *blanc*) wine or red (Fr. *rouge*) wine and whole butter (not clarified). The shallots and wine provide flavor, while the butter becomes the sauce. A good beurre blanc or beurre rouge is rich and buttery, with a neutral flavor that responds well to other seasonings and flavorings, thereby lending itself to the addition of herbs, spices and vegetable purées to complement the dish with which it is served. Its pale color changes depending upon the flavorings added. It should be light and airy yet still liquid, while thick enough to cling to food.

PROCEDURE FOR MAKING BEURRE BLANC OR BEURRE ROUGE

1. Use a nonaluminum pan to prevent discoloring the sauce. Do not use a thin-walled or nonstick pan, as heat is not evenly distributed in a thin-walled pan and a nonstick pan makes it difficult for an emulsion to set.

2. Over medium heat, reduce the wine, shallots and herbs or other seasonings, if used, until *au sec* (i.e., nearly dry). Some chefs add a small amount of heavy cream at this point and reduce the mixture. Although not necessary, the added cream helps stabilize the finished sauce.

3. Whisk in cold butter a small amount at a time. The butter should be well chilled, as this allows the butterfat, water and milk solids to be gradually incorporated into the sauce as the butter melts and the mixture is whisked.

4. When all of the butter is incorporated, strain and hold the sauce in a bain marie.

Temperature

Do not let the sauce become too hot. At 136°F (58°C) some of the emulsifying proteins begin to break down and release the butterfat they hold in emulsion.

Extended periods at temperatures over 136°F (58°C) will cause the sauce to separate. If the sauce separates, it can be corrected by cooling to approximately 110–120°F (43–49°C) and whisking to reincorporate the butterfat.

If the sauce is allowed to cool below 85°F (30°C), the butterfat will solidify. If the sauce is reheated it will separate into butterfat and water; whisking will not re-emulsify it. Cold beurre blanc can be used as a soft, flavored butter, however, simply by whisking it at room temperature until it smooths out to the consistency of mayonnaise.

◆◆◆

RECIPE 10.16

BEURRE BLANC

Yield: 1 qt. (1 lt)

White wine	1 oz.	30 g
White wine vinegar	4 oz.	120 g
Salt	1-1/2 tsp.	7 ml
White pepper	1/2 tsp.	2 ml
Shallots, minced	3 Tbsp.	45 ml
Whole butter, chilled	2 lb.	1 kg

1. Combine the white wine, white wine vinegar, salt, white pepper and shallots in a small saucepan. Reduce the mixture until approximately 2 tablespoons (30 milliliters) of liquid remain. If more than 2 tablespoons of liquid are allowed to remain the resulting sauce will be too thin. For a thicker sauce, reduce the mixture *au sec.*

2. Cut the butter into pieces approximately 1 ounce (30 grams) in weight. Over low heat, whisk in the butter a few pieces at a time, using the chilled butter to keep the sauce between 100° and 120°F (43–49°C).

3. Once all of the butter has been incorporated, remove the saucepan from the heat. Strain through a chinois and hold the sauce between 100° and 130°F (38–54°C) for service.

VARIATIONS: *Lemon-Dill*—Heat 2 tablespoons (30 milliliters) lemon juice and whisk it into the beurre blanc. Stir in 4 tablespoons (60 milliliters) chopped fresh dill.

Pink Peppercorn—Add 2 tablespoons (30 milliliters) coarsely crushed pink peppercorns to the shallot-wine reduction when making beurre rouge. Garnish the finished sauce with whole pink peppercorns.

1. Reducing the shallots and wine *au sec.*

2. Whisking in the cold butter a little at a time.

3. Straining the sauce.

Compound Butters

A compound butter is made by incorporating various seasonings into softened whole butter. These butters, also known as *beurres composés*, give flavor and color to small sauces or may be served as sauces in their own right. For example, a slice of maître d'hôtel butter (parsley butter) is often placed on a grilled steak or piece of fish at the time of service. The butter quickly melts, creating a sauce for the beef or fish.

Butter and flavoring ingredients can be combined with a blender, food processor or mixer. Using parchment paper or plastic wrap, the butter is then rolled into a cylinder, chilled and sliced as needed. Or it can be piped into rosettes and refrigerated until firm. Most compound butters will keep for two to three days in the refrigerator, or they can be frozen for longer storage.

1. Placing the butter on the plastic wrap.

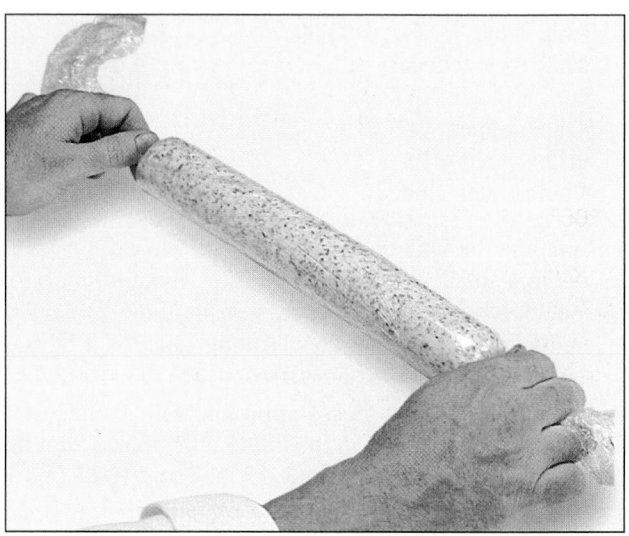

2. Rolling the butter in the plastic wrap to form a cylinder.

Recipes for Compound Butters

For each of the following butters, add the listed ingredients to 1 pound (500 grams) of softened, unsalted butter. The compound butter should then be seasoned with salt and pepper to taste.

Basil Butter   Mince 2 ounces (60 grams) basil, 2 ounces (60 grams) shallots and add to butter with 2 teaspoons (10 milliliters) lemon juice.

Herb Butter   Add to the butter up to 1 cup (250 milliliters) of mixed chopped fresh herbs such as parsley, dill, chives, tarragon or chervil.

Lobster or Crayfish Butter   Grind 8 ounces (250 grams) cooked lobster or crayfish meat, shells and/or coral with 1 pound (500 grams) butter. Place in a saucepan and clarify. Strain the butter through a fine chinois lined with cheesecloth. Refrigerate, then remove the butterfat when firm.

Maître d'Hôtel   Mix into the butter 4 tablespoons (60 milliliters) finely chopped parsley, 3 tablespoons (45 milliliters) lemon juice and a dash of white pepper.

Montpelier   Blanch 1 ounce (30 grams) parsley, 1 ounce (30 grams) chervil, 1 ounce (30 grams) watercress and 1 ounce (30 grams) tarragon in boiling water. Drain thoroughly. Mince two hard-boiled egg yolks, two garlic cloves and two gherkin pickles. Blend everything into the butter.

Red Pepper Purée 8 ounces (250 grams) roasted, peeled red bell peppers until liquid, then add to the butter.

Shallot Butter Blanch 8 ounces (250 grams) of peeled shallots in boiling water. Dry and finely dice them and mix with the butter.

Pan Gravy

Pan gravy is aptly named: It is made directly in the pan used to roast the poultry, beef, lamb or pork the gravy will accompany. Pan gravy is actually a sauce; it is a liquid thickened with a roux. Pan gravy gains additional flavors from the drippings left in the roasting pan and by utilizing a portion of the fat rendered during the roasting process to make the roux. This technique is used in Recipe 17.3, Roast Turkey with Giblet Gravy.

A properly made pan gravy should have all the characteristics of any brown sauce except that it has a meatier flavor as the result of the pan drippings.

PROCEDURE FOR MAKING PAN GRAVY

1. Remove the cooked meat or poultry from the roasting pan.
2. If mirepoix was not added during the roasting process, add it to the pan containing the drippings and fat.
3. Place the roasting pan on the stove top and clarify the fat by cooking off any remaining moisture.
4. Pour off the fat, reserving it to make the roux.
5. Deglaze the pan using an appropriate stock. The deglazing liquid may be transferred to a saucepan for easier handling or the gravy may be finished directly in the roasting pan.
6. Add enough stock or water to the deglazing liquid to yield the proper amount of finished gravy.
7. Determine the amount of roux needed to thicken the liquid and prepare it in a separate pan, using a portion of the reserved fat.
8. Add the roux to the liquid and bring the mixture to a simmer. Simmer until the mirepoix is well cooked, the flavor is extracted and the flour taste is cooked out.
9. Strain the gravy and adjust the seasonings.

Coulis

The term *coulis* most often refers to a sauce made from a purée of vegetables or fruit. A vegetable coulis can be served either as a hot or cold accompaniment to other vegetables, starches, meat, poultry, fish or shellfish. It is often made from a single vegetable base (popular examples include broccoli, tomatoes and sweet red peppers) cooked with flavoring ingredients such as onions, garlic, shallots, herbs and spices and then puréed. An appropriate liquid (stock, water or cream) may be added to thin the purée if necessary. Vegetable coulis are often prepared with very little fat and served as a healthy alternative to a heavier, classic sauce.

A fruit coulis, often made from fresh or frozen berries, is generally used as a dessert sauce. It is usually as simple as puréed fruit thinned to the desired consistency with sugar syrup.

Typically, both vegetable and fruit coulis have a texture similar to that of thin tomato sauce. But their textures can range from slightly grainy to almost lumpy, depending on their intended use. The flavor and color of a coulis should be that of the main ingredient. The flavors of herbs, spices and other flavoring ingredients should only complement and not dominate the coulis.

PROCEDURE FOR MAKING COULIS

Here, we include a procedure for making a vegetable coulis. Procedures for making fruit coulis are included as recipes in Chapter 31, Custards, Creams, Frozen Desserts and Dessert Sauces.

1. Cook the main ingredient and any additional flavoring ingredients with an appropriate liquid.
2. Purée the main ingredient and flavoring ingredients in a food mill, blender or food processor.
3. Combine the purée with the appropriate liquid and simmer to blend the flavors.
4. Thin and season the coulis as desired.

◆◆◆

RECIPE 10.17
RED PEPPER COULIS

Yield: 1 qt. (1 lt)

Vegetable oil	1 oz.	30 g
Garlic, chopped	2 tsp.	10 ml
Onion, small dice	3 oz.	90 g
Red bell pepper, medium dice	3 lb.	1.25 kg
White wine	8 oz.	250 g
Chicken stock	1 pt.	450 ml
Salt and pepper	TT	TT

1. Heat the oil and sauté the garlic and onion until translucent, without browning.
2. Add the red pepper and sauté until tender.
3. Deglaze the pan with the white wine.
4. Add the chicken stock, bring to a simmer and cook for 15 minutes. Season with salt and pepper.
5. Purée in a blender or food processor and strain through a china cap.
6. Adjust the consistency and seasonings and hold for service.

Nutritional values per 2-ounce (60 g) serving:

Calories	57	Protein	1 g
Calories from fat	32%	Vitamin A	4851 IU
Total fat	2 g	Vitamin C	162 mg
Saturated fat	0 g	Sodium	132 mg
Cholesterol	0 mg		

Salsa and Relish

Many people think of salsa (Spanish for sauce) as a chunky mixture of raw vegetables and chiles eaten with chips or ladled over Mexican food; they think of relish as a sweet green condiment spooned on a hot dog. But salsas and relishes—generally, cold chunky mixtures of herbs, spices, fruits and/or vegetables—can be used as sauces for many meat, poultry, fish and shellfish items. They can include ingredients such as oranges, pineapple, papaya, black beans, jicama, tomatillos and an array of vegetables.

Although not members of any classic sauce family, salsas and relishes are currently enjoying great popularity because of their intense fresh flavors, ease of preparation and low fat and calorie content. Salsas and relishes are often a riot of colors, textures and flavors, simultaneously cool and hot, spicy and sweet.

Chutney—*a sweet-and-sour condiment made of fruits and/or vegetables cooked in vinegar with sugar and spices until it has a consistency of jam. Some chutneys are reduced to a purée; others retain recognizable pieces of their ingredients.*

PROCEDURE FOR MAKING A SALSA OR RELISH

1. Cut or chop the ingredients.
2. Precook and chill items as directed in the recipe.
3. Toss all ingredients together and refrigerate, allowing the flavors to combine for at least 30 minutes before service.

◆◆◆

RECIPE 10.18

TOMATO SALSA (PICO DE GALLO)

Yield: 1 qt. (1 lt)

Tomatoes, seeded, small dice	5	5
Green onions, sliced	1 bunch	1 bunch
Garlic cloves, minced	3	3
Cilantro, chopped	1/2 bunch	1/2 bunch
Jalapeño peppers, chopped fine	3	3
Lemon juice	2 oz.	60 g
Cumin, ground	1/2 tsp.	2 ml
Salt and pepper	TT	TT

1. Combine all ingredients and gently toss. Adjust seasonings and refrigerate.

Nutritional values per 2 ounce (60 g) serving:

Calories	13	Protein	0 g
Calories from fat	0%	Vitamin A	338 IU
Total fat	0 g	Vitamin C	12 mg
Saturated fat	0 g	Sodium	232 mg
Cholesterol	0 mg		

TABLE 10.5   USING SAUCES

Sauce	Qualities	Small Sauce or Flavorings	Use
Béchamel	Smooth, rich and creamy; no graininess; cream-colored with rich sheen	Cream sauce Cheddar Mornay Nantua Soubise	Vegetables, pasta, eggs, fish Vegetables, pasta Fish, shellfish, poultry, vegetables Fish, shellfish Veal, pork, eggs

Velouté	Smooth and rich; ivory-colored; good flavor of the stock used; not pasty or heavy	Fish velouté
		  Bercy
		  Cardinal
		  Normandy
		Allemande (veal or chicken)
		  Aurora
		  Horseradish
		  Mushroom
		  Poulette
		Suprême (chicken)
		  Albufera
		  Hungarian
		  Ivory
			
			Poached fish
			Lobster, white fish, crab, eggs
			Delicate white fish, oysters
			
			Eggs, chicken, sweetbreads
			Roast beef, corned beef, baked ham
			Sautéed poultry, white meats
			Vegetables, sweetbreads
			
			Braised poultry, sweetbreads
			Eggs, chicken, chops, sweetbreads
			Eggs, braised poultry

Espagnole	Smooth and rich; dark brown color; good meat flavor	Bordelaise Chasseur Chateaubriand Chevreuil Madeira/Port Mushroom Périgueux/Périgourdine Piquant Poivrade Robert	Sautéed or grilled meats Sautéed or grilled meats and poultry Broiled meats Roasted meats and game Grilled or roasted meats and game, ham Sautéed or grilled meats and poultry Sautéed poultry, grilled meats and game, sweetbreads Pork Grilled or roasted meats, game Pork
Tomato	Thick and rich; slightly grainy; full-flavored	Tomato Creole Spanish Milanaise	Meats, poultry, vegetables, pasta and for making small sauces Fish, eggs, chicken Eggs, fish Pasta, grilled or sautéed poultry and white meats
Hollandaise	Smooth and rich; buttery flavor; light and slightly frothy; pale yellow color; no signs of separating	Béarnaise Choron Foyot Grimrod Mousseline Maltaise	Grilled or sautéed meats and fish Grilled meats and fish Grilled meats and fish Eggs, poached fish Poached fish, eggs, vegetables Poached fish
Beurre blanc and beurre rouge	Rich and buttery; thinner than hollandaise; light and airy; pale-colored	Wide variety of seasonings and flavorings may be used	Steamed, grilled or poached fish, chicken or vegetables
Compound butter	Flavor ingredients should be evenly distributed	Wide variety of seasonings and flavorings may be used	Grilled meats, poultry and fish; finishing sauces
Pan gravy	Smooth; deep rich color; meaty flavor	Made from pan drippings	Roasted meats and poultry
Coulis	Rich color; moderately thin, grainy texture; strongly flavored	Made with a wide variety of vegetables or fruits	Vegetables, grilled or poached meats, poultry and fish
Salsa and relish	Chunky; bright colors; not watery	Made with a wide variety of vegetables, fruits and seasonings	Meats, fish, vegetables and poultry; used as a sauce or condiment

USING SAUCES

Although many classic sauces were designed for or intended to be used with specific dishes, modern chefs often mix and match sauces with foods in unique or nontraditional ways. Nonclassic sauces, such as a beurre blanc, salsa or relish, may be prepared in a range of flavors using a wide variety of ingredients.

The uses shown in Table 10.5 for classic and nonclassic sauces are just suggestions. Most sauces can be used in many different dishes. It depends on your taste, creativity and judgment.

CONCLUSION

In *Le Guide culinaire*, Auguste Escoffier wrote "Indeed, stock is everything in cooking…without it, nothing can be done. If one's stock is good, what remains of the work is easy; if, on the other hand, it is bad or merely mediocre, it is quite hopeless to expect anything approaching a satisfactory result." Because stocks and the sauces made from them are still the basis for much of contemporary cuisine, Escoffier's words are as true today as when he wrote them.

Both the classic mother sauces and the small sauces derived from them as well as sauces such as beurre blanc and beurre rouge, coulis, salsas and relishes that are not based on classic recipes all share two goals: to complement the foods with which they are served and neither mask nor disguise poorly prepared foods. With practice and care (and the right ingredients), you will be able to make great sauces.

QUESTIONS FOR DISCUSSION

1. Why are the bones of younger animals preferred for making stocks?
2. Why should a stock made from beef or veal bones cook longer than a stock made from fish bones? What is the result if a stock does not cook long enough?
3. What can cause a stock to become cloudy? How can you prevent this from happening?
4. List three differences in the production of a white stock and a brown stock.
5. List the five classic mother sauces and explain how they are used to prepare small sauces.
6. Why is demi-glace preferred when making brown sauces? Is jus lié different from classic demi-glace? Can they be used interchangeably?
7. Why are temperatures important when making hollandaise sauce? What precautions must be taken when holding hollandaise for service?
8. Compare a beurre blanc and a hollandaise sauce. How are they similar? How are they different?
9. How are compound butters used in making sauces? What are the ingredients for a traditional maître d'hôtel butter?
10. What are the differences between a salsa, chutney and relish? Can these items be used in place of classic sauces? Explain your answer.

 *A*dditional Sauce Recipes

RECIPE 10.19

Mushroom Tarts with Garlic Cream

Note: *This dish appears in the Chapter Opening photograph.*

CITRUS, LOS ANGELES, CA
Chef Michel Richard

Yield: 6 Servings

GARLIC CREAM

Garlic cloves, peeled	30	30
Heavy cream	1 pt.	500 ml
Salt and pepper	TT	TT

1. Place the garlic in a saucepan. Cover with 3 inches (8 cm) of cold water and bring to a boil. Drain and rinse with cold water. Repeat the process two more times. Then thinly slice the garlic and return it to the saucepan.

2. Add cream. Bring to a boil. Reduce the heat and simmer gently until reduced by half or to a thick, saucelike consistency, stirring occasionally.

3. Season with salt and pepper.

PUFF PASTRY

Puff pastry	8 oz.	225 g

1. Line a large baking sheet with parchment paper. Roll the pastry into a 10- × 9-inch (25 × 22.5 cm) rectangle on a lightly floured surface.

2. Cut into six 3- × 5-inch (7.5 × 12.5 cm) squares using a fluted pastry cutter. Transfer to a baking sheet and dock the dough with a fork.

3. Cover and refrigerate at least 1 hour before baking.

4. Bake at 350°F (180°C) until puffed, browned and baked through, approximately 30 minutes.

MUSHROOMS

Fresh shiitake mushrooms	1-1/2 to 2 lb.	750 to 1000 g
Olive oil	2 Tbsp.	30 ml
Salt and pepper	TT	TT

1. Trim the ends of the mushrooms. Heat a sauté pan over medium-high heat and film with oil. Add the mushrooms and cook until lightly brown and tender, approximately 5 minutes, stirring frequently.

2. Season with salt and pepper.

3. To serve the tart, slice each piece of puff pastry in half horizontally, using a serrated knife. Arrange on six plates.

4. Rewarm the garlic cream and mushrooms. Spoon cream onto the bottom of each piece of pastry. Overlap the mushrooms on top of cream, alternating light and dark pieces. Set the top pieces of pastry at an angle over the mushrooms so the filling is visible.

5. Serve with red wine sauce (p. 211) and garnish with an herb sprig, if desired.

✦✦✦

RECIPE 10.20
DUXELLES SAUCE

Yield: 1-1/2 pt. (750 ml)

Mushrooms, chopped fine	8 oz.	250 g
Shallots, chopped fine	3 oz.	90 g
Clarified butter	1 oz.	30 g
Olive oil	1 oz.	30 g
Dry white wine	12 oz.	700 g
Demi-glace	1 pt.	500 ml
Heavy cream	2 oz.	60 g
Salt and pepper	TT	TT
Parsley, chopped fine	1 Tbsp.	15 ml

1. Sauté the mushrooms and the shallots in the butter and oil. The mushrooms will release their liquid and darken. Cook until completely dry.

2. Deglaze with the white wine and reduce by two thirds.

3. Add the demi-glace. Bring to a boil, then simmer for five minutes.

4. Stir in the cream. Adjust seasonings. Garnish with parsley.

✦✦✦

RECIPE 10.21
BARBECUE SAUCE

Yield: 1-1/2 qt. (1.5 lt)

Onion, small dice	8 oz.	250 g
Garlic, chopped	1 oz.	30 g
Vegetable oil	1 oz.	30 g
Red wine vinegar	6 oz.	180 g
Brown sugar	1 oz.	30 g
Honey	2 oz.	60 g
Beef stock	8 oz.	250 g
Ketchup	10 oz.	300 g
Dry mustard	1 oz.	30 g
Worcestershire sauce	2 Tbsp.	30 ml
Salt and pepper	TT	TT
Cayenne pepper	TT	TT

1. Sweat the onions and garlic in the oil until tender.

2. Combine the remaining ingredients and simmer for 30 minutes.

✦✦✦

RECIPE 10.22
MIGNONETTE SAUCE

Yield: 1 pt. (500 ml)

White pepper	2 tsp.	10 ml
Red wine vinegar	16 oz.	500 g
Shallots, minced	4 oz.	120 g
Salt	TT	TT

1. Combine all ingredients.

◆◆◆

RECIPE 10.23

FRESH TOMATO SAUCE
FOR PASTA

Yield: 2-1/2 qt. (2.5 lt)

Onion, small dice	8 oz.	250 g
Carrot, small dice	4 oz.	120 g
Garlic, minced	1 Tbsp.	15 ml
Olive oil	2 oz.	60 g
Tomato concasse	7 lb.	3.1 kg
Fresh oregano	1 Tbsp.	15 ml
Fresh thyme	2 tsp.	10 ml
Salt	1 tsp.	5 ml
Pepper	1/2 tsp.	2 ml
Fresh basil, chopped	1/2 oz.	15 g

1. Sweat the onion, carrot and garlic in the olive oil until tender.
2. Add the concasse and herbs. Simmer for approximately 1 hour or until the desired consistency is reached.
3. Pass the sauce through a food mill if a smooth consistency is desired. Do not purée if a chunkier sauce is desired.
4. Adjust seasonings and add the chopped basil.

Nutritional values per 4-oz. (120 g) serving:

Calories	87	Protein	2 g
Calories from fat	43%	Vitamin A	3090 IU
Total fat	4 g	Vitamin C	46 mg
Saturated fat	1 g	Sodium	165 mg
Cholesterol	0 mg		

◆◆◆

RECIPE 10.24

APPLE HORSERADISH SAUCE

Yield: 1 pt. (500 ml)

Granny Smith apples	4	4
Cider vinegar	2 oz.	60 g
Fresh horseradish, grated	2 oz.	60 g
Paprika	1 tsp.	5 ml
White wine	1 oz.	30 g

1. Grate the apples and moisten them with vinegar.
2. Add the horseradish and paprika.
3. Add wine to thin to the desired consistency.

◆◆◆

RECIPE 10.25

THAI MELON SALSA

Yield: 1 qt. (1 lt)

Assorted melons such as honeydew, cantaloupe, crenshaw	1 qt.	1 lt
Garlic, chopped	1 tsp.	5 ml
Brown sugar	2 Tbsp.	30 ml
Thai fish sauce	1 oz.	30 g
Serrano chiles, minced	1 Tbsp.	15 ml
Lime juice	2 oz.	60 g
Unsalted peanuts, roasted, chopped fine	4 Tbsp.	60 ml
Fresh mint	4 Tbsp.	60 ml

1. Cut the melons into small dice or shape into small balls using a parisienne scoop.
2. Combine remaining ingredients and toss with the melon pieces. Chill thoroughly. Serve with fish, shellfish or chicken.

Nutritional values per 2-oz. (60 g) serving:

Calories	46	Protein	1 g
Calories from fat	25%	Vitamin A	744 IU
Total fat	1 g	Vitamin C	17 mg
Saturated fat	0 g	Sodium	240 mg
Cholesterol	0 mg		

◆◆◆

RECIPE 10.26

STAR FRUIT CHUTNEY

Yield: 2 lb. (900 g)

Limes	3	3
Fresh ginger, julienne	4 oz.	120 g
Sugar	3 oz.	90 g
Apples, peeled, medium dice	2	2
Golden raisins	2 oz.	60 g
Dark raisins	2 oz.	60 g
Star fruit, peeled, medium dice	1-1/2 lb.	1.3 kg
Cider vinegar	1 Tbsp.	15 ml
Salt and pepper	TT	TT
Cayenne pepper	TT	TT

1. Zest 2 limes.
2. Squeeze the limes to make 4 ounces (120 grams) of juice.
3. Combine the lime juice, zest, ginger and sugar. Bring to a boil and simmer until the sugar is caramelized.
4. Add the apples and raisins; simmer until the apples are soft but not mushy.
5. Add the star fruit and bring back to a boil. Remove from heat. Add the vinegar. Season to taste with salt, pepper and cayenne pepper.

CHAPTER 11 SOUPS

Many classic soups are successfully prepared only if recipes are followed strictly. The successful preparation of other soups depends upon the mastery of specialized techniques. But where classic recipes need not be followed nor special techniques employed, perhaps no other area of the kitchen allows the chef to use his or her imagination and creativity as much as the soup station.

The variety of ingredients, seasonings and garnishes that can be used for soups is virtually endless, provided you understand the basic procedures for making different kinds of soup. Great soups can be made using the finest and most expensive ingredients or leftovers from the previous evening's dinner service and trimmings from the day's production.

This chapter extends to soups the skills and knowledge learned in Chapter 10, Stocks and Sauces. In Chapter 10 we discussed making stocks, thickening liquids, using a liaison and skimming impurities, techniques that apply to soup making as well. Here we discuss techniques such as clarifying consommés and thickening soups with vegetable purées. This chapter also covers cream soups, cold soups and guidelines for garnishing and serving a variety of soups.

Most soups can be classified by cooking technique and appearance as either clear or thick.

Clear soups include **broths** made from meat, poultry, game, fish or vegetables as well as **consommés**, which are broths clarified to remove impurities.

Thick soups include cream soups and purée soups. The most common **cream soups** are those made from vegetables cooked in a liquid that is thickened with a starch and puréed; cream is then incorporated to add richness and flavor. **Purée soups** are generally made from starchy vegetables or legumes. After the main ingredient is simmered in a liquid, the mixture—or a portion of it—is puréed.

Some soups (notably **bisques** and **chowders** as well as **cold soups** such as gazpacho and fruit soup) are neither clear nor thick soups. Rather, they use special preparation methods or a combination of the methods mentioned above.

A soup's quality is determined by its flavor, appearance and texture. A good soup should be full flavored, with no off or sour tastes. Flavors from each of the soup's ingredients should blend and complement, with no one flavor overpowering another. Consommés should be crystal clear. The vegetables in vegetable soups should be brightly colored, not gray. Garnishes should be attractive and uniform in size and shape. The soup's texture should be very precise. If it is supposed to be smooth then it should be very smooth and lump-free. If the soft and crisp textures of certain ingredients are supposed to contrast, the soup should not be overcooked, as this causes all the ingredients to become mushy and soft.

Garnishing is an important consideration when preparing soups. When applied to soups, the word *garnish* has two meanings. The first is the one more typically associated with the word. It refers to foods added to the soup as decoration—for example, a broccoli floret floated on a bowl of cream of broccoli soup. The second refers to foods that may serve not only as decorations but also as critical components of the final product—for example, noodles in a bowl of chicken noodle soup. In this context, the noodles are not ingredients because they are not used to make the chicken soup. Rather they are added to chicken soup to create a different dish. These additional items are still referred to as garnishes, however.

CLEAR SOUPS

All clear soups start as broth. Broths may be served as finished items, used as the base for other soups or refined (clarified) into consommés.

Broths

The techniques for making stocks discussed in Chapter 10 are identical to those used for making broths. Like stocks, broths are prepared by simmering flavoring ingredients in a liquid for long periods of time. Broths and stocks differ, however, in two ways. First, broths are made with meat instead of just bones. Second, broths (often with a garnish) can be served as finished dishes, while stocks are generally used to prepare other items.

Broths are made from meat, poultry, fish or vegetables cooked in a liquid. An especially full-flavored broth results when a stock and not just water is used as the liquid. Cuts of meat from the shank, neck or shoulder result in more flavorful broths, as will the flesh of mature poultry. Proper temperature, skimming and straining help produce well-flavored, clear broths.

PROCEDURE FOR PREPARING BROTHS

1. Truss or cut the main ingredient.
2. Brown the meat; brown or sweat the mirepoix or vegetables as necessary.
3. Place the main ingredient and mirepoix or vegetables in an appropriate stockpot and add enough cold water or stock to cover. Add a bouquet garni or sachet d'epices if desired.
4. Bring the liquid slowly to a boil; reduce to a simmer and cook, skimming occasionally, until the main ingredient is tender and the flavor is fully developed.
5. Carefully strain the broth through a china cap lined with cheesecloth; try to disturb the flavoring ingredients as little as possible in order to preserve the broth's clarity.
6. Cool and store following the procedures for cooling stocks. Or bring to a boil, garnish as desired and hold for service.

◆ ◆ ◆
ESCOFFIER'S
CLASSIFICATION OF SOUPS

In his 1903 culinary treatise *Le Guide culinaire*, Auguste Escoffier recognized many more categories of soups than we do today. They include:

Clear soups, which are always "clear consommés with a slight garnish in keeping with the nature of the consommé."

Purées, which are made from starchy vegetables and are thickened with rice, potato or soft bread crumbs.

Cullises, which use poultry, game or fish for a base and are thickened with rice, lentils, espagnole sauce or bread soaked in boiling salted water.

Bisques, which use shellfish cooked with a mirepoix as a base and are thickened with rice.

Veloutés, which use velouté sauce as a base and are finished with a liaison of egg yolks and cream.

Cream soups, which use béchamel sauce as a base and are finished with heavy cream.

Special soups, which are those that do not follow the procedures for veloutés or creams.

Vegetable soups, which are usually *paysanne* or peasant-type and "do not demand very great precision in the apportionment of the vegetables of which they are composed, but they need great care and attention, notwithstanding."

Foreign soups, "which have a foreign origin whose use, although it may not be general, is yet sufficiently common."

Because of changes in consumer health consciousness and kitchen operations, many of the distinctions between Escoffier's classic soups have now become blurred and, in some cases, eliminated. As discussed in this chapter, for example, clear consommés and vegetable soups are now made with stocks or broths; most cream soups use velouté as a base and are finished with milk or cream rather than a liaison. But not everything has changed: The procedures for making purées and bisques are essentially the same today as they were when Escoffier haunted the great kitchens of Europe.

◆◆◆

RECIPE 11.1
BEEF BROTH

Yield: 8 qt. (8 lt)

Beef shank, neck or shoulder cut in 2 in. (5 cm) thick pieces	12 lb.	5.5 kg
Vegetable oil	8 oz.	250 g
Cold water or stock	2 gal.	8 lt
Mirepoix	2 lb.	900 g
Turnip, medium dice	8 oz.	250 g
Leek, medium dice	8 oz.	250 g
Tomato, seeded and diced	8 oz.	250 g
Sachet:		
Bay leaf	1	1
Dried thyme	1/2 tsp.	2 ml
Peppercorns, crushed	1/2 tsp.	2 ml
Parsley stems	8	8
Garlic cloves, crushed	2	2
Salt	TT	TT

1. Brown the meat in 4 ounces (120 grams) of oil, then place it in a stockpot. Add the stock or water and bring to a simmer. Simmer gently for 2 hours, skimming the surface as necessary.

2. After the meat has simmered for 2 hours, caramelize the mirepoix in the remaining oil and add it to the liquid. Add the turnips, leeks, tomato and sachet.

3. Simmer until full flavor has developed, approximately 1 hour. Skim the surface as necessary.

4. Carefully strain the broth through cheesecloth and season to taste. Cool and refrigerate.

Broth-Based Soups

Broths are often used as bases for such familiar soups as vegetable, chicken noodle or beef barley.

Transforming a broth into a broth-based vegetable soup, for example, is quite simple. While a broth may be served with a vegetable (or meat) garnish, a broth-based vegetable soup is a soup in which the vegetables (and meats) are cooked directly in the broth, adding flavor, body and texture to the finished product. Any number of vegetables can be used to make a vegetable soup; it could be a single vegetable as in onion soup or a dozen different vegetables for a hearty minestrone. Making a mixed vegetable soup allows the chef to use his or her imagination and whatever produce may be on hand.

When making broth-based vegetable soups, each ingredient must be added at the proper time so that all ingredients are cooked when the soup is finished. The ingredients must cook long enough to add their flavors and soften sufficiently but not so long that they lose their identity and become too soft or mushy.

Because broth-based vegetable soups are made by simmering ingredients directly in the broth, they are generally not as clear as plain broths. But appearance is still important. So, when cutting ingredients for the soup, pay particular attention so that the pieces are uniform and visually appealing. Small dice, julienne, batonnet or paysanne cuts are recommended.

PROCEDURE FOR PREPARING BROTH-BASED VEGETABLE SOUPS

1. Sweat long-cooking vegetables in butter or fat.
2. Add the appropriate stock or broth and bring to a simmer.
3. Add seasonings such as bay leaves, dried thyme, crushed peppercorns, parsley stems and garlic, in a sachet, allowing enough time for the seasonings to fully flavor the soup.
4. Add additional ingredients according to their cooking times.
5. Simmer the soup to blend all the flavors.
6. If the soup is not going to be served immediately, cool and refrigerate it.
7. Just before service add any garnishes that were prepared separately or do not require cooking.

◆◆◆

RECIPE 11.2
HEARTY VEGETABLE BEEF SOUP

Yield: 5 qt. (5 lt)

Butter or beef fat	6 oz.	170 g
Mirepoix, small dice	3 lb.	1.5 kg
Turnip, small dice	8 oz.	250 g
Garlic cloves, chopped	2	2
Beef broth or beef stock	4 qt.	4 lt
Beef, small dice	1 lb.	450 g
Sachet:		
Bay leaf	1	1
Dried thyme	1/2 tsp.	2 ml
Peppercorns, crushed	1/2 tsp.	2 ml
Parsley stems	8	8
Tomato concasse	12 oz.	350 g
Corn kernels, fresh, frozen or canned	12 oz.	350 g
Salt and pepper	TT	TT

Tomato concasse—*peeled, seeded and diced tomato.*

1. In a soup pot, sweat the mirepoix and turnip in the butter or fat until tender.
2. Add the garlic and sauté lightly.
3. Add the beef broth or stock and the diced beef; bring to a simmer. Add the sachet. Skim or degrease as necessary.
4. Simmer until the beef and vegetables are tender, approximately 1 hour.
5. Add the tomato concasse and corn; simmer for 10 minutes. Season to taste with salt and pepper.
6. Cool and refrigerate or hold for service.

VARIATIONS: A wide variety of vegetables can be added or substituted in this recipe. If leeks, rutabagas, parsnips or cabbage are used, they should be sweated to bring out their flavors before the liquid is added. Potatoes, fresh beans, summer squash and other vegetables that cook more quickly should be added according to their cooking times. Rice, barley and pasta garnishes should be cooked separately and added just before service.

Consommés

A consommé is a stock or broth that has been clarified to remove impurities so that it is crystal clear. Traditionally, all clear broths were referred to as consommés; a clear broth further refined using the process described below was referred to as a double consommé. The term *double consommé* is still used occasionally to describe any strongly flavored consommé.

Well-prepared consommés should be rich in the flavor of the main ingredient. Beef and game consommés should be dark in color; consommés made from poultry should have a golden to light amber color. They should have substantial body as a result of their high gelatin content, and all consommés should be perfectly clear with no trace of fat.

Because a consommé is a refined broth, it is absolutely essential that the broth or stock used be of the highest quality. Although the clarification process adds some flavor to the consommé, the finished consommé will be only as good as the stock or broth from which it was made.

The Clarification Process

To make a consommé, you clarify a stock or broth. The stock or broth to be clarified must be cold and grease-free. To clarify, the cold degreased stock or broth is combined with a mixture known as a **clearmeat** or **clarification**. A clearmeat is a mixture of egg whites; ground meat, poultry or fish; mirepoix, herbs and spices; and an acidic product, usually tomatoes, lemon juice or wine. (An **onion brûlée** is also often added to help flavor and color the consommé.)

The stock or broth and clearmeat are then slowly brought to a simmer. As the albumen in the egg whites and meat begins to coagulate, it traps impurities suspended in the liquid. As coagulation continues, the albumen-containing items combine with the other clearmeat ingredients and rise to the liquid's surface, forming a **raft**. As the mixture simmers, the raft ingredients release their flavors, further enriching the consommé.

After simmering, the consommé is carefully strained through several layers of cheesecloth to remove any trace of impurities. It is then completely degreased, either by cooling and refrigerating, then removing the solidified fat or by carefully ladling the fat from the surface. The result is a rich, flavorful, crystal-clear consommé.

Onion brûlée—*literally, burnt onion, made by charring onion halves; used to flavor and color stocks and sauces.*

Procedure for Making Consommés

1. In a suitable stockpot (one with a spigot makes it much easier to strain the consommé when it is finished), combine the ground meat, lightly beaten egg white and other clearmeat ingredients.
2. Add the cold stock or broth and stir to combine with the clearmeat ingredients.
3. Over medium heat, slowly bring the mixture to a simmer, stirring occasionally.
4. As the raft forms, make a hole in its center so that the liquid can bubble through, cooking the raft completely and extracting as much flavor as possible from the raft ingredients.
5. Simmer the consommé until full flavor develops, approximately 1 to 1-1/2 hours.
6. Carefully strain the consommé through several layers of cheesecloth and degrease completely.

7. If the consommé will not be used immediately, it should be cooled and refrigerated, following the procedures for cooling stocks discussed in Chapter 10. When the consommé is completely cold, remove any remaining fat that solidified on its surface.

8. If, after reheating the consommé, small dots of fat appear on the surface, they can be removed by blotting with a small piece of paper towel.

1. Combining the ingredients for the clearmeat.

◆◆◆

RECIPE 11.3

BEEF CONSOMMÉ

Yield: 4 qt. (4 lt)

Egg whites	10	10
Ground beef, lean, preferably shank, neck or shoulder	2 lb.	1 kg
Mirepoix	1 lb.	450 g
Tomato, seeded and diced	12 oz.	340 g
Brown beef stock or broth, cold	5 qt.	5 lt
Onion brûlée	2	2
Sachet:		
Bay leaves	2	2
Dried thyme	1/2 tsp.	2 ml
Peppercorns, crushed	1/2 tsp.	2 ml
Parsley stems	8	8
Cloves, whole	2	2
Salt	TT	TT

2. Making a hole in the raft to allow the liquid to bubble through.

1. Whip the egg whites until slightly frothy.

2. Combine the egg whites, beef, mirepoix and tomatoes in an appropriate stockpot.

3. Add the cold beef stock or broth; mix well and add the onion brûlée and sachet.

4. Bring the mixture to a simmer over moderate heat, stirring occasionally. Stop stirring when the raft begins to form.

5. Break a hole in the center of the raft to allow the consommé to bubble through.

6. Simmer until full flavor develops, approximately 1-1/2 hours.

7. Strain through several layers of cheesecloth, degrease and adjust the seasonings. Cool and refrigerate or hold for service.

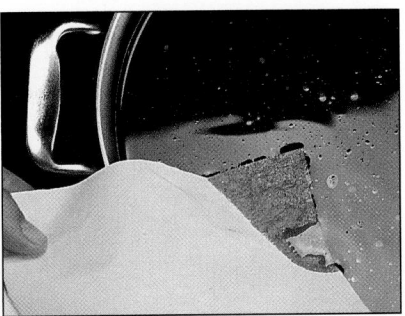

3. Degreasing the consommé with a paper towel.

NOTE: Guidelines for garnishing consommés as well as some classic garnishes are listed on page 245.

4. The finished consommé.

Correcting a Poorly Clarified Consommé

A clarification may fail for a variety of reasons. For example, if the consommé is allowed to boil or if it is stirred after the raft has formed, a cloudy consommé can result. If the consommé is insufficiently clear, a second clarification can be performed using the following procedure. This second clarification should be performed only once, however, and only if absolutely necessary, because the eggs not only remove impurities but also some of the consommé's flavor and richness.

1. Thoroughly chill and degrease the consommé.
2. Lightly beat four egg whites per gallon (4 liters) of consommé and combine with the cold consommé.
3. Slowly bring the consommé to a simmer, stirring occasionally. Stop stirring when the egg whites begin to coagulate.
4. When the egg whites are completely coagulated, carefully strain the consommé.

THICK SOUPS

There are two kinds of thick soups: cream soups and purée soups. In general, cream soups are thickened with a roux or other starch, while purée soups rely on a purée of the main ingredient for thickening. But in certain ways the two soups are very similar: Some purée soups are finished with cream or partially thickened with a roux or other starch.

Cream Soups

Most cream soups are made by simmering the main flavoring ingredient (for example, broccoli for cream of broccoli soup) in a white stock or thin velouté sauce to which seasonings have been added. The mixture is then puréed and strained. After the consistency has been adjusted, the soup is finished by adding cream. In classic cuisine, thin béchamel sauce is often used as the base for cream soups and can be substituted for velouté in many cream soup recipes, if desired.

Both hard vegetables (e.g., celery and squash) and soft or leafy vegetables (e.g., spinach, corn, broccoli and asparagus) are used for cream soups. Hard vegetables are generally sweated in butter without browning before the liquid is added. Soft and leafy vegetables are generally added to the soup after the liquid is brought to a boil. Because cream soups are puréed, it is important to cook the flavoring ingredients until they are soft and can be passed through a food mill easily.

All cream soups are finished with milk or cream. Using milk thins the soup while adding richness; using the same amount of cream adds much more richness without the same thinning effect. Cold milk and cream curdle easily if added directly to a hot or acidic soup. But there are several steps that can be taken to prevent curdling:

1. Never add cold milk or cream to hot soup. Bring the milk or cream to a simmer before adding it to the soup. Or, temper the milk or cream by gradually adding some hot soup to it and then incorporating the warmed mixture into the rest of the soup.
2. If possible, add the milk or cream to the soup just before service.
3. Do not boil the soup after the milk or cream has been added.
4. The presence of roux or other starch helps prevent curdling. Therefore, béchamel or cream sauce is often used instead of milk or cream to finish cream soups.

(Recall from Chapter 10 that a béchamel sauce is made by thickening milk with a roux, and a cream sauce is made by adding cream to a béchamel sauce.)

PROCEDURE FOR MAKING CREAM SOUPS

1. In a soup pot, sweat hard vegetables such as squash, onions, carrots and celery in oil or butter without browning.

2. In order to thicken the soup:
   (a) add flour and cook to make a blond roux, then add the cooking liquid (i.e., the stock), or
   (b) add the stock to the vegetables, bring the stock to a simmer and add a blond roux that was prepared separately, or
   (c) add a thin velouté or béchamel sauce to the vegetables.

3. Bring to a boil and reduce to a simmer.

4. Add any soft vegetables such as broccoli or asparagus, and a sachet or bouquet garni as desired.

5. Simmer the soup, skimming occasionally, until the vegetables are very tender.

6. Purée the soup by passing it through a food mill, blender, food processor or vertical chopper mixer (VCM) and strain through a china cap. If the soup is too thick, adjust the consistency by adding boiling white stock.

7. Finish the soup by adding hot milk or cream or a thin béchamel or cream sauce. Adjust the seasonings and serve.

RECIPE 11.4
CREAM OF BROCCOLI SOUP

Yield: 6 qt. (6 lt)

Whole butter	3 oz.	90 g
Onion, medium dice	12 oz.	340 g
Celery, medium dice	3 oz.	90 g
Broccoli, chopped	3 lb.	1.4 kg
Chicken velouté sauce, hot	4 qt.	4 lt
Chicken stock, hot	approx. 2 qt.	approx. 2 lt
Heavy cream, hot	24 oz.	700 g
Salt and white pepper	TT	TT
Broccoli florets	8 oz.	250 g

1. Sweat the onions, celery and broccoli in the butter, without browning, until they are nearly tender.

2. Add the velouté sauce. Bring to a simmer and cook until the vegetables are tender, approximately 15 minutes. Skim the surface periodically.

3. Purée the soup, then strain it through a fine china cap or chinois.

4. Return the soup to the stove and thin it to the correct consistency with the hot chicken stock.

5. Bring the soup to a simmer and add the hot cream. Season to taste with salt and white pepper.

6. Garnish with blanched broccoli florets just before service.

VARIATIONS: To make cream of asparagus, cauliflower, corn, pea or spinach soup, substitute an equal amount of the chosen vegetable for the broccoli. If using fresh spinach, precook the leaves slightly before proceeding with the recipe.

◆◆◆

CROUTONS

A crouton is simply a piece of bread that is toasted, sautéed or dried. Two types are often used.

The more familiar ones are small seasoned cubes of bread that are baked or toasted and sprinkled over soups or salads.

A more classic variety is made by sautéing slices of bread in clarified butter or olive oil until brown and crisp. The bread may be rough slices from a baguette or cut into shapes (such as hearts, diamonds or circles) from larger slices. Sautéed croutons have two advantages over the toasted variety: They stay crisp longer after coming in contact with moist foods, and they gain flavor from the butter or olive oil in which they are cooked. Sautéed croutons can be used to decorate the border of a serving dish, as a base for canapés, a garnish for soups, an accompaniment to spreads or caviar or as a base under some meat and game dishes.

Purée Soups

Purée soups are hearty soups made by cooking starchy vegetables or legumes in a stock or broth, then puréeing all or a portion of them to thicken the soup. Purée soups are similar to cream soups in that they both consist of a main ingredient that is first cooked in a liquid, then puréed. The primary difference is that unlike cream soups, which are thickened with starch, purée soups generally do not use additional starch for thickening. Rather, purée soups depend on the starch content of the main ingredient for thickening. Also, purée soups are generally coarser than cream soups and are typically not strained after puréeing. When finishing purée soups with cream, follow the guidelines discussed above for adding cream to cream soups.

Purée soups can be made with dried or fresh beans such as peas, lentils and navy beans, or with any number of vegetables including cauliflower, celery root, turnips and potatoes. Diced potatoes or rice are often used to help thicken vegetable purée soups.

Procedure for Making Purée Soups

1. Sweat the mirepoix in butter without browning.
2. Add the cooking liquid.
3. Add the main ingredients and a sachet or bouquet garni.
4. Bring to a boil, reduce to a simmer and cook until all the ingredients are soft enough to purée easily. Remove and discard the sachet or bouquet garni.
5. Reserve a portion of the liquid to adjust the soup's consistency. Purée the rest of the soup by passing it through a food mill, food processor, blender or VCM.
6. Add enough of the reserved liquid to bring the soup to the correct consistency. If the soup is still too thick, add hot stock as needed.
7. Return the soup to a simmer and adjust the seasonings.
8. Add hot cream to the soup if desired.

◆◆◆

RECIPE 11.5

PURÉE OF SPLIT PEA SOUP

Yield: 4 qt. (4 lt)

Bacon, diced	3 oz.	90 g
Mirepoix, medium dice	1 lb.	450 g
Garlic cloves, chopped	2	2
Chicken stock	3 qt.	3 lt
Split peas, washed and sorted	1 lb.	450 g
Ham hocks or meaty ham bones	1-1/2 lb.	650 g
Sachet:		
Bay leaves	2	2
Dried thyme	1/2 tsp.	2 ml
Peppercorns, crushed	1/2 tsp.	2 ml
Salt and pepper	TT	TT
Croutons, sautéed in butter	as needed for garnish	

Render—*to melt and clarify fat.*

1. In a stockpot, **render** the bacon by cooking it slowly and allowing it to release its fat; sweat the mirepoix and garlic in the fat without browning them.

2. Add the chicken stock, peas, ham hocks or bones and sachet. Bring to a boil, reduce to a simmer and cook until the peas are soft, approximately 1 to 1-1/2 hours.
3. Remove the sachet and ham hocks or bones. Pass the soup through a food mill and return it to the stockpot.
4. Remove the meat from the hocks or bones. Cut the meat into a medium dice and add it to the soup.
5. Bring the soup to a simmer and, if necessary, adjust the consistency by adding hot chicken stock. Adjust the seasonings with salt and pepper and serve, garnished with croutons.

VARIATIONS: White beans, yellow peas, and other dried beans can be soaked overnight in water and used instead of split peas.

Adjusting the Consistency of Thick Soups

Cream and purée soups tend to thicken when made in advance and refrigerated. To dilute a portion being reheated, add a small amount of stock, broth, water or milk.

If the soup is too thin, additional roux, beurre manié or cornstarch mixed with cool stock can be used to thicken it. If additional starch is added to thicken the soup it should be used sparingly and the soup should be simmered a few minutes to cook out the starchy flavor. A liaison of egg yolks and heavy cream can be used to thicken cream soups when added richness is also desired. Remember, the soup must not boil after the liaison is added or it may curdle.

OTHER SOUPS

Several popular types of soup do not fit the descriptions of or follow the procedures for clear or thick soups. Soups such as bisques and chowders as well as many cold soups use special methods or a combination of the methods used for clear and thick soups.

Bisques

Traditional bisques are shellfish soups thickened with cooked rice. Today bisques are prepared using a combination of the cream and purée soup procedures. They are generally made from shrimp, lobster or crayfish and are thickened with a roux instead of rice for better stability and consistency.

Much of a bisque's flavor comes from crustacean shells, which are simmered in the cooking liquid, puréed (along with the mirepoix), returned to the cooking liquid and strained after further cooking. Puréeing the shells and returning them to the soup also adds the thickness and grainy texture associated with bisques.

Bisques are enriched with cream, following the procedures for cream soups, and can be finished with butter for additional richness. The garnish should be diced flesh from the appropriate shellfish.

PROCEDURE FOR MAKING BISQUES

1. Caramelize the mirepoix and main flavoring ingredient in fat.
2. Add a tomato product and deglaze with wine.

3. Add the cooking liquid (stock or velouté).

4. Incorporate roux if needed.

5. Simmer, skimming as needed.

6. Strain the soup, reserving the solids and liquid. Purée the solids in a food chopper or processor and return them to the liquid. Return to a simmer.

7. Strain the soup through a fine chinois or a china cap lined with cheesecloth.

8. Return the soup to a simmer and finish with hot cream.

To add even more richness to the bisque, monté au beurre with whole butter or a compound butter such as shrimp or lobster butter just before the soup is served. Also, if desired, add 3 ounces (90 milliliters) of sherry to each gallon (4 liters) of soup just before service.

◆◆◆

RECIPE 11.6

SHRIMP BISQUE

Yield: 4 qt. (4 lt)

Clarified butter	3 oz.	90 g
Mirepoix, small dice	1 lb.	450 g
Shrimp shells and/or lobster or crayfish shells and bodies	2 lb.	1 kg
Garlic cloves, chopped	2	2
Tomato paste	2 oz.	60 g
Brandy	4 oz.	120 g
White wine	12 oz.	350 g
Fish velouté (made with shrimp stock)	4 qt.	4 lt
Sachet:		
Bay leaf	1	1
Dried thyme	1/2 tsp.	2 ml
Peppercorns, crushed	1/2 tsp.	2 ml
Parsley stems	8	8
Heavy cream, hot	1 pt.	500 ml
Salt and white pepper	TT	TT
Cayenne pepper	TT	TT
Shrimp, peeled and deveined	1 lb.	450 g

1. Caramelize the mirepoix and shrimp shells in the butter.

2. Add the garlic and tomato paste and sauté lightly.

3. Add the brandy and flambé.

4. Add the white wine. Deglaze and reduce the liquid by half.

5. Add the velouté and sachet and simmer for approximately 1 hour, skimming occasionally.

6. Strain, discarding the sachet and reserving the liquid and solids. Purée the solids and return them to the liquid. Return to a simmer and cook for 10 minutes.

7. Strain the bisque through a fine chinois or china cap lined with cheesecloth.

8. Return the bisque to a simmer and add the hot cream.

9. Season to taste with salt, white pepper and cayenne pepper.

10. Cook the shrimp and slice or dice them as desired. Garnish each portion of soup with cooked shrimp.

Chowders

Although chowders are usually associated with the eastern United States where fish and clams are plentiful, they are of French origin. Undoubtedly the word *chowder* is derived from the Breton phrase *faire chaudière*, which means to make a fish stew in a caldron. The procedure was probably brought to Nova Scotia by French settlers and later introduced into New England.

Chowders are hearty soups with chunks of the main ingredients (including, virtually always, diced potatoes) and garnishes. With some exceptions (notably, Manhattan clam chowder), chowders contain milk or cream. Although there are thin chowders, most chowders are thickened with roux. The procedures for making chowders are similar to those for making cream soups except that chowders are not puréed and strained before the cream is added.

PROCEDURE FOR MAKING CHOWDERS

1. Render finely diced salt pork over medium heat.
2. Sweat mirepoix in the rendered pork.
3. Add flour to make a roux.
4. Add the liquid.
5. Add the seasoning and flavoring ingredients according to their cooking times.
6. Simmer, skimming as needed.
7. Add milk or cream.

RECIPE 11.7

NEW ENGLAND STYLE CLAM CHOWDER

Yield: 3 qt. (3 lt)

Canned clams with juice*	2 qt.	2 lt
Water or fish stock	approx. 1-1/2 qt.	approx. 1.5 lt
Potato, small dice	1 lb. 4 oz.	600 g
Salt pork, small dice	8 oz.	250 g
Onion, small dice	1 lb.	500 g
Celery, small dice	8 oz.	250 g
Flour	4 oz.	120 g
Milk	1 qt.	1 lt
Heavy cream	8 oz.	250 g
Salt and pepper	TT	TT
Tabasco sauce	TT	TT
Worcestershire sauce	TT	TT
Fresh thyme	TT	TT

1. Drain the clams, reserving both the clams and their liquid. Add enough water or stock so that the total liquid equals 2 quarts (2 liters).
2. Simmer the potatoes in the clam liquid until nearly cooked through. Strain and reserve the potatoes and the liquid.
3. Render the salt pork without browning it. Add the onions and celery and sweat until tender.
4. Add the flour and cook to make a blond roux.
5. Add the clam liquid to the roux, whisking away any lumps.
6. Simmer for 30 minutes, skimming as necessary.

Continued

7. Bring the milk and cream to a boil and add to the soup.

8. Add the clams and potatoes and season to taste with salt, pepper, Tabasco, Worcestershire and thyme.

* If using fresh clams for the chowder, wash and steam approximately 1/2 bushel of chowder clams in a small amount of water to yield 1-1/4 quarts (1.25 liters) of clam meat. Chop the clams. Strain the liquid through several layers of cheese-cloth to remove any sand that may be present. Add enough water or stock so the total liquid is 2 quarts (2 liters). Continue with the recipe, starting at step 2.

Cold Soups

Cold soups can be as simple as a chilled version of a cream soup or as unique as a cold fruit soup blended with yogurt. Other than the fact that they are cold, cold soups are difficult to classify because many of them use unique or combination preparation methods. Regardless, they are divided here into two categories: cold soups that require cooking and those that do not.

Cooked Cold Soups

Many cold soups are simply a chilled version of a hot soup. For example, consommé madrilène and consommé portugaise are prepared hot and served cold. Vichyssoise, probably the most popular of all cold soups, is a cold version of purée of potato-leek soup. When serving a hot soup cold, there are several considerations:

1. If the soup is to be creamed, add the cream at the last minute. Although curdling is not as much of a problem as it is with hot soups, adding the cream at the last minute helps extend the soup's shelf life.

2. Cold soups should have a thinner consistency than hot soups. To achieve the proper consistency, use less starch if starch is used as the thickener, or use a higher ratio of liquid to main ingredient if the soup is thickened by puréeing. Consistency should be checked and adjusted at service time.

3. Cold dulls the sense of taste, so cold soups require more seasoning than hot ones. Taste the soup just before service and adjust the seasonings as needed.

4. Always serve cold soups as cold as possible.

◆◆◆

RECIPE 11.8

VICHYSSOISE
(COLD POTATO-LEEK SOUP)

Yield: 4 qt. (4 lt)

Leek, white part only	2 lb.	1 kg
Whole butter	8 oz.	250 g
Potato, large dice	2 lb.	1 kg
Chicken stock	3-1/2 qt.	3-1/2 lt
Salt and white pepper	TT	TT
Heavy cream	24 oz.	700 g
Chives, snipped	as needed	as needed

1. Split the leeks lengthwise and wash well to remove all sand and grit. Slice them thinly.

2. Sweat the leeks in the butter without browning them.

3. Add the potatoes and chicken stock, season with salt and pepper and bring to a simmer.

4. Simmer until the leeks and potatoes are very tender, approximately 45 minutes.

5. Purée the soup in a food processor, blender or food mill; strain through a fine sieve.

6. Chill the soup well.

7. At service time, incorporate the heavy cream and adjust the seasonings. Serve in chilled bowls, garnished with snipped chives.

Many cooked cold soups use fruit juice (typically apple, grape or orange) as a base and are thickened with cornstarch or arrowroot as well as with puréed fruit. For additional flavor, wine is sometimes used in lieu of a portion of the fruit juice. Cinnamon, ginger and other spices that complement fruit are commonly added, as is lemon or lime juice, which adds acidity as well as flavor. Crème fraîche, yogurt or sour cream can be used as an ingredient or garnish to add richness.

RECIPE 11.9
CHILLED CHERRY SOUP

Yield: 4 qt. (4 lt)

Cherries, pitted	5 lb.	2.25 kg
Apple juice	approx. 2 qt.	approx. 2 lt
Sachet:		
Cinnamon sticks	2	2
Cloves, whole	4	4
Honey	6 oz.	170 g
Cornstarch	1 oz.	30 g
Lemon juice	TT	TT
Dry champagne or sparkling wine	8 oz.	250 g
Crème fraîche	as needed for garnish	
Toasted almonds	as needed for garnish	

1. Combine the cherries, apple juice, sachet and honey. Bring to a simmer and cook for 30 minutes. Remove the sachet.

2. Dilute the cornstarch with a small amount of cold apple juice. Add it to the soup for thickening. Simmer the soup for 10 minutes to cook out the starchy taste.

3. Purée the soup in a food processor or blender and strain if desired.

4. Chill the soup thoroughly.

5. At service, adjust the seasoning with the lemon juice. Stir in the chilled champagne or sparkling wine and serve garnished with crème fraîche and toasted, slivered almonds.

Uncooked Cold Soups

Some cold soups are not cooked at all. Rather they rely only on puréed fruits or vegetables for thickness, body and flavor. Cold stock is sometimes used to adjust the soup's consistency. Dairy products such as cream, sour cream or crème fraîche are sometimes added to enrich and flavor the soup.

Because uncooked cold soups are never heated, enzymes and bacteria are not destroyed and the soup can spoil quickly. When preparing uncooked cold soups, always prepare small batches as close to service time as possible.

◆◆◆

RECIPE 11.10
GAZPACHO

Yield: 4 qt. (4 lt)

Tomato, peeled and diced	2 lb. 8 oz.	1.2 kg
Onion, medium dice	8 oz.	250 g
Green pepper, medium dice	1	1
Red pepper, medium dice	1	1
Cucumber, peeled, seeded, medium dice	1 lb.	500 g
Garlic, minced	1 oz.	30 g
Red wine vinegar	2 oz.	60 g
Lemon juice	2 oz.	60 g
Olive oil	4 oz	120 g
Salt and pepper	TT	TT
Cayenne pepper	TT	TT
Fresh bread crumbs (optional)	3 oz.	90 g
Tomato juice	3 qt.	3 lt
White stock	as needed	as needed
Garnish:		
Tomato, peeled, seeded, small dice	8 oz	250 g
Red pepper, small dice	4 oz.	120 g
Green pepper, small dice	4 oz.	120 g
Yellow pepper, small dice	4 oz.	120 g
Cucumber, peeled, seeded, small dice	3 oz.	90 g
Green onion, sliced fine	2 oz.	60 g
Croutons	as needed	as needed

1. Combine and purée all ingredients except the tomato juice, stock and garnish in a VCM, food processor or blender.
2. Stir in the tomato juice.
3. Adjust the consistency with stock.
4. Stir in the vegetables, the garnishes and adjust the seasonings.
5. Serve in chilled cups or bowls garnished with croutons.

GARNISHING SOUPS

Garnishes can range from a simple sprinkle of chopped parsley on a bowl of cream soup to tiny profiteroles stuffed with foie gras adorning a crystal-clear bowl of consommé. Some soups are so full of attractive, flavorful and colorful foods that are integral parts of the soup (for example, vegetables and chicken in chicken vegetable soup) that no additional garnishes (as either decoration or component) are necessary. In others, the garnish determines the type of soup. For example, a beef broth garnished with cooked barley and diced beef becomes beef barley soup.

Guidelines for Garnishing Soups

Although some soups (particularly consommés) have traditional garnishes, many soups depend on the chef's imagination and the kitchen's inventory for the finishing garnish. The only rules are:

1. The garnish should be attractive.
2. The meats and vegetables used should be neatly cut into an appropriate and uniform shape and size. This is particularly important when garnishing a clear soup such as a consommé, as the consommé's clarity highlights the precise (or imprecise) cuts.
3. The garnish's texture and flavor should complement the soup.
4. Starches and vegetables used as garnishes should be cooked separately, reheated and placed in the soup bowl before the hot soup is added. If they are cooked in the soup, they may cloud or thicken the soup or alter its flavor, texture and seasoning.
5. Garnishes should be cooked just until done; meat and poultry should be tender but not falling apart, vegetables should be firm but not mushy and pasta and rice should maintain their identity. These types of garnishes are usually held on the side and added to the hot soup at the last minute to prevent overcooking.

Garnishing Suggestions

◆ Clear soups—any combination of julienne cuts of the same meat, poultry, fish or vegetable that provides the dominant flavor in the stock or broth, vegetables (cut uniformly into any shape), pasta (flat, small tortellini or tiny ravioli), gnocchi, quenelles, barley, spaetzle, white or wild rice, croutons, crepes, tortillas, or won tons.

◆◆◆ CLASSIC CONSOMMÉS

Many classic consommés are known by their garnishes:

Consommé brunoise—blanched or sautéed brunoise of turnip, leek, celery and onion.

Consommé julienne—blanched or sautéed julienne of carrot, turnip, leek, celery, cabbage and onion.

Consommé paysanne—blanched or sautéed paysanne of leek, turnip, carrot, celery and potato.

Consommé bouquetière—assorted blanched vegetables.

Consommé royale—cooked custard cut into tiny shapes.

Angels' hair consommé—cooked angel hair (vermicelli) pasta.

Consommé with profiteroles—tiny profiteroles (pâté à choux rounds) stuffed with foie gras.

TABLE 11.1   SOUPS, THEIR THICKENING AGENTS AND FINISHES

Category	Type	Thickening Agent or Method	Finish
Clear soups	Broths	None	Assorted garnishes
	Consommés	None	Assorted garnishes
Thick soups	Cream soups	Roux and/or puréeing	Assorted garnishes, cream or béchamel sauce
	Purée soups	Puréeing	Assorted garnishes; cream is optional
Other soups	Bisques	Roux or rice and puréeing	Garnish of main ingredient, cream and/or butter
	Chowders	Roux	Cream
Cold soups	Cooked cold soups	Roux, arrowroot, cornstarch, puréeing, sour cream, yogurt	Assorted garnishes, cream, crème fraîche or sour cream
	Uncooked cold soups	Puréeing	Assorted garnishes, cream, crème fraîche or sour cream

◆ Cream soups, hot or cold—toasted slivered almonds, sour cream or crème fraîche, croutons, grated cheese or puff pastry fleurons; cream vegetable soups are usually garnished with slices or florets of the main ingredient.

◆ Purée soups—julienne cuts of poultry or ham, sliced sausage, croutons, grated cheese, bacon bits.

◆ Any soup—finely chopped fresh herbs, snipped chives, edible flower blossoms or petals, parsley or watercress.

Soup Service

Preparing Soups in Advance

Most soups can be made ahead of time and reheated as needed for service. To preserve freshness and quality, small batches of soup should be heated as needed throughout the meal service.

Clear soups are quite easy to reheat because there is little danger of scorching. If garnishes are already added to a clear soup, care should be taken not to overcook the garnishes when reheating the soup. All traces of fat should be removed from a consommé's surface before reheating.

Thick soups present more of a challenge. To increase shelf life and reduce the risk of spoilage, cool and refrigerate a thick soup when it is still a base (that is, before it is finished with milk or cream). When needed, carefully reheat the soup base just before service using a heavy-gauge pot over low heat. Stir often to prevent scorching. Then finish the soup (following the guidelines noted above) with boiling milk or cream, a light béchamel sauce or a liaison and adjust the seasonings. Always taste the soup after reheating and adjust the seasonings as needed.

Temperatures

The rule is simple: Serve hot soup hot and cold soup cold. Hot clear soups should be served near boiling; 210°F (99°C) is ideal. Hot cream soups should be served at slightly lower temperatures; 190–200°F (90–93°C) is acceptable. Cold soups should be served at a temperature of 40°F (4°C) or below, and are sometimes presented in special serving pieces surrounded by ice.

Conclusion

Soup, often served as the first course, may determine the success or failure of an entire meal. Although a wide variety of ingredients can be used to make both clear and thick soups, including trimmings and leftovers, poor-quality ingredients make poor-quality soups. By using, adapting and combining the basic techniques described in this chapter with different ingredients, you can create an infinite number of new and appetizing hot or cold soups. But exercise good judgment when combining flavors and techniques; they should blend well and complement each other. Moreover, any garnishes that are added should contribute to the appearance and character of the finished soup. And remember, always serve hot soups hot and cold soups cold.

QUESTIONS FOR DISCUSSION

1. What are the differences between a stock and a broth?
2. What are the differences between a beef consommé and a beef-based broth? How are they similar?
3. What are the differences between a cream soup and a purée soup? How are they similar?
4. Create a recipe for veal consommé.
5. Discuss several techniques for serving soup. What can be done to ensure that soups are served at the correct temperature?
6. Explain how and why soups are garnished. Why is it sometimes said that the noodles in a chicken noodle soup are actually a garnish?

ADDITIONAL SOUP RECIPES

RECIPE 11.11

WILD MUSHROOM SOUP WITH FOIE GRAS

NOTE: *This recipe appears in the Chapter Opening photo.*

CHRISTOPHER'S AND CHRISTOPHER'S BISTRO, PHOENIX, AZ
Chef/Owner Christoper Gross

Yield: 8 servings

Port	6 oz.	180 g
Duck stock	2 qt.	2 lt
Chanterelles	4 oz.	120 g
White mushroom caps	4 oz.	120 g
Olive oil	1 Tbsp.	15 ml
Shallots, chopped fine	1 Tbsp.	15 ml
Fresh tarragon or chervil, chopped	3 Tbsp.	45 ml
Tomato concasse	4 oz.	120 g
Foie gras, sinew and veins trimmed	12 oz.	350 g
Fresh truffle (winter or summer)	1	1
White truffle oil	1 tsp.	5 ml

1. Reduce the port to 2 ounces (60 grams). Bring the stock to a boil and add the port and any mushroom stems or peels. Simmer 5 minutes; strain and reserve in a warm place.
2. Trim the stems from the chanterelles and sauté the caps with the white mushroom caps in the olive oil. Add the shallots and cook until they become soft and translucent.
3. Place the mushrooms, tomato concasse and tarragon or chervil in the bottom of eight shallow soup bowls.
4. Portion the foie gras into 8 slices and sear briefly in a very hot, dry pan.
5. Place a slice of the foie gras on top of the mushrooms in the center of each bowl.
6. Julienne the truffle and arrange a portion in each bowl.
7. Pour the hot soup into the bowls and add a drop of truffle oil to each bowl.

◆◆◆

RECIPE 11.12
WILD MUSHROOMS AND VEAL SOUP

Yield: 1 qt. (1 lt)

Garlic, minced	2 tsp.	10 ml
Olive oil	4 oz.	120 g
Assorted wild mushrooms, such as shiitake, oyster, cèpes and morels	8 oz.	250 g
Brown veal stock	24 oz.	700 g
Fresh parsley, minced	2 Tbsp.	30 ml
Fresh mint, minced	4 Tbsp.	60 ml
Salt and pepper	TT	TT
French bread croutons	as needed for garnish	
Fresh parsley, chopped fine	as needed for garnish	

1. Briefly sauté the garlic in the olive oil. Add the mushrooms and cook until tender and the liquid has evaporated.
2. Add the veal broth, parsley and mint; simmer for 15 minutes.
3. Place one crouton in each soup bowl. Ladle in the soup and garnish with finely chopped parsley.

◆◆◆

RECIPE 11.13
CHICKEN SOUP WITH MATZO BALLS

MATZO BALLS

Yield: 48 balls

Eggs	4	4
Water	2 oz.	60 g
Chicken fat or butter, softened	2 oz.	60 g
Matzo meal	4 oz.	120 g
Salt and white pepper	TT	TT

1. Beat the eggs with the water. Stir in the fat.
2. Add matzo meal, salt and pepper. The batter should be as thick as mashed potatoes.
3. Chill for at least 1 hour.
4. Bring 2 quarts of water to a gentle boil. Using a #70 portion scoop, shape the batter into balls. Carefully drop each ball into the hot water. Cover and simmer until fully cooked, approximately 30 minutes. Remove matzo balls from the water and serve in hot chicken soup.

RICH CHICKEN BROTH

Yield: 2 gal. (8 lt)

Chicken pieces	8–10 lb.	4–4.4 kg
Chicken stock	10 qt.	10 lt

Mirepoix	1 lb.	500 g
Sachet:		
Bay leaf	1	1
Dried thyme	1/2 tsp.	2 ml
Peppercorns, crushed	1/2 tsp.	2 ml
Parsley stems	10	10
Salt and pepper	TT	TT
Fresh Parsley, chopped	as needed for garnish	

1. Simmer the chicken in the stock for 2 hours, skimming as necessary.

2. Add the mirepoix and sachet. Simmer for another hour.

3. Strain and degrease the broth. Adjust seasonings.

4. Bring to a boil at service time. Portion into heated bowls, garnish with one or two matzo balls and chopped parsley.

◆◆◆

RECIPE 11.14

MOROCCAN HARIRA
(LAMB, CHICKEN AND LENTIL SOUP)

Yield: 4 qt. (4 lt)

Olive oil	5 oz.	140 g
Stewing lamb, cubed	2 lb. 8 oz.	1.2 kg
Chicken pieces	3–4 lb.	1.3–1.8 kg
Garlic cloves	5	5
Onion, chopped fine	2 lb.	1 kg
Chickpeas, canned	8 oz.	250 g
Chicken stock	5 qt.	5 lt
Turmeric	1-1/2 tsp.	7 ml
Ginger, ground	1-1/2 tsp.	7 ml
Coriander	1-1/2 tsp.	7 ml
Cinnamon	1-1/2 tsp.	7 ml
Tomatoes, canned, chopped	2 lb. 8 oz.	1.2 kg
Lentils, washed	9 oz.	250 g
Rice	4 oz.	120 g
Salt and pepper	TT	TT
Parsley, chopped	5 Tbsp.	75 ml
Whole eggs, beaten	5	5
Lemon juice	5 Tbsp.	75 ml

1. Heat the oil in a large, heavy sauté pan. Lightly brown the lamb, then transfer it to a large saucepot. Repeat for the chicken, garlic and onions.

2. Add the chickpeas, stock, spices, tomatoes and lentils. Cover and simmer for 40 minutes.

3. Add the rice and simmer 20 minutes longer.

Continued

4. Remove the chicken pieces from the soup. Skin them and remove the meat. Dice the meat and return it to the soup.

5. Adjust the seasonings, add the parsley and return to a simmer.

6. Immediately before service, whisk the eggs and lemon juice together. Then slowly pour them into the soup, stirring to create strands of egg throughout the soup.

7. Serve in heated bowls with lemon wedges and harissa on the side.

HARISSA

Yield: 6 Tbsp. (90 ml)

Dried chile peppers, crushed	1 Tbsp.	15 ml
Cayenne pepper	1 Tbsp.	15 ml
Cumin, ground	2 tsp.	10 ml
Caraway seeds	2 tsp.	10 ml
Garlic cloves	2	2
Olive oil	3 Tbsp.	45 ml
Salt	1 tsp.	5 ml

1. Grind the spices and garlic together in a mortar and pestle, blender or spice grinder.

2. Heat the oil. Stir in the spices and salt and cook over a low flame, stirring constantly, for 3 minutes.

◆◆◆

RECIPE 11.15

FRENCH ONION SOUP

Yield: 4 qt. (4 lt)

Yellow onion, thinly sliced	10 lb.	4.4 kg
Clarified butter	8 oz.	250 g
Beef stock	4 qt.	4 lt
Chicken stock	4 qt.	4 lt
Fresh thyme	1/2 oz.	14 g
Salt and pepper	TT	TT
Sherry	8 oz.	250 g
Toasted French bread slices	as needed for garnish	
Gruyère cheese, grated	as needed for garnish	

1. Sauté the onions in the butter over low heat. Carefully caramelize them thoroughly without burning.

2. Deglaze the pan with 8 oz. (250 g.) of the beef stock. Cook au sec. Repeat this process until the onions are a very dark, even brown.

3. Add the remaining beef stock, the chicken stock and thyme.

4. Bring to a simmer and cook 20 minutes to develop flavor. Adjust the seasonings and add the sherry.

5. Serve in warm bowls. Top each portion with a slice of toasted French bread and a thick layer of cheese. Place under the broiler or salamander until the cheese is melted and lightly browned.

✦✦✦

RECIPE 11.16

MINESTRONE

Minestrone is a rich vegetable soup of Italian heritage. Northern Italian versions are made with beef stock, butter, rice and ribbon-shaped pasta. Southern Italian versions, such as the one given here, contain tomatoes, garlic, olive oil and tubular-shaped pasta. The vegetables should be fresh and varied. Substitute or change those listed as necessary to reflect the season.

Yield: 2 gal. (8 lt)

Dry white beans	1 lb.	450 g
Olive oil	2 Tbsp.	30 ml
Onion, diced	10 oz.	300 g
Garlic cloves, minced	2	2
Celery, diced	1 lb.	450 g
Carrot, diced	12 oz.	340 g
Zucchini, diced	1 lb.	450 g
Green beans, cut in		
1/2-inch (1.25 cm) pieces	10 oz.	300 g
Cabbage, diced	1 lb.	450 g
Vegetable stock	5 qt.	5 lt
Tomato, concasse	1 lb.	450 g
Tomato paste, low-sodium	12 oz.	340 g
Fresh oregano, chopped	1 Tbsp.	15 ml
Fresh basil, chopped	2 Tbsp.	30 ml
Fresh chervil, chopped	1 Tbsp.	15 ml
Fresh parsley, chopped	2 Tbsp.	30 ml
Salt and pepper	TT	TT
Elbow macaroni, cooked	4 oz.	120 g
Parmesan cheese, grated	as needed for garnish (optional)	

1. Soak the beans in cold water overnight, then drain.
2. Cover the beans with water and simmer until tender, about 40 minutes.
3. Sauté the onions in the oil. Add garlic, celery and carrots and cook for three minutes.
4. Add the remaining vegetables, one type at a time, cooking each briefly.
5. Add the stock, tomatoes and tomato paste. Cover and simmer for 2-1/2–3 hours.
6. Stir in the chopped herbs and season to taste with salt and pepper.
7. Add the drained beans and cooked macaroni.
8. Bring the soup to a simmer and simmer 15 minutes. Serve in warm bowls, garnished with parmesan cheese.

Nutritional values per 6-ounce (180 grams) serving without cheese:

Calories	79	Protein	2 g	
Calories from fat	21%	Vitamin A	2764 IU	
Total fat	2 g	Vitamin C	14 mg	
Saturated fat	0 g	Sodium	923 mg	
Cholesterol	0 mg			

✦✦✦

RECIPE 11.17

SEAFOOD BOUILLABAISSE

GOTHAM BAR AND GRILL, NEW YORK, NY
Chef/Owner Alfred Portale

Yield: 8 Servings

Olive oil	as needed	as needed
Spanish onion, julienne	10 oz.	300 g
Fennel bulb, small dice, reserve tops for stock	1	1
Leek, julienne	3 oz.	90 g
Cayenne Pepper	TT	TT
Garlic, chopped	1 oz.	30 g
Fresh tomato, chopped	2 qt.	2 lt
Fresh thyme	8 sprigs	8 sprigs
Fish Stock (recipe follows)	3 qt.	3 lt
Saffron	1 pinch	1 pinch
Salt and white pepper	TT	TT
Lobsters, 1 lb. 8 oz. (680 g) each	2	2
Mussels	24	24
Littleneck clams, scrubbed	24	24
Large shrimp, peeled, reserve shells	6	6
Sea scallops	1 lb. 8 oz.	680 g
Squid	1 lb. 8 oz.	680 g
Pernod	6 oz.	170 g
New potatoes, small	16	16
Parsley, chopped	3 Tbsp.	45 ml
Rouille (recipe follows)		

1. In a pot large enough to hold all the shellfish comfortably, heat the olive oil. Add the onions, fennel, leeks and cayenne pepper; cook for 15 minutes over low heat. Add the garlic and continue cooking for one minute.

2. Add the tomatoes, thyme, 3 quarts (3 liters) of fish stock and saffron. Bring to a boil, reduce the heat and simmer until the stock is slightly reduced and intensely flavored. Adjust the seasonings.

3. While the soup is cooking, cook the lobsters in rapidly boiling salted water for 6 minutes. When cool enough to handle, shell them over a bowl to catch juices. Dice the meat and reserve.

4. To serve, bring the soup to a boil. Add the mussels and clams and cook for 2–3 minutes. Add the shrimp and scallops and cook until the mussels open.

5. Add the cooked lobster and reserved lobster juices. Add the squid. Heat thoroughly. Add the Pernod to taste.

6. Steam the potatoes, and arrange in the serving dish. Arrange the seafood over the potatoes.

7. Sprinkle the bouillabaisse with chopped parsley and serve with the rouille.

FISH STOCK

Yield: 3 qt. (3 lt)

Spanish onion, medium	1	1
Fennel top, chopped	1	1
Celery stalk	1	1
Tomatoes, large	3	3
Olive oil	as needed	as needed
Garlic cloves	10	10
Fish bones	3 lb.	1.3 kg
Shrimp shells	6	6
Fresh thyme	2 sprigs	2 sprigs
Orange peel	from 1 orange	from 1 orange
Coriander seed	1 Tbsp.	15 ml
White pepper, cracked	1 Tbsp.	15 ml
Bay leaves	2	2
Dry white wine	26 oz.	750 ml
Water	3 qt.	3 lt

1. Coarsely chop the vegetables and tomatoes. Heat the olive oil in a stock-pot. Add the onions, fennel tops, celery and tomatoes. Sauté for 15 minutes over low heat.

2. Add the garlic. Cook an additional 5 minutes.

3. Add the fish bones, shrimp shells, seasonings and white wine. Raise the heat and reduce the wine for 20 minutes.

4. Add 3 quarts (3 liters)of water. Simmer slowly for 45 minutes. Strain and reserve. This should be made one or two days in advance.

ROUILLE

White bread, crust removed	1 slice	1 slice
Heavy cream	2 oz.	60 g
Egg yolks	3	3
Garlic cloves, minced	6	6
Salt and white pepper	TT	TT
Olive oil	6 oz.	180 g
Cayenne pepper	TT	TT

1. In a bowl, soften the bread in the cream. Whisk in the egg yolks. Add the garlic, salt and white pepper.

2. Add the olive oil in a steady stream. Whisk constantly until the rouille is thick and fluffy. Season with cayenne pepper.

3. Serve in a separate bowl to drizzle over soup.

◆◆◆

RECIPE 11.18
CHEDDAR AND LEEK SOUP

Yield: 2 qt. (2 lt)

Whole butter	1 oz.	30 g
Mirepoix, chopped fine	8 oz.	250 g
Leek, chopped fine	8 oz.	250 g
Flour	2 oz.	60 g
Chicken stock	1-1/2 qt.	1-1/2 lt
Sachet:		
Bay leaf	1	1
Dried thyme	1/4 tsp.	1 ml
Peppercorns, crushed	1/4 tsp.	1 ml
Dry white wine or flat beer	4 oz.	120 g
Half-and-half	4 oz.	120 g
Cheddar cheese, grated	1 lb.	500 g
Salt	TT	TT
Cayenne pepper	TT	TT
Fresh parsley, chopped	as needed for garnish	
Croutons	as needed for garnish	

1. Sweat mirepoix and leeks in the butter until tender.
2. Stir in the flour and cook to make a blond roux.
3. Add stock and sachet and bring to a boil. Add wine (or beer), half-and-half and cheese. Simmer for 1 hour.
4. Strain; adjust seasonings with salt and cayenne pepper. Thin with additional warm half-and-half, if necessary.
5. Serve in warm bowls, garnished with parsley and croutons.

◆◆◆

RECIPE 11.19
SPELT SOUP

REX IL RISTORANTE, LOS ANGELES, CA
Executive Chef Odette Fada

Yield: 6 Servings

Extra-virgin olive oil	5 Tbsp.	75 ml
Mirepoix	10 oz.	300 g
Shallot, minced	1	1
Leek, small, chopped fine	1	1
Garlic cloves, minced	2	2
Bay leaves	2	2
Dried rosemary	1/2 tsp.	2 ml
Dried thyme	1 tsp.	5 ml
Spelt (whole, toasted wheat berries)	4 oz.	120 g
Vegetable stock	1-1/2 qt.	1-1/2 lt
Salt and pepper	TT	TT
Prosciutto	2 slices	2 slices
Spinach leaves	10	10

1. Sauté the mirepoix, shallot, leek, garlic and herbs in 3 tablespoons (45 milliliters) olive oil for 5 minutes.

2. Add the spelt and stock; simmer for 50 minutes. Remove the bay leaves.

3. Purée the soup, adding more stock to thin if necessary. Adjust seasonings.

4. Julienne the prosciutto. Cut the spinach in a chiffonade.

5. Serve the soup in hot bowls. Top each portion with some of the prosciutto and spinach and 1 teaspoon (5 milliliters) of olive oil.

◆◆◆

RECIPE 11.20

SOUTHWESTERN BLACK BEAN SOUP

Yield: 4 qt. (4 lt)

Dried black beans, soaked	1 lb.	500 g
Vegetable stock or water	5 qt.	5 lt
Sachet:		
Bay leaves	2	2
Dried thyme	1/2 tsp.	2 ml
Peppercorns, cracked	10	10
Canola oil	1 Tbsp.	15 ml
Onion, diced	4 oz.	120 g
Garlic cloves, minced	2	2
Anaheim chiles, diced	1 oz.	30 g
Jalapeño or Serrano chiles, minced	1 Tbsp.	15 ml
Cumin, ground	1 tsp.	5 ml
Coriander, ground	1 tsp.	5 ml
Dried oregano	1 tsp.	5 ml
Salt and pepper	TT	TT
Lime wedges	as needed for garnish	
Cilantro	as needed for garnish	

1. Combine the beans and stock or water and bring to a simmer. Add the sachet.

2. Sauté the onions, garlic and chiles in the oil. Add to the saucepot.

3. Stir in the cumin, coriander and oregano.

4. Simmer the soup, uncovered, approximately 2–3 hours. The beans should be very soft, just beginning to fall apart. Add additional water or stock if necessary.

5. Puree about half of the soup, then stir it back into the remaining soup. Season to taste with salt and black pepper.

6. Serve in warmed bowls garnished with lime wedges and chopped cilantro.

Nutritional Values per 6-ounce (180 gram) serving:

Calories	81	Protein	2 g
Calories from fat	31%	Vitamin A	302 IU
Total fat	3 g	Vitamin C	3 mg
Saturated fat	1 g	Sodium	1804 mg
Cholesterol	0 mg		

◆◆◆

RECIPE 11.21

ROASTED CORN CHOWDER

Yield: 1 qt. (1 lt)

Corn, unshucked	10 ears	10 ears
Milk, warmed	3 pt.	1500 ml
Salt pork, small dice	4 oz.	120 g
Celery, small dice	5 oz.	150 g
Onion, small dice	10 oz.	300 g
Garlic cloves, minced	4	4
Flour	2 oz.	60 g
Cream, warmed	4 oz.	120 g
Worcestershire sauce	1 Tbsp.	15 ml
Fresh thyme	1 tsp.	5 ml
Nutmeg, ground	TT	TT
Salt and white pepper	TT	TT
Parsley, chopped fine	as needed for garnish	

1. Roast the ears of corn, in their husks, in a 400°F (200°C) oven for 45 minutes. Cool, shuck the corn and cut off the kernels. Purée half the corn kernels in a blender, adding a small amount of milk if necessary.
2. Render the salt pork. Add the celery, onions and garlic and sauté lightly.
3. Stir in the flour and cook to make a blond roux.
4. Add the remaining warm milk and bring to a simmer.
5. Add the puréed corn and the remaining corn kernels. Simmer 10 minutes.
6. Add the warm cream; adjust the seasonings with Worcestershire sauce, thyme, nutmeg, salt and white pepper.
7. Serve in warm bowls garnished with chopped parsley.

◆◆◆

RECIPE 11.22

CHICKEN AND SAUSAGE GUMBO

Gumbo, a thick, spicy stew, is traditional fare in the delta region of the American South. Gumbo is usually made with poultry, fish, shellfish or sausage and is thickened with dark roux. Okra or filé powder (ground sassafras leaves) may also be added for thickening. Filé powder is sometimes added at the time of service for additional flavor. Gumbo is traditionally served over white rice.

Yield: 3 qt. (3 lt)

Chicken pieces	3–4 lb.	1.3–1.8 kg
Flour	as needed	as needed
Onion powder	as needed	as needed
Salt	as needed	as needed
Cayenne pepper	as needed	as needed
Vegetable oil	8 oz.	250 g
Flour	4 oz.	120 g
Onion, medium dice	6 oz.	170 g
Celery, medium dice	3 oz.	90 g
Green bell pepper, medium dice	6 oz.	170 g

Garlic, minced	1 tsp.	5 ml
Okra, sliced and blanched	5 oz.	140 g
Chicken stock, hot	2 qt.	2 lt
Jalapeño pepper, minced	1 tsp.	5 ml
Dried thyme	1/2 tsp.	2 ml
Dried oregano	1 tsp.	5 ml
Tomato paste	4 oz.	120 g
Andouille sausage	8 oz.	250 g
Filé powder, optional	as needed	as needed
White rice, boiled	as needed	as needed

1. Dredge the chicken in flour seasoned with onion powder, salt and cayenne pepper.

2. Pan-fry in the oil until done; drain.

3. Degrease the pan, reserving 4 ounces (120 milliliters) of the oil.

4. Add the flour to the pan and cook to make a very dark brown roux.

5. Add the onions, celery, green pepper and garlic and sauté briefly. Add the okra.

6. Add the chicken stock. Stir in the jalapeños, thyme, oregano and tomato paste. Simmer uncovered for 30 minutes.

7. Bone the cooked chicken and cut the meat into 1/2-inch (1.2 cm) pieces.

8. Slice the sausage on a diagonal into thin pieces and sauté. Remove and drain.

9. Add the chicken and sausage pieces to the gumbo. Adjust seasoning and simmer 30 minutes.

10. If filé powder is used, stir 1–2 teaspoons (5–10 milliliters) into each portion at service time.

11. Serve ladled over bowls of white rice.

◆◆◆

RECIPE 11.23

FRESH PEACH AND YOGURT SOUP

Yield: 2 qt. (2 lt)

Fresh peaches	4 lb.	1.8 kg
Dry white wine	24 oz.	700 g
Honey	4 oz.	120 g
Lemon juice	2 oz.	60 g
Cinnamon, ground	1/4 tsp.	1 ml
Plain yogurt	8 oz.	225 g
Heavy cream	TT	TT
Pistachios, finely chopped	as needed for garnish	

1. Pit and coarsely chop the peaches without peeling. Place in a nonreactive saucepan. Add wine, honey and lemon juice. Cover and simmer for 30 minutes.

2. Purée the peach mixture in a blender. Strain and chill.

3. Stir in cinnamon, yogurt and heavy cream.

4. Chill thoroughly. Serve in chilled bowls, garnished with finely chopped pistachio nuts.

CHAPTER 12

PRINCIPLES OF MEAT COOKERY

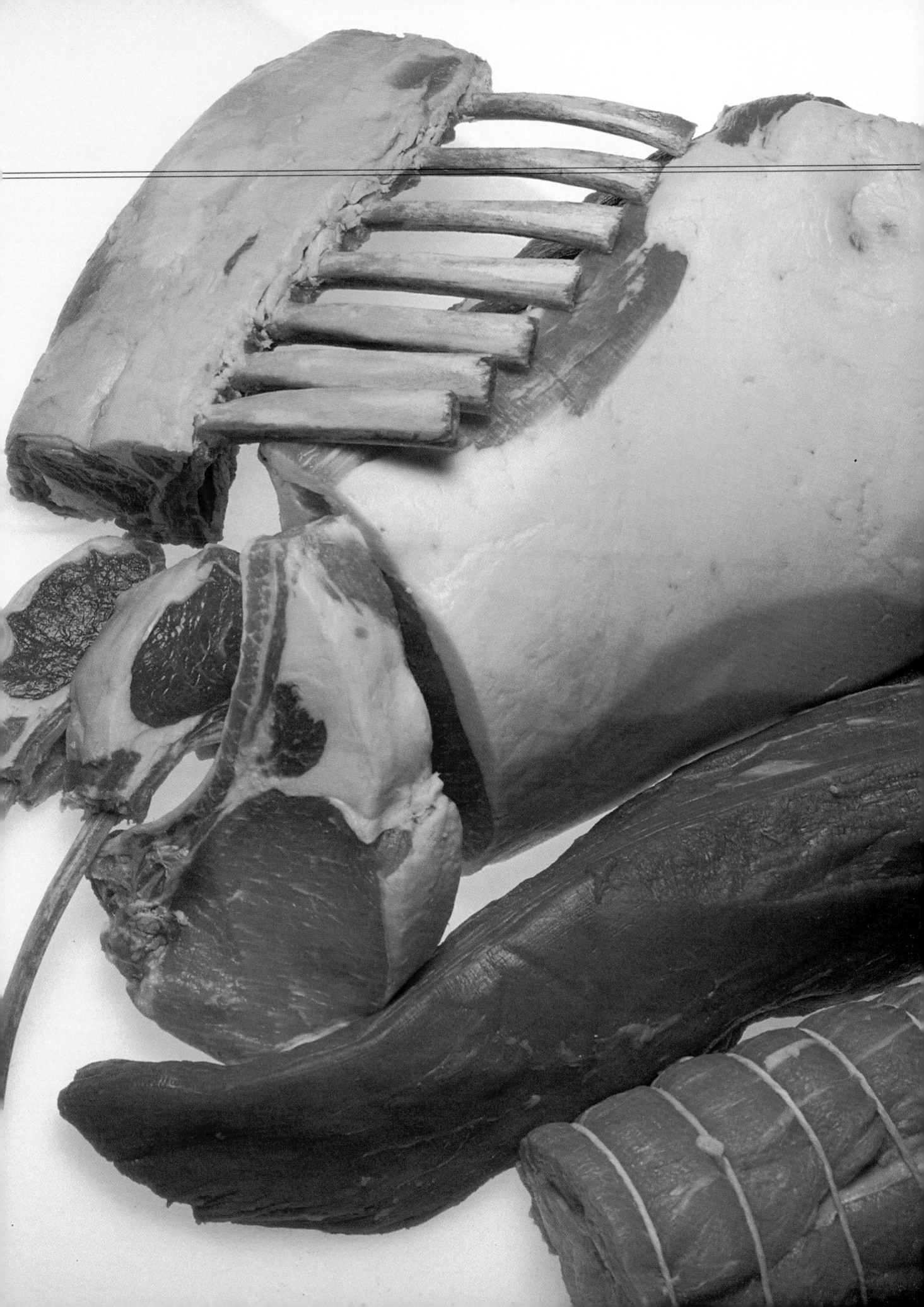

After studying this chapter you will be able to:

◆ understand the structure and composition of meats
◆ understand meat inspection and grading practices
◆ purchase meats appropriate for your needs
◆ store meats properly
◆ prepare meats for cooking
◆ apply various cooking methods to meats

*M*eats—*beef, veal, lamb and pork—often consume the largest portion of your food purchasing dollar. In this chapter we discuss how to protect your investment. You will learn how to determine the quality of meat, how to purchase meat in the form that best suits your needs and how to store it. We also discuss several of the dry-heat, moist-heat and combination cooking methods introduced in Chapter 9, Principles of Cooking, and how they can best be used so that a finished meat item is appealing to both the eye and palate. Although each of the cooking methods is illustrated with a single beef, veal, lamb or pork recipe, the analysis is intended to apply to all meats.*

In Chapters 13 through 16 you will learn about the specific cuts of beef, veal, lamb and pork typically used in food service operations, as well as some basic butchering procedures. Recipes using these cuts and applying the various cooking methods are included at the end of each of those chapters.

MUSCLE COMPOSITION

The carcasses of cattle, sheep, hogs and furred game animals consist mainly of edible lean muscular tissue, fat, connective tissue and bones. They are divided into large cuts called **primals**. Primal cuts are rarely cooked; rather, they are usually reduced to **subprimal cuts** which, in turn, can be cooked as is or used to produce **fabricated cuts**. For example, the beef primal known as a short loin can be divided into subprimals including the strip loin. The strip loin can be fabricated into other cuts including New York steaks. The primals, subprimals and fabricated cuts of beef, veal, lamb and pork are discussed in Chapters 13 through 16, respectively; game is discussed in Chapter 18.

Muscle tissue gives meat its characteristic appearance; the amount of connective tissue determines the meat's tenderness. Muscle tissue is approximately 72% water, 20% protein, 7% fat and 1% minerals. A single muscle is composed of many bundles of muscle cells or fibers held together by connective tissue. The thickness of the cells, the size of the cell bundles and the connective tissues holding them together form the grain of the meat and determine the meat's texture. When the fiber bundles are small, the meat has a fine grain and texture. Grain also refers to the direction in which the muscle fibers travel. When an animal fattens, some of the water and proteins in the lean muscle tissue are replaced with fat, which appears as **marbling**.

Connective tissue forms the walls of the long muscle cells and binds them into bundles. It surrounds the muscle as a membrane and also appears as the tendons and ligaments that attach the muscles to the bone. Most connective tissue is composed of either collagen or **elastin**. Collagen breaks down into gelatin and water when cooked using moist heat. Elastin, on the other hand, will not break down under normal cooking conditions. Because elastin remains stringy and tough, tendons and ligaments should be trimmed away before meat is cooked.

Primal Cuts—*the primary divisions of muscle, bone and connective tissue produced by the initial butchering of the carcass.*

Subprimal Cuts—*the basic cuts produced from each primal.*

Fabricated Cuts—*individual portions cut from a subprimal.*

Marbling—*whitish streaks of inter- and intra-muscular fat.*

Subcutaneous fat—*the fat layer between the hide and muscles, also known as* ***exterior fat****.*

Elastin—*a protein found in connective tissues, particularly ligaments and tendons; it often appears as the white or silver covering on meats known as* ***silverskin****.*

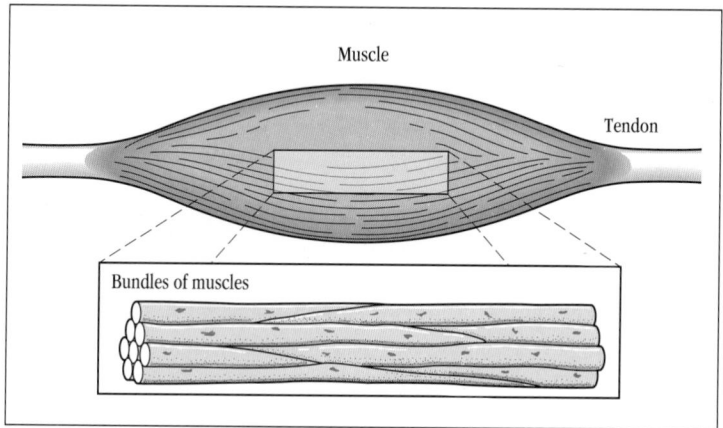

FIGURE 12.1 *Muscle Tissue*

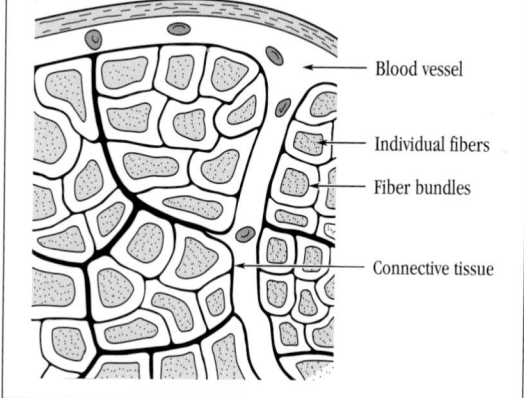

FIGURE 12.2 *Crosscut of a Bundle of Muscle Fibers*

Connective tissue develops primarily in the frequently used muscles. Therefore, cuts of meat from the shoulder (also known as the chuck), which the animal uses constantly, tend to be tougher than those from the back (also known as the loin), which are used less frequently. As an animal ages, the collagen present within the muscles becomes more resistant to breaking down through moist heat cooking. Therefore, the meat of an older animal tends to be tougher than that of a younger one. Generally, the tougher the meat, the more flavorful it is.

Butcher—*to slaughter and dress or fabricate animals for consumption.*

Dress—*to trim or otherwise prepare an animal carcass for consumption.*

Fabricate—*to cut a larger portion of raw meat (for example, a primal or subprimal), poultry or fish into smaller portions.*

Carve—*to cut cooked meat or poultry into portions.*

NUTRITION

Although nutritional content of beef, veal, pork and lamb differs, generally, all are high in protein, saturated fats and cholesterol. See Table 12.1. Consumed in moderate quantities, however, meat can be part of a healthful diet.

TABLE 12.1 NUTRITIONAL VALUES OF MEATS

For 1 ounce (28 grams) Uncooked Lean Meat	Kcal	Protein (g)	Total Fat (g)	Saturated Fat (g)	Cholesterol (mg)	Sodium (mg)
Beef—brisket	94	4.6	8.2	3.4	22	18
Beef—T-bone steak	77	5.0	6.2	2.5	19	14
Beef—ground lean	75	5.0	5.9	2.4	21	20
Veal—chop	46	5.4	2.6	1.1	23	25
Veal—ground leg and shoulder	41	5.5	1.9	0.8	23	23
Lamb—leg	36	5.8	1.3	0.5	18	18
Lamb—chop	106	4.1	9.8	4.3	22	16
Pork—spareribs	81	4.9	6.7	2.7	22	21
Pork—shoulder (picnic)	40	5.6	1.8	0.6	18	23

The Encyclopedia of Food Values by Corrine T. Netzer, 1992.

◆◆◆
Domestication of Animals

Early humans were hunter-gatherers, dependent on what their immediate environment offered for food. As "opportunistic" meat eaters, they ate meat when they could obtain it.

Anthropologists believe that the cultivation of grains and the birth of agriculture, which took place sometime around 9000 B.C., led directly to the domestication of animals. Sheep and goats were attracted to the fields of grain, and dogs and pigs to the garbage heaps of the new communities. Rather than allow these animals to interfere with food produc-

tion, they were tamed, thus providing a steadier supply of meat. The first animals to be domesticated were most likely sheep, soon followed by goats. These animals—ruminants—can digest cellulose (humans cannot), so they could feed on stalks instead of valuable grains. Dogs and pigs, which prefer the same foods as humans, were tamed later, once there was a more certain food supply. Cattle were the most recently domesticated food animal, probably coming under control between 6100 and 5800 B.C.

Inspection and Grading of Meats

Inspection

All meat produced for public consumption in the United States is subject to USDA inspection. Inspections ensure that products are processed under strict sanitary guidelines and are wholesome and fit for human consumption. Inspections do not indicate a meat's quality or tenderness, however. Whole carcasses of beef, pork, lamb and veal are labeled with a round stamp identifying the slaughterhouse. See Figure 12.3. The stamp shown in Figure 12.4 is used for fabricated or processed meats and is found either on the product or its packaging.

FIGURE 12.3 *USDA Inspection Stamp for Whole Carcasses*

FIGURE 12.4 *USDA Inspection Stamp for Fabricated or Processed Meats*

Grading

USDA grading provides a voluntary, uniform system by which producers, distributors and consumers can measure differences in the quality of meats and make price/quality comparisons. There are two parts to this grading system: quality grades and yield grades.

Quality grades, established in 1927, are a guide to the eating qualities of meat: its tenderness, juiciness and flavor. Based on an animal's age and the meat's color, texture and degree of marbling, the USDA quality grades are:

◆ Beef—USDA Prime, Choice, Select, Standard, Commercial, Utility, Cutter and Canner
◆ Veal—USDA Prime, Choice, Good, Standard, Utility
◆ Lamb—USDA Prime, Choice, Good, Utility
◆ Pork—USDA No. 1, No. 2, No. 3, Utility

USDA Prime meats are produced in limited quantities for use in the finest restaurants, hotels and gourmet markets. They are well marbled and have thick coverings of firm fat.

USDA Choice meat is the most commonly used grade in quality food service operations and retail markets. Choice meat is well marbled (but with less fat than Prime) and will produce a tender and juicy product.

FIGURE 12.5 *Grade Stamp for USDA Prime*

FIGURE 12.6 *Grade Stamp for USDA Choice*

Although lacking the flavor and tenderness of the higher grades, beef graded USDA Select or USDA Standard, and lamb and veal graded USDA Good, are also used in food service operations and retail outlets.

The lower grades of beef, lamb and veal are usually used for processed, ground or manufactured items such as meat patties or canned meat products.

Yield grades, established in 1965, measure the amount of usable meat (as opposed to fat and bones) on a carcass and provide a uniform method of identifying cutability differences among carcasses. Yield grades apply only to beef and lamb and appear in a shield similar to that used for the quality grade stamp. The shields are numbered from 1 to 5, with number 1 representing the greatest yield and number 5 the smallest. Beef and lamb can be graded for either quality or yield or both.

Grading is a voluntary program. Many processors, purveyors and retailers (especially pork and veal producers) develop and use their own labeling systems to provide quality assurance information. These private systems do not necessarily apply the USDA's standards.

◆◆◆

A HISTORY OF MEAT SAFETY MEASURES

Ancient times: The biblical books of Exodus, Leviticus and Deuteronomy set forth strict instructions about the kinds of animals that should be eaten and how they should be slaughtered.

13–14th centuries: The first laws regarding meat hygiene were enacted in Florence (Italy). They required butchers to be licensed and to renew their licenses annually, prohibited misrepresentations, substitutions and unsanitary practices; and provided for inspections.

1706: New France (Canada) enacted the first meat inspection laws in North America. They required butchers to notify authorities when animals were to be slaughtered so that the meat could be inspected. Farmers were required to certify that animals destined for slaughter were healthy.

1880s: During this period of rising American meat exports, rumors circulated in Europe that American beef was diseased. Partially to allay these fears, Congress enacted laws providing for final product inspection upon the request of a buyer, seller or exporter.

1891 and 1895: United States meat inspection laws were strengthened. They did not, however, establish a national meat inspection system.

1906: Fueled in part by Upton Sinclair's novel *The Jungle*, in which he describes the horrendous working and sanitary conditions in Chicago slaughterhouses, public pressure persuaded Congress to pass the Comprehensive Meat Inspection Act. The Act strengthened requirements for sanitary conditions in packinghouses and required inspection of meat sold in interstate commerce.

1938: National legislation prohibited on-the-farm slaughter of animals and restricted commercial slaughter operations to packing plants.

1967: The Wholesome Meat Act enabled the USDA to regulate transporters, processors of meat byproducts, cold storage warehouses and animal food manufacturers. Hygiene requirements for imported meats were toughened and inspection of all animals before slaughter became mandatory.

1978: The Humane Methods of Slaughter Act amended previous laws to require that humane methods be used when slaughtering livestock.

Present: Meat inspection has been administered by the USDA's Food Safety and Inspection Service (FSIS) since 1981. The current deregulatory trend places heightened quality-control responsibility on the management of slaughter facilities. This reflects the belief that the wholesomeness of the final product is the responsibility of both industry and government.

Vacuum Packaging—*a food preservation method in which fresh or cooked food is placed in an airtight container (usually plastic). Virtually all air is removed from the container through a vacuum process, and the container is then sealed.*

AGING MEATS

When animals are slaughtered their muscles are soft and flabby. Within 6 to 24 hours rigor mortis sets in, causing the muscles to contract and stiffen. Rigor mortis dissipates within 48 to 72 hours under refrigerated conditions. All meats should be allowed to rest, or age, long enough for rigor mortis to dissipate completely. Meats that have not been aged long enough for rigor mortis to dissipate, or that have been frozen during this period, are known as "green meats." They will be very tough and flavorless when cooked.

Typically, initial aging takes place while the meat is being transported from the slaughterhouse to the supplier or food service operation. Beef and lamb are sometimes aged for longer periods to increase their tenderness and flavor characteristics. Pork is not aged further because its high fat content turns rancid easily, and veal does not have enough fat to protect it during an extended aging period.

Wet Aging

Today, most pre-portioned or precut meats are packaged and shipped in vacuum-sealed plastic packages (sometimes known generically by the manufacturer's trade name, Cryovac®). Wet aging is the process of storing vacuum-packaged meats under refrigeration for up to six weeks. This allows natural enzymes and microorganisms time to break down connective tissue, which tenderizes and flavors the meat. As this chemical process takes place, the meat develops an unpleasant odor that is released when the package is opened and dissipates in a few minutes.

Dry Aging

Dry aging is the process of hanging fresh meats in an environment of controlled temperature, humidity and air flow for up to six weeks. This allows enzymes and microorganisms to break down connective tissues. Dry aging is actually the beginning of the natural decomposition process. Dry aged meats can lose from 5% to 20% of their weight through moisture evaporation. They can also develop mold, which adds flavor but must be trimmed off later. Moisture loss combined with additional trimming can substantially increase the cost of dry aged meats. Dry aged meats are generally available only through smaller distributors and specialty butchers.

PURCHASING AND STORING MEATS

Several factors determine the cuts of meat your food service operation should use:

1. Menu—The menu identifies the types of cooking methods used. If meats are to be broiled, grilled, roasted, sautéed or fried, more tender cuts should be used. If they are to be stewed or braised, flavorful cuts with more connective tissue can be used.

2. Menu price—Cost constraints may prevent an operation from using the best-quality meats available. Generally, the more tender the meat, the more expensive it is. But the most expensive cuts are not always the best choice for a particular cooking method. For example, a beef tenderloin is one of

the most expensive cuts of beef. Although excellent grilled, it will not necessarily produce a better braised dish than the fattier brisket.

3. Quality—Often, several cuts of meat can be used for a specific dish, so each food service operation should develop its own quality specifications.

Purchasing Meats

Once you have identified the cuts of meat your operation needs, you must determine the forms in which they will be bought. Meats are purchased in a variety of forms: as large as an entire carcass that must be further fabricated or as small as an individual cut (known as portion control or P.C.) ready to cook and serve. You should consider the following when deciding how to purchase meats:

1. Employee skills: Do your employees have the skills necessary to reduce large pieces of meat to the desired cuts?
2. Menu: Can you use the variety of bones, meat and trimmings that result from fabricating large cuts into individual portions?
3. Storage: Do you have ample refrigeration and freezer space so that you can be flexible in the way you purchase your meats?
4. Cost: Considering labor costs and trim usage, is it more economical to buy larger cuts of meat or P.C. units?

IMPS/NAMP

The USDA publishes Institutional Meat Purchasing Specifications (IMPS) describing products customarily purchased in the food service industry. IMPS identifications are illustrated and described in *The Meat Buyers Guide*, published by the National Association of Meat Purveyors (NAMP). The IMPS/NAMP system is a widely accepted and useful tool in preventing miscommunications between purchasers and purveyors. Meats are indexed by a numerical system: Beef cuts are designated by the 100 series, lamb by the 200 series, veal by the 300 series, pork by the 400 series, and portion cuts by the 1000 series. Commonly used cuts of beef, veal, lamb and pork and their IMPS numbers, as well as applicable cooking methods and serving suggestions, are discussed in Chapters 13 through 16.

Storing Meats

Meat products are highly perishable, so temperature control is the most important thing to remember when storing meats. Fresh meats should be stored at temperatures of 30–35°F (minus 1–+2°C). Vacuum-packed meats should be left in their packaging until they are needed. Under proper refrigeration, vacuum-packed meats with unbroken seals have a shelf life of three to four weeks. If the seal is broken, shelf life is reduced to only a few days. Meats that are not vacuum packed should be loosely wrapped or wrapped in air-permeable paper. Do not wrap meats tightly in plastic wrap, as this creates a good breeding ground for bacteria and will significantly shorten a meat's shelf life. Store meats on trays and away from other foods to prevent cross-contamination.

Meats freeze at about 28°F (minus 2°C). When freezing meats, the faster the better. Slow freezing produces large ice crystals that tend to rupture the muscle tissues, allowing water and nutrients to drip out when the meat is thawed. Most commercially packaged meats are frozen by blast freezing, which quickly cools by blasting minus 40°F (minus 40°C) air across the meat. Most food service facilities, however, use a slower and more conventional method known as still-air freezing. Still-air freezing is the common practice of placing meat in a standard freezer at about 0°F (minus 18°C) until it is frozen.

The ideal temperature for maintaining frozen meat is minus 50°F (minus 45°C). Frozen meat should not be maintained at any temperature warmer than 0°F (minus 18°C). Moisture- and vaporproof packaging will help prevent **freezer burn**. The length of frozen storage life varies with the species and type of meat. As a general rule, properly handled meats can be frozen for six months. Frozen meats should be thawed at refrigerator temperatures, not at room temperature or in warm water.

Freezer Burn—*the surface dehydration and discoloration of food that results from moisture loss at below-freezing temperatures.*

PREPARING MEATS

Certain procedures are often applied to meats before cooking to add flavor and/or moisture. These include marinating, barding and larding.

Marinating

Marinating is the process of soaking meat in a seasoned liquid to flavor and tenderize it. Marinades can be simple blends (herbs, seasonings and oil) or a complicated cooked recipe (red wine, fruit and other ingredients). Mild marinades should be used on more delicate meats, such as veal. Game and beef require strongly flavored marinades. In wine-based marinades, white wine is usually used for white meats and red wine for red meats. Not only does the wine add a distinctive flavor, the acids in it break down connective tissues and help tenderize the meat.

Veal and pork generally require less time to marinate than game, beef and lamb. Smaller pieces of meat take less time than larger pieces. When marinating, be sure to cover the meat completely and keep it refrigerated. Stir or turn the meat frequently to ensure that the marinate penetrates evenly.

Barding

Barding is the process of covering the surface of meat or poultry with thin slices of pork fatback and tying them in place with butcher's twine. Barded meat or poultry is usually roasted. As the item cooks, the fatback continuously bastes it, adding flavor and moisture. A drawback to barding is that the fatback prevents the meat or poultry from developing the crusty exterior associated with roasting.

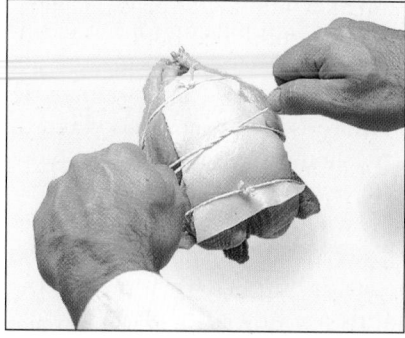

Barding a Pheasant

Larding

Larding is the process of inserting small strips of pork fat into meat with a larding needle. Larded meat is usually cooked by braising. During cooking, the added fat contributes moisture and flavor. Although once popular, larding is rarely used today because advances in selective breeding produce consistently tender, well-marbled meat.

Larding Meat

APPLYING VARIOUS COOKING METHODS

In Chapter 9, Principles of Cooking, you learned the basic techniques for broiling, grilling, roasting, sautéing, pan-frying, poaching, simmering, braising and stewing. In Chapters 13 through 16 you will learn more about applying these cooking methods to beef, veal, lamb and pork. Here we apply these methods to meat cookery in general. Deep-frying is covered in Chapter 20, Deep-Frying.

Dry-Heat Cooking Methods

Dry-heat cooking methods subject food directly to the heat of a flame (broiling and grilling), hot air (roasting) or heated fat (sautéing and pan-frying). These cooking methods firm proteins without breaking down connective tissue. They are not recommended for tougher cuts or those high in connective tissue.

Broiling and Grilling

To serve a good-quality broiled or grilled product you must start with good-quality meat. The broiling or grilling process adds flavor; additional flavors are derived from seasonings. The broiler or grill should brown the meat, keeping the interior juicy. The grill should leave appetizing crosshatch marks on the meat's surface.

Selecting Meats to Broil or Grill

Only the most tender cuts should be broiled or grilled because direct heat does not tenderize. Fat adds flavor as the meat cooks, so the meat should be well marbled. Some external fat is also beneficial. Too much fat, however, will cause the broiler or grill to flare up, burning or discoloring the meat and adding objectionable flavors. Connective tissue toughens when meat is broiled or grilled. Trim away as much of it as possible.

Cooking Temperatures

Red meats should be cooked at sufficiently high temperatures to caramelize their surface, making them more attractive and flavorful. At the same time, the broiler or grill cannot be too hot or the meat's exterior will burn before the interior is cooked.

Because veal and pork are normally cooked to higher internal temperatures than beef and lamb, they should be cooked at slightly lower temperatures so their exteriors are not overcooked when their interiors are cooked properly. The exterior of white meats should be a deep golden color when finished.

Seasoning Meats to be Broiled or Grilled

Meats that have not been marinated should be well seasoned with salt and pepper just before being placed on the broiler or grill. If they are preseasoned

FIGURE 12.7 **Degrees of Doneness** *Meat cooked rare, medium rare, medium and medium well.*

and allowed to rest, the salt will dissolve and draw out moisture, making it difficult to brown the meat properly. Some chefs feel so strongly about this that they season broiled or grilled meats only after they are cooked. Pork and veal, which have a tendency to dry out when cooked, should be basted with seasoned butter or oil during cooking to help keep them moist. Meats can be glazed or basted with barbecue sauce as they cook.

Degrees of Doneness

Consumers request and expect meats to be properly cooked to specific degrees of doneness. It is your responsibility to understand and comply with these requests. Meats can be cooked very rare (or bleu), rare, medium rare, medium, medium well or well done. Figure 12.7 shows the proper color for these different degrees of doneness. This guide can be used for red meats cooked by any method.

Larger cuts of meat, such as a chateaubriand or thick chops, are often started on the broiler or grill to develop color and flavor and then finished in the oven to ensure complete, even cooking.

Determining Doneness

Broiling or grilling meat to the proper degree of doneness is an art. Larger pieces of meat will take longer to cook than smaller ones, but how quickly a piece of meat cooks is determined by many other factors: the temperature of the broiler or grill, the temperature of the piece of meat when placed on the broiler or grill, the type of meat and the thickness of the cut. Because of these variables, timing alone is not a useful tool in determining doneness.

The most reliable method of determining doneness is by pressing the piece of meat with a finger and gauging the amount of resistance it yields. Very rare (bleu) meat will offer almost no resistance and will feel almost the same as raw meat. Meat cooked rare will feel spongy and offer slight resistance to pressure. Meat cooked medium will feel slightly firm and springy to the touch. Meat cooked well done will feel quite firm and will spring back quickly when pressed. See Table 12.2.

Accompaniments to Broiled and Grilled Meats

Because a broiler or grill cannot be deglazed to form the base for a sauce, compound butters or sauces such as béarnaise are often served with broiled

TABLE 12.2	DETERMINING DONENESS	
Degree of Doneness	Color	Degree of Resistance
Very rare (bleu)	Very red and raw-looking center (the center is cool to the touch)	Almost no resistance
Rare	Large deep red center	Spongy; very slight resistance
Medium rare	Bright red center	Some resistance; slightly springy
Medium	Rosy pink to red center	Slightly firm; springy
Medium well	Very little pink at the center, almost brown throughout	Firm; springy
Well done	No red	Quite firm; springs back quickly when pressed

or grilled meats. Brown sauces such as bordelaise, chasseur, périgueux or brown mushroom sauce also complement many broiled or grilled items. Additional sauce suggestions are found in Table 10.5.

PROCEDURE FOR BROILING OR GRILLING MEATS

1. Heat the broiler or grill.
2. Use a wire brush to remove any charred or burnt particles that may be stuck to the broiler or grill grate. The grate can be wiped with a lightly oiled towel to remove any remaining particles and help season it.
3. Prepare the item to be broiled or grilled by trimming off excess fat and connective tissue and marinating or seasoning as desired. The meat may be brushed lightly with oil to help protect it and keep it from sticking to the grate.
4. Place the item in the broiler or on the grill. Following the example in Chapter 9, turn the meat to produce the attractive crosshatch marks associated with grilling. Use tongs to turn or flip the meat without piercing the surface in order to prevent valuable juices from escaping.
5. Cook the meat to the desired doneness while developing the proper surface color. To do so, adjust the position of the meat on the broiler or grill or adjust the distance between the grate and heat source.

❖❖❖

RECIPE 12.1

GRILLED LAMB CHOPS WITH HERB BUTTER

Yield: 2 Servings

Lamb chops, loin or rib,		
approx. 1 in. (2.5 cm) thick	6	6
Salt and pepper	TT	TT
Oil	as needed	as needed
Herb butter	6 thin slices or 6 small rosettes	

1. Preheat the grill for 15 minutes.
2. Season the lamb chops with salt and pepper; brush with oil.
3. Place the lamb chops on the grill, turning as necessary to produce the proper crosshatching. Cook to the desired doneness.
4. Remove the lamb chops from the grill and place a slice or rosette of herb butter on each chop.
5. Serve immediately as the herb butter melts. The plate can be placed under the broiler for a few seconds to help melt the herb butter.

Roasting

Properly roasted meats should be tender, juicy and evenly cooked to the appropriate degree of doneness. They should have a pleasant appearance when whole as well as when sliced and plated.

Selecting Meats to Roast

Because roasting is a dry-heat cooking method and will not tenderize the finished product, meats that are to be roasted should be tender and well marbled. They are usually cut from the rib, loin or leg sections.

1. Brushing the lamb chops with oil.

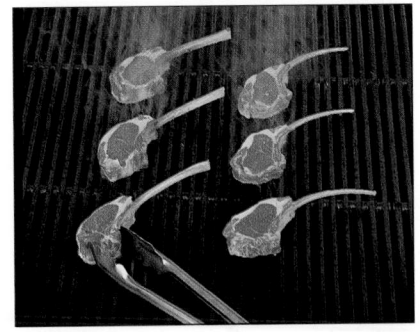

2. Placing the lamb chops on the grill.

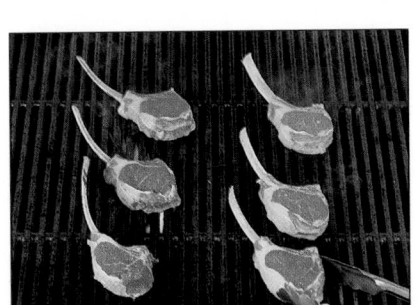

3. Rotating the lamb chops 90 degrees to create crosshatch marks.

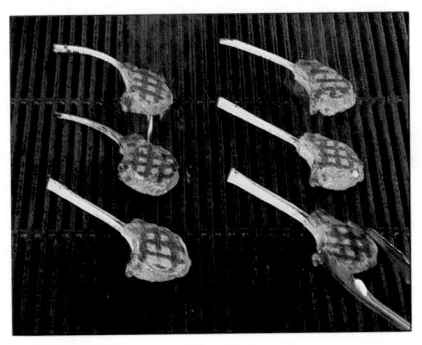

4. Turning the chops over to finish them on the other side.

TABLE 12.3

Degree of Doneness	Internal Temperature	Minutes per Pound*
Very rare	125–130°F 52–54°C	12–15
Rare	130–140°F 54–60°C	15–18
Medium	140–150°F 60–66°C	18–20
Well done	150–165°F 66–74°C	20–25

*Assumes meat was at room temperature before roasting and cooked at a constant 325°F (162°C).

FIGURE 12.8 *The Proper Placement of an Instant-Read Thermometer*

Cooking Temperatures

Small roasts such as a rack of lamb or a beef tenderloin should be cooked at high temperatures, 375–450°F (190–230°C), so that they develop good color during their short cooking times.

Traditionally, large roasts were started at high temperatures to sear the meat and seal in the juices; they were then finished at lower temperatures. Studies have shown, however, that roasts cooked at constant, low temperatures provide a better yield with less shrinkage than roasts that have been seared. Temperatures between 275° and 325°F (120–160°C) are ideal for large roasts. These temperatures will produce a large, evenly cooked pink center portion.

Seasoning Meats to be Roasted

Seasonings are especially important with smaller roasts and roasts with little or no fat covering. With these roasts, some of the seasonings penetrate the meat while the remainder help create the highly seasoned crust associated with a good roast. A large roast with heavy fat covering (for example, a steamship round or prime rib) does not benefit from being seasoned on the surface because the seasonings will not penetrate the fat layer, which is trimmed away before service.

When practical, a roast with excess fat should be trimmed, leaving just a thin fat layer so that the roast bastes itself while cooking. A lean roast can be barded or larded before cooking to add richness and moisture. Lamb legs are sometimes studded with garlic cloves by piercing the meat with a paring knife and then pressing slivers of raw garlic into the holes.

A roast is sometimes cooked on a bed of mirepoix, or mirepoix is added to the roasting pan as the roast cooks. The mirepoix raises the roast off the bottom of the roasting pan, preventing the bottom from overcooking. This mirepoix, however, does not add any flavor to the roast. Rather, it combines with the drippings to add flavor to the jus, sauce or gravy that is made with them.

Determining Doneness

The doneness of small roasts such as a rack of lamb is determined in much the same as with broiled or grilled meats. With experience, the chef develops a sense of timing as well as a feel for gauging the amount of resistance by touching the meat. These techniques, however, are not infallible, especially with large roasts.

Although timing is useful as a general guide for determining doneness, there are too many variables for it to be relied upon exclusively. With this caution in mind, Table 12.3 lists general cooking times for roasted meats.

The best way to determine the doneness of a large roast is to use an instant-read thermometer as shown in Figure 12.8. The thermometer is inserted into the center or thickest part of the roast and away from any bones. The proper finished temperatures for roasted meats are listed in Table 12.3.

Carryover Cooking and Resting

Cooking does not stop the moment a roast is removed from the oven. Through conduction, the heat applied to the outside of the roast continues to penetrate, cooking the center for several more minutes. Indeed, the internal temperature of a small roast can rise by as much as 5–10°F (3–6°C) after being removed from the oven. With a larger roast, such as a 50-pound steamship round, it can rise by as much as 20°F (11°C). Therefore, remove roasted meats before they reach the desired degree of doneness and allow carryover cooking to complete the cooking process. The temperatures listed in Table 12.3 are internal temperatures after allowing for carryover cooking.

As meat cooks, its juices flow toward the center. If the roast is carved immediately after it is removed from the oven, its juices would run from the meat, causing it to lose its color and become dry. Letting the meat rest before slicing allows the juices to redistribute themselves evenly throughout the roast, so the roast will retain more juices when carved. Small roasts, like a rack of lamb, need to rest only 5–10 minutes; larger roasts such as a steamship round of beef require as much as an hour.

Accompaniments to Roasted Meats

Roasts may be served with a sauce based on their natural juices (called *au jus*), as described in Recipe 12.2, Roast Prime Rib of Beef Au Jus, or with a pan gravy made with drippings from the roast. Additional sauce suggestions are found in Table 10.5.

PROCEDURE FOR ROASTING MEATS

1. Trim excess fat, tendons and silverskin from the meat. Leave only a thin fat covering, if possible, so the roast bastes itself as it cooks.
2. Season the roast as appropriate and place it in a roasting pan. The roast may be placed on a bed of mirepoix or on a rack.
3. Roast the meat, uncovered, at the desired temperature (the larger the roast, the lower the temperature), usually 275–425°F (135–220°C).
4. If a jus or pan gravy is desired and a mirepoix was not added at the start of cooking, it may be added 30–45 minutes before the roast is done, thus allowing it to caramelize while the roast finishes cooking.
5. Cook to the desired temperature.
6. Remove the roast from the oven, allowing carryover cooking to raise the internal temperature to the desired degree of doneness. Allow the roast to rest before slicing or carving it. As the roast rests, prepare the jus, sauce or pan gravy.

◆◆◆

RECIPE 12.2

ROAST PRIME RIB OF BEEF AU JUS

Yield: 18 8-oz. (250-g) boneless Servings

Oven-ready rib roast		
IMPS #109, approx. 16 lbs. (7.5 kg)	1	1
Salt and pepper	TT	TT
Garlic, chopped	TT	TT
Mirepoix	1 lb.	500 g
Brown stock	2 qt.	2 lt

1. Pull back the netting, fold back the fat cap and season the roast well with the salt, pepper and chopped garlic. Replace the fat cap and netting; place the roast in an appropriate-sized roasting pan. Roast at 300–325°F (160–165°C).
2. Add the mirepoix to the pan approximately 45 minutes before the roast is

Continued

finished cooking. Continue cooking until the internal temperature reaches 125°F (52°C), approximately 3–4 hours. Carryover cooking will raise the internal temperature of the roast to approximately 138°F (59°C).

3. Remove the roast from the pan and allow it to rest in a warm place for 30 minutes.

4. Drain the excess fat from the roasting pan, reserving the mirepoix and any drippings in the roasting pan.

5. Caramelize the mirepoix on the stove top; allow the liquids to evaporate, leaving only brown drippings in the pan.

6. Deglaze the pan with brown stock. Stir to loosen all the drippings.

7. Simmer the jus, reducing it slightly and allowing the mirepoix to release its flavor; season with salt and pepper if necessary.

8. Strain the jus through a china cap lined with cheesecloth. Skim any remaining fat from the surface with a ladle.

9. Remove the netting from the roast. Trim and slice the roast as described below and serve with approximately 1 to 2 ounces (30 to 60 milliliters) jus per person.

1. Draining off the excess fat.

2. Caramelizing the mirepoix.

3. Deglazing the pan with brown stock.

4. Simmering the jus, reducing it slightly and allowing the mirepoix to release its flavors.

5. Straining the jus through a china cap and cheesecloth.

Carving Roasts

All the efforts that went into selecting and cooking a perfect roast will be wasted if the roast is not carved properly. Roasts are always carved against the grain; carving it with the grain produces long stringy, tough slices. Cutting across the muscle fibers produces a more attractive and tender portion. Portions may be cut in a single thick slice, as with Roast Prime Rib of Beef, or in many thin slices. The photographs below illustrate several different carving procedures.

CARVING PRIME RIB

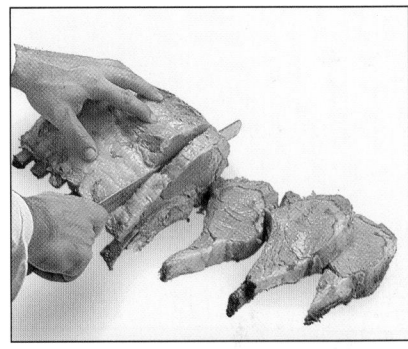

1. Removing the netting, cap fat and chine bones.

2. Trimming the excess fat from the eye muscle.

3. Slicing the rib in long, smooth strokes, the first cut (end cut) without a rib bone, the second cut with a rib bone, and so on.

CARVING PRIME RIB ON THE SLICER

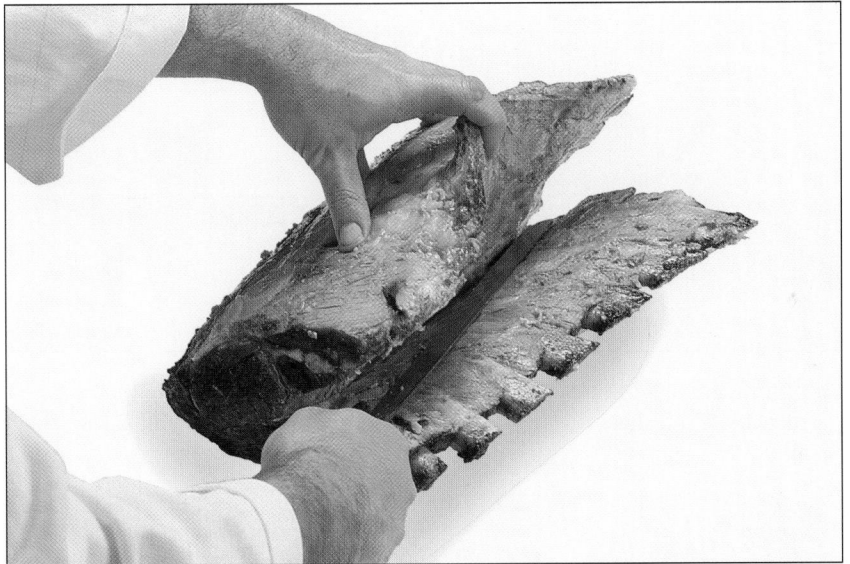
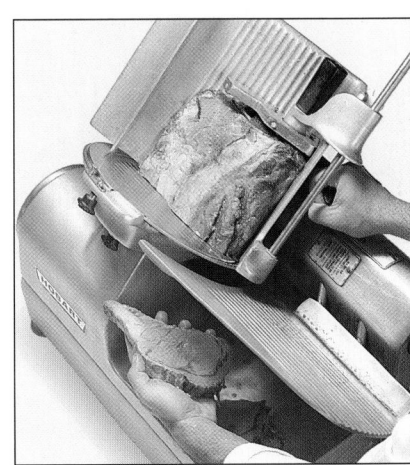

1. When producing large quantities of prime rib, it is often more practical to slice it on a slicing machine. Following the steps illustrated above, remove the netting, cap fat and chine bone; trim excess fat from the eye muscle. Then use a long slicer and completely remove the rib eye from the rib bones, being careful to stay as close as possible to the bones to avoid wasting any meat.

2. After placing the rib on the slicing machine, set the machine to the desired thickness. The blade will have to be adjusted often because a roast's thickness fluctuates.

CARVING A STEAMSHIP ROUND OF BEEF

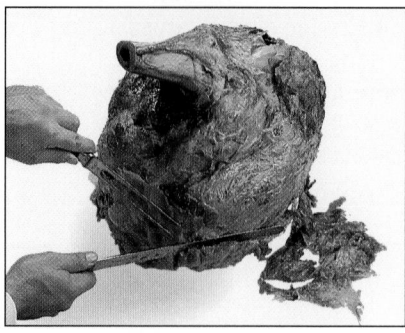

1. After setting the roast on the cutting board with the exposed femur bone (large end of the roast) down and the tibia (shank bone) or "handle" up, trim the excess exterior fat to expose the lean meat.

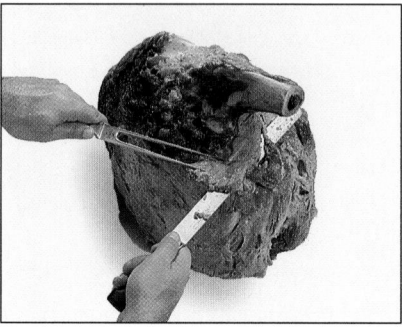

2. Begin slicing with a horizontal cut toward the shank bone, then make vertical cuts to release the slices of beef.

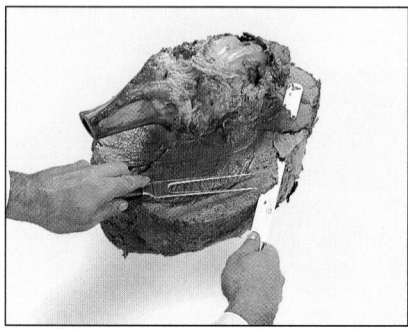

3. Keeping the exposed surface as level as possible. Continue carving, turning the roast as necessary to access all sides.

CARVING A LEG OF LAMB

1. Holding the shank bone firmly, cut toward the bone.

2. Cutting parallel to the shank bone to remove the slices.

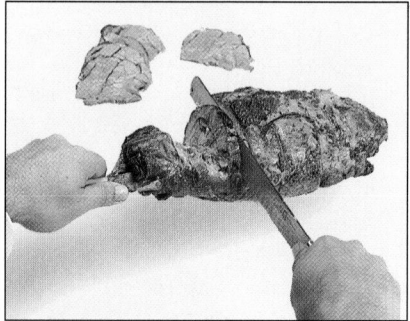

3. Rotating the leg as needed to access the meat on all sides.

Sautéing

Sautéing is a dry-heat cooking method in which heat is conducted by a small amount of fat. Sautéed meats should be tender (a reflection of the quality of the raw product), of good color (determined by proper cooking temperatures) and have a good overall flavor. Any accompanying sauce should be well seasoned and complement the meat without overpowering it.

Selecting Meats to Sauté

As with broiling, grilling and roasting, you should use tender meats of the highest quality in order to produce good results when sautéing. The cuts should be uniform in size and shape to promote even cooking.

Seasoning Meats to be Sautéed

The sauces that almost always accompany sautéed meats provide much of the seasoning. The meat, however, can be marinated or simply seasoned with salt and pepper. If marinated, the meat must be patted dry before cooking to ensure proper browning. Some meats are dusted with flour before cooking to seal in juices and promote even browning.

Determining Doneness

As with broiled and grilled meats, the doneness of sautéed meats is determined by touch and timing. Red meats should be well browned; veal and pork should be somewhat lighter.

Accompaniments to Sautéed Meats

Sauces served with sautéed meats are usually made directly in the sauté pan, utilizing the **fond**. They often incorporate a previously thickened sauce. Additional sauce suggestions for sautéed meats are found in Table 10.5.

Fond—*(1) French for* stock *or* base; *(2) the concentrated juices, drippings and bits of food left in pans after foods are roasted or sautéed; it is used to flavor sauces made directly in the pans in which foods were cooked.*

PROCEDURE FOR SAUTÉING MEATS

1. Heat a sauté pan and add enough oil or clarified butter to just cover the bottom. The pan should be large enough to hold the meat in a single layer. A pan that is too large may cause the fat or meat to burn.
2. Cut the meat into **cutlets, scallops, émincés, medallions, mignonettes, noisettes, chops** or small even-sized pieces. Season the meat and dredge in flour if desired.
3. Add the meat to the sauté pan in a single layer. Do not crowd the pan.
4. Adjust the temperature so that the meat's exterior browns properly without burning and the interior cooks. The heat should be high enough to complete the cooking process before the meat begins to stew in its own juices.
5. Small items may be tossed using the sauté pan's sloped sides to flip them back on top of themselves. Do not toss the meat more than necessary, however. The pan should remain in contact with the heat source as much as possible to maintain proper temperatures. Larger items should be turned using tongs or a kitchen fork. Avoid burns by not splashing hot fat.
6. Larger items can be finished in an oven. Either place the sauté pan in the oven or transfer the meat to another pan. The latter procedure allows a sauce to be made in the original pan as the meat continues to cook.

Cutlet—*a relatively thick, boneless slice of meat.*

Scallop—*a thin, boneless slice of meat.*

Émincé—*a small, thin, boneless piece of meat.*

Paillard—*a scallop of meat pounded until thin, usually grilled.*

Medallion—*a small, round, relatively thick slice of meat.*

Mignonette—*a medallion.*

Noisette—*a small, usually round, portion of meat cut from the rib.*

Chop—*a cut of meat including part of the rib.*

PROCEDURE FOR MAKING SAUCE IN THE SAUTÉ PAN

1. If a sauce is to be made in the pan, hold the meat in a warm spot while preparing the sauce. When the meat is removed from the pan, leave a small amount of fat as well as the fond. If there is excessive fat, degrease the pan, leaving just enough to cover its bottom. Add ingredients such as garlic, shallots and mushrooms that will be used as garnishes and sauce flavorings; sauté them.

2. Deglaze the pan with wine or stock. Scrape the pan, loosening the fond and allowing it to dissolve in the liquid. Reduce the deglazing liquid by approximately three quarters.

3. Add jus lié or stock to the pan. Cook and reduce the sauce to the desired consistency.

4. Add any ingredients that do not require cooking such as herbs and spices. Adjust the seasonings with salt and pepper.

5. For service, the meat may be returned to the pan for a moment to reheat it and coat it with the finished sauce. The meat should remain in the sauce just long enough to reheat. Do not attempt to cook the meat in the sauce.

◆◆◆

RECIPE 12.3

SAUTÉED VEAL SCALLOPS WITH WHITE WINE LEMON SAUCE

Yield: 6 Servings

Veal scallops, 3 oz. (90 g) each	12	12
Clarified butter	2 oz.	60 g
Flour	4 oz.	120 g
Salt and pepper	TT	TT
Shallots, chopped	2 Tbsp.	30 me
White wine	6 oz.	180 g
Lemon juice	2 oz.	60 g
Brown veal stock	4 oz.	120 g
Unsalted butter	2 oz.	60 g
Lemon wedges	12	12

1. Pound the scallops to a uniform thickness, as described in Chapter 14, Veal.

2. Heat a sauté pan and add the clarified butter.

3. Dredge the scallops in seasoned flour and add to the pan in a single layer. Sauté on each side for 1–2 minutes. As the first scallops are done, remove them to a warm platter and sauté the remaining scallops.

4. Add the chopped shallots to the pan and sauté.

5. Deglaze the pan with the white wine and lemon juice.

6. Add the brown veal stock and reduce by half.

7. Swirl in the butter (monte au beurre).

8. Adjust the seasonings with salt and pepper.

9. Serve 2 scallops per person with approximately 1 ounce (30 grams) of sauce. Garnish with lemon wedges.

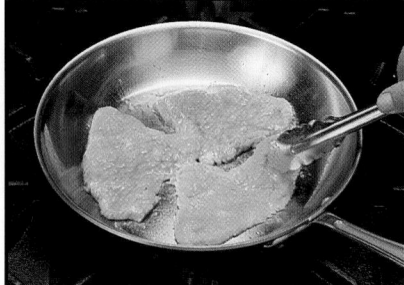

1. Adding the veal scallops to the pan. Note the relationship of scallops to pan size.

2. Adding the chopped shallots to the pan and sautéing them.

3. Deglazing the pan with white wine and lemon juice.

4. Adding the brown veal stock and reducing by half.

5. Swirling in the butter and adjusting the seasonings.

Pan-Frying

Pan-frying uses more fat than sautéing to conduct heat. Pan-fried meats should be tender (a reflection of the quality of the raw product), of good color (determined by proper cooking temperatures) and with a good overall flavor. Meats to be pan-fried are usually breaded. In addition to providing flavor, breading seals the meat. The breading should be free from breaks, thus preventing the fat from coming into direct contact with the meat or collecting in a pocket formed between the meat and the breading. Pan-fried items should be golden in color and the breading should not be soggy.

Selecting Meats to Pan-Fry

As with other dry-heat cooking methods, tender meats of high quality should be used because the meat will not be tenderized by the cooking process. Meats that are pan-fried are often cut into cutlets or scallops.

Seasoning Meats to be Pan-Fried

Pan-fried meats are usually seasoned lightly with salt and pepper either by applying them directly to the meat or adding them to the flour and bread crumbs used in the breading procedure.

Determining Doneness

The most accurate way to determine the doneness of a pan-fried item is by timing. The touch method is difficult to use because of the large amounts of hot fat. It also may not be as accurate as with broiled or grilled meats because pan-fried meats are often quite thin.

Accompaniments to Pan-Fried Meats

Any sauce served with pan-fried meats is usually made separately because there is no fond created during the pan-frying process. Sauce suggestions are listed in Table 10.5.

PROCEDURE FOR PAN-FRYING MEATS

1. Slice and pound out the meat into scallops as described in Chapter 14, Veal.
2. Bread the meat using the standard breading procedure detailed in Chapter 20, Deep-Frying.
3. Heat a moderate amount of fat or oil in a heavy pan. The temperature

should be slightly lower than that used to sauté so that the breading will be nicely browned when the item is fully cooked.

4. Place the meat in the pan, being careful not to splash the hot fat. The fat should come one third to one half way up the side of the meat. Fry until brown. Turn and brown the other side. Ideally, pan-fried meats should be fully cooked when they are well browned on both sides.

5. Remove the meat from the pan; drain it on absorbent paper before serving.

◆◆◆

RECIPE 12.4

BREADED VEAL CUTLETS

Yield: 10 Servings

Veal cutlet, 4 oz. (120 g) each	10	10
Salt and pepper	TT	TT
Standard breading:	as needed	as needed
Flour		
Eggs		
Milk		
Bread crumbs		
Vegetable oil	as needed	as needed
Butter	6 oz.	180 g
Lemon wedges	20	20

1. Using a mallet, pound the cutlets to an even thickness, approximately 1/4 inch (6 millimeters).

2. Season the cutlets with salt and pepper.

3. Bread the cutlets using the standard breading procedure described in Chapter 20, Deep-Frying.

4. Heat a heavy pan to moderate heat; add approximately 1/4 inch (6 millimeters) of oil.

5. Add the cutlets in a single layer. Do not crowd the pan. Brown on one side, then the other. Total cooking time should be approximately 4 minutes.

6. Remove the cutlets and drain on absorbent paper.

7. Melt the butter in a small pan until it foams.

8. Place one cutlet on each plate and pour approximately 1/2 ounce (15 milliliters) butter over each portion. Garnish with lemon wedges.

1. Adding the breaded cutlets to the hot pan. Note the amount of oil in the pan.

2. Turning the cutlets to brown on the second side.

3. Melting the butter in a separate pan until it foams.

4. Pouring the butter over the cutlet.

Moist-Heat Cooking Methods

Moist-heat cooking methods subject food to heat and moisture. Moist heat is often, but not always, used to tenderize tougher cuts of meat through long, slow cooking. Simmering is the only moist-heat cooking method discussed here as it is the only one frequently used with meat.

Simmering

Simmering is usually associated with specific tougher cuts of meat that need to be tenderized through long, slow, moist cooking. Quality simmered meats have good flavor and texture. The flavor is determined by the cooking liquid; the texture is a result of proper cooking temperatures and time.

Selecting Meats to Simmer

Meats such as fresh or corned beef brisket, fresh or cured hams and tongue are often simmered. Beef briskets and tongues, pork butts and hams are often simmered whole.

Cooking Temperatures

Moist-heat cooking methods generally use lower temperatures than dry-heat cooking methods. Meats are normally simmered at temperatures between 180° and 200°F (82–85°C). In larger food service operations, meats such as hams and corned beef are cooked at temperatures as low as 150°F (66°C) for up to 12 hours. Although lower cooking temperatures result in less shrinkage and a more tender finished product, cooking times can be increased to the point that very low cooking temperatures may not be practical.

Seasoning Meats To Be Simmered

If the meat to be simmered was cured by either smoking (as with cured hams, ham hocks and smoked pork butt) or pickling (as with corned beef and pickled tongue), the cooking liquid will not be used to make a sauce and should not be seasoned. Indeed, simmering cured meats helps leach out some of the excess salt, making the finished dish more palatable.

Determining Doneness

Simmered meats are always cooked well done, which is determined by tenderness. The size and quality of the raw product determines the cooking time. Undercooked meats will be tough and chewy. Overcooked meats will be stringy and may even fall apart.

To test large cuts of meat for doneness, a kitchen fork should be easily inserted into the meat and the meat should slide off the fork. Smaller pieces of meat should be tender to the bite or easily cut with a table fork.

Accompaniments to Simmered Meats

Simmered meats are often served with boiled or steamed vegetables, as in the cases of corned beef and cabbage. Pickled meats are usually served with mustard or horseradish sauce on the side.

PROCEDURE FOR SIMMERING MEATS

1. Cut, trim or tie the meat according to the recipe.
2. Bring an adequate amount of liquid to a boil. There should be enough liquid to cover the meat completely. Too much liquid will leach off much of the meat's flavor; too little will leave a portion of the meat exposed, preventing it from cooking. Because the dish's final flavor is determined by the flavor of the liquid, use plenty of mirepoix, flavorings and seasonings.

3. When simmering smoked or cured items, start them in cold water. This helps draw off some of the strong pickled or smoked flavors.

4. Add the meat to the liquid.

5. Reduce the heat to the desired temperature and cook until the meat is tender. Do not allow the cooking liquid to boil. Boiling results in a tough or overcooked and stringy product. If the simmered meat is to be served cold, a moister and juicier product can be achieved by removing the pot from the stove before the meat is fully cooked. The meat and the liquid can be cooled in a water bath like that for a stock, as described in Chapter 10, Stocks and Sauces. This allows the residual heat in the cooking liquid to finish cooking the meat.

1. Placing the corned beef and sachet in an appropriate pot and covering with stock.

2. Carving the beef and presenting it with the vegetable garnish.

◆◆◆

RECIPE 12.5

New England Boiled Dinner

Yield: 12 6-oz (180-g) Servings

Corned beef brisket, 8 lb. (6.5 kg)	1	1
White stock	as needed	as needed
Sachet:		
Bay leaves	2	2
Dried thyme	1/2 tsp.	2 ml
Peppercorns, cracked	1/2 tsp.	2 ml
Parsley stems	10	10
Mustard seeds	1 Tbsp.	15 ml
Cinnamon sticks	2	2
Allspice berries	4	4
Baby red beets	24	24
Baby turnips	24	24
Baby carrots	24	24
Brussels sprouts	24	24
Pearl onions	24	24
Potatoes, Red Bliss	24	24

1. Place the beef in a pot and add enough stock to cover it. Add the sachet, bring to a boil and reduce to a simmer.

2. Simmer until the beef is tender, approximately 3 hours. Remove the beef and hold in a hotel pan in a small amount of the cooking liquid.

3. Peel or prepare the vegetables and potatoes as needed and cook separately in a portion of the cooking liquid.

4. Carve the beef and serve with 2 of each of the vegetables and horseradish sauce (page 208).

Combination Cooking Methods

Braising and stewing are referred to as combination cooking methods because both dry heat and moist heat are used to achieve the desired results.

Braising

Braised meats are first browned and then cooked in a liquid that serves as a sauce for the meat. A well-prepared braised dish has the rich flavor of the meat in the sauce and the moisture and flavor of the sauce in the meat. It should be almost fork tender but not falling apart. The meat should have an attractive color from the initial browning and final glazing.

Selecting Meats to Braise

Braising can be used for tender cuts (such as those from the loin or rib) or tougher cuts (such as those from the chuck or shank). Any meat to be braised should be well marbled with ample fat content to produce a moist finished product.

If tender cuts such as veal chops or pork chops are braised, the finished dish has a uniquely different flavor and texture than if they were cooked by a dry-heat method. Tender cuts require shorter cooking times than tougher cuts because lengthy cooking is not needed to break down connective tissue.

More often, braising is used with tougher cuts that are tenderized by the long, moist cooking process. Cuts from the chuck and shank are popular choices, as they are very flavorful and contain relatively large amounts of collagen, which adds richness to the finished product.

Large pieces of meat can be braised, then carved like a roast. Portion control cuts and diced meats can also be braised.

Cooking Temperatures

Braised meats are always browned before simmering. As a general rule, smaller cuts are floured before browning; larger cuts are not. Flouring seals the meat, promotes even browning and adds body to the sauce that accompanies the meat. Whether floured or not, the meat is browned in fat. After browning, white meats should be golden to amber in color; red meats should be dark brown. Do not brown the meat too quickly at too high a temperature, as it is important to develop a well-caramelized surface. The caramelized surface adds color and flavor to the final product.

The meat and the braising liquid are brought to a boil over direct heat. The temperature is then reduced below boiling and the pot is covered. Cooking can be finished in the oven or on the stove top. The oven provides gentle, even heat without the risk of scorching. If the braise is finished on the stove top, proper temperatures must be maintained carefully throughout the cooking process and great care must be taken to prevent scorching or burning. Lower temperatures and longer cooking times result in more even cooking and thorough penetration of the cooking liquid, providing a more flavorful final product.

Seasoning Meats to be Braised

The seasoning and overall flavor of a braised dish is largely a function of the quality of the cooking liquid and the mirepoix, herbs, spices and other ingredients that season the meat as it cooks. However, braised meats can be marinated before they are cooked to tenderize them and add flavor. The marinade is then sometimes incorporated into the braising liquid. Salt and pepper may be added to the flour if the meat is dredged before it is browned, or the meat may be seasoned directly (although the salt may draw out moisture and inhibit browning).

A standard sachet and a tomato product are usually added at the start of cooking. The tomato product adds flavor and color to the finished sauce as well as acid to tenderize the meat during the cooking process. Final seasoning should not take place until cooking is complete and the sauce will not be reduced further.

Finishing Braised Meats

Near the end of the cooking process, the lid may be removed from oven-braised meats. Finishing braised meats without a cover serves two purposes. First, the meat can be glazed by basting it often. (As the basting liquid evaporates, the meat is browned and a strongly flavored glaze is formed.) Second, removing the lid allows the cooking liquid to reduce, thickening it and concentrating its flavors for use as a sauce.

Determining Doneness

Braised meats are done when they are tender. A fork inserted into the meat should meet little resistance. Properly braised meats should remain intact and not fall apart when handled gently.

Braised meats that fall apart or are stringy are overcooked. If the finished product is tough, it was probably undercooked or cooked at too high a temperature. If the entire dish lacks flavor, the meat may not have been properly browned or the cooking liquid may have been poorly seasoned.

Accompaniments to Braised Meats

Large braised items are often served like roasts. They are carved against the grain in thin slices and served with their sauce. Vegetables can be cooked with the braised meat, cooked separately and added when the main items has finished cooking or added at service. If the vegetables are cooked with the main item they should be added at intervals based on their individual cooking times to prevent overcooking.

PROCEDURE FOR BRAISING MEATS

The liquid used for braising is usually thickened in one of three ways:

1. With a roux added at the start of the cooking process; the roux thickens the sauce as the meat cooks.
2. Prethickened before the meat is added.
3. Thickened after the meat is cooked either by puréeing the mirepoix or by using roux, arrowroot or cornstarch.

The procedure for braising meats includes variations for whichever thickening method is selected.

1. Heat a small amount of oil in a heavy pan.
2. Dredge the meat to be braised in seasoned flour, if desired, and add it to the oil.
3. Brown the meat well on all sides and remove from the pan.
4. Add a mirepoix to the pan and caramelize it well. If using roux, it should be added at this time.
5. Add the appropriate stock or sauce so that when the meat is returned to the pan the liquid comes approximately one third of the way up the side of the meat.
6. Add aromatics and seasonings.
7. Return the meat to the sauce. Tightly cover the pot and bring it to a simmer. Cook slowly either on the stove top or by placing the covered pot directly in an oven at 250–300°F (120–150°C).
8. Cook the item, basting or turning it often so that all sides of the meat benefit from the moisture and flavor of the sauce.
9. When the meat is done, remove it from the pan and hold it in a warm place while the sauce is finished.
10. The sauce may be reduced on the stove top to intensify its flavors. If the meat was braised in a stock, the stock may be thickened using a roux, arrowroot or cornstarch. Strain the sauce or, if desired, purée the mirepoix and other ingredients and return them to the sauce. Adjust the sauce's consistency as desired.

♦♦♦

RECIPE 12.6
AUNT RUTHIE'S POT ROAST

Yield: 12 6-oz. (180-g) meat and
4-oz. (120-g) sauce Servings

Vegetable oil	3 oz.	90 g
Beef brisket	6 lb.	2.7 kg
Onion, thinly sliced	3 lb.	1.4 kg
Garlic, minced	2 Tbsp.	30 ml
Brown veal stock	1 qt.	1 lt
Tomato sauce	1 pt.	450 ml
Brown sugar	4 oz.	120 g
Paprika	1 tsp.	5 ml
Dry mustard	2 tsp.	10 ml
Lemon juice	8 oz.	250 g
Tomato catsup	8 oz.	250 g
Red wine vinegar	8 oz.	250 g
Worcestershire sauce	2 oz.	60 g
Salt and pepper	TT	TT

1. Browning the brisket.

1. Heat the oil in a large skillet. Add the beef and brown thoroughly. Remove and reserve the brisket.
2. Add the onions and garlic to the pan; sauté.
3. Add the stock and tomato sauce to the pan.
4. Return the brisket to the pan, cover tightly and bring to a boil. Braise at 325°F (160°C) for 1-1/2 hours, basting or turning the brisket often.
5. Combine the remaining ingredients and add to the pan.
6. Continue cooking and basting the brisket until tender, approximately 1 hour.
7. Remove the brisket, degrease the sauce and adjust its consistency and seasonings. Do not strain the sauce.
8. Slice the brisket against the grain and serve with the sauce.

2. Sautéing the onions and garlic.

3. Basting the brisket. Note the proper amount of cooking liquid.

Stewing

Stewing, like braising, is a combination cooking method. In many ways the procedures for stewing are identical to those for braising, although stewing is usually associated with smaller or bite-sized pieces of meat.

There are two main types of stews: brown stews and white stews.

When making **brown stews**, the meat is first browned in fat; then a cooking liquid is added. The initial browning adds flavor and color to the finished product. The same characteristics apply to a good brown stew that apply to a good braised dish: It should be fork tender, have an attractive color and rich flavor.

There are two types of **white stews**: **fricassees**, in which the meat is first cooked in a small amount of fat without coloring, then combined with a cooking liquid; and **blanquettes**, in which the meat is first blanched, then rinsed and added to a cooking liquid. White stew should have the same flavor and texture characteristics as a brown stew, but should be white or ivory in color.

STEW TERMINOLOGY

Ragout—A general term that refers to white or brown stews in which the meat is cooked by dry heat before liquid is added. In French, ragout means "to bring back the appetite."

Fricassee—A white ragout usually made from white meat or small game, seared without browning and garnished with small onions and mushrooms.

Navarin—A brown ragout generally made with turnips, other root vegetables, onions, peas and lamb.

Blanquette—A white stew in which the meat is first blanched, then added to a stock or sauce to complete the cooking and tenderizing process. Blanquettes are finished with a liaison of egg yolks and heavy cream.

Chili con carne—A ragout of ground or diced meat cooked with onions, chile peppers, cumin and other spices. Despite the objections of purists, chili sometimes contains beans.

Goulash—A Hungarian beef stew made with onions and paprika and garnished with potatoes.

Selecting Meats to Stew

Stewing uses moist heat to tenderize meat just as braising does, therefore many of the same cuts can be used. Meats that are to be stewed should be trimmed of excess fat and connective tissue and cut into 1- to 2-inch (2.5- to 5-cm) cubes.

Cooking Temperatures

Meats for brown stews are first cooked at high temperatures over direct heat until well browned. Meats for fricassees are first sautéed at low temperatures so they do not develop color.

Once the cooking liquid has been added and the moist-heat cooking process has begun, do not allow the stew to boil. Stews benefit from low-temperature cooking. If practical, stews can be covered and finished in the oven.

Seasoning Meats To Be Stewed

Stews, like braised meats, get much of their flavor from their cooking liquid. A stew's seasoning and overall flavor is a direct result of the quality of the cooking liquid and the vegetables, herbs, spices and other ingredients added during cooking.

Determining Doneness

Stewed meats are done when they are fork tender. Test them by removing a piece of meat to a plate and cutting it with a fork. Any vegetables that are cooked with the meat should be added at the proper times so that they and the meat are completely cooked at the same time.

Accompaniments to Stewed Meats

Stews are often complete meals in themselves, containing meat, vegetables and potatoes in one dish. Stews that do not contain a starch are often served with pasta or rice.

PROCEDURE FOR STEWING MEATS—*BROWN STEWS*

Red meats, lamb or game are used in brown stews. The procedure for making a brown stew is very similar to braising.

1. Trim the meat of excess fat and silverskin and cut into 1- to 2-inch (2.5- to 5-cm) pieces.
2. Dredge the meat in flour if desired. Heat an appropriate-sized pan and add enough oil to cover the bottom. Cook the meat in the oil, browning it well on all sides. Onions and garlic can be added at this time and browned.
3. Add flour to the meat and fat and cook to make a brown roux.
4. Gradually add the liquid to the roux, stirring to prevent lumps. Bring the stew to a boil and reduce to a simmer.
5. Add a tomato product and a sachet or a bouquet garni. Cover and place in the oven or continue to simmer on the stove top until the meat is tender. Add other ingredients such as vegetables or potatoes at the proper time so that they will be done when the meat is tender.
6. When the meat is tender, remove the sachet or bouquet garni. The meat may be strained out and the sauce thickened with roux, cornstarch or arrowroot or reduced to concentrate its flavors.
7. If not added during the cooking process, vegetables and other garnishes may be cooked separately and added to the finished stew.

◆◆◆

RECIPE 12.7

BROWN BEEF STEW

Yield: 8 8-oz. (250-g) Servings

Oil	2 oz.	60 ml
Beef chuck or shank, trimmed and cut into 1-1/2-in. (3.5-cm) cubes	4 lb. 8 oz.	2 kg
Salt	2 tsp.	10 ml
Pepper	1/2 tsp.	2 ml
Onion, small dice	10 oz.	300 g
Garlic, chopped	1 tsp.	5 ml
Flour	1-1/2 oz.	45 g
Red wine	8 oz.	250 g
Brown stock	1 qt.	1 lt
Tomato purée	4 oz.	120 g
Sachet:		
Bay leaves	2	2
Dried thyme	1/2 tsp.	2 ml
Peppercorns, crushed	1/2 tsp.	2 ml
Parsley stems	10	10

1. Browning the beef.

2. Sautéing the garlic and onions until slightly browned.

3. Adding the flour and making a roux.

1. Heat a heavy pot until very hot and add the oil.
2. Season the beef and add it to the pot, browning it well on all sides. Do not overcrowd the pot. If necessary, cook the beef in several batches.
3. Add the onions and garlic and sauté until the onions are slightly browned.
4. Add the flour and stir to make a roux. Brown the roux lightly.
5. Add the red wine and brown stock slowly, stirring to prevent lumps.
6. Add the tomato purée and the sachet.
7. Bring to a simmer and cook until the beef is tender, approximately 1-1/2–2 hours.
8. Optional: Remove the cooked beef from the sauce and strain the sauce. Return the beef to the sauce.
9. Degrease the stew by skimming off the fat.

VARIATION: Vegetables such as turnips, carrots, celery and pearl onions can be cooked separately and added to the stew as garnish.

4. Adding the red wine and beef stock.

5. Adding the tomato purée and sachet.

6. Degreasing the stew.

PROCEDURE FOR STEWING MEATS—*BRAISED WHITE STEWS (FRICASSEES)*

The procedure for making fricassees is similar to the procedure for brown stews. The primary difference is that the meat is sautéed but not allowed to brown. The braised white stew (fricassee) procedure outlined below is the basis for Recipe 14.12, Veal Fricassee.

1. Trim meat of excess fat and silverskin and cut into 1- to 2-inch (2.5- to 5-cm) pieces.
2. Heat an appropriate-sized pan and add enough oil to cover the bottom. Add the meat (and often an onion) to the pan and cook without browning.
3. Sprinkle the meat (and onion) with flour and cook to make a blond roux.
4. Gradually add the liquid, stirring to prevent lumps. Bring the stew to a boil and reduce to a simmer.
5. Add a bouquet garni and seasonings. Cover the stew and place in the oven or continue to simmer on the stove top, being careful not to burn or scorch the stew.
6. Continue to cook until the meat is tender. If the sauce is too thin, remove the meat from the sauce and hold the meat in a warm place. Reduce the sauce to the proper consistency on the stove top or thicken it by adding a small amount of blond roux, cornstarch or arrowroot.

PROCEDURE FOR STEWING MEATS—*SIMMERED WHITE STEWS (BLANQUETTES)*

Unlike fricassees, blanquettes contain meat that was blanched, not sautéed. (Because the meat is cooked only by moist heat and never by dry heat, the blanquette cooking process is not a true combination cooking method; nevertheless, because of its striking similarities to stewing, it is included here.) The most common blanquette is made with veal and is known as blanquette de veau, but any white meat or lamb can be prepared in this manner using a variety of garnishes. The simmered white stew (blanquette) procedure outlined below is the basis for Recipe 15.14, Blanquette of Lamb.

1. Trim meat of excess fat and silverskin and cut into 1- to 2-inch (2.5- to 5-cm) pieces.
2. Blanch the cubed meat by placing the meat in an appropriate pot, covering with cool water, adding salt, and bringing it rapidly to a boil. Drain the water. Rinse the meat to remove any impurities.
3. Return the meat to the pot and add enough stock to cover. Add a bouquet garni, salt and pepper. Simmer until the meat is tender, approximately 1–1-1/2 hours.
4. Strain the meat from the stock. Discard the bouquet garni. Bring the stock to a boil, thicken it with a blond roux and simmer for 15 minutes.
5. Return the meat to the thickened stock. Add a liaison of cream and egg yolks to enrich and thicken the stew. Heat the stew to a simmer. Do not boil or the egg yolks will curdle.
6. If any vegetables are to be added they should be cooked separately and added to the thickened stock with the meat.
7. Adjust the seasoning with a few drops of lemon juice, nutmeg or salt and pepper as needed.

CONCLUSION

Because meat may account for the largest portion of your food-cost dollar, it should be purchased carefully, stored properly and fabricated appropriately. The various cuts and flavors of meat (beef, veal, lamb and pork) can be successfully broiled, grilled, roasted, sautéed, pan-fried, simmered, braised or stewed, provided you follow a few simple procedures and learn which cuts respond best to the various cooking methods.

QUESTIONS FOR DISCUSSION

1. Explain the difference between primals, subprimals and fabricated cuts of meat. Why is it important to be skilled in meat fabrication?

2. What is connective tissue composed of and where is it found? What happens to connective tissues at normal cooking temperatures?

3. Discuss the government's role in regulating the marketing and sale of meat.

4. At what temperature should fresh meat be stored? At what temperature should frozen meat be stored?

5. Would it be better to grill or braise a piece of meat that contains a great deal of connective tissue? Explain your answer.

6. List three ways to improve the cooking qualities of lean meats. What techniques can be used to compensate for the lack of fat?

7. Describe the similarities between sautéing meats and pan-frying them. Describe the differences.

8. Describe the similarities between braising meats and stewing them. Describe the differences.

CHAPTER 13 BEEF

*B*eef is the meat of domesticated cattle. Most of the beef Americans eat comes from steers, which are male cattle castrated as calves and specifically raised for beef. Although Americans are consuming less beef today than we once did, we still consume far more beef than any other meat. The beef we are eating is leaner than that of years past, thanks to advances in animals husbandry and closer trimming of exterior fat.

PRIMAL AND SUBPRIMAL CUTS OF BEEF

After the steer is slaughtered it is cut into four pieces (called quarters) for easy handling. This is done by first splitting the carcass down the backbone into two bilateral halves. Each half is divided into the forequarter (the front portion) and hindquarter (the rear portion) by cutting along the natural curvature between the twelfth and thirteenth ribs. The quartered carcass is then further reduced into the primal cuts and the subprimal and fabricated cuts.

The primal cuts of beef are the chuck, brisket and shank, rib, short plate, short loin, sirloin, flank and round. Figure 13.1 shows the relationship between a steer's bone structure and the primal cuts. It is important to know the location of bones when cutting or working with meats. This makes meat fabrication and carving easier and aids in identifying cuts. Figure 13.2 shows the primal cuts of beef and their location on the carcass. An entire beef carcass can range in weight from 500 to more than 800 pounds (225–360 kg).

Forequarter

Chuck

The primal chuck is the animal's shoulder; it accounts for approximately 28% of carcass weight. It contains a portion of the backbone (which, in turn, consists of feather, finger and chine bones), five rib bones and portions of the blade and arm bones.

Because an animal constantly uses its shoulder muscles, chuck contains a high percentage of connective tissue and is quite tough. This tough cut of beef, however, is one of the most flavorful.

The primal chuck is used less frequently than other primal cuts in food service operations. If cooked whole, the chuck is difficult to cut or carve because of the large number of bones and relatively small muscle groups which travel in different directions.

The primal chuck produces several fabricated cuts: cross rib pot roast, chuck short ribs, cubed or tenderized steaks, stew meat and ground chuck. Because the meat is tough, the fabricated cuts usually benefit from moist-heat cooking or combination cooking methods such as stewing and braising.

Brisket and Shank

The brisket and shank are located beneath the primal chuck on the front half of the carcass. Together, they form a single primal that accounts for approximately 8% of the carcass weight. This primal consists of the steer's breast (the

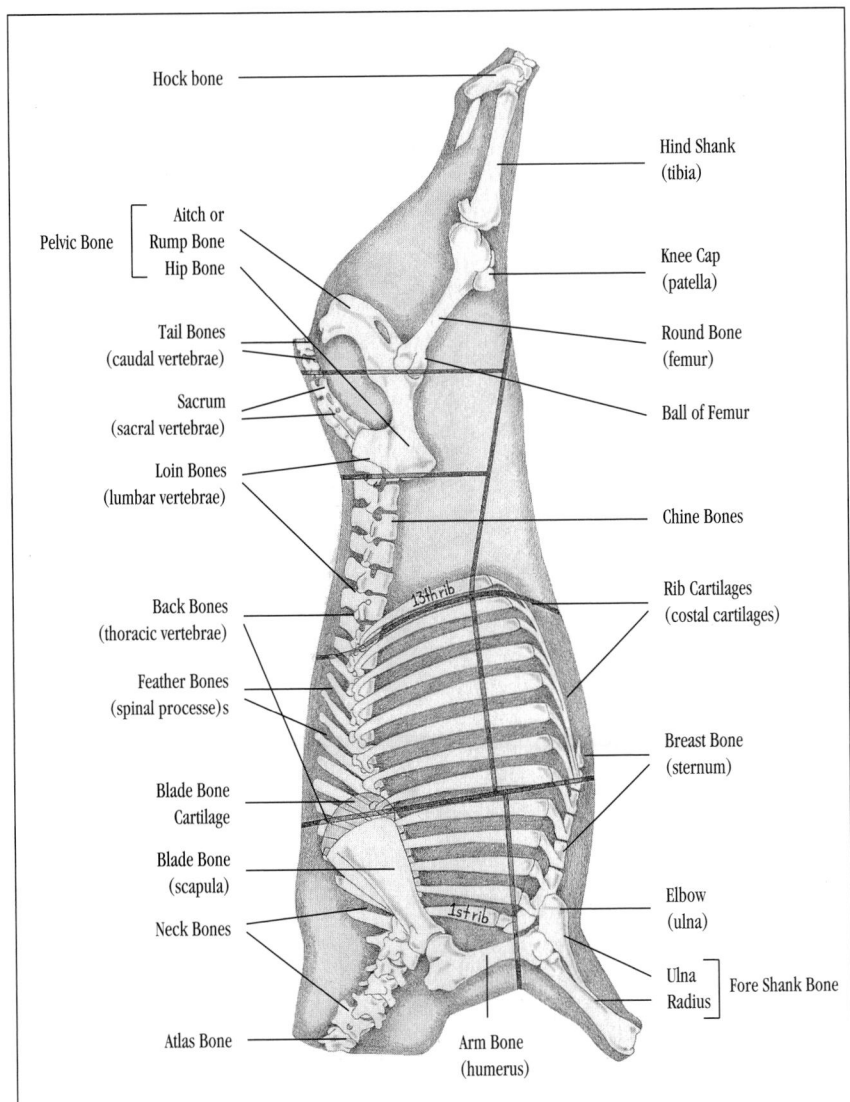

FIGURE 13.1   *The Skeletal Structure of a Steer*

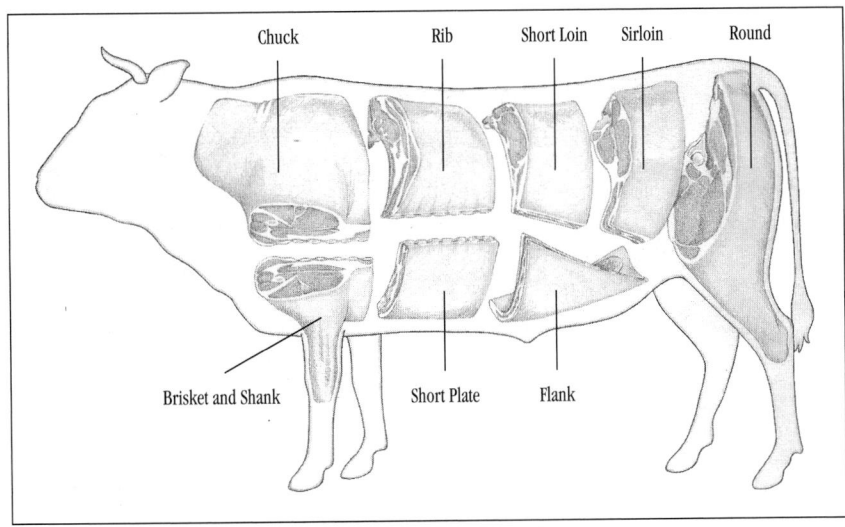

FIGURE 13.2   *The Primal Cuts of Beef*

brisket), which contains ribs and breast bone, and its arm (the foreshank), which contains only the shank bone.

The ribs and breast bone are always removed from the brisket before cooking. The boneless brisket is very tough and contains a substantial percentage of fat, both intermuscular and subcutaneous. It is well suited for moist-heat and combination cooking methods such as simmering or braising. It is often pickled or corned to produce corned beef brisket, or cured and peppered to make pastrami.

Beef foreshanks are very flavorful and high in collagen. Because collagen converts to gelatin when cooked using moist heat, foreshanks are excellent for making soups and stocks. Ground shank meat is often used to help clarify and flavor consommés because of its rich flavor and high collagen content.

Rib

The primal beef rib accounts for approximately 10% of carcass weight. It consists of ribs 6 through 12 as well as a portion of the backbone.

This primal is best known for yielding roast prime rib of beef. Prime rib is not named after the quality grade USDA Prime. Rather, its name reflects the fact that it constitutes the majority of the primal cut. The eye meat of the rib (the center muscle portion) is not a well-exercised muscle and therefore is quite tender. It also contains large amounts of marbling compared to the rest of the carcass and produces rich, full-flavored roasts and steaks. Although roasting the eye muscle on the rib bones produces a moister roast, the eye meat can be removed to produce a boneless rib eye roast or cut into rib eye steaks. The rib bones that are separated from the rib eye meat are quite meaty and flavorful and can be served as barbecued beef ribs. The ends of the rib bones that are trimmed off the primal rib to produce the rib roast are known as beef short ribs. They are meaty and are often served as braised beef short ribs.

Oven-ready Rib Roast

Beef Rib Eye Roll

Short Plate

The short plate is located directly below the primal rib on a side of beef; it accounts for only a small portion of the overall weight of the carcass, approximately 9%. The short plate contains rib bones and cartilage and produces the meaty plate short ribs and skirt steak.

Short ribs are meaty, yet high in connective tissue, and are best when braised. Skirt steak is often marinated and grilled as fajitas. Other, less meaty portions of the short plate are trimmed and ground.

Skirt Steak

Hindquarter

Short Loin

The short loin is the anterior (front) portion of the beef loin. It is located just behind the rib and becomes the first primal cut of the hindquarter when the side of beef is divided into a forequarter and hindquarter. It accounts for approximately 8% of carcass weight.

Porterhouse or T-bone Steaks

The short loin contains a single rib, the thirteenth, and a portion of the backbone. With careful butchering, this small primal can yield several subprimal and fabricated cuts, all of which are among the most tender, popular and expensive cuts of beef.

The loin eye muscle, a continuation of the rib eye muscle, runs along the top of the T-shaped bones that form the backbone. Beneath the loin eye muscle on the other side of the backbone is the tenderloin, the most tender cut of all.

When the short loin is cut in cross sections with the bone in, it produces—starting with the rib end of the short loin—club steaks (which do not contain any tenderloin), T-bone steaks (which contain only a small portion of tenderloin) and porterhouse steaks (which are cut from the sirloin end of the short loin and contain a large portion of tenderloin).

Strip Loin

The whole tenderloin also can be removed and cut into chateaubriand, filet mignon and tournedos. A portion of the tenderloin is located in the sirloin portion of the loin. When the entire beef loin is divided into the primal short loin and primal sirloin, the large end of the tenderloin (the butt tenderloin) is separated from the remainder of the tenderloin and remains in the sirloin; the smaller end of the tenderloin (the short tenderloin) remains in the short loin. If the tenderloin is to be kept whole, it must be removed before the short loin and sirloin are separated. The loin eye meat can be removed from the bones, producing a boneless strip loin, which is very tender and can be roasted or cut into boneless strip steaks.

Tenderloin

Sirloin

The sirloin is located in the hindquarter, between the short loin and the round. It accounts for approximately 7% of carcass weight and contains part of the backbone as well as a portion of the hip bone.

The sirloin produces bone-in or boneless roasts and steaks that are flavorful and tender. With the exception of the tenderloin portion, however, these subprimals and fabricated cuts are not as tender as those from the strip loin. Cuts from the sirloin are cooked using dry-heat methods such as broiling, grilling or roasting.

Top Sirloin Butt

Flank

The flank is located directly beneath the loin, posterior to (behind) the short plate. It accounts for approximately 6% of carcass weight. The flank contains no bones.

Although quite flavorful, it is tough meat with a good deal of fat and connective tissue. Flank meat is usually trimmed and ground, with the exception of the flank steak or London broil. The flank also contains a small piece of meat known as the hanging tenderloin. Although not actually part of the tenderloin, it is very tender and can be cooked using any method.

Flank Steak

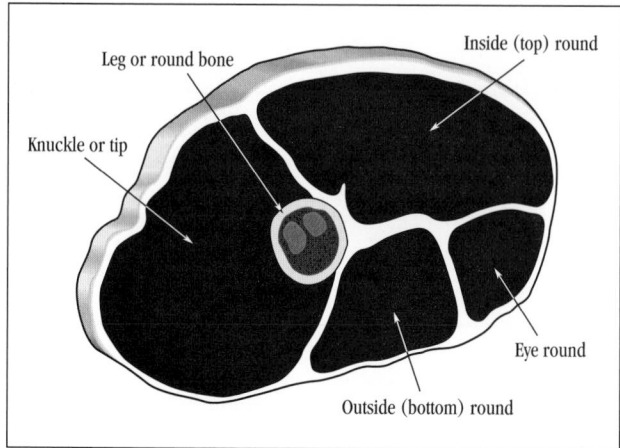

FIGURE 13.3   *Cross Cut of Muscles in a Whole Round*

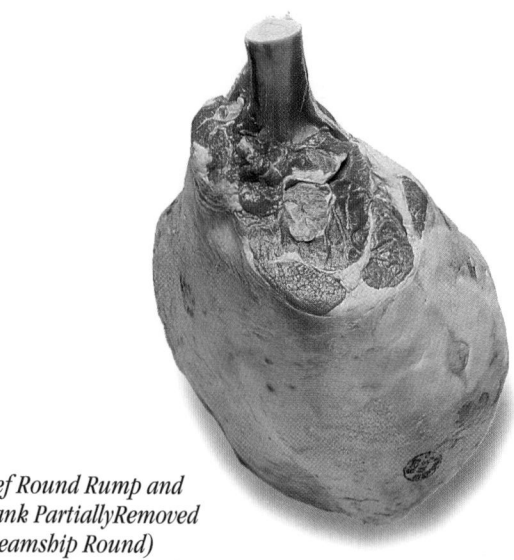

*Beef Round Rump and
Shank PartiallyRemoved
(Steamship Round)*

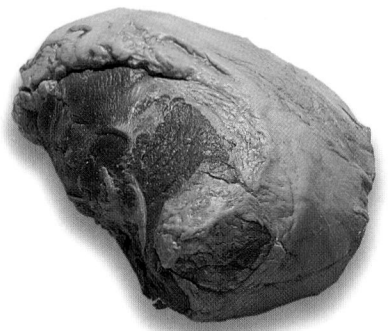

Top (or Inside) Round

Round

The primal round is very large, weighing as much as 200 pounds (90 kg) and accounting for approximately 24% of carcass weight. It is the hind leg of the animal and contains the round, aitch, shank and tail bones.

Meat from the round is flavorful and fairly tender. The round yields a wide variety of subprimal and fabricated cuts: the top round, outside round, eye round (the outside round and the eye round together are called the bottom round), knuckle and shank. See Figure 13.3. Steaks cut from the round are tough, but because they have large muscles and limited intermuscular fat, the top round and knuckle make good roasts. The bottom round is best when braised. The hindshank is prepared in the same fashion as the foreshank.

♦♦♦

BEEF:
FROM COLUMBUS TO CATTLE DRIVES

Although cattle have been domesticated for several thousand years, they have been in the New World only since 1493, when Columbus brought them along on his second expedition to the West Indies. During the succeeding decades, the Spanish brought cattle to Florida and Texas, where they thrived in the dry, hot climates.

The New World's desire for beef steadily grew from the 1500s to the early 1800s. By the mid-1800s, America's demand for beef outpaced the supply available from local family farms, and so cattle ranching was born. Based princi-

pally in the Southwest and West, ranchers used the open range to support large cattle herds. Texas longhorns, descended from the original Spanish cattle stock, were the animal of choice. Prized for the quality of their meat, longhorns are hardy animals that live off the range and demand little care. They grow rapidly on forage such as mesquite beans, prickly pear, weeds, shrubs and buffalo grass. Ranchers brought the cattle from the range to slaughterhouses near consumer markets or to places like Kansas City with rail links to the populous East Coast.

The open range, so vital to the 19th-century cattle industry, began to disappear rapidly after the signing of the Homestead Act of 1862. Squabbles with sheep ranchers further eroded the range land available for the great cattle herds to roam. And, as the railroads expanded westward, the cattle drives shortened and the economies of scale that supported cattle ranching began to dwindle. Although there are still many large cattle ranches, by the early 20th century great cattle drives had become nothing more than fodder for Hollywood.

Organ Meats

Several organ meats are used in food service operations. This group of products is known as **offal**. It includes the heart, kidney, tongue, tripe (stomach lining) and oxtail. Offal benefit from moist-heat cooking and are often used in soup, stew or braised dishes.

> **Offal**— *also called variety meats, edible entrails (for example, the heart, kidneys, liver, sweetbreads and tongue) and extremities (for example, oxtail and pig's feet) of an animal.*

BUTCHERING PROCEDURES

Although many food service operations buy their beef previously cut and portioned, you still should be able to fabricate cuts of beef and perform basic butchering tasks.

PROCEDURE FOR CUTTING A NEW YORK STEAK FROM A BONELESS STRIP LOIN

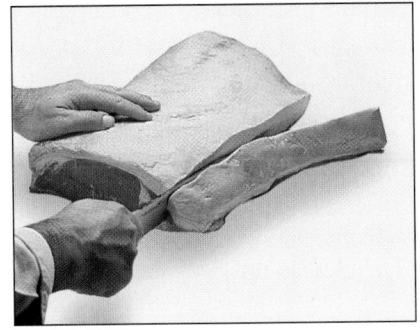

1. Square up the strip loin by trimming off the lip so it extends 1 to 2 inches (2.5 to 5 cm) from the eye muscle.

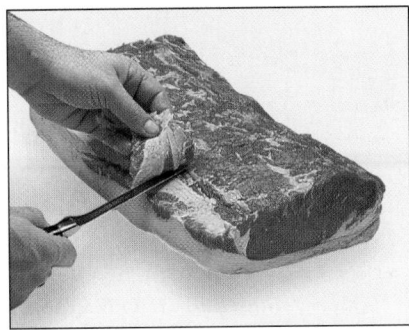

2. Turn the strip over and trim off any fat or connective tissue.

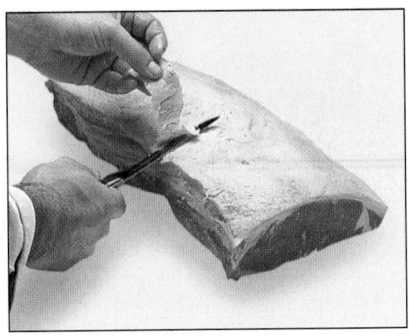

3. Turn the strip back over and trim the fat covering to a uniform thickness of 1/4 inch (6 mm).

4. Cut the steaks to the thickness or weight desired.

5. The eye meat of steaks located on the sirloin end of the strip is divided by a strip of connective tissue. Steaks cut from this area are called vein steaks and are inferior to steaks cut from the rib end of the strip.

PROCEDURE FOR TRIMMING A FULL BEEF TENDERLOIN AND CUTTING IT INTO CHATEAUBRIAND, FILET MIGNON AND TENDER TIPS

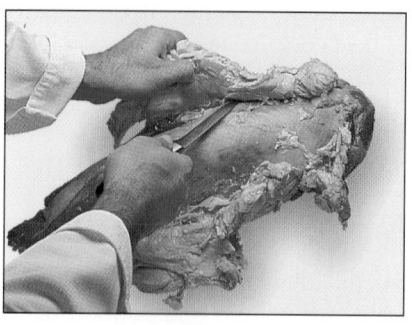

1. Cut and pull the excess fat from the entire tenderloin to expose the meat.

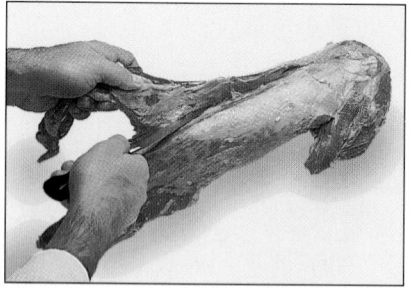

2. Remove the chain muscle from the side of the tenderloin. (Although it contains much connective tissue, the chain muscle may be trimmed and the meat used as tenderloin trimmings in various dishes.)

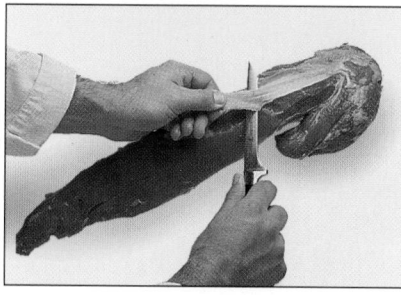

3. Trim away all the fat and silverskin. Do so by loosening a small piece of silverskin, then, holding the loosened silverskin tightly with one hand, cut it away in long strips, angling the knife up toward the silverskin slightly so that only the silverskin is removed and no meat is wasted.

4. Cut the tenderloin as desired into (left to right) tips, chateaubriand, filet mignon, tournedo tips, and tenderloin tips.

PROCEDURE FOR BUTTERFLYING MEATS

Many cuts of boneless meats such as tenderloin steaks and boneless pork chops can be butterflied to create a thinner cut that has a greater surface area and cooks more quickly.

1. Make the first cut nearly all the way through the meat, keeping it attached by leaving approximately 1/4 inch (6 mm) uncut.

2. Make a second cut, this time cutting all the way through, completely removing the steak from the tenderloin .

TABLE 13.1   USING COMMON CUTS OF BEEF

Primal	Subprimal or Fabricated Cut	IMPS	Cooking Methods	Serving Suggestions
Chuck	Chuck roll tied	116A	Combination (braise; stew)	Pot roast; beef stew
	Stew meat	135A	Combination (stew)	Beef stew
	Ground beef	136	Dry heat (broil or grill; roast) Combination (braise; stew)	Hamburgers; meatloaf Chili con carne; beef stews
Brisket and Shank	Brisket	120	Moist heat (simmer)	Corned beef; New England boiled dinner
			Combination (braise)	Pot roast
	Shank	117	Combination (braise)	Shredded beef for tamales or hash
Rib	Oven ready rib roast	109	Dry heat (roast)	Roast prime rib
	Rib eye roll	112	Dry heat (roast)	Roast prime rib
Short Plate	Skirt steak	121D	Dry heat (broil or grill)	Steak; fajitas
	Short ribs	123A	Combination (braise)	Braised short ribs
Short Loin	Porterhouse or T-bone steaks	173, 174	Dry heat (broil or grill)	Steaks
	Strip loin	180	Dry heat (broil or grill; roast; sautée)	New York steak; minute steak entrecôtes bordelaise
	Tenderloin	189	Dry heat (broil or grill; roast)	Tournedos Rossini; beef Wellington
Flank	Flank steak	193	Dry heat (broil or grill) Combination (braise)	London broil Braised stuffed flank steak
Round	Steamship round	160	Dry heat (roast)	Roast beef
	Top (inside) round	168	Dry heat (roast) Combination (braise)	Roast beef Braised beef roulade

CONCLUSION

Antonin Carême once said that "beef is the soul of cooking." It is also the most popular meat consumed in the United States and undoubtedly will play an important role on almost any menu. Beef's assertive flavor stands up well to most any sauce and seasonings.

Prefabricated products are readily available. But preforming some basic fabrication procedures in your own kitchen saves money and allows you to cut the meat to your exact specifications. Each primal and subprimal cut has its own distinct characteristics. The primal rib, short loin and sirloin produce the most popular and most expensive cuts of beef. Once the beef is properly fabricated, choose the appropriate dry-heat, moist-heat or combination cooking method for that cut.

QUESTIONS FOR DISCUSSION

1. List each beef primal cut and describe its location on the carcass. For each primal cut, identify two subprimal or fabricated cuts taken from it.

2. Would it be better to use the chuck for grilling or stewing? Explain your answer.

3. Which fabricated cuts contain a portion of the tenderloin? What cooking methods are best suited for these cuts? Explain your answer.

4. Name four cuts that can be produced from a whole beef tenderloin. Describe a preparation procedure for each cut.

5. Most steaks are cut from the hindquarter. What popular steak is cut from the forequarter, and why is it tender when other cuts from the forequarter are relatively tough?

ADDITIONAL BEEF RECIPES

RECIPE 13.1
T-BONE STEAK

NOTE: *This dish appears in the Chapter Opening photograph.*

RUTH'S CHRIS STEAK HOUSE, PHOENIX, AZ

Yield: 1 Serving   **Method:** Broiling

T-bone steak, 24 oz. (700 g)	1	1
Salt and pepper	TT	TT
Whole butter, melted	1 oz.	30 g
Parsley, chopped	as needed	as needed

1. Season both sides of the steak with the salt and pepper.
2. Broil the steak to the desired degree of doneness and place on a very hot serving platter.
3. Ladle the melted butter over the steak and sprinkle with chopped parsley.

◆◆◆

RECIPE 13.2
MARINATED LONDON BROIL

Yield: 6 5-8 oz. (150- 250-g) Servings   **Method:** Grilling

Marinade:		
Olive oil	4 oz.	120 g
Balsamic vinegar	4 oz.	120 g
Fresh rosemary, chopped	2 Tbsp.	30 ml
Garlic, minced	2 oz.	60 g
Pepper	1 tsp.	5 ml
Beef flank steak, 2–3 lb. (1 to 1-1/2 kg)	1	1

1. Combine the marinade ingredients in a hotel pan.
2. Add the flank steak to the marinade and coat completely. Allow the meat to marinate for at least 4 hours.
3. Grill the steak rare to medium rare. If cooked further, the meat will become extremely tough.
4. Carve into 1/4-inch (6 millimeter) think slices, cutting diagonally across the grain.

♦♦♦

RECIPE 13.3

CHATEAUBRIAND

ANA WESTIN HOTEL, WASHINGTON D.C.
Chef Leland Atkinson

Yield: 2 Servings

Method: Roasting

Beef filet, cut from the "head" of the tenderloin, 16–24 ounces (500–750 grams)	1	1
Salt and pepper	TT	TT
Clarified butter	as needed	as needed

1. Tie the beef with butcher's twine and season with salt and pepper.

2. Sauté the beef in clarified butter until it is well browned.

3. Transfer the beef to a 450°F (230°C) oven and roast until done, approximately 10–12 minutes for rare (internal temperature of 125°F/52°C), or 15–18 minutes for medium (140°F/60°C).

4. Remove the beef from the oven and allow it to rest for at least 5 minutes before carving.

5. At service time, slice the beef evenly on a slight diagonal bias.

Chateaubriand is traditionally served with béarnaise sauce and a bouquetiére of vegetables.

♦♦♦

RECIPE 13.4

HOME-STYLE MEATLOAF

Yield: 16 8-oz. (250-g) Servings

Method: Baking

Onion, small dice	1 lb.	450 g
Celery, small dice	8 oz.	250 g
Garlic, chopped	2 Tbsp.	30 ml
Oil	2 oz.	60 g
Fresh bread crumbs	6 oz.	180 g
Tomato juice	12 oz.	350 g
Ground beef	4 lb.	1.8 kg
Ground pork	4 lb.	1.8 kg
Eggs, beaten	6	6
Salt	1 Tbsp.	15 ml
Pepper	1 tsp.	5 ml
Parsley, chopped	2 Tbsp.	30 ml

1. Sauté the onions, celery and garlic in the oil until tender. Remove from the heat and cool.

2. Combine all ingredients; mix well.

3. Form into loaves of the desired size and place in loaf pans.

4. Bake at 350°F (180°C) until the meatloaf reaches an internal temperature of 165°F (74°C), approximately 1 to 1-1/2 hours.

5. Allow the loaves to rest 15 minutes before slicing. Cut slices of the desired thickness and serve with a tomato or mushroom sauce.

◆◆◆

RECIPE 13.5

TOURNEDOS ROSSINI

Yield: 4 Servings   Method: Sautéing

Tournedos, 3 oz. (90 g) each	8	8
Clarified butter	as needed	as needed
Croutons	8	8
Foie gras, 1-oz. (30-g) slices	8	8
Truffle slices	8	8
Madeira	4 oz.	120 g
Demi-glace	8 oz.	225 g
Salt and pepper	TT	TT

1. Sauté the beef in clarified butter to the desired doneness. Place each tournedo on top of a crouton. Top each with a slice of foie gras, then a slice of truffle. Hold in a warm place.
2. Degrease the pan. Deglaze the pan with the madeira and add the demi-glace.
3. Reduce the sauce to the desired consistency and adjust the seasonings.
4. Warm the tournedos briefly under a broiler or in the oven. Pour the sauce around the tournedos. Garnish with watercress, sautéed asparagus and château potatoes.

◆◆◆

RECIPE 13.6

MINUTE STEAK DIJONAISE

Yield: 2 Servings   Method: Sautéing

Sirloin steak, trimmed, 6 oz. (170 g)	2	2
Dijon mustard	1 oz.	30 g
Onion, small dice	2 oz.	60 g
Clarified butter	1 oz.	30 g
Heavy cream	3 oz.	90 g
Whole butter	1 oz.	30 g
Salt and pepper	TT	TT

1. Pound the steaks to a 1/4-inch (6-mm) thickness.
2. Cover one side of each sirloin first with 1-1/2 teaspoons (8 ml) of the mustard and then half the onions, pressing the onions firmly into the steak.
3. Sauté the steaks in the clarified butter, presentation (onion) side down first. Remove and hold in a warm place.
4. Degrease the pan. Add the cream and reduce by half. Add the rest of the Dijon mustard.
5. Monte au beurre. Adjust the seasonings and serve the steaks with the sauce.

◆◆◆

RECIPE 13.7

BEEF STROGANOFF

Yield: 8 8-oz. (250-g) Servings   Method: Sautéing

Tenderloin tips, émincé	2 lb.	1 kg
Clarified butter	1-1/2 oz.	45 g
Onion, medium dice	4 oz.	120 g

Mushrooms, halved	1 lb.	450 g
Demi-glace	10 oz.	300 g
Heavy cream	10 oz.	300 g
Sour cream	8 oz.	250 g
Dijon mustard	1 Tbsp.	15 ml
Fresh dill, chopped	1 Tbsp.	15 ml
Fresh parsley, chopped	1 Tbsp.	15 ml
Salt and pepper	TT	TT
Egg noodles, cooked	24 oz.	700 g

1. Sauté the tenderloin tips in the butter, searing on all sides. Remove the meat and set aside.

2. Add the onion to the pan and sauté lightly. Add the mushrooms and sauté until dry.

3. Add the demi-glace. Bring to a boil, reduce to a simmer and cook 10 minutes.

4. Add the cream, sour cream, mustard and any meat juices that accumulated while holding the meat.

5. Return the meat to the sauce to reheat. Stir in the dill and parsley. Adjust the seasonings and serve over egg noodles.

◆◆◆

RECIPE 13.8
ENTRECÔTES BORDELAISE

Yield: 4 Servings   **Method:** Sautéing

Beef marrow	4 oz.	120 g
Entrecôtes, 14 oz. (400 g) each	2	2
Salt and pepper	TT	TT
Clarified butter	2 oz.	60 g
Shallots, chopped	2 Tbsp.	30 ml
Red wine	8 oz.	250 g
Demi-glace	12 oz.	340 g
Whole butter	1 oz.	30 g

1. Slice the marrow into rounds and poach in salt water for 3 minutes. Drain the marrow and set it aside.

2. Season the steaks and sauté them in the clarified butter to the desired doneness. Finish in the oven if desired. Remove to a platter and hold in a warm place.

3. Sauté the shallots in the same pan.

4. Deglaze the pan with the wine and reduce by half. Add the demi-glace; simmer for 5 minutes.

5. Monte au beurre.

6. Add the marrow to the sauce. Adjust the seasonings and serve the steaks with the sauce.

◆◆◆

RECIPE 13.9
PEPPER STEAK

Yield: 2 Servings   **Method:** Sautéing

Boneless strip steaks,		
approx. 8 oz. (250 g) each	2	2

Continued

Salt	TT	TT
Peppercorns, cracked	3 Tbsp.	45 ml
Clarified butter	1 oz.	30 g
Cognac	2 oz.	60 g
Heavy cream	4 oz.	120 g
Whole butter	2 oz.	60 g

1. Season the steaks with salt. Spread the peppercorns in a hotel pan and press the steaks into them, lightly coating each side.

2. Sauté the steaks in the clarified butter over high heat for 2 to 3 minutes on each side.

3. Remove the pan from the heat. Pour the cognac over the steaks, return the pan to the heat and flambé. When the flames subside, remove the steaks from the pan and keep them warm on a plate.

4. Add the cream to the pan. Bring to a boil and reduce for 2 minutes over high heat; monte au beurre. Pour this sauce over the steaks and serve immediately.

======= ◆◆◆ =======

RECIPE 13.10

SWISS STEAK

Yield: 10 Servings   **Method:** Braising

Beef bottom round steaks, 6 oz. (180 g) each	10	10
Flour	as needed	as needed
Salt and pepper	TT	TT
Oil	2 oz.	60 g
Onion, small dice	1 lb.	450 g
Garlic cloves, crushed	3	3
Celery	8 oz.	250 g
Flour	4 oz.	120 g
Brown stock	5 pt.	2.2 lt
Tomato purée	6 oz.	180 g
Sachet:		
Bay leaves	2	2
Dried thyme	1/2 tsp.	2 ml
Peppercorns, crushed	1/2 tsp.	2 ml
Parsley stems	8	8

1. Dredge the steaks in flour seasoned with salt and pepper.

2. Heat the oil in a braiser and brown the steaks well on both sides. Remove the steaks.

3. Add the onions, garlic and celery; sauté until tender.

4. Add the flour and cook to a brown roux.

5. Gradually add the brown stock, whisking until the sauce is thickened and smooth. Add the tomato purée and sachet.

6. Return the steaks to the braising pan, cover and cook in a 300°F (150°C) oven until tender, approximately 2 hours.

7. Remove the steaks from the sauce. Discard the sachet. Strain the sauce and adjust the seasonings. Serve the steaks with the sauce.

◆◆◆

RECIPE 13.11

BRAISED SHORT RIBS OF BEEF

Yield: 8 8-oz. (230-g) Servings   **Method:** Braising

Flour	4 oz.	120 g
Salt	1 Tbsp.	15 ml
Pepper	1 tsp.	5 ml
Dried rosemary	1/2 tsp.	2 ml
Short ribs of beef,		
cut in 2-in. (5 cm) portions	6 lbs.	2.7 kg
Vegetable oil	1 oz.	30 g
Onion, chopped	6 oz.	170 g
Celery, chopped	4 oz.	120 g
Brown beef stock	24 oz.	700 g
Roux	as needed	as needed
Salt and pepper	TT	TT

1. Combine the flour, salt, pepper and rosemary. Dredge the ribs in the seasoned flour.
2. Heat the oil and brown the ribs well in a heavy brazier. Remove and hold in a warm place.
3. Add the vegetables to the brazier and sauté lightly.
4. Return the ribs to the pan, add the stock and braise in an oven until done, approximately 2-1/2 hours.
5. Remove the ribs from the liquid and skim off the excess fat.
6. Bring the liquid to a boil on the stove top; thicken it with roux to the desired consistency and simmer 15 minutes. Strain the sauce and adjust the seasonings. Return the ribs to the sauce and simmer for 5 minutes.

◆◆◆

RECIPE 13.12

HUNGARIAN GOULASH

Yield: 10 8-oz. (250-g) Servings   **Method:** Stewing

Lard or vegetable oil	2 oz.	60 g
Onion, medium dice	2 lb.	900 g
Hungarian paprika	4 Tbsp.	60 ml
Garlic, chopped	1 Tbsp.	15 ml
Caraway seeds	1/2 tsp.	2 ml
Salt	TT	TT
Pepper	1/2 tsp.	2 ml
White stock	1 qt.	1 lt
Tomato paste	4 oz.	120 g
Beef stew meat,		
cut in 1-1/2-in. (4-cm) cubes	5 lb.	2.2 kg

1. Sauté the onions in the lard or oil, browning lightly.
2. Add the paprika, garlic, caraway seeds, salt and pepper; mix well.
3. Add the white stock and tomato paste. Bring to a boil, then reduce to a simmer.
4. Add the meat and braise until the meat is very tender, approximately 1-1/2 hours. Adjust the seasonings and serve.

◆◆◆

RECIPE 13.13

BEEF BOURGUIGNON

Yield: 10 8-oz. (250-g) Servings   **Method:** Stewing

Marinade:		
Garlic cloves, crushed	3	3
Onions, sliced	3	3
Carrots, sliced	2	2
Parsley stems	10	10
Bouquet garni:		
Carrot stick, 4 in. (10 cm)	1	1
Leek, split, 4-in. (10-cm) piece	1	1
Fresh thyme	1 sprig	1 sprig
Bay leaf	1	1
Peppercorns, crushed	10	10
Salt	TT	TT
Dry red wine, preferably Burgundy	26 oz.	750 ml
Beef chuck, cubed for stew	4 lb.	1.8 kg
Vegetable oil	2 oz.	60 g
Flour	2 Tbsp.	30 ml
Tomato paste	1 Tbsp.	15 ml
Tomatoes, quartered	4	4
Brown stock	1 pint	450 ml
Mushrooms, quartered	1 lb.	450 g
Unsalted butter	1-1/2 oz.	45 g
Pearl onions, boiled and peeled	30	30
Salt and pepper	TT	TT

1. Combine the garlic, onions, carrots, parsley, bouquet garni, peppercorns, salt and wine to make a marinade.

2. Marinate the meat several hours under refrigeration.

3. Remove and drain the meat. Reserve the marinade.

4. Dry the beef and sauté it in the oil until well browned. Do this in several batches if necessary.

5. Return all the meat to the pot. Sprinkle with flour and cook to make a blond roux.

6. Stir in the tomato paste and cook for 5 minutes.

7. Add the reserved marinade, tomatoes and brown stock. Cook in a 350°F (180°C) oven until the meat is tender, approximately 2-1/2 hours.

8. Remove the meat from the sauce. Strain the sauce through a china cap, pressing to extract all of the liquid. Discard the solids. Return the liquid and beef to the pot.

9. Sauté the mushrooms in the butter and add them to the meat and sauce. Add the onions and adjust the seasonings. Simmer for 10 minutes to blend the flavors.

◆◆◆

RECIPE 13.14

CHILI CON CARNE

Yield: 1 gal. (4 lt)   **Method:** Braising

Onion, medium dice	1 lb.	450 g
Vegetable oil	1 Tbsp.	15 ml

Garlic, chopped	1/2 oz.	15 g
Ground beef	2 lb. 8 oz.	1.2 kg
Tomato, crushed	2 lb.	1 kg
Tomato, diced	4 lb.	1.8 kg
Tomato paste	4 oz.	120 g
Brown stock	1 pt.	450 ml
Chili powder	1 oz.	30 g
Cumin	2 tsp.	10 ml
Bay leaves	4	4
Salt and pepper	TT	TT
Dry kidney beans, soaked and simmered in water until tender	12 oz.	350 g

1. Sauté the onions in the oil until tender. Add the garlic and sauté one minute.
2. Add the beef and brown, stirring occasionally. Drain off the excess fat.
3. Add the remaining ingredients, bring to a simmer, cover and cook for 1 hour.
4. Remove the bay leaves and adjust the seasonings.

◆◆◆

RECIPE 13.15

OXTAIL RAGOUT

Yield: 8 10-oz. (300-g) Servings   **Method:** Stewing

Oxtail pieces, 2 in. (5 cm)	4 lb.	1.8 kg
Flour	as needed	as needed
Salt and pepper	TT	TT
Oil	2 oz.	60 g
Mirepoix	1 lb.	450 g
Fatty prosciutto, small dice	4 oz.	120 g
Garlic cloves, crushed	4	4
Sachet:		
Bay leaf	1	1
Dried thyme	1/2 tsp.	2 ml
Peppercorns, crushed	1/2 tsp.	2 ml
Parsley stems	10	10
Tomato concasse	1 lb.	450 g
White wine	8 oz.	250 g
Lemon zest, julienne	1 tsp.	5 ml
Brown stock	2 qt.	2 lt

1. Trim the excess fat from the oxtail pieces and dredge them in flour seasoned with salt and pepper.
2. Brown the oxtail in the oil. Add the mirepoix, prosciutto and garlic; sauté until the vegetables are tender.
3. Add the sachet, tomato concasse, white wine, lemon zest and brown stock. Cover and bring to a simmer on the stove top or place in a 325°F (160°C) oven and cook until the oxtails are tender, approximately 2 hours.
4. Remove the oxtails from the sauce. Strain and degrease the sauce. Adjust the seasonings. Return the oxtails to the sauce.
5. Serve the ragout with buttered noodles; garnish with batonnet carrots and turnips that have been cooked separately.

CHAPTER 14 VEAL

they account for approximately 16% of carcass weight. This primal contains rib bones and rib cartilage, breast bones and shank bones. Because the calf is slaughtered young, many of the breast bones are cartilaginous rather than bony.

This cartilage, as well as the ample fat and connective tissue also present in the breast, breaks down during long moist cooking, thus making the flavorful breast a good choice for braising. Veal breast can also be cubed for stews such as veal fricassee and veal blanquette, rolled and stuffed, or trimmed and ground.

The foreshank is also very flavorful but tough. It can be braised whole or sliced perpendicular to the shank bone and braised to produce osso buco.

Rib

The double rib, also known as a veal hotel rack, is a very tender, relatively small cut accounting for approximately 9% of carcass weight. It is very popular and very expensive. The double rack consists of two racks, each with seven rib bones and a portion of the backbone.

Veal racks can be roasted either whole or split into two sides. Veal racks can be boned out; each side produces a veal rib eye and a small piece of tenderloin known as the short tenderloin, both of which make excellent roasts. More often, veal racks are trimmed and cut into chops, which can also be bone-in or boneless, to be grilled, sautéed or braised.

Veal Hotel Rack, Split

Hindsaddle

Loin

The veal loin is posterior to the primal rib, contains two ribs (numbers 12 and 13) and accounts for approximately 10% of carcass weight. The loin consists of the loin eye muscle on top of the rib bones and the tenderloin under them.

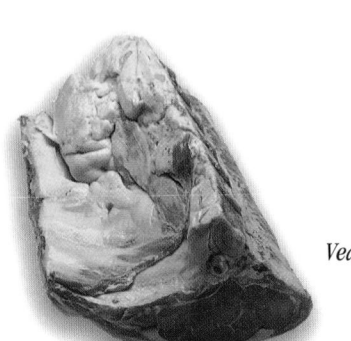

Veal Loin

The veal loin eye is very tender and the tenderloin is, without a doubt, the most tender cut of veal. If the primal veal loin is separated from the primal leg before the tenderloin is removed, the tenderloin will be cut into two pieces. The small portion (short tenderloin) remains in the primal loin and the large portion (butt tenderloin) remains in the sirloin portion of the primal leg. The tenderloin is sometimes removed and cut into medallions. The veal loin is often cut into chops, bone-in or boneless. It is usually cooked using dry heat such as broiling, grilling, roasting or sautéing.

Loin Chops

Boneless Strip Loin

Leg

The primal veal leg consists of both the sirloin and the leg. Together they account for approximately 42% of carcass weight. The primal leg is separated from the loin by a cut perpendicular to the backbone immediately anterior to the hip bone, and it contains portions of the backbone, tail bone, hip bone, aitch bone, round bone and hind shank.

Although it is tender enough to be roasted whole, the veal leg is typically fabricated into cutlets and scallops. To fabricate these cuts, the leg is first broken down into its major muscles: the top round, eye round, knuckle, sirloin, bottom round (which includes the sirloin) and butt tenderloin. Each of these muscles can be reduced to scallops by trimming all fat and visible connective tissue and slicing against the grain to the desired thickness. The scallops then should be pounded carefully to tenderize them further and to prevent them from curling when cooked.

The hindshank is somewhat meatier than the foreshank but both are prepared and cooked in the same manner.

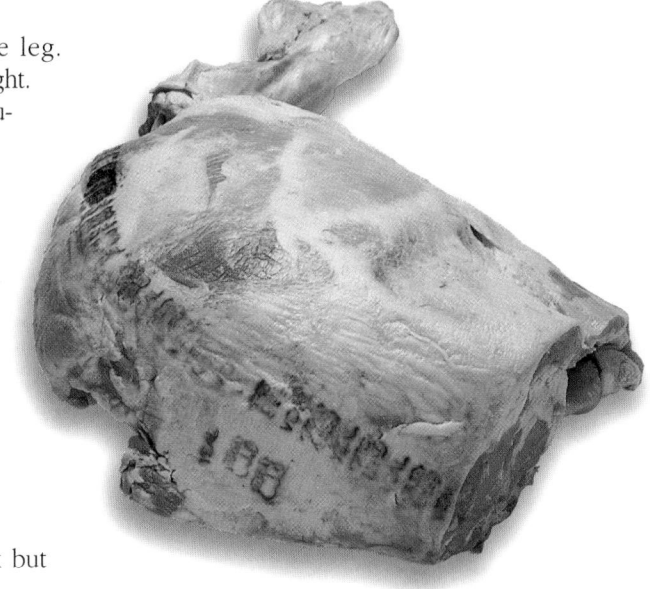

Veal Leg

Because the veal carcass is small enough to be handled easily, it is sometimes purchased in forms larger than the primal cuts described above. Depending on employee skill, available equipment and storage space and an ability to utilize fully all the cuts and trimmings that fabricating meat produces, you may want to purchase veal in one of the following forms:

◆ *Foresaddle:* The anterior portion of the carcass after it is severed from the hindsaddle by a cut following the natural curvature between the eleventh and twelfth ribs. It contains the primal shoulder, foreshank and breast, and rib.
◆ *Hindsaddle:* The posterior portion of the carcass after it is severed from the foresaddle. It contains the primal loin and leg.
◆ *Back:* The trimmed rib and loin sections in one piece. The back is particularly useful when producing large quantities of veal chops.
◆ *Veal side:* One bilateral half of the carcass, produced by cutting lengthwise thorough the backbone.

Top Round

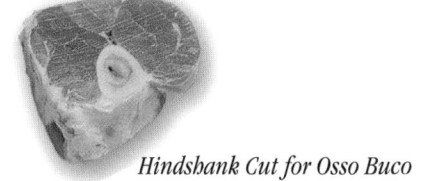

Hindshank Cut for Osso Buco

Organ Meats

Several calf organ meats are used in food service operations.

Sweetbreads

Sweetbreads are the thymus glands of veal and lamb. As an animal ages, its thymus gland shrinks; therefore sweetbreads are not available from older cattle or sheep. Veal sweetbreads are much more popular than lamb sweetbreads in this country. Good-quality sweetbreads should be plump and firm, with the exterior membrane intact. Delicately flavored and tender, they can be prepared by almost any cooking method.

Sweetbreads

Calves' Liver

Calves' liver is much more popular than beef liver because of its tenderness and mild flavor. Good quality calves' liver should be firm and moist, with a shiny appearance and without any off-odor. It is most often sliced and sautéed or broiled and served with a sauce.

Calves' Liver

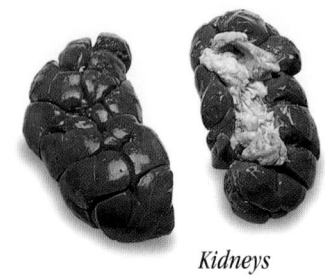

Kidneys

Kidneys

Kidneys are more popular in other parts of the world than in the United States. Good-quality kidneys should be plump, firm and encased in a shiny membrane. Properly prepared kidneys have a rich flavor and firm texture; they are best prepared by moist-heat cooking methods and are sometimes used in stew or kidney pie.

BUTCHERING PROCEDURES

Many food service operations purchase veal in primal or other large cuts and fabricate it in-house to their own specifications. There are several important veal fabrication and butchering techniques you should master.

PROCEDURE FOR BONING A LEG OF VEAL

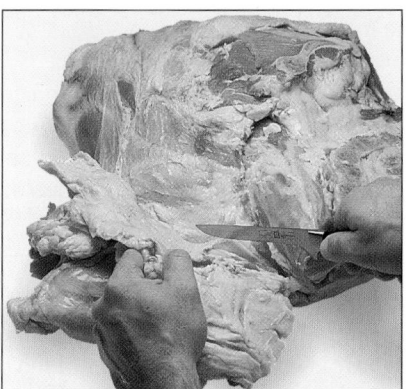

1. Remove the shank by cutting through the knee joint. Remove the excess fat and flank meat.

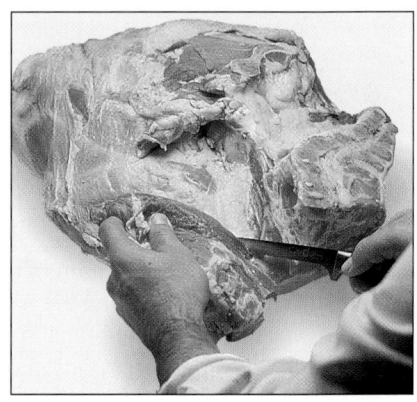

2. Remove the butt tenderloin from the inside of the pelvic bone.

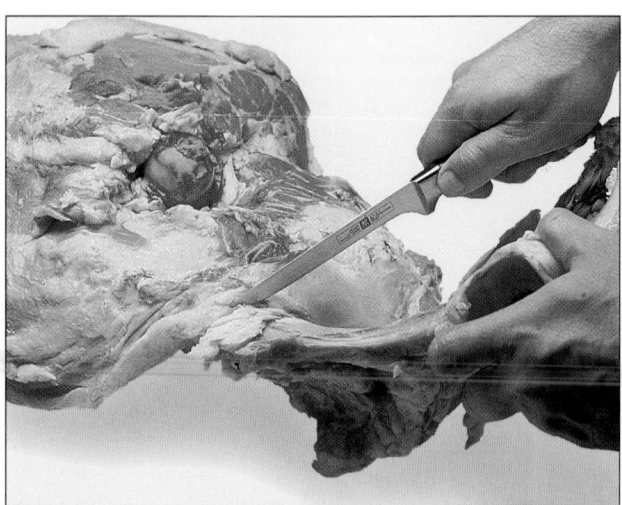

3. Remove the pelvic bone by carefully cutting around the bone, separating it from the meat. Continue until the bone is completely freed from the meat.

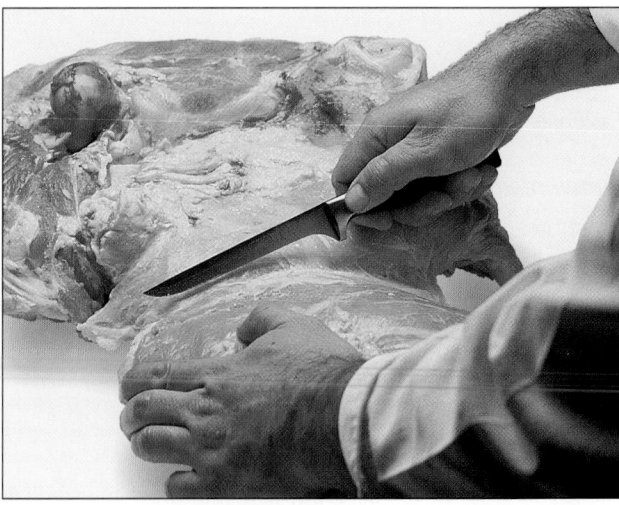

4. With the inside of the leg up, remove the top round by cutting along the natural seam.

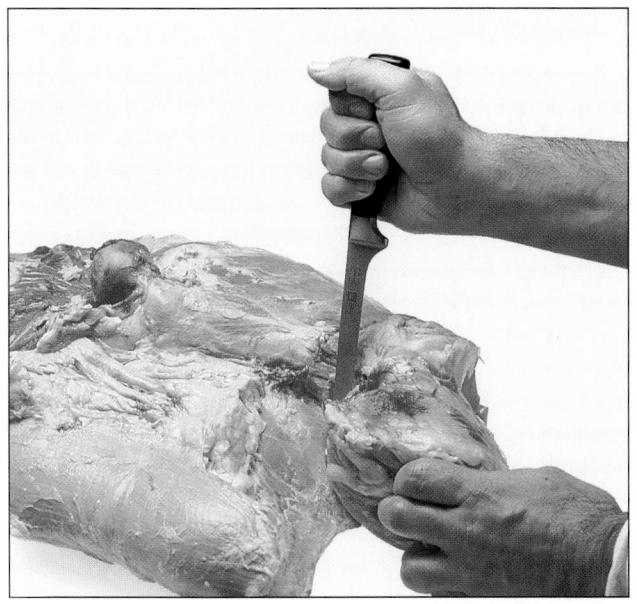

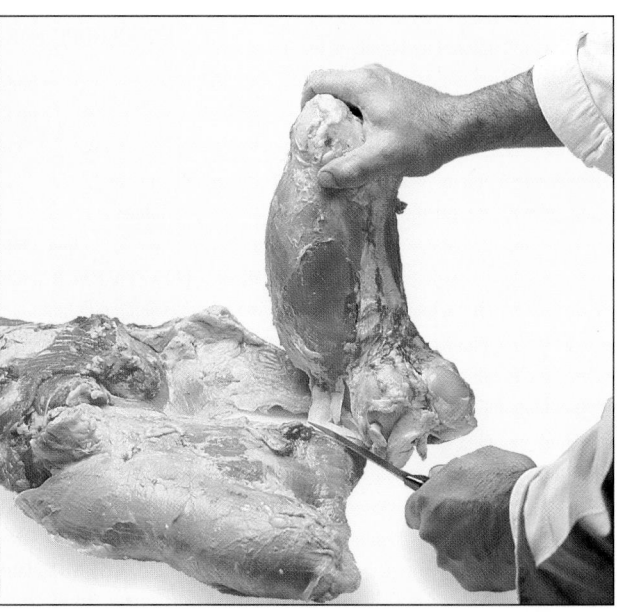

5. Remove the shank meat. (It is the round piece of meat lying between the eye round and the bone, on the shank end of the leg.)

6. Remove the round bone and the knuckle together by cutting around the bone and through the natural seams separating the knuckle from the other muscles. Separate the knuckle meat from the bone.

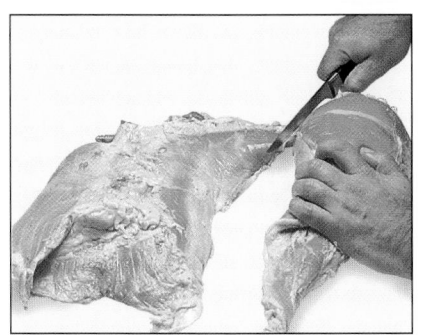

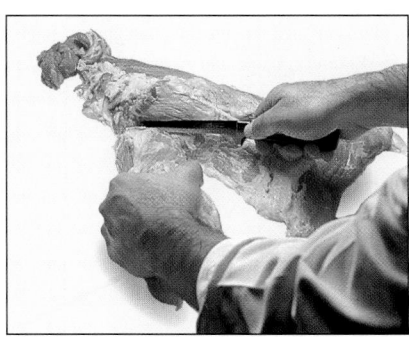

7. Remove the sirloin.

8. Remove the eye round from the bottom round.

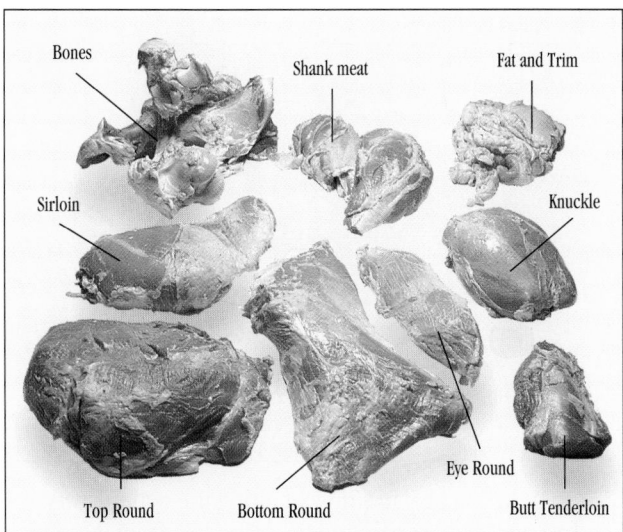

9. The completely boned-out veal leg, producing a top round, eye round, knuckle, shank meat, butt tenderloin, sirloin, bottom round bones and trimmings.

PROCEDURE FOR CUTTING AND POUNDING SCALLOPS

 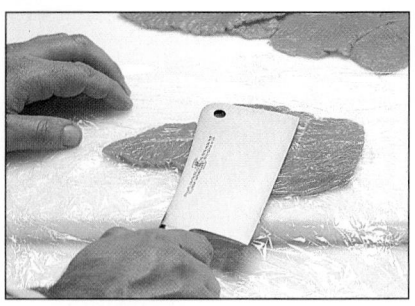

1. Veal scallops are cut from relatively large pieces of veal (here, a portion of the top round). All fat and silverskin must be trimmed. Going against the grain, cut slices approximately 1/4 inch (3 millimeter) thick; cut on the bias to produce larger pieces.

2. Place the scallops between two pieces of plastic wrap and pound lightly to flatten and tenderize the meat. Be careful not to tear or pound holes in the meat.

PROCEDURE FOR CUTTING ÉMINCÉ

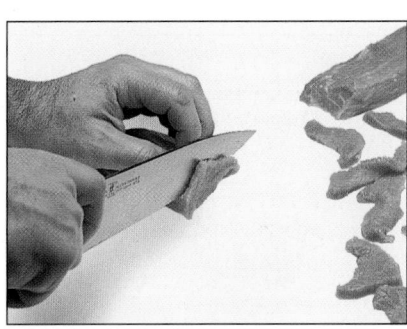

1. Émincé is cut from relatively small, lean pieces of meat. Here veal is cut across the grain into small, thin slices.

PROCEDURE FOR BONING A VEAL LOIN AND CUTTING IT INTO BONELESS VEAL CHOPS

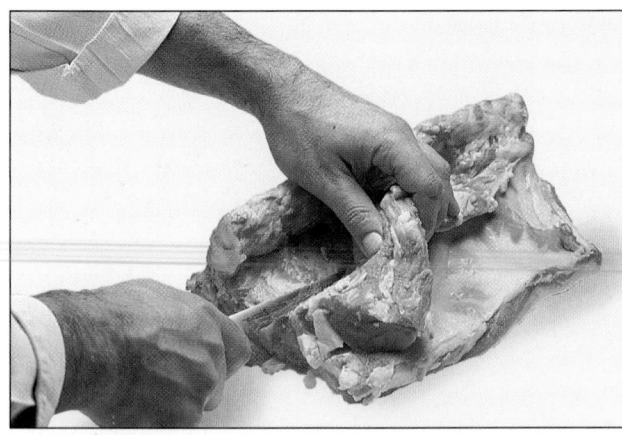 

1. Remove the tenderloin in a single piece from the inside of the loin by following the vertebrae and cutting completely around the tenderloin.

2. From the backbone side, cut along the natural curve of the backbone, separating the loin meat from the backbone.

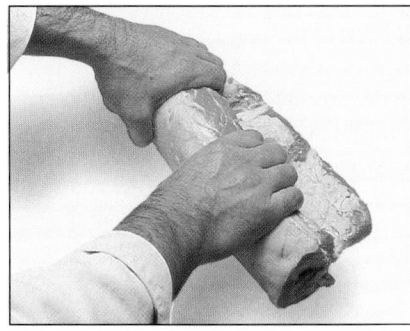

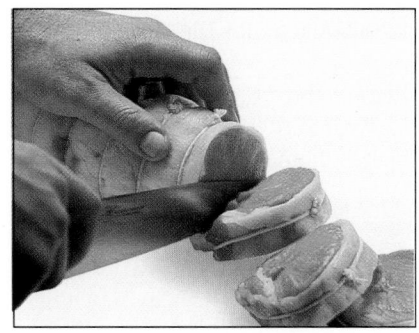

3. Trim any excess fat from the loin, and trim the flank to create a 3-inch (7.5-centimeter) lip. Tightly roll up the loin with the flank on the outside.

4. Tie the loin, using the procedure described below, at 1-inch (2.5-centimeter) intervals. Cut between the pieces of twine for individual boneless loin chops.

PROCEDURE FOR TYING MEATS

Here we apply the tying procedure to a boneless veal loin; the same procedure can be used on any type of meat.

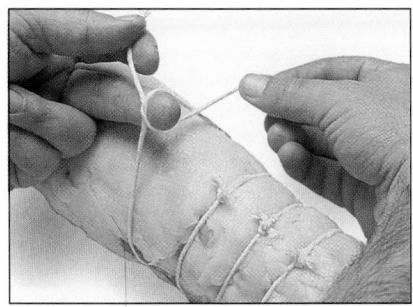

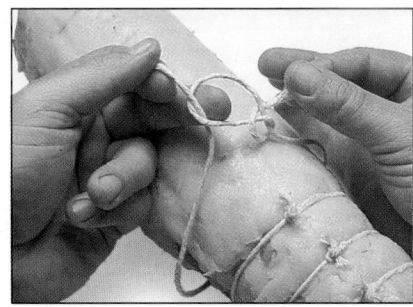

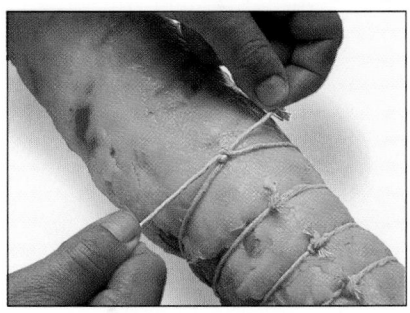

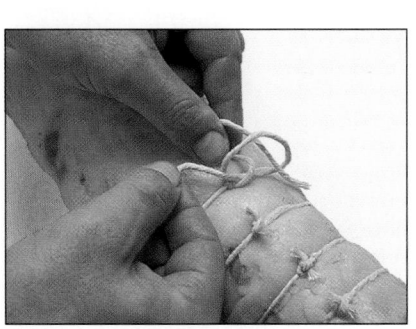

1. Cut a piece of string long enough to wrap completely around the loin. Holding one end between the thumb and forefinger, pass the other end around it and cross the strings. Loop the loose end of the string around your finger.

2. Wrap the string around itself and pass the loose end back through the hole.

3. Pull to tighten the knot. Adjust the string so it is snug against the meat.

4. Loop one end of the string around your thumb and forefinger. Reach through with your thumb and forefinger and pull the other string back through the loop. Pull both strings to tighten the knot, thus preventing the first knot from loosening. Trim the ends of the strings.

5. Continue in this fashion until the entire loin is tied. The strings should be tied at even intervals, just snug enough to hold the shape of the loin; they should not dig into or cut the meat.

PROCEDURE FOR CLEANING AND PRESSING SWEETBREADS

Before fabrication, you should submerge the sweetbreads in cold water, cover and place them in the refrigerator overnight to soak out any blood. Then blanch them in a court bouillon for 20 minutes.

1. Remove the sweetbreads from the poaching liquid and allow them to cool.

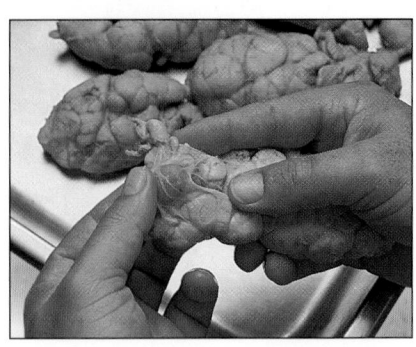

2. Using your hands, pull off any sinew or membranes that may be present on the surface of the sweetbreads.

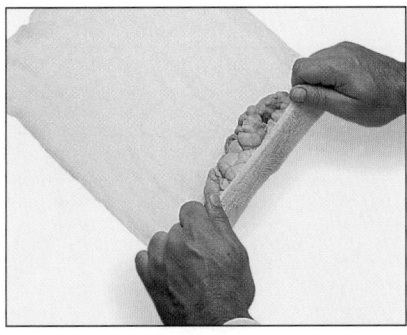

3. Wrap the sweetbreads in cheese-cloth.

4. Tie the ends with butcher's twine.

5. Place the wrapped sweetbreads in a half hotel pan or similar container.

6. Place another half hotel pan on top of the sweetbreads; place a weight in the pan to press the sweetbreads. Pressing sweetbreads in this manner improves their texture.

PROCEDURE FOR CLEANING CALVES' LIVER

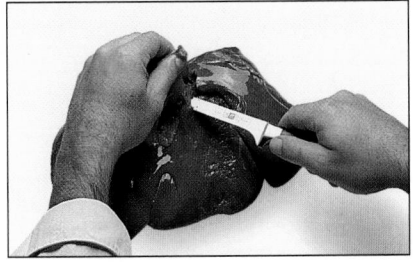

1. Trim the large sinew and outer membrane from the bottom of the liver.

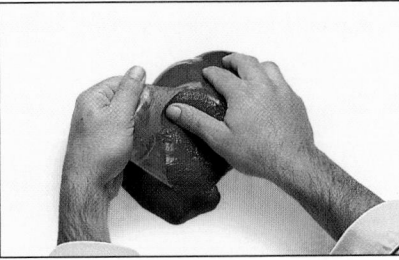

2. Turn the liver over and peel the membrane off with your hands.

3. The liver can be cut into thick or thin slices as needed.

TABLE 14.1   USING COMMON CUTS OF VEAL

Primal	Subprimal or Fabricated Cut	IMPS	Cooking Methods	Serving Suggestions
Shoulder	Cubed veal	1395	Combination (stew)	Blanquette or fricassee
	Ground veal	1396	Dry heat (broil or grill)	Veal patties
			Combination (braise)	Stuffing; meatballs
Foreshank and breast	Foreshank	312	Combination (braise)	Osso buco
	Breast	313	Combination (braise)	Stuffed veal breast
Rib	Hotel rack	306	Dry heat (broil or grill; roast)	Grilled veal chop; roast veal with porcini mushrooms
	Rib chops	1306	Dry heat (broil or grill)	Grilled veal chop
			Combination (braise)	Braised veal chop with risotto
	Rib eye	307	Dry heat (broil or grill; roast)	Broiled veal rib eye with chipotle sauce; roasted veal rib eye marchand de vin
			Combination (braise)	Braised rib eye
Loin	Veal loin	331	Dry heat (broil or grill; roast; sauté)	Roasted veal loin with wild mushrooms; Sautéed veal medallions with green peppercorn sauce;
	Loin chops	1332	Dry heat (broil or grill; sauté)	Broiled or sautéed veal chops with mushroom sauce
			Combination (braise)	Braised veal chops lyonnaise
	Boneless strip loin	344	Dry heat (broil or grill; roast; sauté)	Roasted veal loin sauce poulette
	Veal tenderloin	346	Dry heat (broil or grill; roast; sauté)	Grilled tenderloin; roasted tenderloin; sautéed tenderloin with garlic and herbs
Leg	Leg	334	Dry heat (roast; sauté)	Veal scallopini
			Combination (stew)	Blanquette
	Top round	349A	Dry heat (roast; sauté)	Veal marsala
	Bottom round	NA	Dry heat (sauté)	Sautéed scallops with Calvados
			Combination (braise)	Stuffed veal scallops
	Hindshank	337	Moist heat (simmer)	Veal broth
			Combination (braise)	Osso buco
Offal	Sweetbreads	715	Dry heat (pan-fry; sauté)	Sautéed sweetbreads beurre noisette
			Combination (braise)	Braised sweetbreads madeira
	Calves' liver	704	Dry heat (broil or grill; sauté)	Broiled or sautéed calves' liver with onion and bacon
	Kidneys	NA	Combination (braise)	Kidney pie

PROCEDURE FOR CLEANING VEAL KIDNEYS

1. Split the kidneys lengthwise, exposing the fat and sinew.

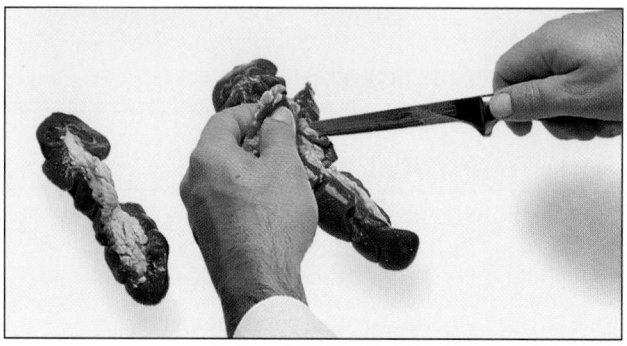

2. With a sharp knife, trim away the fat and sinew. The kidney is now ready for cooking.

CONCLUSION

Although veal may not be as popular as beef or pork, it is versatile, easy to cook and adds variety to menus. Veal is much more delicately flavored than beef, with a finer texture and lighter color. Its flavor blends well with a variety of sauces and other ingredients without overpowering them. Veal can be cooked by almost any dry-heat, moist-heat or combination cooking method.

Veal quality varies greatly among purveyors. Purchase only from reputable companies to be sure you are receiving a consistently high quality product. Because veal carcasses are relatively small, they are sometimes purchased as primal cuts for your further fabrication.

QUESTIONS FOR DISCUSSION

1. Compare and contrast the appearance and flavor of beef and veal.
2. What are the differences between milk-fed veal and free-range veal?
3. Describe two differences between a beef carcass and a veal carcass.
4. List each veal primal and describe its location on the carcass. For each primal, identify two subprimals or fabricated cuts taken from it.
5. Would it better to use a veal loin for grilling or braising? Explain your answer.
6. What are veal sweetbreads? Describe how sweetbreads should be prepared for cooking.

ADDITIONAL VEAL RECIPES

RECIPE 14.1

PAN-SEARED VEAL TENDERLOIN WITH MAINE LOBSTER AND BRAISED ARTICHOKES, MERLOT-THYME PAN JUS

NOTE: *This dish appears in the Chapter Opening photograph.*

ARIZONA BILTMORE HOTEL, PHOENIX, AZ

Yield: 6 Servings   **Method:** Sautéing

Ingredient		
Carrot, sliced	4 oz.	120 g
Onion, sliced	6 oz.	180 g
Garlic head, crushed	1	1
Fresh thyme	9 sprigs	9 sprigs
Bay leaves	2	2
Sea salt	TT	TT
White pepper	TT	TT
Sugar	1 Tbsp.	15 ml
Olive oil	3 Tbsp.	45 ml
Artichokes, small, trimmed, stem on	6	6
White wine	4 oz.	120 g
Chicken stock	1 pt.	450 ml
Carrots, small, tournéed	12	12
Rutabagas, small, tournéed	12	12
Turnips, small, tournéed	12	12
White potatoes, small, tournéed	12	12
Green asparagus tips, small	12	12
Unsalted butter	8 oz.	250 g
Veal medallions, 3 oz. (90 g) each	12	12
Garlic, chopped	1 tsp.	5 ml
Merlot	8 oz.	250 g
Brown veal stock	12 oz.	350 g
Lobster claws	6	6

1. Sauté the sliced carrots, onions and crushed garlic with 1 sprig of thyme, the bay leaves, salt, pepper and sugar in the olive oil. Add the artichokes and deglaze with the white wine. After 2 minutes, add the chicken stock; cover and simmer until tender.

2. Blanch the tournéed vegetables and asparagus tips. Then sauté them in a portion of the butter until tender.

3. In a separate pan, sauté the veal medallions in a portion of the butter. Season with salt and pepper and cook to the desired degree of doneness.

4. To make the sauce, sauté the chopped garlic in 1 tablespoon (15 milliliters) of the butter. Add the merlot and reduce by three quarters. Add the veal stock and 2 thyme sprigs. Monte au beurre with the remaining butter and adjust the seasonings.

5. Steam the lobster claws, remove the meat from the shells in one piece and keep warm.

6. To serve, place the whole artichoke in the top middle part of the plate. Place the tournéed vegetables inside the "trumpet" of the artichoke and the veal medallions crosswise over the stem of the artichoke. Stand the lobster claw between the two medallions. Finish with the sauce. Garnish each plate with a sprig of thyme.

◆◆◆

RECIPE 14.2
ROSEMARY-ROASTED VEAL CHOPS WITH PORCINI MUSHROOMS

THE FOUR SEASONS, NEW YORK, NY
Chef Christian Albin

Yield: 4 Servings   **Method:** Roasting

Veal chops, 12–14 oz. (350–400 g) each	4	4
Salt and pepper	TT	TT
Fresh rosemary	4 sprigs	4 sprigs
Flour	as needed	as needed
Paprika	TT	TT
Clarified butter	4 oz.	120 g
White wine	4 oz.	120 g
Brown veal stock	1 pt.	450 ml
Unsalted butter	2 oz.	60 g

1. Season the veal chops with salt and pepper. Press a rosemary sprig onto one side of each chop. Mix the flour and paprika and dredge the chops (both sides) in this mixture.

2. Heat the clarified butter in a sauté pan. Place the chops in the pan, rosemary side down. Roast in a preheated 375°F (190°C) oven for 7 minutes. Turn the chops carefully to keep the rosemary sprigs intact. Roast for 5–6 minutes more. Remove the chops and keep warm.

3. To make the sauce, degrease the pan and deglaze with the white wine. Add the veal stock and any juices that have accumulated under the chops. Simmer to reduce to 8 ounces (250 grams). Monte au beurre, strain and adjust the seasonings.

4. Serve the chops with grilled porcini mushrooms.

◆◆◆

RECIPE 14.3
VEAL KEBABS

Yield: 4 Servings		Method: Grilling
Onion	1	1
Green pepper	1	1
Boneless veal leg, cut in 1-in. (2.5-cm) cubes	2 lb.	1 kg
Marinade:		
Olive oil	4 oz.	120 g
White wine	2 oz.	60 g
Lemon juice	2 oz.	60 g
Assorted fresh herbs such as parsley, tarragon, sage and dill, chopped	2 Tbsp.	60 ml
Salt and pepper	TT	TT

1. Cut the onion and green pepper into 1-inch (2.5-centimeter) chunks.
2. Prepare the kebabs by threading the veal, onions and peppers onto each of four skewers, alternating the items.
3. Prepare the marinade by combining the oil, wine, lemon juice, herbs, salt and pepper.
4. Marinate the skewers, refrigerated, for 3 hours.
5. Drain the kebabs; season with salt and pepper and grill to the desired doneness.

◆◆◆

RECIPE 14.4
ROAST VEAL LOIN

Yield: 6-oz. (180-g) Servings		Method: Roasting
Boneless veal loin roast, 3 lb. (1.5 kg)	1	1
Salt and pepper	TT	TT
Onions, chopped medium	2	2
Carrots, chopped medium	2	2
Garlic cloves, chopped	4	4
Fresh thyme	3 sprigs	3 sprigs
Bay leaves	2	2
Jue lié	1 pt.	500 ml

1. Tie the veal loin roast with butcher's twine.
2. Season the meat with salt and pepper and place it in a roasting pan. Scatter the onions, carrots, garlic, thyme and bay leaves around it.
3. Roast at 425°F (220°C) for approximately 45 minutes.
4. Remove the meat from the roasting pan and cut away the twine. Hold in a warm place for service.
5. Deglaze the roasting pan with the jue lié. Strain the vegetables and liquid through a chinois into a small saucepan. Discard the solids.
6. Bring the sauce to a boil and skim as much fat as possible from the surface. Season with salt and pepper. Spoon a portion of the sauce over the veal; serve the remainder on the side.

◆◆◆

RECIPE 14.5

SAUTÉED VEAL SCALLOPS WITH CALVADOS

Yield: 6 Servings   **Method:** Sautéing

Mushrooms, sliced	12 oz.	340 g
Clarified butter	4 oz.	120 g
Golden Delicious apples	3	3
Veal scallops, pounded, 6 oz. (170 g) each	6	6
Salt and pepper	TT	TT
Shallots, minced	2	2
Calvados	2 oz.	60 g
Crème fraîche	8 oz.	250 g
Fresh parsley, chopped	1 Tbsp.	15 ml

1. Sauté the mushrooms in a portion of the clarified butter until dry. Remove and reserve.
2. Peel and core the apples. Cut each into 12 wedges.
3. Sauté the apple wedges in a portion of the clarified butter until slightly browned and tender. Remove and reserve.
4. Season the veal scallops with salt and pepper. Sauté in the remaining clarified butter. (This may be done in two or three batches.) Remove and reserve.
5. Add the shallots to the pan and sauté without browning.
6. Deglaze with the Calvados. Flambé the Calvados.
7. Add the sautéed mushrooms and crème fraîche. Bring to a boil and reduce until it thickens slightly.
8. Return the scallops to the pan to reheat. Serve each scallop with sauce, garnished with six apple slices and chopped parsley.

◆◆◆

RECIPE 14.6

SAUTÉED CALVES' LIVER WITH ONIONS

Yield: 10 Servings   **Method:** Sautéing

Onion, julienne	1 lb. 8 oz.	700 g
Clarified butter	3 oz.	90 g
Salt and pepper	TT	TT
White wine	8 oz.	250 g
Fresh parsley, chopped	1 Tbsp.	15 ml
Calves' liver, 6-oz. (180-g) slices	10	10
Flour	as needed	as needed

1. Sauté the onions in 1 ounce (30 grams) of butter until golden brown. Season with salt and pepper.
2. Add the white wine, cover and braise until the onions are tender, approximately 10 minutes. Stir in the chopped parsley.
3. Dredge the liver in flour seasoned with salt and pepper.
4. In a separate pan sauté the liver in the remaining clarified butter until done. The liver should be slightly pink in the middle.
5. Serve the liver with a portion of the onions and their cooking liquid.

◆◆◆

RECIPE 14.7

VEAL MARENGO

Yield: 6 10-oz. (300-g) Servings   **Method:** Braising

Lean boneless veal,		
cut in 2-in. (5-cm) cubes	2 lb. 8 oz.	1.1 g
Salt and pepper	TT	TT
Flour for dredging the veal	as needed	as needed
Vegetable oil	1-1/2 oz.	45 g
Clarified butter	3 oz.	90 g
Onion, sliced fine	12 oz.	350 g
Carrot, sliced fine	10 oz.	300 g
Garlic cloves, crushed	2	2
Tomato paste	1 oz.	30 g
Flour	2 Tbsp.	30 ml
Dry white wine	6 oz.	170 g
Brown veal stock	1 pt.	450 ml
Bouquet garni:		
Carrot stick, 4 in. (10 cm)	1	1
Leek, split, 4-in. (10-cm) piece	1	1
Fresh thyme	1 sprig	1 sprig
Bay leaf	1	1
Mushrooms, washed and quartered	8 oz.	250 g
Tomato, diced	1 lb.	500 g
Pearl onions, boiled and peeled	24	24

1. Season the veal cubes with salt and pepper and dredge in flour.

2. Sauté the veal in 1 ounce (30 grams) of oil and 1 ounce (30 grams) of butter, browning well on all sides. Remove the meat and set aside.

3. Add 1-1/2 ounces (45 grams) of butter and sauté the onions, carrots and garlic without coloring. Stir in the tomato paste and return the veal to the pan. Sprinkle with the 2 tablespoons (30 milliliters) flour and cook to make a blond roux.

4. Add the wine, stock and bouquet garni to the pan; bring to a boil. Cover and braise until the meat is tender, approximately 1-1/2 hours.

5. Sauté the mushrooms until dry in 1 tablespoon (15 milliliters) of oil and 1/2 ounce (15 grams) of butter without browning. Add the tomatoes to the pan and sauté over high heat for 3 minutes. Season with salt and pepper. Remove from the heat and reserve.

6. When the veal is tender, remove it from the pan with a slotted spoon and set aside. Strain the sauce.

7. Return the veal to the sauce along with the mushrooms, tomatoes and pearl onions. Bring to a boil and simmer for 5 minutes. Adjust the seasonings.

◆◆◆

RECIPE 14.8

GRILLED VEAL SWEETBREADS WITH WILD MUSHROOM RAGOUT AND RED WINE THYME SAUCE

VINCENT ON CAMELBACK, PHOENIX, AZ
Chef Vincent Guerathault

Yield: 6 Servings		Method: Grilling
Veal sweetbreads	2 lb.	1 kg
Water	1 gal.	4 lt
Lemons, cut in half	2	2
Bay leaves	4	4
Garlic cloves	5	5
Salt and pepper	TT	TT
Peppercorns	2 Tbsp.	30 ml
Olive oil	as needed	as needed

1. Soak the sweetbreads in water for 24 hours. Change the water at least every 8 hours.
2. Bring 1 gallon (4 lt) of fresh water to a boil with the lemons, bay leaves, garlic, salt and peppercorns. Add the sweetbreads. Simmer until the sweetbreads are firm yet slightly soft in the center, approximately 10 minutes.
3. Remove the sweetbreads; refresh in ice water and allow to cool.
4. Under running water, peel the membrane away from each sweetbread and discard. Place the sweetbreads between 2 hotel pans and press for at least 2 hours.
5. Divide the sweetbreads into 6 portions. Rub each with olive oil and season with salt and pepper.
6. Over a medium-hot grill, cook the sweetbreads for 3–4 minutes on each side.

WILD MUSHROOM RAGOUT

Oyster mushrooms	1 lb.	450 g
Olive oil	1 tsp.	5 ml
Unsalted butter	1 Tbsp.	15 ml
Garlic, chopped	1/2 tsp.	2 ml
Shallots, chopped	1 tsp.	5 ml
Brandy	1 Tbsp.	15 ml
Veal glaze	1 Tbsp.	15 ml
Heavy cream	4 oz.	120 g
Fresh thyme	1 tsp.	5 ml

1. Wash the mushrooms in cold water and pat dry.
2. Heat the olive oil in a sauté pan over medium-high heat. Add the mushrooms and cook for approximately 4 minutes. Add the butter, garlic and shallots and cook for an additional 3 minutes.
3. Add the brandy and ignite. When the flames die down, add the veal glaze and cream and simmer for 5 minutes. Remove from the heat and add the fresh thyme. Serve around the sweetbreads.

RED WINE THYME SAUCE

Red wine	8 oz.	250 g
Garlic, chopped	1 Tbsp.	15 ml
Shallots, chopped	2 oz.	60 g
Veal stock	1 qt.	1 lt
Fresh rosemary	1 sprig	1 sprig
Fresh thyme	1 sprig	1 sprig
Bay leaves	2	2
Unsalted butter	2 Tbsp.	30 ml

1. Reduce the red wine, garlic and shallots by one quarter.
2. Add the veal stock, rosemary, thyme and bay leaves and reduce by one quarter.
3. Remove from the heat and strain. Monte au beurre.
4. Serve with the grilled sweetbreads and mushroom ragout.

RECIPE 14.9
Osso Buco

ANA WESTIN HOTEL, Washington, D.C.
Chef Leland Atkinson

Yield: 4 Servings　　　　　　　　　　　　　　　　**Method:** Braising

Veal shank, cut in 1-in. (2.5-cm) pieces	8–12 pieces	8–12 pieces
Salt and pepper	TT	TT
Flour	4 oz.	120 g
Olive oil	as needed	as needed
Garlic clove, minced	1	1
Carrot, diced	4 oz.	120 g
Lemon zest, grated	1 Tbsp.	15 ml
White wine	8 oz.	250 g
Brown veal stock	1 qt.	1 lt
Tomato purée	2 Tbsp.	30 ml
Gremolada:		
Garlic clove, chopped fine	1	1
Lemon zest	1 Tbsp.	15 ml
Fresh Italian parsley, chopped	1 Tbsp.	15 ml

1. Season the veal with salt and pepper and dredge the pieces in flour. Sauté them in olive oil until brown on both sides.
2. Add the garlic and carrot and sauté briefly.
3. Add the lemon zest, wine, stock and tomato purée. Bring to a boil and reduce to a simmer. Braise on the stove top or in a 325°F (160°C) oven until the meat is tender but not falling from the bone, approximately 40–60 minutes.
4. Remove the cover and reduce the sauce until thick. Adjust the seasonings.
5. At service time, transfer the meat to a serving platter and ladle the sauce over it. Combine the gremolada ingredients and sprinkle over the meat and sauce.

◆◆◆

RECIPE 14.10

STUFFED BREAST OF VEAL

Yield: 12 8-oz. (250-g) Servings   **Method:** Braising

Stuffing:

Onion, small dice	8 oz.	250 g
Garlic, chopped	2 tsp.	10 ml
Whole butter	1 oz.	30 g
Ground veal	1 lb.	450 g
Fresh bread crumbs	4 oz.	120 g
Nutmeg	TT	TT
Salt and pepper	TT	TT
Eggs, beaten	2	2
Mushrooms, sliced	1 lb.	450 g
Clarified butter	2 oz.	60 g
Spinach leaves, stemmed and washed	4 oz.	120 g
Veal breast, approx. 8 lb. (3.6 kg)	1	1
Mirepoix, large dice	1 lb.	450 g
White wine	8 oz.	250 g
Brown veal stock	3 pt.	1.5 lt
Garlic, chopped	1 tsp.	5 ml
Bouquet garni:		
Carrot stick, 4 in. (10 cm)	1	1
Leek, split, 4-in. (10-cm) piece	1	1
Fresh thyme	1 sprig	1 sprig
Bay leaf	2	2

1. To make the stuffing, sauté the onions and garlic in the butter until tender. Cool. Combine with the remaining stuffing ingredients and mix well.
2. Sauté the mushrooms in 1 ounce (30 grams) of the clarified butter and cool.
3. Blanch the spinach and cool.
4. Bone the veal breast. Reserve the bones.
5. Butterfly the veal breast and open it into a large rectangular shape.
6. Spread the stuffing over the breast; leave a 1-inch (2.5-centimeter) border around the edges.
7. Open the spinach leaves and carefully lay them on top of the stuffing. Sprinkle the mushrooms on top of the spinach leaves.
8. Roll the breast up in a cylindrical shape so the spinach leaves form a spiral in the center. Tie with butcher's twine.
9. Brown the breast in the remaining clarified butter.
10. Remove the breast and pour off all but 1 ounce (30 milliliters) of the grease. Add the mirepoix to the pan and sauté.
11. Add the reserved veal bones and place the veal breast on top of the bones.
12. Add the wine, stock, garlic and bouquet garni.
13. Cover and braise the breast until tender, approximately 2-1/2 hours.
14. Remove the breast from the pan and remove the twine. Skim any fat from the sauce.
15. Reduce the sauce and, if desired, thicken it slightly with a small amount of roux or beurre manié. Strain it through a fine chinois and adjust the seasonings.
16. Slice the veal breast and serve with the sauce.

◆◆◆

RECIPE 14.11

VEAL MARSALA

Yield: 6 Servings   **Method**: Sautéing

Veal scallops, pounded, 3 oz. (90 g) each	12	12
Salt and pepper	TT	TT
Flour	approx. 2 oz.	approx. 60 g
Clarified butter	2 oz.	60 g
Olive oil	2 oz.	60 g
Dry marsala	6 oz.	170 g
Brown veal stock	4 oz.	120 g
Whole butter	1-1/2 oz.	45 g

1. Season the scallops with salt and pepper. Dredge in flour and sauté the scallops in a mixture of the clarified butter and oil, a few at a time, until all are cooked.

2. Remove the scallops and set aside. Degrease the pan and deglaze with marsala. Add the stock and reduce until it begins to thicken.

3. Return the scallops to the sauce to reheat. Remove the scallops to plates or a serving platter.

4. Reduce the sauce until it becomes syrupy; adjust the seasonings. Monte au beurre and spoon the sauce over the veal.

◆◆◆

RECIPE 14.12

VEAL FRICASSEE

Yield: 16 8-oz. (250-g) Servings   **Method**: Stewing

Veal stew meat, cut in 2-in. (5-cm) cubes	8 lb.	3.5 kg
Salt and white pepper	TT	TT
Butter	6 oz.	180 g
Onion, small dice	12 oz.	350 g
Garlic, chopped	1 tsp.	5 ml
Flour	6 oz.	180 g
White wine	4 oz.	120 g
White stock	3 qt.	3 lt
Bouquet garni:		
Carrot stick, 4 in. (10 cm)	1	1
Leek, split, 4-in. (10-cm) piece	1	1
Fresh thyme	1 sprig	1 sprig
Bay leaf	1	1
Heavy cream, hot	1 pt.	450 ml

1. Season the veal with salt and pepper and sauté in the butter without browning, approximately 2 minutes.

2. Add the onions and garlic and sauté without coloring, approximately 2 minutes.

3. Add the flour and cook to make a blond roux, approximately 3 minutes.

4. Add the white wine and white stock, stir well to remove any lumps of roux and bring to a boil. Add the bouquet garni, cover and braise until the veal is tender, approximately 30 minutes.

5. Remove the veal from the sauce and reserve. Strain the sauce through a fine chinois and return it to the pan. Degrease the sauce.

6. Add the heavy cream to the sauce. Reduce slightly to thicken if necessary. Return the veal to the sauce and adjust the seasonings.

7. Serve the fricassee with rice pilaf.

CHAPTER 15
LAMB

◆◆◆

RECIPE 15.9

HONEY-MUSTARD DENVER RIBS

Yield: 14 lb. (6.2 kg)   **Method:** Roasting

Lamb ribs, trimmed	20 lb.	9 kg
Salt	4 oz.	120 g
Pepper	2 oz.	60 g
Honey	4 lb.	1.8 kg
Dijon-style mustard	3 lb.	1.4 kg
Lemon juice	1 pt.	450 ml

1. Rub the ribs with salt and pepper.
2. Place the ribs on a rack and roast at 375°F (190°C) for 30 minutes.
3. Combine the honey, mustard and lemon juice.
4. Baste the ribs generously with the honey-mustard mixture. Roast an additional 30 minutes, basting every 10 minutes.

◆◆◆

RECIPE 15.10

SAUTÉED LAMB LOIN
WITH STUFFED RÖSTI POTATOES AND CHERRY CONFIT

ANA WESTIN HOTEL, Washington, D.C.
Chef Leland Atkinson

Yield: 6 5-oz. (150-g) Servings   **Method:** Sautéing

Idaho potatoes, large	2	2
Parmesan, grated	5 oz.	150 g
Salt and pepper	TT	TT
Clarified butter	as needed	as needed
Goat cheese	6 oz.	180 g
Fresh rosemary, chopped	1 tsp.	5 ml
Fresh chives, chopped	1 tsp.	5 ml
Lamb, eye of loin, trimmed, 2 lb. 4 oz. (1 kg)	1	1
Clarified butter	2 oz.	60 g
Port	4 oz.	120 g
Lamb jus lié	12 oz.	350 g
Whole butter	1 oz.	30 g
Cherry Confit (Recipe 25.13)	as needed	as needed

1. Peel and julienne the potatoes.
2. Combine the potatoes with the Parmesan, salt and pepper.
3. Heat the clarified butter in an 8-inch (20-centimeter) nonstick pan. Add the potato mixture and pack it tightly with the back of a spoon. Cook over moderate heat until the potatoes begin to brown.
4. Flip the rösti potatoes and place the pan in a 350°F (180°C) oven. Flipping once, cook until the potatoes are crisp and evenly browned on the outside and soft in the center, approximately 20 minutes on each side.
5. Transfer the rösti potatoes to a wire cooling rack to rest.

6. Slice the rösti horizontally into 2 round halves. Spread the bottom half with the room temperature goat cheese. Grind black pepper over the cheese, sprinkle the herbs evenly over the surface and carefully replace the top.

7. Season the lamb and sauté it in the 2 ounces (60 grams) of clarified butter, turning frequently, until the desired doneness is achieved, approximately 8–12 minutes.

8. Remove the lamb and allow it to rest before slicing.

9. Deglaze the pan with the port and add the lamb jus lié. Reduce by half and monte au beurre.

10. At service time, ladle the sauce onto 6 warm plates, slice the lamb and arrange over the sauce. Cut the rösti into wedges and arrange on the plate. Spoon cherry confit (Recipe 25.13) around the lamb and serve at once.

◆◆◆

RECIPE 15.11
CAROUSEL OF SONOMA LAMB

ARIZONA BILTMORE, PHOENIX, AZ
Executive Chef Peter Hoefler

Yield: 4 Servings　　　　　　　　　　　Method: Sautéing

Lamb loin, trimmed, approx. 1 lb. 8 oz. (700 g)	1	1
Salt and pepper	TT	TT
Unsalted butter	6 oz.	180 g
Fresh chanterelles	8 oz.	250 g
Shallots, chopped	1 tsp.	5 ml
Fresh basil, chopped	1 Tbsp.	15 ml
Fresh spinach	8 oz.	250 g
Garlic, chopped	1 Tbsp.	15 ml
Tomato concasse	8 oz.	250 g
Fresh thyme, chopped	1 tsp.	5 ml
Russet potatoes	2	2
Merlot	4 oz.	120 g
Lamb stock	1 pt.	450 ml
Fresh rosemary	4 sprigs	4 sprigs
Savory Hippen Masse (Recipe 35.1)	as needed	as needed
Fresh Italian parsley	as needed	as needed

1. Season the lamb with salt and pepper. Brown well in 1 ounce (30 grams) of butter and roast at 375°F (190°C) to medium rare, approximately 10 minutes.

2. In a separate pan, sauté the chanterelles and shallots in 1 tablespoon (15 milliliters) of butter, until tender. Add the basil, season with salt and pepper, remove from the pan and reserve.

3. Sauté the spinach with 1 teaspoon (5 milliliters) garlic in 1 tablespoon (15 milliliters) of butter. Season with salt and pepper, remove from the pan and reserve.

4. Sauté the tomato concasse in 1 tablespoon (15 milliliters) of butter with 1 teaspoon (5 milliliters) of garlic and the thyme and set aside.

5. Peel the potatoes and cut them into 16 1-1/2 inch (3.7 centimeter) diameter circles, approximately 1/4 inch (6 millimeters) thick. Trim one edge of each

Continued

slice so that the pieces will stand upright. Sauté the potatoes in 1 ounce (30 grams) of butter until brown and cooked and set aside.

6. Remove the lamb from the pan. Add 1 teaspoon (5 milliliters) garlic and sauté for 15 seconds. Deglaze the pan with the merlot and add the lamb stock. Reduce the sauce until slightly thickened. Strain the sauce and season to taste with salt and pepper. Monte au beurre with the remaining butter.

7. To serve, layer the spinach, chanterelles and tomatoes inside four, 4-inch (20-centimeter) ring molds positioned in the center of four plates. Remove the molds. Slice the lamb and arrange approximately 4 to 5 ounces (120 to 150 grams) of the slices in a spiral on top of each circle of vegetables. Insert the rosemary sprig and the hippen masse decoration in the center of the lamb spiral. Spoon 3 ounces (90 grams) of the sauce around the lamb and vegetables and arrange four potato slices on each plate.

═══════════════ ◆◆◆ ═══════════════

RECIPE 15.12
LAMB SHANK WITH PERSILLADE

Yield: 6 Servings   **Method:** Braising

Lamb shanks, trimmed, 2 lb.–2 lb. 8 oz. (.9–1.1 kg) each	6	6
Salt and pepper	TT	TT
Olive oil	as needed	as needed
Shallots, minced	8 oz.	250 g
Carrot, chopped	8 oz.	250 g
Celery, chopped	8 oz.	250 g
Peppercorns, crushed	6	6
Fresh thyme	2 tsp.	10 ml
Garlic, chopped	2 tsp.	10 ml
Dry white wine	12 oz.	350 g
Lamb stock	1 qt.	1 lt
Demi-glace	1 pt.	450 ml
Dijon mustard	as needed	as needed
Persillade:		
Garlic, minced	1 tsp.	5 ml
Fresh parsley, chopped	1 oz.	30 g
Fresh bread crumbs	2 oz.	60 g
Butter, melted	2 oz.	60 g

1. Season the shanks with salt and pepper; brown in olive oil.
2. Remove the shanks and add the vegetables, peppercorns, thyme and garlic to the pan. Sauté until tender.
3. Place the shanks on top of the vegetables.
4. Add the wine, lamb stock and demi-glace.
5. Bring to a simmer, cover and braise in a 350°F (180°C) oven until tender, approximately 2 hours, adding more lamb stock if necessary.
6. Remove the shanks and hold for service.
7. Degrease the sauce and reduce to the desired consistency.
8. Strain the sauce and adjust the seasonings.
9. To make the persillade, combine all ingredients and toss together.
10. Warm the shanks thoroughly. Brush with mustard and sprinkle with the persillade. Brown under a broiler and serve with the sauce.

◆◆◆

RECIPE 15.13
IRISH LAMB STEW

Yield: 12 8-oz. (250-g) Servings   **Method:** Stewing

Lamb shoulder, 1-1/2-in. (4-cm) cubes	4 lb.	1.8 kg
White stock	3 pt.	1.5 lt
Sachet:		
Bay leaf	1	1
Dried thyme	1/2 tsp.	2 ml
Peppercorns, crushed	1/2 tsp.	2 ml
Parsley stems	10	10
Garlic cloves, crushed	4	4
Onion, sliced	1 lb.	450 g
Leek, sliced	8 oz.	225 g
Potato, peeled, large dice	1 lb. 8 oz.	700 g
Salt and white pepper	TT	TT
Carrots, tournéed or batonnet	20	20
Turnips, tournéed or batonnet	20	20
Potatoes, tournéed or batonnet	20	20
Pearl onions, peeled	20	20
Fresh parsley, chopped	1 Tbsp.	15 ml

1. Combine the lamb, stock, sachet, onions, leeks and potatoes. Season with salt and white pepper. Bring to a simmer and skim the surface. Simmer the stew on the stove or cover and cook in the oven at 350°F (180°C) until the lamb is tender, approximately 1 hour.

2. Degrease the stew; remove and discard the sachet.

3. Remove the pieces of potato and purée them in a food mill or ricer. Use the potato purée to thicken the stew to the desired consistency.

4. Simmer the stew for 10 minutes to blend the flavors.

5. Cook the tournéed or batonnet vegetables, potatoes and pearl onions separately. At service, heat the vegetable garnishes and add to each portion of stew.

6. Garnish with chopped parsley and serve.

◆◆◆

RECIPE 15.14
BLANQUETTE OF LAMB

Yield: 10 8-oz. (250-g) Servings   **Method:** Stewing

White beans, dried	1 lb.	500 g
Onion piquet	2	2
Bouquet Garni:	2	2
Carrot stick, 4 in. (10 cm)	1	1
Leek, split, 4-in. (10-cm) piece	1	1
Fresh thyme	1 sprig	1 sprig
Bay leaf	1	1
Lamb leg or shoulder, cut in 1-1/2-inch (4-cm) cubes	4 lb.	1.8 kg
White stock	1-1/2 qt.	1-1/2 lt

Continued

Sachet:		
Bay leaf	1	1
Dried thyme	1/2 tsp.	2 ml
Peppercorns, crushed	1/2 tsp.	2 ml
Parsley stems	10	10
Garlic cloves, crushed	4	4
Salt	TT	TT
Blond roux	2 oz.	60 g
Heavy cream	10 oz.	280 g
Dijon mustard	3 Tbsp.	45 ml
Egg yolks	4	4

1. Soak the beans in cold water for 12 hours. Drain, then add enough fresh water to cover the beans by 2–4 inches (5–10 centimeters).
2. Add one onion piquet and one bouquet garni and cook until the beans are tender, approximately 1-1/2 hours. Remove and discard the onion piquet and bouquet garni.
3. Blanch the lamb cubes in boiling salted water.
4. Place the blanched lamb in a pot. Add the stock and the second onion piquet, the second bouquet garni, the sachet and salt. Simmer until the meat is tender, approximately 1-1/2 hours.
5. Remove the meat from the liquid and reserve. Reduce the cooking liquid to 1 quart (1 liter). Incorporate the roux.
6. Combine the heavy cream, mustard and egg yolks and add to the reduced stock as a liaison.
7. Return the lamb to the sauce and adjust the seasonings. Heat the sauce and meat thoroughly but do not allow it to boil. Serve the blanquette with the cooked beans.

◆◆◆

RECIPE 15.15

LAMB NAVARIN

Yield: 10 10-oz. (300-g) Servings   **Method:** Stewing

Olive oil	3 Tbsp.	45 ml
Lean lamb shoulder, large dice	3 lb.	1.5 kg
Sugar	1 Tbsp.	15 ml
Salt and pepper	TT	TT
Flour	3 Tbsp.	45 ml
White stock	1 qt.	1 lt
White wine	4 oz.	120 g
Tomato concasse	8 oz.	250 g
Bouquet garni:		
Carrot stick, 4 in. (10 cm)	1	1
Leek, split, 4-in. (10-cm) piece	1	1
Fresh thyme	1 sprig	1 sprig
Bay leaf	1	1
Potato, peeled, medium dice	1 lb. 8 oz.	650 g
Carrot, medium dice	1 lb.	450 g
White turnip, peeled, medium dice	1 lb.	450 g
Pearl onions, peeled	12	12
Fresh green peas	6 oz.	170 g

1. In a braiser, brown the meat in the olive oil.

2. Sprinkle the meat with the sugar and season with salt and pepper.

3. Add the flour and cook to make a blond roux.

4. Add the stock and wine. Add the tomatoes and bouquet garni; bring to a boil. Cover and cook in the oven at 375°F (190°C) until the meat is almost tender, approximately 1 to 1-1/2 hours.

5. Remove the meat and hold in a warm place. Strain the sauce and skim off any excess fat.

6. Combine the sauce, meat, potatoes, carrots, turnips and onions. Cover and cook until the vegetables are almost tender, approximately 25 minutes.

7. Add the peas and cook for 10 minutes more.

RECIPE 15.16
NOISETTES OF LAMB WITH GARLIC SAUCE

Yield: 4 Servings **Method:** Sautéing

Lamb noisettes, 2–3 oz. (60–90 g) each	8	8
Salt and pepper	TT	TT
Fresh thyme	1 tsp.	5 ml
Garlic heads	3	3
Fresh rosemary	1 sprig	1 sprig
Olive oil	2 oz.	60 g
Red wine	4 oz.	120 g
Jus lié	1 pt.	450 ml

1. Season the noisettes with salt, pepper and thyme.

2. Break the garlic into cloves. Cook the cloves with the rosemary in 1 ounce (30 grams) of oil over low heat until they are very soft, approximately 10 minutes.

3. Deglaze with the wine. Add the jus lié; simmer and reduce by half.

4. Strain the sauce through a china cap, pushing to extract some of the garlic. Return the sauce to the saucepan and adjust the consistency and seasonings.

5. Sauté the noisettes to the desired degree of doneness in the remaining oil; serve with the sauce.

CHAPTER 16
PORK

After studying this chapter you will be able to:

◆ identify the primal, subprimal and fabricated cuts of pork
◆ perform basic butchering procedures
◆ apply appropriate cooking methods to several common cuts of pork

𝒫ork is the meat of hogs usually butchered before they are one years old. With the exception of beef, Americans consume more pork than any other meat. The pork we eat is leaner and healthier than it once was because of advances in animal husbandry.

Since hogs are butchered at a young age their meat is generally very tender and has a delicate flavor. It is well suited to a variety of cooking methods. Over two thirds of the pork marketed in the United States is cured to produce products such as smoked hams and smoked bacon. Cured pork products are discussed in Chapter 21, Charcuterie.

PRIMAL AND SUBPRIMAL CUTS OF PORK

After a hog is slaughtered, it is generally split down the backbone, dividing the carcass into bilateral halves. Like the beef carcass, each side of the hog carcass is then further broken down into the primal cuts: shoulder, Boston butt, belly, loin and fresh ham.

Hogs are bred specifically to produce long loins: The loin contains the highest-quality meat and is the most expensive cut of pork. Pork is unique in that the ribs and loin are considered a single primal cut. They are not separated into two different primals as are the ribs and loin of beef, veal and lamb.

Figure 16.1 shows the relationship between the hog's bone structure and the primal cuts. As with all meats, it is important to know the location of bones when cutting or working with pork. This makes meat fabrication and carving easier and aids in identifying cuts. Figure 16.2 shows the primal cuts of pork and their location on the carcass. A hog carcass generally weighs in a range of 120 to 210 pounds (55–110 kg).

Shoulder

The primal shoulder, known as the picnic ham, is the lower portion of the hog's foreleg; it accounts for approximately 20% of carcass weight. The shoulder contains the arm and shank bones and has a relatively high ratio of bone to lean meat.

Because all pork comes from hogs slaughtered at a young age, the shoulder is tender enough to be cooked by any method. It is, however, one of the toughest cuts of pork. It is available smoked or fresh. The shoulder is fairly inexpensive and, when purchased fresh, it can be cut into shoulder butt steaks or boned and cut for chop suey or stew.

The foreshank is called the shoulder hock and is almost always smoked. Shoulder hocks are often simmered for long periods in soups, stews and braised dishes to add flavor and richness.

Boston Butt

The primal Boston butt is a square cut located just above the primal pork shoulder. It accounts for approximately 7% of carcass weight.

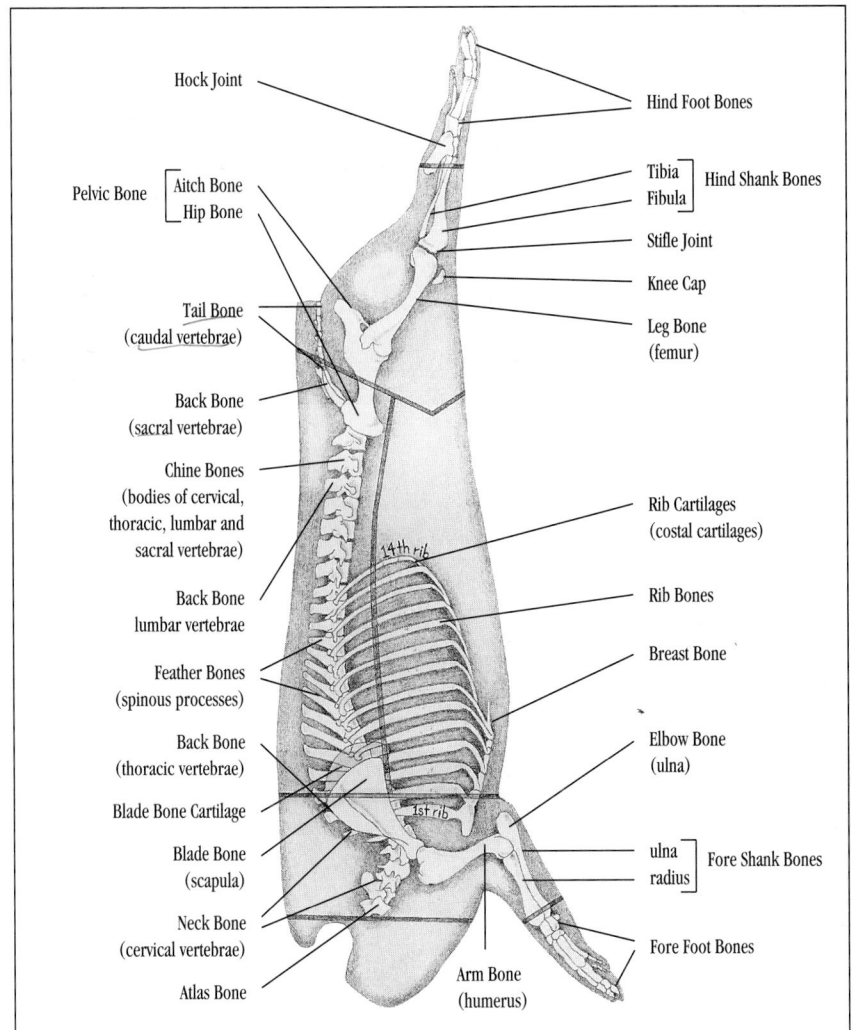

Hock Joint

Hind Foot Bones

Pelvic Bone

Aitch Bone
Hip Bone

Tibia
Fibula   Hind Shank Bones

Stifle Joint

Knee Cap

Tail Bone
(caudal vertebrae)

Leg Bone
(femur)

Back Bone
(sacral vertebrae)

Chine Bones
(bodies of cervical,
thoracic, lumbar and
sacral vertebrae)

Rib Cartilages
(costal cartilages)

14th rib

Back Bone
lumbar vertebrae

Rib Bones

Breast Bone

Feather Bones
(spinous processes)

Back Bone
(thoracic vertebrae)

Elbow Bone
(ulna)

Blade Bone Cartilage

1st rib

Blade Bone
(scapula)

ulna
radius   Fore Shank Bones

Neck Bone
(cervical vertebrae)

Fore Foot Bones

Atlas Bone

Arm Bone
(humerus)

FIGURE 16.1   *The Skeletal Structure of a Hog*

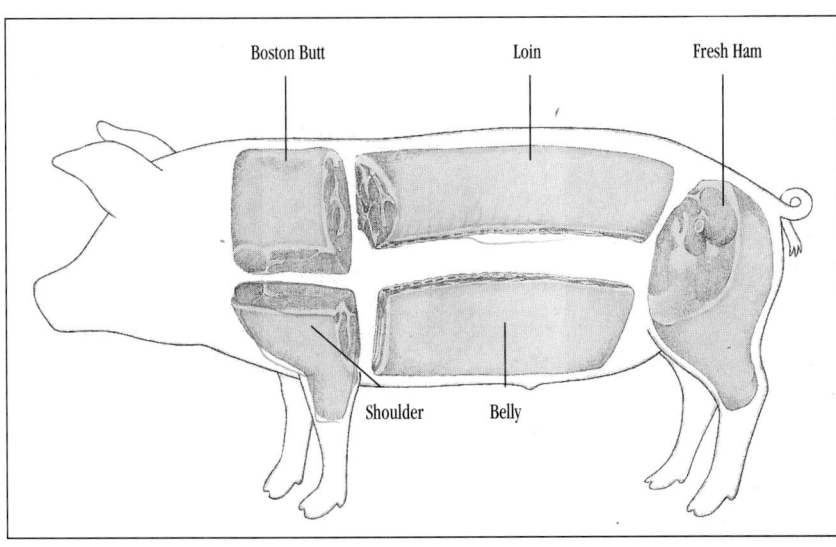

Boston Butt   Loin   Fresh Ham

Shoulder   Belly

FIGURE 16.2   *The Primal Cuts of Pork*

The Boston butt is very meaty and tender, with a good percentage of fat to lean meat. Containing only a small portion of the blade bone, the Boston butt is a good choice when a recipe calls for a solid piece of lean pork. The fresh Boston butt is sometimes cut into steaks or chops to be broiled or sautéed. When the Boston butt is smoked it is usually boneless and called a cottage ham.

Boston Butt

Belly

The primal pork belly is located below the loin. Accounting for approximately 16% of carcass weight, it is very fatty with only streaks of lean meat. It contains the spareribs, which are always separated from the rest of the belly before cooking.

Spareribs usually are sold fresh but can also be smoked. Typically they are simmered and then grilled or baked while being basted with a spicy barbecue sauce. The remainder of the pork belly is nearly always cured and smoked to produce bacon.

Pork Spareribs

Loin

The loin is cut from directly behind the Boston butt and includes the entire rib section as well as the loin and a portion of the sirloin area. The primal loin accounts for approximately 20% of carcass weight. It contains a portion of the blade bone on the shoulder end, a portion of the hip bone on the ham end, all of the ribs and most of the backbone.

The primal pork loin is the only primal cut of pork not typically smoked or cured. Most of the loin is a single, very tender eye muscle. It is quite lean but contains enough intramuscular and subcutaneous fat to make it an excellent choice for a moist-heat cooking method such as braising. Or, it can be prepared with dry-heat cooking methods such as roasting or sautéing. The loin also contains the pork tenderloin, located on the inside of the rib bones on the sirloin end of the loin. The tenderloin is the most tender cut of

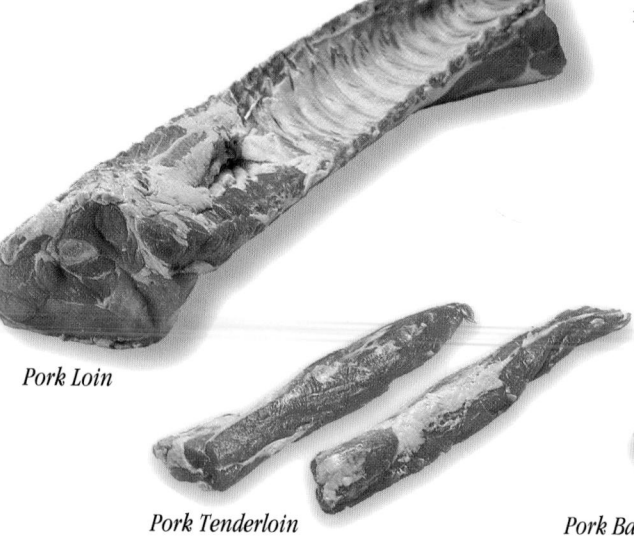

Pork Loin

Pork Tenderloin

Pork Backribs

Pork Loin Chops

Hogs were first brought to Florida by Spanish explorers in 1539, and they thrived in this heavenly new environment. The British shipped hogs to the colonies and as early as 1639 Virginia's colonists were supplying England with ham and bacon. During colonial days, pork was packed in barrels for shipment, giving rise to the term "meat packing."

During the War of 1812, the United States government shipped pork to American soldiers in barrels stamped with the letters "US" and the name of the meat packer, Sam Wilson. The soldiers referred to the meat as "Uncle Sam's meat," thus giving birth to the national government's nickname, Uncle Sam.

pork; it is very versatile and can be trimmed, cut into medallions and sautéed or the whole tenderloin can be roasted or braised. The most popular cut from the loin is the pork chop. Chops can be cut from the entire loin, the choicest being center-cut chops from the primal loin after the blade bone and sirloin portions at the front and rear of the loin are removed. The pork loin can be purchased boneless or boned and tied as a roast. A boneless pork loin is smoked to produce Canadian bacon. The rib bones, when trimmed from the loin, can be served as barbecued pork back ribs.

Although not actually part of the primal loin, fatback is the thick layer of fat—sometimes more than an inch (2.5 centimeters) thick—between the skin and the lean eye muscle. It has a variety of uses in the kitchen, especially in the preparation of charcuterie items.

Fresh Ham

The primal fresh ham is the hog's hind leg. It is a rather large cut accounting for approximately 24% of carcass weight. The ham contains the aitch, leg and hind shank bones. Fresh ham, like the legs of other meat animals, contains large muscles with relatively small amounts of connective tissue.

Like many other cuts of pork, hams are often cured and smoked. But fresh hams also produce great roasts and can be prepared using almost any cooking method. When cured and smoked, hams are available in a variety of styles; they can be purchased bone-in, shankless or boneless, partially or fully cooked. Fully cooked hams are also available canned. There is a specific ham for nearly every use and desired degree of convenience. The shank portion of the ham is called the ham hock. It is used in the same manner as the shoulder hock.

Fresh ham

BUTCHERING PROCEDURES

Other than suckling pigs (which are very young, very small whole pigs used for roasting or barbecuing whole), pork products generally are not purchased in forms larger than the primal cuts described above. There are a few important pork fabrication and butchering techniques that you should master, however.

PROCEDURE FOR BONING A PORK LOIN

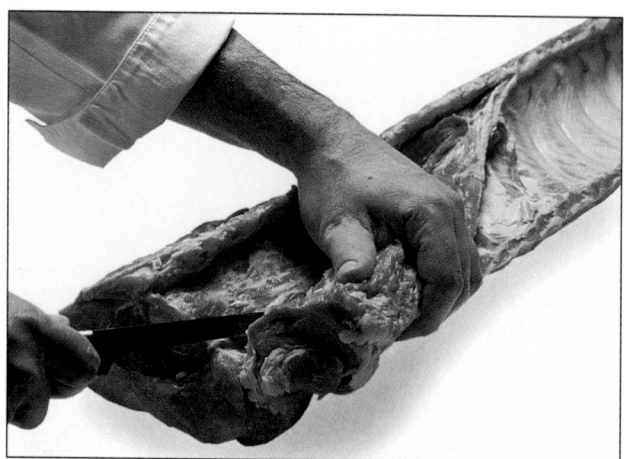

1. Starting on the sirloin end of a full pork loin, remove the tenderloin in one piece by making smooth cuts against the inside of the rib bones. Pull gently on the tenderloin as you cut.

2. Turn the loin over and cut between the ribs and the eye meat. Continue separating the meat from the bones, following the contours of the bones, until the loin is completely separated from the bones.

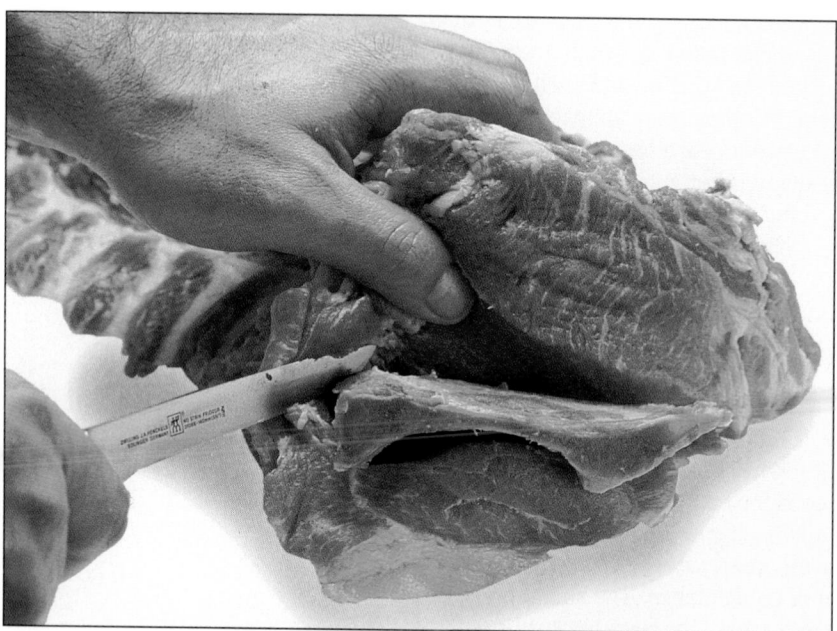

4. The fully boned loin will consist of (from left to right) the tenderloin, boneless loin and loin bones.

3. Trim around the blade bone on the shoulder end of the loin and remove it.

PROCEDURE FOR TYING A BONELESS PORK ROAST WITH THE HALF-HITCH METHOD

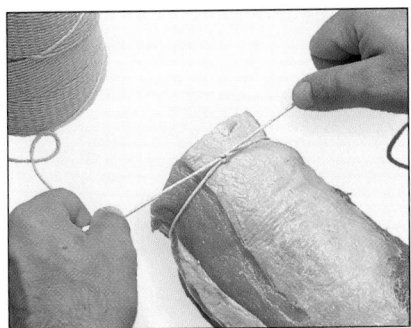

1. Wrap the loose end of the string around the pork loin and tie it with a double knot.

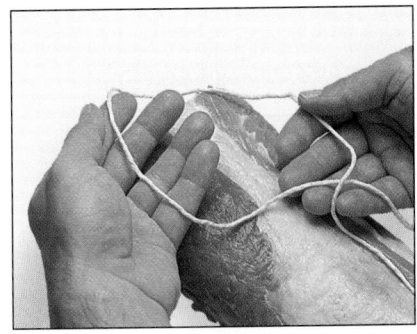

2. Make a loop and slide it down over the roast to approximately 1 inch (2.5 centimeters) from the first knot.

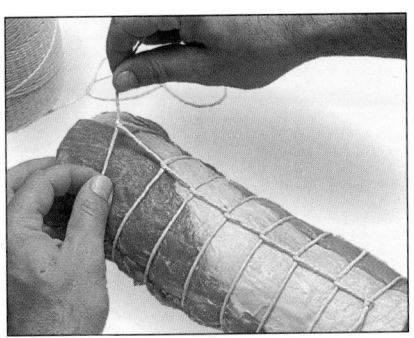

3. Make another loop and slide it down. Continue in this fashion until the whole roast has been tied.

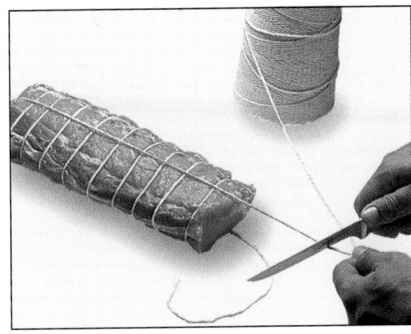

4. Turn the roast over and cut the string, leaving enough to wrap lengthwise around the roast to the original knot.

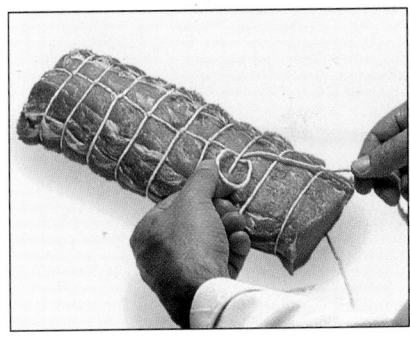

5. Wrap the string around the end of the roast, then around the string that formed the last loop. Continue in this fashion for the length of the roast, pulling the string tight after wrapping it around each loop.

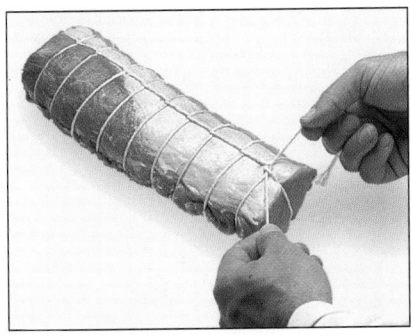

6. Turn the roast back over. Wrap the string around the front end of the roast and secure it to the first loop at the point where you tied the first knot.

7. The finished roast. Note the even intervals at which the strings are tied. They should be just snug enough to hold the shape of the roast; they should not dig in or cut the meat.

PROCEDURE FOR CUTTING A CHOP FROM A PORK LOIN

Center-cut pork chops can be cut from the center portion of a bone-in pork loin without the aid of a saw by using a boning knife and a heavy cleaver. Trim the excess fat from the loin, leaving a 1/4-inch (6-millimeter) layer to protect the meat during cooking.

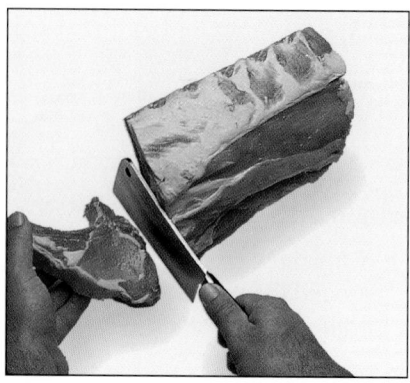

1. Cut through the meat with the knife.

2. Use the cleaver to chop through the chine bone.

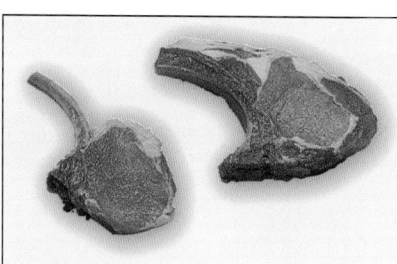

3. To produce a cleaner chop, trim the meat from the end of the rib bone. Then, with the boning knife, separate the loin meat from the chine bones and separate the chine bone from the rib with the cleaver.

PROCEDURE FOR CUTTING A POCKET IN A PORK CHOP

To make a pocket in a pork chop for stuffing, start with a thick chop or a double rib chop. Cut the pocket deep enough to hold ample stuffing, but be careful not to puncture either surface of the chop.

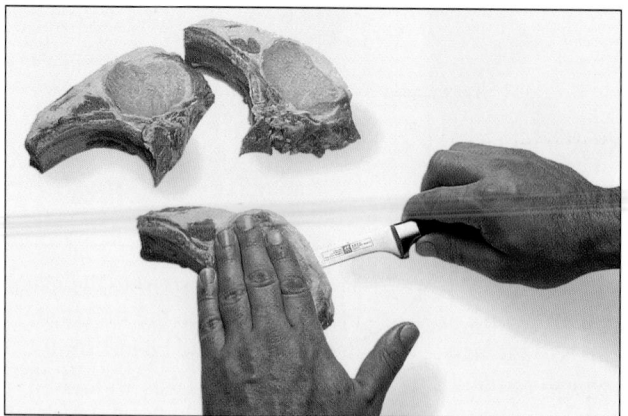

1. Use the tip of a boning knife to cut a pocket.

TABLE 16.1   USING COMMON CUTS OF PORK

Primal	Subprimal or Fabricated Cut	IMPS	Cooking Methods	Serving Suggestions
Shoulder	Picnic shoulder	405	Dry (baked)	Smoked picnic shoulder
Boston butt	Boston Butt	406	Dry heat (broil or grill; sauté) Moist heat (simmer)	Broiled Boston butt steaks Choucroute
Belly	Bacon	539	Dry heat (sauté) Moist heat (simmer) Combination (braise)	Breakfast meat Seasoning Seasoning
	Spare ribs	416A	Combination (steam then grill)	Barbecued spare ribs
Loin	Pork loin	410	Dry heat (roast) Combination (braise)	Roast pork Braised pork chops
	Pork tenderloin	415	Dry heat (broil or grill; sauté; roast)	Roast pork tenderloin
	Pork back ribs	422	Combination (steam then grill)	Barbecued back ribs
	Pork loin chops	1410	Dry heat (broil or grill) Combination (braise)	Broiled loin chop with mushroom sauce Braised loin chop with leeks and fennel
Fresh ham	Fresh Ham	401A	Dry heat (roast)	Roast pork with apricots and almonds

PROCEDURE FOR TRIMMING A PORK TENDERLOIN

As with a beef tenderloin, the pork tenderloin must be trimmed of all fat and silverskin. Follow the procedures outlined in Chapter 13, Beef, for trimming a beef tenderloin.

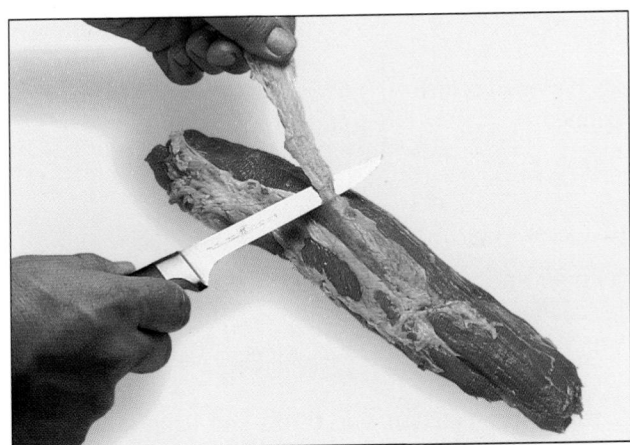

1. Use a boning knife to remove the silverskin from a pork tenderloin.

$\mathcal{C}$ONCLUSION

Pork can be enjoyed cured, processed or fresh. The mild flavor of fresh pork blends well with many different seasonings, making it a popular menu item. It is naturally tender and can be prepared by almost any dry-heat, moist-heat or combination cooking method. Properly fabricated and prepared, it can be a nutritious meat.

$\mathcal{Q}$UESTIONS FOR DISCUSSION

1. List each pork primal and describe its location on the carcass. Identify two subprimals or fabricated cuts taken from each primal.
2. What is unique about the primal pork loin as compared to the beef or veal loin?
3. Are fatback and bacon taken from the same primal? How are they different?
4. What is the only primal cut of pork that is not typically smoked or cured? How is it best cooked? Explain your answer.

$\mathcal{A}$DDITIONAL PORK RECIPES

RECIPE 16.1

CAROLINA BARBECUED RIBS

NOTE: *This dish appears in the Chapter Opening photograph.*

Yield: 6 Servings, approx. 4 ribs each   **Method:** Baking

Salt and pepper	TT	TT
Crushed red pepper flakes	1 Tbsp.	30 ml
Pork backribs, 3–4 lb. (1.3–1.8 kg) slab	2	2
White vinegar	1 pt.	450 ml
Sauce:		
Onion, chopped coarse	5 oz.	150 g
Garlic cloves	3	3
Green bell pepper, chopped coarse	4 oz.	120 g
Plum tomatoes, canned	1 pt.	450 ml
Red Devil hot sauce	8 oz.	225 g
Brown sugar	10 oz.	300 g
Lemon juice	2 oz.	60 g

1. Combine the salt, pepper and red pepper flakes. Rub this mixture over both sides of the ribs, coating them well.
2. Place the ribs in a non-reactive pan and add the vinegar. Cover and refrigerate several hours or overnight.
3. Uncover the ribs, turn the presentation side down and bake in a 375°F (190°C) oven for 1-1/2 hours.
4. Remove the ribs from the liquid and place on a clean sheet pan, turning them so the presentation side is up. Increase the oven temperature to 400°F (200°C) and bake for an additional 30 minutes.
5. Prepare the sauce by puréeing the onion, garlic, green pepper and tomatoes in a food processor or blender. Pour this mixture into a non-reactive saucepan and add the remaining sauce ingredients.
6. Simmer the sauce over low heat until it thickens, approximately 15 to 20 minutes.
7. Brush the ribs with the sauce and serve additional sauce on the side. Serve with Creamy Cole Slaw, Recipe 24.33 and Baked Beans, Recipe 22.23.

♦♦♦

RECIPE 16.2

GRILLED MEDALLIONS OF PORK ON A CORNCAKE WITH BOURBONED APPLE BUTTER

ANA WESTIN HOTEL, WASHINGTON, D.C.
Chef Leland Atkinson

Yield: 4 Servings   **Method:** Grilling

Loin medallions, 3 oz. (90 g) each	8	8
Salt and pepper	TT	TT
Lemon juice	1 oz.	30 g
Garlic, minced	1 tsp.	5 ml
Jalapeño, minced	1 tsp.	5 ml
Corncakes (recipe follows)	4	4
Apple Butter (recipe follows)	as needed	as needed
Fresh cilantro	as needed	as needed

1. Season the pork with salt and pepper and marinate it in the lemon juice, garlic and jalapeño for 2–4 hours.
2. Grill the medallions until done, approximately 4–5 minutes per side.
3. Place the corncakes on four warm plates, top them with a dollop of warm Apple Butter and two pork medallions. Garnish with fresh cilantro and serve.

APPLE BUTTER

Yield: 24 oz. (700 g)

Onion, chopped fine	4 oz.	120 g
Sugar	2 oz.	60 g
Cider vinegar	1 oz.	30 g
Granny Smith apples, peeled and chopped coarse	3	3
Bourbon	6 oz.	180 g
Demi-glace	8 oz.	250 g
Cinnamon, ground	2 tsp.	10 ml
Cloves, ground	1 pinch	1 pinch
Whole butter	1 Tbsp.	15 ml
Salt and pepper	TT	TT

1. Combine the onion, sugar and vinegar; simmer for 5 minutes.
2. Add the apples, bourbon, demi-glace and spices. Simmer until the apples are completely tender.
3. Purée the mixture in a blender or food processor.
4. Strain and monte au beurre. Adjust the seasonings and keep warm for service.

CORNCAKES

Yield: 4 4-oz. (120-g) cakes

Green onion, sliced	2 Tbsp.	30 ml
Red bell pepper, small dice	2 Tbsp.	30 ml
Jalapeño, minced	1	1
Olive oil	1 oz.	30 g
Fresh corn kernels	8 oz.	250 g

Continued

Milk	3 oz.	90 g
Flour	2 oz.	60 g
Cornmeal	2 oz.	60 g
Eggs	2	2
Egg yolk	1	1
Fresh cilantro, chopped	1 tsp.	5 ml
Salt and pepper	TT	TT
Clarified butter	as needed	as needed

1. Sauté the onions, bell peppers and jalapeño in the olive oil. Drain and cool to room temperature.

2. In a food processor, blend the corn kernels with a little milk until the mixture is not quite smooth.

3. Remove the corn mixture to a bowl and stir in the remaining milk, the flour and cornmeal.

4. Beat the eggs with the yolk; add the pepper mixture to them. Add the cilantro and combine this mixture with the corn mixture. Season with salt and pepper.

5. Heat a portion of the clarified butter in a sauté pan or on a griddle. Add 4 ounces (120 grams) of the batter to form 5-inch (12-centimeter) pancakes; lightly brown them on each side.

◆◆◆

RECIPE 16.3

CHINESE BARBECUED SPARERIBS

Yield: approximately 24 ribs

Method: Roasting

Sparerib racks, 2 lb. 8 oz. (1.1 kg) each	2	2
Garlic cloves, crushed	2	2
Tomato catsup	2 Tbsp.	30 ml
Soy sauce	2 Tbsp.	30 ml
Hoisin sauce	2 Tbsp.	30 ml
Red wine	2 Tbsp.	30 ml
Fresh ginger, grated	1 Tbsp.	15 ml
Honey	1 Tbsp.	15 ml

1. Cut the spareribs into individual ribs and arrange them on a rack in a baking pan. Roast for 45 minutes at 300°F (150°C).

2. Combine the remaining ingredients into a sauce. Brush the spareribs lightly with the sauce. Roast for 30 minutes more.

3. Turn the spareribs and brush with more sauce. Roast until the ribs are well browned, approximately 30 minutes.

◆◆◆

RECIPE 16.4

PORK LOIN WITH PRUNES

Yield: 6 6-oz. (180-g) Servings

Method: Roasting

Boneless pork loin roast, 3 lb. (1.5 kg)	1	1
Salt and pepper	TT	TT
Prunes, pitted	1 lb. 8 oz.	750 g
Carrot, chopped coarse	3 oz.	90 g
Onion, chopped coarse	6 oz.	170 g
Vegetable oil	1 Tbsp.	15 ml
Clarified butter	1 Tbsp.	15 ml

Fresh rosemary	1 tsp.	5 ml
Fresh thyme	1 tsp.	5 ml
Bay leaf, crushed	1	1
Garlic cloves	2	2
Apple juice	8 oz.	250 g
White stock	8 oz.	250 g
Sugar	2 oz.	60 g
Vinegar	2 oz.	60 g

1. Trim and butterfly the pork loin; reserve the trimmings. (To butterfly the loin, slice it partway through the center and open it like a book, then flatten it into a rectangular shape.) Season with salt and pepper.

2. Reserve 12 prunes and arrange the remaining prunes along the length of the loin. Roll up the loin and tie with butcher's twine.

3. Brown the pork roll and pork trimmings, carrots and onions in the oil and butter.

4. Add the herbs and garlic and roast the pork on the bed of trimmings and vegetables at 350°F (170°C), basting frequently with the fat that accumulates in the pan, until done, approximately 45–60 minutes.

5. Poach the reserved prunes in the apple juice until plump; set aside.

6. Remove the roast from the pan and keep it warm. Degrease the pan and deglaze with white stock. Simmer for 15 minutes, then strain.

7. Combine the sugar and vinegar in a saucepan. Bring to a boil and cook without stirring until the mixture turns a caramel color. Immediately remove from the heat and add the juices from the roasting pan. When the sputtering stops, return the pan to the heat and skim any fat from the surface; keep the sauce warm over low heat.

8. Drain the prunes. Remove the twine from the roast. Slice and serve the meat with the sauce and prunes.

◆◆◆

RECIPE 16.5

BOURBON BAKED HAM

Yield: 16 6-oz (180-g) Servings   **Method:** Roasting

Ham, fully cooked, bone in, 12–14 lb. (5.4–6.3 kg)	1	1
Brown sugar	6 oz.	170 g
Cloves, ground	1/2 tsp.	2 ml
Crushed pineapple, with juice	16 oz.	500 g
Bourbon	8 oz.	250 g
Orange marmalade	8 oz.	250 g

1. Peel the skin from the ham and trim the exterior fat to an even thickness of 1/4 inch (6 millimeters).

2. Combine the sugar and cloves and pat this mixture evenly over the top of the ham. Roast the coated ham at 350°F (170°C) for 30 minutes.

3. Combine the pineapple, bourbon and marmalade in a saucepan over medium heat. Do not allow the bourbon to flame.

4. Pour the sauce over the ham and cook until done, basting frequently, approximately 3 hours.

5. Remove the ham from the roasting pan. Keep it warm and allow it to rest 30 minutes before carving.

RECIPE 16.6
GRILLED PORK TENDERLOIN
WITH CASCABEL CHILE AND HONEY GLAZE

VINCENT ON CAMELBACK, PHOENIX, AZ
Chef Vincent Guerathault

Yield: 6 6-oz. (180-g) Servings   **Method:** Grilling

Pork tenderloins, approx. 14 oz. (400 g) each	3	3
Olive oil	1 Tbsp.	15 ml
Salt	1 tsp.	5 ml
Black pepper, coarsely ground	2 tsp.	10 ml
Cascabel Chile and Honey Glaze (recipe follows)		

1. Rub the tenderloins with oil and season with salt and pepper.
2. Grill the tenderloins on all sides, a total of approximately 5 minutes. Brush with the Cascabel Chile and Honey Glaze and cook an additional 2 minutes on each side.
3. Remove the pork from the grill and allow it to rest for 5 minutes before slicing.
4. Slice each tenderloin on the bias into 12 slices. Drizzle the remaining Cascabel Chile and Honey Glaze over the sliced pork.

CASCABEL CHILE AND HONEY GLAZE

Yield: 12 oz. (350 g)

Cascabel chiles (if not available, substitute 2 jalapeños)	4	4
Honey	8 oz.	250 g
Chicken stock	4 oz.	120 g
Tomato purée	3 Tbsp.	45 ml
Paprika	1 tsp.	5 ml
Cumin, ground	1 tsp.	5 ml

1. Soften the cascabel chiles by soaking them in warm water for approximately 2 hours.
2. Combine all ingredients in a sauce pan and simmer over medium heat for approximately 10 minutes.
3. Remove from the heat and purée in a blender.

RECIPE 16.7
SAUTÉED PORK MEDALLIONS
WITH RED PEPPER AND CITRUS

Yield: 8 Servings   **Method:** Sautéing

Pork loin, boneless, 3 lb. (1.4 kg)	1	1
Salt and pepper	TT	TT
Olive oil	6 oz.	180 g
Orange juice	6 oz.	180 g

Lemon juice	2 Tbsp.	30 ml
Green onion, sliced	4 oz.	120 g
Oranges	4	4
Flour	as needed	as needed
Red bell pepper, julienne	12 oz.	350 g
Grand Marnier	4 oz.	120 g
Demi-glace	1 pt.	450 ml

1. Season the pork with salt and pepper and marinate overnight in 4 ounces (120 grams) of the olive oil, 4 ounces (120 grams) of the orange juice, 1 tablespoon (15 milliliters) of the lemon juice and 2 ounces (60 grams) of the green onions.
2. Zest the oranges. Blanch and refresh the zest. Peel and section the oranges.
3. Cut the pork into 3-ounce (90-gram) medallions and pound lightly.
4. Dredge the medallions in flour seasoned with salt and pepper.
5. Sauté the medallions in the remaining olive oil until done, approximately 5 minutes. Remove from the pan and reserve.
6. Add the red peppers and remaining green onions to the pan and sauté lightly.
7. Remove the pan from the flame and deglaze with Grand Marnier.
8. Add the demi-glace, orange zest, and remaining orange and lemon juices. Adjust the seasonings.
9. Serve two medallions of pork per portion with sauce. Garnish with the orange sections.

========= ◆◆◆ =========

RECIPE 16.8

STUFFED PORK CHOPS

Yield: 10 Servings   Method: Braising

Thick-cut pork chops, approx. 8 oz. (250 g) each	10	10
Celery, small dice	4 oz.	120 g
Onion, small dice	6 oz.	170 g
Whole butter, melted	6 oz.	170 g
Fresh bread cubes, 1/2 in. (1.2 cm)	8 oz.	250 g
Parsley, chopped	1 Tbsp.	15 ml
Salt and pepper	TT	TT
White stock	approx. 8 oz.	approx. 250 g
Olive oil	2 oz.	60 g
Demi-glace	1 qt.	1 lt

1. Cut pockets in the chops.
2. Sauté the celery and onions in 2 ounces (60 grams) of butter until tender.
3. Combine the celery, onions and remaining butter with the bread cubes, parsley, salt and pepper. Add enough stock to moisten the dressing.
4. Stuff the mixture into each of the pork chops. Seal the pockets with toothpicks and tie with butcher's twine.
5. In a braiser, brown the stuffed chops well on each side in the olive oil.
6. Add the demi-glace. Bring to a simmer, cover and place in a 325°F (160°C) oven. Cook until tender, approximately 45 minutes.
7. Remove the chops from the pan. Degrease the sauce and reduce to the desired consistency. Strain the sauce and adjust the seasonings.

✦✦✦

RECIPE 16.9

CHOUCROUTE

Yield: 12 Servings, 4 oz. (120 g) sauerkraut,   **Method:** Braising
1 sausage and 7 oz. (200 g) pork

Bacon, medium dice	8 oz.	250 g
Onion, medium dice	12 oz.	340 g
Garlic, chopped fine	1-1/2 oz.	45 g
Granny Smith apples, medium dice	8 oz.	250 g
Sauerkraut	2 lb. 8 oz.	1 kg
Dry white wine	4 oz.	120 g
White wine vinegar	4 oz.	120 g
Chicken stock	1 pt.	500 ml
Sachet:		
Juniper berries	6	6
Bay leaves	3	3
Cloves	2	2
Caraway seeds	1 tsp.	5 ml
Boneless pork butt, 4 lb. (1.8 kg)	1	1
Smoked pork loin	2 lb.	1 kg
Red potatoes, peeled and quartered	3 lb.	1.4 kg
Bratwurst	12 links	12 links
Salt and pepper	TT	TT

1. Render the bacon.
2. Sauté the onions, garlic and apples in the bacon fat without browning.
3. Rinse the sauerkraut and squeeze out the liquid. Add the sauerkraut to the pan.
4. Stir in the wine, vinegar, stock and sachet.
5. Place the pork butt on the sauerkraut. Cover and braise in a 325°F (160°C) oven for 1 hour.
6. Add the smoked pork loin and potatoes and braise an additional 30 minutes.
7. Add the bratwurst and braise until all the meats are tender and the potatoes are done, approximately 30 minutes. Remove and discard the sachet. Season to taste with salt and pepper.
8. Carve the meats and serve with a portion of the sauerkraut and potatoes.

✦✦✦

RECIPE 16.10

CASSOULET

ANA WESTIN HOTEL, WASHINGTON, D.C.
Chef Leland Atkinson

Yield: 8 Servings, 8 oz. (250 g) pork stew,   **Method:** Stewing
1-1/2 oz. (45 g) sausage and
1 piece of duck each

White beans	1 lb.	450 g
White stock	2 qt.	2 lt
Smoked ham, large dice	8 oz.	250 g

Bouquet garni:		
Carrot stick, 4 in. (10 cm)	1	1
Leek, split, 4-in. (10-cm) piece	1	1
Fresh thyme	1 sprig	1 sprig
Bay leaf	1	1
Lamb or other sausage	1 lb.	450 g
Onion, medium dice	6 oz.	180 g
Garlic, chopped	1/2 oz.	15 g
Pork butt, cut in 2-in. (5 cm) cubes	1 lb. 8 oz.	700 g
Salt and pepper	TT	TT
Olive oil	1 oz.	30 g
Mirepoix	8 oz.	250 g
White wine	6 oz.	180 g
Tomato concasse	1 lb.	250 g
Demi-glace	1 pt.	450 ml
Brown stock	8 oz.	250 g
Sachet:		
Bay leaf	1	1
Dried thyme	1/2 tsp.	2 ml
Peppercorns, cracked	1/2 tsp.	2 ml
Parsley stems	8	8
Garlic cloves, crushed	2	2
Duck Confit (Recipe 20.16)	8 pieces	8 pieces

1. To make the bean stew, soak the white beans overnight in water. Drain and combine with the white stock, ham and bouquet garni. Bring to a simmer and cook for 30 minutes. Add the lamb sausage, onions and garlic; simmer until the beans are tender.
2. Remove and reserve the sausage.
3. Drain the beans, reserving both the beans and the cooking liquid. Reduce the cooking liquid by half and combine with the beans.
4. To make the meat stew, season the pork with salt and pepper and brown it in olive oil. Remove and reserve the meat.
5. Add the mirepoix to the pan and sauté. Deglaze with the white wine and add the tomato concasse, demi-glace, brown stock and sachet. Cover and simmer the pork until tender, approximately 45 minutes.
6. Remove the meat from the sauce and reserve. Discard the sachet. Reduce the sauce until thick; return the meat to the sauce.
7. To serve, scrape the excess fat from the duck confit. Place the duck in a roasting pan and roast at 350°F (180°C) until the meat is hot and the skin is crisp, approximately 20 minutes.
8. Place a portion of hot beans in a soup plate. Place a portion of the duck confit in the plate. Arrange a portion of the meat stew on top of the beans and around the duck.
9. Slice the lamb sausage and add it to the plate. Garnish with fresh herbs.

CHAPTER 17
POULTRY

After studying this chapter you will be able to:

- ◆ understand the structure and composition of poultry
- ◆ identify various kinds and classes of poultry
- ◆ understand poultry inspection and grading practices
- ◆ purchase poultry appropriate for your needs
- ◆ store poultry properly
- ◆ prepare poultry for cooking
- ◆ apply various cooking methods to poultry

*P*oultry is the collective term for domesticated birds bred for eating. They include chickens, ducks, geese, guineas, pigeons and turkeys. (Game birds such as pheasant, quail and partridge are described in Chapter 18, Game.) Poultry is generally the least expensive and most versatile of all main dish foods. It can be cooked by almost any method and its mild flavor goes well with a wide variety of sauces and accompaniments.

In this chapter we discuss the different kinds and classes of poultry and how to choose those that best suit your needs. You will learn how to store poultry properly to prevent food-borne illnesses and spoilage; how to butcher birds to produce the specific cuts you need and how to apply a variety of cooking methods properly.

Many of the cooking methods discussed here have been applied previously to meats. Although there are similarities with these methods, there are also many distinct differences. As you study this chapter, review the corresponding cooking methods for meats and note the similarities and differences.

MUSCLE COMPOSITION

The muscle tissue of poultry is similar to that of mammals in that it contains approximately 72% water, 20% protein, 7% fat and 1% minerals; it consists of bundles of muscle cells or fibers held together by connective tissue. Unlike red meat, poultry does not contain the intramuscular fat known as marbling. Instead, a bird stores fat in its skin, abdominal cavity and the fat pad near its tail. Poultry fat is softer and has a lower melting point than other animal fats. It is easily rendered during cooking.

As with red meats, poultry muscles that are used more often tend to be tougher than those used less frequently. Also, the muscles of an older bird

FREE-RANGE CHICKENS

Chicken has become increasingly popular in recent years, in part because it is inexpensive, versatile and considered healthier than meat. Indeed, more than 100 million chickens are processed weekly in this country. To meet an ever-increasing demand, chickens are raised indoors in huge chicken houses that may contain as many as 20,000 birds. They are fed a specially formulated mixture composed primarily of corn and soybean meal. Animal protein, vitamins, minerals and small amounts of antibiotics are added to produce quick-growing, healthy birds.

Many consumers feel that chickens raised this way do not have the flavor of chickens that are allowed to move freely and forage for food. Some consumers are concerned about the residual effects of the vitamins, minerals and antibiotics added to the chicken feed. To meet the demand for chickens raised the "old-fashioned way," some farmers raise (and many fine establishments offer) free-range chickens.

Although the USDA has not standardized regulations for free-range chicken, generally the term *free-range* applies to birds that are allowed unlimited access to the area outside the chicken house. Often they are raised without antibiotics, fed a vegetarian diet (no animal fat or byproducts), processed without the use of preservatives and raised under more humane growing methods than conventionally grown birds. Most free-range chickens are marketed at 9–10 weeks old and weigh 4-1/2 to 5 pounds (2 to 2-1/2 kilograms)—considerably more mature and heavier than conventional broilers. They are generally sold with heads and feet intact and are more expensive than conventionally raised chickens.

Many consumers (in both the dining room and the kitchen) feel that free-range chicken is superior in flavor and quality. Others find no perceptible differences. As a consumer you will have to decide whether any difference is worth the added expense.

tend to be tougher than those of a younger one. Because the majority of poultry is marketed at a young age, however, it is generally very tender.

The breast and wing flesh of chickens and turkeys is lighter in color than the flesh of their thighs and legs. This color difference is due to a higher concentration of the protein myoglobin in the thigh and leg muscles. Myoglobin is the protein that stores oxygen for the muscle tissues to use. More-active muscles require more myoglobin and tend to be darker than less-active ones. Because chickens and turkeys generally do not fly, their breast and wing muscles contain little myoglobin and are therefore a light color. Birds that do fly have only dark meat. Dark meat also contains more fat and connective tissue than light meat, and its cooking time is longer.

Skin color may vary from white to golden yellow, depending on what the bird was fed. Such color differences are not an indication of overall quality.

Rock Cornish Game Hen

IDENTIFYING POULTRY

The USDA recognizes six categories or **kinds** of poultry: chicken, duck, goose, guinea, pigeon and turkey. Each poultry kind is divided into **classes** based predominantly on the bird's age and tenderness. The sex of young birds is not significant for culinary purposes. It does matter, however, with older birds: Older male birds are tough and stringy and have less flavor than older female birds. Tables 17.1 through 17.6 list identifying characteristics and suggested cooking methods for each of the various kinds and classes of poultry.

Chicken Broiler/Fryer

Chicken

Chicken (Fr. *poulet*) is the most popular and widely eaten poultry in the world. It contains both light and dark meat and has relatively little fat. A young, tender chicken can be cooked by almost any method; an older bird is best stewed or braised. Chicken is extremely versatile and may be flavored, stuffed, basted or garnished with almost anything. Chicken is inexpensive and readily available, fresh or frozen, in a variety of forms.

Capon

TABLE 17.1   CHICKEN CLASSES

Class	Description	Age	Weight	Cooking Method
Game hen	Young or immature progeny of Cornish chickens or of a Cornish chicken and a White Rock chicken; very flavorful	5–6 weeks	2 lb. (1 kg) or less	Split and broil or grill; roast
Broiler/fryer	Young with soft, smooth-textured skin; relatively lean; flexible breastbone	13 weeks	3 lb. 8 oz. (1.5 kg) or less	Any cooking method; very versatile
Roaster	Young with tender meat and smooth-textured skin; breastbone is less flexible than broiler's	3–5 months	3 lb. 8 oz.–5 lb. (1.5–2 kg)	Any cooking method
Capon	Surgically castrated male; tender meat with soft, smooth-textured skin; bred for well-flavored meat; contains a high proportion of light to dark meat and a relatively high fat content	Under 8 months	6–10 lb. (2.5–4.5 kg)	Roast
Hen/stewing	Mature female; flavorful but less tender meat; nonflexible breastbone	Over 10 months	2 lb. 8 oz.–8 lb. (1–3.5 kg)	Stew or braise

TABLE 17.2   DUCK CLASSES

Class	Description	Age	Weight	Cooking Method
Broiler/fryer	Young bird with tender meat; a soft bill and windpipe	8 weeks or less	3 lb. 8 oz.–4 lb. (1.5–1.8 kg)	Roast at high temperature
Roaster	Young bird with tender meat; rich flavor; easily dented windpipe	16 weeks or less	4–6 lb. (1.8–2.5 kg)	Roast
Mature	Old bird with tough flesh; hard bill and windpipe	6 months or older	4–6 lb. (1.8–2.5 kg)	Braise

Roaster Duckling

Duck

The duck (Fr. *canard*) used most often in commercial food service operations is a roaster duckling. It contains only dark meat and large amounts of fat. In order to make the fatty skin palatable, it is important to render as much fat as possible. Duck has a high percentage of bone and fat to meat; for example, a four-pound duck will serve only two people, while a four-pound roasting chicken will serve four people.

Goose

A goose (Fr. *oie*) contains only dark meat and has very fatty skin. It is usually roasted at high temperatures to render the fat. Roasted goose is popular at holidays and is often served with an acidic fruit-based sauce to offset the fattiness.

Young Goose

TABLE 17.3   GOOSE CLASSES

Class	Description	Age	Weight	Cooking Method
Young	Rich, tender dark meat with large amounts of fat; easily dented windpipe	6 months or less	6–12 lb. (2.5–5.5 kg)	Roast at high temperature, accompany with acidic sauces
Mature	Tough flesh and hard windpipe	Over 6 months	10–16 lb. (4.5–7 kg)	Braise or stew

Young Guinea

Guinea

A guinea or guinea fowl (Fr. *pintade*) is the domesticated descendant of a game bird. It has both light and dark meat and a flavor similar to pheasant. Guinea is tender enough to sauté. Because it contains little fat, a guinea is usually barded prior to roasting. Guinea, which is relatively expensive, is not as popular here as it is in Europe.

TABLE 17.4   GUINEA CLASSES

Class	Description	Age	Weight	Cooking Method
Young	Tender meat; flexible breastbone	3 months	12 oz.–1 lb. 8 oz. (.3–.7 kilo)	Bard and roast; sauté
Mature	Tough flesh; hard breastbone	Over 3 months	1–2 lb. (.5–1 kg)	Braise or stew

TABLE 17.5   PIGEON CLASSES

Class	Description	Age	Weight	Cooking Method
Squab	Immature pigeon; very tender, dark flesh and a small amount of fat	4 weeks	12 oz.–1 lb. 8 oz. (.3–.7 kg)	Broil, roast or sauté
Pigeon	Mature bird; coarse skin and tough flesh	Over 4 weeks	1–2 lb. (.5–1 kg)	Braise or stew

Pigeon

The young pigeon (Fr. *pigeon*) used in commercial food service operations is referred to as squab. Its meat is dark, tender and well suited for broiling, sautéing or roasting. Squab has very little fat and benefits from barding.

Squab

Turkey

Turkey (Fr. *dinde*) is the second most popular poultry kind in the United States. It has both light and dark meat and a relatively small amount of fat. Younger turkey is economical and can be prepared in almost any manner.

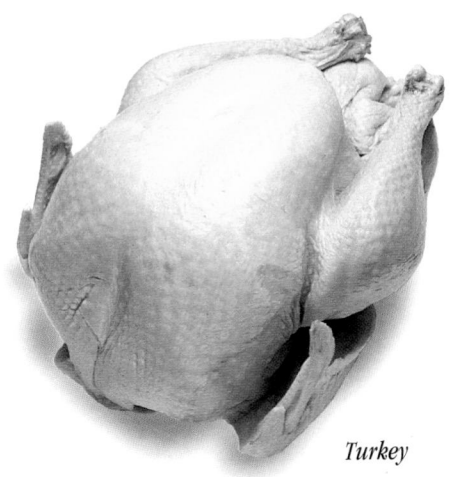

Turkey

TABLE 17.6   TURKEY CLASSES

Class	Description	Age	Weight	Cooking Method
Fryer/roaster	Immature bird of either sex (males are called toms); tender meat with smooth skin; flexible breastbone	16 weeks or less	4–9 lb. (2–4 kg)	Roast or cut into scallops and sauté or pan-fry
Young	Tender meat with smooth skin; less-flexible breastbone	8 months or less	8–22 lb. (3.5–10 kg)	Roast or stew
Yearling	Fully matured bird; reasonably tender meat and slightly coarse skin	15 months or less	10–30 lb. (4.5–13 kg)	Roast or stew
Mature	Older bird with coarse skin and tough flesh	15 months or older	10–30 lb. (4.5–13 kg)	Stew, ground or used in processed products

Livers, Gizzards, Hearts and Necks

Livers, gizzards, hearts and necks are commonly referred to as **giblets**. Although most poultry kinds are sold with giblets, chickens can be purchased with or without them, depending on your needs.

Giblets can be used in a variety of ways. Gizzards (a bird's second stomach), hearts and necks are most often used to make giblet gravy. Gizzards are sometimes trimmed and deep-fried; hearts are sometimes served sautéed and creamed. Necks are very flavorful and can be added to stocks for flavor and richness. Livers, hearts and gizzards are not added to stocks, however, because of their strong flavors.

Chicken livers are often used in pâtés, sautéed or broiled with onions and served as an entree.

Foie Gras

Foie gras is the enlarged liver of a duck or goose. Considered a delicacy since Roman times, it is now produced in many parts of the world, including the United States. Foie gras is produced by methodically fattening the birds by force-feeding them specially prepared corn while limiting their activity. Fresh foie gras consists of two lobes that must be separated, split and deveined. Good foie gras will be smooth, round and putty-colored. It should not be yellow or grainy. Goose foie gras is lighter in color and more delicate in flavor than that of duck. Duck foie gras has a deeper, winy flavor and is far more common than goose foie gras. Fresh foie gras can be grilled, roasted, sautéed or made into pâtés or terrines. No matter which cooking method is used, care must be taken not to overcook the liver. Foie gras is so high in fat that overcooking will result in the liver actually melting away. Most foie gras used in this country is pasteurized or canned.

Duck Foie Gras

Canned foie gras may consist of solid liver or small pieces of liver compacted to form a block. Canned foie gras mousse is also available. Truffles are a natural accompaniment to foie gras and are used in many canned preparations.

TABLE 17.7   NUTRITIONAL VALUES OF POULTRY

For 1 oz. (28 g) uncooked poultry with skin	Kcal	Protein (g)	Total fat (g)	Saturated fat (g)	Cholesterol (mg)	Sodium (mg)
Chicken, breast	49	5.9	2.6	0.8	18	18
Chicken, thigh	60	4.9	4.3	1.2	24	22
Duck	115	3.3	11.2	3.7	22	18
Goose	105	4.5	9.5	2.8	23	21
Squab	83	5.2	6.7	2.4	mq	mq
Turkey, breast	45	6.2	2.0	0.5	18	17
Turkey, leg	41	5.5	1.9	0.6	20	21

The Corinne T. Netzer Encyclopedia of Food Values 1992
mq = measurable quantity, but data is unavailable

NUTRITION

Poultry is an economical source of high-quality protein. Poultry's nutritional value is similar to other meats, except that chicken and turkey breast meat is lower in fat and higher in niacin than other lean meats. (Compare Table 12.1 with Table 17.7.) Generally, dark meat contains more niacin and riboflavin than white meat.

INSPECTION AND GRADING OF POULTRY

Inspection

All poultry produced for public consumption in the United States is subject to USDA inspection. Inspections ensure that products are processed under strict sanitary guidelines and are wholesome and fit for human consumption. Inspections do not indicate a product's quality or tenderness. The round inspection stamp illustrated in Figure 17.1 can be found either on a tag attached to the wing or included in the package labeling.

FIGURE 17.1   *USDA Inspection Stamp for Poultry*

Grading

Grading poultry is voluntary but virtually universal. Birds are graded according to their overall quality with the grade (USDA A, B or C) shown on a shield-shaped tag affixed to the bird or on a processed product's packaging. See Figure 17.2.

According to the USDA, Grade A poultry is free from deformities, with thick flesh and a well-developed fat layer; free of pinfeathers, cuts or tears and broken bones; the carcass is free from discoloration and, if it is frozen, free from defects that occur during handling or storage. Nearly all poultry used in wholesale and retail outlets is Grade A. Grade B and C birds are used primarily for processed poultry products.

Quality grades have no bearing on the product's tenderness or flavor. A bird's tenderness is usually indicated by its class (for example, a "young

FIGURE 17.2   *Grade Stamp for USDA Grade A Poultry*

turkey" is younger and more tender than a yearling). Its grade (USDA A, B or C) within each class is determined by its overall quality.

PURCHASING AND STORING POULTRY

Purchasing Poultry

Poultry can be purchased in many forms: fresh or frozen, whole or cut up, bone-in or boneless, portion controlled (P.C.), individually quick frozen (IQF) or ground. Chicken and turkey are also widely used in prepared and convenience items and are available fully cooked and vacuum-wrapped or boned and canned. Although purchasing poultry in a ready-to-use form is convenient, it is not always necessary: Poultry products are easy to fabricate and portion. Whole fresh poultry is also less expensive than precut or frozen products.

As with meats, you should consider your menu, labor costs, storage facilities and employee skills when deciding whether to purchase whole fresh poultry or some other form.

Storing Poultry

Poultry is highly perishable and particularly susceptible to contamination by salmonella bacteria. It is critical that poultry be stored at the correct temperatures.

Fresh chickens and other small birds can be stored on ice or at 32–34°F (0–2°C) for up to two days; larger birds can be stored up to four days at these temperatures. Frozen poultry should be kept at 0°F (–18°C) or below (the colder the better) and can be held for up to six months. It should be thawed gradually under refrigeration, allowing two days for chickens and up to four days for larger birds. Never attempt to cook poultry that is still partially frozen: It will be impossible to cook the product evenly and the areas that were still frozen may not reach the temperatures necessary to destroy harmful bacteria. Never partially cook poultry one day and finish cooking it later: Bacteria are more likely to grow under such conditions.

Sanitation and Cross-Contamination

Review the information in Chapter 2, Food Safety and Sanitation, before butchering any poultry. Be sure that all work surfaces, cutting boards, knives, hands and other equipment used to prepare poultry products are clean and sanitary. Be careful that juices and trimmings from poultry do not come in contact with other foods. Anything coming in contact with raw poultry should be cleaned and sanitized before it comes in contact with any other food. Cooked foods should never be placed in containers that were used to hold the raw product. Kitchen towels that are used to handle poultry or clean up after butchering should be sanitized before being reused to prevent cross-contamination.

BUTCHERING PROCEDURES

Poultry is easier to butcher than meats and is often processed on-site. You should be able to perform the following commonly encountered procedures. Because the different kinds of poultry are similar in structure, these procedures apply to a variety of birds.

Procedure for Cutting a Bird in Half

Often the first step in preparing poultry is to cut the bird in half. Broiler and fryer chickens are often split to make two portions. This procedure removes the backbone and breast bone (also known as the keel bone) for a neat finished product.

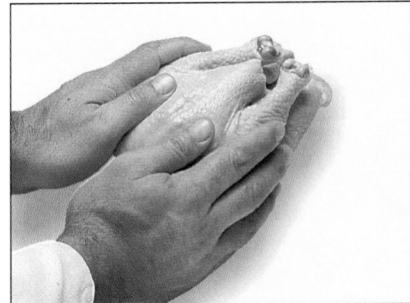

1. Square up the bird by placing it on its back and pressing on the legs and breast to create a more uniform appearance.

2. Place the bird on its breast and hold the tail tightly with the thumb and forefinger of one hand. Using a rigid boning knife and in a single swift movement, cut alongside the backbone from the bird's tail to head.

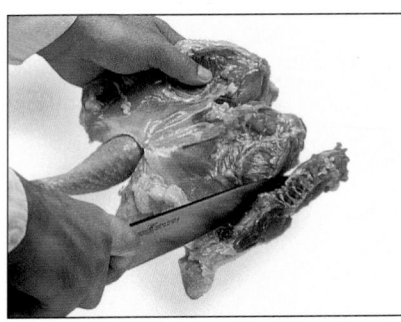

3. Lay the bird flat on the cutting board and remove the backbone by cutting through the ribs connecting it to the breast.

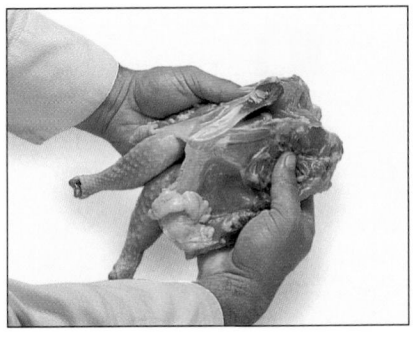

4. Bend the bird back, breaking the breast bone free.

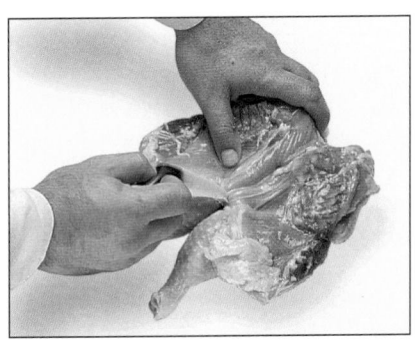

5. Run your fingers along the bone to separate the breast meat from it; pull the bone completely free. Be sure to remove the flexible cartilage completely.

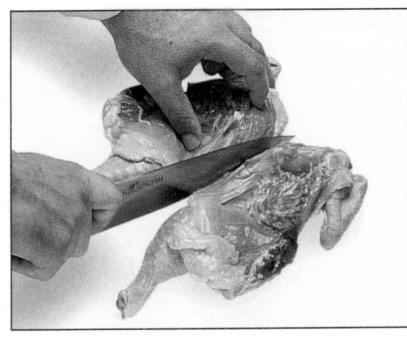

6. Cut through the skin to separate the bird into two halves. The halves are ready to be cooked; for a more attractive presentation, follow steps 7 and 8.

7. Trim off the wing tips and the ends of the leg bone.

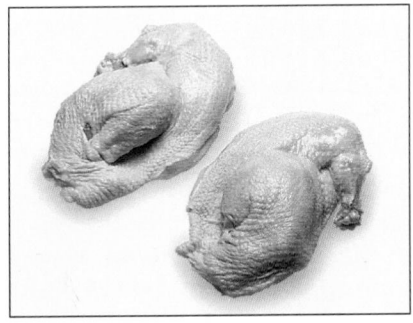

8. Make a slit in the skin below the leg and tuck the leg bone into the slit.

PROCEDURE FOR CUTTING A BIRD INTO PIECES

This is one of the most common butchering procedures. It is also very simple once you understand the bird's structure and are able to find each of its joints.

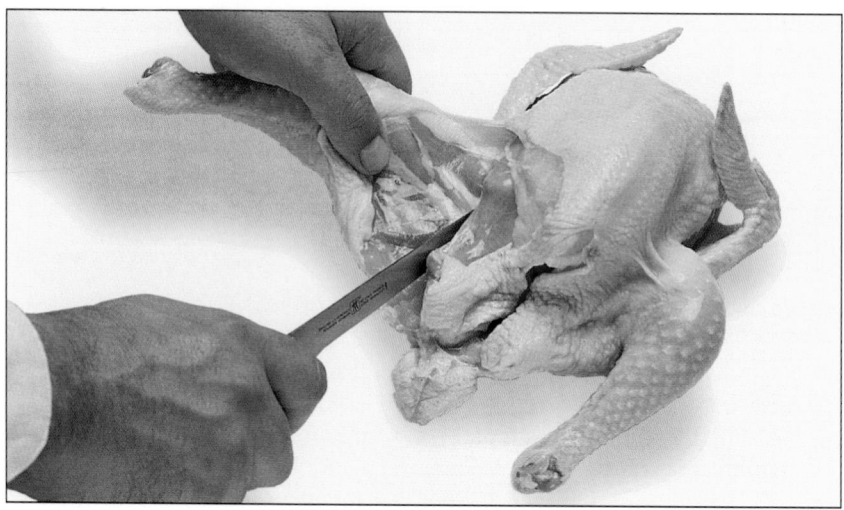

1. Remove the leg by pulling the leg and thigh away from the breast and cutting through the skin and flesh toward the thigh joint.

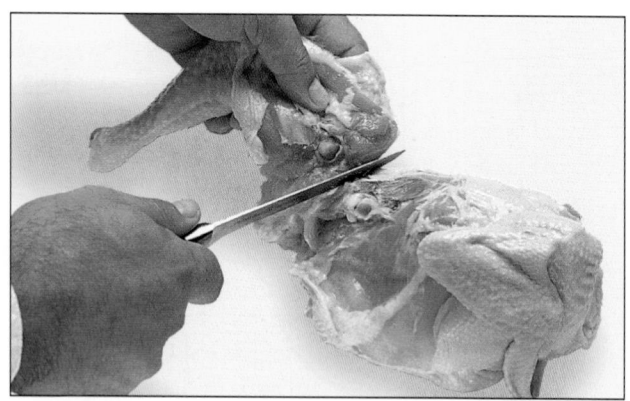

2. Cut down to the thigh joint, twist the leg to break the joint and cut the thigh and leg from the carcass. Be careful to trim around the oyster meat (the tender morsel of meat located next to the backbone); leave it attached to the thigh. Repeat with the other leg.

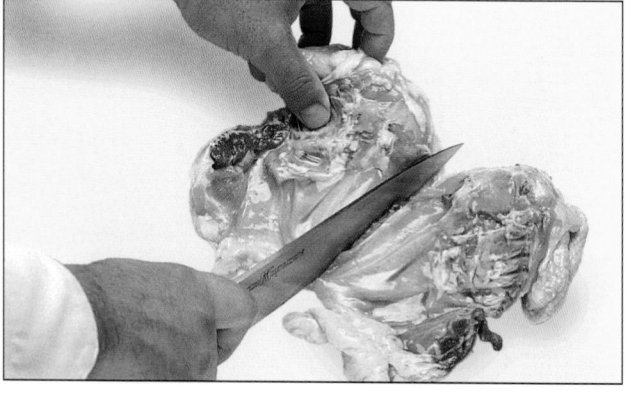

3. To split the breast, follow steps 2 through 6 for cutting a bird in half. Cut the breast into two halves.

4. The bird is now cut into four pieces.

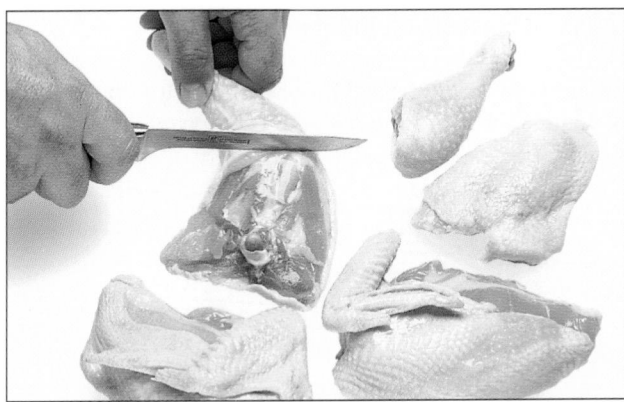

5. To cut the bird into six pieces, separate the thigh from the leg by making a cut guided by the line of fat on the inside of the thigh and leg.

6. To cut the bird into eight pieces, separate the wing from the breast by cutting through the joint, or split the breast, leaving a portion of the breast meat attached to the wing.

PROCEDURE FOR PREPARING A BONELESS BREAST

A boneless chicken breast is one of the most versatile and popular poultry cuts. It can be broiled, grilled, baked, sautéed, pan-fried or poached. Boneless turkey breast can be roasted or sliced and sautéed as a substitute for veal. The skin can be removed or left intact.

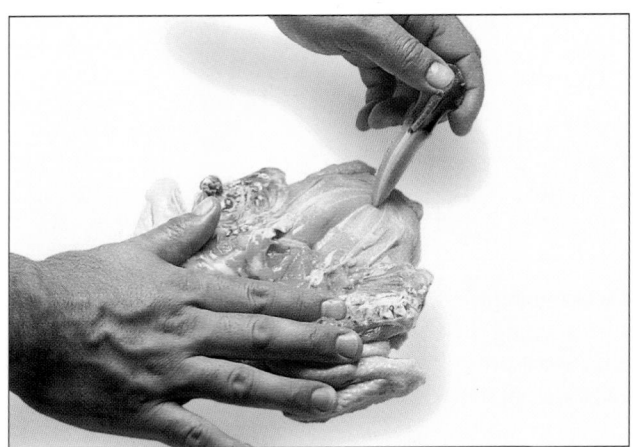

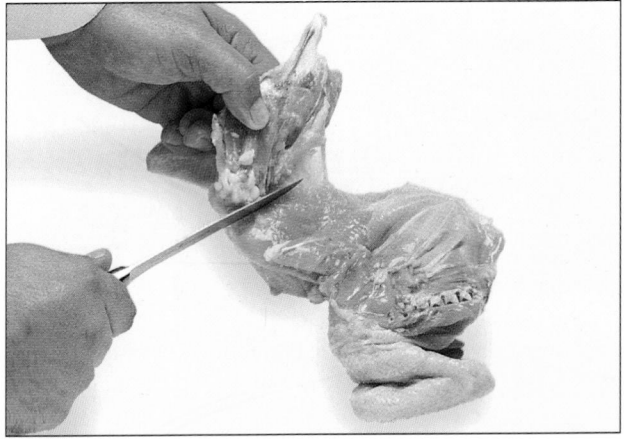

1. Remove the keel bone from the bone-in breast, following steps 4, 5 and 6 for cutting a bird in half.

2. With the chicken breast lying skin side down, separate the rib bones, wing and wishbone from the breast. Leave the two tender pieces of meat known as the tenderloins attached to the breast. Repeat the procedure on the other side, being sure to remove the small wishbone pieces from the front of the breast.

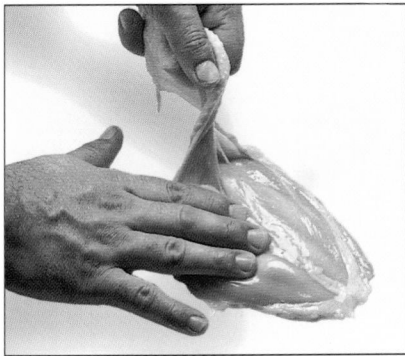

3. The skin may be left intact or removed to produce a skinless boneless breast.

PROCEDURE FOR PREPARING A SUPRÊME OR AIRLINE BREAST

A chicken suprême or airline breast is half of a boneless chicken breast with the first wing bone attached. The tip of the wing bone is removed, yielding a neat and attractive portion that can be prepared by a variety of cooking methods. The skin can be left on or removed.

1. Remove the legs from a chicken following steps 1 and 2 for cutting a bird into pieces. Place the bird on its back. Locate the wishbone, trim around it and remove it.

2. Cut along one side of the breast bone, separating the meat from the bone.

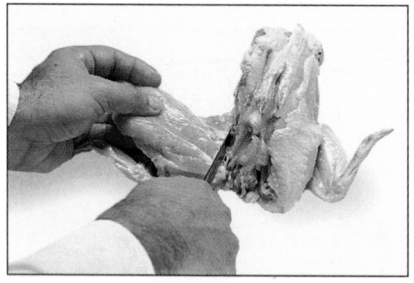 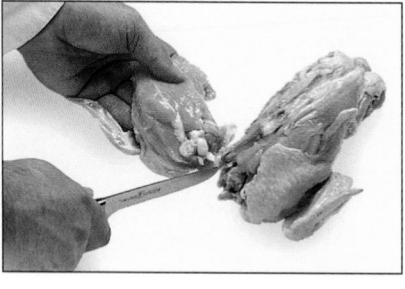 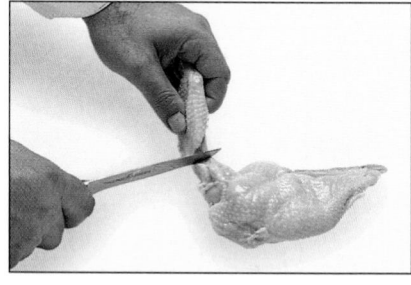

3. Following the natural curvature of the ribs, continue cutting to remove the meat from the bones.

4. When you reach the wing joint, cut through the joint, keeping the wing attached to the breast portion. Cut the breast free from the carcass.

5. Make a cut on the back of the joint between the first and second wing bones.

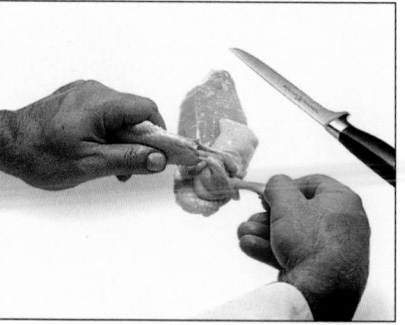 

6. Break the joint and pull the meat and skin back to expose a clean bone. Trim the wing bone.

7. The suprême can be prepared skin-on or skinless.

Procedure for Boning a Chicken Leg

Chicken breasts are usually more popular than legs and thighs. There are, however, uses for boneless, skinless leg and thigh meat; they can be stuffed or used for ballotines, for example.

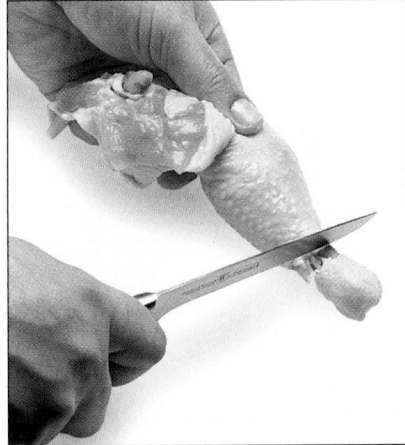

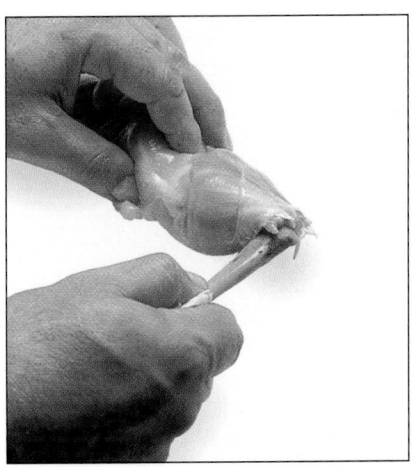

1. Carefully cut through the skin, meat and tendons at the base of the leg. Be sure to cut through completely to the bone.

2. Pull the skin off the leg with your hands, then break the joint between the leg and thigh. Twist and pull out the leg bone.

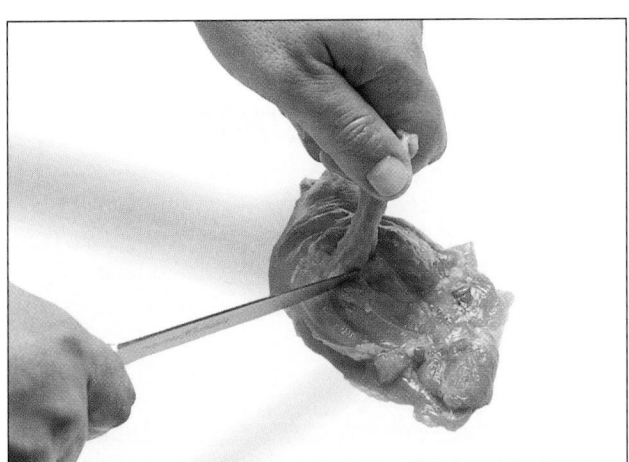

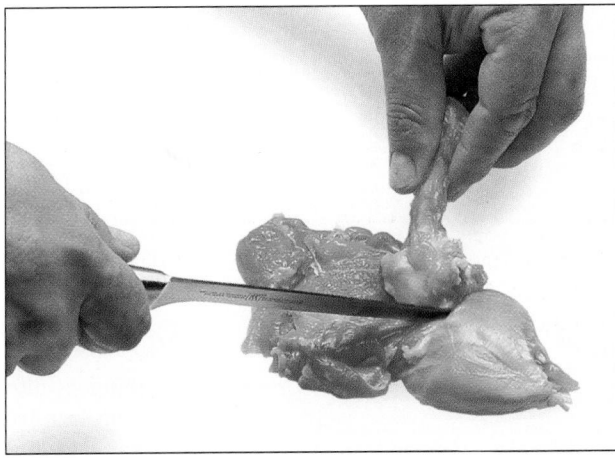

3. Working from the inside of the thigh, cut along both sides of the thigh bone, separating it from the meat.

4. Cut around the cartilage at the joint between the leg and thigh and remove the thigh bone and cartilage.

MARINATING POULTRY

Most poultry is quite mild in flavor, so a marinade is often used to add flavor and moisture, especially to poultry that will be broiled or grilled. Barbecued chicken is one of the simplest and best-known forms of marinated poultry. Poultry is often marinated in a mixture of white wine or lemon juice, oil, salt, pepper, herbs and spices, such as that given in Recipe 17.1.

♦♦♦

RECIPE 17.1

WHITE WINE MARINADE

Yield: 1 qt. (1 lt)

Garlic, minced	2 tsp.	10 ml
Onion, small dice	5 oz.	150 g
Dry white wine	24 oz.	750 g
Bay leaves	2	2
Dried thyme	2 tsp.	10 ml
White pepper	1 tsp.	5 ml
Salt	1 Tbsp.	15 ml
Lemon juice	1 oz.	30 g
Vegetable oil	4 oz.	120 g

1. Combine all ingredients.

Poultry absorbs flavors quickly, so if pieces are left too long in an acidic marinade they may take on undesirable flavors. Two hours is often sufficient, with smaller pieces requiring less time in the marinade than larger ones.

If the marinade contains oil, drain it well to avoid flare-up when the item is placed on the broiler or grill. Use a clean kitchen towel or a paper towel to wipe excess moisture from the poultry's surface so that it browns more easily. The marinade can be used to baste the item during cooking, but leftover marinade should not be served uncooked or reused because of the danger of bacterial contamination from the raw poultry.

APPLYING VARIOUS COOKING METHODS

The principles of cooking discussed in Chapter 9 and applied to meats in earlier chapters also apply to poultry. Dry-heat methods are appropriate for young, tender birds. Moist-heat methods should be used with older, less-tender products. In this section the various cooking methods are applied to poultry.

Dry-Heat Cooking Methods

Cooking poultry with dry-heat methods—broiling and grilling, roasting, sautéing, pan-frying and deep frying—presents some unique challenges. Large birds such as turkeys benefit from low-heat cooking but are better when served with the crispy skin gained through higher temperatures. Duck and goose skin contains a great deal of fat that must be rendered during the cooking process. Small birds such as squab must be cooked at sufficiently high temperatures to crisp their skins but can be easily overcooked. Boneless chicken breasts, particularly flavorful and popular when broiled or grilled, are easily overcooked and dried out because they do not contain bones to help retain moisture during cooking. Proper application of the following dry-heat cooking methods will help meet these challenges and ensure a good-quality finished product.

Broiling and Grilling

Broiled and grilled poultry should have a well-browned surface and can show crosshatched grill marks. It should be moist, tender and juicy throughout. It may be seasoned to enhance its natural flavors or marinated or basted with any number of butters or sauces.

Selecting Poultry to Broil or Grill

Smaller birds such as Cornish hens, chickens and squab are especially well suited for broiling or grilling. Whole birds should be split or cut into smaller pieces before cooking; their joints may be broken so they lie flat. Quail and other small birds can be skewered before being broiled to help them cook evenly and retain their shape. Be especially careful when cooking breast portions or boneless pieces: The direct heat of the broiler or grill can overcook the item very quickly.

Seasoning Poultry to be Broiled or Grilled

Poultry is fairly neutral in flavor and responds well to marinating. Poultry may also be basted periodically during the cooking process with flavored butter, oil or barbecue sauce. At the very least, broiled or grilled poultry should be well seasoned with salt and pepper just before cooking.

Determining Doneness

With the exception of duck breasts and squab, which are sometimes left pink, broiled or grilled poultry is always cooked well done. This makes the poultry particularly susceptible to becoming dry and tough because it contains little fat and is cooked at very high temperatures. Particular care must be taken to ensure that the item does not become overcooked.

Four methods are used to determine the doneness of broiled or grilled poultry:

1. *Touch*—When the item is done it will have a firm texture, resist pressure and spring back quickly when pressed with a finger.
2. *Temperature*—Use an instant read-thermometer to determine the item's internal temperature. This may be difficult, however, because of the item's size and the heat from the broiler or grill. Insert the thermometer in the thickest part of the item away from any bones. It should read 165–170°F (74–77°C) at the coolest point.
3. *Looseness of the joints*—When bone-in poultry is done, the leg will begin to move freely in its socket.
4. *Color of the juices*—Poultry is done when its juices run clear or show just a trace of pink. This degree of doneness is known in French as ***a point***.

Accompaniments to Broiled and Grilled Poultry

If the item was basted with an herb butter it can be served with additional butter; if the item was basted with barbecue sauce, it should be served with the same sauce. Be careful, however, that any marinade or sauce that came in contact with the raw poultry is not served unless it is cooked thoroughly to destroy harmful bacteria. Additional sauce suggestions are found in Table 10.5.

Broiled or grilled poultry is very versatile and goes well with almost any side dish. Seasoned and grilled vegetables are a natural accompaniment, and deep-fried potatoes are commonly served.

PROCEDURE FOR BROILING OR GRILLING POULTRY

As with meats, broiled or grilled poultry can be prepared by placing it directly on the grate. Poultry is also often broiled using a rotisserie.

1. Heat the broiler or grill.
2. Use a wire brush to remove any charred or burnt particles that may be stuck to the broiler or grill grate. The grate can be wiped with a lightly oiled towel to remove any remaining particles and help season it.
3. Prepare the item to be broiled or grilled by marinating or seasoning as desired; it may be brushed lightly with oil to keep it from sticking to the grate.

4. Place the item on the grate, presentation side (skin side) down. Following the example in Chapter 9, turn the item to produce the attractive cross-hatch marks associated with broiling or grilling. Baste the item often. Use tongs to turn or flip the item without piercing the surface so that valuable juices do not escape.

5. Develop the proper surface color while cooking the item until it is done *a point*. To do so, adjust the position of the item on the broiler or grill or adjust the distance between the grate and heat source. Large pieces and bone-in pieces that are difficult to cook completely on the broiler or grill can be finished in the oven.

A commonly used procedure to cook a large volume of poultry is to place the seasoned items in a broiler pan or other shallow pan and then place the pan directly under the broiler. Baste the items periodically, turning them once when they are halfway done. Items begun this way can be easily finished by transferring the entire pan to the oven.

♦♦♦

RECIPE 17.2

GRILLED SQUAB WITH BASIL BUTTER

Yield: 4 Servings

Squab, whole	4	4
Fresh basil leaves	16	16
White Wine Marinade (Recipe 17.1)	1 pt.	450 g
Salt and pepper	TT	TT
Basil butter	6 oz.	170 g

1. Remove the backbone and breast bone from each squab. The birds will lie flat and remain in one piece.
2. Make a slit below each leg and tuck the leg bone into the slit.
3. Carefully slide two basil leaves under the skin over each breast to cover the meat.
4. Marinate the squab in the white wine marinade for 1–2 hours.
5. Heat and prepare the grill.
6. Remove the squab from the marinade and pat dry.
7. Melt approximately 4 ounces (120 grams) of the basil butter, leaving enough for eight thin slices to be served with the finished dish.
8. Brush the squab with basil butter and place it skin side down on the grill. Grill the squab, turning once and basting periodically with the melted basil butter. Finish in the oven if necessary.
9. Serve the squab with a slice of basil butter melting over each breast.

1. Marinating the squab in white wine marinade.

2. Drying the squab.

3. Brushing the squab with the melted basil butter.

4. Grilling the squab.

5. Serving the squab with a slice of basil butter.

Roasting

Properly roasted (or baked) poultry is attractively browned on the surface and tender and juicy throughout. Proper cooking temperatures ensure a crisp exterior and juicy interior. Most roasted poultry is cooked until its juices run clear. Squab and duck breasts are an exception: They are often served medium rare or pink.

Selecting Poultry to Roast

Almost every kind of poultry is suitable for roasting, but younger birds produce a more tender finished product. Because of variations in fat content, different kinds of poultry require different roasting temperatures and procedures.

PROCEDURE FOR TRUSSING POULTRY

Trussing is tying a bird into a more compact shape with thread or butcher's twine. This allows the bird to cook more evenly, helps the bird retain moisture and improves the appearance of the finished product. There are many methods for trussing poultry, some of which require a special tool called a trussing needle. Here we show a simple method using butcher's twine.

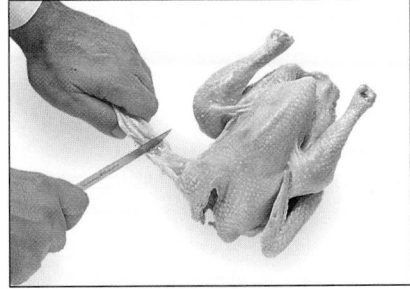

1. Square up the bird by pressing it firmly with both hands. Tuck the first joint of the wing behind the back or trim off the first and second joints as shown.

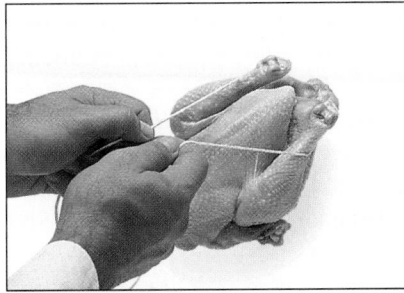

2. Cut a piece of butcher's twine approximately three times the bird's length. With the breast up and the neck toward you, pass the twine under the bird approximately one inch (2.5 centimeters) in front of the tail.

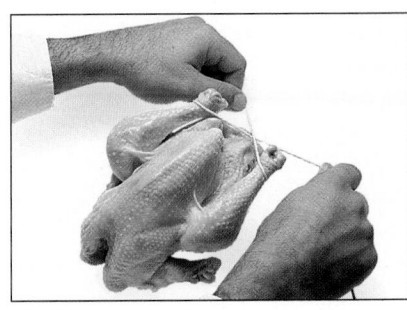

3. Bring the twine up around the legs and cross the ends, creating an X between the legs. Pass the ends of the twine below the legs.

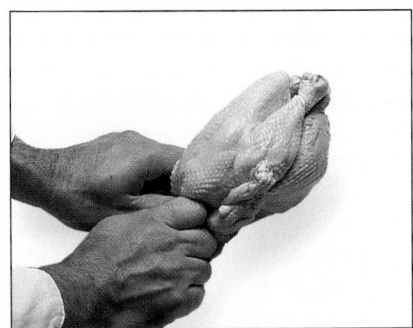

4. Pull the ends of the twine tightly across the leg and thigh joint and across the wing if the first and second joint were trimmed off or just above the wings if they are intact.

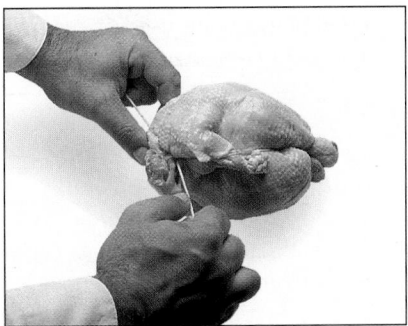

5. Pull the string tight and tie it securely just above the neck.

6. Two examples of properly trussed birds: one with the wings intact and one with the first and second wing joints removed.

Cooking Temperatures

Small birds such as squab and Cornish game hens should be roasted at the relatively high temperatures of 375–400°F (190–200°C). These temperatures help produce crisp, well-colored skins without overcooking the flesh. Chickens are best roasted at temperatures between 350 and 375°F (180–190°C). This temperature range allows the skin to crisp and the flesh to cook without causing the bird to stew in its own juices. Large birds such as capons and turkeys are started at high temperatures of 400–425°F (200–220°C) to brown the skin, then finished at lower temperatures of 275–325°F (135–160°C) to promote even cooking and produce a moister product. Ducks and geese, which are very high in fat, must be roasted at the high temperatures of 375–425°F (190–220°C) to render as much fat from the skin as possible. Duck and goose skin is often pricked before roasting so the rendered fat can escape, helping to create crispy skin.

Seasoning Poultry to be Roasted

Although the mild flavor of most poultry is enhanced by a wide variety of herbs and spices, roasted poultry is often only lightly seasoned with salt and pepper. Poultry that is roasted at high temperatures should never be seasoned with herbs on its surface because the high cooking temperatures will burn them. If herbs or additional spices are used they should be stuffed into the cavity. A mirepoix or a bouquet garni may also be added to the cavity for additional flavor. The cavities of dark-meated birds such as ducks and geese are often stuffed with fresh or dried fruits.

Barding Poultry to be Roasted

Guineas, squabs or any skinless birds without an adequate fat covering to protect them from drying out during roasting can be barded. Bard the bird by covering its entire surface with thin slices of fatback, securing them with butcher's twine. See page 266.

Basting Roasted Poultry

With the exception of fatty birds such as ducks and geese, all poultry items should be basted while they roast to help retain moisture. To baste a bird, spoon or ladle the fat that collects in the bottom of the roasting pan over the bird at 15-to-20-minute intervals. Lean birds that are not barded will not produce enough fat for basting and may be brushed with butter in the same manner.

Determining Doneness

Four methods are used to determine the doneness of roasted poultry. It is best to use a combination of these methods.

1. *Temperature*—Test the internal temperature of the bird with an instant-read thermometer. The thermometer should be inserted in the bird's thigh, which is the last part to become fully cooked. It should not touch the bone and should read 165–170°F (74–77°C) at the coolest point. This method works best with large birds such as capons and turkeys. Large birds are subject to some degree of carryover cooking. This is not as much of a concern with poultry as it is with meat because large birds are always cooked well done.

2. *Looseness of the joints*—The thigh and leg will begin to move freely in their sockets when the bird is done.

3. *Color of juices*—This method is used with birds that are not stuffed. Use a kitchen fork to tilt the bird, allowing some of the juices that have collected

TABLE 17.8   ROASTING TEMPERATURES AND TIMES

Poultry Kind or Class	Cooking Temperatures		Minutes
Capons	350–375°F	180–190°C	18–20 min. per lb.
Chickens	375–400°F	190–200°C	15–18 min. per lb.
Ducks and geese	375–425°F	190–220°C	12–15 min. per lb.
Game hens	375–400°F	190–200°C	45–60 min. total
Guineas	375–400°F	190–200°C	18–20 min. per lb.
Squab	400°F	200°C	30–40 min. total
Turkeys (large)	325°F	160°C	12–15 min. per lb.

in the cavity to run out. Clear juices indicate that the bird is done. If the juices are cloudy or pink, the bird is undercooked.

4. *Time*—Because there are so many variables, timing alone is less reliable than other methods. It is useful, however, for planning production when large quantities are roasted and as a general guideline when used with other methods. Table 17.8 gives some general timing guidelines for roasting several kinds of poultry.

Accompaniments to Roasted Poultry

The most common accompaniments to roasted poultry are bread stuffing and gravy. Large birds, such as capons and turkeys, produce adequate drippings for making sauce or pan gravy. Small birds, such as squab and Cornish game hens, are often stuffed with wild rice or other ingredients and served with a sauce that is made separately.

Ducks and geese are complemented by stuffings containing rice, fruits, berries and nuts. They are very fatty and if stuffed, they should be roasted on a rack or mirepoix bed to ensure that the fat that collects in the pan during roasting does not penetrate the cavity, making the stuffing greasy. Ducks and geese are often served with a citrus- or fruit-based sauce. Its high acid content complements these rich, fatty birds.

PROCEDURE FOR STUFFING POULTRY

Small birds such as Cornish game hens, small chickens and squab can be stuffed successfully. Stuffing larger birds, especially for volume production, is impractical and can be dangerous for the following reasons:

1. Stuffing is a good bacterial breeding ground and because it is difficult to control temperatures inside a stuffed bird, there is a risk of food-borne illness.
2. Stuffing poultry is labor intensive.
3. Stuffed poultry must be cooked longer to cook the stuffing properly; this may cause the meat to be overcooked, becoming dry and tough.

When stuffing any bird, use the following guidelines.

1. Always be aware of temperatures when mixing the raw ingredients. All ingredients should be cold when they are mixed together, and the mixture's temperature should never be allowed to rise above 45°F (7°C).
2. Stuff the bird as close to roasting time as possible.

3. The neck and main body cavities should be loosely stuffed. The stuffing will expand during cooking.

4. After the cavities are filled, their openings should be secured with skewers and butcher's twine or by trussing.

5. After cooking, remove the stuffing from the bird and store separately.

PROCEDURE FOR ROASTING POULTRY

1. Season, bard, stuff and/or truss the bird as desired.

2. Place the bird in a roasting pan. It may be placed on a rack or mirepoix bed to prevent scorching and promote even cooking.

3. Roast uncovered, basting every 15 minutes.

4. Allow the bird to rest before carving to allow even distribution of juices. As the bird rests, prepare the pan gravy or sauce.

◆◆◆

RECIPE 17.3

ROAST TURKEY
WITH CHESTNUT DRESSING
AND GIBLET GRAVY

Yield: 16 portions—4 oz. (120 g) turkey,
3 oz. (90 g) dressing, 4 oz. (120 ml) gravy.

Young turkey, 12–15 lb. (5.5–6.5 kg) with giblets	1	1
Salt and pepper	TT	TT
Mirepoix	20 oz.	600 g
Onion, small dice	8 oz.	225 g
Celery, small dice	6 oz.	180 g
Whole butter	4 oz.	120 g
Dried bread cubes	2 lb.	1 kg
Eggs, beaten	2	2
Fresh parsley, chopped	1 Tbsp.	15 ml
Chicken stock	2-1/4 qt.	2 lt
Chestnuts, cooked and peeled, chopped coarse	8 oz.	225 g
All-purpose flour	3 oz.	90 g

1. Placing the turkey in the roasting pan.

2. Adding the mirepoix to the roasting pan.

1. Remove the giblets from the turkey's cavity and set aside. Season the turkey inside and out with salt and pepper. Truss the turkey.

2. Place the turkey in a roasting pan. Roast at 400°F (200°C) for 30 minutes. Reduce the temperature to 325°F (160°C) and continue cooking the turkey to an internal temperature of 160°F (71°C), approximately 2-1/2 to 3 hours. Baste the turkey often during cooking. Approximately 45 minutes before the turkey is done, add the mirepoix to the roasting pan. If the turkey begins to overbrown, cover it loosely with aluminum foil.

3. To make the dressing, sauté the diced onion and celery in the butter until tender.

4. In a large bowl, toss together the bread cubes, salt, pepper, eggs, parsley,

sautéed onions and celery, 4 ounces (120 grams) of chicken stock and the chestnuts.

5. Place the dressing in a buttered hotel pan and cover with aluminum foil or buttered parchment paper. Bake at 350°F (180°C) until done, approximately 45 minutes.

6. As the turkey roasts, simmer the giblets (neck, heart and gizzard) in 1 quart (1 liter) of the chicken stock until tender, approximately 1-1/2 hours.

7. When the turkey is done, remove it from the roasting pan and set aside to rest. Degrease the roasting pan, reserving 3 ounces (90 grams) of the fat to make a roux.

8. Place the roasting pan on the stove top and brown the mirepoix.

9. Deglaze the pan with a small amount of chicken stock. Transfer the mirepoix and stock to a saucepot and add the remaining stock and the broth from the giblets. Bring to a simmer and degrease.

10. Make a blond roux with the reserved fat and the flour. Add the roux to the liquid, whisking well to prevent lumps. Simmer 15 minutes. Strain the gravy through a china cap lined with cheesecloth.

11. Remove the meat from the turkey neck. Trim the gizzard. Finely chop the neck meat, heart and gizzard and add to the gravy. Adjust the seasonings.

12. Carve the turkey and serve with a portion of chestnut dressing and giblet gravy.

3. Tossing the dressing ingredients together.

4. Browning the mirepoix.

5. Deglazing the roasting pan.

6. Transferring the mirepoix and stock to a saucepot.

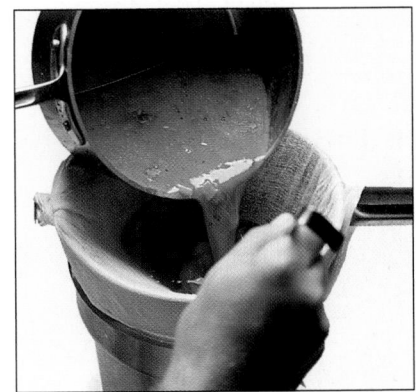

7. Straining the gravy through a china cap and cheesecloth.

Carving Roasted Poultry

Poultry can be carved in the kitchen, at tableside or on a buffet in a variety of manners. The carving methods described below produce slices of both light and dark meat.

PROCEDURE FOR CARVING A TURKEY, CAPON OR OTHER LARGE BIRD

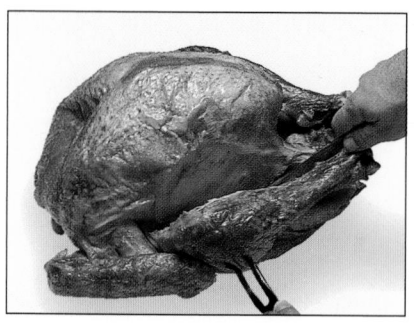

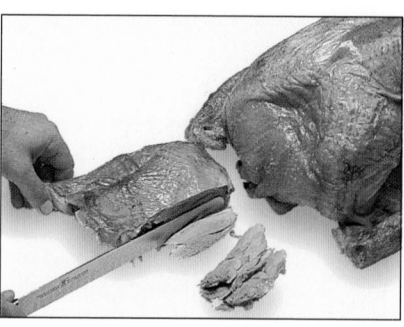

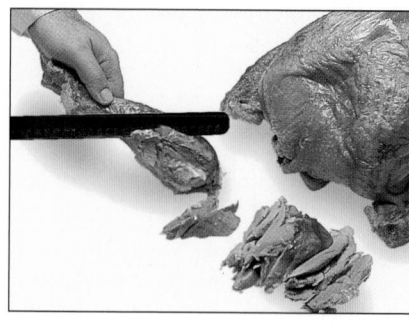

1. After roasting, allow the turkey to stand for 20 minutes so the juices can redistribute themselves. Holding the turkey firmly with a carving fork, pry a leg outward and locate the joint. Remove the leg and thigh in one piece by cutting through the joint with the tip of a knife.

2. Repeat the procedure on the other side. Once both legs and thighs have been removed, slice the meat from the thigh by holding the leg firmly with one hand and slicing parallel to the bone.

3. Separate the thigh from the leg bone by cutting through the joint. Slice the meat from the leg by cutting parallel to the bone.

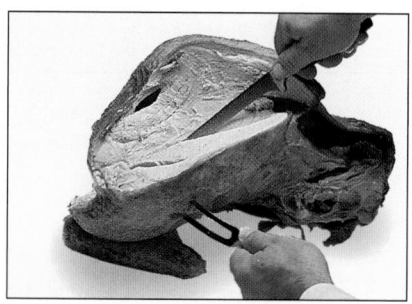

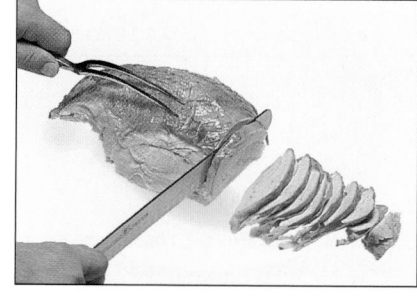

4. Cut along the backbone, following the natural curvature of the bones separating the breast meat from the ribs.

5. Remove an entire half breast and slice it on the cutting board as shown. Cut on an angle to produce larger slices.

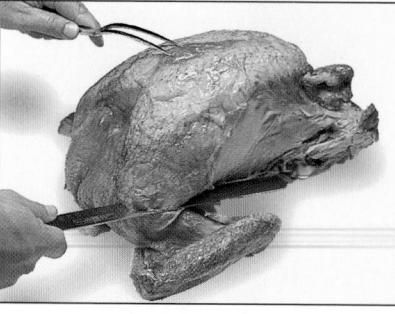

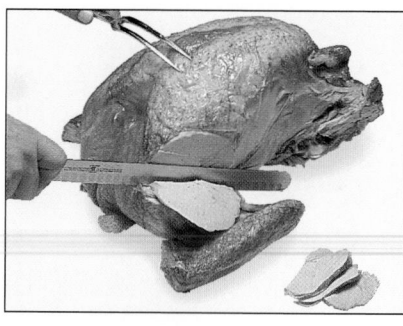

6. Alternatively, the breast can be carved on the bird. Make a horizontal cut just above the wing in toward the rib bones.

7. Slice the breast meat as shown.

PROCEDURE FOR CARVING A CHICKEN OR OTHER SMALL BIRD

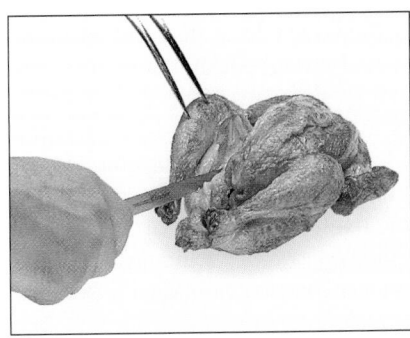

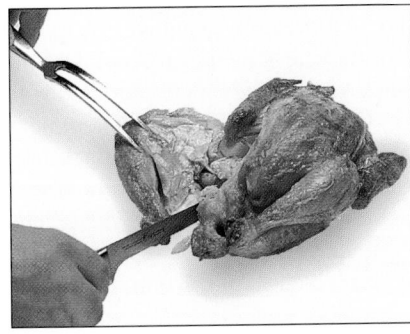

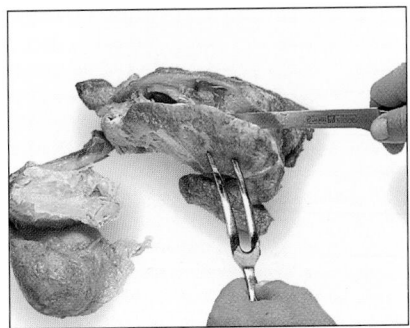

1. After allowing the chicken to rest for 15 minutes so the juices can redistribute themselves, cut through the skin between the leg and breast.

2. Use a kitchen fork to pry the leg and thigh away from the breast. Locate the thigh's ball joint and cut through it with the knife tip, separating it completely from the rest of the chicken. Be sure to cut around the delicate oyster meat, leaving it attached to the thigh.

3. With the knife tip, cut through the skin and meat on one side of the breast bone. Cut and pull the meat away from the bones with the knife.

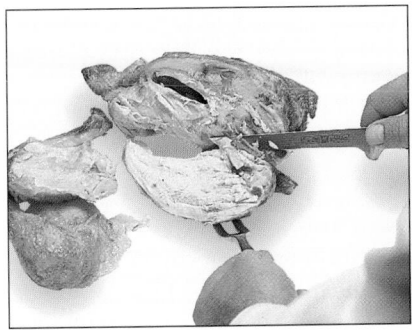

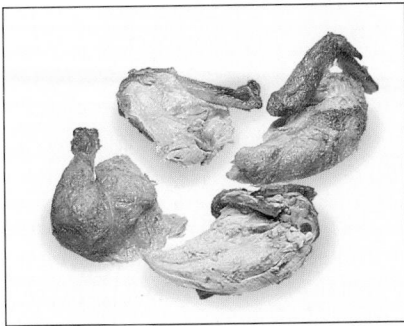

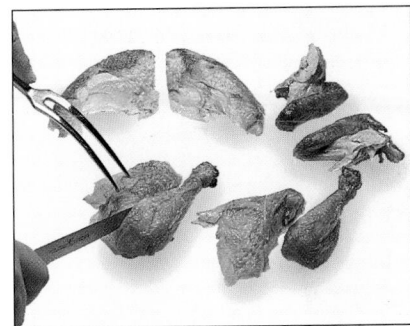

4. Cut through the wing joint, separating the breast and wing from the carcass. Repeat this procedure on the other side of the bird.

5. The chicken is now quartered.

6. To cut it into eight pieces, separate the wings from the breasts and the thighs from the legs.

Sautéing

Sautéed poultry should be tender and juicy, its flavor developed by proper browning. Additional flavors come from a sauce made by deglazing the pan, usually with wine, and adding garnishes, seasonings and liquids. Stir-frying is a popular method of sautéing poultry; boneless pieces are cut into strips and quickly cooked with assorted vegetables and seasonings.

Selecting Poultry to Sauté

Most poultry is quite tender and well suited for sautéing. Although small birds such as squab can be sautéed bone-in, large pieces and bone-in cuts from larger birds should not be sautéed. Boneless breasts, suprêmes, scallops and cutlets are the most common and practical cuts for sautéing. Because they are high in fat, boneless duck breasts (called *magrets*) can be sautéed without additional fat.

Cooking Temperatures

The sauté pan and the cooking fat must be hot before the poultry is added. The temperature at which the poultry is then sautéed is determined by its thickness and the desired color of the finished product. A thin, boneless slice requires relatively high temperatures so that its surface is browned before the center is overcooked. A thicker cut such as a suprême requires lower temperatures so that neither its surface nor the fond are burned before the item is fully cooked. Adjust the temperature throughout the cooking process to achieve the desired results, never letting the pan become too cool.

If the pan is overcrowded or otherwise allowed to cool, the poultry will cook in its own juices and absorb oil from the pan, resulting in a poor-quality product.

Seasoning Poultry to be Sautéed

Poultry has a delicate flavor that is enhanced by a wide variety of herbs, spices, condiments and marinades. Flavor combinations are limited only by your imagination. When poultry items are dusted with flour before sautéing, the seasonings may first be added to the flour.

Determining Doneness

Thin cuts of poultry cook very quickly, so timing is a useful tool; it is less useful with thicker cuts. Experienced cooks can tell the doneness of an item by judging the temperature of the sauté pan and the color of the item being cooked.

A more practical method is to press the item with your finger and judge the resistance. Very undercooked poultry will offer little resistance and feel mushy. Slightly underdone poultry will feel spongy and will not spring back when your finger is removed. Properly cooked poultry will feel firm to the touch and will spring back when your finger is removed. Overcooked poultry will feel very firm, almost hard, and will spring back quickly when your finger is removed.

Accompaniments to Sautéed Poultry

Sautéed poultry is usually served with a sauce made directly in the pan in which the item was cooked. The sauce uses the fond for added flavor. A wide variety of ingredients, including garlic, onions, shallots, mushrooms and tomatoes, are commonly added to the pan as well as wine and stock. Table 10.5 suggests several sauces for sautéed poultry.

Sautéed items are often served with a starch such as pasta, rice or potatoes.

PROCEDURE FOR SAUTÉING POULTRY

1. Heat a sauté pan and add enough fat or oil to just cover the bottom.
2. Add the poultry item, presentation side down, and cook until browned.
3. Turn the item, using tongs or by tossing the item back upon itself using the pan's sloped sides.
4. Larger items can be finished in an oven. Either place the sauté pan in the oven or transfer the poultry to another pan. The latter procedure allows a sauce to be made in the original pan as the poultry cooks in the oven. Hold smaller pieces that are thoroughly cooked in a warm place so that the pan can be used for making the sauce.

PROCEDURE FOR MAKING SAUCE IN THE SAUTÉ PAN

1. Pour off any excess fat or oil from the sauté pan, leaving enough to sauté the sauce ingredients.
2. Add ingredients such as garlic, shallots and mushrooms that will be used as garnishes and sauce flavorings; sauté them.

3. Deglaze the pan with wine, stock or other liquids. Scrape the pan, loosening the fond and allowing it to dissolve in the liquid. Reduce the liquid.

4. Add any ingredients that do not require long cooking times such as herbs and spices. Adjust the sauce's consistency and seasonings.

5. For service, the poultry can be returned to the pan for a moment to reheat and coat it with the sauce. The poultry should remain in the sauce just long enough to reheat. Do not attempt to cook the poultry in the sauce.

6. Serve the poultry with the accompanying sauce.

◆◆◆

RECIPE 17.4

CHICKEN SAUTÉ WITH ONIONS, GARLIC AND BASIL

Yield: 6 Servings

Chicken breasts, boneless, skinless, approx. 8 oz. (250 g) each	3	3
Salt and pepper	TT	TT
Flour	as needed	as needed
Clarified butter	1 oz.	30 g
Onion, small dice	2 oz.	60 g
Garlic cloves, chopped	6	6
Dry white wine	4 oz.	120 g
Lemon juice	1 Tbsp.	15 ml
Tomato concasse	6 oz.	180 g
Chicken stock	4 oz.	120 g
Fresh basil leaves, chiffonade	6	6

1. Sautéing the breasts in butter.

2. The fond left in the pan after sautéing the chicken.

3. Sautéing the onions and garlic.

1. Split the chicken breasts and remove the cartilage connecting the two halves.

2. Season the chicken with salt and pepper; dredge in flour.

3. Sauté the breasts in the butter, browning them and cooking *a point.* Hold in a warm place.

4. Add the onions and garlic to the fond and butter in the pan; sauté until the onions are translucent.

5. Deglaze the pan with the white wine and lemon juice.

6. Add the tomato concasse and chicken stock. Sauté to combine the flavors; reduce the sauce to the desired consistency.

7. Add the basil to the sauce and return the chicken breasts for reheating. Adjust the seasonings and serve 1/2 breast per portion with a portion of the sauce.

4. Deglazing the pan with white wine and lemon juice.

5. Adding the tomatoes and chicken stock and sautéing to combine the flavors.

6. Returning the chicken to the pan to reheat.

Pan-Frying

Pan-fried poultry should be juicy. Its coating or batter should be crispy, golden brown, not excessively oily and free from any breaks that allow fat to penetrate. Both the poultry and the coating should be well seasoned.

Selecting Poultry to Pan-Fry

The most common pan-fried poultry is fried chicken. Young tender birds cut into small pieces produce the best results. Other cuts commonly pan-fried are boneless portions such as chicken breasts and turkey scallops.

Cooking Temperatures

The fat should always be hot before the poultry is added. The temperature at which it is cooked is determined by the length of time required to cook it thoroughly. Pan-frying generally requires slightly lower temperatures than those used for sautéing. Within this range, thinner items require higher temperatures to produce good color in a relatively short time. Thicker items and those containing bones require lower cooking temperatures and longer cooking times.

Seasoning Poultry to be Pan-Fried

Pan-fried poultry is usually floured, breaded or battered before cooking. (Breadings and batters are discussed in Chapter 21, Deep-Frying). Typically, the seasonings are added to the flour, breading or batter before the poultry item is coated. Seasonings can be a blend of any number of dried herbs and spices. But often only salt and pepper are required because the poultry will be served with a sauce or other accompaniments for additional flavors.

Determining Doneness

Even the largest pan-fried items may be too small to be accurately tested with an instant-read thermometer, and using the touch method can be difficult and dangerous because of the amount of fat used in pan-frying. So, timing and experience are the best tools to determine doneness. Thin scallops cook very quickly, so it is relatively easy to judge their doneness. On the other hand, fried chicken can take as long as 30–45 minutes to cook, requiring skill and experience to determine doneness.

Accompaniments to Pan-Fried Poultry

Because pan-frying does not produce fond or drippings that can be used to make a sauce, pan-fried poultry is usually served with lemon wedges, a vegetable garnish or a separately made sauce. Fried chicken is an exception; it is sometimes served with a country gravy made by degreasing the pan, making a roux with a portion of the fat and adding milk and seasonings.

PROCEDURE FOR PAN-FRYING POULTRY

1. Heat enough fat in a heavy sauté pan to cover the item to be cooked one quarter to halfway up its side. The fat should be at approximately 325°F (160°C).
2. Add the floured, breaded or battered item to the hot fat, being careful not to splash. The fat must be hot enough to sizzle and bubble when the item is added.
3. Turn the item when the first side is the proper color; it should be half cooked at this point. Larger items may need to be turned more than once to brown them properly on all sides.
4. Remove the browned poultry from the pan and drain it on absorbent paper.

◆◆◆

RECIPE 17.5
PAN-FRIED CHICKEN WITH PAN GRAVY

Yield: 8 2-piece Servings

Frying chickens, 2 lb. 8 oz.–3 lb. each (1.1–1.4 kg), cut in 8 pieces	2	2
Salt and pepper	TT	TT
Garlic powder	2 tsp.	10 ml
Onion powder	2 tsp.	10 ml
Dried oregano	1 tsp.	5 ml
Dried basil	1 tsp.	5 ml
Flour	9-1/2 oz.	270 g
Buttermilk	8 oz.	250 g
Oil	as needed	as needed
Onion, small dice	4 oz.	120 g
Half-and-half or chicken stock	1-1/2 pt.	750 ml

1. Season the chicken with salt and pepper.
2. Add the herbs and spices to 8 ounces (250 grams) of the flour.
3. Dip the chicken pieces in the buttermilk.
4. Dredge the chicken in the seasoned flour.
5. Pan-fry the chicken in 1/4 to 1/3 inch (1 centimeter) oil until done, approximately 40 minutes, turning so it cooks evenly. Reduce the heat as necessary to prevent the chicken from becoming too dark. Or remove the chicken when well browned, drain it and finish cooking it in the oven.
6. To make the pan gravy, pour off all but 1-1/2 ounces (45 grams) of oil from the pan, carefully reserving the fond.
7. Add the diced onions and sauté until translucent.
8. Add 1-1/2 ounces (45 grams) of flour and cook to make a blond roux.
9. Whisk in the liquid and simmer approximately 15 minutes.
10. Strain through cheesecloth and adjust the seasonings.
11. Serve 1/4 chicken (2 pieces) per person with 4 ounces (120 milliliters) gravy.

1. Dipping the chicken pieces in the buttermilk.

2. Dredging the chicken in the flour mixture.

3. Adding the chicken to the oil. The bubbling fat indicates the proper cooking temperature.

4. Turning the chicken so it cooks evenly.

5. Sautéing the diced onions until translucent.

6. Adding the liquid to the roux.

Moist-Heat Cooking Methods

The moist-heat cooking methods most often used with poultry are poaching and simmering. Poaching is used to cook tender birds for short periods of time. Simmering is used to cook older, tougher birds for longer periods to tenderize them. Poaching and simmering are similar procedures, the principal differences being the temperature of the cooking liquid and the length of cooking time.

Poaching and Simmering

Poached or simmered poultry should be moist, tender and delicately flavored. Although cooked in water, overcooking will cause the poultry to be dry and tough. During cooking, some of the poultry's flavor is transferred to the cooking liquid, which can be used to make a sauce for the finished product.

Selecting Poultry to Poach or Simmer

Young birds are best suited for poaching; boneless chicken pieces are the most commonly used parts. Older, tougher birds are usually simmered. Duck and geese are rarely poached or simmered because of their high fat content.

Cooking Temperatures

For best results, poultry should be poached at low temperatures, between 160° and 175°F (70–80°C). Cooking poultry to the proper doneness at these temperatures produces a product that is moist and tender.

Simmering is done at slightly higher temperatures, between 185°F (85°C) and the boiling point. When simmering, do not allow the liquid to boil, as this may result in a dry, tough and stringy finished product.

Seasoning Poultry to be Poached or Simmered

When poaching poultry it is especially important to use a well-seasoned and highly flavored liquid in order to infuse as much flavor as possible into the item being cooked. Either strong stock with a sachet or a mixture of stock or water and white wine with a bouquet garni or onion piquet produces good results. The poultry should be completely covered with liquid so that it cooks evenly. However, if too much liquid is used and it is not strongly flavored, flavors may be leached out of the poultry, resulting in a bland finished product.

Poultry is often simmered in water instead of stock. A sachet and a generous mirepoix should be added to help flavor it. Typically, simmering birds results in a strong broth that may be used to complete the recipe or reserved for other uses.

Determining Doneness

Poached poultry, whether whole or boneless, is cooked just until done. An instant-read thermometer inserted in the thigh or thicker part of the bird should read 165°F (74°C). Any juices that run from the bird should be clear or show only a trace of pink.

Simmered poultry is usually cooked for longer periods to allow the moist heat to tenderize the meat. A chicken that weighs 3 pounds 8 ounces (1.5 kilograms), for example, may take 2-1/2 hours to cook.

Accompaniments to Poached and Simmered Poultry

Poached or simmered poultry can be served hot or cold. The meat from these birds can be served cold in salads, hot in casseroles or used in any dish that calls for cooked poultry.

Poached items are typically served with a flavored mayonnaise or a sauce made from the reduced poaching liquid, such as sauce suprême. Poultry is also often poached as a means of producing a low-calorie dish. If so, a vegetable coulis makes a good sauce or the poultry can be served with a portion of its cooking liquid and a vegetable garnish.

Simmered poultry to be served cold will be moister and more flavorful if it is cooled in its cooking liquid. To do so, remove the pot containing the bird and the cooking liquid from the heat when the bird is still slightly undercooked. Cool the meat and broth in a water bath following the procedures in Chapter 10, Stocks and Sauces. Once cooled, remove the meat and wipe off any congealed broth before proceeding with the recipe.

PROCEDURE FOR POACHING OR SIMMERING POULTRY

1. Cut or truss the item to be cooked as directed in the recipe.
2. Prepare the cooking liquid and bring it to a simmer. Submerge the poultry in the cooking liquid, or arrange the items to be poached in an appropriate pan and add the poaching liquid to the pan.
3. Poach or simmer the item to the desired doneness in the oven or on the stove top. Maintain the proper cooking temperature throughout the process.
4. Remove the item and hold it for service in a portion of the cooking liquid or, using an ice bath, cool the item in its cooking liquid.
5. The cooking liquid may be used to prepare an accompanying sauce or reserved for use in other dishes.

◆◆◆

RECIPE 17.6

POACHED BREAST OF CHICKEN WITH TARRAGON SAUCE

Yield: 8 Servings

Chicken breasts, boneless, skinless, approx. 8 oz. (250 g) each	4	4
Whole butter	1-1/2 oz.	45 g
Salt and white pepper	TT	TT
White wine	4 oz.	120 g
Chicken stock	1 pt.	450 ml
Bay leaf	1	1
Dried thyme	1/4 tsp.	1 ml
Dried tarragon	1 tsp.	5 ml
Flour	1 oz.	30 g
Heavy cream	4 oz.	120 g
Fresh tarragon sprigs	as needed	as needed

1. Trim any rib meat and fat from the breasts. Cut the breasts into two pieces, removing the strip of cartilage that joins the halves.
2. Select a pan that will just hold the breasts when they are placed close together. Rub the pan with approximately 1/2 ounce (15 grams) of butter.

Continued

3. Season the chicken breasts with salt and pepper and arrange them in the buttered pan, presentation side up.

4. Add the white wine, stock, bay leaf, thyme and dried tarragon.

5. Cut and butter a piece of parchment paper and cover the chicken breasts.

6. Bring the liquid to a simmer and reduce the temperature to poach the chicken.

7. Make a blond roux with 1 ounce (30 grams) of butter and 1 ounce (30 grams) of flour; set aside to cool.

8. When the breasts are done, remove them from the liquid. Thicken the liquid with the roux. Add the cream. Simmer and reduce to the desired consistency.

9. Strain the sauce through cheesecloth and adjust the seasonings.

10. Serve each half breast napped with approximately 2 fluid ounces (60 milliliters) of sauce; garnish each portion with a sprig of fresh tarragon.

1. Arranging the breasts in an appropriate pan.

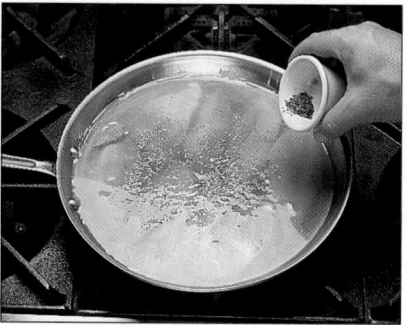

2. Adding the white wine, chicken stock and seasonings to the pan.

3. Covering the breasts with a piece of buttered parchment paper.

4. Adding the cream to the thickened sauce.

5. Plating the poached chicken breast.

Combination Cooking Methods

Braising and stewing use both dry and moist heat to produce a moist, flavorful product. The principal difference between braising and stewing when applied to meats is the size of the cut being cooked: Large cuts of meat are braised; smaller ones are stewed. Because most poultry is relatively small, this distinction does not readily apply in poultry cookery; therefore, the two cooking methods are discussed together here.

Braising and Stewing

Braised or stewed poultry should be moist and fork tender. The poultry is always served with the liquid in which it was cooked. Ducks and geese are braised or stewed in much the same way as red meats. Chicken cacciatore, coq au vin and chicken fricassee are examples of braised or stewed chicken dishes.

Selecting Poultry to Braise or Stew

Braising and stewing, being slow, moist cooking processes, are often thought of as means to tenderize tough meats. Although they can be used to tenderize older, tougher birds, these cooking methods are more often selected as a means to add moisture and flavor to poultry that is inherently tender, such as young ducks and chickens. Typically, the birds are disjointed and cooked bone-in, just until done, so that they retain their juiciness.

Cooking Temperatures

Some recipes, such as chicken cacciatore and coq au vin, require the main item to be thoroughly browned during the initial stages; others, such as chicken fricassee, do not. In either case, after the addition of the liquid it is important to maintain a slow simmer rather than a rapid boil. This can be done on the stove top or in the oven. Low temperatures control the cooking and produce a tender, juicy finished product.

Seasoning Poultry to be Braised or Stewed

Braised or stewed items obtain much of their flavor from the cooking liquid and other ingredients added during the cooking process. The main item and the cooking liquid should be well seasoned. If other seasonings such as an onion piquet, sachet, bouquet garni or dried herbs and spices are required, they should be added at the beginning of the cooking process rather than at the end. This allows the flavors to blend and penetrate the larger pieces of poultry. If the poultry is dredged in flour prior to browning, seasonings may be added directly to the flour. As with all dishes using combination cooking methods, the finished dish should have the flavor of the poultry in the sauce and the moisture and flavor of the sauce in the poultry.

Determining Doneness

Tenderness is the key to determining doneness. It can be determined by inserting a kitchen fork into the poultry. There should be little resistance and the poultry should freely fall off the fork. The pieces should retain their shape, however; if they fall apart they are overdone. Small boneless pieces can be tested by cutting into them with a fork.

Accompaniments to Braised or Stewed Poultry

All braises and stews are cooked in a liquid that results in a sauce or broth served as part of the finished dish. Rice, pasta or boiled potatoes are natural accompaniments to almost any braised or stewed dish, as are boiled vegetables.

PROCEDURE FOR BRAISING OR STEWING POULTRY

1. Sear the main item in butter or oil, developing color as desired.
2. Add vegetables and other ingredients as called for in the recipe and sauté.
3. Add flour or roux if used.
4. Add the appropriate liquid.

5. Cover and simmer on the stove top or in the oven until done.
6. Add seasonings and garnishes at the appropriate times during the cooking process.
7. Finish the dish by adding cream or a liaison to the sauce or by adjusting its consistency. Adjust the seasonings.
8. Serve a portion of the main item with the sauce and appropriate garnish.

RECIPE 17.7

CHICKEN FRICASSEE

Yield: 8 2-piece Servings

Frying chickens, 2 lb. 8 oz.–3 lb. each (1.1–1.4 kg), cut into 8 pieces	2	2
Salt and white pepper	TT	TT
Clarified butter	3 oz.	90 g
Onion, medium dice	10 oz.	300 g
Flour	3 oz.	90 g
Dry white wine	8 oz.	250 g
Chicken stock	1 qt.	1 lt
Sachet:		
Bay leaf	1	1
Dry thyme	1/2 tsp.	2 ml
Peppercorns, cracked	1/2 tsp.	2 ml
Parsley stems	8	8
Garlic clove, crushed	1	1
Heavy cream	8 oz.	250 g
Nutmeg	TT	TT

1. Season the chicken with salt and white pepper.
2. Sauté the chicken in the butter without browning. Add the onions and continue to sauté until they are translucent.
3. Sprinkle the flour over the chicken and onions and stir to make a roux. Cook the roux for two minutes without browning.
4. Deglaze the pan with white wine. Add the chicken stock and sachet; season with salt. Cover the pot and simmer until done, approximately 30–45 minutes.

1. Sautéing the chicken and onions in butter.

2. Sprinkling the flour over the chicken.

3. Deglazing the pan with white wine.

4. Removing the chicken from the pot.

5. Straining the sauce through cheesecloth.

6. Returning the chicken to the sauce to reheat it for service.

5. Remove the chicken from the pot and hold in a warm place. Strain the sauce through cheesecloth and return it to a clean pan.

6. Add the cream and bring the sauce to a simmer. Add the nutmeg and adjust the seasonings. Return the chicken to the sauce to reheat it for service.

CONCLUSION

The renowned French gastronome and author Jean-Anthelme Brillat-Savarin (1755–1826) once observed that "poultry is for the cook what canvas is for the painter." He meant, of course, that poultry, including chicken, duck, goose, guinea, pigeon and turkey, are wonderfully versatile foods that can be cooked by almost any method and with almost any seasonings, and can be served with many accompaniments and garnishes.

QUESTIONS FOR DISCUSSION

1. List the six categories or kinds of poultry recognized by the USDA. How are these categories then divided into classes?

2. How should fresh poultry be stored? Discuss several procedures that should be followed carefully when working with poultry to prevent cross-contamination.

3. What is a suprême? Describe the step-by-step procedure for preparing a chicken suprême.

4. What is trussing? Why is this technique used with poultry?

5. Which poultry items are best suited for broiling or grilling? Explain your answer.

6. Describe the characteristics of properly roasted poultry. Which classes of poultry are recommended for roasting?

7. What is foie gras? Why must you be extremely careful when cooking foie gras?

*A*DDITIONAL *P*OULTRY *R*ECIPES

RECIPE 17.8

*R*OAST *D*UCK WITH *R*ÖSTI *P*OTATOES

NOTE: *This dish appears in the Chapter Opening photograph.*

THE FOUR SEASONS, NEW YORK, NY
Chef Christian Albin

Yield: 4 Servings   **Method:** Roasting

Ducks, 4-1/2 lb. (2 kg) each	2	2
Marinade:		
Fresh ginger, peeled and sliced thin	1 oz.	30 g
Garlic cloves, unpeeled and halved	2	2
Orange zest, julienne	1/2 orange	1/2 orange
Coriander seeds, crushed	2 tsp.	10 ml
Black peppercorns	1 1/2 tsp.	8 ml
Soy sauce	8 oz.	250 g
Honey	2 Tbsp.	30 ml
Jasmine tea leaves, loose	4 Tbsp.	60 ml
Szechuan pepper	1 Tbsp.	15 ml
Sugared Orange Zest and Orange		
Sauce (recipe follows)	as needed	as needed

1. Cut the wings off the ducks at the second joint and reserve. Remove the fat from the ducks' cavities.

2. Place the ducks on a rack in the refrigerator, breast sides up, a few inches apart. Air must circulate around the ducks so that the skin will dry. Leave the birds for 3 days.

3. Combine all of the marinade ingredients and refrigerate for 3 days, stirring daily.

4. Prick the duck skin with a knife point, except for the skin on the breast. Avoid touching or pressing on the breasts, as this will leave dark spots after roasting.

5. Place the ducks on a rack over a shallow pan. Strain the marinade and brush it liberally over the entire surface of both ducks. Spoon the remaining marinade into the ducks' cavities.

6. Let the ducks dry, breast side up, on the rack for 15 minutes. Scrape any marinade drippings from the pan into the cavities.

7. Adjust the oven racks so that one is at the lowest level and the other is directly above the first.

8. Place 3 quarts (3 liters) water in a roasting pan and add the tea leaves. Place the pan on the lower rack of a 350°F (180°C) oven.

9. Position the ducks on the higher oven rack directly over the roasting pan (the ducks should not be touching). Roast undisturbed for 1-1/2 hours.

10. Remove the ducks from the oven. Drain and reserve the juices that have accumulated in the cavity.

11. Sprinkle the ducks with the Szechuan pepper; allow them to rest, then carve.

12. To serve, spoon a layer of Orange Sauce over the bottom of a warmed serving platter.

13. Arrange a pair of drumsticks, wing bones and thighs at each end of the platter. Place the breast in the center and garnish with orange segments. Sprinkle with the Sugared Orange Zest. Serve the duck with rösti potatoes (Recipe 23.13) and the remaining sauce on the side.

SUGARED ORANGE ZEST AND ORANGE SAUCE

Yield: 12 oz. (350 g)

Oranges	2	2
Sugar	3 oz.	90 g
Sugar	as needed	as needed
Grand Marnier	2 Tbsp.	30 ml
Currant jelly	2 Tbsp.	30 ml
Basic Duck Sauce, hot (recipe follows)	12 oz.	350 g
Lightly salted butter	2 Tbsp.	30 ml
Kosher salt and black pepper	TT	TT

1. Remove the zest from the oranges and julienne. Blanch for 3 minutes in boiling water; drain.

2. Squeeze the oranges and boil the juice until reduced by one quarter.

3. Place 3 ounces (90 grams) of sugar and 8 ounces (250 grams) of water in a saucepan and bring to a boil. Add the julienned zest. Boil until the syrup begins to caramelize, turning light brown.

4. Have a bowl ready with a layer of granulated sugar. Remove the zest from the syrup and toss in the sugar until the zest is completely coated. Set the zest aside to cool.

5. Continue cooking the syrup until it becomes a dark caramel syrup. Stir in the Grand Marnier, currant jelly and reduced orange juice. Whisk until smooth.

6. Pour in the Basic Duck Sauce and whisk until smooth. Cook for a few minutes to thicken slightly. Monte au beurre and season with salt and pepper.

BASIC DUCK SAUCE

Yield: 1-1/2 pt. (700 ml)

Vegetable oil	1 Tbsp.	15 ml
Necks and wing tips from 2 ducks		
Celery, chopped	3 oz.	90 g
Carrot, chopped	3 oz.	90 g
Onion, chopped	6 oz.	180 g
Bay leaf	1	1
Mushrooms, large, halved	3	3
Garlic cloves	4	4
Black pepper, crushed	1 Tbsp.	15 ml
Whole cloves	6	6
Tomato purée	2 Tbsp.	30 ml
Flour	2 Tbsp.	30 ml
Dry red wine	8 oz.	250 g
Brown veal stock	2 pt.	900 ml
Cavity juices reserved from 2 roasted ducks		

1. Heat the oven to 400°F (200°C).

2. Heat the oil in a large sauté pan. Add the duck pieces and sauté until they are well caramelized. Place the pan in the oven and roast the duck pieces for 25 minutes at 350°F (180°C), stirring occasionally.

Continued

3. Add the celery, carrot, onion, bay leaf, mushrooms, garlic, pepper and cloves. Roast for 5 minutes.

4. Place the sauté pan on the stove top and add the tomato purée. Sprinkle the flour over the mixture and stir.

5. Add the red wine and brown stock. Stir; bring to a boil. Reduce the heat and simmer for 3 hours.

6. Stir in the cavity juices and cook for 10 minutes more.

7. Strain the sauce through a china cap into a saucepan. Press a ladle against the solids to remove as much liquid as possible.

8. Degrease the sauce and reduce until thick.

◆◆◆

RECIPE 17.9
ROAST CORNISH GAME HEN WITH WILD RICE STUFFING

Yield: 6 Servings　　　　　　　　　　　　　　　**Method:** Roasting

Whole butter, melted	6 oz.	180 g
Onion, fine dice	3 oz.	90 g
Mushrooms, chopped	6 oz.	180 g
Wild rice, cooked	1-1/2 c.	350 ml
Dried thyme, crushed	1/2 tsp.	2 ml
Dried marjoram, crushed	1/2 tsp.	2 ml
Salt and pepper	TT	TT
Rock Cornish game hens	6	6

1. Sauté the onions and mushrooms in 2 ounces (60 grams) of melted butter until tender. Cool.

2. Stir in the rice and herbs and season to taste with salt and pepper.

3. Stuff the cavity of each hen loosely with the rice mixture. Truss and place in a roasting pan.

4. Brush the hens with the remaining butter and season with salt and pepper. Roast at 400°F (200°C) for 15 minutes.

5. Reduce the oven temperature to 300°F (150°C) and roast until the juices run clear, approximately 30 minutes. Baste two or three times with melted butter.

6. Serve the hens with a pan gravy or a sauce made separately such as mushroom sauce.

◆◆◆

RECIPE 17.10
COQ AU VIN

Yield: 8 2-piece Servings　　　　　　　　　　　　　**Method:** Braising

Chickens, 2 lb. 8 oz.–3 lb. (1–1.4 kg)	2	2
Flour for dredging	as needed	as needed
Salt and pepper	TT	TT
Clarified butter	2 oz.	60 g
Brandy	4 oz.	120 g
Bouquet garni:		
Carrot stick, 4 in. (10 cm)	1	1
Leek, split, 4-in. (10-cm) piece	1	1
Fresh thyme	1 sprig	1 sprig
Bay leaf	1	1
Garlic cloves, peeled and crushed	6	6
Red wine	24 oz.	700 g

Chicken stock	8 oz.	250 g
Bacon **lardons**	4 oz.	120 g
Pearl onions, peeled	18	18
Mushrooms, medium, quartered	10	10
Beurre manie	as needed	as needed
Large triangular croutons	8	8

Lardon—*bacon cut into 1/4 inch × 1/4 inch × 2 inch (6 mm × 6 mm × 5 cm) strips; used to moisten braised dishes and stews.*

1. Cut each chicken into 8 pieces and dredge in flour seasoned with salt and pepper.
2. Heat the clarified butter in a braising pan; brown the chicken.
3. Add the brandy and ignite. When the flame dies, add the bouquet garni, garlic, red wine and chicken stock. Bring to a boil, then reduce to a simmer.
4. Cover the pan and simmer until the chicken is tender, approximately 40 minutes.
5. In a separate pan, sauté the bacon until the fat begins to render. Add the onions and sauté until they begin to brown. Cook the bacon and onions covered, over low heat, until the onions are tender. Add the mushroom caps and cook them until tender.
6. Remove the chicken from the pan and adjust the sauce's consistency with the beurre manie. Strain the sauce through a china cap and adjust the seasonings.
7. Spoon the bacon, onions and mushrooms onto a serving platter, place the chicken over them and ladle the sauce over the finished dish. Serve with triangular croutons.

◆◆◆

RECIPE 17.11

CHICKEN CACCIATORE

Yield: 8 2-piece Servings　　　　　　　　**Method:** Braising

Frying chickens, 2 lb. 8 oz.–3 lb. each (1.1–1.4 kg)	2	2
Flour	2 oz.	60 g
Salt and pepper	TT	TT
Olive oil	2 oz.	60 g
Onion, medium dice	4 oz.	120 g
Garlic cloves, chopped	3	3
Mushrooms, sliced	8 oz.	250 g
Dried thyme	1/4 tsp.	1 ml
White wine	2 oz.	60 g
Brandy	1 oz.	30 g
Demi-glace	16 oz.	450 g
Tomato concasse	12 oz.	340 g

1. Cut each chicken into 8 pieces and dredge in flour seasoned with salt and pepper.
2. Heat the oil in a heavy braiser and brown the chicken well. Remove the chicken from the pan. Degrease the pan, leaving 1 tablespoon (15 milliliters) of fat.
3. Add the onions and garlic and sauté lightly. Add the mushrooms and thyme and continue sautéing until the mushrooms are tender.
4. Deglaze the pan with the white wine and brandy. Add the demi-glace and tomato concasse.
5. Return the chicken to the pan and season with salt and pepper. Cover and cook until the chicken is done, approximately 30 minutes.
6. Serve 2 pieces of chicken with a portion of sauce.

◆◆◆

RECIPE 17.12
CHICKEN WITH 40 CLOVES OF GARLIC

Yield: 4 2-piece Servings   Method: Braising

Chicken, 2 lb. 8 oz. (1.2 kg) cut in eight pieces	1	1
Dry white wine	26 oz.	750 g
Flour	as needed	as needed
Salt and pepper	TT	TT
Olive oil	2 Tbsp.	30 ml
Garlic cloves, unpeeled	40	40
Fresh thyme	4 sprigs	4 sprigs
Fresh rosemary	1 sprig	1 sprig
French bread croutons	8	8
Fresh parsley, chopped	as needed for garnish	

1. Marinate the chicken pieces in the white wine for 1–2 hours under refrigeration. Remove and pat dry.
2. Dredge the chicken in flour and season lightly with salt and pepper. Sauté the chicken in the olive oil.
3. Remove the chicken from the pan and sauté the garlic until it begins to brown. Place the chicken on top of the garlic in a single layer. Add the wine marinade and herbs and cover.
4. Braise in a 325°F (160°C) oven until tender, approximately 45 minutes.
5. Remove the chicken and garlic from the pan and reserve. Remove and discard the herbs. Place the pan on the stove top and reduce the wine until slightly thick. Season with salt and pepper.
6. Serve 2 pieces of chicken and several of the garlic cloves resting on 2 French bread croutons. Top with a portion of the sauce and garnish with chopped parsley.

Nutritional values for each 2-piece portion:

Calories	493	Protein	56 g
Calories from fat	46%	Vitamin A	2084 IU
Total fat	48 g	Vitamin C	16 mg
Saturated fat	13 g	Sodium	341 mg
Cholesterol	243 mg		

◆◆◆

RECIPE 17.13
GRILLED BREAST OF CHICKEN FLORENTINE
WITH BRUDER BASIL CHEESE
AND ROASTED GARLIC SAUCE

ANA WESTIN HOTEL, WASHINGTON, D.C.
Chef Leland Atkinson

Yield: 4 Servings   Method: Grilling

Marinade:

Extra virgin olive oil	4 oz.	120 g
Garlic, chopped	1 Tbsp.	15 ml
Fresh basil, chopped	1 Tbsp.	15 ml

Fresh oregano, chopped	1 Tbsp.	15 ml
Lemon juice	2 Tbsp.	30 ml
Salt and pepper	TT	TT
Airline chicken breast, skinless	8	8
Bruder basil cheese (smoked havarti)	8 slices	8 slices
Fresh spinach, cleaned	4 bunches	4 bunches
Unsalted butter	1 oz.	30 g
Roasted Garlic Sauce (recipe follows)	as needed	as needed
Roasted Garlic Garnish (recipe follows)	as needed	as needed
Tomato concasse	2 oz.	60 g

1. Combine the marinade ingredients, add the chicken and marinate for 1 hour.

2. Remove the chicken from the marinade, drain well and pat dry. Grill the chicken until done, approximately 5–6 minutes on each side.

3. Place one slice of cheese over each breast and allow it to melt. Remove the chicken from the grill.

4. Sauté the spinach in butter, season and drain thoroughly. Divide the spinach evenly among 4 warm plates, mounding it in the center.

5. Spoon the Roasted Garlic Sauce around the spinach. Place 2 breasts on top and garnish with the Roasted Garlic Garnish and tomato concasse.

ROASTED GARLIC SAUCE

Shallots, minced	4 Tbsp.	60 ml
Clarified butter	1 Tbsp.	15 ml
Madeira	4 oz.	120 g
Fresh thyme	1 sprig	1 sprig
Bay leaf	1	1
Garlic head, trimmed and roasted	1	1
Demi-glace	1 pt.	450 ml
Salt and pepper	TT	TT

1. Sauté the shallots lightly in the clarified butter until slightly caramelized.

2. Add the Madeira, thyme and bay leaf and reduce by one third.

3. Squeeze in the garlic, discarding the skins and root.

4. Add the demi-glace and reduce by one third.

5. Thicken slightly with roux if desired, adjust the seasonings and force through a fine strainer.

ROASTED GARLIC GARNISH

Garlic heads	4	4
Whole butter	2 oz.	60 g
Salt and pepper	TT	TT
Chicken stock	8 oz.	250 g
Fresh thyme	1/2 bunch	1/2 bunch

1. Remove the tops from the garlic and trim the bottoms. Place the garlic in a shallow buttered baking dish. Season with salt and pepper; place a dollop of butter on top of each.

2. Add the chicken stock to the pan until it reaches halfway up the garlic. Lay the thyme over the garlic, cover and bake at 350°F (180°C) until tender, approximately 30 minutes. Uncover during the last 5 minutes of cooking to allow the garlic to brown slightly.

◆◆◆

RECIPE 17.14

CHICKEN STUFFED WITH SPINACH AND RICOTTA CHEESE IN SAFFRON SAUCE

ANA WESTIN HOTEL, Washington, DC
Chef Leland Atkinson

Yield: 4 Servings		**Method**: Sautéing
Spinach, stemmed	1 lb.	450 g
Ricotta cheese	4 oz.	120 g
Egg whites, lightly beaten	2	2
Salt and pepper	TT	TT
Airline chicken breast		
skin on, 9 oz. (250 g) each	4	4
Clarified butter	2 Tbsp.	30 ml
White wine	1 pt.	450 ml
Saffron	1 pinch	1 pinch
Chicken velouté	8 oz.	250 g
Heavy cream, hot	2 oz.	60 g

1. Blanch, refresh and drain the spinach. Squeeze it tightly to remove as much moisture as possible, then chop it finely.
2. To make the stuffing, combine the cheese, egg whites and spinach in a mixing bowl; season to taste.
3. Place the chicken breasts on a cutting board, skin side down. Using a boning knife, carefully make a pocket that runs the length of each breast.
4. Put the stuffing in a pastry bag and pipe the stuffing into each pocket. Do not overfill the chicken breasts because the stuffing expands as it cooks.
5. Sauté the chicken in the clarified butter until well browned. Transfer the chicken to a sheet pan and finish in a 350°F (180°C) oven, approximately 10–12 minutes.
6. Deglaze the sauté pan with the white wine.
7. Add the saffron, bring to a boil and reduce by half.
8. Add the velouté and the cream. Adjust the seasonings and consistency; strain.
9. Ladle the sauce onto 4 warm plates. Slice and then arrange the chicken in the sauce; garnish as desired.

✦✦✦

RECIPE 17.15
ROMAN-STYLE FREE-RANGE CHICKEN

REX IL RISTORANTE, Los Angeles, CA
Executive Chef Odette Fada

Yield: 4 Servings   **Method:** Sautéing

Extra virgin olive oil	2 Tbsp.	30 ml
Free-range chicken breast halves, boneless	4	4
Salt	TT	TT
Vegetable or chicken broth	8 oz.	225 g
Garlic cloves, chopped fine	4	4
Anchovy fillets in oil, chopped fine	3	3
Fresh rosemary, chopped fine	TT	TT
White wine vinegar	2 Tbsp.	30 ml

1. Sauté the chicken breasts in the olive oil; skin side down. Season with salt.
2. Cook until the chicken begins to brown, then turn it and cook for an additional 2 minutes.
3. Add the broth and reduce by two-thirds, approximately 5 minutes.
4. Combine the garlic, anchovies, rosemary and vinegar.
5. When the chicken is done, add the vinegar mixture to the cooking liquid.
6. Remove the chicken from the heat, slice each breast in 6 pieces and arrange on a hot plate. Pour the sauce over the sliced chicken.

✦✦✦

RECIPE 17.16
SAUTÉED CHICKEN WITH KENTUCKY BOURBON

Method: Sautéing   **Yield:** 1 Serving

Chicken breast, boneless, skinless	1	1
Salt and pepper	TT	TT
Flour	as needed	as needed
Olive oil	as needed	as needed
Garlic, minced	1/2 tsp.	2 ml
Shallots, chopped	1 tsp.	5 ml
Spinach	1 oz.	30 g
Kentucky bourbon	1 Tbsp.	15 ml
Chicken stock	1 oz.	30 g
Heavy cream	2 oz.	60 g

1. Season the chicken breast with salt and pepper and dredge it in flour. Sauté in olive oil until done and remove from the pan.
2. Add the garlic and shallots to the pan and sauté until tender. Add the spinach and sauté until wilted.
3. Add the bourbon and flame. Then add the chicken stock and cream and reduce until slightly thickened.
4. Return the chicken to the sauce to reheat.
5. Pour the spinach and sauce on a plate and arrange the chicken on top.

RECIPE 17.17
CHICKEN STUFFED WITH SPINACH AND CRAB IN LOBSTER BEURRE BLANC

ANA WESTIN HOTEL, WASHINGTON, DC
Chef Leland Atkinson

Yield: 4 Servings   **Method:** Roasting

Spinach	1 bunch	1 bunch
Lump crabmeat	8 oz.	250 g
Heavy béchamel	3 oz.	90 g
Parmesan cheese	1 oz.	30 g
Fresh tarragon, chopped	2 tsp.	10 ml
Chives, chopped	1 tsp.	5 ml
Egg yolk	1	1
Salt and white pepper	TT	TT
Cayenne pepper	TT	TT
Chicken breasts, boneless, skin on 8 oz. (250 g) each	4	4
Unsalted butter	1 Tbsp.	15 ml
Lobster Beurre Blanc (recipe follows)	as needed	as needed

1. Lay the spinach leaves flat on a wire rack or perforated hotel pan. Steam them until they are just wilted, then chill.
2. Combine the crab, béchamel, cheese, herbs and egg yolk in a mixing bowl. Season to taste with salt, white pepper and cayenne pepper.
3. Lay the chicken breasts on a cutting board, skin side down, and remove the tenderloins. Cover the breasts with plastic wrap and lightly pound them with a mallet.
4. Lay the spinach over each chicken breast, one leaf thick, leaving 1/4 inch (6 millimeters) of meat uncovered around the edges.
5. Divide the crab mixture evenly among the breasts, placing it in a cylindrical mound down the center of each breast.
6. Roll each breast into a tight, fat cigar shape and place on a buttered sheet pan, seam side down.
7. Brush the tops with butter, season with salt and pepper and roast at 375°F (190°C) until they reach an internal temperature of 145°F (63°C), approximately 15–18 minutes.
8. At service time, pool the Lobster Beurre Blanc on each plate, slice the breasts and arrange on the sauce. Garnish as desired.

LOBSTER BEURRE BLANC

Shallots, peeled and sliced	2 Tbsp.	30 ml
Clarified butter	1 Tbsp.	15 ml
Fresh tarragon	1 sprig	1 sprig
Bay leaf	1	1
White wine	8 oz.	250 g
Lobster stock	1 pt.	450 ml
Champagne vinegar	1 Tbsp.	15 ml
Lemon juice	2 tsp.	10 ml
Ginger, peeled, chopped coarse	2 Tbsp.	30 ml
Heavy cream, hot	6 oz.	180 g
Unsalted butter	4 oz.	120 g
Salt and white pepper	TT	TT

1. Sauté the shallots in clarified butter until lightly caramelized.

2. Add the tarragon, bay leaf, white wine, lobster stock, vinegar, lemon juice and ginger. Bring to a boil and reduce to approximately 8 ounces (250 grams).

3. Add the cream and reduce by half or until thick.

4. Monte au beurre, adjust the seasonings and strain. Hold in a warm place until service.

$\blacklozenge\blacklozenge\blacklozenge$

RECIPE 17.18

Braised Chicken with Apple Cider and Cashew Butter

ANA WESTIN HOTEL, Washington, DC
Chef Leland Atkinson

Yield: 4 Servings   Method: Braising

Clarified butter	2-1/2 oz.	75 g
Shallots, minced	2 oz.	60 g
Calvados	12 oz.	375 g
Fresh thyme, chopped	2 tsp.	10 ml
Cashews	3 oz.	90 g
Honey	1 Tbsp.	15 ml
Unsalted butter	1 lb.	450 g
Salt and pepper	TT	TT
Chickens, 3 lb. 8 oz. (1.6 kg) each, quartered	2	2
Flour for dredging	as needed	as needed
Mirepoix	12 oz.	350 g
Garlic head, cut in half	1	1
Apple cider	1 pt.	450 ml
Cider vinegar	1 Tbsp.	15 ml
Chicken stock	3 pt.	1350 ml
Bay leaves	2	2
Fresh thyme	1 sprig	1 sprig
Blond roux	as needed	as needed

1. To make the cashew butter, lightly sauté the shallots in 1 tablespoon (15 milliliters) of the clarified butter. Add 4 ounces (120 grams) of the Calvados and the chopped thyme and reduce au sec. Remove from the heat and cool.

2. Place the cashews in a food processor and process to a medium-fine consistency. Add the cooled shallots, honey and unsalted butter. Season with salt and pepper and process well.

3. Season the chicken with salt and pepper and dredge in flour.

4. Brown the chicken evenly in the remaining clarified butter.

5. Remove the chicken. Add the mirepoix and garlic to the pan; sauté for 1 minute.

6. Add the remaining Calvados, cider and vinegar; reduce by half.

7. Return the chicken to the pan and add the chicken stock and herbs. Cover and braise until done, approximately 15 minutes. Remove the chicken from the pan. (The breasts and wings will cook more quickly and must be removed before the thigh and leg pieces.)

8. Reduce the stock by one half. Use the roux to thicken to a light sauce consistency.

9. Strain the sauce, monte au beurre with the cashew butter and season to taste with salt and pepper. Ladle the sauce over the chicken and serve at once.

◆◆◆

RECIPE 17.19
WARM DUCK BREAST SALAD WITH ASIAN SPICES AND HAZELNUT VINAIGRETTE

FETZER VINEYARDS, HOPLAND, CA
Culinary Director John Ash

Yield: 4 Servings **Method:** Sautéing

Whole boneless duck breasts, 12 oz. (350 g) each	2	2
Marinade:		
Garlic, minced	1 tsp.	5 ml
Green onions, minced	2 Tbsp.	30 ml
Oyster sauce	2 tsp.	10 ml
Light soy sauce	1 tsp.	5 ml
Rice wine or dry sherry	1 tsp.	5 ml
Sugar	1 tsp.	5 ml
Five spice powder	1/2 tsp.	3 ml
Hazelnut Vinaigrette:		
Garlic, minced	1 Tbsp.	15 ml
Hazelnut oil	3 oz.	90 g
Walnut or light olive oil	3 oz.	90 g
Chives, minced	1 Tbsp.	15 ml
Balsamic vinegar	2 Tbsp.	30 ml
Light soy sauce	1 tsp.	5 ml
Sugar	1/4 tsp.	1 ml
Mixed baby greens	4–6 oz.	120–180 g
Hazelnuts, toasted, skinned and chopped coarse	2 oz.	60 g

1. Trim the excess fat from the duck breasts and separate the breasts into halves.
2. Combine the marinade ingredients. Thoroughly coat the duck with the marinade and marinate for at least 2 hours.
3. Combine the hazelnut vinaigrette ingredients at least 2 hours before service so that the flavors will develop.
4. Wipe the marinade from the breasts and sauté them, skin side down first, in a dry sauté pan until medium rare, approximately 2-1/2 minutes per side. Do not overcook.
5. Arrange a mixture of baby greens on 4 plates. Slice the breasts on the diagonal and arrange on the plates with the greens. Drizzle the hazelnut vinaigrette over the greens, sprinkle with hazelnuts and serve.

✦✦✦

RECIPE 17.20
DUCK À L'ORANGE

ANA WESTIN HOTEL, WASHINGTON, DC
Chef Leland Atkinson

Yield: 4 Servings

Method: Roasting

Duckling, 5–6 lb. (2.2–2.8 kg)	1	1
Salt and pepper	TT	TT
Duck or chicken stock	8 oz.	250 g
Sugar	1 Tbsp.	15 ml
Champagne vinegar	1 Tbsp.	15 ml
Brandy	2 Tbsp.	30 ml
Orange juice	12 oz.	350 g
Lemon juice	from 1 lemon	from 1 lemon
Whole butter	1 tsp.	5 ml
Oranges, peeled and sectioned	4	4
Orange zest, julienne	4 Tbsp.	60 ml

1. Prick the duck with a fork and season well with salt and pepper.
2. Roast the duck at 400°F (200°C) for 15 minutes. Reduce the heat to 350°F (180°C) and cook until done, approximately 45–60 minutes. Remove the duck from the roasting pan and hold in a warm place.
3. Degrease the roasting pan. Place the pan on the stove top and deglaze with the stock.
4. Melt the sugar and vinegar together in a saucepan and lightly caramelize the mixture.
5. Remove the pan from the stove top and add the brandy.
6. Add the stock, pan drippings and juices and reduce until the sauce is slightly thickened, approximately 10 minutes. Monte au beurre. Strain and degrease the sauce.
7. Place the duck on a warm serving platter. Arrange the orange sections around it. Blanch the orange zest and sprinkle over the duck. Pour the sauce over the duck and serve additional sauce on the side.

✦✦✦

RECIPE 17.21
ROAST GOOSE WITH CABBAGE AND APPLES

Yield: 8 6-oz. (180-g) Servings

Method: Roasting

Goose, approx. 12 lb. (6 kg)	1	1
Salt and pepper	TT	TT
Caraway seeds	1 Tbsp.	15 ml
Onion, large dice	6 oz.	180 g
Carrot, large dice	3 oz.	90 g
Celery, large dice	3 oz.	90 g
Green cabbage, shredded	1 lb.	450 g
Potato, large dice	3 lb.	1.4 kg
Tart apple, cored and diced	1 lb.	450 g
Apple cider	1 qt.	1 lt

1. Remove the giblets from the goose; remove the fat from its cavity. Rinse the goose and pat dry. Sprinkle its interior and exterior with salt, pepper

Continued

and caraway seeds. Truss the goose and place breast side up on a rack in a roasting pan.

2. Roast in a 425°F (220°C) oven for 30 minutes. Prick the skin all over with a fork to release fat.

3. Reduce the oven temperature to 350°F (180°C) and continue roasting for another 45 minutes. Baste the bird occasionally with the fat accumulating in the pan.

4. Meanwhile, combine the vegetables and apple and season with salt and pepper.

5. After roasting for 1-1/4 hours, remove the goose from the pan and drain off all but 3 tablespoons (45 milliliters) of fat. Place the vegetable mixture in the roasting pan and toss to coat with the fat.

6. Place the goose on top of the vegetable mixture and pour the apple cider over all. Return to the oven and continue roasting until done, approximately 1-1/2 hours.

7. Remove the bird from the roasting pan and allow it to rest for 20–30 minutes before carving. Serve with the cooked vegetables.

RECIPE 17.22
SQUAB SALAD WITH MELON

REX IL RISTORANTE, LOS ANGELES, CA
Executive Chef Odette Fada

Yield: 6 servings   **Method:** Sautéing

Squab	3	3
Salt and pepper	TT	TT
Extra virgin olive oil	as needed	as needed
Dry black currants	2 Tbsp.	30 ml
Tahitian squash, thin slices	18	18
Mâche lettuce, small bunches	6	6

1. Bone the squab breasts and remove the thighs and legs. Season with salt and pepper and sauté the breasts and thighs in olive oil until done, approximately 10–15 minutes.

2. Place the currants in a bowl and cover with hot water.

3. Cook the squash slices in boiling water for 40 seconds. Cut the slices in half and arrange them on each of 6 plates as fans opening toward the plate's border.

4. On the other side of each plate, arrange some mâche lettuce; season with salt and pepper.

5. Slice the breasts; arrange the meat with the legs on the squash. Keep the plates in a warm place.

6. Drain the currants and sauté in 2 tablespoons (30 milliliters) of olive oil. Sprinkle the currants around the plates and serve.

◆◆◆

RECIPE 17.23

TURKEY SCALLOPINE WITH CAPERS AND LEMON

Yield: 4 servings   **Method:** Sautéing

Turkey breast, cut into 1/8-in. (3-mm) scallopines, 3 oz. (90 g) each	8	8
Salt and white pepper	TT	TT
Flour	as needed	as needed
Clarified butter	2 oz.	60 g
Dry white wine	4 oz.	120 g
Fresh lemon juice	2 oz.	60 g
Capers	3 Tbsp.	45 ml

1. Gently pound each turkey slice with a meat mallet. Season with salt and pepper and dredge in flour.
2. Sauté the turkey in the clarified butter until golden brown. Remove and hold in a warm place.
3. Deglaze the pan with the wine, then add the lemon juice and capers. Return the turkey to the pan to coat with the sauce and reheat.
4. Serve 2 slices with a portion of the sauce.

◆◆◆

RECIPE 17.24

SAUTÉED CHICKEN LIVERS

Yield: 4 4-oz. (120-g) Appetizer Servings   **Method:** Sautéing

Chicken livers, trimmed	1 lb.	450 g
Salt and pepper	TT	TT
Flour	as needed	as needed
Vegetable oil	1 oz.	30 g
Shallots, minced	2 Tbsp.	60 g
Raspberry vinegar	4 oz.	120 g
Raspberry jam	2 Tbsp.	60 g
French bread croutons	4	4
Watercress	as needed for garnish	

1. Rinse the livers and pat dry. Season with salt and pepper and dredge in flour.
2. Sauté in the oil until just barely pink, approximately 3–4 minutes. Remove the livers from the pan and hold in a warm place.
3. Using the fat remaining in the pan, sauté the shallots until tender. Deglaze with the vinegar.
4. Add the jam. Simmer until thickened. Return the livers to the pan and toss to coat with the sauce.
5. Serve on warm plates with French bread croutons; garnish with watercress.

CHAPTER 18
GAME

*G*ame *(Fr.* gibier*) are animals hunted for sport or food. Traditionally, game supplies depended upon the season and the hunter's success. But game's increasing popularity in food service operations has led to farm-raising techniques. As a result, pheasant, quail, deer, rabbit and other animals, although still considered game, are now ranch-raised and commercially available throughout the year.*

The life of game creatures is reflected in their flesh's appearance, aroma, flavor and texture. Generally, game flesh has a dark color and strong but not unpleasant aroma. It has a robust flavor, less fat than other meats or poultry and is more compact, becoming quite tough in older animals.

Selecting the best cooking methods for game depends on the animal's age and the particular cut of flesh. Younger animals will, of course, be more tender than older ones. Flesh from the loin or less-used muscles will also be tender and therefore can be prepared with dry-heat cooking methods. Flesh from much-used muscles, such as the leg and shoulder, will be tougher and should be prepared with combination cooking methods. Less-tender cuts can also be used in sausages, pâtés and forcemeats as discussed in Chapter 20, Charcuterie.

IDENTIFYING GAME

Furred or Ground Game

Furred game includes large animals such as deer, moose, bear, wild boar and elk as well as smaller animals such as rabbit, squirrel, raccoon and opossum. Although each of these animals (and many others) are hunted for sport and food, only antelope, deer and rabbit are widely available to food service operations.

Large game animals are rarely sold whole or in primal portions. Instead, the meat is available precut into subprimals or portions. So, except for those that are used for rabbits, this chapter does not provide butchering techniques.

Antelope

The blackbuck antelope, about half the size of a large deer, is ranch-raised in this country. Although it has almost no body fat, the meat retains a high amount of moisture. The meat is fine-grained, with a flavor that is only slightly stronger than deer meat (venison). It should be butchered and cooked in a manner similar to venison.

Bison (American Buffalo)

Once found in huge herds roaming the plains states, bison or buffalo were hunted into near extinction during the 19th century. Buffalo now live on reser-

---

MEAT OF THE FUTURE:
BEEFALO

Beefalo is produced by cross-breeding a bison with a domestic beef animal. To be a registered full-blooded beefalo, the animal has to be three-eighths bison and five-eighths domestic beef. The five-eighths domestic beef portion is not restricted to any breed; it is often a combination of two or more breeds such as Hereford, Angus or Charolais. In 1985 the USDA approved a special label for beefalo; it is labeled as either "Beef from Beefalo" or "Beefalo Beef."

Beefalo looks and tastes much like modern beef. The animal itself is hard to distinguish from any other beef animal. Beefalo meat is tender because the animals gain weight faster and go to market at younger ages. The meat is slightly sweeter in taste than beef.

Beefalo is lower in cholesterol than beef, fish or chicken and lower in calories and fat than beef. It offers a great alternative to beef for the diet- and health-conscious guest. The per-pound cost of beefalo may be slightly higher than beef cuts, but its low amount of interior and exterior fat gives it a higher yield with a price per usable pound comparable to beef.

Because of beefalo's finer fiber and low fat content, it cooks in one-third to one-half the time of beef and should be cooked to either rare or medium-rare.

JAMES J. MUTH, *MBA, CFBE*
Chef Instructor,
GRAND RAPIDS COMMUNITY COLLEGE

---

vations or ranches, where they are raised like beef cattle. Their meat is juicy, flavorful and may be prepared in the same manner as lean beef.

Deer

The deer family includes elk, moose, reindeer, red-tailed deer, white-tailed deer (Fr. *chevreuil*) and mule deer. Meat from any of these animals is known as venison (Fr. *venaisan*). Farm-raised venison, particularly from the Scottish red deer bred in New Zealand and the United States, is commercially available all year. Venison is typically dark red with a mild aroma. It is leaner than other meats, having almost no intramuscular fat or marbling.

The most popular commercial venison cuts are the loin, leg and rack. The loin is tender enough to roast, sauté or grill to medium rare. It can be left attached along the backbone to form a cut known as the saddle. The leg is often marinated in red wine and prepared with combination cooking methods. Other cuts can also be stewed or braised or used in sausages and pâtés. Butchering procedures for venison are similar to those for lamb discussed in Chapter 15.

Venison Saddle

Rabbit

Rabbits (Fr. *lapin*) are small burrowing animals that have long been raised for food. Rabbit has mild, lean and relatively tender flesh. Its taste and texture are similar to chicken. Ranch-raised rabbit is available all year, either whole or cut, fresh or frozen. The average weight of a whole dressed rabbit is 2 pounds 8 ounces to 3 pounds (1.2–1.4 kilograms). Young rabbit can be roasted, pan-fried, stewed or braised and is popular in rustic "country-style" dishes, especially casseroles and pâtés.

Procedure for Butchering Rabbit

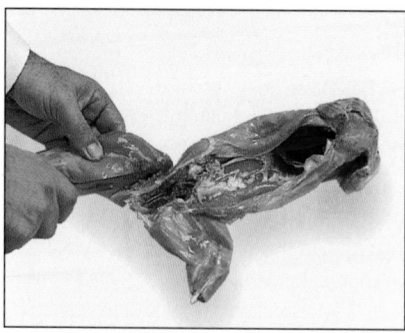

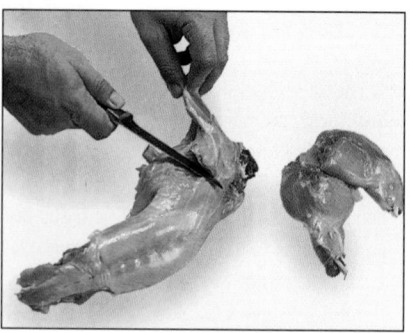

1. Place the rabbit on its back. Remove the hind legs by cutting close to the backbone and through the joint on each side. Each thigh and leg can be separated by cutting through the joint.

2. Remove the forelegs by cutting beneath the shoulder blades.

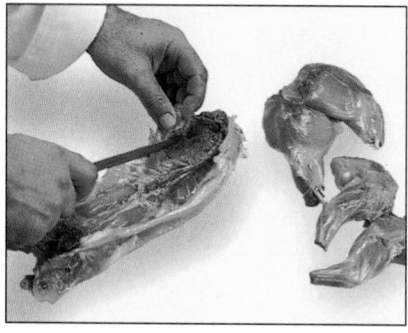

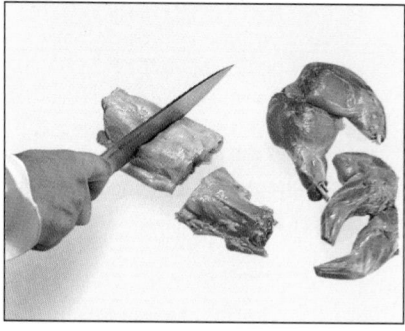

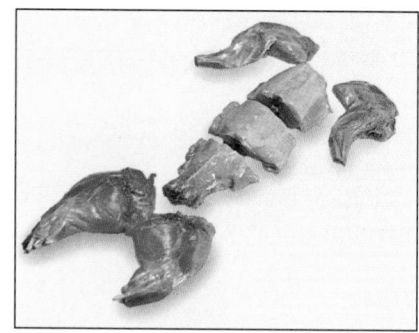

3. Cut through the breast bone and spread open the rib cage. Using a boning knife, separate the flesh from the rib bones and remove the bones.

4. Cut through the backbone to divide the loin into the desired number of pieces.

5. The cut-up rabbit: hind legs, thighs, loin in three pieces, forelegs.

TABLE 18.1   USING FURRED GAME

Animal	Commonly Purchased Cuts	Cooking Methods	Suggested Use
Antelope	Purchased and prepared in the same manner as deer.		
Bison	Purchased and prepared in the same manner as lean beef.		
Deer	Loin	Dry heat (roast; sauté; grill)	Sautéed medallions; whole roast loin; grilled steaks
	Leg	Combination (braise; stew)	Marinate and braise; pot roast with cranberries; chili; sausage; forcemeat
	Rack	Dry heat (roast; grill)	Grilled chops
Rabbit	Full carcass	Dry heat (sauté; pan-fry; roast; grill) Combination (braise; stew)	Pan-fried rabbit with cream gravy; Braised rabbit with mushrooms
Wild Boar	Loin	Dry heat (roast)	Roast loin with mustard crust
	Chops	Combination (braise)	Marinate and braise; stew with red wine and sour cream; sausage; forcemeat

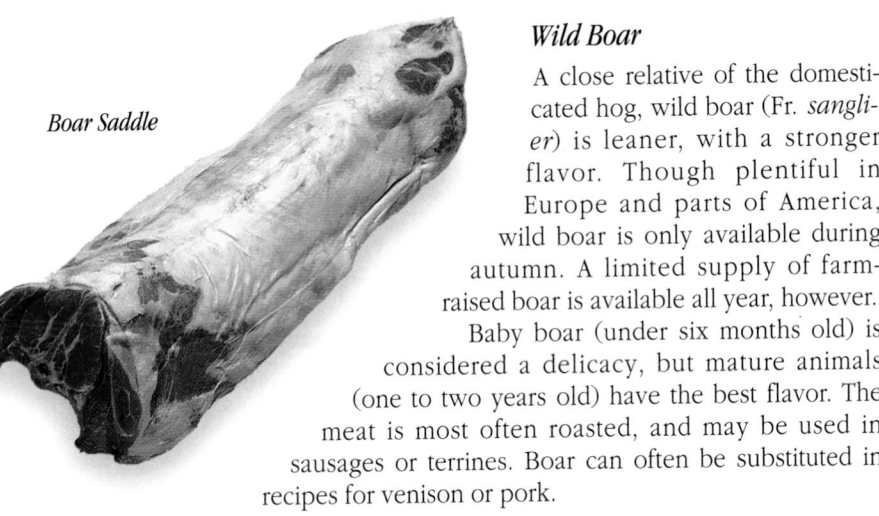

Boar Saddle

Wild Boar

A close relative of the domesticated hog, wild boar (Fr. *sanglier*) is leaner, with a stronger flavor. Though plentiful in Europe and parts of America, wild boar is only available during autumn. A limited supply of farm-raised boar is available all year, however. Baby boar (under six months old) is considered a delicacy, but mature animals (one to two years old) have the best flavor. The meat is most often roasted, and may be used in sausages or terrines. Boar can often be substituted in recipes for venison or pork.

Feathered or Winged Game

Feathered game includes upland birds such as wild turkeys, pheasants, quails, doves and woodcocks; songbirds such as larks, and waterfowl such as wild geese and ducks. Wild birds cannot be sold in the United States. An ever-increasing number of these birds are being farm-raised to meet increased consumer demand, however.

Game birds are available whole or precut into pieces, fresh or frozen. Butchering techniques will not be shown in this chapter as they are the same as those for domesticated poultry discussed in Chapter 17.

Because game birds tend to have less fat than other poultry, they are often barded with fat and cooked to medium rare. If cooked well done they become dry and stringy.

Partridge

The Hungarian and chukar partridges (Fr. *perdrix*) of Europe were introduced to the United States and Canada during the 19th century. Now found principally in the prairie and western mountain states, partridges are widely raised on game preserves and farms, producing a good commercial supply.

Their flavor is less delicate than pheasant and the meat tends to be tougher. Partridge may be roasted or cut into pieces and sautéed or braised. Each bird weighs about 1 pound (450 grams) dressed.

Chukar Partridge

FAISAN À LA SAINTE-ALLIANCE

Any dish prepared *à la sainte-alliance* evokes the festivities surrounding the 1815 signing of the Treaty of Paris, which ended the reign of Napoleon Bonaparte, forcing him into exile on Elba. *Faisan à la sainte-alliance* is a roast pheasant stuffed with woodcock and served on toast topped with woodcock purée. The renowned gastronome Brillat-Savarin gives the following recipe in his *Physiologie du Gout*, published in 1825:

When the pheasant has reached [its peak of ripeness], it is plucked, and not before, and it is larded carefully, with the freshest and firmest of material.... [T]he time has come to stuff it, and in the following manner:

Bone and draw a brace of woodcock, in such a way that you have one supply of the flesh, and another of the entrails.

Take the flesh and make a forcemeat of it by chopping it with some steamed beef marrow, a little scraped bacon, pepper, salt, fresh herbs, and enough fine truffles to make just the amount of stuffing needed to fill the pheasant.

Prepare a slice of bread that will be about two inches bigger on every side than the bird laid lengthwise. Then take the woodcock livers and entrails, and grind them in a mortar with two large truffles, an anchovy, a little finely minced bacon, and a sizeable lump of the best fresh butter.

Spread this paste evenly on the bread slice, and place it under the pheasant, already stuffed ... so that it will catch every drop of juice which will appear while the bird is roasting.

When the bird is done, serve it lying gracefully upon this crisp little couch; surround it with bitter oranges, and be assured of the fortunate outcome.

BRILLAT-SAVARIN,
THE PHYSIOLOGY OF TASTE,
translated and annotated by M. F. K. FISHER
(North Point Press, 1986),
pp. 374–75.

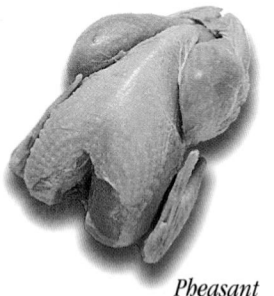

Pheasant

Pheasant

The most popular of game birds, the pheasant (Fr. *faisan*) was introduced into Europe from Asia during the Middle Ages. Its mild flavor is excellent for roasting, stewing or braising. The hen is smaller and more tender than the cock. Stock made from the carcass is often used for consommé or sauce.

Farm-raised birds are available fresh or frozen. A dressed bird weighs about 1 pound 8 ounces to 2 pounds 4 ounces (680 grams to 1 kilogram) and serves two people.

Quail

The quail (Fr. *caille*) is a migratory game bird related to the pheasant. The more popular European and Californian species are farm-raised and available all year.

Quail are rather small, with only about 1–2 ounces (30–60 grams) of breast meat each. Quail may be grilled (especially on skewers), roasted, broiled or sautéed and are often boned and served whole with a stuffing of forcemeat or rice. Because they are so lean, roasted quail benefit from barding.

Quail

NUTRITION

Even ranch-raised game animals live in the wild and are generally more active and less well fed than domesticated animals. This lifestyle produces animals whose meat has less fat than domesticated animals. Most game is also lower in cholesterol and has approximately one third fewer calories than beef. Game is also generally high in protein and minerals. Compare Table 18.2 with Tables 12.1 (Meats) and 17.7 (Poultry).

TABLE 18.2 NUTRITIONAL VALUES OF GAME

For 1 oz. (28 g) Uncooked Lean Meat	Kcal	Protein (g)	Total Fat (g)	Saturated Fat (g)	Cholesterol (mg)	Sodium (mg)
Beefalo	41	6.6	1.4	0.6	13	22
Bison (American buffalo)	31	6.1	0.5	0.2	18	15
Deer (venison)	34	6.5	0.7	0.3	24	15
Rabbit	39	5.7	1.6	0.5	16	12
Wild boar	35	6.1	1.0	0.3	mq	mq
Pheasant	51	6.4	2.6	0.8	mq	11
Quail	54	5.6	3.4	1.0	mq	15

mq = measurable quantity but data is unavailable The Corinne T. Netzer Encyclopedia of Food Values 1992

◆◆◆

WILD GAME—
DELICIOUS, NUTRITIOUS AND AVAILABLE

Wild game is now widely available for use in restaurants and at home. The best of wild game provides a safe, delicious and nutritious dining experience.

In almost all states, our native game animals are protected from harvesting for commercial purposes. It is a violation of state wildlife laws to kill and sell the meat from native species such as the whitetail deer, mule deer, pronghorn antelope, etc. These laws were written when only native game was present in America. Since then, a growing number of non-native species of deer and antelope have been introduced to ranches in America and this has made it possible to harvest deer and antelope legally for meat production.

Oddly enough, however, meats such as antelope, venison, rabbit, and most other game meats are not subject to inspection under federal and most state meat inspection regulations. This is not because the authorities do not believe the meat should be inspected. When the meat inspection laws were written, these meats were not legally available and therefore were not included in the Federal Meat Act. County and city health codes, however, do require that any meat served to the public must be from "an approved source" which is interpreted as "inspected." Therefore, any game meat served in a restaurant should be certified as inspected by either state or federal meat inspection authorities.

Game meat is available from farmed (domesticated) deer and from free-ranging (ranched) deer and antelope. Most farmed deer are taken to a fixed conventional slaughterhouse where they are slaughtered and processed in the same way as cattle, sheep, and goats. Ranched deer can be properly harvested only by an elaborate procedure which involves taking a mobile slaughter facility and meat inspector to the field where the animals are killed by shooting them with a high powered rifle under the supervision of the meat inspector. The carcass is then processed inside the mobile facility to avoid any contamination of the meat. This field harvesting eliminates any stress which might occur in transport of farmed deer to the slaughterhouse.

Farmed deer tend to be relatively more uniform in size and flavor. Free-ranging deer and antelope produce meat of more complex flavor due to the variety of their diet. The difference is somewhat like the difference in cultivated mushrooms and wild mushrooms, or pen-raised chickens compared with free-range chickens. Meat from free-range animals is more expensive due to higher labor and inspection costs.

Meat from both deer and antelope can be legally labeled "venison." All venison is relatively lean when compared with conventional red meats and requires special attention when cooking to avoid drying out the meat and toughening it. Tender cuts should be cooked as little as possible (rare to medium rare) to retain the maximum amount of moisture. Quick sautéing, grilling or roasting to retain a medium rare center is most satisfactory for tender cuts such as the loin, tenderloin, and leg.

Braising is the most effective method for cooking the less tender cuts such as the shoulder, ribs and shanks. Beef broth or red wine are good liquids for braising. The toughest cut of meat will be very satisfactorily tenderized if braised for a sufficient period of time (which may be as long as two or three hours). When properly cooked, these cuts can surpass the more tender cuts in flavor.

MIKE HUGHES,
Broken Arrow Ranch, Ingram, Texas

INSPECTION OF GAME

The USDA and most states restrict the sale of wild game. Truly wild game can only be served by those who hunt and share their kill.

Domestic Game

As opposed to mandatory federal and state inspections for beef, veal, lamb, pork and poultry, farm- or ranch-raised game is only subject to voluntary inspections for wholesomeness. Generally, however, game is processed under the same federal inspection requirements as domesticated meats and poultry. State regulations vary and are constantly being expanded and improved in response to consumer demands. Also unlike meat and poultry from domesticated animals, game is not graded for quality.

Imported Game

The USDA and the FDA work together to ensure the wholesomeness of imported game. Only USDA-approved countries are permitted to export game to the United States. Upon arrival in this country, game shipments are subject to USDA spot inspections.

PURCHASING AND STORING GAME

Purchasing Game

Furred game meats are available fresh, usually in vacuum-sealed packaging, or frozen. Game birds are available cleaned and boned, fresh or frozen. Use the same criteria to determine the freshness of game as you would any other meat or poultry: The flesh should be firm, without slime or an off-odor.

Fresh game is sometimes **hung** before cooking to allow the meat to mature or age. During hanging, carbohydrates (glycogen) stored in muscle tissues are converted to lactic acid. This process tenderizes the flesh and strengthens its flavor. But hanging is not necessary, especially if you object to "gamy" flavors. Commercially sold game is generally fully aged and ready to use when delivered. It does not need nor will it benefit from hanging.

Storing Game

As with any fresh or frozen meat, game should be well wrapped and stored under refrigeration at temperatures below 40°F (4°C). Because the flesh is generally dry and lean, frozen game should be used within four months. Thaw frozen game slowly under refrigeration to prevent moisture loss.

MARINATING FURRED GAME

Tradition calls for marinating game, particularly furred game, in strong mixtures of red wine, herbs and spices. Commercially raised game does not necessarily have to be marinated. Modern animal husbandry techniques used at game ranches assure the cook of receiving meat from young, tender animals.

♦♦♦
HOW TO HANG GAME

The following information may be useful if you find yourself with a need to hang freshly killed game. Most game should be eviscerated (drawn or gutted) as soon as possible, then suspended by either the hind legs or the head in a dry, well-ventilated place. Because the fur or feathers help prevent bacterial contamination, they should be left intact during hanging; game should be skinned or plucked just before butchering. The length of time necessary for hanging depends on the species and age of the animal. Two days may be sufficient for a rabbit, while up to three weeks may be necessary for a deer or boar. Hanging is generally complete when the first whiff of odor is detected (although traditionalists prefer pheasant to be hung until extremely ripe).

Farm-raised game animals also have a naturally milder flavor than their truly wild cousins.

For those preferring the flavors imparted by traditional marinades, the following red wine marinade is included. After the meat is removed, the marinade may be added to the cooking liquid or reduced and used in a sauce. Do not serve uncooked marinade.

◆◆◆

RECIPE 18.1

RED-WINE GAME MARINADE

Yield: 1-1/2 qt. (1.5 lt)

Carrot, chopped fine	2 oz.	60 g
Onion, chopped fine	2 oz.	60 g
Garlic, minced	1 Tbsp.	15 ml
Dried thyme	1 tsp.	5 ml
Bay leaves	2	2
Juniper berries, whole	2 tsp.	10 ml
Peppercorns, whole	1 Tbsp.	15 ml
Sage, ground	1/2 tsp.	2 ml
Red wine	1 qt.	1 lt
Red wine vinegar	4 oz.	120 g

1. Combine all ingredients.
2. Place the meat in the marinade and marinate for the desired time. Tender, farm-raised game may need only 30 minutes; older, wild animals may need 1–2 days.

CONCLUSION

Game is becoming increasingly popular because of consumer desires for leaner, healthier meats. Only farm-raised game can be used in food service operations. Luckily, many popular game items are now farm-raised, government-inspected and readily available. Generally, game flesh has a dark color, strong but not unpleasant aroma and a robust flavor. You should butcher, prepare and cook game according to the comparable guidelines for other meats and poultry.

QUESTIONS FOR DISCUSSION

1. Explain the differences between truly wild game and ranch-raised game.
2. What is hanging? Is it necessary for modern food service operations to hang game?
3. Which cuts of furred game are best suited to dry-heat cooking methods? Which are best for combination cooking methods?
4. Can game birds be purchased whole? How are they fabricated?
5. What degree of doneness is best suited for game birds? Explain your answer.

RECIPE 18.2

Marinated Loin of Venison Roasted with Mustard, Served with Creamy Polenta with Wild Mushrooms

Note: *This dish appears in the Chapter Opening photograph.*

FETZER VINEYARDS, Hopland, CA
John Ash, Culinary Director

Yield: 8–10/6–8 oz. (180–250 g) Servings   **Method:** Roasting

Marinade:		
Carrots, medium	3	3
Yellow onion, large	1	1
Shallots, whole	3	3
Garlic cloves	3	3
Olive oil	2 Tbsp.	30 ml
Hearty red wine	40 oz.	1200 g
Red wine vinegar	4 oz.	120 g
Bay leaves	4	4
Parsley stalks	6	6
Juniper berries, whole	16	16
Sea salt	2 tsp.	10 ml
Peppercorns	12	12
Mustard coating:		
Garlic cloves	3	3
Green onion, chopped	2 oz.	60 g
Chardonnay	3 oz.	90 g
Fresh sage	1 tsp.	5 ml
Fresh thyme	1 tsp.	5 ml
Dijon mustard	1 c.	250 ml
Olive oil	2 oz.	60 g
Sea salt	1 tsp.	5 ml
Venison loin, 5 lb. (2.2 kg), well-trimmed	1	1

1. For the marinade, coarsely chop the vegetables and sauté in the oil until lightly browned.

2. Add the wine, vinegar and remaining marinade seasonings and bring to a boil.

3. Reduce the heat and simmer 10 minutes. Cool before using.

4. For the mustard coating, place all ingredients in a food processor or blender and quickly process until smooth. The mixture should be very thick. Cover and refrigerate.

5. In a nonreactive pan, pour the cooled marinade over the loin and marinate, covered, in the refrigerator for up to 24 hours. Turn occasionally.

6. Remove the meat from the marinade, pat dry and quickly sear the meat in a hot sauté pan or on the grill.

7. Place loin in a roasting pan and coat well with the mustard coating. Roast at 450°F (230°C) for 5 minutes; reduce heat to 375°F (190°C) and roast for an additional 10–15 minutes, until the meat is medium rare.

8. Serve on warm plates with Creamy Polenta with Wild Mushrooms.

CREAMY POLENTA WITH WILD MUSHROOMS

Yield: 8–10 Servings

Yellow onion, chopped coarse	12 oz.	340 g
White mushrooms, chopped coarse	4 oz.	120 g
Garlic, chopped fine	2 Tbsp.	30 ml
Dried porcini or cèpes mushrooms, rinsed, soaked in water and chopped coarse	2 oz.	60 g
Olive oil	5 oz.	150 g
Fresh basil, chopped fine	4 tsp.	20 ml
Fresh oregano, chopped fine	1 tsp.	5 ml
Chicken or vegetable stock	2 qt.	2 lt
Coarse polenta cornmeal	2 c.	450 ml
Salt and pepper	TT	TT
Heavy cream	1 pt.	450 ml
Aged Asiago or Fontina cheese, grated fine	4 oz.	120 g
Fresh wild mushrooms	8–10	8–10
Fresh basil sprigs	as needed for garnish	

1. Sauté the onion, white mushrooms, garlic and porcini in 4 ounces (120 grams) olive oil until lightly colored. Add the basil, oregano and stock; bring to a boil.

2. Slowly stir in the polenta. Simmer 10 minutes, stirring regularly. The polenta should be thick and creamy. Add more stock if necessary. Adjust the seasonings and keep warm.

3. Just before serving, add the cream and cheese and stir vigorously.

4. Sauté the fresh wild mushrooms in the remaining olive oil until tender. Spoon the polenta onto warm plates and garnish with the wild mushrooms and a sprig of fresh basil.

◆◆◆

RECIPE 18.3

BRAISED ANTELOPE IN SOUR CREAM

Yield: 8 Servings, 6–8 oz. (180–250 g) each   Method: Braising

Salt pork	3 oz.	90 g
Bottom round of antelope, 4–5 lb. (2–2.5 kg)	1	1
Onion, small dice	12 oz.	350 g
Garlic cloves, sliced	2	2
Carrot, sliced	8 oz.	250 g
Red wine	24 oz.	700 g

Continued

Veal or game stock	3 pt.	1.5 lt
Bay leaves	2	2
Fresh rosemary, chopped	1 tsp.	5 ml
Fresh thyme	1/2 tsp.	2 ml
Juniper berries, crushed	10	10
Tomato paste	2 Tbsp.	30 ml
Clarified butter	2 Tbsp.	30 ml
Flour	2 Tbsp.	30 ml
Sour cream	1 pt.	500 ml
Salt and Pepper	TT	TT

1. Render the salt pork. Brown the meat well in the fat.
2. Add the onions, garlic and carrots; sauté until the vegetables are tender.
3. Add the red wine, stock, herbs, juniper berries and tomato paste. Braise in a 325°F (160°C) oven until the meat is tender, approximately 1-1/2 to 2 hours.
4. Remove the meat from the pan. If necessary, make a blond roux with the butter and flour and use to thicken the sauce. Bring to a simmer then strain the sauce.
5. Add the sour cream, heat thoroughly and season to taste with salt and pepper.

========= ◆◆◆ =========

RECIPE 18.4

SCALLOPINE OF VENISON WITH CHESTNUTS

Yield: 6 Servings   **Method:** Sautéing

Venison scallopine, cut from leg, 2 oz. (60 g) each	12	12
Salt and pepper	TT	TT
Flour	as needed	as needed
Clarified butter	3 oz.	90 g
White wine	8 oz.	250 g
Heavy cream	8 oz.	250 g
Chestnut purée	3 oz.	90 g
Fresh dill, chopped	1 Tbsp.	15 ml

1. Pound the scallopine to a thickness of 1/4 inch (6 millimeters).
2. Season with salt and pepper; dredge in flour.
3. Sauté the scallopine in the clarified butter; remove to a warm platter.
4. Deglaze the pan with the wine. Add the cream and bring to a boil. Whisk in the chestnut purée. Thin with additional wine or cream if necessary.
5. Return the scallopine to the pan to reheat. Adjust the seasonings and add the chopped dill.
6. Serve 2 slices of venison per portion with 3 ounces (90 milliliters) sauce.

✦✦✦

RECIPE 18.5

VENISON MEDALLIONS GRAND VENEUR

Yield: 2 Servings   **Method:** Sautéing

Venison medallions, 3 oz. (90 g) each	4	4
Salt and pepper	TT	TT
Clarified butter	1 oz.	30 g
White wine	1 oz.	30 g
Poivrade sauce (pg 211)	6 oz.	180 g
Red currant jelly	2 tsp.	10 ml
Heavy cream	1 oz.	30 g

1. Season the medallions with salt and pepper and sauté in the clarified butter to the desired doneness. Remove and reserve.

2. Degrease the pan and deglaze with the white wine.

3. Add the poivrade sauce and bring to a simmer. Stir in the currant jelly, add the cream and adjust the seasonings.

4. Return the medallions to the sauce to reheat. Serve 2 medallions per person with a portion of the sauce.

✦✦✦

RECIPE 18.6

VENISON AND BLACK BEAN CHILI

Yield: 4 qt. (4 lt)   **Method:** Braising

Dried black beans	1 lb.	450 g
Water	2 qt.	2 lt
Peanut oil	3 oz.	90 g
Venison round, trimmed, medium dice	3 lb.	1.3 kg
Garlic cloves, minced	6	6
Onion, small dice	1 lb. 8 oz.	680 g
Jalapeños, seeded and chopped fine	3	3
Masa harina (corn flour)	2 oz.	60 g
Chilli powder	1 oz.	30 g
Cayenne pepper	1 tsp.	5 ml
Cumin, ground	3 Tbsp.	45 ml
Peeled tomatoes, canned	1 lb. 8 oz.	680 g
Veal stock	1 qt.	1 lt
Salt and pepper	TT	TT
Tabasco sauce	TT	TT

1. Soak the beans in water overnight. Drain and simmer in 2 quarts (2 lt) of water until tender, approximately 30–40 minutes.

2. Sauté the venison in the oil until brown. Remove and reserve.

3. Sauté the garlic, onions and jalapeño in the same pan until tender. Add the masa harina, chilli powder, cayenne and cumin. Cook 5 minutes.

4. Add the tomatoes, stock and reserved meat. Cover and braise on the stove top or in a 325°F (160°C) oven for 30–40 minutes.

5. Add the beans and cook an additional 15 minutes. Season to taste with salt, pepper and Tabasco sauce. Thin with additional stock if necessary.

◆◆◆

RECIPE 18.7

RABBIT RACK AND LOIN

STANFORD COURT HOTEL, SAN FRANCISCO, CA
Chef Ercolino Crugnale

Yield: 4 Servings		Method: Sautéing
Rabbits	2	2
Pearl onions	12	12
Chicken or rabbit stock	10 oz.	300 g
Salt and pepper	TT	TT
Olive oil	1 oz.	30 g
Hazelnuts, skinned, cut in half	4 oz.	120 g
White wine	4 oz.	120 g
Pomegranate seeds	2 oz.	60 g
Turnip purée (recipe follows)	8 oz.	250 g
Taro root chips	4	4
Frisee	2 oz.	60 g
Japanese pear, peeled, julienne	1/2	1/2
Basic vinaigrette dressing	1 oz.	30 g

1. Separate the rabbit legs, racks and loins. Remove the eye muscle from the loins. Split the racks into two by cutting them along the backbone and trimming the rib ends so they extend 1/2 inch (1.2 centimeters) past the eye muscle. Use the legs in another recipe.

2. Peel the onions. Simmer them in 6 ounces (180 grams) of stock until tender, reducing the stock to a glaze as they cook. If the onions are not tender when the liquid is gone add a little more stock and continue cooking until they are done. Remove from the heat and reserve.

3. Season the rabbit racks and boneless loins with salt and pepper and sauté in olive oil until well browned and medium rare, approximately 3 minutes. Remove from the pan and reserve.

4. Add the onions and hazelnuts to the pan and sauté briefly. Add the white wine and 4 ounces (120 grams) of stock and reduce by one-third. Adjust the seasonings and add the pomegranate seeds.

5. Spoon 2 ounces (60 grams) of turnip purée on each plate and top with a taro chip. Place one piece of rabbit loin and one piece of rack on each chip.

6. Combine the frisee, pear and vinaigrette. Season and place one-fourth of the salad on each of the plates. Spoon the sauce around the plate and serve.

TURNIP PURÉE

Yield: 8 oz. (250 g)

Russet potato, peeled, large dice	2 oz.	60 g
Turnip, peeled, large dice	6 oz.	180 g
Garlic, chopped	1/2 tsp.	2 ml
Whole butter	1 oz.	30 g
Heavy cream	1-1/2 oz.	45 g
Salt and pepper	TT	TT

1. Cook the potatoes and turnips separately in salted water until tender. Drain and purée in a food mill.

2. Combine the garlic, butter and cream and bring to a boil. Add to the potato and turnip mixture and season with salt and pepper.

◆◆◆

RECIPE 18.8

Grilled Loin of Rabbit with Spinach, Fennel and White Beans

GOTHAM BAR AND GRILL, New York, NY
Chef/Owner Alfred Portale

Yield: 6 Servings   **Method:** Grilling

Rabbit saddles	6	6
Bacon slices	6	6
Lemon, sliced thin	1	1
Shallots, minced	1 Tbsp.	15 ml
Fresh sage	1 bunch	1 bunch
Fresh rosemary	3 sprigs	3 sprigs
Fresh thyme	3 sprigs	3 sprigs
Garlic cloves, sliced thin	2	2
White peppercorns, cracked	1 Tbsp.	15 ml
Olive oil	as needed	as needed
Baby fennel, steamed until tender	12 heads	12 heads
Fresh spinach, steamed	1 lb.	450 g
White Beans (recipe follows)	as needed	as needed
Rabbit Sauce (recipe follows)	as needed	as needed

1. Bone the saddles, removing the two loins and tenderloins.
2. Tightly wrap each loin and tenderloin together with half of a slice of bacon.
3. Place the rolled loins and tenderloins in a shallow container. Sprinkle with the lemon, shallots, herbs, garlic and cracked pepper and drizzle with olive oil; cover and refrigerate for 6–8 hours.
4. Bring the rabbit to room temperature. Remove from the marinade and grill over a medium fire until golden, approximately 6–8 minutes.
5. Cut each loin into medallions and arrange on the plates. Serve with fennel, spinach, White Beans and Rabbit Sauce.

WHITE BEANS

Yield: 2 lb. (.9 kg)

Dried Great Northern beans, soaked	8 oz.	250 g
Sachet:		
Onion, small	1	1
Carrot, 3-in. (8-cm.) piece	1	1
Celery, 2-in. (5-cm.) piece	1	1
Fresh thyme	1 sprig	1 sprig
Fresh rosemary	1 sprig	1 sprig
Black peppercorns	1 tsp.	5 ml
Garlic clove, minced	1	1
Parsley, chopped	1 Tbsp.	15 ml
Fresh rosemary	TT	TT
Fresh thyme	TT	TT
Whole butter, softened	4 oz.	120 g
Salt and white pepper	TT	TT
Heavy cream	2 oz.	60 g

Continued

1. Place the beans and the sachet in a large pot and cover with cold water. Bring to a simmer and cook until tender, approximately 45 minutes.
2. Cream together the garlic, parsley, rosemary, thyme and butter. Season with salt and white pepper.
3. Remove the sachet from the cooked beans and pour off all but 3–4 table-spoons (45–60 milliliters) of the cooking liquid. Return to the heat and swirl in the herb butter and cream. Keep warm.

RABBIT SAUCE

Yield: 1 pt. (450 ml)

Shallots, chopped	1 oz.	30 g
White peppercorns	1 Tbsp.	15 ml
Clarified butter	2 tsp.	10 ml
White wine	4 oz.	120 g
Brown stock, made from chicken and rabbit bones	24 oz.	700 g
Salt and white pepper	TT	TT
Whole butter	3 Tbsp.	45 ml

1. Sauté the shallots and peppercorns in the clarified butter over low heat until browned.
2. Add the white wine and reduce by one third. Add the stock and reduce by one third.
3. Season with salt and white pepper. Monte au beurre just before service.

◆◆◆

RECIPE 18.9
BRAISED RABBIT WITH CAVATELLI PASTA

FETZER VINEYARDS, HOPLAND, CA
John Ash, Culinary Director

Yield: 4 Servings   **Method:** Braising

Rabbit, 4 lb. (1.8 kg), cut into quarters	1	1
Salt and pepper	TT	TT
Olive oil	2 oz.	60 g
Chantrelle or shiitake mushrooms, stemmed and sliced	8 oz.	250 g
Yellow onion, sliced	6 oz.	170 g
Garlic, slivered	3 Tbsp.	45 ml
Carrot, small dice	3 oz.	90 g
Celery, sliced thin	3 oz.	90 g
Sun-dried tomatoes, sliced	1 pt.	500 ml
Zinfandel wine	1 pt.	500 ml
Tomato concassé	1 pt.	500 ml
Fresh thyme	1 tsp.	5 ml
Fresh sage, minced	1 tsp.	5 ml
Rabbit or chicken stock	1 qt.	1 lt
Parsley, chopped fine	4 Tbsp.	60 ml
Fresh basil, chopped	4 Tbsp.	60 ml
Cavatelli, cooked	24 oz.	700 g

Fresh basil sprigs	as needed for garnish
Asiago, Parmesan or	
Dry Jack cheese, shaved	as needed for garnish

1. Season the rabbit pieces with salt and pepper.
2. In a large saucepan, heat the oil and quickly brown the rabbit. Remove and reserve.
3. Add the mushrooms, onion, garlic, carrots and celery and sauté until very lightly browned.
4. Return the rabbit to the pan and add the sun-dried tomatoes, wine, tomatoes, thyme, sage and stock. Cover and simmer until the rabbit is tender and begins to pull away from the bones, approximately 45–50 minutes.
5. Remove the rabbit, separate the meat from the bones, discard the bones, and cut the meat into bite-sized pieces.
6. Strain the sauce, reserving the vegetables, and return the sauce to the saucepan. Bring to a boil and cook over high heat for 8–10 minutes to reduce and thicken slightly.
7. Adjust the seasonings. Add the reserved meat and vegetables and heat. Stir in the basil and parsley just before serving.
8. Toss the hot pasta with the rabbit sauce. Garnish with basil sprigs and cheese.

◆◆◆

RECIPE 18.10

MUSTARD-ROASTED LOIN OF BOAR WITH PAN GRAVY

Yield: 10 6-oz. (180-g) Servings   **Method:** Roasting

Crust:		
Flour	3 Tbsp.	45 ml
Brown sugar	2 Tbsp.	30 ml
Dry mustard	2 tsp.	10 ml
Dried thyme	2 tsp.	10 ml
Sage, rubbed	1 tsp.	5 ml
White wine	1 oz.	30 g
White wine vinegar	1 oz.	30 g
Boar loin, boneless, 4–6 lb. (2–2.7 kg)	1	1
Garlic cloves, sliced	3	3
Salt and pepper	TT	TT
Flour	2 oz.	60 g
Veal or game stock	1-1/2 qt.	1-1/2 lt

1. Combine the crust ingredients to make a paste.
2. Puncture the loin with a paring knife in several places and press a slice of garlic into each hole. Season the loin with salt and pepper.
3. Coat the loin with an even layer of the crust mixture. Roast at 450°F (230°C) for 10 minutes. Reduce the temperature to 325°F (160°C) and roast until done, approximately 1 hour.
4. Remove the roast from the roasting pan. Degrease the pan, leaving about 2 ounces (60 grams) of fat. Stir in 2 ounces (60 grams) of flour and cook to make a blond roux. Add the stock to make a pan gravy. Strain the gravy through a chinois and adjust the seasonings.
5. Carve the boar and serve with the sauce.

✦✦✦

RECIPE 18.16

GRILLED BUFFALO STEAK

Yield: 1 Serving   **Method:** Grilling

Buffalo strip loin steak, 8 oz. (250 g)	1	1
Salt and pepper	TT	TT
Oil	1 Tbsp.	15 ml

1. Season the steak well with salt and pepper.
2. Brush with oil and grill to the desired degree of doneness.
3. Serve the steak with a full-flavored sauce such as a bordelaise (pg 210) or poivrade sauce (pg 211).

Nutritional values without sauce:

Calories	368	Protein	49 g
Calories from fat	44%	Vitamin A	n/a
Total fat	18 g	Vitamin C	n/a
Saturated fat	2.6 g	Sodium	120 mg
Cholesterol	144 mg		

✦✦✦

RECIPE 18.12

BRAISED PARTRIDGE
WITH RED CABBAGE

Yield: 4 Servings   **Method:** Braising

Bacon, medium dice	8 oz.	250 g
Partridges, halved	2	2
Salt and pepper	TT	TT
Onion, chopped coarse	6 oz.	180 g
Red cabbage, chopped	1 lb.	450 g
Red wine	8 oz.	250 g
Red wine vinegar	2 oz.	60 g

1. Cook the bacon until crisp. Remove the bacon from the pan and reserve. Pour off all but 4 ounces (120 grams) of fat. Reserve the excess fat.
2. Season the partridge halves with salt and pepper and brown in the pan with the bacon fat. Remove the partridge from the pan.
3. Add the onion to the pan and sauté until tender, approximately 5 minutes.
4. Stir in the cabbage. Season with salt and pepper. Add the wine and vinegar and bring to a simmer.
5. Place the partridges on top of the cabbage. Brush with the reserved bacon fat.
6. Cover and braise at 300°F (150°C) until done, approximately 1 hour.
7. Serve half of a partridge per person with a portion of the cabbage.

♦♦♦

RECIPE 18.13

ROAST PHEASANT WITH COGNAC AND APPLES

Yield: 2 Servings   **Method:** Roasting

Pheasant	1	1
Salt and pepper	TT	TT
Fatback	as needed	as needed
Mirepoix	12 oz.	350 g
Tart apples	2	2
Whole butter	1 oz.	30 g
Cognac	3 oz.	90 g
Crème fraîche	4 oz.	120 g

1. Season the pheasant with salt and pepper. Bard the body with fatback.
2. Roast on a bed of mirepoix at 350°F (170°C) until done, approximately 1-1/2 hours.
3. Peel, core and slice each apple into eight pieces. Sauté the apples in butter just until tender.
4. When the pheasant is done, remove it from the pan and reserve in a warm place. Deglaze the pan with the cognac, add the crème fraîche and bring to a simmer. Strain the sauce and adjust the seasonings.
5. Serve one half pheasant per person, accompanied by the sliced apples and sauce.

♦♦♦

RECIPE 18.14

STUFFED BREAST OF PHEASANT

Yield: 4 Servings   **Method:** Roasting

Stuffing:		
Prunes, chopped fine	4 oz.	120 g
Apple, chopped fine	4 oz.	120 g
Dried apricots, chopped fine	1 oz.	30 g
Walnuts, chopped fine	2 oz.	60 g
Onion, chopped fine	2 oz.	60 g
Salt	1/4 tsp.	1 ml
Pepper	1/4 tsp.	1 ml
Fresh thyme	1/2 tsp.	3 ml
Pheasant breast, boneless	4	4
Bacon, thin slices	8	8
Ivory sauce (pg. 208)	8 oz.	250 g

1. Combine the stuffing ingredients and set aside.
2. Separate each pheasant breast into two pieces. Pound each to a thickness of 1/4 inch (6 millimeters).
3. Place a portion of the stuffing in the center of four of the pieces of breast meat. Place a second piece of breast meat over the stuffing. Wrap each parcel tightly with two slices of bacon and tie with butcher's twine.
4. Bake at 325°F (160°C) until done, approximately 45 minutes.
5. Remove the twine, carve each bundle into slices and serve with 2 ounces (60 milliliters) of ivory sauce.

♦♦♦

RECIPE 18.15
Grilled Quail
with Potato Galette, Artichoke Wedges and Balsamic Raspberries

STANFORD COURT HOTEL, SAN FRANCISCO, CA
Chef Ercolino Crugnale

Yield: 6 Servings		Method: Grilling
Bobwhite quail	6	6
Salt and pepper	TT	TT
Asparagus tips, 2 in. (5 cm) long, peeled and blanched	18 pieces	18 pieces
Artichoke Wedges (recipe follows)	18 pieces	18 pieces
Roma tomatoes, concasse	3	3
Cipolline onions, peeled and glazed with chicken stock and whole butter	12	12
Pure olive oil	3 oz.	90 g
Chicken stock	6 oz.	180 g
Dry white wine	6 oz.	180 g
Shallots, minced	2 Tbsp.	30 ml
Fresh tarragon, chopped	2 Tbsp.	30 ml
Fresh parsley, chopped	2 Tbsp.	30 ml
Potato Galette (recipe follows)	6 pieces	6 pieces
Mixed greens such as butter lettuce, yellow frisee and radicchio, torn into 1-in. (2.5-cm) pieces	1-1/2 c.	375 ml
Basic vinaigrette dressing	4 Tbsp.	60 ml
Balsamic Raspberries (recipe follows)		
Extra virgin olive oil	3 oz.	90 g

1. Season the quail with slt and pepper and grill on both sides until cooked just under medium.
2. Sauté the asparagus, artichoke wedges, tomatoes and onions in the pure olive oil.
3. Deglaze the pan with chicken stock and white wine. Add the shallots, tarragon and parsley. Season with salt and pepper.
4. To serve, place a potato galette on each plate. Arrange the vegetables around the potato.
5. Dress the mixed greens with the basic vinaigrette dressing and place a small amount in the center of each plate. Place the quail on greens.
6. Place raspberries around the plate; drizzle with extra virgin olive oil.

POTATO GALETTE

Yield: 6 Galettes

Clarified butter	as needed	as needed
Idaho potatoes, peeled and sliced thin on a mandoline	3	3
Salt and pepper	TT	TT

1. For each galette, completely line the bottom of a buttered 8-inch (20-centimeter) pan with potato slices, arranging the slices in a circular, overlapping pattern.
2. Season with salt and pepper and sauté until golden brown on each side. Hold at room temperature.

ARTICHOKE WEDGES

Yield: 20 Pieces

Olive oil	4 oz.	120 g
Artichoke bottoms, turned and cleaned, cut in quarters	5	5
Garlic, minced	2 Tbsp.	30 ml
Fresh thyme, chopped	1 Tbsp.	15 ml
Chicken stock	1 pt.	500 ml
Lemon juice	2 oz.	60 g
White wine	4 oz.	120 g
Salt and white pepper	TT	TT

1. Over high heat, sauté the artichokes in the olive oil for 2 minutes.
2. Add the garlic, thyme and 4 ounces (120 grams) chicken stock; reduce au sec.
3. Add the lemon juice, white wine and seasonings; reduce au sec.
4. Add another 6 ounces (170 grams) chicken stock, reduce au sec.
5. Add the remaining chicken stock; reduce au sec. The artichokes should be glazed, crisp and tender.

BALSAMIC RASPBERRIES

Raspberries, ripe but firm	1 qt.	1 lt
Balsamic vinegar	6 oz.	170 g
Pepper	1 tsp.	5 ml

1. Gently combine all ingredients.
2. Let the raspberries macerate for 15 minutes.
3. Strain off the vinegar and reserve.

CHAPTER 19 FISH AND SHELLFISH

After studying this chapter you will be able to:

♦ understand the structure and composition of fish and shellfish
♦ identify a variety of fish and shellfish
♦ purchase fish and shellfish appropriate for your needs
♦ store fish and shellfish properly
♦ prepare fish and shellfish for cooking
♦ apply various cooking methods to fish and shellfish

ᚎish are aquatic vertebrates with fins for swimming and gills for breathing. Of the more than thirty thousand species known, most live in the seas and oceans; freshwater species are far less numerous. Shellfish are aquatic invertebrates with shells or carapaces. They are found in both fresh and salt water.

Always an important food source, fish and shellfish have become increasingly popular in recent years, due in part to demands from health-conscious consumers. Because of increased demand and improved preservation and transportation techniques, good-quality fish and shellfish, once found only along seacoasts and lakes, are now readily available to almost every food service operation.

Many fish and shellfish species are very expensive; all are highly perishable. Because their cooking times are generally shorter and their flavors more delicate than meat or poultry, special attention must be given to fish and shellfish to prevent spoilage and to produce high-quality finished products.

In this chapter you will learn how to identify a large assortment of fish and shellfish as well as how to properly purchase and store them, fabricate or prepare them for cooking and cook them by a variety of dry-heat and moist-heat cooking methods. This chapter presents many of the cooking methods applied to meats and poultry in the previous chapters. Review the corresponding procedures for meats and poultry and note the similarities and differences.

STRUCTURE AND MUSCLE COMPOSITION

The fish and shellfish used in food service operations can be divided into three categories: fish, mollusks and crustaceans.

Fish (Fr. *poisson*) include both fresh- and saltwater varieties. They have fins and an internal skeleton of bone and cartilage. Based upon shape and skeletal structure, fish can be divided into two groups: round fish and flatfish. **Round fish** swim in a vertical position and have eyes on both sides of their heads. Their bodies may be truly round, oval or compressed. **Flatfish** have asymmetrical, compressed bodies, swim in a horizontal position and have both eyes on top of their heads. Flatfish are bottom dwellers; most are found in deep ocean waters around the world. The skin on top of their bodies is dark, to camouflage them from predators, and can change color according to their surroundings. Their scales are small and their dorsal and anal fins run the length of their bodies.

Mollusks (Fr. *mollusque*) are shellfish characterized by soft, unsegmented bodies with no internal skeleton. Most mollusks have hard outer shells. Single-shelled mollusks such as abalone are known as **univalves**. Those with two shells, such as clams, oysters and mussels, are known as **bivalves**. Squid and octopus, which are known as **cephalopods**, do not have a hard outer shell. Rather, they have a single thin internal shell called a *pen* or *cuttlebone*.

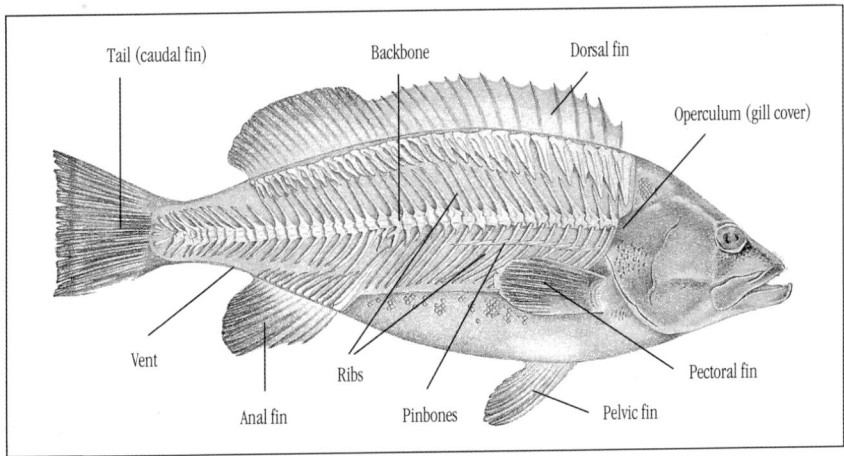

FIGURE 19.1   *Bone Structure of a Round Fish*

Crustaceans (Fr. *crustacé*) are also shellfish. They have a hard outer skeleton or shell and jointed appendages. Crustaceans include lobsters, crabs and shrimp.

The flesh of fish and shellfish consists primarily of water, protein, fat and minerals. Fish flesh is composed of short muscle fibers separated by delicate sheets of connective tissue. Fish, as well as most shellfish, are naturally tender, so the purpose of cooking is to firm proteins and enhance flavor. The absence of the oxygen-carrying protein myoglobin makes fish flesh very light or white in color. (The orange color of salmon and some trout comes from pigments found in their food.) Compared to meats, fish do not contain large amounts of intermuscular fat. But the amount of fat a fish does contain affects the way it responds to cooking. Fish containing a relatively large amount of fat, such as salmon and mackerel, are known as fatty or oily fish. Fish such as cod and haddock contain very little fat and are referred to as lean fish. Shellfish are also very lean.

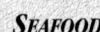

◆◆◆
SEAFOOD

Seafood means different things to different people. For some, the term applies just to shellfish or to shellfish and other small edible marine creatures. For others it is limited to saltwater shellfish or to saltwater shellfish and fish. For yet others, it refers to all fish and shellfish, both freshwater and saltwater. Because of the term's vagueness, it is not used here.

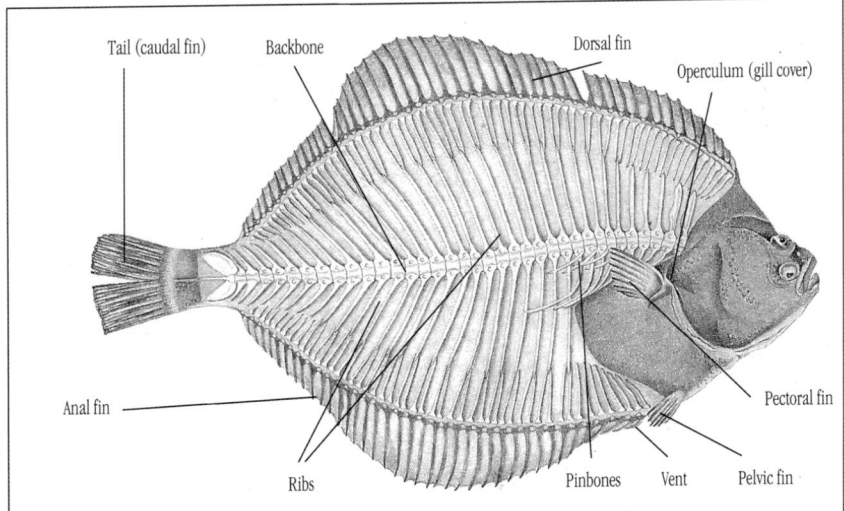

FIGURE 19.2   *Bone Structure of a Flatfish*

IDENTIFYING FISH AND SHELLFISH

Identifying fish and shellfish properly can be difficult because of the vast number of similar-appearing fish and shellfish that are separate species within each family. Adding confusion are the various colloquial names given to the same fish or the same name given to different fish in different localities. Fish with an unappealing name may also be given a catchier name or the name of a similar but more popular item for marketing purposes. Moreover, some species are referred to by a foreign name, especially on menus.

The FDA publishes a list of approved market names for food fish in *The Fish List: FDA Guide to Acceptable Market Names for Food Fish Sold in Interstate Commerce* 1988, available from the U.S. Government Printing Office, Washington D.C. Deviations from this list are strongly discouraged but difficult to enforce. We attempt to list the most commonly used names for each item, whether they are zoologically accurate or not.

Fish

Round Fish

Bass (Fr. *bar*) commonly refers to a number of unrelated fish. The better-known freshwater bass varieties (largemouth, smallmouth, redeye and black) are actually members of the sunfish family. They are lean and delicate but, as game, not commercially available in the United States. The saltwater bass varieties (black sea bass and striped bass) are popular commercial items.

Black sea bass are sometimes referred to as rock sea bass. They have a lean, firm white flesh with a mild flavor and flaky texture. They usually weigh from 1-1/2 to 3 pounds (680–1360 grams) and are most prevalent in the Atlantic Ocean between New York and North Carolina. Black sea bass can be prepared by almost any cooking method and are often served whole in Chinese and Italian cuisines.

Striped bass, often erroneously referred to as rockfish, are ocean fish that depend on freshwater rivers to reproduce. True striped bass cannot be marketed because pollution and overfishing have damaged the supply. A hybrid of striped bass and either white bass or white perch is being **aquafarmed** for commercial use, however. It is this hybrid that food service operations receive as striped bass. Whole fish weigh from 1 to 5 pounds (450 grams to 2.2 kilograms). Striped bass have a rich, sweet flavor and firm texture. They can be steamed, baked, poached or broiled.

Catfish are scaleless freshwater fish common in southern lakes and rivers and now aquafarmed extensively. Aquafarm raising eliminates the "muddy" taste once associated with catfish and ensures a year-round supply. The flesh is pure white with a moderate fat content, a mild, sweet flavor and firm texture. Channel catfish are the most important commercially. They usually weigh from 1-1/2 to 5 pounds (650 grams to 2.2 kilograms). The smaller of these fish are known as **fiddlers**; they are often deep-fried and served whole. Catfish may be prepared by almost any cooking method, but are especially well suited to frying.

The **cod** (Fr. *cabillaud*) family includes Atlantic and Pacific cod as well as pollock, haddock, whiting and hake. Cod have a mild, delicate flavor and lean, firm white flesh that flakes apart easily. Cod can be prepared by most

Black Sea Bass

Striped Bass

Aquafarming—*also known as aquaculture, is the business, science and practice of raising large quantities of fish and shellfish in tanks, ponds or ocean pens; used especially for catfish, trout, salmon, shrimp and other popular fish and shellfish.*

Catfish

◆◆◆
SURIMI

Surimi is made from a highly processed fish paste colored, flavored and shaped to resemble shrimp, lobster, crab or other shellfish. Most surimi is based on Alaskan pollock, but some blends include varying amounts of real crab, shrimp or other items. Available chilled or frozen, surimi is already fully cooked and ready to add to salads, pasta, sauces or other dishes. Surami is very low in fat and relatively high in protein. Because of processing techniques, however, it has more sodium and fewer vitamins and minerals than the real fish or shellfish it replaces. Americans now consume over 100 million pounds of surimi each year and its popularity continues to grow. The FDA requires that all surimi products be labeled "imitation."

cooking methods, although grilling is not recommended because the flesh is too flaky.

Atlantic cod are the best-selling fish in America. They are available fresh, whole or drawn, or cut into fillets or steaks. They are also available frozen and are often used for precooked or prebreaded sticks or portions. Smoked cod and salt cod are also available. While cod may reach 200 pounds (90 kilograms), most market cod weigh 10 pounds (4.4 kilograms) or less. **Scrod** is a marketing term for cod weighing less than 2-1/2 pounds (1.1 kilograms).

Atlantic Cod

Haddock, the second most commercially important fish, look like thin, small Atlantic cod and weigh about 2 to 5 pounds (900 grams to 2.3 kilograms). They have a stronger flavor and more delicate texture than Atlantic cod.

Pacific cod, also known as gray cod, are found in the northern Pacific Ocean and are not as abundant as their Atlantic cousins. Pacific cod are most often available frozen; they should be labeled "true cod" to distinguish them from rock cod and black cod, which are unrelated.

Pollock, also known as Boston bluefish or blue cod, are plentiful in the northern Atlantic and Pacific Oceans. Their flesh is gray-pink when raw, turning white when cooked. Pollock are often frozen at sea, then reprocessed into surimi. They can also be salted or smoked.

Pollock

Eels (Fr. *anguille*) are long, snakelike freshwater fish with dorsal and anal fins running the length of their bodies. (The conger eel is from a different family and has little culinary significance.) American and European eels are available live, whole, gutted or as fillets. Eels have a high fat content and firm flesh; they are sweet and mildly flavored. Their tough skin should be removed before cooking. Eels may be steamed, baked, fried or used in stews. Baby eels are a springtime delicacy, especially in Spain, where they are pan-fried in olive oil and garlic with hot red peppers. Smoked eels are also available.

Eel

The **grouper** family includes almost 400 varieties found in temperate waters worldwide. The more common Atlantic Ocean varieties are the yellowfin grouper, black grouper, red grouper and gag; the Pacific Ocean varieties are the sea bass (also known as jewfish and different from the black sea bass) and spotted cabrilla. Although some species can reach 800 pounds or more, most commercial varieties are sold in the 5 to 20-pound (2.2 to 8.8-kilogram) range. They have lean white flesh with a mild to sweet flavor and very firm texture. Their skin, which is tough and strongly flavored, is generally removed before cooking. Grouper fillets may be baked, deep-fried, broiled or grilled.

Grouper

Herring (Fr. *hareng*) are long, silvery-blue fish found in both the northern Atlantic and Pacific Oceans. Their strongly flavored flesh has a moderate to high fat content. Whole herring weigh up to 8 ounces (225 grams). Fresh herring may be butterflied or filleted and roasted, broiled or grilled. But because herring are very soft and tend to spoil quickly, they are rarely available fresh. More often, they are smoked (known as kippers) or cured in brine.

Sardines (Fr. *sardine*) are young, small herring with fatty, oily flesh that has a flaky texture. Sardines are usually sold canned, whole or as skinned and boned fillets, or fried or smoked and packed in oil or sauce. Sardines are used primarily for sandwiches and salads.

John Dory, also known as St. Peter's fish, have a distinctive round, black spot with a yellow halo on each side of the body. Their flesh is white, firm and finely flaked. They may be filleted and prepared like flounder and are a classic bouillabaisse ingredient.

John Dory

Mackerel

Mackerel (Fr. *maquereau*) of culinary importance include king and Spanish mackerel as well as tuna and wahoo, which are discussed separately below. The species known as Atlantic and Pacific mackerel are not generally used for food because of their small size and high fat content. Mackerel flesh has a high fat content, gray to pink coloring, a mild flavor and flaky texture. The flesh becomes firm and off-white when cooked. Mackerel are best broiled, grilled, smoked or baked.

Mahi-mahi is the more commonly used name for dolphin or dolphinfish; this Hawaiian name is used to distinguish them from the marine mammal of the same name. (Dolphins and porpoises are marine mammals.) Also known by their Spanish name, *dorado*, mahi-mahi are brilliantly colored fish found in tropical seas. Mahi-mahi weigh about 15 pounds (6.6 kilograms) and are sold whole or as fillets. Their flesh is off-white to pink, lean and firm with a sweet flavor. Dolphinfish can be broiled, grilled or baked. The meat may become dry when cooked, however, so sauce or marinade is recommended.

Mahi-Mahi

Monkfish are also known as angler fish, goosefish, rape and lotte. These extraordinarily ugly fish are rarely seen whole, for the large head is usually discarded before reaching market. Only the tail is edible; it is available in fillets, fresh or frozen. The scaleless skin must be removed. The flesh is lean, pearly white and very firm. Its texture and flavor have earned monkfish the nickname of "poor man's lobster." Monkfish absorb flavors easily and are baked, steamed, fried, grilled or broiled. They are also used for stews and soups.

Orange roughy are caught in the South Pacific off the coasts of New Zealand and Australia. They have bright orange skin and firm, pearly-white flesh with a low fat content and extremely bland flavor. Fresh-frozen fillets are widely available year round. Orange roughy are almost always marketed as skinless, boneless frozen fillets, averaging 6 to 8 ounces (140 to 225 grams) each. They can be broiled, steamed, grilled or prepared in the same manner as cod.

Red snapper is also known as the American or northern red snapper. Although there are many members of the snapper family, only one is the true red snapper. Red-skinned rockfish are often mislabeled as the more popular red snapper or Pacific snapper, a practice that is currently legal only in California. True red snapper has lean, pink flesh that becomes white when cooked; it is sweet-flavored and flaky. They are sold whole or as fillets with the skin left on for identification.

Red Snapper

Red snapper may reach 35 pounds, but most are marketed at only 4 to 6 pounds (1.8 to 2.7 kilograms) or as 1 to 3-pound (450 grams to 1.3 kilograms) fillets. Red snapper can be prepared using almost any cooking method. The head and bones are excellent for stock.

Salmon (Fr. *saumon*) flourish in both the northern Atlantic and Pacific Oceans, returning to the freshwater rivers and streams of their birth to spawn. Salmon flesh gets its distinctive pink-red color from fat-soluble carotenoids found in the crustaceans on which they feed.

Atlantic salmon is the most important commercially, accounting for one quarter of all salmon produced worldwide. Extensive aquafarms in Norway, Canada and Scotland produce a steady supply of Atlantic salmon. For marketing purposes, the fish's point of origin is often added to the name (for example, Norwegian, Scottish or Shetland Atlantic salmon). Atlantic salmon have a rich pink color and moist flesh. Their average weight is from 4 to 12 pounds (1.8 to 5.4 kilograms). Wild Atlantic salmon are almost never available.

Atlantic Salmon

Chinook or **king salmon** from the Pacific are also highly desirable. They average from 5 to 30 pounds (2.2 to 13.2 kilograms) and have red-orange flesh with a high fat content and rich flavor. Like other salmon, their flesh separates into large flakes when cooked. Chinooks are often marketed by the name of the river from which they are harvested (for example, Columbia, Yukon or Copper Chinook salmon). They are distinguished by the black interior of their mouth.

Chinook or King Salmon

Coho or **silver** salmon have pinkish flesh and are available fresh or frozen, wild or from aquafarms. Wild coho average from 3 to 12 pounds (1.3 to 5.4 kilograms), while aquafarmed coho are much smaller, usually less than 1 pound (450 grams).

Other varieties, such as chum, sockeye, red, blueback and pink salmon, are usually canned but may be available fresh or frozen.

Mini Coho Salmon

Salmon can be prepared by many cooking methods: broiling, grilling, poaching, steaming or baking. Frying is not recommended, however, because of their high fat content. Salmon fillets are often cured or smoked. **Gravlax** is salmon that has been cured for one to three days with salt, sugar and dill. **Lox** is salmon that is cured in a salted brine and then typically cold-smoked. **Nova** is used in the eastern U.S. to refer to a less-salty, cold-smoked salmon.

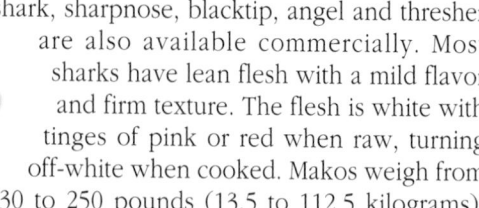

Blacktip Shark

Sharks provide delicious eating, despite their less-than-appealing appearance and vicious reputation. Mako and blue sharks are the most desirable, with mako often being sold as swordfish. Sand shark, sharpnose, blacktip, angel and thresher are also available commercially. Most sharks have lean flesh with a mild flavor and firm texture. The flesh is white with tinges of pink or red when raw, turning off-white when cooked. Makos weigh from 30 to 250 pounds (13.5 to 112.5 kilograms); other species may reach as much as 1000 pounds (450 kilograms). All sharks have cartilaginous skeletons and no bones; therefore, they are not actually fish, but rather marine invertebrates. Sharks are usually cut into loins or wheels, then into steaks or cubes. They can be broiled, grilled, baked or fried. An ammonia smell indicates that the shark was not properly treated when caught. Do not buy or eat it.

Swordfish take their name from the long, swordlike bill extending from their upper jaw. These popular fish average about 250 pounds (112.5 kilograms). Their flesh is lean and sweet with a very firm, meatlike texture; it may be gray, pink or off-white when raw, becoming white when cooked. Swordfish are most often available cut into wheels or portioned into steaks perfect for grilling or broiling.

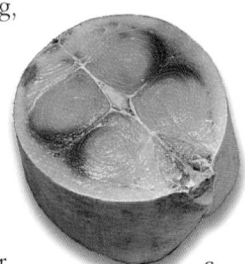

Swordfish Wheel

Tilapia

Tilapia is the name given to several species of freshwater, aquafarm-raised fish bred worldwide. They grow quickly in warm water, reaching about 3 pounds (1.3 kilograms); they are available whole or filleted, fresh or frozen. The flesh is similar to catfish—lean, white and sweet, with a firm texture. Tilapia are sometimes marketed as cherry snapper or sunshine snapper, even though they are not members of the snapper family.

Trout (Fr. *truite*) are members of the salmon family. Most of the freshwater trout commercially available are aquafarm-raised rainbow trout, although brown trout and brook trout are also being aquafarmed. Some trout species spend part of their lives at sea, returning to fresh water to spawn. On the West Coast, these are called salmon trout or steelhead. Trout have a low to moderate fat content, a flaky texture and a delicate flavor that can be easily overwhelmed by strong sauces. The flesh may be white, orange or pink. Trout are usually marketed at 8 to 10 ounces (225 to 280 grams) each, just right for an individual portion. Lake trout, sometimes known as char, are not aquafarmed and have little commercial value because of their extremely high fat content. Trout can be baked, pan-fried, smoked or steamed.

Red Mountain Trout

Rainbow Trout

Tuna (Fr. *thon*) varieties include the bluefin, yellowfin, bonito, bigeye and blackfin. Ahi is the popular market name for either yellowfin or bigeye tuna. All are members of the mackerel family and are found in tropical and subtropical waters around the world. Tuna are large fish, weighing up to several hundred pounds each. Bluefin, the finest and most desirable for sashimi, are becoming very scarce because of overfishing. Regular canned tuna is usually prepared from yellowfin or skipjack; canned white tuna is prepared from albacore, also known as longfin tuna. Pacific tuna that is frozen at sea to preserve its freshness is referred to as clipper fish. Any of these species may be found fresh or frozen, however. Tuna is usually cut into four boneless loins for market. The loins are then cut into steaks, cubes or chunks. The flesh has a low to moderate fat content (a higher fat content is preferred for sashimi) and a deep red color. The dark, reddish-brown muscle that runs along the lateral line is very fatty and can be removed. Tuna flesh turns light gray when cooked and is very firm, with a mild flavor. Tuna work well for grilling or broiling and may be marinated or brushed with seasoned oil during cooking. Tuna are often prepared medium rare to prevent dryness.

Yellowfin Tuna

Wahoo, also known as ono, are found throughout tropical and subtropical waters, but are particularly associated with Hawaii (*ono* even means "good to eat" in Hawaiian). They are actually a type of mackerel and are cooked like any other mackerel.

Wahoo

Whitefish species inhabit the freshwater lakes and streams of North America. Lake whitefish, the most important commercially, are related to salmon. They are marketed at up to 7 pounds (3.2 kilograms) and are available whole or filleted. The flesh is firm and white, with a moderate amount of fat and a sweet flavor. Whitefish may be baked, broiled, grilled or smoked and are often used in processed fish products.

Whitefish

♦♦♦

TRASH FISH

Ocean pout are considered a "trash fish," or fish that fishermen throw away because there is little or no consumer demand and therefore no market value.

Long ago, lobster were considered trash and good for nothing but chicken feed. More recently, monkfish was a trash fish in the U.S., and now we can't get enough. Obscure species are often trash fish until someone somewhere tastes them and realizes that they offer some incredible flavors and textures.

Searobins, dogfish, skate, and whiting are still considered trash fish in America, though they are gradually becoming more popular and will someday be readily available at fish markets.

from THE GREAT AMERICAN SEAFOOD COOKBOOK *by* SUSAN HERRMANN LOOMIS

Flatfish

Flounder (Fr. *flet*) have lean, firm flesh that is pearly or pinkish-white with a sweet, mild flavor. Although they are easily boned, most are deheaded and gutted at sea and sold as fresh or frozen fillets. These fillets are very thin and can dry out or spoil easily, so extra care should be taken in handling, preparing and storing them. Recipes that preserve moisture work best with flounder; poaching, steaming or frying are recommended. Many types of flounder are marketed as sole, perhaps in an attempt to cash in on the popularity of true sole. The FDA permits this practice.

English sole are actually flounder caught off the West Coast of the United States. They are usually marketed simply as "fillet of sole." They are a plentiful species of fair to average quality.

Petrale sole, another West Coast flounder, are generally considered the finest of the domestic "soles." They are most often available as fillets, which tend to be thicker and firmer than other sole fillets.

English Sole

Petrale Sole

TABLE 19.1   FLOUNDER (ALSO KNOWN AS SOLE)

Atlantic Ocean	Pacific Ocean
blackback/winter flounder/lemon sole	arrowtooth
fluke/summer flounder	petrale sole
starry flounder	rex sole
yellowtail	English sole
windowpane flounder	rock sole
gray sole/witch flounder	sand sole
	yellowfin sole
	domestic Dover sole/Pacific flounder
	butter sole

Lemon Sole

Alaskan Halibut

True Dover Sole

Turbot

Domestic Dover sole are also Pacific flounder. They are not as delicate or flavorful as other species of sole or flounder. Moreover, they are often afflicted with a parasite that causes the meat to have a slimy, gelatinous texture. Domestic Dover sole are not recommended if other sole or flounder are available.

Lemon sole are the most abundant and popular East Coast flounder. They are also known as blackback or winter flounder (during the winter they migrate close to shore from the deeper, colder waters). They average 2 pounds (900 grams) in weight.

Halibut are among the largest flatfish; they often weigh up to 300 pounds (135 kilograms). The FDA recognizes only two halibut species: Atlantic (eastern) and Pacific (northern, Alaskan, western) halibut. Both have lean, firm flesh that is snow-white with a sweet, mild flavor. California halibut, which are actually flounder, are similar in taste and texture but average only 12 pounds (5.4 kilograms) each. Halibut may be cut into boneless steaks or skewered on brochettes. The flesh, which dries out easily, can be poached, baked, grilled or broiled and is good with a variety of sauces.

Sole (Fr. *sole*) are probably the most flavorful and finely textured flatfish. Indeed, because of the connotations of quality associated with the name, "sole" is widely used for many species that are not members of the sole (*Soleidae*) family. Even though the FDA allows many species of flatfish to be called "sole" for marketing purposes, no true sole is commercially harvested in American waters. Any flatfish harvested in American waters and marketed as sole is actually flounder.

True **Dover sole**, a staple of classic cuisine, are a lean fish with pearly-white flesh and a delicate flavor that can stand up to a variety of sauces and seasonings. They are a member of the *Soleidae* family and come only from the waters off the coasts of England, Africa and Europe. They are imported into this country as fresh whole fish or fresh or frozen fillets.

Turbot are a Pacific flatfish of no great culinary distinction. In Europe, however, the species known as turbot (Fr. *turbot*) are large diamond-shaped fish highly prized for their delicate flavor and firm, white flesh. They are also marketed as brill.

Mollusks

Univalves

Univalves are mollusks with a single shell in which the soft-bodied animal resides. They are actually marine snails with a single foot, used to attach the creature to fixed objects such as rocks.

Abalone have brownish-gray, ear-shaped shells. They are harvested in California, but California law does not permit canning abalone or shipping it out of state. Some frozen abalone is available from Mexico; canned abalone is imported from Japan. Abalone are lean with a sweet, delicate flavor similar to that of clams. They are too tough to eat unless tenderized with a mallet or rolling pin. They may then be eaten raw or prepared seviche-style. Great care must be taken when grilling or sautéing abalone as the meat becomes very tough when overcooked.

Conch are found in warm waters off the Florida Keys and in the Caribbean. The beautiful peachy-pink shell of the queen conch is prized by beachcombers. Conch meat is lean, smooth and very firm with a sweet-smoky flavor and chewy texture. It can be sliced and pounded to tenderize it, eaten raw with lime juice, or slow-cooked whole.

Bivalves

Bivalves are mollusks with two bilateral shells attached by a central hinge.

Clams (Fr. *clovisses*) are harvested along both the East and West Coasts, with Atlantic clams being more significant commercially. Atlantic Coast clams include hard-shell, soft-shell and surf clams. Clams are available all year, either live in the shell or fresh-shucked (meat removed from the shell). Canned clams, whether minced, chopped or whole, are also available.

Atlantic hard-shell clams or **quahogs** have hard, blue-gray shells. Their chewy meat is not as sweet as other clam meat. Quahogs have different names, depending upon their size. **Littlenecks** are generally under 2 inches (5 centimeters) across the shell and usually are served on the half shell or steamed. They are the most expensive clams. **Cherrystones** are generally under 3 inches (7.5 centimeters) across the shell and are sometimes eaten raw but are more often cooked. **Topnecks** are usually cooked and are often served as stuffed clams. **Chowders**, the largest quahogs, are always eaten cooked, especially minced for chowder or soup.

Soft-shell clams, also known as Ipswich, steamer and long-necked clams, have thin, brittle shells that do not completely close because of the clam's protruding black-tipped siphon. Their meat is tender and sweet. They are sometimes fried but are more often served steamed.

Surf clams are deep-water clams that reach sizes of 8 inches (20 centimeters) across. They are most often cut into strips for frying or are minced, chopped, processed and canned.

Pacific clams are generally too tough to eat raw. The most common is the **Manila clam**, which was introduced along the Pacific coast during the 1930s. Resembling a quahog with a ridged shell, it can be served steamed or on the half shell. **Geoducks** are the largest Pacific clam, sometimes weighing up to 10 pounds (4.5 kilograms) each. They look like huge soft-shell clams with a large, protruding siphon. Their tender, rich bodies and briny flavor are popular in Asian cuisines.

♦♦♦
SNAILS

Although snails (more politely known by their French name, *escargots*) are univalve land animals, they share many characteristics with their marine cousins. They can be poached in court bouillon or removed from their shells and boiled or baked briefly with a seasoned butter or sauce. They should be firm but tender; overcooking makes snails tough and chewy. The most popular varieties are the large white Burgundy snail and the small garden variety called *petit gris*. Fresh snails are available from snail ranches through speciality suppliers. The great majority of snails, however, are purchased canned; most canned snails are produced in France or Taiwan.

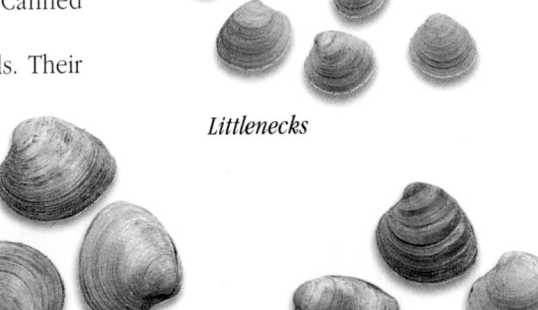

Littlenecks

Cherrystones

Topnecks

Soft-shell Clams

Manila Clams

Cockles

Greenshell Mussels

Gulf Oysters

European Flat Oysters

Hamma-hamma Oysters

Cockles are small bivalves, about 1 inch (2.5 centimeters) long, with ridged shells. They are more popular in Europe than the United States and are sometimes used in dishes such as paella and fish soups or stews.

Mussels (Fr. *moule*) are found in waters worldwide. They are excellent steamed in wine or seasoned broth and can be fried or used in soups or pasta dishes.

Blue mussels are the most common edible mussel. They are found in the wild along the Atlantic Coast and are aquafarmed on both coasts. Their meat is plump and sweet with a firm, muscular texture. The orangish-yellow meat of cultivated mussels tends to be much larger than that of wild mussels and therefore worth the added cost. Blue mussels are sold live in the shell and average from 10 to 20 per pound. Although available all year, the best-quality blue mussels are harvested during the winter months.

Greenshell (or greenlip) **mussels** from New Zealand and Thailand are much larger than blue mussels, averaging 8–12 mussels per pound. Their shells are paler gray, with a distinctive bright-green edge.

Blue Mussels

Oysters (Fr. *huître*) have a rough gray shell; their soft, gray, briny flesh can be eaten raw or cooked. Most oysters available in this country are commercially grown and sold either live in the shell or shucked. Oysters are excellent live, eaten directly from the shell. They can also be steamed or baked in the shell or shucked and fried, sautéed or added to stews or chowders. There are four main domestic species.

Atlantic oysters, also called American or Eastern oysters, have darker, flatter shells than other oysters.

Blue Point Oysters

European flat oysters are often incorrectly called Belon (true Belon oysters live only in the Belon river of France); they are very round and flat and look like giant brownish-green Olympias.

Olympias are the only oysters native to the Pacific Coast; they are tiny (about the size of a 50-cent coin).

Olympias

Pacific oysters, also called Japanese oysters, are aquafarmed along the Pacific Coast; they have curly, thick striated shells and silvery-gray to gold to almost-white meat.

Although it may seem like there are hundreds of oyster species on the market, there are only two that are commercially significant: the Atlantic oyster and the Pacific oyster. These two species yield dozens of different varieties, however, depending on their origin. For example, Atlantic oysters may be referred to as bluepoints, Chesapeake Bay, Florida Gulf, Long Island and so on, while Pacific oysters include Penn Cove Select, Westcott Bay, Hamma-hamma, Kumamoto and Portuguese, among others. An oyster's flavor reflects the minerals, nutrients and salts in its water and mud bed, so a Bristol from Maine and an Apalachicola from Florida will taste very different, even though they are the same Atlantic species.

Scallops contain an edible white adductor muscle that holds together the fan-shaped shells. Because they die quickly, they are almost always shucked and cleaned on-board ship. The sea scallop and the bay scallop, both cold-water varieties, and the calico scallop, a warm-water variety, are the most important commercially. Sea scallops are the largest, with an average count of 20–30 per pound. Larger sea scallops are also available. Bay scallops average 70–90 per pound; calico scallops average 70–110 per pound. Fresh or frozen shucked, cleaned scallops are the most common market form, but live scallops in the shell and shucked scallops with roe attached (very popular in Europe) are also available. Scallops are sweet, with a tender texture. Raw scallops should be a translucent ivory color, nonsymmetrically round and should feel springy. They can be steamed, broiled, grilled, fried, sautéed or baked. When overcooked, however, scallops quickly become chewy and dry. Only extremely fresh scallops should be eaten raw.

Sea Scallops

Cephalopods

Cephalopods are marine mollusks with distinct heads, well-developed eyes, a number of arms that attach to the head near the mouth and a saclike fin-bearing mantle. They do not have an outer shell; instead, there is a thin internal shell called a *pen* or *cuttlebone*.

Octopus is generally quite tough and requires mechanical tenderization or long, moist-heat cooking to make it palatable. Most octopuses are imported from Portugal, though fresh ones are available on the East Coast during the winter. Octopus is sold by the pound, fresh or frozen, usually whole. Octopus skin is gray when raw, turning purple when cooked. The interior flesh is white, lean, firm and flavorful.

Squid, known by their Italian name, *calamari*, are becoming increasingly popular in this country. Similar to octopuses but much smaller, they are harvested along both American coasts and elsewhere around the world (the finest are the East Coast loligo or winter squid). They range in size from an average of 8–10 per pound to the giant South American squid that is sold as tenderized steaks. The squid's tentacles, mantle (body tube) and fins are edible. Squid meat is white to ivory in color, turning darker with age. It is moderately lean, slightly sweet, firm and tender, but it toughens quickly if overcooked. Squid are available either fresh, or frozen and packed in blocks.

Squid

Crustaceans

Crustaceans are found in both fresh and salt water. They have a hard outer shell and jointed appendages, and they breathe through gills.

Crayfish (Fr. *écrevisse*), generally called *crayfish* in the North and *crawfish* or *crawdad* in the South, are freshwater creatures that look like miniature lobsters. They are harvested from the wild or aquafarmed in Louisiana and the Pacific Northwest. They are from 3-1/2 to 7 inches (8 to 17.5 centimeters) in length when marketed and may be purchased live or precooked and frozen. The lean meat, found mostly in the tail, is sweet and tender. Crayfish can be boiled whole and served hot or cold. The tail meat can be deep-fried or used in soups, bisque or sauces. Crayfish are a staple of Cajun cuisine, often used in gumbo, étouffée and jambalaya. Whole crayfish become brilliant red when cooked and may be used as a garnish.

Crabs (Fr. *crabe*) are found along the North American coasts in great numbers and are shipped throughout the world in fresh, frozen and canned forms. Crab meat varies in flavor and texture and can be used in a range of prepared dishes, from chowders to curries to casseroles. Crabs purchased live should last up to five days; dead crabs should not be used.

King crabs are very large crabs (usually around 10 pounds or 4.4 kilograms) caught in the very cold waters of the North Pacific. Their meat is very sweet and snow-white. King crabs are always sold frozen, usually in the shell. In-shell forms include sections or clusters, legs and claws or split legs. The meat is also available in "fancy" packs of whole leg and body meat, or shredded and minced pieces.

Dungeness Crab

Dungeness crabs are found along the West Coast. They weigh 1-1/2 to 4 pounds (680 grams to 1.8 kilograms), and have delicate, sweet meat. They are sold live, precooked and frozen, or as picked meat, usually in 5-pound (2.2-kilogram) vacuum-packed cans.

Blue crabs are found along the entire eastern seaboard and account for approximately 50% of the total weight of all crab species harvested in the United States. Their meat is rich and sweet. Blue crabs are available as hard-shell or soft-shell. Hard-shell crabs are sold live, precooked and frozen, or as picked meat. Soft-shell crabs are those harvested within six hours after molting and are available live (generally only from May 15 to September 15) or frozen. They are often steamed and served whole. Soft-shells can be sautéed, fried, broiled or added to soups or stews. Blue crabs are sold by size, with an average diameter of 4–7 inches (10–18 centimeters).

Blue Crab

Soft-Shell Crabs

Snow or **spider crabs** are an abundant species, most often used as a substitute for the scarcer and more expensive king crab. They are harvested from Alaskan waters and along the eastern coast of Canada. Snow crab is sold precooked, usually frozen. The meat can be used in soups, salads, omelettes or other prepared dishes. Legs are often served cold as an appetizer.

Stone crabs are generally available only as cooked claws, either fresh or frozen (the claws cannot be frozen raw because the meat sticks to the shell). In stone-crab fishery only the claw is harvested. After the claw is removed, the crab is returned to the water, where in about 18 months it regenerates a new claw. Claws average 2-1/2 to 5-1/2 ounces (75 to 155 grams) each. The meat is firm, with a sweet taste similar to lobster. Cracked claws are served hot or cold, usually with cocktail sauce, lemon butter or other accompaniments.

Lobsters have brown to blue-black outer shells and firm, white meat with a rich, sweet flavor. Lobster shells turn red when cooked. They are usually poached, steamed, simmered, baked or grilled, and can be served hot or cold. Picked meat can be used in prepared dishes, soups or sautés. Lobsters must be kept alive until just before cooking. Dead lobsters should not be eaten. The Maine, also known as American or clawed lobster, and the spiny lobster are the most commonly marketed species.

Maine Lobster

Maine lobsters have edible meat in both their tails and claws; they are considered superior in flavor to all other lobsters. They come from the cold waters along the Northeast Coast and are most often sold live. Maine lobsters may be purchased by weight (i.e., 1-1/4 pound [525 grams], 1-1/2 pound [650 grams] or 2 pounds [900 grams] each), or as chix (i.e., less than one pound [450 grams]). Maine lobsters may also be purchased as culls (lobsters with only one claw) or bullets (lobsters with no claws). They are available frozen or as cooked, picked meat.

Figure 19.3 shows a cross section of a Maine lobster and identifies the stomach, tomalley (the olive-green liver) and coral (the roe). The stomach is not eaten; the tomalley and coral are very flavorful and are often used in the preparation of sauces and other items.

Spiny lobsters have very small claws and are valuable only for their meaty tails, which are notched with short spines. Nearly all spiny lobsters marketed in this country are sold as frozen tails, often identified as rock lobster. Harvested in many parts of the world, those found off Florida, Brazil and in the Caribbean are marketed as warm-water tails; those found off South Africa, Australia and New Zealand are called cold-water tails. Cold-water spiny tails are considered superior to their warm-water cousins.

Slipper lobster, lobsterette and **squat lobster** are all clawless species found in tropical, subtropical and temperate waters worldwide. Although popular in some countries, their flavor is inferior to both Maine and spiny lobsters. **Langoustine** are small North Atlantic lobsters.

Shrimp (Fr. *crevette*) are found worldwide and are widely popular. Gulf whites, pinks, browns and black tigers are just a few of the dozens of shrimp varieties used in food service operations. Although fresh, head-on shrimp are available, the most common form is raw, head-off (also called green headless) shrimp with the shell on. Most shrimp are deheaded and frozen at sea to preserve freshness. Shrimp are available in many forms: raw, peeled and deveined; cooked, peeled and deveined; individually quick frozen; as well as in a variety of processed, breaded or canned products. Shrimp are graded by size, which can range from 400 per pound (titi) to 8 per pound (extra-colossal), and are sold in counts per pound. For example, shrimp marketed as "21–26 count" means that there is an average of 21 to 26 shrimp per pound; shrimp marketed as "U-10" means that there are under 10 shrimp per pound.

Prawn is often used interchangeably with the word *shrimp* in English-speaking countries. Although it is perhaps more accurate to refer to freshwater species as prawns and marine species as shrimp, in commercial practice prawn refers to any large shrimp. Equally confusing, *scampi* is the Italian name for the Dublin Bay prawn (which is actually a species of miniature lobster), but in this country *scampi* refers to shrimp sautéed in garlic butter.

Shrimp

Green Headless Shrimp

FIGURE 19.3

NUTRITION

Fish and shellfish are low in calories, fat and sodium, and are high in vitamins A, B and D and protein. Fish and shellfish are also high in minerals, especially calcium (particularly in canned fish with edible bones), phosphorus, potassium and iron (especially mollusks). Fish are high in a group of polyunsaturated fatty acids called omega-3, which may help combat high blood cholesterol levels and aid in preventing some heart disease. Shellfish are not as high in cho-

TABLE 19.2   NUTRITIONAL VALUES OF FISH AND SHELLFISH

Per 1 oz. (28 g) Raw	Kcal	Protein (g)	Total Fat (g)	Saturated Fat (g)	Cholesterol (mg)	Sodium (mg)
Abalone	30	4.8	0.2	<0.1	24	85
Clam, mixed species	21	3.6	0.3	<0.1	10	16
Cod, Atlantic	23	5.0	0.2	<0.1	12	15
Crab, Alaska king	24	5.2	0.2	mq	12	237
Flatfish	26	5.3	0.3	0.1	14	23
Lobster	26	5.3	0.3	mq	27	mq
Oyster, eastern	20	20	0.7	0.2	16	32
Salmon	40	5.6	1.8	0.3	16	113
Sea bass	27	5.2	0.6	0.1	12	19
Shrimp, mixed species	30	5.7	0.5	0.1	43	42
Surimi	28	4.3	0.3	mq	9	41
Tuna, yellowfin	31	6.6	0.3	0.1	13	10
Whitefish	38	5.4	1.7	0.3	17	14

The Corinne T. Netzer Encyclopedia of Food Values 1992
mq = measurable quantity, but data is unavailable

lesterol as was once thought. Crustaceans are higher in cholesterol than mollusks, but both have considerably lower levels than red meat or eggs.

The cooking methods used for fish and shellfish also contribute to their healthfulness. The most commonly used cooking methods—broiling, grilling, poaching and steaming—add little or no fat.

INSPECTION AND GRADING OF FISH AND SHELLFISH

Inspection

Unlike mandatory meat and poultry inspections, fish and shellfish inspections are voluntary. They are performed in a fee-for-service program supervised by the United States Department of Commerce (USDC).

Type 1 inspection services cover plant, product and processing methods from the raw material to the final product. The "Packed Under Federal Inspection" (PUFI) mark or statement shown in Figure 19.4 can be used on product labels processed under Type 1 inspection services. It signifies that the product is safe and wholesome, properly labeled, has reasonably good flavor and odor, and was produced under inspection in an official establishment.

Type 2 inspection services are usually performed in a warehouse, processing plant or cold storage facility on specific product lots. See Figure 19.5. A lot inspection determines whether the product complies with purchase agreement criteria (usually defined in a spec sheet) such as condition, weight, labeling and packaging integrity.

Type 3 inspection services are for sanitation only. Fishing vessels or plants that meet the requirements are recognized as official establishments and are

FIGURE 19.4   *PUFI Mark and Statements*

included in the *USDC Approved List of Fish Establishments and Products*. The list is available to governmental and institutional purchasing agents as well as to retail and restaurant buyers.

Grading

Only fish processed under Type 1 inspection services are eligible for grading. Each type of fish has its own grading criteria, but because of the great variety of fish and shellfish, the USDC has been able to set grading criteria for only the most common types.

The grades assigned to fish are A, B or C. Grade A products are top quality and must have good flavor and odor and be practically free of physical blemishes or defects. The great majority of fresh and frozen fish and shellfish consumed in restaurants is Grade A. See Figure 19.6. Grade B indicates good quality; Grade C indicates fairly good quality. Grade B and C products are most often canned or processed.

PURCHASING AND STORING FISH AND SHELLFISH

Determining Freshness

Because fish and shellfish are highly perishable, an inspection stamp does not necessarily ensure top quality. A few hours at the wrong temperature or a couple of days in the refrigerator can turn high-quality fish or shellfish into garbage. It is important that you be able to determine for yourself the freshness and quality of the fish and shellfish you purchase or use. Freshness should be checked before purchasing and again just before cooking.

Freshness can be determined by:

1. *Smell*—By far the easiest way to determine freshness, fresh fish should have a slight sea smell or no odor at all. Any off-odors or ammonia odors are a sure sign of aged or improperly handled fish.
2. *Eyes*—The eyes should be clear and full. Sunken eyes mean the fish is drying out and is probably not fresh.
3. *Gills*—The gills should be intact and bright red. Brown gills are a sign of age.
4. *Texture*—Generally, the flesh of fresh fish should be firm. Mushy flesh or flesh that does not spring back when pressed with a finger is a sign of poor quality or age.
5. *Fins and scales*—Fins and scales should be moist and full without excessive drying on the outer edges. Dry fins or scales are a sign of age; damaged fins or scales may be a sign of mishandling.
6. *Appearance*—Fish cuts should be moist and glistening, without bruises or dark spots. Edges should not be brown or dry.
7. *Movement*—Shellfish should be purchased alive and should show movement. Lobsters and other crustaceans should be active. Clams, mussels and oysters that are partially opened should snap shut when tapped with a finger. (Exceptions are geoduck, razor and steamer clams whose siphons protrude, preventing the shell from closing completely.) Ones that do not close are dead and should not be used. Avoid mollusks with broken shells or heavy shells that might be filled with mud or sand.

FIGURE 19.5 *Product Inspection Stamps*

FIGURE 19.6 *Grade A Stamp*

Purchasing Fish and Shellfish

Fish are available from wholesalers in a variety of market forms:

+ **Whole** or **round**—as caught, intact.
+ **Drawn**—viscera (internal organs) is removed; most whole fish are purchased this way.
+ **Dressed**—viscera, gills, fins and scales are removed.
+ **Pan-dressed**—viscera and gills are removed; fish is scaled and fins and tail are trimmed. The head is usually removed, although small fish, such as trout, may be pan-dressed with the head still attached. Pan-dressed fish are then pan-fried.
+ **Butterflied**—a pan-dressed fish, boned and opened flat like a book. The two sides remain attached by the back or belly skin.

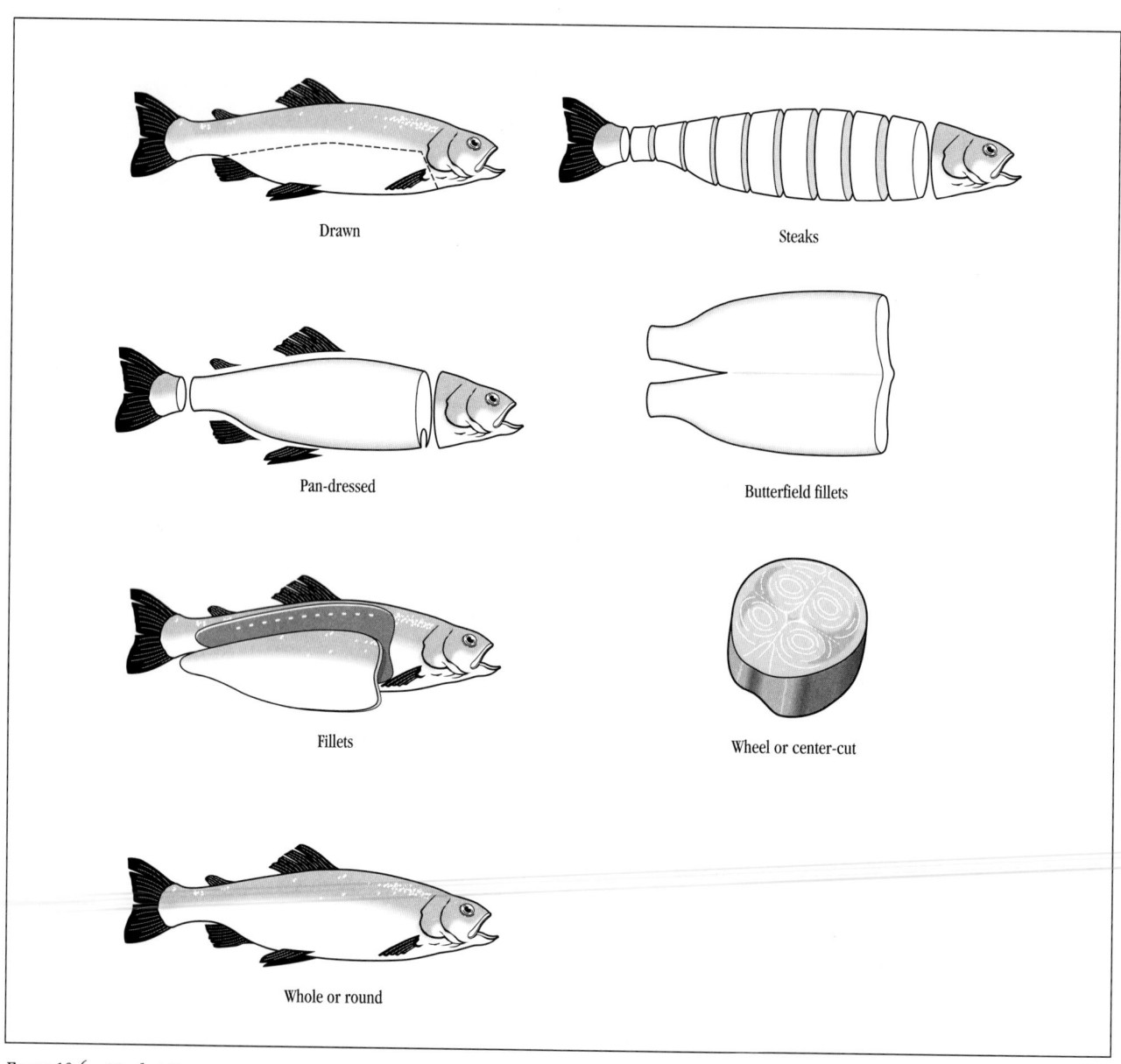

FIGURE 19.6   *Market Forms*

+ **Fillet**—the side of a fish removed intact, boneless or semi-boneless, with or without skin.
+ **Steak**—cross-section slice, with a small section of backbone attached; usually prepared from large round fish.
+ **Wheel** or **center-cut**—used for swordfish and sharks, which are cut into large boneless pieces from which steaks are then cut.

You should purchase fish in the market forms most practical for your operation. Although fish fabrication is a relatively simple chore requiring little specialized equipment, before you decide to cut your own fish you should consider

1. the food service operation's ability to utilize the bones and trim that cutting whole fish produces,
2. the employees' ability to fabricate fillets, steaks or portions as needed,
3. the storage facilities and
4. the product's intended use.

Most shellfish can be purchased live in the shell, shucked (the meat removed from the shell) or processed. Both live and shucked shellfish are usually purchased by counts (i.e., the number per volume). For example, standard live Eastern oysters are packed 200–250 (the count) per bushel (the unit of volume); standard Eastern oyster meats are packed 350 per gallon. Crustaceans are sometimes packed by size based on the number of pieces per pound; for example, crab legs or shrimp are often sold in counts per pound. Or, they are sold either by grades based on size (whole crabs) or by weight (lobsters).

Storing Fish and Shellfish

The most important concern when storing fish and shellfish is temperature. All fresh fish should be stored at temperatures between 30° and 34°F (-1 to 1°C). Fish stored in a refrigerator at 40°F (4°C) will have approximately half the shelf life of fish stored at 32°F (0°C).

Most fish are shipped on ice and should be stored on ice in the refrigerator as soon as possible after receipt. Whole fish should be layered directly in crushed or shaved ice in a perforated pan so that the melted ice water drains away. If crushed or shaved ice is not available, cubed ice may be used provided it is put in plastic bags and gently placed on top of the fish to prevent bruising and denting. Fabricated and portioned fish may be wrapped in moisture-proof packaging before icing to prevent the ice and water from damaging the exposed flesh. Fish stored on ice should be drained and re-iced daily.

Fresh scallops, fish fillets that are purchased in plastic trays, and oyster and clam meats should be set on or packed in ice. Do not let the scallops, fillets or meats come in direct contact with the ice.

Clams, mussels and oysters should be stored at 40°F (4°C), at high humidity and left in the boxes or net bags in which they were shipped. Under ideal conditions, shellfish can be kept alive for up to one week. Never store live shellfish in plastic bags and do not ice them.

If a saltwater tank is not available, live lobsters, crabs and other crustaceans should be kept in boxes with seaweed or damp newspaper to keep them moist. Most crustaceans circulate salt water over their gills; icing them or placing them in fresh water will kill them. Lobsters and crabs will live for several days under ideal conditions.

♦♦♦
HOW FRESH IS FROZEN FISH?

Fresh—the item is not and has never been frozen.

Chilled—now used by some in the industry to replace the more ambiguous "fresh"; indicates that the item was refrigerated, that is, held at 30 to 34°F (-1 to 1°C).

Flash-frozen—the item was quickly frozen on-board ship or at a processing plant within hours of being caught.

Fresh-frozen—the item was quick-frozen while still fresh but not as quickly as flash-frozen.

Frozen—the item was subjected to temperatures of 0°F (-18°C) or lower to preserve its inherent quality.

Glazed—a frozen product dipped in water; the ice forms a glaze that protects the item from freezer burn.

Fancy—code word for "previously frozen."

Like most frozen foods, frozen fish should be kept at temperatures of 0°F (-18°C) or colder. Colder temperatures greatly increase shelf life. Frozen fish should be thawed in the refrigerator; once thawed, they should be treated like fresh fish.

Fabricating Procedures

As discussed, fish and shellfish can be purchased in many forms. Here we demonstrate several procedures for cutting, cleaning and otherwise fabricating or preparing fish and shellfish for cooking and service.

Procedure for Scaling Fish

This procedure is used to remove the scales from fish that will be cooked with the skin on.

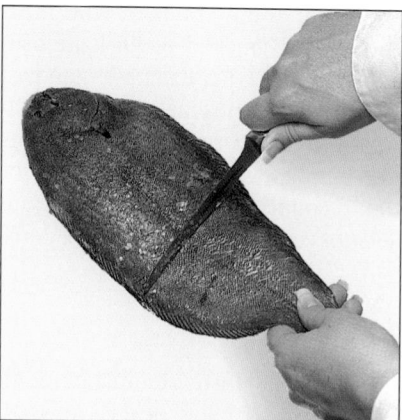

1. Place the fish on a work surface or in a large sink. Grip the fish by the tail and, working from the tail toward the head, scrape the scales off with a fish scaler or the back of a knife. Be careful not to damage the flesh by pushing too hard. Turn the fish over and remove the scales from the other side. Rinse the fish under cold water.

Procedure for Pan-Dressing Flatfish

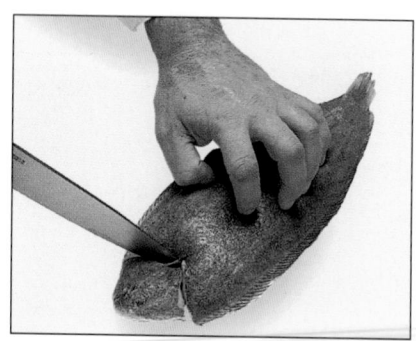

1. Scale the flatfish. Place the fish on a cutting board and remove the head by making a V-shaped cut around it with a chef's knife. Pull the head away and remove the viscera.

2. Rinse the fish under cold water, removing all traces of blood and viscera from the cavity.

3. Using a pair of kitchen shears, trim off the tail and all of the fins.

PROCEDURE FOR FILLETING ROUND FISH

Round fish produce two fillets, one from either side.

1. Using a chef's knife, cut down to the backbone just behind the gills. Do not remove the head.

2. Turn the knife toward the tail; using smooth strokes, cut from head to tail parallel to the backbone. The knife should bump against the backbone so that no flesh is wasted; you will feel the knife cutting through the small pin bones. Cut the fillet completely free from the bones. Repeat on the other side.

3. Trim the rib bones from the fillet with a flexible boning knife.

4. The finished fillet.

PROCEDURE FOR FILLETING FLATFISH

Flatfish produce four fillets: two large bilateral fillets from the top and two smaller bilateral fillets from the bottom. If the fish fillets are going to be cooked with the skin on, the fish should be scaled before cooking (it is easier to scale the fish before it is filleted). If the skin is going to be removed before cooking, it is not necessary to scale the fish.

1. With the dark side of the fish facing up, cut along the backbone from head to tail with the tip of a flexible boning knife.

2. Turn the knife and, using smooth strokes, cut between the flesh and the rib bones, keeping the flexible blade against the bone. Cut the fillet completely free from the fish. Remove the second fillet, following the same procedure.

3. Turn the fish over and remove the fillets from the bottom half of the fish, following the same procedure.

PROCEDURE FOR SKINNING DOVER SOLE

Dover sole is unique in that its skin can be pulled from the whole fish by following this procedure. The flesh of other small flatfish such as flounder, petrale sole and other types of domestic sole is more delicate; pulling the skin away from the whole fish could damage the flesh. These fish should be skinned after they are filleted.

1. Make a shallow cut in the flesh perpendicular to the length of the fish, just in front of the tail and with the knife angled toward the head of the fish. Using a clean towel, grip the skin and pull it toward the head of the fish. The skin should come off cleanly, in one piece, leaving the flesh intact.

PROCEDURE FOR SKINNING FISH FILLETS

Here we use a salmon fillet to demonstrate the procedure for skinning fish fillets. Use the same procedure to skin all types of fish fillets.

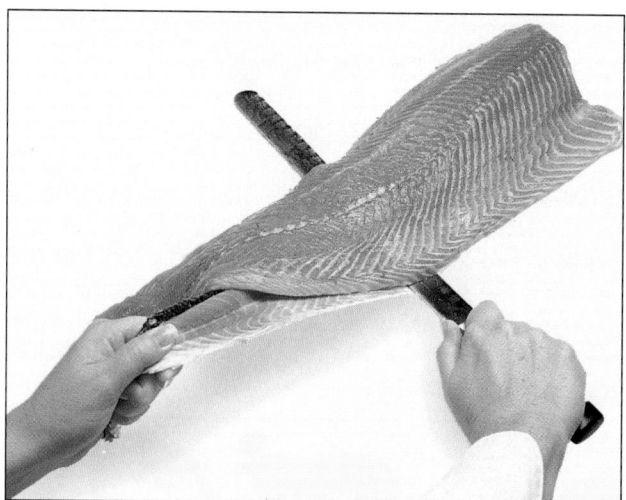

1. Place the fillet on a cutting board with the skin side down. Starting at the tail, use a meat slicer or a chef's knife to cut between the flesh and skin. Angle the knife down toward the skin, grip the skin tightly with one hand and use a sawing motion to cut the skin cleanly away from the flesh.

PROCEDURE FOR PULLING PIN BONES FROM A SALMON FILLET

Round fish fillets contain a row of intramuscular bones running the length of the fillet. Known as pin bones, they are usually cut out with a knife to produce boneless fillets. In the case of salmon, they can be removed with salmon tweezers or small needle-nose pliers.

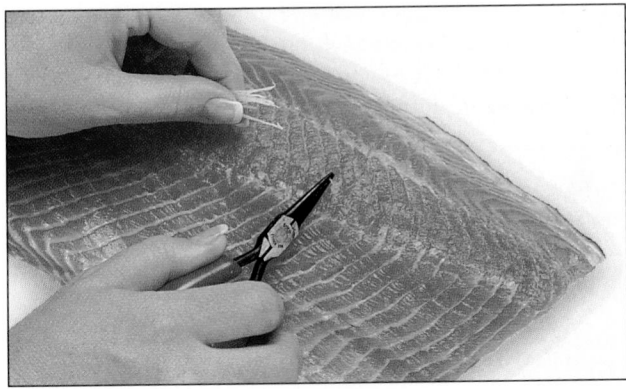

1. Place the fillet (either skinless or not) on the cutting board, skin side down. Starting at the front or head end of the fillet, use your fingertips to locate the bones and pull them out one by one with the pliers.

PROCEDURE FOR CUTTING TRANCHES

A **tranche** is a slice cut from fillets of large flat or round fish. Usually cut on an angle, tranches look large and increase plate coverage.

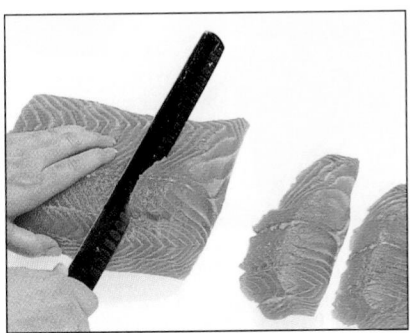

1. Place the fillet on the cutting board, skin side down. Using a slicer or chef's knife, cut slices of the desired weight. The tranche can be cut to the desired size by adjusting the angle of the knife. The greater the angle, the greater the surface area of the tranche.

PROCEDURE FOR CUTTING STEAKS FROM SALMON AND SIMILARLY SIZED ROUND FISH

Steaks are produced from salmon and similarly sized round fish by simply making crosscuts of the whole fish. First scale, gut and remove the fins from the fish. Then:

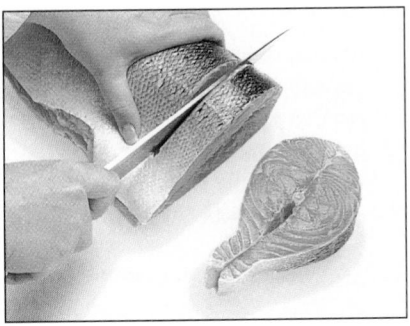

1. Using a chef's knife, cut through the fish, slicing steaks of the desired thickness. The steaks will contain some bones that are not necessarily removed.

PROCEDURE FOR PEELING AND DEVEINING SHRIMP

Peeling and deveining shrimp is a simple procedure done in most commercial kitchens. The tail portion of the shell is often left on the peeled shrimp to give it an attractive appearance or make it easier to eat. This procedure can be used on both cooked and uncooked shrimp.

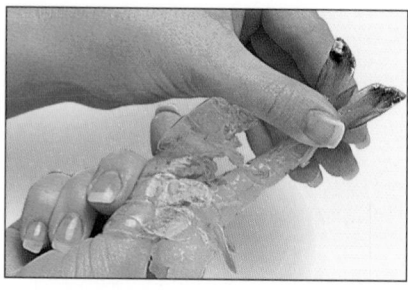

1. Grip the shrimp's tail between your thumb and forefinger. Use your other thumb and forefinger to grip the legs and the edge of the shell.

2. Pull the legs and shell away from the flesh, leaving the tail and first joint of the shell in place if desired.

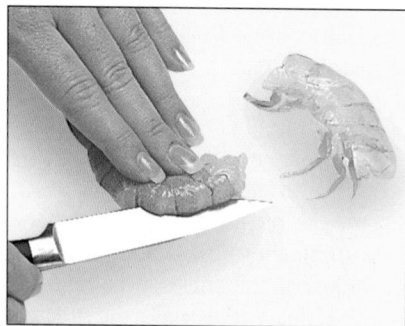

3. Place the shrimp on a cutting board and use a paring knife to make a shallow cut down the back of the shrimp, exposing the digestive tract or "vein."

4. Pull the vein out while rinsing the shrimp under cold water.

PROCEDURE FOR BUTTERFLYING SHRIMP

Butterflying raw shrimp improves their appearance and increases their surface area for even cooking. To butterfly shrimp, first peel them using the procedure outlined above, then:

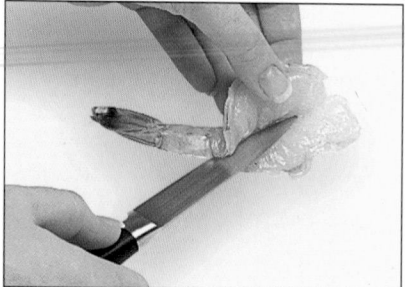

1. Instead of making a shallow cut to expose the vein, make a deeper cut that nearly slices the shrimp into two bilateral halves. Pull the vein out while rinsing the shrimp under cold water.

PROCEDURE FOR PREPARING LIVE LOBSTER FOR BROILING

A whole lobster can be cooked by plunging it into boiling water or court bouillon. If the lobster is to be broiled, it must be split lengthwise before cooking.

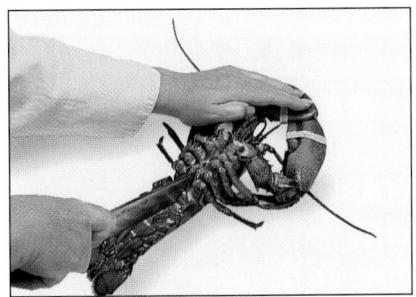

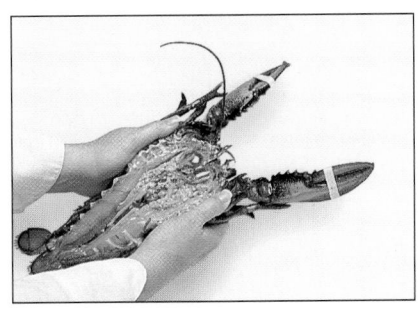

1. Place the live lobster on its back on a cutting board and pierce its head with the point of a chef's knife. Then, in one smooth stroke, bring the knife down and cut through the body and tail without splitting it completely in half.

2. Use your hands to crack the lobster's back so that it lies flat. Crack the claws with the back of a chef's knife.

3. Cut through the tail and curl each half of the tail to the side. Remove and discard the stomach. The tomalley (the olive-green liver) and, if present, the coral (the roe) may be removed and saved for a sauce or other preparation.

PROCEDURE FOR PREPARING LIVE LOBSTER FOR SAUTÉING

A whole lobster may also be cut into smaller pieces for sautéing or other preparations.

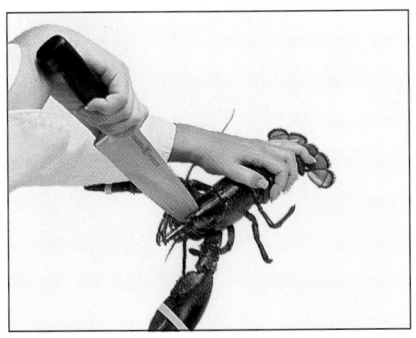

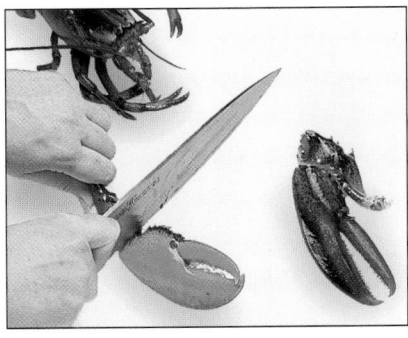

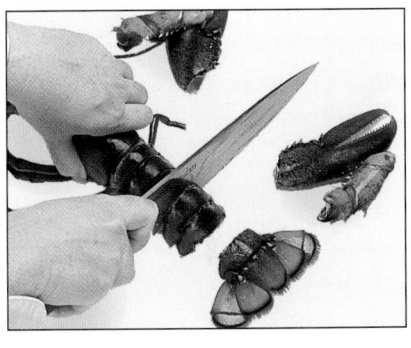

1. Using the point of a chef's knife, pierce the lobster's head.

2. Cut off the claws and arms.

3. Cut the tail into cross sections.

4. Split the head and thorax in half. The tomalley and coral (if present) may be removed and saved for further use. The head and legs may be added to the recipe for flavor, but there is very little meat in them and they are often discarded.

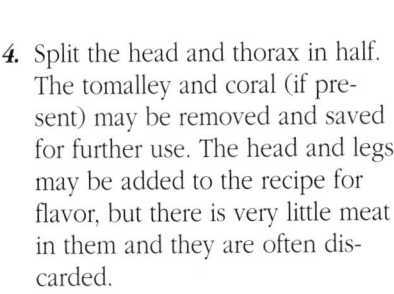

5. Crack the claws with a firm blow, using the back of a chef's knife.

PROCEDURE FOR REMOVING COOKED LOBSTER MEAT FROM THE SHELL

Many recipes call for cooked lobster meat. Cook the lobster by plunging it into a boiling court bouillon and simmering for 6–8 minutes per pound. Remove the lobster and allow it to cool until it can be easily handled. Then:

1. Pull the claws and large legs away from the body. Break the claw away from the leg. Split the legs with a chef's knife and remove the meat, using your fingers or a pick.

2. Carefully crack the claw with a mallet or the back of a chef's knife without damaging the meat. Pull out the claw meat in one piece.

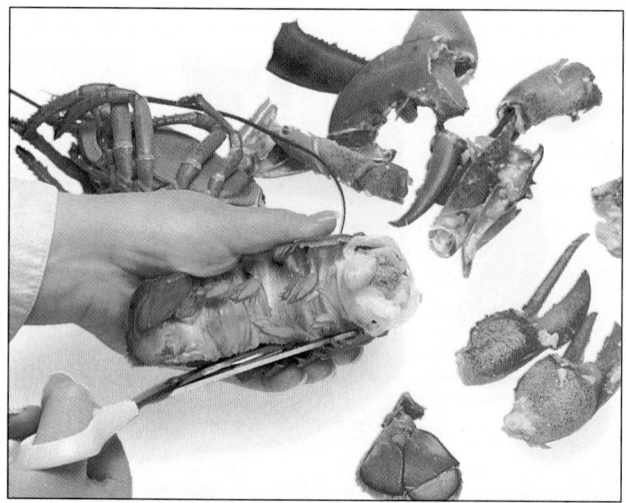

3. Pull the lobster's tail away from its body and use kitchen shears to trim away the soft membrane on the underside of the tail.

4. Pull the meat out of the shell in one piece.

PROCEDURE FOR OPENING CLAMS

Opening raw clams efficiently requires practice. Like all mollusks, clams should be cleaned under cold running water with a brush to remove all mud, silt and sand that may be stuck to their shells. A knife may be more easily inserted into a clam if the clam is washed and allowed to relax in the refrigerator at least an hour before it is opened.

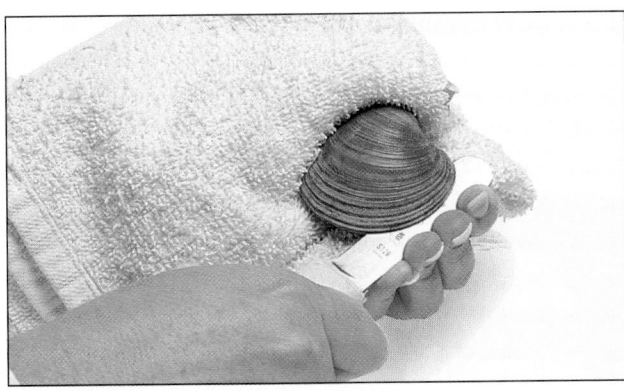
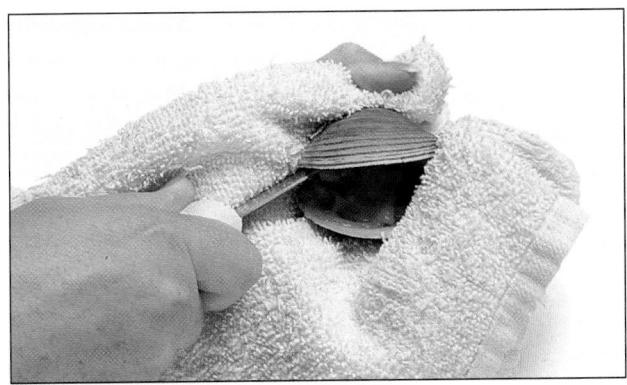

1. Hold the clam firmly in a folded towel in the palm of your hand; the notch in the edge of the shell should be toward your thumb. With the fingers of the same hand, squeeze and pull the blade of the clam knife between the clamshells. Do not push on the knife handle with your other hand; you will not be able to control the knife if it slips and you can cut yourself.

2. Pull the knife between the shells until it cuts the muscle. Twist the knife to pry the shells apart. Slide the knife tip along the top shell and cut through the muscle. Twist the top shell, breaking it free at the hinge; discard it.

3. Use the knife tip to release the clam from the bottom shell.

Procedure for Opening Oysters

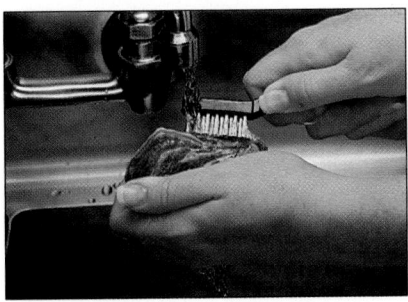
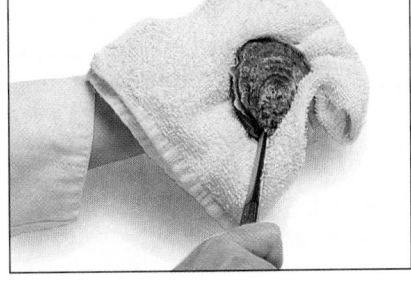
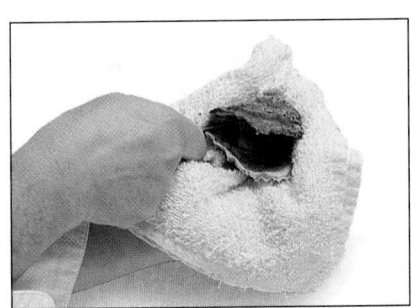

1. Clean the oyster by brushing it under running water.

2. Hold the cleaned oyster firmly in a folded towel in the palm of your hand. Insert the tip of an oyster knife in the hinge and use a twisting motion to pop the hinge apart. Do not use too much forward pressure on the knife; it can slip and you could stab yourself.

3. Slide the knife along the top of the shell to release the oyster from the shell. Discard the top shell.

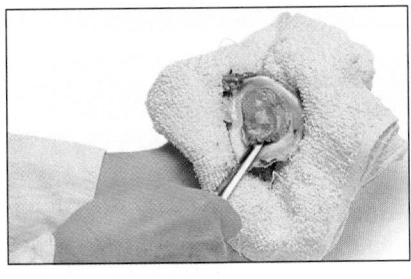

4. Use the knife tip to release the oyster from the bottom shell.

PROCEDURE FOR CLEANING AND DEBEARDING MUSSELS

Mussels are not normally eaten raw. Before cooking, a clump of dark threads called the beard must be removed. Because this could kill the mussel, cleaning and debearding must be done as close to cooking time as possible.

1. Clean the mussel with a brush under cold running water to remove sand and grit.

2. Pull the beard away from the mussel with your fingers or a small pair of pliers.

APPLYING VARIOUS COOKING METHODS

Fish and shellfish can be prepared by the dry-heat cooking methods of broiling and grilling, roasting (baking), sautéing, pan-frying and deep-frying, as well as the moist-heat cooking methods of steaming, poaching and simmering. Other than deep-frying, which is discussed in Chapter 21, these cooking methods are discussed below.

Determining Doneness

Unlike most meats and poultry, nearly all fish and shellfish are inherently tender and should be cooked just until done. Indeed, overcooking is the most common mistake made when preparing fish and shellfish. The Canadian Department of Fisheries recommends that all fish be cooked 10 minutes for every inch (2.5 centimeters) of thickness, regardless of cooking method. Although this may be a good general policy, variables such as the type and form of fish and the exact cooking method used suggest that one or more of the following methods of determining doneness are more appropriate for professional food service operations.

1. *Translucent flesh becomes opaque*—The raw flesh of most fish and shellfish appears somewhat translucent. As the proteins coagulate during cooking, the flesh becomes opaque.

2. *Flesh becomes firm*—The flesh of most fish and shellfish firms as it cooks. Doneness can be tested by judging the resistance of the flesh when pressed with a finger. Raw or undercooked fish will be mushy and soft. As the fish cooks, the flesh offers more resistance and springs back quickly.

3. *Flesh separates from the bones easily*—The flesh of raw fish remains firmly attached to the bones. As the fish cooks, the flesh and bones separate easily.

4. *Flesh begins to flake*—Fish flesh consists of short muscle fibers separated by

thin connective tissue. As the fish cooks, the connective tissue breaks down and the groups of muscle fibers begin to flake, that is, separate from one another. Fish is done when the flesh *begins* to flake. If the flesh flakes easily the fish will be overdone and dry.

Remember, fish and shellfish are subject to carryover cooking. Because fish cooks quickly and at low temperatures, it is better to undercook the item and allow carryover cooking or residual heat to finish the cooking process.

Dry-Heat Cooking Methods

Dry-heat cooking methods are those that do not require additional moisture at any time during the cooking process. The dry-heat cooking methods used with fish and shellfish are broiling and grilling, roasting (usually referred to as baking when used with fish and shellfish), sautéing, pan-frying and deep-frying.

Broiling and Grilling

After brushing with oil or butter, fish can be grilled directly on the grate or placed on a heated platter under the broiler. Broiled or grilled fish should have a lightly charred surface and a slightly smoky flavor as a result of the intense radiant heat of the broiler or grill. The interior should be moist and juicy. Broiled or grilled shellfish meat should be moist and tender with only slight coloration from the grill or broiler.

Selecting Fish and Shellfish to Broil or Grill

Nearly all types of fish and shellfish can be successfully broiled or grilled. Salmon, trout, swordfish and other oily fish are especially well suited to grilling, as are lean fish such as bass and snapper. Fillets of lean flatfish with delicate textures, such as flounder and sole, are better broiled. They should be placed on a preheated broiling (sizzler) platter before being placed under the broiler.

Oysters and clams are often broiled on the half shell with flavored butters, bread crumbs or other garnishes and served sizzling hot. Squid can be stuffed, secured with a toothpick and broiled or grilled. Brushed with butter, split lobsters, king crabs and snow crabs are often broiled or grilled. Whole lobsters can be split and broiled or grilled, or their tails can be removed, split and cooked separately. Large crab legs can also be split and broiled or grilled. Shrimp and scallops are often broiled in flavored butters or grilled on skewers for easy handling.

Seasoning Fish and Shellfish to be Broiled or Grilled

All fish should be brushed lightly with butter or oil before being placed on the grill or under the broiler. The butter or oil prevents sticking and helps leaner fish retain moisture. For most fish, a simple seasoning of salt and pepper suffices. But most fish do respond well to marinades, especially those made with white wine and lemon juice. Because most fish are delicately flavored, they should be marinated for only a brief period of time. (Even marinated fish should be brushed with butter or oil before cooking.) Herbs should be avoided because they will burn from the intense heat of the broiler or grill.

Clams, oysters and other shellfish that are stuffed or cooked with butters, vegetables, bacon or other accompaniments or garnishes gain flavor from these ingredients. Be careful, however, not to overpower the delicate flavors of the shellfish with the addition of too many strong flavorings.

Accompaniments to Broiled and Grilled Fish and Shellfish

Broiled fish and shellfish are served with sauces made separately. Butter sauces such as a beurre blanc are popular, as the richness of the sauce complements the lean fish. Vegetable coulis are a good choice for a healthier, lower-fat accompaniment. Additional sauce suggestions are found in Table 10.5. If the item is cooked on a broiler platter with a seasoned butter, it is often served with that butter. Lemon wedges are the traditional accompaniment to any broiled or grilled fish.

Almost any side dish goes well with broiled or grilled fish or shellfish. Fried or boiled potatoes, pasta and rice are all good choices. Grilled vegetables are a natural choice.

PROCEDURE FOR BROILING OR GRILLING FISH AND SHELLFISH

All fish is delicate and must be carefully handled to achieve an attractive finished product. When broiling whole fish or fillets with their skin still on, score the skin by making several diagonal slashes approximately 1/4 inch (6 millimeters) deep at even intervals. This prevents the fish from curling during cooking, promotes even cooking and creates a more attractive finished product. Be especially careful not to overcook the item. It should be served as hot as possible as soon as it is removed from the broiler or grill.

1. Heat the broiler or grill.
2. Use a wire brush to remove any charred or burnt particles that may be stuck to the broiler or grill grate. The grate can be wiped with a lightly oiled towel to remove any remaining particles and help season it.
3. Prepare the item to be broiled or grilled. For example, cut the fish into steaks or tranches of even thickness; split the lobster; peel and/or skewer the shrimp. Season or marinate the item as desired. Brush the item with oil or butter.
4. Place the item under the broiler or on the grill presentation side down. If using a broiler, place the item directly on the grate or on a preheated broiler platter. Tender fish are usually broiled presentation side up on a broiler platter.
5. If practical, turn the item to produce the attractive crosshatch marks associated with grilling that are discussed in Chapter 9, Principles of Cooking. Items less than 1/2 inch (12 millimeters) thick cooked on a preheated broiler platter do not have to be turned over.
6. Cook the item to the desired doneness and serve immediately.

◆◆◆

RECIPE 19.1

BROILED BLACK SEA BASS WITH HERB BUTTER AND SAUTÉED LEEKS

Yield: 1 Serving

Black sea bass fillet, skin on, approx. 8 oz. (225 g)	1	1
Salt and pepper	TT	TT
Whole butter, melted	as needed	as needed
Leek, julienne	1	1
Lemon juice	2 tsp.	10 ml
Herb butter (pg. 218)	2 slices	2 slices

1. Score the skin of the bass with three diagonal cuts approximately 1/4 inch (6 millimeters) deep.
2. Season the bass fillet with salt and pepper and brush with melted butter.
3. Place the fillet on a preheated broiler platter, skin side up, and place under the broiler.
4. Blanch the julienned leeks in boiling water until nearly tender.
5. Drain the leeks and sauté them in 1 tablespoon (15 milliliters) of whole butter until tender. Add the lemon juice; season with salt and pepper.
6. Remove the fish from the broiler when done. Top with the herb butter and serve on a bed of sautéed leeks.

1. Scoring the skin of the fish.

2. Broiling the fish on a broiler platter.

3. Serving the fish on a bed of sautéed leeks.

Baking

The terms *baking* and *roasting* are used interchangeably when applied to fish and shellfish. One disadvantage of baking fish is that the short baking time does not allow the surface of the fish to carmalize. To help correct this problem, fish can be browned in a sauté pan with a small amount of oil to achieve the added flavor and appearance of a browned surface, and then finished in an oven.

Selecting Fish and Shellfish to Bake

Fatty fish produce the best baked fish. Fish fillets and steaks are the best market forms to bake, as they cook quickly and evenly and are easily portioned. Although lean fish can be baked, it tends to become dry, and must be basted often.

Seasoning Fish and Shellfish to be Baked

The most popular seasonings for baked fish are lemon, butter, salt and pepper. Fish can also be marinated before baking for added flavor. But baked fish usually depend on the accompanying sauce for much of their flavor.

Shellfish are often stuffed or mixed with other ingredients before baking. For example, raw oysters on the half shell can be topped with spinach, watercress and Pernod (oysters Rockefeller) and baked. Shrimp are often butterflied, stuffed and baked; lobsters are split, stuffed and baked. Many food service operations remove clams from their shells; mix them with bread crumbs, seasonings or other ingredients; refill the shells and bake the mixture.

Accompaniments to Baked Fish and Shellfish

Baked fish is often served with a flavorful sauce such as a creole sauce (pg 212) or a beurre blanc (pg 217). Additional sauce suggestions are found in

Table 10.5. Almost any type of rice, pasta or potato is a good accompaniment, as is any variety of sautéed vegetable.

PROCEDURE FOR BAKING FISH AND SHELLFISH

1. Portion the fish and arrange on a well-oiled or buttered pan, presentation side up.
2. Season as desired and brush the surface of the fish generously with melted butter; add garnishes or flavorings as desired or directed in the recipe.
3. Place the pan in a preheated oven at approximately 400°F (200°C).
4. Baste periodically during the cooking process (more often if the fish is lean). Remove from the oven when the fish is slightly underdone.

◆◆◆

RECIPE 19.2
BAKED RED SNAPPER WITH STAR FRUIT CHUTNEY

Yield: 4 Servings

Red snapper fillets, 8 oz. (250 g) each	4	4
Salt and white pepper	TT	TT
Whole butter, melted	2 oz.	60 g
Mint leaves, chopped	1 Tbsp.	15 ml
Garlic, minced	1 tsp.	5 ml
Tomato concasse	4 oz.	120 g
White wine	2 oz.	60 g
Lemon juice	2 oz.	60 g
Star Fruit Chutney (Recipe 10.29)	12 oz.	350 g

1. Place the snapper on a buttered baking pan. Season the fillets with salt and white pepper; brush with butter.
2. Top each portion with chopped mint and 1 ounce (30 grams) of tomato concasse.
3. Add the white wine and lemon juice to the pan.
4. Bake at 400°F (200°C), basting once halfway through the cooking process, until done, approximately 15 minutes.
5. Serve each portion on a bed of 3 ounces (90 grams) of star fruit chutney.

1. Brushing the fillets with butter.

2. Topping each portion with mint and tomato concasse.

3. The finished fish.

Sautéing

Sautéing is a very popular cooking method for fish and shellfish. It lightly caramelizes the food's surface, giving it additional flavor. Typically, other ingredients such as garlic, onions, vegetables, wine and lemon juice are added to the fond to make a sauce.

Selecting Fish and Shellfish to Sauté

Both oily and lean fish may be sautéed. Flatfish are sometimes dressed and sautéed whole, as are small round fish such as trout. Larger fish such as salmon can be cut into steaks or filleted and cut into tranches. The portions should be relatively uniform in size and thickness and fairly thin to promote even cooking. Although clams, mussels and oysters are not often sautéed, scallops and crustaceans are popular sauté items.

Cooking Temperatures

The sauté pan and cooking fat must be hot before the fish or shellfish are added. Do not add too much fish or shellfish to the pan at one time or the pan and fat will cool, letting the foods simmer in their own juices. Thin slices and small pieces of fish and shellfish require a short cooking time, so use high temperatures in order to caramelize their surfaces without overcooking. Large, thick pieces of fish or shellfish being cooked in the shell may require slightly lower cooking temperatures to ensure that they are cooked without over-browning their surfaces.

Seasoning Fish and Shellfish to be Sautéed

Many types of fish—especially sole, flounder and other delicate, lean fish fillets—are often dredged in flour before sautéing. Seasoned butter is used to sauté some items, such as scampi-style shrimp. These items derive their flavor from the butter; additional seasonings should not be necessary.

Accompaniments to Sautéed Fish and Shellfish

Sautéed fish and shellfish are nearly always served with a sauce made directly in the sauté pan. This sauce may be as simple as browned butter (beurre noisette) or a complicated sauce flavored with the fond. In some cases, seasoned butter is used to sauté the fish or shellfish and the butter is then served with the main item. See Table 10.5 for additional sauce suggestions.

Mildly flavored rice and pasta are good choices to serve with sautéed fish or shellfish.

PROCEDURE FOR SAUTÉING FISH AND SHELLFISH

1. Cut or portion the fish or shellfish.
2. Season the item and dredge in seasoned flour if desired.
3. Heat a suitable sauté pan over moderate heat; add enough oil or clarified butter to cover the bottom to a depth of about 1/8 inch (3 millimeters).
4. Add the fish or shellfish to the pan (fish should be placed presentation side down); cook until done, turning once halfway through the cooking process. Add other foods as called for in the recipe.
5. Remove the fish or shellfish. If a sauce is to be made in the sauté pan, follow the procedures discussed in Chapter 17, Poultry.

◆◆◆

RECIPE 19.3

SAUTÉED HALIBUT
WITH THREE-COLOR PEPPERS AND SPANISH OLIVES

Yield: 4 Servings

Halibut fillets, 6 oz. (170 g) each	4	4
Salt and pepper	TT	TT
Olive oil	2 oz.	60 g
Onion, sliced	3 oz.	90 g
Garlic, minced	2 tsp.	10 ml
Green bell pepper, julienned	3 oz.	90 g
Red bell pepper, julienned	3 oz.	90 g
Yellow bell pepper, julienned	3 oz.	90 g
Tomato concasse	8 oz.	250 g
Spanish olives, pitted and quartered	2 oz.	60 g
Fresh thyme, chopped	2 tsp.	10 ml
Lemon juice	2 oz.	60 g
Fish stock	2 oz.	60 g

1. Season the fillets with salt and pepper.
2. Heat a sauté pan and add the olive oil.
3. Sauté the halibut, turning once. Remove and reserve in a warm place.
4. Add the onions and garlic to the same pan and sauté for approximately 1 minute. Add the peppers and sauté for 1–2 minutes more.
5. Add the tomato concasse, olives and thyme; sauté briefly.
6. Add the lemon juice and deglaze the pan. Add the fish stock, simmer 2 minutes to blend the flavors and adjust the seasonings.
7. Return the fish to the pan to reheat. Serve each fish fillet on a bed of vegetables with sauce and an appropriate garnish.

1. Sautéing the halibut fillets.

2. Sautéing the onions, garlic and peppers.

3. Adding the fish stock.

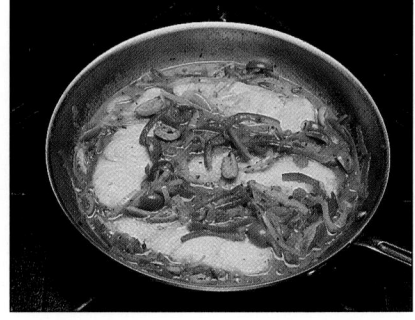

4. Returning the fish to the pan to reheat.

Pan-Frying

Pan-frying is very similar to sautéing, but it uses more fat to cook the main item. Pan-fried fish is always coated with flour, batter or breading to help seal the surface and prevent the flesh from coming in direct contact with the cooking fat. Properly prepared pan-fried fish and shellfish should be moist and tender with a crisp surface. If battered or breaded, the coating should be intact with no breaks.

Selecting Fish and Shellfish to Pan-Fry

Both fatty and lean fish may be pan-fried. Trout and other small fish are ideal for pan-frying, as are portioned fillets of lean fish such as halibut. Pan-fried fish and shellfish should be uniform in size and relatively thin so they cook quickly and evenly.

Cooking Temperatures

The fat should always be hot before the fish or shellfish are added. Breaded or battered fish fillets cook very quickly, and the fat should be hot enough to brown the coating without overcooking the interior. Whole pan-fried fish take longer to cook and therefore require a slightly lower cooking temperature so the surface does not become too dark before the interior is cooked.

Seasoning Fish and Shellfish to be Pan-Fried

Although fish and shellfish can be marinated or seasoned directly, it is more common to season the flour, batter or breading that will coat them. Batters, for example, can contain cheese, and breadings can contain nuts and other ingredients to add different flavors to the fish or shellfish. Review the battering and breading procedures discussed in Chapter 21, Deep-Frying. Additional seasonings come from sauces and other accompaniments served with the pan-fried fish or shellfish.

Accompaniments to Pan-Fried Fish and Shellfish

Lemon wedges are the classic accompaniment to pan-fried fish and shellfish. Sauces that accompany pan-fried items are made separately. Mayonnaise-based sauces such as tartar sauce (Recipe 24.19) and rémoulade sauce are especially popular; rich wine-based sauces should be avoided. Vegetable coulis, such as tomato, also complement many pan-fried items. Additional sauce suggestions are found in Table 10.5.

PROCEDURE FOR PAN-FRYING FISH AND SHELLFISH

1. Heat enough clarified butter or oil in a heavy sauté pan so that it will come one third to half-way up the side of the item. The fat should be at a temperature between 325° and 350°F (160–180°C).
2. Add the floured, breaded or battered item to the pan, being careful not to splash the hot fat. Cook until done, turning once halfway through the cooking process.
3. Remove the food and drain on absorbent paper.
4. Serve it promptly with an appropriate sauce.

◆◆◆

RECIPE 19.4

BLUE CRAB CAKES WITH FRESH SALSA

Yield: 15 2-oz. (60-g) Cakes

Blue crab meat	1 lb.	450 g
Heavy cream	6 oz.	180 g
Red bell pepper, small dice	2 oz.	60 g

Continued

Green bell pepper, small dice	2 oz.	60 g
Clarified butter	as needed	as needed
Green onions, sliced	1 bunch	1 bunch
Fresh bread crumbs	6 oz.	180 g
Salt and pepper	TT	TT
Dijon mustard	1 Tbsp.	15 ml
Worcestershire sauce	TT	TT
Tabasco sauce	TT	TT
Egg, slightly beaten	1	1
Tomato Salsa (Recipe 10.18)	1 pt.	500 ml

1. Carefully pick through the crab meat, removing any pieces of shell. Keep the lumps of crab meat as large as possible.

2. Place the cream in a saucepan and bring to a boil. Reduce by approximately one half. Chill the cream well.

3. Sauté the red and green bell peppers in a small amount of clarified butter until tender.

4. Combine the crab meat, reduced cream, peppers, green onions and approximately 3 ounces (90 grams) of the bread crumbs along with the salt, pepper, Dijon mustard, Worcestershire sauce, Tabasco sauce and egg. Mix to combine all ingredients, trying to keep the lumps of crab meat intact.

5. Form the crab mixture into cakes of the desired size.

6. Place the remaining bread crumbs in an appropriately sized hotel pan. Place the crab cakes, a few at a time, in the hotel pan and cover with the bread crumbs. To help them adhere, press the crumbs lightly into the cakes.

7. Heat a sauté pan over moderate heat and add enough clarified butter to cover the bottom approximately 1/4 inch (1/2 centimeter) deep.

8. Add the crab cakes to the pan and cook until done, turning once when the first side is nicely browned. Remove and drain on absorbant paper.

9. Serve the crab cakes with fresh tomato salsa.

1. Mixing all ingredients for the crab cakes.

2. Forming the crab cakes.

3. Pan-frying the crab cakes.

Moist-Heat Cooking Methods

Fish and shellfish lend themselves well to moist-heat cooking methods, especially steaming, poaching and simmering. Steaming best preserves the food's natural flavors and cooks without adding fat. Poaching is also popular; especially for fish. Poached fish can be served hot or cold, whole or as steaks, fillets or portions. Boiling, which is actually simmering, is most often associated with crustaceans.

Steaming

Steaming is a very natural way to cook fish and shellfish without the addition of fats. Fish are steamed by suspending them over a small amount of boiling liquid in a covered pan. The steam trapped in the pan gently cooks the food while preserving its natural flavors and most nutrients. The liquid used to steam fish and shellfish can be water or a court bouillon with specific herbs, spices, aromatics or wine added to infuse the item with the desired flavors. Mussels and clams can be steamed by placing them directly in a pan, adding a small amount of wine or other liquid and covering them. Their shells will hold them above the liquid as they cook. Fish and shellfish can also be steamed by wrapping them in parchment paper together with herbs, vegetables, butters or sauces as accompaniments and baking them in a hot oven. This method of steaming is called **en papillote**.

Steamed fish and shellfish should be moist and tender. They should have clean and delicate flavors. Any accompaniments or sauces should complement the main item without masking its flavor. Fish and shellfish cooked en papillote should be served piping hot so the aromatic steam trapped by the paper escapes as the paper is cut open tableside.

Selecting Fish and Shellfish to Steam

Mollusks (e.g., clams and mussels), fatty fish (e.g., salmon and sea bass) and lean fish (e.g., sole) all produce good results when steamed. The portions should be of uniform thickness and no more than 1 inch (2.5 centimeters) thick to promote even cooking.

Seasoning Fish and Shellfish to be Steamed

Steamed fish and shellfish rely heavily on their natural flavors and often require very little seasoning. Nevertheless, salt, pepper, herbs and spices can be applied directly to the raw food before steaming. Flavored liquids used to steam fish and shellfish will contribute additional flavors. If the liquid is served with the fish or shellfish as a broth or used to make a sauce to accompany the item; it is especially important that the liquid be well seasoned. Lemons, limes and other fruits or vegetables can also be cooked with the fish or shellfish to add flavors. Clams and mussels often do not require additional salt as the liquor released when they open during cooking is sufficiently salty.

Accompaniments to Steamed Fish and Shellfish

Steamed fish and shellfish are popular partly because they are low in fat. In keeping with this perception, a low or nonfat sauce or a simple squeeze of lemon and steamed fresh vegetables are good accompaniments. If fat is not a concern, then an emulsified butter sauce such as beurre blanc (Recipe 10.16) or hollandaise (Recipe 10.15) may be a good choice. Table 10.5 lists several sauce suggestions.

Classic New England steamed clams are served with a portion of the steaming liquid; steamed mussels are served with a sauce that is created from the wine and other ingredients used to steam them.

PROCEDURE FOR STEAMING FISH AND SHELLFISH

1. Portion the fish to an appropriate size. Clean the shellfish.
2. Prepare the cooking liquid. Add seasoning and flavoring ingredients as desired and bring to a boil.

3. Place the fish or shellfish in the steamer on a rack or in a perforated pan and cover tightly.
4. Steam the fish or shellfish until done.
5. Serve the fish or shellfish immediately with the steaming liquid or an appropriate sauce.

◆◆◆

RECIPE 19.5

STEAMED SALMON WITH LEMON AND OLIVE OIL

Yield: 1 Serving

Lemon zest, blanched	1 Tbsp.	15 ml
Lemon juice	2 Tbsp.	30 ml
Salt and pepper	TT	TT
Virgin olive oil	2 Tbsp.	30 ml
White wine	8 oz.	250 g
Bay leaf	1	1
Leek, chopped	2 oz.	60 g
Fresh thyme	1 sprig	1 sprig
Peppercorns, cracked	1 tsp.	5 ml
Salmon tranche or steak, approx. 6 oz. (180)g	1	1

1. Placing the fish in the steamer.

2. Spooning the dressing over the fish.

1. To make the dressing, combine the lemon zest, lemon juice, salt and pepper. Whisk in the olive oil.
2. Combine the wine, bay leaf, leeks, thyme and pepercorns in the bottom of a steamer.
3. Season the salmon with salt and pepper and place it in the steamer basket.
4. Cover the steamer and bring the liquid to a boil. Cook the fish until done, approximately 4–6 minutes.
5. Plate the salmon and spoon the dressing over it.

◆◆◆

RECIPE 19.6

RED SNAPPER EN PAPILLOTE

Yield: 6 Servings

Clarified butter	as needed	as needed
Leek, julienne	3 oz.	90 g
Fennel, julienne	4 oz.	120 g
Carrot, julienne	3 oz.	90 g
Celery, julienne	3 oz.	90 g
Red bell pepper, julienne	3 oz.	90 g
Red snapper fillets, skin on, 6 oz. (170 g) each	6	6
Salt and pepper	TT	TT
Basil Butter (pg 218)	9 oz.	270 g

1. Cut six heart-shaped pieces of parchment paper large enough to contain the fish and vegetables when folded in half.

2. Brush each piece of parchment paper with clarified butter.

3. Toss the vegetables together. Place one sixth of the vegetables on half of each piece of the buttered parchment paper.

4. Place one portion of red snapper on each portion of vegetables, skin side up; season with salt and pepper.

5. Top each portion of fish with 1-1/2 ounces (45 grams) of basil butter.

6. Fold each piece of paper over and crimp the edges to seal it.

7. Place the envelopes (papillotes) on sheet pans and bake in a preheated oven at 450°F (230°C) for 8–10 minutes.

8. When baked, the parchment paper should puff up and brown. Remove from the oven and serve immediately. The envelope should be carefully cut open tableside to allow the aromatic steam to escape.

1. Cutting heart-shaped pieces of parchment paper.

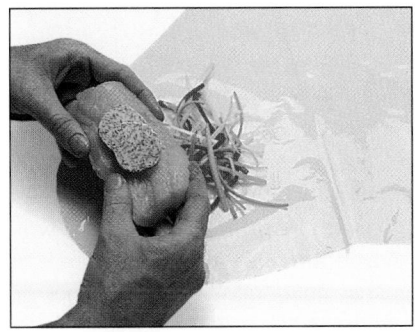

2. Placing the vegetables, red snapper and compound butter on the parchment paper.

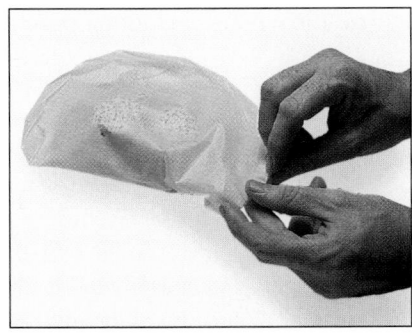

3. Crimping the edge of the parchment paper to seal it.

4. The finished papillotes.

Poaching

Poaching is a versatile and popular method for cooking fish. Shellfish are rarely poached, however. The exception is squid, which can be quickly poached and chilled for use in salads and other preparations.

There are two distinct poaching methods.

The first is the **submersion method**, in which the fish is completely covered with a liquid, usually a court bouillon, fish stock or fish fumet. It is cooked until just done. The poached fish is then served (either hot or cold) with a sauce sometimes made from a portion of the cooking liquid but more often made separately. Whole fish (wrapped in cheesecloth to preserve its shape during cooking), tranches and steaks can all be cooked by submersion poaching.

The second method, called **shallow poaching**, combines poaching and steaming to achieve the desired results. The main item, usually a fillet, tranche or steak, is placed on a bed of aromatic vegetables in enough liquid to come approximately halfway up its sides. The liquid, called a cuisson, is brought to a simmer on the stove top. The pan is then covered with a piece of buttered parchment paper or a lid, and cooking is completed either on the stove top or in the oven. Shallow-poached fish is usually served with a sauce made with the reduced cooking liquid. (Sometimes the main item is sautéed lightly before the cooking liquid is added. If so, the cooking method is more accurately braising, as both dry- and moist-heat cooking methods are used.)

Selecting Fish to Poach

Lean white fish such as turbot, bass and sole are excellent for poaching. Some fatty fish such as salmon and trout are also excellent choices.

Seasoning Fish to be Poached

Fish poached by either submersion or shallow poaching gain all of their seasonings from the liquid in which they are cooked and the sauce with which they are served. Therefore, it is very important to use a properly prepared court bouillon, fish fumet or a good-quality fish stock well seasoned with vegetables such as shallots, onions or carrots as well as ample herbs, spices and other seasonings. Many poached fish recipes call for wine. When using wine either in the cooking liquid or sauce, be sure to choose a wine of good quality. Most fish are very delicately flavored, and using poor-quality wine might ruin an otherwise excellent dish. Citrus, especially lemon, is always a popular seasoning; lemon juice or zest may be added to the poaching liquid, the sauce or the finished dish.

Accompaniments to Poached Fish

Poached fish cooked by submersion go well with rich sauces like hollandaise and beurre blanc. If fat is a concern, a better choice may be a vegetable coulis (for example, broccoli or red pepper). Cold poached fish are commonly served with mayonnaise-based sauces such as sauce vert or rémoulade. Shallow-poached fish are served with sauces such as a white wine sauce or beurre blanc made from a reduction of the liquids in which the fish were poached. See Table 10.5 for additional sauce suggestions.

Poached fish are often served with rice or pasta and steamed or boiled vegetables.

PROCEDURE FOR SUBMERSION POACHING

1. Prepare the cooking liquid. Whole fish should be started in a cold liquid; gradually increasing the liquid's temperature helps preserve the appearance of the fish. Portioned fish should be started in a simmering liquid to preserve their flavor and more accurately estimate cooking time.
2. Use a rack to lower the fish into the cooking liquid. Be sure the fish is completely submerged.
3. Poach the fish at 175–185°F (79–85°C) until done.

4. Remove the fish from the poaching liquid, moisten with a portion of the liquid and hold in a warm place for service. Or, remove the fish from the poaching liquid, cover it to prevent drying and allow it to cool, then refrigerate.
5. Serve the poached fish with an appropriate sauce.

◆◆◆

RECIPE 19.7

WHOLE POACHED SALMON

Yield: 4 Servings

Salmon, drawn, 4–5 lb. (1.8–2.2 kg)	1	1
Court bouillon	as needed	as needed

1. Place the fish on a lightly oiled rack or screen and secure with butcher's twine.
2. Place the rack or screen in a pot and cover with cold court bouillon.
3. Bring the court bouillon to a simmer over moderate heat. Reduce the heat and poach the fish at 175–180°F (79–85°C) until done, approximately 30–45 minutes.
4. If the fish is to be served hot, remove it from the court bouillon, draining well, and serve immediately with an appropriate garnish. If it is to be served cold, remove it from the court bouillon, draining well, cool and refrigerate for several hours before decorating and garnishing as desired.

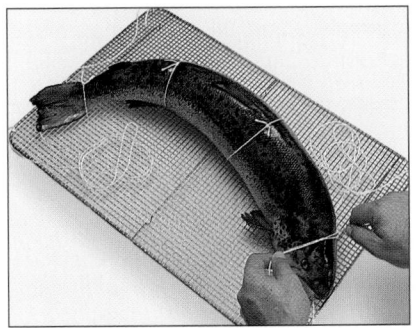  

1. Arranging the whole fish on a rack.

2. Preparing the court bouillon.

3. Removing and draining the fish.

PROCEDURE FOR SHALLOW POACHING

1. Butter a sauteuse and add aromatic vegetables as directed in the recipe.
2. Add the fish to the pan.
3. Add the cooking liquid to the pan.
4. Cover the pan with buttered parchment paper or a lid.
5. Bring the liquid to a simmer and cook the fish on the stove top or in the oven until done.
6. Remove the fish from the pan, moisten with a portion of the liquid and hold in a warm place for service.
7. Reduce the cuisson and finish the sauce as directed in the recipe.
8. Serve the poached fish with the sauce.

1. Arranging the sole on the bed of shallots and mushrooms.

2. Covering the fish with buttered parchment paper after the liquid is added.

3. Adding the velouté to the cuisson.

♦♦♦

RECIPE 19.8
FILLETS OF SOLE BONNE FEMME

Yield: 2 Servings

Sole fillets, approx. 2-1/2 oz. (75 g) each	4	4
Salt and pepper	TT	TT
Whole butter	2 tsp.	10 ml
Shallots, minced	1 tsp.	5 ml
Mushrooms, sliced	4 oz.	120 g
White wine	3 oz.	90 g
Fish stock	4 oz.	120 g
Fish velouté	4 oz.	120 g
Lemon juice	TT	TT
Parsley, chopped	1 tsp.	5 ml

1. Season the sole with salt and pepper.

2. Melt the butter in a sauté pan. Add the shallots and mushrooms and arrange the sole fillets over them. Add the wine and fish stock.

3. Bring the liquid to a simmer. Cover the fish with buttered parchment paper and cook on the stove top or in a 350°F (180°C) oven until done, approximately 5–8 minutes.

4. Remove the sole and reserve in a warm place.

5. Reduce the cuisson until approximately 1 ounce (30 milliliters) remains. Add the velouté. Add lemon juice to taste and adjust the seasonings. Serve the sauce with the fish, sprinkled with chopped parsley.

Simmering

"Boiled" lobster, crab and shrimp are not actually boiled; rather, they are cooked whole in their shells by simmering. Although they are not as delicate as some fish, these crustaceans can become tough and are easily overcooked if the cooking liquid is allowed to boil.

Selecting Shellfish to Simmer

Lobsters, crabs and shrimp are commonly cooked by simmering. Their hard shells protect their delicate flesh during the cooking process.

Seasoning Shellfish to be Simmered

The shellfish being simmered are not seasoned. Rather, they gain flavor by being cooked in a seasoned or flavored liquid, typically salted water or court bouillon. A sachet of pickling spice or Old Bay Seasoning is sometimes used for additional flavor.

Determining Doneness

Timing is the best method for determining the doneness of simmered shellfish. This varies depending on the size of the shellfish and how quickly the liquid returns to a simmer after the shellfish is added. Shrimp cook in as little as 3–5 minutes, crabs cook in 5–10 minutes and it can take as little as 6–8 minutes for a 1-pound (450-gram) lobster to cook and 15–20 minutes for a 2-1/2-pound (1.1- kilogram) lobster.

Accompaniments to Simmered Shellfish

The standard accompaniments to simmered shellfish are lemon wedges and melted butter. If the shellfish is being eaten cold, the traditional sauce is a tomato-based cocktail sauce. Nearly any type of vegetable or starch goes well with simmered shellfish, the most common being fresh corn on the cob and boiled potatoes.

PROCEDURE FOR SIMMERING SHELLFISH

1. Bring court bouillon or water to a boil.
2. Add the shellfish to the liquid. Bring the liquid back to a boil and reduce to a simmer. (Whenever an item is added to boiling water, it lowers the water's temperature. The greater the amount of water, however, the faster it will return to a boil. So, to accelerate the time within which the water returns to a boil after the shellfish is added, use as much water as possible.)
3. Cook until done.
4. Remove the shellfish from the liquid and serve immediately. Or cool by dropping them in ice water if they are to be eaten cold.

$$\diamond \diamond \diamond$$

RECIPE 19.9
BOILED LOBSTER

Yield: 1 Serving

Lobster, 1 lb. 8 oz. (650 g)	1	1
Boiling salted water	4 gal.	16 lt
Lemon wedges	4	4
Whole butter, melted	2 oz.	60 g

1. Drop the lobster into the boiling water. Bring the water back to a boil, reduce to a simmer and cook the lobster until done, approximately 12 minutes.
2. Remove the lobster from the pot, drain and serve immediately with lemon wedges and melted butter on the side.
3. If the lobster is to be eaten cold, drop it in a sink of ice water to stop the cooking process. When cool enough to handle, remove the meat from the shell following the procedures discussed earlier.

Combination Cooking Methods

Combination cooking methods are used with meats, game and poultry in part to tenderize them. Because fish and shellfish are inherently tender, they do not necessarily benefit from such procedures. As noted above in the section on shallow poaching, fish can, on occasion, be lightly sautéed or browned and then poached. Although this procedure is a combination cooking method, it is used to enhance flavors and not to tenderize the product.

You may encounter fish or shellfish recipes with the word "braised" or "stew" in the title. Note, however, that these recipes rarely follow the traditional combination cooking methods discussed in this book.

CONCLUSION

In part because of consumers' increased health awareness, more and more food service operations are expanding their selections of fish and shellfish. Their task is aided by the tremendous variety of high-quality fish and shellfish now available. A variety of dry-heat and moist-heat cooking methods can be used with these products and a variety of sauces and accompaniments can be served with them. Regardless of how they are served, care and attention are required in order to select, store and avoid overcooking fish and shellfish.

QUESTIONS FOR DISCUSSION

1. Discuss six techniques for determining the freshness of fish and shellfish.
2. What are the physical differences between a flatfish and a roundfish? How do fabrication techniques vary for these fish?
3. List four market forms for fish and discuss several factors that may determine the form most appropriate for an operation to purchase.
4. List the three categories of mollusks and give an example of a commonly used food from each category.
5. Discuss four methods for determining the doneness of fish or shellfish. Why is it important not to overcook fish and shellfish?
6. Explain the differences between shallow poaching and submersion poaching. Why is poaching a commonly used method for preparing fish and shellfish?
7. Why are combination cooking methods rarely used with fish and shellfish? Why is boiling rarely used?

ADDITIONAL FISH AND SHELLFISH RECIPES

RECIPE 19.10

SHRIMP WITH BLOOD ORANGE SAUCE

NOTE: *This dish appears in the Chapter Opening photograph.*

TAVERN ON THE GREEN, NEW YORK, NY
Chef Marc Poidevin

Yield: 4 Servings   **Method:** Broiling or grilling

Sauce:

Ingredient		
Blood-orange juice (fresh or frozen)	1 pt.	450 ml
Shallots, sliced	2 oz.	60 g
Fresh tarragon leaves	2 Tbsp.	30 ml
Fresh rosemary, chopped	1 Tbsp.	15 ml
Heavy cream	4 oz.	120 g
Whole butter	12 oz.	340 g
Kosher salt and white pepper	TT	TT
Orange	1	1
Sugar	1 Tbsp.	15 ml

U-15 shrimp	28	28
Basmati rice, cooked	1 lb.	450 g
Fresh chives, chopped	4 Tbsp.	60 ml
Fresh chervil	4 sprigs	4 sprigs

1. To make the sauce, combine the juice, shallots, tarragon and rosemary in a saucepan. Reduce by three quarters over high heat.

2. Add the cream and reduce by half. Add the butter a little at a time to make a beurre blanc. Strain through a chinois. Adjust the seasonings and keep warm.

3. Meanwhile, zest the orange and cut it julienne. Combine the zest with the sugar in a small saucepan with enough water to cover the mixture. Simmer, uncovered, until the water has evaporated. Set aside.

4. Peel and devein the shrimp, leaving the tails intact. Season with salt and pepper and grill on a preheated grill or broiler until done, approximately 4–5 minutes.

5. Place a 4-ounce (120-gram) serving of rice in the center of each of four individual plates. Ladle the sauce around the rice. Place one shrimp on top of the rice and arrange the other shrimp around it and on top of the sauce. Sprinkle with the orange zest and chives. Top with a sprig of chervil and serve.

◆◆◆

RECIPE 19.11
PANACHE OF SEAFOOD

STOUFFER STANFORD COURT HOTEL, SAN FRANCISCO, CA
Chef Ercolino Crugnale

Yield: 1 Serving

Method: Sautéing

Scallop, U-10, halved	1	1
Shrimp, head on, large	1	1
Olive oil	1 oz.	30 g
Lobster claw meat, intact	1	1
Salt and pepper	TT	TT
Dry white wine	1 Tbsp.	15 ml
Chicken stock	1 Tbsp.	15 ml
Shallots, minced	1 tsp.	5 ml
Garlic, minced	1 tsp.	5 ml
Orange zest	2 tsp.	10 ml
Potato Basket (recipe follows)	1	1
Potato-Ginger Purée (recipe follows)	3 oz.	90 g
Frisée	1 oz.	30 g
Chives, 2-in. (5-cm) pieces	1 Tbsp.	15 ml
Iced Red Peppers (recipe follows)	2 Tbsp	30 ml
Basic vinaigrette dressing	1 tsp.	5 ml
Yellow Pepper Saffron Juice (recipe follows)	1 oz.	30 g
Herb Oil (recipe follows)	approx. 1 Tbsp.	15 ml

1. Sauté the scallop and shrimp in the olive oil until brown.

2. Add the lobster claw and season the shellfish with salt and pepper. Cook until the shellfish is just slightly undercooked.

Continued

3. Deglaze the pan with white wine. Add the chicken stock, shallots, garlic and orange zest; adjust the seasonings. Remove the shellfish from the pan.
4. Place the Potato Basket on a plate and fill with the Potato-Ginger Purée.
5. In a small bowl, combine the frisée, chives and Iced-Red Peppers with the vinaigrette dressing. Place to the side of the potato basket.
6. Pour the Yellow Pepper Saffron juice on the plate.
7. Arrange the shellfish around the Potato Basket; drizzle the Herb Oil around the plate.

POTATO BASKETS

Yield: 10 Baskets

Idaho potatoes, large, peeled	10	10
Zucchini	10	10

1. Cut the potatoes on the wide cutter of a Japanese cutter. Wrap the potato slices around a zucchini and fasten with toothpicks.
2. Deep-fry until golden brown. Discard the zucchini.

POTATO-GINGER PURÉE

Yield: 2 lb. (1 kilogram)

Potato, peeled, 1-in. (2.5-cm) pieces	1 lb. 8 oz.	650 g
Heavy cream	4 oz.	120 g
Fresh ginger, grated	1 Tbsp.	15 ml
Whole butter	8 oz.	250 g
Salt and pepper	TT	TT

1. Boil the potatoes in salted water until tender. Drain and set aside.
2. While the potatoes cook, bring the cream to a boil, add the ginger and let steep for 15 minutes. Purée and strain through a fine chinois.
3. Purée the potatoes, add the butter and ginger cream. Season to taste with salt and pepper. Adjust the consistency with additional hot cream as needed.

ICED RED PEPPERS

Yield: 5 oz. (150 g)

Red bell peppers, cored and seeded	5 oz.	150 g

1. Cut the red peppers julienne.
2. Place in a container and add water and lots of ice. Store overnight if possible.
3. Drain and rinse well. Pat dry with a towel.

YELLOW PEPPER SAFFRON JUICE

Yield: 10 oz. (300 g)

Yellow pepper purée, strained	1 pt.	450 ml
Saffron threads	pinch	pinch
Shallots, minced	1-1/2 Tbsp.	45 ml
White wine	5 oz.	150 g
Salt	TT	TT
Tabasco sauce	TT	TT

1. Combine all ingredients and reduce by half.
2. Strain through a fine china cap. Adjust the seasonings. Serve chilled.

HERB OIL

Yield: 4 oz. (120 g)

Fresh parsley	2 oz.	60 g
Fresh tarragon	1 oz.	30 g
Fresh thyme	1 oz.	30 g
Olive oil	approx. 4 oz.	approx. 120 g

1. Blanch the herbs in hot water for 10 seconds. Cool and dry thoroughly.

2. Measure the volume of the herbs and put them in a blender. Add an equal volume of olive oil.

3. Purée and strain through a mesh strainer.

◆◆◆

RECIPE 19.12

RATATOUILLE CRUSTED SALMON

CITRUS, LOS ANGELES, CA
Chef Michel Richard

Yield: 4 Servings

Method: Baking

Red bell pepper, roasted and peeled, brunoise	2 oz.	60 g
Yellow bell pepper, roasted and peeled, brunoise	2 oz.	60 g
Garlic, chopped	1/2 tsp.	3 ml
Olive oil	as needed	as needed
Zucchini, brunoise	4 oz.	120 g
Black olives	1 oz.	30 g
Scallops, 12–16 count	2	2
Salt and white pepper	TT	TT
Heavy cream	1 Tbsp.	15 ml
Salmon fillets, 5 oz. (140 g) each	4	4

1. Sauté the peppers and garlic in a small amount of olive oil until tender. Remove and spread in a pan to cool.

2. Sauté the zucchini in a small amount of olive oil until tender. Remove and spread in a pan to cool.

3. Remove the pits from the black olives and cut brunoise.

4. To make the scallop mousseline, process the scallops in the bowl of a chilled food processor. Season with salt and white pepper. With the motor running, add the cream and mix until incorporated.

5. Remove the mousseline to a bowl and stir in the sautéed vegetables and olives.

6. Place one fourth of the mixture between two sheets of plastic and roll out in a rectangle slightly larger than the surface of the salmon fillets.

7. Remove the top layer of plastic. Season the salmon fillets with salt and pepper. Turn the vegetable mixture over onto a salmon fillet and press so it adheres to the fish. Peel off the second layer of plastic. Repeat for each fillet.

8. Bake the salmon, ratatouille side up, at 350°F (180°C) until done, approximately 8–10 minutes. Serve with an appropriate sauce such as a red pepper coulis (Recipe 10.17).

✦✦✦

RECIPE 19.15
CHILLED POACHED SALMON ROULADE WITH THAI NOODLE SALAD AND SOY MOLASSES VINAIGRETTE

ANA WESTIN HOTEL, WASHINGTON, D.C.
Chef Leland Atkinson

Yield: 5 Servings

Method: Poaching

Red bell pepper, julienne	6 oz.	180 g
Yellow bell pepper, julienne	6 oz.	180 g
Onion, julienne	5 oz.	150 g
Olive oil	1 oz.	30 g
Salmon fillet, skin off, pin bones removed, approx. 2 lb. (1 kg)	1	1
Salt and pepper	TT	TT
Fresh cilantro, chopped	2 bunches	2 bunches
Thai Noodle Salad (recipe follows)	as needed	as needed
Soy Molasses Vinaigrette (recipe follows)	as needed	as needed

1. Quickly sauté the peppers and onions in the olive oil; drain and cool.
2. Trim the fat and dark flesh from the skin side of the fillet. Carefully butterfly the fillet, cover it with plastic and pound gently.
3. Place the salmon, skin side up, on a rectangular piece of plastic wrap that extends at least 3 inches (7.5 centimeters) beyond each end of the fillet.
4. Season the fish with salt and pepper; sprinkle the cilantro over it. Distribute the cooled onions and peppers over the cilantro, leaving at least a 2-inch (5-centimeter) edge of salmon uncovered on all sides.
5. Roll the salmon and peppers into a tight pinwheel and firmly knot the ends of the plastic.
6. Tightly roll the fish in aluminum foil, twisting the ends to form a tight cylinder.
7. Poach or steam the fish until it reaches an internal temperature of 110°F (43°C). Remove from the poaching liquid and chill.
8. At service time, unwrap the chilled salmon and carefully slice it. Arrange the sliced salmon on plates with the Thai Noodle Salad. Pour 3 ounces (90 grams) of the Soy Molasses Vinaigrette around the salmon at the last moment.

THAI NOODLE SALAD

Yield: 5 Servings

Cellophane noodles	3.4 oz.	100 g
Fresh cilantro, chopped	2 bunches	2 bunches
Oyster sauce	2 Tbsp.	30 ml
Sesame oil	1 Tbsp.	15 ml
Garlic, minced	1/2 Tbsp.	8 ml
Soy sauce	2 Tbsp.	30 ml
Red pepper, crushed	1 pinch	1 pinch

1. Pour boiling water over the noodles and allow them to steep until they are al dente, approximately 5 minutes. Refresh in cold water. Drain well.
2. Toss the noodles with the other ingredients. Adjust the seasonings to taste.

SOY MOLASSES VINAIGRETTE

Yield: 1 pt. (450 ml)

Molasses	4 oz.	120 g
Rice vinegar	2 oz.	60 g
Soy sauce	8 oz.	250 g
Fresh ginger, chopped coarse	1 tsp.	5 ml
Olive oil	as needed	as needed

1. Combine the molasses, rice vinegar, soy sauce and fresh ginger in a saucepan. Bring to a boil and remove from the heat immediately. Allow the mixture to rest, undisturbed, for 1 hour.
2. Strain and chill the molasses mixture. Add the olive oil at service time.

◆◆◆

RECIPE 19.16

SALMON IN RICE PAPER WITH A FRESH HERB MOSAIC AND SOY BEURRE BLANC

ANA WESTIN HOTEL, WASHINGTON, D.C.
Chef Leland Atkinson

			Method: Sautéing
Yield: 4 Servings			
Salmon fillet portions, 6 oz. (180 g) each	4	4	
Salt and pepper	TT	TT	
Extra virgin olive oil	2 Tbsp.	30 ml	
Rice vinegar	2 Tbsp.	30 ml	
Rice paper circles, 8 in. (20 cm) in diameter	4	4	
Fresh basil	4 leaves	4 leaves	
Fresh dill	4 sprigs	4 sprigs	
Fresh cilantro	4 leaves	4 leaves	
Soy Beurre Blanc (recipe follows)	as needed	as needed	

1. Season the skin side of the salmon with salt and pepper; drizzle the top with the olive oil and vinegar.
2. Soak the rice paper in warm water, one sheet at a time, for 30 seconds.
3. Transfer each paper to a work surface and let it stand until pliable.
4. Arrange a portion of the fresh herbs in a mosaic pattern in the center of the rice paper.
5. Place the salmon skin side down, centered over the mosaic.
6. Tightly fold in all four sides of the rice paper to enclose the fish.
7. Sauté the salmon, presentation side down first, in olive oil until the rice paper is golden brown. Use caution, as the rice paper browns quickly.
8. Transfer the fish to a 350°F (180°C) oven and cook for 2–3 minutes. Do not overcook.
9. Ladle the Soy Beurre Blanc onto four warm plates and center the fish on it.

Continued

◆◆◆

RECIPE 19.20

BRAISED EEL WITH RAISINS

Yield: 4 Servings   **Method:** Braising

Olive oil	2 oz.	60 g
Porcini mushrooms	8 oz.	250 g
Salt and pepper	TT	TT
Lemon juice	1 oz.	30 g
Whole butter	1 Tbsp.	15 ml
Eel, skinned, 2-in. (5-cm) pieces	2 lb.	1 kg
Mirepoix, small dice	1 lb.	450 g
Garlic, chopped	1 tsp.	5 ml
Flour	1 Tbsp.	15 ml
Red wine	8 oz.	250 g
Brandy	1 oz.	30 g
Brown stock	8 oz.	250 g
Bouquet garni:		
Carrot stick 4 in. (10 cm)	1	1
Leek, split, 4-in. (10-cm) piece	1	1
Fresh thyme	1 sprig	1 sprig
Bay leaf	1	1
Golden raisins	4 oz.	120 g

1. Sauté the mushrooms in half the oil. Season with salt and pepper and add the lemon juice. Remove and reserve in a warm place.
2. Add the remaining oil and the whole butter to the pan. Add the eel and sauté until browned. Remove and reserve the eel.
3. To make the sauce, add the mirepoix and garlic and sauté for 1 minute. Add the flour and cook to make a blond roux. Stir in the wine, brandy and brown stock. Add the bouquet garni and simmer for 30 minutes.
4. Plump the raisins in a small amount of warm water, then drain.
5. Strain the sauce though a chinois. Combine the sauce, mushrooms, raisins and eel and simmer to blend the flavors, approximately 15 minutes.

◆◆◆

RECIPE 19.21

SESAME SWORDFISH

Yield: 1 Serving   **Method:** Sautéing

Leek, julienne	4 oz.	120 g
Swordfish steak, 6 oz. (170 g)	1	1
Sesame oil	1 oz.	30 g
Sesame seeds	1 oz.	30 g
Fish stock	2 oz.	60 g
Tamari sauce	1 Tbsp.	30 ml

1. Deep-fry the leeks at 280°F (140°C) until golden brown. Drain well.
2. Brush both sides of the fish with sesame oil. Coat both sides of the fish with the sesame seeds, pressing to make a solid, even coating.
3. In a very hot pan, sauté the fish in the remaining oil. Turn the fish and finish cooking it in a 375°F (190°C) oven.

4. Remove the fish from the pan and hold on a warm plate. Deglaze the pan with the fish stock. Add the tamari sauce and heat thoroughly.

5. Place the fish on a bed of fried leeks, then pour the sauce over the fish and serve immediately.

VARIATIONS: Substitute a tuna or shark steak for the swordfish steak.

================= ◆◆◆ =================

RECIPE 19.22
PAN-SEARED SEA BASS WITH BEET VINAIGRETTE

STOUFFER STANFORD COURT HOTEL, SAN FRANCISCO, CA
Chef Ercolino Crugnale

Yield: 10 Servings   **Method:** Sautéing

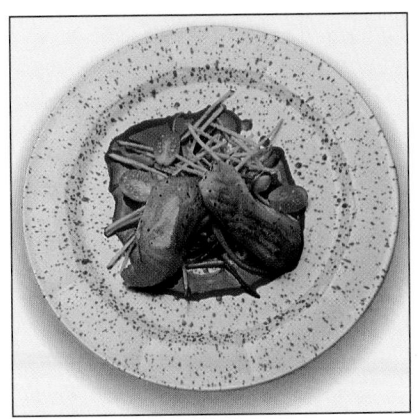

Chilean sea bass, diamond-cut fillets, 3 oz. (90 g) each	20	20
Salt and pepper	TT	TT
Olive oil	as needed	as needed
Shiitake mushrooms, sliced	10 oz.	300 g
Zucchini, julienne	10 oz.	300 g
Yellow squash, julienne	10 oz.	300 g
Red bell pepper, julienne	5 oz.	150 g
Chicken stock	10 oz.	300 g
Beet Vinaigrette (recipe follows)	3 oz.	90 g
Potato, peeled, julienne and deep-fried crisp	20 oz.	600 g

1. Season the fish on both sides. Sauté in olive oil until fully cooked.

2. Meanwhile, sauté the shiitake mushrooms in olive oil for 30 seconds. Add the zucchini, squash and red peppers.

3. Deglaze the pan with chicken stock and adjust the seasonings.

4. To serve, pool the Beet Vinaigrette onto warm plates. For an interesting effect, drizzle the sauce drop by drop into the middle of the plate from a height of 3 feet (1 meter), then pool the remaining sauce on the plate. Place the vegetables in the center with the fried potatoes on top. Arrange the fish on the vegetables.

BEET VINAIGRETTE

Yield: 1 qt. (1 lt)

Beet juice	3 pts.	1.5 lt
Fresh horseradish, grated	3 Tbsp.	45 ml
Shallots, minced	2 Tbsp.	30 ml
Garlic, minced	1 Tbsp.	15 ml
Fresh thyme	1 bunch	1 bunch
Black peppercorns	10	10
Apple cider vinegar	8 oz.	250 g
White wine	4 oz.	120 g
Poultry demi-glace	4 oz.	120 g
Cornstarch	2 Tbsp.	30 ml
Water	2 Tbsp.	30 ml
Salt	TT	TT

1. Combine the beet juice, horseradish, shallots, garlic, thyme and black peppercorns. Reduce to 1-1/2 pints (700 milliliters).

2. Add the vinegar, white wine and demi-glace; simmer 20 minutes.

3. Combine the cornstarch and water until smooth. Whisk into the sauce and bring to a boil. Strain through a fine-mesh china cap and season to taste.

◆◆◆

RECIPE 19.23

STEAMED BLACK BASS
WITH SANSHO PEPPER

THE FOUR SEASONS, NEW YORK, NY
Chef Christian Albin

Yield: 6 Servings			Method: Steaming
Black bass fillets, skin on, approx. 5 oz. (150 g) each	6	6	
Leek, large, cut into strips	1	1	
Sansho pepper and sea salt	TT	TT	
Lime	1	1	
Lemon	1	1	
Olive oil	3 Tbsp.	45 ml	
Pommeray mustard	1 tsp.	5 ml	
Salt and pepper	TT	TT	

1. Place the fish fillets, skin side up, and the leek medallions in a steamer basket. Season with sansho pepper and sea salt. Steam for approximately 5 minutes.
2. To make the vinaigrette, zest and juice the lime and lemon. Blanch the zests in water. Drain and mix the zests and juices with the olive oil and Pommeray mustard; season to taste with salt and pepper.
3. Plate the fish fillets and garnish with the leeks. Drizzle the vinaigrette over the fish and leeks.

◆◆◆

RECIPE 19.24

BAKED MONKFISH
WITH BACON

Yield: 8 Servings			Method: Baking
Bacon, thin slices	4	4	
Monkfish fillets, 6 oz. (180 g) each	8	8	
Whole butter, melted	as needed	as needed	
Salt and pepper	TT	TT	
Lemon juice	2 Tbsp.	30 ml	

1. Partially cook the bacon on a sheet pan in a 350°F (180°C) oven for 5 minutes.
2. Cut each slice of bacon in half. Wrap each portion of fish with bacon and secure with a toothpick.
3. Butter a baking pan and place the fish in it. Season with salt and pepper.
4. Brush the fish with butter and sprinkle with lemon juice.
5. Bake the fish at 450°F (230°C) until done, approximately 12–15 minutes.
6. Serve the fish with an appropriate sauce such as tomato coulis or a tomato-based sauce such as Spanish or creole (Recipe 10.13).

◆◆◆

RECIPE 19.25

SAUTÉED HALIBUT WITH CITRUS BEURRE BLANC

VINCENT ON CAMELBACK, PHOENIX, AZ
Chef Vincent Guerithault

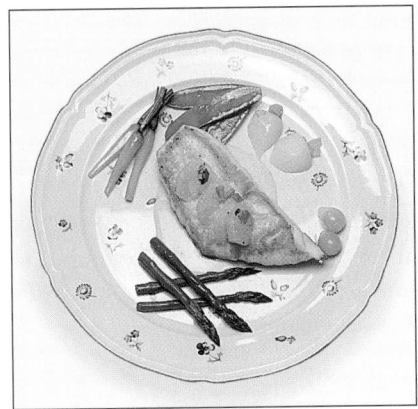

Yield: 4 Servings   **Method**: Sautéing

Halibut fillets, 8 oz. (225 g) each	4	4
Salt and pepper	TT	TT
Olive oil	1 Tbsp.	15 ml
Citrus Beurre Blanc (recipe follows)	as needed	as needed

1. Season the fillets with salt and pepper.
2. Sauté in olive oil for three minutes on each side. Serve in a pool of Citrus Beurre Blanc.

CITRUS BEURRE BLANC

Yield: 4 servings

Orange juice	8 oz.	225 g
Lime juice	1 Tbsp.	15 ml
Lemon juice	1 Tbsp.	15 ml
White wine	8 oz.	225 g
White wine vinegar	8 oz.	225 g
Shallots, chopped fine	1 Tbsp.	15 ml
Heavy cream	1 Tbsp.	15 ml
Unsalted butter	1 lb.	450 g
Salt and pepper	TT	TT
Orange rind, grated and blanced	1 Tbsp.	15 ml
Lime rind, grated and blanched	1 Tbsp.	15 ml
Lemon rind, grated and blanched	1 Tbsp.	15 ml

1. Combine the citrus juices, wine, vinegar and shallots and reduce au sec over moderate heat.
2. Whisk in the cream, then whisk in the butter 2 ounces (60 grams) at a time.
3. Strain the sauce, season with salt and pepper and stir in the citrus rinds. Keep hot for service.

◆◆◆

RECIPE 19.26

WALNUT SOLE

Yield: 4 Servings   **Method:** Sautéing

Flour	4 oz.	120 g
Egg wash	4 oz.	120 g
Walnuts, chopped fine	12 oz.	350 g
Sole fillets, 6 oz. (170 g) each	4	4
Whole butter	4 oz.	120 g

1. Prepare a standard breading station with the flour, egg wash and walnuts. (See Chapter 21, Deep-Frying.)
2. Bread the sole fillets, pressing the walnuts onto only one side of each fillet.
3. Sauté the fish in the butter, presentation (walnut-coated) side down. Turn and finish cooking in a 375°F (190° C) oven, approximately 5–8 minutes.
4. Serve with a citrus beurre blanc.

◆◆◆

RECIPE 19.27

PAUPIETTES OF SOLE
WITH MOUSSELINE OF SHRIMP

Yield: 6 Servings   **Method:** Poaching

Shrimp meat	12 oz.	360 g
Egg white	1	1
Heavy cream	6 oz.	180 g
Salt and white pepper	TT	TT
Lemon sole fillets,		
skinless, 4 oz. (120 g) each.	12	12
Whole butter	as needed	as needed
Shallots, chopped	2 oz.	60 g
Parsley stems, chopped	6	6
White vermouth	6 oz.	180 g
Shrimp stock	12 oz.	360 g
Beurre manié	approx. 1-1/2 oz.	approx. 45 g

1. Purée the raw shrimp meat in a food processor.
2. Add the egg white and pulse to incorporate.
3. Slowly add 2 ounces (60 milliliters) of the cream to the shrimp while pulsing the processor. Season the mousseline with salt and white pepper.
4. Place the sole fillets skin side up on a cutting board and flatten lightly with a mallet.
5. Spread each fillet with a portion of the mousseline. Roll up the fillets, starting with the thickest part and finishing with the tail portion.
6. Butter a sauteuse and sprinkle with the chopped shallots and parsley stems.
7. Place the sole paupiettes in the sauteuse and add the vermouth and shrimp stock.

8. Bring the liquid to a boil, cover with a piece of buttered parchment paper and place in a 350°F (180°C) oven. Poach until nearly done.

9. Remove the sole from the sauteuse and reserve in a warm place.

10. Return the sauteuse to the heat and reduce the cuisson slightly.

11. Thicken the cuisson to the desired consistency with the beurre manié.

12. Add the remaining cream, bring the sauce to a boil and strain through a fine chinois. Adjust the seasonings.

13. Serve two paupiettes per portion on a pool of sauce.

1. Flattening the fillets slightly with a mallet.

2. Spreading the fillets with the prepared mousseline.

3. Rolling the paupiettes.

♦♦♦

RECIPE 19.24

CHILLED SHELLFISH PLATTER

THE FOUR SEASONS, NEW YORK, NY
Chef Christian Albin

Yield: 2 Appetizer Servings   **Method:** Simmering

Lobster, boiled	1	1
Oysters	4	4
Shrimp, U-10, boiled and peeled, tails intact	4	4
Crab meat, lump	3 oz.	90 g
Carrots	as needed	as needed
Celery	as needed	as needed
Scallions	2	2
Baby fennel, split and blanched	1	1
Red oak leaf lettuce	as needed	as needed

1. Remove the tail from the lobster. Remove the meat from the tail in one piece and cut it in half lengthwise.

2. Clean and open the oysters, leaving the oyster meat on the half-shell.

3. Mound crushed ice on a large serving platter. Position the lobster head and body in the center of the ice. Place the pieces of lobster tail around the lobster body. Arrange the remaining shellfish over the ice, using the carrots, celery, scallions, fennel and red oak leaf lettuce as garnish.

◆◆◆

RECIPE 19.25
PAELLA

ANA WESTIN HOTEL, Washington, D.C.
Chef Leland Atkinson

Yield: 4 Servings   **Method:** Steaming

Chicken thighs	4	4
Salt and pepper	TT	TT
Olive oil	2 oz.	60 g
Onion, medium dice	2 oz.	60 g
Garlic, chopped	1 Tbsp.	15 ml
Red bell pepper, medium dice	2 oz.	60 g
Green bell pepper, medium dice	2 oz.	60 g
Rice, long grain	12 oz.	350 g
Saffron	pinch	pinch
Chicken stock, well seasoned, hot	26 oz.	750 g
Chorizo, cooked, sliced	4 oz.	120 g
Clams, scrubbed	12	12
Cockels, scrubbed	12	12
Shrimp, 16–20 count	12	12
Lobster, cut up	1	1
Mussels, debearded and scrubbed	12	12

1. Season the chicken with salt and pepper. Pan-fry it in the olive oil, browning it well. Cook until done, approximately 20 minutes. Remove the chicken and reserve.
2. Add the onions, garlic and peppers to the pan and sauté until tender.
3. Add the rice and sauté until it turns translucent.
4. Add the saffron to the chicken stock. Stir the chicken stock into the rice and bring to a boil.
5. Add the sliced chorizo, clams and cockles to the pan. Cover and place in a 375°F (190°C) oven for 20 minutes.
6. Add the shrimp, lobster and cooked chicken to the pan. Cover and cook for an additional 15 minutes.
7. Add the mussels to the pan and cook until the shrimp and lobster are done, the chicken is hot and all the shellfish are opened, approximately 5 minutes.

◆◆◆

RECIPE 19.26
CLAMS CASINO

Yield: 36 clams   **Method:** Baking

Bacon, diced	4 slices	4 slices
Onion, minced	1 oz.	30 g
Red bell pepper, minced	1 oz.	30 g

Green bell pepper, minced	1 oz.	30 g
Whole butter	6 oz.	180 g
Lemon juice	1 Tbsp.	15 ml
Worcestershire sauce	2 tsp.	10 ml
Tabasco sauce	TT	TT
Clams, scrubbed	36	36
Fresh bread crumbs	2 oz.	60 g

1. Fry the bacon until well done. Drain the fat, reserving 2 tablespoons (30 milliliters).
2. Sauté the onions and peppers in the bacon fat until tender; remove from the heat and cool.
3. Combine 4 ounces (120 grams) of the butter, the lemon juice, Worcestershire sauce, Tabasco sauce, bacon pieces and sautéed vegetables and chill.
4. Open the clams, leaving the meat in the bottom shell. Top each clam with 1 teaspoon (5 milliliters) of the butter mixture.
5. Melt 2 ounces (60 grams) of butter in a sauté pan and toss the bread crumbs in the butter. Top each clam with a portion of the bread crumbs.
6. Bake at 400°F (200°C) until light brown and bubbling approximately 10 minutes. Serve immediately.

◆◆◆

RECIPE 19.27
STEAMED MUSSELS WITH LEEKS AND CARROTS

ANA WESTIN HOTEL, WASHINGTON, D.C.
Chef Leland Atkinson

Yield: 2 Servings   **Method:** Steaming

Mussels, debearded and scrubbed	2 lb.	900 g
Dry white wine	8 oz.	250 g
Garlic, chopped	1 oz.	30 g
Black pepper	1/2 tsp.	2 ml
Fresh thyme	4 sprigs	4 sprigs
Bay leaves	2	2
Leek, julienne	2 oz.	60 g
Carrot, julienne	2 oz.	60 g
Whole butter	4 oz.	120 g
Fresh parsley, chopped	1 Tbsp.	15 ml

1. Combine the mussels, wine, garlic, pepper, thyme, bay leaves, leeks and carrots in a large sautoir.
2. Cover the pan and bring to a boil. Steam until the mussels open.
3. Remove the mussels and arrange them in 2 large soup plates.
4. Reduce the cooking liquid by half, monte au beurre and pour the sauce over the mussels. The carrots and leeks should remain on top of the mussels as garnish.
5. Sprinkle with chopped parsley and serve with French bread.

◆◆◆

RECIPE 19.32
OYSTERS ROCKEFELLER

Yield: 36 Oysters   **Method:** Baking

Unsalted butter	8 oz.	250 g
Fresh parsley, chopped	1 oz.	30 g
Celery, chopped	2 oz.	60 g
Fennel, chopped	2 oz.	60 g
Shallots, chopped	2 oz.	60 g
Garlic, chopped	1 tsp.	5 ml
Watercress, chopped	4 oz.	120 g
Pernod	2 oz.	60 g
Fresh bread crumbs	2 oz.	60 g
Salt and pepper	TT	TT
Oysters, on the half shell	36	36
Rock salt	as needed	as needed

1. Heat the butter in a sauté pan. Add the parsley, celery, fennel, shallots and garlic and cook for 5 minutes.
2. Add the watercress and cook for 1 minute.
3. Add the Pernod and bread crumbs; season with salt and pepper.
4. Transfer the mixture to a food processor and purée.
5. Top each oyster with approximately 2 teaspoons (10 milliliters) of the vegetable mixture; it should coat the oyster's entire surface.
6. Bake the oysters on a bed of rock salt at 450°F (230°C) until the mixture bubbles, approximately 6–7 minutes.

◆◆◆

RECIPE 19.33
FRIED OYSTERS
WITH HERBED CRÈME FRAÎCHE

Yield: 4 Appetizer Servings   **Method:** Deep-Frying

Leeks, julienne	3	3
Oysters, scrubbed	24	24
Flour	4 oz.	120 g
Eggs	2	2
Egg yolks	2	2
Fresh bread crumbs	8 oz.	240 g
Sauce:		
Cornichons, chopped fine	1 Tbsp.	15 ml
Capers, chopped fine	2 Tbsp.	30 ml
Dijon mustard	1 tsp.	5 ml
Paprika	1/2 tsp.	2 ml
Parsley, minced	2 Tbsp.	30 ml
Crème fraîche	4 oz.	120 g

1. Deep-fry the leeks at 280°F (140°C) until golden brown. Drain and set aside.
2. Open the oysters. Strain and reserve the liquor.

3. Poach the oysters in the liquor for 30 seconds. Drain, reserving the liquid. Cool the liquid and oysters separately.

4. Set up a standard breading station with the flour, eggs, egg yolks and bread crumbs. (See Chapter 21, Deep-Frying.)

5. Bread the oysters, then deep-fry them at 375°F (190°C) until browned, approximately 1 minute.

6. Prepare the sauce by combining all remaining ingredients except the crème fraîche. Whip the crème fraîche until stiff. Fold in the cornichon mixture. Chill until service.

7. Serve the oysters on a nest of leeks with the sauce.

◆◆◆

RECIPE 19.34

STEAMED SCALLOPS WITH GINGER, BASIL AND ORANGE

VINCENT ON CAMELBACK, PHOENIX, AZ
Chef Vincent Guerithault

Yield: 1 Serving   **Method**: Steaming

Oranges	2	2
Lime	1	1
Flour tortilla, 8-in. (20-cm)	1	1
Scallops, large	3	3
Ginger, grated	1 tsp.	5 ml
Carrot, julienne	2 oz.	60 g
Celery, julienne	1 oz.	30 g
Tomato, small dice	2 Tbsp.	30 ml
Fresh basil, chopped	1 Tbsp.	15 ml
Olive oil	1 Tbsp.	15 ml
Salt and pepper	TT	TT
White wine	8 oz.	250 g
Shallot, chopped	1 tsp.	5 ml

1. Zest the oranges and then cut them in 1/2-inch (1.2-centimeter) slices. Peel the lime and cut into 1/4-inch (6-millimeter) slices.

2. Line a small bamboo steamer with the flour tortilla.

3. Place the scallops on top of the tortilla. Add the orange zest, ginger, carrot, celery, tomato, basil, olive oil, two slices of lime and a dash of salt and pepper. Cover.

4. Place the white wine, chopped shallots, orange slices and remaining lime slices in the bottom of the steamer pan. Steam the scallops over the seasoned wine until done, approximately 5 minutes.

Nutritional values per serving:

Calories	470	Protein	25 g
Calories from fat	36%	Vitamin A	16216 Iu
Total fat	19 g	Vitamin C	19 mg
Saturated fat	3 g	Sodium	465 mg
Cholesterol	30 mg		

♦♦♦

RECIPE 19.35

SCALLOPS AND SHRIMP SAMBUCA

Yield: 1 9-oz. (270-g) Serving   **Method:** Sautéing

Fennel, julienne	1 oz.	30 g
Carrot, julienne	1 oz.	30 g
Celery, julienne	1 oz.	30 g
Shrimp, U-10, butterflied	3	3
Whole butter	1 Tbsp.	15 ml
Bay scallops	3 oz.	90 g
Salt and white pepper	TT	TT
Sambuca	1 oz.	30 g
Heavy cream	3 oz.	90 g
Puff pastry fleurons	2	2
Fresh dill	1 sprig	1 sprig

1. Blanch the fennel, carrots and celery. Refresh in cold water, drain and reserve.
2. Sauté the shrimp in the butter over high heat for 1 minute. Add the scallops and sauté for 30 more seconds. Season the shellfish with salt and pepper, remove and reserve in a warm place.
3. Deglaze the pan with Sambuca. Add the cream. Boil and reduce until the sauce thickens. Add the vegetables, scallops and shrimp to the pan and simmer until the shellfish is done, approximately 2 minutes. Adjust the seasonings.
4. Serve the vegetables and shellfish mounded on a warm plate, garnished with the fleurons and dill.

♦♦♦

RECIPE 19.36

GRILLED STUFFED SQUID

Yield: 6 Servings   **Method:** Grilling

Squid	12	12
Eggplant	8 oz.	250 g
Olive oil	2 Tbsp.	30 ml
Garlic, chopped	1 tsp.	5 ml
Fresh bread crumbs	1 oz.	30 g
Parmesan cheese, grated	1 oz.	30 g
Egg, beaten	1	1
Fresh oregano, chopped	1 tsp.	5 ml
Salt and pepper	TT	TT
Clarified butter	as needed	as needed

1. Separate the squid bodies and tentacles. Wash both and pat dry.
2. Slice the unpeeled eggplant 1/3 inch (1 centimeter) thick. Season the slices with salt and allow to drain for 30 minutes.

3. Pat the eggplant slices dry and brush with olive oil. Grill the slices over hot coals until browned and tender. Cool and cut the eggplant into small dice.

4. Sauté the garlic in the remaining oil. Add the tentacles and cook until done, approximately 3 minutes. Cool and chop the tentacles and combine with the eggplant, bread crumbs, Parmesan cheese, egg and oregano; season with salt and pepper.

5. Stuff each squid body with approximately 1 tablespoon (15 milliliters) of stuffing. Secure the open end with a toothpick.

6. Brush the squid with clarified butter and grill over hot coals for 10–12 minutes. Slice and serve two squid per portion.

◆◆◆

RECIPE 19.37

Spicy Calamari Salad

THE BAMBOO CLUB, Phoenix, AZ
Benny Chan, President

Yield: 4 6-oz (180-g) Servings   **Method:** Deep-Frying

Squid, cleaned and cut into rings	1 lb.	450 g
Marinade:		
Lemon juice	4 oz.	120 g
Red wine vinegar	1 pt.	450 ml
Garlic powder	1 Tbsp.	15 ml
Whole butter	1 Tbsp.	15 ml
Red bell pepper, sliced thin	3 oz.	90 g
Green bell pepper, sliced thin	3 oz.	90 g
Oyster mushrooms, sliced	12 oz.	350 g
Garlic, chopped	1 Tbsp.	15 ml
Oyster sauce	4 Tbsp.	60 ml
Chile pepper flakes	TT	TT
Flour	6 oz.	170 g
Baking powder	1-1/2 Tbsp.	22 ml
Cornstarch	1-1/2 Tbsp.	22 ml
Boston lettuce, torn into small pieces	8 oz.	250 g
Fresh cilantro or Italian parsley	as needed for garnish	

1. Marinate the squid in the lemon juice, vinegar and garlic powder for three days.

2. Sauté the peppers and mushrooms in the butter. Add the garlic, oyster sauce and chile peppers. Set aside.

3. Drain the squid, pressing out as much liquid as possible. Combine the flour, baking powder and cornstarch; toss with the squid until well coated.

4. Deep-fry the squid at 350°F (180°C) until crispy and golden brown. Drain and toss with the peppers and mushrooms. Serve on a bed of lettuce, garnished with cilantro or Italian parsley.

◆◆◆

RECIPE 19.40

CRAB MEAT FLAN
WITH RED PEPPER COULIS AND CHIVES

THE WHITE HOUSE, WASHINGTON, D.C.
Executive Sous Chef John Moeller

Yield: 6 Servings   **Method:** Baking

Lump crab meat	8 oz.	250 g
Fresh chives, chopped	1 bunch	1 bunch
Salt and white pepper	TT	TT
Eggs	5	5
Heavy cream	1 pt.	500 ml
Sherry	1 oz.	30 g
Whole butter, melted	as needed	as needed
Beurre Blanc (Recipe 10.16)	18 oz.	560 g
Red Pepper Coulis (Recipe 10.17)	3 oz.	90 g
Fresh chives	12 stems	12 stems
Caviar or lumpfish roe	as needed for garnish	

1. Clean the crab meat and toss with the chopped chives. Season with salt and white pepper.
2. Beat the eggs together lightly and add the cream. Add the sherry and the crab meat mixture. Adjust the seasonings.
3. Coat six ramekins with melted butter and fill with the flan mixture. Place the ramekins in a water bath and bake at 350° F (180° C) until set, approximately 45–50 minutes.
4. Pool the Beurre Blanc on six serving plates. Unmold the flans and place in the center of each plate. Decorate the plates with the Red Pepper Coulis and garnish with the chive stems and caviar.

◆◆◆

RECIPE 19.38

GRILLED LOBSTER WITH YELLOW HOT CHILES
AND CHIPOTLE PASTA WITH CHIPOTLE BEURRE BLANC

VINCENT ON CAMBELBACK, PHOENIX, AZ
Chef Vincent Guerathault

Yield: 4 Servings   **Method:** Grilling

Lobsters, 1 lb. (450 g) each	4	4
Olive oil	as needed	as needed
Yellow hot chile peppers, roasted, peeled and seeded	8	8
Shallots, peeled and chopped	2	2
Dry white wine	8 oz.	250 g
Heavy cream	4 oz.	120 g
Unsalted butter	1 tsp.	5 ml
Fresh basil, chopped	1 tsp.	5 ml
Fresh lemon	1/4	1/4

Salt and pepper	TT	TT
Chipotle Pasta (recipe follows)	as needed	as needed
Chipotle Beurre Blanc (recipe follows)	as needed	as needed

1. Cut each lobster in half lengthwise and remove the stomach, tomalley and coral.
2. Brush the meat with olive oil and grill over a very hot fire, meat side down, for approximately 7–8 minutes. Turn and grill for 5 minutes more. Crack the claws and set aside.
3. To make the sauce, combine 4 chopped yellow hot chiles, the shallots and the white wine. Bring to a boil and reduce au sec. Add the cream and simmer for approximately 8 minutes. Remove from the heat and monte au beurre. Strain, add the basil and the juice from 1/4 lemon and season to taste with salt and pepper.
4. Serve the sauce over the lobster and garnish with the remaining yellow chile peppers. Serve with Chipotle Pasta and Chipotle Beurre Blanc.

CHIPOTLE PASTA

Yield: 4 6-oz. (180-g) (cooked weight) Servings

All-purpose flour	10 oz.	300 g
Chipotle chile purée	2 Tbsp.	30 ml
Eggs, extra large	2	2
Olive oil	2 tsp.	10 ml
Salt	TT	TT
Fresh cilantro, chopped	as needed	as needed

1. Combine the flour with the chipotle purée in a food processor; add the eggs and mix.
2. Add the olive oil and salt, then process until the mixture forms a small ball around the blade. It may be necessary to add a few drops of water.
3. Run the dough through a pasta machine until the desired thinness, then cut. Hang the cut pasta on a rack to dry.
4. When ready to serve, cook the dried pasta in boiling salted water for approximately 15 seconds; drain. Add salt to taste and toss with Chipotle Beurre Blanc.
5. Garnish with chopped cilantro and serve hot.

CHIPOTLE BEURRE BLANC

Yield: 4 4-oz. (120-g) Servings

White wine	8 oz.	250 g
White wine vinegar	8 oz.	250 g
Shallots, chopped	1 Tbsp.	15 ml
Heavy cream	1 Tbsp.	15 ml
Unsalted butter, softened	1 lb.	450 g
Chipotle chile, pickled	1 Tbsp.	15 ml
Salt and pepper	TT	TT

1. Combine the wine, vinegar and shallots in a skillet and reduce au sec.
2. Whisk in the cream and slowly add the softened butter, 2 ounces (60 grams) at a time, whisking constantly.
3. Purée the chile and add it to the sauce. Season to taste with salt and pepper.

✦✦✦

RECIPE 19.39
LOBSTER À L'AMÉRICAINE

Yield: 4 4-5 oz. (120-130 g) Lobster and 4 oz. (120 g) Sauce Servings

Method: Sautéing

Lobsters, 1 lb. 12 oz. (750 g) each	2	2
Clarified butter	2 oz.	60 g
Shallots, chopped	1 oz.	30 g
Garlic, chopped	1 tsp.	5 ml
Brandy	4 oz.	120 g
Dry white wine	8 oz.	250 g
Fish stock	16 oz.	450 g
Tomato concasse	8 oz.	250 g
Sachet:		
Bay leaf	1	1
Dry thyme	1/2 tsp.	2 ml
Peppercorns, cracked	1/2 tsp.	2 ml
Parsley stems	6	6
Cayenne	TT	TT
Heavy cream, hot	8 oz.	250 g
Whole butter, softened	2 oz.	60 g
Salt and pepper	TT	TT

1. Cut the lobster for sautéing. Reserve the tomalley and coral if present.
2. Heat the clarified butter and sauté the lobster pieces for 30 seconds.
3. Add the shallots and garlic to the pan and sauté for 30 seconds more.
4. Remove the pan from the stove and add the brandy. Return the pan to the flame, ignite the brandy and allow it to burn a few seconds. Add the white wine, fish stock, tomato concasse, sachet and cayenne.
5. Simmer for 5 minutes. Remove the lobster from the sauce. Remove the meat from the shells and reserve. Return the shells to the sauce.
6. Add the cream to the sauce. Bring to a boil and reduce by half.
7. Strain the sauce. Return to a simmer and thicken with beurre manié if needed.
8. Combine the whole butter with the reserved tomalley and coral and blend well. Monte au beurre with the tomalley and coral butter. Adjust the seasonings and serve the sauce over the lobster meat.

✦✦✦

RECIPE 19.41
LANGOUSTINE SALAD WITH ARTICHOKES

TAVERN ON THE GREEN, NEW YORK, NY
Chef Marc Poidevin

Yield: 6 Servings

Method: Sautéing

Artichoke bottoms	6 medium	6 medium
Lemon juice	1 Tbsp.	15 ml
Olive oil	3 Tbsp.	45 ml
Salt and pepper	TT	TT
Beefsteak tomato concasse	10 oz.	300 g
Dried thyme	1/2 tsp.	2 ml

Langoustines	30	30
Mesclun salad	1 lb.	450 g
Dressing:		
Balsamic vinegar	4 oz.	120 g
Extra virgin olive oil	8 oz.	250 g
Fresh basil	6 sprigs	6 sprigs

1. Cook the artichoke bottoms in water with lemon juice, 1 tablespoon (15 millimeters) of olive oil and salt until tender, approximately 20 minutes. Drain and set aside.

2. Cook the tomato concasse in 1 tablespoon (15 milliliters) of olive oil with the thyme for 10 minutes. Season to taste with salt and pepper and set aside.

3. Clean the langoustines; save six heads for decoration. Sauté the tails and six heads in 1 tablespoon (15 milliliters) of olive oil for 3–4 minutes. Set aside.

4. Place a layer of mesclun salad on six individual plates. Put an artichoke bottom in the center of each plate. Fill with tomatoes and hang five langoustines around the rim. Arrange the head on top of the center. Combine the vinegar and extra virgin olive oil and sprinkle it over the salad. Garnish with basil.

◆◆◆

RECIPE 19.42

FILET MIGNON STUFFED WITH CRAYFISH

Yield: 4 Servings   **Method:** Simmering

Court bouillon	2 qt.	2 lt
Crayfish	36	36
Clarified butter	3 Tbsp.	45 ml
Shallots, chopped	1 Tbsp.	15 ml
Green onion, sliced	1 Tbsp.	15 ml
Garlic, minced	1 tsp.	5 ml
Fresh oregano, chopped	1 tsp.	5 ml
Fresh thyme, chopped	1 tsp.	5 ml
Salt and pepper	TT	TT
Cayenne pepper	TT	TT
Filet mignon steaks, 8 oz. (250 g) each	4	4
Red wine	6 oz.	180 g
Demi-glace	12 oz.	350 g
Whole butter	2 oz.	60 ml

1. Bring the court bouillon to a boil. Add the crayfish and cook until done, approximately 2–3 minutes. Remove and cool. Remove and peel the crayfish tails, reserving the shells from the tails and all of the juices, to yield approximately 3 ounces (90 grams) of meat. Reserve 4 large tails for garnish and coarsely chop the remaining meat.

2. Heat 1 ounce (30 grams) of the butter and sauté half the shallots, all of the green onions and the garlic for 30 seconds.

3. Add the chopped crayfish, oregano and thyme and season with salt, pepper and cayenne. Cool.

Continued

4. Cut a pocket in each of the steaks.

5. Season the steaks inside and out with salt and pepper. Stuff each filet with a portion of the crayfish mixture.

6. Sauté the remaining shallots in 1 tablespoon (15 milliliters) of clarified butter for 30 seconds. Add the red wine and reduce by half. Add the reserved crayfish shells and juice and bring to a boil. Add the demi-glace, bring to a boil and simmer for 5 minutes. Strain the sauce and adjust the seasonings. Return to the stove and monte au beurre.

7. Broil the steaks to the desired doneness and serve with the sauce. Garnish each steak with a large crayfish tail.

═══════════ ◆◆◆ ═══════════

RECIPE 19.43

SHRIMP WITH OLIVE OIL AND GARLIC

Yield: 4 Servings   **Method:** Sautéing

Garlic, chopped	4 Tbsp.	60 ml
Extra virgin olive oil	4 oz.	120 g
Shrimp, 26–30 count, in shell	2 lb. 8 oz.	1 kg
Coarse sea salt	1 Tbsp.	15 ml
Lemon juice	2 Tbsp.	30 ml

1. Sauté the garlic in the olive oil until translucent.

2. Add the shrimp and salt. Toss to coat the shrimp with the oil and cook just until the shrimp are pink, approximately 5 minutes. Add the lemon juice.

3. Arrange the shrimp on warm serving plates; top with the oil, garlic and lemon juice left in the pan. Serve immediately.

═══════════ ◆◆◆ ═══════════

RECIPE 19.44

SEVICHE

In a seviche, the fish and shellfish are "cooked" by the acids in the citrus juice. While a variety of fish or shellfish may be used, it is extremely important that the products be absolutely fresh. Use a nonreactive container such as stainless steel or plastic for mixing or storing the seviche. Aluminum and other metals may react with the acids in the lime juice, giving the food a metallic flavor.

Yield: 3 lb. (1.4 kg)

Raw scallops or shrimp	1 lb.	450 g
Raw firm white fish	1 lb.	450 g
Fresh lime juice	8 oz.	240 g
Serrano pepper, minced	4	4
Red onion, fine dice	6 oz.	170 g
Fresh cilantro, minced	4 Tbsp.	60 ml
Olive oil	2 Tbsp.	30 ml
Tomato concasse	8 oz.	250 g
Garlic, chopped	2 tsp.	10 ml
Salt and pepper	TT	TT

1. Chop the scallops or shrimp and fish coarsely but evenly. Place in a nonreactive container and add the lime juice. Cover and marinate in the refrigerator for four hours. The fish should turn opaque and become firm.

2. Toss in the remaining ingredients and season to taste with salt and pepper. Chill thoroughly and serve as a salad or with tortilla chips.

3. If the seviche is going to be held for more than 2 hours, drain the liquid and refrigerate separately. The reserved liquid can then be tossed with the other ingredients at service time.

Nutritional values per 4 oz. (120 g) serving:

Calories	117	Protein	16 g
Calories from fat	27%	Vitamin A	1919 IU
Total fat	4 g	Vitamin C	49 mg
Saturated fat	1 g	Sodium	114 mg
Cholesterol	89 mg		

CHAPTER 20

CHARCUTERIE

After studying this chapter you will be able to:

+ prepare a variety of forcemeats
+ assemble and cook a variety of pâtés, terrines and sausages
+ understand the proper methods for brining, curing and smoking meats and fish
+ identify several cured pork products

*T*raditionally, charcuterie was limited to the production of pork-based pâtés, terrines and galantines. Over the years, however, it has come to include similar products made with game, poultry, fish, shellfish and even vegetables. Many of these are discussed here.

Charcuterie is an art and science in itself. This chapter is not intended to be a complete guide to the charcutier's art. Instead, we focus on procedures for making common charcuterie items that can be prepared easily in most kitchens. We also discuss the preparation of sausages as well as curing methods, including salt curing, brining, and both cold and hot smoking. The chapter ends with information about several cured pork products.

FORCEMEATS AND THEIR USES

A **forcemeat** is a preparation made from uncooked ground meats, poultry, fish or shellfish, seasoned, then emulsified with fat. Forcemeats are the primary ingredient used to make pâtés, terrines, galantines and sausages.

The word *forcemeat* is derived from the French word *farce*, meaning stuffing. Depending on the preparation method, a forcemeat can be very smooth and velvety, well-textured and coarse, or anything in between. Regardless of its intended use, it has a glossy appearance when raw and will slice cleanly when cooked. A properly emulsified forcemeat provides a rich taste and a comforting texture on the palate.

Forcemeats are emulsified products. Emulsification is the process of binding two ingredients that ordinarily would not combine. (Emulsified sauces are discussed in Chapter 10, Stocks and Sauces; emulsified salad dressings are discussed in Chapter 24, Salads and Salad Dressings.) The proteins present in the meat, poultry, fish and shellfish combine easily with both fat and liquids. In forcemeats, these proteins act as a stabilizer that allows the fat and liquids, which ordinarily would not combine, to bind. When improperly emulsified forcemeats are cooked, they lose their fat, shrink and become dry and grainy. To ensure proper emulsification of a forcemeat:

1. the ratio of fat to other ingredients must be precise,
2. temperatures must be maintained below 40°F (4°C) and
3. the ingredients must be mixed properly.

Forcemeat Ingredients

Forcemeats are usually meat, poultry, fish or shellfish combined with binders, seasonings and sometimes garnishes. Selections from each of these basic categories are used to make an array of forcemeats. All ingredients must be of the finest quality and added in just the right proportions.

Meats

The **dominant meat** is the meat that gives the forcemeat its name and essential flavor. The dominant meat does not have to be beef, veal, lamb, pork or game. It can be poultry, fish or shellfish. When preparing meats, poultry or fish for forcemeat, it is important to trim all silverskin, gristle and small bones so that the meat will be more easily ground and will produce a smoother finished product.

Many forcemeats contain some pork. Pork adds moisture and smoothness to the forcemeat. Without it, poultry-based forcemeats tend to be rubbery, while venison and other game-based forcemeats tend to be dry. The traditional ratio is one part pork to two parts dominant meat.

Many forcemeats also contain some liver. Pork liver is commonly used, as is chicken liver. Liver contributes flavor as well as binding to the forcemeat. For a finer texture, grind the livers and then force them through a drum sieve before incorporating them into the forcemeat.

Fats

Here, **fat** refers to a separate ingredient, not the fat in the dominant meat or pork, both of which should be quite lean in order to ensure the correct ratio of fat to meat. Usually pork fatback or heavy cream is used to add moisture and richness to the forcemeat. Because fat carries flavor, it also promotes the proper infusion of flavors and smoke.

Binders

There are two principal types of binders: panadas and eggs.

A **panada** is something other than fat that is added to a forcemeat to enhance smoothness (especially in fish mousselines, which tend to be slightly grainy in texture), to aid emulsification (especially in vegetable terrines, where the protein levels are insufficient to bind on their own) or both (for example, in liver mousses). It should not make up more than 20% of the forcemeat's total weight. Usually a panada is nothing more than crustless white bread soaked in milk or, more traditionally, a heavy béchamel or rice.

Eggs or egg whites are used as a primary binding agent in some styles of forcemeat. If used in forcemeats that have a large ratio of liver or liquids, they also add texture.

Seasonings

Forcemeats are seasoned with salt, curing salt, marinades and various herbs and spices.

Salt not only adds flavor to a forcemeat but also aids in the emulsification of the meat and fat. As with other foods, a forcemeat that lacks salt will taste flat.

Curing salt is a mixture of salt and sodium nitrite. Sodium nitrite controls spoilage by inhibiting bacterial growth. Equally important, curing salt preserves the rosy pink colors of some forcemeats that might otherwise oxidize to an unappetizing gray. Although currently regarded as substantially safer than the previously used potassium nitrate (saltpeter), some studies suggest that sodium nitrite is a carcinogen. For a typical consumer, however, the amount of sodium nitrite consumed from cured meats should not pose a substantial health threat.

Traditionally, ingredients for forcemeats were marinated for long periods of time, sometimes days, before grinding. The trend today is for a shorter marinating times so that the true flavors of the main ingredients shine through. Both classic and contemporary marinades include herbs, citrus zest, spices and liquors, all of which lend flavor, character and nuance to the forcemeat.

Pâté spice is a mixture of several spices and herbs that can be premixed and used as needed.

◆◆◆

RECIPE 20.1
PATÉ SPICE

Yield: 7-2/3 oz. (220 g)

Cloves	1 oz.	30 g
Dried ginger	1 oz.	30 g
Nutmeg	1 oz.	30 g
Paprika	1 oz.	30 g
Dried basil	2/3 oz.	20 g
Black pepper	2/3 oz.	20 g
White pepper	2/3 oz.	20 g
Bay leaf	1/3 oz.	10 g
Dried thyme	1 oz.	30 g
Dried marjoram	1/3 oz.	10 g

1. Grind all ingredients in a spice grinder. Pass through a sieve to remove any large pieces.

NOTE: This mixture can be used as is, or mix 1 ounce (30 grams) (or any amount desired) with 1 pound (450 grams) of salt. The salt and spice mixture can then be used to season forcemeats; 1/3 ounce (10 grams) per pound of forcemeat usually suffices for most pâtés.

A forcemeat's seasoning and texture can be tested by cooking a small portion before the entire forcemeat is cooked. (Unlike sauces, stews and other dishes, you cannot taste and adjust a forcemeat's flavoring during the cooking process.) A small portion of a hearty forcemeat can be sautéed; a small portion of a more delicate forcemeat should be poached for 3–5 minutes. When cooked, the forcemeat should hold its shape and be slightly firm but not rubbery. If it is too firm, add a little cream.

Garnishes

Forcemeat garnishes are meats, fat, vegetables or other foods added in limited quantities to provide contrasting flavors and textures and to improve appearance. The garnishes are usually diced, chopped or more coarsely ground than the dominant meat. Common garnishes include pistachio nuts, diced fatback, truffles or truffle peelings and diced ham or tongue.

Equipment for Preparing Forcemeats

To properly prepare forcemeats you should have a food chopper or food processor and a heavy-duty drum sieve with a metal band. You will also need a standard meat grinder or meat-grinding attachment with various-size grinding dies (see Figure 20.1).

FIGURE 20.1 *A blade and assorted dies for a standard grinder.*

Preparing Forcemeats

The three common forcemeat preparations are **country-style**, **basic** and **mousseline**. Each can be produced easily in a typical food service operation. Other types of forcemeat preparations such as the emulsified mixture used to make hot dogs and bratwurst are not commonly encountered in food service operations and are not discussed here.

When preparing any forcemeat certain guidelines must be followed:

1. Forcemeat preparations include raw meats, liver, eggs and dairy products. If improperly handled, these potentially hazardous foods create a good environment for the growth of microorganisms. To avoid the risk of food-borne illness, temperatures must be carefully controlled and all cutting boards and food contact surfaces must be as sanitary as possible at all times.
2. To ensure a proper emulsification, the forcemeat must be kept cold— below 40°F (4°C)—at all times. Refrigerate all moist ingredients and keep forcemeats in progress in an ice bath. Chilling or freezing metal grinder and food processor parts helps keep the ingredients as cold as possible.
3. Cut all foods into convenient sizes that fit easily into grinder openings. Do not overstuff grinders or overfill food processors. When grinding items twice, always begin with a larger die, followed by a medium or small die. For exceptional smoothness, press the forcemeat through a sieve after grinding to remove any lumps or pieces of membrane.

Country-Style Forcemeats

A traditional country-style forcemeat is heavily seasoned with onions, garlic, pepper, juniper berries and bay leaves. It is the simplest of the forcemeats to prepare and yields the heartiest and most distinctive pâtés and sausages.

The dominant meat for a country-style forcemeat is usually ground once through the grinder's large die, then ground again through the medium die. This produces the characteristic coarse texture. As with most forcemeats, the dominant meat for a country-style forcemeat is usually marinated and seasoned prior to grinding and then mixed with some liver.

PROCEDURE FOR PREPARING A COUNTRY-STYLE FORCEMEAT

1. Chill all ingredients and equipment thoroughly. Throughout preparation they should remain at temperatures below 40°F (4°C).
2. Cut all meats into an appropriate size for grinding.
3. Marinate, under refrigeration, the dominant meat and pork with the desired herbs, spices and liquors.
4. If using liver, grind it and force it through a sieve.
5. Cut the fatback into an appropriate size and freeze.
6. Prepare an ice bath for the forcemeat. Then grind the dominant meat, pork and fat as directed in the recipe, usually once through the grinder's largest die and a second time through the medium die.
7. If using liver, eggs, panada or garnishes, fold them in by hand, remembering to keep the forcemeat over an ice bath at all times.
8. Cook a small portion of the forcemeat; adjust the seasonings and texture as appropriate.
9. Refrigerate the forcemeat until needed.

◆◆◆

COUNTRY-STYLE FORCEMEAT

Yield: 5 lb. (2.2 kg)

Lean pork, diced	2 lb.	900 g
Pâté spice	2 Tbsp.	30 ml
Salt	1 Tbsp.	15 ml
Pepper	TT	TT
Brandy	2 oz.	60 g
Pork liver, cleaned and diced	1 lb.	450 g
Fatback, diced	1 lb.	450 g
Onion, small dice	3 oz.	90 g
Garlic, minced	1 Tbsp.	15 ml
Fresh parsley, chopped	3 Tbsp.	45 ml
Eggs	6	6

1. Combine the diced pork with the pâté spice, salt, pepper and brandy; marinate under refrigeration for several hours.
2. Grind the liver and force it through a drum sieve. Reserve.
3. Grind the marinated pork and fatback through the grinder's large die.
4. Grind half the pork and fatback a second time through the medium die along with the onions, garlic and parsley.
5. Working over an ice bath, combine the coarse and medium ground pork with the liver and eggs.
6. Cook and taste a small portion of the forcemeat and adjust the seasonings as necessary.

The forcemeat is now ready to use as desired in the preparation of pâtés, terrines, galantines and sausages.

1. Marinating the meat with herbs and spices.

2. Forcing the ground liver through a sieve.

3. Grinding half the meat a second time.

4. Incorporating the liver and eggs into the ground mixture over an ice bath to keep the forcemeat cold.

Basic Forcemeats

Smoother and more refined than a country-style forcemeat, a basic forcemeat is probably the most versatile of all. It should be well seasoned, but the seasonings should not mask the dominant meat's flavor. Examples of basic forcemeats are most game pâtés and terrines as well as traditional pâtés en croûte.

A basic forcemeat is made by grinding the meat and fat separately—the meat twice and the fat once. The fat is then worked into the meat, either by hand or in a food processor or chopper. A quicker method involves grinding the fat and meat together and then blending them in a food processor. Whichever method is used, some recipes call for the incorporation of crushed ice to minimize friction, reduce temperature and add moisture.

PROCEDURE FOR PREPARING A BASIC FORCEMEAT

1. Chill all ingredients and equipment thoroughly. Throughout preparation they should remain at temperatures below 40°F (4°C).

2. Cut all meats into an appropriate size for grinding.

3. Marinate, under refrigeration, the dominant meat and pork with the desired herbs, spices and liquors.

4. If using liver, grind it and force it through a sieve.

5. Cut the fatback into an appropriate size and freeze.

6. Grind the meats twice, once through the grinder's large die and then through the medium die; hold on an ice bath.

7. Grind the chilled or frozen fat once through the medium die and add it to the meat mixture.

8. Work the fat into the meat over an ice bath or in a well-chilled food processor or chopping machine.

9. Over an ice bath, add any required eggs, panada and/or garnishes and work them into the mixture.

10. Cook a small portion of the forcemeat in stock or water; adjust the seasonings and texture as appropriate.

11. Refrigerate the forcemeat until needed.

An alternative method for preparing a basic forcemeat replaces steps 6 to 9 with the following procedures:

6A. Grind the meats and fats together twice.

7A. Place them in a food processor or chopper and blend until smooth.

8A. Add any required eggs or panada while the machine is running and blend them in with the meat and fat.

9A. Remove the forcemeat from the machine and, working over an ice bath, fold in any garnishes by hand.

Whichever method is used, a particularly warm kitchen or a lengthy running time in the food processor or chopping machine may necessitate the addition of small quantities of crushed ice to properly emulsify the forcemeat. Add the ice bit by bit while the machine is running.

━━━━━ ♦♦♦ ━━━━━

RECIPE 20.3

BASIC FORCEMEAT

Yield: 4 lb. 8 oz. (2 kg)

Veal, diced	1 lb. 8 oz.	650 g
Lean pork, diced	1 lb. 8 oz.	650 g
Brandy	2 oz.	60 g
Pâté spice	2 tsp.	10 ml
Salt	1-1/2 tsp.	7 ml
White pepper	TT	TT
Fatback, diced	1 lb. 8 oz.	650 g
Eggs	4	4
Ham, medium dice	4 oz.	120 g
Pistachio nuts	2 oz.	60 g
Black olives, chopped coarse	2 oz.	60 g

1. Combine the veal and pork with the brandy, pâté spice, salt and white pepper; marinate under refrigeration for several hours.

2. Grind the meats through the grinder's large die and again through the small die.

3. Grind the fatback through the grinder's small die.

4. Combine the meat and fat in the bowl of a food processor and blend until they are emulsified.

5. Work in the eggs until the forcemeat is smooth and well emulsified. Do not overprocess the forcemeat.

1. Grinding the meat through the chilled grinder.

2. Combining the fat with the meat in the food processor.

3. Adding the eggs to the meat.

4. Folding the garnishes into the forcemeat.

6. Fold in the ham, pistachio nuts and olives.

7. Cook a small portion of the forcemeat by poaching or sautéing it. Taste and adjust the seasonings as necessary.

The forcemeat is now ready to use as desired in the preparation of pâtés, terrines, galantines or sausages.

Mousseline Forcemeats

A properly made mousseline forcemeat is light, airy and delicately flavored. It is most often made with fish or shellfish but sometimes with veal, pork, feathered game or poultry. (A mousseline forcemeat is not the same as a mousse, which usually contains gelatin and is discussed below.)

A mousseline forcemeat is prepared by processing ground meats and cream in a food processor; often egg whites are added to lighten and enrich the mixture. The proportion of fish to eggs to cream is very important. Too many egg whites and the mousseline will be rubbery; too few and it may not bind together. If too much cream is added, the mousseline will be too soft or will fall apart during cooking.

A mousseline forcemeat can be served hot or cold. It can be used to make fish sausages and a variety of timbales and terrines. Or it can be used to make quenelles, which are discussed below. A shrimp mousseline is used with the Paupiettes of Sole, Recipe 19.27.

PROCEDURE FOR PREPARING A MOUSSELINE FORCEMEAT

1. Chill all ingredients and equipment thoroughly. Throughout preparation they should remain at temperatures below 40°F (4°C).
2. Cut all meats into an appropriate size for processing.
3. Grind the meat in a cold food processor until smooth. Do not overprocess.
4. Add eggs and pulse until just blended.
5. Add cream and seasonings in a steady stream while the machine is running. Stop the machine and scrape down the sides of the bowl once or twice during the processing. Do not run the machine any longer than necessary to achieve a smooth forcemeat.

6. If desired, pass the forcemeat through a drum sieve to remove any sinew or bits of bone.
7. Over an ice bath, fold in any garnishes by hand.
8. Poach a small amount of the mousseline in stock or water. Taste and adjust the seasonings and texture as necessary.
9. Refrigerate until ready for use.

RECIPE 20.4

MOUSSELINE FORCEMEAT

Yield: 4 lb. (1.8 kg)

Fish, scallops, skinless chicken breast or lean veal	2 lb.	900 g
Egg whites	4	4
Salt	1 Tbsp.	15 ml
White pepper	TT	TT
Nutmeg	TT	TT
Cayenne pepper	TT	TT
Heavy cream	1 qt.	1 lt

1. Grind the dominant meat through a large die.
2. Process the meat in a food processor until smooth.
3. Add the egg whites one at a time and pulse the processor until they are incorporated.
4. Scrape down the sides of the processor's bowl and add the spices.
5. With the machine running, add the cream in a steady stream.
6. Scrape down the bowl again and process the mousseline until it is smooth and well mixed. Do not overprocess.
7. Remove the mousseline from the machine and hold in an ice bath. If additional smoothness is desired, force the mousseline through a drum sieve in small batches using a plastic scraper or rubber spatula.
8. Cook a small portion of the forcemeat. Taste and adjust the seasonings and texture as necessary.

The forcemeat is now ready to use as desired in the preparation of pâtés, terrines, galantines or sausages.

1. Processing the ground meat in a cold food processor just until smooth.

2. Adding the eggs and pulsing until blended.

3. Adding the cream in a steady stream while the machine runs.

4. Passing the forcemeat through a drum sieve to ensure a smooth finished product.

Quenelles

Quenelles are small dumpling-shaped portions of a mousseline forcemeat poached in an appropriately flavored stock. Quenelles are a traditional garnish for many soups and a popular appetizer usually accompanied by a tomato coulis or a fish velouté-based sauce such as sauce nantua. The technique used for making and poaching quenelles is also used for testing the seasoning and consistency of a mousseline forcemeat.

PROCEDURE FOR PREPARING QUENELLES

1. Prepare a mousseline forcemeat.
2. Bring an appropriately flavored poaching liquid to a simmer.
3. Use two spoons to form the forcemeat into oblong-shaped dumplings. For small quenelles use small spoons; for larger quenelles use larger spoons.
4. Poach the quenelles until done. Test by breaking one in half to check the center's doneness.
5. Small soup-garnish-sized quenelles can be chilled in ice water, drained and held for service. Reheat them in a small amount of stock before garnishing the soup.

Forming the quenelles using two spoons; poaching gently until done.

USING FORCEMEATS

Forcemeats are used as basic components in the preparation of other foods, including terrines, pâtés, galantines and sausages. Aspic jelly is also an important component of these products.

Terrines, Pâtés and Galantines

Traditionally, a **pâté** was a fine savory meat filling wrapped in pastry, baked and served hot or cold. A **terrine** was considered more basic, consisting of coarsely ground and highly seasoned meats baked in an earthenware mold and always served cold. (The mold is also called a terrine, derived from the French word *terre*, meaning earth.) Pâtés baked in pastry are called **pâtés en croûte**. Many types of pâté are baked in loaf-type pans, without a crust, which according to tradition would make them terrines. Today, the terms *pâté* and *terrine* are used almost interchangeably. **Galantines** are made from forcemeats of poultry, game or suckling pig wrapped in the skin of the bird or animal and poached in an appropriate stock.

♦♦♦

ASPIC JELLY

Aspic jelly is a savory jelly produced by increasing the gelatin content of a strong stock and then clarifying the stock following the process for preparing consommé discussed in Chapter 11, Soups. Brown stock produces an amber aspic jelly; white stock produces a light aspic jelly.

Although gelatin is a natural ingredient present in all good stocks, its concentration level is not normally high enough to produce a firm aspic jelly. Additional gelatin is usually added to the stock in order to assist gelling (setting). This can be done in two ways. The first is to produce a stock with an extremely high gelatin content by using gelatinous meats and bones such as calves' feet, pigs' ears and pork skin; the second is to add plain gelatin to a finished stock. An easier method of preparing aspic jelly is to add gelatin directly to a flavorful finished consommé.

Aspic jelly has many applications throughout the kitchen. In addition to adding flavor and shine, a coating of aspic jelly prevents displayed foods from drying out and inhibits the oxidation of sliced red meats. Aspic jelly is often lightly flavored with liquors such as madeira and cut into decorative garnishes for both plated presentations and buffet displays. It is also used to bind savory mousses, glaze slices of pâté and coat molded mousse. Aspic jelly is funneled into cooked pâtés en croûte to fill the gaps created when the forcemeat shrinks during the cooking process. Aspic jelly is also the basis of aspic molds or terrines (often simply called *aspics*), in which layers of cooked meats or vegetables are bound together and held in place by the aspic jelly. Many of these uses are discussed below.

The gelatin content of aspic jelly varies depending upon its intended use. Aspic jelly to be used only on a display can have a very high gelatin content for easier handling. Aspic jelly to be eaten should be fairly firm when cold, gelled at room temperature but tender enough to melt quickly in the mouth when eaten. To test the gelatin content of a liquid pour a teaspoon (5 milliliters) onto a plate and refrigerate the plate for a few minutes. If the liquid does not gel firmly, additional gelatin can be softened in a small amount of cool liquid then added to the hot liquid.

TABLE 20.1   GELATIN CONCENTRATIONS

Type of Gel	Amount of Gelatin per Gallon (4 lt) of Water	Typical Use
Soft	2 oz. (60 g)	Cubed aspic jelly for edible garnishes.
Firm	4 oz. (120 g)	Brushing slices of pâté or galantine; glazing edible centerpieces; molding terrines, aspics and brawns that will be sliced.
Very Firm	8 oz. + (225 g +)	Nonedible purposes such as coating nonedible centerpieces or trays for presentations.

Terrines, pâtés and galantines are often made with forcemeats layered with garnishes to produce a decorative or mosaic effect when sliced. A wide variety of foods can be used as garnishes including strips of ham, fatback or tongue; mushrooms or other vegetables; truffles and pistachio nuts. Garnishes should always be cooked before they are added to the pâté, terrine or galantine or they will shrink during cooking, creating air pockets.

Pâté Pans, Molds and Terrines

Pâté pans, molds and terrines come in a variety of shapes and sizes. Pâtés that are not baked in a crust can be prepared in standard metal loaf pans of any shape, although rectangular ones make portioning the cooked pâté much easier. For pâtés en croûte, the best pans are collapsible or hinged, thin-metaled ones. They make it easier to remove the pâté after baking. Collapsible and hinged pans come in various shapes and sizes from small plain rectangles to large intricately fluted ovals. Traditional earthenware molds and terrines as well as ones made from enamel, metal, glass or even plastic are available. Most terrines are rectangular or oval in shape. Several of these pans are illustrated in Chapter 5, Tools and Equipment.

Terrines

Terrines are forcemeats baked in a mold without a crust. The mold can be the traditional earthenware dish or some other appropriate metal, enamel or glass mold. Any type of forcemeat can be used to make a terrine. The terrine can be as simple as a baking dish filled with a forcemeat and baked until done. A more attractive terrine can be constructed by layering the forcemeat with garnishes to create a mosaic effect when sliced. A terrine can even be layered with different forcemeats; for example, a pink salmon mousseline may be layered with a white pike mousseline.

PROCEDURE FOR PREPARING A TERRINE

1. Prepare the desired forcemeat and garnishes and keep refrigerated until needed.
2. Line a mold with thin slices of fatback, blanched leafy vegetables or other appropriate liner. (Some chefs claim that the fatback keeps the terrine moist during cooking; most modern chefs do not agree but nevertheless use it for aesthetic purposes.) The lining should overlap slightly, completely covering the inside of the mold and extending over the edge of the mold by approximately 1 inch (2.5 centimeters). Alternatively, line the mold with plastic wrap.
3. Fill the terrine with the forcemeat and garnishes, being careful not to create air pockets. Tap the mold several times on a solid work surface to remove any air pockets.
4. Fold the liner or plastic wrap over the forcemeat and, if necessary, use additional pieces to completely cover its surface.
5. If desired, garnish the top of the terrine with herbs that were used in the preparation of the forcemeat.
6. Cover the terrine with its lid or aluminum foil and bake in a water bath in a 350°F (180°C) oven. Regulate the oven temperature so the water stays between 170° and 180°F (77–82°C).
7. Cook the terrine to an internal temperature of 150°F (66°C) for meat-based forcemeats or 140°F (60°C) for fish- or vegetable-based forcemeats.
8. Remove the terrine from the oven and allow it to cool slightly. If desired, pour off any fat and liquid from around the terrine and cover it with cool liquid aspic jelly.

Several types of terrines are not made from traditional forcemeats; many others are not made from forcemeats at all. But all are nonetheless called terrines because they are molded or cooked in the earthenware mold called a terrine. These include liver (and foie gras) terrines, vegetable terrines, brawns or aspic terrines, mousses, rillettes and confits.

Liver terrines are popular and easy to make. Puréed poultry, pork or veal livers are mixed with eggs and a panada of cream and flour, then baked in a fatback-lined terrine. Although most livers purée easily in a food processor, a smoother finished product is achieved if the livers are forced through a drum sieve after or in lieu of puréeing them in the processor.

Foie gras terrines are made with the fattened geese or duck livers called foie gras. Foie gras is unique, even among other poultry livers, in that it consists almost entirely of fat. (See Chapter 17.) It requires special attention during cooking; if it is cooked improperly or too long it turns into a puddle of very expensive fat.

Vegetable terrines can be made with a relatively low fat content and are becoming increasingly popular. Beautiful vegetable terrines are made by lining

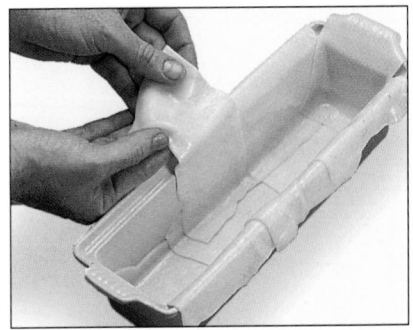

1. Lining a mold with thin slices of fatback.

2. Filling the terrine with the forcemeat and garnish.

3. Decorating the top of the terrine with herbs and placing the terrine in a water bath.

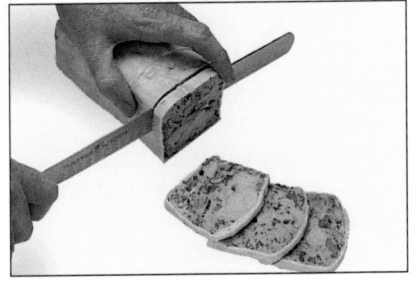

4. Slicing the finished terrine.

a terrine with a blanched leafy vegetable such as spinach, then alternating layers of two or three separately prepared vegetable fillings to create contrasting colors and flavors. A different style of vegetable terrine is made by suspending brightly colored vegetables in a mousseline forcemeat to create a mosaic pattern when sliced.

Brawns or **aspic terrines** are made by simmering gelatinous cuts of meat (most notably, pigs' feet and head, including the tongue) in a rich stock with wine and flavorings. The stock is enriched with gelatin and flavor from the meat, creating an unclarified aspic jelly. The meat is then pulled from the bone, diced and packed into the terrine mold. The stock is reduced to concentrate its gelatin content, strained through cheesecloth and poured over the meat in the terrine. After the terrine has set, it is removed from the mold and sliced for service. The finished product is a rustic and flavorful dish.

A more elegant-appearing brawn is made by lining a terrine mold with aspic jelly, arranging a layer of garnish (for example, sliced meats, vegetables or low-acid fruits) along the mold's bottom, adding aspic jelly to cover the garnish and repeating the procedure until the mold is full.

A **mousse** can be sweet or savory. Sweet mousses are described in Chapter 31, Custards, Creams, Frozen Desserts and Dessert Sauces. A savory mousse—which is not a mousseline forcemeat—is made from fully cooked meats, poultry, game, fish, shellfish or vegetables that are puréed and combined with a béchamel or other appropriate sauce, bound with gelatin and lightened with whipped cream. A mousse can be molded in a decorated, aspic-jelly-coated mold such as that described immediately below, or it can be formed in molds lined with plastic wrap, which is peeled off after the mousse is unmolded. A small mousse can be served as an individual portion; a larger molded mousse can be displayed on a buffet.

PROCEDURE FOR PREPARING AN ASPIC-JELLY-COATED CHILLED MOUSSE

A mold can be lined with aspic jelly, then decorated and filled with cold mousse. The aspic-jelly-coated mousse is then unmolded for an attractive presentation.

1. Set a metal mold in ice water and add 8 ounces (250 grams) of cool liquid aspic jelly. Swirl the mold so the aspic jelly adheres to all sides. Pour out the excess aspic jelly. Repeat as needed to achieve the desired thickness; 1/4 inch (6 millimeters) or less is usually sufficient.

2. Garnish the mold by dipping pieces of vegetable or other foods in the liquid aspic jelly and placing them carefully inside the aspic-jelly-coated mold. The mold can now be filled with a cold filling such as a mousse.

3. Refrigerate the mold until it is well chilled. Unmold the aspic by dipping the mold in warm water, then inverting and tapping the mold on a plate.

Rillettes and **confits** are actually preserved meats. Rillettes are prepared by seasoning and slow-cooking pork or fatty poultry such as duck or goose in generous amounts of their own fat until the meat falls off the bone. The warm meat is mashed and combined with a portion of the cooking fat. The mixture is then packed into a crock or terrine and rendered fat is strained over the top to seal it. Rillettes are eaten cold as a spread accompanied by bread or toast.

Confit is prepared in a similar manner except before cooking the meat or poultry is often lightly salt-cured to draw out some moisture. The confit is then cooked until very tender but not falling apart. Confits are generally served hot. Like rillettes, confits can be preserved by sealing them with a layer of strained rendered fat. Properly prepared and sealed rillettes and confits will keep for several weeks under refrigeration.

Although it is sometimes incorrectly called chicken liver pâté, **chopped chicken liver** is prepared in a similar fashion to a rillette. Chopped chicken liver, however, will not have the keeping qualities of traditional rillettes or confits because it is not normally sealed in a crock or terrine with rendered fat. It should be eaten within a day or two of its preparation.

Pâtés en Croûte

Considered by some to be the pinnacle of the charcutier's art, pâtés en croûte are forcemeats baked in a crust. The forcemeat can be country-style, basic or mousseline, but a basic forcemeat is most commonly used. Although pâtés en croûte can be baked without using a mold, a mold helps produce a more attractive finished product.

Pâté Dough (Pâte au Pâté)

The crust surrounding a baking forcemeat must be durable enough to hold in the juices produced as the pâté bakes and to withstand the long baking process. Unfortunately, some of the more durable crusts are tough and unpleasant to eat.

The goal is to achieve a balance so that the crust will hold the juices of the baking pâté and still be relatively pleasant to the palate. Some pâtés, especially more delicate ones such as fish mousselines, can be wrapped in brioche dough (Recipe 28.16).

◆◆◆

RECIPE 20.5
PÂTÉ DOUGH

Yield: 1 lb. 8 oz. (680 g)

All-purpose flour	1 lb.	450 g
Shortening	7 oz.	200 g
Salt	1-1/2 tsp.	7 ml
Water	5 oz.	150 ml
Egg	1	1

1. Place the flour in the bowl of a mixer. Add the shortening and mix on low speed until smooth.
2. Combine the salt, water and egg; add them to the flour and shortening mixture.
3. Knead until smooth and refrigerate. The dough will be easier to work with if allowed to rest for at least 1 hour.

Procedure for Assembling and Baking Pâtés en Croûte

After preparing a forcemeat and pastry dough, all that remains is to assemble and bake the pâté en croûte. The amount of pastry dough and forcemeat needed is determined by the size of the mold or pan chosen.

1. Prepare the pâté dough and the forcemeat, keeping the forcemeat refrigerated until needed.
2. Roll out the dough into a rectangular shape 1/8 inch (3 millimeters) thick.
3. Using the pâté mold as a pattern, determine how much dough is needed to line its inside; allow enough dough along each side of the mold's length to cover the top when folded over. Mark the dough. Cut the dough slightly larger than the marked lines. Cut a second rectangular piece of dough that is slightly larger than the top of the mold; it will be used as a lid.
4. Lightly butter the inside of the mold.
5. Lightly dust the large rectangle of dough with flour, fold it over and transfer it to the mold.
6. Use your thumbs and a dough ball made from dough trimmings to form the dough neatly into the corners of the mold. Continue until the dough is of even thickness on all sides and in the corners.
7. Trim the dough, leaving 3/4 inch (2 centimeters) on the ends and enough dough to cover the top along the sides.
8. Line the mold with thin slices of fatback or ham, allowing 3/4 inch (2 centimeters) extra around the top of the mold, or as directed in the recipe. This layer helps protect the pastry crust from coming in contact with the moist forcemeat, which would make it soggy.
9. Fill the lined mold with the forcemeat to 1/2 inch (1.2 centimeters) below the top of the mold, pressing it well into the corners to avoid air pockets. Layer and garnish as appropriate.
10. Fold the fatback or ham over the top of the forcemeat, using additional pieces if necessary to cover its entire surface. Fold the pastry over the forcemeat.
11. Brush the exposed surface of the pastry with egg wash; carefully cap with the top piece of dough. Press any overlapping dough down inside the sides of the mold with a small spatula.
12. Using round cutters, cut one or two holes in the top to allow steam to escape during cooking. Egg-wash the surface. Place a doughnut-shaped piece of dough around each of the holes. Egg-wash the decorations.

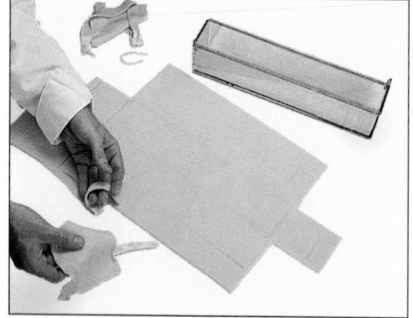

1. Cutting the dough into a large rectangle.

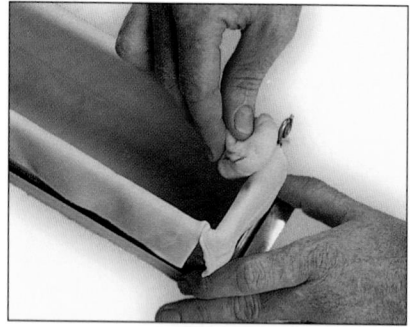

2. Pressing the dough into the mold with a floured dough ball and your thumbs.

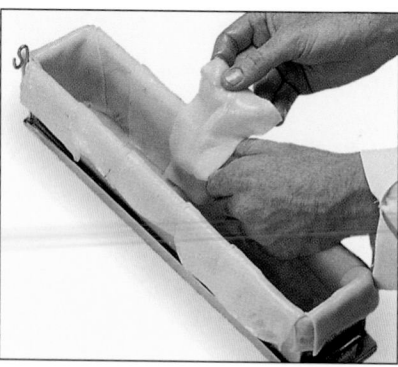

3. Lining the mold with thin slices of fatback.

4. Filling the lined mold with the forcemeat and garnish.

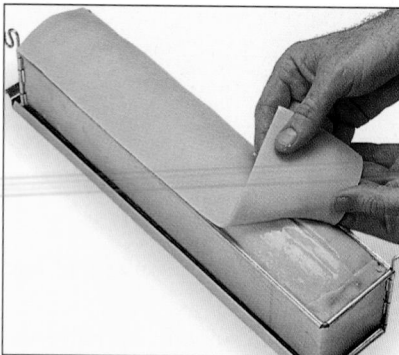

5. Using egg wash on the surface and placing the top on the pâté.

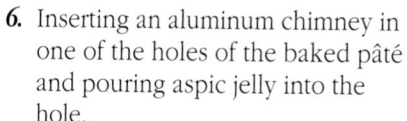

6. Inserting an aluminum chimney in one of the holes of the baked pâté and pouring aspic jelly into the hole.

7. Slicing the pâté with a thin-bladed knife.

13. Bake the pâté in a preheated 450°F (230°C) oven for 15 minutes. Then cover the surface of the pâté with aluminum foil. Reduce the heat to 350°F (180°C) and continue baking until the internal temperature reaches 150°F (66°C) for meat pâtés or 140°F (60°C) for fish and vegetable pâtés.

14. Allow the pâté to cool for at least 1 hour or overnight. Using a funnel, pour cool liquid aspic jelly through the holes to fill the space created when the pâté shrank during cooking. Allow the pâté en croûte to cool overnight before slicing.

Procedure for Glazing Pâté Slices with Aspic Jelly

Slices of chilled terrines, pâtés en croûte or gallantines (discussed below) may be garnished and coated with aspic to preserve their color, prevent drying and create a more attractive presentation.

1. Stirring slowly to cool the clarified aspic jelly.

2. Brush or spoon the aspic jelly over slices of chilled pâté arranged on a cooling rack. Repeat the process until the coating reaches the desired thickness.

Galantines

A classic **galantine** is a boned chicken stuffed with a chicken-based force-meat to resemble its original shape and then poached. Today, galantines are still most often prepared from whole ducks or chickens, but they can also be made from game, veal, fish or shellfish. When appropriate, the forcemeat is stuffed in the skin, which has been removed in one piece, sometimes with flesh still attached. When the skin is not available, its use is inappropriate or in the case of fish and shellfish where there is no skin, the galantine is made by forming the forcemeat into a cylindrical shape and wrapping it in cheesecloth or plastic wrap and foil before poaching. Galantines are always served cold and are often displayed on buffets, sliced and glazed with aspic jelly.

A **ballottine** is similar to a galantine. It is made by removing the bones from a poultry leg, filling the cavity with an appropriate forcemeat and poaching or braising the leg with vegetables. Ballottines are often served hot with a sauce made from the cooking liquid.

PROCEDURE FOR PREPARING A POULTRY GALANTINE

1. Bone the chicken by cutting through the skin along the length of the backbone and then following the natural curvature of the carcass. Keep all the meat attached to the skin. Remove the legs and wings by cutting through the joints when you reach them; leave the legs and wings attached to the skin. Then cut off the wings. Bone the thighs and legs, leaving the skin and meat attached to the rest of the bird. Trim the skin to form a large rectangle.
2. Prepare a forcemeat using the meat from the skinned bird or any other appropriate meat. Reserve a portion of the meat as garnish if desired. Prepare any other garnishes. Refrigerate the forcemeat and garnishes until ready for use.
3. Spread out the skin and meat on plastic wrap or several layers of cheesecloth with the skin side down and the flesh up.
4. Remove the chicken tenderloins and pull the tendon out of each. Butterfly the breasts and tenderloins and cover the entire skin with a thin layer of meat.
5. Arrange the forcemeat and garnishes in a cylindrical shape across the center of the skin.
6. Using the plastic or cheesecloth to assist the process, tightly roll the skin around the forcemeat and garnishes to form a tight cylinder.

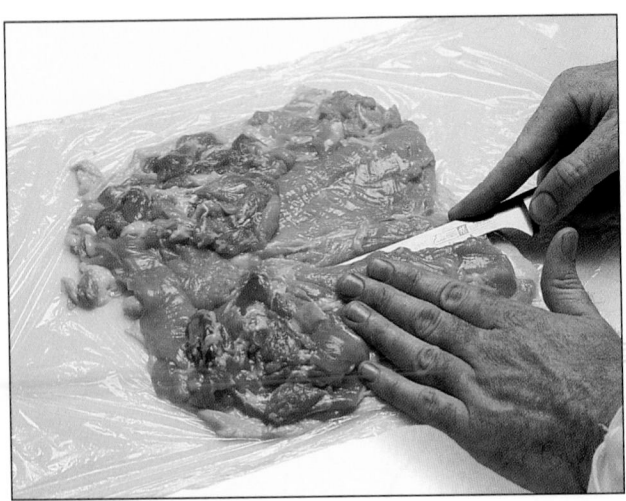

1. Butterflying the breasts and tenderloins and placing a thin layer of meat over the skin.

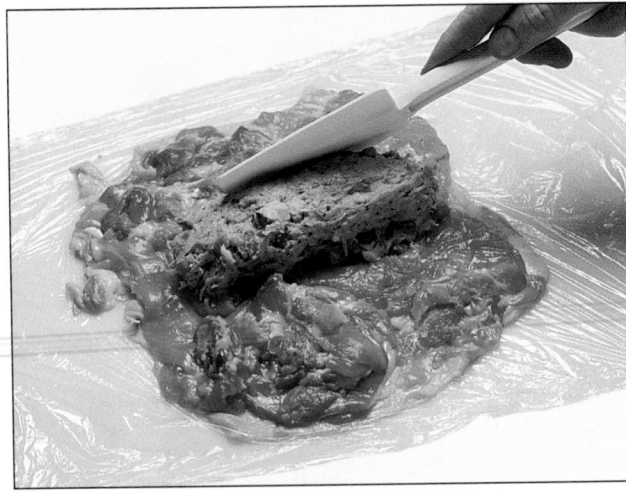

2. Arranging the forcemeat and garnishes in a cylindrical shape across the center of the skin.

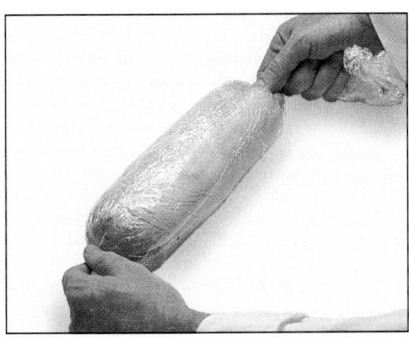

3. Using the plastic wrap to roll the galantine into a tight cylinder.

4. Securing the galantine with heavy-duty aluminum foil.

5. Slicing the finished product.

7. Tie the ends of the cheesecloth with butcher's twine and secure the galantine at even intervals using strips of cheesecloth. If plastic wrap was used, wrap the galantine with heavy-duty aluminum foil.

8. Poach the galantine in a full-flavored stock to an internal temperature of 150°F (66°C) for meat-based forcemeats or 140°F (60°C) for fish- or vegetable-based forcemeats.

9. Cool the galantine in its cooking liquid until it can be handled. Remove the cheesecloth or plastic wrap and aluminum foil and rewrap the galantine in clean cheesecloth or plastic wrap. Refrigerate overnight before decorating or slicing.

Sausages

Sausages are forcemeats stuffed into casings. For centuries, sausages consisted of ground meat, usually pork, and seasonings. Today not only are sausages made from pork, but also from game, beef, veal, poultry, fish, shellfish and even vegetables.

There are three main types of sausages:

1. Fresh sausages include breakfast sausage links and Italian sausages. They are made with fresh ingredients that have not been cured or smoked.

2. Smoked and **cooked sausages** are made with raw meat products treated with chemicals, usually the preservative sodium nitrite. Examples are kielbasa, bologna and hot dogs.

3. Dried or **hard sausages** are made with cured meats, then air-dried under controlled conditions. Dry sausages may or may not be smoked or cooked. Dried or hard sausages include salami, pepperoni, Lebanon bologna and landjäger.

Smoked and cooked sausages and dry or hard sausages are rarely prepared in typical food service operations. They are produced by specialty shops and will not be discussed here. We do discuss the ingredients and procedures for a variety of fresh sausages that can be prepared in almost any kitchen.

Sausage Components

Sausage Meats

Sausage meats are forcemeats with particular characteristics and flavorings. Course Italian and lamb sausages, for example, are simply a country-style forcemeat without liver and with different seasonings, stuffed into casings and formed into links. Hot dogs, bratwurst and other fine-textured sausages are variations of basic forcemeats stuffed into casings and formed into links.

Sausage Casings

Although sausage mixtures can be cooked without casings, most sausages are stuffed into casings before cooking. Two types of sausage casings are commonly used in food service operations:

1. **Natural casings** are portions of hog, sheep or cattle intestines. Their diameters are measured in millimeters and they come in several sizes depending upon the animal or portion of the intestine used. Hog casings are the most popular; sheep casings are considered the finest-quality small casings. Both hog and sheep casings are used to make hot dogs and many types of pork sausage. Beef casings are quite large and are used to make sausages such as ring bologna and Polish sausage. Most natural casings are purchased in salt packs. In order to rid them of salt and impurities, the casings must be carefully rinsed in warm water and allowed to soak in cool water for at least 1 hour or overnight before use.

2. **Collagen casings** are manufactured from collagen extracted from cattle hides. They are generally inferior to natural casings in taste and texture, but they do have advantages: Collagen casings do not require any washing or soaking prior to use and they are uniform in size.

Preparing Sausages

Equipment for Sausage Making

Sausage-stuffing machines are best if you engage in large-scale sausage production. Otherwise, all you need is a grinder with a sausage nozzle attachment such as the ones shown in Figure 20.2. Nozzles are available in several sizes to accommodate the various casing sizes.

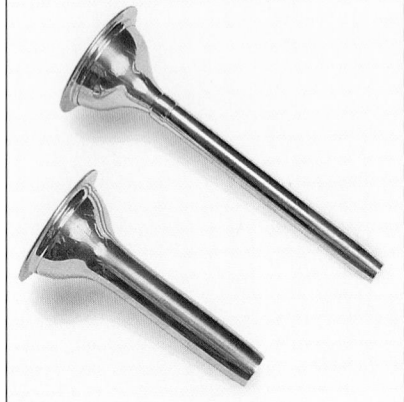

FIGURE 20.2 *Sausage nozzles*

PROCEDURE FOR MAKING SAUSAGES

1. Prepare a forcemeat.
2. Thoroughly chill all parts of the sausage stuffer that will come in contact with the forcemeat.
3. Rinse and soak the casings if using natural ones. Cut the casings into 4–6-foot (1.2–1.8-meter) lengths.
4. Put the sausage in the sausage stuffer.
5. Slide the casing over the nozzle of the sausage stuffer. Tie the end in a knot and pierce with a skewer to prevent an air pocket.

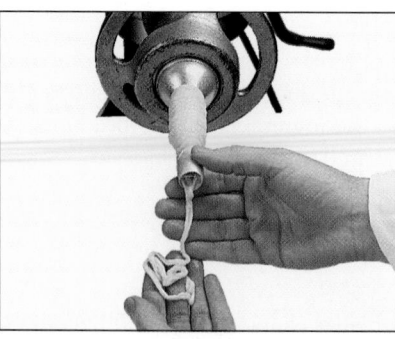

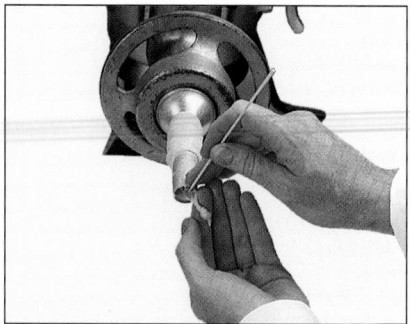

1. Sliding the casing over the nozzle of the sausage stuffer.

2. Knotting and piercing the casing with a skewer.

3. Supporting and guiding the casing off the end of the nozzle as the sausage is extruded from the machine into the casing.

4. Twisting or tying the sausage into uniform links.

6. Support and guide the casing off the end of the nozzle as the sausage is extruded from the nozzle into the casing.

7. After all the sausage has been stuffed into the casing, twist or tie the sausage into uniform links of the desired size.

SALT-CURING, BRINING AND SMOKING

Curing, brining and smoking are ancient techniques for preserving food. Today, foods such as hams, corned beef and smoked salmon are salt-cured, brined or smoked primarily for flavor. Cured meats have a characteristic pink color caused by the reaction of sodium nitrite, which is added during processing, with the naturally occurring myoglobin protein in the meat.

Salt-Curing

Salt-curing is the process of surrounding a food with salt or a mixture of salt, sugar, nitrite-based curing salt, herbs and spices. Salt-curing dehydrates the food, inhibits bacterial growth and adds flavor. It is most often used with pork products and fish. Salt-curing is not a quick procedure—and the time involved adds money to production costs. For example, country-style hams are salt-cured. Proper curing requires approximately 1-1/2 days per pound of ham, which means 3 weeks for the average ham.

Some salt-cured hams such as Smithfield and prosciutto are not actually cooked. The curing process preserves the meat and makes it safe to consume raw.

Gravlax is a well-known salmon dish prepared by salt-curing salmon fillets with a mixture of salt, sugar, pepper and dill. A recipe for gravlax (Recipe 20.22) is included at the end of this chapter.

Brining

A brine is actually a very salty marinade. Most brines have approximately 20% salinity, which is equivalent to 1 pound (450 grams) of salt per gallon (4 liters) of water. As with dry-salt cures, brines can also contain sugar, nitrites, herbs and spices. Brining is sometimes called pickling.

Today, most cured meats are prepared in large production facilities where the brine is injected into the meat for rapid and uniform distribution. Commercially brined corned beef is cured by this process, as are most common hams. After brining, hams are further processed by smoking.

Smoking

There are two basic methods of smoking foods: cold smoking and hot smoking. The principal difference is that hot smoking actually cooks the food, cold smoking does not.

Both are done in a **smoker** specifically designed for this purpose. Smokers can be gas or electric; they vary greatly in size and operation. But they have several things in common. All consist of a chamber that holds the food being smoked, a means of burning wood to produce smoke and a heating element.

Different types of wood can be used to smoke food. Specific woods are selected to impart specific flavors. Hickory is often used for pork products; alder is excellent for smoked salmon. Maple, chestnut, juniper, mesquite and many other woods are also used. Resinous woods such as pine give food a bitter flavor and should be avoided.

Cold smoking is the process of exposing foods to smoke at temperatures of 50–85°F (10–29°C). Meat, poultry, game, fish, shellfish, cheese, nuts and even vegetables can be cold-smoked successfully. Most cold-smoked meats are generally salt-cured or brined first. Salt-curing or brining adds flavor, allows the nitrites (which give the ham, bacon and other smoked meats their distinctive pink color) to penetrate the flesh and, most importantly, extracts moisture from the food, allowing the smoke to penetrate more easily. Cold-smoked foods are actually still raw. Some, like smoked salmon (lox), are eaten without further cooking. Others, such as bacon and hams, must be cooked before eating.

Hot smoking is the process of exposing foods to smoke at temperatures of 200–250°F (93–121°C). As with cold smoking, a great variety of foods can be prepared by hot smoking. Meats, poultry, game, fish and shellfish that are hot-smoked also benefit from salt-curing or brining. Although most hot-smoked foods are fully cooked when removed from the smoker, many are used in other recipes that call for further cooking.

Pork Products

Preparing hams and curing and smoking pork products are a traditional part of charcuterie. Although most bacon and ham are now produced in large commercial facilities, the chef still works with these products and must be able to identify them properly.

Most **bacon** comes from a hog's fatty belly.

Common bacon is produced by brining and cold smoking trimmed pork belly. It is available in slab or sliced form. Sliced bacon is purchased by count (number of slices) per pound; thick-sliced bacon runs 10–14 slices per pound, while thin-sliced bacon may contain as many as 28–32 slices per pound.

Canadian bacon is produced from a boneless pork loin, trimmed so that only a thin layer of fat remains on its surface. It is then brined and smoked.

Pancetta is an Italian pork-belly bacon that is not smoked. It is salt-cured, peppered and often rolled into a cylinder

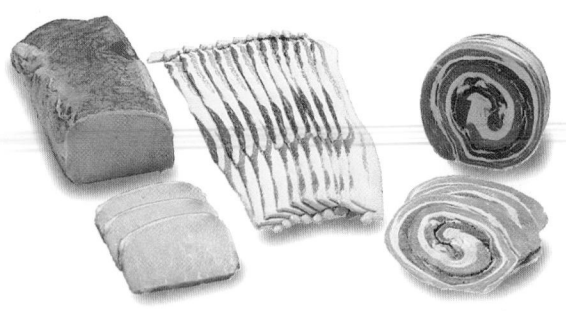

FIGURE 20.3 *Canadian Bacon, Sliced Bacon, and pancetta*

shape. It can be sliced into rounds and fried; it is diced, rendered and combined with sauce to make fettuccine carbonara.

A **fresh ham** is a hog's hind leg; it is a primal cut. Many processed products produced from the primal fresh ham are also called ham.

Ham, in the United States, describes a variety of processed pork products, most of which come from the primal fresh ham. **Boneless** or **formed hams** are produced by separating a primal ham into its basic muscles, defatting the meat, curing it, stuffing the meat into various-sized and -shaped casings and cooking it. Boneless or formed hams are either smoked or chemical smoke flavoring is added during the curing process. The quality of boneless or formed hams varies greatly. The best hams are formed from only one or two large muscles, have low fat content and no added water other than that used during the curing process. Hams of lesser quality are formed from many small pieces of muscle and have a higher fat and water content. Many boneless or formed hams are listed in *The Meat Buyers Guide* and are indexed by the NAMP/IMPS system.

IMPS No. 501, Ham short shank, cured and smoked.

IMPS No. 510, Ham, boneless, skinless, cured and smoked, fully cooked.

Country ham is a specialty of the southeastern United States. Country hams are dry-cured, smoked and hung to air-dry for a period ranging from several weeks to more than a year. During drying, a mold develops on the ham rind that must be scrubbed off before the ham is cooked. It is best cooked by first soaking, then slow simmering. The most famous country hams are Virginia hams; those from Smithfield, Virginia, are considered the finest. Only hams produced in rural areas can be called country hams; others must be labeled country-style ham.

Prosciutto is Italian for ham. What we call prosciutto in this country is called **Parma** in Italy. Parma ham, produced near that Italian city, is made from hogs fed on the whey of cheese processed nearby. It is salt-cured and air-dried but not smoked. The curing process makes it safe and wholesome to consume raw. Several domestic varieties of prosciutto are produced, varying widely in quality. Imported prosciuttos are much larger than the domestic varieties because Italian hogs are larger when butchered.

Westphalian ham is dry-cured, brined and then smoked with beechwood. Authentic Westphalian hams are produced in the Westphalia region of Germany and are quite similar to prosciutto. They are sold bone-in or boneless. Their characteristic flavor is derived from the juniper berries used in the curing process and the beechwood used for smoking.

ONCLUSION

The classic art of charcuterie is as popular today as ever. Consumers regularly enjoy high-quality pâtés, sausages, hams and other charcuterie products.

Although production procedures have changed as new technologies and equipment have developed, the basic principles remain the same: Terrines, pâtés and sausages can only be produced from high-quality forcemeats, and temperature control is fundamental to the proper production of forcemeats and other charcuterie products.

Armed with a basic knowledge of the procedures used for charcuterie, you can use your imagination and creativity to produce a variety of charcuterie products.

QUESTIONS FOR DISCUSSION

1. Explain why the art of charcuterie is relevant to the training of modern chefs.
2. Compare and contrast the three styles of forcemeat.
3. In what way is a terrine different from a pâté? How does a pâté differ from a pâté en croûte?
4. Describe the differences and the similarities between a ballottine and a galantine.
5. Describe the typical procedure for making sausages. Why is the selection of casings important?
6. Explain the difference between hot smoking and cold smoking. Describe a food typically prepared by each of these methods.

ADDITIONAL CHARCUTERIE RECIPES

RECIPE 20.6

SMOKED DUCK AND FOIE GRAS GALANTINE ON A PEAR GALETTE

NOTE: *This dish appears in the Chapter Opening photograph.*

ANA WESTIN HOTEL, WASHINGTON, D.C.
Chef Leland Atkinson

Yield: 1 Galantine

Duck breast, 10 oz. (300 g), boneless, skinless	1	1
Duck meat, lean	1 lb.	450 g
Pork butt, boneless, cubed	8 oz.	240 g
Pâté spice	2 tsp.	10 ml
Salt	1 Tbsp.	15 ml
Orange zest	1 Tbsp.	15 ml
Fresh thyme	1 tsp.	5 ml
Fresh ginger	1 tsp.	5 ml
Juniper berries, crushed	10	10

Port	4 oz.	120 g
Olive oil	1 oz.	30 g
Fatback, cubed	8 oz.	240 g
Foie gras pâté, diced	3 oz.	90 g
Ham, medium dice	2 oz.	60 g
Pistachio meats, chopped	2 oz.	60 g
Fatback, slab	as needed	as needed
Smoker marinade:		
Brown sugar	2 oz.	60 g
Garlic, chopped	1 tsp.	5 ml
Lemon juice	3 oz.	90 g
Walnut oil	6 oz.	180 g
Salt and pepper	TT	TT
Galette (per order)		
Pears	1	1
Clarified butter	1 tsp.	5 ml
Sugar	1/2 tsp.	3 ml
Italian parsley	as needed	as needed

1. Cut the duck breast into several long strips.

2. Marinate the duck breast, duck meat and pork in the pâté spice, salt, orange zest, ginger, thyme, juniper berries and port for 2 days.

3. Remove the strips of duck breast from the marinade and sauté in the olive oil to brown. Remove, drain and reserve.

4. Grind the remaining duck meat, pork butt, marinade ingredients and the cubed fatback in a chilled grinder, first through the large die then through the small die.

5. Place the ground meat in a stainless steel bowl over an ice bath. Fold in the foie gras, ham and pistachios.

6. Slice the fatback into thin sheets. Spread a piece of plastic wrap on the work surface and lay out the slices of fatback in a large rectangle with the edges overlapping slightly.

7. Place the forcemeat and duck breast strips along the length of the fatback rectangle so that when the galantine is rolled up the strips of duck will be arranged in the center. Use the plastic wrap to roll the galantine into a large cylinder.

8. Roll the cylinder in heavy-duty aluminum foil and poach until it reaches an internal temperature of 140°F (60°C). Remove and chill the galantine for at least 6 hours.

9. Combine the ingredients for the smoker marinade in a blender. Unwrap the galantine, brush it with the smoker marinade and chill for 1 hour. Place the galantine in a smoker and cold smoke for 2 hours. Remove and chill before slicing.

10. For each galette, core the pear and slice 1/8 inch (3 millimeters) thick. Add the clarified butter to a warm sauté pan and arrange the pears in the pan by overlapping the slices to form a circle. Sprinkle the pears with the sugar. Sauté the galette, using a spatula to carefully turn it over when browned on the first side.

11. Place a pear galette on a plate and place a slice of galantine directly in the center of the galette. Garnish with Italian parsley or as desired. May be accompanied by Cherry Confit (Recipe 25.13).

◆◆◆

RECIPE 20.7
LAMB SAUSAGE WITH TRICOLOR BEAN SALAD

NOTE: *This dish appears in the Chapter Opening photograph.*

ANA WESTIN HOTEL, WASHINGTON, D.C.
Chef Leland Atkinson

LAMB SAUSAGE

Yield: 12 4-oz. (120-g) Links

Lamb shoulder	3 lb.	1.5 kg
Salt	1 Tbsp.	15 ml
Garlic, chopped	2 tsp.	10 g
Paprika	1 Tbsp.	15 ml
Cayenne pepper	1/2 tsp.	2 ml
Black pepper	1/2 tsp.	2 ml
Cumin	1 Tbsp.	15 ml
Fresh cilantro, chopped	2 Tbsp.	30 ml
Tricolor Bean Salad (recipe follows)	as needed	as needed
Baby lettuces, assorted	12 heads	12 heads
Belgian endive	2 heads	2 heads
Olive oil	as needed	as needed
Red wine vinegar	as needed	as needed

1. Cut the meat in small cubes.
2. Combine the meat with the seasonings and herbs and refrigerate for 1 hour.
3. Grind the meat through a medium die directly into casings.
4. Grill or sauté the sausage links. Present the cooked links with a portion of the Tricolor Bean Salad garnished with baby greens and Belgian endive. Accent with drizzled olive oil and red wine vinegar.

TRICOLOR BEAN SALAD

Yield: 24 oz. (700 g)

Dijon mustard	2 Tbsp.	30 ml
Garlic, minced	1 tsp.	5 ml
Red onion, small dice	1 oz.	30 g
Jalapeños, seeded and minced	2	2
Red wine vinegar	2 Tbsp.	30 ml
Olive oil	3 Tbsp.	45 ml
Black beans, cooked	4 oz.	120 g
Black-eyed peas, cooked	4 oz.	120 g
Plum tomatoes, concasse	3	3
Fresh cilantro, chopped	1 bunch	1 bunch
Salt and pepper	TT	TT

1. Combine the mustard, garlic, onions, jalapeños and red wine vinegar in a mixing bowl.
2. Slowly whisk in the olive oil in a steady stream.
3. Add the beans, black-eyed peas, tomato concasse and cilantro and season with salt and pepper. Refrigerate 1 hour to allow the flavors to blend.

‡ ◆◆◆ ‡

RECIPE 20.8

VEGETABLE TERRINE IN BRIOCHE

NOTE: *This dish appears in the Chapter Opening photograph.*

ANA WESTIN HOTEL, WASHINGTON, D.C.
Chef Leland Atkinson

Yield: 1 12 in. x 4 in. x. 3 in.
(30 cm x 10 cm x 7.5 cm) Terrine

Chicken breast meat, lean	2 lb.	900 g
Egg whites	3	3
Heavy cream	4 oz.	120 g
Brandy	2 oz.	60 g
Salt and pepper	TT	TT
Carrot, medium dice	3 oz.	90 g
Broccoli florets	8 oz.	250 g
Shiitake mushrooms, trimmed	12–18	12–18
Olive oil	1 oz.	30 ml
Red bell pepper, medium dice	2 oz.	60 g
Leek, white part only, medium dice	2 oz.	60 g
Fresh chives, basil and parsley, chopped	4 Tbsp.	60 ml
Nutmeg	TT	TT
Brioche dough, rolled out to approximately 1/8 in. (3 mm), well chilled	1 lb.	450 g
Egg yolks, beaten	2	2
Eggs	2	2
Water	1 oz.	30 g
Madeira aspic	as needed	as needed

1. Dice or grind the chicken; place it in the bowl of a cold food processor and process.

2. Add the egg whites and then the cream and brandy in a steady stream while the motor is running.

3. Season the mousseline and poach a small amount to test for texture and seasonings.

4. Adjust the seasonings and transfer to a metal mixing bowl in an ice bath.

5. Separately blanch the carrots and broccoli; drain and blot dry on a paper towel.

6. Sauté the shiitakes in olive oil. Drain and chill. In the same pan, sauté the red peppers and leeks. Remove from the stove and add the herbs. Fold the carrots, peppers, leeks and herbs into the mousseline.

7. Line a buttered pâté mold with the chilled brioche, reserving the excess for the top and garnish.

8. Fill the mold one-fourth full with the mousseline. Layer the shiitakes over the mousseline, cover them with another layer of mousseline, followed by the dry broccoli. Repeat this process until the mold is filled, finishing with a layer of mousseline.

9. Fold the ends of the brioche over the filling and brush with beaten egg yolk.

10. Make a top from the remaining brioche and place it over the mold; cut a vent and insert a foil funnel into the vent.

11. Beat the eggs with the water to make an egg wash. Brush the exposed

Continued

brioche with the egg wash and bake at 425°F (220°C) until the internal temperature reaches 125°F (52°C), approximately 35–40 minutes.

12. When cold, fill the pâté with madeira aspic, if needed.

◆◆◆

RECIPE 20.9

BASIC GAME FORCEMEAT

Yield: 4 lb. 8 oz. (2 kg)

Venison or antelope, cubed	1 lb. 8 oz.	675 g
Veal, cubed	1 lb. 8 oz.	675 g
Brandy	4 oz.	120 g
Salt and pepper	TT	TT
Dried thyme	1 tsp.	5 ml
Pork fatback, cubed	1 lb.	450 g
Eggs	3	3
Game stock, cold	1 pt.	450 ml
Fresh parsley, chopped	1 oz.	30 g
Green peppercorns	1/2 oz.	15 g

1. Combine the venison or antelope and veal with the brandy, salt, pepper and thyme; marinate for several hours or overnight.
2. Grind the marinated meat and marinade ingredients in a chilled meat grinder once through a large die and then once through a small die; refrigerate.
3. Grind the fatback once through the small die.
4. Emulsify the fat with the ground meats in the bowl of a cold food processor. This can be done in several batches. Place the forcemeat in a stainless steel bowl over an ice bath.
5. Add the eggs, stock, parsley and green peppercorns to the forcemeat in several batches; work them in by hand.
6. Additional garnishes may be added as desired. The forcemeat can be used to make a variety of pâtés or terrines.

◆◆◆

RECIPE 20.10

SALMON AND SEA BASS TERRINE
WITH SPINACH AND BASIL

Yield: 1 12 in. x 4 in. x. 3 in.
(30 cm x 10 cm x 7.5 cm) Terrine

Salmon fillet, boneless, skinless	1 lb. 8 oz.	700 g
Egg whites	3	3
Salt and white pepper	TT	TT
Cayenne pepper	TT	TT
Heavy cream	24 oz.	700 g
Basil leaves	12	12
Truffle, brunoise (optional)	3/4 oz.	22 g
Spinach leaves, cleaned	6 oz.	180 g
Sea bass fillet	12 oz.	350 g

1. Grind the salmon through the large die of a well-chilled meat grinder.

2. Place the salmon in the bowl of a food processor and process until smooth.

3. Add the egg whites, one at a time, pulsing the processor to incorporate. Scrape down the bowl and season with salt, white pepper and cayenne pepper.

4. With the machine running, add the cream in a steady stream. Scrape down the bowl again and process the mousseline until it is smooth and well mixed.

5. Blanch the basil leaves and refresh. Chop them finely.

6. Remove the mousseline from the bowl of the processor. Fold in the basil leaves and truffles and refrigerate.

7. Blanch and refresh the spinach leaves.

8. Spread the spinach leaves on a piece of plastic wrap, completely covering a rectangle approximately the length and width of the terrine mold.

9. Cut the sea bass fillet into strips approximately 1 inch (2.5 centimeters) wide and place end to end on the spinach leaves. Season with salt and white pepper.

10. Use the plastic wrap to wrap the spinach leaves tightly around the fish fillets.

11. Butter a terrine and line it with plastic wrap.

12. Half-fill the lined terrine with salmon mousseline.

13. Carefully unwrap the spinach and sea bass fillets and place them down the center of the terrine. Fill the terrine with the remaining mousseline.

14. Tap the terrine mold firmly to remove any air pockets, then fold the plastic wrap over the top.

15. Cover and bake the terrine in a water bath at 300°F (150°C) to an internal temperature of 140°F (60°C), approximately 1-1/2 hours.

16. Cool the terrine well, unmold, slice or decorate and serve as desired.

◆◆◆

RECIPE 20.11
SWEETBREAD TERRINE

Yield: 1 12 in. x 4 in. x 3 in.
(30 cm x 10 cm x 7.5 cm) Terrine

Lean veal, cubed	2 lb.	1 kg
Pork butt, cubed	1 lb.	450 g
Pâté spice	1 Tbsp.	15 ml
Salt and pepper	TT	TT
Brandy	6 oz.	180 g
Fatback	1 lb.	450 g
Eggs	4	4
Sweetbreads	2 lb.	1 kg
Morels	4 oz.	120 g
Chanterelles	4 oz.	120 g
Shiitake mushrooms	4 oz.	120 g
Clarified butter	1 oz.	30 g
Fresh thyme, chopped	1 Tbsp.	15 ml
Rosemary	2 tsp.	10 ml
Fresh chives, chopped	2 Tbsp.	30 ml

Continued

1. Combine the veal and pork butt with the pâté spice, salt, pepper and brandy; marinate for several hours or overnight.

2. Dice and freeze the fatback.

3. Grind the veal, pork and marinade ingredients in a well-chilled grinder, once through the large die, then once through the medium die. Hold in an ice bath.

4. Grind the fatback once through the medium die; add to the ground meat mixture.

5. Place the meat mixture and fatback in a chilled food processor and process until emulsified.

6. Over an ice bath, incorporate the eggs into the forcemeat. Refrigerate the forcemeat while preparing the garnishes.

7. Blanch the sweetbreads. Remove the connective tissue and cut the sweetbreads into large dice.

8. Wash the mushrooms, sauté them in the butter; season with the thyme and rosemary. Chill them well.

9. Fold the sweetbreads, mushrooms and chives into the forcemeat and follow the procedures for preparing a terrine.

◆◆◆

RECIPE 20.12

LIVER TERRINE

Yield: 1 12 in. x 4 in. x 3 in.
(30 cm x 10 cm x 7.5 cm) Terrine

Pork liver	1 lb. 4 oz.	600 g
Fatback, diced	12 oz.	350 g
Onion, diced	6 oz.	180 g
Eggs	2	2
Salt	1 Tbsp.	15 ml
Green peppercorns	1/2 tsp.	2 ml
Allspice, ground	1/2 tsp.	2 ml
Cloves, ground	1/4 tsp.	1 ml
Ginger, ground	1/4 tsp.	1 ml
Cream sauce	8 oz.	250 g
Brown veal stock	6 oz.	180 g
Fatback, sliced	as needed	as needed

1. Trim and dice the liver.

2. Grind the liver and diced fatback through a grinder with a fine die.

3. Add the onion and pass the liver and fatback through the grinder again.

4. Beat together by hand the eggs, salt, green peppercorns, allspice, cloves and ginger.

5. Combine the cream sauce and brown veal stock, add the egg mixture and mix well.

6. Add the ground liver mixture and beat until smooth.

7. Line a terrine with slices of fatback. Fill the mold with the forcemeat and cover with the overhanging slices of fatback.

8. Cover the terrine with its lid or aluminum foil and bake in a water bath at

350° F (180° C) to an internal temperature of 150° F (66° C), approximately 1-1/2 hours.

9. Cool, unmold, slice and serve as desired.

=== ◆◆◆ ===

RECIPE 20.13

VEGETABLE TERRINE

Yield: 1 12 in. x 4 in. x 3 in.
(30 cm x 10 cm x 7.5 cm) Terrine

Carrots, batonnet	6 oz.	180 g
Green beans	4 oz.	120 g
Leeks, small, white part only	4 oz.	120 g
Shiitake mushrooms	6 oz.	180 g
Whole butter	1 oz.	30 g
Artichoke hearts, cooked and chilled	5	5
Red bell peppers, roasted and peeled, julienne	4 oz.	120 g
Gruyère cheese, shredded	6 oz.	180 g
Heavy cream	1-1/2 pt.	700 ml
Egg yolks	9	9
Nutmeg	TT	TT
Salt and pepper	TT	TT
Fresh chives, chopped	1 Tbsp.	15 ml
Granulated gelatin	1 Tbsp.	15 ml
Red Pepper Coulis (Recipe 10.17)	as needed	as needed

1. Boil the carrots in salted water until tender, approximately 3 minutes. Refresh and reserve.

2. Clean the green beans and boil in salted water until tender, approximately 5 minutes. Refresh and reserve.

3. Trim the roots from the leeks and boil in salted water until tender, approximately 3 minutes. Refresh and reserve.

4. Trim the stems from the shiitake mushrooms. Sauté the caps in butter until tender. Remove from the heat and set aside.

5. Line a terrine mold with plastic wrap, allowing the wrap to extend over the top of the mold.

6. Dry the vegetables well and arrange them in the terrine in loose layers, adding the gruyère cheese between each layer.

7. Whisk the cream and egg yolks together and season with nutmeg, salt and pepper. Stir in the chives.

8. Soften the gelatin in 2 ounces (60 grams) of cool water. Gently warm the softened gelatin, stirring until completely dissolved. Stir the gelatin into the cream mixture.

9. Pour the cream mixture over the layered vegetables. Tap the terrine firmly against the work surface to remove any air pockets. Fold the plastic wrap over the top of the terrine and cover with the lid. Cook the terrine in a water bath at 325° F (160° C) until the custard reaches 145° F (63° C), approximately 1-1/2 hours. Cool the terrine for several hours or overnight.

10. Unmold the terrine and portion into 1/2-inch (12-millimeter) slices. Serve with chilled Red Pepper Coulis.

◆◆◆

RECIPE 20.14

ROASTED RED PEPPER MOUSSE

Yield: 1-1/2 pt. (700 ml)

Onion, small dice	3 oz.	90 g
Garlic, chopped	1 tsp.	5 ml
Olive oil	1 oz.	30 g
Red bell pepper, roasted and peeled, small dice	10 oz.	300 g
Salt and pepper	TT	TT
Chicken stock	8 oz.	225 g
Granulated gelatin	1 Tbsp.	15 ml
Dry white wine	2 oz.	60 g
Heavy cream, whipped	6 oz.	180 g

1. Sauté the onions and garlic in the olive oil until tender, approximately 2 minutes.
2. Add the bell pepper, salt, pepper and chicken stock. Bring to a boil, reduce to a simmer and cook 5 minutes.
3. Soften the gelatin in the white wine, then add to the pepper mixture. Purée the pepper mixture in a blender or food processor and strain through a china cap.
4. Place the pepper purée over an ice bath. Stir until cool but do not allow the gelatin to set. Fold in the whipped cream. Pour the mousse into aspic-lined or well-oiled timbales or molds and refrigerate several hours or overnight.
5. Unmold the mousse and serve as desired.

VARIATIONS: Substitute yellow or green bell peppers for part or all of the red bell peppers.

Broccoli Mousse: Substitute 8 ounces (225 grams) of blanched, chopped broccoli for the red bell peppers.

◆◆◆

RECIPE 20.15

SALMON MOUSSE

Yield: 1 lb. 8 oz. (650 g)

Salmon, boneless, skinless	12 oz.	350 g
Fish velouté, warm	8 oz.	250 g
Heavy cream	8 oz.	250 g
Granulated gelatin	1-1/2 Tbsp.	23 ml
White wine	4 oz.	120 g
Salt and white pepper	TT	TT
Cayenne pepper	TT	TT

1. Steam the salmon and transfer it to the food processor while still warm. Add the warm velouté in a steady stream while the machine is running.
2. Whip the cream to soft peaks and reserve.
3. Add the gelatin to the wine and allow it to rest for 5 minutes. Heat the gelatin mixture to a simmer.
4. Transfer the salmon and velouté to a mixing bowl and stir in the gelatin mixture. Season with salt, pepper and cayenne.

5. When the mixture has cooled to near room temperature, fold in the whipped cream with a rubber spatula until just mixed.

6. The mousse is now ready to be formed into timbales, or molded into various shapes as desired.

◆◆◆

RECIPE 20.16
DUCK CONFIT

Yield: 4 Servings

Duck, 4 lb. (1.8 kg), cut into 4 pieces	1	1
Kosher salt	2 Tbsp.	30 ml
Black pepper, cracked	1 tsp.	5 ml
Bay leaves	4	4
Fresh thyme	6 sprigs	6 sprigs
Garlic cloves, crushed	6	6
Duck or goose fat, melted	2 lb.	900 g

1. Rub the duck with the salt. Place skin side down in a roasting pan just large enough to hold the pieces in one layer; season with the black pepper, crumbled bay leaves, thyme and garlic. Cover and refrigerate overnight.

2. Bake the duck at 325°F (160°C) until brown, approximately 15–20 minutes. Add enough melted duck or goose fat to cover the pieces completely.

3. Cover the pan and cook in a 300°F (150°C) oven until the duck is very tender, approximately 2 hours.

4. Remove the duck from the fat and place in a deep hotel pan. Ladle enough of the cooking fat over the pieces to cover them completely. Be careful not to add any of the cooking juices.

5. Cover the pan and refrigerate for 2 days to allow the flavors to mellow.

6. To serve, remove the duck from the fat and scrape off the excess fat. Bake at 350°F (180°C) until the skin is crisp and the meat is hot, approximately 30 minutes.

◆◆◆

RECIPE 20.17
CHOPPED CHICKEN LIVER

Yield: 20 oz. (600 g)

Chicken livers, trimmed	1 lb.	450 g
Chicken fat or butter	2 oz.	60 g
Kosher salt	TT	TT
Eggs, hard-cooked	2	2
Onion, small dice	6 oz.	170 g
Salt and pepper	TT	TT

1. Sauté the livers in the chicken fat or butter until lightly browned with a slightly pink interior. Season with kosher salt.

2. Chop the livers with a chef's knife, blending in the eggs and onions. Season to taste with salt and pepper.

3. The final product should be slightly coarse and peppery. Blend in additional chicken fat or butter if necessary to make the mixture hold together.

4. Pack into a serving bowl, cover well and chill for 24 hours. Serve with crackers, toast or matzos and sliced radishes.

◆◆◆

RECIPE 20.18
RABBIT PÂTÉ
EN CROÛTE

Yield: 1 3 in x 3.5 in. x 16 in.
(7.5 cm x 8.7 cm x 40 cm) Pâté

Rabbit meat, boneless, large dice	2 lb.	1 kg
Pork butt, large dice	1 lb.	450 g
Marinade:		
Pâté spice	1 Tbsp.	15 ml
Orange zest	2 Tbsp.	30 ml
Lime zest	1 Tbsp.	15 ml
Brandy	4 oz.	120 g
Fresh thyme	1 bunch	1 bunch
Juniper berries	6	6
Salt and pepper	TT	TT
Fatback, large dice	1 lb.	450 g
Eggs	4	4
Pistachios, chopped coarse	8 oz.	250 g
Ham, diced	6 oz.	180 g
Black olives, chopped coarse	2 oz.	60 g
Rabbit loins, browned lightly in oil	4	4
Rabbit livers, browned lightly in oil	6	6
Pâté dough	1 lb. 8 oz.	700 g

1. Combine the rabbit meat and pork butt with the marinade ingredients and marinate several hours or overnight.
2. Freeze the fatback.
3. Remove the thyme and juniper berries from the marinated meat mixture and grind the meat in a well-chilled grinder once through the large die, then through the medium die. Hold the mixture in an ice bath.
4. Grind the fatback through the medium die and add to the meat mixture.
5. Place the meat mixture and fat in a chilled food processor and process until emulsified.
6. Over an ice bath, incorporate the eggs into the forcemeat.
7. Fold the pistachios, ham and olives into the forcemeat.
8. Follow the procedure for preparing a pâté en croûte using the rabbit loins and livers as garnishes running the length of the pâté.

◆◆◆

RECIPE 20.19
TEX-MEX

TURKEY SAUSAGE

Yield: 4 lb. (1.8 kg)

Canola oil	4 Tbsp.	60 ml
Onion, chopped fine	12 oz.	340 g
Garlic, minced	1 Tbsp.	15 ml

Jalapeño, chopped	1 Tbsp.	15 ml
Turkey breast meat, trimmed of fat	2 lb.	1 kg
Veal, lean	8 oz.	250 g
White wine vinegar	2 oz.	60 g
Water	8 oz.	250 g
Fresh cilantro, chopped	4 oz.	120 g
White pepper	1 tsp.	5 ml
Chile powder	1 tsp.	5 ml
Cumin, ground	1/2 tsp.	2 ml
Salt	1 tsp.	5 ml

1. Heat the oil and sauté the onion, garlic and jalapeño until the onions are translucent; remove and chill well.
2. Grind the turkey and veal in a cold meat grinder, once through the large die and then through the medium die. Working over an ice bath, combine the meats, vinegar, water and seasonings. Add the sautéed vegetables.
3. Blend well, then cook a small portion to test the flavor and texture. Adjust the seasonings.
4. Stuff into casings or portion into 2-ounce (60-gram) patties and broil. Serve with papaya salsa.

Nutritional values per 2-ounce (60-gram) patty:

Calories	81	Protein	11 g
Calories from fat	36%	Vitamin A	175 IU
Total fat	3 g	Vitamin C	2 mg
Saturated fat	0 g	Sodium	138 mg
Cholesterol	31 mg		

◆◆◆

RECIPE 20.20
SPICY ITALIAN SAUSAGE

Yield: 5 lb. (2.2 kg)

Pork butt	5 lb.	2.2 kg
Salt	1-1/2 Tbsp.	23 ml
Black pepper	1-1/2 tsp	7 ml
Fennel seeds	1-1/2 tsp.	7 ml
Paprika	1 Tbsp.	15 ml
Red pepper, crushed	1-1/2 tsp.	7 ml
Coriander, ground	3/4 tsp.	4 ml
Cold water	5 oz.	150 g

1. Cut the meat into 2-inch (5-centimeter) cubes.
2. Combine the pork with the remaining ingredients except the water.
3. Grind the meat once through the coarse die of a well-chilled grinder.
4. Add the cold water and mix well.
5. Stuff the sausage into casings.

◆◆◆

RECIPE 20.21
CHORIZO

Yield: 7-1/2 lb. (3.4 kg)

Pork, lean	5 lb.	2.2 kg
Fatback	2 lb. 8 oz.	1.1 kg
Red pepper flakes	1 tsp.	5 ml
Garlic, chopped	1 oz.	30 g
Cumin	3 Tbsp.	45 ml
Cayenne pepper	2 Tbsp.	30 ml
Salt	4 tsp.	20 ml
Paprika	5 Tbsp.	75 ml
Red wine vinegar	3 oz.	90 g

1. Cut the pork and fatback in 1-inch (2.5-centimeter) pieces. Grind the pork once using a medium die. Grind half of the pork a second time together with the fatback through a fine die.

2. Combine all the ingredients in the bowl of a mixer using the paddle attachment. The sausage may be used in bulk or formed into links as desired.

RECIPE 20.22
GRAVLAX

Yield: Approximately 5 lb. (2.2 kg)

Salmon, drawn, 10–12 lb.	1	1
Kosher salt	8 oz.	240 g
White peppercorns, cracked	1 oz.	30 g
Fresh dill, chopped	2 bunches	2 bunches
Sugar	8 oz.	250 g

1. Fillet the salmon, following the procedure discussed in Chapter 19, Fish and Shellfish. Remove the pin bones but leave the skin attached.

2. To make the salt cure, combine the salt, white peppercorns, dill and sugar.

3. Coat the salmon fillets with the salt cure and wrap each fillet separately in plastic wrap.

4. Place the fillets in a hotel pan and place another hotel pan on top. Place two #10 cans in the top hotel pan to weigh it down and press the fish.

5. Refrigerate the salmon 2–3 days.

6. Unwrap the gravlax, scrape off the salt cure and slice it very thin.

◆◆◆

RECIPE 20.23
Smoked Salmon with Tuna

CHRISTOPHER'S AND **CHRISTOPHER'S BISTRO**, PHOENIX, AZ
Chef/Owner Christopher Gross

Yield: 4 Servings

Smoked salmon	8 oz.	225 g
Fresh tuna, cut into 4-oz. (120-g) squares	2	2
Salt and white pepper	TT	TT
Butter, melted	as needed	as needed
Fresh parsley, chopped fine	1 bunch	1 bunch
Fresh thyme, chopped fine	1 bunch	1 bunch
Fresh chervil, chopped fine	1 bunch	1 bunch
Fresh tarragon, chopped fine	1 bunch	1 bunch
Fresh basil leaves, chopped fine	5	5
Saffron	pinch	pinch
Crème fraîche	1 pt.	450 ml
Fresh dill	1 sprig	1 sprig
Fresh spinach	8 oz.	225 g
Caviar (Osetra)	1 oz.	30 g
Baby lettuces, assorted	4 heads	4 heads
Olive oil	2 Tbsp.	30 ml
Brioche	4 slices	4 slices

1. Thinly slice the salmon and arrange it in a single-layer circle on four plates. Leave a 1-inch (2.5-centimeter) border around the edge of each plate.

2. Season the tuna with salt and pepper and coat with a small amount of butter. Roll in an assortment of chopped herbs.

3. Sear the tuna in a hot sauté pan, keeping it rare. Refrigerate until ready to serve.

4. To make the yellow sauce, add a pinch of saffron to 6 ounces (180 grams) of the crème fraîche and simmer until the crème turns yellow, approximately 10 minutes. Strain the sauce, season with salt and white pepper and refrigerate.

5. To make the green sauce, add the dill to another 6 ounces (180 grams) of crème fraîche and simmer for 10 minutes. Place the spinach in a blender. Add the dilled crème fraîche and blend for several seconds. Strain, season with salt and white pepper and cool quickly to preserve the color.

6. Whip the remaining crème fraîche until stiff.

7. Cut the two squares of tuna in half diagonally, creating four triangles. Place a triangle of tuna in the center of each plate of salmon.

8. Form a small quenelle of whipped crème fraîche and place it at the edge of the salmon. Spoon caviar onto the crème fraîche.

9. Toss the baby greens with the olive oil and place a small mound next to the tuna.

10. Garnish the border of each plate with small dots of the yellow and green sauces.

11. Cut the slices of brioche into mushroom shapes and toast. Place one slice against each piece of tuna.

♦♦♦

RECIPE 20.24
THOUSAND-LAYER SMOKED SALMON TERRINE WITH CAVIAR SAUCE

CITRUS, Los Angeles, CA
Chef Michel Richard

Yield: 12 Servings

Smoked salmon, sliced	3 lb.	1.4 kg
Salmon mousse:		
Smoked salmon slices or trimmings	8–9 oz.	225–250 g
Basil leaves	1 oz.	30 g
Chilled cream cheese,		
coarsely chopped	8 oz.	225 g
Unsalted butter, chilled,		
coarsely chopped	4 oz.	120 g
Tabasco sauce	TT	TT
Olive oil	2 oz.	60 g
Chicken stock, unsalted	3-1/2 oz.	100 g
Lemon juice, fresh	2 oz.	60 g
Unflavored gelatin	1/2 oz.	15 g
Flying fish roe, salmon roe		
or other caviar	2 Tbsp.	30 ml
Caviar Sauce (recipe follows)	as needed	as needed
Cucumber slices for garnish (optional)	as needed	as needed

1. Line three identical 12-x-17-inch (30-x-43-centimeter) baking sheets with parchment paper and cover completely with the smoked salmon slices, overlapping if necessary. Top each tray with parchment paper. Freeze for 30 minutes.

2. For the salmon mousse, process the smoked salmon trimmings and basil in a food processor until smooth. With the machine running, add the cream cheese and then the butter, several pieces at a time. Add the Tabasco and process until smooth. With the machine running, pour in the olive oil in a slow, thin stream.

3. Place the stock and lemon juice in a small pot and sprinkle the gelatin over the liquids. Stir over low heat until the gelatin is dissolved, then cool until tepid. With the food processor running, slowly pour the gelatin mixture into the mousse. Transfer to a bowl and stir in the roe.

4. To assemble the terrine, remove the top pieces of parchment paper from the trays of salmon. Spread one third of the mousse evenly over 1 tray, covering the salmon completely. Take the salmon layer from the second tray and invert it over the salmon on the first tray, paper side up, forming 2 layers. Rub and press the paper so that the 2 layers adhere. Remove the paper. Spread one third of the mousse over this second layer. Invert the third tray over the salmon layers, paper side up. Rub and press the paper so that the 3 layers adhere. Invert the tray onto a work surface and remove the tray. Rub the top layer of paper, pressing the salmon layers together.

5. Using a sharp knife and a ruler as a guide, divide the layers equally into five 12-inch (30-centimeter) strips, each just short of 3-1/2 inches (9 centimeters) wide. Remove the top paper. Invert 1 strip onto a cutting board or tray, paper side up. Remove the paper and cover completely with a thin

layer of the remaining salmon mousse. Repeat, stacking the remaining strips. Spread any remaining salmon mousse evenly over the top and sides of the terrine. Cover with plastic wrap. Place in the freezer until firm but not frozen, approximately 30 minutes.

6. Cut the terrine crosswise in half. Stack one half on top of the other. Smooth and square off the edges using a metal spatula dipped in hot water. Freeze until firm, approximately 1 hour, or refrigerate until well chilled, approximately 4 hours or overnight.

7. To serve, cut into 1/2-inch- (1.2-centimeter-) thick slices. If desired, cut each slice in half again, diagonally, forming 2 triangles. Transfer the slices to 12 plates. Let sit for 30 minutes. Ladle caviar sauce alongside. Garnish with cucumber slices and serve immediately.

CAVIAR SAUCE

Mayonnaise	1 pt.	450 ml
Chicken stock, unsalted	2 oz.	60 g
Lemon juice, fresh	TT	TT
Tabasco sauce	10 drops	10 drops
Flying fish roe, salmon roe or other caviar	6 oz.	180 g
Fresh chives, minced	1 oz.	30 g
Tomato paste or beet juice	2 Tbsp.	30 ml

1. Place the mayonnaise in a small bowl. Stir in the chicken stock, lemon juice, Tabasco sauce, roe and chives.

2. Mix in enough tomato paste or beet juice to tint the mayonnaise a slightly lighter shade than the salmon.

CHAPTER 21

DEEP-FRYING

After studying this chapter you will be able to:

◆ select and maintain the proper equipment and fats for deep-frying
◆ use breadings and batters
◆ prepare fritters and croquettes

*D*eep-frying has a bad reputation. Too many consumers think of deep-fried foods as greasy convenience items with thick breadings or batters masking the principal ingredient's inferior quality. But properly prepared deep-fried foods can be deliciously tender and juicy—and their contrasting crispy crusts and moist interiors add to eating enjoyment.

Perhaps no other cooking method can be applied to such a wide variety of foods. Meats, poultry, fish and shellfish, vegetables, potatoes and other starches, fruits, pastries and even ice cream can be deep-fried successfully. That is why we devote a separate chapter to the process.

This versatile procedure is relatively simple provided a few basic guidelines are followed. This chapter explains those guidelines and provides recipes for breading and batters. Also included are illustrative recipes utilizing deep-frying techniques. Other recipes that use deep-frying are found in the various chapters on vegetables, fish, starches and quick breads.

Deep-frying is a dry-heat cooking method using fat as the cooking medium. Boiling and deep-frying are conceptually similar. For both cooking methods, food is placed in a liquid and heat is transferred from the hot liquid (water or fat, respectively) to the food being cooked through conduction (the transfer of heat by direct contact) and convection (the transfer of heat through the currents in a liquid or gas).

The principal difference between boiling and deep frying is the temperature of the cooking medium. The boiling point, 212°F (100°C), is the hottest temperature at which food can be cooked in water. At this temperature, most foods require a long cooking period and surface sugars cannot caramelize. With deep-frying, temperatures up to 400°F (200°C) are used. These high temperatures cook food more quickly and allow the food's surface to brown. Even though the food is cooked in a liquid, deep-frying is not a moist-heat cooking method because the liquid fat contains no moisture.

SELECTING EQUIPMENT FOR DEEP-FRYING

Unlike most kitchen equipment, a deep-fat fryer has only one purpose: to cook foods in a large amount of hot fat. Fryers are sized by the amount of fat they hold. Most commercial fryers range between 15 and 82 pounds. Fryers can be either gas or electric and are thermostatically controlled for temperatures between 200° and 400°F (90–200°C).

When choosing a fryer, look for a fry tank with curved, easy-to-clean sloping sides. Some fryers have a cold zone (an area of reduced temperature) at the bottom of the fry tank to trap particles. This prevents them from burning, creating off-flavors and shortening the life of the fryer fat.

Deep-fryers usually come with steel wire baskets to hold the food during cooking. Fryer baskets are usually lowered into the fat and raised manually, although some models have automatic basket mechanisms controlled by timers.

As with any piece of equipment, read the operator's manual or have an experienced colleague show you how to operate any deep-fryer before using or cleaning it.

The most important factor when choosing a deep-fryer is **recovery time**. Recovery time is the length of time it takes the fat to return to the desired cooking temperature after food is submerged in it. When food is submerged, heat is immediately transferred to the food from the fat. This heat transfer lowers the fat's temperature. The more food added at one time, the greater the drop in the fat's temperature. If the temperature drops too much or does not return quickly to the proper cooking temperature, the food may absorb excess fat and become greasy.

Deep-frying foods in a sauce pot on the stove top is discouraged because it is both difficult and dangerous. Recovery time is usually very slow and temperatures are difficult to control. Also the fat can spill easily, leading to injuries or creating a fire hazard.

SELECTING FATS FOR DEEP-FRYING

Many types of fats can be used for deep-frying. (In this chapter, the term *fat* applies to both solid fats and liquid oils.) Although animal fats, such as rendered beef fat, are sometimes used to impart their specific flavors to deep-fried foods, by far the most common fats used for deep-frying are vegetable oils such as soybean, safflower and canola oil.

Specially formulated deep-fat frying compounds are also available. These are usually composed of a vegetable oil or oils to which antifoaming agents, antioxidants and preservatives have been added. These additives increase usable life and raise smoke points.

A fat's **smoke point** is the temperature at which it visibly begins to smoke and chemically begins to break down. Animal fats generally have low smoke points of about 350°F (180°C), making them unsuitable for deep-frying. Vegetable oils generally have higher smoke points of about 475°F (250°C), thus providing the high temperatures desired for deep-frying. (See Chapter 7, Kitchen Staples, for a list of fat smoke points.)

Some frying fats are also hydrogenated. Hydrogenation is a chemical process that adds hydrogen to oils and turns a liquid oil into a solid (margarine is hydrogenated vegetable oil). Hydrogenated fats are more resistant to oxidation and chemical breakdown.

When fats break down, their chemical structure is altered; the triglyceride molecules that make up fat are converted into individual fatty acids. These acids add undesirable flavors to the fat and can ruin the flavor of the food being cooked. When a fat becomes very dark, foams excessively or adds off-flavors to foods, it has broken down and should be changed.

To choose the right fat, consider flavor, smoke point and resistance to chemical breakdown. High-quality frying fat should have a clean or natural flavor, a high smoke point and, when properly maintained, be resistant to chemical breakdown.

Maintaining Fryer Fat

Properly maintaining fryer fat greatly extends its useful life. To do so:

1. Store the fat in tightly sealed containers away from strong light; cover the fat in the fryer when not in use. Prolonged exposure to air and light turns fat rancid.

2. Skim and remove food particles from the fat's surface during frying. Food particles cause fat to break down; if they are not removed they will accumulate in the fryer and burn.

3. Do not salt food over the fat. Salt causes fat to break down chemically.

4. Prevent excessive water from coming into contact with the fat; pat-dry moist foods as much as possible before cooking and dry the fryer, baskets and utensils well after cleaning. Water, like salt, causes fat to break down.

5. Do not overheat the fat (turn the fryer down or off if not in use). High temperatures break down the fat.

6. Filter the fat each day or after each shift if the fryer is heavily used. Best results are obtained by using a filtering machine designed specifically for this purpose. Many large commercial fryers even have built-in filter systems. Less well equipped operations can simply pour the hot fat through a paper cone filter.

TABLE 21.1

Fryer fat can be damaged by:	Change fryer fat when it:
Salt	Becomes dark
Water	Smokes
Overheating	Foams
Food particles	Develops off-flavors
Oxygen	

PROCEDURES FOR DEEP-FRYING

The temperature of the fat is critical to successful deep-frying. The fat must be hot enough to quickly seal the surface of the food so it does not become excessively greasy, yet it should not be so hot that the food's surface burns before the interior is cooked.

Nearly all deep-fried foods are cooked at temperatures between 325° and 375°F (160–190°C). The fat's temperature can be adjusted within this range to allow the interior of thicker foods or frozen foods to cook before their surfaces become too dark.

Try not to fry delicately flavored foods in the same fat used for more strongly flavored ones. For example, do not deep-fry fruit fritters in the same fat used for catfish. If the fritters are fried in the catfish fat, they could develop an odd taste from the residual flavors left from the catfish.

Deep-Frying Methods

There are two distinct deep-frying methods for standard electric or gas fryers: the basket method and the swimming method. Which is used depends upon the food being fried.

The **basket method** of deep-frying uses a basket to hold foods that are breaded, individually quick frozen or otherwise do not tend to stick together during cooking. The basket is removed from the fryer and filled as much as two-thirds full of product. (Do not fill the basket while it is hanging over the fat as this allows unnecessary crumbs, salt and food particles to fall into the fat, shortening its life.) The filled basket is then submerged in the hot fat. When cooking is completed, the basket is used to remove the food from the fat.

Basket Method of Deep-Frying

A variation on this procedure is the **double-basket method**. This variation is necessitated by the fact that many fried foods float as they cook. This may produce undesirable results because the section of the food not submerged may not cook. To prevent this and to promote even cooking, a second basket is used to keep the foods submerged in the fat.

Most battered foods initially sink to the bottom when placed in hot fat, then rise to the top as they cook. Because they would stick to a basket, the **swimming method** of deep-frying is used for these foods. With the swimming method, battered foods are carefully dropped directly into the hot fat. (Baskets are not used.) They will rise to the top as they cook. When the surface that is in contact with the fat is properly browned, the food is turned over with a spider or a pair of tongs so that it can cook evenly on both sides. When done, the product is removed and drained, again using a spider or tongs.

Double-Basket Method of Deep-Frying

Draining and Holding Deep-Fried Foods

All deep-fried foods must be drained of excess oil before they are served. When removing foods from the deep-fryer, allow excess fat to drain into the fryer. Then transfer the foods to a hotel pan that is either lined with absorbent paper or fitted with a rack.

Deep-fried foods should be kept under a heat lamp. Steam tables do not keep deep-fried foods hot because very little of the crisp foods' surface actually touches the hot surface of the steam table's pan.

Swimming Method of Deep-Frying

SELECTING FOODS FOR DEEP-FRYING

Only tender foods should be deep-fried. Deep-frying cooks foods at relatively high temperatures for short periods of time and does not have a tenderizing effect. Young tender poultry is ideal, as are most types of lean fish and shellfish. Fruits and vegetables can also be deep-fried. Probably the most popular deep-fried foods of all are potatoes, which are cooked in an endless variety of shapes and forms. (Several of the recipes found in Chapter 23, Potatoes, Grains and Pasta, require deep-frying.) Foods that are deep-fried together should be of the same size or thickness so they cook evenly. Slow-cooking vegetables such as broccoli, cauliflower and okra can be blanched first so they deep-fry more quickly.

PREPARING FOODS FOR DEEP-FRYING

With some exceptions (french fries, for example), most foods to be deep-fried are first breaded or battered. Breading and batter coat the food, keeping it moist and preventing it from becoming excessively greasy during cooking.

Seasoning Foods to be Deep-Fried

Breaded and battered foods can be seasoned before the breading or batter is applied. Seasonings may also be added to the flour, bread crumbs or batter before the main item is coated.

Many types of deep-fried food are salted after they are removed from the fat. This should be done immediately after the food is removed from the fryer so the salt will cling more readily.

Breading Foods to be Deep-Fried

A breaded item is any food that is coated with bread crumbs, cracker meal, cornmeal or other dry meal to protect it during cooking. Breaded foods are generally cooked by deep-frying or pan-frying. The breading makes a solid coating that seals during cooking to prevent the fat from coming in direct contact with the food and making it greasy.

Standard Breading Procedure

Whether breading meats, poultry, fish, shellfish or vegetables, a three-step process is typically used. Called the **standard breading procedure**, it gives foods a relatively thick, crisp coating.

1. Pat the food dry and dredge it in seasoned flour. The flour adds seasoning to the food, helps seal it, and allows the egg wash to adhere.
2. Dip the floured food in an egg wash. The egg wash should contain whole eggs whisked together with approximately 1 tablespoon (15 milliliters) milk or water per egg. The egg wash will cause the crumbs or meal to completely coat the item and form a tight seal when the food is cooked.
3. Coat the food with bread crumbs, cracker crumbs or other dry meal. Shake off the excess crumbs and place the breaded item in a pan. As additional breaded items are added to the pan, align them in a single layer; do not stack them or the breadings will get soggy and the foods will stick together.

Figure 21.1 shows the proper setup for breading foods using the standard breading procedure.

The following procedure helps to bread foods more efficiently:

1. Assemble the mise en place as depicted in Figure 21.1.
2. With your left hand, place the food to be breaded in the flour and coat it evenly. With the same hand, remove the floured item, shake off the excess flour and place it in the egg wash.
3. With your right hand, remove the item from the egg wash and place it in the bread crumbs or meal.
4. With your left hand, cover the item with crumbs or meal and press lightly to make sure the item is completely and evenly coated. Shake off the excess crumbs or meal and place the breaded food in the empty pan for finished product.

The key is to use one hand for the liquid ingredients and the other hand for the dry ingredients. This prevents your fingers from becoming coated with layer after layer of breading.

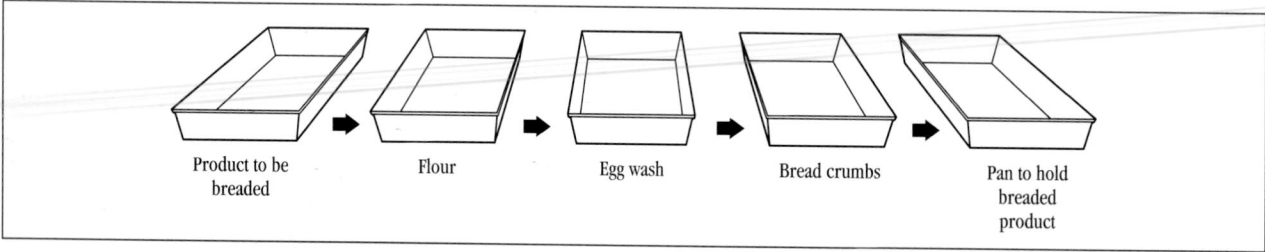

| Product to be breaded | Flour | Egg wash | Bread crumbs | Pan to hold breaded product |

FIGURE 21.1   *Setup for the Standard Breading Procedure*

◆◆◆

RECIPE 21.1

DEEP-FRIED CATFISH FILLETS WITH TARTAR SAUCE

Yield: 8 Servings

Catfish fillets, cut into uniform-size pieces	3 lb.	1.5 kg
Salt and pepper	TT	TT
Flour	as needed	as needed
Egg wash	as needed	as needed
White cornmeal	as needed	as needed
Tartar Sauce (Recipe 24.19)	12 oz.	360 ml

1. Season the fillets with salt and pepper.
2. Bread the fillets using the standard breading procedure (the white cornmeal is the final coating).
3. Using the basket method, deep-fry the fillets until done. Drain well and serve with the tartar sauce.

1. Flouring the seasoned fish fillets.

2. Passing the floured fillets through the egg wash.

3. Coating the fillets with white cornmeal.

4. Deep-frying the fillets using the basket method.

Croquettes

Croquettes are cooked meats, poultry, vegetables, fish or potatoes, usually bound with a heavy béchamel or velouté sauce and seasoned. They are then breaded and deep-fried.

◆◆◆

RECIPE 21.2

SALMON CROQUETTES

Yield: 12 Croquettes

Onion, small dice	2 oz.	60 g
Whole butter	3 oz.	90 g
Flour	3 oz.	90 g
Milk	8 oz.	250 g
Salmon, poached and flaked	1 lb.	450 g
Fresh dill, chopped	TT	TT
Salt and pepper	TT	TT
Lemon juice	1 Tbsp.	15 ml

1. Sauté the onion in the butter until translucent.
2. Add the flour and cook to make a white roux.
3. Add the milk to make a heavy béchamel sauce. Cook the sauce until very thick, approximately 5 minutes.
4. Remove the sauce from the heat and transfer it to a mixing bowl. Add the flaked salmon. Season the mixture with dill, salt, pepper and lemon juice and mix well.
5. Spread the mixture in a hotel pan, cover and refrigerate until cold.
6. Portion the mixture using a #20 portion scoop. Form each portion into a cone shape. Bread the croquettes using the standard breading procedure.
7. Using the basket method, deep-fry the breaded croquettes until done.

1. Portioning the croquette mixture with a portion scoop.

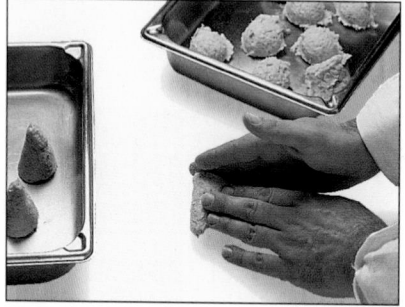

2. Forming the mixture into cone shapes.

3. Deep-frying the croquettes using the basket method.

Battering Foods to be Deep-Fried

Batters, like breading, coat the food being cooked, keeping it moist and preventing it from becoming excessively greasy.

Batters consist of a liquid such as water, milk or beer, combined with a starch such as flour or cornstarch. Many batters also contain a chemical leavening agent such as baking powder. Two common batters are beer batter, which uses the beer for leavening as well as for flavor, and tempura batter.

PROCEDURE FOR BATTERING FOODS

1. Pat the food dry and dredge in flour if desired.

2. Dip the item in the batter and place it directly in hot fat.

=== ◆◆◆ ===

RECIPE 21.3

BEER-BATTERED ONION RINGS

Yield: 1 qt. (1 lt), enough for approx. 4 lb. (1.8 kg) rings

Flour	10 oz.	300 g
Baking powder	2 tsp.	10 ml
Salt	2 tsp.	10 ml
White pepper	1/4 tsp.	1 ml
Egg	1	1
Beer	1 pt.	450 ml
Flour, for dredging	as needed	as needed
Onions, whole	4 lb.	1.8 kg

1. Sift the dry ingredients together.

2. Beat the egg in a separate bowl. Add the beer to the beaten egg.

3. Add the egg-and-beer mixture to the dry ingredients; mix until smooth.

4. Peel the onions and cut in 1/2-inch-(2-centimeter-) thick slices.

5. Break the slices into rings and dredge in flour.

6. Dip the rings in the batter a few at a time and fry at 375°F (190°C) until done. Drain on absorbent paper, season with additional salt and white pepper and serve hot.

1. Dredging the onion rings in flour.

2. Dipping the floured rings in batter.

3. Frying the onion rings using the swimming method.

◆◆◆

RECIPE 21.4

TEMPURA SHRIMP AND VEGETABLES WITH DIPPING SAUCE

Yield: 1 qt. (1 lt), enough for 4 lb. (1.8 kg) vegetables or shrimp

Sweet potato	8 oz.	250 g
Dipping Sauce		
Mirin	2 oz.	60 g
Soy sauce	4 oz.	120 g
Rice wine vinegar	2 oz.	60 g
Lemon juice	1 Tbsp.	15 ml
Wasabi powder	1 tsp.	5 ml
Tempura Batter:		
Eggs	2	2
Sparkling water, cold	1 pt.	500 ml
Flour	10 oz.	300 g
Shrimp, 21–25 count, butterflied with tails on	2 lb.	1 kg
Mushrooms, small, whole	1 lb.	450 g
Zucchini, batonnet	8 oz.	250 g

1. Peel the sweet potato and cut in 1/4-inch-(6-millimeter-) thick slices. If the potato is large, cut each slice in half to make semicircles.
2. Combine all ingredients for the dipping sauce. Set aside.
3. To prepare the batter, beat the eggs and add the cold water.
4. Add the flour to the egg-and-water mixture and mix until the flour is incorporated. There should still be small lumps in the batter. Overmixing develops gluten, which is undesirable.
5. Dry the shrimp well. Holding them by the tail, dip them into the batter and drop them into the deep-fryer using the swimming method. Cook until done.
6. Drop the vegetables in the batter a few at a time. Remove them from the batter one at a time and drop into the deep-fryer using the swimming method. Cook until done.
7. Arrange the tempura shrimp and vegetables on a serving platter. Serve the dipping sauce on the side.

Fritters

Fritters contain diced or chopped fish, shellfish, vegetables or fruits bound together with a thick batter and deep-fried. The main ingredient is usually precooked. Fritters are spooned or dropped directly into the hot fat; they form a crust as they cook. Popular examples are clam fritters, corn fritters, artichoke fritters and apple fritters.

◆◆◆

RECIPE 21.5

APPLE FRITTERS

Yield: 100 2-in. (5-cm) Fritters

Eggs, separated	6	6
Milk	1 pt.	500 ml
Flour	1 lb.	450 g

Baking powder	1 Tbsp.	15 ml
Salt	1 tsp.	5 ml
Sugar	2 oz.	60 g
Cinnamon	1/2 tsp.	2 ml
Apples, peeled, cored, medium dice	1 lb. 8 oz.	700 g
Powdered sugar	as needed	as needed

1. Combine the egg yolks and milk.
2. Sift together the flour, baking powder, salt, sugar and cinnamon. Add the dry ingredients to the milk-and-egg mixture; mix until smooth.
3. Allow the batter to rest 1 hour.
4. Stir the apples into the batter.
5. Just before the fritters are to be cooked, whip the egg whites to soft peaks and fold into the batter.
6. Scoop the fritters into 350°F (180°C) deep fat, using the swimming method. Cook until done.
7. Dust with powdered sugar and serve hot.

1. Adding the dry ingredients to the liquids.

2. Folding the egg whites into the batter.

3. Dropping the fritters into the deep fat.

4. Dusting the fritters with powdered sugar.

DETERMINING DONENESS

It is difficult to determine the doneness of deep-fried foods, especially breaded or battered ones. The keen sense of timing that develops with experience is a useful tool. Otherwise:

1. Color is the most commonly used method for determining doneness. Most fried foods should be deep golden brown when done. But color can be deceiving. If the temperature of the fat is too high, the food's surface will darken quickly and appear done while the center remains raw. Also, fat becomes dark with use; dark fat prematurely darkens food, again allowing foods to appear done before they are. Similarly, foods with high sugar content darken quickly in hot fat.

2. Large items such as fried chicken can be removed from the fat and checked with an instant-read thermometer. The internal temperature should be 165–170°F (74–77°C).

3. Fish and shellfish cook quickly and are easily overcooked. If practical, remove a piece and cut it open to determine its doneness. Then rely on timing and color for the remaining batches.

4. Vegetables should be tender when their surfaces are the proper color.

5. Potatoes should be attractively browned and cooked to the desire crispness.

Generally, deep-fried foods must be completely cooked in the deep-fryer. It is possible, however, to finish some deep-fried foods (for example, fried chicken) in the oven after being browned in the fat. But there is a problem to doing so. As the food cooks in the oven, moisture is released that may cause the breading to become soggy on the bottom.

CONCLUSION

Deep-frying is a useful and versatile dry-heat cooking method. To produce high-quality deep-fried foods it is important to understand which foods respond well to deep-frying and how to prepare them for cooking. You must also understand how to prevent deep-fried food from becoming excessively greasy by properly coating them with batters or breadings and controlling cooking temperatures. Finally, you must understand how to determine doneness. By following the guidelines discussed in this chapter you will be able to consistently produce the desired results.

QUESTIONS FOR DISCUSSION

1. What qualities should be considered when choosing a fat for deep-frying?
2. Name and describe two styles of deep-frying.
3. List three signs that fryer fat has broken down and should be replaced. What causes fryer fat to break down? What can you do to extend the life of fryer fat?
4. Explain the differences between breading and battering foods for deep-frying.
5. Describe the correct mise en place for the standard breading procedure.
6. Explain several similarities and differences between fritters and croquettes.

*A*DDITIONAL *D*EEP-*F*RYING *R*ECIPE

RECIPE 21.6
*W*HOLE *S*IZZLING *C*ATFISH *WITH* *G*INGER *AND* *P*ANZU *S*AUCE

NOTE: *This dish appears in the Chapter Opening photograph.*

CHINOIS ON MAIN, SANTA MONICA, CA
Chef Wolfgang Puck

Yield: 4 Servings

Catfish, cleaned, 3 lb. (1.3 kg)	1	1
Salt and pepper	TT	TT
Fresh ginger, sliced and blanched	6 pieces	6 pieces
Peanut oil	as needed	as needed
Lemon juice	as needed	as needed
Panzu Sauce:		
Soy sauce	4 oz.	120 g
Mirin	4 oz.	120 g
Rice vinegar	4 oz.	120 g
Lemon juice	4 oz.	120 g
Fresh wood ear mushrooms	as needed for garnish	
Fresh cilantro	as needed for garnish	
Green onions	as needed for garnish	

1. Season the catfish with salt and pepper. Make three 2-inch (5-centimeter) incisions on each side of the fish and stuff each incision with blanched ginger.

2. Deep-fry the catfish in peanut oil, being careful to submerge the entire fish. Cook until golden-colored and crispy.

3. Squeeze fresh lemon juice over the top of the fish.

4. Make the sauce by combining the listed ingredients.

5. Serve the whole catfish on a platter garnished with wood ear mushrooms, cilantro and green onions. Serve the Panzu Sauce on the side.

CHAPTER 22 VEGETABLES

After studying this chapter you will be able to:

+ identify a variety of vegetables
+ purchase vegetables appropriate for your needs
+ store vegetables properly
+ understand how vegetables are preserved
+ prepare vegetables for cooking or service
+ apply various cooking methods to vegetables

*L*ong overcooked and underrated, vegetables are enjoying a welcome surge in popularity. Gone are the days when a chef included vegetables as an afterthought to the "meat and potatoes" of the meal. Now, properly prepared fresh vegetables are used to add flavor, color and variety to almost any meal. Many restaurants are featuring vegetarian entrees, an extensive selection of vegetable side dishes or an entire vegetarian menu. This trend reflects the demands of more knowledgeable and health-conscious consumers as well as the increased availability of high-quality fresh produce.

In this chapter we identify many of the vegetables typically used by food service operations. (Potatoes, although vegetables, are discussed in Chapter 23, Potatoes, Grains and Pasta, while salad greens are discussed in Chapter 24, Salads and Salad Dressings.) Here we also discuss how fresh and preserved vegetables are purchased, stored and prepared for service or cooking. Many of the cooking methods analyzed in Chapter 9, Principles of Cooking, are then applied to vegetables.

The term **vegetable** refers to any herbaceous plant that can be partially or wholly eaten. An herbaceous plant has little or no woody tissue. The portions we consume include the leaves, stems, roots, tubers, seeds and flowers. Vegetables contain more starch and less sugar than fruits. Therefore vegetables tend to be savory, not sweet. Also unlike fruits, vegetables are most often eaten cooked, not raw.

IDENTIFYING VEGETABLES

This book presents fruits and vegetables according to the ways most people view them and use them, rather than by rigid botanical classifications. Although produce such as tomatoes, peppers and eggplants are botanically fruits, they are prepared and served like vegetables and are included here under the category we call "fruit-vegetables." Potatoes, although botanically vegetables, are discussed with other starches in Chapter 23, Potatoes, Grains and Pasta.

We divide vegetables into nine categories based upon either botanical relationship or edible part. They are: cabbages, fruit-vegetables, gourds and squashes, greens, mushrooms and truffles, onions, pods and seeds, roots and tubers, and stalks. A vegetable may have several names, varying from region to region or on a purveyor's whim. The names given here follow generally accepted custom and usage.

Cabbages

The *Brassica* or cabbage family includes a wide range of vegetables used for their heads, flowers or leaves. They are generally quick-growing, cool-weather crops. Many are ancient plants with unknown origins. They are inexpensive, readily available and easy to prepare.

Bok Choy

Bok choy, also known as pok choy, is a white-stemmed variety of southern Chinese cabbage. The relatively tightly packed leaves are dark green, with long white ribs attached at a bulbous stem. The stalks are crisp and mild with a flavor similar to romaine lettuce. Although bok choy may be eaten raw, it is most often stir-fried or used in soups.

Choose heads with bright white stalks and dark green leaves; avoid those with brown, moist spots. Fresh bok choy is available all year. Jars of pickled and fermented bok choy (known as Korean kim chee) are also available.

Bok Choy

Broccoli

Broccoli, a type of flower, has a thick central stalk with grayish-green leaves topped with one or more heads of green florets. Broccoli may be eaten raw or steamed, microwaved or sautéed and served warm or cold. Broccoli stalks are extremely firm and benefit from blanching. Stems are often slow-cooked for soups. Generally, broccoli leaves are not eaten.

Choose firm stalks with compact clusters of tightly closed dark green florets. Avoid stalks with yellow flowers. Broccoli is available all year.

Broccoli

PROCEDURE FOR CUTTING BROCCOLI SPEARS

1. Cut off the thick, woody portion of the stalk, then cut the florets and stems into spears.

Brussels Sprouts

Brussels sprouts (Fr. *choux de Bruxelles*) were first cultivated around 1700. The plant produces numerous small heads arranged in neat rows along a thick stalk. The tender young sprouts are similar to baby cabbages and are usually steamed or roasted. Brussels sprouts have a strong, nutty flavor that blends well with game, ham, duck or rich meats.

Choose small, firm sprouts that are compact and heavy. The best size is 3/4 to 1-1/2 inches (2 to 4 centimeters) in diameter. They should be bright green and free of blemishes. Their peak season is from September through February.

Brussels Sprouts

Cauliflower

Cauliflower (Fr. *chou-fleur*) is the king of the cabbage family. Each stalk produces one flower or head surrounded by large green leaves. The head, composed of creamy white florets, can be cooked whole or cut into separate florets for steaming, blanching or stir-frying.

Cauliflower

Choose firm, compact heads. Any attached leaves should be bright green and crisp. A yellow color or spreading florets indicate that the vegetable is overly mature. Cauliflower is available all year, especially from the late fall through the spring.

PROCEDURE FOR CUTTING CAULIFLOWER FLORETS

1. Cut off the stem and leaves.

2. Cut the florets off the core.

Green and Red Cabbages

Cabbage (Fr. *chou*) has been a staple of northern European cuisine for centuries. The familiar green cabbages have large, firm, round heads with tightly packed pale green leaves. Flat and conical-shaped heads are also available. Red (or purple) cabbages are a different strain and may be tougher than green cabbages. Cabbage can be eaten raw (as in coleslaw) or used in soups or stews; it can be braised, steamed or stir-fried. The large, waxy leaves can also be steamed until soft, then wrapped around a filling of seasoned meat.

Choose firm heads without dried cores. Cabbages are available all year.

Kale

Kale has large ruffled, curly or bumpy leaves. Its rather bitter flavor goes well with rich meats such as game, pork or ham. Kale is typically boiled, stuffed or used in soups.

Choose leaves that are crisp, with a grayish-green color. Kale is available all year, with peak season during the winter months.

Ornamental or flowering kale, sometimes marketed as "savoy," is edible, but its pink, purple, yellow or white-and-green variegated leaves are best used for decoration and garnish.

Green and Red Cabbages

Kale

Ornamental Kale

Kohlrabi

Although it looks rather like a round root, kohlrabi is actually a bulbous stem vegetable created by cross-breeding cabbages and turnips. When purchased, both the leaves (which are attached directly to the bulbous stem) and roots are generally removed. Depending on the variety, the skin may be light green, purple or green with a hint of red. The interior flesh is white, with a sweet flavor similar to turnips. (Kohlrabies can be substituted for turnips in many recipes.) Younger plants are milder and more tender than large, mature ones. The outer skin must be removed from mature stems; young stems only need to be well scrubbed before cooking. Kohlrabi can be eaten raw, or it can be cooked (whole, sliced or diced) with moist-heat cooking methods such as boiling and steaming. The stems may also be hollowed out and stuffed with meat or vegetable mixtures.

Kohlrabi

Choose small, tender stems with fresh, green leaves. Peak season for kohlrabi is from June through September.

Napa Cabbage

Napa cabbage, also known as Chinese cabbage, is widely used in Asian cuisines. It has a stout, elongated head with relatively tightly packed, firm, pale green leaves. It is moister and more tender than common green and red cabbages, with a milder, more delicate flavor. Napa cabbage may be eaten raw but is particularly well suited for stir-frying or steaming.

Choose heads with crisp leaves that are free of blemishes. Napa cabbage is available fresh all year.

Savoy

Savoy cabbage has curly or ruffled leaves, often in variegated shades of green and purple. (The term "savoyed" is used to refer to any vegetable with bumpy, wavy or wrinkled leaves.) Savoy cabbage tends to be milder and more tender than regular cabbages and can be substituted for them, cooked or uncooked. Savoy leaves also make an attractive garnish.

Choose heads that are loose or tight, depending on the variety, with tender, unblemished leaves. Peak season is from August through the spring.

Napa Cabbage

Savoy

Fruit-Vegetables

Botanists classify avocados, eggplants, peppers and tomatoes as fruits because they develop from the ovary of flowering plants and contain one or more seeds. Chefs, however, prepare and serve them like vegetables; therefore they are discussed here.

Avocados

Avocados include several varieties of pear-shaped fruits with rich, high-fat flesh. This light golden-green flesh surrounds a large, inedible, oval-shaped seed (pit). Some varieties have smooth, green skin; others have pebbly, almost black skin. Avocados should be used at their peak of ripeness, a condition

Avocados

that lasts only briefly. Firm avocados lack the desired flavor and creamy texture. Ripe avocados should be soft to the touch but not mushy. Ripe Haas avocados have almost-black skins; the skins of the other varieties remain green when ripe. Firm avocados can be left at room temperature to ripen, then refrigerated for one or two days. Avocados are most often used raw to garnish salads, mashed or puréed for sauces, sliced for sandwiches or diced for omelets. Avocado halves are popular containers for chilled meat, fish, shellfish or poultry salads. Because avocado flesh turns brown very quickly once cut, dip avocado halves or slices in lemon juice and keep unused portions tightly covered with plastic wrap.

Choose avocados that are free of blemishes or moist spots. The flesh should be free of dark spots or streaks. Available all year, the peak season for Haas avocados is April through October; for Fuertes avocados it is November through April.

PROCEDURE FOR CUTTING AND PITTING AVOCADOS

1. Cut the avocado in half lengthwise. Separate the two halves with a twisting motion.

2. Insert a chef's knife into the pit and twist to remove.

3. Scoop the flesh out of the skin with a large spoon.

Eggplants

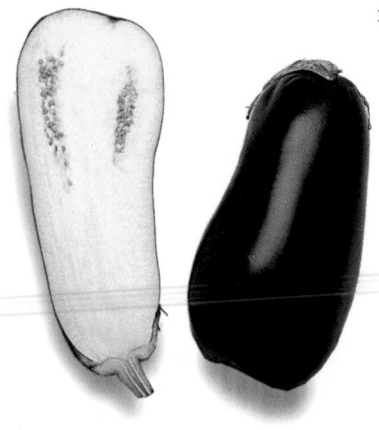

Western Eggplant

Two types of eggplants (Fr. *aubergine*) are commonly available: Asian and western. Asian varieties are either round or long and thin, with skin colors ranging from creamy white to deep purple. Western eggplants, which are more common in the United States, tend to be shaped like a plump pear with shiny lavender to purple-black skin. Both types have a dense, khaki-colored flesh with a rather bland flavor that absorbs other flavors well during cooking. Eggplants can be grilled, baked, steamed, fried or sautéed. They are commonly used in Mediterranean and East Indian cuisines (especially in vegetarian dishes), but also appear in European and North American dishes. The skin may be left intact or removed before or after cooking, as desired.

Sliced eggplants may be salted and left to drain for 30 minutes to remove moisture and bitterness before cooking.

Choose plump, heavy eggplants with a smooth, shiny skin that is not blemished or wrinkled. Asian varieties tend to be softer than western. Eggplants are available all year, with peak season during the late summer.

Asian Eggplants

Peppers

Members of the *Capsicum* family are native to the New World. When "discovered" by Christopher Columbus he called them "peppers" because of their sometimes fiery flavor. These peppers, which include sweet peppers and hot peppers (chiles), are unrelated to peppercorns, the East Indian (Asian) spice for which Columbus was actually searching. Interestingly, New World peppers were readily accepted in Indian and Asian cuisines, in which they are now considered staples.

Fresh peppers are found in a wide range of colors—green, red, yellow, orange, purple or white—as well as shapes, from tiny teardrops to cones to spheres. They have dense flesh and a hollow central cavity. The flesh is lined with placental ribs (the white internal veins), to which tiny white seeds are attached. A core of seeds is also attached to the stem end of each pepper.

Chile peppers get their heat from capsaicin, which is found not in the flesh or seeds, but in the placental ribs. Thus a pepper's heat can be greatly reduced by carefully removing the ribs and attached seeds. Generally, the smaller the chile, the hotter it is. The amount of heat varies from variety to variety, however, and even from one pepper to another depending on growing conditions. Hot, dry conditions result in hotter peppers than do cool, moist conditions. A pepper's heat can be measured by Scoville Heat Units, a subjective rating in which the sweet bell pepper usually rates 0 units, the jalapeño rates from 2500 to 5000 units, the tabasco rates from 30,000 to 50,000 units and the habanero rates a whopping 100,000 to 300,000 units.

When selecting peppers, choose those that are plump and brilliantly colored with smooth, unblemished skins. Avoid wrinkled, pitted or blistered peppers. A bright green stem indicates freshness.

Green Bell Pepper

Sweet Peppers

Common sweet peppers, known as bell peppers, are thick-walled fruits available in green, red, yellow, purple, orange and other colors. They are heart-shaped or boxy, with a short stem and crisp flesh. Their flavor is warm, sweet (red peppers tend to be the sweetest) and relatively mild. Raw bell peppers may be sliced or diced and used in salads or sandwiches. Bell peppers may also be stuffed and baked, grilled, fried, sautéed or puréed for soups, sauces or condiments. Green bell peppers are available all year; other colors are more readily available during the summer and fall.

Red and Yellow Bell Peppers

PROCEDURE FOR CUTTING PEPPERS JULIENNE

1. Trim off the ends of the pepper; cut away the seeds and core.

2. Cut away the pale ribs, trimming the flesh to the desired thickness.

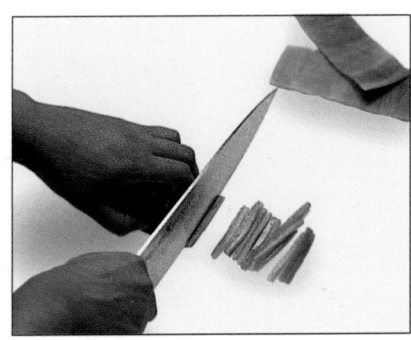

3. Slice the flesh in julienne.

Hot Peppers

Hot peppers, also known as chiles, are also members of the *Capsicum* family. Although a chile's most characteristic attribute is its pungency, each chile actually has a distinctive flavor, from mild and rich to spicy and sweet to fiery hot.

Chiles are commonly used in Asian, Indian, Mexican and Latin American cuisines. The larger (and milder) of the hot peppers, such as Anaheim and poblano, can be stuffed and baked or sautéed as a side dish. Most chiles, however, are used to add flavor and seasoning to sauces and other dishes. Fresh chiles are available all year and are also available canned in a variety of processed forms such as whole or diced roasted, pickled or marinated.

(clockwise from bottom left) Red and Green Serrano; Green and Red Jalapeño; Yellow Hot; Poblano; and Anaheim chiles.

PROCEDURE FOR CORING JALAPEÑOS

1. Cut the jalapeño in half lengthwise. Push the core and seeds out with your thumb. You can avoid burning your fingers by wearing rubber gloves when working with hot chiles.

Dried chiles are widely used in Mexican, Central American and southwestern cuisines. They may be ground to create a powdered spice called chilli or soaked in liquid, then puréed, for sauces or condiments. Drying radically alters the flavor of chiles, making them stronger and more pungent. Dried chiles are often called by names different from those of their fresh versions. For example, the fresh poblano becomes the dried ancho; the fresh jalapeño becomes the dried, smoked chipotle.

Choose dried chiles that are clean and unbroken, with some flexibility. Avoid any with white spots or a stale aroma.

PROCEDURE FOR ROASTING PEPPERS

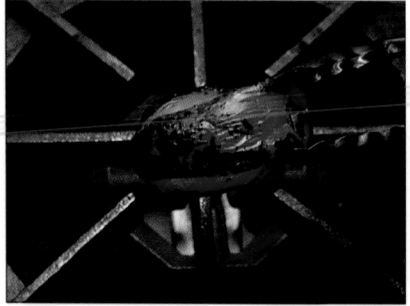

1. Roast the pepper over an open flame until completely charred.

2. Remove the burnt skin and rinse under running water.

Tomatillos

Tomatillos, also known as Mexican or husk tomatoes, grow on small, weedy bushes. They are bright green, about the size of a small tomato, and are covered with a thin, papery husk. They have a tart, lemony flavor and crisp, moist flesh. Although an important ingredient in southwestern and northern Mexican cuisines, tomatillos may not be readily available in other areas. Tomatillos can be used raw in salads, puréed for salsa or cooked in soups, stews or vegetable dishes.

Choose tomatillos whose husks are split but still look fresh. The skin should be plump, shiny and slightly sticky. They are available all year, with peak season during the summer and fall.

Tomatillos

Tomatoes

Tomatoes (Fr. *tomate* or *pomme d'amour*, It. *pomodoro*) are available in a wide variety of colors and shapes. They vary from green (unripe) to golden yellow to ruby red; from tiny spheres (currant tomatoes) to huge, squat ovals (beefsteak). Some, such as the plum tomato, have lots of meaty flesh with only a few seeds; others, such as the slicing tomato, have lots of seeds and juice, but only a few meaty membranes. All tomatoes have a similar flavor, but the levels of sweetness and acidity vary depending on the species, growing conditions and ripeness at harvest.

(clockwise from lower right) Pear, Cherry, Plum and Beefsteak Tomatoes

---

♦♦♦

THREE TREASURES OF THE NEW WORLD

In lieu of many spices, golden treasures and precious gems, early Spanish explorers returned to Spain with items of much greater significance: tomatoes, potatoes and corn. Unfortunately for those who financed the voyagers, the value of this produce was not immediately appreciated.

The Spanish and the Italians hailed the tomato (whose name comes from the Aztec name *tomatl*) as an aphrodisiac—perhaps because of its resemblance to the human heart—when it arrived from the New World during the 16th century. But even though tomatoes soon became part of Spanish and Italian cuisines, most other Europeans, New World colonists and, later, Americans considered tomatoes poisonous. (There is some truth to this notion: tomato vines and leaves contain tomatine, an alkaloid that can cause health problems.) Thus for many years and in many societies, only the adventurous ate tomatoes. Tomato historians consider September 26, 1820, a red-letter day marking the popular acceptance of the tomato. On that day, the then-well-known eccentric Colonel Robert Gibbon Johnson ate an entire bushel of toma-

toes on the Salem, New Jersey, courthouse steps before a crowd of thousands—and lived. Tomatoes soon became one of the most popular of all vegetables.

Similarly, the potato, first delivered to Europe from its native Peru by Francisco Pizarro in the 16th century, did not win wide acceptance in haute cuisine until Antoine-Augustin Parmentier (1737–1813), a French army pharmacist, induced King Louis XVI of France (reign 1775–1793) to try one. He and his courtiers liked them so much they even began wearing potato blossom boutonnières. Parmentier was ultimately honored for his starchy contribution to French cuisine by having several potato dishes named for him. Indeed, the French still call potato soup *potage Parmentier* in his honor. Not only did Parmentier lobby for the acceptance of the potato as a food fit for a king, he also prophesied that the potato would make starvation impossible. Potatoes ultimately did become a staple of many diets. But, sadly, the converse of Parmentier's prophecy came true during the Irish Potato Famine of 1846–48, when a terrible blight destroyed the potato crop. Nearly 1.5

million people died and an equal number emigrated to the United States. They brought with them a cuisine that incorporated potatoes; thus an appreciation of the common potato was reintroduced to its native land.

When returning from his second voyage to the New World, Columbus took corn with him. Called *mahiz* or *maize* by West Indian natives, corn had been a staple of Central American diets for at least 5000 years. Although Europeans did not actively shun corn as they did tomatoes and potatoes, corn never really caught on in most of Europe. (As with another famous New World import, corn's origin was mistakenly attributed by the British, Dutch, Germans and Russians to Turkey. They called corn "Turkish wheat"; the Turks simply called it "foreign grain.") Grown for human consumption mostly in Italy, Spain and southwestern France, corn was and still is usually eaten ground and boiled as polenta. But despite an unenthusiastic European reception, corn's popularity quickly spread well beyond Europe: Within 50 years of Columbus's journey, corn was being cultivated in lands as distant from the New World as China, India and sub-Saharan Africa.

Because tomatoes are highly perishable, they are usually harvested when mature but still green (unripe), then shipped to wholesalers who ripen them in temperature- and humidity-controlled rooms. The effect on flavor and texture is unfortunate.

Tomatoes are used widely in salads, soups, sauces and baked dishes. They are most often eaten raw, but can be grilled, pickled, pan-fried, roasted or sautéed as a side dish.

Choose fresh tomatoes that are plump with a smooth, shiny skin. The color should be uniform and true for the variety. Tomatoes are available all year, with a summer peak season for most varieties. Many canned tomato products are also available (for example, purée, paste, sauce or stewed whole), as are dried tomatoes.

PROCEDURE FOR MAKING TOMATO CONCASSE

1. With a paring knife, mark an X on the bottom of the tomato just deep enough to penetrate the skin.

2. Blanch the tomato in boiling water for 20 seconds; refresh in ice water.

3. Using a paring knife, cut out the core and peel the tomato.

4. Cut the tomato in half horizontally and squeeze out the seeds and juice.

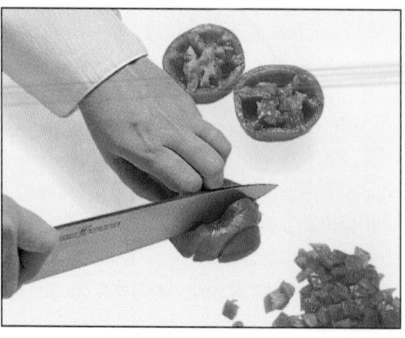

5. Chop or dice the tomato as desired for the recipe.

Gourds and Squashes

The *Cucurbitaceae* or gourd family includes almost 750 species; its members are found in warm regions worldwide. Gourds are characterized by large, complex root systems with quick-growing, trailing vines and large leaves. Their flowers are often attractive and edible. Although some members of the gourd family originated in Africa, chayotes and most squashes are native to the Americas.

Chayotes

The chayote, also known as merliton or vegetable pear, is a food staple throughout Central America. The vine bears slightly lumpy, pear-shaped fruits with a smooth, light green skin and a paler green flesh. There is a single white, edible seed in the center. Chayotes are starchy and very bland and are usually combined with more flavorful ingredients. They may be eaten raw, but their flavor and texture benefit from roasting, steaming, sautéing or grilling.

Chayotes

Choose chayotes that have well-colored skin with few ridges. Avoid those with very soft spots or bruises. Their peak season is the late fall and winter.

Cucumbers

Cucumbers can be divided into two categories: pickling and slicing. The two types are not interchangeable. Pickling cucumbers include the cornichon, dill and gherkin. They are recognizable by their sharp black or white spines and are quite bitter when raw. Slicing cucumbers include the burpless, the seedless English (or hothouse), the lemon (which is round and yellow) and the common green market cucumber. Most have relatively thin skins and may be marketed with a wax coating to prevent moisture loss and improve appearance. Waxed skins should be peeled. All cucumbers are valued for their refreshing cool taste and astringency. Slicing cucumbers are usually served raw, in salads or mixed with yogurt and dill or mint as a side dish, especially for spicy dishes. Pickling cucumbers are generally served pickled, without any further processing.

Choose cucumbers that are firm but not hard. Avoid those that are limp, yellowed or have soft spots. The common varieties are available all year, although peak season is from April through October.

(from left to right)
Pickling, Green and
Hothouse Cucumbers

Squashes

Squashes are the fleshy fruits of a large number of plants in the gourd family. Many varieties are available in a range of colors, shapes and sizes. Squashes can be classified as winter or summer based on their peak season and skin type. All squashes have a center cavity filled with many seeds, although in winter varieties the cavity is more pronounced. Squash blossoms are also edible: They may be added to salads raw, dipped in batter and deep-fried or filled with cheese or meat and baked.

Choose squashes with unbroken skins and good color for the variety. Avoid any squash with soft, moist spots.

Spaghetti

Acorn

Banana

Butternut

Pumpkin

Winter Squashes

Winter squashes include the acorn, banana, butternut, Hubbard, pumpkin and spaghetti varieties. They have hard skins (shells) and seeds, neither of which are generally eaten. The flesh, which may be removed from the shell before or after cooking, tends to be sweeter and more strongly flavored than that of summer squash. Winter squashes should not be served raw; they can be baked, steamed or sautéed. Most winter squashes can also be puréed for soups or pie fillings. Their peak season is October through March.

Summer Squashes

Summer squashes include the pattypan, yellow crookneck and zucchini varieties. They have soft edible skins and seeds that are generally not removed before cooking. Most summer squashes may be eaten raw, but are also suitable for grilling, sautéing, steaming or baking. Although summer squashes are now available all year, their peak season is April through September.

Yellow Crookneck

Zucchini

Greens

The term *greens* refers to a variety of leafy green vegetables that may be served raw, but are usually cooked. Greens have long been used in the cuisines of India, Asia and the Mediterranean and are an important part of regional cuisine in the southern United States. Most have strong, spicy flavors. Mustard, sorrel, spinach, Swiss chard, dandelion and turnip greens fall into this category. The milder varieties of greens that are eaten almost always raw include the lettuces discussed in Chapter 24, Salads and Salad Dressings.

Greens have an extremely high water content, which means that cooking causes drastic shrinkage. As a general rule, allow 8 ounces (250 grams) per portion before cooking.

Choose young, tender greens with good color and no limpness. Avoid greens with dry-looking stems or yellow leaves. Most greens are available fresh all year, especially from November through June. The more popular greens are also available canned or frozen.

Mustard

Mustard, a member of the cabbage family, was brought to America by early European immigrants. Mustard has large, dark green leaves with frilly edges. It is known for its assertive, bitter flavor. Mustard greens can be served raw in salads or used as garnish. Or they can be cooked, often with white wine, vinegar and herbs.

Choose crisp, bright green leaves without discoloration.

Mustard

Sorrel

Sorrel is an abundant and rather ordinary wild member of the buckwheat family. Its tartness and sour flavor are used in soups and sauces and to accent other vegetables. It is particularly good with fatty fish or rich meats. Sorrel leaves naturally become the texture of a purée after only a few minutes of moist-heat cooking.

Choose leaves that are fully formed, with no yellow blemishes.

Sorrel

Spinach

Spinach (Fr. *épinard*) is a versatile green that grows rapidly in cool climates. It has smooth, bright green leaves attached to thin stems. Spinach may be eaten raw in salads, cooked by almost any moist-heat method, microwaved or sautéed. It can be used in stuffings, baked or creamed dishes, soups or stews. Spinach grows in sandy soil and must be rinsed repeatedly in cold water to remove all traces of grit from the leaves. It bruises easily and should be handled gently during washing. Stems and large mid-ribs should be removed.

Choose bunches with crisp, tender, deep green leaves; avoid yellow leaves or those with blemishes.

Spinach

Swiss Chard

Chard—the reference to "Swiss" is inexplicable—is a type of beet that does not produce a tuberous root. It is used for its wide, flat, dark green leaves. Chard can be steamed, sautéed or used in soups. Its tart, spinachlike flavor blends well with sweet ingredients such as fruit.

Choose leaves that are crisp, with some curliness or savoying. Ribs should be an unblemished white or red.

Swiss Chard

Turnip Greens

The leaves of the turnip root have a pleasantly bitter flavor, similar to peppery mustard greens. The dark green leaves are long, slender and deeply indented. Turnip greens are best eaten steamed, sautéed, baked or microwaved.

Turnip Greens

Black Trumpet

Clam Shell

Pom Pom Blanc

Mushrooms and Truffles

Mushrooms

Mushrooms (Fr. *champignon;* It. *funghi*) are members of a broad category of plants known as fungi. (Fungi have no seeds, stems or flowers; they reproduce through spores.) Mushrooms have a stalk with an umbrellalike top. Although not actually a vegetable, mushrooms are used and served in much the same manner as vegetables.

Several types of cultivated mushroom are available. They include the common (or white), shiitake, straw, enokidake (also called enoki) and cloud ear (also known as wood ear or Chinese black). Button mushrooms are the smallest, most immature form of the common mushroom.

Many wild mushrooms are gathered and sold by specialty purveyors. Because wild mushroom spores are spread around the world by air currents, the same item may be found in several areas, each with a different common name. Wild mushrooms have a stronger earthy or nutty flavor than cultivated mushrooms, and should generally be cooked before eating.

Mushrooms, whether cultivated or gathered from the wild, are available fresh, canned or dried. Because mushrooms are composed of up to 80% water, dried products are often the most economical, even though they may cost hundreds of dollars per pound. Dried mushrooms can be stored in a cool, dry place for months. When needed, they are rehydrated by soaking in warm water until soft, approximately 10–20 minutes.

Choose fresh mushrooms that are clean, without soft or moist spots or blemishes. Fresh cultivated mushrooms are generally available all year; fresh wild mushrooms are available seasonally, usually during the summer and fall. Cultivated mushrooms with exposed gills (the ridges on the underside of the umbrellalike top) are old and should be avoided. Fresh mushrooms can be refrigerated in an open container for up to five days. Normally, it is not necessary to peel mushrooms; if they are dirty, they should be quickly rinsed (not soaked) in cool water just before use.

Porcini (cèpe or cep)

Hen of the Woods

Morel

Shiitake

White

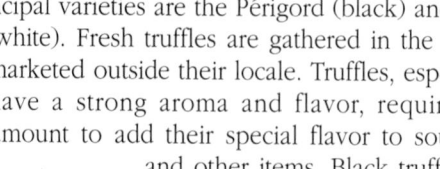

Oyster

Enokidake

Truffles

Truffles are actually tubers that grow near the roots of oak or beech trees. They can be cultivated only to the extent that oak groves are planted to encourage truffle growth. The two principal varieties are the Périgord (black) and the Piedmontese (white). Fresh truffles are gathered in the fall and are rarely marketed outside their locale. Truffles, especially white ones, have a strong aroma and flavor, requiring only a small amount to add their special flavor to soups, sauces, pasta and other items. Black truffles are often used as a garnish or to flavor pâtés, terrines or egg

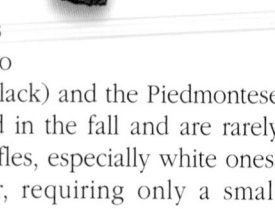

Black Truffles

dishes. Because fresh imported truffles can cost several hundred dollars per pound, most kitchens purchase truffles canned, dried or processed.

Onions

Onions are strongly flavored, aromatic members of the lily family. Most have edible grasslike or tubular leaves. Almost every culture incorporates them into its cuisine as a vegetable and for flavoring.

Bulb Onions

Common or bulb onions (Fr. *oignons*) may be white, yellow (Bermuda or Spanish) or red (purple). Medium-sized yellow and white onions are the most strongly flavored. Larger onions tend to be sweeter and milder. Widely used as a flavoring ingredient, onions are indispensable in mirepoix. Onions are also prepared as a side dish by deep-frying, roasting, grilling, steaming or boiling.

Pearl onions are small, about 1/2 inch (1.25 centimeters) in diameter, with yellow or white skins. They have a mild flavor and can be grilled, boiled, roasted or sautéed whole as a side dish, or used in soups or stews.

Choose onions that are firm, dry and feel heavy. The outer skins should be dry and brittle. Avoid onions that have begun to sprout. They should be stored in a cool, dry, well-ventilated area. Do not refrigerate onions until they are cut. Onions are available all year.

Red Onion

Pearl Onion

Yellow Onion

Shallots

Garlic

Garlic (Fr. *ail*; Sp. *ajo*) is also used in almost all of the world's cuisines. A head of garlic is composed of many small cloves. Each clove is wrapped in a thin husk or peel; the entire head is encased in several thin layers of papery husk. Of the 300 or so types of garlic known, only three are commercially significant. The most common is pure white, with a sharp flavor. A Mexican variety is pale pink and more strongly flavored. Elephant garlic is apple-sized and particularly mild. Although whole bulbs can be baked or roasted, garlic is most often separated into cloves, peeled, sliced, minced or crushed and used to flavor a wide variety of dishes. When using garlic remember that the more finely the cloves are crushed, the stronger the flavor will be. And, cooking reduces garlic's pungency; the longer it is cooked, the milder it becomes.

Choose firm, dry bulbs with tightly closed cloves and smooth skins. Avoid bulbs with green sprouts. Store fresh garlic in a cool, well-ventilated place; do not refrigerate. Fresh garlic is available all year. Jars of processed and pickled garlic products are also available.

White Onions

Garlic

Leeks

Leeks (Fr. *poireaux*) look like large, overgrown scallions with a fat white tip and wide green leaves. Their flavor is sweeter and stronger than scallions, but milder than common bulb onions. Leeks must be carefully washed to remove the sandy soil that gets between the leaves. Leeks can be baked, braised or grilled as a side dish, or used to season stocks, soups or sauces.

Choose leeks that are firm, with stiff roots and stems. Avoid those with dry leaves, soft spots or browning. Leeks are available all year.

Leeks

Scallions

Scallions

Scallions, also known as green onions or bunch onions, are the immature green stalks of bulb onions. The leaves are bright green with either a long and slender or slightly bulbous white base. Green onions are used in stir-fries and as a flavoring in other dishes. The green tops can also be sliced in small rings and used as a garnish.

Choose scallions with bright green tops and clean white bulbs. Avoid those with limp or slimy leaves. Scallions are available all year, with a peak summer season.

Shallots

Shallots (Fr. *échalotes*) are shaped like small bulb onions with one flat side. When peeled, a shallot separates into multiple cloves, similar to garlic. They have a mild yet rich and complex flavor. Shallots are the basis of many classic sauces and meat preparations; they can also be sautéed or baked as a side dish.

Choose shallots that are plump and well shaped. Avoid those that appear dry or have sprouted. They should be stored in a cool, dry, unrefrigerated place. Shallots are available all year.

Pods and Seeds

Pod and seed vegetables include corn, legumes and okra. They are grouped together here because the parts consumed are all the seeds of their respective plants. In some cases only the seeds are eaten; in others, the pod containing the seeds is eaten as well. Seeds are generally higher in protein and carbohydrates (starch and fiber) than other vegetables.

Corn

Yellow and White Corn

Sweet corn (Fr. *maïs*; Sp. *maíz*) is actually a grain, a type of grass. Corn kernels, like peas, are plant seeds. (Dried corn products are discussed in Chapter 23, Potatoes, Grains and Pasta.) The kernels, which may be white or yellow, are attached to a woody, inedible cob. The cob is encased by strands of hairlike fibers called silks and covered in layers of thin leaves called husks. The silks and husks should be shucked prior to cooking, although the husks may be left on for roasting or grilling. Shucked ears can be grilled, boiled, microwaved or steamed. The kernels can be cut off the cob before or after cooking. Corn on the cob is available fresh or frozen; corn kernels are available canned or frozen.

Choose freshly picked ears with firm, small kernels. Avoid those with mold or decay at the tip of the cob or brownish silks. Summer is the peak season for fresh corn.

PROCEDURE FOR CUTTING KERNELS OFF EARS OF CORN

1. Hold the cob upright and use a chef's knife to slice off the kernels.

Legumes

Beans (Fr. *haricots*; It. *fagiolio*) and peas (Fr. *pois*) are members of the legume family, a large group of vegetables with double-seamed pods containing a single row of seeds. Of the hundreds of known varieties of beans, some are used for their edible pods, others for shelling fresh and some only for their dried seeds. Dried beans are actually several varieties of seeds or peas left in the pod until mature, then shelled and dried.

Fresh Beans

Beans used for their edible pods, commonly referred to as green beans, string beans, runner beans or snap beans, are picked when immature. Except for the stem, the entire pod can be eaten. This category includes the American green bean, the yellow wax bean and the French haricot vert, a long, slender pod with an intense flavor and tender texture. If there are any strings along the pod's seams, they should be pulled off before cooking. Beans may be left whole, cut lengthwise into thin slivers (referred to as French cut) or cut crosswise on the diagonal.

Shelling beans are those grown primarily for the edible seeds inside the pod. Common examples are flageolets, lima beans and fava (broad) beans. Their tough pods are not usually eaten.

All beans can be prepared by steaming, microwaving or sautéing. They can be added to soups or stews and they blend well with a variety of flavors, from coconut milk to garlic and olive oil. Cooked beans can be chilled and served as a salad or crudité.

Choose beans that have a bright color without brown or soft spots. Large pods may be tough or bitter. The peak season for fresh beans is from April through December. Most bean varieties are available frozen or canned, including pickled and seasoned products.

Dried Beans

Anthropologists report that for thousands of years cultures worldwide have preserved some members of the legume family by drying. Common dried beans include kidney beans, pinto beans, chickpeas, lentils, black beans, black-eyed peas and split green peas. Shape is the clearest distinction among these products: Beans are oval or kidney-shaped; lentils are small, flat disks; peas are round.

Beans and peas destined for drying are left on the vine until they are fully matured and just beginning to dry. They are then harvested, shelled and quickly dried with warm air currents. Some dried legumes are sold split, which means the skin is removed, causing the seed's two halves to separate.

Most dried beans need to be soaked in water before cooking. Soaking softens and rehydrates the beans, thus reducing cooking time. Lentils and split peas generally do not require soaking, however, and will cook faster than beans. After soaking, beans are most often simmered or baked in a liquid until soft and tender. One type may be substituted for another in most recipes, although variations in color, starch content and flavor should be considered.

Dried beans and peas are available in bulk or in poly-bags. They should be stored in a cool, dry place, but not refrigerated. Many of these beans are also available fully cooked, then canned or frozen. Some dried beans may be fermented or processed into flour, oil or bean curd.

Green Beans

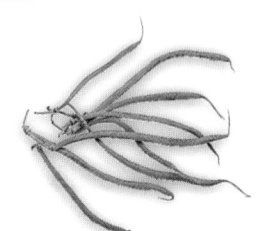
Haricots Verts

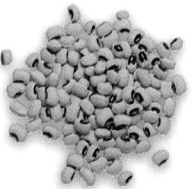
Dried Black-eyed Peas

Lentils

Red Kidney Beans

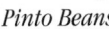
Pinto Beans

Great Northern Beans

PROCEDURE FOR SOAKING DRIED BEANS

1. Pick through the dried beans and remove any grit, pebbles or debris.
2. Place the beans in a bowl and cover with cold water; remove any skins or other items that float to the surface.
3. Drain the beans in a colander, then rinse under cold running water.
4. Return the beans to a bowl and cover with fresh cold water. Allow approximately 3 cups (750 milligrams) of water for each cup of beans.
5. Soak the beans in the cold water for the time specified in the recipe, usually several hours or overnight. Drain through a colander, discarding the water.

PROCEDURE FOR QUICK-SOAKING DRIED BEANS

The soaking procedure can be accelerated by the following technique:

1. Rinse and pick through the beans.
2. Place the beans in a saucepan and add enough cool water to cover them by 2 inches (5 centimeters).
3. Bring to a boil and simmer for 2 minutes.
4. Remove from the heat, cover and soak for 1 hour.
5. Drain and discard the soaking liquid. Proceed with the recipe.

Fresh Shelling Peas

Fresh Shelling Peas

Of the shelling peas that are prepared fresh, the most common are green garden peas (English peas) and the French petit pois. Because they lose flavor rapidly after harvest, most shelling peas are sold frozen or canned. Shelling peas have a delicate, sweet flavor best presented by simply steaming until tender but still al dente. Peas may also be braised with rich meats such as ham or used in soups. Cooked peas are attractive in salads or as garnish.

Choose small fresh pea pods that are plump and moist. Peak season is April and May.

Snow Peas

Edible Podded Peas

Snow peas, also known as Chinese pea pods, are a common variety of edible pea pod. They are very flat and have only a few very small green peas. Snow peas have a string along their seams which can be removed by holding the leafy stem and pulling from end to end. The pods can be eaten raw, lightly blanched or steamed, or stir-fried.

Another variety of edible pea pod is the sugar snap pea, a cross between the garden pea and snow pea, which was developed during the late 1970s. They are plump, juicy pods filled with small, tender peas. The entire pod is eaten; do not shell the peas before cooking.

Choose pea pods that are firm, bright green and crisp. Avoid those with brown spots or a shriveled appearance. Pea pods are available all year, with a peak season in March and April.

Okra

Okra

Okra, a common ingredient in African and Arab cuisines, was brought to the United States by slaves and French settlers. It is now integral to Creole, Cajun, southern and southwestern cuisines. Its mild flavor is similar to asparagus. Okra is not eaten raw; it is best pickled, boiled, steamed, or deep-fried. Okra develops a gelatinous texture when cooked for long periods, so it is used to

TOFU

Tofu or bean curd (Fr. *fromage de soja*) is a staple of Japanese and Chinese cuisines and is gaining acceptance in American kitchens because of its high nutritional value, low cost and flavor adaptability. Tofu is made by processing soybeans into "milk," which is then coagulated (nowadays with calcium sulfate). The curds are then placed in a perforated mold lined with cloth and pressed with a weight to remove the liquid. The result is a soft, creamy-white substance similar to cheese. Tofu is easy to digest, very high in protein, with very little fat and sodium and no cholesterol.

Tofu is an ancient foodstuff, probably created in China during the 2nd century A.D. It was introduced to Japan by Buddhist priests during the 8th century and was "discovered" by Western travelers during the 17th century. Today Japanese tofu is said to be the finest, perhaps because of the superiority of the soybeans grown in the Yamato region, near the city of Kyoto. Japanese cuisine values the natural flavor and texture of tofu and uses it in a tremendous variety of ways. Chinese cuisine uses it as an additive, not as a principal ingredient.

Tofu may be eaten fresh; added to soup, broth or noodle dishes; tossed in cold salads; grilled; deep-fried or sautéed. Its flavor is bland, but it readily absorbs flavors from other ingredients.

Two types of tofu are widely available: cotton and silk. Cotton tofu is the most common. Its texture is firm, with an irregular surface caused by the weave of the cotton fabric in which it is wrapped for pressing. Silk tofu has a silky-smooth appearance and texture, and a somewhat more delicate flavor. Unlike cotton tofu, the water has not been pressed out of silk tofu. Consequently, silk tofu should not be cooked at high temperatures or for a long time, as it falls apart easily. The use of either type in most recipes is simply a matter of personal preference.

Fresh tofu is usually packaged in water. It should be refrigerated and kept in water until used. If the water is drained and changed daily, the tofu should last for one week.

thicken gumbos and stews. To avoid the slimy texture some find objectionable, do not wash okra until ready to cook, then trim the stem end only. Cook okra in stainless steel as other metals cause discoloration.

Choose small to medium pods (1 to 1/2–2 inches; 3.75 to 5 centimeters) that are deep green, without soft spots. Pale spears with stiff tips tend to be tough. Okra's peak season is from June through September. Frozen okra is widely available.

Roots and Tubers

Taproots (more commonly referred to as roots) are single roots that extend deep into the soil to supply the above-ground plant with nutrients. Tubers are fat underground stems. Most roots and tubers can be used interchangeably. All store well at cool temperatures, without refrigeration. Potatoes, the most popular tuber, are discussed in Chapter 23, Potatoes, Grains and Pasta.

Beets

Although records suggest that they were first eaten in ancient Greece, beets are most often associated with the colder northern climates, where they grow for most of the year. Beets can be boiled, then peeled and used in salads, soups or baked dishes.

Choose small to medium-sized beets that are firm, with smooth skins. Avoid those with hairy root tips, as they may be tough. Beets are available all year, with a peak season from March to October.

Beets

Carrots

Carrots, (Fr. *carotte*) among the most versatile of vegetables, are large taproots. Although several kinds exist, the Imperator is the most common. It is long and pointed, with a medium to dark orange color. It has a mild, sweet flavor. Carrots can be cut into a variety of shapes and eaten raw, used for a mirepoix or prepared by moist-heat cooking methods, grilling, microwaving or roasting. They are also grated and used in baked goods, particularly cakes and muffins.

Choose firm carrots that are smooth and well shaped, with a bright orange color. If the tops are still attached, they should be fresh-looking and bright green. Carrots are available all year.

Carrots

Celery Root

Celery root, also known as celeriac, is a large, round root, long popular in northern European cuisines. It is a different plant from stalk celery, and its stalks and leaves are not eaten. Celery root has a knobby brown exterior; a creamy white, crunchy flesh and a mild, celerylike flavor. Its thick outer skin must be peeled away; the flesh is then cut as desired. Often eaten raw, celery root can be baked, steamed or boiled. It is used in soups, stews or salads and goes well with game and rich meats. Raw celery root may be placed in acidulated water to prevent browning.

Choose small to medium-sized roots that are firm and relatively clean, with a pungent smell. Their peak season is October through April.

Celery Root

Jicama

Jicama is actually a legume that grows underground as a tuber. It is becoming increasingly popular because of its sweet, moist flavor; crisp texture; low calorie content and long shelf life. After its thick brown skin is cut away, the crisp, moist white flesh can be cut as desired. Jicama is often eaten raw in salads, with salsa or as a crudité. It is also used in stir-fried dishes.

Choose firm, well-shaped jicamas that are free of blemishes. Size is not an indication of quality or maturity. They are available all year, with a peak season from January through May.

Jicama

Parsnips

Parsnips (Fr. *panais*) are taproots that look and taste like white carrots and have the texture of sweet potatoes. Parsnips should be 5 to 10 inches (12.5 to 25 centimeters) in length, with smooth skins and tapering tips. Parsnips, peeled like carrots, can be eaten raw or cooked by almost any method. When steamed until very soft, they can be mashed like potatoes.

Choose small to medium-sized parsnips that are firm, smooth and well shaped; avoid large, woody ones. Parsnips are available all year, with peak supplies from December through April.

Parsnips

Radishes

Radishes (Fr. *radis*) are used for their peppery flavor and crisp texture. Radishes are available in many colors, including white, black and all shades of red; most have a creamy to pure white interior. Asian radishes, known as daikons, produce roots 2 to 4 inches (5 to 10 centimeters) in diameter and 6 to 20 inches (15 to 20 centimeters) long. Radishes can be steamed or stir-fried, but most often are eaten raw, in salads or used as garnish. Radish leaves can be used in salads or cooked as greens.

Choose radishes that are firm, not limp. Their interior should be neither dry nor hollow. Radishes are available all year.

Red Radishes

Daikon

Rutabagas

Rutabagas are a root vegetable and a member of the cabbage family. Their skin is purple to yellow and they have yellow flesh with a distinctive starchy, cabbagelike flavor. Rutabagas and turnips are similar in flavor and texture when cooked and may be used interchangeably. Rutabaga leaves are not eaten. Rutabagas should be peeled with a vegetable peeler or chef's knife, then cut into quarters, slices or cubes. They are often baked, boiled and then puréed, or sliced and sautéed. They are especially flavorful when seasoned with caraway seeds, dill or lemon juice.

Choose small to medium-sized rutabagas that are smooth, firm and feel heavy. Their peak season is January through March.

Rutabagas

Turnips

Also a root vegetable from the cabbage family, turnips have white skin with a rosy-red or purple blush and white interior. Their flavor, similar to that of a radish, can be rather hot. Turnips should be peeled, then diced, sliced or julienned for cooking. They may be baked or cooked with moist-heat cooking methods, and are often puréed like potatoes.

Choose small to medium-sized turnips that have smooth skin and feel heavy. They should be firm, not rubbery or limp. Any attached leaves should be bright green and tender. Spring is their peak season.

Turnips

Stalks

Stalk vegetables are plant stems with a high percentage of **cellulose** fiber. These vegetables should be picked while still young and tender. Tough fibers should be trimmed before cooking.

Cellulose—*A complex carbohydrate found in the cell wall of plants; it is indigestible by humans.*

Artichokes

Artichokes (Fr. *artichaut*) are the immature flowers of a thistle plant introduced to America by Italian and Spanish settlers. Young, tender globe artichokes can be cooked whole, but more mature plants need to have the fuzzy center (known as the choke) removed first. Whole artichokes can be simmered, steamed or microwaved; they are often served with lemon juice, garlic butter or hollandaise sauce. The heart may be cooked separately, then served in salads, puréed as a filling or served as a side dish. Artichoke hearts and bottoms are both available canned.

Artichokes

Choose fresh artichokes with tight, compact heads that feel heavy. Their color should be solid green to gray-green. Brown spots on the surface caused by frost are harmless. Artichoke's peak season is March through May.

PROCEDURE FOR PREPARING FRESH ARTICHOKES

1. Using kitchen shears or scissors, trim the barbs from the large outer leaves of the artichoke.

2. With a chef's knife, cut away the stem and the top of the artichoke. Steam or boil the artichoke as desired.

Asparagus

Asparagus (Fr. *asperges*), a member of the lily family, has bright green spears with a ruffle of tiny leaves at the tip. Larger spears tend to be tough and woody, but can be used in soups or for purée. Asparagus are eaten raw or steamed briefly, stir-fried, microwaved or grilled. Fresh spring asparagus is excellent with nothing more than lemon juice or clarified butter; asparagus with hollandaise sauce is a classic preparation.

Choose firm, plump spears with tightly closed tips and a bright green color running the full length of the spear. Asparagus should be stored, refrigerated at 40°F (4°C), upright in 1/2 inch (1.25 centimeter) of water or with the ends wrapped in moist paper toweling. They should not be washed until just before use. Canned and frozen asparagus are also available. Peak season is March through June.

A European variety of white asparagus is sometimes available fresh, or readily available canned. It has a milder flavor and soft, tender texture. It is produced by covering the stalks with soil as they grow; this prevents sunlight from reaching the plant and retards the development of chlorophyll.

Asparagus

Celery

Once a medicinal herb, stalk celery (Fr. *céleri*) is now a common sight in kitchens worldwide. Stalk celery is pale green with stringy curved stalks. Often eaten raw in salads or as a snack, it can be braised or steamed as a side dish. Celery is also a mirepoix component.

Choose stalks that are crisp, without any sign of dryness. Celery is available all year.

Celery

Fennel

Fennel (Fr. *fenouil*) is a Mediterranean favorite used for thousands of years as a vegetable (the bulb), an herb (the leaves) and a spice (the seeds). The bulb (often incorrectly referred to as sweet anise) has short, tight, overlapping celerylike stalks with feathery leaves. The flavor is similar to anise or licorice, becoming milder when cooked. Fennel bulbs may be eaten raw or grilled, steamed, sautéed, baked or microwaved.

Choose fairly large, bright white bulbs on which the cut edges appear fresh, without dryness or browning. The bulb should be compact, not spreading. Fresh fennel's peak season is September through May.

Fennel

Nopales

The pads of a prickly pear cactus can be prepared as a vegetable known as nopales. Cactus pads have a flavor similar to green bell peppers. Their texture tends to be rather gelatinous or mucilaginous, making them good for stews or sauces. To prepare fresh nopales, hold the pad with tongs and cut off the thorns and "eyes" with a sharp knife or vegetable peeler. Trim off the edge all the way around. Slice the pad into julienne strips or cubes. The pieces can be boiled or steamed and served hot, or chilled and added to salads. Nopales can also be sautéed with onions, peppers and seasonings for a side dish or added to southwestern-style casseroles.

Nopales

Some cultivated varieties have thin, thornless pads. Choose pads that are stiff and heavy without blemishes. They should not be dry or soggy. Fresh cactus pads are available all year, with peak season in the late spring. Canned and pickled nopales are also available.

Baby Vegetables

Many fine restaurants serve baby vegetables: tiny turnips, finger-length squash, miniature carrots and petite heads of cauliflower. First cultivated in Europe but now widely available throughout the United States, baby vegetables include both hybrids bred to be true miniatures as well as regular varieties that are picked before maturity. Baby vegetables are often marketed with blossoms or greens still attached. They tend to be easily bruised and are highly perishable. Many baby vegetables can be eaten raw, but they are usually left whole, then steamed or lightly sautéed and attractively presented as an accompaniment to meat, fish or poultry entrees.

Baby Yellow Squash with Blossoms

Baby Globe Carrots

Chiogghi Beets

Baby Zucchini with Blossoms

◆◆◆

ANCIENT PLANTS AND
ANCIENT WAYS VANISH

Since the days of Columbus, half of all native American crop varieties have become extinct. If this trend continues, several hundred more will become extinct in our lifetimes. Similarly, ancient farming practices have all but been abandoned. As late as the 1920s, the Tohono O'odham Indians of Arizona still used traditional methods to cultivate more than 10,000 acres without pumping groundwater. Today, only a few scattered floodwater fields remain.

When species disappear we lose an irreplaceable source of genetic diversity—a source of extraordinary genes that could someday improve modern hybrid crops. When native desert crops vanish, so does the ancient tradition of native agriculture, which has selected these crops over millennia to thrive in extreme temperatures, in alkaline soils without millions of gallons of precious water and without expensive, ecologically destructive chemicals.

Today, six highly bred species—wheat, rice, corn, sorghum, potatoes and cassava—supply most of the world's nutrition. As food crops become more and more homogeneous, they often lose their natural ability to tolerate pests, disease and drought. In the past, farmers grew thousands of food crop varieties. These traditional crop varieties contain a storehouse of genetic diversity that enables them to flourish in the most difficult environments. This broad spectrum of genetic variability is a cushion against natural predators and diseases. Wild chiles from the Sierra Madre, for example, are highly disease resistant. Their virus-tolerant genes have been bred into commercial varieties of bell pepper and jalapeños.

Native Seeds/SEARCH, one of the country's first regional seed banks, was founded to keep ancient desert plants and traditional farming methods from disappearing forever. Since 1983

we've ridden mules into remote areas and made more than 1200 collections of desert-adapted crops and wild relatives. We've gathered the seeds of chapalote (a brown popcorn), blue indigo (used for dyes), tepary (a heat- and drought-tolerant bean), teosinte (a wild relative of corn), wild chiles and other plants. These seeds are available to researchers, gardeners, farmers and seed banks. Seeds are offered free to Native Americans.

Each loss of biological and cultural diversity alters and damages the balance of life on earth, often in ways we do not understand. Each loss of leaf, stem and flower diminishes our earth's richness and beauty in ways we often don't appreciate until they're gone.

DR. GARY PAUL NABHAN
Native Seeds/SEARCH
Tucson, Arizona

TABLE 22.1   NUTRITIONAL VALUES OF SELECTED VEGETABLES

Per 4-oz. (112-g) serving, fresh, trimmed and prepared as noted	Kcal	Protein (g)	Carbohydrates (g)	Fiber (g)	Total Fat (g)	Vitamin A (I.U.)	Vitamin C (mg)	Calcium (mg)	Iron (mg)
Asparagus, boiled and drained	28	2.9	5	0.9 c	0.4	896	28.8	39.6	1
Broccoli, boiled and drained	32	3.4	5.7	2.9 d	0.4	1586	85	52	0.9
Cabbage, green, boiled and drained	24	1.1	5.4	0.7 c	0.3	96	27	37.5	0.4
Carrots, raw	48	1.2	11.6	3.6 d	0.4	32,404	11.2	30.4	0.6
Corn, boiled and drained	122	3.8	28.5	4.2 d	1.5	247	6.9	2.8	0.7
Mushrooms, white, raw	28	2.4	5.2	1.6 d	0.4	0	5.8	5.8	1.3
Onions, raw	44	1.2	9.6	2 d	0.3	0	6.7	21.3	0.2
Peppers, bell, green or red, raw	32	1.2	7.2	2 d	0.4	585	56.3	8.7	0.4
Pinto beans, boiled and drained	155	9.3	29.1	4.5 d	0.6	2.6	2.6	53.3	2.9
Snow peas, raw	48	3.2	8.4	2.8 d	0.4	42	17.2	12.4	0.6
Spinach, boiled and drained	26	3.4	4.3	2.5 d	0.3	7371	9	122	3.2
Tomatoes, raw	24	0.8	5.2	1.6 d	0.4	645	20.2	5	0.5
Zucchini, raw	16	1.2	3.2	0.4 d	0.3	100	2.7	4.5	0.1

Corinne T. Netzer Encyclopedia of Foods 1992
c = crude fiber (a designation given to a less-accurate measurement of fiber content)
d = dietary fiber (a designation given to a newer and more accurate measurement of fiber content)

NUTRITION

Most vegetables are more than 80% water; the remaining portions consist of carbohydrates (primarily starches) as well as small amounts of protein and fat. The relative lack of protein and fat makes most vegetables especially low in calories.

Much of a vegetable's physical structure is provided by generally indigestible substances such as cellulose and lignin, also known as fiber. This fiber produces the characteristic stringy, crisp or fibrous textures associated with vegetables.

Vegetables are also a good source of vitamins and minerals. Care must be taken during preparation to preserve their nutritional content, however. Once peeled or cut, vegetables lose nutrients to the air, or to any liquid in which they are allowed to soak. Vitamins are concentrated just under the skin, so peel vegetables thinly, if at all.

PURCHASING AND STORING FRESH VEGETABLES

Fresh vegetables should be selected according to seasonal availability. Using a vegetable at the peak of its season has several advantages: Price is at its lowest, selection is at its greatest and the vegetable's color, flavor and texture are at their best.

Grading

The USDA has a voluntary grading system for fresh vegetables traded on wholesale markets. The system is based on appearance, condition and other factors affecting waste or eating quality. Grades for all vegetables include, in descending order of quality, U.S. Extra Fancy, U.S. Fancy, U.S. Extra No. 1 and U.S. No. 1. There are also grades that apply only to specific vegetables, for example, U.S. No. 1 Boilers for onions.

Consumer or retail grading is currently required only for potatoes, carrots and onions. It uses alphabetical listings, with Grade A being the finest.

Purchasing

Fresh vegetables are sold by weight or count. They are packed in cartons referred to as cases, lugs, bushels, flats or crates. The weight or count packed in each of these containers varies depending on the size and type of vegetable as well as the packer. For example, celery is packed in 55-pound cartons containing 18–48 heads depending on the size of each head.

Some of the more common fresh vegetables (e.g., onions, carrots, celery and lettuces) can be purchased from wholesalers trimmed, cleaned and cut according to your specifications. Although the unit price will be higher for diced onions than for whole onions, for example, the savings in time, labor, yield loss and storage space can be substantial. Processed vegetables may suffer a loss of nutrients, moisture and flavor, however.

Ripening

Although vegetables do not ripen in the same manner as fruits, they do continue to breathe (respire) after harvesting. The faster the respiration rate, the faster the produce ages or decays. This decay results in wilted leaves and dry, tough or woody stems and stalks. Respiration rates vary according to the vegetable variety, its maturity at harvest and its storage conditions after harvest.

Ripening proceeds more rapidly in the presence of ethylene gas. Ethylene gas is emitted naturally by fruits and vegetables and can be used to encourage further ripening in some produce, especially fruit-vegetables such as tomatoes. Items harvested and shipped when mature but green (unripe) can be exposed to ethylene gas to induce color development (ripening) just before sale.

Storing

Some fresh vegetables are best stored at cool temperatures, between 40° and 60°F (4–16° C), ideally in a separate produce refrigerator. These include winter squash, potatoes, onions, shallots and garlic. If a produce refrigerator is not available, store these vegetables at room temperature in a dry area with good ventilation. Do not store them in a refrigerator set at conventional temperatures. Colder temperatures convert the starches in these vegetables to sugars, changing their texture and flavor.

Most other vegetables benefit from cold storage at temperatures between 34° and 40°F (2–4°C) with relatively high levels of humidity. Greens and other delicate vegetables should be stored away from apples, tomatoes, bananas and melons, as the latter give off a great deal of ethylene gas.

PURCHASING AND STORING PRESERVED VEGETABLES

Preservation techniques are designed to extend the shelf life of vegetables. These methods include irradiation, canning, freezing and drying. Except for drying, these techniques do not substantially change the vegetable's texture or flavor. Canning and freezing can also be used to preserve cooked vegetables.

Irradiated Vegetables

The irradiation process uses ionizing radiation (usually gamma rays of cobalt 60 or cesium 137) to sterilize foods. When foods are subjected to radiation, parasites, insects and bacteria are destroyed, ripening is slowed and sprouting is prevented. Irradiation works without a noticeable increase in temperature; consequently, the flavor and texture of fresh foods are not affected. Some nutrients, however, may be destroyed. Irradiated vegetables do not need to be sprayed with post-harvest pesticides and they have an extended shelf life.

The FDA classifies irradiation as a food additive. Although not yet approved for all foods, grains, fruits and vegetables may be treated with low-dose radiation. Irradiated foods must be labeled "Treated with radiation" or "Treated by irradiation." The symbol shown in Figure 22.1 may also be used. Irradiated produce is purchased, stored and used like fresh produce.

FIGURE 22.1 **Irradiation Symbol**

Canned Vegetables

Canned vegetables are the backbone of menu planning for many food service operations. In commercial canning, raw vegetables are cleaned and placed in a sealed container, then subjected to high temperatures for a specific period of time. Heating destroys the microorganisms that cause spoilage, and the sealed environment created by the can eliminates oxidation and retards decomposition. But the heat required by the canning process also softens the texture of most vegetables and alters their nutritional content; many vitamins and minerals may be lost through the canning process. Green vegetables may also suffer color loss, becoming a drab olive hue.

Canned vegetables are graded by the USDA as U.S. Grade A or Fancy, U.S. Grade B or Extra-Select, and U.S. Grade C or Standard. U.S. Grade A vegetables must be top quality, tender and free of blemishes. U.S. Grade C vegetables may lack uniformity or flavor, but can be used in casseroles or soups if cost is a concern.

Combinations of vegetables as well as vegetables with seasonings and sauces are available canned. For example, corn kernels are available canned in water, in seasonings and sauces, combined with other vegetables or creamed. Canned vegetables are easy to serve because they are essentially fully cooked during the canning process.

Canned vegetables are purchased in cases of standard-sized cans (see Appendix II). Canned vegetables can be stored almost indefinitely at room temperature. Once a can is opened, any unused contents should be transferred to an appropriate storage container and refrigerated. Cans with bulges should be discarded immediately, without opening.

Frozen Vegetables

Frozen vegetables are almost as convenient to use as canned. However, they often require some cooking, and expensive freezer space is necessary if an inventory is to be maintained. Regardless, freezing is a highly effective method for preserving vegetables. It severely inhibits the growth of microorganisms that cause spoilage without destroying many nutrients. Generally, green vegetables retain their color, although the appearance and texture of most vegetables may be somewhat altered because of their high water content: Ice crystals form from the water in the cells and burst the cells' walls.

Some vegetables are available individually quick frozen (IQF). This method employs blasts of cold air, refrigerated plates, liquid nitrogen, liquid air or other techniques to chill the vegetables quickly. By speeding the freezing process, the formation of ice crystals can be greatly reduced.

Combinations of vegetables as well as vegetables with seasonings and sauces are available frozen. Some frozen vegetables are raw when frozen; others are blanched before freezing so final cooking time is reduced. Many others are fully cooked before freezing and only need to be thawed or heated for service. Frozen vegetables generally do not need to be thawed before being heated. Once thawed or cooked, they should be stored in the refrigerator and reheated in the same manner as fresh vegetables. Do not refreeze previously frozen vegetables.

Frozen vegetables are graded in the same manner as canned vegetables. They are usually packed in cases containing 1- to 2-pound (450 grams–1.8 kilograms) boxes or bags. All frozen vegetables should be sealed in moisture-proof wrapping and kept at a constant temperature of 0°F (–18°C) or below. Temperature fluctuations can draw moisture from the vegetables, causing poor texture and flavor loss. Adequate packaging also prevents freezer burn, an irreversible change in the color, texture and flavor of frozen foods.

Dried Vegetables

Except for beans, peas, peppers and tomatoes, few vegetables are commonly preserved by drying. Unlike other preservation methods, drying dramatically alters flavor, texture and appearance. The loss of moisture concentrates flavors and sugars and greatly extends shelf life.

APPLYING VARIOUS COOKING METHODS

Vegetables are cooked in order to break down their cellulose and gelatinize their starches. Cooking gives vegetables a pleasant flavor; creates a softer, more tender texture; and makes them more digestible. Ideally, most vegetables should be cooked as briefly as possible in order to preserve their flavor, nutrients and texture. Unfortunately, sometimes you must choose between emphasizing appearance and maintaining nutrition, because cooking methods that preserve color and texture often remove nutrients.

Acid/Alkali Reactions

The acid or alkaline content of the cooking liquid affects the texture and color of many vegetables. This is of greater concern with moist-heat cooking methods, but it is also a consideration with dry-heat cooking methods, as they often call for blanched or parboiled vegetables.

Texture

The acidity or alkalinity of the vegetable's cooking liquid influences the finished product's texture. If an acid such as lemon juice, vinegar or wine is added to the liquid for flavoring, the vegetable will resist softening and will require a longer cooking time. On the other hand, an alkaline cooking medium will quickly soften the vegetable's texture and may cause it to become mushy. Alkalinity also causes nutrient loss (especially thiamin) and may impart a bitter flavor. Alkalinity can be caused by tap water, detergent residue on utensils or the addition of baking soda (a base) to the cooking liquid. (You could add, for example, 1/8 teaspoon (.6 milliliter) of baking soda per cup (225 ml) of beans to speed the softening of dried beans.)

Color

The acidity or alkalinity of the liquid also affects the plant's pigments, causing both desirable and undesirable color changes. There are three principal pigment categories: chlorophyll, carotenoid and flavonoid. A plant's unique color is the

TABLE 22.2	ACID/ALKALI REACTIONS					
		Effect of Acid on:		Effect of Alkali on*:		
Vegetable	Pigment Family	Color	Texture	Color	Texture	Cook Covered?
Spinach, Broccoli	chlorophyll	drab olive green	firm	bright green	mushy	no
Carrots, Rutabagas	carotenoid	no change	firm	no change	mushy	no difference
Cauliflower	flavonoid	white	firm	yellow	mushy	yes
Red Cabbage	flavonoid	red	firm	blue	mushy	yes

*Alkalinity always causes a loss of thiamin and other nutrients.

result of a combination of these pigments. Chlorophyll pigments predominate in green vegetables such as spinach, green beans and broccoli. Carotenoid pigments predominate in orange and yellow vegetables such as carrots, tomatoes, red peppers and winter squashes. Flavonoid pigments predominate in red, purple and white vegetables such as red cabbage, beets and cauliflower.

Initially, as vegetables are cooked, their original colors intensify. Exposure to heat makes pigments, especially chlorophyll, appear brighter. Exposure to acids and bases affects both chlorophyll and flavonoid pigments. Acids will gradually turn green vegetables an olive-drab color, while a slight alkalinity promotes chlorophyll retention. The opposite occurs with vegetables containing flavonoids: They retain desirable colors in a slightly acidic environment while losing colors in an alkaline one. (Carotenoid is not affected by either acidity or alkalinity.) Color changes alone do not affect flavor; but the altered appearance can make the product so visually unappealing as to become inedible.

Colors also change as the naturally occurring acids in vegetables are released during cooking. If the cooking pan is kept covered, the acids can concentrate, creating richer flavonoid pigments but destroying chlorophyll pigments.

Thus, if color is the *one and only* concern, vegetables with a high amount of chlorophyll should be cooked in an alkaline liquid, and vegetables with a high amount of flavonoids should be cooked in an acidic liquid. Just remember, the improvement in color usually comes at the expense of texture and nutrients.

Guidelines for Vegetable Cookery

The following general guidelines for vegetable cookery should be considered regardless of the cooking method used.

1. Vegetables should be carefully cut into uniform shapes and sizes to promote even cooking and provide an attractive finished product.

2. Cook vegetables for as short a time as possible to preserve texture, color and nutrients.

3. Cook vegetables as close to service time as possible. Holding vegetables in a steam table continues to cook them.

4. When necessary, vegetables may be blanched in advance, refreshed in ice water and refrigerated. They can then be reheated as needed.

5. White and red vegetables (those with flavonoid pigments) may be cooked with a small amount of acid such as lemon juice, vinegar or white wine to help retain their color.

6. When preparing an assortment of vegetables, cook each type separately, then combine them. Otherwise some items would be overcooked in the time required to properly cook others.

Determining Doneness

There are so many types of vegetables, with such varied responses to cooking, that no one standard for doneness is appropriate. Each item should be evaluated on a recipe-by-recipe basis. Generally, however, most cooked vegetables are done when they are just tender when pierced with a fork or the tip of a paring knife. Leafy vegetables should be wilted but still have a bright color.

You can avoid overcooking vegetables by remembering that some carryover cooking will occur through the residual heat contained in the foods. Always rely on objective tests—sight, feel, taste and aroma—rather than the clock.

Dry-Heat Cooking Methods

Broiling and Grilling

Broiling and grilling use high heat to cook vegetables quickly. This preserves their nutritional content and natural flavors. The radiant heat of the broiler or grill caramelizes the vegetables, creating a pleasant flavor that is not generally achieved when vegetables are cooked by other methods.

Selecting and Preparing Vegetables to Broil or Grill

Broiling is often used to cook soft vegetables such as tomatoes or items that might not rest easily on a grill rack. Broiling is also used to warm and brown items just before service. If necessary, the vegetables can be basted to prevent them from drying out under the broiler's direct heat. Sometimes a cooked vegetable is napped with sauce or clarified butter and placed briefly under the broiler as a finishing touch at service time.

A large range of vegetables can be grilled. Carrots, peppers, squashes, eggplants and similar vegetables should be cut into broad, thin slices. They can then be placed on the grill in the same manner as a portion of meat or fish to create attractive crosshatchings. (See Chapter 9, Principles of Cooking.) Smaller vegetables such as mushrooms, cherry tomatoes and pearl onions can be threaded onto skewers for easy handling.

Seasoning Vegetables to be Broiled or Grilled

Vegetables contain little fat and therefore benefit greatly from added fat when being broiled or grilled. The added fat can be a brushing of clarified butter or a marinade such as one made from olive oil and herbs. Some vegetables may be brushed with butter and coated with bread crumbs or parmesan cheese before broiling.

PROCEDURE FOR BROILING OR GRILLING VEGETABLES

1. Heat the grill or broiler.
2. Use a wire brush to remove any charred or burnt particles that may be stuck to the broiler or grill grate. The grate may be wiped with a lightly oiled towel to remove any remaining particles and help season it.
3. Prepare the vegetables to be broiled or grilled by cutting them into appropriate shapes and sizes, then seasoning, marinating or otherwise preparing them as desired or directed in the recipe.
4. Place the vegetables on the broiler grate, broiler platter or grill grate and cook to the desired doneness while developing the proper surface color.

♦♦♦

RECIPE 22.1

GRILLED VEGETABLE SKEWERS

Yield: 12 Skewers

Marinade:

Rice wine vinegar	4 oz.	120 g
Vegetable oil	8 oz.	250 g
Garlic, chopped	1 oz.	30 g
Dried thyme	2 tsp.	10 ml
Salt	1 Tbsp.	15 ml
Pepper	1/2 tsp.	2 ml

Zucchini	6 oz.	180 g
Yellow squash	6 oz.	180 g
Broccoli florets, large	12	12
Cauliflower florets, large	12	12
Onion, large dice	24 pieces	24 pieces
Red bell pepper, large dice	12 pieces	12 pieces
Mushroom caps, medium	12	12

1. Combine all ingredients for the marinade and set aside.

2. Cut the zucchini and yellow squash into 1/2-inch- (1.2-centimeter-) thick semicircles.

3. Blanch and refresh the zucchini, yellow squash, broccoli florets, cauliflower florets, onions and red bell pepper as discussed below (Moist-Heat Cooking Methods).

4. Drain the vegetables well and combine them with the marinade. Add the mushroom caps to the marinade. Marinate the vegetables for 30–45 minutes, remove and drain well.

5. Skewer the vegetables by alternating them on 6-inch (10-centimeter) bamboo skewers.

6. Place the vegetable skewers on a hot grill and cook until done, turning as needed. The vegetables should brown and char lightly during cooking. Serve hot.

1. Grilling skewers of marinated vegetables.

Roasting and Baking

The terms *roasting* and *baking* are used interchangeably when referring to vegetables. Roasting or baking is used to bring out the natural sweetness of many vegetables while preserving their nutritional values. The procedures are basically the same as those for roasting meats.

Selecting and Preparing Vegetables to Roast or Bake

Hearty vegetables such as winter squash and eggplant are especially well suited for roasting or baking. Vegetables such as onions, carrots and turnips are sometimes cooked alongside roasting meats or poultry. The vegetables add flavor to the finished roast and accompanying sauce, and the fats and juices released from the cooking roast add flavor to the vegetables.

Vegetables can be baked whole or cut into uniform-size pieces. Squash, for example, is usually cut into large pieces. Vegetables may be peeled or left unpeeled, depending on the desired finished product.

Seasoning Vegetables to be Roasted or Baked

Vegetables may be seasoned with salt and pepper and rubbed with butter or oil before baking, or they may be seasoned afterward with a wide variety of herbs and spices. Some vegetables, such as winter squashes and sweet potatoes, may be seasoned with brown sugar or honey as well.

PROCEDURE FOR ROASTING OR BAKING VEGETABLES

1. Wash the vegetables. Peel, cut and prepare them as desired or directed in the recipe.

2. Season the vegetables and rub with oil or butter if desired.

3. Place the vegetables in a baking dish and bake in a preheated oven until done.

♦♦♦

RECIPE 22.2

BAKED BUTTERNUT SQUASH

Yield: 4 4-oz. (120-g) Servings

Butternut squash, medium dice	1 lb.	450 g
Salt and pepper	TT	TT
Cinnamon	1/4 tsp.	1 ml
Cardamom, ground	1/8 tsp.	1/2 ml
Brown sugar	2 Tbsp.	30 ml
Lemon juice	2 Tbsp.	30 ml
Whole butter, melted	2 oz.	60 g

1. Place the squash in a buttered pan. Season with salt, pepper, cinnamon, cardamom and brown sugar.
2. Drizzle the lemon juice and butter over the top of the squash.
3. Bake, uncovered, in a 350°F (180°C) oven until tender, approximately 50 minutes.

Sautéing

Sautéed vegetables should be brightly colored and slightly crisp when done and show little moisture loss. When sautéing vegetables, all preparation must be complete before cooking begins because timing is important and cooking progresses rapidly. Have all vegetables, herbs, spices, seasonings and sauces ready before you begin.

Selecting and Preparing Vegetables to Sauté

A wide variety of vegetables can be sautéed. Whatever vegetables are used, they should be cut into uniform-size pieces to ensure even cooking.

Quick-cooking vegetables such as summer squashes, onions, greens, stalks, fruit-vegetables and mushrooms can be sautéed without any preparation except washing and cutting. Other vegetables such as Brussels sprouts, green beans, winter squashes, broccoli, cauliflower and most root vegetables are usually first blanched or otherwise partially cooked by baking, steaming or simmering. They are then sautéed to reheat and finish. Carrots, squash and other vegetables are sometimes finished by sautéing in butter and then adding a small amount of honey or maple syrup to glaze them. Some cooked vegetables are reheated by simply sautéing them in a small amount of stock or sauce.

Seasoning Vegetables to be Sautéed

Sautéed vegetables can be seasoned with a great variety of herbs and spices. Seasonings should be added toward the end of the cooking process after all other ingredients have been incorporated in order to accurately evaluate the flavor of the finished dish.

Because sautéing vegetables uses slightly lower temperatures than sautéing meats and poultry, usually whole butter can be used in place of clarified butter. For additional flavors, fats such as bacon fat, olive oil, nut oils or sesame oil can be used in lieu of butter.

PROCEDURE FOR SAUTÉING VEGETABLES

1. Wash and cut the vegetables into uniform shapes and sizes.

2. Heat a sauté pan and add enough fat to just cover the bottom. The pan should be large enough to hold the vegetables without overcrowding.

3. When preparing an assortment of vegetables, add the ingredients according to their cooking times (first add the vegetables that take the longest to cook). Plan carefully so that all vegetables will be done at the same time. Do not overcrowd the pan; maintain high enough heat so the vegetables do not cook in their own juices.

4. Toss the vegetables using the sloped sides of the sauté pan or wok to flip them back on top of themselves. Do not toss more than necessary. The pan should remain in contact with the heat source as much as possible to maintain proper temperatures.

5. Add any sauces or vegetables with high water content, such as tomatoes, last.

6. Season the vegetables as desired with herbs or spices, or add ingredients for a glaze.

◆◆◆

RECIPE 22.3

STIR-FRIED ASPARAGUS WITH SHIITAKE MUSHROOMS

Yield: 1 lb. (450 g)

Asparagus	1 lb.	450 g
Shiitake mushrooms, fresh	6 oz.	180 g
Vegetable oil	1 Tbsp.	15 ml
Sesame oil	1 Tbsp.	15 ml
Garlic, chopped	2 tsp.	10 ml
Oyster sauce	4 oz.	120 g
Crushed red chiles, optional	TT	TT

1. Wash the asparagus, trim the ends and slice on the bias into 1- to 2-inch (2.5–5-centimeter) pieces.

2. Wash the mushrooms, trim off the stems and slice the caps into 1/2-inch- (1.2-centimeter-) thick slices.

3. Heat the oils in a wok or sauté pan.

4. Add the garlic and stir-fry for a few seconds.

5. Add the mushrooms and asparagus and stir-fry for 1 minute.

6. Add the oyster sauce and crushed red chiles (if used) and continue to stir-fry until the asparagus is nearly tender, approximately 3 minutes.

1. Stir-frying mushrooms and asparagus.

Pan-Frying and Deep-Frying

Pan-frying is not as popular as other techniques for cooking vegetables. Green tomatoes, however, are sometimes seasoned, floured and pan-fried; eggplant slices are seasoned, floured, pan-fried and used for eggplant parmesan. When pan-frying vegetables, follow the procedures outlined in Chapter 9, Principles of Cooking.

Deep-frying is a popular method of preparing vegetables such as potatoes, squashes and mushrooms. They can be served as hors d'oeuvre, appetizers or accompaniments to a main dish. Starchy vegetables may be deep-fried plain. Most other vegetables are first breaded or battered. Vegetables can also be grated or chopped and incorporated into fritters or croquettes. Any deep-fried item should have a crisp, golden exterior with a tender, nongreasy center. See Chapter 21, Deep-Frying, for additional information.

Moist-Heat Cooking Methods

Blanching and Parboiling

Blanching and parboiling are variations on boiling; the difference between them is the length of cooking time. Blanched and parboiled vegetables are often finished by other cooking methods such as sautéing.

Blanching is the partial cooking of foods in a large amount of boiling water for a very short period of time, usually only a few seconds. Besides preparing vegetables for further cooking, blanching is used to remove strong or bitter flavors, soften firm foods, set colors or loosen skins for peeling. Kale, chard, snow peas and tomatoes are examples of vegetables that are sometimes blanched for purposes other than preparation for further cooking.

Parboiling is the same as blanching, but the cooking time is longer, usually several minutes. Parboiling is used to soften vegetables and shorten final cooking times. Parboiling is commonly used for preparing root vegetables, cauliflower, broccoli and winter squashes.

Boiling

Vegetables are often boiled. Boiled vegetables can be served as is, or they can be further prepared by quickly sautéing with other ingredients, puréeing or mashing. Boiled vegetables are also chilled, then used in salads.

Starchy root vegetables are generally not boiled but rather simmered slowly so that the heat penetrates to their interiors and cooks them evenly. Green vegetables should be boiled quickly in a large amount of water in order to retain their color and flavor.

Refreshing

Unless the boiled, blanched or parboiled vegetables will be eaten immediately, they must be quickly chilled in ice water after they are removed from the cooking liquid. This prevents further cooking and preserves (sets) their colors. This process is known as **refreshing** or **shocking** the vegetables. The vegetables are removed from the ice water as soon as they are cold. Never soak or hold the vegetables in the water longer than necessary or valuable nutrients and flavor will be leached away.

PROCEDURE FOR REFRESHING VEGETABLES

1. Blanch, parboil or boil the vegetables to the desired doneness.

2. Remove the vegetables from the cooking liquid and submerge them in ice water just until they are cold.

Selecting and Preparing Vegetables to Boil

Nearly any type of vegetable can be boiled. Carrots, cabbages, green beans, turnips and red beets are just a few of the most common ones. Vegetables can be large or small, but they should be uniform in size to ensure even cooking. Some vegetables are cooked whole and only require washing before boiling. Others must be washed, peeled and trimmed or cut into smaller or more manageable sizes.

Seasoning Vegetables to be Boiled

Often vegetables are boiled in nothing more than salted water. Lemon juice, citrus zest, wine and other acidic ingredients are sometimes added to white and red vegetables; if so, they should be added to the liquid before the vegetables. Herbs and spices in a sachet or a bouquet garni are often used to add flavor to boiled vegetables and should be added according to the recipe.

After boiling, vegetables are sometimes finished with herbs, spices, butter, cream or sauces.

PROCEDURE FOR BOILING VEGETABLES

1. Wash, peel, trim and cut the vegetables into uniform shapes and sizes.
2. Bring an adequate amount of water, stock, court bouillon or other liquid to a boil. The liquid should cover the vegetables and they should be able to move around freely without overcrowding.
3. Add seasonings if desired or directed in the recipe.
4. Add the vegetables to the boiling liquid. If more than one vegetable is to be cooked and they have different cooking times, they should be cooked separately to ensure that all are cooked to the proper doneness. The pot may be covered if cooking white, red or yellow vegetables. Do not cover the pot when boiling green vegetables.
5. Cook the vegetables to the desired doneness.
6. Remove the vegetables from the water with a slotted spoon or a spider or drain through a colander.
7. Refresh the vegetables in ice water, drain and refrigerate until needed, or finish the hot boiled vegetables as desired and serve immediately.

◆◆◆

RECIPE 22.4

BRUSSELS SPROUTS IN PECAN BUTTER

Yield: 6 3-oz. (90-g) Servings

Brussels sprouts	1 lb.	450 g
Whole butter	2 oz.	60 g
Pecans, chopped	4 oz.	120 g
Salt and pepper	TT	TT

1. Trim the Brussels sprouts and mark an X in the bottom of each with a paring knife to promote even cooking.
2. Boil the sprouts in salted water until tender, approximately 10 minutes.
3. Drain and hold the sprouts in a warm place.

Continued

1. Marking an X in the bottom of each Brussels sprout.

2. Boiling the Brussels sprouts in the appropriate amount of water.

3. Tossing the Brussels sprouts with the butter.

Beurre noisette—*(Fr.) whole butter heated until it turns light brown and gives off a nutty aroma.*

4. Heat the butter in a sauté pan until it turns nut brown; this is called **beurre noisette**. Add the pecans and toss to brown them.

5. Add the Brussels sprouts and toss to reheat and blend flavors. Adjust the seasonings and serve.

PROCEDURE FOR COOKING DRIED BEANS

Dried beans are best rehydrated by soaking as discussed above and then cooking in a boiling (actually simmering) liquid. After rehydration and cooking, the beans can be served or further cooked in baked, sautéed or puréed dishes.

1. After soaking, place the drained beans in a heavy saucepan and cover with cold water or stock. Allow approximately three times as much liquid as there are beans. Add flavoring ingredients as directed in the recipe, but do not add acids or salt until the beans have reached the desired tenderness. Acids and salt cause the exterior of beans to toughen and resist any further efforts at tenderizing.

2. Slowly bring the liquid to a boil. Boil uncovered for 10 minutes or as directed in the recipe. Use a ladle to remove any scum that rises to the surface.

3. Cover and reduce the heat. Allow the mixture to simmer until the beans are tender. Whole beans generally require 1 to 2-1/2 hours, lentils 20–35 minutes and split peas 30–60 minutes. Add additional hot liquid if necessary. Do not stir the beans during cooking.

4. Drain the cooked beans through a colander.

RECIPE 22.5

CHICKPEAS

WITH OLIVE OIL AND LEMON

Yield: 3 lb. (1.3 kg)

Chickpeas, dried	1 lb.	450 g
Chicken stock	3 pt.	1.5 lt
Onion, medium dice	10 oz.	300 g

Bouquet garni:		
Carrot stick, 4 in. (10 cm)	1	1
Leek, split, 4-in. (10-cm) piece	1	1
Fresh thyme	1 sprig	1 sprig
Bay leaves	2	2
Salt	1 tsp.	5 ml
Lemon juice	2 oz.	60 g
Olive oil	4 oz.	120 g
Garlic, minced	1 oz.	30 g
Fresh oregano, chopped	1 tsp.	5 ml
Lemon zest, grated	2 Tbsp.	30 ml
Pepper	TT	TT

1. Soak the chickpeas in water for 4 hours or overnight.

2. Drain the chickpeas and combine with the chicken stock, onion and bouquet garni. Simmer, uncovered, until the chickpeas are tender, approximately 2-1/2 hours. Add the salt to the chickpeas; cook for 5 minutes.

3. Combine the lemon juice, olive oil, garlic, oregano and lemon zest to make a dressing.

4. Remove the peas from the heat; drain. Combine with the dressing and season to taste with pepper. Serve the peas hot or refrigerate and serve cold.

Steaming

Vegetables can be steamed in a convection steamer or by suspending them over boiling liquid on a rack set over a wok, saucepan or hotel pan. Vegetables can also be pan-steamed by cooking them in a covered pan with a small amount of liquid. Although the food will be touching the cooking liquid, most of the cooking is done by steam because only a small portion of the food is submerged in the liquid. Steamed vegetables can be eaten plain, partially cooked and sautéed lightly to finish, incorporated into casseroles or puréed. If they are not served immediately, they must be refreshed and refrigerated until used.

Properly steamed vegetables should be moist and tender. They generally retain their shape better than boiled vegetables. Vegetables cook very rapidly in steam and overcooking is a common mistake.

Selecting and Preparing Vegetables to Steam

Nearly any vegetable that can be boiled can also be steamed successfully. All vegetables should be washed, peeled and trimmed if appropriate and cut into uniform-size pieces. Pan-steaming is appropriate for vegetables that are small or cut into fairly small pieces such as peas and beans or broccoli and cauliflower florets.

Seasoning Vegetables to be Steamed

Steaming produces vegetables with clean, natural flavors. Foods cooked in convection steamers can be seasoned with herbs and spices; but convection steamers use water to produce steam and the foods being cooked do not gain flavor from the cooking liquid. Vegetables steamed over liquids or pan-steamed in small amounts of liquids can be flavored by using stocks or court bouillon as the cooking liquid. Herbs, spices and aromatic vegetables can be added to any liquid for additional flavor.

Procedure for Steaming Vegetables

1. Wash, peel, trim and cut the vegetables into uniform shapes and sizes.
2. If a convection steamer is not being used, prepare a steaming liquid and bring it to a boil in a covered pan or double boiler.
3. Place the vegetables in a perforated pan in a single layer; do not crowd the pan. Place the pan over the boiling liquid, or add the vegetables to the liquid.
4. Cover the pan and cook to the desired doneness.
5. Remove the vegetables from the steamer and serve, or refresh and refrigerate until needed.

✦✦✦

RECIPE 22.6

BROCCOLI ALMONDINE

Yield: 6 Servings

Broccoli, fresh	2 lb.	1 kg
Salt and pepper	TT	TT
Whole butter	2 oz.	60 g
Almonds, sliced	1 oz.	30 g
Garlic clove, minced	1	1
Lemon juice	2 oz.	60 g

1. Placing the broccoli spears in a perforated pan.

1. Cut the broccoli into uniform spears. Rinse and sprinkle lightly with salt and pepper.
2. Place the broccoli in a single layer in a perforated hotel pan and cook in a convection steamer until tender but slightly crisp, approximately 3 minutes.
3. Melt the butter in a sauté pan. Add the almonds and garlic and cook just until the nuts are lightly browned.
4. Arrange the broccoli on plates for service and sprinkle with the lemon juice. Drizzle the almonds and butter over the broccoli and serve immediately.

2. Drizzling the browned almonds and butter over the broccoli.

Combination Cooking Methods

Braising and Stewing

Braised and stewed vegetables are cooked slowly in a small amount of liquid. The liquid, including any given off by the vegetables, is reduced to a light sauce, becoming part of the finished product. Generally, a braised dish is prepared with only one vegetable; a stew is a mixture of several vegetables. The main ingredients are sometimes browned in fat before the liquid is added in order to enhance flavor and color.

Both braises and stews can be exceptionally flavorful because they are served with all of their cooking liquid. (Boiled vegetables lose some of their flavor to the cooking liquid.) Braised and stewed vegetables generally can be held hot for service longer than vegetables prepared by other cooking methods.

Selecting and Preparing Vegetables to Braise or Stew

Various lettuces, especially romaine and Boston, are often braised. Cabbages, Belgium endive, leeks and many other vegetables are also commonly braised. Stews may contain a wide variety of vegetables such as summer squashes, eggplant, onions, peppers, tomatoes, carrots, celery and garlic. Leafy green vegetables and winter squashes are less commonly braised or stewed.

The vegetables should be washed and peeled or trimmed if appropriate. Vegetables to be braised may be left whole, cut into uniform pieces or shredded, as desired. Lettuces are usually cut into halves or quarters; cabbage is usually shredded.

Seasoning Vegetables to be Braised or Stewed

Both braises and stews usually include flavoring ingredients such as garlic, herbs, bacon or mirepoix. The liquid may consist of water, wine, stock or tomato juice. Vegetables can even be braised in butter and sugar or honey to create a glazed dish.

Both braises and stews can be seasoned with a variety of herbs and spices. Add the seasonings before covering the pot to finish the cooking process. Strongly flavored vegetables such as celery root and turnips are usually parboiled first in order to reduce their strong presence.

PROCEDURE FOR BRAISING AND STEWING VEGETABLES

1. Wash, peel, trim and cut the vegetables.
2. Sauté or sweat the flavoring ingredients in fat to release their flavors. Or, sauté or sweat the main ingredients in fat.
3. For a braise, add the main ingredient in a single layer. For a stew, add the ingredients according to their cooking times or as directed in the recipe.
4. Add the cooking liquid; it should partially cover the vegetables. Bring the liquid to a boil, reduce to a simmer, cover and cook in the oven or on the stove top until done.
5. If desired, remove the main ingredients from the pan and reduce the sauce or thicken it with beurre manié, cornstarch or arrowroot. Then return the main ingredients to the sauce.

◆◆◆

RECIPE 22.7

BRAISED CELERY WITH BASIL

Yield: 12 Servings

Celery	3 heads	3 heads
Onion, small dice	8 oz.	250 g
Garlic, minced	2 tsp.	10 ml
Whole butter	2 oz.	60 g
Olive oil	1 oz.	30 g

Continued

Fresh thyme	1 tsp.	5 ml
Fresh basil, chiffonade	20 leaves	20 leaves
Dry white wine	8 oz.	250 g
Chicken stock	1 pt.	500 ml
Salt and pepper	TT	TT

1. Trim the outer ribs from the celery heads, leaving only the tender hearts. Trim the heads to 6-inch (15-centimeter) lengths. Trim the root slightly, leaving each head together. Cut each head lengthwise into quarters.
2. Sauté the onions and garlic in the butter and olive oil, without coloring, until tender. Add the celery quarters to the pan and sauté, turning occasionally.
3. Add the thyme, basil, wine and chicken stock. Bring to a boil, reduce to a simmer, cover and braise in the oven at 350°F (180°C) until tender, approximately 1 hour.
4. Remove the celery and reserve. Reduce the cooking liquid on the stove top until it thickens. Adjust the liquid's seasonings and return the celery to the pan to reheat. Serve the celery with a portion of the sauce.

1. Trimming and cutting the celery.

2. Adding the liquid to the celery.

3. Reducing the sauce.

Microwaving

Fresh vegetables are among the few foods that can be consistently well prepared in a microwave oven. Often microwave cooking can be accomplished without any additional liquid, thus preserving nutrients. With microwaving, colors and flavors stay true and textures remain crisp.

Microwave cooking is actually a form of steaming. As explained in Chapter 9, Principles of Cooking, microwaves agitate water molecules, thus creating steam. The water may be the moisture found naturally in the food or may be added specifically to create the steam.

Cooking time depends on the type of microwave oven as well as on the freshness, moisture content, maturity and quantity of vegetables being prepared.

Selecting and Preparing Vegetables to Microwave

Any vegetable that can be steamed successfully can be microwaved with good results. Because typical microwave ovens are relatively small, they are impractical for producing large quantities of food. They are most useful for reheating small portions of vegetables that have been blanched or partially cooked using another cooking method.

Seasoning Vegetables to be Microwaved

Microwaving, like steaming, brings out the natural flavors of food and produces a clean, unadulterated flavor. Herbs and spices can be added to the vegetables before they are microwaved. Or, after microwaving, the vegetables can be tossed with butter, herbs and spices or combined with a sauce.

PROCEDURE FOR MICROWAVING VEGETABLES

1. Wash, peel, trim and cut the vegetables into uniform shapes and sizes.
2. Place the vegetables in a steamer designed for microwave use or arrange the vegetables on a microwavable dish. Cover the vegetables with the lid or plastic wrap. If using plastic wrap, it should be punctured to allow some steam to escape during cooking.
3. Cook the vegetables to the desired doneness, allowing for some carryover cooking. Or, reheat the previously cooked vegetables until hot. Stir or turn the vegetables as necessary to promote even cooking.
4. Serve the vegetables or refresh and refrigerate until needed.

Puréeing

Puréeing is a technique often used with vegetables. Cooked vegetable purées can be served as is, or they can be used as an ingredient in other preparations such as pumpkin pie, mashed potatoes or vegetable soufflés. Purées can also be bound with eggs, seasoned and used to make vegetable timbales and terrines.

Puréed vegetables are generally first cooked by baking, boiling, steaming or microwaving. White, red and yellow vegetables should be cooked until quite soft. They are more easily puréed when hot or warm; this also helps ensure a smooth finished purée. For most preparations, green vegetables must be refreshed after cooking and puréed while cold or they will overcook and become discolored.

Seasoning Vegetables to be Puréed

Vegetables for purées can be seasoned before they are puréed following the guidelines for the cooking procedure used. They can also be seasoned after they are puréed with a wide variety of ingredients such as herbs or spices, cheese, honey or brown sugar.

Finishing Puréed Vegetables

Purées can be finished with stocks, sauces, butter or cream to add richness and flavor. First purée the main ingredient, then add additional liquids to obtain the desired consistency.

PROCEDURE FOR PURÉEING VEGETABLES

1. Cook the vegetables. White, red and yellow vegetables should be cooked until very soft. Green vegetables should be cooked until tender but not overcooked to the point of being discolored.
2. Purée the vegetables in a VCM, food processor or blender or by passing them through a food mill.
3. Season or finish the puréed vegetables as desired or directed in the recipe, or use them in another recipe.

◆◆◆

RECIPE 22.8
PARSNIP PURÉE

Yield: 2 qt. (2 lt)

Parsnips	4 lb.	1.8 kg
Russet potatoes	1 lb. 8 oz.	650 g
Heavy cream, hot	8 oz.	250 g
Whole butter, melted	4 oz.	120 g
Salt and white pepper	TT	TT

1. Peel the parsnips and potatoes and cut into large pieces of approximately the same size.
2. Boil the parsnips and potatoes separately in salted water until tender.
3. Drain the parsnips and potatoes well. Purée them together through a food mill.
4. Add the cream and butter and mix to combine. Adjust the consistency by adding cream as desired. Season the mixture with salt and white pepper and serve hot.

CONCLUSION

Vegetables are an essential part of the human diet. They provide the body with vitamins, minerals and fiber and appeal to the appetite with taste, color and texture. Increasing market availability of fresh, high-quality vegetables as well as new hybrids gives you an ever-increasing variety of vegetables from which to choose. Vegetables are a relatively inexpensive food that can be prepared in limitless ways. They can be served as an entire meal or as an accompaniment to or part of a wide variety of other dishes. And when cooking vegetables, remember what James Beard (1903–1985), the great American food consultant, culinary educator and writer once said: "No vegetable exists which is not better slightly undercooked."

QUESTIONS FOR DISCUSSION

1. Explain how season affects the price, quality and availability of vegetables.
2. List and describe three processing techniques commonly used to extend the shelf life of vegetables.
3. What special concerns exist regarding the storage of fresh vegetables? Explain why some vegetables should not be refrigerated.
4. Why is it important to cut vegetables into a uniform size before cooking?
5. Discuss several techniques used for determining the doneness of vegetables. Is carryover cooking a concern when preparing vegetables? Explain your answer.
6. Discuss the role of acid in a cooking liquid used for preparing vegetables. Which vegetables, if any, benefit from an acidic cooking environment?
7. Describe the necessary mise en place and procedure for refreshing vegetables.

ADDITIONAL VEGETABLE RECIPES

RECIPE 22.9

SUMMER VEGETABLES WITH TARRAGON AIOLI

NOTE: *This dish appears in the Chapter Opening photograph.*

GREENS, SAN FRANCISCO, CA
Executive Chef Annie Somerville

Yield: 6 Servings   **Method:** Boiling

Baby artichokes	6	6
Carrots	8 oz.	250 g
Yellow or green zucchini	1 lb.	500 g
Sunburst squash	1 lb.	500 g
Blue lake green beans	8 oz.	250 g
Yellow wax beans	8 oz.	250 g
Broccoli florets	1 lb.	500 g
Cauliflower florets	1 lb.	500 g
Red radishes	1 bunch	1 bunch
Cherry tomatoes	1/2 pt.	250 ml
Niçoise or Gaeta olives	8 oz.	250 g
Tarragon Aioli (recipe follows)	8 oz.	250 g

1. Trim the artichokes. Steam or boil them until tender; refresh.
2. Cut the carrots, zucchini and squash as desired. Snip the ends from the beans. Parboil the vegetables (except the radishes, tomatoes and olives), one variety at a time, in salted water until nearly tender but still crisp. Refresh each and drain well.
3. Wash the radishes. Trim the root end but leave the green tops attached.
4. Wash the cherry tomatoes and remove the stems.
5. Loosely arrange the vegetables on a platter, leaving room for the aioli unless it is to be served separately in a small bowl.

TARRAGON AIOLI

Yield: 1/2 pt. (250 ml)

Egg yolk, large	1	1
Fresh lemon juice	1 Tbsp.	15 ml
Light olive oil	8 oz.	250 g
Garlic clove, chopped	1	1
Champagne vinegar	1 tsp.	5 ml
Fresh tarragon, chopped	2 tsp.	10 ml
Salt	TT	TT

1. Whisk the yolk and 1/2 teaspoon (3 milliliters) of lemon juice together until smooth.
2. Whisk in the oil, very slowly at first, until the aioli begins to emulsify. Add a few drops of lemon juice as necessary to thin the sauce. Continue until all the oil and lemon juice have been incorporated.
3. Season with the garlic, vinegar, tarragon and salt. If the aioli is too thick, thin it with a little warm water.

◆◆◆

RECIPE 22.10

SPINACH AU GRATIN

RUTH'S CHRIS STEAK HOUSE, PHOENIX, AZ

Yield: 8 8-oz. Servings (250 g)   **Method:** Boiling

Clarified butter	1 oz.	30 g
Flour	1 oz.	30 g
Half-and-half	1 pt.	450 ml
Frozen chopped spinach, thawed	2 lb. 8 oz.	2.4 kg
Salt and pepper	TT	TT
Cheddar cheese, shredded	1 lb. 8 oz.	700 g

1. Heat the butter in a saucepan. Add the flour and cook to make a blond roux.

2. Add the half-and-half, whisking to remove any lumps of roux. Bring to a simmer and cook for 15 minutes.

3. Drop the spinach into boiling salted water and cook for 2 minutes. Remove from the heat and drain well.

4. Combine the hot spinach with the cream sauce and adjust the seasonings.

5. Fill eight 10-ounce gratin dishes with the creamed spinach. Top each with 3 ounces (90 grams) shredded cheddar cheese and place under the broiler until the cheese is melted and browned and the spinach is very hot. Serve immediately.

◆◆◆

RECIPE 22.11

BROILED TOMATO

NOTE: *This dish appears in the Beef Chapter Opening photograph.*

RUTH'S CHRIS STEAK HOUSE, PHOENIX, AZ

Yield: 1 Serving   **Method:** Broiling

Tomato, large	1	1
Sugar	2 tsp.	10 ml
Whole butter, melted	1 oz.	30 g
Fresh parsley, chopped	1 Tbsp.	15 ml

1. Core and halve the tomato.

2. Sprinkle sugar on top of each half. Place on a broiler platter and broil until tender.

3. Drizzle with butter and garnish with parsley.

◆◆◆

RECIPE 22.12

GRILLED PORTOBELLO CAPS

Yield: 3 4-oz. (120-g) Servings   **Method:** Grilling

Portobello mushroom caps	1 lb.	500 g
Olive oil	1 Tbsp.	15 ml
Garlic, chopped	1 tsp.	5 ml

Salt and pepper	TT	TT
Fresh thyme	1 tsp.	5 ml

1. Wipe the mushroom caps clean with a damp towel.
2. Combine the olive oil and garlic and brush the mixture on the mushroom caps.
3. Season the mushrooms with salt, pepper and thyme.
4. Grill or broil the mushrooms until tender, approximately 8 minutes, depending on the size of the caps.

◆◆◆

RECIPE 22.13

DUXELLES

Yield: 12 oz. (350 g) **Method:** Sautéing

Mushrooms	1 lb.	500 g
Whole butter	1 Tbsp.	15 ml
Shallots, minced	2 Tbsp.	30 ml
Garlic, chopped	1 tsp.	5 ml
Salt and pepper	TT	TT
Fresh parsley, chopped	1 Tbsp.	15 ml

1. Chop the mushrooms very finely.
2. Sauté the shallots and garlic in butter until tender. Add the mushrooms and sauté until dry.
3. Season with salt and pepper and add the parsley. Cool.
4. Use the duxelles as a stuffing for vegetables or as a flavoring ingredient in other recipes.

◆◆◆

RECIPE 22.14

STIR-FRIED SNOW PEAS WITH DRIED SHRIMP

Yield: 6 3-oz. (90-g) Servings **Method:** Sautéing

Dried shrimp	1 oz.	30 g
Snow peas	1 lb.	500 g
Garlic, chopped	2 tsp.	10 ml
Vegetable oil	2 oz.	60 g
Sesame oil	1 tsp.	5 ml
Water chestnuts, sliced	4 oz.	120 g
Salt	TT	TT

1. Soak the dried shrimp in hot water for 15 minutes. Drain well.
2. Snap the snow peas and remove the strings.
3. Blanch the snow peas and refresh.
4. Stir-fry the garlic and shrimp in the vegetable and sesame oils for 10 seconds. Add the water chestnuts.
5. Add the snow peas and stir-fry until tender, approximately 1 minute. Season to taste with salt.

♦♦♦

RECIPE 22.15
GLAZED PEARL ONIONS

Yield: 1 lb. (450 g)   **Method:** Boiling

Pearl onions, peeled	1 lb.	500 g
Whole butter	1-1/2 oz.	45 g
Sugar	1 Tbsp.	15 ml
Salt and pepper	TT	TT

1. Place the onions, butter and sugar in a sauté pan and add enough water to barely cover.
2. Boil the onions, allowing the water to evaporate. As the water evaporates, the butter-and-sugar mixture will begin to coat the onions. When the water is nearly gone, test the doneness of the onions. If they are still firm, add a small amount of water and continue to boil until the onions are tender.
3. Sauté the onions in the butter-and-sugar mixture until they are glazed.

VARIATIONS: Vegetables such as carrots, turnips, zucchini and other squashes can also be glazed with this procedure. They should be cut into appropriate shapes such as a tourné and be large enough so they glaze properly without overcooking. When preparing a mix of glazed vegetables, cook each type separately because each has a different cooking time.

♦♦♦

RECIPE 22.16
HARVARD BEETS

Yield: 8 4-oz. (120-g) Servings   **Method:** Boiling

Sugar	4 oz.	120 g
Cornstarch	2 tsp.	10 ml
Red wine vinegar	2 oz.	60 g
Salt and pepper	TT	TT
Whole butter	1 oz.	30 g
Beets, boiled, peeled, medium dice	2 lb.	1 kg

1. Combine the sugar, cornstarch, vinegar, salt and pepper in a heavy saucepan. Whisk until the cornstarch and sugar dissolve.
2. Bring to a boil, then cook, stirring constantly, until the mixture is thick and clear.
3. Add the butter and the beets, tossing gently. Serve warm.

♦♦♦

RECIPE 22.17
MAPLE-GLAZED CARROTS

Yield: 16 4-oz. (120-g) Servings   **Method:** Sautéing

Carrots	4 lb.	1.8 kg
Whole butter	4 oz.	120 g
Salt and pepper	TT	TT

Maple syrup	4 oz.	120 g
Fresh parsley, chopped	2 Tbsp.	30 ml

1. Peel the carrots and cut into a shape such as oblique, tourné or rondelle.
2. Parboil the carrots in salt water and refresh. The carrots should be very firm.
3. Sauté the carrots in butter until nearly tender.
4. Season with salt and pepper and add the maple syrup. Garnish with the parsley.

=== ◆◆◆ ===

RECIPE 22.18

CREAMED CORN WITH BASIL

Yield: 10 4-oz. (120-g) Servings   **Method:** Sautéing

Corn	12 ears	12 ears
Whole butter	2 oz.	60 g
Onion, small dice	4 oz.	120 g
Heavy cream	8 oz.	250 g
Basil leaves, chopped	2 Tbsp.	30 ml
Salt and white pepper	TT	TT

1. Cut the kernels from the ears.
2. Sauté the onions in the butter without browning.
3. Add the corn and sauté until hot.
4. Add the cream. Bring to a boil and reduce slightly. Add the basil and season with salt and white pepper.

=== ◆◆◆ ===

RECIPE 22.19

RATATOUILLE

Yield: 16 4-oz. (120-g) Servings   **Method:** Sautéing

Onion, medium dice	12 oz.	360 g
Garlic, chopped	1 Tbsp.	15 ml
Olive oil	4 oz.	120 g
Green bell pepper, medium dice	6 oz.	180 g
Red bell pepper, medium dice	6 oz.	180 g
Eggplant, medium dice	12 oz.	360 g
Zucchini, medium dice	8 oz.	250 g
Tomato concasse	24 oz.	620 g
Fresh basil, chiffonade	1 oz.	30 g
Salt	1 oz.	30 g
Pepper	TT	TT

1. Sauté the onion and garlic in the olive oil.
2. Add the peppers, eggplant and zucchini and sauté until tender, approximately 10 minutes.
3. Add the tomatoes, fresh basil and seasonings. Sauté for 5 minutes. Adjust the seasonings.

✦✦✦

RECIPE 22.20

GARLIC TIMBALES

Yield: 8 2-oz. (60-ml) Timbales   **Method:** Baking

Garlic cloves, peeled	10	10
Milk	3 oz.	90 g
Heavy cream	8 oz.	250 g
Eggs	2	2
Dried thyme	1 tsp.	5 ml
Salt and pepper	TT	TT

1. Butter 8 small ramekins or timbales.
2. Place the garlic in a small saucepan, add enough water to cover and bring to a boil. Drain. Repeat this blanching procedure two more times.
3. Place the garlic in a blender with the milk and blend. Add the cream, eggs and thyme; blend until smooth. Season with salt and pepper.
4. Divide the custard among the timbales and place in a water bath. Bake for 30–45 minutes at 325°F (160°C).
5. Run a paring knife around the rim and unmold onto the serving plate.

VARIATIONS: Broccoli or cauliflower timbales. Place 1 ounce (30 grams) of blanched broccoli or cauliflower in each buttered timbale before adding the garlic custard mixture.

✦✦✦

RECIPE 22.21

ARTICHOKES STUFFED WITH ITALIAN SAUSAGE

Yield: 8 Servings   **Method:** Braising

Artichokes	8	8
Bulk sausage meat	1 lb.	500 g
Onion, chopped fine	1 lb.	500 g
Garlic, chopped fine	2 Tbsp.	30 ml
Cumin, ground	1 tsp.	5 ml
Fresh cilantro, chopped	4 oz.	120 g
Fresh thyme	2 tsp.	10 ml
Fresh bread crumbs	4 oz.	120 g
Tabasco sauce	TT	TT
Salt and pepper	TT	TT
Olive oil	2 oz.	60 g
Chicken stock	1 qt.	1 lt

1. Trim the stem and barbs from the artichokes. Using a tablespoon, scoop out the choke from the center of each artichoke.
2. Cook the sausage meat, breaking it up into small pieces. Pour off the fat. Add the onions and garlic and sauté until tender.
3. Add the cumin, cilantro, thyme and bread crumbs. Season with Tabasco sauce, salt and pepper.
4. Stuff the artichokes with the sausage mixture.
5. Place the artichokes in a braising pan and drizzle with olive oil. Add the chicken stock.
6. Bring the stock to a boil. Cover and braise until the artichokes are tender, approximately 1 hour.

◆◆◆

RECIPE 22.22
MIXED BEAN SALAD

Yield: 12 3-oz. (90-g) Servings   **Method:** Boiling

Green beans, cut in 1/2-in. (1.2-cm) pieces	4 oz.	120 g
White wine vinegar	2 oz.	60 g
Olive oil	3 oz.	90 g
Lemon juice	1 Tbsp.	15 ml
Lemon peel, grated	1 tsp.	5 ml
Garlic cloves, crushed	2	2
White wine	1 Tbsp.	15 ml
Dried red chile, chopped fine	1	1
Red kidney beans, soaked and cooked	8 oz.	250 g
Chickpeas, soaked and cooked	8 oz.	250 g
Lima or cannellini beans, soaked and cooked	8 oz.	250 g
Green onions, chopped	1 bunch	1 bunch
Salt and pepper	TT	TT

1. Steam the green beans until done but still crisp, approximately 3–4 minutes.

2. To make the dressing, combine the white wine vinegar, olive oil, lemon juice, lemon peel, garlic, white wine and chile.

3. Mix together all the drained beans and peas and pour the dressing over them. Add the green onions, season with salt and pepper and toss to combine. Marinate several hours before serving.

◆◆◆

RECIPE 22.23
BAKED BEANS

NOTE: *This dish appears in the Pork Chapter Opening photograph.*

Yield: 1-1/2 qt. (1.5 lt)   **Method:** Baking

Great Northern beans, soaked	1 lb.	450 g
Onion, small dice	4 oz.	120 g
Anaheim chile, small dice	1 oz.	30 g
Molasses	3 oz.	90 g
Brown sugar	3 oz.	90 g
Catsup	8 oz.	250 g
Prepared mustard	2 Tbsp.	30 ml
Cider vinegar	1 Tbsp.	15 ml
Worcestershire sauce	2 Tbsp.	30 ml
Tabasco sauce	TT	TT
Salt and pepper	TT	TT

1. Simmer the beans in water until almost tender, approximately 45 minutes. Drain well.

2. Combine the remaining ingredients, blending well.

3. Add the sauce to the beans, tossing to coat thoroughly. Adjust the seasonings.

4. Place the beans in a hotel pan or a 2-quart (2-liter) baking dish. Cover and bake in a 350°F (180°C) oven until the beans are completely tender, approximately 30–40 minutes.

◆◆◆

RECIPE 22.24

FENNEL AND MUSHROOMS À LA GRECQUE

Yield: 18 3-oz. (90-g) Servings   **Method:** Boiling

Mushrooms, small	1 lb.	500 g
Pearl onions, peeled	4 oz.	120 g
Olive oil	2 oz.	60 g
White wine	4 oz.	120 g
White stock	1 pt.	500 ml
Tomato concasse	12 oz.	360 g
Tomato paste	1 oz.	30 g
Lemon juice	1 oz.	30 g
Coriander, ground	1 tsp.	5 ml
Bouquet garni:		
Carrot stick, 4 in. (10 cm)	1	1
Leek, split, 4-in. (10-cm) piece	1	1
Fresh thyme	1 sprig	1 sprig
Bay leaf	2	2
Salt and pepper	TT	TT
Fennel, batonnet	1 lb.	500 g

1. Wash the mushrooms and trim the stems.
2. Sauté the onions in the olive oil, browning lightly. Add the white wine, stock, tomato concasse, tomato paste, lemon juice, coriander and bouquet garni. Season to taste with salt and pepper and bring to a boil.
3. Add the fennel and mushrooms and simmer for 15 minutes.
4. Remove from the heat and allow to cool to room temperature. Remove the bouquet garni. Adjust the seasonings and refrigerate. Serve chilled.

◆◆◆

RECIPE 22.25

SORREL SAUCE

Yield: 1 qt. (1 lt)   **Method:** Puréeing

Shallots, chopped coarsely	1 Tbsp.	15 ml
Whole butter	1 oz.	30 g
White wine	8 oz.	250 g
Heavy cream	1 pt.	500 g
Sorrel, stemmed	8 oz.	250 g
Spinach, stemmed	8 oz.	250 g
Salt and white pepper	TT	TT
Lemon juice	1 oz.	30 ml

1. Sauté the shallots in the butter until tender.
2. Add the white wine and reduce by half.
3. Add the cream and reduce until it begins to thicken.
4. Add the sorrel and spinach leaves to the cream and cook just until the leaves are wilted.
5. Purée the sauce in a blender or food processor and season with salt, pepper and lemon juice. Serve the sauce with egg, chicken, veal or rich fish dishes.

♦♦♦

RECIPE 22.26
SWISS CHARD
WITH LEMON AND PINE NUTS

Yield: 8 3-oz. (90-g) Servings   **Method:** Simmering

Swiss chard, trimmed,		
stems and leaves separated	2 lb.	1 kg
Water	1 pt.	500 g
Lemon juice	2 oz.	60 g
Extra virgin olive oil	2 oz.	60 g
Salt and pepper	TT	TT
Pine nuts, toasted and chopped	2 oz.	60 g

1. Cut the chard into 1 to 2-inch (2.5 to 5-centimeter) strips on a diagonal.

2. Combine the chard, water and 1 ounce (30 grams) lemon juice in a nonreactive pan. Simmer until tender, stirring frequently, approximately 10–15 minutes.

3. Drain. Toss with the remaining lemon juice and the olive oil. Season with salt and pepper and arrange on plates. Garnish with the pine nuts.

♦♦♦

RECIPE 22.27
BRAISED RED CABBAGE
WITH APPLES AND WINE

Yield: 16 4-oz. (120-g) Servings   **Method:** Braising

Red cabbage	3 lb.	1.4 kg
Bacon, medium dice	12 oz.	360 g
Onions, medium dice	8 oz.	250 g
Salt and pepper	TT	TT
Red wine	8 oz.	250 g
White stock	8 oz.	250 g
Cinnamon sticks	2	2
Apples, tart, cored and diced	12 oz.	360 g
Brown sugar	1 oz.	30 g
Cider vinegar	2 oz.	60 g

1. Shred the cabbage.

2. Render the bacon. Add the onions and sweat in the bacon fat until tender.

3. Add the cabbage and sauté for 5 minutes. Season with salt and pepper. Add the wine, stock and cinnamon sticks. Cover and braise until the cabbage is almost tender, approximately 20 minutes.

4. Add the apples, brown sugar and vinegar and mix well.

5. Cover and braise until the apples are tender, approximately 5 minutes.

◆◆◆

RECIPE 22.28

BRAISED ROMAINE LETTUCE

Yield: 12 Servings

Method: Braising

Romaine lettuce	3 heads	3 heads
Onions, small dice	8 oz.	250 g
Celery, small dice	8 oz.	250 g
Carrots, small dice	8 oz.	250 g
Bacon ends and pieces, small dice	8 oz.	250 g
Brown stock	24 oz.	700 g
Salt and pepper	TT	TT

1. Trim the lettuce heads. Blanch them in salted boiling water and refresh.
2. Combine the onions, celery, carrots, bacon pieces and brown stock in a sauce pot and simmer for 10 minutes.
3. Quarter the heads of romaine and trim off most of the core, leaving just enough to hold the leaves together.
4. Pour the brown stock mixture into a hotel pan and arrange the lettuce portions in the pan. Season with salt and pepper.
5. Cover the pan and braise in a 350°F (180°C) oven for approximately 1 hour. Serve each portion with vegetables, bacon and a portion of the cooking liquid.

◆◆◆

RECIPE 22.29

CUCUMBER-YOGURT SALAD

Yield: 1 qt. (1 lt)

Plain yogurt	1 lb.	500 g
Cucumber, peeled and grated	12 oz.	360 g
Cumin	1 tsp.	5 ml
Salt and pepper	TT	TT
Sugar	1/2 oz.	15 g
Lime juice	1/2 oz.	15 g
Fresh cilantro, chopped	2 Tbsp.	30 ml
Jalapeño, minced	1 tsp.	5 ml
Paprika	as needed	as needed

1. Stir together all ingredients except the paprika. Chill for several hours before service.
2. Dust the top lightly with paprika at the time of service.

Nutritional values per 4 oz. (120 g) serving:

Calories	51	Protein	2 g
Calories from fat	35%	Vitamin A	125 IU
Total fat	2 g	Vitamin C	3 mg
Saturated fat	1 g	Sodium	34 mg
Cholesterol	7 mg		

◆◆◆

RECIPE 22.30

TOMATILLO SALSA

Yield: 2 qt. (2 lt)

Tomatillos	5 lb.	2 kg
Water	8 oz.	250 g
Jalapeños	3	3
Salt	1 Tbsp.	15 ml
Pepper	1/2 tsp.	2 ml
Garlic	2 Tbsp.	30 ml
Onions, chopped	4 oz.	120 g
Cilantro, chopped	2 oz.	60 g

1. Remove the husks from the tomatillos.
2. Combine the tomatillos with the water, jalapeños, salt, pepper, garlic and onions. Bring to a boil and simmer until tender, approximately 20 minutes.
3. Chop all ingredients in a food chopper or purée them in a blender for a smoother sauce.
4. Add the cilantro and adjust the seasonings. The sauce may be served warm or cold.

Nutritional values per 2 oz. (60 g) serving:

Calories	24	Protein	1 g
Calories from fat	7%	Vitamin A	316 IU
Total fat	0 g	Vitamin C	18 mg
Saturated fat	0 g	Sodium	291 mg
Cholesterol	0 mg		

CHAPTER 23

POTATOES, GRAINS AND PASTA

After studying this chapter you will be able to:

- identify a variety of potatoes
- apply various cooking methods to potatoes
- identify a variety of grains
- apply various cooking methods to grains
- identify pasta products
- make fresh pasta
- cook pasta

*P*otatoes, grains (corn, rice, wheat and others) and pastas are collectively known as starches. Some of these foods are vegetables; others are grasses. Pastas, of course, are prepared products made from grains. Starches are, for the most part, staple foods: foods that define a cuisine and give it substance. All are high in starchy carbohydrates, low in fat and commonly used as part of a well-balanced meal.

Today's chefs are rediscovering traditional and ethnic dishes that rely on grains seldom used in typical American food service operations. Pasta, made from a variety of grains in numerous shapes and flavors and accompanied by countless sauces and garnishes, now regularly appears on many menus alongside the ubiquitous potato prepared in many classic and modern manners.

POTATOES

Potatoes (Fr. *pommes de terre*) are one of the few vegetables native to the New World, probably originating in the South American Andes. Botanically, potatoes are succulent, nonwoody annual plants. The portion we consume is the tuber, the swollen fleshy part of the underground stem. Potatoes are hardy and easy to grow, making them inexpensive and widely available.

Identifying Potatoes

Discussed below are some of the more commonly used types of potatoes. Other varieties are regularly being developed or rediscovered and tested in the marketplace.

Choose potatoes that are heavy and very firm with clean skin and few eyes. Avoid those with many eyes, sprouts, green streaks, soft spots, cracks or cut edges. Most varieties are available all year.

Purple Potatoes

Red Potatoes

Purple Potatoes

Purple (or blue) potatoes have a deep purple skin. The flesh is bright purple, becoming lighter when cooked. They are mealy, with a flavor and texture similar to russets. The most common varieties are All Blue and Caribe, which were also quite popular in the mid-19th century.

Red Potatoes

Red potatoes have a thin red skin and crisp, white, waxy flesh, best suited to boiling or steaming. They do not have the dry, mealy texture successful baking requires. **New potatoes** are small, immature red potatoes usually marketed during the early summer. When ordering red-skinned new potatoes, size A is larger than size B.

Russet Potatoes

Russet potatoes, commonly referred to as Idaho potatoes, are the standard baking potato. They are long with rough, reddish-brown skin and mealy flesh.

Russets are excellent baked and are the best potatoes for frying. They tend to fall apart when boiled. They are marketed in several size categories and should be purchased in the size most appropriate for their intended use.

Russet Potatoes

White Potatoes

White potatoes are available in round or long varieties. They have a thin, tender skin with a tender, waxy yellow or white flesh. The smaller ones are sometimes marketed as new potatoes (not to be confused with new red potatoes). Round white potatoes are also referred to as chef or all-purpose potatoes. Yukon Gold and White Rose are common varieties. Finnish Yellow (or Yellow Finn) is an increasingly popular variety; it has a golden skin, creamy flesh and buttery flavor. White potatoes are usually cooked with moist heat or used for sautéing.

White Potatoes

Sweet Potatoes

Sweet potatoes are from a different botanical family than ordinary potatoes, although they are also tubers that originated in the New World. Two types are commonly available. One has yellow flesh and a dry, mealy texture; it is known as a boniato, white or Cuban sweet potato. The other has a darker orange, moister flesh and is high in sugar; it is known as a red sweet potato. Both types have thick skins ranging in color from light tan to brownish red. (Sometimes dark-skinned sweet potatoes are erroneously labeled *yams.*) Sweet potatoes should be chosen according to the desired degree of sweetness. They are best suited for boiling, baking and puréeing, although the less sweet varieties can be deep-fried. The cooked flesh can also be used in breads, pies and puddings. Sweet potatoes are available canned, often in a spiced or sugary sauce.

Sweet Potatoes

Yams

Yams are a third type of tuber, botanically different from both sweet and common potatoes. Yams are less sweet than sweet potatoes, but they can be used interchangeably. The flesh of yams ranges from creamy white to deep red. Yams are Asian in origin and are now found in Africa, South America and the southern United States.

Nutrition

Potatoes contain a high percentage of easily digested complex carbohydrates and little or no fat. They are also a good source of many minerals and some vitamins.

TABLE 23.1   NUTRITIONAL VALUES OF SELECTED POTATOES

Per 4 oz. (112 g), baked in skin	Kcal	Protein (g)	Carbohydrates (g)	Fiber (g)	Total Fat (g)	Niacin (g)	Phosphorous (mg)	Potassium (mg)
Russet	124	2.6	28.6	0.7	0.1	1.9	64.8	475.5
Sweet potato	93	1.6	21.7	2.4	<0.1	mq	mq	mq
Yam	132	1.7	31.2	mq	0.2	0.4	33	455

The Corinne T. Netzer Encyclopedia of Food Values 1992
mq = measurable quantity, but data is unavailable

Purchasing and Storing Potatoes

Mealy Versus Waxy

One of the most important considerations in selecting potatoes is choosing between the mealy and waxy varieties. You should understand the differences and purchase the type best suited to your needs.

Mealy potatoes (also known as starchy potatoes) have a high starch content and thick skin. They are best for baking and are often ordered from suppliers simply as "bakers." Their low sugar content also allows them to be deep-fried long enough to fully cook the interior without burning the exterior. Mealy potatoes tend to fall apart when boiled, making them a good choice for whipped or puréed potatoes.

Waxy potatoes have a low starch content and thin skin. They are best for boiling. They will not develop the desired fluffy texture when baked. They tend to become limp and soggy when deep-fried because of their high moisture content.

TABLE 23.2	COMPARISON OF MEALY AND WAXY POTATOES						
	Content of:			Best to:			
	Starch	Moisture	Sugar	Bake	Boil	Sauté	Deep-fry
Mealy: russet, white rose, purple	high	low	low	✓			✓
Waxy: red, new (red), Finnish yellow	low	high	high		✓	✓	

Grading

Like other vegetables, potatoes are subject to the voluntary USDA grading system. Although U.S. Fancy is the highest grade, most potatoes sold on the wholesale market are U.S. No. 1. Potatoes sold on the retail market can also be graded as either U.S. Grade A or U.S. Grade B.

Purchasing

Potatoes are usually packed in 50-pound cartons. Counts vary depending on average potato size. For example, in a 100-count carton, each potato would weigh an average of 8 ounces. Eighty-, 90- and 100-count cartons are the most common. Generally, larger-sized potatoes (i.e., smaller counts) are more expensive. Size does not affect quality, however, and selection should be based on intended use.

Storing

Temperatures between 50° and 65°F (10–18°C) are best for storing potatoes. Do not store potatoes in the refrigerator. At temperatures below 40°F (4°C) potato starch turns to sugar, making the cooked product too sweet and increasing the risk that the potato will turn gray or streaky when cooked. Potatoes with a high sugar content also burn more easily when fried.

Potatoes should be stored in a dark room, as light promotes chlorophyll production, turning them green and bitter. Any green patches indicate the possible presence of solanine, a toxin harmful if eaten in large amounts, and should be peeled away. Solanine is also present in the eyes and sprouts and they, too, should be removed and discarded before cooking.

Under proper conditions, fresh potatoes should last for two months. Do not wash potatoes until ready to use, as washing promotes spoilage.

Applying Various Cooking Methods

Potatoes have a relatively neutral flavor, making them a perfect accompaniment to many savory dishes. They can be prepared with almost any dry- or moist-heat cooking method: baking, sautéing, pan-frying, deep-frying, boiling or steaming. They can be combined with other ingredients in braises and stews. Potatoes are used in soups (vichyssoise), dumplings (gnocchi), breads, pancakes (latkes), puddings, salads and even vodka.

Many potato dishes, both classic and modern, employ more than one cooking method. For example, lorette potatoes require boiling and deep-frying; hash browns require parboiling, then sautéing. Even french fries are best when first blanched in hot oil.

Determining Doneness

Most potatoes are considered done when they are soft and tender or offer little resistance when pierced with a knife tip. Fried potatoes should have a crisp, golden-brown surface; the interior should be moist and tender.

Roasting and Baking

Potatoes are often roasted with meat or poultry, becoming coated with the fat and drippings released from the main item as it cooks. Either mealy or waxy potatoes, peeled or unpeeled, can be roasted successfully.

Mealy potatoes such as russets are ideal for baking. The skin is left intact, although it may be pierced with a fork to allow steam to escape. A true baked potato should not be wrapped in foil or cooked in a microwave; this changes the cooking method to steaming and prevents a crisp skin from forming. A properly baked potato should be white and fluffy, not yellowish or soggy. Once baked, potatoes can be eaten plain (or with butter, sour cream and other garnishes) or used in other recipes.

PROCEDURE FOR BAKING POTATOES

1. Scrub the potatoes well.
2. Using a fork, pierce the potato skins.
3. Rub the potatoes with oil and salt if desired. Do not wrap them in foil.
4. Bake the potatoes until done. A paring knife should penetrate them easily.

◆◆◆

RECIPE 23.1

BAKED POTATOES

Yield: 8 Servings

Russet potatoes	8	8
Vegetable oil	3 Tbsp.	45 ml
Kosher salt	3 Tbsp.	45 ml

1. Scrub the potatoes well, but do not peel. Pierce the skin of each potato to allow steam to escape.
2. Rub the potatoes with the oil, then sprinkle with kosher salt.
3. Place the potato on a rack over a sheet pan. Bake in a 400°F (200°C) oven until done, approximately 1 hour. The potatoes should yield to gentle pressure and a paring knife inserted in the thickest part should meet little resistance.
4. Hold uncovered in a warm spot and serve within 1 hour.

Baking en Casserole

Many classic potato dishes require baking either raw or parboiled potatoes with sauce, cheese, meat or other seasonings in a baking dish or casserole. Well-known examples include scalloped potatoes, which are baked in béchamel sauce, and au gratin, which are topped with cheese and baked. These dishes usually develop a crisp, brown crust, which is part of their appeal.

The casserole should hold its shape when cut; the potatoes should be tender and the sauce should be smooth, not grainy.

Potato casseroles can be fully baked, then held loosely covered in a steam table for service. Portions can be reheated or browned briefly under a broiler or salamander at service time.

PROCEDURE FOR BAKING POTATOES EN CASSEROLE

1. Prepare the potatoes by washing, peeling, slicing or partially cooking as desired or as directed in the recipe.
2. Add the potatoes to the baking pan in layers, alternating with the sauce, cream, cheese or other ingredients. Or combine the potatoes with the other ingredients and place in a buttered baking pan.
3. Bake the potatoes until done.

◆◆◆

RECIPE 23.2

GRATIN DAUPHINOISE

Yield: 4–5 lb. (1.8 – 2.2 kg)

Potatoes	3 lb.	1.3 kg
Whole butter	as needed	as needed
Salt and white pepper	TT	TT
Nutmeg	1/4 tsp.	2 ml

Gruyère cheese, grated	8 oz.	250 g
Half-and-half	24 oz.	700 ml
Egg yolks	3	3

1. Peel the potatoes and cut into very thin slices.
2. Place a single layer of potatoes in a well-buttered, full-size hotel pan.
3. Season with salt, pepper and a small amount of nutmeg. Sprinkle on a thin layer of cheese.
4. Add another layer of potatoes and cheese and repeat until all the potatoes and about three quarters of the cheese are used.
5. Heat the half-and-half to a simmer. Whisk the egg yolks together in a bowl, then gradually add the hot half-and-half.
6. Pour the cream-and-egg mixture over the potatoes. Top with the remaining cheese.
7. Bake uncovered at 350°F (180°C) until the potatoes are tender and golden brown, approximately 50–60 minutes.

Sautéing and Pan-Frying

Waxy potatoes, such as red- and white-skinned varieties, are best for sautéing or pan-frying. Often they are first parboiled or even fully cooked—a convenient way to use leftover boiled potatoes. They are then cooked in fat following the general procedures for sautéing and pan-frying discussed in Chapter 9, Principles of Cooking.

The fat can be clarified butter, oil, bacon fat or lard, depending on the desired flavor of the finished dish. The fat must be hot before the potatoes are added so that they will develop a crust without absorbing too much fat. Sautéed potatoes should have a crisp, well-browned crust and tender interior. They should be neither soggy nor greasy.

Potatoes can be sautéed or pan-fried by two methods: tossing and still-frying. The **tossing method** is used to cook relatively small pieces of potatoes in a small amount of fat. The potatoes are tossed using the pan's sloped sides so that they brown evenly on all sides. The **still-frying method** is used to create a disc-shaped potato product. The shredded or sliced potatoes are added to the pan, usually covering its bottom, and allowed to cook without stirring or flipping until they are well browned on the first side. The entire mass is then turned and cooked on the second side. When the potatoes are done, they can be cut into wedges for service.

PROCEDURE FOR SAUTÉING AND PAN-FRYING POTATOES

1. Wash, trim, peel, cut and/or cook the potatoes as desired or as directed in the recipe.
2. Heat the pan, add the fat and heat the fat. Add the potatoes to the hot fat. Do not overcrowd the pan. Use enough fat to prevent the potatoes from sticking to the pan. Depending on the recipe, use either the tossing method or still-frying method.
3. Add garnishes, seasonings and other ingredients as desired or as directed in the recipe.
4. Cook the potatoes until done.

MORE THAN A FRENCH FRY

Thanks to the genius of Carême, Escoffier and others, few vegetables have as extensive a classic repertoire as potatoes. Some of these dishes begin with the duchesse potatoes mixture; in this regard, duchesse potatoes can be considered the mother of many classic potato preparations. For example,

Duchesse + Tomato concasse = *Marquis*

Duchesse + Chopped truffles + Almond coating + Deep-frying = *Berny*

Duchesse + Pâte à choux = *Dauphine*

Dauphine + Grated Parmesan + Piped shape + Deep-frying = *Lorette*

Dauphine + Shaping + Breading + Deep-frying = *Croquettes*

Other classic potato preparations not based on duchesse potatoes include:

Anna—thin slices are arranged in several circular layers in a round pan coated with clarified butter; additional butter is brushed on and the potatoes are baked until crisp, then cut into wedges for service.

Boulangère—onions and potatoes are sautéed in butter, then transferred to a baking pan or added to a partially cooked roast in a roasting pan; stock is added and the potatoes are cooked uncovered until done.

Château—tournéed potatoes are sautéed in clarified butter until golden and soft.

Parisienne—small spheres are cut from raw, peeled potatoes with a parisienne scoop; they are seasoned and sautéed in clarified butter, then tossed with a meat glaze and garnished with chopped parsley.

Rösti—potatoes are shredded, seasoned and pan-fried in the shape of a pie, then cut into wedges for service.

♦♦♦

RECIPE 23.3

LYONNAISE POTATOES

Yield: 8 4-oz. (120-g) Servings

Potatoes, waxy variety	2 lb.	1 kg
Onion, julienne	8 oz.	250 g
Clarified butter	4 oz.	120 g
Salt and pepper	TT	TT

1. Partially cook the potatoes by baking, boiling or steaming. Allow to cool.
2. Peel and cut the potatoes into 1/4-inch- (1/2-centimeter-) thick slices.
3. Sauté the onions in half the butter until tender. Remove the onions from the pan with a slotted spoon and set aside.
4. Add the remaining butter to the pan. Add the potatoes and sauté, tossing as needed, until well browned on all sides.
5. Return the onions to the pan and sauté to combine the flavors. Season to taste with salt and pepper.

Deep-Frying

Potato chips and french fries (Fr. *pomme frites*) are extremely popular in a variety of shapes, sizes and seasonings. While a wide range of shapes, sizes and preseasoned frozen products are available, fresh fried potatoes can be a delicious, economical menu item.

Top-quality russet potatoes are recommended for deep-frying. The peel may be removed or left attached. If peeled, the potatoes should be soaked in clear, cold water until ready to cut and cook. This keeps them crisp and white by leaching some of the starch that might otherwise make the potatoes gummy or cause smaller cuts to stick together when cooked.

Deep-fried potatoes are usually blanched in oil ranging in temperature from 250° to 300°F (120–150°C) until tender and translucent. They are then drained and held for service, at which time they are finished in hotter oil, usually at a temperature between 350° and 375°F (180–190°C).

Deep-frying is also used to finish cooking several classic potato dishes such as croquettes and dauphine, in which fully cooked potatoes are puréed, seasoned, shaped and fried.

Deep-fried potatoes should be drained on absorbent paper briefly and served immediately.

In general, the procedures for deep-frying found in Chapter 21 also apply here. Specific recipes for several types of deep-fried potatoes are given at the end of this chapter.

Boiling

Waxy potatoes are best for all moist-heat cooking methods. Boiled potatoes (which are actually simmered) may be served as is or used in multistep preparations such as purées, salads, soups and baked casseroles. Potatoes are usually boiled in water, although stock may be used or milk added for flavor. Always begin cooking potatoes in cold liquid to ensure even cooking. Unlike other vegetables, potatoes should not be refreshed in cold water; it makes them soggy.

PROCEDURE FOR BOILING POTATOES

1. Wash, peel or trim the potatoes as desired.
2. Cut the potatoes into uniform-size pieces. The pieces should not be too small or they will absorb a large amount of water as they cook, making the final product soggy.
3. Add the potatoes to enough cool liquid to cover them by several inches. Bring to a boil, reduce to a simmer and cook until done. If a slightly firm finished product is desired, remove and drain the potatoes when they are slightly underdone and allow carryover cooking to finish cooking them.
4. Drain the potatoes in a colander and serve or use for further preparation.

◆◆◆

RECIPE 23.4

DUCHESSE POTATOES

Yield: 2 lb. (1 kg)

Potatoes, peeled and quartered	2 lb.	1 kg
Butter	1 oz.	30 g
Nutmeg	TT	TT
Salt and pepper	TT	TT
Eggs	1	1
Egg yolks	2	2

1. Boil the potatoes in salted water until tender. Drain and immediately turn out onto a sheet pan to allow the moisture to evaporate.
2. While still warm, press the potatoes through a ricer or food mill, or grind through a grinder's medium die. Blend in the butter and season to taste with nutmeg, salt and pepper.
3. Mix in the eggs and egg yolks, blending well.
4. Place the duchesse mixture in a piping bag fitted with a large star tip. Pipe single portion-sized spirals onto a parchment-lined sheet pan. Brush with clarified butter and bake at 375°F (190°C) until the edges are golden brown, approximately 8–10 minutes. Serve immediately.

USAGE: Duchesse potatoes are often used to decorate platters used for buffets, tableside preparations or to present chateaubriand. To create borders and garnishes, the standard mixture for duchesse potatoes is forced through a piping bag while still very hot and relatively soft.

1. Passing boiled potatoes through a food mill.

2. Piping duchesse potatoes.

3. The finished potatoes.

GRAINS

Botanically, grains are grasses that bear edible seeds. Corn, rice and wheat are the most significant. Both the fruit (i.e., the seed or kernel) and the plant are called a grain.

Most grain kernels are protected by a **hull** or husk. All kernels are composed of three distinct parts: the **bran**, **endosperm** and **germ**. The bran is the tough outer layer covering the endosperm. Bran is a good source of fiber and B vitamins. The endosperm is the largest part of the kernel and is a source of protein and carbohydrates (starch). It is the part used primarily in milled products such as flour. The germ is the smallest portion of the grain and is the only part that contains fat. It is also rich in thiamin. The bran, endosperm and germ can be separated by milling.

Identifying Grains

This section presents information on corn, rice and wheat as well as several minor grains that are nutritionally significant and gaining popularity.

Some products are available in a stone-ground form. This means that the grains were ground with a stone mill rather than by the steel blades typically used for **cracking**, **grinding**, **hulling** and **pearling**. Stone grinders are gentler and more precise, so they are less likely to overgrind the grain. Stone-ground products will always be labeled as such and are usually more expensive than steel-ground ones.

Corn

Corn (Sp. *maíz*; It. *granturco*) is the only grain that is also eaten fresh as a vegetable. (Fresh corn is discussed in Chapter 22, Vegetables.) Its use as a dried grain dates back several thousand years in Central America and long preceded its use as a vegetable.

Cracking—*a milling process in which grains are broken open.*

Grinding—*a milling process in which grains are reduced to a powder; the powder can be of differing degrees of fineness or coarseness.*

Hulling—*a milling process in which the hull is removed from grains.*

Pearling—*a milling process in which all or part of the hull, bran and germ are removed from grains.*

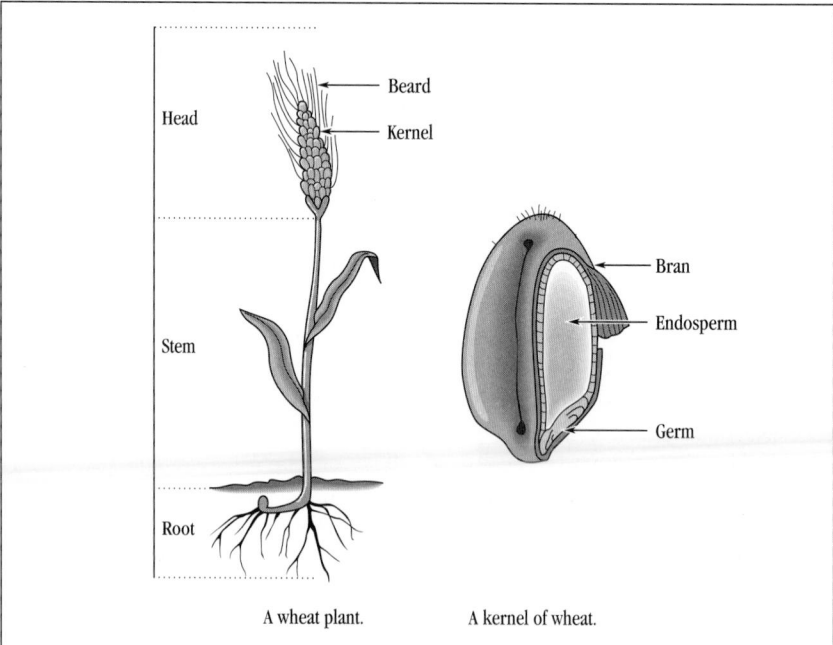

A wheat plant.   A kernel of wheat.

FIGURE 23.1

Cornmeal

Cornmeal is made by drying and grinding a special type of corn known as *dent*, which may be yellow, white or blue. Cornmeal is most often used in breads, as a coating for fried foods or cooked as polenta or mush. Products made with cornmeal have a gritty texture and a sweet but starchy flavor.

Hominy

Hominy, also known as posole or samp, is dried corn that has been soaked in hydrated lime or lye. This causes the kernels to swell, loosening the hulls. The hulls and germs are removed and the kernels dried. These white or yellow kernels resemble popcorn, but with a soft, chewy texture and smoky-sour flavor. Hominy is available dried or cooked and canned. It may be served as a side dish or used in stews or soups. **Masa harina**, a finely ground flour made from hominy, is used for making breads, tortillas, tamales and other Mexican and southwestern dishes.

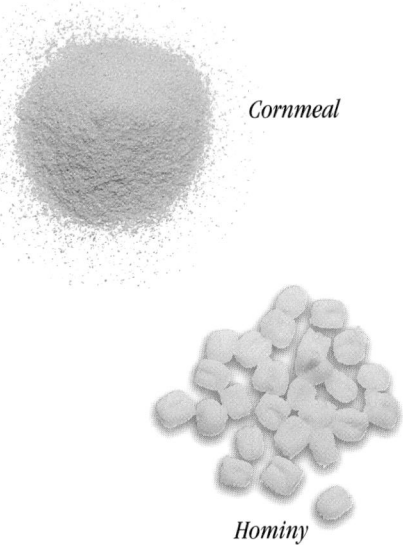

Cornmeal

Hominy

Grits

Grits are traditionally made by grinding dried hominy. These tiny white granules may be used in baked dishes but are most often served as a hot breakfast cereal, usually topped with butter or cheese. Quick-cooking and instant grits are available.

Rice

Rice (Fr. *riz*; It. *riso*; Sp. *arroz*) is the starchy seed of a semiaquatic grass. Probably originating on the Indian subcontinent or in Southeast Asia, rice is used as a staple by more than half of the world's population.

Rice can be incorporated into almost any cuisine, from Asian to Spanish to classic French. Its flavor adapts to the foods and seasonings with which the rice is cooked or served. Its texture adds an appealing chewiness to meat and poultry dishes, salads, breads and puddings. Rice is not limited to a side dish, but may be used in stews or curries, for stuffing vegetables or game birds, in puddings, salads, beverages (such as *horchata*) and breads.

Rice is divided into three types based on seed size: **long-grain, medium-grain** and **short-grain**. Long-grain rice is the most versatile and popular worldwide. The grains remain firm, fluffy and separate when cooked. (Long-grain rice can, however, become sticky if overcooked or stirred frequently during cooking.) Short-grain rice has more starch and becomes quite tender and sticky when cooked. Italian risotto, Japanese sushi and Spanish paella are all traditionally made with short-grain rice. The appearance and starch content of medium-grain rice falls somewhere in between. Medium-grain rice becomes sticky when cool, so it is best eaten freshly made and piping hot.

Long-grain, medium-grain and short-grain rice are available in different processed forms. All rice is originally brown. The grains can be left whole, with the bran attached, for **brown rice**. Or they can be pearled for the more familiar polished **white rice**. Both brown rice and white rice can be processed into Converted rice and instant rice.

Converted rice is parboiled to remove the surface starch. This procedure also forces nutrients from the bran into the grain's endosperm. Therefore, converted rice retains more nutrients than regular milled white rice, although the flavor is the same. Converted rice is neither precooked nor instant; in fact, it cooks more slowly than regular milled white rice.

Instant or **quick-cooking rice** is widely available and useful if time is a concern. Instant rice is created by fully cooking then flash-freezing milled rice. Unfortunately, this processing removes some of the nutrients and flavor.

Converted Rice

Arborio Rice

Basmati Rice

Wild Rice

Wild Pecan Rice

Arborio Rice

Arborio is a round, short-grain rice used primarily in Italian dishes such as risotto. It is very sticky, with a white color and mild flavor.

Basmati Rice

Basmati is one of the finest long-grain rices in the world. It grows in the Himalayan foothills and is preferred in Indian cuisine. It is highly aromatic, with a sweet, delicate flavor and a creamy yellow color. Basmati rice is usually aged to improve its aromatic qualities and should be washed well before cooking.

Brown Rice

Brown rice is the whole natural grain of rice. Only the husk has been removed. Brown rice has a nutty flavor; its chewy texture is caused by the high-fiber bran. Brown rice absorbs more water and takes longer to cook than white rice.

Brown Rice

Wild Rice

Wild rice is prepared in the same manner as traditional rice, although it is actually the seed of an unrelated reedlike aquatic plant. Wild rice has long, slender grains with a dark brown to black color. It has a nuttier flavor and chewier texture than traditional rice. Three grades are available: giant (the best quality, with very long grains); fancy (a medium-sized grain, suitable for most purposes); and select (a short grain, suitable for soups, pancakes or baked goods). Cultivated in California, Idaho and Washington, it is generally served with game, used as a stuffing for poultry or combined with regular rice for a side dish. Wild rice is expensive, but small quantities are usually sufficient.

Wild Pecan Rice

Wild pecan rice is neither wild nor made with pecans. It is a unique long-grain rice grown only in the bayou country of southern Louisiana. Wild pecan rice has a nutty flavor and exceptionally rich aroma.

Guidelines for Cooking Rice

Rice may be rinsed before cooking to remove dirt and debris, but doing so also removes some nutrients. It is not necessary to rinse most American-grown rice as it is generally clean and free of insects. Rice may also be soaked before cooking. Soaking softens the grains, removes some starch and speeds cooking.

TABLE 23.3   GUIDELINES FOR COOKING RICE

Type of Rice	Ratio Rice: Water (by Volume)	Preparation	Cooking Time (simmering)	Yield from 1 Cup Raw Rice
Arborio	1 : 2.5–3	Do not rinse or soak	15–20 min.	2.5–3 c.
Basmati	1 : 1.75	Rinse well; soak	15 min.	3 c.
Brown, long-grain	1 : 2.5	Do not rinse; can soak	45–50 min.	3–4 c.
Converted	1 : 2.5	Do not rinse	20–25 min.	3–4 c.
White, long-grain (regular milled)	1 : 2	Do not rinse	15 min.	3 c.
Wild	1 : 3	Rinse	35–60 min., depending on grade	3–4 c.

The standard ratio for cooking rice is 2 parts liquid to 1 part rice. The actual ratio varies, however, depending on the type of rice. Guidelines for cooking rice are found in Table 23.3.

Once cooked, rice is highly perishable. Because of its neutral pH and high protein content, cooked rice is a potentially hazardous food. To avoid the risk of food-borne illnesses, be sure to store cooked rice out of the temperature danger zone.

Wheat

Wheat (Fr.: *blé*) is most often milled into the wide range of flours discussed in Chapter 26, Principles of the Bakeshop. But wheat and products derived from it are also used as starchy side dishes or ingredients in soups, salads, ground meat dishes and breads. These products include cracked wheat, bulgur and couscous. When cooked they are slightly chewy with a mild flavor. All should be fluffy; none should be soggy or sticky.

Wheat germ and *wheat bran* are widely available and highly touted for their nutritional values. Bran and germ are not generally used plain, but may be added to bread or other cooked dishes.

Cracked Wheat

Cracked wheat is the whole wheat kernel (known as a **berry**) broken into varying degrees of coarseness. It is not precooked, and the kernel's white interior should be visible. The bran and germ are still intact, so cracked wheat has a great deal of fiber but a short shelf life. Whole wheat berries must be soaked for several hours before cooking. Cracked wheat can be fully cooked by long, gentle simmering.

Bulgur

Bulgur is a wheat berry that has had the bran removed; it is then steam-cooked, dried and ground into varying degrees of coarseness. Bulgur has a nutlike flavor and texture; it is a uniform golden-brown color (uncooked cracked wheat is not) and requires less cooking time than cracked wheat. Generally, cracked wheat and bulgur cannot be substituted for one another in recipes.

Bulgur only needs to be soaked in water, then drained, for use in salads, or briefly cooked when used in stews or pilafs. Bulgur is good with grilled meats and as an alternative to rice in stuffings and other dishes. The fine grind is most often used in packaged mixes such as tabouli; the medium grind is most often available in bulk.

Couscous

Couscous is made by removing the bran and germ from **durum wheat** berries. The endosperm is then steamed, pressed to form tiny pellets and dried. Couscous is available in varying degrees of coarseness; medium-fine is the most popular. Couscous is prepared by steaming over water or stock in a pot called a couscousier. Couscous, traditionally served with North African stews, can be used or served like rice.

Other Grains

Barley

Barley is one of the oldest culinary grains, used by humans since prehistoric times. Barley is extremely hardy, growing in climates from the tropics to the near-Arctic. Although much of the barley crop is used to make beer or

Bulgur

Couscous

Durum wheat—*a species of very hard wheat with a particularly high amount of protein; it is milled into* **semolina**, *which is used for making pasta.*

Barley

feed animals, some does find its way into soups, stews and stuffings. The most common type is pearled to produce a small, round white nugget of endosperm. It has a sweet, earthy flavor similar to oats, and goes well with onions, garlic and strong herbs. Barley's texture ranges from chewy to soft, depending on the amount of water in which it is cooked. Its starchiness can be used to thicken soups or stews.

Buckwheat/Kasha

Buckwheat/Kasha

Buckwheat is not a type of wheat; it is not even a grain. Rather, it is the fruit of a plant distantly related to rhubarb. Buckwheat is included here, however, because it is prepared and served in the same manner as grains.

The whole buckwheat kernel is known as a **groat**. The product most often sold as buckwheat is actually kasha, which is a hulled, roasted buckwheat groat. Kasha is reddish brown with a strong, nutty, almost scorched flavor. It is available whole or ground to varying degrees of coarseness. Whole kasha remains in separate grains after cooking; the finer grinds become rather sticky. Kasha can be served as a side dish, usually combined with pasta or vegetables, or it can be chilled and used in salads.

Raw buckwheat groats are ground into flour typically used in pasta, blini and other pancakes. Buckwheat flour contains no gluten-forming proteins and it tends to remain grainy, with a sandy texture. Therefore, it should not be substituted for all of the white or whole wheat flour in breads or baked goods.

Oats

Oats

After rice, oats are probably the most widely accepted whole-grain product in the American diet. Oats are consumed daily as a hot breakfast cereal (oatmeal) and are used in breads, muffins, cookies and other baked goods.

An oat groat is the whole oat kernel with only the husk removed. It contains both the bran and germ. *Steel-cut oats*, sometimes known as Irish oats, are groats that are toasted then cut into small pieces with steel blades. *Rolled oats*, marketed as "old-fashioned oats," are groats that have been steamed, then rolled into flat flakes. *Quick-cooking oats* are simply rolled oats cut into smaller pieces to reduce cooking time. *Instant oats* are partially cooked and dried before rolling so they only need to be rehydrated in boiling water. Several flavored versions are also marketed as breakfast cereal. Rolled oats and quick-cooking oats can be used interchangeably, but instant oats should not be substituted in most recipes.

Oat bran is the outer covering of a hulled oat. It is available as a separate product, although rolled and cut oats do contain some oat bran.

The term *oatmeal* is commonly used to refer to both processed groats and the cooked porridge made from them. The processed groats known as oatmeal are a gray-white color with a starchy texture and sweet flavor. They cook into the soft, thick porridge with a robust flavor called oatmeal.

Nutrition

Grains are an excellent source of vitamins, minerals, proteins and fiber. The amount of milling or refining and the method of preparation affects their nutritional values, however. Unrefined and less-refined grains are excellent sources of dietary fiber. Rice is also quite nutritious: It is low in sodium and calories and contains all the essential amino acids. Some grains, especially white rice and oats, are usually enriched with calcium, iron and B vitamins.

TABLE 23.4 NUTRITIONAL VALUES OF SELECTED GRAINS

Per 4 oz. (112 g), cooked	Kcal	Protein (g)	Carbohydrates (g)	Fiber (g)	Total Fat (g)	Niacin (g)	Phosphorous (mg)	Potassium (mg)
Barley, pearled	139	2.6	32	0.3	0.5	1.6	42.5	72.5
Bulgur	94	3.5	21.1	0.4	0.3	0.9	36.5	62
Grits	68	1.6	14.7	0.1	0.2	0.8	15	27
Kasha	104	3.8	22.6	0.6	0.7	1.2	80	95
Oats	45	3.6	13	0.4	1	0.2	89	66
Rice, brown, long-grain	126	2.9	26	1.9	1	1.5	81	42
Rice, Converted	90	1.5	21.1	mq	0.7	mq	mq	mq
Rice, white, long-grain	146	3.1	31.6	0.1	0.3	1.5	47	40
Wheat germ (toasted)	432	33.2	56.4	14.8	12	6.4	1280	1076

The Corinne T Netzer Encyclopedia of Food Values 1992

mq = measurable quantity, but data is unavailable   c = crude fiber   d = dietary fiber

Purchasing and Storing Grains

Purchasing

When buying grains, look for fresh, plump ones with a bright, even color. Fresh grains should not be shriveled or crumbly; there should be no sour or musty odors.

Grains are sold by weight. They come in bags or boxes ranging from 1 to 100 pounds. Ten-, 25- and 50-pound units are usually available.

Storing

All grains should be stored in air-tight containers placed in a dark, cool, dry place. Air-tight containers prevent dust and insects from entering. Air-tight containers and darkness also reduce nutrient loss caused by oxidation or light. Coolness inhibits insect infestation; dryness prevents mold.

Vacuum-sealed packages will last for extended periods. Whole grains, which contain the oily germ, should be refrigerated to prevent rancidity.

Applying Various Cooking Methods

Three basic cooking methods are used to prepare grains: simmering, risotto and pilaf. Unlike simmered grains, those cooked by either the risotto or pilaf method are first coated with hot fat. The primary distinction between the pilaf and risotto methods is the manner in which the liquid is then added to the grains. When grains are used in puddings, breads, stuffings and baked casseroles, they are almost always first fully cooked by one of these methods.

Determining Doneness

Most grains should be cooked until tender, although some recipes do require a chewier or more al dente product. Doneness can usually be determined by cooking time and the amount of liquid remaining in the pan. Some grains, such as wild rice, are fully cooked when they puff open.

In general, grains will be fully cooked when almost all of the cooking liquid is absorbed. This is indicated by the appearance of tunnel-like holes between the grains. Grains can be cooked until almost all of the liquid is absorbed, then removed from the heat and left to stand, covered, for 5–10 minutes. This allows the cooked grains to absorb the remaining moisture without burning.

Simmering

The most commonly used method for preparing grains is simmering. To do so, simply stir the grains into a measured amount of boiling salted water in a saucepan on the stove top. When the liquid returns to a boil, lower the heat, cover, and simmer until the liquid is absorbed and the grains are tender. The grains are not stirred during cooking.

The grains can be flavored by using stock as the cooking liquid. Herbs and spices can also be added.

PROCEDURE FOR SIMMERING GRAINS

1. Bring the cooking liquid to a boil.
2. Stir in the grains. Add herbs or spices as desired or as directed in the recipe.
3. Return the mixture to a boil, cover and reduce to a simmer.
4. Simmer the grains until tender and most of the liquid is absorbed.
5. Remove the grains from the heat.
6. Drain if appropriate or keep covered and allow the excess moisture to evaporate, approximately 5 minutes. Fluff the grains with a fork before service.

◆◆◆

RECIPE 23.5

BASIC SIMMERED RICE

Yield: 3 c. (750 ml)

Water	1 pt.	500 ml
Salt	1/2 tsp.	2 ml
White rice	1 c.	250 ml

1. Bring the water and salt to a boil in a heavy saucepan. Slowly add the rice.
2. Cover the pan and reduce the heat so that the liquid simmers gently. Cook until the rice is tender and the water is absorbed, approximately 15–20 minutes.
3. Remove from the heat and transfer to a hotel pan. Do not cover. Allow any excess moisture to evaporate for approximately 5 minutes.
4. Fluff the rice and serve, or refrigerate for use in another recipe.

Risotto Method

Risotto is a classic Northern Italian rice dish in which the grains remain firm but merge with the cooking liquid to become a creamy, almost puddinglike dish. True risotto is made with a short-grain starchy rice such as Arborio, but the risotto method can also be used to cook other grains such as barley and oats.

The grains are not rinsed before cooking, as this removes the starches needed to achieve the desired consistency. The grains are coated, but not cooked, in a hot fat such as butter or oil. A hot liquid is then gradually added to the grains so that the mixture is kept at a constant simmer. The cooking liquid should be a rich, flavorful stock. Unlike simmering and the pilaf method, the risotto method requires frequent, sometimes constant, stirring.

When finished, the grains should be creamy and tender, but still al dente in the center. Grated cheese, heavy cream, cooked meat, poultry, fish, shellfish, herbs and vegetables can be added to create a flavorful side dish or a complete meal.

PROCEDURE FOR PREPARING GRAINS BY THE RISOTTO METHOD

1. Bring the cooking liquid to a simmer.
2. Heat the fat in a heavy saucepan over moderate heat. Add any onions, garlic or other flavoring ingredients and sauté for 1–2 minutes without browning.
3. Add the grains to the saucepan. Stir well to make sure the grains are well coated with fat. Do not allow the grains to brown.
4. Add any wine and cook until it is fully absorbed.
5. Begin to add the simmering stock 4 ounces (120 milliliters) at a time, stirring frequently. Wait until each portion of cooking liquid is almost fully absorbed before adding the next.
6. Test for doneness after the grains have cooked for approximately 18–20 minutes.
7. Remove the saucepan from the heat and stir in any butter, grated cheese, herbs or other flavoring ingredients as directed. Serve immediately.

1. Sautéing the rice and onions in butter.

◆◆◆

RECIPE 23.6

RISOTTO MILANESE

Yield: 24 4-oz. (120-g) Servings

Chicken stock	2-1/2 qt.	2.5 lt
Whole butter	4 oz.	120 g
Onions, minced	5 oz.	150 g
~~Arborio rice~~	1 lb. 8 oz.	700 g
Dry white wine	8 oz.	250 ml
Saffron threads, crushed	1/2 tsp.	2 ml
Parmesan cheese, grated	4 oz.	120 g

1. Bring the chicken stock to a simmer.
2. Heat 3 ounces (90 grams) of the butter in a large, heavy saucepan. Add the onion and sauté without browning until translucent.
3. Add the rice to the onion and butter. Stir well to coat the grains with butter but do not allow the rice to brown. Add the wine and stir until it is completely absorbed.
4. Add the saffron. Add the simmering stock, 4 ounces (120 milliliters) at a time, stirring frequently. Wait until the stock is absorbed before adding the next 4-ounce (120-milliliter) portion.
5. After approximately 18–20 minutes all of the stock should be incorporated and the rice should be tender. Remove from the heat and stir in the remaining 1 ounce (30 grams) of butter and the grated cheese. Serve immediately.

Continued

2. Adding the stock gradually while stirring frequently.

3. Stirring in the butter and grated cheese.

VARIATIONS: Risotto with Radicchio (*al Radicchio*)—Omit the saffron and Parmesan. Just before the risotto is fully cooked, stir in 4 ounces (120 milliliters) heavy cream and 3 ounces (90 grams) finely chopped radicchio leaves.

Risotto with Four Cheeses (*al Quattro Formaggi*)—Omit the saffron. When the risotto is fully cooked, remove from the heat and stir in 2 ounces (60 grams) each of grated Parmesan, gorgonzola, fontina and mozzarella cheeses. Garnish with toasted pine nuts and chopped parsley.

Risotto with Smoked Salmon (*al Salmone Affumicato*)—Omit the butter, saffron and Parmesan. Sauté the onion in 3 ounces (90 milliliters) of corn or safflower oil instead of butter. When the risotto is fully cooked, remove from the heat and stir in 8 ounces (240 milliliters) half-and-half, 3 ounces (90 milliliters) fresh lemon juice and 8–10 ounces (240–300 grams) good-quality smoked salmon. Garnish with chopped fresh parsley and dill. Serve with lemon wedges.

Pilaf Method

With the pilaf method, the raw grains are lightly sautéed in oil or butter, usually with onions or seasonings for additional flavor. Hot liquid, often a stock, is then added. The pan is covered and the mixture left to simmer until the liquid is absorbed.

PROCEDURE FOR PREPARING GRAINS BY THE PILAF METHOD

1. Bring the cooking liquid (either water or stock) to a boil.
2. Heat the fat in a heavy saucepan over moderate heat. Add any onions, garlic or other flavorings and sauté for 1–2 minutes without browning.
3. Add the grains to the saucepan. Stir well to make sure the grains are well coated with fat. Do not allow the grains to brown.
4. All at once, add the hot cooking liquid to the sautéed grains.
5. Return the liquid to a boil, reduce to a simmer and cover.
6. Allow the mixture to simmer, either in the oven or on the stove top, until the liquid is absorbed.

◆◆◆

RECIPE 23.7

BULGUR PILAF

Yield: 8 4-oz. (120-g) Servings

Whole butter	2 oz.	60 g
Onions, fine dice	4 oz.	120 g
Bulgur	10 oz.	300 g
Bay leaf	1	1
Chicken stock, hot	1 qt.	1 lt
Salt and pepper	TT	TT

1. Melt the butter in a large, heavy saucepan over moderate heat. Add the onions and cook until translucent.
2. Add the bulgur and bay leaf. Sauté until the grains are well coated with butter.
3. Add the hot stock and season to taste with salt and pepper. Reduce the heat until the liquid barely simmers.

1. Sautéing the bulgur in butter.

2. Adding the hot stock to the bulgur.

4. Cover and continue cooking until all of the liquid is absorbed and the grains are tender, approximately 18–20 minutes.

5. Fluff with a fork and adjust the seasonings before service.

VARIATION: Barley pilaf—Substitute 2 cups of pearled barley for the bulgur. Cooking time may increase by 10–15 minutes.

3. Fluffing the finished bulgur.

PASTA

Pasta is made from an unleavened dough of liquid mixed with flour. The liquid is usually egg and/or water. The flour can be from almost any grain: wheat, buckwheat, rice or a combination of grains. The dough can be colored and flavored with puréed vegetables, herbs or other ingredients and it can be cut or **extruded** into a wide variety of shapes and sizes.

Pasta can be cooked fresh while the dough is still moist and pliable, or the dough can be allowed to dry completely before cooking. Pasta can be filled or sauced in an endless variety of ways. It can stand alone or be used in salads, desserts, soups or casseroles.

Pasta is widely used in the cuisines of Asia, North America and Europe. In Italy, pasta dishes are usually served as a separate course, referred to as the *minestre*; in other European countries, Asia and the United States, pasta dishes may be served as an appetizer, entree or side dish.

Extrusion—*the process of forcing pasta dough through perforated plates to create various shapes; pasta dough that is not extruded must be rolled and cut.*

Identifying Pastas

The better-known pastas are based on the Italian tradition of kneading wheat flour with water and eggs to form a smooth, resilient dough. This dough is rolled very thin and cut into various shapes before being boiled in water or dried for longer storage.

Macaroni—*any dried pasta made with wheat flour and water; only in America does the term refer to elbow-shaped tubes.*

◆◆◆

THE MACARONI MYTH

The popular myth holds that noodles were first invented in China and discovered there by the Venetian explorer Marco Polo during the 13th century. He introduced the food to Italy and from there the rest of Europe. While there is little doubt that the Chinese were making noodles by the 1st century A.D., it is now equally clear that they were not alone.

Middle Eastern and Italian cooks were preparing macaroni long before Marco Polo's adventures. A clear reference to boiled noodles appears in the *Jerusalem Talmud* of the 5th century A.D. There, rabbis debate whether noodles violate Jewish dietary laws (they do, but only during Passover). Tenth-century Arabic writings refer to dried noodles purchased from

vendors. Literary references establish that dishes called lasagna, macaroni and ravioli were all well known (and costly) in Italy by the mid-13th century.

Pasta's current popularity dates from the 18th century, when mass production by machine began in Naples, Italy. English gentlemen on their Grand Tours of the Continent developed a fondness for pasta; the word *macaroni* became a synonym for a dandy or a vain young man. Macaroni arrived in America with English colonists, who preferred it with cream sauce and cheese or in a sweet custard. Domestic factories soon opened, and by the Civil War (1861–1865) macaroni was available to the working class. Pasta became a staple of the

American middle-class diet following the wave of Italian immigrants in the late 19th century.

During the 1980s pasta became ubiquitous. Restaurants began serving it in ways previously unimagined. Corner grocery stores and local supermarkets began offering at least a dozen different shapes, often fresh and sometimes flavored. Dedicated cooks began to make pasta from scratch, though they sometimes tossed it with bottled sauce. Many also became interested in Asian noodles. Chinese, Japanese, Korean and Thai restaurants expanded their menu offerings to include traditional noodle dishes eagerly ordered by curious consumers. Pasta's popularity continues to grow as chefs discover the versatility of this inexpensive, nutritious food.

Commercially prepared dried pasta products are usually made with semolina flour. Semolina flour, ground from hard durum wheat and available from specialty purveyors, has a rich cream color and produces a very smooth, durable dough. Semolina dough requires a great deal of kneading, however, and bread flour is an acceptable substitute when preparing fresh pasta by hand.

Asian pasta, generally known as noodles, is made from wheat, rice, bean or buckwheat flour. It is available fresh or dried from commercial purveyors and at specialty markets.

Italian-Style Pasta

Although all Italian-style pasta is made from the same type of dough, the finest commercial pastas are those made with pure semolina flour, which gives the dough a rich, yellow color. Gray or streaked dough probably contains softer flours. Dried pasta should be very hard and break with a clean snap. The surface should be lightly pitted or dull. (A smooth or glossy surface will not hold or absorb sauces as well.)

Dried pasta, both domestic and imported, is available in a wide range of flavors and shapes. In addition to the traditional white (plain), green (spinach) and red (tomato) pastas, manufacturers are now offering such unusual flavor combinations as lemon–peppercorn, whole wheat–basil, jalapeño–black bean and carrot–ginger. Small pieces of herbs or other flavorings are often visible in these products.

There are hundreds of recognized shapes of pasta, but only two or three dozen are generally available in the United States. When experimenting with unusual flavors and shapes, be sure to consider the taste and appearance of the final dish after the sauce and any garnishes are added.

Italian-style pasta can be divided into three groups based on the shape of the final product: ribbons, tubes and shapes. There is no consistent English nomenclature for these pastas; the Italian names are recognized and applied virtually worldwide. (A specific shape or size may be given different names in different regions of Italy, however. These distinctions are beyond the scope of this text.)

Ribbons

Pasta dough can be rolled very thin and cut into strips or ribbons of various widths. All ribbon shapes work well with tomato, fish and shellfish sauces. Thicker ribbons, such as spaghetti and fettuccine, are preferred with cream or cheese sauces. Sheets of fresh pasta dough can be filled and shaped to create ravioli, cappelletti and tortellini. Filled pasta is usually served with a light cream- or tomato-based sauce that complements the filling's flavors.

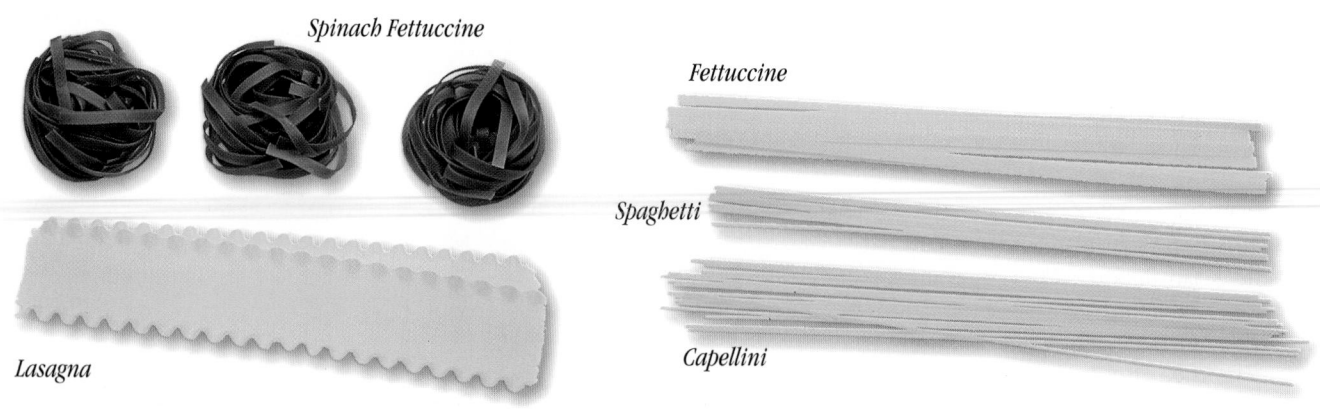

Spinach Fettuccine

Fettuccine

Spaghetti

Lasagna

Capellini

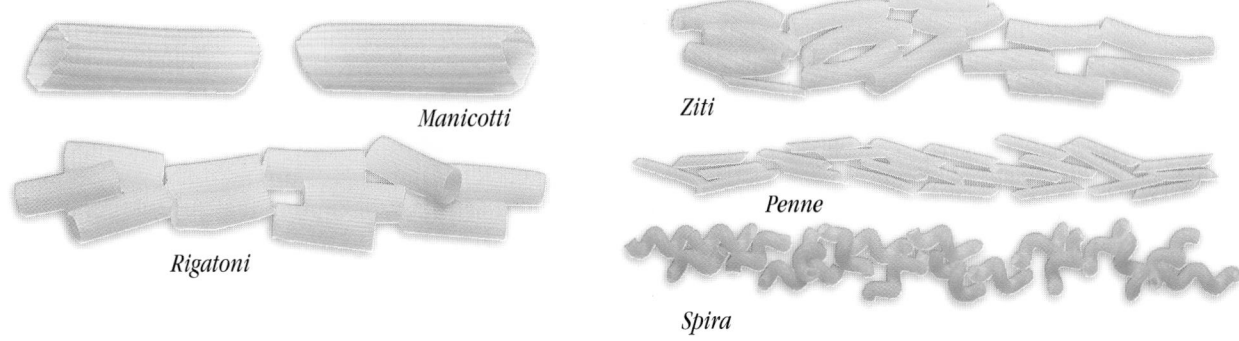

Manicotti

Ziti

Penne

Rigatoni

Spira

Tubes

Cylindrical forms or tubes are made by extrusion. The hollow tubes can be curved or straight, fluted or smooth. Tubes are preferred for meat and vegetable sauces and are often used in baked casseroles.

Shapes

The extrusion process can also be used to shape pasta dough into forms. The curves and textures produced provide nooks and crevices that hold sauces well. Shaped pastas, such as conchiglie, farfalle and fusilli, are preferred with meat sauces and oil-based sauces such as pesto. Larger shaped pastas can be cooked, then stuffed with meat or cheese fillings and baked or served as a casserole.

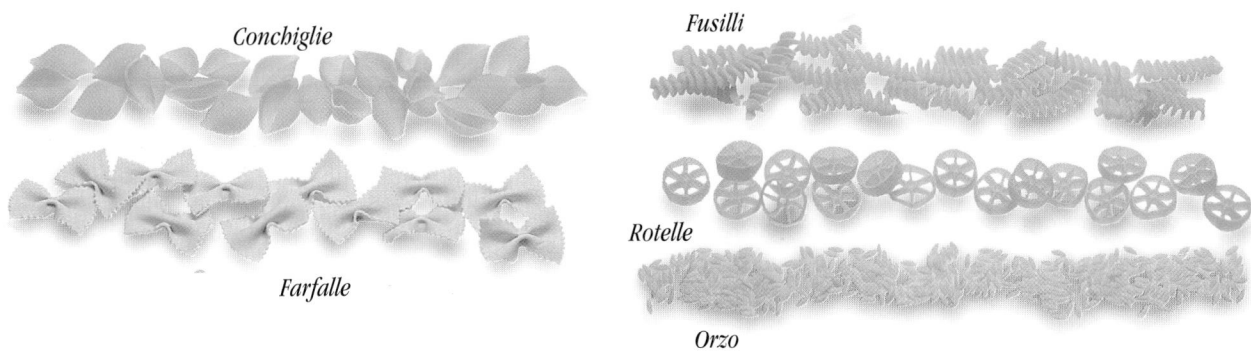

Conchiglie

Fusilli

Farfalle

Rotelle

Orzo

Asian Noodles

Asian noodles are not cut into the same wealth of shapes and sizes as Italian-style pasta, nor are they flavored or colored with vegetable purées, herbs or other ingredients.

Virtually all Asian noodles are ribbons—some thin, some thick—folded into bundles and packaged. Differences arise because of the flours used for the dough.

Most dried Asian noodles benefit by soaking in hot water for several minutes before further preparation. The water softens the noddle strands; the bundles separate, and the noodles cook more evenly.

Flour Stick Wheat Noodles (without egg)

Fresh Wheat and Egg Noodles

Rice Vermicelli

Cellophane Noodles

Japanese Wheat Somen

Wheat Noodles

Wheat noodles, also known as egg noodles, are the most popular and widely available of the Asian noodles. They are thin, flat noodles with a springy texture; they are available fresh or dried. Dried egg noodles can be deep-fried after boiling to create crisp golden noodles (chow mein) used primarily as a garnish.

Japanese wheat noodles, know as somen (if thick) and udon (if thin), may be round, square or flat. They are eaten in broth or with a dipping sauce.

Rice Noodles

Rice noodles are dried thin noodles made with rice flour. They should be soaked in hot water before cooking and rinsed in cool running water after boiling to remove excess starch and prevent sticking. Rice noodles are often served in soups or sautéed.

Rice vermicelli, which has very fine strands, can be fried in hot oil without presoaking. In only a few seconds the strands will turn white, puff up and become crunchy. Mounds of crunchy rice noodles can be used as a base for sautéed dishes or for presenting hors d'oeuvres.

Bean Starch Noodles

Bean starch noodles are also known as spring rain noodles, bean threads, bean noodles or cellophane noodles. They are thin, transparent noodles made from mung beans. Dried bean noodles can be fried in the same manner as rice vermicelli. Otherwise, they must be soaked in hot water before using in soups, stir-fries or braised dishes.

Buckwheat Noodles

Buckwheat flour is used in the noodles of Northern Japan and the Tokyo region, known as soba noodles. Soba noodles are available fresh or dried and do not need soaking before cooking. They are traditionally served in broth or with a dipping sauce, but may be substituted for Italian-style pasta if desired.

Nutrition

Pastas are very low in fat and are an excellent source of vitamins, minerals, proteins and carbohydrates. Also, the processed products are sometimes enriched with additional nutrients.

Purchasing and Storing Pasta Products

Pasta products are purchased by weight, either fresh or dried. Tubes and shapes are not generally available fresh. Dried products, by far the most common, are available in boxes or bags, usually in 1-, 10- and 20-pound units. They can be stored in a cool, dry place for several months. Fresh pasta can be stored in an airtight wrapping in the refrigerator for a few days or in the freezer for a few weeks.

TABLE 23.5 NUTRITIONAL VALUES OF SELECTED PASTA

Per 4 oz. (112 g), cooked	Kcal	Protein (g)	Carbohydrates (g)	Fiber (g)	Total Fat (g)	Niacin (g)	Phosphorous (mg)	Potassium (mg)
Noodle, Japanese soba (buckwheat)	113	5.8	24.4	mq	0.1	0.6	29	40
Pasta, wheat, dried	186	9.2	35.9	0.3	0.2	1.2	38	22
Pasta, wheat, spinach and egg, fresh	147	5.7	28.4	mq	1.10	1.2	65	42

The Corinne T. Netzer Encyclopedia of Food Values 1992
mq = measurable quantity, but data is unavailable

Preparing Fresh Pasta

Making Fresh Pasta

Fresh pasta is easy to make, requiring almost no special equipment and only a few staples. The basic form is the **sfoglia**, a thin, flat sheet of dough that is cut into ribbons, circles or squares.

Although pasta dough can be kneaded by hand, stretched and rolled with a rolling pin and cut with a chef's knife, pasta machines make these tasks easier. Pasta machines are either electric or manual. Some electric models mix and knead the dough, then extrude it through a cutting disk. An extrusion machine is most practical in a food service operation regularly serving large quantities of pasta. The pasta machine more often encountered is operated manually with a hand crank. It has two rollers that knead, press and push the dough into a thin, uniform sheet. Adjacent cutting rollers slice the thin dough into various widths for fettuccine, spaghetti, capellini or the like.

◆◆◆

RECIPE 23.8

BASIC PASTA DOUGH

Yield: 4 lb. (1.8 kg)

Eggs	15	15
Olive oil	1 oz.	30 ml
Salt	1 Tbsp.	15 ml
Bread flour*	2 lb. 8 oz.	1.1 kg

1. Place the eggs, oil and salt in a large mixer bowl. Use the paddle attachment to combine.
2. Add one third of the flour and stir until the mixture begins to form a soft dough. Remove the paddle attachment and attach the dough hook.
3. Gradually add more flour until the dough is dry and cannot absorb any more flour.
4. Remove the dough from the mixer, wrap it well with plastic wrap and set it aside at room temperature for 20–30 minutes.
5. After the dough has rested, roll it into flat sheets by hand or with a pasta machine. Work with only a small portion at a time, keeping the remainder well covered to prevent it from drying out.
6. While the sheets of dough are pliable, cut them into the desired width with a chef's knife or pasta machine. Sheets can also be used for making ravioli, as illustrated below.

VARIATIONS: Garlic-Herb—Roast 1 head of garlic. Peel and purée the cloves and add to the eggs. Add up to 2 ounces (60 grams) of finely chopped assorted fresh herbs just before mixing is complete.

Spinach—Add 8 ounces (250 grams) of cooked, puréed and well-drained spinach to the eggs. Increase the amount of flour slightly if necessary.

Tomato—Add 4 ounces (120 grams) of tomato paste to the eggs; omit the salt. Increase the amount of flour slightly if necessary.

*Semolina flour can be substituted in this recipe, although it makes a tougher dough that is more difficult to work with.

1. Adding flour to the mixing bowl and using the paddle until the mixture forms a soft dough.

2. The finished dough.

Procedure for Rolling and Cutting Pasta Dough

1. Work with a small portion of the dough. Leave the rest covered with plastic wrap to prevent it from drying out.
2. Flatten the dough with the heel of your hand.
3. Set the pasta machine rollers to their widest setting. Insert the dough and turn the handle with one hand while supporting the dough with the other hand. Pass the entire piece of dough through the rollers.
4. Dust the dough with flour, fold it in thirds and pass it through the pasta machine again.
5. Repeat the folding and rolling procedure until the dough is smooth. This may require 4–6 passes.
6. Tighten the rollers one or two marks, then pass the dough through the machine. Without folding it in thirds, pass the dough through the machine repeatedly, tightening the rollers one or two marks each time.
7. When the dough is thin enough to see your hand through, but not so thin that it begins to tear, it is ready to use or cut into ribbons. This sheet is the *sfoglia.*
8. To cut the sfoglia into ribbons, gently feed a manageable length of dough through the desired cutting blades.
9. Lay out the pasta in a single layer on a sheet pan dusted with flour to dry. Layers of pasta ribbons can be separated with parchment paper.

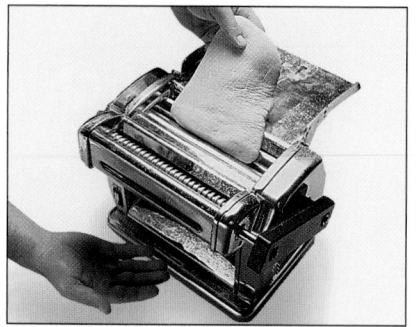

1. Passing the entire piece of dough through the pasta machine.

2. Folding the dough in thirds.

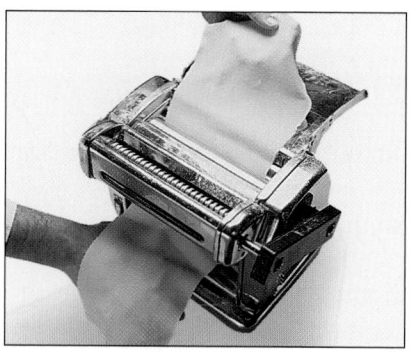

3. Passing the dough through the pasta machine to achieve the desired thickness.

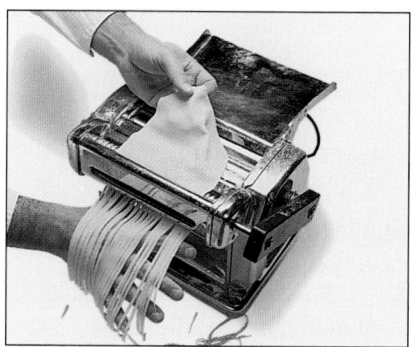

4. Using the pasta machine to cut the pasta into the desired width.

Filling Pasta

Sheets of raw pasta dough can be filled or folded to create ravioli (squares), tortellini (round "hats" with a brim of dough), lunettes (circles of dough folded into half-moons), agnolotti (squares of dough folded into rectangles) and other shapes. The filled pieces of dough are then cooked in boiling water using the procedure for cooking pasta ribbons discussed below. The filling can include almost anything—cheese, herbs, vegetables, fish, shellfish, meat or poultry. It can be uncooked or precooked. But any meat filling should be fully cooked before the pasta is assembled, as the time it takes for the dough to cook may not be sufficient to cook the filling.

Cannelloni is a different type of filled pasta: a large square of cooked dough is wrapped around a meat or cheese filling and baked. Popular lasagna dishes are similar. Lasagna pasta, which consists of wide, flat sheets, are cooked then layered with cheese, tomato sauce and meat or vegetables as desired. The finished casserole is baked and cut into portions.

Some of the larger, commercially prepared pasta shapes such as large shells (conchigloni or rigate) or large tubes (manicotti) can be partially cooked in boiling water, then filled, sauced and baked as a casserole.

Asian noodle dough is also made into filled items such as dumplings, wontons, egg rolls (made with egg noodle dough) and spring rolls (made with rice paper). These items are usually steamed, pan-fried or deep-fried.

When making filled pasta, consider the flavors and textures of the filling, dough and sauce. Each should complement the others. Combinations can range from traditional unflavored semolina pasta with herb and ricotta filling in a tomato sauce to an elegant escargot in garlic-and-herb pasta served with a beurre blanc to pork, ginger, soy and scallions in Asian egg noodle dough served with a soy-based dipping sauce.

PROCEDURE FOR MAKING RAVIOLI

1. Prepare a basic pasta dough of the desired flavor.
2. Prepare and chill the desired filling.
3. Roll out two thin sheets of dough between the rollers of a pasta machine. Gently lay the dough flat on the work surface.
4. Using a piping bag or a small portion scoop, place small mounds of filling on one of the dough pieces. Space the fillings evenly, allowing approximately 2 inches (5 centimeters) between each mound.
5. Brush the exposed areas of dough with water.
6. Gently place the second sheet of dough over the mounds and press firmly around each mound to remove air pockets and seal the dough.
7. Cut between the mounds with a chef's knife, pastry wheel or circular cutter.

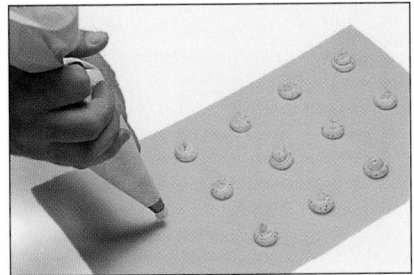
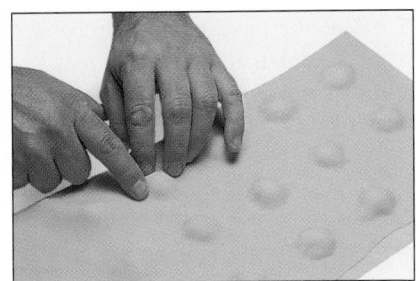

1. Piping the filling onto the dough.

2. Pressing around the mounds of filling to seal the dough and remove any air pockets.

3. Cutting around the mounds with a circular cutter.

Cooking Method

Determining Doneness

Italian-style pastas are properly cooked when they are al dente, firm but tender. Cooking times vary depending on the shape and quantity of pasta, the amount of water used, the hardness of the water and even the altitude. Fresh pasta cooks rapidly, sometimes in seconds. Noodles and dried pasta may require several minutes.

Although package or recipe directions offer some guidance, the only way to accurately test doneness is to bite into a piece. When the pasta is slightly firmer than desired, remove it from the stove and drain. It will continue to cook through residual heat.

Unlike Italian pasta, Asian noodles are not served al dente. Rather, they are either boiled until very soft or stir-fried until very crisp.

Boiling

All Italian-style pasta and most Asian noodles are cooked by just one method: boiling. The secret to boiling pasta successfully is to use ample water. Allow 1 gallon (4 liters) of water for each pound (450 grams) of pasta.

Use a saucepan or stockpot large enough to allow the pasta to move freely in the boiling water, otherwise the starch released by the dough will make the pasta gummy and sticky. The water should be brought to a rapid boil, then all the pasta should be added at once.

Salt should be added to the water. Pasta absorbs water and salt during cooking. Adding salt to the pasta after it is cooked will not provide the same seasoning effect.

Chefs disagree on whether to add oil to the cooking water. Purists argue against adding oil, on the theory that it makes the dough absorb water unevenly. Others think oil should be added to reduce surface foam. Another theory is that oil keeps the pasta from sticking, although this only works when added to cooked, drained pasta.

Asian noodles may be prepared by boiling until fully cooked, or they may be parboiled then stir-fried with other ingredients to finish cooking.

PROCEDURE FOR COOKING PASTA TO ORDER

1. Bring the appropriate amount of water to a boil over high heat.
2. Add oil to the water if desired.
3. Add the pasta and salt to the rapidly boiling water.
4. Stir the pasta to prevent it from sticking together. Bring the water back to a boil and cook until the pasta is done.
5. When the pasta is properly cooked, immediately drain it through a colander. A small amount of oil may be gently tossed into the pasta if desired to prevent it from sticking together.
6. Serve hot pasta immediately, or refresh in cold water for use in salads or other dishes. (Do not rinse pasta that is to be served hot.)

PROCEDURE FOR COOKING DRIED PASTA IN ADVANCE

Fresh pasta is so delicate and cooks so rapidly (sometimes in as little as 15 seconds) that it should be cooked to order. Dried pasta, however, can be cooked in advance for quantity service.

1. Follow the above directions for cooking pasta, but stop the cooking process when the pasta is about two-thirds done.
2. Drain the pasta, rinse it lightly and toss it in a small amount of oil.
3. Divide the pasta into appropriate-sized portions. Individual portions can be wrapped in plastic or laid on a sheet pan and covered. Refrigerate until needed.
4. When needed, place a portion in a china cap and immerse in boiling water to reheat. Drain, add sauce and serve immediately.

Accompaniments to Pasta

Pasta is widely accepted by consumers and easily incorporated in a variety of cuisines—from Italian and Chinese to Thai and spa. It is used in broths; as a bed for stews, fish, shellfish or meat; or tossed with sauce. Today's creative chefs are constantly developing nontraditional but delicious ways of serving pasta.

TABLE 23.6 COMBINING SAUCES, PASTA AND GARNISHES

Sauce	Pasta Shape	Garnish
Ragu	Ribbons, tubes, shapes, filled	Grated cheese
Seafood	Ribbons (fettuccine and capellini)	Fish or shellfish
Vegetable	Ribbons, tubes, filled	Meatballs, sausage, grated cheese
Cream	Thick ribbons (spaghetti and fettuccine), filled	Ham, peas, sausage, mushrooms, smoked salmon, nuts, grated cheese
Garlic-oil	Ribbons, shapes, filled	Grated cheese (if uncooked or cold), herbs
Uncooked	Ribbons, shapes	Cubed or grated cheese, fresh vegetables, herbs

Pasta and Broths

Small shapes can be cooked in the broth with which they are served, or cooked separately, then added to the hot liquid at service time. Soups such as cappelletti in brodo and chicken noodle are examples of these techniques.

Pasta Sauces

There are hundreds of Italian pasta sauces as well as sauces for Italian-style pasta, but most can be divided into six categories: ragus, seafood sauces, vegetable sauces, cream sauces, garlic-oil sauces and uncooked sauces. Recipes for a selection of pasta sauces are included at the end of this chapter.

Although there are no firm rules governing the combinations of sauces and pasta, Table 23.6 offers some of the more common combinations.

◆◆◆

PASTA SAUCES

Ragus are braised dishes used as a sauce. Usually, several flavoring ingredients and meat or poultry are browned, then a liquid and often a tomato product are added. The liquid can be a combination of stock, wine, water, milk or cream.

Seafood sauces can be white or red. White seafood sauces are most often made with white wine or stock and rarely use cream. They are often flavored with herbs. Red seafood sauces are tomato-based. Traditionally, these sauces are not garnished with cheese.

Vegetable sauces often use tomatoes as the base and a stock as the liquid. Mirepoix, garlic and red pepper flakes are commonly used for flavorings. Vegetable sauces include the traditional tomato sauce as well as primavera.

Cream sauces are based on milk or cream and are sometimes thickened with roux. Cheese is often included for flavor and richness.

Garlic-oil sauces (It. *aglio-olio*) consist mainly of garlic and oil; often herbs are added. Garlic-oil sauces can be hot or cold, cooked or uncooked. Pesto is a well-known example of an uncooked, cold garlic-oil sauce.

Uncooked sauces include a variety of dressings such as fresh tomatoes, basil and olive oil; or olive oil, lemon juice, parsley, basil and hot red pepper flakes. Other flavoring ingredients include capers, anchovies, garlic and olives as well as fresh herbs, fresh vegetables, flavored oils and cubed cheeses.

CONCLUSION

Most meals would seem incomplete without a starch. The most popular starches are potatoes, grains (especially rice) and pasta. All are low in fat and a good source of energy. Most can be prepared with several dry- and moist-heat cooking methods. Starches can be sauced, seasoned or flavored in limitless ways.

QUESTIONS FOR DISCUSSION

1. Explain the differences between mealy and waxy potatoes. Give two examples of each.
2. Describe the two methods of sautéing or pan-frying potatoes.
3. Explain why duchesse potatoes are regarded as the "mother" of many classic potato dishes. Name and describe two such dishes.
4. All grains are composed of three parts. Name and describe each of these parts.
5. Describe and compare the three general cooking methods used to prepare grains.
6. Name the three categories of Italian-style pasta shapes and give an example of each.
7. Why is it necessary to use ample water when cooking pasta? Should pasta be cooked in salted water? Should oil be added to the cooking water? Explain your answers.
8. Discuss the differences between cooking fresh pasta and cooking dried, factory-produced pasta.

ADDITIONAL STARCH RECIPES

RECIPE 23.9

VEGETABLE CANNELLONI

NOTE: *This dish appears in the Chapter Opening photograph.*

STOUFFER STANFORD COURT HOTEL, SAN FRANCISCO, CA
Executive Chef Ercolino Crugnale

Yield: 1 Serving

Pasta square of striped beet and saffron fettucine, 5 in. × 5 in. (12.5 cm × 12.5 cm), blanched	1	1
Braised Fennel and Cipolline Onions (recipe follows)	3 oz.	90 g
Thyme-scented Celery Broth (recipe follows)	2 oz.	60 g
Asparagus spears, peeled and blanched	6	6
Black truffles, shaved thin	2 Tbsp.	30 ml

1. Warm the pasta in boiling water; remove and dry.

2. Heat the Braised Fennel and Cipolline Onions and fill one side of the pasta square. Roll up the pasta to form the cannelloni.

3. Place the cannelloni on a dinner plate and ladle the Thyme-scented Celery Broth around it. Garnish with the warm asparagus and truffle shavings.

BRAISED FENNEL AND CIPOLLINE ONIONS

Yield: 3 lb. (1.6 kg)

Whole butter	8 oz.	250 g
Cipolline onions, sliced thin	12 oz.	360 g
Chicken stock	1 pt.	500 ml
Madeira	8 oz.	250 g
Yellow bell peppers, julienne	1 lb.	500 g
Fennel, sliced thin	20 oz.	600 g
Garlic, minced	2 Tbsp.	30 ml
Fresh parsley, chopped	3 Tbsp.	45 ml

1. Heat the butter over medium heat.

2. Add the onions and caramelize well. Deglaze with the chicken stock and add the madeira.

3. Add the peppers, fennel and garlic. Cover and sweat until tender. Add additional stock or Madeira if necessary.

4. Remove from the heat and add the parsley.

5. Spread on a sheet pan and cool.

THYME-SCENTED CELERY BROTH

Yield: 1 qt. (1 lt)

Celery juice	1 qt.	1 lt
Tomato juice	1 pt.	500 ml
Fresh thyme, chopped	1/2 oz.	15 g
Whole butter	6 oz.	180 g
Salt	TT	TT
Tabasco sauce	TT	TT

1. Combine the celery juice, tomato juice and thyme. Bring to simmer and reduce to 1-1/2 pints (750 milliliters).

2. Whisk in the butter and adjust the seasonings with salt and Tabasco sauce.

3. Strain through a chinois.

◆◆◆

RECIPE 23.10

GRILLED POTATO SALAD

GREENS RESTAURANT, SAN FRANCISCO, CA
Executive Chef Annie Somerville

Yield: 4 Servings **Method:** Baking/Grilling

New potatoes	2 lb.	1 kg
Light olive oil	as needed	as needed
Salt and pepper	TT	TT
Cherry tomatoes, sweet one hundreds or pear cherry tomatoes	4 oz.	120 g
Frisée or salad greens (optional)	4 oz.	120 g

Continued

Red and yellow bell peppers, roasted, seeded and cut into strips	1 lb.	500 g
Basil Vinaigrette (recipe follows)		
Champagne vinegar	as needed	as needed
Niçoise or Gaeta olives	12	12

1. Toss the potatoes with the olive oil in a baking dish; sprinkle with a few pinches of salt and pepper.
2. Cover the potatoes and place in a 400°F (200°C) oven. Cook until tender, approximately 35–40 minutes. Set aside to cool.
3. Cut the cooled potatoes in half or quarters if they are large. Thread onto skewers for grilling. (Skewers are not necessary if the grill grating is close together.) Grill the potatoes cut side down until they are golden and crisp with defined grill marks.
4. Cut the tomatoes in half or leave whole if small.
5. Prepare, wash and spin-dry the salad greens.
6. To assemble the salad, slide the grilled potatoes from the skewers and toss with the peppers, cherry tomatoes and vinaigrette. Adjust the seasoning, if necessary, with a splash of champagne vinegar and salt and pepper.
7. Loosely arrange the greens on plates or a platter, spoon the potatoes and other vegetables over the greens and garnish with the olives.

BASIL VINAIGRETTE

Yield: 4 oz. (120 g)

Champagne vinegar	1 oz.	30 g
Extra virgin olive oil	3 oz.	90 g
Fresh basil leaves	1/2 c.	250 ml
Salt	1/2 tsp.	3 ml
Garlic clove, chopped	1	1

1. Combine the ingredients in a blender or food processor until smooth.

RECIPE 23.11

CANDIED SWEET POTATOES

Yield: 6 4-oz. (120-g) Servings   **Method:** Baking

Sweet potatoes	2 lb.	1 kg
Brown sugar	5 oz.	150 g
Water	2 oz.	60 g
Whole butter	2 oz.	60 g
Vanilla extract	1 tsp.	5 ml

1. Wash the sweet potatoes and cut as necessary to promote even cooking.
2. Bake the sweet potatoes on a sheet pan at 350°F (180°C) until cooked but still firm, approximately 30 minutes.
3. Combine the brown sugar, water and butter and bring to a boil. Add the vanilla and remove from the heat.
4. Peel the potatoes and slice or cut as desired. Arrange the potatoes in a baking dish and pour the sugar mixture over them.
5. Sprinkle the potatoes with additional brown sugar if desired and bake for 20 minutes, basting occasionally with the sugar mixture.

◆◆◆

RECIPE 23.12

POTATO PANCAKES

Yield: 12 2-1/2 oz. (75 g) Pancakes   **Method:** Pan-frying

Potatoes, all purpose	2 lb.	1 kg
Eggs, beaten	2	2
Onion, minced	6 oz.	180 g
Flour	2 oz.	60 g
Baking powder	1 Tbsp.	15 ml
Nutmeg	1 tsp.	5 ml
Salt and pepper	TT	TT
Vegetable oil	4 oz.	120 ml

1. Peel and coarsely grate the potatoes.
2. Transfer the grated potatoes to a bowl and add the beaten eggs, onion, flour and baking powder. Season with nutmeg, salt and pepper. Blend well.
3. Heat the oil. Add the potato mixture to the oil in uniform-size pancakes. Pan-fry the pancakes until tender, turning once when well browned on the first side. Remove from the pan and drain well.

◆◆◆

RECIPE 23.13

RÖSTI POTATOES

THE FOUR SEASONS, NEW YORK, NY
Chef Christian Albin

Yield: 6 Servings   **Method:** Pan-frying

Boiling potatoes, large	4	4
Bacon fat	2 oz.	60 g
Lard	2 oz.	60 g
Kosher salt and pepper	TT	TT
Whole butter	1 oz.	30 g

1. Partially cook the potatoes in salted water until almost done.
2. Drain and cool the potatoes, then peel and coarsely grate them.
3. Heat the bacon fat and lard in a heavy, shallow 10-inch (25-cm) skillet with sloping sides until quite hot. Spread half the potatoes over the bottom of the pan; sprinkle with salt and pepper. Cover with the remaining potatoes and cook over medium-high heat until the bottom turns brown and crusty, approximately 10 minutes.
4. Turn the potatoes in one piece. This is easiest to do by placing a large plate over the pan and turning both together so that the potatoes fall onto the plate. Slip the turned-over potatoes off the plate back into the pan, browned side up. Cook until the bottom is browned.
5. Before serving, smooth the edges of the potatoes with a spatula. Sprinkle with salt and brush the edge of the pan with whole butter. It will melt and run into the potatoes.

VARIATION: Cheddar Cheese Rösti Potatoes—Make two thin potatoes cakes. Top one with a layer of 7 ounces (210 grams) sour cream, 2 ounces (60 grams) cubed sharp cheddar cheese and 2 tablespoons (30 milliliters) chopped chives. Top with the other cake. Dot with 1 tablespoon (15 milliliters) whole butter and bake in a 400°F (200°C) oven for 15 minutes.

Cottage fries.

Shoestring potatoes.

French fries.

Steak fries.

◆ ◆ ◆

RECIPE 23.14

COTTAGE FRIES, SHOESTRING POTATOES, FRENCH FRIES, STEAK FRIES

RUTH'S CHRIS STEAK HOUSE, PHOENIX, AZ

Method: Deep-frying

Idaho potatoes, 70 count	as needed
Hot fat	as needed
Parsley, chopped	as needed for garnish

1. Cut each potato into the desired shape:

   Cottage fries—circles 1/4-inch (60-millimeters) thick

   Shoestring potatoes—long juliennes (allumettes)

   French fries—sticks 3/8 inch × 3/8 inch × 3 inches (1 centimeter × 1 centimeter × 7 centimeters)

   Steak fries—four large wedges

2. Deep-fry in 250°F (120°C) fat until lightly brown, approximately 2–3 minutes. Remove and drain.

3. For service, deep-fry the partially cooked potatoes in 350°F (180°C) fat until golden in color and done.

4. Garnish with parsley if desired.

◆ ◆ ◆

RECIPE 23.15

POLENTA

Yield: 1 lb. 12 oz. (800 g)   **Method:** Simmering

Shallots, chopped	2 tsp.	10 ml
Whole butter	as needed	as needed
Milk, white stock or water	2 lb.	950 g
Cornmeal, yellow or white	6 oz.	180 g
Salt and pepper	TT	TT

1. Sauté the shallots in 1 tablespoon (15 milliliters) of butter for 30 seconds. Add the liquid and bring to a boil.

2. Slowly add the cornmeal while stirring constantly to prevent lumps, then simmer for 30 minutes.

3. Scrape the polenta into a buttered nonaluminum dish; spread to an even thickness with a spatula that has been dipped in water. Refrigerate the polenta until well chilled.

4. To serve, unmold the polenta and cut into shapes following the procedure discussed in Chapter 35, Presentation. Sauté or grill the polenta for service, or sprinkle with grated Parmesan cheese and heat under a broiler or salamander.

VARIATIONS: Wild Mushroom Polenta—Sauté 6 ounces (180 grams) cleaned, sliced wild mushrooms such as shiitake, chanterelles or morels in 1 tablespoon (15 milliliters) whole butter with 1 tablespoon (15 milliliters) chopped shallots until dry. Add to the polenta after it has simmered; stir to incorporate.

Wild Rice Polenta—Add 4 ounces (120 grams) cooked wild rice to the polenta after it has simmered; stir to incorporate.

◆◆◆

RECIPE 23.16

GRITS AND CHEDDAR SOUFFLÉ

Yield: 8 Servings | **Method:** Simmering/Baking

Grits	1-1/2 c.	350 ml
Water	1-1/2 pt.	700 ml
Milk	1-1/2 pt.	700 ml
Unsalted butter	4 oz.	120 g
Salt	TT	TT
Sharp cheddar cheese, grated	8 oz.	225 g
Tabasco sauce	1/2 tsp.	2 ml
Eggs, separated	6	6
Sugar	2 tsp.	10 ml

1. Combine the grits, water, milk, butter and salt in a heavy saucepan. Bring to a simmer and cook, stirring constantly, until thick, approximately 5–10 minutes.
2. Remove from the heat and stir in 6 ounces (180 grams) of the cheese and the Tabasco sauce.
3. Whisk the egg yolks together, then stir them into the grits mixture.
4. Whip the egg whites to soft peaks, add the sugar and whip to stiff peaks. Fold the egg whites into the grits mixture.
5. Pour the soufflé into a well-buttered 2-quart casserole or soufflé dish. Top with the remaining 2 ounces (60 grams) of cheese. Bake at 350°F (180°C) until set and browned, approximately 30 minutes. Serve immediately.

◆◆◆

RECIPE 23.17

BROWN RICE PILAF WITH PINE NUTS

Yield: 10 3-oz. (90-g) Servings | **Method:** Pilaf

Saffron threads	1/2 tsp.	2 ml
Chicken stock, hot	1 pt.	500 ml
Sesame oil	1 Tbsp.	15 ml
Vegetable oil	1 Tbsp.	15 ml
Pine nuts	2 oz.	60 g
Onion, medium dice	6 oz.	180 g
Red bell pepper, medium dice	6 oz.	180 g
Garlic, chopped	2 tsp.	10 ml
Brown rice	1 c.	250 ml
Salt	1 tsp.	10 ml
Pepper	TT	TT
Currants, dry	2 oz.	60 ml

1. Steep the saffron threads in the hot stock for 5 minutes.
2. Heat the oils and sauté the pine nuts until lightly browned.
3. Add the onion, red pepper and garlic and sauté without browning.
4. Add the rice and stir to coat the rice with the oil.
5. Add the salt and stock to the rice. Season with pepper, bring to a boil, reduce the heat and cover. Cook on the stove top or in the oven until done, approximately 30 minutes.
6. Stir in the currants, cover and allow them to soften for 5 minutes.

◆◆◆

RECIPE 23.18
WILD RICE AND CRANBERRY STUFFING

Yield: 5 pints (2.5 lt) **Method:** Simmering

Dried morels	1 oz.	30 g
Wild rice	12 oz.	340 g
Onion, minced	8 oz.	225 g
Butter or chicken fat	2 oz.	60 g
Chicken stock, hot	approx. 1 qt.	approx. 1 lt
Dried cranberries	6 oz.	180 g
Salt and pepper	TT	TT
Fresh parsley, chopped fine	4 Tbsp.	60 ml

1. Soak the dried morels overnight in lightly salted water. Drain, reserving the liquid. Rinse well, drain again and chop coarsely.
2. Rinse the wild rice well in cold water.
3. Sauté the onion in the butter or chicken fat until tender. Add the mushrooms and wild rice.
4. Strain the reserved liquid from the mushrooms through several layers of cheesecloth to remove all sand and grit. Add enough chicken stock so that the liquid totals 3 pints (1.5 lt). Add the stock mixture and cranberries to the rice. Cover and simmer until the rice is dry and fluffy, approximately 45 minutes.
5. Season to taste with salt and pepper and stir in the parsley. This rice may be served as a side dish or used for stuffing duck or game hens.

◆◆◆

RECIPE 23.19
TABOULI (BULGUR WHEAT) SALAD

Yield: 15 3-oz. (90-g) Servings

Bulgur	10 oz.	300 g
Onions, brunoise	8 oz.	250 g
Green onions, sliced	2 oz.	60 g
Fresh parsley, chopped	6 oz.	180 g
Fresh mint, chopped	2 oz.	60 g
Olive oil	8 oz.	250 g
Lemon juice	8 oz.	250 g
Tomato, concasse	1 lb.	500 g
Salt and pepper	TT	TT
Pine nuts, toasted	4 oz.	120 g

1. Place the bulgur in a bowl and cover with cold water. Soak the bulgur until tender, approximately 2 hours.
2. Drain the bulgur and squeeze out all of the excess water.
3. Add the onions, green onions, parsley, mint, olive oil and lemon juice. Mix well.
4. Add the tomatoes; mix to combine. Season with salt and pepper.
5. Garnish with the toasted pine nuts.

◆◆◆

RECIPE 23.20
KASHA VARNISHKES
WITH WILD MUSHROOMS

Yield: 4 lb. (1.8 kg)   **Method:** Pilaf

Onion, medium dice	8 oz.	250 g
Kasha	2 c.	450 ml
Chicken fat or clarified butter	4 oz.	120 g
Mushrooms—shiitake, morels, white or		
a combination, sliced	4 oz.	120 g
Garlic, chopped	1 Tbsp.	15 ml
Chicken stock	1 qt.	1 lt
Salt and pepper	TT	TT
Bow tie pasta (farfalle)	10 oz.	300 g

1. Sauté the onions and kasha in 2 ounces (60 grams) of the fat or butter.
2. Add the mushrooms and garlic and stir in the stock. Season with salt and pepper. Bring to a boil, reduce to a simmer and cover. Cook until done, approximately 10–12 minutes.
3. Cook the bow tie pasta; refresh and drain.
4. Sauté the pasta in the remaining fat or butter.
5. Combine the kasha and pasta. Adjust the seasonings and serve.

◆◆◆

RECIPE 23.21
FETTUCCINE CON PESTO
ALLA TRAPANESE

REX IL RISTORANTE, LOS ANGELES, CA
Executive Chef Odette Fada

Yield: 4 8-oz (250-g) Servings

Fresh fettuccine	1 lb.	500 g
Salt	TT	TT
Fresh basil leaves	1/2 oz.	15 g
Garlic cloves, chopped fine	4	4
Bread crumbs	2 Tbsp.	30 ml
Almonds, chopped	1 oz.	30 g
Extra virgin olive oil	approx. 3 oz.	approx. 90 g
Roma tomatoes, peeled, seeded and julienned	8 oz.	250 g

1. Boil the pasta in salted water until almost done.
2. Lightly sauté the basil, garlic, bread crumbs and almonds in the oil.
3. Add the tomatoes and sauté to blend the flavors.
4. Drain the pasta, add it to the pan and sauté for a minute over a low flame.
5. Add more olive oil and salt as needed.

◆◆◆

RECIPE 23.22

GOAT-CHEESE RAVIOLI IN HERBED CREAM SAUCE

Yield: 72 2-in. (5-cm) Ravioli
and 1-1/2 pt. (1.5 lt) Sauce

Fresh goat cheese	11 oz.	330 g
Cream cheese	8 oz.	250 g
Fresh basil, chopped fine	3 Tbsp.	45 ml
Fresh thyme, chopped fine	2 tsp.	10 ml
Fresh parsley, chopped	3 Tbsp.	45 ml
Pepper	TT	TT
Pasta, fresh	2 lb.	1 kg
Heavy cream	1 qt.	1 lt
Parmesan cheese, grated	2 oz.	60 ml
Salt	TT	TT

1. To make the cheese filling, combine the goat and cream cheeses with 2 tablespoons (30 milliliters) basil, 1 teaspoon (5 milliliters) thyme and the parsley; season to taste with pepper.
2. Make ravioli using the cheese mixture and pasta.
3. To make the sauce, combine the cream with the remaining herbs and bring to a boil. Reduce by one third and add the Parmesan cheese. Season with salt and pepper.
4. Boil the ravioli until done. Drain, toss gently with the sauce and serve.

◆◆◆

RECIPE 23.23

FETTUCCINE ALFREDO

Yield: 4 6-oz. (180-g) Servings

Fresh fettuccine	8 oz.	250 g
Whole butter	2 oz.	60 g
Heavy cream	12 oz.	350 g
Parmesan cheese, grated	2 oz.	60 g
Salt and white pepper	TT	TT

1. Boil the pasta, keeping it slightly undercooked. Refresh and drain.
2. To make the sauce, combine the butter, cream and cheese in a sauté pan. Bring to a boil and reduce slightly.
3. Add the pasta to the pan and boil the sauce and pasta until the sauce is thick and the pasta is cooked. Adjust the seasonings and serve.

◆◆◆

RECIPE 23.24

PASTA WITH SHRIMP AND SCALLOPS

Yield: 20 8-oz. (250-g) Servings

Onion, small dice	6 oz.	180 g
Garlic, chopped	1 Tbsp.	15 ml

Olive oil	2 oz.	60 g
Whole butter	2 oz.	60 g
Mushrooms, sliced	8 oz.	250 g
Salt and pepper	TT	TT
White wine	4 oz.	120 g
Tomato, concasse	8 oz.	250 g
Shrimp, peeled and deveined	1 lb.	500 g
Bay scallops	1 lb.	500 g
Mussels or clams, steamed and shucked, including 8 oz. (250 g) of their cooking liquid	2 lb.	1 kg
Fresh parsley, chopped	2 oz.	60 g
Spaghetti	2 lb.	1 kg

1. Sauté the onions and garlic in the oil and butter until tender. Add the mushrooms, season with salt and pepper and sauté.
2. Add the white wine. Boil and reduce by half.
3. Add the tomatoes and simmer for 2 minutes.
4. Add the shrimp and scallops and simmer for 2 minutes.
5. Add the mussels or clams, their cooking liquid and the chopped parsley.
6. Boil the spaghetti. Drain the spaghetti and toss it with the shellfish and sauce, adjust the seasonings and serve.

◆◆◆

RECIPE 23.25

BOLOGNESE SAUCE

Yield: 1 qt. (1 lt)

Mirepoix, fine dice	8 oz.	250 g
Olive oil	2 oz.	60 g
Whole butter	1 oz.	30 g
Ground beef	1 lb.	500 g
White wine	8 oz.	250 g
Milk	6 oz.	180 g
Nutmeg	TT	TT
Tomato, concasse	2 lb.	1 kg
White stock	approx. 8 oz.	approx. 250 g
Salt and pepper	TT	TT

1. Sauté the mirepoix in the olive oil and butter until tender. Add the beef and cook until no pink remains. Drain fat if necessary.
2. Add the wine. Cook and reduce the wine until nearly dry.
3. Add the milk and season with nutmeg. Cook and reduce the milk until nearly dry.
4. Add the tomatoes and 8 ounces. (250 grams) of stock; season with salt and pepper. Simmer for 3–4 hours, adding stock as needed to prevent scorching. Adjust the seasonings.

♦♦♦

RECIPE 23.26
TOMATO VINAIGRETTE

Yield: 4 8-oz. (250-g) Servings

Vinaigrette:

Tomato, concasse	8 oz.	250 g
Fresh basil, thyme or marjoram	1 oz.	30 g
Balsamic vinegar	3 oz.	90 g
Shallots, minced	2 Tbsp.	30 ml
Olive oil	8 oz.	250 g
Salt and pepper	TT	TT
Pasta, cooked	1 lb.	500 g

1. Combine all vinaigrette ingredients. Season to taste with salt and pepper. Set aside for 20–30 minutes to allow the flavors to blend.
2. Toss the sauce with 1 pound (500 grams) warm or cold cooked pasta such as spaghetti or fettuccine. Adjust the seasonings. Serve immediately or refrigerate and serve chilled.

♦♦♦

RECIPE 23.27
PESTO SAUCE

Yield: 1-1/2 pt. (750 ml)

Olive oil	12 oz.	360 g
Pine nuts	3 oz.	90 g
Fresh basil leaves	6 oz.	180 g
Garlic, chopped	1 Tbsp.	15 ml
Parmesan cheese, grated	4 oz.	120 g
Romano cheese, grated	4 oz.	120 g
Salt and pepper	TT	TT

1. Place one third of the olive oil in a blender or food processor and add all the remaining ingredients.
2. Blend or process until smooth. Add the remaining olive oil and blend a few seconds to incorporate.

VARIATION: Walnut Pesto—Substitute walnuts for pine nuts in the above recipe.

♦♦♦

RECIPE 23.28
CAPPELLETTI IN BRODO

Yield: 10 1-pt. (450-ml) Servings
with 12 cappelletti each

Filling:

Pork loin, roasted	6 oz.	180 g
Mortadella	4 oz.	120 g
Ricotta cheese	6 oz.	180 g
Parmesan cheese, finely grated	6 oz.	180 g
Egg	1	1
Nutmeg	TT	TT

Basic Pasta Dough (Recipe 23.8)	1 lb. 8 oz.	750 g
Beef Broth (Recipe 11.1)	5 qt.	5 lt
Parmesan cheese, shredded	8 oz.	250 g
Fresh parsley, chopped fine	3 Tbsp.	45 ml

1. To prepare the cappelletti filling, place the meats and cheeses in a food processor fitted with the metal blade. Process until finely ground. Add the egg and season lightly with nutmeg. Process until blended but not smoothly puréed.

2. Work with one quarter of the pasta dough at a time, keeping the rest covered to prevent it from drying out. Roll out a portion of the dough until it is very thin. Cut the dough into 2-inch (5-cm) squares using a fluted pasta wheel.

3. Place 1 teaspoon (5 milliliters) of filling in the center of each square. Fold the dough over the filling to form a rectangle, pinching the edges together to seal. Bring the ends of each rectangle together, overlapping them and pressing to seal.

4. Place the finished cappelletti on a paper-lined sheet pan. Leave them uncovered and turn them over once or twice so that they dry evenly. Continue working until all of the filling is used. The cappelletti may be cooked immediately or refrigerated for later use.

5. Heat the beef broth to a gentle boil. Drop the cappelletti in and cook until tender, approximately 3–5 minutes.

6. Portion the broth and cappelletti into warmed soup bowls and garnish with the shredded Parmesan and parsley.

◆◆◆

RECIPE 23.29
SOBA NOODLES IN BROTH

Yield: 6 1-pt. (450-ml) Servings

Soba noodles	1 lb.	500 g
Dashi* or chicken broth	1-1/2 qt.	1-1/2 lt
Soy sauce	3 Tbsp.	45 ml
Mirin	1 Tbsp.	15 ml
Sugar	1 Tbsp.	15 ml
Green onions, chopped	4 Tbsp.	60 ml
White sesame seeds	1 Tbsp.	15 ml

1. Boil the noodles in salted water until tender. Drain, rinse in hot water and rinse again. Set aside.

2. Heat the dashi or chicken broth with the soy sauce, mirin and sugar. Add the noodles to the hot broth, simmering just until thoroughly reheated.

3. Portion into warmed bowls and top with the green onions and sesame seeds.

*Dashi is a stock made with dried bonito flakes and dried kelp. It is used extensively in Japanese cuisine and is available as an instant powder or a concentrate.

◆◆◆

RECIPE 23.30

MACARONI AND CHEESE

Yield: 24 8-oz. (250-g) Servings

Cheese sauce (page 205)	2 qt.	2 lt
Worcestershire sauce	TT	TT
Tabasco sauce	TT	TT
Elbow macaroni, boiled and refreshed	2 lb.	1 kg
Cheddar cheese	2 lb.	1 kg
Bread crumbs	8 oz.	250 g
Whole butter	1 oz.	30 g

1. Season the cheese sauce with Worcestershire and Tabasco.
2. Mix the macaroni with the cheese sauce and the cheese.
3. Pour into a buttered full-size hotel pan. Sprinkle with bread crumbs.
4. Bake uncovered at 350°F (180°C) until hot, approximately 30 minutes.

VARIATIONS: Macaroni and cheese with ham and tomato—Stir 2 pounds (1 kilogram) each diced cooked ham and tomato concasse into the macaroni and cheese before pouring it into the hotel pan.

◆◆◆

RECIPE 23.31

BAKED ZITI WITH FRESH TOMATO SAUCE

Yield: 30 Servings

Eggs	6	6
Ricotta cheese	4 lb.	1.8 kg
Fresh thyme	2 Tbsp.	30 ml
Fresh oregano	2 Tbsp.	30 ml
Fresh basil	2 Tbsp.	30 ml
Salt and pepper	TT	TT
Italian sausage links	3 lb.	1.4 kg
Ziti, cooked, refreshed and drained	4 lb.	1.8 kg
Parmesan cheese, grated	8 oz.	250 g
Fresh Tomato Sauce (Recipe 10.23)	3 qt.	3 lt
Mozzarella cheese, shredded	2 lb.	1 kg

1. Combine the eggs, ricotta cheese, thyme, oregano, basil, salt and pepper. Mix well and reserve.
2. Place the sausage links in a 2-inch-deep (5-centimeter) full-sized hotel pan; cook in a 350°F (180°C) oven for 20 minutes. Remove and cool. Drain the sausage. Slice the links into rounds and reserve.
3. Place the ziti in the hotel pan that was used to cook the sausage. Top with an even coating of the cheese mixture, sausage slices and Parmesan cheese.
4. Pour the tomato sauce over the top layer and stir slightly to distribute the sauce.
5. Bake at 375°F (190°C) for 1 hour. Sprinkle the mozzarella evenly over the pasta and return to the oven for 10 minutes. Serve.
6. Ziti may also be prepared in individual casseroles. Decrease baking time as necessary.

RECIPE 23.32

Spinach and Ricotta Lasagna with Bolognese Sauce

Yield: 28 8-oz. (250-g) Servings

Fresh spinach pasta dough, rolled into sheets	2 lb.	1 kg
Spinach, stemmed	2 lb.	1 kg
Whole butter	2 oz.	60 g
Ricotta cheese	1 lb.	500 g
Parmesan cheese, grated	6 oz.	180 g
Eggs	2	2
Salt and pepper	TT	TT
Bolognese sauce (Recipe 23.25)	3 qt.	3 lt
Béchamel sauce (Recipe 10.7)	1 qt.	1 lt

1. Cut the pasta dough into 4-inch (10-centimeter) strips. Boil in salted water until done and drain well.

2. Sauté the spinach in the butter. Drain well and cool.

3. Combine the spinach with the ricotta cheese, 4 ounces (120 grams) of the Parmesan cheese and eggs. Season to taste with salt and pepper.

4. Ladle a small amount of the Bolognese sauce in to the bottom of a standard full-size hotel pan. Cover the sauce with a layer of cooked pasta. Spread a thin layer of the spinach-and-cheese mixture on the pasta. Ladle a portion of the Béchamel sauce over the spinach and spread in a thin even layer. Ladle a portion of the Bolognese sauce over the Béchamel sauce and spread in an even layer.

5. Add another layer of pasta and repeat the process until all of the ingredients are used, finishing with a layer of Béchamel sauce. Sprinkle the remaining Parmesan cheese on top and bake covered at 350°F (180°C) until heated through, approximately 40 minutes. Uncover the lasagna for the last 15 minutes so it browns.

RECIPE 23.33

Chilled Chinese Noodle Salad

Yield: 8 4-oz. (120-g) Servings

Dressing:		
Dark soy sauce	2 Tbsp.	30 ml
White vinegar	2 Tbsp.	30 ml
Salt	1 tsp.	5 ml
Sugar	1 Tbsp.	15 ml
Peanut oil	1 Tbsp.	15 ml
Sesame oil	1 Tbsp.	15 ml
Orange zest	1 tsp.	5 ml
Red chile flakes	1/2 tsp.	2 ml
Chinese egg noodles, fresh	8 oz.	250 g
Bean sprouts, blanched	8 oz.	250 g

Continued

Carrot, finely shredded	6 oz.	180 g
Daikon, finely shredded	3 oz.	90 g
Green onion, sliced	2 oz.	60 g
Black sesame seeds	1 Tbsp.	15 ml
Fresh cilantro leaves	as needed	as needed

1. Combine the dressing ingredients and whisk thoroughly.
2. Cook the egg noodles in rapidly boiling salted water until tender, approximately 2 minutes. Drain and refresh; drain again.
3. Toss the noodles with the bean sprouts, carrots, daikon, green onion and sesame seeds. Add the dressing and toss gently until the noodles and vegetables are thoroughly coated.
4. Chill well. Serve mounds of this noodle salad as an appetizer or an accompaniment for grilled fish or chicken. Garnish with cilantro.

◆◆◆

RECIPE 23.34
GNOCCHI

Yield: 2 lb. 4 oz. (1 kg)

Milk	1 qt.	1 lt
Whole butter	2 oz.	60 g
Salt	2 tsp.	10 ml
Semolina	5 oz.	150 g
Egg yolks	2	2
Parmesan cheese, grated	approx. 6 oz.	approx. 180 g

1. Combine the milk, butter and salt and bring to a boil.
2. Add the semolina in a steady stream while stirring constantly.
3. Cook the mixture over low heat for 15 minutes. The mixture will be thick—be careful not to scorch it.
4. Remove the mixture from the heat and stir in the egg yolks and 4 ounces. (120 grams) of Parmesan cheese.
5. Form the mixture into quenelles, using two spoons, and arrange them in a buttered baking dish. Alternatively, spread the mixture in a pan with a spatula to the thickness of 1/2 inch (12 millimeters) and refrigerate until firm. Cut the desired shapes from the mixture and place them in a buttered baking dish.
6. Sprinkle the gnocchi with Parmesan cheese and place under the salamander or broiler or bake in a hot oven until hot and lightly browned on top.

◆◆◆

RECIPE 23.35
SPAETZLE

Yield: 30 3-oz. (90-g) Servings

Eggs	12	12
Water	1 qt.	1 lt
Flour	3 lb.	1.4 kg
Salt	2 tsp.	10 ml
Nutmeg	1/2 tsp.	2 ml

Whole butter	8 oz.	250 g
Fresh parsley, chopped	as needed	as needed

1. Whisk the eggs to blend. Add the water, flour, salt and nutmeg. Mix until well blended; do not overmix.

2. Place the batter in a colander suspended over a large pot of boiling water. Work the batter through the colander's holes using a plastic bowl scraper or rubber spatula. The batter should drop into the boiling water.

3. Cook the dumplings in the boiling water for approximately 3–4 minutes. Remove them with a skimmer and refresh.

4. For service, sauté the dumplings lightly in butter, just until hot. Garnish with chopped parsley.

CHAPTER 24

SALADS AND SALAD DRESSINGS

After studying this chapter you will be able to:

◆ identify a variety of salad greens
◆ prepare a variety of salad dressings
◆ prepare a variety of salads
◆ present salads attractively

*T*his chapter discusses all types of salads: the small plate of crisp iceberg lettuce with tomato wedges, cucumber slices and ranch dressing; the dinner plate of sautéed duck breast fanned across bright red grilled radicchio and toothy green arugula, sprayed with a vinaigrette dressing; the scoop of shredded chicken, mango chutney and seasonings, bound with mayonnaise; and the bowl of artichokes and mushrooms marinated in olive oil and lemon juice.

Each of these dishes fits the definition of a salad: a single food or a mix of different foods accompanied or bound by a dressing. A salad can contain meat, grains, fruits, nuts or cheese and absolutely no lettuce. It can be an appetizer, a second course served after the appetizer, an entree (especially at lunch) a course following the entree in the European manner or even dessert.

The color, texture and flavor of each salad ingredient should complement those of the others, and the dressing should complement all of the ingredients. Harmony is critical to a salad's success—no matter what type of salad is being prepared.

This chapter opens with a section identifying greens commonly used in salads. A discussion of salad dressings follows. Finally, techniques for preparing green salads (both tossed and composed), bound salads, vegetable salads and fruit salads are discussed.

SALAD GREENS

Identifying Salad Greens

Salad greens are not necessarily green: Some are red, yellow, white or brown. They are all, however, leafy vegetables. Many are members of the lettuce or chicory families.

Lettuce

Lettuce (Fr. *laitue*; It. *lattuga*) has been consumed for nearly as long as people have kept records of what they and others ate. Archaeologists found that Persian royalty were served lettuce at their banquets more than 2500 years ago. Now grown and served worldwide, lettuces are members of the genus *Lactuca*. The most common types of lettuce are butterhead, crisp head, leaf and romaine.

Boston

Boston and bibb are two of the most popular butterhead lettuces. Their soft, pliable, pale green leaves have a buttery texture and flavor. Boston is larger and paler than bibb. Both Boston and bibb lettuce leaves form cups when separated from the heads; these cups make convenient bases for holding other foods on cold plates.

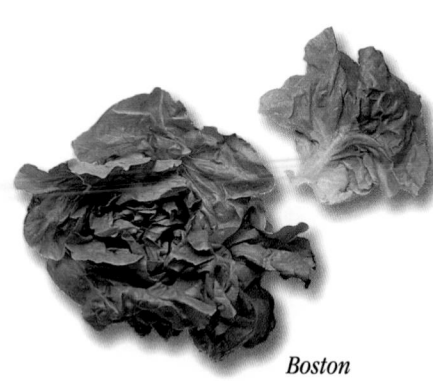

Boston

Iceberg

Iceberg

Iceberg lettuce is the most common of all lettuce varieties in the United States; it outsells all other varieties combined. Its tightly packed spherical head is comprised of crisp, pale green leaves with a very mild flavor. Iceberg lettuce remains crisp for a relatively long period of time after being cut or prepared. Select heads that are firm but not hard and leaves that are free of burnt or rusty tips.

Leaf

Leaf lettuce grows in bunches. It has separate, ruffle-edged leaves branching from a stalk. Because it does not grow into a firm head, it is easily damaged during harvest and transport. Both red and green leaf lettuce have bright colors, mild flavors and tender leaves. Good-quality leaf lettuce should have nicely shaped leaves free of bruises, breaks or brown spots.

Red and Green Leaf Lettuces

Romaine

Romaine lettuce, also known as cos, is a loosely packed head lettuce with elongated leaves and thick midribs. Its outer leaves are dark green and although they look coarse, they are crisp, tender and tasty without being bitter. The core leaves are paler and more tender but still crisp. Romaine has enough flavor to stand up to strongly flavored dressings such as the garlic and Parmesan cheese used in a Caesar salad. A good-quality head of romaine has dark green outer leaves that are free of blemishes or yellowing.

Baby Lettuces

Innovative chefs are always looking for new and different foods to add a twist or flair to their dishes. This has led to the popularity of baby lettuces and other specialty greens. Baby greens have similar but more subtle flavors than their mature versions. They are often less bitter and are always more tender and delicate. Because of their size and variety, they are perfect for composed salads. **Mesclun** is a mixture of several kinds of baby lettuce.

Romaine

Brune d'Hiver

Lola Rosa

Red Sails

Baby Green Bibb

Baby Red Bibb

Baby Red Oak Leaf

Pirate

Baby Red Romaine

Belgian Endive

Curly Endive

Escarole

Radicchio

Arugula

Dandelion

Chicory

Chicories come in a variety of colors, shapes and sizes; most are slightly bitter. Chicories are quite hearty and can also be cooked, usually grilled or braised.

Belgian Endive

Belgian endive grows in small, tight heads with pointed leaves. It is actually the shoot of a chicory root. The small sturdy leaves are white at the base with yellow fringes and tips. (A purple-tipped variety is sometimes available.) Whole leaves can be separated, trimmed and filled with soft butters, cheeses or spreads and served as an hors d'oeuvre. Or they can be used for composed salads. The leaves, cut or whole, can also be added to cold salads. Heads of Belgian endive are often braised or grilled and served with meat or poultry. As the name suggests, Belgian endive is imported from Belgium.

Curly Endive

In this country, curly endive is often called by its family name, chicory, or its French name, frisée. The dark green outer leaves are pointed, sturdy and slightly bitter. The yellow inner leaves are more tender and less bitter. Curly endive has a strong flavor that goes well with strong cheeses, game and citrus. It is often mixed with other greens to add texture and flavor.

Escarole

Escarole, sometimes called broadleaf endive, has thick leaves and a slightly bitter flavor. It has green outer leaves and pale green or yellow center leaves. Escarole is very sturdy and is often mixed with other greens for added texture. Its strong flavor stands up to full-flavored dressings and is a good accompaniment to grilled meats and poultry.

Radicchio

Radicchio resembles a small red cabbage. It retains its bright reddish color when cooked and is popular braised or grilled and served as a vegetable side dish. Because of its attractive color, radicchio is popular in cold salads, but it has a very bitter flavor and should be used sparingly and mixed with other greens in a tossed salad. The leaves form cups when separated and can be used to hold other ingredients when preparing composed salads. Radicchio is quite expensive and availability is sometimes limited.

Other Salad Greens and Ingredients

Leafy vegetables besides lettuce and chicory, as well as other ingredients, are used to add texture, flavor and color to salads. A partial listing follows.

Arugula

Arugula, also known as rocket, is a member of the cabbage family. Available as individual leaves, they are similar to dandelion leaves in size and shape. The best are 2 to 4 inches (5 to 10 centimeters) long. Arugula has a very strong, spicy, peppery flavor—so strong, in fact, that it is rarely served by itself. It is best when used to add zip to salads by combining it with other greens.

Dandelion

Dandelion grows as a weed throughout most of the United States. It has long, thin, toothed leaves with a prominent midrib. When purchasing dandelion for salads, look for small leaves. They are more tender and less bitter. Older, tougher leaves can be cooked and served as a vegetable.

Mâche

Mâche or lamb's lettuce is very tender and very delicately flavored. Its small, cuplike pale to dark green leaves have a slightly nutty flavor. Because its flavor is so delicate, mâche should only be combined with other delicately flavored greens such as Boston or bibb lettuce and dressed sparingly with a light vinaigrette dressing.

Mâche

Sorrel

Sorrel, sometimes called sourgrass, has leaves similar to spinach in color and shape. Sorrel has a very tart, lemony flavor that goes well with fish and shellfish. It should be used sparingly and combined with other greens in a salad. Sorrel can also be made into soups, sauces and purées.

Sorrel

Spinach

Like sorrel, spinach can be cooked or used as a salad green. As a salad green, it is popularly served wilted and tossed with a hot bacon dressing. Spinach is deep green with a rich flavor and tender texture. Good-quality spinach should be fairly crisp. Avoid wilted or yellowed bunches.

Sprouts

Sprouts are not salad greens but are often used as such in salads and sandwiches. Sprouts are very young alfalfa, daikon or mustard plants. Alfalfa sprouts are very mild and sweet. Daikon and mustard sprouts are quite peppery.

Spinach

Sprouts

Watercress

Watercress has tiny, dime-sized leaves and substantial stems. It has a peppery flavor and adds spice to a salad. Good-quality fresh watercress is dark green with no yellowing. To preserve its freshness, watercress must be kept very cold and moist. It is normally packed topped with ice. Individual leaves are plucked from the stems and rinsed just before service.

Watercress

Edible Flowers

Many specialty produce growers offer edible, pesticide-free blossoms. They are used for salads and as garnishes wherever a splash of color would be appreciated. Some flowers such as nasturtiums, calendulas and pansies are grown and picked specifically for eating. Others, such as yellow cucumber flowers and squash blossoms, are byproducts of the vegetable industry.

Nasturtiums

Calendulas

Squash blossoms and other very large flowers should be cut in julienne strips before being added to salads. Pick petals from large and medium-sized flowers. Smaller whole flowers can be tossed in a salad or used as a garnish when composing a salad. Very small flowers or petals can be sprinkled on top of a salad so they are not hidden by the greens.

Pansies

Fresh Herbs

Basil, thyme, tarragon, oregano, dill, cilantro, marjoram, mint, sage, savory and even rosemary are used to add interesting flavors to otherwise ordinary salads. Because many herbs have strong flavors, use them sparingly so the delicate flavors of the greens are not overpowered. Leafy herbs such as basil and sage can be cut chiffonade. Other herbs can be picked into sprigs or chopped before being tossed with the salad greens. Flowering herbs such as chive blos-

> ♦♦♦
> #### FLOWER SAFETY
>
> Many flowers and blossoms are toxic, especially those grown from bulbs. Even flowers that would otherwise be edible may contain pesticides that can be harmful if ingested. Use only flowers grown specifically for use as food; purchase edible flowers only from reputable purveyors.

TABLE 24.1   NUTRITIONAL VALUES OF SELECTED SALAD GREENS AND DRESSINGS

Salad greens per 4-oz. (112-g) serving, trimmed; Salad dressings per 1-oz. (28-g) serving	Kcal	Protein (g)	Carbohydrates (g)	Fiber (g)	Total Fat (g)	Vitamin A (I.U.)	Vitamin C (mg)	Calcium (mg)	Iron (mg)
Belgian endive	20	1.6	3.6	1.2	0.4	2052	8	52	0.8
Boston lettuce	16	1.6	2.8	1.2	0.4	816	6.7	mq	0.2
Chicory greens	28	2	5.2	0.8	0.4	14,400	88	360	3.2
Dandelion greens	52	3.2	10.4	2	0.8	mq	mq	mq	mq
Iceberg lettuce	16	1.2	2.4	1.2	0.4	383	5.8	23	0.6
Romaine lettuce	20	2	2.8	2	0.4	2912	28	40	1.2
Blue cheese dressing	143	1.4	2.1	<0.1	14.8	32	<1	12	tr
Mayonnaise	110	0.3	6.8	0	9.5	32	0	2	tr
Vinaigrette	67	<0.1	2.3	mq	6.5	0	0	0	0

The Corinne T. Netzer Encyclopedia of Food Values 1992

mq = measurable quantity, but data is unavailable   tr = trace amounts

soms are used like other edible flowers to add color, flavor and aroma. Refer to Chapter 7, Kitchen Staples, for more information on herbs.

Nutrition

Salad greens are an especially healthful food. Greens contain virtually no fat and few calories and are high in vitamins A and C, iron and fiber. But when garnished with meat and cheese and tossed with a dressing (many of which are oil-based), fat and calories are added. In an attempt to maintain the healthful nature of greens, low-fat or fat-free dressings should be available to customers.

Purchasing and Storing Salad Greens

Purchasing

Lettuces are grown in nearly every part of the United States; nearly all types are available year-round. Principal salad greens such as spinach are available all year; many of the specialty greens are seasonal.

Lettuce is generally packed in cases of 24 heads with varying weights. Other salad greens are packed in trays or boxes of various sizes and weights.

Because salad greens are simply washed and eaten, it is extremely important that they be as fresh and blemish-free as possible. Try to purchase salad greens daily. All greens should be fresh-looking, with no yellowing. Heads should be heavy, with little or no damage to the outer leaves.

Many types of salad greens are available precut and prewashed. These greens are often vacuum-packed to increase shelf life, although delicate greens are sometimes loosely packaged in 5–10-pound (2–5-kilo) boxes. Precut and prewashed greens are relatively expensive, but can reduce labor costs dramatically.

Storing

Although some types of salad greens are hearty enough to keep for a week or more under proper conditions, all salad greens are highly perishable.

Generally, softer-leaved varieties such as Boston and bibb tend to perish more quickly than the crisper-leaved varieties such as iceberg and romaine.

Greens should be stored in their original protective cartons in a specifically designated refrigerator. Ideally, greens should be stored at temperatures between 34° and 38°F (1–3°C) (most other vegetables should be stored at warmer temperatures of 40–50°F [4–10°C]). Greens should not be stored with tomatoes, apples or other fruits that emit ethylene gas, which causes greens to wilt and accelerates spoilage.

Do not wash greens until you need them, as excess water causes them to deteriorate quickly.

Preparing Salad Greens

Unless salad greens are purchased precut and prewashed, they will need to undergo some preparation before service, principally tearing, cutting, washing and drying.

Tearing and Cutting

Some chefs want all salad greens torn by hand. Delicate greens such as butterhead and baby lettuces look nicer and it is less likely they will be bruised if hand-torn. But often it is not practical to hand-tear all greens. It is perfectly acceptable to cut hardy greens with a knife.

PROCEDURE FOR CUTTING ROMAINE LETTUCE

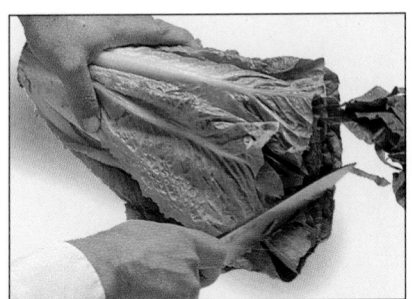

1. To cut romaine lettuce, trim the outer leaves and damaged tips with a chef's knife and split the head lengthwise.

2. Make one or two cuts along the length of the head, leaving the root intact, then cut across the width of the head.

Alternative method:

1A. Trim the outer leaves and damaged tips with a chef's knife. Pull the leaves from the core and cut the rib out of each leaf. The leaf can then be cut to the desired size.

PROCEDURE FOR CORING ICEBERG LETTUCE

1. Loosen the core by gripping the head and smacking the core on the cutting board. (Do not use too much force or you may bruise the lettuce.)

2. Remove the core and cut the lettuce as desired.

PROCEDURE FOR REMOVING THE MIDRIB FROM SPINACH

1. Fold the leaf in half and pull off the stem and midrib. Only the tender leaf should remain.

Washing

All lettuce and other salad greens should be washed before use. Even though they may look clean, greens may harbor hidden insects, sand, soil and pesticides. All greens should be washed after they are torn or cut. Whole heads can be washed by repeatedly dipping them in cold water and allowing them to drain. But washing whole heads is not recommended: It will not remove anything trapped near the head's center, and water trapped in the leaves can accelerate spoilage.

PROCEDURE FOR WASHING SALAD GREENS

1. Fill a sink with very cold water. Place the cut or torn greens in the water.

2. Gently stir the water and greens with your hands and remove the greens. Do not allow the greens to soak. Using fresh water each time, repeat the procedure until no grit can be detected on the bottom of the sink after the greens are removed.

Drying

Salad greens should be dried after washing. Wet greens do not stay as crisp as thoroughly dried ones. Also, wet greens tend to repel oil-based dressings and dilute their flavors. Greens may be dried by draining them well in a colander and blotting them with absorbent cloth or paper towels, or, preferably, they can be dried in a salad spinner, which uses centrifugal force to remove the water.

PROCEDURE FOR DRYING GREENS

1. After washing the greens, place them in the basket of a salad spinner and spin for approximately 30 seconds.

SALAD DRESSINGS

A dressing is a sauce for a salad. Just as sauces for hot foods should complement rather than mask the flavor of the principal food, the sauce (dressing) for a salad should complement rather than mask the flavors of the other ingredients. Although a great many ingredients can be used to make salad dressings, most are based on either a mixture of oil and vinegar, called a vinaigrette, or a mayonnaise or other emulsified product.

♦♦♦

RECIPE 24.30

NEW POTATO SALAD
WITH MUSTARD AND DILL

Yield: 5 lb. (2.2 kg)

New potatoes	4 lb.	1.8 kg
Mayonnaise	4 oz.	120 g
Sour cream	4 oz.	120 g
Garlic, chopped	1-1/2 tsp.	7 ml
Salt	TT	TT
Black pepper	1-1/2 tsp.	7 ml
Fresh dill, chopped	2 Tbsp.	30 ml
Dijon-style mustard	2 Tbsp.	30 ml
Green bell pepper, julienne	1	1
Red bell pepper, julienne	1	1
Red onion, julienne	6 oz.	180 g
Celery, julienne	4 oz.	120 g

1. Boil the potatoes in salted water until done but still firm. Chill well and cut into quarters.
2. Combine the mayonnaise, sour cream, garlic, salt, pepper, dill and Dijon-style mustard; mix well.
3. Combine all ingredients and adjust the seasonings with salt and pepper.

♦♦♦

RECIPE 24.31

POTATO SALAD

Yield: 6 lb. 8 oz. (3 kg)

Potatoes, chef	4 lb.	1.8 kg
Eggs, hard-cooked	6	6
Celery, medium dice	8 oz.	250 g
Green onions, sliced	1 bunch	1 bunch
Radishes, chopped coarse	6 oz.	180 g
Mayonnaise	1 lb.	450 g
Dijon-style mustard	2 oz.	60 g
Fresh parsley, chopped	1 oz.	30 g
Salt and pepper	TT	TT

1. Boil the potatoes in salted water until nearly cooked. Drain the potatoes, spread them on a sheet pan and refrigerate until cold.
2. Peel and cut the cold potatoes into large dice.
3. Peel and chop the eggs.
4. Combine all ingredients and adjust the seasonings with salt and pepper.

RECIPE 24.32

CREAMY COLESLAW

NOTE: This dish appears in the Pork Chapter Opening photograph.

Yield: 2 lb. (1 kg)

Mayonnaise	8 oz.	250 g
Sour cream or crème fraîche	4 oz.	120 g
Sugar	1 oz.	30 g
Cider vinegar	1 oz.	30 g
Garlic clove, minced	1	1
Green cabbage, shredded	1 lb.	450 g
Red cabbage, shredded	8 oz.	250 g
Carrot, shredded	4 oz.	120 g
Salt and white pepper	TT	TT

1. Combine the mayonnaise, sour cream or crème fraîche, sugar, vinegar and garlic in a bowl; whisk together.

2. Add the shredded cabbages and carrots to the dressing and mix well. Season to taste with salt and pepper.

RECIPE 24.33

COUSCOUS SALAD

Yield: 3 lb. (1.4 kg)

Couscous	6 oz.	180 g
Red bell pepper, medium dice	1	1
Green bell pepper, medium dice	1	1
Green onions, sliced on the bias	1 bunch	1 bunch
Cucumbers, peeled, seeded, medium dice	6 oz.	180 g
Black olives, pitted	4 oz.	120 g
Red onion, julienne	6 oz.	180 g
Dressing:		
Orange juice concentrate	3 oz.	90 g
Water	2 oz.	60 g
Rice vinegar	2 oz.	60 g
Garlic, chopped	1 tsp.	5 ml
Salt	1 tsp.	5 ml
Pepper	1 tsp.	5 ml
Fresh oregano, chopped	2 tsp.	10 ml
Salad oil	3 oz.	90 ml
Honey	1 oz.	30 g
Fresh thyme, chopped	2 tsp.	10 ml

1. Steam the couscous until tender; set aside to cool.

2. Combine the couscous with the vegetables.

3. Whisk together all dressing ingredients.

4. Combine the salad ingredients with the dressing. Chill thoroughly before serving.

CHAPTER 25
FRUITS

*B*otanically, a fruit is an organ that develops from the ovary of a flowering plant and contains one or more seeds. Culinarily, a fruit is the perfect snack food; the basis of a dessert, colorful sauce or soup; or an accompaniment to meat, fish, shellfish or poultry. No food group offers a greater variety of colors, flavors and textures than fruit.

This chapter identifies many of the fruits typically used by food service operations. It then addresses general considerations in purchasing fresh and preserved fruits. A discussion follows about some of the cooking methods presented in Chapter 9, Principles of Cooking, as they apply to fruits. Recipes in which a fruit is the primary ingredient are presented at the chapter's end.

IDENTIFYING FRUITS

This book presents fruits according to the ways most people view them and use them, rather than by rigid botanical classifications. Fruits are divided here into eight categories: berries, citrus, exotics, grapes, melons, pomes, stone fruits and tropicals, according to either their shape, seed structure or natural habitat. Botanically, tomatoes, beans, eggplant, capsicum peppers and other produce are fruits. But in ordinary thinking they are not; they are vegetables and are discussed in Chapter 22, Vegetables.

A fruit may have several names, varying from region to region or on a purveyor's whim. Botanists are also constantly reclassifying items to fit new findings. The names given here follow generally accepted custom and usage.

Berries

Berries are small, juicy fruits that grow on vines and bushes worldwide. Berries are characterized by thin skins and many tiny seeds that are often so small they go unnoticed. Some of the fruits classified here as berries do not fit the botanical definition (for example, raspberries and strawberries), while fruits that are berries botanically (for example, bananas and grapes) are classified elsewhere.

Berries may be eaten plain or used in everything from beer to bread, soup to sorbet. They make especially fine jams and compotes.

Berries must be fully **ripened** on the vine, as they will not ripen further after harvesting. Select berries that are plump and fully colored. Avoid juice-stained containers and berries with whitish-gray or black spots of mold. All berries should be refrigerated and used promptly. Do not wash berries until you are ready to use them, as washing removes some of their aroma and softens them.

Blackberries

Blackberries are similar to raspberries, but are larger and shinier, with a deep purple to black color. Thorny blackberry vines are readily found in the wild; commercial production is limited. Peak season is mid-June through August. Loganberries, ollalie berries and boysenberries are blackberry hybrids.

Ripe — *fully grown and developed; the fruit's flavor, texture and appearance are at their peak and the fruit is ready to use as food.*

Blackberries

Blueberries

Blueberries (Fr. *myrtilles*) are small and firm, with a true blue to almost black skin and a juicy, light gray-blue interior. Cultivated berries (high-bush varieties) tend to be larger than wild (low-bush) ones. Blueberries are native to North America and are grown commercially from Maine to Oregon and along the Atlantic seaboard. Peak season is short, from mid-June to mid-August.

Blueberries

Cranberries

Cranberries, another native North American food, are tart, firm fruit with a mottled red skin. They grow on low vines in cultivated bogs (swamps) throughout Massachusetts, Wisconsin and New Jersey. Rarely eaten raw, they are made into sauce or relish or are used in breads, pies or pastries. Cranberries are readily available frozen or made into a jelly-type sauce and canned. Although color does not indicate ripeness, cranberries should be picked over before cooking to remove those that are soft or bruised. Peak harvesting season is from Labor Day through October, leading to the association of cranberries with Thanksgiving dinner.

Cranberries

Currants

Currants are tiny, tart fruits that grow on shrubs in grapelike clusters. The most common are a beautiful, almost translucent red, but black and golden (or white) varieties also exist. All varieties are used for jams, jellies and sauces, and black currants are made into a liqueur, crème de cassis. Although rarely grown in the United States, currants are very popular and widely available in Europe, with a peak season during the late summer. (The dried fruits called currants are not produced from these berries; they are a special variety of dried grapes.)

White Currants

Red Currants

Raspberries

Raspberries (Fr. *framboises*) are perhaps the most delicate of all fruits. They have a tart flavor and velvety texture. Red raspberries are the most common, with black, purple and golden berries available in some markets. When ripe, the berry pulls away easily from its white core, leaving the characteristic hollow center. Because they can be easily crushed and are susceptible to mold, most of the raspberries grown are marketed frozen. They grow on thorny vines in cool climates from Washington State to western New York and are imported from New Zealand and South America. The peak domestic season is from late May through November.

Raspberries

Strawberries

Strawberries (Fr. *fraises*) are brilliant red, heart-shaped fruits that grow on vines. Actually a perennial herb, the berry's flesh is covered by tiny black seeds called achenes, which are the plant's true fruits. Select berries with a good red color and intact green leafy hull. (The hulls can be easily removed with a paring knife.) Avoid berries with soft or brown spots. Huge berries may be lovely to look at but they often have hollow centers and little flavor or juice. Although available to some extent all year, fresh California strawberries are at their peak from April through June.

Strawberries

The tiny wild or Alpine berries, known by their French name *fraises des bois*, have a particularly intense flavor and aroma. They are not widely available in the United States.

Citrus (genus Citrus*)*

Citrus fruits include lemons, limes, grapefruits, tangerines, kumquats, oranges and several hybrids. They are characterized by a thick rind, most of which is a bitter white pith (albedo) with a thin exterior layer of colored skin known as the zest. Their flesh is segmented and juicy. Citrus fruits are acidic, with a strong aroma; their flavors vary from bitter to tart to sweet.

Citrus fruits grow on trees and shrubs in tropical and subtropical climates worldwide. All citrus fruits are fully ripened on the tree and will not ripen further after harvesting. They should be refrigerated for longest storage.

Select fruits that feel heavy and have thin, smooth skins. Avoid those with large blemishes or moist spots.

Grapefruits

White Grapefruits

Grapefruits (Fr. *pamplemousse*) are large and round with a yellow skin, thick rind and tart flesh. They are an 18th-century hybrid of the orange and pummelo (a large, coarse fruit used mostly in Middle and Far Eastern cuisines). Two varieties of grapefruit are widely available all year: white-fleshed and pink- or ruby-fleshed. White grapefruits produce the finest juice, although pink grapefruits are sweeter. Fresh grapefruits are best eaten raw or topped with brown sugar and lightly broiled. Grapefruit segments are available canned in syrup.

Ruby Grapefruits

Kumquats

Kumquats are very small, oval-shaped, orange-colored fruits with a soft, sweet skin and slightly bitter flesh. They can be eaten whole, either raw or preserved in syrup, and may be used in jams and preserves.

Lemons

The most commonly used citrus fruits, lemons (Fr. *citrons*), are oval-shaped, bright yellow fruits available all year. Their strongly acidic flavor makes them unpleasant to eat raw but perfect for flavoring desserts and confections. Lemon juice is also widely used in sauces, especially for fish, shellfish and poultry. Lemon zest is candied or used as garnish.

Limes

Limes (Fr. *limons*) are small fruits with thin skins ranging from yellow-green to dark green. Limes are too tart to eat raw and are often substituted for lemons in prepared dishes. They are also juiced or used in cocktails, curries or desserts. Lime zest can be grated and used to give color and flavor to a variety of dishes. Limes are available all year, with a peak season during the summer.

Oranges

Oranges are round fruits with a juicy, orange-colored flesh and a thin, orange skin. They can be either sweet or bitter.

Valencia oranges and navel oranges (a seedless variety) are the most popular sweet oranges. They can be juiced for beverages or sauces and the flesh may be eaten raw, added to salads, cooked in desserts or used as a garnish. The zest may be grated or julienned for sauces or garnish. Sweet oranges are

Kumquats

Lemons

Limes

Valencia Oranges

available all year, with peak season from December to April. Blood oranges are also sweet but are small, with a rough, reddish skin. Their flesh is streaked with a blood-red color. Blood oranges are available primarily during the winter months and are eaten raw, juiced or used in salads or sauces. When selecting sweet oranges, look for fruits that feel plump and heavy, with unblemished skin. The color of the skin depends on weather conditions; a green rind does not affect the flavor of the flesh.

Bitter oranges include the Seville and bergamot. They are used primarily for the essential oils found in their zest. Oil of bergamot gives Earl Gray tea its distinctive flavor; oil of Seville is essential to curaçao, Grand Marnier and orange flower water. Seville oranges are also used in marmalades and sauces for meats and poultry.

Navel Oranges

Blood Oranges

Tangerines

Tangerines, sometimes referred to as mandarins, are small and dark orange. Their rind is loose and easily removed to reveal sweet, juicy, aromatic segments. Tangerines are most often eaten fresh and uncooked, but are available canned as mandarin oranges.

Tangelos are a hybrid of tangerines and grapefruits. They are the size of a medium orange; they have a bulbous stem end and few to no seeds.

Tangerines

PROCEDURE FOR SEGMENTING CITRUS FRUITS

1. Citrus segments, known as *supremes*, are made by first carefully cutting off the entire peel (including the bitter white pith) in even slices.

2. Individual segments are then removed by gently cutting alongside each membrane.

PROCEDURE FOR ZESTING CITRUS FRUITS

1. A five-hole zester is used to remove paper-thin strips of the colored rind.

PROCEDURE FOR CUTTING CITRUS PEELS

1. Large strips of citrus zest may be used as a garnish or to flavor soups or sauces.

Exotics

Improved transportation has led to the increasing availability (although sporadic in some areas) of exotic or unusual fresh fruits such as figs, persimmons, pomegranates, prickly pears, rhubarb and star fruits. Other exotic fruits, such as breadfruit, lychee, guava, feijoa and loquat, are still only available on a limited basis from specialty purveyors and are not discussed here.

Figs

Figs (Fr. *figues*) are the fruit of ficus trees. They are small, soft, pear-shaped fruits with an intensely sweet flavor and rich, moist texture made crunchy by a multitude of tiny seeds. Fresh figs can be sliced and served in salads or with cured meats such as prosciutto. They can also be baked, poached or used in jams, preserves or compotes.

Dark-skinned figs, known as Mission figs, are a variety planted at Pacific Coast missions during the 18th century. They have a thin skin and small seeds and are available fresh, canned or dried. The white-skinned figs grown commercially include the White Adriatic, used principally for drying and baking, and the all-purpose Kadota. The most important domestic variety, however, is the Calimyrna. These large figs have a rich yellow color and large nutty seeds. Fresh Calimyrna figs are the finest for eating out of hand; they are also available dried.

For the best flavor, figs should be fully ripened on the tree. Unfortunately, fully ripened figs are very delicate and difficult to transport. Most figs are in season from June through October; fresh Calimyrna figs are only available during June.

Persimmons

Persimmons

Persimmons, sometimes referred to as kaki or Sharon fruits, are a bright orange, acorn-shaped fruit with a glossy skin and a large papery blossom. The flesh is bright orange and jellylike, with a mild but rich flavor similar to honey and plums. Persimmons should be peeled before use; any seeds should be discarded. Select bright orange fruits and refrigerate only after they are completely ripe. When ripe, persimmons will be very soft and the skin will have an almost translucent appearance.

Ripe persimmons are delicious eaten raw; halved and topped with cream or soft cheese; or peeled, sliced and added to fruit salads. Persimmon bread, muffins, cakes and pies are also popular. Underripe persimmons are almost inedible, however. They are strongly tannic with a chalky or cottony texture.

Persimmons are tree fruits grown in subtropical areas worldwide, although the Asian varieties—now grown in California—are the most common. Fresh persimmons are available from October through January.

Pomegranates

An ancient fruit native to Persia (now Iran), pomegranates have long been a subject of poetry and a symbol of fertility. Pomegranates are round, about the size of a large orange, with a pronounced calyx. The skin forms a hard shell with a pinkish-red color. The interior is filled with hundreds of small, red seeds (which are, botanically, the actual fruits) surrounded by juicy red pulp. An inedible yellow membrane separates the seeds into compartments. Pomegranates are sweet-sour and the seeds are pleasantly crunchy. The bright red seeds make an attractive garnish. Pomegranate juice is a popular beverage in Mediterranean cuisines and grenadine syrup is made from concentrated pomegranate juice.

Pomegranates

Select heavy fruits that are not rock-hard, cracked or heavily bruised. Whole pomegranates can be refrigerated for several weeks. Pomegranates are available from September through December, with peak season in October.

Prickly Pears

Prickly pear fruits, also known as cactus pears and barbary figs, are actually the berries of several varieties of cactus. They are barrel- or pear-shaped, about the size of a large egg. Their thick, firm skin is green or purple with small sharp pins and nearly invisible stinging fibers. Their flesh is spongy, sweet and a brilliant pink-red, dotted with small black seeds. Prickly pears have the aroma of watermelon and the flavor of sugar-water.

Prickly Pears

Once peeled, prickly pears can be diced and eaten raw, or they can be puréed for making jams, sauces, custards or sorbets, to which they give a vivid pink color. Prickly pears are especially common in Mexican and southwestern cuisines.

Select fruits that are full-colored, heavy and tender, but not too soft. Avoid those with mushy or bruised spots. Ripe prickly pears can be refrigerated for a week or more. Prickly pears are grown in Mexico and several southwestern states and are available from September through December.

PROCEDURE FOR PEELING PRICKLY PEARS

1. To avoid being stung by a prickly pear, hold it steady with a fork, then use a knife to cut off both ends.

2. Cut a lengthwise slit through the skin. Slip the tip of the knife into the cut and peel away the skin by holding it down while rolling the fruit away.

Rhubarb

Rhubarb

Although botanically a vegetable, rhubarb is most often prepared as a fruit. It is a perennial plant that grows well in temperate and cold climates. Only the pinkish-red stems are edible; the leaves contain high amounts of oxalic acid, which is toxic.

Rhubarb stems are extremely acidic, requiring large amounts of sugar to create the desired sweet-sour taste. Cinnamon, ginger, orange and strawberry are particularly compatible with rhubarb. It is excellent for pies, cobblers, preserves or stewing. Young, tender stalks of rhubarb do not need to be peeled. When cooked, rhubarb becomes very soft and turns a beautiful light pink color.

Fresh rhubarb is sold as whole stalks, with the leaves removed. Select crisp, unblemished stalks. Peak season is during the early spring, from February through May. Frozen rhubarb pieces are readily available and are excellent for pies, tarts or jams.

Star Fruits

Star fruits, also known as carambola, are oval, up to 5 inches (12.5 centimeters) long, with five prominent ribs or wings running their length. A cross-section cut is shaped like a star. The edible skin is a waxy orange-yellow; it covers a dry, paler yellow flesh. Its flavor is similar to plums, sweet but bland. Star fruits do not need to be peeled or seeded. They are most often sliced and added to fruit salad or used as a garnish. Unripe fruits can be cooked in stews or chutneys.

Color and aroma are the best indicators of ripeness. The fruits should be a deep golden-yellow and there should be brown along the edge of the ribs. The aroma should be full and floral. Green fruits can be kept at room temperature to ripen, then refrigerated for up to two weeks. Star fruits are cultivated in Hawaii, Florida and California, though some are still imported from the Caribbean. Fresh fruits are available from August to February.

Star Fruit

Grapes *(*Vitis vinifera*)*

Grapes are the single largest fruit crop in the world, due, of course, to their use in wine making. This section, however, discusses only table grapes, those grown for eating. Grapes are berries that grow on vines in large clusters. California is the world's largest producer, with more than a dozen varieties grown for table use. Grapes are classified by color as white (which are actually green) or black (which are actually red). White grapes are generally blander than black ones, with a thinner skin and firmer flesh.

The grape's color and most of its flavor are found in the skin. Grapes are usually eaten raw, either alone or in fruit salads. They are also used as a garnish or accompaniment to desserts and cheeses. Dried grapes are known as raisins (usually made from Thompson Seedless or muscat grapes), currants (made from Black Corinth grapes and labeled as Zante currants) or sultanas (made from sultana grapes).

Grapes are available all year because the many varieties have different harvesting schedules. Look for firm, unblemished fruits that are firmly attached to the stem. A surface bloom or dusty appearance is caused by yeasts and indicates recent harvesting. Wrinkled grapes or those with brown spots around the stem are past their prime. All grapes should be rinsed and drained prior to use.

GRAPES INTO WINE

Virtually all the fine wine made in the world comes from varieties of a single grape species, *Vitis vinifera*. Although a European species, it is also grown in the United States, South Africa, South America, the Middle East, Australia and wherever fine wine is made. The variety of grapes used in any given wine determines the wine's character, and most wine-producing countries carefully regulate the growing areas and production of grapes.

American wines are known by their varietal names, whereas European wines are generally known by the vineyard's location. The major varietals of wine grapes and the wines in which they are used are listed below.

Grape Varietal	Wine
Pinot Noir	red Burgundy and champagne
Chardonnay	white Burgundy, Chablis and champagne
Syrah	Côte Rotie and Hermitage
Cabernet Sauvignon	Bordeaux and red Graves
Sauvignon Blanc	Sauterne, white Graves, fumé blanc and Sancerre
Merlot	Saint-Emilion and for blending with Cabernet Sauvignon
Zinfandel	red and white zinfandel (California claims a virtually monopoly)
Chenin Blanc	Vouvray

Red Flame Grapes

Thompson Seedless Grapes

Red Flame Grapes

Red Flame grapes are a seedless California hybrid, second only in importance to the Thompson Seedless. Red Flame grapes are large and round with a slightly tart flavor and variegated red color.

Thompson Seedless Grapes

The most commercially important table grapes are a variety known as Thompson Seedless, which are pale green with a crisp texture and sweet flavor. Peak season is from June to November. Many are dried in the hot desert sun of California's San Joaquin Valley to produce dark raisins. For golden raisins, Thompson Seedless grapes are treated with sulfur dioxide to prevent browning, then dried mechanically.

Of the table grapes containing seeds, the most important varieties are the Concord, Ribier and Emperor. They range from light red to deep black in color, and all three are in season during the autumn. Concord grapes, one of the few grape varieties native to the New World, are especially important for making juices and jellies.

Melons

Like pumpkins and cucumbers, melons are members of the gourd family (*Cucurbitaceae*). The dozens of melon varieties can be divided into two general types: sweet (or dessert) melons and watermelons. Sweet melons have a tan, green or yellow netted or farrowed rind and dense, fragrant flesh. Watermelon has a thick, dark green rind surrounding crisp, watery flesh.

Melons are almost 90% water, so cooking destroys their texture, quickly turning the flesh to mush. Most are served simply sliced, perhaps with a bit of lemon or lime juice. Melons also blend well in fruit salads or with rich, cured meats such as prosciutto. Melons may be puréed and made into soups or sorbets.

Melons should be vine-ripened. A ripe melon should yield slightly and spring back when pressed at the blossom end (opposite the stem). It should also give off a strong aroma. Avoid melons that are very soft or feel damp at the stem end. Ripe melons may be stored in the refrigerator, although the flavor will be better at room temperature. Slightly underripe melons can be stored at room temperature to allow flavor and aroma to develop.

Cantaloupes

Cantaloupes

American cantaloupes, which are actually muskmelons, are sweet melons with a thick, yellow-green netted rind, a sweet, moist, orange flesh and a strong aroma. (European cantaloupes, which are not generally available in this country, are more craggy and furrowed in appearance.) As with all sweet melons, the many small seeds are found in a central cavity. Cantaloupes are excellent for eating alone and are especially good with ham or rich meats.

Avoid cantaloupes with the pronounced yellow color or moldy aroma that indicates overripeness. Mexican imports ensure a year-round supply, although their peak season is summer.

Casaba Melons

Casaba Melons

Casaba melons are a teardrop-shaped sweet melon. They have a coarse, yellow skin and a thick, ridged rind; their flesh is creamy white to yellow. Casaba melons are used like cantaloupes. Casaba melons do not have an aroma, so selection must be based on a deep skin color and the absence of dark or moist patches. Peak season is during September and October.

Crenshaw Melons

Crenshaw Melons

Crenshaw (or cranshaw) melons have a mottled, green-yellow ridged rind and orange-pink flesh. Crenshaws are large and pear-shaped, with a strong aroma. The flesh has a rich, spicy flavor and may be used like cantaloupe. Crenshaws are available from July through October, with peak season during August and September.

Honeydew Melons

Honeydew melons are large oval melons with a smooth rind that ranges from white to pale green. Although the flesh is generally pale green, with a mild, sweet flavor, pink- or gold-fleshed honeydews are also available.

Gold Honeydews

Green Honeydews

Like casaba melons, honeydew melons have no aroma. They are available almost all year, with peak season from June through October.

Santa Claus Melons

Santa Claus or Christmas melons are large, elongated melons with a green-and-yellow-striped, smooth rind. The flesh is creamy white or yellow and tastes like casaba. They are a winter variety, with peak availability during December, which explains the name.

Santa Claus Melons

Watermelons

Watermelons are large (up to 30 pounds or 13.5 kilograms) round or oval-shaped melons with a thick rind. The skin may be solid green, green-striped or mottled with white. The flesh is crisp and extremely juicy with small, hard, black seeds throughout. Seedless hybrids are available, although they are relatively expensive. Most watermelons have pink to red flesh, although golden-fleshed varieties are becoming more common.

Watermelons are of a different genus from the sweet melons described above. They are native to tropical Africa and are now grown commercially in Texas and several southern states.

Red Seedless Watermelon

Gold watermelon

Pomes *(family* Rosaceae*)*

Pomes are tree fruits with thin skin and firm flesh surrounding a central core containing many small seeds called pips or carpels. Pomes include apples, pears and quince.

Apples

Apples (Fr. *pommes*), perhaps the most common and commonly appreciated of all fruits, grow on trees in temperate zones worldwide. They are popular because of their convenience, taste, variety and availability.

Rome   *Red Delicious*

Granny Smith   *Golden Delicious*

McIntosh

Apples can be eaten raw out of hand, or they can be used in a wide variety of cooked or baked dishes. They are equally useful in breads, desserts or vegetable dishes and go well with game, pork and poultry. Classic dishes prepared with apples are often referred to as *à la Normande*. Apple juice (cider) produces alcoholic and nonalcoholic beverages and cider vinegar.

Of the hundreds of known apple varieties, only 20 or so are commercially significant in the United States. Several varieties and their characteristics are noted in Table 25.1. Most have a moist, creamy white flesh with a thin skin of yellow, green or red. They range in flavor from very sweet to very tart, with an equally broad range of textures, from firm and crisp to soft and mealy.

In Europe, apples are divided into distinct cooking and eating varieties. Cooking varieties are those that disintegrate to a purée when cooked. American varieties are less rigidly classified. Nevertheless, not all apples are appropriate for all types of cooking. Those that retain their shape better during cooking are the best choices where slices or appearance are important. Varieties with a higher malic acid content break down easily, making them more appropriate for applesauce or juicing. Either type may be eaten out of hand, depending on personal preference.

Although not native to North America, apples are now grown commercially in 35 states, with Washington and New York leading in production. Apples are harvested when still sightly underripe, then stored in a controlled atmosphere (temperature and oxygen are greatly reduced) for extended periods until ready for sale. Modern storage techniques make fresh apples available all year, although peak season is during the autumn.

When selecting apples, look for smooth, unbroken skins and firm fruits, without soft spots or bruises. Badly bruised or rotting apples should be discarded immediately. They emit quantities of ethylene gas that speed spoilage of nearby fruits. (Remember the saying about "one bad apple spoils the barrel.") Store apples chilled for up to six weeks. Apple peels (the skin) may be eaten or removed as desired, but in either case, apples should be washed just prior to use to remove pesticides and any wax that was applied to improve appearance. Apple slices may be frozen (often with sugar or citric acid added to slow spoilage) or dried.

TABLE 25.1   APPLE VARIETIES

Variety	Skin Color	Flavor	Texture	Peak Season	Use
Golden Delicious	Glossy, greenish-gold	Sweet	Semifirm	Sept.– Oct.	In tarts; with cheese; in salads
Granny Smith	Bright green	Tart	Firm and crisp	Oct.– Nov.	Eating; in tarts
Jonathan	Brilliant red	Tart to acidic	Tender	Sept.– Oct.	Eating; all-purpose
McIntosh	Red with green background	Tart to acidic	Soft	Fall	Applesauce; in closed pies
Pippin (Newton)	Greenish-yellow	Tart	Semifirm	Fall	In pies; eating; baking
Red Delicious	Deep red	Sweet but bland	Soft to mealy	Sept.– Oct.	Eating
Rome	Red	Sweet-tart	Firm	Oct.– Nov.	Baking; pies; sauces
Winesap	Dark red with yellow streaks	Tangy	Crisp	Oct.– Nov.	Cider; all-purpose

Procedure for Coring Apples

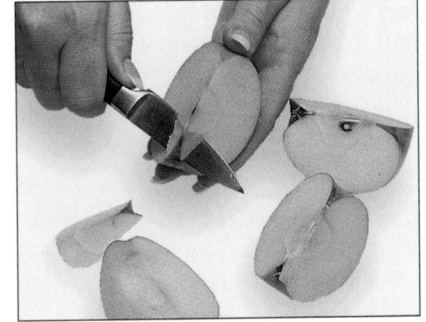

1. Remove the core from a whole apple with an apple corer by inserting the corer from the stem end and pushing out the cylinder containing the core and seeds.

2. Alternatively, first cut an apple into quarters, then use a paring knife to cut away the core and seeds.

Pears

Pears (Fr. *poires*) are an ancient tree fruit grown in temperate areas throughout the world. Most of the pears marketed in this country are grown in California, Washington and Oregon.

Although literally thousands of pear varieties have been identified, only a dozen or so are commercially significant. Several varieties and their characteristics are noted in Table 25.2. Pear varieties vary widely in size, color and flavor. They are most often eaten out of hand, but can be baked or poached. Pears are delicious with cheese, especially blue cheeses, and can be used in fruit salads, compotes or preserves.

Asian pears, also known as Chinese pears or apple-pears, are of a different species than common pears. They have the moist, sweet flavor of a pear and the round shape and crisp texture of an apple. They are becoming increasingly popular in this country, particularly those known as Twentieth Century or Nijisseiki.

Anjou

Red d'Anjou

Bartlett

Bosc

Asian Pears

TABLE 25.2	PEAR VARIETIES				
Variety	Appearance	Flavor	Texture	Peak Season	Use
Anjou (Beurre d'Anjou)	Greenish-yellow skin; egg-shaped with short neck; red variety also available	Sweet and juicy	Firm, keeps well	Oct.– May	Eating; poaching; baking
Bartlett (Williams)	Thin yellow skin; bell-shaped; red variety also available	Very sweet, buttery, juicy	Tender	Aug.– Dec.	Eating; canning; in salads
Bosc	Golden-brown skin; long, tapered neck	Buttery	Dry, holds its shape well	Sept.– May	Poaching; baking
Comice	Yellow-green skin; large and chubby	Sweet, juicy	Smooth	Oct.– Feb.	Eating
Seckel	Tiny; brown to yellow skin	Spicy	Very firm, grainy	Aug.– Dec.	Poaching; pickling

Quince

When selecting pears, look for fruits with smooth, unbroken skin and an intact stem. Pears will not ripen properly on the tree, so they are picked while still firm and should be allowed to soften before use. Underripe pears may be left at room temperature to ripen. A properly ripened pear should have a good fragrance and yield to gentle pressure at the stem end. Pears can be prepared or stored in the same way as apples.

Quince

Common quince (Fr. *coing*) resemble large, lumpy yellow pears. Their flesh is hard, with many pips or seeds, and they have a wonderful fragrance. Too astringent to eat raw, quince develop a sweet flavor and pink color when cooked with sugar. Quince are used in meat stews, jellies, marmalades and pies. They have a high **pectin** content and may be added to other fruit jams or preserves to encourage gelling.

Fresh quince, usually imported from South America or southeast Europe, are available from October through January. Select firm fruits with a good yellow color. Small blemishes may be cut away before cooking. Quince will keep for up to a month under refrigeration.

Stone Fruits (genus Prunus)

Stone fruits, also known as drupes, include apricots, cherries, nectarines, peaches and plums. They are characterized by a thin skin, soft flesh and one woody stone or pit. Although most originated in China, the shrubs and trees producing stone fruits are now grown in temperate climates worldwide.

The domestic varieties of stone fruits are in season from late spring through summer. They tend to be fragile fruits, easily bruised, difficult to transport and with a short shelf life. Do not wash them until ready to use, as moisture can cause deterioration. Avoid ingesting the pits—most contain toxic acids. Stone fruits are excellent dried and are often used to make liqueurs or brandies.

Apricots

Apricots

Apricots (Fr. *abricots*) are small, round stone fruits with a velvety skin that varies in color from deep yellow to vivid orange. Their juicy orange flesh surrounds a dark, almond-shaped pit. Apricots can be eaten out of hand, poached, stewed, baked or candied. They are often used in fruit compotes or savory sauces for meat or poultry, and are also popular in quick breads, fruit tarts or puréed for dessert sauces, jams, custards or mousses.

Apricots enjoy a short season, peaking during June and July, and do not travel well. Select apricots that are well shaped, plump and fairly firm. Avoid ones that are greenish-yellow or mushy. Fresh apricots will last for several days under refrigeration, but the flavor is best at room temperature. If fresh fruits are unavailable, canned apricots are usually an acceptable substitute. Dried apricots and apricot juice (known as nectar) are readily available.

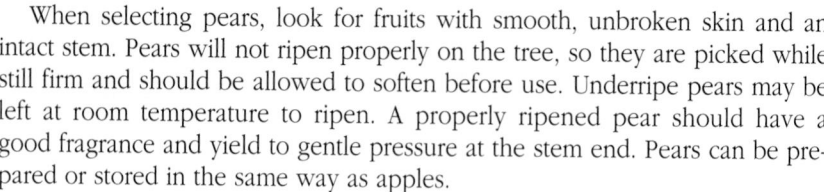

Rainier Cherries

Cherries

From the northern states, particularly Washington, Oregon, Michigan and New York, come the two most important types of cherry: the sweet cherry and the sour (or tart) cherry.

Sweet cherries (Fr. *cerises*) are round to heart-shaped, about 1 inch (2.5 centimeters) in diameter, with skin that ranges in color from yellow to deep red to nearly black. The flesh, which is sweet and juicy, may vary from yellow to dark red. The most common and popular sweet cherries are the dark red Bings. Yellow-red Royal Ann and Rainier cherries are also available in some areas.

Bing Cherries

Sweet cherries are often marketed fresh, made into maraschino cherries or candied for use in baked goods. Fresh sweet cherries have a very short season, peaking during June and July. Cherries will not ripen further after harvesting. Select fruits that are firm and plump with a green stem still attached. There should not be any brown spots around the stem. A dry or brown stem indicates that the cherry is less than fresh. Once the stem is removed, the cherry will deteriorate rapidly. Store fresh cherries in the refrigerator and do not wash them until ready to use.

Sour cherries are light to dark red in color and are so acidic they are rarely eaten uncooked. The most common sour cherries are the Montmorency and Morello. Most sour cherries are canned or frozen, or cooked with sugar and starch (usually cornstarch or tapioca) and sold as prepared pastry and pie fillings.

Both sweet and sour varieties are available dried.

PROCEDURE FOR PITTING CHERRIES

1. Remove the stem and place the cherry in the pitter with the indentation facing up. Squeeze the handles together to force out the pit.

Peaches and Nectarines

Peaches (Fr. *pêches*) are moderate-sized, round fruits with juicy, sweet flesh. Nectarines are a variety of peach, the main difference between the two being their skin. Peaches have a thin skin covered with fuzz, while nectarines have a thin, smooth skin. The flesh of either fruit ranges from white to pale orange. Although their flavors are somewhat different, they may be substituted for each other in most recipes.

Peaches

Peaches and nectarines are excellent for eating out of hand or in dessert tarts or pastries. They are also used in jams, chutneys, preserves and savory relishes, having a particular affinity for Asian and Indian dishes. Although the skin is edible, peaches are generally peeled before being used. (Peaches are easily peeled if blanched first.)

Peaches and nectarines are either freestones or clingstones. With freestones, the flesh separates easily from the stone; freestone fruits are commonly eaten out of hand. The flesh of clingstones adheres firmly to the stone; they hold their shape better when cooked and are the type most often canned.

Nectarines

Select fruits with a good aroma, an overall creamy, yellow or yellow-orange color and an unwrinkled skin free of blemishes. Red patches are not an indication of ripeness; a green skin indicates that the fruit was picked too early and it will not ripen further. Peaches and nectarines will soften but do not become sweeter after harvesting.

The United States, especially California, is the world's largest producer of peaches and nectarines. Peak season is through the summer months, with July and August producing the best crop. South American peaches are sometimes available from January to May. Canned and frozen peaches are readily available.

Plums

Santa Rosa Plums

Plums (Fr. *prunes*) are round to oval-shaped fruits that grow on trees or bushes. Dozens of plum varieties are known, although only a few are commercially significant. Plums vary in size from very small to 3 inches (7.5 centimeters) in diameter. Their thin skin can be green, red, yellow or various shades of blue-purple.

Damson Plums

Plums are excellent for eating out of hand. Plums can also be used in pies, cobblers or tarts, or be baked or poached; they are often used in jams or preserves, and fresh slices can be used in salads or compotes.

Fresh plums are widely available from June through October, with a peak season in August and September. When selecting plums, look for plump, smooth fruits with unblemished skin. Generally, they should yield to gentle pressure, although the green and yellow varieties remain quite firm. Avoid plums with moist, brown spots near the stem. Plums may be left at room temperature to ripen, then stored in the refrigerator. Prunes, discussed below, are produced by drying special plum varieties, usually the French Agen.

Tropicals

Tropical fruits are native to the world's hot, tropical or subtropical regions. Most are now readily available throughout the United States thanks to rapid transportation and distribution methods. All can be eaten fresh, without cooking. Their flavors complement each other and go well with rich or spicy meat, fish and poultry dishes.

Bananas

Common Yellow Bananas

Common yellow bananas (Fr. *bananes*) are actually the berries of a large tropical herb. Grown in bunches called hands, they are about 7–9 inches (17.5–22.5 centimeters) long, with a sticky, soft, sweet flesh. Their inedible yellow skin is easily removed.

Properly ripened bananas are excellent eaten out of hand or used in salads. Lightly bruised or overripe fruits are best used for breads or muffins. Bananas blend well with other tropical fruits and citrus. Their unique flavor is also complemented by curry, cinnamon, ginger, honey and chocolate.

Fresh bananas are available all year. Bananas are always harvested when still green, because the texture and flavor will be adversely affected if the fruits are allowed to turn yellow on the tree. Unripe bananas are hard, dry and starchy. Because bananas ripen after harvesting, it is acceptable to purchase green bananas if there is sufficient time for final ripening before use. Bananas should be left at room temperature to ripen. A properly ripened banana has a yellow peel with brown flecks. The tip should not have any remaining green coloring. As bananas continue to age, the peel darkens and the starches turn to sugar, giving the fruits a sweeter flavor. Avoid bananas that have large brown bruises or a gray cast (a sign of cold damage).

Plantains

Plantains, also referred to as cooking bananas, are larger but not as sweet as common bananas. They are frequently cooked as a starchy vegetable in tropical cuisines.

Dates

Dates are the fruit of the date palm tree, which has been cultivated since ancient times. Dates are about 1–2 inches (2.5–5 centimeters) long, with a paper-thin skin and a single grooved seed in the center. Most are golden to dark brown when ripe.

Although dates appear to be dried, they are actually fresh fruits. They have a sticky-sweet, almost candied texture and rich flavor. Dates provide flavor and moisture for breads, muffins, cookies and tarts. They can also be served with fresh or dried fruits, or stuffed with meat or cheese as an appetizer.

Pitted dates are readily available in several packaged forms: whole, chopped or extruded (for use in baking). Whole unpitted dates are available in bulk. Date juice is also available for use as a natural sweetener, especially in baked goods. Although packaged or processed dates are available all year, peak season for fresh domestic dates is from October through December. When selecting dates, look for those that are plump, glossy and moist.

Medjool

Kiwis

Kiwis, sometimes known as kiwifruits or Chinese gooseberries, are small oval fruits, about the size of a large egg, with a thin, fuzzy brown skin. The flesh is bright green with a white core surrounded by hundreds of tiny black seeds.

Kiwis are sweet, but somewhat bland. They are best used raw, peeled and eaten out of hand or sliced for fruit salads or garnish. Although kiwis are not recommended for cooking because heat causes them to fall apart, they are a perfect addition to glazed fruit tarts and can be puréed for sorbets, mousses or Bavarians. Kiwis contain an enzyme similar to that in fresh pineapple or papaya, which has a tenderizing effect on meat and prevents gelling.

Kiwis

◆◆◆

FRIEDA AND THE KIWIFRUIT

How did a fuzzy brown unknown become a media darling and a hugely viable crop? The answer is thanks to Frieda Caplan. In 1962 Frieda, founder of Frieda's Inc., launched her historical worldwide promotion of kiwifruit. Acting on a suggestion that Chinese gooseberries, then grown only in New Zealand, might sell better under the name kiwifruit (the kiwi is the national bird of New Zealand), Frieda unleashed a produce giant. This story of the kiwifruit is studied throughout the world as one of the great successes in food marketing.

In 1980, after 18 years of Frieda's continual, creative, aggressive and expensive marketing, the kiwifruit became a North American star when nouvelle cuisine chefs prominently featured it in their mixes of strawberry, banana, melon and pineapples. Since that time, the question asked most commonly of Frieda's Inc. is "What will be the next kiwifruit?"

The answer is that there will never be another kiwifruit. When the kiwifruit was accepted into the world's fruit vernacular, there was an unconditional paradigm shift. Today, new specialty produce does not have to go through the rigorous acceptance process inflicted on the kiwifruit. There can never be another kiwifruit because the marketing climate and consumer palate have shifted in a wonderful, irreversible way. Now when a new fruit like red bananas or yellow seedless watermelon comes onto the market, the consuming public does not react with fear and say "Bananas are supposed to be yellow" or "It really isn't watermelon if there aren't any seeds and it's not red." They respond with positive open minds (much the same as Frieda did when she purchased her first flat of kiwifruit in 1962) and a new-found knowledge that new foods will bring quality and variety, not discord, to their diets.

—KAREN CAPLAN
*Frieda's eldest daughter and
president of FRIEDA'S, INC.*

Mangoes

Mangoes

Mangoes are oval or kidney-shaped fruits that normally weigh between 6 ounces and 1 pound (180–500 grams). Their skin is smooth and thin but tough, varying in color from yellow to orange-red, with patches of green, red or purple. As mangoes ripen, the green disappears. The juicy, bright orange flesh clings to a large, flat pit.

A mango's unique flavor is spicy-sweet, with an acidic tang. Mangoes can be puréed for use in drinks or sauces, or the flesh can be sliced or cubed for use in salads, pickles, chutneys or desserts. Mangoes go well with spicy foods such as curry and with barbecued meats.

Although Florida produces some mangoes, most of those available in this country are from Mexico. Peak season is from May through August. Select fruits with good color that are firm and free of blemishes. Ripe mangoes should have a good aroma, and should not be too soft or shriveled. Allow mangoes to ripen completely at room temperature, then refrigerate for up to one week.

PROCEDURE FOR PITTING AND CUTTING MANGOES

1. Cut along each side of the pit to remove two sections.

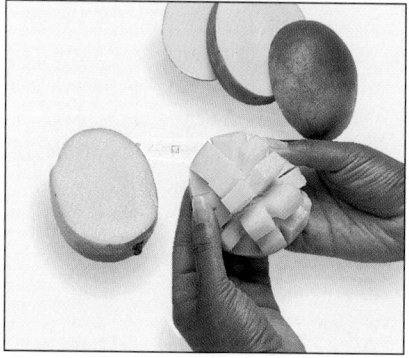

2. Each section can then be cubed using the "hedgehog" technique: Make crosswise cuts through the flesh, just to the skin; press up on the skin side of the section, exposing the cubes.

3. The mango may be served like this, or the cubes can be cut off to use in salads or other dishes.

Papayas

Regular Papayas

Papain—*an enzyme found in papayas that breaks down proteins; used as the primary ingredient in many commercial meat tenderizers.*

Papayas, also known as pawpaws, are greenish-yellow fruits shaped rather like large pears and weighing 1–2 pounds (500–1000 grams). When halved, they resemble a melon. The flesh is golden to reddish-pink; its center cavity is filled with round, silver-black seeds resembling caviar. Ripe papayas can be eaten raw, with only a squirt of lemon or lime juice. They can also be puréed for sweet or spicy sauces, chilled soups or sorbets.

Papayas contain **papain**, which breaks down proteins, and therefore papayas are an excellent meat tenderizer. Meats can be marinated with papaya juice or slices before cooking. Papain, however, makes fresh papayas unsuitable for use in gelatins because it inhibits gelling. Unripe (green) papayas are often used in pickles or chutneys, and can be baked or stewed with meat or poultry.

Papaya seeds are edible, with a peppery flavor and slight crunch. They are occasionally used to garnish fruit salads or add flavor to fruit salsas and compotes.

Papayas are grown in tropical and subtropical areas worldwide. Although available year round, peak season is from April through June. Select papayas that are plump, with a smooth, unblemished skin. Color is a better determinant of ripeness than is softness: The greater the proportion of yellow to green skin color, the riper the fruit. Papayas may be held at room temperature until completely ripe, then refrigerated for up to one week.

Red Papayas

Passion Fruits

Passion fruits (It. *granadillas*) have a firm, almost shell-like purple skin with orange-yellow pulp surrounding large, black, edible seeds. They are about the size and shape of large hen eggs, with a sweet, rich and unmistakable citrusy flavor. The pulp is used in custards, sauces and ice creams.

Select heavy fruits with dark, shriveled skin and a strong aroma. Allow them to ripen at room temperature, if necessary, then refrigerate. Passion fruits are in season only during February and March. Bottles or frozen packs of purée are readily available, however, and provide a strong, true flavor.

Passion Fruits

Pineapples

Pineapples (Fr. *ananas*) are the fruit of a shrub with sharp spear-shaped leaves. Each fruit is covered with rough, brown eyes, giving it the appearance of a pine cone. The pale yellow flesh, which is sweet and very juicy, surrounds a cylindrical woody core that is edible but too tough for most uses. Most pineapples weigh approximately 2 pounds (1 kilogram), but dwarf varieties are also available.

Pineapples are excellent eaten raw, alone or in salads. Slices can be baked or grilled to accompany pork or ham. The cuisines of Southeast Asia incorporate pineapple into various curries, soups and stews. Pineapple juice is a popular beverage, often used in punch or cocktails. Canned or cooked pineapple can be added to gelatin mixtures, but avoid using fresh pineapple, as an enzyme (bromelin) found in fresh pineapple breaks down gelatin.

Pineapples do not ripen after harvesting. They must be left on the stem until completely ripe, at which time they are extremely perishable. The vast majority of pineapples come from Hawaii. Fresh pineapples are available all year, with peak supplies in March through June. Select heavy fruits with a strong, sweet aroma and rich color. Avoid those with dried leaves or soft spots. Pineapples should be used as soon as possible after purchase. Pineapples are also available canned in slices, cubes or crushed, dried or candied.

Pineapples

PROCEDURE FOR TRIMMING AND SLICING PINEAPPLES

1. Slice off the leaves and stem end. Stand the fruit upright and cut the peel off in vertical strips.

2. Cut the peeled fruit in quarters, then cut away the woody core.

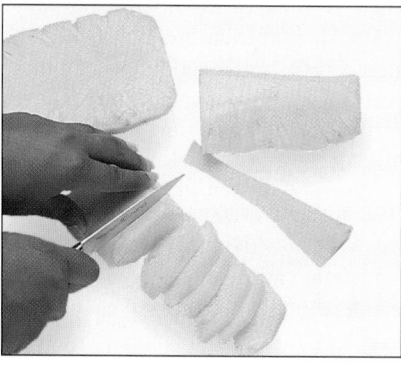

3. The flesh can then be cut as desired.

NUTRITION

Most fruits are quite nutritious. They have a high water content (usually 75% to 95%) and low protein and fat contents, all of which makes them low in calories. They are also an excellent source of fiber, and the sugar content of ripe fruits is a good source of energy. Some fruits, such as citrus, melons and strawberries, contain large amounts of vitamin C (which may be destroyed, however, by cooking or processing). Deep yellow and green fruits, such as apricots, mangoes and kiwis, are high in vitamin A; bananas, raisins and figs are a good source of potassium.

PURCHASING FRESH FRUITS

Fresh fruits have not been subjected to any processing (such as canning, freezing or drying). Fresh fruits may be ripe or unripe, depending on their condition when harvested or the conditions under which they have been stored. In order to use fresh fruits to their best advantage, it is important to make careful purchasing decisions. The size of each piece of fruit, its grade or quality, its ripeness on delivery and its nutritional content may affect your ability to use the fruit in an appropriate and cost-effective manner.

TABLE 25.3 NUTRITIONAL VALUES OF SELECTED FRUITS

Per serving, fresh, raw and/or as noted	Kcal	Protein (g)	Carbohydrates (g)	Fiber (g)	Total Fat (g)	Vitamin A (I.U.)	Vitamin C (mg)	Phosphorous (mg)	Potassium (mg)
Apple, 1 medium 2-3/4″ diameter, unpeeled	81	0.3	21.1	3	0.5	74	8	10	159
Banana, peeled 4 oz. (112 g)	104	1.2	26.4	2	0.4	59.4	6.4	14.2	290
Cantaloupe, 1/2 of 5″ diameter melon, approx. 7 oz. (210 g) of flesh	94	2.3	22.3	2.1	0.7	8608	113	45	825
Cherries, Bing, 10 medium, approx. 2.6 oz. (73 g)	49	0.8	11.3	1	0.7	146	5	13	152
Figs, 10 dried, approx. 6.6 oz. (185 g)	477	5.7	122.2	17.4	2.2	248	2	128	1332
Grapes, Thompson Seedless, 20, approx. 3.5 oz. (98 g)	72	0.6	17.8	0.8	0.6	72	10	12	186
Orange, navel, 1/2 medium, approx. 3.6 oz. (101 g)	35.6	0.8	8.9	0.3	<0.1	128	40	13.5	125
Pineapple, trimmed, 4 oz. (112 g)	56	0.4	14	1.2	0.4	25	17	8.5	125
Raisins, seedless, 4 oz. (112 g)	340	3.6	89.6	6	0.4	8	4	108	852
Strawberries, trimmed, 4 oz. (112 g)	36	0.8	8	2.5	0.4	28.7	60	19.8	175

The Corinne T. Netzer Encyclopedia of Food Values 1992

Grading

Fresh fruits traded on the wholesale market may be graded under the USDA's voluntary program. The grades, based on size and uniformity of shape, color and texture as well as the absence of defects, are: U.S. Fancy, U.S. No. 1, U.S. No. 2 and U.S. No. 3. Most fruits purchased for food service operations are U.S. Fancy. Fruits with lower grades are suitable for processing into sauces, jams, jellies or preserves.

Ripening

Several important changes take place in a fruit as it ripens. The fruit reaches its full size; its pulp or flesh becomes soft and tender; its color changes. In addition, the fruit's acid content declines, making it less tart, and its starch content converts into the sugars fructose and glucose that provide the fruit's sweetness, flavor and aroma.

Unfortunately, these changes do not stop when the fruit reaches its peak of ripeness. Rather, they continue, deteriorating the fruit's texture and flavor and eventually causing spoilage.

Depending upon the species, fresh fruits can be purchased either fully ripened or unripened. Figs and pineapples, for example, ripen only on the plant and are harvested at or just before their peak of ripeness then rushed to market. They should not be purchased unripened as they will never attain full flavor or texture after harvesting. On the other hand, some fruits, including bananas and pears, continue to ripen after harvesting and can be purchased unripened.

With most harvested fruits, the ripening time as well as the time during which the fruits remain at their peak of ripeness can be manipulated. For instance, ripening can be delayed by chilling. Chilling slows down the fruit's respiration rate (fruits, like animals, consume oxygen and expel carbon dioxide). The slower the respiration rate, the slower the conversion of starch to sugar. For quicker ripening, fruit can be stored at room temperature.

Ripening is also effected by ethylene gas, a colorless, odorless hydrocarbon gas. Ethylene gas is naturally emitted by ripening fruits and can be used to encourage further ripening in most fruits. Apples, tomatoes, melons and bananas give off the most ethylene and should be stored away from delicate fruits and vegetables, especially greens. Fruits that are picked and shipped unripened can be exposed to ethylene gas to induce ripening just before sale. Conversely, if you want to extend the life of ripe fruits a day or two, isolate them from other fruits and keep them well chilled.

Fresh fruits will not ripen further once they are cooked or processed. The cooking or processing method applied, however, may soften the fruits or add flavor.

Purchasing

Fresh fruits are sold by weight or by count. They are packed in containers referred to as crates, bushels, cartons, cases, lugs or flats. The weight or count packed in each of these containers varies depending on the type of fruit, the purveyor and the state in which the fruits were packed. For example, Texas citrus is packed in cartons equal to 7/10 of a bushel; Florida citrus is packed in cartons equal to 4/5 of a bushel. Sometimes fruit size must be specified when ordering. A 30-pound case of lemons, for example, may contain 96, 112 or 144 individual lemons, depending on their size.

Some fresh fruits, especially melons, pineapples, peaches and berries, are available trimmed, cleaned, peeled or cut. Sugar and preservatives are sometimes added. They are sold in bulk containers, sometimes packed in water. These items offer a consistent product with a significant reduction in labor costs. The purchase price may be greater than that for fresh fruits and flavor, freshness and nutritional qualities may suffer somewhat from the processing.

PURCHASING AND STORING PRESERVED FRUITS

Preserving techniques are designed to extend the shelf life of fruits in essentially fresh form. These methods include irradiation, acidulation, canning, freezing and drying. Except for drying, these techniques do not substantially change the fruits' texture or flavor. Canning and freezing can also be used to preserve cooked fruits.

Preserves such as jellies and jams are cooked products and are discussed later in this chapter.

Irradiated Fruits

As described in Chapter 22, Vegetables, some fruits can be subjected to ionizing radiation to destroy parasites, insects and bacteria. The treatment also slows ripening without a noticeable effect on the fruits' flavor and texture. Irradiated fruits must be labeled "treated with radiation," "treated by irradiation" or with the symbol shown in Figure 22.1.

Acidulation

Apples, pears, bananas, peaches and other fruits turn brown when cut. Although this browning is commonly attributed to exposure to oxygen, it is actually caused by the reaction of enzymes.

Enzymatic browning can be retarded by immersing cut fruits in an acidic solution such as lemon or orange juice. This simple technique is sometimes referred to as **acidulation**. Soaking fruits in water or lemon juice and water (called acidulated water) is not recommended. Unless a sufficient amount of salt or sugar is added to the water, the fruits will just become mushy. But if enough salt or sugar is added, the flavor will be affected.

Canned Fruits

Almost any type of fruit can be canned successfully; pineapple and peaches are the largest sellers. In commercial canning, raw fruits are cleaned and placed in a sealed container, then subjected to high temperatures for a specific amount of time. Heating destroys the microorganisms that cause spoilage, and the sealed environment created by the can eliminates oxidation and retards decomposition. But the heat required by the canning process also softens the texture of most fruits. Canning has little or no effect on vitamins A, B, C and D because oxygen is not present during the heating process. Canning also has no practical effect on proteins, fats or carbohydrates.

In *solid pack* cans, little or no water is added. The only liquid is from the fruits' natural moisture. *Water pack* cans have water or fruit juice added, which must be taken into account when determining costs. *Syrup pack* fruits have a sugar syrup—light, medium or heavy—added. The syrup should also be taken into account when determining food costs, and the additional sweetness should be considered when using syrup-packed fruits. Cooked fruit products such as pie fillings are also available canned.

Canned fruits are purchased in cases of standard-size cans (see Appendix II). Canned fruits can be stored almost indefinitely at room temperature. Once a can is opened, any unused contents should be transferred to an appropriate storage container and refrigerated. Cans with bulges should be discarded immediately, without opening.

Frozen Fruits

Freezing is a highly effective method for preserving fruits. It severely inhibits the growth of microorganisms that cause fruits to spoil. Freezing does not destroy nutrients, although the appearance or texture of most fruits can be affected because of their high water content. This occurs when ice crystals formed from the water in the cells burst the cells' walls.

Many fruits, especially berries and apple and pear slices, are now individually quick frozen (IQF). This method employs blasts of cold air, refrigerated plates, liquid nitrogen, liquid air or other techniques to chill the produce quickly. By speeding the freezing process, the formation of ice crystals can be greatly reduced.

Fruits can be trimmed and sliced before freezing and are also available frozen in sugar syrup, which adds flavor and prevents browning. Berries are frozen whole, while stone fruits are usually peeled, pitted and sliced. Fruit purées are also available frozen.

Frozen fruits are graded as U.S. Grade A (Fancy), U.S. Grade B (Choice or Extra Standard), or U.S. Grade C (Standard). The "U.S." indicates that a government inspector has graded the product, but packers may use grade names without an actual inspection if the contents meet the standards of the grade indicated.

IQF fruits can be purchased in bulk by the case. All frozen fruits should be sealed in moistureproof wrapping and kept at a constant temperature of 0°F (–18°C) or below. Temperature fluctuations can cause freezer burn.

Dried Fruits

Drying is the oldest-known technique for preserving fruits, having been used for over 5000 years. When ripe fruits are dried they lose most of their moisture. This concentrates their flavors and sugars and dramatically extends shelf life. Although most fruits can be dried, plums (prunes), grapes (raisins, sultanas and currants), apricots and figs are the fruits most commonly dried. The drying method can be as simple as leaving ripe fruits in the sun to dry naturally or the more cost-efficient technique of passing fruits through a compartment of hot, dry air to quickly extract moisture.

Golden Raisins

Currants

Apricots

Persimmons

Apples

Pears

Kiwis

Dried fruits actually retain from 16% to 25% residual moisture, which leaves them moist and soft. They are often treated with sulfur dioxide to prevent browning (oxidation) and to extend shelf life.

Dried fruits may be eaten out of hand; added to cereals or salads; baked in muffins, breads, pies or tarts; stewed for chutneys or compotes; or used as a stuffing for roasted meats or poultry. Before use, dried fruits may be softened by soaking them for a short time in a hot liquid such as water, wine, rum, brandy or other liquor. Some dried fruits should be simmered in a small amount of water before use.

Store dried fruits in air-tight containers to prevent further moisture loss; keep in a dry, cool area away from sunlight. Dried fruits may mold if exposed to both air and high humidity.

JUICING

Fruit juice is used as a beverage, alone or mixed with other ingredients, and as the liquid ingredient in other preparations. Juice can be extracted from fruits (and some vegetables) in two ways: pressure and blending.

Pressure is used to extract juice from fruits such as citrus that have a high water content. Pressure is applied by hand-squeezing or with a manual or electric reamer. All reamers work on the same principle: A ribbed cone is pressed against the fruit to break down its flesh and release the juice. Always strain juices to remove seeds, pulp or fibrous pieces.

A blender or an electric juice extractor can be used to liquify less juicy fruits and vegetables such as apples, carrots, tomatoes, beets and cabbage. The extractor pulverizes the fruit or vegetable, then separates and strains the liquid from the pulp with centrifugal action.

Interesting and delicious beverages can be made by combining the juice of one or more fruits or vegetables: Pineapple with orange, apple with cranberry, strawberry with tangerine and papaya with orange. Color should be considered when creating mixed-juice beverages, however. Some combinations can cause rather odd color changes. Although yellow and orange juices are not a problem, those containing red and blue flavonoid pigments (such as Concord grapes, cherries, strawberries, raspberries and blueberries) can create some unappetizing colors. Adding an acid such as lemon juice helps retain the correct red/blue hues.

Juice—*the liquid extracted from any fruit or vegetable.*

Nectar—*the diluted, sweetened juice of peaches, apricots, guavas, black currants or other fruits, the juice of which would be too thick or too tart to drink straight.*

Cider—*mildly fermented apple juice, although nonalcoholic apple juice may also be labeled cider.*

Applying Various Cooking Methods

Although most fruits are edible raw and typically served that way, some fruits can also be cooked. Commonly used cooking methods are broiling and grilling, baking, sautéing, deep-frying, poaching, simmering and preserving.

When cooking fruits, proper care and attention are critical. Even minimal cooking can render fruits overly soft or mushy. To combat this irreversible process, sugar can be added. When fruits are cooked with sugar, the sugar will be absorbed slowly into the cells, firming the fruits. Acids (notably lemon juice) also help fruits retain their structure. (Alkalis, such as baking soda, cause the cells to break down more quickly, reducing the fruits to mush.)

Determining Doneness

There are so many different fruits with such varied responses to cooking that no one standard for doneness is appropriate. Each item should be evaluated on a recipe-by-recipe basis. Generally, however, most cooked fruits are done when they are just tender when pierced with a fork or the tip of a paring knife. Simmered fruits, such a compotes, should be softer, cooked just to the point of disintegration.

You can avoid overcooking fruits by remembering that some carryover cooking will occur through the residual heat contained in the foods. Always rely on objective tests—sight, feel, taste and aroma—rather than the clock.

Dry-Heat Cooking Methods

Broiling and Grilling

Fruits are usually broiled or grilled just long enough to caramelize sugars. But cooking must be done quickly in order to avoid breaking down the fruits' structure. Good fruits to broil or grill are pineapples, apples, grapefruits, bananas, persimmons and peaches. The fruits may be cut into slices, chunks or halves as appropriate. A coating of sugar, honey or liqueur adds flavor, as do lemon juice, cinnamon and ginger.

When broiling fruits, use an oiled sheet pan or broiling platter. When grilling fruits, use a clean grill grate or thread the pieces onto skewers. Only thick fruit slices will need to be turned or rotated to heat fully. Broiled or grilled fruits can be served alone, as an accompaniment to meat, fish or poultry or as topping for ice creams or custards.

PROCEDURE FOR BROILING OR GRILLING FRUITS

1. Select ripe fruits and peel, core or slice as necessary.
2. Top with sugar or honey to add flavor and aid caramelization.
3. Place the fruits on the broiler platter, sheet pan or grill grate.
4. Broil or grill at high temperatures, turning as necessary to heat the fruits thoroughly but quickly.

RECIPE 25.1

BROILED GRAPEFRUIT

Yield: 8 Servings

Ruby grapefruits	4	4
Sweet sherry	2 Tbsp.	30 ml
Brown sugar	4 Tbsp.	60 ml

1. Cut each grapefruit in half (perpendicular to the segments), then section with a sharp knife, carefully removing any visible seeds.
2. Sprinkle the grapefruit halves with the sherry and sugar.
3. Arrange on a baking sheet and place under a preheated broiler. Cook briefly, only until well heated and the sugar caramelizes. Serve immediately.

Baking

After washing, peeling, coring or pitting, most pomes, stone fruits and tropicals can be baked to create hot, flavorful desserts. Fruits with sturdy skins, particularly apples and pears, are excellent for baking alone as their skin (peel) holds in moisture and flavor. They can also be used as edible containers by filling the cavity left by coring with a variety of sweet or savory mixtures.

Combinations of fruits can also be baked successfully. Try mixing fruits for a balance of sweetness and tartness (for example, strawberries with rhubarb, apples with plums).

Several baked desserts are simply fruits (fresh, frozen or canned) topped with a crust (and called a *cobbler*), strudel (and called a *crumple* or *crisp*) or batter (and called a *buckle*). (See Recipe 29.17 Blackberry Cobbler.) Fruits, sometimes poached first, can also be baked in a wrapper of puff pastry, flaky dough or phyllo dough to produce an elegant dessert.

PROCEDURE FOR BAKING FRUITS

1. Select ripe but firm fruits and peel, core, pit or slice as necessary.
2. Add sugar or any flavorings.

3. Wrap the fruits in pastry dough if desired or directed in the recipe.
4. Place the fruits in a baking dish and bake uncovered in a moderate oven until tender or properly browned.

◆◆◆

RECIPE 25.2

BAKED APPLES

Yield: 8 Servings

Apples, Red or Golden Delicious	8	8
Raisins	6 oz.	170 g
Orange zest	1-1/2 Tbsp.	20 g
Brown sugar	4 oz.	120 g

1. Rinse and core each apple. The peels should be scored or partially removed to allow the pulp to expand without bursting the skin during baking.
2. Plump the raisins by soaking them in boiling water for 10 minutes. Drain the raisins thoroughly.
3. Combine the raisins, orange zest and brown sugar. Fill the cavity of each apple with this mixture.
4. Stand the apples in a shallow baking dish. Add enough water to measure about 1/2 inch (1.25 centimeters) deep.
5. Bake the apples at 375°F (190°C) for 15 minutes. Reduce the temperature to 300°F (150°C) and continue baking until the apples are tender but still hold their shape, approximately 1 hour. Occasionally baste the apples with liquid from the baking dish.

Sautéing

Fruits develop a rich, syrupy flavor when sautéed briefly in butter, sugar and, if desired, spices or liqueur. Cherries, bananas, apples, pears and pineapples are good choices. They should be peeled, cored and seeded as necessary and cut into uniform-size pieces before sautéing.

For dessert, fruits are sautéed with sugar to create a caramelized glaze or syrup. The fruits and syrup can be used to fill crêpes or to top spongecakes or ice creams. Liquor may be added and the mixture flamed (flambéed) in front of diners, as with Bananas Foster (Recipe 25.14).

For savory mixtures, onions, shallots or garlic are often added.

In both sweet and savory fruit sautés, the fat used should be the most appropriate for the finished product. Butter and bacon fat are typical choices.

PROCEDURE FOR SAUTÉING FRUITS

1. Peel, pit and core the fruits as necessary and cut into uniform-size pieces.
2. Melt the fat in a hot sauté pan.
3. Add the fruit pieces and any flavoring ingredients. Do not crowd the pan, as this will cause the fruit to stew in its own juices.
4. Cook quickly over high heat.

◆◆◆

RECIPE 25.3

SAVORY FRUIT
FOR ROAST PORK

Yield: 1 pt. (500 ml)

Onion, fine dice	6 oz.	170 g
Butter or bacon fat	1 oz.	30 g
Apricots	3	3
Apples (tart) or		
peaches, peeled	3	3
Granulated sugar	4 oz.	120 g
Hot paprika	TT	TT
Salt and white pepper	TT	TT

1. Sweat the onions in the butter or bacon fat without browning.
2. Slice the apricots and apples into thin, even pieces. Add the apples to the onions and cook for 1–2 minutes. Add the apricots.
3. Sprinkle the sugar over the fruits and cook, uncovered, over medium heat until tender. Season with paprika, salt and white pepper.
4. Serve warm as an accompaniment to roast pork.

Deep-Frying

Few fruits are suitable for deep-frying. Apples, bananas, pears, pineapples and firm peaches mixed in or coated with batter, however, produce fine results. These fruits should be peeled, cored, seeded and cut into evenly sized slices or chunks. They may also need to be dried with paper towels so that the batter or coating can adhere. The procedures for deep-frying are found in Chapter 21, Deep-Frying.

Moist-Heat Cooking Methods

Poaching

One of the more popular cooking methods for fruits is poaching. Poaching softens and tenderizes fruits and infuses them with additional flavors such as spices or wine. Poached fruits can be served hot or cold and used in tarts, pastries or as an accompaniment to meat or poultry dishes.

The poaching liquid can be water, wine, liquor or sugar syrup. (As noted above, sugar helps fruits keep their shape, although it takes longer to tenderize fruits poached in sugar syrup.) The low poaching temperature (185°F/85°C) allows fruits to soften gradually. The agitation created at higher temperatures would damage them.

Cooked fruits should be allowed to cool in the flavored poaching liquid or syrup. Most poaching liquids can be used repeatedly. If they contain sufficient sugar, they can be reduced to a sauce or glaze to accompany the poached fruits.

PROCEDURE FOR POACHING FRUITS

1. Peel, core and slice the fruits as necessary.

2. In a sufficiently deep, nonreactive saucepan, combine the poaching liquid (usually water or wine) with sugar, spices, citrus zest and other ingredients as desired or as directed in the recipe.

3. Submerge the fruits in the liquid. Place a circle of parchment paper over the fruits to help them stay submerged.

4. Place the saucepan on the stove top over a medium-high flame; bring to a boil.

5. As soon as the liquid boils, reduce the temperature. Simmer gently.

6. Poach until the fruits are tender enough for the tip of a small knife to be easily inserted. Cooking time depends on the type of fruit used, its ripeness and the cooking liquid.

7. Remove the saucepan from the stove top and allow the liquid and fruits to cool.

8. Remove the fruits from the liquid and then refrigerate. The liquid can be returned to the stove top and reduced until thick enough to use as a sauce or glaze or refrigerated for further use.

RECIPE 25.4

PEARS POACHED IN RED WINE

NOTE: *This dish appears in the Chapter Opening photograph.*

SCOTTSDALE COMMUNITY COLLEGE, SCOTTSDALE, AZ
Pastry Chef Sarah Labensky

Yield: 8 Servings

Ripe pears, Anjou or Bartlett	8	8
Zinfandel wine	52 oz.	1500 ml
Whole peppercorns	8–10	8–10
Vanilla bean	1	1
Granulated sugar	12 oz.	340 g
Fresh basil, chopped	1 oz.	30 g
Zest of one orange		

1. Peel and core the pears, leaving the stems intact.

2. Combine the remaining ingredients in a large nonreactive saucepan. Arrange the pears in the liquid in a single layer.

3. Place the pears on the stove top over a medium-high flame. Bring to just below a boil, then immediately reduce the heat and allow the liquid to simmer gently. Cover with a round of parchment paper if necessary to keep the pears submerged.

4. Continue poaching the pears until tender, approximately 1 to 1-1/2 hours. Remove the saucepan from the stove and allow the pears to cool in the liquid.

5. Remove the pears from the poaching liquid and return the liquid to the stove top. Reduce until the liquid is thick enough to coat the back of a spoon, then strain.

6. Serve the pears chilled or at room temperature in a pool of the reduced wine syrup.

Simmering

Simmering techniques are used to make stewed fruits and compotes. Fresh, frozen, canned and dried fruits can be simmered or stewed. As with any moist-heat cooking method, simmering softens and tenderizes fruits. The liquid used may be water, wine or the juices naturally found in the fruits. Sugar, honey and spices may be added as desired. Stewed or simmered fruits can be served hot or cold, as a first course, a dessert or an accompaniment to meat or poultry dishes.

PROCEDURE FOR SIMMERING FRUITS

1. Peel, core, pit and slice the fruits as necessary.
2. Bring the fruits and cooking liquid, if used, to a simmer. Cook until the fruit is tender.
3. Add sugar or other sweeteners as desired or as directed in the recipe.

♦♦♦

RECIPE 25.5

DRIED FRUIT COMPOTE

Yield: 2 lb. (1 kg)

Dried apricots	5 oz.	150 g
Prunes, pitted	5 oz.	150 g
Dried pears or apples	5 oz.	150 g
Dried peaches	5 oz.	150 g
Hot water	24 oz.	720 g
Cinnamon stick	1	1
Light corn syrup	12 oz.	340 g
Cointreau	2 oz.	60 g

1. Coarsely chop the fruits. Place the pieces in a nonreactive saucepan and add the water and cinnamon stick.
2. Bring the mixture to a simmer, cover and cook until tender, approximately 12–15 minutes.
3. Add the corn syrup and Cointreau. Simmer uncovered until thoroughly heated. Serve warm or refrigerate for longer storage.

Preserving

Fresh fruits can be preserved with sugar if the fruit and sugar mixture is concentrated by evaporation to the point that microbial spoilage cannot occur. The added sugar also retards the growth of, but does not destroy, microorganisms.

Pectin, a substance present in varying amounts in all fruits, can cause cooked fruits to form a semisolid mass known as a **gel**. Fruits that are visually unattractive but otherwise of high quality can be made into gels, which are more commonly known as **jams**, **jellies**, **marmalades** and **preserves**.

The essential ingredients of a fruit gel are fruit, pectin, acid (usually lemon juice) and sugar. They must be carefully combined in the correct ratio for the gel to form. For fruits with a low pectin content (such as strawberries) to form gels, pectin must be added, either by adding a fruit with a high pectin content (for example, apples or quinces) or by adding packaged pectin.

Concentrate—*also known as a fruit paste or compound, is a reduced fruit purée, without a gel structure, used as a flavoring.*

Jam—*a fruit gel made from fruit pulp and sugar.*

Jelly—*a fruit gel made from fruit juice and sugar.*

Marmalade—*a citrus jelly that also contains unpeeled slices of citrus fruit.*

Preserve—*a fruit gel that contains large pieces or whole fruits.*

Procedure for Making Fruit Preserves

1. Clean, peel, core, pit and cut the fruits as necessary.
2. Firm fruits should be simmered in water or juice until tender.
3. Add sugar and other flavorings to the fruits as desired or as directed in the recipe.
4. Simmer until the mixture thickens.

◆◆◆

RECIPE 25.6
Quince Jam

Yield: 1 qt. (1 lt)

Water	1 qt.	1 lt
Lemon juice	1 oz.	30 g
Fresh quince	3 lb.	1.3 kg
Granulated sugar	12 oz.	340 g
Vanilla bean	1/2	1/2

1. Combine the water and 1/2 ounce (15 grams) of lemon juice in a large, nonreactive saucepan.
2. Peel, quarter and core the quince. Cut each quarter into small cubes and add to the water.
3. Bring the water to a boil, reduce the heat, cover and simmer until the quince is tender, approximately 30 minutes.
4. Remove about half the quince with a slotted spoon and set aside. Purée the remaining quince and the cooking liquid.
5. Return the purée and the quince pieces to the saucepan and bring to a simmer. Add the remaining 1/2 ounce (15 grams) of lemon juice, the sugar and vanilla bean.
6. Simmer uncovered, stirring frequently, until the jam holds its shape, approximately 15 minutes. Remove from the heat and cool over an ice bath.

Conclusion

Fruits, whether fresh, frozen, canned or dried, are one of the most versatile and popular of foods. Fruits can be used uncooked or incorporated into a soup, salad, bread, meat dish or dessert. When selecting fresh fruits it is important to consider seasonal availability, storage conditions and ripeness. When using them, it is important that they be at their peak of ripeness for the best flavor, texture, aroma and appearance.

Questions for Discussion

1. Define ripeness and explain why ripe fruits are most desirable. How does the ripening process affect the availability of some fruits?
2. Describe the proper storage conditions for most fruits. Which fruits emit ethylene gas and why is this a consideration when storing fruits?

3. Explain why some apple varieties are preferred for cooking, while other varieties are preferred for eating. Which variety is generally preferred for making applesauce?

4. Which types of fruits are best for dry-heat cooking methods? Explain your answer. Why is sugar usually added when cooking any type of fruit?

5. List and describe three ways to prepare fruits for extended storage.

*A*DDITIONAL FRUIT RECIPES

RECIPE 25.7
TROPICAL FRUIT WITH PASSION FRUIT PURÉE

CAMPTON PLACE RESTAURANT, KEMPINSKI HOTELS, SAN FRANCISCO, CA
Executive Chef Jan Birnbaum

Yield: 6 Servings

Mangoes	2	2
Papayas	2	2
Brazilian red bananas	2	2
Fresh coconut	1	1
Lime	1	1
Cherimoya (optional)	1	1
Guavas	2	2
Pineapple, medium, trimmed	1/3	1/3
Passion fruit	12	12
Sugar	4 oz.	120 g
Honey	6 oz.	180 g

1. Trim, peel and slice or cut all of the fruit, except the passion fruit, into interesting shapes. Hold in the refrigerator for service.

2. Cut the passion fruit in half and scoop out the seeds and membrane into a nonreactive saucepan. Add any fleshy trimmings from the mango, papaya, guava and pineapple. Add the sugar and honey and cook to a sauce consistency. Strain and cool.

3. Ladle 1-1/2 ounces (45 g) of the sauce onto a cold plate or bowl. Arrange the sliced fruit attractively on the sauce.

◆◆◆

RECIPE 25.8
FIGS WITH BERRIES AND HONEY MOUSSE

GREENS RESTAURANT, SAN FRANCISCO, CA
Executive Chef Annie Somerville

Yield: 4 Servings

Raspberries or blackberries	1 pt.	450 ml
Fresh figs such as Black Mission, Kadota or Calmyrna	1 pt.	450 ml
Honey	6 oz.	170 g
Egg yolks	4	4

| Salt | TT | TT |
| Heavy cream | 1 pt. | 450 g |

1. Pick through the berries, but do not rinse them because water will dilute their flavor.
2. Rinse the figs and cut them in half, leaving the stem attached.
3. To make the mousse, whisk the honey, yolks and salt together in a bowl over a pan of barely simmering water. Whisk the mixture continuously for 8 minutes. After 5 minutes, the mousse will begin to thicken and the texture will become creamy. Whisk vigorously until the mousse leaves thick ribbons on its surface when poured over itself. Set aside to cool. The texture of the cooled mousse will be stiff and sticky.
4. Whisk 2 tablespoons (30 milliliters) of cream into the mousse, working it until it loosens.
5. Whip the remaining cream until it is firm, fold it into the mousse until it is just incorporated, then whisk the two together. The texture will be light and creamy.
6. Loosely arrange the figs on a platter, sprinkle with the berries and serve with the mousse.

◆◆◆

RECIPE 25.9

PINEAPPLE PAPAYA SALSA

Yield: 2 qt. (2 lt)

Tomatoes	3	3
Pineapple, fresh	1	1
Papaya, fresh	1	1
Green onions, sliced	1 bunch	1 bunch
Fresh cilantro, chopped	1 bunch	1 bunch
Jalapeños, seeded, minced	2	2
Lemon juice	3 Tbsp.	45 ml
Garlic, chopped	1 tsp.	5 ml
Salt	2 tsp.	10 ml

1. Core and dice the tomatoes.
2. Peel and dice the pineapple.
3. Peel, seed and dice the papaya.
4. Combine all ingredients and chill well.

Nutritional values per 2-ounce (60-gram) portion:

Calories	43	Protein	1 g
Calories from fat	7 %	Vitamin A	474 Iu
Total fat	< 1 g	Vitamin C	28 mg
Saturated fat	0 g	Sodium	150 mg
Cholesterol	0 g		

♦♦♦

RECIPE 25.10

TROPICAL FRUIT SALAD
WITH YOGURT DRESSING

Yield: 4 Small Salads

Mango, cut into 1/2-in. (12-mm) cubes	6 oz.	170 g
Pineapple, cut into 1/2-in. (12-mm) cubes	6 oz.	170 g
Papaya, cut into 1/2-in. (12-mm) cubes	4 oz.	120 g
Grapefruit segments	16	16
Pineapple or grapefruit juice	2 oz.	60 g
Plain, nonfat yogurt	4 oz.	120 g
Honey	2 Tbsp.	30 ml
Fresh lime juice	1 Tbsp.	15 ml
Butterhead lettuce, large leaves, separated and cleaned	4	4
Kiwi, peeled and sliced	1	1
Poppy seeds	1 tsp.	5 ml

1. Mix the mango, pineapple, papaya and grapefruit together with the pineapple or grapefruit juice.
2. To make the dressing, whisk the yogurt, honey and lime juice together.
3. Line the plates with the butterhead lettuce. Arrange the kiwi slices and the fruit salad over the lettuce.
4. Drizzle the dressing over the fruits and top with poppy seeds.

Nutritional values per serving:

Calories	187	Protein	5 g
Calories from fat	6 %	Vitamin A	3623 IU
Total fat	1 g	Vitamin C	109 mg
Saturated fat	0 g	Sodium	34 mg
Cholesterol	1 mg		

♦♦♦

RECIPE 25.11

GRATIN OF FRESH BERRIES
WITH CRÈME FRAÎCHE

Yield: 1 Serving

Assorted fresh berries, such as raspberries, blueberries and blackberries	4 oz.	120 g
Crème fraîche	2 oz.	60 g
Orange liqueur	1 tsp.	5 ml
Brown sugar	1 Tbsp.	15 ml

1. Arrange the berries in an even layer in a shallow, heatproof serving dish.

2. Stir the crème fraîche and orange liqueur together. Spoon this mixture over the berries.

3. Sprinkle the brown sugar over the creme. Place under a broiler or salamander just until the sugar melts. Serve immediately.

===== ♦♦♦ =====

RECIPE 25.12

GRILLED FRUIT KEBABS

Yield: 8 Skewers

Cantaloupe	6 oz.	170 g
Honeydew melon	6 oz.	170 g
Pineapple	6 oz.	170 g
Strawberries	8	8
Brown sugar	2 oz.	60 g
Lime juice	4 oz.	120 g
Cinnamon, ground	1/4 tsp.	1 ml

1. Remove the rind and cut the melons and pineapple into 1-inch (2.5-cm) cubes. Hull the strawberries and leave whole.

2. To make the sugar glaze, combine the sugar, lime juice and cinnamon, stirring until the sugar dissolves.

3. Heat the grill and clean the grate thoroughly.

4. Thread the fruits onto kebab skewers, alternating colors for an attractive appearance.

5. Brush the fruits with the sugar glaze. Grill, rotating the skewers frequently to develop an evenly light brown surface.

6. Serve immediately as an appetizer, a garnish for ice cream or an accompaniment to rich meats such as pork or lamb.

===== ♦♦♦ =====

RECIPE 25.13

CHERRY CONFIT

Yield: 4 oz. (120 g)

Red onion, small dice	2 Tbsp.	30 ml
Whole butter	2 tsp.	10 ml
Dried cherries	3 oz.	90 g
Brandy	1 Tbsp.	15 ml
Port	1 Tbsp.	15 ml
Sherry vinegar	1/2 tsp.	3 ml

1. Sauté the onions in butter without coloring.

2. Add the cherries. Add the brandy and flambé.

3. Add the port and sherry vinegar; cook until almost dry. Serve warm or at room temperature with charcuterie items, or grilled or roasted meats.

♦♦♦

RECIPE 25.14

BANANAS FOSTER

Bananas Foster is an American classic, created in New Orleans during the 1950s and named for a local celebrity. It is usually prepared for customers tableside, using a portable burner known as a réchaud.

Yield: 1 Serving

Banana, medium	1	1
Unsalted butter	1/2 oz.	15 g
Brown sugar	1/2 oz.	15 g
Fresh orange juice	1 oz.	30 g
Dark rum	1/2 oz.	15 g
Brandy or crème de banana	1/2 oz.	15 g
Cinnamon	TT	TT
Vanilla ice cream	1 portion	1 portion

1. Peel the banana and cut in half lengthwise. Cut each half into three chunks and set aside.
2. Melt the butter in a sauté pan. Add the brown sugar and stir until the sugar melts.
3. Add the bananas and stir to coat them completely with the sauce. Cook until tender, approximately 1–2 minutes.
4. Stir in the orange juice. Add the rum and brandy, then flame the mixture. Sprinkle the cinnamon onto the bananas.
5. When the flames die, spoon the bananas and sauce over the ice cream and serve immediately.

♦♦♦

RECIPE 25.15

BANANA FRITTERS

Yield: 40 Fritters

Egg, beaten	1	1
Milk	8 oz.	250 g
Unsalted butter, melted	2 oz.	60 g
Vanilla extract	1 tsp.	5 ml
Orange zest, finely grated	2 Tbsp.	30 ml
Orange juice	2 oz.	60 g
Ripe banana, large	1	1
Pastry flour, sifted	12 oz.	340 g
Granulated sugar	4 oz.	120 g
Baking powder	1 Tbsp.	15 ml
Salt	1/2 tsp.	2 ml
Confectioner's sugar	as needed for garnish	

1. Whisk together the egg, milk, butter and vanilla. Add the orange zest and juice.
2. Peel and dice the banana and add to the egg mixture.
3. Sift together the flour, sugar, baking powder and salt. Gently stir in the banana-egg mixture to form a thick batter.

4. Heat deep-fryer oil to 350°F (180°C). Fry 1-tablespoon (15-milliliter) portions of the batter until the fritters are brown and crisp, approximately 5 minutes.

5. Drain on paper towels, dust with confectioner's sugar and serve hot.

$\blacklozenge\blacklozenge\blacklozenge$

RECIPE 25.16

LEMON CURD

Yield: 1-1/2 qt. (1.5 lt)

Whole eggs	12	12
Egg yolks	4	4
Granulated sugar	2 lb.	900 g
Unsalted butter, cubed	1 lb.	450 g
Lemon zest	from 8 lemons	from 8 lemons
Fresh lemon juice	12 oz.	340 g

1. Whisk everything together in a large bowl.
2. Place the bowl over a pan of simmering water and cook, stirring frequently, until very thick, approximately 20–25 minutes.
3. Strain, cover and chill completely. Serve with scones or use as a filling for tartlets or layer cakes.

$\blacklozenge\blacklozenge\blacklozenge$

RECIPE 25.17

BRAISED RHUBARB

Yield: 10 lb. (4.5 kg)

Tart green apples, peeled and cubed	2 lb. 8 oz.	1.1 kg
Rhubarb, IQF pieces	7 lb.	3.2 kg
Unsalted butter	4 oz.	120 g
Sweet white wine	8 oz.	250 g
Brown sugar	14 oz.	400 g
Vanilla extract	2 tsp.	10 ml
Cinnamon	1 Tbsp.	15 ml
Nutmeg	1/4 tsp.	1 ml
Orange juice	2 oz.	60 g
Salt	1/2 tsp.	2 ml

1. Sauté the apples and rhubarb in the butter until they begin to soften.
2. Add the wine and reduce by half. Add the remaining ingredients. Simmer until the rhubarb is very tender.
3. Serve at room temperature in prebaked pastry cups, topped with crème chantilly or serve warm over ice cream.

◆◆◆

RECIPE 25.18
BERRY COMPOTE

Yield: 1 pt. (450 ml)

Berries, fresh or frozen	1 pt.	500 ml
Granulated sugar	4 oz.	120 g
Oranges, juice and zest	2	2
Honey	3 oz.	90 g
Cinnamon stick	1	1
Brandy	3 Tbsp.	45 ml

1. Select an assortment of fresh or frozen berries—strawberries, blueberries, raspberries, blackberries and cherries can be used, depending on availability.

2. Place the fruits and sugar in a nonreactive saucepan. Add the juice of two oranges. Bring to a simmer over low heat; cook until the fruits are soft but still intact.

3. Strain the mixture, saving both the fruits and the liquid. Return the liquid to the saucepan. Add the finely grated zest from one orange, the honey, cinnamon and brandy.

4. Bring to a boil and reduce until the mixture thickens enough to coat the back of a spoon. Remove from the heat and cool to room temperature.

5. Gently stir the reserved fruits into the sauce, cover and chill.

◆◆◆

RECIPE 25.19
APPLESAUCE

Yield: 1 qt. (1 lt)

McIntosh apples	4 lb.	1.8 g
Granulated sugar	5 oz.	150 g
Lemon juice	1 Tbsp.	15 ml
Cinnamon sticks	2	2

1. Peel, core and quarter the apples. Place in a saucepan with just enough cold water to cover the bottom of the pan. Add the cinnamon sticks.

2. Bring to a simmer, cover and cook until the apples are tender, approximately 15 minutes.

3. Add the sugar and lemon juice. Simmer 10 minutes more.

4. Remove the cinnamon stick and press the apples through a food mill.

◆◆◆

RECIPE 25.20
FRESH CRANBERRY-ORANGE SAUCE

Yield: 3 qt. (3 lt)

Granulated sugar	1 lb.	450 g
Orange juice	4 oz.	120 g
Water	8 oz.	225 g
Fresh or frozen cranberries	1 lb. 8 oz.	700 g
Cinnamon stick	1	1
Orange liqueur	2 oz.	60 g

| Orange zest, finely grated | 2 Tbsp. | 30 ml |
| Orange segments | 20 | 20 |

1. Combine the sugar, juice and water in a nonreactive saucepan; bring to a boil.

2. Add the cranberries and cinnamon stick and simmer uncovered until the berries begin to burst, approximately 15 minutes. Skim off any foam that rises to the surface.

3. Add the orange liqueur and zest and simmer for another 5 minutes.

4. Remove from the heat and remove the cinnamon stick. Add the orange segments. Cool and refrigerate.

◆◆◆

RECIPE 25.21

MANGO CHUTNEY

Yield: 1-1/2 qt. (1-1/2 lt)

Mango, peeled and diced	2 lb.	900 g
Onion, fine dice	4 oz.	120 g
Garlic cloves, minced	2	2
Cider vinegar	8 oz.	250 g
Dark brown sugar	8 oz.	250 g
Golden raisins	2-1/2 oz.	75 g
Crystallized ginger	4 oz.	120 g
Salt	1/2 tsp.	2 ml
Cinnamon sticks	2	2
Red pepper flakes	1/2 tsp.	2 ml
Mustard seeds	1/2 tsp.	2 ml
Fresh ginger	1 tsp.	5 ml
Lime juice	1 oz.	30 g

1. Combine the mango, onion, garlic, vinegar and sugar in a large, heavy saucepan. Cook until the sugar dissolves.

2. Stir in the raisins, crystallized ginger, salt and spices. Simmer until the onions and raisins are very soft, approximately 45 minutes. Skim foam from the surface as necessary.

3. Stir in the lime juice and adjust the seasonings.

4. Remove from the heat and cool uncovered. The chutney will thicken somewhat as it cools but should be thinner than fruit preserves.

◆◆◆

RECIPE 25.22

SWEET ORANGE MARMALADE

Yield: 1-1/4 qt. (1-1/4 lt)

Lemon	1	1
Valencia oranges	4	4
Water	as needed	as needed
Granulated sugar	as needed	as needed

1. Cut the lemon and oranges in half lengthwise, then slice very thinly. Remove all seeds. Measure the volume of the fruits and then place them in

Continued

a nonreactive pan. Add 12 ounces (360 grams) of cold water for each cup of fruit and allow to soak several hours or overnight.

2. Place the fruits and water in a heavy saucepan and bring to a boil over medium-high heat. Allow to boil gently for 2 hours. Skin foam from the surface as necessary.

3. Remeasure the volume of fruit and liquid. Add 6 ounces (180 grams) of sugar for each cup of the boiled fruit and liquid. Return to the stove and boil until the temperature reaches 218°F (103°C), approximately 30 minutes. Remove from heat and cool uncovered.

PART FOUR
BAKING

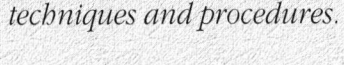

Like cooking, learning to bake fresh breads and to prepare both classic and contemporary pastries and desserts is not simply a matter of following written directions. You must understand the baking process as well as fundamental techniques and procedures.

In order to provide you with a thorough introduction to the skills needed in a bakeshop, we focus on preparing the types of breads and desserts usually found in a small retail shop or restaurant. Because this book is not designed for large wholesale or commercial bakeries, mixes, stabilizers and mechanical preparation and shaping skills are not included.

Part IV begins with a chapter on preparation and ingredients, then presents chapters on quick breads and yeast breads. We then shift to desserts with chapters on pies, pastries and cookies (including classic doughs such as puff pastry and éclair paste), cakes and frostings (including brownies), and creams, custards, frozen desserts and dessert sauces. Many of the recipes found at the end of these chapters are assembled using components from one or more other chapters.

Throughout this portion of the book, you will see the word formula used in place of recipe. This is standard terminology in the industry.

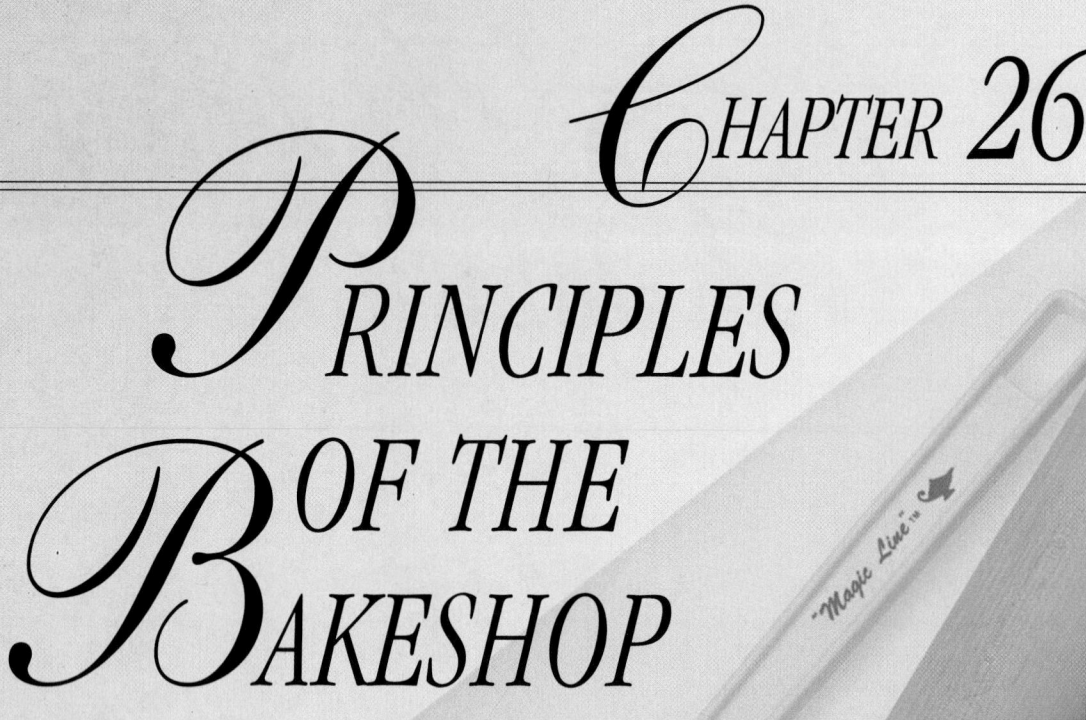

CHAPTER 26

PRINCIPLES OF THE BAKESHOP

CHAPTER 27
QUICK BREADS

CHAPTER 28
YEAST BREADS

After studying this chapter you will be able to:

- select and use yeast
- perform the 10 steps involved in yeast bread production
- mix yeast doughs using the straight dough method and sponge method
- prepare rolled-in doughs

Although few baked goods intimidate novice bakers as much as yeast breads, few baked goods are actually as forgiving or as comforting to prepare as yeast breads. By mastering a few basic procedures and techniques, you can offer your customers delicious, fresh yeast products.

Yeast breads can be divided into two categories: lean doughs and rich doughs. Lean doughs, such as those used for French and Italian breads, contain little or no sugar or fat. Rich doughs, such as brioche and some multigrain breads, contain significantly more sugar and fat. Rolled-in doughs, so-called because the fat is rolled into the dough in layers, are a type of rich dough used for baked goods such as croissants and sweetened danish.

The study of yeast breads could well occupy this entire text and an entire course. The focus here is narrowed to an understanding of fundamental techniques and procedures for making the most common styles of yeast breads for a small retail shop or restaurant. Most of the formulas in this chapter yield only one or two loaves or a few dozen rolls. Although most of these formulas can be increased successfully if necessary, you can best develop proper judgment skills by first preparing small quantities. We discuss hands-on mixing and make-up techniques, leaving the science of commercial (i.e., mechanical) bread production to others.

YEAST

Yeast is a living organism: a one-celled fungus. Various strains of yeast are present virtually everywhere. Yeast feeds on carbohydrates, converting them to carbon dioxide and alcohol in an organic process known as **fermentation**:

Yeast + Carbohydrates = Alcohol + Carbon Dioxide

When yeast releases carbon dioxide gas during bread making, the gas becomes trapped in the dough's gluten network. The trapped gas leavens the bread, providing the desired rise and texture. The small amount of alcohol produced by fermentation evaporates during baking.

As with most living things, yeast is very sensitive to temperature. It prefers temperatures between 90°F and 110°F (32–43°C). At temperatures below 34°F (2°C) it becomes dormant; above 138°F (59°C) it dies.

Salt is used in bread making because it conditions gluten, making it stronger and more elastic. Salt also affects yeast fermentation. Because salt inhibits the growth of yeast, it helps control the dough's rise. Too little salt and not only will the bread taste bland, it will rise too rapidly. Too much salt, however, and the yeast will be destroyed. By learning to control the amount of food for the yeast and the temperatures of fermentation, you can learn to control the texture of your yeast-leavened products.

Fermentation—*the process by which yeast converts sugar into alcohol and carbon dioxide; it also refers to the time that yeast dough is left to rise— that is, the time it takes for carbon dioxide gas cells to form and become trapped in the gluten network.*

TABLE 28.1	TEMPERATURES FOR YEAST DEVELOPMENT	
Temperature		Yeast Development
34°F	2°C	Inactive
60–70°F	16–21°C	Slow action
70–90°F	21–32°C	Best temperature for growth of fresh yeast
105–115°F	41–46°C	Best temperature for growth of dry yeast
125–130°F	52–54°C	Best temperature for activating instant yeast
138°F	59°C	Yeast dies

Types of Yeast

Baker's yeast is available in two forms: compressed and active dry. (You may also encounter a product called brewer's yeast; it is a nutritional supplement with no leavening ability.)

Compressed Yeast

Compressed yeast is a mixture of yeast and starch with a moisture content of approximately 70%. Also referred to as **fresh yeast**, compressed yeast must be kept refrigerated. It should be creamy white and crumbly with a fresh, yeasty smell. Do not use compressed yeast that has developed a sour odor, brown color or slimy film.

Compressed yeast is available in 0.6-ounce (17-gram) cubes and 1-pound (450-gram) blocks. Under proper storage conditions, compressed yeast has a shelf life of 2–3 weeks.

Active Dry Yeast

Active dry yeast differs from compressed yeast in that virtually all of the moisture has been removed by hot air. The absence of moisture renders the organism dormant and allows the yeast to be stored without refrigeration for several months. When preparing doughs, dry yeast is generally rehydrated in a lukewarm (approximately 110°F [43°C]) liquid before being added to the other ingredients.

Dry yeast is available in 1/4-ounce (7-gram) packages and 1- or 2-pound (450-gram or 1-kilogram) vacuum-sealed bags. It should be stored in a cool, dry place and refrigerated after opening.

Instant Yeast

Instant or **quick-rise dry yeast** is also available. It must be blended with the dry ingredients in a bread formula, then activated with hot (approximately 125–130°F [52–54°C]) water. It dramatically speeds the rising process. Instant yeast can be substituted measure for measure for regular dry yeast. Instant yeast is still a living organism and will be destroyed at temperatures above 138°F (59°C).

The flavors of dry and compressed yeasts are virtually indistinguishable, but dry yeast is approximately twice as strong. Because too much yeast can ruin bread, always remember to halve the specified weight of compressed yeast when substituting dry yeast in a formula. Likewise, if a formula specifies dry yeast, double the amount when substituting compressed yeast. All of the formulas in this text requiring yeast use regular active dry yeast.

Sourdough Starter

Prior to commercial yeast production, bakers relied on starters to leaven their breads. Early starters were simple but magical mixtures of flour and liquid (water, potato broth, milk) left to capture wild yeasts from the air and then ferment. Only a portion of the starter was used at a time. The rest was kept for later use, replenished periodically with additional flour and liquid so the magic could continue.

Today, starters are generally fortified with yeast to provide consistency and reliability; they are prized for the unique, sour flavors they impart. Prepared dry cultures are often used commercially to give bread a "sourdough" flavor without requiring the time and space necessary to develop and maintain an active starter.

◆◆◆

RECIPE 28.1

SOURDOUGH STARTER

Yield: 1 qt. (1 lt)

Active dry yeast	1 tsp.	5 ml
Water, warm	4 oz.	120 g
Water, room temperature	14 oz.	400 g
All-purpose flour	2 lb.	1 kg

1. Combine the yeast and warm water. Let stand until foamy, approximately 10 minutes.
2. Stir in the 14 ounces (400 grams) of room-temperature water, then add the flour, 2 ounces (60 grams) at a time.
3. Blend by hand or with the paddle attachment of an electric mixer on low speed for 2 minutes.
4. Place the starter in a warmed bowl and cover with plastic wrap. Let stand at room temperature overnight. The starter should triple in volume but still be wet and sticky. Refrigerate until ready to use.
5. Each time a portion of the starter is used, it must be replenished. To replenish the starter, stir in equal amounts by volume of flour and warm water. Then allow the mixture to ferment at room temperature for several hours or overnight before refrigerating.

NOTE: If liquid rises to the top of the starter it should be stirred back into the mixture. If the starter develops a pink or yellow film it has been contaminated and must be discarded.

Sourdough Starter

PRODUCTION STAGES FOR YEAST BREADS

The production of yeast breads can be divided into 10 stages:

1. scaling ingredients
2. mixing and kneading dough
3. fermenting dough

4. punching down dough
5. portioning dough
6. rounding portions
7. shaping portions
8. proofing products
9. baking products
10. cooling and storing finished products

Stage 1: Scaling Ingredients

As with any other bakeshop product, it is important to scale or measure ingredients accurately when making a yeast bread. Be sure that all necessary ingredients are available and at the proper temperature before starting.

The amount of flour required in a yeast bread may vary depending upon the humidity level, storage conditions of the flour and the accuracy with which other ingredients are measured. The amount of flour stated in most formulas is to be used as a guide; experience teaches when more or less flour is actually needed.

Stage 2: Mixing and Kneading Dough

The way ingredients are combined affects the outcome of the bread. A dough must be mixed properly in order to combine the ingredients uniformly, distribute the yeast and develop the gluten. If the dough is not mixed properly, the bread's texture and shape suffer.

Yeast breads are usually mixed by either the **straight dough method** or the **sponge method**. A third method used for rich, flaky doughs is discussed below in the section on **rolled-in doughs**.

Once ingredients are combined, the dough must be kneaded to develop gluten, the network of proteins that gives a bread its shape and texture. Kneading can be done by hand or by an electric mixer with its dough hook

✦✦✦
THE RISE OF YEAST BREADS

How and when the first yeast-leavened bread came into being no one knows. Perhaps some wild yeasts—the world is full of them—drifted into a dough as it awaited baking. Perhaps some ancient baker substituted fermented ale or beer for water one day. In any case, the resulting bread was different, lighter and more appetizing.

Based on models, images and writings found in excavated tombs, we can be fairly certain that the ancient Egyptians saved a bit of fermented dough from one day's baking to add to the next day's. This use of sourdough starter continues today, enjoying widespread popularity.

Other cultures developed their own leavening methods. The Greeks and Romans prepared a wheat porridge with wine, which caused their doughs to ferment. The Gauls and Iberians added the foamy head from ale to their doughs. Both methods resulted in lighter breads that retained their fresh textures longer.

Since ancient times, bread baking has been one of the first household tasks readily turned over to professionals. The first cooks to work outside homes during the Greek and Roman empires were bakers. The bakery trade flourished during the Middle Ages, with a wide variety of breads being produced. Yeast-leavened breads remained the exception, not the norm, until well into the 17th century, however.

The first real collection of bread recipes is found in Nicolas Bonnefon's *Les Délices de la campagne*, published in 1654. Bonnefon's instructions, meant for those dissatisfied with commercial products of the time, included the use of beer yeast. By the end of the 17th century, published works included recipes for breads leavened with sourdough starter and the yeasts used in breweries.

Louis Pasteur finally identified yeast as a living organism in 1857. Soon after, a process for distilling or manufacturing baker's yeast was developed. By 1868, commercial baking yeast was available in stores.

attachment. Dough should be kneaded until it is smooth and moderately elastic. The presence of a few blisterlike air bubbles on the dough's surface also signals that kneading is complete. Because fat and sugar slow gluten development, rich, sweet doughs are generally kneaded longer than lean doughs. Overkneading results in dough that is, at best, difficult to shape and, in extreme cases, sticky and inelastic. Overkneading is rarely a problem, however, except when using a high-speed mixer or food processor.

PROCEDURE FOR KNEADING DOUGH BY HAND

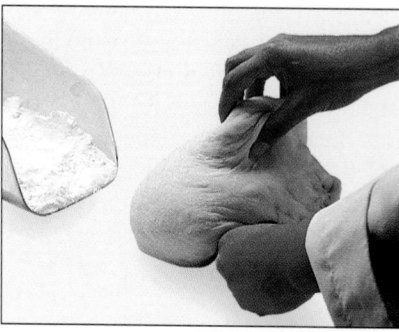

1. First, bring a portion of the dough toward you.

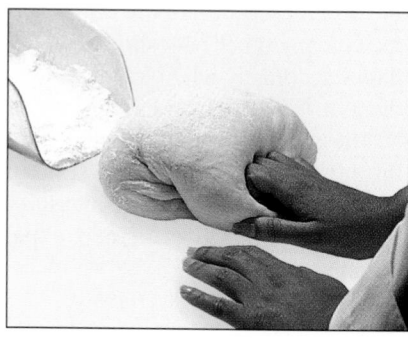

2. Then push the dough away from you with your fist.

3. Repeat until the dough is properly kneaded.

Straight Dough Method

The simplest and most common method for mixing yeast doughs is known as the straight dough method. With this method, all ingredients are simply combined and mixed. The yeast may or may not be combined first with a warm liquid. Be careful that the temperature of the liquid ingredients does not exceed 138°F (59°C) or the yeast will die.

Once the ingredients are combined, the dough is kneaded until it is smooth and elastic. Kneading time varies according to the kneading method used and the type of dough being produced. The straight dough method is illustrated with Recipe 28.2, Soft Yeast Dinner Rolls.

Sponge Method

The sponge method of mixing yeast doughs has two stages. During the first stage the yeast, liquid and approximately one half of the flour are combined to make a thick batter known as a **sponge**. The sponge is allowed to rise until bubbly and doubled in size. During the second stage the fat, salt, sugar and remaining flour are added. The dough is kneaded and allowed to rise again.

These two fermentations give sponge method breads a somewhat different flavor and a lighter texture than breads made with the straight dough method.

Do not confuse sponge method breads with sourdough starters. The sponge method is most often used to improve the texture of heavy doughs such as rye. Unlike a sourdough starter, the first-stage sponge is prepared only for the specific formula and is not reserved for later use. The sponge method is illustrated with Recipe 28.3, Light Rye Bread.

Stage 3: Fermenting Dough

As mentioned earlier, fermentation is the process by which yeast converts sugar into alcohol and carbon dioxide. Fermentation also refers to the time that yeast dough is left to rise—that is, the time it takes for carbon dioxide gas to form and become trapped in the gluten network. Note that **fermentation** refers to the rise given to the entire mass of yeast dough, while **proofing** refers to the rise given to shaped yeast products just prior to baking.

For fermentation, place the kneaded dough into a lightly oiled container large enough to allow the dough to expand. The surface of the dough may be oiled to prevent drying. Cover the dough and place it in a warm place—that is, at temperatures between 75° and 85°F (24–29°C). It is better to allow the dough to rise slowly in a cool place than to rush fermentation.

Fermentation is complete when the dough has approximately doubled in size and no longer springs back when pressed gently with two fingers. The time necessary varies depending on the type of dough, the temperature of the room and the temperature of the dough.

Stage 4: Punching Down Dough

After fermentation, the dough is gently folded down to expel and redistribute the gas pockets with a technique known as **punching down**. Punching down dough also helps even out the dough's temperature and relaxes the gluten.

Stage 5: Portioning Dough

The dough is now ready to be divided into portions. For loaves, the dough is scaled to the desired weight. For individual rolls you can first shape the dough into an even log, then cut off portions with a chef's knife or dough cutter. Weighing the cut dough pieces on a portion scale ensures even-sized portions. When portioning, work quickly and keep the dough covered to prevent it from drying out.

Stage 6: Rounding Portions

The portions of dough must be shaped into smooth, round balls in a technique known as **rounding**. Rounding stretches the outside layer of gluten into a smooth coating. This helps hold in gases and makes it easier to shape the dough. Unrounded rolls rise unevenly and have a rough, lumpy surface.

Stage 7: Shaping Portions

Lean doughs and some rich doughs can be shaped into a variety of forms: large loaves, small loaves, free-form or country-style rounds or individual dinner rolls. Table 28.2 identifies common pan sizes and the approximate weight of the dough used to fill them. Some shaping techniques are diagrammed below. Other doughs, particularly brioche, croissant and danish, are usually shaped in very specific ways. Those techniques are discussed and illustrated with their specific formulas.

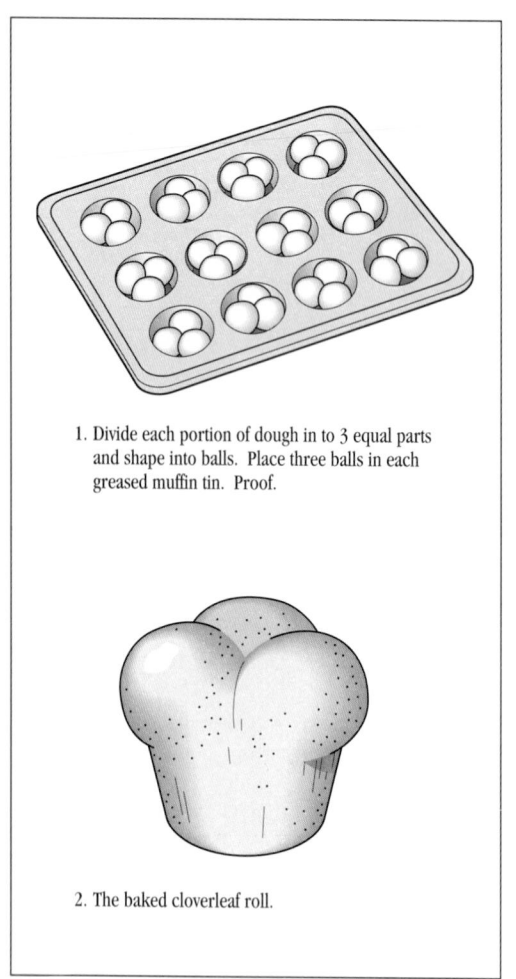

1. Divide each portion of dough in to 3 equal parts and shape into balls. Place three balls in each greased muffin tin. Proof.

2. The baked cloverleaf roll.

FIGURE 28.1 *Cloverleaf Rolls*

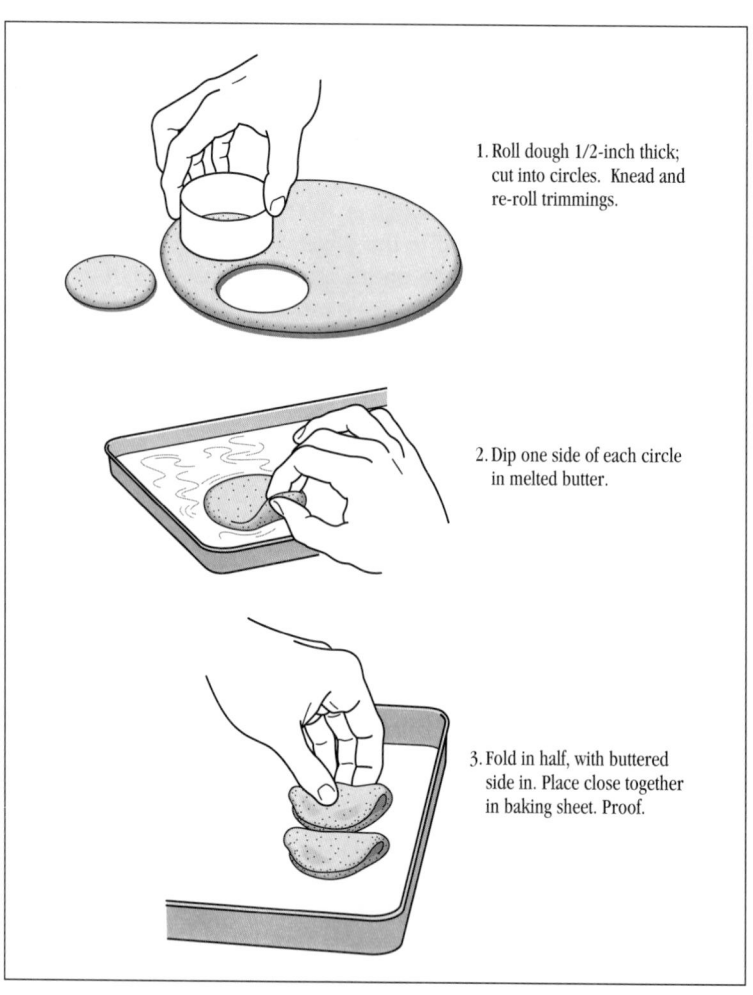

1. Roll dough 1/2-inch thick; cut into circles. Knead and re-roll trimmings.

2. Dip one side of each circle in melted butter.

3. Fold in half, with buttered side in. Place close together in baking sheet. Proof.

FIGURE 28.2 *Parker House Rolls*

TABLE 28.2   PAN SIZES

Pan	Approximate Size	Weight of Dough*
Sandwich Loaf	16 in. × 4 in. × 4-1/2 in.	4 lb.
Pullman	13 in. × 4 in. × 3 in.	3 lb.
Large	9 in. × 5 in. × 3 in.	2 lb.
Medium	8 in. × 4 in. × 2 in.	1 lb. 8 oz.
Small	7 in. × 3 in. × 2 in.	1 lb.
Miniature	5 in. × 3 in. × 2 in.	8 oz.

*Weights given are approximate; variations may occur based on the type of dough used as well as the temperature and time of proofing.

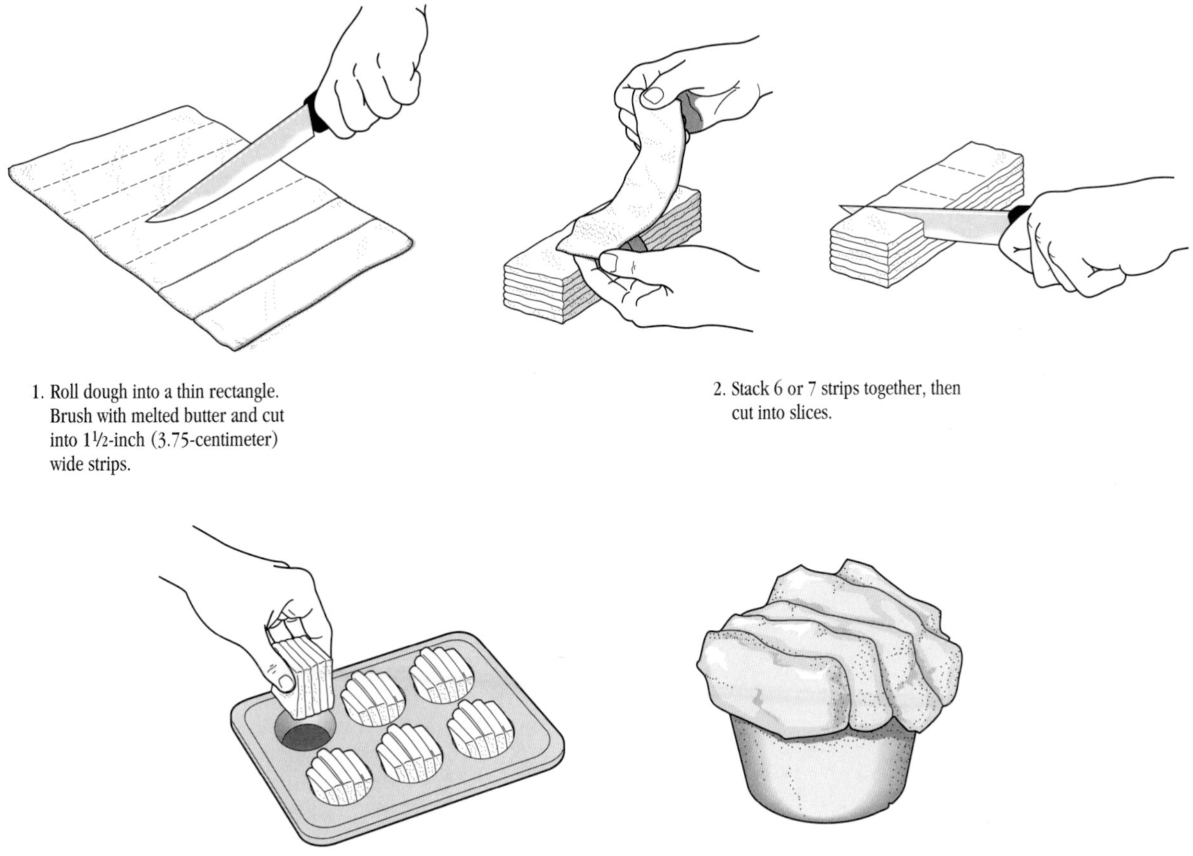

1. Roll dough into a thin rectangle.
   Brush with melted butter and cut
   into 1½-inch (3.75-centimeter)
   wide strips.

2. Stack 6 or 7 strips together, then
   cut into slices.

3. Place each slice into a greased
   muffin tin, cut side up. Proof.

4. The baked butterflake roll.

FIGURE 28.3   *Butterflake Rolls*

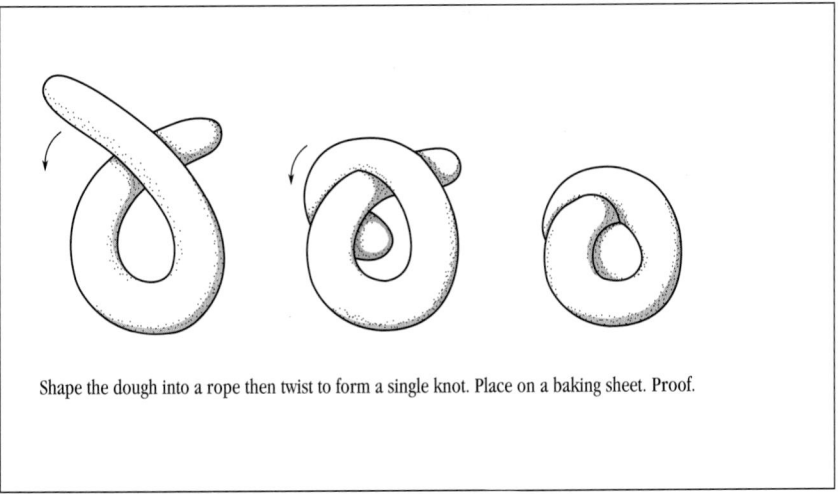

Shape the dough into a rope then twist to form a single knot. Place on a baking sheet. Proof.

FIGURE 28.4   *Bow Knot Rolls*

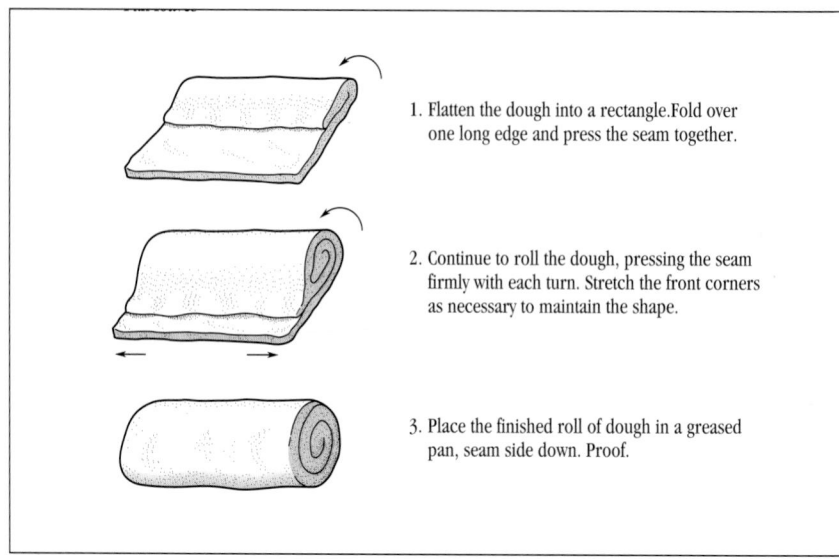

1. Flatten the dough into a rectangle.Fold over one long edge and press the seam together.

2. Continue to roll the dough, pressing the seam firmly with each turn. Stretch the front corners as necessary to maintain the shape.

3. Place the finished roll of dough in a greased pan, seam side down. Proof.

FIGURE 28.5   *Pan Loaves*

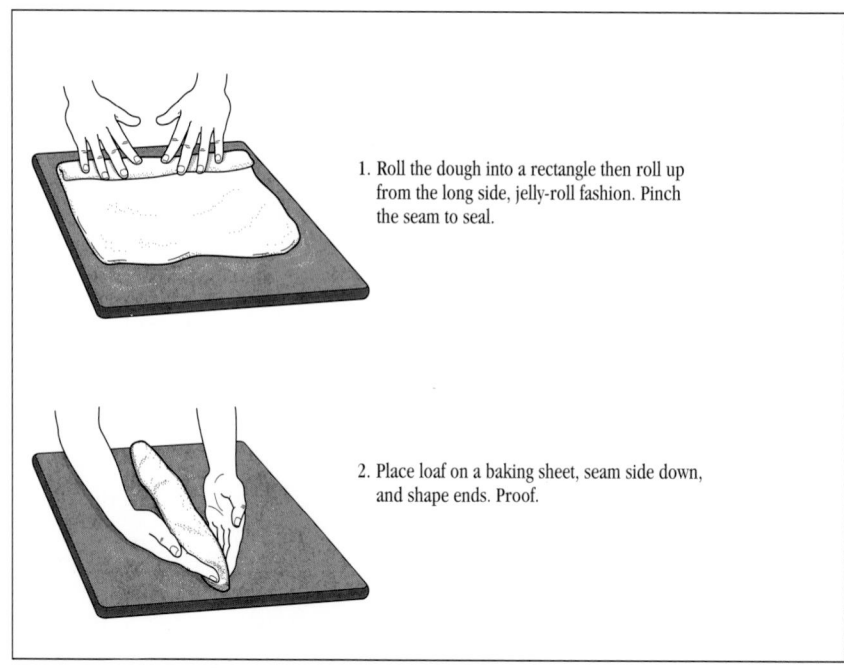

1. Roll the dough into a rectangle then roll up from the long side, jelly-roll fashion. Pinch the seam to seal.

2. Place loaf on a baking sheet, seam side down, and shape ends. Proof.

FIGURE 28.6   *Free-Form Loaves*

Stage 8: Proofing Products

Proofing—*the final rise of shaped yeast products just prior to baking.*

Proofing is the final rise of shaped or panned yeast products before baking. The temperatures should be between 95° and 115°F (35–46°C), slightly higher than the temperatures for fermentation. Some humidity is also desirable to prevent the dough from drying or forming a crust. Temperature and humidity can be controlled with a special cabinet known as a **proof box**.

Proofing should continue until the product doubles in size and springs back slowly when lightly touched. Underproofing results in poor volume and texture. Overproofing results in a sour taste, poor volume and a paler color after baking.

Stage 9: Baking Products

As yeast breads bake, a variety of chemical and physical changes turn the dough into an edible product. These changes are discussed in Chapter 26, Principles of the Bakeshop.

Because of the expansion of gases, yeast products experience a sudden rise when first placed in a hot oven. This rise is known as **oven spring**. As the dough's temperature increases, the yeast dies, the gluten fibers become firm, the starches gelatinize, the moisture evaporates and, finally, the crust forms and turns brown.

Before baking, products can be washed and then, if desired, slashed.

Washes

The appearance of yeast breads can be altered by applying a glaze or **wash** to the dough before baking. The crust is made shiny or matte, hard or soft, darker or lighter by the proper use of washes. Washes are also used to attach seeds, wheat germ, oats or other toppings to the dough's surface.

The most commonly used wash is an egg wash, composed of whole egg and water. Yeast products can also be topped with plain water, a mixture of egg and milk, plain milk or richer glazes containing sugar and flavorings. Even a light dusting of white flour can be used to top dough. (This is commonly seen with potato rolls.)

Avoid using too much wash, as it can burn or cause the product to stick to the pan. Puddles or streaks of egg wash on the dough will cause uneven browning.

Washes may be applied before or after proofing. If applied after proofing, be extremely careful not to deflate the product.

Occasionally a formula will specify that melted butter or oil be brushed on the product after baking. Do not, however, apply egg washes to already baked products, as the egg will remain raw and the desired effect will not be achieved.

TABLE 28.3	WASHES FOR YEAST PRODUCTS
Wash	Use
Whole egg and water	Shine and color
Whole egg and milk	Shine and color with a soft crust
Egg white and water	Shine with a firm crust
Water	Crisp crust
Flour	Texture and contrast
Milk or cream	Color with a soft crust

Slashing

The shape and appearance of some breads can be improved by cutting their tops with a sharp knife or razor just before baking. This is referred to as **slashing** or **docking**. Hard-crusted breads are usually slashed to allow for continued rising and the escape of gases after the crust has formed. Breads that are not properly slashed will burst or break along the sides. Slashing can also be used to make an attractive design on the product's surface.

Steam Injection

The crisp crust desired for certain breads and rolls is achieved by introducing moisture into the oven during baking. Professional bakers' ovens have built-in steam injection jets to provide moisture as needed. To create steam in any oven you can spray or mist the bread with water several times during baking, place ice cubes on the oven floor to melt or keep a pan of hot water on the oven's lowest rack. Rich doughs, which do not form crisp crusts, are baked without steam.

Determining Doneness

Baking time is determined by a variety of factors: the product's size, the oven thermostat's accuracy and the desired crust color. Larger items require a longer baking time than smaller ones. Lean dough products bake faster and at higher temperatures than rich dough products.

Bread loaves can be tested for doneness by tapping them on the bottom and listening for a hollow sound. This indicates that air, not moisture, is present inside the loaf. If the bottom is damp or heavy, the loaf probably needs more baking time. The texture and color of the crust are also a good indication of doneness, particularly with individual rolls. As you bake a variety of yeast products you will develop the experience necessary to determine doneness without strict adherence to elapsed time.

Stage 10: Cooling and Storing Finished Products

The quality of even the finest yeast products suffers if they are cooled or stored improperly. Yeast products should be cooled at room temperature and away from drafts. Yeast breads and rolls should be removed from their pans for cooling. Allow loaves to cool completely before slicing.

Once cool, yeast products should be stored at room temperature or frozen for longer storage. Do not refrigerate baked goods, as refrigeration promotes staling. Do not wrap Italian or French loaves, as this causes crusts to lose the desired crispness.

◆◆◆

RECIPE 28.2
SOFT YEAST DINNER ROLLS

Yield: 75 Rolls   **Method:** Straight Dough

Water, warm	1 lb. 4 oz.	560 g
Active dry yeast	2 oz.	60 g
Bread flour	2 lb. 12 oz.	1.2 kg
Salt	1 oz.	30 g
Sugar	4 oz.	120 g
Dried milk powder	2 oz.	60 g
Shortening	2 oz.	60 g
Unsalted butter, softened	2 oz.	60 g
Eggs, whole	4 oz.	120 g
Egg wash	as needed	as needed

1. Combine the water and yeast in a small bowl. Combine the remaining ingredients (except the egg wash) in the bowl of an electric mixer.
2. Add the water-and-yeast mixture to the remaining ingredients; stir to combine.
3. Knead with a dough hook on second speed for 10 minutes.
4. Transfer the dough to a lightly greased bowl, cover and place in a warm spot. Let rise until doubled, approximately 1 hour.
5. Punch down the dough. Let it rest a few minutes to allow the gluten to relax.
6. Divide the dough into 1-1/4-ounce (35-gram) portions and round. Shape as desired and arrange on paper-lined sheet pans. Proof until doubled in size.
7. Carefully brush the proofed rolls with egg wash. Bake at 400°F (200°C) until medium brown, approximately 12–15 minutes.

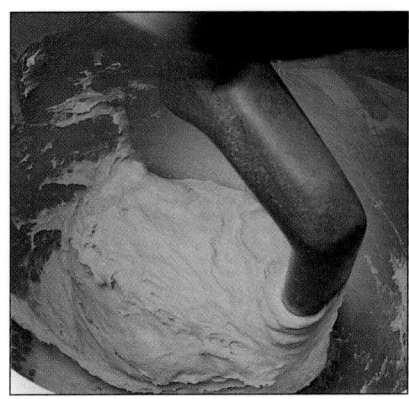

1. Mixing the soft yeast dough:

   a) Combining the ingredients in a mixer bowl with the dough hook attached.

   b) Adding the yeast-and-water mixture.

2. Kneading the dough.

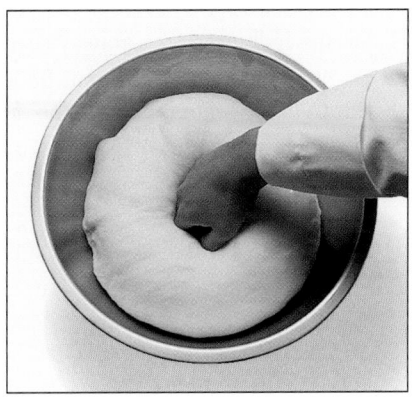

3. The dough before rising.

4. Punching down the dough:

   a) Pressing down on the center of the dough with your fist.

   b) Folding the edges of the dough in toward the center.

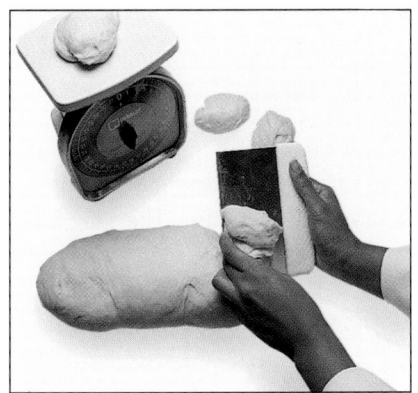

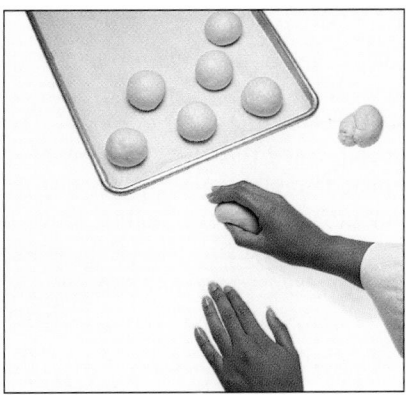

5. Scaling the dough.

6. Rounding the rolls.

7. Egg-washing the rolls.

1. Rye bread starter.

2. Mixing the rye dough.

3. Shaping the rye loaves.

◆◆◆

RECIPE 28.3

LIGHT RYE BREAD

Yield: 2 Large Loaves   **Method:** Sponge

Unbleached wheat flour	1 lb.	450 g
Medium rye flour	8 oz.	225 g
Dark molasses	3 oz.	90 g
Water, warm	1 lb. 4 oz.	600 g
Active dry yeast	1/2 oz.	15 g
Nonfat dry milk	1-1/2 oz.	45 g
Caraway seeds, crushed	2 Tbsp.	30 ml
Kosher salt	1 Tbsp.	15 ml
Unsalted butter, melted	1 Tbsp.	15 ml
Egg wash	as needed	as needed

1. Stir the flours together and set aside.

2. To make the sponge, combine the molasses, water and yeast. Add 8 ounces (225 grams) of the flour mixture. Stir vigorously for 3 minutes. Cover the bowl and set aside to rise until doubled and very bubbly, approximately 1 hour.

3. Stir the milk powder, caraway seeds, salt and butter into the sponge.

4. Gradually add the remaining flour to the sponge. When the dough is too stiff to mix by hand, transfer the dough to a mixer fitted with a dough hook.

5. Continue adding flour until the dough is stiff but slightly tacky. Knead for 5 minutes on low speed.

6. Transfer the dough to a lightly greased bowl, cover and place in a warm place until doubled, approximately 45–60 minutes.

7. Punch down the dough and divide into two pieces. Shape each piece into a round loaf and place on a sheet pan that has been dusted with cornmeal or lightly oiled. Brush the loaves with egg wash and let rise until doubled, approximately 45 minutes.

8. Slash the tops with a razor or knife. Bake at 375°F (190°C) until golden brown and crusty, approximately 25 minutes.

ROLLED-IN DOUGHS

Baked goods made with rolled-in doughs include croissants, Danish pastries and the non-yeast-leavened puff pastry. (Puff pastry is discussed in Chapter 29, Pies, Pastries and Cookies.) The dough is so named because the fat is incorporated through a process of rolling and folding. Products made with a rolled-in dough have a distinctive flaky texture created by the repeated layering of fat and dough. As the dough bakes, moisture is released from the fat in the form of steam. The steam is then trapped between the layers of dough, causing them to rise and separate.

Making Rolled-In Doughs

Rolled-in doughs are made following most of the 10 production stages discussed above. The principal differences are that the butter is incorporated through a turning process after the dough base is fermented and punched down; rolled-in doughs are portioned somewhat differently than other yeast doughs and the portions are then shaped without rounding.

Butter is often used for rolled-in products because of its flavor. Unfortunately, butter is hard to work with because it cracks and breaks when cold and becomes too soft to roll at room temperature. Margarine, shortening or specially formulated high-moisture fats can be used, sometimes in combination with butter, to reduce costs or make the dough easier to work with.

The dough base should not be kneaded too much as gluten will continue to develop during the rolling and folding process. Commercial bakeries, hotels and larger restaurants generally use an electric dough sheeter to roll the dough. This saves time and ensures a more consistent product.

PROCEDURE FOR MAKING ROLLED-IN DOUGHS

1. Mix the dough and allow it to rise.
2. Shape the butter or shortening, then chill it.
3. Roll out the dough evenly, then top with the chilled butter.
4. Fold the dough around the butter, enclosing it completely.
5. Roll out the dough into a rectangle, about 1/2 to 1 inch (1.25 to 2.5 centimeters) thick. Always be sure to roll at right angles; do not roll haphazardly or in a circle as you would pastry doughs.
6. Fold the dough in thirds. Be sure to brush off any excess flour from between the folds. This completes the first turn. Chill the dough for 20 to 30 minutes.
7. Roll out the dough and fold it in the same manner a second and third time, allowing the dough to rest between each turn. After completing the third turn, wrap the dough carefully and allow it to rest for several hours or overnight before shaping and baking.

◆◆◆

RECIPE 28.4
CROISSANTS

Yield: 60 Rolls   **Method:** Rolled-in

Bread flour	2 lb. 4 oz.	1 kg
Salt	1 oz.	30 g
Sugar	6 oz.	170 g
Milk	1 lb. 6 oz.	625 g
Active dry yeast	1 oz.	30 g
Unsalted butter, soft	1 lb. 8 oz.	680 g
Egg wash	as needed	as needed

1. Stir the flour, salt and sugar together in a mixer bowl fitted with a dough hook.
2. Warm the milk to approximately 90°F (32°C). Stir in the yeast.
3. Add the milk-and-yeast mixture to the dry ingredients. Stir until combined, then knead on second speed for 10 minutes.
4. Place the dough in a large floured bowl, cover and let rise until doubled in size, approximately 1 hour.
5. Prepare the butter while the dough is rising. Place the butter in an even layer between two large pieces of plastic wrap and roll into a flat rectan-

Continued

◆◆◆
THE CULTURED CROISSANT

A croissant brings to mind a Parisian sidewalk café and a steaming cup of café crème. It is, however, a truly international delicacy. Created by bakers in Budapest (Hungary) to celebrate the city's liberation from Turkey in 1686, its shape was derived from the crescent moon of the Turkish flag. The delicacy was soon adopted as a breakfast pastry by both the French and the Italians. The first machine for mass-producing croissants was designed by a Japanese firm and manufactured in Italy. Although croissants became popular in this country only during the last decade or so, Americans now consume millions of croissants each year.

gle, approximately 8 inches × 11 inches (20 centimeters × 27.5 centimeters) and chill.

6. After the dough has risen, punch it down. Roll out the dough into a large rectangle, about 1/2 inch (1.25 centimeters) thick and large enough to enclose the rectangle of butter. Place the unwrapped butter in the center of the dough and fold the dough around the butter, enclosing it completely.

7. Roll out the block of dough into a long rectangle, about 1 inch (2.5 centimeters) thick. Fold the dough in thirds, as if you were folding a letter. This completes the first turn. Wrap the dough in plastic and chill for approximately 20–30 minutes.

8. Repeat the rolling and folding process two more times, chilling the dough between each turn. When finished, wrap the dough well and chill it overnight before shaping and baking.

9. To shape the dough into croissant rolls, cut off one quarter of the block at a time, wrapping and returning the rest to the refrigerator. Roll each quarter of dough into a large rectangle, about 1/4 inch (6 millimeters) thick.

10. Cut the dough into uniform triangles. Starting with the large end, roll each triangle into a crescent and place on a paper-lined sheet pan.

11. Brush lightly with egg wash. Proof until doubled, but do not allow the dough to become so warm that the butter melts.

12. Bake at 375°F (190°C) until golden brown, approximately 12–15 minutes.

1. Rolling out the butter between two sheets of plastic wrap.

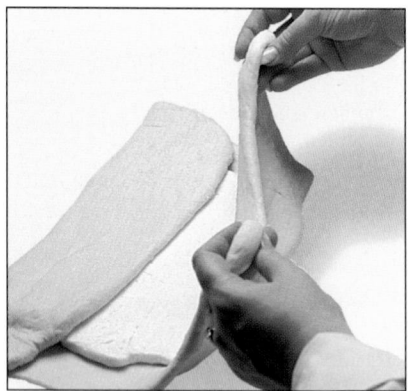

2. After positioning the butter on the rolled-out dough, folding the dough around the butter.

3. Brushing the excess flour from the rolled-out dough.

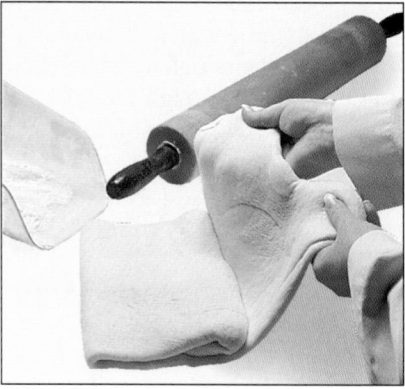

4. Folding the dough in thirds.

5. The finished croissant dough.

6. Cutting the dough into triangles.

7. Baked croissants.

TABLE 28.4   TROUBLESHOOTING CHART

Problem	Cause	Solution
Cannonball of dough	Too much flour forced into the dough	Gradually add water; adjust formula
Crust too pale	Oven temperature too low	Adjust oven
	Dough overproofed	Proof only until almost doubled, then bake immediately
Crust too dark	Oven too hot	Adjust oven
	Too much sugar in dough	Adjust formula or measure sugar carefully
Top crust separates from rest of loaf	Dough improperly shaped	Shape dough carefully
	Crust not slashed properly	Slash dough to a depth of 1/2 in. (1.25 cm)
	Dough dried out during proofing	Cover dough during proofing
Sides of loaf are cracked	Bread expanded after crust had formed	Slash top of loaf before baking
Dense texture	Not enough yeast	Adjust formula or measure yeast carefully
	Not enough fermentation time	Let dough rise until doubled or as directed
	Too much salt	Adjust formula or measure salt carefully
Ropes of undercooked dough running through the product	Insufficient kneading	Knead dough until it is smooth and elastic or as directed
	Insufficient rising time	Allow adequate time for rising
	Oven too hot	Adjust oven
Free-form loaf spreads and flattens	Dough too soft	Add flour
Large holes in bread	Too much yeast	Adjust formula or measure yeast carefully
	Overkneaded	Knead only as directed
	Inadequate punch-down	Punch down properly to knead out excess air before shaping
Blisters on crust	Too much liquid	Measure ingredients carefully
	Improper shaping	Knead out excess air before shaping
	Too much steam in oven	Reduce amount of steam or moisture in oven

CONCLUSION

Fresh yeast breads are a popular and inexpensive addition to any menu and are surprisingly easy to prepare. By understanding and appreciating the importance of each of the ten production stages described above, you will be able to create and adapt formulas to suit your specific operation and needs.

QUESTIONS FOR DISCUSSION

1. Describe the characteristics of lean and rich doughs and give an example of each.
2. Explain the differences between active dry yeast and compressed yeast. Describe the correct procedures for working with these yeasts.
3. Explain the differences between a sponge and a sourdough starter. How are each of these items used?

4. Describe the straight dough mixing method and give two examples of products made with this procedure.

5. Briefly describe the procedure for making a rolled-in dough and give two examples of products made from rolled-in doughs.

6. List the ten production stages for yeast breads. Which of these production stages would also apply to quick bread production? Explain your answer.

Additional Yeast Bread Formulas

RECIPE 28.5

Basic French Bread

Yield: 5 lb. (2.2 kg)   **Method:** Straight Dough

Water, warm	1 qt.	1 lt
Active dry yeast	1 oz.	30 g
Bread flour	2 lb. 12 oz.	1.2 kg
Salt	1 oz.	30 g

1. Combine the water and yeast in a mixer bowl. Add the remaining ingredients and mix on low speed with a dough hook until all of the flour is incorporated.

2. Increase to second speed and knead the dough until it is smooth and elastic.

3. Let the dough rise until doubled. Punch down, divide and shape as desired. Let rise again until doubled.

4. Place a pan of water in the oven to generate steam while the dough rises.

5. Bake at 400°F (200°C) until the crust is well developed and golden brown and the bread is baked through, approximately 12 minutes for rolls and 30 minutes for small loaves.

Nutritional values per 1 oz. (30 g) roll:

Calories	56	Protein	2 g
Calories from fat	4%	Vitamin A	0 IU
Total fat	< 1 g	Vitamin C	0 mg
Saturated fat	0 g	Sodium	138 mg
Cholesterol	0 mg		

◆◆◆

RECIPE 28.6

White Sandwich Bread

Yield: 2 Large Loaves   **Method:** Straight Dough

Water, warm	12 oz.	340 g
Dry milk	1-1/4 oz.	35 g
Sugar	1 oz.	30 g

Salt	2 tsp.	10 ml
Active dry yeast	1/2 oz.	15 g
Bread flour	1 lb. 8 oz.	680 g
Unsalted butter, soft	1 oz.	30 g
Eggs	2	2

1. Combine the water, milk, sugar, salt, yeast and 12 ounces (340 grams) of flour. Blend well. Add the butter and eggs and beat for 2 minutes.

2. Stir in the remaining flour, 2 ounces (60 grams) at a time. Knead for 8 minutes.

3. Place the dough in a lightly greased bowl, cover and let rise at room temperature until doubled, approximately 1 to 1-1/2 hours.

4. Shape into loaves and let rise until doubled.

5. Bake at 400°F (200°C) if free-form or small loaves; bake at 375°F (190°C) if larger loaves. Bake until brown and hollow sounding, approximately 35 minutes for small loaves and 50 minutes for large loaves.

VARIATION: *Whole wheat*—Substitute up to 12 ounces (340 grams) of whole wheat flour for an equal portion of the bread flour.

RECIPE 28.7
POTATO CHEDDAR CHEESE BREAD

STOUFFER STANFORD COURT, San Francisco, CA
Executive Chef Ercolino Crugnale

Yield: 7 1 lb. 4 oz. (600 g) Loaves   **Method:** Straight Dough

Water, warm (100°F/38°C)	8 oz.	225 g
Active dry yeast	2 oz.	60 g
Bread flour	4 lb. 8 oz.	2.2 kg
Potatoes, boiled, peeled and puréed	2 lb.	1 kg
Kosher salt	1-1/2 oz.	45 g
Cracked pepper	1 oz.	30 g
Unsalted butter, melted	3 oz.	90 g
Cheddar cheese, grated	1 lb.	500 g
Water, room temperature	1 pt.	500 ml

1. Dissolve the yeast in the warm water and set aside.

2. Combine the flour, potatoes, salt, pepper, butter and cheese. Blend on low speed for 2–3 minutes.

3. Slowly add the room temperature water and the yeast mixture. Mix on medium speed for 8–10 minutes.

4. Allow the dough to rise in a warm spot until doubled, approximately 2 hours. Punch down the dough and divide into loaves.

5. Proof until doubled in size, approximately 45 minutes. Bake at 350°F (180°C) until brown, approximately 20–30 minutes.

◆◆◆

RECIPE 28.8

WHOLE WHEAT BREAD

Yield: 2 Large Loaves or 35 Dinner Rolls   **Method:** Straight Dough

Salt	2 tsp.	10 ml
Nonfat dry milk	1-1/4 oz.	35 g
Whole wheat flour	1 lb. 10 oz.	780 g
Water, hot	1 lb. 2 oz.	540 g
Active dry yeast	1/2 oz.	15 g
Honey	3 oz.	90 g
Unsalted butter, soft	1 oz.	30 g

1. In a large mixer bowl, combine the salt and dry milk with 12 ounces (340 grams) of flour.
2. Stir in the hot water, yeast, honey and butter. Beat until combined into a thick batterlike dough.
3. Add the remaining flour 2 ounces (60 grams) at a time. Knead about 8 minutes.
4. Place the dough in a lightly greased bowl and cover. Let rise in a warm place until doubled.
5. Punch down, portion and shape as desired.
6. Let the shaped dough rise until doubled. Bake at 375°F (190°C) until firm and dark brown, approximately 1 hour for loaves and 20 minutes for rolls. Brush the top of the loaves or rolls with melted butter after baking if desired.

◆◆◆

RECIPE 28.9

MULTIGRAIN DATE BREAD

Yield: 2 Small Loaves   **Method:** Straight Dough

Dates, chopped	8 oz.	225 g
Bread flour	1 lb. 8 oz.	680 g
Active dry yeast	1/2 oz.	15 g
Water, warm	1 pt.	450 ml
Honey	4 oz.	120 g
Unsalted butter, melted	2 oz.	60 g
Nonfat dry milk	1-1/4 oz.	35 g
Salt	1 Tbsp.	15 ml
Whole wheat flour	6 oz.	180 g
Rye flour	2 oz.	60 g
Wheat germ	2 oz.	60 g
Bran flakes, toasted	2 oz.	60 g
Sesame seeds	2 Tbsp.	30 ml
Egg wash	as needed	as needed
Poppy or sesame seeds	2 Tbsp.	30 ml

1. In a small bowl, combine the dates with 2 ounces (60 grams) of the bread flour; toss to coat and set aside.

2. In a large mixer bowl, dissolve the yeast in the warm water. Add the honey, butter, milk powder, salt and whole wheat flour. Beat at medium speed for 2 minutes.

3. Stir in the rye flour, wheat germ, bran flakes, sesame seeds and date mixture.

4. Slowly add enough of the remaining bread flour to make a soft dough. Knead until smooth and elastic, approximately 5 minutes.

5. Place the dough in a lightly greased bowl and cover. Allow to rise until doubled, approximately 1-1/2 hours.

6. Punch down the dough and knead for a few seconds.

7. Divide the dough in half. Shape each piece and place in a lightly greased loaf pan. Cover and allow to rise until almost doubled, approximately 45 minutes.

8. Slash the top of the loaves as desired and top with egg wash and poppy or sesame seeds. Bake at 375°F (190°C) until golden brown and firm, approximately 40 minutes. Loaves should be dry and sound hollow when tapped on the bottom. Remove the loaves from the pans to cool.

◆◆◆

RECIPE 28.10

BREADSTICKS

Yield: 24 Breadsticks **Method:** Straight Dough

Active dry yeast	1/2 oz.	15 g
Water, warm	10 oz.	300 g
Sugar	1 oz.	30 g
Olive oil	4 oz.	120 g
Salt	2 tsp.	10 ml
Bread flour	1 lb. 2 oz.	540 g
Egg wash	as needed	as needed
Sesame seeds	3 Tbsp.	45 ml

1. Stir the yeast, water and sugar together in a mixer bowl.

2. Blend in the oil, salt and 8 ounces (225 grams) of the flour.

3. Gradually add the remaining flour. Knead the dough until it is smooth and cleans the sides of the bowl, approximately 5 minutes.

4. Remove the dough from the bowl and allow it to rest for a few minutes. Roll the dough into a rectangle, about 1/4 inch (6 millimeters) thick.

5. Cut the dough into 24 even pieces. Roll each piece into a rope and twist; bring the ends together, allowing the sides to curl together. Place on a paper-lined sheet pan.

6. Brush with egg wash and top with sesame seeds. Let the sticks rise until doubled, approximately 20 minutes.

7. Bake at 375°F (190°C) until golden brown, approximately 12–15 minutes.

VARIATIONS: *Garlic breadsticks*—Knead 1 ounce (30 grams) grated Parmesan cheese and 2 tablespoons (30 milliliters) minced garlic into the dough.
Herbed breadsticks—Knead 3 tablespoons (45 milliliters) chopped fresh herbs such as basil, parsley, dill and oregano into the dough.

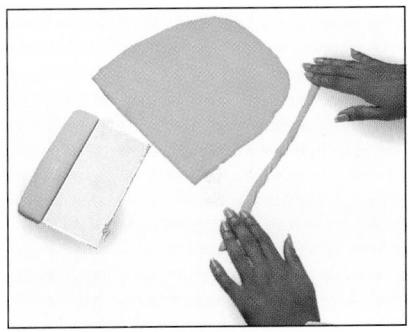

1. Rolling breadstick dough.

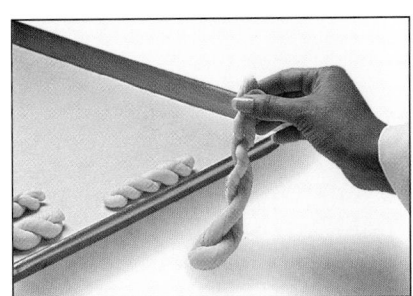

2. Twisting breadstick dough.

◆◆◆

RECIPE 28.11

ROMAN FLATBREAD

Yield: 1 Sheet Pan, 12 in. × 18 in.   **Method:** Straight Dough
(30 cm × 45 cm)

Sugar	1 Tbsp.	15 ml
Active dry yeast	1 Tbsp.	15 ml
Water, lukewarm	12 oz.	340 g
All-purpose flour	1 lb. 2 oz.	540 g
Kosher salt	2 tsp.	10 ml
Onion, chopped fine	3 oz.	90 g
Olive oil	2 tsp.	10 ml
Fresh rosemary, crushed	2 Tbsp.	30 ml

1. Topping the flatbread dough with crushed rosemary.

1. Combine the sugar, yeast and water. Stir to dissolve the yeast. Stir in the flour 4 ounces (120 grams) at a time.

2. Stir in 1-1/2 teaspoons (7 milliliters) of salt and the onion. Mix well, then knead on a lightly floured board until smooth.

3. Place the dough in an oiled bowl, cover and let rise until doubled.

4. Punch down the dough, then flatten it onto an oiled sheet pan. It should be no more than 1 inch (2.5 centimeters) thick. Brush the top of the dough with the olive oil. Let the dough proof until doubled, about 15 minutes.

5. Sprinkle the crushed rosemary and remaining 1/2 teaspoon (2 milliliters) of salt on top of the dough. Bake at 400°F (200°C) until lightly browned, approximately 20 minutes.

◆◆◆

RECIPE 28.12

PIZZA DOUGH

Yield: 1 Large or 8 Individual Pizzas   **Method:** Straight Dough

Water, warm	2 oz.	60 g
Active dry yeast	1 Tbsp.	15 ml
Bread flour	14 oz.	420 g
Water, cool	6 oz.	180 g
Salt	1 tsp.	5 ml
Olive oil	1 oz.	30 g
Honey	1 Tbsp.	15 ml

1. Stir the yeast into the warm water to dissolve. Add the flour.

2. Stir the cool water, salt, olive oil and honey into the flour mixture. Knead with a dough hook or by hand until smooth and elastic, approximately 5 minutes.

3. Place the dough in a lightly greased bowl and cover. Allow the dough to rise in a warm place for 30 minutes. Punch down the dough and divide into portions. The dough may be wrapped and refrigerated for up to two days.

4. On a lightly floured surface, roll the dough into very thin rounds and top as desired. Bake at 400°F (200°C) until crisp and golden brown, approximately 8–12 minutes.

◆◆◆

RECIPE 28.13

BASIC SOURDOUGH BREAD

Yield: 2 Large Loaves   **Method:** Sponge

Active dry yeast	1 Tbsp.	15 ml
Water, warm	12 oz.	340 g
Sourdough starter (Recipe 28.1)	1 cup	225 ml
Honey	1 Tbsp.	15 ml
Bread flour	1 lb. 6 oz.	660 g
Kosher salt	1-1/2 tsp.	7 ml
Distilled vinegar	1 oz.	30 g
Baking soda	1/2 tsp.	2 ml

1. Prepare a sponge by mixing the yeast, water, sourdough starter and honey. Stir in 4 ounces (120 grams) of flour. Beat vigorously by hand or in a mixer on second speed for 3 minutes.

2. Place the sponge in a clean bowl and cover. Set aside until doubled, approximately 1–2 hours.

3. Place the risen sponge into the bowl of a mixer fitted with a dough hook. Add the salt, vinegar and baking soda. Gradually add enough bread flour to make a stiff dough. Knead for 3 minutes on second speed. The dough should clean the bowl, forming a ball around the dough hook.

4. Allow the dough to rest for 5 minutes. Then shape into 2 round or oval loaves and place on a baking sheet that has been dusted with cornmeal.

5. Cover the dough and set aside to proof until doubled, approximately 45 minutes. Slash the top of the loaf with a razor or sharp knife.

6. Bake the bread for 10 minutes in a 450°F (230°C) oven with steam added. Reduce the oven temperature to 375°F (190°C) and continue baking until golden brown and firm, approximately 30–40 minutes.

◆◆◆

RECIPE 28.14

SAN FRANCISCO SOURDOUGH BREAD

STOUFFER STANFORD COURT, SAN FRANCISCO, CA
Executive Chef Ercolino Crugnale

Yield: 1 Loaf   **Method:** Straight Dough

Water, warm (120°F/49°C)	8 oz.	225 g
Active dry yeast	1/2 oz.	15 g
Sourdough starter (recipe follows)	1 cup	225 ml
Bread flour	1 lb.	450 g
Kosher salt	1 Tbsp.	15 ml
Egg white, beaten	1	1

1. Sprinkle the dry yeast over 2 ounces (60 grams) of the warm water and set aside until dissolved and foamy.

2. Combine the sourdough starter and the remaining warm water. Add 6 ounces (180 grams) of bread flour.

Continued

3. Stir until a dough forms then add the yeast mixture. Knead 5 minutes on medium speed.

4. Add the remaining flour and salt. Knead until the dough is smooth and elastic, approximately 10 minutes.

5. Place the dough in a lightly greased bowl and cover with a damp cloth. Let rise in a warm place, about 80–90°F (27–32°C), until doubled.

6. Punch down the dough and shape it into a round loaf. Place the loaf on a greased and cornmeal-dusted sheet pan.

7. Let the loaf rise in a warm place, covered with a damp cloth, until increased to 2-1/2 times its original size.

8. Brush the risen loaf with the beaten egg white and score the top of the loaf with a sharp knife.

9. Bake at 450°F (230°C), with a pan of boiling water underneath the oven rack, for 10 minutes.

10. Reduce the oven temperature to 375°F (190°C), remove the water and continue baking until the loaf is well browned, approximately 35–45 minutes.

SOURDOUGH STARTER

Grapes, off the stem	1 lb.	450 g
Water, warm (100°F/30°C)	as needed	as needed
Bread flour	12 oz.	340 g

1. Mash the grapes thoroughly and place in a covered container. Set aside at room temperature for 48 hours. (Red grapes will give some coloring to the juice; this will be eliminated gradually with continued feeding.)

2. Strain off the fermented juice and discard the pulp. Add enough warm water to the juice to make 1 pint (450 milliliters).

3. Stir in the flour, cover and leave at room temperature overnight.

4. Replenish with 1 pint (450 milliliters) of warm water and 12 ounces (340 grams) of flour daily if starter is kept at room temperature. If kept refrigerated, replenish twice weekly.

◆◆◆

RECIPE 28.15

CHALLAH

Challah is the traditional bread for Jewish Sabbaths and celebrations. Rich with eggs and flavored with honey, it is braided into oval loaves and topped with poppy or sesame seeds. Challah is excellent for toast or sandwiches.

Yield: 2 Large Loaves   **Method:** Straight Dough

Honey	6 oz.	180 g
Salt	1 Tbsp.	15 ml
Bread flour	1 lb. 12 oz.	800 g
Active dry yeast	1/2 oz.	15 g
Water, warm	14 oz.	400 g
Eggs	4	4
Unsalted butter, melted	4 oz.	120 g
Egg wash	as needed	as needed
Sesame or poppy seeds	as needed	as needed

1. Stir together the honey, salt and 8 ounces (225 grams) of flour in a mixer bowl. Add the yeast, water, eggs and butter. Stir until smooth.

2. Using the dough hook, knead the dough on second speed, adding the remaining flour 2 ounces (60 grams) at a time until smooth and elastic, approximately 5 minutes.

3. Place the dough in a lightly greased bowl, cover and let rise until doubled, approximately 1 to 1-1/2 hours.

4. Punch down the dough and divide into six equal portions. Roll each portion into a long strip, about 1 inch (2.5 centimeters) in diameter and 12 inches (30 centimeters) long. Lay three strips side by side and braid. Pinch the ends together and tuck them under the loaf. Place the loaf on a paper-lined sheet pan. Braid the three remaining pieces of dough in the same manner.

5. Brush the loaves with egg wash and sprinkle with sesame or poppy seeds. Proof until doubled, approximately 45 minutes.

6. Bake at 350°F (170°C) until the loaves are golden brown and sound hollow when thumped, approximately 40 minutes.

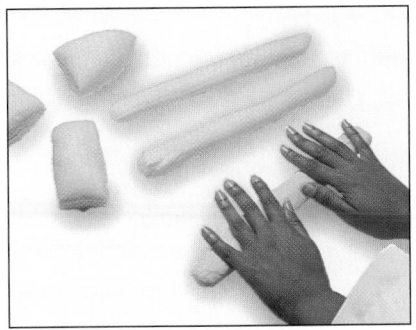 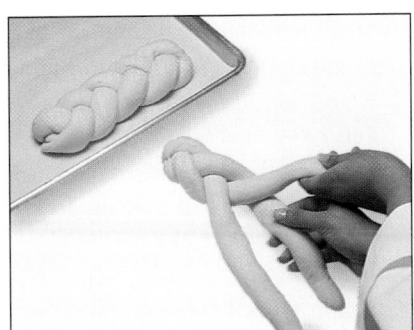

1. Rolling challah dough into ropes. **2.** Braiding challah dough.

◆◆◆

RECIPE 28.16

BRIOCHE

Brioche is a rich, tender bread made with an abundance of eggs and butter. The high ratio of fat makes this dough difficult to work with, but the flavor is well worth the extra effort. Brioche is traditionally made in fluted pans and has a cap or topknot of dough; this shape is known as brioche à tête. The dough may also be baked in a loaf pan, making it perfect for toast or canapés.

Yield: 3 Large Loaves or 60 3-in. (7.5-cm) Rolls

Method: Straight Dough

All-purpose flour	4 lb. 7 oz.	2 kg
Eggs	24	24
Salt	1-3/4 oz.	50 g
Sugar	7 oz.	210 g
Active dry yeast	1-3/4 oz.	50 g
Water, warm	7 oz.	210 g
Unsalted butter, room temperature	3 lb.	1.3 kg

Continued

1. Combining the ingredients for brioche.

2. Adding the yeast-and-water mixture to the dough.

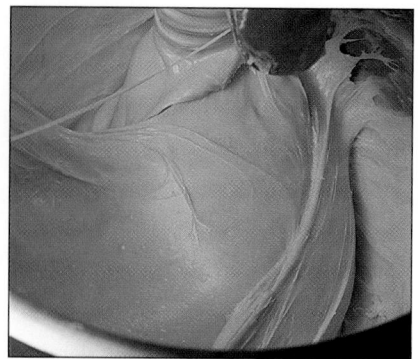

3. Brioche dough after kneading for 20 minutes.

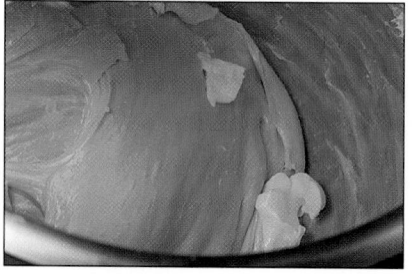

4. Adding the butter to the brioche dough.

5. The finished brioche dough ready for fermentation.

1. Place the flour, eggs, salt and sugar into the bowl of a large mixer fitted with the dough hook. Stir the ingredients together.

2. Combine the yeast and water and add to the other ingredients.

3. Knead for 20 minutes on second speed. The dough will be smooth, shiny and moist. It should not form a ball.

4. Slowly add the butter to the dough. Knead only until all the butter is incorporated. Remove the dough from the mixer and place it into a bowl dusted with flour. Cover and let rise at room temperature until doubled.

5. Punch down the dough, cover well and refrigerate overnight.

6. Shape the chilled dough as desired. Place the shaped dough in well-greased pans and proof at room temperature until doubled. Do not proof brioche in a very warm place; the butter may melt out of the dough before proofing is complete.

7. Bake at 375°F (190°C) until the brioche are a dark golden brown and sound hollow. Baking time will vary depending on the temperature of the dough and the size of the rolls or loaves being baked.

VARIATION: *Raisin brioche*—Gently warm 3 ounces (90 milliliters) rum with 6 ounces (180 grams) raisins. Set aside until the raisins are plumped. Drain off the remaining rum and add the raisins to the dough after the butter is incorporated.

6. Shaping the brioche à tête.

7. Panning the rolls.

8. A finished loaf of brioche baked in a pullman pan.

◆◆◆

RECIPE 28.17
PECAN
STICKY BUNS

Yield: 12–15 Buns   **Method:** Straight Dough

Active dry yeast	1 oz.	30 g
Sugar	2 oz.	60 g
Salt	1/2 tsp.	2 ml
Milk	1 Tbsp.	15 ml
Buttermilk	5-1/2 oz.	165 g
Vanilla	1 tsp.	5 ml
Lemon zest, grated	1 Tbsp.	15 ml
Lemon juice	1 tsp.	5 ml
Egg yolks	2	2
All-purpose flour	14 oz.	420 g
Unsalted butter, very soft	8 oz.	225 g
Topping:		
Honey	6 oz.	180 g
Brown sugar	6 oz.	180 g
Pecans, chopped	3 oz.	90 g
Filling:		
Cinnamon	1 tsp.	5 ml
Pecans, chopped	3 oz.	90 g
Brown sugar	4 oz.	120 g
Unsalted butter, melted	3 oz.	90 g

1. Brushing melted butter over the sticky bun dough.

2. Rolling up the filling in sticky bun dough.

3. Cutting and panning the sticky buns.

1. Stir the yeast, sugar, salt and milk together in a small bowl. Set aside.

2. Stir the buttermilk, vanilla, lemon zest and lemon juice together and add to the yeast mixture.

3. Add the eggs, flour and softened butter to the liquid mixture. Turn out onto a lightly floured board and knead until the butter is evenly distributed and the dough is smooth. Cover and let rise until doubled.

4. Prepare the topping and filling mixtures while the dough is rising. To make the topping, cream the honey and sugar together. Stir in the nuts. This mixture will be very stiff. To make the filling, stir the cinnamon, pecans and sugar together.

5. Lightly grease muffin cups, then distribute the topping mixture evenly, about 1 tablespoon (15 milliliters) per muffin cup. Set the pans aside at room temperature until the dough is ready.

6. Punch down the dough and let it rest 10 minutes. Roll out the dough into a rectangle about 1/2 inch (1.25 centimeters) thick. Brush with the melted butter and top evenly with the filling mixture.

7. Starting with either long edge, roll up the dough. Cut into slices about 3/4–1 inch (1.8–2.5 centimeters) thick. Place a slice in each muffin cup over the topping.

8. Let the buns proof until doubled, approximately 20 minutes. Bake at 350°F (170°C) until very brown, approximately 25 minutes. Immediately invert the muffin pans onto paper-lined sheet pans to let the buns and their topping slide out.

❖❖❖

RECIPE 28.18
DANISH PASTRIES

Danish pastry was actually created by a French baker more than 350 years ago. He forgot to knead butter into his bread dough and attempted to cover the mistake by folding in softened butter. This rich, flaky pastry is now popular worldwide for breakfasts, desserts and snacks. The dough may be shaped in a variety of ways and is usually filled with jam, fruit, cream or marzipan.

DOUGH FOR DANISH PASTRIES

Yield: 36 Pastries   **Method:** Rolled-in

Active dry yeast	1/2 oz.	15 g
All-purpose flour	1 lb. 4 oz.	600 g
Sugar	4 oz.	120 g
Water, warm	4 oz.	120 g
Milk, warm	4 oz.	120 g
Eggs, room temperature	2	2
Salt	1 tsp.	5 ml
Vanilla extract	1 tsp.	5 ml
Cinnamon, ground	1/2 tsp.	2 ml
Unsalted butter, melted	1-1/2 oz.	45 g
Unsalted butter, cold	1 lb.	450 g
Egg wash	as needed	as needed

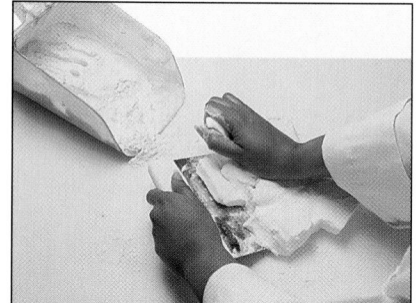

1. Kneading the butter with the flour.

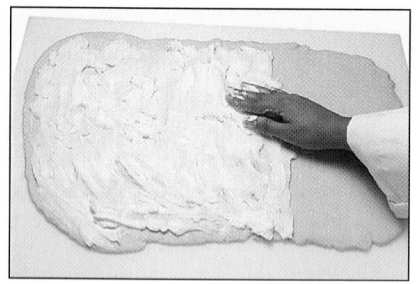

2. Spreading the butter over the rolled-out dough.

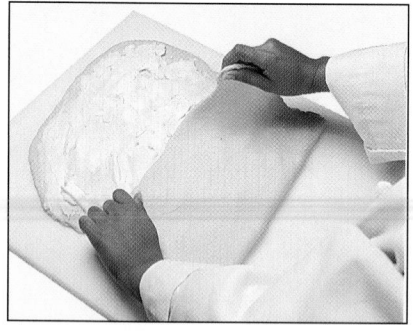

3. Folding the dough in thirds to cover the butter.

1. In a large bowl, stir together the yeast and 12 ounces (340 grams) of flour. Add the sugar, water, milk, eggs, salt, vanilla, cinnamon and melted butter. Stir until well combined.

2. Adding the remaining flour gradually, kneading the dough by hand or with a mixer fitted with a dough hook. Knead until the dough is smooth and only slightly tacky to the touch, approximately 2–3 minutes.

3. Place the dough in a bowl that has been lightly dusted with flour. Cover and refrigerate for 1 to 1-1/2 hours.

4. Prepare the remaining butter while the dough is chilling. Start by sprinkling flour over the work surface and placing the cold butter on the flour. Then pound the butter with a rolling pin until the butter softens. Using a pastry scraper or the heel of your hand, knead the butter and flour until the mixture is spreadable. The butter should still be cold. If it begins to melt, refrigerate it until firm. Set the butter aside until the dough is ready.

5. On a lightly floured surface, roll out the dough into a large rectangle about 1/2 inch (1.25 centimeters) thick. Brush away any excess flour.

6. Spread the butter evenly over two thirds of the dough. Fold the unbuttered third over the center, then fold the buttered third over the top. Press the edges together to seal in the butter.

7. Roll the dough into a rectangle about 12 inches × 18 inches (30 centimeters × 45 centimeters). Fold the dough in thirds as before. This rolling and folding (called a turn) must be done a total of six times. Chill the dough between turns as necessary. After the final turn, wrap the dough well and refrigerate for at least 4 hours or overnight.

8. Shape and fill the danish dough as desired. Place the shaped pastries on a paper-lined baking sheet and allow to proof for approximately 15–20 minutes.

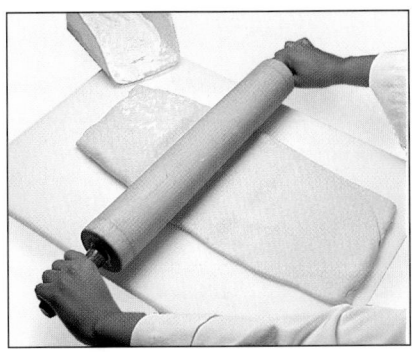

4. Rolling out the dough.

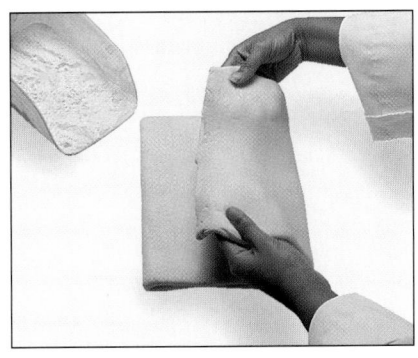

5. Folding the dough in thirds to complete a turn.

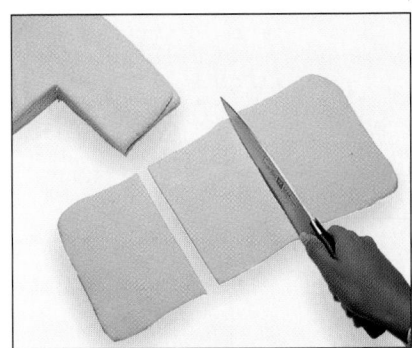

6. Cutting rectangles of danish dough.

9. Brush the pastries with egg wash and sprinkle lightly with sugar if desired. Bake at 400°F (200°C) for 5 minutes. Decrease the oven temperature to 350°F (170°C) and bake until light brown, approximately 12–15 minutes.

FILLINGS FOR DANISH PASTRIES

CREAM CHEESE

Cream cheese	1 lb.	450 g
Sugar	8 oz.	225 g
Salt	1/4 tsp.	1 ml
Vanilla	1 tsp.	5 ml
Flour	2 Tbsp.	30 ml
Egg yolk	1	1
Lemon extract	1 tsp.	5 ml
Lemon zest	2 tsp.	10 ml

1. Beat the cream cheese until light and fluffy. Stir in the remaining ingredients.

ALMOND CREAM

Almond paste	10 oz.	300 g
Unsalted butter, soft	4 oz.	120 g
Salt	1/4 tsp.	1 ml
Vanilla	1 tsp.	5 ml
Egg whites	2	2

1. Blend the almond paste and butter until smooth. Add the salt and vanilla, then the egg whites. Blend well.

APRICOT

Dried apricots	8 oz.	225 g
Orange juice	1 pt.	450 ml
Sugar	6 oz.	180 g
Salt	1/4 tsp.	1 ml
Unsalted butter	2 oz.	60 g

1. Place the apricots and orange juice in a small saucepan. Cover and simmer until the apricots are very tender, approximately 25 minutes. Stir in the sugar and salt. When the sugar is dissolved, add the butter and remove from the heat.

2. Purée the mixture in a blender until smooth. Cool completely before using.

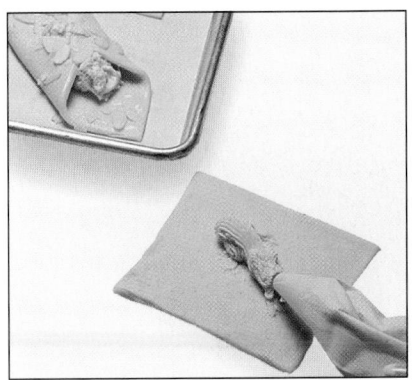

7. Piping the cream cheese filling onto the danish dough.

8. Shaping snails from danish dough.

CHAPTER 29
PIES, PASTRIES AND COOKIES

After studying this chapter you will be able to:

◆ prepare a variety of pie crusts and fillings
◆ prepare a variety of classic pastries
◆ prepare a variety of meringues
◆ prepare a variety of cookies
◆ prepare a variety of dessert and pastry items, incorporating components from other chapters

*M*ention pastry to diners and most conjure up images of buttery dough baked to crisp flaky perfection and filled or layered with rich cream, ripe fruit or smooth custard. Mention pastry to novice chefs and most conjure up images of sophisticated, complex and intimidating work. Although the diners are correct, the novice chefs are not. Pastry making is the art of creating containers for a variety of fillings. Taken one step at a time, most pastries are nothing more than selected building blocks or components assembled in a variety of ways to create traditional or unique desserts.

Perhaps the most important (and versatile) building block is the dough. Pastries can be made with flaky dough, mealy dough, sweet dough, puff pastry, eclair dough or meringue. See Table 29.1. Because pies, tarts and cookies are constructed from some of these same doughs (principally pie dough and sweet dough), they, as well as pie fillings, are discussed in the section on pies and tarts; puff pastry, eclair paste and baked meringue are discussed in the section on classic pastries. The cream, custard and mousse fillings used in some of the recipes at the end of this chapter are discussed in Chapter 31, Custards, Creams, Frozen Desserts and Dessert Sauces. Cakes and frostings are covered in Chapter 30.

PIES AND TARTS

A **pie** is composed of a sweet or savory filling in a baked crust. It can be open-faced (without a top crust) or, more typically, topped with a full or lattice crust. A pie is generally made in a round, slope-sided pan and cut into wedges for service. A **tart** is similar to a pie except it is made in a shallow, straight-sided pan, often with fluted edges. A tart can be almost any shape; round, square, rectangular and petal shapes are the most common. It is usually open-faced and derives much of its beauty from an attractive arrangement of glazed fruit.

TABLE 29.1 CLASSIFICATION OF PASTRY DOUGHS

Dough	French Name	Characteristics After Baking	Use
Flaky dough	Pâte brisée	Very flaky; not sweet	Prebaked pie shells; pie top crusts
Mealy dough	Pâte brisée	Moderately flaky; not sweet	Custard, cream or fruit pie crusts; quiche crusts
Sweet dough	Pâte sucrée	Very rich; crisp; not flaky	Tart and tartlet shells
Eclair paste	Pâte à choux	Hollow with crisp exterior	Cream puffs; eclairs; savory products
Puff pastry	Pâte feuilletée	Rich but not sweet; hundreds of light, flaky layers	Tart and pastry cases; cookies; layered pastries; savory products
Meringue	Meringue	Sweet; light; crisp or soft depending on preparation	Topping or icing; baked as a shell or component for layered desserts; cookies

Crusts

Pie crusts and tart shells can be made from several types of doughs or crumbs. **Flaky dough, mealy dough** and **crumbs** are best for pie crusts; **sweet dough** is usually used for tart shells. A pie crust or tart shell can be shaped and completely baked before filling (known as **baked blind**) or filled and baked simultaneously with the filling.

Flaky and Mealy Doughs

Flaky and mealy pie doughs are quick, easy and versatile. Flaky dough, sometimes known as pâte brisée, takes its name from its final baked texture. It is best for pie top crusts and lattice coverings and may be used for prebaked shells that will be filled with a cooled filling shortly before service. Mealy dough takes its name from its raw texture. It is used whenever a soggy crust would be a problem (for example, as the bottom crust of a custard or fruit pie) because it resists soaking better than flaky dough. Both flaky and mealy doughs are too delicate for tarts that will be removed from the pan for service. Sweet dough, described below, is better for these types of tarts.

Flaky and mealy doughs contain little or no sugar and can be prepared from the same formula with only a slight variation in mixing method. For both types of dough a cold fat, such as butter or shortening, is cut into the flour. The amount of flakiness in the baked crust depends on the size of the fat particles in the dough. The larger the pieces of fat, the flakier the crust will be. This is because the flakes are actually the sides of fat pockets created during baking by the melting fat and steam. When preparing flaky dough, the fat is left in larger pieces, about the size of peas or peanuts. When preparing mealy dough, the fat is blended in more thoroughly, until the mixture resembles coarse cornmeal. Because the resulting fat pockets are smaller, the crust is less flaky.

The type of fat used affects both the dough's flavor and flakiness. Butter contributes a delicious flavor, but does not produce as flaky a crust as other fats. Butter is also more difficult to work with than other fats because of its lower melting point and its tendency to become brittle when chilled. All-purpose vegetable shortening produces a flaky crust but contributes nothing to its flavor. The flakiest pastry is made with lard. Because some people dislike its flavor for sweet pies, lard is more often used for pâté en croûte or other savory preparations. Some chefs prefer to use a combination of butter with either shortening or lard. Oil is not an appropriate substitute as it disperses too thoroughly through the dough; when baked, the crust will be stiff and crisp.

After the fat is cut into the flour, water or milk is added to form a soft dough. Less water is needed for mealy dough because more flour is already in contact with the fat, reducing its ability to absorb liquid. Cold water is normally used for both flaky and mealy doughs. The water should be well chilled to prevent softening the fat. Milk may be used to increase richness and nutritional value. It will produce a darker, less crisp crust, however. If dry milk powder is used, it should be dissolved in the water first.

Hand mixing is best for small to moderate quantities of dough. You retain better control over the procedure when you can feel the fat being incorporated. It is very difficult to make flaky dough with an electric mixer or food processor, as they tend to cut the fat in too thoroughly. Overmixing develops too much gluten, making the dough elastic and difficult to use. If an electric mixer must be used for large quantities, use the paddle attachment at the lowest speed and be sure the fat is well chilled, even frozen.

Bake blind—*to bake a pie shell before it is filled. The dough is often lined with parchment paper and filled with dried beans or pie weights to prevent the crust from rising.*

✦✦✦
Of Tarts and Tortes

The names given to desserts can be rather confusing. One country or region calls an item a *torte* while another region calls the same item a *gâteau*. The following definitions are based on classic terms. You will, no doubt, encounter variations depending on your location and the training of those with whom you work.

Cake—In American and British usages, *cake* refers to a broad range of pastries, including layer cakes, coffee cakes and gâteaux. *Cake* may refer to almost everything that is baked, tender, sweet and sometimes frosted. But to the French, *le cake* is a loaf-shaped fruitcake, similar to an American pound cake with the addition of fruit, nuts and rum.

Gâteau—(pl. *gâteaux*) To the French, *gâteau* refers to various pastry items made with puff pastry, eclair paste, short dough or sweet dough. In America, *gâteau* often refers to any cake-type dessert.

Pastry—*Pastry* may refer to a group of doughs made primarily with flour, water and fat. *Pastry* can also refer to foods made with these doughs or to a large variety of fancy baked goods.

Tart—A tart is a pastry shell filled with sweet or savory ingredients. Tarts have straight, shallow sides and are usually prepared open-face. In France and Britain the term **flan** is sometimes used to refer to the same items. A **tartlet** is a small, individual-sized tart.

Torte—In Central and Eastern European countries a *torte* (pl. *torten*) is a rich cake in which all or part of the flour is replaced with finely chopped nuts or bread crumbs. Other cultures refer to any round sweet cake as a torte.

PROCEDURE FOR MAKING FLAKY AND MEALY DOUGHS

1. Sift flour, salt and sugar (if used) together in a large bowl.
2. Cut the fat into the flour.
3. Gradually add cold liquid, mixing gently until the dough holds together. Do not overmix.
4. Cover the dough with plastic wrap and chill thoroughly before using.

◆◆◆

RECIPE 29.1

BASIC PIE DOUGH

Yield: 5 lb. (2.2 kg)

Pastry flour	3 lb.	1300 g
Salt	4 tsp.	20 g
Sugar (optional)	2 oz.	60 g
All-purpose shortening	1 lb. 8 oz.	680 g
Water, cold*	8 oz.	250 ml

1. Sift the flour, salt and sugar together in a large bowl.
2. Cut the shortening into the flour mixture until the desired consistency is reached.
3. Gradually add the cold water, mixing gently until the dough holds together. Do not overmix or add too much water.
4. Cover the dough with plastic wrap and chill thoroughly before using.

*The amount of water needed varies depending upon the manner in which the fat is incorporated. Mealy dough will probably not require the entire 8 ounces (250 milliliters).

1. Cutting the fat into the flour coarsely for flaky dough.

2. Cutting the fat into the flour finely for mealy dough.

3. The finished dough.

Sweet Dough

Sweet dough or **pâte sucrée** is a rich, nonflaky dough used for sweet tart shells. It is sturdier than flaky or mealy dough because it contains egg yolks and the fat is thoroughly blended in. It is also more cookielike than classic pie dough and has the rich flavor of butter. It creates a crisp but tender crust and is excellent for tartlets as well as for straight-sided tarts that will be removed from their pans before service. Sweet dough crusts may be prebaked then filled, or filled and baked simultaneously with the filling. The raw dough may be kept refrigerated up to two weeks or frozen up to three months.

PROCEDURE FOR MAKING SWEET DOUGH

1. Cream softened butter. Add sugar and beat until the mixture is light and fluffy.
2. Slowly add eggs, blending well.
3. Slowly add flour, mixing only until incorporated. Overmixing toughens the dough.
4. Cover the dough with plastic wrap and chill thoroughly before using.

RECIPE 29.2

SWEET DOUGH

Yield: 7 lb. (3.1 kg)

Unsalted butter, softened	1 lb. 8 oz.	675 g
Powdered sugar	1 lb. 5 oz.	580 g
Egg yolks	1 lb.	450 g
Whole eggs	2	2
All-purpose flour	3 lb. 8 oz.	1600 g

1. Cream the butter and powdered sugar in a large mixer bowl using the paddle attachment.
2. Combine the egg yolks and whole eggs. Slowly add the eggs to the creamed butter. Mix until smooth and free of lumps, scraping down the sides of the bowl as needed.
3. With the mixer on low speed, slowly add the flour to the butter-and-egg mixture. Mix only until incorporated; do not overmix. The dough should be firm, smooth and not sticky.
4. Dust a half-sheet pan with flour. Pack the dough into the pan evenly. Wrap well in plastic wrap and chill until firm.
5. Work with a small portion of the chilled dough when shaping tart shells or other products.

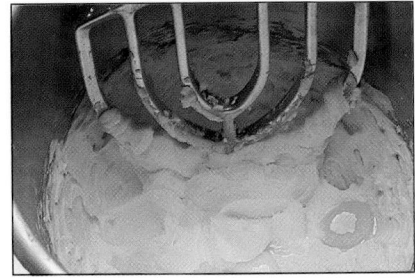

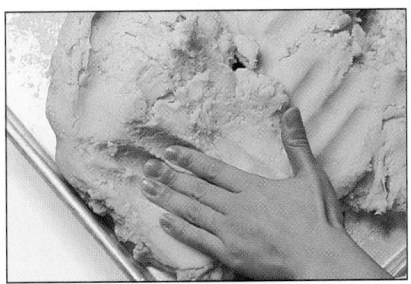

1. Mixing sweet dough.

2. The finished sweet dough.

Shaping Crusts

Crusts are shaped by rolling out the dough to fit into a pie pan or tart shell (mold) or to sit on top of fillings. Mealy, flaky and sweet doughs are all easier to roll out and work with if well chilled, as chilling keeps the fat firm and prevents stickiness. When rolling and shaping the dough, work on a clean, flat surface (wood or marble is best). Lightly dust the work surface, rolling pin and dough with pastry flour before starting to roll the dough. Also, work only with a manageable amount at a time: usually one crust's worth for a pie or standard-sized tart or enough for 10–12 tartlet shells.

Roll out the dough from the center, working toward the edges. Periodically, lift the dough gently and rotate it. This keeps the dough from sticking and helps produce an even thickness. If the dough sticks to the rolling pin or work surface, sprinkle on a bit more flour. Too much flour, however, makes the crust dry and crumbly and causes gray streaks.

PROCEDURE FOR ROLLING AND SHAPING DOUGH FOR A PIE CRUST OR TART SHELL

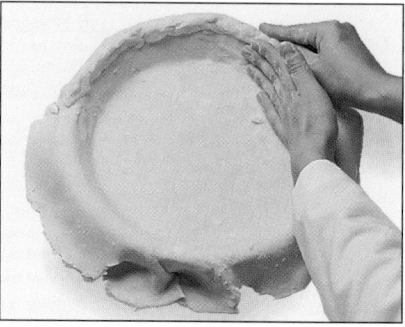

1. A typical pie crust or tart shell should be rolled to a thickness of approximately 1/8 inch (3 millimeters); it should also be at least 2 inches (5 centimeters) larger in diameter than the baking pan.

2. Carefully roll the dough up onto a rolling pin. Position the pin over the pie pan or tart shell and unroll the dough, easing it into the pan or shell. Trim the edges as necessary and flute as desired. Bake or fill as desired.

PROCEDURE FOR ROLLING AND SHAPING DOUGH FOR TARTLET SHELLS

1. A typical crust for tartlets should be approximately 1/4 inch (6 millimeters) thick.
2. Roll the dough out as described above. Then roll the dough up onto the rolling pin.

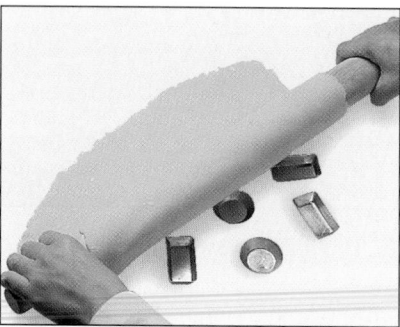
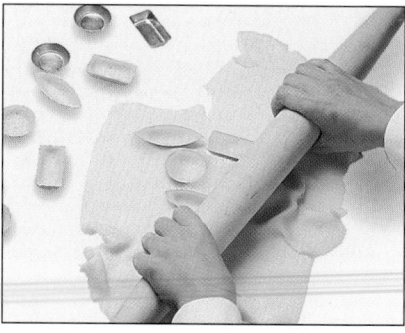

3. Lay out a single layer of tartlet molds. Unroll the dough over the molds, pressing the dough gently into each mold.

4. Roll the rolling pin over the top of the tartlet shells. The edge of the molds will cut the dough. Be sure the dough is pressed against the sides of each mold. Bake or fill as desired.

PROCEDURE FOR ROLLING AND SHAPING DOUGH FOR A TOP CRUST

1. Roll the dough out as before, making the circle large enough to hang over the pan's edge. The dough may be lifted into place by rolling it onto the rolling pin, as with the bottom crust. Slits or designs can be cut from the top crust to allow steam to escape.

2. Seal the top crust to the bottom crust with egg wash or water. Crimp as desired.

PROCEDURE FOR ROLLING AND SHAPING DOUGH FOR A LATTICE CRUST

1. Roll the dough out as described above. Using a ruler as a guide, cut even strips of the desired width, typically 1/2 inch (1.25 centimeters).

2. Using an over-under-over pattern, weave the strips together on top of the filling. Be sure the strips are evenly spaced for an attractive result. Crimp the lattice strips to the bottom crust to seal.

Streusel topping is also used for some pies, particularly fruit pies. A standard recipe is given in Chapter 27, Quick Breads.

Baking Crusts

Pie crusts can be filled and then baked, or baked and then filled. Unfilled baked crusts can be stored at room temperature for two to three days or wrapped in plastic wrap and frozen for as long as three months.

PROCEDURE FOR BAKING UNFILLED (BAKED BLIND) PIE CRUSTS

Dock—*Pricking small holes in an unbaked dough or crust to allow steam to escape and to prevent the dough from rising when baked.*

1. Roll the dough out to the desired thickness and line the pie pan or tart shell. A crimped edge or border can be added.
2. **Dock** the dough with a fork.

3. Cover the dough with baking parchment or greased aluminum foil. Press the paper or foil against the edge or walls of the shell. Allow a portion of the paper or foil to extend above the pan.
4. Fill the pan with baking weights, dry rice or beans. These will prevent the crust from rising.
5. Bake the weighted crust at 350°F (180°C) for 10–15 minutes.

6. Remove the weights and paper and return the crust to the oven. Bake until golden brown and fully cooked, approximately 10–15 minutes.
7. Allow to cool, then fill as desired or store.

Crumb Crusts

A quick and tasty bottom crust can be made from finely ground crumbs moistened with melted butter. Crumb crusts can be used for unbaked pies such as those with cream or chiffon fillings, or they can be baked with their fillings, as with cheesecakes.

Chocolate cookies, graham crackers, gingersnaps, vanilla wafers and macaroons are popular choices for crumb crusts. Some breakfast cereals such as corn flakes or bran flakes are also used. Ground nuts and spices can be added for flavor. Whatever cookies or other ingredients are used, be sure they are ground to a fine, even crumb. If packaged crumbs are unavailable, a food processor, blender or rolling pin can be used.

The typical ratio for a crumb crust is one part melted butter, two parts sugar and four parts crumbs. For example, 8 ounces (250 grams) graham crackers mixed with 4 ounces (120 grams) sugar and 2 ounces (60 grams) melted butter produce enough crust to line one 9-to-10-inch (22- to 25-centimeter) pan. The amount of sugar may need to be adjusted depending on the type of crumbs used, however; for example, chocolate sandwich cookies need

1. Making a crumb crust.

less sugar than graham crackers. If the mixture is too dry to stick together, gradually add more melted butter. Press the mixture into the bottom of the pan and chill or bake it before filling.

Fillings

Fillings make pies and tarts distinctive and flavorful. Four types of fillings are discussed here: **cream**, **fruit**, **custard** and **chiffon**. There is no one correct presentation or filling-and-crust combination. The apples in an apple pie, for example, may be sliced, seasoned and topped with streusel; caramelized, puréed and blended with cream; chopped and covered with a flaky dough lattice; or poached, arranged over pastry cream and brushed with a shiny glaze. Only an understanding of the fundamental techniques for making fillings—and some imagination—ensures success.

Cream Fillings

A cream filling is really nothing more than a flavored pastry cream. Pastry cream is a type of starch-thickened egg custard discussed in Chapter 31, Custards, Creams, Frozen Desserts and Dessert Sauces. When used as a pie filling, pastry cream should be thickened with cornstarch so that it is firm enough to hold its shape when sliced. Popular flavors are chocolate, banana, coconut and lemon.

A cream filling is fully cooked on the stove top, so a prebaked or crumb crust is needed. The crust can be filled while the filling is still warm, or the filling can be chilled and later placed in the crust. A cream pie is often topped with meringue, which is then browned quickly in an over or under a broiler.

═══ ◆◆◆ ═══

RECIPE 29.3

Basic Cream Pie

Yield: 3 9-inch (22-cm) Pies

Granulated sugar	1 lb.	500 g
Milk	2 qt.	2 lt
Egg yolks	8	8
Eggs	4	4
Cornstarch	5 oz.	150 g
Unsalted butter	4 oz.	120 g
Vanilla extract	1 oz.	30 g

1. In a heavy saucepan, dissolve 8 ounces (250 grams) of sugar in the milk. Bring just to a boil.
2. Meanwhile, whisk the egg yolks and whole eggs together in a large bowl.
3. Sift the cornstarch and remaining sugar (8 ounces/250 grams) onto the eggs. Whisk until smooth.
4. Temper the egg mixture with approximately one half of the hot milk. Stir the warmed egg mixture back into the remaining milk and return it to a boil, stirring constantly.
5. Stirring constantly and vigorously, allow the cream to boil until thick, approximately 30 seconds. Remove from the heat and stir in the butter and vanilla. Stir until the butter is melted and incorporated.

Continued

6. Pour the cream into prebaked pie crusts.

7. The pies may be topped with meringue while the filling is still warm. The meringue is then lightly browned in a 425°F (210°C) oven. Chill the pies for service.

VARIATIONS: *Chocolate*—Melt 12 ounces (340 grams) bittersweet chocolate. Fold the melted chocolate into the hot cream after adding the butter and vanilla.

Banana—Fold 12 ounces (340 grams) coarsely mashed bananas (about 3 medium bananas) into the warm cream. The juice of one lemon may be added to the bananas to help prevent browning.

Coconut I—Substitute 12 ounces (340 grams) cream of coconut for 12 ounces (340 grams) of milk and 4 ounces (120 grams) of sugar. Top the pie with meringue and shredded coconut.

Coconut II—Stir 8 ounces (250 grams) toasted coconut into the warm cream.

1. Filling a pie shell with chocolate custard.

2. Topping with meringue.

Fruit Fillings

A fruit filling is a mixture of fruit, fruit juice, spices and sugar thickened with starch. Apple, cherry, blueberry and peach are traditional favorites. The fruit can be fresh, frozen or canned. (See Chapter 25, Fruits, for comments on selecting the best fruits for fillings.) The starch can be flour, cornstarch, tapioca or a packaged commercial instant or pregelatinized starch. The ingredients for a fruit filling are most often combined using one of three methods: **cooked fruit**, **cooked juice** or **baked**.

Cooked Fruit Fillings

The cooked fruit filling method is often used when the fruits need to be softened by cooking (for example, apples or rhubarb) or are naturally rather dry. (Poaching fruit, discussed in Chapter 25, Fruits, is a variation of this procedure.) A cooked fruit filling should be combined with a prebaked or crumb crust.

PROCEDURE FOR MAKING COOKED FRUIT FILLINGS

1. Combine the fruit, sugar and some juice or liquid in a heavy, nonreactive saucepan and bring to a boil.

2. Dissolve the starch (usually cornstarch) in cold liquid, then add to the boiling fruit.

3. Stirring constantly, cook the fruit-and-starch mixture until the starch is clear and the mixture is thickened.

4. Add any other flavorings and any acidic ingredients such as lemon juice. Stir to blend.

5. Remove from the heat and cool before filling a prebaked pie or crumb crust.

◆◆◆

RECIPE 29.4

APPLE-CRANBERRY PIE

Yield: 1 9-inch (22-cm) Pie   **Method:** Cooked Fruit Filling

Fresh tart apples such as Granny Smiths, peeled, cored and cut in 1-inch (2.5-centimeter) cubes	1 lb.	450 g
Brown sugar	4 oz.	120 g
Granulated sugar	4 oz.	120 g
Orange zest	1 Tbsp.	15 ml
Ground cinnamon	1 tsp.	5 ml
Salt	1/4 tsp.	1 ml
Cornstarch	2 tsp.	10 ml
Orange juice	3 oz.	90 g
Fresh cranberries, rinsed	1 pt.	500 ml
Partially baked pie shell	1	1
Streusel Topping (Recipe 27.4)	4 oz.	120 g

1. Combine the apples, brown sugar, granulated sugar, orange zest, cinnamon and salt in a large, nonreactive saucepan.

2. Dissolve the cornstarch in the orange juice and add it to the apples.

3. Cover and simmer until the apples begin to soften, stirring occasionally. Add the cranberries, cover and continue simmering until the cranberries begin to soften, approximately 2 minutes.

4. Place the apple-cranberry mixture in the pie shell and cover with the prepared streusel topping. Bake at 400°F (200°C) until the filling is bubbling hot and the topping is lightly browned, approximately 20 minutes.

VARIATION: *Apple-rhubarb pie*—Substitute cleaned rhubarb, cut into 1-inch (2.5-centimeter) chunks, for the cranberries. Add 1/8 teaspoon (0.5 milliliter) nutmeg.

Cooked Juice Fillings

The cooked juice filling method is used for juicy fruits such as berries, especially when they are canned or frozen. This method is also recommended for delicate fruits that cannot withstand cooking such as strawberries, pineapple or blueberries. Because only the juice is cooked, the fruit retains its shape, color and flavor better. A cooked juice filling should be combined with a prebaked or crumb crust.

PROCEDURE FOR MAKING COOKED JUICE FILLINGS

1. Drain the juice from the fruit. Measure the juice and add water if necessary to create the desired volume.
2. Combine the liquid with sugar in a nonreactive saucepan and bring to a boil.
3. Dissolve the starch in cold water, then add it to the boiling liquid. Cook until the starch is clear and the juice is thickened.
4. Add any other flavoring ingredients.
5. Pour the thickened juice over the fruit and stir gently.
6. Cool the filling before placing it in a precooked pie shell.

RECIPE 29.5

BLUEBERRY PIE FILLING

Yield: 8 lb. (3.6 kg) Filling   **Method:** Cooked Juice Filling

Canned blueberries, unsweetened	1 #10 can	1 #10 can
Sugar	1 lb. 12 oz.	840 g
Cornstarch	4-1/2 oz.	135 g
Water	8 oz.	225 g
Cinnamon	1/2 tsp.	2 ml
Lemon juice	2 Tbsp.	30 ml
Lemon zest, grated fine	1 Tbsp.	15 ml

1. Drain the juice from the canned blueberries, reserving both the fruit and the juice.
2. Measure the juice and, if necessary, add enough water to provide 1 quart (1 liter) of liquid. Bring to a boil, add the sugar and stir until dissolved.
3. Dissolve the cornstarch in 8 ounces (225 grams) of water.
4. Add the cornstarch to the boiling juice and return to a boil. Cook until the mixture thickens and clears. Remove from the heat.
5. Add the cinnamon, lemon juice, lemon zest and reserved blueberries. Stir gently to coat the fruit with the glaze.
6. Allow the filling to cool, then use it to fill prebaked pie shells or other pastry items.

Baked Fruit Fillings

The baked fruit filling method is a traditional technique in which the fruit, sugar, flavorings and starch are combined in an unbaked shell. The dough and filling are then baked simultaneously. Almost any type of fruit and starch can be used. The results are not always consistent, however, because thickening is difficult to control.

PROCEDURE FOR MAKING BAKED FRUIT FILLINGS

1. Combine the starch, spices and sugar.
2. Peel, core, cut or drain the fruit as desired or as directed in the recipe.
3. Toss the fruit with the starch mixture, coating well.
4. Add a portion of juice to moisten the fruit. Small lumps of butter are also often added.

5. Fill an unbaked shell with the fruit mixture. Cover with a top crust, lattice or streusel and bake.

◆◆◆

RECIPE 29.6

CHERRY PIE

Yield: 2 9-inch (22-cm) Pies   **Method:** Baked Fruit Filling

Tapioca	1-1/2 oz.	45 g
Salt	pinch	pinch
Granulated sugar	1 lb.	450 g
Almond extract	1/2 tsp.	2 ml
Canned pitted cherries, drained		
(reserve the liquid)	3 lb.	1.3 kg
Unbaked pie shells	2	2
Unsalted butter	1 oz.	30 g
Egg wash	as needed	as needed
Sanding sugar	as needed	as needed

1. Stir the tapioca, salt and sugar together. Add the almond extract and cherries.

2. Stir in up to 8 ounces (250 grams) of the liquid drained from the cherries, adding enough liquid to moisten the mixture thoroughly.

3. Allow the filling to stand for 30 minutes. Then stir gently and place the filling in an unbaked pie shell.

4. Cut the butter into small pieces. Dot the filling with the butter.

5. Place a top crust or a lattice crust over the filling; seal and flute the edges. Cut several slits in the top crust to allow steam to escape. Brush with an egg wash and sprinkle with sanding sugar.

6. Place on a preheated sheet pan and bake at 400°F (200°C) for 50–60 minutes.

1. Dotting the cherry filling with butter.

Custard Fillings

A custard pie has a soft filling that bakes along with the crust. Popular examples include pumpkin, egg custard and pecan pies. As explained in Chapter 31, Custards, Creams, Frozen Desserts and Dessert Sauces, custards are liquids thickened by coagulated egg proteins. To make a custard pie, an uncooked liquid containing eggs is poured into a pie shell. When baked, the egg proteins coagulate, firming and setting the filling.

The procedure for making custard pies is simple: Combine the ingredients and bake. But there is often a problem: baking the bottom crust completely

◆◆◆
CONVENIENCE PRODUCTS

Prepared or canned pie fillings are available in a variety of fruit and custard flavors. These products offer convenience and the ability to serve fruit pies out of season. The ratio of fruit to pregelled liquid varies greatly from brand to brand, however. Most commercial fillings are stabilized to permit any additional cooking needed to assemble the final product. Shelf life tends to be extremely long, often without the need for refrigeration. Dry custard mixes are also available, needing only the addition of water or milk. Despite the convenience, most prepared pie fillings are a disappointing substitute for a well-made fresh fruit or custard filling.

without overcooking the filling. For the best results, start baking the pie near the bottom of a hot oven at 400°F (200°C). After 10 minutes, reduce the heat to 325–350°F (160–180°C) to finish cooking the filling slowly.

To determine the doneness of a custard pie:

1. Shake the pie gently. It is done if it is no longer liquid. The center should show only a slight movement.
2. Insert a thin knife about 1 inch (2.5 centimeters) from the center. The filling is done if the knife comes out clean.

◆◆◆
RECIPE 29.7
PUMPKIN PIE

Yield: 4 9-inch (22-cm) Pies   **Method:** Baked Custard Filling

Eggs, beaten slightly	4	4
Pumpkin purée	2 lb.	900 g
Granulated sugar	12 oz.	340 g
Salt	1 tsp.	5 ml
Nutmeg, ground	1/2 tsp.	2 ml
Cloves, ground	1/2 tsp.	2 ml
Cinnamon, ground	2 tsp.	10 ml
Ginger, ground	1 tsp.	5 ml
Evaporated milk	24 oz.	700 g
Unbaked pie shells	4	4

1. Combine the eggs and pumpkin. Blend in the sugar.
2. Add the salt and spices, then the evaporated milk. Whisk until completely blended and smooth.
3. Allow the filling to rest for 15–20 minutes before filling the pie shells. This allows the starch in the pumpkin to begin absorbing liquid, making it less likely to separate after baking.
4. Pour the filling into unbaked pie shells. Place in the oven on a preheated sheet pan at 400°F (220°C). Bake for 15 minutes. Lower the oven temperature to 350°F (180°C) and bake until a knife inserted near the center comes out clean, approximately 40–50 minutes.

Chiffon Fillings

A chiffon filling is created by adding gelatin to a stirred custard or a fruit purée. Whipped egg whites are then folded into the mixture. The filling is placed in a prebaked crust and chilled until firm. These preparations are the same as those for chiffons, mousses and Bavarians discussed in Chapter 31, Custards, Creams, Frozen Desserts and Dessert Sauces.

Assembling Pies and Tarts

The various types of pie fillings can be used to fill almost any crust or shell, provided the crust is prebaked as necessary. The filling can then be topped with meringue or whipped cream as desired. Garnishes such as toasted coconut, cookie crumbs and chocolate curls are often added for appearance and flavor.

TABLE 29.2   SUGGESTIONS FOR ASSEMBLING PIES

Filling	Crust	Topping	Garnish
Vanilla or lemon cream	Prebaked flaky dough or crumb	None, meringue or whipped cream	Crumbs from the crust
Chocolate cream	Prebaked flaky dough or crumb	None, meringue or whipped cream	Crumbs from the crust or shaved chocolate
Banana cream	Prebaked flaky dough	Meringue or whipped cream	Dried banana chips
Coconut cream	Prebaked flaky dough	Meringue or whipped cream	Shredded coconut
Fresh fruit	Unbaked mealy dough or sweet dough if shallow tart	Lattice, full crust or streusel	Sanding sugar or cut-out designs if lattice or top crust is used
Canned or frozen fruit	Unbaked mealy dough	Lattice, full crust or streusel	Sanding sugar or cut-out designs if lattice or top crust is used
Chiffon or mousse	Crumb or prebaked, sweetened flaky dough	None or whipped cream	Crumbs, fruit or shaved chocolate
Custard (e.g., pecan or pumpkin)	Unbaked mealy dough	None	Whipped cream
Vanilla pastry cream	Prebaked sweet dough	Fresh fruit	Glaze

Storing Pies and Tarts

Pies and tarts filled with cream or custard must be kept refrigerated to retard bacterial growth. Baked fruit pies may be held at room temperature for service.

Unbaked fruit pies or unbaked pie shells may be frozen for up to two months. Freezing baked fruit pies is not recommended. Custard, cream and meringue-topped pies should not be frozen, as the eggs will separate, making the product runny.

TABLE 29.3   TROUBLESHOOTING CHART FOR PIES

Problem	Cause	Solution
Crust shrinks	Overmixing	Adjust mixing technique
	Overworking dough	Adjust rolling technique
	Not enough fat	Adjust formula
Soggy crust	Wrong dough used	Use mealier dough
	Oven temperature too low	Adjust oven
	Not baked long enough	Adjust baking time
Crumbly crust	Not enough liquid	Adjust formula
	Too much fat	Adjust formula
Tough crust	Not enough fat	Adjust formula
	Overmixing	Adjust mixing technique
Runny filling	Insufficient starch	Adjust formula
	Starch insufficiently cooked	Allow starch to gelatinize completely
Lumpy cream filling	Starch not incorporated properly	Stir filling while cooking
	Filling overcooked	Adjust cooking time
Custard filling weeps or separates	Too many eggs	Reduce egg content or add starch to the filling
	Eggs overcooked	Reduce oven temperature or baking time

Classic Pastries

Puff pastry, **éclair paste** and **meringue** are classic components of French pastries; they are used to create a wide variety of dessert and pastry items. Many combinations are traditional. Once you master the skills necessary to produce these products, however, you will be free to experiment with other flavors and assembly techniques.

Puff Pastry

Puff pastry is one of the bakeshop's most elegant and sophisticated products. Also known as **pâte feuilletée**, it is a rich, buttery dough that bakes into hundreds of light, crisp layers.

Puff pastry is used for both sweet and savory preparations. It can be baked and then filled or filled first and then baked. Puff pastry may be used to wrap beef (for beef Wellington), pâté (for pâté en croûte) or almond cream (for an apple tart). It can be shaped into shells or cases known as vol-au-vents or bouchées and filled with shellfish in a cream sauce or berries in a pastry cream. Puff pastry is essential for napoleons, pithiviers and tartes tatin.

Like croissant and danish dough (discussed in Chapter 28, Yeast Breads), puff pastry is a rolled-in dough. But unlike those doughs, puff pastry does not contain any yeast or chemical leavening agents. Fat is rolled into the dough in horizontal layers; when baked, the fat melts, separating the dough into layers. The fat's moisture turns into steam, which causes the dough to rise and the layers to further separate.

Butter is the preferred fat because of its flavor and melt-in-the-mouth quality. But butter is rather difficult to work with as it becomes brittle when cold and melts at a relatively low temperature. Therefore, specially formulated puff pastry shortenings are used to compensate for butter's shortcomings. They do not, however, provide the true flavor of butter.

Raw, frozen, commercially prepared puff pastry is readily available in sheets or precut in a variety of shapes. Some convenience products, especially those made with butter, provide excellent, consistent results. Their expense may be offset by the savings in time and labor. Keep these frozen doughs well wrapped to prevent drying and freezer burn, and prepare according to package directions.

Making Puff Pastry

The procedure described here for making puff pastry is just one of many. Each chef will have his or her own formula and folding method. All methods, however, depend upon the proper layering of fat and dough through a series of turns to give the pastry its characteristic flakiness and rise.

Some chefs prefer to prepare a dough called *blitz* or *quick puff pastry*. It does not require the extensive rolling and folding procedure used for true puff pastry. Blitz puff pastry is less delicate and flaky but may be perfectly acceptable for some uses. A formula for it is given at the end of this chapter.

Procedure for Making Puff Pastry

Detrempe—*a paste made with flour and water during the first stage of preparing a pastry dough, especially rolled-in doughs.*

1. Prepare the dough base (**detrempe**) by combining the flour, water, salt and a small amount of fat. Do not overmix. Overmixing results in greater gluten formation; too much gluten can make the pastry undesirably tough.

2. Wrap the detrempe and chill for several hours or overnight. This allows the gluten to relax and the flour to absorb the liquid.
3. Shape the butter into a rectangle of even thickness; wrap and chill until ready to use.
4. Allow the detrempe and butter to sit at room temperature until slightly softened and of the same consistency.
5. Roll out the detrempe into a rectangle of even thickness.
6. Place the butter in the center of the dough. Fold the dough around the butter, enclosing it completely.
7. Roll out the block of dough and butter into a long, even rectangle. Roll only at right angles so that the layered structure is not destroyed.
8. Fold the dough like a business letter: Fold the bottom third up toward the center so that it covers the center third, then fold the top third down over the bottom and middle thirds. This completes the first turn.
9. Rotate the block of dough one-quarter turn (90 degrees) on the work surface. Roll out again into a long, even rectangle.
10. Fold the dough in thirds again, like a business letter. This completes the second turn. Wrap the dough and chill for approximately 30 minutes. The resting period allows the gluten to relax; the chilling prevents the butter from becoming too soft.
11. Repeat the rolling and folding process, chilling between every one or two turns, until the dough has been turned a total of five times.
12. Wrap well and chill overnight. Raw dough may be refrigerated for a few days or frozen for two to three months.
13. Shape and bake as needed. Baked, unfilled puff pastry can be stored at room temperature for two to three days.

◆◆◆

RECIPE 29.8
PUFF PASTRY

Yield: 2 lb. (1 kg)   **Method:** Rolled-In Dough

All-purpose flour	13 oz.	390 g
Salt	1-1/2 tsp.	7 ml
Unsalted butter, cold	3 oz.	90 g
Water, cold	7 oz.	210 ml
Unsalted butter, softened	10 oz.	300 g

1. To form the detrempe, sift the flour and salt together in a large bowl. Cut the 3 ounces (90 grams) of cold butter into small pieces and then cut the pieces into the flour until the mixture resembles coarse cornmeal.
2. Make a well in the center of the mixture and add all the water at once. Using a rubber spatula or your fingers, gradually draw the flour into the water. Mix until all of the flour is incorporated. Do not knead the dough. The detrempe should be sticky and shaggy-looking.

NOTE: The detrempe can be made in a food processor. To do so, combine the flour, salt and pieces of butter in a food processor bowl fitted with the metal blade. Process until a coarse meal is formed. With the processor running, slowly add the water. Turn the machine off as soon as the dough comes together to form a ball. Proceed with the remainder of the recipe.

Continued

1. Mise en place for puff pastry. The detrempe is shown on the left.

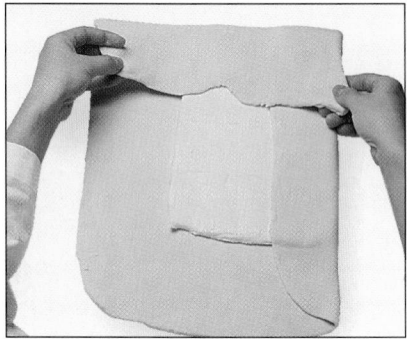

2. Folding the dough around the butter.

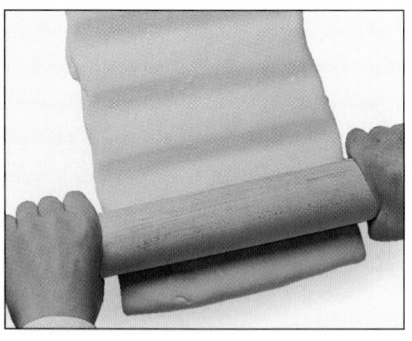

3. Rolling out the dough.

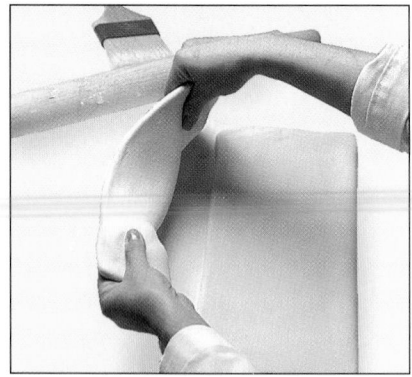

4. Folding the dough in thirds.

3. Turn the detrempe out onto a lightly floured surface. Knead the dough a few times by hand, rounding it into a ball. Wrap the dough tightly in plastic and chill overnight.

4. To roll in the butter, first prepare the 10-ounce (300-gram) piece of butter by placing it between two sheets of plastic wrap. Use a rolling pin to roll the softened butter into a rectangle approximately 5 inches × 8 inches (12.5 centimeters × 20 centimeters). It is important that the detrempe and butter be of almost equal consistency. If necessary, allow the detrempe to sit at room temperature to soften or chill the butter briefly to harden.

5. On a lightly floured board, roll the detrempe into a rectangle approximately 12 inches × 15 inches (30 centimeters × 37.5 centimeters). Lift and rotate the dough as necessary to prevent sticking.

6. Use a dry pastry brush to brush away any flour from the dough's surface. Loose flour can cause gray streaks and can prevent the puff pastry from rising properly when baked.

7. Peel one piece of plastic wrap from the butter. Position the butter in the center of the rectangle and remove the remaining plastic. Fold the four edges of the detrempe over the butter enclosing it completely. Stretch the dough if necessary; it is important that none of the butter be exposed.

8. With the folded side facing up, press the dough several times with a rolling pin. Use a rocking motion to create ridges in the dough. Place the rolling pin in each ridge and slowly roll back and forth to widen the ridge. Repeat until all of the ridges are doubled in size.

9. Using the ridges as a starting point, roll the dough out into a smooth, even rectangle approximately 8 inches × 24 inches (20 centimeters × 60 centimeters). Be careful to keep the corners of the dough as right angles.

10. Use a dry pastry brush to remove any loose flour from the dough's surface. Fold the dough in thirds, like a business letter. If one end is damaged or in worse condition, fold it in first; otherwise start at the bottom. This completes the first turn.

11. Rotate the block of dough 90 degrees, so that the folded edge is on your left and the dough faces you like a book. Roll the dough out again, repeating the ridging technique. Once again, the dough should be in a smooth, even rectangle of approximately 8 inches × 24 inches (20 centimeters × 60 centimeters).

12. Fold the dough in thirds again, completing the second turn. Cover the dough with plastic wrap and chill for at least 30 minutes.

13. Repeat the rolling and folding technique until the dough has had a total of five turns. Do not perform more than two turns without a resting and chilling period. Cover the dough completely and chill overnight before shaping and baking.

NOTE: It is not necessary to work with the entire block of dough when making bouchées, cookies or the like. Cut the block into thirds or quarters and work with one of these portions at a time, keeping the rest chilled until needed.

Shaping Puff Pastry

Once puff pastry dough is prepared, it can be shaped into containers of various sizes and shapes. Classic shapes are bouchées, vol-au-vents and feuilletées. **Bouchées** are small puff pastry shells often used for hors d'oeuvres or appetizers. **Vol-au-vents** are larger, deeper shells, often filled with savory mixtures for a main course. Although they are most often round or square, special vol-au-vent cutters are available in the shape of fish, hearts or petals. **Feuilletées** are square, rectangular or diamond-shaped puff pastry boxes. They can be filled with a sweet or savory mixture.

When making straight cuts in puff pastry, press the tip of your knife into the dough and cut by pressing down on the handle. Do not drag the knife through the dough or you will crush the layers and deform the pastry.

Procedure for Shaping Vol-Au-Vents and Bouchées

1. Roll out the puff pastry dough to a thickness of approximately 1/4 inch (6 millimeters).
2. Cut the desired shape and size using a vol-au-vent cutter or rings.

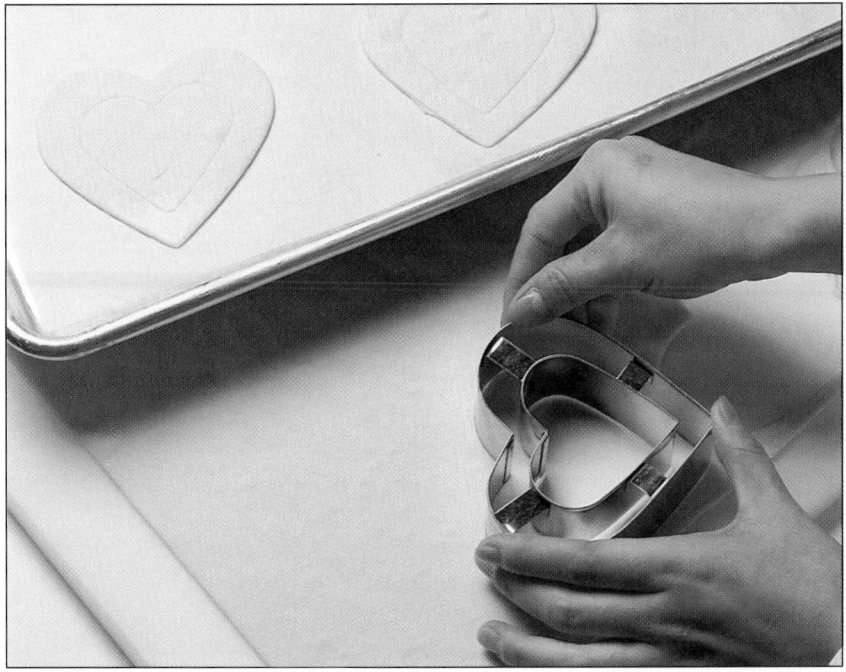

a. A vol-au-vent cutter looks like a double cookie cutter with one cutter about 1 inch (2.5 centimeters) smaller than the other. To cut the pastry, simply position the cutter and press down.

b. To shape with rings, use two rings, one approximately 1 inch (2.5 centimeters) smaller in diameter than the other. The larger ring is used to cut two rounds. One will be the base and is set aside. The smaller ring is then used to cut out an interior circle from the second round, leaving a border ring of dough. (The scrap of dough from the dough ring's center has no further use in making vol-au-vents.)

3. Place the vol-au-vent or bouchée on a paper-lined sheet pan. If you used rings, place the base on the paper-lined sheet pan, brush lightly with water, then top it with the dough ring; score the edge with the back of a paring knife. Chill for 20–30 minutes to allow the dough to relax before baking.
4. Egg-wash if desired and dock the center with a fork.

Procedure for Shaping Feuilletées

1. Roll out the puff pastry dough into an even rectangle approximately 1/8 to 1/4 inch (3 to 6 millimeters) thick.
2. Using a sharp paring knife or chef's knife, cut squares that are about 2 inches (5 centimeters) larger than the desired interior of the finished feuilletée.

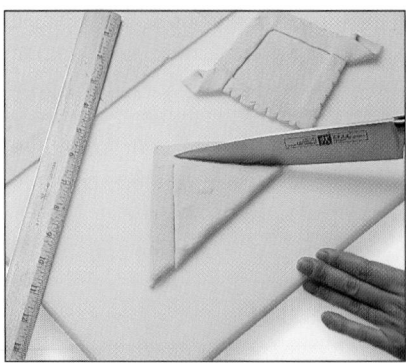

3. Fold each square in half diagonally. Cut through two sides of the dough, about 1/2 inch (1.25 centimeters) from the edge. Cut a "V," being careful not to cut through the corners at the center fold.

4. Open the square and lay it flat. Lift opposite sides of the cut border at the cut corners and cross them.

5. Brush water on the edges to seal the dough. Place the feuilletées on a paper-lined sheet pan.

6. Score the edges with the back of a paring knife. Chill for 20 to 30 minutes to allow the dough to relax before baking.

7. Egg-wash if desired and dock the center with a fork.

Puff pastry scraps cannot be rerolled and used for products needing a high rise. The additional rolling destroys the layers. Scraps (known as *rognures*), however, can be used for cookies such as palmiers (Recipe 29.26), turnovers, decorative crescents (fleurons), tart shells, napoleons (Recipe 29.24) or any item for which rise is less important than flavor and flakiness.

Most puff pastry products bake best in a hot oven, about 400–425°F (200–220°C).

Cream Puffs—*baked rounds of éclair paste cut in half and filled with pastry cream, whipped cream, fruit or other filling.*

Profiteroles—*small baked rounds of éclair paste filled with ice cream and topped with chocolate sauce.*

Croquembouche—*a pyramid of small puffs, each filled with pastry cream; a French tradition for Christmas and weddings, it is held together with caramelized sugar and decorated with spun sugar or marzipan flowers.*

Éclairs—*baked fingers of éclair paste filled with pastry cream; the top is then coated with chocolate glaze or fondant.*

Paris-Brest—*rings of baked éclair paste cut in half horizontally and filled with light pastry cream and/or whipped cream; the top is dusted with powdered sugar or drizzled with chocolate glaze.*

Beignets—*squares or strips of éclair paste deep-fried and dusted with powdered sugar.*

Churros—*a Spanish and Mexican pastry in which sticks of eclair paste flavored with cinnamon are deep-fried and rolled in sugar while still hot.*

Crullers—*a Dutch pastry in which a loop or strip of twisted éclair paste is deep-fried.*

Éclair Paste

Éclair paste, also known as **pâte à choux**, bakes up into golden brown, crisp pastries. The inside of these light pastries are mostly air pockets with a bit of moist dough. They can be filled with sweet cream, custard, fruit or even savory mixtures. The dough is most often piped into rounds for **cream puffs**, fingers for **éclairs** or rings for **Paris-Brest**. Éclair paste may also be piped or spooned into specific shapes and deep-fried for doughnut-type products known as **beignets**, **churros** and **crullers**.

Making Éclair Paste

Éclair paste is unique among doughs because it is cooked before baking. The cooking occurs when the flour is added to a boiling mixture of water, milk and butter. This process breaks down the starches in the flour, allowing them to absorb the liquid, speeding gelatinization. Eggs are added to the flour mixture for leavening. The dough produced is batterlike with a smooth, firm texture; it does not have the dry, crumbly texture of other doughs. Without this technique the dough would not puff up and develop the desired large interior air pockets when baked.

PROCEDURE FOR MAKING ÉCLAIR PASTE

1. Combine liquid ingredients and butter and bring to a boil.

2. Add all of the flour to the saucepan as soon as the water-and-butter mixture comes to a boil. If the liquid is allowed to boil, evaporation occurs; this can create an imbalance in the liquid-to-flour ratio.

3. Stir vigorously until the liquid is absorbed. Continue cooking the dough until it forms a ball that comes away from the sides of the pan, leaving only a thin film of dough in the pan.

4. Transfer the dough to a mixing bowl. Add eggs one at a time, beating well after each addition. This may be done in a mixer with the paddle attachment or by hand. The number of eggs used varies depending on the size of each egg and the moisture content of the flour mixture. Stop adding eggs when the dough just begins to fall away from the beaters.

5. The finished dough should be smooth and pliable enough to pipe through a pastry bag; it should not be runny.

6. Pipe the dough as desired and bake immediately. A high oven temperature is necessary at the start of baking; it is then reduced gradually to finish baking and dry the product. Do not open the oven door during the first half of the baking period.

7. Allow the dough to bake until completely dry. If the products are removed from the oven too soon, they will collapse.

8. Baked éclair paste can be stored, unfilled, for several days at room temperature or frozen for several weeks. Once filled, the pastry should be served within two or three hours, as it quickly becomes soggy.

◆◆◆

RECIPE 29.9

BASIC ÉCLAIR PASTE

Yield: 2 lb. (1 kg) Dough

Milk*	8 oz.	225 g
Water	8 oz.	225 g
Salt	1-1/2 tsp.	7 ml
Granulated sugar	2 tsp.	10 ml
Butter	7-1/2 oz.	210 g
All-purpose flour	8 oz.	450 g
Eggs	7–9	7–9

1. Preheat the oven to 425°F (220°C). Line a sheet pan with parchment. Have a pastry bag with a large plain tip ready.

2. Place the milk, water, salt, sugar and butter in a saucepan. Bring to a boil. Make sure the butter is fully melted.

3. Remove from the heat and immediately add all the flour. Vigorously beat the dough by hand. Put the pan back on the heat and continue beating the dough until it comes away from the sides of the pan. The dough should look relatively dry.

4. Transfer the dough to a mixing bowl and allow it to cool briefly to a temperature of approximately 130°F (54°C) or lower. Using the mixer's paddle attachment, being beating in the eggs one at a time.

---

* For a crisper product, replace the milk with water.

Continued

5. Continue to add the eggs until the mixture is shiny but firm. It may not be necessary to use all nine eggs. The dough should pull away from the sides of the bowl in thick threads; it will not clear the bowl.

6. Put a workable amount of dough into the pastry bag and pipe onto the sheet pan in the desired shapes at once.

7. Bake immediately, beginning at 425°F (220°C) for 10 minutes, then lowering the heat to 375°F (190°C) for another 10 minutes. Continue gradually lowering the oven temperature until the shapes are brown and dry inside. Open the oven door as little as possible to prevent rapid changes in the oven's temperature.

8. Cool completely, then fill as desired. Leftovers can be frozen or stored at room temperature.

1. Heating the butter and milk.

2. Adding the flour to the hot liquid.

3. Stirring the dough to dry it.

4. The finished batter after the eggs are incorporated.

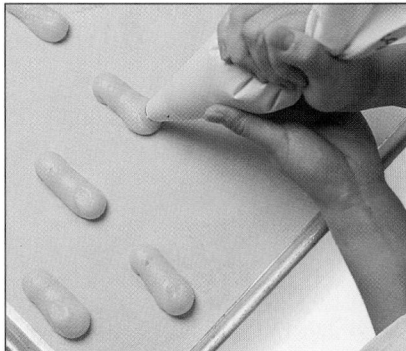

5. Piping éclairs.

Meringues

Meringues are egg whites whipped with sugar. The texture—hard or soft—depends on the ratio of sugar to egg whites.

A low sugar content in comparison with the egg whites creates a **soft meringue**. Soft meringues can be folded into a mousse or Bavarian to lighten it or used in a spongecake or soufflé. Meringues with only a small amount of sugar will always be soft; they will not become crisp no matter how they are used.

TABLE 29.4   MERINGUES

Type	Ratio of Sugar to Egg Whites	Preparation	Use
Common—hard	Twice as much or more	Whip or fold sugar into whipped egg whites	Baked
Common—soft	Equal parts or less	Whip or fold sugar into whipped egg whites	Pie toppings; soufflés; cake ingredient
Swiss	Varies	Warm egg whites with sugar, then whip	Buttercream; pie topping; baked
Italian	Varies	Hot sugar syrup poured into whipped egg whites	Buttercream; frosting; crèmet Chiboust; baked.

Hard meringues are made with egg whites and an equal part or more of sugar. They can be incorporated into a butter cream or pastry cream or used to top a pie or baked Alaska. These toppings are usually placed briefly under a broiler to caramelize the sugar, creating an attractive brown surface.

Hard meringues with twice as much sugar as egg whites can be piped into disks or other shapes and dried in an oven. A low oven temperature evaporates the eggs' moisture, leaving a crisp, sugary, honeycomblike structure. Disks of baked meringue can be used as layers in a torte or cake. Cups or shells of baked meringue can be filled with cream, mousse, ice cream or fruit. Often baked meringues also contain ground nuts (and are then known as *dacquoise*), cocoa powder or other flavorings.

Making Meringues

There are three methods for making meringues: **common**, **Swiss** and **Italian**. Regardless of which preparation method is used, the final product should be smooth, glossy and moist. A meringue should never be dry or spongelike. You should review the procedure for whipping egg whites given in Chapter 8, Eggs and Dairy Products.

Common Meringues

Common meringues are made by first beating egg whites to a soft foam (soft peaks). Granulated sugar is then slowly beaten or folded into the egg whites. The final product may be hard or soft depending on the ratio of sugar to egg whites.

Swiss Meringues

Swiss meringues are made by combining unwhipped egg whites with sugar and warming the mixture over a bain marie to a temperature of approximately 100°F (38°C). The syrupy solution is then whipped until cool and stiff. The final product may be hard or soft depending on the ratio of sugar to egg whites. Swiss meringues are extremely stable but rather difficult to prepare. If the mixture gets too hot it will not whip properly; the result will be syrupy and runny. Swiss meringue is often used as a topping or in buttercream.

Italian Meringues

Italian meringues are made by slowly pouring a hot sugar syrup into whipped egg whites. The heat from the syrup cooks the egg whites, adding stability. Be sure that the sugar syrup reaches the correct temperature and that

TABLE 29.5   TROUBLESHOOTING CHART FOR MERINGUES

Problem	Cause	Solution
Weeps or beads of sugar syrup are released	Old eggs	Use fresher eggs or add starch or stabilizer
	Egg whites overwhipped	Whip only until stiff peaks form
	Not enough sugar	Increase sugar
	Not baked long enough	Increase baking time
	Browning too rapidly	Do not dust with sugar before baking; reduce oven temperature
	Moisture in the air	Do not refrigerate baked meringue
Fails to attain any volume or stiffness	Fat present	Start over with clean bowls and utensils
	Sugar added too soon	Allow egg whites to reach soft peaks before adding sugar
Lumps	Not enough sugar	Add additional sugar gradually or start over
	Overwhipping	Whip only until stiff peaks form
Not shiny	Not enough sugar	Add additional sugar gradually or start over
	Overwhipping	Whip only until stiff peaks form

it is added to the egg whites in a slow, steady stream. Italian meringues are used in buttercream (see Chapter 30, Cakes and Frostings) or folded into pastry cream to produce crème Chiboust. They may be flavored and used as a cake filling and frosting called boiled icing.

COOKIES

Cookies are small, flat pastries usually eaten alone (although not singularly) and rarely used as a component in other desserts. The recent proliferation of cookie shops in malls and office buildings attests to the popularity of freshly baked cookies. They are indeed among the world's best-loved foods.

Part of the pleasure of cookies comes from their versatility. They may be eaten as a midmorning snack or as the elegant end to a formal dinner. Cookies also provide the finishing touch to a serving of ice cream, custard or fruit. Flavors are limited only by the baker's imagination; chocolate, oatmeal, cornmeal, fresh and dried fruit and nuts all find their way into several types of cookies. Several cookie formulas are given at the end of this chapter.

Mixing Methods

Most cookie doughs are mixed by the creaming method used for quick breads and cake batters. (See Chapters 27, Quick Breads, and 30, Cakes and Frostings.) Because cookie dough contains less liquid than these batters, the liquid and flour need not be added alternately, however. Cookies may be leavened with baking soda, baking powder or just air and steam. Most cookies are high in fat, which contributes taste and tenderness and extends shelf life. Overdevelopment of gluten is usually not a problem with cookies because of their high fat and low moisture contents. But careless mixing can cause the dough to become tough and dense instead of tender and flaky.

Procedure for Mixing Cookie Doughs

1. Cream the fat and sugar together to incorporate air and to blend the ingredients completely.
2. Add the eggs gradually, scraping down the bowl as needed.
3. Stir in the liquid ingredients.
4. Stir in the flour, salt, spices and leaveners.
5. Fold in any nuts, chocolate chips or chunky ingredients by hand.

Drop Cookies

Makeup Methods

Cookie varieties are usually classified by the way in which the individual cookies are prepared. This section describes six preparation or makeup techniques: **drop**, **icebox**, **bar**, **cut-out** or **rolled**, **pressed** and **wafer**. Some doughs can be made up by more than one method. For example, chocolate chip cookie dough can be (a) baked in sheets and cut into bars, (b) dropped in mounds or (c) rolled into logs, chilled and sliced like icebox cookies. Regardless of the makeup method used, uniformity of size and shape is important for appearance and baking time. Cookies should also be evenly spaced on sheet pans for proper air circulation and crust formation.

Drop Cookies

Drop cookies are made from a soft dough that is spooned or scooped into mounds for baking. Chunky cookies such as chocolate chip, oatmeal raisin and nut jumbles are common examples. Although a uniform appearance is not as important for drop cookies as for other types, uniform size and placement results in uniform baking time. A portion scoop is recommended for portioning the dough. Drop cookies tend to be thick with a soft or chewy texture.

Icebox Cookies

Icebox Cookies

Icebox cookies are made from dough that is shaped into logs or rectangles, chilled thoroughly, then sliced into individual pieces and baked as needed. Icebox cookies can be as simple as a log of chocolate chip dough or as sophisticated as elegant pinwheel and checkerboard cookies assembled with two colors of short dough. This method usually produces uniform, waferlike cookies with a crisp texture.

Bar Cookies

Bar cookie dough is pressed or layered in shallow pans and cut into portions after baking, usually squares or rectangles to avoid waste or scraps. This category, also known as sheet cookies, contains a wide variety of layered or fruit-filled products. Brownies, often considered a bar cookie, are discussed in Chapter 30, Cakes and Frostings.

Bar Cookies

Cut-Out or Rolled Cookies

Cut-out or rolled cookies are made from a firm dough that is rolled out into a sheet and then cut into various shapes before baking. A seemingly infinite selection of cookie cutters is available, or you can use a paring knife or pastry wheel to cut the dough into the desired shapes. Always start cutting cookies from the edge of the dough, working inward. Cut the cookies as close to each other as possible to avoid scraps. Cut-out cookies are usually baked on an ungreased pan to keep the dough from spreading.

Cut-Out or Rolled Cookies

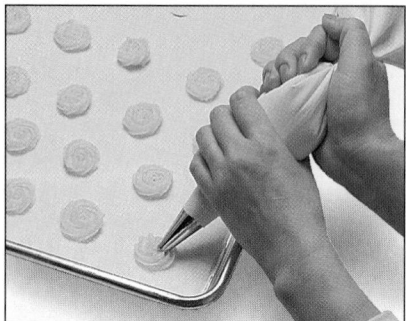

Pressed Cookies

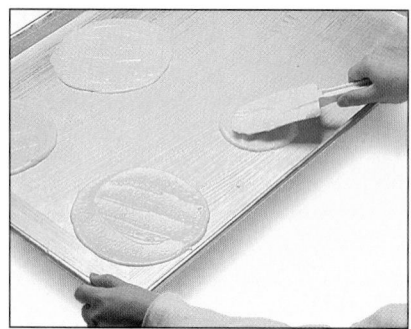

Wafer Cookies

Cut-out cookies are often garnished or decorated with nuts, glaze, fruit or candies. Raw cookies should be decorated as soon as they are placed on the pan. If the dough is allowed to stand, the surface will dry out and the garnish will not adhere properly.

Pressed Cookies

Also referred to as bagged or spritz cookies, these products are made with a soft dough that is forced through a pastry tip or cookie gun. Pressed cookies are usually small, with a distinct, decorative shape. The task of piping out dozens of identical cookies may seem daunting, but the skill can be mastered with practice and an understanding of doughs. Doughs for pressed cookies often include eggs as their only liquid. Eggs, which are a toughener, contribute body and help the cookies retain their shape. Using too much fat or too-soft flour (i.e., one low in protein) can cause the cookies to spread and lose their shape.

Wafer Cookies

Wafer cookies are extremely thin and delicate. They are made with a thin batter that is poured or spread onto a baking sheet and baked. Then, while still hot, the wafer is molded into a variety of shapes. The most popular shapes are the tightly rolled cigarette, the curved tuile and the cup-shaped tulipe. Wafer batter is sweet and buttery and is often flavored with citrus zest or ground nuts. The recipe for the tulipe shown in the photograph that introduces Chapter 31, Custards, Creams, Frozen Desserts and Dessert Sauces, is an example of a wafer cookie used as a pastry container.

Cookie Textures

The textures associated with cookies—crispness, softness, chewiness or spread—are affected by various factors, including the ratio of ingredients in the dough, the oven's temperature and the pan's coating. Understanding these factors allows you to adjust formulas or techniques to achieve the desired results. See Table 29.6.

TABLE 29.6   COOKIE TEXTURES

		Content of				
Desired Texture	Fat	Sugar	Liquid	Flour	Size or Shape	Baking
Crispness	High	High; use granulated sugar	Low	Strong	Thin dough	Well done; cool on baking sheet
Softness	Low	Low; use hydroscopic sugars	High	Weak	Thick dough portion	Use parchment-lined pan; underbake
Chewiness	High	High; use hydroscopic sugars	High	Strong	Not relevant; chilled dough	Underbake; cool on rack
Spread	High	High; use coarse granulated sugar	High; especially from eggs	Weak	Not relevant; room-temperature dough	Use greased pan; low temperature

◆◆◆

THE STORY BEHIND THE CHIP

History was made in 1930 when Ruth Wakefield, innkeeper of the Toll House Inn in Whitman, Massachusetts, cut up a semisweet chocolate bar and added the pieces to cookie dough. She was disappointed, however, that the pieces kept their shape when baked—until her first bite, that is.

Mrs. Wakefield contacted Nestlé Foods Corporation, which published her cookie recipe on the wrapper of their semisweet chocolate bars. The recipe's popularity led Nestlé's to market chocolate chips in 1939.

Under terms of its agreement with the Toll House Inn, Nestlé could not alter the recipe for Original Toll House® Cookies for 40 years. When the agreement expired in 1979, Nestle simplified the recipe. The original Original Toll House® Cookie recipe is no longer published by Nestlé Foods, but is reprinted here for the sake of tradition.

◆◆◆

RECIPE 29.10
ORIGINAL
ORIGINAL TOLL HOUSE® COOKIES

Yield: 50 2-inch Cookies

1 c. + 2 Tbsp.	Sifted cake flour
1/2 tsp.	Baking soda
1/2 tsp.	Salt
1/2 c.	Butter, softened
6 Tbsp.	Granulated sugar
6 Tbsp.	Packed brown sugar
1/2 tsp.	Vanilla extract
1/4 tsp.	Water
1	Egg
1 package (6 oz. or 1 c.)	Nestlé Toll House® Semi-Sweet Chocolate Morsels
1/2 c.	Nuts, chopped coarse

1. Sift the flour, baking soda and salt together and set aside.
2. Combine butter, sugars, vanilla and water; beat until creamy. Beat in egg. Add the flour mixture; mix well. Stir in Nestlé Toll House® Semi-Sweet Chocolate Morsels and nuts.
3. Drop well-rounded half teaspoons of cookie dough onto greased cookie sheets. Bake at 375°F for 10–12 minutes.

Storing Cookies

Most cookies can be stored for up to one week in an airtight container. Do not store crisp cookies and soft cookies in the same container, however. The crisp cookies will absorb moisture from the soft cookies, ruining the texture of both. Do not store strongly flavored cookies, such as spice, with those that are milder, such as shortbread.

Most cookies freeze well if wrapped airtight to prevent moisture loss or freezer burn. Raw dough can also be frozen, either shaped or unshaped.

CONCLUSION

Pastry making is the backbone of dessert preparation. A wide variety of pastry doughs can be prepared from flour, fat and a liquid. Proper mixing, rolling and shaping techniques are crucial to the success of the finished product. With a selection of properly prepared doughs and fillings, you can prepare an endless variety of endlessly tempting desserts.

QUESTIONS FOR DISCUSSION

1. How does the type of pie filling influence the selection of a pie crust? What type of crust would be best for a fresh uncooked fruit pie? Explain your answer.

2. How does rolling fat into a dough in layers (as with puff pastry) produce a flaky product? Why isn't sweet dough (which contains a high ratio of butter) flaky?

3. Explain the difference between a cream pie filling and a custard pie filling. Give two examples of each type of filling.

4. List and describe three ways of preparing fruit fillings for pies.

5. Why is it said that éclair paste is the only dough that is cooked before it is baked? Why is this step necessary? List three ways for using éclair paste in making classic desserts.

6. Explain the differences and similarities between common, Swiss and Italian meringues.

7. List and describe four makeup methods for cookie doughs.

ADDITIONAL PIE, PASTRY AND COOKIE FORMULAS

Several of the formulas given below are combinations of the pastry items presented in this chapter and the creams, custards and other dessert products covered in other chapters. For example, the Strawberry Napoleon is made with the puff pastry discussed in this chapter, the pastry cream and crème Chantilly discussed in Chapter 31, Custards, Creams, Frozen Desserts and Dessert Sauces, and the fondant glaze discussed in Chapter 30, Cakes and Frostings.

◆◆◆

RECIPE 29.11

GATEAU ST. HONORÉ

NOTE: *This dish appears in the Chapter Opening photograph.*

CITY RESTAURANT, Los Angeles, CA
Chef/Owners Susan Feniger and Mary Sue Milliken

Yield: 10 Servings

Puff pastry	1 lb.	450 g
Milk	4 oz.	120 g

Unsalted butter	1-3/4 oz.	50 g
Salt	1/8 tsp.	1/2 ml
All-purpose flour	2-1/2 oz.	75 g
Eggs	2	2
Pastry Cream (recipe follows)	as needed	as needed
Sugar	10 oz.	300 g
Water	4 oz.	120 g
City Chocolate (recipe follows)	as needed	as needed
Heavy cream, cold	1 pt.	450 ml
Semisweet chocolate, melted	3 oz.	90 g

1. Roll out the puff pastry to form a 10-inch (25-centimeter) square; reserve in the refrigerator.

2. Make the cream puff dough by combining the milk, butter and salt in a medium-heavy saucepan. Bring to a boil. Add the flour all at once. Mix quickly with a wooden spoon until a ball forms on the spoon and the flour is evenly moistened. Transfer to a bowl and add the eggs one at a time, beating well after each addition.

3. Fit a piping bag with a large plain tip; fill it with cream puff dough. Line a baking sheet with parchment paper. Pipe dough onto the baking sheet to form small circles about the size of quarters. With a finger dipped in cold water, flatten the point on top of each puff. Drop the pan on the counter to set the puffs.

4. Bake at 450°F (230°C) until uniformly puffed and golden, approximately 10 minutes. Reduce heat to 375°F (190°C) and bake an additional 15–20 minutes. Test for doneness by opening a puff. The inside should be totally dry. Set aside to cool on a rack.

5. Place the puff pastry on a parchment-paper-lined baking sheet and, with a 10-inch (25-centimeter) round cake pan inverted over the dough, trace a circle using a sharp knife. This will be the base for the cake. Prick the circle of puff pastry all over with a fork and set in the refrigerator to rest for 15 minutes.

6. Bake the puff pastry at 425°F (220°C) until puffed and golden, approximately 20 minutes. Reserve at room temperature.

7. Fit a piping bag with a #2 tip; fill it with pastry cream. Make a hole in the bottom of each puff using a small paring knife. Fill each puff with pastry cream and reserve.

8. To make the caramel, combine the sugar and water in a saucepan and cook until golden brown. Immediately remove from heat. Using a fork, dip half of each cream puff into the warm caramel and place on a tray lined with parchment paper. When the caramel has set, turn each puff and dip the uncoated half in the caramel. Immediately arrange the puffs, flat side up, along the edge of the cooled puff pastry to form the wall.

9. Fill the center of the pastry with a even layer of City Chocolate.

10. Whip the cold cream until soft peaks form. Fold half of this cream into the 3 ounces (90 grams) of melted chocolate and set aside.

11. Spoon the remaining whipped cream into a pastry bag fitted with a #8 plain tip. Pipe about five rows of Hershey's Kiss-shaped domes over the chocolate filling, leaving even spaces between the rows. Fill the bag with the chocolate-flavored cream and repeat, filling the spaces between rows. Chill until serving time.

Continued

PASTRY CREAM

Yield: 1-1/4 pt. (600 ml)

Sugar	4 oz.	120 g
Cornstarch	4 Tbsp.	60 ml
Egg yolks	4	4
Milk	1 pt.	450 ml
Vanilla extract	1/2 tsp.	2 ml

1. Mix 2 ounces (60 grams) of sugar and all of the cornstarch in a bowl. Add the egg yolks and mix until a paste is formed. Stir in 4 ounces (120 grams) of milk.

2. Combine the remaining milk and sugar in a saucepan and bring to a boil. Pour the hot milk into the egg yolk mixture, whisking constantly. Then pour the mixture back into the pan.

3. Cook over moderate heat, stirring constantly, until smooth and thick. Remove from the heat and stir for an additional minute. Stir in the vanilla and transfer to a bowl.

4. Cover with buttered parchment paper touching the top and chill a minimum of 2 hours or as long as 2 days.

CITY CHOCOLATE

Brandy	1-1/2 Tbsp.	20 ml
Golden raisins	1-1/2 oz.	45 g
Semisweet chocolate	9 oz.	270 g
Unsalted butter	7 oz.	210 g
Eggs, separated	5	5

1. Combine the brandy and raisins in a small saucepan and warm over low heat. Reserve.

2. Chop the chocolate into small pieces and melt with butter over a bain marie. Remove from the heat and stir in the raisins and brandy. Whisk in the yolks until combined.

3. Whisk the egg whites until soft peaks form. Gently fold the whites into chocolate mixture in two stages.

◆◆◆

RECIPE 29.12

Cannoli Alla Siciliana

REX IL RISTORANTE, Los Angeles, CA
Executive Chef Odette Fada

Yield: 12 Pieces

Dough:		
All-purpose flour	2 oz.	60 g
Granulated sugar	1/2 oz.	15 g
Cocoa powder	1/2 oz.	15 g
Red Wine	1 Tbsp.	15 ml
Filling:		
Orange zest, candied, chopped	1 oz.	30 g
Chocolate chips	1 oz.	30 g
Pistachio nuts, chopped	1 oz.	30 g
Confectioner's sugar, sifted	1-1/2 oz.	45 g
Fresh ricotta cheese	12 oz.	360 g

1. To make the cannoli, sift the dry ingredients together, then stir in the wine. Add more wine if necessary to produce a stiff dough. Chill the dough for at least 1 hour.

2. Roll the dough very thin and cut it into 2-inch (5-centimeter) squares.

3. Roll each square of dough around a dowel and deep-fry until crisp, approximately 1 minute. Drain on absorbent paper.

4. To make the filling, stir all filling ingredients together and chill until ready to use.

5. To assemble, fit a piping bag with a large plain tip; fill with the filling mixture and pipe it into each of the fried cannoli shells.

6. Serve with a pool of dark chocolate sauce, garnished with candied fruits.

═══════════ ✦✦✦ ═══════════

RECIPE 29.13
LINZER TART

CITY RESTAURANT, Los Angeles, CA
Chef/Owners Susan Feniger and Mary Sue Milliken

Yield: 8–10 Servings

Unsalted butter, softened	8 oz.	225 g
Sugar	8 oz.	225 g
Egg yolks	2	2
Orange zest	2 Tbsp.	30 ml
Lemon zest	1 Tbsp.	15 ml
All-purpose flour	11 oz.	330 g
Hazelnuts, ground fine	6 oz.	180 g
Baking powder	1 tsp.	5 ml
Cinnamon, ground	2 tsp.	10 ml
Cloves, ground	1/2 tsp.	2 ml
Salt	1/4 tsp.	1 ml
Raspberry preserves	6 oz.	180 g

1. To make the dough, cream together the butter and sugar until light and fluffy. Add the egg yolks, lemon and orange zests. Beat until well combined.

2. In another bowl, mix together the remaining ingredients except the preserves. Add the dry mixture all at once to the creamed mixture and mix briefly, until just combined. (This dough looks more like cookie dough than pastry.) Wrap in plastic and chill until firm, about 4 hours or overnight.

3. Divide the dough in half. On a generously floured board, briefly knead one piece of dough and flatten it with the palm of your hand. Gently roll the dough out 1/4 inch (6 millimeters) thick and use it to line a 9- or 10-inch (20–25 centimeter) tart pan with a removable bottom. This rich dough patches easily. Chill about 10 minutes.

4. Roll out the second piece of dough to form a 12-inch- × 4-inch (30 × 10 centimeter) rectangle. Using a sharp knife or pastry wheel, cut lengthwise strips, about 1/3 inch (.8 centimeters) wide.

5. Remove the lined tart shell from the refrigerator and spread the raspberry preserves evenly over it. To create the lattice pattern with the pastry strips, first lay some strips in parallel lines, 1/2 inch (12 millimeters) apart. Then lay a second row of strips at a 45-degree angle to the first. Press the strips to the edge of the crust to seal.

6. Bake at 350°F (180°C) until the crust is golden brown and the filling is bubbly in center, approximately 45 minutes. Set aside to cool.

◆◆◆

RECIPE 29.14

QUICHE DOUGH

Yield: 8 lb. (3.6 kg)

All-purpose flour	4 lb. 7 oz.	2 kg
Salt	1-1/2 oz.	45 g
Unsalted butter, cold	2 lb. 3 oz.	1 kg
Eggs	12	12

1. Combine the flour and salt in a mixer bowl fitted with the paddle attachment. Cut in the butter until the mixture looks like coarse cornmeal.
2. Whisk the eggs together to blend, then add them slowly to the dry ingredients. Blend only until the dough comes together in a ball.
3. Remove from the mixer, cover and chill until ready to use.

◆◆◆

RECIPE 29.15

LEMON MERINGUE PIE

Yield: 2 9-inch (22-cm) Pies

Granulated sugar	1 lb. 4 oz.	600 g
Cornstarch	3 oz.	90 g
Salt	pinch	pinch
Water, cold	24 oz.	750 g
Egg yolks	10	10
Fresh lemon juice	8 oz.	250 g
Lemon zest, grated	2 Tbsp.	60 ml
Prebaked pie shells	2	2
Butter	2 Tbsp.	60 ml
Egg whites	8 oz.	250 g
Granulated sugar	8 oz.	250 g

1. To make the filling, combine the 1 lb. 4 oz. (600 grams) of sugar, cornstarch, salt and water in a heavy saucepan. Cook over medium-high heat, stirring constantly, until the mixture becomes thick and almost clear.
2. Remove from the heat and slowly whisk in the egg yolks. Stir until completely blended. Return to the heat and cook, stirring constantly, until thick and smooth.
3. Stir in the lemon juice and zest. When the liquid is completely incorporated, remove the filling from the heat. Add the butter and stir until melted.
4. Set the filling aside to cool briefly. Fill two prebaked pie shells with the lemon filling.
5. To prepare the meringue, whip the egg whites until soft peaks form. Slowly add the 8 ounces (250 grams) of sugar while whisking constantly. The meringue should be stiff and glossy, not dry or spongy looking.
6. Mound the meringue over the filling, creating decorative patterns with a spatula. Be sure to spread the meringue to the edge of the crust, so that all of the filling is covered.
7. Place the pie in a 400°F (200°C) oven until the meringue is golden brown, approximately 5–8 minutes. Let cool at room temperature, then refrigerate. Serve the same day.

VARIATION: *Key lime pie*—Substitute 7 ounces (200 milliliters) key lime juice for the lemon juice and zest. Pour the filling into two prebaked pie shells and chill. Top with whipped cream.

◆◆◆

RECIPE 29.16
FRESH STRAWBERRY PIE

Yield: 2 9-inch (22-cm) Pies

Sugar	1 lb. 7 oz.	700 g
Water	8 oz.	450 g
Cornstarch	2-1/2 oz.	75 g
Water, cold	12 oz.	360 g
Salt	1/2 tsp.	2 ml
Lemon juice	4 Tbsp.	60 ml
Red food coloring	as needed	as needed
Fresh strawberries, rinsed and sliced in half	2 qt.	2 lt
Prebaked pie shells	2	2
Whipped cream	as needed	as needed

1. Bring the sugar and 8 ounces (225 grams) water to a boil.

2. Dissolve the cornstarch in the cold water and add to the boiling liquid. Cook over low heat until clear, approximately 5 minutes.

3. Stir in the salt, lemon juice and enough red food coloring to produce a bright red color.

4. Pour this glaze over the strawberries and toss gently to coat them. Spoon the filling into the prepared pie shells. Chill thoroughly and top with whipped cream for service.

◆◆◆

RECIPE 29.17
BLACKBERRY COBBLER

A cobbler is a home-style baked fruit dessert, usually made with a top crust of flaky pie dough, biscuit dough or streusel topping. The finished product will be slightly runny and is often served warm in a bowl or rimmed dish, accompanied by whipped cream or ice cream.

Yield: 10 Servings

IQF blackberries	2 qt.	2 lt
Sugar	8 oz.	450 g
Tapioca	2 oz.	60 g
Water	10 oz.	300 g
Unsalted butter	2 oz.	60 g
Lemon zest	1 Tbsp.	15 ml

1. Combine all ingredients, tossing the berries gently until well coated with the other ingredients.

2. Transfer to a lightly buttered half-size hotel pan, then set aside for at least 30 minutes before baking.

3. The cobbler can be topped with flaky pie dough (Recipe 29.1), biscuit dough (Recipe 27.1) or streusel topping (Recipe 27.4) before baking.

4. Bake at 350°F (180°C) until the berry mixture bubbles and the crust is appropriately browned, approximately 40–50 minutes.

♦♦♦

RECIPE 29.18

PECAN PIE

Yield: 1 9-inch (22-cm) Pie

Eggs	3	3
Sugar	3 1/2 oz.	110 g
Corn syrup	8 oz.	225 g
Unsulfured molasses	2 oz.	60 g
All-purpose flour	1 Tbsp.	15 ml
Unsalted butter, melted	2 Tbsp.	30 ml
Vanilla extract	1 tsp.	5 ml
Salt	1/4 tsp.	2 ml
Pecans, chopped	4 oz.	120 g
Unbaked pie shell	1	1

1. Whisk the ingredients together in the order listed, stirring in the nuts with a spatula last.
2. Pour the filling into the unbaked pie crust.
3. Place the pie on a preheated sheet pan in a 375°F (190°C) oven. Bake until golden brown and almost set, approximately 40 minutes. Chill completely before slicing.

♦♦♦

RECIPE 29.19

FRENCH APPLE TART

*NOTE: The amount of each ingredient needed and the yield will depend on the capacity and number of tart molds used. This procedure may be followed using individual tartlets or with large round, rectangular or daisy-shaped tart pans.

Sweet dough (Recipe 29.2)	as needed
Almond Cream (Recipe 29.23)	as needed
Tart apples, peeled, cored and sliced thin	as needed
Unsalted butter, melted	as needed
Granulated sugar	as needed
Apricot glaze	as needed

1. Line the tart forms with pâte sucrée. Do not prick the dough.
2. Pipe in an even layer of almond cream.
3. Arrange the apples in overlapping rows covering the almond cream completely.
4. Brush the top of the apples with melted butter and sprinkle lightly with granulated sugar.
5. Bake at 375°F (190°C) until the crust is done and the apples are light brown.
6. Allow the tart to cool to room temperature. Brush the top with apricot glaze.

◆◆◆

RECIPE 29.20
Fresh Berry Tart

Yield: 1 9-inch (22-cm) Tart

Sweet dough tart shell, fully baked (Recipe 29.2)	1	1
Pastry cream (Recipe 31.2)	1 pt.	500 ml
Fresh berries such as strawberries, blackberries, blueberries or raspberries	3 pt.	1.5 lt
Apricot glaze	as needed	as needed

1. Fill a cool tart shell with pastry cream.

2. Arrange the berries over the pastry cream in an even layer. Be sure to place the berries so that the pastry cream is covered.

3. Heat the apricot glaze and brush over the fruit to form a smooth coating.

1. Arranging the fruit over the pastry cream.

2. Brushing the apricot glaze over the fruit.

◆◆◆

RECIPE 29.21
Quick Puff Pastry

Adapted From *NICK MALGIERI'S PERFECT PASTRY*

Yield: 1 lb. 4 oz. (560 g)

Unbleached all-purpose flour	6-1/4 oz.	180 g
Cake flour	1-1/4 oz.	37 g
Unsalted butter	8 oz.	225 g
Salt	1/2 tsp.	2 ml
Water, very cold	4 oz.	120 g

1. To mix the dough, place the all-purpose flour in a 2-quart mixer bowl and sift the cake flour over it. Thoroughly stir the two flours together.

2. Slice 1 ounce (30 grams) of the butter into thin pieces and add to the

Continued

bowl. Rub in the butter by hand, tossing and squeezing in the butter until no visible pieces remain.

3. Cut the remaining butter into 1/2-inch (12-millimeter) cubes. Add the butter cubes to the flour mixture. Toss with a rubber spatula just to separate and distribute the butter. Do not rub the butter into the flour.

4. Dissolve the salt in the water. Make a well in the flour-butter mixture and add the water. Toss gently with the spatula until the dough is evenly moistened. Add drops of water, if necessary, to complete the moistening. Press and squeeze the dough in a bowl to form a rough cylinder.

5. To turn the dough, first lightly flour the work surface and the dough. Using the palm of your hand, press down on the dough three or four times to shape the dough into a rough rectangle.

6. Press and pound the dough with a rolling pin to form an even rectangle about 1/2 inch (12 millimeters) thick. Roll the dough back and forth along its length once or twice until it is an even rectangle about 1/4 inch (6 millimeters) thick. At this stage, pieces of butter are likely to stick to the work surface. If the dough does stick, loosen it with a long spatula or scraper. Clean the surface to minimize further sticking.

7. Fold both ends of the dough in toward the center, then fold them in toward the center again to make four layers. The folded package of dough will resemble a book, with a spine on one side and the cover opening opposite it. Position the package of dough so that the spine is on the left.

8. Lightly flour the work surface and the dough and repeat the pressing as before. Roll the dough along its length as before, then roll several times along its width to form a rectangle approximately 6 inches × 18 inches (15 × 45 centimeters). Fold the dough, both ends in toward the center, then over again as before. Repeat the process once more so that the dough will have three double turns.

9. Wrap the dough well in plastic and chill for at least one hour before using.

10. The dough can be refrigerated for about three days or frozen for up to one month. Defrost frozen dough in the refrigerator over night before using it.

◆◆◆

RECIPE 29.22

APPLE TART WITH VANILLA ICE CREAM

CHRISTOPHER'S AND **CHRISTOPHER'S BISTRO,** PHOENIX, AZ
Chef/Owner Christopher Gross

Yield: 8 Servings

Cake flour	9 oz.	260 g
Salt	1/8 tsp.	.5 ml
Unsalted butter, cut into small pieces	4-1/2 oz.	135 g
Egg	1	1
Water, very cold	2 oz.	60 g
Green apples, peeled, cored and sliced thin	12	12
Unsalted butter, melted	4 oz.	120 g
Granulated sugar	4 oz.	120 g
Caramel sauce	as needed	as needed
Vanilla Ice Cream (recipe follows)	as needed	as needed

1. Combine the flour, salt, pieces of butter and egg in a food processor. Process for a few seconds, until the mixture looks like coarse meal.

2. With the processor running, add the cold water. Stop the machine as soon as the dough comes together, then knead briefly by hand if necessary. Do not overmix the dough. Cover the dough and refrigerate for one hour.

3. Roll the dough out very thin and cut into eight 7-inch (17-centimeter) diameter circles. Place the dough circles on a sheet pan lined with parchment paper.

4. Arrange the apple slices in a fan pattern on top of the tart dough. Brush with melted butter and top each tart with approximately 1 tablespoon (15 milliliters) of sugar.

5. Bake at 350°F (180°C) until brown, approximately 10 minutes. Serve warm with caramel sauce and vanilla ice cream.

VANILLA ICE CREAM

Yield: 2 qt. (2 lt)

Half-and-half	1 pt.	500 ml
Milk	1 pt.	500 ml
Vanilla bean	1	1
Egg yolks	16	16
Granulated sugar	8 oz.	225 g

1. Bring the half and half, milk and vanilla bean to a boil.

2. Whisk the egg yolks and sugar together in a medium bowl. Temper the eggs with a portion of the hot milk mixture.

3. Return the warmed eggs to the hot milk and cook, stirring constantly, until the custard coats the back of a spoon.

4. Strain, chill and process in an ice cream machine according to the manufacturer's directions.

◆◆◆

RECIPE 29.23

FRESH PEACH TART WITH ALMOND CREAM

VINCENT ON CAMELBACK, Phoenix, AZ
Chef Vincent Guerithault

Yield: 8 Servings

Puff pastry	6 oz.	180 g
Almond Cream (recipe follows)	1 lb. 8 oz.	750 g
Fresh peaches, peeled, pitted and sliced	6–8	6–8
Unsalted butter, melted	3 oz.	90 g
Granulated sugar	2 Tbsp.	30 ml
Powdered sugar	as needed	as needed

1. Roll out the puff pastry into a thin strip, approximately 6 inches × 22 inches (the length of a sheet pan) (15 cm × 55 cm). Lay the dough on a sheet pan lined with parchment paper.

2. Using a large plain tip, pipe four rows of almond cream down the length of the puff pastry. Leave a 3/4-inch (18-millimeter) margin along both long edges of the dough.

Continued

3. Arrange the peach slices over the almond cream, overlapping slightly.

4. Brush the peaches with melted butter and evenly sprinkle the granulated sugar over them.

5. Bake at 400°F (200°C) until the dough is done and the peaches are lightly browned, approximately 20–30 minutes.

6. Serve warm, dusted with powdered sugar and accompanied by vanilla ice cream.

ALMOND CREAM (FRANGIPANE)

Yield: 3 lb. (1.3 kg)

Unsalted butter, softened	8 oz.	225 g
Granulated sugar	1 lb.	450 g
Eggs	8 oz.	225 g
All-purpose flour	5 oz.	150 g
Almonds, ground	12 oz.	360 g

1. Cream the butter and sugar. Slowly add the eggs, scraping down the sides of the bowl as necessary.

2. Stir the flour and ground almonds together, then add to the butter mixture. Blend until no lumps remain.

3. Almond cream may be stored under refrigeration up to three weeks.

◆◆◆

RECIPE 29.24

STRAWBERRY NAPOLEON

Yield: 10 Servings

Puff pastry, cut into 4-inch- × 15-inch (10- × 37-centimeter) strips, docked and baked	3	3
Pastry cream (Recipe 31.2)	1 pt.	500 ml
Fresh strawberries, sliced	1 qt.	1 lt
Crème Chantilly (Recipe 31.6)	1 pt.	500 ml
Sugar Glaze (Recipe 30.12)		
Dark chocolate, melted	1 oz.	30 g

1. Allow the puff pastry to cool completely before assembling.

2. Place a strip of puff pastry on a cake cardboard for support. Pipe on a layer of pastry cream, leaving a clean margin of almost 1/2 inch (12 millimeters) on all four sides.

3. Top the cream with a layer of berries.

4. Spread on a thin layer of crème Chantilly. Repeat the procedure for the second layer of puff pastry.

5. Chill while you prepare the sugar glaze. When ready to glaze, place the third strip of puff pastry on an icing rack, flat side up. Pour the sugar glaze down the length of the pastry and spread evenly with a metal cake spatula. Allow the excess to drip over the sides.

6. Immediately pipe thin lines of chocolate across the glaze. Use a toothpick to pull a spiderweb pattern in the glaze. Chill to set the glaze, then place the top in position on the napoleon.

◆◆◆

RECIPE 29.25

Crème Brûlée Napoleons with Hazelnuts

CITRUS, Los Angeles, CA
Chef Michel Richard

Yield: 8 Servings

Crème Brûlée (recipe follows)		
Caramel Sauce (recipe follows)		
Hazelnuts	6 oz.	180 g
Granulated sugar	6 oz.	180 g
Phyllo dough, defrosted	8 sheets	8 sheets
Unsalted butter, melted	4 oz.	120 g
Powdered sugar	2 oz.	60 g

1. Prepare the crème brulée and caramel sauce up to two days in advance; refrigerate.

2. Place the hazelnuts on a small baking sheet and toast in a 350°F (180°C) oven until brown, approximately 15 minutes. Rub the nuts in a sieve or dry towel to remove their skins.

3. Coarsely grind the nuts with the sugar in a food processor, pulsing on/off.

4. For the pastry, line two large baking sheets with parchment paper. Unroll the phyllo dough and remove one sheet; cover the remaining phyllo with plastic wrap and a damp towel. Brush the sheet with melted butter and sprinkle generously with the hazelnut-sugar mixture. Top with a second sheet of phyllo, pressing to seal. Brush with butter and sprinkle with the nut mixture. Repeat with a third and fourth sheet.

5. Using a ruler as a guide, trim the edges of the phyllo dough with a knife or pastry wheel to form a 12-inch × 16-inch (30-centimeter × 40-centimeter) rectangle. Cut the pastry into three strips lengthwise and four strips crosswise, forming twelve 4-inch (10-centimeter) squares.

6. Transfer the squares to prepared baking sheets in a single layer using a large spatula. Bake until brown, approximately 10 minutes.

7. Make and bake twelve more 4-inch squares using the remaining phyllo, butter and nut mixture.

Continued

8. Place as many phyllo squares as will fit under a broiler at one time on a baking sheet. Sieve powdered sugar generously over the squares. Watching carefully, broil the squares several inches below the heat source until golden brown, approximately 1 minute. Transfer to racks in a single layer. Repeat with the remaining squares.

9. To serve, divide the crème brûlée among the 16 pastry squares, nut side up, spreading evenly. Make eight napoleons by stacking two crème brûlée-filled squares and topping with one unfilled square, nut side up. Place the napoleons in the center of eight large plates.

10. Reheat the caramel sauce and ladle around the napoleons. Serve immediately.

CRÈME BRÛLÉE

Yield: 1 pt. (500 ml)

Milk	4 oz.	120 g
Heavy cream	1 pt.	500 ml
Granulated sugar	4 oz.	120 g
Vanilla beans, slit lengthwise	1 or 2	1 or 2
Egg yolks, blended with a fork	2	2

1. Place the milk, cream and sugar in a heavy medium saucepan. Scrape the seeds from the vanilla beans into the milk mixture. Add the beans and bring to a boil over medium-high heat. Remove from the heat and let the beans steep for at least 1 hour or until the mixture cools to room temperature.

2. To prepare the water bath, place a 9-inch × 13-inch (22-centimeter × 32-centimeter) baking dish in a larger baking pan. Pour enough water into the larger pan to come three quarters of the way up the sides of the baking dish. Remove the baking dish and place the baking pan of water in an oven to preheat.

3. Whisk the egg yolks into the cooled custard mixture. Strain through a fine sieve into the baking dish.

4. Place the baking dish with the custard in the baking pan with the water and bake at 300°F (150°C) until the custard is set and a knife inserted into the center comes out dry, approximately 45 minutes to 1 hour. Remove the baking dish from the water bath. Cool, then cover and refrigerate until 15 minutes before assembling the napoleons.

CARAMEL SAUCE

Yield: 14 oz. (400 g)

Granulated sugar	12 oz.	360 g
Water	as needed	as needed
Heavy cream	10 oz.	300 g

1. Place the sugar in a heavy medium saucepan. Cover with water and cook over low heat until the sugar dissolves, occasionally swirling the pan.

2. Increase the heat and boil until the sugar caramelizes and turns a deep mahogany brown. Watch carefully so that the mixture does not burn.

3. Standing back to avoid splatter, gradually pour in the cream. Simmer the sauce, stirring occasionally, until the caramel dissolves and the sauce is smooth and thick, approximately 3 minutes. Cool and refrigerate.

✦✦✦

RECIPE 29.26
PALMIERS

Puff pastry	as needed
Granulated Sugar	as needed

1. Roll out the puff pastry into a very thin rectangle. The length is not important but the width should be at least 7 inches (17.5 centimeters).
2. Using a rolling pin, gently press the granulated sugar into the dough on both sides.
3. Make a 1-inch (2.5-centimeter) fold along the long edges of the dough toward the center. Sprinkle on additional sugar.
4. Make another 1-inch (2.5-centimeter) fold along the long edges of the dough toward the center. The two folds should almost meet in the center. Sprinkle on additional sugar.
5. Fold one side on top of the other. Press down gently with a rolling pin or your fingers so that the dough adheres. Chill for 1 hour.
6. Cut the log of dough in thin slices. Place the cookies on a paper-lined sheet pan and bake at 400°F (200°C) until the edges are brown, approximately 8–12 minutes.

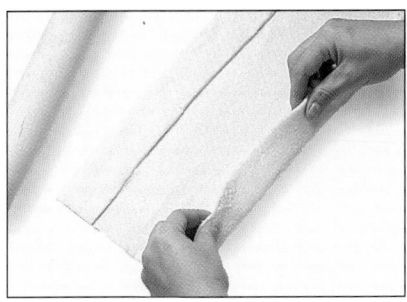

1. Folding the dough toward the center from both edges.

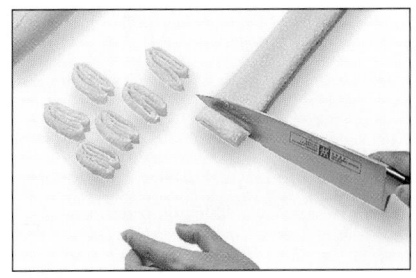

2. Slicing the log of dough into individual cookies.

✦✦✦

RECIPE 29.27
CHOCOLATE ÉCLAIRS

Yield: 20 Eclairs

Baked Éclair Shells,		
4 inches (10 cm) long, made from		
Éclair Paste (Recipe 29.9)	20	20
Vanilla Pastry Cream (Recipe 31.2)	1 qt.	1 lt
Chocolate glaze:		
Unsweetened chocolate	4 oz.	120 g
Semisweet chocolate	4 oz.	120 g
Unsalted butter	4 oz.	120 g
White corn syrup	4 tsp.	20 ml
White chocolate, melted (optional)	as needed	as needed

1. Use a paring knife or skewer to cut a small hole into the end of each baked, cooled, éclair shell.
2. Pipe the pastry cream into each shell using a piping bag fitted with a small plain tip. Be sure that the cream fills the full length of each shell. Refrigerate the filled éclairs.
3. Prepare the glaze by melting all ingredients together over a bain marie. Remove from the heat and allow to cool until slightly thickened, stirring occasionally.
4. In a single, smooth stroke, drag the top of each filled éclair through the glaze. Only the very top of each pastry should be coated with chocolate.
5. Melted white chocolate may be piped onto the wet glaze, then pulled into patterns using a toothpick. (See sauce-pulling techniques in Chapter 35, Plate Presentation.) Keep finished éclairs refrigerated and serve within 8–12 hours.

1. Filling the éclairs with pastry cream using a piping bag.

2. Dipping the éclairs in chocolate glaze.

◆◆◆

RECIPE 29.28

BAKED MERINGUE

Yield: 6 lb. 8 oz. (3 kg)

Egg whites	2 lb. 3 oz.	1 kg
Sugar	4 lb. 6 oz.	2 kg
Coffee extract (optional)	2-1/2 oz.	75 g

1. Whip the egg whites to soft peaks. With the mixer running at medium speed, slowly add the sugar and continue whipping until very stiff and glossy.
2. Whip in the coffee extract if desired.
3. Spread or pipe the meringue into the desired shapes on parchment-lined sheet pans.
4. Bake at 200°F (120°C) for 5 hours or overnight in a nonconvection oven. The baked meringues should be firm and crisp but not browned.
5. Use in assembling dessert or pastry items.

◆◆◆

RECIPE 29.29

CHOCOLATE DÉLICE

Yield: 1 8-inch (20-cm) Cake

Classic Dacquoise (recipe follows)
Ganache (recipe follows)
Creme Chantilly (recipe follows)
Candied Almonds (recipe follows)

1. Spread an even layer of ganache over two of the dacquoise disks.
2. Top one disk with about 3/4 cup (170-millileters) of crème Chantilly. Place the second disk on top, chocolate side up. Top with another 3/4 cup (170- millileters) of crème Chantilly. Position the third disk on top, flat side up.
3. Spread the remaining crème Chantilly over the top and sides.
4. Sprinkle candied almonds over the top and sides of the cake.
5. Freeze to firm the cream, approximately 1 hour. Remove from freezer and refrigerate for service.

CLASSIC DACQUOISE

Blanched almonds	2 oz.	60 g
Granulated sugar	6 oz.	180 g
Egg whites	3 oz.	90 g

1. Preheat oven to 225°F (110°C). Line a baking sheet with parchment. Draw three 8-inch (20-centimeter) circles on the parchment.
2. Grind the nuts in a food processor. They should be the consistency of cornmeal and as dry as possible. Combine with 2 ounces (60 grams) of the sugar and set aside.
3. Whip the egg whites on medium speed until foamy. Increase the speed and gradually add 1 ounce (30 grams) of the sugar.

4. Continue whipping until the egg whites form soft peaks. Gradually add the remaining sugar.

5. Continue whipping until smooth and glossy, about 2 minutes.

6. Sprinkle the almond-sugar mixture over the meringue and fold together by hand.

7. Using a pastry bag with a plain tip, pipe the meringue into 3 8-inch (20-centimeter) disks.

8. Bake until firm and crisp but not brown, approximately 60–75 minutes. Cool completely.

GANACHE

Semisweet chocolate	4 oz.	120 g
Heavy cream	3 oz.	90 g

1. Chop the chocolate into small pieces and place in a bowl.

2. Heat the cream just to boiling. Pour the cream over the chocolate and stir until the mixture is glossy and smooth. Allow to cool slightly before using.

CRÈME CHANTILLY

Heavy cream	1 qt.	1 lt
Sugar	3 oz.	90 g
Vanilla extract	1 tsp.	5 ml

1. Whip the ingredients together until soft peaks form.

CANDIED ALMONDS

Egg whites	2	2
Granulated sugar	2 oz.	60 g
Sliced almonds	8 oz.	250 g

1. Preheat oven to 325°F (160°C).

2. Whisk the egg whites and sugar together. Add the almonds. Toss with a rubber spatula to coat the nuts completely.

3. Spread the nuts in a thin layer on a lightly greased baking sheet. Bake until lightly toasted and dry, approximately 15–20 minutes. Watch closely to prevent burning.

4. Stir the nuts with a metal spatula every 5–7 minutes during baking.

5. Cool completely. Store in an airtight container for up to 10 days.

◆◆◆

RECIPE 29.30

CHEWY DATE BARS

CITY RESTAURANT, LOS ANGELES, CA
Chef/Owners Susan Feniger and Mary Sue Milliken

Yield: 12 Large Squares   **Method:** Bar Cookies

Dates, pitted and chopped	1 lb.	450 g
Water	8 oz.	225 g
Granulated sugar	8 oz.	225 g
Lemon juice, fresh	4 oz.	120 g

Continued

Rolled oats	1-1/2 pt.	700 ml
All-purpose flour	10 oz.	300 g
Brown sugar, packed	9 oz.	270 g
Baking soda	3/4 tsp.	4 ml
Salt	3/4 tsp.	4 ml
Unsalted butter, melted	14 oz.	400 g

1. Combine the dates and water in a saucepan. Cook at a low boil until the mixture is as thick as mashed potatoes, approximately 5 minutes. Stir in the granulated sugar and remove from the heat. Add the lemon juice and set aside to cool.

2. In a large bowl, mix together the oats, flour, brown sugar, baking soda and salt. Add the melted butter. Stir to moisten evenly.

3. Spread half of the oat mixture in a well-buttered 9-inch × 12-inch (22-centimeters × 30-centimeters) pan to form an even layer. Cover evenly with all of the date mixture. Spread the remaining oat mixture over the top.

4. Bake at 350°F (180°C) until the top is golden brown and pebbly, approximately 40 minutes. The edges should start caramelizing. Set aside to cool, in the pan on a rack, for about 1 hour. Run a sharp knife along the inside edges to loosen. Invert, trim the edges, and cut into squares. Serve with Caramel Ice Cream, Recipe 31.27.

◆◆◆

RECIPE 29.31

MADELEINES

Yield: 15 Large Cookies

Unsalted butter	4 oz.	120 g
Eggs	2	2
Sugar	3 oz.	90 g
Lemon zest, grated fine	1 tsp.	5 ml
Lemon juice	1/4 tsp.	1 ml
Vanilla extract	1/4 tsp.	1 ml
Baking powder	1/8 tsp.	.5 ml
Cake flour, sifted	3 oz.	90 g

1. Melt the butter over medium heat; continue cooking until the milk solids turn a golden-brown color. Set aside to cool.

2. Whisk the eggs and sugar over a bain marie until warm (98°F/38°C). Remove from the heat and whisk in the lemon zest, lemon juice and vanilla.

3. Sift the baking powder and flour together; stir into the egg mixture. Stir in the melted and cooled butter. Cover the bowl and allow to rest for 1 hour at room temperature.

4. Butter and flour the madeleine shells. Spoon the batter into the shells, filling each three-fourths full.

5. Bake at 450°F (230°C) until the cookies rise in the center and are very light brown on the bottom and edges, approximately 3–4 minutes for 1-1/2-inch (3.7-centimeter) madeleines and 10–12 minutes for 3-inch (7.5-centimeter) madeleines. They should spring back when touched lightly in the center. Remove the madeleines from the oven, invert the pan over a wire cooling rack, and tap lightly to release the cookies from the pan.

◆◆◆

RECIPE 29.32

SUGAR COOKIES

Yield: 3 Dozen   **Method:** Cut-out Cookies

All-purpose flour	12 oz.	360 g
Baking powder	2 tsp.	10 ml
Mace, ground	1/4 tsp.	1 ml
Unsalted butter, softened	4 oz.	120 g
Granulated sugar	8 oz.	250 g
Vanilla extract	1 tsp.	5 ml
Egg	1	1

1. Stir together the flour, baking powder and mace. Set aside.
2. Cream the butter and sugar until light and fluffy. Blend in the vanilla. Add the egg and beat again until fluffy. Gradually add the flour mixture, beating just until well combined.
3. Wrap the dough in plastic wrap and refrigerate until firm, about 1–2 hours.
4. Work with about half the dough at a time, keeping the remainder refrigerated. On a lightly floured board, roll out the dough to a thickness of about 1/8 inch (3 millimeters). Cut as desired with cookie cutters. Carefully transfer the cookies to lightly greased baking sheets.
5. Bake at 325°F (160°C) until golden brown, approximately 10–12 minutes. Let stand for about 1 minute, then transfer to wire racks to cool.

◆◆◆

RECIPE 29.33

GINGERBREAD COOKIES

Yield: 1 Dozen   **Method:** Cut-out Cookies

Unsalted butter, softened	4 oz.	120 g
Brown sugar	4 oz.	120 g
Molasses	6 oz.	180 g
Egg	1	1
All-purpose flour	12 oz.	360 g
Baking soda	1 tsp.	5 ml
Salt	1/2 tsp.	2 ml
Ginger	2 tsp.	10 ml
Cinnamon	1 tsp.	5 ml
Nutmeg	1/2 tsp.	2 ml
Cloves	1/2 tsp.	2 ml

1. Cream the butter and sugar until light and fluffy. Add the molasses and egg and beat to blend well; set aside.
2. Stir together the flour, baking soda, salt, ginger, cinnamon, nutmeg and cloves. Gradually add the flour mixture to the butter mixture, beating until just blended. Gather the dough into a ball and wrap in plastic wrap; refrigerate at least 1 hour.
3. On a lightly floured board, roll out the gingerbread to a thickness of 1/4 inch (6 millimeters). Cut out the cookies with a floured cutter and transfer to greased baking sheets.
4. Bake at 325°F (160°C) until the cookies are lightly browned around edges and feel barely firm when touched, approximately 10 minutes. Transfer to wire racks to cool. Decorate as desired with Royal Icing (Recipe 30.13).

◆ ◆ ◆

RECIPE 29.34
SPRITZ COOKIES

Yield: 7 Dozen   **Method:** Pressed Cookies

Unsalted butter, softened	8 oz.	250 g
Granulated sugar	4 oz.	120 g
Salt	1/4 tsp.	1 ml
Vanilla extract	1 tsp.	5 ml
Egg	1	1
Cake flour, sifted	10 oz.	300 g

1. Cream the butter and sugar until light and fluffy. Add the salt, vanilla and egg; beat well.
2. Gradually add the flour, beating until just blended. The dough should be firm but neither sticky nor stiff.
3. Press or pipe the dough onto an ungreased sheet pan using a cookie press or a piping bag fitted with a large star tip.
4. Bake at 350°F (177°C) until lightly browned around edges, approximately 10 minutes. Transfer to wire racks to cool.

◆ ◆ ◆

RECIPE 29.35
SPICED OATMEAL COOKIES

Yield: 3 Dozen   **Method:** Drop Cookies

All-purpose shortening	6 oz.	180 g
Brown sugar	6 oz.	180 g
Granulated sugar	6 oz.	180 g
Eggs	2	2
Orange juice concentrate	2 Tbsp.	30 ml
All-purpose flour	7 oz.	210 g
Baking soda	1 tsp.	5 ml
Baking powder	1 tsp.	5 ml
Salt	1 tsp.	5 ml
Cinnamon	1 tsp.	5 ml
Allspice	1/2 tsp.	2 ml
Nutmeg	1/2 tsp.	2 ml
Regular oats	1 pt.	500 ml
Dark raisins	6 oz.	180 g
Golden raisins	6 oz.	180 g

1. Cream the shortening and sugars until light and fluffy. Add the eggs and orange juice concentrate.
2. Sift the dry ingredients together and add them to the creamed mixture.
3. Blend in the oats and raisins.
4. Portion the dough onto lightly greased sheet pans and bake at 325°F (160°C) until almost firm, approximately 12 minutes.

✦✦✦

RECIPE 29.36
Lacy Pecan Cookies

Yield: 100 3-inch Cookies   **Method:** Wafer Cookies

Brown sugar	3 lb.	1.3 kg
Unsalted butter	2 lb. 8 oz.	1.1. kg
Dark corn syrup	3 lb. 12 oz.	1.7 kg
All-purpose flour	3 lb.	1.3 kg
Pecans, chopped	2 lb. 8 oz.	1.1 kg

1. Combine the sugar, butter and corn syrup in a large, heavy saucepan. Bring to a full boil.

2. Mix the flour and nuts together.

3. As soon as the sugar mixture comes to a boil, start timing it. Let it boil for a full 3 minutes. Remove from the heat and stir in the flour-nut mixture. Pour into a hotel pan to cool.

4. Let cool completely before baking. Use a small portion scoop to make equal-size balls of dough. Flatten out the balls of dough and place on flat paper-lined sheet pans.

5. Bake at 325°F (160°C) until very dark brown and no longer moist in center, approximately 15–18 minutes. Remove from oven and shape as desired.

CHAPTER 30

CAKES AND FROSTINGS

After studying this chapter you will be able to:

◆ prepare a variety of cakes
◆ prepare a variety of frostings
◆ assemble cakes using basic finishing and decorating techniques

akes are popular in most bakeshops because a wide variety of finished products can be created from only a few basic cake, filling and frosting formulas. Many of these components can even be made in advance and assembled into finished desserts as needed. Cakes are also popular because of their versatility: They can be served as unadorned sheets in a high-volume cafeteria or as the elaborate centerpiece of a wedding buffet.

Cake making need not be difficult or intimidating, but it does require an understanding of ingredients and mixing methods. This chapter begins by explaining how typical cake ingredients interact. Each of the traditional mixing methods is then explained and illustrated with a recipe. Information on panning batters, baking temperatures, determining doneness and cooling methods follows. The second portion of this chapter presents mixing methods and formulas for a variety of frostings and icings. The third section covers cake assembly and presents some simple and commonly used cake decorating techniques. A selection of popular cake formulas concludes the chapter.

Chapter 29 covers Pies, Pastries and Cookies; Chapter 31 covers Custards, Creams, Frozen Desserts and Dessert Sauces. Some of the desserts presented in those chapters use cake or frosting formulas presented here.

CAKES

Most cakes are created from liquid batters with high fat and sugar contents. The baker's job is to combine all of the ingredients to create a structure that will support these rich ingredients, yet keep the cake as light and delicate as possible. As with other baked goods, it is impossible to taste a cake until it is fully cooked and too late to alter the formula. Therefore, it is extremely important to study any formula before beginning and to follow it with particular care and attention to detail.

Ingredients

Good cakes begin with high-quality ingredients (see Chapter 26, Principles of the Bakeshop). However, even the finest ingredients must be combined in the proper balance. Too much flour and the cake may be dry; too much egg and the cake will be tough and hard. Changing one ingredient may necessitate a change in one or more of the other ingredients.

Each ingredient performs a specific function and has a specific effect on the final product. Cake ingredients can be classified by function as tougheners, tenderizers, moisteners, driers, leaveners and flavorings. Some ingredients fulfill more than one of these functions. For example, eggs contain water, so they are moisteners, and they contain protein, so they are tougheners. By understanding the function of various ingredients you should be able to understand why cakes are made in particular ways and why a preparation sometimes fails. With additional experience, you should be able to recognize and correct flawed formulas and develop your own cake formulas.

Tougheners

Flour, milk and eggs contain protein. Protein provides structure and toughens the cake. Too little protein and the cake may collapse; too much protein and the cake may be tough and coarse-textured.

Tenderizers

Sugar, fats and egg yolks shorten gluten strands, making the cake tender and soft. These ingredients also improve the cake's keeping qualities.

Moisteners

Liquids such as water, milk, juice and eggs bring moisture to the mixture. Moisture is necessary for gluten formation and starch gelatinization, as well as improving a cake's keeping qualities.

Driers

Flour, starches and milk solids absorb moisture, giving body and structure to the cake.

Leaveners

Cakes rise because gases in the batter expand when heated. Cakes are leavened by the air trapped when fat and sugar are creamed together, by carbon dioxide released from baking powder and baking soda and by air trapped in beaten eggs. All cakes rely on natural leaveners—steam and air—to create the proper texture and rise. Because baking soda and baking powder are also used in some cake formulas, you should review the material on chemical leaveners in Chapter 27, Quick Breads.

Flavorings

Flavorings such as extracts, cocoa, chocolate, spices, salt, sugar and butter provide cakes with the desired flavors. Acidic flavoring ingredients such as sour cream, chocolate and fruit also provide the acid necessary to activate baking soda.

Cake ingredients should be at room temperature, approximately 70°F (21°C), before mixing begins. If one ingredient is too cold or too warm it may affect the batter's ability to trap and hold the gases necessary for the cake to rise.

Mixing Methods

Even the finest ingredients will be wasted if the cake batter is not mixed correctly. When mixing any cake batter your goals are to combine the ingredients uniformly, incorporate air cells and develop the proper texture.

All mixing methods can be divided into two categories: *high fat*—those that create a structure that relies primarily on **creamed fat**, and *egg foam*—those that create a structure that relies primarily on **whipped eggs**. Within these broad categories are several mixing methods or types of cakes. Creamed-fat cakes include **butter cakes** (also known as **creaming method cakes**) and **high-ratio cakes**. Whipped-egg cakes include **genoise**, **spongecakes**, **angel**

TABLE 30.1 CAKES

Category	Mixing Method/Type of Cake	Key Formula Characteristics	Texture
Creamed Fat (High Fat)	Butter (creaming method)	High-fat formula; chemical leavener used	Fine grain; air cells of uniform size; moist crumb; thin and tender crust
	High-ratio (two-stage)	Emulsified shortening; two-part mixing method	Very fine grain; moist crumb; relatively high rise
Whipped Egg (Egg Foam)	Genoise	Whole eggs are whipped with sugar; no chemical leaveners	Dry and spongy
	Sponge	Egg yolks are mixed with other ingredients, then whipped egg whites are folded in	Moister and more tender than genoise
	Angel food	No fat; large quantity of whipped egg whites; high percentage of sugar	Tall, light and fluffy
	Chiffon	Vegetable oil used; egg yolks mixed with other ingredients, then whipped egg whites folded in; baking powder may be added	Tall, light and fluffy; moister and richer than angel food

food cakes and **chiffon cakes**. See Table 30.1. Although certain general procedures are used to prepare each cake type, there are, of course, variations. Follow specific formula instructions precisely.

Creamed Fat

Creamed-fat cakes include most of the popular American-style cakes: poundcakes, layer cakes, coffeecakes and even brownies. All are based on high-fat formulas containing chemical leaveners. A good high-fat cake has a fine grain, cells of uniform size and a crumb that is moist rather than crumbly. Crusts should be thin and tender.

Creamed-fat cakes can be divided into two classes: butter cakes and high-ratio cakes.

Butter Cakes

Butter cakes, also known as creaming method cakes, begin with softened butter or shortening creamed to incorporate air cells. Because of their high fat content, these cakes usually need the assistance of a chemical leavener to achieve the proper rise.

Modern-day butter cakes—the classic American layer cakes, popular for birthdays and special occasions—are made with the creaming method. These cakes are tender yet sturdy enough to handle rich buttercreams or fillings. High-fat cakes are too soft and delicate, however, to use for roll cakes or to slice into extremely thin layers.

When making butter cakes, the fat should be creamed at low to moderate speeds to prevent raising its temperature. An increased temperature could cause a loss of air cells.

PROCEDURE FOR PREPARING BUTTER (CREAMING METHOD) CAKES

1. Preheat the oven and prepare the pans.
2. Sift the dry ingredients together and set aside.

♦♦♦

POUNDCAKES

Poundcakes are the original high-fat, creaming method cake. They are called poundcakes because early formulas specified one pound each of butter, eggs, flour and sugar. Poundcakes should have a close grain and compact texture but still be very tender. They should be neither heavy nor soggy.

As bakers experimented with poundcake formulas they reduced the amount of eggs and fat, substituting milk instead. These changes led to the development of the modern butter cake.

3. Cream the butter or shortening until it is light and fluffy. Add the sugar and cream until the mixture is fluffy and smooth.

4. Add the eggs slowly, beating well after each addition.

5. Add the dry and liquid ingredients alternately.

6. Divide the batter into prepared pans and bake immediately.

RECIPE 30.1

Classic Poundcake

Yield: 2 8 × 4 inch (20 × 10 cm) Loaves   **Method:** Creaming

Cake flour	1 lb.	500 g
Baking powder	2 tsp.	10 ml
Salt	1/2 tsp.	2 ml
Unsalted butter, softened	1 lb.	500 g
Granulated sugar	12 oz.	340 g
Eggs	9	9
Vanilla extract	1 tsp.	5 ml
Lemon extract	1 tsp.	5 ml

1. Sift the cake flour, baking powder and salt together; set aside.

2. Cream the butter and sugar until light and fluffy. Add the eggs one at a time, beating well after each addition. Stir in the extracts.

3. Fold in the dry ingredients by hand. Divide the batter into greased loaf pans.

4. Bake at 325°F (160°C) until golden brown and springy to the touch, approximately 1 hour and 10 minutes.

Variation: *French-style fruitcake:* Add 6 ounces (180 grams) finely diced nuts, raisins and candied fruit to the batter. Substitute vanilla extract for the lemon extract and add 3 tablespoons (45 milliliters) rum to the batter. After baking, brush the warm cake with additional rum.

1. Creaming the butter.

2. Folding in the flour.

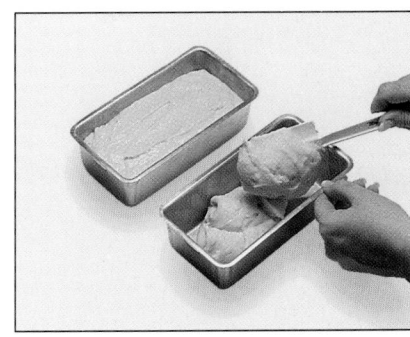

3. Panning the batter.

High-Ratio Cakes

Commercial bakers often use a special two-stage mixing method to prepare large quantities of a very liquid cake batter. These formulas require emulsified shortenings and are known as two-stage cakes because the liquids are added in two stages or portions. If emulsified shortenings are not available, do not substitute all-purpose shortening or butter as they cannot absorb the large amounts of sugar and liquid in the formula.

Because they contain a high ratio of sugar and liquid to flour, these cakes are often known as high-ratio cakes. They have a very fine, moist crumb and relatively high rise. High-ratio cakes are almost indistinguishable from modern butter cakes and may be used interchangeably.

PROCEDURE FOR PREPARING HIGH-RATIO CAKES

1. Preheat the oven and prepare the pans.
2. Place all the dry ingredients and emulsified shortening into a mixer bowl. Blend on low speed for several minutes.
3. Add approximately one half of the liquid and blend.
4. Scrape down the mixer bowl and add the remaining liquid ingredients. Blend into a smooth batter, scraping down the bowl as necessary.
5. Pour the batter into prepared pans using liquid measurements to ensure uniform division.

◆◆◆

RECIPE 30.2

HIGH-RATIO YELLOW CAKE

Yield: 3–4 Sheet Pans   Method: High-Ratio

Cake flour	5 lb.	2.2 kg
Granulated sugar	5 lb. 4 oz.	2.3 kg
Emulsified shortening	2 lb. 8 oz.	1.1 kg
Salt	2 oz.	60 g
Baking powder	4 oz.	120 g
Powdered milk	8 oz.	225 g
Light corn syrup	12 oz.	340 g
Water, cold	1 qt.	1 lt
Eggs	2 lb. 8 oz.	1.1 kg
Water, cold	2-1/4 qt.	2.25 lt
Lemon extract	1 oz.	30 g

1. Combine the flour, sugar, shortening, salt, baking powder, powdered milk, corn syrup and 1 quart (1 liter) cold water in a large bowl of a mixer fitted with the paddle attachment. Beat for 5 minutes on low speed.
2. Combine the remaining ingredients in a separate bowl. Add these liquid ingredients to the creamed-fat mixture in three additions. Scrape down the sides of the bowl after each addition.
3. Beat for 2 minutes on low speed.
4. Divide the batter into greased and floured pans. Pans should be filled only halfway. One gallon of batter is sufficient for an 18-inch × 24-inch × 2-inch (45- × 60- × 5- centimeter) sheet pan. Bake at 340°F (180°C) until a cake tester comes out clean and the cake springs back when lightly touched, approximately 12–18 minutes.

Whipped Egg

Cakes based on whipped egg foams include European-style genoise as well as spongecakes, angel food cakes and chiffon cakes. Some formulas contain chemical leaveners, but the air whipped into the eggs (whether whole or separated) is the primary leavening agent. Egg-foam cakes contain little or no fat.

Genoise

Genoise is the classic European-style cake. It is based on whole eggs whipped with sugar until very light and fluffy. Chemical leaveners are not used. A small amount of oil or melted butter is sometimes added for flavor and moisture. Genoise is often baked in a thin sheet and layered with buttercream, puréed fruit, jam or chocolate filling to create multilayered specialty desserts. Because genoise is rather dry, it is usually soaked with a flavored sugar syrup (see Chapter 26, Principles of Baking) or liquor for additional flavor and moisture.

PROCEDURE FOR PREPARING GENOISE

1. Preheat the oven and prepare the pans.
2. Sift the flour with any additional dry ingredients.
3. Combine the whole eggs and sugar in a large bowl and warm over a double boiler to a temperature of 100°F (38°C).
4. Whip the egg-and-sugar mixture until very light and tripled in volume.
5. Fold the sifted flour into the whipped eggs carefully but quickly.
6. Fold in oil or melted butter if desired.
7. Divide into pans and bake immediately.

1. Whipped eggs.

◆◆◆

RECIPE 30.3

CLASSIC GENOISE

Yield: 3 Full Sheet Pans **Method:** Whipped Egg

Cake flour	1 lb. 8 oz.	680 g
Eggs	30	30
Granulated sugar	1 lb. 8 oz.	680 g
Unsalted butter, melted (optional)	4 oz.	120 g

1. Sift the flour and set aside.
2. Whisk the eggs and sugar together in a large mixer bowl. Place the bowl over a bain marie and warm the eggs to about 100°F (38°C). Stir frequently to avoid cooking the eggs.
3. When the eggs are warm, remove the bowl from the bain marie and attach to a mixer fitted with a whip attachment. Whip the egg-and-sugar mixture at medium speed until tripled in volume.
4. Quickly fold the flour into the egg mixture by hand. Be careful not to deflate the batter.
5. Pour the melted, cooled butter around the edges of the batter and fold in quickly.
6. Divide the batter immediately into parchment-lined pans. Bake at 350°F (180°C) until light brown and springy to the touch, approximately 8 minutes.

VARIATION: *Chocolate genoise*—Sift 3-1/2 ounces (100 grams) of cocoa powder with the flour.

2. Folding in the flour.

3. Adding the melted butter.

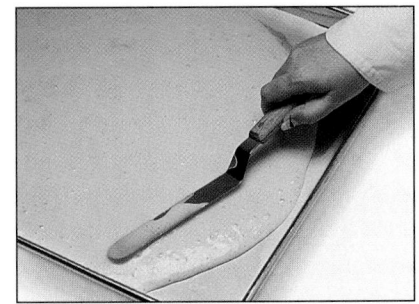

4. Panning the batter.

Spongecakes

Spongecakes (Fr. *biscuits*) are made with whole separated eggs. A batter is prepared with the egg yolks and other ingredients, then the egg whites are whipped to firm peaks with a portion of the sugar and folded into the batter. Spongecakes are primarily leavened with air, but baking powder may be included in the formula. As with genoise, oil or melted butter may be added if desired.

Spongecakes are extremely versatile. They can be soaked with sugar syrup or a liquor and assembled with buttercream as a traditional layer cake. Or, they can be sliced thinly and layered, like genoise, with jam, custard, chocolate or cream filling.

PROCEDURE FOR PREPARING SPONGECAKES

1. Preheat the oven and prepare the pans.
2. Separate the eggs. Whip the egg whites with a portion of the sugar.
3. Sift the dry ingredients together and combine with liquid ingredients, including the egg yolks, as directed.
4. Carefully fold the whipped egg whites into the batter.
5. Pour the batter into the pans and bake immediately.

◆◆◆

RECIPE 30.4

CLASSIC SPONGECAKE

Yield: 2 9-inch (22-cm) Rounds   **Method:** Whipped Egg

Cake flour, sifted	6 oz.	180 g
Granulated sugar	11 oz.	300 g
Eggs	10	10
Vanilla extract	1-1/2 tsp.	7 ml
Cream of tartar	1-1/2 tsp.	7 ml

1. Line the bottom of two springform pans with parchment. Do not grease the sides of the pans.
2. Sift the flour and 6 ounces (150 grams) of the sugar together and set aside.
3. Separate the eggs, placing the yolks and the whites in separate mixing bowls. Whip the yolks on high speed for 3–5 minutes, until thick, pale and at least doubled in volume. Whip in the vanilla extract. The yolks should be whipped "to ribbon," that is, until they fall from the beater in thick ribbons that slowly disappear into the batter's surface.
4. Place the bowl of egg whites on the mixer and, using a clean whip attachment, beat until foamy. Add the cream of tartar and 2 tablespoons (30 grams) of sugar. Whip at medium speed until the whites are glossy and stiff but not dry.
5. Remove the bowl from the mixer. Pour the egg yolks onto the whipped whites. Quickly fold the two mixtures together by hand. Sprinkle the remaining sugar over the mixture and fold in lightly.
6. Sprinkle one third of the sifted flour over the batter and fold in. Repeat the procedure until all of the flour is incorporated. Do not overmix; fold just until incorporated.

7. Pour the batter into the prepared pans, smoothing the surface as needed. Bake immediately at 375°F (190°C) until the cake is golden brown and spongy, approximately 30 minutes. A toothpick inserted in the center will be completely clean.

8. Allow the cakes to rest in their pans until completely cool, approximately 2 hours.

9. To remove the cakes from their pans, run a thin metal spatula around the edge of each pan. When the cake is completely cool it can be frosted or wrapped in plastic wrap and frozen for 2–3 months.

1. The eggs whipped to ribbon stage.

2. Folding the flour into the batter.

3. Panning the batter.

Angel Food Cakes

Angel food cakes are tall, light cakes made without fat and leavened with a large quantity of whipped egg whites. Angel food cakes are traditionally baked in ungreased tube pans, but large loaf pans can also be used. The pans are left ungreased so that the batter can cling to the sides as it rises. The cakes should be inverted as soon as they are removed from the oven and left in the pan to cool. This technique allows gravity to keep the cakes from collapsing or sinking as they cool.

Although they contain no fat, angel food cakes are not low in calories as they contain a high percentage of sugar. The classic angel food cake is pure white, but flavorings, ground nuts or cocoa powder may be added for variety. Although angel food cakes are rarely frosted, they may be topped with a fruit-flavored or chocolate glaze. They are often served with fresh fruit, a fruit compote or whipped cream.

PROCEDURE FOR PREPARING ANGEL FOOD CAKES

1. Preheat the oven.
2. Sift the dry ingredients together.
3. Whip the egg whites with a portion of the sugar until stiff and glossy.
4. Gently fold the dry ingredients into the egg whites.
5. Spoon the batter into an ungreased pan and bake immediately.
6. Allow the cake to cool inverted in its pan.

❖❖❖

RECIPE 30.5
Chocolate Angel Food Cake

Yield: 1 10-inch (25-cm) Tube Cake　　　　　**Method:** Whipped Egg

Cocoa powder, alkalized	1 oz.	30 g
Water, warm	2 oz.	60 g
Vanilla extract	2 tsp.	10 ml
Granulated sugar	12 oz.	340 g
Cake flour, sifted	3-1/2 oz.	100 g
Salt	1/4 tsp.	1 g
Egg whites	16	16
Cream of tartar	2 tsp.	10 ml

1. Combine the cocoa powder and water in a bowl. Add the vanilla and set aside.

2. In another bowl, combine 5 ounces (150 grams) of the sugar with the flour and salt.

3. Whip the egg whites until foamy, add the cream of tartar and beat to soft peaks. Gradually beat in the remaining sugar. Continue beating until the egg whites are stiff but not dry.

4. Whisk approximately 1 cup (225 millileters) of the whipped egg whites into the cocoa mixture. Fold this into the remaining egg whites.

5. Sift the dry ingredients over the whites and fold in quickly but gently.

6. Pour the batter into an ungreased tube pan and smooth the top with a spatula. Bake immediately at 350°F (180°C) until the cake springs back when lightly touched and a cake tester comes out clean, approximately 40–50 minutes. The cake's surface will have deep cracks.

7. Remove the cake from the oven and immediately invert the pan onto the neck of a bottle. Allow the cake to rest upside down until completely cool.

8. To remove the cake from the pan, run a thin knife or spatula around the edge of the pan and the edge of the interior tube. If a two-piece tube pan was used, the cake and tube portion are lifted out of the pan. Use a knife or spatula to loosen the bottom of the cake, then invert it onto a cake cardboard or serving platter.

1. Folding the cocoa mixture into the whipped egg whites.

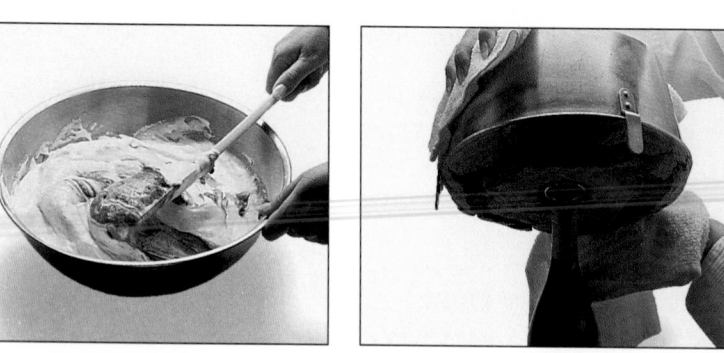

2. Folding in the flour.

3. Cooling the cake upside down in its pan.

4. Removing the cake from the pan.

Chiffon Cakes

Although chiffon cakes are similar to angel food cakes in appearance and texture, the addition of egg yolks and vegetable oil makes them moister and richer. Chiffon cakes are usually leavened with whipped egg whites but may contain baking powder as well. Like angel food cakes, chiffon cakes are baked in an ungreased pan to allow the batter to cling to the pan as it rises. Chiffon cakes can be frosted with a light buttercream or whipped cream or topped with a glaze. Lemon and orange chiffon cakes are the most popular, but formulas containing chocolate, nuts or other flavorings are also common.

PROCEDURE FOR PREPARING CHIFFON CAKES

1. Preheat the oven.
2. Whip the egg whites with a portion of the sugar until almost stiff. Set aside.
3. Sift the dry ingredients together. Add the liquid ingredients, including oil.
4. Fold the whipped egg whites into the batter.
5. Spoon the batter into an ungreased pan and bake immediately.
6. Allow the cake to cool inverted in its pan.

♦♦♦

RECIPE 30.6

ORANGE CHIFFON CAKE

Yield: 1 10-inch (25-cm) Tube Cake   **Method:** Whipped Egg

Cake flour, sifted	8 oz.	225 g
Sugar	12 oz.	340 g
Baking powder	1 Tbsp.	15 ml
Salt	1 tsp.	5 ml
Vegetable oil	4 oz.	120 g
Egg yolks	6	6
Water, cool	2 oz.	60 g
Orange juice	4 oz.	120 g
Orange zest	1 Tbsp.	15 ml
Vanilla extract	1 Tbsp.	15 ml
Egg whites	8 oz.	250 g

1. Sift together the flour, 6 ounces (170 grams) of sugar, the baking powder and salt.

2. In a separate bowl mix the oil, yolks, water, juice, zest and vanilla. Add the liquid mixture to the dry ingredients.

3. In a clean bowl beat the egg whites until foamy. Slowly beat in the remaining 6 ounces (170 grams) of sugar. Continue beating until the egg whites are stiff but not dry.

4. Stir one third of the egg whites into the batter to lighten it. Fold in the remaining egg whites.

5. Pour the batter into an ungreased 10-inch (25-centimeter) tube pan. Bake at 325°F (160°C) until a toothpick comes out clean, approximately 1 hour.

6. Immediately invert the pan over the neck of a wine bottle. Allow the cake to hang upside down until completely cool, then remove from the pan.

Continued

♦♦♦
A BAKER CREATED CHIFFON CAKES

Chiffon cake is one of the few desserts whose history can be traced with absolute certainty. According to Gerry Schremp in her book *Kitchen Culture: Fifty Years of Food Fads*, a new type of cake was invented by Henry Baker, a California insurance salesman, in 1927. Dubbed *chiffon*, it was as light as angel food and as rich as poundcake. For years he kept the formula a secret, earning fame and fortune by selling his cakes to Hollywood restaurants. The cake's secret ingredient—vegetable oil—became public knowledge in 1947 when Baker sold the formula to General Mills, which promoted it on packages of cake flour. Chiffon cakes, in a variety of flavors, became extremely popular nationwide.

ORANGE GLAZE

Powdered sugar	3 oz.	90 g
Orange juice	2 Tbsp.	30 ml
Orange zest	2 tsp.	10 ml

1. Sift the sugar, then stir in the juice and zest.
2. Drizzle the glaze over the top of the cooled cake.

VARIATION: *Lemon chiffon cake*—Substitute 2 ounces (60 grams) fresh lemon juice and 2 ounces water for the orange juice. Substitute lemon zest for the orange zest. Top with Basic Sugar Glaze, Recipe 30.12.

Panning, Baking and Cooling

Preparing Pans

In order to prevent cakes from sticking, most baking pans are coated with fat or a nonstick baking parchment. Pans should be prepared before the batter is mixed, so that they may be filled and the cakes baked as soon as the batter is finished. If the batter stands while the pans are prepared, air cells within the batter will deflate and volume may be lost.

Solid shortening is better than butter for coating pans because it does not contain any water; butter and margarine do contain water and this may cause the cake to stick in places. Solid shortening is also less expensive, tasteless and odorless. Finally, solid shortening does not burn as easily as butter and it holds a dusting of flour better.

Pan release sprays are useful but must be applied carefully and completely. Although relatively expensive, sprays save time and are particularly effective when used with parchment pan liners.

In kitchens where a great deal of baking is done, it may be more convenient to prepare quantities of pan coating to be kept available for use as needed. Pan coating is a mixture of equal-parts oil, shortening and flour that can be applied to cake pans with a pastry brush. It is used whenever pans need to be greased and floured. Pan coating will not leave a white residue on the cake's crust as a dusting of flour often does.

TABLE 30.2   NUTRITIONAL VALUES OF SELECTED CAKES

Per 1/12 Portion of a 9-inch Cake, Unfrosted	Kcal	Protein (g)	Carbohydrates (g)	Total Fat (g)	Saturated Fat (g)	Sodium (mg)
Angel food	130	3	30	0	0	170
Butter cake	260	3	37	11	6	350
Chiffon, lemon	200	4	36	5	mq	200
Devil's food	260	4	35	12	3	450
Sponge (2-in. square)	80	1	11	3	1	125

All cakes are prepared from a typical mix according to package directions.
The Corinne T. Netzer Encyclopedia of Food Values 1992
mq = measurable quantity but data is unavailable

TABLE 30.3 PAN PREPARATIONS

Pan Preparation	Used For
Ungreased	Angel food and chiffon cakes
Ungreased sides; paper on bottom	Genoise layers
Greased and papered	High-fat cakes, sponge sheets
Greased and coated with flour	High-fat cakes, chocolate cakes, anything in a bundt or shaped pan
Greased, floured and lined with paper	Cakes containing melted chocolate, fruit chunks or fruit or vegetable purées

=== ◆◆◆ ===

RECIPE 30.7

PAN COATING

Yield: 1-1/2 qt. (1.5 lt)

Vegetable oil	1 lb.	500 g
All-purpose shortening	1 lb.	500 g
Bread flour	1 lb.	500 g

1. Combine all ingredients in a mixer fitted with the paddle attachment. Blend on low speed for 5 minutes or until smooth.

2. Store in an airtight container at room temperature for up to two months.

3. Apply to baking pans in a thin, even layer using a pastry brush.

Pan coating is not appropriate for all cakes, however. Those containing chocolate, raisins or fruit should still be baked in pans lined with parchment paper to prevent sticking.

Angel food and chiffon cakes are baked in ungreased, unlined pans because these fragile cakes need to cling to the sides of the pan as they rise. Spongecakes and genoise are often baked in pans with a paper liner on the

◆◆◆

BROWNIES

Where do you draw the line between cakes and brownies? The decision must be a matter of texture and personal preference, for the preparation methods are nearly identical. Brownies are generally chewy and fudgy, sweeter and denser than even the richest of butter cakes.

Brownies are a relatively inexpensive and easy way for a food service operation to offer its customers a fresh-baked dessert. Although not as sophisticated as an elaborate gâteau, a well-made brownie can always be served with pride (and a scoop of ice cream).

Brownies are prepared using the same procedures as those for high-fat cakes. Good brownies are achieved with a proper balance of ingredients: A high percentage of butter to flour produces a dense, fudgy brownie; less butter produces a more cakelike brownie. Likewise, the higher the ratio of sugar, the gooier the finished brownie. In some formulas, the fat is creamed to incorporate air, as with butter cakes. In others, the fat is first melted and combined with other liquid ingredients. Brownies are rarely made with whipped egg whites, however, as this makes their texture too light and cakelike.

Each customer and cook has his or her own idea of the quintessential brownie. Some are cloyingly sweet, with a creamy texture and an abundance of chocolate; others are bitter and crisp. Baked brownies can be frozen for 2–3 months if well wrapped.

bottom and ungreased sides. While the ungreased sides give the batter a surface to cling to, the paper liner makes removing the cake from the pan easier.

Filling Pans

Pans should be filled no more than one-half to two-thirds full. This allows the batter to rise during baking without spilling over the edges.

Pans should be filled to uniform depths. High-fat and egg-foam cake batters can be ladled into each pan according to weight. High-ratio cake batter is so liquid that it can be measured by volume and poured into each pan. Filling the pans uniformly prevents both uneven layers and over- or underfilled pans. If you are baking three 8-inch layers to be stacked for one presentation and the amount of batter is different in each pan, the baking times will vary and the final product will suffer.

The cake batter should always be spread evenly in the pan. Use an offset spatula. Do not work the batter too much, however, as this destroys air cells and prevents the cake from rising properly.

Baking

Temperatures

Always preheat the oven before preparing your batter. If the finished batter must wait while the oven reaches the correct temperature, valuable leavening will be lost and the cake will not rise properly.

Most cakes are baked at temperatures between 325° and 375°F (160–190°C). The temperature must be high enough to create steam within the batter and cause that steam and other gases in the batter to expand and rise quickly. If the temperature is too high, however, the cake may rise unevenly and the crust may burn before the interior is completely baked. The temperature must also be low enough that the batter can set completely and evenly without drying out. If the temperature is too low, however, the cake will not rise sufficiently and may dry out before baking completely.

If no temperature is given in a formula or you are altering the dimensions of the baking pan from those specified, use common sense in setting the oven temperature. The larger the surface area, the higher the temperature can usually be. Tall cakes, such as bundt or tube cakes, should be baked at a lower temperature than thin layer or sheet cakes. Tube or loaf cakes take longer to bake than thin sheet cakes; butter cakes, because they contain more liquid, take longer to bake than genoise or spongecake.

Altitude Adjustments

As you learned in Chapter 9, Principles of Cooking, altitude affects the temperatures at which foods cook. The decreased atmospheric pressure at altitudes above 3000 feet affects the creation of steam and the expansion of hot air in cake batters. These factors must be considered when making cakes. Because gases expand more easily at higher altitudes, your cake may rise so much that its structure cannot support it and the cake collapses.

Therefore, the amount of leavening should be decreased at higher altitudes. Chemical leaveners should usually be reduced by one third at 3500 feet and by two thirds at altitudes over 5000 feet. Eggs should be underwhipped to avoid incorporating too much air, which would also create too much rise. In general, oven temperatures should also be increased by 25°F (4°C) at altitudes over 3500 feet to help set the cake's structure rapidly.

Because the boiling point decreases at higher altitudes, more moisture will evaporate from your cake during baking. This may cause dryness and an excessive proportion of sugar, which shows up as white spots on the cake's surface. Correct this by reducing every 8 ounces (225 grams) of sugar by 1/2 ounce (15 grams) at 3000 feet and by 1-1/2 ounces (45 grams) at 7000 feet.

Attempting to adjust typical (i.e., sea level) formulas for high altitudes is somewhat risky, especially in a commercial operation. Try to find and use formulas developed especially for your area or contact the local offices of your state's Department of Agriculture or the Agricultural Extension Service for detailed assistance.

Determining Doneness

In addition to following the baking time suggested in a formula, several simple tests can be used to determine doneness. Whichever test or tests are used, avoid opening the oven door to check the cake's progress. Cold air or a drop in oven temperature can cause the cake to fall. Use a timer to note the minimum suggested baking time. Then, and only then, should you use the following tests to evaluate the cake's doneness:

◆ Appearance—The cake's surface should be a light to golden brown. Unless noted otherwise in the formula, the edges should just begin to pull away from the pan. The cake should not jiggle or move beneath its surface.
◆ Touch—Touch the cake *lightly* with your finger. It should spring back quickly without feeling soggy or leaving an indentation.
◆ Cake tester—If appearance and touch indicate that the cake is done, test the interior by inserting a toothpick, bamboo skewer or metal cake tester into the cake's center. With most cakes, the tester should come out clean. If wet crumbs cling to the tester the cake probably needs to bake a bit longer.

If a formula provides particular doneness guidelines, they should be followed. For example, some flourless cakes are fully baked even though a cake tester will not come out clean.

Cooling

Generally, a cake is allowed to cool for 10–15 minutes in its pan after taking it out of the oven. This helps prevent the cake from cracking or breaking after it is removed from its pan.

To remove the partially cooled cake from its pan, run a thin knife or spatula blade between the pan and the cake to loosen it. Place a wire rack, cake cardboard or sheet pan over the cake and invert. Then remove the pan. The cake can be left upside down to cool completely or inverted again to cool top side up. Wire racks are preferred for cooling cakes because they allow air to circulate, speeding the cooling process and preventing steam from making the cake soggy.

Angel food and chiffon cakes should be turned upside down immediately after they are removed from the oven. They are left to cool completely in their pans to prevent the cake from collapsing or shrinking. The top of the pan should not touch the countertop so that air can circulate under the inverted pan.

All cakes should be left to cool away from drafts or air currents that might cause them to collapse. Cakes should not be refrigerated to speed the cooling process, as rapid cooling can cause cracking. Prolonged refrigeration also causes cakes to dry out.

TABLE 30.4   TROUBLESHOOTING CHART FOR CAKES

Problem	Cause	Solution
Batter curdles during mixing	Ingredients too warm or too cold	Eggs must be room temperature and added slowly
	Incorrect fat used	Use correct ingredients
	Fat inadequately creamed before liquid was added	Add a portion of the flour, then continue adding the liquid
Cake lacks volume	Flour too strong	Use a weaker flour
	Old chemical leavener	Replace with fresh leavener
	Egg foam underwhipped	Use correct mixing method, do not deflate eggs during folding
	Oven too hot	Adjust oven temperature
Crust burst or cracked	Too much flour or too little liquid	Adjust formula
	Oven too hot	Adjust oven temperature
Cake shrinks after baking	Weak internal structure	Adjust formula
	Too much sugar or fat for the batter to support	Adjust formula
	Cake not fully cooked	Test cake for doneness before removing from oven
	Cake cooled too rapidly	Cool away from drafts
Texture is dense or heavy	Too little leavening	Adjust formula
	Too much fat or liquid	Cream fat or whip eggs properly
	Oven too cool	Adjust oven temperature
Texture is coarse with an open grain	Overmixing	Alter mixing method
	Oven too cool	Adjust oven temperature
Poor flavor	Poor ingredients	Check flavor and aroma of all ingredients
	Unclean pans	Do not grease pans with rancid fats
Uneven shape	Butter not incorporated evenly	Incorporate fats completely
	Batter spread unevenly	Spread batter evenly
	Oven rack not level	Adjust oven racks
	Uneven oven temperature	Adjust oven temperature

FROSTINGS

Frosting, also known as **icing**, is a sweet decorative coating used as a filling between the layers or as a coating over the top and sides of a cake. It is used to add flavor and to improve the cake's appearance. Frosting can also extend a cake's shelf life by forming a protective coating.

There are seven general types of frosting: **buttercream**, **foam**, **fudge**, **fondant**, **glaze**, **royal icing** and **ganache**. See Table 30.5. Each type can be produced with a number of formulas and in a range of flavorings.

TABLE 30.5   FROSTINGS

Frosting	Preparation	Texture/Taste
Buttercream	Mixture of sugar and fat (usually butter); can contain egg yolks or egg whites	Rich but light; smooth, fluffy
Foam	Meringue made with hot sugar syrup	Light, fluffy; very sweet
Fudge	Cooked mixture of sugar, butter and water or milk; applied warm	Heavy, rich and candylike
Fondant	Cooked mixture of sugar and water; applied warm	Thick; opaque; sweet
Glaze	Confectioner's sugar with liquid	Thin
Royal icing	Uncooked mixture of confectioner's sugar and egg whites	Hard and brittle when dry
Ganache	Blend of melted chocolate and cream	Rich, smooth, intense flavor

Because frosting is integral to the flavor and appearance of many cakes, it should be made carefully using high-quality ingredients and natural flavors and colors. A good frosting is smooth; it is never grainy or lumpy. It should complement the flavor and texture of the cake without overpowering it.

Buttercream

A buttercream is a light, smooth, fluffy mixture of sugar and fat (butter, margarine or shortening). It may also contain egg yolks for richness or whipped egg whites for lightness. A good buttercream will be sweet, but not cloying; buttery, but not greasy.

Buttercreams are popular and useful for most types of cakes and may be flavored or colored as desired. They may be stored, covered, in the refrigerator for several days but must be softened before use.

Although there are many types of buttercream and many formula variations, we discuss the three most popular styles: **simple**, **Italian** and **French**.

Simple Buttercream

Simple buttercream, sometimes known as **American-style buttercream**, is made by creaming butter and powdered sugar together until the mixture is light and smooth. Cream, eggs (whole, yolks or whites) and flavorings may be added as desired. Simple buttercream requires no cooking and is quick and easy to prepare.

If cost is a consideration, hydrogenated all-purpose shortening can be substituted for a portion of the butter, but the flavor and mouth-feel will be different. Buttercream made with shortening tends to feel greasier and heavier because shortening does not melt on the tongue like butter. It will be more stable than pure butter buttercream, however, and is useful for products that will be on display.

PROCEDURE FOR MAKING SIMPLE BUTTERCREAM

1. Cream softened butter or shortening until the mixture is light and fluffy.
2. Beat in egg, if desired.
3. Beat in sifted powdered sugar, scraping down the sides of the bowl as needed.
4. Beat in the flavoring ingredients.

♦♦♦

RECIPE 30.8
SIMPLE BUTTERCREAM

Yield: 2 lb. (1 kg)

Lightly salted butter, softened	1 lb.	450 g
Egg (optional)	1	1
Powdered sugar, sifted	2 lb.	900 g
Vanilla extract	2 tsp.	10 ml

1. Using a mixer fitted with the paddle attachment, cream the butter until light and fluffy.
2. Beat in the egg if desired. Gradually add the sugar, frequently scraping down the sides of the bowl.
3. Add the vanilla and continue beating until the frosting is smooth and light.

VARIATIONS: *Light chocolate*—Dissolve 1 ounce (30 grams) sifted cocoa powder in 2 ounces (60 grams) cool water. Add to the buttercream along with the vanilla.

Lemon—Decrease the vanilla extract to 1 teaspoon (5 milliliters). Add 1 teaspoon (5 milliliters) lemon extract and the finely grated zest of one lemon.

Italian Buttercream

Italian buttercream, also known as **meringue buttercream**, is based on an Italian meringue, that is, whipped egg whites cooked with hot sugar syrup. (See Chapter 29, Pies, Pastries and Cookies.) Softened butter is then whipped into the cooled meringue and the mixture is flavored as desired. This type of buttercream is extremely soft and light. It can be used on most types of cakes and is particularly popular for multilayered genoise or spongecakes.

PROCEDURE FOR MAKING ITALIAN BUTTERCREAM

1. Whip the egg whites until soft peaks form.
2. Beat granulated sugar into the egg whites and whip until firm and glossy.
3. Meanwhile, combine additional sugar with water and cook to soft ball stage (238°F/115°C).
4. With the mixer on medium speed, pour the sugar syrup into the whipped egg whites. Pour slowly and carefully to avoid splatters.
5. Continue whipping the egg-white-and-sugar mixture until completely cool.
6. Whip softened, but not melted, butter into the cooled egg-white-and-sugar mixture.
7. Add flavoring ingredients as desired.

♦♦♦

RECIPE 30.9
ITALIAN BUTTERCREAM

Yield: 5 lb. (2.2 kg)

Egg whites	14 oz.	400 g
Sugar	1 lb. 11 oz.	750 g
Lightly salted butter, softened but not melted	2 lb. 12 oz.	1250 g

1. All ingredients should be at room temperature before beginning.
2. Place the egg whites in a mixer bowl. Have 9 ounces (250 grams) of sugar nearby.
3. Place 1 pound 2 ounces (500 grams) of sugar in a heavy saucepan with enough water to moisten. Bring to a boil over high heat.
4. As the sugar syrup's temperature approaches a soft ball stage (238°F/115°C), begin whipping the egg whites. Watch the sugar closely so that the temperature does not exceed 238°F (115°C).
5. When soft peaks form in the egg whites, gradually add the 9 ounces (250 grams) of sugar to them. Reduce mixer speed to medium and continue whipping the egg whites to stiff peaks.
6. When the sugar syrup reaches soft ball stage, immediately pour it into the whites while the mixer is running. Pour the syrup in a steady stream between the side of the bowl and the beater. If the syrup hits the beater it will splatter and cause lumps. Continue beating at medium speed until the egg whites are completely cool. At this point the product is known as Italian meringue.
7. Gradually add the softened butter to the Italian meringue. When all of the butter is incorporated, add flavoring ingredients as desired.

VARIATION: *Chocolate:* Add 1 tablespoon (15 milliliters) vanilla extract and 10 ounces (300 grams) melted and cooled bittersweet chocolate.

1. Adding the sugar syrup to the whipped egg whites.

2. Adding the softened butter to the cooled Italian meringue.

3. Finished Italian buttercream.

French Buttercream

French buttercream, also known as **mousseline buttercream**, is similar to Italian buttercream except that the hot sugar syrup is whipped into beaten egg yolks (not egg whites). Softened butter and flavorings are added when the sweetened egg yolks are fluffy and cool. An Italian meringue such as the one created in the above formula is sometimes folded in for additional body and lightness. French buttercream is perhaps the most difficult type of buttercream to master, but it has the richest flavor and smoothest texture. Like a meringue buttercream, mousseline buttercream may be used on almost any type of cake.

PROCEDURE FOR MAKING FRENCH BUTTERCREAM

1. Prepare a sugar syrup and cook to soft ball stage (238°F/115°C).
2. Beat egg yolks to a thin ribbon.

3. Slowly beat the sugar syrup into the egg yolks.
4. Continue beating until the yolks are pale, stiff and completely cool.
5. Gradually add softened butter to the cooled yolks.
6. Fold in Italian meringue.
7. Stir in flavoring ingredients.

RECIPE 30.10
FRENCH BUTTERCREAM

Yield: 2 qt. (2 lt)

Granulated sugar	1 lb. 10 oz.	800 g
Water	8 oz.	250 g
Egg yolks	16	16
Lightly salted butter, softened but not melted	3 lb.	1500 g
Italian Meringue (Recipe 30.9)	1 qt.	1 lt

1. Combine the sugar and water in a small saucepan and bring to a boil. Continue boiling until the syrup reaches 238°F (115°C).

2. Meanwhile, beat the egg yolks in a mixer fitted with a wire whisk on low speed. When the sugar syrup reaches 238°F (115°C), pour it slowly into the egg yolks, gradually increasing the speed at which they are whipped. Continue beating at medium-high speed until the mixture is very pale, stiff and cool.

3. Gradually add the softened butter to the egg mixture, frequently scraping down the sides of the bowl.

4. Fold in the Italian meringue with a spatula. Stir in flavoring extracts as desired.

Foam Frosting

Foam frosting, sometimes known as **boiled icing**, is simply a meringue made with hot sugar syrup. Foam frosting is light and fluffy but very sweet. It may be flavored with extract, liqueur or melted chocolate.

Foam frosting is rather unstable. It should be used immediately and served the day it is prepared. Refrigeration often makes the foam weep beads of sugar. Freezing causes it to separate or melt.

An easy foam frosting can be made by following the formula for Italian Buttercream (Recipe 30.9), but omitting the butter. As soon as the meringue has cooled to room temperature it should be flavored with extract as desired, then used.

Fudge Frosting

A fudge frosting is a warmed mixture of sugar, butter and water or milk. It is heavy, rich and candylike. It is also stable and holds up well. A fudge frosting should be applied warm and allowed to dry on the cake or pastry. When dry, it will have a thin crust and a moist interior. A fudge frosting can be vanilla- or chocolate-based and is used on cupcakes, layer cakes and sheet cakes.

PROCEDURE FOR MAKING FUDGE FROSTING

1. Blend sifted powdered sugar with corn syrup, beating until the sugar is dissolved and the mixture is smooth.
2. Blend in warm melted shortening and/or butter.
3. Blend in hot liquids. Add extracts or flavorings.
4. Use fudge frosting while still warm.

◆◆◆

RECIPE 30.11

BASIC FUDGE FROSTING

Yield: 3 lb. (1500 g)

Powdered sugar, sifted	3 lb.	1500 g
Salt	1/4 tsp.	1 ml
Light corn syrup	2 oz.	60 g
Shortening, melted	4 oz.	120 g
Water, hot (140°F/60°C)	10 oz.	300 g
Vanilla extract	2 Tbsp.	30 ml

1. Blend the sugar, salt and corn syrup. Beat until smooth.
2. Add the melted shortening and blend well.
3. Add the hot water and vanilla and blend well. If the fudge is too stiff it may be thinned with a simple sugar syrup. Use before the icing cools.

VARIATION: *Cocoa fudge frosting:* Sift 4 ounces (120 grams) cocoa powder with the powdered sugar. Add 2 ounces (60 grams) melted unsalted butter with the shortening.

1. Cocoa fudge frosting.

Fondant

Fondant is a thick, opaque sugar paste commonly used for glazing napoleons, petit fours and other pastries as well as some cakes. It is a cooked mixture of sugar and water, with **glucose** or corn syrup added to encourage the correct type of sugar crystallization. Poured onto the surface being coated, fondant quickly dries to a shiny, nonsticky coating. It is naturally pure white and can be tinted with food coloring. Fondant may also be flavored with melted chocolate.

Glucose—*a thick, sweet syrup made from cornstarch, composed primarily of dextrose. Light corn syrup can usually be substituted for it in baked goods or candy making.*

Fondant is rather difficult to make, so it is almost always purchased prepared. To use, thin it with water or simple syrup and carefully warm to 100°F (38°C). Commercially prepared fondant will keep for several months at room temperature in an airtight container. The surface of the fondant should be coated with simple syrup, however, to prevent a crust from forming.

Glaze

A glaze is a thin coating meant to be poured or dripped onto a cake or pastry. A glaze is usually too thin to apply with a knife or spatula. It is used to add moisture and flavor to cakes on which a heavy frosting would be undesirable—for example, a chiffon or angel food cake.

Flat icing is a specific type of glaze used on danish pastries and coffeecakes. It is pure white and dries to a firm gloss.

PROCEDURE FOR MAKING GLAZE

1. Blend sifted powdered sugar with a small amount of liquid and flavorings.
2. Use immediately.

═══════════ ◆◆◆ ═══════════

RECIPE 30.12

BASIC SUGAR GLAZE

Yield: 12 oz. (340 g)

Powdered sugar, sifted	9-1/2 oz.	270 g
Light cream or milk	2 oz.	60 g
Unsalted butter, melted	1 oz.	30 g
Vanilla extract	2 tsp.	10 ml

1. Stir the ingredients together in a small bowl until smooth.
2. Adjust the consistency by adding more cream or milk to thin the glaze if necessary.
3. Adjust the flavor as necessary. (Another extract, such as lemon or almond, may be used if desired.)
4. Use immediately, before the glaze begins to dry.

Royal Icing

Royal icing, also known as **decorator's icing**, is similar to flat icing except it is much stiffer and becomes hard and brittle when dry. It is an uncooked mixture of powdered sugar and egg whites. It may be dyed with food coloring pastes.

Royal icing is used for making decorations, particularly intricate flowers or lace patterns. Prepare royal icing in small quantities and always keep any unused portion covered with a damp towel to prevent hardening.

PROCEDURE FOR MAKING ROYAL ICING

1. Combine egg white and lemon juice, if used.
2. Beat in sifted powdered sugar until the correct consistency is reached.

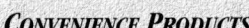

CONVENIENCE PRODUCTS

A wide selection of prepared icings, glazes and toppings are available. Often, chocolate and vanilla fudge icing bases are purchased, then flavored or colored as needed. Foam frostings can be purchased in powder form, to which you add water and then whip. Even prepared "buttercreams" are available, although they contain little or no real butter.

Prepared icings are often exceedingly sweet and overpowered by artificial flavors and chemical preservatives. These products save time but often cost more than their counterparts made from scratch. They should be used only after balancing the disadvantages against the benefits for your particular operation.

3. Beat until very smooth and firm enough to hold a stiff peak.
4. Color as desired with paste food colorings.
5. Store covered with a damp cloth and plastic wrap.

◆◆◆

RECIPE 30.13

ROYAL ICING

Yield: 6 oz. (180 g)

Powdered sugar	6 oz.	180 g
Egg white, room temperature	1	1
Lemon juice	1/4 tsp.	1 ml

1. Sift the sugar and set aside.
2. Place the egg white and lemon juice in a stainless steel bowl.
3. Add 4 ounces (120 grams) of sugar and beat with an electric mixer or metal spoon until blended. The mixture should fall from a spoon in heavy globs. If it pours, it is too thin and will need the remaining 2 ounces (60 grams) of sugar.
4. Once the consistency is correct, continue beating for 3–4 minutes. The icing should be white, smooth and thick enough to hold a stiff peak. Food coloring paste can be added at this time if desired.
5. Cover the icing with a damp towel and plastic wrap to prevent it from hardening.

Ganache

Ganache is a blend of chocolate and cream. It may also include butter, liquor or other flavorings. Any bittersweet, semisweet or dark chocolate may be used; the choice depends on personal preference and cost considerations.

Depending on its consistency, ganache may be used as a filling, frosting or glaze-type coating on cakes or pastries. The ratio of chocolate to cream determines how thick the cooled ganache will be. Equal parts chocolate and cream generally are best for frostings and fillings. Increasing the percentage of chocolate produces a thicker ganache. Warm ganache can be poured over a cake or pastry and allowed to harden as a thin glaze, or the ganache may be cooled and whipped to create a rich, smooth frosting. If it becomes too firm, ganache can be remelted over a bain marie.

PROCEDURE FOR MAKING GANACHE

1. Pouring the hot cream over the chopped chocolate.

2. Cool, firm ganache.

1. Melt finely chopped chocolate with cream in a double broiler. Or,
2. Bring cream just to a boil. Then pour it over finely chopped chocolate and allow the cream's heat to gently melt the chocolate.
3. Whichever method is used, cool the cream and chocolate mixture over an ice bath.

Do not attempt to melt chocolate and then add cool cream. This will cause the chocolate to resolidify and lump.

◆◆◆

RECIPE 30.14
CHOCOLATE GANACHE

Yield: 2.2 lb. (1 kg)

Bittersweet chocolate	1 lb. 1 oz.	500 g
Heavy cream	1 lb. 1 oz.	500 ml
Almond or coffee liqueur	1 oz.	30 ml

1. Chop the chocolate into small pieces and place in a large metal bowl.
2. Bring the cream just to a boil, then immediately pour it over the chocolate, whisking to blend. Stir gently until all the chocolate has melted.
3. Stir in the liqueur.
4. Allow to cool, stirring frequently until the desired consistency is achieved. An ice bath may be used to speed the cooling process.

TABLE 30.6   **TROUBLESHOOTING CHART FOR FROSTINGS**

Problem	Cause	Solution
Frosting breaks or curdles	Fat added too slowly or eggs too hot when fat was added	Add shortening or sifted confectioner's sugar
Frosting is lumpy	Confectioner's sugar not sifted	Sift dry ingredients
	Ingredients not blended	Use softened fat
	Sugar syrup lumps in frosting	Add sugar syrups carefully
Frosting is gritty	Granulated sugar not dissolved	Cook sugar syrups properly; cook fudge frostings as directed
Frosting is too stiff	Not enough liquid	Adjust formula; add small amount of water or milk to thin frosting
	Too cold	Bring frosting to room temperature
Frosting will not adhere to cake	Cake too hot	Cool cake completely
	Frosting too thin	Adjust frosting formula

◆◆◆

CHOCOLATE TRUFFLES

Ganache, a sublime mixture of pure chocolate and cream, is the foundation of one of the world's most sophisticated candies: the chocolate truffle. Truffles take their name from the rough, black, highly prized food they resemble, but there the similarity ends. Chocolate truffles should have a rich, creamy ganache center with a well-balanced, refined flavor.

Chocolate truffles are surprisingly simple to make. Fine chocolate is melted with cream and perhaps butter. The mixture is flavored as desired with liqueur, extracts, fruit or coffee and allowed to harden. Once firm, the ganache is scooped into balls and rolled in cocoa powder, confectioner's sugar or melted chocolate. The classic French truffle is a small, irregularly shaped ball of bittersweet chocolate dusted with cocoa powder. Americans, however, seem to prefer larger candies, coated with melted chocolate and decorated with nuts or additional chocolate. The following recipe can be prepared in either style.

1. Shaping chocolate truffles.

◆◆◆

RECIPE 30.15

DARK CHOCOLATE TRUFFLES

Yield: 150 medium-sized Truffles

Dark chocolate	2 lb.	1 kg
Unsalted butter	1 lb.	500 g
Cream	1 pt.	500 ml
Brandy	4 oz.	120 ml

1. Chop the chocolate and butter into small pieces and place in a large metal bowl.

2. Bring the cream to a boil. Immediately pour the hot cream over the chocolate and butter. Stir until the chocolate and butter are completely melted.

3. Stir in the brandy. Pour the ganache into a flat, shallow, ungreased pan and chill until firm.

4. Shape the ganache into rough balls using a melon ball cutter. Immediately drop each ball into a pan of sifted cocoa powder or confectioner's sugar, rolling it around to coat completely.

5. Truffles can be stored in the refrigerator for 7–10 days. Allow them to soften slightly at room temperature before serving.

ASSEMBLING AND DECORATING CAKES

Much of a cake's initial appeal lies in its appearance. This is true whether the finished cake is a simple sheet cake topped with swirls of buttercream or an elaborate wedding cake with intricate garlands and bouquets of royal icing roses. Any cake assembled and decorated with care and attention to detail is preferable to a carelessly assembled or garishly overdecorated one.

◆◆◆

ADVANCED PATISSERIE

Sugar can be used to create a number of doughs, pastes and syrups used for artistic and decorative work. Mastering even some of these products takes years of experience and practice. Although formulas and preparation methods are beyond the scope of this book, it is important that all pastry cooks be able to recognize and identify certain decorative sugar products.

Blown sugar—a boiled mixture of sucrose, glucose and tartaric acid that is colored and shaped (in a manner very similar to glass blowing) using an air pump. It is used for making pieces of fruit and containers such as bowls and vases.

Gum paste—a smooth dough made of sugar and gelatin; it dries relatively slowly, becoming very firm and hard. The paste can be colored and rolled out, cut and shaped, or molded. It is used for making flowers, leaves and small figures.

Marzipan—a mixture of almond paste and sugar that may be colored and used like modeling clay for sculpting small fruits, flowers or other objects. Marzipan may also be rolled out and cut into various shapes or used to cover cakes or pastries.

Nougat—a candy made of caramelized sugar and almonds that can be molded into shapes or containers. Unlike other sugar decorations, nougat remains deliciously edible.

Pastillage—a paste made with sugar, cornstarch and gelatin. It can be rolled into sheets, then cut into shapes. It dries in a very firm and sturdy form, like plaster. Naturally pure white, it can be painted with cocoa or food colorings. Pastillage is used for showpieces and large decorative items.

Pulled sugar—a doughlike mixture of sucrose, glucose and tartaric acid that is colored, then shaped by hand. Pulled sugar is used for making birds, flowers, leaves, bows and other items.

Spun sugar—made by flicking dark caramelized sugar rapidly over a dowel to create long, fine, hairlike threads. Mounds or wreaths of these threads are used to decorate ice cream desserts, croquembouche and gâteaux.

Thousands of decorating styles or designs are possible, of course. This section describes a few simple options that can be prepared by beginning pastry cooks using a minimum of specialized tools. In planning your cake's design consider the flavor, texture and color of the components used as well as the number of guests or portions that must be served. Consider who will be cutting and eating the cake and how long the dessert must stand before service.

Assembling Cakes

Before a cake can be decorated, it must be assembled and coated with frosting. Most cakes can be assembled in a variety of shapes and sizes: sheet cakes, round layer cakes and rectangular layer cakes are the most common. When assembling any cake, the goal is to fill and stack the cake layers evenly and to apply an even coating of frosting that is smooth and free of crumbs.

Most of the photographs used in this section show the assembly and decoration of a wedding cake. The finished cake is shown in the photograph that introduces this chapter. The complete formula is found in Recipe 30.16.

PROCEDURE FOR ASSEMBLING CAKES

1. Begin by leveling the cake and trimming the edges as needed with a serrated knife.

2. Split the cake horizontally into thin layers if desired. Use cake boards to support each layer as it is removed. Brush away any loose crumbs with a dry pastry brush or your hand.

3. Position the bottom layer on a cake board. Place the layer on a revolving cake stand, if available. Top the layer with a mound of frosting or filling, then use a cake spatula to spread it evenly to the edges.

4. Position the next cake layer over the filling and continue layering and filling the cake as desired.

5. Place a mound of frosting in the center of the cake top. Push it to the edge of the cake with a cake spatula. Do not drag the frosting back and forth or lift the spatula off the frosting, as these actions tend to pick up crumbs.

6. Cover the sides with excess frosting from the top, adding more as necessary. Hold the spatula upright against the side of the cake and, pressing gently, turn the cake stand slowly. This smooths and evens the sides. When the sides and top are smooth, the cake is ready to be decorated as desired.

Simple Decorating Techniques

An extremely simple yet effective way to decorate a frosted cake is with a garnish of chopped nuts, fruit, toasted coconut, shaved chocolate or other foods arranged in patterns or sprinkled over the cake. Be sure to use a garnish that complements the cake and frosting flavors or reflects one of the cake's ingredients. For example, finely chopped pecans would be an appropriate garnish for a carrot cake that contains pecans; shaved chocolate would not.

Side masking is the technique of coating only the sides of a cake with garnish. The top may be left plain or decorated with icing designs or a message. Be sure to apply the garnish while the frosting is still damp enough for it to adhere.

Stencils can be used to apply finely chopped garnishes, confectioner's sugar or cocoa powder to the top of a cake in patterns. A design can be cut from cardboard, or thin plastic forms can be purchased. Even simple strips of parchment paper can be used to create an attractive pattern. If using a stencil on a frosted cake allow the frosting to set somewhat before laying the stencil on top of it. After the garnishes have been sprinkled over the stencil, carefully lift the stencil to avoid spilling the excess garnish and messing the pattern.

Side masking—coating the sides of a carrot cake with chopped pecans.

Stencils—creating a design with confectioner's sugar and strips of parchment paper.

Piped-On Decorating Techniques

Instead of leaving the sides of a frosted cake smooth or coating them with chopped nuts or crumbs, you can pipe on frosting designs and patterns. A simple but elegant design is the basket weave, shown below.

Normally a border pattern will be piped around the base of the cake and along the top edge. Borders should be piped on after nuts or any other garnishes are applied.

Each slice or serving of cake can be marked with its own decoration. For example, a rosette of frosting or a whole nut or piece of fruit could be used as shown below. This makes it easier to portion the cake evenly.

Delicate flowers such as roses can be piped, allowed to harden, then placed on the cake in attractive arrangements. Royal icing is particularly useful for making decorations in advance because it dries very hard and lasts indefinitely.

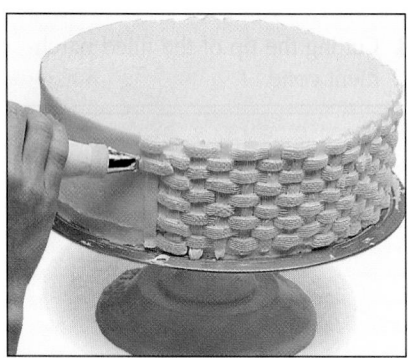

Applying a basket weave pattern to the sides of the wedding cake.

Applying a shell border to the wedding cake.

Placing royal icing flowers onto cake portions.

PROCEDURE FOR PIPING A BUTTERCREAM ROSE

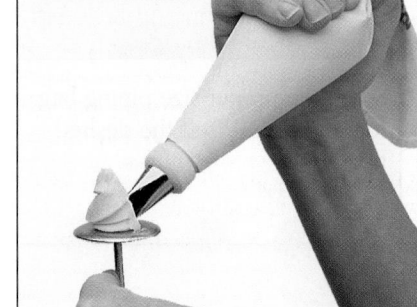

1. Using a #104 tip, pipe a mound of icing onto a rose nail.

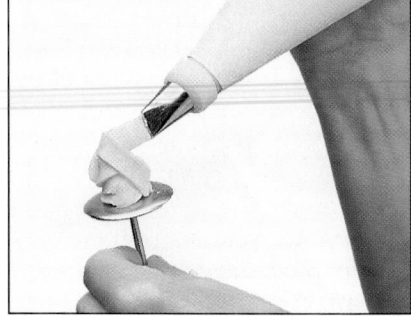

2. Pipe a curve of icing around the mound to create the center of the rose.

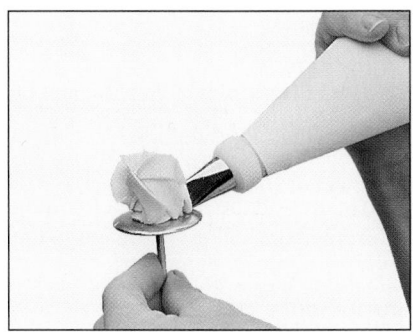 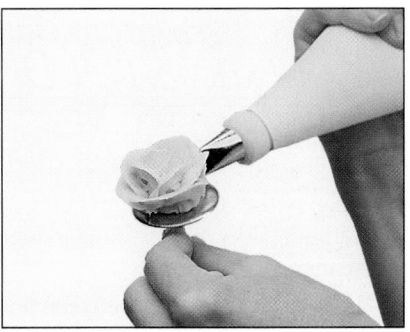 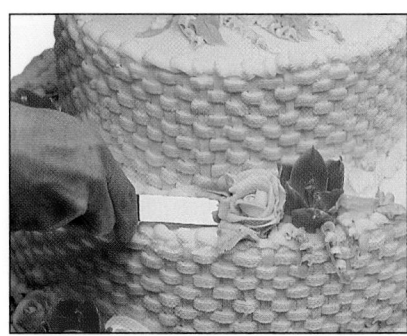

3. Pipe three overlapping petals around the center.

4. Pipe five more overlapping petals around the first three petals.

5. The finished rose is placed on the cake.

The key to success with a piping bag is practice, practice, practice. Use plain all-purpose shortening piped onto parchment paper to practice and experiment with piping techniques. Once you are comfortable using a piping bag, you can apply these newfound skills directly to cakes and pastries.

Storing Cakes

Unfrosted cake layers or sheets can be stored at room temperature for two or three days if well covered. Frosted or filled cakes are usually refrigerated to prevent spoilage. Simple buttercreams or sugar glazes, however, can be left at room temperature for one or two days. Any cake containing custard filling or whipped cream must be refrigerated. Cakes made with foam-type frosting should be eaten the day they are prepared.

Cakes can usually be frozen with great success; this makes them ideal for baking in advance. Unfrosted layers or sheets should be well covered with plastic wrap and frozen at 0°F (-18°C) or lower. High-fat cakes will keep for up to six months; egg foam cakes begin to deteriorate after two or three months.

Frostings and fillings do not freeze particularly well, often losing flavor or changing texture when frozen. Buttercreams made with egg whites or sugar syrups tend to develop crystals and graininess. Foam frostings weep, expelling beads of sugar and becoming sticky. Fondant will absorb moisture and separate from the cake. If you must freeze a filled or frosted cake, it is best to freeze it unwrapped first, until the frosting is firm. The cake can then be covered with plastic wrap without damaging the frosting design. Leave the cake wrapped until completely thawed. It is best to thaw cakes in the refrigerator if time permits. Do not refreeze thawed cakes.

ONCLUSION

The ability to produce good cakes and frostings depends on using the right balance of high-quality ingredients and combining them with the proper techniques. When preparing cakes and frostings, always combine flavors and textures with care; apply frostings, garnishes and decorations with care also. Avoid overly rich, cloyingly sweet or garishly decorated products. With study and practice, you can learn the mixing techniques and assembly skills necessary for producing good cakes. Additional practice will develop the decorating and garnishing skills of a fine pastry chef.

QUESTIONS FOR DISCUSSION

1. Cake ingredients can be classified by function into six categories. List them and give an example of each.
2. What is the primary leavening agent in cakes made with the foaming method? How is this similar to or different from cakes made with the creaming method?
3. What is the difference between a spongecake and a classic genoise?
4. Describe the procedures for making three types of frosting or icing as discussed in this chapter.
5. List the steps employed in assembling and frosting a three-layer cake.

ADDITIONAL CAKE AND FROSTING FORMULAS

RECIPE 30.16

VANILLA RASPBERRY LAYER CAKE WITH WHITE CHOCOLATE BUTTERCREAM

NOTE: *This dish appears in the Chapter Opening photograph.*

HYATT REGENCY SCOTTSDALE AT GAINEY RANCH, SCOTTSDALE, AZ
Executive Pastry Chef Judy Doherty

VANILLA CAKES

Yield: 1 8-inch (20-cm), 1 10-inch (25-cm) and 1 14-inch (35-cm) tier for Wedding Cake   **Method:** Two-Stage

Cake flour	1 lb. 14 oz.	850 g
Sugar	2 lb. 8 oz.	1130 g
Baking powder	2-1/2 oz.	70 g
Eggs	28	28
Salt	1 oz.	28 g
Fluid Flex	1 lb. 4 oz.	570 g
Milk	1 pt.	450 ml

1. Prepare pans by spraying with pan release and lining with parchment paper.
2. Combine the flour, sugar, baking powder, eggs and salt in a large mixer bowl. Whip on high speed for 8 minutes.
3. Add Fluid Flex (an emulsifier for spongecakes) and milk. Mix for 8 more minutes at medium speed.
4. Divide the batter between one 8-inch (20-cm), one 10-inch (25-cm) and one 14-inch (35-cm) cake pan. Fill each pan halfway.
5. Bake at 350°F (180°C) for 35–60 minutes, depending upon tier size. The cake is done when it springs back when lightly touched in the center. Allow to cool, then remove from the pans and freeze.

RASPBERRY SYRUP

Water	1 pt.	450 ml
Sugar	1 lb.	450 g
Raspberry liqueur	2 oz.	60 g

1. Bring the sugar and water to a boil, then cool to room temperature. Add the raspberry liqueur.

DIPLOMAT CREAM FILLING

Pastry cream, chilled	1 gal.	4 lt
Raspberry liqueur	4 oz.	120 g
Gelatin	1-1/2 oz.	42 g
Water	6 oz.	170 g
Whipped cream	1 qt.	1 lt

1. Place the pastry cream in a large mixer bowl and whip on high speed until smooth. Add the raspberry liqueur.
2. Soften the gelatin in the water, then place over a low flame and heat to dissolve.
3. Add 1 pint (450 milliliters) of the raspberry flavored pastry cream to the gelatin. Place over a low flame and whip by hand until smooth and the gelatin is incorporated. Add this mixture to the remainder of the pastry cream.
4. Fold in the whipped cream.

WHITE CHOCOLATE BUTTERCREAM

Sugar	5 lb. 8 oz.	2500 g
Water	1 pt. 6 oz.	625 ml
Egg whites	1 lb. 12 oz.	800 g
Unsalted butter, softened	7 lb.	3150 g
White crème de cacao	9 oz.	260 g
White chocolate, melted	1 lb. 8 oz.	680 g

1. Cook the sugar and water to 242°F (117°C), then pour into a measuring container with a handle for easier pouring.
2. Start whipping the egg whites when the sugar reaches 235°F (113°C).
3. When the whites are whipped to firm peaks, add the hot sugar syrup slowly while continuing to whip at low speed. Whip until completely cool.
4. Add the butter and whip until smooth.
5. Add the crème de cacao to the white chocolate. Whip until smooth, then add to the buttercream.

ASSEMBLY: Each cake tier is sliced horizontally into three layers. The layers are brushed with the raspberry syrup, then filled with diplomat cream and fresh raspberries. The top and sides of each tier are coated with the white chocolate buttercream; the sides are coated with a basketweave design; and the tiers are decorated with pulled sugar and royal icing roses. The assembly is illustrated with the photographs appearing throughout this chapter.

◆◆◆

RECIPE 30.17

POPPY SEED CAKE WITH LEMON GLAZE

CITY RESTAURANT, LOS ANGELES, CA
Chefs Susan Feniger and Mary Sue Milliken

Yield: 8–10 Servings   **Method:** Creaming

Poppy seeds	5 oz.	150 g
Honey	4 oz.	120 g
Water	2 oz.	60 g
Unsalted butter, softened	6 oz.	180 g
Granulated sugar	6 oz.	180 g
Lemon zest, grated	1 Tbsp.	15 ml
Vanilla extract	1 tsp.	5 ml
Eggs	2	2
All-purpose flour	9 oz.	270 g
Baking soda	1 tsp.	5 ml
Baking powder	1 tsp.	5 ml
Salt	1 tsp.	5 ml
Lemon juice, fresh	2-1/2 Tbsp.	35 ml
Sour cream	8 oz.	225 g
Lemon Glaze (recipe follows)	as needed	as needed

1. Combine the poppy seeds, honey and water in a medium saucepan. Cook over moderate heat, stirring frequently, until the water evaporates and the mixture looks like wet sand, approximately 5 minutes. Set aside to cool.
2. Cream the butter and sugar until light and fluffy. Mix in the lemon zest and vanilla. Add the eggs, one at a time, beating well after each addition.
3. In another bowl, combine the flour, baking soda, baking powder and salt. Set aside.
4. When the poppy seed mixture has cooled, stir in the lemon juice. Pour into the creamed-butter mixture and stir until combined.
5. By hand, add the dry ingredients and sour cream to the creamed butter in three stages, alternating liquid and dry, and ending with sour cream.
6. Spoon the batter into a greased and floured 10-inch (25-centimeter) tube pan. Smooth the top with a spatula and tap vigorously on a counter to eliminate air pockets.
7. Bake at 325°F (160°C) until a toothpick inserted near the center comes out clean, approximately 1 hour and 15 minutes. Set aside to cool, in the pan on a rack, about 15 minutes. Invert onto a platter and prepare the Lemon Glaze.
8. Brush the hot Lemon Glaze all over the bottom, top and sides of the cake to flavor it and seal in moisture. Serve with whipped cream.

LEMON GLAZE

Yield: 12 oz. (340 g)

Granulated sugar	8 oz.	225 g
Lemon juice, fresh	4 oz.	120 g

1. Combine the sugar and lemon juice in a small saucepan. Bring to a boil over moderate heat and cook until the sugar is dissolved, approximately 1–2 minutes.

RECIPE 30.18

CARROT CAKE WITH CREAM CHEESE FROSTING

Yield: 5 Sheet Cakes or 16 10-inch (25-cm) Rounds   **Method:** Creaming

Vegetable oil	3 lb. 8 oz.	1750 g
Granulated sugar	3 lb. 11 oz.	1850 g
Eggs	1 lb. 12 oz.	875 g
Carrots, shredded	5 lb.	2500 g
Crushed pineapple, with juice	3 lb. 4 oz.	1625 g
Baking soda	1-1/2 oz.	45 g
Cinnamon	2 oz.	60 g
Pumpkin pie spice	1-1/2 oz.	45 g
Salt	1-1/2 oz.	45 g
Baking powder	1-1/4 oz.	40 g
Cake flour	4 lb. 10 oz.	2300 g
Coconut, shredded	1 lb.	500 g
Walnut pieces	1 lb.	500 g

1. Blend the oil and sugar in a large mixer bowl fitted with the paddle attachment. Add the eggs, beating to incorporate.
2. Blend in the carrots and pineapple.
3. Sift the dry ingredients together, then add them to the batter. Stir in the coconut and walnuts.
4. Divide the batter into greased and floured pans, scaling at 5 pounds per sheet pan or 1 pound 8 ounces (680 grams) per 10-inch (25-centimeter) round.
5. Bake at 340°F (180°C) until springy to the touch and a cake tester comes out almost clean.

CREAM CHEESE FROSTING

Unsalted butter, softened	12 oz.	350 g
Cream cheese, softened	3 lb.	1500 g
Margarine	12 oz.	350 g
Vanilla extract	1 oz.	30 ml
Powdered sugar, sifted	6 lb.	3000 g

1. Cream the butter and cream cheese until smooth. Add the margarine and beat well.
2. Beat in the vanilla extract. Slowly add the sugar, scraping down the bowl frequently. Beat until smooth.

RECIPE 30.19

FRESH STRAWBERRY SHORTCAKE

THE FOUR SEASONS, NEW YORK, NY

Yield: 6 Servings

Flour	10 oz.	300 g
Salt	1/2 tsp.	2 ml
Sugar	3 Tbsp.	45 ml

Continued

Baking powder	1/2 Tbsp.	7 ml
Unsalted butter, cold	2-1/2 oz.	75 g
Shortening	2 Tbsp.	30 ml
Zest of one orange		
Milk	2 oz.	60 g
Egg	1	1
Vanilla extract	1 tsp.	5 ml
Heavy cream	1 pt.	450 ml
Confectioner's sugar	3 oz.	90 g
Fresh strawberries, sliced	3 pt.	1350 ml

1. Combine the dry ingredients. Add the butter and shortening and cut in until the mixture looks like cornmeal. Add the orange zest.

2. Combine the milk, egg and vanilla and add to the dry ingredients. Turn out the dough on a board and knead a few times.

3. Divide the dough into six portions. Shape each portion into a circle with your hands. Bake at 450°F (230°C) until lightly browned, about 12–15 minutes. Cool on a rack.

4. Whip the cream with 2 ounces (60 grams) of confectioner's sugar. Split the shortcakes in the middle and fill with the whipped cream and strawberries. Sprinkle confectioner's sugar on top and serve with strawberry sauce.

RECIPE 30.20

SOUR CREAM COFFEECAKE

Yield: 1 10-inch (25-cm) Tube Cake **Method:** Creaming

Filling:		
Flour	1-1/2 Tbsp.	20 ml
Cinnamon	1 Tbsp.	15 ml
Brown sugar	6 oz.	180 g
Chopped pecans	4 oz.	120 g
Unsalted butter, melted	1 oz.	30 g
Unsalted butter	4 oz.	120 g
Granulated sugar	8 oz.	225 g
Eggs	2	2
Sour cream	8 oz.	225 g
Cake flour, sifted	7 oz.	210 g
Salt	1/4 tsp.	1 ml
Baking powder	1 tsp.	5 ml
Baking soda	1 tsp.	5 ml
Vanilla extract	1 tsp.	5 ml

1. To make the filling, blend all filling ingredients together in a small bowl. Set aside.

2. To make the cake batter, cream the butter and sugar. Add the eggs, one at a time, beating well after each addition. Add the sour cream. Stir until smooth.

3. Sift the presifted flour, salt, baking powder and baking soda together twice. Stir into the batter. Stir in the vanilla extract.

4. Spoon half of the batter into a greased tube pan. Top with half the filling. Cover the filling with the remaining batter and top with the remaining filling. Bake at 350°F (180°C) for 35 minutes.

◆◆◆

RECIPE 30.21

MARBLE SHEET CAKE
WITH FUDGE FROSTING

Yield: 1 18- × 24-inch (45- × 60-cm) Sheet Cake   **Method:** Creaming

Cake flour, sifted	1 lb. 11 oz.	1300 g
Baking powder	2-1/2 Tbsp.	35 ml
Salt	1-1/2 tsp.	7 ml
Unsalted butter	12 oz.	360 g
Granulated sugar	1 lb. 11 oz.	1300 g
Milk	24 oz.	720 g
Vanilla extract	1 tsp.	5 ml
Dark chocolate, melted	4-1/2 oz.	135 g
Baking soda	1/4 tsp.	1 ml
Coffee extract	2 tsp.	10 ml
Egg whites	12	12
Cocoa Fudge Frosting (Recipe 30.11)	as needed	as needed

1. Sift the flour, baking powder and salt together; set aside.
2. Cream the butter and sugar until light and fluffy.
3. Combine the milk and vanilla.
4. Add the dry ingredients to the creamed butter alternately with the milk. Stir the batter only until smooth.
5. Separate the batter into two equal portions. Add the melted chocolate, baking soda and coffee extract to half the batter.
6. Whip the egg whites until stiff but not dry. Fold half the whites into the vanilla batter and half into the chocolate batter.
7. Spoon the batter onto a greased sheet pan, alternating the two colors. Pull a paring knife through the batter to swirl the colors together.
8. Bake at 350°F (180°C) until a tester comes out clean, approximately 25 minutes.
9. Allow the cake to cool, then cover the top with Cocoa Fudge Frosting.

◆◆◆

RECIPE 30.22

FRESH COCONUT CAKE

Yield: 1 9-inch (22-cm) Cake   **Method:** Creaming

All-purpose shortening	8 oz.	225 g
Granulated sugar	1 lb.	450 g
Egg yolks	4	4
All-purpose flour	14 oz.	420 g
Salt	1 tsp.	5 ml
Baking powder	4 tsp.	20 ml
Milk	10 oz.	300 g
Vanilla extract	1 tsp.	5 ml
Egg whites	7 oz.	210 g
Coconut milk	4 oz.	120 g

Continued

Frosting (recipe follows)
Fresh coconut, grated   8 oz.   225 g

1. Cream the shortening and sugar together until light and fluffy. Add the egg yolks one at a time, blending well.

2. Sift the dry ingredients together, then add to the creamed mixture alternately with the milk.

3. Stir in the vanilla.

4. Whip the egg whites until firm peaks form. Fold the whites into the batter. Portion into two 9-inch (22-cm) cake pans that have been greased and lined with parchment paper.

5. Bake at 350°F (180°C) until a cake tester comes out clean, approximately 25–30 minutes.

6. Remove the cakes from the oven and prick the top with a toothpick. Brush the coconut milk over the cakes, allowing it to be absorbed completely. Cool on a rack, then remove from the pans.

7. Top one cake layer with frosting, then sprinkle on 2 ounces of the grated coconut. Top with the second cake layer. Coat the top and sides with the remaining frosting, then sprinkle on the remaining coconut.

FROSTING

Granulated sugar	1 lb.	450 g
Light corn syrup	11 oz.	330 g
Egg whites	5	5
Salt	pinch	pinch

1. Bring the sugar and corn syrup to a boil. Cook to 238°F (115°C).

2. Meanwhile, beat the egg whites with the salt until stiff. With the mixer on second speed, add the hot sugar syrup to the whites in a slow, steady stream. Continue whipping until the frosting is cool.

◆◆◆

RECIPE 30.23

SACHER TORTE

Yield: 2 9-inch (22-cm) Cakes

All-purpose flour	10 oz.	280 g
Cocoa powder, alkalized	3 oz.	80 g
Unsalted butter	12-1/2 oz.	360 g
Granulated sugar	18 oz.	520 g
Eggs, separated	14	14
Hazelnuts, toasted and ground	3 oz.	80 g
Apricot jam	18 oz.	520 g
Apricot glaze	as needed	as needed
Chocolate Glaze (Recipe 29.27)	as needed	as needed

1. Grease two 9-inch (22-cm) springform pans lightly with butter and line with parchment paper.

2. Sift the flour and cocoa powder together twice; set aside.

3. Cream the butter and 7 ounces (200 grams) of the sugar together until light and fluffy. Gradually add the egg yolks and beat well.

4. Fold in the sifted flour and cocoa and the hazelnuts by hand.

5. Whip the egg whites to soft peaks, then gradually add the remaining sugar and continue whipping until stiff, glossy peaks form.

6. Lighten the batter with about one fourth of the egg whites, then fold in the remaining whites.

7. Pour the batter into the prepared pans and bake at 350°F (180°C) until the cakes are set, approximately 35–45 minutes.

8. Cool the cakes for 5 minutes before removing from the pans.

9. Cool completely, then cut each cake horizontally into three layers. Spread apricot jam on each layer and restack them, creating two 3-layer cakes.

10. Heat the apricot glaze until spreadable. Pour it over the top and sides of each cake.

11. Allow the apricot glaze to cool completely, then pour the chocolate glaze over the top and sides of each cake to create a smooth, glossy coating.

◆◆◆

RECIPE 30.24
DEVIL'S FOOD CAKE

Yield: 5 Sheet Pans or 30 8-inch (20-cm) Rounds   **Method:** High-Ratio

Cake flour	5 lb.	2500 g
Granulated sugar	6 lb.	3000 g
Emulsified shortening	3 lb.	1500 g
Cocoa powder	1 lb.	500 g
Salt	2-1/2 oz.	75 g
Baking powder	3 oz.	90 g
Baking soda	1-1/2 oz.	45 g
Nonfat dry milk powder	9-1/2 oz.	270 g
Vanilla extract	1-1/2 oz.	45 ml
Corn syrup	1 lb.	500 g
Water, cold	2 qt. 8 oz.	2.25 lt
Eggs	4 lb.	2000 g

1. Mix the cake flour, sugar and emulsified shortening in a large mixer bowl on low speed for 5 minutes.

2. Add the cocoa powder, salt, baking powder, baking soda, milk powder, vanilla, corn syrup and 1 quart (1 liter) cold water. Blend well, then scrape down the bowl.

3. Combine the eggs with the remaining 1 quart 8 ounces (1250 milliliters) cold water and add to the batter in three equal parts, blending well and scraping down the bowl after each addition.

4. After all ingredients are incorporated, blend on low speed for 2 minutes.

5. Divide into greased and floured pans, scaling 1 gallon (4 liters) of batter for each sheet pan or 1 pound (450 grams) for each 8-inch (20-centimeter) round layer.

6. Bake at 340°F (180°C) until springy and a toothpick inserted in the center comes out clean.

♦♦♦

RECIPE 30.25
BÛCHE DE NOËL

Yield: 10–12 Servings

Genoise, Recipe 30.3, freshly baked	one-half sheet	one-half sheet
Simple syrup	as needed	as needed
Buttercream—coffee, chocolate		
or vanilla	1 qt.	1 lt

1. Roll up the genoise in a spiral, starting with the long side. Wrap in parchment paper and cool.
2. Carefully unroll the cake. Brush the interior with simple syrup and coat with buttercream, leaving a 1-inch (2.5 centimeter) unfrosted rim around each edge.
3. Reroll the cake tightly and position it with the seam down on a cake cardboard.
4. Cut one end from the cake on a diagonal. Place the cut piece on top of the log, securing with toothpicks.
5. Pipe additional buttercream onto the cake log using a large star tip. Pipe the buttercream onto the ends in a spiral pattern. Decorate as desired with buttercream flowers, baked meringue mushrooms or marzipan figures.

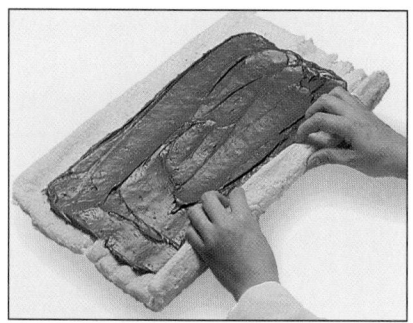

1. Rolling the cake filled with buttercream.

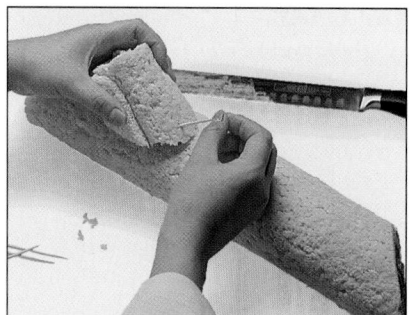

2. Attaching the cut end to the log.

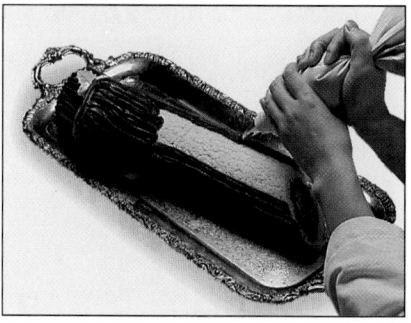

3. Piping on the buttercream.

♦♦♦

RECIPE 30.26
LADYFINGERS

Yield: 80 4-inch (10-cm) Cookies

Cornstarch	3 oz.	90 g
Bread flour	4 oz.	120 g
Eggs, separated	6	6
Granulated sugar	6 oz.	180 g
Lemon juice	1/2 tsp.	2 ml

1. Sift the cornstarch and bread flour together.
2. Whip the egg yolks with 2 ounces (60 grams) of sugar until thick and creamy.
3. Whip the egg whites until foamy. Gradually add 2 ounces (60 grams) of the sugar and the lemon juice. Continue whipping to soft peaks, then add the remaining sugar gradually and whip to stiff peaks.
4. Fold approximately one quarter of the egg whites into the whipped yolks

to lighten them, then gently fold in the remaining whites. Fold in the flour mixture.

5. Place the batter into a pastry bag fitted with a large plain tip. Pipe 4-inch-long (10-cm) cookies onto paper-lined sheet pans.

6. Bake immediately at 425°F (220°C) until lightly browned, approximately 8 minutes.

===== ◆◆◆ =====

RECIPE 30.27
GÂTEAU BENOIT

CITY RESTAURANT, Los Angeles, CA
Chefs Susan Feniger and Mary Sue Milliken

Yield: 8 Servings

Semisweet chocolate, chopped	7-1/2 oz.	220 g
Unsalted butter	5-1/2 oz.	165 g
Eggs, separated	4	4
Granulated sugar	4 oz.	120 g
All-purpose flour	2 oz.	60 g
Chocolate Curls (recipe follows)	as needed	as needed
Confectioner's sugar	as needed	as needed

1. Melt the chocolate and butter together over a bain marie. Set aside to cool.

2. Beat the egg yolks until light and fluffy, then slowly add the sugar, beating constantly until pale yellow. Fold in the melted chocolate mixture.

3. Sift the flour over the chocolate mixture and fold just until the flour disappears.

4. Whisk the egg whites to soft peaks. Fold the whites into the chocolate mixture in two parts. Pour the batter into a 10-inch (25-centimeter) cake pan that is buttered, floured and lined with parchment paper. Spread the batter evenly and tap once or twice on a counter to remove air pockets.

5. Bake at 350°F (180°C) until a toothpick inserted in the center comes out with a few flakes clinging to it, approximately 20–25 minutes. Set aside to cool, in the pan on a rack, about 1 hour.

6. To release the cake, run a knife along the inside edge of the pan to loosen. Invert onto a serving platter, peel off parchment, and invert again. Prepare the chocolate curls.

7. Pile the curls on top of the cake in a circular pattern pointing outward from the center. Dust with confectioner's sugar.

CHOCOLATE CURLS

Semisweet chocolate, block	1 lb. or larger	500 g or larger

1. The key to making chocolate curls or cigarettes, is the right temperature. Place the chocolate in an oven with only the pilot light on until it softens slightly, approximately 10–20 minutes. Or place the chocolate in an oven that is off but still warm, until the chocolate just begins to soften. In warm weather, this step may not be necessary.

2. Holding a heavy chef's knife between both hands and applying even pressure, pull the blade across the surface of the block, toward you, at about a 60-degree angle.

3. With some practice you can make either tight cigarette rolls or free-form ruffles. Leftover chocolate can be wrapped in plastic and used again.

◆◆◆

RECIPE 30.28
CHOCOLATE FLOURLESS CAKE

VINCENT ON CAMELBACK, PHOENIX, AZ
Chef Vincent Guerithault

Yield: 21 Servings

Unsalted butter	1 lb.	450 g
Chocolate	27 oz.	800 g
Eggs, separated	20	20
Sugar	7 oz.	200 g
Powdered sugar	as needed	as needed

1. Melt the chocolate and butter over a bain marie.
2. Whisk the yolks into the melted chocolate.
3. Whip the egg whites until shiny. Add the sugar and whip until very stiff. Fold into the chocolate. Pour the batter into a full size hotel pan that is lined with buttered parchment.
4. Bake at 400°F (200°C) for 10 minutes. Reduce oven temperature to 350°F (180°C) and continue baking until done, approximately 40 minutes. A cake tester will not come out clean, even though the cake will be done.
5. Invert the cake onto the back of a sheet pan. Cool completely; then dust with powdered sugar.

◆◆◆

RECIPE 30.29
CONTINENTAL BROWNIES

Yield: 1 Sheet Pan   **Method:** Egg Foam

Unsweetened chocolate	2 lb.	1000 g
Unsalted butter	2 lb.	1000 g
Eggs	20	20
Sugar	5 lb. 12 oz.	2.6 kg
Vanilla extract	2 oz.	60 g
All-purpose flour	1 lb. 10 oz.	800 g
Pecan pieces	1 lb.	500 g

1. Melt the chocolate with the butter over a double boiler.
2. While the chocolate is melting, whip the eggs and sugar in a large mixer bowl fitted with the paddle attachment for 10 minutes.
3. Add the melted chocolate and vanilla to the eggs. Stir to blend completely. Stir in the flour and nuts.
4. Spread the batter evenly onto a parchment-lined and buttered sheet pan. The pan will be very full. Bake at 325°F (160°C) for 40 minutes, rotating the pan after the first 20 minutes.
5. Allow to cool completely before cutting. Dust the brownies with confectioner's sugar if desired.

◆◆◆

RECIPE 30.30

APPLESAUCE BROWNIES

Yield: One Sheet Pan

Unsweetened chocolate	4 oz.	120 g
Cake flour, sifted	1 lb.	450 g
Cocoa powder	9 oz.	270 g
Salt	2 tsp.	10 ml
Egg whites	12	12
Whole eggs	8	8
Granulated sugar	2 lb. 2 oz.	1 kg
Light corn syrup	2 lb.	900 g
Unsweetened applesauce	1-1/2 pt.	670 ml
Canola oil	7 oz.	210 g
Vanilla extract	2 Tbsp.	30 ml

1. Coat a sheet pan with spray pan release.
2. Melt the chocolate over a bain marie and set aside.
3. Sift the flour, cocoa powder and salt together and set aside.
4. Whisk the egg whites and eggs together. Add the sugar, corn syrup, applesauce, oil and vanilla. Whisk in the chocolate.
5. Fold the flour mixture into the egg mixture. Pour into the prepared pan and bake at 350°F (180°C) until a cake tester comes out clean, approximately 25 minutes.

Nutritional value per 2-inch (5-cm) square:

Calories	133	Protein	2 g
Calories from fat	24%	Vitamin A	30 IU
Total fat	3 g	Vitamin C	0
Saturated fat	1 g	Sodium	38 mg
Cholesterol	18 mg		

CHAPTER 31

CUSTARDS, CREAMS, FROZEN DESSERTS AND DESSERT SAUCES

*T*he bakeshop is responsible for more than just quick breads, yeast breads, pies, pastries, cookies and cakes. It also produces many delightfully sweet concoctions that are not baked and often not even cooked. These include sweet custards, creams, frozen desserts and dessert sauces. Sweet custards are cooked mixtures of eggs, sugar and milk; flour or cornstarch may be added. Sweet custards can be flavored in a variety of ways and eaten hot or cold. Some are served alone as a dessert or used as a filling, topping or accompaniment for pies, pastries or cakes. Creams include whipped cream and mixtures lightened with whipped cream such as Bavarians, chiffons and mousses. Frozen desserts include ice cream and sorbet as well as the still-frozen mousses called semifreddi.

Sauces for these desserts, including fruit purées, caramel sauces and chocolate syrup, are also made in the bakeshop and are discussed in this chapter. Indeed, many of the items presented in this chapter are components, meant to be combined with pastries (Chapter 29) or cakes (Chapter 30) to form complete desserts. Guidelines for assembling desserts are given at this chapter's end.

After studying this chapter you will be able to:

- prepare a variety of custards and creams
- prepare a variety of ice creams, sorbets and frozen dessert items
- prepare a variety of dessert sauces
- use these products in preparing and serving other pastry and dessert items

---

EGGS AND SANITATION

Eggs are high-protein foods that are easily contaminated by bacteria such as salmonella that cause food-borne illnesses. Because custards cannot be heated to temperatures high enough to destroy these bacteria without first curdling the eggs, it is especially important that sanitary guidelines be followed in preparing the egg products discussed in this chapter.

1. Cleanliness is important: Wash your hands thoroughly before beginning; be sure to use clean, sanitized bowls, utensils and storage containers.

2. When breaking or separating eggs, do not allow the exterior of the eggshell to come into contact with the raw egg.

3. Heat the milk to just below a boil before combining it with the eggs. This reduces the final cooking time.

4. Chill the finished product quickly in an ice bath and refrigerate immediately.

5. Do not use your fingers to taste the custard.

6. Do not store any custard mixture, cooked or uncooked, at room temperature.

CUSTARDS

A **custard** is any liquid thickened by the coagulation of egg proteins. A custard's consistency depends on the ratio of eggs to liquid and the type of liquid used. The more eggs used, the thicker and richer the final product will be. The richer the liquid (cream versus milk, for example), the thicker the final product. Most custards, with the notable exception of pastry creams, are not thickened by starch.

A custard can be stirred or baked. A **stirred custard** tends to be soft, rich and creamy. A **baked custard**, typically prepared in a bain marie, is usually firm enough to unmold and slice.

Stirred Custards

A stirred custard is cooked on the stove top either directly in a saucepan or over a double boiler. It must be stirred throughout the cooking process to prevent curdling (overcooking).

A stirred custard can be used as a dessert sauce, incorporated into a complex dessert or eaten alone. The stirred custards most commonly used in food service operations are **vanilla custard sauce** and **pastry cream**. Other popular stirred custards are lemon curd (Recipe 25.16) and **sabayon** (Recipe 31.3).

Vanilla Custard Sauce

A custard sauce is made with egg yolks, sugar and milk or half-and-half. Usually flavored with vanilla bean or pure vanilla extract, a custard sauce can also be flavored with liquor, chocolate, ground nuts or other extracts.

It is prepared on the stove top over direct heat. When making custard sauce, be extremely careful to stir the mixture continually and not allow it to boil, or it will curdle. A properly made custard sauce should be smooth and thick enough to coat the back of a spoon. It should not contain any noticeable bits of cooked egg.

Vanilla custard sauce (Fr. *crème anglaise*) is served with cakes, pastries, fruits and soufflés and is often used for decorating dessert plates. It may be served hot or cold. It is also used as the base for many ice creams.

A very thick version of custard sauce can be made using heavy cream and additional egg yolks. Its consistency is more like a pudding than a sauce. This custard is often served over fruit in a small ramekin or other container and then topped with caramelized sugar for a dessert known as **crème brûlée** (burnt cream). See Recipe 31.15.

Pastry Cream

Pastry cream (Fr. *crème pâtissière*) is a stirred custard made with egg yolks, sugar and milk and thickened with starch (flour, cornstarch or a combination of the two). Because starch protects the egg yolks from curdling, pastry cream can be boiled. In fact, it must be boiled to fully gelatinize the starch and eliminate the taste of raw starch.

Pastry cream can be flavored with chocolate, liquors, extracts or fruits. (Pudding is nothing more than flavored pastry cream.) It is used for filling éclairs, cream puffs, napoleons, fruit tarts and other pastries. Pastry cream thickened with cornstarch is also the filling for cream pies (see Chapter 29, Pies, Pastries and Cookies). Pastry cream is thick enough to hold its shape without making pastry doughs soggy.

Pastry cream can be rather heavy. It can be lightened by folding in whipped cream to produce a **mousseline**, or Italian meringue can be folded in to produce a **crème Chiboust**.

PROCEDURE FOR MAKING VANILLA CUSTARD SAUCE AND PASTRY CREAM

1. Place milk and/or cream in a heavy, nonreactive saucepan; add vanilla bean if desired.
2. In a mixing bowl, whisk together the egg yolks, sugar and starch (if used). Do not use an electric mixer as it incorporates too much air.
3. Bring the liquid just to a boil. **Temper** the egg mixture with approximately one third of the hot liquid.
4. Pour the tempered eggs into the remaining hot liquid and return the mixture to the heat. The stove's temperature can be as hot as you dare: The lower the temperature, the longer the custard will take to thicken; the higher the temperature, the greater the risk of curdling.
5. Cook, stirring constantly, until thickened. Custard sauce should reach a temperature of 185°F (85°C). Pastry cream should be allowed to boil for a few moments.
6. Immediately remove the cooked custard from the hot saucepan to avoid overcooking. Butter or other flavorings can be added at this time.
7. Cool over an ice bath. Store in a clean, shallow container, cover and refrigerate.

Temper—*to heat gently and gradually; refers to the process of slowly adding a hot liquid to eggs to raise their temperature without causing them to curdle.*

PROCEDURE FOR SALVAGING CURDLED VANILLA CUSTARD SAUCE

1. Strain the sauce into a bowl. Place the bowl over an ice bath and whisk vigorously.
2. If this does not smooth out the overcooked sauce, place the sauce in a blender and process for a few moments.

◆◆◆

RECIPE 31.1

VANILLA SAUCE

Yield: 40 oz. (1200 g)

Half-and-half	1 qt.	1 lt
Vanilla bean, split	1	1
Egg yolks	12	12
Granulated sugar	10 oz.	300 g

1. Using a heavy, nonreactive saucepan, bring the half-and-half and vanilla bean just to a boil.
2. Whisk the egg yolks and sugar together in a mixing bowl. Temper the egg mixture with approximately one third of the hot half-and-half, then return the entire mixture to the saucepan with the remaining half-and-half.
3. Cook the sauce over medium heat, stirring constantly, until it is thick enough to coat the back of a spoon. Do not allow the sauce to boil.
4. As soon as the sauce thickens, remove it from the heat and pour it through a fine mesh strainer into a clean bowl. Chill the sauce over an ice bath, then cover and keep refrigerated. The sauce should last 3–4 days.

1. Mise en place for vanilla sauce.

2. Tempering the eggs.

3. The properly cooked sauce.

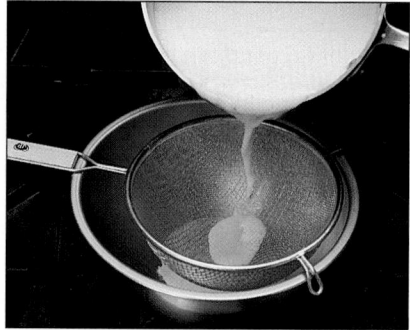

4. Straining the sauce into a bowl over an ice bath.

◆◆◆

RECIPE 31.2

PASTRY CREAM

Yield: 1 qt. (1 lt)

Cake flour	4 oz.	120 g
Sugar	12 oz.	340 g
Milk	1 qt.	1 lt
Egg yolks	12	12
Vanilla bean	1	1
Unsalted butter	2 oz.	60 g

1. Sift the flour and sugar together.
2. Whisk 8 ounces (225 grams) of the milk into the egg yolks. Then add the flour and sugar and whisk until completely smooth.
3. Heat the remaining milk with the vanilla bean in a heavy, nonreactive

saucepan. As soon as the milk comes to a boil, whisk approximately one third of it into the egg-and-flour mixture and blend completely. Pour the egg mixture into the saucepan.

4. Stir constantly until the custard thickens. As it thickens, the custard will go through a lumpy stage. Although you should not be alarmed, you should increase the speed of your stirring. Continue to stir vigorously and it will smooth out and thicken just before coming to a boil.

5. Allow the pastry cream to boil for approximately 1 minute, stirring constantly.

6. Remove the pastry cream from the heat and immediately pour it into a clean mixing bowl.

7. Fold in the butter until melted. Do not overmix, as this will thin the custard.

8. Cover by placing plastic wrap on the surface of the custard. Chill over an ice bath. Remove the vanilla bean just before using the pastry cream.

1. Stirring the pastry cream as it comes to a boil.

2. Folding butter into the cooked pastry cream.

Sabayon

Sabayon (It. *zabaglione*) is a foamy, stirred custard sauce made by whisking eggs, sugar and wine over low heat. The egg proteins coagulate, thickening the mixture, while the whisking incorporates air to make it light and fluffy. Usually a sweet wine is used; marsala and champagne are the most popular choices.

The mixture can be served warm, or it can be chilled and lightened with whipped cream or whipped egg whites. Sabayon may be served alone or as a sauce or topping with fruit or pastries such as spongecake or ladyfingers.

PROCEDURE FOR MAKING SABAYON

1. Combine egg yolks, sugar and wine in the top of a double boiler.
2. Place the double boiler over low heat and whisk constantly until the sauce is foamy and thick enough to form a ribbon when the whisk is lifted.
3. Remove from the heat and serve immediately, or whisk over an ice bath until cool. If allowed to sit, the hot mixture may separate.
4. Whipped egg whites or whipped cream may be folded into the cooled sabayon.

◆◆◆

RECIPE 31.3
CHAMPAGNE SABAYON

Yield: 1 qt. (1 lt)

Egg yolks	8	8
Granulated sugar	4 oz.	120 g
Salt	1/4 tsp.	1 ml
Marsala wine	2 oz.	60 g
Dry champagne	6 oz.	180 g
Heavy cream (optional)	8 oz.	225 g

1. Combine the egg yolks, sugar and salt in a stainless steel bowl.
2. Add the marsala and champagne to the egg mixture.
3. Place the bowl over a pan of barely simmering water. Whisk vigorously until the sauce is thick and pale yellow, approximately 10 minutes. Serve immediately.
4. To prepare a sabayon mousseline, place the bowl of sabayon over an ice bath and continue whisking until completely cold. Whip the cream to soft peaks and fold it into the cold sabayon.

1. The thickened sabayon.

Baked Custards

A baked custard is based on the same principle as a stirred custard: A liquid thickens by the coagulation of egg proteins. However, with a baked custard, the thickening occurs in an oven. The container of custard is usually placed in a water bath (bain marie) to protect the eggs from curdling. Even though the water bath's temperature will not exceed 212°F (100°C), care must be taken not to bake the custards for too long or at too high a temperature. An over-baked custard will be watery or curdled; a properly baked custard should be smooth-textured and firm enough to slice.

Baked custards include simple mixtures of egg yolks, sugar and milk such as **crème caramel** as well as custard mixtures in which other ingredients are suspended, for example, **cheesecake**, rice pudding, **bread pudding** and quiche.

Crème Caramel

Crème caramel, crème renversée and flan all refer to an egg custard baked over a layer of caramelized sugar and inverted for service. The caramelized sugar produces a golden-brown surface on the inverted custard and a thin caramel sauce.

◆◆◆

RECIPE 31.4
TOFFEE CARAMEL FLAN

Yield: 10-6-ounce (180-ml) Ramekins

Granulated sugar	1 lb. 4 oz.	600 g
Water	8 oz.	250 g
Milk	24 oz.	750 g
Heavy cream	24 oz.	750 g
Cinnamon sticks	2	2

Vanilla bean, split	1	1
Whole eggs	8	8
Egg yolks	4	4
Brown sugar	6 oz.	180 g
Molasses	1 Tbsp.	15 ml
Amaretto liqueur	2 Tbsp.	30 ml

1. Combine the granulated sugar with the water in a small, heavy saucepan; bring to a boil. Cook until the sugar reaches a deep golden brown. Immediately pour about 2 tablespoons (30 milliliters) of the sugar into each of the lightly greased ramekins. Tilt each ramekin to spread the caramel evenly along the bottom. Arrange the ramekins in a 2-inch-deep hotel pan and set aside.

2. Combine the milk, cream, cinnamon sticks and vanilla bean in a large saucepan. Bring just to a boil, cover and remove from the heat. Allow this mixture to **steep** for about 30 minutes.

3. Whisk the eggs, egg yolks, brown sugar, molasses and amaretto together in a large bowl.

4. Uncover the milk mixture and return it to the stove top. Bring just to the boil. Temper the egg-and-sugar mixture with approximately one third of the hot milk. Whisk in the remaining hot milk.

5. Strain the custard through a fine mesh strainer. Pour into the caramel-lined ramekins, filling to just below the rim.

6. Pour enough warm water into the hotel pan to reach halfway up the sides of the ramekins. Bake at 325°F (160°C) for approximately 30–40 minutes. The custards should be almost set, but still slightly soft in the center.

7. Completely chill the baked custards before serving. To unmold, run a small knife around the edge of the custard, invert onto the serving plate and give the ramekin a firm sideways shake. Garnish with fresh fruit or caramelized almonds.

Steep—*to soak food in a hot liquid in order to either extract its flavor or soften its texture.*

1. Filling the ramekins for flans.

Cheesecake

Cheesecakes, which are almost as old as western civilization, have undergone many changes and variations since the ancient Greeks devised the first known recipe. Americans revolutionized the dessert with the development of cream cheese in 1872.

Cheesecake is a baked custard that contains a smooth cheese, usually a soft, fresh cheese such as cream, ricotta, cottage or farmer cheese. A cheesecake may be prepared without a crust or it may have a base or sides of short dough, cookie crumbs, ground nuts or spongecake. The filling can be dense and rich (New York style) or light and fluffy (Italian style). Fruit, nuts and flavorings may also be included in the filling. Cheesecakes are often topped with fruit or sour cream glaze. Recipes for both dense and light cheesecakes are at the end of this chapter.

Some cheesecakes are unbaked and rely on gelatin for thickening; others are frozen. These are not really custards, however, but are more similar to the chiffons or mousses discussed below.

Bread Pudding

Bread pudding is a home-style dessert in which chunks of bread, flavorings and raisins or other fruit are mixed with an egg custard and baked. The result is somewhat of a cross between a cake and a pudding. It is often served with custard sauce, ice cream, whipped cream or a whiskey-flavored butter sauce. Bread pudding is a delicious way to use stale or leftover bread or overripe fruit. A recipe for bread pudding with bourbon sauce appears at the end of this chapter.

Soufflés

A soufflé is made with a custard base that is lightened with whipped egg whites and then baked. The air in the egg whites expands to create a light, fluffy texture and tall rise. A soufflé is not as stable as a cake or other pastry item, however, and will collapse very quickly when removed from the oven.

Soufflés can be prepared in a wide variety of sweet and savory flavors. The flavorings may be incorporated into the custard, as in the following recipe. Alternatively, an unflavored pastry cream can be used as the base; the liqueur, fruit or chocolate are then added to each portion separately.

When making a soufflé, the custard base and egg whites should be at room temperature. First, the egg whites will whip to a better volume, and second, if the base is approximately the same temperature as the egg whites, the two mixtures can be more easily incorporated. The egg whites are whipped to stiff peaks with a portion of the sugar for stability. The whipped egg whites are then gently folded into the base immediately before baking.

A soufflé is baked in a straight-sided mold or individual ramekin. The finished soufflé should be puffy with a lightly browned top. It should rise well above the rim of the baking dish. A soufflé must be served immediately, before it collapses. A warm custard sauce (crème anglaise) is often served as an accompaniment to a sweet soufflé.

A frozen soufflé is not a true soufflé. Rather, it is a creamy custard mixture thickened with gelatin, lightened with whipped egg whites or whipped cream and placed in a soufflé dish wrapped with a tall paper collar. When the paper is removed, the mixture looks as if it has risen above the mold like a hot soufflé.

PROCEDURE FOR MAKING BAKED SOUFFLÉS

1. Butter the mold or ramekins and dust with granulated sugar. Preheat the oven to approximately 425°F (220°C).
2. Prepare the custard base. Add flavorings as desired.
3. Whip the egg whites and sugar to stiff peaks. Fold the whipped egg whites into the base.
4. Pour the mixture into the prepared mold or ramekins and bake immediately.

◆◆◆

RECIPE 31.5

CHOCOLATE SOUFFLÉS

Yield: 8 Servings

Orange juice	1 pt.	500 ml
Eggs, separated	8	8
Sugar	4 oz.	120 g
All-purpose flour	3 oz.	90 g
Bittersweet chocolate, chopped fine	8 oz.	225 g
Orange liqueur	2 oz.	60 g

| Butter, melted | as needed | as needed |
| Granulated sugar | as needed | as needed |

1. To prepare the base, heat the orange juice to lukewarm in a heavy saucepan.

2. Whisk the egg yolks with 3 ounces (90 grams) of the sugar in a large mixing bowl. Whisk in the flour and warm orange juice, then return the mixture to the saucepan.

3. Cook over medium-low heat, stirring constantly, until the custard is thick. Do not allow it to boil. Remove from the heat.

4. Stir in the chocolate until completely melted. Stir in the liqueur. Cover the base mixture with plastic to prevent a skin from forming. Hold for use at room temperature. (Unused base can be keep overnight in the refrigerator; it should be brought to room temperature before mixing with the egg whites.)

5. To prepare the soufflés, brush individual-serving-sized ramekins with melted butter and dust with granulated sugar.

6. Preheat the oven to 425°F (220°C). Place a sheet pan in the oven, onto which you will place the soufflés for baking. (This makes it easier to remove the hot soufflé cups from the oven.)

7. Whip the egg whites to stiff peaks with the remaining 1 ounce (30 grams) of sugar. Fold the whites into the chocolate base and spoon the mixture into the prepared ramekins. The ramekins should be filled to within 1/4 inch (6 millimeters) of the rim. Smooth the top of each soufflé with a spatula and bake immediately.

8. The soufflés are done when well risen, golden brown on top and the edges appear dry. Do not touch a soufflé to test doneness.

9. Sprinkle the soufflés with powdered sugar if desired and serve immediately.

1. Folding the whipped egg whites into the chocolate base.

2. Filling the ramekins.

3. The finished soufflé, ready for service.

CREAMS

Creams (Fr. *crèmes*) include light, fluffy or creamy-textured dessert items made with whipped egg whites or cream. Some, such as **Bavarian creams** and **chiffons**, are thickened with gelatin. Others, such as **mousses** and **crèmes Chantilly**, are softer and lighter. The success of all, however, depends on the proper whipping and incorporation of egg whites or heavy cream.

You should review the material on whipping cream found in Chapter 8, Eggs and Dairy Products. Note that whipping cream has a butterfat content of 30–40 percent. When preparing any whipped cream be sure that the cream, the mixing bowl and all utensils are well chilled and clean. A warm bowl can melt the butterfat, destroying the texture of the cream. Properly whipped cream should increase two to three times in volume.

Crème Chantilly

Crème Chantilly is simply heavy cream whipped to soft peaks and flavored with sugar and vanilla. It can be used for garnishing pastry or dessert items, or it can be folded into cooled custard or pastry cream and used as a component in a pastry.

When making crème Chantilly, the vanilla extract and sugar should be added after the cream begins to thicken. Either granulated or powdered sugar may be used; there are advantages and disadvantages to both. Granulated sugar assists in forming a better foam than powdered sugar, but it may cause the cream to feel gritty. Powdered sugar dissolves more quickly and completely than granulated sugar, but does nothing to assist with foaming. Whichever sugar is used, it should be added just before the whipping is complete to avoid interfering with the cream's volume and stability.

◆◆◆

RECIPE 31.6

CRÈME CHANTILLY (CHANTILLY CREAM)

Yield: 2 to 2-1/2 qt. (2 to 2-1/2 lt)

Heavy cream, chilled	1 qt.	1 lt
Powdered sugar	3 oz.	90 g
Vanilla extract	2 tsp.	10 ml

1. Place the cream in a chilled mixing bowl. Using a balloon whisk, whisk the cream until slightly thickened.
2. Add the sugar and vanilla and continue whisking to the desired consistency. The cream should be smooth and light, not grainy. Do not overwhip.
3. Crème Chantilly may be stored in the refrigerator for several hours. If the cream begins to soften, gently rewhip as necessary.

1. Properly whipped crème Chantilly

Bavarian Cream

A Bavarian cream (Fr. *bavarois*) is prepared by first thickening custard sauce with gelatin, then folding in whipped cream. The final product is poured into a mold and chilled until firm enough to unmold and slice. Although a Bavarian cream can be molded into individual servings, it is most often poured into a round mold lined with spongecake or ladyfingers to create the classic dessert known as a **charlotte**.

Bavarians may be flavored by adding chocolate, puréed fruit, chopped nuts, extracts or liquors to the custard sauce base. Layers of fruit or liquor-soaked spongecake may also be added for flavor and texture.

When thickening a dessert cream with gelatin, it is important to use the correct amount of gelatin. If not enough gelatin is used or it is not incorporated completely, the cream will not become firm enough to unmold. If too much gelatin is used, the cream will be tough and rubbery. The recipes given here use sheet gelatin, although an equal amount by weight of granulated gelatin can be substituted. Refer to Chapter 26, Principles of the Bakeshop, for information on using gelatin.

PROCEDURE FOR MAKING BAVARIAN CREAMS

1. Prepare a custard sauce of the desired flavor.
2. While the custard sauce is still quite warm, stir in softened gelatin. Make sure the gelatin is completely incorporated.

3. Chill the custard until almost thickened, then fold in the whipped cream.

4. Pour the Bavarian into a mold or charlotte form. Chill until set.

◆ ◆ ◆

RECIPE 31.7

FRESH FRUIT BAVARIAN

Yield: 1 1-qt. (1-lt) Mold

Fresh fruit such as 2 kiwis, 1 banana
or 1/2 pint (225 ml) raspberries, blueberries or wild strawberries

Honey	1 Tbsp.	15 ml
Kirsch	2 Tbsp.	30 ml
Egg yolks	4	4
Sugar	4 oz.	120 g
Milk	8 oz.	250 g
Vanilla bean	1/2	1/2
Gelatin, softened	1/2 oz.	14 g
Heavy cream	12 oz.	340 g

1. Lightly spray the bottom of a 1-quart (1-liter) mold with pan release spray. If a smooth mold is being used, line it with a sheet of plastic wrap, allowing the wrap to extend beyond the mold's edges.

2. Peel and thinly slice the fruit if necessary. Mix the honey and kirsch and pour over the fruit. Chill while preparing the Bavarian cream.

3. Prepare a vanilla custard sauce using the yolks, sugar, milk and vanilla. Remove from the saucepan.

4. Add softened gelatin to the hot custard. Chill until thick, but do not allow the custard to set.

5. Whip the cream until stiff and fold it into the chilled and thickened custard. Pour about one third of this mixture (the Bavarian cream) into the mold. Arrange one half of the fruit on top. Pour half of the remaining Bavarian cream on top of the fruit and top with the remaining fruit. Fill with the rest of the Bavarian cream. Chill until completely set, approximately 2 hours.

6. Unmold onto a serving dish. Garnish the top with additional fruit and whipped cream as desired.

NOTE: Gelatin may separate in the freezer, so quick chilling is not recommended. Products made with gelatin keep well for 1–2 days but stiffen with age.

VARIATION: *Charlotte*—Line a 1- to 1-1/2-quart (1- to 1.5-liter) charlotte mold with ladyfingers (Recipe 30.26) before filling with layers of fruit and Bavarian. Invert onto a serving platter when firm and garnish with whipped cream.

◆ ◆ ◆

CHARLOTTE, SWEET CHARLOTTE

The original charlotte was created during the 18th century and named for the wife of King George III of England. It consisted of an apple compote baked in a round mold lined with toast slices. A few decades later, the great French chef Carême adopted the name but altered the concept in response to a kitchen disaster. When preparing a grand banquet for King Louis XVIII, he found that his gelatin supply was insufficient for the Bavarian creams he was making, so Carême steadied the sides of his sagging desserts with ladyfingers. The result became known as charlotte russe, probably due to the reigning fad for anything Russian. A fancier version, known as charlotte royale, is made with pinwheels or layers of spongecake and jam instead of ladyfingers. The filling for either should be a classic Bavarian cream.

1. Adding gelatin to the custard base.   **2.** Folding in the whipped egg whites.

Chiffon

A chiffon is similar to a Bavarian except that whipped egg whites instead of whipped cream are folded into the thickened base. The base may be a custard or a fruit mixture thickened with cornstarch. Although a chiffon may be molded like a Bavarian, it is most often used as a pie or tart filling.

PROCEDURE FOR MAKING CHIFFONS

1. Prepare the base, which is usually a custard or a fruit mixture thickened with cornstarch.
2. Add gelatin to the warm base.
3. Fold in whipped egg whites.
4. Pour into a mold or pie shell and chill.

◆◆◆

RECIPE 31.8

LIME CHIFFON

Yield: 1 10-inch (25-cm) Pie or 8 Servings

Granulated gelatin	1/4 oz.	7 g
Water	5 oz.	150 g
Granulated sugar	7 oz.	210 g
Fresh lime juice	3 oz.	90 g
Lime zest	1 Tbsp.	15 ml
Eggs, separated	4	4

1. Soften the gelatin in 1 ounce (30 grams) of the water.
2. Combine 4 ounces (120 grams) of the sugar, the remaining water, lime juice, zest and egg yolks in a bowl over a pan of simmering water.
3. Whisk the egg-and-lime mixture together vigorously until it begins to thicken. Add the softened gelatin and continue whipping until very thick and foamy.
4. Remove from the heat, cover and refrigerate until cool and as thick as whipping cream.
5. Meanwhile, whip the egg whites to soft peaks. Whip in the remaining sugar (3 ounces/90 grams) and continue whipping until stiff but not dry.
6. Fold the whipped egg whites into the egg-and-lime mixture. Pour into a prepared pie crust or serving dishes and chill for several hours, until firm.

VARIATIONS: *Lemon Chiffon*—Substitute lemon juice and lemon zest for the lime juice and zest.

Orange Chiffon—Substitute orange juice for the lime juice and for 4 ounces (120 grams) of the water. Substitute orange zest for the lime zest. Reduce the amount of sugar in the egg yolk mixture to 1 ounce (30 grams).

Mousse

The term *mousse* applies to an assortment of dessert creams not easily classified elsewhere. A mousse is similar to a Bavarian or chiffon in that it is lightened with whipped cream, whipped egg whites or both. A mousse is generally softer than these other products, however, and only occasionally contains a small amount of gelatin. A mousse is generally too soft to mold.

A mousse may be served alone as a dessert or used as a filling in cakes or pastry items. Sweet mousses may be based on a custard sauce, melted chocolate or puréed fruit.

PROCEDURE FOR MAKING MOUSSES

1. Prepare the base, which is usually a custard sauce, melted chocolate or puréed fruit.
2. If gelatin is used, it is softened first, then dissolved in the warm base.
3. Fold in whipped egg whites, if used. If the base is slightly warm when the egg whites are added, their proteins will coagulate making the mousse firmer and more stable.
4. Allow the mixture to cool completely, then fold in whipped cream, if used. Note that the egg whites are folded in before any whipped cream. Although the egg whites may deflate somewhat during folding, if the cream is added first it may become overwhipped when the egg whites are added, creating a grainy or coarse product.

◆◆◆

RECIPE 31.9
CLASSIC CHOCOLATE MOUSSE

Yield: 1-1/2 to 2 qt. (1.5 to 2 lt)

Bittersweet chocolate	15 oz.	440 g
Unsalted butter	9 oz.	280 g
Egg yolks	7	7
Egg whites	11	11
Granulated sugar	2-1/2 oz.	70 g
Heavy cream	8 oz.	250 g

1. Melt the chocolate and butter in a double boiler over low heat. Stir until no lumps remain.
2. Allow the mixture to cool slightly, then whisk in the egg yolks one at a time.
3. Beat the egg whites until soft peaks form. Slowly beat in the sugar and continue beating until stiff peaks form. Fold the whipped egg whites into the chocolate mixture.
4. Whip the cream to soft peaks. Allow the mousse to cool, then fold in the whipped cream. Make sure no streaks of egg white or cream remain.
5. Spoon the mousse into serving bowls or chill completely and pipe into bowls or baked tartlet shells. The mousse may be used as a cake or pastry filling.

◆◆◆

CONVENIENCE PRODUCTS

Commercially prepared powders and mixes can be used to make a wide assortment of puddings, custards, mousses, gelatin desserts and creams. Although these mixes are not recommended for fine dining facilities, pastry cooks in mass feeding institutions such as schools and hospitals base much of their dessert preparation on them. The advantages are speed, cost, quality control and the ability to use semiskilled assistants. Packaged mixes are simply prepared according to the directions provided by the manufacturer, then portioned for service. The pastry cook can often improve on the final product by adding whipped cream, fruit or an appropriate garnish. As with other convenience products, quality varies from merely adequate to very good. Sample and experiment with several brands to select the best for your operation.

TABLE 31.1   CREAM (CRÈME) COMPONENTS

For a:	Begin with a base of:	Thicken with:	Then fold in:
Bavarian	Custard	Gelatin	Whipped cream
Chiffon	Custard or starch-thickened fruit	Gelatin	Whipped egg whites
Mousse	Melted chocolate, puréed fruit or custard	Nothing or gelatin	Whipped cream, whipped egg whites or both

FROZEN DESSERTS

Frozen desserts include **ice cream** and **gelato** and desserts assembled with ice cream such as baked Alaska, bombes and parfaits. Frozen fruit purées, known as **sorbets** and **sherbets**, are also included in this category. Still-frozen desserts, known as **semifreddi**, are made from custards or mousses that are frozen without churning.

When making any frozen mixture, remember that cold dulls flavors. Although perfect at room temperature, flavors seem weaker when the mixture is cold. Thus, it may be necessary to oversweeten or overflavor creams or custards that will be frozen for service. Although liquors and liqueurs are common flavoring ingredients, alcohol drastically lowers a liquid mixture's freezing point. Too much alcohol will prevent the mixture from freezing; thus any liqueurs or liquors must be used in moderation.

Ice Cream and Gelato

Ice cream and gelato are custards that are churned during freezing. They can be flavored with a seemingly endless variety of fruits, nuts, extracts, liqueurs and the like. Gelato is an Italian-style ice cream. It is denser than American-style products because less air is incorporated during churning.

Overrun—*the amount of air churned into an ice cream.*

The USDA requires that products labeled "ice cream" contain not less than 10% milk fat and 20% milk solids, and have no more than 50% **overrun**. "Ice milk" refers to products that do not meet the standards for ice cream. Low-fat products made without cream or egg yolks are also available for the calorie

♦♦♦

ICE CREAM:
FROM ANCIENT CHINA TO DOUBLE FUDGE BROWNIE CHOCOLATE CHIP WITH COOKIE DOUGH AND TOASTED ALMOND SLIVERS

Despite claims to the contrary, it is impossible to identify any one country as having invented ice cream. More likely, it was invented in several places around the world at various times.

Early ancestors of today's ice creams were flavored water ices, which have been popular in China since prehistoric times. They have also been popular in the Mediterranean and Middle East since the Golden Age of Greece. In fact, Alexander the Great had a penchant for wine-flavored ices, made with ice brought down from the mountains by runners. The Roman Emperor Nero served his guests mixtures of fruit crushed with snow and honey. The Saracens brought their knowledge of making flavored ices with them when they migrated to Sicily in the 9th century. And 12th-century Crusaders returned to western Europe with memories of Middle Eastern sherbets.

The Italians are said to have developed gelato from a recipe brought back from China by Marco Polo in the 13th century. Somehow the dish spread to England by the 15th century, where it was recorded that King Henry V served it at his coronation banquet. Catherine de Medici brought the recipe with her when she married the future king of France in 1533. A different flavor was served during each of the 34 days of their marriage festivities.

Ice cream was first served to the public in Paris during the late 17th century. It was available at fashionable cafés serving another new treat: coffee. French chefs quickly developed many elaborate desserts using ice creams including bombes, coupes and parfaits.

Many of this country's founders—Thomas Jefferson, Alexander Hamilton, James and Dolly Madison—were confirmed ice cream addicts.

George Washington spent over $200, a very princely sum, for ice cream during the summer of 1790.

The mechanized ice cream freezer was invented in 1846, setting the stage for mass production and wide availability. By the late 19th century ice cream parlors were popular gathering places. (Many of today's ice cream parlors take their décor from "Gay Nineties" motifs.)

Despite the disappearance of most ice cream wagons, soda fountains and lunch counters, all of which were popular ice cream purveyors for much of the 20th century, ice cream sales have never waned. Today, over 80% of all ice cream is sold in supermarkets or convenience stores. The public's demand for high-fat, homemade-style "super-premium" ice creams with rich and often-elaborate flavor combinations shows no sign of declining.

conscious. Frozen yogurt uses yogurt as its base. Although touted as a nutritious substitute for ice cream, frozen yogurt may have whole milk or cream added for richness and smoothness.

One hallmark of good ice cream and gelato is smoothness. The ice crystals that would normally form during freezing can be avoided by constant stirring or churning. Churning, usually accomplished mechanically, also incorporates air into the product. The air causes the mixture to expand. Gelato has little incorporated air. Good-quality ice creams and sorbets have enough air to make them light; inferior products often contain overrun. The difference becomes obvious when equal volumes are weighed.

Many food service operations use ice cream makers that have internal freezing units to chill the mixture while churning it. Most commercial machines are suitable for churning either ice cream or sorbet. Follow the manufacturer's directions for using and cleaning any ice cream maker.

PROCEDURE FOR MAKING ICE CREAMS

1. Place the milk and/or cream in a heavy saucepan. If vanilla bean is being used it may be added at this time.
2. Whisk the egg yolks and sugar together in a mixing bowl.
3. Bring the liquid just to a boil. Temper the egg mixture with approximately one third of the hot liquid.
4. Pour the tempered eggs into the remaining hot liquid and return the mixture to the heat.
5. Cook, stirring constantly, until warm.
6. Remove the cooked custard sauce from the hot saucepan immediately. If left in the hot saucepan, it will overcook. Flavorings may be added at this time.
7. Cool the cooked custard sauce over an ice bath. Store covered and refrigerated until ready to process.
8. Process according to the machine manufacturer's directions.

◆◆◆

RECIPE 31.10

ICE CREAM BASE

Yield: 2 qt. (2 lt)

Whole milk	1-1/2 qt.	1500 ml
Heavy cream	1 pt.	500 ml
Vanilla bean, optional	1	1
Egg yolks	16	16
Granulated sugar	20 oz.	600 g

1. Combine the milk and cream in a heavy saucepan and bring to a boil. Add the vanilla bean if desired.
2. Whisk the egg yolks and sugar together in a mixing bowl.
3. Temper the eggs with one third of the hot milk. Return the egg mixture to the saucepan.
4. Cook over medium heat until slightly thickened. Pour through a fine mesh strainer into a clean bowl.
5. Chill the cooked custard sauce completely before processing.

Continued

VARIATIONS: *Chocolate*—Add approximately 9 ounces (250 grams) of finely chopped bittersweet chocolate per quart (liter) of ice cream base. Add the chocolate to the hot mixture after it is strained. Stir until completely melted.

Cappuccino—Steep the hot milk and cream with the vanilla bean and 2–3 cinnamon sticks. After the ice cream base is made, stir in 2 tablespoons (30 milliliters) coffee extract.

Brandied Cherry—Drain the liquid from one 16-ounce (500-gram) can of tart, pitted cherries. Soak the cherries in three tablespoons (45 milliliters) brandy. Prepare the ice cream base as directed, omitting the vanilla bean. Add the brandy-soaked cherries to the cooled custard before processing.

Sherbets and Sorbets

Sherbet and sorbet are frozen mixtures of fruit juice or fruit purée. Sherbet contains milk and/or egg yolks for creaminess; sorbet contains neither.

Sorbet can be prepared in a wide variety of fruit (and even some vegetable) flavors; it is often flavored with an alcoholic beverage. It is served as a first course, a palate refresher between courses or a dessert. Because of its milk content, sherbet tends to be richer than a sorbet, so it is generally reserved for dessert.

Sorbet and sherbet may be made with fresh, frozen or canned fruit. Granulated sugar or sugar syrup is added for flavor and body. The ratio of sugar to fruit purée or juice depends to some extent on the natural sweetness of the specific fruit as well as personal preference. If too much sugar is used, however, the mixture will be soft and syrupy. If too little sugar is used, the sorbet will be very hard and grainy. Egg whites may also be added during churning for body.

◆◆◆

RECIPE 31.11

GRAPEFRUIT SORBET

Yield: 1-1/2 qt. (1.5 lt)

Fresh grapefruit juice	1 qt.	1 lt
Granulated sugar	8 oz.	250 g

1. Combine the juice and sugar.

2. Process in an ice cream maker according to the manufacturer's directions.

3. Pack into a clean container and freeze until firm.

Serving Suggestions for Ice Creams and Sorbets

Ice creams and sorbets are usually served by the scoop, often in cookie cones. Or they can be served as **sundaes**. More formal presentations include **baked Alaska**, **bombes**, **coupes** and **parfaits**.

Still-Frozen Desserts

Still-frozen desserts (It. *semifreddi*) are made with frozen mousse, custard or cream. Layers of spongecake and/or fruit may be added for flavor and texture. Because these mixtures are frozen without churning, air must be incorporated

Sundae—*a great and gooey concoction of ice cream, sauces (hot fudge, marshmallow and caramel, for example), toppings (nuts, candies, and fresh fruit to name a few) and whipped cream.*

Baked Alaska—*ice cream set on a layer of spongecake and encased in meringue, then baked until the meringue is warm and golden.*

Bombe—*two or more flavors of ice cream, or ice cream and sherbet shaped in a spherical mold; each flavor is a separate layer that forms the shell for the next flavor.*

Coupe—*ice cream served with a fruit topping.*

Parfait—*ice cream served in a long, slender glass with alternating layers of topping or sauce.*

by folding in relatively large amounts of whipped cream or meringue. The air helps keep the mixture smooth and prevents it from becoming too hard. Still-frozen desserts develop ice crystals quicker than churned products, so they tend to have a shorter shelf life than ice creams or sorbets.

Still-frozen products include frozen soufflés, **marquis**, mousses and **neapolitans**. The Chocolate Hazelnut Marquis recipe at the end of this chapter (Recipe 31.29) is an example of a still-frozen dessert.

Marquis—*a frozen mousse-like dessert, usually chocolate.*

Neapolitan—*a three-layered loaf or cake of ice cream; each layer is a different flavor and a different color, a typical combination being chocolate, vanilla and strawberry.*

Dessert Sauces

Pastries and desserts are often accompanied by sweet sauces. Dessert sauces provide flavor and texture and enhance plate presentation. Vanilla custard sauce (Recipe 31.1) is the principal dessert sauce. It can be flavored and colored with chocolate, coffee extract, liquor or fruit compound as desired. Other dessert sauces include fruit purées, caramel sauces and chocolate syrups. Techniques for decorating plates with sauces are discussed in Chapter 35, Plate Presentation.

Fruit Purées

Many types of fruit can be puréed for dessert sauces: Strawberries, raspberries, blackberries, apricots, mangoes and papayas are popular choices. They produce thick sauces with strong flavors and colors. Fresh or individually quick frozen (IQF) fruits are recommended.

Puréed fruit sauces, also known as **coulis**, can be cooked or uncooked. Cooking thickens the sauces by reduction and allows any starch thickener to gelatinize. They can also be sweetened with granulated sugar or a sugar syrup. The amount of sweetener will, of course, vary depending upon the fruit's natural sweetness and personal preference.

◆◆◆

RECIPE 31.12
Raspberry Sauce

Yield: 1 qt. (1 lt)

Raspberries, fresh or IQF	2 lb.	1 kg
Granulated sugar	1 lb.	500 g
Lemon juice	1 oz.	30 g

1. Purée the berries and strain through a fine chinois.
2. Stir in the sugar and lemon juice. Adjust the flavor with additional sugar if necessary.

Raspberry sauce.

Caramel Sauce

Caramel sauce is a mixture of caramelized sugar and heavy cream. A liqueur or citrus juice may be used for added flavor. Review the material on caramelizing sugar in Chapter 26, Principles of the Bakeshop, before making caramel sauce.

♦♦♦

RECIPE 31.13
CARAMEL SAUCE

Yield: 4 qt. (4 lt)

Granulated sugar	4 lb. 8 oz.	2 kg
Water	1 pt.	500 g
Lemon juice	2 oz.	60 g
Heavy cream, room temperature	2 qt.	2 lt
Unsalted butter, cut into pieces	5 oz.	150 g

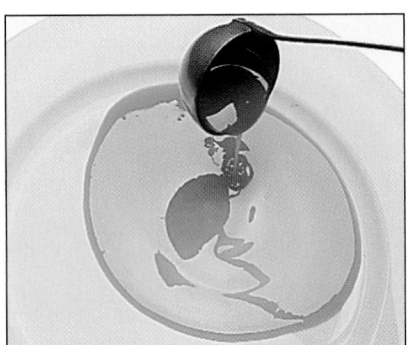

Caramel sauce.

1. Combine the sugar and water in a large, heavy saucepan. Stir to moisten the sugar completely. Place the saucepan on the stove top over high heat and bring to a boil. Brush down the sides of the pan with water to remove any sugar granules.
2. When the sugar comes to a boil, add the lemon juice. Do not stir the sugar, as this may cause lumping. Continue boiling until the sugar caramelizes, turning a dark golden brown and producing a rich aroma.
3. Remove the saucepan from the heat. Gradually add the cream. Be extremely careful, as the hot caramel may splatter. Whisk in the cream to blend.
4. Add the pieces of butter. Stir until the butter melts completely. If necessary, return the sauce to the stove to reheat enough to melt the butter.
5. Strain the sauce and cool completely at room temperature. The sauce may be stored for several weeks under refrigeration. Stir before using.

Chocolate Syrup

Chocolate syrup or sauce can be prepared by adding finely chopped chocolate to warm vanilla custard sauce. A darker syrup can also be made with unsweetened chocolate or cocoa powder. Fudge-type sauces, like the one at the end of this chapter, are really just variations on ganache, discussed in Chapter 30, Cakes and Frostings.

♦♦♦

RECIPE 31.14
DARK CHOCOLATE SYRUP

Yield: 1 pt. (500 ml)

Cocoa powder	2 oz.	60 g
Water	12 oz.	340 g
Granulated sugar	8 oz.	250 g
Unsalted butter	3 oz.	90 g
Heavy cream	1 oz.	30 g

Dark chocolate syrup.

1. Mix the cocoa powder with just enough water to make a smooth paste.
2. Bring the sugar and remaining water to a boil in a small, heavy saucepan. Immediately add the cocoa paste, whisking until smooth.
3. Simmer for 15 minutes, stirring constantly, then remove from the heat.
4. Stir the butter and cream into the warm cocoa mixture. Serve warm or at room temperature.

ASSEMBLING DESSERTS

As noted previously, many pastries and other desserts are assembled from the baked doughs discussed in Chapter 29, Pies, Pastries and Cookies; the cakes, icings and glazes discussed in Chapter 30, Cakes and Frostings; and the creams, custards and other products discussed in this chapter. Many of these desserts are classic presentations requiring the precise arrangement of specific components. Formulas for some of these desserts are found at the end of the chapters in this part. But once you begin to master the basic skills presented in these chapters, you can use your creativity, taste and judgment to combine these components into a wide selection of new, unique and tempting desserts.

Assembled pastries and other desserts generally consist of three principal components: the base, the filling and the garnish. The **base** is the dough, crust or cake product that provides structure and forms the foundation for the final product. The **filling** refers to whatever is used to add flavor, texture and body to the final product. The **garnish** is any glaze, fruit, sauce or accompaniment used to complete the dish.

GUIDELINES FOR ASSEMBLING DESSERTS

1. There should be a proper blend of complementary and contrasting flavors. For example, pears, red wine and blue cheese go well together, as do chocolate and raspberries. Do not combine flavors simply for the sake of originality, however.
2. There should be a proper blend of complementary and contrasting textures. For example, crisp puff pastry, soft pastry cream and tender strawberries are combined for a strawberry napoleon.
3. There should be a proper blend of complementary and contrasting colors. For example, a garnish of red raspberries and green mint looks great.
4. Garnishes should not be overly fussy or garish.
5. The base should be strong enough to hold the filling and garnish without collapsing, yet thin or tender enough to cut easily with a fork.
6. The filling or garnish may cause the base to become soft or even soggy. This may or may not be desirable. If you want a crisp base, assemble the product very close to service. If you want this softening to occur, assemble the product in advance of service.
7. Consider the various storage and keeping qualities of the individual components. It may be best to assemble or finish some products at service time.
8. The final construction should not be so elaborate or fragile that it cannot be portioned or served easily or attractively.
9. Consider whether the product would be better prepared as individual portions or as one large item. This may depend on the desired plate presentation and the ease and speed with which a large product can be cut and portioned for service.

CONCLUSION

If pastry doughs are the backbone of dessert preparations, then custards, creams, mousses and the like are the heart. The skills and techniques presented in this chapter are essential to successful pastry production. Many of these skills, such as whipping cream or preparing custards, will be useful in other areas of the kitchen as well. Once you have mastered these skills as well as those discussed in Chapter 29, Pies, Pastries and Cookies, and Chapter 30, Cakes and Frostings, you will be able to prepare a wide variety of tempting desserts.

⟨uestions for Discussion

1. Eggs and dairy products are susceptible to bacterial contamination. What precautions should be taken to avoid food-borne illnesses when preparing custards?
2. Explain why pastry cream should be boiled and why custard sauce should not be boiled.
3. Identify three desserts that are based on a baked custard.
4. Compare a classically prepared Bavarian, chiffon, mousse and souffle. How are they similar? How are they different?
5. Describe the procedure for making a typical still-frozen dessert. What is the purpose of including whipped cream or whipped egg whites?
6. Explain three ways in which sweet sauces can be used in preparing or presenting a dessert.

⟨dditional Custard, Cream, Frozen Dessert and Dessert Sauce Formulas

RECIPE 31.15
CRÈME BRÛLÉE

NOTE: *This dish appears in the Chapter Opening photograph.*

VINCENT ON CAMELBACK, PHOENIX, AZ
Chef Vincent Guerithault

Yield: 3-1/2 qt. (3.5 lt)

Heavy cream	2 qt.	2 lt
Vanilla beans	2	2
Egg yolks	50	50
Granulated sugar	20 oz.	600 g
Fresh berries	as needed	as needed
Tulipe Cookie Cups (recipe follows)		
Granulated sugar	as needed for caramelized topping	

1. Place the cream and the vanilla beans in a large, heavy saucepan. Heat just to a boil.
2. Whisk the egg yolks and sugar together until smooth and well blended.
3. Temper the eggs with one third of the hot cream. Return the egg mixture to the saucepan and cook, stirring constantly, until very thick. Do not allow the custard to boil.
4. Remove from the heat and strain into a clean bowl. Cool over an ice bath, stirring occasionally.

5. To serve, place fresh berries in the bottom of each cookie cup. Top with several spoonfuls of custard.

6. Sprinkle granulated sugar over the top of the custard and caramelize with a propane torch. Serve immediately.

TULIPE COOKIE CUPS

Yield: 4-1/2 lb. (2 kg) Batter

Unsalted butter	1 lb.	500 g
Powdered sugar	1 lb.	500 g
All-purpose flour	1 lb.	500 g
Egg whites	1 lb. 8 oz.	750 ml

1. Melt the butter and place in a mixer bowl fitted with the paddle attachment. Add the sugar and blend until almost smooth.

2. Add the flour and blend until smooth. With the mixer running, add the egg whites very slowly. Beat until blended, but do not incorporate air into the batter.

3. Strain the dough through a china cap and set aside to cool completely.

4. Coat several sheet pans with melted butter. Spread the dough into 6-inch (15-centimeter) circles on the pans. Bake at 400°F (200°C) until the edges are brown and the dough is dry, approximately 12–18 minutes.

5. To shape into cups, lift the hot cookies off the sheet pan one at a time with an offset spatula. Immediately place over an inverted glass and top with a ramekin or small bowl. The cookies cool very quickly, becoming firm and crisp.

◆◆◆

RECIPE 31.16

PASTRY CREAM CHIBOUST

Yield: 1 pt. (500 ml)

Gelatin	3 sheets	3 sheets
Milk	6 oz.	180 g
Vanilla bean	1/2	1/2
Egg yolks	3	3
Granulated sugar	3 Tbsp.	45 ml
Cornstarch	2 Tbsp.	30 ml
Granulated sugar	6 oz.	180 g
Water	3 Tbsp.	45 ml
Egg whites	3	3
Cream of tartar	1/8 tsp.	0.5 ml

1. Soak the gelatin in ice water.

2. Prepare a pastry cream by heating the milk and vanilla bean just to a boil. Whisk the egg yolks, 3 tablespoons (45 milliliters) of sugar and the cornstarch together. Temper with one third of the hot milk, then return the mixture to the saucepan and cook over moderate heat until thick. The pastry cream should be allowed to boil briefly to properly gelatinize the starch. Remove the cream from the heat and transfer to a clean bowl.

3. Stir the softened gelatin into the hot cream. Cover and set aside but do not chill or allow the cream to set while preparing the Italian meringue.

4. Prepare an Italian meringue using the remaining ingredients.

5. Quickly and thoroughly incorporate one third of the meringue into the warm pastry cream with a spatula. Gently fold in the remaining meringue.

◆◆◆

RECIPE 31.17

CHOCOLATE POT AU CRÈME

Yield: 8 4-oz. (120-ml) Servings

Milk	1 pt.	500 g
Bittersweet chocolate	8 oz.	225 g
Granulated sugar	7 oz.	210 g
Vanilla extract	1 tsp.	5 ml
Coffee liqueur	2 Tbsp.	30 ml
Egg yolks	7	7

1. Heat the milk just to a simmer. Add the chocolate and sugar. Stir constantly until the chocolate melts; do not allow the mixture to boil. Remove from the heat and add the vanilla and liqueur.
2. Whisk the egg yolks together, then slowly whisk them into the chocolate mixture.
3. Pour the custard into ramekins. Place the ramekins in a hotel pan and add enough hot water to reach halfway up the sides of the ramekins.
4. Bake at 325°F (160°C) until custards are almost set in the center, approximately 30 minutes. Remove from the water bath and refrigerate until thoroughly chilled. Serve garnished with whipped cream and chocolate shavings.

◆◆◆

RECIPE 31.18

PISTACHIO CITRUS CHEESECAKE

Yield: 4 10-inch (25-cm) Cakes

Unsalted butter, melted	as needed	as needed
Pistachios, chopped fine	8 oz.	250 g
Cream cheese, softened	6 lb. 10 oz.	3.7 kg
All-purpose flour	3-1/2 oz.	100 g
Granulated sugar	2 lb. 5 oz.	1 kg
Eggs	18	18
Heavy cream	10 oz.	300 g
Lemon zest, grated fine	4 Tbsp.	60 ml
Orange zest, grated fine	4 Tbsp.	60 ml

1. Brush the sides and bottoms of four cake pans (do not use springform pans) with melted butter. Coat with an even layer of pistachio nuts.
2. Beat the cream cheese until smooth. Add the flour and sugar and beat to incorporate completely.
3. Add the eggs slowly, then stir in the cream. Stir in the zest and pour the batter into prepared pans.
4. Place the cake pans in a water bath and bake at 325°F (160°C) until set, approximately 45 minutes.
5. Cool to room temperature before inverting onto a serving tray or cake cardboard. The nut crust becomes the top of the cakes.

♦♦♦

RECIPE 31.19

NEW YORK-STYLE CHEESECAKE

Yield: 2 10-inch (25-cm) Cakes

Cream cheese, softened	3 lb. 6 oz.	1.6 kg
Cake flour	2 oz.	60 g
Granulated sugar	18 oz.	540 g
Eggs	8	8
Heavy cream	5 oz.	150 g
Vanilla extract	1 Tbsp.	15 ml

1. Beat the cheese until smooth. Beat in the flour and sugar.

2. Blend in the eggs slowly, then add the cream and vanilla.

3. Pour the batter into well-buttered springform pans. Bake at 300°F (150°C) until set, approximately 1 to 1-1/2 hours.

4. Cool completely before removing the sides of each pan.

♦♦♦

RECIPE 31.20

BREAD PUDDING WITH BOURBON SAUCE

Yield: 20 Servings

Raisins	8 oz.	250 g
Brandy	4 oz.	120 g
Unsalted butter, melted	2 oz.	60 g
White bread, day-old	24 oz.	720 g
Heavy cream	2 qt.	2 lt
Eggs	6	6
Granulated sugar	1 lb. 10 oz.	800 g
Vanilla extract	2 oz.	60 g
Bourbon Sauce (recipe follows)	as needed	as needed

1. Combine the raisins and brandy in a small saucepan. Heat just to a simmer, cover and set aside.

2. Use a portion of the butter to thoroughly coat a 2-inch-deep (5 centimeter) hotel pan. Reserve the remaining butter.

3. Tear the bread into chunks and place in a large bowl. Pour the cream over the bread and set aside until soft.

4. Beat the eggs and sugar until smooth and thick. Add the remaining ingredients, including the melted butter, raisins and brandy.

5. Toss the egg mixture with the bread gently to blend. Pour into the hotel pan and bake at 350°F (180°C) until browned and almost set, approximately 45 minutes.

6. Serve warm with 2–3 tablespoons (30–45 milliliters) of the Bourbon Sauce.

Continued

BOURBON SAUCE

Unsalted butter	8 oz.	250 g
Granulated sugar	1 lb.	500 g
Eggs	2	2
Bourbon	8 oz.	250 g

1. Melt the butter; stir in the sugar and eggs and simmer to thicken.
2. Add the bourbon and hold in a warm place for service.

♦♦♦

RECIPE 31.21

CHERRY CLAFOUTI

Yield: 1 10-inch (25-cm) Cake

Clafouti—*a country-style French dessert similar to a quiche, in which dark cherries are baked in an egg custard.*

Dark cherries, fresh or canned, pitted	1 lb.	500 g
Eggs, large	4	4
Milk	12 oz.	340 g
Granulated sugar	2 oz.	60 g
Vanilla extract	1 tsp.	5 ml
All-purpose flour	2 oz.	60 g
Powdered sugar	as needed	as needed

1. Drain the cherries and pat them completely dry with paper towels. Arrange them evenly on the bottom of a buttered 10-inch (25-centimeter) pan. Do not use a springform pan or removable-bottom tartlet pan.
2. Make the custard by whisking the eggs and milk together. Add the sugar, vanilla and flour and continue whisking until all the lumps are removed.
3. Pour the custard over the cherries and bake at 325°F (160°C) for 1 to 1-1/2 hours. The custard should be lightly browned and firm to the touch when done.
4. Dust with powdered sugar and serve the clafouti while still warm.

♦♦♦

RECIPE 31.22

WHITE CHOCOLATE FRANGELICO BAVARIAN

Yield: 4 qt. (4 lt)

Heavy cream	2 qt.	2 lt
White chocolate, chopped	2 lb.	1 kg
Gelatin	8 sheets	8 sheets
Frangelico liqueur	10 oz.	300 g
Vanilla extract	2 tsp.	10 ml

1. Bring 1 quart (1 liter) of cream just to a boil. Immediately pour over the chopped chocolate. Stir until the chocolate melts.
2. Place the gelatin in ice water to soften.
3. Gently heat the liqueur just to a simmer. Remove from the heat and stir in the gelatin, one softened sheet at a time.

4. Add the gelatin mixture to the chocolate. Stir to blend well. Cool over an ice bath, stirring frequently.

5. Whip the remaining 1 quart (1 liter) of cream with the vanilla to stiff peaks.

6. Fold the whipped cream into the chocolate mixture. Chill until ready to use.

◆◆◆

RECIPE 31.23
CHOCOLATE CHIFFON PIE

Yield: 2 9-inch (22-cm) Pies

Gelatin	1/2 oz.	15 g
Milk	20 oz.	600 g
Unsweetened chocolate	4 oz.	120 g
Granulated sugar	6 oz.	180 g
Salt	1/4 tsp.	1 ml
Eggs, separated	6	6
Vanilla extract	2 tsp.	10 ml
Crumb-crust pie shells	2	2

1. Soften the gelatin and set aside.

2. Combine the milk and chocolate in a heavy saucepan and warm over low heat until the chocolate melts.

3. Add 4 ounces (120 grams) of the sugar, the salt and the egg yolks. Continue cooking, stirring constantly, until the mixture thickens.

4. Remove from the heat and add the gelatin, stirring until completely dissolved. Pour the mixture into a bowl and chill until very thick.

5. Whip the egg whites to soft peaks. Add the vanilla and the remaining sugar and whip to stiff peaks. Fold the whites into the chocolate.

6. Mound the chiffon into the pie shells and chill for several hours before serving. Garnish with unsweetened whipped cream and chocolate shavings.

◆◆◆

RECIPE 31.24
WHITE CHOCOLATE MOUSSE CAKE
WITH GRAND MARNIER SAUCE

THE FOUR SEASONS, NEW YORK, NY

Yield: 6 Servings

Mousse:

White chocolate, cut into small pieces	8 oz.	250 g
Heavy cream	8 oz.	250 g
Unsalted butter	1 oz.	30 g
Rum	1 Tbsp.	15 ml
Egg whites	2	2
Sugar	1 Tbsp.	15 ml

Decoration:

White chocolate, tempered	10 oz.	300 g
Dark chocolate, melted	2 oz.	60 g

Continued

Sauce:

Orange marmalade	10 oz.	300 g
Grand Marnier liqueur	3 oz.	90 g
Lemon juice	2 Tbsp.	30 ml

1. To make the mousse, melt the chocolate with 3 ounces (90 grams) of the heavy cream and the butter in a double boiler. Remove from the heat and stir until smooth.

2. Stir in the rum and let the mixture cool to room temperature.

3. Whip the remaining cream and chill.

4. Whip the egg whites, adding the sugar gradually until they hold stiff peaks. Gently fold the egg whites into the chocolate mixture, then fold in the whipped cream.

5. Spoon the mousse into six 2-1/2-inch (6.25-centimeter) rings or soufflé molds and chill until firm.

6. To make the decorations, spread thin layers of tempered white chocolate onto a piece of plastic film. Let the chocolate set until firm. With a sharp knife, cut six 2-1/2-inch-diameter (6.25-centimeter) circles and six long strips the same height as the mousse cakes. (Make sure you cut through the plastic film.)

7. Remove the white chocolate mousse cakes from their molds and keep chilled.

8. Warm the white chocolate strips slightly, just enough to bend them, then wrap the side of the cakes, placing the chocolate side against the mousse. Place the circles on top of the cakes. Chill again for 10 minutes and then pull off the plastic wrap.

9. Apply a design of your choice with the melted dark chocolate. Keep the cakes well chilled.

10. To make the sauce, warm the marmalade, liqueur and juice in a saucepan, stirring frequently.

11. Serve the cakes on a pool of the Grand Marnier sauce.

◆◆◆

RECIPE 31.25

RASPBERRY MOUSSE

Yield: 1 qt. (1 lt)

Gelatin	6 sheets	6 sheets
Raspberries, puréed	12 oz.	360 g
Granulated sugar	3 oz.	90 g
Raspberry brandy	2 Tbsp.	30 ml
Heavy cream	8 oz.	250 g

1. Soften the gelatin in ice water and set aside.

2. Place the raspberry purée, sugar and brandy in a nonreactive saucepan and warm just to dissolve the sugar. Remove from the heat and strain through a fine chinois.

3. Add the gelatin, stirring until it is dissolved. Chill the mixture until thick but not set.

4. Whip the cream to soft peaks and fold it into the raspberry mixture.

= ◆◆◆ =

RECIPE 31.26

Parnassienne de Mousse au Chocolat (Chocolate Tower)

CHRISTOPHER'S AND CHRISTOPHER'S BISTRO, PHOENIX, AZ
Chef/Owner Christopher Gross

Yield: 8 Servings

Parchment paper molds	8	8
Dark chocolate, chopped	5-1/2 oz.	165 g
Unsalted butter	3 Tbsp.	45 ml
Heavy cream	2 oz.	60 g
Egg whites	10	10
Superfine sugar	4 Tbsp.	60 ml
Dark chocolate, melted	2 oz.	60 g
White chocolate, melted	5 oz.	150 g
Espresso Sauce (recipe follows)	as needed	as needed
Fresh berries	as needed	as needed

1. To make the molds, cut parchment paper into sixteen strips, each 3-1/2 inches (8.75 centimeters) high and 5 inches (12.5 centimeters) long. Roll eight of these strips into tubes and tape closed. Stand these eight tubes upright on a parchment lined sheet pan. Reserve the remaining strips for the tower coating.

2. To make the mousse, melt the 5-1/2 ounces (165 grams) of chocolate and the butter in a medium bowl over a bain marie.

3. Whip the cream to stiff peaks and refrigerate.

4. Whip the egg whites and the superfine sugar to stiff peaks.

5. Fold the egg whites into the melted chocolate, then fold in the whipped cream.

6. Using a large piping bag fitted with a plain tip, pipe the mousse into the eight parchment paper tubes. Freeze until completely solid, several hours or overnight.

7. To make the tower coating, pipe a pattern of melted dark chocolate onto the 8 remaining strips of parchment paper. When the dark chocolate hardens, coat the same side of the parchment with the melted white chocolate. Immediately remove a tube of mousse from the freezer. Remove the paper wrapping and wrap the chocolate-coated parchment strip around the frozen mousse, placing the chocolate next to the mousse. Refreeze for 5 minutes, then carefully peel the paper off the tower. The dark and white chocolate coating will remain wrapped around the mousse.

8. Repeat the procedure for wrapping the frozen mousse with chocolate-coated paper for the remaining pieces.

9. For service, ladle espresso sauce onto eight plates, place a mousse tower in the center of each plate and garnish with fresh berries.

ESPRESSO SAUCE

Yield: 1-1/2 pt. (700 ml)

Egg yolks	8	8
Granulated sugar	3-1/2 oz.	100 g

Continued

Half-and-half	1 pt.	450 ml
Espresso beans	3 oz.	90 g
Vanilla bean	1/2	1/2

1. Whisk the egg yolks and sugar together in a medium bowl.
2. Bring the half-and-half, espresso beans and vanilla bean to a simmer in a heavy saucepan.
3. Temper the egg yolks with a portion of the hot half-and-half, then return the mixture to the saucepan. Cook over low heat, stirring constantly, until the sauce is thick enough to coat the back of a spoon. Strain and cool over an ice bath.

◆◆◆

RECIPE 31.27
CARAMEL ICE CREAM

CITY RESTAURANT, LOS ANGELES, CA
Chef/Owners Susan Feniger and Mary Sue Millikin

Yield: 1-1/2 qt. (1-1/2 lt)

ICE CREAM

Half-and-half	20 oz.	600 g
Heavy cream	12 oz.	360 g
Egg yolks	9	9
Granulated sugar	6 oz.	180 g
Vanilla extract	2 tsp.	10 ml
Sour cream	8 oz.	225 g
Caramel Chunks (recipe follows)	as needed	as needed

1. Combine the half-and-half and cream in a medium-heavy saucepan. Bring to a boil.
2. Whisk together the egg yolks and sugar until thick and pale yellow. Pour in the boiling liquid and stir to combine. Remove from the heat.
3. Add the vanilla and stir. Strain into an large container and chill over an ice bath, stirring occasionally.
4. Stir in the sour cream and pour into an ice cream maker. Process according to the manufacturer's directions.
5. When the ice cream is done, fold in the reserved Caramel Chunks. Store in the freezer for 1–2 days.

CARAMEL CHUNKS

Granulated sugar	8 oz.	225 g
Water	4 oz.	120 g

1. Combine the sugar and water in a heavy saucepan. Cook over moderate heat until the color turns deep brown and the aroma is strong, approximately 10–15 minutes.
2. Immediately, and with great care, pour the hot caramel onto a greased sheet pan. Set aside until cool, then crack into 1/2-inch (12-millimeter) pieces.

✦✦✦

RECIPE 31.28
LEMON SORBET

VINCENT ON CAMBELBACK, Phoenix, AZ
Chef Vincent Guerithault

Yield: 1-1/2 qt. (1.5 lt)

Lemon juice	1 pt.	500 ml
Water	1 pt.	500 ml
Granulated sugar	1 lb.	500 g

1. Combine the juice, water and sugar in a large bowl. Stir until the sugar dissolves completely.
2. Pour the lemon mixture into the ice cream/sorbet machine and process according to the manufacturer's directions.
3. The finished sorbet will be rather soft. Pack it into a storage container and freeze at a temperature of 0°F (-18°C) or lower until firm.

✦✦✦

RECIPE 31.29
CHOCOLATE HAZELNUT MARQUIS WITH FRANGELICO SAUCE

Yield: 12 Servings

Dark chocolate	1 lb.	500 g
Unsalted butter	4 oz.	120 g
Hazelnuts, roasted, skinned and chopped coarse	4 oz.	120 g
Eggs, separated	6	6
Frangelico (hazelnut liqueur)	2 oz.	60 g
Salt	pinch	pinch
Frangelico Sauce (Recipe follows)	as needed	as needed
Hazelnuts, roasted and chopped coarse	as needed	as needed
Raspberries	as needed	as needed
Mint	as needed	as needed

1. Line a terrine mold with melted butter and parchment paper.
2. Melt the chocolate and butter over a bain marie. Remove from the heat and stir in the nuts, egg yolks and hazelnut liqueur. Set aside to cool to room temperature but do not use an ice bath as the chocolate will solidify.
3. Whip the egg whites with the salt until stiff but not dry. Fold the whipped whites into the chocolate mixture.
4. Pour the mixture into the pan and freeze overnight.
5. Remove the marquis from the pan and peel off the paper. (Work quickly because this melts quickly.) While still frozen, use a hot knife to slice the loaf into 1/3-inch-thick (8-millimeter) slices. Return the marquis to freeze until just before service.
6. Serve two slices on a pool of frangelico sauce. Garnish with coarsely chopped hazelnuts, fresh raspberries and mint.

FOR THE FRANGELICO SAUCE: Prepare a crème anglaise (Recipe 31.1), omitting the vanilla bean. Stir in 1/2 teaspoon (2 millimeters) vanilla and 2–3 tablespoons (30-45 millimeters) of frangelico, to taste.

♦♦♦

RECIPE 31.30
HOT AND COLD CHOCOLATE

CHRISTOPHER'S AND CHRISTOPHER'S BISTRO, PHOENIX, AZ
Chef/Owner Christopher Gross

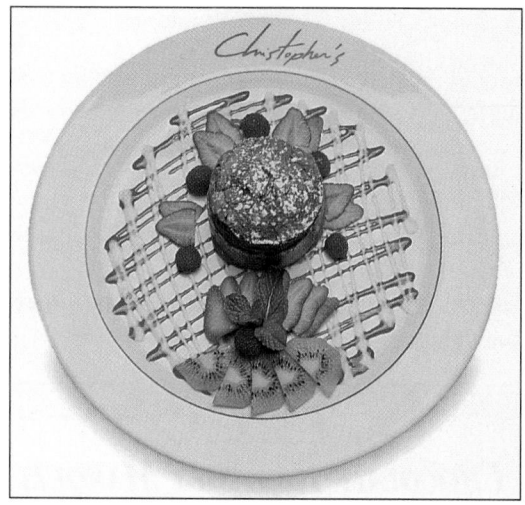

Yield: 1 Serving

Chocolate Ice Cream (recipe follows)	1 portion	
Chocolate Tart Batter (recipe follows)	1 portion	
Espresso Sauce (recipe follows)	as needed	
Dark Chocolate Sauce (recipe follows)	as needed	

1. Mold the chocolate ice cream in a 3-inch-diameter (7.5-centimeter) ring mold and refreeze.
2. Coat another ring mold with melted butter or pan-release spray and place on a sheet pan lined with parchment paper. Fill this ring with the Chocolate Tart batter to a depth of 1 inch (2.5 centimeters).
3. Bake the tart batter at 375°F (190°C) for 3 minutes. The center should still be liquid.
4. Unmold the circle of ice cream in the center of a chilled plate. Carefully unmold the hot chocolate tart and place it on top of the ice cream. Decorate the plate with Espresso and Dark Chocolate Sauces and serve immediately.

CHOCOLATE ICE CREAM

Yield: 10 Servings

Egg yolks	5	5
Granulated sugar	5 oz.	150 g
Cocoa powder	1-1/2 oz.	45 g
Milk	1 pt.	500 ml
Heavy cream	3 oz.	90 g
Semi-sweet chocolate, chopped	4 oz.	120 g

1. Whisk the egg yolks, sugar and cocoa together.
2. Combine the milk and cream and bring to a boil. Temper the egg mixture

with a portion of the hot milk; return the mixture to the saucepan and continue cooking, stirring constantly, until the custard thickens.

3. Remove from the heat and add the chocolate. Stir until the chocolate melts, then strain and chill.

4. Process the custard in an ice cream maker according to the manufacturer's directions.

CHOCOLATE TART BATTER

Yield: 10 Servings

Eggs	5	5
Granulated sugar	6-1/2 oz.	195 g
Unsalted butter, melted	5 oz.	150 g
Dark chocolate, melted	5 oz.	150 g
Pastry flour	1-1/4 oz.	38 g

1. Whisk the eggs and sugar together until thick. Stir in the melted butter and chocolate then fold in the flour.

2. Allow the batter to rest at room temperature for approximately 1 hour before baking.

ESPRESSO AND DARK CHOCOLATE SAUCES

Yield: 6 oz. (180 g) of Each Sauce

Heavy cream	8 oz.	250 g
Vanilla bean	1/2	1/2
Espresso beans	2 oz.	60 g
Egg yolks	4	4
Dark chocolate, chopped	2 oz.	60 g

1. Combine the cream, vanilla bean and espresso beans in a saucepan and bring to a boil.

2. Whisk the egg yolks together in a mixing bowl and temper with one-third of the hot cream.

3. Return the egg-and-cream mixture to the remaining cream and continue cooking, stirring constantly, until thick. Strain.

4. Divide the espresso sauce in half while still warm. Add the chocolate to one half of the warm sauce and stir until melted.

═══════════ ♦♦♦ ═══════════

RECIPE 31.31

BUTTERSCOTCH SAUCE

Yield: 2 qt. (2 lt)

Granulated sugar	1 lb. 8 oz.	720 g
Light corn syrup	2 lb. 4 oz.	1 kg
Unsalted butter	4 oz.	120 g
Heavy cream	10 oz.	300 g
Scotch	4 oz.	120 g

1. Cook the sugar to a dark brown caramel. Add the corn syrup.

2. Remove the sugar from the heat and slowly add the butter and the cream, stirring until the butter is completely melted.

3. Stir in the scotch and cool.

═══════════════ ◆◆◆ ═══════════════

RECIPE 31.32

CHOCOLATE FUDGE SAUCE

Yield: 1 gl. (4 lt)

Heavy cream	2 qt.	2 lt
Light corn syrup	6 oz.	180 g
Granulated sugar	8 oz.	225 g
Bittersweet chocolate	4 lb.	2 kg

1. Combine the cream, corn syrup and sugar in a saucepan and bring just to a boil, stirring frequently.
2. Chop the chocolate and place in a large bowl.
3. Pour the hot cream over the chocolate and stir until completely melted.
4. Store well covered and refrigerated. Gently rewarm over a bain marie if desired.

PART FIVE

MEAL SERVICE AND PRESENTATION

Part V begins with a chapter on Breakfast and Brunch and another on Hors d'Oeuvres and Appetizers. In each, we discuss the preparation and presentation of foods typically associated with these categories. This information is designed to synthesize many of the skills presented earlier in the book.

We then present material on several international cuisines. We emphasize each cuisine's distinguishing flavors and cooking procedures; we do not attempt to provide an array of representative recipes.

Part V concludes with a chapter on plate presentation in which we demonstrate simple yet effective techniques for making foods visually appealing.

CHAPTER 32
BREAKFAST AND BRUNCH

Overcooking or cooking at too high a temperature causes the eggs to become tough and rubbery.

Scrambled eggs are often flavored by sautéing other foods (for example, onions, mushrooms or diced ham) in the pan before adding the eggs or by adding other foods (for example, grated cheeses or herbs) to the eggs just before cooking is complete. Suggested additions include finely diced bell peppers, onions, mushrooms, zucchini or tomatoes; cottage cheese or any variety of shredded firm cheese; crumbled bacon; diced ham, turkey or beef; bits of smoked salmon, cooked shrimp or cooked sausage; and fresh herbs.

PROCEDURE FOR MAKING SCRAMBLED EGGS

1. Break the eggs into a mixing bowl. Season lightly with salt and pepper. Add 1 scant tablespoon (12 milliliters) of milk or cream per egg and whisk everything together.
2. Heat a sauté pan, add clarified butter or oil and heat until the fat begins to sizzle.
3. Sauté any additional ingredients in the hot fat.
4. Pour the eggs into the pan all at once. As the eggs begin to set, slowly stir the mixture with a spatula. Lift cooked portions to allow uncooked egg to flow underneath.
5. Sprinkle on additional ingredients such as cheese or herbs.
6. Cook just until the eggs are set, but still shiny and moist. Remove from the pan and serve immediately.

◆◆◆

RECIPE 32.3

GREEK-STYLE SCRAMBLED EGGS

Yield: 6 6-oz. (180-g) Servings

Eggs	12	12
Heavy cream	2 oz.	60 ml
Salt and pepper	TT	TT
Onion, fine dice	2 oz.	60 g
Clarified butter	3 oz.	90 g
Spinach, chiffonade	2 oz.	60 g
Feta cheese, crumbled	4 oz.	120 g
Greek olives, pitted and chopped	3 Tbsp.	45 ml

1. Combine the eggs, cream, salt and pepper in a mixing bowl. Whisk until well blended.
2. Sauté the onion in the butter until translucent but not brown.
3. Pour the egg mixture into the pan and cook, stirring frequently, until half cooked, approximately 1 minute.
4. Add the spinach to the eggs and continue cooking. Just before the eggs are fully cooked, sprinkle on the cheese.
5. Spoon the cooked egg mixture onto serving plates and garnish with the olives. Serve immediately.

Omelets

Omelets are needlessly intimidating egg creations that begin as scrambled eggs. They are usually prepared as individual servings using two or three eggs. The cooked eggs are then folded around a warm filling.

The filling may contain vegetables, cheeses or meats. Any filling ingredient that needs cooking should be cooked before being added to the omelet. Because the eggs cook relatively quickly, raw fillings would not be properly cooked until the eggs were overcooked.

PROCEDURE FOR MAKING FOLDED OMELETS

1. Fully cook any meats and blanch or otherwise cook any vegetables that will be incorporated into the omelet.
2. Heat an omelet pan over moderately high heat and add clarified butter.
3. Whisk the eggs together in a small bowl. Season with salt and pepper if desired.
4. Pour the eggs into the pan and stir until they begin to set, approximately 10 seconds.
5. Pull cooked egg from the sides of the pan toward the center, allowing raw egg to run underneath. Continue doing so for 20–30 seconds.
6. Spoon any fillings on top of the eggs or add any other garnishes.
7. When cooked as desired, flip one side of the omelet toward the center with a spatula or a shake of the pan. Slide the omelet onto the serving plate so that it lands folded in thirds with the seam underneath.
8. Spoon any sauce or additional filling on top, garnish as desired and serve immediately.

1. Lifting the edge of the eggs to allow them to cook evenly.

2. Adding the filling to the eggs.

◆◆◆

RECIPE 32.4

SHRIMP AND AVOCADO OMELET

Yield: 1 Serving

Shrimp, peeled, deveined and cut into pieces	3 oz.	90 g
Green onion, sliced	1 Tbsp.	15 ml
Clarified butter	1 oz.	30 g
Eggs	3	3
Salt and pepper	TT	TT
Avocado, peeled and diced	1/4	1/4
Cilantro, chopped	2 tsp.	10 ml

1. Sauté the shrimp and onion in half of the butter for 1 minute. Remove from the heat and set aside.
2. Heat an omelet pan and add the remaining butter.
3. Whisk the eggs together in a small bowl, season with salt and pepper and pour into the omelet pan.
4. Stir the eggs as they cook. Stop when they begin to set. Lift the edges as the omelet cooks to allow the raw eggs to run underneath.
5. When the eggs are nearly set, add the shrimp filling, avocado and cilantro. Fold the front of the eggs over and roll the omelet onto a plate.

3. Folding the eggs.

4. Rolling the omelet onto the plate.

Frittatas

Frittatas are essentially open-faced omelets of Spanish-Italian heritage. They may be cooked in small pans as individual portions or in large pans, then cut into wedges for service. A relatively large amount of hearty ingredients are mixed directly into the eggs. The eggs are first cooked on the stove top, then the pan is transferred to an oven or placed under a salamander or broiler to finish cooking.

PROCEDURE FOR MAKING FRITTATAS

1. Fully cook any meats and blanch or otherwise prepare any vegetables that will be incorporated into the frittata.
2. Heat a sauté pan and add clarified butter.
3. Whisk the eggs, flavorings and any other ingredients together; pour into the pan.
4. Stir gently until the eggs start to set. Gently lift the cooked eggs at the edge of the frittata so that the raw eggs can run underneath. Continue cooking until the eggs are almost set.
5. Place the pan in a hot oven or underneath a salamander or broiler to finish cooking and lightly brown the top.
6. Slide the finished frittata out of the pan onto a serving platter.

◆◆◆

RECIPE 32.5

GARDEN FRITTATA

Yield: 1 Serving

Chicken breast, 4 oz. (120 g), boneless, skinless	1	1
Garlic, chopped	1 tsp.	5 ml
Cumin	TT	TT
Salt and pepper	TT	TT
Mushrooms, sliced	2 oz.	60 g
Unsalted butter	3 Tbsp.	45 g
Jalapeño, seeded, minced	1 tsp.	5 ml
Red bell pepper, roasted, seeded, peeled, julienne	2 oz.	60 g
Green onions, sliced	1 oz.	30 g
Cilantro	2 tsp.	10 ml
Eggs, beaten	2	2
Monterey Jack or cheddar cheese	2 oz.	60 g

1. Rub the chicken breast with the garlic, cumin, salt and pepper. Grill or broil the chicken until done. Allow it to rest briefly, then cut into strips.
2. In a well-seasoned 9-inch (23-centimeter) sauté pan, sauté the mushrooms in the butter until tender. Add the jalapeños and sauté for 30 seconds. Add the chicken, roasted pepper, green onions and cilantro and sauté until hot.
3. Add the eggs and season with salt and pepper. Cook the mixture, stirring and lifting the eggs to help them cook evenly, until they begin to set.
4. Sprinkle the cheese over the eggs and place under a salamander or broiler to melt the cheese and finish cooking the eggs. Slide the frittata onto a plate or cut into wedges for smaller portions.

Pan-Frying

Pan-fried eggs are commonly referred to as sunny-side-up or over-easy, over-medium or over-hard. These are visibly different products produced with proper timing and technique. Very fresh eggs are best for pan-frying as the yolk holds its shape better and the white spreads less.

Sunny-side-up eggs are not turned during cooking; their yellow yolks remain visible. They should be cooked over medium-low heat long enough to firm the whites and partially firm the yolks: approximately 4 minutes if cooked on a 250°F (120°C) cooking surface.

For "over" eggs, the egg is partially cooked on one side, then gently flipped and cooked on the other side until done. The egg white should be firm and its edges should not be brown. The yolk should never be broken regardless of the degree of doneness. Not only is a broken yolk unattractive, the spilled yolk will coagulate on contact with the hot pan, making it difficult to serve.

For over-easy eggs, the yolk should remain very runny; on a 250°F (120°C) cooking surface, the egg should cook for about 3 minutes on the first side and 2 minutes on the other. Eggs fried over-medium should be cooked slightly longer, until the yolk is partially set. For over-hard eggs, the yolk should be completely cooked.

PROCEDURE FOR PAN-FRYING EGGS

1. Select a sauté pan just large enough to accommodate the number of eggs being cooked. (An 8-inch-diameter [20-centimeter] pan is appropriate for up to three eggs.)

2. Add a small amount of clarified butter and heat until the fat just begins to sizzle.

3. Carefully break the eggs into the pan.

4. Continue cooking over medium-low heat until the eggs reach the appropriate degree of firmness. Sunny-side-up eggs are not flipped during cooking; "over" eggs are flipped once during cooking.

5. When done, gently flip the "over" eggs once again so that the first side is up, then gently slide the cooked eggs out of the pan onto the serving plate. Serve immediately.

Basted eggs are a variation of sunny-side-up eggs. Basted eggs are cooked over low heat with the hot butter from the pan spooned over them as they cook. Another version of basted eggs is made by adding 1–2 teaspoons (5–10 milliliters) of water to the sauté pan and then covering the pan. The steam cooks the top of the eggs.

Moist-Heat Cooking Methods

In-Shell Cooking (Simmering)

The difference between **soft-cooked eggs** (also called soft-boiled) and **hard-cooked eggs** (also called hard-boiled) is time. Both styles refer to eggs cooked in their shell in hot water. Despite the word "boiled" in their names, eggs cooked in the shell should never be boiled. Boiling toughens eggs and causes discoloration. Instead, eggs should be simmered. Soft-cooked eggs are usually simmered for 3–5 minutes; hard-cooked eggs may be simmered for as long as 12–15 minutes.

Sometimes it is difficult to remove the shell from very fresh eggs. Eggs that are a few days old are better for cooking in the shell.

PROCEDURE FOR MAKING SOFT-COOKED EGGS

1. Fill a saucepan or stockpot with sufficient water to cover the eggs. Bring the water to a simmer.
2. Carefully lower each egg into the simmering water. Simmer uncovered for 3–5 minutes, depending on the firmness desired.
3. Lift each egg out of the water with a slotted spoon or spider. Crack the large end of the shell carefully and serve immediately.

PROCEDURE FOR MAKING HARD-COOKED EGGS

1. Repeat steps 1 and 2 for soft-cooked eggs, simmering the eggs for 12–15 minutes.
2. Lift each egg out of the water with a slotted spoon or spider and place in an ice bath.
3. When the eggs are cool enough to handle, peel them and use as desired or cover and refrigerate for up to 5 days.

Poaching

Eggs that are to be poached should always be very fresh. They should also be kept very cold until used. Cold egg whites stay together better when dropped into hot water. Poached eggs should be soft and moist; the whites should be firm enough to encase the yolk completely, but the yolk should still be runny.

Some chefs add salt to the poaching water for flavor; others feel the salt causes the egg whites to separate. To help the egg whites cling together, add 2 tablespoons (30 milliliters) of white vinegar per quart (liter) of water.

PROCEDURE FOR POACHING EGGS

1. Fill a saucepan or stockpot with at least 3 inches (7.5 centimeters) of water. Add salt and vinegar if desired. Bring the water to a simmer and hold at a temperature of approximately 200°F (90°C).
2. One at a time, crack the eggs into a small ramekin or cup. If a piece of shell falls into the egg, it can be removed; if the yolk breaks, the egg can be set aside for some other use.
3. Gently slide each egg into the simmering water and cook for 3–5 minutes.
4. Lift the poached egg out of the water with a slotted spoon. Trim any ragged edges with a paring knife. Serve immediately.

For quantity service, eggs can be poached in advance and held for up to one day. To do so, cook the eggs as described above. As each egg is removed from the hot water, set it in a hotel pan filled with ice water. This stops the cooking process. The eggs can be stored in the ice water until needed. For banquet-style service, all of the eggs can be reheated at once by placing the entire pan on the stove top. Or, the eggs can be reheated one or two at a time by placing them in a pan of barely simmering water until they are hot.

◆◆◆

RECIPE 32.6

POACHED EGGS

Yield: 1 Serving

Water	as needed	as needed
Salt	1 tsp.	5 ml
Vinegar	2 Tbsp.	30 ml
Eggs	2	2

1. Bring the water to a simmer; add the salt and vinegar.

2. Crack one egg into a cup and carefully add it to the water. Repeat with the other egg.

3. Cook the eggs to the desired doneness, approximately 3–5 minutes. Remove them from the water with a slotted spoon and serve as desired or carefully lower them into ice water and refrigerate for later use.

1. Adding an egg to a pot of simmering water.

2. Lowering the eggs into ice water to cool them for future use.

BREAKFAST MEATS

At other meals, meat is typically the principal food, but at breakfast it is usually an accompaniment. Breakfast meats tend to be spicy or highly flavored. A hearty breakfast menu may include a small beef steak (usually sirloin and often pan-fried) or pork chop. Corned beef, roast beef or roast turkey can be diced or shredded, then sautéed with potatoes and other ingredients for a breakfast hash. Fish, particularly smoked products, are also served at breakfast.

But the most popular breakfast meats are bacon (including Canadian-style bacon), ham and sausages. They are all discussed in Chapter 20, Charcuterie. Bacon can be cooked on a flat griddle, in a heavy skillet or baked on a sheet pan. Regardless of the method used, the cooked bacon should be drained on absorbent paper towels to remove excess fat. Canadian-style bacon is very lean and requires little cooking, although slices are usually sautéed briefly before serving. The round slices may be served like ham and are essential for eggs Benedict. A ham steak is simply a thick slice ideal for breakfast. Fully cooked ham only needs to be heated briefly on a griddle or in a sauté pan before service. The most popular breakfast sausages are made from uncured, uncooked meats. They can be mild to spicy, slightly sweet or strongly seasoned with is still popular, especially with toppings such as cream, brown sugar, fresh or dried fruit or fruit preserves. Grits, made from ground corn, are another grain product served hot at breakfast. Grits may be topped with butter and presented as a starch side dish or served in a bowl as a porridge with cream and brown sugar. Oats and oatmeal, grits and other grains are discussed in Chapter 23, Potatoes, Grains and Pasta.

Ready-to-eat (cold) cereal is usually topped with milk or light cream and sugar. Fresh or dried fruits may be added. Many products are enriched or fortified with vitamins and minerals to compensate for the nutrients lost during processing. Creative cooks can avoid overly sweet, artificially flavored commercial products by making their own ready-to-eat breakfast cereals such as granola, a toasted blend of whole grains, nuts and dried fruits. The results are less expensive, more nutritious and far more interesting.

◆◆◆

RECIPE 32.10
CRUNCHY GRANOLA

Yield: 12 c. (3 lt)

Brown sugar	8 oz.	250 g
Water, hot	4 oz.	120 g
Canola oil	6 oz.	180 g
Old-fashioned oats	18 oz.	500 g
Wheat germ	4 oz.	120 g
Coconut, shredded	2-1/2 oz.	75 g
Salt (optional)	1 Tbsp.	15 ml
Whole wheat flour	2 oz.	60 g
Amaranth flour	2 oz.	60 g
Unbleached all-purpose flour	2 oz.	60 g
Yellow cornmeal	2 oz.	60 g
Pecans, chopped	4 oz.	120 g

1. Dissolve the brown sugar in the hot water. Add the oil.
2. Combine the dry ingredients in a large bowl. Mix thoroughly by hand.
3. Add the brown-sugar-and-oil mixture to the dry ingredients; toss to combine.
4. Spread out the granola in a thin layer on a sheet pan. Bake at 200°F (90°C) until crisp, approximately 1-1/2 to 2 hours. Toss lightly with a metal spatula every 30 minutes.
5. Let the baked granola cool completely at room temperature, then store in an airtight container. Chopped dried fruits, additional nuts or fresh fruits can be added at service time.

NUTRITION

Most nutritionists agree that you and your customers should start the day with a nutritious breakfast. Depending upon what is eaten, a breakfast can supply a good percentage of the day's proteins, carbohydrates, fats, vitamins and minerals.

TABLE 32.1   NUTRITIONAL VALUES OF SELECTED BREAKFAST FOODS

Per portion as noted	Kcal	Protein (g)	Carbohydrates (g)	Total Fat (g)	Saturated Fat (g)	Cholesterol (mg)	Sodium (mg)
Coffee, brewed, 6 oz. (180 ml)	4	0.1	0.8	0	0	0	4
Cream, light, 1 oz. (30 ml)	55	0.8	1	5.5	3.4	19	11
Sugar, granulated, 1 Tbsp. (15 ml)	46	0	11.9	0	0	0	trace
Orange juice, fresh, 6 oz. (180 ml)	83	1.3	19.3	0.4	<0.1	0	2
Egg, hard-cooked, 1 large	77	6.3	0.6	5.3	1.6	213	62
Egg, pan-fried in margarine, 1 large	91	6.2	0.6	6.9	1.9	211	162
Bacon, cooked, 3 slices (20 slices per lb)	109	5.8	0.1	9.4	3.3	16	303
English muffin, 1	130	4.3	25.4	1.3	na	0	206
Corn flakes, 1 oz. (28 g)	100	2	24	0	0	0	250
Milk, 8 oz. (240 ml)	88	7.2	11.2	1.6	0.8	8	240

The Corrine T. Netzer Encyclopedia of Food Values 1992
na = not available

CONCLUSION

Breakfast is an important meal for consumers and food service operations alike. Breakfast menus may offer a variety of items, including fruits, cereals, eggs, pancakes and cured meats, or they can be devoted to one or two specialty items such as coffee and cinnamon rolls. Whatever is served should be prepared and served with care.

QUESTIONS FOR DISCUSSION

1. Explain the differences between a typical breakfast and a typical brunch. Create a sample menu for each of these meals.
2. Explain the difference between an omelet and a frittata.
3. Describe four different types of fried eggs and explain how each is prepared.
4. What is the difference between a soft-cooked egg and a hard-cooked egg? Why are these eggs simmered instead of boiled?
5. List three types of griddlecakes and explain how they are prepared.
6. What problems might be encountered when preparing French toast with very thick slices of bread? How can you avoid these problems?
7. Should meats be fully cooked before being incorporated in egg dishes such as omelettes and quiches? Explain your answer.

*A*DDITIONAL *B*REAKFAST *R*ECIPES

RECIPE 32.11

CAMPTON PLACE BAGELS
WITH SMOKED TROUT CREAM CHEESE

NOTE: *This dish appears in the Chapter Opening photograph.*

CAMPTON PLACE RESTAURANT, KEMPINSKI HOTELS, SAN FRANCISCO, CA
Chef Jan Birnbaum

Yield: 24 Bagels;
24-oz. (720-g) Spread

Dry yeast	1 Tbsp.	15 ml
Water (95°F/35°C)	8 oz.	250 g
Granulated sugar	3 Tbsp.	45 ml
Malt	3 Tbsp.	45 ml
Flour	1 lb.	450 g
Salt	1 Tbsp.	15 ml
Vegetable oil	2 Tbsp.	30 ml
Egg wash	as needed	as needed
Cream cheese	1 lb.	450 g
Crème fraîche or sour cream	4 oz.	120 g
Pepper, cracked	1/2 tsp.	3 g
Chives, cut	4 Tbsp.	60 ml
Smoked trout	1 lb.	450 g

1. To make the bagels, dissolve the yeast in the water.
2. Thoroughly combine the sugar, malt, flour and salt.
3. Add the oil to the yeast solution, then add the liquid ingredients to the dry ingredients. Mix thoroughly and knead the dough until hands and board come clean. Cover with a moist towel and allow to proof in a warm place (70–85°F/21–29°C) until doubled.
4. Punch down and cut into 1-ounce (30-gram) pieces. Roll into doughnut shapes. Proof the bagels for 15 minutes.
5. Blanch the bagels in simmering water for 4 minutes, turning once. Remove and place on a sheet pan lined with parchment paper.
6. Brush with egg wash and bake at 350°F (180°C) until golden, approximately 20 minutes.
7. To make the cream cheese with smoked trout, whisk the cream cheese in an electric mixer with the paddle attachment for approximately 5 minutes to incorporate air.
8. Add the crème fraîche and whisk for 2–3 minutes.
9. Add the pepper and chives and mix until incorporated, approximately 30 seconds.
10. Fold in 4 ounces (120 g) of the trout by hand.
11. To assemble, spread 2 ounces (60 grams) of smoked trout on one half of each bagel. Top with two or three thin slices of smoked trout.
12. Place a poached or basted egg on the other half of the bagel.
13. Garnish the plate with fresh tomatoes and baby greens. Serve immediately.

✦✦✦

RECIPE 32.12

HOT CHOCOLATE MOUSSE

Yield: 2 Servings

Milk	8 oz.	250 g
Heavy cream	8 oz.	250 g
Chocolate Fudge Sauce, Recipe 31.32	3 oz.	90 g

1. Heat the milk with 4 ounces (120 grams) of the heavy cream and the fudge sauce over moderate heat, stirring constantly, until almost boiling.

2. Whip the remaining heavy cream to soft peaks.

3. Portion the hot chocolate into warmed cups. Serve the whipped cream on the side.

✦✦✦

RECIPE 32.13

SPICED CIDER

Yield: 2 qt. (2 lt)

Apple cider	1 qt.	1 lt
Orange or cranberry juice	1 qt.	1 lt
Brown sugar	2 oz.	60 g
Cinnamon sticks	2	2
Cloves, whole	5	5
Allspice, whole	5	5

1. Combine all ingredients in a nonreactive saucepan over medium-low heat.

2. Bring the mixture to a simmer, cover and remove from the heat. Let steep for 10–15 minutes. Strain and serve garnished with sliced lemon or a cinnamon stick.

✦✦✦

RECIPE 32.14

ARTICHOKE FRITTATA

THE INN OF THE WHITE SALMON, WHITE SALMON, WA

Yield: 1 9-inch-round (22-cm) frittata

Artichoke hearts, cooked, fresh or canned	8 oz.	250 g
Unsalted butter	1 oz.	30 g
Parmesan cheese, grated	2 oz.	60 g
Eggs	10	10
Half-and-half	6 oz.	180 g
Monterey Jack cheese, grated	4 oz.	120 g

1. Quarter the artichoke hearts.

2. Melt the butter in a sauté pan. Add the artichokes and sauté until heated through but not browned.

3. Distribute the artichokes in an even layer on the bottom of a 9-inch-round

Continued

(22 centimeter) nonstick pan. Sprinkle with 1 ounce (30 grams) of the Parmesan cheese.

4. In a small mixing bowl, whisk the eggs together with the half-and-half. Pour over the artichokes.

5. Sprinkle the Monterey Jack cheese over the entire pan.

6. Bake for 30 minutes at 350°F (180°C). Remove from the oven and sprinkle the remaining 1 ounce (30 grams) of Parmesan cheese over the frittata. Return to the oven until the cheese is melted and light brown, approximately 5 minutes.

RECIPE 32.15

LOBSTER SCRAMBLED EGGS WITH SOFT-SHELL CRAB

CAMPTON PLACE RESTAURANT, KEMPINSKI HOTELS, SAN FRANCISCO, CA
Executive Chef Jan Birnbaum

Yield: 4 Servings

Fresh soft-shell crabs	2	2
Lobster, 1-1/4 lb. (.5 kg)	1	1
Eggs	10	10
Half-and-half	8 oz.	250 g
Salt and white pepper	TT	TT
New potatoes	1 lb.	500 g
Vegetable oil	5 Tbsp.	75 ml
Onion, medium dice	8 oz.	250 g
Flour, seasoned with salt and white pepper	5 oz.	150 g
Unsalted butter	1 Tbsp.	15 ml

1. Clean the soft-shell crabs. Cut in half and reserve.

2. Cook the lobster in salted water for 3 to 4 minutes and refresh in ice water. Remove the meat from the shells and cut it into 1/2-inch (1.2-centimeter) pieces.

3. In a separate bowl, vigorously whisk together the eggs and half-and-half. Season with salt and white pepper.

4. Wash and dry the potatoes. Toss them in 1 tablespoon (15 milliliters) oil, season with salt and white pepper and roast at 350°F (180°C) for 15 to 25 minutes. They should be undercooked and still very firm. Cut them in half.

5. Sauté the onions in 1 tablespoon (15 milliliters) of oil until soft and translucent. Add 1 tablespoon (15 milliliters) of oil and the potatoes, placing them in the pan with the cut side down. Sauté 1 minute without turning the potatoes. Place in a 300°F (150°C) oven while finishing eggs.

6. Dust the crabs in seasoned flour and sauté them in 2 tablespoons (30 milliliters) of oil. Drain and reserve in warm place.

7. Melt the butter in a nonstick pan. Add the egg mixture and cook over low to medium heat, stirring vigorously and constantly with a rubber spatula. When the eggs begin to set, add the lobster. When the eggs are nearly set, pour them into four 4-inch (10-centimeter) buttered circular rings placed on a nonstick pan. Place in preheated 325°F (160°C) oven and bake for 3 to 4 minutes.

8. Place one ring of eggs in the center of each plate and remove the ring.

9. Place the potatoes around the baked eggs. Stand one crab half on the side of each plate.

✦✦✦

RECIPE 32.16

HOMINY CORNCAKES WITH HAM AND POACHED EGGS IN PIPERADE SAUCE

CAMPTON PLACE RESTAURANT, KEMPINSKI HOTELS, San Francisco, CA
Executive Chef Jan Birnbaum

Yield: 6 Servings

Milk	1 qt.	1 lt
Corn cobs, chopped coarse	2	2
Unsalted butter	2 oz.	60 g
Salt and pepper	TT	TT
Dry grits	1 c.	250 ml
Fresh corn kernels, sautéed	4 oz.	120 g
Chives, cut fine	2 bunches	2 bunches
Red bell peppers, julienne	2	2
Yellow bell peppers, julienne	2	2
Yellow onion, julienne	1	1
Olive oil	2 oz.	60 g
White wine	8 oz.	225 g
Fresh thyme	2 Tbsp.	30 ml
Eggs, poached	12	12
Prosciutto, sliced very thin	12 pieces	12 pieces

1. To make the hominy cakes, bring the milk to a boil with the corn cobs. Remove from the heat and allow to steep for 10 minutes. Strain out the cobs.

2. Return the milk to a boil and add the butter, salt and pepper. As soon as the butter melts, add the grits to the boiling liquid.

3. Cook over low heat, stirring often, for approximately 15–20 minutes. Add the cooked corn kernels and the chives.

4. Spread the mixture out on a lightly greased sheet pan. Cool at least 2 hours in the refrigerator. Cut out 6-inch (15-centimeter) circles of the mixture and cook on a griddle to brown and reheat at time of service.

5. To make the Piperade, sauté the peppers and onion in the olive oil until tender. Deglaze the pan with the wine and allow to reduce. Season with the thyme and salt and pepper.

6. To assemble, place one freshly griddled corncake on a warm plate. Top with the warm Piperade. Arrange two slices of prosciutto and two poached eggs on the plate. Serve immediately.

Salt	1/2 tsp.	2 ml
Flour	4 oz.	120 g
Clarified butter	as needed	as needed
Ricotta cheese	12 oz.	350 g
Egg yolk	1	1
Salt	1/4 tsp.	1 ml
Lemon juice	1 tsp.	5 ml
Vanilla extract	1 tsp.	5 ml
Butter	2 oz.	60 g

1. To make the batter, whisk together the eggs, milk and oil. Add the salt. Stir in the flour and mix until smooth. Allow the batter to rest for 30 minutes.
2. Heat a crepe pan and add a small amount of clarified butter.
3. Add 1 ounce (30 grams) of the batter to the pan. Tip the pan so the batter coats the entire surface in a thin layer.
4. Cook the pancake until browned on the bottom. Remove it from the pan.
5. To make the filling, drain the cheese in a china cap. Combine the remaining ingredients (except the butter) with the cheese and mix well.
6. To assemble, place a pancake on the work surface with the cooked side down. Place 1 ounce (30 grams) of the filling in the center of the pancake. Fold the opposite ends in and then roll up to form a small package.
7. Sauté each blintz in butter until hot. Serve with sour cream or fruit compote as desired.

RECIPE 32.21
BANANA BRIOCHE FRENCH TOAST

CAMPTON PLACE RESTAURANT, KEMPINSKI HOTELS, SAN FRANCISCO, CA
Executive Chef Jan Birnbaum

Yield: 4 Servings

Bananas, sliced	3	3
Lemon juice	2 Tbsp.	30 ml
Zest of two lemons		
Brioche, sliced 1-1/2 inches (3.7 cm) thick	12 slices	12 slices
Eggs	10	10
Heavy cream	11 oz.	330 g
Salt	pinch	pinch
Cinnamon, ground	1/2 tsp.	2 ml
Nutmeg	1/4 tsp.	1 ml
Granulated sugar	3 oz.	90 g
Vanilla extract	1 tsp.	5 ml
Unsalted butter	as needed	as needed
Powdered sugar	as needed	as needed
Mango preserves	as needed	as needed
Macadamia nuts, chopped	as needed	as needed

1. Toss the bananas with the lemon juice and zest.
2. Cut into one side of each slice of bread to create a deep pocket. Stuff the pocket with the banana slices.
3. Whisk together the eggs, cream, salt, cinnamon, nutmeg, sugar and vanilla.

Soak the stuffed bread in this mixture until very soggy. Remove from the egg mixture and drain briefly.

4. Sauté the soaked bread in butter until golden brown on each side. Place in a 375°F (190°C) oven and bake until the bread puffs, approximately 3–4 minutes.

5. Dust with powdered sugar and top with mango preserves and macadamia nuts.

CHAPTER 33

HORS d'Oeuvres
AND
Appetizers

After studying this chapter you will be able to:

♦ prepare and serve a variety of cold and hot hors d'oeuvres
♦ prepare a variety of appetizers
♦ choose hors d'oeuvres and appetizers that are appropriate for the meal or event

*H*ors d'oeuvres, whether hot or cold, are very small portions of foods served before the meal to stimulate the appetite. Hors d'oeuvres can be passed elegantly by waiters or displayed on buffets. Appetizers, whether hot or cold, are generally the first course or introduction to a meal; they are more typically served with dinner than with lunch. Sometimes there is very little difference between an hors d'oeuvre and an appetizer.

Preparing hors d'oeuvres and appetizers uses skills from almost every work station. Because they can consist of meat, poultry, fish, shellfish, vegetables, potatoes, grains, pasta, fruits, baked goods and sauces, they require a detailed knowledge of these foods and how they are prepared.

Although both hors d'oeuvres and appetizers can be divided into hot and cold varieties, it is difficult (and unnecessary) to further categorize them because of the vast variety possible and the absence of any one dominant food type or style.

HORS D'OEUVRES

The French term *hors d'oeuvre* translates as "outside the work." Its usage was correct under the classic kitchen brigade system, for it was the service staff's responsibility to prepare small tidbits for guests to enjoy while the kitchen prepared the meal. Today, however, the kitchen staff prepares the hors d'oeuvres as well as the meals. Cold hors d'oeuvres are usually prepared by the *garde-manger*; hot ones are prepared in the main kitchen.

There are really only two limitations on the type of food and manner of preparation that can be used for hors d'oeuvres: the chef's imagination and the foods at his or her disposal. There are, however, a few guidelines.

GUIDELINES FOR PREPARING HORS D'OEUVRES

1. They should be small, one to two bites.
2. They should be flavorful and well seasoned without being overpowering.
3. They should be visually attractive.
4. They should complement the foods to follow without duplicating their flavors.

Cold Hors d'Oeuvres

Cold hors d'oeuvres are divided here into five broad categories based upon preparation method, principal ingredient or presentation style. They are: canapés, caviars, crudités, dips and sushi. These categories may vary somewhat from classical teachings, but they are completely appropriate for modern menus and food service operations.

Canapés

Canapés are tiny, open-faced sandwiches. They are constructed from a base, a spread and one or more garnishes.

The most common **canapé base** is a thin slice of bread cut into an interesting shape and toasted. Although most any variety of bread can be used, spiced, herbed or otherwise flavored breads may be inappropriate for some spreads or garnishes. Melba toasts, crackers or slices of firm vegetables such as cucumbers or zucchini are also popular canapé bases. The base must be strong enough to support the weight of the spread and garnish without falling apart when handled.

The **canapé spread** provides much of the canapé's flavor. Spreads are usually flavored butters, cream cheese or a combination of the two. Several examples of spreads are listed in Table 33.1. Each of the spreads is made by adding the desired amount of the main ingredient (chopped or puréed as appropriate) and seasonings to softened butter or cream cheese and mixing until combined. Quantities and proportions vary according to individual tastes. Other canapé spreads include bound salads (for example, tuna or egg), finely chopped shrimp or liver mousse. Any of a number of ingredients can be combined for spreads, provided the following guidelines are followed.

GUIDELINES FOR MAKING CANAPÉ SPREADS

1. The spread's texture should be smooth enough to produce attractive designs if piped through a pastry bag fitted with a decorative tip.
2. The spread's consistency should be firm enough to hold its shape when piped onto the base, yet soft enough to stick to the base and hold the garnishes in place.
3. The spread's flavor should complement the garnishes and be flavorful enough to stimulate the appetite without being overpowering.

A spread may be a substantial portion of the canapé as well as its distinguishing characteristic. Or it can be applied sparingly and used more as a means of gluing the garnish to the base than as a principal ingredient.

Canapés with bread bases tend to become soggy quickly from both the moisture in the spread and the moisture in the refrigerator where they are stored. Using a spread made with butter will help keep the bread bases crispier, as will buttering the base with a thin coat of softened plain butter before piping on the spread. The best way to ensure a crisp base is to make the canapés as close to service time as possible.

The variety of **canapé garnishes** is vast. The garnish can dominate or complement the spread, or it can be a simple sprig of parsley intended to provide visual appeal but little flavor. Although several ingredients can be used to garnish the same canapé, remember the limitations imposed by the canapé's size and purpose.

PROCEDURE FOR MAKING CANAPÉS

This procedure can be adapted and used with a variety of ingredients to produce a variety of canapés. If the canapé base is a bread crouton, begin with step 1. If some other product is used as the base, prepare that base and begin with step 4.

1. Trim the crust from an unsliced loaf of bread. Slice the bread lengthwise approximately 1/3 inch (8 millimeters) thick.

TABLE 33.1   A SELECTION OF CANAPÉ SPREADS AND SUGGESTED GARNISHES

Spread	Suggested Garnishes
Anchovy butter	Hard-cooked eggs, capers, green or black olive slices
Blue cheese	Grape half, walnuts, roast beef roulade, pear slice, currants, watercress
Caviar butter	Caviar, lemon, egg slice, chives
Deviled ham	Cornichons, mustard butter, sliced radish
Horseradish butter	Smoked salmon, roast beef, smoked trout, marinated herring, capers, parsley
Lemon butter	Shrimp, crab, caviar, salmon, chives, parsley, black olive slices
Liver pâté	Truffle slice, cornichon
Mustard butter	Smoked meats, pâté, dry salami coronet, cornichon
Pimento cream cheese	Smoked oyster, sardine, pimento, parsley
Shrimp butter	Poached bay scallops, shrimp, caviar, parsley
Tuna salad	Capers, cornichons, sliced radish

2. Cut the bread slices into the desired shapes using a serrated bread knife or canapé cutter.
3. Brush the bread shapes with melted butter and bake in a 350°F (180°C) oven until they are toasted and dry. Remove and cool.
4. If desired, spread each base with a thin layer of softened plain butter.
5. Apply the spread to the base. If a thin layer is desired, use a palette knife. If a thicker or more decorative layer is desired, pipe the spread onto the base using a pastry bag and decorative tip.
6. Garnish the canapé as desired.
7. If desired, glaze each canapé with a thin coating of aspic jelly. The aspic jelly can be applied with a small spoon or a spray bottle designated for that purpose.

Barquettes, Tartlets and Profiteroles

Barquettes, tartlets and profiteroles are all adaptations of the basic canapé. A **barquette** is a tiny boat-shaped shell made from a savory dough such as pâte brisée. A **tartlet** is simply a round version of a barquette. A **profiterole** is a small puff made from pâte à choux. These three items can be prepared like canapés by filling them with flavored spreads and garnishing as desired.

Other Types of Canapés

Vegetables such as cherry tomatoes, blanched snow peas, mushroom caps and Belgian endive leaves are sometimes used as canapé bases. They are filled and garnished in the same manner as barquettes, tartlets and profiteroles.

Caviar

Caviar, considered by many to be the ultimate hors d'oeuvre, is the salted roe (eggs) of the sturgeon fish. In the United States, only sturgeon roe can be labeled as simply "caviar." Roe from other fish must be qualified as such on the label (e.g., salmon caviar or lumpfish caviar).

Most of the world's caviar comes from sturgeon harvested in the Caspian Sea and imported from Russia and Iran. Imported sturgeon caviar, classified according to the sturgeon species and the roe's size and color, includes **beluga**, **osetra** and **sevruga** as well as **pressed caviar**. Most of the caviar consumed in this country, however, comes from either domestic sturgeon or other fish and is labeled **American sturgeon caviar**, **golden whitefish caviar**, **lumpfish caviar** or **salmon caviar**.

Purchasing and Storing Caviars

Although all caviar is processed with salt, the best caviar is labeled **malassol**, which means "little salt." Caviar should smell fresh, with no off odors. The eggs should be whole, not broken, and they should be crisp and pop when pressed with the tongue. Excessive oiliness may be caused by a large number of broken eggs. The best way to test caviar's quality is to taste it. Remember, price alone does not necessarily indicate quality.

Most caviar can be purchased fresh or pasteurized in tins or jars ranging from one ounce (28 grams) to over four pounds (2 kilograms). Some caviars are also available frozen. (Frozen caviar should be used only as a garnish and should not be served by itself.) In order to ensure the freshest possible product, always purchase caviar in small quantities as often as possible based on your needs.

Fresh caviar should be stored at 32°F (0°C). Because most refrigerators are considerably warmer than that, store the caviar on ice in the coldest part of the refrigerator and change the ice often. If properly handled, fresh caviar will last one to two weeks before opening and several days after opening. Pasteurized caviar does not require refrigeration until it is opened and will last several days in the refrigerator after opening.

Serving Caviars

Fine caviar should be served in its original container or a nonmetal bowl on a bed of crushed ice, accompanied only by lightly buttered toasts or blinis and sour cream. Connoisseurs prefer china, bone or other nonmetal utensils for serving caviar because metal reacts with the caviar, producing off flavors.

Lesser-quality caviars are often served on ice, accompanied by minced onion, chopped hard-cooked egg whites and yolks (separately), lemon, sour cream and buttered toasts.

Lumpfish and other nonsturgeon caviars are usually not served by themselves. Rather, they are used as ingredients in or garnishes for other dishes.

Crudités

Crudité, a French word meaning "raw thing," generally refers to raw or slightly blanched vegetables served as an hors d'oeuvre. Although almost any vegetable will do, the most commonly used are broccoli, cauliflower, carrots, celery, asparagus and green beans, all of which are often blanched, and cucumbers, zucchini, yellow squash, radishes, green onions, cherry tomatoes, Belgian endive leaves, mushrooms, peppers and jicama, which are served raw.

When preparing crudités, use only the freshest and best-looking produce available. Because they are displayed and eaten raw, blemishes and imperfections cannot be disguised. Vegetables, both blanched and raw, should be cut into attractive shapes. Crudités are usually served with one or more dips.

Dips

Dips can be served hot or cold and as an accompaniment to crudités, crackers, chips, toasts, breads or other foods.

Beluga—*the most expensive caviar, it comes from the largest species (the sturgeon can weigh up to 1750 pounds/800 kilograms); the dark gray and well separated eggs are the largest and most fragile kind.*

Osetra—*considered by some connoisseurs to be the best caviar, the eggs are medium-sized, golden yellow to brown in color and quite oily.*

Sevruga—*harvested from small sturgeon, the eggs are quite small and light to dark gray in color.*

Pressed caviar—*a processed caviar made from osetra and sevruga roes. The eggs are cleaned, packed in linen bags and hung to drain; as salt and moisture drain away, the natural shape of the eggs is destroyed and the eggs are pressed together. Approximately 3 pounds (1.3 kilograms) of roe produce only 1 pound (450 grams) of pressed caviar; pressed caviar has a spreadable, jamlike consistency.*

American sturgeon caviar—*not considered of the same quality as Russian or Iranian caviars, nevertheless, roe from sturgeon harvested in the coastal waters of the American northwest and the Tennessee River is becoming increasingly popular, due in part to its relatively low price.*

Golden Whitefish caviar—*the small and very crisp eggs are a natural golden color and come from whitefish native to the northern Great Lakes.*

Lumpfish caviar—*readily available and reasonably priced, is produced from lumpfish harvested in the North Atlantic. The small and very crisp eggs are dyed black, red or gold; the food coloring is not stable, however, and when used to garnish foods, colored lumpfish caviar has a tendency to bleed.*

Salmon caviar—*the eggs of the chum and silver salmon, a very popular garnish, are large with a good flavor and natural orange color.*

Artful array of crudités and dip.

Cold dips often use mayonnaise, sour cream or cream cheese as a base. The methods for preparing mayonnaise- and sour-cream based dips are identical to those for making mayonnaise-based salad dressings discussed in Chapter 24, Salads and Salad Dressings. The principal difference is that dips are normally thicker than dressings.

To use cream cheese as a base, first soften it by mixing it in an electric mixer with a paddle attachment. Then add the flavoring ingredients such as chopped cooked vegetables, chopped cooked fish or shellfish, herbs, spices, garlic or onions. Adjust the consistency of the dip by adding milk, buttermilk, cream, sour cream or other appropriate liquid.

Some cold dips such as guacamole and hummus use purées of fruits, vegetables or beans as the base.

Hot dips often use a béchamel, cream sauce or cheese sauce as a base and usually contain a dominant flavoring ingredient such as chopped spinach or shellfish. The traditional Italian bagna cauda is an example of a hot, oil-based dip. It is made with olive oil, garlic and anchovies and is kept hot over a small burner while guests dip raw vegetables in it.

Dips can be served in small bowls or hollowed-out cabbages, squash, pumpkins or other vegetables. Hot dips are often served in **chafing dishes**.

The combinations of ingredients and seasonings that can be used to make dips as well as the foods that are dipped in them are limited only by the chef's imagination.

Chafing dish—*a metal dish with a heating unit (flame or electric) used to keep foods warm at tableside or during buffet service.*

◆ ◆ ◆

RECIPE 33.1

CLAM DIP

Yield: 3 pt. (1.5 lt)

Cream cheese	1 lb.	450 g
Worcestershire sauce	1 oz.	30 g
Dijon mustard	1 Tbsp.	15 ml
Sour cream	1 lb.	450 g
Canned clams, drained	1 lb.	450 g
Lemon juice	1 oz.	30 g
Salt and pepper	TT	TT
Tabasco sauce	TT	TT
Green onions, sliced	2 oz.	60 g

1. Soften the cream cheese in the bowl of an electric mixer, using the paddle attachment.
2. Add the Worcestershire sauce, Dijon mustard and sour cream; mix until smooth.
3. Add the clams and lemon juice and season with salt, pepper and Tabasco.
4. Add the green onions and mix well.

Sushi

Generally, **sushi** refers to cooked or raw fish and shellfish rolled in or served on seasoned rice. **Sashimi** is raw fish eaten without rice. In Japan, the word sushi (or **zushi**) refers only to the flavored rice. Each combination of rice and another ingredient or ingredients has a specific name. These include: *nigiri zushi* (rice with raw fish), *norimaki zushi* (rice rolled in seaweed), *fukusa* *zushi* (rice wrapped in omelet), *inari zushi* (rice in fried bean curd) and *chirashi zushi* (rice with fish, shellfish and vegetables). Although a Japanese sushi master spends years perfecting style and technique, many types of sushi can be produced in any professional kitchen with very little specialized equipment.

Ingredients

Fish—The key to good sushi and sashimi is the freshness of the fish. All fish must be of the highest quality and absolutely fresh, preferably no more than one day out of the water. Ahi and yellowfin tuna, salmon, flounder and sea bass are typically used for sushi. Cooked shrimp and eel are also popular.

Rice—Sushi rice is prepared by adding seasonings such as vinegar, sugar, salt and rice wine (sake or mirin) to steamed short-grain rice. The consistency of the rice is very important. It must be sticky enough to stay together when formed into finger-shaped oblongs, but not too soft.

Seasonings—These include:

◆ Shoyu—Japanese soy sauce, which is lighter and more delicate than the Chinese variety.
◆ Wasabi—A strong aromatic root, purchased as a green powder. It is sometimes called green horseradish although it is not actually related to the common horseradish.
◆ Pickled ginger—fresh ginger pickled in vinegar, which gives it a pink color.
◆ Nori—a dried seaweed purchased in sheets; it adds flavor and is sometimes used to contain the rolled rice and other ingredients.

RECIPE 33.2
ZUSHI
(SUSHI RICE)

Yield: 2 lb. (1 kg)

Short-grain rice	1 lb.	450 g
Water	20 oz.	600 g
Rice vinegar	2 oz.	60 g
Sugar	3 Tbsp.	45 ml
Salt	2-1/2 tsp.	12 ml
Mirin	1 oz.	30 g

1. Wash the rice and allow it to drain for 30 minutes.
2. Combine the rice and water in a saucepan. Bring to a boil, reduce to a simmer, cover and steam for 20 minutes.
3. Combine the rice vinegar, sugar, salt and mirin and add to the rice. Mix well and cool to room temperature.

RECIPE 33.3
NIGIRI ZUSHI

Yield: 24 Pieces

Sushi-quality fish fillets such as ahi, salmon, flounder or sea bass	1 lb.	450 g
Wasabi powder	1 oz.	30 g

Continued

Water	1 oz.	30 g
Sushi rice	2 lb.	900 g
Pickled ginger, sliced	2 oz.	60 g
Shoyu	3 oz.	90 g

1. Trim the fish fillets of any skin, bone, imperfections or blemishes. Cut the fillets into 24 thin slices approximately 2 inches long by 1 inch wide (5 centimeters by 2.5 centimeters).
2. Mix the wasabi powder and water to form a paste.
3. With your hands, form a 1-1/2-ounce (50-gram) portion of rice into a finger-shaped mound.
4. Rub a small amount of wasabi on one side of a slice of fish.
5. Holding the rice mound in one hand, press the fish, wasabi side down, onto the rice with the fingers of the other hand.
6. Serve with additional wasabi, pickled ginger and shoyu.

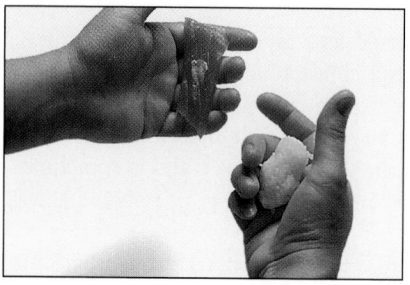

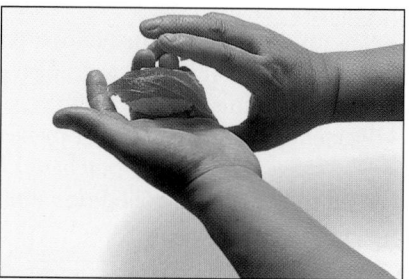

1. Forming a finger-shaped rice mound.

2. Pressing the fish onto the rice.

◆◆◆

RECIPE 33.4

NORIMAKI ZUSHI

Yield: 36 Pieces

Dried shiitake mushrooms	4	4
Shoyu	4 oz.	120 g
Brown sugar	1 Tbsp.	15 ml
Cucumber	1/2	1/2
Sushi-quality fish fillets such as ahi, salmon, flounder or sea bass	5 oz.	150 g
Nori	3 sheets	3 sheets
Sushi rice	18 oz.	500 g
Pickled ginger	2 oz.	60 g
Wasabi paste	2 oz.	60 g

1. Soak the mushrooms in hot water for 20 minutes. Remove the mushrooms and reserve 4 ounces (120 grams) of the liquid. Trim off the mushroom stems.
2. Julienne the mushroom caps. Combine the reserved soaking liquid with 2 tablespoons (30 milliliters) of the shoyu and the brown sugar. Simmer the caps in this liquid and reduce au sec. Remove from the heat and refrigerate.

3. Peel and seed the cucumber; cut it into strips the size of pencils, approximately 6 inches (15 centimeters) long.

4. Trim the fish fillets of any skin, bone, imperfections or blemishes. Cut the fillets into strips the same size as the cucumbers.

5. Cut the sheets of nori in half and place one half sheet on a napkin or bamboo rolling mat. Divide the rice into six equal portions; spread one portion over each half sheet of nori, leaving a half inch (12 millimeters) border of nori exposed.

6. Spread 1 teaspoon (5 milliliters) of wasabi evenly on the rice.

7. Lay one sixth of the mushrooms, cucumber and fish strips in a row down the middle of the rice.

8. Use the napkin or bamboo mat to roll the nori tightly around the rice and garnishes.

9. Slice each roll into six pieces and serve with the remaining shoyu, pickled ginger and wasabi.

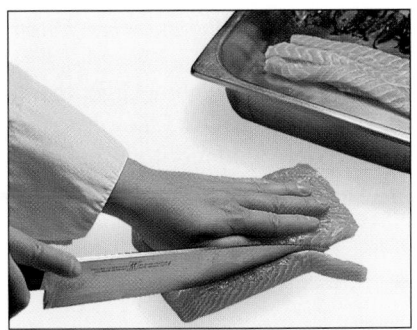

1. Preparing the garnishes for the sushi roll.

2. Spreading the rice over the nori.

3. Adding the garnishes in a row down the middle of the rice.

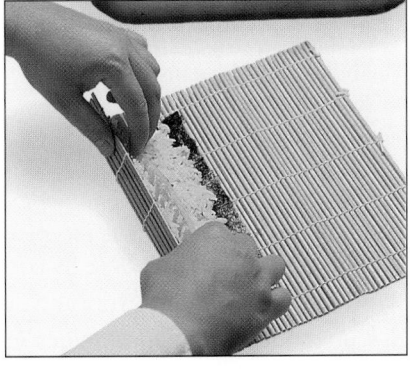

4. Rolling the nori around the rice and garnishes.

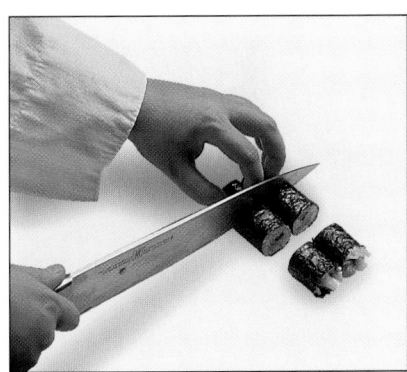

5. Slicing the roll into six pieces.

Hot Hors d'Oeuvres

To provide a comprehensive list of hot hors d'oeuvres would be virtually impossible; therefore we discuss just a few of the more commonly encountered ones that can be easily made in most any kitchen.

Filled Pastry Shells

Because savory (unsweetened) barquettes and tartlets, choux puffs and bouchées can hold a small amount of liquid, they are often baked then filled with warm meat, poultry or fish purées or ragouts, garnished and served hot. They become soggy quickly, however, and must be prepared at the last possible minute before service.

Brochettes

Hors d'oeuvre brochettes are small skewers holding a combination of meat, poultry, game, fish, shellfish or vegetables. They are normally baked, grilled or broiled and are often served with a dipping sauce. Brochettes can be small pieces of boneless chicken breast marinated in white wine and grilled; beef cubes glazed with teriyaki sauce; lamb or chicken satay (saté) with peanut sauce or rabbit and shiitake mushrooms skewered on a sprig of fresh rosemary. (See recipes at the end of this chapter.)

In order to increase visual appeal, the main ingredients should be carefully cut and consistent in size and shape. The ingredients are normally diced, but strips of meat and poultry can also be threaded onto the skewers. Often, ingredients are first marinated.

As hors d'oeuvres, the skewers should be very small, slightly larger than a toothpick. When assembling brochettes, leave enough exposed skewer so diners can pick them up easily. Wooden skewers have a tendency to burn during cooking. Soaking them in water before assembling helps reduce the risk of burning.

RECIPE 33.5

RABBIT AND SHIITAKE SKEWERS

Yield: 12 Skewers

Rabbit	1	1
Shiitake mushrooms	2 lb.	1 kg
Rosemary sprigs	12	12
Salt and pepper	TT	TT
Olive oil	2 oz.	60 g

1. Bone the rabbit and cut the pieces into 1/2-inch (1.2-centimeter) cubes. One rabbit should produce 36 cubes.
2. Wash the mushrooms. Trim and discard the stems.
3. Cut enough of the mushrooms into 1/2-inch (1.2-centimeter) dice to produce 24 pieces.
4. Skewer three pieces of rabbit and two pieces of mushroom alternately onto each rosemary sprig.
5. Season the skewers and the remaining mushrooms with salt and pepper and brush with olive oil. Grill the skewers and the mushroom caps over medium heat, being careful not to burn the rosemary sprigs.
6. Slice the mushroom caps and arrange a portion of sliced mushrooms and two rabbit skewers on each plate.

Meatballs

Meatballs made from ground beef, veal, pork or poultry and served in a sauce buffet-style are a popular hot hors d'oeuvre. One of the best known is the Swedish meatball. It is made from ground beef, veal and pork bound with eggs and bread crumbs and served in a velouté or cream sauce seasoned with dill. Other sauces that can be used in the same manner are mushroom sauce, red wine sauce or any style of tomato sauce.

◆◆◆

RECIPE 33.6

SWEDISH MEATBALLS

Yield: 4 lb. 8 oz. (2 kg)

Onions, small dice	8 oz.	250 g
Whole butter	2 oz.	60 g
Ground beef	2 lb.	1 kg
Ground pork	2 lb.	1 kg
Bread crumbs, fresh	4 oz.	120 g
Eggs	3	3
Salt	1 Tbsp.	15 ml
Pepper	TT	TT
Nutmeg	TT	TT
Allspice	TT	TT
Lemon zest, grated	1 tsp.	5 ml
Demi-glace, hot	1 qt.	1 lt
Heavy cream, hot	8 oz.	250 g
Fresh dill, chopped	2 Tbsp.	30 ml

1. Sauté the onions in butter without coloring. Remove and cool.
2. Combine the onions with all the ingredients except the demi-glace, cream and dill. Mix well.
3. Portion the meat with a #20 scoop; form into balls with your hands and place on a sheet pan.
4. Bake the meatballs at 400°F (200°C) until firm, approximately 15 minutes. Remove the meatballs from the pan with a slotted spoon, draining well, and place in a hotel pan.
5. Combine the demi-glace, cream and dill; pour over the meatballs.
6. Cover the meatballs and bake at 350°F (180°C) until done, approximately 20 minutes. Skim off the grease from the surface and serve.

Rumaki

Traditionally, rumaki were made by wrapping chicken livers in bacon and broiling or baking them. Today, however, many other foods prepared in the same fashion are called rumaki. For example, blanched bacon can be wrapped around olives, pickled watermelon rind, water chestnuts, pineapple, dates or scallops. These morsels are then broiled, baked or fried and served piping hot.

━━━━━━━━━━━━━━ ✦✦✦ ━━━━━━━━━━━━━━

RECIPE 33.7

DATE AND CHORIZO RUMAKI

Yield: 32 Pieces

Bacon, thin-cut slices	16	16
Chorizo (Recipe 20.21)	8 oz.	250 g
Cream cheese	4 oz.	120 g
Whole dates, pitted	32	32

1. Partially cook the bacon on a sheet pan in a 350°F (180°C) oven, approximately 5 minutes.
2. Cook the chorizo to render the excess fat. If the chorizo is in links, remove the meat from the casings before cooking.
3. Remove the cooked chorizo from the pan and drain in a mesh strainer or china cap to remove excess fat. Then blend the cream cheese into the meat.
4. Cut the dates open, butterfly style. Stuff each date with a portion of the chorizo mixture.
5. Wrap each date with a half slice of bacon, securing with a toothpick.
6. Arrange the rumaki on a rack placed over a sheet pan. Bake at 350°F (180°C) until the bacon is crisp and the dates are hot, approximately 15–20 minutes.

Stuffed Wonton Skins

Wonton skins are an Asian noodle dough used to produce a wide variety of hors d'oeuvres such as a miniature version of the traditional egg roll or a puff filled with a mixture of seasoned cream cheese and crab. Or they can be stuffed with a wide variety of pork, chicken, shellfish and vegetables before cooking. As hors d'oeuvres, stuffed wonton skins can be steamed, but they are more often pan-fried or deep-fried.

━━━━━━━━━━━━━━ ✦✦✦ ━━━━━━━━━━━━━━

RECIPE 33.8

STUFFED WONTONS WITH APRICOT SAUCE

Yield: 24 Pieces

Cream cheese	8 oz.	250 g
Crab meat	8 oz.	250 g
Garlic, chopped	1 tsp.	5 ml
Green onion, sliced	1 oz.	30 g
Salt and pepper	TT	TT
Worcestershire sauce	TT	TT
Sesame oil	TT	TT
Wonton skins	24	24
Apricot Sauce (recipe follows)	as needed	as needed

1. Place the cream cheese in the bowl of a mixer and mix until soft.

2. Add the crab, garlic and green onion. Season with salt and pepper, Worcestershire sauce and a drop or two of sesame oil.

3. Place several wonton skins on a work surface. Brush the edges with water. Place 1 tablespoon (15 milliliters) of the cream cheese mixture in the center of each skin. Fold the wonton skin in half to form a triangle; seal the edges.

4. Deep-fry the wontons using the swimming method, at 350°F (180°C) for 10 seconds. Remove the wontons, drain well and refrigerate.

5. At service, deep-fry the wontons at 350°F (180°C) until crisp, approximately 1 minute. Serve with Apricot Sauce.

APRICOT SAUCE

Yield: 8 oz. (250 g)

Apricot preserves	8 oz.	250 g
Fresh ginger, grated	1 Tbsp.	15 ml
Dry mustard	1 tsp.	5 ml
Red wine vinegar	1 Tbsp.	15 ml

1. Combine all ingredients and heat until the preserves melt and the flavors blend.

Other Hot Hors d'Oeuvres

Other types of hot hors d'oeuvres include layers of phyllo dough wrapped around various fillings; vegetables such as mushrooms that are stuffed and baked; tiny red potatoes filled with sour cream and caviar or Roquefort cheese and walnuts; tiny artichoke or clam fritters or any of the hundreds of varieties of chicken wings that are seasoned or marinated, baked, fried, broiled or grilled and served with a cool and soothing or outrageously spicy sauce.

The secret is to let your imagination be your guide, to keep the ingredients harmonious and, if the hors d'oeuvres are to precede dinner, not to allow them to duplicate the foods to be served or overpower them with excessively spicy flavors.

Serving Hors d'Oeuvres

Hors d'oeuvres are not only served as a precursor to dinner. At many events the only food served may be butlered hors d'oeuvres, an hors d'oeuvre buffet or a combination of the two. Whether the hors d'oeuvres are being served before dinner or as dinner, butler style or buffet style, they must always be attractively prepared and displayed.

All events have themes and varying degrees of formality. Long buffets with overflowing baskets of cruditées and sweet potato chips with dips presented in hollowed squashes and cabbages may be appropriate for one event, while elegant silver trays of carefully prepared canapés passed among guests by white-gloved, tuxedoed service staff may be appropriate for another. When preparing and serving hors d'oeuvres, always keep the event's theme in mind and plan accordingly.

When choosing hors d'oeuvres, select an assortment that contrasts flavors, textures and styles. There are no limits to the variety of hors d'oeuvres that can be served, but three to four cold and three to four hot selections are sufficient for most occasions. The following is a small selection of hot and cold hors d'oeuvres that contrast flavors, textures and styles as well as types of food.

Cold:

+ Canapés of smoked salmon on brioche
+ Barquettes filled with Roquefort cheese and garnished with grapes
+ Tiny tortilla cups filled with grilled chicken and spicy tomato salsa

Hot:

+ Tiny pouches of shrimp wrapped in phyllo dough (Recipe 33.21)
+ Date and chorizo rumaki (Recipe 33.7)
+ Rabbit and shiitake mushroom brochettes on rosemary sprigs (Recipe 33.5)
+ Small chevre tarts (Recipe 33.16)

Butler Service

Butler service hors d'oeuvres or "passed" hors d'oeuvres are presented to guests on trays by the service staff. The hors d'oeuvres can be hot or cold and should be very small to make it easier for the guests to eat them without the aid of a knife or fork. Hot and cold hors d'oeuvres should be passed separately so that they can be kept at the correct temperatures. For a one-hour cocktail reception before a dinner, three to five hors d'oeuvres per person is usually sufficient.

Buffet Service

An hors d'oeuvre buffet should be beautiful and appetizing. It may consist of a single table to serve a small group of people or several huge multilevel displays designed to feed thousands. Colors, flavors and textures must all be taken into account when planning the menu.

Both hot and cold hors d'oeuvres may be served on buffets. Hot hors d'oeuvres are often kept hot by holding them in chafing dishes. Alternatively, hot hors d'oeuvres can be displayed on trays or platters; the trays and platters, however, must be replaced frequently to ensure that the food stays hot. Cold hors d'oeuvres can be displayed on trays, mirrors, platters, baskets, leaves, papers or other serving pieces to create the desired look.

Arranging Buffet Platters

When displaying hors d'oeuvres and other foods on mirrors, trays or platters, the foods should be displayed in a pattern that is pleasing to the eye and flows toward the guest or from one side to the other. An easy and attractive method for accomplishing this is to arrange the items on a mirror or tray with an attractive centerpiece. The food can be placed in parallel diagonal lines, alternating the various styles and shapes. Be careful not to make the tray or mirror too fussy or cluttered, however; often the best approach is to keep it simple. The diagrams in Figure 33.1 may be used as guides for arranging canapés and other foods on trays.

APPETIZERS OR FIRST COURSES

Because eating habits have changed over the years, the types of foods chefs prepare have also changed. Today, even the most elaborate banquets rarely include hors d'oeuvres, an appetizer, soup, salad, entree and dessert, let alone

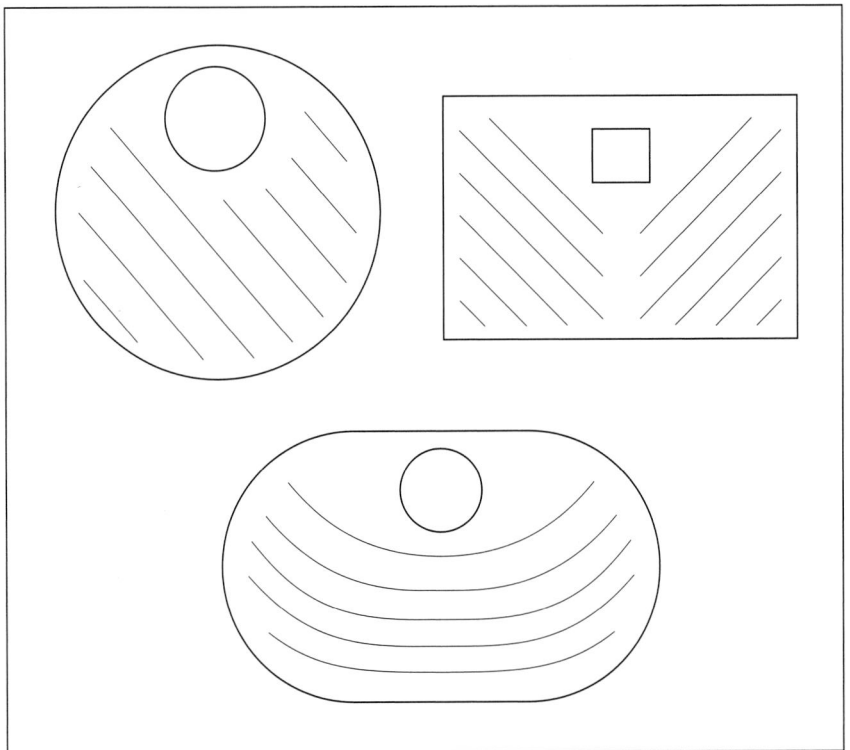

FIGURE 33.1   *Simple patterns that can be used to effectively display canapés and other foods on trays or mirrors.*

separate fish and cheese courses. A more likely progression may be soup (which serves as the appetizer), salad, entree and dessert, or a salad with a small portion of grilled meat or fish that doubles as both appetizer and salad, followed by an entree and dessert. Because of these changes the term **first course** may be more fitting than appetizer.

Generally, appetizers and first courses are small portions of foods intended to whet the appetite in anticipation of more substantial courses to follow. Unlike foods prepared as entrees, appetizers rarely contain the traditional combination of meat or other main item, vegetable and starch. More often, appetizers consist only of the main item accompanied by a sauce and/or garnish. Appetizers do not need to contain any meat, poultry, fish or shellfish, however. Soups, salads, charcuterie items, vegetables, pizzas, pastas and other starch dishes may be served as appetizers. Because they are very rich, some foods such as foie gras and escargots are traditionally served as appetizers. These foods are generally consumed in small amounts and are rarely served as entrees.

Although there are few limitations on what can be served as an appetizer or first course, a few guidelines should be followed to ensure that whatever is served will be well received.

GUIDELINES FOR PREPARING APPETIZERS

1. The first course should be small. Remember, there are other, more substantial courses to follow. As the name implies, an appetizer should stimulate the appetite rather than satisfy it. Remember that rich cream-based sauces tend to satisfy appetites quickly, even when the portions are small. Two to 3 ounces (60–90 grams) of pasta and 2 ounces (60 grams) of sauce is an ample appetizer portion. Many recipes, such as Ahi Tuna Seared with Lavender and Pepper with Whole Grain Mustard Sauce (Recipe 24.24) and Chinese Barbecued Spareribs (Recipe 16.3), can be prepared as an appetizer by simply serving smaller portions.

2. Avoid very spicy foods that may deaden the palate and detract from any more delicate flavors that follow.

3. The first course should be harmonious with the rest of the meal with respect to the types of foods as well as the style. For example, an appetizer of a roasted Anaheim chile stuffed with grilled corn and goat cheese followed by an entree of paupiettes of sole vin blanc would be a poor combination: The strong spices and flavors of the chile would overpower the delicate flavors of the sole; while the chile has strong southwestern ties, the sole is a classic French dish.

4. Avoid duplication of foods within the meal. If fish or shellfish is served as the first course, do not serve fish or shellfish as the main course.

5. For more variety, use several methods of preparation within the meal. If the entree will be grilled or roasted, serve a first course that is poached or sautéed.

6. A first course should always be attractively presented. Remember that often it is the first food the customer sees. It should set the standard for the rest of the meal.

CONCLUSION

The preparation of hors d'oeuvres and appetizers provides an opportunity for the chef to demonstrate his or her creativity, knowledge of food and skills in presentation and garnishing. Because hors d'oeuvres and appetizers often serve as the guests' introduction to the foods you serve, it is especially important that these foods be properly prepared and of the highest quality.

QUESTIONS FOR DISCUSSION

1. Discuss four guidelines that should be followed when preparing hors d'oeuvres.
2. Identify and describe the three parts of a canapé.
3. Describe the differences between beluga, osetra and sevruga caviars and explain how these foods differ from domestic caviars.
4. Create an hors d'oeuvre menu for a small cocktail party. Include three hot and three cold items and explain the reasons for your selections.
5. List and explain five guidelines that should be followed when preparing appetizers or first courses.

Additional Hors d'Oeuvre and Appetizer Recipes

RECIPE 33.9

Stuffed Squash Blossoms and Buckwheat Blini with Smoked Salmon and Caviar

Yield: 24 Servings

Chevre cheese	8 oz.	250 g
Cream cheese	4 oz.	120 g
Assorted fresh herbs, chopped	2 tsp.	10 ml
Garlic cloves, minced	2	2
Black pepper	TT	TT
Baby squash with blossoms	24	24
Tempura Batter (Recipe 21.4)	24 oz.	700 g
Olive oil	1 Tbsp.	15 ml
Bell peppers, red, yellow		
and green, julienne	12 oz.	360 g
Salt	TT	TT
Buckwheat Blinis (recipe follows)	24	24
Blackberry preserves	3 oz.	90 g
Smoked salmon, sliced	1 lb.	500 g
Caviar	2 oz.	60 g
Fresh basil sprigs	24	24

1. Blend the chevre cheese and cream cheese in the bowl of an electric mixer until smooth. Fold in the herbs and garlic and season with black pepper.
2. Using a pastry bag fitted with a round tip, fill each of the squash blossoms with the cheese mixture and pinch the flowers shut.
3. Dip each of the squash in tempura batter and deep fry until lightly browned, approximately 1 minute. Remove and drain well.
4. Sauté the peppers in olive oil until tender. Season with salt and pepper.
5. Carefully split each squash and blossom in half. Arrange two squash halves on each plate and garnish with the julienne peppers.
6. Spread each of the blini with blackberry preserves. Form rosettes out of the salmon slices and place one on each blini.
7. Place the blini on the plate with the squash and peppers and garnish with two dollops of caviar and a sprig of basil.

BUCKWHEAT BLINI

Yield: 24 Blini

Granulated sugar	2 tsp.	10 ml
Dry yeast	1/4 oz.	7 g
Milk, lukewarm	14 oz.	420 g
Buckwheat flour	4 oz.	120 g
All-purpose flour	3 oz.	90 g

Continued

Salt	1/2 tsp.	2 ml
Unsalted butter, melted	3 Tbsp.	45 ml
Vegetable oil	2 Tbsp.	30 ml
Egg yolks	3	3
Egg whites	2	2

1. Stir the sugar and yeast into the warmed milk and let stand until foamy, approximately 5 minutes.

2. Whisk in the flours, salt, butter, oil and egg yolks. Beat until smooth.

3. Cover the batter and allow it to rise in a warm place until doubled, approximately 1 hour.

4. Beat the egg whites to stiff peaks, then fold them into the risen batter.

5. Lightly oil and pre-heat a large sauté pan. Drop 2 tablespoons (30 milliliters) of batter into the sauté pan, spacing the blini at least 1 inch (2.5 centimeters) apart. Cook until the bottom of each blini is golden, approximately 1 minute. Turn the blini and cook an additional 30 seconds. Remove from the pan and keep warm for service.

◆◆◆

RECIPE 33.10

GRAPEFRUIT AND OYSTER HORS D'OEUVRE

Yield: 6 Servings

Grapefruit	1	1
Olive oil	1 oz.	60 g
Fresh ginger, minced	1/4 tsp.	1 ml
Black pepper	TT	TT
Heavy cream	8 oz.	250 g
Horseradish, grated	1 tsp.	5 ml
Salt	TT	TT
Russet potato	1	1
Red tomato	1	1
Yellow tomato	1	1
Oysters	12	12

1. Peel the grapefruit and cut 12 thin segments from it. Squeeze the juice from the remaining grapefruit pulp.

2. Combine the grapefruit juice with the olive oil and ginger and season with black pepper.

3. Whip the cream until stiff and stir in the horseradish. Season with salt and pepper.

4. Peel the potato. Use a mandoline to cut 12 waffle patterned chips. Deep fry the chips at 350°F (180°C) until crisp. Drain on absorbent paper.

5. Core, blanch and peel the red and yellow tomatoes. Cut each tomato into four wedges. Cut thin strips of flesh from each wedge of tomato to resemble leaves.

6. Shuck the oysters. Place one grapefruit segment on each oyster and spoon 1 teaspoon (5 milliliters) of the grapefruit dressing over each oyster.

7. Arrange two oysters per serving. Garnish with 1 tablespoon (15 milliliters) creamed horseradish, one potato chip, one red tomato leaf, one yellow tomato leaf and a sprig of thyme.

♦♦♦

RECIPE 33.11
SANTA BARBARA PRAWN HORS D'OEUVRE

Yield: 6 Servings

Fresh prawns, head-on	6	6
Sea salt	TT	TT
Pepper	TT	TT
Lime juice	1 oz.	30 g
Ratatouille, chilled (Recipe 22.19)	6 oz.	180 g

1. Arrange the prawns in a hotel pan. Season them with sea salt and pepper and sprinkle with the lime juice.
2. Cover the pan and place in a 400°F (200°C) oven until the prawns are just cooked, approximately 5 minutes. Remove from the oven and cool.
3. Place 1 ounce (30 grams) of ratatouille on each plate and arrange one prawn on top of the ratatouille. Garnish as desired.

♦♦♦

RECIPE 33.12
HUMMUS

Yield: 1 qt. (1 lt)

Chickpeas, cooked	1 lb.	450 g
Tahini paste	8 oz.	225 g
Garlic, chopped	2 tsp.	10 ml
Cumin	1/2 tsp.	2 ml
Lemon juice	4 oz.	120 g
Salt	1 tsp.	5 ml
Cayenne pepper	TT	TT
Olive oil	2 oz.	60 g
Fresh parsley, chopped	2 tsp.	10 ml

Tahini paste—*a paste made from crushed sesame seeds.*

1. Combine the chickpeas, tahini, garlic, cumin and lemon juice in a food processor; process until smooth. Season with salt and cayenne.
2. Spoon the hummus onto a serving platter and smooth the surface. Drizzle the olive oil over the hummus and garnish with the chopped parsley. Serve with warm pita bread that has been cut into quarters.

♦♦♦

RECIPE 33.13
GUACAMOLE

Yield: 1 qt. (1 lt)

Avocados	6	6
Lemon juice	2-1/2 oz.	75 g
Green onion, sliced	4 Tbsp.	60 ml
Cilantro, chopped	3 Tbsp.	45 ml

Continued

Tomatoes, seeded, diced	3 Tbsp.	45 ml
Garlic, chopped	1 tsp.	5 ml
Dried oregano	1/2 tsp.	2 ml
Jalapeños, seeded, chopped	1	1
Salt	TT	TT

1. Cut each avocado in half. Remove the seed and scoop out the pulp.

2. Add the lemon juice to the avocado pulp and mix well, mashing the avocado pulp.

3. Add the remaining ingredients. Season with salt and mix well.

RECIPE 33.14

SUN-DRIED TOMATO AND BASIL AIOLI

Yield: 1 qt. (1 lt)

Garlic cloves, mashed to a paste	4	4
Egg yolks	4	4
Lemon juice	2 Tbsp.	30 ml
Olive oil	1-1/2 pt.	700 ml
Sun-dried tomatoes, packed in olive oil	4 oz.	120 g
Fresh basil, chopped	4 Tbsp.	60 ml
Salt	1 tsp.	5 ml
Pepper	1/2 tsp.	2 ml

1. Combine the garlic, egg yolks and a few drops of the lemon juice in a bowl and whip until frothy.

2. While whipping the egg yolk mixture, slowly add the olive oil until an emulsion begins to form. Continue adding the oil while whipping until all of the oil is incorporated. A few drops of lemon juice may be added from time to time to thin the sauce.

3. Finely chop the sun-dried tomatoes. Add them, a portion of the olive oil in which they were packed, and the basil to the aioli.

4. Season with salt, pepper and lemon juice.

RECIPE 33.15

BAGNA CAUDA

Yield: 1 qt. (1 lt)

Anchovy fillets	6 oz.	180 g
Garlic	2 oz.	60 g
Olive oil	24 oz.	700 g
Black pepper	1 tsp.	5 ml

1. Rinse the anchovy fillets under cool water to remove the excess salt. Purée the anchovy fillets and garlic in a food processor.

2. Add the olive oil and season with black pepper.

3. Warm the sauce in a saucepan over low heat.

4. Serve the warm sauce in a fondue pot or casserole accompanied by crudités.

✦✦✦

RECIPE 33.16
Chevre Tarts

Yield: 12 Tarts

Tomato concasse	4 oz.	120 g
Pepper	TT	TT
Parmesan cheese, grated	3 oz.	90 g
Puff pastry	8 oz.	250 g
Olive oil	as needed	as needed
Pesto sauce (Recipe 23.27)	2 oz.	60 g
Goat cheese (chevre), Montrachet style	4 oz.	120 g
Zucchini, shredded	1 lb.	450 g

1. Season the tomato with fresh-ground pepper; sprinkle with 1 ounce (30 grams) of the Parmesan cheese.
2. Roll out the puff pastry until it is approximately 1/4 inch (6 millimeters) thick, then cut it into 12 circles approximately 2-1/2 inches (6.25 centimeters) in diameter.
3. Brush a mini-muffin tin with olive oil and line with the puff pastry circles.
4. Add 1 teaspoon (5 milliliters) pesto sauce to each tart.
5. Add 1/3 ounce (10 grams) goat cheese to each tart.
6. Add enough shredded zucchini to each tart to nearly fill it.
7. Top each tart with the tomato and sprinkle with the remaining Parmesan cheese.
8. Bake at 375°F (190°C) until the tarts are brown on top and the dough is cooked, approximately 15–20 minutes.

✦✦✦

RECIPE 33.17
Lamb Satay with Peanut Sauce

Yield: 16 Skewers

Lamb leg meat, boned, trimmed	2 lb.	1 kg
Vegetable oil	2 oz.	60 g
Lemon grass, chopped	2 Tbsp.	30 ml
Garlic, chopped	1 Tbsp.	15 ml
Red pepper flakes, crushed	1 tsp.	5 ml
Curry powder	1 Tbsp.	15 ml
Honey	1 Tbsp.	15 ml
Fish sauce	1 Tbsp.	15 ml
Peanut Sauce (recipe follows)	as needed	as needed

1. Cut the lamb into 2-ounce (60-gram) strips approximately 4 inches (10 centimeters) long. Lightly pound the strips with a mallet. Thread the strips onto 6-inch (15-centimeter) bamboo skewers which have been soaked in water.
2. To make the marinade, combine the remaining ingredients in the bowl of a food processor and purée until smooth.
3. Brush the meat with the marinade and allow to marinate for 1 hour.
4. Grill the skewers until done, approximately 2 minutes. Serve with Peanut Sauce.

Continued

PEANUT SAUCE

Yield: 28 oz. (800 g)

Garlic, chopped	1 tsp.	5 ml
Onion, small dice	6 oz.	180 g
Red pepper flakes, crushed	1 tsp.	5 ml
Kaffir lime leaves (optional)	4	4
Curry powder	2 tsp.	10 ml
Lemon grass, minced	1 oz.	30 g
Vegetable oil	1 oz.	30 g
Coconut milk	8 oz.	250 g
Cinnamon sticks	2	2
Bay leaves	4	4
Lime juice	1 oz.	30 g
Rice wine vinegar	4 oz.	120 g
Chicken stock	10 oz.	300 g
Peanut butter	10 oz.	300 g

1. Sauté the garlic, onion, red pepper flakes, lime leaves, curry powder and lemon grass in the vegetable oil for 5 minutes.

2. Add the remaining ingredients and simmer for 30 minutes. Stir often, as the sauce can easily burn. Serve warm.

VARIATIONS: Beef or chicken satay can be made by substituting well-trimmed beef or boneless, skinless chicken meat for the lamb.

◆◆◆

RECIPE 33.18

SPINACH AND ARTICHOKE DIP

Yield: 4 lb. 6 oz. (2 kg)

Onion, medium dice	3 oz.	90 g
Garlic, chopped	2 tsp.	10 ml
Clarified butter	1 oz.	30 g
Frozen chopped spinach, thawed	1 lb. 8 oz.	700 g
Artichoke hearts, canned, chopped coarse	1 lb.	450 g
Cream sauce	1 qt.	1 lt
Worcestershire sauce	2 tsp.	10 ml
Salt and pepper	TT	TT
Tabasco sauce	TT	TT
Parmesan cheese, grated	6 oz.	180 g

1. Sauté the onion and garlic in the butter until tender without coloring.

2. Add the spinach and sauté until hot.

3. Add the artichoke hearts, cream sauce, Worcestershire and 4 ounces (120 grams) of the Parmesan cheese. Mix well.

4. Season with salt, pepper and Tabasco.

5. Transfer the dip to a half hotel pan. Top with the remaining 2 ounces (60 grams) of Parmesan cheese and bake at 350°F (180°C) until hot and browned on top, approximately 20 minutes.

◆◆◆

RECIPE 33.19

KALAMATA OLIVE AND ASIAGO CHEESE CROSTINI

LES GOURMETTES COOKING SCHOOL, PHOENIX, AZ
Barbara Fenzl

Yield: 12 Pieces

French bread	1/2 loaf	1/2 loaf
Basil leaves, chopped	50	50
Tomato concasse	4 oz.	120 g
Garlic, chopped	2 tsp.	10 ml
Kalamata olives, pitted, chopped	15	15
Asiago cheese, grated	2 oz.	60 g

1. Slice the bread 1/4-inch (6-millimeters) thick.

2. Combine the remaining ingredients and mix well.

3. Spread 1/2 tablespoon (8 milliliters) of the mixture on each slice of bread. Place under the broiler or salamander until hot and the cheese is melted, approximately 2 minutes.

◆◆◆

RECIPE 33.20

SPANAKOPITTA

Yield: 90 Triangles

Onion, small dice	4 oz.	120 g
Unsalted butter, melted	6 oz.	180 g
Fresh spinach, cooked and cooled, or frozen spinach, thawed	24 oz.	700 g
Fresh mint, chopped	1 Tbsp.	15 ml
Feta cheese, crumbled	1 lb.	450 g
Eggs, beaten	3	3
Salt and pepper	TT	TT
Phyllo dough	1 lb.	450 g

1. Sauté the onions in 1 tablespoon (15 milliliters) of butter until tender. Remove and cool.

2. Combine the cooled onions, spinach, mint, feta cheese and beaten eggs. Season with salt and pepper and mix well.

3. Spread one sheet of phyllo dough on the work surface; brush with melted butter. Place another sheet of phyllo on top of the first; brush it with butter. Place a third sheet of phyllo on top of the second and brush it with butter as well.

4. Cut the dough into 2-inch-wide (5 centimeter) strips.

5. Place 1 tablespoon (15 milliliters) of the spinach on the end of each strip of phyllo.

6. Starting with the end of the dough strip with the spinach, fold one corner of the dough over the spinach to the opposite side of the strip to form a triangle. Continue folding the dough, keeping it in a triangular shape, like point-folding a flag.

7. Place the phyllo triangles on a sheet pan and brush with melted butter. Bake at 375°F (190°C) until brown and crispy, approximately 20 minutes.

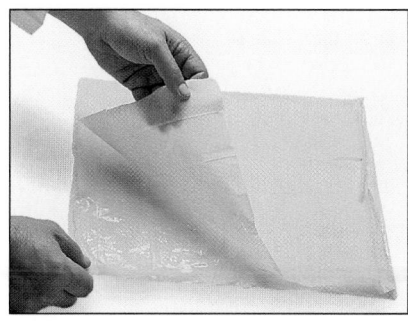

1. Brushing and stacking the layers of phyllo pastry with butter.

2. Placing the filling on the pastry.

3. Folding the pastry and filling into triangles.

♦♦♦

RECIPE 33.21

SHRIMP CRUMPLE

Yield: 24 Pieces

Rice vinegar	1 Tbsp.	15 ml
Cayenne pepper	TT	TT
Garlic, minced	1 tsp.	5 ml
Ginger, minced	1 tsp.	5 ml
Orange juice	1 Tbsp.	15 ml
Salt and pepper	TT	TT
Fresh thyme	TT	TT
Papaya	1/2	1/2
Shrimp, 16–20 count, peeled and deveined	12	12
Phyllo dough	6 sheets	6 sheets
Whole butter, melted	as needed	as needed

1. To make the marinade, combine the vinegar, cayenne, garlic, ginger and orange juice in a bowl. Stir to combine; season with salt, pepper and thyme.
2. Peel, seed and cut the papaya into medium dice. Place the papaya in a bowl and pour a small amount of marinade over it.
3. Split the shrimp and add them to the marinade.
4. Spread one sheet of phyllo dough on a work surface and brush it with butter. Lay another sheet on top of the first and brush it with butter. Place a third sheet of phyllo on top of the second and brush it with butter as well.
5. Prepare a second stack of phyllo with the three remaining sheets. Cut each stack of phyllo dough into 12 squares.
6. Place one half shrimp in the center of each square of phyllo dough and place several pieces of papaya on each shrimp. Wrap the dough around the shrimp and papaya to form a small pouch.
7. Repeat with remaining shrimp.
8. Bake the phyllo pouches at 350°F (180°C) until the phyllo is browned and the shrimp is cooked, approximately 15–20 minutes.

♦♦♦

RECIPE 33.22

RED POTATOES
WITH WALNUTS AND GORGONZOLA CHEESE

Yield: 80 Pieces

New red potatoes	40	40
Salt and pepper	TT	TT
Fresh thyme	2 tsp.	10 ml
Olive oil	2 oz.	60 g
Cream cheese	8 oz.	250 g
Gorgonzola cheese	3 oz.	90 g

Bacon, medium dice, cooked	1 oz.	30 g
Sour cream	4 oz.	120 g
Walnuts, chopped coarse	1-1/2 oz.	45 g
Worcestershire sauce	TT	TT
Tabasco sauce	TT	TT
Chives, minced	3 Tbsp.	45 ml

1. Cut the new potatoes in half and scoop out a portion of the inside with a parisienne scoop.

2. Toss the potatoes with the salt, pepper, thyme and olive oil. Arrange the potatoes on a sheet pan with their flat surfaces down and bake at 400°F (200°C) until brown and cooked through, approximately 15 minutes.

3. Soften the cream cheese in the bowl of an electric mixer. Add the Gorgonzola cheese, bacon bits, sour cream and walnuts. Mix until smooth. Season with the Worcestershire and Tabasco sauces.

4. Using a pastry bag and plain tip, fill each hot potato half with the cold cheese mixture and sprinkle with chopped chives.

VARIATION: Fill the cooked potatoes with crème fraîche, top with caviar and sprinkle with sliced chives instead of using the bacon-and-cheese mixture.

◆◆◆

RECIPE 33.23

STUFFED MUSHROOM CAPS

Yield: 48 Pieces

White mushrooms, medium	60	60
Clarified butter	2 oz.	60 g
Onion, minced	4 oz.	120 g
Flour	1 Tbsp.	15 ml
Heavy cream	4 oz.	120 g
Ham, chopped, cooked	4 oz.	120 g
Fresh parsley, chopped	2 Tbsp.	30 ml
Salt and pepper	TT	TT
Swiss cheese, shredded	2 oz.	60 g

1. Wash the mushrooms. Remove and chop the stems and 12 of the caps.

2. Sauté the whole mushroom caps in 1 ounce (30 grams) of clarified butter until partially cooked but still firm. Remove from the pan and reserve.

3. Add the remaining butter to the pan. Sauté the onion and chopped mushrooms until dry.

4. Add the flour and cook 1 minute. Add the cream; bring to a simmer and cook for 2 minutes.

5. Add the ham and parsley, season to taste with salt and pepper; stir to combine. Remove from the pan and cool slightly.

6. Stuff the mushroom caps with the ham mixture and sprinkle with shredded Swiss cheese.

7. Bake the mushrooms at 350°F (180°C) until hot, approximately 10–15 minutes.

◆◆◆

RECIPE 33.24

CROWN ROAST
OF FROG LEGS

CHRISTOPHER'S AND CHRISTOPHER'S BISTRO, PHOENIX, AZ
Chef/Owner Christopher Gross

Yield: 2 Servings

Frog legs	3 pairs	3 pairs
Garlic cloves	20	20
White wine	8 oz.	250 g
Fresh tarragon	6 sprigs	6 sprigs
Heavy cream	approx. 20 oz.	approx. 600 g
Fresh parsley	4 bunches	4 bunches
Chicken stock	8 oz.	250 g
Salt and pepper	TT	TT
Russet potatoes	4	4
Flour	as needed	as needed
Olive oil	1 oz.	30 g
Currant tomatoes	as needed	as needed

1. Separate each set of legs into single legs. Cut the calf meat off the bone and wipe the bones clean. Refrigerate the legs until service.

2. To prepare the sauce, combine five cloves of garlic with the white wine and tarragon and reduce au sec. Add 1 pint (500 milliliters) of heavy cream and reduce until thick. Strain through a chinois and set aside.

3. Blanch the parsley in boiling water for 30 seconds. Remove, drain and refresh. Purée the parsley and chicken stock in a blender. Strain through a chinois and combine with the garlic-cream sauce. Adjust the seasonings and keep warm for service.

4. To prepare the garlic purée, place 15 cloves of garlic in a small saucepan and cover with cold water. Bring the water to a boil. Drain off the water and repeat this process five more times. The garlic will be very soft and cooked. Peel and dice two potatoes. Simmer the potatoes in salted water until very soft. Purée the potatoes with the garlic in a food processor until smooth; pass through a china cap. Warm the potato purée in a small saucepan, adding enough heavy cream to make it the consistency of mashed potatoes. Keep warm for service.

5. To prepare the potato tower, use a Japanese potato spinner to cut two potatoes into long strands. Spray two short lengths of 1-1/2 inch- (3.75-centimeter-) diameter pipe with non-stick coating. Wrap the potato strands evenly around the pipes to create two towers. Deep-fry the potatoes, while still on the pipes, until golden brown.

6. To serve the frog legs, season them with salt and pepper and dredge in flour, leaving the bone clean. Sauté them in 1 ounce (30 grams) of olive oil until done. Place three frog legs inside a potato tower on each plate. Form quenelles from the potato-garlic purée and place two on each plate. Pool the warm sauce on the plate. Garnish with currant tomatoes.

RECIPE 33.25

GRILLED SHRIMP WITH PROSCIUTTO AND BASIL

Yield: 12 Pieces

Shrimp, 16–20 count, peeled and deveined, tails removed	12	12
Dry white wine	4 oz.	120 g
Rice wine vinegar	2 oz.	60 g
Thyme	2 tsp.	10 ml
Onion, minced	2 oz.	60 g
Cumin, ground	1 Tbsp.	15 ml
Salt and pepper	TT	TT
Vegetable oil	6 oz.	180 g
Dried basil	2 tsp.	10 ml
Garlic cloves, chopped	2	2
Prosciutto slices	3	3
Fresh basil leaves	6	6

1. Combine all of the ingredients except the prosciutto and fresh basil in a stainless steel bowl. Marinate for 30 minutes.

2. Remove the shrimp from the marinade and drain them well.

3. Cut each slice of prosciutto into quarters.

4. Wrap each shrimp first with 1/2 leaf of basil, then a piece of prosciutto; secure with a toothpick.

5. Grill until done, remove the toothpick and serve hot or cold.

RECIPE 33.26

SMOKED SALMON ROULADE

THE FOUR SEASONS, NEW YORK, NY
Chef Christian Albin

Yield: 4 Servings

Smoked salmon, sliced	10 oz.	300 g
Wasabi powder	1 tsp.	5 ml
Celery root (or celery), small dice	8 oz.	250 g
Sour cream	3 oz.	90 g
Chives, blanched and refreshed	1 bunch	1 bunch
Black caviar	4 oz.	120 g
Radish, cut into strips (placed in ice water to crisp)	4	4
Cucumber, cut in rounds (placed in ice water to crisp)	1/2	1/2

1. Form the slices of smoked salmon into four rectangles. Reserve any salmon trimmings for the stuffing.

2. To make the stuffing, dilute the wasabi powder with 2 teaspoons (10 milliliters) of water. Mix the celery root with the sour cream, diluted wasabi and smoked salmon trimmings.

Continued

3. To make the roulades, place an equal portion of stuffing on each smoked salmon rectangle. Roll up each piece of salmon, neatly locking the stuffing in place.

4. Tie each roulade with a chive "string" at each end. Trim the strings.

5. Place each roulade on a plate. Garnish with caviar, radish strips and cucumber rounds.

♦♦♦

RECIPE 33.27

ESCARGOT IN GARLIC BUTTER

Yield: 6- 8 piece Servings

Snails, canned	48	48
Butter, softened	1 lb.	450 g
Shallots, minced	2 Tbsp.	30 ml
Garlic, chopped	2 tsp.	10 ml
Parsley, chopped	3 Tbsp.	45 ml
Salt and pepper	TT	TT
Mushroom caps, medium	48	48

1. Drain and rinse the snails.

2. Combine the butter, shallots, garlic, parsley, salt and pepper in a mixer or food processor and mix or process until well blended.

3. Sauté the mushroom caps in a small amount of the butter mixture until cooked but still firm. Remove from the heat and place six caps in each of eight shallow ramekins.

4. Place a snail in each cap and top with a generous amount of the garlic butter.

5. Bake the mushrooms and snails at 450°F (230°C) for 5 to 7 minutes and serve hot.

VARIATIONS:

1. If snail shells are available, place a small amount of the butter in each shell. Push a snail into the buttered shell and add more butter to completely cover the snail. Place the shells in a specially designed escargot dish or a shallow ramekin with 1/2 inch (12 millimeters) of rock salt to hold them in place and cook as above.

2. Prepare 48 small bouchées from puff pastry. Sauté the snails in a generous amount of the garlic butter and place one snail in each bouchée. Drizzle the snail with the garlic butter and serve as an hors d'oeuvre.

♦♦♦

RECIPE 33.28

TERIYAKI SALMON
WITH PINEAPPLE-PAPAYA SALSA

Yield: 4 Servings

Soy sauce	8 oz.	250 g
Garlic, crushed	1 tsp.	5 ml
Ginger, minced	1 tsp.	5 ml
Brown sugar	2 oz.	60 g
Sake	4 oz.	120 g

Salmon, tranches, 4 oz. (120 g) each	4	4
Vegetable oil	as needed	as needed
Pineapple-Papaya Salsa (Recipe 25.9)	16 oz.	450 g

1. To make the marinade, combine the soy sauce, garlic, ginger, brown sugar and sake.

2. Marinate the salmon tranches in the sauce for 15 minutes.

3. Remove the salmon from the marinade and pat dry. Brush them with vegetable oil and broil or grill until done.

4. Serve the salmon on a bed of warmed Pineapple-Papaya Salsa.

RECIPE 33.29
SOFT SHELLED CRAB HORS D'OEUVRE

Yield: 12 Servings

Carrots	1 lb.	450 g
Zucchini	2 lb.	1 kg
Soft shelled crabs	12	12
Red tomato	1	1
Yellow tomato	1	1
Assorted fresh herbs, chopped	1 Tbsp.	15 ml
Éclair Paste (Recipe 29.9)	12 oz.	350 g
Olive oil	1 oz.	30 g
Salt and pepper	TT	TT
Flour	as needed	as needed
Beurre Blanc Sauce (Recipe 10.16), infused with 1/2 tsp. (3 ml) saffron threads	4 oz.	120 g
Beurre Blanc Sauce (Recipe 10.16) with the addition of 1 Tbsp. (15 ml) puréed roasted red pepper	4 oz.	120 g

1. Cut the carrots into elongated julienne strips using a mandoline. Cut the unpeeled zucchini in the same fashion.

2. Clean the soft shelled crabs using the following procedure: Lift up the skirt or tail and twist it off, the intestinal tract should remain attached to the tail when you remove it. Cut off the head, including the eyes and antennae. Lift up the top shell on each side where it is pointed and pull out the soft spongy gills.

3. Core, blanch and peel the red and yellow tomatoes. Cut each tomato into four wedges. Cut thin strips of flesh from each tomato wedge to resemble leaves.

4. Stir the chopped fresh herbs into the éclair paste. Pipe the batter through a pastry bag fitted with a small round tip into a 350°F (180°C) fryer in a circular pattern to make garnishes.

5. Sauté the carrots and zucchini in 1 ounce (30 grams) of olive oil until tender, approximately 2 minutes. Season with salt and pepper.

6. Dredge the crabs in flour seasoned with salt and pepper and sauté in 2 ounces (60 grams) of olive oil until done, approximately 4 minutes.

7. Place each crab on a plate. Garnish with the sautéed vegetables, éclair paste and tomato leaves. Decorate the plates with drops of each of the Beurre Blanc Sauces.

◆◆◆

RECIPE 33.30

BLUE CORN AND SHRIMP TAMALES

Yield: 16 Pieces

Fresh blue corn masa	1 lb.	450 g
Baking powder	1/2 tsp.	2 ml
Shortening	4 oz.	120 g
Salt	TT	TT
Onion, small dice	5 oz.	150 g
Red bell pepper, small dice	2 oz.	60 g
Green bell pepper, small dice	2 oz.	60 g
Garlic, chopped	1 tsp.	5 ml
Vegetable oil	1 oz.	30 g
Salt and pepper	TT	TT
Shrimp, 16–20 count, peeled and deveined	16	16
Dried corn husks	as needed	as needed

1. Combine the masa, baking powder and shortening in a bowl of an electric mixer, season with salt and mix until the masa pulls away from the sides of the bowl.
2. Sauté the onion, peppers and garlic in the vegetable oil until tender, season with salt. Remove from the heat and cool.
3. Cut the shrimp in half lengthwise.
4. To assemble the tamales, use a rubber spatula to spread 5 ounces (150 grams) of the masa mixture lengthwise on a 16-inch-by-12-inch (40-centimeter-by-30-centimeter) piece of parchment paper to form a 4-inch-by-12-inch (10-centimeter-by-30-centimeter) band of masa. Spread 1-1/2 ounces (45 grams) of the vegetable mixture in a line lengthwise down the center of the masa.
5. Place eight shrimp halves, end to end, on top of each row of onion-pepper-and-garlic mixture. Roll the mixture in the parchment paper so the masa completely encircles the shrimp and vegetable mixture. Twist the ends of the paper to seal. Repeat three more times to make four rolls. Freeze the rolls.
6. Unwrap each frozen roll and cut into four pieces. Wrap each piece tightly in dry corn husks that have been soaked in water, tying each end with thin strands of husk. Steam the tamales for 30–45 minutes. Allow the steamed tamales to rest 10 minutes after cooking so the masa becomes firm. Serve warm.

◆◆◆

RECIPE 33.31

POTATO RAVIOLI WITH LOBSTER

Yield: 32 Ravioli

Lobster meat	4 oz.	120 g
Salt and pepper	TT	TT
Lemon juice	TT	TT
Baking potatoes, 80 count	2	2
Clarified butter	4 oz.	120 g

1. Dice the lobster and season with salt, pepper and a few drops of lemon juice.

2. Peel the potatoes and slice them very thin (almost translucent) on an electric slicer or mandoline.

3. Place a small piece of lobster between two slices of potato and press the potato slices together with your fingers.

4. Place the ravioli immediately into a hot sauté pan with 1/4 inch (6 millimeters) of clarified butter. Fry until the potato begins to brown. Turn and finish on the other side.

5. Serve the ravioli accompanied by greens or an appropriate sauce such as mushroom sauce.

━━━━━ ◆◆◆ ━━━━━

RECIPE 33.32
SAUTÉED FOIE GRAS ON WILD MUSHROOM DUXELLES WITH TOASTED BRIOCHE

ANA WESTIN HOTEL, WASHINGTON D.C.
Chef Leland Atkinson

Yield: 4 Servings

Fresh foie gras, A grade	1 lb.	450 g
Wild mushrooms	1 lb.	450 g
Shallots, chopped	2 Tbsp.	30 ml
Garlic, chopped	1 tsp.	5 ml
Butter	1 Tbsp.	15 ml
Tomato paste	1 tsp.	5 ml
Brandy	1 Tbsp.	15 ml
Fresh thyme	1 tsp.	5 ml
Salt and pepper	TT	TT
Madeira sauce (Recipe 10.12)	8 oz.	250 g
Brioche (Recipe 28.16)	8 slices	8 slices

1. Allow the foie gras to come to near room temperature. With a sharp knife, scrape the thin membrane from the outside of the liver. Gently pull the pieces apart. Gently pull out any visible veins. Slice the liver on a slight bias into slices approximately 1 inch (2.5 centimeters) thick. Cover and chill until service.

2. To make the duxelles, clean and chop the wild mushrooms.

3. Sauté the shallots and garlic in the butter.

4. Add the mushrooms and cook until they first release their moisture and then begin to dry, approximately 5 minutes.

5. Add the tomato paste and brandy and cook until dry, stirring often.

6. Add the thyme and adjust the seasonings with salt and pepper. Remove the duxelles from the heat.

7. Quickly sauté the foie gras in a hot dry pan until it is browned on both sides but still bright pink in the middle, approximately 2 minutes.

8. Portion the duxelles onto four warm serving plates. Ladle the Madeira sauce around the duxelles. Blot the foie gras on a dry towel and arrange it over the top of the duxelles. Serve with toasted brioche and fresh thyme garnish.

◆◆◆

RECIPE 33.33
CARPACCIO

Yield: 8 Servings

Beef tenderloin, trimmed of all silverskin and fat	1 lb.	450 g
Mayonnaise, fresh	8 oz.	250 g
Dijon mustard	1 Tbsp.	15 ml
Salt and pepper	TT	TT
Onion	4 oz.	120 g
Capers, chopped	4 tsp.	20 ml
Cracked black pepper	TT	TT
Olive oil	8 tsp.	40 ml

1. Place the tenderloin in the freezer until nearly frozen.
2. Combine the fresh mayonnaise with the mustard. Season with salt and pepper.
3. Peel the onion and cut it in half from the stem to the root end. Slice it very thin.
4. Slice the nearly frozen tenderloin on an electric slicer very thin, almost transparent. On a very cold plate, arrange one slightly overlapping layer of thin slices of beef.
5. Sprinkle each plate of beef with 1/2 teaspoon (2.5 milliliters) of capers, a generous amount of cracked black pepper, salt and 1/2 ounce (15 grams) of shaved onion. Drizzle with 1 teaspoon (5 milliliters) of the olive oil and spoon 1/2 ounce (15 grams) of the mayonnaise in the center of each plate. Serve very cold.

◆◆◆

RECIPE 33.34
EGGPLANT AND SUN-DRIED TOMATO PIZZA

GREENS RESTAURANT, SAN FRANCISCO, CA
Executive Chef Annie Somerville

Yield: 1 15-in. (37-cm) or
2 9-in. (22-cm) Pizzas

Japanese eggplants	2	2
Extra virgin olive oil	2 oz.	60 g
Garlic, chopped	2 tsp.	10 ml
Salt and pepper	TT	TT
Pizza dough (Recipe 28.12)	1 lb.	450 g
Sun-dried tomatoes, packed in oil	5	5
Provolone cheese, grated	4 oz.	120 g
Mozzarella cheese, grated	2 oz.	60 g
Parmesan cheese, grated	1/2 oz.	15 g
Fresh basil, chiffonade	12 leaves	12 leaves

1. Slice the eggplant diagonally into 1/2-inch (1.2-centimeters) slices.
2. Toss the eggplant with 1 ounce (30 grams) of olive oil and the garlic; season with salt and pepper.

3. Place the eggplant slices on a baking sheet and roast at 375°F (190°C) until soft in the center, approximately 15–20 minutes. Cool and slice into strips.

4. Preheat the oven to 500°F (260°C). Roll out the dough and place it on a lightly oiled pizza pan or well-floured wooden peel; brush it lightly with the remaining olive oil. Lay the eggplant and sun-dried tomatoes on top. Toss the provolone and mozzarella cheeses together and sprinkle on the pizza.

5. Bake the pizza until the crust is golden and crisp, approximately 8–12 minutes. Remove from the oven and sprinkle with the Parmesan cheese and basil.

========= ◆◆◆ =========

RECIPE 33.35

SPRING ROLLS

Yield: 36 Rolls

Peanut oil	2 oz.	60 g
Sesame oil	3 Tbsp.	45 ml
Onions, julienne	12 oz.	350 g
Red bell peppers, julienne	12 oz.	350 g
Snow peas, julienne	12 oz.	350 g
Fresh ginger, grated	1 Tbsp.	15 ml
Garlic, chopped	1 Tbsp.	15 ml
Napa cabbage, julienne	8 oz.	250 g
Bean sprouts	1 lb.	450 g
Cashews, unsalted, crushed	1 lb.	450 g
Cayenne pepper	1 tsp.	5 ml
Salt and pepper	TT	TT
Rice paper wrappers	36	36

1. Heat the oils and sauté the onions and peppers for 30 seconds.

2. Add the snow peas, ginger and garlic; sauté for 15 seconds.

3. Add the cabbage, bean sprouts, cashews, cayenne, salt and pepper. Cook for 15 seconds more.

4. Remove from the heat, cool and refrigerate.

5. Soak the rice paper wrappers in water for a few seconds to soften them. Place 2 ounces (60 grams) of filling in each wrapper, fold the sides over toward the middle and roll up into a cigar shape. Brush the edge with water and press to seal.

6. Deep-fry the spring rolls at 350°F (180°C) until hot and crispy, approximately 45 seconds.

CHAPTER 34

INTERNATIONAL FLAVOR PRINCIPLES

After studying this chapter you will be able to:

◆ understand the flavor principles of several cuisines
◆ prepare chicken and starch dishes incorporating the flavor principles and representative cooking methods of each of these cuisines

*P*eople worldwide share a love of food. But the ingredients, flavorings, seasonings and cooking methods they use are not the same. Whether defined by geography, history, ethnicity, politics or religion, various societies eat different foods seasoned and prepared in distinctive manners. These differences shape and define their particular cuisine.

Because this book is a guide to understanding the hows and whys of cooking and is not simply a collection of recipes, we will not explore here all of the world's cuisines nor provide a comprehensive selection of recipes illustrating the cuisines discussed. Instead, we delve into the flavor principles that distinguish several important cuisines from European and American traditions.

Once you understand these principles, you should be able to prepare a variety of dishes that reflect a particular cuisine's flavor principles and cooking methods. To illustrate this point, and because most societies eat chicken, we include a chicken and starch recipe from each of the cuisines discussed.

Cookery—*the art, practice or work of cooking.*

Cuisine—*the ingredients, seasonings, cooking procedures and styles and eating habits attributable to a particular group of people; the group can be defined by geography, history, ethnicity, politics, culture or religion.*

National cuisine—*the characteristic cuisine of a nation.*

Regional cuisine—*a set of recipes based upon local ingredients, traditions and practices; within a larger geographical, political, cultural or social unit, regional cuisines are often variations of each other that blend together to create a national cuisine.*

Ethnic cuisine—*the cuisine of a group of people having a common cultural heritage as opposed to the cuisine of a group of people bound together by geography or political factors.*

Professional cooking—*a system of cooking based upon a knowledge of ingredients and procedures.*

◆◆◆
RECIPES FOR ETHNIC CUISINES

In *Ethnic Cuisine: The Flavor Principle Cookbook*, Elisabeth Rozin writes: "Every culture tends to combine a small number of flavoring ingredients so frequently and so consistently that they become definitive of that particular cuisine" (p. xiv). She calls these defining flavors "flavor principles" and notes that they are "designed to abstract what is absolutely fundamental about a cuisine and, thus, to serve as a guide in cooking and developing new recipes" (p. xvii). She identifies the following flavor principles for European cuisines:

Greek:
tomato, cinnamon *or* olive oil, lemon, oregano

Italian:
generally—olive oil, garlic, basil
Northern Italy—wine vinegar, garlic
Southern Italy—olive oil, garlic, parsley and/or anchovy plus tomato as a variation

French:
generally—olive oil, garlic, basil *or* wine, herb *or* butter and/or cream and/or cheese plus wine and/or stock
Southern France—olive oil, garlic, parsley and/or anchovy plus tomato as a variation
Provence—olive oil, thyme, rosemary, marjoram, sage plus tomato as a variation
Normandy—apple, cider, Calvados

Spanish:
olive oil, garlic, nut *or* olive oil, onion, pepper, tomato

Hungarian:
onion, lard, paprika

Eastern European Jewish:
onion, chicken fat

Eastern and Northern European:
sour cream, dill or paprika or allspice or caraway

CHINESE CUISINES

China, a large, geographically diverse country, nurtures several distinctive regional cuisines, the most prominent of which are called here Northern, Southern, Western and Eastern. All Chinese cuisines emphasize a sophisticated contrast and harmony of flavors (sweet, sour, bitter, spicy and salty) and textures (crisp, crunchy, chunky, chewy, smooth and liquid) and rely on the quick cooking of attractively cut, bite-sized pieces of food. Reducing all foods to bite-sized pieces promotes the quick infusion of flavorings. Most cooking is done in a wok that can be used for stir-frying, deep-frying and steaming. Anthropologists suggest that the reliance on quick cooking methods was the result of chronic fuel shortages. Although these quick cooking methods can produce fully cooked foods in minutes, the careful cutting and preparation techniques often require far more time.

Staples include several varieties of rice, noodles (made from rice, beans and wheat) and soy beans (eaten as seeds, beans, sprouts and curd, and used for oil and sauce). Pork, poultry (particularly chicken and duck), fish (particularly pike, carp and bass) and shellfish are regularly consumed, as are a large assortment of vegetables (including varieties of mushrooms, several cabbages, bamboo shoots, water chestnuts and snow peas) and fruits (including litchi, pears, plums and various citrus fruits).

Common spices are star anise, cinnamon, cloves, fennel and Szechuan peppercorns (these are sometimes blended for five spice powder), lemon balm, tangerine peel, coriander, sesame seeds and oil, lotus nut paste, lotus root and hot chiles (a New World import). Commonly used sauces include plum, oyster, hoisin and both light and dark soy.

Chinese - (clockwise from top left) chicken in black bean sauce, white rice, rolls of moo shu chicken, plum sauce, moo shu chicken

Northern China

Northern China includes Beijing, the capital. Some consider this region's cuisine to be the most aristocratic of the regional cuisines; indeed, it is sometimes referred to as Mandarin cuisine, named for the centuries-old Chinese aristocratic and bureaucratic classes.

Northern Chinese dishes are generally lightly spiced and contain little residual oil. Because northern China is relatively dry, rice is not a regional staple, as rice needs an abundance of water to grow. Instead, wheat and millet, eaten as noodles, dumplings and pancakes, are popular. *Chao mian* is a dish of thin wheat noodles stir-fried with other ingredients. Freshwater fish are regularly consumed, as is lamb, a meat rarely eaten elsewhere in china. Meats and poultry are most often roasted or barbecued; Peking duck is a well-known example. Mongol influence still exists in the form of the Mongolian hot pot: a simmering broth into which each diner submerges bits of meat, poultry, vegetables or bean curd.

A classic Northern Chinese dish is Moo Shu Chicken: The wood ears (mushrooms) and bamboo shoots provide contrasting textures, the duck sauce (also known as plum sauce) is a delicate condiment and the pancakes are classically Mandarin. The dish is best enjoyed by spreading 1/2 teaspoon (3 milliliters) of the duck sauce on each pancake, then topping with green onions and 2–3 tablespoons (30–45 milliliters) of the moo shu. The pancake is then rolled up with the ends folded in.

RECIPE 34.1
MOO SHU CHICKEN

Yield: 4 Servings

Chicken breast, boneless, skinless	8 oz.	250 g
Marinade:		
Chinese rice wine	1 tsp.	5 ml
Salt	TT	TT
Egg white, beaten	1	1
Soy sauce	1/2 tsp.	3 ml
Wood ear mushrooms, dried	5	5
Eggs	3	3
Vegetable oil	4 oz.	120 g
Garlic, chopped	1 tsp.	5 ml
Hoisin sauce	2 oz.	60 g
Bamboo shoots, shredded	3 oz.	90 g
Bok choy, shredded	3 oz.	90 g
Carrot, shredded	3 oz.	90 g
Salt	1 tsp.	5 ml
Chicken stock	2 oz.	60 g
Green onions, shredded	1 oz.	30 g

1. Slice the chicken into thin strips, approximately 1-1/2 inches by 1/4 inch (4 centimeters by .6 centimeters), and marinate in the rice wine, salt, egg white and soy sauce for 15 minutes.
2. Soak the wood ears in hot water until soft. Break off the hard stems and shred the mushrooms.
3. Beat the eggs. Heat 1 tablespoon (15 milliliters) of the oil in a wok and cook the eggs. Do not let them brown. Remove the eggs, shred and set aside.

4. Stir-fry the garlic in 2 ounces (60 grams) of oil until golden. Add the chicken and stir-fry until the chicken is very lightly browned. Remove the chicken, drain and set aside.

5. Add the hoisin sauce and 2 tablespoons (30 milliliters) of oil to the wok; quickly stir-fry the sauce. Add the bamboo shoots, bok choy, carrots and shredded mushrooms and cook for 5 minutes.

6. Add the chicken, salt, chicken stock and shredded eggs. Stir-fry over high heat for 1 minute.

7. Serve hot, garnished with green onions.

━━━ ◆◆◆ ━━━

RECIPE 34.2

DUCK SAUCE

Yield: 4 oz. (110 g)

Sweet bean sauce	3 Tbsp.	45 ml
Hoisin sauce	3 Tbsp.	45 ml
Sugar	1 tsp.	5 ml
Sesame oil	1 Tbsp.	15 ml

1. Combine and stir all the ingredients until smooth. Serve at room temperature.

━━━ ◆◆◆ ━━━

RECIPE 34.3

MANDARIN PANCAKES

Yield: 16 5-inch (12.5-centimeter) Pancakes

All-purpose flour	8 oz.	250 g
Sesame oil	1 Tbsp.	15 ml
Salt	pinch	pinch
Boiling water	6 oz.	180 g

1. Place the flour, 1/2 teaspoon (2 milliliters) of sesame oil and a pinch of salt in a bowl. Add the boiling water and gradually mix by hand to make a soft dough.

2. On a lightly floured surface, gently knead the dough until smooth. Cover with a damp cloth and let rest for 15 minutes.

3. Shape the dough into a cylinder about 1 inch (2.5 centimeters) in diameter, adding more flour if necessary. Slice the log into 16 equal pieces; roll each piece into a ball and then flatten each to make a disk.

4. Brush the tops of eight disks with the remaining sesame oil. Then place an unoiled disk on top of each oiled disk. Using a rolling pin, flatten each pair of disks into a 5-inch (12.5-centimeter) circle. Cover the pancakes with a dry towel.

5. Heat an ungreased 8-inch (20-centimeter) skillet over high heat for 30 seconds to 1 minute. Reduce the heat to medium.

6. Place one pancake pair into the skillet. When it puffs and bubbles appear on its surface, turn it over and cook the other side until it is speckled brown, approximately 1 minute. Then turn the pancake and cook the first side until it too is speckled brown, approximately 30 seconds. Remove the pancake and wrap it in a clean, dry towel.

Continued

7. Repeat until each pancake pair is cooked.

8. Just before service, separate each pancake pair by gently pulling apart at the edges. Serve warm.

Southern China

Southern Chinese cuisine is centered in and around Canton, a fertile area rich with rice paddies, vegetable farms and fruit orchards. All these ingredients are found in the cuisine, along with an abundance of saltwater and freshwater fish and shellfish as well as more exotic ingredients such as abalone, sea urchin, snake, shark fins, turtle, snails and eel. Both rice and wheat noodle dishes are very popular.

Southern Chinese cuisine emphasizes the freshness of its local ingredients; therefore stir-frying is a popular cooking method. When stir-frying, most of the spices and nonliquid flavoring ingredients are added at the start. Their flavors are released by quickly sautéing them in hot oil. The liquid flavoring ingredients are usually mixed with a thickening agent (often cornstarch) and added toward the end of cooking. This mixture then boils and thickens, coating the foods with the flavoring sauce.

◆◆◆

RECIPE 34.4
CHICKEN AND SNOW PEAS IN BLACK BEAN SAUCE

Yield: 4 Servings

Chicken breasts, boneless, skinless	2 lb.	1 kg
Egg white	1	1
Chinese rice wine	6 oz.	180 g
Cornstarch	2 Tbsp.	30 ml
Soy sauce	2 oz.	60 g
Granulated sugar	2 tsp.	10 ml
Onions, small	2	2
Peanut oil	4 oz.	120 ml
Garlic, minced	1 Tbsp.	15 ml
Fresh ginger, minced	2 tsp.	10 ml
Fermented black beans, mashed	3 Tbsp.	45 ml
Snow peas, fresh	4 oz.	120 g

1. Slice the chicken into thin strips, approximately 1-1/2 inches by 1/4 inch (4 centimeters by .6 centimeters).

2. Combine the egg white, one third of the wine and 1 tablespoon (15 milliliters) of the cornstarch. Add the chicken and refrigerate for 2 hours.

3. For the sauce, mix the soy sauce, sugar and the remaining wine and cornstarch.

4. Quarter the onions and separate the layers.

5. Stir-fry the chicken in 3 ounce (90 grams) of oil. Remove and set aside.

6. If necessary, add all the remaining oil and stir-fry the garlic and ginger for 30 seconds. Add the onions and mashed beans and stir-fry for 30 seconds. Add the snow peas and cook for 1 minute.

7. Return the chicken to the wok, add the sauce mixture and stir-fry until hot and the sauce has thickened.

8. Serve immediately with short-grain white rice.

VARIATION: Add 2 ounces (60 grams) sliced mushrooms and reduce the amount of snow peas by half.

Western China

Encompassing the cookery of both Szechuan and Hunan provinces, Western Chinese cuisine is distinguished by its spiciness. Favorite seasonings include ginger, vinegar, garlic, sesame oil, green onions and hot chiles. Szechuan recipes usually incorporate chiles in paste form, while Hunan dishes use fresh chiles. Hunan cuisine is typically more sweet and sour than Szechuan cuisine. Both, however, include countless dishes that offer diners several competing spices. After the first fiery sensation passes, these multiple flavors should be recognizable and savored.

Both rice and wheat are grown in western China. Fresh and dried freshwater fish, pork, beef and poultry are common ingredients, as are several types of mushrooms. Often the meats are subjected to several preparations for one dish.

♦♦♦

RECIPE 34.5

JAR GAI
(SZECHUAN-STYLE FRIED CHICKEN)

Yield: 4 Servings

Chicken breasts, boneless, skinless	1 lb.	500 g
Cornstarch	5 Tbsp.	75 ml
Salt	1 tsp.	5 ml
Five spice powder	3/4 tsp.	4 ml
Chicken stock	8 oz.	250 g
Granulated sugar	2 tsp.	10 ml
Light soy sauce	1 Tbsp.	15 ml
Sesame oil	1/2 tsp.	3 ml
Rice wine vinegar	1 tsp.	5 ml
Chinese rice wine	2 tsp.	10 ml
Black pepper, ground	1/4 tsp.	2 ml
Cold water	1 Tbsp.	15 ml
Canola or corn oil	4 oz.	120 g
Red chiles, dried and seeded	15	15
Garlic, chopped fine	2 tsp.	10 ml
Fresh ginger, peeled and chopped fine	2 tsp.	10 ml
Green onions, trimmed and cut into 2-in. (5-cm) lengths	4	4

1. Slice the chicken into thin strips, approximately 1-1/2 inches by 1/4 inch (4 centimeters by .6 centimeters).

2. Combine 4 tablespoons (60 milliliters) of the cornstarch, the salt and 1/2

Continued

A CHINESE MEAL

In traditional Chinese culture, little separates philosophy, religion and food, and certain rituals are associated with all meals. Meals are also full of symbolism: Braised turtle, for instance, signifies long life; round foods are consumed on holidays dedicated to the full moon.

Just as each dish should provide contrasting flavors and textures, an entire meal should be composed of several complementary and contrasting dishes. A festive Chinese dinner often starts with a cold dish, followed by several hot dishes, then a light soup, usually clear with a few uncooked or undercooked garnishes. Normally, no one hot dish is meant as the main course, and each should offer a different dominant flavor or texture. Rice, noodles or pancakes are served as an accompaniment; tea is the principal beverage and fresh or crystallized fruit constitutes dessert.

American and European eating habits have given rise to a first course of small, usually hot appetizers such as steamed or fried pork dumplings (*chiao-tzu*), steamed yeast-risen wheat buns with various fillings (*bao*) or spring rolls. (Traditionally, all manner of stuffed dumplings and other small dishes, known collectively as *dim sum*—Cantonese for "heart's delight"—are served as a mid-morning meal.) The appetizers are then followed by soup. Fortune cookies are an American invention; moon cakes (*yue bing*), pastries with various sweet fillings made of bean pastes, nuts or fruits surrounding a piece of salted duck egg yolk, are a more traditional sweet served as dessert.

Although the Chinese knew of forks for centuries, they viewed their use at the table as barbaric, preferring the more delicate chopsticks.

teaspoon (3 milliliters) of the five spice powder. Toss the chicken pieces in the mixture; dust off any excess cornstarch.

3. Mix 4 ounces (120 grams) of the stock with the sugar, soy sauce, sesame oil, vinegar, wine, pepper and the remaining five spice powder.

4. In a separate bowl, mix the water and remaining cornstarch.

5. Heat the oil and stir-fry the chicken in small batches.

6. Degrease the pan, reserving 2 tablespoons (30 milliliters) of the oil. Add the chiles, garlic and ginger; stir-fry until the garlic and ginger are golden and the chiles turn dark.

7. Add the green onions and toss for a few seconds. Add the stock mixture and bring to a boil.

8. Thicken the sauce with the remaining cornstarch-and-water mixture.

9. Return the chicken to the pan and toss to heat thoroughly.

10. Serve immediately with short-grain white rice.

Eastern China

Shanghai, a large city on China's east coast, has been the principal point of contact between foreigners and Chinese since the 19th century. Its cuisine reflects this contact. For example, dairy products, which rarely appear in Chinese cuisine, are sometimes used in Eastern Chinese recipes. Similarly, meats are often subjected to slow cooking methods more typical of Europe, such as red-cooking, a form of simmering named for the rich, red-brown sauce that results from cooking the meat in soy sauce. Wine, soy sauces, vinegars (especially an aged vinegar known as Chinkiang) and sugar are the predominant flavorings.

Eastern Chinese cuisine also reflects the fertile area's year-round growing season, many rivers and long shoreline. While most other regional Chinese cuisines incorporate only one or two vegetables in a dish, Shanghai chefs will blend six or more, often cutting them into different shapes.

◆◆◆

RECIPE 34.6

SEE YO GAI
(RED-COOKED CHICKEN)

Yield: 4 Servings

Roasting chicken, 3–4 lb. (1.3–1.8 kg)	1	1
Cold water	12 oz.	350 g
Dark soy sauce	12 oz.	350 g
Chinese rice wine	2 oz.	60 g
Fresh ginger, peeled and sliced thin	2 oz.	60 g
Garlic, chopped	1 tsp.	5 ml
Star anise	10	10
Granulated sugar	1-1/2 Tbsp.	23 ml
Sesame oil	2 tsp.	10 ml

1. Place the washed chicken, breast side down, in a lidded saucepan small enough so that the liquid ingredients will cover it completely.

2. Add all other ingredients except the sesame oil and slowly bring to a boil. Reduce the heat and simmer for 15 minutes. Turn the chicken and simmer for 20 minutes, basting the bird every 5 minutes.

3. Remove the pot from the heat and leave covered until cool.*

4. Remove the chicken and brush it with the sesame oil. The chicken can be carved in joints or, in the traditional Chinese manner, split lengthwise and chopped into strips 1-1/2 inches (4 centimeters) wide.

5. Serve the chicken at room temperature* with the leftover sauce for dipping and a noodle dish as an accompaniment.

*Allowing cooked chicken to cool in this manner and then serving it at room temperature is not consistent with sound food-handling procedures; it is, however, an authentic practice.

JAPANESE CUISINE

As with their arts, the Japanese strive for a cuisine that reflects *sappari*: clarity, lightness, simplicity and order. Small portions of subtly combined ingredients, flavors and textures beautifully presented on dishes that complement the food are its hallmarks.

Rice, both sweet and savory, is the staple of the Japanese diet; indeed, *gohan*, a Japanese word for rice, also refers to a meal. Rice is served steamed, pressed into cakes or made into noodles. Other staples are soybean products

Japanese - (clockwise from top left) sake, white rice, chicken yakitori with dipping sauce, ebi sushi

◆◆◆

A JAPANESE MEAL

The aesthetics of a Japanese meal are of great importance. The aesthetic considerations relate to both the beauty of the food as well as to its presentation. Great care is often taken to cut, carve and form foods into delightful shapes: a carrot slice can be cut like a blossom for spring and a maple leaf in the autumn; a nigiri zushi can be tied with a bow of green onion; a choice morsel of raw fish can be formed into the shape of a rose. Lacquered and porcelain trays, dishes and covered bowls are commonly used for service, and care is taken to make sure the shape, material, size, color and pattern complement the food.

Traditional dinners cooked by highly trained chefs known as *kappo* consist of at least four different courses. They combine liquid, crisp and simmered foods, some spicey and others bland. Alternating consistencies and tastes is a golden rule of Japanese cuisine. Generally tofu and invariably rice are served. Bites of rice are often eaten along with the other foods. Tea and sake are common dinner drinks.

including bean curd (tofu), bean paste (miso), sprouts, seeds and sauce. Japanese cuisine also relies on a variety of noodles, including ones made from wheat (the thin ramen, the thicker somen and the very thick udon), buckwheat (soba) and mung beans.

Fish and shellfish play important roles in Japanese cuisine for two reasons. First, Japan is a nation of mountainous islands that depends on the sea as the source for much of its protein. And, second, until the 19th century much of the Japanese population followed Buddhist teachings that prescribed a vegetarian diet supplemented with fish and shellfish. During this century, however, there has been a marked increase in the consumption of meat (especially beef) and poultry (especially chicken).

Typical seasonings—used, for the most part, quite judiciously—include rice wine vinegar, wasabi (a pungent green root erroneously called green horseradish), daikon (a white radish), pepper, sesame oil and seeds, ginger, soy sauce (known as *shoyu*, generally lighter and more delicate than Chinese soy sauce), rice wine (mirin, which is light and sweet and used only for cooking, and sake, a finer product used for cooking and drinking), tamari sauce, seaweed and pressed algae products (from the delicate to the very fishy), dried fish and shellfish and a variety of pickled foods (collectively known as *zuke*) as well as fresh herbs. Many dishes are marinated before cooking.

Yakitori, a classic Japanese flavoring combination of soy sauce, rice wine and sugar, is often used for broiled or grilled dishes.

◆◆◆

RECIPE 34.7

CHICKEN YAKITORI

Yield: 8 Servings

Soy sauce	8 oz.	250 g
Sake	8 oz.	250 g
Granulated sugar	2 oz.	60 g
Chicken breasts, boneless	2 lb.	1 kg
Cornstarch	1 Tbsp.	15 ml
Sesame seeds	1 Tbsp.	15 ml

1. Combine the soy sauce, sake and sugar. Reserve 8 ounces (250 grams) of the mixture.
2. Brush the chicken with a portion of the reserved soy sauce mixture and grill over hot charcoal until done, basting regularly.
3. To make the sauce, combine 2 ounces (60 grams) of the soy sauce mixture with the cornstarch. Bring the remainder to a boil in a small saucepan and stir in the cornstarch slurry. Stirring constantly, continue boiling until the sauce thickens. Simmer 1 minute.
4. Serve with short-grain white rice and garnish with sesame seeds.

Japanese cooking generally relies on quick cooking of bite-sized pieces of food. Foods can be grilled (called *yakimono*; if done tableside, as is typical, they are referred to as *nabemon*), steamed (*mushimono*), simmered in an aromatic broth (these liquid-based dishes often start with *dashi*, a fish-flavored stock made from kelp and bonito; the cooking process is referred to as *nimono*) or deep-fried (*agemono*). The deep-frying technique and batter known as tempura are actually derived from cooking techniques and recipes Portuguese Jesuits introduced to the Japanese during the late 16th century.

Japanese cuisine also offers a variety of raw foods, collectively known as *namamono*. Sashimi, small slices of fresh fish served with a soy sauce spiked with mustard and wasabi, is popular; as are *nigiri zushi* (small balls of sushi—vinegar-flavored rice—topped with a slice of raw fish or shellfish) and *maki zushi* (raw fish or shellfish rolled in sushi and crisp seaweed). Recipes and techniques for these are given in Chapter 33, Hors d'Oeuvres and Appetizers.

INDIAN CUISINES

Indian cuisine offers more than curry. The Indian subcontinent is home to many peoples, including Hindus, Buddhists and Muslims; each has a distinctive cuisine, and each cuisine has influenced the others, giving rise to several regional cuisines. Kasmir in the far north is famous for its meat and chickpeas, while the northern areas of Delhi and Bengal are famous for their tandoori and intensely sweet desserts, respectively. The western seaport of Bombay is known for its pork and vinegar, while vegetarian dishes made with tamarind, semolina and coconut are popular in the southern seaport of Madras.

The heart of Indian cookery is the masala, the combination of spices that gives each dish its distinctive taste. A masala's preparation, subtlety and sophistication are the tests by which chefs are often judged. The timing of its incorporation into the dish is critical. Common spices for masalas are turmeric, cumin seeds, coriander seeds, fenugreek, saffron, fennel seeds, mace, nutmeg, cardamom, clove, cinnamon, mustard seeds, sesame seeds, and black, red and white peppercorns. Garlic, onions and chiles are also popular flavorings, as are several herbs including coriander leaves, mint leaves and sweet basil. Souring agents include vinegar, lemon juice and imli (water with extract of tamarind). Curry powder is really nothing more than a commercial masala typically containing fenugreek, coriander, cumin, turmeric, ginger, celery seeds,

Indian - (clockwise from top) naan, chicken tandoor, mango chutney, saffron rice

mace and pepper. The word *curry* is probably derived from the Tamil word *kari*, meaning sauce or combination of seasonings; the product is considered an inferior British invention never used in true Indian cooking.

◆◆◆

RECIPE 34.8

MASALA

Yield: 3 oz. (90 g)

Coriander seeds	4 Tbsp.	60 ml
Cumin seeds	2 Tbsp.	30 ml
Black peppercorns, whole	1 Tbsp.	15 ml
Cardamom seeds (measure after		
removing pods)	2 tsp.	10 ml
Cinnamon sticks, 3 in. (7.5 cm) long	4	4
Cloves, whole	1 tsp.	5 ml
Nutmeg, whole	1	1

1. In a small saucepan, separately dry-roast the coriander seeds, cumin seeds, peppercorns, cardamom seeds, cinnamon and cloves. As each begins to smell fragrant, remove from the pan to cool. After dry-roasting the cardamom, peel it, remove the seeds and discard the pods.

2. With a mortar and pestle or spice grinder, blend all the roasted spices to a fine powder.

3. Finely grate the nutmeg and mix it in with the other spices.

4. Store tightly covered and away from light.

The staples of Indian cuisine are rice, dals and bread. The rice is usually long-grain and served steamed and mixed with flavorings and garnishes. For special occasions, aromatic rices such as basmati are eaten. Dals are pulses such as lentils, beans and peas; nearly 60 varieties of protein-rich pulses are used in Indian cookery. These include the small, sweet yellow *chana dal, moong dal* (mung beans) and the salmon-colored split pea called *masoor dal*. Breads, called *roti*, include *capitis* (flat, unleavened rounds made of whole wheat flour), *naan* (one of the few leavened breads), *paratha* (a flaky bread fried on a pan called a *tava*) and *poori* (a deep-fried puffy bread). Many pan-fried breads are stuffed with savory mixtures or dusted with flavorings. Rice and lentil flours are also used for breads.

Devout Muslims do not eat pork; devout Hindus do not eat beef and devout Buddhists do not eat any meat, poultry, fish, shellfish or dairy product.

For those who do eat meat and poultry, the most commonly eaten are mutton and chicken, prepared in a variety of ways: stewed with spices; marinated and grilled; braised in yogurt or cream (called *kormas*); sautéed and baked (called *bhoona*) or formed into meatballs (called *koftas*). A wide variety of freshwater and saltwater fish and shellfish are also consumed. Dairy products include a mild white fresh cheese known as *paneer*.

The long tradition of vegetarianism and the variety of vegetables and spices available have made for a vegetarian cuisine rich in flavors and textures. Vegetables are usually fried with spices and served without any sauce. These pungent dishes are known as *foogath* in the South and *bhujia* in the North. Vegetables can be puréed and delicately spiced (called *bharta*); or mashed, shaped into balls and fried.

Chutneys are relishes made from fruits, vegetables and herbs. Sometimes their flavors are tempered by marinating or cooking, although most fresh chutneys are nothing more than a mixture of raw foods, ground or finely cut and blended with seasonings. Chutneys are used to add contrast to the highly spiced dishes that dominate Indian cuisines.

Clarified butter made from water buffalo milk, known as *ghee*, is an important cooking medium, although ghee's expense has made a hydrogenated vegetable fat called *vanaspati* more popular. Usually, only meat is cooked in ghee; vegetable oils are used for vegetables.

The *degchi* is a commonly used cooking vessel. Traditionally made of brass but now also made of aluminum, it is a tall, straight-sided, flat-rimmed pot used for boiling, stewing, braising or steaming. When lidded, it can be used as an oven by placing coals below the pot as well as on the lid.

Northern India

The cuisine of Northern India reflects the strong Muslim presence found in northern and central India since the 16th-century Mogul invasions. This presence has given rise to a regional cuisine using meat. The area's geography favors wheat, not rice, so capitis is a dietary staple. Generally, Northern Indian cuisine produces dryer foods with thick sauces. A typical Northern masala calls for cumin, fenugreek, ginger and garlic. After the spices are ground and mixed, they are added to the dish without further preparation.

One of the best-known Northern Indian dishes is tandoori chicken. The tandoor is a jar-shaped clay oven usually buried in the earth and heated by placing hot coals inside. The meat or poultry is threaded on skewers and placed inside the oven to cook. The finished product has a wonderfully dry, crusty surface. Although it is difficult to reproduce the surface in a conventional oven, it is possible to reproduce the flavors.

◆◆◆

RECIPE 34.9

TANDOORI MURGH (CHICKEN TANDOOR)

Yield: 4 Servings

Roasting chicken, 3 lb. (1.3 kg)	1	1
Saffron strands	1/2 tsp.	3 ml
Boiling water	1 Tbsp.	15 ml
Garlic, chopped	2 Tbsp.	30 ml
Fresh ginger, peeled and minced	1 Tbsp.	15 ml
Lemon juice	2 Tbsp.	30 ml
Chilli powder	1 tsp.	5 ml
Paprika	1-1/2 tsp.	8 ml
Masala (Recipe 34.8)	2 tsp.	10 ml
Salt	1 tsp.	5 ml
Ghee (or clarified butter or canola oil)	3 Tbsp.	45 ml
Lemons, wedged	2	2

1. Quarter and skin the chicken, making slits in the drumsticks, thighs and breasts to allow the spices to penetrate.
2. Steep the saffron in boiling water for 10 minutes. Then combine it with the garlic, ginger, lemon juice, chilli powder, paprika, masala and salt; blend until smooth.
3. Season the chicken with the spice mixture, covering the entire surface, especially the slits. Cover and marinate, under refrigeration, for at least two hours or overnight.
4. Roast the chicken on a rack at 350°F (180°C), basting periodically with ghee, until done, approximately 45 minutes.
5. Serve hot, garnished with lemon wedges and accompanied by naan.

Southern India

The cuisine of Southern India is heavily influenced by Hindus. It offers a wide range of meatless dishes with rich, spicy sauces. Rice is the principal crop and it is eaten with almost every meal, as plain or flavored rice or as rice-flour breads such as *idli* and *dosa*. Southern Indian cuisine uses more fresh herbs than Northern Indian cuisine and its masalas are wet; that is, the ground spices are mixed into a paste with vinegar, water or coconut milk. (Wet masalas must be used immediately.) Typical spices used in Southern Indian masalas include mustard seed, tamarind and asafetida (a fennel-like resin). Chiles are more popular in the south than in the north, as is garlic.

◆◆◆

RECIPE 34.10

MURGHI KARI (CHICKEN CURRY)

Yield: 4 Servings

Onions, small dice	8 oz.	250 g
Garlic, crushed	2 tsp.	10 ml

Ghee (or clarified butter)	2 Tbsp.	30 ml
Fresh ginger, fine dice	2 oz.	60 g
Turmeric	1-1/2 tsp.	8 ml
Coriander seeds, ground	1-1/2 tsp.	8 ml
Cumin seeds, ground	1 tsp.	5 ml
Cayenne pepper	1 tsp.	5 ml
Fenugreek, ground	1/2 tsp.	3 ml
Coconut milk	20 oz.	575 g
Roasting chicken, 3 lb. (1.3 kg), cut into 8 pieces	1	1
Salt	1 tsp.	5 ml
Green chiles, slit lengthwise	3	3
Lemon juice	1 oz.	30 ml

1. Stir-fry the onions and garlic in the ghee until the onions are golden brown.

2. To make the wet masala, mix the ginger, turmeric, coriander, cumin, cayenne pepper and fenugreek; add just enough of the coconut milk to form a paste.

3. Add the wet masala to the onions and stir-fry for 8 minutes.

4. Add the chicken pieces and cook, turning them frequently, for 6–8 minutes.

5. Add the remaining coconut milk, salt and chiles. Bring to a boil, cover and reduce to a simmer. Cook until the chicken is done, approximately 45 minutes.

6. Just before service, stir in the lemon juice and adjust the seasonings. Serve with saffron rice and a chutney.

◆◆◆

RECIPE 34.11

KESAR CHAVAL (SAFFRON RICE)

Yield: 6 Servings

Basmati rice	1 pt.	450 ml
Saffron threads	1 tsp.	5 ml
Boiling water	1 qt.	900 ml
Ghee (or clarified butter)	3 oz.	90 g
Cinnamon sticks, 2 in. (5 cm) long	1	1
Cloves, whole	4	4
Onion, fine dice	5 oz.	150 g
Dark brown sugar	1 Tbsp.	15 ml
Salt	2 tsp.	10 ml
Cardamom seeds	1/4 tsp.	2 ml

1. Wash the rice and drain thoroughly.

2. Steep the saffron in 2 ounces (60 grams) of the boiling water.

3. In a saucepan, heat the ghee, add the cinnamon and cloves. Add the onions and stir-fry until they are soft and slightly brown.

4. Add the rice and stir until it is well coated with the ghee and the grains are a light golden color.

Continued

5. Stirring constantly, add the remaining boiling water, brown sugar, salt and cardamom seeds. Bring to a boil and reduce to a simmer.
6. Gently stir in the saffron and its water, cover and simmer until the rice has absorbed all the liquid.
7. Fluff with a fork and serve at once.

Throughout India, many foods are eaten in the form of savory snacks (collectively known as *chat*) which are served as appetizers or at teatime. Examples include *chanachur* (made from split peas, peanuts, lemon, peppers and lentil flour, all the ingredients being fried separately), *samosas* (deep-fried tidbits like turnovers, stuffed with meat, potatoes or vegetables), *pakoras* (vegetables or other foods dipped in chickpea flour and deep-fried), spiced fish balls and eggplant fritters served with chutney.

Sweet snacks (collectively known as *meethai*) are also an integral part of Indian cuisines. Many are made from milk that is condensed into a thick mass called *mawa*. *Mawa* is then cooked with sugar and flavorings such as coconut, almond, pistachio or kewra (a perfumed flower essence). *Jelebis* are pretzel-like sweets made from a batter of wheat and chickpea flour, oil and curds that is deep-fried and then dipped into a sugar syrup.

NORTH AFRICAN AND MIDDLE EASTERN CUISINES

Stretching from Morocco at the northwest tip of Africa, along the southern and eastern portions of the Mediterranean Sea and north to Lebanon, is a land primarily populated by Arabs. It is rich in religious and culinary traditions and offers a range of national cuisines. These various cuisines can be divided into two main groups: North African and Middle Eastern.

All of the cuisines, however, share certain staples, seasonings and a fondness for sweets. Wheat in various forms is eaten throughout the area. Legumes, including lentils, beans and peas, provide starch. Pork is virtually nonexistent for religious reasons; lamb is the principal meat, chicken the principal poultry. Fish from the Mediterranean is also popular. Garlic, onions, peppers, tomatoes and citrus are commonly used flavoring ingredients. Spices include cumin, ginger and peppercorns; herbs include mint, coriander and parsley. Eggplants, cucumbers, squash, okra, tomatoes, quinces, dates, figs, melons, pomegranates, mangoes and bananas are popular. A consistent theme among the various cuisines is a combination of fruits and nuts cooked with savory meat dishes.

North African

The cuisines of North Africa include those of Morocco, Algeria and Tunisia as well as those of the more nomadic Bedouin tribes. This area, often referred to as the Maghreb, was once the granary for Imperial Rome. More recently, France was the dominant foreign influence. North African cuisine is based on cereals, vegetables, dried fruits and grilled meats. The national cuisines differ to a degree: Foods are more highly seasoned in Algeria and Tunisia and more subtly spiced in Morocco.

A principal spice mixture (known as *ras al hanout* in Morocco) consists of cinnamon, cumin, coriander, ginger and turmeric. Other North African season-

*Middle Eastern - (clockwise from top left) baklava, medjool dates, pita bread, harissa,
Tangier couscous*

ings and flavoring ingredients include garlic, onions, tomatoes, olives, fresh
coriander leaves, fresh mint leaves, parsley and dried limes or lemons.

Many North African meat dishes include fruit or other sweet foods. For
example, *tajine*, a type of slow-cooked ragout, may be made with mutton or
rabbit with prunes and accompanied by fennel with lemon; chicken is cooked
with cinnamon, kumquats and onions, and mutton is cooked with quinces
and honey. Meats, often reduced to bite-sized chunks or ground balls, are
often grilled or spit-roasted as kebabs. Fish can be grilled or fried. Vegetables
are cooked in a sauce and frequently served with scrambled eggs, marinated
and served in a salad or stuffed with sweet and savory foods. Soups are
always highly aromatic and often associated with religious festivities. The
soups often combine dried vegetables or cereals (lentils, beans, chickpeas,
unripe wheat) with meat (diced mutton or chicken) or fish.

Wheat is the principal grain and it is used to make one of the better-known
North African dishes: couscous. Couscous refers to both the starch and the
completed dish. The starch is made of semolina flour produced from hard
durum wheat. It is steamed over a watery stew of lamb, chicken, beef (usually
in the form of meatballs), fish or tripe and vegetables in a couscousier. A
couscousier consists of two bulbous pots. The bottom one sits on the heat
and holds the watery stew. The second sits on top of the first; it has a perforated bottom and holds the couscous. As the stew simmers, steam rising from
it gently cooks the couscous and infuses flavors. The dish can be flavored
with saffron (Morocco), tomato purée (Algeria) or ginger and pepper
(Tunisia). Traditionally mixed with smeun fat, a sort of rancid butter, the couscous and stew are more typically served with harissa, a hot and pungent

sauce (see Recipe 11.14). Couscous is eaten by taking a small amount of the couscous along with a morsel of meat or vegetable, rolling it into a ball and popping it into the mouth. This entire action should be accomplished with only the first three fingers of the right hand.

━━━ ◆◆◆ ━━━

RECIPE 34.12
TANGIER COUSCOUS (SEKSU TANJAOUI)

Yield: 4 Servings

Roaster chicken, quartered with giblets, 3–4 lb. (1.3–1.8 kg)	1	1
Salt	2 tsp.	10 ml
Pepper	1 Tbsp.	15 ml
Ginger, ground	2-1/2 tsp.	12 ml
Saffron, pulverized and mixed with turmeric	1/2 tsp.	3 ml
Cayenne pepper	pinch	pinch
Onions, medium, quartered	3	3
Bouquet garni:		
Fresh coriander	4 sprigs	4 sprigs
Fresh parsley	4 sprigs	4 sprigs
Whole butter	8 oz.	250 g
Water	5 pt.	2.5 lt
Couscous	1 lb. 8 oz.	700 g
Onion, large, julienne	1	1
Raisins	3 oz.	90 g
Chicken stock	as needed	as needed

1. Place the chicken, salt, pepper, ginger, saffron, cayenne, onion quarters, bouquet garni and half the butter in the bottom of the couscousier. Melt the butter and stir the ingredients to coat them with the melted butter. Add 5 pints (2.5 liters) of water; bring to a boil, reduce to a simmer and cook 1 hour.

2. Combine the couscous with 3 quarts (3 liters) cold water; mix and drain. Gently break apart any lumps.

3. After the stew has simmered for 1 hour, place the couscous in the top pot or a metal colander suspended over the pot, lower the heat and steam for 20 minutes. Do not cover the couscous while it steams.

4. Remove the colander and add the sliced onions and raisins to the stew; adjust its consistency with water or chicken stock if necessary. Replace the colander and steam for 15 minutes. Dot the couscous with the remaining butter and steam for 5 minutes. Fluff the couscous with a fork to distribute the melted butter.

5. Serve the couscous with the stew and Harissa, Recipe 11.14.

Middle Eastern

The cuisines of the Middle East include those of Egypt, Jordan, Syria and Lebanon. This is the southern portion of the Levant, an area that stretches from Egypt through Israel, north to Turkey and east through Greece. Now predominantly Arab, the area has been ruled by the Egyptians, Romans, Turks, British and French, to name a few. Each nationality has left its mark.

Generally, rice and wheat (wheat for bread flour and bulgur) are the principal staples, as are legumes, especially chickpeas. Chickpeas are used in many dishes, most notably *hummus*, in which they are mashed with sesame seed paste, and *ful medames*, an ancient Egyptian dish in which the beans are flavored with garlic and dressed with lemon juice and oil. Important spices include cinnamon, cumin, ginger, coriander, allspice and hot peppers, as well as some more unusual spices such as *mahlab* (ground black-cherry pits, which gives food a slightly fruity flavor), *zatar* (a variety of thyme that tastes like a cross between thyme and oregano) and *sumac* (which gives meats a woody taste). Dried whole limes and verjuice are also used for flavorings.

Yogurt is used as a beverage, pudding and flavoring ingredient. Olive oil is a typical cooking medium as well as a dressing and a basic ingredient in many of the vegetable dishes called *yakhni*. Sesame seed oil is also used, especially in Lebanese dishes. Tahini is a popular paste made from crushed sesame seeds. Produce of importance includes garlic, okra, cucumbers, eggplants and lemons as well as tomatoes and peppers (New World imports).

Several varieties of freshwater and saltwater fish are enjoyed grilled, baked or poached. Little beef is consumed, although camel is eaten (hump meat is the choicest). Lamb, however, dominates Middle Eastern cuisine. It can be grilled, roasted, braised, stewed with vegetables or made into a variety of meatballs (called *kofta*) and kebabs. It is also the basic ingredient in the Lebanese and Syrian dish known as *kibbeh*. For kibbeh, ground lamb is mixed with onion-flavored bulgur, parsley and pine nuts. It is then shaped into cakes and grilled, deep-fried or baked, or stuffed with savory ingredients and deep-fried. Chicken is also popular, whether spit-roasted, marinated in oil and citrus or stuffed with rice and pine nuts and baked in an earthenware casserole.

◆◆◆

RECIPE 34.13

DAJAJ MAHSHY
(CHICKEN STUFFED WITH RICE, CURRANTS AND PINE NUTS)

Yield: 4 Servings

Long-grain white rice	1 c.	250 ml
Whole butter	4 oz.	120 g
Onions, fine dice	3 oz.	90 g
Pine nuts	3 Tbsp.	45 ml
Water	1 pt.	500 ml
Dried currants	2 Tbsp.	30 ml
Salt	2 Tbsp.	30 ml
Pepper	TT	TT
Fryer chicken, 3 to 3-1/2 lb. (1.3 to 1.5 kg), including coarsely chopped giblets	1	1
Yogurt	2 oz.	60 g

1. Wash the rice and set aside.
2. Sauté the onions in the butter until transparent.
3. Add the coarsely chopped giblets and pine nuts and sauté until the pine nuts are browned.

Continued

4. Stir in the rice and cook until the grains are coated with butter.

5. Add the water, currants, 1 tablespoon (15 milliliters) of the salt and pepper to taste; cover and cook until the rice is done.

6. Remove from the heat and mix in the remaining butter.

7. Stuff the chicken's cavity with the rice mixture and truss.

8. Season the yogurt with the remaining salt and pepper. Brush half of the mixture over the chicken. Roast the chicken at 350°F (180°C), basting periodically with the yogurt mixture until done, approximately 1 hour.

9. Carve the chicken and serve it with the rice.

Middle Eastern sweets are very sweet; they include *ataif* (pancakes drenched with syrup and topped with chopped nuts and thick clotted cream), *muhallabia* (a milk pudding flavored with orange flower water) and *ma'amoul* (pastries stuffed with dates or nuts and coated with powdered sugar or served in cream) as well as the more familiar halva, candied dates, baklava and Turkish delight.

MEXICAN CUISINE

Mexican cuisine is rooted in its pre-Columbian past and nurtured by centuries of Spanish influence. For thousands of years before Columbus's arrival, the people of Mexico lived on a diet of squash, corn (maize) and beans supplemented with fresh vegetables (avocados, peppers, tomatoes), fruit (manioc and bananas) and occasionally fish, shellfish, game and wild poultry. The population relied on steaming and slow cooking methods such as wrapping meats, poultry and fish in leaves and slow-roasting them over hot embers or stewing foods with little liquid in tightly lidded earthenware pots.

In the wake of Hernan Cortes's conquest of Mexico in 1521 came pigs, cattle and dairy products, chicken, wheat, rice, sesame seeds, citrus and almonds. The Spanish also brought with them a new manner of cooking: rendering fat from meat and using the rendered fat and vegetable oils to fry foods. All of these foods, to one degree or another, were soon integrated into the local cuisines; sautéing and pan-frying became standard cooking methods. (Although the people of Mexico quickly adopted European foods and cooking methods, Europeans waited centuries before adopting Mexican foods and appreciating Mexican cuisine.)

Mexico has given rise to several regional cuisines of note. Unfortunately, many consumers in this country erroneously believe that Mexican cuisine starts and ends with tacos and refried beans.

The most characteristic feature of Mexican cookery is the widespread use of chiles. There are about 100 varieties, many of which have a hot, pungent taste. (Unlike English, Mexican Spanish differentiates between the word *hot* as applied to a food's temperature—*caliente*—and *hot* as applied to its degree of spiciness—*chiloso*.) Fresh chiles can be served raw; stuffed and baked; stewed; chopped with tomatoes, herbs and oil for a salsa; or minced and used as a seasoning. Or they can be dried and used whole or ground as a seasoning. Other seasonings include garlic, cinnamon, cumin, oregano, onion, achiote seeds, basil, peppercorns, cilantro and other fresh herbs.

Fresh vegetable salsas accompany many dishes. Guacamole, for example, is an ancient dish made from avocados and flavorings such as onions and tomatoes. The numerous fresh salsas are usually categorized as either red or green. Red salsa, called *salsa roja*, is made from chiles (usually dried), onions

Mexican - (clockwise from top left) poblano rice, poblano chili, coconut candies, chicken mole on corn tortillas, hybiscus water

and tomato. Green salsa, called *salsa verde*, is made from chiles (usually fresh), onions and tomatillos.

Corn flour is used to make a dough called *masa*. Popular throughout Mexico, smooth masa is pressed (traditionally by hand) into flat rounds and quickly cooked on a griddle to make tortillas. Tortillas are eaten like bread, filled with savory mixtures for burritos, fried crisp and topped for tostadas, folded around savory mixtures and fried for tacos, or used for turnovers (quesadillas, empanadas and enchiladas). Tamales are made from a coarser masa dough that is stuffed with a savory mixture of beans, meats or poultry, encased in corn husks and steamed. Many of these masa-based dishes are considered snack foods known as *antojitos*, the traditional portable snacks of the Mexican marketplace.

Wheat flour is also used for tortillas (especially in north Mexico) as well as for a variety of leavened breads. Rice, although not indigenous, is also a staple of Mexican diets.

As they were during pre-Columbian times, beans are still a staple. They are usually dried, then reconstituted in water and served in a soupy fashion, or mashed and fried in lard or oil to make a smooth paste called *frijoles refritos* (refried beans).

Chicken is popular throughout the country. Meat is used somewhat sparingly in most Mexican regional cuisines. Beef and dairy products are more widely consumed in the north, while goat and goat cheese are more typical of the country's central regions. Fish and shellfish are eaten along both coasts.

The ancient manner of slow cooking is still used for meats, poultry and fish; there is a great variety of stews and soups. The ancient cooking method known as *pibil*, in which meats were wrapped in maguey or banana leaves and cooked in a pit lined with hot coals, is often replaced today by steaming banana-leaf wrapped meats. Some meats and vegetables are also grilled (called *al carbon*) or seared and roasted. A popular meat marinade known as *adobado* combines chiles, garlic and herbs.

Sauce making is very different from European traditions and includes a step known as "frying the sauce." Most sauces start with dried peppers that are soaked, seeded and ground to a paste and then mixed with herbs, spices and vegetables. The mixture, sometimes thickened with ground toasted pumpkin seeds or nuts, is then puréed and fried in oil or lard. This sauce is added to partially cooked and drained meat or poultry and the dish is then simmered to blend the flavors.

Moles are dishes made with a classic cooking method that incorporates this sauce-making technique. The meat or poultry is cooked and then steeped or simmered in a sauce made from chiles and other ingredients.

◆◆◆

RECIPE 34.16
MOLE ROJO CON POLLO
(RICH RED MOLE WITH CHICKEN)

Yield: 4 Servings

Chiles, dried, stemmed, seeded and deveined:		
Chiles anchos	2 oz.	60 g
Chiles mulatos	1 oz.	30 g
Chiles pasilla	1/3 oz.	10 g
Vegetable oil	3 oz.	90 g
Tomato, medium, roasted, cored, peeled and diced	1	1
Medium tomatillos, husked, washed and simmered until tender	3	3
Mexican chocolate, chopped	1 oz.	30 g
Oregano, dried	1/2 tsp.	3 ml
Thyme, dried	1/4 tsp.	2 ml
Bay leaf	1	1
Peppercorns	8	8
Cloves	3	3
Cinnamon stick	1 in.	2.5 cm
Sesame seeds	2 Tbsp.	30 ml
Raisins	2 Tbsp.	30 ml
Garlic, chopped	1 tsp.	5 ml
Onion, thickly sliced	2 oz.	60 g
Peanuts	1 oz.	30 g
Plantain, small, peeled and diced (optional)	4 oz.	120 g
Corn tortilla, stale	1/2	1/2
White bread slice, stale	1	1
Chicken stock	1 qt.	900 ml
Chicken, 3-1/2 lb. (1.6 kg), quartered	1	1
Salt	1 tsp.	5 ml
Granulated sugar	1 Tbsp.	15 ml

1. Sauté the chiles in 3 tablespoons (45 milliliters) of oil until nutty brown.

Remove, reserving the oil. Cover the chiles with boiling water and soak for 1 hour. Drain and set aside.

2. Combine the tomatoes, tomatillos, chocolate, oregano and thyme in a large bowl. Pulverize the bay leaf, peppercorns, cloves and cinnamon and combine with the tomato mixture.

3. Toast the sesame seeds and add them to the tomato mixture.

4. Sauté the raisins in the reserved chili oil until they puff; add them to the tomato mixture.

5. In the same oil, sauté the garlic, onion and peanuts until they are well browned; add to the tomato mixture.

6. Sauté the plantain until golden brown; add to the tomato mixture.

7. Sauté the tortilla until brown; shred it and add to the tomato mixture.

8. Lay the bread in the pan and quickly flip it to coat both sides with the fat; then brown it on both sides. Tear it into pieces and add to the tomato mixture.

9. Stir the tomato mixture well. Purée it with 6 ounces (180 grams) of chicken stock and strain through a china cap.

10. Purée the reconstituted chiles with 2 ounces (60 grams) of chicken stock; strain through a china cap in a separate bowl and set aside.

11. Sauté the chicken in oil. Remove and degrease the pan. In the same pan, sauté the chile purée until it is thick and dark. Add the tomato purée and cook until thick.

12. Add 1-1/2 pints (700 milliliters) of chicken stock. Simmer the sauce 45 minutes. Season with salt and sugar. If the sauce is thicker than heavy cream, dilute it with additional chicken stock.

13. Add the chicken to the pan and braise until done.

14. Degrease the sauce. Garnish the chicken with sesame seeds and serve with the sauce and Arroz a la Poblana.

❖❖❖

RECIPE 34.17
Arroz a la Poblana
(Rice with Poblano Chiles)

Yield: 4 Servings

Vegetable oil	1-1/2 Tbsp.	23 ml
Onion, small dice	5 oz.	150 g
Long- or medium-grain rice	1 c.	250 ml
Chicken stock, hot	14 oz.	400 g
Salt	TT	TT
Chiles poblanos, fresh, roasted and peeled, seeded, julienne	3	3
Fresh corn kernels	6 oz.	180 g
Mexican queso fresco (or feta or farmers cheese), crumbled	5 oz.	150 g
Parsley or cilantro sprigs	as needed	as needed

1. Sauté the onion in oil until translucent. Add the rice and sauté without coloring.

Continued

♦♦♦

A Mexican Meal

A typical Mexican meal may start with a hearty soup such as *pozole rojo* (pork and hominy soup with red chile and fresh garnishes) followed by a meat-and-sauce dish served with beans, rice and tortillas. Dessert would be flan. Popular beverages include *horchata* (cinnamon-infused milk with ground rice), *agua de jamaica* (usually served before a meal; a sweetened, hibiscus-flower-infused water), *agua de tamarindo* (a sweetened, tamarind-infused water) and *cerveza* (beer).

2. Add the hot stock, salt, chiles and corn to the rice mixture; bring to a boil, reduce to a simmer, cover and cook until all liquid has evaporated.

3. Add the crumbled cheese to the rice and toss to combine.

4. Serve as a side dish garnished with parsley or cilantro sprigs.

Sweets, especially candies, candied fruits and hard cookies or cakes, are popular throughout Mexico. The more commonly encountered deserts such as flans and caramels are derived from the Spanish tradition.

Mexico is a country rich in regional cuisines. A few observations about them follow.

Central (Mexico City)

Blended with tomatoes, the fiery hot *guajillos* or smoky *chipotles* are the principal chiles used for sauces. Also popular are the common black chile and the *pasilla*. A great variety of beans are used, but the purplish *flor de mayo* and the tan *bayo* are the most popular. Cooking methods include mole. A typical meat dish would be lamb wrapped in maguey or banana leaves cooked in brick pits and served with a sauce of fermented maguey juice and pasilla.

West Central (Guadalajara)

The defining sauce is made with a purée of the very hot *de arbol* chiles, sometimes thickened with tomatillos. De arbol also come bottled, pickled with vinegar. A great variety of beans are used, but as with Central Mexican cuisine, flor de mayo and bayo are the most popular. A typical meat dish would be kid (young goat) marinated in chiles and slow-cooked in a sealed container. From the west coast also comes seviche, a dish of finely chopped fish and shellfish marinated in lime juice, cilantro, tomato chunks and herbs.

Central East Coast (Veracruz)

Although still used in abundance, chiles play a less prominent role. Herbs (especially cilantro, basil, bay leaves, parsley and oregano) and spices (peppercorns and cinnamon) are a vital part of the cuisine. The area is known for its fish and shellfish cooked in a chunky broth of olives, herbs and chiles (usually jalapeños). The basic bean is black and usually cooked with a sprig of epazote.

Northern (Sonora, Chihuahua)

As in West Central Mexico, the defining sauce is made with a purée of the very hot de arbol chiles, sometimes thickened with tomatillos. This region is known for its wheat and beef, which is sometimes dried and called *carne seca*. A typical pork dish is the simmered *carne con chile colorado*. Popular beans are pintos and the yellowish-tan *piruano*.

Southeastern (Yucatan)

This regional cuisine is unique, using achiote seeds as the principal seasoning. Fresh chiles are usually ground with salt and lime or purchased in a bottled form. A vinegary orange-red and a green sauce made with the local *habañero* chiles are especially popular. Seasonings are added to most dishes in the form of a paste that can be brick red (made from achiote seeds ground with oregano, black pepper, cloves and cumin mixed with garlic and vinegar), olive-amber (a mild blend of garlic, allspice, cinnamon and other spices) or coal black (made from burnt chiles, achiote, spices and garlic). A typical pork dish is flavored with achiote and wrapped in banana leaves, then slowly steamed or roasted. The most commonly used bean is black and usually cooked with a sprig of epazote.

Southern (Oaxaca)

A wide range of dried peppers are used in many different stews and sauces, some of which combine sweeter spices such as cloves and cinnamon with savory foods. A typical meat or poultry dish would be kid or chicken marinated in chiles, then wrapped in avocado leaves and steamed. Some consider this region to produce the finest *chorizo*, a pork sausage made with herbs, spices, a touch of vinegar and deep red chiles. The basic black bean is also regularly used throughout the south.

CONCLUSION

Although the foods and flavorings may differ from the cuisine of one culture to the cuisine of another, the fundamentals of cookery do not: Quality ingredients need to be prepared, seasoned and cooked, then presented in an attractive and appropriate manner. With a good purveyor, a little practice and an understanding of the principles discussed throughout this book, a world of great cooking and eating is available to you and your customers.

QUESTIONS FOR DISCUSSION

1. Which of the cuisines discussed rely on slow-cooking methods for meats? Which rely on quick-cooking methods?
2. Identify the flavor principle for each of the cuisines discussed.
3. Which New World product plays an important role in some Asian cuisines?
4. Compare and contrast the cuisines of Japan and North Africa.
5. Compare and contrast one of the cuisines of India and one of the cuisines of China.
6. Explain why there may be several cuisines within a single country.

CHAPTER 35

PLATE PRESENTATION

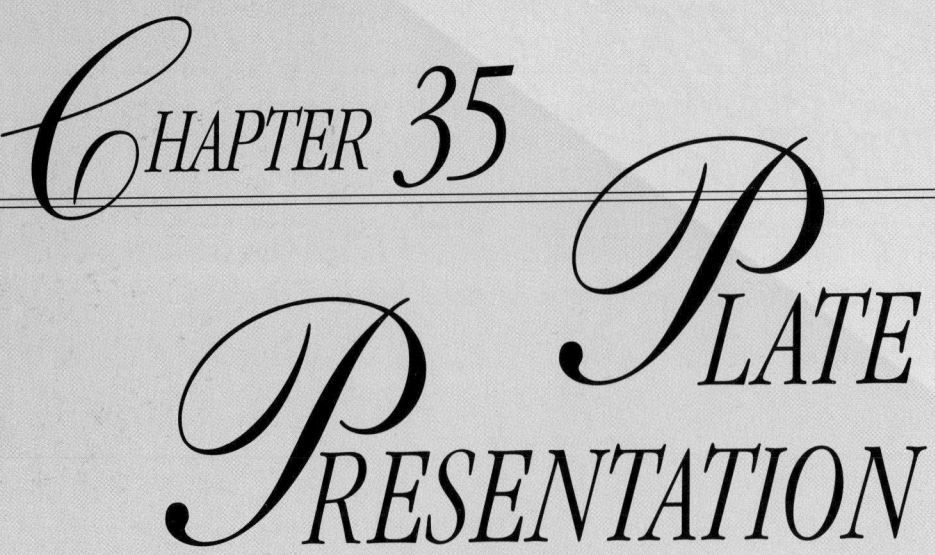

Choosing Plates

Restaurant china is available in many different shapes, sizes, colors and patterns. It is often the chef's responsibility to choose the appropriate piece of china for a particular dish.

Sizes and Shapes

Most plates are round, but oval plates, often referred to as platters, are becoming more common. Plates are available in a variety of sizes from a small 4-inch (10-centimeter) bread plate to a huge 14-inch (35-centimeter) charger or base plate. Plates are typically concave; their depths vary within a limited range of about 1 inch (2.5 centimeters). Most plates have rims; rim diameters also vary. Soup bowls can be rimmed or rimless. Soup plates are usually larger and shallower than soup bowls and have wide rims. Soup cups are also available. There are also dozens of plate designs intended for a specific purpose, such as plates with small indentations for holding escargots, or long, rectangular plates with grooves for holding asparagus.

Choose plates large enough to hold the food comfortably without overcrowding or spilling. Oversized, rimmed soup plates are becoming quite popular for serving any food with a sauce. Be careful when using oversized plates, however, as the food may look sparse, creating poor value perception.

Regardless of whether you choose a round, oval or less-conventionally-shaped plate, be sure to choose one with a size and shape that best highlights the food and supports the composition. For example, in the photo to the left, the rectangular dish with round corners and raised rim accentuates the geometrically simple yet effective composition of the square date bar and spherical scoop of ice cream.

Chewy Date Bars with Caramel Ice Cream
(Recipes 29.30 and 31.27)

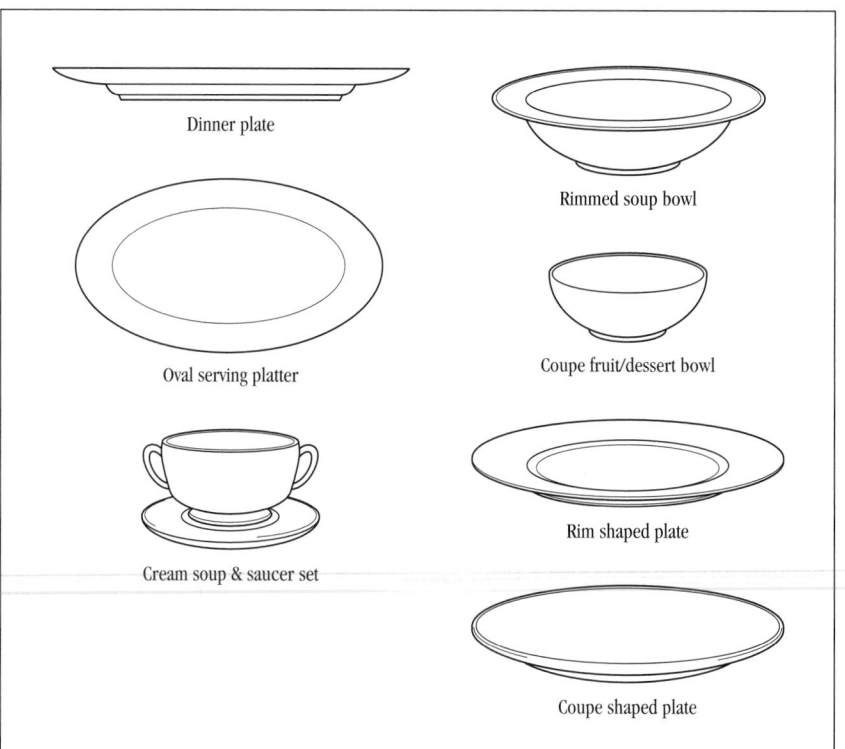

Figure 35.1   *Common Restaurant China*

Colors and Patterns

White and cream are by far the most common colors for restaurant china. Almost any food looks good on these neutral colors.

Colored and patterned plates can be used quite effectively to accent food, however. The obvious choice is to contrast dark plates with bright- or light-colored foods and light plates with dark-colored foods.

The food should always be the focal point of any plate. Be careful in selecting restaurant china with intricate designs and brightly colored patterns that can conflict or compete with the colors, shapes and arrangements of the foods. The colors and shapes in the pattern should blend well and harmonize with the foods served. The swirling patterns of blues, grays, pinks and yellows along the plate rim shown to the right, for example, harmonize well with the colors of the salmon blini and its accompaniments.

Salmon Blini with Stuffed Squash Blossoms (Recipes 33.9 and 33.10)

Arranging Foods on Plates

You should strive for a well-balanced plate composition. This can be achieved by carefully considering colors, textures, shapes and arrangements.

Colors

Foods come in a rainbow of colors and to the extent appropriate, foods of different colors should be presented together. Generally, the colors should provide balance and contrast. But no matter how well prepared or planned, some dishes simply have dull, boring or similar colors. If so, try adding another ingredient or garnish for a splash of color. The vivid red lobster claws and the shiny black mussel shells shown here add striking color notes to a paella dish that would otherwise be dominated by yellow rice, tan chicken, brown sausages and gray clam shells.

Paella (Recipe 19.29)

Textures

Visual texture refers to how smooth or rough, coarse or fine a food looks. Mashed potatoes and carrot purée both look smooth and soft. Salmon mousseline and spinach soufflé both have slightly grainy surfaces. Rösti potatoes and meatloaf both appear coarse. The flavors of each food in these pairs differ; their visual textures do not.

Typically, foods with similar textures look boring together; foods with different textures look more exciting. Serve carrots cut julienne with the mashed potatoes to achieve a balance of hard and soft textures; steamed leaf spinach with the salmon mousseline for a combination of smooth and grainy textures; and a baked potato with the meatloaf for pairing fluffy and coarse textures. These pairs generally maintain the same range of flavors as the first set of pairs while providing different visual textures.

The cassoulet shown to the right harmoniously combines several textures in one dish: the pebbly beans, the slices of smooth slab bacon and coarse sausage and the bumpy skin of the duck leg. Indeed, the variation in textures is so dramatic and appealing that many diners may not even notice that all the principal ingredients are essentially the same color.

Cassoulet (Recipe 16.11)

Shapes

For a more dramatic presentation, combine foods with different shapes on one plate. The plate shown on the next page is an excellent example of simple shapes artfully combined: ovals of evenly sliced lamb loin with cleanly cut

Lamb Loin with Rösti Potatoes (Recipe 15.10)

triangles of crisp potatoes and long, thin spears of asparagus. The three very different shapes lend contrast and character to the dish.

Arrangements

Having decided on the colors, textures and shapes of the foods that will go on the plate, you must next decide where to place each individual item to achieve a balanced and unified composition. Mostly this takes judgment and style, but there are a few general guidelines.

GUIDELINES FOR ARRANGING FOODS ON A PLATE

1. Strike a balance between overcrowding the plate and leaving large gaps of space. Foods should not touch the plate rim nor necessarily be confined to the very center.
2. Choose a focal point for the plate—that is, the point to which the eye is drawn. This is usually the highest point on the plate. Design the plate with the highest point to the rear or center. Avoid placing foods of equal heights around the edge of the plate leaving a hole in the center—the eye will naturally be drawn to that gap.
3. The plate's composition should flow naturally. For example, make the highest point the back of the plate and have the rest of the food become gradually shorter toward the front of the plate. Slicing and fanning foods can attract the eye and help establish a flow.

The grilled duck with roasted vegetables shown below elegantly illustrates these principles. Height is established by a structure composed of the duck leg and thigh, sliced turnips and baby carrots. The structure sits toward the back of the plate. Its height, placement and striking appearance make it the focal point. The neatly sliced duck breast is then fanned across the plate in front of this focal point, drawing the viewer into the plate.

Grilled Duck with Roasted Vegetables

Decorating Plates

The colors, textures, shapes and arrangements of foods on a plate can be improved or highlighted by decorating a plate with herbs, spices and other garnishes, baked hippen masse dough and sauces. If any of these are to be applied after the principal food is placed on the plate, be prepared to do so quickly so that the food is served at its proper temperature.

Plate Dusting

An attractive method for decorating dessert plates is to cover the entire plate with a dusting of powdered sugar, cocoa powder or both before placing the dessert on the plate. Use sugar on dark-colored plates and cocoa on light-colored plates. These items can be dusted onto the plate with a shaker can or sifter in a free-form fashion or into any desired pattern by using a template. The template can be a doily or a stencil placed over the plate before it is dusted.

PROCEDURE FOR DUSTING DESSERT PLATES

1. Place a template over the plate. Dust the sugar or cocoa over the template.

2. Carefully remove the template.

Provided they complement the food, very finely chopped nuts can also be used to decorate plates for sweet or savory foods. See, for example, the plate of French toast garnished with chopped macadamia nuts shown here. Plates for savory foods can be decorated in a similar fashion by sprinkling them with finely chopped herbs such as thyme or minced vegetables such as a combination of brightly colored peppers.

Banana Brioche French Toast (Recipe 32.21)

Garnishing Plates with Herbs

Using fresh herbs is one of the easiest ways to add color, texture and flow to a plate. Whether the herb is an ingredient in the dish or merely a decoration, it should always complement the foods and be consistent with their seasonings. A sprig of fresh rosemary garnishing a beautifully roasted rack of lamb, or tiny leaves of chervil garnishing delicately poached fillets of sole are natural combinations. Sprigs of fresh green mint (often with a fresh berry or two or a strawberry cut in a fan) are often the perfect decoration for a dessert plate.

Using herbs to garnish a plate.

Garnishing Plate Rims with Herbs or Spices

Finely chopped herbs or nuts or whole or ground spices can be used to decorate plate rims. Whatever garnishing items are used, they should complement the main foods and be consistent with their seasonings.

PROCEDURE FOR GARNISHING PLATE RIMS

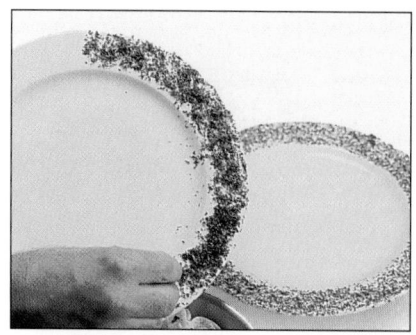

1. Apply a light coating of oil or softened butter to the plate rim with a pastry brush. Be careful to apply the oil or butter only where you want the herbs, spices or other garnishes to stick.

2. Sprinkle the desired amount of garnish over the oiled or buttered area. Then tip the plate to let the excess garnish fall away.

3. Alternatively, a small portion of the plate can be brushed and decorated.

Garnishing Plates with Hippen Masse

An increasingly popular presentation technique is to pipe batters into intricate designs and then bake them to form crisp, rigid, cookielike garnishes. These garnishes are then used to create height and add texture.

◆◆◆

RECIPE 35.1

SAVORY HIPPEN MASSE

ARIZONA BILTMORE, PHOENIX, AZ

Yield: 1 lb. (450 g)

Egg whites, room temperature	8 oz.	250 g
Wondra flour	4 oz.	120 g
Heavy cream	3 oz.	90 g
Granulated sugar	1 oz.	30 g
Salt and white pepper	TT	TT
Dried thyme, crushed	1 tsp.	5 ml

1. Stir the egg whites together to blend. Stir in all of the flour at once.
2. Blend in the heavy cream, then add the remaining ingredients.
3. Strain the batter through a china cap and allow to rest for 30 minutes.
4. Lightly oil the back of a very flat sheet pan. Pipe the hippen masse onto the pan using a plastic squeeze bottle. Pipe the batter into decorative patterns appropriate for the desired plate presentation.
5. Bake at 375°F (190°C) until set and lightly browned. Remove from the oven, then remove the decorations from the sheet pan while still slightly warm.

1. Piping the batter onto an oiled sheet pan.

2. Using the baked batter as a component when composing a plate. Carousel of Sonoma Lamb (Recipe 15.11)

Decorating Plates with Sauces

The sauce is an integral part of most any dish: It adds flavor and moisture; it also adds color, texture and flow to the plate. A rich, glossy bordelaise or Madeira sauce pooled beneath sautéed tournedos of beef is a classic example. A chunky salsa of tomatoes, papaya and pineapple beneath a juicy piece of grilled salmon is a more contemporary approach.

Sauces are also used in other, less traditional ways to add visual appeal. For example, if using a vinaigrette dressing for grilled foods, let the oil and vinegar separate and pool on the plate, creating the interesting effect illustrated here.

One or more colored sauces can also be used to paint plates. One technique is simply to drizzle or splatter the sauce onto the plate. In the photo below, the sauce boldly splattered across the plate is the same rich magenta beet vinaigrette as that pooled beneath the sea bass; the plate's drama is heightened by the contrasting tomato ovals and potato spikes.

Grilled Quail with Balsamic Raspberries (Recipe 18.15)

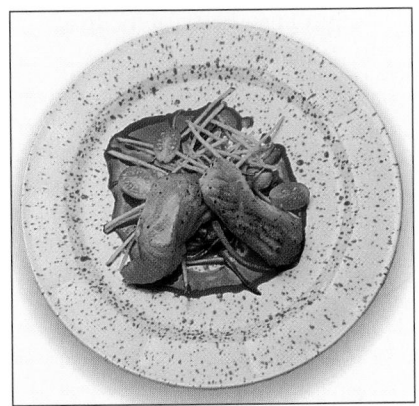

Pan-seared Sea Bass with Beet Vinaigrette (Recipe 19.22)

Alternatively, one or more colored sauces can be applied to a plate using squirt bottles to create abstract patterns or representational designs. Painting plates with different-colored sauces also facilitates flow and adds color. Although this technique can be used with hot sauces, it is more often used with cold sauces (such as vanilla, caramel, chocolate and fruit-flavored ones) for dessert presentations. The sauces must be thick enough to hold the pattern once it is created and they should all be of the same viscosity.

PROCEDURE FOR PAINTING A DESIGN WITH SAUCES

 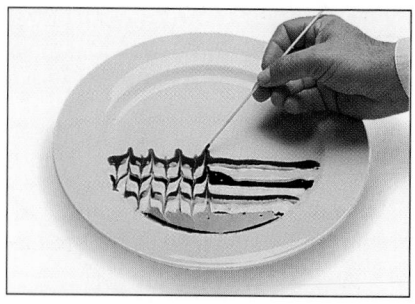

1. Apply the sauces to the plate in parallel lines of alternating colors.

2. Carefully pull a toothpick through the sauces, perpendicular to the parallel lines in the sauces.

PROCEDURE FOR PAINTING A SPIDER WEB DESIGN

1. Pool one sauce evenly across the entire base of the plate, then apply a contrasting sauce onto the base sauce in a spiral.

2. Draw a thin-bladed knife or a toothpick through the sauces from the center point toward the edge. Then, leaving a half inch (1.2 centimeter) space along the edge, draw a knife blade or toothpick from the edge to the center.

Other patterns can be produced by squirting the sauces onto the plate in different patterns or by pulling the knife or toothpick through the sauces in different directions. As shown to the left, a circle of chocolate-sauce dots in a pool of vanilla sauce is pulled to create a leaf wreath.

CONCLUSION

Although the techniques described in this chapter—as well as many other ones—can be used to create a variety of effects, often the most elegant plates are those with the simplest designs. Thoughtful presentation improves the appeal and appearance of any food as well as the completed plate, but it cannot mask poor-quality, poorly prepared or bland-tasting foods.

QUESTIONS FOR DISCUSSION

1. Explain why proper service and presentation are important in food service operations.

2. Distinguish between cutting and molding foods for visual appeal and creating garnishes out of foods.

3. How can the selection of service ware such as bowls and platters affect the visual appeal of the foods served?

4. List and describe four techniques for garnishing plates.

5. Describe how color, texture, shape and arrangement can be used to create a well-balanced plate composition.

Appendix I

Twenty Suggested Menus

The following menus are designed for beginning students. They use basic skills and techniques that students should master before progressing to more difficult items.

Beginning Menu 1:

RECIPE 24.4   *Mesclun Salad with Raspberry Vinaigrette*
RECIPE 13.9   *Pepper Steak*
RECIPE 22.6   *Broccoli Almondine*
RECIPE 27.1   *Country Biscuits*
RECIPE 31.17   *Chocolate Pot Au Crème*

Beginning Menu 2:

RECIPE 24.7   *Tomato and Asparagus Salad with Fresh Mozzarella*
RECIPE 19.1   *Broiled Black Sea Bass with Herb Butter and Sautéed Leeks*
RECIPE 23.5   *Basic Simmered Rice*
RECIPE 25.4   *Pears Poached in Red Wine*

Beginning Menu 3:

RECIPE 11.2   *Hearty Vegetable Beef Soup*
Tossed salad with
    RECIPE 24.17   *Roquefort Dressing* and
    RECIPE 24.20   *Garlic Croutons*
RECIPE 17.23   *Turkey Scallopine*
RECIPE 23.17   *Brown Rice Pilaf with Pinenuts*
RECIPE 31.9   *Classic Chocolate Mousse*

Beginning Menu 4:

RECIPE 11.18   *Cheddar and Leek Soup*
RECIPE 19.6   *Red Snapper en Papillote with Julienne Vegetables and Basil Butter*
RECIPE 23.4   *Duchesse Potatoes*
RECIPE 31.21   *Cherry Clafouti*

Beginning Menu 5:

RECIPE 11.15   *French Onion Soup*
RECIPE 12.1   *Grilled Lamb Chops with Herb Butter*
RECIPE 23.15   *Polenta*
RECIPE 22.14   *Stir-Fried Snow Peas*
RECIPE 25.11   *Gratin of Fresh Berries with Crème Fraîche*

Beginning Menu 6:

RECIPE 11.4   *Cream of Broccoli Soup*
RECIPE 13.1   *T-Bone Steak*
RECIPE 23.14   *Steak Fries*
RECIPE 22.11   *Broiled Tomato*
RECIPE 28.2   *Soft Yeast Dinner Rolls*
RECIPE 31.18   *Pistachio Citrus Cheesecake*

Beginning Menu 7:

RECIPE 11.23   *Fresh Peach and Yogurt Soup*
RECIPE 17.19   *Duck Breast Salad with Hazelnuts*
RECIPE 28.10   *Breadsticks*
RECIPE 29.29   *Chocolate Délice*

Beginning Menu 8:

Tossed salad with
    RECIPE 24.3   *Emulsified Vinaigrette Dressing*
RECIPE 12.2   *Roast Prime Rib of Beef au Jus*
RECIPE 23.1   *Baked Potatoes*
RECIPE 22.17   *Maple Glazed Carrots*
RECIPE 28.5   *Basic French Bread*
RECIPE 29.6   *Cherry Pie*

BEGINNING MENU 9:

RECIPE 12.5   *NEW ENGLAND BOILED DINNER*
RECIPE 28.8   *WHOLE WHEAT BREAD*
RECIPE 25.2   *BAKED APPLES*

BEGINNING MENU 10:

RECIPE 11.5   *PURÉE OF SPLIT PEA SOUP*
RECIPE 13.4   *HOMESTYLE MEATLOAF* with mushroom sauce
RECIPE 22.2   *BAKED BUTTERNUT SQUASH*
RECIPE 23.3   *LYONNAISE POTATOES*
RECIPE 31.10   *CHOCOLATE ICE CREAM*
RECIPE 29.32   *SUGAR COOKIES*

The following menus are designed for intermediate-level students. They include dishes that integrate multiple techniques in order to build upon skills previously learned.

INTERMEDIATE MENU 1:

RECIPE 19.33   *FRIED OYSTERS WITH HERBED CRÈME FRAÎCHE*
RECIPE 24.28   *WARM LAMB SALAD WITH BOURBON VINAIGRETTE*
RECIPE 28.4   *CROISSANTS*
RECIPE 31.29   *CHOCOLATE HAZELNUT MARQUIS*

INTERMEDIATE MENU 2:

RECIPE 20.18   *RABBIT PÂTÉ EN CROÛTE*
RECIPE 11.8   *VICHYSSOISE*
RECIPE 18.12   *BRAISED PARTRIDGE WITH RED CABBAGE*
RECIPE 23.35   *SPAETZLE*
RECIPE 29.4   *APPLE CRANBERRY PIE* with
  RECIPE 31.27   *CARAMEL ICE CREAM*

INTERMEDIATE MENU 3:

RECIPE 20.8   *VEGETABLE TERRINE IN BRIOCHE*
RECIPE 19.27   *PAUPIETTES OF SOLE WITH MOUSSELINE OF SHRIMP*
RECIPE 23.13   *RÖSTI POTATOES*
Salad of baby greens with shaved parmesan cheese and
  RECIPE 24.11   *THREE PEPPERCORN CRANBERRY VINAIGRETTE*
RECIPE 29.27   *CHOCOLATE ÉCLAIRS*

INTERMEDIATE MENU 4:

RECIPE 11.3   *BEEF CONSOMMÉ*
RECIPE 23.22   *GOAT'S CHEESE RAVIOLI IN HERBED CREAM SAUCE*
RECIPE 19.5   *STEAMED SALMON WITH LEMON AND OLIVE OIL*
RECIPE 22.3   *STIR-FRIED ASPARAGUS WITH SHIITAKE MUSHROOMS*
RECIPE 23.7   *BULGAR PILAF*
RECIPE 29.24   *STRAWBERRY NAPOLEON*

INTERMEDIATE MENU 5:

Tossed green salad with
  RECIPE 24.1   *BASIC VINAIGRETTE DRESSING* and
  RECIPE 20.14   *RED PEPPER MOUSSE*
RECIPE 16.10   *CASSOULET*
RECIPE 28.14   *SAN FRANCISCO SOURDOUGH BREAD*
RECIPE 31.22   *WHITE CHOCOLATE FRANGELICO BAVARIAN* served with
  RECIPE 29.36   *LACY PECAN COOKIES*

INTERMEDIATE MENU 6:

RECIPE 19.36   *SQUID STUFFED WITH GRILLED EGGPLANT*
RECIPE 11.16   *MINESTRONE*
RECIPE 17.15   *FREE RANGE CHICKEN*
RECIPE 29.12   *CANNOLI ALLA SICILIANA*

INTERMEDIATE MENU 7:

RECIPE 19.4   *BLUE CRAB CAKES WITH FRESH SALSA*
Romaine lettuce with
  RECIPE 24.12   *RED ONION VINAIGRETTE*
RECIPE 17.14   *CHICKEN STUFFED WITH SPINACH IN SAFFRON SAUCE*
RECIPE 23.2   *GRATIN DAUPHINOISE*
RECIPE 31.7   *FRESH FRUIT BAVARIAN CHARLOTTE* made with
  RECIPE 30.26   *LADYFINGERS*

INTERMEDIATE MENU 8: BRUNCH BUFFET

RECIPE 24.25   *VINE-RIPENED TOMATO SALAD*
RECIPE 32.3   *GREEK-STYLE SCRAMBLED EGGS*
RECIPE 32.5   *GARDEN FRITTATA*
RECIPE 23.16   *GRITS AND CHEESE SOUFFLÉ*
RECIPE 27.2   *BLUEBERRY MUFFINS*
RECIPE 28.18   *DANISH PASTRIES*
RECIPE 30.20   *SOUR CREAM COFFEECAKE*
RECIPE 25.8   *FIGS WITH BERRIES AND HONEY MOUSSE*
RECIPE 32.12   *HOT CHOCOLATE MOUSSE*

INTERMEDIATE MENU 9:

RECIPE 24.21   *WILTED SPINACH SALAD WITH ROASTED PEPPERS*
RECIPE 11.13   *CHICKEN SOUP WITH MATZO BALLS*
RECIPE 12.6   *AUNT RUTHIE'S POT ROAST*
RECIPE 22.4   *BRUSSELS SPROUTS IN PECAN BUTTER*
RECIPE 28.15   *CHALLAH*
RECIPE 30.22   *FRESH COCONUT CAKE*

INTERMEDIATE MENU 10:

RECIPE 24.22   *WHITE ASPARAGUS MOUSSE WITH GARDEN FRESH LETTUCES*
RECIPE 11.17   *SEAFOOD BOUILLABAISSE*
RECIPE 28.11   *ROMAN FLATBREAD*
RECIPE 29.23   *FRESH PEACH TART WITH ALMOND CREAM*

MEASUREMENT AND CONVERSION CHARTS

MEASUREMENT CONVERSION CHART

Formulas for Exact Measures				Rounded Measures for Quick Reference		
	When you know:	Multiply by:	To find:			
Mass (Weight)	ounces	28.35	grams	1 oz.		= 30 g
	pounds	0.45	kilograms	4 oz.		= 120 g
	grams	0.035	ounces	8 oz.		= 225 g
	kilograms	2.2	pounds	16 oz.	= 1 lb.	= 450 g
				32 oz.	= 2 lb.	= 900 g
				36 oz.	= 2 1/4 lb.	= 1000 g (1 kg)
Volume (Capacity)	teaspoons	5.0	milliliters	1/4 tsp.	= 1/24 oz.	= 1 ml
	tablespoons	15.0	milliliters	1/2 tsp.	= 1/12 oz.	= 2 ml
	fluid ounces	29.57	milliliters	1 tsp.	= 1/6 oz.	= 5 ml
	cups	0.24	liters	1 Tbsp.	= 1/2 oz.	= 15 ml
	pints	0.47	liters	1 c.	= 8 oz.	= 250 ml
	quarts	0.95	liters	2 c. (1 pt.)	= 16 oz.	= 500 ml
	gallons	3.785	liters	4 c. (1 qt.)	= 32 oz.	= 1 lt
	milliliters	0.034	fluid ounces	4 qt. (1 gal.)	= 128 oz.	= 3 3/4 lt
Temperature	Fahrenheit	5/9 (after subtracting 32)	Celsius	32°F	= 0°C	
	Celsius	9/5 (then add 32)	Fahrenheit	122°F	= 50°C	
				212°F	= 100°C	

CONVERSION GUIDELINES

1 gallon	=	4 quarts
		8 pints
		16 cups (8 ounces)
		128 ounces
1 fifth bottle	=	approximately 1 1/2 pints or exactly 26.5 ounces
1 measuring cup	=	8 ounces (a coffee cup is generally 6 ounces)
1 large egg white	=	1 ounce (average)
1 lemon	=	1 to 1 1/4 ounces of juice
1 orange	=	3 to 3 1/2 ounces of juice

SCOOP SIZES

Scoop Measure	Level Measure
6	2/3 cup
8	1/2 cup
10	2/5 cup
12	1/3 cup
16	1/4 cup
20	3 1/5 tablespoons
24	2 2/3 tablespoons
30	2 1/5 tablespoons
40	1 3/5 tablespoons

The number scoop determines the number of servings in each quart of a mixture, for example, with a No. 16 scoop, one quart of mixture will yield 16 servings.

LADLE SIZES

Size	Portion of a Cup	Number per Quart	Number per Liter
1 oz.	1/8	32	34
2 oz.	1/4	16	17
2 2/3 oz.	1/3	12	13
4 oz.	1/2	8	8.6
6 oz.	3/4	5 1/3	5.7

CANNED GOOD SIZES

Size	No. of Cans per Case	Average Weight	Average No. Cups per Can
No. 1/2	8	8 oz.	1
No. 1 tall (also known as 303)	2 & 4 doz.	16 oz.	2
No. 2	2 doz.	20 oz.	2 1/2
No. 2 1/2	2 doz.	28 oz.	3 1/2
No. 3	2 doz.	33 oz.	4
No. 3 cylinder	1 doz.	46 oz.	5 2/3
No. 5	1 doz.	3 lb. 8 oz.	5 1/2
No. 10	6	6 lb. 10 oz.	13

BIBLIOGRAPHY AND RECOMMENDED READING

GENERAL INTEREST

Bickel, Walter, ed. and trans. *Hering's Dictionary of Classical and Modern Cookery*. 12th Eng. ed. London: Virtue & Company Limited, 1991.

Culinary Institute of America. *The New Professional Chef*. 5th ed. New York: Van Nostrand Reinhold, 1991.

Dawson, Hannelore. *Great Food for Great Numbers*. New York: Van Nostrand Reinhold, 1991.

Escoffier, Auguste. *Le Guide culinaire*. (Translation entitled *The Escoffier Cookbook and Guide to the Fine Art of Cookery for Connoisseurs, Chefs, Epicures*). New York: Crown Publishers, 1969.

Gisslen, Wayne. *Professional Baking*. New York: John Wiley & Sons, Inc., 1985.

———. *Professional Cooking*. 2nd ed. New York: John Wiley & Sons, Inc., 1989.

The Grand Masters of the French Cuisine. Selected and adapted by Celine Vence and Robert Courtine. New York: G.P. Putnam & Sons, 1978.

Haines, Robert G. *Food Preparation*. Homewood, Ill.: American Technical Publishers, Inc., 1988.

Lang, Jennifer Harvey, ed. *Larousse Gastronomique*. American ed. New York: Crown Publishers, Inc., 1988.

Leith, Prue. *The Cook's Handbook*. New York: A & W Publishers, Inc., 1981.

Pauli, Eugen, *Classical Cooking the Modern Way*. 2nd ed. New York: Van Nostrand Reinhold, 1989.

Pepin, Jacques. *The Art of Cooking*. New York: Alfred A. Knopf, 1987.

———. *La Technique*. New York: Wallaby/Pocket Books, 1976.

Rombauer, Irma von Starkloff and Marion Rombauer Becker. *Joy of Cooking*. New York: The Bobbs-Merrill Co., Inc., Macmillan, 1975.

Shugart, Grace and Mary Molt. *Food for Fifty*. 9th ed. New York: Macmillan, 1993.

Willan, Anne. *La Varenne Pratique*. New York: Crown Publishers, 1989.

FOOD HISTORY

Clair, Colin. *Kitchen & Table: A Bedside History of Eating in the Western World*. New York: Abelard-Schuman Limited, 1965.

Fussell, Betty. *The Story of Corn*. New York: Borzoi Books, Alfred A. Knopf, Inc., 1992.

Hale, William Harlan, and The Editors of Horizon Magazine. *The Horizon Cookbook and Illustrated History of Eating and Drinking Through the Ages*. New York: American Heritage Publishing Co., Inc., 1968.

Mintz, Sidney W. *Sweetness and Power: The Place of Sugar in Modern History*. New York: Penguin Books, 1985.

Norman, Barbara. *Tales of the Table: A History of Western Cuisine*. Englewood Cliffs, N.J.: Prentice-Hall, 1972.

Revel, Jean-François. *Culture and Cuisine*. (Trans. of *Un Festin en paroles*.) New York: Da Capo Press, Inc., 1982.

Rupp, Rececca. *Blue Corn and Square Tomatoes*. Pownal, Vt.: Garden Way Publishing, 1987.

Schremp, Gerry. *Kitchen Culture: Fifty Years of Food Fads*. New York: Pharos Books, A Scripps Howard Co., 1991.

Shapiro, Laura. *Perfection Salad: Women and Cooking at the Turn of the Century*. New York: Farrar, Straus and Giroux, 1986.

Tannahill, Reay. *Food in History*. New York: Crown Publishers, Inc., 1988.

Toussaint-Samat, Maguelonne. *A History of Food*. Translated by Anthea Bell. Cambridge, Mass.: Blackwell Publishers, 1992.

Wheaton, Barbara Ketcham. *Savoring the Past*. Philadelphia: The University of Pennsylvania Press, 1983.

Willan, Anne. *Great Cooks and Their Recipes: From Taillevent to Escoffier*. Boston: Little, Brown and Co., A Bulfinch Press Book, 1992.

SANITATION AND SAFETY

The Educational Foundation of the National Restaurant Association. *Applied Foodservice Sanitation: A Foundation Textbook*. 4th ed. John Wiley & Sons, Inc., 1992.

Guthrie, Rufus K. *Food Sanitation*. 3d ed. New York: Van Nostrand Reinhold, 1988.

National Assessment Institute. *Handbook for Safe Food Service Management*. Englewood Cliffs, N.J.: Regents/Prentice Hall, 1994.

NUTRITION

Brody, Jane E. *Jane Brody's Nutrition Book*. New York: Bantam Books, Inc., 1982.

Freyberg, Nicholas, and Willis A. Gortner. *The Food Additives Book*. New York: Bantam Books, Inc., 1982.

Hamilton, Eva Mae Nunnelley, Eleanor Noss Whitney, and Frances Sienkiewicz Sizer. *Nutrition: Concepts and Controversies*. 4th ed. St. Paul, Minn.: West Publishing Co., 1988.

Netzer, Corinne T. *The Corinne T. Netzer Encyclopedia of Food Values*. New York: Dell Publishing, 1992.

Spiller, Gene. *The Super Pyramid Eating Program: Introducing the Revolutionary Five New Food Groups*. New York: Times Books, Random House, Inc., 1993.

FOOD COSTING AND MENU PRICING

Coltman, Michael M. *Financial Control for Your Foodservice Operation*. New York: Van Nostrand Reinhold, 1991.

Keister, Douglas C. *Food and Beverage Control*. 2nd ed. Englewood Cliffs, N.J.: Prentice Hall, 1990.

McVety, Paul J., and Bradley J. Ware. *Fundamentals of Menu Planning*. New York: Van Nostrand Reinhold, 1989.

Miller, Jack E. *Menu Pricing and Strategy*. 2nd ed. New York: Van Nostrand Reinhold, 1987.

Schmidt, Arno. *Chef's Book of Formulas, Yields, and Sizes*. New York: Van Nostrand Reinhold, 1990.

TOOLS

Bridge, Fred, and Jean F. Tibbetts. *The Well-Tooled Kitchen*. New York: William Morrow and Co., 1991.

GENERAL INGREDIENTS

DeMers, John. *The Community Kitchens Complete Guide to Gourmet Coffee*. New York: Simon & Schuster, 1986.

Dowell, Philip, and Adrian Bailey. *Cook's Ingredients*. New York: William Morrow and Co., 1980.

Jordan, Michele Anna. *The Good Cook's Book of Oil & Vinegar*. Reading, Mass.: Addison-Wesley, 1992.

Norman, Jill. *The Complete Book of Spices*. American ed. New York: Viking Studio Books, 1991.

Ortiz, Elisabeth Lambert. *The Encyclopedia of Herbs, Spices and Flavorings*. 1st American ed. New York: Dorling Kindersley, Inc., 1992.

Schapira, Joel, and Karl Schapira. *The Book of Coffee and Tea*. New York: St. Martin's Press, 1975.

Schuler, Stanley, ed. *Simon & Schuster's Guide to Herbs and Spices*. New York: Fireside and Simon & Schuster, 1990.

Stobart, Tom. *Herbs, Spices and Flavorings*. Woodstock, N.Y.: The Overland Press, 1982.

EGGS, DAIRY AND CHEESE

Eggcyclopedia. 2nd ed. Park Ridge, Ill.: American Egg Board, revised 1989.

Jones, Evan. *The World of Cheese*. New York: Alfred A. Knopf, 1984.

Marquis, Vivienne, and Patricia Haskell. *The Cheese Book*. New York: Simon & Schuster, 1985.

FOOD SCIENCE

Freeland-Graves, H., and Gladys C. Peckham. *Foundations of Food Preparation*. 5th ed. New York: Macmillan, 1987.

McGee, Harold. *On Food and Cooking*. New York: Charles Scribner's Sons, 1984.

McWilliams, Margaret. *Food Fundamentals*. 4th ed. New York: Macmillan, 1985.

Potter, Norman N. *Food Science*. 4th ed. Westport, Conn.: The AVI Publishing Co. Inc., 1986.

STOCKS, SAUCES AND SOUPS

Clayton, Bernard. *The Complete Book of Soups and Stews*. New York: Simon & Schuster, 1984.

Davis, Deidre. *A Fresh Look at Saucing Foods*. Reading, Mass.: Addison-Wesley, 1993.

Larousse, David Paul. *The Sauce Bible: Guide to the Saucier's Craft*. New York: John Wiley & Sons, Inc., 1993.

Peterson, James. *Sauces: Classical and Contemporary Sauce Making*. New York: Van Nostrand Reinhold, 1991.

Sokolov, Raymond A. *The Saucier's Apprentice*. New York: Alfred A. Knopf, 1976.

MEAT

Libby, James A. *Meat Hygiene*. Philadelphia: Lea & Febiger, 1975.

The Meat Buyers Guide. Reston, Va.: National Association of Meat Purveyors, 1990.

Thomas, John R., and P. Thomas Ziegler. *The Meat We Eat*. Danville, Ill.: Interstate Printers & Publishers, Inc., 1985.

The Editors of Time-Life Books. *The Good Cook: Lamb*. London: Time Life International (Nederland) B.V., 1981.

The Editors of Time-Life Books. *The Good Cook: Beef and Veal*. London: Time Life International (Nederland) B.V., 1978.

POULTRY

The Editors of Time-Life Books. *The Good Cook: Poultry*. London: Time Life International (Nederland) B.V., 1978.

GAME

Cameron, Angus, and Judith Jones. *The L.L. Bean Game and Fish Cookbook*. New York: Random House, 1983.

Little, Carolyn. *The Game Cookbook*. Wiltshire, England: The Crowood Press, 1988.

Marrone, Teresa. *Dressing and Cooking Wild Game*. New York: Prentice Hall Press, 1987.

FISH AND SHELLFISH

Cronin, Isaac, Jay Harlow, and Paul Johnson. *The California Seafood Cookbook*. Berkeley, Calif.: Harris Publishing Co., Inc. (Aris Books), 1983.

The Fish List: FDA Guide to Acceptable Market Names for Food Fish Sold in Interstate Commerce. Washington, D.C.: U.S. Government Printing Office, 1988.

Howarth, A. Jan. *The Complete Fish Cookbook*. New York: St. Martin's Press, 1983.

King, Shirley. *Fish, The Basics.* New York: Simon & Schuster, 1990.

———. *Saucing the Fish.* New York: Simon & Schuster, 1976.

Loomis, Susan Herrmann. *The Great American Seafood Cookbook.* New York: Workman Publishing, 1988.

McClane, A. J. *The Encyclopedia of Fish Cookery.* New York: Holt, Rinehart and Winston, 1977.

The Seafood Handbook: Seafood Standards. Rockland, Maine: Seafood Business Magazine, 1991.

CHARCUTERIE

Ehlert, Friedrich W., et al. *Pâtés and Terrines.* Reprint. London: Hearst Books, 1990.

Grigson, Jane. *The Art of Charcuterie.* Reprint. New York: The Echo Press, 1991.

The Editors of Time-Life Books. *The Good Cook: Terrines, Pâtés and Galantines.* London: Time Life International (Nederland) B.V., 1981.

VEGETABLES AND FRUITS

Andrews, Jean. *Peppers: The Domesticated Capsicums.* Austin, Tex.: University of Texas Press, 1984.

Bauer, Cathy, and Juel Andersen. *The Tofu Cookbook.* Emmaus, Pa.: Rodale Press, 1979.

Beck, Bruce. *Produce: A Fruit and Vegetable Lovers' Guide.* New York: Friendly Press, 1984.

Brennan, Georgeanne, Isaac Cronin, and Charlotte Glenn. *The New American Vegetable Cookbook.* Berkeley, Calif.: Harris Publishing Co., 1985.

Brown, Marlene. *International Produce Cookbook and Guide.* Los Angeles: HP Books, 1989.

Davidson, Alan. *Fruit: A Connoisseur's Guide and Cookbook.* New York: Simon & Schuster, 1991.

DeWitt, Dave, and Nancy Gerlach. *The Whole Chile Pepper Book.* Boston: Little, Brown and Co., 1990.

Holthaus, Fusako. *Tofu Cookery.* Tokyo: Kodansha International, 1992.

Miller, Mark, with John Harrisson. *The Great Chile Book.* Berkeley, Calif.: Ten Speed Press, 1991.

Murdich, Jack. *Buying Produce.* New York: William Morrow and Co., 1986.

Payne, Rolce Redard, and Dorrit Speyer Senior. *Cooking With Fruit.* New York: Crown Publishers, Inc., 1992.

Schmidt, Jimmy. *Cooking For All Seasons.* New York: Macmillan, 1991.

Schneider, Elizabeth. *Uncommon Fruits and Vegetables: A Commonsense Guide.* New York: Harper & Row, 1986.

GRAINS AND PASTA

Bugialli, Giuliano. *On Pasta.* New York: Simon & Schuster, 1988.

Della Croce, Julia. *Pasta Classica.* San Francisco: Chronicle Books, 1987.

Gelles, Carol. *The Complete Whole Grain Cookbook.* New York: Donald I. Fine, Inc., 1989.

Greene, Bert. *The Grains Cookbook.* New York: Workman Publishing, 1988.

Kummer, Corby. "Pasta." *The Atlantic,* 258, no. 1 (July 1986): 35–47.

Leblang, Bonnie Tandy, and Joanne Lamb Hayes. *Rice.* New York: Harmony Books, 1991.

Scott, Marisa Luisa, and Jack Denton Scott. *Rice.* New York: Times Books, 1985.

Spier, Carol. *Food Essentials: Grains and Pasta.* New York: Crescent Books, 1993.

SALADS AND SALAD DRESSINGS

Blair, Eulalia. C. *Salads for Foodservice Menu Planning.* New York: Van Nostrand Reinhold, 1988.

Idone, Christopher. *Christopher Idone's Salad Days.* New York: Random House, 1989.

Muller, Veronika. *Salads.* New York: Van Nostrand Reinhold, 1989.

Nathan, Amy. *Salad.* San Francisco: Chronicle Books, 1985.

BREADS

Albright, Barbara, and Leslie Weiner. *Mostly Muffins.* New York: St. Martin's Press, 1984.

Alston, Elizabeth. *Biscuits and Scones.* New York: Clarkson N. Potter, Inc., 1988.

Amendola, Joseph. *The Bakers' Manual.* 4th ed. New York: Van Nostrand Reinhold, 1993.

Clayton, Bernard. *Bernard Clayton's New Complete Book of Breads.* Rev. ed. New York: Simon & Schuster, 1987.

Cunningham, Marion. *The Fannie Farmer Baking Book.* New York: Alfred A. Knopf, 1984.

David, Elizabeth. *English Bread and Yeast Cookery.* Notes by Karen Hess. American ed. New York: The Viking Press, 1980.

Jones, Judith, and Evan Jones. *The Book of Bread.* New York: Harper & Row, 1982.

Ortiz, Joe. *The Village Baker: Classic Regional Breads from Europe and America.* Berkeley, Calif.: Ten Speed Press, 1993.

Weiner, Leslie, and Barbara Albright. *Simply Scones.* New York: St. Martin's Press, 1988.

PASTRIES AND DESSERTS

Bernachon, Maurice, and Jean-Jacques Bernachon. *A Passion for Chocolate.* Translated and adapted for the American kitchen by Rose Levy Beranbaum. New York: William Morrow and Co., Inc., 1989.

Braker, Flo. *The Simple Art of Perfect Baking.* Shelburne, Vt.: Chapters Publishing, Ltd., 1992.

Fletcher, Helen S. *The New Pastry Cook.* New York: William Morrow and Co., Inc., 1986.

Friberg, Bo. *The Professional Pastry Chef.* 2nd ed. New York: Van Nostrand Reinhold, 1990.

Healy, Bruce, and Paul Bugat. *Mastering the Art of French Pastry.* Woodbury, N.Y.: Barron's, 1984.

Hyman, Philip, and Mary Hyman, trans. *The Best of Gaston Lenotre's Desserts.* Woodbury, N.Y.: Barron's, 1983.

London, Sheryl, and Mel London. *Fresh Fruit Desserts: Classic and Contemporary.* New York: Prentice Hall Press, 1990.

Purdy, Susan G. *A Piece of Cake.* New York: Macmillan, 1989.

Roux, Michel, and Albert Roux. *The Roux Brothers on Pâtisserie.* New York: Prentice Hall Press, 1986.

Silverton, Nancy. *Desserts by Nancy Silverton.* New York: Harper & Row, 1986.

Sultan, William J. *The Pastry Chef.* New York: Van Nostrand Reinhold, 1983.

Sultan, William J. *Practical Baking.* 5th ed. New York: Van Nostrand Reinhold, 1990.

MEAL SERVICE

Alston, Elizabeth. *Breakfast with Friends: Seasonal Menus to Celebrate the Morning.* New York: McGraw-Hill, 1989.

Bristow, Linda Kay. *Bread and Breakfast.* San Ramon, Calif.: 101 Productions, 1985.

Janericco, Terence. *The Book of Great Hors d'Oeuvre.* New York: Van Nostrand Reinhold, 1990.

Kolpas, Norman. *Breakfast and Brunch Book.* Los Angeles: HP Books, 1988.

Kotschevar, Lendal H. *Short Order Cooking.* New York: Van Nostrand Reinhold, 1990.

INTERNATIONAL CUISINES

Bayless, Rick, with Deann Groen Bayless. *Authentic Mexican: Regional Cooking from the Heart of Mexico.* New York: William Morrow and Co., Inc., 1987.

Bugialli, Giuliano. *The Fine Art of Italian Cooking.* New York: Random House, 1990.

Casas, Penelope. *The Foods and Wines of Spain.* New York: Alfred A. Knopf, 1991.

Curnonsky [Maurice Edmond Sailland]. *Traditional French Cooking.* Translation of *Cuisine et vins de France,* English ed. Jeni Wright. New York: Doubleday, 1989.

Devi, Yamuna. *The Art of Indian Vegetarian Cooking.* New York: E.P. Dutton, 1987.

Downer, Lesley. *At the Japanese Table.* San Francisco: Chronicle Books, 1993.

Efrain, Martinez. *Classic Spanish Cooking with Chef Ef.* Los Angeles: Lowell House, 1993.

Field, Carol. *Celebrating Italy.* New York: William Morrow & Co., Inc., 1990.

Gin, Maggie. *Regional Cooking of China.* San Francisco: 101 Productions, 1984.

Grigson, Jane. *Jane Grigson's Book of European Cookery.* New York: Atheneum, 1983.

Hazan, Marcella. *Essentials of Classic Italian Cooking.* New York: Alfred A. Knopf, 1993.

Jaffrey, Madhur. *An Invitation to Indian Cooking.* New York: Vintage Books, 1973.

———. *A Taste of India.* New York: Atheneum, 1986.

Kasper, Lynn Rossetto. *The Splendid Table: Recipes from Emilia-Romagna the Heartland of Northern Italian Food.* New York: William Morrow & Co., Inc., 1992.

Kennedy, Diana. *The Cuisines of Mexico.* Rev. ed. New York: Harper & Row, 1986.

Lo, Kenneth. *The Encyclopedia of Chinese Cooking.* New York: Bristol Books, 1979.

McDermott, Nancie. *Real Thai: The Best of Thailand's Regional Cooking.* San Francisco: Chronicle Books, 1992.

Olaore, Ola. *Traditional African Cooking.* London: Foulsham & Company Ltd., 1990.

Randelman, Mary Urrutia, and Joan Schwartz. *Memories of a Cuban Kitchen.* New York: Macmillan, 1992.

Richie, Donald. *A Taste of Japan.* New York: Kodansha, 1985.

Roden, Claudia. *A Book of Middle Eastern Food.* New York: Vintage Books, 1972.

Rojas-Lombardi, Felipe. *The Art of South American Cooking.* New York: HarperCollins, 1991.

Rose, Evelyn. *The New Complete International Jewish Cookbook.* New York: Carroll & Graf Publishers, Inc., 1992.

Routhier, Nicole. *The Foods of Vietnam.* New York: Stewart, Tabori & Chang, 1989.

Rozin, Elisabeth. *Ethnic Cuisine; The Flavor-Principle Cookbook.* Lexington, Mass.: S. Green Press, 1983. Reprint. New York: Penguin Books USA Inc., Viking Penguin, 1992.

Sandler, Bea. *The African Cookbook.* New York: World Publishing, 1970.

Scharfenberg, Horst. *The Cuisines of Germany: Regional Specialties and Traditional Home Cooking.* New York: Poseidon Press, 1980.

Solomon, Charmaine. *The Complete Asian Cookbook.* New York: McGraw-Hill, 1976.

———. *Charmaine Solomon's Thai Cookbook.* Rutland, Vt.: Charles E. Tuttle Co., 1991.

Toomre, Joyce. *Classic Russian Cooking: Elena Molokhovets' A Gift to Young Housewives.* Translated, introduced, and annotated by Joyce Toomre. Bloomington, Ind.: Indiana University Press, 1992.

Volokh, Anne, with Mavis Manus. *The Art of Russian Cuisine.* New York: Collier Books, 1983.

Von Bremzen, Anya, and John Welchman. *Please To The Table: The Russian Cookbook.* New York: Workman Publishing Co., 1990.

Wolfert, Paula. *Couscous and Other Good Food from Morocco.* New York: Harper & Row, 1973.

PRESENTATION AND GARNISHING

Budgen, June. *The Book of Garnishes.* Los Angeles: HP Books, 1986.

Grotz, Peter. *Successful Cold Buffets.* New York: Van Nostrand Reinhold, 1990.

Haydock, Robert, and Yukiko Haydock. *Japanese Garnishes.* New York: Holt, Rinehart and Winston, 1980.

Larousse, David Paul. *Edible Art: Forty-Eight Garnishes for the Professional.* New York: Van Nostrand Reinhold, 1987.

Lynch, Francis Talyn. *Garnishing: A Feast for Your Eyes.* Los Angeles: HP Books, 1987.

BOOKS BY CONTRIBUTING CHEFS

Ash, John, and Sid Goldstein. *American Game Cooking.* Reading, Mass.: Addison-Wesley (Aris Books), 1991.

Beranbaum, Rose Levy. *The Cake Bible.* New York: William Morrow and Co., Inc., 1988.

Carpenter, Hugh, and Teri Sandison. *Chopstix: Quick Cooking with Pacific Flavors.* New York: Stewart, Tabori & Chang, 1990.

Golden, Harris. *Golden's Kitchen: The Artistry of Cooking and Dining on the Light Side.* Rev. 2nd ed. Phoenix, Ariz.: Quail Run Books, 1989.

Kerr, Graham. *Graham Kerr's Minimax Cookbook.* New York: Doubleday, 1992.

Malgieri, Nick. *Nick Malgieri's Perfect Pastry.* New York: Macmillan, 1989.

Medrich, Alice. *Cocolat.* New York: Warner Books, 1990.

Milliken, Mary Sue, and Susan Feniger. *City Cuisine.* New York: William Morris and Co., Inc., 1989.

Miller, Mark. *Coyote Cafe.* Berkeley, Calif.: Ten Speed Press, 1989.

Puck, Wolfgang. *Adventures in the Kitchen: 175 New Recipes from Spago, Chinois on Main, Postrio and Eureka.* New York: Random House, 1991.

———. *The Wolfgang Puck Cookbook.* New York: Random House, 1986.

Richard, Michel. *Michel Richard's Home Cooking with a French Accent.* New York: William Morrow and Co., Inc., 1993.

Roberts, Michael. *Secret Ingredients.* New York: Bantam Books, 1988.

Somerville, Annie. *Fields of Greens: New Vegetarian Recipes from the Celebrated Greens Restaurant.* New York: Bantam Books, 1993.

Tropp, Barbara. *China Moon Cookbook.* New York: Workman Publishing Co., 1992.

GLOSSARY

Acid—foods such as citrus juice, vinegar and wine that have a sour or sharp flavor (most foods are slightly acidic); acids have a pH of less than 7.

Acidulation—the browning of cut fruit caused by the reaction of an enzyme (polyphenoloxidase) with the phenolic compounds present in these fruits; this browning is often mistakenly attributed to exposure to oxygen.

Additives—substances added to foods to prevent spoilage or to improve appearance, texture, taste or nutritional value.

Aerobic bacteria—those that thrive on oxygen.

Aging—(1) the period of time during which freshly killed meat is allowed to rest so that the effects of rigor mortis dissipate; (2) the period during which freshly milled flour is allowed to rest so that it will whiten and produce less sticky doughs; the aging of flour can be chemically accelerated.

Airline breast—a boneless chicken breast with the first wing bone attached.

À la carte—(1) a menu on which each food and beverage is listed and priced separately; (2) foods cooked to order as opposed to foods cooked in advance and held for later service.

Albumen—the principal protein found in egg whites.

Al dente—(ahl den-tay) cooked foods (usually vegetables and pasta) that are prepared firm to the bite, not soft or mushy.

Alkali—also known as a base, any substance with a pH higher than 7; baking soda is one of the few alkaline foods.

Alkaloid—a number of bitter organic substances with alkaline properties; found most often in plants and sometimes used in drugs.

Allemande—(ah-luh-mahnd) a sauce made by adding lemon juice and a liaison to a velouté made from veal or chicken stock; used to make several small sauces of the velouté family.

Allumette—(al-u-met) (1) a matchstick cut of 1/8 inch × 1/8 inch × 1–2 inches (3 millimeters × 3 millimeters × 2.5–5 centimeters) usually used for potatoes; (2) a strip of puff pastry with a sweet or savory filling.

American service—restaurant service where the waiter takes the orders and brings the food to the table; the food is placed on dishes (plated) in the kitchen, making it a relatively fast method for seated service.

Amino acid—the basic molecular component of proteins; each of the approximately two dozen amino acids contain oxygen, hydrogen, carbon and nitrogen atoms.

Anaerobic bacteria—those that are able to live and grow without the presence of oxygen.

Animal husbandry—the business, science and practice of raising domesticated animals.

Anterior—at or toward the front of an object or place; opposite of posterior.

Appetizers—also known as first courses, usually small portions of hot or cold foods intended to whet the appetite in anticipation of the more substantial courses to follow.

Aquafarming—also known as aquaculture, the business, science and practice of raising large quantities of fish and shellfish in tanks, ponds or ocean pens.

Aromatic—a food added to a preparation to enhance the flavor and aroma; includes herbs and spices as well as some vegetables.

Aspic or **aspic jelly**—a clear jelly usually made from a clarified stock thickened with gelatin; used to coat foods, especially charcuterie items, and for garnish.

As-purchased (A.P.)—the condition or cost of an item as it is purchased or received from the supplier.

As-served (A.S.)—the weight or size of a food product as sold or served after processing or cooking.

Au gratin—(ah graw-ton) foods with a browned or crusted top; often made by browning a food with a bread crumb, cheese, and/or sauce topping under a broiler or salamander.

Au jus—(ah zhew) roasted meats, poultry or game served with their natural, unthickened juices.

Au sec—(ah sec) cooked until nearly dry.

Bacteria—single-celled microorganisms, some of which can cause diseases, including food-borne diseases.

Bain marie—(bane mah-ree) (1) a hot water bath used to gently cook food or keep cooked food hot; (2) a container for holding food in a hot water bath.

Baking—a dry-heat cooking method in which foods are surrounded by hot, dry air in a closed environment; similar to roasting, the term baking is usually applied to breads, pastries, vegetables and fish.

Baking powder—a mixture of sodium bicarbonate and one or more acids, generally cream of tartar and/or sodium aluminum sulfate, used to leaven baked goods; it releases carbon dioxide gas if moisture is present in a formula. Single-acting baking powder releases carbon dioxide gas in the presence of moisture only; double-acting baking powder releases some carbon dioxide gas upon contact with moisture, more gas is released when heat is applied.

Baking soda—the chemical sodium bicarbonate, an alkaline compound that releases carbon dioxide gas when combined with an acid and moisture; used to leaven baked goods.

Ballotine—(bahl-lo-teen) similar to a galantine, it is usually made by stuffing a deboned poultry leg with forcemeat; it is then poached or braised and normally served hot.

Barbecue—(1) to cook foods over dry heat created by the burning of hardwood or hardwood charcoals; (2) a tangy tomato- or vinegar-based sauce used for grilled foods; (3) foods cooked by this method and/or with this sauce.

Barding—tying thin slices of fat, such as bacon or pork fatback, over meats or poultry that have little to no natural fat covering in order to protect and moisten them during roasting.

Basting—moistening foods during cooking (usually roasting, broiling or grilling) with melted fat, pan drippings, sauce or other liquids to prevent drying and to add flavor.

Batonnet—(bah-toh-nah) foods cut into matchstick shapes of 1/4 inch × 1/4 inch × 2–2 1/2 inches (6 millimeters × 6 millimeters × 5–6 centimeters).

Batter—(1) a semiliquid mixture containing flour or other starch used to make cakes and breads. The gluten development is minimized and the liquid forms the continuous medium in which other ingredients are disbursed; generally contains more fat, sugar and liquids than a dough; (2) a semiliquid mixture of liquid and starch used to coat foods for deep-frying.

Baumé scale—(boh-may) see **Hydrometer**.

Bavarian cream—a sweet dessert mixture made by thickening custard sauce with gelatin and then folding in whipped cream; the final product is poured into a mold and chilled until firm.

Beard—a clump of dark threads found on a mussel.

Béarnaise—(bare-naze) a sauce made of butter and egg yolks and flavored with a reduction of vinegar, shallots, tarragon and peppercorns.

Beating—a mixing method in which foods are vigorously agitated to incorporate air or develop gluten; a spoon or electric mixer with its paddle attachment is used.

Béchamel—(bay-shah-mell) a leading sauce made by thickening milk with a white roux and adding seasonings.

Beef—the meat of domesticated cattle.

Beefalo—the product of crossbreeding a bison (American buffalo) and a domestic beef animal.

Berry—(1) the kernel of certain grains such as wheat; (2) small, juicy fruits that grow on vines and bushes.

Beurre blanc—(burr blanhk) (Fr. for white butter) an emulsified butter sauce made from shallots, white wine and butter.

Beurre composé—(burr kom-poz-a) see **Compound butter**.

Beurre manié—(burr man-yay) a combination of equal amounts by weight of flour and soft, whole butter; it is whisked into a simmering sauce at the end of the cooking process for quick thickening and added sheen and flavor.

Beurre noir—(burr nwar) (Fr. for black butter) whole butter heated until dark brown; sometimes flavored with vinegar.

Beurre noisette—(burr nwah-zett) whole butter heated until it turns light brown, giving off a nutty aroma.

Beurre rouge—(burr rooge) (Fr. for red butter) an emulsified butter sauce made from shallots, red wine and butter.

Bilateral—symmetrical halves arranged along a central axis.

Biscuit method—a mixing method used to make biscuits, scones and flaky doughs; it involves cutting cold fat into the flour and other dry ingredients before any liquid is added.

Bisque—(bisk) a soup made from shellfish; classic versions are thickened with rice.

Bivalves—mollusks such as clams, oysters and mussels that have two bilateral shells attached at a central hinge.

Blanching—very briefly and partially cooking a food in boiling water or hot fat; usually used to assist preparation (for example, to loosen peels from vegetables), as part of a combination cooking method, to remove undesirable flavors or to prepare a food for freezing.

Blanquette—(blang-kett) a white stew made of a white sauce and meat or poultry that is simmered without first browning.

Blending—a mixing method in which two or more ingredients are combined just until they are evenly distributed; a spoon, rubber spatula, whisk or electric mixer with its paddle attachment is used.

Bloom—(1) a white, powdery layer that sometimes appears on chocolate if the cocoa butter separates; (2) a measure of gelatin's strength.

Blown sugar—a boiled mixture of sucrose, glucose and tartaric acid colored and shaped using an air pump; used to make fruits and containers.

Boiling—a moist-heat cooking method that uses convection to transfer heat from a hot (approximately 212°F [100°C]) liquid to the food submerged in it; the turbulent waters and higher temperatures cook foods more quickly than do poaching or simmering.

Bordelaise—(bor-da-lays) a brown sauce flavored with a reduction of red wine, shallots, pepper and herbs and garnished with marrow.

Bouchées—(boo-shays) small puff pastry shells often filled with a savory mixture and used for hors d'oeuvres.

Bound salad—a salad composed of cooked meats, poultry, fish, shellfish, pasta or potatoes combined with a dressing.

Bouquet garni—(boo-kay gar-nee) fresh herbs and vegetables tied into a bundle with twine and used to flavor stocks, sauces, soups and stews.

Bouquetiere—(buk-a-tyer) a garnish (bouquet) of carefully cut and arranged fresh vegetables.

Braising—a combination cooking method in which foods are first browned in hot fat, then covered and slowly cooked in a small amount of liquid over low heat; braising uses a combination of simmering and steaming to transfer heat from the liquid (conduction) and the air (convection) to the foods.

Bran—the tough outer layer of a cereal grain and the part highest in fiber.

Brandy—an alcoholic beverage made by distilling the fermented mash of grapes or other fruits.

Brawn—also called an aspic terrine, made from simmered meats packed into a terrine and covered with aspic.

Brazier or **brasier**—a pan designed for braising; usually round with two handles and a tight-fitting lid.

Breading—(1) a coating of bread or cracker crumbs, cornmeal or other dry meal applied to foods that will typically be deep-fried or pan-fried; (2) the process of applying this coating.

Brigade—also known as the kitchen brigade, a system of staffing a kitchen so that each worker is assigned a set of specific tasks; these tasks are often related by cooking method, equipment or the type of foods being produced.

Brine—a mixture of salt, water and seasonings used to preserve foods.

Brioche—(bree-yohsh) a rich yeast bread containing large amounts of eggs and butter.

Brochettes—(bro-shetts) skewers, either small hors d'oeuvre or large entree size, threaded with meat, poultry, fish, shellfish and/or vegetables and grilled, broiled or baked; sometimes served with a dipping sauce.

Broiling—a dry-heat cooking method in which foods are cooked by heat radiating from an overhead source.

Broth—a flavorful liquid obtained from the long simmering of meats and/or vegetables.

Browning—see **Caramelization**.

Brown sauce—see **Espagnole**.

Brown stew—a stew in which the meat is first browned in hot fat.

Brown stock—a richly colored stock made of chicken, veal, beef or game bones and vegetables, all of which are caramelized before they are simmered in water with seasonings.

Brunch—a late morning to early afternoon meal that takes the place of both breakfast and lunch; a brunch menu often offers breakfast foods as well as almost anything else.

Brunoise—(broo-nwah) (1) foods cut into cubes of 1/8 inch × 1/8 inch × 1/8 inch (3 millimeters × 3 millimeters × 3 millimeters); (2) foods garnished with vegetables cut in this manner.

Buffet service—diners generally serve themselves foods arranged on a counter or table or are served by workers assigned to specific areas of the buffet. Usually buffet-service-style restaurants charge by the meal; restaurants offering buffet service that charge by the dish are known as cafeterias.

Butcher—(1) to slaughter and dress or fabricate animals for consumption; (2) the person who slaughters and fabricates animals.

Butler service—the use of servers to pass foods (typically hors d'oeuvres) or drinks arranged on trays.

Buttercream—a light, smooth, fluffy frosting of sugar, fat and flavorings; egg yolks or whipped egg whites are sometimes added. There are three principal kinds: simple, Italian and French.

Butterflying—slicing boneless meat, fish or shrimp nearly in half lengthwise so that they spread open like a book; used to increase surface area and speed cooking.

Cafeteria—see **Buffet service**.

Caffeine—an alkaloid found in coffee beans, tea leaves and cocoa beans that acts as a stimulant.

Cake—in American usage, refers to a broad range of pastries including layer cakes, coffeecakes and gâteaux; can refer to almost anything that is baked, tender, sweet and sometimes frosted.

Calf—(1) a young cow or bull; (2) the meat of calves slaughtered when they are older than five months.

Calorie—the unit of energy measured by the amount of heat required to raise 1000 grams of water one degree Celsius; it is also written as *kilocalorie* or *kcal* and is used as a measure of food energy.

Canapé—(kahn-ah-pay) tiny open-faced sandwich served as an hors d'oeuvre; usually composed of a small piece of bread or toast topped with a savory spread and garnish.

Canning—a preservation method in which the food is sealed in a glass or metal container and subjected to high temperatures for a specific period of time in order to destroy microorganisms that cause spoilage; the sealed environment eliminates oxidation and retards decomposition.

Capon—(kay-pahn) the class of surgically castrated male chickens; they have well-flavored meat and soft, smooth skin.

Capsaicin—(kap-say-ih-sin) an alkaloid found in a chile pepper's placental ribs that provides the pepper's heat.

Caramelization—the process of cooking sugars; the browning of sugar enhances the flavor and appearance of foods.

Carbohydrates—a group of compounds composed of oxygen, hydrogen and carbon that supply the body with energy (4 calories per gram); carbohydrates are classified as simple (including certain sugars) and complex (including starches and fiber).

Carotenoid—a naturally occurring pigment that predominates in red and yellow vegetables such as carrots and red peppers.

Carryover cooking—the cooking that occurs after a food is removed from a heat source; it is accomplished by the residual heat remaining in the food.

Cartilage—also known as gristle, a tough, whitish elastic connective tissue that helps give structure to an animal's body.

Carve—to cut cooked meat or poultry into portions.

Casings—membranes used to hold forcemeat for sausages; they can be natural animal intestines or manufactured from collagen extracted from cattle hides.

Casserole—(1) a heavy dish, usually ceramic, for baking foods; (2) foods baked in a casserole dish.

Caul fat—a fatty membrane from pig or sheep intestines; it resembles fine netting and is used to bard roasts and pâtés and to encase forcemeat for sausages.

Cellulose—a complex carbohydrate found in the cell wall of plants; it is edible but indigestible by humans.

Cephalopods—mollusks with a single, thin internal shell called a pen or cuttlebone, well-developed eyes, a number of arms that attach to the head and a saclike fin-bearing mantle; include squid and octopus.

Chafing dish—a metal dish with a heating unit (flame or electric) used to keep foods warm at tableside or during buffet service.

Chalazae cords—thick, twisted strands of egg white that anchor the yolk in place.

Charcuterie—the production of pâtés, terrines, galantines, sausages and similar foods.

Cheesecloth—a light, fine mesh gauze used to strain liquids and make sachets.

Chef de partie—also known as station chef, produces the menu items under the direct supervision of the chef or sous-chef.

Chef du cuisine—also known simply as chef, the person responsible for all kitchen operations, developing menu items and setting the kitchen's tone and tempo.

Chef's knife—an all-purpose knife used for chopping, slicing and mincing; its tapering blade is 8–14 inches long.

Chemical hazards—a danger to the safety of food caused by chemical substances, especially cleaning agents, pesticides and toxic metals.

Chemical leavening agents—see **Baking powder** and **Baking soda**; through chemical reactions between acids and bases, these products release gases used to leaven baked goods.

Chevre—(shev-ruh) (Fr. for goat) generally refers to a cheese made from goat's milk.

Chiffonade—(cheh-fon-nahd) (1) to finely slice or shred leafy vegetables or herbs; (2) the finely cut leafy vegetables or herbs often used as a garnish or bedding.

Chile—a member of the capsicum plant family.

Chili—the stewlike dish containing chiles.

Chilled—a food that has been refrigerated.

Chilli—a commercial spice powder containing a blend of seasonings.

China cap—a cone-shaped strainer made of perforated metal.

Chinoise—(shen-wasz) a conical strainer made of fine mesh, used for straining and puréeing foods.

Chlorophyll—a naturally occurring pigment that predominates in green vegetables such as cabbage.

Cholesterol—a fatty substance found in foods derived from animal products and in the human body; it has been linked to heart disease.

Chop—(1) a cut of meat including part of the rib; (2) to cut an item into small pieces where uniformity of size and shape is neither feasible nor necessary.

Chowder—a hearty soup made from fish, shellfish and/or vegetables, usually containing milk and potatoes and often thickened with roux.

Chutney—a sweet-and-sour condiment made of fruits and/or vegetables cooked in vinegar with sugar and spices; some chutneys are reduced to a purée, while others retain recognizable pieces of their ingredients.

Cider—mildly fermented apple juice; nonalcoholic apple juice may also be labeled cider.

Citrus—fruits characterized by a thick rind, most of which is a bitter white pith (albedo) with a thin exterior layer of colored skin (zest); their flesh is segmented, juicy and varies from bitter to tart to sweet.

Clarification—(1) the process of transforming a broth into a clear consommé by trapping impurities with a clearmeat consisting of the egg white protein albumen, ground meat, an acidic product, mirepoix and other ingredients; (2) the clearmeat used to clarify a broth.

Clarified butter—purified butterfat; the butter is melted and the water and milk solids are removed.

Classes—the subdivisions of poultry kinds based on the bird's age and tenderness.

Classic cuisine—a late 19th- and early 20th-century refinement and simplification of French grande cuisine. Classic (or classical) cuisine relies upon the thorough exploration of culinary principles and techniques and emphasizes the refined preparation and presentation of superb ingredients.

Clean—to remove visible dirt and soil.

Clearmeat—see **Clarification**.

Clear soups—unthickened soups including broths, consommés and broth-based soups.

Coagulation—the irreversible transformation of proteins from a liquid or semi-liquid state to a drier, solid state; usually accomplished through the application of heat.

Cocoa butter—the fat found in cocoa beans and used in fine chocolates.

Colander—a perforated bowl, with or without a base or legs, used to strain foods.

Collagen—a protein found in nearly all connective tissues; it dissolves when cooked with moisture.

Combination cooking methods—cooking methods, principally braising and stewing, that employ both dry-heat and moist-heat procedures.

Composed salad—a salad prepared by arranging each of the ingredients (the base, body, garnish and dressing) on individual plates in an artistic fashion.

Compound butter—also known as a beurre composé, a mixture of softened whole butter and flavorings used as a sauce or to flavor and color other sauces.

Compound sauces—see **Small sauces**.

Concasse—(kon-kaas say) peeled, seeded and diced tomatoes.

Concasser—(kon-kaas-say) to pound or chop coarsely; usually used for tomatoes or parsley.

Condiment—traditionally, any item added to a dish for flavor, including herbs, spices and vinegars; now also refers to cooked or prepared flavorings such as prepared mustards, relishes, bottled sauces or pickles.

Conduction—the transfer of heat from one item to another through direct contact.

Confit—meat or poultry (often lightly salt-cured) slowly cooked and preserved in its own fat and served hot.

Connective tissues—tissues found throughout an animal's body that hold together and support other tissues such as muscles.

Consommé—a rich stock or broth that has been clarified with clearmeat to remove impurities.

Contaminants—biological, chemical or physical substances that can be harmful when consumed in sufficient quantities.

Contamination—the presence, generally unintentional, of harmful organisms or substances.

Convection—the transfer of heat caused by the natural movement of molecules in a fluid (whether air, water or fat) from a warmer area to a cooler one. Mechanical convection is the movement of molecules caused by stirring.

Cookery—the art, practice or work of cooking.

Cookies—small, sweet, flat pastries; usually classified by preparation or makeup techniques as drop, icebox, bar, cutout, pressed and wafer.

Cooking—the transfer of energy from a heat source to a food; this energy alters the food's molecular structure, changing its texture, flavor, aroma and appearance.

Cooking medium—the air, fat, water or steam in which a food is cooked.

Coring—the process of removing the seeds or pit from a fruit or fruit-vegetable.

Cost of goods sold—the total cost of food items sold during a given period; calculated as beginning inventory plus purchases minus ending inventory.

Cost per portion—the cost of one serving; calculated as the total recipe cost divided by the number of portions produced from that recipe.

Coulis—(koo-lees) a sauce made from a purée of vegetables or fruit; may be hot or cold.

Count—the number of individual items in a given measure of weight or volume.

Court bouillon—(cort boo-yon) water simmered with vegetables, seasonings and an acidic product such as vinegar or wine; used for simmering or poaching fish, shellfish or vegetables.

Couscoussier—two bulbous pots, the top one has a perforated bottom and sits snugly on the bottom pot; used to cook couscous.

Cows—female cattle after their first calving, principally raised for milk and calf production.

Cream filling—a pie filling made of flavored pastry cream thickened with cornstarch.

Creaming—a mixing method in which softened fat and sugar are vigorously combined to incorporate air; used for making some quick breads, cookies and high-fat cakes.

Creams—also known as crèmes, include light, fluffy or creamy-textured dessert foods made with whipped cream or whipped egg whites, such as Bavarian creams, chiffons, mousses and crème Chantilly.

Cream soup—a soup made from vegetables cooked in a liquid that is thickened with a starch and puréed; cream is then incorporated to add richness and flavor.

Crème Anglaise—(crem ahn-glas) or crème a l'anglaise; see **Vanilla custard sauce**.

Crème caramel—(crem cah-rah-mel) like crème renversée and flan, a custard baked over a layer of caramelized sugar and inverted for service.

Crème Chantilly—(crem shan-tee) heavy cream whipped to soft peaks and flavored with sugar and vanilla; used to garnish pastries or desserts or folded into cooled custard or pastry cream for fillings.

Crème Chiboust—(crem chee-boos) a pastry cream lightened by folding in Italian meringue.

Crème patissière—(crem pah-tees-syehr) see **Pastry cream**.

Crepe—(krayp) a thin, delicate unleavened griddlecake made with a very thin egg batter cooked in a very hot sauté pan; used in sweet and savory preparations.

Critical control point—under the HACCP system, it is any step during the processing of a food when a mistake can result in the transmission, growth or survival of pathogenic bacteria.

Croissant—(krwah-san) a crescent-shaped roll made from a rich, rolled-in yeast dough.

Croquette—(crow-kett) a food that has been puréed or bound with a thick sauce (usually béchamel or velouté), made into small shapes, then breaded and deep-fried.

Cross-contamination—the transfer of bacteria or other contaminants from one food, work surface or equipment to another.

Croute, en—(awn croot) a food encased in a bread or pastry crust.

Crouton—a bread or pastry garnish, usually toasted or sautéed until crisp.

Crudités—(croo-dee-tays) generally refers to raw or blanched vegetables served as an hors d'oeuvre and often accompanied by a dip.

Crustaceans—shellfish characterized by a hard outer skeleton or shell and jointed appendages; include lobsters, crabs and shrimp.

Cuisine—the ingredients, seasonings, cooking procedures and styles attributable to a particular group of people; the group can be defined by geography, history, ethnicity, politics, culture or religion.

Cuisson—(kwee-zon) the liquid used for shallow poaching.

Curdle—the separation of milk or egg mixtures into solid and liquid components; caused by overcooking, high heat or the presence of acids.

Curing salt—a mixture of salt and sodium nitrite that inhibits bacterial growth; used as a preservative, often for charcuterie items.

Custard—any liquid thickened by the coagulation of egg proteins; its consistency depends on the ratio of eggs to liquid and the type of liquid used. Custards can be baked in the oven or cooked in a bain marie or on the stove top.

Cutlet—a relatively thick boneless slice of meat.

Cutting—(1) reducing a food to smaller pieces; (2) a mixing method in which solid fat is incorporated into dry ingredients until only lumps of the desired size remain.

Cutting loss—the unavoidable and unrecoverable loss of food during fabrication; the loss is usually the result of food particles sticking to the cutting board or the evaporation of liquids.

Cuttlebone—also known as the pen, the single, thin internal shell of cephalopods.

Cycle menu—a menu that changes every day for a certain period and then repeats the same daily items in the same order (e.g., on a seven-day cycle, the same menu is used every Monday).

Dairy products—include cow's milk and foods produced from cow's milk such as butter, yogurt, sour cream and cheese.

Decline phase—a period during which bacteria die at an accelerated rate, also known as the negative growth phase.

Decoction—(1) boiling a food until its flavor is removed; (2) a procedure used for brewing coffee.

Decorator's icing—see **Royal icing**.

Deep-frying—a dry-heat cooking method using convection to transfer heat to a food submerged in hot fat; foods to be deep-fried are usually first coated in batter or breading.

Deglaze—to swirl or stir a liquid (usually wine or stock) in a sauté pan or other pan to dissolve cooked food particles remaining on the bottom; the resulting mixture often becomes the base for a sauce.

Degrease—to skim the fat from the top of a liquid such as a sauce or stock.

Demi-glace—(deh-me glass) (Fr. for half-glaze) a mixture of half brown stock and half brown sauce reduced by half.

Detrempe—(day-trup-eh) a paste made with flour and water during the first stage of preparing a pastry dough, especially rolled-in doughs.

Deveining—the process of removing a shrimp's digestive tract.

Deviled—meat, poultry or other food seasoned with mustard, vinegar and other spicy seasonings.

Diagonals—elongated or oval-shaped slices of cylindrical vegetables or fruits.

Dice—(1) to cut foods into cubes: 1/4 inch (6 millimeters) for small, 3/8 inch (9 millimeters) for medium and 5/8 (1.5 centimeters) for large; (2) the cubes of cut food.

Dietary fiber—see **Fiber**.

Dip—a thick, creamy sauce, served hot or cold, to accompany crudités, crackers, chips or other foods, especially as an hors d'oeuvre; dips are often based on sour cream, mayonnaise or cream cheese.

Direct contamination—the contamination of raw foods in their natural setting or habitat.

Docking—pricking small holes in an unbaked dough or crust to allow steam to escape and prevent the dough from rising when baked.

Dough—a mixture of flour and other ingredients used in baking; has a low moisture content and gluten forms the continuous medium into which other ingredients are embedded; it is often stiff enough to cut into shapes.

Drawn—a market form for fish in which the viscera is removed.

Dredging—coating a food with flour or finely ground crumbs; usually done prior to sautéing or frying or as the first step of the standardized breading procedure.

Dressed—(1) an animal carcass trimmed or otherwise prepared for consumption; (2) a market form for fish in which the viscera, gills, fins and scales are removed.

Drupes—see **Stone fruits**.

Dry-heat cooking methods—cooking methods, principally broiling, grilling, roasting and baking, sautéing, pan-frying and deep-frying, that use air or fat to transfer heat through conduction and convection; dry-heat cooking methods allow surface sugars to caramelize.

Drying—a preservation method in which the food's moisture content is dramatically reduced; drying changes the food's texture, flavor and appearance.

Duchesse potatoes—(duh-shees) a purée of cooked potatoes, butter and egg yolks, seasoned with salt, pepper and nutmeg; can be eaten as is or used to prepare several classic potato dishes.

Dumpling—any of a variety of small starchy products made from doughs or batters that are simmered or steamed; can be plain or filled.

Durum—a type of hard wheat milled into semolina flour which is used for making pasta.

Duxelles—(duke-sell) a coarse paste made of finely chopped mushrooms sautéed with shallots in butter.

Éclair paste—(ay-clahr) also known as pâte à choux, a soft dough that produces hollow baked products with crisp exteriors; used for making éclairs, cream puffs and savory products.

Edible portion (E.P.)—the amount of a food available for consumption after trimming or fabrication.

Egg wash—a mixture of beaten eggs (whole eggs, yolks or whites) and a liquid, usually milk or water, used to coat doughs before baking to add sheen.

Elastin—a protein found in connective tissues, particularly ligaments and tendons, it often appears as the white or silver covering on meats known as silverskin; elastin does not dissolve when cooked.

Émincé—(eh-manss) a small, thin boneless piece of meat.

Emulsification—the process by which generally unmixable liquids, such as oil and water, are forced into a uniform distribution.

Emulsion—(1) a uniform mixture of two unmixable liquids; (2) flavoring oils such as orange and lemon, mixed into water with the aid of emulsifiers.

Endosperm—the largest part of a cereal grain and a source of protein and carbohydrates (starch); it is the part used primarily in milled products.

Entree—(ahn-tray) the main dish of an American meal, usually meat, poultry, fish or shellfish accompanied by a vegetable and starch; in France, the first course, served before the fish and meat courses.

Enzymatic browning—see **Acidulation**.

Enzyme—proteins that aid specific chemical reactions in plants and animals.

Escalope—(ess-cal-lop) see **Scallop**.

Espagnole—(ess-spah-nyol) also known as brown sauce, a leading sauce made of brown stock, mirepoix and tomatoes thickened with brown roux; often used to produce demi-glace.

Essential nutrients—nutrients that must be provided by food because the body cannot or does not produce them in sufficient quantities.

Ethnic cuisine—generally, the cuisine of a group of people having a common cultural heritage, as opposed to the cuisine of a group of people bound together by geography or political factors.

Ethylene gas—a colorless, odorless hydrocarbon gas naturally emitted from fruits and fruit-vegetables that encourages ripening.

Evaporation—the process by which heated water molecules move faster and faster until the water turns to a gas (steam) and vaporizes; evaporation is responsible for the drying of foods during cooking.

Extracts—concentrated mixtures of ethyl alcohol and flavoring oils such as vanilla, almond and lemon.

Extrusion—the process of forcing pasta dough through perforated plates to create various shapes; pasta dough that is not extruded must be rolled and cut.

Fabricate—to cut a large item into smaller portions; often refers to the butchering of fish or shellfish.

Fabricated cuts—individual portions of meat cut from a subprimal.

Facultative bacteria—those that can adapt and will survive with or without oxygen.

Fancy—(1) fish that has been previously frozen; (2) a quality grade for fruits, especially canned or frozen.

Fatback—fresh pork fat from the back of the pig, used primarily for barding.

Fats—(1) a group of compounds composed of oxygen, hydrogen and carbon atoms that supply the body with energy (9 calories per gram); fats are classified as saturated, monounsaturated or polyunsaturated; (2) the general term for butter, lard, shortening, oil and margarine used as cooking media or ingredients.

Fermentation—(1) the process by which yeast converts sugar into alcohol and carbon dioxide; (2) the period of time that yeast bread dough is left to rise.

Feuillettes—(fuh-yuh-lyeth) square, rectangular or diamond-shaped puff pastry boxes that can be filled with a sweet or savory mixture.

Fiber—also known as dietary fiber, indigestible carbohydrates found in grains, fruits, and vegetables; fiber aids digestion.

FIFO (First In, First Out)—an inventory storage and utilization process in which the oldest product is always used first.

Filé—(fee-lay) a seasoning and thickening agent made from dried, ground sassafras leaves.

Filet, fillet—(fee-lay) (1) filet: the boneless tenderloin of meat; (2) fillet: the side of a fish removed intact, boneless or semiboneless, with or without skin; (3) to cut such a piece.

Fish scaler—an inflexible, rasplike tool used to remove scales from fish.

Fish velouté—a velouté sauce made from fish stock.

Flambé—(flahm-bay) food served flaming; produced by igniting brandy, rum or other liquor.

Flash-frozen—food that has been frozen very rapidly using metal plates, extremely low temperatures or chemical solutions.

Flatfish—fish with asymmetrical, compressed bodies that swim in a horizontal position and have both eyes on the top of the head; include sole, flounder and halibut.

Flat icing—a white, glossy glaze used on danish pastries.

Flavonoid—a naturally occurring pigment that predominates in red, purple and white vegetables such as cauliflower, red cabbage and beets.

Flavoring—an item that adds a new taste to a food and alters its natural flavors; flavorings include herbs, spices, vinegars and condiments.

Fleuron—(floor-ahn) a crescent-shaped piece of puff pastry used as a garnish.

Flour—a powdery substance of varying degrees of fineness made by milling grains such as wheat, corn or rye.

Foie gras—(fwah grah) liver of specially fattened geese.

Fold—a measurement of the strength of vanilla extract.

Folding—a mixing method used to gently incorporate light, airy products into heavier ingredients (for example, mixing dry ingredients with whipped eggs).

Fond—(fahn) (1) Fr. for stock; (2) Fr. for bottom; the concentrated juices, drippings and bits of food left in pans after foods are roasted or sautéed; used to flavor sauces made directly in the pans in which the foods were cooked.

Fondant—(fahn-dant) a sweet, thick opaque sugar paste commonly used for glazing pastries such as napoleons or making candies.

Fond lié—(fahn lee-ay) See **Jus lié**.

Food cost—the cost of the materials that go directly into the production of menu items.

Food cost percentage—the ratio of the cost of foods served to the food sales dollars during a given period.

Food danger zone—the temperature range of 40–140°F (5–60°C) which is most favorable for bacterial growth.

Food Pyramid—a dietary guide that prioritizes and proportions food choices among six general food groups.

Forcemeat—a preparation made from uncooked ground meats, poultry, fish or shellfish, seasoned, and emulsified with fat; commonly prepared as country-style, basic and mousseline and used for pâtés, sausages and other charcuterie items.

Formula—a recipe; the term is most often used in the bakeshop.

Frangipane—(fran-juh-pahn) a sweet almond and egg filling cooked inside pastry.

Free-range chickens—chickens allowed to move freely and forage for food; as opposed to chickens raised in coops.

Free-range veal—the meat of calves that are allowed to roam freely and eat grasses and other natural foods; this meat is pinker and more strongly flavored than that of milk-fed calves.

Freezer burn—the surface dehydration and discoloration of food that results from moisture loss at below-freezing temperatures.

French service—restaurant service where one waiter (a captain) takes the order, does the tableside cooking and brings the drinks and food, the secondary or back waiter serves bread and water, clears each course, crumbs the table and serves the coffee.

Fresh—a food that is not and has never been frozen.

Fresh-frozen—a food that has been frozen while still fresh.

Fricassee—(frick-a-see) a white stew in which the meat is cooked in fat without browning before the liquid is added.

Frittata—(free-tah-ta) an open-faced omelet of Spanish-Italian heritage.

Frosting—also known as icing, a sweet decorative coating used as a filling

between the layers or as a coating over the top and sides of a cake.

Fruit—refers to the edible organ that develops from the ovary of a flowering plant and contains one or more seeds (pips or pits).

Fruit-vegetables—foods such as avocados, eggplants, chile peppers and tomatoes that are botanically fruits but are most often prepared and served like vegetables.

Frying—a dry-heat cooking method in which foods are cooked in hot fat; includes sautéing and stir-frying, pan-frying and deep-frying.

Fumet—(foo-may) a stock made from fish bones or shellfish shells and vegetables simmered in a liquid with flavorings.

Fungi—a large group of plants ranging from single-celled organisms to giant mushrooms; the most common are molds and yeasts.

Galantine—similar to a ballottine, it is a charcuterie item made from a forcemeat of poultry, game or suckling pig usually wrapped in the skin of the bird or animal and poached in an appropriate stock; often served cold, usually in aspic.

Game—birds and animals hunted for sport or food; many game birds and animals are now ranch-raised and commercially available.

Game hen—the class of young or immature progeny of Cornish chickens or of a Cornish chicken and White Rock chicken; they are small and very flavorful.

Ganache—(ga-nosh) a rich blend of chocolate and heavy cream and, optionally, flavorings, used as a pastry or candy filling or frosting.

Garde-manger—(gar mawn-zhay) (1) also known as the pantry chef, the cook in charge of cold food production, including salads and salad dressings, charcuterie items, cold appetizers and buffet items; (2) the work area where these foods are prepared.

Garnish—(1) food used as an attractive decoration; (2) a subsidiary food used to add flavor or character to the main ingredient in a dish (for example, noodles in chicken noodle soup).

Gastronomy—the art and science of eating well.

Gâteau—(ga-toe) (1) in American usage, refers to any cake-type dessert; (2) in

French usage, refers to various pastry items made with puff pastry, éclair paste, short dough or sweet dough.

Gelatin—a tasteless and odorless mixture of proteins (especially collagen) extracted from bones, connective tissues and other animal parts; when dissolved in a hot liquid and then cooled, it forms a jellylike substance; used as a thickener and stabilizer.

Gelatinization—the process by which starch granules are cooked. They absorb moisture when placed in a liquid and heated; as the moisture is absorbed, the product swells, softens and clarifies slightly.

Gelato—(jah-laht-to) an Italian-style ice cream that is denser than American-style ice cream.

Genoise—(zhen-waahz) (1) a form of whipped-egg cake that uses whole eggs whipped with sugar; (2) a French sponge cake.

Germ—the smallest portion of a cereal grain and the only part that contains fat.

Giblets—the collective term for edible poultry viscera including gizzards, hearts, livers and necks.

Gizzard—a bird's second stomach.

Glace de poisson—(glahss duh pwah-sawng) a syrupy glaze made by reducing a fish stock.

Glace de viande—(glahss duh vee-awnd) a dark, syrupy meat glaze made by reducing a brown stock.

Glace de volaille—(glahss duh vo-lahy) a light brown, syrupy glaze made by reducing a chicken stock.

Glaze—(1) any shiny coating applied to food or created by browning; (2) the dramatic reduction and concentration of a stock; (3) a thin, flavored coating poured or dripped onto a cake or pastry.

Gliaden—see **Gluten**.

Glucose—an important energy source for the body; also known as blood sugar.

Gluten—a tough elastic substance created when flour is moistened and mixed; it gives structure and strength to baked goods and is responsible for their volume, texture and appearance. The proteins necessary for gluten formation are glutenin and gliaden.

Glutenin—see **Gluten**.

Grading—a series of voluntary programs offered by the United States Department of Agriculture to designate a food's overall quality.

Grains—(1) grasses that bear edible seeds, including corn, rice and wheat; (2) the fruit (i.e., seed or kernel) of such grasses.

Gram—the basic unit of weight in the metric system; equal to approximately one-thirtieth of an ounce.

Grande Cuisine—the rich, intricate and elaborate cuisine of the 18th- and 19th-century French aristocracy and upper classes. It is based upon the rational identification, development and adoption of strict culinary principles.

Grate—to cut a food into small, thin shreds by rubbing it against a serrated metal plate known as a grater.

Green meats—freshly slaughtered meats that have not had sufficient time to age and develop tenderness and flavor.

Gremolada—(greh-moa-lah-dah) an aromatic garnish of chopped parsley, garlic and lemon zest used for osso buco.

Grilling—a dry-heat cooking method in which foods are cooked by heat radiating from a source located below the cooking surface; the heat can be generated by electricity or by burning gas, hardwood or hardwood charcoals.

Grind—to pulverize or reduce food to small particles using a mechanical grinder or food processor.

Grinding—a milling process in which grains are reduced to a powder; the powder can be of differing degrees of fineness or coarseness.

Gristle—see **Cartilage**.

Gross profit—or gross margin, the difference between the cost of goods sold and sales during a given period of time.

Gum paste—a smooth dough of sugar and gelatin that can be colored and used to make decorations, especially for pastries.

HACCP—see **Hazard Analysis Critical Control Points**.

Hanging—the practice of allowing eviscerated (drawn or gutted) game to age in a dry, well-ventilated place; hanging helps tenderize the flesh and strengthen its flavor.

Hazard Analysis Critical Control Points (HACCP)—a rigorous system of self-inspection used to manage and maintain sanitary conditions in all types of food service operations; it focuses on the flow of food through the food service facility to identify any point or step in preparation (known as a critical control point) where some action must be taken to prevent or minimize a risk or hazard.

Heifers—young cows; cows before their first calving.

Heimlich maneuver—the first aid procedure for choking victims in which sudden upward pressure is applied to the upper abdomen in order to force any foreign object from the windpipe.

Herbs—any of a large group of aromatic plants whose leaves, stems or flowers are used to add flavors to other foods.

High-ratio cakes—a form of creamed-fat cake that uses emulsified shortening and has a two-stage mixing method.

Hollandaise—(holl-uhn-daze) an emulsified sauce made of butter, egg yolks and flavorings (especially lemon juice).

Homogenization—the process by which milk fat is prevented from separating out of milk products.

Hors d'oeuvres—(ohr durvs) very small portions of hot or cold foods served before the meal to stimulate the appetite.

Hotel pan—a rectangular, stainless steel pan with a lip allowing it to rest in a storage shelf or steam table; available in several standard sizes.

Hull—also known as the husk, the outer covering of a fruit, seed or grain.

Hybrid—the result of crossbreeding different species that are genetically unalike; it is often a unique product.

Hybrid menu—a menu combining features of a static menu with a cycle menu or a market menu of specials.

Hydrogenation—the process used to harden oils: Hydrogen atoms are added to unsaturated fat molecules, making them partially or completely saturated and thus solid at room temperature.

Hydrometer—a device used to measure specific gravity; it shows degrees of concentration on the Baumé scale.

Hygroscopic—the characteristic of a food to readily absorb moisture from the air.

Icing—see **Frosting**.

IMPS/NAMP—see **NAMP/IMPS**.

Induction cooking—a cooking method that uses a special coil placed below the stove top's surface in combination with specially designed cookware to generate heat rapidly with an alternating magnetic field.

Infection—in the food safety context, a disease caused by the ingestion of live pathogenic bacteria that continue their life processes in the consumer's intestinal tract.

Infrared cooking—a heating method that uses an electric or ceramic element heated to such a high temperature that it gives off waves of radiant heat that cook the food.

Infusion—(1) the extraction of flavors from a food at a temperature below boiling; (2) a group of coffee brewing techniques including steeping, filtering and dripping; (3) the liquid resulting from this process.

Instant-read thermometer—a thermometer used to measure the internal temperature of foods; the stem is inserted in the food, producing an instant temperature readout.

Intoxication—in the food safety context, a disease caused by the toxins that bacteria produce during their life processes.

Inventory—the listing and counting of all foods in the kitchen, storerooms and refrigerators.

IQF (Individually Quick Frozen)—the technique of rapidly freezing each individual item of food such as slices of fruit, berries or pieces of fish before packaging; IQF foods are not packaged with syrup or sauce.

Irradiation—a preservation method used for certain fruits, vegetables and grains in which ionizing radiation sterilizes the food, slows ripening and prevents sprouting; irradiation has little effect on the food's texture, flavor or appearance.

Jam—a fruit gel made from fruit pulp and sugar.

Jelly—a fruit gel made from fruit juice and sugar.

Juice—the liquid extracted from any fruit or vegetable.

Julienne—(ju-lee-en) (1) to cut foods into stick-shaped pieces, approximately 1/8 inch × 1/8 inch × 1–2 inches (3 millimeters × 3 millimeters × 2.5–5 centime-

ters); (2) the stick-shaped pieces of cut food.

Jus lié—(zhew lee-ay) also known as fond lié, a sauce made by thickening brown stock with cornstarch or similar starch; often used like a demi-glace, especially to produce small sauces.

Kinds—the categories of poultry recognized by the United States Department of Agriculture: chickens, ducks, geese, guineas, pigeons and turkeys

Kitchen brigade—see **Brigade**.

Kneading—working a dough to develop gluten.

Kosher—Prepared in accordance with Jewish dietary laws.

Lag phase—a period, usually following transfer from one place to another, during which bacteria do not experience much growth.

Lamb—the meat of sheep slaughtered under the age of one year.

Lard—the rendered fat of hogs.

Larding—inserting thin slices of fat, such as pork fatback, into low-fat meats in order to add moisture.

Leading sauces—also known as mother sauces, the foundation for the entire classic repertoire of hot sauces; the five leading sauces (béchamel, velouté, espagnole [also known as brown], tomato and hollandaise) are distinguished by the liquids and thickeners used to make them. They can be seasoned and garnished to create a wide variety of small or compound sauces.

Lean doughs—yeast doughs that contain little or no sugar or fat; used for French or Italian breads.

Leavener—an ingredient or process that produces or incorporates gases in a baked product in order to increase volume, provide structure and give texture.

Lecithin—a natural emulsifier found in egg yolks.

Legumes—(lay-gyooms) (1) Fr. for vegetables; (2) a large group of vegetables with double-seamed seed pods; depending upon the variety, the seeds, pod and seeds together, or the dried seeds are eaten.

Liaison—(lee-yeh-zon) a mixture of egg yolks and heavy cream used to thicken and enrich sauces.

Liqueur—a strong, sweet, syrupy alco-

holic beverage made by mixing or redistilling neutral spirits with fruits, flowers, herbs, spices or other flavorings; also known as a cordial.

Liquor—an alcoholic beverage made by distilling grains, vegetables or other foods; includes rum, whiskey and vodka.

Liter—the basic unit of volume in the metric system, equal to slightly more than a quart.

Log phase—a period of accelerated growth for bacteria.

Macaroni—(1) any dried pasta made with wheat flour and water; (2) in American usage, an elbow-shaped pasta tube.

Macerate—to soak foods in a liquid, usually alcoholic, to soften them.

Macronutrients—the nutrients needed in large quantities: carbohydrates, proteins, fats and water.

Madeira—a Portuguese fortified wine heated during aging to give it a distinctive flavor and brown color.

Maître d'hotel (maître d')—(may-tr dohtel) (1) the leader of the dining room brigade, also known as the dining room manager, he oversees the dining room or "front of the house" staff; (2) a compound butter flavored with chopped parsley and lemon juice.

Mandoline—a stainless steel, hand-operated slicing device with adjustable blades.

Marbling—Whitish streaks of inter- and intramuscular fat.

Marinade—the liquid used to marinate foods; it generally contains herbs, spices and other flavoring ingredients as well as an acidic product such as wine, vinegar or lemon juice.

Marinate—to soak a food in a seasoned liquid in order to tenderize the food and add flavor to it.

Market menu—a menu based upon product availability during a specific time period; it is written to use foods when they are in peak season or readily available.

Marmalade—a citrus jelly that also contains unpeeled slices of citrus fruit.

Marsala—a flavorful fortified sweet-to-semidry Sicilian wine.

Marzipan—a paste of ground almonds, sugar and egg whites used to fill and decorate pastries.

Matzo—thin, crisp unleavened bread made only with flour and water; can be ground into meal that is used for matzo balls and pancakes.

Mayonnaise—a thick, creamy sauce consisting of oil and vinegar emulsified with egg yolks, usually used as a salad dressing.

Mealy potatoes—also known as starchy potatoes, those with a high starch content and thick skin; they are best for baking.

Medallion—a small, round piece of meat or fish.

Melt—the process by which certain foods, especially those high in fat, gradually soften then liquefy when heated.

Menu—a list of foods and beverages available for purchase.

Meringue—(muh-reng) a foam made of beaten egg whites and sugar.

Metabolism—all of the chemical reactions and physical processes that occur continuously in living cells and organisms.

Meter—the basic unit of length in the metric system, equal to slightly more than one yard.

Mezzaluna—a two-handled knife with one or more thick, crescent-shaped blades used to chopped and mince herbs and vegetables.

Micronutrients—the nutrients needed only in small amounts: vitamins and minerals.

Microorganisms—single-celled organisms as well as tiny plants and animals that can be seen only through a microscope.

Microwave cooking—a heating method that uses radiation generated by a special oven to penetrate the food. It agitates water molecules, creating friction and heat; this energy then spreads throughout the food by conduction (and by convection in liquids).

Mignonette—a small cut or medallion of meat.

Milk-fed veal—also known as formula-fed veal, it is the meat of calves fed only a nutrient-rich liquid and kept tethered in pens; this meat is whiter and more mildly flavored than that of free-range calves.

Milling—the process by which grain is ground into flour or meal.

Mince—to cut a food item into very small pieces.

Mineral—inorganic micronutrients necessary for regulating body functions and proper bone and teeth structures.

Mirepoix—(meer-pwa) a mixture of coarsely chopped onions, carrots and celery used to flavor stocks, stews and other foods; generally, a mixture of 50% onions, 25% carrots and 25% celery, by weight, is used.

Mise en place—(meez on plahs) (Fr. for putting in place) refers to the preparation and assembly of all necessary ingredients and equipment.

Mix—to combine ingredients in such a way that they are evenly dispersed throughout the mixture.

Moist-heat cooking methods—cooking methods, principally simmering, poaching, boiling and steaming, that use water or steam to transfer heat through convection; moist-heat cooking methods are used to emphasize the natural flavors of foods.

Molding—the process of shaping foods, particularly grains and vegetables bound by sauces, into attractive, hard-edged shapes by using metal rings, circular cutters or other forms.

Molds—(1) algaelike fungi that form long filaments or strands; for the most part, molds affect only food appearance and taste; (2) containers used for shaping foods.

Mollusks—shellfish characterized by a soft, unsegmented body, no internal skeleton and a hard outer shell.

Monounsaturated fats—see **Unsaturated fats**.

Monter au beurre—(mohn-tay ah burr) to finish a sauce by swirling or whisking in butter (raw or compound) until it is melted; used to give sauces shine, flavor and richness.

Mortar and pestle—a hard bowl (the mortar) in which foods such as spices are ground or pounded into a powder with a club-shaped tool (the pestle).

Mother sauces—(Fr. *sauce mère*), see **Leading sauces**.

Mousse—(moose) a soft, creamy food, either sweet or savory, lightened by adding whipped cream, beaten egg whites or both.

Mousseline—(moose-uh-leen) (1) a delicately flavored forcemeat based on white meat, fish or shellfish lightened with cream and egg whites; (2) a sauce or cream lightened by folding in whipped cream.

Muffin method—a mixing method used to make quick bread batters; it involves combining liquid fat with other liquid ingredients before adding them to the dry ingredients.

Muscles—animal tissues consisting of bundles of cells or fibers that can contract and expand; they are the portions of a carcass usually consumed.

Mushrooms—members of a broad category of plants known as fungi; they are often used and served like vegetables.

Mutton—the meat of sheep slaughtered after they reach the age of one year.

NAMP/IMPS—the Institutional Meat Purchasing Specifications (IMPS) published by the United States Department of Agriculture; the IMPS are illustrated and described in *The Meat Buyer's Guide* published by the National Association of Meat Purveyors (NAMP).

Nappe—(nap) (1) the consistency of a liquid, usually a sauce, that will coat the back of a spoon; (2) to coat a food with sauce.

National cuisine—the characteristic cuisine of a nation.

Nectar—the diluted, sweetened juice of peaches, apricots, guavas, black currants or other fruits, the juice of which would be too thick or too tart to drink straight.

Net cost—a food's total cost after subtracting the value of the trim and cutting loss.

Noisette—(nwah-zet) (1) a small, usually round, portion of meat cut from the rib or loin; (2) Fr. for hazelnut.

Noodles—flat strips of pasta-type dough that contains eggs; may be fresh or dried.

Nouvelle cuisine—(Fr. for new cooking) a mid-20th-century movement away from many classic cuisine principles and toward a lighter cuisine based on natural flavors, shortened cooking times and innovative combinations.

Nut—(1) the edible single-seed kernel of a fruit surrounded by a hard shell; (2) generally refers to any seed or fruit with an edible kernel in a hard shell.

Nutrients—the chemical substances found in food that nourish the body by promoting growth, facilitating body functions and providing energy; there are six categories of nutrients: proteins, carbohydrates, fats, water, minerals and vitamins.

Nutrition—the science that studies nutrients.

Oblique cuts—also known as roll cuts, small pieces of food, usually vegetables, with two angle-cut sides.

Offal—also called variety meats, edible entrails (for example, the heart, kidneys, liver, sweetbreads and tongue) and extremities (for example, oxtail and pig's feet) of an animal.

Oignon brûlée—(ohn-nawng brew-lay) (Fr. for burnt onion) charred onion halves; used to flavor and color stocks and sauces.

Oignon piqué—(ohn-nawng pee-kay) (Fr. for pricked onion) a bay leaf tacked with a clove to a peeled onion; used to flavor sauces and soups.

Oil—a type of fat that remains liquid at room temperature.

Organic farming—a method of farming that does not rely on synthetic pesticides, fungicides, herbicides or fertilizers.

Oven spring—the rapid rise of yeast goods in a hot oven, resulting from the production and expansion of trapped gases.

Paillarde—(pahy-lahrd) a scallop of meat pounded until thin; it is usually grilled.

Panada or **panade**—(1) something other than fat added to a forcemeat to enhance smoothness, aid emulsification or both; it is often béchamel, rice or crustless white bread soaked in milk; (2) a mixture for binding stuffings and dumplings, notably quenelles, often choux pastry, bread crumbs, frangipane, puréed potatoes or rice.

Pan-broiling—a dry-heat cooking method that uses conduction to transfer heat to a food resting directly on a cooking surface; no fat is used and the food remains uncovered.

Pan-dressed—a market form for fish in which the viscera, gills and scales are removed and the fins and tail are trimmed.

Pan-frying—a dry-heat cooking method in which food is placed in a moderate amount of hot fat.

Pan gravy—a sauce made by deglazing pan drippings from roast meat or poultry

and combining them with a roux or other starch and stock.

Papillote, en—(awn poppy-yote) a cooking method in which food is wrapped in paper or foil and then heated so that the food steams in its own moisture.

Parboiling—partially cooking a food in a boiling or simmering liquid; similar to blanching but the cooking time is longer.

Parchment (paper)—heat-resistant paper used throughout the kitchen for tasks such as lining baking pans, wrapping foods to be cooked en papillote and covering foods during shallow poaching.

Parcooking—partially cooking a food by any cooking method.

Paring knife—a short knife used for detail work, especially cutting fruits and vegetables; it has a rigid blade approximately 2–4 inches long.

Parstock or par—the amount of stock necessary to cover operating needs between deliveries.

Pasta—(1) an unleavened paste or dough made from wheat flour (often semolina), water and eggs; the dough can be colored and flavored with a wide variety of herbs, spices or other ingredients and cut or extruded into a wide variety of shapes and sizes; it can be fresh or dried and is boiled for service; (2) general term for any macaroni product or egg noodle.

Pasteurization—the process of heating a liquid to a prescribed temperature for a specific period of time in order to destroy pathogenic bacteria.

Pastillage—a paste made of sugar, cornstarch and gelatin; it may be cut or molded into decorative shapes.

Pastry cream—also known as crème patissière, a stirred custard made with egg yolks, sugar and milk and thickened with starch; used for pastry and pie fillings.

Pâte—(paht) Fr. for dough.

Pâté—(pah-tay) traditionally, a fine savory meat filling wrapped in pastry, baked and served hot or cold as opposed to a terrine, which was a coarsely ground and highly seasoned meat mixture baked in an earthenware mold and served cold; today the words *pâté* and *terrine* are generally used interchangeably.

Pâte à choux—(paht ah shoe) see **Éclair paste**.

Pâte au pâté—(paht ah pah-tay) a specially formulated pastry dough used for wrapping pâté when making pâté en croûte.

Pâte brisée—(paht bree-zay) a dough that produces a very flaky baked product containing little or no sugar; flaky dough is used for prebaked pie shells or pie top crusts; mealy dough is a less flaky product used for custard, cream or fruit pie crusts.

Pâté en croute—(pah-tay awn croot) a pâté baked in pastry dough such as pâte au pâté.

Pâte feuilletée—(paht fuh-yuh-tay) also known as puff pastry, it is a rolled-in dough used for pastries, cookies and savory products, it produces a rich and buttery but not sweet baked product with hundreds of light, flaky layers.

Pâte sucrée—(paht sew-kra) a dough containing sugar that produces a very rich, crisp (not flaky) baked product; also known as sweet dough, it is used for tart shells.

Pathogen—any organism that causes disease; usually refers to bacteria.

Patissier—(pah-tees-sir-yair) a pastry chef, the person responsible for all baked items, including breads, pastries and desserts.

Paupiette—(po-pee-et) thin slices of meat, poultry or fish spread with a savory stuffing and rolled, then braised or poached.

Paysanne—(pahy-sahn) foods cut into flat squares of 1/2 inch × 1/2 inch × 1/4 inch (1.2 centimeters × 1.2 centimeters × 6 millimeters).

Pearling—a milling process in which all or part of the hull, bran and germ are removed from the grain.

Pectin—a gelatinlike carbohydrate obtained from certain fruits, used to thicken jams and jellies.

Persillade—(payr-se-yad) (1) a food served with or containing parsley; (2) a mixture of bread crumbs, parsley and garlic used to coat meats, usually lamb.

pH—a symbol for the level of acidity or alkalinity of a solution; expressed on a scale of 0 to 14.0; 7.0 is considered neutral or balanced acid/alkaline. The lower the pH value, the more acidic the substance.

Phyllo—(fee-low) pastry dough made

with very thin sheets of a flour and water mixture; several sheets are often layered with melted butter and used in sweet or savory preparations.

Physical hazards—a danger to the safety of food caused by particles such as chips, metal shavings, bits of wood or other foreign matter.

Picked—refers to the crab or lobster meat removed from the shell with a fine, needle-like tool called a pick.

Pigment—any substance that gives color to an item.

Pilaf—a cooking method for grains in which the grains are lightly sautéed in hot fat and then a hot liquid is added; the mixture is simmered without stirring until the liquid is absorbed.

Poaching—a moist-heat cooking method that uses convection to transfer heat from a hot (approximately 160–180°F [71–82°C]) liquid to the food submerged in it.

Polyunsaturated fats—See **Unsaturated fats**.

Pomes—members of the Rosaceae family, they are tree fruits with a thin skin and firm flesh surrounding a central core containing many small seeds (called pips or carpels); include apples, pears and quince.

Pork—the meat of hogs usually slaughtered under the age of one year.

Posterior—at or toward the rear of an object or place; opposite of anterior.

Potentially hazardous foods—foods on which bacteria thrive.

Poultry—the collective term for domesticated birds bred for eating; they include chickens, ducks, geese, guineas, pigeons and turkeys.

Preserve—(1) a fruit gel that contains large pieces or whole fruits; (2) to extend the shelf life of a food by subjecting it to a process such as irradiation, canning, vacuum-packing, drying or freezing and/or by adding preservatives.

Primal cuts—the primary divisions of muscle, bone and connective tissue produced by the initial butchering of the carcass; primals are further broken down into smaller, more manageable cuts.

Prime cost—the combination of food costs and direct labor.

Prix fixe—(pree feks) (Fr. for fixed price) refers to a menu offering a com-plete meal for a set price, also known as table d'hôte.

Professional cooking—a system of cooking based upon a knowledge of and appreciation for ingredients and procedures.

Profiterole—(pro-feet-uh-roll) small round pastry made from éclair paste filled with a savory filling and served as an hors d'oeuvre or filled with ice cream and served as a dessert.

Proofing—the rise given shaped yeast products just prior to baking.

Proteins—a group of compounds composed of oxygen, hydrogen, carbon and nitrogen atoms necessary for manufacturing, maintaining and repairing body tissues and as an alternative source of energy (4 calories per gram); protein chains are constructed of various combinations of amino acids.

Puff pastry—see **Pâte feuilletée**.

Pulled sugar—a doughlike mixture of sucrose, glucose and tartaric acid that can be colored and shaped by hand.

Pulses—dried seeds from a variety of legumes.

Pumpernickel—(1) coarsely ground rye flour; (2) bread made with this flour.

Purée—(pur-ray) (1) to process food to achieve a smooth pulp; (2) food that is processed by mashing, straining or fine chopping to achieve a smooth pulp.

Purée soup—a soup usually made from starchy vegetables or legumes; after the main ingredient is simmered in a liquid, the mixture, or a portion of it, is puréed.

Putrefactives—bacteria that spoil food without rendering it unfit for human consumption.

Quenelle—(cuh-nell) a small, dumpling-shaped portion of a mousseline forcemeat poached in an appropriately flavored stock; it is shaped by using two spoons.

Quiche—a savory tart or pie consisting of a custard baked in a pastry shell with a variety of flavorings and garnishes.

Quick bread—a bread, including loaves and muffins, leavened by chemical leaveners or steam rather than yeast.

Radiation cooking—a heating process that does not require physical contact between the heat source and the food being cooked; instead, energy is transferred by waves of heat or light striking the food. Two kinds of radiant heat used in the kitchen are infrared and microwave.

Raft—formed during the clarification process from the clearmeat and impurities from the stock; it rises to the top of the simmering stock and releases additional flavors.

Ragout—(rah-goo) (1) traditionally, a well-seasoned, rich stew containing meat, vegetables and wine; (2) any stewed mixture.

Ramekin—a small, ovenproof dish, usually ceramic.

Rancidity—a chemical change in fats caused by exposure to air, light or heat that results in objectionable flavors and odors.

Recipe—a set of written instructions for producing a specific food or beverage; also known as a formula.

Recommended Dietary Allowance (RDA)—a standard for the daily intake of various nutrients established by the National Food and Nutrition Board.

Recovery time—the length of time it takes hot fat to return to the desired cooking temperature after food is submerged in it.

Reduce—to cook a liquid mixture, often a sauce, until its quantity decreases because of evaporation; typically done to concentrate flavors and thicken liquids.

Refreshing—submerging a food in cold water to quickly cool it and prevent further cooking, also known as shocking; usually used for vegetables.

Regional cuisine—a set of recipes based on local ingredients, traditions and practices; within a larger geographical, political, cultural or social unit, regional cuisines are often variations of each other that blend together to create a national cuisine.

Relishes—cooked or pickled sauces usually made with vegetables or fruits and often used as a condiment.

Remouillage—(Fr. for rewetting) a stock produced by reusing the bones from another stock.

Render—(1) to melt and clarify fat; (2) to cook meats in order to remove the fat.

Ricer—a sieve-like utensil with small holes through which soft food is forced; it produces particles about the size of a grain of rice.

Rich doughs—yeast doughs such as those used for brioche and some multigrain breads that contain a significant amount of sugar and fat.

Rillette—(ree-yet) meat or poultry slowly cooked, mashed and preserved in its own fat and served cold and usually spread on toast.

Ripe—(1) fully grown and developed fruit; the fruit's flavor, texture and appearance are at their peak and the fruit is ready to eat; (2) an unpleasant odor indicating that a food, especially meat, poultry, fish or shellfish, may be past its prime.

Risotto—(re-zot-toe) (1) a cooking method for grains in which the grains are lightly sautéed in butter and then a liquid is gradually added; the mixture is simmered with near-constant stirring until the still-firm grains merge with the cooking liquid; (2) a Northern Italian rice dish prepared this way.

Roasting—a dry-heat cooking method that heats food by surrounding it with hot, dry air in a closed environment or on a spit over an open fire; similar to baking, the term roasting is usually applied to meats, poultry, game and vegetables.

Roe—(roh) fish eggs.

Roll cuts—see **Oblique cuts**.

Rolled-in dough—a dough in which a fat is incorporated in many layers by using a rolling and folding procedure; it is used for flaky baked goods such as croissants, puff pastry and danish.

Rondeau—(ron-doe) a shallow, wide, straight-sided pot with two loop handles.

Rondelles—(ron-dells) or rounds, disk-shaped slices of cylindrical vegetables or fruits.

Rotisserie—cooking equipment that slowly rotates meat or other foods in front of a heating element.

Roulade—(roo-lahd) (1) a slice of meat, poultry or fish rolled around a stuffing; (2) a filled and rolled spongecake.

Round fish—fish with round, oval or compressed bodies that swim in a vertical position and have eyes on both sides of their heads; includes salmon, swordfish and cod.

Rounding—the process of shaping dough into smooth, round balls; used to stretch the outside layer of gluten into a smooth coating.

Roux—(roo) a cooked mixture of equal parts flour and fat, by weight, used as a thickener for sauces and other dishes; cooking the flour in fat coats the starch granules with the fat and prevents them from lumping together or forming lumps when introduced into a liquid.

Royal icing—also known as decorator's icing, an uncooked mixture of confectioner's sugar and egg whites that becomes hard and brittle when dry; used for making intricate cake decorations.

Russian service—restaurant service in which the entree, vegetables and starches are served from a platter onto the diner's plate by a waiter.

Sabayon—(sa-by-on) also known as zabaglione, a foamy, stirred custard sauce made by whisking eggs, sugar and wine over low heat.

Sachet d'épices or **sachet**—(sah-shay day-pea-say) (Fr. for bag of spices) aromatic ingredients tied in a cheesecloth bag and used to flavor stocks and other foods; a standard sachet contains parsley stems, cracked peppercorns, dried thyme, bay leaf, cloves and, optionally, garlic.

Salad—a single food or a mix of different foods accompanied or bound by a dressing.

Salad dressing—a sauce for a salad; most are based on a vinaigrette, mayonnaise or other emulsified product.

Salad greens—a variety of leafy vegetables that are usually eaten raw.

Salamander—a small broiler used primarily for browning or glazing the tops of foods.

Salsa—(sahl-sah) (Sp. for sauce) (1) generally, a cold chunky mixture of fresh herbs, spices, fruits and/or vegetables used as a sauce for meat, fish or shellfish; (2) in Italian usage, a general term for pasta sauces.

Salt curing—the process of surrounding a food with salt or a mixture of salt, sugar, nitrite-based curing salt, herbs and spices; salt curing dehydrates the food, inhibits bacterial growth and adds flavor.

Sanitation—the creation and maintenance of conditions that will prevent food contamination or food-borne illness.

Sanitize—to reduce pathogenic organisms to safe levels, usually with heat or chemical disinfectants.

Sashimi—(sah-shee-mee) raw fish eaten without rice; usually served as the first course of a Japanese meal.

Saturated fats—fats found mainly in animal products and tropical oils; they are usually solid at room temperature. The body has more difficulty breaking down saturated fats than either monounsaturated or polyunsaturated fats.

Sauce—generally, a thickened liquid used to flavor and enhance other foods.

Sausage—a seasoned forcemeat usually stuffed into a casing; a sausage can be fresh, smoked and cooked, dried or hard.

Sautéing—(saw-tay-ing) a dry-heat cooking method that uses conduction to transfer heat from a hot pan to food with the aid of a small amount of hot fat; cooking is usually done quickly over high temperatures.

Sauteuse—(saw-toose) the basic sauté pan with sloping sides and a single long handle.

Sautoir—(saw-twahr) a sauté pan with straight sides and a single long handle.

Savory—(1) spiced or seasoned, as opposed to sweet, foods; (2) (savoury) a highly seasoned last course of a traditional English dinner.

Scald—to heat a liquid, usually milk, to just below the boiling point.

Scallop—(Fr. escalope) a thin, boneless slice of meat.

Score—to cut shallow gashes across the surface of a food before cooking.

Scoville Heat Units—a subjective rating for measuring a chile's heat; the sweet bell pepper usually rates 0, the tabasco rates from 30,000 to 50,000 and the habañera rates from 100,000 to 300,000 units.

Seafood—an inconsistently used term encompassing some or all of the following: saltwater fish, freshwater fish, saltwater shellfish, freshwater shellfish, other edible marine life.

Sear—to brown food quickly over high heat; usually done as a preparatory step for combination cooking methods.

Season—(1) traditionally, to enhance flavor by adding salt; (2) more commonly, to enhance flavor by adding salt and/or pepper as well as herbs and spices; (3) to mature and bring a food (usually beef or game) to a proper condition by aging or special preparation; (4) to prepare a pot, pan or other cooking surface to prevent sticking.

Seasoning—traditionally, an item added to enhance the natural flavors of a food without dramatically changing its taste; salt is the most common seasoning although all herbs and spices are often referred to as seasonings.

Semi à la carte—a menu on which some foods (usually appetizers and desserts) and beverages are priced and ordered separately, while the entree is accompanied by and priced to include other dishes such as a salad, starch or vegetable.

Semifreddi—(seh-mee-frayd-dee) also known as still-frozen desserts, made with frozen mousse, custard or cream into which large amounts of whipped cream or meringue are folded in order to incorporate air; layers of spongecake and/or fruits may be added for flavor and texture; they include frozen soufflés, marquis, mousses and neapolitans.

Semolina—see **Durum**.

Sfoglia—(sfo-glee-ah) a thin, flat sheet of pasta dough that can be cut into ribbons, circles, squares or other shapes.

Shallow poaching—a moist-heat cooking method that combines poaching and steaming; the food (usually fish) is placed on a vegetable bed and partially covered with a liquid (cuisson) and simmered.

Shellfish—aquatic invertebrates with shells or carapaces.

Sherbet—a frozen mixture of fruit juice or fruit purée that contains milk and/or egg yolks for creaminess.

Shocking—see **Refreshing**.

Shortening—(1) a white, tasteless, solid fat formulated for baking or deep-frying; (2) any fat used in baking to tenderize the product by shortening gluten strands.

Shred—to cut into thin but irregular strips.

Shuck—(1) a shell, pod or husk; (2) to remove the edible portion of a food (e.g., clam meat, pea and ear of corn) from its shell, pod or husk.

Side Masking—the technique of coating only the sides of a cake with garnish.

Sift—(1) to shake a dry, powdered substance through a sieve or sifter to remove lumps and incorporate air; (2) to mix together powdery substances by sifting.

Silverskin—the tough connective tissue that surrounds certain muscles; see **Elastin**.

Simmering—(1) a moist-heat cooking method that uses convection to transfer heat from a hot (approximately 185–205°F [85–96°C]) liquid to the food submerged in it; (2) maintaining the temperature of a liquid just below the boiling point.

Skim—to remove fat and impurities from the surface of a liquid during cooking.

Slice—to cut an item into relatively broad, thin pieces.

Slurry—a mixture of raw starch and cold liquid used for thickening.

Small sauces—also known as compound sauces, made by adding one or more ingredients to a leading sauce; they are grouped together into families based on their leading sauce. Some small sauces have a variety of uses; others are traditional accompaniments for specific foods.

Smoke point—the temperature at which a fat begins to break down and emit smoke.

Smoking—any of several methods for preserving and flavoring foods by exposing them to smoke, includes cold smoking (in which the foods are not fully cooked) and hot smoking (in which the foods are cooked).

Solid pack—canned fruits or vegetables with little or no water added.

Sorbet—(sore-bay) a frozen mixture of fruit juice or fruit purée; similar to sherbet but without milk products.

Soufflé—(soo-flay) either a sweet or savory fluffy dish made with a custard base lightened with whipped egg whites and then baked; the whipped egg whites cause the dish to puff when baked.

Sous-chef—(soo-shef) a cook who supervises food production and who reports to the executive chef; he is second in command of a kitchen.

Specifications or **specs**—standard requirements to be followed in procuring items from suppliers.

Spices—any of a group of strongly flavored or aromatic portions of plants (other than leaves) used as flavorings, condiments or aromatics.

Springform pan—a circular baking pan with a separate bottom and a side wall held together with a clamp which is released to free the baked product.

Spring lamb—the meat of sheep slaughtered before they have fed on grass or grains.

Spun sugar—a decoration made by flicking dark caramelized sugar rapidly over a dowel to create long, fine, hairlike threads.

Squab—the class of young pigeon used in food service operations.

Staling—also known as starch retrogradation, a change in the distribution and location of water molecules within baked products; stale products are firmer, drier and more crumbly than fresh baked goods.

Standard breading procedure—the procedure for coating foods with crumbs or meal by passing the food through flour, then an egg wash and then the crumbs; it gives foods a relatively thick, crisp coating when deep-fried or pan-fried.

Standardized recipe—a recipe producing a known quality and quantity of food for a specific operation.

Staples—(1) certain foods regularly used throughout the kitchen; (2) certain foods, usually starches, that help form the basis for a regional or national cuisine and are principal components in the diet.

Starch—(1) complex carbohydrates from plants that are edible and either digestible or indigestible (fiber); (2) a rice, grain, pasta or potato accompaniment to a meal.

Starch retrogradation—see **Staling**.

Starchy potatoes—see **Mealy potatoes**.

Static menu—a menu offering patrons the same foods every day.

Station chef—the cook in charge of a particular department in a kitchen.

Steak—(1) a cross-section slice of a round fish with a small section of the bone attached; (2) a cut of meat, either with or without the bone.

Steamer—(1) a set of stacked pots with perforations in the bottom of each pot, they fit over a larger pot filled with boiling or simmering water and are used to steam foods; (2) a perforated insert made of metal or bamboo placed in a pot and used to steam foods; (3) a type of soft-shell clam from the East Coast; (4) a piece of gas or electric equipment in which foods are steamed in a sealed chamber.

Steaming—a moist-heat cooking method in which heat is transferred from steam to the food being cooked by direct contact; the food to be steamed is placed in a basket or rack above a boiling liquid in a covered pan.

Steel—a tool, usually made of steel, used to hone or straighten knife blades.

Steep—to soak a food in a hot liquid in order to extract its flavor or impurities or to soften its texture.

Steers—male cattle castrated prior to maturity and principally raised for beef.

Sterilize—to destroy all living microorganisms.

Stewing—a combination cooking method similar to braising but generally involving smaller pieces of meat that are first blanched or browned, then cooked in a small amount of liquid which is served as a sauce.

Stir-frying—a dry-heat cooking method similar to sautéing in which foods are cooked over very high heat using little fat while stirring constantly and briskly; often done in a wok.

Stirring—a mixing method in which ingredients are gently mixed until blended using a spoon, whisk or rubber spatula.

Stock—(Fr. fond) a clear, unthickened liquid flavored by soluble substances extracted from meat, poultry or fish and their bones as well as from a mirepoix, other vegetables and seasonings.

Stone fruits—members of the genus Prunus and also known as drupes, they are tree or shrub fruits with a thin skin, soft flesh and one woody stone or pit; include apricots, cherries, nectarines, peaches and plums.

Straight dough method—a mixing method for yeast breads in which all ingredients are simply combined and mixed.

Strain—to pour foods through a sieve, mesh strainer or cheesecloth to separate or remove the liquid component.

Streusel—(stroo-zel) a crumbly mixture of fat, flour, sugar and sometimes nuts and spices; used to top baked goods.

Subcutaneous fat—also known as exterior fat; the fat layer between the hide and muscles.

Submersion poaching—a poaching method in which the food is completely covered with the poaching liquid.

Subprimal cuts—the basic cuts produced from each primal.

Sucrose—the chemical name for refined or table sugar, it is refined from the raw sugars found in the large tropical grass called sugar cane and the root of the sugar beet; it is available as white or brown granules, molasses or powdered sugar.

Sugar—a carbohydrate that provides the body with energy and gives a sweet taste to foods.

Sugar syrups—either simple syrups (thin mixtures of sugar and water) or cooked syrups (melted sugar cooked until it reaches a specific temperature).

Suprême—(su-prem) (1) a sauce made by adding cream to a velouté made from chicken stock; it is used to make several compound sauces of the velouté family; (2) a boneless, skinless chicken breast with the first wing segment attached.

Sushi—(szu-she) cooked or raw fish or shellfish rolled in or served on seasoned rice.

Sweating—cooking a food (typically vegetables) in a small amount of fat, usually covered, over low heat without browning until the food softens and releases moisture; sweating allows the food to release its flavor more quickly when cooked with other foods.

Sweetbreads—the thymus glands of a calf or lamb.

Sweet dough—see **Pâte sucrée**.

Syrup—sugar that is dissolved in liquid, usually water, and often flavored with spices or citrus zest.

Syrup pack—cans of fruits with a light, medium or heavy syrup added.

Table d'hôte—(tab-bluh dote) see **Prix fixe**.

Tang—the portion of a knife's blade that extends inside the handle.

Taproots—more commonly referred to as roots, includes edible single roots that extend deep into the ground to provide the above-ground plant with nutrients.

Tart—a sweet or savory filling in a baked crust made in a shallow, straight-sided pan without a top crust.

Tartlet—a small, single-serving tart.

Temperature danger zone—the broad range of temperatures between 40° and 140°F (4–60°C) at which bacteria multiply rapidly.

Tempering—(1) heating gently and gradually; (2) refers to the process of slowly adding a hot liquid to eggs or other foods to raise their temperature without causing them to curdle; (3) refers to a process for melting chocolate.

Terrine—(1) traditionally, a loaf of coarse forcemeat cooked in a covered earthenware mold and without a crust; today, the word is used interchangeably with pâté; (2) the mold used to cook such items, usually a rectangle or oval shape and made of ceramic.

Thickening agents—ingredients used to thicken sauces, include starches (flour, cornstarch and arrowroot), gelatin and liaisons.

Timbale—(tim-bull) (1) a small pail-shaped mold used to shape foods; (2) a preparation made in such a mold.

Tisanes—(teh-zahns) beverages made from herbal infusions that do not contain any tea.

Tomato sauce—a leading sauce made from tomatoes, vegetables, seasonings and white stock; it may or may not be thickened with roux.

Toque—(toke) the tall white hat worn by chefs.

Torte—in Central and Eastern European usage, refers to a rich cake in which all or part of the flour is replaced with finely chopped nuts or bread crumbs.

Tossed salad—a salad prepared by placing the greens, garnishes and salad dressing is a large bowl and tossing to combine.

Tourner—(toor-nay) (Fr. for to turn), to cut foods, usually vegetables, into football-shaped pieces with seven equal sides and blunt ends.

Toxins—byproducts of living bacteria that can cause illness if consumed in sufficient quantities.

Tranche—(tranch) an angled slice cut from fish fillets.

Trim loss—the amount of a food item removed when preparing it for consumption.

Tripe—the edible lining of a cow's stomach.

Truffles—(1) flavorful tubers that grow near the roots of oak or beech trees; (2) rich chocolate candies made with ganache.

Truss—to tie poultry with butcher's twine into a compact shape for cooking.

Tube pan—a deep round baking pan with a hollow tube in the center.

Tuber—the fleshy root, stem or rhizome of a plant from which a new plant will grow; some, such as potatoes, are eaten as vegetables.

Tunneling—the holes that may form in baked goods as the result of overmixing.

Unit cost or **price**—the price paid to acquire one specified unit.

Univalves—single-shelled mollusks with a single muscular foot, such as abalone.

Unsaturated fat—fats that are normally liquid (oils) at room temperature; they may be monounsaturated (from plants such as olives and avocados) or polyunsaturated (from grains and seeds such as corn, soybeans and safflower as well as from fish).

Vanilla custard sauce—also known as crème anglaise, a stirred custard made with egg yolks, sugar and milk or half-and-half and flavored with vanilla; served with or used in dessert preparations.

Vanillin—(1) whitish crystals of vanilla flavor that often develop on vanilla beans during storage; (2) synthetic vanilla flavoring.

Variety—the result of breeding plants of the same species that have different qualities or characteristics; the new plant often combines features from both parents.

Variety meats—see **Offal**.

Veal—the meat of calves under the age of nine months.

Vegetable—refers to any herbaceous plant (one with little or no woody tissue) that can be partially or wholly eaten; vegetables can be classified as cabbages, fruit-vegetables, gourds and squashes, greens, mushrooms and truffles, onions, pods and seeds, roots and tubers, and stalks.

Velouté—(veh-loo-tay) a leading sauce made by thickening a white stock (either fish, veal or chicken) with roux.

Venison—meat from any member of the deer family including elk, moose, reindeer, red-tailed deer, white-tailed deer and mule deer; it is typically a lean, dark red meat with a mild aroma.

Vent—(1) to allow circulation or escape of a liquid or gas; (2) to cool a pot of hot liquid by setting the pot on blocks in a cold water bath and allowing cold water to circulate around it.

Vinaigrette—(vin-nay-greht) a temporary emulsion of oil and vinegar (usually three parts oil to one part vinegar) seasoned with herbs, salt and pepper; used as a salad dressing or sauce.

Vinegar—a thin, sour liquid used as a preservative, cooking ingredient and cleaning solution.

Viruses—the smallest known form of life; they invade the living cells of a host and take over those cells' genetic material, causing the cells to produce more viruses; some viruses can enter a host through the ingestion of food contaminated with those viruses.

Viscera—internal organs.

Vitamins—compounds present in foods in very small quantities; they do not provide energy but are essential for regulating body functions.

Vol-au-vent—(vul-oh-van) a large, deep puff pastry shell often filled with a savory mixture for a main course.

Volume—the space occupied by a substance; volume measurements are commonly expressed as liters, teaspoons, tablespoons, cups, pints and gallons.

Wash—a glaze applied to dough before baking; a commonly used wash is made with whole egg and water.

Water bath—see **Bain marie**.

Water pack—canned fruits with water or fruit juice added.

Waxy potatoes—those with a low starch content and thin skin; they are best for boiling.

Weight—the mass or heaviness of a substance; weight measurements are commonly expressed as grams, ounces and pounds.

Wheel—(1) a large boneless piece of fish (such as swordfish or tuna) from which steaks are cut, also known as a center cut; (2) a cylindrical-shaped cheese.

Whetstone—a dense, grained stone used to sharpen or hone a knife blade.

Whipping—a mixing method in which foods are vigorously beaten in order to incorporate air; a whisk or an electric mixer with its whip attachment is used.

White stew—see **Fricassee** and **Blanquette**.

White stock—a light-colored stock made from chicken, veal, beef or fish bones simmered in water with vegetables and seasonings.

Whitewash—a thin mixture or slurry of flour and cold water used like cornstarch for thickening.

Wine—an alcoholic beverage made from the fermented juice of grapes; may be sparkling (effervescent) or still (noneffervescent) or fortified with additional alcohol.

Work section—see **Work station**.

Work station—a work area in the kitchen dedicated to a particular task, such as broiling or salad making; work stations using the same or similar equipment for related tasks are grouped together into work sections.

Yeasts—microscopic fungi whose metabolic processes are responsible for fermentation; they are used for leavening bread and in cheese, beer, and wine making.

Yield—(1) the total amount of a food item created or remaining after trimming or fabrication; (2) the total amount of a product made from a specific recipe.

Yield factor or **percentage**—the ratio of the edible portion to the amount purchased.

Yield grades—a grading program for meat that measures the amount of usable meat on a carcass.

Zest—the thin, colored part of a citrus peel.

Zushi—(zhoo-she) the seasoned rice used for sushi.

RECIPE INDEX

◆ *indicates a healthful recipe.*

1059

goat's-milk, 170
hard, 169–70
nutritional values of, 165
semisoft, 166–67
soft, 165–66
Natural convection, 177
Navarin, definition of, 284
Neapolitan, 917
Necks, poultry, 372
Nectar, 721
Nectarines, 711–12
Negative growth phase, 24
New potatoes, 618
New York steak, cutting from a
boneless strip loin, 295
Niacin, 42
Nick Malgieri's Perfect Pastry, 843
Noisettes, definition of, 275
Noncost-based pricing, 74
Nonstick coatings, cookware, 92
Nonwheat flour, 742–43
Nopales, 585
North African cuisine, 1010–12
Norwalk virus, 26
Nougat, 882
Nouvelle cuisine, 7–8
Nova, 443
NSF International (NSF), 82–83
Nutmeg, 133, 135
Nut oils, 142
Nutrasweet®, 45
Nutrition, 36–55
additives, 48
and the chef, 53–55
essential nutrients, definition
of, 38
Food Pyramid, 52–53
ingredient substitutes/alterna-
tives, 44–48
macronutrients, 38–41
micronutrients, 41–44
nutritional information, 51
package labeling, 48–51
Recommended Dietary
Allowance (RDA), 44–45, 52
Nuts, 138–41
nutritional value of, 140

Oat bran, 630
Oats, 630
Oblique cut, 122
Occupational Safety and Health
Act (OSHA), 33–34
Octopus, 449
Offal, 395
Oils, 141–43, 750
canola, 141
flavored, 142
hazelnut, 142
infused, 142
nut, 142
olive, 142
vegetable, 141
in vinaigrette dressings, 670
Okra, 580–81
Old Bay® seasoning, 145

Olestra®, 45
Olive oil, 142
Olives, 142
Olympias (oysters), 448
Omelets, 941
*On Food and Cooking, The
Sci;ence and Lore of the
Kitchen* (McGee), 163
Onion brûlée, 234
Onion piquet, 136–37
Onion(s), 577–78
bulb onions, 577
dicing, 120
garlic, 577
leeks, 577
scallions, 578
shallots, 578
Oolong tea, 150
Opal basil, 126
Orange roughy, 443
Oranges, 700–701
Ordering, and food cost control,
75
Oregano, 128
Organically grown products, 48
Organ meats, 295
Osetra caviar, 965
Ounces, converting, 64
Outhier, Louis, 7–8
Ovens, 99–100
Oven spring, 789
Overproofing, 788
Overrun, 914
Oxidation, 147
Oyster knife, 86, 87
Oysters, 448
Oyster sauce, 145

Pacific clams, 447
Pacific cod, 441
Pacific oysters, 448
Package labeling, 48–51
approved health claims for, 50
FDA requirements, 48
reading, 48–51
product claims, 49–51
product identification, 48–49
Pain de Pyrenees, 166
Panada, 511
Pancakes, 946–47
Pancetta, 530–31
Pan coating, 868–69
Pan-dressed fish, 454
Pan-frying, 182
eggs, 943
fish/shellfish, 470–71
meat, 278–79
potato(es), 623–24
vegetables, 595
Pan gravy, 199, 219, 222
Pan loaves, shaping technique,
788
Pan release sprays, 868
Pans, 92
paté, 520
Papain, 714

Papayas, 714–15
Paprika, 131
Parasites, 26
Parboiling, vegetables, 596
Parfait, 916
Paring knife, 85, 86
Paris-Brest, 828
Parker House rolls, shaping tech-
nique, 786
Parmentier, Augustin, 571
Parmigiano-Reggiano (Parmesan),
170
Parsley, 128
chopping, 116
Parsnips, 582
Parstock (par), 75
Partridge, 419
Passion fruits, 715
Pasta, 635–43
accompaniments to, 642
Asian noodles, 637
bean starch noodles, 638
boiling, 642
and broths, 643
buckwheat noodles, 638
cooking to order, 642
doneness, determining, 641
dough, rolling/cutting, 640
dried, cooking in advance, 642
filling, 640–41
fresh, preparing, 639–40
Italian-style, 636
macaroni, 635
nutritional value of, 638
purchasing, 638
ravioli, making, 641
ribbons, 636
rice noodles, 638
sauces, 643
shapes, 637
storing, 638
tubes, 637
wheat noodles, 637–38
See also Grains
Pasteurization, 158
egg(s), 156
milk, 158
Pasteurized processed cheese, 170
Pastillage, 882
Pastries, 824–32
éclair paste, 828–30
meringues, 830–31
puff pastry, 824–28
troubleshooting chart, 832
Pastry chef, 14
Pastry cream, 902, 903
Pastry doughs, classifications of,
710
Pastry tips, 884
Pâté dough (pâté au pâté), 523
Pâté en choux, *See* Éclair paste
Pâté en croûte, 519, 520, 523–25
assembling/baking, procedure
for, 524–25
pâté dough, 523
Pâté en croûte molds, 92, 93

Pâte feuilletée, 824
Pâté pans/molds/terrines, 520
Pâtés, 519–20
Pâté spice, 511–12
Pathogenic, 22
Patissier royal partisian, le, 6
Patissiers, 4, 12
Paysanne, 118, 119
Peaches, 711–12
Peanuts, 140
Pearling, 626
Pearl onions, 577
Pears, 709–10
Peas, 580
Pecans, 140
Pecorino romano, 170
Pectin, 710
Peppercorn, 133
Peppermint, 128
Peppers, 569–70
hot peppers, 570
roasting, 570
sweet peppers, 569
Peppers Julienne, cutting, 569
Perceived value pricing, 74
Persimmons, 702–3
Personal cleanliness, 29–30
Pest management, 31–32
Petrale sole, 445
pH, 24–25
Pheasant, 420, 421
Phosphorus, 43
Physical contamination, 20, 28
Physiology of Taste, The
(Brillat-Savarin), 420
Pickapeppa® sauce, 145
Pickling cucumbers, 573
Pickling spice, 134
Pies/tarts, 810–24
assembling, 822–23
crusts, 811–17
definition of, 810
fillings, 817–22
storing, 823
troubleshooting chart, 823
See also Crusts; Pastry
Pigeon, 371
Pineapples, 715–16
Pine nuts, 140
Pink peppercorns, 133
Pinto beans, 579
Piping bag, 885
Piping techniques, 884–87
Pistachios, 140
Plastic cookware, 91
Plate presentation, 1020–33
food, 1022–25
cutting, 1023–24
molding, 1024–25
preparing properly, 1023
plates, 1025–32
presentation, 1022
service, 1022
Plates, 1025–32
arranging foods on, 1027–28
arrangements, 1028

Visual Basic™ 4
Expert Solutions

Steve Potts
Michael McKelvy
Edward B. Toupin
Michael Marchuk
James A. Dooley
Joseph Armitage
Elisabeth Boonin

Andrew Dean
Steven List
S. Rama Ramachandran
J.D. Evans, Jr.
Brian Blackman
Jon Oelschlaeger
Dr. David Fullerton

Visual Basic 4 Expert Solutions

Copyright © 1995 by Que® Corporation

Library of Congress Catalog No.: 95-71042

ISBN: 0-7897-0073-5

97   96   95   6   5   4   3   2   1

Interpretation of the printing code: the rightmost double-digit number is the year of the book's printing; the rightmost single-digit number, the number of the book's printing. For example, a printing code of 95-1 shows that the first printing of the book occurred in 1995.

All terms mentioned in this book that are known to be trademarks or service marks have been appropriately capitalized. Que cannot attest to the accuracy of this information. Use of a term in this book should not be regarded as affecting the validity of any trademark or service mark.

Screen reproductions in this book were created using Collage Plus from Inner Media, Inc., Hollis, NH.

Credits

President and Publisher
Roland Elgey

Associate Publisher
Joseph B. Wikert

Editorial Services Director
Elizabeth Keaffaber

Managing Editor
Sandy Doell

Director of Marketing
Lynn E. Zingraf

Senior Series Editor
Chris Nelson

Title Manager
Bryan Gambrel

Acquisitions Editor
Fred Slone

Product Director
Nancy D. Price

Production Editor
Jeff Riley

Editors
Kelli M. Brooks
Elizabeth Bruns
Patrick Kanouse
Jeanne Terheide Lemen
Diana Moore
Nanci Sears Perry
Hugh Vandivier

Assistant Product Marketing Manager
Kim Margolius

Technical Editors
Jeff Bankston
Brian Blackman
Steve Caudill
J.D. Evans, Jr.
Thomas Kiehl

Acquisitions Coordinator
Angela C. Kozlowski

Operations Coordinator
Patty Brooks

Editorial Assistant
Michelle R. Newman

Book Designer
Dan Armstrong

Cover Designer
Dan Armstrong

Production Team
Angela D. Bannan, Becky Beheler,
Chad Dressler, Jennifer Eberhardt,
Jason Hand, John Hulse,
Damon Jordan, Clint Lahnen,
Bob LaRoche, Julie Quinn,
Laura Robbins, Bobbi Satterfield,
Clair Schweinler, Craig Small,
Mike Thomas, Todd Wente

Indexer
Kathy Venable

Composed in *Utopia* and *MCPdigital* by Que Corporation.

About the Authors

Steve Potts received a degree in Computer Science from Georgia Tech. He has been designing and writing software systems for 12 years. He is a consultant in Windows-based technologies and owns NoBoredom Classes, a computer education firm in Atlanta, Ga.

Michael McKelvy is president of McKelvy Software Systems, a firm specializing in the development of custom computer software. Mike has written a variety of engineering and financial analysis programs for a number of businesses. Mike has two degrees in Nuclear Engineering and has been writing computer applications since college.

Degreed in Mathematics, Computer Science, and Electronics Technology, **Edward B. Toupin** is an automation engineer for a Denver-based engineering firm. Edward designs and develops applications under various platforms for industrial control, expert system applications, database management, GIS, mobile satellite applications, integration solutions, and network management and communications.

Michael Marchuk has been working in the computer industry since 1979, when he started as a part-time BASIC programming instructor. Along with his bachelor's degree in Finance from the University of Illinois, he has received certification as a Netware CNE and a Compaq Advanced Systems Engineer. He has designed and built an international multi-protocol wide area network for a Fortune 500 company and now serves as an Integration Engineer and as the Network Security Chairman for a Forbes 400 corporation. Michael can be contacted via CompuServe at 73321,3606.

James A. Dooley is an independent systems consultant who holds several degrees. He has more than 10 years of experience in software design and implementation for multi-national companies—particularly in the area of client/server and Windows applications. James can be contacted via CompuServe at 100034,3627.

Joseph Armitage is president of Montare International, a computer consulting and education company based in Dallas, Texas. Joseph has implemented data-processing systems for banking, manufacturing, retail, oil, and gas industries throughout the U.S. and Great Britain. He is a nationally recognized speaker on application design and development, CASE, and implementing business systems using leading-edge technologies. He can be contacted via CompuServe at 72203,1317.

Elisabeth Boonin holds a B.A. in math from Reed College and an M.S. in math from the University of Oregon. She has developed and presented training seminars on various Microsoft products and contributed to the user interface designs of Windows 3.1, QuickC, and other products. Elisabeth spends her time in the Pacific Northwest as a writer, computer consultant, and paraglider pilot.

Andrew Dean is president of Advanced Digital Solutions, Inc., a software development and consulting firm specializing in integrating Visual Basic with other development tools using techniques such as multiple language development, DLLs, OLE automation, DDE, and Visual Basic for Applications. Much of his work is related to developing Geographic Information Systems for business mapping, logistics, and schedule optimization applications. Andy is also a cofounder and President of the Atlanta Visual Basic Users Group. He can be contacted via CompuServe at 71233,1412.

Steven List is the president and founder of Transact Software, Inc., which designs and builds custom software primarily using Visual Basic. Steven has indulged himself and learned many of the leading custom controls available for application development. He can be contacted via CompuServe at 70153,1735.

S. Rama Ramachandran is a senior consultant with TechWorks International, a Westport, Connecticut-based Microsoft Solution Provider Partner. He specializes in the design and development of custom GUI-based stand-alone, network, and client/server database systems. He has been developing database systems on Windows, Windows NT, and Win95 using Visual Basic, Access, FoxPro, and PowerBuilder. Rama, who has contributed numerous articles in VBPJ, can be contacted via CompuServe at 73313,3030.

J.D. Evans, Jr., the author of four Visual Basic books, has worked on projects ranging from software configuration management for the NASA Space Shuttle Mission Simulation System to designing and programming Windows DLL parsing functions for Microsoft SQL Server stored procedures at Bachman Information Systems. He is actively involved in the Microsoft Certified Professional program and he participates in various aspects of examination construction and testing.

Brian Blackman is a Charter Member of the Microsoft Certified Solution Developer program and a Microsoft Certified Trainer currently teaching Windows development and Windows NT Server courses. Brian is a software design engineer with an engineering firm in the Great Smoky Mountains in East Tennessee. Formerly he was with Microsoft as a premier developer support engineer supporting ISVs in Windows software development using Visual C++, Visual Basic, and Microsoft Access.

Jon Oelschlaeger is founder and president of Ensemble Systems Corporation, a San Francisco-area consulting firm specializing in business applications, technical training, and courseware development using Microsoft products. He is a Microsoft-certified engineer and instructor in Visual Basic, VBA Programming, and Windows—including Windows 3.x, Windows NT, and Windows 95. He provides services in the design and development of application-specific custom computer systems and programs. Jon can be contacted at jonoel@ix.netcom.com or via CompuServe at 76550,2632.

Dr. David Fullerton has more than 25 years of experience developing computer solutions for business problems, including several years of mainframe database management and application development. David, who has been a Visual Basic beta tester from release 1.0, is a Microsoft Certified Professional in Windows 3.1, Visual Basic, Access, and Word. He is MES certified as an instructor in Visual Basic. He has had several articles and reviews published in *Visual Basic Programmers Journal* and *Data Based Advisor*. David has a Ph.D. in Theoretical Chemistry from Georgia Tech University, where he also served as an instructor.

We'd Like to Hear from You!

As part of our continuing effort to produce books of the highest possible quality, Que would like to hear your comments. To stay competitive, we *really* want you, as a computer book reader and user, to let us know what you like or dislike most about this book or other Que products.

You can mail comments, ideas, or suggestions for improving future editions to the address below, or send us a fax at (317) 581-4663. For the online inclined, Macmillan Computer Publishing has a forum on CompuServe (type **GO QUEBOOKS** at any prompt) through which our staff and authors are available for questions and comments. The address of our Internet site is **http://www.mcp.com** (World Wide Web).

In addition to exploring our forum, please feel free to contact me personally to discuss your opinions of this book: I'm at 75767,2543 on CompuServe and I'm **nprice@que.mcp.com** on the Internet.

Thanks in advance—your comments will help us to continue publishing the best books available on computer topics in today's market.

Nancy D. Price
Product Development Specialist
Que Corporation
201 W. 103rd Street
Indianapolis, Indiana 46290
USA

Contents at a Glance

Contents

Part II: Adding Client/Server Database Capabilities   141

Part III: Enhancing Your Application   413

Part IV: Checking the Efficiency of Your Application   821

Introduction

by Steve Potts

Microsoft's Visual Basic has become one of the most dynamic Windows development tools in existence. It is evolving rapidly and replacing traditional development methods and tools for an ever larger set of applications. Because of the speed at which Visual Basic development occurs, it is a popular tool with management. Now that it has become integrated with C++ through the use of custom controls, many of the past performance complaints can be silenced.

If you run a profiler on any application, you will find that, at most, 20% of the code accounts for 80% of the time that an application requires. In the past, a decision would be made to implement a whole system in a third-generation language like C or C++ to attack performance problems that result from the 20% of the code that is on the critical path of the response time. While this strategy worked well to speed execution, it slowed development to a crawl. What businesses need is a tool that supports rapid development as well as Visual Basic, but generates finished applications that perform like C++.

With this version of Visual Basic, a company can have its cake and eat it, too. By the ancient practice of division of labor, a company can assign one group of programmers to develop the user interface, and another group to develop the performance-critical parts of the system in C++. If done correctly, the system can be integrated seamlessly, using the principles taught in this book, into a Windows application.

From the birth of the computer, serious programming had been the province of the professional programmers. With the introduction of fourth-generation languages, some freedom from the user/programmer paradigm was possible. A certain class of applications could now be created by the end users, if they would learn a language. A new class of end user/programmer hybrids emerged to create applications. These developers normally started their careers in the functional organization, but then migrated to the computer tools as the need for systems arose. Many of these programmers discovered a natural interest in computing, and welcomed the chance to specialize.

The majority of Visual Basic programmers come from this functional world. As a new-wave fourth generation language, it allows the users to go beyond the character cell, green screen applications of the mainframe, and create visually interesting programs in the premier operating environment—Microsoft Windows.

Visual Basic 4 goes beyond the capabilities of earlier versions. It provides the user with new tools, like the bound data controls, OLE support, and better custom-control support. These new features increase the power of systems built using Visual Basic. In fact, by developing custom controls and Dynamic Link Libraries, a company can remove the remaining limitations of the language.

This new complexity, however, pushes Visual Basic out of the end-user computing arena and into the full-blown programming language classification. A new class of Visual Basic gurus must now provide the support that traditional Visual Basic programmers need to complete their applications. These new ranks will be filled by both the most technical Visual Basic programmers and by traditional computer science experts defecting from the mainframe, UNIX, and C++ specialties. This book has been written for these people.

Who Should Read This Book

This book is written for those who want to make things happen in Visual Basic. Specifically, the following people will benefit greatly from the knowledge between these covers:

➤ The Visual Basic programmer who wants to be more independent of the experts in the office.

➤ The Visual Basic programmer who has no experts to call upon.

➤ The Visual Basic programmer who wants to become the expert in the office.

➤ The mainframe programmer who wants to find a niche in the PC world by providing support to the Visual Basic programmers.

➤ The C++ programmer who wants to use Visual Basic for the front end and C++ for the "down-and-dirty" routines.

➤ The independent consultant who is looking for better ways to service his clients. As the easy development is more commonly done in-house, the consultant must sound the depths of the hard development to ensure a steady demand for service.

These users will find what they are looking for in this book. For the programming novice, this book will prove to be some very strong material. A more appropriate starting point would be Que's *Visual Basic 4 by Example*, which walks you through each menu, control, and each feature in the language, providing examples of how they are used. When you have mastered that material, you will be ready for this book.

What This Book Is About

This book is designed to make an expert out of a very good Visual Basic programmer. It contains answers to questions that will make you the most popular programmer in the building when the hard questions come up. The following is a list of questions that you will find answers to in this book:

➤ How do I put a really good user interface on my applications? See Chapter 1, "User Interface Design," and Chapter 4, "Advanced Database Front Ends."

➤ How do I write a program that opens many documents or bitmaps at the same time? See Chapter 2, "Multiple Document Interface (MDI)."

➤ How do I use Windows API functions that are not supported by Visual Basic controls? See Chapter 3, "Using the Windows API."

➤ How can I do data-driven programming with Visual Basic? See Chapter 5, "Data Management and Data-Driven Programming."

➤ What is the relationship between Visual Basic and ODBC? See Chapter 6, "Working with ODBC."

➤ How does the Jet engine fit into the ODBC approach? See Chapter 7, "The Jet Engine and ODBC."

➤ What does client/server computing mean? See Chapter 8, "Modern Client/Server Computing."

➤ What do I do when my application gets too large and services too many users for the Jet engine to handle? See Chapter 9, "Client/ Server Databases."

➤ How do I create more powerful SQL commands? See Chapter 10, "SQL."

➤ How can I use OLE automation in my programs? See Chapter 11, "OLE Automation."

➤ When can creating an OLE server enhance my programs? See Chapter 12, "OLE Servers."

➤ What does the container class do and how can I use it? See Chapter 13, "OLE Container Classes."

➤ How is the Media Control Interface used? See Chapter 14, "Media Control Interface."

➤ How can I incorporate multimedia into my applications? See Chapter 15, "Multimedia in Action."

➤ How do the advanced graphics features of Visual Basic work? See Chapter 16, "Graphics: Data Analysis."

➤ How do I use the MSComm custom control to run the modem? See Chapter 17, "Communications Basics."

➤ How do I develop a help system that is as good, or better, than those in the applications that I buy? See Chapter 18, "Developing Online Help."

➤ How do I develop applications that run over the network? See Chapter 19, "Networkable Apps."

➤ How do third-party controls fit into the Visual Basic development environment and strategy? See Chapter 20, "OLE Controls, Add-Ins, and 32-bit DLLs."

➤ How can I make my Visual Basic application float like a butterfly and sting like a bee? See Chapter 21, "Optimizing VB Code."

➤ What is this new Visual Basic for Applications? See Chapter 22, "VB Versus VBA."

➤ How can DLLs improve my applications? See Chapter 23, "Mixed Language Development with DLLs."

How This Book Is Organized

This book is organized around the following four main themes:

➤ Part I, "Designing the Ideal Program." As an expert, you want to design quality into the system. This section will give you the advice that you need to design a program that fits the business need. It helps you decide whether to use a single- or multiple-document interface. It also shows you how to design and lay-out the interface to match your client's need. It also helps you to bridge the gap between the capabilities of Win95 and the limitations of the built-in Visual Basic controls by teaching you how to call the Windows application programming interface (API) from within Visual Basic.

➤ Part II, "Adding Client/Server Database Capabilities." Most business applications need to store a lot of data and retrieve it at random. This section will help you decide where and how to store it so as to create the lowest cost solution to the business problem.

➤ Part III, "Enhancing Your Application." Boring applications have followed leisure suits in going out of style. Today's users want their applications to be interesting and innovative. This section will show you how to spice up your forms with graphics, multimedia, modem and network communications, and third-party controls.

➤ Part IV, "Checking the Efficiency of Your Application." Applications that run like molasses are not going to win you the Coder-Boy of the Year award. This section teaches you how to avoid certain practices and features when application performance is inadequate.

How to Use This Book

This book will be read from front to back by a only few hardy souls. The majority of you will want to use it as an encyclopedia of solutions on an as-needed basis. This approach will be the most useful because you will have the question clearly placed in your mind before you read the answer.

Those of you who really thirst for advanced Visual Basic knowledge would be well-served by skimming the book from cover to cover to become familiar with the types of problems that are solved in these pages. You will be surprised at how smart you will look when you start explaining the approach outlined in the book to your colleagues. The fact that your knowledge is not very deep is a small one, because the book is on your desk and you have confidence in your ability to teach yourself the details when the need arises.

When you are faced with the task of turning the principles of a chapter into a piece of a system, give yourself time to get it to work. Unlike the built-in Visual Basic controls, the solutions in this book usually are not trivial. Experienced programmers fully expect to read a chapter several times before fully understanding it. The best strategy is to find a quiet spot, fill a cooler with your favorite soft drinks, open the book, and start coding. Experiment with the examples after you get them to work. Change colors, add objects—above all, have fun.

Few experiences in life afford the level of satisfaction that mastering a difficult topic provides. Your standing in the programming community rises with each new technique that you add to your repertoire.

What's on the CD

An iridescent disk, commonly known as a CD, is neatly tucked inside the back flap of this book. It contains the code used in each chapter, as well as a number of sample VBX and OCXs—each provided for your examination by its respective vendor. These samples help you understand what kind of custom controls are available, and give you a flavor of what to expect when you purchase them.

Custom controls are truly the best things since interactive debuggers. While they usually cost several hundred dollars for a full version with distribution rights, a good one is worth 50 times the price. When you consider that a programmer costs your company at least $50 an hour, you realize that you break even if you save four hours of coding time by buying a custom control. After that, every minute that you save is money in the pocket of the shareholders. Even if your product sells millions of copies or is distributed worldwide, you never pay an additional penny.

Make sure that you follow what kinds of custom controls are available. As more and more companies are forming to provide these tools, you will see more controls written for niche markets. A good programmer and/or business person should never spend time developing functionality that is available at a reasonable price.

Part I
Designing the
Ideal Program

1

User Interface Design

by Elisabeth Boonin

Sometimes programmers think of user interface design as a purely cosmetic exercise. They believe the real guts of a program is its feature set and performance level. However, creating a good user interface is of the utmost importance. The best features in the world will be ignored by many users if they are difficult to find or cumbersome to use.

The user interface is your primary mode of communication with the user. Like other forms of communication, whether your ideas will be appreciated depends on how well they are presented. With a good interface design, your program can be efficient and user-friendly. This chapter discusses how to design interfaces with the work habits and learning styles of different kinds of users in mind.

Interface design in Visual Basic is largely a matter of dragging and dropping various icons into place and making them work together. The goal of this chapter is to give an overview of good design, rather than explaining in great detail how to set properties and write code for various controls. We will cover the following:

- ➤ Designing with the user in mind
- ➤ When to be innovative and when to be traditional in interface design

- ➤ Standard formats for menus and dialog boxes

- ➤ Choosing the right controls for the right tasks

- ➤ How to determine if your interface design really works

Understanding a Good User Interface

There are certain elements that good user interfaces share, even in very different environments. Keeping these in mind as general goals will help you empathize with the user and will put the specifics of interface design in Visual Basic into perspective.

The successful interface designer learns to see a program from a very different vantage than the norm: that of the user. It can be difficult to put yourself in the shoes of naive users and try to anticipate their needs and the potential pitfalls they will encounter. This is particularly true since, as a programmer, you are several steps removed from most users in terms of computer expertise.

Compounding this difficulty is the fact that programming is an exercise in explaining things to the computer. Programmers are used to organizing according to the logic of the computer, rather than the logic of a user. Objects that are alike to the computer may not seem so to the user and vice versa.

Consider a typical user's desktop in the Windows 95 environment. Graphical objects representing entirely different types of data and commands are presented side by side. Application shortcuts, folders, documents, the recycle bin, a printer icon for drag/drop printing, and the taskbar can all occupy the desktop simultaneously. From the computer's point of view, these objects are not only unrelated, they aren't even in the same category. Programs, files, folders, commands, and other objects are all presented together on-screen. An icon that launches a program and one designating the Network Neighborhood sit side by side, as if they are in some way equivalent. In terms of the internal organization of the computer, this makes little or no sense. Now, consider it from the user's point of view. The user wants commonly used files, tasks, folders, and commands to be easily accessible. In terms of the user's work patterns, it makes perfect sense.

This philosophy can be transferred to many elements of program design. Examples include choosing items for a toolbar, organizing menus, and designing a dialog box. All aspects should try to reflect the way the user works rather than the way the program was written. Keep in mind, however, that users have become accustomed to finding certain things in certain situations. Relocating standard commands is not a good idea. The Print command belongs on the File menu, regardless of whether it seems more appropriate to include it on another menu. Leave the major interface revisions to the industry giants.

Visual Appeal in the Long Run

There is absolutely no question that the look of a program affects its popularity. When Windows 3.0 was released, most users were thrilled with the three dimensional buttons that looked like they were being pressed. Screen saver programs are a perennial best seller, despite the fact that simple ones come free with Windows. Users are interested in having programs look nice.

On the other hand, programs that employ non-standard graphic elements can work against a user. It is frustrating to learn a program with new and unfamiliar dialog boxes or buttons that don't look like buttons. Also, fancy graphics and animation that slow down the performance or loading time of an application are generally not worth it unless they serve some other purpose.

The design goal, then, is to produce an interface that is attractive, conforms to the standards of the Windows environment, and uses graphics in a way that enhances the usability and appeal of the program.

Learning Ease and Efficiency

For almost any program, there are different types of users to be considered. The new user wants an interface as simple and self explanatory as possible. Ideally, the menu and command names should make it obvious what function they perform, and the interface should mirror other Windows applications so that objects can be found in their expected places. Keep in mind that it is not only the brand-new user, but the experienced, occasional user as well who will need an interface that requires little or no memorization.

On the other hand, the proficient or power user wants to interact quickly with the program. If he is typing and needs to use a command, he doesn't want to have to reach for his mouse. The screen should not be cluttered with icons that reduce his work space too much. Frequently used menu commands should have short-cuts to reduce the number of keystrokes or eliminate the need to use the mouse.

Balancing the needs of both kinds of users can be challenging. However, some of the elements of a good UI design are beneficial to everyone. Good menu and dialog box design allow the beginner to see which aspects of an application are essential while providing the power user with clear routes to take to delve more deeply into the more advanced features. Good organization in your menus and dialog boxes will blaze a trail for the user, making it easy to determine which path to choose to find a feature, and how to return to an earlier position without making changes.

Allowing the user to customize the program helps to address different levels of expertise. When you create a highly customizable program, however, you need to create it so that the initial installation is one that is appropriate for the beginning user. Remember, it may be a while before the beginning user learns *how* to customize a program, while the advanced user will quickly seek out the Options or Preferences menu commands and start changing whatever settings she can to brand the application as hers. Examples of good customization options are: menus that allow items to be added or removed, View options that allow palettes, toolbars, and other windows to be made visible or invisible, and user definable shortcuts.

There are no strict laws to finding the balance between ease of learning and efficiency; your options depend on the particular application. Just remember to keep the needs of your users in mind.

Allowing Users to Make Mistakes

One of the great advantages of the Windows environment is the ability to learn new software by exploring. Rather than being faced with a command line prompt with no idea of what to type, the Windows user can browse through menus and dialog boxes, seeing what commands are available and trying them out. Your programs should both encourage users to take this approach and protect them from damaging data or painting themselves into corners. When users make mistakes, your program should be forgiving enough to allow them to correct themselves.

Some ways to make programs allow for user mistakes are as follows:

➤ The use of a confirmation dialog box whenever the user invokes a command that involves deleting or overwriting data

➤ Not providing shortcuts to "dangerous" commands

➤ Making it clear how to exit a dialog box without making changes, usually with a cancel button

➤ Providing a full featured Undo command that will reverse the last action taken

Designing Main Application Window

Almost every program has a main application window. It serves as the home base for all actions taken. Visual Basic takes care of some of the more tedious aspects of designing the window. Scroll bars, title bars, and sizing controls are all produced automatically. Your task is to add the features and controls that are specific to your application.

Figure 1.1 shows a simple text editing application. The main portion of the screen is a the area for the user's work. From the top down, you see the title bar, menu bar, and toolbar. On the bottom, is the status bar.

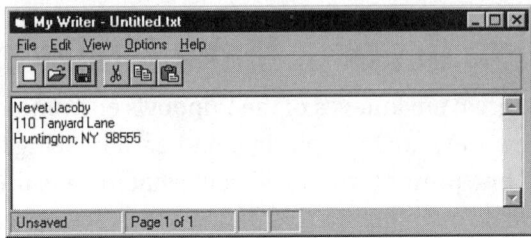

Fig. 1.1 The parts of an application window.

The title and menu bar are necessary features for almost any application. For most applications, you will want the main window to be sizable. If you want to give your user a larger work area than the screen provides, scroll bars can be added. For your main application window, you'll generally want to use the default control menu and max and min buttons. All of these features are shown in figure 1.1.

Toolbars and status bars are an addition to many applications. Frequently used menu and dialog box choices can be included on the Toolbar and information about the current state of the application along with some basic online help can be given on the status bar.

Toolbars

Toolbars are the result of a kind of grass roots software movement. More and more software designers included them in their application. Microsoft finally took the hint and included a Toolbar control in most versions of VB 4. There was nothing to bar the programmer from creating Toolbars from scratch in earlier versions of Visual Basic, but the new Toolbar control provides a standard look and a great deal of built in functionality. For VB versions that do not include the Toolbar control, you can still create them from scratch.

There are many different customization options that you can offer in conjunction with Toolbars. For tool heavy applications, you can create different Toolbars and allow the user to select which ones to display. The individual Toolbars can be made customizable as well.

Note: The Toolbar control also includes Tooltip functionality. Tooltips are the small text boxes that pop up when you leave the mouse pointer on a Toolbar icon for a second. They are an excellent and unobtrusive way to provide context-sensitive help to the user. If you include Tooltips in your application, include an option where they can be disabled as well, since some advanced users may find them distracting.

Status Bars

The status bar is a good place to present helpful, but non-essential, information to the user. In Fig 1.1, for example, the status bar indicates the total number of pages and the current page, as well as whether or not the document has been saved. Avoid putting essential information here because many users don't notice the status bar at all. Never use the status bar as a substitute for alert dialog boxes.

Note: With all of the various bars taking up screen space, allow the user to choose not to display them in order to get a larger working area. Be careful about hiding the menu bar, however, since users may not remember how to get it back.

Exploring Menus

Menus are the roadmap to your application. When looking at a new application, most users will go right for the mouse and start clicking on menus to get a feel for what the software does and how it is organized. Menus can make a program easy to use and efficient, or they can make navigation a chore. Poor menu design will frustrate even the most advanced users. For example, users may remember a command for changing the default directory but must search through the Preferences, Options, and Settings dialog boxes to find it.

Experienced users are conditioned to expect some standard features in menus. You should strive to conform to these standards of menu names, contents, and shortcuts. Menus are not the best place to become creative. You may have extensive user testing to prove that "Write File" is a more descriptive command than "Save" but those familiar with other programs will curse you for such ingenuity. Almost as important as familiarity is conforming to the standard shortcut keys. Keyboard oriented users expect to zoom through options they know (pressing Alt+F then X to leave a program, for instance) without needing to learn new conventions for each program. The most common standards are shown in figures 1.3, 1.4, and 1.5 shown later in this chapter.

For less standard options, including those that are specific to your program, careful thought should be put into menu organization, menu titles and item names. Both the new and experienced users should be considered. Concise, well organized menus can keep the choices from being overwhelming for the novice and should provide obvious routes of progression to the user who is ready to explore the more advanced options offered in dialog boxes. On the other hand, making the menus too concise can later trap the user in excessively complicated dialog boxes.

Adding to the complexity but providing excellent functionality in the right situations are additional menu formats: cascaded and pop-up menus. Used correctly, they can be of great benefit to more advanced users who will understand how to use them. However, they have a tendency to be awkward to use, or even go unnoticed by novice users.

Creating and Organizing Drop-Down Menus

Menu organization has the following components:

➤ What menu names to use and where to place them

➤ Deciding which items to include in menus

➤ Choosing menu item names

➤ How to organize the items within a menu

When choosing menu names, first and foremost consider the established standards. All programs, even if they don't write or read files, must have at least one menu with the minimum requirement being an Exit item in this menu. In most applications, this is called the File menu. For applications that do not involve files, this menu is often given another name, such as Game or the name of the program. Whenever possible, use the name File for this menu, even if it means "cheating" a little for applications that don't use files, since most users will expect to use the Alt+F mnemonic to access the first menu.

Any program with Cut, Copy, and Paste commands or an Undo command needs an Edit menu. MDI programs should have a Window menu, and every program should have a Help menu. Even if you do not provide online help, the Help menu should contain an About... item leading to an About dialog box.

Note: When creating a Window menu for an MDI application, just check the Window List box in the Menu Editor dialog box. Visual Basic will automatically add a separator bar and a list of the open documents to the bottom of the Window menu. Giving a menu the name "Window" automatically activates this feature.

There are also standards for menu positions. The control menu is placed on the far left of the title bar by the system. Visual Basic takes care of this automatically. The first named menu should be File, then Edit and View if used. The last menu is always the Help menu.

The Help menu used to be placed to the far right of the screen, but now should placed like the other menus as the rightmost one. In a MDI application, the Window menu should immediately precede the Help menu. There is leeway for the placement of other menu names but some rough guidelines can be obtained by looking at a few of software best-sellers. Figure 1.2 shows a MDI application with a maximized child window (note the two control menu icons). The figure displays good menu names and placement.

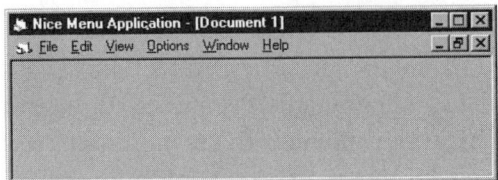

Fig. 1.2 Standard menu placement and menu names.

Some menu items have become standard in name and placement. Figures 1.3, 1.4, and 1.5 show typical File, Edit, and Help menus.

Note: A menu item that leads to a dialog box *must* be followed by an ellipsis (...), as seen in the Open and Save As items in figure 1.3.

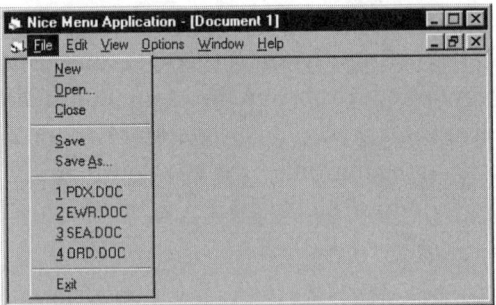

Fig. 1.3 The typical File menu.

The underlined mnemonic characters and shortcut keystrokes are discussed later in this chapter in the "Shortcuts" section.

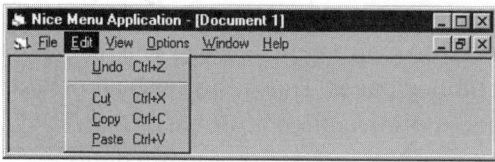

Fig. 1.4 The typical Edit menu.

Grouping similar menu items together and then using a horizontal separator line helps the user in a number of ways. First, it makes it easier to assimilate a large amount of data at once if it is organized into smaller sections. Second, the user will be able to better understand less familiar commands by analogy if they are grouped with more familiar ones. Note the placement of the separator bars in figures 1.3 through 1.5.

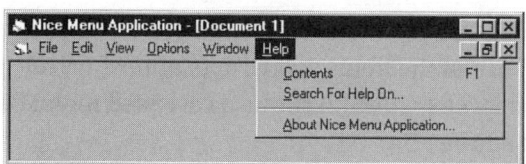

Fig. 1.5 The typical Help menu.

Naming original menu items is an art. What seems to be a completely self explanatory name to a developer can mystify a user. Strive for names that are descriptive and unambiguous. Having different items in the same menu called Options and Preferences is sure to confuse.

Note: When presented with a situation of too many similar sounding names or several items that belong together but seem to make a menu too long or confusing, consider the option of a tabbed dialog box. One menu item can lead to a dialog box with several different tabbed pages. This design also allows the user to browse the different options much more easily than having to back out of a dialog box and choose another menu option.

Using Cascaded and Pop-up Menus

Cascaded menus appear adjacent to a standard drop-down menu when items marked with a right pointing triangle are selected. Pop-up menus appear when the user clicks the right mouse button (for right-handed users) over an area that has a pop-up menu associated with it. Both add versatility and can be time-savers for the advanced user, but neither is without its drawbacks.

To create a cascaded menu, create the main menu item in the menu editor. Then, list the items you wish to appear on the cascaded menu indented a level. Figure 1.6 shows a cascaded menu being defined in the menu editor.

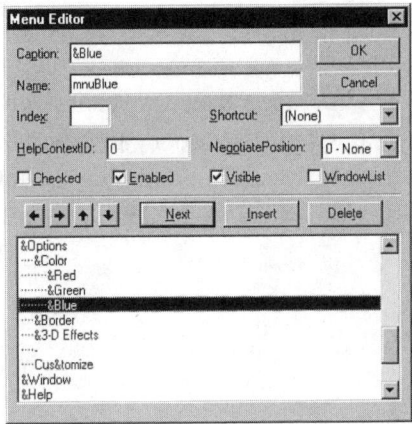

Fig. 1.6 Defining a cascaded menu with the menu editor.

Cascaded menus are considered a standard interface feature and their
extensive use in the Start Menu on the Windows 95 taskbar has made
users more comfortable with them. They are, however, more awkward
to manipulate than drop-down menus, both for mouse and keyboard
users. Multiple layers of cascaded menus are generally not a good idea.
Users will find themselves running out of mouse space making it difficult to navigate back and forth between levels. When having a hierarchy of commands is desirable, consider using a tabbed dialog box or
creating an additional menu to group commands. Cascaded menus
can be very useful if kept manageable and short and are good for picking tools, colors, and fonts. Figure 1.7 shows a well-implemented,
single-level cascaded menu. It is the one that was defined in figure 1.6.

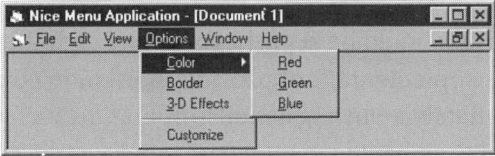

Fig. 1.7 A single-level cascaded menu.

Pop-up menus are useful as a supplemental way to get to features offered elsewhere. Because of the infrequent use of the right mouse button, many users will never realize that pop-up menus are available so it
is important that they only duplicate functionality available in other
menus, command buttons or dialog boxes. Windows 95 uses the right
mouse button far more than any previous version of the operating
system, however, so your pop-up menus will be found and appreciated
by many users.

Because of their context sensitivity, pop-up devices are wonderful for
frequently used commands on certain objects. A pop-up menu that
gives formatting options for selected text is a good example of an effective use. Figure 1.8 shows such a pop-up menu. Notice the position of
the pointer; the menu appears at the pointer when the right mouse
button is clicked.

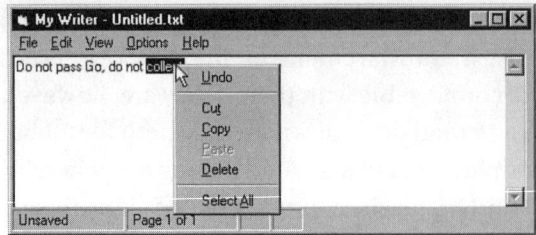

Fig. 1.8 A pop-up menu.

Visual Basic includes several standard pop-up menus for different controls. The one shown in figure 1.8 is automatically generated for text boxes. Check to see what VB has included for a control before creating a pop-up menu of your own.

Pop-up menus should be kept short: around eight items or fewer. The most useful implementations provide shortcut to commands that are used immediately following a mouse operation such as selection. Then, rather than having to move the mouse to the menu or switch to the keyboard, the user can keep the mouse stationary and simply click the right mouse button to access the desired command.

Note: Most pop-up menus don't appear as drop-down menus. When this is the case, create a menu in the menu editor with the Visible property unchecked. The menu title will not appear in the pop-up menu, but the items of that menu will appear when the menu is called as a pop-up in your code.

Both pop-up and cascaded menu items can lead to dialog boxes. Remember that these menu items should be followed by an ellipsis, just as in drop-down menus.

Changing Menus at Runtime

There are several ways that menus can change while an application is running. Menu items or even entire menus can appear or disappear, items can become grayed, indicating they are not currently available, or a check mark can appear alongside menu a item to show it is selected or active. These changes can occur in response to a user action, or they may be induced deliberately when the user customizes a program.

Menus can disappear when their context is not relevant. Many MDI applications will drop-down to just a File and Help menu when all documents are closed. Some applications will use one window for very different modes and have different menus as appropriate. For example, a game might use the same window for playing and later to display the high scores. While the high scores are being displayed, the Weapons menu could disappear. Only cause menus to vanish when the reason for their absence is wholly apparent by the current circumstances. If nothing is in your Clipboard and nothing is selected, don't make the Edit menu disappear just because none of its commands are currently useful. Frustrated users will remember a menu title or menu item and go hunting for it.

An alternative to removing menus or reducing their contents is to disable choices when they are not available. The user will see that the choice exists but is not currently available. Figure 1.9 shows an Edit menu with the Cut and Copy items disabled. When options are not available, they should be dimmed to avoid the confusion of selecting an item and seeing no results.

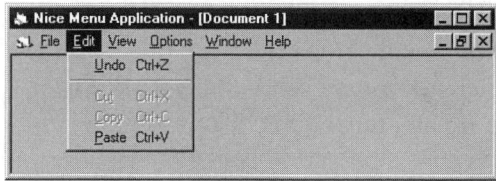

Fig. 1.9 Dimmed menu items indicate commands that are not currently available

It has become nearly mandatory for MDI applications to include the four most recently used documents in the File menu. The File menu in figure 1.3 gives an example of this. The application must recall these documents after it is closed, so this data must be stored in a separate file. If your application has an *.ini file, this is a good place for it. This is a different feature than the Window menu which will list all currently *open* documents, as opposed to the most recently used ones, and which can be implemented automatically by checking the Window List box in the Menu Editor.

Many applications allow users to customize menus. Being able to add commonly used fonts or remove infrequently used commands can help the user become more efficient with the program. Be careful not to give the user too much control, though. Imagine a user removing all useful menu items and then also removing the menu item that leads to the customization!

> **Note:** To allow the user to add menu items at runtime, create the menu items in their proper places with the visible property set to false. When the user invokes the command to add the menu items, change the visible property to true.

Finally, menus can change by modifying names or putting check marks next to options to reflect the current status. For example, "Undo" can change to "Redo" immediately after the Undo command is selected, or formatting commands like Bold can be checked to indicate they are currently selected.

Keep in mind that the object is to provide helpful information to the user and then ask yourself, or better yet ask a user, if these changes in the menus are helpful and not disorienting.

Dialog Boxes

Dialog boxes are the primary way an application presents information and solicits feedback from the user. The very name "Dialog" suggests an ongoing conversation, and in the familiar context of the Windows environment, the user expects dialog boxes to be where most information exchanges take place. If the menu structure is the roadmap of your application, the dialog boxes are the primary destinations.

Dialog boxes appear in a variety of circumstances. Menus do not provide enough space to list all possible alternatives, and a dialog box can be presented upon selecting a menu item. To indicate that further options follow a particular menu selection, the item command must be followed by an ellipsis. Thus, selecting a menu item entitled "Print" will cause the print job to start immediately. Selecting an item called "Print…" will bring up a Print dialog box.

Note: When a dialog box is called through a menu item, give the dialog box the same name as the menu item. When necessary for clarity, the menu name can precede the name of the menu item. For example, the dialog box called by the Page item of the Format menu can be titled Page or Format Page.

The simplest dialog boxes are ones that solely provide feedback to the user. These appear when the application wishes to alert the user of some status change (such as a file transfer completed). Other dialog boxes can ask the user to make a simple choice in response to a command. For instance, clicking Close without having saved the latest revisions of a document should always produce the familiar "Do you want to save changes to…" dialog box.

Visual Basic provides you with several ways to implement dialog boxes. The easiest is to use the `MsgBox` or `InputBox` functions. Although limited in scope, they are extremely handy and can be used to keep the user informed or solicit simple decisions or information. Often, much more is required in the way of user input. A File Open dialog box, for instance, requires many controls and quite a bit of code to implement. Fortunately, the Common Dialog control allows a quick way to create five commonly used dialog boxes: Open, Save As, Print, Font and Color.

Modality

Some dialog boxes require you to take action within the dialog box before returning to the rest of the program. Some allow you to have the dialog box open while performing other tasks. This attribute is called modality.

A modeless dialog box allows the user to perform other actions while the dialog box is present. Typically, the dialog box remains on the top layer, though, so that it is not obscured by other parts of the application. A good example of this type of dialog box is a Search/Replace dialog box in a word processing application. It allows the user to edit the text without first closing the dialog box.

An application modal dialog box requires that the dialog box be closed before any action can be taken within the application. A system modal dialog box requires that the dialog box be closed before any other action can be taken at all.

The order of preference for choice of modality is: modeless, application modal, system modal. Use the least degree of modality whenever practical. System modal dialog boxes should be saved for data or system stability endangering situations.

MsgBox and InputBox

There are a host of situations for which the `InputBox` and especially the `MsgBox` functions provide a quick and easy way to give information to or request information from the user. `MsgBox` can be called as a function or a statement. Use it as a function when you need to get a response from the user. `InputBox` is always used as a function and the value it returns is the text entered by the user into its text box.

`MsgBox` can be used simply to display information such as warnings, alerts, simple "About this Application…" information, and error messages. These typically contain a single OK button and it is implied that no action is being taken; pressing OK acknowledges that the user has read the message.

The MsgBox function is far more versatile than this, however. It can be used to solicit information from the user. Upon selecting Close, the MsgBox function can generate a confirmation dialog box like the one shown in figure 1.10. It will return a numeric value to indicate which button the user pressed. Appropriate action can be taken based on the user's choice.

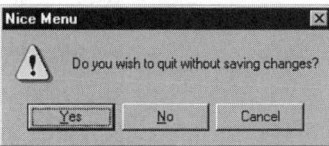

Fig. 1.10 A confirmation dialog box created with MsgBox.

Message boxes have several options that can be specified when the function is called. You can define which buttons to include and which to use as the default, what icon to use, and the level of modality.

The options for MsgBox each have a numeric value. To use several of the options, simply add the values together. For instance, to call the message box displayed in figure 1.10, use the statement:

```
UserAnswer = MsgBox("Do you wish to save changes before_
    closing?", 51)
```

The 51 is equal to the sum of 3 and 48 where the 3 indicates you wish to use Yes, No, and Cancel Buttons and the 48 produces the exclamation icon. The default button is the first and the dialog box is application modal because higher values weren't added. If no value is specified, the message box defaults to 0, which produces an application modal dialog box with an OK button and no icon.

The various options for MsgBox are listed in Table 1.1.

Table 1.1 Various Options for MsgBox

Option Type	Number	Use
Buttons	0	OK
	1	OK and Cancel
	2	Abort, Retry and Ignore (especially useful for error trapping)
	3	Yes, No and Cancel
	4	Yes and No (forces a decision from the user)
	5	Retry and Cancel
⊗	16	Stop (for critical problems)
⑦	32	Question (can often use exclamation instead)
⚠	48	Exclamation
ⓘ	64	Information (accompanied by an OK button only)
Default Buttons	0	Makes the first button the default
	256	Makes the second button the default
Modality	0	Application modal
	4096	System modal (use very sparingly!)

For more readable code, you may wish to use constants rather than numbers for the `MsgBox` options. These constants are included as part of the Visual Basic language. Using constants, your statement would read as follows:

```
UserAnswer = MsgBox("Do you wish to save changes_
    before closing?", vbYesNoCancel + vbQuestion)
```

There are four icons that can accompany a message box: the information, question, exclamation, and stop icons. Using them appropriately will help the user understand the significance of the information. The information icon should be used when the message box only contains an OK button and no changes will result from any action the user takes with respect to the message box. It should give information about some status but not require further action. If the message box contains only an OK button, but requires further action on the part of the user, the exclamation icon should be used instead. An example of such a situation could be: "Please insert the Setup disk before continuing."

Intuitively, the question icon is to alert the user that a question is being posed, but some interface designers prefer to reserve the question mark to denote online help. The exclamation and question icon are sometimes used interchangeably for situations such as the message box shown in figure 1.10. It is acceptable to avoid the use of the question icon and use the exclamation icon whenever posing a question to the user. Make sure you are consistent throughout your application, whatever you decide.

The Stop icon alerts the user that a critical problem has occurred. If something has gone wrong and it is too late to be corrected, the Stop icon is appropriate. It can also be used to warn the user that continuing an action will cause such a problem to occur. An accepted but less obvious use is to alert the user that a problem (usually hardware related) must be corrected before work can continue. Some designers prefer to use the exclamation icon for this purpose, but again consistency is the key.

Message boxes also allow several options for the buttons you wish to display. Information boxes should include the OK button only and make it clear that no action will be taken. Use the Yes/No option when its meaning is clearer than OK/Cancel.

Finally the `MsgBox` function allows you to choose a level of modality. Message boxes are all modal to some degree but you may choose between application and system modality. Application modality requires the user to respond to the message box before taking other actions in the application, but allows the user to switch to other applications before dealing with the message box. System modal message boxes require a response to the message box before any other action at all can be taken. Application modality is sufficient for almost all situations. There should be a very good reason for a system modal dialog box: one which threatens data or system stability.

The `InputBox` function is a quick and dirty way to get simple information from the user—such as a login name or a password. Although easy to implement, it is not the most aesthetically pleasing of dialog boxes and its range of uses are limited.

Common Dialog boxes

If you've ever designed a File Open dialog box (see fig. 1.11) from scratch, you know what an involved process it is. A multitude of controls are required to sort through the file system on the computer. Code must be written to update the status of one control based on selections made in the others. The dialog box needs to look nice, too, and lining up the various list boxes, combo boxes, command buttons, and other controls can be a headache.

Fortunately, the wheel need not be reinvented. Some of the most used and most useful dialog boxes can be generated automatically within Visual Basic by using the Common Dialog control. A moderate amount of customization can be specified when displaying the dialog box, and all of the grunt work of laying out the controls and making them work together properly is already handled.

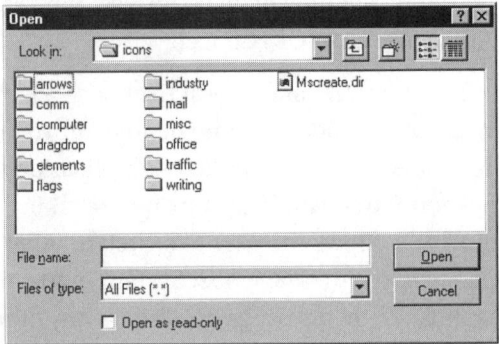

Fig. 1.11 The Open common dialog box.

The common dialog boxes are a boon to programmers and should be used whenever practical. Not only do they save development time, they are also the dialog boxes with which users are already comfortable. In fact, if your program demands that you write an Open dialog box from scratch, due to some special ways in which your program can open files, it is best to try to copy the physical layout of the common Open dialog box as closely as possible.

> **Note:** When creating filters for your common dialog boxes, be sure to include an option for All Files *.* along with whatever other extension types are appropriate. Often, the file the user is looking for will not have the correct extension.

Designing Original Dialog Boxes

When an original dialog box is needed, one can be created from scratch from a form. Although they can vary from simple windows with only one or two controls to large ones with many different controls, all dialog boxes share some common properties.

> ➤ They do not take up entire screen; if the application is maximized, it should be visible behind the dialog box.

> ➤ They are not sizable and lack the maximize and minimize buttons. Set the `Border` property of the form to `Fixed Dialog` and the `Max Button` and `Min Button` properties to `False`.

> ➤ The dialog box may or may not include a control menu. If a control menu is included, it contains only the move and close options.

> ➤ Dialog boxes should have a title bar. If the dialog box is the result of a menu selection, the title should be that of the menu item minus the ellipsis. If it is an alert or information dialog box, use the name of the application for the dialog box title.

> ➤ A dialog box generally includes a minimum of one button. Except in the case of unrecoverable errors, one button must show the user how to get rid of the dialog box without changing the status

of the program. (Some objects such as Toolbars or palettes can be thought of as modeless dialog boxes and do not necessarily contain a "go away" button.

Visual Basic makes a wide range of dialog box controls available. The user can issue a command by pressing a command button or selecting a menu item. Options can be selected with check boxes, option buttons, or by selecting menu items. Which control you choose to use will affect the functionality and ease of use of your program.

> **Note:** Visual Basic 4 allows you to create an automatic 3D style for your dialog boxes. Most Windows 95 applications use this 3D style and it is fast becoming standard.

Maneuvering Through Dialog Boxes

When a dialog box appears on the screen, the user must switch to working in a different window. To keep the user from becoming lost, make it easy to enter, exit, move within, and go between your various dialog boxes.

Dialog boxes can have buttons that lead to other dialog boxes. This is particularly useful for more in-depth or advanced features. When implementing this, make sure the original dialog box can be seen when the new one comes up. Then the user will understand the hierarchy of the two boxes.

Buttons can also lead laterally to other dialog boxes which are not merely extended options of the first one. This tends to lose users in a maze of dialog boxes. A better design is to include the two or more dialog boxes as tabbed pages under one heading.

Command buttons should be lined up along the bottom or right side of the dialog box. They should read in a natural order from left to right or top to bottom. The OK button should be first, and the Cancel button last. Set the default button to the OK button in most cases, but for particularly dangerous options, make the Cancel button the default.

To allow users to tab to the various parts of the dialog box, set the `TabIndex` properties for each of the controls on the dialog box that the user will wish to access. The tab order should follow some logical progression, usually based on the location of the controls: generally moving from left to right, then top to bottom.

Note: The tab order of controls usually reflects the orientation of written language. When creating software for use in a country where the language reads from right to left, you may want to adjust the tab order to move from right to left as well.

Tabbed Dialog Boxes

Tabbed dialog boxes provide a solution to the problem of overcrowded and bewildering dialog boxes. Rather than cluttering one dialog box with too many options, or creating chains of dialog boxes that can access each other, the tabbed dialog box allows you to roll several dialog boxes into one. Moreover, they are visually appealing and correspond to real life objects with which the user is familiar.

Any time you need a dialog box to contain more than one category of controls, consider using a tabbed dialog box. Don't worry if one of the pages on such a dialog box seems sparse. Figure 1.12 shows a page with only four text boxes. It is also acceptable to create a page with fewer controls: even a single check box! The question to ask is whether or not breaking these controls down into small categories will help the user.

The time to combine controls onto one page is when they affect each other or when knowledge of one is required to make decisions about another. So, if you have a check box indicating whether or not a password is required and a control button for changing the password, these belong together.

Tabbed dialog boxes have not yet become standardized. In figure 1.12, the OK and Cancel buttons appear outside of the tab pages. This approach is recommended because the buttons apply to all three pages.

You might notice that many of the major software releases put these buttons on the tabbed pages themselves. Instead, save this area for buttons that are specific to the page.

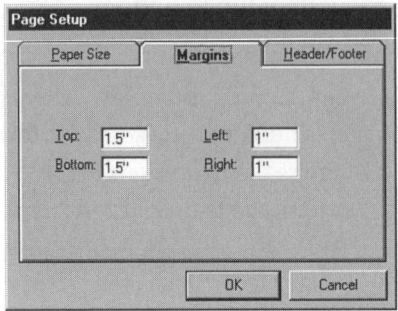

Fig. 1.12 A tabbed dialog box.

Dialog Box Controls

An entire book could be written about the various kind of dialog box controls and their uses. In addition to the standard and custom controls that come with Visual Basic, many third-party developers have created controls of their own.

Some controls are found in virtually every program: command buttons, list boxes, option buttons, etc. Others are essential for some programs, useful in others, and extraneous in most. There's nothing wrong with using a control because it looks great, as long as it doesn't hinder the user. Just be judicious in selecting your controls, especially in productivity applications.

Command Buttons

Command buttons are perhaps the most versatile control. The most obvious home for command buttons is in a dialog box. Dialog boxes rely on command buttons for all user directives since they lack menus (other than the control menu). However, they can also appear on the main application form itself and on Toolbars.

Smaller programs, particularly non-MDI applications, will often use a variety of command buttons in the main application window. Usually these buttons duplicate commands found on the menus. This may seem like an unnecessary waste of resources but in a utility program which only has a few commands, this lets the user see all the available options. Access to button commands is simplified for both the keyboard and mouse user as well. The keyboard user will be able to use the accelerator keys to go directly to the command without having to use the menu accelerator key combination. The button can also be reached by tabbing to highlight it, then pressing enter. The mouse user will be able to press the button directly, without having to maneuver through menus.

Note: Command button names are much like menu items. They should include an accelerator key, indicated by an underlined letter (except for Cancel buttons, which are activated by the Esc key).

In larger programs or any program for which screen real estate is an issue, it becomes impractical to litter the screen with command buttons. Their usefulness led to the compromise of the Toolbar, where some of the most popular command buttons are given in miniature form. Toolbars are discussed in their own section earlier in this chapter.

Check Boxes and Option Buttons

Usually found in dialog boxes, check boxes and option buttons (also called "Radio Buttons") both allow the user to specify options (see fig. 1.13). The purpose for which they are intended should determine which of the two is used.

Check boxes can exist alone or in groups. Each one, however, is an independent entity representing an On/Off status. A good example would be check boxes for Bold, Italic, and Underline. Any or all could be checked and changing one would not affect the others.

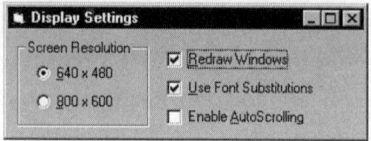

Fig. 1.13 Check boxes and option buttons.

Option buttons always occur in a group and operate as mutually exclusive. If one is selected, the others are not. Selecting one will change the status of the others. An example of where this would be used is often found in word processors in choosing a kind of tab stop, such as Left, Right, or Center. The tab stop would have to be exactly one of those. Option buttons should be grouped together in a frame whose title reflects their function.

Note: The simplest way to handle a group of option buttons in your code is to create a control array. Then, when one is selected it is easy check the state of all the others with a for/next loop on the array index.

With check boxes and option buttons, the question of which one will work for a certain purpose is automatically determined by the nature of the use. However, whether such a control should be used at all is a more complicated decision facing the programmer. For example, option button groups can be replaced by list boxes. Check boxes can be replaced or supplemented by menu items.

Use a group of option buttons over a list box when the number of options is fairly small. Choose between check boxes, menu items, or a combination based on the organization of your program, the available menu space, and the amount of clutter in your dialog boxes.

There are no hard and fast rules about choosing one kind of control over another. Try to anticipate the needs of different kinds of users and design accordingly.

List and Combo Boxes

The different types of combo boxes can be a confusing aspect of Visual Basic interface design. The first two styles of combo box, drop-down and Simple, are very similar. The third style of combo box, drop-down list, is actually not a combo box at all but a kind of list box.

Drop-down and Simple combo boxes are combination text and list boxes. They present the user with a list of suggested choices but allow the user to type an entry that is not on the list. Simple combo boxes always have their list displayed. Drop-down combo boxes wait until the user clicks on the attached arrow before displaying the list. Since any displayed list should show at least 3 items, the simple combo box takes up significantly more space on a form than the drop-down combo. However, the simple combo has the advantage of showing more information at first glance.

Combo boxes have a tendency to confuse users. If space permits, the most user-friendly way to implement a combo box is to use a simple combo with instructions above it, such as: "Type a name or select one from the list."

To make the user choose from a predetermined list of choices, you can use a list box or a drop-down list combo box. The purpose of a list box is more immediately obvious to the user but takes up more space.

List boxes and simple combo boxes should be sized so that between three and eight items can be seen. Drop-down boxes will automatically size themselves and will even drop up if positioned too close to the bottom of the screen.

Using Controls to Represent Numeric Data

A variety of controls exists for inputting and displaying numeric data. How do you choose among spin buttons, sliders, gauges, text boxes, scroll bars and other possibilities?

Often, although a value is really numerical to the computer, its meaning to the user may be less so. A program that plays music may use a numerical setting for volume. Thus, it could be represented as a number alone. However, a scroll bar in its rightmost position will tell the user that the volume is turned up high better than a text box showing the number 11.

Use graphical controls to supplement or replace numeric displays when it will help the user to better understand or better manipulate values. Avoid using them to be cute or just for looks, except when simulation is the point, as in game programming.

Spin buttons allow the user to click up and down buttons to increase or decrease a setting. Spin buttons are input only controls, and thus are usually used together with some kind of display that indicates the value that they control: generally a text box. The spin button itself has no value property, that must be stored elsewhere. In figure 1.14, the SpinUp and SpinDown events control the value property of the text box.

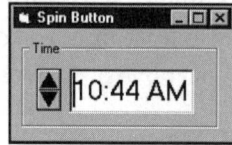

Fig. 1.14 Spin buttons used in conjunction with a text box.

Spin buttons are often used for date or time settings. Often the value affected by the spin buttons can vary depending on what value is selected. For example, the spin buttons in figure 1.14 can change the hour, minutes or AM/PM settings of the clock, depending on which is selected.

Because spin buttons only allow you to change a value one unit at a time, some other method of changing the value should be used as well. Trying to change the minutes setting of a clock from 00 to 30 by clicking on spin buttons is not a good design feature. For this situation, let the user choose between using the spin button and typing the value directly into the text box.

Spin buttons are good to use for "wraparound" values: where you wish the top value to be followed by the bottom one. For example, in using spin buttons to set the minutes of a clock, make 00 follow 59.

Sliders (see fig. 1.15) and *scroll bars* (see fig. 1.16) both can accept and display values to the user.

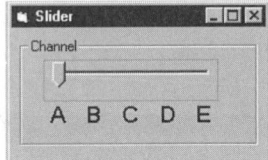

Fig. 1.15 A slider can accept and display values to the user.

They also have the advantage of presenting a visual idea of how big a value is relative to a maximum value.

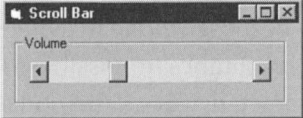

Fig. 1.16 A scroll bar also can accept and display values to the user.

Scroll bars are often used for setting values along a continuum. Volume controls and brightness level are good uses. A slider can be used the same way by removing its tick marks and setting its maximum value to a high number. Sliders can be used to good effect when emulating physical controls with which the user is familiar. They have a nice "real world" look to them.

Sliders with tick marks are best used with a limited number of values: around 15 or fewer. For choosing among discrete values, like channel settings or lines per inch, a slider can be used where a scroll bar cannot.

Progress Bars

Another control worth mentioning is the *progress bar* (see fig. 1.17) available in most versions of VB 4. Any operation that requires more than a second or two for the computer to complete can leave the user wondering if things are progressing as they should. If your program saves or loads lengthy files, or performs calculations that can take a while, you will want to include feedback on the progress of these operations.

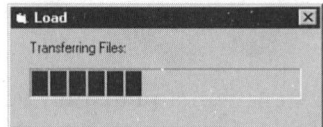

Fig. 1.17 A progress bar should be used to provide the user with feedback about time-consuming tasks.

The progress bar is best used alone in a dialog box, as shown in figure 1.17. Although it is sometimes impossible to gauge what percentage of an operation is completed, it is still helpful to give the user the impression that progress is being made.

Shortcuts

The following are several categories of shortcuts for Windows applications:

➤ Mnemonic letters that provide keyboard routes to all menu items and command buttons (used with the Alt key)

➤ Shortcut keystrokes for commonly used commands (usually used with the Ctrl key)

➤ Alternate ways of accepting choices in dialog boxes (indicated by double-clicking on the choice)

Some of these shortcuts are mandatory and some are optional. It is important to follow the standards and de facto standards that have evolved both for where to provide a shortcut and which one to use.

Applying Menu and Command Button Mnemonics

Theoretically, a user should be able to negotiate a Windows application without touching a mouse. In reality, this is usually impractical, if not impossible, but keyboard access to every menu item is a necessary part of a well-designed interface. The Visual Basic implementation is very simple. When entering the caption in the menu editor, precede the mnemonic character with an ampersand. Thus, entering a caption of "`&File`" will produce the menu name <u>F</u>ile.

Each menu name and menu item must have an underlined letter which, when typed with the Alt key, will have the same effect as clicking on that item. These are called mnemonic or access characters. Generally, the first letter of the name is used when possible. Duplication of first letters sometimes makes it impossible to use the first letter. There are also some cases where a different letter will provide a better mnemonic, such as the "x" in E<u>x</u>it.

Each menu must have a unique mnemonic character. Within a menu, each item must have a mnemonic character unique to that menu. When the first letter is unavailable, try to pick a significant consonant in the name. When that isn't possible, use any consonant or a vowel.

Similar mnemonic characters can be used for command buttons as well. Remember to check that the mnemonic character used does not duplicate one used on any of the menu names. The cancel button does not receive a mnemonic character. Instead, it is activated by pressing the Esc key. To implement this in Visual Basic, set the `Cancel Button` property to `True`.

Implementing Shortcut Keystrokes

In addition to the mnemonic character, certain menu commands should have a shortcut keystroke. These are usually implemented as Ctrl key combinations but the function keys (Del and Esc) are also used. Shortcut keystrokes differ from mnemonics in that they do not require negotiation through menu or dialog boxes to use. To use a mnemonic character, you must be able to see the title or menu item it is associated with. Shortcut keystrokes do not have this limitation.

Shortcut keystrokes are listed on the menu itself, providing an on-line reference for the user. Visual Basic implements the functionality of the keystroke and puts it on the menu for you when you enter the keystroke in the Menu Editor.

Some commands, Cut and Copy for instance, must have a shortcut keystroke. You may wish to provide shortcuts for other ones, especially those that the user will use frequently especially if the command will immediately precede or follow typing. There are, however, some commands which should not have a shortcut keystroke. Consider the possible consequences of setting Ctrl+S as a shortcut for Save. After cutting out a large section of a document and repositioning the cursor, the user could mistakenly type Ctrl+B instead of Ctrl+V to paste. Now the document has been saved minus the cut text. In general, avoid creating shortcut keystrokes for commands that cannot be revoked with the Undo command.

The standards and recommended standards for some commonly used shortcut keystrokes are listed in Table 1.2.

Table 1.2   Mnemonic Characters and Shortcut Keystrokes for Commands

Command & Mnemonic Character	Shortcut Keystroke
Bold	Ctrl+B
Cancel	Esc
Cut	Ctrl+X
Copy	Ctrl+C
Find	Ctrl+F
Help	F1
Italic	Ctrl+I
New	Ctrl+N
Open	Ctrl+O
Paste	Ctrl+V

Command & Mnemonic Character	Shortcut Keystroke
Print	Ctrl+P
Save As	Ctrl+S
Undo	Ctrl+Z

Using Double-Clicks

Instead of selecting an item in a list box or on an option button and then clicking an OK command button, most designers choose to implement the shortcut of double-clicking on the desired item to both select and then approve the choice. This is considered to be an optional shortcut but most major programs utilize it and users have come to expect it.

This shortcut is useful on Option buttons, list boxes and Simple combo boxes. Drop-down list and combo boxes do not support a double-click event since the first click makes the drop-down section disappear.

If the dialog box in question has several different controls, using this shortcut should accept all changes that were made in the dialog box, not just the one that is double-clicked. This is easy to implement by simply running the click event of the OK button when the option button or list item is double-clicked.

Helping the User at Runtime

Many users, including some real computer novices, consider paper documentation to be a last resort. They learn new programs by exploration and experimentation with occasional dips into the online help system.

A well designed interface facilitates this kind of learning. A liberal use of message boxes for information, alerts and error trapping makes a program both forgiving and more comprehensible. Providing useful online help, while not a quick or easy job, should be given as much, if not more, attention as more traditional written documentation.

Message boxes are a useful way to communicate with the user at runtime. They can be used to provide context sensitive help and information, alerts and error traps. A program with too few message boxes leaves the user wondering what is going on: How long is this sort going to take? What does "Device Error" mean? Did I remember to save that file? On the other hand, too many message boxes can frustrate the experienced user.

Try to anticipate any runtime error that the user could generate. The most common one is the user selecting a drive that is not available in drive list box. Create informative message boxes that explain to the user in clear language what is wrong and what steps need to be taken to correct it.

Any time the user is going to perform a task that will result in permanent loss of data, an alert dialog box should appear giving the user an explanation of what will happen and the option to cancel the operation. Make sure that the command button names on the alert dialog box reflect what will happen. In a message box with the text: "Installing this program will erase the file GERBIL.DOC. Do you wish to continue?" the labels "Yes" and "No" are more informative than using "OK" and "Cancel." Users sometimes associate OK buttons in message boxes as merely the button that makes the box go away.

Sometimes it is necessary to include a way to skip alert messages. In a database program that confirms whether the user wants to delete a record, it is impractical for the user to respond to this dialog box for each of 100 records being deleted. In such a case, the option to turn off the feature altogether could be included. The disadvantage is that the user will probably neglect to turn it back on, or the next user may not even realize that such an option exists. An alternative is to include an additional "Yes to All" button on the confirmation dialog box that accepts the deletion for all the chosen records. This provides a kind of one time exemption from the confirmation dialog box but it is effective the next time the user chooses to delete.

Usability Testing

Once scorned by most major software companies, usability testing has finally come of age. In rooms with one way mirrors, users are videotaped as they work their way through beta versions of software programs. Clearly, this approach is unfeasible for smaller companies and individuals writing software, but the goals of the large companies in usability testing are shared by all programmers who want their software to be used and appreciated.

Usability testing can take a very simple form. Perhaps one of the easiest and most effective ways to test a new piece of software is to sit down with an inexperienced user, and ask him to perform certain tasks. Watching where he looks for certain functions may be telling. If you instruct him to create a title and center it on the page and he tries out all of the options in the Format menu, never noticing the Alignment menu, then you may have an indication that the menu titles are not as informative as you had hoped.

A more extensive method of usability testing involves a technique called "metering." Special code is added to the beta version of your application to record the different actions taken by the user, writing it to a log file. This allows you to track wrong turnings and dead ends that the user encounters. It also allows the user to work without being observed, something that often affects user behavior.

When using this technique, you will usually want to come up with a script of tasks for the user to perform. This allows you to compare the actions of several users and also keeps the data you accumulate within manageable levels. Remember, by writing a script of actions to follow, you may overlook something that users find puzzling. Use a variety of testing methods, including soliciting free-form feedback from some "guinea-pig" users.

Of course, too much stake should not be set on one or even on a few users. The long term working habits of those who will be using the program regularly must also be considered. But, in general, usability testing can provide helpful and often surprising insight for the programmer.

From Here...

This chapter discussed some of the fundamentals of interface design, including the mindset required of a programmer to design effectively. You learned many of the standards of layout and choice of controls, as well as ways to make the program more efficient for experienced users. By designing with the user in mind, using the appropriate tools, your interfaces will be easy-to-learn, effective, and streamlined.

➤ For more information on designing applications that support several open documents, see Chapter 2, "Multiple Document Interface (MDI)."

➤ For a discusion of designing and implementing online help systems, see Chapter 18, "Developing Online Help."

➤ For information on some of the additional controls available, see Chapter 20, "OLE Controls, Add-Ins, and 32-bit DLLs."

2

Multiple Document Interface (MDI)

by Steve Potts

The *Multiple Document Interface (MDI)* is a powerful feature of Windows programming that is fully supported in Visual Basic 4. MDI programs differ from ordinary programs in that a hierarchical relationship exists between one of the forms, the MDI form, and some or all of the other forms, instead of the common peer-to-peer form relationships in ordinary Visual Basic programs. These subordinate forms are called *child forms*.

In a MDI program, one form is designated as the *MDI form,* also known as the *parent form.* This form provides the workspace for the rest of the application's forms. The most common use of MDI is to provide multiple documents of the same type without having to decide how many of them to create in advance.

This chapter describes the distinguishing features of MDI applications and possible uses of this technology. The topics covered in this chapter are:

➤ Creating an MDI application

➤ Managing icons to the application

➤ Using object variables for child forms

➤ Using New and Me keywords

➤ Adding a list of the child windows to the MDI form's menu

➤ Adding a Toolbar, status bar, and Tooltips to the MDI form

At the end of the chapter, you will see some of the uses of MDI technology in two sample applications.

MDI Application Behavior

Programs like Microsoft Word and Excel are MDI applications. When using Microsoft Word, a user creates a document. He may also want to create additional documents without closing the first one.

MDI child forms become windows at runtime and obey the following rules:

➤ All child windows are displayed with the parent window's internal area or workspace. They cannot be moved outside of this area.

➤ When a child window is minimized, its icon appears in the parent window, not on the desktop.

➤ When an MDI parent window is minimized, the parent window and all of its child windows are represented by a single icon that is placed on the desktop. When the MDI application is restored, the parent window and all of the child windows are restored to exactly the same layout as when it was minimized.

➤ When you maximize a child form, it fills the entire work area of the parent window, and the parent's title bar displays both the name of the parent and the name of the maximized child form.

➤ If the child window has a menu, it will be displayed in the parent window's menu bar when it is activated but not in the child's.

➤ You cannot directly place controls on the MDI form unless they support the `Align` property. Only the Picture control among the standard Visual Basic 4 controls qualifies in this way.

These rules allow for a tighter integration between child windows and their parent than would be possible using simple peer forms.

Using Visual Basic to Create MDI Applications

Visual Basic 4 fully supports the creation of MDI applications. The following example creates a very simple MDI program.

To create an MDI application, follow these steps:

1. Choose New Project from the File menu.

2. Choose MDI Form from the Insert menu to create the parent form. A new form appears with the word "`MDIForm1`" in the title bar. The Project window will now contain the original form and one MDI form, as shown in figure 2.1.

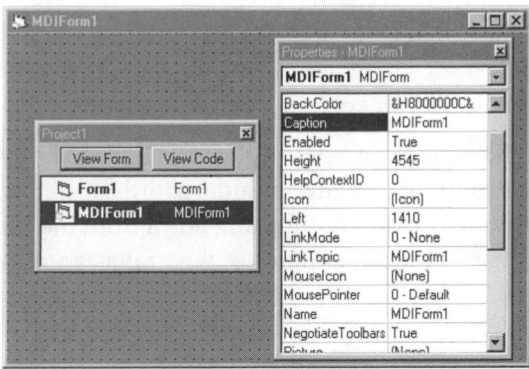

Fig. 2.1 The Project window shows MDI forms differently.

Observe that the icon next to the original form `Form1` is different from the MDI form `MDIForm1` in the Project window. The MDI icon has an extra little window beside the big one. This lets you differentiate at a glance between the two types of forms.

3. Set the MDIChild property of Form1 to True. This establishes the parent/child relationship between MDIForm1 and Form1. This occurs because only one MDI parent form can exist in an application. Therefore, if a form's MDIChild property is set to True, it must be a child of the one and only MDI form in the application. Notice in figure 2.2 that Form1's icon in the Project window has changed from what it was in figure 2.1.

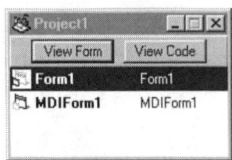

Fig. 2.2 The icon for Form1 has changed.

The icon for Form1 looks a lot like the icon for MDIForm1. The only difference is that the large part of the icon is grayed out in the child form, and the small part of the icon is grayed out in the parent form.

4. Run the application and prove to yourself that Form1 is contained within MDIForm1 and cannot be moved outside of its boundaries, except when you are in development mode.

5. Not all forms in an MDI application have to be child forms. Your application may include standard forms also. To illustrate this, create a new form by choosing Form from the Insert menu. This will change the appearance of the Project window to look like figure 2.3.

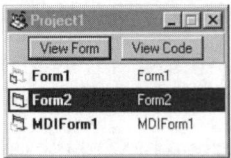

Fig. 2.3 Non-child forms have different icons in the Project window.

Notice that Form2 has a traditional icon beside it in the Project window. This indicates that no parent-child relationship exists between Form2 and MDIForm1. Run the application again to prove that Form2 behaves differently from Form1 in that you can move it freely outside the work area of MDIForm1. To do this, you will need to add a command button to Form1 and add the following code to its event procedure:

```
Private Sub Command1_Click()
    Form2.Show
End Sub
```

Observe that Form1 displayed inside of MDIForm1 immediately when you started the application. The reason for this is that Form1 is listed as the Startup Form in the Project Options dialog box, as shown in figure 2.4.

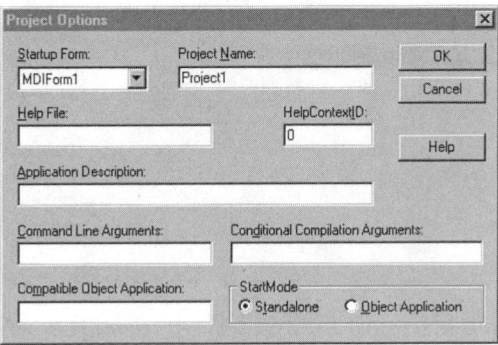

Fig. 2.4 The Project Options dialog box specifies which form appears first.

When Windows obtains the command to load an MDI child form, it automatically loads the MDI parent form so that the MDI rules are observed. When the MDI parent form is loaded as the Startup form, Windows does not need to load Form1 until instructed to do so by the code.

Managing Icons in MDI Applications

As stated earlier, MDI child forms live entirely within the boundaries of their MDI parent forms. This is true even when the child form becomes an icon. Note that `Form2`'s `MDIChild` property was changed to `True` before figure 2.5 was created. You can place these icons that represent child forms anywhere in the MDI parent's window, as shown in figure 2.5.

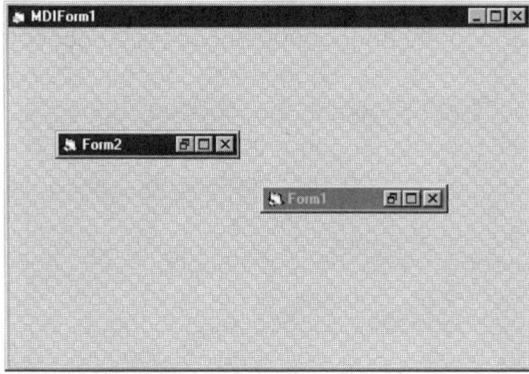

Fig. 2.5 Place MDI child icons anywhere in the MDI parent form's workspace.

The behavior of the MDI parent form is interesting when it becomes an icon. The entire application collapses into one icon that is placed at the bottom of the screen. All of the MDI child windows and icons disappear, leaving only an icon for the MDI parent form. This can give the illusion that the child windows or processes have terminated. When the MDI parent form is restored, however, all of the child forms and icons return to their places on the MDI parent form exactly as they were before.

Using Object Variables

Thus far, the MDI applications that we've shown have been fairly simple and offer little advantage over simple forms. By using an Object variable, you can create any number of MDI child forms at runtime. This is important because it lets your users decide how many MDI child windows they need to open without having to worry about some arbitrary limitations that you've placed on them. For example, suppose you create an MDI parent form to perform simple word processing. Each document will be contained in one MDI child form. If you allow few of them, you risk user frustration when users can't open as many forms as they really need. If you make the number huge, you bloat the size of your application and hurt performance (see Chapter 21, "Optimizing VB Code," for more on this).

Visual Basic 4 provides a solution to this problem through a special kind of variable called the *Object variable*. An Object variable can be either a `Form` object or `Control` object. In order to create a `Form` object at runtime, the syntax is as follows:

```
Dim Form1 as New Form1
```

The New Keyword

This `New` keyword is used to create an instance of a specific form type. Notice that, in the previous section, the `Dim` statement referred to `Form1`, and not to the generic form. The reason for this is to specify which controls, properties, event procedures, and subroutines will be created for this form. Generic forms are not useful at runtime because they have nothing associated with them. In the case of a word processing application, the new MDI child forms that the user creates need to be word processing application forms, not just blank forms with no code.

Likewise, you can create an array of `Form1` by the following syntax:

```
Dim FormArr(5) As New Form1
```

This code creates five forms at runtime. The following application creates an array of forms at runtime and displays them when the MDI parent form is loaded at startup:

1. Create a new project by choosing New Project from the File menu.

2. Create the MDI parent form by choosing MDI Form from the Insert menu.

3. Change the `MDIChild` property of `Form1` to `True`.

4. Add a command button to `Form1` with the following code:

```
Private Sub Command1_Click()
 Form1.Caption = "Form X"
End Sub
```

5. Add the following code to the `Form_Load` event procedure on the MDI parent form:

```
Private Sub MDIForm_Load()
    Dim Frm_Array(5) As New Form1
    Dim I As Integer
    For I = 1 To UBound(Frm_Array)
      Frm_Array(I).Show
    Next I
End Sub
```

Notice the use of the `UBound` function, which takes an array as its argument and returns the largest valid subscript for that array.

6. Run the program.

7. Click on a command button on one of the five forms that are arranged in a cascaded fashion. Observe that the caption in the Form on the upper-left changes but that none of the other forms' captions changes at all. This occurs because all of the command button event procedures refer to `Form1` by name. The original `Form1` is known by this name at runtime.

The Me Keyword

`Me` is a reserved word in Visual Basic 4 and is known to every subroutine and procedure in a form. For C++ programmers, it is the same as the

This operator. When several instances of the same form exist, it represents the instance that is currently being executed in code. We can modify the New keyword example to take advantage of the Me keyword.

The following application creates an array of forms at runtime, displays them when the MDI parent form is loaded at Startup, and employs the Me keyword to allow each form's code to apply to itself:

1. Create a new project by choosing New Project from the File menu.

2. Create the MDI parent form by choosing MDI Form from the Insert menu just as you did in the previous example.

3. Change the MDIForm property of Form1 to True.

4. Add a command button to Form1 with the following code:

```
Private Sub Command1_Click()
 Me.Caption = "Form X"
End Sub
```

Notice the Me keyword before the property caption.

5. Add the following code to the Form_Load event procedure on the MDI parent form.

```
Private Sub MDIForm_Load()
    Dim Frm_Array(5) As New Form1
    Dim I As Integer
    For I = 1 To UBound(Frm_Array)
      Frm_Array(I).Show
    Next I
End Sub
```

6. Run the program and observe that each form's code now changes the caption of its own form and not Form1's caption as in the previous example. The output looks like figure 2.6.

7. Click on one of the command buttons on one of the five forms that are arranged in a cascaded fashion. Observe that the caption in the form on the upper-left remains unchanged but that Form X appears on the other forms' captions as each command button is clicked.

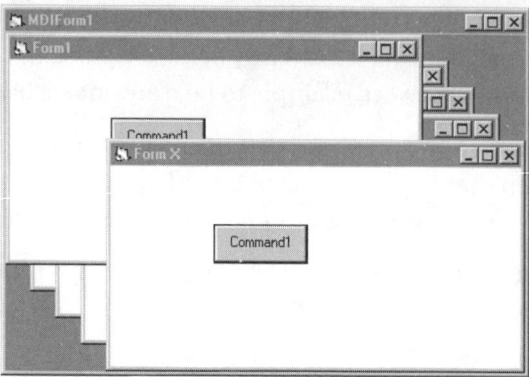

Fig. 2.6 MDI child forms can use the `Me` keyword.

Enhancing MDI Applications

Now that you understand how to create child forms, you will want to produce full-scale professional applications. This section will show you how to add additional features that add power to your applications. These features flatten the learning curve for new users.

Adding Menus

Most of the Windows applications that you buy contain a menu structure. The menu bar provides a compact way to provide numerous commands to the user.

When using MDI applications like Microsoft Word, you will notice some unique menu behavior. When no child window is open, one set of menus is present as shown in figure 2.7.

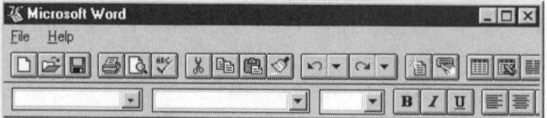

Fig. 2.7 Microsoft Word has a small menu when no document is open.

When a document is opened, however, the menu changes to show a full complement of functionality. This kind of program behavior distinguishes professional applications from the ones written by a guy who just bought a computer. In fact, this is just another feature of MDI applications. Figure 2.8 shows the MDI child's menu bar.

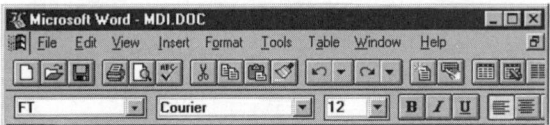

Fig. 2.8 The MDI child's menu bar takes over.

Active Windows

When an MDI child window is active, its menu bar will appear on the MDI parent window instead of the MDI parent's own menu bar. The following example shows how this works:

1. Create a new project by choosing New Project from the File menu.

2. Create the MDI parent form by choosing MDI Form from the Insert menu just as you did in the previous example.

3. Change the MDIChild property of Form1 to True.

4. Add a menu to Form1 with the following items on it:

        &Draw
        &Write
        &Paint

5. Add the following menu to MDIForm1:

        &File
        &Window
        &Help

   In Design mode, your program will look like figure 2.9.

   Notice that both the MDI parent window and the MDI child window have normal menus on them.

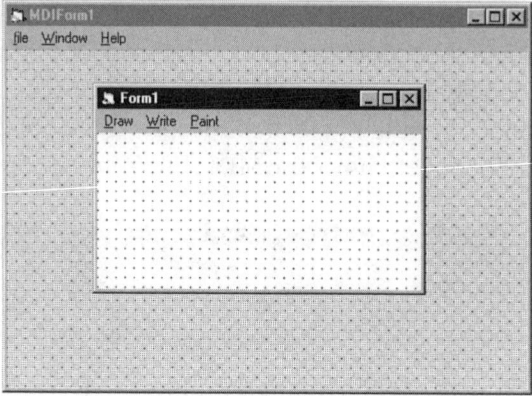

Fig. 2.9 In Design mode, the menus appear on the MDI child forms.

6. Run the application and observe that when `Form1` is loaded, it takes over the menu of the MDI parent with its own menu as shown in figure 2.10.

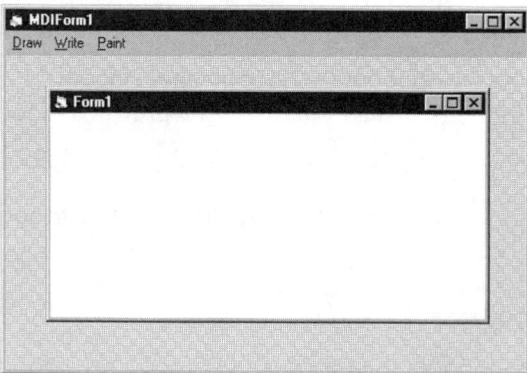

Fig. 2.10 The MDI child window menu takes over the MDI parent window menu when activated.

7. Next, add a second MDI child form, `Form2`, to the application by choosing Form from the Insert menu.

8. Add the following menu to `Form2`:

```
&Import
&Export
&Transport
```

In Development mode, your application now looks like figure 2.11.

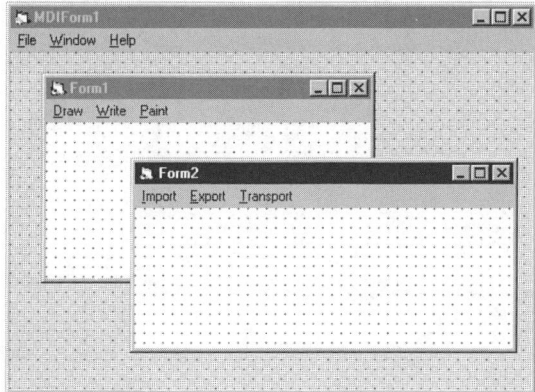

Fig. 2.11 MDI child forms can use different menus.

Notice that all three forms have a different menu bar.

9. Run the program with the following code added to the MDI parent form:

```
Private Sub MDIForm_Load()
      Form2.Show
End Sub
```

This code is necessary to display both forms at the same time. Notice that when `Form1` had the focus, the screen looked like figure 2.10. When the focus changed to `Form2`, however, the menu on `MDIForm1` changed to contain the menu from `Form2`.

This mapping of all menus to one location on the MDI parent form preserves precious window real estate. As applications become more ambitious, this becomes more important.

Window Lists

You have probably used the Window List provided by Microsoft Word or other MDI applications This is a location on a menu that lists all of the MDI child windows currently in memory. Figure 2.12 shows the Window List for Microsoft Word 6.0.

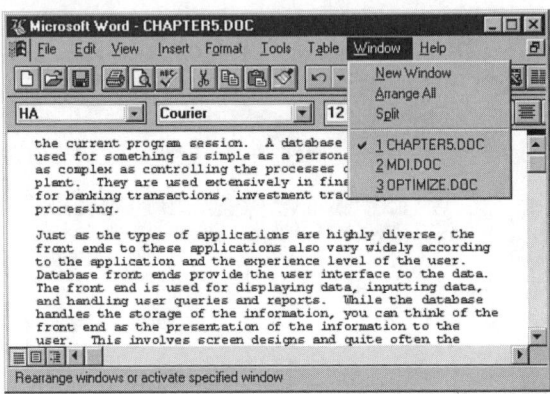

Fig. 2.12 The Window List shows active MDI child windows.

This list gives your users a quick way to switch back and forth between active MDI child windows whenever they need to do so. As we've come to expect, there is an easy way to add this feature to MDI applications. You can add this feature to your application by following these simple steps:

1. Continue with the same application that you were working with in the previous exercise. Add a Window menu item to both `Form1` and `Form2`.

2. While still in the Menu Editor, click on the check box labeled WindowList with `&Window` selected, as shown in figure 2.13.

   Notice that the WindowList box is checked. You must do this for each MDI child window's menu bar. This is because any of these menus could be in control of the MDI parent window's menu bar when your user wants to use this feature.

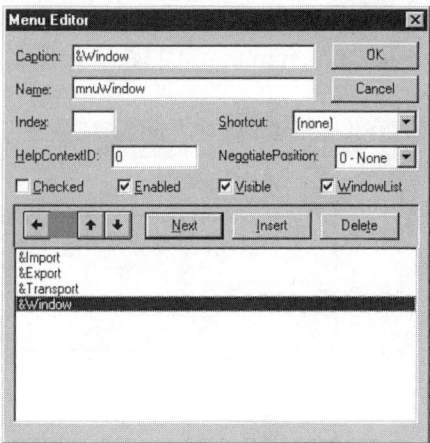

Fig. 2.13 Check the WindowList box in the Menu Editor.

3. Run the program and choose Window. Your program now contains a list of all active MDI child windows, as shown in figure 2.14.

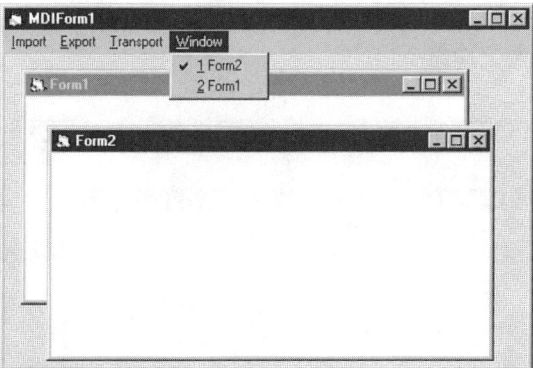

Fig. 2.14 You can change an MDI child window by using WindowList on the Menu Editor.

The menu selection chosen to hold the WindowList may list any other menu selections that you choose to provide. The following exercise will demonstrate how this works:

1. Modify the previous example's forms. De-select the WindowList check box, as shown in figure 2.15.

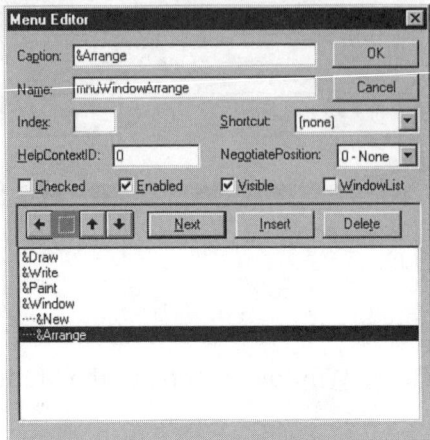

Fig. 2.15 The WindowList menu can contain other selections.

2. Run the program and observe that the Window menu now contains other selections as well as the Window list, as shown in figure 2.16.

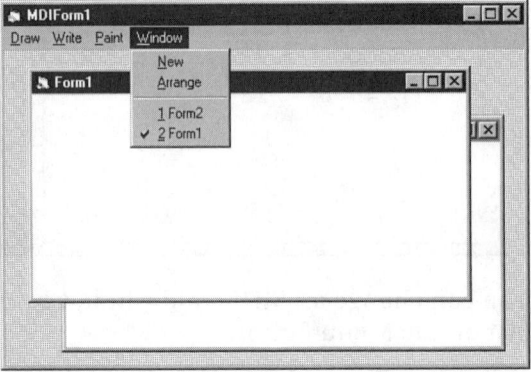

Fig. 2.16 The Window menu has other menu selections as well as the Window list.

Adding this Window list to your applications' menus will make your programs look and feel more professional.

Adding Toolbars

The addition of a Toolbar to your application will also enhance its appearance and utility for your users. Toolbars provide a quick invocation of a subset of the items in the menu bar. They use icons instead of words to help the users learn how to use your application more quickly.

When deciding which icons to use in your Toolbars, be sure to look at some of the more popular applications like Word, Excel, Borland C++, and Visual Basic itself for ideas. One of the current problems with Toolbars is that each vendor picks icons independent of the other vendors. Thus, users must learn many more icons. You can do your part by making your applications look like one of the other major vendor's applications whenever practical.

To risk stating the obvious, make sure your icons also have some association to the action that will occur. This seems fundamental, but a surprising number of icons confuse users by their lack of intuitive quality. Another must for Toolbars are *Tooltips*. These are the little yellow flags that magically appear over icons in Visual Basic 4 and other leading software packages. In the section "Adding Tooltips" later in this chapter, we will create a set of Tooltips to show you how.

MDI parent forms place severe restrictions on what kind of controls you can place on its workspace. Only those controls, stock or custom, that support the `Align` property can be used in this way. Of the stock properties of Visual Basic 4, only the Picture control qualifies. Because the Picture control can serve as a container for other controls, we will place one of them on the MDI parent form and then place the other controls on it. Follow these steps to accomplish this:

1. Create an MDI application with a parent form, `MDIForm1`, and three child forms `Form1`, `Form2`, and `Form3`.

2. Add a Picture Box control to MDIForm1 named Toolbar and set its Align property to 1 - Align Top.

3. Add the following four Image controls to the Toolbar:

Image1	1 – Fixed Single	True	HANDSHAK.ICO
Image2	1 – Fixed Single	True	NET01.ICO
Image3	1 – Fixed Single	True	PHONE.ICO
Image4	1 – Fixed Single	True	NET09A.ICO

All of the icons are in the C:\VB\ICONS\COMM directory in which C: is the drive where you installed Visual Basic 4.

4. Add the Listing 2.1 code to each Image control (buttons 1–4):

Listing 2.1 PICBOX1.BAS—Adding a Toolbar

```
   The code for each image control
Private Sub Image1_Click()
    Form1.Show
End Sub

Private Sub Image2_Click()
    Form2.Show
End Sub

Private Sub Image3_Click()
    Form3.Show
End Sub

Private Sub Image4_Click()
    Form1.Hide
    Form2.Hide
    Form3.Hide
End Sub
```

5. Run the program and prove to yourself that these Image controls now behave like buttons. When you click on them, their corresponding child form receives the focus. When you click on the fourth one, all of the child windows are hidden. Figure 2.17 shows the program running with Form3 displayed.

Fig. 2.17 The icons on the Toolbar act as buttons.

Child windows can also contain working Toolbars. To create one, follow the steps from the previous example to create an application with an MDI parent that contains a Toolbar. Add a Toolbar to the MDI child form. The result will be a form that contains a working Toolbar, as shown in figure 2.18.

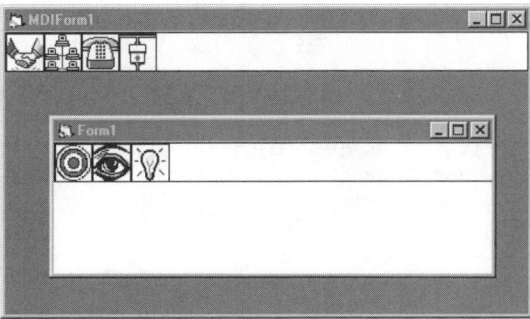

Fig. 2.18 MDI child forms may also contain Toolbars.

Adding a Status Bar

Another common feature of commercial systems is the status bar at the bottom of the window. This feature is so common that many people assume it is part of the window like the minimize button. The status bar can be a very useful device. For example, the status bar in

Microsoft Word 6.0 tells the user the page number, section number, number of pages, line number, column number, the time, and the status of several Word 6.0 flags. To add a status bar to a form, follow these steps:

1. Create a new project by choosing New from the File menu.

2. Add a Picture Box control to the form.

3. Set the `Align` property of the Picture Box to `2 - At Bottom`.

4. Add a text box that completely covers the Picture Box. Set the `Backcolor` property to the same gray used in Windows 95 for the window border (`&H000000C&`) to make it the same color as the rest of the window.

5. Set the `Borderstyle` property to `0 - None`. This will blend the status bar's sides into the window seamlessly.

6. Add three forms to the application: `Form1`, `Form2`, and `Form3`. Notice that the status bar on the `MDIForm` has nothing on it.

7. Add the Listing 2.2 code to the application:

Listing 2.2   STATBAR1.BAS—A Status Bar Program

```
Private Sub MDIForm_Load()
   Form2.Show
   Form3.Show
End Sub

Private Sub Form_Load()
  MDIForm1.Text1 = "Form1 Now Active"
End Sub

Private Sub Form_GotFocus()
    MDIForm1.Text1 = "Form1 Now Active"
End Sub

Private Sub Form_GotFocus()
    MDIForm1.Text1 = "Form2 Now Active"
End Sub

Private Sub Form_GotFocus()
    MDIForm1.Text1 = "Form3 Now Active"
End Sub
```

8. Run the application and see that whenever a form is loaded, a message to that effect appears on the MDIForm status bar, as shown in figure 2.19.

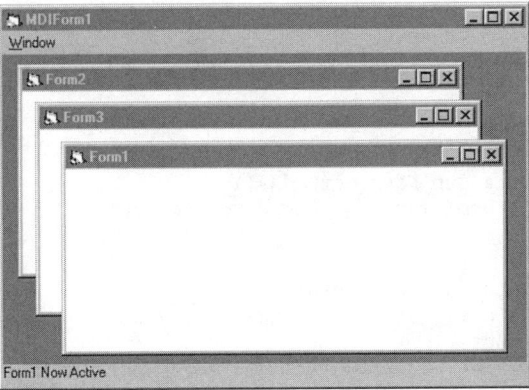

Fig. 2.19 The status bar displays messages to the user.

As in Microsoft Word 6.0, many different pieces of information are on the same status bar. You can accomplish this by placing several Text Box controls on the same Picture Box control. Add three additional Text Box controls (Text2, Text3, and Text4) to the application. Then add the following code to the Picture Box control:

The code for MDIForm1:

```
Private Sub MDIForm_Load()
    Form2.Show
    Form3.Show
End Sub
```

The code for Form1:

```
Private Sub Form_GotFocus()
    MDIForm1.Text1 = "Form1 Now Active"
End Sub

Private Sub Form_Load()
    MDIForm1.Text1 = "Form1 Now Active"
    MDIForm1.Text2 = "Form1 is Loaded"
End Sub
```

The code for Form2:

```
Private Sub Form_GotFocus()
    MDIForm1.Text1 = "Form2 Now Active"
End Sub

Private Sub Form_Load()
    MDIForm1.Text3 = "Form2 is Loaded"
End Sub
```

The code for Form3:

```
Private Sub Form_GotFocus()
  MDIForm1.Text1 = "Form3 Now Active"
End Sub

Private Sub Form_Load()
  MDIForm1.Text4 = "Form3 is Loaded"
End Sub
```

Running this program displays the status of all forms at all times at the bottom of the screen, along with information about which form is active or has focus. Figure 2.20 shows this application running.

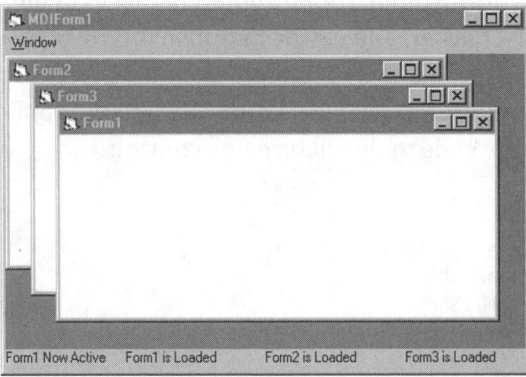

Fig. 2.20 The status bar can display numerous messages.

Take care not to turn the status bar into another piece of clutter on the screen. However, judicious use of status bars to display important information can really make your software valuable to your users.

Changing Form Captions

Several improvements to this application are needed. First, the caption on all of the MDI child forms is Form1. Showing the filename would be more useful instead. To make this happen, just change the following code in Form1:

```
Private Sub Form_Load()
    CommonDialog1.Action = 1
    Me.Caption = CommonDialog1.FileName
    Me.Image1.Picture = LoadPicture(CommonDialog1.FileName)
End Sub
```

The value returned by the Open dialog box is assigned to the caption of the Me form. In both cases where Me is used in the Form_Load event procedure, the program behaves the same way whether the Me keyword is present or not. Many programmers prefer to insert it to avoid any confusion over which Caption (or Image1) control that this line of code is really affecting. Figure 2.21 shows the result of this change, which enhances the usefulness of the program.

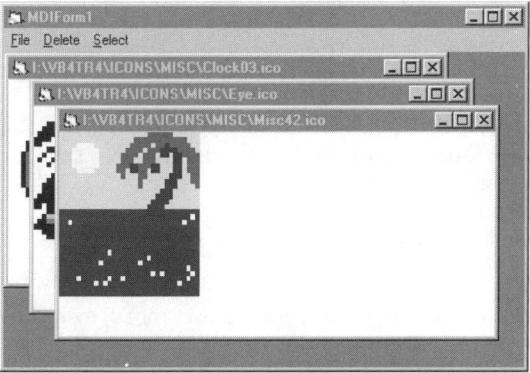

Fig. 2.21 The filename is displayed in the form's title bar.

Adding Tooltips

Adding Tooltips to your Toolbars is almost a requirement in a world with no standards for Toolbar icons. Tooltips normally pop-up after the mouse pointer has rested over an icon for one second or more. You have probably been pleased to find those little yellow hints popping up at least once in the Visual Basic 4 user interface. Windows 95 makes good use of these aids also.

The following steps demonstrate how to add Tooltips to a Toolbar:

1. Create an MDI application that has a Toolbar with three icons.

   These icons are found in the directory C:\VB\ICONS\INDUSTRY. Their names are FACTORY.ICO, PLANE.ICO, ROCKET.ICO.

2. Add three Label controls (Label1, Label2, and Label3).

3. Add the Listing 2.3 code to MDIForm1:

Listing 2.3   TOOLTIP1.BAS—Adding Tooltips to a Program

```
Dim intButton As Integer

'When the mouse pointer is positioned over the factory
Private Sub Image1_MouseMove(Button As Integer, Shift As _
  Integer, X As Single, Y As Single)
  intButton = 1
  Timer1.Enabled = True
End Sub

'When the mouse pointer is positioned over the plane
Private Sub Image2_MouseMove(Button As Integer, Shift As _
  Integer, X As Single, Y As Single)
  intButton = 2
  Timer1.Enabled = True
End Sub

'When the mouse pointer is positioned over the rocket
Private Sub Image3_MouseMove(Button As Integer, Shift As _
  Integer, X As Single, Y As Single)
  intButton = 3
  Timer1.Enabled = True
End Sub

'When the mouse moves off of a button, clear all Tooltips
Private Sub Picture1_MouseMove(Button As Integer, _
Shift As Integer, X As Single, Y As Single)
```

```
 TipClear
 Timer1.Enabled = False
End Sub

'When the timer goes off, call the sub which displays
Private Sub Timer1_Timer()
 DisplayToolTip
End Sub

Sub DisplayToolTip()
' Clear Tooltips so two don't show at once
  TipClear
'Display the right Tooltip based on the mouse position
  Select Case intButton
  Case Is = 1
     Label1.Visible = True
  Case Is = 2
     Label2.Visible = True
  Case Is = 3
     Label3.Visible = True
  End Select
End Sub

' Clear all Tooltips from the screen
Sub TipClear()
 Label1.Visible = False
 Label2.Visible = False
 Label3.Visible = False
End Sub
```

The strategy behind this code is to react to all mouse events and display a Tooltip if the mouse sits over a button for one second or more. In a production system, you would probably use one label for the whole screen and change both its screen position and caption whenever necessary. The principle is the same with either strategy. The running program looks like figure 2.22.

Tooltips add another professional touch to your programs. They also flatten the learning curve for new users by allowing them a quick way to discover what the icons on the Toolbar mean.

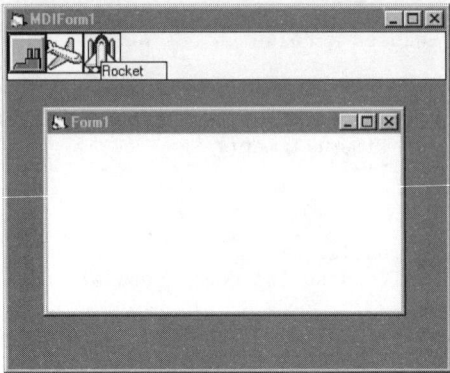

Fig. 2.22 Tooltips are displayed because of `MouseMove` events.

Creating an Icon Selection Program

Now that we have covered the fundamental approach to creating MDI applications and some enhancements, we are ready for some almost real examples of useful MDI applications. The first of these is an icon selection program. It is "almost real" because it contains the code to work well, but it does not have any of the error handling code that a commercial application would require. Start by following these steps:

1. Create a new project by choosing New Project from the File menu.

2. Add an MDI form by choosing MDI Form from the Insert menu.

3. Make `Form1` an MDI child form by changing the `MDIChild` property to `True`.

4. Make `MDIForm1` the Startup form by Choosing Project Options from the Tools menu.

5. Set the `AutoShowChild` property of `MDIForm1` to `False`. This property tells Visual Basic to load in `Form1` in automatically. In this case, we don't want to load any forms until we are ready.

6. Add the following menu structure to `MDIForm1`:

```
&File        mnuFile
----&New        mnuFileNew
----&End        mnuFileEnd
```

7. Add the following code to `MDIForm1`:

```
' When the New menu selection is selected, create a new
' form and show it.
Private Sub MnuFileNew_Click()
    Dim NewIconForm As New Form1
    NewIconForm.Show
End Sub

' When the End menu selection is selected, terminate the
' application
Private Sub mnuFileEnd_Click()
    End
End Sub
```

The MDI parent form simply creates a new form and then displays it. The MDI child forms do the rest of the work. `MDIForm1` now has a File New and End.

The next task will be to add the MDI child form, menu, and code.

8. Add the following controls to `Form1` adding the property values on the right to the control named on the left:

Control Name	Type	Properties
Image1	Image	Stretch = True Height = 2000 Width = 2000
CommonDialog1	CommonDialog	(none)

9. Add the Listing 2.4 code to Form1:

Listing 2.4   ICONSEL1.BAS—Selecting an Icon

```
' As soon as the form loads, find out which icon the user
' wants in it
Private Sub Form_Load()
```

continues

Listing 2.4   Continued

```
' Action = 1 means show the open common dialog
  CommonDialog1.Action = 1

' Load the icon into the Image1 control using the result
' of the common dialog session
' The LoadPicture function retrieves a picture file from
' disk and puts it on the control
' The keyword Me refers to the instance of Form1 that is
' under execution
  Me.Image1.Picture = LoadPicture(CommonDialog1.FileName)

End Sub


'End this program
Private Sub mnuFileEnd_Click()
     End
End Sub

'Create a new form
Private Sub MnuFileNew_Click()

' The new form allocates memory dynamically for a form
  Dim NewIconForm As New Form1

' Showing the form causes it to be created and loaded
' onto the screen
  NewIconForm.Show
End Sub

' Unload the active form from memory
Private Sub mnuDelete_Click()
   Unload Me
End Sub

' When the Select menu selection is chosen, display the
' filename of the chosen icon in a message box
Private Sub mnuSelect_Click()
x = MsgBox("You Selected " + CommonDialog1.FileName)
End Sub
```

10. Run the program and observe its behavior. When New is chosen from the File menu, a dialog box appears as shown in figure 2.23.

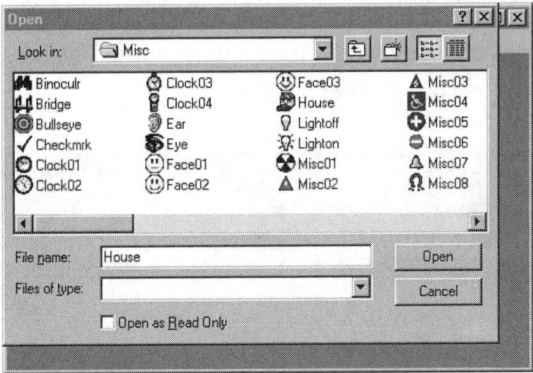

Fig. 2.23 The Open dialog box is used to choose an icon.

The icon directory displayed is located at C:\VB\ICONS\MISC where C: is the installation drive for Visual Basic 4. Pick an icon that you want to display and click the Open button. This will load an icon into the `Image1` control on `Form1`, or more exactly the `Me` form. The result of this is displayed in figure 2.24.

Fig. 2.24 The selected icon is loaded into the `Image1` control.

The advantage of the MDI application is its capability to create a user-defined number of MDI child forms that hold enlarged icons in this application. This is operationally superior to preallocating a certain number of them. Figure 2.25 shows the application with three MDI child forms open at the same time. This is the normal usage of this application, and it gives the user a way of looking at several icons in order to choose one of them.

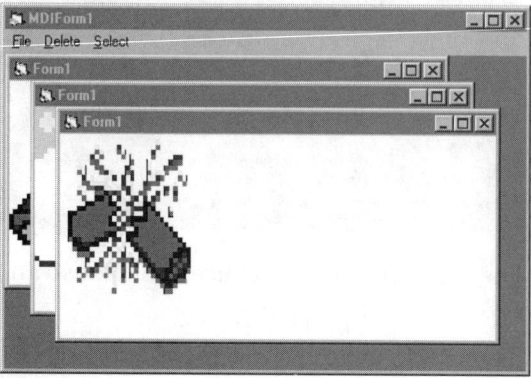

Fig. 2.25 The user can examine several icons to choose the one that he wants.

Finally, the user selects one of the icons. In this case, a stub is used that displays the name of the icon file which the user selected in a message box, as shown in figure 2.26.

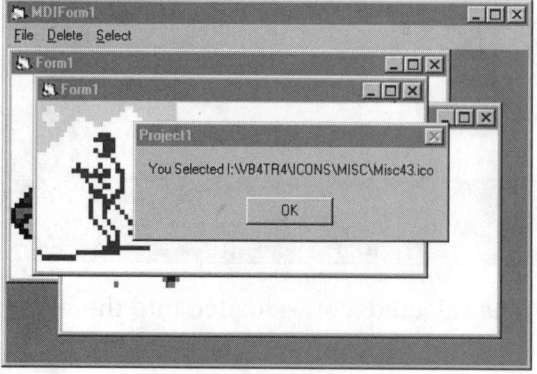

Fig. 2.26 The name of the selected icon file is available for use in your application.

Matching Icon and Window Size

Another problem with this program is that the MDI child window size doesn't match the size of the icon. The reason for this is that the `BorderStyle` property of `Form1` is set to `2 - Sizeable`. This means that Windows sets the size of the window and that the `Height` and `Width` properties of the MDI child form are ignored. Change the `BorderStyle` of `Form1` to `1 - Fixed Single`. Set `Form1`'s `Height` property to `3,000` and the `Width` to `2,000`. Figure 2.27 shows the result.

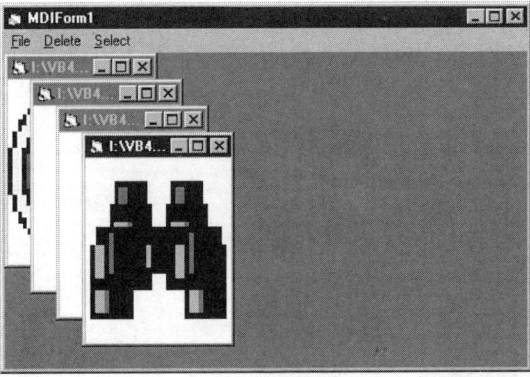

Fig. 2.27 The size of the MDI child window now matches the size of the enlarged icons.

This improves the appearance of the application significantly. For systems with so many windows, users need a mechanism for arranging icons, tiling, and cascading the windows. To add this functionality to the program, you need to add a <u>W</u>indow menu to the MDI parent form that has the following selections:

&Cascade	mnuWindowCascade
&Tile	mnuWindowTile
&ArrangeIcons	mnuWindowArrangeIcons

Just for laughs, check the <u>W</u>indowList selection for the <u>W</u>indow menu. Now add the following code to the `Form1` code window:

```
Private Sub mnuWindowArrangeIcons_Click()
    MDIForm1.Arrange vbArrangeIcons
End Sub

Private Sub mnuWindowCascade_Click()
    MDIForm1.Arrange vbCascade
End Sub

Private Sub mnuWindowTile_Click()
    MDIForm1.Arrange vbTileVertical
End Sub
```

All three of these event procedures use the same method: `Arrange`. The words `vbTileVertical`, `vbCascase`, and `VbArrangeIcons` are all constants defined by the system. The <u>W</u>indow menu provides a convenient place to invoke this method. Figure 2.28 shows the result when you tile the MDI application.

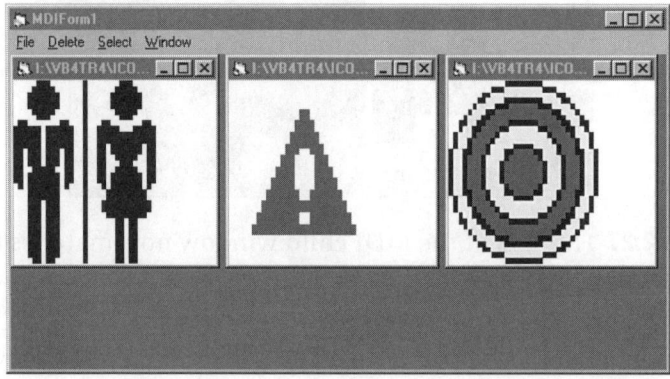

Fig. 2.28 You can tile the application using the `Arrange` method.

Figure 2.29 shows many interesting features of this application. Notice the <u>W</u>indowList at the bottom of the <u>W</u>indow menu. This resulted from checking the <u>W</u>indowList check box on the Menu Editor dialog box. Notice also that the cascaded MDI child windows look like they do normally. In other words, the child windows are cascaded, by default, upon creation.

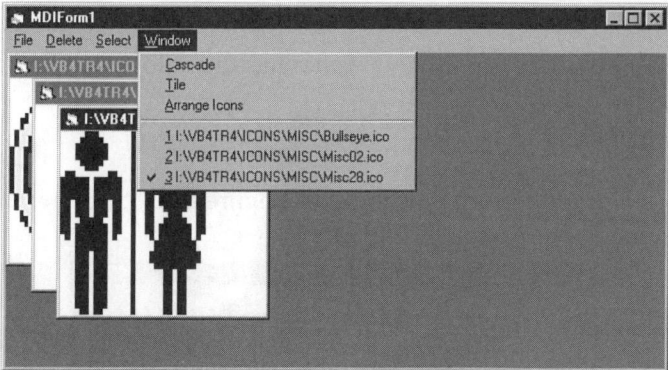

Fig. 2.29 Cascading the MDI child windows can also be done with the `Arrange` method.

Finally, when you iconify the child windows by clicking the iconify button (the one next to the X), the icons appear on the MDI parent form along the bottom of the window and not on your Windows workspace.

Creating a Text Editor

Another type of application that often needs several identical window types is a word processing system, in which a user commonly cuts text from one document and pastes it to another on the same screen.

The next application we'll create will be an MDI word processor also, but with far fewer features. To create this application, follow these steps:

1. Choose New Project from the File menu.

2. Choose MDI Form from the Insert menu.

3. Turn `Form1` into a child form by changing the value of the MDIChild property to `True`.

4. Create a text box on `Form1` called `Text1`. Set its `Text` property to blanks, its `MultiLine` property to `True`, and its position (`Top`, `Left`) to `0,0`.

5. Set the `Caption` property of both forms to blank.

6. Add a menu to MDI`Form1` that has the following items:

```
&File              mnuFile

---&New            mnuFileNew
```

The application now looks like figure 2.30.

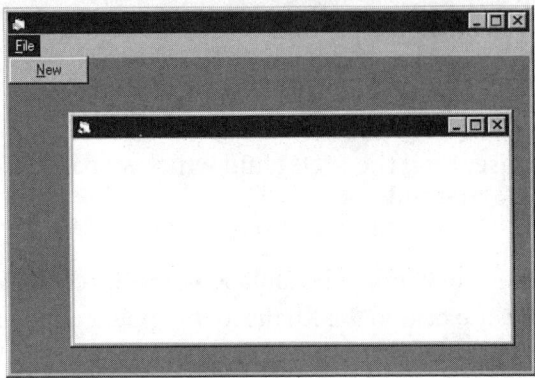

Fig. 2.30 The application has one MDI child form.

7. Add the following code to the application:

```
' This event procedure creates a new instance of Form1
Private Sub mnuFileNew_Click()
    Dim NewForm As New Form1
    NewForm.Show
End Sub

' This event procedure causes the text box to fill the
' whole window upon creation
Private Sub Form_Resize()
    Text1.Height = ScaleHeight
    Text1.Width = ScaleWidth
End Sub
```

8. Run the program, create three new forms, and type something different on each of them. You can see how this application is starting to look like a real word-processing system. Figure 2.31 shows what the system should look like at this point.

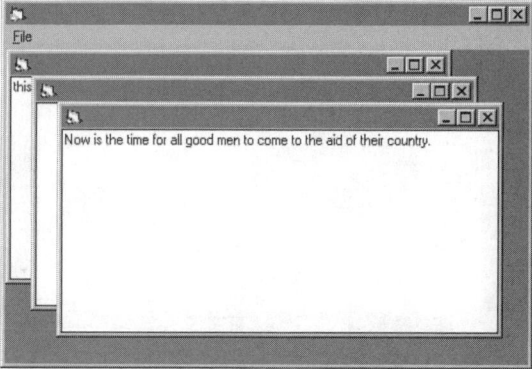

Fig. 2.31 The text box acts like a word-processing document when it fills the form.

One feature of a word-processing system is its capability to copy text to a Clipboard. We can add this capability to this application via a menu selection.

1. Add the following menu to the `&File` menu on your form:

```
----&Copy   mnuFileCopy
```

2. Add the following code to this menu selection:

```
Private Sub mnuFileCopy_Click()
    Clipboard.SetText ActiveForm.ActiveControl.SelText
End Sub
```

Now, your user can highlight a piece of text and copy it to the Clipboard by choosing Edit, Copy or by pressing Ctrl+C to copy and Ctrl+V to Paste. This is illustrated in figure 2.32.

This application shows what is possible with MDI technology.

Fig. 2.32 You can copy text to the Clipboard using the Copy menu selection.

From Here...

In this chapter, you were introduced to concepts and strategies associated with the Multiple Document Interface. You learned how to add an MDI parent form to an application. You also learned how to specify that another form in the application is a child of the MDI parent form.

The concepts of object variables were introduced along with the New and Me keywords. Using these devices, you can create an indefinite number of MDI child forms.

We also covered the topic of menus in MDI applications. You learned that all menus display on the MDI parent's menu bar during program execution. You also learned how to add a list of all child windows to the menu bar.

We then covered the creation of a Toolbar. In this section, you learned how Toolbars are created and what code is required to implement them.

The status bar and Tooltips were explained next. These features make your programs more desirable to a user. The status bar allows your applications to send information to the screen on a continuous basis.

Tooltips are indispensable when a Toolbar is added. These little messages assist the user in learning the meaning of the icons in your application.

We created two applications that combined many of the concepts learned earlier into a useful program. The icon finder application made use of child forms to display icons to the user for selection. In the final example, you saw how some of the features of a text editor are created.

➤ For a thorough discussion of databases, see Chapter 1, "User Interface Design."

➤ For more information on graphics, see Chapter 16, "Graphics: Data Analysis."

➤ For more information on optimizing Visual Basic, see Chapter 21, "Optimizing VB Code."

3

Using the Windows API

by S. Rama Ramachandran

Visual Basic 4 incorporates many new features over previous versions, chief among them being the use of OLE custom controls, the capability to create reusable objects, 32-bit support, the use of resource files, and Data Access Objects (DAO). However, as an experienced programmer, you will frequently need to go beyond the power that Visual Basic provides and tap into the power of Windows API functions. Even if you are a beginning programmer, you will find out how the Windows API can help you accomplish tasks faster and more efficiently. And Visual Basic provides the ease of using virtually all of the Windows API functions. As you will see in this chapter, the Windows API can effectively manage Windows (or forms), handle menus creatively, and create dazzling special effects with the Windows API graphics routines.

Many programmers balk at using the Windows API. The main fear, and a well-justified one, stems from encountering the dreaded GPF (General Protection Fault) from Windows because of improper use of API calls. But once you know the basics of declaring a procedure or function in a DLL and the technique of initiating a call and interpreting its results, you will find that Windows API makes the programmer's task much easier. Unlike the code you write with Visual Basic to accomplish a task, the code is much tighter and compact in the DLLs where the API function is written (usually in C or C++). This results in faster processing of the routine and quicker results. Not only that, as a programmer, you will need to supply just a few parameters to perform a routine within a DLL without having to bother how it's done. This will save you on development time and effort.

The Windows API contains more than a thousand useful functions and routines. A single chapter will not do justice to all of them. In fact, entire books are being written on it. This chapter is meant to whet your appetite and offer a sampling of what you can do with the Windows API. Consequently, you will find that this chapter touches on the most popular of the API routines.

To begin with, you need to understand the basics of the Windows API. We introduce the Windows API and the ways in which you can declare functions and statements within Visual Basic in order to use the API calls. Parameter passing is one of the most important and least understood areas of using the Windows API (this is covered next). The Windows API routines fall into broad categories. Once the groundwork has been laid, the rest of the chapter is divided into sections, each of which concentrates on a single area of the Windows API. These sections explain a little of the Windows API in question, how it needs to be declared, what it does, and so forth, and then jumps into a small application that illustrates the live, hands-on usage of the specific Windows API being discussed. In this chapter, you learn the following:

➤ How to make calls to the Windows API without encountering General Protection Faults (GPFs)

➤ How to use the Window Control API functions to create a parent-child list of all open windows

➤ How to display custom bitmaps in a menu instead of menu strings by making a few well-placed calls to the Menu Control API

➤ How to create a Slide Show viewer to display bitmaps using special effects by utilizing the power of the Windows Graphics API calls

➤ How to use the Multimedia API calls to manipulate sound and video

➤ What to consider when programming with the 32-bit APIs

Understanding the Windows API

What is the *Windows API*? The API stands for "Application Programming Interface." The Windows API is a set of procedures available to Windows (and Visual Basic) programmers that allow you to manipulate Windows' Graphical User Interface and other aspects of the Windows operating environment (such as virtual memory). All these procedures reside as functions in the various DLLs that Windows uses. These functions are powerful, fast, and most important of all: free. They come with Windows, and every user that uses your VB application under Windows is guaranteed to have them residing in his Windows/System directory.

The Major Windows DLLs are KERNEL.EXE, GDI.EXE, and USER.EXE. These three DLLs alone provide hundreds of functions. KERNEL.EXE holds functions responsible for core Windows operations: managing memory, multitasking, and handling virtual memory. In addition, it contains functions to handle Initialization (.INI) files.

GDI.EXE contains functions that handle output to devices: the screen, the printer, memory blocks, and so on. Windows provides for Graphic DCs that shield the programmer from having to write code specific for a single printer or a single monitor. Windows handles all the conversions so that your code (in Windows or VB) will run irrespective of the type of monitor the user has or the type of printer connected to the computer. All drawing functions reside in this DLL, and we will be making use of it extensively in this chapter.

The USER.EXE DLL contains functions related to the Windows environment: managing windows, menus, cursors, timers, and so on.

Dynamic Link Libraries

All Windows API functions reside in *Dynamic Link Libraries* (DLLs). These are typically files with a .DLL or an .EXE extension. Conceptually, a DLL is a collection of procedures and functions placed inside a Windows recognizable file. Multiple procedures or functions can exist within a DLL. Each procedure or function is similar to the procedure or function that you create within your Visual Basic code. When you write a function, you declare the function and its arguments and then write the code that is executed when the function is called. At another place in your code, you will make a call to the function, passing the correct parameters in the right order. If you pass the wrong parameters or they are in the wrong order, you receive a runtime error (or most probably a compile-time error). In the case of a DLL function, in addition to letting Visual Basic know of the function name and its arguments, you also have to indicate where the function is residing, usually the name of a Windows .DLL file or .EXE file. This is done by the immensely popular `Declare` statement in Visual Basic.

Declaring a DLL Routine

The Visual Basic keyword `Declare` is the way you indicate to Visual Basic that an external function or subroutine is present within a Dynamic Link Library. The syntax for declaring a function or subroutine is provided in the Visual Basic manual with a full explanation. In a simplified form, the syntax is as follows:

```
Declare Sub <name> Lib "<libname>" Alias <alias name> _
    (<argument list>)
Declare Function <name> Lib "<libname>" Alias <alias name> _
    (<argument list>) As type
```

In the previous syntax declaration, `<name>` is either the sub or function name, or if the `Alias` clause is used, it can be any valid routine name.

This is a useful feature, as you will see later. If the `Alias` clause is used, the `<alias name>` is the real name of the sub or function as it exists within the library `<libname>`. This could either be the character string name of the function (like `SetWindowPos`) or could be the ordinal position of the function within the library (like `#123`).

In the case of declaring a function, `As type` indicates the return type of the function. The type that functions can return may be `Boolean`, `Byte`, `Currency`, `Date`, `Double`, `Integer`, `Long`, `Object`, `Single`, `String` (variable-length only), a user-defined type, or `Variant` type.

You can declare a sub or a function to be either `Private` or `Public`. A `Private` sub/function is visible to all routines within the same module only, whereas a `Public` sub/function is visible to all routines within the project. You can declare an API call in a module (.BAS file) or in the declarations section of a form (.FRM file). When you declare it at the module level, the API function/routine has a global scope and can be called from any routine within your application. When you declare it at the form level, however, its scope lies within the form only. With Visual Basic 4, when you declare an API call at the form level, you have to use the `Private` keyword to explicitly declare its scope.

For example, the `GetDC` function declared at the module level would be as follows:

```
Declare Function GetDC Lib "User" (ByVal hWnd As Integer) _
    As Integer
```

When placed in the declarations section of a form you need to add the keyword `Private` as follows:

```
Private Declare Function GetDC Lib "User" _
    (ByVal hWnd As Integer) As Integer
```

The `Declare` statement is usually placed at the very beginning of a module, usually following the global type and constant declarations. If you follow this style of programming, you will more easily locate and maintain your code than if all API calls were bunched together in a single module.

Note: Unlike the previous versions of Visual Basic that required you to type the entire line of the `Declare` statement in a single line of code within the module, with Visual Basic 4, you can use the line-continuation characters " _" (a space followed by an underscore) to break up the `Declare` statement anywhere but within a quoted string.

Passing Arguments

Like in any other subroutine or function within Visual Basic, you need to pass arguments (if any are required) to the routines and functions within a DLL also. However, you have to be careful when you make your declarations and also while passing arguments. Remember, that the functions inside the DLL were written in a non-VB language, usually C or C++, and the arguments it expects can be of a different data type from what you think you are passing to it. In addition to this, Visual Basic can't verify that you are passing the correct number and type of arguments to a function residing in an external DLL.

Note: Because Visual Basic cannot verify whether the number and type of arguments you declare for a function residing in an external DLL are correct, it will ignore them, compile cleanly, and allow you to run the program. VB just takes it as you give it, and if the function fails because of incorrect arguments, you will encounter a GPF causing your program to hang up and lose data. The only remedy is to make sure you are passing the correct arguments and to save your work often. In fact, to prevent code loss, you should set your project parameters to always prompt you to save before running your application.

Passing by Value or Reference

By default, Visual Basic passes all its arguments by reference. That is, when you pass an argument to a function, what is actually passed is a

32-bit pointer to the address where the data is stored. This is alright for most DLL functions, but some C functions require you to pass arguments by value: a copy of the argument is passed to the function. In such cases, you can use the `ByVal` keyword. You can use the `ByRef` keyword to indicate a value passed by reference if you wish; this will make your code easier to read.

For example, the function that provides the dimensions of the client area of a window on-screen requires its first argument to be passed by value and the second one (which is returned back stuffed with the dimension for you) to be passed by reference:

```
Declare Sub GetClientRect Lib "User" (ByVal hWnd As Integer, _
    lpRect As RECT)
```

Using Ordinal Numbers

Sometimes, the functions inside a DLL have names that would be considered invalid as a procedure name in Visual Basic. For example, they may contain an invalid character (like a hyphen) as in the case of the functions `"_lread"` and `"_lwrite"` that perform file read and write procedures. Other DLLs may not have function names for their functions but may use numbers (called as ordinal numbers) to declare and use their functions. The creator of the DLL has done it in this way to consume less memory resources, but it poses a problem when declaring such a function from within Visual Basic. The answer to both cases is to use the `Alias` keyword. You can rename a DLL function to any valid function name and use your user-defined function name to refer to it throughout your code. For example, you can code the `"_lread"` and `"_lwrite"` functions as follows:

```
Declare Function FileRead% Lib "Kernel" Alias "_lread" _
    (ByVal hFile As Integer, ByVal lpBuffer As String, ByVal _
    wBytes As Integer)
Declare Function FileWrite% Lib "Kernel" Alias "_lwrite" _
    (ByVal hFile As Integer, ByVal lpBuffer As String, _
    ByVal wBytes As Integer)
```

Now, when you refer to these functions in your Visual Basic code, you use `FileRead` and `FileWrite` as their names. In the previous example, we have called the functions `FileRead` and `FileWrite` because they are easier to understand. You could have called the functions `LRead` and `LWrite` (or anything else) for simplicity.

You would use the following similar process to handle a DLL using ordinal numbers (provided you know the ordinal numbers beforehand):

```
Declare Function SomeFunctionName Lib "LibName" Alias "#123" _
    (arguments) as Integer
```

Passing Strings

Passing strings to functions inside a DLL is perhaps the most frustrating and confusing area to the Windows API VB programmer. The reason for this is that Visual Basic handles strings in a manner different from C or C++. In C or C++, a string identified as an `LPSTR` structure is a long pointer to a string data type, the string that a DLL function expects to receive. In this case, the `LPSTR` structure is a pointer to an address in memory that contains a set of characters terminated by the Null (\0) character.

In Visual Basic, a `String` type has a structure called `BSTR`, which is a data type defined by OLE Automation. A `BSTR` is a pointer to an address in memory that contains a piece of information called the Header plus the actual set of characters that make up the string, terminated by the Null character. The `BSTR` ignores this header that contains data used by Visual Basic and points to the first data byte in the string. Therefore, a `BSTR` is actually a pointer to the string, just like an `LPSTR` structure. However, Visual Basic passes all strings by reference unless you specifically tell it not to. This means that Visual Basic passes a pointer to the `BSTR` structure (which itself is a pointer to the string).

If you pass a string to a DLL function expecting an `LPSTR` type (just a simple pointer to the data), it will receive a pointer to the `BSTR` type (a pointer to a pointer) and you will end up with disastrous results. To avoid this, when a DLL function is expecting a string via a `LPSTR` type, pass the string explicitly by value using the `ByVal` keyword.

For example, when you are using the `GetPrivateProfileInt` function to read in values from your own private .INI file, it is best to declare all strings with the `ByVal` keyword and then pass the strings to avoid unexpected crashes.

Say you want to retrieve the value in your .INI file that looks like the following:

```
[Preferences]
VBBookEdition=2
```

Declare the function at the module level, as follows:

```
Declare Function GetPrivateProfileInt Lib "Kernel" _
    (ByVal lpApplicationName As String, ByVal lpKeyName _
    As String, ByVal nDefault As Integer, ByVal lpFileName _
    As String) As Integer
```

And use the following in your code to retrieve the value:

```
'----- Declare variables
Dim MyIniFile as string
Dim sAppName as string
Dim sKeyWord as string
Dim I as integer
' ----- Initialize variables
MyIniFile = App.Path & "\MYAPP.INI"
sAppName = "Preferences"
sKeyWord = "VBBookEdition"
' ----- Call the function, default value expected is '1'
I = GetPrivateProfileInt(sAppName,sKeyWord,1,MyIniFile)
```

When you pass strings to a DLL function, expect the function to modify your string, and have it passed back to you, you need to take special precautions. Remember that the actual string is not passed to the DLL function; what you are passing is a pointer to a location in memory that contains the string data. If the DLL modifies the string and the resultant string is bigger than the original one, the DLL does not know that and simply writes to the portion in memory where the string pointer points to, overwriting other portions in memory when it runs out of space. This could lead to unpredictable results. The remedy to this is to make sure that the string that you are passing to the DLL is sufficiently large to fit any value you expect the DLL to return. For example, to retrieve a string from an .INI file using the

`GetPrivateProfileString` function, make sure that the string you pass is at least 255 characters long by actually stuffing it with characters—Null or binary zero is a good choice.

To retrieve the string from the following .INI file:

```
[Preferences]
VBBookName=Visual Basic 4 Expert Solutions
```

Add the following declaration in your module level code:

```
Declare Function GetPrivateProfileString Lib "Kernel" _
    (ByVal lpApplicationName As String, lpKeyName As Any, ByVal _
    lpDefault As String, ByVal lpReturnedString As String, _
    ByVal nSize As Integer, ByVal lpFileName As _
    String) As Integer
```

And use the following code to retrieve the string:

```
' ----- Declare variables
Dim MyIniFile as string
Dim sAppname as string
Dim sKeyWord as string
Dim sDefault as string
Dim sBuf as string
Dim L as integer
Dim sBookName as string
' ----- Initialize variables
MyIniFile = App.path & "\MYAPP.INI"
sAppName = "Preferences"
sKeyWord = "VBBookName"
sDefault = "None"
' ----- Stuff the buffer with nulls, forcing its size
sBuf = String$(255,0)
' ----- Call the function and get the size of the string
L = GetPrivateProfileString(sAppName, sKeyWord, sDefault, _
    sBuf, Len(sBuf), MyIniFile)
' ----- Get the book name from the buffer
sBookName = Left$(sBuf,L)
```

Passing Structures

In addition to passing strings, integers, and other data types, you can also pass entire user-defined types to DLL functions. C functions recognize these user-defined types as structures: the ones you define in Visual Basic using the `Type` or `End Type` statements.

You can pass individual elements of a user-defined type as an argument to a DLL function with no problems. However, if you intend to pass the entire structure, it can only be passed by reference. User-defined types cannot be passed by value. For example, in our `GetClientRect` example described previously, the second argument is of the type RECT defined, as follows:

```
Type RECT
    left as integer
    top as integer
    right as integer
    bottom as integer
End Type
```

You can then define a variable of type RECT as follows:

```
Dim rc as RECT
```

And pass it to the function as follows:

```
GetClientRect Form1.hWnd, rc
```

Win32 API Considerations

With Visual Basic 4, you can now create and compile applications for a 32-bit operating system like Windows NT and Windows 95. You can use the same source code to create applications to run on 16-bit and 32-bit systems—provided you are aware of the slight differences to take into account when writing for the two platforms.

In most cases, your code will run without modifications as the general data types are the same in both versions of Visual Basic: an Integer is an Integer on both the systems and VB will take care of any translations for you. However, the biggest difference between the 16-bit and 32-bit versions of Visual Basic is the way in which they handle character data. This area is also transparent to the developer/user, and VB can handle most of the data conversions. However, if you are manipulating character data at the byte level, you should be aware of the differences and how to handle them.

The main difference arises because of the different character sets that can be used on 32-bit systems. The ANSI character set uses one byte per character, the standard that 16-bit applications use. In this case, each byte represents a single character. The Unicode character set uses two bytes for each character and is defined by the International Standards Organization (ISO). This is the set used by 32-bit OLE and is supported by Windows NT. The DBCS character set, or *Double Byte Character Set*, is used to represent far eastern languages that use non-Latin characters: for example, the Kanji characters of the Japanese language use DBCS format. In this case, each character is represented by two bytes. However, unlike Unicode character sets, the entire two bytes do not refer to a single character. DBCS uses the numbers zero through 128 to represent normal ASCII characters. Numbers greater than 128 are "*lead byte characters*" and represent special formatting characteristics for the character that follows.

When coding for DBCS character sets, a string manipulation function like `Mid$` will return a character reading from the beginning of the string. Therefore, if you wanted the third character in a string initialized to "Hello," you can use the `Mid$(stringname, 3,1)` to return the character "l" under ANSI. However, under DBCS, the same `Mid$` function would now return the "lead byte character" for the second character and it will represent gibberish. Instead, a byte manipulation equivalent of `Mid$` called `MidB$` needs to be used, which understands the byte position of each character and returns the proper one.

When it comes to using the Windows API, the 32-bit version of Visual Basic assumes that all external DLLs use ANSI characters and make the necessary conversions when passing or retrieving string variables. All 32-bit Windows API files use ANSI characters so this is not a problem. Windows NT offers both ANSI and Unicode functions as 32-bit Windows API functions, but you can only use the ANSI version with Visual Basic. ANSI versions of common Windows API functions under the 32-bit system are differentiated by the character "A" at the end of the function name. You can still use the old function name if you `Alias` the function to represent the correct one.

Using Window Control Functions

Now that we have cleared up the issue of declaring routines within a DLL to Visual Basic, it's time we actually used the Windows API. First and foremost, Windows API routines concern controlling Windows.

Handling Windows

All windows under the Microsoft Windows operating system are identified by their handles. Visual Basic provides a `hWnd` property to each form that represents the handle of the form when it is opened as a window. You cannot create a handle, and you should not manipulate the handle of a window. However, the `hWnd` property comes in very handy when we need to manipulate the windows themselves. Because every window has a handle, we can manipulate windows belonging to other applications using their handles.

The `GetActiveWindow` function can be used to retrieve the handle of the currently active window, the top-level window that has the input focus.

```
Declare Function GetActiveWindow Lib "User" () As Integer
```

For example, the following code activates the Notepad application and retrieves the handle of the Notepad window. This code checks to make sure Notepad is active also:

```
Dim hWindow As Integer
On Error Resume Next
Err = 0
AppActivate "Notepad"
If Err <> 0 Then
    MsgBox "Notepad not found"
Else
    hWindow = GetActiveWindow()
    MsgBox "Notepad window handle = " & Str$(hWindow)
End If
```

To obtain the handle of a specific window, we need to know either its title or its class name. The *title* is the string that the window displays on its caption, and the *class name* is the string name by which the window was registered with MS Windows when it was created. Even the desktop in Windows on which all other windows are placed has a handle and can be retrieved.

```
Declare Function FindWindow Lib "User" (ByVal lpClassName As _
        Any, ByVal lpWindowName As Any) As Integer
```

If you know the value of only one of the two arguments, use a Null string as a value for the other. Do not use the keyword Null, but instead pass zero as a Long data type (0&).

To find the handle of the notepad window, whose title we know to be "Notepad - (Untitled)", use the following:

```
hWindow = FindWindow (0&, "Notepad - (Untitled)")
```

To find the handle of another Visual Basic EXE application window, whose class name we know to be "ThunderForm", use the following:

```
hWindow = FindWindow("ThunderForm", 0&)
```

Obtaining Window Information

MS Windows maintains a lot of information regarding all open windows, including their class names, title, sizes, locations, hierarchies, and so on. It is easy to obtain this information and manipulate it. Be careful in manipulating values, however, because some properties cannot be modified while modifying others could be disastrous. We shall see some of the more interesting functions that provide window information in this section. The small application that will conclude this section will provide you with more hands-on experience.

The GetWindowRect function returns the dimensions of the window on-screen including the title and border areas. The GetClientRect function returns the dimensions of the client area alone.

```
Declare Sub GetWindowRect Lib "User" (ByVal hWnd As Integer, _
        lpRect As RECT)
Declare Sub GetClientRect Lib "User" (ByVal hWnd As Integer, _
        lpRect As RECT)
```

The MoveWindow function allows you to move and change the size of the window in a single stroke. SetWindowPos allows you to set the position and size of a window on-screen as well as alter the window's order within the internal list of windows that MS Windows maintains.

```
Declare Sub MoveWindow Lib "User" (ByVal hWnd As Integer, ByVal _
    X As Integer, ByVal Y As Integer, ByVal nWidth As Integer, _
    ByVal nHeight As Integer, ByVal bRepaint As Integer)

Declare Sub SetWindowPos Lib "User" (ByVal hWnd As Integer, _
    ByVal hWndInsertAfter As Integer, ByVal X As Integer, ByVal _
    Y As Integer, ByVal cx As Integer, ByVal cy As Integer, _
    ByVal wFlags As Integer)
```

Using the previously mentioned functions, we can write a small piece of code that will allow our application window to have an "Always on Top" property.

Declare the type RECT at the module level, as follows:

```
Type RECT
    left as integer
    top as integer
    right as integer
    bottom as integer
End Type
```

And add the following code to a form:

```
Const SWP_SHOWWINDOW = &h40
Const HWND_TOPMOST = -1
Private Declare Sub GetWindowRect Lib "User" _
    (ByVal hWnd As Integer, lpRect As RECT)
Private Declare Sub SetWindowPos Lib "User" (ByVal hWnd As _
    Integer, ByVal WndInsertAfter As Integer, ByVal X As _
    Integer, ByVal Y As Integer, ByVal cx As Integer, _
    ByVal cy As Integer, ByVal wFlags As Integer)

Private Sub Form_Load()
    Dim rc As RECT
    GetWindowRect Me.hWnd, rc
    Call SetWindowPos(Me.hWnd, HWND_TOPMOST, 0, 0, _
    (rc.right - rc.left),  (rc.bottom - rc.top), SWP_SHOWWINDOW)
End Sub
```

In addition, the functions GetClassName and GetWindowText return the class name and title caption of a window, as we shall see used in our application.

```
Declare Function GetClassName Lib "User" (ByVal hWnd As
Integer, _
     ByVal lpClassName As String, ByVal nMaxCount As Integer) _
     As Integer
hWnd : Handle of the Window
lpClassName : String Buffer to fill in with the Class Name
nMaxCount : Size of the string buffer

Declare Function GetWindowText Lib "User" (ByVal hWnd As Integer, _
     ByVal lpString As String, ByVal aint As Integer) As Integer
hWnd : Handle of the Window
lpString : String buffer to fill in with the Window's title caption
aint : Size of the string buffer
```

Generating Window Parent-Child Hierarchies

Using the Windows API, we can easily build a parent-child hierarchy between all the windows open on the desktop, and, selecting any one at random, we can investigate its properties more clearly. All this is possible because Windows itself maintains a list of windows and their relations to each other. Remember, to Windows, a window is not only the "form" in Visual Basic but even objects such as combo boxes, list boxes, command buttons, and so on. A hierarchy list like this provides a lot of illumination as to how commercial applications were developed. For example, you may open up Microsoft Word, load a document, and then this application to see the various child windows that MS Word uses to manage itself (see fig. 3.1).

We have used a new project PARCHILD.MAK (see Listing 3.1) to build a parent-child hierarchy list of our own. This system includes two files: PARCHILD.FRM is the main form and PARCHILD.BAS contains global declarations.

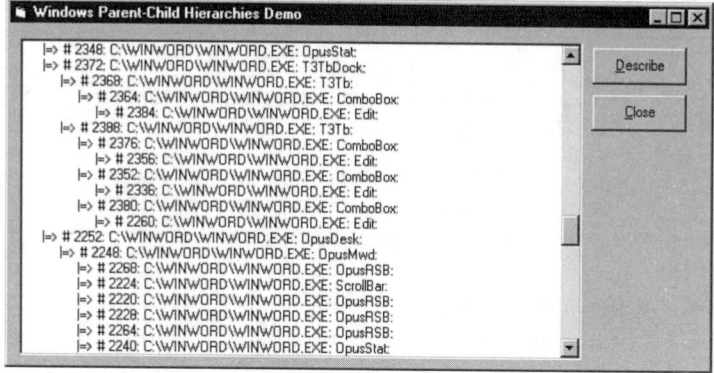

Fig. 3.1 PARCHILD.EXE displays parent-child hierarchies within Windows.

Listing 3.1   PARCHILD.MAK—Building a Parent-Child Hierarchy List with PARCHILD.MAK

```
PARCHILD.FRM
PARCHILD.BAS
 Object={F9043C88-F6F2-101A-A3C9-08002B2F49FB}#1.0#0; _
   COMDLG16.OCX
 Object={FAEEE763-117E-101B-8933-08002B2F4F5A}#1.0#0; _
   DBLIST16.OCX
ProjWinSize=160,352,248,215
ProjWinShow=2
IconForm="Form1"
HelpFile=""
Title="PARCHILD"
ExeName="PARCHILD.exe"
Command=""
Name="ParChild"
HelpContextID="0"
StartMode=0
VersionCompatible="0"
MajorVer=1
MinorVer=0
RevisionVer=0
AutoIncrementVer=0
VersionComments="Parent Child Hierarchy demo"
VersionCompanyName="Que Publishing"
VersionLegalCopyright="Que Publishing"
```

continues

Listing 3.1 Continued

```
Reference=*\G{00025E01-0000-0000-C000-000000000046}#0.0#0# _
    C:\VB4\PRODUCT\DAO2516.DLL#Microsoft DAO 2.5 Object _
    Library
Reference=*\G{BEF6E001-A874-101A-8BBA-00AA00300CAB}#1.0#0# _
    C:\WINDOWS\SYSTEM\OC25.DLL#Standard OLE Types
```

Create a form called PARCHILD.FRM and retain its name of `Form1`. Add a list box named `WinList` covering most of the window and insert two command buttons, one with a caption of Describe called `cmdDescribe` and one with a caption of Close called `cmdClose`. When you have done so, your form should look like the one shown in figure 3.2.

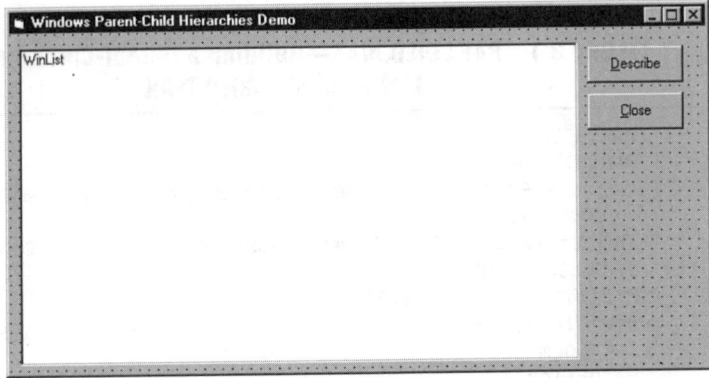

Fig. 3.2 PARCHILD.FRM at designtime.

The accompanying CD-ROM contains the complete source code for the PARCHILD.MAK project. You can refer to it at any time; however, I point out the key features in this project.

This project puts the following API declarations to use. All these declarations are included in the previous PARCHILD.FRM form (included on the enclosed CD-ROM) in its `declarations` section.

```
Private Declare Function IsWindowEnabled% Lib "User" (ByVal hWnd%)
Private Declare Function IsWindowVisible% Lib "User" (ByVal hWnd%)
```

```
Private Declare Function GetClassName Lib "User" (ByVal hWnd As _
    Integer, ByVal lpClassName As String, ByVal nMaxCount _
    As Integer) As Integer
Private Declare Function GetDesktopWindow Lib "User" () As Integer
Private Declare Function GetModuleFileName Lib "Kernel" _
    (ByVal hModule As Integer, ByVal lpFilename As String, _
    ByVal nSize As Integer) As Integer
Private Declare Function GetWindow Lib "User" (ByVal hWnd As _
    Integer, ByVal wCmd As Integer) As Integer
Private Declare Function GetWindowLong& Lib "User" (ByVal hWnd%, _
    ByVal nIndex%)
Private Declare Sub GetWindowRect Lib "User" (ByVal hWnd%, _
    lpRect As RECT)
Private Declare Function GetWindowWord Lib "User" (ByVal hWnd As _
    Integer, ByVal nIndex As Integer) As Integer
```

There are three main routines in this application that perform the
functions of populating the list box on-screen with all open windows,
providing individual details of any window, and describing each window selected by the user in detail.

The LoadListBox routine accepts the handle of a top-level window—
usually the desktop window, and then proceeds to walk through the list
of all open windows. For each window it finds, the routine proceeds to
walk through a list of all open child windows, calling itself recursively
to perform the same task on the parent and the child window and any
grandchild windows, ad infinitum. Listing 3.2 shows you how this is
done.

Listing 3.2   PARCHILD.FRM—The LoadListBox Routine that Walks through All Open Windows

```
Private Sub LoadListBox(iWin As Integer)
'
' This is a recursive sub LoadListBox. For every window, a
' description is pasted into the List box. If the window has
```

continues

Listing 3.2 Continued

```
' children, this sub is recursively called. If the window has
' siblings, this sub is again recursively called. The recur-
' sive
' call ends when there are no more siblings at any level - to
' be precise, we have a list of all windows with all their
' children nested deep.
'

    Static Level As Integer
    Dim hChild As Integer
    Dim hSibling As Integer

    ' ----- Load this window's description into the list box
    WinList.AddItem GetWindowDetails(iWin, Level)
    WinList.ItemData(WinList.NewIndex) = CLng(iWin)

    ' ----- Does it have a child
    hChild = 0
    hChild = GetWindow(iWin, GW_CHILD)
    If hChild Then
        ' -- Child found, increment level and call sub
        ' recursively
        Level = Level + 1
        LoadListBox hChild
        Level = Level - 1
    End If

    ' ----- Does it have a sibling
    hSibling = 0
    hSibling = GetWindow(iWin, GW_HWNDNEXT)
    If hSibling Then
        ' ----- Sibling found, call sub recursively
        LoadListBox hSibling
    End If



End Sub
```

As you can see, the LoadListBox routine makes a call to the routine GetWindowDetails that actually returns a string containing the properly formatted window handle, the window's module name as well as its class name. Listing 3.3 shows how it is done.

Listing 3.3   PARCHILD.FRM—The GetWindowDetails Routine

```
Private Function GetWindowDetails(hWindow As Integer, _
    iLevel As Integer)
'
' Provides a string to paste into the ListBox with details
' of a single window
'
    Dim ResultStr As String         ' String returned
    Dim sBuf As String              ' Buffer string
    Dim L As Integer                ' Misc integer

    ' ----- Construct our string piece by piece with information
    ' ----- Initial simple graphic to display hierarchy
    ResultStr = Space$(iLevel * 5) + "¦=> "

    ' ----- The Window handle
    ResultStr = ResultStr & "#" & Str$(hWindow) & ": "

    ' ----- The Window Application Name
    sBuf = String$(255, 0)
    L = GetModuleFileName(GetWindowWord(hWindow, _
      GWWHINSTANCE), _
     sBuf, Len(sBuf))
    sBuf = left$(sBuf, L)
    ResultStr = ResultStr & sBuf & ": "

    ' ----- The Window Class Name
    sBuf = String$(255, 0)
    L = GetClassName(hWindow, sBuf, Len(sBuf))
    sBuf = left$(sBuf, L)
    ResultStr = ResultStr & sBuf & ": "

    GetWindowDetails = ResultStr


End Function
```

And finally, the `DescribeWindow` routine in Listing 3.4 displays a message box containing detailed information about the window that the user selects from the list box. This routine interrogates the window for its characteristics and displays them to the user.

Listing 3.4   PARCHILD.FRM—The DescribeWindow Routine

```
Private Sub DescribeWindow(hWind As Integer)
'
' Provide the description of a single window in a message
' box to the user
'

    Dim ResultStr As String      ' The string to be
                                  ' displayed
    Dim rc As RECT                ' Window dimensions
                                  ' rectangle
    Dim CrLf As String            ' Carriage return and
                                  ' line feed string
    Dim LStyle As Long            ' Style flag

    CrLf = Chr$(13) + Chr$(10)

    ' ----- Build up our string, piece by piece
    ResultStr = "Window description " & CrLf

    ' ----- Window handle
    ResultStr = ResultStr & "Handle # = " & Str$(hWind) & _ CrLf

    ' ----- Window Dimensions
    GetWindowRect hWind, rc
    ResultStr = ResultStr & "Position (" & Str$(rc.left) & ", " _
     & Str$(rc.top) & ") - (" & Str$(rc.right) & ", " _
     & Str$(rc.bottom) & ") " & CrLf
    ResultStr = ResultStr & "Dimensions " & Str$(rc.right - _
     rc.left) & "x" & Str$(rc.bottom - rc.top) & " pixels" & _
     CrLf
    ' ----- Window Condition
    If IsWindowEnabled(hWind) Then
        ResultStr = ResultStr & "Is Enabled" & CrLf
    Else
        ResultStr = ResultStr & "Is Disabled" & CrLf
    End If

    If IsWindowVisible(hWind) Then
        ResultStr = ResultStr & "Is Visible" & CrLf
    Else
        ResultStr = ResultStr & "Is Invisible" & CrLf
    End If
```

```
'  ----- Window Style
LStyle = GetWindowLong(hWind, GWL_STYLE)

If LStyle And WS_BORDER Then ResultStr = ResultStr & _
  "WS_BORDER" & CrLf
If LStyle And WS_CAPTION Then ResultStr = ResultStr & _
  "WS_CAPTION" & CrLf
If LStyle And WS_CHILD Then ResultStr = ResultStr & _
  "WS_CHILD" & CrLf
If LStyle And WS_CLIPCHILDREN Then ResultStr = ResultStr & _
  "WS_CLIPCHILDREN " & CrLf
If LStyle And WS_CLIPSIBLINGS Then ResultStr = ResultStr & _
  "WS_CLIPSIBLINGS " & CrLf
If LStyle And WS_DISABLED Then ResultStr = ResultStr & _
  "WS_DISABLED " & CrLf
If LStyle And WS_DLGFRAME Then ResultStr = ResultStr & _
  "WS_DLGFRAME " & CrLf
If LStyle And WS_HSCROLL Then ResultStr = ResultStr & _
  "WS_HSCROLL " & CrLf
If LStyle And WS_MAXIMIZE Then ResultStr = ResultStr & _
  "WS_MAXIMIZE " & CrLf
If LStyle And WS_MINIMIZE Then ResultStr = ResultStr & _
  "WS_MINIMIZE " & CrLf
If LStyle And WS_OVERLAPPED Then ResultStr = ResultStr & _
  "WS_OVERLAPPED " & CrLf
If LStyle And WS_POPUP Then ResultStr = ResultStr & _
  "WS_POPUP " & CrLf
If LStyle And WS_SYSMENU Then ResultStr = ResultStr & _
  "WS_SYSMENU " & CrLf
If LStyle And WS_THICKFRAME Then ResultStr = ResultStr & _
  "WS_THICKFRAME " & CrLf
If LStyle And WS_VISIBLE Then ResultStr = ResultStr & _
  "WS_VISIBLE " & CrLf
If LStyle And WS_VSCROLL Then ResultStr = ResultStr & _
  "WS_VSCROLL " & CrLf

'  ----- Display the string in a message box
MsgBox ResultStr, 48, gsAPPNAME


End Sub
```

When you run PARCHILD.MAK, you get a screen listing all open windows with parent-child hierarchies built in (see fig. 3.3). Click on any window and click OK to obtain more information about the window selected.

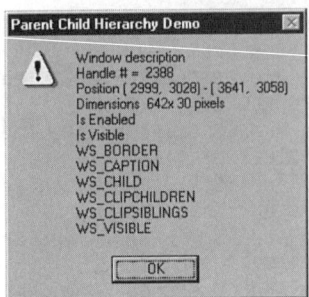

Fig. 3.3 PARCHILD.EXE displays details of a single selected window in a message box.

Incorporating Menu Functions

Visual Basic provides a robust Menu Editor where you can create your own top-level menus containing sub menus. This feature in Visual Basic should be able to provide you with all the functionality you desire from menus. Because this chapter deals with using the Windows API to accomplish tasks that Visual Basic otherwise may not provide, we shall look at a few Windows API menu manipulation functions.

Customizing Menus with Bitmaps

One of the ways in which you can liven up your menus is to provide graphic images in menus instead of text. For example, you may want to have a small graphic of a fax machine next to the menu caption "Fax this document," or a small caption of a modem next to the e-mail menu. The Windows API function `ModifyMenu` allows you to modify an existing menu by adding a bitmap of your own. The declaration for the function is as follows:

```
Declare Function ModifyMenu% Lib "User" (ByVal hMenu%, ByVal _
    nPosition%, ByVal wFlags%, ByVal wIDNewItem%, ByVal _
    lpString As Any)
hMenu : Handle to the Menu being manipulated obtained from _
    GetMenu/GetSubMenu
nPosition : Position of menu item being manipulated - _
    numbered from zero
wFlags : Windows Flags to indicate how modification can be done
lpString : String used as caption for menu item, or Long _
    identifying a bitmap
```

In the previous function, hMenu is the handle of the menu you wish to modify, and nPosition is the specific menu item number you wish to change. You can retrieve this hMenu handle by using the API function GetMenu and GetSubMenu repeatedly until you reach the menu item you need. The GetMenu function returns a handle to the top-level menu (if it exists) of a window. GetMenu is declared with the following:

```
Declare Function GetMenu% Lib "User" (ByVal hWnd%)
hWnd : Handle to the Window
```

Once you get the handle of the menu, you can obtain the handle of any pop-up menu or sub menu within it using the GetSubMenu function. Submenus begin with 0 so you should remember to pass the right parameter to the nPos argument as follows:

```
Declare Function GetSubMenu% Lib "User" (ByVal hMenu%, ByVal nPos%)
hMenu : Handle to the Menu
nPos : Position of the sub Menu within hMenu, numbered from zero
```

Each menu item is associated with a unique menu ID in Windows, and when you modify a menu, you can keep the existing ID or provide a new one. You can obtain the current menu ID for a menu item by using the GetMenuItemID function. Menu items begin with a 0, so remember to pass the correct position of the item you want.

```
Declare Function GetMenuItemID% Lib "User" (ByVal hMenu%, _
        ByVal nPos%)
hMenu : Handle to the Menu
nPos : Position of the menu item within hMenu, numbered from zero
```

Using the previous set of functions, we can modify a menu to incorporate a custom bitmap within a menu item. The handle to the bitmap is passed as the last argument to the `ModifyMenu` function. Let's see how we can use it for a real-world application. One of the menu types found mostly on the Macintosh version of word processors is the capability to display font names available to the user. Each menu item displaying the font name appears in the actual font of the menu item. Our application for this section duplicates this procedure by using `ModifyMenu` to load bitmaps into the menu items. But before we begin with our application, Displaying Bitmaps in Menus, there is one more API functionality that you may find interesting: pop-up menus.

Using Pop-Up Menus

Pop-up menus are menus that are not attached to the horizontal menu on the top of the window. Traditionally, pop-up windows appear at the click of a mouse button (usually the right mouse button), and the pop-up menu is displayed at the current cursor position. For example, in the design mode in VB 4, you can click your right mouse button on an OLE Control to bring up a context-sensitive pop-up menu.

With Visual Basic 3.0 onward, VB has this feature built-in with the `Pop-upMenu` command. To use this effectively, create a menu as you normally would with the Menu Editor. For the last menu item in a top-level menu, change the caption to a Null string "", and create a submenu for this item. This will make the menu item invisible to the user but will still retain the submenu in memory that you can bring up anywhere on the form using the VB `Pop-upMenu` command. We shall use this functionality in our application for this section.

The Windows API function `TrackPop-upMenu` provides a similar functionality.

```
Declare Function TrackPop-upMenu% Lib "User" (ByVal hMenu%, _
ByVal
    wFlags%, ByVal x%, ByVal y%, ByVal nReserved%, ByVal _
hWnd%, lpRect As Any)
```

In the previous function, hMenu is the handle of the pop-up menu, and wFlags refers to position and mouse tracking flags similar to the VB Pop-upMenu flags. X and y refer to the screen coordinates where the pop-up menu will be displayed. nReserved is not used and should be passed as 0. hWnd is the handle of the window to receive the pop-up menu commands. lpRect refers to the rectangular area on-screen beyond which, if the user clicks with the mouse, the pop-up menu will be closed. Pass this as zero long (0&) to make the pop-up menu close any time the user clicks the mouse anywhere on the screen.

Displaying Bitmaps in Menus

Let's now build an application that puts into practice what we have discussed about menus. We shall create a single form project that contains a text box. This text box allows you to type in text and with a right mouse click displays a list of fonts available for the text box's text (see fig. 3.4). When the user selects a font, the text box text changes to display in the selected font. The available fonts are displayed in their original fonts using bitmaps, and VB's own Pop-upMenu command is used to bring up the pop-up menu.

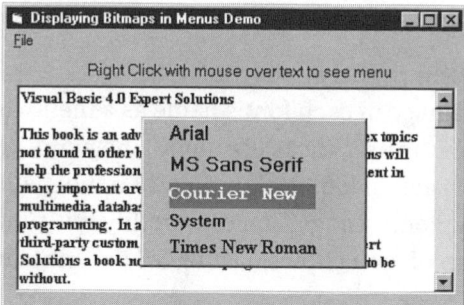

Fig. 3.4 MENU4.EXE displays a pop-up menu of available fonts.

Create a new project called MENU4.MAK. Create a new form MENU4.FRM and retain its name as Form1. Add a text box to fill almost the entire form, add a label to indicate "Click the right mouse button to view menu," and add a Picture box. Give the Picture box an index of 0 to create a control array. Use the Menu Editor to create a menu that has two menu items: `"File"` and `"Fonts"`. Create a submenu containing `"Exit"` under `"File"`, and a submenu containing `"First Font"` under `"Fonts"`. When you are done, your screen should look like the one shown in figure 3.5.

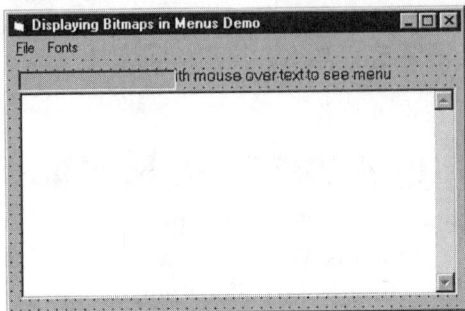

Fig. 3.5 MENU4.FRM in design mode.

Remember that you have access to the complete source code on the accompanying CD-ROM. In this project MENU4.MAK, you make use of all the Menu Control APIs discussed earlier, including `GetMenu`, `GetMenuItemID`, `ModifyMenu`, and `GetSubMenu`.

The key routine in this application is `LoadMenuFonts`. This routine places the bitmap image of each font's name as a menu item within the Font menu. When the user clicks the menu, the name of the font is displayed in the actual font itself rather than the menu names dropping as standard menu strings. You can modify this routine to include any other bitmap of your choice. Listing 3.5 describes the `LoadMenuFonts` routine.

Listing 3.5   MENU4.FRM—The LoadMenuFonts Routine in the MENU4.MAK Application

```
Sub LoadMenuFonts()
'
' For each font in the  array, create a bitmap and load it
```

```
' into the menu using API calls
'
    Dim hMenu As Integer                ' Handle to the menu
    Dim hSubMenu As Integer             ' Handle to the sub
                                        ' menu
    Dim i As Integer, J As Integer      ' Misc counters
    Dim menuID As Integer               ' Menu item ID

    ' ----- Load Font Names into Array
    FontList(0) = "Arial"
    FontList(1) = "MS Sans Serif"
    FontList(2) = "Courier New"
    FontList(3) = "System"
    FontList(4) = "Times New Roman"


    ' ----- Change "Font" menuitem to null string: This will
    ' cause
    ' ----- it to be invisible to the user, yet loaded for our
    ' use
    mnuFont.Caption = ""

    ' ----- Get a handle to the Form Menu
    hMenu = GetMenu(hWnd)

    ' ----- Get a handle to Form Menu's Sub Menu
    ' - at position 1 = "Font"
    hSubMenu = GetSubMenu(hMenu, 1)

    ' ----- Load items in control array - this ensures that
    ' they
    ' ----- are loaded in memory and are made available to us.
    For i = 1 To 4
        ' ----- Menu item control array that holds a font name
        Load mnuFontList(i)
        ' ----- Picture box control array that holds a bitmap
        Load Picture1(i)
    Next

    For i = 0 To 4
        ' ----- Place new font in picture box
        Picture1(i).FontName = FontList(i)
        Picture1(i).FontSize = 14
        Picture1(i).Width = Picture1(i).TextWidth(FontList(i))
        ' ----- Provide enough space for the name to be
        ' visible
        Picture1(i).Height = Picture1(i).TextHeight(FontList(i)) _
```

continues

Listing 3.5   Continued

```
    * 1.5

        ' ----- Print the name in the Picture box
        Picture1(i).Print FontList(i)

        ' ----- Create a Persistent Bitmap in the Picture Box
        Picture1(i).Picture = Picture1(i).Image

        ' ----- Get the Menu ID for this sub menu
        menuID = GetMenuItemID(hSubMenu, i)

        ' ----- Place the Persistent Bitmap on the menu
        '   at the same location
        J = ModifyMenu(hMenu, menuID, MF_BYCOMMAND Or _
        MF_BITMAP, _
    menuID, CLng(Picture1(i).Picture))
    Next

End Sub
```

When this application runs, the user sees a screen containing a text box with some text. When the user clicks on the text with the right mouse button, the Font menu pops up displaying a choice of fonts for the text box. Once the user makes a choice, the text box font changes to the selected font. Listing 3.6 shows the code that handles this event.

Listing 3.6   MENU4.FRM—The MouseDown Event Displays a Pop-up Menu

```
Private Sub Text1_MouseDown(button As Integer, Shift As
Integer, _
    x As Single, Y As Single)
'
' If the button pressed is the right mouse button,
' then display pop-up menu
'
    If button And RIGHT_BUTTON Then Pop-upMenu mnuFont
End Sub
```

Note: The previous application uses the right mouse button to pop up a menu displaying bitmaps. If you are running VB 4 under Windows 95, when you click the right mouse button, Windows 95 puts up its own context-sensitive pop-up menu. Just ignore it and click the right mouse button once again to display the application pop-up menu.

Graphics Functions

Probably the most appealing of all Windows API functions are the graphics routines available to the VB programmer. Windows is a graphical operating system and provides a rich set of graphics routines. However, in order to use these effectively, the VB programmer has to understand about graphic device interface objects or GDI objects. In this section, we shall see how to use GDI routines to create special graphical effects.

GDI Objects—The Device Contexts

One of the advantages of programming under Windows is that Windows performs most of the hardware-related processing under the hood. Different users could run your Visual Basic program by running Windows with different monitors and different screen resolutions. When you write VB code, you are not bothered about the actual hardware that the application is to run on—Windows will handle any hardware specific issues. For example, when printing out a report, your code will work no matter what printer the user is connected to: provided Windows has been configured to write to that printer.

In the same way, when we use graphic routines to draw to the screen, Windows provides us with an object called as a *device context* (DC). A DC can represent a window, a hardware device such as a printer, or even a portion of memory that, to us, acts as the device. When a DC refers to a block of memory, it is called as a *memory DC*. When we use graphic routines, we do all our drawing to these DCs. This way, all our code is written to the DC and Windows is left with the job of figuring out any translations and the actual process of displaying it on your user's monitor.

Windows provides us with other structures that control how graphic routines are handled and how graphics are displayed on-screen. These form the collection of GDI objects or objects belonging to the GDI of Windows. We have already seen the DC that is a key GDI object. When you display lines on-screen, you use the `Pen` object. When you fill an area on-screen with color or with a pattern, you use the `Brush` object. Color palettes determine what colors are visible on a window. Bitmaps store information about an image including color within an object called as the `Bitmap` object.

> **Note:** Before you start to use graphic routines in Windows, you must select the proper GDI object to draw with, and the correct DC to draw onto.

Creating and Selecting GDI objects

You can use DCs by either obtaining it from Windows or creating your own new one. You can obtain the DC of an existing window or device or even the screen by using the `GetDC` API function. You can pass the handle of a window to obtain the DC for the window, or you can pass a 0 to retrieve the DC of the screen itself.

```
Declare Function GetDC Lib "User" (ByVal hWnd As Integer) _
    As Integer
```

Once you have a handle to the DC, you can then perform graphic routines directly onto the DC. Sometimes, it is beneficial to create a copy of an existing DC in memory. To do so, we use the `CreateDC` and `CreateCompatibleDC` functions.

```
Declare Function CreateDC Lib "GDI" (ByVal lpDriverName _
    As String, ByVal lpDeviceName As String, ByVal lpOutput _
```

```
        As String, ByVal lpInitData As String) As Integer
Declare Function CreateCompatibleDC Lib "GDI" (ByVal hDC _
        As Integer) As Integer
```

To create a DC compatible with the screen, you can use the `CreateDC` function as follows:

```
Dim hScrDC as integer
hScrDC = CreateDC("DISPLAY", Null, Null, Null)
```

To create a DC in memory that is compatible with the DC of an existing window, you can use the `CreateCompatibleDC` function as follows:

```
Dim hCompatDC as integer
hCompatDC = CreateCompatibleDC(MyWinHwnd)
```

Once you have a handle to either the DC of a window, or the memory DC, you can perform graphic routines like drawing lines, circles, arcs, and rectangles to the DCs. You can also draw entire bitmaps as we shall see. By manipulating both memory DCs and window DCs, we can create graphic special effects, as our application for this section will show.

In the same way in which you create a DC, Windows also supplies functions to create Pens, Brushes, Bitmaps, Color Palettes, Fonts, and so on. Once you create these objects and are ready to apply them to the DC, you need to select the object into the DC using the `SelectObject` API.

```
Declare Function SelectObject Lib "GDI" (ByVal hDC As Integer, _
        ByVal hObject As Integer) As Integer
```

This ensures that the object you desire is currently the active object within the DC and subsequent graphic routines can access that object.

Displaying Bitmaps with Special Effects

Bitmaps or BMP files are the format in which Windows stores information about an Image. You can store bitmaps either as BMP files on disk, in a Picture control, or in an Image control within your application. For our application, we are going to provide the user with the capability to display any bitmap of choice. We can either use API routines to read individual bytes from a Bitmap structure on disk or take the easy way out and use the Visual Basic LoadPicture routine. We'll take the easy way out.

Once we have a bitmap stored in a Picture control, we can then use the Windows API functions BitBlt and StretchBlt to copy portions of it onto a form or even the screen. BitBlt copies a bitmap from a source DC to a destination DC rectangle without any change in image size. StretchBlt goes one step further and is capable of stretching or shrinking the source image to fit in the destination rectangle you require.

BitBlt takes nine arguments. The first one is the destination DC to display the image. The next four are the destination rectangle dimensions. This is followed by the source DC and the origin of the source rectangle. BitBlt will start copying the image from the origin specified in the source rectangle and will fill an area pointed to by the destination rectangle. The last argument for BitBlt is a Raster Operation flag that determines how the function copies the bitmap from source to destination DCs. The simplest flag is SRCCOPY that copies the source to the destination. Other operations allow you to invert the image, do an XOR and AND copy, and so on.

```
Declare Function BitBlt Lib "GDI" (ByVal hDestDC As Integer, _
    ByVal X As Integer, ByVal Y As Integer, ByVal nWidth _
    As Integer, ByVal nHeight As Integer, ByVal hSrcDC _
    As Integer, ByVal XSrc As Integer, ByVal YSrc _
    As Integer, ByVal dwRop As Long) As Integer
```

StretchBlt is similar to BitBlt in that it requires the source rectangle dimensions to figure out how much stretching or shrinking needs to be done.

```
Declare Function StretchBlt% Lib "GDI" (ByVal hDC%, ByVal X%, _
    ByVal Y%, ByVal nWidth%, ByVal nHeight%, ByVal hSrcDC%, _
    ByVal XSrc%, ByVal Ysrc%, ByVal nSrcWidth%, ByVal _
    nSrcHeight%, ByVal dwRop&)
```

Have you wished to create presentations that display a series of images one on top of the other with professional dissolves? Do you like the way that Microsoft PowerPoint presents its slides? Well, with a little help from the Windows API, we can create our own BMP F/X application (see fig. 3.6).

Fig. 3.6 BMPFX4.MAK illustrates how you can display bitmaps with special effects.

We shall create a simple application for this chapter, and you can easily modify it to do more. Our application will use a form to display bitmaps of choice. For each bitmap to be displayed, we need to know the name of the bitmap file, the particular special effect to use to display it, the speed with which a bitmap will be displayed, and the time to wait in between bitmap displays. We can also let the user determine whether we should use the original size of the bitmap or fill the entire window with the bitmap, stretching or shrinking the bitmap as desired. And lastly, we need to know if the bitmap has to replace an existing image on-screen or if we should paint the screen white before displaying the bitmap. For each bitmap (or slide) to be displayed, we will store all this information in a user-defined type called `SlideType`.

```
Type SlideType       ' Structure holding a single slide
                     ' display
    information
    szFileName As String       ' Graphic file to be
                               ' displayed
```

```
    iFX As Integer              ' Special effect to use
    iSpeed As Integer           ' Speed of transition
                                ' effect
    iWait As Integer            ' Milliseconds to wait
                                ' before yielding
    fClearBG As Integer         ' Flag to clear back-
                                ' ground before display
    fFillWindow As Integer      ' Flag to indicate
                                ' whether entire window
                                ' is filled
End Type
```

For this application, we shall let the user decide all this by supplying information in an .INI file which we can read, again by using Windows API calls. Our .INI file will indicate the total number of slides to display, and for each slide, will present all information.

Before you proceed, you need to create an .INI file as shown in Listing 3.7. Your application uses this .INI file to display bitmaps. You can change the settings in this .INI file to experiment with different special effects for displaying bitmaps.

Listing 3.7   BMPFX4.INI—Creating an INI File

```
; BMPFX4.INI
; INI file containing Slide information

[SlideInfo]
MaxSlides=5

[Slide1]
FileName=bmpfx1.bmp
SpecialFX=1
Speed=2
Wait=1
ClearBG=
FillWindow=0

[Slide2]
FileName=bmpfx2.bmp
SpecialFX=2
Speed=2
Wait=1
ClearBG=
FillWindow=0

[Slide3]
FileName=bmpfx3.bmp
```

```
SpecialFX=3
Speed=1
Wait=1
ClearBG=
FillWindow=0

[Slide4]
FileName=bmpfx4.bmp
SpecialFX=5
Speed=4
Wait=1
ClearBG=
FillWindow=0

[Slide5]
FileName=bmpfx5.bmp
SpecialFX=6
Speed=4
Wait=1
ClearBG=
FillWindow=0
```

In this application, the function LoadPDetails first identifies how many slides are displayed by looking at MaxSlides under SlideInfo in the .INI file. For each slide, it obtains information to fill in the SlideType structure: the name, the special effect to use, the speed, the wait time, and so forth. The RunPresentation routine displays each slide one by one. The DisplayPic routine displays a single slide with the desired special effect. The actual Bitmap Special Effects (or FX) are as follows:

```
0 = Normal display, no effect.
1 = Push Bitmap from Left to Right
2 = Push Bitmap from Right to Left
3 = Push Bitmap from Top to Bottom
4 = Push Bitmap from Bottom to Top
5 = Display as Horizontal blinds
6 = Display as Vertical blinds
```

As you see, for the first five effects, you use the window's DC and draw on it directly, and for the last two, you use a memory DC.

Create a new project called BMPFX4.MAK with one form BMPFX.FRM and one module BMPFX.BAS. Create the form BMPFX.FRM with one

Picture box and one common dialog box control. The form
BMPFX.FRM has a menu with three options. The first loads slide
data from an .INI file, the second displays the slides using special
effects, and the third exits the system. Figure 3.7 shows what your
form looks like in design mode.

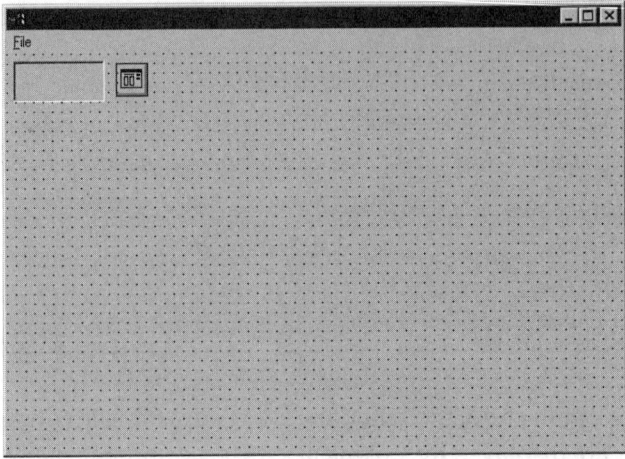

Fig. 3.7 This is what your form should look like in design mode.

Note that the common dialog box control has its properties set as
follows:

```
defaultext    =   "*.INI"
dialogtitle   =   "Choose Presentation Data file to Open"
filename      =   "*.INI"
filter        =   "Presentation Data (*.INI)¦*.INI¦All _
                  Files (*.*)¦*.*¦"
```

As usual, you can refer to the actual code on the accompanying
CD-ROM. In this application, you make use of the following API calls
declared within the BAS file BMPFX.BAS.

```
Declare Function BitBlt Lib "gdi" (ByVal hDC1 As Integer, _
    ByVal x1 As Integer, ByVal y1 As Integer, ByVal wd As _
    Integer, ByVal ht As Integer,  ByVal hDC2 As Integer, _
    ByVal x2 As Integer, ByVal y2 As Integer, ByVal _
    pattern As Long) As Integer
```

```
Declare Function GetDC Lib "user" (ByVal hWnd As Integer) _
    As Integer
Declare Function GetDesktopWindow Lib "user" () As Integer
Declare Function ReleaseDC Lib "user" (ByVal hWnd As Integer, _
    ByVal hDC As  Integer) As Integer
Declare Function CreateCompatibleDC% Lib "gdi" (ByVal hDC%)
Declare Function SelectObject% Lib "gdi" (ByVal hDC%, _
    ByVal hObject%)
Declare Function StretchBlt% Lib "gdi" (ByVal hDC%, ByVal X%, _
    ByVal Y%, ByVal nWidth%, ByVal nHeight%, ByVal hSrcDC%, _
    ByVal XSrc%, ByVal YSrc%, ByVal nSrcWidth%, ByVal _
    nSrcHeight%, ByVal dwRop&)
Declare Sub GetClientRect Lib "user" (ByVal hWnd%, lpRect As RECT)
Declare Function DeleteDC% Lib "gdi" (ByVal hDC%)
Declare Function DeleteObject% Lib "gdi" (ByVal hObject%)
Declare Function CreateCompatibleBitmap Lib "gdi" (ByVal hDC _
    As Integer, ByVal nWidth As Integer, ByVal nHeight As _
    Integer) As Integer
Declare Function GetPrivateProfileInt Lib "Kernel" (ByVal _
    lpApplicationName As String, ByVal lpKeyName As String, _
    ByVal nDefault As Integer, ByVal lpFileName As String) _
    As Integer
Declare Function GetPrivateProfileString% Lib "Kernel" (ByVal _
    lpApplicationName$, ByVal lpKeyName As Any, ByVal _
    lpDefault$, ByVal lpReturnedString$, ByVal nSize%, _
    ByVal lpFileName$)
Declare Function PatBlt Lib "gdi" (ByVal hDC As Integer, ByVal X _
    As Integer, ByVal Y As Integer, ByVal nWidth As Integer, _
    ByVal nHeight As Integer, ByVal dwRop As Long) As Integer
```

This BAS file also contains all the code to create the special effects. The special effects themselves are enumerated using global constants.

```
' ----- Special Effects defined
Global Const BMPFX_NORMAL = 0
Global Const BMPFX_LEFT_TO_RIGHT = 1
Global Const BMPFX_RIGHT_TO_LEFT = 2
Global Const BMPFX_TOP_TO_BOTTOM = 3
Global Const BMPFX_BOTTOM_TO_TOP = 4
Global Const BMPFX_HORIZONTAL_BLINDS = 5
Global Const BMPFX_VERTICAL_BLINDS = 6
```

The actual grunt work of displaying a bitmap using a special effect is done by the `DisplayPic` routine. This routine loads the correct bitmap into a hidden VB picture box and then proceeds to paint it on to the form using the desired effect. Listing 3.8 shows the code for this routine.

Listing 3.8   BMPFX4.BAS—The DisplayPic Routine Displays a Bitmap with a Desired Special Effect

```
Sub DisplayPic(iCurSlide As Integer)
    Dim i As Integer
    Dim retval As Integer          ' Value returned by functions
    Dim ScreenhWnd As Integer, ScreenDC As Integer
    Dim hShadowDC%
    Dim OldBM%
    Dim hShadowBMP%
    Dim hTempBitmap%
    Dim rc As RECT
    Dim dyFactor%, j%, dx%, dy%, result%
    Dim fOriginalSize As Integer

    Dim nWidth%, nHeight%, X%, Y%
    Dim nSrcWidth%, nSrcHeight%, XSrc%, YSrc%

    Dim hCompatDC%
    Dim iPropFactor%
    Dim Start As Long

    ' ----- Load the file into picture1 -
    ' use VB LoadPicture for simplicity
    BmpFX.Picture1.Picture = _
    LoadPicture(ArySlides(iCurSlide). szFileName)

    ' ----- Create a compatible DC for our form
    hCompatDC% = CreateCompatibleDC(BmpFX.hDC)

    ' ----- Select the bitmap into the compatible DC
    OldBM% = SelectObject(hCompatDC%, BmpFX.Picture1.Picture)


    ' ----- Dimensions of source bitmap
    GetClientRect BmpFX.Picture1.hWnd, rc
    nSrcWidth% = rc.right - rc.Left
    nSrcHeight% = rc.bottom - rc.Top
    XSrc% = rc.Left
    YSrc% = rc.Top
```

```
' ----- Dimensions of destination
GetClientRect BmpFX.hWnd, rc
If ArySlides(iCurSlide).fFillWindow Then
    ' ----- Destination is entire window client area
    nWidth% = rc.right - rc.Left
    nHeight% = rc.bottom - rc.Top
    X% = rc.Left
    Y% = rc.Top
Else
    ' ----- Destination is bitmap centered in client area
    nWidth% = nSrcWidth%
    nHeight% = nSrcHeight%
    X% = rc.Left + Abs((rc.right - rc.Left) - nWidth%) / 2
    Y% = rc.Top + Abs((rc.bottom - rc.Top) - nHeight%) / 2
End If


' ----- Do we need to clear the background first ?
If ArySlides(iCurSlide).fClearBG Then
    retval = PatBlt(BmpFX.hDC, X%, Y%, nWidth%, nHeight%, _
 WHITENESS)
End If

' ----- Carry out the Special Effects
Select Case ArySlides(iCurSlide).iFX
    Case BMPFX_NORMAL
        ' ----- display without any effect
        result = StretchBlt(BmpFX.hDC, X%, Y%, nWidth%, _
 nHeight%, hCompatDC, 0, 0, nSrcWidth%, nSrcHeight%, _
 SRCCOPY)
    Case BMPFX_LEFT_TO_RIGHT
        ' ----- Push Left to Right
        iPropFactor% = nWidth% / nSrcWidth%
        For i% = 0 To nSrcWidth% Step _
        (ArySlides(iCurSlide). _
 iSpeed * iPropFactor)
            retval% = StretchBlt%(BmpFX.hDC, X%, Y%, (i% * _
 iPropFactor), nHeight%, hCompatDC%, XSrc%, YSrc%, i%, _
 nSrcHeight%, SRCCOPY)
        Next i%

    Case BMPFX_RIGHT_TO_LEFT
        ' ----- Push Right to Left
        iPropFactor% = nWidth% / nSrcWidth%
        For i% = 0 To nSrcWidth% Step _
        (ArySlides(iCurSlide). _
 iSpeed * iPropFactor)
            retval% = StretchBlt%(BmpFX.hDC, X% + _
```

continues

Graphics Functions **127**

Listing 3.8 Continued

```
(nSrcWidth% - i%) * iPropFactor%, Y%, i% * iPropFactor%, _
nHeight%, hCompatDC%, nSrcWidth% - i%, YSrc%, i%, _
nSrcHeight%, SRCCOPY)
        Next i%

    Case BMPFX_TOP_TO_BOTTOM
        ' ----- Push Top to Bottom
        iPropFactor% = nHeight% / nSrcHeight%
        For i% = 0 To nSrcHeight% Step _
        (ArySlides(iCurSlide). _
iSpeed * iPropFactor)
            retval% = StretchBlt%(BmpFX.hDC, X%, Y%, _
            nWidth%, _
i% * iPropFactor%, hCompatDC%, XSrc%, YSrc%, nSrcWidth%, _
i%, SRCCOPY)
        Next i%

    Case BMPFX_BOTTOM_TO_TOP
        ' ----- Push Bottom to Top
        iPropFactor% = nHeight% / nSrcHeight%
        For i% = 0 To nSrcHeight% Step _
        (ArySlides(iCurSlide). _
iSpeed * iPropFactor)
            retval% = StretchBlt%(BmpFX.hDC, X%, Y% + _
(nSrcHeight% - i%) * iPropFactor%, nWidth%, i% * _
iPropFactor, hCompatDC%, XSrc%, nSrcHeight% - i%, _
nSrcWidth%, i%, SRCCOPY)
        Next i%

    Case BMPFX_HORIZONTAL_BLINDS
        ' ----- Display as Horizontal Blinds
        ' ----- We need a third DC as our workspace -
        ' create it now
        hShadowDC = CreateCompatibleDC(BmpFX.hDC)
        ' ----- Create a compatible bitmap as working area
        hShadowBMP = CreateCompatibleBitmap(BmpFX.hDC, _
nWidth%, nHeight%)
        ' ----- Select the bitmap into the Shadow DC
        hTempBitmap = SelectObject(hShadowDC, hShadowBMP)

        ' ----- How many slats will we be having:
        dyFactor = nSrcHeight% / 10

        ' ----- For each row of pixels in each slat

        For j = 1 To dyFactor Step _
        ArySlides(iCurSlide).iSpeed
```

```
            ' ----- Copy the screen image into shadow dc.
            result = BitBlt(hShadowDC, 0, 0, nWidth%, _
nHeight, BmpFX.hDC, X%, Y%, SRCCOPY)

            ' ----- For each slat
            For i = 1 To dyFactor
                ' ----- Now manipulate the ShadowDC image
                result = StretchBlt(hShadowDC, 0, (i * _
dyFactor), nSrcWidth%, j, hCompatDC, 0, (i * dyFactor), _
nSrcWidth%, j, SRCCOPY)
            Next i

            ' ----- And copy the reconstructed image
            ' back to screen
            result = StretchBlt(BmpFX.hDC, X%, Y%, _
nSrcWidth%, nSrcHeight, hShadowDC, 0, 0, nSrcWidth%, _
nSrcHeight%, SRCCOPY)

        Next j
        ' ----- Make sure entire bitmap has been copied
        result = StretchBlt(BmpFX.hDC, X%, Y%, nWidth%, _
nHeight%, hCompatDC, 0, 0, nSrcWidth%, _ nSrcHeight%, _
SRCCOPY)

        ' ----- Delete objects and restore resources
        i% = SelectObject(hShadowDC, hTempBitmap)
        i% = DeleteObject(hShadowBMP)
        i% = DeleteDC(hShadowDC)

    Case BMPFX_VERTICAL_BLINDS
        ' ----- Display as Vertical Blinds
        ' ----- We need a third DC as our workspace -
        ' create it now
        hShadowDC = CreateCompatibleDC(BmpFX.hDC)
        ' ----- Create a compatible bitmap as working area
        hShadowBMP = CreateCompatibleBitmap(BmpFX.hDC, _
nWidth%, nHeight%)
        ' ----- Select the bitmap into the Shadow DC
        hTempBitmap = SelectObject(hShadowDC, hShadowBMP)

        ' ----- How many slats will we be having:
        dyFactor = nSrcWidth% / 10

        ' ----- For each row of pixels in each slat

        For j = 1 To dyFactor Step _
        ArySlides(iCurSlide).iSpeed
```

continues

Listing 3.8   Continued

```
                       ' ----- Copy the screen image into shadow dc.
               result = BitBlt(hShadowDC, 0, 0, nWidth%, _
        nHeight, BmpFX.hDC, X%, Y%, SRCCOPY)

                   ' ----- For each slat
               For i = 1 To dyFactor
                   ' ----- Now manipulate the ShadowDC image
                   result = StretchBlt(hShadowDC, (i * _
        dyFactor), 0, j, nSrcHeight%, hCompatDC, (i * dyFactor), _
        0, j, nSrcHeight%, SRCCOPY)
               Next i

                   ' ----- And copy the reconstructed image
                   ' back to screen
               result = StretchBlt(BmpFX.hDC, X%, Y%, _
        nSrcWidth%, nSrcHeight, hShadowDC, 0, 0, nSrcWidth%, _
        nSrcHeight%, SRCCOPY)

           Next j
           ' ----- Make sure entire bitmap has been copied
           result = StretchBlt(BmpFX.hDC, X%, Y%, nWidth%, _
        nHeight%, hCompatDC, 0, 0, nSrcWidth%, nSrcHeight%, _
        SRCCOPY)

               ' ----- Delete objects and restore resources
               i% = SelectObject(hShadowDC, hTempBitmap)
               i% = DeleteObject(hShadowBMP)
               i% = DeleteDC(hShadowDC)

    End Select

    ' ----- Reselect old object into shadow DC
    i% = SelectObject(hCompatDC%, OldBM%)

    ' ----- Delete DC, free up resources
    i% = DeleteDC(hCompatDC%)
    If OldBM% <> 0 Then
        i% = DeleteObject(OldBM%)
    End If

    ' ----- Wait for the time required
    Start = Timer    ' Set start time.
    Do While Timer < Start + ArySlides(iCurSlide).iWait
        DoEvents     ' Yield to other processes.
    Loop

End Sub
```

For the first five special effects, we create a DC compatible with the form's DC and select the bitmap into the compatible DC. We then use the StretchBlt function to blast bits from the bitmap onto the form using different widths and heights as the destination. For the last two special effects, it is not sufficient that we copy the image from the picture box to the form. Because we are creating a horizontal or vertical blinds effect, after drawing each blind, or a portion of it, we need the image now on the form to work with. That is, after drawing each portion of a blind, we need a copy of what is visible on the form. Therefore, we need to copy the image from the picture box to the form, and copy the image from the form to a temporary storage space with which we can then work. This is done by creating a memory DC compatible to the form's DC as follows:

```
' ----- We need a third DC as our workspace -
' create it now
  hShadowDC = CreateCompatibleDC(BmpFX.hDC)
  ' ----- Create a compatible bitmap as working area
  hShadowBMP = CreateCompatibleBitmap(BmpFX.hDC, _
   nWidth%, nHeight%)
  ' ----- Select the bitmap into the Shadow DC
  hTempBitmap = SelectObject(hShadowDC, hShadowBMP)
```

Once we have a memory DC and have selected a bitmap object into it, we can now copy the image from the form DC into the memory DC:

```
' -----  Copy the screen image into shadow dc.
        result = BitBlt(hShadowDC, 0, 0, nWidth%, nHeight, _
     BmpFX.hDC, X%, Y%, SRCCOPY)
```

We then proceed to draw portions of our horizontal or vertical blinds onto the hShadowDC. And when we are satisfied, we copy the entire hShadowDC back to the form DC.

```
' ----- And copy the reconstructed image back to screen
        result = StretchBlt(BmpFX.hDC, X%, Y%, nSrcWidth%, _
     nSrcHeight, hShadowDC, 0, _
       0, nSrcWidth%, nSrcHeight%, SRCCOPY)
```

This way, we can use the memory DC to perform fast BitBlt or StretchBlt operations and then copy the entire memory DC image onto the form DC with one stroke.

You can see the potential to modify the application. You can add a variety of different special effects in a similar manner. You can have menu options that allow the user to modify the presentation data and view the results immediately. You can have a flag in the .INI file to cycle through the presentation so that all the slides are shown over again.

Multimedia Functions

Windows provides us with a set of rich multimedia functions through the Windows Multimedia System built into Windows. With these multimedia functions, you can manipulate sound, graphics, and video. The sound recorder that comes with Windows 3.1 and Windows for Workgroups 3.1x versions lets you add digitized sounds to your documents and applications. The Media Player utility plays WAVE files, MIDI sequencer files, or AVI video files.

The functions that provide multimedia Windows API are present in the MMSYSTEM.DLL file. And like any other API call, you can also declare and use these functions. The entire gamut of multimedia functions available and their usage is too large for the scope of this chapter. We will, however, discuss a small sampling of how to use sound, video, and multimedia text in your applications.

Using Sound

The simplest way to incorporate sound in your applications is, of course, to use the Visual Basic Beep statement. However, if you wish to provide professional quality sound, you need to be able to play sound files (with a .WAV extension). To do so, you can use the mciExecute API function.

```
Declare Function mciExecute Lib "MMSystem" (ByVal lpString _
    as String) as Integer
```

Then, in your application, you can have the following code to play the .WAV file TADA.WAV:

```
Dim x as integer
x = mciExecute("play c:\windows\tada.wav")
```

You can test out the code only if you have a multimedia PC (or at least have a sound card installed and configured under Windows).

If you wish to have a wave audio file (.WAV file) playing in the background as your application proceeds with its tasks, you can use the sndPlaySound API function. To do so, you must have the waveform audio device driver installed.

```
Declare Function sndPlaySound Lib "MMSYSTEM" (ByVal _
    lpszSoundName As String, ByValuFlags As Integer) As Integer
```

In the previous function, lpszSoundName is the filename of the wave audio file to play. uFlags refers to the Windows flag that determines how you want the function to behave. The valid values for uFlags are as follows:

➤ SND_SYNC (&H0): The function plays the sound and then returns.

➤ SND_ASYNC(&H1): The function starts playing the sound and immediately returns. The sound continues to play in the background. To stop the sound from playing, call the function again by passing Null as the filename.

➤ SND_NODEFAULT (&H2): If the function does not find filename, it does not play anything.

➤ SND_MEMORY (&H4): The filename does not point to a file on disk but rather points to an in-memory image of the waveform sound.

➤ SND_LOOP (&H8): Used along with SND_ASYNC to keep playing the WAVE file continuously in a loop until canceled by a call to the same function with Null as the filename.

➤ SND_NOSTOP (&H10): If another sound is currently being played, do not interrupt it, return immediately instead.

You can find numerous other functions included in MMSYSTEM.DLL to help you play .WAV files and .MID files and to control sound.

Using Video

You can use the Media Control Interface VBX (MCI.VBX) that comes with the pro edition of Visual Basic to display video files (.AVI files) in your application. However, if you wish, you can directly manipulate the multimedia functions within MMSYSTEM.DLL to accomplish the same thing.

In order to run .AVI files, you need to have software such as Video for Windows (from Microsoft) or QuickTime for Windows (from Apple) loaded on your machine. This software comes in runtime versions and is available from numerous bulletin board services and on CompuServe. They provide an extension for Windows that enables applications to play video clips.

You can play an .AVI file in your VB application by using the same `mciExecute` command we saw earlier.

```
Declare Function mciExecute Lib "MMSystem" (ByVal _
    lpString as String) as Integer
```

And, in your application, you can call the previous function to play an AVI file:

```
Dim x as integer
x = mciExecute("play MyAVI.AVI")
```

This code causes Windows to open a new window, title it with the name of the AVI file and play it. When the file is done playing, the window is automatically closed.

Using WinHelp Functions

If you are using your own Help file with your application, you can activate it and have it perform different actions by using the `WinHelp` API function.

```
Declare Function WinHelp Lib "User" (ByVal hWnd As Integer, _
    ByVal lpHelpFile As String, ByVal wCommand As Integer, _
    dwData As Any) As Integer
```

You can call the function as the response to the user pressing the F1 key or for any other action. In the previous function, `hWnd` is the handle of the window requesting help. Windows keeps track of which application requested what help and needs this parameter. `lpHelpFile` is the fully qualified name of your Help file. `wCommand` is the action you desire from Windows Help engine, and `dwData` is the data supporting the action you request. The valid values for `wCommand` and its corresponding `dwData` type are as follows:

➤ `HELP_CONTEXT (&H1)`: Open the Help file and display a particular topic. `dwData` is a long integer containing the context number of the topic to be displayed. The topic Index has a value of –1.

➤ `HELP_QUIT (&H2)`: Quit displaying Help. `dwData` is ignored and can be passed as 0.

➤ `HELP_INDEX (&H3)`: Open the Help file and display the main Help Index. `dwData` is ignored.

➤ `HELP_HELPONHELP (&H4)`: Open the Help file and display the Using Help topic.

➤ `HELP_SETINDEX (&H5)`: Open the Help file and set a particular topic as the Index topic. `dwData` contains a long value of the topic to be set as the Index topic.

➤ `HELP_KEY (&H101)`: Open the Help file and display the first topic that matches the data in `dwData` within the keyword list in the help file. `dwData` is a string containing the key requested.

➤ `HELP_MULTIKEY (&H201)`: Displays help for a topic identified by a keyword in an alternate keyword file. `dwData` is a structure of type `MULTIKEYHELP`. This structure identifies the table footnote character and the keyword within your Help file.

```
Type MULTIKEYHELP
    mkSize As Integer
    mkKeylist As String * 1
    szKeyphrase As String * 253 ' Array length is _
    arbitrary; may be changed
End Type
```

Create a new project called TESTHELP.MAK (see fig. 3.8) and create a new form called TESTHELP.FRM with two text boxes, a label, and three command buttons. Figure 3.9 shows your form at designtime.

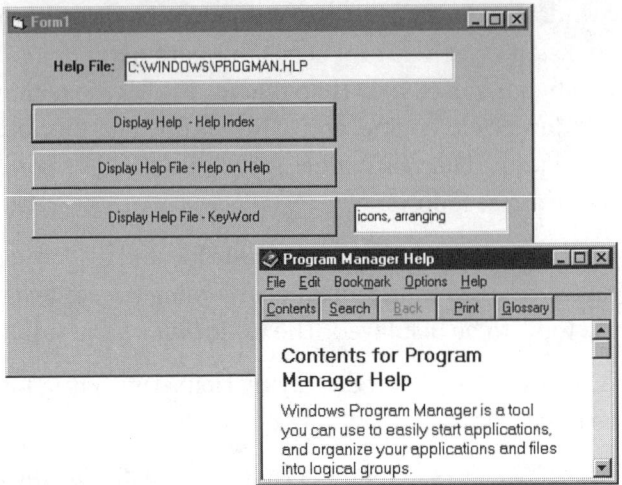

Fig. 3.8 TESTHELP.MAK demonstrates how the `WinHelp` API can display Help files.

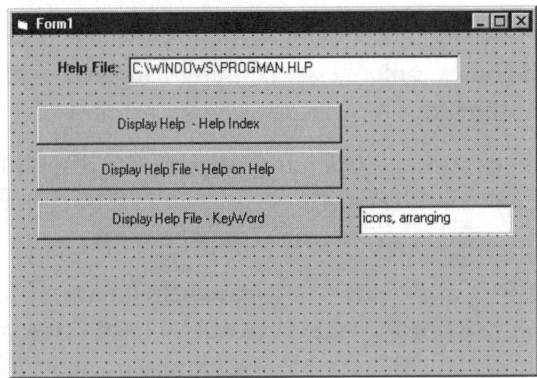

Fig. 3.9 TESTHELP.FRM in design mode.

The source code for this small application is included on the accompanying CD-ROM. Compile and run this application. When you use the default text box strings, you can see the Program Manager Help file displayed with different starting options when you click on each of the three command buttons.

Using the Windows API under Win32 Systems

Visual Basic 4 now provides you with the option of writing applications that will work in a 32-bit environment such as Windows NT or Windows 95. The advantage is that you can now write code that can utilize the power and speed of a 32-bit operating system. Your copy of VB 4 will be optimized to work under 32-bit systems. However, if you are delving into the Windows API you are on your own and need to keep a few things in mind.

For the 32-bit operating system, Windows provides a 32-bit API with its own new functions. Most of the changes in the Windows 32-bit API fall into one of four categories: functions that have been dropped, 16-bit values that have been widened to 32 bits, modified functions, and new APIs for file I/O and new features.

Microsoft has taken care to change very little from the 16-bit API to the 32-bit API, and this change has been well managed, with Microsoft employing strict rules to ensure minimum differences. For example, names of symbolic constants you use in your 16-bit API have not changed. Similarly, data structure names and members remain the same as do function names and argument orders.

To make a smooth transition from 16-bit API usage to 32-bit API usage, keep the following in mind:

> ➤ Window handling is different under 32-bit systems. Because multiple applications now occupy their own private worlds, each 32-bit Windows program will run as a separate process and not as a second instance of another process. A handle to `PrevInstance` therefore may not be valid: you will need to use `FindWindow` to locate a previously loaded application.

> ➤ When you are using bitmaps, use device-independent bitmaps or DIBS and the functions that accompany them. Device-dependent bitmaps are not portable and should be avoided.

➤ If you are using functions/routines that use Windows messages and especially the `wParam` and `lParam` structures, remember to break them down and store their values immediately to prevent maintenance problems when parameter values are changed.

➤ When you are porting your code from 16-bit to 32-bit systems, and if you are using API calls, most of your code should be portable. There are certain categories of functions, though, where you may need to change your API calls and incorporate new functions if needed.

Graphic Routines

The 16-bit API calls `MoveTo`, `ScaleViewPortExt`, `ScaleWindowExt`, `SetBitmapDimension`, `SetViewPortExt`, `SetWindowExt`, and a few others handle graphic routines and include packed x and y coordinates for graphics. In Windows 3.x, the x and y coordinates are 16 bits each and are packed into a 32-bit return value. In Win32, they are 32 bits each and the return value is 64 bits long and cannot be handled by the previous function calls. You need to use their equivalent Win32 API calls, each of which has the same name as the previously mentioned functions with the characters "Ex" appended to the end. So `MoveTo` becomes `MoveToEx`. The Ex provides an additional parameter that points to the location from where you can retrieve data. If you do not wish to use this data, you can pass `Null`. For example, in a call to `MoveTo`, we would not be concerned with knowing where we actually moved to, so the call under Windows 3.x as `MoveTo (hDC, x, y)` can be changed to `MoveToEx(hDC,x,y,Null)` under Win32 without any problem.

Other graphic routines have now included the `POINT` structure to obtain the values of x and y coordinates instead of passing x and y as return values. For these functions, the characters `"Point"` are appended to the end of the function name to denote the use of a `POINT` structure. In addition, these new `"Point"` functions now accept an argument of type `POINT` in which the return values are placed.

DOS System Calls

If you are using DOS system calls (using the `DOS3Call` API function) to perform file I/O, they need to be replaced with Win32 file I/O calls. For example, the functions that retrieve the system date and time, obtain disk free space, and create and remove directories have to be changed to their corresponding Win32 API equivalent: `GetDateAndTime`, `SetDateAndTime`, `GetDiskFreeSpace`, `CreateDirectory`, and `RemoveDirectory`.

Because Windows NT supports filenames of up to 256 characters, fixed-length buffers for filenames, and environment strings need to be increased in size.

From Here...

As you can see, we have carried out a whirlwind tour of the Windows API. We managed to glimpse briefly at the power and ease of using the Windows API. The only way you can master it fully is by practice. Learn to pass parameters the right way, use the API to perform activities that Visual Basic does not provide, and you will be developing applications that your users will marvel at, and your peers will be wondering how that was done in VB.

Now that you have mastered the basics of using the Windows API with Visual Basic, you can round out your knowledge and use it in your applications. To do so, you should also review the material in the following chapters of this book:

➤ For more information on using the Windows Help API calls, see Chapter 18, "Developing Online Help."

➤ For more information on using the Windows API calls to make your applications run faster, see Chapter 21, "Optimizing VB Code."

➤ For a more detailed discussion on what to consider when using the Windows API and how to use it effectively, see Chapter 23, "Mixed-Language Development with DLLs."

Part II
Adding Client /Server Database Capabilities

4

Advanced Database Front Ends

by Michael McKelvy

Database applications can be used for a wide variety of programming needs. Their particular strength is the ability to store data in a manner that makes data retrieval and maintenance easy. A database application can be used for something as simple as a personal mailing list or as complex as controlling the processes of a manufacturing plant. They are used extensively in financial applications for banking transactions, investment tracking, and loan processing.

Just as the types of applications are highly diverse, the front ends to these applications also vary widely according to the application and the experience level of the user. Database front ends provide the user interface to the data. The front end is used for displaying data, inputting data, and handling user queries and reports. While the database handles the storage of the information, you can think of the front end as the presentation of the information to the user. This involves screen designs and, quite often, the design of reports.

This chapter will focus specifically on the design of various screens for data input and data display. In this chapter, you will learn the following:

➤ How to create a simple data-entry form.

➤ How to enhance the basic functionality of the simple form.

➤ How to use multiple windows for data-entry.

➤ How to implement non-standard input techniques.

➤ How to use different data display methods, including graphics.

One of the advantages of working with Visual Basic to develop database front ends is that you are not constrained to a single database type. Visual Basic is designed to work best with Access databases, but the Jet engine used in Visual Basic also allows you to use other database formats such as FoxPro or Paradox. This means that, in addition to creating new databases, you can also link to existing databases on your machine or on database servers.

In designing the database front end, you should always keep the user's task in mind. Your design should be one that makes it as easy as possible for the user to perform his work. For example, if the user's function is to monitor warehouse inventory levels as items are sold, he may not need the capability to page through individual records. Or, if your user needs to be able to call up and modify specific records, he will need a search capability built into the application.

Visual Basic provides a variety of controls and methods for you to use in designing your database front end. For most applications, your only limitations are the task for which you are designing the application and your own imagination.

There are two methods of accessing databases from Visual Basic. These are as follows:

➤ Using the Data control and bound controls

➤ Using the Data Access Objects

In this chapter, a combination of these methods will be used to achieve the desired results for the front ends being designed. For an introduction to database design and using these data access methods, see Que's *Special Edition Using Visual Basic 4.*

A Simple Front End

Any discussion of advanced topics needs to begin with a brief discussion of the basics. This is to ensure that everyone is communicating from a common knowledge base. In this discussion, the starting point is an example of a simple database front end. For this front end and for many of the other elements of this chapter, a sample application will be used. This sample case tracks information about the participants in a youth group and their attendance at various events and functions. If you wish to view the sample application, you may access it in Visual Basic by loading the YOUTH.VBP project file on the companion CD.

> **Note:** In the interest of saving space, most of the information about the structure of the database and tables used in the sample case are omitted from the chapter text. If you want such a description, you may look at or print the YOUTHDAT.TXT file on the companion CD. Or, if you want a challenge, you can map the structure of the database using the Data Access Objects.

Starting with a Simple Data-Entry Form

A good starting point is a simple, one-form display of the participant information. If you have done any database programming, you have probably developed a form like this at some point. This first panel is developed with the Data control and the bound controls. It contains basic information about the group member such as name, address, and phone number. The form also contains command buttons to add new records and delete existing records. This sample form is shown in figure 4.1.

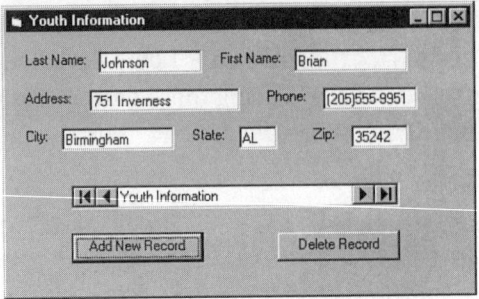

Fig. 4.1 A simple input form can be developed with the Data control and bound controls.

As previously stated, front ends can be developed with the Data Access Objects as well as the Data control and the bound controls. To illustrate this point, figure 4.2 shows a form with the same functionality as the one in figure 4.1—but developed without the Data control and bound controls. Both of these forms are available in the sample application, as Youth-1 and Youth-2, respectively.

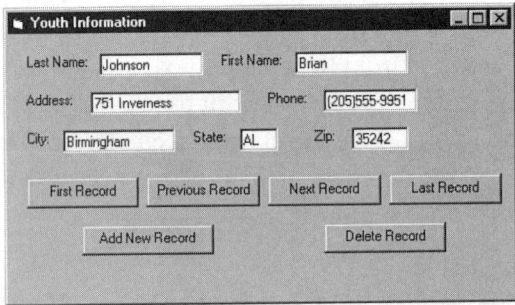

Fig. 4.2 A simple input form can also be developed with just the Data Access Objects.

Enhancing with Navigation Keys

One of the most useful enhancements for a database front end is to add navigation keys. These keys allow the user to move through the records by pressing keys on the keyboard instead of having to use the mouse to click on the control buttons of the Data control or the command buttons of the data-entry form. If you have ever entered a long series of records, you know how time-consuming it can be to constantly move your hand from the keyboard to the mouse and back. Fortunately, this enhancement is also one of the easiest to implement.

To illustrate the use of navigation keys, support for the following keys will be added to the data-entry form of figure 4.1:

➤ Ctrl+Page Up—Move to the first record in the database.

➤ Page Up—Move to the previous record in the database.

➤ Page Down—Move to the next record in the database.

➤ Ctrl+Page Down—Move to the last record in the database.

➤ Ctrl+A—Add a new record to the database.

➤ Ctrl+D—Delete the current record from the database.

> **Note:** You may wonder why we don't use the Insert and Delete keys to add or delete a record. The reason is that these have meaning in the editing of text in a field. That is, the Insert key toggles between the insert and overwrite edit modes and the Delete key is used for character deletion.

To implement the use of keys to navigate the database, the keystrokes must be intercepted and checked against an action list before they are passed to the active control (for example, a text box). Intercepting the keystrokes is done by setting the `KeyPreview` property to True for the current form. This is shown in the following code:

```
Form1.KeyPreview = True
```

This code allows events in the form to examine the keystrokes to determine if any action is necessary. There are three form events where keystrokes can be examined. These are the `KeyPress`, `KeyDown`, and `KeyUp` events. (This discussion will not use the `KeyUp` event, but it works the same as the `KeyDown` event for our purposes.) The `KeyPress` event can be used if you do not need to know the shift state of the key being pressed.

Note: Shift state refers to whether the Shift, Ctrl, or Alt keys were held down when a key was pressed.

When the `KeyPress` event is triggered, it passes an argument to the event subroutine that specifies an integer value for the key. This value is compared against key code constants to determine if the desired key was pressed. These constants are defined in Visual Basic's help system.

If you need to know the shift state of the key, you should use the `KeyDown` event. When the `KeyDown` event is triggered, it passes the integer value of the key just like the `KeyPress` event did. However, the `KeyDown` event passes a second variable that indicates the shift state of the key. The possible values of this variable are summarized in Table 4.1.

Table 4.1   Shift, Ctrl, and Alt Keys Pass Different Values to the Event

Held Key	Value
(None)	0
Shift	1
Ctrl	2
Alt	4

Note: In addition to the values of the individual keys, the values may be combined to indicate a key combination. The value for the combination is just the sum of the individual keys (for example, the value for Ctrl+Alt is 6).

To process the desired keystrokes, a set of nested `Case` statements is placed in the form's `KeyDown` event. These statements check the key code and shift state values against desired values, then process the keystrokes accordingly. The code to process the keystrokes for the data-entry form is shown in Listing 4.1. The code shown sets up the outer Case statement on the value of the shift state, then uses inner Case statements to process individual keys. You can, of course, change things around to suit your programming style. Setting the code up in this manner also allows you to easily add other keys such as Ctrl+F for a seek function.

Listing 4.1   Case Statements Allow the Processing of Different Keystrokes

```
****************************************************
'Outer Select statement checks for the shift state
****************************************************
    Select Case Shift
        Case 0
            Select Case Keycode
                Case vbKeyNext
                    Data1.Recordset.MoveNext
                Case vbKeyPrior
                    Data1.Recordset.MovePrevious
            End Select
        Case 1
        Case 2
            Select Case Keycode
                Case vbKeyNext
                Data1.Recordset.MoveLast
                Case vbKeyPrior
                Data1.Recordset.MoveFirst
                Case vbKeyA
                Data1.Recordset.AddNew
                Case vbKeyD
                Data1.Recordset.Delete
                Data1.Recordset.MovePrevious
            End Select
        Case 4
End Select
```

Setting up this functionality has no effect on the appearance of the data-entry form. The form looks the same to the user, but it can help the user accomplish his data-entry tasks more easily.

Caution: Certain controls such as command buttons and list boxes do not pass specific keystrokes to the form even with the `KeyPreview` property set. These keys include the Enter key and arrow keys. You should be careful when trying to process these keys if you have command or list controls present.

Multiple Window Front Ends

Single-form database front ends are very useful for simple databases, typically where tables are not highly dependent on one another. Many applications require the user to be able to look at and modify data from multiple tables during the course of a data-entry session. When this is the case, it is usually desirable to present the data in multiple windows. While it might be possible to present all of the information on a single form, this is often confusing to the user and usually results in a very cluttered form. Using multiple windows allows you to place data in logical groupings in separate windows.

For example, in the sample case, when a new youth is added to the database, you usually need to add information about his parents (unless he is the sibling of another youth in the group). You would typically want information such as the parents' names, places of employment, and work phone numbers. Trying to pack all this on the same form with the youth information would yield a screen like the one shown in figure 4.3. This screen is very cluttered and is difficult to use.

A better solution is to put the parent information in a separate data-entry window. This can be done in several ways. This section will look at the following:

➤ Using frames

➤ Using multiple forms

➤ Using Multiple Document Interface (MDI) forms

➤ Connecting the data in forms

➤ Maximizing screen real estate

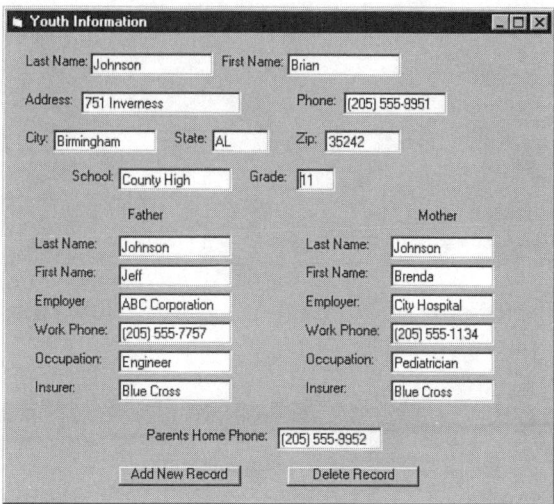

Fig. 4.3 Too much data on a single form creates a cluttered data-entry screen.

Using Frames for Creating Pages

If you have done much programming with Visual Basic, you know that you can use a Frame control as a container for other controls. This is convenient if you have a group of controls that you want to be able to hide or move during your application. With the controls contained by the Frame control, you have to set only the visible or position properties of the frame instead of each control in the group.

This behavior can be used to present different pieces of related data to the user. For instance, you could place a command button on the youth data part of the form (which causes the parent data to be shown), and a button on the parent data part of the form (which returns to the youth data view). Using this method would allow us to eliminate some of the clutter on the form but still get to both sets of data fairly easily. This approach is shown in figures 4.4 and 4.5.

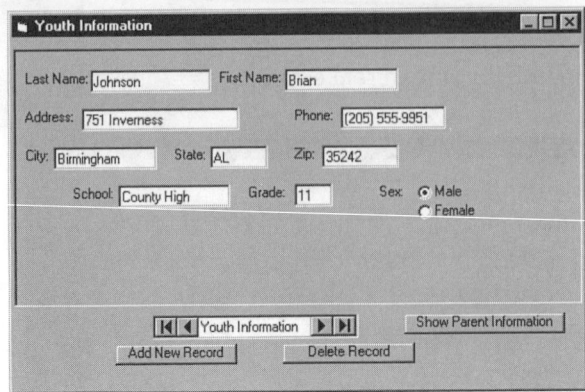

Fig. 4.4 Putting the youth data in a frame allows it to be swapped with the parent data.

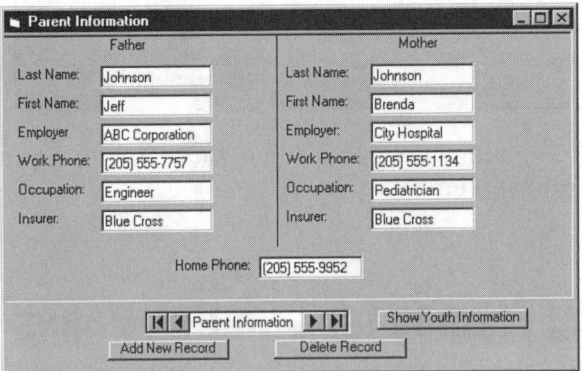

Fig. 4.5 Putting the parent data in a second frame eliminates the clutter on the screen.

The swap function for these frames is easy to implement. Each command button hides one control and displays the other. The statements for this are shown below.

```
'****************************************
'Hide youth data and display parent data
'****************************************
Frame1.Visible = False
Frame2.Visible = True
'****************************************
```

```
'Hide parent data and display youth data
'*****************************************
Frame2.Visible = False
Frame1.Visible = True
```

You do not have to place all the information inside the frames. For instance, if you wanted to leave the youth name on the screen while the parent data was shown, you could leave the name on the main form outside the frame. You would also need to size both frames so that they did not cover this part of the form.

There are other ways to use the frames to control what is presented to the user on the screen. One of these is to use the frames to swap between a single record mode and a browse mode. The browse mode uses the data-bound grid to display information about multiple records in a spreadsheet-like form. The data-bound grid will be discussed further in the section "Using Other Controls" later in this chapter.

Another way to use frames is to put data on multiple "pages." Creating multiple pages is an extension of the method of swapping two screens, as was shown with the youth and parent data swap. This method will be shown in the section "Optimizing the Use of Available Screen Space" later in this chapter.

There are several drawbacks to using the method of multiple frames.

➤ Frames cannot be moved on the form the way forms can be moved on the desktop. This means that your users cannot move one group of data out of the way momentarily to view other data.

➤ The second drawback is that you can't resize a frame by dragging a corner or side. This means that the user doesn't have the flexibility to size or position a data window so that only a part of it shows.

➤ You also cannot minimize a frame the way you can a form.

Multiple Forms

Another way of presenting data in multiple windows is to use multiple forms. With multiple forms, you can segregate the information you need to present into two or more windows. You can set the forms up so that all of them are displayed at the same time, or you can call one form from another.

Using multiple forms to display and edit information can provide the following advantages to your users:

➤ Both forms can be shown at the same time, allowing users to view related information on one form while editing the information on the second form.

➤ Users can quickly toggle back and forth between the forms to edit information on either one. To move from one form to the other, the user just needs to click on the desired form with the mouse.

➤ Users can move or resize the forms that they are not currently using so that only pertinent information is shown on the screen. Or, if desired, the user can close the form completely if it is no longer needed.

Continuing with the example of youth group membership, figure 4.6 shows how the youth data and the parent data would be presented on separate forms. The data shown on each form is the same as the separate frames used in the last section; however, with the two forms, all information is displayed at the same time.

Since it is desirable to have both the youth and parent data shown on the screen at the same time, you need to load both forms when the application is invoked. To do this, you can use one of two methods. With the first method, your program starts by loading the first form (Form1). Then, in the Load event of Form1, you place the code to show the second form as shown below.

```
Form2.Show
```

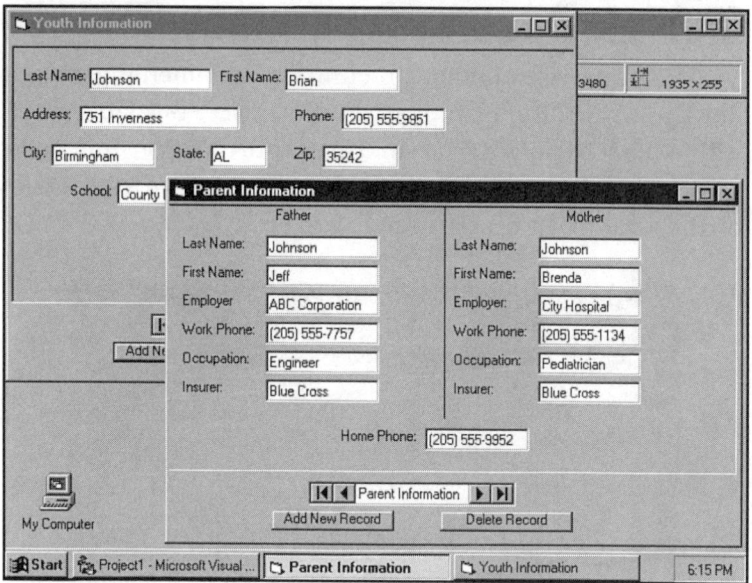

Fig. 4.6 Using multiple forms allows you to place data in separate windows, yet display all the data at the same time.

Using the second method, a program module or menu choice would contain the code to load both forms. This code is shown below. Note in the code listing that the form you want active should be the last one loaded.

```
Form2.Show
Form1.Show
```

If your application needs access to the second form but does not need it present all the time, you may wish to call the second form from a command button on the first form. In this case, you define the command button and place the `Form.Show` statement in the `Click` event of the command button. You might also want to use this method even if you typically display both forms at once. That way the user can call a form back up if he accidentally closed it.

Multiple Document Interface (MDI) Forms

MDI forms provide another structure for implementing multiple windows. With MDI forms, your application places the data on child forms within the MDI parent. The child forms are then constrained to the boundaries of the MDI parent instead of being able to move anywhere on the desktop. This is illustrated in figure 4.7.

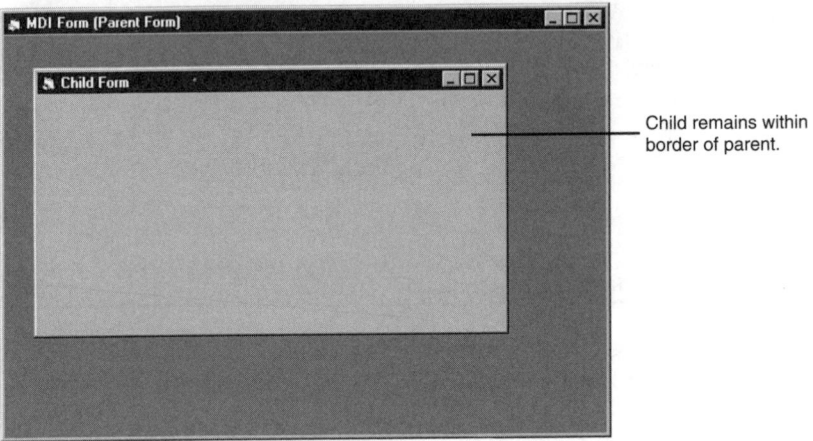

Child remains within border of parent.

Fig. 4.7 An MDI child form can only be moved and resized within the boundaries of the parent form.

Note: For the MDI discussion, *parent* and *child* refer to the relationship of the forms, not the people that are included in the youth tracking application.

Using MDI forms can be an advantage in situations where your application will be used in conjunction with several others. The MDI form provides the common container for all your application's forms. That way, if users switch from your application to another and then switch back, none of your application's open forms will be hidden. They will be brought back up as a unit. Similarly, if your users need to minimize the application, they have to minimize only the parent form, not each individual form in your application.

The MDI form also provides a convenient means of incorporating a menu with multiple sub-forms. The menu, and possibly even a Toolbar, can be placed on the parent form, then the child forms can be called as necessary.

A key benefit to using MDI forms is the ability to create multiple instances of a child form. Most of you are probably familiar with calling up multiple documents in a word processor. This is an example of using multiple instances of a child form. Each document is a new instance of the same basic form.

For a database application, being able to create multiple instances of a form allows you to look at multiple views of the data. Consider the youth application; you could run two queries that showed different groups of youth. One query could show youth in grades 6–8, while the other would show youth in grades 9–12. Or you could run the queries based on interests such as choir or mission work. Being able to look at different groupings of the data side-by-side often provides greater insight into the data than just looking at a single view.

Another possibility of using multiple instances would be with graphs. Using an MDI child form containing a Graph control, you could place a bar chart of total sales by region in one instance of the form. Then in a second instance, you could place a pie chart that showed each region's contribution to total sales. Again, this allows you to analyze your data in different ways.

To create an instance of an MDI child form, the form must first be defined in the design mode. To create the new form, you place the following code in the event from which the form is launched:

```
Dim newgrid As New Form2
newgrid.Show
```

In this code, you identify the name of the new instance of the form (newgrid) and the form that is the basis of the new instance (Form2). Once the new form is dimensioned, the Show method loads it and places it on the screen. If you want to learn more about using MDI forms, you should refer to Chapter 2, "Multiple Document Interface (MDI)."

Connecting the Data in Forms

The key to making a multi-window interface work is being able to maintain the proper relationship between the data elements in each window. For example, with the youth data in one window and the parent data in another window, you need to make sure that the parent information shown corresponds with the youth record you are editing. This means that you have to set up the link between the youth data and the parent data when the forms are first opened, and maintain that link each time you change youth records.

To set up the example, a form is created containing the youth information. This form uses the Data control and a set of bound controls to access the data. A second form is created containing the parent information, also using the Data control and bound controls.

> **Note:** You do not have to use the Data control and bound controls for this method to work. They are used for the example because their use simplifies the display of information and recordset navigation. This allows the explanation to focus on the link between the two forms.

The structure of the database defines a `ParentID` field in both the Youth table and the Parents table. (Examine the file YOUTHDAT.TXT to see the database structure.) This field provides the link between the two tables. To make this link work on the forms, a Label control bound to the `ParentID` is placed on the youth information form. Each time the record pointer is moved, this control will change to the new value of the `ParentID`. Placing the following code in the `Change` event of the Label control makes the link between the forms:

```
fndcode = Form1.Data1.Recordset("ParentID")
Form2.Data1.Recordset.FindFirst "ParentID = " & fndcode
```

The first line of this code assigns the value of the `ParentID` for the current youth record to a variable. The second line of the code then searches the recordset in `Form2` for the corresponding `ParentID` in the parent table. When the record in the parent table is found, its contents are displayed in the appropriate fields on `Form2`. This link is initialized when the two forms are loaded. The link is maintained each time the record pointer is moved because the record movement triggers the `Change` event containing the code.

Caution: It is possible to use a similar technique to provide a simultaneous link in the other direction, that is, from the parent form to the youth form. However, care must be exercised to avoid an infinite loop. For example, a change in the youth record triggers the first `Change` event. This causes the record pointer in the Parents recordset to move, causing a `Change` event on the parent form. This then causes the record pointer for the Youth recordset to move, and so on. To avoid this situation, set a global variable that indicates which form is in control. Then place an `If` statement around the code in the `Change` event. If the form containing the `Change` event is not in control, the code is not executed.

Optimizing the Use of Available Screen Space

A major concern in managing the use of multiple information screens is optimizing the use of available screen space. Only so much information will be visible on the computer screen at any one time, no matter how many windows you use. In fact, as you add more forms to the desktop, the amount of visible information decreases because each form has borders and a header that take up screen space.

There are several ways to maximize your use of available screen space. Some of these are as follows:

➤ Shrinking forms that are not in use

➤ Moving forms that are not in use

➤ Creating multiple pages

Shrinking and Moving a Form

Shrinking and moving a form that is not in use will be covered together since they are variations on the same technique and are often used together. The purpose behind shrinking a form is to show only the essential information on the form in the smallest format possible. In the sample application, the parent information form might show only the parents' names while the youth form is being edited. Likewise, the youth form might only show the youth's name while the parents' information is being edited.

In addition to shrinking the form when it is not in use, it is often desirable to move the form to an edge of the screen. (I prefer moving it to the bottom.) This provides the maximum amount of contiguous space on the screen for the active form. Figures 4.8 and 4.9 show the two data views where the active form is full-size and the inactive form is reduced-size.

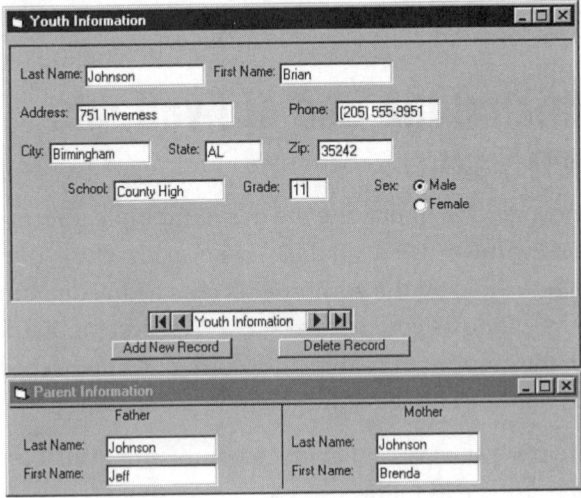

Fig. 4.8 Shrinking the Parent Information form while the youth data is being edited saves screen space.

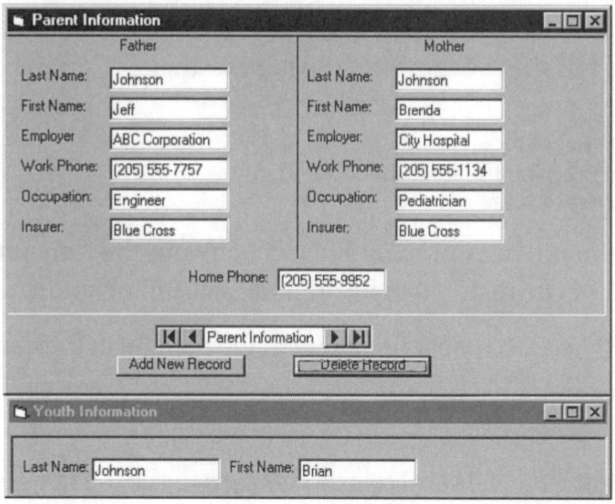

Fig. 4.9 Activating the Parent Information form reverses the form sizes and positions.

Invoking this technique involves placing code in the `Activate` and `Deactivate` events of each form. To get the position and size of the inactive form, you should create the desired look of the form while in the design mode. When the form is positioned and sized to your liking, read the form's `Top` and `Left` position properties and the `Height` and `Width` size properties. (For the example, the following values will be assumed: `Top = 5760, Left = 1245, Height = 1410, Width = 6840`.) Then, in the `Deactivate` event of the form, place code that will set the position and size to the desired values as shown below.

```
Form2.Top = 5760
Form2.Left = 1245
Form2.Height = 1410
Form2.Width = 6840
```

This code will be invoked whenever another form is made active, thereby shrinking and moving the current form.

To restore the form to its full size, get the `Top`, `Left`, `Height`, and `Width` properties of the form as you want it to appear when it is active. (Example: `Top = 1170, Left = 1080, Height = 4335, Width = 7710`.)

Then place these values in the `Activate` event of the form to restore the form to full size, as shown in the next listing.

```
Form2.Top = 1170
Form2.Left = 1080
Form2.Height = 4335
Form2.Width = 7710
```

This code will be run when the user activates the form and will cause the form to be restored to its original size and position.

You will need to repeat this process for each form that you want to shrink.

Caution: You will want to exercise care in setting the sizes and positions of your forms to ensure that they do not overlap. If your active form completely covers any of your reduced forms, the user will not be able to see the information on the form, nor will he be able to activate the form with a mouse click.

Note: Your user may want the ability to move and resize the active form. In this case, you will want to preserve the size and position of the form when it is reduced and then restored. For this, you will need to set global variables for the four size and position properties of each form. Then, in the form's `Deactivate` event, read the current values of the properties prior to reducing the form. To restore the form, you will need to reset the properties to the previous values. The next listing shows the code for the `Activate` and `Deactivate` events.

```
'Deactivate event
Sub Form_Deactivate()
F2T = Form2.Top
F2L = Form2.Left
F2H = Form2.Height
F2W = Form2.Width
Form2.Top = 1170
Form2.Left = 1080
Form2.Height = 4335
Form2.Width = 7710
```

```
End Sub
'Activate event
Sub Form_Activate()
Form2.Top = F2T
Form2.Left = F2L
Form2.Height = F2H
Form2.Width = F2W
```

The user will not be able to change the size and position of the reduced form. Because, as soon as the user clicks on the form to move it or change its size, the Activate event is triggered.

Creating Multiple Pages

Some applications may have a large amount of data that the user needs to process, but the data does not all have to be on the screen at the same time. In this case, you can present the information in pages using multiple frames to represent the pages. An example of this type of program would be one that handles mortgage applications. If you've ever applied for a mortgage, you know how much information they want about you—your name, address, employer, income, whether any of your ancestors arrived on the *Mayflower*, and so on.

To efficiently set up multiple pages, you need to have a way to easily navigate from one page to another. You will also probably need to keep some information on the screen that is constant for all pages (such as a borrower's name). Other information that would be beneficial to your users would be the number of the current page and the total number of pages for the application. This can be placed in a group of Label controls to exhibit something like "Page 1 of 5."

When you are developing pages, you will need to work with your user to determine the most efficient arrangement of the information on the pages. For the mortgage example, you might want separate pages for borrower information, spouse information, employment history, and credit history.

Sequential Page Navigation

Once the pages are set up, you will need to give the user a means of moving from one page to the next. The easiest way to do this is to provide two command buttons, one for Next Page and one for Previous Page. Choosing these buttons moves the user forward or backward through the available pages in sequential order. This is good for applications with a small number of pages. The first page of a mortgage application with the two command buttons is shown in figure 4.10.

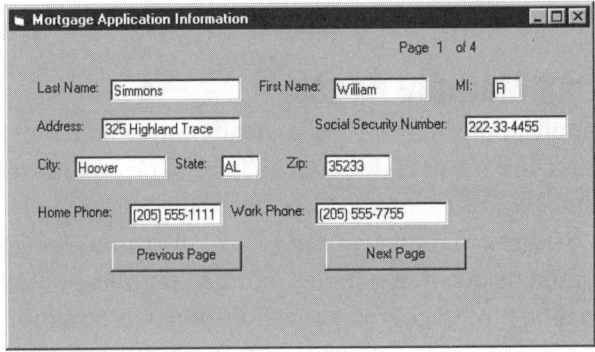

Fig. 4.10 A multi-page form requires a way to move between pages.

To implement the movement between pages, we place code in the `Click` event of the command buttons. This code will hide the current Frame control and show the frame for the next (or previous) page. This code is shown in Listing 4.2. The listing assumes that there are four pages of information. (Also, the command buttons are named `NextPage` and `PrevPage`.)

Listing 4.2   MORTGAGE.FRM—These Subroutines Enable the Page Movement Buttons

```
Sub NextPage_Click
Select Case ipage
    Case 1
        Frame1.Visible = False
```

```
         Frame2.Visible = True
         ipage = 2
      Case 2
         Frame2.Visible = False
         Frame3.Visible = True
         ipage = 3
      Case 3
         Frame3.Visible = False
         Frame4.Visible = True
         ipage = 4
End Select
PageNo.Caption = ipage
If ipage = 4 Then
   NextPage.Enabled = False
Else
   NextPage.Enabled = True
End Sub

Sub PrevPage_Click
Select Case ipage
   Case 2
      Frame2.Visible = False
      Frame1.Visible = True
      ipage = 1
   Case 3
      Frame3.Visible = False
      Frame2.Visible = True
      ipage = 2
   Case 4
      Frame4.Visible = False
      Frame3.Visible = True
      ipage = 3
End Select
PageNo.Caption = ipage
If ipage = 1 Then
   PrevPage.Enabled = False
Else
   PrevPage.Enabled = True
End If
End Sub
```

You should note two things about Listing 4.2. The first is that the code updates the label caption that contains the page number. This is so the user knows the current page number. The second item of note is that the code disables the Next Page button when the last page is reached, and disables the Previous Page button when the first page is reached. This is for the convenience of the user. Disabling the buttons provides an additional visual indication of the user's position in the application. Adding this type of visual indicator is good programming practice.

Direct Page Navigation

Next Page and Previous Page buttons are sufficient for applications with a small number of pages (2–4). However, moving through several pages to get to the information you need can be frustrating. Also, the Next Page and Previous Page buttons provide the user with no information about what is on other pages.

Therefore, if you have a larger number of pages, you might want to provide the user with a means to go directly to any given page. This can be done by creating a Toolbar of command buttons on your form. Each command button is assigned to a specific page of the form. You can use either text descriptions, or, if your application is amenable to it, icons to identify each button. The text on the command buttons can be used to identify the information on the page it accesses. Figure 4.11 shows a redesign of the mortgage application with the Toolbar added.

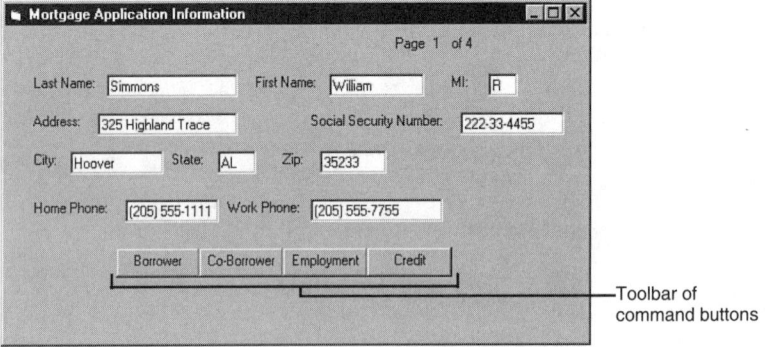

Fig. 4.11 A Toolbar allows the user to access any page at any time.

Along with adding the Toolbar to the form, another change was made to the application—namely, the way in which frames are defined. Instead of using individually named frames for each page, a Frame control array is used. This simplifies the implementing code of each command button by using the current page number to determine which page to hide.

In this case, the current page number corresponds to an index of the Frame control array. When a command button is pressed, an array index is generated from the current page number. This frame of the array is then hidden. Next, the new page number is set along with the array index of its corresponding page. The new page is then shown, and the current page display is updated. This process is shown in the next code listing for the Page 3 command button.

```
ipict = ipage-1
Frame(ipict).Visible = False
ipage = 3
ipict = ipage-1
Frame(ipict).Visible = True
PageNo.Caption = ipage
```

Note that in the listing, the array index is one less than the page number. This is because the index for a control array starts with 0.

Creating Tab Pages

An interface that is gaining a lot of popularity lately is the use of tab pages. These pages look like a series of file folders lined up behind each other. You will often find this type of interface used for accessing multiple pages of a three-dimensional spreadsheet or in the option setting dialog boxes of many programs. The advantage of using this method is that it provides a familiar metaphor for the user to access information.

Visual Basic comes with a custom control that allows you to add a tabbed interface to your program. You can add this control to your Toolbox by selecting the control from the Custom Controls dialog box. The individual tabs on the control work like a series of frames to allow you to present information on separate pages of the control.

To set up the Tab interface, you must first draw the control on your form. You do this like you would for any other control, drawing the Tab to the size and shape that you want. The initial Tab control will contain three tab pages on a single row. By setting the Tabs and TabsPerRow properties of the control, you can adjust the number of tabs and control how many rows will be presented. Figure 4.12 shows how the control would look with five tabs arranged in two rows (Tabs = 5, TabsPerRow = 3).

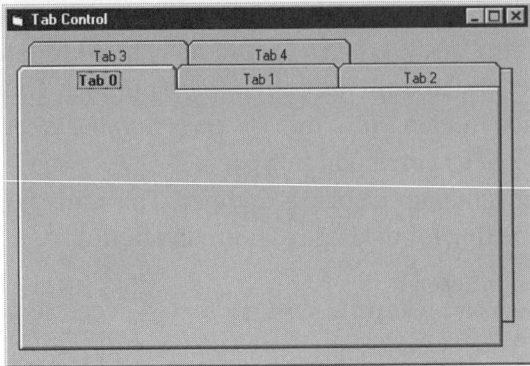

Fig. 4.12 The Tab control allows you to present information on a series of pages.

You can also control other aspects of the appearance of the Tab control using the following five properties:

➤ Style—Controls whether the tabs look like those in Microsoft Office applications or the ones in Windows 95.

➤ TabHeight—Controls the height (in twips) of the tab portion of each page. A larger height allows more information to be printed on the tab.

➤ TabMaxWidth—Sets the maximum width of each tab in twips. If this property is set to zero, the tabs will be sized to fit the space on a row.

➤ TabOrientation—Controls whether the tabs appear on the top, bottom, left, or right of the control.

➤ WordWrap—Controls whether the text in the Caption property can use multiple lines to print.

After you have set the appearance of the Tab control to your liking, it is time to add information to the pages. For each tab page, you select the page by clicking on page's tab. You can then add any controls to that tab page. To add the controls, you just draw them on the tab page as you would on a frame, picture box, or a form. You can also set the

`Caption` property of the tab page to indicate the type of information that appears on the page. As you move from page to page in the Tab control, only the controls on that page will be shown. All other controls on other pages will be hidden.

One caveat with using the Tab control: the individual tab pages cannot be used to group option buttons. That is, the control considers all option buttons on all tab pages to be part of the same group. Therefore, if you need separate groups of option buttons within the Tab control, you will need to place a frame on the tab page containing the option buttons, then place the buttons on the frame.

Figure 4.13 shows how the Tab control could be used in presenting information for the Mortgage Application.

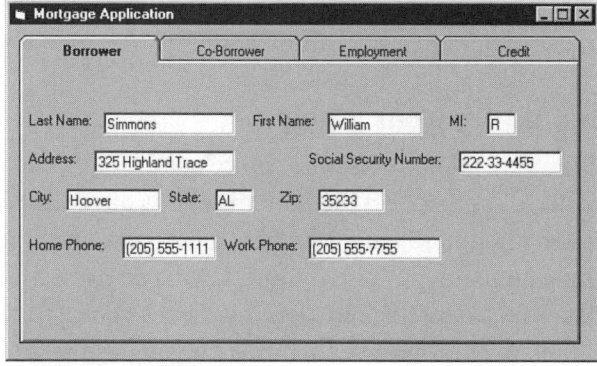

Fig. 4.13 The Mortgage Application makes good use of the Tab control.

Other Input Methods

In addition to the standard input form with Text and Label controls to show the data, there are ways of getting data into a database. There are other controls that can be used to enter, edit, and display data. Several of these controls can be used as bound controls, meaning that they will work with the Data control. Other controls cannot be bound, but they can be used with the Data Access Objects and, with a little work, can be made to function with the Data control.

Using Other Controls

For many applications, the Text Box and Label controls are sufficient for handling data display and entry functions. These controls handle a wide variety of data types. They are also commonly used because they can be bound to a Data control, making many data editing operations automatic.

Another bound control that is used less often is the Check Box. The check box only works with True/False data fields. There are times, however, when these controls are not sufficient to handle all of your data-entry needs. This section will look at several other controls that you can use to enhance your application.

Picking Items from a List

For many applications, you will want to use a list of valid options from which your user can select. In earlier versions of Visual Basic, the List control was not bound, and data from a list had to be input using assignment statements. In Visual Basic 4, you can use a list to directly enter data into a data field. In fact, you have a choice of two bound List controls and two bound combo boxes for your application. Only list boxes will be covered in this section, but the combo boxes work the same way. Figure 4.14 shows a screen that uses both types of list boxes. This screen is from a library system.

The first type of list box is known as a Data-Aware List Box. The list box is drawn on a form just like any other control. The items available for selection in the list box are set up using the AddItem method. To initially set up the list, place a series of AddItem statements in the Load event of the form. For the library screen shown in figure 4.14, the Data-Aware List Box is used to select the type of media for the resource (for example, book, audio tape, video, or CD). The code to set up the list is shown below.

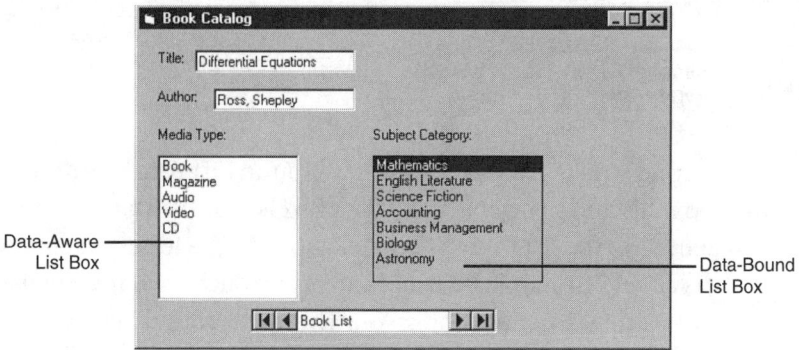

Fig. 4.14 This screen uses both the Data-Aware List Box and the Data-Bound List Box controls.

```
Media.AddItem "Book"
Media.AddItem "Magazine"
Media.AddItem "Audio"
Media.AddItem "Video"
Media.AddItem "CD"
```

For use in a database application, this list box may be bound to a single field in a recordset. When a list box is bound to a field, the user's selection is automatically stored to the bound field. For instance, if the user chose Book from the media type list, the value Book would be stored in the Media field of the recordset. The list box can be bound to a recordset by setting its DataSource and DataField properties. The DataSource property specifies the Data control for the recordset being edited. The DataField property specifies the actual field in the recordset that will accept the selection from the list box.

If you are using the Data Access Objects instead of the Data control, you will need to determine the user's selection manually. To do this, you check the ListIndex and List properties of the list box. The ListIndex tells you the index number of the selected item, then the list value for that index gives you the text of the selected item. The code below shows how the Media data field would be updated from the media selection list. The Media field is in a recordset named MyDyn.

```
MyDyn.Edit
slitm = List1.ListIndex
psnm = List1.List(slitm)
MyDyn("Media") = psnm
MyDyn.Update
```

The second type of list box is the Data-Bound List Box. The difference between this and the Data-Aware List Box is that the Data-Bound List Box generates the list from a field in a table. In the library example, there is a table containing a list of categories such as math, English literature, science fiction, and so on. The Data-Bound List Box uses the records in this table to set up the list for the user's selection. Three properties of the Data-Bound List Box are used to set up the list:

➤ `RowSource`—Specifies the Data control of the recordset containing the list of choices.

➤ `ListField`—Specifies the field of the recordset that will be displayed in the list.

➤ `BoundColumn`—Specifies the field whose value will be used as the selected value of the list.

Two other properties of the Data-Bound List Box determine where the selection from the list will be stored. These are:

➤ `DataSource`—Specifies the Data control of the output recordset.

➤ `DataField`—Specifies the output field.

All five of these parameters must be specified or an error will be generated when the application is loaded. In setting up the list, the same Data control (and therefore the same recordset) can be used for both the `RowSource` and `DataSource` properties. Also, the `BoundColumn` and `DataField` properties must both reference the same *type* of field (for example, both-character or both-integer).

When a user makes a selection from the list, the value of the `BoundColumn` field of the source recordset is stored to the `DataField` field in the target recordset. This control and its `ComboBox` counterpart cannot be used with the Data Access Objects.

Using Option Buttons

Another very useful control is the option button. Unfortunately, it is not a bound control that can be used directly with the Data control. However, this does not have to stop you from using the control. Option buttons come in handy for allowing the user to select between a small number of choices. A typical use would be for selecting gender in a membership application, as shown in figure 4.15.

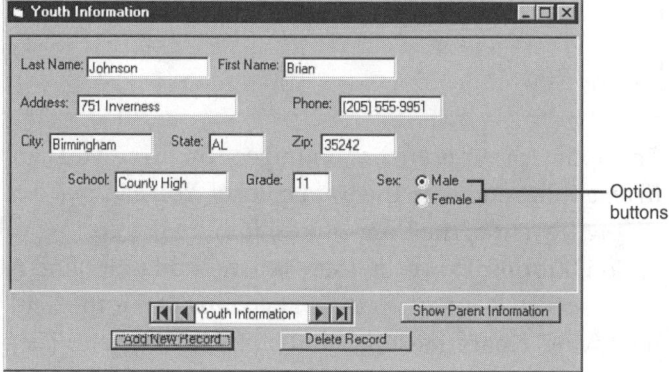

Fig. 4.15 Option buttons can be used to present the user with choices.

In code, you determine which option button was chosen by checking the `Value` property of each one. If the value of a button is `True`, then this was the selected button. Only one option button of a group may be selected. Option buttons may be grouped on a form, in a picture box, or in a frame. It is a good practice to set up each group of option buttons in a picture box or frame to avoid conflicts with other groups.

Once you have determined which option button was selected, you can assign the desired value for your data field based on the selection. For the membership case, either an `M` (male) or `F` (female) is stored, depending on the option button selected.

Note: If you have more than two option buttons, you might want to put them in a control array. Then you can use a loop to look for the selected option, as shown in this code listing.

```
isel = 0
'Loop through five option buttons
For I = 0 To 4
    If Option(I).Value Then
        isel = I
        'Exit the loop when the selection is found
        Exit For
    End If
Next I
```

The option buttons are not bound controls, but you can still use them in an application with the Data control. You can place code in the `Validate` event of the Data control to store the desired value from the option buttons. However, there is a method that I find easier to use. (It's a sneaky way to trick the Data control.) For the field that you are modifying, create a text box and bind it to the field. Then set the `Visible` property of the text box to `False`. This will keep the box from being seen by the user. Then, in the `Click` event of each option button, place a line of code that changes the contents of the text box to the value represented by the option button. Then, when the Data control is invoked to move the record pointer, the field bound to the hidden box is updated along with all other bound fields. For the membership case, the following code would be used:

```
Sub Male_Click()
    Gender.Text = 'M'
End Sub
Sub Female_Click()
    Gender.Text = 'F'
End Sub
```

Using this hidden box method has an additional benefit. You can use the `Change` event of the box to mark the proper option box for each record that is accessed. The code for this would be:

```
If Gender.Text = 'M' Then
    Male.Value = True
```

```
Else
    Female.Value = True
End If
```

While this discussion has focused on how to use the option buttons with the Data control, you can also use them when you program with just the Data Access Objects. In this case, you use an assignment statement to set the value of your field just like you do any other field. For the membership case (assuming the field is named Gender), you would use the following code:

```
OldTbl.Edit
If Male.Value Then
    OldTbl("Gender") = 'M'
Else
    OldTbl("Gender") = 'F'
End If
OldTbl.Update
```

Using Spin Button Controls

Spin Button controls are another control that is not a bound control, but can be useful in a database application. The spin buttons are really a modifier for a Text or Label control. To use a spin button, you use a Text or Label control to hold the contents of a numeric field. Then you place a Spin Button control next to the Text or Label control. Finally, you place code in the SpinUp and SpinDown events of the Spin Button control to increment or decrement the value of the Text or Label control. The following code would add one to or subtract one from the value in a text box named Price; you can set the values of the spin button to any increments that you need:

```
Private Sub SpinButton1_SpinDown()
    Price.Text = Price.Text - 1
End Sub

Private Sub SpinButton1_SpinUp()
    Price.Text = Price.Text + 1
End Sub
```

Once the value of the text box has been set, the field in the database is updated the same as any other text box. This is handled by the Data control if you are using it or with an assignment statement if you are using the Data Access Objects. Figure 4.16 shows the youth data application with a spin box that is used in conjunction with the Grade text box.

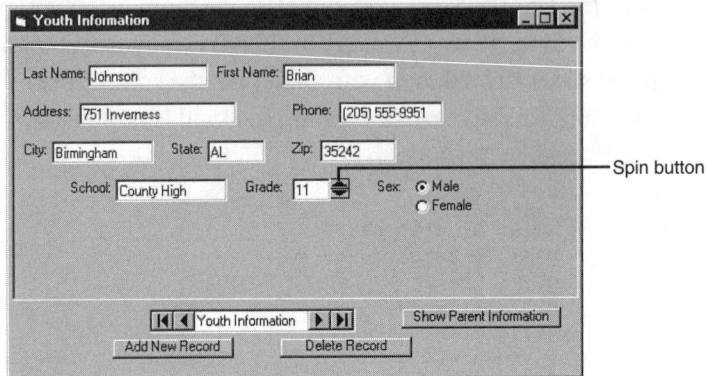

Fig. 4.16 You can use a spin button to increment the value of a number.

You can also use the spin button to manipulate date information. This is slightly more complex than working with numbers because you cannot add a number directly to the `Text` property that represents a number. If the text box represents a date, the following code in the `SpinUp` event will add one day to the date:

```
Dim Oldate As Date
Oldate = Text1.Text
Text1.Text = Oldate + 1
```

If you want to add a month at a time to the date (or a year at a time), you can use the `DateAdd` function. This function allows you to specify the date interval (day, week, month, quarter, or year) and number of intervals to be added to the current date. The following code shows how to add a week at a time to the date:

```
Dim Oldate As Date
Oldate = Text1.Text
Text1.Text = DateAdd("ww", 1, Oldate)
```

Using the Data-Bound Grid

The Data-Bound Grid is a new control for Visual Basic 4. This control only works with the Data control. It cannot be used with the Data Access Objects. The Data-Bound Grid provides a spreadsheet-like view of the records in your recordset. This view is similar to the Table mode in Access or the Browse mode in FoxPro.

Setting Up the Data-Bound Grid

As stated, the Data-Bound Grid may only be used with the Data control. The Data-Bound Grid is one of the custom controls provided with Visual Basic. You must add the DBGrid control to the Toolbar by selecting it from the Custom Controls dialog box. To use the grid, select it from the Toolbar and size it on the form just like you would any other control. Add a Data control to the form and set it up to access the desired recordset. Then set the DataSource property of the DBGrid to the Data control. The grid is then set up. When activated, the grid can show all fields in all records of the recordset. If all of the information will not fit on the screen, the grid will display scroll bars to allow the user to view additional data.

Using the Grid as a Primary Input Method

The Data-Bound Grid can be used for input by setting up the grid and setting the AllowAddNew and AllowUpdate properties to True. Used in this manner, the grid provides your users with access to a number of records at a time. They can then use the cells of the grid to edit individual fields in any record shown. Scroll bars allow the user to move through fields and records that do not fit on the screen.

If the AllowAddNew property has been set to True, an asterisk (*) will be shown in the last row of the grid. Entering information in this row will add a new record to the grid.

As an additional option for your users, you may wish to place the Data-Bound Grid in a frame. Then, in a second frame, place the controls necessary to edit a single record of the recordset. By hiding one frame and providing a command button to switch the frames, you can provide your user with a means of viewing records in either a single-record mode or a browse mode. This is useful if the users want to do most of their editing in the browse mode but like the additional information (specifically labels used as input prompts) that can be placed on the single-record view.

User-Defined Queries

The data-bound grid is also useful for displaying the results of developer-defined queries or, if you include a query builder in your application, user-defined queries. An example of this method is included in the project contained in the SAMPLQRY.VBP file on the companion CD. The example allows the user to choose from a number of queries on the youth data table. The user may filter the youth shown by grade, gender, or school attended. Figure 4.17 shows the selection form for the queries. Once the user has selected the query he wants, he clicks the Execute Query button to display the results.

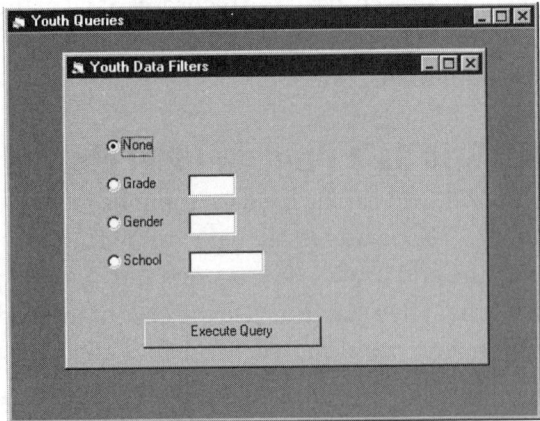

Fig. 4.17 The user may select from several filters in the query selection form.

In the example, an MDI parent form is used to contain the query selection form and the query results forms. An MDI child form contains the Data control and the Data-Bound Grid. When a query is run, a new instance of the child form is created and the database name and the SQL statement to create a recordset are passed to the child window. These variables are then used to set the DatabaseName and RecordSource properties of the Data control. The code to invoke the query results form is shown in Listing 4.3. This listing shows the query with no filter condition. Figure 4.18 shows the results of one of the queries from the example project.

Listing 4.3   YOUTHFIT.FRM—A Child Form Containing a Data-Bound Grid Is Loaded to Display the Results of a Query

```
'****************************************************
'These statements set the database name and recordset
'****************************************************
MydbName = "YOUTH.MDB"
MyrcSource = "SELECT * FROM Youth"
'*********************************************************************
'These statements create a new instance of the form and
'display it
'*********************************************************************
Dim newgrid As New Form2
newgrid.Show
'************************************************************
'The form load event sets the properties of the data control
'The size and position of the child form are also set.
'************************************************************
Private Sub Form_Load()
    Me.Height = 5985
    Me.Width = 8610
    Me.Left = 1
    Me.Top = 1
    Data1.DatabaseName = MydbName
    Data1.RecordSource = MyrcSource
End Sub
```

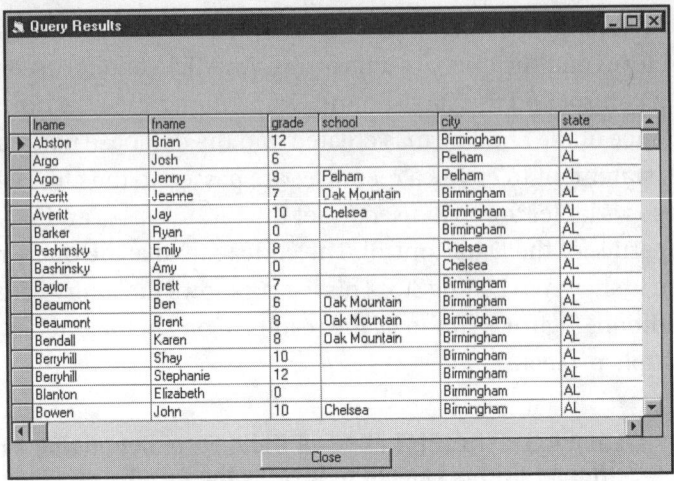

Fig. 4.18 The query results are displayed in a Data-Bound Grid.

Two-Column Pick List

There are times in applications when it is desirable to add a group of records at one time. In the youth group membership application, an attendance-tracking module is included to keep track of which youth were at a particular event. One method of inputting this information would be to set up a form where the youth names are entered one-at-a-time on the form, and an attendance record is created with each selection. This method works but is inefficient for several reasons. First, a user may accidentally enter a youth more than once. Second, there is no easy method of checking the list of attendees prior to adding the information to the database. Finally, the method is slow because the processing of each attendance record is done individually instead of as a batch.

There is, of course, a better method. (You knew there was or this section wouldn't be here.) By using two List Box controls and a command button, you can set up what is called a two-column pick list. You are probably familiar with these if you have ever chosen options for setting up a windows program. The two-column pick list for the attendance example is shown in figure 4.19.

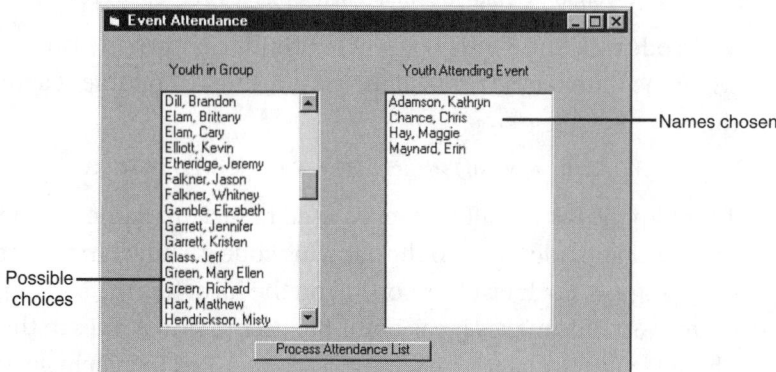

Fig. 4.19 A two-column pick list provides an easy way to enter multiple records.

With the two-column pick list, the user selects youth names from the first list by double-clicking the name with the mouse. The name is then removed from the first list (Youth in Group) and added to the second list (Youth Attending Event). Removing the name from the first list prevents the user from accidentally adding a name twice. After all the attendees have been added to the attendance list, the user can review the list to look for any omissions or people who were added accidentally. If necessary, the user can remove a name from the attendance list by double-clicking on the name. This removes the name from the attendance list and adds it back to the first list. After the user is satisfied with the list, he can click the Process Attendance List button to create the actual attendance records in the database.

Since you don't want to constrain the user to just using the mouse, you will also want to add keyboard functionality to this input method. This is easily accomplished using the `KeyDown` event of each list. While a list has focus, the user may press the arrow or page keys to move through the list. This is an inherent behavior of the list box. The only thing you need to do is set up a keystroke for the user to make a selection.

The natural key for this is the Enter key. To activate the Enter key for List1, add the following line of code to the KeyDown event:

```
If KeyCode = vbKeyReturn Then Call List1_DblClick
```

This code calls the DblClick event subroutine shown in Listing 4.4 when the Enter key is pressed in List1. A similar statement activates the Enter key for List2.

```
If KeyCode = vbKeyReturn Then Call List2_DblClick
```

To set up the list initially, a loop is used to pick up names from the recordset and add them to the list. This code is shown in the first part of Listing 4.4. Each List Box control on the form has the Sorted property set to True. This makes it easier for the user to find names in the list. The selection process for each list box is enabled by placing code in the DblClick event of the control. The code determines the item number of the selection, removes it from one list and adds it to the other list. This code is shown in the second part of Listing 4.4. Finally, when the user clicks the Process Attendance List button, the actual attendance records are created. This is done using a loop to scan the contents of the attendance list and create a record for each name on the list. This code is shown in the third section of Listing 4.4.

Listing 4.4 ATTEND.FRM—These Code Segments Handle All the Processing for the Two-Column Pick List

```
'**********************************************************
'Code in the form load event sets up the initial list.
'**********************************************************
Sub Form_Load()
    Dim OldWs As Workspace, OldDb As Database, OldTbl As _
      Recordset
    Set OldWs = DBEngine.Workspaces(0)
    Set OldDb = OldWs.OpenDatabase("A:\YOUTH.MDB")
    Set OldTbl = OldDb.OpenRecordset("Youth",dbOpenTable)
    Do Until OldTbl.EOF
        List1.AddItem OldTbl("Lastname") & ", " &
OldTbl("Firstname")
        OldTbl.MoveNext
    Loop
End Sub
'****************************************************************
```

```
'Code in the double-click event of each list handles user
'selections
'*********************************************************************
Private Sub List1_DblClick()
    slitm = List1.ListIndex
    psnm = List1.List(slitm)
    List2.AddItem psnm
    List1.RemoveItem slitm
End Sub

Private Sub List2_DblClick()
    slitm = List2.ListIndex
    psnm = List2.List(slitm)
    List1.AddItem psnm
    List2.RemoveItem slitm
End Sub
'*******************************************************
'Code in the click event of the process button creates
'attendance records
'*******************************************************
Dim Tbl2 As Recordset
Set Tbl2 = OldDb.OpenRecordset("Attend",dbOpenTable)
OldWs.BeginTrans
For I = 1 to List2.ListCount
   Tbl2.AddNew
   Tbl2("Event") = evntname
   Tbl2("Name") = List2.List(I-1)
   Tbl2.Update
Next I
OldWs.CommitTrans
```

Several notes should be mentioned about this method. First, in the code to create the attendance records, transaction-processing statements were used so that all attendance records could be added at once. This increases the performance of the application. Second, the name used in the List Box control was used in the attendance record. In most cases, you would probably use a member's ID to reduce the space required for the records. The name was used here to simplify the code listing.

> **Caution:** The two-column pick list should probably be used only for relatively small recordsets (less than 200 records) since the list controls store each list item in memory. A large recordset would probably exceed available resources.

Output Methods

The previous sections of this chapter have focused primarily on ways to get data into a database. However, part of a database front end involves the presentation of data to the user. Information in text form can be displayed to the user with the same types of controls and forms used for data-entry. In fact, one of the examples of use of the Data-Bound Grid involved displaying the results of queries. Another method of presenting data is by using pictures. Access databases can store pictures in a Long Binary field. These pictures can be displayed in a picture box on a form.

Note: You cannot directly edit a picture in the picture box.

Another powerful way of presenting information to the user is through the use of graphs. Two ways to create graphs on your forms are:

➤ Using the Graph control

➤ Using the graphics methods

Creating graphics is covered in detail in Chapter 16, "Graphics: Data Analysis." The following sections will make use of these methods, but will focus on the purpose of creating the graph—rather than the details of how to create them.

Static Graphs

Static graphs can be used to show all types of information and can be presented in many forms. Examples include: a pie chart to show expense distributions, a bar chart showing weekly sales levels, or a high/low/close chart for stock quotes. Static graphs are meant to show data at a specific point in time (for example, at the end of a month). Figure 4.20 shows an example of a bar chart displaying a company's sales levels by region for the previous week.

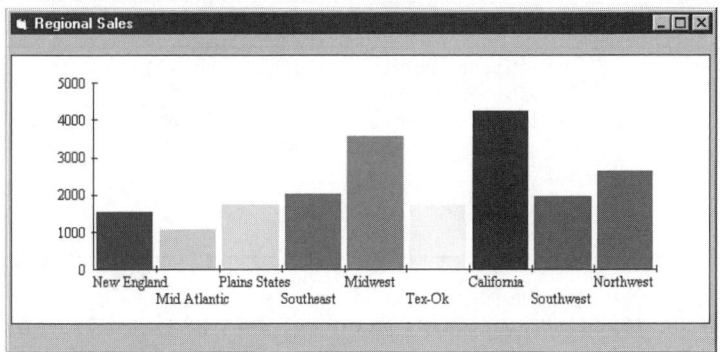

Fig. 4.20 Data charts provide the user with a visual aid in analyzing data.

To create this chart, a Graph control was placed on the form with its GraphType property set to 3 (2D - Bar). To set up the rest of the graph, data is accessed from the sales table in the sales database. The code to set up the graph is shown in Listing 4.5. The first lines of the listing set up the table to access the data. The code then uses a MoveLast method to set the RecordCount property of the recordset to the number of records accessed. This value is then used to set the NumPoints property of the graph. Next, a For...Next loop is used to set the values of the LabelText and GraphData properties for each point, based on the contents of the fields of the recordset. Once this code is completed, the graph is displayed.

Listing 4.5 SALESGR.FRM—Data Is Entered into the Graph's Data Array from the Sales Table

```
Dim OldWs As Workspace, OldDb As Database, OldTbl As Table
    Set OldWs = DBEngine.Workspaces(0)
    Set OldDb = OldWs.OpenDatabase("A:\SALES.MDB")
    Set OldTbl = OldDb.OpenRecordset("Sales", dbOpenTable)
    OldTbl.MoveLast
    J = OldTbl.RecordCount
    Graph1.NumPoints = J
    OldTbl.MoveFirst
    For I = 1 To J
        Graph1.ThisPoint = I
```

continues

Listing 4.5   Continued

```
        Graph1.GraphData = OldTbl("Gross")
        Graph1.ThisPoint = I
        Graph1.LabelText = OldTbl("Region")
        If I < J Then OldTbl.MoveNext
    Next I
    OldTbl.Close
    OldDb.Close
```

By looking at a chart, users can quickly get a feel for the average sales per region and which regions are the best and worst performers. Combining the chart with supporting data, such as actual sales figures in a grid, gives the user even greater insight into the information. This combination is shown in figure 4.21.

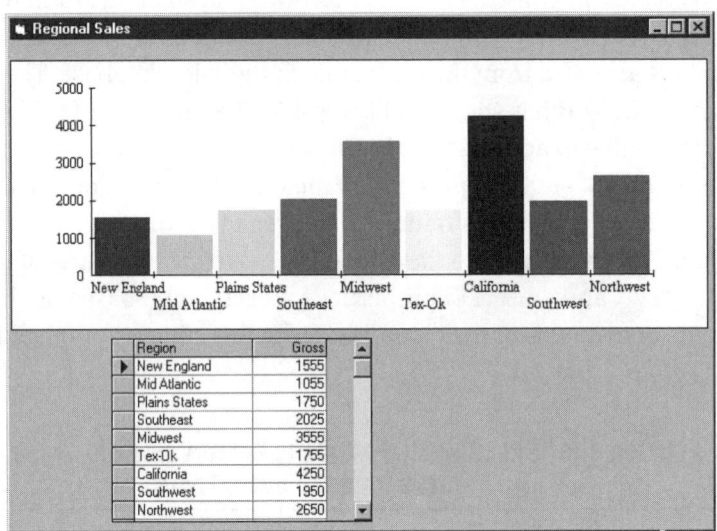

Fig. 4.21 Combining a graph with detail data gives the user more information than either one alone.

Dynamic Graphs

Dynamic graphs are those that change with time. They are typically used to analyze ongoing processes. An example would be to view the output of a manufacturing operation. A particular process produces pellets that range in diameter from 0.45 inches to 0.50 inches. Any pellets outside that dimension must be rejected. The user wants to monitor the process to be able to spot any trends that might show the process heading toward a rejectable condition. If the trends are spotted soon enough, adjustments can be made to the process. The measurements from the process are automatically stored in a database.

One approach to this application would be to show the actual values of the last 10 samples. This would provide some benefit to the user but would not provide as much information as he needs. A better approach would be to set up a chart that has the upper and lower bounds of the range on it, then plot each of the last 50 measurements on the chart. The chart would be updated with each new measurement so that the latest 50 measurements are always shown. A chart of this type is shown in figure 4.22.

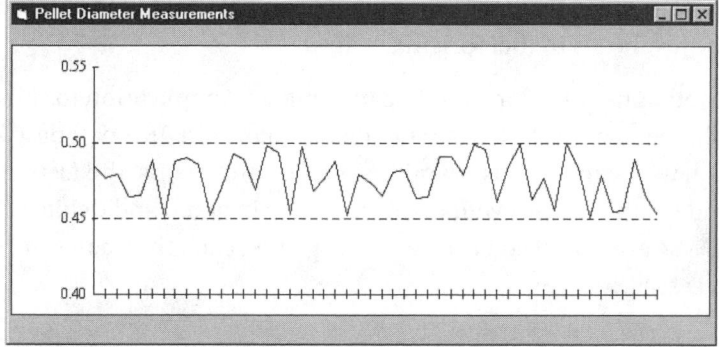

Fig. 4.22 A time-dependent chart can show data trends.

By using a continuously updated chart, the user can spot trends as they are occurring. Then, if necessary, he can take action to adjust the process before a problem occurs. This type of data presentation provides real value for the user. The creation of dynamic graphs is covered in detail in Chapter 16, "Graphics: Data Analysis."

Using Color

Color is another consideration in the presentation of data to a user. Color can be used to provide visual clues to the user about the data itself, or about the status of the data. For instance, you could place code in the Change event of a text box to notify the user that the data has been changed. The following code changes the text from black to blue as soon as any change is made to the data in the text box.

```
Private Sub Text1_Change()
    Text1.ForeColor = &hff0000
End Sub
```

You might also want to use a color change to indicate that information is available for editing. This is very useful when using the Data Access Objects, since you have to specifically invoke the edit method. In this case, you could have a button on your form that invokes the edit method and changes the foreground color of all text boxes. Then when the user saves the data, code is run to restore the foreground color of the text boxes to their original values.

Another use of color would be in a financial application to show whether a number was greater or less than zero. In a database application where the user is examining credits and debits, the Listing 4.6 code in the Change event displays credits in green and debits in red. The Change event is used because it is triggered each time a new record is accessed.

Listing 4.6   Using Color to Provide the User with Information About His or Her Data

```
Private Sub Text1_Change()
    If Text1.Text < 0# Then
        Text1.ForeColor = &hff
    Else
        Text1.ForeColor = &hff00&
    End If
End Sub
```

From Here...

This chapter has presented several ideas for input and output user interfaces for accessing databases. There are, of course, several ways that you can design a database front end. Hopefully, the ideas presented here will provide you with the basis for more advanced interfaces for your own applications.

➤ For more information about many of the controls discussed in this chapter, you can refer to Que's *Special Edition Using Visual Basic 4.*

➤ For more information on using MDI forms in your application, see Chapter 2, "Multiple Document Interface (MDI)."

➤ For more information about creating graphics in your application, see Chapter 16, "Graphics: Data Analysis."

For a discussion of other database topics, see the following chapters:

➤ For more information about manipulating data in a database, see Chapter 5, "Data Management and Data-Driven Programming."

➤ To learn about Open Database Connectivity operations, see Chapter 6, "Working with ODBC."

➤ To find out how Jet handles ODBC databases, see Chapter 7, "The Jet Engine and ODBC."

➤ To learn about connecting to database servers, see Chapter 8, "Modern Client/Server Computing," and Chapter 9, "Client/Server Databases."

5

Data Management and Data-Driven Programming

by Michael McKelvy

Visual Basic 4 is a very powerful programming language. With it, you can create applications to balance your checkbook, chart daily temperature changes, or calculate the stress load on an airplane's landing gear. Most applications you create have to handle data in some form. A program typically needs to get input from and deliver output to the user. The program may also need to store results for later use.

Advanced programs may handle a lot of data from various sources: data from the primary user, data from other users, data from previous calculations, data from other applications, or data from outside sources. With all this data flying around inside the computer, you need an efficient way to handle it. This is where data management comes in.

If you need to know how to manage data better, stay tuned. This chapter discusses the following topics:

➤ Data management and relational database management systems

➤ How to organize your data in a database management system

➤ Data validation and data integrity

➤ Structured Query Language (SQL) and how it can help with database management

➤ Advanced data-management concepts

Most of the concepts put forth in this chapter may be applied to any data-management situation and can be used with a variety of database management systems. Discussion and examples in this chapter, however, will focus on the use of the Jet database engine, particularly Access databases.

Explaining Data Management

Data management is a process primarily concerned with the following three objectives:

➤ Storing data

➤ Retrieving data

➤ Ensuring data integrity

In addition to these primary objectives, your particular application may need to meet other business objectives. These can include speed of data retrieval, minimizing storage space, and ease of programming.

These objectives are not completely independent, and in many cases, tradeoffs between them must be made. Which objective has priority is determined by the tasks that the system must accomplish and the applications that it must support.

Data management is a process or logical approach to handling the objectives outlined above. It is not the physical means by which information is stored. Data management can be applied to any type of file system. If you have previously written programs that store data in a file and have given any thought to the logical layout of that data, then you have done some data management. In fact, if you are an overly ambitious programmer, you can apply data-management concepts to the writing of your own database management system. (Actually, by writing a small file storage and record indexing system, I gained a great appreciation for the complexity and power of commercial database management systems.)

A *relational database management system* (RDBMS) facilitates the storage and retrieval of data. The RDBMS is made up of a file system and an engine that handles the accesses to the data. The beauty of an RDBMS is that it frees the programmer from the details of reading data and writing data on the disk. It also provides a consistent interface with the data. This is illustrated in figure 5.1.

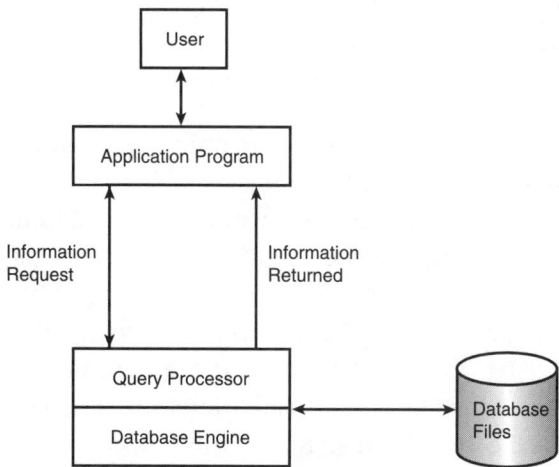

Fig. 5.1 Data access is simplified with a relational database management system.

With a system of flat files, you have to define the file structure of your data in every program that accesses the file. With an RDBMS, the file structure is defined once, then stored in the database itself. When you need to access a particular piece of data (a *field*), you send a request to the database engine asking for the field by name. If you store name data in a flat file, for example, you need to tell your program that a person's last name is contained in the first 20 bytes of each record (or wherever it is located). With an RDBMS, you specify the field name (*Lastname*) to retrieve the data. Listing 5.1 shows the difference between these two approaches. Both code segments assume that all the appropriate file open functions have been performed.

Listing 5.1   The Difference Between Code Used to Retrieve a Field from a Text File and a Database File

```
'**************************************
'Get the last name from an ASCII file.
'**************************************
Line Input #1, Inpdat$
Lname = Mid(Inpdat$, 1, 20)
'******************************
'Get the last name from an RDBMS
'******************************
Lname = OldTbl("Lastname")
```

If you are going to use the data with only one program and the format of the data is never going to change—no new fields, the fields don't change size—either method will work. But what if things do change? (They always do, right?) Then an RDBMS makes things much easier. Suppose the length of your last name field changed because you didn't allow enough characters, for example. With sequential file access, you have to change the code for obtaining the last name in every program that accessed the file. This is in addition to actually changing the format of the file itself. With an RDBMS, all you change is the length of the field in the database structure. All programs that access the file remain unchanged because they never knew the field length to start with.

Using a Database Management System

OK, now you're convinced that you can't live without an RDBMS for your next project. How do you get your data into it and use it?

Follow these steps to set up the database (or databases) in an RDBMS for your project:

1. Organize your data into logical groups (*tables*).

2. Determine the *relationships* between the tables.

3. Create the database file and define the structure of your tables to the database.

4. Load your data.

The first two items of the list are the design phase of database management. Good design is extremely important. If the design is a good one, other aspects of data management are made much easier. If the design is bad, operations performed on the database are inefficient and can potentially lead to errors in your data.

Sample Case Definition

A sample case will be used for discussing the data-management concepts presented in this chapter. This sample case calculates the cost and delivery information for fuel assemblies for a nuclear power plant. The production of the fuel assemblies requires several stages of material deliveries and process services, as shown in figure 5.2.

The production and delivery of one component must be completed prior to the start of production for the next component with each process or material delivery being handled by a separate vendor. Each vendor has its own contract with the utility receiving the fuel. The production of each component requires a specific amount of time to complete. Since the target delivery date of the final product (the assemblies) is known, and the production time requirement for each component is known, a schedule for the start and completion of each stage of production can be calculated. In addition, since each component is produced by a separate vendor, a cost calculation is required for each component. The final cost of the assemblies is the sum of the component costs.

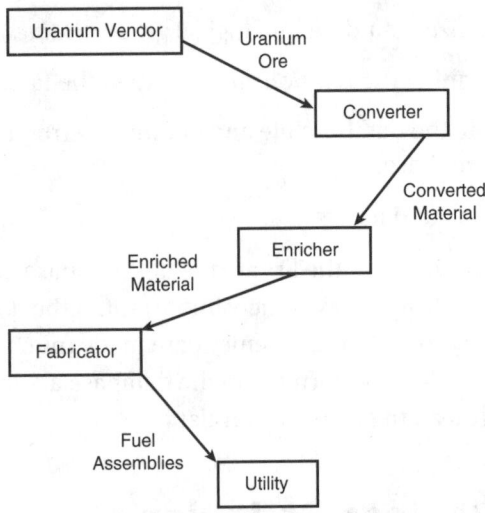

Fig. 5.2 Producing fuel assemblies requires multiple processes performed by multiple vendors.

Therefore, the application developed for the utility must calculate the demand for each raw material or service, the timing of deliveries of materials from each vendor, and the cost of each component. For the remainder of the chapter, the application is referred to as CostPlan. The data flow for the application is shown in figure 5.3.

The main business objective of CostPlan is to minimize the cost of the fuel assemblies. This means getting material at the lowest price from competing vendors, and minimizing the amount of time that the fuel is in production. To determine a minimum cost requires multiple scenarios to be run. The management of all the input and output for the multiple scenarios is what makes an RDBMS so valuable to the calculation.

The information used by `CostPlan` comes from a variety of sources. Much is input by the application's users, but two databases come from outside sources. One is a fuel type database, which is generated by another department in the company. The other is a table of raw material and service quantities provided by one of the vendors. Because of the source of these databases, the design of the data-management system needs to account for any special needs, such as security or data access modes.

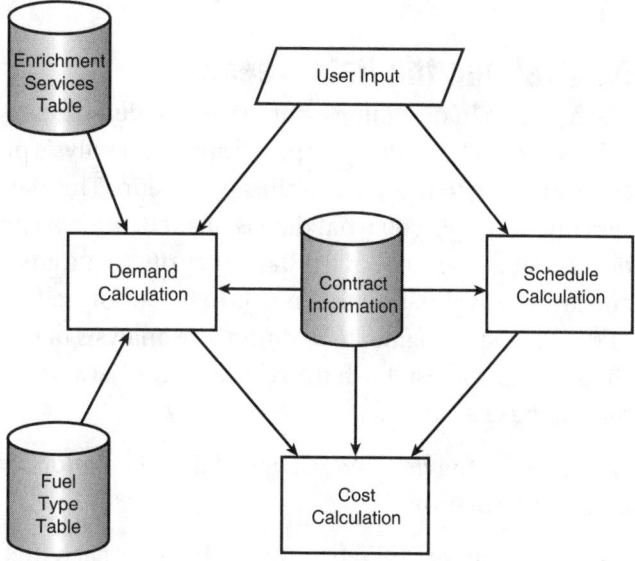

Fig. 5.3 The data flow for the calculation illustrates the complexity of the data-management tasks.

Database Design

The design of the database(s) for an application depends on the task the application performs, the sources of the data, and specific requirements of the user. While the topic of database design is much too extensive for a complete treatment in this chapter, we will present some of the basics of good design as a foundation for other data-management topics.

The main activities in the design of a database are as follows:

➤ Determining the data needs of the application

➤ Determining the sources of the data

➤ Organizing the data into logical groups

➤ Data normalization and relations

➤ Determining how the tables will be used

Determining the Data Needs

The first step in designing a database is to determine what data needs to be stored. This is done by performing an analysis of the application and by talking to the users of the application. This determination process not only tells you what data is needed, but also provides information about the sources of the data, security requirements for the data, and any data validation that needs to be performed by the application or the database engine. In addition, the analysis of data requirements should help you establish the relationships between different parts of the database.

For `CostPlan`, the *demand portion* of the calculation requires the following information:

➤ The number and type of assemblies for each fuel batch (`CostPlan` will calculate the cost of multiple batches in each run)

➤ The physical characteristics of each assembly type (weight and enrichment)

➤ A table of enrichment process inputs and outputs (for example, the amount of raw material and services input to the process to produce a given amount of product)

The *delivery portion* of `CostPlan` requires information about the final delivery date of the assemblies and the lead times required for each step of the manufacturing process.

Finally, *cost calculation* needs information about the cost of each process on a per unit basis and payment schedule information. The *cost information* is further broken down into base cost and escalation factors (how much the cost increases over time).

Data Sources

Determining the sources of the data also provides you with essential design information. If the data is from an outside source, the design of that particular database or table may be beyond your control. In this case, you must tailor the design of your database and application to mesh efficiently with the external data. Also, because the users of your application are not responsible for maintaining or updating the data, this will determine the access level that your application uses for the data. Typically, if your application has no data maintenance functions for a database, read-only access should be used for that database.

`CostPlan` uses two outside information sources.

➤ The first is the table of enrichment process information. This table is provided by the enrichment vendor; the users of the application need only to access it in read mode.

➤ The second outside source is the fuel type information. This data is created and maintained by another department in the company. Again, `CostPlan`'s users need read-only access to the data.

The remaining data, batch requirements information, and vendor contract information will be entered and maintained by the `CostPlan` users. The rest of the design discussion will focus on this information.

Grouping Data in Tables

After determining what data is needed and which data is to be created and maintained by your application, you will need to group the data into separate tables and possibly separate databases. One reason for placing some data in separate databases is to segregate data that is used only internally from data that is created by your application, but shared with other applications or users. Placing this shared information in separate databases makes access control easier. This was done with the enrichment and fuel type information for CostPlan.

For all the data you are maintaining, you will want to store related information in tables. Each table should correspond to a particular topic, and data in the table should be easily identifiable as belonging to that topic.

From CostPlan, two major information topics are not provided by outside sources. These topics will be the basis of two tables: BATCHINF for the batch requirements information and CONTRACT for the vendor contract information. The structures of these two data tables are presented in Tables 5.1 and 5.2. The Batch Information table (see Table 5.1) contains user input about batch requirements. The Contract table (see Table 5.2) contains information about material deliveries and pricing for each vendor.

Table 5.1   Batch Requirements Information

Field Name	Type	Size	Description
BatchID	Text	6	Unique identification for the batch
FuelTp	Text	6	Fuel type identifier
NumAsm	Numeric	Integer	Number of assemblies in the batch
DelvDate	Date	N/A	Required delivery date for the batch

Table 5.2 Material Delivery and Pricing Information for Each Vendor

Field Name	Type	Size	Description
CompType	Text	3	Type of component being delivered
Quantity	Numeric	Integer	Amount of material being delivered
Price	Numeric	Single	Unit price of material
CompDate	Date	N/A	Delivery date for the material
Vendor	Text	6	Vendor identifier
ContractID	Text	6	Identifier for the contract

Data Normalization

Once the data has been grouped for inclusion in tables, review the tables for redundant data. Even if all the information in a table is related to the same topic, you may have repetitive records in the table. In this case, further separate the data into other tables to eliminate the redundancy. Separating the information into multiple, related tables to eliminate data redundancy is called *data normalization.*

As an example, consider the youth program from Chapter 4, "Advanced Database Front Ends." It would be possible to store all the information about each youth in a single record of one table. This information would include the youth's name, address, phone number, parents' names, and so on. Figure 5.4 shows a table of information organized in this manner.

This design will work fine as long as there is only one youth per family (no brothers or sisters). If there are siblings in the youth group, there will be redundant information—address, phone number, and parents' names—for the related youth. Instead of allowing this redundant information, a better design is to separate the information into two tables: one for the youths' names (and other personal information) and one for the family information (the data that might be common to two or more youth). These tables are then related by a key field, in this case, an ID assigned to each parent record. Figure 5.5 shows the two tables resulting from the elimination of redundant data.

Lname	Fname	FFname	MFname	City	State
Able	Brian	Sam	Jane	Birmingham	AL
Armond	Josh	Terry	Cathy	Pelham	AL
Armond	Jenny	Terry	Cathy	Pelham	AL
Avery	Jennifer	Jim	Sherry	Birmingham	AL
Avery	Jack	Jim	Sherry	Birmingham	AL
Baker	Ryan	Ron	Patti	Birmingham	AL
Bayley	Brett	Bill	Sherry	Birmingham	AL
Beaulieu	Brad	Larry	Kathy	Birmingham	AL
Beaulieu	Ben	Larry	Kathy	Birmingham	AL
Bennning	Karen	Robert	Anne	Birmingham	AL
Berry	Shannon	Steve	Sharon	Birmingham	AL
Berry	Stephanie	Steve	Sharon	Birmingham	AL
Bowman	John	John	Brenda	Birmingham	AL
Bowler	Marrianne	Chuck	Barbara	Birmingham	AL
Brinkley	Daniel	Danny	Carol	Birmingham	AL
Chancelor	Chris	Allen	Kate	Birmingham	AL
Cordele	James	Jim	Janice	Birmingham	AL
Cordele	Tommy	Jim	Janice	Birmingham	AL

Record: 1 of 74

Fig. 5.4 Youth and parent data stored in a single table is an inefficient design.

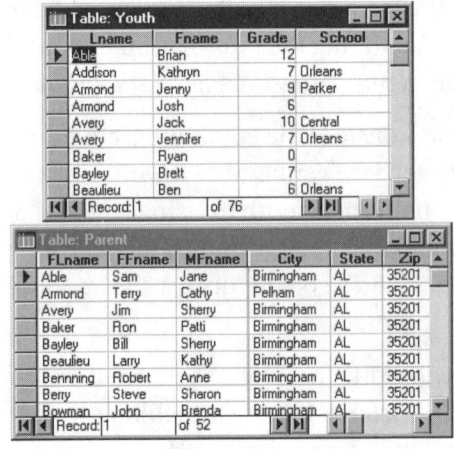

Fig. 5.5 Using separate tables for the parent and youth data eliminates redundancy.

For the CostPlan data, looking at the contract information shows that there can be several prices for materials over the life of the contract.

Using a single table for all the contract information results in repeating much of the information for each different price level. It is therefore necessary to create a different table to contain the price information. The same problem exists with the delivery and payment information for the contract. The final design for `CostPlan` results in three tables for contract information. These tables and their relationships are illustrated in figure 5.6. The detailed data structure of the tables can be found in the COSTPLAN.TXT file on the companion CD.

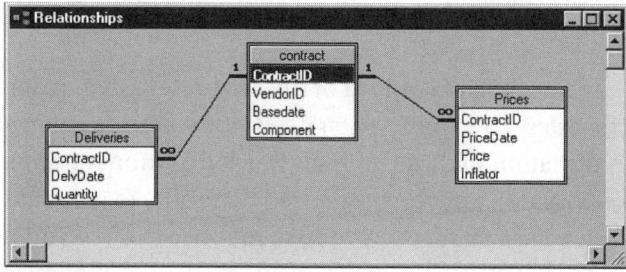

Fig. 5.6 Creating multiple, related tables eliminates redundant data in `CostPlan`.

Types of Tables

A final consideration in the design of the database is the type of tables used for the information. In this discussion, we are specifically talking about two types of tables, temporary and permanent. A *permanent table* is one that contains data that is necessary for multiple calculations or reports, and is not easily reproducible from a calculation. A *temporary table* is one that is needed only for the current calculation (or other task) and may be discarded upon completion of the calculation.

In the design process, you must decide what information needs to be permanently maintained and what can be stored in temporary tables. Typically, if the data can be obtained by a quick calculation from a single source, it should be stored in a temporary table and reproduced for each calculation. On the other hand, if the data is user input or is created by a complex and time-consuming calculation, you should create a permanent table for it.

You may also want to use a temporary table to hold a copy of the information in another table. In the `CostPlan` application, for example, we want to maintain the inventory information on a permanent basis. However, for some of the calculations, the inventory data needs to be modified as the calculation proceeds. By using a temporary copy of the data for the calculation, the original inventory data is preserved for future use.

For `CostPlan`, the final output of the calculation (batch demands, delivery schedules, and batch costs) needs to be kept as a permanent table. The information in these tables is needed as input to other parts of the `CostPlan` system, and the users need to be able to generate a variety of reports from the data. `CostPlan` also makes use of a temporary table for the tracking of material inventory during the calculation. The use of this table will be covered later in the section "Using Temporary Tables."

Creating the Database

Creating the database for an application involves creating the actual database file, then defining the tables and fields of the database structure. These tables and fields come from the design information you developed using the methods described in the design section of this chapter.

The database, tables, and fields are created with the Jet engine using the data access objects (DAOs). These objects are like handles that enable you to access and manipulate data. The DAOs have methods associated with them that enable you to perform the operations on the database. Listing 5.2 demonstrates how the DAOs are used to create the database and one of the tables of the sample case.

> **Note:** A *workspace* provides an area in which the database engine can work. Within each workspace, you can have multiple databases and tables open, but you may have only one user and one set of transactions. By using multiple workspaces, you can handle multiple transaction sets.

Listing 5.2   DAOCOST.TXT—How to Create the CostPlan Database

```
'*****************************
'Dimension data access objects
'*****************************
Dim Ws As Workspace, NewDb As Database
Dim NewTbl As TableDef, F1 As Field, F2 As Field, F3 As Field
Dim F4 As Field,F5 As Field, F6 As Field
'*****************
'Set up workspace
'*****************
Set Ws = DBEngine.Workspaces(0)
'***************
'Create database
'***************
Set NewDb = Ws.CreateDatabase("A:\COSTPLAN.MDB",_
dbLangGeneral)
'**********************
'Create tabledef object
'**********************
Set NewTbl = NewDb.CreateTableDef("Contract")
'********************
'Create field objects
'********************
Set F1 = NewTbl.CreateField("CompType", dbText, 6)
Set F2 = NewTbl.CreateField("Quantity", dbInteger)
Set F3 = NewTbl.CreateField("Price", dbSingle, 30)
Set F4 = NewTbl.CreateField("CompDate", dbDate)
Set F5 = NewTbl.CreateField("Vendor", dbText, 6)
Set F6 = NewTbl.CreateField("ContractID", dbText, 3)
'*********************
'Add fields to tabledef
'*********************
NewTbl.Fields.Append F1
NewTbl.Fields.Append F2
NewTbl.Fields.Append F3
```

continues

Listing 5.2   Continued

```
NewTbl.Fields.Append F4
NewTbl.Fields.Append F5
NewTbl.Fields.Append F6
'************************
'Add tabledef to database
'************************
NewDb.TableDefs.Append NewTbl
NewDb.Close
```

As an alternative to using DAOs to create tables in a database, you can use SQL statements. With SQL, you can create, alter, or delete tables in a database. The code in Listing 5.3 uses an SQL statement to create a new table in an existing database.

Listing 5.3   SQLCOST.TXT—Using SQL Statements to Create the Table

```
'*****************************
'Dimension data access objects
'*****************************
Dim OldWs As Workspace, OldDb As Database
'*****************************
'Set up workspace and database
'*****************************
Set OldWs = DBEngine.Workspaces(0)
Set OldDb = OldWs.OpenDatabase("A:\COSTPLAN.MDB")
'*********************************************
'Set up SQL statement to create a new table
'*********************************************
SQLCreate = "CREATE TABLE Batchinf (BatchID TEXT (6),FuelTp_
Text"
SQLCreate = SQLCreate + "(6), NumAsm INTEGER, DelvDate DATE)"
'*********************
'Execute SQL statement
'*********************
OldDb.Execute SQLCreate
OldDb.Close
```

Entering Your Data

Once the database and all its associated tables have been created, you can enter data into the database. If part of your application includes a user interface for data entry, this is one way for you to enter data as well. If you already have existing data in electronic form, you could also write a short program to import the data.

As part of the sample application, a data entry form is needed to enable the user to enter batch information. This form is shown in figure 5.7.

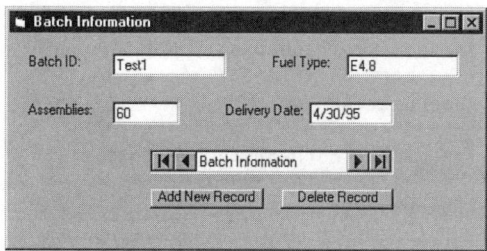

Fig. 5.7 A data-entry form enables the user to enter and modify batch information.

The data-entry form shown in figure 5.7 was created using the data control and bound controls. These are design objects that simplify the development of some data entry and display screens. (A more detailed discussion of database front ends may be found in Chapter 4, "Advanced Database Front Ends.") The form is set up as follows:

1. Draw the data control on the form.

2. Set the `DatabaseName` and `RecordSource` properties of the control to attach it to a database and recordset. For the sample case, `DatabaseName` is set to `A:\COSTPLAN.MDB` and `RecordSource` is set to `Batchinf`.

3. Draw a text box on the screen for each field in the recordset—a total of four.

4. Set the `DataSource` property of each text box to `Data1`.

5. Set the Datafield property of each box to the fields in the recordset, as shown in Table 5.3.

6. Place label controls on the form as prompts for the fields.

7. Place two command buttons on the form, one to add new records and one to delete the current record. The code to attach to the `Click` events of these two buttons is shown in Listing 5.4.

Listing 5.4   Using Program Code to Add or Delete Records in a Database

```
'*******************************
'Code for add new record button
'*******************************
Data1.Recordset.AddNew
'************************************
'Code for delete current record button
'************************************
Data1.Recordset.Delete
```

Table 5.3   DataField Settings for the Four Text Boxes

Text Box Name	DataField Setting
Text1	BatchID
Text2	FuelTp
Text3	NumAsm
Text4	DelvDate

Data Validation

Data validation is concerned with ensuring the accuracy of the data in the database. Validation is usually performed by checking a given piece of data against a list or range of acceptable values. This is *data field validation*. There are, however, some validation requirements that are applied to an entire record (such as comparisons between two fields), or to groups of records.

Data validation can be implemented in three different processes:

➤ Engine-level validation

➤ Program input validation

➤ Batch or offline validation

Each validation technique is covered in this section.

> **Note:** Validation of groups of records is typically handled by a batch process only. Field and record validation can be handled by any of the three processes. The process used depends on the particular situation.

Engine-Level Validation

Engine-level validation is performed at the field and record level by the database engine. The validation rules for fields and records are embedded in the definitions of the tables in the database. When data is added to or changed in a field or record, the engine checks the entry against the validation rule. If the data meets the criterion of the rule, the data is stored to the database. Otherwise, the user is informed that a rule has been violated and is given the opportunity to correct the data.

Field validation rules typically compare the contents of a field to a value or set of values. The rules are usually expressed in terms that will return either a True or False value. An example of this type of rule is `Price > 1.00`.

Record validation rules are typically used to compare two fields in the same record. For example, you might have a rule that verifies that the retail price of an item is greater than the wholesale price.

For Access databases used in Visual Basic, the validation rules are simple value checks. These rules cannot contain any user-defined functions or comparisons to variables.

The advantage of engine-level validation is that the rules are enforced whether the data is changed by your application, by another application, or by someone directly manipulating the database with Access or another product. Therefore, the rules are consistently applied for any data transactions.

Program Validation

Program validation of data is performed by your application as users enter data or as data is added by a calculation. The field and record validation rules can include a greater complexity than is possible with engine-level validation rules. You can either include user-defined functions in the validation rule or compare the contents of a field to a variable within the application.

Program validation can also accomplish some tasks that are difficult with engine-level validation. You may have a data entry function where either of two fields may be left blank, but both fields cannot be blank. This rule is hard to code in the engine validation, but easy to set up in a program.

Program validation can also be used to compare the value of a field in one table to the contents of another table. This cannot be accomplished with engine-level validation. For CostPlan, program validation would be used to ensure that the fuel types entered by the user in the batch requirements information exist in the fuel type database.

> **Note:** With Access databases, you can establish a relationship between two tables in the same database and tell the Jet engine to enforce referential integrity. This performs the same function as the program validation of comparing one table to another. This is not possible for CostPlan because the data resides in separate databases. Also, referential integrity cannot be enforced by Jet on non-Access databases. Referential integrity is further discussed later in the section "Data Integrity."

Another use of program validation is to check a value against a list of valid entries. Then if the entry is invalid, pop up the list of valid entries from which the user may choose. You may wonder, "Why not just use a List control for the user input?" If the user is familiar with the data being entered, it is often faster to type an entry than to navigate a list of values each time the field is edited. By checking the input value against the list, then showing the list if the entry is invalid, you give the user the best of both worlds—rapid data entry and good data validation.

> **Note:** While a combo box combines the capabilities of a list and a text box, it does not restrict the user to entering only items that are contained in the list portion of the control.

Offline or Batch Data Validation

Offline or batch data validation carries program validation one step further. This validation technique is actually a program that checks the contents of an entire table against a set of validation rules. The rules can be for individual fields or records, or they may be used to test a group of records. For example, you may want to verify that the average value of a field is within a certain range, even if some individual records are outside the range.

In the `CostPlan` application, one calculation (not part of the sample case) needs to verify that the total number of assemblies in a group of batches exactly matches the number of assemblies used in the reactor. This verification (or validation) is performed prior to the remainder of the calculations in the module.

Batch validation can also be used in situations where a data entry operator is putting data in the database, but another person is verifying the data before it is posted. The data entry operator may not know how to correct an invalid entry. For example, someone transcribing medical notes may input an invalid diagnosis, but if given a list of valid entries would not know which to choose. A batch validation could be used to create a report of invalid entries, along with the record number containing the entry. Then a more knowledgeable person could review the report and input the correct information.

Data Integrity

Like data validation, *data integrity* is concerned with maintaining the accuracy of the information in a database. In this case, it is concerned with maintaining the references between tables. This is called *referential integrity*. A reference is a link between two tables, such as the parent ID that links the youth and parent tables in the youth information system shown in Chapter 4, "Advanced Database Front Ends." The main threat to referential integrity in that example occurs when a parent record is deleted or the parent ID of a record is changed. If the parent ID listed in a youth record refers to a parent record that no longer exists, the youth record is said to be orphaned. What this means for an application is that some of the information about the youth is no longer available.

For Access databases, referential integrity may be enforced at the engine-level. You can specify in the set up of the relationship between two tables whether referential integrity will be enforced. If you choose to have it enforced, you may also choose to allow updates and deletions to be cascaded. Cascading means that a change to a parent record will also be made in the child records related to it. Also, if a parent record is deleted, the related child records will be deleted. Figure 5.8 shows the relationship between two tables and shows an orphaned record.

Engine-level enforcement of referential integrity can be performed by the Jet engine only on Access databases, and only between related tables in the same database. For all other relationships, enforcing referential integrity is the responsibility of the application.

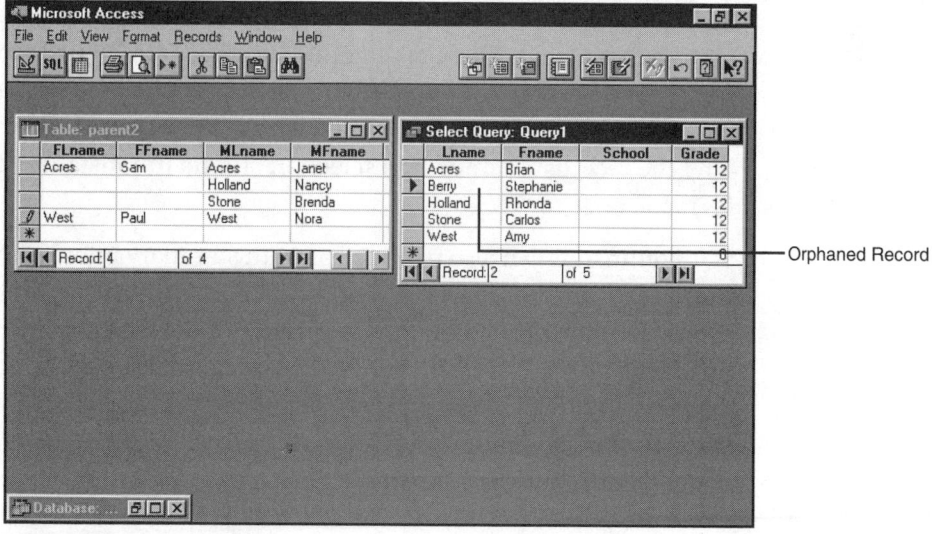

Fig. 5.8 Referential integrity maintains the relationship between two tables.

Structured Query Language (SQL)

Structured Query Language (SQL) is a set of commands that is used to manipulate information in a database. SQL commands can be used to do the following:

> ➤ Retrieve records from a table or set of tables

> ➤ Delete records from a table

> ➤ Insert records into a table

> ➤ Modify records in a table

> ➤ Create a new table in a database

> ➤ Alter the structure of a table in a database

> ➤ Delete a table from a database

SQL commands for retrieving records are the heart of many data-management tasks. These commands enable you to set up recordsets from a single table, or combine fields from a group of tables. They also enable you to specify the order in which the records are presented, and filter the records returned by a selection criteria (for instance, deliveries made after 10/31/94).

SQL commands can also provide you with summary information about the records in a recordset. The commands can be used to provide record counts, summations and averages of a field, maximum and minimum values of a field, or the standard deviation of the values of a field. For these functions, one SQL command can take the place of many lines of equivalent program code and can perform the functions many times faster than the program could.

Database Maintenance

If you create a database application, you will at some time need to perform maintenance on the database. This is not maintenance of the records or everyday housekeeping, but occasional operations that are required to keep your database operating at peak efficiency.

The main task to be performed on your database is compacting. This operation eliminates any wasted space in the database and reduces the database file size. The reason this operation needs to be performed is that when records or tables are deleted, the Jet engine does not automatically recover the space that was previously used by those records. Other records may be written into the space, but over time, you end up with a fair amount of unused space in the database file. This takes up disk space and can slow the performance of data access operation. Wasted space can become a big problem if an application uses a number of temporary tables (discussed later in the chapter). The way to get rid of unused space in the database is by using the `CompactDatabase` method. This method copies the information from the current database to a new database. The old database may then be deleted, and the new database renamed to the old name. The following code shows how the COSTPLAN.MDB database would be compacted and the original database kept as a backup.

```
DBEngine.CompactDatabase "COSTPLAN.MDB", "TEMPCOST.MDB"
Kill "COSTPLBK.MDB"
Name "COSTPLAN.MDB", "COSTPLBK.MDB"
Name "TEMPCOST.MDB", "COSTPLAN.MDB"
```

Note: If you are attempting to compact a database, you must have exclusive access to it. That is, no other users may be working with the database. Also, the Jet engine can compact Access databases only. If you are working with other database formats, you need to use other methods to recover unused space.

The other database maintenance operation that you may have to perform (unless you are extremely lucky) is a database repair. Database management systems are reasonably stable, but from time to time, something will occur that will corrupt your database. You usually find this out when a user attempts to open a database and gets a message that there is a problem with the database. If this occurs, you will need to attempt to repair the database using the RepairDatabase method as shown in the code below.

```
DBEngine.RepairDatabase "COSTPLAN.MDB"
```

A typical problem encountered when a database is corrupt is that the record count for a table does not match the physical number of records stored. This can occur if processing is interrupted while a record is being added. In this case, the repair function resets the record counter to the physical number of records.

One final note about database maintenance. As with all other files, you should back up your database on a regular basis. This is your best protection against a number of threats to your data. It is also about the only way to recover your data if a repair operation fails.

Advanced Data-Management Concepts

While many types of applications benefit from the use of data-management techniques, calculation applications may gain the most benefit. These applications often require a means of setting up the initial condition from a variety of data sources; creating, maintaining, and deleting temporary tables; and managing the output of the calculations. For many calculation applications, the volume of data handled can seem almost overwhelming. This section looks at several aspects of a calculation program to show how data management is used to make the program more efficient and potentially more flexible.

Setting Up the Input Tables

Once the user has started a calculation, an application needs to set up the input data from individual tables. This means pulling information from external tables and setting up the proper recordsets for processing in the calculation. Often, only a portion of a table is needed, and the application sets the appropriate filters for the recordset. Or if a specific processing order is required, the application creates the recordset with a sort order specified. When using a table, the application must set or create the proper index to establish the desired order. Setting up the input data is one area where SQL statements are invaluable. These statements enable the application to combine data from multiple tables, filter the data, and set the sort order for the recordset.

For the demand calculation, `CostPlan` opens DAOs to set up the enrichment information table, the fuel type table, the batch information table, and the demand output table. Batch information is sorted by final delivery date so that batches will be processed in chronological order. The other setup operation is to delete the results of previous studies from the demand output table—so that the results of the current study don't get mixed in with previous runs. Listing 5.5 shows the code that set up all the tables for the demand calculation. Note that the initial table setup is performed using SQL statements and data access objects.

Listing 5.5 OPENCALC.TXT—Opening all the Necessary Tables for the Demand Calculation

```
'*****************************
'Dimension data access objects
'*****************************
Dim OldWs As Workspace, Fltp As Database, Cstpln As Database
Dim Enrsrv As Database
Dim FlTbl As Recordset, Btch As Recordset, Dmnd As Recordset
Dim EnrTbl As Recordset
'Set up workspace and open databases
'***********************************
Set OldWs = DBEngine.Workspaces(0)
Set Fltp = OldWs.OpenDatabase("C:\COSTPLAN\FUELTYPE.MDB")
Set Cstpln = OldWs.OpenDatabase("C:\COSTPLAN\COSTPLAN.MDB")
Set Enrsrv = OldWs.OpenDatabase("C:\COSTPLAN\ENRICHER.MDB")
'***********************
'Open fuel type recordset
'***********************
Set FlTbl = Fltp.OpenRecordset("TypeData", dbOpenDynaset)
'*********************************
'Open enrichment services recordset
'*********************************
Set EnrTbl = Enrsrv.OpenRecordset("Services", dbOpenDynaset)
'*****************************************************
'Set up SQL statement for batch information recordset
'*****************************************************
SqlQry = "SELECT * FROM BatchInf ORDER BY DelvDate"
 '*********************************************
'Open batch data recordset using SQL statement
'*********************************************
Set Btch = Cstpln.OpenRecordset(SqlQry, dbOpenDynaset)
'*********************************************
'Delete results from previous demand calculation
'*********************************************
DelQry = "DELETE FROM Demand"
Cstpln.Execute DelQry
'Open demand output recordset
'***************************
Set Dmnd = Cstpln.OpenRecordset("Demand", dbOpenDynaset)
```

The use of database functions doesn't end with the setup of the data. For each batch in the study, the program looks up information in the fuel type table to get the weight and enrichment of the assemblies. Then the enrichment value is used to look up an entry in the enrichment services table to get the quantities of raw materials and services needed for the batch. This calculation flow is outlined in Listing 5.6. The listing shows only the use of the DAOs. Other calculation steps are indicated by a comment line only.

Listing 5.6   DMDCALC.TXT—Showing the Data Retrieval Used in the Demand Calculation

```
'***************************
'Start batch processing loop
'***************************
Btch.MoveFirst
Do
    '**********************************
    'Get information about current batch
    '**********************************
    asmtype = Btch("FuelTp")
    asmy = Btch("NumAsm")
    btid = Btch("BatchID")
    '**********************************
    'Find fuel type and get information
    '**********************************
    FlTbl.FindFirst "FuelTp = '" & asmtype & "'"
    enrtype = FlTbl("Enrich")
    flweight = FlTbl("AsmWeight")
    '***********************************
    'Find enrichment type and get constants
    '***********************************
    EnrTbl.FindFirst "Enrichment = '" & enrtype & "'"
    uf6unit = EnrTbl("Feed")
    swunit = EnrTbl("SWUReq")
    '*******************************************************
    'Calculate component demands for current batch.
    'Demands will be stored to variables uox, cnv, enr, fab
    '*******************************************************
    '*************************************************
    'Generate output demand record for current batch
    '*************************************************
    Dmnd.AddNew
    Dmnd("UOXdmd") = uox
    Dmnd("CNVdmd") = cnv
```

```
        Dmnd("ENRdmd") = enr
        Dmnd("FABdmd") = fab
        Dmnd("BatchID") = btid
        Dmnd.Update
        '************************
        'Move to next batch record
        '************************
        Btch.MoveNext
Loop Until Btch.EOF  'Continue until all batches are
processed
```

Using Temporary Tables

Temporary data tables are those that are needed for a part of a calculation, but whose contents are not needed on a permanent basis. A temporary table can be an exact copy of a table, a portion of a table, or the combination of multiple tables. A temporary table is actually stored in a database for the duration of the calculation. It should not be confused with dynaset or snapshot recordsets that do not exist physically in the database.

If you can create a dynaset type recordset to access part of a table or multiple tables, why do you need a temporary table? You need a temporary table when your calculation has to modify data in the table, but you also want to preserve the original information in the table.

In CostPlan, for example, materials are delivered in discrete quantities. Then the materials are assigned to batches based on the material needs. Because the quantities delivered don't exactly match the quantities needed by a batch, a batch may require multiple deliveries, and a delivery may be a part of several batches. This is illustrated in figure 5.9.

From a calculation standpoint, it means that the quantity of material in a delivery record must be reduced each time part of it is used to fill a demand. However, the original delivery quantity information needs to be retained for use in the next calculation. Therefore, a copy of the information needs to be created in a temporary table.

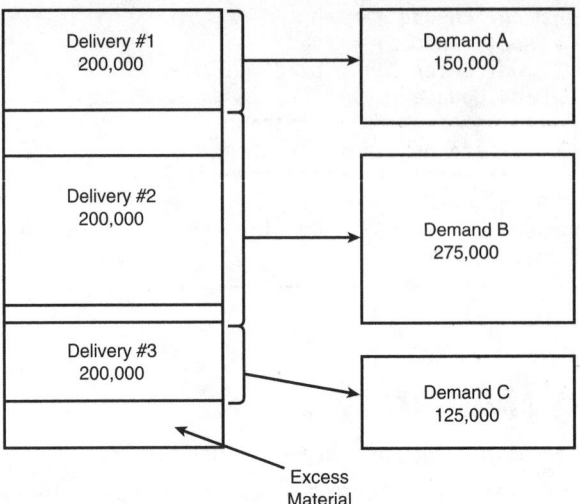

Fig. 5.9 Deliveries of material can be used in several batches.

Creating a Temporary Table

The easiest way to create a new table is with an SQL statement. The INTO clause of the SELECT statement enables you to store the results of the query to another table. Because this is a physical table in the database, it can be handled like any other table with the DAOs. Because it is a copy of the required information, the data can be modified without any effect on the original table or tables. Listing 5.7 shows how a temporary delivery information table can be created for the CostPlan application.

Listing 5.7   Creating a Temporary Table Using an SQL Statement

```
Dim OldWs As Workspace, OldDb As Database
Set OldWs = DBEngine.Workspaces(0)
Set OldDb = OldWs.OpenDatabase("A:\COSTPLAN.MDB")
SqlQry = "SELECT * INTO TempDelv FROM Deliveries"
OldDb.Execute SqlQry
```

Once created, the new table can be accessed with standard DAO methods as shown in the following code:

```
Dim OldTbl As Table
Set OldTbl = OldDb.OpenRecordset("TempDelv",dbOpenTable)
```

Deleting the Temporary Tables

Deleting a temporary table is easily accomplished using an SQL statement. For the preceding table, the following lines of code will close and delete the table:

```
OldTbl.Close
SqlQry = "DROP TABLE TempDelv"
OldDb.Execute SqlQry
```

One problem with creating and deleting temporary tables is that it can increase the size of your database, even though you end up with the same amount of information in the database that you started with. This is because the database size is increased when the table is created, but the space is not recovered when the table is deleted. You can recover the space by running the CompactDatabase function as part of your database maintenance.

Putting Temporary Tables in a Separate Database

One way to avoid the size increase in your database when using temporary tables is to place the temporary tables in a separate database. This way you can simply delete the entire database when the calculation is finished. The SQL statement used to create a table can be modified to direct the table to a different database. The other database must already exist; it will not be created by the SQL statement. The code in Listing 5.8 shows how you can create a new database and store your temporary table in it.

Listing 5.8 TEMPDATA.TXT—Storing the Temporary Table in a Separate Database

```
Dim OldWs As Workspace, OldDb As Database, NewDb As Database
Set Ws = DBEngine.Workspaces(0)
'***********************
```

continues

Listing 5.8   Continued

```
'Create the new database
'***********************
Set NewDb =
Ws.CreateDatabase("A:\COSTTEMP.MDB",dbLangGeneral)
'**********************************************************
'Open the source database and create the temporary table
'**********************************************************
Set OldDb = Ws.OpenDatabase("A:\COSTPLAN.MDB")
SqlQry = "SELECT * INTO TempDelv IN Costtemp FROM Deliveries"
OldDb.Execute SqlQry
'***********************
'Open the temporary table
'***********************
Dim OldTbl As Table
Set OldTbl = OldDb.OpenRecordset("TempDelv",dbOpenTable)
```

After the calculation has been completed, you can close and delete the temporary database. The space used by the database is then released for use by any other files. Your original database will not have been impacted by the use of the temporary table. The following code closes and deletes the temporary database.

```
NewDb.Close
Kill "A:\COSTTEMP.MDB"
Kill "A:\COSTTEMP.LDB"
```

Note that in the above code, two `Kill` statements were used. This is because Access databases consist of two files, one with the LDB extension, and one with the MDB extension. If you are using other database types, you may encounter a similar situation.

> **Note:** LDB files keep track of the record locks in the database file. The information in the LDB file is not accessible by your programs.

Duplicating with the Clone Method

You may have noticed at some point in reviewing the user's manuals or help files for Visual Basic that the recordset object supports a `Clone` method that makes a duplicate of the recordset. The duplicate recordset created in this manner is not a separate table. It is a duplicate handle or entry into the same base information. Therefore, if you change the data in either the original or cloned recordset, the data in the underlying table is changed. This method then does not accomplish the objective of preserving the original data, which is why a temporary table is used in the first place.

Output Data Tables

As previously stated, a calculation program generally produces an output table or set of tables. These tables are usually already in existence when the calculation is run, but you may want to include code in your application that creates the table(s) the first time the calculation is run. Optionally, you may want your application to check for the existence of the table before the run and create the table if it doesn't exist. This is good practice if your users may be creating multiple sets of data for different studies.

You can check for the existence of the table in either of two ways. First, you can use the `TableDefs` collection of the database to see if it contains the table. This method is shown in Listing 5.9.

Listing 5.9   CHKTABLE.TXT—Determining if a Specific Table Exists

```
Dim OldWs As Workspace, OldDb As Database
Dim TblDf As TableDef
Set OldWs = DBEngine.Workspaces(0)
Set OldDb = OldWs.OpenDatabase("C:\COSTPLAN\COSTPLAN.MDB")
tblcrt = True
'**************************************************
'Scan table definitions for the desired table name
'**************************************************
For Each TblDf In OldDb.TableDefs
    If TblDf.Name = "Costout" Then
        tblcrt = False
        '***********************************
        'Exit the loop when the table is found
        '***********************************
        Exit For
```

continues

Listing 5.9   Continued

```
    End If
Next TblDf
If tblcrt Then
    '********************************
    'Create table if it does not exist
    '********************************
Else
    '*********************
    'Open the output table
    '*********************
End If
```

With the second method, you just try to open the table. If the table does not exist, an error will be generated, and you can create the table as part of your error-handling routine. If you have multiple tables that you are handling in this manner, you need to be able to tell the error handler which table to create. This can be done by setting a global variable to the name of the table you are trying to open. Listing 5.10 shows the components of this type of file checking.

Listing 5.10   ERROR.TXT—Using an Error Handler to Create a Table When it Doesn't Exist

```
Sub OpnTables()
Dim OldWs As Workspace, OldDb As Database, OldRc As Recordset
Set OldWs = DBEngine.Workspaces(0)
Set OldDb = OldWs.OpenDatabase("C:\COSTPLAN\COSTPLAN.MDB")
'*********************
'Set up error handler
'*********************
On Error GoTo HandlErr
'************************
'Try to open output table
'************************
Set OldRc = OldDb.OpenRecordset("Costout", dbOpenTable)
On Error GoTo 0
Exit Sub

HandlErr:    ' Error-handling routine.
    Select Case Err.Number   ' Check error number.
        Case 3011
            '*********************************************
            'If output table does not exist, create it.
            '*********************************************
```

```
      End Select
      '********************************
      'Return to statement opening table
      '********************************
      Resume
Exit Sub
```

Case Management

Complex applications are never built to run a calculation once and then be discarded. They are built to enable the user to analyze many cases of a problem or run new cases on a regular basis. Many times an application is used to handle parametric studies. A parametric study is a series of cases where only certain data is changed and the changes in the output are analyzed. Whatever the reason, users will typically build input data and run a calculation many times over the life of the application.

Users also will usually want to keep the data from each case they run. The data can be archived to a tape or a diskette (if the amount of data is small), or stored in a separate directory on the disk. However, much of the data in each case is unchanged, and storing multiple copies of the data wastes a lot of space.

> **Note:** For some applications, you may need to archive and store the complete information for a case to meet record retrieval or regulatory requirements for the data.

Data currency is another problem that is introduced when users frequently change the input data for an application. It often becomes difficult to keep straight which input belongs to which case. This can lead to errors in the data analysis being performed.

Storing Multiple Cases

Storing multiple cases in the same database and tables provides a solution to many data-management problems associated with multiple runs of an application. Adding a case ID field to the databases enables your application to track the data belonging to each case. This provides the following advantages:

➤ Redundant data is eliminated; data that is common to all cases is not entered more than once.

➤ Data that differs from case to case is explicitly identified, eliminating confusion about the input for a particular case.

➤ Multiple output cases can be stored in the application's output tables, making it possible to write comparison programs for the studies.

➤ A case description table can be added to help identify the particular conditions of each case. This is really helpful when you go back a year later asking, "Why did I run this case?"

By adding a `CaseID` field to each table in the `CostPlan` application (except those provided by outside sources) and adding a case description table, the user's task of running many cases is simplified. For each new case, a new ID is entered and data is changed for the item of interest. For `CostPlan`, a typical change is the number of assemblies per batch.

Handling Case-Specific Data

Without the benefit of a database system, case management would be extremely difficult. With a database system, recordsets can be easily set up for the case. The user tells the application which case to run, and the system does the rest. The behind-the-scenes handling of the data for case management is just about as easy. Case management takes advantage of SQL's ability to retrieve selected records based on a conditional expression. In an SQL statement, this is handled by the `WHERE` clause.

In a particular `CostPlan` run, the user has requested the case identified as `"ShortRun"`. As part of the setup for the run, the program sets up information from the `BatchInf` table, using only data for the `"ShortRun"` case ID. Figure 5.10 shows the original `BatchInf` table and the recordset returned by the setup code. The code for the task is shown in Listing 5.11.

Listing 5.11   Retrieving the Information Needed
for a Specific Case

```
Dim NewDyn As Recordset
inpcas = "ShortRun"
'**********************************************
'Set up SQL statement for creating recordset
'**********************************************
SqlQry = "SELECT BatchID,FuelTp,NumAsm,DelvDate FROM_
Batchinf"
SqlQry = SqlQry + " WHERE CaseID = '" & inpcas & "'"
'***************************************************
'Create dynaset type recordset using SQL statement
'***************************************************
Set NewDyn = OldDb.OpenRecordset(SqlQry, dbOpenDynaset)
```

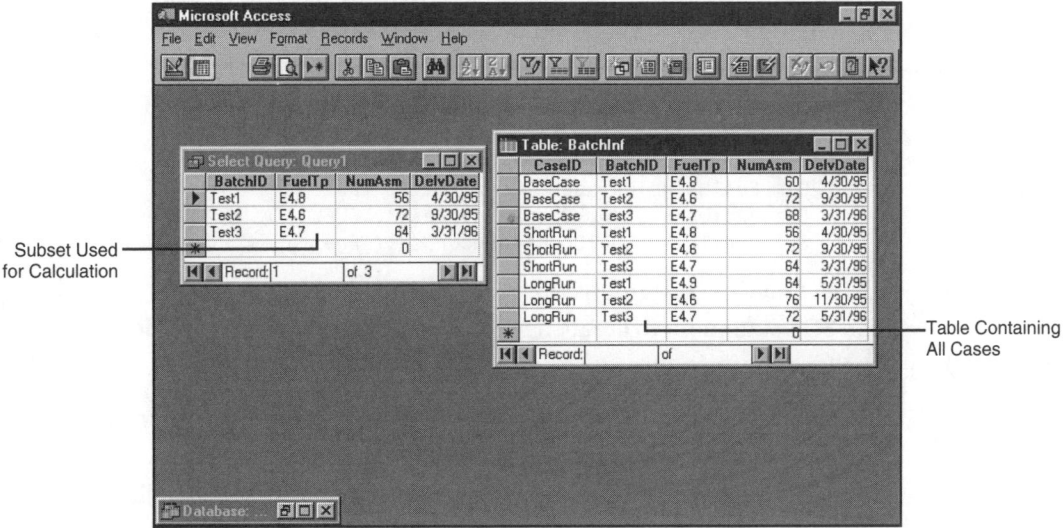

Subset Used for Calculation

Table Containing All Cases

Fig. 5.10 The program builds a recordset from the base table for the requested case.

Once the recordset is created for the desired case data, the calculation is ready to run. Most, if not all, other references or calls to the recordset in the program are unchanged. Therefore, for many applications, the only code change necessary to enable case management is in the setup of recordsets.

Handling Generic Data

As stated previously, much of the data for a calculation remains unchanged between cases. This data can be referred to as generic data. The generic data can be further divided into the following two types:

> ➤ Data that will never change between cases, such as materials constants or information in external databases

> ➤ Data that can be changed, but is held constant for the current series of cases

Each type of generic data requires different handling in an application.

If data is truly constant and will never change, no case information needs to be added to the data table. When the data is set up for the calculation, recordsets based on these tables will be set up the same as if case management didn't exist. One table of this type in the CostPlan application is the fuel type table. This table is set up for a calculation using the following code:

```
Dim FuelDb As Database, FuelTbl As Table
Set FuelDb = OldWs.OpenDatabase("A:\FUELDATA.MDB")
Set FuelTbl = FuelDb.OpenRecordset("Fueltypes",dbOpenTable)
```

Note that this code opens the table directly. It is not necessary to use an SQL statement to create a recordset, nor is any filter condition needed for the table.

Handling data that can change is a little trickier. You want your program to look for data specific to the case that the user specified. If that data is available, a recordset is created based on the case specific data. If there is no data for the specified case, you want the program to look for generic data. The best way to indicate generic data of this type in a table is to leave the case ID blank, or if you are using numeric IDs, make the case ID 0. This way, your generic data is treated like any other case data but with a special ID.

Listing 5.12 is used to set up contract price information for the CostPlan application. The code uses the RecordCount property of the recordset to determine if any case specific data was found. If not, the code looks for generic data by searching for a blank case ID. If no generic data is found, an error message is presented to the user. In Listing 5.12, the case ID is represented by the variable Rnid.

Listing 5.12   CASE.TXT—Retrieving Either Case-Specific or Generic Data

```
Dim PriceTbl As Recordset
SqlQry = "SELECT * FROM Price WHERE CASEID = '" & Rnid & "'"
Set PriceTbl = OldDb.OpenRecordset(SqlQry,dbOpenDynaset)
PriceTbl.MoveLast
If PriceTbl.RecordCount = 0 Then
   PriceTbl.Close
   Blnk = "        "
   SqlQry = "SELECT * FROM Price WHERE CASEID = '" & Blnk &_
"'"
   Set PriceTbl = OldDb.OpenRecordset(SqlQry,dbOpenDynaset)
   PriceTbl.MoveLast
   If PriceTbl.RecordCount = 0 Then
      MsgBox "No price data available"
      End
   End If
End If
```

Comparison Programming

Another benefit of storing information from multiple cases is that re-sults comparisons are made easier. You can include methods in your application that provide your users with comparison tables or graphs to enable them to further analyze the results of their studies. More sophisticated users can even use query tools in Access or Excel (or other programs) to develop their own comparisons.

Without case management, users would have to store copies of the output files or write critical information down for each case. Then to perform a comparison between cases, the data would have to be im-ported from the various files, or re-entered from the written data. This is an awkward and time-consuming task, and in the case of reentering data, prone to errors.

With case management, a single SQL statement using the GROUP BY clause can be used to retrieve summary information for the desired fields. If detailed information is needed, a series of SQL queries can be used to retrieve the data for the different cases. In this case an MDI form could be used to create multiple instances of the data display form, one for each case considered. Listing 5.13 shows the SQL statement used to retrieve the total component costs for each case in a CostPlan study. The listing also shows how the results of the query were then fed to a graph control for display as a bar chart. The resultant chart is shown in figure 5.11.

Listing 5.13   COMPARE.TXT—Using a Graph to Display Summary Information for Component Costs

```
'***************************
'Set up data access objects
'***************************
Dim OldWs As Workspace, OldDb As Database, OldRc As Recordset
Dim Cases As Recordset
Set OldWs = DBEngine.Workspaces(0)
Set OldDb = OldWs.OpenDatabase("C:\COSTPLAN\COSTPLAN.MDB")
'*****************************************************
'Set up SQL statement to obtain summary information
'*****************************************************
SqlQry = "SELECT CaseID, SUM(Uoxcst) AS Uox,SUM(Cnvcst) AS_
Cnv,"
SqlQry = SqlQry & " SUM(Enrcst) AS Enr,SUM(Fabcst) AS Fab_
FROM "
SqlQry = SqlQry & "Costout GROUP BY CaseID"
'************************
'Create summary recordset
'************************
Set OldRc = OldDb.OpenRecordset(SqlQry, dbOpenDynaset)
OldRc.MoveFirst
curset = 1
'*****************************************************************
'Create one set of data points for each case in the recordset
'*****************************************************************
Do
     Graph1.ThisSet = curset
     '*********************************************
     'Input cost information for the four components
     '*********************************************
     Graph1.ThisPoint = 1
     Graph1.GraphData = OldRc("Uox")
     Graph1.ThisPoint = 2
     Graph1.GraphData = OldRc("Cnv")
```

```
        Graph1.ThisPoint = 3
        Graph1.GraphData = OldRc("Enr")
        Graph1.ThisPoint = 4
        Graph1.GraphData = OldRc("Fab")
        Graph1.ThisPoint = curset
        '**************************************************
        'Set the legend for the set to the current case ID
        '**************************************************
        Graph1.LegendText = OldRc("CaseID")
        OldRc.MoveNext
        curset = curset + 1
    Loop Until OldRc.EOF
    '*******************************
    'Set the X-axis label text values
    '*******************************
    Graph1.ThisPoint = 1
    Graph1.LabelText = "Uranium"
    Graph1.ThisPoint = 2
    Graph1.LabelText = "Conversion"
    Graph1.ThisPoint = 3
    Graph1.LabelText = "Enrichment"
    Graph1.ThisPoint = 4
    Graph1.LabelText = "Fabrication"
```

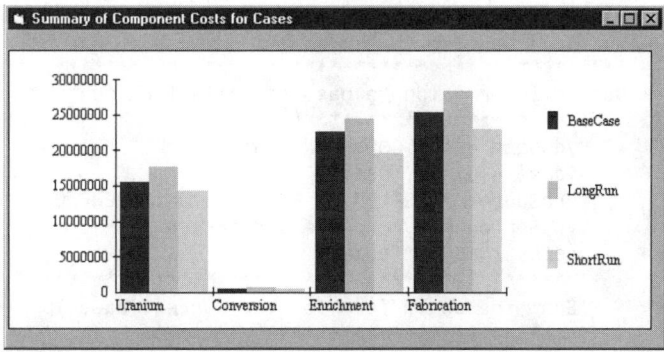

Fig. 5.11 Summary results of multiple cases can be displayed in a graph.

Listing 5.14 shows how the detail information for multiple cases would be retrieved and displayed in a series of MDI child windows. Figure 5.12 shows the results of the code for three cases.

Listing 5.14   DETAILS.TXT—Using the Data-Bound Grid Control to Show Detail Information in Multiple Child Forms of a MDI Form

```
'***************************
'Dimension child form array
'***************************
Dim NewGrid() As New Form2
'***************************
'Set up data access objects
'***************************
Dim OldWs As Workspace, OldDb As Database, OldRc As Recordset
Set OldWs = DBEngine.Workspaces(0)
Set OldDb = OldWs.OpenDatabase("C:\COSTPLAN\COSTPLAN.MDB")
'*************************************************
'Create a recordset with just the unique case IDs
'*************************************************
SqlQry = "SELECT DISTINCT CaseID FROM CostOut"
Set OldRc = OldDb.OpenRecordset(SqlQry, dbOpenDynaset)
OldRc.MoveLast
cases = OldRc.RecordCount
'********************************************************
'Set the number of child forms to the number of cases
'********************************************************
ReDim NewGrid(cases)
OldRc.MoveFirst
csidx = 1
Do
'***********************************************************
'Set up information to pass to child form containing grid
'***********************************************************
    MydbName = "C:\COSTPLAN\COSTPLAN.MDB"
    Mycase = OldRc("CaseID")
    MyrcSource = "SELECT * FROM Costout WHERE CaseID='"
    MyrcSource = MyrcSource & Mycase & "'"
    posmov = 150 * (csidx - 1)
    '*********************************************
    'Show the child form for the current case ID
    '*********************************************
    NewGrid(csidx).Show
    csidx = csidx + 1
    OldRc.MoveNext
Loop Until OldRc.EOF
```

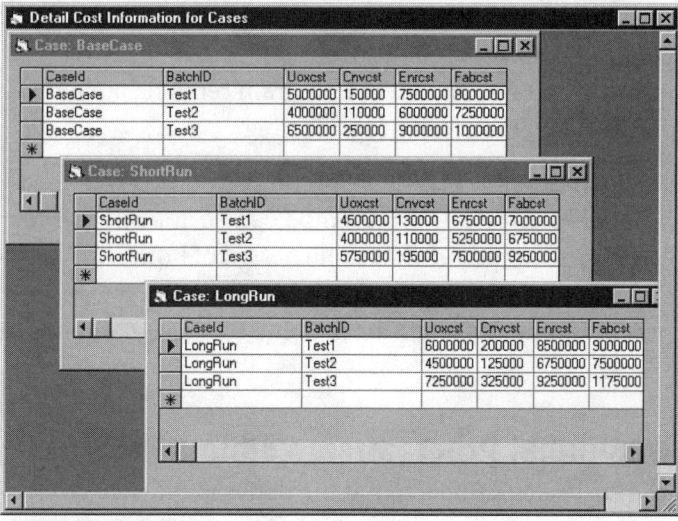

Fig. 5.12 Detail information for multiple cases can be displayed in multiple child forms.

Data-Driven Programming

Another area where data management can be useful is in enhancing program flexibility and reducing program maintenance. This is done by taking some of the task management functions of the program and designing them into the data itself.

To illustrate the concept, consider a simple example. Banks handle a wide variety of loans, including mortgage loans, car loans, boat loans, home equity loans, and others. From a marketing standpoint, these loans are all different and are targeted at different borrowers. However, from the standpoint of the calculations of payments and amortization schedules, the loans are the same. That is, all use the same equations for their calculations. If you had a different program segment for each type of loan, you would be constantly updating the program as new loan types came out. Instead, one calculation module is created for all loans, and the data contains all the necessary information to drive the calculation, including interest rate, term of the loan, and compounding period. Then when a new loan is created, data for the new loan is added to the system, but the program remains unchanged. This is the essence of data-driven programming.

The loan example is probably intuitively obvious to most people. What is not obvious is how this method can be applied to other situations, and how the method affects the design of both your database and your application program. To further develop this concept of data-driven programming, let's look again at the cost calculation portion of CostPlan.

Traditional Programming Approach

The cost calculation looks at the demand for each component of the production process and matches that to deliveries and their associated costs. This matching process, called *allocation*, was illustrated in figure 5.9. The demand table used as input for the cost calculation contains a field for the batch ID and a demand quantity and required delivery date field for each fuel component. This type of table structure is referred to as a horizontal table. The demand table is shown in figure 5.13.

BatchID	UOXDmd	UOXDate	CNVDmd	CNVDate	ENRDmd	ENRDate	FABDmd	FABDate
Test1	500000	10/31/94	450000	11/30/94	250000	12/31/94	85000	3/31/95
Test2	750000	2/28/95	625000	3/31/95	375000	4/30/95	125000	7/31/95
*	0		0		0		0	

Record: 1 of 2

Fig. 5.13 The original demand table contains fields for each fuel component.

As each batch is processed, a separate calculation has to be performed for each of the fuel components. This requires setting up a separate deliveries recordset for each of the components, even though all the delivery information is contained in the same table. The code to set up these recordsets and run the calculation is shown in Listing 5.15.

Listing 5.15 FUELCOMP.TXT—Performing a Separate Calculation for Each Fuel Component

```
Dim OldWs As Workspace, OldDb As Database, Uoxdlv As_
  Recordset
Dim Cnvdlv As Recordset, EnrDlv As Recordset
Dim Fabdlv As Recordset
Dim Dmnd As Recordset, Costs As Recordset
Set OldWs = DBEngine.Workspaces(0)
Set OldDb = OldWs.OpenDatabase("C:\COSTPLAN\COSTPLAN.MDB")
'**************************************************************
'Four recordsets are required for the material deliveriesdata
'**************************************************************
SqlQry = "SELECT * FROM Deliveries WHERE CompType = 'UOX'"
Set Uoxdlv = OldDb.OpenRecordset(SqlQry, dbOpenDynaset)
SqlQry = "SELECT * FROM Deliveries WHERE CompType = 'CNV'"
Set Cnvdlv = OldDb.OpenRecordset(SqlQry, dbOpenDynaset)
SqlQry = "SELECT * FROM Deliveries WHERE CompType = 'ENR'"
Set EnrDlv = OldDb.OpenRecordset(SqlQry, dbOpenDynaset)
SqlQry = "SELECT * FROM Deliveries WHERE CompType = 'FAB'"
Set Fabdlv = OldDb.OpenRecordset(SqlQry, dbOpenDynaset)
Set Dmnd = OldDb.OpenRecordset("Demand", dbOpenTable)
Set Costs = OldDb.OpenRecordset("CostOut", dbOpenTable)
Dmnd.MoveFirst
Do
'**************************************************************
'A separate calculation section is required for each
component
'**************************************************************
    'Assign UOX material to demand
    uox = Dmnd("UOXdmd")
    'Material assignment from Uoxdlv recordset

    'Assign CNV material to demand
    cnv = Dmnd("CNVdmd")
    'Material assignment from Cnvdlv recordset

    'Assign ENR material to demand
    enr = Dmnd("ENRdmd")
    'Material assignment from Enrdlv recordset

    'Assign FAB material to demand
    fab = Dmnd("FABdmd")
    'Material assignment from Fabdlv recordset

    Dmnd.MoveNext
Loop Until Dmnd.EOF
```

The code in Listing 5.15 will perform the calculation for each component even if the demand for the component is zero. This is one inefficiency of the program. Now consider what would happen if another component was introduced into the production process. This would require a change to the demand table to accommodate the new information and a change to the program to add a new calculation step for the component.

Data-Driven Programming Approach

Now take a look at how this would be handled using a data-driven approach. Because the allocation of delivered material to demands is the same for each component of the process, it would be more efficient to use just one calculation routine. The key to doing this is a redesign of the demand data table. Instead of a pair of fields for each component, the table is changed so that each record contains only four fields: the batch identifier, the component identifier, the demand quantity, and the required delivery date. This type of table is called a *vertical table*. Figure 5.14 shows this new demand table structure.

BatchID	CompType	Quantity	DelvDate
Test1	UOX	500000	10/31/94
Test1	CNV	450000	11/30/94
Test1	ENR	250000	12/31/94
Test1	FAB	85000	3/31/95
Test2	UOX	750000	2/28/95
Test2	CNV	625000	3/31/95
Test2	ENR	375000	4/30/95
Test2	FAB	125000	7/31/95
		0	

Fig. 5.14 The revised demand table contains only four fields.

During the initial setup of the calculation, this demand table is sorted by component type. This enables all the batch demands for a single component to be processed at once. This enables the program to set up only one deliveries recordset at a time, instead of having to create four. Then each time a different component is encountered, the deliveries recordset is re-created to handle the different component. This process is no more time-consuming than creating four recordsets initially. The program for the data-driven method of handling allocation is shown in Listing 5.16. The data-driven programming approach simplifies code maintenance and increases flexibility.

Listing 5.16   DATADRV.TXT—Code that is More Flexible and Easier to Maintain than Listing 5.15

```
Dim OldWs As Workspace, OldDb As Database, Delvry As_
Recordset
Dim Dmnd As Recordset, Costs As Recordset
Set OldWs = DBEngine.Workspaces(0)
Set OldDb = OldWs.OpenDatabase("C:\COSTPLAN\COSTPLAN.MDB")
'*************************************************************
'Demand recordset is sorted by component type and delivery
'date
'*************************************************************
SqlQry = "SELECT * FROM Compdmd ORDER BY CompType, DelvDate"
Set Dmnd = OldDb.OpenRecordset(SqlQry, dbOpenDynaset)
Set Costs = OldDb.OpenRecordset("CostOut", dbOpenTable)
Dmnd.MoveFirst
cmptp = "    "
Do
'*************************************************************
'The deliveries recordset is re-created for each new
'component
'*************************************************************
    If Dmnd("CompType") <> cmptp Then
        cmptp = Dmnd("CompType")
        SqlQry = "SELECT * FROM Deliveries WHERE CompType =_
        ' "
        SqlQry = SqlQry & cmptp & "'"
        Delvry.Close
        Set Delvry = OldDb.OpenRecordset(SqlQry,_
        dbOpenDynaset)
    End If
'*************************************************
'Only one generic calculation is required
'*************************************************
    'Assign material to demand
    qty = Dmnd("Quantity")
    'Material assignment from deliveries recordset

    Dmnd.MoveNext
Loop Until Dmnd.EOF
```

Using this data-driven approach, if a component is not needed for a particular batch, no demand record will exist for the component. If there is no demand record, the calculation will not be run for that component. This can make the program run more efficiently.

More importantly, this new table structure and program design can much more easily handle new components in the process. Instead of having to change the table structure to accommodate new fields and adding another calculation step to the program, demand data for the new component is just added to the demand table. No program changes would be required.

From Here...

By necessity, several topics in this chapter were only discussed briefly. The following references will help you learn more about these topics.

➤ For more about presenting data to the user, see Chapter 4, "Advanced Database Front Ends."

➤ To learn about open database connectivity operations, see Chapter 6, "Working with ODBC."

➤ To find out how Jet handles ODBC databases, see Chapter 7, "The Jet Engine and ODBC."

➤ To learn about connecting to database servers, see Chapter 8, "Modern Client/Server Computing," and Chapter 9, "Client/Server Databases."

➤ Database design and basic database programming concepts are covered in detail in Que's *Special Edition Using Visual Basic 4*.

Working with ODBC

by James A. Dooley

In some ways, building a client/server application can be very similar to building a desktop application: most of the user interface development is the same, database design has to be done, and so on. Differences start to crop up when you consider the data access component of the application; the data is physically located on another machine, and, as a result, it will require a different data access strategy than that of a desktop application. The key to developing successful client/server application is to recognize that there are two cooperative processes, the client and the server, involved in the delivery of such an application. Accordingly, you design your application to take advantage of both features.

This chapter adopts a hands-on approach to working with ODBC. Where examples are used to demonstrate a point, they are done in the context of moving the now famous Northwind Traders database from MS Access to client/server using Visual Basic and MS SQL Server. In designing our solutions, we will aim to provide a reasonable performance on an overloaded network. We do this because, more often than not, this is the type of environment that companies use to take a look at this "client/server stuff."

This chapter will cover the following information:

➤ How to design a client/server application

➤ How to configure ODBC

➤ How to attach ODBC tables

➤ How to access remote data

➤ How to create action queries

➤ The creation of new tables

➤ How to create stored procedures

After completing this chapter, you will be able to design and implement client/server applications using Visual Basic and a Database Management System (DBMS) that supports an ODBC connection.

Client/Server Application Design

Broadly speaking, most business applications consist of three layers, as depicted in figure 6.1.

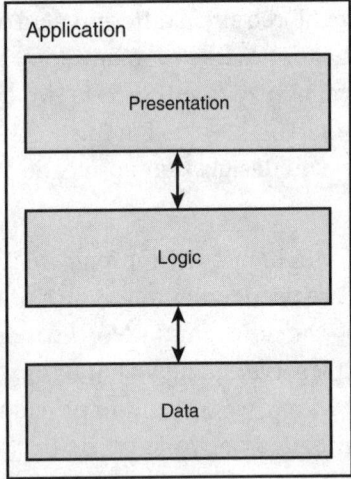

Fig. 6.1 The three application layers.

Presentation Layer: The presentation layer consists of the application's user interface, reports, and so on.

Logic Layer: The logic layer is the heart of the application. It consists of all the modules necessary to implement the functionality of the application.

Data Layer: The data layer contains all the data used by the application, as well as various validation rules required to ensure the integrity of the data.

While most applications consist of these three layers, the architecture used to implement them can vary greatly ranging from a dumb terminal to a complex cooperative processing system. Figure 6.2 has been adopted from work done by the Gartner Group and depicts a wide range of architectures used to implement this three-layered model. In this figure, H represents a host system, and W represents a workstation or PC.

	Time Share	UI	C/S I	C/S II	Co-Op
Presentation	H	W	W	W	W
Logic	H	H	W	H	H/W
Data	H	H	H	H	H

H : Host
W : Workstation or PC

Fig. 6.2 This application architecture depicts a wide range of architectures.

On the left of this diagram, you see what might be described as a typical mainframe application, with the host managing the data, logic, and presentation. On the extreme right, we have a cooperative processing application where the workstation is responsible for the presentation and also contains some for the processing logic or business rules. Between these two extremes we have various systems that represent transitions from one to the other. The first, titled UI, recognizes that the power of the workstation can be used to manage the user interface.

C/S I is what is commonly termed client/server today. The workstation carries out the presentation and logic, and the back-end, or server, carries out data management. C/S II is almost a reversal of C/S I, whereby the logic and data are located on the server, and the workstation does the presentation and some light processing. What distinguishes C/S II from UI is the light processing being done on the workstation, such as calculating totals.

Among the key issues facing the designer of a client/server application is deciding how to split the processing and how to locate the data. The basic idea is for the client and the server to do the work that they are best suited to do. Thus, the client should concentrate on the user interface, whereas the server handles the data integrity, transaction management, and so on. We'll come back to this issue later, in the section entitled "Using Remote data," as we consider how to implement various aspects of the Northwind Traders System.

Understanding ODBC

Over the years, corporations have invested in diverse platforms for strategic, technical, financial, and—dare we say—political reasons. Thus, we find in most cases a combination of mainframe, mid-range, and PC systems are being used to manage the corporation. Each system brings its own method of data storage, ranging from VSAM files to hierarchical and relational databases. These systems store critical data for their corporations, and they can't be tossed aside in the race to client/server. Instead, they must be integrated into the new environment. But how? Each platform provides its own means of data access; thus, to integrate them would require considerable effort on our part.

This was the challenge that Microsoft set out to solve with its Open Database Connectivity (ODBC) standard. In developing ODBC, Microsoft wanted to provide a single Application Programming Interface (API) that could be used to access data on a variety of database management systems. Two of the main advantages of using ODBC are as follows:

➤ ODBC provides a single interface for access to a wide number of databases, thus reducing the learning curve for you, the developer.

➤ ODBC enables the development of client applications, which are independent of the back-end server.

The documentation on ODBC runs to some 800 pages, most of which you need not concern yourself with as a Visual Basic developer. However, you should understand the basic principles of ODBC because it is the critical element enabling you to use Visual Basic for developing client/server applications.

ODBC Architecture

The architecture consists of four major components, as shown in figure 6.3.

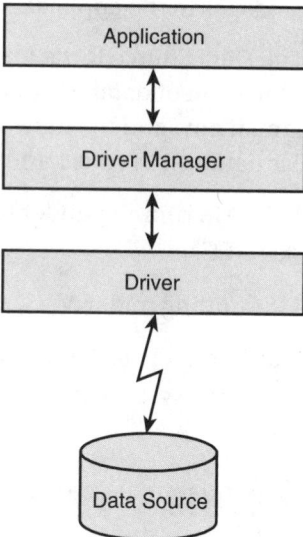

Fig. 6.3 ODBC architecture consists of these four major components.

Application: As its name suggests, the application is the front end you develop to work with the database. It uses ODBC API calls to establish a connection to the database and then uses SQL commands to manipulate the data.

Driver Manager: The driver manager acts as the middleman between the application and the specific driver needed to access a particular database. You should realize that the application does not request a connection to a specific driver; instead it requests access to a logical, known as the *Data Source.* The driver manager maps the logical to a physical driver and database. For example, if an application requests access to a Data Source called MyPubs, the manger maps this to the PUBS demo database in MS SQL Server and determines that the driver needed is the MS SQL Server driver. The manager then loads and initializes the driver.

Driver: The driver actually implements the ODBC API for a particular database management system. It establishes the connection to the server, submits the SQL queries, and returns the result sets or error messages to the application.

Data Source: The Data Source is the term Microsoft uses to describe the combination of database management system; remote operating system, if any; and the network, if any, required to access a particular database. Typical examples are as follows:

➤ An Oracle DBMS running under Open VMS, accessed via PathWorks/DECNet.

➤ DB2 DBMS running under MVS, accessed via a gateway.

➤ A local database such as Paradox or FoxPro, where no remote operating system or network is required.

Conformity Levels

Unfortunately, the ODBC standard is not as straightforward as we would like. Instead of providing a single standard for drivers, it classifies drivers conformity along two lines, their support for the ODBC API and their support for the SQL standard. An understanding of this issue is critical because it determines whether you can use a particular driver with your Visual Basic application.

API Conformance Levels

For API purposes, drivers are classified into three categories: Core, Level 1, and Level 2. Categories are incremental; thus, Level 1 supports Core plus Level 1, and Level 2 supports Core plus Level 1 and Level 2. As the name suggests, Core provides a very basic level of functionality, such as the capability to do the following:

- ➤ Establish a connection to the database
- ➤ Prepare and execute SQL statements
- ➤ Retrieve data from result sets
- ➤ Commit and Rollback transactions
- ➤ Provide error information

In addition to the previous items, a Level 1 driver provides the following:

- ➤ Connection to a data source with driver specific dialog boxes so that the user can complete the connection information in cases where the application provides insufficient information to establish the connection
- ➤ Handle long data types (such as LONG VARCHAR and LONG VARBINARY)
- ➤ Retrieve catalog information, such as table structures
- ➤ Retrieve information about the capabilities of the driver

A Level 2 driver represents a top of the range ODBC driver. In addition to the previous items, it can do the following:

- ➤ Perform LEFT OUTER JOIN and RIGHT OUTER JOIN
- ➤ Process batch SQL statements
- ➤ Execute stored procedures

 **Note:** Most applications that provide access to data via ODBC require a driver that supports the full Level 1 API.

SQL Conformity

As with API conformity, ODBC defines three levels for SQL conformity: Minimum, Core, and Extended. The differences between these three are defined in terms of the Data Definition Language (DDL), the Data Manipulation Language (DML), expressions, and data types they support. Table 6.1 highlights the differences.

Table 6.1   SQL Conformity

DDL	DML	Expressions	Data Types
	Minimum		
CREATE TABLE, DROP TABLE	SELECT, INSERT, UPDATE VARCHAR, SEARCHED, DELETE SEARCHED	Simple	CHAR, or LONG, VARCHAR
	Core		
CREATE TABLE, DROP TABLE, ALTER TABLE, CREATE INDEX, DROP NUMERIC, SMALLINT, INDEX, CREATE VIEW DROP VIEW, GRANT, REVOKE	SELECT (full), INSERT, UPDATE SEARCHED, DELETE SEARCHED	simple, subquery,	CHAR, VARCHAR, LONG, DECIMAL, set functions INTEGER, REAL, FLOAT, DOUBLE PERCISION
	Extended		
CREATE TABLE, DROP TABLE ALTER TABLE,	outer joins, unions, positioned	simple, subquery	CHAR, VARCHAR, set

DDL	DML	Expressions	Data Types
	Extended		
LONG, DECIMAL, CREATE INDEX, DROP NUMERIC, SMALLINT, INDEX, CREATE VIEW, DROP VIEW, GRANT, REVOKE	UPDATE, positioned		functions
	DELETE, SELECT FOR UPDATE, SELECT (full), INSERT, UPDATE SEARCHED, DELETE SEARCHED		INTEGER, FLOAT, DOUBLE PERCISION

Single-Tier and Multi-Tier Drivers

In addition to classifying drivers based on their conformity to the ODBC standard, you can define drivers as *single-tier* or as *multi-tier*.

➤ Single-Tier Drivers: In addition to accessing remote databases, you can use ODBC drivers to access local databases such as Xbase or Paradox. Such drivers not only process the API calls but also process the SQL commands, thus having to perform file I/O and so on, on the files containing the data.

➤ Multi-Tier Drivers: In a typical client/server application, the database is located on a server, and each user runs the client application on his workstation. The client application sends SQL commands to the database, which returns the requested data. The multi-tier driver processes the ODBC API calls and submits the SQL commands to the server.

Configuring ODBC

Having seen an overview of ODBC in the previous section, we'll look at how ODBC is implemented and how to configure it for use with our applications.

ODBC is implemented as a series of executable files, Dynamic Link Libraries (DLLs), and INI files, as follows:

ODBC Administrator (ODBCADM.EXE): This is the control panel applet that enables you to install new ODBC drivers and define new Data Sources. Details of the installed drivers are stored in ODBCINST.INI, while details of the Data Sources are stored in ODBC.INI.

Drive Manager (ODBC.DLL): As already described, the driver manager is responsible for mapping the Data Sources to the drivers, loading the various ODBC drivers, and other initialization activities.

Drivers: The drivers themselves can consist of one or more DLLs as well as supporting INI files, depending on the particular vendor's implementation.

Before we can access a database via ODBC, we must define the Data Source so that the ODBC knows how to establish the connection for us when we make the request. In our case, you can do this in the following two ways:

➤ Use the ODBC Administrator to define the Data Source.

➤ Use the Visual Basic function `RegisterDatabase` to programmatically define the Data Source.

Regardless of which method you use, you'll need to know several things about the database before you can define the Data Source. The exact information required depends on the ODBC driver, so you'll need to refer to the vendor's documentation. In our case, because we're working with MS SQL Server, we need to know the following:

➤ The Data Source name.

➤ The Description of Data Source.

➤ The name of the server on the network where our database is located.

➤ The name of the database.

In the following two subsections, we'll examine how to define the Data Source required to access the Northwind database. For our examples, the information required to define the Data Source is as follows:

➤ Data Source name: NWIND.

➤ Description of Data Source: Northwind Database.

➤ The name of the server: QUE_1.

➤ The name of the database: Northwind.

Using the ODBC Administrator

To define the Data Source using the ODBC Administrator do the following:

1. Launch the ODBC Administrator applet by double-clicking it from the Control Panel.

2. From the ODBC Administrator main window (see fig. 6.4) click Add to add the new Data Source.

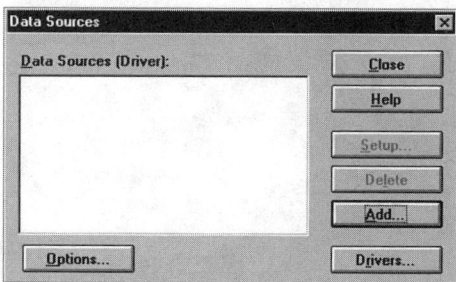

Fig. 6.4 The ODBC Administrator is used to add data sources.

3. The ODBC manager provides you with the list of installed drivers, which you can use to connect to various databases (see fig. 6.5). Because we want to connect to MS SQL Server, select SQL Server and click OK.

4. You are now asked to provide driver-specific information via the dialog box shown in figure 6.6. Complete this dialog box as shown and click OK to complete the task.

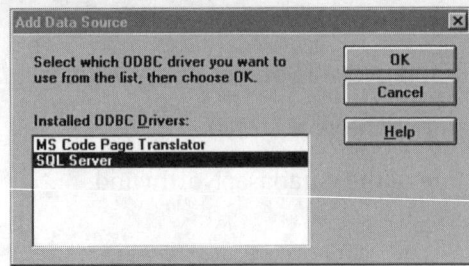

Fig. 6.5 A list of installed drivers.

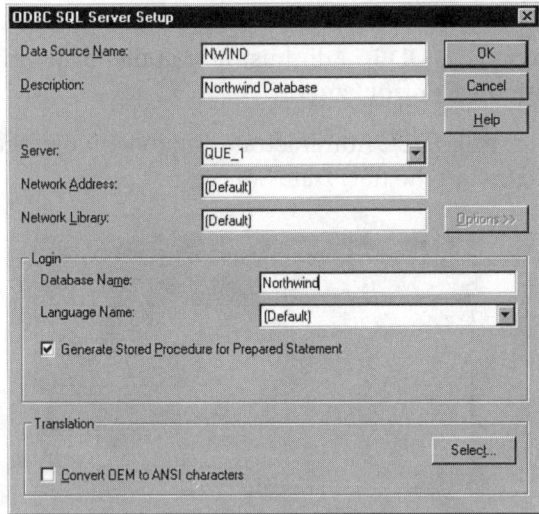

Fig. 6.6 Specify your ODBC driver information here.

After completing the task, you return to the main window, where you can see your Data Source displayed in the list box (see fig. 6.7).

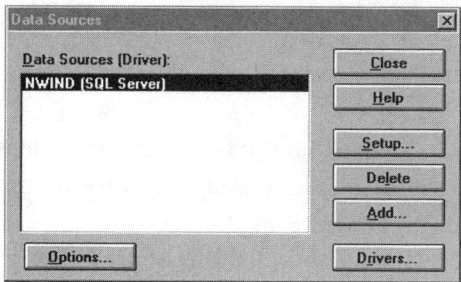

Fig. 6.7 The SQL Server Data Source is defined in the ODBC Administrator main window.

Using the RegisterDatabase Method

Visual Basic provides the `RegisterDatabase` method so that developers can programmatically define Data Sources. The `RegisterDatabase` method takes the following four parameters:

➤ The Data Source Name.

➤ The driver to be used to connect to the database.

➤ A numeric expression, indicating whether the ODBC driver dialog boxes should be displayed. (Use this option if you wish to have the user provide additional information needed to establish the connection.)

➤ A carriage-return delimited string containing all additional information required by the driver.

The easiest way to determine all the values for the various parameters is to define the Data Source first using the ODBC Administrator and then examine the ODBC.INI file. Examining the INI file for our NWIND Data Source, you'll see the following entries:

```
[NWIND]
Driver=C:\WIN31\SYSTEM\sqlsrvr.dll
Description=Northwind Database
Server=QUE_1
```

```
FastConnectOption=No
UseProcForPrepare=Yes
Database=Northwind
OEMTOANSI=No
```

From this, you can see that the Data Source name is NWIND, the driver is
C:\WIN31\SYSTEM\sqlsrvr.dll, and that the remaining attributes are
Description, Server, FastConnectOption, UseProcForPrepare, Database,
and OEMTOANSI. Having obtained this information, you are now ready to
create the code required to define the Data Source (see Listing 6.1).

Listing 6.1   REGDB.BAS—Registering the Database

```
Private Sub cmdRegDatabase_Click()
    Dim Attribs As String
    ' Build keywords string.
    Attribs = "Description=Northwind Database" & Chr$(13)
    Attribs = Attribs & "Server=QUE_1" & Chr$(13)
    Attribs = Attribs & "FastConnectOption=No" & Chr$(13)
    Attribs = Attribs & "UseProcForPerpare=Yes" & Chr$(13)
    Attribs = Attribs & "OEMTOANSI=No"
    Attribs = Attribs & "Database=Northwind"

    ' Update ODBC.INI.
    DBEngine.RegisterDatabase "NWIND", "SQL Server", True,
Attribs
End Sub
```

Note: In the previous code, you will notice the driver name being
passed to the RegisterDatabase function is "SQL Server" and not
sqlsrvr.dll. The driver is known to ODBC as "SQL Server", which
is responsible for determining the DLL that matches the logical
name. To obtain this entry, I had to examine the ODBCINST.INI
file, where a list of installed drivers is maintained. The relevant
entries are shown as follows:

```
[SQL Server]
Driver=C:\WIN31\SYSTEM\sqlsrvr.dll
Setup=C:\WIN31\SYSTEM\sqlsrvr.dll
```

Attaching ODBC Tables

The most common way to access data stored in tables located on a remote database is to attach the tables to a local Jet database and then use the DAO model to work with the tables. With Visual Basic, you can programmatically attach remote tables to a local database. In this section, we're going to examine these features by building a simple application that allows the user to attach remote tables to a Jet database and view the attached tables.

In the context of our examination of ODBC, there are two key features to the application:

1. Allow the user to select a Data Source from those defined on his workstation.

2. Attach the remote table to the database.

Selecting the Data Source

We'll begin by implementing the dialog box to display a list of the Data Sources defined on the user's workstation. The dialog box will provide the following functionality:

➤ Display a list of Data Sources, as defined on the workstation.

➤ As a Data Source is selected, display the following information: Database name, Description, Driver used to access the database, and last user ID.

➤ Allow the user to enter his user ID and password for accessing the Data Source.

➤ Return to the calling program, via form properties, the selected database name, and the ODBC connect string required to access it.

Let's begin by implementing the user interface; figure 6.8 shows the completed dialog box.

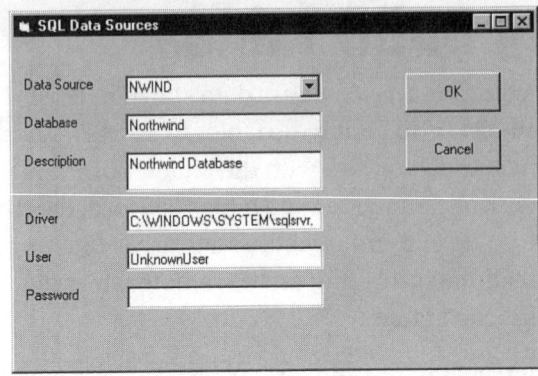

Fig. 6.8 The SQL Data Sources selection dialog box.

The form properties that need to be changed are set out in Table 6.2.

Table 6.2 Data Source Selection Form Properties

Property	Setting
Auto3D	True
BackColor	&H00C0C0C0& (light gray)
BorderStyle	Fixed Double
Caption	SQL Data Sources
ControlBox	False
MaxButton	False
MinButton	False
Name	frmODBCDataSources

All other properties should be left at their default. Once you have set the form properties, you can add the required controls, as shown in figure 6.8. Details of the controls and their property settings are set out in Table 6.3 (label controls take default properties).

Table 6.3   Control Settings for the Data Sources Dialog Box

Control	Property	Setting
ComboBox	Name	cboDSN
	Sorted	True
	Style	Dropdown List
TextBox	Name	txtDatabase
TextBox	MultiLine	True
	Name	txtDesc
TextBox	Name	txtDriver
TextBox	Name	txtUser
TextBox	Name	txtPassword
	PasswordChar	*
CommandButton	Caption	OK
	Default	True
	Name	cmdOK
CommandButton	Cancel	True
	Caption	Cancel
	Name	cmdCancel

Now that you've completed the user interface, it's time to start adding the code. The most difficult part of implementing this feature is to obtain a list of the Data Sources that are defined on the user's workstation. To do this, you'll have to drop down to the ODBC API. Included in the ODBC API is a function called SQLDataSources, which we can use to obtain a list of the Data Sources. To use this function, we need to allocate some ODBC environment space, which is done via another ODBC function called SQLAllocEnv. Listing 6.2 shows the necessary Visual Basic declarations.

Listing 6.2 SQLENV.BAS—Allocating the Environment Space

```
Private Declare Function SQLAllocEnv Lib "odbc.dll" _
                         (env As Long) As Integer
Private Declare Function SQLDataSources Lib "odbc.dll" _
                         (ByVal henv As Long, _
                          ByVal fdir As Integer, _
                          ByVal szDSN As String, _
                          ByVal cbDSNMAx As Integer, _
                          pcbDSN As Integer, _
                          ByVal szDesc As String, _
                          ByVal cbDescMax As Integer, _
                          pcbDesc As Integer) As Integer
```

Now that we're figured out the API calls we need to make, we're ready to use the code in Listing 6.3 to write a subroutine to load the list of Data Sources into the list box on the dialog box.

Listing 6.3 GETDSRC.BAS—Listing the Data Sources

```
Private Sub GetDataSources(listctrl As Control)

    ' Gets ODBC data sources and displays then in a list box

    Dim strDataSrc As String
    Dim strDesc As String
    Dim intDataSrcLen As Integer
    Dim intDescLen As Integer
    Dim intRetCode As Integer
    Dim henv As Long

    If SQLAllocEnv(henv) <> -1 Then
        strDataSrc = String$(32, 32)
        strDesc = String$(255, 32)

        'get the first one
        intRetCode = SQLDataSources(henv, 2, strDataSrc, _
                        Len(strDataSrc), intDataSrcLen, _
                        strDesc, Len(strDesc), intDescLen)
        While intRetCode = 0 Or intRetCode = 1
            listctrl.AddItem Mid(strDataSrc, 1, intDataSrcLen)
            strDataSrc = String$(32, 32)
            strDesc = String$(255, 32)
```

```
                  'get all the others
                  intRetCode = SQLDataSources(henv, 1, strDataSrc, _
                                              Len(strDataSrc), _
                                              intDataSrcLen, _
                                              strDesc,
    Len(strDesc), _
                                              intDescLen)
            Wend
       End If
End Sub
```

After defining the required variables, you allocate the required ODBC
environment space. Once this is done, you begin to obtain a list of the
Data Sources by making successive calls to the SQLDataSources function. As you retrieve each Data Source, you add it to the list box until
you have obtained all Data Sources.

Once you have written the routine for retrieving the Data Sources,
you're in a position to use Listing 6.4 to complete the Form_Load
method.

Listing 6.4   LOADFRM!.BAS—Loading the Form

```
Private Sub Form_Load()

    MousePointer = vbHourglass

    ' Center form
    Move (Screen.Width - Width) \ 2, _
            (Screen.Height - Height) \ 2

    ' Load ODBC Sources
    GetDataSources cboDSN

    MousePointer = vbDefault

End Sub
```

Once you have displayed the list of data sources, all that's left is to
retrieve the information about each Data Source as the user selects it.
This is done by reading the ODBC.INI file using the Windows API call

`GetPrivateProfileString`. The code itself is added to the list box's click method as shown in Listing 6.5.

Listing 6.5   GETDSINF.BAS—Getting Data Source Information

```
Private Sub cboDSN_Click()

    ' Display info about DSN
    txtDatabase = GetAppINIString(cboDSN, "Database", "", _
    "ODBC.INI")
    txtDesc = GetAppINIString(cboDSN, "Description", "", _
    "ODBC.INI")
    txtDriver = GetAppINIString(cboDSN, "Driver", "", _
    "ODBC.INI")
    txtUser = GetAppINIString(cboDSN, "LastUser",
GetUserID(), "ODBC.INI")

    ' Set focus
    If Len(txtUser) Then
        txtPassword.SetFocus
    Else
        txtUser.SetFocus
    End If

End Sub
```

Having written the most difficult functions, you only need to add the supporting code.

Having provided the user with a means for selecting the Data Source, all that remains is to add the code for attaching the table to the local database and the supporting code. The function in Listing 6.6 attaches the table to the database.

Listing 6.6   TBLATTCH.BAS—Attaching the Table

```
Public Sub AttachTable(dbODBC As Database, strSourceTable _
    As String, fSavePassword As Integer)

    ' Attach the ODBC table to the Jet database
    Dim tbl As New TableDef
```

```
Dim strTableName As String

Dim intLoc As Integer

' First build a table name to use
' in Jet database by removing any full stops
' from source table name
strTableName = strSourceTable
intLoc = InStr(strTableName, ".")
While intLoc <> 0
    Mid$(strTableName, intLoc, 1) = "_"
    intLoc = InStr(strTableName, ".")
Wend

' Confirm table name
strTableName = InputBox$("Enter name for attached table", _
frmMainWnd.Caption, strTableName)

' Attach the table
Set tbl = DB.CreateTableDef(strTableName, dbAttachedODBC, _
strSourceTable, dbODBC.Connect)
If fSavePassword Then
    tbl.Attributes = tbl.Attributes + dbAttachSavePWD
End If
DB.TableDefs.Append tbl

' Add table to list box
lstTables.AddItem strTableName

End Sub
```

Using Server Data

Most business applications can be split into types: transaction process-ing and decision support or reporting. While you will use the same elements of Visual Basic to build both types of application, they differ greatly in one aspect: the location of the data.

In a transaction type system, the data needs to be updated immedi-ately on the server so that it reflects the current situation at any given time. For example, if I have only one item on a particular product in stock and I accept an order for it, I need to update the stock records to reflect this so that no one else will accept an order for the same item.

In a decision support type of system, the data tends to be at least a day old, if not longer. Normally, users are looking at trends, so up-to-the-minute data is not required.

Using Visual Basic to develop such applications allows us to take advantage of this fact. In developing the application, we can copy the data once from the server to the user's workstation before the user begins to work with it. This will free up the server to handle other requests and also means that the user will normally experience better performance in screen updates and so forth. In this section, we'll look at the techniques used to implement such an application.

In our example, you'll implement a screen for the Northwind Traders database, which allows users to view a graph of product sales for the year. In this case, you need to extract the product sales from the Orders and Order Details tables and store them locally. The first thing you need to do, then, is to create a table in our local database to store the data. The structure of this table is shown in Table 6.4.

Table 6.4   Structure of the Local Sales Table

Field	Type	Length	Comment
Month	Text	2	Month indicator for product sales
Product_id	Number		Product's ID number
NetSales	Number		Net sales of product

In order to access the data stored in the remote database, you'll need to attach the tables to our local database.

Once you have created the local table and attached the remote tables, you need to write some queries to copy the data between the tables.

The first query needs to join the Orders table with the Order Details table to extract the date, the product, and the net sales. The SQL to do this is as follows:

```
SELECT DISTINCTROW Orders.[Order Date], [Order Details]._
[Product ID], Sum(LNG((([Quantity]*[Unit Price])*(1-[Discount])))) _
    AS NetSales
FROM Orders INNER JOIN [Order Details] ON Orders.[Order ID] = _
[Order Details].[Order ID]
GROUP BY Orders.[Order Date], [Order Details].[Product ID]
HAVING (((Year([Order Date]))=1992));
```

Once you have extracted this information, you add a second query that summarizes the information and enters it in the local table. This query is as follows:

```
INSERT INTO locMonthlyProductSales ( Month, [Product ID], _
    NetSales )
SELECT DISTINCTROW Month([Order Date]) AS Month,
GetDailySales1992.[Product ID],
Sum(GetDailySales1992.NetSales) AS NetSales
FROM GetDailySales1992
GROUP BY Month([Order Date]), GetDailySales1992.[Product ID];
```

Now that you have all the basic components in place, you need to provide the user with the means to execute the copy. Each time you copy down the remote data, you need to do two things: first, you need to delete the existing data, and second, you need to copy down the new data. To allow for future growth in the system, we'll develop a dynamic method of handling this. The idea is to create a batch job consisting of the several queries, which when executed in sequence, provides the required functionality. In order to store information about the batch process, you need to add two tables to our local database: one to hold general information about the batch jobs and one to hold the detailed steps of each job. The structure of these tables is shown in Table 6.5 and Table 6.6.

Table 6.5   Structure of Batch Description Table

Field	Type	Length	Comment
BatchNo	Text	3	Batch number
BatchName	Text	50	Name of batch
BatchDesc	Text	50	Description of what batch does

Table 6.6   Structure of Batch Detail Table

Field	Type	Length	Comment
BatchNo	Text	3	Batch number
StepNo	Number		Step in batch
SQLQuery	Text	50	Name of query to be executed

Having provided a means for storing the batch information, all you need to do now is add a user interface that will allow the user to execute the batch. The user interface can be a simple dialog box, like the one in figure 6.9, which lists the batch jobs and their descriptions.

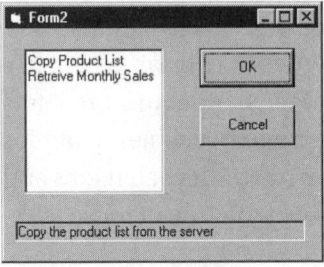

Fig. 6.9 The batch execution dialog box.

When the user clicks OK, the batch is executed via the routine shown in Listing 6.7.

Listing 6.7   RUNBATC1.BAS—Running a Batch Query

```
Private Sub cmdOK_Click()

    Dim rec As Recordset
    Dim qry As QueryDef

    ' Execute the batch
    Set qry = frmMainWnd.gdb.OpenQueryDef("GetBatch")
    qry!BatchNum = Format$( _
                lstBatches.ItemData(lstBatches.ListIndex), _
                "000")
    Set rec = qry.OpenRecordset(dbOpenSnapshot)
    qry.Close

    While Not rec.EOF
        Set qry = frmMainWnd.gdb.OpenQueryDef(rec!SQLQuery)
        qry.Execute
        qry.Close
        rec.movenext
    Wend

End Sub
```

Once the data has been copied to the local table, we're back to standard Visual Basic to create the decision support screen.

Action Queries

Up to this stage, you have worked exclusively with Visual Basic's DAO model. Using the model, you have created recordsets and worked on the data returned in these sets. While this method of working with data has been adequate in dealing with the Northwind situation, it does have one major disadvantage: it is not very well suited for carrying out operations on large tables. Consider the following problem.

On your server, you have a table that contains a summary of your company's product sales by day. This table contains over 100,000 rows. Each day you receive a file containing 6,000 transactions, which either replace existing rows or add new rows to the table. How would you go about performing the required updates/additions?

Using the DAO model, our first attempt might be to use a design such as this:

1. Attach the sales summary table to a Jet database.

2. Open the sales summary table as a Dynaset.

3. Open the update file for input.

4. Read in the rows from the update file until the EOF marker is reached.

5. With each row that is read in, use the `FindFirst` method to locate the old record in the sales summary table and update it with the new data.

6. For rows read that we fail to find an existing record in the sales summary table, we add it as a new record.

While this solution will work fine on a small table, it will fail in our case because our Dynaset contains over 100,000 rows and the `FindFirst` method performs a liner search. Thus, it will take hours to perform the required updates. (Take my word, I've tried it.)

Because we have identified the performance hog as such a large Dynaset, our second attempt might be to try and reduce the size of the Dynaset. One way we can do this is to retrieve all the sales summary records for a particular day, update them or add new ones, and move on to the next day. Our refined design might look like the following:

1. Attach the sales summary table to a Jet database.

2. Sort the update file by date order.

3. Open the update file for input.

4. Read in the rows from the update file until the EOF marker is reached.

5. For each change of date in the update file, create a new Dynaset from the sales summary table based on update record date.

6. With each row that is read in, use the `FindFirst` method to locate the old record in the sales summary Dynaset and update it with the new data.

7. For rows read in that we fail to find an existing record in the sales summary table, we add it as a new record.

While this solution does improve the situation, it still does not reach our expectations. We're still moving thousands of records from the server to the workstation.

What this problem requires is the capability to carry out operations on the data located in the remote database without having to transfer the records to the workstation. The solution lies in an action query. The `Execute` method of the database object allows us to submit SQL commands to manipulate data stored in a table without first having to create a recordset. Using the `Execute` method, our final solution would be as follows:

1. Connect to the ODBC database directly.

2. Open the update file for input.

3. Read in the rows from the update file until the EOF marker is reached.

4. For each row that is read in, build an update query based on the primary key, and submit it to the server using the `Execute` method.

5. Check the number of rows that the update query affects; if it is zero, build an insert query to add the record to the table because it must be a new record.

For comparison, testing the first and final solutions on my server showed that the final solution took only one-sixth the time of the first solution.

In addition to using action queries to insert or update records, you can use them to do the following:

➤ Delete records

➤ Create new tables and indexes

Creating Tables on a Server Database

At times, you will need to create tables and indexes on the server database from the desktop application. This section discusses how this is done and the challenges associated with this activity.

Creating tables and indexes in a C/S environment is almost the same as doing so in a typical desktop database application, with one exception: you need to have been granted the correct security privileges on the server before you can perform the task.

In the first example, you'll build a simple utility to create tables on any database for which ODBC drivers are available.

The utility's functionality can be summarized as follows:

1. Connect to the database via the standard ODBC sign-on screen.

2. Once signed on, display a list of the tables in the database.

3. When the user selects a table, display a list of the fields in the table.

4. When the user clicks the New button, a dialog box is displayed, which will enable him to create a new table.

Before building the application, let's take it for a test drive so that we understand how it works.

1. Start the application.

2. Once started, the application will present you with the standard ODBC logon dialog box. Select a Data Source and complete the logon sequence.

3. Once you have completed the logon, you'll find yourself at the main window of the application.

4. From the main window, click the New button in the dialog box shown in figure 6.10.

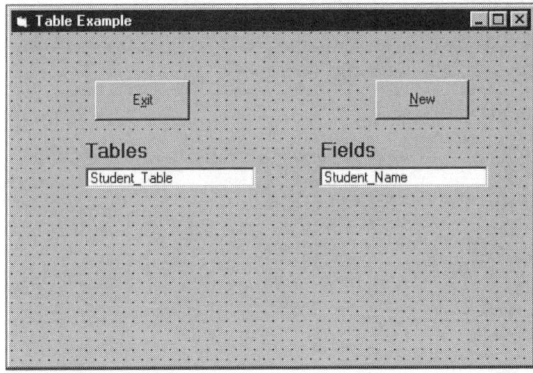

Fig. 6.10 The New button allows you to add a new table to a database.

5. Complete the dialog box as shown in figure 6.11 and click the Create button to add the new table.

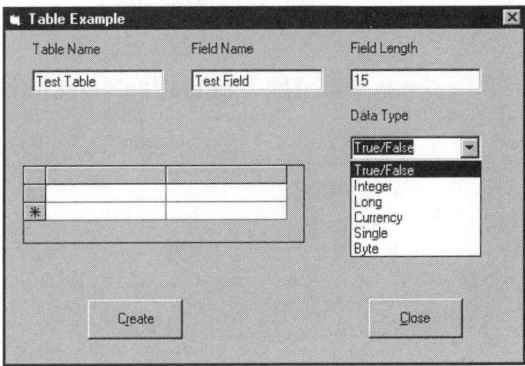

Fig. 6.11 An application can be written to add a new table to a server database using Visual Basic.

Now it's time to start coding. We'll begin by developing the user interface. After opening a new project, set the form's properties to the values set out in Table 6.7.

Table 6.7 The Form Property Settings

Property	Setting
Auto3D	True
BackColor	&H00C0C0C0& (light gray)
BorderStype	Fixed Double
Caption	Table Example
ControlBox	False
MaxButton	False
MinButton	False
Name	fMainWnd

All other properties should be left at their default. Once you have set the form properties, you can add the required controls, as shown in figure 6.11. Details of the controls and their property settings are set out in Table 6.8 (Label controls take default properties).

Table 6.8 The Application's Controls

Control	Property	Setting
ListBox	Columns	3
	Name	lstTables
	Sorted	True
ListBox	Columns	3
	Name	lstFields
	Sorted	True
Button	Caption	E&xit
	Name	cmdExit
Button	Caption	&New...
	Name	cmdNew

After building the main form, we turn our attention to the Create Table dialog box. Add a new form to the project, and set its properties as set out in Table 6.9.

Table 6.9   The Dialog Box Settings

Property	Setting
Auto3D	True
BackColor	&H00C0C0C0& (light gray)
BorderStype	Fixed Double
Caption	Table Example
ControlBox	False
MaxButton	False
MinButton	False
Name	fNew

Add controls to the form as shown in figure 6.11, and set the properties as shown in Table 6.10.

Table 6.10   The Dialog Box Control Settings

Control	Property	Setting
TextBox	Name	txtTable
Grid	Cols	4
	Name	grd
	Rows	20
Frame	Name	fraNewField
TextBox	Name	txtName
ComboBox	List	True/False
		Byte
		Integer
		Long
		Currency
		Single

continues

Table 6.10   Continued

Control	Property	Setting
		Double
		Name cboType
TextBox	Name	txtLength
Button	Caption Name	&Add cmdAdd
Button	Caption Name	C&reate cmdCreate
Button	Caption Name	&Close cmdClose

This completes the interface, now let's start adding the code. We'll handle the application startup first. The code executed at the start of the application is located in the main form's Form_Load, as shown in Listing 6.8.

Listing 6.8   DSPMAIN.BAS—Displaying the Main Form

```
Private Sub Form_Load()

    MousePointer = Hourglass

    ' Locate and display form
    Move (Screen.Width - Width) \ 2, (Screen.Height - Height) \ 2
    Show
    Refresh

    ' Open the database
    Set gdb = Workspaces(0).OpenDatabase("", False, False, _
    "ODBC;")
    DisplayTables

    MousePointer = Default

End Sub
```

The first block of code simply centers the form on the user's screen. The second block of code opens the database and displays its list of tables. Note the way the OpenDatabase method is used. Entering just "ODBC;" as the last parameter causes the ODBC manager to display the list of data sources and enables the user to log on to any data source. The function DisplayTables simply loops through the database's TableDefs and adds the name of the table to the tables list box in the main screen. The code is provided in Listing 6.9.

Listing 6.9 DSPTBL.BAS—Displaying the Existing Tables

```
Private Sub DisplayTables()

    Dim strTable As String   ' hold table name
    Dim tbl As TableDef      ' curret table def

    MousePointer = Hourglass

    ' Display Tables
    lstTables.Clear
    lstFields.Clear
    For Each tbl In gdb.TableDefs
        If (tbl.Attributes And dbSystemObject) = 0 Then
            strTable = tbl.Name
            lstTables.AddItem strTable
        End If
    Next

    MousePointer = Default

End Sub
```

Moving to the new table form, you use its Load method to configure the grid and locate the form, as shown in Listing 6.10.

Listing 6.10 CNFGRID1.BAS—Configuring the Grid and Locating the Form

```
Private Sub Form_Load()

    ' Locate and display form
    Move (Screen.Width - Width) \ 2, (Screen.Height - Height) \ 2
    Show
    Refresh

    ' Config grid
    grd.Col = 1
    grd.Row = 0
    grd.Text = "Name"
    grd.ColWidth(1) = (grd.ColWidth(1) * 5)
    grd.Col = 2
    grd.Text = "Type"
    grd.ColWidth(2) = (grd.ColWidth(2) * 2)
    grd.Col = 3
    grd.Text = "Width"

    ' Init variables
    iLastUsedRow = 0
    fFieldsAdded = False

End Sub
```

In review of the code, you will note that the form uses two variables at the form level: `iLastUsedRow` indicates the number of rows used in the grid, whereas `fFieldsAdded` acts as a flag to indicate if fields have been added.

The most interesting code in the new table form is in the `Click` method of the Create button (see Listing 6.11).

Listing 6.11 ADDTBL1.BAS—Adding a Table

```
Private Sub cmdCreate_Click()

    ' Add a new table
    Dim i As Integer
    Dim gdb As Database
    Dim tbl As TableDef      ' New table
    Dim fld As Field         ' New field
```

```
Dim strFldName As String
Dim fType As Integer
Dim iLen As Integer

' Create new table def
Set tbl = gdb.CreateTableDef(txtTable)

' Add new fields
For i = 1 To iLastUsedRow
    grd.Row = i
    grd.Col = 1
    strFldName = grd.Text

    grd.Col = 2
    Select Case grd.Text
        Case "True/False"
            fType = dbBoolean
        Case "Byte"
            fType = dbByte
        Case "Integer"
            fType = dbInteger
        Case "Long"
            fType = dbLong
        Case "Currency"
            fType = dbCurrency
        Case "Single"
            fType = dbSingle
        Case "Double"
            fType = dbDouble
        Case "Date/Time"
            fType = dbDate
        Case "Text"
            fType = dbText
        Case "Long Binary"
            fType = dbLongBinary
        Case "Memo"
            fType = dbMemo
    End Select

    If fType = dbText Then
        grd.Col = 3
        iLen = CInt(grd.Text)
    Else
        iLen = 0
    End If

      ' Create field def
     Set fld = tbl.CreateField(strFldName, fType, iLen)
     tbl.Fields.Append fld
```

continues

Creating Tables on a Server Database   **273**

Listing 6.11 Continued

```
    Next i

    ' Create the table, by adding it to the
    ' tabledefs
    gdb.TableDefs.Append tbl

End Sub
```

As you can see, there are several steps involved in adding a table to the database. First, a new `TableDef` must be created. Then, the table's fields need to be created and added to the new `TableDef`. Finally, the new `TableDef` must be added to the database's `TableDefs` collection.

This completes the utility. As you can see, there really is no difference in creating a table on a C/S database as opposed to a desktop database from a code point of view. From a process point of view there is one major difference: security. Before you can create the table you must possess the required security level.

While server databases are normally managed by a Database Administrator, there are situations where users are allowed to add tables themselves. This section showed you how to use Visual Basic to accomplish this.

From Here...

This chapter taught you how to use ODBC technology in Visual Basic applications. To round out your knowledge on using Visual Basic for developing client/server database applications, you should also review the material in the following chapters:

➤ To learn more about designing front ends, read Chapter 4, "Advanced Database Front Ends."

➤ To learn more about using the Jet Database Engine, see Chapter 7, "The Jet Engine and ODBC."

➤ To learn more about client/server, read Chapter 8, "Modern Client/Server Computing."

➤ To learn more about SQL Server, see Chapter 9, "Client/Server Databases."

7

The Jet Engine and ODBC

by James A. Dooley

The Microsoft Jet Database Engine (or *Jet* for short) provides Visual Basic with all its database access capabilities. Jet is responsible for all aspects of database management. It also provides the DAO (Data Access Objects), an object-based model used to operate upon the database and its contents.

A good analogy is that you don't have to be a motor mechanic to drive a car. Once you learn to drive, you can tour the countryside to your heart's content. But if your car breaks down in some out-of-the-way place, your knowledge of motor mechanics can help you get back on the road. Like a car, Visual Basic implements many powerful features that allow you to develop professional applications quickly. And like motor mechanics, your knowledge of the Jet Database Engine can help you optimize the performance of your application and troubleshoot problems when they arise.

Jet is an advanced database engine, offering many features that are found only on mid-range and mainframe database systems. This chapter concentrates on those aspects of Jet that enable you to write professional applications using Visual Basic. This chapter will provide you with the following:

➤ An understanding of the various Jet Database Engine components

➤ An insight into how Jet provides access to data stored in databases such as dBASE and Paradox

➤ An understanding of how Jet uses ODBC to access database servers such as SQL Server and Oracle

➤ An insight into how Jet supports attached tables

➤ An overview of how Jet processes database queries

Jet Engine Components

Jet Database Engine is the database management system (DBMS) included with the Visual Basic programming environment. Jet has no user interface of its own. Instead, users and developers interface with Jet via an application. Figure 7.1 shows how a Visual Basic application interacts with Jet.

One of the difficulties in understanding how Jet works is that there is currently little documentation available on the versions of Jet that are delivered with Visual Basic 4. However, we can learn a lot from white papers released by Microsoft on earlier versions of the engine and by drawing conclusions from our observations of tests we carry out in this chapter. To help us better understand Jet, we're going to break it down into a number of components, naming them as indicated in figure 7.2.

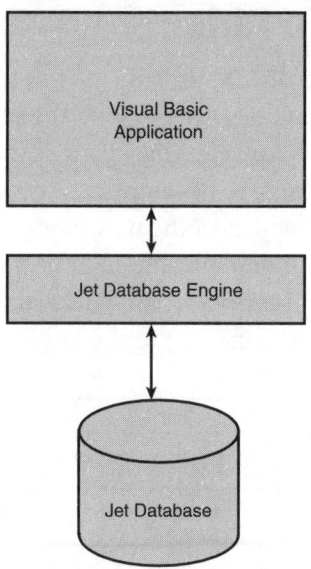

Fig. 7.1 The Jet Database Engine applications interface.

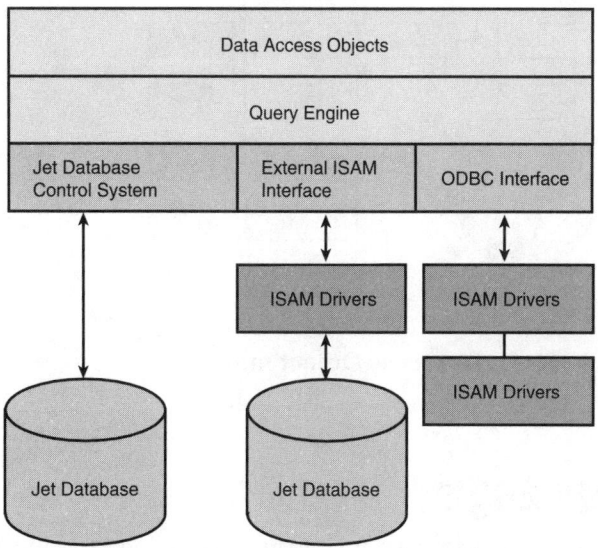

Fig. 7.2 The Jet Database Engine components.

Data Access Objects

Data Access Objects (DAOs) provide the interface to Jet functionality from Visual Basic and MS Access. With the release of Visual Basic 4, Microsoft has made considerable changes to the DAO object model. The new DAO available to developers is shown in light gray in figure 7.3. With the introduction of the new model, Microsoft dropped some components of the model presented in Visual Basic 3 (although these components are still supported for backwards compatibility). In figure 7.3, the dropped components are shown in dark gray.

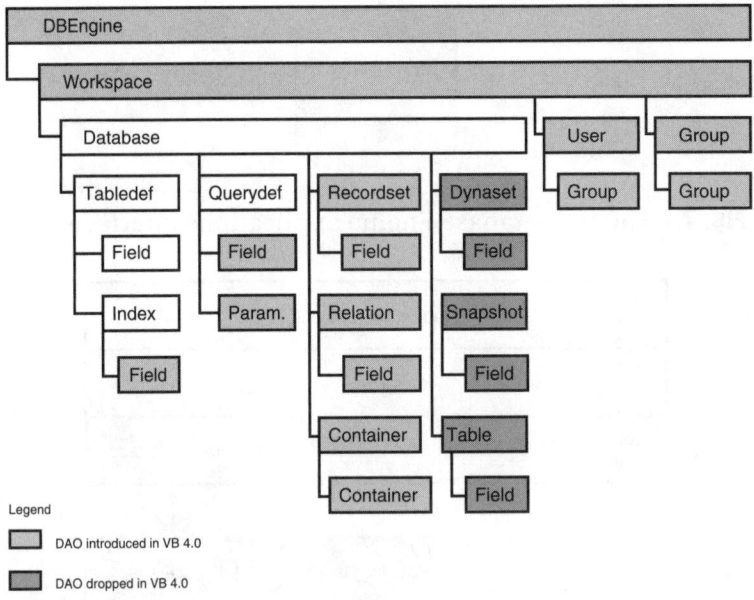

Fig. 7.3 The Data Access Object model.

Query Engine

The *Query Engine* is responsible for processing SQL queries submitted to it via the DAO. While Microsoft has not documented the internal workings of the Query Engine, we can make the following educated assumptions about how it handles queries.

1. The Query Engine examines our query to ensure that it complies with the version of SQL supported by Jet.

2. If a query complies with the SQL standard, the Engine binds the column names referenced in the query to the tables in the database to ensure that it can process the query.

3. Next the Engine generates all possible strategies it can use to satisfy the query.

4. Once the Engine has a series of possible strategies, it must decide which one to use. It does this by costing each strategy. This means that it calculates the amount of computer resources required to execute each strategy and selects the one that makes optimal use of the resources.

5. When the Engine has decided on a strategy, it stores it together with the query, ready to be executed.

For further information on how the Query Engine works, please refer to the "Query Processing" section later in this chapter.

When you store a query in the database, the Query Engine determines the execution plan for the query and stores it together with the query. The Engine uses the database statistics available to it at the time—such as number of records and indexes on the table—to determine how to execute the query.

When you execute the query subsequently it uses this plan to process the query. This has both a positive and negative side. On the positive side, Jet can execute your query faster because it does not have to go through the procedure outlined above to decide on an execution plan. On the negative side, any changes to the database structure—such as adding an index—will not be taken into account. For this reason, have the Query Engine recompile your query after you make significant changes to the database or when the size of the table has grown significantly. To have the Jet Engine recompile your query and you need to adopt a two-phase approach: first delete the query and then re-create it. This causes Jet to generate a new execution plan for the query.

Jet Database Control System

The *Jet Database Control System* is the subsystem that manages databases stored in the Jet format. In particular it is responsible for data integrity, security, and basic file I/O.

Record locking for Jet format databases is implemented via a page locking concept, in this case pages of 2K. A *page* is the technical term for a block of memory or disk space. When Jet needs to lock a record, it locks the entire page containing the record. This can have a major side effect on tables with a short record length because all records in the locked page are unavailable to other users.

External ISAM Interface

The *External ISAM Interface* is the subsystem that interfaces with the External ISAM Drivers (DLLs) that Jet uses to access data stored in formats such as Xbase, Paradox, and Btrieve.

One primary use of the External ISAM Interface is to enable its applications using Jet to coexist with other database applications. The interface allows Jet to access data stored in the following formats:

➤ Microsoft FoxPro, versions 2.0, 2.5, and 2.6

➤ dBASE III, dBASE IV, and dBASE 5

➤ Paradox, versions 3.x, 4.x, and 5.x

➤ Btrieve, versions 5.1x and 6.0

➤ Microsoft Excel, versions 3.0, 4.0, and 5.0

➤ Lotus WKS, WK1, and WK3

➤ Text data

Transparent access to data is a key concept in the design of Jet. While Jet makes great efforts to ensure that external tables appear as native Jet tables, it falls short on a number of occasions.

➤ When conducting a search on an external database, Jet adopts the native search rules of that database. Because many such databases are case-sensitive, this leads to Jet's own searches also being case-sensitive.

➤ DAOs and methods intended for use with database stored in the Jet format are not supported.

➤ Deleted records in FoxPro and dBASE tables are not removed from the FoxPro or dBASE file until the file is packed using either FoxPro or dBASE. Instead, they are simply marked as deleted and no longer appear in recordsets. However, the record remains in the database, occupying disk space.

➤ Paradox Graphic, Binary, and formatted memo types are not supported.

➤ Jet cannot open a password-protected Paradox table if it is already opened by a Paradox user.

➤ When working with rows from a speadsheet such as Excel, it is not possible to delete rows.

➤ Jet does not support multi-user access to Excel worksheets.

➤ It is not possible to create indexes on Excel worksheets.

➤ It is not possible to delete or update data stored in a text file, nor is it possible to create indexes on it.

➤ As with Excel worksheets, text files are not supported in a multi-user environment.

Because of these restrictions, most users convert existing databases to the Jet format wherever possible.

Regardless of the external database type, the steps involved in attaching the table are the same:

1. Open the Jet database.

2. Create a new `TableDef` object for the attached table.

3. Provide the connection information for the database and table.

4. Attach the table by adding it to the Jet database's `TableDef` collection.

Attaching an Excel 5.0 Worksheet

As previously indicated, we can attach a table from many external sources; the following example shows how to attach an Excel 5.0 worksheet. For the purpose of this example we're going to attach the Excel worksheet shown in figure 7.4. This worksheet contains the product table for the Northwind traders database.

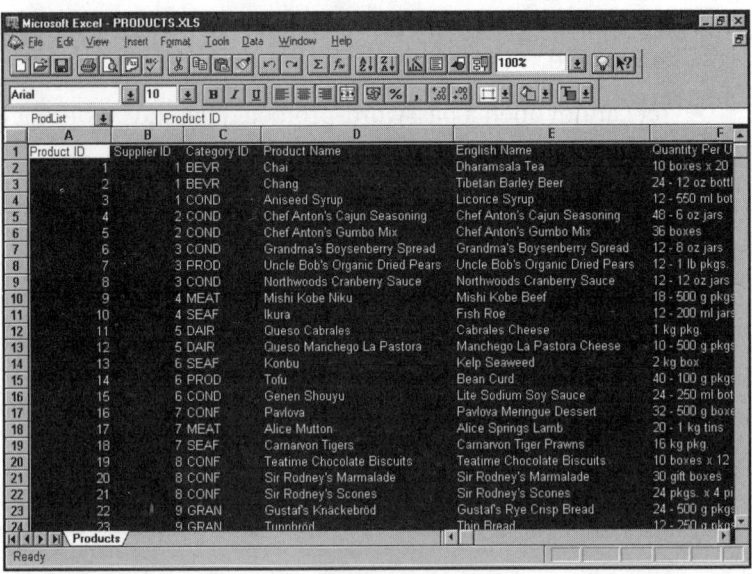

Fig. 7.4 The Northwind product table.

Before we can attach a worksheet, we need to name the range containing the data we want to make available to Jet. If the range has not already been named, then follow these steps in MS Excel:

1. Select the data range.

2. From the Insert menu, choose Name, Define.

3. After choosing Define, the Define Name dialog box appears (see fig. 7.5).

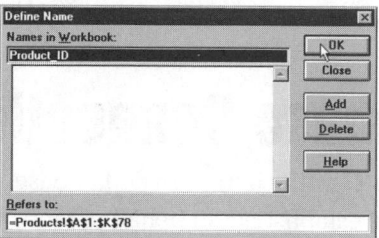

Fig. 7.5 The Define Name dialog box.

4. Type ProdList in the text box and click OK to define the data range name.

Once you have named the data range in the Excel Worksheet, you're ready to attach it to a Jet database. The following code in Listing 7.1 is used to attach the product table:

Listing 7.1 The Attach Table Source Code

```
Dim db As Database
Dim tbl As TableDef
' Open database
Set db = DBEngine.Workspaces(0).OpenDatabase(App.Path & _
  "\ATTACH.MDB")
' Attach Excel worksheet
Set tbl = db.CreateTableDef("MSE_Product")
tbl.Connect =
"Excel5.0;database=c:\book\source\jet\attach\product.xls"
tbl.SourceTableName = "ProdList"
db.TableDefs.Append tbl
```

ODBC Interface

The *ODBC Interface* is the subsystem that interfaces with the ODBC Manager to establish connections with database servers, such as SQL Server and Oracle. When Jet communicates with a database server via ODBC, it needs to make several ODBC API calls. This subsystem manages these calls.

ODBC Database Connections

Jet communicates with client/server databases via database connections. These are established on behalf of Jet by the ODBC Driver Manager. The engine not only shields the Visual Basic developer from the complexities of the ODBC Application Programming Interface (API), but also provides sophisticated features for managing these connections.

During the development cycle, it is unlikely that more than a few users will be connected to the database at any one time. As a result, problems associated with database connections may not arise until intensive user testing begins. At this stage the developer may be faced with the prospect of having to redesign any code changes necessary to overcome these problems. Having to make such changes so late in a project can be a costly experience. Much better then, to factor in the management of connections early in the design and avoid the problems. This section deals with three aspects of connection management featured in the development process: connection management on the server and client and optimizing connection usage.

Connection Management on the Server

When first connected to an ODBC data source, Jet looks for a table called MSysConf. Apart from this special significance to ODBC, this table is like any other in the database. It is normally created by the Database Administrator to assist in managing the connections to the database.

If you have Table Create and Update privileges on the database you are accessing, you can create and maintain this table. The structure of MSysConf is set out in Table 7.1.

Table 7.1   Structure of the MSysConf Table

Column Name	Datatype	Description
Config	SNALLINT	The number of the configuration option.
chValue	VARCHAR(255)	The text value of the configuration option.
nValue	INTEGER	The integer value of the configuration option.
Comment	VARCHAR(255)	A description of the configuration option.

If Jet finds this table, it examines the entries to determine how to manage the connection. The current version of Jet examines the table with a View to determine the following:

➤ Whether it should allow the user to store his/her user ID and password when attaching tables to a Jet database

➤ The strategy it should adopt to optimize the usage of database connections when retrieving data from the database server

While Jet's ability to store the user's ID and password with an attachment enables the development of transparent data access applications, it also introduces a security risk. If you attach a table from a server to a Jet database that is not itself password protected, for example, then anyone who opens the Jet database gets access to your server table without being authenticated. For this reason it is recommended that you turn off this feature in databases containing sensitive data by making the appropriate entry in the MSysConf table. Table 7.2 lists all the possible entries for MSysConf.

Table 7.2 Valid Entries for the MSysConf Table

Config	nValue	Explanation
101	0	Do not let the user save his ID and password in attachments.
101	1	Allow the user to have his ID and password in attachments (default).
102	D	Jet delays D seconds between each background chunk fetch (default = 10).
103	N	Jet fetches N rows on each background chunk fetch (default = 100).

When Jet is asked to return a result set as a Dynaset, it does not retrieve all records in the set before returning control to the requesting program. Instead it retrieves a chunk of these records, returns control to the calling program, and retrieves the remaining records as a background task. Entries 102 and 103 control how Jet carries out this task. There are no recommended settings for these entries. Test your system with various entries to determine the best settings for your network configuration.

Jet issues the following query to access the MSysConf table:

```
Select Config, nValue from MSysConf
```

Caution: When setting up security on your database, ensure that the above query can be executed from the user's account. If it can't be executed as typed above, then Jet will be unable to find the table and will ignore your table entries.

Including the MSysConf table in your database design and documenting its entries enables your Database Administrators to actively manage the database connections.

Connection Management on the Client

Jet provides an extensive array of options for managing the database connection on the client side. Most significant for our purposes are as follows:

➤ Defining the length of time to allow for connecting to the database server

➤ Defining the length of time to allow for a query to finish processing

➤ Restricting the type of objects that a user can attach to the Jet database

➤ Instructing Jet to attempt to connect to the database server, using the user's Jet sign-on ID and password, before asking the user to supply authentication information for the connection

➤ Requesting Jet to provide trace information to assist in debugging an application

Depending on the version of Jet you are using, when your application first starts, Jet will try to locate an [ODBC] section in your application's INI file or alternatively try to find similar entries in the Windows Registration database. If it finds this section, it uses the entries for the section to determine how it should manage all database connections for your application. Table 7.3 has been adopted from an earlier white paper by Microsoft on Jet and lists all entries for the [ODBC] section.

Table 7.3   [ODBC] Section Entries

Entry	Value	Effect
TraceSQLMode	1	Trace SQL Jet send to ODBC into file SQLOUT.TXT
TraceODBCAPI	1	Trace ODBC API calls into file ODBCAPI.TXT
DisableAsync	0	Use asynchronous query execution if possible (default)
	1	Force synchronous query execution

continues

Table 7.3   Continued

Entry	Value	Effect
LoginTimeout	S	Cancel login attempts that don't finish in S seconds (default = 20)
QueryTimeout	S	Cancel queries that don't finish in S seconds (default = 60)
ConnectionTimeout	S	Close cached connections after S seconds idle time (default 600)
AsyncRetryInterval	M	Ask server "Is query done?" every M milliseconds (default = 500)
AttachCaseSensitive	0	Attach to first table matching specified names, regardless of case (default)
SnapshotsOnly	0	Allow the creation of Dynasets (default)
	1	Return all result sets as Snapshots
AttachableObjects	*string*	List of server object types to allow attaching to (default = 'TABLE','VIEW','SYSTEM TABLE','ALIAS','SYNONYM')
TryJetAuth	1	Try Jet User ID and password before prompting
	0	Don't try Jet User ID and password before prompting
PreparedInsert	0	Use custom INSERT that only inserts non-NULL values (default)
	1	Use prepared INSERT that inserts all columns
PreparedUpdate	0	Use custom UPDATE that only SETs columns that changed (default)
	1	Use prepared UPDATE that updates all columns

In most cases, where you are accessing a database server on a local area network (LAN), the default values are satisfactory. However, if you have to access a database over a wide area network (WAN), via modem, or over a busy LAN, you can use the time-out related settings to overcome poor network performance. Regardless of whether you use the default settings or customized settings, document the settings in your user documentation so that people using your application on a slow network can take advantage of them.

During the development phase, the `TraceSQLMode` can be very useful in assisting you to optimize the SQL queries being used to access the remote data. For example, if you have two attached tables in your database, both located on an Oracle server, use the following query to access the tables:

```
Select PUBS.Name, TITLES.Title From PUBS, TITLES _
Where PUBS.PubID=TITLES.PubID
```

You can find out about how Jet processes the query by setting `TraceSQLMode=1` and issuing the query. After processing we find that the log file contains the following entry:

```
SQLExecDirect: SELECT `PUBS`.`Name` ,`TITLES`.`Title`
FROM `TITLES`,`PUBS` WHERE (`PUBS`.`PubID` = `TITLES`.`PubID` )
```

In this situation we can see that Jet submits the entire query to the Oracle server for processing. If we now move the PUBS table to SQL Server and execute the query again, we see that the query execution plan has changed:

```
SQLExecDirect: SELECT `PubID` ,`Name`  FROM _
`PUBS` ORDER BY `PubID`
SQLExecDirect: SELECT `Title` ,`PubID`  FROM _
`TITLES` ORDER BY `PubID`
```

In this case Jet sends one query to SQL Server to get the required data from the PUBS table and another query to Oracle to get the required data from the TITLES table. It then carries out the Join on the workstation. Thus, you can use the `TraceSQLMode` option to help you understand how Jet processes your query.

Optimizing Connection Usage

All database connections are equal, right? Wrong! Some database servers support powerful connections that can handle multiple partially complete queries at the same time, while other servers can only process a single query at a time. Regardless of whether the connection supports multiple or single queries, Jet allows multiple queries and manages the connections automatically. Let's look at an example:

Assume we're building a data browser to allow a user to view tables on an SQL Server database, which is configured to allow for 20 concurrent connections. We decide to build the application using a MDI interface so that the user can view more than one table at a time. We code and test our application, and when we're satisfied, we give it to a group of 10 users for testing. Shortly after testing begins, our users complain that they are not able to connect to the server because the number of concurrent connections have been exhausted.

The cause of the problem is that SQL Server supports only a single query per connection. As a result, Jet was opening additional database connections in order to support the multiple queries. The number of connections that Jet opened depended on the status of the current connection. If it contained a partially completed query, then Jet had to open a new connection to run the new query. As a result, the 10 users were exceeding the maximum number of concurrent connections being supported by SQL Server.

If your server does not support multiple partially completed queries on a single database connection, use the following tips to reduce the number of connections your application requires:

➤ Limit Dynasets to 100 records. A Dynaset containing less than 100 records requires only a single connection. A Dynaset containing more than 100 records, however, requires two connections, one to fetch the key values from the server and one to fetch the data associated with the keys for the records being processed.

➤ Release connections that are no longer required by your application. You can do this by executing a recordset's `MoveLast` method immediately after opening it.

➤ Use a `TOP 100 PERCENT` query to return all records in the result set.

➤ Set Jet's connection time-out value to a short period, thus forcing Jet to close the connections earlier.

When you begin working with remote database servers, you will notice that the first time you access a remote table takes much longer than subsequent accesses. This is because Jet caches and shares the database connections as much as possible. Jet will share two connections where the data source name (DSN) and the DATABASE name are the same. Jet also shares the database connection, in the absence of a DATABASE name, where the DSN is the same. Furthermore, Jet maintains the connections even when they are not explicitly in use.

When you use a database's `Close` method, Jet does not in fact close the database connection. Instead, Jet maintains a persistent connection in case the user reopens the database later in the application. If the user does not reopen the database, a connection time-out will occur and Jet will close the connection. To force Jet to close a connection try this:

➤ In the application's INI file, create an [ODBC] section as described above and set `ConnectionTimeout=1`.

➤ Immediately after calling the database's `Close` method, add the code in Listing 7.2.

Listing 7.2 Closing a Connection

```
db.close
Start = Timer
Do
     FreeLocks
     DoEvents
While Timer <= Start + 1
```

While you cannot reduce connection time without first improving network performance, you can improve the perceived performance of the application by taking advantage of the fact that Jet caches and shares database connections. The trick is to establish a dummy database connection during application startup. As part of your startup routine, open the database and close it. Jet will cache the connection and use it later when the user attempts to access the database.

Attached Data

Traditionally, database servers hold corporate-wide data, which supports many applications. Accessing data on such servers is very different from accessing a database located on your PC. In particular, you will find that the databases are under the supervision of a Database Administrator (DBA).

Database Administrators are responsible for granting access to the data stored on the server and creating new databases, tables, and indexes. They also optimize the performance of the server and back up the databases. In addition to this added level of administration, the methods used to provide access to the data are different.

Jet provides the following two methods of accessing data stored on a database server:

➤ Attach the tables to a Jet database and access the tables as if they were Jet tables.

➤ Connect to the ODBC data source and access the tables.

> **Note:** Microsoft recommends that you use attached tables rather than connecting directly to the ODBC data source because it appears to offer better performance in most cases.

Attaching Tables

Attaching an ODBC data source table to a local Jet database requires the following steps:

1. Open the database.

2. Create a new `TableDef`.

3. Complete the `TableDef` connection and `SourceTableName` properties.

4. Append the new `TableDef` to the databases `TableDefs` collection.

The code in Listing 7.3 illustrates these steps.

Listing 7.3   Example of Attaching an ODBC Table

```
Dim curDB as Database
Dim tblDef as TableDef
' Open database
Set curDB = DBEngine.Workspaces(0).OpenDatabase
  ("ACCOUNTS.MDB")'
' Create table
set tblDef = curDB.CreateTableDef("SQLSRVR_Accounts")'
tblDef.Connect = "ODBC;DSN=Accounts;UID=sa;PWD=LetMeIn"
tblDef.SoruceTableName = "Accounts"
curDB.TableDefs.Append tblDef
```

When you attempt to update or add new records to some attached tables, you may receive an error message stating that the Dynaset is read-only. The following are two common reasons for this:

➤ Jet requires that a table to be updated must have a unique index. If the table you are attempting to update does not have a unique index, then Jet opens it as read-only.

➤ You do not have the required permission to update or insert records into the table. To update a table, you need UPDATE permission on the table from the DBA. To add new records to the table, you need the DBA's INSERT permission.

In most cases there is not a one-to-one relationship between the data types supported by the ODBC data source and Jet. When attaching a table, Jet calls several ODBC APIs to determine the data type, precision, and scale of each column in the table. It then uses this information to map the ODBC data sources to Jet data types. This mapping, together with the connection information, is stored in the attached table definition. Thereafter, Jet uses this information to communicate with the server to obtain data from the table.

Note: In situations where Jet does not support a particular ODBC data type, it must select an appropriate Jet data type. When this conversion fails, the value is treated as NULL. Zero-length text retrieved from a server is also treated as NULL. As a result, the user cannot always distinguish between a NULL value and a data-conversion failure.

Attaching Views

In some environments, access to data is provided via what is known as a View. From a user perspective, a View is very much like a table, with one exception: you cannot normally update a View. In the database, however, a View is actually stored as a predefined SELECT query that is executed every time the user queries the View. Because a View is in fact a query, it can span more than one table, restrict the records returned via a WHERE clause, and so on.

For example, suppose you wanted to allow the sales force to view the sales data for the state in which they operate but not for any other state. One way to do this would be to create a table containing only the sales data for each state and grant the salesperson access to the table for their state. While this solution would work for the sales force, it will cause problems later when others want to view the data. Suppose you now want to let the Marketing Manager view the sales data for the Eastern Region. To do this, you'd have to grant him access to the table for each state in the Eastern region and then he would have to create queries to join the tables before he could see the data at region level. The best way to handle such situations is to store all the data in one table and then create different Views over it, to meet each group's needs. For example, to let the sales force for CA see their data, you create a CA View using the following SQL:

```
Select * from SalesData Where State = 'CA'
```

The code required to attach a View is exactly the same as that used to attach a table. Jet treats a View as if it were a table without indexes. In other words, when you open it, it will be opened as read-only.

While Views normally are treated as read-only, you can have Jet open them as updatable if your server allows you to update Views. Because Jet requires a unique index to update records, you need to tell Jet which field or fields can be used to uniquely identify the records returned by the View. To do this, issue a data definition query (not a Pass-Through Query) to define a unique index on the View. This will not create an index on the server nor will it create an index in the local Jet database. It simply tells Jet which fields it can use to uniquely identify the records when communicating with the server.

Query Processing

Understanding how Jet processes your ODBC-related queries is a prerequisite for optimization. Users who are familiar with Oracle or SQL Server know that these systems provide facilities to enable them to ascertain how the system intends to process the query submitted. Unfortunately, Jet does not provide such facilities, at least not directly. To understand more about how Jet processes an ODBC based query, you can use the `TraceSQLMode=1` option to cause Jet to log the SQL commands it sends to the server. This output is logged to a file called SQLOUT.TXT. Using this log, we can draw some conclusions about how Jet is handling our query.

The key to understanding this output is to understand the commands on the left-hand side. An explanation of these commands is provided in Microsoft's white paper and has been reproduced in Table 7.4.

Table 7.4   Explanation of the SQL Trace Commands

Command	Explanation
SQLExecDirect : <SQL-String>	Execute non-parameterized user query
SQLPrepare : <SQL-String>	Prepare parameterized query
SQLExecute : (PARAMETERIZED QUERY)	Execute prepared, parameterized user query

continues

Table 7.4 Continued

Command	Explanation
SQLExecute : (GOTO BOOKMARK)	Fetch single row based on bookmark
SQLExecute : (MULTI-ROW FETCH)	Fetch 10 rows based on 10 bookmarks
SQLExecute : (MEMO FETCH)	Fetch Memos for single row based on bookmark
SQLExecute : (GRAPHIC FETCH)	Fetch OLE Objects for a single row based on bookmark
SQLExecute : (ROW-FIXUP SEEK)	Fetch single row based on some index key (not necessarily bookmark index)
SQLExecute : (UPDATE)	Update single row based on bookmark
SQLExecute : (DELETE)	Delete single row based on bookmark
SQLExecute : (INSERT)	Insert single row (Dynaset mode)

This section examines how Jet processes a number of common types of query. To carry out this investigation, assume you have set up two databases on an SQL server and a local database on the workstation. The structure of these databases are the same as the Northwind database shipped with Visual Basic. Figure 7.6 illustrates the test environment.

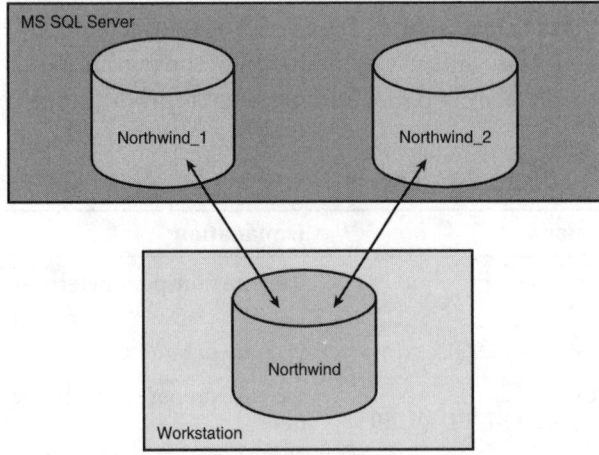

Fig. 7.6 The Query Processing environment.

ORDER BY

Although Jet will parse all queries, we'd expect that if we issue simple
SELECT queries on a remote table, Jet is smart enough to let the server
do the work. Let's see what happens when we issue the following query:

```
SELECT DISTINCTROW
     dbo_Customers.Customer_ID,
     dbo_Customers.Company_Name,
     dbo_Customers.City
FROM dbo_Customers
ORDER BY dbo_Customers.Customer_ID
```

When we examine SQLOUT.TXT we find the entries in Listing 7.4.

Listing 7.4   SQL Trace Output

```
SQLExecDirect: SELECT dbo.Customers.Customer_ID
                  FROM dbo.Customers ORDER BY Customer_ID
SQLPrepare: SELECT Customer_ID,Company_Name,City
                  FROM dbo.Customers  WHERE Customer_ID = ? OR_
                  Customer_ID = ?
                  OR Customer_ID = ? OR Customer_ID = ? OR _
                  Customer_ID = ? OR
                  Customer_ID = ? OR Customer_ID = ? OR _
                  Customer_ID = ? OR
                  Customer_ID = ? OR Customer_ID = ?
SQLExecute: (MULTI-ROW FETCH)
SQLExecute: (MULTI-ROW FETCH)
SQLExecute: (MULTI-ROW FETCH)
SQLExecute: (MULTI-ROW FETCH)
SQLExecute: (MULTI-ROW FETCH)
SQLExecute: (MULTI-ROW FETCH)
SQLExecute: (MULTI-ROW FETCH)
SQLExecute: (MULTI-ROW FETCH)
```

As you can see, our single query has produced a lot of activity. Because
the result set is a Dynaset, the first thing seen is that Jet has issued a
single query to retrieve the key information about the customer
records. It then prepares a parameterized query, which it uses to
return the records in sets of 10.

GROUP BY

As with our ORDER BY query, we'd expect to find that Jet also passes our GROUP BY query to the server.

```
SELECT DISTINCTROW dbo_Orders.Customer_ID,
      Sum(dbo_Orders.Order_Amount) AS SumOfOrder_Amount
FROM dbo_Orders
GROUP BY dbo_Orders.Customer_ID;
```

Examining the trace file, we find that there was not as much activity as before because this result will be returned as a Snapshot:

```
SQLExecDirect: SELECT Customer_ID ,_
               SUM(Order_Amount )  _
               FROM dbo.Orders GROUP BY Customer_ID
```

TOP N

How does Jet handle Access SQL supported features when dealing with a remote database server? Let's begin by issuing the TOP N query in Listing 7.5.

Listing 7.5   Top 10 Percent Query

```
SELECT DISTINCTROW TOP 10 PERCENT dbo_Customers.Company_Name,
      Sum(dbo_Orders.Order_Amount) AS SumOfOrder_Amount
FROM dbo_Orders INNER JOIN dbo_Customers
      ON dbo_Orders.Customer_ID = dbo_Customers.Customer_ID
GROUP BY dbo_Customers.Company_Name
ORDER BY Sum(dbo_Orders.Order_Amount) DESC;
```

From the trace file we see that because the server does not implement a TOP N capability, Jet must handle it, itself. To do this, Jet has sent a standard GROUP BY/ORDER BY query to the server (see Listing 7.6).

Listing 7.6   SQL Trace Output

```
SQLExecDirect: SELECT dbo.Customers.Company_Name
               SUM(dbo.Orders.Order_Amount )
               FROM dbo.Customers,dbo.Orders WHERE _
```

```
        (dbo.Orders.Customer_ID = _
                dbo.Customers.Customer_ID )
        GROUP BY dbo.Customers.Company_Name
        ORDER BY SUM(dbo.Orders.Order_Amount )    DESC
```

So although Jet returned only 10% of the records to the application, we discover that it in fact retrieved all records from the server. In our case this was not really a problem because the table was small. If the table had contained several million records, however, Jet would have had major problems.

Query on Query

One interesting thing about Jet queries is that they can be based on another query in the database. To see how Jet handles such queries, execute the query in Listing 7.7, which is based on the previous GROUP BY and ORDER BY queries.

Listing 7.7   SQL Query

```
SELECT DISTINCTROW OrderBy.Customer_ID,
        OrderBy.Company_Name,
        GroupBy.SumOfOrder_Amount
FROM GroupBy INNER JOIN OrderBy ON
      GroupBy.Customer_ID = OrderBy.Customer_ID
WHERE ((OrderBy.City='Seattle'))
```

When we examine the trace file, we find that Jet has had to handle this itself, executing both queries and carrying out the join locally.

```
SQLExecDirect: SELECT Customer_ID ,Company_Name
                FROM dbo.Customers WHERE (City = 'Seattle' )
SQLExecDirect: SELECT Customer_ID ,SUM(Order_Amount )
                FROM dbo.Orders GROUP BY Customer_ID
```

The conclusion to be drawn from these last queries is that in cases where a particular feature of Access SQL is not supported on the server, Jet takes over and processes it. This will have a major impact on performance if the tables being processed are large.

Having examined these simple queries, we're now going to move up a gear and examine how Jet deals with joining various tables in a result set.

LEFT JOIN

In a LEFT JOIN, all records from the table in the left are included, while records from the right table are included only if there is a match. Let's see how Jet handles the following query:

```
SELECT DISTINCTROW dbo_Customers.Customer_ID,
       dbo_Customers.Company_Name,
       dbo_Orders.Order_Date,
       dbo_Orders.Order_Amount
FROM dbo_Orders LEFT JOIN dbo_Customers ON
       dbo_Orders.Customer_ID = dbo_Customers.Customer_ID;
```

After executing the query, we examine the SQLOUT.TXT log through Listing 7.8 to see how the query was processed:

Listing 7.8   SQL Trace Output

```
SQLExecDirect: SELECT dbo.Orders.Order_ID,
               dbo.Customers.Customer_ID
               FROM {oj dbo.Orders LEFT OUTER JOIN
               dbo.Customers ON (dbo.Orders.Customer_ID
               = dbo.Customers.Customer_ID ) }
SQLPrepare: SELECT Customer_ID,Company_Name
            FROM dbo.Customers
            WHERE Customer_ID = ? OR Customer_ID = ?
            OR Customer_ID = ? OR Customer_ID = ? OR
            Customer_ID = ? OR Customer_ID = ? OR
            Customer_ID = ? OR Customer_ID = ? OR
            Customer_ID = ? OR Customer_ID = ?
SQLExecute: (MULTI-ROW FETCH)
SQLPrepare: SELECT Order_ID,Customer_ID,Order_Date,
            Order_Amount  FROM dbo.Orders   WHERE
            Order_ID = ? OR Order_ID = ? OR
            Order_ID = ? OR Order_ID = ? OR
            Order_ID = ? OR Order_ID = ? OR
            Order_ID = ? OR Order_ID = ? OR
            Order_ID = ? OR Order_ID = ?
SQLExecute: (MULTI-ROW FETCH)
SQLExecute: (MULTI-ROW FETCH)
```

```
SQLExecute: (MULTI-ROW FETCH)
SQLExecute: (MULTI-ROW FETCH)
SQLExecute: (MULTI-ROW FETCH)
SQLExecute: (MULTI-ROW FETCH)
SQLExecute: (MULTI-ROW FETCH)
SQLExecute: (MULTI-ROW FETCH)
```

In this case, Jet has taken the following steps:

1. Submitted a query to the server to join the orders and customer table, returning only the key information—in other words, the IDs of the orders and customers that meet the join criteria.

2. Retrieved the customer information for the customer IDs returned by step 1.

3. Retrieved the order information for the order IDs returned by step 1.

4. Joined the two result sets locally and returned the final result to the calling application.

By the way, {oj is the instruction to carry out an outer join.

Heterogeneous Joins

A *heterogeneous join* is the name given to the process where two tables located in different databases are joined to form a result set. Let's try to join the Orders table in one server database to the Order Details table in the other server database (see Listing 7.9).

Listing 7.9   An SQL Heterogeneous Join Query

```
SELECT DISTINCTROW dbo_Orders1.Customer_ID,
     dbo_Orders1.Order_ID, dbo_Orders1.Order_Date,
dbo_OrderDetails.Product_ID, dbo_OrderDetails.Quantity
FROM dbo_Orders1 INNER JOIN dbo_OrderDetails
     ON dbo_Orders1.Order_ID = dbo_OrderDetails.Order_ID;
```

On examining the trace file, we find the activity shown in Listing 7.10.

Listing 7.10   An SQL Trace Output for Heterogeneous Join

```
SQLExecDirect: SELECT Order_ID ,dbo.OrderDetails.Order_
               ID,dbo.OrderDetails.Product_ID FROM dbo._
               OrderDetails
SQLExecDirect: SELECT Order_ID ,dbo.Orders.Order_ID FROM _
               dbo.Orders
SQLPrepare: SELECT Order_ID,Customer_ID,Order_Date  FROM _
            dbo.Orders
            WHERE Order_ID = ?              OR Order_ID = ? OR_
            Order_ID = ? OR Order_ID = ? OR
            Order_ID = ? OR Order_ID = ? OR Order_ID = ?
            OR Order_ID = ?
            OR Order_ID = ? OR Order_ID = ?
SQLExecute: (MULTI-ROW FETCH)
SQLPrepare: SELECT Order_ID,Product_ID,Quantity
            FROM dbo.OrderDetails  WHERE Order_ID = ?
            AND Product_ID = ? OR Order_ID = ? AND
            Product_ID = ? OR Order_ID = ? AND Product_ID = ?
            OR Order_ID = ? AND Product_ID = ?
            OR Order_ID = ? AND Product_ID = ? OR Order_ID = ?
            AND Product_ID = ? OR Order_ID = ? AND _
            Product_ID = ?
            OR Order_ID = ? AND Product_ID = ? OR Order_ID = ?
            AND Product_ID = ? OR Order_ID = ? AND _
            Product_ID = ?
SQLExecute: (MULTI-ROW FETCH)
SQLExecute: (MULTI-ROW FETCH)
SQLExecute: (MULTI-ROW FETCH)
```

This output appears more complex than it actually is because the two databases use the same underlying table names and column names. Filtering out this, we find that Jet has done the following:

➤ Executed a local join on the key information

➤ Retrieved the key information for the Orders file

➤ Based on the local join, requested record details from each table that matches the join

➤ Retrieved the key information for the Order Details file

This concludes our review of Jet's query processor. To summarize, we have learned to do the following:

➤ Restrict the amount of data requested by using WHERE clauses. This reduces the network traffic and speeds up local joins.

➤ Avoid using Jet-specific extensions to SQL. Where servers do not support these functions, Jet is forced to implement then locally.

➤ Avoid heterogeneous joins, which force Jet to perform the join locally.

➤ Index all columns used to join tables.

Our investigation of Jet's query processing capability is not comprehensive. Jet's execution plan is based on several factors: the complexity of the query, the content and structure of the tables, and the indexes available. For this reason, it is strongly recommended that you undertake an exercise similar to what we have done here, as you strive to gain optimal performance. Bear in mind, however, that the execution plan Jet uses in evaluating your queries may change over time, as the structure and content of your server databases change.

Pass-Through Queries

So far, all our queries have been processed by Jet. It has been responsible for ensuring that our query has been formulated correctly and decided on how to execute it. But there is another type of query—known as a *Pass-Through Query*—in which Jet plays only a minor role. As its name suggests, this type of query passes right through the Jet Database Engine to the database server for processing. Jet is responsible only for providing the database connection and for returning any result sets or errors to the Visual Basic application. This is depicted in figure 7.7.

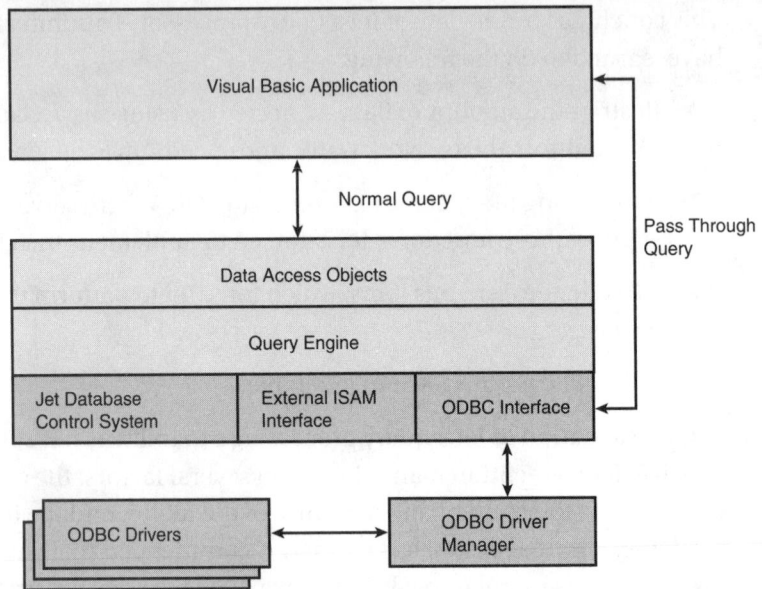

Fig. 7.7 The processing of Pass-Through Queries.

In addition to being able to select and change data, such queries can carry out database administrative tasks, such as changing roles on an Oracle database, adding users or groups on an SQL Server database, and so on. The following example in Listing 7.11 shows how to use a Pass-Through Query to add a user to the current database on an SQL Server:

Listing 7.11   An Example Pass-Through Query

```
Dim db as Database
Set db = DBEngine.WorkSpaces(0).OpenDatabase
        ("NWIND", False, False, _
        "ODBC;DSN=NWIND;UID=James;PWD=")
db.Execute "sp_adduser James, James, UserGroup",
        dbSQLPassThrough
db.Close
```

Pass-Through Queries offer a number of advantages over standard Jet queries:

➤ Pass-Through UPDATE, DELETE, and APPEND queries tend to be faster than those dealing with Jet attached tables and the DAOs.

➤ Pass-Through Queries can call stored procedures on the server.

➤ Pass-Through Queries can make use of SQL extensions that are supported by the server.

➤ Pass-Through Queries can carry out administrative tasks on the server, assuming you have the correct permissions.

However there are also some disadvantages.

➤ Pass-Through Queries, by their very nature, tend to be database-server specific and, as a result, can make it difficult to port your database application to another database platform.

➤ Result sets returned by Pass-Through Queries are read-only.

➤ Results sets are returned as Snapshots and, as such, perform badly on a WAN. Remember, Jet retrieves all records in a Snapshot before returning control to your application. As a result, the user must wait until all records have been dragged across the network before continuing work. Contrast this with a Dynaset, where Jet retrieves some of the records, returns control to your application, and then continues to retrieve the remaining records in the background.

Clearly the biggest disadvantage of using Pass-Through Queries is that they may be server-specific and, as a result, cause difficulty in porting the application later. If you do decide to use Pass-Through Queries, then you need to adopt a strategy that will allow you to port your application easily should you need to at a later stage. The following are a few ideas to consider:

➤ Try to localize your Pass-Through Queries to one module. Encapsulate each call into a function and, if necessary, have the function return any recordsets or error messages to the rest of the program.

➤ Use stored procedures rather than embedding the SQL in your application.

➤ If your stored procedures do not require parameters, you might consider storing their names in a lookup table in your database, rather than hard-coding the names into your code.

From Here...

Developing professional database applications with Visual Basic requires an understanding of the Jet Database Engine. In this chapter you have gained an understanding of the various activities performed by Jet. By examining the Query-Processing capabilites of Jet, you have learned how to optimize your queries and, by using the trace option, you have learned how to debug a query.

➤ For more information on working with ODBC, see Chapter 6, "Working with ODBC."

➤ For more information on developing client/server applications, see Chapter 8, "Modern Client/Server Computing."

➤ For more information on client/server databases, see Chapter 9, "Client/Server Databases."

➤ For more information on SQL, see Chapter 10, "SQL."

8

Modern Client/Server Computing

by Steve Potts

Client/server computing is a topic of great importance to everyone in the computing field. It is also the object of considerable hype by the trade press. Much of what you read about client/server computing is factually correct but misses the point. Sometimes client/server is treated like a kind of database management system akin to hierarchical and relational database. In truth, the database vendors are early adopters of client/server, but the topic is bigger than just database access. At other times, we see client/server treated as another category of computer science, like multimedia or artificial intelligence. This ignores the fundamental nature of client/server as a link in the evolution of computers, not a feature of applications.

There is a sea change taking place in the computing world as we shift away from single-vendor mainframe computing toward small, single purpose computing. There are still more mainframe and midrange applications than client/server applications, but the preponderance of new development is taking place in the new client/server paradigm.

This shift is the topic of this chapter. Its goal is to lead your thoughts through the next 10 years of computing changes in order to prepare you for the future. This chapter will cover the following topics:

➤ Understanding the different types of computing

➤ The distinction between clients and servers

➤ Advantages of client/server computing

➤ Obstacles to implementation

➤ The role of enabling technologies

➤ The nature of distributed objects

➤ The future of client/server computing

At the conclusion of this chapter, you will be aware of the direction that the computing industry is heading.

Understanding Computing History

Client/server is not a type of computer or a feature of an application, but rather it is simply the next generation of computing technology. To understand what this means, we have to look at the history of the information industry. The invention of the computer marks the beginning of the computer age but not of the information age. Man has been processing data, mostly by hand, for the past 500 years. As companies began to form and grow, they identified, cataloged, processed, and summarized data about their activities in support of the decision-making process. Double-entry bookkeeping dates from the time of Columbus. An examination of the books of any large company in the nineteenth century reveals an extremely sophisticated business approach complete with process and procedures. These processes and data were scattered throughout the enterprise and maintained by people who understood their origin, use, and value.

In the early 1950s, businesses began learning about computers. These early machines could perform certain tasks far better than humans and could potentially reduce the cost of certain activities. Two attributes dominated the understanding of computers of this era: their complexity and their cost. A computer center could cost millions of dollars and required a whole staff of computer experts to keep it going.

The expense and complexity of those computers suggested that a centralized organization was required to feed these new wonders. Because of the relative expense of the computing hardware, it was not cost effective to take the computers to where the business data naturally resided, so the early adopters brought the "mountains to Mohammed." In effect, they brought their mountains of data to the programmer/ analysts of the computer room. These people transformed this data into information by putting it into the computer and running programs against it. Over the ensuing decade, businesses found themselves investing tons of money and reaping tons of benefit from this arrangement.

The biggest problem with this was that the programmer/analysts lack of understanding of the data that they were throwing about with such deftness. They knew something about what it meant, but this knowledge was far inferior to that of the functional workers in each part of the company. This was recognized by everyone, but the resulting savings was so great that everyone just lived with it. This era was dominated by the "big iron" vendors like Honeywell, Control Data, IBM, Burroughs, and Sperry. In the late 1970s, several changes began to take place:

➤ The price of computing power began to decline.

➤ The quality of the system software that ran these computers began to mature and, therefore, required less maintenance.

➤ The knowledge of how computers work began to proliferate into technical fields like engineering and accounting.

This brought about a drastic change in the way people used the computer. Departments began to buy computers for themselves and to create programs that addressed their problems. This was especially true in design and manufacturing organizations that had a large number of engineers on staff. The mainframe companies were not nimble enough to react properly to this change, and new companies like Digital Equipment, Hewlett-Packard, and Data General emerged from obscurity to become household names.

Nothing lasts forever, and in the late 1980s, another set of changes began to fall into place:

➤ The price of computing power accelerated its decline.

➤ The quality of the software that ran these computers began to mature and "ease of use" became an important metric.

➤ The personal computer penetrated the homes of workers in every field. These simple machines were great laboratories for risk-free experimentation, which led to a huge increase in the general workforce's understanding of computer science. Before long, nearly every department in every company had one or two serious computer hobbyists on staff. While some of these people were hackers, a lot of them were not.

Now, functional workers began to ask why they couldn't have a computer on their desks at work. This created a demand for the personal workstation that dominates the business computing landscape of the 1990s.

In reality, all that the computer professionals are doing is relinquishing the ownership of data to its rightful owners (the department that created the data) who now bear responsibility for its completeness and correctness. For a business to remain competitive, data must flow freely between these departments to shed light on the decisions that must be made every day.

For example, the engineering department needs to know what the consequences of its design would be on the manufacturing department. What changes to the design could it make to lower the cost? How much would an extra wingding on the side of the widget cost? How much more does marketing project that customers will be willing to pay for the extra wingding? How much capital investment will be required to purchase the wingding mold and press? How much can we buy the wingding part for if we give the specification to a supplier?

The answers to all of these questions require data from multiple organizations. Engineering owns the part design model data. Manufacturing data is required to project the fabrication cost. Marketing data contains the price projections. Procurement has data about suppliers, their capabilities, and their prices. Finance knows how much capital will be required and what other projects are competing for this investment capital.

The solution to this problem of integrating these "islands of automation" is commonly referred to as "client/server" computing. The person or program that wants a service performed is the *client*, and the person or program that provides that service is the *server*. The "/" in the middle is the responsibility of the computer scientist. Your job, should you choose to accept it, is to set up the infrastructure so that these functional experts can obtain the services that they need to do their jobs and thereby earn the money to create paychecks for everyone.

Clients

The generic concept of a client is fairly simple: it is someone or something that wants service. This basic client/server relationship is repeated billions of times each day, everywhere on the planet. The majority of these transactions take place with the heavy involvement of humans, although more of these are being transferred to computers.

Each of the transactions of your day that involves the participation of resources other than yourself is a client/server relationship. Some of these transactions, like getting a haircut, involve only people while others, like withdrawing money from the bank via an electronic teller, involve only computers. Most services, like eating at a restaurant, have a human component as well as a computing component.

The client/server computing evolution is not anything new in a logical sense. It is just the automation of relationships that already exist.

From the standpoint of the Visual Basic programmer, the client is the application that needs data or services from another program, often running on another computer. An example of this is a Visual Basic program that allows a user to browse through a library of presentation graphics stored on a centralized server. This front-end client makes requests to the presentation graphics server for specific slides. The server sends the requested slides back to the client who then displays them for the user.

Servers

What types of servers will this brave new world need in order to function properly? The correct answer is probably not known at this time. Mankind usually requires a decade or more to realize the best use of a technology. A few categories have already emerged. We will look at these server types in this section.

Remember that a server is defined as a program that services multiple clients who are interested in the resources that the server owns. By definition, a restaurant is a server, but the kitchen in your home is not. To use a restaurant, you make functional requests to cook some ribs. The kitchen, on the other hand, just sits there when you give it orders. It has resources but no process to use them, so it is not a server.

In Visual Basic, the server is usually a repository of information that could potentially be of interest to a number of different clients. The Jet Database Engine can implement this server, but often the server requires a more robust platform like Microsoft SQL Server. A database of current budget allocations might be kept by the accounting department on a server. Other departments can write client programs in Visual Basic that access this budget data over the network. This data can be displayed in the desired format by the using department.

File Servers

The earliest example of one computer providing services to another is in the area of file sharing. One computer was typically purchased with a very large (by the standards of the day) hard disk drive. This drive would be made to appear as if it were local to the rest of the computers on the same local area network. An application's files could be loaded on this hard drive that was seen by every computer. Whenever another computer needed this program loaded into its own memory, the network would perform its magic and the program would be loaded on the local computer. Figure 8.1 illustrates this concept.

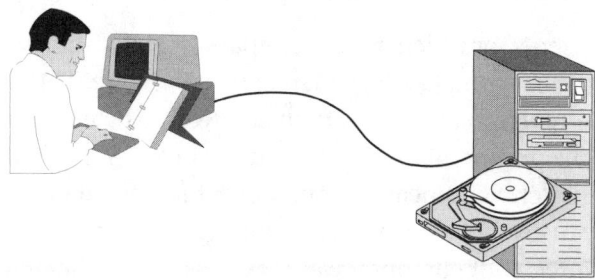

Fig. 8.1 File servers make data and programs available over the network.

Print Servers

In the mid-1980s, printers were dumb devices. They were nothing more than a print head, a simple processor to drive the print head, a power cord, and a communications line. Each type of printer responded to a set of commands that were sent to it over the serial or parallel line. These commands were processed sequentially as they were received. The computer program was responsible for running on the host computer to generate the commands needed to print a page.

Some computers had special programs written for a specific printer called *printer drivers*. These printer drivers accepted files as input and translated them into a stream of characters that the printer understood. Every computer that needed to print to that printer needed to install the printer driver or write its own printer control code.

Every computer had to have a printer attached to one of its hardware ports. For mainframe computing, this was not a problem because scores of people shared the computer and hence the printer. For personal computers and workstations, however, this situation was intolerable because of the expense of providing everyone with a printer. Organizations began to designate one computer as the printing computer. Users would walk over to this computer with a diskette containing the file that they wanted to print and would use the designated printing machine to produce hard copy.

This lessened productivity, so companies next installed a commercially available network, like LAN Manager or NetWare. This allowed that one computer to be hooked to the network. The network software made the printer on the designated PC look like it was attached to a local printer. Your local computer became a client of this printer server. Instead of using your computer to send instructions directly to the printer, your computer was really asking another computer to provide this connection and actually send the commands down the wire to the printer.

The next step in the evolution of the printer was the merging of the controlling computer and the printer into network nodes. Network-attached printers contained all of the computing power needed to drive the print engine in the same box. These printers had addresses on the network and looked like ordinary nodes on the network. However, because this node was a special printing computer and not a general purpose computing machine, it could use RISC processors and run software that was tuned for the purpose of processing printouts as quickly as possible. These print servers removed the need for every computer to drive the printer. If an application could create an output file in PostScript or HPPCL languages, it could be translated at the printer and printed out.

These printers were and still are important to client/server computing because they were truly service devices that offloaded significant work from the local computers. Because of the sophisticated processing that they could do, they caused the industry to think of other uses for servers. Figure 8.2 illustrates this architecture.

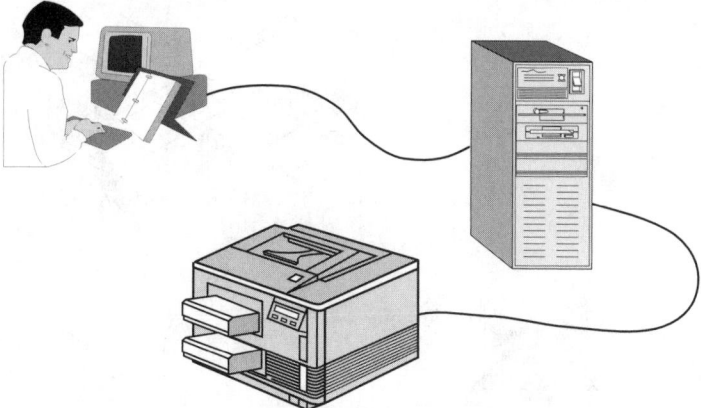

Fig. 8.2 Attaching a printer to a network removes the need for a computer to manage it.

Graphical User Interface Servers

Two different kinds of GUI servers appeared in the late 1980s: mainframe screen scrapers and X Windows terminals. They both provided graphics services to the user locally but displayed data that was being retrieved from another machine.

The mainframe scrapers attached to the big computer by making the workstation look like a dumb terminal to the application. Whenever the mainframe application sent what it thought was instruction on how to paint a terminal screen, the screen scraper would intercept it, transfer it to a personal computer, put a pretty face on it, and display it on the screen. Whenever the user entered data on this GUI screen, the scraper would then package it up to look like an ugly terminal, and send it to the mainframe. The application was none the wiser. Figure 8.3 shows how this works.

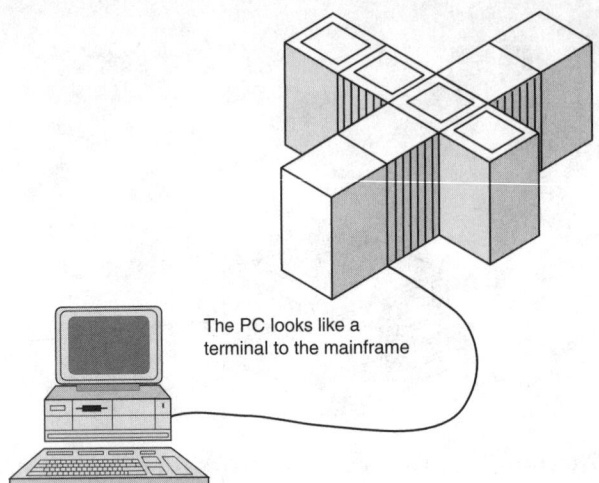

The PC looks like a
terminal to the mainframe

Fig. 8.3 The computer does not know that the screen scraper is not an ordinary terminal.

X Windows terminals were designed to allow a graphical user interface to be displayed on a terminal. As workstations began to proliferate, a problem arose: organizations could not afford to let everyone have a $25,000 computer on the desktop. Whenever they did foot the bill for one of these prizes, the owner still spent much of his time in meetings, thereby wasting the resources on his desk.

X Windows terminals relieved this problem pretty well. They moved much of the GUI work to a terminal that provided a workstation look and feel for a quarter of the cost. They did this without burdening the main computer with a lot of screen handling work.

These special terminals were also popular for centralized database applications written with a GUI front end. These applications provided a beautiful user interface to each terminal without having to deal with the issues of distributed databases and without clogging the network with GUI screen painting commands.

Image Servers

The next server type, in this progression from the simple to the complex, is the image server. At the time of this writing, images consume considerable disk space and can be stored in more formats than you can count without taking off your shoes. Image servers can assist in dealing with both of these problems.

For example, suppose that a travel agency wants to really jazz up face-to-face meetings with its customers. It wants to display pictures of the great vacation destinations that it offers. Instead of loading these huge files onto everyone's local machine, the agency purchases an array of CD-ROM photographs from these places. These pictures come from a variety of sources and come in a variety of formats. Whenever a session requires that a photo be displayed, the client program makes a request to the print server for that picture. The print server locates the photo, and converts it to the format, (.BMP, .TIF, .PCX, and so on) and sends it to the client for display.

Database Servers

Everyone immediately thinks of distributed databases when the words "client/server" are used. There are already mature products in this niche: Oracle, Microsoft SQL Server, Sybase, and Ingres to name a few.

Earlier, when file sharing was being discussed, we mentioned how all users in a local area network could access files on the server's hard disk drive. Certainly, within five minutes of this network features introduction, someone wrote some data to a file so that another user could access it. Immediately, the issues of security, concurrent access, logical schema independence, and every other mainframe database problem came to the desktop computer. These DBMS vendors set about solving these problems, as well as a host of others dealing with distributed data.

These database vendors benefited tremendously from the existence of a de facto standard database manipulation language, IBM's structured query language, SQL. SQL was designed to provide a functional user interface to database access. Fortunately, it was designed when distributed database was a hot research topic, if not yet a reality. As a result, the designers of SQL considered the importance of set-oriented processing and its effect on network performance in their design.

Set-oriented processing means that instead of asking for a row that meets the criteria of the search, you ask for all rows at once. This provides four advantages:

➤ The transport mechanism can transfer entire blocks of data as a group across the network. This is much more efficient than transferring one row at the time over the wire.

➤ The server filters out rows that fail the criteria, which avoids a lot of network transmission of uninteresting data.

➤ Programmers can gain an efficiency improvement by coding with set operations.

➤ Query optimization is possible when the database is told about all of the rows that the user needs at this time.

The downside of the SQL issue is that every vendor produced a slightly different flavor of SQL than what the standard says. So, while the learning curve is shorter than it would be otherwise, applications are really not completely portable across multiple vendor offerings. Chapter 10, "SQL," discusses SQL in more detail.

The big advantage of client/server databases is that they fit the model of modern data ownership better than a mainframe database does. Typically, the business unit that creates the data understands how to use it best. It wants to be able to increase the database as it sees fit. It is also the best qualified to determine what constitutes invalid data and to set up the rules to prevent it from entering the database. Add to this the fact that functional units often have the political power required to keep the data in their organizations, and you'll understand why mainframe database types are changing sides and declaring victory in record numbers. The focus of wise database gurus has shifted to helping these data owners deal with the pure computer science problems of performance, concurrency, security, and so on. Figure 8.4 shows how these client/server databases are linked together.

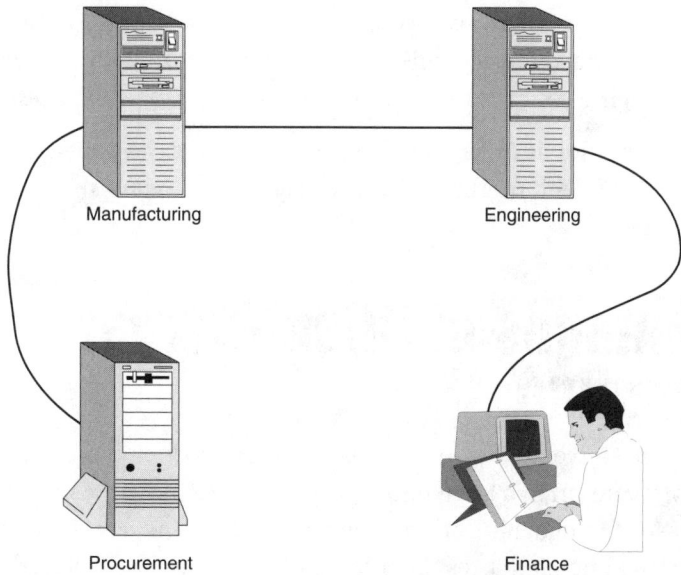

Fig. 8.4 The client/server databases are owned by the departments that created them, but everyone with permission can access the data.

Wrapped Servers

An important enabling technology that makes the evolution of computing practical is the wrapper. A *wrapper* is a layer of code, hopefully thin, that allows an existing system, written in another epoch, to imitate a modern application. In order to accomplish this task, an old application is "wrapped" in a disguise that makes it look like something it isn't.

For example, suppose you have a very important database on a mainframe that contains critical data. Surrounding this database is an army of people who control the data that goes into this database very well. If you rewrite this application and move it to another platform, you will have to redesign the control structure. Because everyone that you suggest this to turns pale, you choose to avoid the issue by accessing the data in place. However, you cannot use the old development tools that normally accompany this ancient environment without permanently damaging your resume, not to mention your mental health.

The solution is to write a wrapper that makes the application look like an object with methods. Now, you can use modern tools to access this data.

Advantages of Client/Server Computing

Client/server computing saves money by reducing the need for human intervention in a large number of transactions. In a centralized database of budget allocations, each client can send a request to the server for the budget figures that it needs. These can be displayed on a screen for the user. This is much less expensive than having either a written request or a telephone call retrieve the data.

The key strategy of every enterprise is to lower its cost to either drive demand or improve its margins. Therefore, in the business world, lowering costs is a primary motive.

Labor costs are the largest cost component of almost every product and service on the planet. Even if the cost of raw materials is high, it is normally due to the amount of touch labor that manufacturing requires. Therefore, a key strategy of most cost reduction efforts has to focus on the reduction of labor costs. Client/server computing holds great promise in this labor-cost-reduction strategy.

Another advantage of client/server computing is the speed at which data can be accessed. Even if a company doesn't mind paying people to call each other with questions, it probably minds waiting for the response if the person who knows the answer is unavailable. A server can be configured for 24-hour availability if necessary. This means that the speed at which a request can be fulfilled is improved, and normally the entire project is completed more quickly. In many businesses, the company which calls back the customer first with the answer gets the order.

A third advantage of the client/server model is in the division of labor. While becoming a client/server expert requires considerable aptitude and training, becoming a Visual Basic front-end programmer requires much less. If all of the difficult issues like data integrity and multi-user access are handled at the server, the job of creating the client program is simplified and can be done either by a lower salaried person or, most often, by a worker whose primary job is not programming.

The Obstacles of an Ideal System

Implementing the next generation of computing systems is another insurmountable opportunity for the quick and the brave. While it is conceptually simple to think about allowing all of the data to be maintained by the best qualified people, and then made available to whomever needs it to do his job, the details are kind of hard.

One requirement of our ideal system is that the delivery mechanism needs to be transparent to the client. This transparency takes several forms:

➤ The client should be able to communicate transparently with every server in the enterprise.

➤ The programmers should be able to access a resource on a remote server as if it were local to his computer.

➤ The client should not have to know the physical address of a resource. He should be able to refer to it by name.

➤ The client should be able to find a service, even if you moved it to a different disk or even a different server.

➤ The user should be able to log on once and access every resource that he is authorized to access.

➤ A resource located in another time zone should display the local time of the client.

➤ A disk drive crash or CPU meltdown on one of the servers should be transparent to the client.

➤ The organization that owns the data should not be asked to sacrifice the autonomy of its system to a centralized autocracy.

Though this is a lot of information, if you master the art of solving all these problems, you will be gainfully employed at least until the kids are out of college. You probably started estimating how much code will be required to satisfy these requirements. It will take a lot of programming to make this a reality. This is good news for those with skill at creating and implementing systems.

As you ponder that list, you can probably think of many more requirements such as:

➤ The data in the servers must be protected from unauthorized access and alteration.

➤ The server should be able to handle multiple requests at the same time and avoid making a client wait.

➤ The server should not allow bad data to be entered into it.

➤ Small additional amounts of computing power must be affordable. The company should not have to invest millions when it only wants to add 10 users.

➤ The architecture must be scaleable. You should not be required to move to a new network technology or operating system simply because of the increasing popularity of the service that you provide.

> Equipment purchased from different vendors must work together seamlessly.

> The architecture must handle peak demand periods without degradation of services.

> License and billing issues must be handled in a way that doesn't annoy the users.

For the next generation of systems to be usable, most of these obstacles must be overcome. In order for the system to fulfill the huge potential of truly distributed computing, it must overcome them all.

Enabling Technologies

For a client/server application to be successful, it must have a reliable connection to the server involving both hardware and software, sometimes called *middleware*. For example, the physical connection between the client and the server can be as simple as a wire or as complex as a wide area network (WAN). The software may be as simple as a communications program, or it may involve military-style security.

Many of these technologies have matured to the point where they are already in everyday use, while others have a ways to go.

Hardware

The stand-alone personal computer of the 1980s had a huge gulf between it and client/server computing: the lack of a physical connection to the other computers in the world. The hardware and operating system software engineers of that day did a fine job of solving this problem. Now, the vast majority of serious business computers are linked to some form of network.

The simplest piece of equipment purchased in the hardware world was the wire. Normally, these wires are shielded metal, have a specific resistance, and connectors on the end. They had to be connected to something, and so a device called the network interface card had to be installed in the computer. The problem of connecting computers together via wire was not hard. The main challenge of the late 1980s was the affordability of these devices for personal computers.

The next piece of the puzzle was in the area of network operation systems. For a time, Novel NetWare looked like it would be the dominant system in this market, but innovations by other vendors and a desire to interconnect the PC networks into the larger networks have kept the jury out on which architectures will win out. As of this writing, multiple protocol stacks support a coexistence of architectures, although not without some pain.

Soon after, every computer in the company was filling these new wires with happy sounds. Before long, everyone learned the meaning of the word *bandwidth*, and how little of it there seems to be when a whole company was sharing it. They also learned that their computers did not always speak the same language as the computers that they want to talk to. Computers attached to local networks wanted to have access to the other computers in the company when they needed it, but they had to have good response time when communicating with their own departments. To address this problem, bridges, routers, and gateways were introduced.

Bridges are devices that interconnect LANs. They listen to the traffic going across the network and filter out traffic that is local to one side of the bridge, thereby lowering the traffic on the other side. Figure 8.5 illustrates how bridges work.

Routers interconnect the LANs using protocol-dependent information gleaned from the packets on the network. They lower the amount of traffic on a part of the network by filtering out protocols that are not supported on a LAN. Devices that both bridge and route, sometimes called *brouters*, are the most popular.

Gateways are devices that translate one protocol into another. The SNA gateway has been in use for years. It translates other network packets into SNA compatible packets in order to talk to the IBM mainframe.

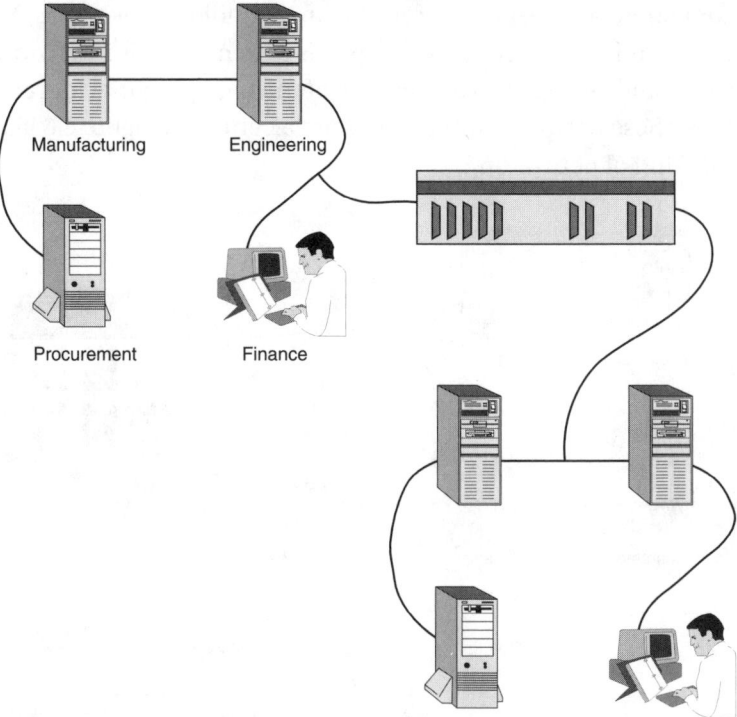

Fig. 8.5 Bridges interconnect networks and filter unwanted traffic.

All of these devices introduce delays in the movement of data across the network. This lowers the user's satisfaction when the data is time-dependent, like video transmission.

This niche has produced a few millionaires and will certainly produce a few dozen more in the next decade. As a result, the rate of innovation is very fast, and new products appear every month. This progress, when combined with more standardization between service providers will continue to improve the connectivity between computers.

For the vision of global client/server computing to be a reality, every computer in the world needs to be able to talk to every other computer in the world, (if it has permission) in much the same way that any telephone can talk to any other telephone. The large communications companies are spending a fortune on technologies like ATM, X.25, ISDN, and other acronyms that promise to make this interconnection easier and less expensive. Because of the high potential for revenue from these networks, innovations are a certainty. Figure 8.6 illustrates this kind of networking.

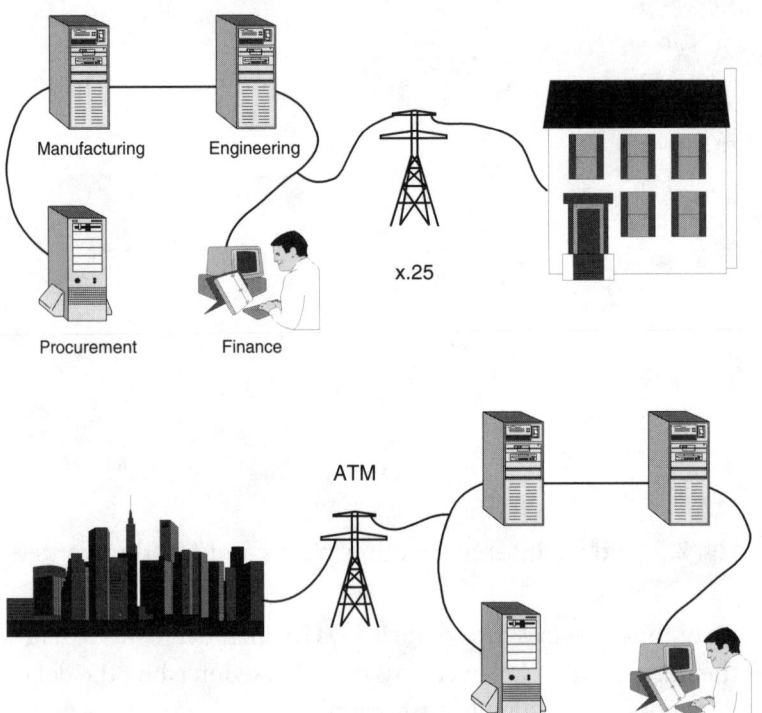

Fig. 8.6 A large mix of technologies are required to interconnect a large number of computers.

The challenges associated with creating a hardware infrastructure are formidable but well on the way to solution. The challenges associated with the software interoperability are not nearly as mature.

Middleware

The hardware solutions of the previous section addressed a few of the obstacles to implementing a global client/server computing vision. The rest of the obstacles will be left to a software layer often called middleware. Products find themselves classified as middleware when they are neither application nor operating system software.

The middleware field is interesting because it is so immature. Standards are plentiful and fluid, and new requirements are still being discovered. Five main categories of middleware are currently under development:

➤ Database middleware addresses the problem of connecting database servers to clients. It attempts to solve the problems of incompatible SQL dialects and normally works with the network to hide network access issues from the programmer. The major players are de facto standards like ODBC, IDAPI, and Oracle Glue. Progress in this area improves the transparency of distributed data for the client.

➤ Transaction-oriented RPC middleware deals with the issues involving multisite transactions. The simplest example of a multisite transaction is that of transferring money from one bank to another. If the system fails after deducting the amount from your bank account on one computer before adding it to your account on the other computer, the system must restore the first account and try again. This problem has long been solved on a single computer but presents new challenges when it involves multiple computers. The standards in this field are called ATMI, /WS, Transactional RPC, TxRPC, and XATMI. Progress in this area will enable electronic commerce to take place better.

➤ Group middleware provides standards *du jour* for mail-enabled and groupware applications. This area is the most fluid and includes electronic mail, group calendaring, compound documents, and so forth. Lotus Notes API, MAPI, VIM, and VIC are all jockeying for position. Progress in this area promotes the use of geographically dispersed teams that compose the basic units of the "virtual corporations" that are popular in business literature.

➤ System management middleware allows one management station to perform system management tasks such as defragmentation, database administration, monitoring, and the like on all of the machines in his charge, regardless of their physical location. The standards are SNMP and CMIP. Progress in this area lowers the cost of system management.

➤ Distributed Objectware allows a client to run software (invoke methods) that resides on servers. This area is a key to the next generation client/server applications and the subject of the next section.

All of these middleware layers perform important functions, without which client/server computing would either be impossible or impractical. The evolution of the computing field is more dependent on the evolution of middleware than on any other factor.

Distributed Objects

Nearly everyone in the computing field agrees that objects are the wave of the future, even if they aren't really sure what an object is. Simply, an object is a piece of code that has characteristics, or *attributes*, and provides services through functions called *methods*. Object technology has facilitated the development of large complex software systems by hiding the complexity of software components behind simpler object interfaces. The next logical step in object technology is to implement the advantages of object technology across platforms and geographic locations.

Distributed objects allow a client to run software (invoke methods) that resides on another computer. Logically, this activity is very similar to accessing data on another computer, except for the fact that the interaction between the objects in the two processes will be more complex.

Instead of sending an SQL statement to a server which sends back a set of rows, a distributed object client might send a geometric model of an aircraft part to a server that optimizes part models for weight and strength. These complexities must be addressed in order to make the whole scheme work properly. The main complexities are as follows:

➤ Location: The client must figure out where this service will be performed. If the location changes, then the client must still be able to find it. If the first service that the client tries is busy or out of service, then it should try another.

➤ Authorization: The server must protect itself from unauthorized access. When the client attempts a connection to the application object, the server must decide whether to allow it. Given the number of servers in the world, it is not practical to issue every client a logon ID and password on every server that it might want to communicate with. This processing involves the invocation of another server application.

➤ Interface: Data normally flows across networks as packets. These packets are made up of a core of application data wrapped in an envelope of address identifiers as shown in figure 8.7.

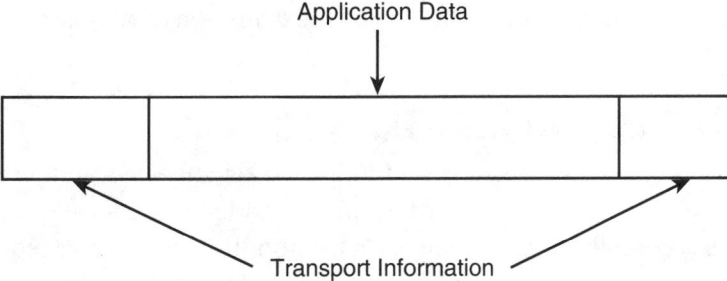

Fig. 8.7 Data travels in packets across the network from the client to the server and from the server to the client.

This packet acts like a box. The network doesn't care what you send, as long as it fits into a packet. The disposition of the stuff is the job of the addressee. In computer terms, the server application must parse the data in the packet as it receives it. The format of this data must be in some form that the receiver can understand. An agreement must exist between the sending and receiving application as to the format of this data. This format specification is called the *interface*.

When applications call functions, they are sending information via an application programming interface (API). The function called is normally located inside the same address space as the calling routine, and located by a pointer to the start of the code in memory. What is needed is a pointer to the function on the other computer. The middleware and the network must redirect what the application thinks is a local pointer to a function for calling a function on a remote computer.

Armed with an interface definition, the client can arrange the data into a string to be sent to the server. The server must now react appropriately to process the request. Having done this, the server would like to pass the output back to the client. At this point, the server must call some function in its address space to pass the data back to the client. It also needs an interface to bridge this gap.

Finally, the clients in the scenario need to say goodbye to the servers and resume their own work. This is another application interface need. These problems are addressed by the definition of an object model.

The Object Model

The goal of distributed computing is to exchange data and services between computers, regardless of type and physical location. In order to accomplish this exchange, each computer must receive requests for action that it can understand. In past and current implementations of distributed computing systems, one vendor of hardware or software would publish an interface, normally in the form of an application programming interface, and other programmers and vendors would write programs to this standard. This was a step in the correct direction but not the final solution.

When one computer requests data or services from another, it must use an interface. This interface must provide exact details of what method performs what function and what the data types of the parameters that each method will accept are. It must be exact enough to allow coding to take place. It must also be easy for a programmer to connect to other server objects. The specification is called the object model because it describes the object in such a way that all software conforming to this model can communicate with all other conforming software.

Two main camps have published object models and proposed them as standards for everyone to use. One of them is the Common Object Requester Broker Architecture (CORBA) proposed by a consortium called the Object Management Group (OMG). The other is called the Component Object Model (COM) and is favored by Microsoft.

Common Object Requester Broker Architecture (CORBA)

In 1989, an industry consortium was formed to develop standards for objects to interoperate in the heterogeneous global client/server world. This group was called the Object Management Group (OMG) and was joined by most of the vendors in the industry including Microsoft.

The OMG has published and revised the Object Management Architecture Guide (OMA Guide). This guide describes four main components as shown in figure 8.8.

The functions of these services are as follows:

➤ *The Object Request Broker (ORB)* is a piece of middleware responsible for managing the interconnection of a client with a server, regardless of its hardware platform or where the object and services are located. To make this possible, an Interface Definition Language (IDL) is used to describe the interface to the ORB.

➤ *The Object Services* provide services like object naming, event notification, persistence, and lifecycle management. Eventually, this category will include transaction management, security, licensing, and other similar services.

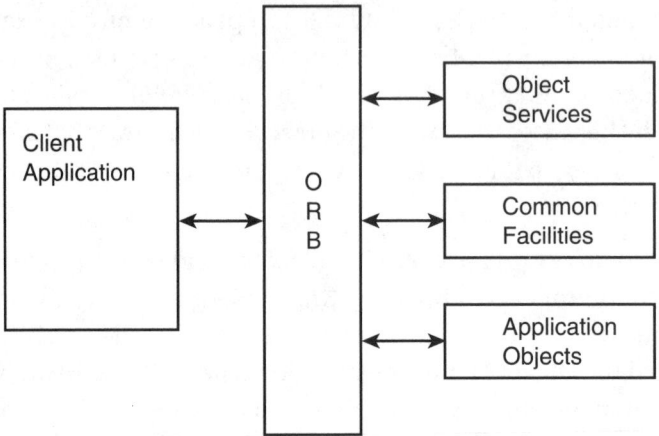

Fig. 8.8 There are four major components of the CORBA architecture.

➤ *The Common Facilities* are a group of specified end-user services that fall outside the scope of the object model specification but which are generally useful. These include e-mail, database access, compound documents, and so forth. The CORBA spec lists these services as optional.

➤ *Application Objects* are objects written specifically to be part of an application. They must define an interface using the IDL if they are to connect to services via the ORB.

The operation of the client/server request is fairly simple. The ORB is a piece of middleware that accepts a request for a service from a client. The ORB then looks to find the object that provides that service in its directories. The ORB then completes the circuit between the client and the server and passes the request to the server. The server performs the requested action and passes the output parameters back to the ORB, which then communicates them back to the original client.

Component Object Model (COM)

Microsoft designed COM so that applications could be built from components supplied by different vendors. Encouraged by the successful third-party developer industry that has sprung up to write VBXs, Microsoft wanted to generalize this effort to include all languages and all operating systems. The model sustains higher level services like those provided by OLE 2.0. Because this is a *Microsoft* Visual Basic book, COM piques a particular interest.

COM offers a set of services to the application provider. Microsoft claims that the following features of an object standard should exist if it is to be taken seriously:

➤ Binary Interoperability: The objects created must be able to interoperate without recompiling.

➤ Language Independence: The object types should be created with a variety of programming languages, not with just one language like C++.

➤ Transparent cross-process interoperability: The objects can be called across process boundaries and across physical machine boundaries using the same programming model.

➤ Versioning: Allows for the evolution of the components over time without causing systems that used to work to quit because an interface changed.

➤ Performance: Application performance must not be sacrificed.

Briefly, COM deals with the problem of calling a function outside of its own address space by specifying that a small piece of code (called a proxy) be linked into the local application. In order to call a function in the interface of another object, the application calls that function in the local proxy. The job of the proxy is to capture the calling parameters, package them in a way to travel across the network intact, and send them to its counterpart on the other machine, the *stub*.

The stub resides in the same address space as the server application and can therefore access all of the server's functions via a normal C or

Pascal style pointer. The stub unpacks the call that was sent by the proxy, and makes the call to the local method or function. The method then passes the returning parameters to the stub, which then packages them and transmits them back to the client's proxy. The proxy unpackages the results and hands them back to the client. Figure 8.9 shows what this looks like.

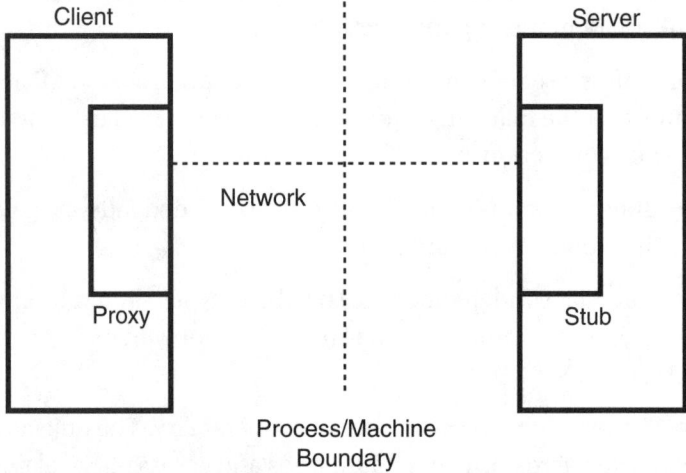

Fig. 8.9 The proxy and stub do the communications work for the client and server application.

The proxy and stub work fine as messengers, but they do not concern themselves with the calls made to the methods of the server object. How is this coordinated between the client and server? COM specifies that any objects worthy to be called a COM object must be able to answer the following question: "Do you speak the XYZ language?" (or in computer terms: "Do you support the XYZ interface?"), where XYZ is any interface that the client speaks (has implemented).

The server must either pass back a pointer to the interface in question, or NULL, which indicates that it cannot speak XYZ. The details of the XYZ interface are beyond the interest of COM except to pass calls back and forth between client and server for the duration of the conversation.

The value of this strategy is based in three simple features:

➤ The programmer only needs to learn how the methods in the object work in order to use it. Windows and Visual Basic programmers are very adept at doing exactly that.

➤ Anyone at any time can write a new interface and load it into COM immediately without any committee meetings or votes. If Company A wants to provide an interface spec to Company B, it can. Company A servers then support this interface, and Company B clients can use it immediately. In practice, the companies in this niche market will soon arrive at a small number of interfaces to support in an attempt to lower support costs. But the minute a company develops a better interface, it can implement it and try to get others to follow suit. This fits well with a free market like the one that surrounds the computer business.

➤ The overhead for the COM process is low when compared to other approaches.

These objects are compiled and loaded onto a computer. They can be communicated with at the binary level and, therefore, can be accessed by any language that can call a function via a pointer to a pointer.

Version management is unnecessary because the rule of COM is that once an interface has been defined, the interface specification cannot be changed. The implementation may be improved over and over, but the definition of how the client application calls its methods is fixed. If a change is needed, a new interface spec is written, and the interface receives a new name.

COM has the advantage of being used commercially in OLE 2.0. This means that every developer who writes the next generation of VBXs, called OCX, will be somewhat familiar with COM. This gives COM some early momentum in the race for universal adoption. Because Visual Basic provides such a large market for these OCXs, the number of developers likely to learn how to code to the COM model is likely to number in the thousands in the next several years.

Comparing COM and CORBA

By closely examining the details of both COM and CORBA, you can understand that the differences are not cosmetic or petty, but rather each represents a different set of goals. CORBA has a certain beauty and completeness about it. It attempts to solve the problem of interoperability in its general form, in a complete and elegant way.

COM, however, is for the pragmatic at heart. It is simple enough to be immediately usable without waiting on anyone or anything, at least on homogeneous systems. It has a "quick to market" orientation that emphasizes "getting it done" as opposed to "getting it right."

So who is right? Neither. Depending on what you are trying to accomplish, one approach is better than the other. In some ways CORBA is reminiscent of the Open Database Connection (ODBC), which attempted to solve the client/server database interconnection problem generally. ODBC, however, pays a performance penalty for the flexibility, and so it is bypassed for the pragmatic version, pass-through mode, more often than not. In time, however, this performance penalty may be less important as machines become more powerful. Many old-timers can remember a time when languages like Fortran and COBOL wore the same "too slow to be practical" label and were bypassed by those who wrote assembly language.

The Future of Client/Server Computing

Plenty of consumers are telling their hardware and software vendors in plain English, Spanish, French, and every other known language that they want improvement. The vendors themselves have begun to talk about interoperability as a good thing, but some of their behavior still causes us to blink twice.

This need for interoperability brought about an age of ad hoc solutions. This is the situation that the computer business faces now. Because of the lack of agreement on what the right answer is, we are implementing technologies like ODBC and CORBA that mask differences but at a price. Routers and gateways perform similar services on network packets. Wrappers fill this niche in the object-oriented world. While these solutions don't truly satisfy, they allow a certain level of interoperability to take place while the industry experts ponder the deep question of what we really need to solve the fundamental problem.

Predicting the future is easy, but getting it right is the hard part. Having said that, the following seem likely to occur:

➤ The large communications conglomerates of today will dominate the delivery of bandwidth in the future, perhaps even between two points in the same building. The young upstart companies will do well, but their technology will be absorbed by the giants as they are bought out.

➤ SQL differences will not be tolerated in the future, and it will become hard to tell whose database server you are going against. These database servers will become commodities.

➤ The COM standard will prosper in the short term because of its low overhead. In the long run, it is too limited in its present form to prevail. The CORBA camp will struggle but will, over time, build up steam. Performance complaints will vex them just as they have vexed ODBC. In the long run, COM will move in the CORBA direction, and the two will meld together. This will likely cause yet another surge in the demand for applications driven by lower costs.

➤ The OLE versus OpenDoc race has started with OLE in the lead by two furlongs. OpenDoc has about two years to turn the corner or surrender.

➤ The demand for applications will continue to grow but will increasingly be filled by end-users using Visual Basic's descendants. The demand for computer science wizards to build better tools and to turn the end-user written systems into production class systems will soar. Several people will leave the computing field even as this demand soars because they fail to make the transition from application developer to system integrator.

➤ The difference between client processes and server processes will blur beyond distinction and become time-dependent. Instead of saying that a program is a server, we will say that it is acting as a server, at this moment.

From Here...

In this chapter, we defined client/server computing in a broad sense as any process that receives services from another process. This definition allows us to view the future of computing from a better perspective.

We examined the kinds of servers from simple print servers to complex object servers. We looked at the future of computing with objects and object standards. Finally, we looked to the future to see what it might look like.

In order to increase your understanding of databases and client/server, you should examine the following chapters:

➤ For more information on Visual Basic database interfaces, see Chapter 4, "Advanced Database Front Ends."

➤ For information about data management, see Chapter 5, "Data Management and Data-Driven Programming."

➤ For information about connecting to remote databases, see Chapter 6, "Working with ODBC."

➤ For information about Microsoft SQL Server, see Chapter 9, "Client/Server Databases."

9

Client/Server Databases

by Steve Potts

The most common use of client/server technology is in the database field. Client/server databases are very popular in nonmainframe-based companies because they provide most of the advantages of mainframe databases, like security and transaction processing, while maintaining the ease of use and lower life-cycle cost of distributed hardware and software.

This chapter will use Microsoft SQL Server 4.21 running under Windows NT/Advanced Server for its examples. SQL Server is, as its name implies, a database server. It was designed to be a powerful and reliable back-end server and it relies on front-end tools like Visual Basic to provide the user interface for the applications.

In this chapter, we will learn how to build applications using Visual Basic and SQL Server. The following topics will be covered:

- Understanding the client/server database architecture

- The role of Microsoft SQL Server

- How to install SQL Server

- How to create a table

- How to add data to the table

- How to query the table

- How to create a stored procedure

- How to call a stored procedure

You will create a simple, but real application using Visual Basic and SQL Server.

Client/Server Databases

The client/server architecture is an important step in the evolution of computing. Data exists everywhere in the enterprise: in desks, in file cabinets, on purchase orders, in spreadsheets, etc. In years past, a small subset of this data was transferred into mainframe databases where it could be widely viewed. The expense of this approach and its regimented nature limited the amount of data that could be managed in this manner. The other data remained in the functional units of companies.

As desktop computers proliferated throughout the organization, single user databases were created using dBASE, Lotus 1-2-3, Access, and other desktop databases. These databases produced a cost savings over paper systems, and made some data available electronically for the first time.

Once data is stored electronically, it begins to attract attention. Other departments perceive that an integration of this data with their own internal data could yield some very interesting information. They start by asking first for reports, then for diskettes, and finally for online access to this data.

This is wonderful for the enterprise because it improves the ability of the organization to make sound decisions, but it is difficult for the person with the desktop database. They now must deal with issues such as data integrity, concurrent access, security, and performance. These issues are the province of computer scientists, not of functional experts.

Ten years ago, the universal answer would have been to port the database to the mainframe. Now, an alternative has appeared: the client/server database.

This architecture moves the desktop database to a departmental server where a database administrator can maintain it. Because server databases like SQL Server are fully functional in the areas of transaction processing, crash recovery, and performance, they have the advantages of a mainframe database. They reside on a departmental server and are normally maintained by an employee of that department, so they better fit the political reality of companies and governmental organizations.

Performing this conversion of a desktop database to a server database is a booming business. Those computer specialists who can master the art of performing these tasks will be in demand both inside traditional companies, and in consulting firms which specialize in this type of conversion.

Microsoft SQL Server

One of the most popular client/server database platforms is Microsoft SQL Server. It provides a symmetric server architecture that multi-processes at the thread level. This allows for the efficient use of multi-processing servers that are becoming common. It uses the additional CPUs without any intervention by either the user or the database administrator.

Optional components provide gateways to mainframe and minicomputer database management systems, including IBM DB2, AS/400, and

ORACLE. In addition, it can interoperate with SYBASE SQL Server running on UNIX or VMS.

ODBC drives are widely available to connect SQL server to any front-end development tool that supports ODBC. For more information on ODBC, see Chapter 6, "Working with ODBC."

SQL Server is a back-end processor, and is designed to perform back-end tasks such as fast updates and retrieval. It is an engine whose sole purpose is to store and retrieve data as quickly as possible while protecting the data from disaster.

Separating the front end from the back end in this way allows the customer to receive the advantages of both the mainframe and the PC world. The multiuser support, centralized administration, and security features of a mainframe are combined with the low-cost graphical interactive tools from the PC.

Installing SQL Server

Microsoft SQL Server runs under the Microsoft Windows NT/Server network operating system. It requires 16 MB of memory and can be loaded in about 35 MB of hard disk space.

Installation is not difficult, and normally proceeds without any problem. Upon completion of the installation, the workgroup will be added to your Windows NT desktop.

These icons serve the following purposes:

➤ *SQL Setup*—Allows you to run setup and install additional components.

➤ *SQL Service Manager*—Allows you to start and stop the database server.

➤ *SQL Tape Utility*—Provides a graphical front end for managing tape backups.

➤ *ISQL/w*—Allows you to execute SQL commands interactively against the database.

➤ *SQL Security Manager*—Provides a dialog to set up password-protection requirements. It also allows you to grant and revoke privileges.

➤ *SQL Client Configuration Utility*—Gives you the tools needed to prepare client files for the computers that will access the database.

➤ *SQL Transfer Manager*—Allows you to transfer objects and data from SQL Server to another database or from the other database into SQL Server.

➤ *SQL Administrator Win32*—Empowers the database administrator to manage devices, databases, logins, remote servers, and system resources.

➤ *SQL Object Manager Win32*—Provides a graphical user interface for Database administrator duties such as table, index, rule, and trigger creation.

➤ *SQL Performance*—Allows the administrator to monitor the performance of the servers in the domain.

➤ *SQL Help*—Provides a Help utility for the Transact SQL language. Help for other utilities is provided on the menu bar of each utility.

➤ *Release Notes*—Contains last-minute information about this release of SQL Server.

Through this user interface, the database administrator can perform all of the tasks required to support production systems. It is the existence of these additional support services that makes SQL Server a robust departmental server that is capable of handling a large number of users.

Using the SQL Service Manager, we can now start the database server by following these steps:

1. Double-click the SQL Service Manager icon in the SQL Server program group. This will bring up the dialog box to perform server start, pause, and stop.

2. Click Start/Continue to start up the server.

3. Look at the bottom of the SQL Service Manager window at the status line. It should say, `The service is starting` for a few seconds, then say `The service is running`.

The server is now ready to receive commands from the database administrator and later from user applications (once they are written).

Creating a Database

With the server running, you are ready to create a database. To perform this task, SQL Server contains a utility called the Microsoft SQL Administrator. This utility provides a user interface to facilitate device and database creation.

Prerequisite to creating a database, you must create a device for the database to reside in. Devices are files that can hold one or more databases and transaction logs. Devices can be thought of as named logical disk drives. When SQL Server is first installed, several devices are created which hold system information and a few sample databases. To create a device to hold the database for this chapter's examples, follow these steps:

1. Start the SQL Administrator by double-clicking its icon.

2. Click the Toolbar button labeled Devices then choose Create from the Manage Devices menu. The Create Device dialog box appears, as shown in figure 9.1.

3. In the Logical Name box, type `QUEDevice`.

4. Type the path for the device file's location. One will be suggested by the system, but you may choose a different name and path.

5. In the Type area, select Database as the type of device that you want to create.

6. In the Size (MB) box, type 2. This is the minimum database size, but it will be more than adequate for this chapter's examples.

7. Click the OK button. The device will be created and an entry representing it will be added to the Device Management list as shown in figure 9.2.

Fig. 9.1 Devices are required to hold databases and transaction logs.

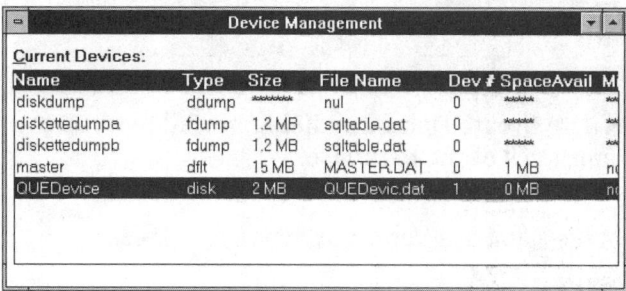

Fig. 9.2 The Device Management list contains a listing of all the devices defined for this server.

You are now the proud owner of a device suitable to contain a test database. You create databases using the same SQL Administrator utility that you used to create the device to contain it. You create this database by following these steps:

1. Start the SQL Administrator by double-clicking its icon.

2. Click the Toolbar button labeled <u>D</u>B. The Database Management window appears and lists all of the current databases on this server, as shown in figure 9.3.

3. From the <u>M</u>anage menu, choose Database, Create Database. The Create Database dialog box appears, as shown in figure 9.4.

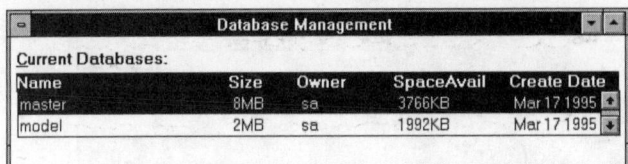

Fig. 9.3 The Database Management window lists all of the databases on this server.

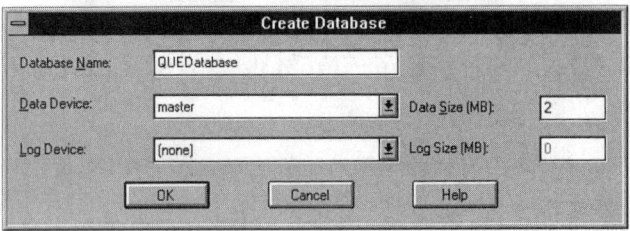

Fig. 9.4 The Create Database dialog box allows you to specify the characteristics of the database.

4. In the Database Name box, type QUEDatabase.

5. In the Data Device box, choose QUEDevice. This is the device that we created earlier.

6. In the Data Size (MB) box, type 2.

7. In the Log Device box, choose (none). The purpose of the log device is to allow for rollback and recovery in case of a system crash. For our test database, this can be ignored because we are not storing any real data.

8. Click the OK button. This will create the database and a listing in the Database Management window.

Armed with a real database, you are now ready to begin building objects.

Creating a Table

Once the database is created, the next task will be to create a table. The Transact SQL language contains commands to create tables using the

SQL syntax. The SQL Object Manager, however, is more convenient because it provides a graphical way of accomplishing the same task. SQL Object Manager manipulates the objects of a database such as tables, indexes, triggers, views, keys, rules, defaults, datatypes, and stored procedures. SQL Object Manager allows you to create, alter, and delete database objects, as well as grant and revoke object permissions.

To create a new table in the database, follow these steps:

1. Double-click the SQL Object Manager icon in the SQL Server program group. The Connect Server dialog box appears, as shown in figure 9.5.

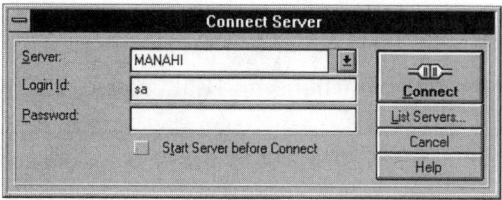

Fig. 9.5 The SQL Server Object Manager will connect to the server called MANAHI.

The sa in the Login Id text box indicates that you are the system administrator. No password is required if you are using the default-integrated security features of Windows NT.

2. Click the Connect button to make the connection. The name of the server that you are connected to is shown in a combo box on the SQL Object Manager window. It is possible to be connected to several databases at the same time, but for the sake of clarity, we will limit this discussion to one connection.

3. In the Current Database combo box, select QUEDatabase (the database that you created).

4. From the Manage menu, choose Tables and the Manage Tables window appears (see fig. 9.6).

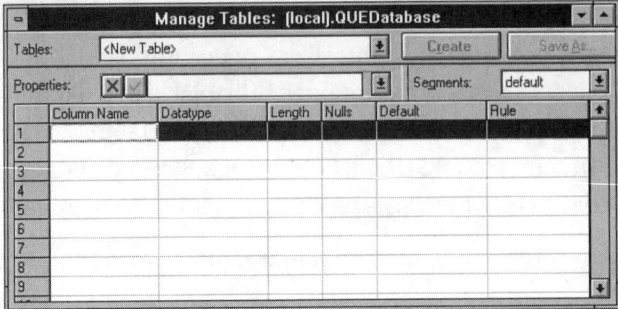

Fig. 9.6 The Manage Tables window allows you to specify the characteristics of the table that you are creating.

5. In the Tables box, choose `<New Table>`.

6. Enter the following fields and data types in the table:

Column Name	Datatype	Length	Nulls	Default	Rule
SSN	text		no		
LastName	varchar		no		
FirstName	varchar		no		
Age	int		yes		
Balance	Money		no		

7. Click the Create button and a dialog box appears, asking for a table name (see fig. 9.7).

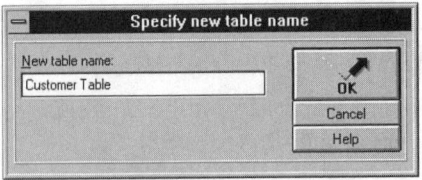

Fig. 9.7 The Specify New Table Name dialog box appears when you click Create.

8. In the <u>N</u>ew Table Name box, type `CustomerTable` and click OK. SQL Server will add this table to the database.

With a table in the database, we are ready to store and retrieve data.

Adding Data to the Table

Now you need to add data to the table in order to make it useful. The easiest way to do this is with a utility called ISQL/W. This is an interactive SQL front-end program that allows you to enter SQL commands in a window. It shows you the results of that query immediately. It is useful as a quick way to query and update a database, and to test SQL statements before including them in your code.

You invoke ISQL/W by double-clicking the ISQL/W icon in the SQL Server program group. When you first invoke ISQL/W, the window is set to go against the default database, normally `master`. You change that by choosing Change <u>D</u>atabase from the Query menu. This will direct all queries to the database containing the sample data. In your case, set the database to `QUEDatabase`. With the database set, you are now ready to enter data into the table. The following code will add one row of data into the table:

```
INSERT INTO Customer_Table
    VALUES (       '234-56-7890',
              'Banks',
              'Dusty',
              49,
              123.45 )
```

The syntax is fairly obvious, even if you are new to SQL. `INSERT INTO` specifies what table to affect. `VALUES` specifies the data values that you want entered. Because all of the columns in the table will receive a value from this `INSERT` statement, you may omit any reference to the row values by name.

Now, also enter all of these rows into the table at this point:

650-09-9008	Jones	Johnny	15	8.75
650-09-9008	Jones	Johnny	15	8.75
123-45-4321	Hearn	Will	9	45.66

The repeated entry of Johnny Jones was intentional. Next, use ISQL/W to look at the data in the table. We do this using a SELECT statement:

```
SELECT * FROM Customer Table
```

The SELECT * means that you want to see all the fields from Customer Table. The results of this query are shown in figure 9.8.

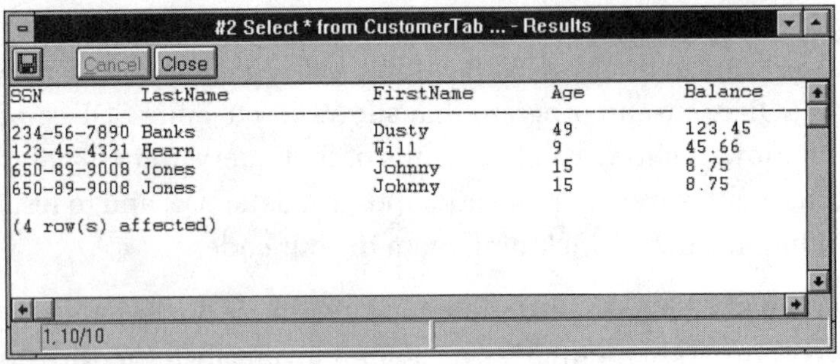

Fig. 9.8 The output of the query appears in a child window.

ISQL/W displays the data along with the field names in the Results window. The practice of verifying that the data is in the table before attempting to do a remote query is important. Often, network problems or ODBC setup problems will prevent the query from working properly from the client side. Being sure that this data is indeed resident in the database on the server can speed up the debugging process by reducing the number of possible causes of the failure.

Making the ODBC Connection

Now that we have a database that contains valid data, we can move to the client side and set up the connection. You do this by choosing the Control Panel icon. Double-clicking this icon will bring up the program group that contains the 32-bit ODBC icon.

When you first bring up the ODBC Data Sources window, you will see no data sources defined. To define one, click the Add button on the Data Sources dialog box (see fig. 9.9).

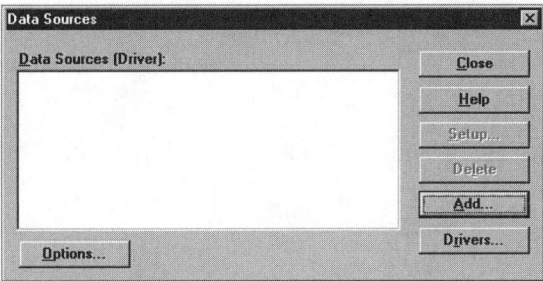

Fig. 9.9 You define data sources through the Add button on the Data Sources dialog box.

The Add button will invoke the Add Data Source dialog box. This dialog box lists all of the ODBC drivers that are currently installed on the client system. The ODBC drivers come from a number of sources. Some of them, like SQL Server, ship with Visual Basic. Another set of them can be obtained from Microsoft directly or through their distributors.

> **Note:** A small industry of ODBC driver writers has emerged who sell drivers which are claimed to be superior to the common drivers. These companies advertise in programming magazines. Finally, the vendor of your DBMS has probably written one also. Contact him for information.

In our case, the driver ships with Visual Basic, so it shows up right away (see fig. 9.10).

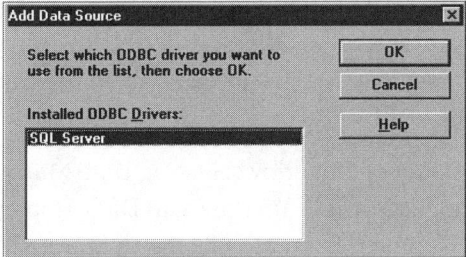

Fig. 9.10 The ODBC drivers installed on your system show up in the Add Data Source dialog box.

Clicking OK brings up the ODBC SQL Server Setup dialog box. It contains the following important text input boxes that gather critical information:

➤ Data Source Name—This is a name that will identify the data source.

➤ Description—This is a free format description of the source.

➤ Server—This is the name of the server where the database is located.

➤ Database Name—This is the name of the database as it is known on the server.

Having completed the definition, the data source can now be seen in the Data Sources dialog box. The only data source defined is QUEDatabase. The SQL Server shown in parentheses beside the Data Source Name indicates the driver that will be used to implement the accesses to this database will be the Microsoft SQL Server Database. This client has only one ODBC data source that can be accessed by Visual Basic, C++, or other application development tools.

Accessing the SQL Server

Accessing the SQL Server from within Visual Basic can be done in a number of ways. In this text, we will use the recommended way, which is to attach the SQL Server table that we wish to access to a table in a Microsoft Access Database. This sounds convoluted, but it is the way that Microsoft says will yield the best performance. To do this, we need to create a dummy Access database. This could be done in Microsoft Access, but it can be done just as easily from the Data Manager product in Visual Basic itself.

You start the Data Manager by selecting Data Manager from the Add-ins menu. This brings up the main Data Manager window. Next, choose New Database from the File menu in Data Manager. This will bring up the New Database dialog box (see fig. 9.11).

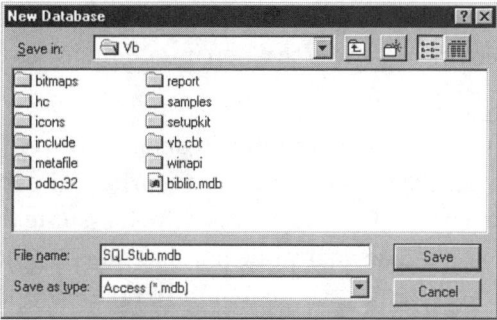

Fig. 9.11 The Data Manager can be used to create a new database in the Microsoft Access database format.

Name the new database `SQLStub` to signify that it exists to attach SQL Server tables to. Click OK to bring up the dialog box that manages the creation and attachment of tables. This dialog box contains the fully qualified name of the database in its title bar, as shown in the upper half of figure 9.12. Click the Attach button, as shown in the lower half of figure 9.12, to invoke the Attach Tables dialog box.

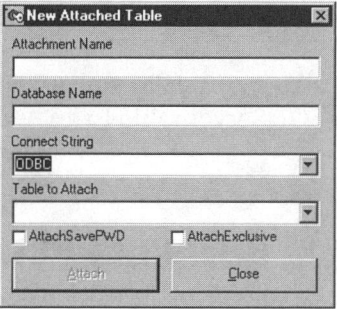

Fig. 9.12 The Data Manager Add-in can be used to create and attach tables from ODBC data sources.

Choose ODBC as the data source type in the Attach Tables dialog box and click OK. This brings up the SQL Data Sources dialog box, which contains a listing of all of the data sources that are available to your Visual Basic program as a result of the work done with the ODBC tools.

In this case, only one choice appears, QUEDatabase. This is because you only defined one data source when interacting with ODBC directly earlier in the chapter.

A common problem encountered in dealing with a client/server database management system concerns security and permissions. In contrast to ordinary PC DBMS systems (which assume that only one user will be accessing data at any one point in time) client/server database management systems assume that the whole enterprise will be trying to access the data. It also assumes that some unauthorized accesses will be attempted, and must be guarded against. As a result, SQL Server requires a login and password before granting access to the data in one of its databases. To address this requirement, the SQL Server Login dialog box (see fig. 9.13) appears during the process of attaching tables to the database. Putting in a login ID and password that is valid to Microsoft SQL Server satisfies part of the requirement.

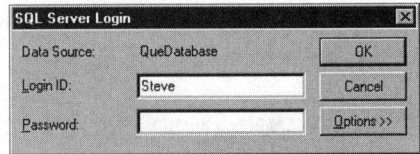

Fig. 9.13 You must supply a valid SQL Server Login ID and Password to attach a SQL Server table to an Access database.

Granting and Revoking Permissions

In addition to the required Login ID and Password, SQL Server controls users at the individual permission level. This means that even if a user attempts to make a connection with the SQL Server database using a valid Login ID and Password, access may still be denied if the Database Administrator (DBA) has not given this user the appropriate permission on the requested table. The procedure used to grant and revoke permissions is as follows:

1. Open the SQL Server for Windows NT program.

2. Double-click the SQL Object Manager icon to bring up the main window of that application. Select the database that you want to modify by pulling down the list box and selecting QUEDatabase. QUEDatabase becomes the current database, which means that all Toolbar and menu requests will be applied to the tables and objects in this database.

3. Click the Objects button on the Toolbar. This brings up a window containing one line for each object in the current database (see fig. 9.14). These objects can be rules, stored procedures, events, or tables. The object of greatest interest to this discussion is the Customer Table, which contains the data that was entered earlier using ISQL/W.

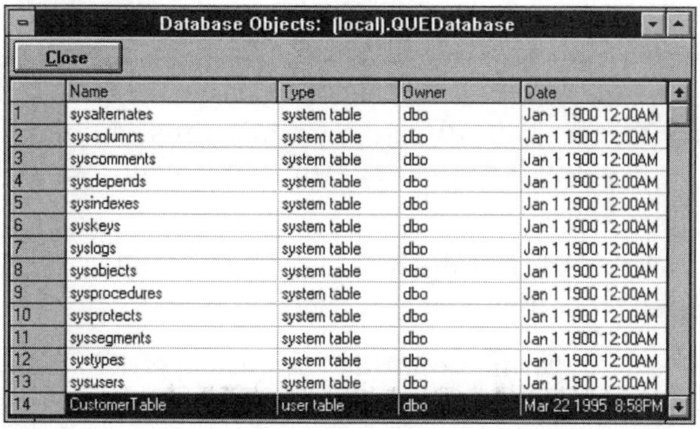

	Name	Type	Owner	Date
1	sysalternates	system table	dbo	Jan 1 1900 12:00AM
2	syscolumns	system table	dbo	Jan 1 1900 12:00AM
3	syscomments	system table	dbo	Jan 1 1900 12:00AM
4	sysdepends	system table	dbo	Jan 1 1900 12:00AM
5	sysindexes	system table	dbo	Jan 1 1900 12:00AM
6	syskeys	system table	dbo	Jan 1 1900 12:00AM
7	syslogs	system table	dbo	Jan 1 1900 12:00AM
8	sysobjects	system table	dbo	Jan 1 1900 12:00AM
9	sysprocedures	system table	dbo	Jan 1 1900 12:00AM
10	sysprotects	system table	dbo	Jan 1 1900 12:00AM
11	syssegments	system table	dbo	Jan 1 1900 12:00AM
12	systypes	system table	dbo	Jan 1 1900 12:00AM
13	sysusers	system table	dbo	Jan 1 1900 12:00AM
14	CustomerTable	user table	dbo	Mar 22 1995 8:58PM

Fig. 9.14 The objects in the QUEDatabase are displayed in a list when the Object button on the Toolbar is clicked.

4. Highlight the Customer Table row in the Database Objects window and choose Object Permissions from the Object menu.

5. Select the permissions that you want the user to have. The granting of permissions can be as simple or as difficult as you need it to be. You can grant all permissions to all users to read, modify, augment, or remove the table from the database by selecting All in the Permissions area (see fig. 9.15). You also can give each user selected permissions.

6. In the Existing Users/Groups box, highlight the users or groups that you want to alter.

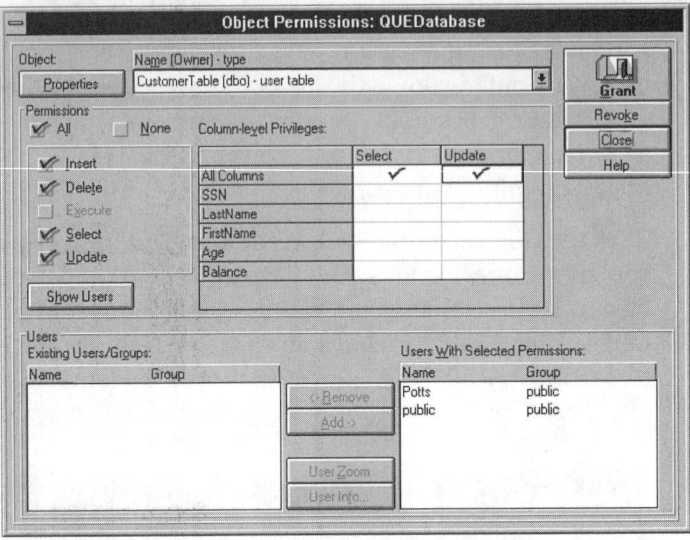

Fig. 9.15 The granularity of the permissions can be controlled at a low level using the Object Permissions window.

7. Click the Add button, which adds the name to the Users With Selected Permissions.

8. Select the permissions that you wish to give to the users and groups in the lower right. For the purpose of this exercise, give your user account all privileges for this table. In the real world, you would only want to grant permission to users on a "need-to-know" basis. This gives your data maximum protection against the inadvertent corruption of data by legal users, and the malicious destruction of important data by hackers. In a world that is dominated by remote database accesses, security is a very big issue.

9. Click the Grant button to make your selections known to the system. This registers the permissions in the database and allows the clients to access data up to the limit of their permissions.

Attaching a Table to a Jet Engine Database

According to Microsoft, attaching ODBC table to Jet Engine tables is the recommended way to connect Visual Basic to a non-Access database. The reason for doing this is one of processing speed. The Jet Database Engine maintains all of the data needed to process transactions in its internal control blocks. This removes the need for Visual Basic to retrieve that information for every transaction.

Having granted the proper permissions to your user account in SQL Server, you are ready to complete the task of attaching an SQL Server table to a Microsoft Jet Engine database. The following steps will accomplish this:

1. Return to Data Manager and click the Attach button again.

2. Next, click ODBC in the Attach Table dialog box as before.

3. Select QUEDatabase as the ODBC data source. The Login Dialog box will appear again.

4. Enter the Login ID and Password for the accounts that have been granted permissions.

5. This brings up a list of all of the ODBC tables that your client can view. Select the one labeled `dbo_CustomerTable`. The `dbo` prefix indicates which user owns the table.

6. Select this table and click the Attach button. This completes the attachment of the table to the Access database called SQLStub. Figure 9.16 shows that the name of the table, `dbo_CustomerTable`, now appears in the Data Manager's Tables dialog box.

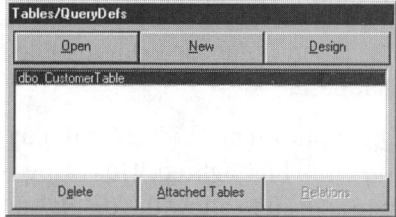

Fig. 9.16 The tables in, or attached to, a database are listed in the Tables dialog box.

While you are still in the data manager, clean up the data in the database a little. Earlier in the chapter, we entered the following data in the Customer Table.

234-56-7890	Banks	Dusty	49	123.45
650-09-9008	Jones	Johnny	15	8.75
650-09-9008	Jones	Johnny	15	8.75
123-45-4321	Hearn	Will	9	45.66

Notice that rows two and three contain identical data. You need to delete them and add one of them back. This can be done easily in the Object Manager using the following procedure:

1. Access the Microsoft SQL Object Manager exactly as you did earlier.

2. Select QUEDatabase as the Current Database.

3. Click the Query button on the Toolbar.

4. Enter the following code in the upper half of the Query window.

```
Delete from CustomerTable Where FirstName = 'Johnny'
```

The result of this action will be displayed as (2 row(s) affected).

Querying the Table

Now that the data in the database is correct, you can use Visual Basic to access it. The easiest way to do this is through the Data Manager.

1. Start Visual Basic and invoke the Data Manager by picking it from the Add-Ins menu. This brings up the Data Manager.

2. Next, choose Open Database from the File menu to open the SQLStub database.

3. Click the Open button on the Tables dialog box with dbo_CustomerTable highlighted. This brings up a form that is automatically configured to allow the display and editing of the fields in the dbo_CustomerTable (see fig. 9.17).

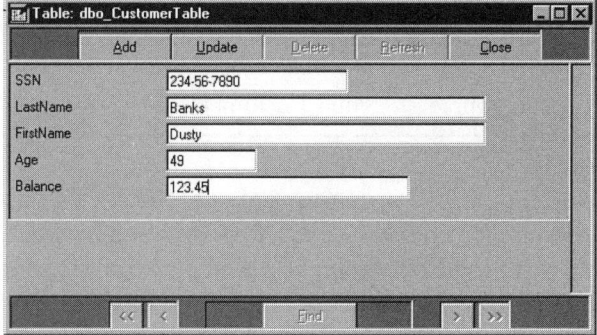

Fig. 9.17 The <u>O</u>pen button on the Tables dialog box generates a data input screen.

The generation of the fields on this form was done automatically by the Data Manager software.

Using the Data Control to View SQL Database Tables

The Data Manager is good for a quick look at the data, but the real power of Visual Basic is in the Data control. You can use this control on an SQL Server table that is attached to an Access database just like you can on native Access database tables. The following procedure illustrates how this is done:

1. Open a Visual Basic form.

2. Double-click the Data control in the toolbox.

3. Set the following properties on the Data control:

Property	Value
Name	Data1
DatabaseName	C:\VB\SQLSTUB.MDB
Connect	Access

continues

Property	Value
Caption	QueCustomer
RecordSource	dbo_CustomerTable

The `DatabaseName` property applies to the Access database and not the database on SQL Server. All interaction between the server and this program is being handled by a combination of the Microsoft Access database engine and the SQL Server ODBC driver in ways that are not visible to the Visual Basic programmer.

4. As always, the Data control needs a Bound control that is capable of displaying the data from the database. In this case, use the Text Box control. To bind the text box to the Data control, set the following `TextBox` properties:

Property	Value
Name	Text1
DataSource	Data1
DataField	LastName

5. Run the program and experiment with the data. Verify that the data being retrieved is the same data that you input into the SQL Server database. Figure 9.18 shows the program with a field from one of the rows displayed.

6. Expand the number of data items to include all of the fields in the database table as shown in figure 9.19. The following table shows how their properties should be set.

Property	Value
Name	Text2, Text3, Text4, etc.
DataSource	Data1
DataField	FirstName, Age, SSN, etc.

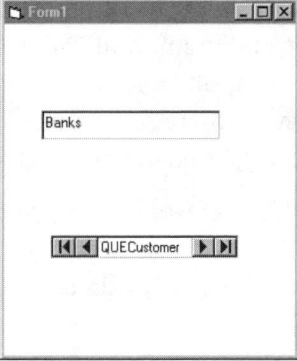

Fig. 9.18 The rows of the SQL Server are accessed by the Data control and displayed using a Bound Text Box control.

Now, run the program and observe that the form that you have created looks a lot like the one created by Data Manager to handle these same fields.

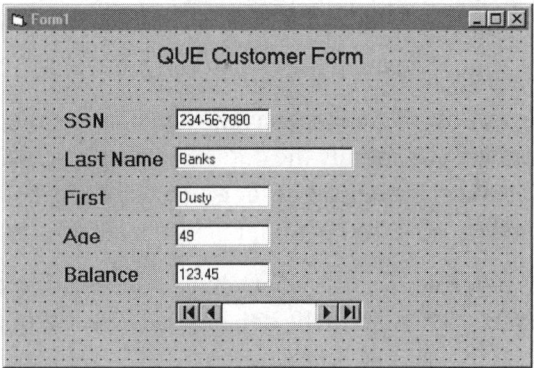

Fig. 9.19 The entire table can be displayed in a professional fashion.

The motivation for going to this much trouble must now be clear. In order to implement a full-blown 100+ user system running over a network, a considerable database engine is required. Issues of performance, concurrent access, and security become huge when a large number of users are accessing a database. The solution in years gone by was to buy a huge mainframe and connect everyone to a terminal. This solved some of the problems, but this architecture does not fit in well with the "data everywhere" enterprises of the 1990s because it requires that all data be stored in a central location.

Visual Basic and SQL Server working together allows users to manipulate remote data as if it were local to their machines, while maintaining data integrity and security as if the data was on a mainframe.

Stored Procedures

Most database management systems include some type of programming language that can be used to manipulate data, produce reports and so on. This language is normally an extension of the SQL language, to include variables, control statements, printing and so on. When you write a program using these languages they are normally compiled and stored in the database as stored procedures. They are executed on the server with the result sets, with messages and errors being returned to the workstation. The main uses for stored procedures are the following:

> *Triggers*—A trigger is a procedure that is executed by the DBMS, whenever you modify the data in a specific table. In a customer order system, when an order is placed, a trigger could be executed to see if the customer has an available line of credit.

> *Rules*—A rule controls what you can or cannot enter in the column of a table. This allows the database administrator to control the data in the database. For example, a rule could be written that rejects Social Security numbers if they contain alphabetic characters.

> *Stored Procedures*—Stored procedures are full blown programs using SQL statements, control statements, variables and so on, to manipulate data on the server. We'll examine these in more detail in the following section.

Since we are working with MS SQL Server, we will be using the Transact SQL Language in our examples.

Calling Procedures from Visual Basic

It is important to remember that stored procedures and calling stored procedures are DBMS specific and as such are outside the scope of the ODBC standard. For this reason, the calling of stored procedures must be done using the SQL Pass-Through option. When you use this option the ODBC does not interpret the query, it simply passes the whole thing directly to the DBMS and lets it deal with it.

Visual Basic provides two methods of executing an SQL Pass-Through query:

➤ The `Execute` (query) method, which can be used to execute queries that do not return a value or record set.

➤ SQL Pass-Through queries, which can be used to execute a procedure, in cases where the procedure returns a value or record set.

In the past, applications consisted of programs and data files. Because the data files were application specific, you were able to incorporate all data validation checks in the applications and thus ensure the integrity of the data. However, when using DBMS like SQL Server this is not enough. While we can still build applications that can carry out all the data validation as before and store the data on the server, our users are free to connect to the server with MS Access or MS Excel and carry out modifications to the data, thus by-passing our data validation routines.

The way to overcome this is to create data validation and triggers in the database. However this falls short when it comes to implementing business rules. For example, assume that Northwind Traders decide that important customers should get an extra discount. An important customer is one to whom we have sold more than $5,000. How would we go about implementing the rule that defines what an important customer is?

We could always code it up in our application, but this would cause a problem, since people using Access or Excel to modify data, would also have to code it up. When the rule changes, you would also have to ensure that all applications using the rule were changed. To avoid all these problems, implement this rule as a stored procedure on the server and have each application call it.

The basic requirement is that we need to total all the orders for a given customer, and if the total is greater than $5,000, then indicate that the customer is an important customer. The first element of our procedure is to write the SQL statement to summarize the orders as follows:

```
SELECT SUM(order_amount) FROM orders WHERE customer_id =
@CUST_ID
```

This statement summarizes the orders for a customer, where the customer_id is equal to the variable CUST_ID (@CUST_ID is the format used to indicate a variable in Transact SQL).

Next we need to add the code to test if the total is over $5,000. As you might have suspected, we use an IF statement as follows:

```
IF (SELECT SUM(order_amount) FROM orders
        WHERE customer_id = @CUST_ID) > 5000
    /* An important customer */
ELSE
    /* A normal customer */
```

The final element of our procedure is to return the value to Visual Basic. Transact SQL provides the following three methods of doing this:

1. A SELECT statement

2. A RETURN statement

3. A PRINT statement

Since Visual Basic cannot retrieve values that are returned via the RETURN statement, we can rule that method out. So using the SELECT statement, our procedure becomes the following:

```
IF (SELECT SUM(order_amount) FROM orders
        WHERE customer_id = @CUST_ID) > 5000
    /* Important Customer */
    SELECT 1
```

```
ELSE
      /* Normal Customer */
      SELECT 0
```

While using the PRINT statement the procedure becomes the following:

```
IF (SELECT SUM(order_amount) FROM orders
         WHERE customer_id = @CUST_ID) > 5000
      /* Important Customer */
      PRINT "Important Customer"
ELSE
      /* Normal Customer */
      PRINT "Normal Customer"
```

The only other task to be carried out from the stored procedure's point of view is to implement it on MS SQL Server. The final code required to create the procedure using the PRINT statement that follows (the code to create the procedure is similar and is not reproduced here):

```
CREATE PROCEDURE IMPORTANT_CUSTOMER @CUST_ID VARCHAR(5)
AS
IF (SELECT SUM(order_amount) FROM orders
         WHERE customer_id = @CUST_ID) > 5000
      /* Important Customer */
      PRINT "Important Customer"
ELSE
      /* Normal Customer */
      PRINT "Normal Customer"
```

This code tells MS SQL Server to create our stored procedure IMPORTANT_CUSTOMER and also tells it that the procedure accepts a parameter CUSD_ID.

Having implemented the procedure on the server, it's now time to take a look at how we can go about calling it. The method we choose depends on whether or not the procedure returns a value. In our case, both procedures return a value, so we'll call it via an SQL Pass-Through query.

Since the query using the SELECT statement is the simpler to call, we'll deal with that first. The code required to create and execute the query is as follows:

```
Private Sub cmdProc_Click
    ' Demo calling stored procedure that returns
    ' a value via a select statement
    Dim db As Database
```

```
    Dim qry As QueryDef
    Dim rsStoredProc As Recordset
    Set db = DBEngine(0).OpenDatabase(App.Path &
"\PROCS.MDB", False, False)
        Set qry = db.CreateQueryDef("ImportantCustomer")
        qry.SQL = "EXEC IMPORTANT_CUSTOMER 'ALWAO'"
        qry.Connect =
"ODBC;DATABASE=Northwind;DSN=NWIND;UID=Sa; PWD="
        qry.ReturnsRecords = True
        Set rsStoredProc = qryTemp.OpenRecordSet()
        MsgBox "Returned value was :" & Str$(rsStoredProc(0))
        qry.Close
        rsStoredProc.Close
    db.Close
end Sub
```

In this segment of code, we create a `QueryDef` **called** `ImportantCustomer`;
set its SQL property to the MS SQL Server-specific command required
to call the stored procedure; set its `Connect` property to the values required to connect to the server; and indicate that it will return records
by setting its `ReturnsRecords` property. Once we have created the query,
we create a record set based on it to obtain the return value.

In the case of our stored procedure that uses the `PRINT` statement,
things are little different. Rather than returning a result set, the query
returns a message. These messages are trapped by Jet and stored in a
table, based on the user's name. Let's first look at the code required to
call the procedure and then examine the database to find out how the
message is stored.

```
Private Sub cmdProc_Click
    ' Demo calling stored procedure that returns
    ' a value via a select statement
    Dim db As Database
    Dim qry As QueryDef
    Set db = DBEngine(0).OpenDatabase(App.Path &
"\PROCS.MDB", False, False)
        Set qry = db.CreateQueryDef("ImportantCustomer")
        qry.CreateProperty("LogMessages", dbBoolean, True)
        qry.SQL = "EXEC IMPORTANT_CUSTOMER 'ALWAO'"
        qry.Connect =
"ODBC;DATABASE=Northwind;DSN=NWIND;UID _
        =Sa;PWD="
        qry.ReturnsRecords = False
```

```
        qry.Execute
        qry.Close
     db.Close
  end Sub
```

In dealing with the PRINT statement, we start out the same way, creating a QueryDef and setting its properties. However, in addition to setting the Default properties, we create one user-defined property, LogMessages. This tells Jet to log the messages returned by the PRINT statement to a table in the local database, PROCS.MDB.

From Here...

In this chapter you were introduced to the details of implementing a Visual Basic program that accesses data stored on a server using a commercial database product, Microsoft SQL Server. This approach adds power to Visual Basic programs by freeing them from the limitations of ordinary PC-based database management products. It will allow you to implement systems that scale to hundreds of users while maintaining the advantages of application development using Visual Basic.

In order to increase your understanding of databases and client/server, you should examine the following chapters:

➤ For more information on Visual Basic database interfaces, see Chapter 4, "Advanced Database Front Ends."

➤ For information about data management, see Chapter 5, "Data Management and Data-Driven Programming."

➤ For information about connecting to remote databases, see Chapter 6, "Working with ODBC."

➤ For information about client/servers, see Chapter 8, "Modern Client/Server Computing."

SQL

by Steve Potts

The Structured Query Language, SQL (pronounced *SEE-kwal*), is the industry standard database manipulation language. This language enables you to manipulate almost every major database management system in widespread use at this writing.

For the Visual Basic programmer, SQL is important because it is the primary means of communication between Visual Basic and both the Jet Database Engine and the Microsoft SQL Server Database Engine that run under Windows NT Server. While it is possible to create some applications with Visual Basic and the Data Access Object, substantial applications will require that you learn SQL.

SQL traces its genealogy back to the "olden" days of relational database theory. In 1970, Dr. E. F. Codd, then an IBM employee, noticed a theoretical similarity between relational mathematics and the problem of manipulating a database. He wrote a famous paper explaining these similarities, and thus invented the relational database. The first language that Dr. Codd and his assistants at the IBM San Jose laboratory created to implement this theory was a primitive form of SQL. While it differs from modern SQL in important ways, it was the seed which later caused the SQL language to be popularized.

Unlike Visual Basic itself, SQL is a published American National Standards Institute (ANSI) standard (X.3.135-1992). Most of the SQL implementations in use today follow this standard fairly closely. However, because the standard doesn't address 100 percent of the issues needed for a complete implementation of a database management system, the different dialects of SQL differ slightly. While these slight differences complicate the porting of your applications from one database management system (DBMS) to another, they do not become an issue often during the learning of the SQL syntax and implementation strategy. Most SQL dialects contain some useful features that are missing from the ANSI standard. For example, Microsoft's SQL Server product uses a dialect of SQL called *Transact SQL*. This language contains many more reserved words than the SQL standard calls out. It even supports conditional execution and loops within the SQL statement. Access SQL supports the `Transform` and `Pivot` statements that process crosstab queries. These features are useful, but they should be avoided if you plan to port your application to another database management platform that supports its own dialect of SQL.

The goal of SQL is to provide a functional interface between the user and the functionality of the database management system. This is an important concept. The inner workings of a modern database management system are extremely complex. Pointers, multiple processes, indexing schemes, and buffers abound. The goal of SQL is to provide the user with a simple way of manipulating the database, while allowing the database management system development team the freedom necessary to create the complex system needed for good performance.

This chapter approaches the SQL language from the perspective of the Visual Basic programmer. We will drive our understanding beyond the superficial level normally found in Visual Basic books. This approach serves the following two purposes:

> ➤ It will make you a stronger Visual Basic programmer.

> ➤ It will help you when working on other, non-Microsoft database management products.

The subject of this chapter is the SQL language. Therefore, the following topics will be addressed:

➤ Overview of SQL

➤ Creating databases and tables

➤ Adding data to the databases

➤ Changing and deleting the data

➤ Getting data from tables

In each section you will create simple, but real applications to illustrate the language concepts.

Global View of SQL

SQL is a text-oriented, *fourth-generation* language. Fourth-generation languages are called *nonprocedural languages* because the statements tell the database management system what you want it to do, without telling it how to do it. The SQL syntax doesn't say, "Go to the first row of the table. Move that row to a buffer. Go to the second row. Move that row into the buffer also. Test if the third field of each row is greater than 17. If it is, delete it from the buffer. Get the next row... " The SQL statement to accomplish this will be `SELECT * FROM Table1 WHERE id < 17;`.

It is true that the computer cannot understand instructions at the SQL level. They must be translated to a level as low as or lower than the instructions in the preceding paragraph. The important thing to understand is that it is the task of the database management system vendor—not the application programmer—to write that code. This greatly increases the speed at which applications can be developed, and also enlarges the pool of people that can develop these applications. Many intelligent people who can enjoy writing SQL statements would not enjoy coding database calls.

This does not mean that SQL is a "wimpy" language that never gets complex. Complex queries are needed at times, but the majority of the SQL routines that you will write are fairly straightforward.

Understanding Set-Orientation

Set-oriented languages differ from traditional *array-oriented* languages in the way that they treat data. Traditional database management systems (such as IMS on the mainframe) assume that the receiver of the data is using the same computer that the database management system is using. These products are built to provide data to the application where the application logic can perform the task of selecting the data that is needed by the application. This strategy breaks down when the database management system is located on a different computer from the application. The strategy of culling out the unwanted data at the application computer can cause a performance problem over the network. For example, if your application wanted to retrieve the record for one of your company's 175,000 employees whose salary was over $30,000, the array-oriented query language would retrieve all 175,000 records, send them to your application, which would then throw away half of them (those employees with salaries under $30,000). This approach would choke a network for half an hour.

A set-oriented database management system is intelligent enough to perform all of the selections before sending the data that passes the test over the wire. If you send a request to the following:

```
SELECT * FROM employee_table WHERE employee_num = "G546897";
```

the SQL-based database management system is smart enough to pass you only the one row that satisfies the request. If the request reads `"SELECT * FROM employee_table WHERE salary > 30,000;"`, then the database management system will cull out all rows in the table which fail this test, and pass the rows that pass the selection criteria over the network.

One of the differentiating skills of the SQL programmer is her ability to make SQL do as much of the work of selecting rows as possible. Always keep network traffic issues in mind when designing your SQL-based applications.

Types of SQL-Based Applications

Most SQL-based database management systems support a variety of ways of accessing their functionality. The primary types are as follows:

➤ *Interactive or direct invocation*—Most vendors provide a way to access the database through the use of a window where the user types SQL commands in one window and observes the results in another. Figure 10.1 shows the ISQL/W product that ships with Microsoft SQL Server.

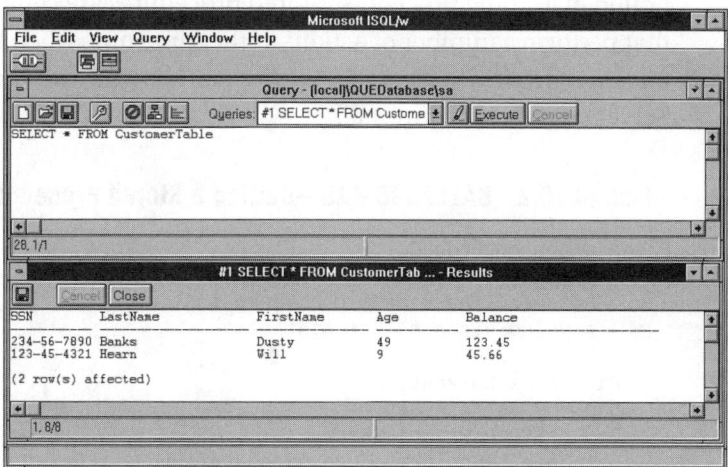

Fig. 10.1 The ISQL/W product in Microsoft SQL Server enables the user to access the data in a database interactively.

➤ *Embedded SQL*—Most dialects of SQL support the insertion of SQL statements into the normal code of their applications. This allows access to the data via SQL without having to use a rigid user interface tool. The host language can be C or Visual Basic. Listing 10.1 shows an example of embedding SQL syntax into Visual Basic code.

Listing 10.1 Embedding an SQL Statement into a Visual Basic Application

```
SQLQuery = "UPDATE Titles SET Title = 'My Right Foot'"
SQLQuery = SQLQuery & " WHERE Title = 'My Right Hand';"

MyDatabase.Execute SQLQuery
' Execute the query.
```

In this example, the object `MyDatabase` is a database. The Execute method executes the SQL string to the right. The `SQLQuery` string variable will contain the phrase *"UPDATE Titles SET Title = 'My Right Foot' WHERE Title = 'My Right Hand';"*

➤ *Stored Procedures or Modules*—Many SQL servers support the notion of a stored procedure. Stored procedures are code blocks that perform a number of actions at the same time when the application invokes it, via a call. Listing 10.2 shows a Microsoft SQL Server stored procedure call.

Listing 10.2 CALLPROC.BAS—Calling a Stored Procedure

```
Private Sub cmdProc_Click

    ' Demo calling stored procedure that returns
    ' a value via a select statement

    Dim db As Database
    Dim qry As QueryDef
    Dim rsStoredProc As Recordset
    Set db = DBEngine(0).OpenDatabase(App.Path & _
    "\PROCS.MDB", False, False)
            Set qry = db.CreateQueryDef("ImportantCustomer")
            qry.SQL = "EXEC IMPORTANT_CUSTOMER 'ALWAO'"
            qry.Connect = "ODBC;DATABASE=Northwind; _
            DSN=NWIND;UID=Sa;PWD="
            qry.ReturnsRecords = True
            Set rsStoredProc = qryTemp.OpenRecordSet()
            MsgBox "Returned value was :" & Str$(rsStoredProc(0))
            qry.Close
            rsStoredProc.Close
        db.Close
    end Sub
```

First, create a `QueryDef` called `ImportantCustomer` and set its SQL property to the Microsoft SQL Server specific command required to call the stored procedure `EXEC IMPORTANT_CUSTOMER 'ALWAO'`. Set its connect property to the values required to connect to the server. Indicate that it will return records by setting its `ReturnsRecords` property. For a more thorough explanation of stored procedures, refer to Chapter 9, "Client/Server Databases."

➤ *Dynamic SQL*—Many of the SQL products support the creation of SQL statements by the code that is executing. Early in the life of SQL, it was common for embedded SQL statements to be passed through a precompiler which translated them into the proper third-generation language subroutine calls. This made dynamic creation of SQL impossible because all SQL translation had to take place by compile time. Visual Basic and SQL Server support dynamic SQL statement creation. In Listing 10.2, the SQL string that was executed was created in the code. It did not have to be precompiled into a third-generation language interface to work properly.

Creating a Database

Database creation is the most product-specific aspect of using an SQL-based database management system. For Visual Basic users, Data Manager can be used to create a Jet database. If you own Microsoft Access, you can create a database using that product, and then use Visual Basic to perform operations on it.

If you are using Microsoft SQL Server, you need to go into the "Microsoft SQL Administrator" application that ships with the product to create a database. Figure 10.2 illustrates how this is accomplished.

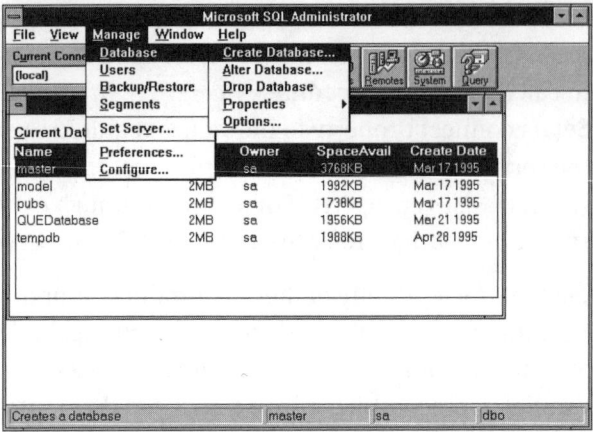

Fig. 10.2 The SQL Server Administrator is where you go to create a database.

If you are using another product, refer to the documentation that ships with the software for specific instructions on how to create a database in that environment. The procedure varies widely from one database management system to another.

Creating Tables

As the proud owner of a new database, you are now ready to add a table to it. In the best textbook tradition, create an example database that manages the enrollment of students in courses. The tables and columns are listed in Table 10.1.

Table 10.1   An Example Student Enrollment Database

Table Name	Column Name	Data Type	Length	Key
students_table	student#	INTEGER		Yes
	student_name	CHARACTER	20	
	address	CHARACTER	30	
	city	CHARACTER	20	
	state	CHARACTER	2	
	zip	CHARACTER	5	
	sex	CHARACTER	1	

Table Name	Column Name	Data Type	Length	Key
teachers_table	teacher#	INTEGER		Yes
	teacher_name	CHARACTER	20	
	phone	CHARACTER	10	
	salary	FLOAT		
courses_table	course#	INTEGER		Yes
	course_name	CHARACTER	20	
	department	CHARACTER	16	
	num_credits	INTEGER		
sections_table	course#	INTEGER		Yes
	section#	INTEGER		Yes
	teacher#	INTEGER		
	num_students	INTEGER		
enrolls_table	course#	INTEGER		Yes
	section#	INTEGER		Yes
	student#	INTEGER		Yes
	grade	INTEGER		

The SQL keywords in this example are all capitalized and the user de-fined words are all in small letters. This is done to help you distinguish which parts of the syntax are literal SQL and which parts are under your control.

These tables are designed to help illustrate the features of the lan-guage. While another example featuring a factory assembly line or a Wall Street brokerage might be more visually interesting than yet an-other student database, the concepts would be harder to comprehend.

The SQL code to create the tables is simple. Listing 10.3 shows the statements needed to create students_table.

Listing 10.3   Statements Needed to Create students_table

```
CREATE TABLE students_table
     (student#         int,
      student_name     char(20),
      address          char(30),
      city             char(20),
      state         char(2),
      zip              char(5),
      sex              char(1)  )
```

The CREATE TABLE keywords indicate, obviously, that this is a new table. The field names along with their data type and length follow. The previous syntax is correct for Transact SQL. Other dialects may place a comma differently or place a semicolon at the end, but this syntax is fairly common.

It has become popular in recent years for database management system vendors to provide utilities to manage tables. These can be more convenient to use and free you from some syntax headaches. Be sure to know how to use SQL to perform these tasks also, because, if you live long enough, you will find yourself working in an environment where SQL is the only method available.

One practical application of the SQL CREATE TABLE method is during testing. Many database administrators create procedures that create and populate the tables using SQL. Each day, the testing process updates and deletes the data in the tables. The administrator will then delete the changed tables and re-create them using the script, thus restoring the tables to their original state, ready for another day of testing.

Listing 10.4 contains the code to create the rest of the tables in the example database.

Listing 10.4   CRETABL1.SQL—Creating SQL Tables

```
CREATE TABLE teachers_table
     (teacher#      int,
      teacher_name     char(20),
      phone            char(10),
      salary           float )

CREATE TABLE courses_table
     (course#      int,
         course_name      char(20),
      department       char(16),
      num_credits      int)

CREATE TABLE sections_table
     (course#      int,
      section#      int,
```

```
        teacher#        int,
        num_students    int)

    CREATE TABLE enrolls_table
        (course#        int,
         section#       int,
          student#      int,
         grade          int)
```

Primary Keys

The primary key of a table is defined as the minimum set of fields that make a row unique. For example, the government administers Social Security by means of your Social Security Number. This is the unique key for an individual that assures that all of the payments made on your behalf are recorded as being from you. No other combination of attributes—name, hair color, place of birth, and so on—could guarantee uniqueness across a set of 100 million people.

In the same fashion, every row in a table must be unique from all other rows in the same table according to the rules set forth by Dr. Codd in his pivotal paper of 1970. The reason for this lies in the need for a row to be updated without error. If you get a raise, you want it to appear in your paycheck, not in your office mate's paycheck.

The mechanism for guaranteeing this in a relational database is the primary key. This field, or fields, when taken as a group must be unique. In some cases, as in the Social Security example, no natural field or set of fields is satisfactory, so an artificial key field, the Social Security Number, was created. Artificial key fields are nice in that it is easy to make them unique, but the chore of assigning them can prove burdensome.

SQL systems use a variety of techniques to designate a field or fields as the primary key of a table. Transact SQL uses the following syntax:

```
sp_primarykey students_table, student#
```

This syntax tells SQL Server that `student#` is the primary key. At a minimum, the database management system must enforce uniqueness for that row based on the primary key. This means that if a user attempts to add another row to the table and that row has the same primary key value as one already in the table, then the system will issue an error message. In addition to this, many systems use the primary key to order the row physically on the disk when they compress the database, but that is the vendor's prerogative.

Listing 10.5   Adding the Primary Keys to the Tables in the Student Database

```
sp_primarykey students_table, student#
sp_primarykey teachers_table, teacher#
sp_primarykey courses_table, course#
sp_primarykey sections_table, course#, section#
sp_primarykey enrolls_table, course#, section#, student#
```

The `sp_primarykey` keyword tells SQL Server that you want to designate the columns after the table name to be the primary key. Notice that on `sections_table` and `enrolls_table` the primary key is compound, meaning that it is made up of multiple columns in the row.

It is sometimes useful to query the server to be sure that the key is defined properly. The `sp_helpkey` command displays this information. The syntax of this command is as follows.

```
sp_helpkey enrolls_table
keytype    object    related_object    object_keys    related_keys
---------- -------------------------------- ------------------------
primary    enrolls_table  — none —  course#, section#, student#,*
```

This report tells that `enrolls_table` has three keys: `courses#`, `section#`, and `student#`.

Adding Data to Tables

Understanding how tables are defined and how keys are designated prepares you for data input into the tables. This is done in SQL using the following syntax:

```
INSERT INTO students_table
    ( student#, student_name, address, city, state, zip,_ sex)
   VALUES (  593, 'Joe Smith', '123 4th St.', 'Auburn', 'AL',_ '32456', 'M')
```

The first set of parentheses encloses the names of the fields that you want to update. This list can be omitted if you want to update all of the columns in a row, and if you provide a data value for each of them. In that case, the database server will assign the first value to the first field in the table, the second value to the second field, and so on. The syntax for the previous example could be written as follows:

```
INSERT INTO students_table
VALUES (  593, 'Joe Smith', '123 4th St.', 'Auburn', 'AL',_
'32456', 'M')
```

Table 10.2 lists all of the data that needs to be loaded into the example tables in order to provide data to the rest of the examples in this chapter.

Table 10.2   Data for students_table

No.	Name	Street	City	State	Zip	Sex
593	Joe Smith	123 4th St.	Auburn	AL	32456	M
594	Pomare Piti	1121 Tahiti St.	Miami	FL	12121	F
595	Ed Oken	1234 Rue de Vallee	Hollywood	CA	21212	M
596	Angel Loon	P.O.Box 657	Amsterdam	GA	31204	F
597	John Byron	4434 London Dr	New York	NY	34565	M
598	J. Roggeveen	876 Honden Rd	Hoorne	RI	34534	M
599	James Cook	7878 Astrolab Ct	OLakes	FL	34545	M
600	Joseph Banks	23 Botany Bay	Brisbaine	CA	87803	M
601	Addison Pratt	78043 Tubai La	Large	OR	43980	M
602	Eliza Pratt	78432 Pahi Rd	Rockville	MD	29796	F

After loading all of these rows into the table, you can run the following command to inspect all of the data in the table.

```
SELECT * FROM students_table
```

This will give you a listing of the rows as shown in figure 10.3.

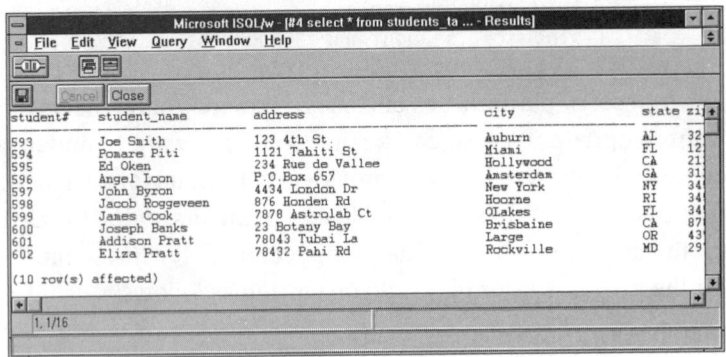

Fig. 10.3 Selecting the rows in a table enables you to inspect them for correctness.

The following tables give you the rest of the data for the other tables.

Table 10.3   Data for teachers_table

No.	Name	Phone Number	Salary
101	Ralph Daniel	798-0989	80000
102	Sandy Turner	897-9089	80001
103	Lantie Hearn	546-0397	65000
104	John Baluch	494-9787	66000
105	Carl Kennedy	777-4981	110000

To put this data into the teachers table, use the following SQL statement once for each row in the table:

```
INSERT INTO teachers_table
      VALUES (101, 'Ralph Daniel', '798-0989', 40000)
```

Table 10.4   Data for courses_table

Course No.	Course Name	Department	Credits
1001	Underwater Basketweaving	Recreation	7
1002	The History of Rap	Music	9
1003	Country Music Theory	Music	7
1004	Paris on 3500 Calories a Day	PE	3
1005	Life after Baseball Strikes	PE	7

To put this data into the teachers table, use the following SQL statement once for each row in the table:

```
INSERT INTO courses_table
     VALUES (1001, 'Underwater Basketweaving', 'Recreation', 7)
```

Table 10.5   Data for sections_table

Course No.	Section No.	Teacher No.	No. of Students
1001	1	105	23
1001	2	104	12
1002	1	101	45
1003	1	101	12
1004	1	102	9
1004	2	103	16
1004	3	105	77
1005	1	101	2

To put this data into the teachers table, use the following SQL statement once for each row in the table:

```
INSERT INTO sections_table
     VALUES (1001,1,105,23)
```

Table 10.6 Data for enrolls_table

Course No.	Section No.	Student No.	Grade
1001	1	593	90
1001	1	594	87
1001	1	595	77
1001	2	596	99
1001	2	597	66
1001	2	598	79
1001	2	599	81
1002	1	600	89
1002	1	601	87
1002	1	602	75
1002	1	603	92
1003	1	603	100
1003	1	595	76
1003	1	596	78
1004	1	593	98
1004	1	594	65
1004	1	595	22
1004	2	596	67
1004	2	597	87
1005	1	593	86
1005	1	603	87
1005	1	600	83
1005	1	601	79
1005	1	599	73
1005	1	598	72
1005	1	597	91
1005	1	596	87

To put this data into the teachers table, use the following SQL statement once for each row in the table:

```
INSERT INTO enrolls_table
    VALUES (1005,1,596,87)
```

At this point, you have five tables in the database, each containing a number of rows to experiment with. The rest of the chapter will be spent learning how to use this data.

Changing the Schema of a Table

One of the inadequacies of the SQL standard is in the area of schema changes. Standard SQL provides no way to change the composition of a table once it is created. Given the nature of real world projects, it is unlikely that even half of the tables in a database are complete and never need to add or remove columns.

Almost every vendor has had to come up with a way of performing this function. Transact SQL, DB/2, Oracle, and others support the ALTER command to provide this functionality. The syntax of the ALTER command is as follows:

```
ALTER TABLE students_table ADD new_column char(8) NULL
```

The only operation that is allowed using the ALTER command is to add a column. The only columns that can be added are those that can contain nulls. The server creates space for the data in the table, but because it does not know what the values will be yet, it inserts nulls in every new field in every existing row.

Deleting a column is occasionally required in the real world to avoid a database filled with obsolete and unused data. There is no easy way to perform this function in SQL. The strategy most often employed is as follows:

1. Create a new table with the schema the way that you want it.

2. Copy the data from one table to the other using a query within an update.

3. Drop the original table after you are sure that the data transfer worked.

4. Finally, rename the new table to the same name as the old one.

The following example shows how this is done. The creation of the new table is a familiar process. Note that the new table name is created with the names of the columns exactly as they will appear in the finished table.

```
CREATE TABLE new_courses_table
     (course#              int,
         new_course_name      char(20),
       num_credits          int)
```

You now have two tables that contain fields about courses: `courses_table`, and `new_courses_table`. If you want a primary key assigned to the `course#` field in the new table, you must execute the `sp_primarykey` command.

```
sp_primarykey new_courses_table, course#
```

Now, the new table is ready for data. There are a number of ways of getting the data from the first table to the second. The first way that comes to mind for most programmers is to select one row at a time, and perform *n* updates for *n* rows. This approach has the following three disadvantages:

➤ It causes data to be moved from the database to the application and back to the database, increasing network traffic.

➤ It is complicated to code.

➤ It is difficult for someone else to maintain.

The preferred approach is to use a SELECT statement within the UPDATE command to choose the columns that you want to update.

```
INSERT INTO new_courses_table (course#,_
    new_course_name, num_credits)
SELECT course#, course_name, num_credits from courses_table
```

This syntax tells the database server to retrieve the rows and columns from the courses table that meet its specifications. This data is then handed to the INSERT statement on a column by column basis. The result is a copying of the data from one table to the other.

If you run a SELECT on the new table, you will see that it worked perfectly. All of the data that was needed in the new_courses_table has been moved into it.

```
SELECT * from new_courses_table
```

The result is listed here:

```
course#       new_course_name       num_credits
-----------   --------------------  -----------
1001          Underwater Basketwea  7
1002          The History of Rap    9
1003          Country Music Theory  7
1004          Paris on 3500 Calori  3
1005          Life after Baseball   7

(5 row(s) affected)
```

Now you have two tables containing similar data. The courses_table has the old schema but the correct name, and the new_courses_table has the new schema and correct data but the old name.

The next step is to delete the original table from the database. This is done so that there will be no name conflict when you rename the new table to the old name.

```
DROP TABLE courses_table
```

Finally, you can rename the new_courses_table as courses_table without a name conflict.

```
sp_rename new_courses_table, courses_table
```

The sp_rename command is specific to Transact SQL. Other dialects provide their own methods for accomplishing this. SQL Server gives the following confirmation that the change was successful:

```
Object name has been changed.
```

In order to convince yourself that this convoluted procedure worked, SELECT all rows and all columns from the courses_table and examine the results. Figure 10.4 shows the results of this procedure. The courses_table now has one fewer column than before, and one of the columns has a new name.

```
select * from courses_table
```

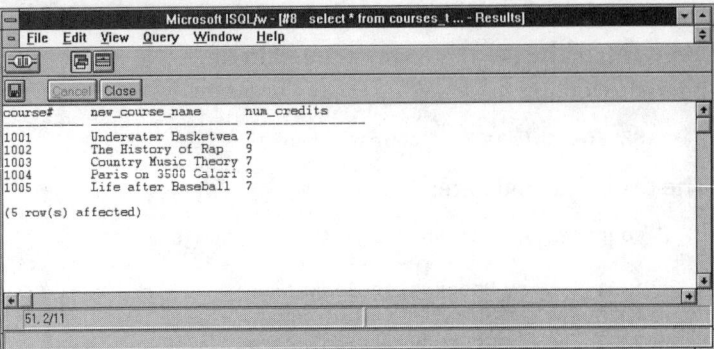

Fig. 10.4 The courses_table now has a new schema that includes one fewer column and one renamed column.

The basis of this procedure was the ability to use the set processing features of SQL to avoid a lot of coding and network traffic. The stronger SQL programmers understand set theory and the set operations of the language and make effective use of them. The result is a simpler system that executes faster as well.

Changing the Data in the Tables

The most common tasks in a database application are updating and retrieving data. Commonplace systems like an order handling system provide screens to a salesperson who uses them to enter data. The warehouse pulls the order up on a screen, fills it, and marks it as complete via another set of screens. The billing department uses the same database to prepare an invoice to be mailed to the customer. Finally, the accounts receivable department enters the payment into the database and the transaction is complete.

The basic flow of this sample system and nearly every database application is the creation of a row in a table, which is then updated several times before it is complete. Systems that handle trouble calls from customers follow a simple pattern. An operator logs a call into a database. A dispatcher sends a crew to perform the repair and logs that fact to the database. The crew completes the repair and logs that also.

These systems rely on the capability of one set of workers to update a common database which will be used by coworkers to perform their functions. These systems rely on the UPDATE command in SQL to change the values of the fields in the database. The syntax of the UPDATE command is as follows:

```
UPDATE teachers_table
SET salary = 71000
WHERE salary < 71000
```

SELECT the data from this table before you execute this command. The values are as follows:

```
teacher#    teacher_name          phone       salary
----------  --------------------  ----------  -------
101         Ralph Daniel          798-0989    80000.0
102         Sandy Turner          897-9089    80001.0
103         Lantie Hearn          546-0397    65000.0
104         John Baluch           494-9787    66000.0
105         Carl Kennedy          777-4981    110000.0
(5 row(s) affected)
```

Next, run the UPDATE above and observe that the values in the table are now changed, as shown here:

```
teacher#    teacher_name          phone       salary
----------  --------------------  ----------  ---------
101         Ralph Daniel          798-0989    80000.0
102         Sandy Turner          897-9089    80001.0
105         Carl Kennedy          777-4981    110000.0
103         Lantie Hearn          546-0397    71000.0
104         John Baluch           494-9787    71000.0

(5 row(s) affected)
```

Notice again that all of the rows in the table were treated as a set by SQL. The WHERE clause tells which rows are to be affected by the command. The UPDATE verb told which columns were to receive what value. Contrast this with the following third-generation language or procedural approach:

1. Read a row.

2. Test the value of the salary field.

3. If the salary < 71000, update it to 71000.

4. Write the row back to the file.

Comparing the simplicity of the UPDATE command with the complexity of the procedural approach highlights the value of the set processing mentality.

The UPDATE command can handle calculations as well. Suppose that in the previous example you wanted to give everyone a 5% raise. This can be done directly in SQL using the following syntax:

```
UPDATE teachers_table
SET salary = (salary * 1.05)
```

The result of this action is the following:

```
teacher#      teacher_name          phone       salary
---------     --------------------  ----------  --------
101           Ralph Daniel          798-0989    84000.0
102           Sandy Turner          897-9089    84001.05
105           Carl Kennedy          777-4981    115500.0
103           Lantie Hearn          546-0397    74550.0
104           John Baluch           494-9787    74550.0
(5 row(s) affected)
```

The absence of a WHERE clause caused the UPDATE to be applied to every row in the table in the same way that omitting a WHERE clause in a SELECT statement causes every row in the table to be retrieved.

UPDATEs are not limited to single values either. Several fields can be updated at the same time.

```
UPDATE teachers_table
SET salary = (salary * 1.01),_
    teacher_name = 'Ralphie Daniel'
WHERE teacher# = 101

teacher#      teacher_name          phone       salary
---------     --------------------  ----------  --------
101           Ralphie Daniel        798-0989    84840.0
```

In this example, two fields in the same row were updated at the same time.

Complex UPDATE commands can be achieved by using a SELECT in the WHERE clause like you did above in the Insert example. In the following example, give the teachers whose salaries are below average a 2% raise. Don't give the ones that are at or above average any raise at all. If you think about how to do this using a procedural approach, it will look hard. Using the power of the set processing mentality, however, it becomes much simpler.

```
UPDATE teachers_table
SET salary = salary * 1.02
WHERE salary < (SELECT AVE(Salary)
FROM teachers_table
```

The before picture of the table shows the old salaries.

```
teacher#     teacher_name           phone        salary
-----------  ---------------------  ----------   --------
102          Sandy Turner           897-9089     84001.05
105          Carl Kennedy           777-4981     115500.0
103          Lantie Hearn           546-0397     74550.0
104          John Baluch            494-9787     74550.0
101          Ralphie Daniel         798-0989     84840.0

(5 row(s) affected)
```

After running the UPDATE, the salaries of four of the teachers have been increased according to the logic of the SQL statement.

```
teacher#     teacher_name           phone        salary
-----------  ---------------------  ----------   --------
105          Carl Kennedy           777-4981     115500.0
102          Sandy Turner           897-9089     85681.071
103          Lantie Hearn           546-0397     76041.0
104          John Baluch            494-9787     76041.0
101          Ralphie Daniel         798-0989     86536.8

(5 row(s) affected)
```

In this example also, you saw how much more powerful the set processing approach is than the procedural approach. In fact, much of the system design of a production application involves finding a strategy to avoid moving any more data than necessary over the network.

Deleting Data and Tables

Deleting data from a table is very simple using SQL. If you want to delete the data in one field in one row, then the strategy would be to assign a 0, blank, or NULL value to that field.

```
UPDATE students_table
SET new_column = NULL
WHERE student# > 600
```

The state of the data in the table before the execution of the table has the string abc in the new_column.

```
student#        student_name          new_column
- - - - - - - - - -   - - - - - - - - - - - - - - - - -   - - - - - - - - - -
593             Joe Smith             abc
594             Pomare Piti           abc
595             Ed Oken               abc
596             Angel Loon            abc
597             John Byron            abc
598             Jacob Roggeveen       abc
599             James Cook            abc
600             Joseph Banks          abc
601             Addison Pratt         abc
602             Eliza Pratt           abc
```

After the execution of the UPDATE command, the values of the last two student rows are changed to NULL according to the logic of the SQL statement.

```
student#        student_name          new_column
- - - - - - - - - -   - - - - - - - - - - - - - - - - -   - - - - - - - - - -
593             Joe Smith             abc
594             Pomare Piti           abc
595             Ed Oken               abc
596             Angel Loon            abc
597             John Byron            abc
598             Jacob Roggeveen       abc
599             James Cook            abc
600             Joseph Banks          abc
601             Addison Pratt         (null)
602             Eliza Pratt           (null)
```

The null values were allowed in new_column because the keyword NULL was used in the ALTER command that added this column.

```
ALTER TABLE students_table ADD new_column char(8) NULL
```

The null value means that data is missing from the table, normally because it is unknown. Whenever a calculation like an average takes place on a column that has nulls, the null value is ignored in both the numerator and the denominator.

Often programmers are tempted to code applications where they store 0 in a numeric field whenever data is unknown. This can cause problems with procedures like the AVG() function. To illustrate this point, take the salaries of the teachers.

```
teacher#      salary
----------    --------
102           85681.07
103           76041.0
104           76041.0
101           86536.8
105           0.0
```

Suppose that you know the salary of every teacher except teacher# 105. In real systems, perhaps that salary hasn't been determined yet. Normally you would put 0 in order to be able to add the teacher to the database. This works fine when people read it because they know that people don't work for free, and so they are correctly able to determine that this data is missing. If they were averaging the numbers by hand, then they would be smart enough to omit that value and calculate the average of the other values. The average that they would calculate would be $81.074.97. But, if they were content to average numbers by hand, they wouldn't be paying you to automate their business, would they?

Next, set the computer to use the AVG() function to calculate this average.

```
Select AVG(salary)  from teachers_table
```

The answer that it gives is as follows (which is incorrect):

```
64859.9742
```

The computer literally averaged all of the fields in the database that it was instructed to average. Thus, the result was wrong.

The first thing to try would be to change the 0.0 to NULL. This is an illegal action because the salary field was defined as the default of NOT NULL when the table was created. SQL Server gives the following error message:

```
Msg 233, Level 16, State 1
The column salary in table teachers_table may not be null.
```

ALTER the table to add a new column that has the NULL attribute, and then copy the data from the salary column to this new column.

```
ALTER TABLE teachers_table ADD new_salary int NULL
```

The table now looks like the following:

```
teacher#        teacher_name            salary       new_salary
----------      --------------------    ----------   -----------
102             Sandy Turner            85681.071    (null)
103             Lantie Hearn            76041.0      (null)
104             John Baluch             76041.0      (null)
101             Ralphie Daniel          86536.8      (null)
105             Carl Kennedy            0.0          (null)
```

Update the table to copy the salaries into the new_salary field.

```
UPDATE teachers_table
SET new_salary = salary
WHERE salary > 0
```

The result is the following table:

```
teacher#        teacher_name            salary       new_salary
----------      --------------------    ----------   -----------
105             Carl Kennedy            0.0          (null)
102             Sandy Turner            85681.071    85681
103             Lantie Hearn            76041.0      76041
104             John Baluch             76041.0      76041
101             Ralphie Daniel          86536.8      86536
```

Now, use the AVG() function again to see what happens.

```
Select AVG(new_salary)  from teachers_tab
```

The result is a much more pleasing average that matches what a person would calculate when performing this task.

```
81074
```

Deleting a row from a table is very easy. It is accomplished by the following syntax:

```
DELETE FROM teachers_table
WHERE salary > 100000
```

The result is a "reengineered" workforce that is absent the highest-paid technical person.

```
teacher#     teacher_name        salary          new_salary
----------   ----------------    -----------     -----------
105          Carl Kennedy        0.0             (null)
102          Sandy Turner        85681.071       85681
103          Lantie Hearn        76041.0         76041
104          John Baluch         76041.0         76041
```

You can see that the expected result was achieved. The offending employee has been dismissed from the teachers table.

Retrieving Data from Tables

By far, the most common operation on a database management system is a query. A query is a transaction whose goal is to retrieve data from the database. In SQL, the query verb is SELECT. SELECT statements follow the form:

```
SELECT <column names> FROM <table name>
```

An example of this would be:

```
SELECT course#, course_name FROM courses_table
```

The result of this query would be:

```
course#      course_name
----------   --------------------
1001         Underwater Basketwea
1002         The History of Rap
1003         Country Music Theory
1004         Paris on 3500 Calori
1005         Life after Baseball
```

Another variation on this simple SELECT statement would be to retrieve all of the columns from all of the rows.

```
SELECT * FROM courses_table
```

The results would be as follows:

course#	course_name	department	num_credits
1001	Underwater Basketwea	Recreation	7
1002	The History of Rap	Music	9
1003	Country Music Theory	Music	7
1004	Paris on 3500 Calori	PE	3
1005	Life after Baseball	PE	7

Be selective in your use of the wildcard (*) in production systems. If you create a report using the * and format it to look just right, adding a row to the schema of the table will make your report look bad. In embedded SQL procedures, it is best to avoid the use of the *, even if you want all of the columns. The * is very useful, however, for interactive sessions where you are testing the data or some SQL syntax.

The Simple WHERE Clause

While you sometimes want to look at every row in a table, you often want only a subset of those rows. The SQL mechanism for telling the system which of these rows you want is the WHERE clause. The syntax of the WHERE clause is as follows:

```
SELECT <column names> FROM <table name>
WHERE <predicate>
```

An example of this would be as follows:

```
SELECT course_name FROM courses_table
WHERE course# = 1003
```

The result of this query is as follows:

```
course_name
-------------------
Country Music Theory
```

The predicate in this SELECT statement is course# = 1003. It is also legal to have a predicate that returns more than one row, as in the following example:

```
SELECT course#, course_name FROM courses_table
WHERE course# > 1003
```

The result of this query is the following two rows:

```
course#      course_name
----------   --------------------
1004         Paris on 3500 Calori
1005         Life after Baseball
```

Developing skill in the writing of predicates is what separates the good SQL programmer from the average one. The rest of this chapter concerns predicate writing.

The Compound WHERE Clause

It is often necessary to satisfy multiple conditions in one SELECT statement. If you wanted all students who lived in Florida you would use the following:

```
SELECT student#, student_name FROM students_table
WHERE state = 'FL'
```

The result is as follows:

```
student#     student_name
----------   -------------
594          Pomare Piti
599          James Cook
```

If you wanted all male students, you would use the following:

```
SELECT student#, student_name FROM students_table
WHERE sex = 'male'
```

The result is as follows:

```
student#     student_name
----------   --------------------
593          Joe Smith
595          Ed Oken
597          John Byron
598          Jacob Roggeveen
599          James Cook
600          Joseph Banks
601          Addison Pratt
```

One strategy would be to retrieve all of the rows from one table into your application, then select the ones that meet the second criteria.

Alternatively, you could use a compound SELECT statement and let the database management system do the work for you before it sends the result over the network.

```
SELECT student#, student_name FROM students_table
WHERE sex = 'M' AND state = 'FL'
```

The result is as follows:

```
student#      student_name
-----------   --------------------
599           James Cook
```

The efficiency of your program is greatly enhanced when you allow the database management system to manage the selection of the rows for you. Modern database servers have rule-based query optimizers that analyze a request and create a strategy of retrieval that they predict would be the fastest to execute. In this case, it would discover that the state field part of the predicate would yield the fewest candidate rows, two. It would then have only two rows to evaluate on the sex = 'M' part of the predicate.

Another flavor of the compound predicate contains the keyword OR. It is used when there are several possible values that would be acceptable. Suppose that a student wanted a ride home for the summer. Because he lives in Georgia, another student from either Georgia or Florida would do, as Florida students drive through Georgia on the way home. This query could be done by brute force or it could be done as follows:

```
SELECT student_name, state from students_table
WHERE state = 'FL' OR state = 'GA'
```

The result of this selection is as follows:

```
student_name           state
--------------------   -----
Pomare Piti            FL
Angel Loon             GA
James Cook             FL
```

Parentheses are sometimes used to clarify the request to the database management system. The following request is ambiguous:

```
SELECT student#, student_name FROM students_table
WHERE state = 'FL' or state = 'GA' AND sex = 'M'
```

Does this SQL statement want students from 'GA' who are male and both male and female students from 'FL', or does it want male students from either state? It is likely that different servers could parse this sentence differently and give different answers. If you rewrite the sentence as follows:

```
SELECT  student_name, state, sex FROM students_table
WHERE (state = 'FL' OR state = 'GA') AND sex = 'M'
```

then the confusion dissipates; the meaning becomes obvious. The result is as follows:

```
student_name              state sex
------------------------- ----- ---
James Cook                FL    M
```

The Not keyword is also part of the legal syntax of the SQL predicate. If you were willing to go anywhere for spring break except 'NY', then you could say:

```
SELECT student_name, state FROM students_table
WHERE NOT (state = 'NY')
```

The result would be as follows:

```
student_name              state
------------------------- -----
Joe Smith                 AL
Pomare Piti               FL
Ed Oken                   CA
Angel Loon                GA
Jacob Roggeveen           RI
James Cook                FL
Joseph Banks              CA
Addison Pratt             OR
Eliza Pratt               MD
```

Notice that all rows are present except the one student from the "Big Apple."

BETWEEN and NOT BETWEEN

It is common to want to select a set of rows with a value of a certain column falling within a certain range, as in the following:

```
SELECT student_name, zip FROM students_table
WHERE zip BETWEEN '30000' AND '40000'
```

The result is as follows:

```
student_name             zip
-------------------- -----
Joe Smith                32456
Angel Loon               31204
John Byron               34565
Jacob Roggeveen          34534
James Cook               34545
```

By the same token, you might want all of the rows that are not in that range:

```
SELECT student_name, zip FROM students_table
WHERE zip NOT BETWEEN '30000' AND '40000'
```

The result is as follows:

```
student_name             zip
-------------------- -----
Pomare Piti              12121
Ed Oken                  21212
Joseph Banks             87803
Addison Pratt            43980
Eliza Pratt              29796
```

As expected, this query chose all of the rows with zip codes outside of that range.

LIKE and NOT LIKE

Many times you want to query data where you have only part of the criteria necessary to completely specify the predicate. This necessitates the use of an approximation in the WHERE clause. The LIKE operator gives us that capability.

```
SELECT student_name FROM students
WHERE student_name LIKE 'Jo%'
```

The result of this query is as follows:

```
student_name
-------------------
Joe Smith
John Byron
Joseph Banks
```

Another variation on the LIKE theme is the NOT LIKE keywords.

```
SELECT student_name FROM students
WHERE student_name NOT LIKE 'Jo%'
```

The result of this query is—as you might predict—as follows:

```
student_name
-------------------
Pomare Piti
Ed Oken
Angel Loon
Jacob Roggeveen
James Cook
Addison Pratt
Eliza Pratt
```

IN and NOT IN

Earlier, you saw how a WHERE clause could be used to find a student from 'GA' or 'FL'. The compound predicate worked well for two values but would become tedious if you needed to find students from 9 or 10 states. To facilitate this type of query, a special keyword called IN is available. Instead of the following:

```
SELECT student_name, state from students_table
WHERE state = 'FL' OR state = 'GA' OR state = 'AL' OR ...
```

You could use the IN keyword, as follows:

```
SELECT student_name, state from students_table
WHERE state IN ( 'FL','GA','AL')
```

The result is the same as if you had strung together a set of OR's in the predicate.

```
student_name          state
-------------------   -----
Joe Smith             AL
Pomare Piti           FL
Angel Loon            GA
James Cook            FL
```

As with the other predicate keywords, IN can be written NOT IN, as follows:

```
SELECT student_name, state from students_table
WHERE state NOT IN ( 'FL','GA','AL')
```

The result will be as follows:

```
student_name              state
--------------------      -----
Ed Oken                   CA
John Byron                NY
Jacob Roggeveen           RI
Joseph Banks              CA
Addison Pratt             OR
Eliza Pratt               MD
```

IS NULL and IS NOT NULL

If a field can contain nulls, there needs to be a way to check for the null value. Because the values actually representing NULL vary from system to system, a way of testing for NULL is required. SQL implements this through the IS NULL and the IS NOT NULL keyword phrases.

```
SELECT student_name, new_column FROM students_table
WHERE new_column IS NULL
```

The result of this query is as follows:

```
student_name              new_column
--------------------      ----------
Addison Pratt             (null)
Eliza Pratt               (null)
```

The opposite effect can be achieved by using the following IS NOT NULL keyword phrase:

```
SELECT student_name, new_column FROM students_table
WHERE new_column IS NOT NULL
```

The result of this query is as follows:

```
student_name              new_column
--------------------      ----------
Joe Smith                 abc
Pomare Piti               abc
Ed Oken                   abc
Angel Loon                abc
John Byron                abc
Jacob Roggeveen           abc
James Cook                abc
Joseph Banks              abc
```

ORDER BY

Relational database theory states that there is no order to the rows in a table. This means that all ordering of rows must be done at retrieval time. Because people can understand ordered data much easier than they can understand unordered data, it is a requirement in some applications to sort data. SQL provides a built-in syntax, ORDER BY, to specify how you want the results of the query sorted.

```
SELECT  teacher_name, salary FROM teachers_table
ORDER BY salary
```

The result of this query is as follows:

```
teacher_name          salary
-------------------- ----------
Carl Kennedy          0.0
John Baluch           76041.0
Lantie Hearn          76041.0
Sandy Turner          85681.071
```

In similar fashion, you can order rows in descending order.

```
SELECT  teacher_name, salary FROM teachers_table
ORDER BY salary DESC
```

The results are now ordered in the opposite fashion.

```
teacher_name          salary
-------------------- ----------
Sandy Turner          85681.071
John Baluch           76041.0
Lantie Hearn          76041.0
Carl Kennedy          0.0
```

Calculated Columns

There are times when you want to retrieve and display a calculation, without changing the data in the database. "What-if" logic is an example of this. What would happen to salaries if you gave everyone a raise of 4% instead of a raise of 5%?

```
SELECT teacher_name, salary, salary4% = salary * 1.04, _
salary5% = salary * 1.05 FROM teachers_table

teacher_name          salary        salary4      salary5
--------------------  --------     -----------   ----------
Carl Kennedy          0.0              0.0           0.0
Sandy Turner          85681.07     89108.31      89965.12
Lantie Hearn          76041.0      79082.64      79843.05
John Baluch           76041.0      79082.64      79843.05
```

In addition to the normal arithmetic operators (+ - * /) there are a number of aggregate operations built into SQL. MIN(), MAX(), SUM(), AVE(), and COUNT() are all supported. In addition, specific database management systems provide other functions.

```
SELECT SUM(salary) FROM teachers_table
```

The result of this query is as follows:

```
----------
237763.071
```

Another interesting query is as follows:

```
SELECT COUNT(course#) FROM sections_table
```

The result of this query is as follows:

```
----------
8
```

If you do a SELECT on those course# fields in sections_table:

```
SELECT course# FROM sections_table
```

You will find that the course# field contains a lot of the same courses:

```
course#
-----------
1001
1001
1002
1003
1004
1004
1004
1005
```

If the question being posed in the query is "How many different courses are being taught?", then the following query would be a better choice:

```
SELECT COUNT(DISTINCT course#) FROM sections_table
```

The result of this query might better serve your purposes.

```
-----------
5
```

Thus, there are five distinct course numbers being taught out of the eight sections.

Joining Tables

Relational database theory states that no redundant data should be stored in the database. In other words, you would not store the name of the student with her student# in the enrolls field. You already have a way of finding out the name of a student given the student# from `students_table`. However, if you do a SELECT on `enrolls_table` to display grades, you will get the following:

course#	section#	student#	grade
1001	1	593	90
1001	1	593	90
1001	1	594	87
1001	1	595	77
1001	2	596	99
1001	2	597	66
1001	2	598	79
1001	2	599	81
1002	1	600	89
1002	1	601	87
1002	1	602	75
1002	1	603	92
1003	1	603	100
1003	1	595	76
1003	1	596	78
1004	1	593	98
1004	1	594	65
1004	1	595	22
1004	2	596	67
1004	2	597	87
1005	1	593	86
1005	1	603	87
1005	1	600	83
1005	1	601	79
1005	1	599	73
1005	1	598	72
1005	1	597	91
1005	1	596	87

This report is accurate enough, but the teacher would rather have the names of the students on the report also. That will require a joining of two tables to accomplish this. The following query shows how SQL uses the WHERE clause to effect a join.

```
SELECT course#, section#, student_name, grade
FROM students_table, enrolls_table
WHERE enrolls_table.student# = students_table.student#
```

The result of this query is as follows:

course#	section#	student_name	grade
1001	1	Joe Smith	90
1001	1	Joe Smith	90
1004	1	Joe Smith	98
1005	1	Joe Smith	86
1001	1	Pomare Piti	87
1004	1	Pomare Piti	65
1001	1	Ed Oken	77
1003	1	Ed Oken	76
1004	1	Ed Oken	22
1001	2	Angel Loon	99
1003	1	Angel Loon	78
1004	2	Angel Loon	67
1005	1	Angel Loon	87
1001	2	John Byron	66
1004	2	John Byron	87
1005	1	John Byron	91
1001	2	Jacob Roggeveen	79
1005	1	Jacob Roggeveen	72
1001	2	James Cook	81
1005	1	James Cook	73
1002	1	Joseph Banks	89
1005	1	Joseph Banks	83
1002	1	Addison Pratt	87
1005	1	Addison Pratt	79
1002	1	Eliza Pratt	75

In order for a join to be successful, at least one field from each table must have the same domain. In the previous example, the student# fields in both the students_table and the enrolls_table both contained student numbers. This is by design. By performing the join, you were able to display the names of the fields next to the grades even though these two fields are in separate tables.

Joins can be combined with other WHERE clauses in order to perform more complicated tasks. In the following example, only a subset of the rows is returned:

```
SELECT course#, section#, student_name, grade
FROM students_table, enrolls_table
WHERE enrolls_table.student# = students_table.student# and _
      grade > 85 and state IN ('FL','GA','CA')
```

The result is as follows:

```
course#       section#      student_name        state grade
-----------   -----------   ------------------   ----- -----------
1001          1             Pomare Piti          FL    87
1001          2             Angel Loon           GA    99
1002          1             Joseph Banks         CA    89
1005          1             Angel Loon           GA    87
```

A join can also be created across three tables.

```
SELECT teacher_name, sections_table.teacher#, _
       sections_table.course#, course_name
FROM teachers_table, sections_table, courses_table
WHERE teachers_table.teacher# = sections_table.teacher#_
AND sections_table.course# = courses_table.course#
```

The result of this query is as follows:

teacher_name	teacher#	course#	course_name
Carl Kennedy	105	1001	Underwater Basketwea
Carl Kennedy	105	1004	Paris on 3500 Calori
Sandy Turner	102	1004	Paris on 3500 Calori
Lantie Hearn	103	1004	Paris on 3500 Calori
John Baluch	104	1001	Underwater Basketwea

In this rather complex example, there are two key elements. The first was the specification of which columns you want displayed. The fact that the sections_table columns were called out explicitly means that these rows will be the anchors and will determine which rows display. The second key point is the WHERE clause. Because you have three tables joined, the relationships between the three have to be specified. That is why two fields from the `sections_table` are in the WHERE clause and only one field each from the other two tables.

Relational theory, if followed strictly, will sometimes cause five tables to be joined together.

```
SELECT teacher_name, course_name, student_name
FROM teachers_table, sections_table, courses_table, _
     enrolls_table, students_table
WHERE teachers_table.teacher# = sections_table.teacher#
AND sections_table.course# = courses_table.course#
AND sections_table.section# = enrolls_table.section#
AND sections_table.course# = enrolls_table.course#
AND enrolls_table.student# =  students_table.student#
ORDER BY teacher_name
```

The result of this nightmare of a SQL sentence is as follows:

```
teacher_name           course_name            student_name
------------------     -------------------    -------------------
Carl Kennedy           Underwater Basketwea   Ed Oken
Carl Kennedy           Underwater Basketwea   Joe Smith
Carl Kennedy           Underwater Basketwea   Joe Smith
Carl Kennedy           Underwater Basketwea   Pomare Piti
John Baluch            Underwater Basketwea   Angel Loon
John Baluch            Underwater Basketwea   Jacob Roggeveen
John Baluch            Underwater Basketwea   James Cook
John Baluch            Underwater Basketwea   John Byron
Lantie Hearn           Paris on 3500 Calori   Angel Loon
Lantie Hearn           Paris on 3500 Calori   John Byron
Sandy Turner           Paris on 3500 Calori   Ed Oken
Sandy Turner           Paris on 3500 Calori   Joe Smith
Sandy Turner           Paris on 3500 Calori   Pomare Piti
```

This join works fine, but would be very hard to maintain. In reality, joins of more than two tables perform poorly in production applications. While relational theory states that there can be no redundant data in a database, real world systems often contain replicated data. In fact, modern systems support replicated data by handling the copying of the data automatically.

From Here...

In this chapter you were introduced to the Structured Query Language (SQL). This language forms the user interface of most modern database management systems.

This chapter also examined how to use SQL to create, modify, and delete tables. You also learned how to add and delete data in the database. Finally, you learned how to retrieve the data in all sorts of clever ways.

➤ For more information about many of the controls discussed in this chapter, you can refer to Que's *Special Edition Using Visual Basic 4.*

➤ For more information on using MDI forms in your application, see Chapter 2, "Multiple Document Interface (MDI)."

➤ For more information about creating graphics in your application, see Chapter 16, "Graphics: Data Analysis."

➤ For more information covering the inclusion of database management into your application, refer to Chapter 7, "The Jet Engine and ODBC."

Part III
Enhancing Your Application

OLE Automation

11

by *Edward B. Toupin*

This chapter introduces you to Object Linking and Embedding version 2.0, otherwise known in Visual Basic 4 as OLEv2.0. As you learn the basics of application integration with OLE, you will see how Visual Basic's tools can be used to give you a fully functional method of information-sharing between Windows-based applications.

We will first delve into OLE and its capabilities under Microsoft Windows 95. This topic provides a brief overview and history of OLE to give you an understanding of the premise for OLEv2.0. Once the basics of OLE are explained, we will take a look at object linking and embedding. This topic will explore the interaction between OLE servers and OLE containers as well as the different methods of integrating applications under Windows.

The remainder of the chapter explains some of the concepts involved in OLE automation and how it is utilized by Windows-based applications. To demonstrate some of the concepts of OLE, we will take a look at a few sample Visual Basic applications that utilize OLE to manipulate objects under Windows.

 **Note:** Unless otherwise specified, all references to OLE and OLEv2.0 refer to Object Link and Embedding version 2.0.

In this chapter we will cover the following:

➤ Overview of OLE

➤ OLE Automation under Windows 95

➤ Object embedding

➤ Object linking

➤ OLE objects and their manipulation

➤ Visual Basic OLE controls

➤ Limitation of OLE

What Is OLE?

Windows 3.0 introduced a whole new method of working with the computer. Everything was at the user's fingertips in a graphical environment. However, the user was still working with many disparate applications. As applications that supported OLE—also known as *OLE enabled applications*—began to appear in the marketplace, the user was able to combine the functionality of different applications into one consolidated document.

OLE was originally developed on top of the Windows Dynamic Data Exchange (DDE) subsystem. DDE allows Windows-based applications to communicate with one another by exchanging simple messages and handles to globally allocated memory. Many applications had requirements that exceeded the capabilities of DDE, so users and vendors needed to develop extensions to support these requirements. The primary problem with DDE was that it was not robust enough to handle the morass of information exchanged between the multitude of evolving Windows-based applications.

To spearhead an endeavor to produce a more robust and efficient means of information exchange between applications, Microsoft and Aldus Corporation set forth a document outlining the initial specifications for OLE. As a result of the specification, Microsoft delivered OLEv1.0. The first applications to support OLEv1.0 were Microsoft Excel and Lotus Notes. As more and more vendors added OLEv1.0 capabilities to their applications, Microsoft found a need to develop a more sophisticated communications interface. Out of this need came the specifications for OLEv2.0.

Because everything under OLEv2.0 is centered around the contents of one document, a new form of computing—known as *document-centric computing*—came about. This new form of computing allows users to be more productive by integrating Windows applications and providing a common interface standard for all Windows applications.

Users and developers benefit considerably from this document-centric, *component software* approach to productivity. Instead of relying on the functionality of a single application, users now can utilize the functionality of many applications, or components, for their documents. For developers, the use of component software reduced the complexity of application development considerably by providing a Plug and Play approach to application development.

Document-Centric Computing

The premise of OLE is to change the view of productivity in the Windows environment. Instead of looking at many different applications and how they contribute to a finished product, document-centric computing focuses on the finished product. This view of computing frees the user from worrying about which application will meet the needs of a given task. The user is able to approach the document from the data standpoint instead.

For example, the user doesn't have to work specifically with a spreadsheet application to manipulate numbers, a drawing application to draw figures, or a word-processing application to manage text. With

OLE, the user can work in any OLE-enabled application and have access to numbers, figures, and text by using the functionality of spreadsheets, graphic applications, and word processors in one container application (see fig. 11.1).

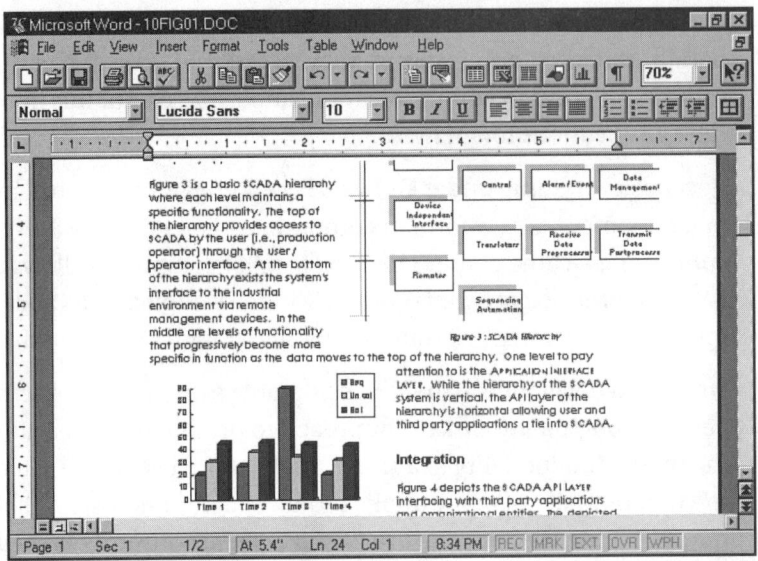

Fig. 11.1 Word for Windows 6.0 acts as a container to incorporate a drawing object and a graph object.

Component Software

Document-centric computing is based on the use of software components to supply functionality to a container application. *Component software* can be compared to a puzzle. The puzzle consists of many pieces of different shapes and colors. By assembling these pieces together you get one complete picture. With component software you have the ability to combine the functionality of many different applications together to produce a result consisting of each application's—or component's—data.

The ideas of component software usage and document-centric computing are very similar to the ideas of *object-oriented* applications. Object-oriented principles are focused on data rather than on function. The operations on data are encapsulated to hide the specifics of the data's functional requirements and provide a common calling interface to manipulate the data.

> **Note:** Object-oriented, document-centric applications focus on data while structured applications are centered around the functionality of one application.

Word for Windows, for example, allows you to incorporate images from Microsoft Draw, spreadsheets from Excel, and numerous other such objects. However, Word for Windows does not have the built-in functionality to manage such objects by itself, but instead uses the functionality of the different software components. Each component provides a means of manipulating data, but all components have a common means of accessing the data. To contrast, a structured application, such as one of the older DOS-based word processors, could manage text only. The functionality of the application was designed to handle word-processing operations and could not handle any other type of information.

OLE Terminology

As with every technological advancement, OLE comes with a dictionary of buzzwords. The following terms are important throughout these next few chapters and are important in understanding the concepts of OLE.

➤ An *OLE server* is an application that provides services to other OLE-enabled applications. Servers can be drawing programs, spreadsheets, communication applications, or any number of applications that provide a service.

➤ A *container* is an application that can contain linked or embedded objects. A container is known also as an OLE client because it can use the services of OLE servers.

➤ An *OLE object* refers to data that is made available, or exposed, by an OLE server application. OLE server applications can expose many different types of objects for use by container applications. For example, a spreadsheet application may expose a worksheet, macrosheet, chart, cell, or range of cells. These types of data are all different types (also known as *classes*) of exposed objects.

➤ *Object linking* is a method of establishing a dynamic connection between OLE objects in different applications. This type of connection essentially parallels hot links in DDE in that all information is updated dynamically. For example, a group of cells located in an Excel spreadsheet are linked into a Word for Windows document. As you view the cells in Word for Windows, they will update automatically if the linked cells in Excel should change.

➤ *Object embedding* is a method where an instance of an OLE object from one application is literally stored into another. In this instance, the cells in the Excel spreadsheet from above would be placed into the Word for Windows document. If you wanted to change the information in the cells, you would double-click the cells to run Excel and have them loaded into Excel for editing. Once the editing is complete, you can update the instance of the cells in Word.

➤ *In-place activation* is a function of object embedding where all editing is accomplished internal to the container application. Instead of having to access the server application to edit the object, the functionality of the server is brought into the container and used to edit the object internal to the container.

➤ *Drag and drop* is a method that allows you to pick up an icon or document with your mouse, drag it to an OLE-enabled server application, and drop the icon or document on the server application. This type of operation allows you to exchange information between applications that previously could be handled by the clipboard only.

➤ *OLE Automation* is a method that enables you to access exposed objects located in another application.

What Is OLE Automation?

OLE Automation is the implementation of OLE that integrates applications through interapplication communications. Applications that support OLE automation expose their OLE objects to allow programming languages and other applications access to these objects.

When an application exposes its objects, you can programmatically manipulate the application from programming tools and other applications. You can develop in Visual Basic applications that can access the objects of OLE server applications as well as utilize the functionality of those applications within container applications.

An example of OLE Automation would be in the contrast of spreadsheet macros and programming languages. In a spreadsheet, such as Microsoft Excel, you can write macros that automatically execute keystrokes that you would otherwise have to execute manually. These keystrokes may sort data or print reports to a printer. With OLE Automation, you can write an application in Visual Basic that can perform operations with the Excel spreadsheet externally.

OLE Automation offers the following advantages over implementations of macro languages included within some applications:

➤ Exposed objects from many applications are available in a single programming environment. In this way, developers can bring together the best pieces from different applications and can create completely new, specialized applications from these existing pieces.

➤ Exposed objects are accessible from any application or programming tool that implements OLE Automation. You may choose a programming tool based on your current knowledge, rather than learning a new language for each application.

➤ Exposed object names can remain consistent across versions of an application. In many cases, the implementation of objects may change drastically while the interface, or the way your application sees the object, does not have to change.

OLE applications that expose their objects to other applications allow other applications to incorporate the functionality of these objects. Because these objects are available, you can use the functionality of OLE servers in your own applications. This approach allows you to bring together the best functionality of multiple applications into one consolidated application. You can take components from different applications and plug them into your own, giving you a Plug and Play approach to development.

Using OLE Automation from Visual Basic you can, for example, print a range of cells within a spreadsheet to a printer or change the values of a range of cells in a spreadsheet. Operations such as these are useful, for example, when you have an application that collects data from the stock market to provide up-to-the-minute information on market activity. You can incorporate the data of the stock market server application into Excel and use it to periodically update a graph for trending the market's activity for the day.

Prior to OLE, developers had to be concerned about the interfaces to applications as the applications were upgraded from one version to the next. With OLE, the object interfaces remain the same to give you a consistent calling convention for all versions of an application. In this way, container applications that you develop using OLE will not have to change drastically every time a server application is upgraded. This not only reduces the amount of time spent in development but also reduces the learning curve that would otherwise be involved in re-learning the new server's interface calling methods.

OLE Automation Objects

An *OLE Automation object* is an instance of a class within your application that you can manipulate programmatically. In an application that manages documents, the OLE Automation objects might look like the diagram in figure 11.2.

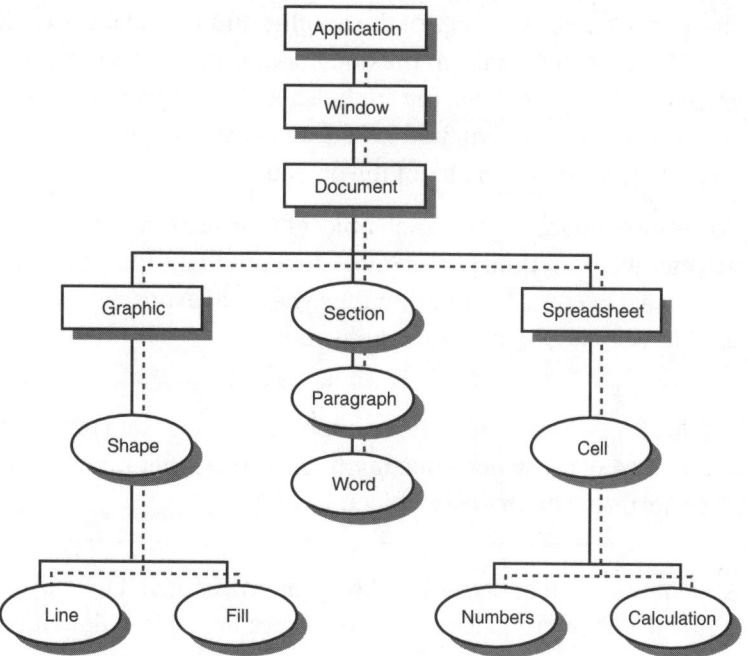

Fig. 11.2 With an application object at the base of a hierarchy, objects contained within OLE-enabled applications constitute an application's OLE object hierarchy.

Figure 11.2 depicts a word-processing application that contains windows to manage documents for your word-processing activity. Each document contains characteristic sections, paragraphs, and words. These characteristics are also known as the *properties* of the document. Just as your hair, eyes, nose, and ears are your unique properties that describe you, the properties of the document describe the document to an application.

The document in figure 11.1 also contains other OLE objects, such as graphics and spreadsheets. These objects are created by two other applications and are stored in the document by a method known as *embedding*. Because the document application does not have the resources available to manage the graphic and spreadsheet objects alone, it uses the resources of the graphic and spreadsheet applications. The graphic image in the document is drawn and managed by a graphic application while the spreadsheet is managed by a spreadsheet application. As is shown, both of the objects contain properties that describe the characteristics of the objects.

To perform operations on each object in the illustration, each object has member functions, or *methods*, that uniquely apply to that object. The object becomes programmable when you expose those member functions for access by other applications.

> **Note:** Properties contain information about the state (or characteristics) of an object while methods are member functions that perform an action on an object.

As demonstrated in figure 11.2, the properties for an OLE object describe the characteristics of the object. For example, a document can have sections, paragraphs, and words as well as dimensions, fonts, and color. A graphic can have shape, line, and fill properties as well as color. The methods of an OLE object allow you to perform actions on the object. The document object may include `Print` to print the document to a printer and `Resize` to adjust for different printer page sizes. The graphic object may include `Scale` to resize the graphic and `Redraw` to update the graphic.

OLE and the System Registration Database

When using OLE, container applications require information that describe the server applications and services available for an object. This type of information is supplied by the system registration database, or *system registry*. All OLE server applications must register themselves with the system registry before they can be used by any container applications. When registering themselves, they provide information as to the type of objects they provide, the file extensions they service, and the directory paths to the server.

The system registry contains information about applications stored on the computer for use by OLE as well as configuration information for the Windows environment on the current machine. This information replaces the INI files that accompanied many earlier applications and is a central store for all OLE applications as well as the Program Manager and File Manager.

For example, the File Manager uses the system registry to locate the server application of the file selected. When you double-click a file in a file list, the File Manager looks for the extension of the selected file in the system registry. Once located, the File Manager runs the server listed in the registry that services this file and loads the file into the server. For example, selecting a file named TEST.TXT would run Notepad and load TEST.TXT into Notepad for editing.

The database for the system registry is a binary file called REG.DAT and is located in the Windows directory. The application REGEDIT allows you to view and edit the information in the database to manage your machine. REGEDIT allows you to view all configuration information in a tree structure by using the following command:

```
REGEDIT
```

As seen in figure 11.3, the application displays the tree of information for each OLE server class so that you can view and edit information associated with each application class.

Many server applications come with a text file with the extension REG. This file contains vital registration information for the server, which is registered in the system registry. To load this information manually, use the following command:

```
REGEDIT /S filename.REG
```

Many server applications automatically register themselves with the system registry when they are either installed or when they are first run. On occasion a server is not registered automatically. It is a good idea to perform this operation manually if this should occur so that you will have access to the server.

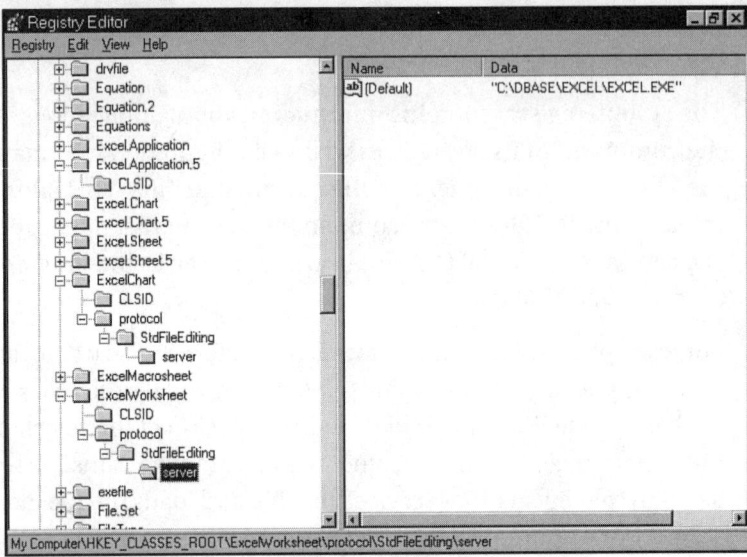

Fig. 11.3 REGEDIT contains a hierarchy of information for applications and OLE objects available in the system.

Object Linking and Embedding

Object linking provides a means of linking an object of a server application into a container application. The linked object is managed by its server application, but the object is used by the container application. The container stores only a reference to the object of the server application.

Object embedding involves the placement of an object into a container application. Similar to linking, the object is still managed by a server application, but it resides wholly in the container application. To follow object embedding is *in-place activation*. This method allows you edit an embedded object within a container application by incorporating the object's server's functionality within the container.

The OLE Control provides an interface for OLE in Visual Basic and allows you to incorporate data into an application by linking or embedding that data from another application. The control can manage linked and embedded data as well as in-place activation and OLE Automation either programatically or manually.

Linked Objects

When you link an object into a container application you are inserting a placeholder for the object but not the actual object itself. This placeholder is a reference to the server application and object name that are used in the container application. For example, you can link a range of spreadsheet cells into a Visual Basic application. The data associated with the cells is stored in another file. The only reference to the spreadsheet information is a link to the data and an image of the data stored in an OLE Control.

If you want to edit the linked spreadsheet cells, double-click the linked object in the OLE Control. If not already running, the spreadsheet server application starts automatically and loads the linked cells. You can then edit those spreadsheet cells using the server application. The edited cells of the spreadsheet are then updated in the Visual Basic container application and stored in the OLE object.

The information stored in the spreadsheet server application is accessible not only by the Visual Basic application but also by any other application that has a link to the data. The linked information in the spreadsheet server application can be changed by any of the linked containers. For example, in figure 11.4, a spreadsheet is linked to a Visual Basic application and a Microsoft Word document. If the spreadsheet's data is changed by either application, the modified data appears in both the Visual Basic application and the Microsoft Word document.

Linking an object from a server application into one or more container applications enables you to maintain a common data object for access by multiple container applications. Object linking is beneficial where you have multiple applications that use a central store of information. You have to edit the information one time only, and all containers that use the information are updated.

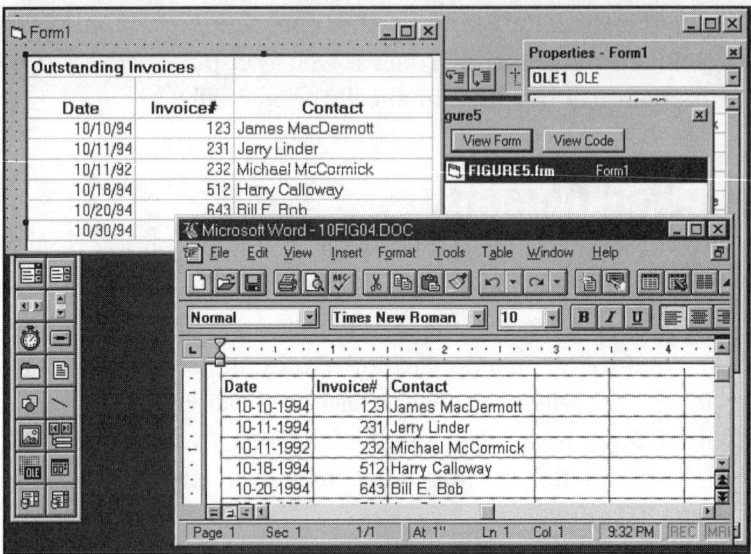

Fig. 11.4 Linked objects are centrally available for access by multiple applications.

Embedded Objects

When you create an embedded object in an OLE Control of a Visual Basic container application, the data associated with the embedded object is stored in the container application. When you save the contents of the container application to a file, the file contains the name of the application that produced the object, the object's data, and a Metafile image of the object.

When an object is embedded in an application, no application except for the container has access to the data in the embedded object. Embedding is useful when you want your container application to maintain data that is produced and edited in another application. When the user activates the object, the server application that created the object is invoked by the container application, and the object's data is opened for editing.

For example, in figure 11.5 we are opening the Microsoft Graph server application from a Visual Basic container application. The server is used to create the object, which is then stored, embedded, into the container application. The graph from Microsoft Graph is now native to Visual Basic and can be treated as though it were part of the Visual Basic container application.

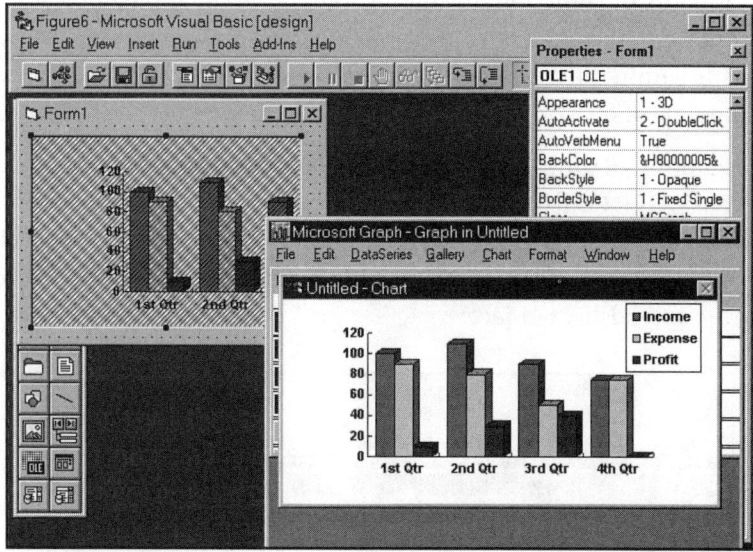

Fig. 11.5 Embedded objects are wholly contained within container applications.

In-Place Activation

A variation to object embedding is called *in-place activation*, also known as *visual editing*. In-place activation enables you to edit an embedded object within the container application. As with embedding, the capabilities of the server application are used to edit the object; the functionality of the server application is incorporated into the container for the editing process. The one requirement for using in-place activation is that the container and server applications support OLE

Automation. If either of the two applications does not support OLE Automation, then you will not be able to use in-place activation on an embedded object.

With in-place activation, when you double-click an embedded object, the menus and toolbars of the server application replace the menus and toolbars of the container application. The container application inherits the functionality of the object's server application so that you may edit the object in-place—that is, you may edit the object where it sits within the container. When you complete editing the object, all menus of the container application are restored to the original state.

Figure 11.6 shows an Excel worksheet being edited in-place in a Visual Basic OLE Control. The form in the figure contains an Excel spreadsheet object in a Visual Basic OLE Control. Notice the menu is in the form inherited from the spreadsheet application to allow you to edit the spreadsheet object.

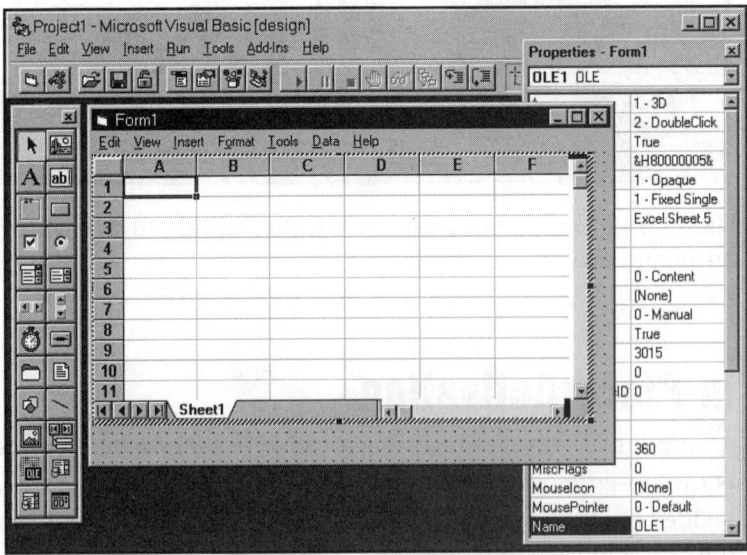

Fig. 11.6 In-place activation allows you to inherit the functionality of an embedded object's server application.

By incorporating OLE Automation and in-place activation, you can add numbers, text, and equations to the cells as though you were actually working in the Excel application.

> **Note:** If a server application supports in-place activation, its menus and functions will supersede the container application's menu and functions. If it does not support in-place activation, the server is loaded, and the object you are to edit is loaded into the server.

Visual Basic OLE Control

Visual Basic OLE Control is an object within Visual Basic that provides an interface to the OLEv2.0 subsystem. The OLE Control allows you to incorporate objects from server applications for use in a Visual Basic application. You can link, embed, and visually edit the object located in the OLE Control.

The Plug and Play approach discussed earlier is made possible with the OLE object by allowing you to incorporate the functionality from many different applications into one container application. Not only can you incorporate the spreadsheet capabilities of Excel, but you can also access the word-processing capabilities of Word for Windows and the drawing capabilities of Microsoft Draw into one consolidated application. This keeps you from having to write all of the base code otherwise required to perform operations already available in the many server applications that support OLEv2.0.

The OLE Control at Designtime

Designtime OLE Controls in Visual Basic are specifically for editing and creating OLE objects within a Visual Basic container application. At designtime, you can place an OLE Control into a form using the OLE tool of the toolbox, as shown in figure 11.7. Once you position the OLE Control on the form, Visual Basic will load the Insert Object dialog box, shown in figure 11.8, so that you may select a class to add to the object.

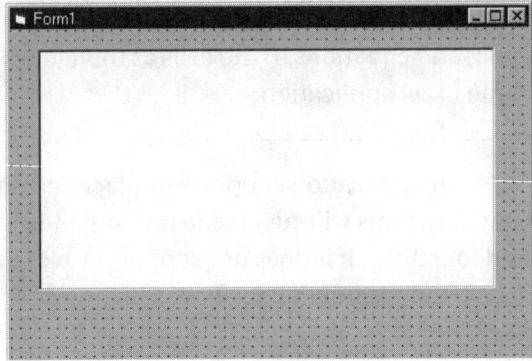

Fig. 11.7 The OLE Control at designtime allows you to link or embed objects into Visual Basic applications.

The Insert Object dialog box (see fig. 11.8) allows you to embed or link an object in the OLE Control. If you select the Create New radio button of the dialog box, you will be embedding an object in your container application.

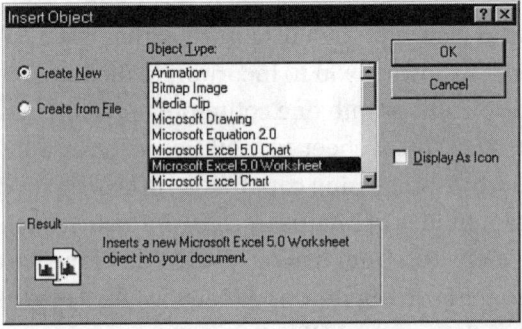

Fig. 11.8 The Insert Object dialog box contains a list of objects available for insertion into the OLE Control.

You may select a class from the Object Type list by double-clicking the class or clicking the OK button. If the class supports in-place activation, the form in which the OLE Control is contained will acquire a menu from that class server, and an image of the selected class will appear in the OLE Control. If the class does not support in-place activation, the server for the selected class will be executed and appear for you to edit your object. For example, selecting the Microsoft Excel 5.0 Worksheet places an image of a spreadsheet in the control; selecting Microsoft Graph, however, executes the graph application.

As shown in figure 11.9, if you select the Create from File radio button, you will be selecting a particular file from your hard disk to load as the object.

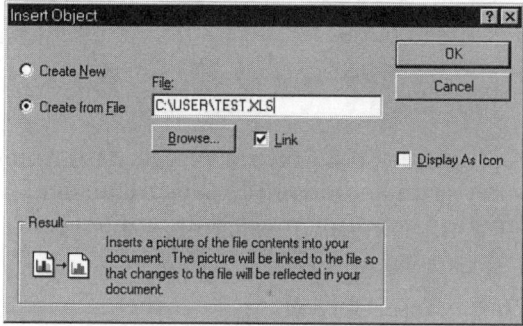

Fig. 11.9 The Insert Object dialog box also selects files for linking into the OLE Control of a Visual Basic application.

If you select the Link check box, a reference to the object will be placed into your container so that it will be updated whenever it is changed by the server application of the object. If you do not select the Link check box, the image from the file will be loaded into the OLE Control. Changes will not be reflected, however, if the object's file should be changed by the server. The latter is similar to embedding an object in that the object from the file is wholly contained in the container. As with object embedding, you may edit the object by double-clicking that object to access the object's server.

OLE Control at Runtime

At runtime there are several methods of the OLE Control that you can use to embed and link an object into a container application. As you can see in figure 11.10, three command buttons on the form are programmed to manipulate the control.

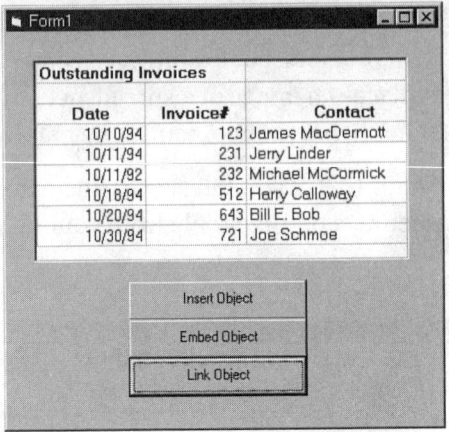

Fig. 11.10 A runtime OLE Control can contain different types of objects, such as an embedded Excel spreadsheet object, to provide automation support within your application.

The first button, Insert Object, executes the `Insert_Click()` subroutine in Listing 11.1 and accesses the Insert Object dialog box that you worked with at designtime. The method `OLE1.InsertObjDlg` opens the dialog box so that you may select an object to link or embed in the same manner as you did at runtime.

The second button, Embed Object, executes the `Link_Click()` subroutine in Listing 11.1 and allows you to dynamically embed an object into the `OLE1` Control of the form. You must provide the name of a source document that you want to embed into the application. This function bypasses the Insert Object dialog box and performs the embedding operation on the values you pass to the method. For example, `OLE1.CreateEmbed "C:\USER\TESTSHT.XLS"` loads the file TESTSHT.XLS and embeds it into the `OLE1` Control on the form.

To edit the embedded object, select the object with the right mouse button or double-click the object. Using the right mouse button accesses a floating menu from which you can select to edit or open the object's server. Double-clicking goes straight to the editing function of the object. If the server supports in-place activation, you can edit the object within the OLE Control; otherwise, the server is started and you edit the object within the server application.

The third button, Link Object, executes the `Embed_Click()` subroutine in Listing 11.1 and allows you to dynamically link an object into the `OLE1` Control of the form. As with `OLE1.CreateEmbed`, `OLE1.CreateLink "C:\USER\TESTSHT.XLS"` uses the name of a source document that you want to link into the application. As with embedding, you can select the object with the right mouse button or double-click the object to edit. You cannot edit a linked object in-place because the object is not contained within the container as it is with embedding. When you edit the object, the server application for the object is started and the object is loaded into the server for editing.

Listing 11.1   FIGURE.MAK—Creating an Embedded and a Linked Object

```
Private Sub Insert_Click()
    OLE1.InsertObjDlg
End Sub

Private Sub Embed_Click()
    OLE1.CreateEmbed "C:\USER\TESTSHT.XLS"
End Sub

Private Sub Link_Click()
    OLE1.CreateLink "C:\USER\TESTSHT.XLS"
End Sub
```

Using OLE Automation to Manage Objects

OLE automation is an industry standard that applications use to expose their OLE objects to development tools, macro languages, and other applications that support OLE Automation. A spreadsheet application, for example, may expose a worksheet, chart, cell, or range of cells all as different types of objects. A word processor might expose objects such as an application, document, paragraph, or sentence.

When an application supports OLE Automation, the objects it exposes can be accessed by Visual Basic. You can use Visual Basic to manipulate these objects by invoking methods on the object or by getting and setting the object's properties. For example, if you created an OLE Automation object named `MyObj`, you might write code such as this to manipulate the object:

```
MyObj.Insert "Hello, world." 'Place text.
MyObj.Bold = True 'Format text.
MyObj.SaveAs  "C:\TEMP\TESTOBJ.DOC" 'Save the object.
```

To access another application's OLE objects, you have to provide a reference to the application's object library. The objects, functions, properties, and methods supported by an application are usually defined in the application's object library. For more information on the properties and methods supported by an application, refer to an application's documentation. In Visual Basic, shown in figure 11.11, follow these steps to load the object library of an application:

1. Choose Tools, References. The References dialog box appears, allowing you to select which object libraries to include.

2. Select the application reference or, if it is not listed, click Browse and select the appropriate file.

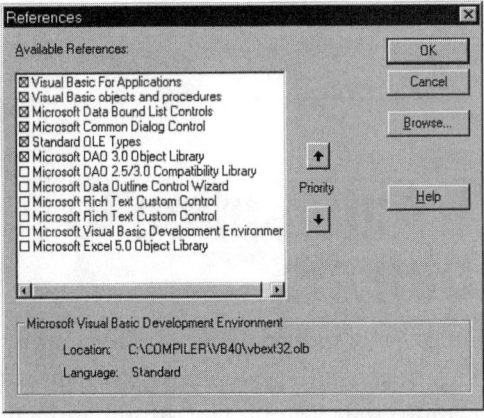

Fig. 11.11 Object library references provide a means of determining the interface to object applications' methods and properties.

An application's objects can be referenced without adding a reference to the application's object library. Adding the object library reference is preferable for the following reasons:

➤ Globally accessible functions may be accessed directly without qualification.

➤ The application will be automatically launched if it has not been previously by the first reference to it.

➤ Invocation of functions, properties, and methods may be checked at compile time for correctness; therefore, they will execute more quickly at runtime.

➤ It is possible to declare variables of the types defined in the library, which increases runtime reliability and readability.

Creating a New Object

To access another application's objects, you must define a variable to use when referencing the methods and properties of the application. The variable is then provided a reference to an object when you open communications with that application. To create a variable, you must dimension a variable of type `Object` as follows:

```
Dim Spread As Object
```

This statement uses the `Object` data type of Visual Basic and creates a variable called `Spread`. Now you must use this variable to initiate a conversation with an application. This can be accomplished with the `CreateObject()` function that creates an object of a specified type and assigns that object to your variable `Spread`. Use the following syntax to specify an object to create:

```
Application.ObjectType
```

Let's say there is a spreadsheet application named SPRDSHT.EXE that supports a worksheet object and a chart object. These objects would be defined as follows:

```
Sprdsht.Worksheet
Sprdsht.Chart
```

For other applications, refer to the application's documentation to get a list of supported objects. You can also look in the system registry, as shown in figure 11.12. As is shown, Excel supports application, chart, and sheet objects.

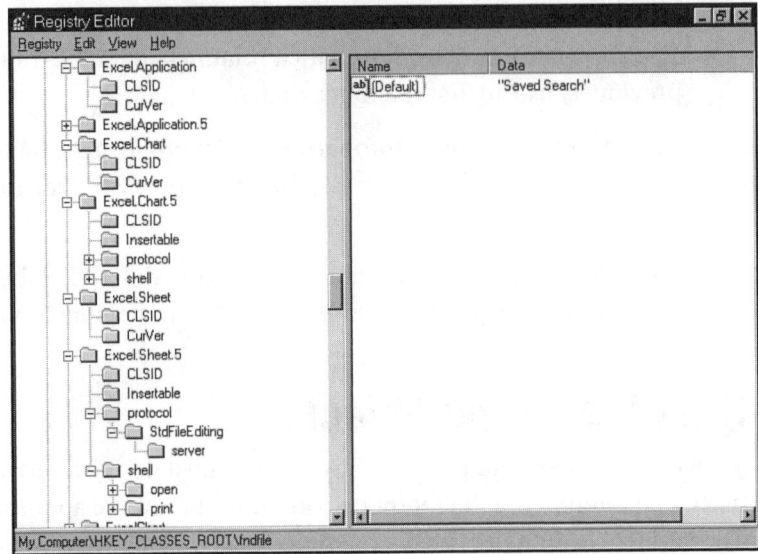

Fig. 11.12 Applications register their objects in the system registry for access by other applications.

Once you know the type of object you want to create, use the `Set` keyword to assign the object returned by the `CreateObject()` function to the object variable. When the following statement is executed, the SPRDSHT application is started and a worksheet object is created:

```
Set Spread = CreateObject("Sprdsht.Worksheet")
```

If the application is already running, the current instance of the application is used. The worksheet object's image is not embedded or linked into the Visual Basic application but instead resides in and is maintained by the spreadsheet application.

Once a class is available, you can access the objects of the class. Accessing these objects involves calling member functions or changing properties of the objects from within Visual Basic. In figure 11.13, the Visual Basic application uses a globally declared object variable named Spread.

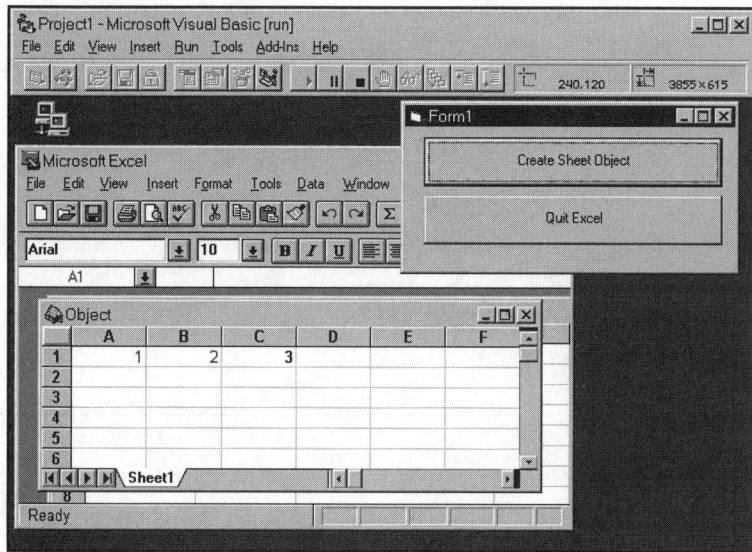

Fig. 11.13 Visual Basic can access classes and create instances of those classes in Microsoft Excel.

When the Create Sheet Object button (refer to fig. 11.13) is clicked, we use CreateObject() from Listing 11.2 to assign a sheet class of Excel to the Spread object variable. Using the Cells method of the sheet class, we place numbers at row 1-column 1 and row 1-column 2 and a formula at row 1-column 3. The final call to the Cells() method sets the Font.Bold property to True to bold the resulting value of the equation. The Quit Excel button uses the Spread.Application.Quit method to exit the Excel application and clear the Spread object.

```
'Dimension a spreadsheet object
Dim Spread As Object

Private Sub Create_Click()
    'Create a sheet object
    Set Spread = CreateObject("Excel.Sheet.5")

    'Set the values of the cells
    Spread.Cells(1, 1).Value = 1
    Spread.Cells(1, 2).Value = 2
    Spread.Cells(1, 3).Value = "=A1+B1"

    'Make the text at row 1, col 3 BOLD
    Spread.Cells(1, 3).Font.Bold = True
End Sub

Private Sub Quit_Click()
    'Quit the spreadsheet application
    Spread.Application.Quit
End Sub
```

Note: In figure 11.13, Excel was already running when the Visual Basic application was executed. Because Excel was running, OLE used the currently executing version. Otherwise, if Excel was not running it would have been started before the remainder of the code executed. If OLE had started the Excel application, it would have been invisible—the default startup state of an OLE Automation server application. To make Excel visible, the `Spread.Application.Visible = True` statement would have been used immediately following the `CreateObject()` function.

Linking to an Existing Object

Similar to object linking, you can access existing objects that reside in files saved by server applications. You can use the `GetObject()` function to activate an object that has been saved to a file.

The `GetObject()` function is similar to the `CreateObject()` function in that it initiates a conversation with an application. However, it does not create a new object. The `GetObject()` function uses an existing object and allows you to manipulate that object from within Visual Basic. For example, the function call `GetObject("C:\EXCEL\FILES\FRATE2.XLS")` will load the Excel spreadsheet application and load the file FRATE2.XLS into the spreadsheet for you. When you call the function with a path and filename, as with C:\EXCEL\FILES\FRATE2.XLS, OLE refers to the registry database to find out which application is associated with a file containing the XLS extension. The application, being Excel, is run and loaded with the file FRATE2.XLS for editing.

To activate an object from a file, first dimension an object variable as you did with `CreateObject()`, then call the `GetObject()` function using the following syntax:

```
GetObject (filename[, class])
```

The `filename` argument is a string containing the full path and name of the file you want to activate. For example, let's use SPRDSHT.EXE again and say that we created an object that was saved in a file called FRATE2.SPD. The following code invokes SPRDSHT.EXE, loads the file FRATE2.SPD, and assigns FRATE2.SPD to an object variable:

```
Dim Spread As Object
Set Spread = GetObject("C:\TEMP\FRATE2.SPD")
```

When you use `GetObject()` to activate an object, OLE determines which application to invoke and which object to activate from the system registry based on the file name you provide. Some files may support more than one class of object and require that you specify which application to use. For example, FRATE2.SPD may support an application object and a worksheet object, both of which are part of the same file. To specify which object in a file you want to activate, you use the optional `class` parameter. Here's an example of activating the worksheet object in the file FRATE2.SPD:

```
Set Spread =GetObject("C:\TEST\FRATE2.SPD","SPRDSHT.Worksheet")
```

If the *filename* argument is set to an empty string (""), the GetObject() function returns the currently active object of the class specified as the second argument. For example, the following code will return a reference to an object of the SPRDSHT.Worksheet class that may be currently running.

```
Set Spread = GetObject(,"SPRDSHT.Worksheet")
```

In figure 11.14, we are using a file that we saved from figure 11.13. As you can see, the basic structure of the code is similar except for the GetObject() function.

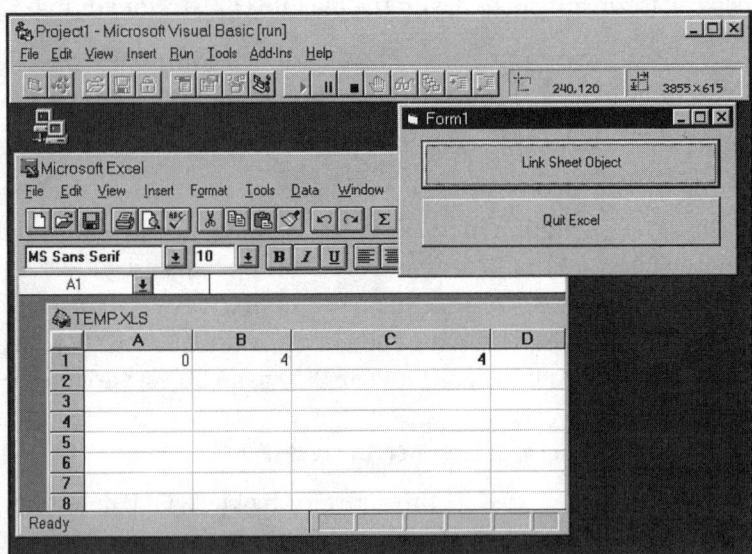

Fig. 11.14 OLE automation allows you to link Visual Basic to an existing object and perform operations on that object.

When the Link Sheet Object button is clicked, we use GetObject() from Listing 11.3 to load the file TEMP.XLS into the Excel application. The resulting sheet reference is assigned to the Spread variable. Using the Cells() method of the Sheet class, we place numbers at row 1-column 1 and row 1-column 2. We are using the equation placed into the spreadsheet from the `CreateObject()` call of figure 11.13 to add the new numbers together and display the result in row 1-column 3. As before, the Quit Excel button uses the `Spread.Application.Quit` method to exit the Excel application and clear the `Spread` object. The primary difference between this application and the one mentioned in the section "Creating a New Object" is that the Visual Basic application is using an object, a sheet in this case, that already exists. The `GetObject()` function uses classes of objects that are readily available and does not create a new object for its specific use.

> **Note:** When you use `GetObject()`, OLE looks in the system registry to locate the server associated with the object you are referencing. OLE uses the extension of a filename you specify, such as XLS or TXT, and runs the server application that services that extension. The object you are referencing is then loaded into the server application for editing.

Listing 11.3   PROJECT1.MAK—Linking an Existing Object with GetObject( )

```
'Dimension a spreadsheet object
Dim Spread As Object

Private Sub Link_Click()
    'Load the TEMP.XLS object
    Set Spread = GetObject("TEMP.XLS")

    'Set the values of the cells
    Spread.Cells(1, 1).Value = 0
    Spread.Cells(1, 2).Value = 4
    Spread.Cells(1, 3).Value = "=A1+B1"
End Sub

Private Sub Quit_Click()
    'Quit the spreadsheet application
    Spread.Application.Quit
End Sub
```

> **Note:** In figure 11.14, Excel was already running when the Visual Basic application was executed. Because Excel was running, OLE used the currently executing version. Otherwise, if Excel was not running, it would have been started before the remainder of the code executed. If OLE had started the Excel application it would have been invisible, the default startup state of an OLE Automation server application. To make Excel visible, use the `Spread.Application.Visible = True` statement immediately following the `GetObject()` function.

Manipulating Objects

Once you have created a variable that references an OLE object, you can use the object in Visual Basic in the same way as any Visual Basic object. You use the `object.property` syntax that is normally used in Visual Basic to get and set the object's properties or to perform methods on an object. By calling to the methods and properties of and object, you can use the resources of the object as well as manipulate it for your application.

Accessing an Object's Properties

Once you initiate a conversation with an application and have an available object, you manipulate the properties of the object from within Visual Basic. After creating the object, for example, you could write code such as the following to change the current cell, insert text, and save the object to a file:

```
Spread.Row = 1
Spread.Column   = 1
Spread.Insert   = "Hello, world."
Spread.SaveAs   "C:\TEMP\TEST.SPD"
```

As you have seen, you can use the OLE Control to create and display linked and embedded objects in a Visual Basic application. Some applications that supply objects support linking and embedding and also support OLE Automation. If you use the OLE Control to create a linked or embedded object and that object does support OLE Automation, you can access that object's properties and methods in Visual Basic using the `Object` property. The `Object` property returns the object in the OLE Control. This property refers to an OLE object in the same way an object variable created using the `CreateObject()` or `GetObject()` functions refers to an object.

For example, let's say an OLE Control named `OLE1` contains an object that supports OLE Automation. Let's also say that this object has an `Insert` method, a `Select` method, and a `Bold` property. In this case, you could write the following code in Listing 11.4 to manipulate the OLE Control's object:

Listing 11.4   Setting the Properties of a Visual Basic OLE Object

```
' Insert text in the object.
OLE1.Object.Insert "Hello, world."
' Select the text.
OLE1.Object.Select
' Format the text as bold.
OLE1.Object.Bold = True
```

You assign values to OLE object properties in the same manner as that of a regular variable in Visual Basic. You place the object's variable and property name on the left side of an equation and the desired property setting on the right side, as in Listing 11.5.

Listing 11.5   Assigning Values to OLE Objects

```
Dim ObjVar As Object
Dim RowPos, ColPos
Set ObjVar = CreateObject("SprdSht.Worksheet")

ObjVar.Cell(RowPos, ColPos) = "This is some test text."
```

The above code creates an object, `ObjVar`, of the class `SprdSht.Worksheet`. The code then sets the text of a cell at the row and position stored in `RowPos` and `ColPos` to the string `"This is some test text."`. This operation will work only if the object we created in

`CreateObject()` supports the `Cell()` method, so it is a good idea to check the documentation of the application to determine which methods are supported by its objects.

Retrieving information from a property is just as simple as setting the value. In the following code, we are retrieving the text from `ObjVar` and storing it into the `Variant` variable `X`.

```
Dim X
X = ObjVar.Text
```

All arguments involved with OLE Automation objects use the `Variant` data type. When retrieving a value from a property or method, OLE Automation objects always return values of the `Variant` data type. If you use a variable with a data type other than `Variant` when assigning a property value or performing a method, the variable is coerced to the `Variant` data type.

Performing Methods

In addition to getting and setting properties, you can manipulate an object by using the methods it supports. In a manner similar to that of executing Visual Basic methods on internal objects, you can access the methods of applications that expose their object for OLE Automation.

Some object methods may return a value to the calling Visual Basic application while others do not return any values. Methods that do not return a value behave like a subroutine. If you assign such a method to a variable, an error occurs.

The code in Listing 11.6 uses a function called `IsBold`, which is a method of the `Text` property of `ObjVar`. The function returns a value to the `Variant X`, which is used to determine execution through the remainder of the application.

Listing 11.6   Performing Methods on OLE Objects

```
X = ObjVar.Text.IsBold
If X Then
     ObjVar.Text = "The text is bold."
```

```
Else
      ObjVar.Text = "The text is not bold."
End If

' This method requires two arguments.
ObjVar.Move XPos, YPos
```

Some OLE Automation objects contain subobjects. A cell could be considered a subobject of a spreadsheet object. You can include multiple
objects, properties, and methods on the same line of code using the
dot syntax, just as you would with a Visual Basic object. For example,
the following code is setting the `FontBold` property of the cell returned
by the method `Cell()` of the `ObjVar` object.

```
ObjVar.Cell(1,1).FontBold = True
```

Closing an Object

All OLE Automation objects support some method that closes the object and the application that created it. Because OLE objects can use a
significant amount of memory in your Visual Basic application, it is a
good idea to explicitly close an object when you no longer need it. To
close an object, use the appropriate method, such as the following
example:

```
' Closes the object.
ObjVar.Close
' Closes the application that created the object.
ObjVar.Application.Quit
```

The user can close an object using the application that created the
object. When an object has been closed, either programmatically or by
the user, any object variables that refer to the object are set to NULL.
This NULL value represents that the object variable is no longer assigned
an object.

If you define an object locally within a procedure and the variable loses
scope when you leave the procedure, the object and its application are
not closed. However, you can no longer use that object variable to refer
to the object. Attempting to use the object variable will return the error

`Object Variable Not Set`. If the application is still running and the object is still active, you can use the `GetObject()` function to assign another object variable to the object.

```
Set Spread = GetObject(,"SPRDSHT.Worksheet")
```

Limitations

Even though you can perform a multitude of OLE operations from within Visual Basic applications, some features of objects supported by OLE cannot be accessed by Visual Basic applications. Such circumstances involve the limits on access to data that is specific or unique to an application. For example, Visual Basic cannot exchange user-defined types effectively with another application because that user-defined type may not be known to the other application. Passing an unknown type to another application can have unforeseen affects since the other application will not know how to handle the unknown data type. The following sections discuss some of these limitations.

Arrays and User-Defined Types

Some OLE objects contain properties and methods that use arrays as arguments. Visual Basic has the following limitations when using arrays with OLE objects:

➤ Visual Basic cannot use an array or a user-defined type as an argument to a method.

➤ Visual Basic cannot set a property using an array or a user-defined type.

➤ Visual Basic cannot assign a variable of an array or of a user-defined type to the return value of a property or method.

If you want to access an array returned from a property or user-defined type, you should use the `LBound()` and `UBound()` functions to determine the size of the array. Once the size is determined, you can access the individual elements of the array one at a time.

The code in Listing 11.7 increments `I` through each element of the array. Using `I`, the value of each array element is placed into `Value`, which can then be used in code that you require to use on the elements of the array.

Listing 11.7   Accessing Arrays within Specified Bounds

```
Dim I, Value
For I = LBound(ObjVar.Selection) To UBound(ObjVar.Selection)
    Value = ObjVar.Selection(I)
    .
    (Your code that uses Value)
    .
Next
```

Named Arguments

When calling an object's methods from Visual Basic you cannot use named arguments. A *named argument* is one that contains the name of the argument followed by the value of the argument. For example, the following lines of code use named arguments:

```
FileOpen Name = "MYDOC.DOC", ReadOnly = 0, Password = "Mahler"
FileOpen ReadOnly = 0, Name = "MYDOC.DOC", Password = "Mahler"
```

When calling a method using named arguments, you can pass the arguments in any order desired because the names of the arguments will correlate the values in the called method. In Visual Basic, however, you cannot use named arguments.

When calling from Visual Basic a method that supports named arguments, you must specify each argument being passed to the method in the order specified in the argument list of the called method. If you want to omit one of the optional arguments for the method you should leave it blank.

```
' Each argument specified in the correct order.
ObjVar.FileOpen "MYDOC.DOC", 0, "Mahler"
' The second argument is omitted.
ObjVar.FileOpen "MYDOC.DOC", , "Mahler"
```

Collections

A *collection* is an object that contains objects of one specific class. Many objects that support collections can be referenced in a singular form and a plural form. For example, a collection of menus for a particular application can be accessed using a `Menu` object and a `Menus` object. Collections are, however, usually accessed using the plural form. A collection of `Row` objects in a spreadsheet is referenced by `Rows` and a collections of a `Cell` object is referenced by `Cells`.

In order to determine the number of elements in a collection, many collections support a property called `Count`. This property returns the number of elements of the specific type in the collection. For example, the property `ObjVar.Rows.Count` returns the number of rows in the object variable `ObjVar`.

To access an individual element of a collection you use an index in a manner similar to that of an array. For example, `Rows(1)` returns the first row of an object while `Rows(Rows.Count)` returns the last row.

When accessing an OLE collection object you may encounter the following two problems:

➤ There is no guarantee the subscripts of the collection are numeric.

➤ If a collection does return a numeric subscript, there is no guarantee that the subscripts are contiguous.

Some OLE collection objects allow access to methods that enable you to iterate through the collections. If an object does not explicitly provide methods for doing this, you may not be able to cycle through an object's collections in your Visual Basic program.

If you know that a collection indeed uses a numeric subscript, you can iterate through it. You'll need to provide error trapping, however, because you don't know if the subscripts are contiguous.

To add a twist to accessing collections, some collections do not use numeric subscripts. For example, if an object has a collection of fonts, instead of using numeric subscripts, the `Fonts` collection might use string subscripts. In code, the collection might look like this:

```
ObjVar.Fonts("Courier")
ObjVar.Fonts("Helvetica")
ObjVar.Fonts("Arial")
```

In essence, collections may be seen as arrays that may be accessed either by numeric offset or by a textual index. In either case, the collection allows you to reference any number of like elements available within a given application.

From Here...

In this chapter we discussed the elements of OLE Automation and how it is implemented with Visual Basic 4. OLE servers (or object applications) provide methods and properties that can be manipulated from OLE clients (or controlling applications). From Visual Basic you can use the OLE Control to embed or link objects as well as perform automation on those objects. You can also create instances of objects programatically to access the members and methods of those objects.

For more information, refer to the following chapters:

➤ For information on OLE server applications, refer to Chapter 12, "OLE Servers."

➤ To examine the use of OLE servers by client applications, refer to Chapter 13, "OLE Container Classes."

➤ To further examine the differences and similarities of Visual Basic and Visual Basic for Applications, refer to Chapter 22, "VB Versus VBA."

12

OLE Servers

by Edward B. Toupin

This chapter introduces you to the concepts of OLE from a server application perspective. We first take a look at exactly what an OLE server is, the different types of servers, and how servers fit into the OLE hierarchy. We then examine some of the capabilities of a Visual Basic OLE server and operations that you can perform under Windows.

Once the basics are covered, we will step through the development of a Visual Basic OLE server application, including debugging and application distribution. The application will give you a taste of OLE development from the ground up. Make sure to keep the server that we develop in this chapter because it will be used in the next chapter when we discuss OLE clients and their development.

The following topics will be covered about OLE servers:

➤ The capabilities of a Visual Basic server

➤ How an OLE server is developed and used

➤ What is a Visual Basic Object Application?

➤ Registering an OLE server with the system registry

➤ Limitations of Visual Basic OLE servers

What Is an OLE Server?

OLE provides a foundation for integration through a set of interfaces. These interfaces are exposed as a set of methods and properties that allow programmatic control of one application by another. Exposing the functionality of applications for access by another makes OLE a very *open* and *extensible* technology. The concept of being open means that the functionality of an application may be shared by many applications. OLE extensibility represents the ability to expand the basic functionality of one application by incorporating the functionality of other applications.

OLE servers are those applications which expose their functionality to allow client applications access to the functionality of the server. A server provides a set of services to container applications including embedding, linking, and visual editing.

Types of Servers

Visual editing servers create OLE objects for use by container applications and allow these container applications to incorporate the functionality of the server into the application itself. Visual editing server applications can support both embedded and linked objects but can perform only visual editing on embedded objects because linked objects are file-based. The one common feature of all visual editing server applications is that they all support activation by container applications when you want to edit an object.

A *full server* is an application that can be run as a standalone application or can be launched by container applications. A full server has the ability to save documents as files on disk when run standalone and can also support linking and embedding when launched by a container. Some full servers can support linking only while others can support embedding only. However, the norm for a full server is to support both methods of object interaction.

A *mini server* is a server application that can be run only when launched by a container application. A mini server cannot save documents as files on a disk but instead uses the objects stored in the container application from which it was launched. As a result, a mini server can support embedding only, not linking. Examples of mini servers are Microsoft Draw, Microsoft Graph, and Microsoft Equation.

An *automation server*, also known as an *object application*, is an application that provides a service other than linking and embedding to other applications. OLE Automation provides a means of taking advantage of extensibility of Windows-based applications by allowing the integration of application functionality. Using OLE Automation, you can create applications that expose objects and their interfaces to programming tools and macro languages to provide a means of incorporating the server's capabilities into one or more applications. Applications that utilize the capabilities of OLE Automation servers are known as *controlling applications* because they control the functions of the OLE Automation servers with which they are communicating.

> **Note:** With regards to linking, embedding, and visual editing, the applications that utilize OLE servers are called containers because they *contain* objects created by the servers. With OLE Automation applications that use OLE Automation, servers are called controllers because they *control* the functions of the automation servers with which they are communicating.

There is a point that is reached during the development of an object application where the requirements of a controlling application exceed the functional capabilities of the object application. In such a situation it is beneficial to move to OLE custom control (OCX) technology.

Windows-based applications take advantage of OLE Automation to use code from other applications. Through Visual Basic, you can obtain references to objects in another application and make calls to the application's internal functions as if the code were located in your application. The syntax, type, and number of parameters for each object and function are defined in the application's object library, which provides a detailed map of each of the applications objects.

Visual Basic OLE Servers

Visual Basic allows you to develop object applications that expose their objects for use by many different controlling applications. As you can see in figure 12.1, the controlling application is using the object library for the Visual Basic object application to locate, or map, the methods and properties of the object application. These mapped methods and properties of the object application can be executed by any Windows controlling applications.

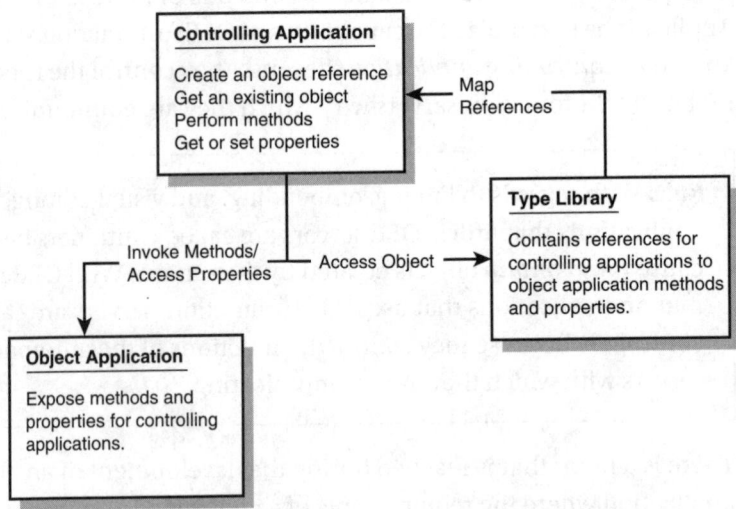

Fig. 12.1 Controlling applications use the Type Library to execute methods and use members of Object applications.

Visual Basic OLE Automation Objects

Objects exposed to controlling applications by object applications are known as OLE Automation objects. Object applications can expose any number of objects to be used by controlling applications. OLE Automation uses what is known as the *component object model* to allow programmers to manipulate an application's objects from outside that object application.

Component Object Model

The *component object model*, the result of a consortium for establishing standards as well as the key to OLE's extensible architecture, defines how objects interact with one another, both within an application and between separate applications. The foundation of the model on which the rest of OLE is built provides mechanisms that support multiple interfaces between an object application and controlling applications (see fig. 12.2). The architecture is divided into services supported by the component object model (interface negotiation, memory management, error and status reporting, and task-to-task communications) and other basic services built on the model.

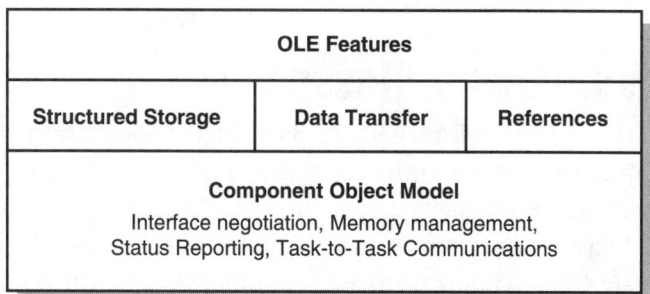

Fig. 12.2 The Component Object Model provides a foundation for communications and data sharing between applications.

The model defines an interface by which a controlling application can communicate with an object application that provides a service for the requesting controlling application. Through the model, each object application can support multiple interfaces to service multiple controlling applications, who may query about support for a specific interface or service.

The model provides a mechanism for task-to-task communications, which provides a means of allowing objects to communicate with controlling applications. This mechanism allows communications to exist across application boundaries so that controlling applications can pass information to the objects of object applications and visa versa.

The model also provides a means of dynamically loading and destroying objects. When an object is requested, the object application in which the requested object exists is loaded or, if the application is already running, the existing object application is accessed.

Each access made by a controlling application increments a reference counter so that the model will know how many interfaces are currently active for an object application. Likewise, as controlling applications release control over an object application, the reference counter is decremented. When all references—and subsequent interfaces—are released, the object application is removed from memory, and that memory is freed by OLE.

Visual Basic Classes

To create objects from a Visual Basic object application, Visual Basic maintains modules known as *classes*. Each class defines a template for the creation of objects that are used by controlling applications. A Visual Basic class is similar to a data type in that it describes what type of object you are referring to. For example, Visual Basic provides an intrinsic integer data type. In order to use that data type, you have to create a variable of type `Integer`. With classes, you create a base class (the data type) but before you can use that class you have to create an object (the variable).

Because most of the discussion in this chapter concerns the behavior of the objects you create, the term *object* is sometimes used in place of *class*—but do not confuse the two terms. Objects are instances of classes where a `Worksheet` object is an instance of a `Worksheet` class. The `Worksheet` class is the template that is used to create multiple instances of the class as `Worksheet` objects. Each instance is a usable object accessible by controlling applications.

Visual Basic classes define methods and properties that are exposed to other applications. The methods of the class are used by controlling applications to perform actions on an object while the properties describe the characteristics of an object. When an object of a particular class is created, certain methods and properties become visible to the accessing application. In some cases properties are accessed by procedures known as *property procedures*. One property procedure might set a particular property's value while the another might retrieve that property's value and return the value to the controlling application.

Designing an Object Hierarchy

An object hierarchy describes the interaction of objects both within an object application and with controlling applications. In object applications that supply more than one object, the application has an object hierarchy. The exposed objects may or may not be related to each other. If they are related, there is often a dependent relationship where the existence of some object cannot exist outside of the context of a higher-level object.

Visual Basic allows you to create object hierarchies in which some objects can be directly created by controlling applications as well as those that cannot. For example, you can set the `Creatable` property of a Visual Basic class to `False` if you don't want controlling applications to create a dependent object directly. You can then define a top-level class that includes a method to produce instances of the dependent classes for the controlling applications. This way, all controlling applications must go through the top-level class to reach the dependent objects.

In figure 12.3, `Class2` is a higher-level class than `Class1`. Because `Class1` is dependent on `Class2` in our hierarchy, you must use the methods of `Class2::Object1` or `Class2::Object2` to access the methods and properties of objects of `Class1`. `Class3::Object1` and `Class3::Object2` are independent objects of `Class3` and can be accessed directly by controlling applications.

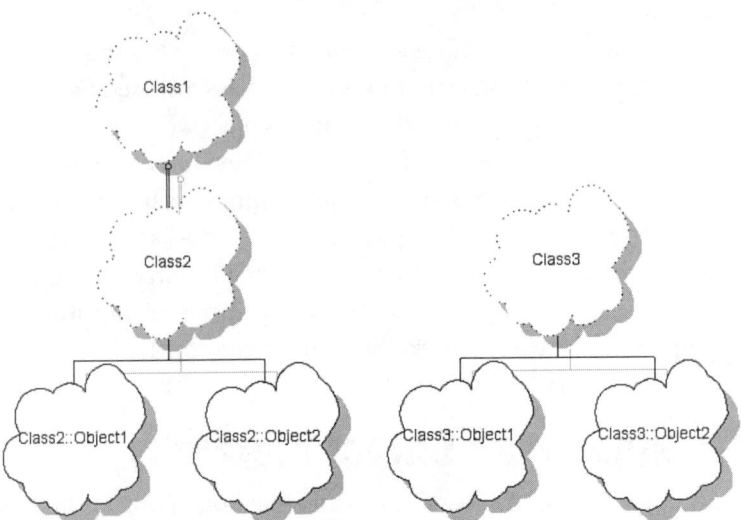

Fig. 12.3 Classes and their objects are arranged into object hierarchies.

As with `Class2` and `Class3` of figure 12.3, a Visual Basic class whose `Instancing` property is set to `Creatable MultiUse` or `Creatable SingleUse` and `Public` property is set to `True` defines an externally creatable object. Such creatable objects are higher-level objects that can be used to navigate to and use the methods and properties of dependent objects. You can make these creatable objects externally using `CreateObject()` from a controlling application to directly create an instance (object) of the class from outside the application.

> **Note:** OLE objects defined in an OLE Automation object hierarchy are actually OLE classes. The best way to remember the difference is that an object is an instance of a class.

To organize your objects into a hierarchy, you need to define in each higher-level object a method that returns a reference to dependent objects. For example, the externally creatable object `Plane` defines an `AddPassenger()` method. The `Passenger` class, dimensioned as `X`, is dependent on the `Plane` class, as shown in Listing 12.1.

Listing 12.1   Accessing Dependent Objects Through Independent Object Methods

```
Public Function AddPassenger As Passenger (NumOfBags as
Integer)
    Dim X As New Passenger
    X.Bags = NumOfBags
    Me.Passenger = X
    AddPassenger = X
End Function
```

In the preceding code, `X` is defined as an object of the `Passenger` class. The `New` keyword allows you to dynamically create an object of an OLE class of the local application in a `Dim` statement. Once the object is instantiated, you have access to the methods and properties of the object. In this instance you are gaining access to the methods and properties of the `Passenger` class.

A controlling application cannot obtain a reference to a `Passenger` object because the object, in this example, is not creatable and is a dependent object of `Plane`. However, a controlling application can use the `Passenger` object indirectly by first accessing the `Plane` object from an application named `Ticketing` and then using the new object referenced by `DC10` to access its `AddPassenger` method.

```
DC10 = CreateObject("Ticketing.Plane")
DC10.AddPassenger(2)
```

Creating an OLE Server in Visual Basic

In addition to the requirements for Windows-based application development in Visual Basic, OLE Automation requires a few additional things of a server. As you can see in figure 12.4, you must execute a logical sequence of actions to create an object application in Visual Basic.

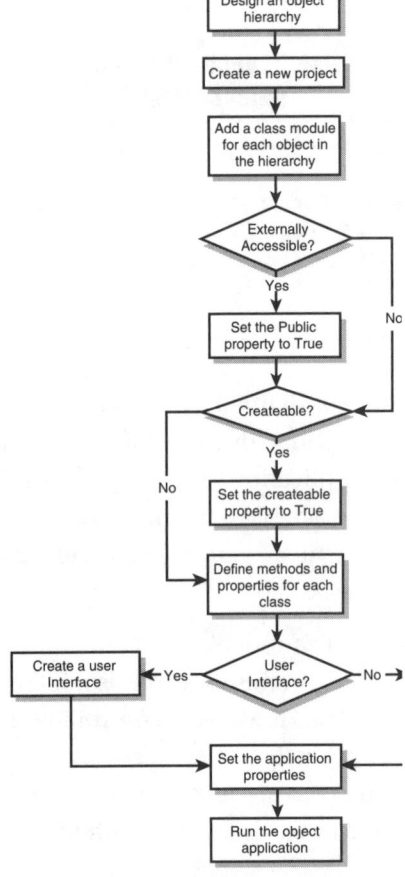

Fig. 12.4 To create an object application, several sequential steps must be taken for proper implementation.

The process is simple and parallels some of the things you already know about Visual Basic programming. When it comes to running and using your application, however, the code will be shared with other applications, and the project will take on a different look and feel.

It is essential that you plan your application's object model, or hierarchy. If you do not have a properly planned hierarchy, your application may not be easy to use by controlling applications and may not fit into the standards established for object application interfacing. We will be discussing some of these standards later in the section "Standards and Guidelines."

First determine which classes you will need for your application. Each object in your hierarchy will correspond to one Visual Basic class with all properties and methods for each object defined in a class module. Determine the visibility of your objects—will they be creatable by a controlling application or will they be dependent upon another internal class of the object application. For each class, determine the properties and methods to be used within the instantiated objects of your classes.

As you can see in figure 12.5, we have two independent classes—`Picture` and `Calc`. The `Picture` class has methods and properties to display a picture on a Visual Basic form when commanded by a controlling application. The `Calc` class contains methods and properties to perform some minor calculations and storage of values.

Note: To create a new project, choose File, New from the Visual Basic menu. Visual Basic will clear its working area and display an empty form to allow you to begin work on the new project.

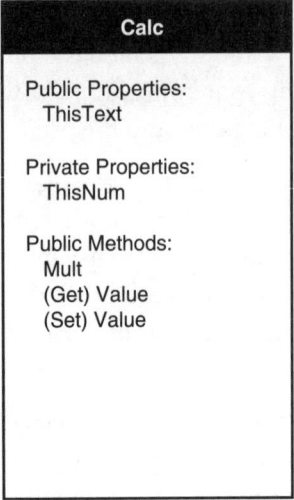

Fig. 12.5 The base classes contain members and methods that are inherited by derived classes and are used by instantiated objects of the classes

Adding Classes

You must add one class module for each class that you defined in your object hierarchy. To create a new class, choose Insert, Class Module from the Visual Basic menu. Each new class module that you add will be the template of each object created and used by controlling applications. In these class modules you will add the methods and properties you defined in the classes of your hierarchy.

For this object application you will want to create two classes—one for Calc and the other for Picture. As in figure 12.6, you set the Name property for one class module to Calc and the other to Picture in the property list for the respective module. Controlling applications use the Name property to create object variables that reference the class. In the following example, an application is creating an object variable, X, that uses the Calc class of the AutoSrvr object application:

```
Set X = CreateObject("AutoSrvr.Calc")
```

Fig. 12.6 The properties of classes provide a means of establishing the operational characteristics of a class.

Class Public Property

In our object hierarchy, both classes are independent classes and should be made accessible to all controlling applications. Referring back to figure 12.6, you will want to set the `Public` property for the `Picture` and `Calc` class modules to `True` so that objects of either class can be used by controlling applications.

All classes whose `Public` property is set to `True` are registered in the system registry to make them visible to all applications who may request access to the object application's classes. If set to `False`, the class is available within the project only, and any instances of that class are not visible nor are they accessible outside of the object application.

Class Creatable Property

To allow controlling applications access to the objects of classes, we must set the `Public` property to `True`. We want to allow controlling applications to be able to create objects of the two classes using

CreateObject(). Referring back to figure 12.6, you will want to set the Instancing property for the Picture and Calc class modules to either Creatable SingleUse or Creatable MultiUse. Creatable SingleUse allows a controlling application to create a single object of the class. Creatable MultiUse allows a controlling application to create multiple instances of a given class.

> **Note:** Classes defined in a class module are always accessible and creatable within your project, even if the class properties of your project are set to False. Setting the Instancing property to any of the mentioned settings except for Not Creatable allows controlling applications access to your classes.

Defining Public Methods and Properties

Now that the class modules are established, we need to write the methods and properties for the two classes. In both class modules, you can declare public and private methods, properties, and constants for the class.

Private declarations to be hidden in your applications—not accessible by controlling applications—can be implemented as private procedures in a standard Visual Basic module or as private members in a class module. OLE Automation objects are public declarations implemented as public methods and properties in public class modules. Class methods are defined as Functions and Sub procedures within the class modules; properties are defined as public variables, constants, or property procedures.

Calc Class

In the Calc class module we define two variables, one Public and one Private. The Public variable, ThisText, is directly accessible by controlling applications while the Private variable, ThisNum, is accessible only from within the class. We can directly set the values of Public variables within the object application and from controlling applications. `Private` variables are accessible through class methods only and not directly by controlling applications.

```
'Properties
Dim ThisNum As Integer
Public ThisText As String
```

We now define the methods specific to our class. The first `Public` method is `Mult()`, which accepts two values from a controlling application, multiplies them together, and returns the result. As you may have noticed, the code for this function is identical to the definition of a function in a standard Visual Basic module. Because the function is defined as `Public` in a public class module the function is accessible by controlling applications. If defined as `Private`, the function would be visible to the class module only (see Listing 12.2).

Listing 12.2 OLESRVR.MAK—Methods in the Calc Class Accessible by External Client Applications

```
'Multiply two values
Public Function Mult(X As Integer, Y As Integer) As Integer
    Mult = X * Y
End Function

'Property function to retrieve values
Public Property Let Value(X)
    ThisNum = X
End Property

Public Property Get Value()
    Value = ThisNum
End Property
```

The two property procedures define operations that occur on properties. Similar to a function, a `Property Let` procedure is a procedure that can take arguments, execute a series of statements, and change the value of class properties as required. Unlike a function, however, you can use a `Property Let` procedure only on the left-hand side of a property assignment expression or `Let` statement. For instance, a controlling application would use a `Property Let Value(X)` procedure as follows:

```
Dim AutoSrvr As Object
Set AutoSrvr = CreateObject("AutoSrvr.Calc")
AutoSrvr.Value = 10
```

As you can see, the `Property Let` procedure is assigned a value as though it were a standard variable. Visual Basic takes the value of `10` from the assignment and passes it to the `Value` procedure as the `x` argument of the procedure.

`Property Get` procedures are similar to functions in that they can be used on the right-hand side of an expression in the same way you use a function to return values. The `Property Get` procedure returns the values of and performs operations on properties of a class. For instance, a controlling application would use a `Property Get Value()` procedure as follows:

```
X = AutoSrvr.Value
```

As is shown in the sample code above, `x` is assigned the value of the property from the value returned by the `Property Get` procedure. Visual Basic gets the value from the `ThisNum` private variable and returns it to be stored in `x`.

Visual Basic determines which property procedure to execute based on the position of that procedure in an expression. The property procedures located on the left-hand side of an expression notify Visual Basic that it is to call a corresponding `Property Let` procedure. Property procedures on the right-hand side of the expression inform Visual Basic to call the corresponding `Property Get` procedure. If you are assigning objects, you can also write statements for a `Property Set` procedure that would be located on the right-hand side of an expression in a controlling application.

Note: In most cases, it is preferable to use property procedures when accessing class properties. Within a property procedure you can write statements that can perform some level of error checking, validation, or calculation before performing a assignment to or retrieval from the respective property of the class.

Picture Class

The `Picture` class is much simpler than the `Calc` class in that we are only defining one `Public Sub` and no properties. The `Sub` creates a new form and loads a picture, specified by the controlling application, into a picture control on the form, shown in Listing 12.3.

Listing 12.3   OLESRVR.MAK—Method of the Picture Class

```
'Load a picture into a new form
Public Sub DispPicture(Picfile As String)
    'Create a new form instance
    Dim PicForm As New Form1

    'Load a picture into the picture control
    PicForm.Picture1.Picture = LoadPicture(Picfile)

    'Show the form
    PicForm.Show
End Sub
```

The `Sub` first creates a new form using the `New` operator and stores the reference to the form in `PicForm`. This form is a new instance of a form containing a picture control created for the object application. The `LoadPicture()` function uses the name of the picture passed by the controlling application in the `Picture` parameter. The loaded picture is stored and displayed in the picture control `Picture1` located on the new form. Each time that this `Sub` is called from a controlling application, a new form is created to display the specified picture.

Scoping Issues

When developing classes for your object application, you should take care when determining the visibility of your methods and properties. Because we are managing class modules and controlling applications, standard Visual Basic modules, and forms, you must properly determine the scoping of your methods and properties throughout your application.

Some general items that you should pay attention to are as follows:

➤ Data that you want to be global to your object application and not accessible by controlling applications should be placed in a standard module and declared `Public`.

➤ Data that you want to be private for each specific instance of a class should be placed in a class module and declared `Private`.

➤ Methods and property procedures declared as `Public` in a public class module cannot have a private argument or return a user-defined type declared as `Private`.

➤ Methods and properties declared as `Public` in a public class module are available to modules within the application and to controlling applications.

➤ User-defined types are supported by Visual Basic 4 in class modules but can be accessible within the object application only.

➤ Methods or property procedures that pass user-defined types as arguments can be declared `Private` only, because the user-defined types are valid within the object application only.

Object application classes can expose properties and methods of any public OLE Automation data type. Some of the public data types include the following:

➤ Classes that are provided as a reference by an object library similar to the references provided to Visual Basic in the Tools, References menu selection.

➤ Objects provided by Visual Basic for Applications (VBA) including the `Error` and `Collection` data types.

➤ All intrinsic data types provided by Visual Basic (such as integer and float).

On the other hand, object applications cannot expose to controlling applications properties and methods of private data type instances within a given object application. The class instances (objects) that cannot be exposed to controlling applications are as follows:

➤ The objects provided in the Visual Basic object library.

➤ Private classes and forms defined in the current object application's project.

➤ Classes defined by a Visual Basic type library.

In object applications, public methods or properties in a public class can have an argument or return a value with a type of a private class. For instance, you can create an object variable of type `RecordSet` that would have the standard set of properties and methods of the Visual Basic `RecordSet` class. However, you cannot declare a public variable of type `Form`, because an object of type `Form` cannot expose public properties, be used as a public return type, or be passed in a public argument list.

> **Note:** Arrays and fixed-length strings must be declared as `Private` in class modules because they are user-defined data types.

In your object application, try to avoid using public variables outside of the class module in which the variable is defined. Because multiple instances of class objects can exist simultaneously, they can also share any application-wide global data. If you make the assumption that a single object is the only object accessing a particular global data, you could run into a situation where each object of the class may change the one global data, producing erroneous results.

Initialization Code

Each class module has `Initialize` and `Terminate` events built-in to allow you to write code to be executed when an object of a class is instantiated or destroyed. When a class is first initialized, Visual Basic executes the `Initialize` procedure to perform operations on the instantiated object before any other code is executed—also known as a *constructor*.

When an object for a given class is terminated, Visual Basic executes the `Terminate` procedure to the class immediately before the class is destroyed—as known as a *destructor*. In Visual Basic 4, you can define additional methods specific to your class only, but you cannot define additional application events in class modules. The event procedures are selected by first selecting `Class` in the Object list then selecting `Initialize` or `Terminate` from the `Proc` list.

Application Object

Each object application should have an `Application` object that maintains information specific to the application. This information is made available to controlling applications in the form of properties or property procedures.

To create an `Application` object for your application, first create a class, `AppClass`, that contains properties to describe your application. To initialize the `Application` object, declare a public variable in a standard module of the object application that references the class.

```
Public GlobalApp As New AppClass
```

In each class you create for your object hierarchy of your object application, you will define the `Application` object. If you decide that a class module in the object application has an `Application` property, include the following declaration at the class module level:

```
Public Application As AppClass
```

In the `Initialize` event procedure of each class module, assign the instance of the `Application` object for your class to an `Application` property for the class.

```
Set Application = GlobalApp
```

Through the above steps, each instance of a class can contain an `Application` property, which is a reference to single instance of the `Application` object. An `Application` object cannot be used to create multiple instances of a Visual Basic object application because the same `Application` object serves all controlling applications that access the object application.

Finalizing the Created OLE Server

Once the classes are created and the methods are completed, you can continue to finalize the application. The first thing to look at when completing an OLE server is to determine whether or not you will require a user interface. This is important since, in some cases, you will need direct interaction with the classes while in other you can simply use the interface of the controlling application. To complete the task, you can select the desired options for compilation of the object application then compile the application for execution.

Developing a User Interface

Although the classes you create in Visual Basic cannot support visual editing, you can have them display forms from your Visual Basic object application. In general, object applications fall into one of the following three categories with regards to user interface:

➤ Object applications that have their own user interface—An Excel spreadsheet, for example, is a complete application, but it also supplies objects that can be used by other applications.

➤ Object applications that provide dialog boxes—Some object applications can display information to the user and maintain a common user interface for all controlling applications.

➤ Object applications that have no user interface but exist strictly to provide objects to other applications—Data access objects in Microsoft Access supplies no user interface at all but instead provides data access functionality to controlling applications.

There is no mandate requiring a user interface for your application. If you want to display a user interface, however, you need to include a form in your object application. For example, the `Picture` class of our object application uses the `Form1` form. For each instance of the `Picture` class you have one instance of `Form1` loaded to display a picture.

An object application must have a designated starting place, whether it is a form (in the form of a user interface) or a procedure. Because this object application has a user interface, the starting place will be `Form1`.

To specify this starting form, the name of the form, `Form1`, is selected in the `Startup Form` field of the Project tab in the Tools, Options dialog box. Because `Form1` is the starting place of the application, that form is going to be displayed the first time the object application is called to create an instance of a class. When the form is displayed, the form's `Load` event will be called before the object's `Initialize` event.

If we were not going to have a visible user interface but only provide objects to other applications, the Startup Form field should be set to `Sub Main` of the Project tab in the Tools, Options dialog box. `Sub Main` is a procedure that you declare in a Visual Basic module that contains initialization code for the application. If necessary, you can leave the procedure empty; however, there must be a `Sub Main` procedure if no form is to be used.

```
Sub Main()
    'Your initialization code goes here
End Sub
```

> **Caution:** A `Sub Main` in a class module is treated as an object method named `Main`, not as a startup procedure. In order for Visual Basic to use a `Sub Main`, it must be defined in a global module. Do not attempt to pass an instance of a form as a return value or as a `ByRef` argument to an object's method. Forms are instances of private classes that cannot be used outside of the project. Forms are not exposed as classes or members of a class.

Choosing Project Options

The Project tab of the Tools, Options dialog box (see fig. 12.7) allows you to set the Project Name, StartMode, and Application Description properties for the project. This information is required for an object application to establish information for the system registry and application operation.

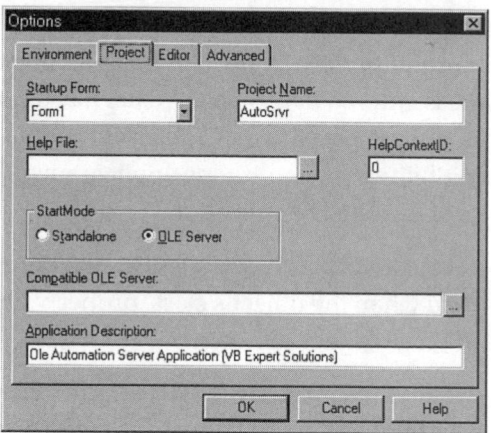

Fig. 12.7 Project properties allow you to establish the characteristics of the resultant application.

➤ The Project Name is used as the `projectname` argument in the `CreateObject()` and `GetObject()` statements. For this object application, set the Project Name to `AutoSrvr`. When controlling applications attempt to access this application, the statements would be as follows:

```
Set variable = CreateObject("AutoSrvr.Calc")
Set variable = CreateObject("AutoSrvr.Picture")
Set variable = GetObject(,"AutoSrvr.Calc")
Set variable = GetObject(,"AutoSrvr.Picture")
```

➤ The StartMode option determines whether your application is a standalone executable or an OLE Automation server. For this application, select the OLE Server option.

➤ The text you enter in the Application Description field will be used in the Tools, References dialog box to identify your object application to controlling applications.

➤ The Help file contains information about object methods and procedures for the application and is used when the ? button of the View, Object Browser is clicked. If a Help file is created, set the Help File field to the name of the help file.

➤ The Compatible Object Application is the name of the .EXE file for the current project, if the .EXE file is an object application. If a file name is entered in this field, Visual Basic verifies that any changes to a project with a public class module will not introduce incompatibilities for controlling applications that used previous versions of the object application.

➤ The `Description` property sets the text that appears in the comments field when the object's class, property, or method is selected in View, Object Browser.

➤ The `HelpContextID` property is used to provide context-sensitive help when the ? button is clicked for a class, property, or method in View, Object Browser.

> **Note:** You can set the `Description` and `HelpContextID` properties for each method and property of a class through View, Object Browser. For each class you can set `Description` and `HelpContextID` values for only public methods, property procedures, and the class itself. You cannot set these values for properties defined simply as data members.

Running the Application

In the Visual Basic environment you can run the object application by choosing Run, Start. Once elected, Visual Basic registers your object application's classes with the system registry for access by controlling applications. You can now run a controlling application to gain access to and manipulate the object application's classes.

Using a Visual Basic OLE Server

The purpose of developing an object application is to expose objects that provide functionality to accessing controlling applications. Controlling applications that access those objects decide which objects to use and when to use them; the object application merely provides the requested objects to the requester. To provide visibility of object applications for use, the object application must first be registered in the system registry. Once registered, OLE Automation starts your object application when a controlling application requests the services of an object from the object application.

> **Note:** With Visual Basic, you can create object applications in the form of executable (EXE) files that supply object libraries. You cannot create object applications as Dynamic Link Libraries (DLLs) with Visual Basic 4.

Registering an OLE Server

You have seen how the system registration database contains information about all object classes and their servers installed on the user's machine. To make this scheme work, all server applications should register themselves in the server registration database, preferably at the time of installation.

To register a Visual Basic application you should run the application with the /REGSERVER on the command line. This will start your object application, have it register its classes with the system registry, then shut down and wait for requests by controlling applications. If you run you object application for the first time without the /REGSERVER on the command line, the server application will register its classes and then remain running.

```
olesrvr /REGSERVER
```

To verify that the application is registered, look in REGEDIT to see registered classes. As shown in figure 12.8, the AutoSrvr object application of this chapter is registered in REGEDIT and can provide its objects, Calc and Picture, for use by controlling applications.

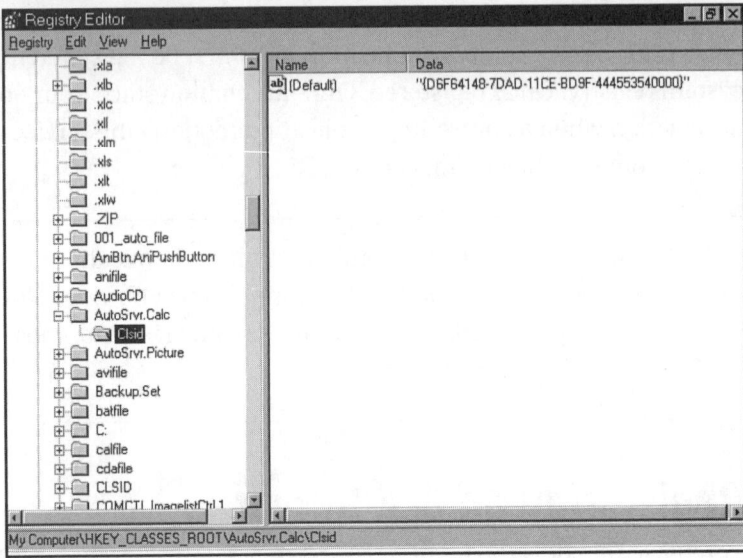

Fig. 12.8 Once registered in the system registry, the `AutoSrvr` server application is available for access by controlling applications.

Removing an Object Application from the System Registry

As you develop your application and run different versions repeatedly, especially when debugging, the OLE system registry may get filled with obsolete entries. It is a good idea to clean out the registry periodically to keep it at a minimum size. You can remove these entries from the registry in the following two ways:

➤ You can run the older versions of your object application with the `/UNREGSERVER` command-line argument.

➤ You can use REGEDIT.EXE periodically to remove entries of obsolete versions of your object application. REGEDIT.EXE includes a Help file with online instructions (see fig. 12.9).

If you run your object application with the /UNREGSERVER option, Visual Basic deletes the following keys in the system registry:

➤ The matching ROOT entry (such as *projectname.class*), regardless of whether the value of the CLSID key in the ROOT entry matches the CLSID of the object application.

➤ The matching CLSID entry.

➤ The matching Interface IDs for the interfaces that the EXE file supports.

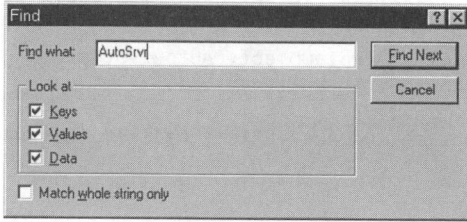

Fig. 12.9 REGEDIT provides a search facility that enables you to rapidly locate entries in the system registry.

Starting an Object Application

OLE Automation automatically starts your object application when a controlling application requests an object from your application. At that point, the object application is started, a new instance of the requested class is created, and OLE passes an object reference to the controlling application after the object's Initialize event has completed.

Once running, the object application provides new objects to all controlling applications that request them. One instance of the object application can supply several objects and multiple copies of those objects to requesting controlling applications.

In Listing 12.4, we are starting the AutoSrvr object application from Excel using Visual Basic for Applications. Applications that support

VBA, such as Microsoft Excel 5.0, can be used to access and manipulate the functionality of object applications.

Listing 12.4   SRVRDBG.XLS—Creating a Calc Object from Excel 5.0 VBA

```
Sub TestAutoSrvr()
    Dim x As Object
    Dim aa As Integer
    Dim bb As Integer

    aa = Application.ActiveSheet.Cells(1, 1).Value
    bb = Application.ActiveSheet.Cells(1, 3).Value

    Set x = CreateObject("AutoSrvr.Calc")
    MsgBox Str(x.Mult(aa, bb))

    Application.ActiveSheet.Cells(1, 5).Value = x.Mult(aa,
bb)

    End Sub
```

From Excel we can access all of the objects' public methods and properties, thus the functionality of the object application's classes. In the application of Listing 12.4, we obtain values from cells within the active worksheet within Microsoft Excel using the `Application.ActiveSheet.Cells(x, y).Value`. The application then creates and instance of our `Calc` class using the `CreateObject("AutoSrvr.Calc")` function.

We then take the values and multiply them using the `x.Mult(aa, bb)` methods of the new object. The resulting value is then stored into a cell within the active Excel worksheet.

Once your object application is started, Visual Basic keeps track of the number of times an object is requested by one or more controlling applications. When the last of these instances is closed, Visual Basic closes your object application. One point to keep in mind is that you cannot close a controlling application from your object application, but you can close an object application from a controlling application.

Debugging Your Object Application

As with any code that you develop, you need to test and debug your object application once it is coded. Testing can be accomplished within the Visual Basic development environment by having two instances of Visual Basic: one instance running the object application, and a second running a controlling application. Figure 12.10 illustrates one Visual Basic instance running a simple controller and another running a server. Visual Basic does not allow you to run separate projects in one instance of Visual Basic, so you have to run multiple instances of Visual Basic, each with a different project, simultaneously.

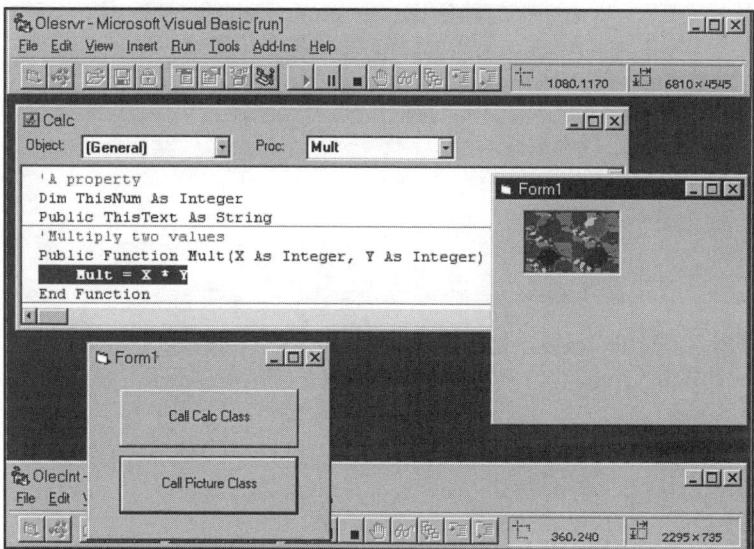

Fig. 12.10 In some circumstances, you may run multiple versions of Visual Basic to debug your object applications.

You are not required to make an executable file of an object application to debug it. However, the object application must be an executable file before it can be permanently registered in the system registry. When debugging your object application, Visual Basic makes temporary entries in the system registry and deletes them when you finish the debugging session.

You can also debug your application from a controlling application other than Visual Basic. As shown in figure 12.11, we are running Microsoft Excel as a controller for a small Visual Basic object application.

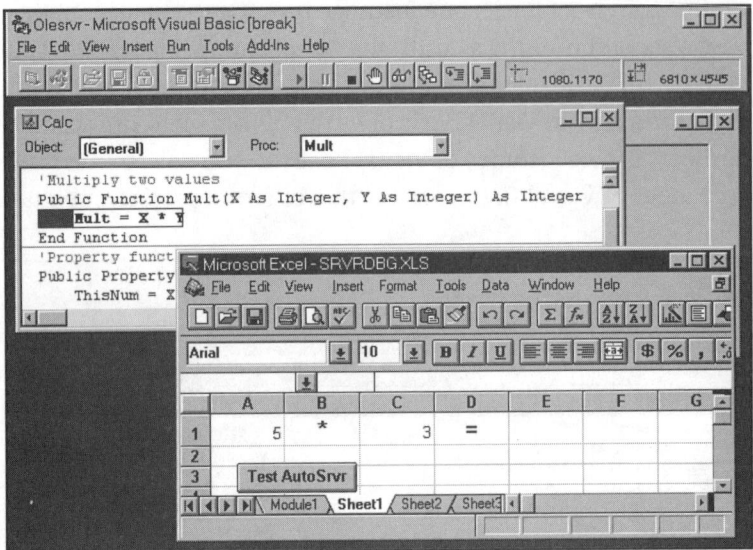

Fig. 12.11 Excel can be used to debug Visual Basic object applications.

The following steps detail how to debug Visual Basic object applications:

1. Using Visual Basic, set breakpoints in your class module code where required and set up watch expressions for class module variables that you want to monitor while your object application is running.

2. Ensure that an existing version of your object application is not already running. If it is, existing references to the object application and the classes it exposes may not be valid and the debugger may not operate properly on the proper version of the application.

Run the object application and, using the debug facility of Visual Basic, verify the operation of the object application.

3. Start a second instance of Visual Basic as the controlling application and open a new project.

4. While in the controlling application project, choose Tools, References from the Visual Basic menu and make sure that the object application, located in the other instance of Visual Basic, is selected.

5. In the controlling application project, choose View, Object Browser to check that all intended public methods and properties from the object application are displayed. If some are not, make sure that you have properly declared them as `Public` members in a public class module.

6. In the controlling project, declare and set a variable of a class defined in the object application. If you try do this using the `CreateObject()` and it fails, make sure that the class module defining that class does not have its `Instancing` property set to `Not Creatable`.

7. In the controlling application project, write code that creates and manipulates objects from the classes of the object application. Make sure that you test all of the functionality intended for the object application.

When the controlling application invokes an action that jumps to a watch expression or breakpoint in the object application, the object application will stop and receive focus. Visual Basic displays the object application's class module in the Debug window of the first instance of Visual Basic. It displays the controlling application's modules in the Debug window of the second instance of Visual Basic.

 **Caution:** Debugging may cause artificial changes in focus that prevent continued execution from behaving as expected. You should be careful to avoid debugging situations that are sensitive to focus or activation events, especially mouse and key events.

Running Multiple Application Versions

Once your object application is fully debugged so that an instance of each class can be successfully created and used, you may want to run several Visual Basic controlling applications simultaneously to simulate multiple instances of classes being created and used.

Visual Basic is capable of running two object application projects simultaneously. If the class names conflict between the applications, however, the second project will overwrite the registry entries of the first object application when the second object application is running. In this case, controlling applications can access OLE Automation objects from the most recently started object application only. To remedy this situation, use different project names and class names if you are going to run two or more versions of an object application simultaneously.

> **Caution:** If the controlling application is in runtime mode and you stop running the object application project, the controlling application will no longer be able to access the object application's objects and a runtime error may occur.

Changing Controller References to the Application

After the class modules are defined and debugged, choose File, Make EXE File from the menu to build an executable version of your object application. Once you have successfully made an executable file, go back to your controlling application and use the References dialog box to change the reference from the debug version of your object application to the executable version. Of course, if you don't plan to use the controlling application again, you don't need to do this. But if you do use it after building the object application executable file, the reference to your object application should point to the executable version, not the debug version.

Caution: Do not build an executable file for your controlling application while the debug version of the object application project is running. If you do, the controlling application will reference the temporarily registered version of the object application. When the object application is made into an executable file, that reference will change, and the controlling application will no longer refer to the executable version of the object application.

Standards and Guidelines

Object application developers have adopted a standardized scheme for organizing and naming OLE Automation objects and their methods and properties. If you follow these standards when creating an object application, controlling applications can better recognize the purpose of a method or property.

The next few sections discuss standard OLE Automation, naming guidelines for creating OLE Automation objects. If your object application does not have a visible interface or supports a single document interface only, you should adapt the standards and guidelines as appropriate.

Standard Objects

Standard objects, a set of objects defined by OLE, should be used as appropriate in your application. The OLE Automation objects described in this chapter are oriented toward document-centric applications. Other applications that don't have a visible user-interface may have requirements different from those described here.

The naming guidelines are recommendations meant to improve consistency across applications. In this way controlling applications can easily interface with many different object applications using a standard naming convention.

The following list has the standard OLE Automation objects and their methods and properties. Although none of these objects is required, it is recommended that applications with dependent objects include an `Application` object.

➤ `Application` is a top-level object that provides a standard way for controlling applications to retrieve and navigate to an application's subordinate objects.

➤ `Collection` provides a way to add, list, and remove objects from a collection.

The following sections describe the standard properties and methods for all objects, and then more specifically for collection objects and the `Application` object. These sections list only standard methods and properties for each object, as well as the standard arguments for those properties and methods.

> **Note:** You may define additional application-specific properties and methods for each object. You may also provide additional optional arguments for any of the listed properties or methods; however, such optional arguments should follow the standards for argument lists.

Properties Required

All objects, including the `Application` object and collection objects, should provide the following properties:

➤ `Application` is read-only and stores the `Application` object.

➤ `Parent` is read-only and stores the creator of the object—usually the `Application` object.

A collection provides a mechanism for storing objects that can be indexed and searched. All collection objects automatically provide the `Count` property, which is read-only and returns an integer data type containing the number of items in the collection.

Collection Methods

The following list describes methods available for the `Collection` object. You cannot extend the members of the `Collection` object, but you can create your own collections in Visual Basic class modules.

➤ `Add` adds an item to a collection.

➤ `Item` sets an indicated item in the collection to a particular value.

➤ `Remove` removes an item from a collection.

The Item Method

All collection objects must provide at least one way of indexing through the items of the collection. Because `Item` is the default method for collection objects, it can be used in the following form:

```
ThirdDef = MyWords(3).Definition
```

`Item` takes one argument, an index, which can be a number, string, or other data type. When declaring the `Item` method, use the following syntax:

```
Function Item (index As Variant) As Variant
DogDef = MyWords("dog").Definition
```

You should take into account the following when using the `Item` method:

➤ If index is an integer, it must be between 1 and the value of the `Count` property, inclusive; otherwise an error is returned.

➤ If index is a key and no item exists in the collection that has the key you specify, then an error is returned.

➤ Because `Item` is the default method, you can use either of the following lines of code:

```
Print MyCollection(1)
Print MyCollection.Item(1)
```

The Add Method

The `Add` method takes four arguments, as shown in the following code:

```
Sub Add (item As Variant [, key As Variant]
[, before As Variant] [, after As Variant] )
```

You can omit the three optional arguments. In Listing 12.5, for example, `MyWord` is an object with the properties `Letters` and `Definition`:

Listing 12.5   Managing Information in a Dictionary

```
Dim MyWord As New Word
Dim MyDictionary as Words
MyWord = "dog"
MyWord.Letters = "Dog"
MyWord.Definition = "My best friend."
MyDictionary.Add MyWord
MyDictionary.Remove("Dog")
```

You should take into account the following when using the `Add` method:

➤ `Item` can be any data type.

➤ Before and after, use the same indexing as described in the `Item` method. That is, if before is specified, it is considered a positional index if it is an integer. Otherwise, it is considered a key.

➤ An error occurs if either before or after is specified and the value is out of bounds. The value is out of bounds if the `Item` method fails to return an object if it is indexed with the same argument.

➤ Before and after are mutually exclusive. It is an error to specify both.

➤ An error is returned if key is an integer.

➤ An error is returned if there is already an item in the collection with the key.

The Remove Method

The `Remove` method takes one argument, index, that points to the item in the collection to remove. You should take into account the following when using the `Remove` method:

➤ Indexing works the same way as it does for the `Item` method.

- If index is an integer, it must be between 1 and *Count*, inclusive. If it is not in this range, an error is returned.

- If index is not an integer, then it must be a key. If there is no item in the collection that has that key, then an error is returned.

Application Object Properties and Methods

For an object application, the `Application` object should have the following standard properties.

- `ActiveDocument` is read-only and returns the active document object or `Nothing` if no documents are active.

- `Application` is read-only and returns the `Application` object.

- `Caption` is read/write and sets or returns the title of the application window.

- `DefaultFilePath` is read/write and sets or returns the default path specification used by the application for opening files.

- `Documents` is read-only and returns a collection object for the open documents.

- `FullName` is read-only and returns the file specification for the application, including path—for example, C:\AUTOSRVR\OLESRVR.EXE.

- `Name` returns the name of the application, such as "Microsoft Excel."

- `Parent` is read-only and returns the `Application` object.

- `Path` is read-only and returns the path specification for the application's executable file—for example, C:\AUTOSRVR if the executable is C:\AUTOSRVR\OLESRVR.EXE.

Naming Guidelines

You should choose names for exposed objects, properties, and methods that can be easily understood by the users of your application. The following guidelines apply to all objects, properties, methods, and constants:

➤ Use entire words or syllables whenever possible.

It is easier for users to remember complete words than to remember whether you abbreviated Window as Wind, Wn, or Wnd. For instance, use the object name `Application` instead of `App` and `SpellCheck` instead of `SpChk`.

When you need to abbreviate because an identifier would be too long, try to use complete initial syllables. For example, use `AltExpEval` instead of either `AlternateExpressionEvaluation` or `AltExpnEvln`.

➤ Use mixed case.

All identifiers should use mixed case, rather than underscores, to separate the words in the identifier.

➤ Use consistent terminology.

Use the same word you use in the interface. Do not use identifier names like HWND, which are based on Hungarian notation. Remember that this code will be accessed by other users, so try to use the same word your users would use to describe a concept. For example, use `Name`, not `Lbl`.

➤ Use the correct plural for collection class names.

Using plurals rather than inventing new names for collections reduces the number of items a user must remember. It also simplifies the selection of names for collections.

If you have a class named `Axis`, for example, a collection of `Axis` objects is stored in an `Axes` class. Similarly, a collection of `Vertex` objects is stored in a `Vertices` class. In rare cases where English uses the same word for the plural, append the word `Collection`.

From Here...

In this chapter we discussed the development and implementation of OLE server applications. We looked at the different types and capabilities of servers and how they fit into the OLE hierarchy. After the discussions of server development we stepped through the debugging process of an OLE server. Finally we discussed some of the standards required by OLE servers to provide a common interface for each distributed object application.

➤ To further examine the development of data-driven applications, refer to Chapter 5, "Data Management and Data-Driven Programming."

➤ To examine the use OLE server's by client applications, refer to Chapter 13, "OLE Container Classes."

➤ To examine the use of custom controls within your Visual Basic application, refer to Chapter 20, "OLE Controls, Add-Ins, and 32-bit DLLs."

13

OLE Container Classes

by Edward B. Toupin

In the previous two chapters, we discussed the basics of OLE, OLE servers, and the implementing of object applications in Visual Basic. Throughout those chapters, references were made to client and controlling applications t o provide you with an understanding of why certain operations are performed in a server. In this chapter, we will take your knowledge of servers and your exposure to clients and delve into the development of Visual Basic client container and controlling applications.

To demonstrate the development of Visual Basic client applications, we will develop several types of clients using different methods of integration between OLE servers and OLE clients. The following is a list of concepts that you will learn as you read through this chapter:

➤ How container applications handle embedded objects

➤ Using linked objects with client container applications

➤ Develop controlling applications to interact with object applications

What Is an OLE Client?

OLE clients are applications that query and use the services of OLE servers. Clients can use these services by incorporating objects from, or the functionality of, server applications. For linking and embedding operations, those clients that incorporate objects are known as *containers*; for automation, those clients that incorporate the functionality are known as *controlling applications*.

In many circumstances, OLE clients, containers, and controlling applications provide a means of integrating multiple applications to supply one single-user interface for the integrated applications. For example, as shown in figure 13.1, you can incorporate the functionality of a Word for Windows document, an Excel worksheet, and an Excel chart. Instead of separately accessing each object in its respective application, you can have access to the functionality of all objects in one single application.

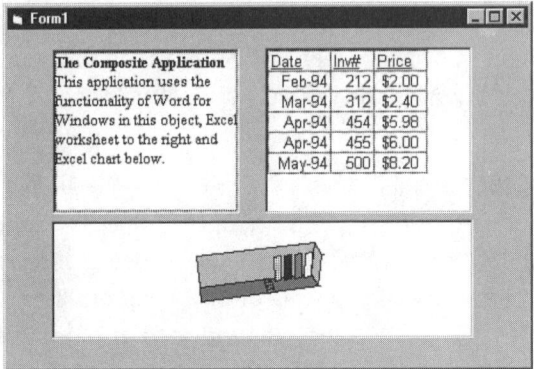

Fig. 13.1 OLE clients can be used to integrate OLE server applications to provide one consolidated application.

OLE container applications that support this single-user interface concept can support object embedding, object linking, or both. To assist in developing OLE container applications, Visual Basic provides you with the OLE Control that gives you a simple means of inserting and manipulating embedded or linked objects. For embedded objects, if the embedded object's server supports in-place activation, visual editing can be performed on objects within the OLE Control.

Controlling applications provide a means of interfacing with the objects of object applications developed in Visual Basic as well as any other Windows applications that expose their objects. You can perform OLE Automation using Object variables programmatically as well as through the OLE Control. Object variables provide you with a means of storing the object of a created automation class with `CreateObject()` and `GetObject()`. You can then manipulate the object referenced by the Object variable you created.

The OLE Control previously mentioned also provides you with a means of manipulating objects that are either embedded or linked into the control itself. In a manner similar to that of any Object variable you may create, you can access the methods and properties of the object within the control.

From your knowledge of server application development you will notice that client application development is much easier to accomplish. Since server applications maintain much of the code used by client applications, all you have to do is access a class, create an object, and access the methods and properties of the server.

The OLE Control and the Client

Container applications and some controlling applications that support linking, embedding, and OLE Automation incorporate objects from server applications using the Visual Basic OLE Control. The OLE Control is a Visual Basic control that provides a programmable interface to embedded and linked objects and their servers. Primarily, this control provides you with a means of embedding and linking objects. Secondly, you can perform automation operations on the object in an OLE control through methods and properties of the control.

To start the development of an OLE container or controlling application, you must load Visual Basic and create a new form by choosing File, New. Once selected, Visual Basic will clear its workspace and create a new, empty form. You then incorporate the OLE Control to manage embedded objects in a Visual Basic application. This control is located in the Toolbox, as shown in figure 13.2.

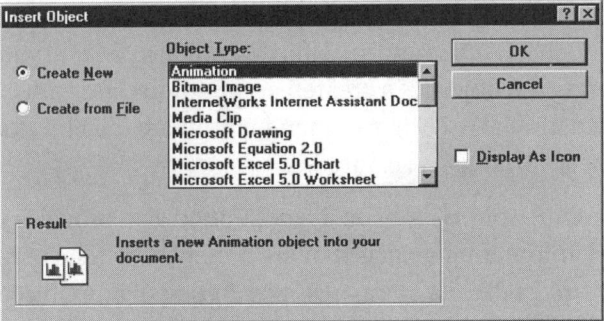

Fig. 13.2 Once an OLE Control is placed into a form, the Insert Object dialog box allows you to select an object to embed into the control.

To place the control, follow these steps:

1. Select it from the Toolbox with your mouse.

2. Move your mouse over to the form and click and hold the left mouse button.

3. Move the mouse until the control is sized appropriately in the form.

4. Once you release the mouse button, the Insert Object dialog box appears, allowing you to select a class of object to embed or link into your OLE Control.

You have access to the verbs of the OLE Control by clicking the right mouse button on the control. With these verbs you can embed or link objects to the OLE Control even after the control is positioned on the form. As you can see in figure 13.3, a menu appears that allows you to select a class to link or embed.

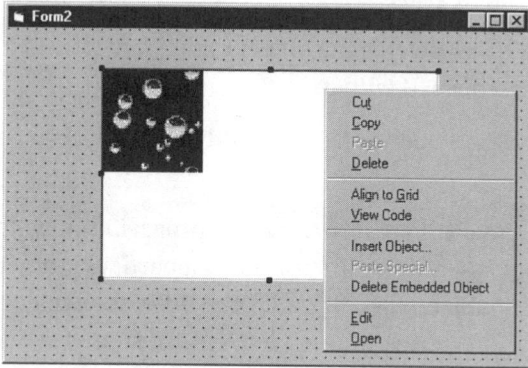

Fig. 13.3 The OLE Control allows you access to the verbs of the embedded or linked object.

You can also perform linking and embedding programmatically using the methods and properties of the OLE Control. The following sections outline some of the methods, properties, and events for the OLE Control and provide some brief explanations for each.

Methods

The methods of the OLE Control are functions that can be called by your application to perform actions on the control and the object within the control. The following list is a partial list of methods available for the OLE Control:

➤ `Close` closes the object in the control and terminates the connection to the server application that provided the object.

➤ `Copy` copies the object within the control to the system Clipboard.

➤ `CreateEmbed` creates an embedded object for the control using a disk-based file. You can also supply the name of a class registered in the system registry.

➤ `CreateLink` establishes a link between the control and a disk-based file. You can also supply the name of a class registered in the system registry.

➤ `Delete` deletes the object in the control and frees the memory associated with it.

➤ `DoVerb` opens an object and performs object-specific verbs.

> **Note:** *Verbs* are the set of programmatically invoked operations supported by a particular object. The set of object-specific verbs can differ for each object type because different verbs make sense for different objects.

➤ `Drag` begins, ends, or cancels a drag operation of any object.

➤ `FetchVerbs` retrieves a list of verbs, or operations, that can be performed on an object within the control.

➤ `InsertObjDlg` displays the Insert Object dialog box, which allows you to select an object that you wish to embed or link into the control.

➤ `Move` allows you to move the control in the form on which it is located.

➤ `Paste` copies data from the system Clipboard into the control.

➤ `PasteSpecialDlg` displays the Paste Special dialog box so you can specify the format of the object that you wish to paste from the system Clipboard.

➤ `ReadFromFile` loads an object from a file created by the `SaveToFile` method.

➤ `Refresh` forces a repaint of the control to update the current drawing in the specified control. Painting, or *refreshing*, a control is handled automatically while no events are occurring. However, there may be situations where you want the form or control updated manually.

➤ `SaveToFile` saves OLE data to an OLE version 2 file, while `SaveToOle1File` saves OLE data to a file compatible with OLE version 1. If the object is linked, only the link information and an image of the data is saved to the specified file since the object's data is maintained by the server application of the object. If the object is embedded, the object's data is maintained by the control and can be saved by your Visual Basic application.

➤ `Update` retrieves the current data from the server application of the object and displays that data as a graphic in the control.

Properties

Properties of the OLE control allow you to set the characteristics as well as determine the operational state of the control programmatically. The following list describes the available properties for the OLE Control:

➤ `Action` allows you to set a value at runtime that determines an action to be performed. The settings for this property determine whether the object within the control is embedded, linked, pasted from the system Clipboard, or loaded from a file.

➤ `AppIsRunning` allows you to determine if the server application of the object in the control is running and also allows you to start that application. Retrieving a `True` from this property means that the creating application is running. Setting the property to `True` starts the application.

➤ `AutoActivate` returns or sets a value that enables you to activate an object by double-clicking the OLE container control or by moving the focus to the OLE container control.

➤ `AutoVerbMenu` returns or sets a value that determines if a pop-up menu containing the object's verbs is displayed when the user clicks the control with the right mouse button.

➤ `Class` is the name of the class of an embedded object in the control.

➤ `DragMode` returns or sets a value that determines whether manual or automatic drag mode is used for a drag-and-drop operation. When `DragMode` is set to Automatic, the control doesn't respond as usual to mouse events. You can use the Manual setting to determine when a drag-and-drop operation begins or ends.

➤ `Format` returns or sets the format when sending data to, and getting data from, a server application for the object in the control.

➤ `Height`, `Width`, `Left`, and `Top` returns or sets the location of the OLE Control in a form.

➤ `Object` is a pointer to the object in the control and is used to access the methods of the object for performing automation tasks.

➤ `ObjectAcceptFormats` and `ObjectAcceptFormatsCount` returns the formats and number of formats that an object in the control can accept.

➤ `ObjectGetFormats` and `ObjectGetFormatsCount` returns the formats and number of formats that an object can provide from the control.

➤ `ObjectVerbFlags` returns the states of the verbs for an object in an OLE Control.

➤ `ObjectVerbs` and `ObjectVerbsCount` returns the verbs and number of verbs supported by an object in an OLE Control.

➤ `OLEDropAllowed` returns or sets the state of an OLE Control to whether or not the control can be a drop target for a drag-and-drop operation.

➤ `OLEType` and `OLETypeAllowed` determines the type of object—whether linked, embedded, or none—allowed in the control.

➤ `Parent` returns the form on which the control is located.

➤ `PasteOK` returns whether the contents of the system Clipboard can be pasted into the control.

➤ `Picture` specifies a picture (for example, bitmap, metafile, or icon) that may be loaded into the OLE Control.

➤ `SourceDoc` and `SourceItem` specify the name and item of a file for a linked or embedded object.

➤ `UpdateOptions` defines how the object in the control is to be updated. You can specify that linked data is updated when changed, updated only when the linked data is saved, or updated only when you execute the `Update` method.

➤ `Verb` allows you to specify which verb of the verb list from `ObjectVerbs` you wish to execute.

> **Note:** The `Action` and `Verb` properties are only available for compatibility with earlier versions. It is suggested that appropriate methods of the OLE Control be used over the assignment of verbs to the `Action` and `Verb` properties.

Events

The following list outlines some of the events that are executed for the OLE control:

➤ `Click` and `DblClick` occur when you click or double-click the OLE Control.

➤ `DragDrop` occurs when a drag-and-drop operation is completed as a result of dragging a control over a form or control and releasing the mouse button or using the `Drag` method with its action argument set to 2 (Drop).

➤ `DragOver` occurs when a drag-and-drop operation is in progress. You can use this event to monitor the mouse pointer as it enters, leaves, or rests directly over a valid target. The mouse pointer position determines the target object that receives this event.

➤ `KeyPress`, `KeyDown`, and `KeyUp` events occur when you press a key on the keyboard when the OLE Control has focus.

➤ `MouseMove`, `MouseDown`, and `MouseUp` events occur when you move the mouse over the control or a mouse button is either pressed or released.

➤ `ObjectMove` occurs immediately after the object within a control is moved or resized while the object is active.

➤ `Updated` occurs when an object's data has been changed, saved, closed, or renamed.

Embedding

Visual Basic provides you with two different methods for embedding objects in an OLE Control. The first method is through the Insert Object dialog box, as you have seen, and the second is programmatically through controls and code. The code for managing embedded objects within the OLE Control allows you to pass object names to functions to incorporate these objects into your application. The two methods available with the OLE Control for managing embedded objects are `InsertObjDlg()` and `CreateEmbed()`.

The `InsertObjDlg()` method of the OLE control programmatically accesses the Insert Object dialog box. In this application, the `Name` property of the OLE Control is `OLEControl`. The statement `OLEControl.InsertObjDlg()` uses the method of `OLEControl` to display the dialog box shown in figure 13.4 so that you can select a class to use for an object in the OLE Control.

```
Private Sub EmbedDialog_Click()
    'Set the allowable OLE type (Embed)
    OLEControl.OLETypeAllowed = 1
```

Note: The dialog box that appears with `InsertDlg()` is the same dialog box that appears when you first place the OLE Control on the form or access the menu with the right mouse button.

The `OLETypeAllowed` property allows you to specify the type of object that can be created for the OLE Control. This application specifies, with a value of 1, that the OLE Control will allow embedded objects only. You can also specify 0 for linked or 2 to allow either type of object for the OLE control.

```
    'Specify how the object is to be activated (Double Click)
    OLEControl.AutoActivate = 2

    'Access the insert dialog box to create an embedded
    'object
    OLEControl.InsertObjDlg
End Sub
```

The AutoActivate property specifies how the object is to be activated by the user. This application specifies, with a value of 2, that the server application for the object be activated by double-clicking on the object in the OLE control (the default). If you specify 0, the server application for the object can be activated manually using the DoVerb(-1) method, or Verb = -1 property, of the OLE Control. A value of 1 specifies that the ser- ver application for the object be activated when the object gains focus. Finally, a value of 3 specifies that the server application for the object be activated based on the object's normal method of activation wheth-er the control receives the focus or the user double-clicks the control.

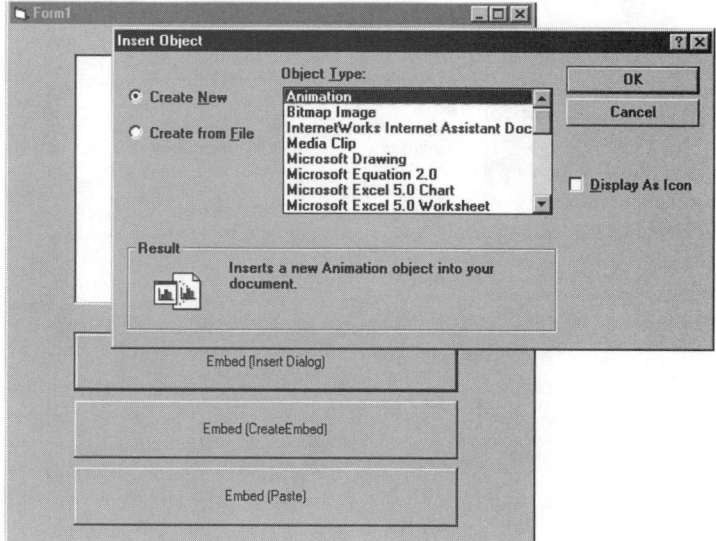

Fig. 13.4 The Insert Object dialog box can be used to select an object for embedding.

The CreateEmbed() method allows you to create an embedded object from a file. The first parameter of CreateEmbed() is the name of the disk-based document that you wish to embed into the OLE Control. The optional second parameter is a class that allows you to specify a class to which you wish the object to be assigned. The class can be, for example, Excel.Sheet or Word.Document.

```
Private Sub EmbedMethod_Click()
    'Set the allowable OLE type (Embed)
    OLEControl.OLETypeAllowed = 1

    'Create an embedded object using the file
    '   specified.
    OLEControl.CreateEmbed "C:\TEMP\TESTSHT.XLS"

    'Display the class of the object in the
    '   OLEControl
    MsgBox OLEControl.Class
End Sub
```

The MsgBox statement uses the Class property of the OLE Control (OLEControl) to display the class of the object embedded in the control. In this application, the MsgBox statement will display the class name of the sheet (Excel.Sheet), as listed in the system registry.

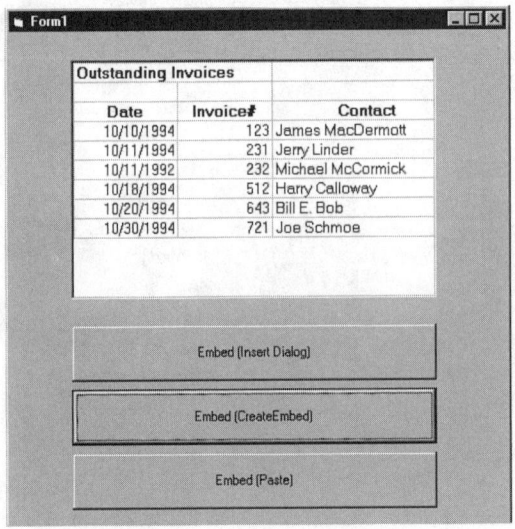

Fig. 13.5 Using the system registry for an Excel worksheet, you can embed a Sheet object into the Visual Basic OLE Control.

Note: Since you can only perform visual editing on embedded objects, in-place activation, visual editing, and embedded objects go hand-in-hand. Performing in-place activation on embedded objects is actually a function of the server application and can be used by the OLE Control.

Using the Clipboard

You can also perform embedding operations using the Clipboard with the Paste method of the OLE Control. The paste operation is similar to the Edit, Paste operation of many Windows-based applications. Any object that resides in the system Clipboard with a format acceptable by the OLE Control can be pasted into the control.

Note: The *formats* used in the system Clipboard specify the type of information located in the Clipboard. For example, you can have text, bitmaps, metafiles, and DDE link formats available for use by container applications.

To perform the paste, we must first establish that we want the control to accept the paste from the Clipboard as an embedded object. This is done by setting the OLETypeAllowed property to 1. As we did in the previous section of this chapter, we set the AutoActivate property to 2 to activate the object's server application when you double-click on the object in the OLE Control.

```
Private Sub EmbedPaste_Click()
    'Set the allowable OLE type (Embed)
    OLEControl.OLETypeAllowed = 1

    'Specify how the object is to be activated (Double Click)
    OLEControl.AutoActivate = 2
```

Once the parameters for the paste operation are established, we have to check to see if the OLE Control will accept the type, or format, of object currently in the Clipboard. By checking to see if the PasteOK property of the OLE Control is `True`, we are letting Visual Basic check to see if it can handle the system Clipboard's data for a paste. Primarily, the OLE Control can handle text, bitmaps, metafiles, and standard OLE types.

```
'If the control allows pasting
If OLEControl.PasteOK = True Then
    'Paste from the clipboard
    OLEControl.Paste
End If
```

If the OLE Control is able to embed the object in the Clipboard into the OLE Control, you can issue a call to the `Paste` method of the OLE Control with `OLEControl.Paste`. This method will retrieve the data from the Clipboard and embed it into the OLE Control (see fig. 13.6).

```
    'If an error occurs issue a msg to the user
    If OLEControl.OLEType = 3 Then
        MsgBox "Unable to Paste"
    End If
End Sub
```

Once the paste operation is complete, we check to see if it was successful by checking the `OLEType` property of the control. If `OLEType` equals the type that you specified in `OLETypeAllowed`, which is a value of `1` in this application, then the operation was successful. If the value of `OLEType` is `3`, the paste was unsuccessful and the control deletes any object that may have previously existed in the control.

Note: You can also use the `Copy` method of the OLE Control to copy the contents of the control to the system Clipboard for use by other applications.

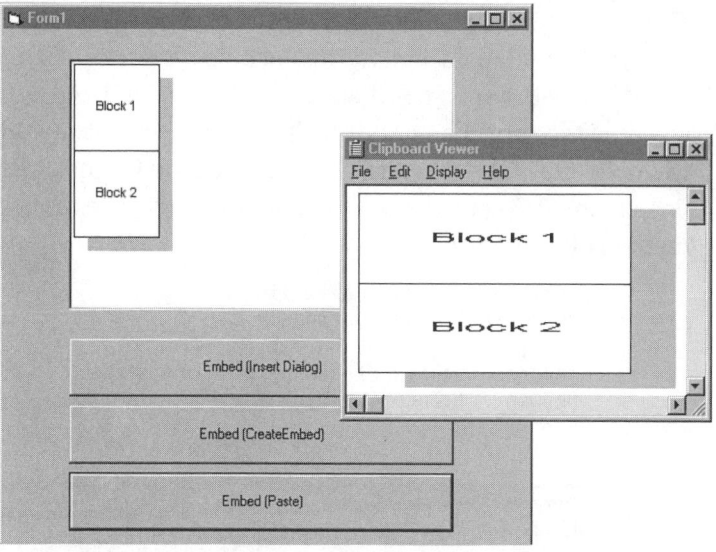

Fig. 13.6 The OLE Control allows you to paste objects that had been copied to the Clipboard by other applications.

Linking

Container applications that support linking provide a means of incorporating files, saved by server applications, into the container application. Developing an application to support linking is similar to that of embedding. The primary difference in the coding has to do with the methods used and the values of the properties.

As with embedding, the Insert Object dialog box can be accessed and used to select a file to link. To specify that linking is to be allowed by the OLE Control, the OLETypeAllowed property is set to a value of 0. We also want the server application for the object to be activated when you double-click the object, so we set the AutoActivate property to 2.

```
Private Sub LinkDialog_Click()
    'Set the allowable OLE type (Link)
    OLEControl.OLETypeAllowed = 0

    'Specify how the object is to be activated (Double Click)
    OLEControl.AutoActivate = 2
```

The UpdateOptions property of the control allows you to specify how the link is to be updated when the linked object's data is changed by the object's server. 0 specifies that the link is to be updated automatically any time the data changes. 1 specifies that the link is updated only when the file is saved by the server application for the object. 2 specifies a manual update that only occurs when you use the Update() method of the control.

```
'Automatic updating of link
OLEControl.UpdateOptions = 0

'Access the insert dialog box to create a linked object
OLEControl.InsertObjDlg
End Sub
```

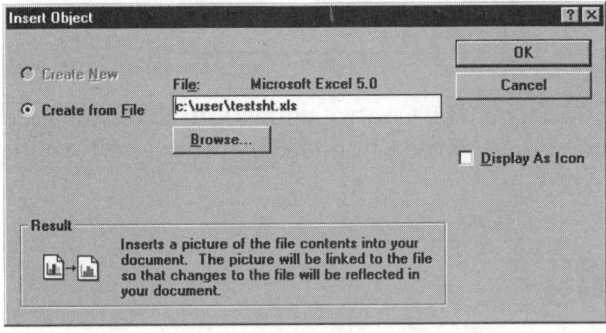

Fig. 13.7 The Insert Object dialog box can be accessed programmatically and used to link objects to the OLE Control.

Notice the difference between the dialog box in figure 13.7 and the dialog box for embedding in figure 13.4. The dialog box in figure 13.7 appears because you set the OLETypeAllowed to allow only linked objects. Since this parameter is set, you can only perform linking to objects of files.

As with embedding and the CreateEmbed() method, you can programmatically link to objects using a method called CreateLink(). CreateLink() creates a link to a file specified as a parameter to the method. As with CreateEmbed(), you specify the source document and, optionally, the class of the object to which you wish to link.

```
Private Sub LinkMethod_Click()
    'Set the allowable OLE type (Link)
    OLEControl.OLETypeAllowed = 0

    'Create a linked object using the file specified.
    OLEControl.CreateLink "c:\temp\TESTSHT.XLS"
End Sub
```

Using the Clipboard

Linking data from the Clipboard is more a function of DDE than it is
of OLE, but it is a feature made part of the Visual Basic OLE Control.
Container applications that support linking with system Clipboard
information allows the user to provide a link to a running server
application.

> **Note:** When you perform a link with an object in the system Clip-
> board, you are actually establishing a link to the object's server.
> In this situation, the object's server should be running and the
> object in the Clipboard would have been placed there using the
> Edit, Copy operation of the server application.

As we discussed with embedding, you should set the OLETypeAllowed
property for the control to accept linked objects. We also set the
AutoActivate property to activate the object's server on a double-click
and the UpdateOptions property to update automatically whenever the
object's data changes.

```
Private Sub LinkPaste_Click()
    'Set the allowable OLE type (Link)
    OLEControl.OLETypeAllowed = 0

    'Specify how the object is to be activated
    '    (Double Click)
    OLEControl.AutoActivate = 2

    'Automatic updating of link
    OLEControl.UpdateOptions = 0
```

The Paste operation for linking is identical to the Paste operation for
embedding. Using the PasteOK property, we check to see if the control

can handle the type of object in the Clipboard as well as determine if the object's server is running. If the format is correct and the server is running, we `Paste` a link to the object into the OLE Control.

```
'If the control allows pasting
If OLEControl.PasteOK = True Then
    'Paste from the clipboard
    OLEControl.Paste
End If

'If an error occurs issue a msg to the user
If OLEControl.OLEType = 3 Then
    MsgBox "Unable to Paste"
End If
End Sub
```

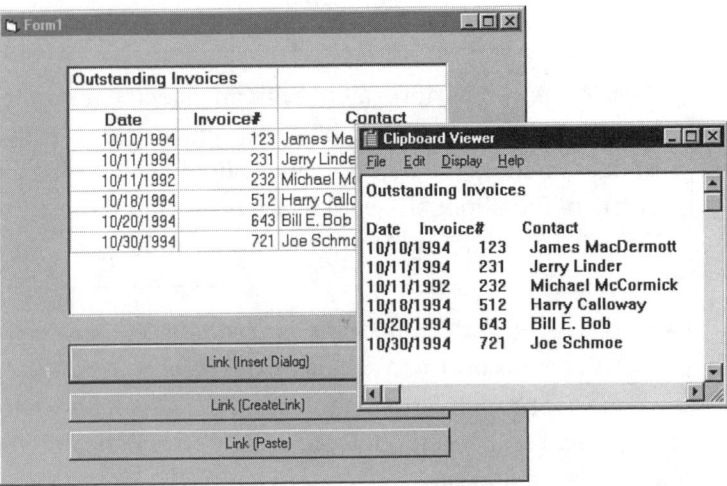

Fig. 13.8 The OLE object allows you to programmatically paste links to objects that have been copied to the Clipboard from other applications.

Pasting Special Objects Using the Clipboard

An alternative to using the `Paste` method of the OLE Control is using the `PasteSpecialDlg` method. This method allows you to specify—using the Paste Special dialog box—the version or format of an object in the Clipboard you want to paste into the OLE Control.

In the following code, we are performing the `Paste` operation on data from a dialog box from which we can select the type of data. By setting the `OLETypeAllowed` to `2` in this application, we are allowing either linked or embedded data to be placed into the control.

```
Private Sub PasteSpecial_Click()
    'Set the allowable OLE type
    OLEControl.OLETypeAllowed = 2

    'Specify how the object is to be activated
    '    (Double Click)
    OLEControl.AutoActivate = 2

    'Automatic updating of link
    OLEControl.UpdateOptions = 0
```

The primary difference between the code used for pasting in the application and in the embedding or linking application is in the call to `PasteSpecialDlg`. This method loads a dialog box (see fig. 13.9) from which you can select the format of the data you wish to paste into the control.

```
    'If the control allows pasting
    If OLEControl.PasteOK = True Then
        'Paste from the clipboard
        OLEControl.PasteSpecialDlg
    End If

    'If an error occurs issue a msg to the user
    If OLEControl.OLEType = 3 Then
        MsgBox "Unable to Paste"
    End If
End Sub
```

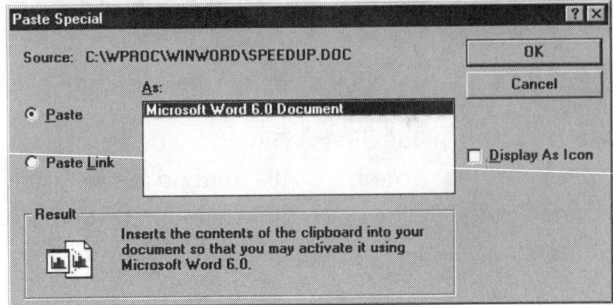

Fig. 13.9 The Paste Special dialog box allows you to select the format of the data that you wish to paste into your OLE Control.

As you can see in figure 13.9, you can either embed or link the object by selecting either the Paste or Paste Link radio button. To paste the object into the OLE Control, simply double-click the desired object or select the object and click OK. If you select Display As Icon, an icon will appear (see fig. 13.10) in the OLE Control representing the server that will load the object (file) named below the icon.

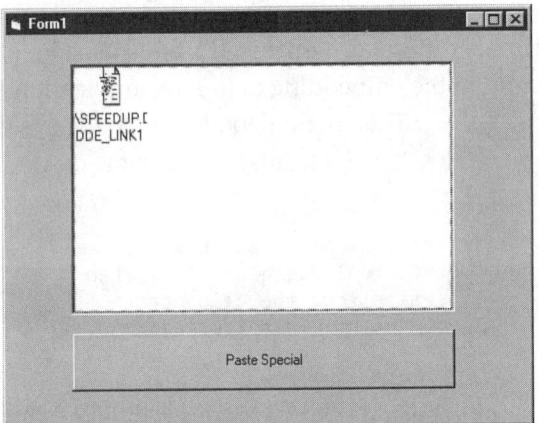

Fig. 13.10 An icon can be placed into the OLE Control to represent the server that will open when you wish to load and edit the linked object.

Verbs

Verbs are the set of programmatically invoked operations supported by a particular object. The set of object-specific verbs can differ for each object type because different verbs make sense for different objects. For example, a video object's verbs might include play and edit, while a text object might only support edit. So that other Windows applications will know what types of verbs are supported, an object application registers object-specific verbs (see fig. 13.11) in the registration database for each type of object supported.

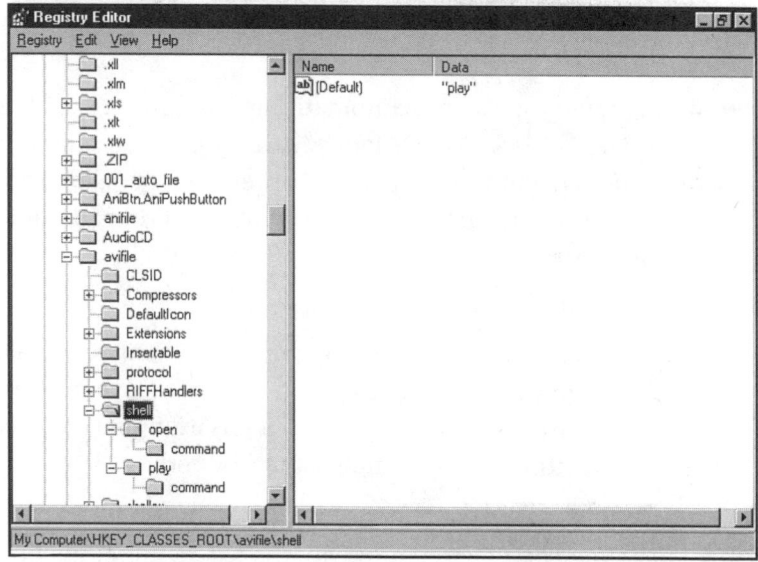

Fig. 13.11 Servers register their verbs in the system registry so that container applications can have access to the available actions of the server.

As you can see in figure 13.12, by clicking the right mouse button over Microsoft Video for Windows in the OLE Control, a small menu appears that contains the verbs specific to the object. Referring back to figure 13.11, you can see that the two verbs are registered as 0 for `Play` and 1 for `Edit`. Selecting Play in figure 13.12 plays the video object in the OLE control while selecting Edit allows you to edit the object in-place.

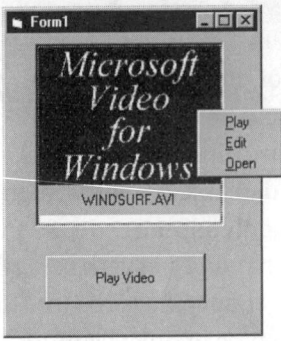

Fig. 13.12 The Microsoft Video for Windows server allows containers to play and edit video objects.

If you prefer, you can programmatically manipulate the object using the method called DoVerb() for OLE Control. As you saw in the list of methods at the beginning of this chapter, DoVerb() allows you to select a verb to be executed based on the verb's position and value in the system registry.

```
OLEControl.DoVerb (0)
```

We know from the system registry that Play is assigned a value of 0 at the 0 offset of the verb list. To execute the specific verb, you merely use the OLE Control (named OLEControl in this example) and call the DoVerb() method with the value of the Play verb.

> **Note:** You can execute verbs with the DoVerb() method or the Verb() property procedure. The syntax for the members are DoVerb(verb_val) and Verb = verb_val. The parameter verb_val is the value of the verb as registered in the system registry.

Controlling Applications

As you saw in the previous chapter, "OLE Servers," object applications allow you to provide a service through exposed objects for use by controlling applications. In this chapter, we will create a controlling application that will access our object application from the previous chapter as well as other applications that expose their objects for use by controlling applications. There are two methods for using OLE Automation on object applications—automation using objects and automation using the OLE Control.

Automation Using Objects

In the previous chapters, we briefly touched on the use of objects to develop controlling applications to perform OLE Automation in Visual Basic. Recall that object applications are registered in the system registry. Through the registry and the library for the object application, you can see what classes, methods, and properties are available with the Object Browser (which is accessible from the View menu in Visual Basic).

In this section, we will develop a controlling application that uses the AutoSrvr object application we developed in the previous chapter. To find out what object, methods, and properties are available to us, we will first use the Object Browser to look at the AutoSrvr object application.

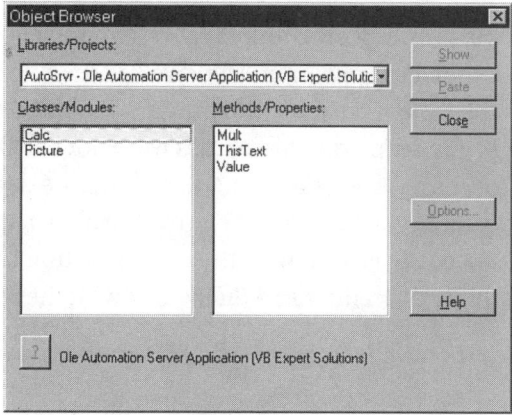

Fig. 13.13 AutoSrvr.Calc's methods and properties, as listed in the Object Browser, allow you to perform automation operations on the object.

As you can see in figure 13.13 and figure 13.14, and as you already know from the previous chapter, the AutoSrvr object application provides us with two classes: Calc and Picture. The Calc class contains three members: Mult(), ThisText, and Value. Selecting the Picture class with your mouse reveals the member DispPicture(). Now that we know what is provided to us by AutoSrvr, we can use these classes in controlling applications.

In the following event procedure, we first declare a variable of type Object that is used throughout the procedure to manage a class instance of Calc. We then create a class instance with the CreateObject() function for the class Calc of the object application AutoSrvr.

```
Private Sub CalcClass_Click()
    'Dim an object variable
    Dim AutoSrvr As Object

    'Create an object of the Calc class
    Set AutoSrvr = CreateObject("AutoSrvr.Calc")
```

To utilize the methods and properties of the object, we use the Mult() method to multiply two times three. The result is converted to a string and printed in a dialog box with the MsgBox statement.

```
    'Display the result of 2 * 3
    MsgBox Str(AutoSrvr.Mult(2, 3))
```

Recall the property procedures Get Value and Let Value from the AutoSrvr object application. Here we use the Let Value procedure to assign the value 10 to a private property. In the Object Browser from figure 13.13, the private properties were not listed; however, the property procedure Value was listed. Recall that we declared ThisNum as a private property when we developed the object application. The Get Value procedure is used with the Str() function to print the result of the property procedure in a dialog box with the MsgBox statement.

```
    'Set the Value to 10 then display
    AutoSrvr.Value = 10
    MsgBox Str(AutoSrvr.Value)

    'Set ThisText the display
    AutoSrvr.ThisText = "This is a test"
    MsgBox AutoSrvr.ThisText
End Sub
```

To end the procedure, we access the `ThisText` public property directly and assign a string to the variable. We then print the value stored in the public variable of `Calc` in a dialog box using the `MsgBox` statement.

The `Picture` class is treated in the same manner as the `Calc` class. As you can see in the following code, we first declare an `Object` variable in which we will store an instance of the class `Picture`. Using the `CreateObject()` function, we create an object so that we can access the methods and properties of the class.

```
Private Sub PictureClass_Click()
    'Dim an object variable
    Dim AutoSrvr As Object

    'Create an object of the Picture class
    Set AutoSrvr = CreateObject("AutoSrvr.Picture")

    'Call the method to display a picture
    AutoSrvr.DispPicture ("C:\WINDOWS\ARCHES.BMP")
End Sub
```

From the Object Browser, we see in figure 13.14 that the `Picture` class maintains only one method: `DispPicture()`. To use this method, we pass the name of the picture we want to display in the parameter line of the method.

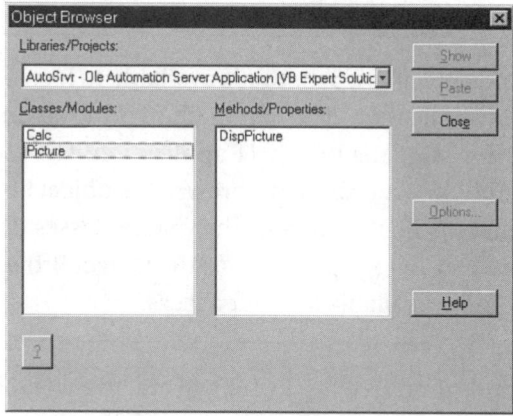

Fig. 13.14 `AutoSrvr.Picture`'s methods and properties, as listed in the Object Browser.

Now let's apply what we accomplished for `AutoSrvr` to Microsoft Excel and take OLE Automation with Visual Basic a few steps further. The first thing that we have to do is look in the Object Browser to find the objects, methods, and properties that are exposed for our use. Since we are going to create a worksheet object, we should look at the exposed methods and properties of the `Worksheet` class (see fig. 13.15).

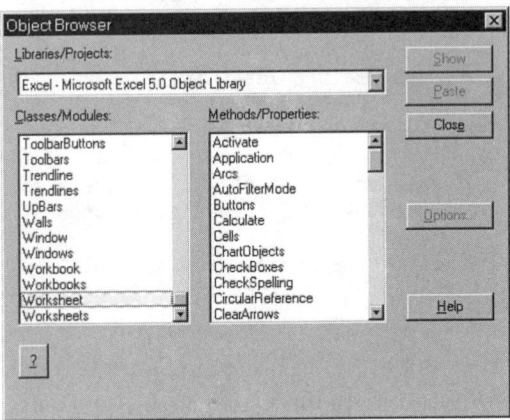

Fig. 13.15 `Excel.Worksheet`'s methods and properties, as listed in Object Browser.

Note: There are two methods available to locate the classes for a given application. The first method is by looking in the system registry using the REGEDIT application. The second method is to use the Object Browser to browse the object library for the application. REGEDIT contains the visible classes that are accessible from controlling applications; the Object Browser shows the public classes available for your access.

Our application (see fig. 13.16) will create a worksheet, set the values of several cells, then calculate the sum of the values and place that sum in a cell.

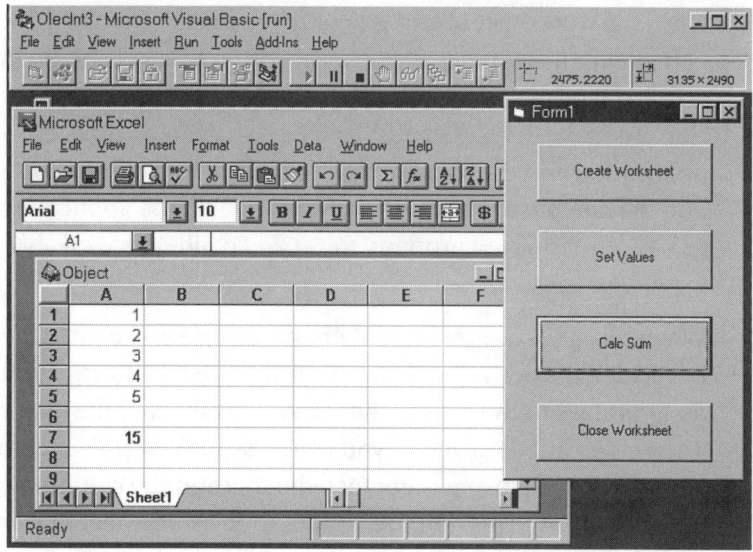

Fig. 13.16 OLE Automation can be performed on Excel from Visual Basic.

In Listing 13.1, we first dimension an object variable globally that will be used to access our worksheet object. When you click the Create Worksheet button control, the event procedure `CreateSheet_Click()` is executed. This event procedure creates an instance of an Excel worksheet and assigns the instance of the worksheet to the Sheet object variable.

Listing 13.1   OLECLNT3.VBP—Creating an Instance of an Excel Worksheet and Assigning it to the Sheet Object Variable

```
'Dim an object variable
Dim Sheet As Object

'Create a new worksheet object
Private Sub CreateSheet_Click()
    Set Sheet = CreateObject("Excel.Sheet")

    'Make the sheet and the application visible
    Sheet.Visible = True
    Sheet.Application.Visible = True
End Sub
```

Once the worksheet object is created, we want to make the Excel application and the instance of the sheet within Excel visible so that we can watch the results of the remainder of the procedures in our application. To make the object visible, we set the Visible property of the application and the sheet to True to make the Excel application and the new sheet visible. If you want to hide the application, set the Application.Visible property to False. To hide the worksheet, set the Sheet.Visible to False.

When the SetValues_Click() event procedure is executed, as a result of clicking the Set Values button control, we use the Sheet object and assign values to the cells of the active worksheet of the application. The Cells() method allows you to access the cell collection of the worksheet using two parameters: the row and the column—Cells(row,col). This method applies to the worksheet that we created with the CreateObject() function. Value is a variant property procedure that allows us to set the values of the cells as well as retrieve the values of cells for use in the application (see Listing 13.2).

Listing 13.2   OLECLNT4.VBP—Using the Value Variant Property Procedure

```
'Set the values of the cells.  Set each value
'   in a column (A1,A2,A3,A4,A5)
Private Sub SetValues_Click()
    'Row 1, Col 1
    Sheet.Cells(1, 1).Value = 1
    'Row 2, Col 1
    Sheet.Cells(2, 1).Value = 2
    'Row 3, Col 1
    Sheet.Cells(3, 1).Value = 3
    'Row 4, Col 1
    Sheet.Cells(4, 1).Value = 4
    'Row 5, Col 1
    Sheet.Cells(5, 1).Value = 5
End Sub
```

In the Listing 13.3, we add something a little different to demonstrate how to use a different OLE automation function—GetObject(). In this event procedure, executed when you click the Calc Sum button control, we first dimension an `Object` variable for use locally within the procedure. This variable is used with the `GetObject()` function to obtain a reference to the active sheet we created with the `CreateObject()` function.

`GetObject()` takes two parameters: a path and a class— `GetObject(path, class)`. If path is a zero-length string (" "), `GetObject()` returns a new object instance of the specified type in a manner similar to that of `CreateObject()`. If the pathname argument is omitted entirely, as in this application, `GetObject()` returns the currently active object of the specified type.

Note: Use the `GetObject()` function when there is a current instance of the object or if you want to create the object with a file already loaded. If there is no current instance, and you don't want the object started with a file loaded, use the `CreateObject()` function.

Caution: If a class has been registered as a single-instance object (for example, the `Word.Basic` class for Microsoft Word for Windows 6.0), only one instance of the object is created regardless of the number of times `CreateObject()` is executed. Note, however, that with a single-instance object, `GetObject()` always returns the same instance when called with the zero-length string syntax (" ") and it causes an error if the path argument is omitted.

Listing 13.3   OLECLNT4.VBP—Using the GetObject( ) OLE Automation Function

```
'Calculate the sum of the values
Private Sub CalcSum_Click()
    Dim XLApp As Object
```

continues

Listing 13.3 Continued

```
        Set XLApp = GetObject(, "Excel.Application")
        XLApp.Cells(7, 1).Value = "=SUM(A1:A5)"
        XLApp.Cells(7, 1).Font.Bold = True
    End Sub
```

Using the worksheet reference we obtained in the `XLApp` object variable, we assign an equation to the cell at row 7, column 1. Since `Value` is a variant variable, we can assign equations as strings as simple as we can assign integers or floating-point decimals. The string equation `"=SUM(A1:A5)"` calculates the sum of the five values that we placed into the worksheet in the previous event procedure.

To emphasize the total of the values, we bold the value of the sum using the `Font.Bold` property of the cell. You can also change fonts, change styles, and change the point of fonts as required by accessing the methods and properties of the exposed objects.

Closing the application is just as simple as starting it and creating an instance of one of its objects. You can access the `Quit` method of the `Application` object for our application, which will quit the Excel application. If unsaved workbooks are open, Excel displays a dialog box asking if you want to save any changes. You can prevent this by saving all workbooks before using the `Quit` method or by setting the `DisplayAlerts` property to `False`. When this property is `False`, Excel does not display the dialog box and it quits without saving them. If you set the `Saved` property to `True` without saving it to the disk, Excel will quit without asking you to save the workbook.

```
    'Quit Excel
    Private Sub CloseSheet_Click()
        Sheet.Application.Quit
    End Sub
```

Automation Using the OLE Control

Now let's use the OLE Control to implement a controlling application for Excel in the same manner we did when using objects. The one thing that is different is the way you access exposed objects with the OLE Control. With the OLE Control, you do not have to programmatically create an object with `CreateObject()`; you instead use the OLE Control as your object interface.

As with objects, you should refer to the Object Browser to find the available methods and procedures that you can access. However, you do not have to consult the system registry to find the class names of the object application since the OLE Control will handle all class references. Recall from our discussions of linking and embedding that you can insert objects into the OLE Control using the Insert Object dialog box or programmatically. If these objects located in the OLE Control support OLE Automation, you can manipulate the classes of the object applications programmatically.

The form for the application (see fig. 13.17) contains an OLE Control called `OLEControl`. This control contains an embedded Excel worksheet that was embedded using the Insert Object dialog box when the OLE Control was placed on the form.

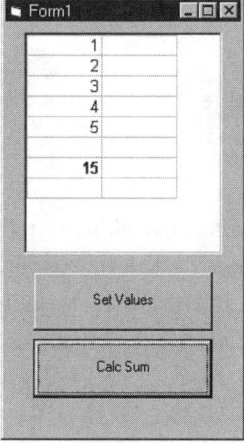

Fig. 13.17 OLE Automation can be performed on an embedded object in the same manner as that of a created object.

This control provides us with a method of accessing the functionality of Excel through the `Object` property of the control. The `Object` property points to the object in the OLE control and provides us with a reference to the object and its methods and properties. This reference is similar to the reference of a dimensioned object provided after a call to `CreateObject("Excel.Sheet")` (see Listing 13.4).

Listing 13.4   OLECLNT4.VBP—Referencing the Object and its Methods and Properties

```
'Set the values of the cells.  Set each value in a column
(A1,A2,A3,A4,A5)
Private Sub SetValues_Click()
    'Row 1, Col 1
    OLEControl.Object.Cells(1, 1).Value = 1
    'Row 2, Col 1
    OLEControl.Object.Cells(2, 1).Value = 2
    'Row 3, Col 1
    OLEControl.Object.Cells(3, 1).Value = 3
    'Row 4, Col 1
    OLEControl.Object.Cells(4, 1).Value = 4
    'Row 5, Col 1
    OLEControl.Object.Cells(5, 1).Value = 5
End Sub
```

As when we used object variables, we reference the `Cells` method of the `Object` from the OLE control and set the value for the cells with the `Value` property.

To calculate the sum of the values that we just placed into the cells, we place the equation using the `OLEControl.Object` reference. As before, the cell in row 7, column 1 is updated with the equation `"=SUM(A1:A5)"` and the font is bolded to emphasize the result.

```
'Calculate the sum of the values
Private Sub CalcSum_Click()
    OLEControl.Object.Cells(7, 1).Value = "=SUM(A1:A5)"
    OLEControl.Object.Cells(7, 1).Font.Bold = True
End Sub
```

One noticeable difference between the use of the OLE control and the use of object variables is that the object in the `OLEControl` is updated to show you the results of the operations. With the object variable, we had to make the application and the sheet visible to view the operations of the code where the OLEControl of this application contains a visible embedded object.

From Here...

In this chapter, we used your knowledge of OLE servers and provided insight into the use of OLE clients. By delving into the development of Visual Basic client container and controlling applications, we discussed several different methods for OLE interaction using Visual Basic. The methods of OLE interaction discussed in this chapter included object embedding, object linking, and OLE Automation.

➤ For more information on the inclusion of controls into your application, see Chapter 20, "OLE Controls, Add-Ins, and 32-bit DLLs."

➤ To investigate the features and functionality of Windows 95 custom controls, see Chapter 20, "OLE Controls, Add-Ins, and 32-bit DLLs."

➤ For information covering the inclusion of database management in your application, see Chapter 7, "The Jet Engine and ODBC."

14

Media Control Interface

by Dr. David Fullerton

With the predominance of fast microprocessors, brilliant, high-resolution color displays, cheap RAM, CD-ROM drives, and sound cards, the multimedia industry is beginning to hit its stride in the mass market. More multimedia CD-ROM titles such as *Microsoft's Encarta Encyclopedia* and *Broderbund's Living Books* are arriving at local computer software dealers daily.

The technology of multimedia presentations is becoming as commonplace as color monitors, and many users have begun to expect to see flashy graphic displays demonstrating the usage of a particular function, or hear their computer explain why they can't press that button. The technology of multimedia is not just for flash, but is a truly useful application of today's newest computer hardware.

As a Visual Basic programmer, you can take advantage of these types of audio-visual presentations in your applications. Conveniently, Microsoft has included the Multimedia Control Interface custom control as an easy way to make use of multimedia commands through Visual Basic.

This chapter will discuss the following information about multimedia the Multimedia Control Interface (MCI):

➤ What constitutes a multimedia application

➤ Terminology regarding multimedia

➤ Properties of the Microsoft MCI control enabling authoring of multimedia applications

➤ Using the Multimedia API

Multimedia Systems

Before learning about programming multimedia applications under Visual Basic in the next chapter, it is helpful to understand some of the hardware and software requirements for this environment. There are two groups of people that have different hardware and software requirements. Programmers like you have far greater hardware and software needs to develop multimedia applications than users who will just be playing back the multimedia files you have created.

> **Note:** Most computer systems being sold today more than exceed the minimum for supporting multimedia. In fact, there are few non-multimedia systems sold. With Windows 95, these systems are becoming even more common.

Development Hardware

For serious development of any multimedia programs, you will need the fastest PC with as much memory as you can afford. Multimedia tends to lean towards heavy processing requirements during the recording phase where real-time audio or video must be sampled, compressed, and saved as quickly as possible to maintain continuity.

> **Note:** Don't skimp on the hardware if you are serious about multimedia development. The extra money you spend on hardware up front will save you many hours in the future. Unless you have too much time on your hands, the investment in better hardware will pay for itself.

Some guidelines on minimum hardware are as follows:

CPU	Intel 486/66, Pentium or better
RAM	16 Megabytes
Hard Drive	1 Gigabyte
CD-ROM	Quad-Speed
Audio	16-bit DAC/ADC such as SoundBlaster
Video	Windows accelerated, 2 Meg Video RAM

Again, these are minimum guidelines on hardware that will only get more intense as time goes on. (Assuming that they aren't obsolete by the time this is printed! 6x and 8x CD-ROM devices are now available.)

If you are planning on recording video, you will also need a video capture-board, such as Truevision's Targa+ 64 or Creative Lab's VideoBlaster. Again, if you are cheap with your hardware, the more likely that you will be disappointed with the results.

Playback Hardware

During development of your application, you should be viewing the results on something more representative of your user's hardware. The Multimedia PC Marketing Council suggests the following minimum requirements for multimedia "compliance."

CPU	Intel 386sx or equivalent
RAM	2 Meg
Storage	Floppy / Hard Drive
CD-ROM	150 KB/s (single-speed)
Audio	Sound card with DAC/ADC
Video	VGA (16-color)

By looking at these requirements, you've probably shaken your head and sighed since you haven't seen a 386sx PC with 2 Meg of RAM since you gave yours away to your mother-in-law. What really matters here is that you can test your system out on a "regular" user's system to see how it will look. Perhaps your minimum requirements will be higher than the listing above. If they are, make sure that your user's know that up-front. The last thing you want is to have an irate user call you because his 386sx isn't performing the way he expected.

 **Note:** To be more realistic, the minimum should be the minimum for an acceptable Windows 95 machine. That is a 496/33 with 8 meg and at least a double-speed CD-ROM. The 4 meg that Microsoft says is the minimum yields unacceptable performance.

Development Software

This section is only meant as a general guideline to prepare a multimedia developer for the costs involved in creating multimedia applications. There are many multimedia authoring packages available depending on the type and quality of the application that you want to build.

The best package for your development will require a little research. Browse through various trade magazines or on-line discussion groups to find out how other people rate the currently available authoring tools. Be aware of which version that a particular article or discussion is reviewing. Often times, the package that may have rated lowest on the charts in one review is highest on the charts in the next review due to the changes that were made between versions of the software. Use the guidelines in Table 14.1 to find the right package for your needs.

Table 14.1   Guidelines for Choosing Multimedia Packages

Guideline	Commentary
Don't use price as the only guideline.	You may find that the best package is not always the most expensive.
Look at the reviewer's comments for the features you'll use most.	An article may discuss how poorly a product performed overall while that same product performed the best in the features that you'll use most.
Look for a commitment to a product line.	Larger companies will often phase out less profitable products after a short time, while smaller companies with a few core products may offer better long-term commitment to upgrades and feature enhancements. Also, smaller companies are more receptive to user suggestions for new features.
Try out the software package.	When you finally choose an authoring tool, purchase it from a local vendor or mail-order outlet that will offer a money-back guarantee. This will insure that you can take back software that doesn't meet your needs.

Note: Of course, you already have a superior multimedia development tool in Visual Basic 4. Other tools may offer some advantages in certain areas. Visual Basic will offer you a strong interface for all aspects of multimedia development.

Manipulating the Multimedia Control Interface

The Multimedia Control Interface (MCI) is a very powerful OLE Control that allows you to manipulate the recording or playing back of multimedia files on various MCI devices. Devices such as audio CDs, VideoDisc, and VCRs can be controlled by MCI. In addition, MCI can manipulate various file formats such as WAV files, AVI files, and MIDI files. While the MCI control can govern the operation of devices and files, it has no control over the data being played.

The basic format of the MCI control is that of a standard VCR. Standard controls include: Previous Track, Next Track, Play, Pause, Back, Step, Stop, Record, and Eject. Figure 14.1 shows the default MCI control buttons for the Visual Basic MCI custom control. Note that only the buttons that can be used are enabled.

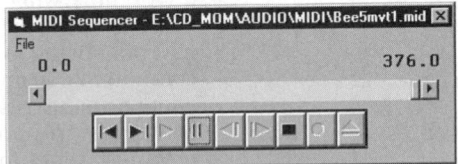

Fig. 14.1 Default MCI Control buttons provide much of the functionality for multimedia devices.

Since many devices that can be managed through the MCI control, it is helpful to know the specifics about the devices before you begin coding. While many applications can be written to make use of the various devices, keep in mind that each manufacturer may or may not support the particular command set that you issue to the device. The following examples list the most popular devices that could be a part in a general user's system.

Audio CD Device

Since most PC manufacturer's have begun shipping CD-ROM drives as "standard equipment," it is possible that the CD drive will become as common on PCs as a hard drive. With the cost of CD-ROM drives dropping to the price of a floppy drive for a single-speed CD-ROM player, it is a good bet that those older PCs that don't currently have a CD-ROM drive will get one soon.

Most people with a multimedia compliant PC also desire to play audio CDs through their computer. The MCI control offers complete control over audio CDs through the default MCI control buttons.

Starting with Windows 3.1, all Windows systems had built-in multimedia support. The only problem you may face is support for older DOS-type programs that use the CD. Windows NT 3.51 and Windows 95 have full multimedia support built-in along with drivers for most devices. Under Windows 95 and Windows NT 3.51, support for CD-ROM uses the 32-bit CD-ROM File System (CDFS). MSCDEX.EXE is included as a last resort for products that use it directly.

Note: If you have an old operating system, the only prerequisite for using the audio CD functions is that the MSCDEX (Microsoft's CD Extensions) driver is loaded and the MCICDA.DRV file is in your Windows SYSTEM directory. These drivers make communication from the CD-ROM device driver to the Windows CD audio driver possible. They are also responsible for providing DOS with a drive letter for the CD-ROM drive. The MSCDEX.EXE file should have been installed by default with your DOS installation if you have MS-DOS version 5.0 or better. If you are using anything less than version 5.0, you should upgrade to the latest version of DOS or move to Windows 95. The MCICDA.DRV file is located on your Windows 3.1 installation diskette number 4 and is usually installed with the default installation.

Animation

Several animation or movie-type formats are supported by the MCI control. The Multimedia Movie format makes reference to the standard that Macromind Director established and that Microsoft adopted. It is based on the Macintosh format of Macromind Director files. Since most of the multimedia files that are available for Windows are not in the Multimedia Movie format, you may not need to utilize this format very often.

Many multimedia animation recordings are available in the AVI format, which stands for *Audio-Video Interleaved*. In this format, a frame of video is followed by a frame of audio. This way, when the segment is played back, even from a slow media such as a CD-ROM drive, the audio and video remain synchronized. The AVI format typically implements some form of compression to both reduce the file sizes and to improve the playback.

One of the most important details of using any animation or full-motion video segment is that of data storage. Since these multimedia files could be 5-10 megabytes for a short clip, you must be very conscious of any other processing that may be going on during the presentation. It is not wise to expect the user of your application to be able to have a full-motion video segment running smoothly while another process is composing three-dimensional ray-traced images in the background. Today's microprocessors are good, but your average user probably won't have that kind of "horsepower" to spare.

Since much of multimedia surrounds the ability to display full-motion video, this topic will be explained in greater detail later on in this chapter and will be demonstrated in Visual Basic code in Chapter 15, "Multimedia in Action."

Wave Audio Files

One of the most common multimedia events that programmers want to take advantage of is the ability to play audio clips. Whether the audio clip is for informational purposes, error condition alerts, or just for fun, the MCI control can make the playback or recording of these files easy.

The Wave format, indicated by files that end in the WAV extension, is the de facto format of choice for Windows. Wave files not only contain the digital sampling information, but also include descriptive information about the format of this audio data. To illustrate, the wave format structure is shown in Listing 14.1

Listing 14.1   Format of a WAV File

```
Type WAVEHDR
        lpData As String
        dwBufferLength As Long
        dwBytesRecorded As Long
        dwUser As Long
        dwFlags As Long
        dwLoops As Long
        lpNext As Long
        Reserved As Long
End Type
Type WAVEFORMAT
        wFormatTag As Integer
        nChannels As Integer
        nSamplesPerSec As Long
        nAvgBytesPerSec As Long
        nBlockAlign As Integer
End Type
Type PCMWAVEFORMAT
        wf As WAVEFORMAT
        wBitsPerSample As Integer
End Type
```

As you can see, information about the number of channels and the sampling rate and depth is included in this structure. A wave file is called a RIFF (Resource Interchange File Format) file.

Graphic Images

Most programmers would like to make their user-interface as slick as possible. They know that a good interface reduces support calls and provides the user with a more intuitive application. To provide some of these functions, many developers have begun using more graphic images. Since image files, like most other forms of multimedia files, require large amounts of storage space, most developers are compressing images to save storage space. Refer to the section on image compression later on in this chapter for more information on saving space using graphic images. Also, Chapter 15, "Multimedia in Action," will go into greater hands-on detail on how to use graphic images in a user-interface.

Fig. 14.2 Flashy user-interfaces use graphic images to spice up the display.

Other Multimedia Devices

Many other multimedia devices can be governed using the MCI control. The MCI control can handle devices of type AVIVideo, CDAudio, DAT, DigitalVideo, MMMovie, Scanner, Sequencer, VCR, Videodisc, or WaveAudio. If you are not running Windows 95 or Windows NT 3.51, you will need the proper DOS device driver and the corresponding Windows driver. (Check your user's manual for guidance on the installation of these drivers.) Devices such as VCRs, Video Disc Players, and MIDI instruments require special hardware. The Plug and Play technology incorporated in Windows 95 should greatly alleviate the problems with getting all those IRQs and DMAs correctly set.

Multimedia Terminology

Each technology has its own set of concepts that are identified with particular verbiage. Multimedia is no exception to this rule. The images and sounds that are encapsulated within a multimedia file need to be indexed for programmers to make better use of them. An audio CD contains many songs, but each title is labeled and indexed so that the choice of which song to play is up to the end user. The same is true for a video-cassette tape. The VCR can record multiple programs, but the counter is necessary to find each individual program.

These ideas can be applied to the indexing of the multimedia files through the MCI custom control. The concepts of tracks, time, sampling, and frames will be explained to provide a better understanding of the usage of these indices.

Understanding CD Tracks

A track is a logical break in the media used to separate certain segments from other segments. In an audio CD, the tracks represent the particular songs on an album. In other media, tracks may have a completely different meaning, but will most likely be used in a similar way. An audio CD may be made up of 53 minutes of music, but the segment of music from 12 minutes 8 seconds to 17 minutes 22 seconds may contain a song that has a logical beginning and ending point. Therefore, it is assigned a track number.

A data CD may contain multiple "sessions" that contain data segments that were recorded together for a particular reason. For example, a roll of film is developed and then processed onto a CD during a session. This session would be seen as a track to the MCI custom control. Figure 14.3 illustrates the tracks on an audio CD being played by the CD player.

Fig. 14.3 CD tracks are logical subdivisions of data on the CD-ROM.

Time Indexing

The concept of time indexing is not new. Just as a calendar is used to mark the passage of time in a global sense, we use our age to mark time in a more personal way. Programmers must make use of time to index the multimedia files for playback and recording.

Wave audio files and CD-ROMs use time as their own "personal" or local way. A wave audio file contains a segment of sound for a particular amount of time. The file's size may not accurately represent the amount of time that was recorded due to differing sampling rates or sampling depths. These will be explained more fully later in this chapter, however, these variables show that bytes alone may not be the most accurate way for measuring time in a wave audio file.

Since time is the indexing method that provides an accurate playback of a recorded segment, the next step is understanding the different time formats that the MCI custom control provides. Just as your age can be measured in years or in seconds since you were born, so the time slices used to index an audio file can be honed to provide the necessary accuracy. For example, a program that only needs to play a file of a recorded "ding" probably doesn't need to utilize the file's time in milliseconds. On the other hand, a file that contains over a hundred different sound effects that have been compiled into one file would need to know the exact start and finish times of any one of the effects to play them back properly.

The MCI control allows the programmer to access the time format of a specific recording. Time is stored as a 4-byte variable whose format represents measurement of time and frame rate from milliseconds to hours, depending on the needs for an application.

> **Note:** Some devices do not recognize particular time formats since they do not make sense. A wave file contains no frames, therefore setting the time format to any of the frame-specific time formats will be ignored.

Sampling

Sampling is the process of recording a sound signal and converting that analog signal into digital code. Sampling is a function of the following three parameters:

> ➤ *Rate*—The frequency at which samples are taken.

> ➤ *Number of Channels*—Stereophonic or Monophonic.

> ➤ *Depth*—The breadth of each sample point usually 8-bit or 16-bit.

The sampling rate is the number of samples that are recorded during a particular time period. Often this value is expressed in samples per second. For example, if a wave audio file is recorded at 11.025kHz that means that 11,025 samples are taken each second to map the analog sound into a digital form.

The accuracy of this digital recording is affected by the number of samples taken per second. The higher the sampling rate, the more accurate the digital representation of the sound and the larger the file size. Figure 14.4 illustrates the recording parameters: Sample Rate, Channels, and Sample. The combination of the three parameters is displayed at the bottom.

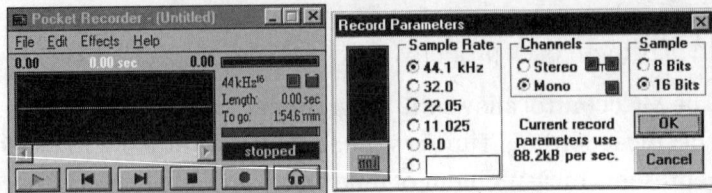

Fig. 14.4 Audio sampling rates provide several levels of quality.

The digital recording accuracy not only depends on sampling rate, but it also relies heavily on sampling depth. For example, if a recording is being made with an 8-bit sampling depth, the value for any particular sample could be one of 256 possible values. If however, the sampling depth was decreased to a two bit sample, the value could only be one of four possible values.

As the sampling rate or depth increases you will get better clarity, a more accurate digital recording, and a larger file. With a smaller sampling depth you will get a recording of poorer quality but a smaller file.

Additionally, the sampling depth could be expanded to multiple channels. A single-channel or mono recording is smaller than the same recording made with two channels or stereo. Depending on the application, the choice of sampling depths can produce widely variable file sizes. This point should be seriously considered when analyzing the application that will be recording or playing back wave audio files.

Understanding Frames

With video or animation sequences, similar quality and size issues arise when sampling rate is considered. Typical sampling rates for video and animation are 24, 25, and 30 frames per second. These speeds are fast enough for our brains to interpret them as "full-motion" images. Frames are merely a segment of time during which a sample is either recorded or played back. A frame-based time format allows the programmer to an index other than time or bytes to determine a position for playback or recording.

When recording or playing back, the sampling or frame rate is extremely important to the throughput of these images. The choice of 30 frames per second (fps) may overload a transport medium with data where a 24 fps animation would not. Each frame is dependent on the rate at which the data for that frame can be displayed or recorded. As with the wave audio files, video or animation files are heavily contingent on the color depth and frame dimensions to determine the amount of data that is being handled.

Using Video Compression

Since raw video frames can contain quite a lot of data, depending on the size and color depth, it is imperative to use some sort of compression scheme to reduce the amount of data that has to be stored. Most video file formats make provisions for compression, including the AVI format, and some are based on industry-standard algorithms that have been exclusively designed to compress full-motion video, such as the MPEG format.

Each format uses somewhat different compression techniques, however most techniques have a general compression style. The style makes reference to a "key" frame from which the next group of frames get their major characteristics. The frames following the key frame are made up of the changes that happen to that frame when compared to the key frame.

Figure 14.5 shows a sequence of frames which illustrate how frames are sequenced and how audio is aligned with the frames. This is using the AVIVIEW in the Video for Windows SDK.

The key-frame technique is fairly good at compressing a series of frames that are similar, however, as time goes on the frames begin to differ more and more significantly from the key frame. This requires a new key frame to begin referencing new changes. The more often a key frame is registered, the better the quality of the following frames and the more storage space that is required for the video segment. The fewer the key frames, the better the compression, but the worse the quality. As you'll quickly find when working with video multimedia files, there are many trade-offs between quality, size, and speed.

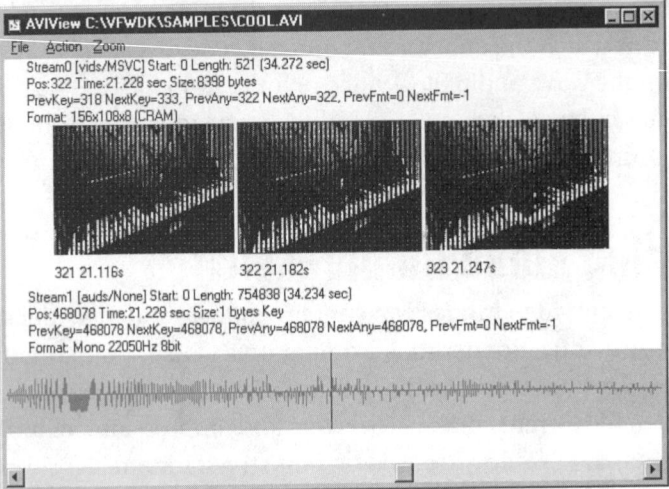

Fig. 14.5 Key frame and changed frames allow a greater compression rate for video streams.

When working with video compression, there are two methods to compress the video stream. Either you buy a video-compression board (hardware) for your system, which could run from several hundred to several thousand dollars, or you use an application's compression (software) to save the video stream into a compressed format. Each compression method has its particular strengths and weaknesses:

➤ Hardware Compression—The video compression boards are an excellent way to off-load the compression task from the main processor and achieve good results. These compression boards have hard-wired circuitry known as an ASIC or "Application Specific Integrated Circuit." They are specifically designed to implement the compression technique that is hard-coded on to the board. While this allows the hardware technology to compress video "on-the-fly," it also comes with a price. The price to buy into the technology, and the price of obsolescence a couple years down the road. If your applications require real-time video compression or high-capacity throughput, then hardware compression is your best choice.

➤ Software Compression—While software compression may be as good as hardware compression in results, the speed typically leaves much to be desired. As with any software implementation, the drawbacks include the memory and processor requirements for the host computer as well as the small capacity for video compression. However, even though software compression is slower on comparable machines than a hardware equivalent, software has the advantage of being easier to upgrade or change when technology changes. Also, since the investment in software is typically less-expensive than a hardware alternative, the choice to change compression technique in the future is somewhat easier on the pocketbook. Also, for developers who do not have a need for high capacity video compression, the software compression method may be a good choice.

Image Compression

Image compression is very common and most users have probably had some sort of contact with the various compression methods. Whether by downloading an image from a bulletin board, or viewing an image off a CD-ROM encyclopedia, most have used a compressed image. But few programmers have a detailed understanding of the various image compression methods.

Image compression is usually separated between "lossy" and "lossless" methods. A *lossless compression technique* takes an image and reduces the size without compromising the integrity of the data. It does this by identifying repeating bytes and storing the byte and count of repeating bytes. Such compressions reduce the size of the file by up to about 60 percent. All of the data that was there before the image is compressed will be there when the image is decompressed for viewing later. A *lossy compression technique* removes small parts of the data to reduce the size of an image. Lossy compression makes an assumption that a given pixel is close to the other 16 pixels around it. Therefore, the redundant 15 pixels are eliminated. Now, since an AVI file is a sequence of DIBs, the remaining data is then compressed using lossless compression. This method does not produce the same image after it is decompressed. This type of compression usually has some parameter which allows the amount of data that is lost to be varied. The more data that is lost, the higher the compression and the less faithful the image will be to the original. With experience, the amount of data lost can be compromised with the image quality to obtain a compression/quality balance. Lossy compression often reduces the size of an AVI file by a factor of 10 or more. You can achieve some effects of lossy compression by reducing the sampling or using a slower frame. However, this does not introduce loss of image. This would simply reduce the number of images and, therefore, file size. You must experiment to ascertain acceptable sampling rates.

Table 14.2 describes the various common graphic image file formats and their corresponding compression techniques.

Table 14.2   Graphic Image File Formats

Image File Format	Compression Type	Comments
BMP	Lossless	Very common with Windows users, but compression is usually low. Run length encoding counts the duplicated pixels to reduce the file size. It is effective in some images with large single-colored areas, but not very effective on photographic images.
PCX	Lossless	Common file format for some older images. Usually not of the preferred image formats for newer images.

Image File Format	Compression Type	Comments
TIFF	Lossless	Common file format for high resolution images, and for images that are transferred between dissimilar operating systems.
GIF	Lossless	Common file format that is limited to 256 colors. Popularized by Compuserve, image compression is good and images are transferable between dissimilar operating systems.
TGA	Lossless	Used primarily for maintaining high-quality images with 24-bit color resolution.
JPEG	Lossy	Provides excellent compression at the price of quality. Many bulletin board systems have begun using this image compression standard to allow users to download images with less on-line time. Compression of 30:1 is common. JPEG is also widely used on the internet to reduce file size.
Fractal	Lossy	Provides superior compression at the price of speed. Compression times are long without special hardware and decompression times are much longer than most other methods. Uses a proprietary mathematical model for image compression that allows for image compression of 100:1.

The standard Visual Basic picture property allows the loading of BMP, RLE, ICO, WMF, or DIB files. To use the other file formats in your Visual Basic application, you need to use the OLE container control or a third-party OLE Control or DLL. You can get a degree of animation with the PICCLIP custom control. If your application requires the storage of large quantities of graphic images, you may want to consider an alternative file format to reduce the storage requirements. Additionally, you may wish to store the images in a resource file and load the images only when the image is needed.

Multimedia Control Interface Commands

Since the MCI custom control can handle many different types of multimedia devices, a programmer needs to configure the control to perform according to the application.

The rest of this chapter will explain the details of the properties and commands to allow you to properly configure the MCI custom control.

DeviceType Property

The `DeviceType` property accepts values for the device that will be manipulated via the MCI custom control. The valid device types are as follows:

AVIVideo	Microsoft Video for Windows Format
CDAudio	Audio Compact Disc
DAT	Digital Audio Tape
DigitalVideo	Digital Video Format
MMMovie	Multimedia Movie Format
Overlay	Overlay Format
Scanner	Scanning Device
Sequencer	MIDI Sequencing Device
VCR	Video Cassette Recorder
VideoDisc	VideoDisc Player

WaveAudio	.WAV File Format
Other	Unlisted Format

The structure for setting the DeviceType property is as follows:

```
[FormName.]MMcontrol.DeviceType [= DeviceName$]
```

DeviceName$ is a string variable with the value of one of the devices listed above.

> **Note:** When giving syntax expressions, the following conventions are used:
>
> []: Items in brackets are optional parts of the expression.
>
> **Bold**: A required name, such as a property or method.
>
> *Italics*: An object with a user-defined name.
>
> $&!…: Indicate the datatype of the argument.

TimeFormat Property

As mentioned earlier, the time format for each device depends upon the media type. Refer to Table 14.3 to choose an appropriate time format. All time is stored as a 4-byte integer where each byte represents one token in the format. Sometimes, not all bytes are used.

Table 14.3   Time Formats for the MCI Control

Media Type	Time Format Setting	4-Byte Position Value
AVI, CD, MIDI, WAV	mciFormatMilliseconds	Milliseconds
AVI, CD, MIDI	mciFormatHms	Hours, minutes, seconds
CD	mciFormatMsf	Minutes, Seconds, Frames
AVI	mciFormatFrames	Frames count
MIDI	mciFormatSmpte24	SMPTE 24-frame format

continues

Table 14.3   Continued

Media Type	Time Format Setting	4-Byte Position Value
MIDI	mciFormatSmpte25	SMPTE 25-frame format
MIDI	mciFormatSmpte30	SMPTE 30-frame format
MIDI	mciFormatSmpte30Drop	SMPTE 30-frame format usi
WAV	mciFormatBytes	Byte count
WAV	mciFormatSamples	Sample count
CD	mciFormatTmsf	Tracks, minutes, seconds

Note: In this table, mciFormatSmpte24, mciFormatSmpte25, mciFormatSmpte30, and mciFormatSmpte30Drop all use the Society of Motion Picture and Television Engineers time format, which uses a 4-byte variable containing Hours, Minutes, Seconds, and Frames. Only the frame count changes between the various formats.

The syntax for the TimeFormat property is as follows:

```
[FormName.]MMControl.TimeFormat [= format&]
```

Note: Use the built-in intrinsic constants from Table 14.3 to specifiy format&.

Position Property

The Position property can be used to read the current position of the media. This is useful as an indicator in a user-interface which displays statistics on the current file or track.

The Position property depends on the value that has been set in the TimeFormat property. If an application will have a display that makes use of the position property, try to choose a time format that will make sense for the type of media that you are using. While milliseconds is a valid time format for an Audio CD, it is not that useful to display a 7-digit value for a display. It is more useful to display minutes and seconds in this case. The `Position` property is read-only at runtime and not available at designtime.

The syntax for obtaining the `Position` property is as follows:

```
x& = [FormName.]MMControl.Position
```

The value of x will be a long integer that must be parsed to display the appropriate value. Use Table 14.3 as a guide to format the `Position` value for display.

From/To Properties

The `From` and the `To` properties allow the media position for playback to be changed. Both properties require an additional command to be issued to function properly. Setting the `From` property not followed by a `Play` command will cause the `From` property to be ignored. In the same way, setting the `To` property not followed by a `Play`, `Record`, or `Seek` command will also be ignored.

The `From` and `To` properties consist of 4-byte values that correspond to the time format chosen for the device and media type. The `To` and `From` properties are not available at design. Use the following syntax to set the `From` and `To` properties at runtime:

```
[FormName.]MMControl.To [= timevalue&]
[FormName.]MMControl.From [= timevalue&]
```

`timevalue` is a 4-byte value using the current time format.

Dealing with Track Information

There are four properties that identify track information. All of these properties are read-only and available only at runtime.

➤ `Tracks` is a read-only value that indicates the total number of tracks of the MCI device media.

➤ The `Track` property specifies which track the information the `TrackPosition` and `TrackLength` properties will reference. The `Track` property does not necessarily indicate the current track.

➤ The `TrackLength` property is typically used in conjunction with the `Track` property. `TrackLength` is returned as a value that conforms with the current time.

➤ The `TrackPosition` property is used to find out the starting position of a particular track in the current time format. The track to be queried is specified using the `Track` property.

To read the `Tracks` property, use the following syntax:

```
x& = [FormName.]MMControl.Tracks
```

`x&` will contain the number of tracks.

To set the `Track` property, use the following syntax:

```
[FormName.]MMControl.Track = x&
```

`x&` is the value of the track for which the length or position will be queried.

To check a track's length, use the following syntax:

```
x& = [FormName.]MMControl.TrackLength
```

`x&` is a 4-byte variable using the current time format.

To find the starting position of a track, use the following syntax:

```
x& = [FormName.]MMControl.TrackPosition
```

`x&` is a 4-byte variable using the current time format.

Mode Property

The `Mode` property provides a method of checking the current state of an MCI device. This is useful for providing error-handling and error-prevention by only allowing state-appropriate commands to be issued. Table 14.4 shows the various values that can be returned as an integer value from the `Mode` property.

MCI Device Mode	Value	Constant
Device Not Open	524	mciModeNotOpen
Device Open and Stopped	525	mciModeStop
Device Open and Playing	526	mciModePlay
Device Open and Recording	527	mciModeRecord
Device Open and Seeking	528	mciModeSeek
Device Open and Paused	529	mciModePause
Device Open and Ready for Commands	530	mciModeReady

Command Property

The Command property provides a general means to control a MCI device via a command list. These commands are often used in conjunction with other MCI properties.

Table 14.5 lists the various commands that can be sent to an MCI device and their uses.

Table 14.5   MCI Commands

Command	Command Usage
Open	Opens the MCI device for use. If a device is currently open by another process, this will return an error. If the MCI device media is a file, the name is specified in the FileName property.
Close	Closes the MCI device that is currently open.
Play	Begins playing the selected MCI device's media from the current position. The starting position can be altered using the From and To properties.
Pause	Suspends the current playback or recording operation of the MCI device media. If a device is already paused, this command will resume the playback or recording from the currently pause position.

continues

Table 14.5   Continued

Command	Command Usage
Stop	Stops the playback or recording of an MCI device's media.
Back	Moves backwards in the media. This command is used in conjunction with the Frames property.
Step	Moves forwards in the media. This command is used in conjunction with the Frames property.
Prev	Moves to the beginning of the current track. If the Prev command is issued within three seconds of another Prev command, the operation moves backwards one track unless the media is at the first track.
Next	Moves to the next track. If the current track is the last track, it will move to the beginning of the last track.
Seek	Moves to the position indicated by the value of the To property.
Record	Begins recording at the current position or at the position indicated by the From or To properties.
Eject	Ejects media from the MCI device.
Sound	Plays the sound indicated by the FileName property.
Save	Saves the current recorded sound to the file indicated by the FileName property.

To use the Command property, use the following syntax:

```
[FormName.]MMControl.Command [= commandstring$]
```

commandstring$ is one of the commands listed in Table 14.5.

The Notify Property and the Done Event

The Notify property is typically used when the time-delay is significant during a particular event. For example, seeking on a CD-ROM is relatively quick compared to seeking on a VCR. Therefore, by setting the Notify property to True before a seek starts, the system can be used to perform other activities until the Done event indicates that the task has finished.

Use the following syntax to set the Notify property:

```
[FormName.]MMControl.Notify [= {True|False}]
```

The Done event will be triggered upon completion of the activity.

The UpdateInterval Property and the StatusUpdate Event

The status of the MCI device can be refreshed by using this specialized timer event. Typically, this is used to update the user-interface with the track number, time, or frame number of the current MCI device's media.

Use the following syntax to set the UpdateInterval property:

```
[FormName.]MMControl.UpdateInterval [= time%]
```

time% is the number of milliseconds between StatusUpdate events. Setting the UpdateInterval value to 0 disables the StatusUpdate event.

Beyond the Visual Basic MCI Control—Using the Multimedia API

There are times when you may want to do things beyond that allowed by the MCI Multimedia control provided with Visual Basic 4. As a Visual Basic programmer, you have full access to the multimedia API. However, there are certain cases in which you may have to move to C++. Those are cases where callbacks are used. In other instances, you may want to build an OLE interface to deal with the capability that you want to provide. For more information, see Chapter 20, "OLE Controls, Add-Ins, and 32-bit DLLs."

In addition to the properties available in Visual Basic's MCI custom control, several other commands that aren't directly accessible are very useful for programming multimedia applications. To use these commands, you will need to make calls to the dynamic linked library (DLL). For more information on using DLLs under Visual Basic, see Chapter 23, "Mixed-Language Development with DLLs." All references in this section will be 32-bit specific.

Note: Visual Basic 4 has two sources to find information about the Multimedia API calls. For the 16-bit environment, the API calls are stored in WINMMSYS.TXT. For the 32-bit operating systems, the Multimedia API is integrated with other Windows API calls in WIN32API.TXT. The API Text Viewer can be used to get specific information from these files.

Controlling the Volume

You may wish to offer the user control over the audio channels from within your application. Since the Visual Basic custom control does not make provisions for this, the DLL must be referenced. The following commands relate specifically to reading the current volume level (waveOutGetVolume) and setting the volume level (waveOutSetVolume).

```
RC& = waveOutGetVolume(deviceID, volumelevel)

deviceID is a Windows Handle (32-bit)
volumelevel is a long integer (32-bit)
```

deviceID is the Windows identification to the audio device that plays back the waveform files and sounds and volumelevel is the 32-bit volume level (16-bits per channel) that is returned by the function. A value of 0x0000 (zero) means that the channel is set to its lowest level while a value of 0xFFFF (65536) means that the channel is at full volume.

The waveOutSetVolume command is similar to the waveOutGetVolume command in its structure, however instead of returning a value, it is used to pass the volume level to the device. The following code line will set the volume of device deviceID to the level specified in VolumeLevel:

```
RC& = waveOutSetVolume(deviceID, volumelevel)
```

> **Note:** Not all devices support 16-bit volume definition per channel nor do all devices support stereo output. Those devices that do not support stereo output return the volume level in the low-order word. Devices that do not support 16-bit per channel volume will still return the 16-bit value that was set.

Multimedia DLL Command Strings

One of the most powerful and easy ways to make use of the multimedia control interface's capabilities is by passing command strings to the DLL. These command strings provide an additional way to control an MCI device without using MCI custom control properties.

One of the easier techniques is to use the `mciExecute` function. The prototype for this function is as follows

```
Declare Function mciExecute Lib "winmm.dll" Alias _
"mciExecute" (ByVal lpstrCommand As String) As Long
```

With this function you can simply execute any MCI command, such as the following:

```
lRC = mciExecute("play cdaudio")
```

or

```
lRC = mciExecute("seek cdaudio to 5"
```

or

```
lRC = mciExecute("play c:\windows\media\tada.wav")
```

The trick to this is the use of specific keywords and the system registry. `cdaudio` is a key word that MCI knows about. WAV is associated with Wave Sound in the registry. `mciExecute` requires that you know exact commands and strings to send to the MCI interface.

Sending a command string through the Multimedia Control Interface involves setting up a command line that can be interpreted by the MCI OLE.

These commands allow the programmer to utilize the multimedia functions without learning more difficult DLL calls. Additionally, debugging applications is much easier when you can read the codes that you are sending to the devices.

The mciExecute function is a variation of the mciSendCommand function that allows you to completely utilize the MCI API. The mciSendCommand function has the following prototype:

```
Declare Function mciSendCommand Lib "winmm.dll" Alias _
"mciSendCommandA" (ByVal wDeviceID As Long, ByVal uMessage _
As Long, ByVal dwParam1 As Long, ByVal dwParam2 As Long) As
Long
```

To use this function, you will need to fill in a set of structures with the information. Chapter 15, "Multimedia in Action," fully explores this concept. Following is the structure to pass for opening a device:

```
Type MCI_OPEN_PARMS
        dwCallback As Long
        wDeviceID As Long
        lpstrDeviceType As String
        lpstrElementName As String
        lpstrAlias As String
End Type
```

Since Visual Basic does not support callbacks, set the first parameter to vbNullChar. You will also need the API call mciGetDeviceID to get the parameter wDeviceID. lpstrDeviceType is the device type and lpstrElementName is the command you are sending. You can also give the name an alias in lpstrAlias.

Note: Most of these parameters are set with a set of predefined constants. You can find all requisite values in the API text viewer for both 32-bit and 16-bit API calls. You simply copy the values along with structures and declarations into your program.

To have complete control over your multimedia environment, there are many other structures and parameters to master. Of course, most of the time `mciExecute` will more than adequately suit your needs. To see everything about the MCI, check out the Multimedia Programmers Guide in the Microsoft Windows SDK.

From Here...

You have learned much of the terminology regarding multimedia and have learned many of the characteristics that make multimedia applications unique. You also saw many of the problems with multimedia and some of the techniques to get around these problems.

You also gained an understanding of the Multimedia Control Interface and the MDI custom control. To look at some of the other advanced techniques using Visual Basic, see the following chapters:

➤ To apply what you learned about the MCI to Multimedia applications, see Chapter 15, "Multimedia in Action."

➤ To learn more about the advanced graphics features of Visual Basic 4, see Chapter 16, "Graphics: Data Analysis."

➤ To find out more information on 32-bit DLLs, see Chapter 20, "OLE Controls, Add-Ins, and 32-bit DLLs."

15

Multimedia in Action

by Brian Blackman

The *Media Control Interface* (MCI) gives you a way of delivering and composing multimedia content using a simple and easy to understand interface to control multimedia devices. The Media Control Interface enables the developer to control devices using a uniform and simple syntax without specific, low-level knowledge of the device. This chapter will focus on the real-world practice of the Media Control Interface concepts.

There are many devices for composing and creating multimedia content. These devices can be very complex and expensive. The software that drives the devices to create the content strains simple computer resources. You must understand that creating multimedia content and viewing that content take two different sets of requirements. Creating the content can take much more horsepower than the personal computer that meets the MPC requirements. The MPC requirements are for the viewing and using of multimedia content. This requires far less computer resources than the creation of multimedia content.

In this chapter, you will learn the following:

➤ How to implement the Multimedia MCI Control in an application with CD audio

➤ How to use the MCI APIs to control devices

➤ How to apply a wave file audio

➤ How to use the AVI file video playback for animation

Multimedia MCI Control

Since the Multimedia MCI control is not one of the default controls listed in your Toolbox, you'll need to add it to your project. To add a custom control to your project choose Tools, Custom Controls. In the Custom Controls dialog box click on the check box next to the custom control you want to add to the project. Figure 15.1 indicates that the Microsoft Multimedia Control has been added to the project.

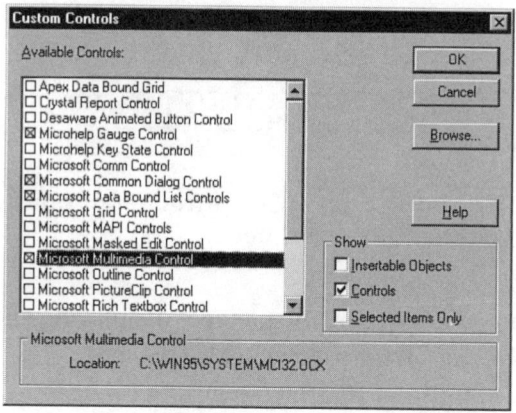

Fig. 15.1 The Multimedia MCI control is not added to your environment by default.

When the custom control has been added, you will see the Toolbox icon shown in figure 15.2.

Fig. 15.2 The Multimedia MCI Control Toolbox icon appears after you add the custom control.

After selecting the Multimedia MCI control and adding it to a form, you will see a button bar similar to that of a tape recorder (see fig. 15.3).

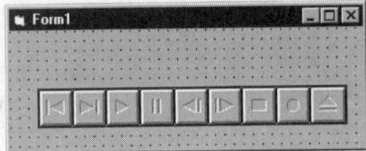

Fig. 15.3 The Multimedia MCI control default button bar contains most of the functions you'll need.

The Multimedia MCI control manages the playing and recording of multimedia files on the following MCI devices:

➤ Audio boards

➤ MIDI sequencers

➤ CD-ROM drives

➤ CD audio players

➤ Videodisc players

➤ Videotape recorders and players

➤ Playback of Video for Windows (*.AVI) files

For a detailed listing of all the properties and events for the Multimedia MCI control, search for "Multimedia MCI control" in the Visual Basic Help file. Many of the properties listed are limited in relevance to the device that is being controlled. For example, a CD-ROM is a read-only medium, therefore any properties relating to recording are not relevant. Of special note are the properties DeviceType, AutoEnable, hWndDisplay, Mode, Notify, Wait, and the events Done and StatusUpDate. The use of these properties and events in the sample application provides specific examples of the implementation details.

The simplicity of the Multimedia MCI control is exemplified in the DeviceType property, which specifies which device will be controlled. Through the use of string specifiers, you set this property to the device type (see Table 15.1).

Table 15.1   Device Types for the DeviceType Property

Device Type	Description
AVIVideo	AVI player
CDaudio	CD Audio
DAT	Digital Audio Tape player
DigitalVideo	Digital video
MMMovie	Multimedia movie player
Other	Undefined device
Overlay	Analog video in a window
Scanner	Image scanning device
Sequencer	MIDI sequencer
VCR	Videotape recorder/player
Videodisc	Videodisc player
WaveAudio	WAV file player

Note: The `Command`, `hWndDisplay`, `Mode`, `Notify`, and `Wait` properties are available only at runtime. Hence you set these properties in your code.

`AutoEnable` allows the MCI control to detect and enable the appropriate buttons on the control. While this is the default implementation, there are circumstances where you want this disabled, such as when you want to prevent the user from performing an action with the media until the application enables the function. The buttons are enabled and disabled individually.

The `Command` property is available only at runtime and setting this property immediately executes the command. You set the property using a string command. This demonstrates the simplicity of MCI and the Multimedia MCI control. You simply set the property to commands such as: `Open`, `Close`, `Play`, `Pause`, `Stop`, and `Eject`.

The `hWndDisplay` property sets and reads the playback window handle to allow the Multimedia Control Interface to redirect output from a default window (handle of zero) to the window you specify. You choose whether to use your own window or let MCI create a stage window. To get the handle of a form, use the control's `SetFocus` method to set the focus to the control, and then call the Windows `GetFocus` API to obtain the handle.

`Mode` allows the application to determine what the MCI device is doing. By reading the `Mode` property, your application can determine the correct operations to perform. The `Mode` status codes appear in Table 15.2:

Table 15.2   Mode Status Codes

Code	Description	Constant
524	Device is not open	mciModeNotOpen
525	Device is stopped	mciModeStop
526	Device is playing the media	mciModePlay
527	Device is recording onto the media	mciModeRecord
528	Device is seeking over the media	mciModeSeek
529	Device is paused	mciModePause
530	Device is ready for MCI commands	mciModeReady

`Notify` enables the device to send messages back to your application when a command has finished. By setting this property to `True`, the device will trigger the `Done` event when the current command has completed.

`Wait` allows your application to protect the device from further input until the current operation is complete. This is useful in an application that controls a VCR. For example, your Visual Basic application could require that, after the playing of the video, the device would not allow the tape to be ejected until the tape was rewound.

The `Done` event allows your application to handle information that is returned after a command is sent to the device with the `Notify` property set. The `Notify` values are 1 - `Successful`, 2 - `Superseded`, 3 - `Aborted`, and 4 - `Failure`. The constants are 1 - `mciNotifySuccessful`, 2 - `mciNotifySuperseded`, 3 - `mciNotifyAborted`, and 4 - `mciNotifyFailure`.

`UpdateInterval` triggers the `StatusUpdate` event. When the `UpdateInterval` time elapses, the application can read the newest statistics about the device. Using these features, you could display the current elapsed time of a media playback or recording.

Jamming with the CD Jammer Sample Application

The CD Jammer application is available on the book's accompanying CD-ROM. You'll find two versions; a 16- and 32-bit named CDJAM16.EXE and CDJAM32.EXE, respectively. For best performance simply copy the executable and CDJAMMER.AVI files to a directory on your hard drive. Then place an audio CD in your CD-ROM drive and run either version of this application.

> **Note:** To run any of the Visual Basic applications on the CD-ROM you need to copy the VB40016.DLL and VB40032.DLL to your Windows, Windows 95, or Windows NT system directory. You can find these DLLs in the Chapter 15 directory on the CD-ROM.

The CD Jammer application was born out of a sense that the shareware versions of CD players were too expensive for the functionality that they provided, and the applications did not begin to explore the potential that was available for a Windows-based audio CD player. So the first versions of CD Jammer, which were written in Visual Basic 3, were released as freeware with the ability to play audio CDs. As the application progressed, other features began to appear, such as the ability to create customized play lists, shuffled play lists, and a database of the user's CD collection. The code from the freeware version of CD Jammer was used to create the examples in this chapter and the application that is on the CD-ROM.

As figure 15.4 shows, the main CD Jammer screen is comprised of a group of buttons that controls the functions of the CD player and it includes an LED-style track and time display.

> **Caution:** The design of the main form requires at least a 256-color display. With most multimedia machines, this is fairly standard. On machines with displays that are less than 256 colors, the palette will dither some colors and may cause some odd colors to appear.

Fig. 15.4 The main screen of CD Jammer shows how the multimedia parts of the application come together.

Choosing Button Controls

In CD Jammer, I chose not to use the Multimedia MCI control and used my own buttons. These buttons are grouped differently from the Multimedia MCI control buttons. This was done largely for aesthetic reasons. By grouping the controls differently and adding new icons, the application gets a fresh look and feel.

Caution: The code in this chapter works only if you have just one CD-ROM. It will not work if you have more than one CD-ROM connected to your computer. If there is more than one CD-ROM, the application makes no attempt to distinguish between the two or more CD-ROM devices. It is assumed that the majority of users of this application have one CD-ROM. Yet, now we have an opportunity to upgrade the feature set once again or to leave this as an exercise for the reader in MCI development!

Listing 15.1 shows the code used to program the new Play Button control.

Listing 15.1   CDJAMMER.FRM—The Play Button Control

```
Private Sub PlayButton_Click()
    Dim lReturnValue As Integer, i As Integer

    PlayButton.Visible = False
    PauseButton.Visible = True
    Timer1.Interval = 900
    TrackPanel.Caption = "Track"
    DiscPanel.Caption = "Elapsed Time"


    If Shuffle.Value = True Then
        For i = 0 To PlayList.ListCount
            lReturnValue = mciSendString("play CD from " + _
    PlayList.List(i) + " wait", vbNullString, 0, 0)
        Next

    Else
        lReturnValue = mciSendString("play CD", _
        vbNullString, 0, 0)
    End If

End Sub
```

Note: In Visual Basic 4, you use the constant `vbNullString` to pass a Null pointer to the Windows API. This is improved over the handling of passing nulls to Dynamic Link Libraries in previous versions of Visual Basic.

You may have noticed the reference to the function `mciSendString`. This is the multimedia "heart" of this application. The `mciSendString` commands provide all of the functionality to control and query the device's operation. This function demonstrates another method for creating multimedia controlling applications. `mciSendString` is a Windows API function and serves us well. By using this function we don't have to include the OLE Multimedia MCI custom control extension and thereby reduce the size of our application and number of redistributable files.

Windows API functions are declared in the `Declarations` section of the form; they must be declared `Private`. Listing 15.2 indicates the declaration of the 16-bit `mciSendString` and the 32-bit `mciSendStringA` functions, which can return error codes to your application. You can choose whether you want to handle and report these errors. The use of the alias feature gives us a way to use only one function name in our code instead of two function calls surrounded with conditional compilation statements.

Listing 15.2   CDJAMMER.FRM—Declaring the Multimedia Control Interaction Functions

```
#If Win16 Then
Private Declare Function mciSendString Lib "mmsystem" (ByVal _
    MCI_Command As String, ByVal ReturnString As String, _
    ByVal ReturnLength As Integer, ByVal Handle _
    As Integer) As Long
#ElseIf Win32 Then
Private Declare Function mciSendString Lib "winmm.dll" Alias _
    "mciSendStringA" (ByVal lpstrCommand As String, ByVal _
    lpstrReturnString As String, ByVal uReturnLength As Long, _
    ByVal hwndCallback As Long) As Long
#End If
```

While there isn't much to the functions declared above, they are responsible for one of the ways for interaction that CD Jammer (or any application) has with the multimedia devices. Since this code is responsible for the core functionality of the application, it is useful to understand how to communicate with the multimedia devices which it controls.

As discussed in Chapter 14, "Media Control Interface," the MCI command string is an extremely useful way to easily control multimedia devices and files. Programming from within Visual Basic requires little preparation or understanding of the strings that can be passed into the multimedia DLL. You have only one MCI API to call, `mciSendString`, with which you pass your string commands and these string commands are simple and self explanatory.

In addition to the declaration functions shown above, the buffers for the messages returned from the DLL must be created. In Visual Basic, a return buffer can be built using the `String` variable type. The following function indicates how a buffer of 1024 bytes or 1K can be created:

```
Dim ReturnString as String * 1024
```

The following is an example of using the `ReturnString` in the `mciSendString` command function:

```
longreturn = mciSendString("open cdaudio",ReturnString,1024,0)
```

This would effectively send the `open` command to the CD audio device. The additional functionality of the `ReturnString` variable is not evident unless your application reads the return information in the buffer. Issuing an `"open the CD device"` type of command does not really yield much useful information from the `ReturnString` other than device status, but other commands pass interesting information such as the device's name and model number. The following function queries the CD audio device for information and then displays the returned information in a message box.

```
Sub QueryIt()
    Dim lReturnVal as Long
    Dim szReturnString as String * 1024
    Rem Open up the device
```

```
lReturnVal = mciSendString("open cdaudio",_
    vbNullString, 0, 0)
lReturnVal = mciSendString("info cdaudio product",_
    szReturnString, 1024, 0)
MsgBox(szReturnString)
lReturnVal = mciSendString("close cdaudio",_
    vbNullString, 0, 0)
End Sub
```

> **Note:** For those of you familiar with 16-bit MCI development, you will note the absence of the use of `mciExecute()`. This is a popular 16-bit MCI API; however, there is no `mciExecute()` in Win32.

Using Track Access Control

Track playback was also enhanced through the use of shuffle play, custom shuffle, and custom play lists. The shuffle play feature basically randomizes the order of the songs to be played from the CD. Listing 15.3 shows the code used to generate the randomized play list for the shuffle play feature.

Listing 15.3   CDJAMMER.FRM—The Shuffle Play Feature

```
Sub ShuffleUpdate()
Dim j As Integer, i As Integer, x As Integer
    Dim k As Integer, e As Integer, y As Integer

    If DiscList.ListCount > 0 Then
        Dim rgszBuffer(99) As String
        j = DiscList.ListCount

        For i = 1 To j
            rgszBuffer(i) = "X"
        Next

        PlayListViewable.Clear
        PlayList.Clear
        Randomize
        k = 1

        For x = 1 To j
            e = Int(Rnd(1) * j)
```

```
        If rgszBuffer = "X" Then
            rgszBuffer(e) = k
            k = k + 1
        Else
            e = e + 1

            For y = 1 To j
                If rgszBuffer(e) <> "X" Then
                    e = e + 1
                    If e > j Then e = 1
                Else
                    rgszBuffer(e) = k
                    k = k + 1
                End If
            Next

        End If
    Next

    For x = 1 To j
        PlayList.AddItem rgszBuffer(x)
        PlayListViewable.AddItem DiscList.List(Val_
    (rgszBuffer(x)) - 1)
    Next

    End If
End Sub
```

Note: For much of the code in this chapter you cannot just type in the code and compile. Most of the code contains interdependencies with other code in the project. If you want to type this code in yourself, use the project on the CD-ROM.

The custom shuffle play feature allows the user to select individual songs to be played in a particular order, and allows the songs to be heard more than once if desired. With custom shuffle play, not all songs need be played. A selection of one song played three times in a row is an example of a custom shuffle play list.

The custom play list allows the user to create custom shuffle play lists and save them. This allows the user to create up to 99 different song sequences for a particular CD. While this may be excessive for most users, you may modify the code in the database saving function to create as many play lists as you think are necessary.

Database Access Control

The database feature allows the user to catalog his CD collection while he plays his CDs. Loading a new disc allows the user to begin the cataloging procedure. He may add information on the album title, the artist, and the titles of each of the songs on that CD. This database does not use the built-in Access database engine for the following two reasons:

➤ The requirements of the data access are not very demanding, as you can see by the code example on the CD-ROM in the DATAFORM.FRM form.

➤ This application was originally created under Visual Basic 3 and distributed as freeware. The size of the various VBX and DLL modules that would have to be sent with the actual application totaled over one megabyte. The application without the Visual Basic 3.0 runtime DLL was only around 60K! It was decided early on that one megabyte was too large of an archive to send over the telephone lines when all that was needed was 1/17th the size.

The basic structure of the database file is that of comma-delimited, end-of-line terminated records. The following shows example data that you would find in a file created by the CD Jammer database engine:

CD Jammer,2.5,2

"Herby's Greatest Hits","Herby Schlonskins Sr.",9,"I Need Love",...

"Wanda's Tunes for Tommorow","Wanda QuaferYokle",12,"Breakfast",...

Special Features of CD Jammer

The CD Jammer application is primarily an audio CD player. However, several features were added to demonstrate the true meaning of multimedia. For example, the application handles and catalogs text data for the audio CD such as artist, title, and song. This lets you build a comprehensive database of your CD collection. In addition to playing and cataloging the audio CD, the application also plays a Video for Windows AVI file and uses an LCD type display. The playing of the AVI file makes for a unique and great splash screen. The LCD display provides familiar application feedback to the user.

The rest of this chapter will focus on the code and the design of these features to demonstrate how multimedia features interact within an application.

Automatically Recognizing the Disc

One of the first features added was the ability to automatically recognize the CD that the user had inserted into the CD-ROM player. This feature ranks highly for its "neat-o" effect. While it is fairly simple to accomplish, it provides a great selling point. An application can make use of this feature for audio CDs like the sample program or, in the case of a CD-ROM data vendor, it can check a data CD-ROM to verify that it's the distribution version that the application is expecting.

Identifying the Disc by Track Sequence

There are tracks on an audio CD that represent songs on an album. These songs have specific lengths that can be used to identify the particular CD by comparing the sequence of track times for a given number of tracks.

What happens if the first couple of tracks for two different albums coincidentally have the same lengths? Well, it may be possible for two or more albums to meet this criteria, but several factors weigh against it. First, a typical user's collection size will be a sufficiently small sample of all audio CDs in existence. This significantly decreases the chances that a user has two albums that register as the same album. Second, the time increments used to measure a track's length are very small. Table 15.3 illustrates how the first two tracks of two albums may appear to match, but in reality, are different.

Table 15.3   Track Length Comparison

Album Title	Track Lengths in Minutes and Seconds	Track Lengths in Milliseconds
Herby's Greatest Hits	Track 1 – 3:24 Track 2 – 4:18	Track 1 – 204020 Track 2 – 257946
Wanda's Tunes for Tomorrow	Track 1 – 3:24 Track 2 – 4:18	Track 1 – 203997 Track 2 – 258094

Notice that the first track has a time of 3 minutes, 24 seconds for both albums, but as the time format changes to a more precise measurement, the difference becomes apparent. Obviously, it would be far more difficult for an album to register incorrectly when track lengths in milliseconds are compared.

There is a particular event that would invalidate this type of comparison. It would be the case that the disc contains only one track that extends to the end of the medium. An audio CD might not have this type of configuration but a data CD could certainly fulfill the requirements. In this scenario, an additional check mechanism should be instituted, such as checking the date of the first file in the root directory of the CD.

Identifying the Disc by Length

Using a CD's recorded length, in milliseconds, can also be a fairly accurate identification routine. The Track Sequence method records the length of each song or track. The Disc by Length method measures the total playing time of the CD. Just like the Track Sequence method, this identification process makes the assumption that a user will have a small enough sample of available CDs to presume that each CD owned will have unique amount of information recorded on it.

Again, this identification routine has the same drawbacks about full media as the Track Sequence method. However, in general, either of these processes should work well when implementing an automatic disc identification routine in your application.

Animating the Splash Screen

The multimedia explosion is being fueled by the availability of full-motion video. To demonstrate this type of functionality, CD Jammer was designed with an introduction screen, or *splash screen*, which plays an AVI video file. Figure 15.5 shows a still image of the splash screen.

Fig. 15.5 A still shot of CD Jammer's splash screen video shows a CD-ROM spinning.

A great deal of time and effort went into designing and creating this video file. If you have never experimented with animation, ray-tracing, or video files, let me warn you that it is addictive. A good portion of a week was used to create the two-second animation that is the splash screen for CD Jammer. It would have taken much longer if I had not been as familiar with the POV-ray tracing application. While you are able to create stunning three-dimensional graphics, you need a lot of patience and a good creative touch.

Caution: It cannot be stressed strongly enough that multimedia applications will take much longer to develop than other types of applications. There is not much difference in the difficulty of coding the application, but there is a huge time factor for producing the "perfect" bitmaps, icons, video files, animation sequences, and audio files that most programmers have never encountered. Again, unless you start out with your eyes open, you will be disappointed with your development times.

Note: Unfortunately for many of us, we don't possess a lot of patience nor any creativity when it comes to graphic arts. However, there are many tools available, such as Autodesk's 3D-Studio and others, that make developing high-quality, ray-traced artwork and animation much easier.

To incorporate the AVI video file, the application must be able to verify the existence of special drivers. Microsoft's Video for Windows driver or some other manufacturer's driver capable of AVI playback must be installed on the user's PC to view the file. If your application will be distributed to the masses as a shareware program, then it is wise to specify that the Video for Windows drivers must be installed on the user's PC before she installs your application. Yet, with Windows 95 and Windows NT, Video for Windows is part of the normal installation and your users will already have the driver.

The code to display the AVI file in the splash screen window is detailed in Listing 15.4. This subroutine is called from the form's `Form_Load` event.

Listing 15.4   CDJAMMER.FRM—AVI Splash Screen Code

```
Sub AboutBox()
    Dim lReturnValue As Long, lhWnd As Long
    Dim szAVIFile As String
    Dim i As Integer
```

```
On Error GoTo Err_AboutBox

About.Show

' This do nothing for loop is to give the form time to process
' paint messages so the author's name will appear on the form
' before the avi file is played. Windows treats WM_PAINT
' messages as low priority.
For i = 0 To 200
    DoEvents
Next

szAVIFile = Dir$(App.Path & "\cdjammer.avi")
If szAVIFile = "" Then
    MsgBox ("Unable to locate the CD-Jammer AVI file in _
    the application's directory.")
    Unload About
    Exit Sub
End If

ChDir (App.Path)

' Open AVI file and give it an alias
lReturnValue = mciSendString("open cdjammer.avi _
 alias cdspin style popup", vbNullString, 0, 0)

If lReturnValue Then Err.Raise 65000 ' Raise our own _
 fictitious error.

' Have MCI create a window for playback
' Windows Handles are integers in 16bit Visual Basic must
' use a long for cross-platform support.

lhWnd = About.hWnd
lReturnValue = mciSendString("window cdspin handle " + _
 Str$(lhWnd), vbNullString, 0, 0)

' Play it...
lReturnValue = mciSendString("play cdspin wait", _
 vbNullString, 0, 0)

' Wait until it's done playing
While Left$(gReturnString, 7) <> "stopped"
        lReturnValue = mciSendString("status cdspin mode", _
    gReturnString, 1024, 0)
            ' Be nice and give some time back while we're waiting
```

continues

Listing 15.4   Continued

```
            DoEvents
    Wend

Exit_AboutBox:
    ' Close AVI file
    lReturnValue = mciSendString("close cdspin", _
    vbNullString, 0, 0)
    Unload About
    Exit Sub

Err_AboutBox:
    ' Report the error
    GetMCIError lReturnValue
    Err = 0
    Resume Exit_AboutBox

End Sub
```

Note that this procedure has the benefit of error checking. While not used throughout the sample application's code, it is added in this procedure for the reader's benefit as a demonstration on how to accomplish error checking using the MCI APIs. The call to the procedure GetMCIError() in the label Err_ABoutBox checks the error and reports it to the user in a message box. The GetMCIError() procedure is in the module GLOBAL.BAS.

While this is not the optimal method of handling the error, it does present to you, the programmer, the way of getting the MCI error. From that point you choose whether you want to handle the error, report the error to the user, or ignore it completely.

Also note that during the actual playback of the file, the status of the device is queried through a While loop. This is done because the application is not using the Multimedia Control Interface custom control, but is using direct calls to the multimedia DLL. Listing 15.5 shows example code that would be used to accomplish the same thing if you were using the Multimedia MCI control.

Listing 15.5 Playing the AVI File through the Custom Control

```
Sub MCIPlayAVI()
    Rem Set the device type
    MMControl1.DeviceType = "avivideo"
    Rem Set the file to play
    MMControl1.FileName = "cdjammer.avi"
    Rem Tell the MCI control to enable the default buttons
    MMControl1.AutoEnable = True
    Rem Open the AVI device
    MMControl1.Command = "open"
    Rem Turn on the notification - enablimg the "Done" event
    MMControl1.Notify = True
    Rem Play the file...
    MMControl1.Command = "play"
End Sub
Private Sub MMControl1_Done(NotifyCode As Integer)
    Rem Close the AVI device after it finishes
    MMControl1.Command = "close"
End Sub
```

Either way that you choose to implement this functionality, the sequence of events is similar. Follow these steps to play a generic multimedia file:

1. Select the file to play.

2. Open the multimedia device that will play the file.

3. Begin playing the file.

4. Wait for the file to end its playback.

5. Close the device.

The last step of closing the device is very important. If your application does not close the multimedia device that closes the file that was being played, the next time that the application returns to use that device or file, it will be in use and unavailable.

Note: The exception to this rule is the CD-Audio device. Typically, the interaction with the user requires that the device is open to switch tracks, begin and end playback, and eject the media.

The next section discusses another form of multimedia file playback using WAV audio files to confirm button-control selections.

Vocalizing Controls

This feature was added as an exercise in WAV audio file recording and playback. The main idea behind the function is to speak the function that was chosen via the control buttons. If the user clicks the Play button, the application says "Play" and begins to play the CD.

The wave audio prompts were created by using the Sound Recorder application found in the accessories section of Windows. After the individual files were created, the sounds were merged back into one large WAV file which contains all of the audio prompts. You may be asking yourself, "Why do such a goofy thing?" In general, it is much easier to open up the WAV audio device with one file, play that file, and close the device. But this is an expert solutions book and the techniques presented here solve a problem you could run into in the future.

Concatenating the WAV File

The basic idea behind this theory is that it is better to send one large file rather than many smaller files that take up the same amount of space. If one file can contain all of the prompts that are necessary, then installation becomes easier to manage and troubleshooting becomes easier.

The additional bonus of concatenating the WAV files is the ability to safeguard your application from tampering. For example, you may have intended your application to be distributed with a word from the author. Your friend takes a picture of you that you scan into your machine. You design an "About" form that tells a little about you and your company and has your picture plastered dead center.

Note: As a neat side note, you add to the WAV files that announce other functions in the program by personally describing your pride in the quality of this application. If the WAV files were separate, your speech could easily be replaced by lewd comments from a teenaged hacker. All of your development efforts were not spent to have your application distributed without your WAV file. To reduce this risk, distributing one WAV file with all of the application's audio prompts and your speech makes tampering more difficult.

The hardest part to concatenation is figuring out where to begin and end each clip. Using the Sound Recorder application will get you pretty close, and if you have a little "dead-air" or periods of silence on either side of the desired audio clip, the positioning is not as critical. Also, depending on the number of audio clips, the task becomes harder the more clips you add.

If you intend to concatenate any audio clips or need a somewhat higher resolution of time-slicing to determine exactly when a clip begins and ends, it is highly recommended that you purchase an audio file management utility. There are several good shareware utilities, such as CoolWave Editor, that allow you to work with WAV files down to the individual sample. These types of utilities will save you a lot of time and effort if you plan on using this technique.

Playing Back Audio Clips

You understand how WAV files can be strung together to build a single file containing multiple audio clips. You also understand how to index those audio clips. Now you need to know how to play an audio clip from within the concatenated WAV file.

The audio file for the CD Jammer application has nine audio clips built into a single concatenated file. The nine clips are show in Table 15.4.

Table 15.4   Audio Clips in CD Jammer

Audio Clip	Start Position (Sample Number)	End Position (Sample Number)
Welcome to CD Jammer	0	16172
Goodbye	18869	24467
Play	29030	34627
Stop	37946	42922
Pause	47277	51423
Next Track	56608	67805
Previous Track	69464	77343
Eject	80869	87504
Thank You Speech	89371	123999

To play the specific clips, the WAV device needs to be opened only once. Then each audio clip can be accessed using the "play" feature bounded by the "from" and "to" fields. Listing 15.6 shows code that accepts the positions as input from the calling function and plays the specified clip. This example shows the Play control calling the audio clip.

Listing 15.6   Audio Clip Playback Example

```
Private Sub Form_Load()
    Dim lReturnValue as Long
    Rem Open the Concatenated Wave File
    lReturnValue = mciSendString("open cdjammer.wav_
      alias waves", vbNullString, 0, 0)
End Sub

Sub PlayIt(PlayFrom As Long, PlayTo As Long)
    Dim lReturnValue as Long
    Rem Reset the time format to samples
    lReturnValue = mciSendString("set waves time format_
      samples", vbNullString, 0, 0)
    Rem Generate MCI command string from parameters
    Play$ = "play waves from " + Str$(PlayFrom) + " to "_
      + Str$(PlayTo)
```

```
    Rem Send the command to play the sound
    lReturnValue = mciSendString(Play$, vbNullString, 0, 0)
End Sub

Private Sub PlayButton_Click()
    Rem Play the audio clip by passing it
    Rem the start and end times
    Call PlayIt(29030, 34627)
End Sub

Private Sub Form_Unload(Cancel As Integer)
    Dim lReturnValue as Long
    Rem Shut down the WAV file device when the program exits
    lReturnValue = mciSendString("close waves", _
      vbNullString, 0, 0)
End Sub
```

The rest of the control buttons are activated in the same way by calling the PlayIt function with the correct values indicated in the table. As you can see, it would be fairly straightforward to create a large concatenated file if it were necessary.

Using LED-Style Displays

Most newer stereo systems have some sort of LED or LCD type of display panel that indicates what station you are listening to, what the volume level is at, and what device you are controlling. Well, the CD Jammer display is taken from the same idea. The panel is made up of several digits that indicate the current track, the total number of tracks, and the playing time of the track and disc. Figure 15.6 shows a close-up view of the LED display.

To create the illusion of an LED display panel, a 4×6 array of circles was created to form a single digit. The digit was then copied several times to create the remaining digits. Making the digits an array has a couple of advantages. First, copying the digits was far simpler than creating new ones. Second, the array allows the application code to take advantage of the placement when activating the digits.

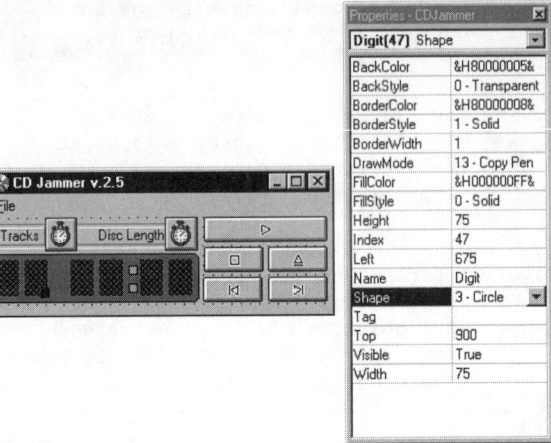

Fig. 15.6 The LED-style display panel is made up of an array of shapes.

To further explore this point, see figure 15.7. The two digits in this example are made up of 48 individual circles. The first digit has circles numbered zero through 23 and the second digit has circles numbered 24 through 47. These circles, when colored in a specific pattern, will display numbers.

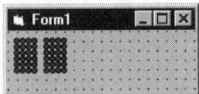

Fig. 15.7 A digit array shows how the shapes are arranged.

By exploiting the arrangement of the array of circles, the same code can be made to activate any one digit with a particular value. For example, if we take a very simple example of the number 1 and chart its pattern according to the array, the binary representation can be gathered (see fig. 15.8).

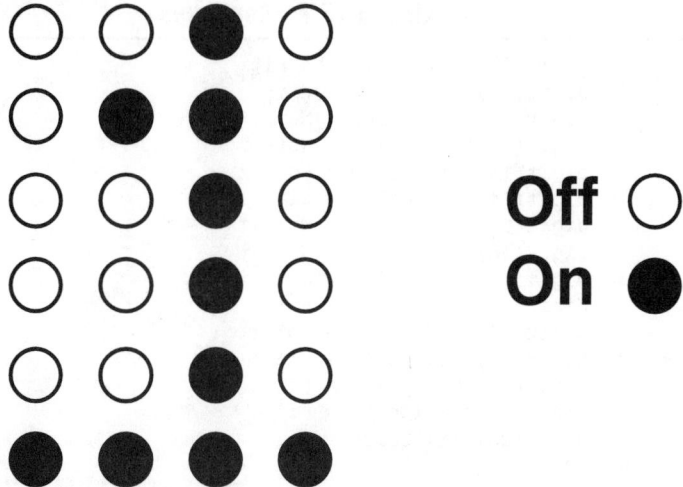

Fig. 15.8 Charting a digit within the shape array will help develop the code to display the number.

After the binary "ons" and "offs" are charted, the code to create the visual representation can be implemented. Listing 15.7 shows how the individual circles are colored appropriately for the number 1. Figure 15.9 shows how the code looks when the program is run.

Listing 15.7   Creating the Number One on the Digit Array

```
Sub DigitOne()
Rem This function builds a number "1"
    Rem Set the colors of On and Off
    Lit = &hffff&     Rem "on"
    NotLit = &h8080&  Rem "off"
    Rem The digit() stands for an array of circles
    digit(0).FillColor = NotLit
    digit(1).FillColor = NotLit
    digit(2).FillColor = Lit
    digit(3).FillColor = NotLit
    digit(4).FillColor = NotLit
    digit(5).FillColor = Lit
    digit(6).FillColor = Lit
    digit(7).FillColor = NotLit
    digit(8).FillColor = NotLit
```

continues

Listing 15.7   Continued

```
        digit(9).FillColor = NotLit
        digit(10).FillColor = Lit
        digit(11).FillColor = NotLit
        digit(12).FillColor = NotLit
        digit(13).FillColor = NotLit
        digit(14).FillColor = Lit
        digit(15).FillColor = NotLit
        digit(16).FillColor = NotLit
        digit(17).FillColor = NotLit
        digit(18).FillColor = Lit
        digit(19).FillColor = NotLit
        digit(20).FillColor = Lit
        digit(21).FillColor = Lit
        digit(22).FillColor = Lit
        digit(23).FillColor = Lit
    End Sub
```

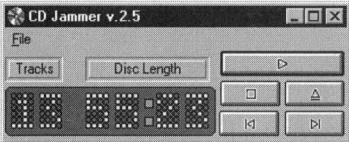

Fig. 15.9 The number 1 created by the sample code is shown displayed in the shape array.

The sample function shown in Listing 15.7 is not very practical if you have more than one digit. Since CD Jammer has six digits, much of the code would be duplicated if a separate function was produced for each number that each digit would display.

To alleviate the repetitive and unnecessary coding, it is useful to create a digit function where your application can pass the digit position and the number that the digit should display. That way, the code for each of the digits would be the same code with different parameters. For a complete listing that shows how the `digits` function performs this operation see the CDJAMMER.FRM module in the CD Jammer sample on the CD.

The `digits` function can now be called to display a number by any function. This function could be extended to include the alphabet or any other special characters. Listing 15.8 show how the tracks, minutes, and seconds are updated and shown in CD Jammer's main form.

Listing 15.8   CDJAMMER.FRM—The LEDUpdate( ) Function Calls the Digits Function

```
Sub LEDUpdate()
    Dim lReturnValue As Long
    Dim CurrentPosition As String
    Dim Track As Integer
    Dim Minutes As Integer, Seconds As Integer
    Dim TrackTens As Integer, TrackOnes As Integer
    Dim MinuteTens As Integer, MinuteOnes As Integer
    Dim SecondTens As Integer, SecondOnes As Integer

    ' Updates the LED Display panel
    ' Update the Current Track

    lReturnValue = mciSendString("status CD position", _
      gReturnString, 1024, 0)

    CurrentPosition = gReturnString
    Track = Val(Left$(CurrentPosition, 2))
    Minutes = Val(Mid$(CurrentPosition, 4, 2))
    Seconds = Val(Mid$(CurrentPosition, 7, 2))

    TrackTens = Int(Track / 10)
    TrackOnes = Int(Track Mod 10)
    MinuteTens = Int(Minutes / 10)
    MinuteOnes = Int(Minutes Mod 10)
    SecondTens = Int(Seconds / 10)
    SecondOnes = Int(Seconds Mod 10)

    Call digits(1, TrackTens)
    Call digits(2, TrackOnes)
    Call digits(3, MinuteTens)
    Call digits(4, MinuteOnes)
    Call digits(5, SecondTens)
    Call digits(6, SecondOnes)

End Sub
```

From Here...

This chapter has shown you how to apply multimedia technology to your applications. We've discussed and presented examples using the Multimedia MCI control and the MCI APIs. This chapter presented various ways in which to entertain your users, store and retrieve data, give yourself deserving recognition, and provide familiar visual user feedback.

Multimedia continues to be a very hot buzzword in both the computer trade journals and the popular press. Building with these tools will become more prevalent as interfaces to noncomputer peripherals such as toasters and microwaves becomes possible. Just remember, it takes a lot of time to perfect your multimedia skills.

For additional topics and some other advanced topics to enhance your multimedia applications check out these chapters as good starting places to investigate and learn more:

➤ For more information about presenting and accessing data, see Chapter 4, "Advanced Database Front Ends."

➤ For more information about storing and manipulating data, see Chapter 5, "Data Management and Data-Driven Programming."

➤ For more information about working with heterogeneous data-bases, see Chapter 6, "Working with ODBC."

➤ For more information about storing and retrieving data in a client-server environment, see Chapters 8, "Modern Client/Server Computing," and 9, "Client/Server Databases."

➤ For more information about using devices over serial ports like modems, see Chapter 17, "Communications Basics."

16

Graphics: Data Analysis

by Michael McKelvy

What do you think of when someone mentions graphics? Do you think of the artistic creations of a graphic designer? Or are you more business-minded and conjure up images of the last sales presentation that you attended? Maybe if you're a very technically oriented person, you think of computer aided design (CAD) or intricate data charts. Graphics encompass a very wide range of images and applications.

Put in simplest terms, graphics is the placement of lines, circles, points, and text on a screen in a specific pattern. These objects can be different sizes, shapes, and colors. The purpose of this chapter is to illustrate how to control the placement and characteristics of these objects to suit the purposes of your applications.

The design and use of graphics is a large and complex subject. There are a number of books that are devoted specifically to various types of graphics. Obviously, this single chapter cannot cover all the bases. Instead, this chapter concentrates on three specific areas of using graphics. In this chapter, you will learn how to do the following:

➤ Enhance the user interface

➤ Display and create simple graphic images

➤ Analyze data

From the material presented in this chapter, you will be able to create graphics to suit many of your needs. Then, combined with some imagination and experimentation, you can create even more advanced graphics applications.

Enhancing the User Interface

A typical user interface for an application consists of labels, text boxes, command buttons, and perhaps a few other controls for specific pieces of data. The interface may also contain a menu. This will provide the user access to the functions of the application and present her with specific data, but it can be quite boring. Graphics can be used to enhance the user interface by:

➤ Highlighting specific information on the screen

➤ Providing a different view of the information

➤ Providing a more intuitive link to the application's functions

These enhancements can be accomplished through the use of the Line and Shape controls, color, pictures, and drawing methods.

Using the Line and Shape Controls

The Line and Shape controls provide the easiest means to add a graphic element to a form. The controls are drawn on the form at designtime and placed where you need them. During the execution of a program, these controls can be hidden or moved, or their colors can be changed by setting the appropriate property values in your code.

As you would guess by its name, the Line control places a line on the form. You can control the width of the line, the line style, the color, and the position of the terminal points of the line through the control's properties. Figure 16.1 shows several Line controls drawn on a form using the various styles.

Fig. 16.1 The Line control lets you place lines of different styles on a form.

> **Note:** If you set the `BorderWidth` property of the Line control greater than one, the `BorderStyle` property will have no effect.

The Line control can be used on a form to separate areas of the form from one another. For instance, you might want to separate the data display portion of a form from the command buttons, as shown in figure 16.2. Or you may want to separate the information on the form into distinct groups. If you are presenting a lot of information on a form, this is a good way of enabling the user to focus on one group of information at a time.

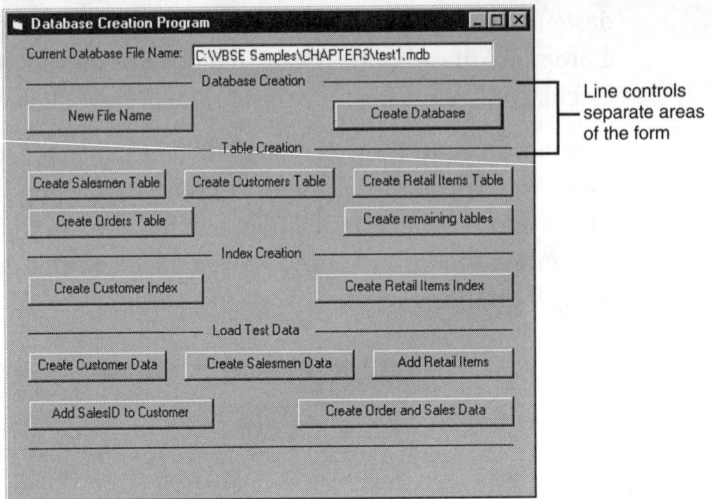

Line controls
separate areas
of the form

Fig. 16.2 The Line control can be used to separate information on a form into distinct groupings.

The Shape control provides another simple means of placing graphics elements on a form. The Shape control can be used to create the following six shapes:

➤ Rectangle

➤ Square

➤ Oval

➤ Circle

➤ Rounded rectangle

➤ Rounded square

These six shapes are shown in figure 16.3.

For any of these shapes, you can set the BorderStyle to any of the six line styles shown in figure 16.1 for the Line control. You can also set a fill pattern and fill color for the shapes. The Shape control can be used to enclose various areas of a form and other controls as shown in figure 16.4.

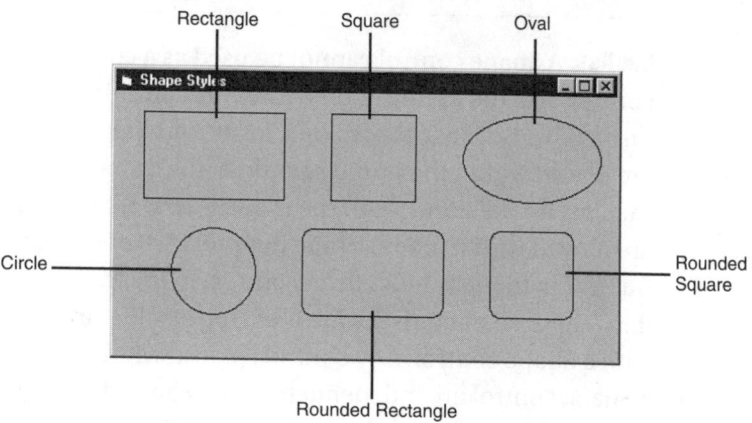

Fig. 16.3 The Shape control can be used to create any of these six shapes on a form.

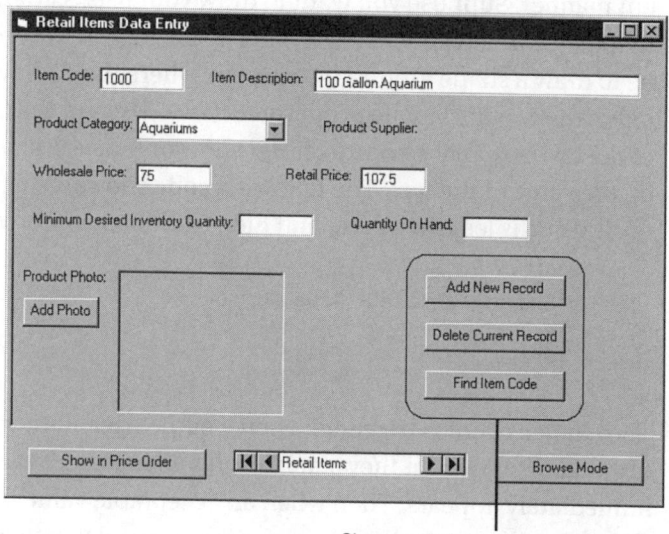

Shape control sets off command buttons

Fig. 16.4 The Shape control can be used to indicate groups of controls or information.

Caution: A Shape control cannot be used as a container for other controls like the Frame and Picture Box controls can. To explain further, if a Frame is placed on a form, and then other controls are placed within the frame's borders, the frame and the controls then act as one unit. When the frame is moved, the other controls are moved with it, maintaining their relative position within the frame. If a frame is hidden, all controls in the frame are also hidden. These characteristics are also true of a Picture Box. Not so with a Shape control. Any controls placed within the border of a Shape control are independent of the shape. If the shape is moved or hidden, the other controls remain unaffected.

The Shape control can also be used to highlight information in a different manner. Suppose you want to draw your user's attention to the fact that they entered an incorrect value in a field. One way to do this would be to draw a shape around the text box where the data would be entered, then set its Visible property to `False`. Then in the Change event of the text box, place code to either show or hide the shape depending on the value of the text. The following code shows a shape when the text's value is less than zero, and hides the shape otherwise.

```
If Text1.Text < 0 Then
    Shape1.Visible = True
Else
    Shape1.Visible = False
End If
```

The change event is triggered whenever the user starts typing in the text box. Therefore, if they start to enter an incorrect value, the shape immediately appears. Then when an acceptable value is entered, the shape disappears. A good shape for this is an oval with a `BorderWidth` of three and a red `BorderColor`.

Pictures on the Form

Another way to enhance your screens with graphics is to place pictures on-screen. A picture is a bitmap file that can contain art, flow diagrams, or photos. The picture can be purely decorative, or it can be used to communicate specific information. You have probably seen pictures used for information in the setup screens of many programs. These pictures tell you about the features and benefits of the program while the installation is running.

There are several ways to add a picture to a form. The picture can be placed on the form itself, or it can be placed in a Picture Box or Image control on the form. There are advantages and drawbacks to each of these methods, as will be addressed in the following paragraphs.

Loading a Picture on the Form

The simplest way to add a picture to your screen is to add it to the form itself. You can do this at designtime by setting the Picture property from the properties dialog box. To load a picture, select the Picture property, and then press the ellipsis button at the far right of the line. This will call up the Load Picture dialog box shown in figure 16.5. From this box, you can select the file containing the desired picture.

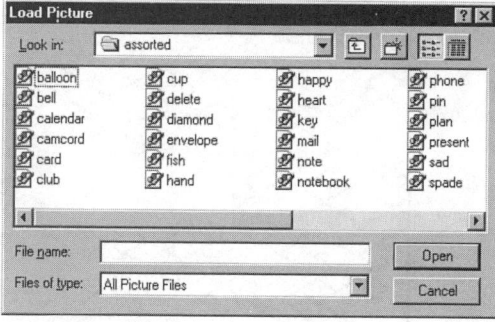

Fig. 16.5 You can select a picture to load on your form from the Load Picture dialog box.

When the picture is loaded on the form, it places the entire picture on the form starting in the upper left corner of the form. If the picture is smaller than the form, space will be left below and to the right of the picture. If the picture is larger than the form, the entire picture will still be loaded, but only part of it will be visible. As the form is resized, the amount of the picture shown will change.

Note: The picture is always placed starting in the upper left corner. It cannot be placed anywhere else on the form. If you want a small picture in another area of the form, you must use either a picture or Image control.

When a picture is loaded on the form, it provides a background for the form. Any other controls added to the form appear on top of the picture. With the exception of the label and shape controls, the picture will not show through the background of the control. The label and shape controls will allow the picture to show through if the `BackStyle` property of the control is set to Transparent. Figure 16.6 shows a simple cross-hatch design picture on a form with other controls placed on it. Notice the background of the controls without the design.

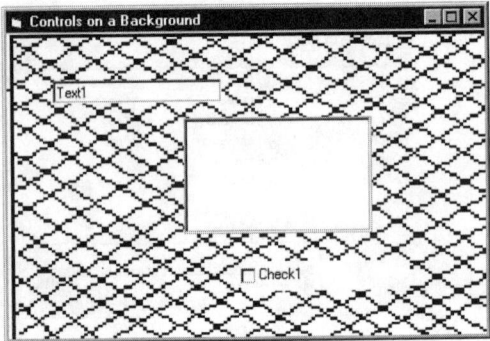

Fig. 16.6 Other controls placed on a form do not allow the picture to show through.

You can also add a picture to a form at runtime. This is done by setting the `Picture` property of the form with the `LoadPicture` function as shown in the following code:

```
Form1.Picture = LoadPicture("C:\MYPICT.BMP")
```

You can also remove the picture from the form by specifying a null argument for the LoadPicture function:

```
Form1.Picture = LoadPicture("")
```

The key advantage to placing your picture directly on the form is that this method uses fewer system resources than placing the picture in a picture or Image control. Another benefit of placing the picture on the form is that you can use drawing methods to annotate the picture if necessary. This capability is available with the Picture Box control as well, but is not available with the Image control.

Placing the picture directly on the form does, however, have several drawbacks, such as the following:

➤ You cannot hide the picture; it can only be loaded or unloaded.

➤ You cannot control the placement of the picture on the form.

➤ You can only place one picture at a time on the form.

These drawbacks can be overcome with the use of the picture or Image control. However, the added flexibility comes at the expense of system resources.

Using the Image Control

A second way of getting pictures on a form is to use an Image control. The Image control provides a frame for a bitmap or other picture on a form. The control can be placed anywhere on the form and can be drawn to any desired size. You assign a picture to the Image control by setting the Picture property of the control. This can be done either at designtime using the properties dialog or at runtime using an assignment statement. Assigning the picture is done the same way as placing a picture directly on the form.

One other property of the Image control is very important to the appearance of any pictures you may use. This is the Stretch property. The Stretch property determines whether the Image control will be sized to fit the picture, or the picture will be sized to fit the control as drawn. If the Stretch property is set to False (the default), the Image control will automatically be resized to fit the picture you assign to it. If the `Stretch` property is set to `True`, the picture will automatically be resized so that the entire picture will fit within the current boundaries of the Image control. This will cause the overall size of the picture to change and can potentially change the aspect ratio of the picture (the ratio of vertical to horizontal size). Figure 16.7 shows the same picture in two Image controls, one with the `Stretch` property set to `True` and the other with the property set to `False`.

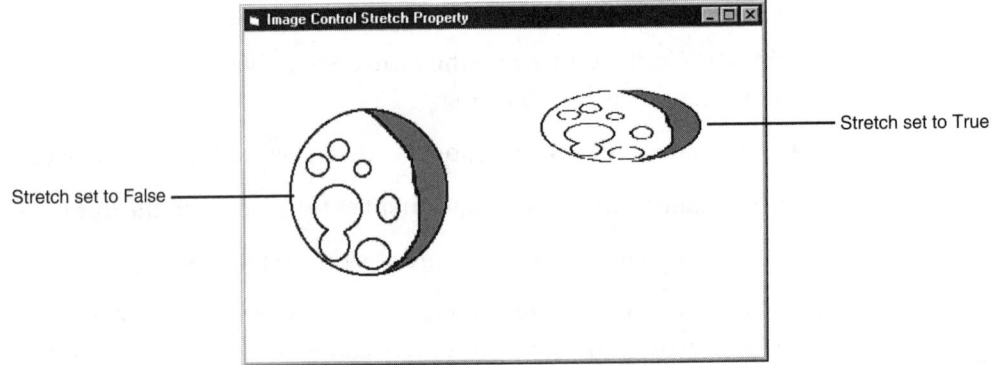

Fig. 16.7 The `Stretch` property affects the appearance of the picture in an Image control.

Note: If you are showing pictures of different sizes in your application, you might want to set the `Stretch` property to `True`. Otherwise, the size of the Image control will change with each picture, and may cause the Image control to overlap other controls on the form. The Image control is anchored at its top left corner, so only objects to the right and below the control would be affected. If the appearance of the pictures is unsuitable due to stretching, you may want to use the Picture Box control instead of the Image control.

The advantages of using the Image control over placing a picture directly on the form are as follows:

➤ You can control the size of the picture's display area.

➤ You can place the picture anywhere on the form.

➤ You can place multiple Image controls on a form.

➤ You can easily hide the picture using the `Visible` property of the Image control.

Using the Image control does have a few drawbacks:

➤ The Image control uses more resources than placing the picture directly on the form.

➤ You cannot use drawing methods to modify the picture in the Image control.

➤ The Image control cannot serve as a container for other controls the way the Picture Box control can.

Using the Picture Box Control

The third and most flexible way to place a picture on a form is with the Picture Box control. This method uses the most resources of the three. Loading a picture in a Picture Box control is accomplished the same way as loading a picture on a form or into an Image control. The picture can either be loaded at designtime or at runtime.

Using the Picture Box control enables you to place a picture anywhere on a form and place multiple pictures on the form. It also enables you to control the size of the picture. The default behavior of the Picture Box control is to show only as much of a picture as will fit in the current boundaries of the control. If the picture is larger than the control, the upper left corner of the picture will be shown (though the entire picture is available if the control is resized). If the picture is smaller than the control, there will be space shown around the edges of the picture. This default behavior occurs with the `AutoSize` property set to `False`. Setting the `AutoSize` property to `True` will cause the Picture Box control to be resized to fit the current picture. As with the Image control, the top left corner of the control is anchored in place, and resizing occurs to the right and down. The Picture Box control always preserves the aspect ratio of the picture being shown. Figure 16.8 shows the same picture in each of two Picture Box controls, one with the `AutoSize` property set to `False`, the other with the `AutoSize` property set to `True`.

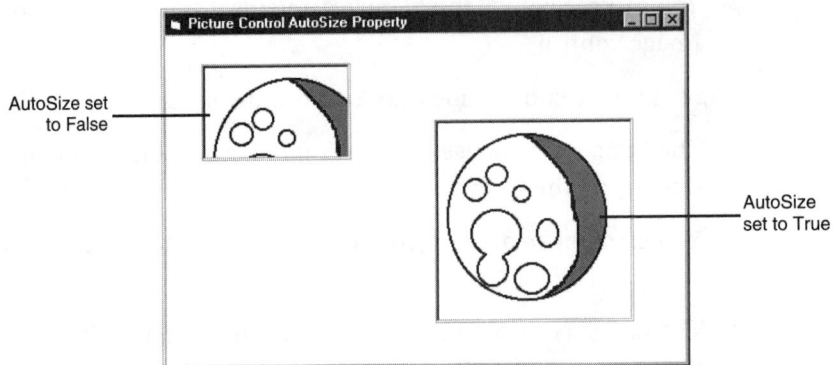

Fig. 16.8 The `AutoSize` property determines whether or not the Picture Box control will change size to fit the picture being displayed.

The Picture Box control also provides you with other capabilities in handling pictures. Like the picture on a form, you can use the drawing methods to make changes to the picture. Like the Image control, you can hide the picture or move it on the screen. But the Picture Box control also has some added benefits. The Picture Box control can be used as a container for other controls. This means that any controls placed on the Picture Box control are treated as a unit with the Picture Box control. If the Picture Box control is hidden or moved, the other controls on it are also hidden or moved. This allows the Picture Box control to be used to display multiple views or portions of data on a single form. This was discussed in detail in Chapter 4, "Advanced Database Front Ends."

Creating Invisible Buttons on Your Form

As useful as it is to be able to display a picture on a form, you probably would like to be able to do more with it. One way to take advantage of the visual information displayed in a picture is to use it to control part of your application's interface.

As an example, consider a flowchart displayed on a form that shows the various input files and calculations in a complex application. A flowchart of this type is shown in figure 16.9.

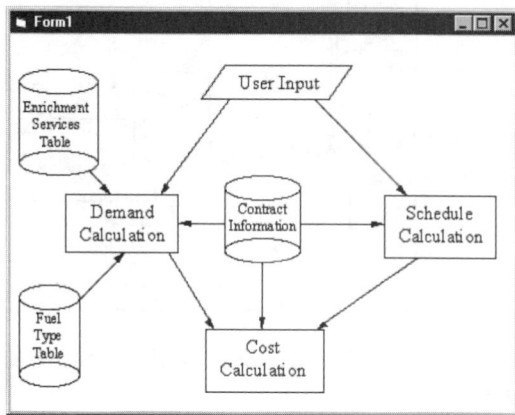

Fig. 16.9 A flowchart can be used to display information about an application.

The flowchart helps the user understand how the information in the application is related. But suppose you could set up your application so that the user could access an input file merely by clicking on the file name in the flowchart. This can be done by superimposing Image controls over the flowchart to create invisible buttons.

To accomplish this, load a picture onto the form or into a Picture Box control. Then, anywhere that you want an invisible button, place an Image control over the region that you want to activate. Finally, place code in the `Click` event of each Image control to accomplish the task you want performed. The Image control is invisible because it has no border, and with no picture assigned to it, the background of the control is transparent. Figure 16.10 shows the flowchart from figure 16.9 with the invisible buttons on it. The `BorderStyle` of the Image controls has been set to a single line to show where the controls are located. Normally, these controls would not be seen. In an actual application, the `BorderStyle` would be set to none.

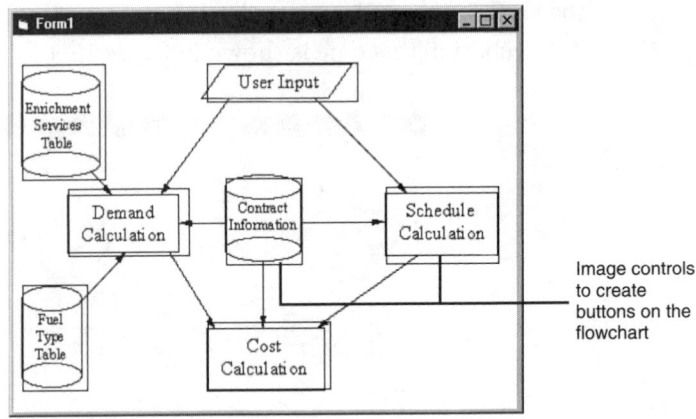

Fig. 16.10 Invisible buttons can make a picture part of your user interface.

This flowchart and invisible button application is contained in the file INVISBTN.VBP. When the buttons are clicked, a message box appears to tell you which button or area you pressed.

Okay, since the buttons are invisible, how do you let the user know where they are? You can use a characteristic of the mouse pointer and the `MouseMove` event of the Image controls to change the mouse pointer to a different picture when it is over one of the invisible buttons. This is done by setting the mouse pointer to an icon as shown in the following code.

```
Image1.MousePointer = 13
Image1.MouseIcon = Image2.Picture
```

This code changes the mouse pointer to the icon for as long as the mouse is over the Image control. When the mouse is moved off the control, the mouse pointer reverts to its original style. Figure 16.11 shows the invisible button with the changed mouse pointer over it.

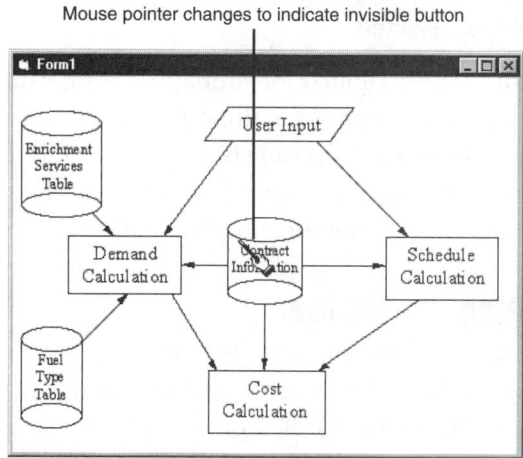

Fig. 16.11 Changing the mouse pointer shows the user where the invisible buttons are located.

This invisible button concept could be used with all types of applications. For example, you could create a demonstration application for a new car. By placing invisible buttons on a picture of the car, you could allow the user to click on the parts of the car to get information about its features (for example, describe the engine capabilities if the user clicks on the hood). The invisible buttons can be made any size you want them.

Creating Toolbars with the Image Control

Another use of the Image control is the creation of Toolbars. Toolbars are a series of buttons that provide access to the functions of your application. Toolbars are used in most commercial Windows applications to provide access to the most commonly used functions.

The buttons on a Toolbar usually contain a graphics image which tells the user the function of the button. In addition, these graphics are usually set up to show several states of the button, such as disabled, enabled, or selected.

You can create a Toolbar for your application using a series of Image controls, each containing a bitmap of a button. You can use the bitmaps provided with Visual Basic (located in the \bitmaps\toolbar subdirectory under the Visual Basic main directory) or create your own with Paintbrush or another graphics package.

Creating the Toolbar

The first step in creating the Toolbar is to place a series of Image controls on the form. To do this, select the Image control from the Visual Basic Toolbar and position it on the form. Add an Image control to the form for each Toolbar button you need to make.

> **Note:** To create a number of Image controls on the form, hold down the Ctrl key while you click the Toolbar. This will enable you to place multiple controls on the form without having to re-select the Image control from the Toolbar each time.

Once you have placed the Image controls on the form, you will need to assign the picture of a button to each of the Image controls. The pictures can be assigned at designtime using the Load Picture dialog box described previously. As the pictures are loaded, the Image controls will automatically be resized to fit the button pictures (remember the default setting of the `stretch` property). You can then rearrange the buttons into their final configuration. Figure 16.12 shows a Toolbar derived from the one used in Microsoft Word.

To activate the buttons, you will need to place code for the desired function in the click event of each Image control. When your application is run, the user will access these functions simply by clicking the button for the function.

Fig. 16.12 A Toolbar can be created using the Image controls and pictures of buttons.

Handling Multiple States of the Button

If you have worked with an application containing a Toolbar, you have probably noticed that many buttons change appearance when they are clicked. Typically, they show one image when the button is "up," then show a different image when the button is pressed. The button is pressed when the mouse button is pushed down. This activity often happens quickly, but if you press and hold the mouse button, you can see the other image.

You can enable this same functionality in your Toolbar by using multiple pictures for each Image control and placing the appropriate code in the MouseDown and MouseUp events of the control. The following discussion will demonstrate this technique for a single button of the Toolbar shown in figure 16.12.

To create this two-state button, you will need to place three Image controls on the form for each button you wish to present to the user. One Image control will be the actual button on the Toolbar. The other two Image controls will contain the pictures for the two button states, one for the "up" state and one for the "down" state. You will need to set the Visible property of these latter two Image controls to False, so that they do not show up in the actual application. Figure 16.13 shows the form as it looks in the design mode and as it looks in the run mode for a single button on a Toolbar.

Changing the state of the button requires changing the picture in the Image control presented to the user. This is done by setting the Picture property of the Image control shown to the user with the picture in one

of the other Image controls. The "down" button is loaded in the
MouseDown event, while the "up" button is loaded in the MouseUp event.
This code is shown in Listing 16.1. Notice that the initial setting of the
button is loaded in the Form_Load event.

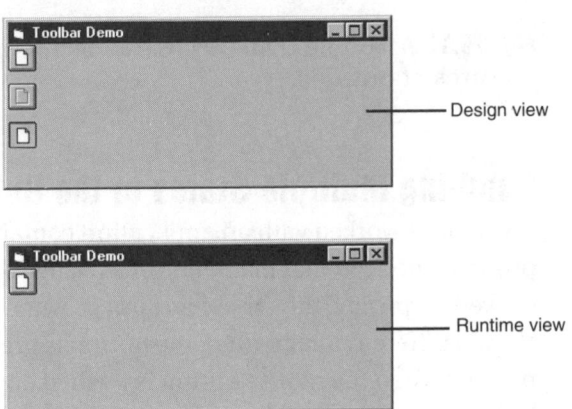

Fig. 16.13 The controls containing the button images need to be
hidden when the application is run.

Listing 16.1   TOOL2.FRM—The Button's Appearance Is Changed by Setting the Picture Property of the Image Control to Different Pictures

```
'******************************************************
'The button is initially loaded with the up picture.
'******************************************************
Private Sub Form_Load()
    Image1.Picture = Image2.Picture
End Sub
'*************************************************************
'When the mouse button is pressed, the down button is shown
'*************************************************************
Private Sub Image1_MouseDown(Button As Integer, Shift As
Integer, X As Single, Y As Single)
    Image1.Picture = Image3.Picture
End Sub
'*****************************************************************
'When the mouse button is released, the up button is shown again
'*****************************************************************
```

```
Private Sub Image1_MouseUp(Button As Integer, Shift As _
Integer, X As Single, Y As Single)
    Image1.Picture = Image2.Picture
End Sub
```

This code and the different pictures provide the appearance that the button is actually being pressed. The up and down appearance of the button is shown in figure 16.14.

Fig. 16.14 Using a two-state button gives the user the impression of actually pressing a button on the screen.

Animating the Button

You can also use multiple pictures to animate a button. The animation can either take the form of showing multiple images after the button is pressed, or the button can be animated while it is just sitting on the form. For the animation, you will need a picture for each frame you want to display, and you will need to use the Timer control. The Timer control provides the events which cause the picture to change at a given interval. For simplicity, this discussion will only deal with the animation of a button while it sits on the form.

To set up the animation, you will need to do the following:

➤ Place one Image control on the form to display the button to the user.

➤ Use an Image control array to contain the frames of the picture. While you can use individual Image controls for this purpose, an array makes the animation programming easier. The `Visible` property of each Image control in the array needs to be set to `False` to keep them from being displayed when the application is run.

➤ Place the Timer control on the form.

➤ Assign a picture to the `Picture` property of each control in the array.

Figure 16.15 shows the Image controls containing the various pictures for the animation.

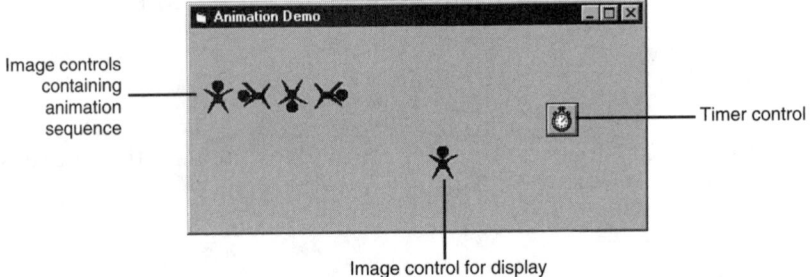

Fig. 16.15 Animation requires the use of several images and the Timer control.

To make the animation work, you will need to set the interval property of the timer to the desired number of milliseconds that you want to elapse between picture changes. A setting of 500 will produce a half-second delay. Each time the interval elapses, the `Timer` event of the Timer control will be triggered. By placing the code to change the picture in your Image control in the `Timer` event, the picture will change. This code is shown below.

```
If btnidx = 3 Then
    btnidx = 0
Else
    btnidx = btnidx + 1
End If
Image1.Picture = Image4(btnidx).Picture
```

In the preceding code, you will notice that the index of the control array is incremented each time the event is triggered. When the last index is reached, the index value is reset to zero, which is the first element of the array. The display Image control and the array index were set to their initial values using the following code placed in the `Form_Load` event.

```
Image1.Picture = Image4(0).Picture
btnidx = 0
```

Managing Pictures with the PicClip Control

As you might guess, loading the images for a large Toolbar can require a lot of Image controls. For instance, the control Toolbar for Visual Basic contains 24 buttons. Using one Image control to display the current button state and two controls to store the button state images would require 72 total Image controls to create the one Toolbar. This would not only clutter your design screen, but more importantly, would use a lot of system resources handling all those pictures.

One possible solution would be to load each picture from a file as needed at runtime. While this would work, it would significantly slow your operations and would require you to distribute a large number of bitmap files with your application. Also, if a user ever deleted one of the bitmap files accidentally, your application would generate an error when it tried to load the file.

Fortunately, there is a control that can help you manage the images needed for a Toolbar or for animation. This is the `PicClip` control. The `PicClip` control stores a single bitmap, and enables you to retrieve pieces of the bitmap to use in the picture property of other controls. The `PicClip` control is one of the custom controls and must be added to your Visual Basic Toolbar from the Tools menu. The `PicClip` control provides you with two methods to retrieve portions of the bitmap it contains—the random-access method and the enumerated method. Both of these will be discussed in this section.

Setting Up the PicClip Control

Before you can use either of the clipping methods to get pieces of a picture, you must set up the PicClip control. This is done by first drawing the control on your form. Then you assign a bitmap to the Picture property of the control using the Load Picture dialog. Figure 16.16 shows a PicClip control with a button bitmap loaded.

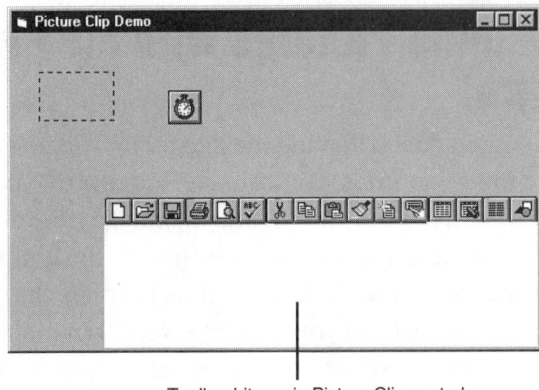

Toolbar bitmap in Picture Clip control

Fig. 16.16 The PicClip control contains a bitmap from which you can retrieve pieces of the image.

In the design mode, you can also assign the number of rows and columns to use for the enumerated access method. Most of the other properties of the PicClip control are only available at runtime. You can also load the picture and assign the number of rows and columns at runtime if you desire.

Using the Random-Access Method

The random-access method of retrieving pieces of the bitmap enables you to specify any size piece located anywhere on the bitmap. You retrieve the desired image by setting the ClipX, ClipY, ClipHeight, and ClipWidth properties of the PicClip control. The ClipX and ClipY properties specify the coordinates of the upper left corner of the area to be retrieved. The ClipHeight and ClipWidth properties specify the vertical and horizontal sizes of the area to be retrieved. After you set the position and size of the region to be retrieved, you place the image in the target control by setting the `Picture` property of the target control (a form, Picture Box control, or Image control) to the `Clip` property of the `PicClip` control. This process is shown in the following code, which loads a portion of a bitmap into an Image control.

```
PictureClip1.ClipX = 10
PictureClip1.ClipY = 20
PictureClip1.ClipWidth = 40
PictureClip1.ClipHeight = 80
Image2.Picture = PictureClip1.Clip
```

> **Caution:** The size of the bitmap in the Picture Clip control is measured in pixels instead of twips as is the default for Visual Basic. Therefore, you must use caution in specifying the starting point and size of the region of the Picture Clip you want to retrieve. If you specify a measurement that exceeds a dimension of the control, an error message will be generated.

Using the Enumerated Method

For storing pictures for a Toolbar, the enumerated method is easier to use than the random-access method. The enumerated method divides the bitmap in the Picture Clip control into a number of equally sized cells. The number of cells is determined by the number of rows and columns that you set. For example, a setting of three rows and five columns would yield 15 cells. Figure 16.17 shows a bitmap in a Picture Clip control with grid lines superimposed to show the cells of the control.

The cells in the Picture Clip control are addressed through the `GraphicCell` property of the Picture Clip control. To retrieve a particular cell, specify the index number of the cell you want, as shown in the following code:

```
Image1.Picture = PictureClip1.GraphicCell(0)
```

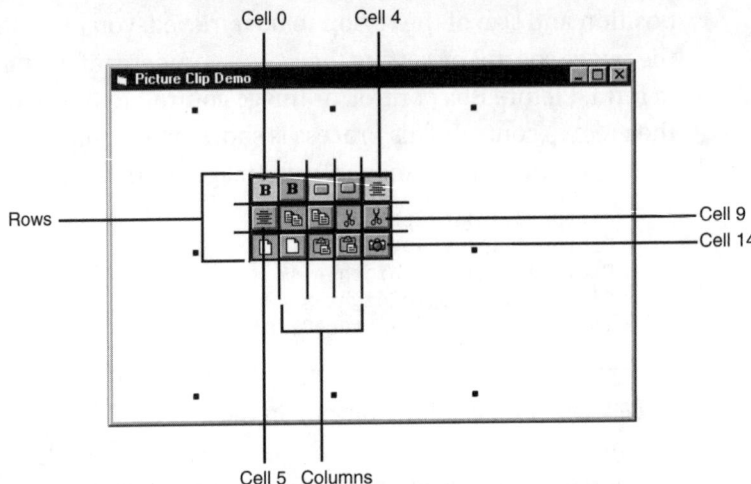

Fig. 16.17 A bitmap in a Picture Clip control can be divided into a number of equally sized cells.

The index number for the cells starts with zero for the cell in the upper left corner of the control. The numbering then proceeds across the row. For example, in a three row by five column bitmap, the last cell on the first row would be cell number four, while the first cell on the second row would be cell number five. The general formula for the index number of any given cell is:

```
(Row - 1) * [Total Columns] + Column - 1
```

This number scheme is illustrated in figure 16.17.

To see how the Picture Clip control works in developing a Toolbar, look again at the code in Listing 16.1. Using the bitmap of the Picture Clip shown in figure 16.17, the code in Listing 16.1 would be updated as shown in Listing 16.2.

Listing 16.2   Using a Picture Clip Control to Manage the Graphics for a Toolbar

```
'**********************************************************
'The button is initially loaded with the up picture.
'**********************************************************
```

```
Private Sub Form_Load()
    Image1.Picture = PictureClip1.GraphicCell(0)
End Sub
'***********************************************************
'When the mouse button is pressed, the down button is shown
'***********************************************************
Private Sub Image1_MouseDown(Button As Integer, Shift As_
Integer, X As Single, Y As Single)
    Image1.Picture = PictureClip1.GraphicCell(5)
End Sub
'*************************************************************
'When the mouse button is released, the up button is shown again
'*************************************************************
Private Sub Image1_MouseUp(Button As Integer, Shift As_
Integer, X As Single, Y As Single)
    Image1.Picture = PictureClip1.GraphicCell(0)
End Sub
```

Note: To avoid having to place code in the events of each Image control, you can use a control array for the Image controls used to display the Toolbar buttons. Then by carefully developing a bitmap with two rows and a number of columns equal to the number of Image controls, you can use the index number of the Image control to determine the necessary cell number of the Picture Clip control. Referring back to the Toolbar shown in figure 16.12, the bitmap needed for the Toolbar is shown in figure 16.18, and the code to implement the entire Toolbar is shown in Listing 16.3.

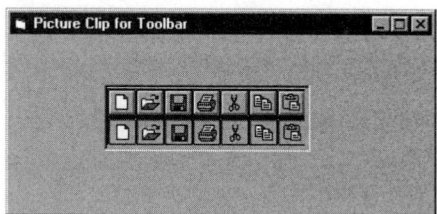

Fig. 16.18 A two-row bitmap can provide all the button images for a Toolbar and simplify the programming.

Listing 16.3   Using an Image Control Array and a Properly Designed Bitmap, You Can Simplify the Code Required to Implement the Entire Toolbar

```
'*************************************************
'Load all buttons with the appropriate up picture
'*************************************************
Private Sub Form_Load()
    For I = 0 To 14
        Toolbar(I).Picture = ToolClip.GraphicCell(I)
    Next I
End Sub
'*****************************************************************
'When the mouse button is pressed, the down button is shown
'*****************************************************************
Private Sub Image1_MouseDown(Index As Integer, Button As _
Integer, Shift As Integer, X As Single, Y As Single)
    Toolbar(Index).Picture = ToolClip.GraphicCell(Index + 16)
End Sub
'*****************************************************************
'When the mouse button is released, the up button is shown again
'*****************************************************************
Private Sub Image1_MouseUp(Index As Integer, Button As _
Integer, Shift As Integer, X As Single, Y As Single)
    Toolbar(Index).Picture = ToolClip.GraphicCell(Index)
End Sub
```

Using the Animated Button Control

In a previous section, animation of a button in an Image control was discussed. The animation consisted of placing different button pictures in the Image control at specified intervals. For some types of animation, the animated button control can be used. This control combines a picture array with a Timer control and handles all the necessary event code for you. While the control cannot be used to animate a button that is sitting idle on the screen, it does provide you with several types of animation for buttons that are clicked. The three types of animated buttons that you can create are as follows:

➤ *Animated,* where the button runs through half of its images when the mouse button is pressed and the other half of the images when the button is released.

➤ *Multistate*, where the image of the button changes each time the button is pressed.

➤ *Two-state animated*, where the button runs through half of its images the first time the button is pressed and the rest of the images the second time the button is pressed.

The animated button is one of the custom controls that comes with Visual Basic. To add it to the Visual Basic Toolbar, you need to select it from the Custom Controls dialog box on the Tools menu. To set up an animated button, you need to draw the control on your form, and then assign a series of pictures to the button. The `Picture` property in the animated button differs from the `Picture` property of other controls in that it is actually a picture array. The index of the array is determined by the value of the `Frame` property. You can load all the necessary pictures for the animated button at designtime using the Frame Settings dialog box as shown in figure 16.19.

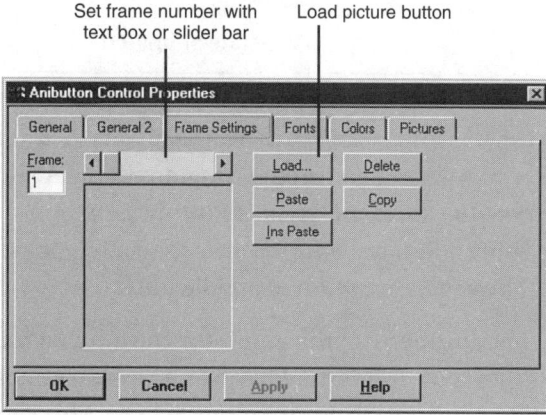

Fig. 16.19 The Frame Settings dialog box enables you to set the pictures for all the frames of the animated button.

Using the Frame Settings dialog box, you specify the frame either in the frame number text box or with the slide bar below the text box.

When you have set the desired frame index, press the Load button to bring up the open dialog where you select the picture file for that frame. You repeat this process until all the frames have been loaded.

To complete the setup of the animated button, you will also need to choose the button type by setting the Cycle property and the Speed property. The Cycle property tells the animated button which of the three types to use. The values of the property for each button type are summarized in Table 16.1. The Speed property determines the number of milliseconds between frames in the animation sequence. A setting between 100 and 500 provides a good animation speed.

Table 16.1   The Cycle Property Determines Which Type of Animated Button Is Created

Cycle Value	Button Type
0	Animated
1	Multi-state
2	Two-state animated

Because it is impossible to show the effects of animation on the printed page, you will need to run the program in the ANIMATED.VBP project file to see the different types of buttons in action. This project file contains three animated buttons (one for each type) and an Image control that shows the animation of an idle button.

One other property of the animated button that may interest you is the ClickFilter property. This property determines what part of the animated button will accept mouse clicks. This can provide you with finer control over the use of the button. The four setting values of the ClickFilter property and their effects on the performance of the button are summarized in Table 16.2.

Table 16.2   The ClickFilter Property Determines Which Part of the Animated Button Responds to Mouse Clicks

ClickFilter Value	Responsive Area
0	A mouse click anywhere on the control will trigger the click event.
1	A mouse click on the image frame or the caption text will trigger the click event. This differs from the "0" setting only if the animated button is larger than the image on the button.
2	The click event will only be triggered if the mouse is clicked on the image in the control, not on the caption text.
3	The click event will only be triggered if the mouse is clicked on the caption text of the control, not on the image in the control.

Creating and Managing Graphics

Earlier sections of this chapter have shown how graphics can be used to enhance the user interface through displayed pictures, Toolbars, invisible buttons, and other devices. To obtain the graphics used in these display elements, you can either use a graphics image from a library or create your own with a package such as Paintbrush.

But what if your application needs to be able to create graphics on its own? Applications that need to be able to create graphics include data analysis programs that create charts, and programs where the user might need a sketch pad for note-taking. This section will discuss how you can create graphics images in your application, and how to store and manage the created graphics.

Creating Graphics

Visual Basic provides several tools that can be used to create graphics. The drawing methods will work on a form or in a Picture Box control.

They can also be used with the printer object to send the output to the printer. This discussion will focus on creating graphics to be stored in files, so the drawing methods will be used with a Picture Box control. If no object is specified with the method, the form that currently has focus will receive the output of the methods.

Visual Basic provides seven basic methods for creating graphics. These methods can be used in combination to create many types of graphics images. The seven methods are as follows:

➤ `Line` method, which draws a line or a box on the target object.

➤ `Circle` method, which draws a circle or oval on the target object.

➤ `PSet` method, which places a single point on the target object.

➤ `PaintPicture` method, which draws an image from another control onto the target object.

➤ `Cls` method, which clears the output area of the target object.

➤ `Print` method, which places text on the target object.

➤ `Point` method, which returns the color of a specific point.

Using the Line Method

The `Line` method is used to draw lines and boxes on the form. To draw a line, you need to provide the `Line` method with the starting and ending points of the line. You can omit the starting point, and the method will draw a line from the current position to the ending point. The code below draws a triangle on a form.

```
Line (1600, 750)-(2000, 750)
Line -(2000, 1250)
Line -(1600, 750)
```

To draw a box on the form, you again use the `Line` method with the starting and ending points, but you also include the optional B argument. This will draw an open box with the top left and bottom right (or bottom left and top right) corners specified by the starting and ending points. (Drawing an open box assumes that the `FillStyle` property of the form is set to transparent.) If you want the box to be filled, you can also specify the optional F argument. This will fill the box with the same color used to draw the border of the box. As with drawing a line, if the starting point is omitted, the box is drawn from the current position to the ending point. The commands to draw boxes are shown in the following code. Figure 16.20 displays the results of the line and box drawing commands, as well as the results of several drawing properties that will be discussed below.

```
Line (2000,2000)-(2500,2500),,B
Line -(3000,3000),,BF
```

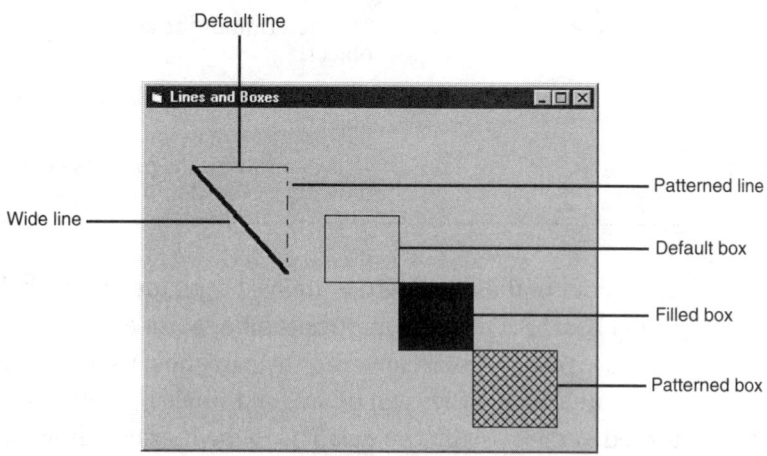

Fig. 16.20 The `Line` method is used to draw lines and boxes on an object.

As you can see, the commands to draw lines and boxes are quite simple. The real trick to controlling the appearance of lines and boxes is setting the drawing properties of the form (or other object that is receiving the graphics). These properties are set for the form, and the graphics methods will use the setting of the properties that is in effect when the method is used. The properties that affect the graphics methods are summarized in Table 16.3. The effects of some of these properties are shown in figure 16.20.

Table 16.3   The Drawing Properties Affect the Appearance of Graphics Drawn with the Graphics Methods

Property Name	Purpose
DrawMode	This determines how the color used to draw the border of the object interacts with objects already on-screen.
DrawStyle	This determines the pattern used to draw the border of the object.
DrawWidth	This determines the width of the line used to draw the border of the object.
FillColor	This determines the color used to fill an object.
FillStyle	This determines the fill pattern used to fill an object.
ForeColor	This determines the primary color used in drawing the border of an object.

The values of these properties are well explained in the help files for Visual Basic. All these properties can be set for a form or Picture Box control at designtime. However, they are most useful when they are set at runtime, where they can be set for a single operation and then returned to their original values. The following code draws a series of boxes and then returns the form's properties to their original settings.

Listing 16.4   DRAW.FRM—Drawing a Series of Lines and Boxes on a Form

```
frmset1 = Form1.DrawStyle
frmset2 = Form1.DrawWidth
frmset3 = Form1.FillColor
frmset4 = Form1.FillStyle
frmset5 = Form1.ForeColor
Line (1000, 1000)-(1600, 1600), , B
Form1.DrawStyle = 2
Form1.FillStyle = 2
Line -(2000, 2000), , B
Form1.FillColor = &hff
Line -(2500, 2500), , B
Form1.DrawWidth = 3
```

```
Form1.ForeColor = &hff0000
Line -(3000, 3000)
Form1.DrawStyle = frmset1
Form1.DrawWidth = frmset2
Form1.FillColor = frmset3
Form1.FillStyle = frmset4
Form1.ForeColor = frmset5
Line (100, 100)-(500, 500), , B
```

Using the Circle Method

The `Circle` method enables you to draw circles, ellipses, arcs, and pies on the form. The simplest form of the method is:

```
Circle (X,Y),R
```

This command draws a circle of radius R with a center at the position specified by X and Y. As with the `Line` method, the pattern and color of the circle's border and fill are determined by the settings of the drawing properties.

There are several optional arguments that can be used with the `Circle` method. The start and end arguments of the method are used to draw an arc on the form. The values of start and end are the angles from horizontal expressed in radians. (The values of an angle in radians are determined by multiplying the angle in degrees by pi/180.) The values of start and end can range from 0 to 2*pi or 0 to -2*pi. If the value of both the start and end arguments is negative, then the method will draw a pie (an arc with lines extending to the center of the circle). If both values are positive, a simple arc is drawn. If one of the values is negative, a line will be drawn from that end of the arc to the center.

The other argument that can be specified is the aspect argument. This argument is used to draw an ellipse or oval. The aspect is the ratio of the vertical size of the ellipse to the horizontal size. An aspect of one draws a circle. If the aspect is greater than one, the ellipse is taller than it is wide. If the aspect is less than one, the ellipse is wider than it is tall. In all cases, the radius specified in the method sets the size of the longer dimension. The code for drawing several shapes with the `Circle` method is shown below. The results of this code are shown in figure 16.21.

```
Circle (500, 500), 500
Circle (1600, 1600), 500, , 1.57, 0
Circle (2500, 2500), 500, , -4.7, -6.2
Circle (3500, 3500), 500, , , , 1.5
Circle (4500, 4500), 500, , -0.01, -1.57, 1.5
```

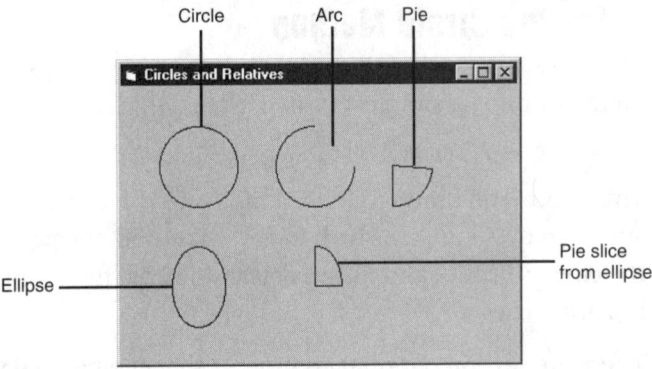

Fig. 16.21 The `Circle` method can be used to draw circles, ellipses, arcs, and pies.

Using the PSet Method

The `PSet` method is used to draw a single point on the form using the color specified by the `ForeColor` property. The size of the point drawn is dependent on the setting of the `DrawWidth` property. A larger `DrawWidth` setting will produce a larger point. The `PSet` method will draw the point at the coordinates specified in the argument of the method. The following code will draw a point at position 100, 100.

```
PSet (100,100)
```

One use of the `PSet` method is to provide a freehand drawing capability for the users of your application. This use will be covered in the "Sketch Pad Application" section later in this chapter.

Using the PaintPicture Method

The PaintPicture method enables you to place all or part of a picture from one object into a specific location in another object. Also, by carefully setting the height and width arguments for the source and target objects, you can enlarge or reduce the size of the source picture. The following code paints part of a picture from a Picture Box control onto the base form.

```
PaintPicture Picture1.Picture, 50, 50, 750, 750, 0, 0, 500, 500
```

The PaintPicture method contains several arguments as shown in this code. The first argument after the name of the method specifies the source of the picture from which a piece is being taken. The first two numerical arguments specify the coordinates of the upper left corner of the region where the picture is to be placed. These three arguments are the only ones that are required for the PaintPicture method. All other arguments are optional. If only the three required arguments are specified, the entire source picture will be copied to the target at full size.

The second pair of numbers in the command specifies the horizontal and vertical size of the target region. If this size is different from the size of the source picture or region, the picture will be stretched or compressed to fit the specified space. The third pair of numbers in the command specifies the upper left corner of the source region, that is, the part of the picture being copied. The final pair of numbers specifies the height and width of the source region. The code shown in the previous listing will take a piece of a picture from the Picture Box control, enlarge it by 50%, and place it on the form. The results of this command are shown in figure 16.22.

Some uses of the PaintPicture method in creating graphics would be:

➤ To provide a zoom feature for looking more closely at specific regions of a picture

➤ To make multiple copies of a picture (or portion of one) on a target object

➤ To clear a specified region of a picture

➤ To print the contents of a Picture Box control

➤ To be able to create data point markers for a chart

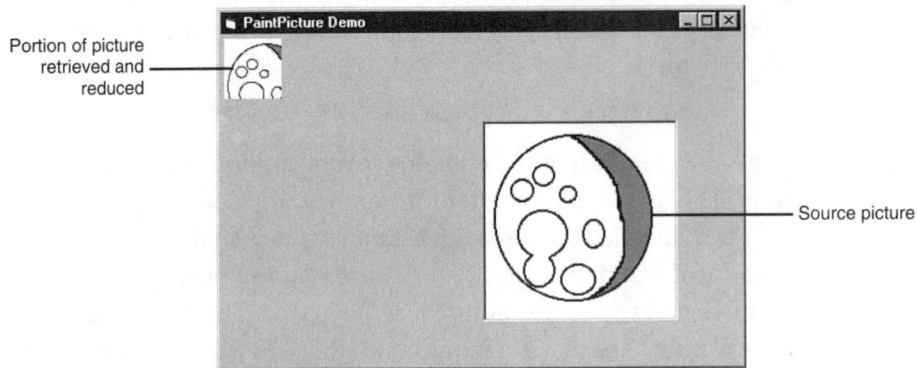

Portion of picture retrieved and reduced

Source picture

Fig. 16.22 The `PaintPicture` method can copy all or part of a picture from one object to another, and enlarge or reduce the picture.

Using the Print Method

While the `Print` method is not technically a graphics method, it is used to place text on a form, Picture Box control, or the printer object. The `Print` method can be used in conjunction with the graphics methods to create charts or drawings, or to annotate existing bitmaps. The `Print` method itself is quite simple. The following code displays a single line of text at the current position on the form.

```
Print "This is a one-line test."
```

The output of the `Print` method is controlled by the settings of five properties of the object being printed on. These properties are as follows:

➤ `CurrentX`: This sets the horizontal position for the starting point of the text.

➤ `CurrentY`: This sets the vertical position for the starting point of the text.

➤ `Font`: This determines the font type and size used for the text.

➤ `ForeColor`: This determines the color of the text.

➤ `FontTransparent`: On a form or Picture Box control, this determines whether or not the background behind the text will show through the spaces in the text.

Point and Cls Methods

The other two graphics methods mentioned at the beginning of this section are the `Point` method and the `Cls` method. These two methods each perform a single function. The `Point` method returns the RGB color setting of a single specified point. The `Cls` method clears all graphics drawn with the graphics methods from a form, or picture, or Image control. The `Cls` method has no effect on any controls that are on the object; it only clears graphics that were drawn at runtime.

Sketch Pad Application

To further illustrate how the different graphics methods work, this section will discuss how to create a sketch pad application. This application will be similar to the Paintbrush application in Windows with which most people are familiar. The starting form for the application is shown in figure 16.23.

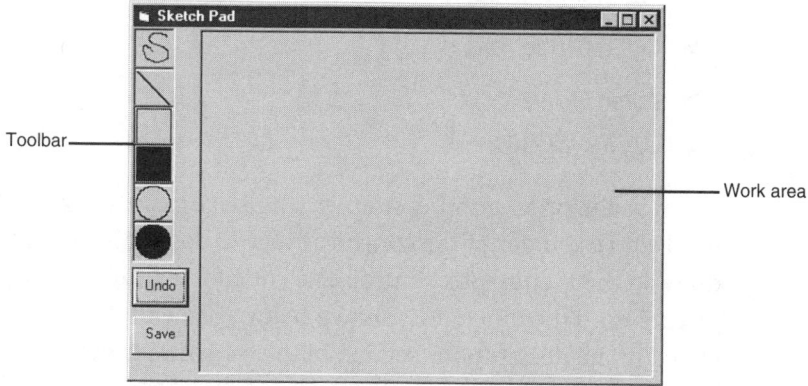

Fig. 16.23 You can create a Paintbrush-style application using the drawing methods.

This sketch pad application only creates drawings that are bitmaps. Any object placed on the screen is handled as simply a series of points after it is created. The objects cannot be selected again later to be resized or moved. In contrast to this application, programs like PowerPoint save information about the size, type, location, and other characteristics of an object. This allows the object to be re-selected and those characteristics to be modified to change the object's appearance at a later time.

Setting Up the Toolbar

For the sketch pad application, a Toolbar is needed to allow the user to select which type of object to draw. The Toolbar is set up by placing an Image control on the form for each of the objects to be drawn. A pair of Image controls is then assigned for each tool to hold the image of the "up" button and the "down" button. When the button for a tool is pressed, two things occur. First, the "down" image of the button is displayed to provide the user with an indication of which tool was se-lected. Second, a variable is set to tell the program which drawing tool to use. The sketch pad application provides the user the ability to draw one of six objects:

- ➤ Line
- ➤ Open Box
- ➤ Filled Box
- ➤ Open Circle
- ➤ Filled Circle
- ➤ Freehand Sketch

To make the programming simpler, an Image control array will be used, and the index of the control array will define the tool used to draw on the Picture Box control. The code for setting the Image control pictures and the tool type is shown below. The variable ToolTp is de-clared in the declarations section of the form and is initially set to zero, the number for the Freehand tool.

```
'*****************************************************************
'Reset the button for the previously used tool to the Up position
'*****************************************************************
 Image1(ToolTp).Picture = Image2(ToolTp).Picture
'*****************************************************************
'Set the button for the newly selected tool to the Down position
'*****************************************************************
 Image1(Index).Picture = Image3(Index).Picture
'*****************************************
'Set the ToolTp variable to the new tool
'*****************************************
 ToolTp = Index
```

Using the Various Drawing Tools

The functionality of the sketch pad enables the user to press the mouse
button, and then drag the mouse to generate the object. As the mouse
is being dragged, the object changes size and shape to give the user an
indication of the appearance of the drawn object. When the mouse
button is released, the object is drawn in its final form. The sketch pad
application provides a Picture Box control on which the user may
draw.

To implement the various drawing tools, you will need to work with
three events: the MouseDown, MouseMove, and MouseUp events. These
events correspond to the actions of the user as he or she is drawing an
object.

The MouseDown event is responsible for telling the program that the user
is drawing on the Picture Box control and to set the initial position of
the object. The purpose of this initial point depends on the type of
object being drawn. Table 16.4 shows the purpose of the initial point
for each of the objects in the sketch pad application.

Table 16.4   The Initial Point of a Drawing Operation Has Different Meanings for Each Object

Object	Use of Initial Point
Line	One of two points defining the line
Box (open or filled)	One of the corners of the box

continues

Table 16.4   Continued

Object	Use of Initial Point
Circle (open or filled)	One corner of a box which would bound the circle
Freehand	The first point drawn

To tell the program whether or not to actually draw objects while the mouse is in motion, a variable has been defined. This variable, DrawNow, will have a value of either True or False. The MouseDown event sets this variable to True. The following code is placed in the MouseDown event to enable the drawing methods. In the code, the variables curX and curY are the coordinates of the initial point. The variables oldX and oldY are the coordinates of the last mouse position. These are important in the MouseMove event as you will see.

```
Private Sub Picture1_MouseDown(Button As Integer, Shift As _
Integer, X As Single, Y As Single)
    DrawNow = -1
    curX = X
    curY = Y
    oldX = X
    oldY = Y
End Sub
```

The MouseMove event is the main workhorse of the sketch pad application. If the mouse button is down (DrawNow is set to True), the code in the MouseMove event draws the selected object between the initial point of the drawing and the current mouse position. The event contains a set of cases to handle the various types of objects that might be drawn. You will note that the open and filled boxes and the open and filled circles use the same code. This is because in the Move event, it is only necessary to show the outline of a filled object while the drawing is in progress. You will also note that, for the Freehand drawing, the Line method is used instead of the PSet method. The reason for this is that the move event is triggered at certain intervals, not as a continuous event. Rapid movements of the mouse will then leave gaps in the lines drawn with the PSet method. By using the Line method, a line is drawn between the last position of the mouse and the current position, thereby providing a continuous line. The code for the MouseMove event is shown in Listing 16.5.

Listing 16.5   SKETCH.FRM—The MouseMove Event Draws the Outline of the Object as the Mouse Is Dragged

```
Private Sub Picture1_MouseMove(Button As Integer, Shift As _
Integer, X As Single, Y As Single)
If DrawNow Then
    Select Case ToolTp
        Case 0
            Picture1.Line (oldX, oldY)-(X, Y)
            oldX = X
            oldY = Y
        Case 1
            Picture1.Line (curX, curY)-(oldX, oldY), _
Picture1.BackColor
            Picture1.Line (curX, curY)-(X, Y)
            oldX = X
            oldY = Y
        Case 2,3
            Picture1.Line (curX, curY)-(oldX, oldY), _
Picture1.BackColor, B
            Picture1.Line (curX, curY)-(X, Y), , B
            oldX = X
            oldY = Y
        Case 4,5
            cntX = curX + Int((X - curX) / 2)
            cntY = curY + Int((Y - curY) / 2)
            radX = Abs(curX - X)
            radY = Abs(curY - Y)
            radcir = IIf(radX > radY, radX, radY) / 2
            If radX = 0 Then
                aspcir = 1
            Else
                aspcir = radY / radX
            End If
            Picture1.Circle (oldX, oldY), oldrad, _
Picture1.BackColor, , , _
                oldasp
            Picture1.Circle (cntX, cntY), radcir, , , , aspcir
```

continues

Listing 16.5   Continued

```
            oldY = cntY
            oldasp = aspcir
            oldrad = radcir
      End Select
   End If
   End Sub
```

When the user is finished drawing and releases the mouse button, the MouseUp event creates the final drawing for the object and turns off the drawing mode. Much of the same code is used in the MouseUp event as in the MouseMove event, but separate cases have been added for the filled boxes and circles. The code for the MouseUp event is shown in Listing 16.6.

Listing 16.6   SKETCH.FRM—The MouseUp Event Renders the Final Drawing and Turns Off the Drawing Mode

```
Private Sub Picture1_MouseUp(Button As Integer, Shift As _
Integer, X As Single, Y As Single)
If DrawNow Then
    Select Case ToolTp
        Case 1
            Picture1.Line (curX, curY)-(oldX, oldY), _
Picture1.BackColor
            Picture1.Line (curX, curY)-(X, Y)
        Case 2
            Picture1.FillStyle = 1
            Picture1.Line (curX, curY)-(oldX, oldY), _
Picture1.BackColor, B
            Picture1.Line (curX, curY)-(X, Y), , B
        Case 3
            Picture1.FillStyle = 0
            Picture1.Line (curX, curY)-(oldX, oldY), _
Picture1.BackColor, B
            Picture1.Line (curX, curY)-(X, Y), , B
            Picture1.FillStyle = 1
        Case 4
            cntX = curX + Int((X - curX) / 2)
            cntY = curY + Int((Y - curY) / 2)
            radX = Abs(curX - X)
            radY = Abs(curY - Y)
            radcir = IIf(radX > radY, radX, radY) / 2
```

```
            If radX = 0 Then
                aspcir = 1
            Else
                aspcir = radY / radX
            End If
            Picture1.FillStyle = 1
            Picture1.Circle (oldX, oldY), oldrad, _
    Picture1.BackColor, , ,  oldasp
            Picture1.Circle (cntX, cntY), radcir, , , , aspcir
        Case 5
            cntX = curX + Int((X - curX) / 2)
            cntY = curY + Int((Y - curY) / 2)
            radX = Abs(curX - X)
            radY = Abs(curY - Y)
            radcir = IIf(radX > radY, radX, radY) / 2
            If radX = 0 Then
                aspcir = 1
            Else
                aspcir = radY / radX
            End If
            Picture1.FillStyle = 0
            Picture1.Circle (oldX, oldY), oldrad, _
    Picture1.BackColor, , , oldasp
            Picture1.Circle (cntX, cntY), radcir, , , , aspcir
            Picture1.FillStyle = 1
    End Select
End If
DrawNow = 0
End Sub
```

Creating an Undo Feature

Most applications that perform drawing functions have an Undo feature that enables the user to restore the picture to its state prior to the last drawing operation. An Undo function can be implemented in the sketch pad application by adding a second Picture Box control to the form, placing some additional code in the MouseDown event, and adding an Undo button. The second Picture Box control will contain a copy of the image in the primary drawing Picture Box control. This Picture Box control will have its Visible property set to False so it is not visible when the application is running. The second picture is updated each time a new drawing operation is started. This update is performed in the `MouseDown` event as shown in the following code.

```
Picture2.Picture = Picture1.Image
```

To undo an operation, the code simply copies the picture in the second Picture Box control back to the main Picture Box control. This returns the drawing area back to the way it was before the last drawing operation. This code is shown in the line below.

```
Picture1.Picture = Picture2.Picture
```

Saving the Picture

Finally, you will want to give your users the capability of saving the pictures they create. The drawings on a Picture Box control can be saved as a bitmap file using the `SavePicture` function. This function requires the name of the source picture and the name of the output file. You will probably want to use the `CommonDialog` control to allow the user to specify a name for the output file. For a drawing, the source of the picture is the Image property of the Picture Box control or form on which the drawing was made. The following code gets a file name using the `CommonDialog` control (named `GetFile`) and stores the drawing created by the sketch pad application.

```
GetFile.Filter = "Bitmap Files (*.BMP)¦*.bmp¦Icon Files ¦
*.ico ¦All Files¦*.*"
GetFile.DefaultExt = "BMP"
GetFile.ShowSave
DataName = GetFile.FileName
SavePicture Picture1.Image, DataName
```

Bitmap Annotation

The sketch pad application showed how you can create graphics with the graphics methods then store the graphics in files. Since the Picture Box control is also capable of displaying an existing graphics file, you can use the sketch pad function to modify graphics from other sources. You might want to use this to annotate fax images before sending them on to another person. You can also use it to make changes to bitmaps created by other people.

To annotate bitmaps, you will need to add a `LoadPicture` function to the sketch pad application to import the picture into the editing area. The code for this operation is shown below. This code again uses the `CommonDialog` control to obtain the name of the file to be edited.

```
GetFile.Filter = "Bitmap Files (*.BMP)¦*.bmp¦Icon Files ¦
*.ico ¦All Files¦*.*"
GetFile.DefaultExt = "BMP"
GetFile.ShowOpen
DataName = GetFile.FileName
Picture1.Picture = LoadPicture(DataName)
```

Using a Database to Store Pictures

You should be aware of one last thing regarding the storage of pictures. An Access database can store pictures in a long binary field. This database can be bound to a data control, and the field containing the pictures can be bound to either a Picture Box control or an Image control. If a Picture Box control is used, the drawing methods discussed in this section can be used to create or edit the pictures in the database. The only thing to be aware of is how to save the changes to the pictures back into the database. The problem arises from the fact that the data field containing the picture is bound to the `Picture` property of the Picture Box control. The drawings that are made with the graphics methods are not part of the `Picture` property, but rather part of the `Image` property of the control. It is therefore necessary to copy the `Image` property to the `Picture` property prior to the update of the database. This is done with the following line of code:

```
Picture1.Picture = Picture1.Image
```

Once the drawing or annotations have been copied to the `Picture` property, the drawing will be stored in the database. An application that requires a number of sketches can benefit from using this technique to store the drawings. By using the database, all the drawings are stored in one file rather than a series of bitmap files. It is also possible to add other fields to the database that would contain a description of the drawing and possibly supporting information or notes.

Analyzing Data with Graphics

The final topic in this chapter deals with analyzing data or information with the use of graphics or charts. Often charts are very useful in giving users a better feel for the information than is possible by looking at just numbers. If you were to look at a pie chart of your household budget, the percentage of your budget devoted to debt reduction is presented far more dramatically than if you only looked at dollar amounts. Charts can also help a user spot trends in the data that would not be possible from viewing only the numeric data.

This section will look at two ways to create data charts—with the Graph control and with the graphics methods. Using the Graph control is far easier than creating your own charts, but there are situations where "rolling your own" is the best solution. Also, if you understand how to create your own charts, you will have a better understanding of the workings of the Graph control and will be able to make better use of it.

Using the Graph Control to Analyze Data

The Graph control is one of the custom controls provided with Visual Basic. This control provides you with the means to create any of the following graph types:

➤ *Pie charts*: used to display a set of values as the percentage of a total.

➤ *Bar charts* or *histograms*: used to display discrete quantities such as sales per month.

➤ *Gantt charts*: usually used to display a time dependence between events in a process.

➤ *Line charts*: used for showing trends such as the increase in consumer prices over a period of time.

➤ *Area charts*: line charts with the area between the line and the horizontal axis (or another line) filled in.

➤ *Scatter charts*: used to display the dependence of one variable on another.

➤ *High/Low/Close (HLC) charts*: used to display stock quotes, or high, low, and average quantities such as daily temperature.

To create a chart, you first need to select the Graph control from the Toolbar, and draw the chart area on your form. You will then need to set the type of graph desired by using the GraphType property. You will also need to use the NumSets and NumPoints properties to tell the control how many sets of data to include in the chart and how many points are in each set. Finally, you will have to input the data that you want displayed on the chart. You can input all this information at designtime through the properties dialog box. After you have drawn the Graph control on your form, click the right mouse to bring up a pop-up menu, then select Properties from the menu. This will bring up the Graph Control Properties dialog box as shown in figure 16.24.

Fig. 16.24 The Graph Control Properties dialog box provides an easy way of entering information for the graphics control.

The first tab in the properties dialog box enables you to specify the type of graph, and the number of sets and points. You can also set the graph style, which provides additional formatting information, and information about the colors to be used on the graph. For illustration purposes, select a 2D pie chart with one data set and five data points. After entering this information for your graph, you can select the Data tab at the top of the properties page to go to the data-entry dialog box shown in figure 16.25.

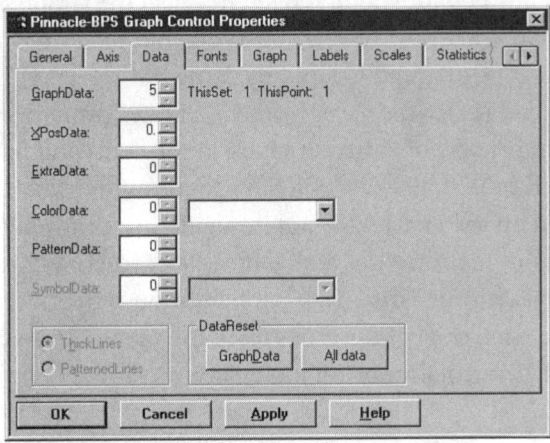

Fig. 16.25 The Data page enables you to enter the data to be displayed on the graph.

For the pie chart, you can enter the data value and the color and pattern of each pie slice from the Data page. Each data point is accessed using the scroll buttons to the right of the data-entry area. When you have finished entering the data, you click the OK button to return to the form design window, and then run your program to show the results of the graph. Figure 16.26 shows the pie chart with values of 1, 2, 3, 4, and 5 for the five pie slices.

If you could only enter data for the Graph control at designtime, the Graph control's usefulness would be pretty limited. You can, however, enter data for the control at runtime. Listing 16.7 will set up the data to produce a pie chart similar to the one in figure 16.26, but with six data points and different values for the data points.

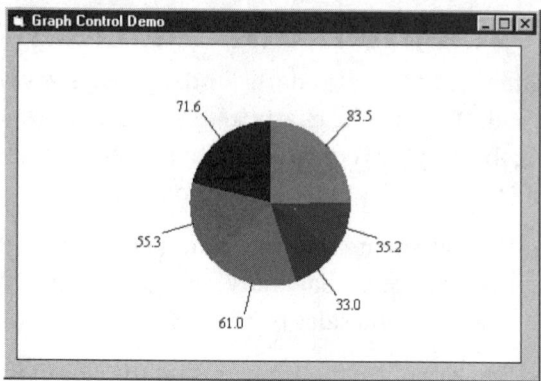

Fig. 16.26 This pie chart is the result of the information entered for the Graph control.

Listing 16.7   PIECHART.FRM—Using the Graphic Control to Create a Pie Chart

```
Graph1.GraphType = 1
Graph1.NumPoints = 6
Graph1.ThisSet = 1
For I = 1 To 6
    Graph1.ThisPoint = I
    Graph1.GraphData = 100 * Rnd + I
    Graph1.ThisPoint = I
    Graph1.ColorData = I
Next I
```

Note: Once the graph is displayed on a form, it cannot be changed. Therefore, the way to pass data to the graph at runtime is to place the Graph control on a second form, then place the code to set up the graph in the `Activate` event of that form. When the form is accessed through the `Load` method, the new information will be displayed on the graph. When the user has finished viewing the graph and is ready to move on, the form containing the Graph control can be unloaded. The same thing can be accomplished through the use of an MDI form.

Creating Your Own Data Analysis Graphics

Another way to create charts for data analysis is with the graphics methods. Generating charts in this manner is much more difficult than using the graphics control, but there are some advantages to the effort. Some of these advantages are as follows:

➤ You can create multiple charts on the same Picture Box control (for example, a bar chart for regional sales by month and a pie chart for total sales by region).

➤ You can place multiple axes on the same chart, allowing you to plot multiple variables (for example, a chart of engine temperature and coolant pressure versus speed).

➤ You can create charts that change with time.

➤ You can superimpose the chart on another graphic for special effects.

This section will discuss the general programming aspects of creating your own charts, and then look in detail at some of the advantages mentioned in the list.

Creating a Simple Chart

To begin the discussion, consider the pie chart created in figure 16.26. To create the same chart in a program, follow these steps:

1. Calculate the total value of all the points.

2. Convert the value of each point to a fraction of the total.

3. Convert the fractional value to the radian values of a circle.

4. Set the `FillColor` property for each point.

5. Draw the pie shape for each of the points.

Listing 16.8 performs these steps for the graph in figure 16.26.

Listing 16.8 PIECHRT2.FRM—Creating a Pie Chart Using the Graphics Methods

```
Dim piedat(6) As Integer
***************
'Set data values
***************
piedat(1) = 5
piedat(2) = 3
piedat(3) = 8
piedat(4) = 2
piedat(5) = 9
piedat(6) = 6
***********************
'Get total of all points
***********************
totpnt = 0
For I = 1 To 6
    totpnt = totpnt + piedat(I)
Next I
*********************************************
'Calculate percent, pie coordinates then plot
*********************************************
strtpt = -0.001
Form1.FillStyle = 0
For I = 1 To 6
    pctpnt = piedat(I) / totpnt
    piesiz = pctpnt * 2 * 3.1416
    endpnt = strtpt - piesiz
    endpnt = IIf(endpnt < -6.2831, -6.2831, endpnt)
    Form1.FillColor = QBColor(I)
    Circle (2000, 2000), 1600, , strtpt, endpnt
    strtpt = endpnt
Next I
```

This is a somewhat generic routine for creating a pie chart. If you needed to add more data points, you would only need to expand the array and the terminal value of the FOR ... NEXT loop. You would also need to change the way colors are handled if you had more than 16 data points.

Using Methods for Different Chart Types

As you saw above, a pie chart can be created using the `Circle` method. Most of the chart types described above for the graphic control can be easily ("easily" being a relative term) created with the graphics methods. Each graphic type will use one or more of the graphics methods to create the charts. Table 16.5 shows several of the most common chart types and the methods used to create them.

Table 16.5   Different Graphics Methods Are Used to Create Different Types of Charts

Chart Type	Graphics Method
Pie	`Circle` method
Bar	`Line` method (drawing boxes)
Gantt	`Line` method (drawing lines or boxes)
Line	`Line` method
Scatter	`PSet` method, `PaintPicture` method, `Print` method
High/Low/Close	`Line` method

Symbols can be drawn on any of the chart types using the `PaintPicture` method, or if the symbols are simple characters, the `Print` method can be used to place the character on the chart. You will also note that the `Print` method was mentioned as one that could produce Scatter charts. This works the same way as placing symbols on the chart. You would establish the necessary position of the symbol using the `CurrentX` and `CurrentY` properties, then print the symbol.

Determining Where to Place Points on the Chart

The section on "Creating a Simple Chart" showed how to use the `Circle` method to create a pie chart. The code used to produce the chart assumed that the size of the form and the position of the chart were predetermined. This may not always be the case. If you are drawing a chart on a form whose size can change, you will need to calculate the position of the chart on the form. In addition, for many chart types such as line or bar, you need to establish the range of the horizontal and vertical coordinates that are available for showing data.

This section will walk through this process using the example of a line chart containing 50 data points with a random value of 0 to 1000. The actual chart is shown in figure 16.27.

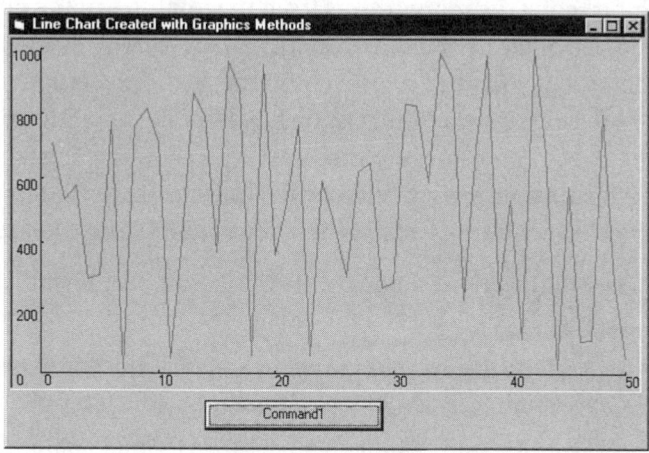

Fig. 16.27 To create a chart, you need to determine the placement of any labels and the area available for drawing the data.

The first step in determining where the data for the chart will be placed is to find the size of the form or Picture Box control that will contain the chart. Horizontal and vertical size are determined using the ScaleWidth and ScaleHeight methods respectively. These properties determine the maximum space available for the output of the chart.

Next, determine the amount of space needed for labels on the two axes. This is handled by the TextHeight and TextWidth properties. You will want the maximum value of these properties for all the labels that will be placed on the chart. For the sample case, the Y-axis will range from 0 to 1000 in increments of 200. Therefore, the maximum TextWidth would be for 1000. Along the X-axis, the values will range from 1 to 50 in increments of 10, but all the values should have the same text height. The TextWidth will determine the margin between the edge of the output object (form or picture box) and the Y-axis. Similarly, the TextHeight gives the margin between the bottom of the output object and the X-axis. If you also want a margin at the top and right of the chart, you will have to establish values for these as well. The code for the sample chart uses half the TextWidth and TextHeight margins for the right and top margins respectively.

Subtracting the margin sizes from the total size of the object gives you the size of the actual drawing area. This size will determine the scaling factor that you need to use to determine the placement of data points. For the Y-axis values, this is the height of the drawing area divided by the maximum value. For the X-axis value, the scaling factor is the width of the drawing area divided by the maximum X value. To obtain the drawing position of any point you will need to do the following:

1. Multiply the X value by the horizontal scaling factor to determine the distance from the Y-axis.

2. Add the distance obtained in Step 1 to the width of the left margin to obtain the actual X position on the output object.

3. Multiply the Y value by the vertical scaling factor to determine the distance from the X-axis.

4. Subtract the distance obtained in Step 3 from the position of the X-axis to obtain the actual Y position on the output object.

You will notice that the last step instructs you to subtract the value obtained in step 3 from the position of the X-axis. This is because the vertical position coordinates of an object increase from top to bottom. Therefore, a point above the X-axis will have a smaller number for the vertical position than the axis itself. The program code for the chart is shown in Listing 16.9.

Listing 16.9   LINECHRT.FRM—Creating a Chart Involves Setting the Position of the Axis and Labels, and Determining the Scaling Factor to Be Used to Position Points

```
********************************
'Determine maximum size of object
********************************
maxX = Chart.ScaleWidth
maxY = Chart.ScaleHeight
**********************
'Determine margin sizes
```

```
*********************
lmarg = Chart.TextWidth("1000")
bmarg = Chart.TextHeight("50")
rmarg = maxX - 0.5 * lmarg
tmarg = 0.5 * bmarg
bmarg = maxY - bmarg
****************************************
'Determine scale factors for each axis
****************************************
SclX = (rmarg - lmarg) / 50
SclY = (bmarg - tmarg) / 1000
*********
'Draw axes
*********
Chart.Line (lmarg, tmarg)-(lmarg, bmarg)
Chart.Line -(rmarg, bmarg)
**************************
'Draw labels and tic marks
**************************
For I = 1 To 6
    Chart.CurrentX = 5
    Ypsn = bmarg - ((I - 1) * 200 * SclY)
    Chart.CurrentY = Ypsn
    Chart.Print Right(Str((I - 1) * 200), 4)
    Chart.Line (lmarg, Ypsn)-(lmarg + 40, Ypsn)
Next I
For I = 1 To 6
    Xpsn = lmarg + ((I - 1) * 10 * SclX)
    Chart.CurrentX = Xpsn
    Chart.CurrentY = bmarg + 5
    Chart.Print Right(Str((I - 1) * 10), 2)
    Chart.Line (Xpsn, bmarg)-(Xpsn, bmarg - 40)
Next I
*********************
'Draw Points on the chart
*********************
Chart.ForeColor = &hff
For I = 1 To 50
    Xpsn = lmarg + (I * SclX)
    Ypsn = bmarg - (1000 * Rnd * SclY)
    If I = 1 Then
        Chart.CurrentX = Xpsn
        Chart.CurrentY = Ypsn
    Else
        Chart.Line -(Xpsn, Ypsn)
    End If
Next I
```

Dynamic (or Time-Dependent) Charts

One of the advantages mentioned for creating your own data-analysis charts is that you can create a chart that changes with time. To create this dynamic (or time-dependent) chart, you will need a way to add points to the chart at specified intervals. A chart such as this would be used in a manufacturing environment to track continuous processes. There are two ways to handle plotting time-dependent information. You can track all the information, adding new points but never removing old points, or you can track some number of points representing the most recent measurements (for example, the last 100 points).

Tracking a number of recent points is usually the preferable method of developing a dynamic chart. The advantages of this method are that you have a limited number of points, which keep system resource requirements down, and you do not have to constantly recalculate the scale factors to account for additional points. The code below shows the use of the Timer event to generate points at half second intervals and place them on a chart. Listing 16.10 produces the chart shown in figure 16.28.

Listing 16.10   DYNCHART.FRM—Code Placed in the Timer Event to Create a Dynamic Chart

```
If drwchrt = 1 Then
    Xpsn = lmarg + (pntidx * SclX)
    Ypsn = Int(bmarg - (1000 * Rnd * SclY))
    chrtpnt(pntidx) = Ypsn
    If pntidx = 1 Then
        Chart.CurrentX = Xpsn
        Chart.CurrentY = Ypsn
    Else
        Chart.Line -(Xpsn, Ypsn)
    End If
    pntidx = pntidx + 1
End If
```

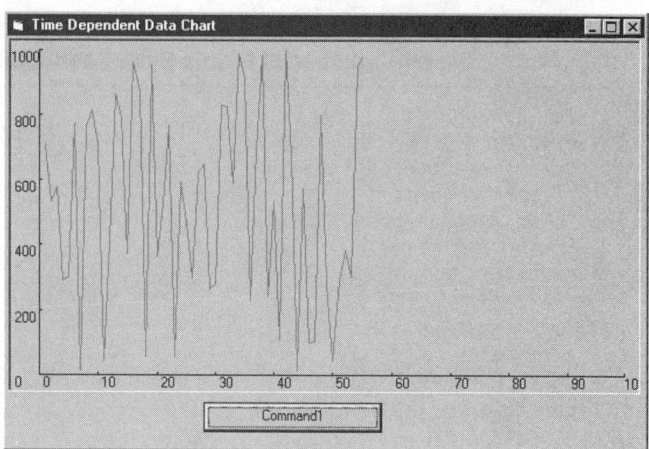

Fig. 16.28 A dynamic chart can be created that changes as new points are added.

This code is set up to track 100 data points. (The array `chrtpnt` was previously dimensioned to that size.) Now the question is, what do you do after the 100th point is reached? You will need to discard the first value in the array, move the rest of the array elements up, and then add the last value to the end of the array. You would then need to replot the entire array. If this were done for each point, your code would be running a lot of operations, and redrawing the chart for every new point. A better way to handle this is to eliminate about one-fourth of the points when the end of the array is reached. This way, the redraw operation is performed much less often, improving the efficiency of your code. For the sample case with 100 points, a redraw would occur only every 25 points. Listing 16.11 shows the subroutine that resets the array and redraws the chart.

Listing 16.11 DYNCHRT.FRM—Redrawing the Chart After a Certain Number of Points Have Been Added

```
Sub RdrwChrt()
drwchrt = 0
Chart.ForeColor = &h0
****************
'Clear chart area
****************
Chart.Cls
*********
'Draw axes
*********
Chart.Line (lmarg, tmarg)-(lmarg, bmarg)
Chart.Line -(rmarg, bmarg)
***********
'Draw labels
***********
For I = 1 To 6
    Chart.CurrentX = 5
    Ypsn = bmarg - ((I - 1) * 200 * SclY)
    Chart.CurrentY = Ypsn
    Chart.Print Right(Str((I - 1) * 200), 4)
    Chart.Line (lmarg, Ypsn)-(lmarg + 40, Ypsn)
Next I
For I = 1 To 11
    Xpsn = lmarg + ((I - 1) * 10 * SclX)
    Chart.CurrentX = Xpsn
    Chart.CurrentY = bmarg + 5
    Chart.Print Right(Str((I - 1) * 10), 3)
    Chart.Line (Xpsn, bmarg)-(Xpsn, bmarg - 40)
Next I
Chart.ForeColor = &hff
*****************************
'Reset array and redraw points
*****************************
For I = 1 To 75
    chrtpnt(I) = chrtpnt(I + 25)
    Xpsn = lmarg + (I * SclX)
    Ypsn = chrtpnt(I)
    If I = 1 Then
        Chart.CurrentX = Xpsn
        Chart.CurrentY = Ypsn
    Else
        Chart.Line -(Xpsn, Ypsn)
    End If
Next I
```

```
*********************************
'Reset point index and restart timer
*********************************
pntidx = 76
drwchrt = 1
End Sub
```

The reset and redraw operations are fairly quick, so if you want to reset a smaller number of points, it should be no problem. The total number of points you use for the chart, and the number of points you reset will depend on your application and the time interval between points. You want to set these so that the chart is not being continuously reset.

From Here...

This chapter has discussed any number of ways that graphics can be used to enhance your applications. Each of the sections discussed an individual area of graphics usage. You can, of course, combine many of these techniques to add even greater sophistication to your applications.

➤ To learn more about using databases for managing graphics, refer to Chapter 5, "Data Management and Data-Driven Programming." Or see Que's *Special Edition Using Visual Basic 4.*

➤ You can also see how graphics are used in multimedia applications in Chapter 15, "Multimedia in Action."

17

Communications Basics

by Steve Potts

Communication between computers is a fundamental requirement of modern systems. Often this subject is treated with an undue amount of respect. Communications between computers is a complex arrangement of simple ideas and functionality.

Many end users are content to purchase a modem and run the applications that they purchase right out of the box. This chapter is written for programmers who are not willing to operate at such a global level. To create communication applications in Visual Basic, you can simply use the MSComm custom control, memorize what properties to set, and include them in your code. This approach creates the following two real problems, however:

➤ Your ability to create applications will be limited by your lack of comprehension of the underlying principles of communications.

➤ Your ability to debug your applications will be limited by the rote method.

To be really good, you must understand what is happening while communication between two computers is taking place. This chapter will attempt to give you an understanding of data communications in general, not just a primer on the MSComm custom control.

Data communications emerged as a field in the 19th century. Samuel F. B. Morse, of Morse code fame, learned of an experiment where an electrical signal was sent over a wire more than 25 miles long. He immediately commented that if that is possible, then intelligence can be transmitted instantaneously over long distances. That statement marks the birth of communications. He next went to work creating the infrastructure necessary to make this concept a reality. Shortly thereafter, he demonstrated how a sender can transmit information to a receiver using the Morse code. The dots and dashes were the protocol of the telegraph when it was the preferred means of communications.

Modern data communications still centers around that idea. In this chapter, you will learn the following:

➤ Data communications theory

➤ Communications hardware

➤ The MSComm custom control

Serial Communications

The simplest form of personal computer communications is called *serial communications*, because it transmits data signals in series, or one-at-a-time over one line. There are often other wires involved in supporting the data line, however. The following is a list of personal computer communication components:

➤ The sender—The input/output card of most personal computers holds the electronics necessary to put the signal on the wire.

➤ The power source—The power supply of your computer provides a source of electrical power.

➤ The physical transmission medium—A cable normally runs between an I/O port and a peripheral device like a printer or modem.

➤ The protocol—Each peripheral device has a set of commands that the developers built into it. These commands are used by applications to tell the device what to do. The AT command set for modems and Hewlett-Packard's printer control language (HPPCL), are examples of this class.

➤ The receiver—The printer interface translates the input stream to mechanical action.

➤ The translator—The I/O card in a personal computer receives signals from a modem and translates them to data.

➤ Persistent storage—The hard drive of a computer stores data after it has been received.

➤ Recording mechanism—The write heads on the hard drive record data to the disk.

This is in contrast to *parallel communications* where multiple signals are sent over multiple lines at the same time. If you have nine data wires in a cable, you could—in theory—send nine bits of information simultaneously. Parallel communications operates on this theory. Figure 17.1 shows a theoretical view of serial communications.

In practice, while there is only data wire in serial communications, there are a number of other wires that are needed to support the data wire.

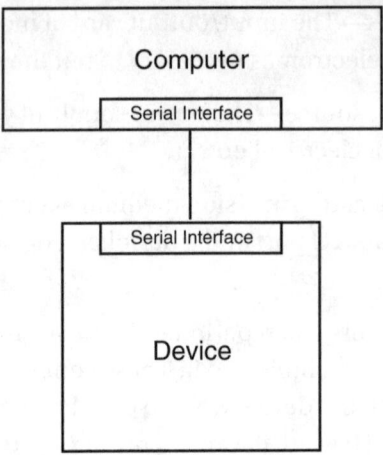

Fig. 17.1 Serial communication theory states that all communication takes place over one wire.

Communication Hardware

These other wires manage the starting and stopping of the transmission of data, as well as other tasks. The Electronics Industries Association (EIA) wrote "Recommended Standard Number 232, Revision C," which gives the specifications for the pin and voltage assignments for an operational serial communication standard. This standard is better known as the *RS-232 standard*. It defines 25 wires and their uses in serial communications. Table 17.1 lists these lines.

Table 17.1   The 25-Pin RS-232 Standard

Pin	Abbreviation	Name
1	AA	Protective Ground
2	BA	Transmitted Data
3	BB	Received Data
4	CA	Request to Send
5	CB	Clear to Send

Pin	Abbreviation	Name
6	CC	Data Set Ready
7	AB	Signal Common
8	CF	Received Line Signal Detect
9	(none)	Reserved for Testing
10	(none)	Reserved for Testing
11	(none)	Unassigned
12	SCF	Secondary Received Line Signal Detect
13	SCB	Secondary Clear to Send
14	SCA	Secondary Transmitted Data
15	DB	Transmission Signal Element Timing
16	SBB	Secondary Received Data
17	DD	Receiver Signal Element Timing
18	(none)	Unassigned
19	SCA	Secondary Request to Send
20	CD	Data Terminal Ready
21	CG	Signal Quality Detector
22	CE	Ring Indicator
23	CH/CI	Data Signal Rate Detector
24	DA	Transmit Signal Element Timing
25	(none)	Unassigned

The total comprehension of the reasons behind the specifying of each pin would be fascinating reading on a stormy night. For the purposes of our discussion, however, there are only a few that we need to understand. Lines 2 and 3 actually send and receive data. If you hook two RS-232 ports together with a cable, it must have these two lines reversed from one end to the other. This is because one port's transmission is the other's reception. Pins 6, 8, 20, 22, and 23 communicate the various status from one device to another. Pins 4 and 5 (Request to Send and Clear to Send) are used to coordinate the timing of the transmissions between the devices. Figure 17.2 shows a female version of this device. The female version accepts the pins of the male version to make the connection.

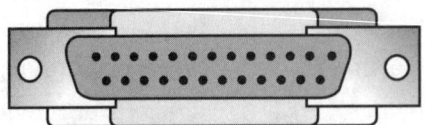

Fig. 17.2 The RS-232 standard specifies the arrangement and use of a 25-pin serial connector.

It is not common on a personal computer to find all 25 pins actually present in a cable. This is because the EIA committee built in a lot of redundant capability to its standard. The budget-minded personal computer marketplace doesn't use these backups in its devices, so it dropped the pins while keeping the plug shape.

Table 17.2   The Pin Assignments for the 9-Pin Plug in a 25-Pin Shell

Pin	Abbreviation	Name
1	-	Protective Ground
2	TD	Transmitted Data
3	RD	Received Data
4	RTS	Request to Send
5	CTS	Clear to Send
6	DSR	Data Set Ready
7	-	Signal Common
8	DCD	Received Line Signal Detect
20	DTR	Data Terminal Ready
22	RI	Ring Indicator
23	DSRD	Data Signal Rate Detector

If you examine the back of the computer at your desk, you will probably discover another plug that is described as a serial port. A smaller plug with nine pins is most likely located right beside the printer port on your machine. This is a *9-pin "D" shell plug*. It was created by IBM in the early personal computer days because it was small enough to fit with a parallel port on the same card, and because so many of the pins on a standard RS-232 plug are not commonly used by devices. They chose the nine pins that had to be present, and placed them in a pin arrangement on their computers. This decision was popular with the clone vendors, who copied the IBM arrangement. Table 17.3 shows the pin assignment for the 9-pin plug.

Table 17.3   The Common 9-Pin Plug

Pin	Abbreviation	Name
1	DCD	Data Carrier Detect
2	RD	Received Data
3	TD	Transmit Data
4	DTR	Data Terminal Ready
5	(none)	Signal Common
6	DSR	Data Set Ready
7	RTS	Request to Send
8	CTS	Clear to Send
9	RI	Ring Indicator

It is common to find both kinds of connectors on the same computer. Often, one is set up as COM1 and the other is called COM2. There is no official standard for the 9-pin plug and pin arrangement, except in the heads of 30 million computer lovers who would beat the tar out of any vendor who wanted to deviate one bit without good reason.

Each pin has a definite purpose in the 9-pin arrangement. These assignments depend on the connection between a computer (called *Data*

Terminal Equipment or *DTE*) and a peripheral device (called *Data Communication Equipment* or *DCE*). These are as follows:

Data Carrier Detect (DCD)	This line carries a positive voltage whenever a device (DCE) is ready to receive data. This is how a modem communicates to a computer that it is ready to accept data.
Received Data (RD)	When data flows from the device (DCE) to the computer (DTE), it uses this line.
Transmit Data (TD)	When data flows from the device (DTE) to the computer (DCE), it uses this line.
Data Terminal Ready (DTR)	When a computer (DTE) is ready to talk to a device (DCE), it places a positive voltage on this line.
Signal Common (–)	This is defined as 0 volts. Electrical engineers tell us that all voltage is relative, not absolute. This line defines what it is compared against.
Data Set Ready (DSR)	The device (DCE) places a positive voltage on this wire when it is ready to communicate with the computer (DTE).
Request to Send (RTS)	This line is given a positive voltage by the computer (DTE) when it wants to transmit data to the device (DCE).
Clear to Send (CTS)	This line is given a positive voltage by the device (DCE) when it is ready to receive data from the computer (DTE).

Ring Indicator (RI)	When a device (DCE)—normally a modem—detects a ring, it places a positive voltage on this wire.

You can see from the description of the pins that each is a wire with one specific purpose. Whenever a device wants to send data to a computer, it follows a procedure of placing a positive voltage on the appropriate lines, then checking the lines that the computer controls for its "answer." If it receives the correct responses, it starts transmitting data. As long as the computer leaves the lines that it controls in the same state, the device continues to pump data. If its buffers become full, or another problem occurs, the computer tells the device to wait a minute through these same wires.

Protocol

Now that we have a physical connection between the two devices, we need to agree on the data that we plan to send across these wires. The first decision to make is the rate of data transfer. Different devices can accept data at different rates. For example, if you have a modem that accepts data at 14,400 baud, then it can accept 14,400 bits per second (bps). At times, one device is capable of faster data transfer than the other. In this case, the lower of the two rates must be used or the communication will fail. For example, if my laptop has a 14,400/28,800 baud modem, and I dial-up my office, which can only accept 14,400 bits per second, the "handshake" between modems will agree on 14,400 bits per second.

Another decision that must be made concerns the extra bits that are sent—but are not part of the data. There are three of these bits:

➤ The Start bit—When a device wants to start transmitting, it wants to be sure that the computer will correctly receive the very first bit. The "protocol" that they use first is the Stop bit, then the Parity bit.

➤ The Stop bit—Just as the Start bit signifies the start of a character, the stop bit signifies the end of a character. The transmitting device always sends a logical 1 for the Stop bit. This is done by placing a positive voltage on the TD line.

➤ The Parity bit—Reliability has always been a concern in serial communications. In the early days of data communications, someone invented a crude form of error detection, call *parity checking*, that is still being used today. Parity checking is done by sending an extra bit that indicates whether there was an even or odd number of logical 1 bits in the character just sent. Even parity places a logical 1 in the last bit sent if an odd number of logical 1 bits were in the character. If an even number of logical 1 bits were sent, then the parity bit is set to logical 0. This means that an even number of bits will always be sent. If an odd number of bits is sent, then that indicates an error condition.

The shortcomings of this scheme are obvious. If two errors occur in the same string, the failure can go undetected. While the odds of this happening are very small in a single character's transmission, the probability increases drastically when multiplied by the 100,000,000 characters that are commonly sent over the Internet to download one file.

The Serial Card

You may be wondering how all of this bit-sending takes place in your computer. The setting of the lines at just the right voltages, sending the bits, and checking the parity of the response are the jobs of the I/O card in your computer. This card contains a number of chips that handle these tasks for you. It plugs into the motherboard of your computer and provides one or more serial plugs to the back of the case.

By plugging into the motherboard, the serial card can receive instructions from a program running on the CPU. Unfortunately, your serial card cannot understand Visual Basic commands. This problem is overcome by the authors of both your operating system and Visual Basic.

The serial card contains a chip called a *Universal Asynchronous Receiver Transmitter (UART)*. This UART has a number of registers that are addressable as memory locations. This means that a program running under Windows 95 can write to one of the addresses in Table 17.4, and the data will be placed in the buffer of the UART.

Table 17.4 Serial Port Base Register Addresses

Serial Port	Base Register Port Address
COM1	3F8H
COM2	2F8H
COM3	3E8H
COM4	2E8H

By sending one of a series of instructions that the UART understands to these registers, your program can control the string of characters that gets sent out of the serial port.

At this point, you should have a feel for what goes on under the covers when you are using a modem. The authors of Visual Basic have provided a custom control for you to use when you need to communicate with devices connected to the serial port on your computer. This custom control interacts with the operating system and, in turn, the operating system interacts with the device—hiding much technical detail from you, the programmer. The use of this custom control is the subject of the next section.

The Communications Control

The communication custom control (MSComm) ships with Visual Basic 4.0, Professional Edition. It is called MSCOMM16.OCX or MSCOMM32.OCX—depending on whether you are running the 16- or 32-bit version of Visual Basic. In order to use the MSComm custom control, choose Custom Controls from the Tools menu. The Custom Controls dialog box appears, as shown in figure 17.3.

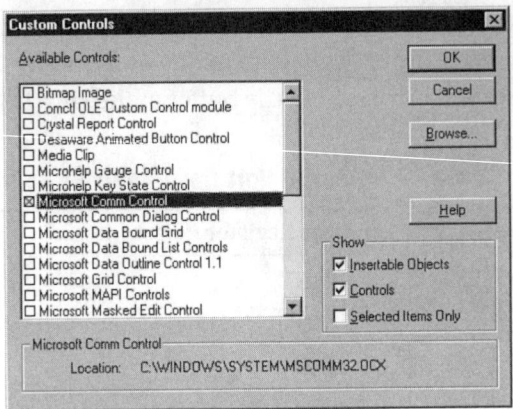

Fig. 17.3 The Custom Controls dialog box is used to place the MSComm custom control in your Visual Basic Toolbox.

After you have indicated via the Custom Controls dialog box that you want to add the MSComm custom control to your project, the MSComm icon is added to your Toolbox, as shown in figure 17.4.

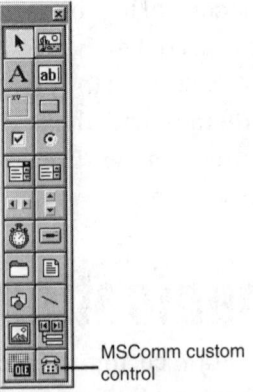

MSComm custom control

Fig. 17.4 The MSComm custom control icon looks like an old-fashioned telephone.

This first step in using the MSComm custom control is to place it on a form, as shown in figure 17.5. This icon on the form will be invisible at runtime. It only appears on the form at designtime to preserve the visual programming paradigm.

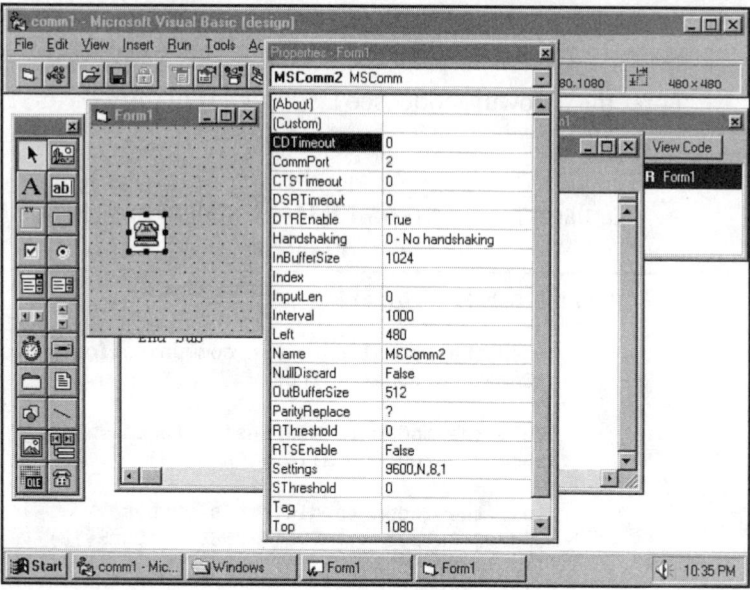

Fig. 17.5 The MSComm custom control appears on the form at runtime so that you can access its properties and code in the same manner as the other Visual Basic controls.

The MSComm custom control works like the standard edition controls using properties, events, and methods. Before delving into the deeper details of how this control operates, run this simple example. The purpose of this experiment is to give you a global feel for the MSComm control. We will discuss this example's details following the code. This example assumes that your modem is properly configured and connected to COM2. If you have used the Windows 95 modem setup, then you should have no problem. If you are using Windows 3.1, follow the instructions that came with your modem to install it. If you are using COM1, COM3, or COM4, substitute that comm port for COM2.

This example sets up the MSComm custom control for use with a modem.

1. Create a Form and add an MSComm custom control to it.

2. Name the control MSComm2.

3. Set the CommPort property to 2, indicating COM2.

4. Set the Settings property to the right settings for your modem. Try `9600,N,8,1` if you are not sure. Many modems can use this setting.

5. Enter the following code (see Listing 17.1) in the `Form_Click` event procedure:

Listing 17.1 TESTCOM1.BAS—A Simple Communication Program

```
Private Sub Form_Click()

        'Open the serial port for communications
        MSComm2.PortOpen = True

        'Tell the modem to dial using tones
        MSComm2.Output = "ATT" + Chr$(13)

        'Tell the Modem to dial this number
        MSComm2.Output = "ATD514-9688" + Chr$(13)

        'Close the port
        MSComm2.PortOpen = False

    End Sub
```

6. Enter a phone number in your home or office (instead of 514-9688). Substitute your own phone number for this sample one.

7. Run the program by single-stepping through your code.

8. Click on the form.

9. Step through the code until you get to the line that reads:

```
MSComm2.Output = "ATD514-9688" + Chr$(13)
```

10. Listen to your modem and watch its indicator lights (if it is so equipped). If the settings are correct, you will hear a dial tone, the tones for the number that you placed on this line, and the phone ring. If you pick up that phone and say something, you will likely hear your voice on the modem's speaker.

Briefly, the example opens the COM2 port with the following statement:

```
MSComm2.PortOpen = True
```

Opening the port means that the driver associated with the hardware port is connected to this program. On many modems, an indicator light will illuminate. The `Output` property takes string data and places it in the output buffer. The modem is looking in this buffer for commands. The commands that it understands are called *AT commands*, because they begin with AT. The command `ATT` tells the modem to dial using tones instead of pulses. You will learn more AT commands in the section "Programming a Modem" later in this chapter.

```
MSComm2.Output = "ATT" + Chr$(13)
```

The command `ATD514-9688` tells the modem to dial this number.

```
MSComm2.Output = "ATD514-9688" + Chr$(13)
```

The `Chr$(13)` appends a carriage return to the end of the command, telling the modem to execute the command.

```
MSComm2.PortOpen = False
```

Having finished with the program, we now close COM2 so that it can be used by another application.

The Designtime Properties

Only about half of the properties of the MSComm custom control are available to you at designtime. The rest expect to be set at runtime. As with other Visual Basic controls, not all of the properties need a static value at program initialization. Figure 17.6 shows the properties in the Properties window at designtime.

The most frequently used of these properties are as follows:

➤ (Custom)—While listed as a property in the Property window, this is really a dialog box that contains the settings of properties for hardware, buffers, and general information. Figure 17.7 shows what the dialog box looks like with different tabs associated with the control properties. You will probably find it simpler to describe your modem using this dialog box than by setting individual property values.

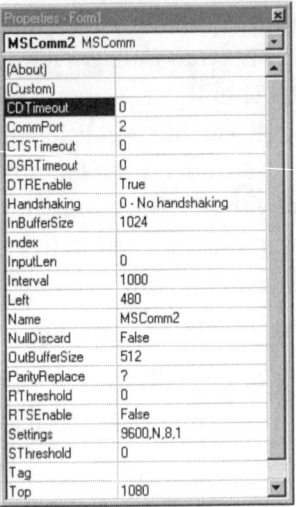

Fig. 17.6 These properties of the MSComm custom control are available at designtime.

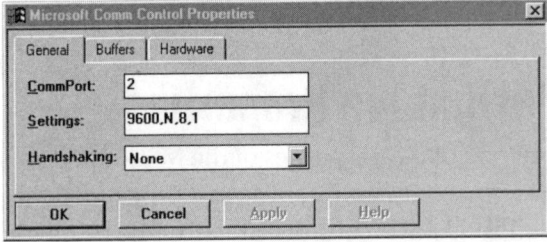

Fig. 17.7 The Custom dialog box allows the designer to specify the values of several properties.

➤ CDTimeout—Sets and returns the amount of time that your program will wait to receive a CD (carrier detect) signal before timing out. Carrier detect is the name of one of the pins on the serial port. When another device connects to the serial port, it places a positive charge (logical 1) on the CD line and keeps it there for the duration. If your serial port attempts a connection and fails to see the CD line go to logical 1, it will give up after the number of milliseconds set in this property. After it gives up, it triggers the OnComm event, which allows you to code what you want your program to do in the event of a timeout. The CommEvent property will be set to CDTO in the event of a timeout. In code, you set the CDTimeout property like this:

```
MSComm2.CDTimeout = 1000
```

To display this setting, you use this syntax:

```
Text1.Text = MSComm2.CDTimeout
```

➤ CommPort—Sets the serial port associated with this control to 1-COM1, 2-COM2, 3-COM3, or 4-COM4. You may set up multiple communications sessions in the same program by creating multiple instances of the MSComm control if you have multiple devices with which to connect.

➤ CTSTimeout—Sets and returns the amount of time that your program will wait to receive a CTS (Clear to Send) signal before timing out. Clear to Send is the name of one of the pins on the serial port. When two devices are connected, one device will send a signal called Request to Send (RTS) to the other. If the second device is ready to receive data, it responds by setting the Clear to Send (CTS) line to logical 1. If your serial port fails to see the CTS line go to logical 1, it will give up after the number of milliseconds set in this property. After it gives up, it triggers the OnComm event, which allows you to code what you want your program to do in the event of a timeout. The CommEvent property will be set to CTSTO in the event of a timeout. In code, you set the CTSTimeout property like this:

```
MSComm2.CTSTimeout = 1000
```

To display this setting, you use this syntax:

```
Text1.Text = MSComm2.CTSTimeout
```

➤ DSRTimeout—This property is useful when writing a Data Set Ready/Data Terminal Ready handshaking routine. It sets and returns the amount of time that your program will wait to receive a DSR (Data Set Ready) signal before timing out. Data Set Ready is the name of one of the pins on the serial port. When two devices are connected, one device will send a signal called Request To Send (RTS) to the other. If the second device is ready to communicate, it responds by setting the Data Terminal Ready (DTR) line to logical 1. If your serial port fails to see the DTR line go to logical 1, it will give up after the number of milliseconds set in this property. After it gives up, it triggers the OnComm event, which allows you to code what you want your program to do in the event of a timeout. The CommEvent property will be set to DSRTO in the event of a timeout. In code, you set the DSRTimeout property like this:

```
MSComm2.DSRTimeout = 1000
```

To display this setting, you use this syntax:

```
Text1.Text = MSComm2.DSRTimeout
```

➤ DTREnable—Allows you to control whether or not your serial port is able to set its DTR line to logical 1. Normally, True is the best setting. In fact, the phone line will often hang if this value is set to False.

➤ Handshaking—Sets and returns the type of handshaking protocol that your program is to use. *Handshaking* is a similar to humans shaking hands. When we meet someone new, especially in an official capacity, we shake hands. If the other person refuses to shake our hand, then we conclude that something is wrong, and friendly communication doesn't begin until the reason for the handshaking problem is resolved. Handshaking, in the data communications sense, refers to the internal communications protocol by which data is transferred from the hardware port to the receive buffer. When a character of data arrives at the serial port, the communications device has to move it into the receive buffer where your Visual Basic program can read it by using the Input property.

A handshaking protocol is used to make sure that data is not lost by coming in so rapidly that your device is not able to move the data into the buffer. The software way of asking the other device to suspend transmission for a moment is done by sending a CHR$(19) (called XOFF) to the other device. When the bottleneck is cleared, a `CHR$(17)` (called `XON`) is sent. In code, you set the `Handshaking` property like this:

```
MSComm2.Handshaking = XOnXOff
```

To display this setting, you use this syntax:

```
Text1.Text = MSComm2.Handshaking
```

The hardware method for communicating this is called *RTS/CTS*. The RTS line in the serial port is used to indicate that a request to send is being sent. The CTS line is used to indicate that all is clear, so send away. If the overrun situation begins to form, the receiver removes the CTS line's signal. The sender, seeing that line go to logical 0, suspends transmission until either the CTS line goes back to logical 1, or the `CTSTimeout` setting expires. The values for the `Handshaking` property shown in Table 17.5.

Table 17.5   The Settings for the Handshaking Property

Setting	Description
None	(Default) No handshaking
XOnXOff	XON/XOFF handshaking
RTS	RTS/CTS handshaking
RTSXOnXOff	Both RTS and XON/XOFF handshaking are used

➤ `InBufferSize`—When a serial port receives data over its RD (received data) line, it has to put it somewhere. If it had to hold the data in a register on the serial card until your program asked for it, the maximum transmission rate would be very low. In order to speed things up, an area of memory is set up to be used by the serial card to unload the data as it is received. If you set a value that is too small, you will have to use handshaking in your program to avoid overrunning the buffer's length and generating an error. If you make it too large, then you make your program larger than it needs to be. In code, you set the `InBufferSize` property like this:

```
MSComm2.InBufferSize = 1024
```

To display this setting, you use this syntax:

```
Text1.Text = MSComm2.InBufferSize
```

➤ InputLen—Sets and returns the number of characters that the Input property reads from the receive buffer. If the value of the InputLen property is set to 0, then the Input property will read all of the characters in the buffer. In code, you set the InputLen property like this:

```
MSComm2.InputLen = 1024
```

To display this setting, you use this syntax:

```
Text1.Text = MSComm2.InputLen
```

> **Note:** The implementation of the MSComm custom control uses two properties to perform tasks normally associated with methods. The Output property places data in the output buffer. The Input property moves data from the buffer into a variable.

➤ Name—Sets the name of the control so that it can be uniquely referenced in code. MSComm2 is the name of the control in the following line:

```
Text1.Text = MSComm2.InputLen
```

➤ NullDiscard—Determines whether or not Chr$(0) nulls are transferred to the input buffer after they are received from a device, or whether they are discarded. A True setting means to discard them. False means to transfer them. In code, you set the NullDiscard property like this:

```
MSComm2.NullDiscard = True
```

To display this setting, you use this syntax:

```
Text1.Text = MSComm2.NullDiscard
```

➤ OutBufferSize—Sets and returns the size of the output buffer. In code, you set the OutBufferSize property like this:

```
MSComm2.OutBufferSize = 1024
```

To display this setting, you use this syntax:

```
Text1.Text = MSComm2.OutBufferSize
```

➤ ParityReplace—The MSComm control can use the parity bit to provide a small bit (no pun intended) of error-checking. If, upon adding the bits, a parity error is detected, a character is placed in the buffer in place of the bad one. By default, the ? character is used for this. If you place @ in this property, the MSComm control disables parity checking because it has nothing to insert even if it finds a problem. In code, you set the ParityReplace property as follows:

```
MSComm2.ParityReplace = "@"
```

To display this setting, you use the following syntax:

```
Text1.Text = MSComm2.ParityReplace
```

➤ RThreshold—Sets and returns the number of characters that must be received in the input buffer before the OnComm event triggers. If the RThreshold property is set at 0 (the default), an OnComm event is generated for every character. In practice, it may be more efficient to program your application to accept a larger number of characters before triggering the OnComm event. In code, you set the RThreshold property like this:

```
MSComm2.RThreshold = 64
```

To display this setting, you use the following syntax:

```
Text1.Text = MSComm2.RThreshold
```

➤ RTSEnable—If you are using the RTS/CTS handshaking protocol in your program, you will want to enable the RTS line. This allows you to use the hardware to transmit status information to the other device. True means that this the RTS line is enabled. In code, you set the RTSEnable property like this:

```
MSComm2.RTSEnable = 64
```

To display this setting, you use the following syntax:

```
Text1.Text = MSComm2.RTSEnable
```

➤ `Settings`—Sets and receives the baud rate, parity, Data bit, and Stop bit parameters for the serial port. The format of the `Settings` property is as follows:

```
MSComm2.Settings = "9600,N,8,1"
```

This means that the baud rate is 9600, no parity checking is desired, there are 8 Data bits, and there is 1 Stop bit in each packet. If the string doesn't contain a valid set of values when the `PortOpen` property is set to `True`, then an `Error 380` is generated. The valid settings for the MSComm custom control are shown in Table 17.6.

Table 17.6   The Valid Settings for the MSComm Custom Control

Baud Rates	
110, 300, 600, 1200	
2400, 9600 (default)	
14400, 19200	

Parity Settings	
Setting	**Description**
E	Even
M	Mark
N (default)	None
O	Odd
S	Space

Data Bits	
4, 5, 6, 7, 8 (8 is the default)	

Stop Bits	
1 (default), 1.5, and 2	

It is more important to match the settings that the other device is expecting than it is to use any particular set. Luckily, the more efficient settings have been gaining in popularity in recent years, improving the performance of communications overall. The default settings are the most common.

The Runtime Properties

As the name implies, the runtime properties only have meaning while the program is running. They tell you the status of your program, serial port, or peripheral device. Earlier, you saw how the `PortOpen` property was used to open the port for communications. This property can also be used to query the system for the status of a port. Listing 17.2 shows this.

Listing 17.2   PORTOPN1.BAS—Checking Port Status

```
Private Sub Form_Click()

        'Open the serial port for communications
        MSComm2.PortOpen = True

        'Tell the modem to dial using tones
        MSComm2.Output = "ATT" + Chr$(13)

        'Tell the Modem to dial this number
        MSComm2.Output = "ATD514-9688" + Chr$(13)

        'Display the status of the port
        Text1.Text = MSComm2.PortOpen

        'Close the port
        MSComm2.PortOpen = False

        'Display the status of the port
        Text1.Text = MSComm2.PortOpen

    End Sub
```

When you run this program, single-step and watch what happens to the value of the `PortOpen` property as it is displayed in the `Text1` Text Box control. The value will be `True` for a time, then after the port is closed (`PortOpen = False`), you can see the value change. While the port is open, you will see the window as it is displayed in figure 17.8.

Fig. 17.8 The status of a port can easily be queried using the `PortOpen` property

This property allows you to keep up with the status of the port during the course of your program's execution.

It is also useful to query the `Settings` property and the `ComPort` property during the course of the program's execution. An example of this would be during a user session where she is changing the settings to those required by the service that she wants to connect with. It is useful to display the current values. Listing 17.3 shows how this is done.

Listing 17.3   WHATSET1.BAS—Checking Modem Settings

```
Private Sub Form_Click()

    'Open the serial port for communications
    MSComm2.PortOpen = True

    'Tell the modem to dial using tones
    MSComm2.Output = "ATT" + Chr$(13)

    'Tell the Modem to dial this number
    MSComm2.Output = "ATD514-9688" + Chr$(13)

    'Display the status of the port
    Text1.Text = MSComm2.PortOpen

    'Display the settings for the port
    Text3.Text = MSComm2.Settings

    'Display the port number
    Text1.Text = MSComm2.CommPort

    'Close the port
    MSComm2.PortOpen = False
```

```
        'Display the status of the port
        Text1.Text = MSComm2.PortOpen

End Sub
```

Run this program and observe a form that looks like the one shown in figure 17.9.

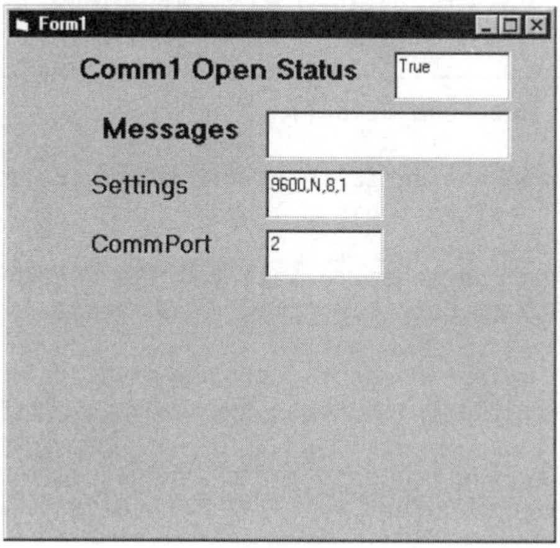

Fig. 17.9 The `Settings` and `CommPort` properties can be queried at runtime.

The real power of a communications control is in its ability to communicate with a device. The MSComm custom control uses properties, curiously, to perform these tasks. Just as we saw how the `Output` property can be used to send the dial command to the modem, the same property can be used to send data to the modem also. The following code shows how this is done by sending a string to the modem when a command button is clicked:

```
Private Sub _Form_KeyPress (KeyAscii as Integer)

'Send the keystroke to the output buffer
    MSComm2.Output = Chr$(KeyAscii)

End Sub
```

In a similar fashion, the Input property can be used to retrieve data from the input buffer. Listing 17.4 shows how this is done. Getting a little ahead of ourselves, we will send an AT command (ATI0) to the modem, instructing the modem to identify itself by model number and also to perform a checksum. In both cases, we will use the Input property to pick up the string out of the buffer and display it on the form.

Listing 17.4   WHATMOD1.BAS—Examining the Modem Model Number

```
Private Sub Form_Click()

    'Open the serial port for communications
    MSComm2.PortOpen = True

    'Ask the modem to tell you its model ID
    MSComm2.Output = "ATIO" + Chr$(13)

    'Display the status of the result
    Text1.Text = MSComm2.Input

    'Ask the modem to perform a checksum
    MSComm2.Output = "ATI1" + Chr$(13)

    'Display the results
    Text2.Text = MSComm2.Input

    'Close the port
    MSComm2.PortOpen = False

End Sub
```

The result of this code is a self-test. The result of this exercise is displayed in figure 17.10.

By way of these commands, your programs can do some automatic detection of models and do the setup for the users. This is the mentality behind the Plug and Play concept. Instead of asking the user to configure a modem, which can be a difficult task even for battle veterans, your software would query the modem and use a database of modem characteristics to configure the port to work correctly.

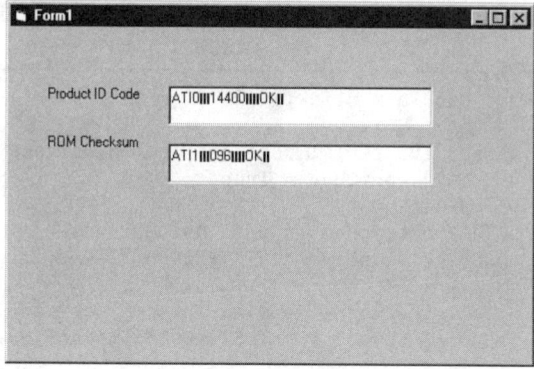

Fig. 17.10 The modem can be instructed to do self-tests.

Note: As a precaution, make sure to flush out the buffer after writing to it and before reading from it.

In figure 17.11, the buffer was read using the `Input` property right after the dialing command was sent to it. You can see that the same information that was just sent using the `Output` property was retrieved using the `Input` property.

Fig. 17.11 The commands sent by your program are stored in the buffer even after they have been executed. Note the example phone number left from another command.

After this has been read, the buffer is now empty and awaiting data.

A query to an external service is far more interesting than data generated by a query to the modem. Listing 17.5 dials-up a local bulletin board and receives a connect message from it.

Listing 17.5   CONNECT1.BAS—Displaying the Connection Success

```
Private Sub Form_Click()

    'Open the serial port for communications
    MSComm2.PortOpen = True

    'Tell the modem to dial using tones
    MSComm2.Output = "ATT" + Chr$(13)

    'Tell the Modem to dial this number
    MSComm2.Output = "ATD514-9688" + Chr$(13)

    'Display the status of the port
    Text1.Text = MSComm2.PortOpen

    'Wait for the carrier to connect and query the buffer
    Text2.Text = MSComm2.Input

    'Close the port
    MSComm2.PortOpen = False

    'Display the status of the port
    Text1.Text = MSComm2.PortOpen

End Sub
```

The result is the standard CONNECT 9600 message, which means that the connection has been established. The verbose message allows you to easily display to the user that the connection was successful. Figure 17.12 shows the result of this program.

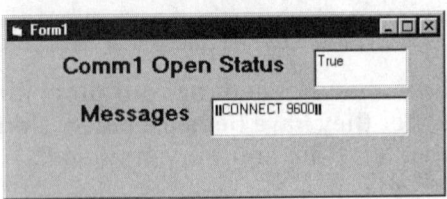

Fig. 17.12 The carrier sends back a connect message that can be displayed to the user.

The status can also be captured and a different message of your own composition can be displayed, such as `You are now connected to the XYZ Online Service`.

Modems and the AT Command Set

Previously in this chapter, in the section "The Communications Control," we used a modem and the `AT` command set to demonstrate the features of the MSComm custom control without defining what they were. The word *modem* is a contraction, of the concatenation of the words *modulator* and *demodulator*. It comes from the fact that data communications first used tones sent over telephone lines to transfer data. *Modulation*, the translation of bits into sounds, occurred at the sending end; *demodulation*, the translation of sounds into bits, occurred at the receiving end. Thus, the pair of modems could move bits from one location to another without a magnetic media.

This remote communication at first involved dialing-up a remote site, telling the person at the other end to put the handset inside a couple of rubber donut-like things called *acoustical couplers*, and doing the same with your handset. The signals moved at a blistering 300 signals per second (300 baud). The result was that the remote computer could cause characters to be printed on a huge roll of paper that fed through a massive terminal.

Over the years, the roll of paper was replaced by the CRT screen, and the mechanical print head was replaced by video cards. The terminal itself has been replaced by attaching a modem to a PC. Not only do short answers pass back and forth, entire books are downloaded. Speeds now reach upwards of 28,800 bits per second and beyond.

Early modems responded to a set of commands that were unique to them. Each vendor created a way of communicating between modems. Hayes Microcomputer Products created a command set for its wildly popular modems in the mid-1980s. This command set started every command with an `AT` (meaning "ATtention"), followed by a string of characters that told the modem what the program wanted it to do next.

Hayes sold so many of these modems that independent software vendors were willing to write programs that ran over these modems. Other modem vendors, anxious to cash-in on the sales generated by these independent software houses, designed their modems to accept the same command set. The result was a defacto standard for the industry. Now, in the mid 1990s, you can hardly buy a modem that doesn't support the AT commands.

While all of these modems support the basic AT commands, many of them—especially the high-speed modems—have considerable extensions to the basic commands. The use of these commands for a specific modem can produce performance that is far superior to the standard AT set.

Programming a Modem

Whenever a modem is turned on, it is in one of two states: the *command mode* or the *online mode*. The online mode is when the modem is connected with another modem. In online mode, the pair of modems is simply a pipeline connecting two programs at opposite ends of a wire. An example of online mode is when you are accessing an online service like CompuServe. You are normally running CIS, a program written for your PC, and connecting to a main CompuServe host over the phone line. Your modem is in command mode when the dialing and handshaking are going on, but when the logo comes up, that means that you are now in online mode.

Command mode is designed for accepting characters from the AT command set. The following code shows how this works. If you want to use pulse (or rotary) dialing instead of touch-tone, you would run the program in Listing 17.6.

Listing 17.6   PULSE1.BAS—Setting a Modem to Send Pulse Tones

```
Private Sub Form_Click()

        'Open the serial port for communications
        MSComm2.PortOpen = True

        'Tell the modem to dial using pulse
```

```
MSComm2.Output = "ATP" + Chr$(13)

'Tell the Modem to dial this number
MSComm2.Output = "ATD514-9688" + Chr$(13)

'Display the status of the port
Text1.Text = MSComm2.PortOpen

'Close the port
MSComm2.PortOpen = False

'Display the status of the port
Text1.Text = MSComm2.PortOpen

End Sub
```

In this example, the command ATP was sent to your modem. If you have the speaker turned on, you will hear a series of irregular tapping sounds instead of the familiar tones. Pulse-type switching equipment counts the number of pulses sent over the line instead of the frequency of the tone.

Another popular use for the AT command set is to test the modem. Listing 17.7 sends a command AT&T6 to the modem, asking it to perform a remote loopback test.

Listing 17.7   LOOP1.BAS—Performing a Loopback Test

```
Private Sub Form_Click()

    'Open the serial port for communications
    MSComm2.PortOpen = True

    'Tell the Modem to dial this number
    MSComm2.Output = "AT&T6" + Chr$(13)

    'Display the status of the port
    Text1.Text = MSComm2.Input

    'Close the port
    MSComm2.PortOpen = False

    'Display the status of the port
    Text1.Text = MSComm2.PortOpen

End Sub
```

Because the test is being run without a connection first being made, we expect it to fail. Figure 17.13 shows what the message looks like.

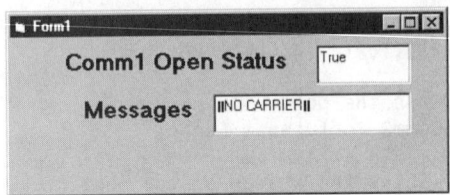

Fig. 17.13 A loopback test will fail if no carrier is connected.

The phrase NO CARRIER means that it couldn't find a connection, or carrier, to perform the test.

The Modem Registers

Another use of the AT command set is to query and set the register values in the modem. In Listing 17.8, a query is made regarding the current setting of register S0. This register controls the number of rings that the modem will wait before auto answering.

Listing 17.8   SETREG.BAS—Setting Register Values

```
Private Sub Form_Click()

    'Open the serial port for communications
    MSComm2.PortOpen = True

    'Tell the Modem to dial this number
    MSComm2.Output = "ATS0?" + Chr$(13)

    'Display the status of the port
    Text1.Text = MSComm2.Input

    'Close the port
    MSComm2.PortOpen = False

    'Display the status of the port
    Text1.Text = MSComm2.PortOpen

End Sub
```

The answer that comes back is displayed in the text box in figure 17.14.

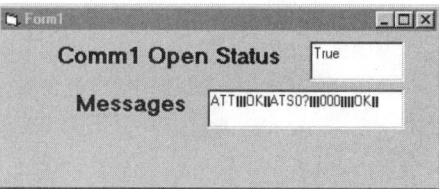

Fig. 17.14 The s registers control the behavior of the modem.

The answer that comes back is 000. This means that the modem is currently not in auto-answer mode.

From Here...

In this chapter you were introduced to the details of communications programming using the MSComm custom control. You learned about how serial ports work and how Visual Basic interfaces with them.

You also learned how to program a modem using the AT command set, which was created by Hayes Microcomputer Products. You learned how to send data to a modem, and how to read data that was sent by a modem.

➤ For more information about how data communications works with applications and networks, see Chapter 19, "Networkable Apps."

➤ To find related topics dealing with communications and enabling technologies, see Chapter 8, "Modern Client/Server Computing."

18

Developing Online Help

by Jon Oelschlaeger

One very visible quality measure of a professionally developed Visual Basic application is advertised by the scope and usability of its Help system. Oftentimes this is an overlooked aspect of an otherwise well crafted program. An application with no Help system, or one that's amateurish, is frequently the result of not understanding how to effectively develop and control a Help system. In this chapter, we'll cover the following:

➤ The concepts involved in developing a Windows Help system and integrating it with your Visual Basic application

➤ The steps required to develop a professional-quality Help system

➤ Some of the available tools and techniques you can use to create your Help system

➤ The mechanics of how you can control and configure the Windows Help engine to suit your needs

Understanding Windows Help

Achieving an understanding of the Windows Help environment begins with a clear-cut definition of the components involved. In this regard there are both runtime components of your Visual Basic program supporting the Help system, and components used during the design phase to develop the Help system.

First, let's look at the relationship between your Visual Basic program, the Windows Help engine, and your application's Help system files (*.HLP files). As shown in figure 18.1, your Visual Basic application will typically have several interfaces to the Windows Help system.

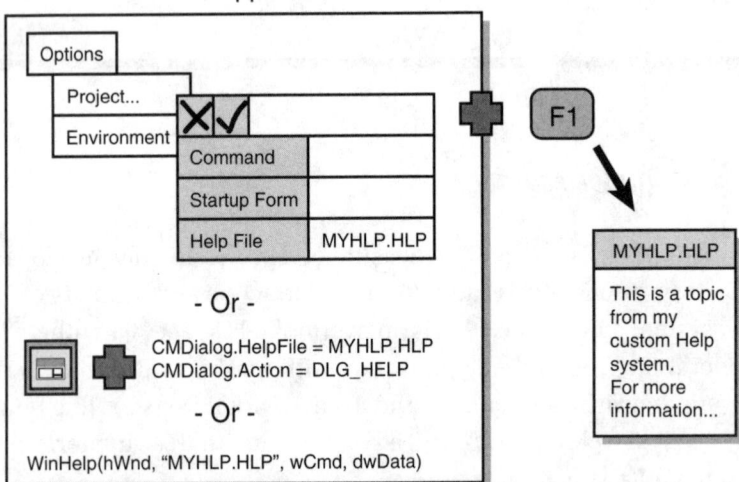

Fig. 18.1 Your Visual Basic application's Help system interfaces can be used to make Help easily accessible from within your application.

Next, let's look at the software components that are used during the design of your Visual Basic application's Help system. The files involved and the Help compiler are shown in figure 18.2. The subsequent sections survey various tools that are designed to create and manage these files.

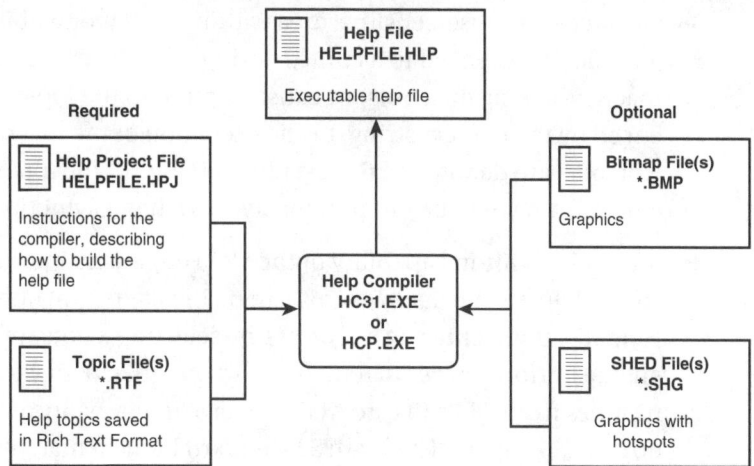

Fig. 18.2 The components of a designtime Help system are compiled into a user-friendly Help system.

Understanding Help System Terms

The remainder of this chapter incorporates some very specific terminology regarding development and use of a Help system. The following is a list of terms and their relationships:

➤ *Topic*—A unit of Help system information, written on one subject. A topic comprises the text that appears within the Help system. Topics are linked to pop-ups, hotspots, and jumps by means of a context string that is associated with the topic.

➤ *Pop-up*—The text of some referenced topic that appears in place in the Help system enclosed within a bounding box. A pop-up is dismissed whenever the user clicks again.

➤ *Context String*—A string referencing a topic that is used like a symbolic variable name within a Help system. All references to topics are made through their context strings.

➤ *Hotspot*—A mouse-sensitive area within the text or within a graphic that is linked to a context string or to the execution of a macro. Clicking on a hotspot causes a jump to the topic referenced by the context string, or the execution of the macro. Hotspots are denoted to the user by a change of the mouse cursor from your current pointer style to a hand symbol.

➤ *Macro*—A built-in capability of the Help engine that performs some Help engine task. Macros can be invoked upon opening a Help file, upon entering a topic, or by selecting a hotspot, Help engine button, or menu item. It is also possible to register custom routines from DLLs to extend the macro functionality of the Windows Help engine. There are 52 standard built-in macro functions within the Help engine.

➤ *Jump*—A jump is a change of topic context initiated by user mouse action. Jumps to other topics can be controlled by hotspot words, hotspots within graphics, or by invocation of a macro.

➤ *RTF Files*—Rich Text Format files produced by any word-processing program that can create and edit files in this format. Microsoft Word for Windows is one such word processor that can create and edit RTF files. RTF files comprise the source code in producing Help systems. RTF topic files are submitted to the Windows Help compiler for conversion into Windows Help resource files (*.HLP).

➤ *Help Project File (*.HPJ)*—Like the "make file" used by most compilers. The help project file contains instructions to the Help compiler concerning the RTF files to compile, the relationships between context strings, the HelpContextIDs, bitmaps to be used, and other Help compiler options and configuration settings that control the compiler. Help Project files are simple ASCII files.

➤ *Help Compiler*—The Windows Help Compiler uses the Help Project File (*.HPJ) with the RTF and other files and options specified in the Help Project file. The Help Compiler generates a Windows Help engine resource file (*.HLP) as its output.

There are several versions of the Help Compiler, supporting different Windows operating system versions. These compilers are:

HC.EXE and HC30.EXE: Support the Windows 3.0 Help engine.

HCP.EXE and HC31.EXE: Support extended features of the Windows 3.1, Windows for Workgroups 3.11, and Windows NT 3.1 and 3.5 Help engine.

WINHELP.EXE: Displays Help files in Windows 95.

Note: As of the writing of this book, the Version of the Help Compiler for HCP or HC is Version 3.10.505. The most current version of the Help Compiler is available from CompuServe on the Windows Development forum. If in doubt, check to see if you have the most current version of the Help compiler.

➤ *Hotspot Editor*—Used to incorporate one or more hotspots into a graphics file. Hotspots are mouse-sensitive areas that can be included within bitmap files (*.BMP and *.DIB) or Windows metafile graphic files (*.WMF). The incorporated hotspot, along with the original graphic, is saved as a segmented hypergraphics file (*.SHG). Hotspots can be used to jump to topics or execute macros.

➤ *HelpContextID*—An integer that is associated with a Help system context string within the [MAP] section of Help Project file (*.HPJ). These integers are used as the value of the HelpContextID property of Visual Basic controls or forms. When the focus is on a control or form, and the F1 key is pressed, the Help system is initiated and the Help topic identified by the context string is automatically shown.

➤ Compiler Codes—A variety of special codes are incorporated into the Help RTF topic files. The Help compiler uses these codes to interpret the topic files. Many of the codes are automatically produced just by creating the Help RTF files. Other specialized codes are incorporated as footnotes or as underlined or hidden text.

The central concept in a Help system is the *topic*. A topic is a sort of modular unit of explanation in the Help system that can stand alone and convey essential information. Physically, topics are delimited from each other in the source text of your Help system by hard page breaks. Topics are identified uniquely throughout the Help system by means of an associated context string.

A *context string* is an arbitrary string that acts as an address or location within the completed and compiled Help system of a Help topic. Context strings, therefore, are used to reference topics.

Context strings are used by pop-ups, jumps, and jump or pop-up hotspots to identify the topics to be displayed in the pop-up window, or the location to which to jump.

And finally, *keywords* are words that are associated with one or more topics (or actually the topic's context string). Keywords are displayed in the upper list portion of the Window's Help Search dialog box, and the associated topics are displayed in the lower list of the dialog box. Thus, keywords act much like the index section of a book.

Invoking Help from Visual Basic Menus

There are two fundamental mechanisms that you can use to invoke your application's Help system. One mechanism is to control the Help system by means of Visual Basic code. The other mechanism is to control the Help system using Visual Basic's built-in context-sensitive jumps into the Help system by using the F1 function key. Both approaches can, and should, be used together within the same application, and are generally complementary to each other.

Note: The Windows Help engine (WINHELP.EXE) can be invoked directly because it is an ordinary Windows executable program. Many people have not had the experience of just starting WINHELP, and should try it at least once. In the startup screen, you should notice some characteristics of WINHELP all by itself. First, if you don't specify Windows Help resources file (*.HLP) when starting WINHELP, Windows Help initializes with only a logo screen and menu bar. In addition, there are only four standard menu bar items—File, Edit, Bookmark and Help. In the section "Setting Up Added Menus" (later in this chapter), you learn how to customize the standard menu bar and drop-down menus associated with each menu bar item to suit your own special purposes.

The next section examines techniques for controlling your Help system using Visual Basic coding techniques.

Controlling Help System Operations

Usually you invoke WINHELP indirectly by using the Windows Common Dialogs capabilities, Windows API calls, or by using context-sensitive Help and Help Context IDs that are associated with objects in your Visual Basic application user interface.

When you invoke the Windows Help engine from your Visual Basic code, you can start it in one of several operating modes. These modes are generally known as:

➤ *Contents Mode*—Shows the Contents Page

➤ *Search Mode*—Shows the Search Dialog

➤ *Index Mode*—Shows an Index Page

Starting the Help engine in one or the other of these modes is typically accomplished by having the menu items as part of your Visual Basic application's menu system, and then using either the Common Dialogs or Windows API calls to invoke the corresponding mode based on the menu item's `Click` event procedure.

Using Windows Common Dialogs

The simplest and most direct way to invoke the Windows Help engine in code is to make use of the Common Dialog Control (CMDIALOG.VBX) provided with Visual Basic. The Common Dialog control enables you to invoke one of six standard Windows dialog boxes. Each of the six dialog boxes has its own unique properties that are set before execution of the dialog box.

To invoke the Help engine, you set some properties of the Common Dialog control, and then invoke the dialog box by setting the `Action` property to `DLG_HELP` (for example, `integer value = 6`).

Let's look a little more closely at how you can get the Windows Help engine started with a particular *.HLP file loaded, and in a specific mode by setting the properties of the Common Dialog control. When invoking the Windows Help system, the Common Dialog uses the properties in Table 18.1.

Table 18.1   The Common Dialog Properties

Property	Purpose and Effect
HelpFile	Sets the *.HLP Help resource file to use in Help engine when it is started.
HelpCommand	Sets the Mode of the Help engine, according to: HELP_CONTEXT—starts with particular Help context displayed. HELP_HELPONHELP—displays Help on the Help engine itself. HELP_INDEX—displays the Index of the Help file. HELP_KEY—displays Help for a specified keyword. HELP_QUIT—terminates use of a Help file and the Help engine. HELP_SETINDEX—starts Help with a specific index key set.
HelpContext	Specifies the Context ID of the desired Help topic; used to invoke a specific Context ID.

Property	Purpose and Effect
HelpKey	Specifies a keyword that identifies the Help topic; sets the index key.
Action	Set to DLG_HELP, invokes the Help engine.

In the section "Understanding the Help Project File" (later in the chapter), we'll discuss how you can control other aspects of the way that the Windows Help engine initializes, by choosing various options at the time you run the Help compiler to produce your Help resources file (*.HLP).

Using the Common Dialog to invoke the Help system appears to limit the modes and options that you can control. This might be inferred if you just refer to the Visual Basic Help topics associated with the search topic WinHelp. However, this impression is misleading.

The principle use of the Common Dialog is to invoke the Windows Help engine. You can, in fact, invoke the Windows Help engine using the Common Dialog control in any way that you can by making direct Windows API WinHelp function calls. For other modes of the Help engine, we'll next investigate using Windows API calls.

Using Windows API Calls

You can use calls to functions in the Windows API to invoke the Help engine and to select its operating modes. The Windows API function that you need to call is the WinHelp function.

The WinHelp function as defined in a Visual Basic formatted external DLL library function declaration is as follows:

```
Declare Function WinHelp Lib "User" (ByVal hWnd As Integer,_
ByVal lpHelpFile As String,
     ByVal wCommand As Integer, dwData As Any) As Integer
```

The purpose and use of each of the function's calling arguments is shown in Table 18.2.

Table 18.2 The Arguments for the WinHelp Function

Argument	Values and Effects
hWnd	Window handle of window requesting Help.
lpHelpFile	String specifying file name of Help file.
wCommand	Integer specifying the operation of the Help system as:
	HELP_CONTEXT—displays Help for a particular topic specified by dwData context ID.
	HELP_CONTENTS—dwData ignored; displays Help Contents topic.
	HELP_SETCONTENTS—dwData ignored; sets Help Content topic.
	HELP_CONTEXTPOPUP—dwData is a pointer to a HelpContextID; displays PopUp with ID number.
	HELP_KEY—dwData is a pointer to string containing a specific keyword; puts Help in Search mode.
	HELP_PARTIALKEY—dwData is a pointer to string for partial keyword; puts Help in Search mode.
	HELP_MULTIKEY—dwData is a pointer to MULTIKEY data structure.
	HELP_COMMAND—dwData is a pointer to string containing a Help macro; executes macro.
	HELP_SETWINPOS—dwData is a pointer to a HELPWININFO structure; sets Help window position and other attributes.
	HELP_FORCEFILE—dwData ignored; changes Windows Help file to a different file.
	HELP_HELPONHELP—dwData ignored; displays Help's Help file.
	HELP_QUIT—dwData ignored; Windows closes WinHelp engine.
dwData	Long specifying additional data depending on wCommand as presented in the list above. Ignored means dwData can be set to 0& (long null pointer).

As mentioned in the previous section, any of the symbolic constants that can be used with the WinHelp API function call can also be used to accomplish the same objectives with the Help Common Dialog control. Any of these symbolic constant values can be set as the HelpCommand property of the Common Dialog. Corresponding values for the HelpKey and HelpContext property also must be set prior to setting the Common Dialog Action property to DLG_HELP.

For example, to invoke the Windows Help engine in the general search mode, you would set the `HelpKey` property to a `NULL` string, and set the `HelpCommand` property to `HELP_PARTIALKEY`. Invoking the Help Common dialog box by setting the Action property to `Dlg_Help` would start the Windows Help engine in the Search mode.

Setting the `HelpKey` property to a partial search string (for example, `HelpKey = "s"`) and then setting the `HelpCommand` property to `HELP_PARTIALKEY` starts the Windows Help engine in the Search mode with the letter "s" as the preset default search key and so forth. The results of using this setting of the `HELP_PARTIALKEY`, and using the CALC.HLP Help file, are shown in figure 18.3.

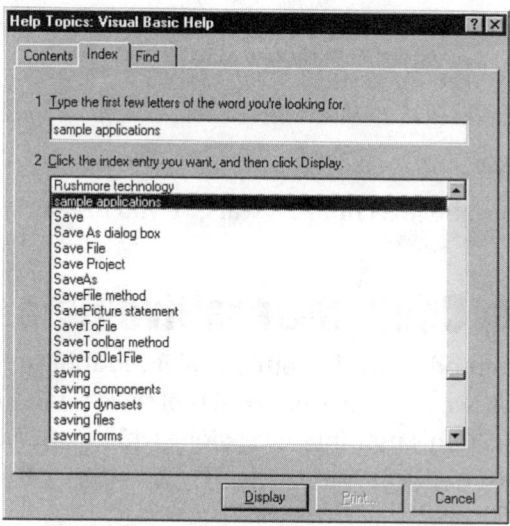

Fig. 18.3 Use the `HELP_PARTIALKEY` property—set to "s" to start the Help engine with a specific value.

The Visual Basic code for invoking the Windows Help engine in the `PARTIALKEY` mode is in Listing 18.1.

Listing 18.1 HELPSRC1.BAS   Using the PARTIALKEY Property

```
Sub mnuHelpSearch_Click ()

    Dim hlpFile As String
    hlpFile = WinDir & "\calc.hlp"
    Dim rc As Integer
    Dim hlpSearch As String
    hlpSearch = "s"

    rc = WinHelp(Form1.hWnd, hlpFile, HELP_PARTIALKEY,_
    ByVal hlpSearch)
```

Alternatively, the `WinHelp` function call can be eliminated by using the Visual Basic Common Dialog VBX, as shown in the following code:

```
    CMDialog1.HelpFile = hlpFile
    CMDialog1.HelpCommand = HELP_PARTIALKEY
    CMDialog1.HelpKey = hlpSearch
    CMDialog1.Action = DLG_HELP

End Sub
```

Either of the above techniques will give you the same results.

Linking Context-Sensitive Help

Another method to invoke your Visual Basic application's Help system is to use the Help Context IDs of the objects that make up your application's user interface, along with the F1 Key. This is called *context-sensitive help*. Support for it is a built-in feature of Visual Basic.

Context-sensitive help is very valuable to the user. When your application is running, the user merely moves the focus to a particular object in any user interface window and presses the F1 key. This causes the Windows Help engine to be loaded and initialized at a specific topic within the Help resources file—the topic assigned to the object that has the focus. Setting up this object-to-topic relationship, and specifying the correct Help resource file, are discussed in this section.

In order to establish the Help file that is used with context-sensitive Help, you need only set the `HelpFile` by choosing Options, Project in Visual Basic. Executing these menu commands invokes the dialog box shown in figure 18.4. Setting the Help File item in this dialog box creates the association between your Visual Basic application and the context-sensitive Help file.

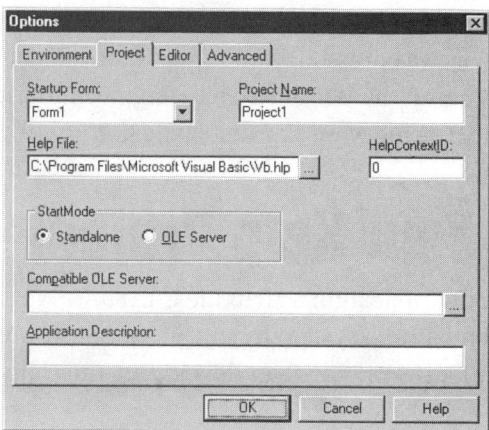

Fig. 18.4 You can set your application's Help File in the Options dialog box.

Mapping Context Strings and HelpContextIDs

Each visible screen object in your Visual Basic application includes the property `HelpContextID`. The value setting of this property determines which Help topic is presented when the user is focused on the object, and then presses F1. The relationship between these values of `HelpContextID` and the corresponding topic is established in the `[MAP]` section of your Help Project file (MYAPP.HPJ).

As an example, assume that the following is part of the `[MAP]` section of your Visual Basic application's MYAPP.HPJ Help Project file:

```
[MAP]
SALARY_FIELD          1
YEARS_FIELD           2
DEPT_FIELD          3
MENU_EDIT_NEW           4
MENU_EDIT_EXIST      5
MENU_INSERT_OBJ      6
'  . . .
'  . . .
' and so forth
```

The string on the left-hand side of each line in the [MAP] section is called a *context string,* which corresponds to some Help topic in your MYAPP.RTF text. The number on the right-hand side of each line is the HelpContextID property value you would assign to the control or menu object. During program execution, when the focus was set to the object and the F1 key was pressed, your application's Help file would be loaded along with the Windows Help engine, and the topic referenced by the context string would be displayed automatically.

Creating Your Help Project

Invoking your application's Help file is in some ways the simplest aspect of adding a Help system to your Visual Basic application. Most of the really hard work involves developing the Help files in the first place.

The central concept in developing your Help files revolves around authoring one or more technical manuals that comprise the raw material from which your Help files are created. This authoring process is quite similar to the process involved in writing any type of technical documentation.

Planning Your Documentation

Without a doubt, the most important step in authoring your Help system is planning. This is true of writing any type of technical documentation, but it is even more important when working on a Help system. Planning is important because at each step you will make decisions that are time-consuming to edit or rework later.

Your best time investment is to develop a fairly detailed schematic of the way you anticipate your Help system needs to work after it is completed. With this detailed schematic, you can then proceed to actually develop the Help topics that comprise the body of your Help system. Even with this advance planning, there will always be the inevitable modifications and changes that crop up during writing of your Help system documentation. However, with a clearly defined plan, incorporating these changes or additions is much easier to manage, because you will have a well-defined frame of reference.

Therefore, suggested planning steps are as follows:

➤ Clearly identify the audience for the Help system. This step is often overlooked. Identify the background, assumed skill level, and task orientation of the presumed Help system user. If necessary, define several different Help systems for the same application if several different types of users will be involved.

➤ Develop a topic hierarchy that depicts the relationship among the subjects that you'll include in your Help system documentation. Start the top of the hierarchy with the most general information, and add successive layers of detail lower down in the hierarchy.

➤ Develop a "storyboard" that outlines the key points to be covered in each Help topic, and the keywords used in each topic, or used to refer to a topic.

➤ If a particular storyboard includes too many key points (that is, more than three or four), carefully consider breaking down the one big topic into a series of smaller-scope additional topics.

➤ Your consistent objective should be to envision a topic as a granule or bite-sized unit of information that fits on a single Help system page (one screenful without vertical scroll bars).

A typical topic hierarchy for a simple application might look something like that shown in figure 18.5.

Once you have a detailed plan for your Help system, you are ready to begin writing the materials used for each of the Help topics. The process involved in this writing step is like writing any other documentation.

At a minimum, you'll need to use a word processor that supports writing documents in RTF (Rich Text Format), and incorporate the specialized codes that provide information for the Windows Help compiler.

There are a number of high-end Windows and DOS-based word processors that can be used to accomplish this task. However, throughout the remainder of this chapter we'll be restricting our attention to Microsoft Word for Windows, because many of the tools to assist you in this process are centered around Word for Windows.

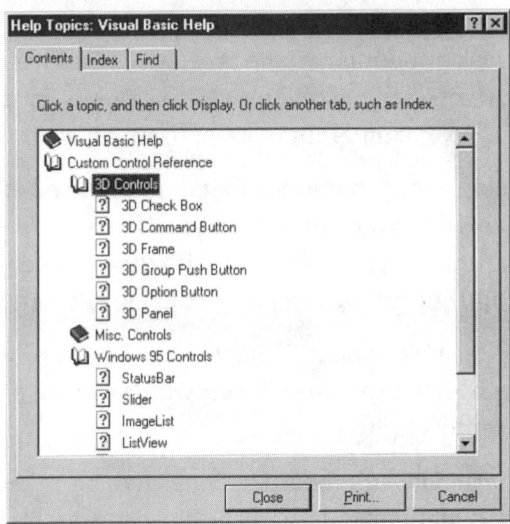

Fig. 18.5 The topic hierarchy of a Help system determines the navigation path through the information.

Incorporating Help Compiler Codes

In addition to the ordinary text that comprises the written materials of your RTF formatted Help materials, you need to embed special codes within your RTF files. These codes are processed by the Help Compiler while it creates the HLP Help resource files used by the Windows Help engine. These special codes are formatted as footnotes, or embedded in-line with the rest of the text in your RTF files. These special codes are listed in Table 18.3.

Table 18.3   The RTF File Codes

Special Code	Name	Purpose
Number Sign (#) Footnote	Context String	String that uniquely identifies a topic. Used for links. Topics without context strings can only be displayed with keywords in a browse sequence.
Dollar Sign ($) Footnote	Title	Defines topic title. Titles appear in list box in Search mode. Titles are optional.
Letter K (K) Footnote	Keyword	Defines keyword for topic using the standard keyword table search. Keywords are optional. Other Letters can be used as such footnotes to provide other alternative keyword search tables.
Plus Sign (+) Footnote	Browse Sequence	Defines a sequence number determining user browse order. Browse sequence numbers are optional.
Asterisk (*) Footnote	Build Tag	Help compiler conditional inclusion tags.
Strikethrough or Double-Underline	Jump Text	Specifies jump to another topic. Jump text is followed by Context String of topic for jump
Underlined Text	Definition	Specifies that a pop-up window is to appear. Underlined text is followed by context string for topic of the pop-up content.
Hidden Text	Context String	Specifies context string for topic to be displayed when user selected text immediately preceding. Embedded jump to a topic.
{command fn.ext}	Graphics	Reference to graphics command—file name and extension, and graphic positioning.

The methodology for coding and using these special Help compiler codes is fairly involved if you just use a word processor to create your RTF files. Using a Help authoring tool can automate the correct insertion of these specialized compiler codes.

Indexing for Searches

Design of the indexing scheme for your Help system is very important. After designing the general topic hierarchy and relationships for your Help system, the indexing scheme is the next highest priority.

The Windows Help engine uses keywords as the mechanism for implementing index searches. The process of selecting keywords, therefore, is identical to the process of developing the index section of any book. Keywords are often the most efficient and direct way for a user to find the Help topic information they need.

There are numerous ways to orient an indexing scheme for Help information. Oftentimes, combinations of one or more orientations proves to be the most effective for the Help system user. Possible orientations are:

- *Procedural Orientation*—The major types of tasks that can be accomplished with the application.

- *Sequential Orientation*—The progression of steps typically used with the application.

- *Conceptual Orientation*—The key ideas or concepts that the application is based upon.

- *Definitional Orientation*—The special terms that must be understood to use the application.

Designing an effective index (or, in this case, *keyword system*) is usually not simple. It deserves a great deal of thought and planning, since the usability of the index scheme will more than anything else determine the effectiveness of the Help system to the end user.

The basic idea of keywords is that a particular keyword is associated with one or more Help system topics. The keywords themselves appear in the upper list box in the Help system Search dialog box. See figure 18.6 for the Search dialog box.

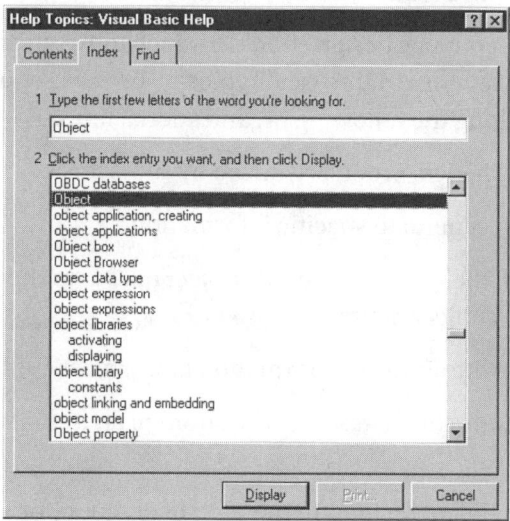

Fig. 18.6 The Help system Search dialog box shows keywords and topics (using Visual Basic Help file).

For each keyword in the upper list box, there are one or more Help topics presented in the lower list box of the dialog box. Selecting one of the topics causes a jump to the selected topic within the Help system.

Incorporating Browse Sequences

Next in importance after a well designed keyword scheme is a well developed browse sequence. The browse sequence defines the order in which Help system topics are presented to the user when she clicks the Browse Forward (>>) and Browse Back (<<) buttons on the Help engine's Toolbar. To the user, these browse buttons present Help system topics in an apparent linear subject order that is similar to reading successive topics in a book. Although the user isn't really browsing in this fashion, she is lead through a succession of related topics determined by the Help system developer. This ordering is called a *browse sequence*.

A browse sequence design should arrange topics in an order that would make sense to the user. Typically, browse sequences are constructed along the following organizational lines:

➤ Alphabetical order, organized by subject

➤ From general to specific information

➤ From the most likely used subject matter to the most infrequently used subject matter

➤ From the simplest information to the most complex information

➤ From top of an item to the bottom of an item (for example, menus)

➤ From left of an item to the right of an item (for example, Toolbars)

Browse sequences consist of a browse sequence group and an order number within the group. For plus-sign (+) footnotes that define browse sequences, the group name string is separated from the order number by a colon, as follows:

```
GroupName:050
```

Browse sequences can also be organized into a hierarchy, using a major topic and minor topic type of structure, like the following:

```
TOPIC_1_MAIN      -      MajorTopics:005
      SubTopic_1    -        TOPIC_1:005
      SubTopic_2    -        TOPIC_1:010
      SubTopic_3    -        TOPIC_1:015
TOPIC_2_MAIN      -      MajorTopics:010
      SubTopic_10   -        TOPIC_2:005
      SubTopic_20   -        TOPIC_2:010
      SubTopic_30   -        TOPIC_2:015
      SubTopic_40   -        TOPIC_2:020
```

In the above example, `Topic_1_Main` and `Topic_2_Main` are members of the `MajorTopics` group, with the order being `Topic_1_Main` first in the browse order, and `Topic_2_Main` second.

Within `Topic_1_Main`, the sub-topics are in the browse order `Topic_1:005`, then `Topic_1:010`, and finally `Topic_1:015`.

Assigning Build Tags

Build tags are strings that control conditional compilation of a particular set of topics. Each topic in the Help source text (*.RTF files) can have one or more associated build tags. These can be used to produce different versions, and therefore different content Help resource files during compilation.

Build tags are associated with the asterisk (*) footnote compiler codes. If more than one build tag is assigned to a topic, the successive build tag strings are separated by a semicolon (;).

At compilation time, all of the topics with the build tag specified in the [BUILD] section of the Help Project file (*.HPJ) are included in the compilation. In addition, all topics for which no build tags are specified are also included in the compilation. Therefore, the use of build tags can be considered to operate in an exclusionary fashion. That is, any topic with a build tag defined for which no corresponding build tag inclusion is specified in the Help Project file's [BUILD] section will be excluded from compilation.

Linking Topics with Jumps and Pop-Ups

The context strings that you define for your Help system topic information provide the mechanism for navigating through your completed Help system. In addition to the keyword and browse navigation previously discussed, the context strings provide the addressing information for the following types of Help system navigation:

➤ *Context-Sensitive Help*—By relating the context string with a `HelpContextID` integer in the Help project `[MAP]` section. Setting your application's focus and pressing the F1 key then jumps the user to the topic specified by the context string.

➤ *Jump Text*—By coding some text as Jump text, the user can jump to a particular new topic. The context string identifies the jump destination. In the compiled Help system, Jump text appears underlined in default green text. The Jump text is a hotspot that can be noted by the user, because the cursor changes.

➤ *Graphic Hotspot*—By embedding a hotspot in a graphic and assigning the hotspot to a particular context string, a jump (or pop-up) is executed by the Help engine. Clicking on the hotspot results in a jump (or pop-up window) to the context string-specified topic.

➤ *Pop-Up Text*—By coding some text as pop-up text, the user can click on the text thus designated, and a specific topic is presented in a pop-up secondary window. The pop-up text is associated with a particular context string, thereby determining what topic is displayed. You should keep the topics used for pop-ups very brief, since all of the topic text will appear in the pop-up window.

These facilities provide the fundamental navigational features of the Windows Help system. More sophisticated types of jumps can also be implemented in your Help system.

Jumping to Topics in Other Help Files

Oftentimes all of the Help topics you might want to use may not be present in a single Help file. There are several circumstances where you might encounter this, for example:

➤ You have sub-divided your Help system into several separate parts based on the type of user audience, or level of detail, or even functional content.

➤ You want to "borrow" Help topics from other Help files that you know are already present on the user's computer. For example, why repeat all of the basics of using the mouse, or selecting a file from a browser? These subjects are well-treated in the basic Windows product Help files.

To jump to a topic in another Help file, just follow the jump's context string with the "@" symbol, and then the path and file name of the Help file that contains the desired topic. An example might be the following:

```
Context_String@d:\path\newfile.hlp
```

Don't forget that once you have jumped out of a Help file, the only way for the user to get back to the original Help file is to use the "Back" button, the "History" list, or through another explicit jump that refers to the original Help file.

Jumping to Secondary Windows

In addition to the basic navigational techniques outlined in the previous section, it is possible to achieve more complex and more sophisticated types of jumps.

Up to this point, we have assumed that any of the jumps that we specify will cause the topic to which you jumped to be presented in the main Help window. It is possible, however, to specify jumps that display the topic in a secondary window. To accomplish this, follow the jump's context string reference with the ">" symbol, and specify a named secondary window within which to display the topic identified by the context string. For example:

```
Context_String>Secondary_WindowName
```

The section entitled "Setting Other Compiler Options" (later in this chapter) examines how to define named secondary windows that can be used for this purpose.

Thus far, you have looked at the basic terms and steps in planning a Help system, as well as the navigational techniques for maneuvering through the Help system topics. Now that you have some idea what the terminology means, and what can be done within a Help system, you can focus on the Help compiler and the all-important Help Project file that gives the Help compiler its marching orders.

Identifying Help Project Components

The components of your Help project consist of one or more RTF (Rich Text Formatted) files, along with the embedded special codes outlined in the previous section. All of the text in an RTF file contains special formatting codes. These codes are what makes an RTF file self-describing, and creates an exchangeable file format between word processors supporting this format. So just by using an RTF-capable word processor you automatically accomplish much of the work of preparing your Help text for the Help compiler.

Additionally, any of the bitmaps and other graphics that you've produced, along with any 'hot spots' you've embedded, will become components of your Help file. These bitmaps, graphics, and hotspots can be part of the user topic selection interface, as well as decoration to add visual interest.

Finally, instructions to the Help compiler, contained in your Help Project file, round out the components of your Help project. The section "Creating the Help Project File" has more information about the Help Project file sections that provide information to the Help compiler.

Using Bitmaps and Graphics with Hotspots

Using bitmaps and graphics as active user interface elements involves embedding "hotspots" within the bitmaps and graphics. Embedded hotspots can be associated with context strings to control jumps, pop-ups, or can be used to invoke macros, thereby making them a mechanism for user interaction. The process of embedding one or more hotspots within a bitmap or graphic involves the use of the Hotspot Editor.

The Hotspot Editor is a software tool that is provided with Visual Basic. It is a Windows application named SHED.EXE. The Hotspot Editor enables you to load a bitmap or graphic and add one or more hotspots to the files before using them in your Help system. Figure 18.7 shows the Hotspot Editor with a bitmap loaded into it, and incorporating a hotspot.

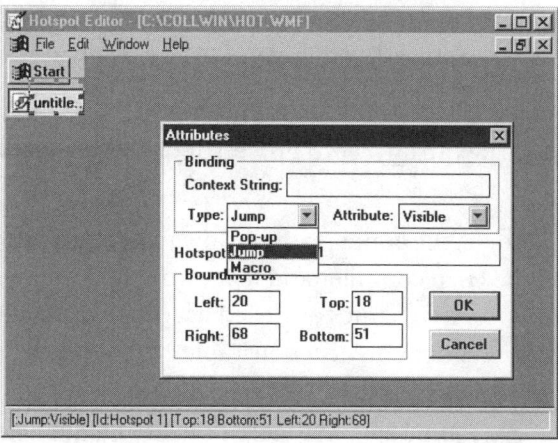

Fig. 18.7 The Hotspot Editor shows a bitmap with a hotspot and the hotspot Attributes dialog box.

As you can see in figure 18.7, the bitmap graphic (SCREEN01.BMP) has one hotspot assigned within it—notice the rectangular box with the sizing handles near the top-left corner of the bitmap image. You will also notice, in the Attributes dialog box near the center of the screen that the selected hotspot can be defined as a jump, pop-up, or macro. If it's a jump or pop-up, it can be assigned to a specific context string.

Multiple hotspots can be incorporated into a bitmap or graphic, each with its own set of attributes. Once the hotspots have been added, the bitmap or graphic is saved as an *.SHG file (*Segmented Hypergraphics file*).

Including these SHG files into your Help system project, and locating them within topic files, enables you to accomplish jumps, pop-ups, and macro execution when the user clicks on the corresponding hotspots in the graphic.

Understanding the Help Project File

The Help Project file is at the crossroads of pulling together all of many pieces of your Help system. It is the road map that identifies to the Windows Help compiler what files and other resources it's supposed to use to generate your Help resource file (*.HLP).

A Help Project file (*.HPJ) is an ordinary ASCII file without formatting. You produce it with any word processor or editor that can edit ASCII files.

The Help Project file contains the following sections that provide information to the Help compiler and tell it what it's to do. Sections are identified by section names enclosed in square brackets (for example, [and]). These sections are listed in Table 18.4.

Table 18.4   The Help Project File Sections

Section	Purpose and Description
[OPTIONS]	Specifies options that control the compilation process. If it is used, it must be the first section.
[FILES]	This section lists all of the RTF text topic files to include in the compilation. This section must be present.
[BUILDTAGS]	Specifies the build tags to be used in the compilation. Build tags selectively specify what topics to include. Topics without build tags are automatically included. This section is optional, and needed only if you intend to use the build tag capability. A maximum of 30 build tags can be specified.
[CONFIG]	Specifies author-defined menus and buttons to be included in the Help file. It is also used to register custom dynamic link libraries (DLLs) and functions in these DLLs that are used as custom macros within the

Section	Purpose and Description
	Help file. This section is required if any such customization is desired.
[BITMAPS]	Specifies bitmap files to be included in the compilation. This section is not required if the Help Project file lists a path for bitmap files in the [OPTIONS] section using the BMROOT or ROOT options. More on this later.
[MAP]	This section associates context strings with HelpContextID integers. This section is optional, but is highly important for Visual Basic programs, since it is these associations that provide the HelpContextID property values for context-sensitive Help system invocation.
[ALIAS]	Assigns one or more context strings to the same Help topic. This section is optional.
[WINDOWS]	Defines the characteristics of the primary Help window, and the types and characteristics of any secondary windows that may be used in the Help system. This section is required if secondary windows are used.
[BAGGAGE]	Lists files that are to be placed within the Help file (*.HLP). The Help file contains its own stand-alone file system that can be used during execution of the Help system. These additional files can be more efficiently accessed from within the Windows Help engine. This section is optional.

The [OPTIONS] section includes settings that control how the Help file is built by the compiler, and what types of information the compiler produces while it is executing. The options that can be specified in this section are listed in Table 18.5.

Table 18.5   The [OPTIONS] Specifiers

Option	Purpose and Description
BMROOT	Specifies the directory where the Help Compiler can find the bitmaps used in the Help topics. The format of this option line is: BMROOT = pathname1, pathname2, and so on.

continues

Table 18.5 Continued

Option	Purpose and Description
BUILD	Determines which topics to include or exclude in the compilation. The format of this option is a logical expression using the following operators and operands: ( ) — group operator & — the AND operator | — the OR operator ~ — the NOT operator tag — a build tag string (operand) An example might be like: `BUILD = PART1 & PART2` which would include PART1 and PART2 build tags, as well as topics with no build tags.
COMPRESS	Specifies the type of compression used during compilation of the Help files. There are three levels of compression that can be specified: COMPRESS = NO No compression COMPRESS = MEDIUM Medium compression (~40%) COMPRESS = HIGH High compression (~50%)
CONTENTS	Specifies the context string for the Help Contents topic of the Help file. An example would be: CONTENTS = context_string
COPYRIGHT	Adds a copyright message to the Help About dialog box: a string of 35 to 75 characters.
ERRORLOG	Places compiler error messages into a file during the compilation process. These can be reviewed after compilation. A file name.
FORCEFONT	Forces fonts used in the RTF files to be remapped into some other font during compilation. A font name.
ICON	Specifies the icon to be displayed when the Help file and Help engine application are minimized. An icon file name (*.ICO).

Option	Purpose and Description
LANGUAGE	Specifies a different sort ordering for Help file authored in a Scandinavian language.
MAPFONTSIZE	Maps a font size used in the RTF topic files into a different font size in the compiled Help files. An example might be: MAPFONTSIZE = 12-24:16, which would map all fonts in the size range of 12 to 24 points into 16 point font. The specification can include a single size or a range of sizes.
MULTIKEY	Specifies an alternate keyword table for mapping topics. The standard keyword footnote table character is "K". Other keyword footnotes using other letters can be used to create additional keyword tables.
OLDKEYPHRASE	Designates whether the Help compiler should use the existing key phrase table or create a new one during compilation.
REPORT	Controls message display during compilation. To turn on message display: REPORT = ON.
ROOT	Designates the root directories used to locate topic and data files listed in the Help Project file. An example would be: ROOT = pathname1, pathname2, and so on.
TITLE	Specifies the text caption that appears in the Help engine's title bar. String of up to about 50 characters.
WARNING	Indicates the desired level of compiler error-level reporting to be used during compilation. Warning levels are: Level 1—Only severe errors Level 2—Moderate number of errors Level 3—All errors and warnings

The [MAP] section also merits some additional attention, because it is used to map context strings to HelpContextID that are used to set the properties of Visual Basic objects to link them to context-sensitive Help invocation.

When you create the [MAP] section of the Help Project file, it is usually a good idea to create and maintain a context string to HelpContextID number catalog when you begin to author the Help topic (*.RTF) files. The assignment of HelpContextID integers is completely arbitrary and up to your discretion.

Creating the Help Project File

This section examines a typical Help Project file, and analyzes the purpose of the specifications in each section. For this analysis we will start with a Help Project file shipped with the Visual Basic product—the Help Project file for IconWorks.

The sample Visual Basic program IconWorks is a browser and editor for Windows Icons. It is a complete Visual Basic application, all the way through to including a Help system. The Help Project file that we are going to investigate is in the HC directory of the installed Visual Basic product.

We will investigate each section, and then correlate the effects of the specifications in each section with the behavior and appearance of the completed Help system for the IconWorks application.

Using Project File Sections

The following listing is the Help Project file for the IconWorks sample Visual Basic program. Most of the lines in the [MAP] section have been eliminated in the interests of brevity, because a few sample lines indicate the concept involved.

```
[OPTIONS]
errorlog = iconwrks.err
title = IconWorks Help
contents = CONTENTS
compress = false
oldkeyphrase = false
warning = 3

[FILES]
```

```
iconwrks.rtf

[MAP]
CONTENTS 1
EDITOR_KEYBOARD 2
EDITOR_COMMANDS 3
VIEWER_KEYBOARD 5
VIEWER_COMMANDS 6
DEFINING_COLORS 1000
EDITOR_FILE_MENU 1100
EDITOR_FILE_MENU 1101
          .
          .
          .
UNDO_ICON 1902
ZOOMING 1903
STATUS_BAR 1904
COLOR_PALETTE 1905
DEFINING_COLORS 1906

[WINDOWS]
main = "IconWorks Help", (0,0,1023,1023 ),,, (192,192,192 )
glossary = "IconWorks Help", (222,206,725,486 ),,, _
(192,192,192 ), 1

[CONFIG]
CreateButton("glossary", "&Glossary","JI(`iconwrks.hlp>glossary'_
, `GLOSSARY')")
BrowseButtons()
```

The initial section of the Help Project file is the [OPTIONS] section. From this section you can see that an error log file has been specified, the title of the completed Help system is to be "IconWorks Help," the contents topics are to correspond to the context string CONTENTS, compression has been turned off, any old key phrase dictionary is not to be used, and the compiler warning level has been set to 3 (that is, show all errors and warnings).

Of course, it would have been possible to specify specialized directory roots for bitmaps and RTF files (using the BMROOT or ROOT parameters), but in this case all bitmap and RTF files are going to be located in the same root directory as the project file, so these optional specifications are not used.

Build tags are also not used, because all of the contents of the topics file are to be compiled in this version of the Help system. Likewise, no copyright notice is specified, nor are any font mappings specified.

Notice the `[FILES]` section of the Help Project file. It contains only one RTF topic file. If additional topic files were needed they could be added as lines in this section.

The next section of the ICONWRKS.HPJ Help Project file is the `[MAP]` section. This section correlates context strings (on the left-hand side of each line) with the `HelpContextID` integer (on the right-hand side of each line). You should notice in particular that the choice of context strings has been done in such a way that the chosen string is evocative of the topic being referenced. This is good practice, and can make your work much easier; choose good context strings.

You can have as many lines as you need to completely specify the context string to `HelpContextID` relationships. It should also be noted that a given context string can be correlated to more than one `HelpContextID`. The effect is that a number of different `HelpContextID` integers will all invoke the same Help topic.

Setting Other Compiler Options

Other sections of our IconWorks sample Help Project file are used to specify other options to be incorporated into the Help resources file (ICONWRKS.HLP) that will be produced by the Help compiler.

The `[WINDOWS]` section characterizes two windows that can be used in the completed Help system. It specifies the "main" window, and a secondary window called "glossary." Remember that any Help topic can be displayed in any named window. If no named window is specified, the default (or main) window is used to display the topic.

The parameters specifying the "main" and "glossary" windows attributes consist of the following information:

```
typename = "caption", (xpos, ypos, width, height), sizing, _
(clientRGB),(nonscrollingRGB), topmost
```

In the case of the "main" window, the attributes specified are that the caption is to be "IconWorks Help," the window is to be positioned at 0,0 (upper-left corner of the screen), and is to be 1,023 units wide and 1,023 units high. The specification then skips over the `sizing` and `clientRGB` fields, and specifies the RGB colors for the non-scrolling area of the main window (192,192,192—or medium gray).

For the "glossary" window, the attributes specified are that the caption is also to be "IconWorks Help," that the window is to be positioned with its upper-left corner at 222 units right of the left-screen edges, and 206 units from the top of the screen. Additionally, this window is to be 725 units wide and 486 units high. The specification then skips over the `sizing` and `clientRGB` fields, and finally specifies the non-scrolling area of the window as medium gray (i.e., 192,192,192). The last field of the specification for this window sets the attributes of this window to topmost (for example, on top of other windows).

It should be noted here that the Windows Help engine uses an internal screen coordinate system that is 1024 x 1024 units in size. This `1coordinate` system is proportionally mapped to the actual screen resolution of the display device being used.

If desired, additional named secondary windows can be specified for other specialized purposes, using the same type of specifications.

Next let's turn our attention to the `[CONFIG]` section of the Help Project file. The first line in this section (`CreateButton`, and so on) creates a custom button that is added to the standard buttons at the top of the Help system window. The form of this line, which is a Window Help engine macro, is as follows:

```
CreateButton("buttonid", "name", "macro")
```

The `buttonid` field is used to specify the internal symbol name used by the Windows Help engine. You may later want to refer to this symbol to invoke the `DisableButton`, `DestroyButton`, or `ChangeButtonBinding` macros to manipulate this resource. In our example, this symbol name is `glossary`.

The `name` field is used to specify the caption used on the additional button. In this example, the caption is `&Glossary` with the usual convention that the character of any caption that is preceded with an "&" character becomes the access key (Alt+G in this case).

Finally, the `macro` field identifies the macro to be invoked when the added custom button is chosen by the user. In this example, the macro invoked is the `JI` macro (short for `JumpId`. The `JumpId` macro causes a jump to another Help file, and topic within that Help file identified by a context string. In our example, the form used causes a jump to the context string `GLOSSARY`, and the Help file is the ICONWRKS.HLP Help file. Note, however, the use of the ">" character and the reference to the `glossary` window. This `JI` macro then would display the topic referenced by the `GLOSSARY` context string, of the ICONWRKS.HLP Help file, and display the referenced topic in the secondary window named `glossary`.

The second line of the `[CONFIG]` section specifies that the macro `BrowseButtons` be invoked. This adds the two browse buttons (Browse Forward ">>" and Browse Back "<<") to the standard default set of command buttons at the top of the Help window.

Finally, the order in which these additional buttons are appended to the default Help window is the same as the order in which they are specified in the `[CONFIG]` section. Furthermore, it is possible to invoke other macros in the `[CONFIG]` section to accomplish such things as registering custom DLLs for use with the Help system, insert custom menu bar items, append menu items to menus, and so on.

Using the Microsoft Help Compiler

Using the Microsoft Help compiler is pretty straightforward. The Help compiler is a DOS command-line compiler that accepts just the Help Project file as a command-line argument.

For any contemporary application Help system, you will typically use the Windows 3.1 (Windows for Workgroups 3.11 and Windows NT 3.1 and 3.5 compatible) Help compiler. This compiler incorporates all of the latest Help system capabilities, and is called HCP.EXE or HC31.EXE. The most current version of the HCP compiler as of this writing is version 3.10.505.

Using our example of the IconWorks Help project from the previous section's example, you would invoke the compiler from a DOS prompt as follows:

```
C:>HCP <pathname>\ICONWRKS.HPJ
```

This would create a file Windows Help resource file, ICONWRKS.HLP in the same directory path that you used for the Project file. It would also create an error log file in the file specified in the [OPTIONS] section of the project file.

> **Note:** The HCP or HC31 Help compiler requires quite a bit or extended memory (XMS) to successfully execute. Alternatively, you can use expanded (EMS) memory using EMM386 from within DOS. Estimates of the memory required range from a low of about 1 MB to more than 2MB, depending on the complexity of your Help project. The easiest way to assure that this memory will be available is to execute the Help compiler from a Windows DOS session. This will provide the needed XMS memory automatically.

Evaluating and Debugging Compiler Errors

If you encounter errors during compilation of your Help project, you will need to review the error log, and interpret the error messages that you find so that you can take corrective action.

To interpret the error log messages you should refer to the Help Compiler Reference, which is contained in the Help file HELPREF.HLP. In this Help system is a comprehensive listing and interpretation of all of the Help compiler error messages.

Whenever possible, the Help compiler error log identifies the topic that caused the error by outputting the topic string, as well as a sequential topic number. The topic number given with an error message refers to the sequential position of that topic in the topic file (first topic, second topic, and so on). Topics within your Help topic RTF files are separated by hard page breaks, even though there is no such thing as a "page" within the Help system itself. By locating the sequential "page" in the appropriate RTF file you can find the topic referenced by the error message.

Error messages beginning with "Error" may indicate fatal errors. Fatal errors are always reported, since no usable Help file results from the compilation. Messages beginning with the word "Warning" are less serious in nature. A compilation with warnings produces a valid Help file that the WinHelp engine can open, but the file may contain operational errors that render it unusable. Remember, you can specify the amount of warning information that you want to be reported by the Help Compiler using the WARNING parameter in the [OPTIONS] section of your Help Project file.

During processing of the .HPJ file, the Help Compiler ignores lines that contain errors and attempts to continue with the compilation. This can have the effect that errors found near the beginning of the compilation may result in an error cascade later as additional errors are reported during the remainder of the compilation process.

Similarly, errors encountered during the processing of the RTF topic files are reported, but if the errors are not serious, the Help Compiler continues with the build.

Testing Compiled Help Files

Once you have successfully corrected the errors and completed a Help resources file (*.HLP) in the Help compiler, you need to test it to make sure that it operates as you intended.

To test your Help file, start up WINHELP.EXE, and choose File, Open. A standard File Browser dialog box opens, and you can select your HLP file to load into the Help engine.

Once loaded, you can try out the topic jumps, pop-ups, hotspot graphics, and search mode keywords to make sure that what you intended when you designed your Help system works correctly. As an example, refer to figure 18.8 showing the IconWorks Help system that we looked at in previous sections after it has been compiled and loaded into the Windows Help engine.

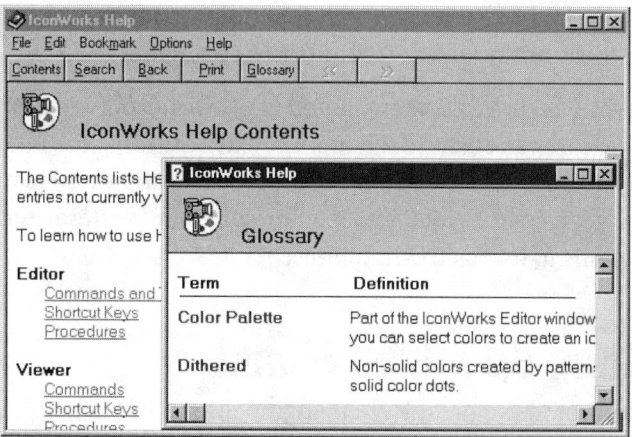

Fig. 18.8 The IconWorks Help system shows a main window Contents topic and a secondary window used for the Glossary.

You also need to set the `HelpContextID` property of all of your Visual Basic applications forms and controls to correspond to the topic you want to display when you press the F1 key in your application. Remember to also set the Help File name in the Visual Basic editor under Tools, Options, and the Project tab.

You should test the link between your Visual Basic application and the completed Help system by setting the focus to each and every control in your application and pressing the F1 key to make sure that the correct context-sensitive Help is displayed.

Make note of any operational errors that you notice, and go back and correct your Help Project file, topic RTF files, hotspot graphics, and `HelpContextID` maps to get the desired changes effected.

Using Help Engine Features

Although we looked at some of the added capabilities of the Windows Help engine briefly in the earlier section "Creating the Help Project File," we did not get a chance at that point to focus on the details of using these optional features of the Help engine.

The sections that follow are aimed at giving additional attention to such features as customized menus, extra buttons, the use of macros, and Help engine initialization techniques. Using these features enables you to get a custom look and feel for your Help system, and to add extensions to its basic capabilities.

Setting Up Added Menus

In addition to the default Help engine menus of File, Edit, Bookmark, and Help, you can create your own customized menus and menu items. You can also manipulate such menus and menu items in response to user interactions with your Help system.

Customizing your Help system's menus and menu items can be accomplished at the time the Windows Help engine is initialized, or at any time during user interaction with the elements of your Help system. Menu and menu-item customization is accomplished using the Help engine macros listed in Table 18.6.

Table 18.6   The Help Engine Macros

Menu Macros	Features and Arguments
InsertMenu	Adds a new menu to the Help engine menu bar. The arguments allow specification of the menuid, menuname, and menuposition.
InsertItem	Adds a new menu item to one of the standard menus or to a custom menu. The arguments allow specification of the menuid where the item is to be inserted, itemid, itemname, macro to execute when the menu item is selected, and position in list of menu items.

Menu Macros	Features and Arguments
AppendItem	Appends a new menu item to the bottom of a menu created with the InsertMenu macro. The arguments allow specification of the menuid, itemid, itemname, and macro.
DeleteItem	Deletes a new menu item that was added with the AppendItem macro. The argument allows specification of the itemid.
DisableItem	Disables a menu item that was added with the AppendItem macro. The argument allows specification of the itemid.
EnableItem	Enables a menu item that was added with the AppendItem macro. The argument allows specification of the itemid.

Any of these menu macros can be executed by placing them in the [CONFIG] section of the Help Project file. This causes the menus and menu items to be initialized when the Windows Help engine is initialized.

The menu items can also be executed from text or graphics hotspots during user interaction with your Help system. The techniques used depend on what you are trying to accomplish with the menu modifications.

Attaching Extra Buttons

You can also incorporate additional command buttons in the Windows Help engine to customize its look and feel. In a manner that is quite parallel to adding menus and menu items, you can invoke Windows Help macros to manipulate command buttons.

Command button customization is accomplished using the Help engine macros listed in Table 18.7.

Table 18.7   Additional Help Engine Macros

Button Macros	Features and Arguments
BrowseButtons	Adds the Browse Back (<<) and Browse Forward (>>) buttons to the standard Toolbar button set of the Windows Help engine.
CreateButton	Adds a new button to the Help engine Toolbar. The arguments allow specification of the buttonid, name, and macro.
DestroyButton	Deletes a new button that was added with the CreateButton macro. The argument allows specification of the buttonid.
DisableButton	Disables a button that was added with the CreateButton macro. The argument allows specification of the buttonid.
EnableButton	Enables a button that was added with the CreateButton macro. The argument allows specification of the buttonid.

Any of these button macros can be executed by placing them in the [CONFIG] section of the Help Project file. This will cause the buttons to be initialized when the Windows Help engine is initialized. It should be noted here that if the BrowseButtons macro is used and also other button macros, the Browse Buttons themselves will appear in the order of the macros in the [CONFIG] section.

As with the menu macros, they can also be executed from text or graphics hotspots during user interaction with your Help system.

Using Custom DLLs

The capabilities of the built-in macros within the Windows Help engine can easily be extended to include your own custom functions. Your external DLL functions can be incorporated by using the RegisterRoutine macro described earlier in this section. The RegisterRoutine macro has the following calling arguments:

```
RegisterRoutine("DLLname", "functionname", "formatspec")
```

Of these the `formatspec` argument requires a bit of explanation. The `formatspec` argument uses single character abbreviations for standard C data types to identify the type of the return value and the calling arguments. These are as follows:

Character	C Data Type
u	Unsigned short
U	Unsigned long
i	Short integer (short int)
I	Long integer (long int)
s	String (or near char *) pointer
S	String (or far char *) pointer
v	Void

A typical `formatspec` might be something like the following:

```
"S=ssU"
```

This example `formatspec` indicates that the Registered Routine returns an s or String (far char *) pointer, and accepts two s or String (near char *) arguments and a single u or unsigned long argument.

From Here...

We have looked closely at invoking and creating Help systems and we've discussed some of the tools that can be used to develop a Help system. You can use this material to improve your applications.

➤ For more information on improving your application, see Chapter 1, "User Interface Design."

➤ For more information calling the API, see Chapter 3, "Using the Windows API."

➤ For a thorough discussion of graphics, see Chapter 16, "Graphics: Data Analysis."

19

Networkable Apps

by Joseph Armitage

Why is writing a networked application different than writing a single desktop application? All you need to do is find some place that everybody can get to your application and put it out there for everybody to use, right? Well, it's not quite that simple. You have a lot of flexibility when writing a desktop application; you have only one user to be concerned about, and relatively speaking, the interaction between the user and his data is fairly simple.

In a networked application you have a conflicting set of requirements. You want your application to appear to perform as fast as and be as easy to use as a desktop application, while ensuring that the actions of one user do not interfere with the work of the other users. This balancing of ease of use and providing a stable and secure environment requires a number of important decisions to be made and trade-offs to be considered.

Let's take a look at some of the issues that we will have to deal with to take a simple desktop application and turn it into a robust networked application. In this chapter you learn how to do the following:

➤ Evaluate the trade-offs between speed and robustness involved in designing networked applications

➤ Understand the differences between and advantages of the different types of network systems

➤ Take a stand-alone system and implement it on a peer-to-peer network and then on a dedicated LAN system

➤ Discuss the advantages and disadvantages of different database engines for networked applications

➤ Add security permissions to your database to protect your data from prying eyes

➤ Discuss the different types of locking mechanisms that you can use to prevent database inconsistencies

➤ Through all of this, you will build on your existing knowledge of developing stand-alone systems. We will take you step-by-step through each added layer of sophistication

Understanding Design Characteristics of Networkable Applications

The overriding design characteristic of a networked application versus a single-user application is robustness. A networked application should be bullet proofed by having thorough and extensive error-checking. This is the most important concept for a programmer new to network programming. In some stand-alone applications, you may be able to skimp on error-checking in the interests of performance by making some assumptions like "the user will never do that." In a networked application some can and will "do that." The actions of one user must not be allowed to negatively affect the work of another user.

➤ **Ensuring Data Consistency:** Let's say you went to an ATM machine at your local bank and transferred $5,000 from your savings account to your checking account. You would not be pleased if—because someone else "crashed" the ATM system—the savings account database was debited $5,000, but somehow the $5,000 credit update was not applied to your checking account. You want to be sure that the information the bank has about you as a whole is consistent even if it is stored in different databases.

➤ **Concurrent Access to the Data:** You won't be pleased if you can't withdraw money from the ATM because someone at the bank is printing statements. You want to be sure that people can have concurrent access to their information.

➤ **Security and Backing Up:** If your bank didn't require you to enter an access code to withdraw money from your account, you probably wouldn't feel safe about keeping your money there. You want to be sure that sensitive information is secure from casual access.

➤ **Performance and Tuning:** You try to withdraw money and find that the ATM programmer decided to print on-screen, full-screen bitmapped graphics of each bill you withdraw. This delay takes 20 minutes. You want timely access to your data and efficient performance.

Now we'll further examine each feature in the following sections.

Ensuring Data Consistency

In a multi-user system, database updates from one user may be interspersed with updates from one or more other users. The goal of a multi-user system is to have the database look as if those transactions had all been executed in a serial fashion, one after the other. If a networked application is not designed correctly, a number of problems can occur that leave the database in an inconsistent state.

For example, see what happens when you try running two separate copies of the ADDRESS application on the accompanying disk as follows.

1. Run the ADDRESS.EXE program from the enclosed disk in directory ADDRESS. The dialog box in figure 19.1 appears.

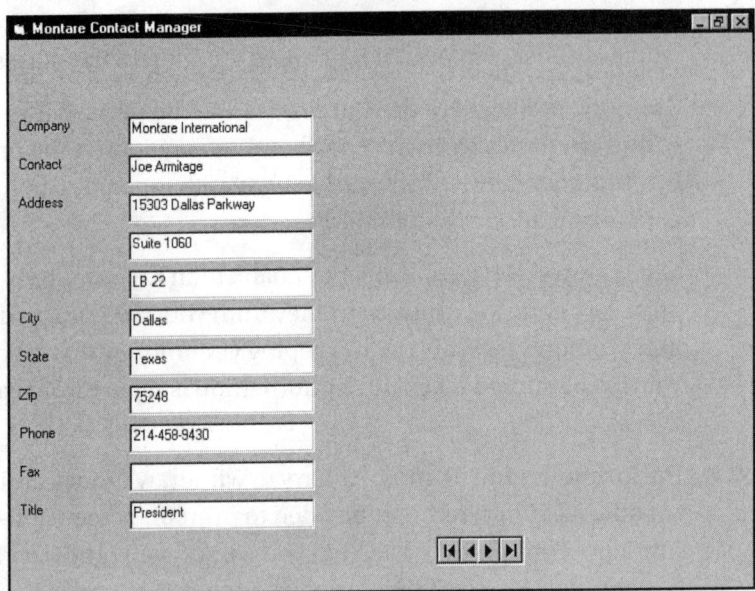

Fig. 19.1 The Montare Contact Manager is a very useful tracking tool that can be used on a network.

2. Now start a second copy of ADDRESS.EXE. The same record appears.

3. Change the name field from Joe Armitage to **John Bradford** and click the Data control to update the record.

4. Switch back to the first version of ADDRESS and change the city to **Austin**. This version of the data still shows Joe Armitage. Now try updating the database from this version of the application. How will the final record be stored in the database? Will John Bradford be in Dallas or will Joe Armitage be in Austin?

This is a failure to communicate, not only between the two users but also between the two copies of the application. The way to prevent conflicts like this is to ensure that only one user at a time can change data. This requires a data-locking strategy. When data is locked, any number of users can read it, but only one user can make changes to it. Data locks ensure that updates to the data are not lost and the database remains in a consistent state. We will discuss implementing an appropriate locking scheme in the sections on database, recordset, and page-level locking later in this chapter.

Allowing Concurrent Access to the Data

If you want to prevent any chance of conflicting updates, you could specify that you wanted exclusive access to the database. This is essentially what happens when you open a database in a stand-alone application. However, no other user can even open this database, let alone use any of the records. While this is desirable for a desktop application because it provides fast access, it is not practical for a networked application because everyone else is locked out.

To complicate matters even more, in Visual Basic you can control how a database is opened, but outside of your application, users can open a database exclusively using the Open Database command and prevent your users from accessing the database. For example, in Microsoft Access the Open Database dialog box defaults to Exclusive access.

Most users won't even see the check mark in the Exclusive box; if they do, they know that they will get faster access if they leave it selected. So in addition to limiting how users can open your database in your application, you need to have database software that can prevent the database from being monopolized by someone using the database software to access the data. An error dialog box (see fig. 19.2) displays when you try to access the MONTARE database using the ADDRESS2 application when it is already opened for exclusive access using Microsoft Access.

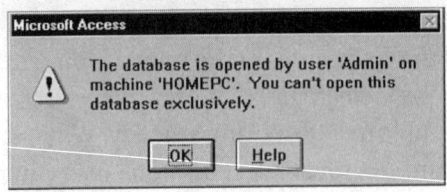

Fig. 19.2 This Access error dialog box informs the user that some-one else is already using the database, so it can't be opened for exclusive access.

The application continues to execute and shows a blank data-entry screen where the fields from the database should be. In an actual ap-plication, you would trap this error and end the application in a more graceful manner. You'll see how to do this in the sections on error trap-ping for database, page, and recordset locking.

A networked application must ensure an appropriate balance between allowing the maximum number of users possible to have concurrent access to the database and still maintain the integrity of that data. If there is contention between users, then the application should provide a graceful way to wait and retry accessing the data and should give the user the option to exit and retry at a less busy time.

Security and Backing Up

In stand-alone applications, you may tend to concentrate on the application's features and not so much on protecting data from unauthorized access. Security in a desktop application is usually either limited to being able to boot the PC containing the application or to a sign-on password for the database or application itself. Once you are signed on you have carte blanche to create, update, and delete records. You can even delete the entire database if you so wish.

Networked applications are more likely to contain information that's critical to you or your users, therefore protecting that information is an important part of application development. In a networked applica-tion you need to make decisions about just exactly who can access this application and the data it uses. By securing your application, you can control what a user or a group of users can do with the objects and data in your application. For example, you can specify that a user or group of users can view but not change the database.

The amount of data-entry/update is typically higher in networked applications, simply because there are more people accessing the application. For many database applications, controlling and managing who can view information and who can change information can be as important as creating the application. Protecting the application itself from being changed or copied may also be a concern. In order to handle this you need a security strategy, and your network and database software must be capable of implementing this strategy.

Along with a security strategy, regular backups of your data become more important because you are dealing with critical data. Backups now have to be scheduled at a time when no one else is accessing the database. Compacting the database (purging deleted records) requires exclusive access to the database, so this is usually scheduled at off hours.

Performance and Tuning

Speeding up performance of a desktop application usually means using a machine with a faster CPU and adding more RAM or a faster and bigger hard drive. You can essentially throw resources at the problem until it goes away.

The Microsoft Jet Database Engine has a stated requirement of six megabytes of RAM to run. In reality this is closer to eight, especially if you are using add-ins, OLE, or interfacing with other products such as Microsoft Mail or Excel. Upgrading one machine to 12 or even 16M of RAM is a simple matter, but upgrading numerous client machines can be expensive.

With a networked application you need to do some detective work to decide where to add hardware. If there is a performance problem with a networked system, it is much more involved to try to track down the source of the problem. Is the client too slow or the server? Is there a problem with the speed of the network wire? How much data is going across the network? Are too many users trying to access too few resources?

In a stand-alone application, database design is done primarily with an eye to providing as many features as possible to the user. In networked applications you need to assess your database design more carefully in terms of trade-offs between ease of access and speed of access. A stand-alone application can simply present as much of the application data as can sensibly fit on a screen. A networked application must be concerned with how much data is being sent back and forth between the server and the workstation. Particularly in a wide area network where data transfer rates may be slow, the goal of a networked application is to send the minimum amount of data, at one time, that the user needs to do his job.

Using Peer-to-Peer Networks

Peer-to-peer networks such as Microsoft Windows for Workgroups, Microsoft Windows 95, Novell Netware Lite, and Artisoft LANtastic are designed primarily for small companies or small workgroups within a large company.

The main emphasis of peer-to-peer networks is on sharing hardware resources such as printers, scanners, fax modems, and CD-ROMs. Peer-to-peer networks also provide basic file- and database-sharing capabilities. Any machine on the network can act as a server, making its resources available to any other machine on the network—or conversely, as a client requesting resources from any other machine on the network—provided those resources have been shared by the server machine.

Peer-to-peer networks can usually support 10 to 15 people, so long as their workload is not high volume and is evenly spread through the work period. Some of the advantages of using a peer-to-peer network are the following:

➤ Setup is a fairly easy and straightforward procedure and requires little maintenance and administration.

➤ The only extra expense incurred is for network cards and cabling. You do not have to buy a new machine to act as a server. You do not have to buy new software; Windows for Workgroups and Windows 95 come with networking capability built in.

➤ If the server for the application goes down, you can restore it to another similar machine (provided you have an up-to-date backup), set up connections to this server, and continue business.

Additionally, peer-to-peer networks are typically informal with no full-time network administrator. This means that there is no one person responsible for coordinating file security and backup or for ensuring that application performance remains within acceptable limits. This can be good, but on the other hand, it can provide the following disadvantages:

➤ Because no one is usually designated as a full-time system administrator, performance monitoring and database maintenance may not be done until a crisis point is reached.

➤ Backup of the application and data are the responsibility of the user who owns the "server" machine; backups may not be done on a regular basis.

➤ Shared passwords tend to not be very secure and usually do not get changed as often as they should because of the work involved in notifying everybody.

➤ Security is enforced only at the directory level, not at the file level. Users who can change application data have access to the application itself and can change or even delete startup and initialization files. Your sharing options are limited to read-only or full. Users can only read the data, or they are free to delete the entire database and your application with it if they wish.

➤ The "server" machine is now forced into double duty as a regular workstation and as a "server" to anyone who wants to run your application. If the user of the server runs disk- or computer-intensive applications, then anyone trying to use your application will be slowed down. If a lot of users try to access the application at the same time, the server disk will be thrashing around trying to get different pieces of data for different users.

Making the Application Networkable

To make an application networkable, first create a path to it from each user's machine. Using Windows 95 as our example, follow these steps:

1. Install appropriate hardware, such as network cards, hub, and cabling. Install Windows 95, if necessary on all machines, and activate the Client for Microsoft Networks option along with File and Print Sharing from Control Panel.

2. Select the machine with the most available hard-disk space and RAM (or with the most peripherals such as a CD-ROM, printer, and so on) to be the "server." Create a directory named ADDRESS on the "server" machine and copy the files from the ADDRESS directory on the accompanying disk to it.

3. Open the Start menu and choose Programs, Windows Explorer.

4. Right-click the mouse button on your new ADDRESS directory to open a shortcut menu for this directory.

5. Choose the Sharing option to bring up the Properties sheet for the directory. If the Sharing option does not appear on your shortcut menu, either the Client for Microsoft Networks has not been installed or the File and Print Sharing option has not been turned on. Select the Sharing tab and click the Shared As radio button to create a share name for this directory. The share name defaults to the directory name. Because you have only 12 characters here, leave it as a directory name. You can describe the application a little better in the comment section.

6. Choose Depends on Password. Enter a password in the Read-Only text box to provide to users whom you only want to be able to read this. Enter a password in the Full Access text box to

provide to users you want to be able to read and write this data. The Password Confirmation dialog box appears. Retype the passwords exactly as you did in the Sharing Properties dialog box.

7. Click OK to complete the share operation. The Windows Explorer file list is redisplayed. You see a little hand grabbing your directory folder file. You have successfully shared control of your application to anyone on the network who knows either the read- only password or the full-access password.

Connecting from the Client Side

To connect from the client side, follow these steps:

1. Open the Start menu and choose Programs, Windows Explorer.

2. Choose Map Network Drive from the Tools menu. This produces the Map Network Drive dialog box showing the next available logical disk-drive letter on your local machine (see fig. 19.3). Click the Path combo box to show a list of UNC names for potential "servers"—other computers attached to the network that are sharing directories. UNC names consist of \\computername\sharename where computername is the name you gave a computer when you set up your network software. sharename is the name you gave the resource when you shared it from the server.

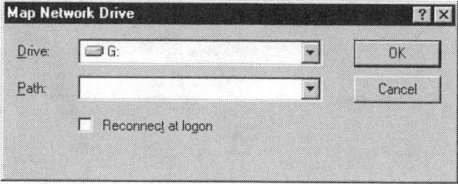

Fig. 19.3 The Map Network Drive dialog box allows you to create a new logical drive letter.

3. Select the UNC name that corresponds to the computer and directory where your application was installed and click OK.

4. The Enter Network Password dialog box appears; enter either the read-only password or the full-access password. The Windows Explorer is redisplayed with the share directory added as a new "virtual" drive with the next available drive letter. Notice that all subdirectories are also available.

Extending Peer-to-Peer Networking Capabilities

You can add extra levels of security to the application itself using your database software. See the section "Setting Up Security for Your Database" later in this chapter.

In addition, you can tune how fast the server machine shares its resources with clients as follows:

1. Open the Start menu and choose Settings, Control Panel. Double-click the System icon to display the File System Properties sheet. Select the Performance tab and double-click the File System button. From the Typical Role Of This Machine drop-down box, select Network Server (see fig. 19.4).

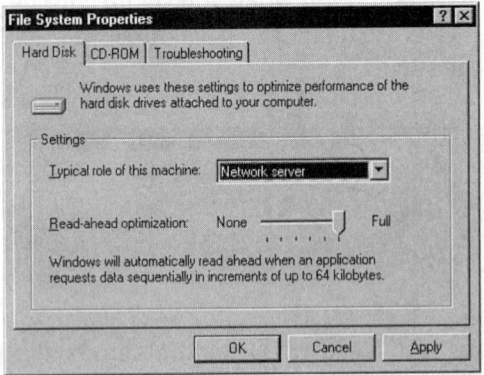

Fig. 19.4 The File System Properties sheet allows you to configure a machine for typical use as either a desktop, mobile, or network server computer.

> **Note:** This slows response for the local user; make sure that this machine is either dedicated as a server or receives only occasional light use.

Provided your client machines are powerful enough and have enough disk space, you can distribute your application. That is, put the application EXE on each client that needs to access the data. The server is now not responsible for actually running the EXE and can potentially serve more clients. Network traffic may be reduced because your EXE does not have to be shipped across the wire.

Down sides to this are that anyone can make a copy of your application from any client and try to run it herself on her machine with unpredictable results. Conversely, every time your application is updated, you have to distribute your EXE to everyone and make sure that everyone gets a copy and installs it. The clients may not be as powerful as the server, so if the server is lightly used, the clients may actually see longer response times. As an alternative you can buy a faster disk and more RAM for the server machine so that it can keep more data in RAM and doesn't have to access the disk as often.

If you have Windows NT workstations, you can use them to run a peer-to-peer network. Windows NT workstations provide better security in that logon IDs and passwords are mandatory in NT; they are optional in Windows for Workgroups. If you use the NTFS file system you can protect individual files rather than granting access to the entire directory.

Note that beginning with the 3.5 release of NT, Microsoft limited the number of connections to 10 concurrent users who can attach to the workstation. This is to ensure that performance remains acceptable for all users. Beyond this level you need to move to a dedicated server like Windows NT Advanced Server for performance and maintainability reasons. Usually machines powerful enough to run an NT workstation are running heavy-duty applications of their own; placing the extra burden of server duty on them would not result in acceptable performance.

Using Dedicated File Server Networks

Dedicated server networks such as Microsoft Windows NT Advanced Server, Novell NetWare, and Banyan Vines are designed to provide a centralized point of control and shareability. They provide a greater ability to support large departments. Dedicated file server networks are also used for small workgroups where security and centralized backup are an important consideration.

Dedicated file servers can be connected together to form a wide area network with hundreds or even thousands of users. They have more robust, feature-rich toolsets with security options to the individual file level, ability to dial in from a remote location to the server, and capability to monitor server and application performance.

Dedicated file servers can also be managed at the workgroup level by partitioning people and resources into domains. This allows users to access databases or hardware resources on a different physical server than the one that they are connected to. Other advantages of this method are as follows:

➤ Each user has her own password and can be assigned individual rights and restrictions.

➤ Security can be enforced at the file level.

➤ The server is dedicated to providing file services to applications.

➤ Dedicated networks have fault tolerance built in; mirror images of data can be written to redundant arrays of inexpensive disks (RAID). Windows NT Server supports RAID levels 0–5; however, the more redundancy you build in, the slower your network will run.

➤ All application files on the server can be backed up automatically from the server.

Note: Windows NT Server has a sophisticated performance monitoring tool built in. You can monitor and tune numerous features of the system. The NT Resource kit devotes a whole book to this subject.

➤ A system administrator is usually assigned and responsible for ensuring availability of the server, backing up files, and monitoring performance levels.

Setting up security for a multiple server configuration involving large numbers of users requires careful planning and coordination. If your network involves this kind of large scale deployment, a formal security structure plan is a must. You will need to work with network administrators from multiple departments to provide a balance between enough security but not so much that it restricts users from doing their jobs. You also need to ensure that adequate resources are available on each server to support your application's demands. What works on one server flawlessly may not work on a similar machine due to differences in configuration. Though there is a good solution for some, there are the following disadvantages to this method:

➤ A dedicated network requires at least a part-time system administrator who requires training to administer the network effectively.

➤ Dedicated network software is an extra expense that is incurred on a per-user basis.

➤ In a dedicated network, if you do not have a backup server, it is fairly complex and time-consuming to switch out the server. Most small organizations do not want to spend the money for a backup server but quickly become upset when they lose business if the server is down for an extended period of time.

The major differences between the two types of networks are summarized in Table 19.1.

Table 19.1   Comparing Peer-to-Peer and Dedicated Server Networks

	# of Users	Security	Cost	Maintainability	Scalability
Peer to Peer	10–15	Controlled to Directory level	Inexpensive, can use existing software, logon password optional	Relatively simple, can be done by end users	Limited to one processor
Dedicated Server	10–?*	Can be Controlled to File level	Requires purchase of additional software	More complex, requires trained administrator	Can use more than one CPU

* limited only by hardware capacity

Sharing an Application on a Dedicated File Server Network

The process for sharing files on an NT Server is similar to that for Windows 95. You must access the server machine and create a directory, if necessary, to contain your application. This directory becomes the share name or access point for the programs and files in the application.

1. Log on to the server using the Admin account or the account that owns the files that you wish to share.

2. Open File Manager from the Windows Program Manager.

3. Select Share As from the Disk menu to create a share name for this directory. The New Share dialog box appears (see fig. 19.5). Enter a meaningful Share Name. Because you have only 12 characters here you may as well leave it as the directory name. You can describe the application a little better in the Comment section.

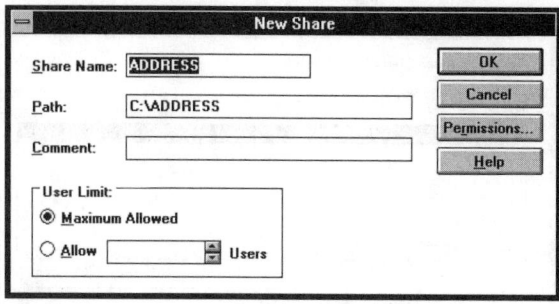

Fig. 19.5 The New Share dialog box allows you to establish a share point for your application from the server.

Note: You can limit the number of users who can access the directory. This gives you the opportunity to trade off, allowing multitudes of people to fight for control of this resource versus limiting the number of people, but gives them a reasonable share of access to the resource. This is something that you can adjust later if people are having problems getting a reasonable response time. So leave the radio button checked at Maximum Allowed for now.

4. Click the Permissions button to set the permissions for the directory. The Access Through Share Permissions dialog box appears.

5. Click the Add button and the Add Users And Groups dialog box appears.

6. Scroll through the list of groups, or click the Show Users button to display individual users. Double-click your selection to add it to the Add Names box; select the type of access you want the user or group to have in the Type of Access box and click OK.

7. The Access Through Share Permissions dialog box appears again (see fig. 19.6), showing your new user/group.

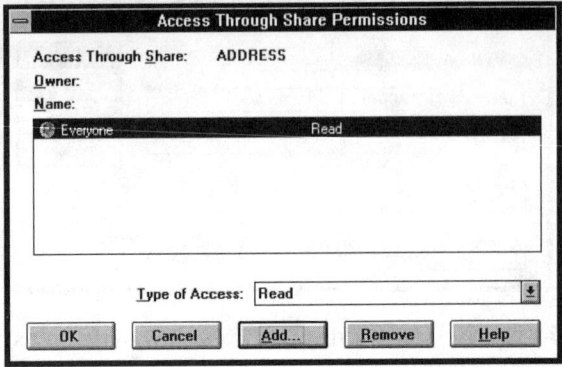

Fig. 19.6 The Access Through Share Permissions dialog box allows you to specify the type of access that client workstations have to the share point.

If your files are created on an NTFS partition, you can enforce security at the file level. The permissions you can grant in an NTFS partition are also more granular. You can assign Read, Write, Delete, Execute, change Permission, and take ownership rights to individual users or groups of users.

Using Desktop Databases

There are a multitude of desktop databases that you can use with Visual Basic. You can select from dBASE, FoxPro, Paradox, Microsoft Access, Btrieve, even Lotus, Excel, or plain old text files. Many desktop databases are adding multi-user capabilities, but quite simply the easiest way to access any of these databases in Visual Basic is through the Microsoft Jet Database Engine provided with the Visual Basic package. The combination of Visual Basic and the Jet Engine make database access largely a matter of point and shoot through the use of Data controls.

In addition, desktop database products are fast because they lock data at the database level and do not provide the extra features provided in multi-user databases. The only down side of this are the following disadvantages:

➤ Desktop databases lock data at the database level, restricting your application to one user at a time even if you have multiple copies of your desktop database software. Everyone else is locked out.

➤ Desktop databases provide no support for multi-user systems. Security and handling consistency issues (locking) are left to either the network software or the operating system software.

Even if you use a single-user desktop database system on a network, you will want to supplement network security with a database security scheme. By default, the Jet Engine allows you to access any database without having to supply a user name or password. This is usually okay in a single-user environment. In a multiple-user environment, you want to require the users to log on with their name and password. You do not have to set up multiple security IDs. Every user who knows the logon password for the application is granted the same permission to add, delete, or update records.

Visual Basic now includes a number of security features that can restrict applications from accessing entire databases or their table, field, user, or group objects. In order to manage which users have permission to access which objects, Jet uses a SYSTEM.MDA file. This file and the application you use to create and maintain files of this type are included with Microsoft Access but not with Visual Basic.

When you install Microsoft Access, a default SYSTEM.MDA with no security is automatically created in your Microsoft Access directory. A tool called the Access WorkGroup Administrator is automatically placed in the program group where you installed Microsoft Access. Until you explicitly set up the security system, neither Access nor Visual Basic knows anything about security. Also, Microsoft Access uses the default workgroup each time you start Microsoft Access.

Setting Up Security for Your Database

Whenever you create or change any security objects, write down their names, including whether letters are upper- or lowercase, and keep them in a safe place. If you ever have to re-create the system database, you must supply the exact same entries. If you forget or lose these entries, you can't recover them unless you have a current copy backed up in a safe place.

Follow these steps to password-protect your database:

1. Create a workgroup system database in which to establish and maintain users and groups of users or join an existing workgroup.

2. Activate the logon procedure for this workgroup.

3. Create an administrator logon account for the workgroup and an owner account for the application database.

You can use the MS Access Workgroup Administrator to create a new Microsoft Access workgroup as follows:

1. Set up the directory on the server machine to hold your application.

2. Double-click the MS Access Workgroup Administrator icon. The Workgroup Administrator dialog box appears.

3. Click the Create button. Microsoft Access displays the Workgroup Owner Information dialog box, which allows you to enter information that identifies the owner of the system database that defines the new workgroup. Type your name and organization in the dialog box if they're not already present.

4. Type a unique workgroup ID using a meaningful name, in this case **SALES**, and click OK. Click OK again when the Confirm Workgroup Information dialog box appears.

5. Click the OK button to display the Workgroup System Database dialog box (see fig. 19.7). Enter the path and name of the system database that defines the new workgroup. It's best to name the database system.mda because there are other utilities that expect your security file to be called that name.

6. Click OK to display a confirmation dialog box that displays the path to your system database. This path is saved in your Microsoft Access initialization file and, until you change it again using the Workgroup Administrator, this will be your default security file.

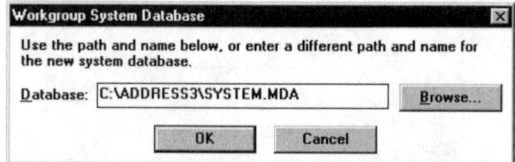

Fig. 19.7 The Workgroup System Database dialog box is where you specify that you want to keep the SYSTEM.MDA security permissions database for your application.

Your new workgroup is now set up. The next time you start Microsoft Access, it uses the new workgroup. Microsoft Access stores any user and group accounts or passwords you create or changes in system option settings in the new workgroup's system database.

Activating the Logon Procedure

Until you establish security for a workgroup, Microsoft Access always logs you on at startup using a default Admin account that does not require you to enter a password. The default password for the Admin account is a zero-length string. To activate the logon procedure, change the Admin user account's password from a zero-length string to another password as follows:

1. Start Microsoft Access using the new workgroup you've chosen (which is the default, unless someone else has used the Workgroup administrator to join a different group).

2. Open any database. Because the security settings are stored in the workgroup system database, you can open any database (.MDB) file.

3. From the Security menu, choose Change Password. The Change Password dialog box appears (see fig. 19.8).

4. In the New Password box, type the new password.

5. Confirm the new password by typing it again in the Verify box and clicking OK.

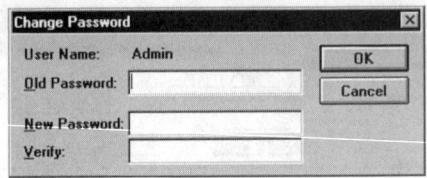

Fig. 19.8 The Change Password dialog box allows you to set up and maintain the password security for your Access databases.

The next time you start Microsoft Access, it will display the Logon dialog box (see fig. 19.9).

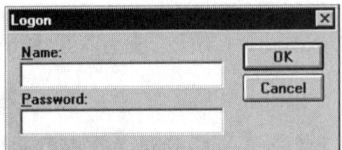

Fig. 19.9 The Microsoft Access Logon dialog box provides logon security to your application database.

Using Workgroup Databases

The Microsoft Jet Engine can also function as a Workgroup database. To make your application into a true multi-user system you need to do a few more things.

Multi-user (Workgroup) databases such as Microsoft Access provide their own security system that acts as a complement to any security provided by the network software. For Access, this is provided via the SYSTEM.MDA database and accompanying Workgroup Administrator program.

Workgroup databases provide flexible and efficient support for locking data that is in the process of being updated. Access has three native locking mechanisms to control multi-user data access in your Visual Basic applications. These locking levels are discussed in the section on database locking.

Note: I do not recommend trying to write your own locking scheme. Workgroup databases locking support, while sophisticated, is not as robust as that of client/server databases, and it requires you to be extremely thorough in your error-checking procedures or your users will get cryptic and unhelpful error messages. Also, the security systems in Workgroup databases must be maintained by someone and the security files must be backed up regularly.

Caution: You have protected the database from the casual user, but if someone wants access, he can get access by using another copy of Microsoft Access and the default Admin account.

Because the default Admin account is exactly the same for every copy of Microsoft Access, it is not enough to password protect the default Admin account. You should set up your own administrator account in place of Admin. Otherwise, anyone with a copy of Microsoft Access can log on to your workgroup using the Admin account and have full permissions for the workgroup's objects. And then, of course, you need to delete that Admin account.

The first step in activating the logon procedure is to create a new administrator account along with the user and group accounts for the application. Then you need to remove default permissions and assign new permissions for the application objects. Finally, you need to create passwords for the necessary accounts and encrypt the database. The following sections take you through this process.

Creating a New Administrator Account

To create a new administrator account, follow these steps:

1. Log on to Access using the default Admin account and the password you set up in the section "Activating the Logon Procedure."

2. Choose Users from the Security menu. The Users dialog box appears (see fig. 19.10).

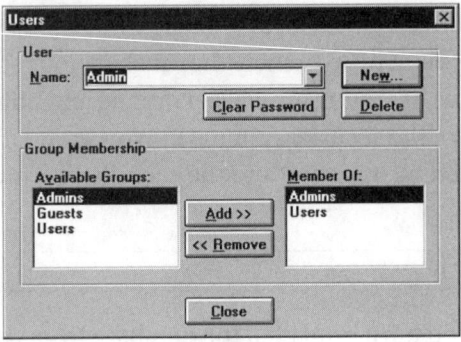

Fig. 19.10 The Microsoft Access Users dialog box allows you to maintain the list of valid users for this application.

3. Click New and the New User/Group dialog box appears (see fig. 19.11). Type the Name of the new account and a Personal ID.

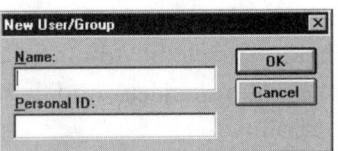

Fig. 19.11 The New User/Group dialog box allows you to add a new user or group of users to the list of valid users/groups for this application.

4. Click OK to create the new account. Microsoft Access returns to the Users dialog box.

5. From the Available Groups list, select the Admins group and click Add. Microsoft Access adds the new account to the Admins group and displays Admins in the Member Of list.

6. Click Close to close the Users dialog box.

An administrator account is a member of the Admins group for a workgroup. An administrator account can always get full permission for all objects created in the workgroup. Therefore, rather than just setting up an Admin account for your database and giving out that password, you want to create an owner account that can do routine maintenance on that particular database only. An owner account is a user or group account you designate to own (have control over) an application's databases and objects. Like an Admin account, an owner account's permissions can't be taken away, even by an administrator.

Changing Database and Object Ownership

If you're creating a secure application from scratch, the best approach is to log on with the account that you want to own the database and its objects, and then create the database and its objects.

In this case, because the database was created using the default Admin account, Admin owns the database and any objects in ADDRESS application and in any other application that hasn't been secured. To secure the application, you must change ownership of the database and its objects to a designated owner account.

You can change ownership of an existing database and all its objects by creating a new database, and then importing the contents of the existing database.

To change ownership of a database and all its objects, follow these steps:

1. Start Microsoft Access using the new workgroup you created and log on using the account that you want to be the new owner.

2. Select New Database from the File menu. This displays the New Database dialog box. Type a name for your database and press Enter.

3. Choose File, Import, and click OK. The Import dialog box appears (see fig. 19.12).

4. Double-click Microsoft Access, which brings up a dialog box listing the available Microsoft Access databases in the current directory.

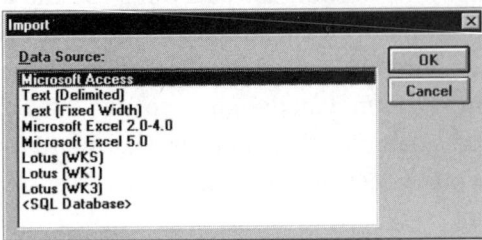

Fig. 19.12 The Import dialog box allows you to specify which database you want to import.

5. Double-click the database you wish to import and the Import Objects dialog box appears (see fig. 19.13).

6. In the Object Type box, select Tables and click Import. Microsoft Access imports all objects for which you have permission from the selected database to the new database you've created.

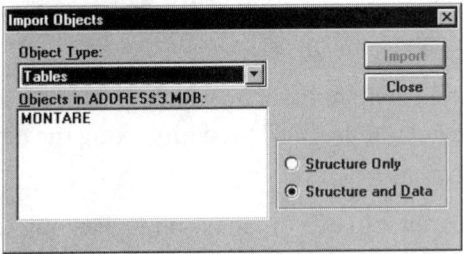

Fig. 19.13 The Import Objects dialog box allows you to select which database objects to import.

Creating and Managing User and Group Accounts

Setting up groups of users makes it easier to manage a secure application. Instead of assigning permissions to each individual user for each object in your application, you can assign permissions to groups, and then add users to the appropriate group. A member of a group inherits the permissions of any groups to which he or she belongs, in addition to any specific permissions you grant to that specific user.

For example, as you secure the ADDRESS application, you can create a Managers group for managers and a Sales group for sales representatives. You can assign one set of permissions to the Managers group, and another set of permissions to the Sales group. To create a new Sales group account, follow these steps:

1. Start Microsoft Access using the workgroup you've chosen.

2. Open a database.

3. Choose Security, Groups. The Groups dialog box appears (see fig. 19.14).

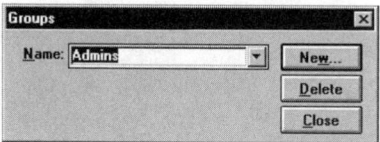

Fig. 19.14 The Groups dialog box allows you to maintain valid groups for your application.

4. Click New and the New User/Group dialog box appears.

5. Type the Name of the new account and a Personal ID.

6. Click OK to create the new account.

7. The Groups dialog box appears again. Click Close.

Assigning and Removing Permissions

To secure an application, you must remove the permissions of the Admin user and Users group, which includes all users in a workgroup. Until you remove those permissions, users may have permissions that you didn't intend for objects. Once the permissions have been removed, users have only the permissions you assign.

After you've created user and group accounts, you can assign permissions to those accounts for the application's objects. To secure the ADDRESS2 application, you can assign permissions to the Sales group you created in the section "Creating and Managing User and Group Accounts."

1. Open the MONTARE database. Choose Security, Permissions. The Permissions dialog box shows a list of valid users (see fig. 19.15).

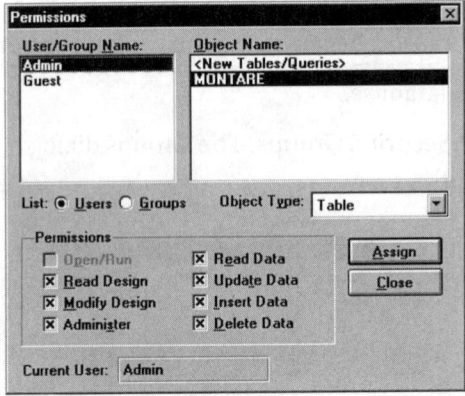

Fig. 19.15 The Permissions dialog box lists valid users/groups for the application and their specific access rights or permissions for individual database objects.

2. Highlight the appropriate user and select or clear the appropriate check boxes to set or revoke permissions and click Assign.

To set permissions for groups, select the Groups option button to display a list of groups in the Permissions dialog box. Then do the same for users.

Encrypting a Database

The final step in protecting your database from unauthorized access is encrypting the database. When you encrypt a database file, Microsoft

Access makes it indecipherable in order to protect it from unauthorized viewing or use by someone using a utility program or a word processor.

1. In the Microsoft Access startup window choose File, Encrypt/Decrypt. The Encrypt/Decrypt Database dialog box appears.

2. Select the database that you want to encrypt or decrypt and click OK. The Encrypt Database As dialog box appears (if the database you selected isn't already encrypted). If the database is encrypted, the Decrypt Database As dialog box appears.

3. Specify a file name, drive, and directory for the destination encrypted or decrypted database using standard MS-DOS naming conventions. Then click OK.

Using Client/Server Databases

By separating the Jet Database Engine from the physical data store (.MDB, .DBF files, etc.), Microsoft made it possible to connect to a number of different back-end physical database file types. You can connect to virtually any database that uses SQL as an access mechanism, such as SQL Server, Oracle, and DB2. You can even use mainframe files in VSAM or ADABAS through third-party ODBC drivers.

The flexibility of the Jet Engine leads to some confusion about what that engine is suited for and, consequently, to misuse and associated performance problems. Even though you can couple the Jet Engine to a database on a remote server, the Jet Database Engine is not a client/server engine.

The Jet Database Engine is dynamically linked to your application, and so each copy of your program will have access to its own local copy of the Jet Database Engine. A thorough understanding of the SQL preprocessor and the results processor can dramatically improve the speed of your client/server application. You can decrease network traffic by structuring your application so that an efficient query that takes advantage of existing indexes is sent to the server and returns the minimum data set that meets your criteria to the client.

When using external data engines such as Microsoft SQL Server, Sybase, or Oracle, the locking methodology is the responsibility of the remote database engine.

The advantages of client/server databases are as follows:

➤ Server-based databases have sophisticated security access routines and flexible locking support methods.

➤ Visual Basic simply acts as a front end to these database servers and does not control the data sharing aspects of the back-end database engines. Much of the error handling can be done by the database server, which results in less complex programs.

The disadvantages of client/server databases are as follows:

➤ The disk space requirements and processing requirements of server-based databases require that you have a dedicated server machine. They are written to be used on dedicated network servers.

➤ The sophisticated security access routines and locking support methods require careful setup and detailed knowledge of how both the server database and network operating system work. This usually means dedicating a full-time person to administering database setup and maintenance.

➤ Your application does not totally control the data in the database. The database administrator may have written stored procedures or triggers that affect what can be done to the database.

For more information on client/server databases, see Chapter 9, "Client/Server Databases."

Locking Levels

In order to prevent the types of problems discussed in the sections on consistency and concurrency in a multi-user system, you need to implement a *locking strategy*. A locking strategy is simply a means to prevent other users from attempting to update a particular record, part of a particular record, or a collection of records while another user is in the middle of updating the same data. In a high-use multi-user system, the typical goal is to lock the minimum number of records possible for the shortest period of time, while ensuring that the database is maintained in a consistent state at the end of our processing.

Access provides three different levels of locking: recordset level, page level, and database level. Recordset locking is the most-often-used type of locking because it is less restrictive than database locking. Using this method, you have the flexibility of locking only the records or tables you are working with at the time, so other records or tables can be used by others who are using the same database.

The default locking level when accessing a Jet Engine database is page-level locking. Unless you specify database- or recordset-level locking, the entire 2K page of data containing the record you're editing is locked. Because entire pages are locked and a given page may contain more than one record, users need not be on the exact same record to cause a locking conflict. For example, if user A locks a record in page 1, and user B attempts to edit another record that is also on page 1, user B will receive a locking error. Other users can read data from locked pages.

Database locking is the most restrictive type of locking. It provides fast access in single-user systems but is rarely used in multi-user situations, except to perform database maintenance or in specialized applications that require a lot of updates done by one user.

> **Caution:** Programmers often overlook the fact that the same locking scheme applies to the index pages. When you use the `Seek` method or you are rebuilding indexes, entire 2K pages of indexes are locked. This can cause locking errors that can affect access to a large number of actual records in the database.

Note: The Jet Engine does not provide for locking at the individual-record level. If your application requires that you lock at the record level, you can force Jet to lock individual records by creating record sizes that are larger than half a page—that is, larger than 1024 bytes. This works because Access won't begin storing a new record on a partially filled page if it can't fit the entire record on that page. Of course, this will also waste a tremendous amount of disk space.

The following programs set locking at the database, page, and recordset levels and demonstrate how to check for possible multi-user locking conflicts with other people trying to access the same data. If there is a conflict, the user receives a message box that describes the type of error. In most cases the code allows the user to retry the operation or cancel. Note that the error handling in the samples is only for the purposes of trapping locking errors, and you will need much more extensive error-handling code in an actual application.

Page Locking

With page-level locking there are two main runtime errors to trap. The first is error 3260 (`Couldn't update; currently locked by user x on machine y`), which indicates that another user locked the page you want to modify.

The second error is 3197 (`Data has changed; operation stopped`), which indicates that someone has modified the record that you are attempting to modify in the database since the last time you retrieved that page from the database.

For example, user A creates a recordset on the Contacts table and pulls in the first page (2K) of records from the database. User B now creates an identical recordset, retrieving the same 2K of records. If User A updates the first record in the recordset, user B will not immediately see this change because User B has already retrieved the first page of the record and will not do so again unless he or she refreshes (re-creates) the recordset.

If user B now attempts to modify the first record of the recordset, she will receive error 3197, warning her that she is about to overwrite new data that she has never retrieved from the database. If you re-execute the operation that caused the Data has changed; operation stopped after receiving the error once, the data will be overwritten without the error being generated a second time. Listing 19.1 is sample code to deal with this situation.

Listing 19.1   PAGELOCK.TXT—Routine to Handle Page-Locking Errors

```
Sub Handle_Lock ()
  Dim Mydb As database
  Dim Myds As dynaset
  Dim ret As Integer, fSuccess As Integer
  Set Mydb = OpenDatabase("MONTARE.MDB")
  Set Mydb = db.CreateDynaset("CONTACTS")
  Do Until Myds.EOF = True
  ' Read records, checking for possible page locking conflicts
    fSuccess = False
  ' Disable any previous error handler and continue
    On Error Resume Next
    While Not fSuccess
      Err = 0
      Myds.Edit
      If Err Then
        If Err = ERR_DATA_CHANGED Then
          ret = MsgBox("Record has been updated. Overwrite?", _
          MB_RETRYCANCEL)
          If ret = IDNO Then fSuccess = True
        ElseIf Err = ERR_RECORD_LOCKED Then
          ret = MsgBox("Record in use by another user.", _
          MB_RETRYCANCEL)
          If ret = IDCANCEL Then Exit Sub
        Else
          MsgBox "Unexpected error" & Str$(Err) & " editing _
          record."
          Exit Sub
        End If
```

continues

Listing 19.1   Continued

```
      Else
        fSuccess = True
      End If
    Wend
' disable error trapping OR place On Error statements
' pointing to a new error handler here
    On Error GoTo 0
    Myds("CONTACT") = Myds("CONTACT")
Myds.Update
    Myds.MoveNext
Loop
    Myds.Close
    Mydb.Close
End Sub
```

Recordset Locking

To update our stand-alone contact manager application, which uses a
Data control, the method is as follows:

1. Open up the ADDRESS.MAK project in the ADDRESS directory on
   the accompanying disk. Open Form1.

2. Right-click on the Data control and select Properties.

3. Scroll to the Recordset Type property, bring up the list box, and
   you can see that you can specify whether you want the recordset
   to be a Dynaset, Table, or Snapshot. Leave it as a Dynaset.

4. Scroll, if necessary, to the Options property, which defaults
   to 0, no locking. Change this to 5, which is a combination of 1
   (dbDenyWrite) + 4 (dbReadOnly). In a multi-user environment
   dbDenyWrite specifies that other users cannot make changes to
   records in the recordset. The other option, dbReadOnly, specifies
   that your process can't make changes to records in the recordset.
   You might use this combination if you wanted to scan through a
   group of records and summarize them and didn't want anyone
   changing them during the process.

   If you set the DatabaseName or RecordSource properties of a Data
   control at designtime, the Data control will automatically attempt

to perform the equivalent of an OpenDatabase and OpenRecordset when the form containing the Data control is first loaded.

If an error occurs when the Data control attempts to automatically open the database or recordset, the Data control will fire its Error event and pass in the appropriate runtime error value. Because no Visual Basic code is executing at this time, you will need to handle any possible locking conflicts in the Error event rather than using On Error. Add the following code:

```
Sub Data1_Error(DataError As Integer, Response As Integer)
   ret = MsgBox("Table(s) in use by another user.",_
   MB_RETRYCANCEL)
    Select Case DataError
        Case 3024    ' If database file not found.
'            CMDialog1.Action = 1    ' Display an Open _
             dialog box.
        ret = MsgBox("Table(s) in use by another user.", _
        MB_RETRYCANCEL)
    End Select
End Sub
```

> **Note:** If you change the Options property at runtime, you must use the Refresh method for the change to have any effect.

5. Compile the program and try running two different instances of it. If another user tries to edit any of the records in your recordset at the same time you are running the previous code, he would get an error message.

6. Save the project as MYADDR if you wish to keep it for future reference.

The OpenRecordSet method gives you more control over your access to the data.

1. Open the ADDRESS4.MAK project in the ADDRESS4 directory on the accompanying disk. Change the line opening the recordset from:

```
Set data1 = db.OpenRecordset("MONTARE")
```

to this:

```
Set data1 = db.OpenRecordset("MONTARE", DB_DENYWRITE Or _
    DB_DENYREAD)
```

Now the entire recordset is being locked for your exclusive use.

Look at the following section of generic error-handling code that gives the user a cryptic error number returned from Visual Basic and an unhelpful message.

```
' Check for errors
If Err Then
MsgBox "Unexpected error" & Str$(Err) & " opening database."
        Exit Sub
Else
        fSuccess = True
    End If
```

The replacement code below performs additional error-checking that indicates if there are any multi-user conflicts. It also displays a message box allowing the user to retry the update or exit gracefully and try his update later.

```
' Check for locking conflicts or other errors
If Err Then
        If Err = ERR_CANT_OPEN_TABLE Then
            ret = MsgBox("Table(s) in use by another user.", _
MB_RETRYCANCEL)
            If ret = IDCANCEL Then Exit Sub
        Else
            MsgBox "Unexpected error" & Str$(Err) & " opening _
            database."
            Exit Sub
        End If
    Else
        fSuccess = True
    End If
```

2. Save the project as MYADDR4 if you wish to keep it for future reference.

3. Choose Run, Start (or press F5) to run the program. Click the Show Me a Record button. If another user tries to access the MONTARE table when you're running the program, he would get an error message.

This method is not normally used for Snapshots because they are read-only and changes to the data will not normally affect a Snapshot (with the exception of memo fields).

Error 3197 (`Data has changed; operation stopped`) can occur for Snapshots that have memo fields. Because memo fields are usually quite large, the Access engine does not pull the entire contents of a memo field into the Snapshot at the time it is created; instead, a reference to the memo field in the database is stored in the Snapshot.

If the data in the memo field is changed by another user between the time a Snapshot is first populated (meaning that you access a given record, using the `Move` or `Find` methods or visit all records, using the `sn.MoveLast` method) and the time that record is revisited or made the current record again, the database engine will signal that your data is out of date by invoking runtime error 3197.

Database Locking

Once again, using our stand-alone application as a starting point that uses a Data control, the method for database locking is as follows:

1. Open the ADDRESS.MAK project in the ADDRESS directory on the accompanying disk. Open Form1.

2. Right-click on the Data control and select Properties.

3. Scroll, if necessary, to the `Exclusive` property that defaults to `False`. To enable database locking, change this to `True` via the list box. As long as this Data control is active, no one else will be able to access any record in the entire database; she will receive an error message explaining that the data is in use by another user.

4. Compile the program and try running two different instances of it. If another user tries to open the MONTARE.MDB database at the same time you are running the code previously listed, she will receive an error message.

5. Save the project as MYADDR if you wish to keep it for future reference.

If you're handling your data access programmatically, as in the ADDRESS4 application, the OpenDatabase method is as follows:

1. Open the ADDRESS4.MAK project in the ADDRESS4 directory on the accompanying disk. The OpenDatabase method is opening the database in non-exclusive mode as follows.

```
Set db = OpenDatabase("MONTARE.MDB")
```

Change this to:

```
Set db = OpenDatabase("MONTARE.MDB", True)
```

Now the entire database is being locked for your exclusive use.

The generic error-handling code below, from the ADDRESS4 application, does not specifically check for multi-user errors.

```
"Check for errors
If Err Then
MsgBox "Unexpected error" & Str$(Err) & " opening database."
        Exit Sub
Else
        fSuccess = True
    End If
```

The replacement code below checks for multi-user conflicts, presents the user with a meaningful message box, and gives them the option of canceling or proceeding.

```
'Check for locking conflicts or other errors
If Err Then
        If Err = ERR_CANT_OPEN_DB Then
            ret = MsgBox("Database in use by another user.",_
            MB_RETRYCANCEL)
            If ret = IDCANCEL Then Exit Sub
        Else
            MsgBox "Unexpected error" & Str$(Err) & " _
            opening database."
            Exit Sub
        End If
Else
        fSuccess = True
    End If
```

2. Save the project as MYADDR4 if you wish to keep it for future reference.

The Jet Engine provides two different approaches to locking: optimistic and pessimistic. In either case, you need to handle errors raised by the

Jet Engine that indicate that someone else has either locked the data or has updated the data in the middle of your attempt to update the data.

Optimistic Locking

You can take the optimistic approach and only lock data at the point where you actually update the data. This approach assumes that the likelihood of another user attempting to access your data to update it is low.

The advantages of using optimistic locking are as follows:

➤ It is simple to use.

➤ It allows more than one user to edit the same record at the same time. (Some may consider this a disadvantage.)

➤ It is less likely to lock other users out of records.

➤ It provides better performance than pessimistic locking.

The disadvantages of optimistic locking are as follows:

➤ It may be confusing to the user when there is a write conflict.

➤ Users can potentially overwrite each other's edits.

Listing 19.2 opens a recordset and sets its LockEdits property to False. This enables optimistic locking so other users can change the database records at any time. Your application triggers a trappable error if the data changes before you use the Update method.

Listing 19.2   OPTLOCKS.TXT—Setting LockEdits Property to False

```
Sub OptLocks()
Dim MyDB As Database, MyRecords As Recordset
Set MyDB = Workspaces(0).OpenDatabase("ADDRESS.MDB")
Set MyRecords = MyDB.OpenRecordset("MONTARE")
MyRecords.LockEdits = False
MyRecords.Edit     ' Start editing.
MyRecords!Name = "Joe Armitage"
OnError Goto MyErrH
MyRecords.Update     ' Try to post the changes.
```

continues

Listing 19.2   Continued

```
MyRecords.Close
Exit Sub
MyErrH:
     If Error = 3197 Then      ' Data changed.
          MsgBox "Data changed by Someone else."
          Resume Next
     Else
          Msgbox "Some other error."
     End If
End Sub
```

In a real application you would allow the user to display the new data and then perhaps attempt his update again.

Using External Database Engines

When using ODBC data sources such as Microsoft SQL Server, Sybase, or Oracle, locking is handled by the remote database engine. Visual Basic simply acts as a front end to these database servers and does not control the locking mechanisms used in the back-end database engines. Therefore, setting `LockEdits` or the `Exclusive` parameter of the `OpenDatabase` method has no effect on ODBC databases.

Caution: In some cases, you can control how the remote server locks data by using back-end–specific SQL statements or administrative options. Do not send commands that lock the entire table or database in a high-volume transaction environment, as this will lock everyone else out, bringing the system to its knees.

Note: Designing thorough error-handling routines that react correctly when locking contention occurs is the only reliable way to allow the back-end database engine to operate its native locking scheme for maximum throughput. Think about what you are trying to achieve before you code and test for a variety of possible locking contention situations.

Pessimistic Locking

Jet by default takes the pessimistic approach and assumes that some-one else will want to update your data and automatically locks the data as soon as you use the `Edit` method on the data. The data is not released until you use the `Update` method, `Close` method, or `Find` or `Move` to another record.

The advantages of pessimistic locking are as follows:

➤ It is simple for the developer and may be less confusing to the user.

➤ It works well for small workgroups or where users are not likely to be editing the same record.

➤ It prevents users from overwriting each other's work.

The disadvantages of pessimistic locking are as follows:

➤ It will usually lock multiple records. (How many depends on the size of the records.)

➤ When a user is at the end of a table (and thus has locked the last page), other users may be prevented from adding new records.

➤ It is not recommended where lots of users will be editing the same records, or where lots of users will be adding new records at the same time.

Caution: Pessimistic locking can potentially prevent your users from being able to edit or add new records for long periods of time if someone places a lock and walks away from his computer or starts a task that updates large amounts of data. Unless you have a dire need to use pessimistic locking, I strongly recom-mend that you use optimistic locking with appropriate error-checking. If you decide to use pessimistic locking in your applications, you will spend a lot of time explaining what locked records are and why the users can't get at their databases.

From Here...

This chapter taught you how to identify the different types of network systems and their unique advantages and disadvantages. It also taught you the importance of thorough, up-front design techniques, and complete error-checking to identify or prevent multi-users errors. You also learned the different roles that single-user, Workgroup, and client/server databases play in the design and development of networked systems.

To round out your knowledge on using Visual Basic for developing networkable and client/server applications, you should also review the material in the following chapters of this book:

➤ For more information on database front ends, see Chapter 4, "Advanced Database Front Ends."

➤ For more information on data management, see Chapter 5, "Data Management and Data-Driven Programming."

➤ For a thorough discussion of ODBC, see Chapter 6, "Working with ODBC."

➤ For details of client/server issues, see Chapter 8, "Modern Client/Server Computing," and Chapter 9, "Client/Server Databases."

20

OLE Controls, Add-Ins, and 32-bit DLLs

by J.D. Evans, Jr.

Windows 95 is a limited, 32-bit operating system, and Visual Basic 4 is designed for Windows 95 programming. Since Windows 95 only provides some of the functionality of the Win32 Application Programming Interface (API), there are restrictions on 32-bit work in Windows 95. However, Visual Basic 4 also is designed for use with Windows NT—where you find no restrictions imposed by the operating system on 32-bit work.

In Utopia, Visual Basic 4 would have no restrictions, but Visual Basic 4 is not so Utopian in its implementation. Unfortunately, some things are not so easy to do with Visual Basic 4. To understand the more difficult aspects of using Visual Basic 4, it is necessary to understand the manner in which Visual Basic 4 implements the general rules imposed in Windows 95 and Windows NT (as well as the more specific rules imposed by OLE technology, the Win32 API, and Unicode).

OLE is a set of technologies that provides a wide range of services. Connectable Objects, the Component Object Model (COM), Structured Storage, Monikers, Uniform Data Transfer, the OLE Clipboard, OLE Drag and Drop, OLE Automation, OLE Documents, and OLE Controls are some of the OLE technologies. In this context, OLE Controls is a technology—not simply a particular control—and, OLE Controls uses (or can use) all the other OLE technologies. The Win32 API provides a wide range of functionality that is necessary for doing work in Windows 95 and Windows NT. Unicode is a universal character set in which each character is described by two bytes of information, and Unicode sets the general standard for the ways in which both OLE and the Win32 API do character work.

For Visual Basic 4 programming, the most important OLE technologies are OLE Controls and OLE Automation. Since OLE Controls can use every other OLE technology, it may appear a bit oxymoronic to focus specifically on everything, but for your Visual Basic 4 work, you will use premade controls that were built using the OLE Controls technology. If you do Visual C++ programming, you may decide to build your premade controls—in which case, you will find yourself working with the OLE Controls technology—hence, everything that OLE does. OLE Automation is particularly important in Visual Basic 4, because Visual Basic 4 can build an OLE Automation server and your Visual Basic 4 applications (and OLE Automation servers) can act as OLE Automation controllers.

In this chapter, the important OLE technologies are OLE Controls and OLE Automation. The goals of this chapter are the following:

➤ Learn to choose 32-Bit OLE Controls for use with Visual Basic 4

➤ Understand how to build an OLE Automation server and use Visual Basic 4

➤ Provide information that helps you build the framework for a Visual Basic 4 Add-In

➤ Understand how to use a 32-Bit, Unicode-aware, Dynamic Link Library (DLL) in your Visual Basic 4 programs

➤ Acquire the information that helps you build a 32-Bit, Unicode-aware, Dynamic Link Library (DLL) when you decide to use Visual C++

Visual Basic 4 supports building OLE Automation servers. That means you can design and program OLE objects that provide various services. OLE Automation servers are very powerful, and they let you become a provider of services to any application (and OLE Automation server) that operates as an OLE Automation controller, including Visual Basic 4.

Working in the 32-bit Environment

The fundamental rules and regulations of the 32-bit world are defined in the Win32 Application Programming Interface (API). First and foremost, Win32 is a 32-bit API. Nevertheless, there also is an OLE API, and the two must work together. With a few exceptions, most of your work does not directly require explicit use of Win32 API and OLE API functions. However, if you are doing international application designing and programming, your work involves Unicode; while Unicode is a fundamental part of both the Win32 and OLE APIs, Windows 95 and Visual Basic 4 do not fully support Unicode. Only Windows NT fully supports Unicode, and learning all the Windows 95 and Visual Basic 4 exceptions to the general rules involving Unicode, the Win32 API, and the OLE API is not a trivial endeavor.

Note: Historically, Unicode is nothing new—at least insofar as being the name for a code. As early as 1886, telegraphers were using a special code in which one word represented an entire phrase or sentence. That code was called Unicode. In more recent times (1988), Apple and Xerox set the foundation for a new incarnation of Unicode. A few years later, everyone in the industry joined the Unicode party and began developing precise definitions and rules. Today, over 100 years after the first Unicode message was delivered, Unicode has been transformed (perhaps,

continues

continued

reinvented) into a special, two-byte character set that Microsoft and other companies promote as the standard for storing character data. The Unicode standard is the work of many companies, and Microsoft is one of the leaders.

The primary reason for Unicode is that many languages have more characters and symbols than can be fully expressed in the one-byte (ANSI) character set. The general idea is that everyone is supposed to begin using Unicode for Windows work; while that is a wonderful idea, moving to the Unicode standard will take time because it is not so easy to abandon the ANSI standard. In the US, most legacy code and nearly all data involves the ANSI standard. Visual Basic 4 supports Unicode internally, but externally Visual Basic 4 makes an effort to convert everything to ANSI. In fact, if you want to use Unicode externally with Visual Basic 4, extra work is required.

For all practical purposes, Visual Basic 4 is ANSI-based, though Visual Basic 4 does use Unicode strings internally, which means that you can view Visual Basic 4 as a framework that moderately tolerates Unicode work. The standard Visual Basic controls are not Unicode-aware. However, an OLE Control can provide Unicode services, so the burden falls on the shoulders of third-party vendors. In fact, an OLE Control should provide Unicode services. If so, Visual Basic 4 is fully capable of joining the Unicode party.

In the arena of working with a 32-bit, Unicode-aware, Win32 Dynamic Link Library (DLL), things are not so pleasant when your application programming language is Visual Basic 4. The reason is that Visual Basic 4 arbitrarily performs a Unicode-to-ANSI conversion when you use a string as a parameter in a DLL function call. Additionally, if the DLL function sends a Unicode string back to its Visual Basic 4 caller, Visual Basic 4 quite arbitrarily performs another Unicode-to-ANSI conversion, followed by putting that converted ANSI string right back into a Unicode string. In other words, it certainly appears that Visual Basic 4 simply wants nothing to do with Unicode—even though it uses Unicode internally for strings.

Of course, there are several techniques that provide adequate workarounds for that particular bit of nonsense, and one of them requires copying Visual Basic strings to a new kind of data type array: the `Byte` array.

Another strategy involves using a special kind of function information file called a `typelib`. If you have a `typelib` for your 32-bit, Unicode-aware DLL, Visual Basic 4 does not perform its arbitrary Unicode-to-ANSI and Unicode-to-ANSI-to-Unicode conversions. However, since Visual Basic for Applications (VBA) neither supports passing a user-defined type variable by reference nor supports using parameters defined `As Any`, if your 32-bit, Unicode-aware DLL requires either of those, you cannot use a `typelib` for the particular function. This restriction originates in the dual interface requirements of OLE (one of several types of interfaces that can be used), so the restriction exists because (a) VBA chose to provide a dual interface and (b) Visual Basic 4 is built around the VBA engine. Therefore, you are restricted to using the traditional, DLL declaration technique when you must use certain types of DLL functions; and, when that is the case, you must provide extra Visual Basic 4 code to ensure that you can both send and receive Unicode data correctly.

> **Note:** The extra code requirements necessary for a Visual Basic 4 application to work with a 32-bit, Unicode-aware DLL are explained in the "32-bit Dynamic Link Libraries" section of this chapter.

One of the most exciting, new features of Visual Basic is the ability to create a special kind of OLE Automation server that is loosely equivalent to a true, Win32 Dynamic Link Library (DLL)—something that is both easy and fun. The Visual Basic 4 technology for building what Microsoft calls an "OLE DLL" is mostly a matter of creative packaging.

The "OLE DLL" that Visual Basic 4 builds is conceptually similar to packaging a Visual Basic 4 application with the Visual Basic 4 runtime engine—all in one file. For those readers who have the 32-bit version of Visual C++, this chapter includes a simple example of a true, 32-bit, Unicode-aware DLL function. The 32-bit version of Visual C++ is both highly usable and totally unrestricted.

OLE Controls

In some respects, OLE Controls are similar to their Visual Basic Extension (VBX) counterparts, but the similarities are only casual. OLE Controls are much more, and they dramatically change the way applications work in Windows 95 and Windows NT. In that respect, OLE Controls are everything. They are the fundamental building blocks of Bill Gates' vision of "Information at Your Fingertips."

At the moment, most third-party vendors are rather overwhelmingly engaged in the development of 32-bit OLE Controls. Consequently, some of the advance information provided in this chapter is based on alpha and beta versions of OLE Controls from a few of my favorite companies. When a feature is mentioned, it is backed by a firm commitment given directly by the respective company president or product manager.

Note: The names and phone numbers for the following third-party control companies are listed at the end of the chapter in the "From Here" section.

FarPoint Technologies, Inc.

In the arena of Unicode-compliant OLE Controls, look to FarPoint Technologies, Inc. for spreadsheet, tab, button, and data-aware custom controls.

In addition to providing index card, file folder, and notebook style tab interfaces (some of which are shown in fig. 20.1), the Tab/Pro OLE Control is data-aware. Complete control is provided for all aspects of the visual appearance of the various styles of tabs. Text alignment, font, and rotation are controlled by properties. When working with the notebook style, properties control the number of rings, the size and appearance of rings, colors, animation of page flipping, and orientation. Tab/Pro is a 32-bit, Unicode-aware OLE Control, as are all the FarPoint OLE Controls for Visual Basic 4 (including Spread, Aware, and ButtonMaker).

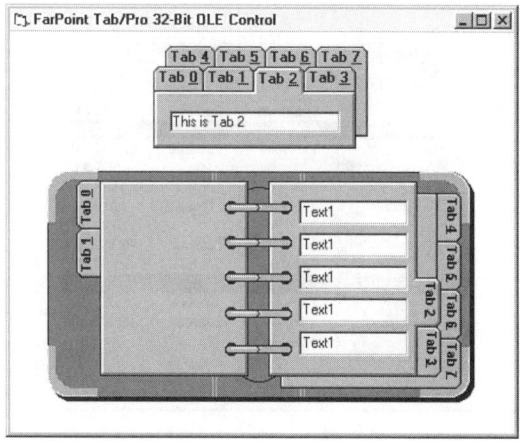

Fig. 20.1 This figure shows two of the many styles of the FarPoint Tab/Pro 32-bit OLE Control.

FarPoint's Spread control is an advanced control that is very easy to use with Visual Basic 4. The Spread OLE Control uses straightforward technologies that make it friendly to Visual Basic 4. Drag and drop, multiple block selection, user formulas, automatic calculations, calculate dependencies, clipboard support, various editing options, virtual mode, and a special designer tool are provided. This is a very usable OLE Control, yet it provides a wide range of advanced capabilities.

FarPoint also provides ANSI versions, 16-bit OLE Controls, and both 16-bit and 32-bit DLL implementations. When compatibility and portability are crucial, these are the OLE Controls and DLLs to use. At press time, FarPoint is the only third-party vendor that provides Unicode-aware, 32-bit OLE Controls for Visual Basic 4.

VideoSoft

Look to VideoSoft for both ANSI and DBCS-aware OLE Controls for spreadsheet, grid, pattern matching, index tab, resizing, parsing, print previewing, and printing custom controls. The VideoSoft product line for Visual Basic 4 includes VS/OCX, VSVIEW/OCX, and VSFLEX/OCX.

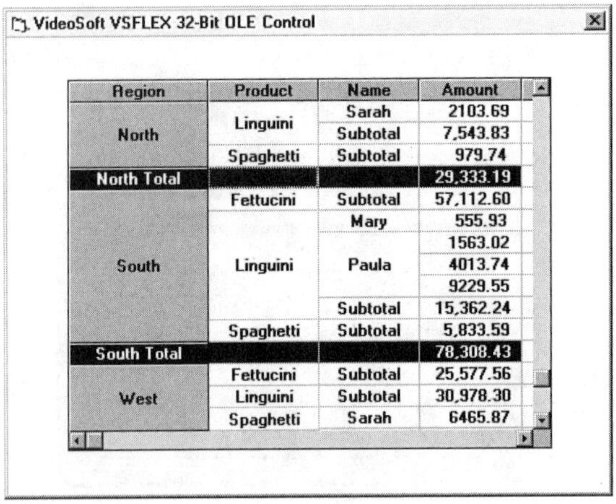

Fig. 20.2 This figure shows one of the many styles of the VideoSoft VSFLEX/OCX 32-bit OLE Control.

VSFLEX (see fig. 20.2) is an interesting, 32-bit OLE Control, because it includes special capabilities for doing SQL work. VideoSoft has developed a technique that separates the SELECT...FROM part of a SQL statement from the SORT BY and GROUP BY clauses. By doing this, sorting and grouping can be done locally by the VSFLEX OLE Control.

This technique makes the query faster, because the server has less work to do. Additionally, this technique gives the user greater flexibility in the different types of sorting and grouping of data. To change the sorting and grouping order, the user simply drags and drops columns and cells. VSFLEX automatically adjusts the sorting and grouping order.

In addition to the more traditional types of grid capabilities, VSFLEX provides `FlexString` pattern matching functions. `FlexString` uses the popular, regular expressions found in UNIX and is well suited to finding and replacing complex string patterns. It also is used for context-sensitive searches and data cleaning.

Sylvain Faust Inc. (SFI)

If you work with SYBASE SQL Server or Microsoft SQL Server, then Sylvain Faust Inc. (SFI) has unique products for doing a wide variety of SQL Server tasks. The SFI product line for Visual Basic 4 includes SQL-Sombrero/OCX for DB-Library, SQL-Sombrero/OCX for CT-Library, and CompressIT/OCX. For the Database Analyst (DBA) and SQL Server Systems Programmer, SFI offers its industry standard, back-end development tool, SQL-Programmer for Windows.

SQL-Sombrero/OCX for DB-Library, available in both 16- and 32-bit versions, contains all the DB-Library functionality and provides that functionality through five objects available with the SQL-Sombrero/OCX for DB-Library Automation component. It provides access to all the DB-Library Bulk Copy functions and is fully compatible with Microsoft SQL Server (including Microsoft SQL Server 6.0) and SYBASE SQL Server (including System 10).

A new version of SQL-Sombrero/OCX that will support WATCOM SQL Server is in development at press time. This version is very important, because it provides an OLE Control that makes the transition from SYBASE SQL Server to Watcom SQL Server very transparent to Visual Basic 4 programs. Sybase recently merged with Powersoft, and since Powersoft previously had purchased Watcom, the entire Sybase strategy now includes a clearly scalable path from standalone desktop systems using Watcom SQL Server to client/server systems using SYBASE SQL Server. Watcom SQL Server now supports Transact-SQL, and that support makes Watcom SQL Server a crucial product for corporate developers who must support multiple environments.

For the Visual Basic 4 Client/Server developer, SQL-Sombrero/OCX is an excellent and very affordable replacement for Microsoft's

VBSQL.VBX custom control. One of the primary advantages of SQL-Sombrero/OCX is that it is a 32-bit OLE Control that provides all the necessary functionality for Visual Basic 4 Client/Server development. Figures 20.3 through 20.5 show some typical forms that are used in database front-end programming.

Figure 20.3 shows how a data-entry form appears in Visual Basic 4 Design mode. Observe the SQL-Sombrero/OCX 32-bit OLE Control parked at the left side of the form.

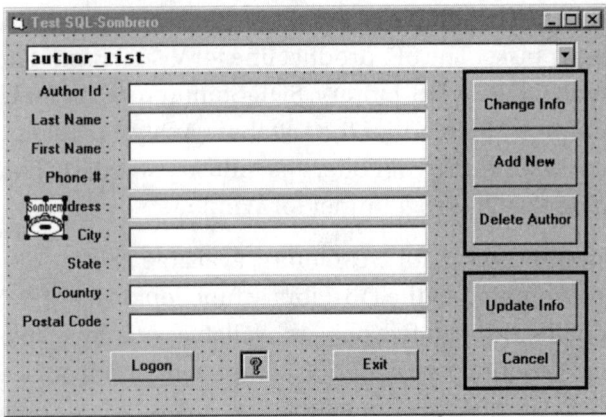

Fig. 20.3 The SQL-Sombrero/OCX 32-bit OLE Control is shown parked on a database form in Design mode.

Figure 20.4 shows a typical database logon form in Visual Basic 4 Run mode. The SQL-Sombrero/OCX 32-bit OLE Control provides all the necessary functions for connecting to a SQL Server database. SQL-Sombrero/OCX includes sample code for typical database forms and procedures.

Figure 20.5 shows the typical data-entry form (refer to fig. 20.3) in Visual Basic 4 Run mode. SQL-Sombrero/OCX provides all the necessary functions for retrieving and updating SQL Server data. If you need to work with large quantities of data, SQL-Sombrero/OCX also provides full support for DB-Library Bulk Copy operations. SFI is both a Microsoft Solution Provider and a SYBASE Open Solutions Partner, and SFI works closely with both major SQL Server vendors. These partnerships ensure that SFI products support the new versions of Microsoft and SYBASE databases and languages.

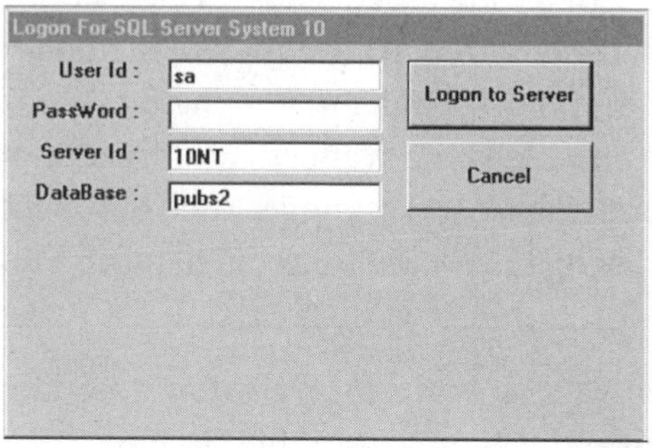

Fig. 20.4 This form is used to log into a SYBASE System 10 server.

One of the most exciting features of SQL-Sombrero/OCX is its ability to store and retrieve Binary Large Object (BLOB) data. Recognizing that working with BLOBs can be a rather complex endeavor, SFI has automated the process, making working with BLOBs an easy task. This functionality is especially useful for developers who need to archive and retrieve document images, multimedia clips, and other types of large data. Unicode data can be stored in BLOBs, even though SQL Server does not currently support Unicode.

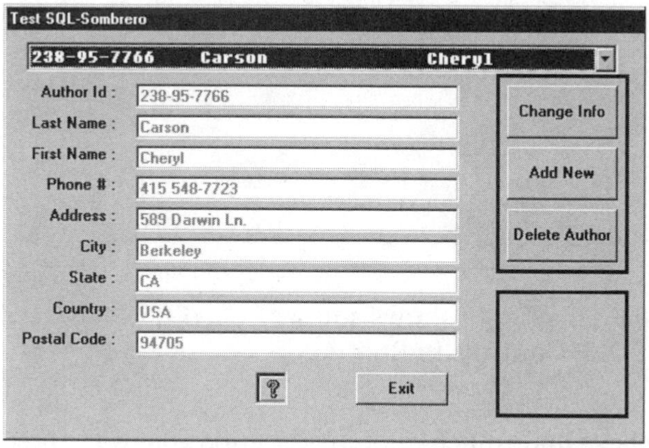

Fig. 20.5 The data retrieved from the PUBS database resides on a SYBASE System 10 server.

Lenel Systems International, Inc.

If you are doing multimedia development, look to Lenel Systems International, Inc. for a wide range of 32-bit OLE Controls for use with Visual Basic. Lenel's MediaDeveloper kit includes controls for playing animations, audio clips, images, and digital video clips. Additional controls are provided for advanced, multimedia-related memory management; for database tasks using a Microsoft Access database for storing and retrieving binary, multimedia data; and for video overlay tasks.

> **Note:** Figure 20.6 shows a form currently working with a PCX image of one of the figures from this chapter. The animation and digital video controls are inactive in this particular screen capture.

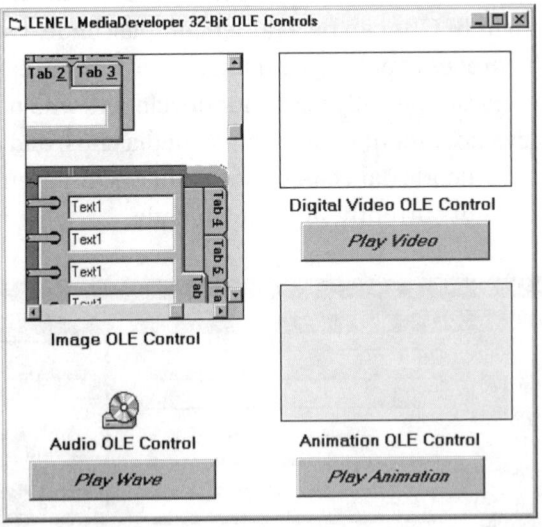

Fig. 20.6 This figure shows some of LENEL's MediaDeveloper 32-bit OLE Controls in Run mode.

If you have done much multimedia work, you will appreciate the advanced capabilities of the MediaDeveloper OLE Controls. The MediaDeveloper manual presumes you have a working knowledge of multimedia, so if you are just beginning your multimedia development work, you want to do a bit of general study before using the Media-Developer OLE Controls.

Nevertheless, once you understand the fundamentals of multimedia development, you will both appreciate and enjoy using the MediaDeveloper OLE Controls. They are advanced and sophisticated controls, and they provide a wide and flexible range of powerful, multimedia services. You can do all the things that Microsoft does in its Encarta product with these multimedia OLE Controls. When you need to do professional quality multimedia work, these are the multimedia controls to use. If you are new to multimedia work, LENEL's free technical support is a big help. The LENEL folks are experts in multimedia work, and their technical support is excellent.

MicroHelp, Inc.

MicroHelp is a leader in custom control collections, and its flagship product, VBTools, has become an industry standard. As Visual Basic 4 moves into the OLE Control arena, so does VBTools.

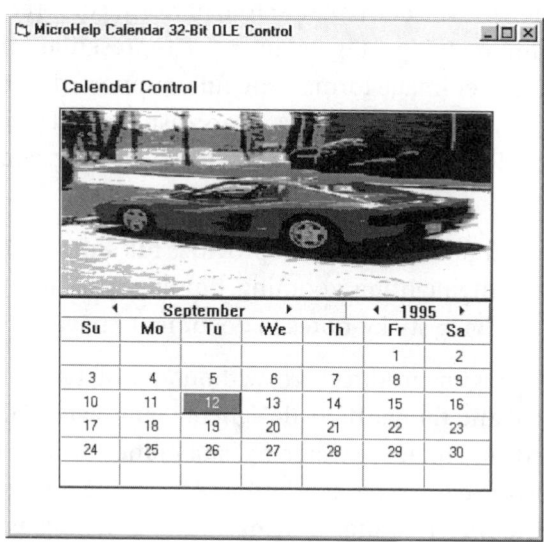

Fig. 20.7 This figure shows the MicroHelp Calendar 32-bit OLE Control.

The MicroHelp Calendar OLE Control provides a convenient way to get date-related information. Users can select a single date, a range of dates, and several individual dates. These capabilities are especially useful for applications that schedule things like conference rooms, equipment, deliveries, appointments, meetings, and so forth. The Calendar OLE Control is one of many controls that come with VBTools.

MicroHelp also provides custom controls and applications for use with communications, networks, word-processing (a spelling checker and a thesaurus), data encryption, fax processing, project management and cross-referencing, file and image viewing, reporting, and data compression. MicroHelp's Muscle provides a library of over 600 functions ranging from advanced string manipulation to system routines.

AccuSoft Corporation

For advanced imaging capabilities, look to AccuSoft Corporation. AccuSoft has a wide range of imaging toolkits, advanced compression technologies, and document-imaging tools.

The AccuSoft Imaging OLE Control provides functions that easily let you rotate, invert, zoom, pan, scroll, perform color reduction, and provide "thumbnails" (postage-stamp-size representations of images). Thirty-six faster image formats are fully supported, and you can import, export, convert, compress, scan, display, and print images. (See fig. 20.8 and 20.9 for examples of image displaying, zooming, and panning.)

The AccuSoft Redlining Toolkit provides full support for redlining, annotating, highlighting, zooming, flipping, scrolling, freehand drawing, and applying sticky-notes to document images.

AccuSoft imaging products are, without doubt, both impressively sophisticated and thoughtfully designed. Eight types of compression are supported, and image-processing capabilities include rotating, filtering, adjusting contrast and brightness, isolating points, converting bit depth, cropping, resizing, blurring, and sharpening. Full control of dither, palette, and color reduction is provided. The AccuSoft imaging products provide complete control over image-scanning hardware.

If it involves imaging, AccuSoft does it in a way that is very easy to program.

Fig. 20.8 An AccuSoft Imaging 32-bit OLE Control is shown displaying an image at its regular size.

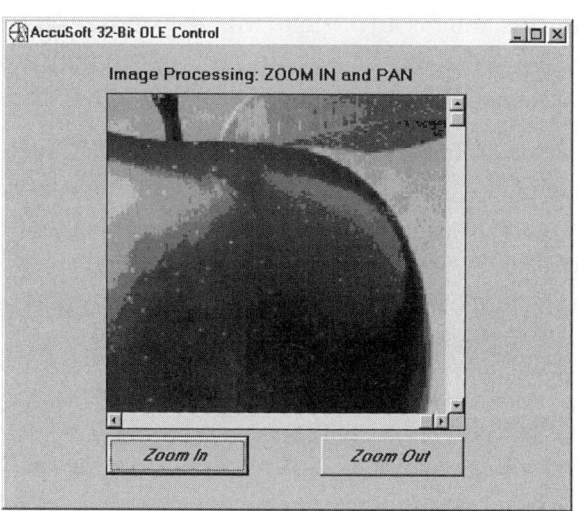

Fig. 20.9 An AccuSoft Imaging 32-bit OLE Control is shown displaying the image from figure 20.8 after being zoomed and panned.

OLE Automation Servers

There will be times when you will want to make some of your application's functionality and data available to other applications. In OLE terminology, this means that you want to expose some of your application so that other applications can use it.

When an OLE Control does something like that, the OLE Control must meet certain criteria. Of those criteria, the most important one is that the exposing be mutual. Some folks call this the "I will show mine, if you show yours" rule. In more practical terms, this rule means that Visual Basic can cause things to happen in the OLE Control and vice versa. It is a bi-directional connection, and some of what an OLE Control does is accomplished by using OLE Automation techniques.

However, OLE Automation does not have to be bi-directional, and in Visual Basic 4, that is the case when you build an OLE Automation server. While it would be convenient if your OLE Automation server could directly trigger events in Visual Basic 4, it cannot. What this means is that when you need to do everything, you must use a development product like Visual C++.

Nevertheless, much can be done with the kinds of OLE Automation servers that Visual Basic 4 creates. You can certainly provide a wide range of services in a unidirectional, OLE Automation server.

When you examine the Add-Ins menu above the Visual Basic 4 toolbar, you will find an Add-In Manager menu item. Add-ins are OLE Automation servers that you and other folks can design and program to do all kinds of useful work. For example, you can build an add-in to generate code using templates. One of the sample add-ins that comes with Visual Basic 4 generates data-aware forms. This new add-in technology is both exciting and puzzling.

This new technology is exciting because it obviously has possibilities and is puzzling because it is so abstrusely documented. In effect, you must deduce many of the expected behaviors. Nevertheless, if you have an abundance of patience and a creative imagination, you can find very useful ways to use your add-ins to automate much of your

Visual Basic 4 work. If you create an especially useful add-in, you can market it and (perhaps) become a millionaire. The opportunities are clearly present—provided you can find them.

Cloning Code

The general practice of cloning is nicely supported by most of the Windows and Visual Basic programming books you are likely to find at your local bookstore, including this book. Microsoft provides a wide range of sample code for Visual Basic 4, and the intent of that code is to make it easier and faster for you to become productive when you choose Visual Basic as your primary development language.

Note: Several years ago, during a discussion of the general fact that Charles Petzold, in one way or another, taught nearly every Windows programmer how to program Windows applications and Dynamic Link Libraries, one of my more astute programmer friends made the not-so-subtle observation that, "...for all practical purposes, after Charles Petzold wrote *Programming Windows*, no further, original Windows coding was ever done." While that is not literally true, it does have a ring of truth in the sense that Windows (and Visual Basic) programmers go to extraordinary lengths to avoid original programming. Put in more simple terms, folks usually clone as much code as possible.

The first rule of cloning is that you can only clone code for which you have permission to clone. Such permission is customarily stated in some reasonably obvious place—often in the code itself, or somewhere in the license that accompanies the code. You can clone your personal code, but if code is written under contract or during your work as an employee of some company, that code is likely considered proprietary, confidential, or a trade secret and as such is not something you can clone without permission from your client or employer. Code that is patented has additional restrictions.

Because the Visual Basic 4 add-in samples are moderately complex and most of their complexity has little to do with designing and programming an OLE Automation server, cloning code when building a very simple add-in is quite useful. Most folks begin with one of the sample add-ins, and then toss everything that is not pertinent. If you begin with the VisData add-in sample and do a bit of cloning and tossing, you can produce a very simple add-in that tells you a new Visual Basic 4 project consists of a grand total of one form. Admittedly, this is not the most useful add-in in the universe, but it provides a simple starting point for later departures that may lead to true utility. This chapter contains the code for a very simple add-in that can be used as a framework for your more sophisticated add-in development.

Understanding Classes

Before looking at the code, it is useful to observe that one of the new features of Visual Basic 4 involves something called a class module. If you are familiar with object-oriented programming, you recognize classes, and a class is what you get when you design and program a Class Module.

In Visual Basic 4, classes are object-based rather than object-oriented. There is no inheritance, no operator overloading, and no "quite a few other things." However, the "yes" list is very adequate, and classes are a very exciting aspect of Visual Basic 4.

> **Note:** Composition is supported in classes, along with recursively cascading instantiations of class objects. The former is good, and the latter is guaranteed to lock-up your machine. Mostly, the latter feature is a bit of object-based humor, and it is only amusing until you encounter it.

Just as OLE Controls and Automation servers expose their functionality (actions) and content (information), so do classes. In fact, you might say that OLE Controls and Automation servers are classes that have been transformed into executable entities. In that regard, it is useful to observe that classes are a bit intangible, whereas objects are very tangible.

An object is what you get when you instantiate an instance of a particular class and then materialize it. You might find it useful to visualize the process of instantiating and materializing an instance of a class—thereby producing an object—as akin to operating the teleporter on the Star Trek Enterprise. When you say, "Beam me aboard, Scotty!" and Scotty sends you a "two-by-four," that board is an instantiated and materialized instance of the class "Board" and is a tangible object.

In Visual Basic 4, classes have a grand total of four things: variables, events, properties, and methods. Internally, classes are derived from the same internal class from which forms are derived, so you will notice many similarities among classes and forms. The primary differences between classes and forms are that classes only have two events (`Initialize` and `Terminate`) and classes do not function as containers for visual objects. The latter difference simply means that you cannot put OLE Controls on a class because there really is no visual place to put them.

For all practical purposes, a form makes a nice alternative to a class. Over the long run, the distinction between classes, forms, and modules will probably diminish. Ultimately, everything will likely just be an object of one type or another. If you want the object to be a form, you might be able to set an `ObjectType` property or something similar. That is a very logical way to proceed, but it has not happened—yet.

> **Note:** The problem regarding "module" is that Microsoft originally called "places where you put non-form, procedural code" by the name "modules." Then, Microsoft decided to call the files "modules," regardless of whether they contained forms or procedures. Now, with VB4, Microsoft introduces a new kind of "module" file that happens to be the place where class stuff resides.
>
> *continues*

> *continued*
>
> Nevertheless, if you select Insert, Module from the menu, you get what VB programmers fully understand to be a "module." It is technical jargon, and it is very specific to VB.

The `Initialize` and `Terminate` events of a class correspond to the `Initialize` and `Terminate` events of a form. These are new events for Visual Basic 4, and there are very subtle distinctions among the states through which a class or form passes along the path to becoming fully materialized. Specifically, in the case of a form, simply referencing the form does not cause the form to be loaded (materialized)—it only causes the form to be instantiated. The same is true of a class, and it is very important that you avoid doing certain things in the `Initialize` event of a class. For this to make sense, you need to understand composition in classes.

Composition is the formal name for the general practice of building one class by using other classes in such a way that those other classes literally become part of the class you are building. In other words, you can build a new class in such a way that it is composed of one or more other classes. In fact, you can build a class that is composed of itself, and while that is fully supported, it must be done very carefully with respect to the `Initialize` event. This kind of composition is accomplished by defining an object variable of the particular class in the General Declarations section of the Class module, but that alone does not cause any particular problem. The problem occurs when you explicitly do something tangible with that object in the `Initialize` event of the class.

Creating an Instance of the Class

When you first begin creating an instance of the class, the `Initialize` event is triggered. If you then do something that explicitly references another object of the same class (an object that is present as a consequence of composition), that object must also be created. When the creation process begins, the `Initialize` event is again triggered and then everything recursively cascades to infinity.

At this point, examining the code for one of the classes of the Simple add-in proves useful (see Listing 20.1).

Listing 20.1   SIMPLE12.CLS—Source Code for the SimpleAddInClass Module

```
VERSION 1.0 CLASS
BEGIN
  MultiUse = -1   'True
END
Attribute VB_Name = "SimpleAddInClass"
Attribute VB_Creatable = True
Attribute VB_Exposed = True
Attribute VB_Description = "Simple Class (c) 1995, Que"
'-------------------------------------------------
' NOTE-> General Declarations Section...
'-------------------------------------------------
Dim objItems     As Object
Dim objSimple    As Object

Sub ConnectAddIn(ByVal VBInst As Object)
On Error GoTo jmpConnectAddInError
Dim lVal As Long
Dim objMenu    As Object
Dim objME      As Object
Set gobjClient = VBInst
Set objMenu = gobjClient.AddInMenu
Set objItems = objMenu.MenuItems
Set objSimple = objItems.Add("&Simple...")
Set objME = Me
lVal = objSimple.ConnectEvents(objME)
Exit Sub
jmpConnectAddInError:
   MsgBox Error$
   Exit Sub
End Sub

Sub DisconnectAddIn(ByVal mode As Integer)
On Error GoTo jmpDisconnectAddInError
objItems.Remove objSimple
Exit Sub
jmpDisconnectAddInError:
```

continues

Listing 20.1   Continued

```
      MsgBox Error$
      Exit Sub
End Sub

Sub AfterClick()
On Error GoTo jmpAfterClickError
Set objNew = CreateObject("Simple.SimpleClass")
objNew.SetAddInSimple gobjClient
Exit Sub
jmpAfterClickError:
    MsgBox Error$
    Exit Sub
End Sub
```

This particular class, SIMPLE12.CLS, does not use self-composition, but if it did, the following line of code would need to be included in the General Declarations section:

```
Dim objSimpleClass    As New SimpleAddInClass
```

If this object definition is added to the General Declarations section of SIMPLE12.CLS, what happens is that an object of the same class is added to the class by self-composition. In other words, the SimpleAddInClass class contains itself. Were it not for the fact that Visual Basic rather astutely separates instantiating an object from materializing the same object, adding the aforementioned self-composition definition to the class would introduce recursion. However, Visual Basic 4 eliminates the immediate introduction of the problem simply by postponing the materialization of the objSimpleClass object until the moment when the objSimpleClass object is actually used in a non-definitional code statement.

As you examine Listing 20.1, observe that no mention whatsoever is made of the Initialize and Terminate events. The explanation is simple: there is no explicit code for those events in the class; consequently, Visual Basic 4 does not include them in the source code file for the class.

In contrast, Listing 20.2 shows how SIMPLE12.CLS might look if recursively cascading, self-composition were present:

Listing 20.2   SIMPLE12.CLS—When Recursively Cascading, Self-Composition Is Present

```
VERSION 1.0 CLASS
BEGIN
  MultiUse = -1   'True
END
Attribute VB_Name = "SimpleAddInClass"
Attribute VB_Creatable = True
Attribute VB_Exposed = True
Attribute VB_Description = "Simple Class (c) 1995, Que"
'---------------------------------------------------
' NOTE-> General Declarations Section...
'---------------------------------------------------
Dim objItems       As Object
Dim objSimple      As Object
'---------------------------------------------------
' NOTE-> self-composition definition
'---------------------------------------------------
Dim objSimpleClass As New SimpleAddInClass

Sub ConnectAddIn(ByVal VBInst As Object)
On Error GoTo jmpConnectAddInError
Dim lVal As Long
Dim objMenu    As Object
Dim objME      As Object
Set gobjClient = VBInst
Set objMenu = gobjClient.AddInMenu
Set objItems = objMenu.MenuItems
Set objSimple = objItems.Add("&Simple...")
Set objME = Me
lVal = objSimple.ConnectEvents(objME)
Exit Sub
jmpConnectAddInError:
   MsgBox Error$
   Exit Sub
End Sub
Property Get Materialize() As String
Materialize = "Cascading"
End Property
Sub DisconnectAddIn(ByVal mode As Integer)
On Error GoTo jmpDisconnectAddInError
objItems.Remove objSimple
Exit Sub
jmpDisconnectAddInError:
   MsgBox Error$
   Exit Sub
End Sub
```

continues

Listing 20.2 Continued

```
Sub AfterClick()
On Error GoTo jmpAfterClickError
Set objNew = CreateObject("Simple.SimpleClass")
objNew.SetAddInSimple gobjClient
Exit Sub
jmpAfterClickError:
   MsgBox Error$
   Exit Sub
End Sub
Private Sub Class_Initialize()
Dim sRecursive As String
'------------------------------------------------
' NOTE-> explicitly using objSimpleClass in the
'        Initialize event triggers recursively
'        cascading self-composition
'------------------------------------------------
sRecursive = objSimpleClass.Materialize
End Sub
```

In Listing 20.2, note that there is code for the Initialize event. There also is code for a Property Get procedure called Materialize. There are three types of Property procedures: Property Let, Property Set, and Property Get. These various types of Property procedures make it possible for your class to expose properties in much the same way that OLE Controls expose their properties. In this particular example of a Property Get, what happens is that the procedure simply returns a value for the property (in this case, the string "Cascading").

However, you are not restricted only to sending and receiving property values. A Property procedure can do other types of work; and, in some cases, it may just perform some action—without needing to return a specific property value. This ability is especially useful when you need to do work but do not want the user of your class to know precisely what that work involves. By hiding the work in a Property procedure, you are doing what is formally called implementation hiding. Insofar as the user of your class is concerned, something simply happens.

For example, the user of your class sets a property value to True and a spreadsheet is recalculated. The user does not know how the recalculation work was done internally—externally, the spreadsheet is presented with recalculated values. In this example, the actual code that performs the recalculation may contain proprietary algorithms about which the user of the class need not know. This is often done to protect trade secrets and proprietary algorithms.

In both listings, you will find three subroutines of particular interest: `ConnectAddIn`, `DisconnectAddIn`, and `AfterClick`. These are the methods of the `SimpleAddInClass` class, and they are used to perform the various actions that are necessary when the add-in is used in the Visual Basic 4 Integrated Development Environment (IDE). As previously mentioned, `Property` procedures can also be used to perform actions, but those actions are hidden from the user of the class. For example, if you did not want the user of a class to know about some method, you could make the method `Private` and then invoke it inside a `Property` procedure. In that example, the user would only know that setting the particular property caused something to happen—the user would not know that the hidden method was used to do the work.

Potential Recursion Problem Introduced by Self-Composition

When you want to force a series of recursively cascading `Initialize` events, one way is to use the self-composition object variable in some expression in the `Initialize` event, and using it to reference the `Materialize` property is more than sufficient.

> **Note:** In this discussion, "self-composition object variable" usually refers specifically to the object variable, `objSimpleClass`, that is defined in the `General Declarations Section` of the class module. It may also be used in a more general sense. In any case, there is no "self-composition" data type or keyword in Visual Basic 4, so remember that "self-composition" is just an arbitrary name used in the discussion.

What happens is that referencing the property causes the object variable to materialize. Since it must be instantiated before it is materialized, the `Initialize` event of the object's class is triggered. In this particular case, that `Initialize` event is the one for the class whose `Initialize` event is already active for another object of the class, so it requires yet another `Initialize` event. Remember that the first `Initialize` event has not finished at this time.

Now, there are two `Initialize` events in progress, and just as soon as the property assignment statement is encountered in the second `Initialize` event, still another `Initialize` event is triggered, and in a short while, there are many such `Initialize` events. Eventually, the Simple add-in overloads the system with `Initialize` events, and the most likely result is that your Windows session comes to a screeching halt.

Caution: Be sure to save your work and close all other applications before attempting this experiment. It will probably lock-up your current Windows 95 session, and you will need to reboot your machine. Neither Visual Basic 4 nor Windows 95 will recover gracefully from this experiment. You should not need to reinstall Visual Basic 4 or Windows 95 after performing this experiment, but if you are unwilling to accept that risk, then do not perform this experiment. Recursively cascading self-composition forces Visual Basic 4 and Windows 95 to do things that are very unpredictable and potentially damaging. Neither Visual Basic 4 nor Windows 95 were designed to run this type of code.

While self-composition makes a good example case, it is not the only case where the cascading problem occurs. The problem also occurs when you have several classes that use composition. For example, if Class A is composed of Class B; Class B is composed of Class C, and Class C is composed of Class A, then you must be careful when you reference any of those objects in the `Initialize` events because Class A can trigger Class B, Class B can trigger Class C, and Class C can trigger Class A; then it all becomes recursive. This is just a variation of the more general cascading problem that often occurs when code in an event of one control triggers an event in a second control that, in turn, triggers the original event in the first control. Diagramming your class design helps identify troublesome compositions and references, and since forms and classes are based on the same internal class, it is reasonable to presume that your form and control development skills will serve you well when adapted to class designing and programming.

Examining the Module File

The next thing to examine is the module file that acts as a helper for SIMPLE12.CLS. It might appear that classes eliminate the need for modules, but that is not the case. There are some things that cannot be done in a class, one of which is providing global variables. That is what SIMPLE11.BAS does.

```
Attribute VB_Name = "SimpleModule"
Global gobjClient As Object
Sub Main()
End Sub
```

When building an add-in, there are two, separate requirements. The first requirement is an OLE Automation server that Visual Basic 4 can use to start the application that does the real work for your add-in. In this particular example, SERVER11.BAS and SERVER12.CLS provide that part of the add-in service. When built into an OLE Automation server, that component is what Visual Basic 4 uses to get things started.

Setting Project Options

After programming the class and module for the `SimpleAddIn` Automation server, the next step is to set the appropriate project options for the OLE Automation server. To do that, choose Tools, Options. Once the Options dialog box appears, select the Project tab and set the various fields as shown in figure 20.10.

Notice that the OLE Server option is selected. Most importantly, the Compatible OLE Server field is blank. The first time you make an OLE Automation server, there is no compatible OLE Automation server. Behind the scenes, a lot of work is being done, and it is very important that all your add-in names match precisely. Everything matters—class names, project name, property names, method names, menu item name, application description, and member name description. Each one of those names plays an important role in your add-in.

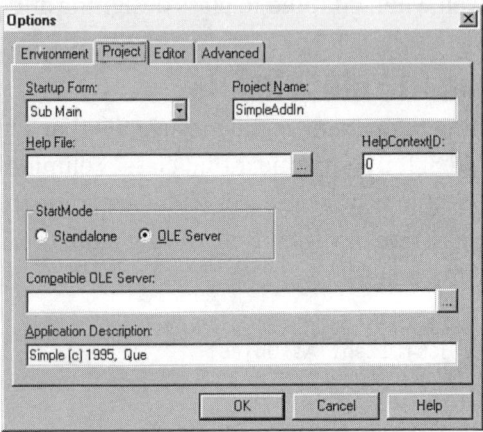

Fig. 20.10 The Project page is shown with the correct settings for the first-time make of an OLE Automation server.

At some point, your OLE Automation server will be registered in the system registry, and the names you specify throughout your project are used to identify your OLE Automation server in the system registry. In addition, Visual Basic 4 creates a Globally Unique Identifier (GUID) for your OLE Automation server.

All of the names are important, and they are almost randomly scattered throughout the code, class properties, project options, and one other place: Member Options. If you look in the Add-Ins Manager dialog box, you will see a description for each add-in, and those descriptions are set via the Object Browser's Options dialog box. However, you should not set a description for everything. Once you have provided a description for your add-in's primary class (the only class in this particular example), you can make your project (see fig. 20.11 and 20.12). For this example, choose to make an EXE by selecting the Make EXE option from the File menu. To get to the Add-Ins Manager dialog box, click on the Add-Ins Manager menu item found in the Add-Ins menu. To get to the Object Browser dialog box, click on the Object Browser menu item found in the View menu. Once the Object Browser dialog box appears, click Options and the Member Options dialog box appears.

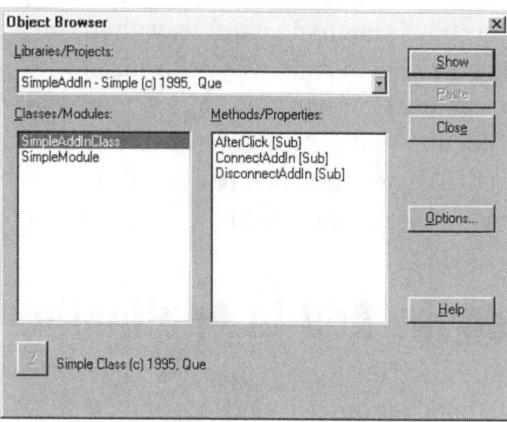

Fig. 20.11 The Object Browser dialog box shows the various member components of your Automation server.

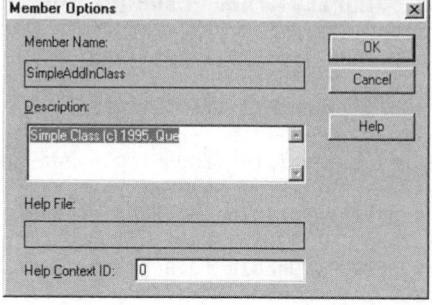

Fig. 20.12 The Member Options dialog box shows the settings for the Description of your OLE Automation server's class.

When you have finished with the first make, revisit the Project page in the Options dialog box and set the Compatible OLE Server field to the

OLE Automation server you just created. Then remake the OLE Automation server. This lets Visual Basic perform reference checks to ensure that later versions of your Automation server remain compatible with earlier versions. It also lets you continue to use the same GUID, and if you are making frequent changes to your OLE Automation server, using the same GUID makes your system registry work much easier. If you choose not to do it this way, then you waste considerable time keeping the system registry synchronized with your current, development version. However, it is important to understand that Visual Basic does not automatically register your OLE Automation server. It does the GUID generation and revision validation, but the registry work is something you must do in the second part of your add-in.

Building the Add-In Application

At this point, half of the work is finished. The next step is to build an application that does the real work of your add-in. Since the Simple add-in needs to display data about your project, it needs a form, and part of the code for that form is shown in Listing 20.3.

Listing 20.3   SIMPLE01.FRM—Excerpts from the frmSimple Form

```
Private Sub mnuFileItems_Click(Index As Integer)
Dim vRetVal As Variant
On Error GoTo jmpmnuFileItemsClickError
'------------------------------------------------
' NOTE-> try to register the Simple add-in stub
'------------------------------------------------
vRetVal = Shell(App.Path & "\Simple" & ".exe /regserver")
If (Err) Then
   MsgBox "ERROR: Unable to Register Simple.EXE", 48
   Exit Sub
End If
'------------------------------------------------
' NOTE-> try to register Simple
'------------------------------------------------
vRetVal = Shell(App.Path & "\" & App.EXEName & _
      ".EXE /regserver")
If (Err) Then
   MsgBox "You must run this from an EXE!", 48
   Exit Sub
End If
```

```
'--------------------------------------------------
' NOTE-> only add it if the registration was successful
'--------------------------------------------------
vRetVal = OSWritePrivateProfileString("Add-Ins32", _
    "SimpleAddIn. SimpleAddInClass", "1", "VB.INI")
frmSimple.mnuFileItems(0).Enabled = False
Exit Sub
jmpmnuFileItemsClickError:
    Resume Next
End Sub

Private Sub pbtExit_Click()
Unload frmSimple
Set frmSimple = Nothing
End
End Sub

Private Sub pbtList_Click()
If (gobjSimpleList Is Nothing) Then
    Set gobjSimpleList = New SimpleList
End If
gobjSimpleList.ListSimple
End Sub
```

For the most part, this form consists of one menu, one menu item, one list box, and two command buttons. Since you need to register your add-in (so that Visual Basic 4 knows it exists), there is special code to register the add-in. This code is run by choosing File, Make Add-In. You must do this when the application is running as an EXE—you cannot do it from Visual Basic 4 Run mode. Remember that you only need to do this one time. After that, the File menu is disabled.

Making the Add-In Available

Two things are necessary to make your Add-In available for use by Visual Basic:

1. The add-in must be registered in the system registry.

2. The add-in must be identified in your VB.INI file.

Both actions are performed in the `Click` event of the Make Add-In menu item. After you have done the first-time registering, the Simple add-in appears in the <u>A</u>dd-Ins menu the next time you start a Visual Basic session.

The class modules code is shown in Listings 20.4 and 20.5.

Listing 20.4 SIMPLE01.CLS—The Source Code for the SimpleClass Module

```
VERSION 1.0 CLASS
BEGIN
  MultiUse = -1  'True
END
Attribute VB_Name = "SimpleClass"
Attribute VB_Creatable = True
Attribute VB_Exposed = True

Sub SetAddInSimple(ByVal objClient As Object)
'---------------------------------------------------
' NOTE-> this method is used as a call from the
'        add-in stub Simple.EXE
'---------------------------------------------------
On Error GoTo jmpSetAddInSimpleError
'---------------------------------------------------
' NOTE-> this sets the VB instance handle...
'---------------------------------------------------
Set gobjClient = objClient
'---------------------------------------------------
' NOTE-> (1) Simple is ALREADY an ADD-IN...
'        (2) DISALLOW add-in creation...
'---------------------------------------------------
frmSimple.mnuFileItems(0).Enabled = False
frmSimple.WindowState = vbNormal
Exit Sub
jmpSetAddInSimpleError:
  MsgBox Error$
  Exit Sub
End Sub

Sub CloseSimple()
'---------------------------------------------------
' NOTE-> this method closes Simple...
'---------------------------------------------------
sbrCloseSimple
End Sub
```

When this application is running as an add-in, choosing the List command button causes the application to do some class work that gets information about your current project and displays it in the list box.

Listing 20.5   SIMPLELIST.CLS—The Source Code for the SimpleList Class Module

```
VERSION 1.0 CLASS
BEGIN
  MultiUse = -1   'True
END
Attribute VB_Name = "SimpleList"
Attribute VB_Creatable = False
Attribute VB_Exposed = False

Public Sub ListSimple()
Dim vComponent As Variant
Dim objClient   As Object
Dim objCollect As Object
Dim nItem%
Dim nCount%
On Error GoTo jmpListSimpleError
frmSimple.lbxItems.Clear
Set objClient = gobjClient
Set objCollect = objClient.ActiveProject.Components
For Each vComponent In objCollect
   nCount% = vComponent.FileCount - 1
   For nItem% = 0 To nCount%
      frmSimple.lbxItems.AddItem vComponent.FileNames(nItem%)
   Next nItem%
Next
Exit Sub
jmpListSimpleError:
   Resume Next
End Sub
```

The procedure module code is shown in Listing 20.6.

Listing 20.6   SIMPLE01.BAS—The Source Code for modSimple01 Procedure Module

```
Attribute VB_Name = "modSimple01"
Global gobjClient      As Object
Global gobjSimpleList As Object
Declare Function OSGetPrivateProfileString% Lib _
```

continues

OLE Automation Servers   **799**

Listing 20.6   Continued

```
        "Kernel32" Alias "GetPrivateProfileStringA" _
        (ByVal AppName$, ByVal KeyName$, ByVal _
        keydefault$, ByVal ReturnString$, ByVal _
        NumBytes As Integer, ByVal FileName$)
    Declare Function OSWritePrivateProfileString% Lib _
        "Kernel32"
        åalias "WritePrivateProfileStringA" (ByVal _
        AppName$, ByVal KeyName$, åByVal keydefault$, _
        ByVal FileName$)
    Declare Function OSGetWindowsDirectory% Lib "Kernel32" _
        Alias "GetWindowsDirectoryA" (ByVal a$, ByVal b%)
    Sub sbrCloseSimple()
    Unload frmSimple
    Set frmSimple = Nothing
    End Sub
```

As figure 20.13 shows, the Simple add-in does not provide a tremendous amount of useful information, but it gives you a starting point for your add-in development work. Once you become familiar with the structure and syntax of the source code files that Visual Basic 4 creates for classes, forms, and modules, you can write code that automatically generates templates that can be added to the project via your "Not So Simple" add-in. It may prove quite useful to have a library of source code procedures, variable names, comments, and so forth, and if you keep them in a local Microsoft Access database, your "Not At All Simple" add-in can be used to search and copy algorithms, descriptions, and so forth into the Clipboard. Once in the Clipboard, you can paste the contents into whichever class, form, or module you desire. You can also generate complete forms and save them as files.

For all practical purposes, your add-in lets you customize Visual Basic 4 in all sorts of ways. Some of the IDE can be accessed from an add-in, but not so much as you would like. There are limitations on the things you can instruct the IDE to do, but if you encounter a limitation, remember that you can work outside the IDE. Essentially, your add-in is an application that can do just about anything that can be done in Windows 95 or Windows NT. Some of that work may be very complex, but it is certainly both possible and practical to do. If you are an entrepreneur and have been looking for new opportunities that synergize your Visual Basic 4 designing and programming skills, then add-in development is a brand-new field. If you look at Visual Basic 4 and find yourself thinking, "I wish it could...," then it probably can if you design and program an add-in that does.

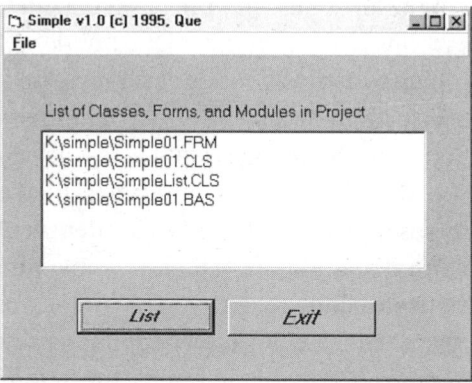

Fig. 20.13 The Simple application is shown running as an add-in in Visual Basic 4 Design mode's Integrated Development Environment (IDE).

32-bit Dynamic Link Libraries

Since Windows 95 and Windows NT provide different implementations of the Win32 API, and since both operating systems are intimately connected with both OLE and Unicode, there are some rather unusual cases that Visual Basic 4 must handle. These cases exist because Visual Basic 4 must run in both Windows 95 and Windows NT, and the way Unicode is handled in the two operating systems is very different. Specifically, Windows 95 does not implement all of the Unicode versions of the Win32 API, and Windows 95 mostly views the world with ANSI eyes. In contrast, Windows NT fully supports Unicode.

The manner in which Visual Basic 4 handles the "Unicode versus ANSI" problem is to choose the lowest common denominator (ANSI) most of the time. In a rather convoluted attempt to protect you from the "Unicode versus ANSI" problem, Visual Basic 4 will very arbitrarily perform certain conversions that garble Unicode strings. However, there are ways to avoid the string garbling.

Another problem involves the way that structures are aligned in a 32-Bit Win32 Dynamic Link Library (DLL). There is a wide range of alignment options for 32-bit DLLs, and the particular alignment is entirely subject to the whims of the particular DLL builder. The DLL builder can choose to align to 1-byte boundaries, 2-byte boundaries, 4-byte boundaries, 8-byte boundaries, or 16-byte boundaries. Recognizing that this might be a problem for Visual Basic 4 developers who must use 32-bit DLLs, Microsoft chose arbitrarily to align all Visual Basic 4 user-defined types (the Visual Basic 4 equivalents of Visual C++ structures) to the natural boundaries of their member items. This alignment is done automatically, and you have no say in the matter. The problem occurs when the 32-bit DLL does not happen to provide the same kind of natural alignment. When that happens, the 32-bit DLL will not recognize the layout of the structure, and your data will (for all practical purposes) be garbled. However, there are ways to avoid the structure garbling.

> **Note:** In fact, the combination of string garbling and structure garbling is rather puzzling, in the sense that one must wonder, "Why was it done this way?" It makes a wonderful topic for this chapter, and providing solutions that solve the problems will make your Visual Basic 4 work considerably easier. The bad news is that the problems clearly exist, but the good news is that there are workaround solutions. This is not a show-stopper—rather, it is a hassle that should never have been allowed to happen. In attempting to make your Visual Basic 4 development work easier, Microsoft has made it more difficult.

The following sections will provide information that will contribute greatly to your overall happiness when you work with Visual Basic 4.

Garbling Unicode

Internally, Visual Basic 4 fully supports Unicode, but externally it is a different matter. The Unicode support ranges from none to some—depending on the particular manner in which work is done. There are simple, clearly defined rules, but there are so many of them that, when combined, they become rather complex.

The general rule is that Visual Basic is Unicode on the inside but ANSI on the outside. However, even that rule has several, major exceptions. 32-bit OLE Controls follow (or should follow) the Unicode standard, and when acting as the dumb framework for 32-bit, Unicode-aware OLE Controls, Visual Basic 4 does not interfere. Similarly, if a 32-bit, Unicode-aware DLL function is used via a `typelib` declaration, Visual Basic 4 does not interfere. However, a `typelib` declaration cannot be used for a 32-bit, Unicode-aware DLL function that requires an `As Any` parameter or requires a user-defined type variable passed by reference. (These latter restrictions are imposed by OLE.)

Additionally, even though Visual Basic 4 automatically converts strings from Unicode to ANSI when calling a DLL function that is not declared using a `typelib`, it does not perform that arbitrary conversion when the string is copied into a `Byte` array. It is important to remember that both individual strings and string items in a user-defined type are converted. If it is a string, it is converted when the declaration is not found in a `typelib`.

The automatic string conversion also occurs when the regularly declared (not using a `typelib`) DLL function sends string data back to Visual Basic 4, and in this case, the automatic conversion is even more bizarre because Visual Basic 4 first converts each byte of the Unicode string to an ANSI character (one byte) and then converts each of those ANSI characters (one byte each) into Unicode characters (two bytes each). The result of this arbitrary Unicode-to-ANSI-to-Unicode conversion is a garbled string.

If you need to send or receive a Unicode string in your Visual Basic program, and if you need to send or receive that Unicode string to or from a 32-bit, Unicode-aware DLL, using a Visual Basic `String` data type variable is not going to work when the DLL function is declared using a regular (non-`typelib`) declaration. Instead of using a `String` data type variable, you need to use a `Byte` data type array.

Aligning User-Defined Types

Visual Basic 4 performs a natural alignment operation on the items in user-defined types. The general idea is that each data type must begin on its natural boundary. For example, an `Integer` is a two-byte data type in Visual Basic 4 and is aligned to a two-byte boundary. A `Byte` is a one-byte data type in Visual Basic 4 and is aligned to a one-byte boundary. If the first item in a user-defined type is (1) a `Byte` and the second item in that user-defined type is (2) an `Integer`, then Visual Basic 4 arbitrarily adds an extra, padding byte following the `Byte` item—thereby causing the `Integer` item to begin on a two-byte boundary.

Since this conversion of user-defined types is done, you must carefully consider the consequences, because Visual Basic 4 pads your user-defined types when it is necessary for natural alignment. For practical purposes, Visual Basic 4 considers it necessary when you use a user-defined type variable or array in a DLL function call, but when you are using the user-defined type variable or array in `Get` and `Put` statements, Visual Basic 4 does not consider the padding necessary and does not interfere.

The following examples help illustrate this concept. In the following examples each single character occupies one byte of storage: B represents a `Byte` data type, I represents an `Integer` data type, L represents a `Long` data type, and P represents a padding byte. Bytes are arranged in groups of two, with spaces provided for clarity, and byte numbers appear above the bytes.

EXAMPLE 1: Consider the following Visual Basic user-defined type:

```
Type udvBIL
  bByte    As Byte
  nInteger As Integer
  lLong    As Long
End Type
```

Since the items in this user-defined type are not naturally aligned, Visual Basic 4 will naturally align them:

01 23 45 67

BP II LL LL

The result of this arbitrary alignment is that Visual Basic 4 has introduced an extra padding byte into the structure. The problem this causes happens when you send this structure to a 32-Bit DLL function that is not expecting the extra padding byte.

EXAMPLE 2: Consider the following Visual Basic user-defined type:

```
Type udvIBL
nInteger As Integer
bByte    As Byte
lLong    As Long
End Type
```

Since the items in this user-defined type are not naturally aligned, Visual Basic 4 will naturally align them: II BP LL LL.

EXAMPLE 3: Consider the following Visual Basic user-defined type:

```
Type udvLBI
lLong    As Long
bByte    As Byte
nInteger As Integer
End Type
```

Since the items in this user-defined type are not naturally aligned, Visual Basic 4 will naturally align them: LL LL BP II.

EXAMPLE 4: Consider the following Visual Basic user-defined type:

```
Type udvBIL
lLong    As Long
nInteger As Integer
bByte    As Byte
End Type
```

Since the items in this user-defined type are naturally aligned, Visual Basic 4 will not interfere: LL LL II B.

Of all the user-defined types in the above examples, only the fourth one is not arbitrarily padded because it already follows the natural alignment of each item. If you are designing and programming your DLL functions for use with Visual Basic 4, you want to observe natural alignment rules.

If you cannot observe natural alignment rules, then there are two useful solutions:

> The first solution uses the "`Byte-Array`" technique, and it involves moving your data entirely to a `Byte` array. Since a `Byte` array is always naturally aligned, Visual Basic 4 will not interfere.

> The second solution involves designing and programming a special, DLL function (called an agent) that acts as a translator between Visual Basic 4 and the actual DLL function you really need to call. In this case, the agent function will do all of the other DLL function calling and communicating, and it will then package whatever data is involved in such a way that Visual Basic 4 does not feel compelled to garble it. This technique requires you to be proficient in both Visual Basic 4 and Visual C++ (or some other language that can build a true 32-Bit DLL—one that lets the builder do everything necessary to make both Visual Basic 4 and the target DLL function speak the same language).

Note: Also, you want to observe another very important rule: In Visual C++ 2.0 (and higher), an integer (in Visual C++, the data type is named `int`) is defined to be four bytes. So if your DLL function has an `int` parameter, your Visual Basic 4 caller needs to use a `Long` data type for that parameter. This also applies to items within a user-defined type (UDT) and to arrays.

Building a Unicode-Aware DLL in Visual C++

If you happen to have Visual C++ 2.0 (or higher), the following code and figures 20.14 through 20.16 enable you to build a simple, 32-bit,

Unicode-aware DLL that sends an astute observation to your Visual Basic 4 program.

Note: If you have read the various documentation that comes with Visual Basic 4, you found that this particular DLL uses different techniques from the ones recommended in the Visual Basic 4 documentation and knowledge base articles. The information provided in this section is intended for use by proficient Visual C++ programmers. Some explanations of the various techniqes are provided, but the overall purpose is to provide a quick overview of the information. If you have no interest in Visual C++, then you may skip this section. The code examples require Visual C++.

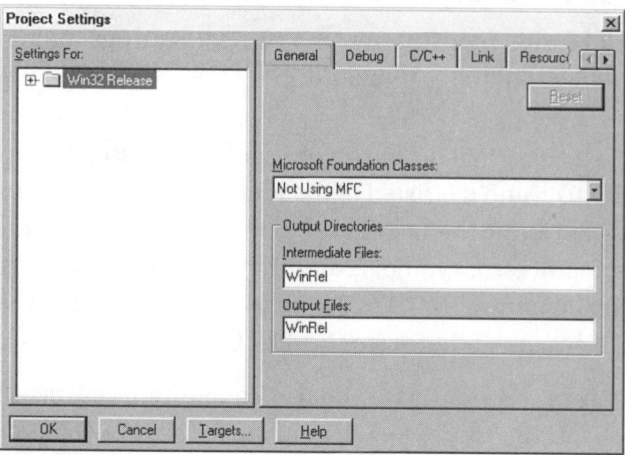

Fig. 20.14 This is the Project Settings dialog box's General page for SDLL32.MAK.

The first thing you need to do when starting a new Visual C++ project is to set the various project options. There are a wide range of options for each aspect of the language, the compiler, the preprocessor, the linker, and several more things. Since this particular DLL is very simple, you do not want to use the Microsoft Foundation Classes (MFC). Therefore, you need to select Not Using MFC in the Microsoft Foundation Classes (refer to fig. 20.14).

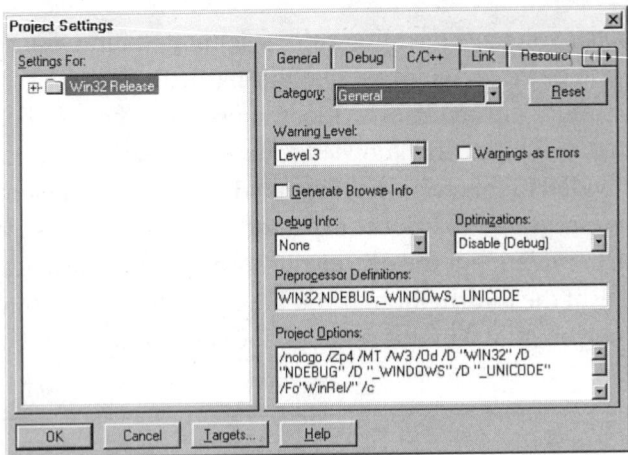

Fig. 20.15 This figure shows the Project Settings dialog box's C/C++ page, General Category for SDLL32.MAK (Visual C++ 2.0).

The next important option involves a preprocessor symbol, _UNICODE, and it is listed in the Preprocessor Definitions field of the C/C++ tab found in the Project Settings dialog box (refer to fig. 20.15). This preprocessor symbol is one of the things that tells Visual C++ that you are building a Unicode-aware DLL. For this DLL, the alignment is set to 4-byte boundaries (see fig. 20.16).

The source code for this 32-Bit, Unicode-aware DLL needs to be built into a DLL. In Visual C++ 2.0, building a DLL involves compiling the source code and then linking it to produce a DLL. As long as you avoid using MFC (done by selecting Not Using MFC, as previously explained), Visual C++ is much easier to use, because you have one less new technology (MFC) to learn. Since much of the work typically done in DLLs involves computations and string manipulations, there is not so much Win32 API work required. Mostly, the work involves using the C programming language, and C is not so different from Visual Basic 4. If you can do Visual Basic 4 programming, then you can learn to do C programming (but not in this chapter).

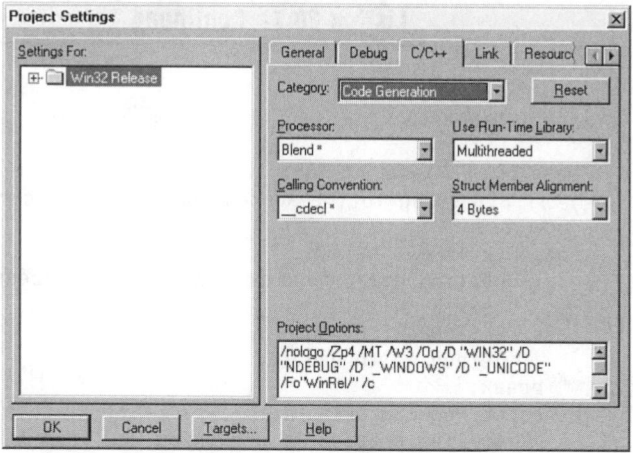

Fig. 20.16 This figure shows the Project Settings dialog box's C/C++ page, Code Generation Category Project settings for SDLL32.MAK (Visual C++ 2.0).

Listing 20.7   SDLL32.C—The source code for SDLL32.C

```
//-------------------------------------------------------------
// PROGRAM: SDLL32.C//
// PURPOSE: 32-Bit, Unicode-aware DLL for compatibility
testing...
// FUNCTIONS:  (1) DllMain - startup and exit...
//             (2) fntPutString - string test...
//-------------------------------------------------------------
//                    >>>  INCLUDES  <<<
//-------------------------------------------------------------
#pragma  comment(lib, "msvcrt " "-subsystem:Windows,4")
     å // Windows 95...
#define  UNICODE          // Unicode switch...
#include "windows.h"    // WINDOWS includes...
#include "tchar.h"        // TCHAR (Unicode compatibility)
     å includes...
#include "sdll32.h"     // local includes and defines...
//-------------------------------------------------------------
// FUNCTION: DllMain (HINSTANCE, DWORD,    LPVOID)
// PURPOSE: startup and exit...
//-------------------------------------------------------------
BOOL WINAPI DllMain (HINSTANCE hinstDll, DWORD fdwReason,
```

continues

Listing 20.7   Continued

```
       åLPVOID lpvReserved)
{
switch (fdwReason)
   {
   case DLL_PROCESS_ATTACH:
     // attaching to the address space of the current process.
     // break;
   case DLL_THREAD_ATTACH:
     // creating new thread in the current process...
        break;
   case DLL_THREAD_DETACH:
     // detaching thread...
     break;
   case DLL_PROCESS_DETACH:
     // calling process is detaching DLL from its address space.
     break;
   }
   return(TRUE);
}


//------------------------------------------------------------
-----
// FUNCTION: fntPutString(LPTSTR)
// PURPOSE:  Unicode string test...
// RETURNS:  test code ...
//------------------------------------------------------------
-----
__declspec(dllexport) int PASCAL fntPutString(LPTSTR
sString){
_tcscpy(sString, (LPCTSTR)_T(
     å"Humpty Dumpty sat on a wall.
     åHumpty Dumpty had a big fall.
     åAll the King's horses
     åand all the King's men
     åcouldn't put Humpty together again!"));
return (BIGGER_THAN_INT16);
}
```

If you have Visual C++ 2.0 or higher, then you can use the code shown in Listings 20.7 through 20.9 for the 32-bit, Unicode-aware DLL. Everything you need is provided in the listings, but you must have Visual C++ 2.0 or higher to do anything with the source code.

Listing 20.8   SDLL32.H—Description of Code

```
#define SUCCESSFUL                          0
#define SMALLER_THAN_INT16              32766
#define JUST_OVER_INT16                 32768
#define BIGGER_THAN_INT16               70000
#define A_LOT_BIGGER_THAN_INT16    2000000000
```

The defines in Listing 20.8 can be used to test the way Visual Basic 4 handles various types of return values. By varying the particular value returned by the DLL function, you can see what Visual Basic 4 does when it receives the return value in an `Integer` or a `Long` data type. In some cases, Visual Basic 4 will receive the correct value, but in other cases Visual Basic 4 will receive a truncated value. It all depends on the value returned by the DLL function and the type of Visual Basic 4 data type to which that value is returned. For example, if the DLL function returns `BIGGER_THAN_INT16` into a Visual Basic 4 Integer variable, the result will be rather unexpected, because that value is larger than the value that can be stored in a Visual Basic 4 `Integer` variable. In that case, the value will be the actual value modula 65,534. It will be seen in Visual Basic 4 as 4,466. In contrast, if you return the value into a Visual Basic 4 `Long` variable, the value will be correctly received as 70,000. There are quite a few combinations that you can test, and those experiments will help you understand some of the new rules involved in 32-bit work.

Listing 20.9   SDLL32.DEF—Description of Code

```
LIBRARY     SDLL32
EXPORTS
    fntPutString       @1
```

Here is what happens when you call `fntPutString` using a Visual Basic 4 `String` variable (see fig. 20.17 and 20.18).

As you examine figures 20.17 and 20.18, several things become apparent. The first thing you may notice is that in figure 20.17, none of the various display controls show anything but an "H" character. There are several reasons, and one of them involves the fact that the regular

Visual Basic 4 controls (the ones that are intrinsic to the language) are not Unicode-aware but are ANSI controls.

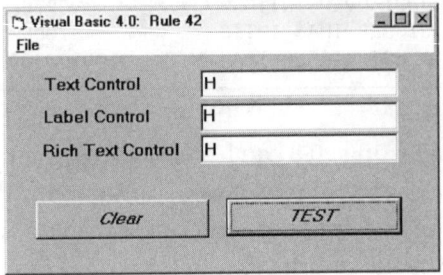

Fig. 20.17 The screen shows what happens when a Unicode string is arbitrarily garbled by the Visual Basic 4 conversion algorithm.

The compiled and linked DLL file for this sample is contained on the CD, so you can run at least one of the experiments regardless of whether you have Visual C++ 2.0 or higher. Sample code for the Visual Basic 4 calling program is also provided. The project will automatically display the Debug Window when you run it from Visual Basic 4. The results of the test will be in the Visual Basic 4 Debug Window, as shown in figure 20.18.

Since Visual Basic 4 has taken a perfectly good Unicode string and converted each of its bytes into ANSI bytes, followed by putting the converted ANSI bytes into separate Unicode characters (two bytes per Unicode character), the second thing you may notice is that the Debug Window shows that each character of the fully converted string is followed by a blank character. While it may be intuitive to suggest that the Debug Window is showing both bytes of each Unicode character in the string, that is not the case.

When the string is sent from the 32-bit, Unicode-aware DLL function (see listings 20.7 through 20.9), the two bytes of each Unicode character in the string are reversed from the way the values are customarily shown in documentation. For example, the Unicode character "H" has the value of 0x0072 when shown in documentation. The "0x" means that it is a decimal value. Internally, these two bytes are stored in reverse order. If you print the first byte of the two-byte Unicode character, that byte will be shown as "72." The second byte will be shown as "0." Visual Basic 4 knows how to work with the bytes in the order they are delivered, and that ordering is standard for Win32 work on Intel machines.

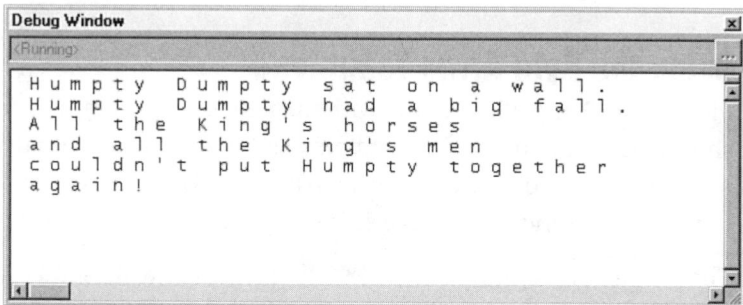

```
Debug Window                                                    x
<Running>                                                     ...
 H u m p t y   D u m p t y   s a t   o n   a   w a l l .
 H u m p t y   D u m p t y   h a d   a   b i g   f a l l .
 A l l   t h e   K i n g ' s   h o r s e s
 a n d   a l l   t h e   K i n g ' s   m e n
 c o u l d n ' t   p u t   H u m p t y   t o g e t h e r
 a g a i n !
```

Fig. 20.18 The Debug Window shows the contents of sString after the Unicode-to-ANSI-to-Unicode conversion has been performed.

What Visual Basic 4 has done is convert the byte with value 72 to an ANSI "H" and then put it into a Unicode character (the one you see in the Debug Window as an "H"). Then Visual Basic 4 converts the next byte (the one with value 0) to an ANSI Null terminator and puts it into a Unicode character, where it becomes the Unicode "double zero" character (the one you see in the Debug Window as the space following the "H").

It is very important to understand that this conversion begins by treating each byte in the Unicode string sent from the DLL as a separate ANSI character. This is the first mistake, because each byte in the Unicode is not sufficient to describe the Unicode character. It takes two bytes to define a Unicode character. The next step is to take each of what Visual Basic 4 now (incorrectly) believes to be ANSI characters and then to convert each of those single bytes to two bytes—thereby creating a completely imaginary Unicode character from each individually misinterpreted ANSI character. The result of this conversion is total garbage. The fact that it vaguely resembles an ANSI string only happens when the Unicode string happens to contain certain characters. If the Unicode string contained Kanji characters (a Japanese character set), then the string would be shown as a series of question marks (e.g., ???,…,???). In any event, when the resulting string is displayed in an ANSI-aware control, the first zeroed byte terminates the string, insofar as the ANSI-aware control is concerned.

Using the Byte Array Technique

Figures 20.19 and 20.20, along with the following program listings, show what happens (and how to make it happen) when you use the `Byte` array technique when talking to a 32-bit, Unicode-aware DLL function that sends a Unicode string to your Visual Basic program.

The `Byte` array technique involves using a `Byte` array to send and receive string data when talking to a DLL function. The source code for the Visual Basic 4 calling application sample (see Listing 20.10) shows how to define a `Byte` array, how to give it a value, and how to get the results of the DLL function all from the `Byte` array into a Visual Basic 4 `String` variable. Pay close attention to everything.

The `Byte` array, `bArray()`, is defined with beginning and ending parentheses. This makes it a variable length `Byte` array. Similarly, the Visual Basic 4 `String` variable is copied from and assigned to the `Byte` array using the `bArray()` notation. However, the DLL function declaration does not use the parenthetical format. When the `Byte` array is passed to the DLL function, you must specify the starting index of the `Byte` array. If you follow these simple rules, it is very easy to send the bytes of a Visual Basic 4 Unicode string to a DLL function in such a way that the "Unicode-to-ANSI-to-Unicode" string garbling is not done.

Getting the results of this experiment is done by running the Visual Basic 4 sample program in `Run` mode. If you install the sample code on any drive and subdirectory other than the one specified in the sample code, you will need to change the name of the library file, because it includes the full path. Once you have made the necessary modification, you can run the program to see what happens.

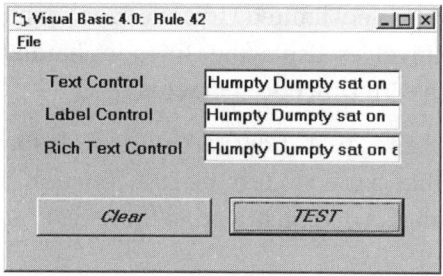

Fig. 20.19 This screen shows a correct ANSI conversion of a Unicode string sent from a DLL.

Examining figures 20.19 and 20.20 shows that everything is working reasonably well.

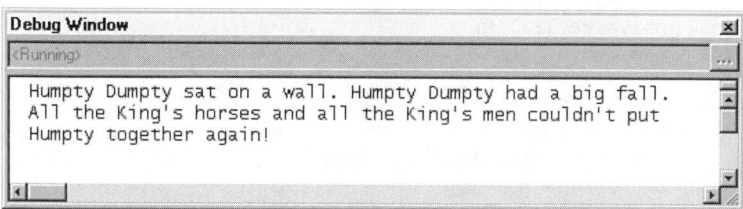

Fig. 20.20 The Debug Window shows the contents of sString after the Byte Array to Unicode conversion has been performed.

The "astute observation" is displayed in the appropriate controls on the form, and the Debug Window shows that the message is in the string. This is wonderful—unless you happen to be working with Unicode strings that contain characters that do not convert correctly to ANSI. If you are working with Unicode characters that do not convert to ANSI, then the Visual Basic 4 Unicode string contains the correct characters, but you cannot display them using the intrinsic Visual Basic 4 controls. Instead, you need to use 32-bit, Unicode-aware OLE Controls and that means you need to rely on third-party vendors whose OLE Controls fully support Unicode. Additionally, it likely means that you are restricted to using Windows NT because Windows

95 only provides very limited Unicode functionality. (The problem with Windows 95 involves displaying Unicode characters rather than internally working with Unicode characters.)

Listings 20.10 and 20.11 show part of the code for the Visual Basic 4 application that is used to test the DLL function. The Byte array technique for strings is demonstrated in these two code listings.

Listing 20.10   SDLL32F.FRM—Excerpts from the Source Code for the frmMain Form

```
Dim sString As String
Dim bArray() As Byte

Private Sub pbtClear_Click()
lblTest.Caption = ""
txtValue.TEXT = ""
rtxValue.TEXT = ""
End Sub

Private Sub pbtTest_Click()
Dim lRetVal&
sString = Space$(499) + Chr$(0)
bArray() = sString
lRetVal& = fntPutString(bArray(0))
sString = bArray()
lblTest.Caption = sString
txtValue.TEXT = sString
rtxValue.TEXT = sString
Debug.Print "Mid$(sString, 1,   58) = >>"; _
    Mid$(sString, 1, 58)
Debug.Print "Mid$(sString, 59,  60) = >>"; _
    Mid$(sString, 59, 60)
Debug.Print "Mid$(sString, 119, 44) = >>"; _
    Mid$(sString, 119, 44)
Debug.Print "Mid$(sString, 163, 46) = >>"; _
    Mid$(sString, 163, 46)
Debug.Print "Mid$(sString, 209, 56) = >>"; _
    Mid$(sString, 209, 56)
Debug.Print "Mid$(sString, 267, 50) = >>"; _
    Mid$(sString, 267, 50)
End Sub
```

Listing 20.11 shows the procedure module file for the Visual Basic 4 test program. The entire purpose of this module is to provide a convenient place to put the declaration of the 32-bit, Unicode-aware DLL function. The rule that applies to using declaration or definition is very simple: You define a function one time, but you declare it when you want to use it. The 32-bit, Unicode-aware DLL function is defined in the Visual C++ source code, but in Visual Basic 4 you are only using the DLL function—so, you can declare it many times. However, only one time is necessary, provided it is global to your program. Putting the declaration in a procedure module file is one way to make the function declaration global (that is, visible everywhere within the Visual Basic 4 program).

Listing 20.11   SDLL32M.BAS—The Source Code for Module1

```
Attribute VB_Name = "Module1"
Declare Function fntPutString Lib "K:\SDLL32\SDLL32.DLL"_
    (ByRef bArray As Byte) As Long
```

If your 32-bit, Unicode-aware DLL function requires structures (the C/C++ equivalents of Visual Basic user-defined types) that contain string members, you must use the Byte Array technique for every single string; and you cannot use a typelib because user-defined types are sent by reference and a typelib cannot handle user-defined type variables when they are sent by reference. Be sure not to forget the automatic padding rule.

From Here...

This chapter introduced you to some excellent third-party OLE Controls, and it showed you how to build a simple (but very useful) framework for a Visual Basic 4 add-in. You also got a glimpse of some very troublesome problems involving DLL functions, and you have seen that there are solutions for those problems.

For those readers who are proficient in Visual C++, there was a bonus section on building a 32-bit, Unicode-aware DLL function. If you do not use Visual C++, you can still have a bit of fun running the sample program. When using Visual Basic 4, be careful when using strings and user-defined types. There are new rules, and it makes good sense to learn them. There are solutions, and once you learn them Visual Basic 4 becomes very friendly.

Additional information on topics related to this chapter can be found in the following chapters:

➤ To learn how to use OLE Automation in your programs, see Chapter 11, "OLE Automation."

➤ To find out how to create an OLE Server to enhance your programs, see Chapter 12, "OLE Servers."

➤ For more information on what the container class does and how to use it, see Chapter 13, "OLE Container Classes."

The following are the third-party vendor names mentioned in the chapter:

➤ *FarPoint Technologies, Inc.* 800-645-5913 and 919-460-4551. Fax: 919-460-7606. ANSI and Unicode-compliant, OLE Controls.

➤ *VideoSoft.* 800-547-7295 (U.S.) and 510-704-8200 (international). Fax. 510-843-0174. ANSI- and DBCS-aware OLE Controls.

➤ *Sylvain Faust Inc. (SFI).* 800-567-9127 (U.S. and Canada) and 819-778-5045 (International). Fax: 819-778-7953. SYSBASE SQL Server, Microsoft SQL Server, and WATCOM SQL Server OLE Controls and DBA support tools.

➤ *Lenel Systems International, Inc.* 800-225-3635 (U.S.) and 716-248-9270 International). Fax. 716-248-9185. Multimedia development, 32-bit OLE Controls.

➤ *MicroHelp, Inc.* 800-922-3383 (U.S.) and 404-516-1099 (International). Fax: 404-516-1099. OLE Control collections, advanced library functions, communication technologies, developer tools.

➤ *AccuSoft Corporation.* 800-525-3577 (U.S.) and 508-898-2770 (International). Fax: 508-898-9662. OLE Controls with advanced imaging capabilities.

Part IV
Checking the Efficiency of Your Application

21

Optimizing VB Code

by *Steve Potts*

For your programs to be successful, they must execute quickly enough to be acceptable to the user. As Visual Basic programs become larger and more sophisticated, the amount of memory that they use and the speed with which they execute becomes extremely important. The goal of this chapter is to highlight features and practices in Visual Basic that make wise use of resources, and therefore perform well.

Programs that are unnecessarily large generally perform poorly. This happens because all of the code and data can't fit in memory, so Windows must use the hard disk to store part of the program during execution. This means that whenever your program needs a part of the application that is on the disk, Windows must perform an I/O operation and load in this part from the disk into memory. The larger the program, the bigger this problem gets.

If your program is really large compared to the available memory on a customer's machine, it will spend most of its time accessing the disk, and very little time running your program. When this happens, the computer is said to be *thrashing*. If you hear your hard drive running after every command, your program is causing your computer to thrash. The antidote to this poison is to shrink your program to a size that fits better in the memory available in the minimum hardware that you intend to support.

Another reason for poor performance is the unwise use of Visual Basic features on your form and in your code. Like every complex application, Visual Basic allows the developer alternative ways of accomplishing the same objective. Both approaches look identical to the user, but they cause Visual Basic to behave much differently. Labels often look like text boxes and images look like picture boxes. Being wise when making these choices is a key to achieving good performance.

This chapter addresses the topics of program size and speed. It presents rules of thumb for using certain techniques. Generally, the key to good performance is a strict adherence to the best programming practices at all stages of development. By following this strategy, you will be assured that the finished application will perform well on the widest possible range of computers, and therefore be marketable to the most potential customers.

The major topics of this chapter are as follows:

➤ Measuring program size and performance

➤ Reducing program size

➤ Improving program performance

➤ Comparing the performance of alternative Visual Basic controls

➤ Improving Visual Basic performance with databases

Measuring Program Performance

Programs that perform poorly sell poorly and frustrate the users. This results in excessive hardware expenditures and reduced productivity.

To improve performance, we must be able to measure it. In the programming field, this means measuring how much memory is being used by a certain feature or practice, and how much time something takes to execute.

Many of the practices that we will discuss in this chapter will involve simple reductions in these two metrics. Others will involve trade-offs between size and speed. These trade-offs require good measurements so that you can make wise choices.

Measuring Program Speed

The first metric that we will need is a measurement of the speed of a program. This is done using a subroutine based on the use of the Time function. This subroutine is shown in Listing 21.1.

Listing 21.1   TIMEDIFF.BAS—Creating a Time-Measuring Subroutine

```
Sub TimeDiff(Time1 As Date, Time2 As Date)
    Dim Seconds1 As Integer
    Dim Minutes1  As Integer
    Dim Seconds2 As Integer
    Dim Minutes2  As Integer
    Dim NumSecs As Integer

    Seconds1 = DatePart("s", Time1)
    Minutes1 = DatePart("n", Time1)
    Seconds2 = DatePart("s", Time2)
    Minutes2 = DatePart("n", Time2)

    MinPart = (Minutes2 - Minutes1) * 60
    NumSecs = MinPart + (Seconds2 - Seconds1)

    msg = "The Elapsed Time was " + Str$(NumSecs) + "_
      Seconds"
    MsgBox (msg)
End Sub
```

This listing accepts two Time variables of type Date as input, the earlier one first. It calculates and displays the number of seconds between the two times. The DatePart() function parses the input and returns the seconds and minutes components of the argument based on the "s" (seconds) or "n" (minutes) value in the first parameter.

Listing 21.2 is an example that shows how to use this subroutine.

Listing 21.2   HOWLONG.BAS—Using the TimeDiff ( ) Subroutine

```
Private Sub Command1_Click()
    Dim Time1 As Date
    Dim Time2 As Date
    Dim NumSecs As Integer

    Time1 = Time

    While j < 300000
        j = j + 1
    Wend

    Time2 = Time
    TimeDiff Time1, Time2

End Sub
```

This simple program used the `Time` built-in function to query the system clock. The first query is stored in the variable `Time1`. After a long `While` loop executes, a second time measure is taken and stored in `Time2`. Then the program calls the `TimeDiff` subroutine, which displays the elapsed time. The output of this program is a message box that displays the following phrase:

```
The Elapsed Time was 3 Seconds
```

All of the measurements in this chapter were made on a homemade 486DX2/66 computer with 8 MB of RAM. The times that you measure on your own computer may vary.

Another technique for measuring performance is the use of an external stopwatch. This works well when you are measuring the efficiency of an operation that takes several minutes or hours.

Measuring Program Size

The second metric that we will need in our programs is program size. One way that we can measure this is by examining the file size after an executable is created using File Manager. It is not difficult to see the difference between these two lines:

```
time1.exe        6544  11/19/94   10:14:42am     a
time1.exe        6304  11/21/94   08:17:02am     a
```

Although execution speed depends on the locality of code as much as raw size, a decrease in the size of the executable file is normally beneficial.

Another metric that we need is memory usage on running programs. Again, we can use a subroutine to measure that for us. We need a program that displays the current amount of available memory, but that doesn't consume more than a little memory itself. We can do this by invoking the Clipboard viewer that comes with Windows, and then sending the Alt+H and A keystrokes to it (this is the About selection on the Help menu). Listing 21.3 shows the routine that does this.

Listing 21.3   A Memory Display Program

```
Private Sub DispMemWin()
  Retco = Shell("C\Program Files\Common_
Files\MSInfo\Msinfo32.exe", 1)

End Sub
```

The shell command loads the MSInfo application in memory, as shown in figure 21.1.

We now have the following four options for measuring programs:

➤ Using the `TimeDiff()` subroutine from within an application to measure its execution time

➤ Using a stopwatch to measure the execution time from outside the computer

➤ Using the File Manager to view the size of the executable on disk when it is not running

➤ Embedding the `DispMemWin()` subroutine in an application and calling it to measure the size of the application while it is running

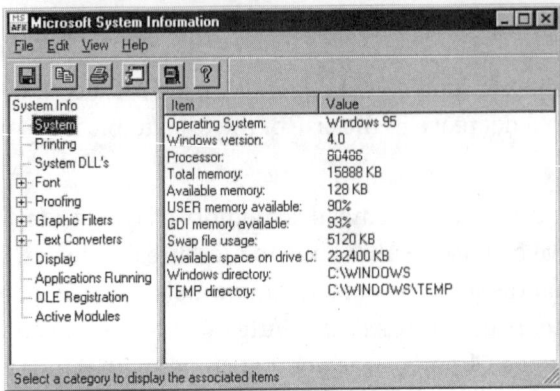

Fig. 21.1 The Msinfo32 applet can be used to display the available memory.

Improving the Performance of Objects

Because Visual Basic performs so much work for you through built-in objects, it's sometimes difficult to understand the performance impact of certain features and practices. The only way to determine the best approach in a given situation is to run tests. In this section, we will set up a number of tests on alternate ways of using objects and properties in order to discover some rules of thumb.

Show/Hide versus Load/Unload

Multiform applications are composed of a number of forms that are displayed to the user and removed from view when appropriate, according to the logic of the program. There are basically two ways to make a form invisible to the user:

➤ The Unload method removes a form from memory completely. The next time a Show method is invoked in the code, Visual Basic must load the form back into memory before it can be displayed onto the screen.

➤ The `Hide` method removes a form from view, but leaves it in memory. The next time a `Show` method is executed, it is simply made visible.

Because these two approaches are functionally equivalent, we need to determine which one to use in a given situation. It should be obvious that the `Unload` method conserves memory, and that the `Hide` method will execute faster. The question is how much more memory is used by the `Hide` method, and how much slower is the `Unload` method. We can run a test to find out the answers to these questions.

A proper test will be one that performs a series of `Show` and `Hide` combinations on a set of fairly complicated forms like the one shown in figure 21.2.

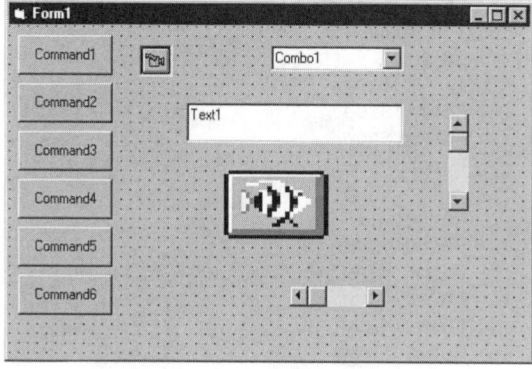

Fig. 21.2 A large sample form will show the difference between the performance of the `Show` and `Hide` methods.

This form is a sort of jumble of bitmaps, metafiles, and controls that were added to make it large enough to measure. This form was duplicated four times in order to create an application that had five fairly large forms to display. Next, the code in Listing 21.4 was added to `Form1`.

Listing 21.4 SHOWHID1.BAS—Hiding Forms

```
Private Sub Form_Load()
    Dim Time1 As Date
    Dim Time2 As Date

' Display memory before loading the other forms
    DispMemWin
' Load all of the Forms into memory
    Formb.Show
    Formc.Show
    Formd.Show
    Forme.Show
' Hide all but Forma
    Formb.Hide
    Formc.Hide
    Formd.Hide
    Forme.Hide

' Take a time measurement
    Time1 = Time
' Show and Hide each form in turn
    For i = 1 To 10
        Forma.Hide
        Formb.Show
        Formb.Hide
        Formc.Show
        Formc.Hide
        Formd.Show
        Formd.Hide
        Forme.Show
        Forme.Hide
        Forma.Show
    Next i
' Take a second time measurement
    Time2 = Time
' Find out how long it took
    TimeDiff Time1, Time2
' Take a memory measurement
    DispMemWin
End Sub
```

After creating an executable file from this project, it ran with an 11-second time lapse between Time1 and Time2.

Next, we need to change the program to use the `Unload` command instead of the `Hide` command and run it again. The code to do this is provided in Listing 21.5.

Listing 21.5   SHOWHID2.BAS—Unloading Forms

```
Private Sub Form_Load()
    Dim Time1 As Date
    Dim Time2 As Date

' Display memory before loading the other forms
    DispMemWin

' Take a time measurement
    Time1 = Time
' Show and Hide each form in turn
    For i = 1 To 10
        Formb.Show
        Unload Formb
        Formc.Show
        Unload Formc
        Formd.Show
        Unload Formd
        Forme.Show
        Unload Forme
    Next i
' Take a second time measurement
    Time2 = Time
' Find out how long it took
    TimeDiff Time1, Time2
' Take a memory measurement
    DispMemWin
End Sub
```

Because `Form1` contains this code, it will be left in memory the entire time. The `Unload` statements completely remove the forms from memory and recover (in theory) all of the memory that was allocated for it. The execution time for this program was 18 seconds.

By comparing the two times, we learn that using `Unload` instead of `Hide` required about seven additional seconds but consumed 127 KB less memory.

The conclusion that we can draw from this experiment is that there are advantages to each strategy. Hiding forms allows your application to execute quickly, but requires more memory. Unloading a form after it has been used significantly reduces the program's memory requirements, but is slower.

> **Note:** Use the `Hide` method whenever execution speed is the highest priority. Use the `Unload` subroutine whenever memory conservation is the higher priority.

A hybrid approach is also possible. This approach would unload the less common forms and hide those that tend to be used more often.

Feedback to the User

Often, it is just as important to give the user visual feedback as it is to give her rapid response. The use of an introductory or logo form and a timer can help you accomplish this. A problem can arise whenever a long `Form_Load` event procedure is employed in an application. Programs that make heavy use of list boxes that are filled by accessing the database fall in this category.

The form doesn't appear until the entire `Form_Load` event procedure is completed. This can cause your user to wonder if the computer is hung up, especially if the delay is for more than a few seconds. You could issue the `Show` method at the top of the `Form_Load` procedure and show the window frame, but the rest of the controls won't be painted until the procedure finishes.

A partial solution is to create a logo screen that becomes the `Startup` form for the application. If, however, you issue the `Show` method for the main form directly as in the following listing, this logo form doesn't paint immediately either.

```
Private Sub Form_Load()
    Formb.Show
End Sub
```

One way around this problem is to create the logo form and place a timer on it. You can enable the timer in the `Form_Load` event for that form. The timer event procedure can issue the `Show` method for the second form without making the logo form wait.

```
Private Sub Form_Load()
    Timer1.Enabled = True
End Sub

Private Sub Timer1_Timer()
    Timer1.Enabled = False
    Formb.Show
End Sub
```

This immediate feedback will allow your users to remain calm while the main form is loading.

The AutoRedraw Property

Forms and picture boxes have a property called `AutoRedraw`. When `AutoRedraw` is set to `True`, all graphics on the object are saved in an area of memory called the *canvas*. The size of this canvas is determined by the size of the area it represents. The advantage of this canvas becomes apparent when the window is covered and then uncovered by another window. The window's graphics repaint automatically only if `AutoRedraw` is set to `True`. These graphics that reappear automatically are said to be "persistent."

Windows 95 takes care of redisplaying the window and controls, but your application must take care of redisplaying graphics in a form or picture box. The easiest way to do this is by setting the `AutoRedraw` property to `True`.

A negative feature of the `AutoRedraw` canvas is that it consumes memory. The size of the canvas is determined by the size of the object that is being redrawn. If your form has no graphics objects on it, always set the `AutoRedraw` property to `False`.

> **Note:** Always set the `AutoRedraw` property of a form to `False` if it contains no graphical objects.

You may want to set `AutoRedraw` to `False` even on a form that has a graphic object on it. If the form's graphics are localized around a part of the form, it is often better to create a Picture Box control, draw the graphics on it, and set its `AutoRedraw` property to `True`. This enables you to set the `AutoRedraw` property of the form to `False` without losing any graphics if it is covered and then uncovered. Since the Picture Box is only a fraction of the size of the whole form, the memory savings can be substantial.

> **Note:** If a form has graphical objects on it, try to localize them into a Picture Box control that has `AutoRedraw` set to `True`. Then set the `AutoRedraw` property for the form to `False`.

If the graphics objects are really simple, you can employ the `Paint` event to redraw them. The `Paint` event is triggered by Windows whenever a part of the form has been covered up and then exposed. You can set all `AutoRedraw` properties to `False` and include the code that draws these objects from scratch in the `Paint` event procedure. This saves all of the memory that would normally be used for the canvas.

Improving Graphics Performance

Because Windows has a graphical user interface, the performance of graphics processing methods is critical to overall application performance. In this section, we will look at several areas where design decisions can have a large impact on the performance of the application as a whole. In this section, we will look at a number of design decisions and their performance impact.

The LoadPicture Method

Whenever you want to include pictures or images to your forms, you have the following decisions to make:

➤ Will you use a Picture Box or Image control?

➤ Will you use the `LoadPicture` function or store the picture in the form itself?

We will examine each issue separately.

Picture Box versus Image Control

There are two controls in the toolbox that are capable of displaying pictures on your forms: the Picture Box control and the Image control. Selecting the correct one to use can save memory and speed execution.

The Picture Box control is really a little window that is placed inside another window. It consumes resources just like another form does. As such, you can use a Picture Box control to group `OptionButtons` and to display output from graphics methods. You can also display text written with the `Print` method. The Picture Box control is the only standard Visual Basic control that can be placed in the client area of an MDI form. It can be used to group controls in order to create a Toolbar. This control can also act as a destination link in a DDE conversation. If you want to accomplish one of these tasks, you will have to use the Picture Box control.

If, however, you only want to display a picture on a form, and you are not interested in the advanced functionality available in the Picture Box control, you can use the Image control. The Image control is a light resource consumer compared to the Picture Box control. We can run a test to see how much resource each of them consumes. Figure 21.3 shows a form with a picture on it. We will create two applications that each have eight of these pictures in them.

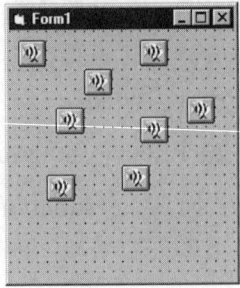

Fig. 21.3 This form contains numerous controls to be measured by the following program.

This test compares an executable that was created with no controls with one that has eight pictures, and to one that has eight images. We can look at the size of the executable file that is produced by Visual Basic for each of these cases in Table 21.1.

Table 21.1   Sizes of Executable Files

Program	Size (Bytes)
Blank Form	5440
Eight Images	121,792
Eight Pictures	121,952

The size of the executable file doesn't show much difference in the size of the executables based on the use of the Image control. When the applications are run, however, we see that the size of the programs differ significantly. Table 21.2 shows the results of this test as compared to the system with a program that displays a blank form running.

Table 21.2   Comparing Sizes of Executable Files

Program	Free Memory(Kbytes)	Difference(Kbytes)
Blank Form	21,532	—
Eight Images	21,419	113
Eight Pictures	21,361	171

In summary, it took 113 KB of memory to add the eight Image controls (about 14 KB per control) to the blank form. It took 171 KB of memory to add the eight Picture Box controls, or about 21 KB per control. Therefore, we conclude that a Picture Box control consumes 50 percent more resources than an Image control.

> **Note:** Use Image controls to display simple bitmaps and metafiles instead of Picture Box controls, unless you need the additional functionality provided by the Picture Box control.

In conclusion, use a Picture Box control to group option buttons, to display output from graphics methods, to display text written with the `Print` method, or to group controls to create a Toolbar. Use the Image control to do all simple picture displays.

Loaded versus Embedded Pictures

The next decision that you must make is whether you will load graphics using the `LoadPicture` function or embed these picture in the form itself. Once again, this is a question of execution speed versus program size—loading is slower, but produces smaller executables. We can run a test to see how much larger and faster an application that stores pictures becomes. Start by creating an application that contains four metafiles in Image controls on two virtually identical forms. Use the metafile called `c:\vb\metafile\business\apptbook.wmf` that is pictured in figure 21.3.

Create an executable file called `storpic1.exe`, and run it from the Windows 95 Run command on the menu. The code for this application will look like Listing 21.6.

Listing 21.6 STORPIC1.BAS—Showing and Hiding a Form that Contains a Metafile

```
Private Sub Command1_Click()
    Form1.Hide
    Form2.Show
```

continues

Listing 21.6   Continued

```
End Sub

Private Sub Command1_Click()
    Form2.Hide
    Form1.Show
End Sub
```

Next, create a similar application that uses the LoadPicture method to load the metafile into the Image controls during the Form_Load event procedure using the Listing 21.7 code.

Listing 21.7   LOADPIC1.BAS—Preloading a Metafile

```
Private Sub Command1_Click()
    Unload Form1
    Form2.Show
End Sub

Private Sub Form_Load()
    Image1.Picture = _
LoadPicture("i:\vb\metafile\business\apptbook.wmf ")
    Image2.Picture = _
LoadPicture("i:\vb\metafile\business\apptbook.wmf ")
    Image3.Picture = _
LoadPicture("i:\vb\metafile\business\apptbook.wmf ")
    Image4.Picture = _
LoadPicture("i:\vb\metafile\business\apptbook.wmf ")
End Sub

Private Sub Form_Unload(Cancel As Integer)
    Image1.Picture = LoadPicture()
    Image2.Picture = LoadPicture()
    Image3.Picture = LoadPicture()
    Image4.Picture = LoadPicture()
End Sub
```

Call this form Form1. The reason that we assign null strings to the Images in the Unload event procedure is to recover the memory that was used to store the pictures. Create another form called Form2 that has identical code for the Load and Unload events, but the following code for the command button:

```
Private Sub Command1_Click()
    Unload Form2
    Form1.Show
End Sub
```

Call this application `loadpic1.exe`. Both of these programs display a form with four pictures and a command button on it. When the command button is pressed, the second form is displayed and it also has four pictures and a command button. Pressing the command buttons toggles between the two forms; functionally, they are identical. However, they are very different internally. The `storpic1` program stores all eight metafiles as pictures in the application. The `loadpic1` application loads the four pictures for each form during `Form_Load`, and then unloads them during `Form_Unload`. It also unloads the forms instead of hiding them.

The results are shown in Table 21.3.

Table 21.3   Executable Size on Disk

Executable Name	Disk File Size
loadpic1	10,432 Bytes
storpic1	124,352 Bytes

As you can see, storing the pictures takes up drastically more space on disk. The size of the programs during execution is also larger as shown in Table 21.4.

Table 21.4   Executable Size at Runtime

Executable Name	Runtime Size
loadpic1	233,000 Bytes
storpics	299,000 Bytes

The reason that this size difference is not as great at runtime is because when the size was measured, one of the forms was loaded with four pictures.

If you examine the code, you will see that the code needed to load and unload the pictures is far more complex than that needed to process the stored picture application. In addition to that, when you distribute the application, you must also distribute the file containing the picture. Then if your user inadvertently deletes the picture file, your application won't run and the user must call for support. To make matters worse, the loading and unloading of pictures takes time and therefore slows down your application. To determine how much slower loading and unloading makes your program, we need to run a test.

Listing 21.8   SHOWUNL1.BAS—Showing and Hiding a Form

```
Private Sub Command1_Click()
    Dim Time1 As Date
    Dim Time2 As Date
    Time1 = Time
    Unload Form2
    Form1.Show
    Unload Form1
    Form2.Show
    Unload Form2
    Form1.Show
    Unload Form1
    Form2.Show
    Unload Form2
    Form1.Show
    Unload Form1
    Form2.Show
    Time2 = Time
    TimeDiff Time1, Time2
End Sub
```

We changed the Command1_Click to Load and Unload the forms three times each. This was done in order to get a large enough elapsed time to measure. Next, change the storpic1 application to contain the code in Listing 21.9.

Listing 21.9   SHOWHID1.BAS—Showing and Hiding the Form

```
Private Sub Command1_Click()
    Dim Time1 As Date
    Dim Time2 As Date
```

```
        Time1 = Time
        Form1.Hide
        Form2.Show
        Form2.Hide
        Form1.Show
        Form1.Hide
        Form2.Show
        Form2.Hide
        Form1.Show
        Form1.Hide
        Form2.Show
        Form2.Hide
        Form1.Show
        Form1.Hide
        Form2.Show
        Form2.Hide
        Form1.Show
        Time2 = Time
        TimeDiff Time1, Time2
    End Sub
```

This code uses the `Show` and `Hide` methods to accomplish the same purpose. Table 21.5 shows the times measured by the two programs.

Table 21.5   The Execution Times

Program	Elapsed Time
ShowHid1	1 Second
ShowUnl1	9 Seconds

What a difference in execution speed! So now you don't like loading pictures because it takes too long, and you don't like storing them because they take up so much room. You are like the customer in the bakery that was too hard to please. One day his bread was raw and he complained. The next day it was burned, and he complained again. The baker protested that some people are impossible to please.

There is another approach that borrows the best from each of these two approaches. It involves creating a form that is never displayed but stores all of the pictures that are needed in Image controls on all forms. This enables a simple assignment of the `Picture` property value instead of a `Form_Load`. Here is how it works. Create a new form called `Form3`. Add one image control to this form. Change the `Load` event procedures in the other two forms to the following:

```
Private Sub Form_Load()
    Image1.Picture = Form3!Image1.Picture
    Image2.Picture = Form3!Image1.Picture
    Image3.Picture = Form3!Image1.Picture
    Image4.Picture = Form3!Image1.Picture
End Sub
```

This code performs an assignment of the `Picture` property value of `Form3!Image1` to the other Image controls in the application. The effect on the size of the application is outstanding (only 231 KB). This is because only one copy of the picture is in memory and all of the Image controls use it to display. The size of the executable grew to 26,208 bytes, which is only slightly larger than the `loadpic1` application. The concern over the inadvertent deletion of the picture file is gone, however, because a copy of the picture is stored in the executable file as part of `Form3`. The time required to execute the six form loads is reduced to around seven seconds. Thus, the dummy form approach gives a reasonably sized executable file somewhat better performance than the `loadpic1` application and a better distribution model. These improvements are based on the fact that the same picture is used in several places in the application. This is often the case in applications that use cell animation or buttons with pictures on them.

In conclusion, load pictures to reduce memory usage, store them in the application to maximize performance, and use a dummy form when the same picture is used in several places in the same application. Table 21.6 lists the different performance characteristics.

Note: Stored pictures provide the fastest execution. Loaded pictures require the least memory and disk space. Performance can be improved by using dummy forms to store pictures that are used in multiple places in the application.

Table 21.6　Summary of Results from Test Programs

Program	Size on Disk	Size in Memory	Time to Run
ShowUnl1	10,432	233KB	9 Seconds
ShowHid1	124,352	299KB	1 Second
Dummy Form	26,208	213KB	7 Seconds

In tuning performance, it's important to wisely choose techniques to use when adding pictures to your Visual Basic applications. By choosing the correct approach, you can optimize on size or speed or balance the two.

Improving Code Performance

Now that you are more familiar with the performance characteristics of built-in objects, you are ready for a discussion of coding techniques and their effects. If you write a program to balance a checkbook that takes too long to calculate the results, your users won't be happy. In this section, you will learn how to avoid this problem.

To appreciate the following discussion, you must understand how memory is managed in Visual Basic 4.

Types of Memory and Their Sizes

In Visual Basic 4, the following memory allocations are available to your program:

➤ *The Stack*—A single stack is allocated for an entire application. This stack can be no larger than 20 KB. If your code performs an operation that attempts to allocate stack space in excess of 20 KB, a runtime error will occur. Because of this limitation, it is essential that you understand what types of variables are allocated on the stack and what kind of variables are given other types of memory allocation. Visual Basic's runtime library and other DLLs that you call explicitly also use stack space. The result is that you never really have even 20 KB of stack memory available to your program. The primary users of stack space are subroutine arguments and local variables.

➤ *Form Data Segment*—Each Visual Basic form and module is given one 64 KB segment in which to store its data. All variables declared as `Static` (including those declared in subroutines and functions) and all module-level variables are allocated in this data segment except variable-length strings and arrays.

➤ *Variable-Length String Data Segment*—All variable-length strings occupy the same data segment.

➤ *Array Data Segments*—Each array element is allocated in a separate data segment with a maximum size of 64 KB.

➤ *User-Defined Type Segments*—Each user-defined type is given a data segment that is 64 KB. The aggregate size of the user-defined type, including nested types, is limited to 64 KB. If your type contains variable-length strings, then they occupy four bytes each in this total.

You must consider these limitations when writing your applications, or you will need a very good runtime error-handler in your code. Don't forget that it's much better to build a guard rail on the edge of a cliff than to park an ambulance at the bottom of it.

Explicit Variable Declarations

One of the great features of Visual Basic is the `Variant` data type. These magic variables handle overflow without a hitch, perform data conversions, and allow all kinds of flexible programming practices. Whenever you are testing out concepts and creating prototypes, use them wherever possible.

When creating production systems, use the `Variant` data type sparingly, or not at all. Because `Variant` is the default data type, avoid using variables that are not declared explicitly.

To help you follow the practice of including a declaration for every variable, include the phrase "Option Explicit" in each module that you create. When you choose Tools, Options, and check the Require Variable Declaration option in the Environment tab, then this phrase will appear automatically whenever you create a new module. This option gives an error message for each undeclared variable.

Run the following example to see that this is important. Create a new project and place one button on the form. In the first part of the experiment, place the Listing 21.10 code in the command button's event procedure.

Listing 21.10   VAR1.BAS—Using the Variant Data Type

```
Private Sub Command1_Click()
    Dim Time1 As Date
    Dim Time2 As Date
    Time1 = Time
    For i = 1 To 10000
        For j = 1 To 500
            k = k + 1
        Next j
    Next i
    Time2 = Time
    TimeDiff Time1, Time2
End Sub
```

In this example, the variables `i`, `j`, and `k` are undeclared and—by default—of type `Variant`. When run, this program took 39 seconds to complete. If, however, you add the following declarations to the example, the `Variant` data type is overridden by the `Integer` and `Long` statements.

```
Dim i As Integer
Dim j As Integer
Dim k As Long
```

Running the application again, it completes in 17 seconds. The only difference was the explicit datatyping of the variables instead of accepting the default Variant type.

> **Note:** Avoid using the Variant data type in production systems. It is simply too slow for large systems.

Each numeric data type is listed here in order, from the fastest to the slowest:

- ➤ Integer
- ➤ Long
- ➤ Single
- ➤ Double
- ➤ Currency
- ➤ Variant

Fixed-Length Strings versus Variable-Length Strings

There are two reasons you should avoid using *fixed-length strings*: they are slow, and they use precious stack memory. To demonstrate how slow they are, we can run the Listing 21.11 code attached to a form with only one command button.

Listing 21.11   FIXLEN.BAS—Fixed-Length Strings

```
Dim i As Integer
Dim FS As String * 1000

Private Sub Command1_Click()
    Dim Time1 As Date
    Dim Time2 As Date
    Time1 = Time
    For i = 1 To 10000
```

```
        FS = "Hello, World "
        Print FS
    Next i
    Time2 = Time
    TimeDiff Time1, Time2
End Sub
```

This code executed in a staggering 39 seconds. Next, we can run a program that uses *variable-length strings* instead. The code in Listing 21.12 uses these.

Listing 21.12   VARSTR1.BAS—Variable-Length String

```
Dim i As Integer

Private Sub Command1_Click()
    Dim Time1 As Date
    Dim Time2 As Date
    V$ = String$(1000, " ")
    Time1 = Time
    For i = 1 To 10000
        V$ = "Hello, World "
        Print V$
    Next i
    Time2 = Time
    TimeDiff Time1, Time2
End Sub
```

Amazingly, this program ran in less than 10 seconds. The only explanation is the fact that stack-processing normally looks at certain memory locations to learn where the top of the stack is located. Variable-length strings follow a pointer to the exact beginning of the string in a separate data segment. This would lead one to expect that the variable-length string would process more quickly, but the magnitude of the difference is surprising.

In addition to this, putting strings on the stack is flirting with danger, because it's difficult to predict the exact amount of stack space that will be needed in production.

> **Note:** Always use variable-length strings instead of fixed-length strings to store your textual data. Variable-length strings are handled more efficiently by Visual Basic.

Given this difference in processing times, it is difficult to envision a situation where a fixed-length string would be preferable.

Fixed-Length Arrays versus Variable-Length Arrays

The performance problems that we encountered with fixed-length strings raise doubt about fixed-length arrays as well. *Fixed-length arrays* are those that are declared with Global or Dim. Memory for them is allocated at that time in a data segment that is given to that array individually.

Variable-length (or *dynamic*) arrays are those whose memory is allocated in a subroutine or function body using the ReDim statement. The ReDim statement allows the same array to change sizes during the execution of the program. One advantage of the variable-length array is that memory for it is allocated at the last possible instant, and by consequence, not allocated when not needed. Additionally, when the procedure ends, the memory allocated to the array is recovered automatically.

Because the size advantage clearly goes to the variable-length array strategy, we only need to test the relative speed of the two approaches.

Listing 21.13 CHKSPD1.BAS—Measuring String-Processing Speed of Fixed-Length Arrays

```
Dim i As Integer
Dim Fl(1 To 10000) As Integer
Private Sub Command1_Click()
    Dim Time1 As Date
    Dim Time2 As Date
    Time1 = Time
    For i = 1 To 10000
```

```
        Fl(i) = i
        Print Fl(i)
    Next i
    Time2 = Time
    TimeDiff Time1, Time2
End Sub
```

This code executed in 11 seconds. Now, modify the code to use a variable-length array instead, as shown in Listing 21.14.

Listing 21.14   CHKSPD2.BAS—Measuring String-Processing Speed of Variable-Length Arrays

```
Dim i As Integer
Dim Fl() As Integer

Private Sub Command1_Click()
    Dim Time1 As Date
    Dim Time2 As Date
    ReDim Fl(1 To 10000) As Integer

    Time1 = Time
    For i = 1 To 10000
        Fl(i) = i
        Print Fl(i)
    Next i
    Time2 = Time
    TimeDiff Time1, Time2
End Sub
```

This code also completed in 11 seconds. Therefore, we conclude that there is a memory size advantage to using variable-length arrays that does not exact any execution-time penalty.

> **Note:** Applications that use variable-length arrays run at the same speed as those that use fixed-length arrays, but require less memory.

One important use of the dynamic array is to create Visual Basic built-in objects at runtime. The following code creates five forms and allocates memory for them at runtime.

```
Global ExtraForms () as New Form1
Sub AllocProcedure()
    NumForms = 3
  ReDim ExtraForms(NumForms)
      .
      .
      .
End Sub
```

No memory is allocated to hold these forms until the `ReDim` statement is
executed. Thus, if you had three sets of five forms that were allocated
in three different subroutines, your application would only allocate
memory for five of them at a time, thereby reducing the running size
of the application by the size of 10 forms in memory.

Calling a Dynamic Link Library Routine

Whenever you run Visual Basic, or any other Windows application, you
are making extensive use of Dynamic Link Libraries (DLLs). Windows
is built upon three of the libraries:

➤ User

➤ Kernel

➤ GDI (Graphics Device Interface)

All of the routines contained in these libraries are available to you as a
Visual Basic developer. Most of the time, developers call the Windows
DLLs to perform some task that is difficult or impossible to do directly
in Visual Basic code. Occasionally, you may bypass an equivalent function in Visual Basic in favor of a faster function in a Windows DLL.

Calling DLL routines is not complicated, but it is more involved than
simple Visual Basic function calls. First, you must declare the Function
that you want to call in the general section of your module. Then you
use the function just like any other function in Visual Basic. Listing
21.15 shows an example program that calls a DLL routine.

Listing 21.15 DLL1.BAS—Calling DLLs

```
Private Declare Function SendMessage% Lib "user" (ByVal_
hWd%, ByVal wMsg%, ByVal wParam%, ByVal lParam&)

Private Declare Function GetFocus% Lib "user" ()

Const EM_GETLINECOUNT = &h40a


Private Sub Command1_Click()
text1.SetFocus
hWd% = GetFocus()
Msg$ = "The Number of Lines: "

Label1.Caption = Str$(SendMessage(hWd%, EM_GETLINECOUNT, 0,_
0))

End Sub
```

The first line on this example is a declaration of the function. This tells Visual Basic what the function call will look like and where to find it. The phrase `Lib "user"` tells Visual Basic that the routine is in the DLL called `user`, which is distributed with every copy of Windows.

The word `ByVal` indicates that a parameter is being passed by value. The statement that begins with `Const` is defining one of the standard constants in Windows. It will be used later in the code.

The purpose of this routine is to learn the number of lines that exist in a text box on the screen. The line that reads `text1.SetFocus` sets the focus on the text box that we want to examine. By setting the focus and then issuing the command `hWd% = GetFocus()`, we get the handle (`hWd%`) of that object. An object's *handle* is how it is known to Windows. It is kind of like a social security number, which is how a person is known to government computers. With the handle stored in `hWd%`, we can find the answer to the question about how many lines are in the text box by executing the following line:

```
Label1.Caption = Str$(SendMessage(hWd%, EM_GETLINECOUNT, 0,_
0))
```

This stores the information in a label that is displayed on the form.

Creating DLLs for yourself is a strategy that some developers use. The actual creation of these libraries is beyond the scope of this book, but we can describe the process in general. Using a C/C++ compiler, you can write routines in C/C++ that normally make Windows Application Programming Interface (API) calls. These routines are then compiled and linked into a special executable library with the suffix .DLL. All of the commonly available compilers support the creation of these libraries. (They can be created using other languages also, but C/C++ is the most common way.)

You store this .DLL file in the Windows system directory. When you `Declare` a function that comes from that library, Windows automatically loads it into memory for you. When you are through with it, Windows automatically unloads it.

The advantage of doing all of this work is simple: speed. Certain kinds of algorithms run much faster if written in C/C++ than they do in Visual Basic. This is because C and C++ are languages that are truly compiled into machine instructions. Additionally, C/C++ designers had performance foremost in their minds when creating the language, whereas the Visual Basic designers were more concerned with ease of use.

> **Note:** Consider coding complex and CPU-intensive routines in C/C++ and making them into a Dynamic Link Library. Call these DLL routines from within Visual Basic.

Label Controls versus Text Box Controls

Many developers confuse Label controls and Text Box controls. While both of them can be used to display text on a screen, a Text Box control also allows multi-line displays and text entry. As a result, it is much larger than a Label control. To demonstrate this, we created an application that contained 32 Text Box controls. When loaded in memory, it occupied 250 KB. Then we created a form that contained 32 Label controls. It only occupied 218 KB of memory. Thus we can conclude that a Text Box control is 1024 bytes larger than a Label control.

In terms of performance, this means that anytime you use a Text Box control where a Label control would have worked, you wasted 1014 bytes of precious memory. As always, this is of little concern in trivial applications, but of real concern in production systems.

> **Note:** Use Labels instead of Text Boxes if possible. Use Text Boxes only when you need the additional functionality.

Improving Database Performance

The performance of the database is critical to the performance of applications that use them. In fact, many applications use the database so heavily that database performance overwhelms all other performance considerations when optimizing the application. Databases introduce considerably more overhead than simple files because they deal with so many problems that files ignore. Among other things, databases are expected to coordinate access by several users at the same time, protect itself from corruption when a system failure occurs, and verify data as it is being entered. Databases are also supposed to operate properly after a new field has been inserted into the schema.

None of these challenges are insurmountable. The number of successful database programs on the market prove that it is achievable. They achieve these goals by adding special code for each new feature. This increases the load on the system and provides performance challenges to you, as an application developer. The database vendors have provided special features that speed up the operation of their products, but most of them work only if you tell them to.

Indexes

The most basic and most important performance improvement that can be made is in the indexes that you put on the tables in the database. *Indexes* are special data files that contain the approximate locations of important data. In Visual Basic, these indexes are normally created using the Data Manager add-in.

To be effective, indexes must be created for the fields that will be used to access the data. For example, an index on the zip code field will not help you if you are searching for everyone who drives a Honda. You instead need to create an index on the make of the car to speed this query.

At times, designers are tempted to index every field. While this certainly would speed queries, it slows down database updates because so many indexes must be updated. In addition, all those indexes take up a lot of disk space. Realistically, you should only create indexes on fields that you know you will use to access data.

> **Note:** Create indexes only on those fields that will be used often to access rows in the database. Otherwise, you will be introducing overhead to the updating process for no benefit.

Some fields, such as gender, may be used quite often as criteria for a query but are not of any value in speeding things up. If half of your rows qualify for membership in the index, it is probably just as fast to process the data by primary key as it is with a special index.

Set-Level Processing

To obtain good performance from a client/server database, it is critical to use set level logic in your program. For example, it is possible to access your data one row at the time and test for a certain condition in your Visual Basic code. If the row passes the test, you display it. If it fails the test, you ignore it. This is a poor way to design an application.

By sending a request for one row at the time, you are preventing the query optimization code in the database management system from working its magic. If the database is physically located on a server on the network, then you will be flooding the wires with data that you don't want. It is far better to include code like the following:

```
SELECT Name, Rank, Serial Number FROM Employee_Table _
WHERE Department=4812
```

By so doing, the database engine will be free to send you only those rows which contain a Department field that equals 4812. None of the other rows will be sent.

Note: Use set-level commands wherever possible. Avoid processing one row at the time because it is a very inefficient way to process data in a client/server environment.

From Here...

In this chapter, you were introduced to concepts and strategies that help speed up the execution and shrink the size of your application at runtime. You learned how to measure both the speed of an application and its size.

In the section on the performance of objects, you saw examples of how to manage multiple forms in the same application. You also learned to manage graphics, particularly in the form of pictures. You also learned when to use Label controls and when to employ Text Box controls instead.

Then you learned how to efficiently allocate variables, strings, and arrays. Then you were introduced to the concept of Dynamic Link Libraries. Finally, you were introduced to the topic of database access. The importance of indexes and set-level processing was discussed in some detail.

➤ For more information on calling DLLs , see Chapter 3, "Using the Windows API."

➤ For more information on databases, see Chapter 9, "Client/Server Databases."

➤ For a thorough discussion of graphics, see Chapter 16, "Graphics: Data Analysis."

VB Versus VBA

by Jon Oelschlaeger

This chapter takes a brief look at some of the similarities and differences between Visual Basic 4 and Visual Basic for Applications. You will explore the impact that these differences might have on the design and development of your Visual Basic application code.

This chapter investigates the following differences between Visual Basic 4 and Visual Basic for Applications:

- ➤ Common program language syntax
- ➤ Programming impact of noncomparable syntactical code
- ➤ User interface and programming object comparisons
- ➤ Data Access Object models
- ➤ Cross-environment code development and porting
- ➤ Singular features of Visual Basic 4

Comparing the Differences Between Visual Basic 4 and VBA

First the good news and then the bad news. The good news is that with the introduction of Visual Basic 4, the degree of conformance between the Visual Basic language syntax and that of Visual Basic for Applications (VBA) has been greatly improved. In addition, the code editors supporting Visual Basic 4 and contemporary VBA implementations have been essentially unified. For those of you who have previously tried to exploit OLE 2 Automation programming using Visual Basic 3, you will notice the following improvements:

➤ Programmers porting code between Visual Basic, and say Microsoft Excel 7 VBA or Microsoft Project 4 VBA, will find that the job is much easier. Bi-directional code reuse or migration between Visual Basic 4 and either of these two Visual Basic for Applications programming environments is much easier, and less prone to require adapting language modifications.

➤ Many syntax language elements used in VBA that previously conflicted with restricted keywords and structures within Visual Basic 3 no longer conflict. This eliminates the need to enclose conflicting keywords in `[…]` when coding OLE 2 Automation features within Visual Basic using other VBA-compliant application object libraries.

➤ Object collection manipulation syntax such as `For Each…Next`, and object manipulation syntax such as `With…End With` which were quite efficient in source code and performance when programming within VBA, specifically using Excel 5, Excel 7, or Project 4, are now also supported in Visual Basic 4.

➤ Code organization and code editing techniques are now nearly identical between Visual Basic and VBA, as are the supporting tools and commands for editing operations.

➤ The scope of variables and code procedures, and the syntax for declaring variable and procedure scope are now used consistently between Visual Basic and VBA.

- Visual Basic 4 and VBA-supporting applications, such as Excel 7 and Project 4, all provide capabilities for menu bar and toolbar negotiations for embedded OLE 2 objects. This now allows both Visual Basic applications and VBA-hosted applications to equally implement OLE 2's edit-in-place capabilities.

- Visual Basic 4 and VBA both provide named argument capabilities in procedure calling conventions. Arguments can be passed using call-by-name techniques, and not just by using position dependent arguments. In a related change to the argument passing conventions, Visual Basic, like VBA, can make use of optional argument specifications when declaring `Sub` and `Function` procedures.

- Code modules, class code, and form-level procedures created in Visual Basic 4 and VBA can now be browsed and managed in a consistent, integrated fashion. Previously, Visual Basic 3 code libraries could not be viewed and accessed using the Object Browser facility provided with Excel 7 and Project 4.

These are the major areas of welcome good news. However, there are still some differences between Visual Basic 4 and VBA applications code. That's sort of the bad news.

Many of the differences are a result of the different programming audiences and level of application detail that the two similar language facilities address. Some of the major differences between Visual Basic 4 and VBA that are likely to impact your applications planning, design, development, and porting are listed below.

- VBA objects, in particular user interface controls (such as text edit boxes, combo boxes, and list boxes), typically only provide a single event (or a limited repertoire of events). This is unlike Visual Basic, where each control provides numerous events, thereby affording detailed program-controlled interaction with the object. VBA controls, in most cases, provide only the equivalent of Visual Basic's `Click` event.

➤ Visual Basic objects provide the Windows Handle (hWnd) and, if appropriate, the Device Context Handle (hDC) properties which are crucial to programming with Windows API calls. VBA objects do not provide the hWnd and hDC properties. It is possible, however, to determine the hWnd and hDC for VBA controls, but the coding required to do this is not necessary when using Visual Basic.

➤ VBA windows control objects typically have a more restricted set of properties that can be retrieved or set than their functionally equivalent Visual Basic counterparts.

➤ Visual Basic enables programmers to directly create several generic classes of windows (for example, MDI Parent, MDI Child, and ordinary windows), and in a variety of styles (like fixed border and sizable border). In addition to creating windows, Visual Basic programmers can create and manipulate the usual window components, such as menu bars and custom toolbars. VBA does not directly provide for creating windows from generic classes, but rather enables the programmer to create windows only from the specialized classes and styles that are supported by the application context within which VBA runs. Additionally, VBA programmers are limited to manipulating the hosting application's menu bars and toolbars.

➤ Visual Basic 4 programs can be designed to define their own Classes and also create multiple instances of Objects of these custom Classes; VBA presently cannot.

➤ Visual Basic 4 programmers can design and create OLE 2 Automation Servers which can be utilized by other Visual Basic and VBA applications as components of larger applications. This capability to create OLE 2 Automation Servers is not available within VBA.

Summarizing Syntax Differences

Previous to the introduction of Visual Basic 4 , there were quite noticeable syntactical differences between Visual Basic 3 and subsequently released applications—such as Microsoft Excel 7, Microsoft Access 2, and Microsoft Project 4—which supported variants of the Visual Basic language (known collectively hereafter as Visual Basic for Applications, or just simply as VBA).

> **Note:** Although Microsoft Access versions 1 and 2 also host a programming facility with extensive similarities in concept and syntax to Visual Basic 3, this language facility is not, strictly speaking, VBA compliant. Instead, the Access 1 and 2 built-in programming language facilities are known as *Access Basic*. Presumably, the forthcoming release of the Microsoft Access 7 will show greater conformance to the VBA language model. However, for the purposes of limiting the scope of discussions here, we will focus mainly on Excel 7 and Project 4 VBA and Visual Basic 4 features when making comparisons.

With the recent introduction of Microsoft Excel 7 and Microsoft Project 4, the syntax differences between VBA and Visual Basic 4 are quite small.

Understanding Common Syntax

For those Microsoft products that are not fully VBA-compliant as of the date of publication of this book, the keywords that reflect the language syntax have for some time been a fairly consistent set, and also include *restricted keywords* specified by Microsoft for eventual future expansion and compatibility purposes.

As a first step in understanding the common syntax and keyword similarities, you should closely compare the language facilities of all Microsoft products which support the Visual Basic language. Such a comparison quickly becomes important when you are contemplating the development of a Visual Basic application that is to be migrated or ported across the listed development or runtime environments.

Analyzing Word 7 Syntax Differences

Word 7 implements the least consistent and compliant version of Basic. In fact, Word 7 is not really a Visual Basic for Applications (VBA) language host facility at all.

Word 7 supports a variation of the Basic language which is known as *Word Basic.* The focus of Word Basic is to provide a language programming facility within Word 7 that is highly tailored to the manipulation of word processing documents, and which operates by itself in a stand-alone setting.

Unlike the other Microsoft products, Word 7 cannot participate as a client or controller in OLE 2 Automation operations, and therefore cannot access and manipulate another application's objects. This state of affairs is most visible in the fact that Word 7 does not support the VBA `CreateObject` and `GetObject` functions which are central to all OLE 2 Automation operations. Word 7 does not support the `Debug` object, the `Me` object, or the `Nothing` object. Finally, the `For Each…` and `With…` constructs which are the hallmark of VBA for efficient collection and object manipulation are also absent in Word Basic.

In fact, Word 7 is not really object-oriented. Word Basic instead relies on cursor positioning and selection-oriented techniques, combined with menu command-equivalent language syntax elements to accomplish its programming purposes. The area of greatest Basic language consistency between Visual Basic, VBA, and Word Basic lies in the realm of string processing functions and variable types. This is pretty much what you would expect, because document content manipulation relies to a significant degree on string processing.

Word 7 does, however, provide support for OLE 2 Automation as a server. That is, Visual Basic and the other truly VBA-compliant host application programming facilities can use Word 7 as an OLE 2 Automation server.

Applications that fully support OLE Automation make their "documents" available as objects. However, with Word 7, you cannot use OLE Automation to directly manipulate a Word 7 document as an object. That is to say, you cannot use the `GetObject` function in Visual

Basic to access a Word 7 document. Moreover, the Word Basic language does not support properties and methods or the syntax structure which would allow for their specification.

Word 7 *does* offer, as an OLE Automation server, an object called the `Word.Basic` object. This object essentially presents all of the programming language elements of Word Basic for use in manipulating the Word 7 application, and any Word documents which Word 7 currently contains. Most of these language elements are statements, or "commands" which manipulate Word document components.

A major difference between using the `Word.Basic` object, and the objects within other VBA-compliant applications like Excel 7 and Project 4, is that the language syntax of Word Basic is such that the "thing" to be acted upon is specified along with the action to be taken within a single line of Word Basic code. The concepts of properties to modify the attributes of objects, and methods to perform some action on objects is absent from Word Basic.

Interestingly, the `Word.Basic` object and its syntax do support one of the key features of the broader VBA syntax; the capability of position-independent named arguments (call-by-name arguments), and the omission of optional arguments in function and statement argument lists.

It is likely that at some point in the not-too-distant future, Microsoft will revamp Word for Windows to:

➤ Fully support OLE 2 Automation with Word functioning as an object-oriented server. Word would offer objects, properties, and methods that could be used by other VBA client code, much as Excel 7 now offers its complete panoply of objects in an object library for external reference.

➤ Integrate a new VBA-compliant language facility into Word. This would provide Word with the capability to act as an OLE 2 Automation client in relationship to other OLE 2 Automation servers.

Of course one of the key considerations in achieving this advancement would be to maintain backward compatibility with the current Word

Basic language syntax, and the `Word.Basic` OLE Automation object. This compatibility would be needed to support existing Word 7 macros written in Word Basic, or Visual Basic, or VBA applications currently using the `Word.Basic` object. Until this revision takes place, the Word 7 product is sort of an odd-man-out in the world of VBA programming in Microsoft's application product lineup.

Analyzing Microsoft Access 2 Syntax Differences

The Basic language variation supported by Microsoft Access 2 is called Access Basic. Access Basic is nearly fully compliant with VBA, but not quite. Again, it is highly likely that Microsoft will implement full VBA compliance with the next release of the Access product, but this is currently not the case. Areas of noncompliance which are likely to have a significant cross-application programming impact include:

➤ Does not support the use of named arguments and omission of optional arguments in function and statement invocations.

➤ Does not support the use of the VBA construct `With...End With` for modifying multiple properties, or invoking multiple methods for a single object.

➤ Does not support the use of the VBA construct `For Each...Next` for looping through the members of a collection, or the elements of a `Variant` array.

When designing Visual Basic code which might be ported later to Access 2, you can employ specific programming strategies to eliminate problems with these noncompliance areas. Here's how to deal with:

➤ *Argument differences*—Do not use named arguments or omit optional arguments. Specify all arguments, and make sure that they are specified in the correct positional order. This will work correctly with Visual Basic, and all variations of VBA, including Access Basic, and the `Word.Basic` object.

➤ *With...End With*—Do not use this approach to multiple specification of properties or invocation of methods for a single object. Instead, spell out each code line's object name and property or method.

➤ *For Each...Next*—Use ordinary `For` loops instead. This requires declaration of an appropriate loop variable, and the range of values of the loop. Usually, the ending value of this loop will be the name of the collection object and the count property of the collection object (`collection.count`).

Another area where Access Basic is not fully VBA-compliant is in the area of default declaration specifications. This is a programming area that, for most typical programs, will have less impact. The specifications for default declaration which are not supported by Access Basic are

➤ `CDecl`—Specifying the use of C language argument conventions in external code resource function declarations; applicable only to the Macintosh

➤ `DefBool`—Default variable letter range automatically defined of the type Boolean

➤ `DefByte`—Default variable letter range automatically defined of the type byte

➤ `DefDate`—Default variable letter range automatically defined of the type date

➤ `DefObj`—Default variable letter range automatically defined of the type object

These declaration-related statements can usually be easily avoided. All variables can be declared explicitly, without the use of the default specification mechanism.

Finally, for compatibility with Macintosh versions of your applications, the following functions are not supported by Access Basic, but are supported in VBA:

➤ `MacID`—Converts a four character constant to a value to be used with the `Dir`, `Kill`, `Shell`, and `AppActivate` functions when executing a VBA application on a Macintosh

➤ `MacScript`—Executes a named Macintosh Script file

Clearly, these areas of nonconformance are not presently a problem, because no implementation of Access 2 exists for the Apple Macintosh. Furthermore, it must be assumed that should an implementation of Access 2 (or higher version) be offered for the Macintosh, then this issue would be resolved by Microsoft.

These points where Access Basic and VBA syntax are not perfectly synchronized represent, in most cases, only minor limitations within Access Basic. The code should function without serious errors at worst and reveal subtle errors at least.

Access 2 itself does not offer OLE 2 Automation library capabilities for external use. That is, Access 2 cannot act as an OLE 2 Automation server. If you were to check the Windows Registry, you would find Access 2 absent. This can most easily be observed by starting up the Windows Registry Editor application REGEDIT.EXE (found in the WINDOWS directory).

If you start the REGEDIT and have the Access 2 product installed on your computer, you will find that Access 2 has a registered association between the file name extensions it supports such as MDB and MDA, but does not register to offer any object libraries.

However, Access 2 *can* function as an OLE 2 Automation client, using and manipulating the objects offered by other OLE 2 Automation server libraries such as those provided by Excel 7, Project 4, and the Word Basic object offered by Word 7, as well as OLE 2 Automation Server Class libraries that are created and registered using Visual Basic.

Access 2 is unlike other VBA-compliant applications in other respects. VBA-compliant products such as Visual Basic itself, Excel 7, and Project 4 have both the capability to reference-link to external OLE 2 Automation server libraries, and have an Object Browser to view the contents of such libraries. Access 2 does not have the capability to reference-link to OLE libraries, nor does it include an Object Browser.

This requires that you know the objects, methods, and properties of any OLE 2 Automation Server libraries that you choose to use from inside of Access 2. Using the Object Browser of some other application like Excel 5 or Visual Basic 4 to get the information you need is about the only way to bridge this lack in Access 2.

Analyzing Excel 7 and Project 4 Differences

When comparing Visual Basic 4 and the core syntax of Excel 7 and Project 4, the level of correspondence between all three of these products is almost complete. That is, Visual Basic 4, Excel 7, and Project 4 all implement the same core language syntax.

It is pretty clear that code which involves only the fundamental core syntax and that has been developed in any of these three environments can be freely transported between any of the others.

What remains unique to each of these three programming environments are the objects, and the objects' attendant properties and methods.

Understanding Visual Basic 4 Extensions

Visual Basic includes some extensions to the core VBA language capabilities which are unique to the Visual Basic product. Some of these Visual Basic extensions involve syntax elements, while others involve capabilities and objects that are not present in any other VBA implementations. These differences are primarily found in the `Command` keyword, device contexts, and object references.

Using the Command Keyword

Visual Basic as well as Access 2 make use of the keyword `Command`, whereas other VBA-compliant applications do not. The keyword `Command` is a function which returns a string containing a command line argument. This function enables you to retrieve and subsequently interpret a string of characters that follows the executable program name which starts a Windows application—in this case a Visual Basic (or Access 2) application.

Excel 7 and Project 4 allow the specification of a startup command-line argument string, but the interpretation of how the command-line argument string should be used is a fixed built-in capability of the application itself, and is therefore not available to any VBA code module which may be associated with an Excel 7 or Project 4 "document" file.

As a practical programming consideration it is therefore advisable not to make use of the `Command` function in code that is used across Visual Basic and the various VBA contexts. Generally, this does not present a serious programming restriction or limitation.

Using Device Contexts in Visual Basic

Another area where Visual Basic and VBA differ is Visual Basic's ability to manipulate Windows device contexts. A Windows device context is an abstract graphical area and the data which characterize the area, such as its dimensions, scaling, aspect ratio, pens, brushes, color palette, and so forth. Visual Basic affords you the capability to programmatically modify, via the Windows API, the device contexts associated with the following objects:

➤ `Printer` *Object*—Where the device context reflects the usable printing area and graphical capabilities of the default Windows printer

➤ `PictureBox` *Object*—Where the device context is formed by the interior area within the outer border of the `PictureBox` object

➤ *Form Objects*—Where the device context consists of the interior area within the form, excluding the border and title bar areas. All styles of Visual Basic forms (regular forms, MDI Parent forms, and MDI Child forms) have associated device contexts

Visual Basic provides corresponding properties, methods, and functions of these device contexts which enables you to manipulate them. All of the methods are graphical methods, since they render some graphical modification of the object's device context. The attendant Visual Basic methods, properties, and functions of a device context are listed below.

➤ `LoadPicture(`*filename*`)`—A function that loads a device context with a bitmap (BMP or RLE file), metafile (WMF file), or icon (ICO file) obtained from disk.

➤ `SavePicture Object.Picture,` *`filename`*—A statement that copies the graphical contents (`Picture` property) of a device context into a bitmap, metafile, or icon file to be saved on disk. You can also use this function to save the device context contents of OLE Container objects, consisting of the graphical rendering within the OLE Container's bounding box.

➤ `PaintPicture Object.Picture,` *`X1, Y1, width1, height1, X2, Y2, width2, height2,`* `opcode`—A method that draws (renders) the contents of one device context onto the another device context, making specified modifications during the drawing process. The `Picture` parameter is the source device context for the drawing, typically specified as the `Picture` property of the object acting as the source device context. The object upon which the `PaintPicture` method operates is used as the destination device context. The x and y coordinates specify offsets from the upper left-hand corner of the destination device context and source device context, respectively. This allows clipping and offsetting in the copy operation. `width` and `height` parameters specify compression or stretching of the device context when copied. Finally, the `opcode` parameter specifies the type of copy operation to be performed when copying bitmap graphics. The `opcode` parameter is as specified in the Windows API function call for the `BitBlt` function.

➤ `PSet [Step]` *`(X, Y)`*, *`color`*—A graphical method that draws a point at the specified x and y locations (or offset from the `CurrentX` and `CurrentY` positions, if the optional `Step` parameter is used). The point drawn is of the color, specified by the *`color`* parameter. The size of the point is determined by the `DrawWidth` property then current for the device context.

➤ `Line [Step]` *`(X1, Y1)`* - `[Step]` *`(X2, Y2)`*, *`color`*, `[B][F]`— A graphical method which draws a line between the point-pair *x1,y1* and *x2,y2* (or offset from the `CurrentX` and `CurrentY` positions, if the optional `Step` parameter is used). The line drawn is of the color specified by the *`color`* parameter. The width of the line is determined by the `DrawWidth` property, the current for the device context. If the optional `B` parameter is used, the coordinates are taken to specify the diagonally opposite corners of a rectangle to be drawn. If the optional `F` parameter is used, the rectangle is filled with color.

➤ `Circle [Step] (X, Y), radius, color, start, end, aspect`—A graphical method that draws a circle or arc segment. The x and y coordinates specify the center of the circle or arc (or offset from the `CurrentX` and `CurrentY` positions, if the optional `Step` parameter is used). The `radius` parameter specifies the radius of the circle or arc, and `color` specifies the color of the circle or arc. The `start` and `end` parameters specify the start and end angles of an arc to be formed (in radians). Finally, the parameter `aspect` specifies the aspect ratio of the circle. If `aspect` is not 1.0, then an ellipse is formed.

➤ `Scale (X1, Y1) - (X2, Y2)`—A method that modifies the metrics and coordinate system of a device context. The point-pair coordinates specify the dimensions of a diagonal of the device context (that is, the upper left-hand corner and lower right-hand corner).

➤ `Point (X, Y)`—A method that returns the RGB color number of the point in the device context specified by the coordinates x and y.

➤ `Print outputlist`—A method that renders printed output in a device context. The type of printing performed is determined by the various Font-related properties of the device context, and the `ForeColor` property. The `outputlist` parameter is any valid printing expression.

➤ `CurrentX`—A property that sets or gets the current x location of the pen position relative to the upper left-hand corner of the coordinate system origin within the device context. Printing or drawing methods applied to the device context also modify the `CurrentX` property.

➤ `CurrentY`—A property that sets or gets the current y location of the pen position relative to the upper left-hand corner of the coordinate system origin within the device context. Printing or drawing methods applied to the device context also modify the `CurrentY` property.

➤ `Picture`—A property that sets or gets the graphical contents of the device context.

➤ `DrawWidth`—A property that sets the drawing pen width to be used in the device context. Specifies the pen width used by the various drawing methods.

➤ `ScaleMode`—A property that sets or gets the scaling and coordinate system used within the device context. Also the properties `ScaleTop`, `ScaleLeft`, `ScaleWidth`, and `ScaleHeight` are related to the `ScaleMode` property, and the `Scale` method when defining custom coordinate systems and scales for a device context.

Additionally, these Visual Basic objects also have a property—`hDC`—the handle of a device context, which enables you to identify the device contexts by their Windows assigned handles. As a consequence, you can invoke most of the Windows API function calls of the GDI.DLL (Graphics Device Interface) library. Declaring and using Windows GDI function calls within your Visual Basic program gives you the opportunity to perform sophisticated transformations and manipulations of the device contents in these objects.

In this regard, it is possible to access a device context by invoking the Windows API function `GetDC(hWnd)`, which returns a handle to a device context (i.e., `hDC`). Of course, unlike the special properties, methods, and functions discussed above for Visual Basic manipulation of device contexts, you would have to thereafter exclusively use other Windows API calls to use the device context referenced in this manner.

A related consideration is that only Visual Basic objects have an `hWnd` property—the handle of a window, which enables you to identify the windows handle of all screen windows objects. Again, to invoke most Windows API function calls of the USER.DLL, and some of the function calls of the GDI.DLL libraries, you need to provide the windows handle as one or more of the calling arguments. For example, to send a message to a Windows window, you need to provide the `hWnd` as a calling parameter in the Windows API `SendMessage(hWnd, Msg, wParam, lParam)` function, or the `PostMessage(hWnd, Msg, wParam, lParam)` function. Note also, that in order to invoke function calls to a device context, you must first obtain its `hDC` using the `GetDC(hWnd)` function, and the `GetDC` function needs the window handle as a calling parameter.

It is of course possible to use the Windows API function `GetActiveWindow()` from within a VBA application to obtain the windows handle (`hWnd`) of whichever window is active within a VBA application, and then proceed from there. Some amount of additional coding work would have to be done in VBA code—activating the desired window—prior to making the `GetActiveWindow()` function call that would not have to be done if you would do the same coding in Visual Basic.

Because Visual Basic alone provides these capabilities, you must carefully consider several issues when developing an application. First, any application that must directly manipulate a device context is best developed as a Visual Basic application, rather than a VBA application. Second, Visual Basic code which manipulates the above listed device contexts cannot be ported into an equivalent VBA application code module.

As a practical matter, it would probably afford the maximum flexibility to develop a set of Class modules in Visual Basic 4 that both create and manipulate the device contexts that your applications might need. Because the Class modules can be registered as OLE Automation servers, both Visual Basic applications and VBA applications can create the objects they need from these classes, along with appropriate methods and properties for the object. The Visual Basic and VBA code that creates instances of objects (that is, instantiates the object) from these classes—using the `CreateObject(registered.classname)` function—can successfully execute unmodified in both the Visual Basic and the VBA contexts.

Using Object References in Visual Basic

Another area of difference between Visual Basic and VBA is in object referencing. Some of the capabilities of Visual Basic to reference and allocate storage for objects are not present in VBA.

Specifically, the following keywords—which are part of Visual Basic's repertoire—are absent within VBA:

➤ `Me`—Acts as an implicitly defined global object variable within the runtime environment of Visual Basic. It is an object variable that references (provides the base memory address of) the object whose code stream is executing at any instant. Various VBA-host environments provide a similar concept. For example, in Excel 7 VBA, the method `ThisWorkbook` returns an object variable which references the workbook object within which the code stream is currently executing.

➤ `New`—A keyword that is used in the syntax of object variable declaration (for example, `Dim objectvar As New class`, where `objectvar` is an object variable, and `class` refers to a class of Visual Basic or externally creatable objects). The keyword `New` invokes the class constructor, thereby creating an instance of an object of the class, and assigns the reference of the object to the object variable.

By invoking the class constructor, the `New` keyword also has the effect of dynamically allocating storage for the member variables of the class (the object's properties), and loading of the member functions of the class (the code library elements which embody the object's methods). The classes used by the `New` keyword can be any Visual Basic intrinsic class (such as controls, forms, and collections), and any externally creatable classes, such as Visual Basic Class module classes, or externally creatable OLE Automation classes.

In VBA-host environments, dynamic memory allocation for object storage is usually handled someplace implicitly buried within a function for an object class. For example, in Excel 7 VBA, the constructors which create an instance of objects of a class are incorporated into an object called a collection. Each class has a corresponding collection—like `Workbooks` is the collection for `Workbook` objects. Within each collection is a function that creates the object(similar to a C++ constructor)—a method of the collection called `Add`. It is this function that actually does the memory allocation.

➤ `TypeOf` *objectname* `Is` *classname*—This is a logical expression that determines if the *objectname* object is an instance of the *classname* class. Use of this syntax is only permitted in `If…Then…Else` expressions as the logical `If` test.

Although no such syntax exists in VBA, there are alternative mechanisms to accomplish much the same thing within VBA-host versions. For example, in Excel 7 VBA, there is function called `TypeName(`*object*`)`, which returns the class name of an object as a string. You can then test the class name using typical logical comparisons.

The primary consequences of these differences between Visual Basic and VBA are strongly influenced by whether the application you are developing is dependent on the capabilities provided by these unique syntax elements.

Again, if your application needs to perform object-class tests, determine within which object the code stream is currently executing, or perform sophisticated instantiation of objects, then such code should be written in Visual Basic. Converting it to another VBA-host environment would require rethinking the code, and then making modifications.

Conversely, if you want to develop and test parts of an application within Visual Basic, and later port the code into a VBA execution environment, you should avoid the use of the above syntax elements, because they are not supported in VBA.

Comparing Environment Differences

One of the key differences that impacts not only language syntax but also behavioral characteristics of Visual Basic programs as compared to VBA programs, is the ability of Visual Basic to create its own generic window objects. The consequences and considerations which these differences entail will be investigated in the subsections that follow.

A second major difference that has a significant impact on the characteristics of Visual Basic when compared to VBA is that Visual Basic controls generally have more extensive event capabilities (that is, a greater number and variety of windows messages are decoded and presented as Visual Basic events) than do corresponding functionality VBA controls. In this regard, the comparison is drawn between the Visual Basic controls of the controls toolbox, and the similar controls of VBA's controls toolbox. Also, many of the properties of functionally comparable controls in Visual Basic and VBA are different. These differences are addressed in following subsections.

Reviewing Object Differences

In the previous major section you focused on language syntax differences between Visual Basic 4 and various implementations of VBA. In this section you will shift your attention to differences among the objects that are part of the Visual Basic and VBA environments.

To accomplish this comparison let's first subdivide the comparison into two major parts—window objects and control objects.

Comparing Visual Basic and VBA Window Objects

One of the chief distinctions between Visual Basic 4 and VBA is just what constitutes a "window" in these different environments. Consider for a moment that in Visual Basic you have a fair degree of control over defining your own generic windows, and that in VBA the windows you can use are more-or-less predefined for you as some part of the VBA host application's object hierarchy.

To clarify this issue of windows a bit you should recall that Visual Basic can statically and dynamically (during design and during execution) create windows of fairly general classes and styles. Visual Basic programs can include general Forms, MDI Parent Forms, and MDI Child Forms. Objects of these fundamental window classes allow the greatest generalized flexibility in defining placement and use of other child windows of these Form-class windows, such as controls, and in determining how the windows themselves can be used.

This is in contrast to VBA windows classes and styles, and how they are specified and used. In a VBA environment, the classes and styles of windows are preordained by the VBA host application itself. That is to say that they are built into the overall fabric of the VBA host application's user interface.

Take as an example VBA as hosted within Excel 7, where there are several classes of user interface windows which are predefined as being within Excel's object hierarchy. The following classes and styles of predefined windows are part of Excel 7:

➤ `Worksheet` *Class*—Window class and style, acting as an MDI Child window, that itself includes a very complex set of child window classes which are contained within its object hierarchy. Examples of child windows are `PivotTable`, `Range`, and `Drawing Objects`.

➤ `DialogSheet` *Class*—Window class and style, also acting as an MDI Child window, that itself incorporates a different set of child window classes, such as `DialogFrame` and `Drawing Objects`.

➤ `Chart` *Class*—Window class and style, again acting as an MDI Child window, that includes yet another set of child window classes as part of its object hierarchy. A representative list of these child windows includes `ChartArea`, `PlotArea`, `Axis`, and `Legend Objects`.

➤ `Workbook` *Class*—Window class and style that acts as a type of MDI Parent window for `Worksheet` and `Chart` child windows during runtime. In design-time mode, the Workbook window also acts as an MDI Parent window for `DialogSheet`, `Module`, and Excel 4 `MacroSheet` window classes which act as MDI Child windows.

A cursory analysis of other VBA host environments such as Project 4 and Access 2 reveals that this same application-customized assortment of user interface windows is provided intrinsically by all host applications. As other Microsoft applications are brought into VBA compliance, the diversity of application-unique window classes and styles will continue to grow.

So, you may well ask, what are some of the consequences of these different window classes and styles when comparing Visual Basic and VBA? Well, the foremost consequence is that if your application requires use of the generalized window styles afforded by Visual Basic 4, then you must design a Visual Basic-centric method for accomplishing your objectives.

You can design a Visual Basic 4 Class that includes the desired generalized windows, and then register the Class. Armed with this registered Class, you can incorporate generalized Forms (windows) within both a Visual Basic application, and any VBA application that can act as an OLE 2 Automation controller (or "client"). Referencing your Visual Basic 4 defined Class enables you to port the code which instantiates the window objects within the Class to any suitable VBA (or of course Visual Basic) host application.

Comparing Visual Basic and VBA Control Objects

Another key area of difference between Visual Basic and VBA pertains to the characteristics of controls and menus. For the purposes of the following discussion, the illustrations again principally reference Excel 7 but are equally applicable to other VBA-hosting applications.

The controls and menus have different object names, and other differences in Visual Basic and across the various VBA implementations. However, at this point you should concentrate on only one characteristic of these objects—their event capabilities.

Evaluating Control Event Differences

As you may or may not realize, the events triggered user interaction with these controls, and menus arise as the result of decoding Windows messages. As users interact with these objects, messages are queued by the Windows operating system and sent to the windows message decoding code which constitutes the message processing loop for these controls' windows.

Within the Visual Basic 4 runtime environment, almost all windows messages for controls and menus are decoded and transformed into events. Typically, most of the code in a Visual Basic program consists of event procedures which execute upon the control or menu receiving a windows message.

By way of contrast, most VBA functionally equivalent user interface controls and menus only support a single (or in some cases a restricted number of) events. Again, using the Excel 7 VBA environment as an example, you will notice that the controls offer only the equivalent of the Visual Basic `Click` event.

Controls in VBA environments do not support the same programming style and automatic construction of event procedure "code stubs" that are present in Visual Basic. Instead, VBA programming environments reflect the "decoding of windows messages" for controls as a property of the control object. It is usually quite apparent which property represents the effect of windows message decoding, since, by convention in VBA, they all have the form "OnXyyyyy." For example in Excel 7, if the user interacts with a Text Box control, the corresponding property is `OnAction`.

The scheme implemented in VBA to invoke execution of the related application code stream when an "event" takes place consists of assigning the name of a code procedure (a `Function` or `Sub` procedure) to this `OnAction` property. When the "event" occurs, execution control is then transferred to the code procedure that responds to the "event."

The sense of the "event" being decoded by VBA with the OnAction property oftentimes does not correspond directly to what you might think of as the Visual Basic event. The VBA `OnAction` property in Excel 5 is not like Visual Basic's `Click` event. However, only in the context of Excel 5 VBA, the `OnAction` property is generally otherwise equivalent to "Click."

On the surface of it, for simple control uses, this seems pretty straightforward—and oftentimes it is. If you are just dealing with Visual Basic menu objects everything works just fine, because menu objects only have a single event—the `Click` event. However, what do you do about Visual Basic code where a given control may have several event procedures? Or, worse yet, what do you do when the logical sense of what constitutes an "event" is different between Visual Basic and VBA? For example, the Visual Basic Text Box control supports the multitude of events listed in Table 22.1.

Table 22.1   The Equivalent Visual and VBA Events

Event	Excel VBA Equivalent	Access VBA Equivalent
Change	OnAction	OnChange
Click	(none)	OnClick
DblClick	(none)	OnDblClick
DragDrop	(none)	(none)
DragOver	(none)	(none)
GotFocus	(none)	OnGotFocus
KeyDown	(none)	OnKeyDown
KeyPress	(none)	OnKeyPress
KeyUp	(none)	OnKeyUp
LinkClose	(none)	(none)
LinkError	(none)	(none)
LinkNotify	(none)	(none)
LinkOpen	(none)	(none)
LostFocus	(none)	OnLostFocus
MouseDown	(none)	OnMouseDown
MouseMove	(none)	OnMouseMove
MouseUp	(none)	OnMouseUp

While investigating the correspondence (or lack thereof) between events in Visual Basic and VBA, it should be noted that there is a great degree of variation in the number of events (or event-equivalent properties) among the various VBA-host environments.

First, the events of the Visual Basic 4 controls, and the event equivalent properties of the Access 2 control are nearly the same. The two consistent areas where there are differences are:

➤ Visual Basic provides `DragOver` and `DragDrop` message decoding for its controls, whereas Access 2 does not. Clearly, Access 2 does not support drag-and-drop programming with its controls.

➤ Visual Basic provides `LinkOpen`, `LinkClose`, `LinkError` and `LinkNotify` message decoding for its controls that can participate in DDE Link operations (Label and Text Box controls), and Access 2 does not.

Secondly, notice that all Excel 7 equivalent controls provide only a single event equivalent property for all decoded messages. Furthermore, the decoded message that provokes the event action varies with each of the controls in Excel 7.

Finally, notice that although Word 7 (in Word Basic) does not have any event (or event-equivalent property), it does support the usual controls. In Word 7 the standard controls are defined during the design phase using the Word Dialog Editor. This is a utility applet that installs with Word 7. The Word Dialog Editor is a specialized Windows applet that provides for the layout and design of dialog forms. Using the Dialog Editor, you can create a form with the listed controls, and set the default design-time properties of the controls. The results of the Dialog Editor are left as a set of Word Basic code on the Clipboard. This automatically generated code can then be pasted into your Word Basic application. If you have knowledge of the Windows API, some functions are accessible via Word Basic.

For example, take a look at figure 22.1, which shows a sample Word dialog box that uses an assortment of controls.

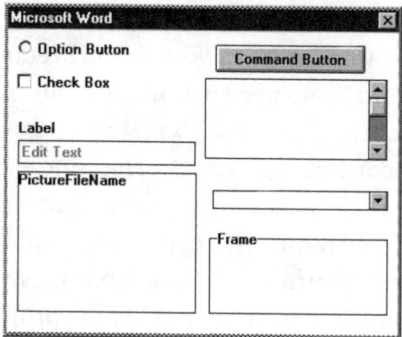

Fig. 22.1 A custom Word dialog box can be created with the Word Dialog Editor using assorted VBA controls.

The resulting Word Basic code reflecting the dialog box is as follows:

```
Begin Dialog UserDialog 446, 234, "Microsoft Word"
        OptionGroup  .OptionGroup1
                OptionButton 10, 6, 133, 16, "Option Button", _
        .OptionButton1
        CheckBox 11, 32, 111, 16, "Check Box", .CheckBox1
        Text 12, 69, 43, 13, "Label", .Text1
        TextBox 12, 85, 203, 18, .TextBox1
        Picture 12, 109, 204, 108, "PictureFileName", 0, _
        .Picture1
        PushButton 237, 10, 171, 21, "Command Button", .Push1
        ListBox 225, 36, 208, 62, ListBox1$(), .ListBox1
        DropListBox 235, 122, 200, 108, DropListBox1$(), _
        .DropListBox1
        GroupBox 230, 153, 204, 64, "Frame"
End Dialog
```

The Word Dialog Editor applet provides a simplified visually-oriented way to design dialog boxes with controls, and automatically generate the Word Basic code required for the execution of the dialog box.

None of the controls used provides any external (programmable) events. Instead, the controls are used within the dialog form to obtain values and inputs from the user. Following dismissal of the dialog box upon which the controls are used, you can use Word Basic code to retrieve the values (properties) of the controls as they might have been manipulated and modified by the user. Notice that this treatment of control objects with Word Basic is quite different from that used in Visual Basic or other VBA-supporting applications.

In many respects, the way in which Excel 7 treats controls is quite similar to the way they are used in Word Basic. Predominantly, controls in Excel 7, as in Word 7, are used within the context of a `DialogSheet` as child windows of the `DialogSheet`'s `DialogFrame` window. However, in Excel 7's use of controls, each control has one event (actually event property equivalent). This allows for dynamic programming within the scope of Dialog execution. This can be accomplished because this single "event" per control can be used to trigger the execution of VBA code streams, which in turn can modify the properties of other controls within the dialog box.

Evaluating Control Property and Method Differences

Although your first concern is probably to understand the event characteristics of controls, your next consideration is typically to note that there are also variations in properties and methods associated with these controls. Differences do indeed exist for the properties and methods of controls when comparing the Visual Basic and various VBA implementations.

Because each control, in each different environment (Visual Basic and multiple VBA variations), has a different number of properties, the best approach to begin with may be to identify those properties that are consistent. Also because of the number of different controls, let's first restrict our comparison to the Text Box control.

The Visual Basic 4 Text Box control is most nearly like the Access 2 Text Box control. You will find this higher degree of similarity for all controls when you compare the Visual Basic and the Access versions.

There are few other general observations that can be made when comparing the Visual Basic 4 Text Box control's properties to those of its VBA counterparts:

1. Properties that are completely unique to the capabilities of Visual Basic 4 are as follows:

   `DataXxxx`: Used for recordset-bound data controls
   `DragXxxx`: Used for drag-and-drop operations
   `LinkXxxx`: Used for Dynamic Data Exchange (DDE)

These specialized capabilities of only the Visual Basic 4 controls should not be used if you hope to make your programs portable across environments.

2. Properties that deal with dimensions and location (`Height`, `Width`, `Top`, and `Left`) are consistent.

3. Properties that deal with fonts and font characteristics (such as `FontName`, `FontSize`, `FontBold`, `FontItalic`, and `FontUnderline`) are used fairly consistently. Any small variations (noted in the table above) can usually be accommodated easily. Some VBA versions of the controls assign default values to these properties and are therefore not programmable. Once again, notice that Word Basic is an exception—using "macro-style" selection and function call techniques to achieve the same effect as Visual Basic's `object.property` approach.

4. Properties that deal with borders and colors (`BorderStyle`, `BackColor`, `ForeColor`, and so forth) are used consistently. Some VBA versions of the controls assign default values to these properties and are therefore not programmable. Again, Word Basic enables you control of most of the "properties" by using its "macro-style" approach.

5. Properties that deal with control status (`Visible` and `Enabled`) are used consistently, with the exception again of Word Basic.

Remaining properties that don't compare well across Visual Basic and the VBA implementations should be avoided if you hope to port your code between environments. And, of course, if you must use control in Word Basic dialogs, count on a lot of back-and-forth conversions. You can accomplish the same effect in most cases with the controls, but only at the expense of major programming conversion efforts.

There are a few observations that can be made from comparing Visual Basic 4 Text Box control's methods to those of its VBA counterparts:

1. Unique methods of Visual Basic 4 dealing with DDE Link or drag-and-drop operations are `Drag`, `LinkExecute`, `LinkPoke`, `LinkRequest`, `Move`, `Refresh`, `SetFocus`, and `ZOrder`.

2. Excel 7 uses two differently named methods—`SendToBack` and `BringToFront`—to accomplish what Visual Basic accomplishes

with a single method—ZOrder—and a parameter specifiying order.

3. The only consistent method is the SetFocus method. However, you will also notice that Word Basic uses a different technique—a language function call that moves the focus to a named object. Again, Word Basic is still "macro language" oriented and not yet VBA oriented.

> **Note:** Similar comparisons can be made for those controls that are common to all programming environments. It would take a great deal of space in this book to exhaustively make such comparisons. This process is left as an exercise for the reader—or until Microsoft comes up with a comparative database. It's on my "wish list" of helpful utilities to be added to the Microsoft Office Developers Kit. For the moment though, comparisons can be made quite easily using the Visual Basic and various products' VBA Help systems information.

Without going to this detailed comparison, as a first approximation you can generally apply the following rules-of-thumb concerning the properties and methods of functionally equivalent controls, and be assured that you have identified shared properties and methods:

➤ *Properties*—If a property deals with dimension and location, fonts, borders, colors, status, or enumeration it is highly likely that the property is common to both the Visual Basic and VBA implementations. As you can notice from the Text Box control comparison above, it is equally likely that Access 2 will be the most nearly comparable to the Visual Basic control, followed by Excel 7, and then Word Basic is a distant third.

➤ *Methods*—If a method deals with an intrinsic behavior of the control, then it is highly likely that the method is common to both the Visual Basic and VBA implementations. Examples of such intrinsic behaviors would be as follows:

> *Manipulating Lists*: AddItem and RemoveItem methods
> *Setting Focus*: SetFocus method

➤ *Word Basic*—Has its own "macro-style" selection and function call approach to accomplishing the same ends. Conversion or porting between VBA into and out of Word 7 is like moving to a completely different programming paradigm and coding environment. Similar control and control capabilities are present, but the mechanization of programming is quite different.

➤ *Microsoft Project*—Notice in the preceding properties and methods comparison tables that Project 4 does not provide any of the standard windows control "widgets" as part of its object libraries. The moral of the story is that if you need to use customized dialog boxes, or any of these usual controls, you need to develop either a Visual Basic 4 Class which can be used from Project, or some other VBA Object library that includes these controls.

As a final piece of practical advice, be careful to analyze any porting or conversion efforts, especially across these various VBA host environments. There is some greater or less degree of consistency among them, but there is no substitute for careful study of whether or not your particular applications will convert easily or with great difficulty. Hopefully, some of the analysis and investigation included in this section will point the way to your own considerations for any specific application you have in mind.

Noticing Database Access Differences

For the majority of Visual Basic and VBA applications there is at least some reliance on the use of databases. In fact, many Visual Basic and VBA applications are almost entirely developed to act as customized "front-ends" for existing (or newly contemplated) corporate database resources.

As in previous sections of this chapter, our goal will be to analyze not only the differing capabilities, but to evaluate the consequences as they influence Visual Basic or VBA software design and implementation.

Using ODBC Facilities

For the greatest generality and breadth of kinds of database access, nothing surpasses using the Microsoft ODBC (Open Database Connectivity) architecture. There are ODBC database drivers available for just about any database ever used by mortal man.

Visual Basic 4 and VBA applications can all access ODBC databases—but the degree of difficulty and the capabilities that are available are strongly dependent on which specific application is acting as the VBA host environment. A summary of these facilities (or lack thereof) is presented in Table 22.2.

Table 22.2   ODBC Facilities

VBA Environment	ODBC Facilities Provided
Visual Basic 4	The Visual Basic 4 built-in database engine (JET Version 2.5) incorporates a direct interface to the ODBC facilities; language syntax features make using this capability quite direct and efficient. The effect is that ODBC access is tightly integrated with Visual Basic, and acts like a native language facility.
Excel 5 VBA	ODBC facility can be obtained by referencing the Visual Basic 4 DAO Model Object library.
Access 2 VBA	Microsoft Access 2 also incorporates a built-in database engine; the Jet 2 Database Engine. The ODBC facilities of Access 2 are most like those found in Visual Basic 4, in that the language syntax of Access Basic includes native language syntax faciliites for ODBC database access. However, at the present time, beware of the subtle differences that exist between the Jet 2.5 Database Engine in Visual Basic 4 and the Jet 2 Database Engine found in Access 2.
Project 4 VBA	Microsoft Project 4 doesn't really support any database (except for dBASE III/IV-compatible tables' import and export) facilities. To use any ODBC facilities in VBA in Project you have to declare and use the ODBC API functions, and perform API-level programming, or reference the Visual Basic 4 DAO model Object library.

VBA Environment	ODBC Facilities Provided
Word 7 VBA	Microsoft Word for Windows 7 and its Word Basic facilities surprisingly do support a useful form of ODBC database access. The form that this takes is the `InsertDatabase` function, which can be accessed by choosing Insert, Database. The `InsertDatabase` function provides parameters for specifying an ODBC "connect string" and suitable SQL language statements that create a query result set from an ODBC database. The result set is treated like a Word Table to be formatted within a document. This bears little or no resemblance to the Visual Basic 4 or Access 2 language mechanisms for accessing an ODBC database and manipulating the result set. Furthermore, modifying and updating an ODBC database is not supported, because the `InsertDatabase` function is a query results-oriented capability.

From a careful reading of the table you can rightly conclude that ODBC database-related code compatibility between Visual Basic 4 and Access 2 VBA environments is very good. Your conclusions would indeed be correct. However, within all of the other VBA variations, there is a different—and non-Visual Basic compatible—approach to ODBC databases.

Other alternatives are not too pleasant, and entail a lot of ODBC API programming. That is, you could declare the requisite ODBC API functions within your VBA program, and thereafter make the direct API function calls to obtain the desired ODBC database access. While this is certainly quite possible, it requires a pretty comprehensive and in-depth knowledge of how to correctly use the ODBC API functions; this is the subject for another book.

Using DAO Model Facilities

Only two of the products—Visual Basic 4 and Access 2—include built-in Data Access Object Models. Previously, Visual Basic 3 had a quite different—and much simpler—DAO model than that present in

Access 2. However, with the release of Visual Basic 4, the DAO models in Visual Basic and in Access 2 are nearly the same.

The consequence of this change in Visual Basic 4 is that Visual Basic and Access VBA code using the DAO model are now pretty much interchangeable. There are few exceptions within Visual Basic 4's Data Access Object model that are not present in Access 2's DAO model. The top-level differences are summarized in the following table, which lists the Visual Basic 4 unique differences:

VB 4 Objects	Summary Description
Columns	Used to store column information for DBGrid
Errors	Information on database object errors
SelBookmarks	Set of selected rows in the DBGrid object

This compatibility is not the major source of good news for VBA programmers. With the introduction of Visual Basic 4, the DAO 2.5 Model is packaged as an OLE 2 Automation server object library. This means that any VBA-host application that can create "references" to the DAO 2.5 Model libraries can also support database access via the DAO 2.5 Object library. Furthermore, the language syntax and programming techniques are identical in all VBA-host environments, because all VBA environments can use the same Object Library.

Referencing the DAO 2.5 Library in VBA

Any VBA-host environment that supports object library references can make use of the Visual Basic 4 DAO 2.5 Object Library, and therefore can use any of the database techniques available in Visual Basic 4. It is quite easy to determine if a particular VBA-host environment supports external library "references." To check for external library reference support, choose Tools, References.

Note: In Excel 7, you must be in a Module sheet to find the References item on the Tools menu. While in a worksheet, the item disappears from this menu.

When you choose References, the application displays a dialog box like that shown in figure 22.2. The dialog box displays a series of external reference object libraries whose functions can be linked into the VBA environment of the host application. In the case illustrated by the two figures, reference linkages are made to Excel 7's VBA environment, the Excel 5.0 Object Library and the Office 95 Document Properties Type Library.

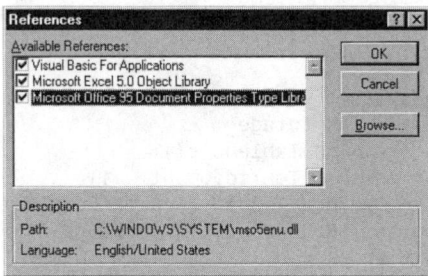

Fig. 22.2 The References dialog box shows the available external object libraries.

Selecting one or more of the available reference libraries is accomplished just by clicking on the desired library—setting the check box to indicate selection.

Once the DAO 2.5 library is referenced, all of the objects, functions, methods and properties within the library are available within the VBA-host application environment.

Testing DAO 2.5 Object Library References

Some simple examples of DAO 2.5 code that serve to illustrate the consistency of database access in Microsoft Project 4, Excel 5, and Visual Basic 4 are shown in code Listings 22.1, 22.2, 22.3 respectively.

The example code just opens a database, and uses some of the objects, collections, and properties of the DAO 2.5 Object Library to enumerate all of the tables within the opened database, and also to determine the number of records in each table in the database.

Listing 22.1   Code Example in Project 4

```
Option Explicit

Dim db As Object 'Module level database object variable
Dim td As Object 'Module level tabledefs object variable

Sub NWindOpen()
    Set db = DBEngine.Workspaces(0).OpenDatabase_
    ("d:\access\sampapps\nwind.mdb")
    MsgBox "Database NWIND.MDB is OPEN"
    EnumTables      'Invoke Enumerate tables
End

Sub EnumTables()      'Enumerate tables in a database
    Dim inx As Integer
    Set td = db.TableDefs()
    For inx = 0 To (td.Count - 1)
        MsgBox "Table [" & td(inx).Name & "] with " _
    & td(inx).RecordCount & " records"
    Next inx
End Sub
```

Listing 22.2   Code Example in Excel 7

```
Option Explicit

Dim db As Object 'Module level database object variable
Dim td As Object 'Module level tabledefs object variable

Sub NWindOpen()
    Set db = DBEngine.Workspaces(0).OpenDatabase_
    ("d:\access\sampapps\nwind.mdb")
    MsgBox "Database NWIND.MDB is OPEN"
    EnumTables      'Invoke Enumerate tables
End

Sub EnumTables()      'Enumerate tables in a database
    Dim inx As Integer
    Set td = db.TableDefs()
    For inx = 0 To (td.Count - 1)
        MsgBox "Table [" & td(inx).Name & "] with " _
    & td(inx).RecordCount & " records"
    Next inx
End Sub
```

Listing 22.3   Code Example in Visual Basic 4

```
Option Explicit

Dim db As Object 'Module level database object variable
Dim td As Object 'Module level tabledefs object variable

Private Sub Command1_Click()

    NWindOpen       'Invoke NWindOpen

Sub NWindOpen()
    Set db = DBEngine.Workspaces(0).OpenDatabase_
    ("d:\access\sampapps\nwind.mdb")
    MsgBox "Database NWIND.MDB is OPEN"
    EnumTables      'Invoke Enumerate tables
End

Sub EnumTables()       'Enumerate tables in a database
    Dim inx As Integer
    Set td = db.TableDefs()
    For inx = 0 To (td.Count - 1)
        MsgBox "Table [" & td(inx).Name & "] with " _
    & td(inx).RecordCount & " records"
    Next inx
End Sub
```

Admittedly, the three exact duplicate code examples in these three VBA-compliant environments do not in any way pass as an "acid test," but you will find that any database application code that was written in any of the three example VBA environments can be ported between any of the others. This really illustrates the power of the OLE 2 Automation object library concepts in practice.

Using OLE Custom Controls

This section examines controls that are implemented as OLE 2 Object Libraries—much like the DAO 2.5 Object Library discussed in the previous section—and the consequences of using such controls.

The Object Library controls are called *OLE Custom Controls*, and are a specialized type of OLE 2 object dubbed a "mini-server." These OLE Custom Controls are contained in files with the OCX filename extensions. They are created using C++, normally with the Visual C++ Control Developer's Toolkit. Several third-party development kits have begun to appear on the market.

One of the chief advantages of these OLE Custom Controls is that they can be used interchangeably in Visual Basic and any VBA environments that supports their use. Like other OLE 2 Objects, the OLE Custom Controls can only be accessed following their registration in the Registry Database (REG.DAT).

If you have already installed Visual Basic 4 on your computer, all of the OLE Custom Controls that are shipped as part of the product are automatically registered in the Registry Database during installation.

In addition to these OLE Custom Controls, there are three more that are shipped by Microsoft as part of the Access 2 Office Development Kit:

➤ *Calendar*—Monthly calendar page

➤ *Scrollbar*—Horizontal and vertical scroll bars

➤ *Data Outline*—Database-bound outline list box

Because these OLE Custom Controls (OCX) are intended by Microsoft to replace the earlier controls (VBX) you'll be seeing more OLE Custom Controls from Microsoft and other Visual Basic product add-on vendors.

Registering OLE Custom Controls

Prior to using OLE Custom Controls you must make sure that they are registered in the registry database (REG.DAT). Usually, registration is handled by the Windows setup program for a product during the installation process. This is the case for the OLE Custom Controls listed above.

However, it is also possible to manually register OCXs using one of several techniques. If you have a copy of Access 2 you can use it to update the registry for new OLE Custom Controls. To update the registry, follow these steps:

1. Open any Access 2 Form in Design mode.

2. Choose Edit, Insert Object.

3. Choose the Insert Control option from the dialog box.

4. Click the Add Control button in the dialog box.

5. Use the dialog box to locate the OCX file.

6. Select your desired OCX file.

7. Click OK.

After clicking OK, there will be a slight delay while the OCX is added to the Registry. Once registered, you can start using the OCX Control. Custom Controls can be deleted from your forms by selecting them and pressing the delete key.

When an OLE Custom Control is registered in the registry database, you can use the REGEDIT.EXE program (found in the Windows directory), to view the registry database. The view that you want to use is the "verbose" view. This can be invoked using the following command line with the /V switch:

```
C:\WINDOWS\REGEDIT.EXE /V
```

This command starts the Win95 RegEdit, which is a pure Windows Applet.

Programming with OLE Custom Controls

Programming with and using OLE Custom Controls is fairly straightforward. There are a few steps that must be observed in all programming environments, including Visual Basic 4 and the various VBA implementations.

In all environments, the first step in using an OLE Custom Control is to create a Reference to the Object Library. This is accomplished by selecting the References command in the VBA host environment. Generally, this command is found under the Tools menu. Choosing the References command displays a dialog box that lists all the registered OLE 2 Object Libraries that are present in the Windows registry database.

You will notice in the References dialog box that all of the registered object libraries are shown in the list box portion of the dialog box. To create a Reference linkage between the object library and say, Excel 7, just select the appropriate option button on the left-hand side of each line.

Once a reference linkage is established, the object libraries' objects are available in the Object Browser. For example, in figure 22.3, the Excel Object Library is selected. In the left-hand list box, the Excel Objects/Modules are listed, and ScrollBar is selected. The right-hand list box accordingly shows the Methods/Properties for ScrollBar.

Note: To access the Excel 7 Object Browser, you must be in a module sheet and then choose View, Object Browser. The Object Browser cannot be accessed through a worksheet.

If you select a different object from the Objects/Modules list box of the Object Browser dialog box, the right-hand Methods/Properties list box displays all of the selected objects methods and properties.

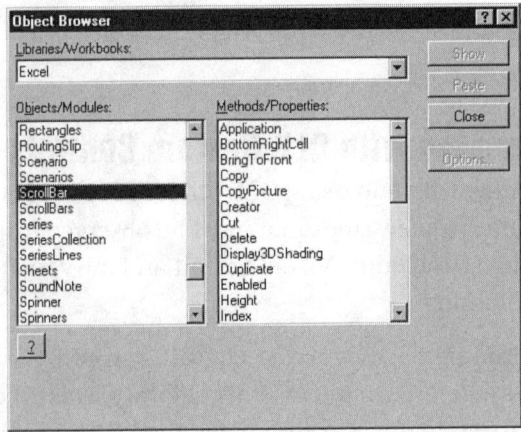

Fig. 22.3 The Excel 7 Object Browser dialog box allows the developer to examine the methods and properties of an object.

In summary, once the object is registered, you can create a reference linkage between the control's library and Visual Basic 4 and VBA applications. Once the reference linkage is defined, the OLE Custom Controls' object library exposes its objects, properties, methods, and events, which can be viewed using Object Browser. This view in the Object Browser provides you with the information you need to incorporate the Custom Control in your application. Don't forget that there are usually Help files that provide additional information about the Custom Control to assist you in your programming efforts.

Porting Code Between Visual Basic and VBA

As you have noticed thus far, there are enough differences between Visual Basic and the various incarnations of VBA environments that porting code from one to another requires some serious study.

There are a variety of conditions which you must pay close attention to in undertaking code migrations from one of these environments to another. In the subsections that follow, we will focus on a couple of the major considerations involved.

Managing Event Limitations

Previously we discussed the fact that control objects have a restricted set of events in the various VBA environments. Therefore, if you plan to use these controls in applications that will be moved across the various VBA platforms and also Visual Basic 4, you should attempt to restrict your code procedures associated with these events to a single event. Typically, this is the equivalent of the Visual Basic 4 `Click` event or the `Change` event, depending on the control.

If, however, your code porting aspirations are less generalized, you should compare the event repertoire of the controls in the actual VBA environments that you are considering. As noticed earlier, designing and developing code that is to execute in both the Visual Basic and the Access Basic environments allows the use of equivalent events in both contexts, with the exception of the following:

➤ Any drag-and-drop rop events (DragOver, DragDrop)

➤ Any DDE-related events (LinkError, LinkNotify)

The conversion between the Visual Basic 4 program and the equivalent Access Basic program requires that the name of the code procedure to be executed be assigned to the OnEvent equivalent property in the Access Basic program. Otherwise you can just copy the code procedures from the Visual Basic module directly into the Access Basic code module, and then assign the name of the Visual Basic code procedure for the event to the OnXxxx property within Access code.

Converting Properties

In a like manner, there are some generalized suggestions that you might adopt for converting properties between Visual Basic and VBA environments. These are as follows:

➤ Properties that deal with such things as colors, dimensions, screen location, and border styles are generally fairly consistently used.

➤ Properties that deal with such things as fonts and font characteristics are also used fairly consistently, although in some VBA environments you are presented with precanned values for these properties which cannot be changed.

➤ Properties that deal with the status of controls such as Visible and Enabled are used consistently.

➤ Properties that deal with recordset-bound data controls, or which are associated with drag-and-drop operations, or which are used for Dynamic Data Exchange operations are not consistently used, and are restricted solely to Visual Basic 4.

If you bear these general rules in mind you can usually devise code that can be moved from environment to environment with ease. You may need to make minor fixes and modifications but usually nothing radical.

Using Visual Basic Class Libraries

One of the greatest enhancements of Visual Basic 4 in comparison to its predecessor Visual Basic 3 is the ability to create Class Libraries in Visual Basic 4. This capability offers the simplest and most direct mechanism to provide consistent programming approaches both in Visual Basic and from VBA in any host environment.

Developing your own custom Class Libraries (or OLE Object Servers if you prefer) in Visual Basic 4 is a powerful technique for achieving these objectives.

There are distinct advantages in using this Class Library approach that you may want to seriously consider, among which are the following:

➤ Consistent references to objects, methods, and properties from any Visual Basic or VBA host programming environment.

➤ The ability to include encapsulated screen objects using any of the Visual Basic techniques, thereby supplementing the native window-type interface of the various VBA host environments.

➤ The ability to exploit the oftentimes more fine-grained Visual Basic event procedures into VBA host environments which otherwise only support limited events for each screen object. For example, Excel 7 VBA only supports one event equivalent for controls, the `OnAction` event.

➤ The capability to use features that are supported in Visual Basic, but that are not accessible in a VBA programming environment. Examples of such features include drag and drop and DDE programming techniques.

> ➤ The capability to easily port code from one VBA environment to another without the need to make code modifications to accommodate VBA host differences.

These are significant advantages and can greatly expedite your development of "universal" applications approaches. Encapsulation of algorithms, object structures, and user interface design in Visual Basic 4 Class Libraries is a highly leveraged programming technique if properly applied.

Developing and Using Components

The key to getting the greatest benefit from Visual Basic 4's new Class Library capability is to begin designing your applications as a series of modular and reusable program components. Each modular component should encapsulate the data structures, screen objects, and code procedures that make it unique and allow it to accomplish one clearly defined functional purpose.

Although these rules of structured program design have been with us for decades now, and sometimes have been espoused as the "Holy Grail" of professional program design and development, their observation in practice has more often than not been honored in the breach—usually because of rigid interpretations of what's the best methodology.

To some degree, the basic nature of Windows programming tends to naturally motivate toward the development of more modular code, because it is an event-driven rather than procedural execution environment. As a result, most Windows code procedures tend to be fairly small and oriented around a single specific purpose. Additionally, more "modern" programming strategies, especially those associated with C++ programming practice, tend toward more modular programming results, although oftentimes older C (and other procedural language) programming practices still persist.

However, none of these really address many of the prime imperatives of modular or encapsulated programming techniques, which include:

➤ *Data Hiding*—Encapsulated procedures should not directly expose Global or Public variables. They should instead externally offer programmatic function interfaces that manipulate data structures within their scope to prevent direct external modification of variables.

➤ *Code Reuse*—More primitive code modules should be combined to create progressively more highly differentiable specialized function code modules. The concept is intended to prevent the proliferation of similar-function but slightly different code streams.

➤ *Self-Contained*—Encapsulated procedures should be designed to be self-protective. They should check externally supplied arguments for validity. They should internally provide for their own error handling and recovery. They should be designed to eliminate reaching outside of their own scope and influencing other code components.

➤ *Singular Purpose*—Encapsulated procedures should be designed to accomplish only a single functional purpose. Procedures which internally perform multiple jobs present confusing external interfaces and are typically difficult to learn and use reliably.

It is certain that other rules could be easily added to the list presented above, but that would be another whole book in its own right. Using just the basic concepts outlined above, you should be able to create Visual Basic Classes that can be used from within any Visual Basic program, or consistently from within any VBA environment.

From Here...

In this chapter, we looked at some of the similarities and differences between Visual Basic 4 and Visual Basic for Applications. You learned to understand the differences in common syntax, extensions, and object references. Along with reviewing environment differences, the chapter compared window objects and control objects.

The database access differences were investigated regarding the Data Access Object model facilities and OLE custom controls. Finally, event limitations and converting properties were discussed concerning porting code between VB and VBA.

The following is a list of chapters that you can refer to for related topics in this book:

➤ To find out how you can enhance your Visual Basic 4 applications and design an ideal program, see Chapter 1, "User Interface Design."

➤ To learn more about databases and how you can apply Visual Basic 4 to client/server applications, see Chapter 9, "Client/Server Databases."

➤ To find out more information on OLE custom controls, see Chapter 20, "OLE Controls, Add-Ins, and 32-bit DLLs."

23

Mixed-Language Development with DLLs

by Andrew Dean

This chapter describes using Windows *Dynamic Link Libraries (DLLs)* written in other programming languages with your Visual Basic programs. DLLs allow you to take advantage of most of the internal system functions in the Windows API as well as incorporate many third-party function libraries. Whether you are programming in Visual Basic and calling DLL functions or writing DLLs that will be called by Visual Basic programs, you need to understand the rules and limitations of mixing Visual Basic with other development languages. This chapter covers the ground rules of mixed-language development with Visual Basic and gives some useful tips on how to avoid the most common problems associated with calling DLLs.

This chapter will teach you the following:

➤ How to take advantage of the Windows API

➤ How to use third-party DLL libraries

➤ How to debug calls to DLL libraries

➤ Tips on writing your own DLLs for VB

What Is a Dynamic Link Library?

Visual Basic is a powerful development tool in its own right. Many useful programs are written using Visual Basic as it comes out of the box. However, if you are a heavy-duty Visual Basic developer, eventually you will find yourself running into the Visual Basic wall. In reality, you cannot really do many things well with Visual Basic alone. The Visual Basic programming language has many limitations in terms of program performance, user interface objects, developer efficiency, and other areas. However, the Visual Basic programming system includes facilities to step beyond the limitations of straight Visual Basic.

Extendibility is one of the primary strengths of Visual Basic. Visual Basic is a very open, flexible development platform, and it has been since its very first release. In fact, Visual Basic has defined the standard for open application development platforms in the Windows environment. Now that Visual Basic for Applications (VBA) is becoming the standard application automation language in the Windows environment, you will have more opportunities to integrate a variety of languages and applications.

You can extend Visual Basic in several different ways, including third-party custom controls, OLE servers, and DLLs. This chapter introduces you to one way to mix other development languages with Visual Basic. We will explore the details of extending Visual Basic programs using DLLs.

DLLs are function libraries that an application can link to at runtime rather than at compiletime. DLLs are very important to the architecture of Windows itself, so learning a little about DLLs in general is worthwhile before learning how you can use them in Visual Basic.

Static Linking

In the DOS world, if you use a function library to develop your application, you must link that library with your program when you create your executable file for distribution. This is known as *static linking* because the library is now part of the executable file and cannot be changed independently. Linking resolves the address references that are made when your program calls one of the library procedures. Essentially, the code, or executable instructions, from the library are copied into your executable file. If your application consists of several executable files, all of which use the same function library, each executable will contain a copy of the function library. When your application is installed, you end up installing multiple copies of the function library, embedded in each of the different executable files. This can significantly waste disk space.

Another characteristic of static linking is that the function library cannot be updated independently from the actual executable files of your application. Suppose you have developed a function library that is used by several applications that you distribute. One day you make some changes to the library that improve its performance. Now you want to distribute updates to your users. You will have to recompile all programs, statically link the updated function library, and redistribute the applications. Your users then must reinstall each of the updated applications.

Dynamic Linking

Wouldn't it be easier if you could simply distribute the updated function library, users could install it once, and all their applications that use the library could automatically take advantage of the improvements? Dynamic link libraries do this by addressing the problems with static linking described above. Dynamic link libraries are linked (the addresses are resolved) at runtime rather than compiletime. The library (DLL) exists as a separate file on disk, distinct from the application's EXE file. Because of this, DLLs have several advantages over static linked libraries. If several applications all use the same library, that library only needs to exist on the disk once, provided that all the applications can find the library file (DLL). This is usually assured by installing the library in either the WINDOWS or WINDOWS\SYSTEM directory. As another advantage, you can update DLLs independently of the application that calls them. Because the DLL is just another file on your hard drive, you can replace it with an updated version. When an application program calls the DLL, it will use the executable instructions contained in the updated disk file.

Dynamic link libraries are a central component of the Windows system architecture. In fact, Windows itself is a collection of DLLs. The GDI.EXE and USER.EXE files that are part of any Windows installation are actually DLLs.

> **Note:** Although DLL is a common file extension for dynamic link library files, it is not required. A DLL can have any file extension. Two of the most common file extensions for Dynamic Link Libraries, besides DLL, are EXE and VBX.

The previous note brings out an interesting point. Visual Basic custom controls, both OCX and VBX controls, are actually DLLs. Yes, it's true. A custom control is simply a Windows DLL that has been written to specifications that allow it to integrate with the Visual Basic development environment. A custom control file may itself also contain functions that can be called directly, in addition to manipulating properties of custom controls. We will explore these possibilities later in this chapter.

Using DLLs with VB

OK, so now we all agree that DLLs are an excellent way to extend the power of Visual Basic. The next question is: Where do you find DLLs that you can use with Visual Basic? The answer is that you can use just about any DLL with Visual Basic. (Many people refer to calling a DLL, when they really mean calling a specific function within a DLL. Remember that a DLL is a library of procedures. Rather than calling a DLL, you actually call a specific procedure within a DLL.)

The truth is, any time you run a Visual Basic program, you are already using DLLs. The Visual Basic runtime library, VBRUN400.DLL, is actually a DLL. VBRUN400.DLL must always be present in order to run a Visual Basic executable program.

> **Note:** Older versions of Visual Basic required runtime libraries VBRUN100.DLL, VBRUN200.DLL, and VBRUN300.DLL.

Because VBRUN400.DLL is a dynamic link library, you only need a single copy of the file no matter how many Visual Basic programs you may have. This makes Visual Basic a very practical development tool in corporate environments where many applications developed in Visual Basic will be deployed.

Although specific technical restrictions prevent some DLL procedures from being called from Visual Basic directly, you can call the vast majority of DLL procedures from Visual Basic. All you need to know is the proper calling sequence to invoke them.

Windows API

The DLLs most commonly used with Visual Basic are the Windows DLLs themselves. Because everybody who uses Visual Basic for Windows will already have these DLLs available to them, we will use the Windows DLLs for our examples in this chapter.

The internal Windows procedures that are available as DLL calls are commonly referred to as the *Windows API* (*Application Programming Interface*). These are the same procedures that programmers using C/C++, Pascal, Fortran, and other development languages use to develop the GUI portions of their programs. As a Visual Basic developer, you do not need to master the Windows API when you first start writing Windows programs because Visual Basic takes care of most of that for you. However, the power of the Windows API is available when you want to start taking advantage of it.

Third-Party Products

Many commercial third-party function libraries are distributed as DLLs. You can find libraries for image processing, financial functions, dBASE file access, and many other specialized application areas. Although many of these libraries were originally written for C/C++, they are increasingly being marketed to Visual Basic developers as well. Some libraries are written specifically for use with Visual Basic, but the vast majority are fairly generic and can be used with any Windows development tools.

Custom DLLs

The final source of DLLs for extending Visual Basic is you. You can write your own DLLs that can be called from your Visual Basic programs. There is nothing special about a DLL procedure that makes it callable from Visual Basic. For this reason, Visual Basic is often used for prototyping and as a testing harness for DLLs that will ultimately be called from systems written in other languages.

Unfortunately, you can call DLLs all you want from Visual Basic, but you will not be able to create your own DLLs with Visual Basic 4.

There are many tools that you can use to create DLLs, including compilers that work with C/C++, Fortran, Pascal, and Basic.

A Simple Windows Resource Monitor

Let's look at a simple example of calling procedures from the Windows API. We'll write a program, SYSMON, to monitor Windows system resources such as memory, using a Timer control to update the resource information once every second. Notice the `Declare` statement that appears in the SYSMON project. `Declare` statements tell Visual Basic that a procedure is located in a dynamic link library. The `Declare` statement will be fully explained later in this chapter. Figure 23.1 shows the system resource monitor as it is running.

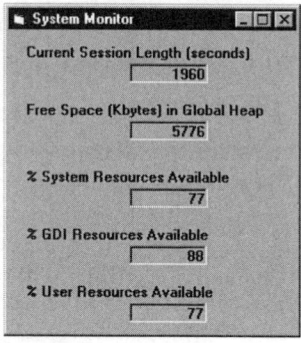

Fig. 23.1 The system resource monitor.

Start a new Visual Basic project. We'll name it SYSMON.MAK. Include a single form, and a single code module, and name the code module SYSMDECS.BAS.

Place five Label controls on the form. Name them `lblTime`, `lblFreeSpace`, `lblSystemResources`, `lblGDIResources`, and `lblUserResources`. For each of these controls, set the `BorderStyle` to 1 (Fixed single) and make the `Caption` property a `Null` string. These label controls will be used to display data that is being updated by our program. Listing 23.1 shows all the property settings from the FRM file for one of the data display labels, `lblUserResources`.

Listing 23.1   Property Settings for a Display Label

```
Begin Label lblUserResources
        Alignment       =    1   'Right Justify
        BorderStyle     =    1   'Fixed Single
        Height          =    240
        Left            =    1545
        TabIndex        =    9
        Top             =    3405
        Width           =    990
End
```

Place five additional Label controls to the left of the above Label controls. Set the captions for these new controls to, respectively, Current session length (seconds), Free space (Kbytes) in Global Heap, % system resources available, % GDI Resources available, and % user resources available. Make sure these labels are positioned appropriately relative to the previous controls.

Place a Timer control on the form.

Listing 23.2 shows the contents of the SYSMDECS.BAS file, which contains declarations of Windows API procedures used by the system resource monitor. These declarations will be described in detail later in the chapter.

Listing 23.2   The Contents of the SYSMDECS.BAS File

```
Option Explicit
Declare Function GetCurrentTime Lib "User" () As Long
Declare Function GetFreeSpace Lib "Kernel" (ByVal wFlags_
    As Integer) As Long
Declare Function GetFreeSystemResources Lib "User" _
    (ByVal fuSysResource As Integer) As Integer
Global Const GFSR_SYSTEMRESOURCES = &H0
Global Const GFSR_GDIRESOURCES = &H1
Global Const GFSR_USERRESOURCES = &H2
```

Listing 23.3 shows the code for the Timer event.

Listing 23.3   The Timer1_Timer Event Handler

```
Sub Timer1_Timer ()
  Dim lSeconds    As Long_
  Dim lSpace      As Long
  lblTime = CInt(GetCurrentTime() / 1000)_
  lblFreeSpace = CInt(GetFreeSpace(0) / 1024)_
  lblSystemResources = _
GetFreeSystemResources(GFSR_SYSTEMRESOURCES)_
  lblGDIResources = _
  GetFreeSystemResources(GFSR_GDIRESOURCES)_
  lblUserResources = _
  GetFreeSystemResources(GFSR_USERRESOURCES)
End Sub
```

Set the Interval property of the Timer control to 1,000. Because the Interval property is in milliseconds, the Timer event will fire once every second.

```
Begin Timer Timer1
      Interval      =   1000
      Left          =   0
      Top           =   3360
   End
```

The Timer event is called once every second. The program calls the Windows API procedures to update the contents of the displayed fields.

Setting Control Properties with Windows API Calls

Sometimes the standard Visual Basic controls do not do what you need. This is the reason for the third-party custom control market. However, there are times when you don't need to use a new custom control to retrieve some missing functionality. One option is always to write Visual Basic code to overcome the shortcomings of a control. Often, the easier option is to take advantage of built-in Windows functionality by calling the Windows API. Instead, a call to the Windows API may let you tweak the behavior of the control enough so that it works the way you want.

An example of this is the Visual Basic Combo Box control. The standard Visual Basic combo box does not have a property that can be used to limit the length of input to the combo box. You can use the SendMessage() function from the Windows API to force the combo box to limit its input. Listing 23.4 shows the declarations that are necessary to call SendMessage() for this purpose.

Listing 23.4   A SendMessage() Declaration

```
Global Const WM_USER = &H400
Global Const CB_LIMITTEXT = (WM_USER + 1)

Declare Function SendMessage Lib "User" (ByVal hWnd As_
  Integer, ByVal wMsg As Integer, ByVal wParam As Integer,_
   lParam As Any) As Long
```

The Visual Basic code that will limit Combo1 to five characters of input is shown in Listing 23.5.

Listing 23.5   Limiting Input in a Combo Box with SendMessage()

```
Dim lRet as Long
lRet = SendMessage(Combo1.hWnd, CB_LIMITTEXT, 5, ByVal 0& )
```

The Declare Statement

The previous examples all included at least one line of Visual Basic code beginning with the keyword Declare. The Declare statement identifies a single DLL procedure to Visual Basic. This section of the chapter will explain the details of the Declare statement. The WIN31API.TXT file that comes with Visual Basic contains all the procedure and type declarations for the Windows API. (Don't be confused by the name of WIN31API.TXT. It works for Windows 95 as well.) Visual Basic also comes with two utilities, APILOD16.EXE and APILOD32.EXE, that you can use to paste Declare statements directly into your project.

In order to use a procedure that is included in a DLL, you must *export* that procedure from the DLL. This means that the developer of the DLL must identify the procedure as one which can be called externally. This is not an action that you as a Visual Basic programmer have any control over (unless, of course, you are also the developer of the DLL). You must identify procedures as exported when the DLL is compiled. If the DLL contains procedures that have not been exported, there is nothing you can do with Visual Basic to gain access to those procedures. For the purposes of this chapter, when we refer to DLL procedures, we mean procedures that have been exported from a DLL.

Utilities such as EXEHDR, which comes with the Microsoft Visual C++ compiler, can be used to list all the exported procedures that are included in a DLL. Listing 23.6 shows a portion of the results from using EXEHDR to list exported functions in the file GDI.EXE.

Listing 23.6 Sample Output from EXEHDR.EXE

```
Exports:
ord seg offset name
 59   1   1ec0  WEP exported, shared data
 46   1   79f4  __GP exported, shared data
474   1   5f6d  GETWINDOWEXTEX exported
 47   1   4d4e  COMBINERGN exported, shared data
482   1   4ef4  SETWINDOWORGEX exported, shared data
480   1   4f28  SETVIEWPORTORGEX exported, shared data
155   7   052d  QUERYABORT exported, shared data
301   6   0560  ENGINEDELETEFONT exported, shared data
232  27   00fe  EXTRACTPQ exported
149   1   515a  GETBRUSHORG exported
```

The first step in using a DLL procedure is to declare the procedure in the Visual Basic program. To do this, we need to identify the procedure, the DLL file that contains it, and any arguments and return values used by the procedure.

Syntax

The declaration of a DLL procedure can go in the Declarations section of a form, standard, or class module. If you put the declaration in a standard module, it is global or public, and code can call the DLL procedure anywhere in your application. If you declare the DLL procedure in the Declarations section of a form or class module, you must use the `Private` keyword. This prevents the procedure from being globally available within your Visual Basic application but allows it to be called only within the scope of that form or class module.

The `Declare` statement has the following syntax:

```
Declare [Private] Sub publicname Lib "libname" [Alias_
 "alias"] [([[ByVal] variable _[As type][,[ByVal]_
 variable [As type]]...]))
```

or

```
Declare [Private] Function publicname Lib "libname" _
 Alias "alias"] [([[ByVal] variable_[As type][,[ByVal]_
 variable [As type]]...])) As type
```

If an exported procedure returns a value, declare that procedure as a `Function`. Otherwise, declare the procedure as a `Sub`. The differences between `Sub` and `Function` procedures are discussed in detail in a later section.

The simplest example of a `Declare` statement is the `ReleaseCapture()` routine, which releases the mouse capture after the mouse has been captured or limited, to a specific window. This procedure has no arguments and no return value. The `Declare` statement for `ReleaseCapture()` simply identifies the name of the subroutine and the disk file where it can be found. The declaration is as follows:

```
Declare Sub ReleaseCapture Lib "User" ()
```

Naming Exported Procedures

The *publicname* specified in a `Declare` statement is the name used to refer to the procedure within your Visual Basic program. This will usually be the name that the DLL developer used when the procedure was exported.

Be aware that the procedure name is not case-sensitive in 16-bit versions of Visual Basic. In 32-bit versions of Visual Basic, the function name is case-sensitive. If there is any chance that your code will be running in 32-bit Windows at some time in the future, always type your procedure names consistently. But you are doing that anyway, aren't you?

Using Aliases

The `Alias` section of a `Declare` statement makes it possible for you to use an identifier for an exported procedure that is different from the name used by the DLL developer when the procedure was exported from the DLL. The string literal that follows the `Alias` keyword is the identifier that Windows will use when attempting to locate the procedure in the DLL. Several occasions pop up when using the `Alias` keyword may be necessary.

Invalid Procedure Names

Some languages that you can use for DLL development follow rules for naming identifiers that are different from the rules used by Visual Basic. For instance, you can name a C/C++ function with a leading underscore. The Windows API includes such a function, `_lopen()`, which is used to open a file. In Visual Basic, underscores can be used in identifier names, with the exception that an underscore cannot be the first character in the name. An identifier with a name that begins with the underscore character will generate syntax errors in your Visual Basic program. Although the `_lopen()` function is exported in a DLL, a Visual Basic program cannot include a reference to a procedure named `_lopen()`. Instead, the procedure name used in Visual Basic is `lopen()`, and the `Alias` section of the `Declare` statement is used to identify the function's name in the DLL. The appropriate declaration would be as follows:

```
Declare Function lopen Lib "Kernel" Alias "_lopen"_
(ByVal lpPathName As String, ByVal iReadWrite As Integer)_
As Integer
```

Duplicate Identifiers

The Alias section is also useful when a DLL procedure name conflicts with a Visual Basic keyword or an identifier that you are already using in your application. For example, the Windows API includes a procedure named SetFocus. This is the same name as a Visual Basic method, SetFocus. To distinguish between the two, the Visual Basic program will refer to the Windows API function by appending API to its name, making it SetFocusAPI. The declaration is as follows:

```
Declare Function SetFocusAPI Lib "User" Alias "SetFocus"_
(ByVal hWnd As Integer) As Integer
```

This declaration indicates that the SetFocusAPI() procedure referenced in your Visual Basic program is actually the SetFocus() procedure in the "User" DLL.

Ordinal Numbers for DLL Procedures

Another way (though less valuable for source code documentation purposes) to specify a function in a DLL is to specify the ordinal number of a DLL procedure as its Alias. Every exported DLL procedure has an associated ordinal number that specifies the position of the procedure in the DLL. In fact, you can export a procedure without specifying the name of the procedure. The ordinal number is then the only way to reference an exported function.

In this case, you use the ordinal number of the procedure, preceded by a pound sign (#) as the literal string following the Alias keyword. Use any name you want as the procedure name for the routine. For example:

```
Declare Sub ReleaseCapture Lib "User" Alias "#19"()
```

The first column of the report produced by EXEHDR gives the ordinal values for exported procedures.

```
Exports:
ord seg offset name
    ...
19  1  28bd  RELEASECAPTURE exported, shared data
```

DLLs and the Windows Search Path

The `Lib` keyword identifies the dynamic link library disk file that contains the exported DLL. If a full path is not specified, the standard Windows path is searched in order to find the appropriate file. If the DLL needs to be installed in a specific directory, the full path of the file should be specified in the `Declare` statement. The most common places to install DLLs are the Windows directory, the Windows system directory, or an application's home directory.

The standard Windows search path is as follows:

1. The current working directory as specified in Program Manager.
2. The Windows directory.
3. The Windows system directory.
4. The default system path.
5. The directory of the calling application's EXE file.

When a Visual Basic application includes calls to DLL procedures, the application does not search for the DLL until one of its procedures is actually invoked. At this time, if the DLL file cannot be found, you will receive an error message.

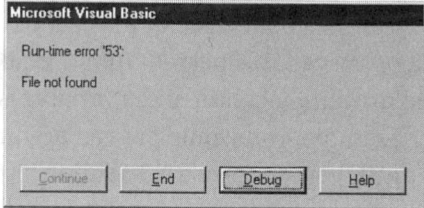

Fig. 23.2 The error message when a DLL file is not found.

Sometimes the DLL may not contain the procedure that is defined in the `Declare` statement, or it may have a significant argument list. In this case, the Visual Basic program will not be able to load the DLL properly to call the procedure, and the error message in figure 23.3 will be displayed.

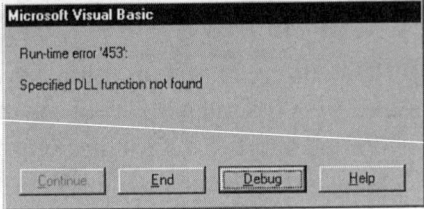

Fig. 23.3 The DLL file did not contain the procedure as specified in the `Declare` statement.

Argument Lists

Each procedure exported from a DLL procedure can have a list of arguments. The simplest argument list is empty; the procedure has no arguments. In this case, a pair of parentheses, with nothing inside, is used. The parentheses cannot be omitted even if there are no arguments to the procedure. If there are arguments, they are listed in order, along with their data types.

Passing Arguments by Reference

In Visual Basic, you can pass arguments to subroutines and functions in two ways. The default is to pass arguments by reference. Passing an argument by reference means that the called routine can change the actual value of the variable passed from the calling routine. A reference to the actual memory location of the variable is passed to the called routine. For example, you would pass an argument by reference to a routine that will then perform a calculation and return the result in the passed argument.

Passing Arguments by Value

Arguments can also be passed to a subroutine by value. This means that a copy of the variable's value is passed to the called subroutine. Any changes made to the argument inside the called subroutine will not be visible to the calling routine once the subroutine returns.

You can think of passing an argument by value as passing a read-only argument, whereas passing an argument by reference is essentially passing a read/write argument.

By default, all arguments are passed to DLL procedures by reference. If an argument is passed by value, the keyword `ByVal` must precede the argument name.

Visual Basic user-defined types, corresponding to user-defined types, structures, or records used in the DLL, can also be used. The user-defined types should be defined in the Visual Basic file containing the `Declare` statements. Any user-defined types should be defined above where they are referenced in a `Declare` statement.

Comparing Functions and Subs

A DLL procedure is not required to have a return value. Procedures that have return values are called *functions*. Procedures that do not return a value are called *subs* (short for subroutines). Every Visual Basic `Declare` statement will be for either a Function or a Sub. One of the two keywords, `Function` or `Sub`, follows the `Declare` keyword in the `Declare` statement.

If a procedure is a Function, the `Declare` statement must also specify the data type of the returned value. The return type of a DLL function is specified at the end of a `Declare` statement. User-defined types cannot be used as return values for DLL functions. You can only use Visual Basic's built-in data types, such as `Integer` and `Double`. However, this does not pose much of a problem because very few functions will return a value that Visual Basic data types cannot handle. If a DLL function returns a pointer, that value should be stored in Visual Basic as a `Long`. Although the pointer value cannot be dereferenced in Visual Basic, it can be returned, stored, or passed back into other DLL procedures that will then be able to dereference the pointer correctly.

Many DLL procedure libraries include functions that allocate objects and return a pointer to the object. The pointer is then used as an input argument to other procedures in the library. You can use these libraries by returning the created pointer in a Long variable and using that Long as the input pointer argument to other procedures in the library.

Translating Between Data Types

The overall structure and syntax of the Visual Basic Declare statement is pretty straightforward. You have the most opportunity for problems when you have to worry about the specific argument data types and function return values. Understanding how the data types of different languages correspond goes a long way to understanding how to call DLL procedures with Visual Basic. Although it helps if you are familiar with other programming languages, such as C/C++ or Pascal, and even have experience with Windows programming, these are by no means prerequisites for using DLL procedures with Visual Basic. Once you master the basic rules, any Visual Basic programmer can use DLL procedures.

Comparing C and VB Data Types

The following tables display how the standard C/C++ data types, as well as some standard Windows data types (such as handles), are used with DLL procedures. For example, if you need to call a DLL routine that has an argument declared as long in C, then you would have to make the corresponding argument as long in the Visual Basic Declare statement for that routine.

Table 23.1 Converting Between C/C++ and Visual Basic Data Types

C++Argument Data Type	VB Data Type	Size (in Bits)	Declaration of Possible VB Argument
void	No arguments	N/A	N/A
char	ByVal x As Byte	8	Dim x as String*1 Dim x as Byte

C++ Argument Data Type	VB Data Type	Size (in Bits)	Declaration of Possible VB Argument
int (16-bit)	ByVal x as Integer ByVal x as Boolean	16	Dim x as Integer Dim x as Boolean Dim x as Variant Any Integer constant Any Boolean constant
int (32-bit)	ByVal x as Long	32	Dim x as Long Dim x as Variant Any Integer constant
long	ByVal x as Long	32	Dim x as Long Dim x as Variant Any Long integer constant
float	ByVal x as Float	32	Dim x as Float Dim x as Variant Any Float constant
double	ByVal x as Double	64	Dim x as Double Dim x as Variant Any double constant
void *	x as Any	32	Dim x as Long Any VB variable
char *	ByVal x as String	32	Dim x as String Dim x as String*10
int *	x as Integer	32	Dim x as Integer
long *	x as Long	32	Dim x as Long
float *	x as Single	32	Dim x as Single
double *	x as Double	32	Dim x as Double
To pass Null pointers, invoke with (...,ByVal 0&,...) as argument	x as Any	32	ByVal 0&

continues

Table 23.1   Continued

C++Argument Data Type	VB Data Type	Size (in Bits)	Declaration of Possible VB Argument
struct MyType *	x as MyType, where MyType is the name of a corresponding VB user-defined type.	32	Dim x as MyType

Table 23.2   Standard Windows C Data Types

C++Argument Data Type	VB Data Type	Size (in Bits)	Declaration of Possible VB Argument
INT UINT WORD constant BOOL	ByVal x as Integer ByVal x as Boolean	16	Dim x as Integer Dim x as Boolean Any Integer
DWORD	ByVal x as Long	32	Dim x as Long
LPWORD	x as Integer	32	Dim x as Integer Dim x as Boolean
LPDWORD	x as Long	32	Dim x as Long
LPSTR	ByVal x as String	32	Dim x as String Dim x as String*256
HWND (16-bit)	ByVal x as Integer	16	Dim x as Integer
HWND (32-bit)	ByVal x as Long	32	Dim x as Long
HDC HMENU	Integer		Any HDC or HWND control property

Working with Variants

The extent to which you can pass Visual Basic Variant variables to a DLL procedure depends on whether the DLL is written to support OLE automation data types. More specifically, the DLL procedure must expect a variable of type OLE Automation `Variant` data structure. If the DLL supports OLE Automation, you can pass `Variant` variables to the DLL procedure the same way you would pass any other data type.

If the DLL procedure does not directly support the `Variant` data type, you cannot pass Visual Basic `Variant`s by reference. You can, however, pass `Variant` variables by value (using the `ByVal` keyword). That is to say, if a DLL procedure expects a pointer to an integer, you should not send the procedure a pointer to a `Variant` data structure. However, if the DLL procedure expects an integer value, you can use a `Variant` as the argument. Before invoking the DLL, Visual Basic will evaluate the `Variant` as an integer and send a copy of the appropriate value to the DLL procedure.

Passing Arrays

Understanding how arrays are passed to DLL functions requires an understanding of how C/C++ programs work with arrays. In C/C++, arrays are closely linked with pointers. So hold on, this section will be getting down into the nitty gritty. However, if you understand this section, you will have survived the toughest section of this chapter, and you will have gained some insight into how Windows and C/C++ programs work as well.

The data, or variables, of a computer program are stored in memory. You can think of this memory as a linear set of cells, each of which holds some small chunk of data. Each cell is the same size (say, for example, eight bits). The cells are often called *bytes*, or words. All the memory is laid out in a single block. Each individual cell can be identified by its position relative to the beginning of the memory block. The position of a cell is called the cell's *memory address.*

A pointer is actually a memory address. Although all programming languages that include variables deal with memory addresses internally, not all languages allow the programmer to manipulate memory addresses directly. Visual Basic is one such language that does not allow direct access to pointers. C/C++, on the other hand, does allow such access.

In C/C++, and therefore in Windows, an array is stored as a set of contiguous data cells. If an array is 10 elements long, 10 adjacent blocks of memory (with each block the size of one element of the array) would be used to store the array. There are no gaps in the memory block used to store the entire array. The memory address of the first element in the array, therefore, is actually the memory address of the entire array. If a C/C++ program can access the address of the first element of an array, the program can access the entire array.

To pass a Visual Basic array to a DLL procedure that expects an array, you must recognize that the DLL expects the address of the first element in the array. All you have to do is pass the first element of the array by reference. Suppose you have an array of integers that you need to pass to a DLL procedure. The procedure's declaration is as follows:

```
Declare Sub PassArray Lib "Test" (IntArray as Integer)
```

The Visual Basic dimension statement for the array is as follows:

```
Dim IntArray(0 to 9) as Integer
```

The invocation of the DLL procedure would be as follows:

```
PassArray IntArray(0)
```

Notice how passing an array to a DLL procedure differs from passing an array to another Visual Basic procedure. In Visual Basic, arrays are referenced as arguments in procedure invocations by specifying the array name followed by an empty set of parentheses. If, in the previous example, the PassArray() procedure were written in Visual Basic, its definition would be as follows:

```
Sub PassArray( IntArray() as Integer)
'...
End Sub
```

The invocation would be as follows:

```
PassArray IntArray().
```

This is an important distinction to keep in mind when you are debugging your application. To pass an array to a DLL procedure, pass an element of that array by reference.

Working with Strings

`String` variables are the most likely to give you trouble when being passed to DLL procedures. The reason is that C/C++, which most DLL procedures are written in, handles character string data much differently than Visual Basic. Let's look at how character strings are stored in both Visual Basic and C/C++ before we look more deeply at how to pass string data between the two.

➤ Visual Basic `String` variables are stored as a header followed by a Null-terminated string of characters. The header contains information used by Visual Basic, such as the length of the `String`.

➤ Visual Basic `String` variables are referenced through a data type called a `BSTR`, which is defined by OLE automation. A `BSTR` is a pointer to the first character of data in a Visual Basic `String`.

In DLL, procedures that use C/C++ style strings (which include all the procedures in the Windows API), a data structure called `LPSTR` is used to store character strings. An `LPSTR` is simply a pointer to the first character in a Null-terminated data string.

When a Visual Basic `String` argument, or `BSTR`, is passed to a DLL procedure, the default is to pass the argument by reference. This means that a pointer to the `BSTR` is passed. Because the `BSTR` is a pointer, this means that a pointer to a pointer is being passed. If the DLL procedure expects an `LPSTR` to be passed as an argument, it is looking for a pointer to a character. Therefore, to pass Visual Basic strings to DLL procedures that expect `LPSTR` arguments, you must pass the string by value, rather than by reference.

With simpler data types such as `Integer`, the way to pass a Visual Basic variable as an argument that a DLL procedure will fill is to pass the argument by reference. The DLL procedure will fill the address pointed to by the argument with the appropriate value. However, we have just learned that strings should always be passed by value. How then do we modify a string by passing it to a DLL procedure?

The trick to remember when passing Visual Basic strings that DLL procedures will fill is to pass in a string that is known to be long enough to handle the result. This is done by passing a fixed-length string into the DLL procedure. You cannot pass an uninitialized variable-length string to a DLL procedure that will fill the string with a value. If the Visual Basic argument is a variable-length string, make sure that it has been initialized longer than any possible result. An easy way to do this is by using the `String()` function from Visual Basic, as follows:

```
Declare Function GetSystemDirectory Lib "Kernel" _
(ByVal lpBuffer as String, ByVal nSize as Integer) as Integer

    Dim Path as String
    Path = String(256,0)
    ReturnLength = GetSystemDirectory(Path, Len(Path))
    Path = Left(Path, ReturnLength)
```

Another approach is to define the target string buffer with a fixed length, as follows:

```
Dim Path as String * 256
ReturnLength = GetWindowsDirectory(Path, Len(Path))
```

Many DLL procedures that return character strings in their arguments require another argument that gives the maximum length of the variable that holds the string. This is useful because it allows the DLL procedure to avoid overwriting the target variable and possibly corrupting other program data. However, not all DLL procedures require such a length argument. In this case, consult your documentation for the DLL to determine if limits exist. If you have no way of knowing, a general rule of thumb for many DLL procedures, including most Windows API procedures, is to allow at least 256 characters to be returned.

Memory Buffers and Binary Data

One difference between Visual Basic and languages such as C/C++ and Pascal is that Visual Basic cannot directly manipulate binary data. Visual Basic cannot dereference pointers to memory addresses. However, you can use Visual Basic to store such data, moving the data back and forth between DLL procedures.

In previous versions of Visual Basic, `String` variables were used to hold buffers of binary data returned by DLL procedures. Visual Basic 4 has a new data type, `Byte`, that you should use to hold generic binary data buffers. Because a `String` customarily contains only characters, binary data may not be interpreted properly if it is passed as a `String` rather than a `Byte` variable.

Handling User-Defined Types

For the most part, user-defined data types are handled the same as simple numeric data types. User-defined data types are always passed by reference. If the DLL procedures you are using already have documentation and `Declare` statements for Visual Basic, you are all set and can call the DLL procedures directly.

If you have only documentation for calling the routines from C/C++ or another language, you will first have to define new data types for Visual Basic and build the corresponding `Declare` statements. This is where passing user-defined types differs from passing standard data types to DLL procedures.

Use Tables 23.1 and 23.2 for matching corresponding Visual Basic and C/C++ data types, and of course, the problem data type is again character strings. If the C/C++ struct definition includes pointers (including `LPSTR`), you should make the corresponding Visual Basic fields in the `Type` statement `Long`. Also, be aware that your Visual Basic code will not be able to dereference the data pointed to.

If you happen to be specifying a Visual Basic user-defined type that will contain strings to be filled by a DLL procedure, use fixed-length strings as fields in the user-defined type. This will allow your Visual Basic program to dereference the strings returned from the DLL procedure.

Passing Arguments to DLL Procedures

Visual Basic control properties can be passed to DLL procedures only if they are passed by value. If the `Declare` statement for the DLL procedure specifies the `ByVal` keyword for an argument, a control property can be used for that argument directly. This is commonly used when passing handles to device contexts (hDC) or windows (hWnd) to DLL procedures.

> **Caution:** If you are passing handles to Windows API functions, be careful on which version of Windows you are going to run your application. On 32-bit Windows versions, handles are Long values. On 16-bit Windows, handles are Integer values.

If you want to modify a property using a DLL procedure, you will have to use an intermediate variable to hold the value. Copy the property to the variable, pass the variable by reference to the DLL procedure, and assign the property the value of the variable.

When a DLL procedure takes pointers as arguments, these are 32-bit long integer values. Although Visual Basic does not have pointer data types, you can use Long variables to store such pointers.

Sometimes a DLL procedure will expect to receive a Null pointer. A *Null pointer* is a pointer with a value of zero. DLL procedures usually interpret this to mean the pointer is uninitialized. DLL procedures often accept Null pointers for String (and other) arguments to indicate that the particular argument is to be ignored. If an argument can be either a Null pointer or a valid pointer to data (frequently a character string), declare the argument with As Any. Then, when the procedure is invoked, pass a Null pointer as ByVal 0&. The ByVal is used to make sure the DLL procedure gets a zero value rather than a (non-Null) pointer to a zero value. The trailing & makes sure a 32-bit zero is passed to the DLL procedure, rather than a 16-bit zero.

Drawing with the Windows API

The Visual Basic Forms and Picture controls have several methods that allow you to draw on them. However, they don't include methods for drawing polygons. For any Visual Basic application that does lots of drawing, using polygon drawing functions will often be more efficient than drawing all the individual line segments separately with the `Line` method.

The Windows API includes functions that will draw polygons. Let's look at an example of a Visual Basic drawing program that uses Windows API procedures for all its low-level graphic output. Instead of using methods such as `.Circle` and `.Line`, we will draw directly with Windows API procedures. In the course of developing DRAWDEMO, we will exercise many of the possible combinations for calling DLL procedures from Visual Basic, including passing arrays and user-defined types. Figure 23.4 shows the finished DRAWDEMO program.

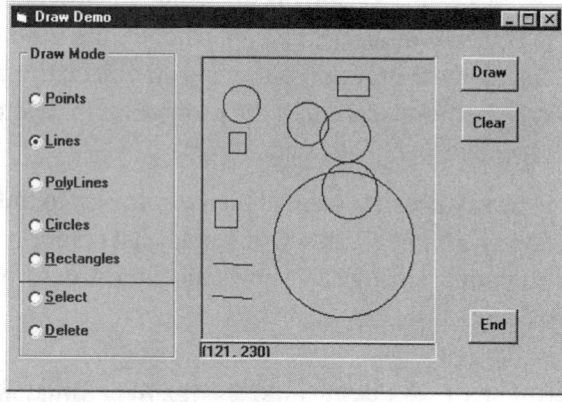

Fig. 23.4 The finished DRAWDEMO program.

`DrawDemo` allows us to draw several different types of graphical objects. Once drawn, you can select these objects and move them around on the screen. Although a fair amount of Visual Basic code is associated with managing the objects that have been drawn, we will focus on the parts of the program that call the DLL procedures of the Windows API.

`DrawDemo` is always in one of three modes. You can either draw objects, move objects, or delete objects. The option buttons on the left side of the screen indicate which mode is current. The drawing area is in the center of the screen.

- When a MouseDown event is detected over the drawing area, the current mode is tested. If the program is in drawing mode, the current mouse cursor location is saved for inclusion in an object definition. If objects are being moved, the program finds the object closest to the cursor location and prepares to move the objects as MouseMove events are generated. If objects are being deleted, the program does nothing with the MouseDown event.

- When a MouseMove event occurs in the drawing area while the program is in Move mode, the selected object is drawn using XOR mode to animate its motion as it follows the cursor.

- When a MouseUp event occurs while the program is in draw mode, the current mouse cursor coordinates are used to define a new object. If the program is moving an object, the object is dropped at its current location. If the program is in delete mode, the closest object will be deleted.

We will use a data structure called a *display list* to hold all the current objects and their attributes. Our display list is simply an array of object data structures. Listing 23.7 shows the data structure used to hold a single object.

Listing 23.7 DRAWDEMO.BAS—The Data Structure for a Drawing Object

```
' Define a single graphical object
Type DisplayObject
        ObjectType as Integer      ' LINE, RECTANGLE, ...
        rectBBox as RECT           ' Bounding box coordinates
        MidPoint as POINTAPI       ' Center point of the
                                   ' object

        iNumPts as Integer         ' Number of points _
        defining the object
        Points(20) as POINTAPI     ' At most 20 points.
End type
```

The ObjectType field of an object indicates whether an object is a LINE, POLYLINE, CIRCLE, or RECTANGLE. The rectBBox field contains the bounding box of the object. MidPoint is the center point of the object.

The MidPoint is used as a hotpoint when selecting an object. The field iNumPts holds how many points are included in the object, and the Points(20) array holds all the points used to define the object. For example, a LINE object is always defined with two points, and a POLYLINE object could have an arbitrary (but less than 20 in our case) number of points.

RECT and POINTAPI are user-defined types used by the Windows API. RECT is used to hold the defining points of rectangles on the screen. POINTAPI defines a single point on the screen. Listing 23.8 shows the definition of RECT and POINTAPI.

Listing 23.8   DRAWDEMO.BAS—Windows API Data Structures for Screen Locations

```
Type RECT
      left As Integer
      top As Integer
      right As Integer
      bottom As Integer
End Type

Type POINTAPI
      x As Integer
      y As Integer
End Type
```

The DrawDemo program uses a global array to hold all the objects in the drawing. At most, you can use 100 objects in the drawing.

```
Global DisplayList(100) as DisplayObject
Global iNumObjects As Integer
```

A more elegant approach would be to use ReDim to redimension the DisplayList() array, rather than hardcoding the value to 100. To avoid obfuscating our example, we will simply dimension the array to a fixed size.

Several Visual Basic routines are used to manipulate objects in the display list:

```
Function AddObject (iMode As Integer, iNumPts As Integer,_
   PointList() As POINTAPI) As IntegerFunction
```

```
Sub DrawDisplayList()
Sub DrawObject (iObject As Integer)
Function FindNearestObject (x as Variant, y as Variant) As_
  Integer
Sub RelMoveObject (iObject As Integer, fDeltaX As Single,_
  fDeltaY As Single)
Sub RemoveObject (iObject As Integer)
```

Listing 23.9 shows the `DrawObject()` routine, which calls several Windows API drawing functions to draw the objects on the screen. Note that you could replace some of the calls to DLL procedures with Visual Basic drawing methods.

Listing 23.9   DRAWDEMO.BAS—The DrawObject() Subroutine

```
''''''''''''''''''''''''''''''''''''''''''''''''''''''''''''
' Draw a single object.
''''''''''''''''''''''''''''''''''''''''''''''''''''''''''''
Sub DrawObject (iObject As Integer)
   Dim lRet As Long
   Dim iRet As Integer

   Select Case DisplayList(iObject).ObjectType

     Case MODE_LINES
         ' MoveTo() and LineTo() are WINAPI functions.
         lRet = MoveTo(Form1.Picture1.hDC,_
 DisplayList(iObject)_
.Points(0).x, DisplayList(iObject).Points(0).y)
         iRet = LineTo(Form1.Picture1.hDC,_
 DisplayList(iObject)._
Points(1).x, DisplayList(iObject).Points(1).y)
     Case MODE_CIRCLES
         ' Arc() is a WINAPI function.
         iRet = Arc(Form1.Picture1.hDC, DisplayList(iObject)._
Points(0).x, DisplayList(iObject).Points(0).y, _
DisplayList(iObject).Points(1).x, DisplayList(iObject)._
Points(1).y, 0, 0, 0, 0)

     Case MODE_RECTANGLES
         'Rectangle() is a WINAPI function.
         iRet = Rectangle(Form1.Picture1.hDC, _
Min(DisplayList(iObject).Points(1).x, DisplayList(iObject)._
Points(0).x), Min(DisplayList(iObject).Points(1).y, _
DisplayList(iObject).Points(0).y), Max(DisplayList(iObject)._
Points(1).x, DisplayList(iObject).Points(0).x), _
Max(DisplayList(iObject).Points(1).y, DisplayList(iObject)._
Points(0).y))
```

```
        Case MODE_POLYLINES
            ' PolyLine() is a WINAPI function.
            ' Note that the second argument is an array of user
            ' defined POINTAPI types.
            iRet = Polyline(Form1.Picture1.hDC, _
    DisplayList(iObject).Points(0), DisplayList(iObject).iNumPts)
        End Select
End Sub
```

Debugging Hints

Using DLL procedures with Visual Basic requires some additional debugging skills and techniques that are not necessary when programming with straight Visual Basic. Not only are you now dealing with
your Visual Basic code, but you must interface with code in the DLL,
which may even be written in a language with which you are not
familiar.

> **Note:** You cannot use the step-through debugging (pressing F8 or
> choosing Debug, Single Step) that is so useful in the Visual Basic
> development environment to step into DLL procedures.

From the point of view of the Visual Basic developer, the DLL procedure is a black box. Program execution enters the DLL procedure and
waits for the procedure to end before moving on. With the tools supplied with Visual Basic, you cannot do anything to debug from inside
the DLL, such as looking at the values that the DLL procedure actually
received. (If you are the developer of the DLL, you can debug the DLL
procedure the same way you would any other DLL, using tools such as
CodeView.) There are some techniques you can use to debug problems
you may have working with DLL procedures. These, though, will have
to assume that the DLL procedure is correct.

Checking the Declare Statement

If you have problems calling a DLL procedure, the first thing you should do is verify that the DLL procedure is correct.

If the DLL procedure expects an array for an argument, make sure that the argument is declared to be passed by reference (not ByVal). By default, Visual Basic programs pass arguments to DLL procedures by reference.

If the DLL procedure expects a single scalar value (such as an integer), make sure that the argument is declared to be passed by value (using the keyword ByVal).

If the DLL procedure expects a pointer to a variable, make sure that the argument is declared to be passed by reference. If the argument is a user-defined structure, the argument is expected to be passed by reference.

If the DLL procedure expects to receive a Null-terminated character string, or LPSTR, make sure that the string is passed by value. Visual Basic will convert constant strings and variable-length strings automatically. If the string is stored in a fixed-length String variable, make sure that the string has Chr$(0) at its end.

If the DLL procedure expects a string buffer (as an LPSTR) that can be used to return a string value, you cannot use a variable-length string. Instead, use a fixed-length string that is bigger than the maximum possible length of the returned string. You can use the Visual Basic procedure in Listing 23.10 to convert the fixed-length string with embedded Null characters back to a Visual Basic variable-length string:

Listing 23.10 Trimming Terminating Null Character from C Strings

```
'
' Trim a terminating Null character from a string.
' This is useful when fixed char buffers have been
' passed into DLL functions.
'
Private Function TrimTerminatingNull (szStr As String) As String
```

```
Dim iPos    As Integer      ' Position of terminating Null.

TrimTerminatingNull = szStr
iPos = InStr(1, szStr, Chr$(0))
If iPos > 0 Then
    TrimTerminatingNull = Left$(szStr, iPos - 1)
End If
End Function
```

If the DLL procedure is a function with a return value that is a pointer, make the return value in the `Declare` statement a `Long` data type.

Checking the Procedure Invocation

If a Visual Basic array is being passed to a DLL procedure, make sure that you pass the first element of the array. If you are using 0-based array indexing, pass the 0th element of the array. It is possible to pass a subset of an array by specifying some element of the array other than the first. Listing 23.11 shows how you would pass just the second half of a 10-element integer array to a DLL procedure.

Listing 23.11   Passing Part of an Array to a DLL Procedure

```
Declare Sub ArrayFunc Lib "Xxxx" ( IntArray As Integer)

Dim iaArray(1 to 10) as Integer
ArrayFunc iaArray(5)
```

If you are passing a value stored in a Visual Basic `Variant`, make sure that the corresponding argument is declared as `ByVal`.

If a DLL procedure expects a pointer as an argument, do not invoke the procedure with a constant value (either a number or `String` variable). Even if you know the value will not be changed by the DLL, the referencing will be incorrect.

If you are having problems with a DLL procedure that is a function returning a floating-point value, check which compiler was used to build the DLL. Microsoft compilers will not cause any problems, but some leading commercial C/C++ compilers return floating-point numbers differently than Visual Basic expects.

Double-Check Arrays

If you are passing an array to a DLL procedure, make sure that you pass the first element of the array, rather than passing the array with empty parentheses as you would if you were passing an array to a Visual Basic routine.

Path Issues Revisited

If the declaration of the DLL procedure is correct and the procedure is being invoked correctly, maybe the DLL file cannot be found. Double-check that the DLL is stored in your WINDOWS directory, Windows system directory, or the directory that is the current directory when your application runs.

DLLs Can Crash Windows

DLLs typically work more closely with Windows internals. Although crashing Windows is not very common when you are working just with Visual Basic, once you start calling DLLs, the potential for a crash becomes much greater. Save your project every time before you test your Visual Basic program that calls DLLs. The easiest way to remember to save is to go to Tools, Options, and select the Save Before Run, Prompt option (or select Save Before Run, Don't Prompt) in the Environment tab.

Stack Space Considerations

Although it is not likely to be a consideration, if a DLL uses a lot of stack space, it may cause problems for your application. The DLL uses the stack of the calling program. A Visual Basic program has a limited amount of stack space available, particularly in 16-bit Windows. Using highly recursive code or lots of local variables in subroutines eats up lots of stack space, whether in a Visual Basic program or in the code of a DLL procedure.

Using INI Files

Many Windows programs use an initialization file to store information about the current status of the program, such as which files have been opened or the positions of various windows on the screen. These files typically are named with the INI file extension and are referred to as profile files, or more commonly INI files. Windows itself includes several INI files that you may be familiar with: WIN.INI and SYSTEM.INI. Visual Basic uses VB.INI as its initialization file.

The general structure of an INI file is as follows:

```
[section]
entry = string
```

A typical section of an INI file looks like the following:

```
[Visual Basic]
MainWindow=31 16 616 76 1
ToolBox=6 82 0 0 1
ProjectWindow=402 152 248 215 9
```

The line with square brackets identifies a section of the INI file. A single INI file can have multiple sections. Each line below the section has a left side and a right side, separated by an equal sign. The left side is the name of some setting, and the right side is the value of the setting. The meaning of the left and right side is interpreted by the application that uses the INI file. There are no rules as to what you may or may not put in an INI file, as long as you follow the structure of identifying sections with square brackets and settings with equal signs.

The Windows API includes several procedures (see Listing 23.12) for manipulating INI files.

Listing 23.12   WIN31API.TXT—Windows API Procedures for INI Files

```
Declare Function GetProfileInt Lib "Kernel" (ByVal lpAppName_
As String, ByVal lpKeyName As String, ByVal nDefault As_
Integer) As Integer
Declare Function GetProfileString Lib "Kernel" (ByVal_
lpAppName As String,lpKeyName As Any, ByVal lpDefault As_
String, ByVal lpReturnedString As String, ByVal nSize As_
Integer) As Integer
Declare Function WriteProfileString Lib "Kernel" (ByVal_
lpAppName As String, lpKeyName As Any, lpString As Any)_
As Integer
Declare Function GetPrivateProfileInt Lib "Kernel"_
(ByVal lpAppName As String, ByVal lpKeyName As String,_
ByVal nDefault As Integer, ByVal lpFileName As String) As_
Integer
Declare Function GetPrivateProfileString Lib "Kernel" _
(ByVal lpAppName As String,_
 lpKeyName As Any, ByVal lpDefault As String, ByVal _
lpReturnedString As String, ByVal nSize As Integer, _
ByVal lpFileName As String) As Integer
Declare Function WritePrivateProfileString Lib "Kernel"_
(ByVal lpAppName As String, lpKeyName As Any, lpString_
As Any, ByVal lpFileName As String) As Integer
```

The argument names used by the Windows API are not the easiest to understand. You can remember the arguments by thinking of the structure of an INI file as follows:

```
[lpAppName]
lpKey = lpString
```

The procedures in Listing 23.12, which include Private as part of their name, are for accessing application-specific INI files. These procedures include an argument, lpFileName, that identifies the INI file to use. The other procedures read and write to the WIN.INI file in your WINDOWS directory.

Note that several of the functions declare lpKeyName as Any, rather than as String, to allow the passage of Null pointers.

As an example, let's write some code to read and write the name of the current file to an application's private INI file. The INI file will be called INIDEMO.INI. Listing 23.13 shows the necessary Visual Basic code.

Listing 23.13   INISAMP.FRM—Writing to an Application's INI File

```
Sub SaveCurFile(szCurFile as String)
    Dim iLen as Integer
    iLen = WritePrivateProfileString("Files",_
 ByVal "CurrentFile", ByVal szCurFile, App.Path + _
"\INIDEMO.INI")
End Sub
```

Two of the arguments in the function invocation of Listing 23.13 are preceded by the ByVal keyword. This is necessary because the WritePrivateProfileString() declaration identifies the data type of those arguments as As Any, passed by reference, rather than As String passed by value. This is to allow Null pointers to be passed as well.

The Declare statements we are using for the INI file declarations are the most general. If you know that you will not be passing Null pointers to the procedures, you can go ahead and use ByVal Xxx as String in the declarations instead of Xxx as Any to avoid having to pass the arguments with the ByVal keyword when the procedures are called.

If szCurFile contains STUDENTS.MDB, after calling the code in Listing 23.13, the INIDEMO.INI file will include the following:

```
[Files]
CurrentFile=STUDENTS.MDB
```

If the INIDEMO.INI file does not already exist, it will be created by the call to WritePrivateProfileString().

You will also want to retrieve any information that you write to a INI file. Listing 23.14 shows a Visual Basic function that retrieves the current file and passes it back as a returned string. This function would be called when your application loads to restore the same file being used when the application was last closed.

Listing 23.14   Reading from an Application's INI File

```
Function GetCurFile() as String
    Dim szCurFile as String
    szCurFile = String(256, 0)
    iLen = GetPrivateProfileString( "Files", ByVal _
"CurrentFile", "", szCurFile,_
 Len(szCurFile),App.Path + "\INIDEMO.INI" )
    GetCurFile = Left$(szCurFile, iLen)
End Function
```

Practical Examples

The rest of this chapter will introduce you to several features you can easily add to your applications by calling Windows API procedures. The examples are all solutions to common problems that you could encounter in just about any Visual Basic programming project.

Waiting for a Shelled Process to Finish

A common technique when using Visual Basic to integrate other applications is to use the Shell() function to start another program running. However, the Shell() command does not wait for the shelled program to finish. If you want your VB application to wait, you can use the GetModuleUsage() function from the Windows API. GetModuleUsage retrieves the usage count for a module. When the usage count drops to zero, the module is no longer running. Your VB program simply needs to call Shell() to start the other application and then wait for the module count to drop to zero. In the polling loop you must call DoEvents so Windows will allow the shelled application to run. Without DoEvents, the shelled program would never get time to use the processor.

Listing 23.15 shows a Visual Basic subroutine, SyncShell(), which starts an application running and waits for the application to finish before returning and allowing the program to proceed.

Listing 23.15 **Running Another Program Synchronously Using GetModuleUsage()**

```
Declare Function GetModuleUsage Lib "Kernel" _
(ByVal hModule As Integer) As Integer

Sub SyncShell(szAppName as String)
    Dim hModule as Integer
    hModule = Shell( szAppName ,1 )
    while GetModuleUsage(hModule) > 0
        DoEvents
    Wend
End Sub
```

Making a Window Stay on Top

You can configure some Windows applications so that they always stay on top of other windows. These are called floating windows because they appear to float on top of the screen in front of other windows. An example is the CLOCK.EXE applet that comes with Windows. Common contexts for floating windows include an application that has a non-modal dialog box that needs to stay on top of the application's windows (such as a tool palette) or resource monitoring programs that should always remain visible to the user.

This technique is easy to incorporate into your applications. Listing 23.16 shows how the SetWindowPos() routine from the Windows API can be used to force a window to stay on top.

Listing 23.16 **SetWindowPos() Can Make a Window Float**

```
Declare Sub SetWindowPos Lib "User" (ByVal hWnd As _
Integer, ByVal hWndInsertAfter As Integer, ByVal X As Integer,_
 ByVal Y As Integer, ByVal cx As Integer, ByVal cy As Integer,_
 ByVal wFlags As Integer)

Global Const SWP_NOSIZE = &H1
Global Const SWP_NOMOVE = &H2
Global Const HWND_TOPMOST = -1
Global Const HWND_NOTOPMOST = -2
```

continues

Listing 23.16   Continued

```
Sub SetFormTopmost( F as Form )
    SetWindowPos F.hWnd, HWND_TOPMOST, 0, 0, 0, 0, _
SWP_NOMOVE or SWP_NOSIZE
End Sub

Sub SetFormNoTopmost( F as Form )
    SetWindowPos F.hWnd, HWND_NOTOPMOST, 0, 0, 0, 0, _
SWP_NOMOVE or SWP_NOSIZE
End Sub
```

Invoking Windows Help Files

Many applications written with Visual Basic include a Windows help file. One way to display a help file to your users is with the Common Dialog custom control that is included with Visual Basic. If your program does not use the Common Dialog control for anything other than to invoke help, including it with your program's installation is a bit of a waste. Instead, you can call the WinHelp procedure from the Windows API (see Listing 23.17). The wCommand argument allows you to specify which topic in the help file you want to display initially, as well as several other possibilities.

Listing 23.17   Invoking Windows Help Files

```
' Commands to pass WinHelp()
Global Const HELP_CONTEXT = &H1 '  Display topic in ulTopic
Global Const HELP_QUIT = &H2    '  Terminate help
Global Const HELP_INDEX = &H3   '  Display index
Global Const HELP_HELPONHELP = &H4      '  Display help _
on using help
Global Const HELP_SETINDEX = &H5         '  Set the current_
  Index for multi index help
Global Const HELP_KEY = &H101             '  Display topic for_
  keyword in offabData
Global Const HELP_MULTIKEY = &H201

Declare Function WinHelp Lib "User" (ByVal hWnd As Integer,_
  ByVal lpHelpFile As String, ByVal wCommand As Integer,_
  dwData As Any) As Integer
```

```
Sub CallForHelp()
    Dim iRV as Integer
    iRV = WinHelp(CurrentForm.hWnd, "PROGMAN.HLP", HELP_INDEX, _
    ByVal 0&)
End Sub
```

From Here...

This chapter described the basic issues involved when writing DLLs with Visual Basic. With well-behaved DLL procedures and the proper declarations and user-defined types, you really don't have much to do.

If you buy a commercial third-party DLL that includes a file containing the necessary declarations, using the library is a simple matter of including the file of declarations in your Visual Basic project and then writing your procedure calls. The procedures behave just like built-in Visual Basic statements and functions.

Sometimes, you have to debug calls to DLL procedures from Visual Basic. If you remember the differences between how data types, strings, and arrays are used in Visual Basic and DLL procedures, you will be able to debug most problems.

Dynamic link libraries offer huge improvements to a Visual Basic application. Whether you will be calling a few Windows API procedures or using Visual Basic simply as a front-end for an extensive library of DLL procedures, Visual Basic can be effectively used with DLLs.

This chapter taught you how to integrate other languages into your Visual Basic program by calling DLLs. You have learned the basic mechanics of how to make the calls to DLLs, as well as some tips on how to debug DLL calls and how to take advantage of the Windows API.

➤ For more information on calling DLLs in the Windows API, see Chapter 3, "Using the Windows API."

➤ For more information on calling third-party DLLs, see Chapter 20, "OLE Controls, Add-Ins, and 32-bit DLLs."

Index

G

P

S

X-Y-Z

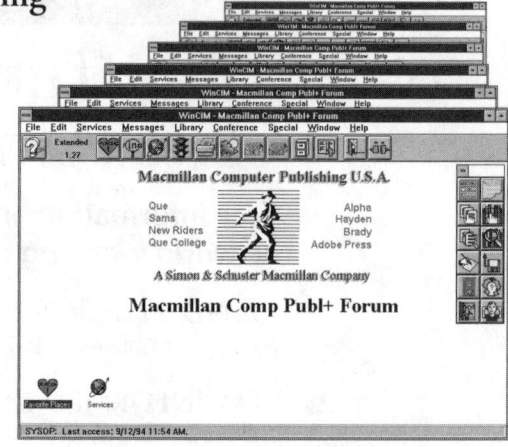

Complete and Return this Card
for a *FREE* Computer Book Catalog

Thank you for purchasing this book! You have purchased a superior computer book written expressly for your needs. To continue to provide the kind of up-to-date, pertinent coverage you've come to expect from us, we need to hear from you. Please take a minute to complete and return this self-addressed, postage-paid form. In return, we'll send you a free catalog of all our computer books on topics ranging from word processing to programming and the internet.

.r. ☐   Mrs. ☐   Ms. ☐   Dr. ☐

ame (first) ☐☐☐☐☐☐☐☐☐☐☐☐   (M.I.) ☐   (last) ☐☐☐☐☐☐☐☐☐☐☐☐☐☐☐☐

.ddress ☐☐☐☐☐☐☐☐☐☐☐☐☐☐☐☐☐☐☐☐☐☐☐☐☐☐☐☐☐☐☐☐

☐☐☐☐☐☐☐☐☐☐☐☐☐☐☐☐☐☐☐☐☐☐☐☐☐☐☐☐☐☐☐☐

.ity ☐☐☐☐☐☐☐☐☐☐☐☐☐   State ☐☐   Zip ☐☐☐☐☐ ☐☐☐☐

.ione ☐☐☐ ☐☐☐ ☐☐☐☐   Fax ☐☐☐ ☐☐☐ ☐☐☐☐

.ompany Name ☐☐☐☐☐☐☐☐☐☐☐☐☐☐☐☐☐☐☐☐☐☐☐☐☐☐☐☐

.-mail address ☐☐☐☐☐☐☐☐☐☐☐☐☐☐☐☐☐☐☐☐☐☐☐☐☐☐☐☐

Please check at least (3) influencing factors for purchasing this book.

.ront or back cover information on book .... ☐
.pecial approach to the content .... ☐
.ompleteness of content .... ☐
.uthor's reputation .... ☐
.ublisher's reputation .... ☐
.ook cover design or layout .... ☐
.dex or table of contents of book .... ☐
.rice of book .... ☐
.pecial effects, graphics, illustrations .... ☐
.ther (Please specify): _____ ☐

. How did you first learn about this book?

.aw in Macmillan Computer Publishing catalog .... ☐
.ecommended by store personnel .... ☐
.aw the book on bookshelf at store .... ☐
.ecommended by a friend .... ☐
.eceived advertisement in the mail .... ☐
.aw an advertisement in: _____ ☐
.ead book review in: _____ ☐
.ther (Please specify): _____ ☐

. How many computer books have you purchased in the last six months?

.his book only .... ☐   3 to 5 books...................... ☐
. books.................. ☐   More than 5...................... ☐

4. Where did you purchase this book?

Bookstore .... ☐
Computer Store .... ☐
Consumer Electronics Store .... ☐
Department Store .... ☐
Office Club .... ☐
Warehouse Club .... ☐
Mail Order .... ☐
Direct from Publisher .... ☐
Internet site .... ☐
Other (Please specify): _____ ☐

5. How long have you been using a computer?

☐ Less than 6 months   ☐ 6 months to a year
☐ 1 to 3 years   ☐ More than 3 years

6. What is your level of experience with personal computers and with the subject of this book?

	With PCs	With subject of book
New	☐	☐
Casual	☐	☐
Accomplished	☐	☐
Expert	☐	☐

Source Code ISBN: 0-7897-0073-5

7. Which of the following best describes your job title?

- Administrative Assistant ☐
- Coordinator ☐
- Manager/Supervisor ☐
- Director ☐
- Vice President ☐
- President/CEO/COO ☐
- Lawyer/Doctor/Medical Professional ☐
- Teacher/Educator/Trainer ☐
- Engineer/Technician ☐
- Consultant ☐
- Not employed/Student/Retired ☐
- Other (Please specify): _____ ☐

8. Which of the following best describes the area of the company your job title falls under?

- Accounting ☐
- Engineering ☐
- Manufacturing ☐
- Operations ☐
- Marketing ☐
- Sales ☐
- Other (Please specify): _____ ☐

9. What is your age?

- Under 20 ☐
- 21-29 ☐
- 30-39 ☐
- 40-49 ☐
- 50-59 ☐
- 60-over ☐

10. Are you:

- Male ☐
- Female ☐

11. Which computer publications do you read regularly? (Please list)

_____
_____
_____
_____
_____
_____
_____
_____
_____
_____

Comments: _____
_____
_____

Fold here and scotch-tape to ma

Read This Before Opening Software

By opening this package, you are agreeing to be bound by the following: